MW00717831

2004 Edition

V.I.P. ADDRESS BOOK

Edited by James M. Wiggins, Ph.D.

Associated Media Companies

Table of Contents

INTRODUCTION

ADDRESS LISTINGS

NECROLOGY

ADDITIONAL ADDRESSES

BIBLIOGRAPHY

ORDER FORMS & ADVERTISEMENTS

INTRODUCTION

The purpose of the V.I.P. ADDRESS BOOK is to provide readers with a means of reaching Very Important People — Celebrities, Government Officials, Business Leaders, Entertainers, Sports Stars, Scientists and Artists.

It is genuinely hoped that people will use this volume to write for information about an entrant's work or to express encouragement. Compliments and praise for one's efforts are always appreciated. Being at the top of one's chosen profession is no exception. And for those who are no longer active in a field, it is especially flattering to be contacted about one's past accomplishments.

Methodology

The determination of candidates for inclusion in this reference work is an on-going process. Committees of prominent and knowledgeable people review those included in the nine major areas (listed in bold below).

Public Service includes World Leaders, Government Officials (both U.S. and International), Law Enforcement Officials and Members of the Legal and Judicial Fields.

Adventure includes Military Leaders (both U.S. and International), Astronauts and Cosmonauts, Heroes and Explorers.

Business, Religion and Education includes Financial and Labor Leaders as well as Businesspeople and Nobel Prize Winners in Economics and Peace.

Life and Leisure includes Fashion Design, Modeling, Beauty and Health Care and Social and Political Activists.

Communications includes Columnists, Commentators, Editors and Publishers, along with Editorial and Comic Book Cartoonists.

Fine Arts includes Architects, Artists, Opera, Ballet and Dance Performers, Conductors, Concert Artists, Composers (both classical and popular), Writers, Photographers and Nobel Literature Laureates.

Science covers Nobel Prize winners in Chemistry, Medicine and Physics, Engineers, Inventors, Earth and Space Scientists, Psychologists and Psychiatrists, Medical and Research Scientists.

Entertainment includes stars of Radio, Stage and Screen, Musicians, Cinematographers, Producers and Directors.

Sports includes all major spectator and participatory sports.

The committees define the parameters of the people included and prepare a list of additions and deletions to the candidate list. The research staff checks and updates information daily.

Occupations and Titles

The category listed after an entrant's name is selected to best describe his/her most noteworthy accomplishment. No distinction is made as to whether the person still holds that position. It is felt that a person who made a name for herself or himself still retains that identity even if it was accomplished in the past.

How Addresses Are Obtained

The editors of the V.I.P. ADDRESS BOOK have made every effort possible to insure that the addresses listed are accurate and current. Once it is determined a person is eligible for inclusion in the book, that person is contacted to determine which address he or she prefers. If a person prefers a home address, it is included. If a person prefers a business address or one in care of an agent or representative, that address is included. If a person specifically asks that their name not be included, their name is omitted. Once an address is listed, we continue efforts to verify that the address has not changed. These efforts include random sampling of the entire database and follow-up on all returned mailings received including those received from users of the book.

Users of the book should realize that people's addresses are in a state of constant change. The U.S. Bureau of Statistics says that almost 20 percent of people move each year. Not only do people change places of residence, they may also change business affiliations. Businesses move their headquarters as well as downsizing, merging or selling portions of their companies. Athletes get traded or retire. Entertainers change agents or personal managers and television shows get canceled. Politicians leave office or run for new positions. In addition, there are deaths almost daily which affect the address listings.

National Change of Address Program

Our staff notes changes on a daily basis by watching television news shows and reading newspapers around the world. But we also take an extra step which no other directory or address book attempts. We match addresses of all U.S. listees with the U.S. Postal Service's National Change of Address program. The National Change of Address match is a process that compares mailing lists with more than 100 million address change cards filed by postal customers over the past three years. Address change information is provided for mailing list records that match with information from address change cards.

If a person/family/business moves, there are several factors which determine whether the National Change of Address program is effective. These include whether the mover filed an address change with the Postal Service, when the change was filed, whether the mover lived in an area covered by the automated address change systems (which includes more than 90 percent of the United States) and whether the name and address information in our files matches the information provided by the mover.

Bad Addresses/Corrections

We keep track of not only current addresses but outdated ones as well. Our files list more than 110,000 people and we have up to 20 addresses for some of the people in the book. We continually update our data base and you can help. While we no longer provide address corrections, we do welcome information about bad addresses from users of the book.

Envelope Markings

On your outgoing letters, you should always write "Address Correction Requested" beneath your return address in a clear and noticeable manner. If you do this, postal workers are supposed to send the forwarding address for a nominal fee.

V.I.P. Address Book Update

Realizing the ever changing aspect of addresses, we also publish the single volume V.I.P. ADDRESS BOOK UPDATE which is available mid-year for an additional fee. The UPDATE lists several thousand address changes and new addresses as well as informing users of the names of celebrities who pass away.

Recommendations for the Book

If you are interested in people who are not listed in the book, send us a letter with their name, address and biographical information. If these people are deemed worthy for inclusion, they may be listed in a future edition of the V.I.P. ADDRESS BOOK.

Until people stop moving or changing jobs, there are going to be address changes. We want to provide the best service possible and we think we have the highest percentage of accuracy of any directory or address book.

If you have suggestions for improving accuracy beyond random follow-ups, following daily news events, checking on all bad address notifications and using the Postal Service's National Change of Address service, let us know your ideas.

Forms of Address

An important part of writing to people - regardless of their positions - is to properly address envelopes and to use the correct salutations in the letters. Although the titles and positions of people listed in this directory are too numerous to cover, there are a number of people whose forms of address are worth noting. The table below is a guide to enhance the likelihood your letter will be received in a favorable light.

POSITION	ENVELOPE/ADDRESS	SALUTATION
Presidents of Countries	The President	Dear Mr/Madam President - - -
Vice Presidents of Countries	The Vice President	Dear Mr/Madam Vice President - - -
Cabinet Officers	The Honorable John/Jane Doe Secretary of - - -	Dear Mr/Madam Secretary - - -
Senators	The Honorable John/Jane Doe US Senator from - - -	Dear Mr/Ms Senator - - -
Representatives	The Honorable John/Jane Doe US Representative from - - -	Dear Mr/Ms Representative - - -
Judges	The Honorable John/Jane Doe, Judge, US - - - Court	Dear Judge - - -
US Ambassadors	The Honorable John/Jane Doe US Ambassador to (Country)	Dear Mr/Ms Ambassador - - -
Foreign Ambassadors	His/Her Excellency John/Jane Doe	Dear Mr/Ms Ambassador - - -
Kings/Queens	His/Her Royal Highness - - - , King/Queen of - - -	Your Royal Highness - - -
Military Leaders (Attention should be given to the actual rank)	General/Admiral John/Jane Doe	Dear General/ Admiral - - -
Governors	The Honorable John/Jane Doe, Governor of - - -	Dear Governor - - -

Continued on page xii

2004 Edition

V.I.P. ADDRESS BOOK

Publisher and Editor
James M. Wiggins, Ph.D.

President and Managing Editor
Adele M. Cooke

Vice President of Technical Affairs
Michael K. Maloy

Design Director
Lee Ann Nelson

Publisher
ASSOCIATED MEDIA COMPANIES
P.O. Box 489
Gleneden Beach, OR 97388
United States of America

TABLE OF ABBREVIATIONS

A

AB	Alberta
ACT	Australian Capital Territory
AFB	Air Force Base
AK	Alaska
AL	Alabama
Aly	Alley
APO	Army Post Office
AR	Arkansas
Arc	Arcade
AS	American Samoa
Assn	Association
Assoc	Associates
Ave	Avenue
AZ	Arizona

B

BC	British Columbia
Bd	Board
Beds	Bedfordshire
Berks	Berkshire
Bldg	Building
Blvd	Boulevard
Br	Branch
Bros	Brothers
Bucks	Buckinghamshire
BWI	British West Indies
Byp	Bypass

C

CA	California
Cambs	Cambridgeshire
Cir	Circle
CM	Mariana Islands
CMH	Congressional Medal of Honor
CO	Colorado
Co	Company
Corp	Corporation
Cres	Crescent
Cswy	Causeway
CT	Connecticut
Ct	Court
Ctr	Center
Ctrl	Central
Cts	Courts
CZ	Canal Zone

D

DC	District of Columbia
DE	Delaware
Dept	Department
Dis	District
Div	Division
Dr	Drive
Drwy	Driveway

E

E	East
Edin	Edinburgh
Ent	Entertainment
Expy	Expressway
Ext	Extended, Extension

F

Fedn	Federation
FL	Florida
FPO	Fleet Post Office
Ft	Fort
Fwy	Freeway

G

GA	Georgia
Gdns	Gardens
Glos	Gloucestershire
Grp	Group
Grv	Grove
Gt	Great
GU	Guam

H

Hants	Hampshire
Herts	Hertfordshire
HI	Hawaii
HOF	Hall of Fame
Hq	Headquarters
Hts	Heights
Hwy	Highway

I

IA	Iowa
ID	Idaho
IL	Illinois
IN	Indiana
Inc	Incorporated
Inst	Institute
Int'l	International
Intercoll	Intercollegiate

J

Jr	Junior

K

KS	Kansas
KY	Kentucky

L

LA	Louisiana
Lab	Laboratory
Lancs	Lancashire
Lincs	Lincolnshire
Ln	Lane
Ltd	Limited

M

MA	Massachusetts
MB	Manitoba
MD	Maryland
Mddx	Middlesex
ME	Maine
Med	Medical
Mgmt	Management
MI	Michigan
MN	Minnesota
MO	Missouri
Mon	Monmouthshire
MS	Mississippi
MT	Montana
Mt	Mount

N

N	North
NB	New Brunswick
NC	North Carolina
ND	North Dakota
NE	Northeast, Nebraska
NF	Newfoundland
NH	New Hampshire
NJ	New Jersey
NM	New Mexico
Northants	Northamptonshire
Notts	Nottinghamshire
NS	Nova Scotia
NSW	New South Wales
NT	Northwest Territories, Northern Territory
NV	Nevada
NW	Northwest
NY	New York

O

OH	Ohio
OK	Oklahoma
ON	Ontario
OR	Oregon
Oxon	Oxfordshire

P

PA	Pennsylvania
PE	Prince Edward Island
Pkwy	Parkway
Pl	Place
Plz	Plaza
PO	Post Office
PR	Puerto Rico
Prof	Professional
Pt	Point

Q

QC	Quebec
QLD	Queensland

R

RD	Rural Delivery
Rd	Road
Rep	Republic
RI	Rhode Island
RR	Rural Route

S

S	South
SA	South Australia
SC	South Carolina
Sci	Science
SD	South Dakota
SE	Southeast
SK	Saskatchewan
Spdwy	Speedway
Sq	Square
St	Saint, Street
SW	Southwest

T

Tas	Tasmania
Ter	Territory
Terr	Terrace
TN	Tennessee
Tpke	Turnpike
Trl	Trail
TX	Texas

U

Univ	University
US	United States
UT	Utah

V

VA	Virginia
VC	Victoria Cross
VI	Virgin Islands
VIC	Victoria
VT	Vermont

W

W	West
WA	Washington, Western Australia
WI	Wisconsin
Worcs	Worcestershire
WV	West Virginia
WY	Wyoming

X-Y-Z

YK	Yukon Territory
Yorks	Yorkshire

Mayors	The Honorable John/Jane Doe, Mayor of - - -	Dear Mayor - - -
The Clergy		
Catholic		
The Pope	His Eminence the Pope - - -	Your Holiness - - -
Cardinals	His Eminence, John Cardinal Doe	Dear Your Eminence Cardinal
Episcopalian	The Rt Rev John Doe	Dear Bishop - - -
Protestant	The Rev John Doe	Dear Mr/Ms - - -
Eastern Orthodox		
Patriarch	His Holiness, the Patriarch - - -	Your Holiness - - -
Jewish	Rabbi John Doe	Dear Rabbi - - -

Forms of addresses can vary to almost impossible proportions. If you are a real stickler for proper protocol, you will need to obtain one of the many excellent reference books on etiquette or consult your local reference librarian for assistance.

Times are less formal so if you are polite and spell names correctly, your letter should be favorably received.

ACKNOWLEDGEMENTS

The Editors would like to thank the following people for their generous assistance in maintaining the accuracy of this publication:

Robert Allen, Jr., Ed Bielucke, III, John Gracen Brown, Gloria & Len Bytnar, Thomas Burford, Douglas Files, Michael Gerstley, Steve Koroknay, Massee McKinley, Jurgen Schwarz, Anders Tvegard and Michael Vallieres

THE DIRECTORY OF ADDRESS LISTINGS

Although we have made every effort to provide current correct addresses, we assume no responsibility for addresses which become outdated.
Neither do we guarantee that people listed in the book will personally answer their mail or that they will respond to correspondence.

Aadland, Beverly *Actress*
27617 Ennismore Ave, Canyon Country, CA 91351, USA
Aaker, Lee *Actor*
PO Box 8013, Mammoth Lakes, CA 93546, USA
Aames, Willie *Actor*
10209 SE Division St, Portland, OR 97266, USA
Aamodt, Kjetil Andre *Alpine Skier*
Holmenkollvn 105, 0391 Oslo, Norway
Aaron, Caroline *Actress*
%Mindel & Donigan, 9057 Nemo St, #C, West Hollywood, CA 90069, USA
Aaron, Chester *Writer*
PO Box 388, Occidental, CA 95465, USA
Aaron, Henry J *Economist*
1326 Hemlock St SW, Washington, DC 20012, USA
Aaron, Henry L (Hank) *Baseball Player, Executive*
1611 Adams Dr SW, Atlanta, GA 30311, USA
Aaron, Paul *Movie, Television Director*
1604 Courtney Ave, Los Angeles, CA 90046, USA
Aaron, Tommy *Golfer*
440 E Lake Dr, Gainesville, GA 30506, USA
Aarsleff, Hans *Linguist*
%Princeton University, English Dept, Princeton, NJ 08544, USA
Aas, Roald *Speed Skater*
Enebakkvn 252, 1187 Oslo 11, Norway
Abair, Mindy *Singer*
PO Box 931513, Los Angeles, CA 90093, USA
Abakanowicz, Magdalena *Artist*
Ul Bzowa 1, 02-708 Warsaw, Poland
Abalakin, Victor K *Astronomer*
%Main Observatory, Pulkovskoye Shosse 65, 196140 Saint Petersburg, Russia
Abalkin, Leonid I *Economist*
%Academy of Sciences, Nakhimovsky Prospekt 32, 117218 Moscow, Russia
Abbado, Claudio *Conductor*
Piazzetta Bossi 1, 20121 Milan, Italy
Abbatiello, Carmine *Harness Racing Driver*
176 Stone Hill Road, Colts Neck, NJ 07722, USA
Abbott, Bruce *Actor*
%Metropolitan Talent Agency, 4526 Wilshire Blvd, Los Angeles, CA 90010, USA
Abbott, D Thomas *Businessman*
%Savin Corp, 333 Ludlow St, Stamford, CT 06902, USA
Abbott, Diahnne *Actress*
460 W Ave 46, Los Angeles, CA 90065, USA
Abbott, James A (Jim) *Baseball Player*
3449 Quiet Cove, Corona del Mar, CA 92625, USA
Abbott, L Kyle *Baseball Player*
24275 Spartan St, Mission Viejo, CA 92691, USA
Abboud, A Robert *Businessman*
%A Robert Abboud Co, 212 Stone Ave, Lake Zurich, IL 60047, USA
Abboud, Joseph M *Fashion Designer*
650 5th Ave, #2700, New York, NY 10019, USA
Abd al-Mohsin Hammad al-Bassam *Cosmonaut, Saudi Arabia*
%Royal Embassy of Saudi Arabia, 22 Holland Park, London W11, England
Abdnor, James *Senator, SD*
PO Box 217, Kennebec, SD 57544, USA
Abdul Ahad Mohmand *Cosmonaut, Afghanistan*
%Potchta Kosmonavtov, Moskovskoi Oblasti, 141160 Syvisdny Goroduk, Russia
Abdul, Paula J *Singer, Dancer*
%Metropolitan Entertainment, 363 US Highway 46, #3F, Fairfield, NJ 07004, USA
Abdul-Jabbar, Kareem *Basketball Player*
5458 Wilshire Blvd, Los Angeles, CA 90036, USA
Abdullah Ahamad Badawi *Prime Minister, Malaysia*
%Prime Minister's Office, Jalan Dato Onn, 50502 Kuala Lumpur, Malaysia
Abdullah Ibn Abdul al-Aziz *Crown Prince, Saudi Arabia*
%Council of Ministers, Murabba, Riyadh 11121, Saudi Arabia
Abdullah II *King, Jordan; Army General*
%Royal Palace, Amman, Jordan
Abdulov, Aleksandr G *Actor*
Peschanaya Str 4, #3, 125252 Moscow, Russia
Abdur-Rahim, Shareef *Basketball Player*
%Atlanta Hawks, 190 Marietta St SW, Atlanta, GA 30303, USA
Abel, Joy *Bowler*
PO Box 296, Lansing, IL 60438, USA
Abelson, John N *Biologist*
1097 Blanche St, #316, Pasadena, CA 91106, USA
Abelson, Philip H *Physicist*
4244 50th St NW, Washington, DC 20016, USA
Abercrombie, Ian *Actor*
1040 N Gardner St, West Hollywood, CA 90046, USA

A

Abercrombie - Ackerman

Abercrombie, John L *Jazz Guitarist*
%Joel Chriss, 300 Mercer St, #3J, New York, NY 10003, USA
Abernathy, Brent *Baseball Player*
508 Cascade Circle, Palm Harbor, FL 34684, USA
Abernathy, Frederick H *Mechanical Engineer*
43 Islington Road, Newton, MA 02166, USA
Abernethy, Robert *Commentator*
%Public Broadcasting System, 1320 Braddock Place, Alexandria, VA 22314, USA
Abiodun Oyewole *Rap Artist (Last Poets)*
%Agency Group Ltd, 370 City Road, London EC1V 2QA, England
Abizaid, John P *Army General*
Commander, US Central Command, MacDill Air Force Base, FL 33621, USA
Ablon, Ralph E *Businessman*
%Ogden Corp, PO Box 2615, Fairfield, NJ 07004, USA
Abourezk, James G *Senator, SD*
21 Dupont Circle NW, #400, Washington, DC 20036, USA
Abraham, E Spencer *Secretary of Energy; Senator, MI*
%Energy Department, 1000 Independence Ave SW, Washington, DC 20585, USA
Abraham, F Murray *Actor*
%Brooklyn College, Theater Dept, 2900 Bedford Ave, Brooklyn, NY 11210, USA
Abrahamian, Emil *Cartoonist (Stumpy Stumbler)*
147 Woodleaf Dr, Winter Spings, FL 32708, USA
Abrahams, Jim S *Movie Director*
501 10th St, Santa Monica, CA 90402, USA
Abrahams, Jonathan *Actor*
%Gersh Agency, 232 N Canon Dr, Beverly Hills, CA 90210, USA
Abrahamson, James A *Air Force General, Businessman*
3557 Havercamp Road, Hibbing, MN 55746, USA
Abramovitz, Max *Architect*
176 Honey Hollow Road, Pound Ridge, NY 10576, USA
Abramowicz, Daniel (Danny) *Football Player*
10018 Evergreen Court N, Minneapolis, MN 55443, USA
Abrams, Elliott *Government Official*
10607 Dogwood Farm Lane, Great Falls, VA 22066, USA
Abramson, Neil *Movie Director, Writer*
%United Talent Agency, 9560 Wilshire Blvd, #500, Beverly Hills, CA 90212, USA
Abreu, Aldo *Concert Recorder Player*
%Concert Artists Guild, 850 7th Ave, #1205, New York, NY 10019, USA
Abrikosov, Alexei A *Nobel Physics Laureate*
804 Houston St, Lemont, IL 60439, USA
Abril, Victoria *Actress*
%JFPM Representation, 11 Rue Chanez, 75016 Paris, France
Abroms, Edward M *Television Director*
%EMA Enterprises, 1866 Marlowe St, Thousand Oaks, CA 91360, USA
Abronzino, Umberto *Soccer Player*
1336 Seattle Ave, San Jose, CA 95125, USA
Abrosimova, Svetlana *Basketball Player*
%Minnesota Lynx, Target Center, 600 1st Ave N, Minneapolis, MN 55403, USA
Abrunhosa, Pedro *Singer, Songwriter*
%Polygram Records, Worldwide Plaza, 825 8th Ave, New York, NY 10019, USA
Abruzzo, Ray *Actor*
20334 Pacific Coast Highway, Malibu, CA 90265, USA
Abshire, David M *Diplomat*
%Strategic/International Studies Center, 1800 K St NW, Washington, DC 20006, USA
Abul-Ragheb, Ali *Prime Minister, Jordan*
%Prime Minister's Office, PO Box 80, 35215 Amman, Jordan
Accardo, Salvatore *Concert Violinist*
%Columbia Artists Mgmt Inc, 165 W 57th St, New York, NY 10019, USA
Accola, Paul *Alpine Skier*
Bolgenstr 17, 7270 Davos Platz, Switzerland
Acconci, Vito *Conceptual Artist*
39 Pearl St, Brooklyn, NY 11201, USA
Achebe, Chinua *Writer*
%Bard College, Language & Literature Dept, PO Box 41, Annandale, NY 12504, USA
Achica, George *Football Player*
3165 Lone Bluff Way, San Jose, CA 95111, USA
Acker, Sharon *Actress*
332 N Palm Dr, #401, Beverly Hills, CA 90210, USA
Ackeren, Robert V *Movie Director*
%Kurfurstendamm 132A, 10711 Berlin, Germany
Ackerman, Bettye *Actress*
100 Sunset Blvd, West Columbia, SC 29169, USA
Ackerman, F Duane *Businessman*
%BellSouth Corp, 1155 Peachtree St NE, Atlanta, GA 30309, USA
Ackerman, Leslie *Actress*
4439 Worster Ave, Studio City, CA 91604, USA
Ackerman, Roger G *Businessman*
%Corning Inc, Houghton Park, Corning, NY 14831, USA

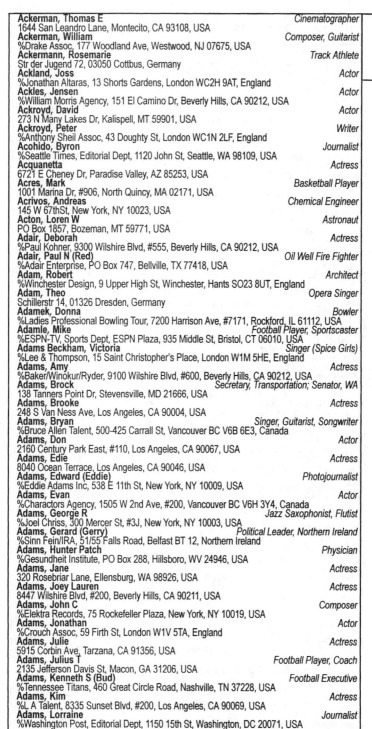

Ackerman, Thomas E *Cinematographer*
1644 San Leandro Lane, Montecito, CA 93108, USA
Ackerman, William *Composer, Guitarist*
%Drake Assoc, 177 Woodland Ave, Westwood, NJ 07675, USA
Ackermann, Rosemarie *Track Athlete*
Str der Jugend 72, 03050 Cottbus, Germany
Ackland, Joss *Actor*
%Jonathan Altaras, 13 Shorts Gardens, London WC2H 9AT, England
Ackles, Jensen *Actor*
%William Morris Agency, 151 El Camino Dr, Beverly Hills, CA 90212, USA
Ackroyd, David *Actor*
273 N Many Lakes Dr, Kalispell, MT 59901, USA
Ackroyd, Peter *Writer*
%Anthony Sheil Assoc, 43 Doughty St, London WC1N 2LF, England
Acohido, Byron *Journalist*
%Seattle Times, Editorial Dept, 1120 John St, Seattle, WA 98109, USA
Acquanetta *Actress*
6721 E Cheney Dr, Paradise Valley, AZ 85253, USA
Acres, Mark *Basketball Player*
1001 Marina Dr, #906, North Quincy, MA 02171, USA
Acrivos, Andreas *Chemical Engineer*
145 W 67thSt, New York, NY 10023, USA
Acton, Loren W *Astronaut*
PO Box 1857, Bozeman, MT 59771, USA
Adair, Deborah *Actress*
%Paul Kohner, 9300 Wilshire Blvd, #555, Beverly Hills, CA 90212, USA
Adair, Paul N (Red) *Oil Well Fire Fighter*
%Adair Enterprise, PO Box 747, Bellville, TX 77418, USA
Adam, Robert *Architect*
%Winchester Design, 9 Upper High St, Winchester, Hants SO23 8UT, England
Adam, Theo *Opera Singer*
Schillerstr 14, 01326 Dresden, Germany
Adamek, Donna *Bowler*
%Ladies Professional Bowling Tour, 7200 Harrison Ave, #7171, Rockford, IL 61112, USA
Adamle, Mike *Football Player, Sportscaster*
%ESPN-TV, Sports Dept, ESPN Plaza, 935 Middle St, Bristol, CT 06010, USA
Adams Beckham, Victoria *Singer (Spice Girls)*
%Lee & Thompson, 15 Saint Christopher's Place, London W1M 5HE, England
Adams, Amy *Actress*
%Baker/Winokur/Ryder, 9100 Wilshire Blvd, #600, Beverly Hills, CA 90212, USA
Adams, Brock *Secretary, Transportation; Senator, WA*
138 Tanners Point Dr, Stevensville, MD 21666, USA
Adams, Brooke *Actress*
248 S Van Ness Ave, Los Angeles, CA 90004, USA
Adams, Bryan *Singer, Guitarist, Songwriter*
%Bruce Allen Talent, 500-425 Carrall St, Vancouver BC V6B 6E3, Canada
Adams, Don *Actor*
2160 Century Park East, #110, Los Angeles, CA 90067, USA
Adams, Edie *Actress*
8040 Ocean Terrace, Los Angeles, CA 90046, USA
Adams, Edward (Eddie) *Photojournalist*
%Eddie Adams Inc, 538 E 11th St, New York, NY 10009, USA
Adams, Evan *Actor*
%Charactors Agency, 1505 W 2nd Ave, #200, Vancouver BC V6H 3Y4, Canada
Adams, George R *Jazz Saxophonist, Flutist*
%Joel Chriss, 300 Mercer St, #3J, New York, NY 10003, USA
Adams, Gerard (Gerry) *Political Leader, Northern Ireland*
%Sinn Fein/IRA, 51/55 Falls Road, Belfast BT 12, Northern Ireland
Adams, Hunter Patch *Physician*
%Gesundheit Institute, PO Box 288, Hillsboro, WV 24946, USA
Adams, Jane *Actress*
320 Rosebriar Lane, Ellensburg, WA 98926, USA
Adams, Joey Lauren *Actress*
8447 Wilshire Blvd, #200, Beverly Hills, CA 90211, USA
Adams, John C *Composer*
%Elektra Records, 75 Rockefeller Plaza, New York, NY 10019, USA
Adams, Jonathan *Actor*
%Crouch Assoc, 59 Firth St, London W1V 5TA, England
Adams, Julie *Actress*
5915 Corbin Ave, Tarzana, CA 91356, USA
Adams, Julius T *Football Player, Coach*
2135 Jefferson Davis St, Macon, GA 31206, USA
Adams, Kenneth S (Bud) *Football Executive*
%Tennessee Titans, 460 Great Circle Road, Nashville, TN 37228, USA
Adams, Kim *Actress*
%L A Talent, 8335 Sunset Blvd, #200, Los Angeles, CA 90069, USA
Adams, Lorraine *Journalist*
%Washington Post, Editorial Dept, 1150 15th St, Washington, DC 20071, USA

Adams, Mark *Artist*
3816 22nd St, San Francisco, CA 94114, USA
Adams, Marla *Actress*
247 S Beverly Dr, #102, Beverly Hills, CA 90212, USA
Adams, Mary Kay *Actress*
%Roe Enterprises, PO Box 2023, Fairfield, IA 52556, USA
Adams, Mason *Actor*
570 Park Ave, #9B, New York, NY 10021, USA
Adams, Maud *Actress*
PO Box 10838, Beverly Hills, CA 90213, USA
Adams, Michael F *Educator*
%University of Georgia, President's Office, Athens, GA 30602, USA
Adams, Noah *Commentator*
%National Public Radio, 635 Massachusetts Ave NW, Washington, DC 20001, USA
Adams, Oleta *Singer*
%Engine Entertainment, 4840 Peninsula Pointe Dr, Hermitage, TN 37076, USA
Adams, Pat *Artist*
370 Elm St, Bennington, VT 05201, USA
Adams, Ranald T, Jr *Air Force General*
1002 Emerald Dr, Alexandria, VA 22308, USA
Adams, Richard G *Writer*
%Benwell's, 26 Church St, Whitechurch, Hants RG28 7AR, England
Adams, Richard N *Anthropologist*
PO Box ZZ, Basalt, CO 81621, USA
Adams, Ryan *Singer, Songwriter*
%High Road, 751 Bridgeway, #300, Sausalito, CA 94965, USA
Adams, Sam E *Football Player*
12010 Holly Stone Dr, Houston, TX 77070, USA
Adams, Scott *Cartoonist (Dilbert)*
%Harper Business Publishers, 10 E 53rd St, New York, NY 10022, USA
Adams, Terry *Pianist, Clarinet Player (NRBQ)*
%Skyline Music, PO Box 31, Lancaster, NH 03584, USA
Adams, Trace *Singer*
%Borman, 1222 16th Ave S, #23, Nashville, TN 37212, USA
Adams, Yolanda *Singer*
%Mahogany Entertainment, PO Box 4367, Upper Marboro, MD 20775, USA
Adams-Sassoon, Beverly *Model*
1923 Selby Ave, #203, Los Angeles, CA 90025, USA
Adamson, James C *Astronaut*
16459 Frederick Road, Woodbine, MD 21797, USA
Adamson, Robert E, Jr *Navy Admiral*
1801 Patriots Colony Dr, Williamsburg, VA 23188, USA
Adderly, Herbert A (Herb) *Football Player*
1058 Tristam Circle, Mantua, NJ 08051, USA
Addis, Don *Cartoonist (Bent Offerings)*
%Creators Syndicate, 5777 W Century Blvd, #700, Los Angeles, CA 90045, USA
Addy, Mark *Actor*
%International Creative Mgmt, 8942 Wilshire Blvd, #219, Beverly Hills, CA 90211, USA
Ade, King Sunny *Singer*
%Monterey International, 200 W Superior, #202, Chicago, IL 60610, USA
Adelman, Kenneth L *Government Official*
%Int'l Contemporary Studies Institute, 4018 27th St N, Arlington, VA 22207, USA
Adelman, Rick *Basketball Player, Coach*
1905 Lane Ave NE, Salem, OR 97314, USA
Adey, Christopher *Conductor*
137 Anson Road, Willesden Green NW2 4AH, England
Adjani, Isabelle *Actress*
%Agence Intertalent, 5 Rue Clement Marot, 75008 Paris, France
Adjodhia, Jules *Prime Minister, Suriname*
%Prime Minister's Office, Kleine Combeweg 1, Paramaribo, Suriname
Adkins, Trace *Singer*
%Borman Entertainment, 1222 16th Ave S, #23, Nashville, TN 37212, USA
Adkisson, Perry L *Etomologist, Educator*
9211 Lake Forest Court N, College Station, TX 77845, USA
Adleman, Leonard *Computer Scientist*
%University of Southern California, Computer Math Dept, Los Angeles, CA 90089, USA
Adler, Brian *Composer*
%Gorfaine/Schwartz, 13245 Riverside Dr, #450, Sherman Oaks, CA 91423, USA
Adler, Charles *Actor*
%Arlene Thornton Assoc, 12001 Ventura Place, #20, Studio City, CA 91604, USA
Adler, Lee *Artist*
Lime Kiln Farm, Climax, NY 12042, USA
Adler, Lou *Actor, Movie Director, Producer*
%Ode Sounds & Visuals, 3969 Villa Costera, Malibu, CA 90265, USA
Adler, Richard *Composer, Lyricist*
PO Box 1151, Southampton, NY 11969, USA
Adler, Stephen L *Physicist*
%Institute for Advanced Study, Einstein Lane, Princeton, NJ 08540, USA

Adler, Steven *Drummer (Guns n' Roses)*
%Big FD Entertainment, 301 Arizona Ave, #200, Santa Monica, CA 90401, USA
Adni, Daniel *Concert Pianist*
64A Menelik Road, London NW2 3RH, England
Adoboli, Koffi Eugene *Prime Minister, Togo*
%Prime Minister's Office, BP 5618, Lome, Togo
Adoor, Gopalakrishnan *Movie Director*
Darsanam, Trivandrum, 695 017 Kerala, India
Adotta, Kip *Actor, Comedian*
PO Box 5734, Santa Rosa, CA 95402, USA
Adria, Ferran *Chef*
%El Bulli, En Cala Montjoi Roses, 17480 Girona, Spain
Adyrkhayeva, Svetlana D *Ballerina*
1 Smolensky Pereulor 9, #74, 121099 Moscow, Russia
Aerle Taree *Soul/Rap Artist (Arrested Development)*
%William Morris Agency, 1325 Ave of Americas, New York, NY 10019, USA
Afanasiyev, Viktor M *Cosmonaut*
%Potchta Kosmonavtov, Moskovskoi Oblasti, 141160 Syvisdny Goroduk, Russia
Affleck, Ben *Actor*
%Endeavor Talent Agency, 9701 Wilshire Blvd, #1000, Beverly Hills, CA 90212, USA
Affleck, Casey *Actor*
%Creative Artists Agency, 9830 Wilshire Blvd, Beverly Hills, CA 90212, USA
Affleck, James G *Businessman*
%American Cyanamid, 5 Giralda Farms, Madison, NJ 07940, USA
Afinogenov, Maxim *Hockey Player*
%Buffalo Sabres, HSBC Arena, 1 Seymour St, Buffalo, NY 14210, USA
Afroman *Rap Artist*
%Crescent Moon, 20 Music Square W, Nashville, TN 37203, USA
Afwerki, Isaias *President, Eritrea*
%State Council, Asmara, Eritrea
Aga Khan IV, Prince Karim *Spiritual Leader*
Aiglemont, 60270 Gouvieux, France
Agajanian, Benjamin (Ben) *Football Player*
5251 E Los Altos Plaza, Long Beach, CA 90815, USA
Agam, Yaacov *Artist*
26 Rue Boulard, 75014 Paris, France
Agase, Alexander G (Alex) *Football Player, Coach*
1281 Pine Ridge Circle E, #G1, Tarpon Springs, FL 34688, USA
Agassi, Andre *Tennis Player*
8921 Andre Dr, Las Vegas, NV 89148, USA
Aghayan, Ray *Costume Designer*
431 S Fairfax Ave, #3, Los Angeles, CA 90036, USA
Agnelli, Umberto *Businessman*
Corsp Mateotti 26, 10121 Turin, Italy
Agnelo, Geraldo Majella Cardinal *Religious Leader*
Rua Martin Alfonso de Souza 270, 40100-050 Salvador BA, Brazil
Agnew, Harold M *Physicist*
322 Punta Baja Dr, Solana Beach, CA 92075, USA
Agoos, Jeff *Soccer Player*
4628 Buckhorn Ridge, Fairfax, VA 22030, USA
Agostini, Didier *Actor*
%Cineart, 36 Rue de Ponthieu, 75008 Paris, France
Agranoff, Bernard W *Biochemist*
1942 Boulder Dr, Ann Arbor, MI 48104, USA
Agre, Bernard Cardinal *Religious Leader*
Archeveche, Ave Jean-Paul II, 01 BP 1287, Abidjan, Ivory Coast
Agre, Peter *Nobel Chemistry Laureate*
7033 Lenleigh Road, Baltimore, MD 21212, USA
Agt, Andries A M Van *Prime Minister, Netherlands*
Europa House, 9-15 Sanbancho, Chiyodaku, Tokyo 102, Japan
Aguilar, Pepe *Singer*
%Agency Group Ltd, 1775 Broadway, #430, New York, NY 10019, USA
Aguilera, Christina *Singer, Songwriter*
%Irving Azoff, 1100 Glendon Ave, #2000, Los Angeles, CA 90024, USA
Aguilera, Richard W (Rick) *Baseball Player*
PO Box 174, Rancho Santa Fe, CA 92067, USA
Aguilera-Hellweg, Max *Photographer*
144 Magazine St, #3, Cambridge, MA 02139, USA
Aguirre, Mark A *Basketball Player, Executive*
%LifeCast.com, Park Central II, 12750 Merit Dr, #1020, Dallas, TX 75251, USA
Agustoni, Gilberto Cardinal *Religious Leader*
Piazzi della Citta Leonina 9, 00193 Rome, Italy
Agutter, Jenny *Actress*
73930 Shadow Lake Dr, Palm Desert, CA 92260, USA
Ahearn, Kevin *Hockey Player*
174 Marlborough St, Boston, MA 02116, USA
Ahern, Bertie *Prime Minister, Ireland*
%Prime Minister's Office, Upper Merrion St, Dublin 2, Ireland

A

Ahmed - Al-Hoss

Ahmed, Kazi Zafar *Prime Minister, Bangladesh*
%Jatiya Sangsad, Dhaka, Bangladesh
Ahmed, Shahabuddin *President, Bangladesh; Judge*
%President's Office, Old Sangsad Bhaban, Bangabhaban, Dhaka 2, Bangladesh
Aho, Esko *Prime Minister, Finland*
%Centre Party, Pursimiehenkatu 15, 00150 Helsinki, Finland
Ahrens, Lynn *Lyricist*
%William Morris Agency, 151 El Camino Dr, Beverly Hills, CA 90212, USA
Ahrens, Thomas J *Geophysicist*
%California Institute of Technology, Seismology Laboratory, Pasadena, CA 91125, USA
Ahronovitch, Yuri *Conductor*
%Stockholm Philharmonic, Hotorget 8, Stockholm, Sweden
Aida, Takefumi *Architect*
1-3-2 Okubo, Shinjukuku, Tokyo 169, Japan
Aiello, Danny *Actor*
30 Chestnut Ridge Road, Saddle River, NJ 07458, USA
Aikman, Laura Holly *Actress*
551 Green Lanes, Palmers Green, London N13 3DR, England
Aikman, Troy K *Football Player, Sportscaster*
325 Brock St, Coppell, TX 75019, USA
Ailes, Roger E *Businessman*
218 Truman Dr, Cresskill, NJ 07626, USA
Aimee, Anouk *Actress*
%ICM France, 37 Rue de Acacias, 75017 Paris, France
Aimi, Milton *Soccer Player*
5703 W Bellfort St, Houston, TX 77035, USA
Ainge, Daniel R (Danny) *Basketball Player, Coach*
140 Wellesley Ave, Wellesley Hills, MA 02481, USA
Ainsleigh, H Gordon *Track Athlete*
17119 Placer Hills Road, Meadow Vista, CA 95722, USA
Ainslie, Ben *Yachtsman*
%RYA House, Romsey Road, Eastleigh, Hampshire S050 9YA, England
Ainsworth, Kurt *Baseball Player*
6317 Hope Estate Dr, Baton Rouge, LA 70820, USA
Aitay, Victor *Concert Violinist*
800 Deerfield Road, #203, Highland Park, IL 60035, USA
Aitken, John *Sculptor*
%University College, Slade Art School, London WC1E 6BT, England
Aitmatov, Chingiz T *Writer*
Ulitsa Toktogulstz 98, #9, 720000 Bishkek, Kyrgyzstan
Aizenberg Selove, Fay *Physicist*
118 Cherry Lane, Wynnewood, PA 19096, USA
Akayev, Askar *President, Kyrgyzstan*
%President's Office, Government House, 720003 Bishkek, Kyrgyzstan
Akbar, Taufik *Astronaut, Indonesia*
Jalan Simp, Pahlawan III/24, Bandung 40124, Indonesia
Akebono *Sumo Wrestler*
%Azumazeki Stable, 4-6-4 Higashi Komagata, Ryogoku, Tokyo, Japan
Akerlof, George A *Nobel Economics Laureate*
%University of California, Economics Dept, Evans Hall, Berkeley, CA 94720, USA
Akers, Fred *Football Coach*
%Purdue University, Athletic Dept, West Lafayette, IN 47907, USA
Akers, John F *Businessman*
PO Box 194, Pebble Beach, CA 93953, USA
Akers, Michelle *Soccer Player*
%SOI, 2875 S Orange Ave, #500, Orlando, FL 32806, USA
Akers, Thomas D (Tom) *Astronaut*
11770 Timberline Dr, Rolla, MO 65401, USA
Akerson, Daniel F *Businessman*
%Nextel Communications, 2001 Edmund Halley Dr, Reston, VA 20191, USA
Akihito *Emperor, Japan*
%Imperial Palace, 1-1 Chiyoda, Chiyodaku, Tokyo 100, Japan
Akins, Rhett *Singer*
%RPM Mgmt, 209 10th Ave S, #229, Nashville, TN 37203, USA
Akiyama, Kazuyoshi *Conductor*
%Columbia Artists Mgmt Inc, 165 W 57th St, New York, NY 10019, USA
Akiyama, Toyohiro *Astronaut, Journalist*
%Tokyo Broadcasting Systems, 3-6-5 Akasaka, Minatoku, Tokyo 107, Japan
Akiyoshi, Toshiko *Jazz Pianist, Composer, Bandleader*
%Berkeley Agency, 2608 9th St, Berkeley, CA 94710, USA
Akoshino *Princess, Japan*
%Imperial Palace, Tokyo, Japan
Aksyonov, Vassily P *Writer*
%Random House, 1745 Broadway, #B1, New York, NY 10019, USA
Aksyonov, Vladimir V *Cosmonaut*
Astrakhansky Per 5, Kv 100, 129010 Moscow, Russia
Al-Hoss, Selim *Prime Minister, Lebanon*
%Premier's Office, Serail, Place de l'Etoile, Beirut, Lebanon

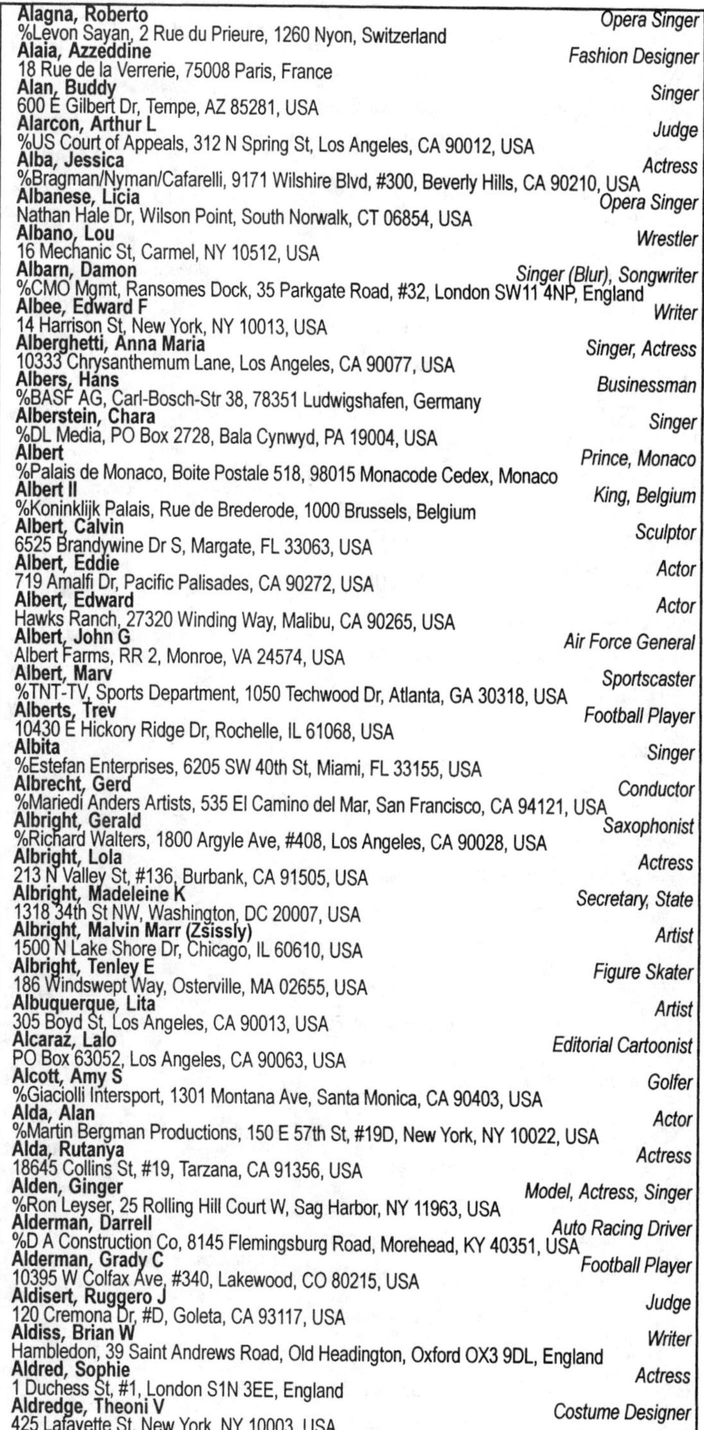

Alagna, Roberto *Opera Singer*
%Levon Sayan, 2 Rue du Prieure, 1260 Nyon, Switzerland
Alaia, Azzeddine *Fashion Designer*
18 Rue de la Verrerie, 75008 Paris, France
Alan, Buddy *Singer*
600 E Gilbert Dr, Tempe, AZ 85281, USA
Alarcon, Arthur L *Judge*
%US Court of Appeals, 312 N Spring St, Los Angeles, CA 90012, USA
Alba, Jessica *Actress*
%Bragman/Nyman/Cafarelli, 9171 Wilshire Blvd, #300, Beverly Hills, CA 90210, USA
Albanese, Licia *Opera Singer*
Nathan Hale Dr, Wilson Point, South Norwalk, CT 06854, USA
Albano, Lou *Wrestler*
16 Mechanic St, Carmel, NY 10512, USA
Albarn, Damon *Singer (Blur), Songwriter*
%CMO Mgmt, Ransomes Dock, 35 Parkgate Road, #32, London SW11 4NP, England
Albee, Edward F *Writer*
14 Harrison St, New York, NY 10013, USA
Alberghetti, Anna Maria *Singer, Actress*
10333 Chrysanthemum Lane, Los Angeles, CA 90077, USA
Albers, Hans *Businessman*
%BASF AG, Carl-Bosch-Str 38, 78351 Ludwigshafen, Germany
Alberstein, Chara *Singer*
%DL Media, PO Box 2728, Bala Cynwyd, PA 19004, USA
Albert *Prince, Monaco*
%Palais de Monaco, Boite Postale 518, 98015 Monacode Cedex, Monaco
Albert II *King, Belgium*
%Koninklijk Palais, Rue de Brederode, 1000 Brussels, Belgium
Albert, Calvin *Sculptor*
6525 Brandywine Dr S, Margate, FL 33063, USA
Albert, Eddie *Actor*
719 Amalfi Dr, Pacific Palisades, CA 90272, USA
Albert, Edward *Actor*
Hawks Ranch, 27320 Winding Way, Malibu, CA 90265, USA
Albert, John G *Air Force General*
Albert Farms, RR 2, Monroe, VA 24574, USA
Albert, Marv *Sportscaster*
%TNT-TV, Sports Department, 1050 Techwood Dr, Atlanta, GA 30318, USA
Alberts, Trev *Football Player*
10430 E Hickory Ridge Dr, Rochelle, IL 61068, USA
Albita *Singer*
%Estefan Enterprises, 6205 SW 40th St, Miami, FL 33155, USA
Albrecht, Gerd *Conductor*
%Mariedi Anders Artists, 535 El Camino del Mar, San Francisco, CA 94121, USA
Albright, Gerald *Saxophonist*
%Richard Walters, 1800 Argyle Ave, #408, Los Angeles, CA 90028, USA
Albright, Lola *Actress*
213 N Valley St, #136, Burbank, CA 91505, USA
Albright, Madeleine K *Secretary, State*
1318 34th St NW, Washington, DC 20007, USA
Albright, Malvin Marr (Zsissly) *Artist*
1500 N Lake Shore Dr, Chicago, IL 60610, USA
Albright, Tenley E *Figure Skater*
186 Windswept Way, Osterville, MA 02655, USA
Albuquerque, Lita *Artist*
305 Boyd St, Los Angeles, CA 90013, USA
Alcaraz, Lalo *Editorial Cartoonist*
PO Box 63052, Los Angeles, CA 90063, USA
Alcott, Amy S *Golfer*
%Giaciolli Intersport, 1301 Montana Ave, Santa Monica, CA 90403, USA
Alda, Alan *Actor*
%Martin Bergman Productions, 150 E 57th St, #19D, New York, NY 10022, USA
Alda, Rutanya *Actress*
18645 Collins St, #19, Tarzana, CA 91356, USA
Alden, Ginger *Model, Actress, Singer*
%Ron Leyser, 25 Rolling Hill Court W, Sag Harbor, NY 11963, USA
Alderman, Darrell *Auto Racing Driver*
%D A Construction Co, 8145 Flemingsburg Road, Morehead, KY 40351, USA
Alderman, Grady C *Football Player*
10395 W Colfax Ave, #340, Lakewood, CO 80215, USA
Aldisert, Ruggero J *Judge*
120 Cremona Dr, #D, Goleta, CA 93117, USA
Aldiss, Brian W *Writer*
Hambledon, 39 Saint Andrews Road, Old Headington, Oxford OX3 9DL, England
Aldred, Sophie *Actress*
1 Duchess St, #1, London S1N 3EE, England
Aldredge, Theoni V *Costume Designer*
425 Lafayette St, New York, NY 10003, USA

A

Aldrich - Alfaro

Aldrich, Lance *Cartoonist*
%Universal Press Syndicate, 4520 Main St, Kansas City, MO 64111, USA
Aldridge, Donald O *Air Force General*
1004 Lincoln Road, #168, Bellevue, NE 68005, USA
Aldridge, Edward C (Pete), Jr *Government Official*
%Aerospace Corp, 2350 E El Segundo Blvd, El Segundo, CA 90245, USA
Aldrin, Edwin E (Buzz), Jr *Astronaut*
%NASA, 400 Maryland Ave SW, Washington, DC 20202, USA
Aleandro, Norma *Actress*
Blanco Encalada 1150, 1428 Buenos Aires, Argentina
Alechinsky, Pierre *Artist*
2 Bis Rue Henri Barbusse, 78380 Bougival, France
Aleksiy II *Religious Leader*
%Moscow Patriarchy, Chisty Per 5, 119034 Moscow, Russia
Alerlof, George *Nobel Economics Laureate*
%University of California, Economics Dept, Berkeley, CA 94720, USA
Alesi, Jean *Auto Racing Driver*
%HWA GmbH, Benzstr 8, 71563 Affalterbach, Germany
Aletter, Frank *Actor*
5430 Corbin Ave, Tarzana, CA 91356, USA
Alexakis, Art *Singer (Everclear)*
%Pinnacle Entertainment, 30 Glenn St, White Plains, NY 10603, USA
Alexander *Crown Prince, Yugoslavia*
36 Park Lane, London W1Y 3LE, England
Alexander of Weedon, Robert S *Financier*
%National Westminster Bank, 41 Lothbury, London EC2P 2BP, England
Alexander, A Lamar *Secretary, Education; Governor; Senator*
2233 Blue Springs Road, Ashland City, TN 37015, USA
Alexander, Bruce E *Football Player*
508 Englewood Dr, Lufkin, TX 75901, USA
Alexander, Christopher W J *Architect*
2701 Shasta Road, Berkeley, CA 94708, USA
Alexander, Clifford L, Jr *Government Official*
412 A St SE, Washington, DC 20003, USA
Alexander, Corey *Basketball Player*
440 Alpha St, Waynesboro, VA 22980, USA
Alexander, Denise *Actress*
270 N Canon Dr, #1919, Beverly Hills, CA 90210, USA
Alexander, Derrick S *Football Player*
18508 Monte Vista St, Detroit, MI 48221, USA
Alexander, Eric *Saxophonist*
%Joel Chriss, 300 Mercer St, #3J, New York, NY 10003, USA
Alexander, Erika *Actress*
%Innovative Artists, 1505 10th St, Santa Monica, CA 90401, USA
Alexander, Jane *Actress, Government Official*
%William Morris Agency, 1325 Ave of Americas, New York, NY 10019, USA
Alexander, Jason *Actor*
%Baker/Winokur/Ryder, 9100 Wilshire Blvd, #600, Beverly Hills, CA 90212, USA
Alexander, Jules *Musician (Association)*
%Variety Artists, 1924 Spring St, Paso Robles, CA 93446, USA
Alexander, Khandi *Actress*
%Innovative Artists, 1505 10th St, Santa Monica, CA 90401, USA
Alexander, Lloyd *Writer*
1005 Drexel Hills Blvd, New Cumberland, PA 17070, USA
Alexander, Monty *Jazz Pianist*
%Bennett Morgan, 1282 RR 376, Wappingers Falls, NY 12590, USA
Alexander, R Minter *Air Force General*
824 Eden Court, Alexandria, VA 22308, USA
Alexander, Robert M *Zoologist*
14 Moor Park Mount, Leeds LS6 4BU, England
Alexander, Sasha *Actress*
%Endeavor Talent Agency, 9701 Wilshire Blvd, #1000, Beverly Hills, CA 90212, USA
Alexander, Shana *Journalist*
PO Box 429, Wainscott, NY 11975, USA
Alexander, Shaun *Football Player*
%Seattle Seahawks, 11220 NE 53rd St, Kirkland, WA 98033, USA
Alexander, Victor *Basketball Player*
8405 Holcomb Bridge Road, Alpharetta, GA 30022, USA
Alexander, Willie *Bassist, Guitarist (Velvet Underground)*
%Toumaline Music Group, 894 Mayville Road, Bethel, PA 04217, USA
Alexandrov, Alexander P *Cosmonaut*
Hovanskaya Ul 3, #27, 129515 Moscow, Russia
Alexie, Sherman *Writer*
PO Box 376, Wellpinit, WA 99040, USA
Alexis, Kim *Model*
2219 W Olive Ave, PO Box 10038, Burbank, CA 91506, USA
Alfaro, Victor *Fashion Designer*
130 Barrow St, New York, NY 10014, USA

Alferov, Zhores *Nobel Physics Laureate*
%Ioffe Institute, 26 Polytekhnicheskaya, 194021 Saint Petersburg, Russia
Alfieri, Janet *Cartoonist (Suburban Cowgirls)*
15 Bumpus Road, Plymouth, MA 02360, USA
Alfonso, Kristian *Actress*
%Metropolitan Talent Agency, 4526 Wilshire Blvd, Los Angeles, CA 90010, USA
Alford, Steve *Basketball Player, Coach*
831 Forest Hill Dr, Coralville, IA 52241, USA
Alford, William *Writer*
150 Federal St, #2600, Boston, MA 02110, USA
Alfredsson, Helen *Golfer*
%Int'l Mgmt Group, 1 Erieview Plaza, 1360 E 9th St, #1300, Cleveland, OH 44114, USA
Algabid, Hamid *Premier, Niger*
%National Assembly, Vice President's Office, Niamey, Niger
Ali, Laila *Boxer*
PO Box 491246, Los Angeles, CA 90049, USA
Ali, Muhammad *Boxer*
Ali Farm, PO Box 187, Berrien Springs, MI 49103, USA
Ali, Tatyana *Singer, Actress*
%Evolution Talent, 1776 Broadway, #1500, New York, NY 10019, USA
Alis, Robert *Cinematographer*
13920 72nd Road, Flushing, NY 11367, USA
Alisha *Singer*
1168 E 73rd St, Brooklyn, NY 11234, USA
Alison, Jane *Writer*
%Farrar Straus Giroux, 19 Union Square W, New York, NY 10003, USA
Alito, Samuel A, Jr *Judge*
%US Court of Appeals, US Courthouse, 50 Walnut St, Newark, NJ 07102, USA
Aliyev, Ilham *President, Azerbaijan*
%President's Office, 370066 Baku, Azerbaijan
Allain, William A *Governor, MS*
970 Morningside St, Jackson, MS 39202, USA
Allais, Maurice *Nobel Economics Laureate*
60 Blvd Saint-Michel, 75006 Paris, France
Allan, Gary *Singer*
%Lytle Management Group, 1101 18th Ave S, Nashville, TN 37212, USA
Allan, Jed *Actor*
76740 Minaret Way, Palm Desert, CA 92211, USA
Allan, Stephen D (Steve) *Golfer*
%Gaylord Sports Mgmt, 14646 N Kierland Blvd, #230, Scottsdale, AZ 85254, USA
Allard, Linda M *Fashion Designer*
%Ellen Tracy Corp, 575 Fashion Ave, New York, NY 10018, USA
Allbaugh, Joseph *Government Official*
%Federal Emergency Management Agency, 500 C St SW, Washington, DC 20472, USA
Allegre, Claude J *Geochemist*
%Recherce/Technolologie Institute, 110 Rue Grenelle, 75700 Paris, France
Allem, Fulton P *Golfer*
%Professional Golfer's Assn, PO Box 109601, Palm Beach Gardens, FL 33410, USA
Allen, Andrew M *Astronaut*
762 Killarney Court, Merritt Island, FL 32953, USA
Allen, Betty *Concert, Opera Singer*
%Harlem School of Arts, 645 Saint Nicholas Ave, New York, NY 10030, USA
Allen, Bruce *Auto Racing Driver*
%Reger-Morrison Racing Engines, 1120 Enterprise Place, Arlington, TX 76001, USA
Allen, C Keith *Hockey Executive*
10000 Highland Ave, Long Beach Township, NJ 08008, USA
Allen, Carl *Harness Racing Driver, Owner*
%Golden Cross Farm, 12662 NY Highway 27, Ocala, FL 32675, USA
Allen, Chad *Actor*
6926 Pacific View Dr, Los Angeles, CA 90068, USA
Allen, Clarence R *Geologist*
1763 Royal Oaks Dr, #F207, Duarte, CA 91010, USA
Allen, Corey *Actor, Director*
8642 Hollywood Blvd, Los Angeles, CA 90069, USA
Allen, Danielle Sherie *Actress*
%Privilege Agency, 9229 Sunset Blvd, Los Angeles, CA 90069, USA
Allen, Debbie *Dancer, Singer, Actress*
607 Marguerita Ave, Santa Monica, CA 90402, USA
Allen, Deborah *Singer*
%Morningstar, 595 Hicks Road, #3B, Nashville, TN 37221, USA
Allen, Duane D *Singer (Oak Ridge Boys)*
88 New Shackle Island Road, Hendersonville, TN 37075, USA
Allen, Frances E *Computer Scientist*
Finney Farm, Croton on Hudson, NY 10520, USA
Allen, George F *Senator, Governor, VA*
PO Box 17704, Richmond, VA 23226, USA
Allen, Geri *Jazz Pianist, Composer*
%Clayton Ross Productions, 307 Lake St, San Francisco, CA 94118, USA

A

Allen, Henry *Critic*
%Washington Post, Editorial Dept, 1150 15th St NW, Washington, DC 20071, USA
Allen, Joan *Actress*
%International Creative Mgmt, 8942 Wilshire Blvd, #219, Beverly Hills, CA 90211, USA
Allen, Joseph P, IV *Astronaut*
%Veridian, 1200 S Hayes St, #1100, Arlington, VA 22202, USA
Allen, Karen *Actress*
PO Box 237, Monterey, MA 01245, USA
Allen, Kevin *Movie Director*
%William Morris Agency, 52/53 Poland Place, London W1F 7LX, England
Allen, Krista *Actress*
%Stone Manners, 6500 Wilshire Blvd, #550, Los Angeles, CA 90048, USA
Allen, Larry C *Football Player*
2001 Piner Road, Santa Rosa, CA 95403, USA
Allen, Lew, Jr *Air Force General*
%Draper Laboratory, 555 Technology Square, Cambridge, MA 02139, USA
Allen, Loy, Jr *Auto Racing Driver*
3197 Steamboat Ridge Road, Port Orange, FL 32128, USA
Allen, Marcus L *Football Player, Sportscaster*
%CBS-TV, Sports Dept, 51 W 52nd St, New York, NY 10019, USA
Allen, Marty *Actor, Comedian*
8704 Carlitas Joy Court, Las Vegas, NV 89117, USA
Allen, Maryon P *Senator, AL*
3215 Cliff Road, Birmingham, AL 35205, USA
Allen, Nancy *Actress*
%Creative Artists Agency, 9830 Wilshire Blvd, Beverly Hills, CA 90212, USA
Allen, Nancy *Concert Harpist*
%Columbia Artists Mgmt Inc, 165 W 57th St, New York, NY 10019, USA
Allen, Pam *Golfer*
809 Delphinium Dr, Billings, MT 59102, USA
Allen, Paul G *Co-Developer (PC Language)*
%Vulcan Northwest, 505 5th Ave S, #900, Seattle, WA 98104, USA
Allen, Ray *Basketball Player, Actor*
2095 Hillside Dr, Storrs Mansfield, CT 06269, USA
Allen, Rex, Jr *Singer*
209 10th Ave, #527, Nashville, TN 37203, USA
Allen, Richard A (Richie) *Baseball Player*
RR 2, Possum Hollow Road, Wampum, PA 16157, USA
Allen, Richard J (Rick) *Drummer (Def Leppard)*
%Q Prime Mgmt, 729 7th Ave, #1400, New York, NY 10019, USA
Allen, Richard V *Government Official*
905 16th St NW, Washington, DC 20006, USA
Allen, Robert E *Businessman*
60 Stewart Road, Short Hills, NJ 07078, USA
Allen, Rosalind *Actress*
%Agency for Performing Arts, 9200 Sunset Blvd, #900, Los Angeles, CA 90069, USA
Allen, Scott *Figure Skater*
40 Brayton St, Englewood, NJ 07631, USA
Allen, Sian Barbara *Actress*
732 S Plymouth Blvd, #E, Los Angeles, CA 90005, USA
Allen, Thomas B *Opera Singer*
%I C M Artists, 40 W 57th St, New York, NY 10019, USA
Allen, Tim *Actor, Comedian*
%Messina Baker Entertainment, 955 Carillo Dr, #100, Los Angeles, CA 90048, USA
Allen, William L *Editor*
%National Geographic Magazine, 17th & M NW, Washington, DC 20036, USA
Allen, Woody *Actor, Comedian, Director*
48 E 92nd St, New York, NY 10128, USA
Allenby, Robert *Golfer*
%Masters Int'l, Hurst Grove, Sanford Lane, Hurts, Berks RG10 0SQ, England
Allende, Fernando *Actor*
%William Morris Agency, 151 El Camino Dr, Beverly Hills, CA 90212, USA
Allende, Isabel *Writer*
92 Fernwood Dr, San Rafael, CA 94901, USA
Alley, Alphonse *President, Benin; Army Officer*
Carre 181-182, BP 48, Cotonou, Benin
Alley, Kirstie *Actress*
%Untitled Entertainment, 8436 W 3rd St, #650, Los Angeles, CA 90048, USA
Alley, L Eugene (Gene) *Baseball Player*
10236 Steuben Dr, Glen Allen, VA 23060, USA
Allimadi, E Otema *Prime Minister, Uganda*
PO Box Gulu, Gulu District, Uganda
Allison, Brooke *Singer, Songwriter*
%2K/EMI America Records, 6920 Sunset Blvd, Los Angeles, CA 90028, USA
Allison, Dave *Hockey Coach*
PO Box 1416, International Falls, MN 56649, USA
Allison, Donnie *Auto Racing Driver*
355 Quail Dr, Salisbury, NC 28147, USA

Allison, Glenn *Bowler*
1844 S Haster St, #138, Anaheim, CA 92802, USA
Allison, Herbert M *Businessman*
%TIAA-CREF, 730 3rd Ave, New York, NY 10017, USA
Allison, Jerry *Drummer (Crickets), Songwriter*
%Gold Mountain, 3575 Cahuenga Blvd W, #450, Los Angeles, CA 90068, USA
Allison, John A, IV *Financier*
%BB&T Corp, 200 W 2nd St, Winston Salem, NC 27101, USA
Allison, John V *Vietnam War Air Force Hero*
2007 Banshore Dr, Niceville, FL 32578, USA
Allison, Mose J, Jr *Jazz Pianist, Composer, Singer*
34 Dogwood Dr, Smithtown, NY 11787, USA
Allison, Richard C *Judge*
24 Circle Dr, Manhasset, NY 11030, USA
Allison, Stacy *Mountaineer*
7003 SE Reed College Place, Portland, OR 97202, USA
Allman, Greg *Singer, Musician, Songwriter*
%Allman Brothers Band Inc, 18 Tamworth Road, Waban, MA 02468, USA
Allnutt, Robert *Space Scientist, Biochemist*
5400 Edgemoor Lane, Bethesda, MD 20814, USA
Allouache, Merzak *Movie Director*
Cite des Asphodeles, Bt D15, 183 Ben Aknoun, Algiers, Algeria
Allport, Chris M *Actor*
1324 Pine St, Santa Monica, CA 90405, USA
Allred, Gloria R *Attorney*
%Allred Maroko Goldberg, 6300 Wilshire Blvd, #1500, Los Angeles, CA 90048, USA
Allsup, Mike *Guitarist (Three Dog Night)*
%McKenzie Accountancy, 5171 Caliente St, #134, Las Vegas, NV 89119, USA
Allsup, Tommy *Guitarist (Crickets)*
%Tophands Talent, PO Box 1547, Arlington, TX 76004, USA
Allyson, June *Actress*
1651 Foothill Road, Ojai, CA 93023, USA
Almodovar, Pedro *Movie Director*
El Deseo SA, Ruiz Perello 25, 28028 Madrid, Spain
Almond, Marc *Singer*
%Take Out Productions, 630 9th Ave, #216, New York, NY 10036, USA
Almunia Amann, Joaquin *Government Official, Spain*
Plaza de las Cortes, #9, 4A Planta, 28014 Madrid, Spain
Alois *Hereditary-Prince, Liechtenstein*
%Schloss Vaduz, 9490 Vaduz, Liechtenstein
Alomar, Roberto V (Robbie) *Baseball Player*
3803 54th Dr W, #103, Bradenton, FL 34210, USA
Alomar, Santos C (Sandy), Jr *Baseball Player*
PO Box 367, Salinas, PR 00751, USA
Alonso, Alicia *Ballerina*
Calzada 510 Entre D & E, CP 10400, El Vedada, Havana, Cuba
Alonso, Maria Conchita *Actress, Singer*
118 S Beverly Dr, #201, Beverly Hills, CA 90212, USA
Alou, Felipe R *Baseball Player, Manager*
80119 Heather Cove Dr, Boynton Beach, FL 33467, USA
Alou, Moises *Baseball Player*
13095 NW 13th St, Pembroke Pines, FL 33028, USA
Alpert, Herb *Musician*
31930 Pacific Coast Highway, Malibu, CA 90265, USA
Alpher, Ralph A *Physicist*
253 Ascot Lane, Schenectady, NY 12309, USA
Alsgaard, Thomas *Cross Country Skier*
Cathinka Guldbergsveg 16, 2034 Holter, Norway
Alston Reeves, Shirley *Singer (Shirelles)*
%GHR Entertainment, 6014 N Pointe Place, Woodland Hills, CA 91367, USA
Alston, Alyce Carolyn *Publisher*
%Oprah Magazine, 224 W 57th St, #900, New York, NY 10019, USA
Alston, Barbara *Singer (Crystals)*
%Superstars Unlimited, PO Box 371371, Las Vegas, NV 89137, USA
Alstott, Mike *Football Player*
7800 9th Ave S, Saint Petersburg, FL 33707, USA
Alt, Carol *Model, Actress*
%Metropolitan Talent Agency, 4526 Wilshire Blvd, Los Angeles, CA 90010, USA
Alt, John M *Football Player*
1 Scotch Pine Road, Saint Paul, MN 55127, USA
Altenberg, Wolfgang *Army General, Germany*
Birkenhof 44, 28759 Brenen-Saint Magnus, Germany
Alter, Hobie *Surfboard, Boat Designer*
PO Box 1008, Oceanside, CA 92051, USA
Alther, Lisa *Writer*
1086 Silver St, Hinesburg, VT 05461, USA
Altman, Jeff *Actor*
4628 Halbrent Ave, Sherman Oaks, CA 91403, USA

A

Altman, Robert B *Movie Director, Producer*
%International Creative Mgmt, 8942 Wilshire Blvd, #219, Beverly Hills, CA 90211, USA
Altman, Scott D *Astronaut*
3011 Harvest Hill Dr, Friendswood, TX 77546, USA
Altman, Sidney *Nobel Chemistry Laureate*
71 Blake Road, Hamden, CT 06517, USA
Altmeyer, Jeannine T *Opera Singer*
Im Muhlader, 8709 Herrliberg, Switzerland
Altobelli, Joseph (Joe) *Baseball Player*
10 Stowell Dr, #3, Rochester, NY 14616, USA
Altschul, Serena *Commentator*
%MTV, News Dept, 1515 Broadway, New York, NY 10036, USA
Alvarado, Natividad (Naty) *Handball Player*
%Equitable of Iowa, 2700 N Main St, Santa Ana, CA 92705, USA
Alvarez Martinez, Francisco Cardinal *Religious Leader*
Arco de Palacio 3, 45002 Toledo, Spain
Alvarez, Barry *Football Coach*
%University of Wisconsin, Athletic Dept, Madison, WI 53711, USA
Alvarez-Buylla, Arturo *Biologist*
%Rockefeller University, Medical Center, 1230 York Ave, New York, NY 10021, USA
Alves, Joe *Movie Director*
4176 Rosario Road, Woodland Hills, CA 91364, USA
Alvina, Anicee *Actress*
41 Rue du l'Echese, 75008 Le Visinet, France
Alworth, Lance D *Football Player*
242 22nd St, Del Mar, CA 92014, USA
Amaker, Tommy *Basketball Player, Coach*
%University of Michigan, Athletic Dept, Ann Arbor, MI 48109, USA
Amalfitano, J Joseph (Joe) *Baseball Player*
265 Bowstring Dr, Sedona, AZ 86336, USA
Amalou, J K *Movie Director*
%William Morris Agency, 52/53 Poland Place, London W1F 7LX, England
Amanar, Simona *Gymnast*
%Gymnastic Federation, Str Vasile Conta 16, 70139 Budapest, Romania
Amandes, Tom *Actor*
%Writers & Artists, 8383 Wilshire Blvd, #550, Beverly Hills, CA 90211, USA
Amanpour, Christiane *News Correspondent*
%Cable News Network, 2 Stephen St, #100, London W1P 1PL, England
Amara, Lucine *Opera Singer*
260 W End Ave, #7A, New York, NY 10023, USA
Amaral, Richard L (Rich) *Baseball Player*
3122 Country Club Dr, Costa Mesa, CA 92626, USA
Amarjargal, Rinchinnyamiyn *Prime Minister, Mongolia*
%Prime Minister's Office, Great Hural, Ulan Bator 12, Mongolia
Amato, Giuliano *Prime Minister, Italy*
%Carmera dei Deputati, Piazza di Montecitorio, 00186 Rome, Italy
Amato, Joe *Auto Racing Driver*
%Amato Racing, 44 Tunkhannuck Ave, Exeter, PA 18643, USA
Amaya, Armando *Sculptor*
Lopex 137, Depto 1, Mexico City 06070 CP, Mexico
Ambasz, Emilio *Architect*
8 E 62nd St, New York, NY 10021, USA
Amber *Singer*
%Artists & Audience Entertainment, PO Box 35, Pawling, NY 12564, USA
Ambro, Thomas L *Judge*
%US Court of Appeals, Federal Building, 844 N King St, Wilmington, DE 19801, USA
Ambrose, Ashley A *Football Player*
2877 Major Ridge Trail, Duluth, GA 30097, USA
Ambrose, Lauren *Actress*
%United Talent Agency, 9560 Wilshire Blvd, #500, Beverly Hills, CA 90212, USA
Ambrosius, Marsha *Singer (Floetry), Songwriter*
%DreamWorks Records, 9268 W 3rd St, Beverly Hills, CA 90210, USA
Ambrozic, Aloysius Matthew Cardinal *Religious Leader*
%Archdiocese, 1155 Yonge St, Toronto ON M4T 1W2, Canada
Ambuehl, Cindy *Actress*
%Paul Kohner, 9300 Wilshire Blvd, #555, Beverly Hills, CA 90212, USA
Amdahl, Gene M *Computer Engineer, Businessman*
4 Hallmark Circle, Menlo Park, CA 94025, USA
Ameling, Elly *Concert Singer*
%Hubstein Artist Services, 65 W 90th St, #13F, New York, NY 10024, USA
Amelio, Gilbert F *Businessman*
13416 Middle Fork Lane, Los Altos, CA 94022, USA
Amend, Bill *Cartoonist (FoxTrot)*
%Universal Press Syndicate, 4520 Main St, Kansas City, MO 64111, USA
Amendola, Tony *Actor*
%J Michael Bloom, 9255 Sunset Blvd, #710, Los Angeles, CA 90069, USA
Ament, Jeff *Bassist (Pearl Jam)*
%Annie Ohayon Media Relations, 525 Broadway, #600, New York, NY 10012, USA

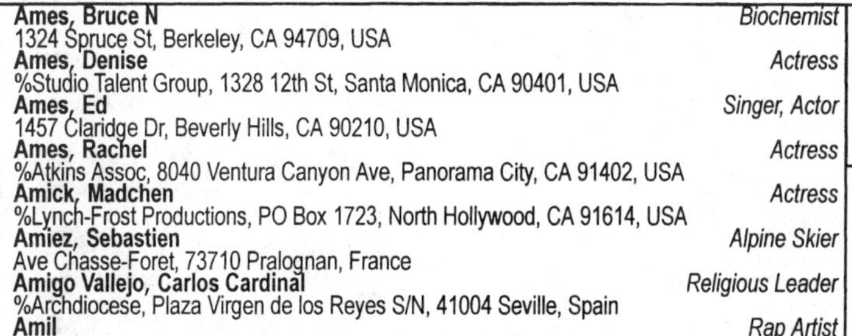

Ames, Bruce N — *Biochemist*
1324 Spruce St, Berkeley, CA 94709, USA

Ames, Denise — *Actress*
%Studio Talent Group, 1328 12th St, Santa Monica, CA 90401, USA

Ames, Ed — *Singer, Actor*
1457 Claridge Dr, Beverly Hills, CA 90210, USA

Ames, Rachel — *Actress*
%Atkins Assoc, 8040 Ventura Canyon Ave, Panorama City, CA 91402, USA

Amick, Madchen — *Actress*
%Lynch-Frost Productions, PO Box 1723, North Hollywood, CA 91614, USA

Amiez, Sebastien — *Alpine Skier*
Ave Chasse-Foret, 73710 Pralognan, France

Amigo Vallejo, Carlos Cardinal — *Religious Leader*
%Archdiocese, Plaza Virgen de los Reyes S/N, 41004 Seville, Spain

Amil — *Rap Artist*
%Sony Records, 2100 Colorado Ave, Santa Monica, CA 90404, USA

Amis, Martin — *Writer, Journalist*
%P F D, Drury House, 34-43 Russell St, London WC2B 5HA, England

Amis, Suzy — *Actress, Model*
%International Creative Mgmt, 8942 Wilshire Blvd, #219, Beverly Hills, CA 90211, USA

Amitri, Del — *Singer*
%Progressive Global Agency, PO Box 50294, Nashville, TN 37205, USA

Amlong, Joe — *Rowing Athlete*
HC 36 Box 73, Sand Coulee, MT 59472, USA

Amlong, Thomas — *Rowing Athlete*
166 Four Mile River Road, Old Lyme, CT 06371, USA

Ammaccapane, Danielle — *Golfer*
13214 N 13th St, Phoenix, AZ 85022, USA

Ammachi — *Religious Leader*
%Amrita Institutions, Ettimadai, Coimbatore, Tamil Nadu 641105, India

Ammann, Simon — *Ski Jumper*
%Ski Verband, Worbstr 52, 3074 Muri, Switzerland

Amonte, Tony — *Hockey Player*
5245 E Saguaro Place, Paradise Valley, AZ 85253, USA

Amorosi, Vanessa — *Singer*
%Mar Jac Productions, PO Box 51, Caulfield South VIC 3162, Australia

Amos, John — *Actor*
%Innovative Artists, 1505 10th St, Santa Monica, CA 90401, USA

Amos, Paul S — *Businessman*
%AFLAC Inc, AFLAC Center, 1932 Wynnton Road, Columbus, GA 31999, USA

Amos, Tori — *Singer, Pianist, Songwriter*
%Spivak Entertainment, 11845 W Olympic Blvd, #1125, Los Angeles, CA 90064, USA

Amos, Wally (Famous) — *Businessman*
%Rosica Mulhern Assoc, 627 Grove St, Ridgewood, NJ 07450, USA

Amoyal, Pierre A W — *Concert Violinist*
%Jacques Thelen, 252 Rue de Faubourg Saint-Honore, 75008 Paris, France

Amplas, John — *Actor*
443 Meridian Dr, Pittsburgh, PA 15228, USA

Amram, David W, III — *Jazz, Classical Composer, Conductor*
Peekskill Hollow Farm, Peekskill Hollow Road, Putnam Valley, NY 10579, USA

Amte, Baba — *Religious Leader*
Maharogi Sewa Samiti, Waora, Anandwan, Dist Chandrapur 442914, India

Ana-Alicia — *Actress*
%S D B Partners, 1801 Ave of Stars, #902, Los Angeles, CA 90067, USA

Anakin, Douglas — *Bobsled Athlete*
PO Box 27, Windermere BC V0B 2L, Canada

Ananiashvili, Nina G — *Ballerina*
%Bolshoi Theatre, 1 Ploschad Sverdlova, 103009 Moscow, Russia

Anastacia — *Singer*
%Helter Skelter, Plaza, 535 Kings Road, London SW10 0S, England

Anastasio, Trey — *Guitarist (Phish, Oysterhead)*
%Dionysian Productions, 431 Pine St, Burlington, VT 05401, USA

Anaya, Rudolfo — *Writer*
5324 Canada Vista NW, Albuquerque, NM 87120, USA

Anaya, Toney — *Governor, NM*
711 E May Ave, Las Cruces, NM 88001, USA

Anchia, Juan-Ruiz — *Cinematographer*
%Sanford-Beckett-Skouras, 1015 Gayley Ave, Los Angeles, CA 90024, USA

Anders, William A — *Astronaut, Air Force General*
1 Aeroview Lane, Eastsound, WA 98245, USA

Andersen Watts, Teresa — *Sychronized Swimmer*
2582 Marsha Way, San Jose, CA 95125, USA

Andersen, Elmer L — *Governor, MN*
1483 Bussard Court, Arden Hills, MN 55112, USA

Andersen, Eric — *Singer, Songwriter*
%Drake, 177 Woodland Ave, Westwood, NJ 07675, USA

Andersen, Greta — *Swimmer*
19332 Brooktrail Lane, Huntington Beach, CA 92648, USA

A

Anderson - Anderson

Andersen, Hjalmar (Hjallis) *Speed Skater*
%Velferden for Handelsflaten, Trondheimsvn 2, 0560 Oslo 5, Norway
Andersen, Ladell *Basketball Coach*
41 W Cedar Dr, Hermiston, OR 97838, USA
Andersen, Linda *Yachtswoman*
Aroysund, 3135 Torod, Norway
Andersen, Mogens *Artist*
Strandagervej 28, 2900 Hellerup, Copenhagen, Denmark
Andersen, Morten *Football Player*
6501 Old Shadburn Ferry Road, Buford, GA 30518, USA
Andersen, Reidar *Ski Jumper*
%National Ski Hall of Fame, PO Box 191, Ishpeming, MI 49849, USA
Anderson Lee, Pamela *Model, Actress*
5699 Kanan Road, #255, Agoura Hills, CA 91301, USA
Anderson, Anthony *Actor*
1619 Broadway, #900, New York, NY 10019, USA
Anderson, Barbara *Actress*
PO Box 10118, Santa Fe, NM 87504, USA
Anderson, Bill *Singer, Guitarist, Songwriter*
PO Box 6721, San Bernardino, CA 92412, USA
Anderson, Brad *Drag Racing Driver*
1240 S Cucamonga Ave, Ontario, CA 91761, USA
Anderson, Brad *Movie Director*
422 Santa Monica Court, Escondido, CA 92029, USA
Anderson, Bradley J (Brad) *Cartoonist (Marmaduke)*
13022 Wood Harbour Dr, Montgomery, TX 77356, USA
Anderson, Brett *Singer (Suede)*
%Interceptor Enterprises, 98 White Lion St, London N1 9PF, England
Anderson, C Neal *Football Player*
%35 Farms, 3351 SE State Road 121, Morriston, FL 32668, USA
Anderson, Chantelle *Basketball Player*
%Cleveland Rockers, Gund Arena, 1 Center Court, Cleveland, OH 44115, USA
Anderson, Christopher *Writer*
%Avon/William Morrow, 1350 Ave of Americas, New York, NY 10019, USA
Anderson, Clayton C *Astronaut*
1909 Summer Reef Dr, League City, TX 77573, USA
Anderson, Daryl *Actor*
24136 Friar St, Woodland Hills, CA 91367, USA
Anderson, David P (Dave) *Sportswriter*
8 Inness Road, Tenafly, NJ 07670, USA
Anderson, Derek *Basketball Player*
%Portland Trail Blazers, Rose Garden, 1 Center Court St, Portland, OR 97227, USA
Anderson, Dion *Actor*
%S D B Partners, 1801 Ave of Stars, #902, Los Angeles, CA 90067, USA
Anderson, Don (Donny) *Football Player*
4516 Lovers Lane, #133, Dallas, TX 75225, USA
Anderson, Don L *Geophysicist*
669 Alameda St, #E, Altadena, CA 91001, USA
Anderson, Duwayne M *Polar Scientist*
PO Box 468, Hamilton, WA 98255, USA
Anderson, Edward G (Ed), III *Army General*
Senior Representative, United Nations Military Committee, Washington, DC 20318, USA
Anderson, Erich *Actor*
%Paradigm Agency, 10100 Santa Monica Blvd, #2500, Los Angeles, CA 90067, USA
Anderson, Erika *Actress, Model*
%Artists Agency, 1180 S Beverly Dr, #301, Los Angeles, CA 90035, USA
Anderson, Ernestine I *Singer*
%Thomas Cassidy, 11761 E Speedway Blvd, Tucson, AZ 85748, USA
Anderson, Garret J *Baseball Player*
11268 Overlook Point, Tustin, CA 92782, USA
Anderson, Gary A *Football Player*
5563 Wingwood Court, Minnetonka, MN 55345, USA
Anderson, Gary L *Marksman*
%National Rifle Assn, 11250 Waples Mill Road, Fairfax, VA 22030, USA
Anderson, George L (Sparky) *Baseball Manager*
PO Box 6415, Thousand Oaks, CA 91359, USA
Anderson, Gerry *Television Director, Puppeteer*
%Gerry Anderson Magazine, 332 Lytham Road, Blackpool FY4 1DW, England
Anderson, Gillian *Actress*
%Creative Artists Agency, 9830 Wilshire Blvd, Beverly Hills, CA 90212, USA
Anderson, Harry *Actor*
100 Bourbon St, PO Box 372, New York, NY 10008, USA
Anderson, Howard A *Actor*
PO Box 2230, Los Angeles, CA 90028, USA
Anderson, Ian *Singer (Jethro Tull), Songwriter*
43 Brook Green, London W6 7EP, England
Anderson, Jack N *Columnist*
PO Box TT, McLean, VA 22101, USA

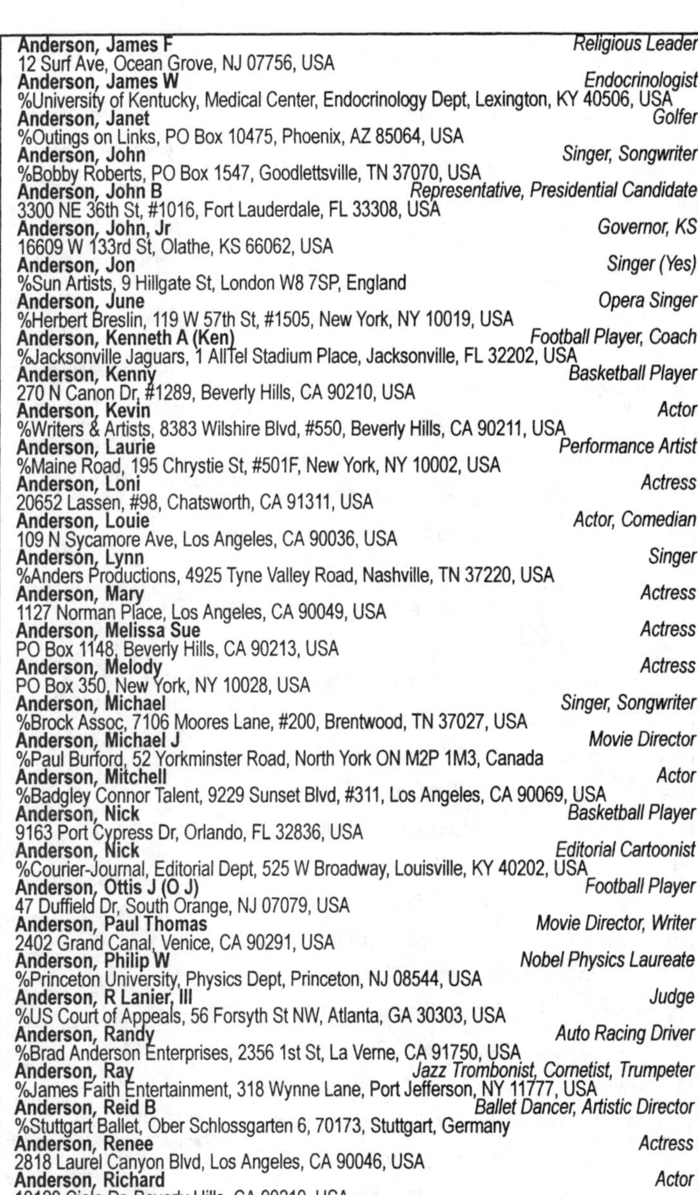

Anderson, James F *Religious Leader*
12 Surf Ave, Ocean Grove, NJ 07756, USA
Anderson, James W *Endocrinologist*
%University of Kentucky, Medical Center, Endocrinology Dept, Lexington, KY 40506, USA
Anderson, Janet *Golfer*
%Outings on Links, PO Box 10475, Phoenix, AZ 85064, USA
Anderson, John *Singer, Songwriter*
%Bobby Roberts, PO Box 1547, Goodlettsville, TN 37070, USA
Anderson, John B *Representative, Presidential Candidate*
3300 NE 36th St, #1016, Fort Lauderdale, FL 33308, USA
Anderson, John, Jr *Governor, KS*
16609 W 133rd St, Olathe, KS 66062, USA
Anderson, Jon *Singer (Yes)*
%Sun Artists, 9 Hillgate St, London W8 7SP, England
Anderson, June *Opera Singer*
%Herbert Breslin, 119 W 57th St, #1505, New York, NY 10019, USA
Anderson, Kenneth A (Ken) *Football Player, Coach*
%Jacksonville Jaguars, 1 AllTel Stadium Place, Jacksonville, FL 32202, USA
Anderson, Kenny *Basketball Player*
270 N Canon Dr, #1289, Beverly Hills, CA 90210, USA
Anderson, Kevin *Actor*
%Writers & Artists, 8383 Wilshire Blvd, #550, Beverly Hills, CA 90211, USA
Anderson, Laurie *Performance Artist*
%Maine Road, 195 Chrystie St, #501F, New York, NY 10002, USA
Anderson, Loni *Actress*
20652 Lassen, #98, Chatsworth, CA 91311, USA
Anderson, Louie *Actor, Comedian*
109 N Sycamore Ave, Los Angeles, CA 90036, USA
Anderson, Lynn *Singer*
%Anders Productions, 4925 Tyne Valley Road, Nashville, TN 37220, USA
Anderson, Mary *Actress*
1127 Norman Place, Los Angeles, CA 90049, USA
Anderson, Melissa Sue *Actress*
PO Box 1148, Beverly Hills, CA 90213, USA
Anderson, Melody *Actress*
PO Box 350, New York, NY 10028, USA
Anderson, Michael *Singer, Songwriter*
%Brock Assoc, 7106 Moores Lane, #200, Brentwood, TN 37027, USA
Anderson, Michael J *Movie Director*
%Paul Burford, 52 Yorkminster Road, North York ON M2P 1M3, Canada
Anderson, Mitchell *Actor*
%Badgley Connor Talent, 9229 Sunset Blvd, #311, Los Angeles, CA 90069, USA
Anderson, Nick *Basketball Player*
9163 Port Cypress Dr, Orlando, FL 32836, USA
Anderson, Nick *Editorial Cartoonist*
%Courier-Journal, Editorial Dept, 525 W Broadway, Louisville, KY 40202, USA
Anderson, Ottis J (O J) *Football Player*
47 Duffield Dr, South Orange, NJ 07079, USA
Anderson, Paul Thomas *Movie Director, Writer*
2402 Grand Canal, Venice, CA 90291, USA
Anderson, Philip W *Nobel Physics Laureate*
%Princeton University, Physics Dept, Princeton, NJ 08544, USA
Anderson, R Lanier, III *Judge*
%US Court of Appeals, 56 Forsyth St NW, Atlanta, GA 30303, USA
Anderson, Randy *Auto Racing Driver*
%Brad Anderson Enterprises, 2356 1st St, La Verne, CA 91750, USA
Anderson, Ray *Jazz Trombonist, Cornetist, Trumpeter*
%James Faith Entertainment, 318 Wynne Lane, Port Jefferson, NY 11777, USA
Anderson, Reid B *Ballet Dancer, Artistic Director*
%Stuttgart Ballet, Ober Schlossgarten 6, 70173, Stuttgart, Germany
Anderson, Renee *Actress*
2818 Laurel Canyon Blvd, Los Angeles, CA 90046, USA
Anderson, Richard *Actor*
10120 Cielo Dr, Beverly Hills, CA 90210, USA
Anderson, Richard Dean *Actor*
1 North Road, Jefferson, NH 03583, USA
Anderson, Richard P (Dick) *Football Player*
4603 Santa Maria St, Coral Gables, FL 33146, USA
Anderson, Robert *Businessman*
%Rockwell International, 5836 Corporate Ave, #100, Cypress, CA 90630, USA
Anderson, Robert G W *Museum Director*
%British Museum, Great Russell St, London WC1B 3DG, England
Anderson, Ross *Journalist*
%Seattle Times, Editorial Dept, 1120 John St, Seattle, WA 98109, USA
Anderson, Shandon *Basketball Player*
8 Oak Valley Lane, Purchase, NY 10577, USA
Anderson, Shelly *Drag Racing Driver*
1240 S Cucamonga Ave, Ontario, CA 91761, USA

A

Anderson - Andrew

Anderson, Stephen H *Judge*
%US Court of Appeals, Federal Building, 125 S State St, Salt Lake City, UT 84138, USA
Anderson, Sunshine *Singer*
%Family Tree, 135 E 57th St, #2600, New York, NY 10022, USA
Anderson, Terence (Terry) *Hostage, Journalist*
17 Sunlight Hill, Yonkers, NY 10704, USA
Anderson, W French *Biochemist, Geneticist*
%USC Medical School, 144 E Lake View Terrace, Los Angeles, CA 90039, USA
Anderson, Webster *Vietnam War Army Hero (CMH)*
3044 US Highway 321 N, Winnsboro, SC 29180, USA
Anderson, Wendell R *Governor, Senator, MN*
%Larkin & Hoffman, 1700 First Bank Plaza W, Minneapolis, MN 55402, USA
Anderson, Wes *Movie Director, Writer*
%United Talent Agency, 9560 Wilshire Blvd, #500, Beverly Hills, CA 90212, USA
Anderson, Wessell *Jazz Saxophonist*
%Fat City Artists, 1906 Chet Atkins Place, #502, Nashville, TN 37212, USA
Anderson, Weston *Physicist*
%Varian Assoc, 611 Hansen Way, Palo Alto, CA 94304, USA
Anderson, Wilford C *WW II Army Hero*
3585 Round Barn Blvd, Santa Rosa, CA 95403, USA
Anderson, William R *Representative, TN; Navy Officer*
10505 Miller Road, Oakton, VA 22124, USA
Anderson, Willie *Basketball Player*
%Toronto Raptors, Air Canada Center, 40 Bay St, Toronto ON M5J 2N8, Canada
Andersson, Benny *Singer (ABBA), Composer*
%Mono Music, Sodra Brobaeken 41-A, 111 49 Stockholm, Sweden
Andersson, Bibi *Actress*
%Royal Dramatic Theater, Box 5037, 112 41 Stockholm, Sweden
Andersson, Harriet *Actress*
Roslagsgatan 15, 113 55 Stockholm, Sweden
Andersson, Henrik *Guitarist (Komeda)*
%MOB Agency, 6404 Wilshire Blvd, #505, Los Angeles, CA 90048, USA
Andersson, Kent-Erik *Hockey Player*
Persiljav 9, Karlstad 65 351, Sweden
Anderszewski, Piotr *Concert Pianist, Conductor*
%Virgin Classics Records, 90 University Plaza, New York, NY 10003, USA
Andes, Karen *Body Builder*
%G P Putnam's Sons, 375 Hudson St, New York, NY 10014, USA
Ando, Tadao *Architect, Pritzker Laureate*
%Tadao Ando Architect, 5-23-2 Toyosaki, Kitaku, Osaka 531, Japan
Andov, Stojan *President, Macedonia*
Sobranje, 11 Oktombri Blvd, 91000 Skopje, Macedonia
Andrade, William T (Billy) *Golfer*
4439 E Brookhaven Dr NE, Atlanta, GA 30319, USA
Andre, Carl *Sculptor*
689 Crown St, Brooklyn, NY 11213, USA
Andre, Maurice *Concert Trumpeter*
Presles-en-Brie, 77220 Tournan-en-Brie, France
Andre-Deshays, Claudie *Spatinaut, France*
%Hopital Cochin, Rhumatologie Dept, 75000 Paris, France
Andreas, Dwayne O *Businessman*
181 Southmoreland Place, Decatur, IL 62521, USA
Andreas, G Allen *Businessman*
%Archer-Daniels-Midland, 4666 Faries Parkway, Decatur, IL 62526, USA
Andreasen, Nancy C *Psychiatrist*
200 Hawkings Dr, Iowa City, IA 52242, USA
Andreason, Larry *Diver*
10874 Kyle St, Los Alamitos, CA 90720, USA
Andreeff, Starr *Actress*
%C N A Assoc, 1925 Century Park East, #750, Los Angeles, CA 90067, USA
Andreessen, Marc *Computer Software Designer*
%Opsware, 599 N Mathilda Ave, Sunnyvale, CA 94085, USA
Andrei, Alessandro *Track Athlete*
Via V Bellini 1, 50018 Scandicci, Firenze, Italy
Andreone, Leah *Singer, Songwriter*
%Metropolitan Entertainment, 363 US Highway 46, #300F, Fairfield, NJ 07004, USA
Andress, Tuck *Jazz Guitarist (Tuck & Patti)*
%Windham Hill Records, PO Box 5501, Beverly Hills, CA 90209, USA
Andress, Ursula *Actress*
Via Francesco Siacci 38, 00186 Rome, Italy
Andretti, John *Auto Racing Driver*
107 Keats Road, Mooresville, NC 28117, USA
Andretti, Mario *Auto Racing Driver*
630 Selvaggio Dr, #340, Nazareth, PA 18064, USA
Andretti, Michael M *Auto Racing Driver*
3310 Airport Road, Allentown, PA 18109, USA
Andrew *Prince, England*
%Buckingham Palace, London SW1A 1AA, England

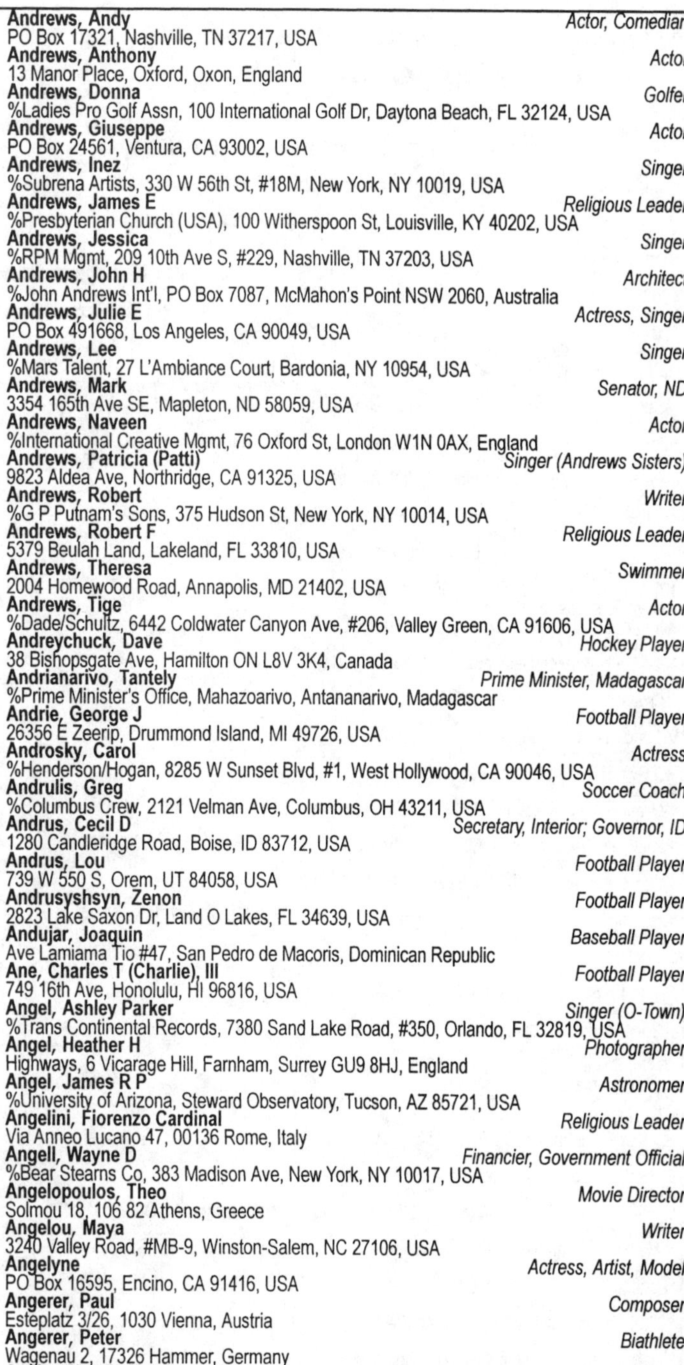

Andrews, Andy *Actor, Comedian*
PO Box 17321, Nashville, TN 37217, USA
Andrews, Anthony *Actor*
13 Manor Place, Oxford, Oxon, England
Andrews, Donna *Golfer*
%Ladies Pro Golf Assn, 100 International Golf Dr, Daytona Beach, FL 32124, USA
Andrews, Giuseppe *Actor*
PO Box 24561, Ventura, CA 93002, USA
Andrews, Inez *Singer*
%Subrena Artists, 330 W 56th St, #18M, New York, NY 10019, USA
Andrews, James E *Religious Leader*
%Presbyterian Church (USA), 100 Witherspoon St, Louisville, KY 40202, USA
Andrews, Jessica *Singer*
%RPM Mgmt, 209 10th Ave S, #229, Nashville, TN 37203, USA
Andrews, John H *Architect*
%John Andrews Int'l, PO Box 7087, McMahon's Point NSW 2060, Australia
Andrews, Julie E *Actress, Singer*
PO Box 491668, Los Angeles, CA 90049, USA
Andrews, Lee *Singer*
%Mars Talent, 27 L'Ambiance Court, Bardonia, NY 10954, USA
Andrews, Mark *Senator, ND*
3354 165th Ave SE, Mapleton, ND 58059, USA
Andrews, Naveen *Actor*
%International Creative Mgmt, 76 Oxford St, London W1N 0AX, England
Andrews, Patricia (Patti) *Singer (Andrews Sisters)*
9823 Aldea Ave, Northridge, CA 91325, USA
Andrews, Robert *Writer*
%G P Putnam's Sons, 375 Hudson St, New York, NY 10014, USA
Andrews, Robert F *Religious Leader*
5379 Beulah Land, Lakeland, FL 33810, USA
Andrews, Theresa *Swimmer*
2004 Homewood Road, Annapolis, MD 21402, USA
Andrews, Tige *Actor*
%Dade/Schultz, 6442 Coldwater Canyon Ave, #206, Valley Green, CA 91606, USA
Andreychuck, Dave *Hockey Player*
38 Bishopsgate Ave, Hamilton ON L8V 3K4, Canada
Andrianarivo, Tantely *Prime Minister, Madagascar*
%Prime Minister's Office, Mahazoarivo, Antananarivo, Madagascar
Andrie, George J *Football Player*
26356 E Zeerip, Drummond Island, MI 49726, USA
Androsky, Carol *Actress*
%Henderson/Hogan, 8285 W Sunset Blvd, #1, West Hollywood, CA 90046, USA
Andrulis, Greg *Soccer Coach*
%Columbus Crew, 2121 Velman Ave, Columbus, OH 43211, USA
Andrus, Cecil D *Secretary, Interior; Governor, ID*
1280 Candleridge Road, Boise, ID 83712, USA
Andrus, Lou *Football Player*
739 W 550 S, Orem, UT 84058, USA
Andrusyshsyn, Zenon *Football Player*
2823 Lake Saxon Dr, Land O Lakes, FL 34639, USA
Andujar, Joaquin *Baseball Player*
Ave Lamiama Tio #47, San Pedro de Macoris, Dominican Republic
Ane, Charles T (Charlie), III *Football Player*
749 16th Ave, Honolulu, HI 96816, USA
Angel, Ashley Parker *Singer (O-Town)*
%Trans Continental Records, 7380 Sand Lake Road, #350, Orlando, FL 32819, USA
Angel, Heather H *Photographer*
Highways, 6 Vicarage Hill, Farnham, Surrey GU9 8HJ, England
Angel, James R P *Astronomer*
%University of Arizona, Steward Observatory, Tucson, AZ 85721, USA
Angelini, Fiorenzo Cardinal *Religious Leader*
Via Anneo Lucano 47, 00136 Rome, Italy
Angell, Wayne D *Financier, Government Official*
%Bear Stearns Co, 383 Madison Ave, New York, NY 10017, USA
Angelopoulos, Theo *Movie Director*
Solmou 18, 106 82 Athens, Greece
Angelou, Maya *Writer*
3240 Valley Road, #MB-9, Winston-Salem, NC 27106, USA
Angelyne *Actress, Artist, Model*
PO Box 16595, Encino, CA 91416, USA
Angerer, Paul *Composer*
Esteplatz 3/26, 1030 Vienna, Austria
Angerer, Peter *Biathlete*
Wagenau 2, 17326 Hammer, Germany
Angier, Natalie M *Journalist*
%New York Times, Editorial Dept, 229 W 43rd St, New York, NY 10036, USA
Angle, Kurt *Wrestler*
%Hawk & Co, PO Box 97007, Pittsburgh, PA 15229, USA

A	**Anglim, Philip**	*Actor*
	2404 Grand Canal, Venice, CA 90291, USA	
	Anglin, Jennifer	*Actress*
	651 N Kilkea Dr, Los Angeles, CA 90048, USA	
	Angus, Michael	*Businessman*
	%Whitbread PLC, Chiswell St, London EC1Y 4SD, England	
	Anikulap-Kuti, Femi	*Singer, Songwriter*
	%MCA Records, 70 Universal City Plaza, Universal City, CA 91608, USA	
	Anissina, Marina	*Figure Skater*
	%Sports de Glace Federation, 35 Rue Felicien David, 75016 Paris, France	
	Aniston, Jennifer	*Actress*
	%Creative Artists Agency, 9830 Wilshire Blvd, Beverly Hills, CA 90212, USA	
	Aniston, John	*Actor*
	3110 Summit Pointe Dr, Topanga, CA 90290, USA	
	Anka, Paul	*Singer, Songwriter, Actor*
	12078 Summit Circle, Beverly Hills, CA 90210, USA	
	Ann-Margret	*Actress, Singer, Dancer*
	2707 Benedict Canyon Road, Beverly Hills, CA 90210, USA	
	Annakin, Kenneth (Ken)	*Movie Director*
	%Denise Denny, 9233 Swallow Dr, Los Angeles, CA 90069, USA	
	Annan, Kofi A	*Secretary-General, United Nations*
	%Secretary-General's Office, 1 United Nations Plaza, New York, NY 10017, USA	
	Annand, Richard Wallace	*WW II British Army Hero (VC)*
	Springwell House, Whitesmocks, Durham City DH1 4ZL, England	
	Annaud, Jean-Jacques	*Movie Director*
	%Reperage, 16 Rue Saint-Vincent, 75018 Paris, France	
	Anne	*Princess, England*
	%Gatecombe Park, Gloucestershire, England	
	Anne of Bourbon-Palma	*Queen, Romania*
	%Villa Serena, 77 Chemin Louis-Degallier, 1290 Versoix-Geneva, Switzerland	
	Annenberg, Wallis	*Publisher*
	10273 Century Woods Dr, Los Angeles, CA 90067, USA	
	Annis, Francesca	*Actress*
	%International Creative Mgmt, 76 Oxford St, London W1N 0AX, England	
	Ansara, Michael	*Actor*
	4624 Park Mirasol, Calabasas, CA 91302, USA	
	Anschutz, Philip F	*Businessman, Sports Executive*
	%Qwest Communications, 700 Qwest Tower, 555 17th St, Denver, CO 80202, USA	
	Anselmo, Philip	*Singer (Pantera)*
	%Concrete Mgmt, 361 W Broadway, #200, New York, NY 10013, USA	
	Anspach, Susan	*Actress*
	PO Box 5605, Santa Monica, CA 90409, USA	
	Anspaugh, David	*Movie Director*
	%Creative Artists Agency, 9830 Wilshire Blvd, Beverly Hills, CA 90212, USA	
	Ant, Adam	*Singer*
	%Kathleen Denney Co, 18685A Main St, #627, Huntington Beach, CA 92648, USA	
	Anthony, Barbara Cox	*Businesswoman*
	%Cox Enterprises, 1400 Lake Hearn Dr NE, Atlanta, GA 30319, USA	
	Anthony, Carl	*Environmentalist*
	%Harvard University, Kennedy Government School, Cambridge, MA 02138, USA	
	Anthony, Carmelo	*Basketball Player*
	%Denver Nuggets, Pepsi Center, 1000 Chopper Circle, Denver, CO 80204, USA	
	Anthony, Greg	*Basketball Player*
	520 S 4th St, Las Vegas, NV 89101, USA	
	Anthony, Jason	*Model*
	%Boss Models, 1 Gansevoort St, New York, NY 10014, USA	
	Anthony, Lysette	*Actresss*
	46 Old Compton St, London WV 5PB, England	
	Anthony, Marc	*Singer, Actor, Songwriter*
	%Marc Anthony Productions, 146 W 57th St, #38C, New York, NY 10019, USA	
	Anthony, Piers	*Writer*
	PO Box 2289, Inverness, FL 34451, USA	
	Anthony, Ray	*Orchestra Leader, Trumpeter*
	9288 Kinglet Dr, Los Angeles, CA 90069, USA	
	Antin, Steve	*Actor, Writer*
	%International Creative Mgmt, 8942 Wilshire Blvd, #219, Beverly Hills, CA 90211, USA	
	Anton, Alan	*Musician (Cowboy Junkies)*
	%Macklam Feldman Mgmt, 1505 W 2nd Ave, #200, Vancouver BC V6H 3Y4, Canada	
	Anton, Craig	*Actor*
	%United Talent Agency, 9560 Wilshire Blvd, #500, Beverly Hills, CA 90212, USA	
	Anton, Susan	*Actress, Singer*
	16830 Ventura Blvd, #1616, Encino, CA 91436, USA	
	Anton, Susan	*Antropologist*
	%Institute of Human Origins, 1288 9th St, Berkeley, CA 94710, USA	
	Antonakakis, Dimitris	*Architect*
	%Atelier 66, Emm Benaki 118, Athens 114-73, Greece	
	Antonakakis, Suzana M	*Architect*
Anglim - Antonakakis	%Atelier 66, Emm Benaki 118, Athens 114-73, Greece	

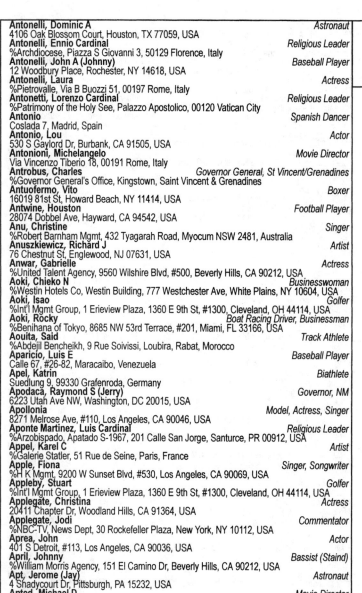

Antonelli, Dominic A *Astronaut*
4106 Oak Blossom Court, Houston, TX 77059, USA
Antonelli, Ennio Cardinal *Religious Leader*
%Archdiocese, Piazza S Giovanni 3, 50129 Florence, Italy
Antonelli, John A (Johnny) *Baseball Player*
12 Woodbury Place, Rochester, NY 14618, USA
Antonelli, Laura *Actress*
%Pietrovalle, Via B Buozzi 51, 00197 Rome, Italy
Antonetti, Lorenzo Cardinal *Religious Leader*
%Patrimony of the Holy See, Palazzo Apostolico, 00120 Vatican City
Antonio *Spanish Dancer*
Coslada 7, Madrid, Spain
Antonio, Lou *Actor*
530 S Gaylord Dr, Burbank, CA 91505, USA
Antonioni, Michelangelo *Movie Director*
Via Vincenzo Tiberio 18, 00191 Rome, Italy
Antrobus, Charles *Governor General, St Vincent/Grenadines*
%Governor General's Office, Kingstown, Saint Vincent & Grenadines
Antuofermo, Vito *Boxer*
16019 81st St, Howard Beach, NY 11414, USA
Antwine, Houston *Football Player*
28074 Dobbel Ave, Hayward, CA 94542, USA
Anu, Christine *Singer*
%Robert Barnham Mgmt, 432 Tyagarah Road, Myocum NSW 2481, Australia
Anuszkiewicz, Richard J *Artist*
76 Chestnut St, Englewood, NJ 07631, USA
Anwar, Gabrielle *Actress*
%United Talent Agency, 9560 Wilshire Blvd, #500, Beverly Hills, CA 90212, USA
Aoki, Chieko N *Businesswoman*
%Westin Hotels Co, Westin Building, 777 Westchester Ave, White Plains, NY 10604, USA
Aoki, Isao *Golfer*
%Int'l Mgmt Group, 1 Erieview Plaza, 1360 E 9th St, #1300, Cleveland, OH 44114, USA
Aoki, Rocky *Boat Racing Driver, Businessman*
%Benihana of Tokyo, 8685 NW 53rd Terrace, #201, Miami, FL 33166, USA
Aouita, Said *Track Athlete*
%Abdejil Bencheikh, 9 Rue Soivissi, Loubira, Rabat, Morocco
Aparicio, Luis E *Baseball Player*
Calle 67, #26-82, Maracaibo, Venezuela
Apel, Katrin *Biathlete*
Suedlung 9, 99330 Grafenroda, Germany
Apodaca, Raymond S (Jerry) *Governor, NM*
6223 Utah Ave NW, Washington, DC 20015, USA
Apollonia *Model, Actress, Singer*
8271 Melrose Ave, #110, Los Angeles, CA 90046, USA
Aponte Martinez, Luis Cardinal *Religious Leader*
%Arzobispado, Apatado S-1967, 201 Calle San Jorge, Santurce, PR 00912, USA
Appel, Karel C *Artist*
%Galerie Statler, 51 Rue de Seine, Paris, France
Apple, Fiona *Singer, Songwriter*
%H K Mgmt, 9200 W Sunset Blvd, #530, Los Angeles, CA 90069, USA
Appleby, Stuart *Golfer*
%Int'l Mgmt Group, 1 Erieview Plaza, 1360 E 9th St, #1300, Cleveland, OH 44114, USA
Applegate, Christina *Actress*
20411 Chapter Dr, Woodland Hills, CA 91364, USA
Applegate, Jodi *Commentator*
%NBC-TV, News Dept, 30 Rockefeller Plaza, New York, NY 10112, USA
Aprea, John *Actor*
401 S Detroit, #113, Los Angeles, CA 90036, USA
April, Johnny *Bassist (Staind)*
%William Morris Agency, 151 El Camino Dr, Beverly Hills, CA 90212, USA
Apt, Jerome (Jay) *Astronaut*
4 Shadycourt Dr, Pittsburgh, PA 15232, USA
Apted, Michael D *Movie Director*
360 N Saltair Ave, Los Angeles, CA 90049, USA
Aquilino, Thomas J, Jr *Judge*
%US Court of International Trade, 1 Federal Plaza, New York, NY 10278, USA
Aquino, Amy *Actress*
9615 Brighton Way, #300, Beverly Hills, CA 90210, USA
Aquino, Corazon C *President, Philippines*
119 de la Rosa Corner, Castro St, Makati City, Manila, Philippines
Arafat, Yasser *President, Palestine; Nobel Laureate*
%President's Office, PO Box 115, Jericho, Palestine, Israel
Aragall Garriga, Giacomo *Opera Singer*
%Stafford Law Assoc, 6 Barham Close, Weybridge, Surrey KT1 9PR, England
Aragon, Art *Boxer*
19050 Wells Dr, Tarzana, CA 91356, USA
Aragones, Sergio *Cartoonist (Mad Comics)*
PO Box 696, Ojai, CA 93024, USA

Araiza, Francisco *Opera Singer*
%Columbia Artists Mgmt Inc, 165 W 57th St, New York, NY 10019, USA
Aramburu, Juan Carlos Cardinal *Religious Leader*
Arzobispado, Suipacha 1034, Buenos Aires 1008, Argentina
Arana Osorio, Carlos M *President, Guatemala; Army General*
%Liberacion Nacional Movimienti, 5-A Calle 1-20, Guatemala City, Guatemala
Arana, Tomas *Actor*
%Paradigm Agency, 10100 Santa Monica Blvd, #2500, Los Angeles, CA 90067, USA
Ararktsyan, Babken G *Chairman of Supreme Council, Armenia*
%National Assembly, Marshal Bagzamyan Prosp 26, 375019 Yerevan, Armenia
Arashi, Qadi Abdul Karim al- *Chairman Presidential Council, Yemen*
%Constituent People's Assembly, Sana'a, Yemen
Araskog, Rand V *Businessman*
%ITT Corp, 1330 Ave of Americas, New York, NY 10019, USA
Arau, Alfonso *Movie Director*
%Productions AA, Privada Rafael Oliva 8, Coyoacan 04120, Mexico
Araujo, Serafim Fernandes de Cardinal *Religious Leader*
%Curia Metropolitana, Av Brasil 2079, 30240-002 Belo Horizonte MG, Brazil
Araya, Zeudy *Actress*
%Carol Levi Co, Via Giuseppe Pisanelli, 00196 Rome, Italy
Arbanas, Frederick V (Fred) *Football Player*
3350 SW Hook Road, Lees Summit, MO 64082, USA
Arbeid, Murray *Fashion Designer*
202 Ebury St, London SW1W 8UN, England
Arber, Werner *Nobel Medicine Laureate*
70 Klingelbergstr, 4056 Basel, Switzerland
Arbour, Louise *Judge*
%Supreme Court of Canada, 301 Wellington St, Ottawa ON K1A 0J1, Canada
Arbulu Galliani, Guillermo *Prime Minister, Peru; Army General*
%Prime Minister's Office, Urb Corpac, Calle 1 Oeste S/N, Lima 27, Peru
Arbus, Alan *Actor*
2208 N Beverly Glen, Los Angeles, CA 90077, USA
Archambault, Lee J *Astronaut*
4318 Sweet Cicely Court, Houston, TX 77059, USA
Archer of Weston-Super-Mare, Jeffrey H *Government Official, England; Writer*
93 Albert Embankment, London SE1 7TY, England
Archer, Anne *Actress*
13201 Old Oak Lane, Los Angeles, CA 90049, USA
Archer, Beverly *Actress*
%Judy Schoen, 606 N Larchmont Blvd, #309, Los Angeles, CA 90004, USA
Archer, George *Golfer*
774 Mays Blvd, #10-184, Incline Village, NV 89451, USA
Archer, Glenn L, Jr *Judge*
%US Court of Appeals, 717 Madison Place NW, Washington, DC 20439, USA
Archer, John *Writer*
10901 176th Circle NE, #3601, Redmond, WA 98052, USA
Archerd, Army *Journalist*
%Variety Magazine, Editorial Dept, 5700 Wilshire Blvd, Los Angeles, CA 90036, USA
Archibald, Nathaniel (Nate) *Basketball Player*
2920 Holland Ave, Bronx, NY 10467, USA
Archibald, Nolan D *Businessman*
%Black & Decker Corp, 701 E Joppa Road, Towson, MD 21286, USA
Archipowski, Ken *Singer (Randy & the Rainbows)*
PO Box 656507, Fresh Meadows, NY 11365, USA
Ard, William D (Bill) *Football Player*
41 Vail Lane, Watchung, NJ 07069, USA
Ardalan, Nader *Architect*
%KEO International Consultants, PO Box 3679, Safat 13037, Kuwait
Ardant, Fanny *Actress*
%Artmedia, 20 Ave Rapp, 75007 Paris, France
Arden, Jann *Singer, Songwriter*
%Macklam Feldman Mgmt, 1505 W 2nd Ave, #200, Vancouver BC V6H 3Y4, Canada
Arden, John *Writer*
%Cassarotto, 60/66 Wardour St, London W1V 4ND, England
Arden, Toni *Singer*
3434 75th St, Jackson Heights, NY 11372, USA
Ardito Barletta, Nicolas *President, Panama*
PO Box 7737, Panama City 9, Panama
Arditti, Irvine *Concert Violinist*
%Lattidue Arts, 109 Boul Saint-Joseph Quest, Montreal PA H2T 2P7, Canada
Ardolino, Todd *Movie Director*
%Creative Artists Agency, 9830 Wilshire Blvd, Beverly Hills, CA 90212, USA
Aregood, Richard L *Journalist*
%Philadelphia Daily News, Editoral Dept, 400 N Broad St, Philadelphia, PA 19130, USA
Arena, Bruce *Soccer Player, Coach*
%DC United, 14120 Newbrook Dr, Chantilly, VA 20151, USA
Arena, Tina *Singer*
%Magnus Entertainment, 5 Darley St, Neutral Bay, NSW 2089, Australia

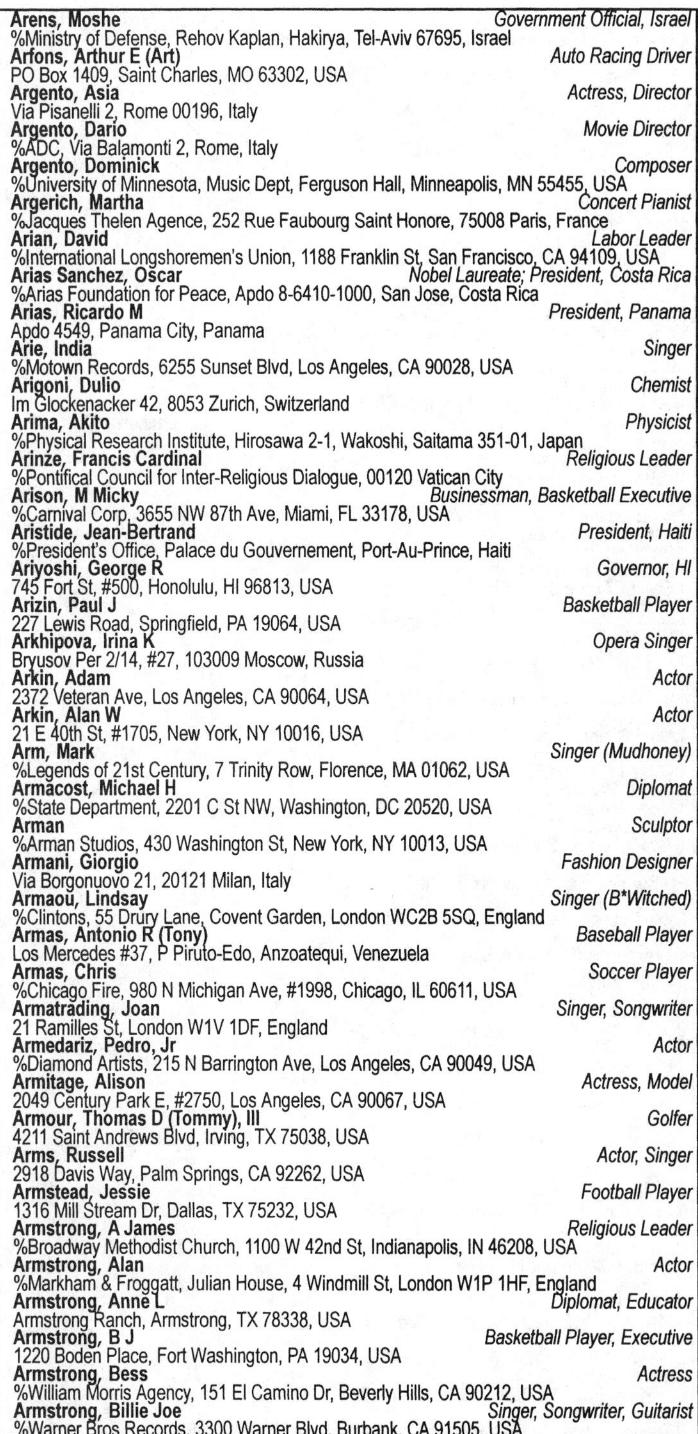

Arens, Moshe *Government Official, Israel*
%Ministry of Defense, Rehov Kaplan, Hakirya, Tel-Aviv 67695, Israel
Arfons, Arthur E (Art) *Auto Racing Driver*
PO Box 1409, Saint Charles, MO 63302, USA
Argento, Asia *Actress, Director*
Via Pisanelli 2, Rome 00196, Italy
Argento, Dario *Movie Director*
%ADC, Via Balamonti 2, Rome, Italy
Argento, Dominick *Composer*
%University of Minnesota, Music Dept, Ferguson Hall, Minneapolis, MN 55455, USA
Argerich, Martha *Concert Pianist*
%Jacques Thelen Agence, 252 Rue Faubourg Saint Honore, 75008 Paris, France
Arian, David *Labor Leader*
%International Longshoremen's Union, 1188 Franklin St, San Francisco, CA 94109, USA
Arias Sanchez, Oscar *Nobel Laureate; President, Costa Rica*
%Arias Foundation for Peace, Apdo 8-6410-1000, San Jose, Costa Rica
Arias, Ricardo M *President, Panama*
Apdo 4549, Panama City, Panama
Arie, India *Singer*
%Motown Records, 6255 Sunset Blvd, Los Angeles, CA 90028, USA
Arigoni, Dulio *Chemist*
Im Glockenacker 42, 8053 Zurich, Switzerland
Arima, Akito *Physicist*
%Physical Research Institute, Hirosawa 2-1, Wakoshi, Saitama 351-01, Japan
Arinze, Francis Cardinal *Religious Leader*
%Pontifical Council for Inter-Religious Dialogue, 00120 Vatican City
Arison, M Micky *Businessman, Basketball Executive*
%Carnival Corp, 3655 NW 87th Ave, Miami, FL 33178, USA
Aristide, Jean-Bertrand *President, Haiti*
%President's Office, Palace du Gouvernement, Port-Au-Prince, Haiti
Ariyoshi, George R *Governor, HI*
745 Fort St, #500, Honolulu, HI 96813, USA
Arizin, Paul J *Basketball Player*
227 Lewis Road, Springfield, PA 19064, USA
Arkhipova, Irina K *Opera Singer*
Bryusov Per 2/14, #27, 103009 Moscow, Russia
Arkin, Adam *Actor*
2372 Veteran Ave, Los Angeles, CA 90064, USA
Arkin, Alan W *Actor*
21 E 40th St, #1705, New York, NY 10016, USA
Arm, Mark *Singer (Mudhoney)*
%Legends of 21st Century, 7 Trinity Row, Florence, MA 01062, USA
Armacost, Michael H *Diplomat*
%State Department, 2201 C St NW, Washington, DC 20520, USA
Arman *Sculptor*
%Arman Studios, 430 Washington St, New York, NY 10013, USA
Armani, Giorgio *Fashion Designer*
Via Borgonuovo 21, 20121 Milan, Italy
Armaou, Lindsay *Singer (B*Witched)*
%Clintons, 55 Drury Lane, Covent Garden, London WC2B 5SQ, England
Armas, Antonio R (Tony) *Baseball Player*
Los Mercedes #37, P Piruto-Edo, Anzoatequi, Venezuela
Armas, Chris *Soccer Player*
%Chicago Fire, 980 N Michigan Ave, #1998, Chicago, IL 60611, USA
Armatrading, Joan *Singer, Songwriter*
21 Ramilles St, London W1V 1DF, England
Armedariz, Pedro, Jr *Actor*
%Diamond Artists, 215 N Barrington Ave, Los Angeles, CA 90049, USA
Armitage, Alison *Actress, Model*
2049 Century Park E, #2750, Los Angeles, CA 90067, USA
Armour, Thomas D (Tommy), III *Golfer*
4211 Saint Andrews Blvd, Irving, TX 75038, USA
Arms, Russell *Actor, Singer*
2918 Davis Way, Palm Springs, CA 92262, USA
Armstead, Jessie *Football Player*
1316 Mill Stream Dr, Dallas, TX 75232, USA
Armstrong, A James *Religious Leader*
%Broadway Methodist Church, 1100 W 42nd St, Indianapolis, IN 46208, USA
Armstrong, Alan *Actor*
%Markham & Froggatt, Julian House, 4 Windmill St, London W1P 1HF, England
Armstrong, Anne L *Diplomat, Educator*
Armstrong Ranch, Armstrong, TX 78338, USA
Armstrong, B J *Basketball Player, Executive*
1220 Boden Place, Fort Washington, PA 19034, USA
Armstrong, Bess *Actress*
%William Morris Agency, 151 El Camino Dr, Beverly Hills, CA 90212, USA
Armstrong, Billie Joe *Singer, Songwriter, Guitarist*
%Warner Bros Records, 3300 Warner Blvd, Burbank, CA 91505, USA

A

Armstrong - Arnold

Armstrong, Clay M *Medical Researcher*
%University of Pennsylvania, Medical School, 3400 Spruce, Philadelphia, PA 19104, USA
Armstrong, Curtis *Actor*
3867 Shannon Road, Los Angeles, CA 90027, USA
Armstrong, Darrell *Basketball Player*
2238 Kettle Dr, Orlando, FL 32835, USA
Armstrong, Deborah (Debbie) *Alpine Skier*
PO Box 710, Taos Ski Valley, NM 87525, USA
Armstrong, Gillian *Movie Director*
%Harry Linstead, 500 Oxford St, Bondi Junction NSW 2022, Australia
Armstrong, Michael *Movie Director*
114 N Doheny Dr, West Hollywood, CA 90048, USA
Armstrong, Murray A *Hockey Player, Coach*
104 Augusta Circle, Saint Augustine, FL 32086, USA
Armstrong, Neil *Hockey Referee*
1169 Sherwood Trail, Sarnia ON N7V 2H3, Canada
Armstrong, Neil A *Astronaut*
%CTA Inc, PO Box 436, Rt 123, Lebanon, OH 45036, USA
Armstrong, Otis *Football Player*
7183 S Newport Way, Centennial, CO 80112, USA
Armstrong, R G *Actor*
3856 Reklaw Dr, Studio City, CA 91604, USA
Armstrong, Robb *Cartoonist (Jump Start)*
%United Feature Syndicate, 200 Madison Ave, New York, NY 10016, USA
Armstrong, Russell P *Vietnam War Marine Corps Hero*
425 Bench Road, Fallon, NV 89406, USA
Armstrong, Spence M *Air Force General*
8714 Bluedale St, Alexandria, VA 22308, USA
Armstrong, Thomas *Auto Racing Driver*
%PacWest Racing Group, 150 Gasoline Alley Road, Indianapolis, IN 46222, USA
Armstrong, Thomas H W *Concert Organist*
1 East St, Olney, Bucks MK46 4AP, England
Armstrong, Tom *Cartoonist (Marvin)*
%North American Syndicate, 235 E 45th St, New York, NY 10017, USA
Armstrong, Trace *Football Player*
18 Oyster Shoals, Alameda, CA 94502, USA
Armstrong, Vaughn *Actor*
4416 Union Ave, La Canada, CA 91011, USA
Armstrong, William L *Senator, CO*
1900 E Girard Place, #1004, Englewood, CO 80113, USA
Arnaud, Jean-Loup *Government Official, France*
55 Rue de Seine, 75006 Paris, France
Arnault, Bernard *Businessman*
%Moet Hennessy Louis Vuitton, 30 Ave Hoche, 75008 Paris, France
Arnaz, Desi, Jr *Actor*
1361 Ridgecrest, Beverly Hills, CA 90210, USA
Arnaz, Lucie *Actress*
PO Box 636, Cross River, NY 10518, USA
Arnell, Richard A S *Composer*
Benhall Lodge, Benhall, Suffolk IP17 1DJ, England
Arnesen, Liv *Polar Skier*
Yourexpedition, 119 N 4th St, #406, Minneapolis, MN 55401, USA
Arness, James *Actor*
PO Box 492163, Los Angeles, CA 90049, USA
Arnett, Jon D *Football Player*
PO Box 4077, Palos Verdes Peninsula, CA 90274, USA
Arnette, Jay *Basketball Player*
2 Hillside Court, Austin, TX 78746, USA
Arnette, Jeanetta *Actress*
466 N Harper Ave, Los Angeles, CA 90048, USA
Arning, Lisa *Actress*
%Chasin Agency, 8899 Beverly Blvd, #716, Los Angeles, CA 90048, USA
Arno, Ed *Cartoonist*
11220 72nd Dr, Flushing, NY 11375, USA
Arnold, Anna Bing *Philanthropist*
%Anna Bing Arnold Foundation, 9700 W Pico Blvd, Los Angeles, CA 90035, USA
Arnold, Brian A *Air Force General*
Commander, Space & Missile Systems Center, Los Angeles Air Force Base, CA 90245, USA
Arnold, Edward (Eddy) *Singer*
PO Box 97, Franklin Road, Brentwood, TN 37024, USA
Arnold, Eve *Photographer*
%Magnum Photographic Agency, 5 Old St, London EC1V 9HL, England
Arnold, Gary H *Movie Critic*
5133 N 1st St, Arlington, VA 22203, USA
Arnold, Jackson D *Navy Admiral, WW II Hero*
Los Pinos, Box 185, Rancho Santa Fe, CA 92067, USA
Arnold, James (Jimmy) *Singer (Four Lads)*
%Thomas Cassidy, 11761 E Speedway Blvd, Tucson, AZ 85748, USA

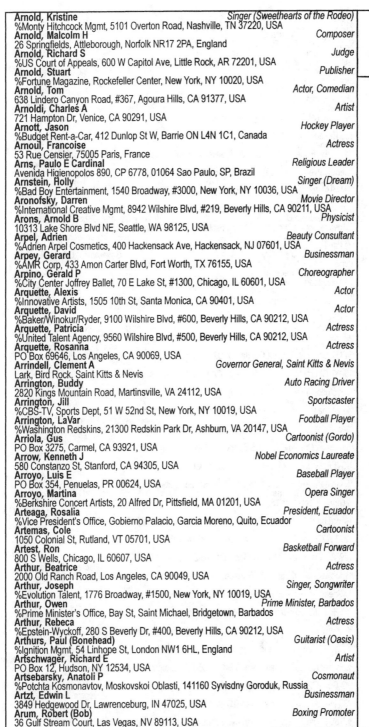

Arnold, Kristine *Singer (Sweethearts of the Rodeo)*
%Monty Hitchcock Mgmt, 5101 Overton Road, Nashville, TN 37220, USA
Arnold, Malcolm H *Composer*
26 Springfields, Attleborough, Norfolk NR17 2PA, England
Arnold, Richard S *Judge*
%US Court of Appeals, 600 W Capitol Ave, Little Rock, AR 72201, USA
Arnold, Stuart *Publisher*
%Fortune Magazine, Rockefeller Center, New York, NY 10020, USA
Arnold, Tom *Actor, Comedian*
638 Lindero Canyon Road, #367, Agoura Hills, CA 91377, USA
Arnoldi, Charles A *Artist*
721 Hampton Dr, Venice, CA 90291, USA
Arnott, Jason *Hockey Player*
%Budget Rent-a-Car, 412 Dunlop St W, Barrie ON L4N 1C1, Canada
Arnoul, Francoise *Actress*
53 Rue Censier, 75005 Paris, France
Arns, Paulo E Cardinal *Religious Leader*
Avenida Higienopolos 890, CP 6778, 01064 Sao Paulo, SP, Brazil
Arnstein, Holly *Singer (Dream)*
%Bad Boy Entertainment, 1540 Broadway, #3000, New York, NY 10036, USA
Aronofsky, Darren *Movie Director*
%International Creative Mgmt, 8942 Wilshire Blvd, #219, Beverly Hills, CA 90211, USA
Arons, Arnold B *Physicist*
10313 Lake Shore Blvd NE, Seattle, WA 98125, USA
Arpel, Adrien *Beauty Consultant*
%Adrien Arpel Cosmetics, 400 Hackensack Ave, Hackensack, NJ 07601, USA
Arpey, Gerard *Businessman*
%AMR Corp, 433 Amon Carter Blvd, Fort Worth, TX 76155, USA
Arpino, Gerald P *Choreographer*
%City Center Joffrey Ballet, 70 E Lake St, #1300, Chicago, IL 60601, USA
Arquette, Alexis *Actor*
%Innovative Artists, 1505 10th St, Santa Monica, CA 90401, USA
Arquette, David *Actor*
%Baker/Winokur/Ryder, 9100 Wilshire Blvd, #600, Beverly Hills, CA 90212, USA
Arquette, Patricia *Actress*
%United Talent Agency, 9560 Wilshire Blvd, #500, Beverly Hills, CA 90212, USA
Arquette, Rosanna *Actress*
PO Box 69646, Los Angeles, CA 90069, USA
Arrindell, Clement A *Governor General, Saint Kitts & Nevis*
Lark, Bird Rock, Saint Kitts & Nevis
Arrington, Buddy *Auto Racing Driver*
2820 Kings Mountain Road, Martinsville, VA 24112, USA
Arrington, Jill *Sportscaster*
%CBS-TV, Sports Dept, 51 W 52nd St, New York, NY 10019, USA
Arrington, LaVar *Football Player*
%Washington Redskins, 21300 Redskin Park Dr, Ashburn, VA 20147, USA
Arriola, Gus *Cartoonist (Gordo)*
PO Box 3275, Carmel, CA 93921, USA
Arrow, Kenneth J *Nobel Economics Laureate*
580 Constanzo St, Stanford, CA 94305, USA
Arroyo, Luis E *Baseball Player*
PO Box 354, Penuelas, PR 00624, USA
Arroyo, Martina *Opera Singer*
%Berkshire Concert Artists, 20 Alfred Dr, Pittsfield, MA 01201, USA
Arteaga, Rosalia *President, Ecuador*
%Vice President's Office, Gobierno Palacio, Garcia Moreno, Quito, Ecuador
Artemas, Cole *Cartoonist*
1050 Colonial St, Rutland, VT 05701, USA
Artest, Ron *Basketball Forward*
800 S Wells, Chicago, IL 60607, USA
Arthur, Beatrice *Actress*
2000 Old Ranch Road, Los Angeles, CA 90049, USA
Arthur, Joseph *Singer, Songwriter*
%Evolution Talent, 1776 Broadway, #1500, New York, NY 10019, USA
Arthur, Owen *Prime Minister, Barbados*
%Prime Minister's Office, Bay St, Saint Michael, Bridgetown, Barbados
Arthur, Rebeca *Actress*
%Epstein-Wyckoff, 280 S Beverly Dr, #400, Beverly Hills, CA 90212, USA
Arthurs, Paul (Bonehead) *Guitarist (Oasis)*
%Ignition Mgmt, 54 Linhope St, London NW1 6HL, England
Artschwager, Richard E *Artist*
PO Box 12, Hudson, NY 12534, USA
Artsebarsky, Anatoli P *Cosmonaut*
%Potchta Kosmonavtov, Moskovskoi Oblasti, 141160 Syvisdny Goroduk, Russia
Artzt, Edwin L *Businessman*
3849 Hedgewood Dr, Lawrenceburg, IN 47025, USA
Arum, Robert (Bob) *Boxing Promoter*
36 Gulf Stream Court, Las Vegas, NV 89113, USA

A

Arvesen - Ashton

Arvesen, Nina *Actress*
412 Culver Blvd, #9, Playa del Rey, CA 90293, USA
Arzu Irigoyen, Alvaro E *President, Guatemala*
%President's Office, Palacio Nacional, Guatemala City, Guatamala
Asay, Chuck *Cartoonist*
%Colorado Springs Gazette, 303 S Prospect St, Colorado Springs, CO 80903, USA
Asbury, Martin *Cartoonist (Garth)*
Stoneworld, Pitch Green, Princes Risborough, Bucks HP27 9QG, England
Aschenbrenner, Frank *Football Player*
16372 E Jacklin Dr, Fountain Hills, AZ 85268, USA
Ash, Roy L *Businessman, Government Official*
655 Funchal Road, Los Angeles, CA 90077, USA
Ashbery, John L *Writer*
326 Belmont Ave, Buffalo, NY 14223, USA
Ashbrook, Dana *Actor*
%Rigberg Roberts Rugolo, 1180 S Beverly Dr, #601, Los Angeles, CA 90035, USA
Ashbrook, Daphne *Actress*
%Innovative Artists, 1505 10th St, Santa Monica, CA 90401, USA
Ashby, Jeffrey S *Astronaut*
%NASA, Johnson Space Center, 2101 NASA Road, Houston, TX 77058, USA
Ashby, Linden *Actor*
639 N Larchmont Blvd, #207, Los Angeles, CA 90004, USA
Ashcroft, John D *Attorney General; Senator/Governor, MO*
%Justice Department, 10th St & Constitution Ave NW, Washington, DC 20530, USA
Ashcroft, Richard *Singer (Verve), Songwriter*
%Little Big Man Booking, 39A Grammercy Park N, #1C, New York, NY 10010, USA
Ashdown, J J D (Paddy) *Government Official, England*
Vane Cottage, Norton Sub Hamdon, Somerset TA14 6SG, England
Ashenfelter, Horace, III *Track Athlete*
100 Hawthorne Ave, Glen Ridge, NJ 07028, USA
Asher, Barry *Bowler*
%Professional Bowlers Assn, 719 2nd Ave, #701, Seattle, WA 98104, USA
Asher, Jane *Actress*
24 Cole St, London SW3 3QU, England
Asher, Peter *Businessman, Singer (Peter & Gordon)*
%Peter Asher Mgmt, 644 N Doheny Dr, Los Angeles, CA 90069, USA
Asher, William *Movie Director, Screenwriter*
54337 Oak Hill Blvd, La Quinta, CA 92253, USA
Ashford Washington, Evelyn *Track Athlete*
38997 Cherry Point Lane, Murrieta, CA 92563, USA
Ashford, Mandy *Singer (Innosense)*
%Evolution Talent, 1776 Broadway, #1500, New York, NY 10019, USA
Ashford, Matthew *Actor*
%J Michael Bloom, 9255 Sunset Blvd, #710, Los Angeles, CA 90069, USA
Ashford, Nicholas (Nick) *Singer (Ashford & Simpson), Songwriter*
%Associated Booking Corp, 1995 Broadway, #501, New York, NY 10023, USA
Ashford, Roslyn *Singer (Martha & Vandellas)*
%Thomas Cassidy, 11761 E Speedway Blvd, Tucson, AZ 85748, USA
Ashida, Jun *Fashion Designer*
1-3-3 Aobadai, Meguroku, Tokyo 153, Japan
Ashihara, Yoshinobu *Architect*
%Ashihara Architects, 31-15 Sakuragaokacho, Shibuyaku, Tokyo 150, Japan
Ashkenazy, Vladimir D *Concert Pianist, Conductor*
Savinka, Kappelistr 15, 6045 Meggen, Switzerland
Ashley *Model*
%Ford Model Agency, 142 Greene St, #400, New York, NY 10012, USA
Ashley, Elizabeth *Actress*
1223 N Ogden Dr, West Hollywood, CA 90046, USA
Ashley, Jennifer *Actress*
129 W Wilson, #202, Costa Mesa, CA 92627, USA
Ashley, John *Hockey Player, Referee*
%Hockey Hall of Fame, BCE Place, 30 Yonge St, Toronto ON M5E 1X8, Canada
Ashley, Laurence *Actress*
%Cineart, 36 Rue de Ponthieu, 75008 Paris, France
Ashley, Leon *Singer*
PO Box 567, Hendersonville, TN 37077, USA
Ashley, Merrill *Ballerina*
%New York City Ballet, Lincoln Center Plaza, New York, NY 10023, USA
Ashmore, Edward B *Navy Admiral, England*
%Naval Secretary, Victory Bldg, HM Naval Base, Portsmouth, Hants, England
Ashrawi, Hanan *Political Leader, Palestine*
%Higher Education Ministry, PO Box 17360, Jerusalem, West Bank, Israel
Ashton, John *Actor*
PO Box 272489, Fort Collins, CO 80527, USA
Ashton, Peter S *Tropical Forest Scientist*
233 Herald Road, Carlisle, MA 01741, USA
Ashton, Susan *Singer*
%Bob Doyle Assoc, 1111 17th Ave S, Nashville, TN 37212, USA

Ashworth, Gerald (Gerry) *Track Athlete*
7 Athena Circle, Andover, MA 01810, USA
Ashworth, Jeanne C *Speedskater*
Whiteface Highway, Wilmington, NY 12997, USA
Askew, Luke *Actor*
%Media Artists Group, 6300 Wilshire Blvd, #1470, Los Angeles, CA 90048, USA
Askew, Reubin O *Governor, FL*
PO Box 1512, Burnsville, NC 28714, USA
Askin, Leon *Actor*
Hutteldorferstr 349, 1140 Vienna, Austria
Asner, Edward *Actor*
3556 Mound View Ave, Studio City, CA 91604, USA
Asomugha, Nnamdi *Football Player*
%Oakland Raiders, 1220 Harbor Bay Parkway, Alameda, CA 94502, USA
Aspen, Jennifer *Actress*
%B&B Entertainment, 1640 S Sepulveda Blvd, #530, Los Angeles, CA 90025, USA
Asphaug, Erik *Astronomer*
%University of California, Astrology Dept, Santa Cruz, CA
Aspromonte, Kenneth J (Ken) *Baseball Player*
2 Derham Parc St, Houston, TX 77024, USA
Assad, Bashar al- *President, Syria*
%Presidential Palace, Muharreem Abu Rumanch, Al-Rashid St, Damascas, Syria
Assante, Armand *Actor*
RR 1 Box 561, Campbell Hall, NY 10916, USA
Assinger, Armin *Skier*
Kuhweg 23, 9620 Hermagor, Austria
Assoumani, Azaly *President, Comoros; Army Colonel*
%President's Office, BP 421, Moroni, Grand Comoro, Comoros
Asti, Adrianna *Actress*
%Carol Levi Co, Via Giuseppe Pisanelli, 00196 Rome, Italy
Astin, John *Actor, Director*
3801 Canterbury Road, #505, Baltimore, MD 21218, USA
Astin, Mackenzie *Actor*
%Metropolitan Talent Agency, 4526 Wilshire Blvd, Los Angeles, CA 90010, USA
Astin, Sean *Actor*
PO Box 57858, Sherman Oaks, CA 91413, USA
Astley, Rick *Singer*
4-7 Vinyard Sanctuary, London SE1 1QL, England
Astor, Brooke *Foundation Executive*
%Vincent Astor Foundation, 405 Park Ave, New York, NY 10022, USA
Asturaga, Nova *Government Official, Nicaragua*
%Permanent Mission of Nicaragua, 820 2nd Ave, #801, New York, NY 10017, USA
Asylmuratova, Altynai *Ballerina*
%Mariinsky Theater, Teatralnaya Pl 1, Saint Petersburg, Russia
Atala, Anthony *Surgeon*
%Harvard Medical School, 25 Shattuck St, Boston, MA 02115, USA
Atchison, Michael *Editorial Cartoonist*
%Associated Press, 50 Rockefeller Plaza, New York, NY 10020, USA
Atherton, David *Conductor*
%Askonas Holt Ltd, 27 Chancery Lane, London W2A 1PF, England
Atherton, William *Actor*
5102 San Feliciano Dr, Woodland Hills, CA 91364, USA
Atiyah, Michael F *Mathematician*
3/8 West Grange Gardens, Edinbergh EH9 2RA, Scotland
Atiyeh, Victor *Governor, OR*
%Victor Atiyeh Co, 519 SW Park Ave, #205, Portland, OR 97205, USA
Atkin, Harvey *Actor*
527 S Curson St, Los Angeles, CA 90036, USA
Atkins, Christopher *Actor*
6934 Bevis Ave, Van Nuys, CA 91405, USA
Atkins, Douglas L (Doug) *Football Player*
PO Box 14007, Knoxville, TN 37914, USA
Atkins, Eileen *Actress*
%Jonathan Altaras, 13 Shorts Gardens, London WC2H 9AT, England
Atkins, Erica *Singer (Mary Mary), Songwriter*
%The Firm, 9100 Wilshire Blvd, #100W, Beverly Hills, CA 90210, USA
Atkins, Sharif *Actor*
%Stone Manners, 6500 Wilshire Blvd, #550, Los Angeles, CA 90048, USA
Atkins, Tina *Singer (Mary Mary), Songwriter*
%The Firm, 9100 Wilshire Blvd, #100W, Beverly Hills, CA 90210, USA
Atkins, Tom *Actor*
%Paradigm Agency, 10100 Santa Monica Blvd, #2500, Los Angeles, CA 90067, USA
Atkinson, Jayne *Actress*
%Innovative Artists, 1505 10th St, Santa Monica, CA 90401, USA
Atkinson, Paul *Guitarist (Zombies)*
%Lustig Talent, PO Box 770850, Orlando, FL 32877, USA
Atkinson, Rick *Journalist, Writer*
%Kansas City Times, Editorial Dept, 1729 Grand Ave, Kansas City, MO 64108, USA

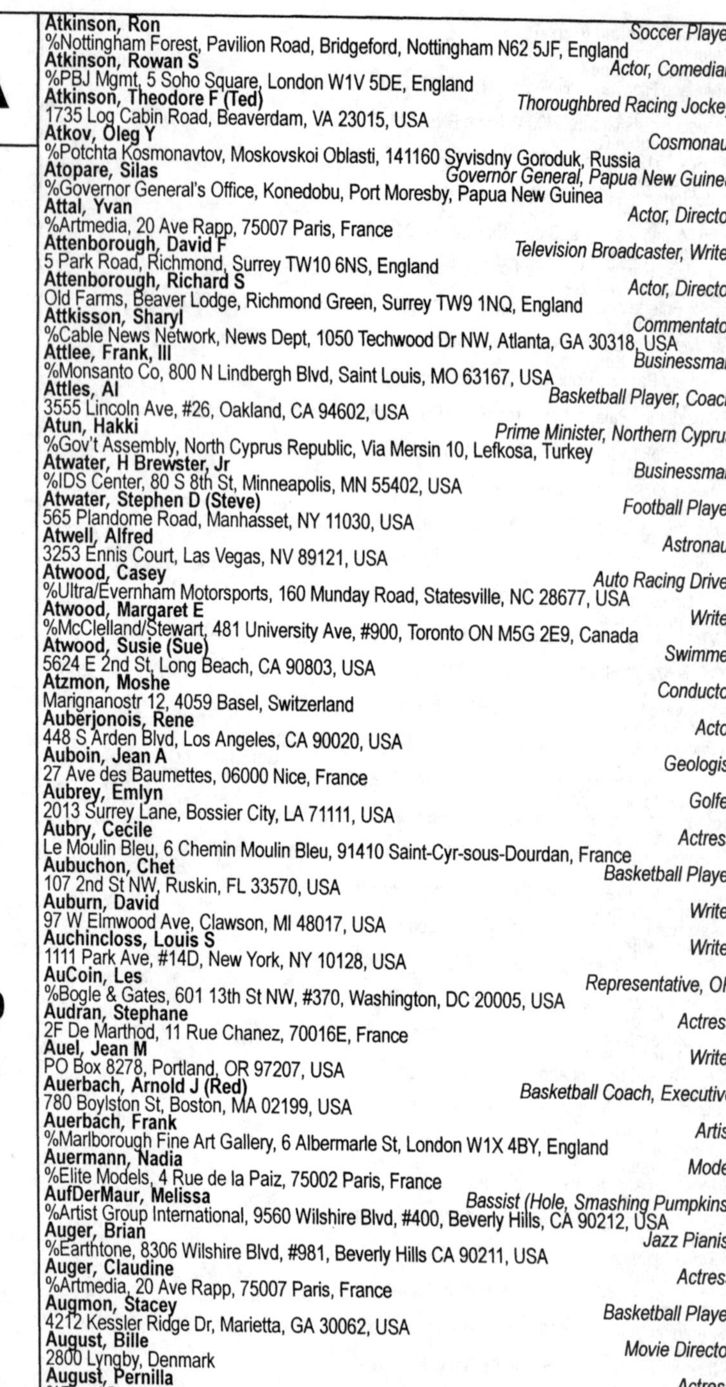

A

Atkinson - Augustain

Atkinson, Ron *Soccer Player*
%Nottingham Forest, Pavilion Road, Bridgeford, Nottingham N62 5JF, England
Atkinson, Rowan S *Actor, Comedian*
%PBJ Mgmt, 5 Soho Square, London W1V 5DE, England
Atkinson, Theodore F (Ted) *Thoroughbred Racing Jockey*
1735 Log Cabin Road, Beaverdam, VA 23015, USA
Atkov, Oleg Y *Cosmonaut*
%Potchta Kosmonavtov, Moskovskoi Oblasti, 141160 Syvisdny Goroduk, Russia
Atopare, Silas *Governor General, Papua New Guinea*
%Governor General's Office, Konedobu, Port Moresby, Papua New Guinea
Attal, Yvan *Actor, Director*
%Artmedia, 20 Ave Rapp, 75007 Paris, France
Attenborough, David F *Television Broadcaster, Writer*
5 Park Road, Richmond, Surrey TW10 6NS, England
Attenborough, Richard S *Actor, Director*
Old Farms, Beaver Lodge, Richmond Green, Surrey TW9 1NQ, England
Attkisson, Sharyl *Commentator*
%Cable News Network, News Dept, 1050 Techwood Dr NW, Atlanta, GA 30318, USA
Attlee, Frank, III *Businessman*
%Monsanto Co, 800 N Lindbergh Blvd, Saint Louis, MO 63167, USA
Attles, Al *Basketball Player, Coach*
3555 Lincoln Ave, #26, Oakland, CA 94602, USA
Atun, Hakki *Prime Minister, Northern Cyprus*
%Gov't Assembly, North Cyprus Republic, Via Mersin 10, Lefkosa, Turkey
Atwater, H Brewster, Jr *Businessman*
%IDS Center, 80 S 8th St, Minneapolis, MN 55402, USA
Atwater, Stephen D (Steve) *Football Player*
565 Plandome Road, Manhasset, NY 11030, USA
Atwell, Alfred *Astronaut*
3253 Ennis Court, Las Vegas, NV 89121, USA
Atwood, Casey *Auto Racing Driver*
%Ultra/Evernham Motorsports, 160 Munday Road, Statesville, NC 28677, USA
Atwood, Margaret E *Writer*
%McClelland/Stewart, 481 University Ave, #900, Toronto ON M5G 2E9, Canada
Atwood, Susie (Sue) *Swimmer*
5624 E 2nd St, Long Beach, CA 90803, USA
Atzmon, Moshe *Conductor*
Marignanostr 12, 4059 Basel, Switzerland
Auberjonois, Rene *Actor*
448 S Arden Blvd, Los Angeles, CA 90020, USA
Auboin, Jean A *Geologist*
27 Ave des Baumettes, 06000 Nice, France
Aubrey, Emlyn *Golfer*
2013 Surrey Lane, Bossier City, LA 71111, USA
Aubry, Cecile *Actress*
Le Moulin Bleu, 6 Chemin Moulin Bleu, 91410 Saint-Cyr-sous-Dourdan, France
Aubuchon, Chet *Basketball Player*
107 2nd St NW, Ruskin, FL 33570, USA
Auburn, David *Writer*
97 W Elmwood Ave, Clawson, MI 48017, USA
Auchincloss, Louis S *Writer*
1111 Park Ave, #14D, New York, NY 10128, USA
AuCoin, Les *Representative, OR*
%Bogle & Gates, 601 13th St NW, #370, Washington, DC 20005, USA
Audran, Stephane *Actress*
2F De Marthod, 11 Rue Chanez, 70016E, France
Auel, Jean M *Writer*
PO Box 8278, Portland, OR 97207, USA
Auerbach, Arnold J (Red) *Basketball Coach, Executive*
780 Boylston St, Boston, MA 02199, USA
Auerbach, Frank *Artist*
%Marlborough Fine Art Gallery, 6 Albermarle St, London W1X 4BY, England
Auermann, Nadia *Model*
%Elite Models, 4 Rue de la Paiz, 75002 Paris, France
AufDerMaur, Melissa *Bassist (Hole, Smashing Pumpkins)*
%Artist Group International, 9560 Wilshire Blvd, #400, Beverly Hills, CA 90212, USA
Auger, Brian *Jazz Pianist*
%Earthtone, 8306 Wilshire Blvd, #981, Beverly Hills CA 90211, USA
Auger, Claudine *Actress*
%Artmedia, 20 Ave Rapp, 75007 Paris, France
Augmon, Stacey *Basketball Player*
4212 Kessler Ridge Dr, Marietta, GA 30062, USA
August, Bille *Movie Director*
2800 Lyngby, Denmark
August, Pernilla *Actress*
%Royal Dramatic Theater, Box 5037, 102 41 Stockholm, Sweden
Augustain, Ira *Actor*
%Diamond Artists, 215 N Barrington Ave, Los Angeles, CA 90049, USA

Augustine, Norman R *Businessman*
24131 Doreen Dr, Gaithersburg, MD 20882, USA
Augustnyiak, Jerry *Drummer (10000 Maniacs)*
%Agency for Performing Arts, 9200 Sunset Blvd, #900, Los Angeles, CA 90069, USA
Auker, Eldon L *Baseball Player*
15 Sailfish Road, Vero Beach, FL 32960, USA
Aulby, Michael (Mike) *Bowler*
1591 Springmill Ponds Circle, Carmel, IN 46032, USA
Aulenti, Gae *Architect*
4 Piazza San Marco, 20121 Milan, Italy
Aung San Suu Kyi *Nobel Peace Laureate*
%National League for Democracy, 97B W Shwegondine Road, Yangon, Myanmar
Auriemma, Geno *Basketball Coach*
%University of Connecticut, 2095 Hillside Road, Storrs Mansfield, CT 06269, USA
Austen, W Gerald *Surgeon*
163 Wellesley St, Weston, MA 02493, USA
Auster, Paul *Writer, Movie Director*
%Henry Holt, 115 W 18th St, New York, NY 10011, USA
Austin, A Woody *Golfer*
705 SE Melody Lane, #B, Lees Summit, MO 64063, USA
Austin, Charles *Track Athlete*
514 Duncan Dr, San Marcos, TX 78666, USA
Austin, Dallas *Actor*
4523 Wieuca Road NE, Atlanta, GA 30342, USA
Austin, Debbie *Golfer*
6733 Bittersweet Lane, Orlando, FL 32819, USA
Austin, Denise *Physical Fitness Instructor*
%Peter Pan Industries, 88 Saint Francis St, Newark, NJ 07105, USA
Austin, Karen *Actress*
3356 Rowena Ave, #3, Los Angeles, CA 90027, USA
Austin, Patti *Singer*
3 Loudon Dr, #8, Fishkill, NY 12524, USA
Austin, Sherrie *Singer, Guitarist, Actress*
PO Box 551, Gallatin, TN 37066, USA
Austin, Stone Cold Steve *Wrestler*
5 Nollkamper Road, Boerne, TX 78006, USA
Austin, Teri *Actress*
4245 Laurel Grove, Studio City, CA 91604, USA
Austin, Tracy *Tennis Player*
1751 Pinnacle Dr, #1500, McLean, VA 22102, USA
Austrian, Robert *Physician*
%Univ of Pennsylvania, Med Center, 36 Hamilton Circle, Philadelphia, PA 19130, USA
Auteuil, Daniel *Actor*
%Artmedia, 20 Ave Rapp, 75007 Paris, France
Auth, Tony *Editorial Cartoonist*
%Philadelphia Inquirer, Editorial Dept, 1830 Town Center Dr, Langhorne, PA 19047, USA
Autolitano, Astrid *Businesswoman*
%Mattel Inc, 333 Continental Blvd, El Segundo, CA 90245, USA
Autry, Alan *Actor*
%David Shapira, 15821 Ventura Blvd, #235, Encino, CA 91436, USA
Autry, Darnell *Football Player*
510 E Greenway Dr, Tempe, AZ 85282, USA
Autry, Jim *Golf Executive*
%Professional Golfer's Assn, PO Box 109601, Palm Beach Gardens, FL 33410, USA
Avalon, Frankie *Singer, Actor*
4303 Spring Forest Lane, Westlake Village, CA 91362, USA
Avdelsayed, Gabriel *Religious Leader*
%Coptic Orthodox Church, 427 West Side Ave, Jersey City, NJ 07304, USA
Avdeyev, Sergei V *Cosmonaut*
%Potchta Kosmonavtov, Moskovskoi Oblasti, 141160 Syvisdny Goroduk, Russia
Avedon, Richard (Dick) *Photographer*
407 E 75th St, New York, NY 10021, USA
Avellini, Robert H (Bob) *Football Player*
1085 Flamingo Dr, Roselle, IL 60172, USA
Averre, Berton *Guitarist (Knack)*
17510 Posetano Road, Pacific Palisades, CA 90272, USA
Avery, James *Actor*
195 S Beverly Drive, #400, Beverly Hills, CA 90212, USA
Avery, Margaret *Actress*
%Artists Agency, 1180 S Beverly Dr, #301, Los Angeles, CA 90035, USA
Avery, Mary Ellen *Physician, Pediatrician*
52 Liberty St, Plymouth, MA 02360, USA
Avery, Phyllis *Actress*
609 Sterling Place, South Pasadena, CA 91030, USA
Avery, Val *Actor*
84 Grove St, #19, New York, NY 10014, USA
Avery, William H *Governor, KS*
PO Box 6, Wakefield, KS 67487, USA

A

Avery - Azzi

Avery, William J *Businessman*
%Crown Cork & Seal, 1 Crown Way, Philadelphia, PA 19154, USA
Avi *Writer*
%Orchard Books, 95 Madison Ave, New York, NY 10016, USA
Avila, Roberto F G (Bobby) *Baseball Player*
Navegantes FR-19, Reforma-Veracruz, Mexico
Avildsen, John G *Movie Director*
2423 Briarcrest Road, Beverly Hills, CA 90210, USA
Avital, Mili *Actress*
%Creative Artists Agency, 9830 Wilshire Blvd, Beverly Hills, CA 90212, USA
Avnet, Jonathan M (Jon) *Movie Director, Producer*
3815 Hughes Ave, Culver City, CA 90232, USA
Avory, Mike *Drummer (Kinks)*
%Larry Page, 29 Rushton Mews, London W11 1RB, England
Awtrey, Dennis *Basketball Player*
509 W Granada, Phoenix, AZ 85003, USA
Ax, Emmanuel *Concert Pianist*
173 Riverside Dr, #12G, New York, NY 10024, USA
Axelrod, Jonathan H *Molecular Biologist*
%Salk Institute, 10100 N Torrey Pines Road, La Jolla, CA 92037, USA
Axelrod, Julius *Nobel Medicine Laureate*
10401 Grosvenor Place, Rockville, MD 20852, USA
Axtell, George C *WW II Marine Corps Air Force Hero*
41 High Bluff Dr, Weaverville, NC 28787, USA
Ay-O *Artist*
2-6-38 Matsuyama, Kiyoseshi, Tokyo, Japan
Ayala, Francisco J *Geneticist, Molecular Biologist*
2 Locke Court, Irvine, CA 92612, USA
Ayala, Paul *Boxer*
7524 Creek Meadow Dr, Fort Worth, TX 76123, USA
Ayanna, Charlotte *Actress*
%Industry Entertainment, 955 Carillo Dr, #300, Los Angeles, CA 90048, USA
Ayckbourn, Alan *Writer, Director*
%M Ramsay, 14A Goodwins Ct, Saint Martin's Lane, London WC2N 4LL, England
Aycock, Alice *Artist*
62 Green St, New York, NY 10012, USA
Ayers, Chuck *Cartoonist (Crankshaft)*
%Universal Press Syndicate, 4520 Main St, Kansas City, MO 64111, USA
Ayers, Dick *Cartoonist (Sgt Fury)*
64 Beech St W, White Plains, NY 10604, USA
Ayers, Randy *Basketball Coach*
%Philadelphia 76ers, 1st Union Center, 3601 S Broad St, Philadelphia, PA 19148, USA
Ayers, Roy E, Jr *Jazz Vibist, Pianist, Singer*
%Associated Booking Corp, 1995 Broadway, #501, New York, NY 10023, USA
Aykroyd, Dan *Actor, Comedian*
%Creative Artists Agency, 9830 Wilshire Blvd, Beverly Hills, CA 90212, USA
Aylwin Azocar, Patricio *President, Chile*
Teresa Salas 786, Providencia, Santiago, Chile
Azar, Steve *Singer*
%Gold Mountain, 2 Music Circle S, #212, Nashville, TN 37203, USA
Azaria, Hank *Actor*
%Endeavor Talent Agency, 9701 Wilshire Blvd, #1000, Beverly Hills, CA 90212, USA
Azimov, Yakhyo *Prime Minister, Tajikistan*
%Prime Minister's Office, Rudaki Prosp 42, 743051 Dushaube, Tajikistan
Azinger, Paul W *Golfer*
%Leader Enterprises, 1101 N Kentucky Ave, #100, Winter Park, FL 32789, USA
Aziz, Tariq *Prime Minister, Iraq*
%Prime Minister's Office, Karadat Mariam, Baghdad, Iraq
Azlan Muhibuddin Shan *Sultan, Malaysia*
%Sultan's Palace, Istana Bukit Serene, Kuala Lumpur, Malaysia
Aznar, Jose Maria *Prime Minister, Spain*
%Prime Minister's Office, Complejo de las Moncloa, 28071 Madrid, Spain
Aznavour, Charles *Singer, Actor, Songwriter*
%Levon Sayan, 76-78 Ave Champs-Elysees, 75008 Paris, France
Azria, Max *Fashion Designer*
%BCBG/Max Azria, 2761 Fruitland Ave, Vernon, CA 90058, USA
Azuma, Takamitsu *Architect*
%Azuma Architects, 3-6-1 Minami-Aoyama Minatoku, Tokyo 107, Japan
Azumah, Jerry *Football Player*
39 King St, Worcester, MA 01610, USA
Azzara, Candice *Actress*
%Meridian Artists, 9229 Sunset Blvd, #310, Los Angeles, CA 90069, USA
Azzi, Jennifer *Basketball Player*
%San Antonio Silver Stars, 1 SBC Center, San Antonio, TX 78219, USA

Baba, Encik Abdul Ghafar Bin *Prime Minister, Malaysia*
%Rural Development Ministry, Jalan Raja Laut, 50606 Kuala Lampur, Malaysia
Babashoff, Jack *Swimmer*
4859 Monroe Ave, San Diego, CA 92115, USA
Babashoff, Shirley *Swimmer*
17254 Santa Clara St, Fountain Valley, CA 92708, USA
Babatunde, Obba *Actor*
%Stone Manners, 6500 Wilshire Blvd, #550, Los Angeles, CA 90048, USA
Babb, Charlie *Football Player*
371 Heron Ave, Naples, FL 34108, USA
Babb-Sprague, Kristen *Synchronized Swimmer*
4677 Pine Valley Dr, Stockton, CA 95219, USA
Babbidge, Homes D, Jr *Educator*
3 Diving St, Stonington, CT 06378, USA
Babbitt, Bruce E *Secretary, Interior; Governor, AZ*
5169 Watson St NW, Washington, DC 20016, USA
Babbitt, Milton B *Composer*
222 Western Way, Princeton, NJ 08540, USA
Babbitt, Natalie *Writer*
%Farrar Straus Giroux, 19 Union Square W, New York, NY 10003, USA
Babcock, Barbara *Actress*
PO Box 222271, Carmel, CA 93922, USA
Babcock, Mike *Hockey Coach*
%Anaheim Mighty Ducks, 2000 E Gene Autry Way, Anaheim, CA 92806, USA
Babcock, Tim M *Governor, MT*
%Ox Bow Ranch, PO Box 877, Helena, MT 59624, USA
Babenco, Hector E *Movie Director*
%International Creative Mgmt, 8942 Wilshire Blvd, #219, Beverly Hills, CA 90211, USA
Babich, Bob *Football Player*
4994 Mount Ashmun Dr, San Diego, CA 92111, USA
Babilonia, Tai *Figure Skater*
13889 Valley Vista Blvd, Sherman Oaks, CA 91423, USA
Babin, Rex *Editorial Cartoonist*
%Sacramento Bee, Editorial Dept, 21st & Q Sts, Sacramento, CA 95852, USA
Baby Oje *Soul/Rap Artist (Arrested Development)*
%William Morris Agency, 1325 Ave of Americas, New York, NY 10019, USA
Baby Peggy *Actress*
2219 Canyon Brook Lane, Newman, CA 95360, USA
Babych, Dave *Hockey Player*
6 Willow Brook Road, Glastonbury, CT 06033, USA
Baca, John P *Vietnam War Army Hero (CMH)*
PO Box 9203, San Diego, CA 92169, USA
Baca, Susana *Singer*
%Todo Mondo, PO Box 652, Cooper Station, New York, NY 10276, USA
Bacall, Lauren *Actress*
%Dakota Hotel, 1 W 72nd St, #43, New York, NY 10023, USA
Bach, Barbara *Actress*
2 Glynde Mews, London SW3 1SB, England
Bach, Catherine *Actress*
%C N A Assoc, 1925 Century Park East, #750, Los Angeles, CA 90067, USA
Bach, Emmanuelle *Actress*
%Artmedia, 20 Ave Rapp, 75007 Paris, France
Bach, Pamela *Actress*
%William Morris Agency, 151 El Camino Dr, Beverly Hills, CA 90212, USA
Bach, Richard *Writer*
%Dell Publishing, 1540 Broadway, New York, NY 10036, USA
Bach, Sebastian *Singer (Skid Row), Actor*
%Premier Talent, 3 E 54th St, #1100, New York, NY 10022, USA
Bacharach, Burt *Composer, Musician*
681 Amalfi Dr, Pacific Palisades, CA 90272, USA
Bachardy, Don *Writer*
145 Adelaide Dr, Santa Monica, CA 90402, USA
Bachman, Randy *Singer, Songwriter, Guitarist*
%Entertainment Services, 6400 Pleasant Park Dr, Chanhassen, MN 55317, USA
Bachman, Tal *Singer, Songwriter, Musician*
%Q Prime, 729 7th Ave, #1600, New York, NY 10019, USA
Bachmann, Maria *Concert Violinist*
%Columbia Artists Mgmt Inc, 165 W 57th St, New York, NY 10019, USA
Bachrach, Louis F, Jr *Photographer*
%Bachrach Inc, 647 Boylston St, #2, Boston, MA 02116, USA
Baciocco, Albert J, Jr *Navy Admiral*
747 Pitt St, Mount Pleasant, SC 29464, USA
Backis, Audrys Juozas Cardinal *Religious Leader*
Sventaragio 4, 2001 Vilnius, Lithuania
Backley, Stephen (Steve) *Track Athlete*
%Cambridge Harriers, 56A-60 Glenhurst Ave, Bexley, Kent DA5 3QN, England
Backus, Billy *Boxer*
308 N Main St, Canastota, NY 13032, USA

B

Backus - Bahr

Backus, Gus *Singer (Del Vikings)*
%Lustig Talent, PO Box 770850, Orlando, FL 32877, USA
Backus, John *Computer Programmer, Mathematician*
91 Saint Germaine Ave, San Francisco, CA 94114, USA
Backus, Sharon *Softball Coach*
%University of California, Athletic Dept, Los Angeles, CA 90024, USA
Bacon, Coy *Football Player*
1017 S 8th St, Ironton, OH 45638, USA
Bacon, Edmund N *Architect*
2117 Locust St, Philadelphia, PA 19103, USA
Bacon, James *Columnist*
10982 Topeka Dr, Northridge, CA 91326, USA
Bacon, Kevin *Actor*
PO Box 668, Sharon, CT 06069, USA
Bacon, Nicky D *Vietnam War Army Hero (CMH)*
%Medal of Honor Society, 40 Patriots Point Road, Mount Pleasant, SC 29464, USA
Bacon, Roger F *Navy Admiral*
24285 Johnson Road NW, Poulsbo, WA 98370, USA
Bacot, J Carter *Financier*
48 Porter Place, Montclair, NJ 07042, USA
Bacs, Ludovic *Conductor, Composer*
31 D Golescu, Sc III, E7 V Ap 87, Bucharest 1, Romania
Bacuicchi, Antonello *Co-Regent, San Marino*
%Co-Regent's Office, Government Palace, 47031 San Marino
Badalamenti, Angelo *Composer*
11 Fidelian Way, Lincoln Park, NJ 07035, USA
Badalucco, Michael *Actor*
%Manhattan Beach Studios, 1600 Rosecrans Ave, #1A, Manhattan Beach, CA 90266, USA
Baddour, Raymond F *Chemical Engineer*
6495 SW 122nd St, Miami, FL 33156, USA
Bader, Diedrich *Actor*
131 N June St, Los Angeles, CA 90004, USA
Badgley, Mark *Fashion Designer*
%Badgley Mischka, 525 Fashion Ave, New York, NY 10018, USA
Badham, John M *Movie Director*
%Badham Company, 344 Clerendon Road, Beverly Hills, CA 90210, USA
Badler, Jane *Actress*
%Melbourne Artists, 21 Cardigan Place, Albert Park VIC 3206, Australia
Badu, Erykah *Singer, Songwriter*
%Motown Records, 6255 Sunset Blvd, Los Angeles, CA 90028, USA
Badura-Skoda, Paul *Concert Pianist, Composer*
Zuckerkandlgass 14, 1190 Vienna, Austria
Baer, Gordy *Bowler*
8577 Tullamore Dr, Tinley Park, IL 60477, USA
Baer, Max, Jr *Actor, Movie Producer, Director*
PO Box 1831, Zephyr Cove, NV 89448, USA
Baer, Robert J (Jacob) *Army General*
6213 Militia Court, Fairfax Station, VA 22039, USA
Baez, Joan *Singer, Songwriter*
%Mark Spector C, 44 Post Road W, Westport, CT 06880, USA
Baeza, Braulio *Thoroughbred Racing Jockey*
650 Huntington Ave, Boston, MA 02115, USA
Bafile, Corrado Cardinal *Religious Leader*
Via P Pancrazio Pfeiffer 10, 00193 Rome, Italy
Bagabandi, Ntsaagiyn *President, Mongolia*
%President's Office, Great Hural, Ulan Bator, Mongolia
Baggetta, Vincent *Actor*
3928 Madelia Ave, Sherman Oaks, CA 91403, USA
Baggio, Roberto *Soccer Player*
%Bologna FC, Via Casteldebole 10, 40132 Bologna, Italy
Baggott, Julianna *Writer*
%Pocket Books, 1230 Ave of Americas, New York, NY 10020, USA
Bagian, James P *Astronaut*
21537 Holmbury Road, Northville, MI 48167, USA
Bagnal, Charles W *Army General*
%Ratchford Assoc, 221 W Springs Road, Columbia, SC 29223, USA
Bagwell, Jeffrey R (Jeff) *Baseball Player*
4 Saddle Creek, Houston, TX 77024, USA
Bahcall, John N *Astrophysicist*
21 Adams Dr, Princeton, NJ 08540, USA
Bahnsen, Stanley R (Stan) *Baseball Player*
PO Box 5414, Lighthouse Point, FL 33074, USA
Bahr, Chris *Football Player*
122 Kaywood Dr, Boalsburg, PA 16827, USA
Bahr, Matthew D (Matt) *Football Player*
53 Parkridge Lane, Pittsburgh, PA 15228, USA
Bahr, Morton *Labor Leader*
%Communications Workers Union, 501 3rd St NW, Washington, DC 20001, USA

Bahr, Walter *Soccer Player*
250 Elks Road, Boalsburg, PA 16827, USA
Bai Ling *Actress*
%Agency for Performing Arts, 485 Madison Ave, New York, NY 10022, USA
Bai Yang *Actress*
978 Huashan Road, Shanghai 200050, China
Bailar, Benjamin F *Government Official, Educator*
410 Walnut Road, Lake Forest, IL 60045, USA
Bailey, Christina (Chris) *Hockey Player*
2749 Rose Hill Road, Marietta, NY 13110, USA
Bailey, David *Photographer*
%Robert Montgomery, 3 Junction Mews, Sale Place, London W2, England
Bailey, Donovan *Track Athlete*
625 Hales Chapel Road, Gray, TN 37615, USA
Bailey, F Lee *Attorney*
%Beverly & Freeman, 823 N Olive Ave, West Palm Beach, FL 33401, USA
Bailey, G W *Actor*
22935 Frisca Dr, Valencia, CA 91354, USA
Bailey, Jim *Actor, Singer*
5909 W Colgate Ave, Los Angeles, CA 90036, USA
Bailey, John *Cinematographer*
%United Talent Agency, 9560 Wilshire Blvd, #500, Beverly Hills, CA 90212, USA
Bailey, Johnny L *Football Player*
1282 Kingsbury Road, Abilene, TX 79602, USA
Bailey, Keith E *Businessman*
%Williams Companies, 1 One Williams Center, Tulsa, OK 74172, USA
Bailey, Maxwell C *Air Force General*
306 2nd St, Paris, KY 40361, USA
Bailey, Norman S *Opera Singer*
84 Warham Road, South Croydon, Surrey CR2 6LB, England
Bailey, Paul *Writer*
79 Davisville Road, London W12 9SH, England
Bailey, Philip *Singer (Earth Wind & Fire)*
%Covenant Agency, 1011 4th St, #315, Santa Monica, CA 90403, USA
Bailey, Razzy *Singer, Songwriter*
%Doc Sedelmeier, PO Box 62, Geneva, NE 68361, USA
Bailey, Thomas H *Financier*
%Janus Capital Corp, 100 Fillmore St, Denver, CO 80206, USA
Bailey, Thurl *Basketball Player*
6406 S Crestmont Circle, Salt Lake City, UT 84121, USA
Bailon, Adrienne *Singer (3LW)*
%Pyramid Entertainment, 89 5th Ave, #700, New York, NY 10003, USA
Bailyn, Bernard *Historian*
170 Clifton St, Belmont, MA 02478, USA
Bain, Barbara *Actress*
1501 Skylark Lane, Los Angeles, CA 90069, USA
Bain, Conrad *Actor*
1230 Chickory Lane, Los Angeles, CA 90049, USA
Bain, William E (Bill) *Football Player*
27661 Paseo Barona, San Juan Capo, CA 92675, USA
Bainbridge, Beryl *Actress, Writer*
42 Albert St, London NW1 7NU, England
Bainbridge, Merril *Singer, Songwriter*
%001 Productions, PO Box 1760, Collingswood VIC 3068, Australia
Baio, Jimmy *Actor*
11662 Duque Dr, Studio City, CA 91604, USA
Baio, Scott *Actor*
4333 Forman Ave, Toluca Lake, CA 91602, USA
Baird, Briny *Golfer*
%Pro's Inc, 9 S 12th St, #300, Richmond, VA 23219, USA
Baird, Butch *Golfer*
PO Box 2633, Carefree, AZ 85377, USA
Baird, James M *Religious Leader*
%Presbyterian Church, PO Box 1428, Decatur, GA 30031, USA
Bairstow, Scott H *Actor*
4333 Forman Ave, Toluca Lake, CA 91602, USA
Baiul, Oksana *Figure Skater*
%Bob Young, PO Box 988, Niantic, CT 06357, USA
Bajanowsky, Louis J *Architect*
%Cambridge Seven Assoc, 1050 Massacuhsuetts Ave, Cambridge, MA 02138, USA
Bajcsy, Ruzena *Electrical Engineer*
%University of California, Electrical Engineering Dept, Berkeley, CA 94720, USA
Bakalyan, Richard *Actor*
1070 S Bedford St, Los Angeles, CA 90035, USA
Bakatin, Vadim V *Government Official, Russia*
Kotelnicheskaya Nab 17, 103240 Moscow, Russia
Baker, Anita *Singer*
%Associated Booking Corp, 1995 Broadway, #501, New York, NY 10023, USA

B

Baker - Bakhtair

Baker, Buddy *Auto Racing Driver*
4860 Moonlite Bay Dr, Sherrills Ford, NC 28673, USA
Baker, Carroll *Actress*
%Abrams Artists, 9200 Sunset Blvd, #1125, Los Angeles, CA 90069, USA
Baker, Diane *Actress*
2733 Outpost Dr, Los Angeles, CA 90068, USA
Baker, Donald K *Cinematographer*
11789 Lakeshore N, Auburn, CA 95602, USA
Baker, Dylan *Actor*
%Paradigm Agency, 10100 Santa Monica Blvd, #2500, Los Angeles, CA 90067, USA
Baker, Earl P, Jr *WW II Navy Hero*
10100 Cypress Cove Dr, Fort Myers, FL 33908, USA
Baker, Ellen Shulman *Astronaut*
2207 Garden Stream Court, Houston, TX 77062, USA
Baker, Frank *Bowling Executive*
13900 W Burleigh Road, Brookfield, WI 53005, USA
Baker, Ginger *Drummer (Cream/Masters of Reality)*
%Twist Mgmt, 4230 Del Rey Ave, #621, Marina del Rey, CA 90292, USA
Baker, Howard H, Jr *Senator, TN; Diplomat*
%US Embassy, 10-1-1 Akasaka, Minatoku, Tokyo 1-7, Japan
Baker, James A, III *Secretary, State*
%Baker & Botts, 1 Shell Plaza, 910 Louisiana, Houston, TX 77002, USA
Baker, Janet A *Opera, Concert Singer*
%Transart Ltd, 8 Bristol Gardens, London W9 2JG, England
Baker, Joe Don *Actor*
23339 Hatteras St, Woodland Hills, CA 91367, USA
Baker, John F, Jr *Vietnam War Army Hero (CMH)*
%Medal of Honor Society, 40 Patriots Point Road, Mount Pleasant, SC 29464, USA
Baker, John H, Jr *Football Player*
5 Farnham Park Dr, Houston, TX 77024, USA
Baker, Johnnie B (Dusty) *Baseball Player, Manager*
40 Livingston Terrace Dr, San Bruno, CA 94066, USA
Baker, Kathy *Actress*
1146 N Central Ave, #163, Glendale, CA 91202, USA
Baker, Kendall L *Educator*
%University of North Dakota, President's Office, Grand Forks, ND 58202, USA
Baker, Kenny *Actor*
51 Mulgrave Ave, Ashton, Preston, Lancashire PR2 1HJ, England
Baker, Laurie *Hockey Player*
67 Prairie St, Concord, MA 01742, USA
Baker, Leslie M, Jr *Financier*
%Wachovia Corp, 301 N Main St, Winston Salem, NC 27150, USA
Baker, Lewis *Singer (Danny & the Juniors)*
%Joe Terry Mgmt, PO Box 1017, Turnersville, NJ 08012, USA
Baker, Mark *Bowler*
11751 Steele Dr, Garden Grove, CA 92840, USA
Baker, Mark-Linn *Actor*
2625 6th St, #2, Santa Monica, CA 90405, USA
Baker, Michael A (Mike) *Astronaut*
%NASA, Johnson Space Center, 2101 NASA Road, Houston, TX 77058, USA
Baker, Paul T *Anthropologist*
1000 Escalon Ave, #A3005, Sunnyvale, CA 94085, USA
Baker, Raymond *Actor*
253A 26th St, #312, Santa Monica, CA 90402, USA
Baker, Robert *Attorney*
%Baker Silberberg Keener, 2850 Ocean Park Blvd, Santa Monica, CA 90405, USA
Baker, Russell W *Columnist*
%New York Times, Editorial Dept, 229 W 43rd St, New York, NY 10036, USA
Baker, Scott Thompson *Actor, Director*
17651 Sidwell, Granada Hills, CA 91344, USA
Baker, Simon *Actor*
Norman House, Cambridge Place, Cambridge CB2 1NS, England
Baker, Terry W *Football Player*
3208 SW Fairmount Blvd, Portland, OR 97239, USA
Baker, Vernon J *WW II Army Hero (CMH)*
650 Vernon Lane, Saint Maries, ID 83861, USA
Baker, Vin *Basketball Player*
PO Box 179, Old Saybrook, CT 06475, USA
Baker, W Thane *Track Athlete*
6704 Saint John Court, Granbury, TX 76049, USA
Baker, William (Bill) *Hockey Player*
6005 Sugarbush Trail, Brainerd, MN 56401, USA
Baker, William O *Chemist*
%AT&T Bell Lucent Laboratory, 600 Mountain Ave, New Providence, NJ 07974, USA
Baker-Finch, Ian *Golfer*
%IBF Enterprises, PO Box 176, Sanctuary Grove QLD 4212, Australia
Bakhtair, Rudi *Commentator*
%Cable News Network, News Dept, 1050 Techwood Dr NW, Atlanta, GA 30318, USA

Bakke, Brenda *Actress*
28128 Pacific Coast Highway, #258, Malibu, CA 90265, USA
Bakken, Earl *Heart Surgeon, Inventor*
68-1399 Mauna Lani Dr, Kamuela, HI 96743, USA
Bakker Messner, Tammy Faye *Religious Leader*
1527 Wood Creek Road, Matthews, NC 28105, USA
Bakker, James O (Jim) *Religious Leader*
123 E End Road, Branson, MO 65616, USA
Bako, Brigitte *Actress*
%Kritzer, 12200 W Olympic Blvd, #400, Los Angeles, CA 90064, USA
Bakshi, Ralph *Animator*
7950 Sunset Blvd, Los Angeles, CA 90046, USA
Bakula, Scott *Actor*
15300 Ventura Blvd, #315, Sherman Oaks, CA 91403, USA
Baladmenti, Angelo *Composer*
4146 Lankershim Blvd, #401, North Hollywood, CA 91602, USA
Balandin, Aleksandr N *Cosmonaut*
%Potchta Kosmonavtov, Moskovskoi Oblasti, 141160 Syvisdny Goroduk, Russia
Balaski, Belinda *Actress*
%Epstein-Wyckoff, 280 S Beverly Dr, #400, Beverly Hills, CA 90212, USA
Balboa, Marcelo *Soccer Player*
13139 Hedda Dr, Cerritos, CA 90703, USA
Baldacci, David *Writer*
%Warner Books, 1271 Ave of Americas, New York, NY 10020, USA
Baldeschwieler, John D *Chemist*
PO Box 50065, Pasadena, CA 91115, USA
Baldessari, John *Conceptual Artist*
2001 1/2 Main St, Santa Monica, CA 90405, USA
Baldinger, Brian *Sportscaster*
%Fox-TV, Sports Dept, 205 W 67th St, New York, NY 10021, USA
Baldock, Bobby R *Judge*
%US Court of Appeals, PO Box 2388, Roswell, NM 88202, USA
Baldrige, Letitia *Businesswoman, Writer*
2339 Massachusetts Ave NW, Washington, DC 20008, USA
Baldwin, Adam *Actor*
1301 Caryle Ave, Santa Monica, CA 90402, USA
Baldwin, Alec *Actor*
%El Dorado Pictures, 725 Arizona Ave, 100, Santa Monica, CA 90401, USA
Baldwin, Burr *Football Player*
2000 Ashe Road, Bakersfield, CA 93309, USA
Baldwin, Daniel *Actor*
%William Morris Agency, 151 El Camino Dr, Beverly Hills, CA 90212, USA
Baldwin, Jack *Auto Racing Driver*
4748 Balmoral Way NE, Marietta, GA 30068, USA
Baldwin, Jack E *Chemist*
%Oxford University, Dyson Perrins Lab, S Parks Rd, Oxford OX1 3QY, England
Baldwin, John A (Jack), Jr *Navy Admiral*
1371 Millersville Road, Millersville, MD 21108, USA
Baldwin, John W *Historian*
%Johns Hopkins University, History Dept, Baltimore, MD 21218, USA
Baldwin, Judy *Actress*
PO Box 4723, Valley Village, CA 91617, USA
Baldwin, Margaret *Writer*
PO Box 1106, Williams Bay, WI 53191, USA
Baldwin, Robert E *Economist*
125 Nautilus Dr, Madison, WI 53705, USA
Baldwin, Stephen *Actor*
%Chris Marsh, 1300 Lucas Ave, Chesapeake, VA 23324, USA
Baldwin, William *Actor*
%P M K Public Relations, 8500 Wilshire Blvd, #700, Beverly Hills, CA 90211, USA
Bale, Christian *Actor*
685 McCowan Road, Box 66534, Toronto ON M1J 3NB, Canada
Balfanz, John C *Ski Jumper*
7770 E Iliff Ave, #G, Denver, CO 80231, USA
Balgimbayev, Nurlan *Prime Minister, Kazakhstan*
%Dom Pravieelstva, Pl im VI Lenina, 148008 Astana, Kazakhstan
Baliga, Bantval Jayant *Electrical Engineer*
2612 Bembridge Dr, Raleigh, NC 27613, USA
Baliles, Gerald L *Governor, VA*
Riverfront Plaza East Tower, 951 E Byrd St, Richmond, VA 23219, USA
Balin, Marty *Singer, Songwriter*
%Joe Buchwald, PO Box 170040, San Francisco, CA 94117, USA
Balitran, Celine *Model*
%Ford Model Agency, 142 Greene St, #400, New York, NY 10012, USA
Balk, Fairuza *Actress*
%Rigberg Roberts Rugolo, 1180 S Beverly Dr, #601, Los Angeles, CA 90035, USA
Balkenende, Jan-Peter *Prime Minister, Netherlands*
%Premier's Office, Binnenhof 20, Postbus 20001, 2500 EA Hague, Netherlands

B

Balkenhol - Bancroft

Balkenhol, Klaus *Equestrian Athlete*
Narzissenweg 11A, 40723 Hilden, Germany
Ball, David *Singer, Songwriter*
%Buddy Lee, 38 Music Square E, #300, Nashville, TN 37203, USA
Ball, Jerry L *Football Player*
3311 Meadowside Dr, Sugar Land, TX 77478, USA
Ball, Michael A *Singer, Actor*
PO Box 2073, Colchester, Essex CO4 3WS, England
Balladur, Edouard *Prime Minister, France*
5 Rue Jean Formige, 75015 Paris, France
Ballard, Carroll *Movie Director*
PO Box 556, Saint Helena, CA 94574, USA
Ballard, Del, Jr *Bowler*
%Ebonite International, PO Box 746, Hopkinsville, KY 42241, USA
Ballard, Donald E *Vietnam War Navy Hero (CMH)*
PO Box 34593, North Kansas City, MO 64116, USA
Ballard, Glenn *Songwriter*
%Gorfaine/Schwartz, 13245 Riverside Dr, #450, Sherman Oaks, CA 91423, USA
Ballard, James Graham (J G) *Writer*
36 Old Charlton Road, Shepperton, Middx TW17 8AT, England
Ballard, Kaye *Actress*
PO Box 922, Rancho Mirage, CA 92270, USA
Ballard, Robert D *Oceanographer (Titanic Discoverer)*
%Institute for Exploration, 55 Coogan Blvd, Mystic, CT 06355, USA
Ballesteros, Seveiano (Seve) *Golfer*
%Fareway SAE, Pasage de Pena 10, Curata Planta, 39008 Santander, Spain
Ballhaus, Florian M *Cinematographer*
115 Berkeley Place, Brooklyn, NY 11217, USA
Ballhaus, Michael *Cinematographer*
11 Elm Place, Rye, NY 10580, USA
Ballmer, Steven A *Businessman*
%Microsoft Corp, 1 Microsoft Way, Redmond, WA 98052, USA
Ballou, Tyson *Model*
%Ford Model Agency, 142 Greene St, #400, New York, NY 10012, USA
Balmaseda, Liz *Journalist*
%Miami Herald, Editorial Dept, 1 Herald Plaza, Miami, FL 33132, USA
Balmer, Jean-Francois *Actor*
%Artmedia, 20 Ave Rapp, 75007 Paris, France
Balsam, Talia *Actress*
1 Bank St, #6H, New York, NY 10014, USA
Balser, Glennon *Religious Leader*
%Advent Christian Church, 6315 Studley Road, Mechanicsville, VA 23116, USA
Balsley, Philip E *Singer (Statler Brothers)*
191 Abbington Road, Swoope, VA 24479, USA
Baltes, Jameson *Actor*
%Hervey/Grimes, PO Box 64249, Los Angeles, CA 90064, USA
Baltimore, David *Nobel Medicine Laureate, Educator*
31460 Beach Park Road, Malibu, CA 90265, USA
Baltray, Charles *Astronomer*
%Yale University, Astronomy Dept, New Haven, CT 06520, USA
Baltron, Donna *Actress*
%C N A Assoc, 1925 Century Park East, #750, Los Angeles, CA 90067, USA
Baltsa, Agnes *Opera Singer*
%Manuela Kursidem, Wasagasse 12/1/3, 1090 Vienna, Austria
Balukas, Jean *Billiards Player*
9818 4th Ave, Brooklyn, NY 11209, USA
Bamberger, George I *Baseball Player, Manager*
455 Bath Club Blvd N, North Redington Beach, FL 33708, USA
Ban Breathnach, Sarah *Writer*
%Warner Books, 1271 Ave of Americas, New York, NY 10020, USA
Bana, Eric *Actor, Comedian*
8-12 Sandilands St, #2, South Melbourne, Victoria 3205, Australia
Banach, Edward (Ed) *Wrestler*
2128 Country Club Blvd, Ames, IA 50014, USA
Banach, Louis (Lou) *Wrestler*
3276 E Fairfax Road, Cleveland Heights, OH 44118, USA
Banachowski, Andy *Volleyball Player, Coach*
%University of California, Athletic Dept, Los Angeles, CA 90024, USA
Banaszak, Pete *Football Player*
612 W Surf Spray Lane, Ponte Vedra Beach, FL 32082, USA
Banaszynski, Jacqui *Journalist*
%Saint Paul Pioneer Press, Editorial Dept, 345 Cedar St, Saint Paul, MN 55101, USA
Banbury, F H Frith *Theater Director*
18 Park Saint James, Prince Albert Road, London NW8 7LE, England
Bancroft, Ann *Explorer, Cross Country Skier*
%Yourexpedition, 119 N 4th St, #406, Minneapolis, MN 55401, USA
Bancroft, Anne *Actress*
23868 Malibu Road, Malibu, CA 90265, USA

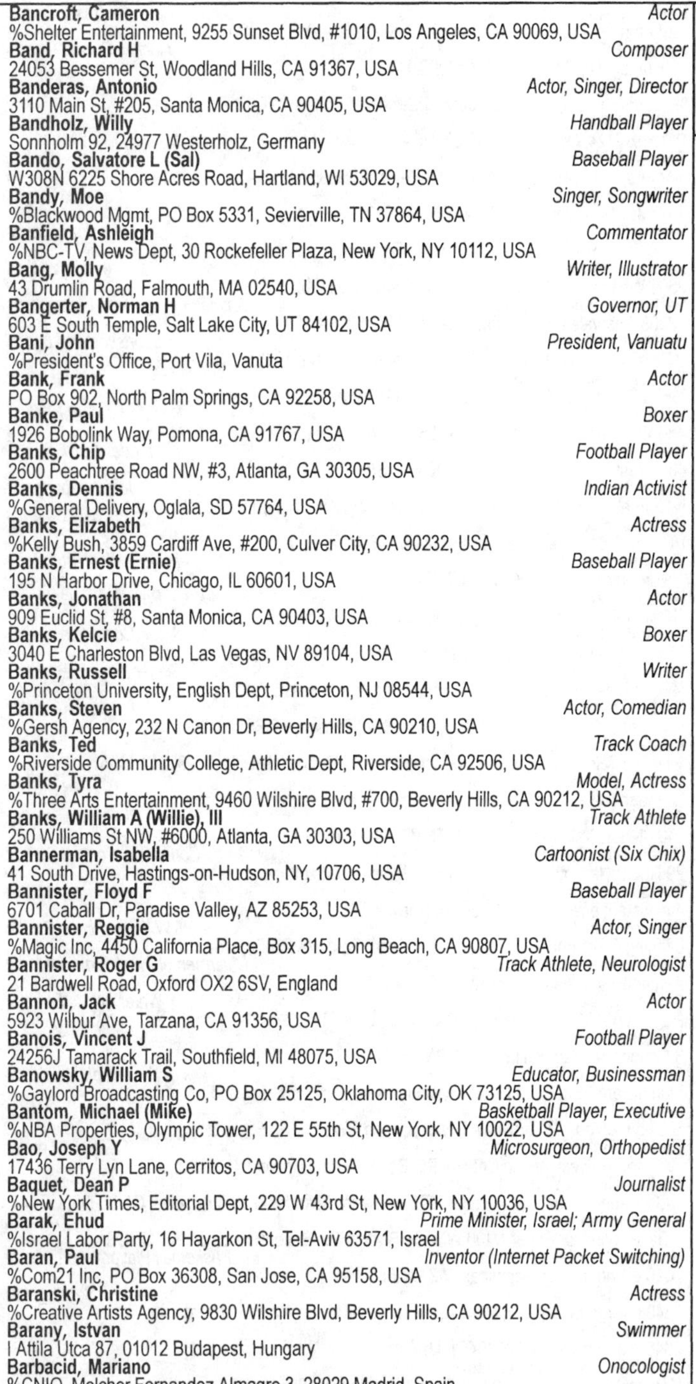

Bancroft, Cameron *Actor*
%Shelter Entertainment, 9255 Sunset Blvd, #1010, Los Angeles, CA 90069, USA
Band, Richard H *Composer*
24053 Bessemer St, Woodland Hills, CA 91367, USA
Banderas, Antonio *Actor, Singer, Director*
3110 Main St, #205, Santa Monica, CA 90405, USA
Bandholz, Willy *Handball Player*
Sonnholm 92, 24977 Westerholz, Germany
Bando, Salvatore L (Sal) *Baseball Player*
W308N 6225 Shore Acres Road, Hartland, WI 53029, USA
Bandy, Moe *Singer, Songwriter*
%Blackwood Mgmt, PO Box 5331, Sevierville, TN 37864, USA
Banfield, Ashleigh *Commentator*
%NBC-TV, News Dept, 30 Rockefeller Plaza, New York, NY 10112, USA
Bang, Molly *Writer, Illustrator*
43 Drumlin Road, Falmouth, MA 02540, USA
Bangerter, Norman H *Governor, UT*
603 E South Temple, Salt Lake City, UT 84102, USA
Bani, John *President, Vanuatu*
%President's Office, Port Vila, Vanuta
Bank, Frank *Actor*
PO Box 902, North Palm Springs, CA 92258, USA
Banke, Paul *Boxer*
1926 Bobolink Way, Pomona, CA 91767, USA
Banks, Chip *Football Player*
2600 Peachtree Road NW, #3, Atlanta, GA 30305, USA
Banks, Dennis *Indian Activist*
%General Delivery, Oglala, SD 57764, USA
Banks, Elizabeth *Actress*
%Kelly Bush, 3859 Cardiff Ave, #200, Culver City, CA 90232, USA
Banks, Ernest (Ernie) *Baseball Player*
195 N Harbor Drive, Chicago, IL 60601, USA
Banks, Jonathan *Actor*
909 Euclid St, #8, Santa Monica, CA 90403, USA
Banks, Kelcie *Boxer*
3040 E Charleston Blvd, Las Vegas, NV 89104, USA
Banks, Russell *Writer*
%Princeton University, English Dept, Princeton, NJ 08544, USA
Banks, Steven *Actor, Comedian*
%Gersh Agency, 232 N Canon Dr, Beverly Hills, CA 90210, USA
Banks, Ted *Track Coach*
%Riverside Community College, Athletic Dept, Riverside, CA 92506, USA
Banks, Tyra *Model, Actress*
%Three Arts Entertainment, 9460 Wilshire Blvd, #700, Beverly Hills, CA 90212, USA
Banks, William A (Willie), III *Track Athlete*
250 Williams St NW, #6000, Atlanta, GA 30303, USA
Bannerman, Isabella *Cartoonist (Six Chix)*
41 South Drive, Hastings-on-Hudson, NY, 10706, USA
Bannister, Floyd F *Baseball Player*
6701 Caball Dr, Paradise Valley, AZ 85253, USA
Bannister, Reggie *Actor, Singer*
%Magic Inc, 4450 California Place, Box 315, Long Beach, CA 90807, USA
Bannister, Roger G *Track Athlete, Neurologist*
21 Bardwell Road, Oxford OX2 6SV, England
Bannon, Jack *Actor*
5923 Wilbur Ave, Tarzana, CA 91356, USA
Banois, Vincent J *Football Player*
24256J Tamarack Trail, Southfield, MI 48075, USA
Banowsky, William S *Educator, Businessman*
%Gaylord Broadcasting Co, PO Box 25125, Oklahoma City, OK 73125, USA
Bantom, Michael (Mike) *Basketball Player, Executive*
%NBA Properties, Olympic Tower, 122 E 55th St, New York, NY 10022, USA
Bao, Joseph Y *Microsurgeon, Orthopedist*
17436 Terry Lyn Lane, Cerritos, CA 90703, USA
Baquet, Dean P *Journalist*
%New York Times, Editorial Dept, 229 W 43rd St, New York, NY 10036, USA
Barak, Ehud *Prime Minister, Israel; Army General*
%Israel Labor Party, 16 Hayarkon St, Tel-Aviv 63571, Israel
Baran, Paul *Inventor (Internet Packet Switching)*
%Com21 Inc, PO Box 36308, San Jose, CA 95158, USA
Baranski, Christine *Actress*
%Creative Artists Agency, 9830 Wilshire Blvd, Beverly Hills, CA 90212, USA
Barany, Istvan *Swimmer*
I Attila Utca 87, 01012 Budapest, Hungary
Barbacid, Mariano *Onocologist*
%CNIO, Melchor Fernandez Almagro 3, 28029 Madrid, Spain
Barbarin, Philippe X I Cardinal *Religious Leader*
%Archdiocese, 1 Place de Fourviere, 69321 Lyon Cedex 05, France

Barbeau, Adrienne *Actress, Singer*
%Shefrin Co, 808 S Ridgeley Dr, Los Angeles, CA 90036, USA
Barber, Bill *Hockey Player, Coach*
12 Hunters Dr, Cherry Hill, NJ 08003, USA
Barber, Glynis *Actress*
%Susan Sharper, Queen's House, 1 Leicester, London WC2H 7BP, England
Barber, Mike *Football Player*
PO Box 2424, DeSoto, TX 75123, USA
Barber, Miller *Golfer*
%Myers, PO Box 11807, Marina del Rey, CA 90295, USA
Barber, Stephen D (Steve) *Baseball Player*
1997 Joy View Lane, Henderson, NV 89012, USA
Barber, Tiki *Football Player*
PO Box 20595, Roanoke, VA 24018, USA
Barber, William *Cinematographer*
2509 White Chapel Place, Thousand Oaks, CA 91362, USA
Barbera, Joseph R (Joe) *Animator (Yogi Bear, Flintstones)*
12003 Briarvale Lane, Studio City, CA 91604, USA
Barberie, Jillian *Sportscaster, Actress*
%Fox-TV, Sports Dept, 205 W 67th St, New York, NY 10021, USA
Barberos, Alessandro *Businessman*
%Fiat Spa, Corso G Marconi 10/20, 10125 Turin, Italy
Barbi, Shane *Model (Barbi Twins)*
480 Westlake Blvd, Malibu, CA 90265, USA
Barbi, Sia *Model (Barbi Twins)*
480 Westlake Blvd, Malibu, CA 90265, USA
Barbieri, Gato *Jazz Saxophonist*
%Central Entertainment Services, 123 Harvard Ave, Staten Island, NY 10301, USA
Barbieri, Paula *Actress, Model*
PO Box 20483, Panama City, FL 32411, USA
Barbot, Ivan *Law Enforcement Official*
4 Rue Marguerite, 75017 Paris, France
Barbour, Ian *Nuclear Physicist, Theologian*
%Carleton College, Theology Dept, Northfield, MN 55057, USA
Barbour, John *Actor, Comedian, Writer*
54 Pine Isle Court, Henderson, NV 89074, USA
Barbour, Ross *Singer (Four Freshmen)*
%Four Freshmen, PO Box 93534, Las Vegas, NV 89193, USA
Barbutti, Pete *Jazz Trumpeter*
%Thomas Cassidy, 11761 E Speedway Blvd, Tucson, AZ 85748, USA
Bardem, Javier E *Actor*
%United Talent Agency, 9560 Wilshire Blvd, #500, Beverly Hills, CA 90212, USA
Bardot, Brigitte *Actress*
La Madrique, 83990 Saint Tropez, Var, France
Bare, Robert J (Bobby) *Singer, Songwriter*
2401 Music Valley Dr, Nashville, TN 37214, USA
Barenboim, Daniel *Conductor, Concert Pianist*
29 Rue de la Coulouvreeniere, 1206 Geneva, Switzerland
Barfod, Hakon *Yachtsman*
Jon Ostensensv 15, 1360 Nesbru, Norway
Barfoot, Van T *WW II Army Hero (CMH)*
Leaning Oaks Farm, 4801 Namozine Road, Ford, VA 23850, USA
Barkauskas, Antanas S *Chairman of Presidium, Lithuania*
Akmenu 71, Vilnus, Lithuania
Barker, Clive *Writer, Movie Director*
PO Box 691885, Los Angeles, CA 90069, USA
Barker, Clyde F *Surgeon*
3 Coopertown Road, Haverford, PA 19041, USA
Barker, David J P *Epidemiologist*
Manor Farm, East Dean near Salisbury, Wilts SP5 1HB, England
Barker, Pat *Writer*
%Gillon Aitken, 29 Fernshaw Road, London SW10 0TG, England
Barker, Richard A *Religious Leader*
%Orthodox Presbyterian Church, PO Box P, Willow Grove, PA 19090, USA
Barker, Robert W (Bob) *Entertainer*
%Goodson-Todman Productions, 5757 Wilshire Blvd, #206, Los Angeles, CA 90036, USA
Barkin, Ellen *Actress*
%Baker/Winokur/Ryder, 9100 Wilshire Blvd, #600, Beverly Hills, CA 90212, USA
Barkley, Charles W *Basketball Player, Sportscaster*
7815 E Vaquero Dr, Scottsdale, AZ 85258, USA
Barkley, Dean M *Senator, MN*
2840 Evergreen Lane N, Minneapolis, MN 55441, USA
Barkley, Iran *Boxer*
2645 3rd Ave, Bronx, NY 10451, USA
Barkman Tyler, Jane (Janie) *Swimmer*
%Princeton University, Athletic Dept, Princeton, NJ 08544, USA
Barksdale, James (Jim) *Businessman*
%Barksdale Group, 2730 Sand Hill Road, Menlo Park, CA 94025, USA

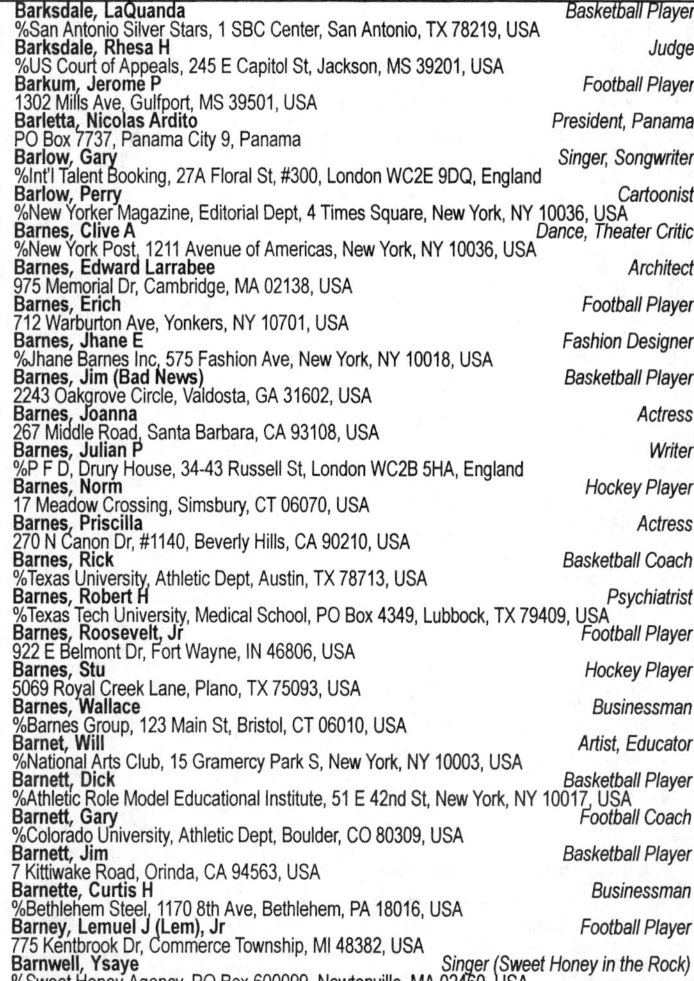

Barksdale, LaQuanda *Basketball Player*
%San Antonio Silver Stars, 1 SBC Center, San Antonio, TX 78219, USA
Barksdale, Rhesa H *Judge*
%US Court of Appeals, 245 E Capitol St, Jackson, MS 39201, USA
Barkum, Jerome P *Football Player*
1302 Mills Ave, Gulfport, MS 39501, USA
Barletta, Nicolas Ardito *President, Panama*
PO Box 7737, Panama City 9, Panama
Barlow, Gary *Singer, Songwriter*
%Int'l Talent Booking, 27A Floral St, #300, London WC2E 9DQ, England
Barlow, Perry *Cartoonist*
%New Yorker Magazine, Editorial Dept, 4 Times Square, New York, NY 10036, USA
Barnes, Clive A *Dance, Theater Critic*
%New York Post, 1211 Avenue of Americas, New York, NY 10036, USA
Barnes, Edward Larrabee *Architect*
975 Memorial Dr, Cambridge, MA 02138, USA
Barnes, Erich *Football Player*
712 Warburton Ave, Yonkers, NY 10701, USA
Barnes, Jhane E *Fashion Designer*
%Jhane Barnes Inc, 575 Fashion Ave, New York, NY 10018, USA
Barnes, Jim (Bad News) *Basketball Player*
2243 Oakgrove Circle, Valdosta, GA 31602, USA
Barnes, Joanna *Actress*
267 Middle Road, Santa Barbara, CA 93108, USA
Barnes, Julian P *Writer*
%P F D, Drury House, 34-43 Russell St, London WC2B 5HA, England
Barnes, Norm *Hockey Player*
17 Meadow Crossing, Simsbury, CT 06070, USA
Barnes, Priscilla *Actress*
270 N Canon Dr, #1140, Beverly Hills, CA 90210, USA
Barnes, Rick *Basketball Coach*
%Texas University, Athletic Dept, Austin, TX 78713, USA
Barnes, Robert H *Psychiatrist*
%Texas Tech University, Medical School, PO Box 4349, Lubbock, TX 79409, USA
Barnes, Roosevelt, Jr *Football Player*
922 E Belmont Dr, Fort Wayne, IN 46806, USA
Barnes, Stu *Hockey Player*
5069 Royal Creek Lane, Plano, TX 75093, USA
Barnes, Wallace *Businessman*
%Barnes Group, 123 Main St, Bristol, CT 06010, USA
Barnet, Will *Artist, Educator*
%National Arts Club, 15 Gramercy Park S, New York, NY 10003, USA
Barnett, Dick *Basketball Player*
%Athletic Role Model Educational Institute, 51 E 42nd St, New York, NY 10017, USA
Barnett, Gary *Football Coach*
%Colorado University, Athletic Dept, Boulder, CO 80309, USA
Barnett, Jim *Basketball Player*
7 Kittiwake Road, Orinda, CA 94563, USA
Barnette, Curtis H *Businessman*
%Bethlehem Steel, 1170 8th Ave, Bethlehem, PA 18016, USA
Barney, Lemuel J (Lem), Jr *Football Player*
775 Kentbrook Dr, Commerce Township, MI 48382, USA
Barnwell, Ysaye *Singer (Sweet Honey in the Rock)*
%Sweet Honey Agency, PO Box 600099, Newtonville, MA 02460, USA
Barocco, Rocco *Fashion Designer*
Via Occhio Marion, 80773 Capri/Napoli, Italy
Baron Crespo, Enrique *Government Official, Spain*
%European Parliament, 97/113 Rue Velliard, 1040 Brussels, Belgium
Barone, Anita *Actress*
1180 S Beverly Dr, #608, Beverly Hills, CA 90212, USA
Barr, Doug *Actor*
PO Box 63, Rutherford, CA 94573, USA
Barr, Julia *Actress*
%Saint Laurent Assoc, Cherokee Station, PO Box 20191, New York, NY 10028, USA
Barr, Nevada *Writer*
%G P Putnam's Sons, 375 Hudson St, New York, NY 10014, USA
Barrasso, Thomas (Tom) *Hockey Player*
40 Alder Lane, North Falmouth, MA 02556, USA
Barratt, Michael R *Astronaut*
2102 Pleasant Palm Circle, League City, TX 77573, USA
Barrault, Marie-Christine *Actress*
%Cineart, 36 Rue de Ponthieu, 75008 Paris, France
Barre, Raymond *Prime Minister, France*
4-6 Ave Emile-Acollas, 75007 Paris, France
Barreto, Bruno *Movie Director*
22 W 68th St, New York, NY 10023, USA
Barrett, Brendon Ryan *Actor*
9255 Sunset Bvd, #1010, West Hollywood, CA 90069, USA

B

Barrett - Barry

Barrett, Craig R *Businessman*
%Intel Corp, 2200 Mission College Blvd, Santa Clara, CA 95054, USA
Barrett, Jacinda *Actress, Model*
1836 Courtney Terrace, Los Angeles, CA 90046, USA
Barrett, James E *Judge*
%US Court of Appeals, 2120 Capitol Ave, Cheyenne, WY 82001, USA
Barrett, Marcia *Singer (Boney M)*
%Psycho Mgmt, 111 Clarence Road, Wimbledon, London SW19 8QB, England
Barrett, Michael (Mike) *Basketball Player*
5721 Templegate Dr, Nashville, TN 37221, USA
Barrett, Shirley *Movie Director*
%Hilary Linstead, 500 Oxford St, Bondi Junction NSW 2022, Australia
Barrett, Stanton *Auto Racing Driver*
Rocking K Ranch, Bishop, CA 93514, USA
Barrett, Stephen *Psychiatrist, Social Activist*
PO Box 1747, Allentown, PA 18105, USA
Barrett, Thomas J *Coast Guard Admiral*
Vice Commandant, US Coast Guard, 2100 2nd St SW, Washington, DC 20593, USA
Barrett, Wade *Soccer Player*
%San Jose Earthquakes, 3550 Stevens Creek Blvd, #200, San Jose, CA 95117, USA
Barrett, William *Philosopher*
34 Harwood Ave, Sleepy Hollow, NY 10591, USA
Barrett-Roddenberry, Majel *Actress*
%Lincoln Enterprises, PO Box 691370, West Hollywood, CA 90069, USA
Barretto, Ray *Jazz Percussionist, Conga Player*
%Pan American Music, 6407 Overbrook Ave, Philadelphia, PA 19151, USA
Barrichello, Rubens *Auto Racing Driver*
%Stewart Grand Prix, Bradbourne Drive, Tilbrook, Bucks MK7 8BJ, England
Barrie, Barbara *Actress*
15 W 72nd St, #2A, New York, NY 10023, USA
Barrileaux, James *Test Pilot*
%Dryden Flight Research Center, PO Box 273, Edwards, CA 93523, USA
Barron, Alex *Auto Racing Driver*
%Gurney Racing, 2334 S Broadway, Santa Ana, CA 92707, USA
Barron, Kenneth (Kenny) *Jazz Pianist, Composer*
%Joel Chriss, 300 Mercer St, #3J, New York, NY 10003, USA
Barron, Steve M *Movie Director*
%William Morris Agency, 52/53 Poland Place, London W1F 7LX, England
Barrowman, John *Actor, Singer*
293 Villas Road, Plumstead, London SE18 7PR, England
Barrowman, Mike *Swimmer*
706 N Warner St, Bay City, MI 48706, USA
Barrs, Jay *Archery Athlete*
6395 Senoma Dr, Salt Lake City, UT 84121, USA
Barry, A L *Religious Leader*
%Lutheran Church Missouri Synod, 1333 S Kirkwood Road, Saint Louis, MO 63122, USA
Barry, Brent *Basketball Player*
2302 4th Ave N, Seattle, WA 98109, USA
Barry, Claudja *Singer*
%Talent Consultants International, 1560 Broadway, #1308, New York, NY 10036, USA
Barry, Daniel T (Dan) *Astronaut*
46 Ashton Lane, South Hadley, MA 01075, USA
Barry, Dave *Journalist, Writer*
%Miami Herald, Editorial Dept, 1 Herald Plaza, Miami, FL 33132, USA
Barry, Gene *Actor*
12178 Ventura Blvd, #205, Studio City, CA 91604, USA
Barry, John *Composer*
540 Centre Island Road, Oyster Bay, NY 11771, USA
Barry, John J *Labor Official*
%Int'l Brotherhood of Electrical Workers, 1125 15th St NW, Washington, DC 20005, USA
Barry, Jon *Basketball Player*
%Detroit Pistons, Palace, 2 Championship Dr, Auburn Hills, MI 48326, USA
Barry, Len *Singer (Dovells)*
%Cape Entertainment, 1161 NW 76th Ave, Plantation, FL 33322, USA
Barry, Lynda *Cartoonist (Ernie Pook's Comeck)*
PO Box 447, Footville, WI 53537, USA
Barry, Marion S, Jr *Mayor*
161 Raleigh St SE, Washington, DC 20032, USA
Barry, Mark *Singer, Flutist (BBMak)*
%DayTime, Crown House, 225 Kensington High St, London W8 8SA, England
Barry, Maryanne Trump *Judge*
%US Court of Appeals, US Courthouse, 50 Walnut St, Newark, NJ 07102, USA
Barry, Patricia *Actress*
12742 Highwood St, Los Angeles, CA 90049, USA
Barry, Raymond J *Actor*
%Metropolitan Talent Agency, 4526 Wilshire Blvd, Los Angeles, CA 90010, USA
Barry, Richard F D (Rick), III *Basketball Player, Sportscaster*
5240 Broadmoor Bluffs Dr, Colorado Springs, CO 80906, USA

Barry, Seymour (Sy) *Cartoonist (Flash Gordon/Phantom)*
34 Saratoga Dr, Jericho, NY 11753, USA
Barrymore, Drew *Actress*
%Flower Films, 9220 W Sunset Blvd, #309, Los Angeles, CA 90069, USA
Barrymore, John, III *Actor*
2825 Forest Hill Blvd, Pacific Grove, CA 93950, USA
Barshai, Rudolf B *Conductor, Concert Viola Player*
Homberg Str 6, 4433 Ramlinsburg, Sweden
Barsotti, Charles *Cartoonist*
419 E 55th St, Kansas City, MO 64110, USA
Barstow, Josephine C *Opera Singer*
%Harold Holt, 31 Sinclair Road, London W14 0NS, England
Barth, Robert *Religious Leader*
%Churches of Christ in Christian Union, PO Box 30, Circleville, OH 43113, USA
Barth, T Fredrik W *Anthropologist*
Rodkleivfaret 16, 0393 Oslo, Norway
Bartholome, Earl *Hockey Player*
6024 W 35th St, Minneapolis, MN 55416, USA
Bartholomeos I *Religious Leader*
Eastern Orthodox Church, Rum Ortoks Patrikhanesi, H Fener, Istanbul,Turkey
Bartholomew, Dave *Jazz Trumpeter, Singer/Bandleader*
4732 Odin St, New Orleans, LA 70126, USA
Bartholomew, Reginald *Diplomat*
%State Department, 2201 C St NW, Washington, DC 20520, USA
Bartiromo, Maria *Commentator*
%CBS-TV, News Dept, 51 W 52nd St, New York, NY 10019, USA
Bartkowski, Steven J (Steve) *Football Player*
10745 Bell Road, Duluth, GA 30097, USA
Bartlett, Bonnie *Actress, Singer*
12805 Hortense St, Studio City, CA 91604, USA
Bartlett, Jennifer L *Artist*
%Paula Cooper Gallery, 534 W 21st St, New York, NY 10011, USA
Bartlett, Thomas A *Educator*
1209 SW 6th St, #904, Portland, OR 97204, USA
Bartletti, Don *Photojournalist*
%Los Angeles Times, Editorial Dept, 202 W 1st St, Los Angeles, CA 90012, USA
Bartley, Robert L *Editor*
%Wall Street Journal, Editorial Dept, 200 Liberty St, New York, NY 10281, USA
Bartoe, John-David F *Astronaut*
2724 Lighthouse Dr, Houston, TX 77058, USA
Bartoli, Cecilia *Opera Singer*
%La Scala, Via Filodrammatici 2, 20100 Milan, Italy
Bartolo, Sal *Boxer*
422 Border St, East Boston, MA 02128, USA
Bartolomew, Ken *Speed Skater*
4820 Bryant Ave S, Minneapolis, MN 55409, USA
Barton, Austin *Sculptor*
100 N Lake, Joseph, OR 97846, USA
Barton, Eileen *Singer*
8740 Holloway Dr, Los Angeles, CA 90069, USA
Barton, Gregory (Greg) *Canoeing Athlete*
6657 58th Ave NE, Seattle, WA 98115, USA
Barton, Harris S *Football Player*
765 Market St, #32E, San Francisco, CA 94103, USA
Barton, Jacqueline K *Chemist*
%California Insitute of Techonolgy, Chemistry Dept, Pasadena, CA 91125, USA
Barton, Mischa *Actress*
%Avante Entertainment, 295 Greenwich St, #246, New York, NY 10007, USA
Barton, Peter *Actor*
2265 Westwood Blvd, #2619, Los Angeles, CA 90064, USA
Barton, Rachel *Concert Violinist*
%I C M Artists, 40 W 57th St, New York, NY 10019, USA
Bartow, Gene *Basketball Coach*
%Memphis Grizzlies, 175 Toyota Plaza, #150, Memphis, TN 38103, USA
Bartz, Carol A *Businesswoman*
%Autodesk Inc, 111 McInnis Parkway, San Rafael, CA 94903, USA
Barucci, Piero *Financier; Government Official, Italy*
%Treasury Ministry, Via XX Settembre 97, 00187 Rome, Italy
Baryshnikov, Mikhail *Ballet Dancer, Actor*
%Creative Artists Agency, 9830 Wilshire Blvd, Beverly Hills, CA 90212, USA
Barzini, Benedetta *Model*
%Donna Karan Co, 361 Newbury St, Boston, MA 02115, USA
Barzun, Jacques M *Educator*
597 5th Ave, New York, NY 10017, USA
Basch, Harry *Actor*
920 1/2 S Serrano Ave, Los Angeles, CA 90006, USA
Basche, David Alan *Actor*
60 W 84th St, #GDX, New York, NY 10024, USA

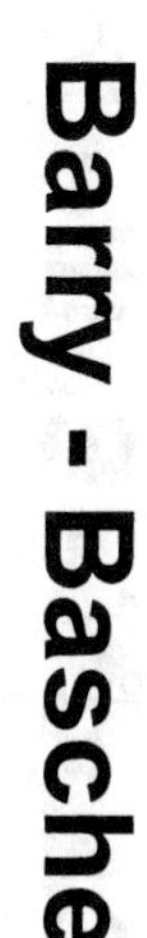

B

Basco, Dante *Actor*
%Don Buchwald, 6500 Wilshire Blvd, #2200, Los Angeles, CA 90048, USA
Bashir, Omar Hassan Ahmed al- *President, Sudan; Army General*
%Prime Minister's Office, Revolutionary Command Council, Khartoum, Sudan
Bashmet, Yuri A *Concert Viola Player*
Briyusov 7, #16, 103009 Moscow, Russia
Basia *Singer*
%Creative Artists Agency, 9830 Wilshire Blvd, Beverly Hills, CA 90212, USA
Basilashuili, Oleg V *Actor*
Borodinskaya Str 13, #58, 196180 Saint Petersburg, Russia
Basilio, Carmen *Boxer*
67 Boxwood Dr, Rochester, NY 14617, USA
Basinger, Kim *Actress*
11288 Ventura Blvd, #414, Studio City, CA 91604, USA
Bass, Fontella *Singer, Keyboardist*
%Cape Entertainment, 1181 NW 76th Ave, Plantation, FL 33322, USA
Bass, George F *Underwater Archaeologist*
1600 Dominik Dr, College Station, TX 77840, USA
Bass, Lance *Singer ('N Sync)*
%Wright Entertainment, 7680 Universal Blvd, #500, Orlando, FL 32819, USA
Bass, Richard L (Dick) *Football Player*
14001 Bayside Dr, Norwalk, CA 90650, USA
Bass, Ronald (Ron) *Writer*
%Creative Artists Agency, 9830 Wilshire Blvd, Beverly Hills, CA 90212, USA
Bassett, Angela *Actress*
%Creative Artists Agency, 9830 Wilshire Blvd, Beverly Hills, CA 90212, USA
Bassett, Brian *Editorial Cartoonist, Cartoonist (Adam)*
%Seattle Times, Editorial Dept, 1120 John St, Seattle, WA 98109, USA
Bassett, Leslie R *Composer*
1618 Harbal Dr, Ann Arbor, MI 48105, USA
Bassett-Seguso, Carling *Tennis Player*
1008 Vista del Mar Dr, Delray Beach, FL 33483, USA
Bassey, Shirley *Singer*
Villa Capricorn, 55 Via Campoine, 6816 Bissone, Switzerland
Bastedo, Alexandra *Actress*
%Charlesworth, 68 Old Brompton Road, #280, London SW7 3LQ, England
Basti, Juli *Actress*
Krecsanyi Utca 6, 1025 Budapest, Hungary
Batali, Mario *Chef*
%Food Network, 1180 Ave of Americas, #1200, New York, NY 10036, USA
Batalov, Aleksey V *Movie Director*
Serafimovicha 2, #91, Moscow 109072, Russia
Batchelor, Joy E *Animator*
%Educational Film Center, 5-7 Kean St, London WC2B 4AT, England
Bate, Anthony *Actor*
%Al Parker, 55 Park Lane, London W1Y 3DD, England
Bate, Jennifer L *Concert Organist*
35 Collingwood Ave, Muswell Hill, London N10 3EH, England
Bateman, Jason *Actor*
8828 Wonderland Park Ave, Los Angeles, CA 90046, USA
Bateman, Justine *Actress*
11288 Ventura Blvd, #190, Studio City, CA 91604, USA
Bateman, Robert M *Artist*
PO Box 115, Fulford Harbour BC V0S 1C0, Canada
Bates, Alan *Actor*
%Chatto & Linnit, Prince of Wales, Coventry St, London W1V 7FE, England
Bates, Alfred *Track Athlete*
4506 Mulberry St, Philadelphia, PA 19124, USA
Bates, Kathy *Actress*
PO Box 472, Culver City, CA 90232, USA
Bates, Patrick J *Football Player*
10101 Harwin D, #298, Houston, TX 77036, USA
Bates, Robert T *Labor Leader*
%Railroad Signalmen Brotherhood, 601 W Golf Road, Mount Prospect, IL 60056, USA
Bathgate, Andrew J (Andy) *Hockey Player*
43 Brentwood Dr, Bramelea ON L6T 1R1, Canada
Bathurst, D Benjamin *Navy Admiral, England*
%Coutts Co, 440 Strand, London WC2B 0QS, England
Batinkoff, Randall *Actor*
1330 4th St, Santa Monica, CA 90401, USA
Batiuk, Thomas M (Tom) *Cartoonist (Crankshaft)*
%Universal Press Syndicate, 4520 Main St, Kansas City, MO 64111, USA
Batiz Campbell, Enrique *Conductor*
Periferico Sur 5141, Col Fabela, Dele Tlalan, Mexico City DF 14030, Mexico
Batliner, Gerard *Head of Government, Liechtenstein*
Am Schragen, Weg 2, 9490 Vaduz, Liechtenstein
Batlle Ibanez, Jorge L *President, Uruguay*
%Casa de Gobierno, Ave Luis Alberto de Herrear 3350, Montevideo, Uruguay

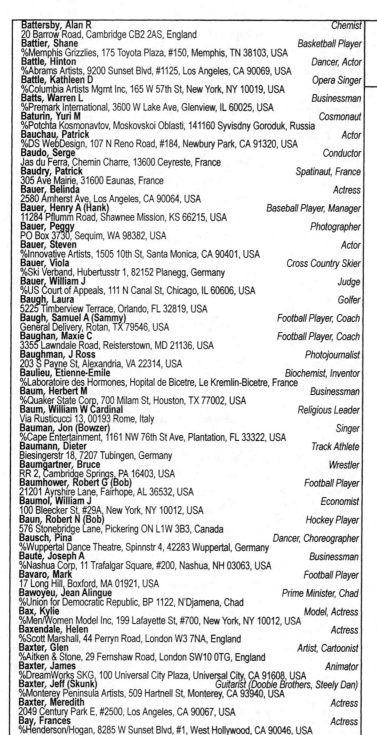

Battersby, Alan R *Chemist*
20 Barrow Road, Cambridge CB2 2AS, England
Battier, Shane *Basketball Player*
%Memphis Grizzlies, 175 Toyota Plaza, #150, Memphis, TN 38103, USA
Battle, Hinton *Dancer, Actor*
%Abrams Artists, 9200 Sunset Blvd, #1125, Los Angeles, CA 90069, USA
Battle, Kathleen D *Opera Singer*
%Columbia Artists Mgmt Inc, 165 W 57th St, New York, NY 10019, USA
Batts, Warren L *Businessman*
%Premark International, 3600 W Lake Ave, Glenview, IL 60025, USA
Baturin, Yuri M *Cosmonaut*
%Potchta Kosmonavtov, Moskovskoi Oblasti, 141160 Syvisdny Goroduk, Russia
Bauchau, Patrick *Actor*
%DS WebDesign, 107 N Reno Road, #184, Newbury Park, CA 91320, USA
Baudo, Serge *Conductor*
Jas du Ferra, Chemin Charre, 13600 Ceyreste, France
Baudry, Patrick *Spatinaut, France*
305 Ave Mairie, 31600 Eaunas, France
Bauer, Belinda *Actress*
2580 Amherst Ave, Los Angeles, CA 90064, USA
Bauer, Henry A (Hank) *Baseball Player, Manager*
11284 Pflumm Road, Shawnee Mission, KS 66215, USA
Bauer, Peggy *Photographer*
PO Box 3730, Sequim, WA 98382, USA
Bauer, Steven *Actor*
%Innovative Artists, 1505 10th St, Santa Monica, CA 90401, USA
Bauer, Viola *Cross Country Skier*
%Ski Verband, Hubertusstr 1, 82152 Planegg, Germany
Bauer, William J *Judge*
%US Court of Appeals, 111 N Canal St, Chicago, IL 60606, USA
Baugh, Laura *Golfer*
5225 Timberview Terrace, Orlando, FL 32819, USA
Baugh, Samuel A (Sammy) *Football Player, Coach*
General Delivery, Rotan, TX 79546, USA
Baughan, Maxie C *Football Player, Coach*
3355 Lawndale Road, Reisterstown, MD 21136, USA
Baughman, J Ross *Photojournalist*
203 S Payne St, Alexandria, VA 22314, USA
Baulieu, Etienne-Emile *Biochemist, Inventor*
%Laboratoire des Hormones, Hopital de Bicetre, Le Kremlin-Bicetre, France
Baum, Herbert M *Businessman*
%Quaker State Corp, 700 Milam St, Houston, TX 77002, USA
Baum, William W Cardinal *Religious Leader*
Via Rusticucci 13, 00193 Rome, Italy
Bauman, Jon (Bowzer) *Singer*
%Cape Entertainment, 1161 NW 76th St Ave, Plantation, FL 33322, USA
Baumann, Dieter *Track Athlete*
Biesingerstr 18, 7207 Tubingen, Germany
Baumgartner, Bruce *Wrestler*
RR 2, Cambridge Springs, PA 16403, USA
Baumhower, Robert G (Bob) *Football Player*
21201 Ayrshire Lane, Fairhope, AL 36532, USA
Baumol, William J *Economist*
100 Bleecker St, #29A, New York, NY 10012, USA
Baun, Robert N (Bob) *Hockey Player*
576 Stonebridge Lane, Pickering ON L1W 3B3, Canada
Bausch, Pina *Dancer, Choreographer*
%Wuppertal Dance Theatre, Spinnstr 4, 42283 Wuppertal, Germany
Baute, Joseph A *Businessman*
%Nashua Corp, 11 Trafalgar Square, #200, Nashua, NH 03063, USA
Bavaro, Mark *Football Player*
17 Long Hill, Boxford, MA 01921, USA
Bawoyeu, Jean Alingue *Prime Minister, Chad*
%Union for Democratic Republic, BP 1122, N'Djamena, Chad
Bax, Kylie *Model, Actress*
%Men/Women Model Inc, 199 Lafayette St, #700, New York, NY 10012, USA
Baxendale, Helen *Actress*
%Scott Marshall, 44 Perryn Road, London W3 7NA, England
Baxter, Glen *Artist, Cartoonist*
%Aitken & Stone, 29 Fernshaw Road, London SW10 0TG, England
Baxter, James *Animator*
%DreamWorks SKG, 100 Universal City Plaza, Universal City, CA 91608, USA
Baxter, Jeff (Skunk) *Guitarist (Doobie Brothers, Steely Dan)*
%Monterey Peninsula Artists, 509 Hartnell St, Monterey, CA 93940, USA
Baxter, Meredith *Actress*
2049 Century Park E, #2500, Los Angeles, CA 90067, USA
Bay, Frances *Actress*
%Henderson/Hogan, 8285 W Sunset Blvd, #1, West Hollywood, CA 90046, USA

B

Bay - Bearden

Bay, Michael *Movie Director*
%Creative Artists Agency, 9830 Wilshire Blvd, Beverly Hills, CA 90212, USA
Baye, Nathalie *Actress*
%Artmedia, 20 Ave Rapp, 75007 Paris, France
Bayes, G E *Religious Leader*
%Free Methodist Church, PO Box 535002, Winona Lake, IN 46590, USA
Bayi, Filbert *Track Athlete*
PO Box 60240, Dar es Salaam, Tanzania
Bayle, Jean-Michel *Motorcycle Racing Rider*
%General Delivery, Manosque, France
Baylor, Don E *Baseball Player, Manager*
56325 Riviera, La Quinta, CA 92253, USA
Baylor, Elgin G *Basketball Player, Executive*
2480 Briarcrest Road, Beverly Hills, CA 90210, USA
Bazell, Robert J *Commentator*
%NBC-TV, News Dept, 4001 Nebraska Ave NW, Washington, DC 20016, USA
Bazer, Fuller W *Animal Scientist*
8600 Creekview Court, College Station, TX 77845, USA
Bazin, Marc L *Prime Minister, Haiti*
%MIDH, 114 Ave Jean Paul II, Port-au-Prince, Haiti
Beach, Adam *Actor*
%Paradigm Agency, 10100 Santa Monica Blvd, #2500, Los Angeles, CA 90067, USA
Beach, Bill *Bowler*
435 Koehler Dr, Sharpsville, PA 16150, USA
Beach, Gary *Actor*
62 W 62nd St, #6F, New York, NY 10023, USA
Beach, Michael *Actor*
1823 Virginia Road, Los Angeles, CA 90019, USA
Beach, Roger C *Businessman*
%Unocal Corp, 2141 Rosecrans Ave, El Segundo, CA 90245, USA
Beacham, Stephanie *Actress*
%P F D, Drury House, 34-43 Russell St, London WC2B 5HA, England
Beachy, Roger N *Agricultural Scientist*
526 W Polo Dr, Saint Louis, MO 63105, USA
Beagle, Ronald G (Ron) *Football Player*
3830 San Ysidro Way, Sacramento, CA 95864, USA
Beal, Jack *Artist*
80 Epps Road, Oneonta, NY 13820, USA
Beal, Jeff *Composer*
%Gorfaine/Schwartz, 13245 Riverside Dr, #450, Sherman Oaks, CA 91423, USA
Beals, Jennifer *Actress*
%Innovative Artists, 1505 10th St, Santa Monica, CA 90401, USA
Beals, Vaughn L, Jr *Businessman, Motorcycle Executive*
%Harley-Davidson Inc, 3700 W Juneau Ave, Milwaukee, WI 53208, USA
Beam, C Arlen *Judge*
%US Court of Appeals, Federal Building, 100 Centennial Mall N, Lincoln, NE 68508, USA
Beaman, Lee Anne *Actress*
%Cavaleri Assoc, 178 S Victory Blvd, #205, Burbank, CA 91502, USA
Beamer, Frank *Football Coach*
%Virginia Polytechnic Institute, Athletic Dept, Blacksburg, VA 24061, USA
Beamon, Autry, Jr *Football Player*
12200 River Ridge Blvd, Burnsville, MN 55337, USA
Beamon, Robert (Bob) *Track Athlete*
%Florida Atlantic University, Athletic Dept, Boca Raton, FL 33431, USA
Bean, Alan L *Astronaut*
9173 Briar Forest Dr, Houston, TX 77024, USA
Bean, Andy *Golfer*
2912 Grasslands Dr, Lakeland, FL 33803, USA
Bean, Dawn Pawson *Synchronized Swimmer*
11902 Red Hill Ave, Santa Ana, CA 92705, USA
Bean, Henry *Movie Director, Writer*
%William Morris Agency, 151 El Camino Dr, Beverly Hills, CA 90212, USA
Bean, Orson *Actor, Comedian*
444 Carrol Canal, Venice, CA 90291, USA
Bean, Sean *Actor*
9100 Wilshire Blvd, #600-W, Beverly Hills, CA 90212, USA
Bearak, Barry *Journalist*
%New York Times, Editorial Dept, 229 W 43rd St, New York, NY 10036, USA
Beard, Alfred (Butch) *Basketball Player, Coach*
3834 Berleigh Hill Court, Burtonsville, MD 20866, USA
Beard, Amanda *Swimmer*
3792 Carmel Ave, Irvine, CA 92606, USA
Beard, Frank *Golfer*
70 Rocio Court, Palm Desert, CA 92260, USA
Beard, Frank *Drummer (ZZ Top)*
%Lone Wolf Mgmt, PO Box 163690, Austin, TX 78716, USA
Bearden, H Eugene (Gene) *Baseball Player*
3701 Dadeville Road, Alex City, AL 35010, USA

Bearse, Amanda *Actress*
15332 Antioch St, #143, Pacific Palisades, CA 90272, USA
Beart, Emmanuelle *Actress*
9 Rue Constant-Coquelin, 75007 Paris, France
Beasley, Allyce *Actress*
639 S Spring St, #4C, Los Angeles, CA 90014, USA
Beatrix *Queen, Netherlands*
Kasteel Drakesteijn, Lage Vuursche 3744 BA, Netherlands
Beattie, Ann *Writer*
%Janklow & Nesbit, 445 Park Ave, #1300, New York, NY 10022, USA
Beattie, Bob *Alpine Skier*
210 Aabc, #N, Aspen, CO 81611, USA
Beattie, Bruce *Editorial Cartoonist*
%Daytona Beach News-Journal, Editorial Dept, 901 6th St, Daytona Beach, FL 32117, USA
Beatty, James T (Jim) *Track Athlete*
1516 LaRochelle Lane, Charlotte, NC 28226, USA
Beatty, Ned *Actor*
2706 N Beachwood Dr, Los Angeles, CA 90068, USA
Beatty, Warren *Actor, Director, Producer*
13671 Mulholland Dr, Beverly Hills, CA 90210, USA
Beaty, Zelmo *Basketball Player*
2808 120th Ave NE, Bellevue, WA 98005, USA
Beauford, Carter *Drummer (Dave Matthews Band)*
%Red Light Mgmt, 3302 Lobban Place, Charlottesville, VA 22903, USA
Beaupre, Don *Hockey Player*
5020 Scriver Road, Edina, MN 55436, USA
Beauvais, Garcelle *Model, Actress*
%Nina Blanchard, 8826 Burton Way, Beverly Hills, CA 90211, USA
Beaver, Jim *Actor*
%Artists Agency, 1180 S Beverly Dr, #301, Los Angeles, CA 90035, USA
Beaver, Joe *Rodeo Rider*
PO Box 1595, Huntsville, TN 77342, USA
Beavogui, Louis Lansana *Prime Minister, Guinea*
%Prime Minister's Office, Conakry, Guinea
Beban, Gary J *Football Player*
20 Timber Lane, Northbrook, IL 60062, USA
Becherer, Hans W *Businessman*
%Deere Co, 1 John Deere Place, Moline, IL 61265, USA
Bechtel, Riley P *Businessman*
%Bechtel Group, 50 Beale St, San Francisco, CA 94105, USA
Bechtel, Stephen D, Jr *Businessman*
%Bechtel Group, 50 Beale St, San Francisco, CA 94105, USA
Bechtol, Hubert E (Hub) *Football Player*
7917 Taranto Dr, Austin, TX 78729, USA
Beck *Singer, Songwriter*
%GAS Entertainment, 8935 Lindblade St, Culver City, CA 90232, USA
Beck Hilton, Kimberly *Actress*
%Badgley Connor Talent, 9229 Sunset Blvd, #311, Los Angeles, CA 90069, USA
Beck, Charles H (Chip) *Golfer*
%Int'l Mgmt Group, 1 Erieview Plaza, 1360 E 9th St, #1300, Cleveland, OH 44114, USA
Beck, Jeff *Singer, Guitarist (Yardbirds)*
%Miracle Prestige, 1 Water Lane, Camden Town, London NW1 8N2, England
Beck, Marilyn M *Columnist*
2152 El Roble Lane, Beverly Hills, CA 90210, USA
Beck, Michael *Actor*
10100 Santa Monica Blvd, #310, Los Angeles, CA 90067, USA
Beck, Ray M *Football Player*
745 N College St, Cedartown, GA 30125, USA
Beckel, Robert D *Air Force General*
%New Mexico Military Institute, Superintendent's Office, Roswell, NM 88201, USA
Beckenbauer, Franz *Soccer Player, Coach*
Am Lutzenberg 15, 6370 Kitzbuhel, Austria
Becker, Boris *Tennis Player*
Grafenau, Grafenauweg, 6300 Zug, Switzerland
Becker, Edward R *Judge*
%US Court of Appeals, US Courthouse, 601 Market St, Philadelphia, PA 19106, USA
Becker, Gary S *Nobel Economics Laureate*
1308 E 58th St, Chicago, IL 60637, USA
Becker, George *Labor Leader*
%United Steelworkers of America, 5 Gateway Center, Pittsburgh, PA 15222, USA
Becker, Gretchen *Actress*
%Acme Talent, 4727 Wilshire Blvd, #333, Los Angeles, CA 90010, USA
Becker, Margaret *Singer, Guitarist*
%Sparrow Communications, 101 Winners Circle, Brentwood, TN 37027, USA
Becker, Quinn H *Army General, Surgeon*
PO Box 2388, Dillon, CO 80435, USA
Becker, Rob *Actor, Comedian*
%William Morris Agency, 151 El Camino Dr, Beverly Hills, CA 90212, USA

B

Becker - Beghe

Becker, Robert J *Allergist*
6 Oakbrook Club Dr, #J101, Oak Brook, IL 60523, USA
Becket, MacDonald G *Architect*
%Becket Group, 2501 Colorado Blvd, Santa Monica, CA 90404, USA
Beckett, Josh *Baseball Player*
%Florida Marlins, Pro Player Stadium, 2269 Dan Marino Blvd, Miami, FL 33056, USA
Beckett, Margaret M *Government Official, England*
%House of Commons, Westminster, London SW1A 0AA, England
Beckett, Sister Wendy *Art Critic*
%BBC TV Center, Wood Lane, London W12 7R3, England
Beckford, Tyson *Model, Actor*
%Bethann Model Mgmt, 36 N Moore St, #36N, New York, NY 10013, USA
Beckham, David *Soccer Player*
%Real Madrid FC, Avda Concha Espina 1, 28036 Madrid, Spain
Beckinsale, Kate *Actress*
%PA One, PO Box 21, Honiton, Devon EX14 1YH, England
Beckley, Gerry *Singer, Guitarist (America)*
%Agency for Performing Arts, 9200 Sunset Blvd, #900, Los Angeles, CA 90069, USA
Beckman, Arnold O *Inventor (Acidity Testing Apparatus)*
100 Academy Dr, Irvine, CA 92612, USA
Becton, Julius W, Jr *Army General, Educator*
%Prairie View A&M University, President's Office, Prairie View, TX 77446, USA
Bedard, Irene *Actress*
%Don Buchwald, 6500 Wilshire Blvd, #2200, Los Angeles, CA 90048, USA
Bedelia, Bonnie *Actress*
2082 Topanga Skyline Dr, Topanga, CA 90290, USA
Bedford, Brian *Actor*
%Arts Management Group, 1133 Broadway, #1025, New York, NY 10010, USA
Bedford, David V *Composer*
39 Shakespeare Road, Mill Hill, London NW7 4BA, England
Bedford, Sybille *Writer*
%Lutyens & Rubinstein, 231 Westbourne Park Road, London W11 1EB, England
Bedi, Bisban Singh *Cricketer*
Ispat Bhawan, Lodhi Road, New Delhi 3, India
Bedi, Kabir *Actor*
%Conway Van Gelder Robinson, 18-21 Jermyn St, London SW1Y 6NB, England
Bednarik, Charles P (Chuck) *Football Player*
6379 Winding Road, Coopersburg, PA 18036, USA
Bednorz, J Georg *Nobel Physics Laureate*
%IBM Research Laboratory, Saumerstr 4, 8803 Ruschlikon, Switzerland
Bedrosian, Stephen W (Steve) *Baseball Player*
3335 Gordon Road, Senoia, GA 30276, USA
Bedser, Alec V *Cricketer*
%Initial Cleaning Services, 33/34 Hoxton Square, London N1 6NN, England
Bedsole, Harold (Hal) *Football Player*
146 Balboa Lane, Tustin, CA 92780, USA
Beem, Rich *Golfer*
%Gaylord Sports Mgmt, 14646 N Kierland Blvd, #230, Scottsdale, AZ 85254, USA
Beene, Geoffrey *Fashion Designer*
%Geoffrey Beene Inc, 1770 W Maine St, Riverhead, NY 11901, USA
Beerbaum, Ludger *Equestrian Rider*
Altvaterweg 5, 86807 Buchloe, Germany
Beering, Steven C *Educator*
%Purdue University, President's Office, West Lafayette, IN 47907, USA
Beers, Gary *Bassist, Singer (INXS)*
8 Hayes St, #1, Neutral Bay 20891 NSW, Australia
Beeson, Jack H *Composer*
18 Seaforth Lane, Lloyd Harbor, NY 11743, USA
Beeson, Paul B *Physician*
7 Riverwoods Dr, #F125, Exeter, NH 03833, USA
Beevers, Harry *Biologist*
26 Hacienda Carmel, Carmel, CA 93923, USA
Beezer, Robert R *Judge*
%US Court of Appeals, US Courthouse, 1010 5th Ave, Seattle, WA 98104, USA
Bega, Leslie *Actress*
%Irv Schechter, 9300 Wilshire Blvd, #410, Beverly Hills, CA 90212, USA
Bega, Lou *Singer*
%Mission Control, Business Center, Lower Road, London SE16 2XB, England
Begay, Notah *Golfer*
%Professional Golfer's Assn, PO Box 109601, Palm Beach Gardens, FL 33410, USA
Begert, William J *Air Force General*
Commander, Pacific Air Force, Hickam Air Force Base, HI 96853, USA
Beggs, James M *Space Engineer, Government Official*
1177 N Great Southwest Parkway, Grand Prairie, TX 75050, USA
Beghe, Jason *Actor*
7473 Mulholland Dr, Los Angeles, CA 90046, USA
Beghe, Renato *Judge*
%US Tax Court, 400 2nd St NW, Washington, DC 20217, USA

B

Begley, Ed, Jr *Actor*
3850 Mound View Ave, Studio City, CA 91604, USA
Behe, Michael *Biochemist, Writer*
%Lehigh University, Biochemistry Dept, Bethlehem, PA 18015, USA
Behle, Petra *Biathlete*
Sonnenhof 1, 34508 Willingen, Germany
Behm, Forrest E *Football Player*
3 Briarcliff Dr, Corning, NY 14830, USA
Behnken, Robert L *Astronaut*
43708 Dejay St, Lancaster, CA 93536, USA
Behr, Dani *Actress*
%Planet 24, Norex, 195 March Wall, London E14 9SG, England
Behr, Jason *Actor*
%Rogers & Cowan, 6340 Breckenridge Run, Rex, GA 30273, USA
Behrend, Marc *Hockey Player*
1808 Savannah Way, Waunakee, WI 53597, USA
Behrendt, Jan *Luge Athlete*
Karl-Zink-Str 2, 96893 Ilmenau, Germany
Behrens, Hildegard *Opera Singer*
%Herbert Breslin, 119 W 57th St, #1505, New York, NY 10019, USA
Behrens, Sam *Actor*
530 Bryant Dr, Canoga Park, CA 91304, USA
Behrensmyer, Anna K *Paleobiologist*
%Amboseli National Park, PO Box 18, Namanga, Kenya
Beickler, Ferdinand *Businessman*
%Adam Opel AG, Bahnhofsplatz 1, 65428 Russelsheim, Germany
Beikirch, Gary B *Vietnam War Army Hero (CMH)*
68 South Ave, Hilton, NY 14468, USA
Beilina, Nina *Concert Violinist*
400 W 43rd St, #7D, New York, NY 10036, USA
Beitz, Berthold *Businessman*
Weg Zur Platte 37, 45133 Essen, Germany
Bejart, Maurice J *Ballet Dancer, Choreographer*
%Bejart Ballet, Case Postale 25, 1000 Lausanne 22, Switzerland
Bela, Magyari *Cosmonaut, Hungary*
18885 P Alffy 7-11, Budapest, Hungary
Belafonte, Harry *Singer, Actor*
%William Morris Agency, 1325 Ave of Americas, New York, NY 10019, USA
Belafonte, Shari *Actress, Model*
%Peter Giagni, 8981 W Sunset Blvd, West Hollywood, CA 90069, USA
Belen, Ana *Actress, Singer*
%Rompeolas Productions, Alabama St, #1761, San Gerardo, Rio Piedras, PR 00926, USA
Belenky, Valery *Gymnast*
Schillerstr 20, 73760 Ostfildern, Germany
Belew, Adrian *Guitarist*
%Umbrella Artists Mgmt, 2612 Erie Ave, Cincinnati, OH 45208, USA
Belford, Christina *Actress*
10635 Santa Monica Blvd, #130, Los Angeles, CA 90025, USA
Belfour, Edward (Ed) *Hockey Player*
%Promo Athlete Inc, 9810 Sarle Road, Freeland, MI 48623, USA
BelGeddes, Barbara *Actress*
PO Box 869, Northeast Harbor, ME 04662, USA
Belichick, Steve *Football Player*
3035 Aberdeen Road, Annapolis, MD 21403, USA
Belichik, William S (Bill) *Football Coach*
%New England Patriots, Gillette Stadium, RR 1, 60 Washington, Foxboro, MA 02035, USA
Belin, Gaspard D *Attorney*
4 Willard St, Cambridge, MA 02138, USA
Belin, Nat *Cartoonist*
%Drawing Board, PO Box 1162, Winston Salem, NC 27102, USA
Belita *Actress*
44 Crabtree Lane, London SW6 6LW, England
Beliveau, Jean A *Hockey Player*
155 Rue Victoria, Longuevil QC J4H 2J4, Canada
Bell, Archie *Singer*
%Speer Entertainment Services, PO Box 49612, Atlanta, GA 30359, USA
Bell, C Gordon *Computer Scientist*
%Microsoft Corp, 1 Microsoft Way, Redmond, WA 98052, USA
Bell, Catherine *Actress*
%Innovative Artists, 1505 10th St, Santa Monica, CA 90401, USA
Bell, Clyde R (Bob) *Navy Admiral, Association Executive*
1301 Harney St, Omaha, NE 68102, USA
Bell, David G (Buddy) *Baseball Player, Manager*
PO Box 11718, Chandler, AZ 85248, USA
Bell, Felicia M *Actress*
1365 Riverside Dr, #317, North Hollywood, CA 91607, USA
Bell, Gary *Baseball Player*
%American Sports, 1436 N Flores St, San Antonio, TX 78212, USA

Bell, Gregory (Greg) *Track Athlete*
831 W Miami Ave, Logansport, IN 46947, USA
Bell, Griffin B *Attorney General*
206 Townsend Place NW, Atlanta, GA 30327, USA
Bell, Jamie *Actor*
PO Box 1116, Belfast B72 7AJ, Northern Ireland
Bell, Jay S *Baseball Player*
PO Box 50249, Phoenix, AZ 85076, USA
Bell, John *Singer (Widespread Panic)*
%Brown Cat Inc, 400 Foundry St, Athens, GA 30601, USA
Bell, Jorge A M (George) *Baseball Player*
Lamiama #14, Bell 2nd Planto, San Pedo de Macoris, Dominican Republic
Bell, Joshua *Concert Violinist*
%I M G Artists, 3 Burlington Lane, Chiswick, London W4 2TH, England
Bell, Larry S *Artist*
PO Box 4101, Taos, NM 87571, USA
Bell, Lynette *Swimmer*
149 Henry St, Merwether NSW 22, Australia
Bell, Madison Smartt *Writer*
%Random House, 1745 Broadway, #B1, New York, NY 10019, USA
Bell, Mike *Motorcyle Racing Rider*
%American Motorcycle Assn, 13515 Yarmouth Dr, Pickerington, OH 43147, USA
Bell, Robert L (Bobby), Sr *Football Player*
208 NW Shagbark St, Lees Summit, MO 64064, USA
Bell, Sam *Track Coach*
2310 E Woodstock Place, Bloomington, IN 47401, USA
Bell, Tom *Actor*
%Shepherd & Ford, 13 Radnor Walk, London SW3 4BP, England
Bell, Tommy *Astronaut*
205 S Redondo Ave, Manhattan Beach, CA 90266, USA
Bell-Lundy, Sandra *Cartoonist (Between Friends)*
255 Northwood Dr, Welland ON L3C 6V1, Canada
Bella, Ivan *Cosmonaut*
%Potchta Kosmonavtov, Moskovskoi Oblasti, 141160 Syvisdny Goroduk, Russia
Bellamy, Bill *Actor, Comedian*
%Talent Entertainment Group, 9111 Wilshire Blvd, Beverly Hills, CA 90210, USA
Bellamy, Carol *United Nations Official*
%United Nations Children's Fund, 3 United Nations Plaza, New York, NY 10017, USA
Bellamy, David *Singer (Bellamy Brothers), Songwriter*
%Webster Assoc, 811 18th Ave S, #200, Nashville, TN 37203, USA
Bellamy, David J *Botanist, Writer, Broadcaster*
Mill House, Bedburn, Bishop Auckland, County Durham DL13 3NN, England
Bellamy, Howard *Singer (Bellamy Brothers), Songwriter*
%Webster Assoc, 811 18th Ave S, #200, Nashville, TN 37203, USA
Bellamy, Walter J (Walt) *Basketball Player*
2884 Lakeshore Dr, College Park, GA 30337, USA
Belle, Albert J *Baseball Player*
9574 E Ann Way, Scottsdale, AZ 85260, USA
Belle, Regina *Singer*
%Green Light, PO Box 3172, Beverly Hills, CA 90212, USA
Beller, Kathleen *Actress*
PO Box 806, Half Moon Bay, CA 94019, USA
Bellingham, Norman *Canoist*
208 Morgan St NW, Washington, DC 20001, USA
Bellini, Mario *Architect*
%Architecture Center, 66 Portland Place, London W1, England
Bellino, Joseph M (Joe) *Football Player*
45 Hayden Lane, Bedford, MA 01730, USA
Bellisario, Donald P *Television Producer*
%Broder Kurland Webb Uffner, 9242 Beverly Blvd, #200, Beverly Hills, CA 90210, USA
Bellmon, Henry *Governor, Senator, OK*
RR 1, Red Rock, OK 74651, USA
Bello, Maria *Actress*
%Creative Artists Agency, 9830 Wilshire Blvd, Beverly Hills, CA 90212, USA
Bellotti, Mike *Football Coach*
%University of Oregon, Athletic Dept, Eugen, OR 97403, USA
Bellovin, Steven M *Computer Scientist*
%AT&T Research Labs, 180 Park Ave, PO Box 971, Florham Park, NJ 07932, USA
Bellow, Saul C *Nobel Literature Laureate*
%Boston University, 745 Commonwealth Ave, Boston, MA 02215, USA
Bellows, Gil *Actor*
%International Creative Mgmt, 8942 Wilshire Blvd, #219, Beverly Hills, CA 90211, USA
Bellson, Louis (Louie) *Jazz Drummer, Composer*
%Ted Schmidt Assoc, 901 Winding River Road, Vero Beach, FL 32963, USA
Bellucci, Monica *Model, Actress*
%Agence Intertalent, 5 Rue Clement Marot, 75008 Paris, France
Bellwood, Pamela *Actress*
1696 San Leandro Lane, Santa Barbara, CA 93108, USA

Belmondo, Jean-Paul *Actor*
9 Rue des Saint Peres, 75007 Paris, France
Belo, Carlos Filipe Ximenes *Nobel Peace Laureate, Religious Leader*
%Catholic Bishop, Dili, East Timor
Belote Hamlin, Melissa *Swimmer*
7311 Exmore St, Springfield, VA 22150, USA
Belousova, Ludmila *Figure Skater*
Chalet Hubel, 3818 Grindelwald, Switzerland
Belov, Sergei *Basketball Player*
%Basket Cassino, Vis Appia Nuova, Cassino, Rome, Italy
Beltran, Robert *Actor*
2210 Talmadge St, Los Angeles, CA 90027, USA
Belushi, James *Actor*
%Borinstein Oreck Bogart, 3172 Dona Susana Dr, Studio City, CA 91604, USA
Belzer, Richard *Actor, Comedian*
%Wolf, Chelsea Pier, 62 W 23rd St & 12th Ave, New York, NY 10010, USA
Beman, Deane R *Golfer, Golf Executive*
255 Deer Haven Dr, Ponte Vedra, FL 32082, USA
Ben Ali, Zine al-Abidine *President, Tunisia; Army General*
%President's Office, Palais Presidentiel, Tunis, Tunisia
Benacerraf, Baruj *Nobel Medicine Laureate*
111 Perkins St, Boston, MA 02130, USA
Benade, Leo Edward *Army General*
417 Pine Ridge Road, #A, Carthage, NC 28327, USA
Benatar, Pat *Singer, Songwriter*
%Sonder, 250 W 57th St, #1830, New York, NY 10107, USA
Benavides, Fortunato P (Pete) *Judge*
%US Court of Appeals, 903 San Jacinto Blvd, Austin, TX 78701, USA
Bench, John L (Johnny) *Baseball Player*
528 4 Mile Road, Cincinnati, OH 45230, USA
Benchley, Peter B *Writer*
35 Boudinot St, Princeton, NJ 08540, USA
Benchoff, Dennis L (Den) *Army General*
380 Arbor Road, Lancaster, PA 17601, USA
Bender, Gary N *Sportscaster*
%TNT-TV, Sports Dept, 1050 Techwood Dr NW, Atlanta, GA 30318, USA
Bender, Thomas *Historian*
54 Washington Mews, New York, NY 10003, USA
Benedek, George B *Physicist*
%Massachusetts Institute of Technology, Physics Dept, Cambridge, MA 02139, USA
Benedict, Dirk *Actor*
PO Box 634, Bigfork, MT 59911, USA
Benedict, Manson *Chemical Engineer*
108 Moorings Park Dr, #206, Naples, FL 34105, USA
Benedict, Paul *Actor*
84 Rockland Place, Newton, MA 02464, USA
Benes, Andrew C (Andy) *Baseball Player*
1127 Highland Point Dr, Saint Louis, MO 63131, USA
Benet, Eric *Singer, Songwriter*
%Family Tree Entertainment, 135 E 57th St, #2600, New York, NY 10022, USA
Benetton, Giuliana *Businesswoman*
%Benetton Group SpA, Via Minelli, 31050 Ponzano Treviso, Italy
Benetton, Luciano *Businessman*
%Benetton Group SpA, Via Minelli, 31050 Ponzano Treviso, Italy
Benflis, Ali *Prime Minister, Algeria*
%Prime Minister's Office, Palais du Gouvernement, Algiers, Algeria
Benglis, Lynda *Artist*
222 Bowery St, New York, NY 10012, USA
Bengston, Billy Al *Artist*
805 Hampton Dr, Venice, CA 90291, USA
Benhima, Mohamed *Prime Minister, Morocco*
Km 5.5, Route des Zaers, Rabat, Morocco
Benigni, Roberto *Actor, Director*
Via Traversa 44, Vergaglio, Provinz di Prato, Italy
Bening, Annette *Actress*
13671 Mulholland Dr, Beverly Hills, CA 90210, USA
Benirschke, Rolf J *Football Player*
4326 Vista de la Tierra, San Diego, CA 92130, USA
Benjamin, Andre (Dre) *Rap Artist*
%LaFace/Arista Records, 3423 Piedmont Road NE, Atlanta, GA 30305, USA
Benjamin, Richard *Actor, Director*
%Bartels Co, PO Box 57593, Sherman Oaks, CA 91413, USA
Benjamin, Stephen *Yachtsman*
40 Quintard Ave, Norwalk, CT 06854, USA
Benkovic, Stepehn J *Chemist*
771 Teaberry Lane, State College, PA 16803, USA
Benmosche, Robert H *Businessman*
%Metropolitan Life Insurance, 1 Madison Ave, New York, NY 10010, USA

B

Benn - Benzali

Benn, Nigel *Boxer*
%Matchroom Boxing, 10 Western Road, Romford Essex RM1 3JT, England
Bennett, Bob *Singer, Songwriter*
%Jeff Roberts Assoc, 909 Meadowland Lane, Goodlettsville, TN 37072, USA
Bennett, Brooke *Swimmer*
2585 Rowe Road, Milford, MI 48380, USA
Bennett, Bruce (Herman Brix) *Actor, Track Athlete*
2702 Forester Road, Los Angeles, CA 90064, USA
Bennett, Clay *Editorial Cartoonist*
%Christian Science Monitor, Editorial Dept, 1 Norway St, Boston, MA 02115, USA
Bennett, Darren *Football Player*
PO Box 705, Solano Beach, CA 92075, USA
Bennett, Donnell *Football Player*
8055 W Leitner Dr, Coral Springs, FL 33067, USA
Bennett, Fran *Actress*
749 N Lafayette Park Place, Los Angeles, CA 90026, USA
Bennett, Hywel *Actor*
%Gavin Barker, 45 S Molton St, London W1Y 3RD, England
Bennett, Joe C *Rheumatologist, Educator*
4101 Altamont Road, Birmingham, AL 35213, USA
Bennett, John *Governor, NJ*
%New Jersey State Senate, 125 W State St, Trenton, NJ 08608, USA
Bennett, Michael *Football Player*
%Minnesota Vikings, 9520 Viking Dr, Eden Prairie, MN 55344, USA
Bennett, Nigel *Actor*
PO Box 14, Rossford, OH 43460, USA
Bennett, Richard Rodney *Composer*
%Novello Co, 8-9 Firth St, London W1V 5TZ, England
Bennett, Robert R *Businessman*
%Home Shopping Network, 2501 118th Ave N, Saint Petersburg, FL 33716, USA
Bennett, Tony *Singer*
%Tony Bennett Enterprises, 130 W 57th St, #9D, New York, NY 10019, USA
Bennett, William J *Secretary, Education*
1701 Pennsylvania Ave NW, #900, Washington, DC 20006, USA
Bennington, Chester *Singer (Linkin Park)*
%Artist Group International, 9560 Wilshire Blvd, #400, Beverly Hills, CA 90212, USA
Bennis, Warren G *Educator, Writer*
%University of Southern California, Management School, Los Angeles, CA 90007, USA
Benoit Samuelson, Joan *Track Athlete*
95 Lower Flying Point Road, Freeport, ME 04032, USA
Benoit, David *Jazz Pianist*
%Fitzgerald-Hartley, 34 N Palm St, #100, Ventura, CA 93001, USA
Benson, George *Jazz Guitarist*
374 Poli St, #205, Ventura, CA 93001, USA
Benson, Harry *Photographer*
181 E 73rd St, #18A, New York, NY 10021, USA
Benson, Johnny, Jr *Auto Racing Driver*
PO Box 150619, Grand Rapids, MI 49515, USA
Benson, Renaldo (Obie) *Singer (Four Tops)*
%William Morris Agency, 151 El Camino Dr, Beverly Hills, CA 90212, USA
Benson, Robby *Actor*
%Innovative Artists, 1505 10th St, Santa Monica, CA 90401, USA
Benson, Stephen R (Steve) *Editorial Cartoonist*
%Arizona Republic, Editorial Dept, 200 E Van Buren St, Phoenix, AZ 85004, USA
Bentley, John *Actor*
Wedgewood House, Peterworth, Sussex, England
Bentley, Ray *Sportscaster*
%Fox-TV, Sports Dept, 205 W 67th St, New York, NY 10021, USA
Bentley, Stacey *Body Builder*
PO Box 26, Santa Monica, CA 90406, USA
Bentley, Wes *Actor*
151 W 74th St, #600, New York, NY 10023, USA
Benton, Andrew K *Educator*
%Pepperdine University, President's Office, Malibu, CA 90263, USA
Benton, Barbi *Model, Actress*
40 N 4th St, Carbondale, CO 81623, USA
Benton, Fletcher *Artist*
250 Dore St, San Francisco, CA 94103, USA
Benton, Robert *Movie Director*
%International Creative Mgmt, 40 W 57th St, #1800, New York, NY 10019, USA
Bentsen, Lloyd M, Jr *Secretary, Treasury; Senator, TX*
%Verner Lipfert Bernhard, 901 15th St NW, #700, Washington, DC 20005, USA
Benvenuti, Giovanni (Nino) *Boxer*
%FPI, Viale Tiziano 70, 00196 Rome, Italy
Benza, A J *Actor*
5670 Wilshire Blvd, #400W, Los Angeles, CA 90036, USA
Benzali, Daniel *Actor*
%The Agency, 1800 Ave of Stars, #400, Los Angeles, CA 90067, USA

Benzer, Seymour *Biologist*
2075 Robin Road, San Marino, CA 91108, USA
Beranek, Josef *Hockey Player*
%Pittsburgh Penguins, Mellon Arena, 66 Mario Lemieux Place, Pittsburgh, PA 15219, USA
Bercaw, John E *Chemist*
%California Institute of Technology, Chemistry Dept, Pasadena, CA 91125, USA
Bercu, Michaela *Model, Actress*
Habaal-Shem Tov #10, Apt 93, Herzelia 46342, Canada
Berdahl, Robert M *Educator*
%University of California, Chancellor's Office, Berkeley, CA 94720, USA
Berendzen, Richard E *Educator*
1300 Crystal Dr, Arlington, VA 22202, USA
Berenger, Tom *Actor*
%Creative Artists Agency, 9830 Wilshire Blvd, Beverly Hills, CA 90212, USA
Berenson, Ken (Red) *Hockey Player, Coach*
3555 Daleview Dr, Ann Arbor, MI 48105, USA
Beresford, Bruce *Movie Director*
3 Marathon Road, #13, Darling Point, Sydney NSW, Australia
Beresford, Meg *Social Activist*
Wiston Lodge, Wiston, Biggar ML12 6HT, Scotland
Berezhnaya, Yelena *Figure Skater*
%Ice House Skating Rink, 111 Midtown Bridge Approach, Hackensack, NJ 07601, USA
Berezovy, Anatoli N *Cosmonaut*
%Potchta Kosmonavtov, Moskovskoi Oblasti, 141160 Syvisdny Goroduk, Russia
Berg, A Scott *Writer*
%G P Putnam's Sons, 375 Hudson St, New York, NY 10014, USA
Berg, Aki-Petteri *Hockey Player*
%Octagon, 1751 Pinnacle Dr, #1500, McLean, VA 22102, USA
Berg, Elizabeth *Writer*
%Random House, 1745 Broadway, #B1, New York, NY 10019, USA
Berg, Matraca *Singer, Songwriter*
%Joe's Garage, 4405 Belmont Park Terrace, Nashville, TN 37215, USA
Berg, Patricia J (Patty) *Golfer*
%William Harvey, PO Box 1607, Fort Myers, FL 33902, USA
Berg, Paul *Nobel Chemistry Laureate*
%Stanford University, Medical School, Beckman Center, Stanford, CA 94305, USA
Berg, Peter *Actor*
%H S I Productions, 3630 Eastham Dr, Culver City, CA 90232, USA
Berganza, Teresa *Opera Singer*
La Rossiniana, Archanda 5, 28200 San Lorenzo del Escorial, Madrid, Spain
Berge, Francine *Actress*
%Cineart, 36 Rue de Ponthieu, 75008 Paris, France
Berge, Ole M *Labor Leader*
%Maintenance of Way Brotherhood, 12050 Woodward Ave, Detroit, MI 48203, USA
Berge, Pierre V G *Businessman*
%Yves Saint Laurent SA, 5 Ave Marceau, 75116 Paris, France
Bergen, Candice P *Actress*
222 Central Park South, New York, NY 10019, USA
Bergen, Polly *Actress*
%Jan McCormack, 1746 S Britain Road, Southbury, CT 06488, USA
Berger, Gerhard *Auto Racing Driver*
%Berger Motorsport, Postfach 1121, 9490 Vaduz, Austria
Berger, Helmut *Actor*
Viale Parioli 50, 00197 Rome, Italy
Berger, John *Writer*
Quincy, Mieussy, 74440 Taninges, France
Berger, Senta *Actress*
%Sentana Films, Gebsattelstr 30, 81541 Munich, Germany
Berger, Thomas L *Writer*
PO Box 11, Palisades, NY 10964, USA
Bergere, Lee *Actor*
57 Fellows Dr, Brentwood, NH 03833, USA
Bergeron, Michel *Hockey Coach*
CHL T630, 25 Rue Bryant, Sherbrooke QC J1J 3Z5, Canada
Bergeron, Tom *Entertainer*
%Creative Artists Agency, 9830 Wilshire Blvd, Beverly Hills, CA 90212, USA
Bergey, John *Inventor (Pulsar Watch)*
1807 Mayflower Circle, Lancaster, PA 17603, USA
Bergey, William E (Bill) *Football Player*
2 Hickory Lane, Chadds Ford, PA 19317, USA
Berggren, Jenny *Singer (Ace of Base)*
%Basic Music Mgmt, Norrtullsgatan 51, 113 45 Stockholm, Sweden
Berggren, Jonas *Singer (Ace of Base)*
%Basic Music Mgmt, Norrtullsgatan 51, 113 45 Stockholm, Sweden
Berggren, Malin *Singer (Ace of Base)*
%Basic Music Mgmt, Norrtullsgatan 51, 113 45 Stockholm, Sweden
Berggren, Thommy *Actor*
%Swedish Film Institute, PO Box 27126, 102 52, Stockholm, Sweden

B

Bergin - Bernal

Bergin, Michael *Model, Actor*
300 Park Ave, #200, New York, NY 10010, USA
Bergin, Patrick *Actor*
%Hyler Mgmt, 25 Sea Colony Dr, Santa Monica, CA 90405, USA
Bergkamp, Dennis *Soccer Player*
%Arsenal FC, Arsenal Stadium, Avenell Road, London N5 1BU, England
Bergl, Emily *Actress*
%Innovative Artists, 1505 10th St, Santa Monica, CA 90401, USA
Bergland, Robert S (Bob) *Secretary, Agriculture*
1104 7th Ave SE, Roseau, MN 56751, USA
Berglund, Paavo A E *Conductor*
Munkkiniemenranta 41, 00330 Helsinki 33, Finland
Bergman, Alan *Lyricist*
714 N Maple Dr, Beverly Hills, CA 90210, USA
Bergman, Andrew C *Writer, Movie Director*
555 W 57th St, #1230, New York, NY 10019, USA
Bergman, Ingmar *Movie Director*
Box 73, 62036 Farosund, Sweden
Bergman, Marilyn K *Lyricist*
714 N Maple Dr, Beverly Hills, CA 90210, USA
Bergman, Martin *Movie Producer*
641 Lexington Ave, New York, NY 10022, USA
Bergman, Peter *Actor*
4799 White Oak Ave, Encino, CA 91316, USA
Bergman, Robert G *Chemist*
501 Coventry Road, Kensington, CA 94707, USA
Bergmann, Arnfinn *Ski Jumper*
Nils Collett Vogtsv 58, 0765 Oslo 7, Norway
Bergoglio, Jose Mario Cardinal *Religious Leader*
%Arzobispado, Rivadavia 415, 1002 Buenos Aires, Argentina
Bergonzi, Carlo *Opera Singer*
%I C M Artists, 40 W 57th St, New York, NY 10019, USA
Bergoust, Eric *Freestyle Aerials Skier*
228 W Main, Missoula, MT 59802, USA
Bergstrom, K Sune *Nobel Medicine Laureate*
%Karolinska Institute, Box 270, 171 77 Stockholm, Sweden
Beristain, Gabriel L *Cinematographer*
%United Talent Agency, 9560 Wilshire Blvd, #500, Beverly Hills, CA 90212, USA
Berkeley, Michael F *Composer*
%Rogers Coleridge White, 20 Powis Mews, London W11 1JN, England
Berkeley, Xander *Actor*
%Writers & Artists, 8383 Wilshire Blvd, #550, Beverly Hills, CA 90211, USA
Berkley, Elizabeth *Actress, Model*
%Handprint Entertainment, 8436 W 3rd St, Los Angeles, CA 90048, USA
Berkoff, David *Swimmer*
%Harvard University, Athletic Dept, Cambridge, MA 02138, USA
Berkowitz, Bob *Entertainer*
%CNBC-TV, 2200 Fletcher Ave, Fort Lee, NJ 07024, USA
Berlin, Mike *Bowler*
12 Coventry Lane, Muscatine, IA 52761, USA
Berlin, Steve *Singer (Los Lobos)*
%Gold Mountain, 3575 Cahuenga Blvd W, #450, Los Angeles, CA 90068, USA
Berling, Clay *Soccer Executive, Publisher*
2935 Franciscan Way, Carmel, CA 93923, USA
Berlinger, Warren *Actor*
10642 Arnel Place, Chatsworth, CA 91311, USA
Berlitz, Charles F *Linguist, Writer, Archaeologist*
7 Mendota Lane, Sea Ranch Lakes, FL 33308, USA
Berlusconi, Silvio *Prime Minister, Italy*
%Premier's Office, Palazzo Chigi, Piazza Colonna 370, 00187 Rome, Italy
Berman, Andy *Actor*
%Gersh Agency, 232 N Canon Dr, Beverly Hills, CA 90210, USA
Berman, Chris *Sportscaster*
%ESPN-TV, Sports Dept, ESPN Plaza, 935 Middle St, Bristol, CT 06010, USA
Berman, Jennifer *Physician*
%University of California, Women's Sexual Health Center, Los Angeles, CA 90024, USA
Berman, Laura *Psychotherapist*
%University of California, Women's Sexual Health Center, Los Angeles, CA 90024, USA
Berman, Lazar N *Concert Pianist*
%World Touring Productions, 26 Middlesex Dr, Dix Hills, NY 11746, USA
Berman, Shelley *Actor, Comedian*
268 Bell Canyon Road, Bell Canyon, CA 91307, USA
Bern, Howard A *Biologist*
1010 Shattuck Ave, Berkeley, CA 94707, USA
Bernabei, Ray *Soccer Player*
541 Woodview Dr, Longwood, FL 32779, USA
Bernal, Gael Garcia *Actor*
%United Talent Agency, 9560 Wilshire Blvd, #500, Beverly Hills, CA 90212, USA

Bernard, Betsy *Businesswoman*
%American Telephone & Telegraph Corp, 32 Ave of Americas, New York, NY 10013, USA
Bernard, Claire M A *Concert Violinist*
53 Rue Rabelais, 69003 Lyon, France
Bernard, Crystal *Actress, Singer, Songwriter*
%Creative Artists Agency, 9830 Wilshire Blvd, Beverly Hills, CA 90212, USA
Bernard, Ed *Actor*
PO Box 7965, Northridge, CA 91327, USA
Berner, Robert A *Geochemist*
15 Hickory Hill Road, North Haven, CT 06473, USA
Berners-Lee, Timothy J *Computer Scientist*
%Massachusetts Institute of Technology, Computer Sci Lab, Cambridge, MA 02139, USA
Bernhard *Prince, Netherlands*
%Soestdijk Palace, Baarn, Netherlands
Bernhard, Ruth *Photographer*
2982 Clay St, San Francisco, CA 94115, USA
Bernhard, Sandra *Actress, Comedienne, Singer*
9465 Wilshire Blvd, #308, Beverly Hills, CA 90212, USA
Bernheim, Emmanuele *Writer*
%Viking Press, 375 Hudson St, New York, NY 10014, USA
Bernheimer, Martin *Music Critic*
17350 Sunset Blvd, #702C, Pacific Palisades, CA 90272, USA
Bernier, Sylvie *Diver*
%Olympic Assn, Cite du Harve, Montreal QC H3C 3R4, Canada
Berning, Susie Maxwell *Golfer*
1701 Rock Springs Dr, Las Vegas, NV 89128, USA
Bernsen, Corbin *Actor*
13535 Hatteras St, Van Nuys, CA 91401, USA
Bernstein, Basil *Sociologist*
90 Farquhar Road, Dulwich SE19 1LT, England
Bernstein, Carl *Journalist*
%William Morris Agency, 151 El Camino Dr, Beverly Hills, CA 90212, USA
Bernstein, Charles *Composer*
%FMA, 6525 Sunset Blvd, #300, Los Angeles, CA 90028, USA
Bernstein, Elmer *Composer*
2715 Pearl St, Santa Monica, CA 90405, USA
Bernstein, Kenny *Auto Racing Driver*
%King Racing, 26231 Dimension Dr, Lake Forest, CA 92630, USA
Berov, Lyuben *Prime Minister, Bulgaria*
%Rights & Freedom Movement, Tzarigradsko Shosse 47/1, 1408 Sofia, Bulgaria
Berra, Lawrence P (Yogi) *Baseball Player, Manager*
19 Highland Ave, Montclair, NJ 07042, USA
Berresford, Susan V *Foundation Executive*
%Ford Foundation, 320 E 43rd St, New York, NY 10017, USA
Berri, Claude *Movie Director, Producer*
%Renn Espace d'Art Contemporain, 7 Rue de Lille, 75007 Paris, France
Berridge, Elizabeth *Actress*
%Judy Schoen, 606 N Larchmont Blvd, #309, Los Angeles, CA 90004, USA
Berridge, Michael J *Zoologist, Biologist*
13 Home Close, Histon, Cambridge CB4 4JL, England
Berrigan, Daniel *Clergyman, Social Activist*
220 W 98th St, #11L, New York, NY 10025, USA
Berruti, Livio *Track Athlete*
Via Avigliana 45, 10138 Torino, Italy
Berry, Bill *Skiing Writer*
839 N Center St, Reno, NV 89501, USA
Berry, Bill *Drummer (REM)*
%REM/Athens Ltd, 170 College Ave, Athens, GA 30601, USA
Berry, Charles E (Chuck) *Singer, Songwriter*
Berry Park, 691 Buckner Road, Wentzville, MO 63385, USA
Berry, Halle *Actress, Model*
%Creative Artists Agency, 9830 Wilshire Blvd, Beverly Hills, CA 90212, USA
Berry, Jan *Singer (Jan & Dean), Songwriter*
221 Main St, #P, Huntington Beach, CA 92648, USA
Berry, Jim *Editorial Cartoonist*
%United Feature Syndicate, 200 Madison Ave, New York, NY 10016, USA
Berry, John *Singer*
%Firstars Mgmt, 14724 Ventura Blvd, #PH, Sherman Oaks, CA 91403, USA
Berry, Ken *Actor*
13911 Fenton Ave, Sylmar, CA 91342, USA
Berry, Kevin *Swimmer*
28 George St, Manly NSW 2295, Australia
Berry, Michael J *Chemist*
PO Box 1421, Pebble Beach, CA 93953, USA
Berry, Raymond E *Football Player, Coach*
1972 Montane Dr E, Golden, CO 80401, USA
Berry, Robert V (Bob) *Hockey Player, Coach, Executive*
640 3rd St, Hermosa Beach, CA 90254, USA

B

Berry, Stephen J (Steve) *Journalist*
6527 Ellenview Ave, West Hills, CA 91307, USA
Berry, Wendell E *Writer, Ecologist*
River Road, Port Royal, KY 40058, USA
Berryman, Michael *Actor*
PO Box 1746, Middletown, CA 95461, USA
Bersia, John *Journalist*
%Orlando Sentinel, Editorial Dept, 633 N Orange Ave, Orlando, FL 32801, USA
Berteotti, Missy *Golfer*
3221 Annandale Dr, Preston, PA 15142, USA
Berthold, Helmut *Handball Player*
Meyerstr 21, 21075 Hamburg, Germany
Bertil *Prince, Sweden*
Hert Av Halland, Kungl Slottet, 111 30 Stockholm, Sweden
Bertinelli, Valerie *Actress*
1850 Pleasant St, Walla Walla, WA 99362, USA
Bertini, Catherine *Association Executive*
%United Nations, 1 United Nations Plaza, New York, NY 10017, USA
Bertolucci, Bernardo *Movie Director*
Via Della Lungara 3, 00165 Rome, Italy
Bertone, Tarcisco Cardinal *Religious Leader*
%Archdiocese, Piazza Matteotti 4, 16123 Genoa, Italy
Berzon, Marsha S *Judge*
%US Court of Appeals, Court Building, 95 7th St, San Francisco, CA 94103, USA
Bessmertnova, Natalia *Ballerina*
Sretenskii Blvd 6/1, #9, 101000 Moscow, Russia
Bessmertnykh, Aleksandr *Government Official, Russia*
Yelizarova Str 10, 103064 Moscow, Russia
Besson, Luc *Movie Director*
%CBC, 11 Rue de la Croix Boissee, 91540 Mennecy, France
Best, George *Soccer Player, Sportscaster*
%British Sky Broadcasting, Grant Way, Middx TW7 5QD, England
Best, James *Actor*
PO Box 621027, Oviedo, FL 32762, USA
Best, John O *Soccer Player*
1065 Lomita Ave, Harbor City, CA 90710, USA
Best, Pete *Singer, Drummer (Beatles)*
8 Hymans Green, West Derby, Liverpool 12, England
Beswicke, Martine *Actress*
%Goldey Co, 1156 S Carmelina Ave, #B, Los Angeles, CA 90049, USA
Bethe, Hans A *Nobel Physics Laureate*
324 Savage Farm Dr, Ithaca, NY 14850, USA
Bethea, Elvin L *Football Player*
16211 Leslie Lane, Missouri City, TX 77489, USA
Bethune, Zina *Actress*
3096 Lake Hollywood Dr, Los Angeles, CA 90068, USA
Bettenhausen, Gary *Auto Racing Driver*
2741 Chesterfield Dr, Bettendorf, IA 52722, USA
Bettis, Angela *Actress*
1122 S Roxbury Dr, Los Angeles, CA 90035, USA
Bettis, Jerome A *Football Player*
17600 Fairway Dr, Detroit, MI 48221, USA
Bettman, Gary B *Hockey Executive*
%National Hockey League, 1251 Ave of Americas, New York, NY 10020, USA
Betts, Austin W *Army General*
6414 View Point, San Antonio, TX 78229, USA
Betts, Dickie *Singer, Guitarist (Allman Brothers Band)*
%FreeFalls, PO Box 604, Chagrin Falls, OH 44022, USA
Betz Addie, Pauline *Tennis Player*
18560 SE Wood Haven Lane, #F, Tequesta, FL 33469, USA
Beuchel, Ted *Musician (Association)*
%Variety Artists, 1924 Spring St, Paso Robles, CA 93446, USA
Beuerlein, Stephen T (Steve) *Football Player*
15624 McCullers Court, Charlotte, NC 28277, USA
Beutel, Bill *Commentator*
%WABC-TV, News Dept, 7 Lincoln Square, New York, NY 10023, USA
Bevan, Timothy H *Financier*
%Barclay's Bank, 54 Lombard St, London EC3P 3AH, England
Beverley, Nick *Hockey Player, Coach, Executive*
%Chicago Blackhawks, United Center, 1901 W Madison St, Chicago, IL 60612, USA
Beverly, Frankie *Singer (Maze)*
115 Cherokee Rose Lane, Fairburn, GA 30213, USA
Bewkes, Jeff *Businessman*
%Time Warner, 75 Rockefeller Plaza, New York, NY 10019, USA
Bey, Turhan *Actor*
Paradisgasse Ave 47, 1190 Vienna XIX, Austria
Beyer, Troy *Actress*
%Don Buchwald, 6500 Wilshire Blvd, #2200, Los Angeles, CA 90048, USA

Beymer, Richard *Actor*
1818 N Fuller Ave, Los Angeles, CA 90046, USA
Bezos, Jeff *Businessman*
%Amazon.com, PO Box 81226, Seattle, WA 98108, USA
Bhan Bhagta Gurung *WW II Nepal Army Hero (VC)*
%Victoria Cross Assn, Old Admiralty Building, London SW1A 2BL, England
Bhattarai, Krishna Prasad *Prime Minister, Nepal*
%Nepali Congress Central Office, Baneshwar, Kathmandu, Nepal
Bhumibol Adulyadej *King, Thailand*
%Royal Residence, Chirtalad a Villa, Bangkok, Thailand
Biagiotti, Laura *Fashion Designer*
%Studio Biagiotti, Via Borgopesco 19, 20121 Milan, Italy
Bialik, Mayim *Actress*
1529 N Cahuenga Blvd, #19, Los Angeles, CA 90028, USA
Bianchi, Alfred (Al) *Basketball Player, Coach*
%Miami Heat, American Airlines Arena, 601 Biscayne Blvd, Miami, FL 33132, USA
Biasucci, Dean *Football Player*
3355 Allegheny Court, Westlake Village, CA 91362, USA
Bibb, Leslie *Actress*
9615 Brighton Way, #300, Beverly Hills, CA 90210, USA
Bibby, Mike *Basketball Player*
%Sacramento Kings, Arco Arena, 1 Sports Parkway, Sacramento, CA 95834, USA
Bichette, A Dante *Baseball Player*
4207 S Atlantic Ave, #2S, New Smyrna, FL 32169, USA
Bickerstaff, Bernard T (Bernie) *Basketball Coach, Executive*
%Charlotte Bobcats, 129 W Trade St, #700, Charlotte, NC 28202, USA
Bidart, Frank *Writer*
%Wellesley College, English Dept, 106 Central St, Wellesley, MA 02481, USA
Biddle, Adrian *Cinematographer*
Whitelands, Saint Georges Hill, Weybridge, Surrey KT13 0LB, England
Biddle, Melvin E *WW II Army Hero (CMH)*
918 Essex Dr, Anderson, IN 46013, USA
Bieber, Owen F *Labor Leader*
%United Auto Workers Union, 8000 E Jefferson Ave, Detroit, MI 48214, USA
Biebl-Prelevic, Heidi *Alpine Skier*
Haus Olympia, 87534 Oberstaufen, Germany
Biederman, Charles J *Artist*
5840 Collischan Road, Red Wing, MN 55066, USA
Biegler, David W *Businessman*
%Texas Utilities Co, Energy Plaza, 1601 Bryan St, Dallas, TX 75201, USA
Biehn, Michael *Actor*
11220 Valley Spring Lane, North Hollywood, CA 91602, USA
Bieka, Silvestre Siale *Prime Minister, Equatorial Guinea*
%Prime Minister's Office, Malabo, Equatorial Guinea
Biel, Jessica *Actress*
%Creative Artists Agency, 9830 Wilshire Blvd, Beverly Hills, CA 90212, USA
Bielecki, J Krzysztof *Prime Minister, Poland*
%Urzad Rady Ministrow, Al Ujazdowskie 9, 00-918 Warsaw, Poland
Biellmann, Denise *Figure Skater*
Im Brachli 25, 8053 Zurich, Switzerland
Bieniemy, Eric *Football Player*
325 Westwood Plaza, Los Angeles, CA 90095, USA
Bierko, Craig *Actor, Singer*
%Talent Entertainment Group, 9111 Wilshire Blvd, Beverly Hills, CA 90210, USA
Bies, Don *Golfer*
1262 NW Blakely Court, Seattle, WA 98177, USA
Bies, Susan Schmidt *Government Official, Economist*
%Federal Reserve Board, 20th St & Constitution Ave, Washington, DC 20551, USA
Bieshu, Mariya L *Opera Singer*
24 Pushkin Str, Chisinau 2012, Moldova
Bietila, Walter *Skier*
%General Delivery, Iron Mountain, MI 49801, USA
Bif Naked *Singer*
%Crazed Mgmt, PO Box 779, New Hope, PA 18938, USA
Biffen, John *Government Official, England*
Tanat House, Llanyblodwel, Oswestry, Shropshire SY10 8NQ, England
Biffi, Giacomo Cardinal *Religious Leader*
Archdiocese of Bologna, Via Altabella 6, 40126 Bologna, Italy
Biffle, Greg *Truck Racing Driver*
122 Knob Hill Road, Mooresville, NC 28117, USA
Biffle, Jerome *Track Athlete*
3205 Monaco Parkway, Denver, CO 80207, USA
Big Boi *Rap Artist (Outkast)*
%Family Tree Entertainment, 135 E 57th St, #2600, New York, NY 10022, USA
Big Daddy Kane *Rap Artist, Lyricist*
%Tough Guy Mgmt, 53 W 23rd St, #1100, New York, NY 10010, USA
Bigeleisen, Jacob *Chemist*
PO Box 217, Saint James, NY 11780, USA

B

Bigelow - Binmore

Bigelow, Kathryn A — *Movie Director*
%Creative Artists Agency, 9830 Wilshire Blvd, Beverly Hills, CA 90212, USA

Biggio, Craig A — *Baseball Player*
6520 Belmont St, Houston, TX 77005, USA

Biggs, Jason — *Actor*
%Innovative Artists, 1505 10th St, Santa Monica, CA 90401, USA

Biggs, John H — *Businessman*
240 E 47th St, #47D, New York, NY 10017, USA

Biggs, Peter M — *Veterinarian*
Willows, London Road, Saint Ives, Huntingdon, Cam PE17 4ES, England

Biggs, Richard — *Actor*
728 W 28th St, Los Angeles, CA 90007, USA

Biggs-Dawson, Roxann — *Actress*
%Innovative Artists, 1505 10th St, Santa Monica, CA 90401, USA

Bigley, Thomas J — *Navy Admiral*
1329 Carpers Ferry Way, Vienna, VA 22182, USA

Bignotti, George — *Auto Racing Mechanic*
9413 Steeplehill Dr, Las Vegas, NV 89117, USA

Bijan — *Fashion Designer*
420 N Rodeo Dr, Beverly Hills, CA 90210, USA

Bikel, Theodore — *Actor, Singer*
94 Honey Hill Road, Wilton, CT 06897, USA

Bila, Lucie — *Singer, Actress*
%Theate Ta Fantastika, Karlova Ul 8, 110 00 Prague 1, Czech Republic

Bilal — *Singer, Songwriter*
%Creative Artists Agency, 9830 Wilshire Blvd, Beverly Hills, CA 90212, USA

Bildt, Carl — *Prime Minister, Sweden*
Sveriges Riksdag, 10012 Stockholm, Sweden

Biletnikoff, Frederick (Fred) — *Football Player, Coach*
516 Iris Lane, San Ramon, CA 94583, USA

Bilheimer, Robert S — *Religious Leader*
15256 Knightwood Road, Cold Spring, MN 56320, USA

Bill, Tony — *Producer, Director, Actor*
%Market Street Productions, 73 Market St, Venice, CA 90291, USA

Billie — *Singer*
%CIA, Concorde House, 101 Shepherds Bush Road, London W6 7LP, England

Billingham, John E (Jack) — *Baseball Player*
8945 Lake Irma Pointe, Orlando, FL 32817, USA

Billings, Marland P — *Geologist*
Westside Road, RFD, North Conway, NH 03860, USA

Billingslea, Beau — *Actor*
6025 Sepulveda Blvd, #201, Van Nuys, CA 91411, USA

Billingsley, Barbara — *Actress, Model*
%Cosden, 129 W Wilson St, #202, Costa Mesa, CA 92627, USA

Billingsley, Hobie — *Diving Coach*
746 Pepperridge Dr, Bloomington, IN 47401, USA

Billingsley, Ray — *Cartoonist (Curtis)*
%King Features Syndicate, 888 7th Ave, New York, NY 10106, USA

Billington, David P — *Civil Engineer*
45 Hodge Road, Princeton, NJ 08540, USA

Billington, Kevin — *Movie Director*
33 Courtnell St, London W2 5BU, England

Billups, Chauncey — *Basketball Player*
%Detroit Pistons, Palace, 2 Championship Dr, Auburn Hills, MI 48326, USA

Bilson, Bruce — *Television Director*
%Downwind Enterprises, 12505 Sarah St, Studio City, CA 91604, USA

Bilson, Malcolm — *Concert Pianist*
132 N Sunset Dr, Ithaca, NY 14850, USA

Binchy, Maeve — *Writer*
%Irish Times, 11-15 D'Olier St, Dublin 2, Ireland

Binder, John — *Religious Leader*
%North American Baptist Conference, 1S210 Summit, Oakbrook Terrace, IL 60181, USA

Binder, Mike — *Actor, Director, Writer*
%Three Arts Entertainment, 9460 Wilshire Blvd, #700, Beverly Hills, CA 90212, USA

Binder, Theodor — *Physician*
Taos Canyon, Taos, NM 87571, USA

Bing, David (Dave) — *Basketball Player*
%Bing Manufacturing, 1111 Rosedale Court, Detroit, MI 48211, USA

Bingham, Barry, Jr — *Editor, Publisher*
%Louisville Courier Journal & Times, 525 W Broadway, Louisville, KY 40202, USA

Bingham, Gregory R (Greg) — *Football Player*
3710 W Valley Dr, Missouri City, TX 77459, USA

Bingham, Traci — *Actress, Model*
%Vincent Cirrincione, 8721 Sunset Blvd, #205, Los Angeles, CA 90069, USA

Binkley, Leslie J (Les) — *Hockey Player*
RR 3, Main Station, Hanover ON N4N 3B9, Canada

Binmore, Kenneth G — *Economist*
Newmills, Whitebrook, Monmouth, Gwent NP5 4TY, England

Binnig, Gerd K *Nobel Physics Laureate*
%IBM Research Laboratory, Saumerstr 4, 8803 Ruschlikon, Switzerland
Binns, Malcolm *Concert Pianist*
233 Court Road, Orpington, Kent BR6 9BY, England
Binoche, Juliette *Actress*
%Artmedia, 20 Ave Rapp, 75007 Paris, France
Bintley, David *Choreographer*
%Royal Ballet, Covent Garden, Bow St, London WC2E 9DD, England
Biondi, Frank J, Jr *Businessman*
%Seagram Co, 1430 Peel St, Montreal QC H3A 1S9, Canada
Biondi, Matthew N (Matt) *Swimmer*
%Nicholas A Biondi, 1404 Rimer Dr, Moraga, CA 94556, USA
Birch, L Charles *Zoologist*
5A/73 Yarranabbe Road, Darling Point NSW 2027, Australia
Birch, Stanley F, Jr *Judge*
%US Court of Appeals, 56 Forsyth St NW, Atlanta, GA 30303, USA
Birch, Thora *Actress*
%Keep the Peace Productions, PO Box 69156, West Hollywood, CA 90069, USA
Birchard, Bruce *Religious Leader*
%Friends General Conference, 1216 Arch St, Philadelphia, PA 19107, USA
Birck, Michael J *Businessman*
%Tellabs Inc, 1415 W Diehl Road, Naperville, IL 60563, USA
Bird, Antonia *Movie Director*
%International Creative Mgmt, 76 Oxford St, London W1N 0AX, England
Bird, Caroline *Writer, Social Activist*
60 Grammercy Park, New York, NY 10010, USA
Bird, Forrest M *Inventor (Medical Respirators)*
212 N Cerritos Dr, Palm Springs, CA 92262, USA
Bird, Larry J *Basketball Player, Coach*
%Indiana Pacers, Conseco Fieldhouse, 125 S Pennsylvania, Indianapolis, IN 46204, USA
Bird, Lester B *Prime Minister, Antigua & Barbuda*
%Prime Minister's Office, Factory Road, Saint John's, Antigua
Bird, R Byron *Chemical Engineer*
%University of Wisconsin, Chemical Engineering Dept, Madison, WI 53706, USA
Bird, Sue *Basketball Player*
%Seattle Storm, Key Arena, 351 Elliott Ave W, #500, Seattle, WA 98119, USA
Bird, Thora *Actress*
Old Loft, 21 Leinster Mews, Lancaster Gate, London W2, England
Birdsong, Carl *Football Player*
1807 Clubview Dr, Amarillo, TX 79124, USA
Birdsong, Otis *Basketball Player*
3202 Farrow Ave, Kansas City, KS 66104, USA
Birk, Roger E *Businessman*
%Federal National Mortgage Assn, 3900 Wisconsin Ave NW, Washington, DC 20016, USA
Birkavs, Valdis *Prime Minister, Latvia*
%Foreign Affairs Ministry, Brivbas Blvd 36, Riga 1395, Latvia
Birkerts, Gunnar *Architect*
%Gunnar Birkerts Assoc, 28105 Greenfield Road, Southfield, MI 48076, USA
Birkin, Jane *Actress*
%Cineart, 36 Rue de Ponthieu, 75008 Paris, France
Birman, Len *Actor*
%Michael Mann Talent, 617 S Olive St, #311, Los Angeles, CA 90014, USA
Birmingham, Stephen *Writer*
%Brandt & Brandt, 1501 Broadway, New York, NY 10036, USA
Birney, David *Actor*
20 Ocean Park Blvd, #118, Santa Monica, CA 90405, USA
Birney, Earle *Writer*
1204-130 Carlton St, Toronto ON M5A 4K3, Canada
Birren, James E *Gerontologist*
%University of California, Borun Gerontology Center, Los Angeles, CA 90024, USA
Birtwistle, Harrison *Composer*
%Allied Artists, 42 Montpelier Square, London SW7 1JZ, England
Bisher, J Furman *Sportswriter*
431 Lester Road, Fayetteville, GA 30215, USA
Bishop, Ed *Actor*
29 Sunbury Court Island, Sunbury-on-Thames, Middx TW16 5PP, England
Bishop, Elvin *Singer, Guitarist*
%DeLeon Artists, 4031 Panama Court, Piedmont, CA 94611, USA
Bishop, J Michael *Nobel Medicine Laureate*
%University of California, Hooper Foundation, San Francisco, CA 94143, USA
Bishop, Joey *Actor, Comedian*
534 Via Lido Nord, Newport Beach, CA 92663, USA
Bishop, Michael *Football Player*
PO Box 168, 113 Philpot St, Willis, TX 77378, USA
Bishop, Robert R *Businessman*
%Silicon Graphics, 1600 Amphitheatre Parkway, Mountain View, CA 94043, USA
Bishop, Stephen *Singer, Songwriter*
2310 Apollo Dr, Los Angeles, CA 90046, USA

B

Bisoglio - Black

Bisoglio, Val *Actor*
%House of Representatives, 400 S Beverly Dr, #101, Beverly Hills, CA 90212, USA
Bisplinghoff, Raymond L *Aeronautical Engineer*
%Tyco Laboratories, 273 Corporate Dr, #100, Portsmouth, NH 03801, USA
Bissell, Charles O *Editorial Cartoonist*
1006 Tower Place, Nashville, TN 37204, USA
Bissell, Charles P (Phil) *Cartoonist*
%Cartoon Corner, 4 Cross Hill Circle, Forestdale, MA 02644, USA
Bissell, Jean G *Judge*
%US Court of Appeals, 717 Madison Place NW, Washington, DC 20439, USA
Bisset, Jacqueline *Actress*
1815 Benedict Canyon Dr, Beverly Hills, CA 90210, USA
Bissett, Josie *Actress*
8033 Sunset Blvd, #4048, West Hollywood, CA 90046, USA
Bista, Kirti Nidhi *Prime Minister, Nepal*
Gyaneshawor, Kathmandu, Nepal
Bittinger, Ned *Illustrator*
410 Graham Ave, Santa Fe, NM 87501, USA
Bittle, Ryan *Actor*
%Hollander Talent, 3518 Cahuenga Blvd, #103, Los Angeles, CA 90068, USA
Bittner, Armin *Alpine Skier*
Rauchbergstr 30, 83334 Izell, Germany
Bivins, Jimmy *Boxer*
3206 E 137th St, Cleveland, OH 44120, USA
Biya, Paul *President, Cameroon Republic*
%Palais Presidentiel, Rue de L'Exploration, Yaounde, Cameroon Republic
Bizzy Bone *Rap Artist (Bone Thugs-N-Harmony)*
%Creative Artists Agency, 9830 Wilshire Blvd, Beverly Hills, CA 90212, USA
Bjedov-Gabrilo, Djurdjica *Swimmer*
Brace Santini 33, 5800 Split, Serbia & Montenegro
Bjork *Singer, Songwriter, Actress*
16 Rue des Fosses Saint Jacques, 75007 Paris, France
Bjork, Anita *Actress*
AB Baggensgatan 9, 111 31 Stockholm, Sweden
Bjorklund, Anders *Neurologist*
%University of Lund, Neurology Dept, Lund, Sweden
Bjorkman, Jonas *Tennis Player*
%Octagon, 1751 Pinnacle Dr, #1500, McLean, VA 22102, USA
Bjorkman, Olle E *Plant Biologist*
3040 Greer Road, Palo Alto, CA 94303, USA
Blachnik, Gabriele *Fashion Designer*
%Blachnik Gabriele KG, Marstallstr 8, 80539 Munich, Germany
Black Thought *Rap Artist (Roots)*
%William Morris Agency, 1325 Ave of Americas, New York, NY 10019, USA
Black, Barbara A *Attorney, Educator*
%Columbia University, Law School, 435 W 116th St, New York, NY 10027, USA
Black, Bibi *Concert Trumpeter*
%Columbia Artists Mgmt Inc, 165 W 57th St, New York, NY 10019, USA
Black, Carole *Businesswoman*
%Lifetime Entertainment, 39 W 49th St, New York, NY 10112, USA
Black, Cathleen P *Publisher*
%Hearst Corp, Magazine Division, 250 W 55th St, New York, NY 10019, USA
Black, Cilla *Singer, Actress*
%Bobsons Productions, 10 Abbet Orchard St, London SW1P 2JP, England
Black, Clint *Singer, Songwriter*
%Fitzgerald-Hartley, 1908 Wedgewood Ave, Nashville, TN 37212, USA
Black, Jack *Actor, Singer, Comedian*
%United Talent Agency, 9560 Wilshire Blvd, #500, Beverly Hills, CA 90212, USA
Black, James W *Nobel Medicine Laureate*
3 Ferrings, Dulwich, London SE21 7LU, England
Black, Jay *Singer (Jay & the Americans)*
%Charles Rapp, 1650 Broadway, #1410, New York, NY 10019, USA
Black, Karen *Actress*
%Contemporary Artists, 610 Santa Monica Blvd, #202, Santa Monica, CA 90401, USA
Black, Larry *Track Athlete*
14401 Pierce St, Miami, FL 33176, USA
Black, Lewis *Actor, Comedian*
%Agency for Performing Arts, 9200 Sunset Blvd, #900, Los Angeles, CA 90069, USA
Black, Lucas *Actor*
%Agency for Performing Arts, 9200 Sunset Blvd, #900, Los Angeles, CA 90069, USA
Black, Mary *Singer*
%International Music Network, 278 S Main St, #400, Gloucester, MA 01930, USA
Black, Michael Ian *Actor, Puppeteer*
%United Talent Agency, 9560 Wilshire Blvd, #500, Beverly Hills, CA 90212, USA
Black, Robert P *Financier, Government Official*
10 Dahlgren Road, Richmond, VA 23233, USA
Black, Shirley Temple *Actress, Diplomat*
%Motion Picture Arts-Sciences Acad, 8949 Wilshire Blvd, Beverly Hills, CA 90211, USA

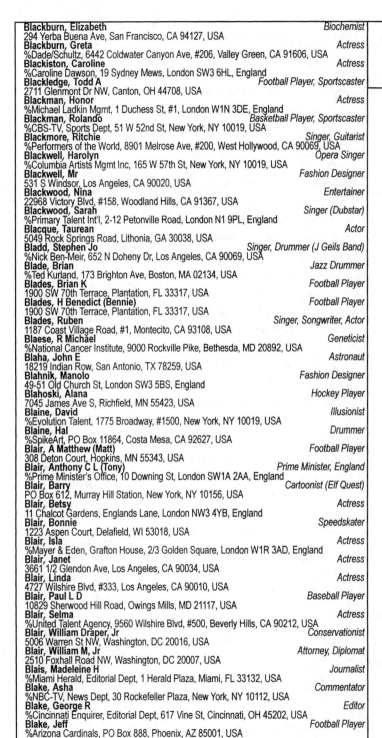

Blackburn, Elizabeth *Biochemist*
294 Yerba Buena Ave, San Francisco, CA 94127, USA
Blackburn, Greta *Actress*
%Dade/Schultz, 6442 Coldwater Canyon Ave, #206, Valley Green, CA 91606, USA
Blackiston, Caroline *Actress*
%Caroline Dawson, 19 Sydney Mews, London SW3 6HL, England
Blackledge, Todd A *Football Player, Sportscaster*
2711 Glenmont Dr NW, Canton, OH 44708, USA
Blackman, Honor *Actress*
%Michael Ladkin Mgmt, 1 Duchess St, #1, London W1N 3DE, England
Blackman, Rolando *Basketball Player, Sportscaster*
%CBS-TV, Sports Dept, 51 W 52nd St, New York, NY 10019, USA
Blackmore, Ritchie *Singer, Guitarist*
%Performers of the World, 8901 Melrose Ave, #200, West Hollywood, CA 90069, USA
Blackwell, Harolyn *Opera Singer*
%Columbia Artists Mgmt Inc, 165 W 57th St, New York, NY 10019, USA
Blackwell, Mr *Fashion Designer*
531 S Windsor, Los Angeles, CA 90020, USA
Blackwood, Nina *Entertainer*
22968 Victory Blvd, #158, Woodland Hills, CA 91367, USA
Blackwood, Sarah *Singer (Dubstar)*
%Primary Talent Int'l, 2-12 Petonville Road, London N1 9PL, England
Blacque, Taurean *Actor*
5049 Rock Springs Road, Lithonia, GA 30038, USA
Bladd, Stephen Jo *Singer, Drummer (J Geils Band)*
%Nick Ben-Meir, 652 N Doheny Dr, Los Angeles, CA 90069, USA
Blade, Brian *Jazz Drummer*
%Ted Kurland, 173 Brighton Ave, Boston, MA 02134, USA
Blades, Brian K *Football Player*
1900 SW 70th Terrace, Plantation, FL 33317, USA
Blades, H Benedict (Bennie) *Football Player*
1900 SW 70th Terrace, Plantation, FL 33317, USA
Blades, Ruben *Singer, Songwriter, Actor*
1187 Coast Village Road, #1, Montecito, CA 93108, USA
Blaese, R Michael *Geneticist*
%National Cancer Institute, 9000 Rockville Pike, Bethesda, MD 20892, USA
Blaha, John E *Astronaut*
18219 Indian Row, San Antonio, TX 78259, USA
Blahnik, Manolo *Fashion Designer*
49-51 Old Church St, London SW3 5BS, England
Blahoski, Alana *Hockey Player*
7045 James Ave S, Richfield, MN 55423, USA
Blaine, David *Illusionist*
%Evolution Talent, 1775 Broadway, #1500, New York, NY 10019, USA
Blaine, Hal *Drummer*
%SpikeArt, PO Box 11864, Costa Mesa, CA 92627, USA
Blair, A Matthew (Matt) *Football Player*
308 Deton Court, Hopkins, MN 55343, USA
Blair, Anthony C L (Tony) *Prime Minister, England*
%Prime Minister's Office, 10 Downing St, London SW1A 2AA, England
Blair, Barry *Cartoonist (Elf Quest)*
PO Box 612, Murray Hill Station, New York, NY 10156, USA
Blair, Betsy *Actress*
11 Chalcot Gardens, Englands Lane, London NW3 4YB, England
Blair, Bonnie *Speedskater*
1223 Aspen Court, Delafield, WI 53018, USA
Blair, Isla *Actress*
%Mayer & Eden, Grafton House, 2/3 Golden Square, London W1R 3AD, England
Blair, Janet *Actress*
3661 1/2 Glendon Ave, Los Angeles, CA 90034, USA
Blair, Linda *Actress*
4727 Wilshire Blvd, #333, Los Angeles, CA 90010, USA
Blair, Paul L D *Baseball Player*
10829 Sherwood Hill Road, Owings Mills, MD 21117, USA
Blair, Selma *Actress*
%United Talent Agency, 9560 Wilshire Blvd, #500, Beverly Hills, CA 90212, USA
Blair, William Draper, Jr *Conservationist*
5006 Warren St NW, Washington, DC 20016, USA
Blair, William M, Jr *Attorney, Diplomat*
2510 Foxhall Road NW, Washington, DC 20007, USA
Blais, Madeleine H *Journalist*
%Miami Herald, Editorial Dept, 1 Herald Plaza, Miami, FL 33132, USA
Blake, Asha *Commentator*
%NBC-TV, News Dept, 30 Rockefeller Plaza, New York, NY 10112, USA
Blake, George R *Editor*
%Cincinnati Enquirer, Editorial Dept, 617 Vine St, Cincinnati, OH 45202, USA
Blake, Jeff *Football Player*
%Arizona Cardinals, PO Box 888, Phoenix, AZ 85001, USA

Blake - Bland

Blake, John C *Artist*
Oz Voorburgwal 131, 1012 ER Amsterdam, Netherlands
Blake, Julian W (Bud) *Cartoonist (Tiger)*
PO Box 146, Damariscotta, ME 04543, USA
Blake, Norman *Guitarist, Mandolin Player*
%Scott O'Malley Assoc, 433 E Cucharras St, Colorado Springs, CO 80903, USA
Blake, Peter *Architect*
80 Cedar St, #311, Branford, CT 06405, USA
Blake, Peter T *Artist*
%Waddington Galleries, 11 Cork St, London W1X 1PD, England
Blake, Rob *Hockey Player*
4 Gooseberry Lane, Englewood, CO 80113, USA
Blake, Rockwell *Opera Singer*
1 Onondaga Lane, Plattsburgh, NY 12901, USA
Blake, Stephanie *Actress*
%First Artists, 1631 N Bristol St, #B20, Santa Ana, CA 92706, USA
Blake, Susan *Commentator*
%News Center 4, 1001 Van Ness Ave, San Francisco, CA 94109, USA
Blake, Tchad *Bassist (Latin Playboys)*
%Monterey International, 200 W Superior, #202, Chicago, IL 60610, USA
Blake, Teresa *Actress*
%Stone Manners, 6500 Wilshire Blvd, #550, Los Angeles, CA 90048, USA
Blakeley, Ronee *Actress, Singer*
8033 Sunset Blvd, #693, West Hollywood, CA 90046, USA
Blakely, Rachel *Actress*
%Melbourne Artists, 21 Cardigan Place, Albert Park VIC 3206, Australia
Blakely, Susan *Actress, Model*
%Jaffe Co, 9663 Santa Monica Blvd, #214, Beverly Hills, CA 90210, USA
Blakemore, Colin B *Neurophysiologist, Physiologist*
%University Laboratory of Physiology, Parks Road, Oxford OX1 3PT, England
Blakemore, Michael H *Theater Director, Actor, Writer*
18 Upper Park Road, London NW3 2UP, England
Blaker, Clay *Singer, Songwriter*
%Texas Sounds Entertainment, 2317 Pecan, Dickinson, TX 77539, USA
Blakey, Marion *Government Official*
%Federal Aviation Agency, 800 Independence Ave SW, Washington, DC 20591, USA
Blalack, Robert *Cinematographer*
12251 Huston St, North Hollywood, CA 91607, USA
Blalock, Jane *Golfer*
Flagship Wharf, 197 8th St, Charlestown, MA 02129, USA
Blalock, Jolene *Actress*
%Don Buchwald, 6500 Wilshire Blvd, #2200, Los Angeles, CA 90048, USA
Blanc, Georges *Chef*
Le Mere Blanc, 01540 Vonnas, Ain, France
Blanc, Jennifer *Actress*
%Writers & Artists, 8383 Wilshire Blvd, #550, Beverly Hills, CA 90211, USA
Blanc, Raymond R A *Chef*
%Le Manoir, Church Road, Great Milton, Oxford OX44 7PD, England
Blancas, Homero *Golfer*
6826 Queensclub Dr, Houston, TX 77069, USA
Blanchard, Felix A (Doc) *Football Player, Army General*
30395 Olympus, Bulverde, TX 78163, USA
Blanchard, George S *Army General*
9110 Belvoir Woods Parkway, #126, Fort Belvoir, VA 22060, USA
Blanchard, James H *Financier*
%Synovus Financial Corp, 901 Front Ave, PO Box 120, Columbus, GA 31902, USA
Blanchard, James J *Governor, MI; Diplomat*
426 4th St NE, Washington, DC 20002, USA
Blanchard, John A *Businessman*
%Deluxe Corp, 3680 Victoria St N, Shoreview, MN 55126, USA
Blanchard, Kenneth *Writer, Business Consultant*
2048 Aldergrove, #B, Escondido, CA 92029, USA
Blanchard, Nina *Model Agency Executive*
3610 Wrightwood Dr, Studio City, CA 91604, USA
Blanchard, Rachel *Actress*
%Creative Artists Agency, 9830 Wilshire Blvd, Beverly Hills, CA 90212, USA
Blanchard, Tammy *Actress*
%International Creative Mgmt, 8942 Wilshire Blvd, #219, Beverly Hills, CA 90211, USA
Blanchard, Terence *Jazz Trumpeter, Composer*
%BMI, 8730 Sunset Blvd, #300W, Los Angeles, CA 90069, USA
Blanchard, Tim *Religious Leader*
%Conservative Baptist Assn, 1501 W Mineral Ave, #B, Littleton, CO 80120, USA
Blanchett, Cate *Actress*
%Robyn Gardiner Mgmt, 397 Riley St, Surrey Hills NSW 2010, Australia
Blanco-Cervantes, Raul *President, Costa Rica*
Apdo 918, San Jose, Costa Rica
Bland, Bobby (Blue) *Singer*
%It's Happening Presents, PO Box 8073, Pittsburg, CA 94565, USA

Blanda, George F *Football Player*
18 Forest Gate Circle, Oak Brook, IL 60523, USA
Blandford, Roger D *Astronomer*
%California Institute of Technology, Astrophysics Dept, Pasadena, CA 91125, USA
Blaney, Dave *Auto Racing Driver*
1751 W Lexington Ave, High Point, NC 27262, USA
Blankers-Koen, Fanny *Track Athlete*
%Olympic Committee, Surinamestraat 33, 2585 La Harve, Netherlands
Blankfield, Mark *Actor*
%Artists Group, 10100 Santa Monica Blvd, #2490, Los Angeles, CA 90067, USA
Blasco, Chuck *Singer (Vogues)*
%Media Promotion Enterprises, 423 6th Ave, Huntington, WV 25701, USA
Blashford-Snell, John N *Explorer*
%Exploration Society, Motcome, Shaftesbury, Dorset SP7 9PB, England
Blasi, Rosa *Actress*
8060 Melrose Ave, Los Angeles, CA 90046, USA
Blass, Stephen R (Steve) *Baseball Player*
1756 Quigg Dr, Pittsburgh, PA 15241, USA
Blatnick, Jeffrey C (Jeff) *Wrestler*
848 Whitney Dr, Schenectady, NY 12309, USA
Blatter, Joseph (Sepp) *Soccer Executive*
%Federation Int'l Football Assn, PO Box 85, 8030 Zurich, Switzerland
Blatty, William Peter *Writer*
7018 Longwood Dr, Bethesda, MD 20817, USA
Blau, Daniel *Artist*
Belgradstr 26, 80796 Munich, Germany
Blazelowski, Carol A *Basketball Player, Executive*
%New York Liberty, Madison Square Garden, 2 Penn Plaza, New York, NY 10121, USA
Bleak, David B *Korean War Army Hero (CMH)*
355 Louise Dr, Arco, ID 83213, USA
Bleaney, Brebis *Physicist*
Garford House, Garford Road, Oxford OX1 3PU, England
Bledel, Alexis *Actress, Model*
%P M K Public Relations, 8500 Wilshire Blvd, #700, Beverly Hills, CA 90211, USA
Bledsoe, Drew *Football Player*
PO Box 786, East Aurora, NY 14052, USA
Bledsoe, Tempestt *Actress*
%Artists Group, 10100 Santa Monica Blvd, #2490, Los Angeles, CA 90067, USA
Bleeth, Yasmine *Actress*
%Creative Artists Agency, 9830 Wilshire Blvd, Beverly Hills, CA 90212, USA
Blegen, Judith *Opera Singer*
91 Central Park West, #1B, New York, NY 10023, USA
Bleier, Robert P (Rocky) *Football Player*
801 Larchmont Road, Pittsburgh, PA 15243, USA
Blessed, Brian *Actor*
%Associated International Mgmt, 5 Denmark St, London WC2H 8LP, England
Blessen, Karen A *Journalist, Illustrator*
%Karen Blessen Illustration, 6327 Vickery Blvd, Dallas, TX 75214, USA
Blethen, Frank A *Publisher*
%Seattle Times, Publisher's Office, 1120 John St, Seattle, WA 98109, USA
Blethyn, Brenda A *Actress*
61-63 Portobello Road, London W1N OAX, England
Bley, Carla B *Composer, Jazz Pianist*
%Watt Works, PO Box 67, Willow, NY 12495, USA
Bley, Paul *Jazz Pianist, Composer*
%Legacy Records, 550 Madison Ave, #1700, New York, NY 10022, USA
Blick, Richard (Dick) *Swimmer*
2505 Tamarack Court, Kingsburg, CA 93631, USA
Blier, Bertrand *Movie Director*
11 Rue Margueritte, 75017 Paris, France
Blige, Mary J *Rap Artist, Singer*
%International Creative Mgmt, 40 W 57th St, #1800, New York, NY 10019, USA
Blim, Richard D *Pediatrician*
304 W 172nd St, Belton, MO 64012, USA
Blinder, Alan S *Government Official, Financier*
%Princeton University, Economics Dept, Princeton, NJ 08544, USA
Blitzer, Wolf *Commentator*
8929 Holly Leaf Lane, Bethesda, MD 20817, USA
Blobel, Gunter K-J *Nobel Medicine Laureate*
%Rockefeller University, Cell Biology Dept, 1230 York Ave, New York, NY 10021, USA
Bloch, Erich *Electrical Engineer, Computer Scientist*
%National Science Foundation, 1800 C St NW, Washington, DC 20550, USA
Bloch, Henry W *Businessman*
%H & R Block Inc, 4410 Main St, Kansas City, MO 64111, USA
Blochwitz, Hans-Peter *Opera Singer*
%Matthew Sprizzo, 477 Durant Ave, Staten Island, NY 10308, USA
Block, John R *Secretary, Agriculture*
%National Wholesale Grocers Assn, 201 Park Washington, Falls Church, VA 22046, USA

B

Block, Lawrence *Writer*
299 W 12th St, #12D, New York, NY 10014, USA
Block, Ned J *Philosopher*
29 Washington Square, New York, NY 10011, USA
Blocker, Dirk *Actor*
5063 La Ramada Dr, Santa Barbara, CA 93111, USA
Bloembergen, Nicolaas *Nobel Physics Laureate*
13835 E Langtree Lane, Tucson, AZ 85747, USA
Blomstedt, Herbert T *Conductor*
%Kunstleragentur Raab & Bohm, Plankengasse 7, 1010 Vienna, Austria
Blood, Edward J *Skier*
2 Beech Hill, Durham, NH 03824, USA
Bloodworth-Thomason, Linda *Television Producer, Screenwriter*
%Badgley Connor Talent, 9229 Sunset Blvd, #311, Los Angeles, CA 90069, USA
Bloom, Alfred H *Educator*
%Swarthmore College, President's Office, Swarthmore, PA 19081, USA
Bloom, Anne *Actress*
%Abrams Artists, 9200 Sunset Blvd, #1125, Los Angeles, CA 90069, USA
Bloom, Brian *Actor*
11 Croydon Court, Dix Hills, NY 11746, USA
Bloom, Claire *Actress*
%Conway Van Gelder Robinson, 18-21 Jermyn St, London SW1Y 6NB, England
Bloom, Floyd E *Physician*
628 Pacific View Dr, San Diego, CA 92109, USA
Bloom, Lindsay *Actress*
PO Box 412, Weldon, CA 93283, USA
Bloom, Luka *Singer*
%Mattie Fox Mgmt, Derryneel, Ballinalee, Longford, Ireland
Bloom, Orlando *Actor*
%The Firm, 9100 Wilshire Blvd, #100W, Beverly Hills, CA 90210, USA
Bloom, Ursula *Writer*
Newton House, Walls Dr, Ravenglass, Cumbria, England
Bloom, Verna *Actress*
327 E 82nd St, New York, NY 10028, USA
Bloomberg, Michael R *Mayor*
%Mayor's Office, Gracie Mansion, New York, NY 10007, USA
Bloomfield, Michael J (Mike) *Astronaut*
14302 Autumn Canyon Trace, Houston, TX 77062, USA
Bloomfield, Sara *Museum Director*
%Holocaust Memorial Museum, 100 Wallenberg Place SW, Washington, DC 20024, USA
Blount, Lisa *Actress*
2060 Paramount Dr, Los Angeles, CA 90068, USA
Blount, Melvin C (Mel) *Football Player, Executive*
6 Mel Blount Dr, Claysville, PA 15323, USA
Blount, Winton M, III *Businessman*
%Blount Inc, 4909 SE International Way, Portland, OR 97222, USA
Blout, Eikan R *Biological Chemist*
1010 Memorial Dr, #12A, Cambridge, MA 02138, USA
Blow, David M *Biophysicist*
1 Meeting St, Appledore, Bideford, North Devon EX39 1RH, England
Blow, Kurtis *Rap Artist*
%Entertainment Artists, 2409 21st Ave S, #100, Nashville, TN 37212, USA
Blucas, Marc *Actor*
%United Talent Agency, 9560 Wilshire Blvd, #500, Beverly Hills, CA 90212, USA
Blue, Vida R *Baseball Player*
PO Box 1449, Pleasanton, CA 94566, USA
Bluford, Guion S (Guy), Jr *Astronaut*
PO Box 549, North Olmsted, OH 44070, USA
Bluhm, Kay *Canoeing Athlete*
Bahnofstr 104, 14480 Potsdam, Germany
Blum, Arlene *Mountaineer*
%University of California, Biochemistry Dept, Berkeley, CA 94720, USA
Blum, H Steven *Army General*
%Chief, National Guard Bureau, HqUSA, Pentagon, Washington, DC 20310, USA
Blumberg, Baruch S *Nobel Medicine Laureate*
324 N Lawrence St, Philadelphia, PA 19106, USA
Blume, Judy S *Writer*
%Tashmdo, 244 5th Ave, #1100, New York, NY 10001, USA
Blume, Martin *Physicist*
%Brookhaven National Laboratory, 2 Center St, Upton, NY 11973, USA
Blumenthal, W Michael *Secretary, Treasury; Financier*
227 Ridgeview Road, Princeton, NJ 08540, USA
Blundell, Mark *Auto Racing Driver*
4001 Methanol Lane, Indianapolis, IN 46268, USA
Blundell, Pamela *Fashion Designer*
%Copperwheat Blundell, 14 Cheshire St, London E2 6EH, England
Blunstone, Colin *Singer (Zombies)*
%Barry Collins, 21A Cliftown, Southend-on-Sea, Sussex SS1 1AB, England

Bluth, Ray *Bowler*
569 Beauford Dr, Saint Louis, MO 63122, USA
Bly, Dre' *Football Player*
4312 Topsail Landing, Chesapeake, VA 23321, USA
Bly, Robert E *Writer, Psychologist*
1904 Girard Ave S, Minneapolis, MN 55403, USA
Blyleven, R Bert *Baseball Player*
1501 McGregor Reserve Dr, Fort Myers, FL 33901, USA
Blyth, Ann *Actress, Singer*
PO Box 9754, Rancho Santa Fe, CA 92067, USA
Blyth, Chay *Yachtsman, Explorer*
Inmans House, 12 London Road, Sheet, Petersfield, Hamps GU31 4BE, England
Boatman, Michael *Actor*
1432 Sunnycrest Dr, Fullerton, CA 92835, USA
Bob, Tim *Bassist (Rage Against the Machine)*
%ArtistDirect, 10900 Wilshire Blvd, #1400, Los Angeles, CA 90024, USA
Bobek, Nicole *Figure Skater*
19220 Seaview Road, #100, Jupiter, FL 33469, USA
Bobko, Karol J *Astronaut*
14214 Lake Scene Trail, Houston, TX 77059, USA
BoBo, D J *Singer*
Postfach, 6242 Wauwil, Switzerland
Bocelli, Andrea *Concert Singer*
Galleria del Corso 4, 201122 Milan, Italy
Bochco, Steven *Television Producer, Writer*
%Steven Bochco Productions, PO Box 900, Beverly Hills, CA 90213, USA
Bochner, Hart *Actor*
%Gersh Agency, 232 N Canon Dr, Beverly Hills, CA 90210, USA
Bochner, Lloyd *Actor*
42 Haldeman Road, Santa Monica, CA 90402, USA
Bock, Charles, Jr *Test Pilot*
PO Box 4197, Incline Village, NV 89450, USA
Bock, Edward J *Football Player, Businessman*
2232 Clifton Forge Dr, Saint Louis, MO 63131, USA
Bock, Jerrold L (Jerry) *Composer*
145 Wellington Ave, New Rochelle, NY 10804, USA
Bocuse, Paul *Restauranteur*
40 Rue de la Plage, 69660 Collonges-au-Mont d'Or, France
Boddicker, Michael J (Mike) *Baseball Player*
11324 W 121st Terrace, Overland Park, KS 66213, USA
Bode, John R *Vietnam War Air Force Hero*
1100 Warm Sands Dr SE, Albuquerque, NM 87123, USA
Bode, Ken *Commentator, Educator*
%Northwestern University, Journalism School, Evanston, IL 60206, USA
Boden, Margaret A *Philosopher, Psychologist*
%Brighton University, Cognitive Science School, Brighton BN1 9QH, England
Bodett, Tom *Writer, Entertainer*
PO Box 3249, Homer, AK 99603, USA
Bodine, Brett *Auto Racing Driver*
%Brett Bodine Racing, 304 Performance Road, Mooresville, NC 28115, USA
Bodine, Geoffrey (Geoff) *Auto Racing Driver*
%Brett Bodine Racing, 304 Performance Road, Mooresville, NC 28115, USA
Bodine, Todd *Auto Racing Driver*
PO Box 2427, Cornelius, NC 28031, USA
Bodison, Wolfgang *Actor*
%J Michael Bloom, 9255 Sunset Blvd, #710, Los Angeles, CA 90069, USA
Bodmer, Walter F *Geneticist*
%Oxford University, Hertford College, Oxford OX1 3BW, England
Boede, Marvin J *Labor Leader*
%Plumbing & Pipe Fitting Union, 901 Massachusetts Ave NW, Washington, DC 20001, USA
Boeheim, James A (Jim), Jr *Basketball Coach*
%Syracuse University, Manley Field House, Syracuse, NY 13244, USA
Boehm, Gottfried K *Architect, Pritzker Laureate, Historian*
Sevogelplatz 1, 4052 Basel, Switzerland
Boehne, Edward G *Financier*
%Federal Reserve Bank, Independence Mall, 100 N 6th St, Philadelphia, PA 19106, USA
Boerner, Jacqueline *Speedskater*
Bernhard-Bastlein-Str 55, 10367 Berlin, Germany
Boeschenstein, William W *Businessman*
10617 Cardiff Road, Perrysburg, OH 43551, USA
Boesel, Raul *Auto Racing Driver*
9181 W Bay Harbor Dr, #2, Bay Harbor Island, FL 33154, USA
Boesen, Dennis L *Astronaut*
6613 Sandra Ave NE, Albuquerque, NM 87109, USA
Boff, Leonardo G D *Theologian*
Pr M Leao 12/204, Alto Vale Encantado, 20531-350 Rio de Janeiro, Brazil
Bofill, Angela *Singer*
1385 York Ave, #6B, New York, NY 10021, USA

B

Bofill - Bolleau

Bofill, Ricardo — *Architect*
%Taller de Arquitectura, 14 Ave de la Industria, 08960 Barcelona, Spain
Bofinger, Heinz — *Architect*
Biebricher Allee 49, 65187 Wiesbaden, Germany
Bogart, Paul — *Television, Movie Director*
1801 Century Park E, #2160, Los Angeles, CA 90067, USA
Bogdanovich, Peter — *Movie Director*
468 N Camden Dr, #200, Beverly Hills, CA 90210, USA
Bogeberg, J B — *Bassist (A-Ha)*
%Bandana Mgmt, 11 Elvaston Place, #300, London SW7 5QC, England
Boggs, Haskell — *Cinematographer*
3710 Goodland Ave, Studio City, CA 91604, USA
Boggs, Wade A — *Baseball Player*
6006 Windham Place, Tampa, FL 33647, USA
Bogguss, Suzy — *Singer, Songwriter, Guitarist*
%Brokaw Co, 9255 Sunset Blvd, #804, Los Angeles, CA 90069, USA
Bogle, John C — *Financier*
612 Shipton Lane, Bryn Mawr, PA 19010, USA
Bogner, Willy — *Fashion Designer*
%Bogner Film GmbH, Saint-Veit-Str 4, 81673 Munich, Germany
Bogosian, Eric — *Performance Artist, Actor*
Ararat Productions, PO Box 24, New York, NY 10013, USA
Bohan, Marc — *Fashion Designer*
35 Rue du Bourg a Mont, 21400 Chatillon Sur Seine, France
Bohay, Heidi — *Actress*
48 Main St, South Bound Brook, NJ 08880, USA
Bohigas Guardiola, Oriol — *Architect*
Calle Calvert, 71 Barcelona 21, Spain
Bohlmann, Ralph A — *Religious Leader*
%Lutheran Church Missouri Synod, 1333 S Kirkwood Road, Saint Louis, MO 63122, USA
Bohn, Parker, III — *Bowler*
25 Pitney Lane, Jackson, NJ 08527, USA
Bohr, Aage N — *Nobel Physics Laureate*
Strangade 34, 1-Sal, 1401 Copenhagen, Denmark
Bohrer, Corinne — *Actress*
%Abrams-Rubaloff Lawrence, 8075 W 3rd St, #303, Los Angeles, CA 90048, USA
Bohrer, Thomas — *Rowing Athlete*
77 Crest St, Concord, MA 01742, USA
Boies, David — *Attorney*
%Cravath Swaine Moore, 1 Chase Manhattan Plaza, New York, NY 10005, USA
Boileau, Linda — *Editorial Cartoonist*
%Frankfort State Journal, Editorial Dept, 321 W Main St, Frankfort, KY 40601, USA
Boisson, Christine — *Actress*
%Artmedia, 20 Ave Rapp, 75007 Paris, France
Boitano, Brian — *Figure Skater*
%Brian Boitano Enterprises, 101 1st St, #370, Los Altos Hills, CA 94022, USA
Boiteux, Jean — *Swimmer*
51 Ave de Merignac, 33200 Bordeaux, Cauderan, France
Boivin, Leo J — *Hockey Player*
PO Box 406, Prescott ON K0E 1T0, Canada
Bok, Bart J — *Astronomer, Educator*
200 N Sierra Vista Dr, Tucson, AZ 85719, USA
Bok, Chip — *Editorial Cartoonist*
709 Castle Blvd, Akron, OH 44313, USA
Bok, Derek C — *Educator*
%Harvard University, Kennedy Government School, Cambridge, MA 02138, USA
Bok, Sissela — *Philosopher*
75 Cambridge Parkway, #E610, Cambridge, MA 02142, USA
Bokamper, Kim — *Football Player*
301 NW 127th Ave, Plantation, FL 33325, USA
Bolanos, Enrique — *President, Nicaragua*
%President's Office, Casa de Gobierno, #2398, Managua, Nicaragua
Bolcom, William E — *Composer*
3080 Whitmore Lake Road, Ann Arbor, MI 48105, USA
Bolden, Charles F, Jr — *Astronaut, Marine Corps General*
2952 Holly Hall St, Houston, TX 77054, USA
Boldon, Ato — *Track Athlete*
PO Box 3703, Santa Cruz, Trinidad, Trinidad & Tobago
Boles, John E — *Baseball Manager, Executive*
7901 Timberlake Dr, West Melbourne, FL 32904, USA
Bolger, James B (Jim) — *Prime Minister, New Zealand*
%New Zealand Embassy, 37 Observatory Circle NW, Washington, DC 20008, USA
Bolin, Bobby D — *Baseball Player*
PO Box 1948, Easley, SC 29641, USA
Bolkiah Mu'izuddin Waddaulah — *Sultan, Brunei Darussalam*
Istana Darul Hana, Brunei Darussalam
Bolleau, Linda — *Editorial Cartoonist*
%Frankfort State Journal, Editorial Dept, 321 W Main St, Frankfort, KY 40601, USA

Bollen, Roger *Cartoonist (Animal Crackers, Catfish)*
%Tribune Media Services, 435 N Michigan Ave, #1500, Chicago, IL 60611, USA
Bolles, Richard N *Writer*
2378 Hagen Oaks Dr, Alamo, CA 94507, USA
Bollettieri, Nick *Tennis Coach*
%Nick Bollettieri Tennis Academy, 5500 34th St W, Bradenton, FL 34210, USA
Bolling, Claude *Jazz Pianist, Composer*
20 Ave de Lorraine, 92380 Garches, France
Bolling, Tiffany *Actress*
12483 Braddock Dr, Los Angeles, CA 90066, USA
Bollinger, Lee C *Educator*
%Columbia University, President's Office, New York, NY 10027, USA
Bologna, Joseph *Actor*
16830 Ventura Blvd, #326, Encino, CA 91436, USA
Bolt, John F *WW II Marine Corps Air Force Hero*
705 N Atlantic Ave, #303, New Smyrna Beach, FL 32169, USA
Bolt, Mae *Bowler*
1321 Highland Ave, Berwyn, IL 60402, USA
Bolt, Tommy *Golfer*
%Cherokee Village Public Golf Course, Cherokee Village, AR 72525, USA
Bolten, Joshua *Government Official*
%Office of Management/Budget, Executive Office Building, Washington, DC 20503, USA
Bolton, Michael *Singer, Songwriter*
130 W 57th St, #10B, New York, NY 10019, USA
Bolton-Holifield, Ruthie *Basketball Player*
%Sacramento Monarchs, Arco Arena, 1 Sports Parkway, Sacramento, CA 95834, USA
Bombassaro, Gerald *Labor Leader*
%Tile Marble & Granite Cutters Union, 801 N Pitt St, Alexandria, VA 22314, USA
Bon Jovi, Jon *Singer (Bon Jovi), Songwriter, Actor*
%Bon Jovi Mgmt, 248 W 17th St, #501, New York, NY 10011, USA
Bonaduce, Danny *Actor, Singer*
2651 La Cuesta Dr, Los Angeles, CA 90046, USA
Bonaly, Surya *Figure Skater*
35 Rue Felicien David, 75016 Paris, France
Bonamy, James *Singer*
%Hallmark Direction, 15 Music Square W, Nashville, TN 37203, USA
Bonanno, Louis *Actor*
PO Box 583, Laguna Beach, CA 92652, USA
Bond, Alan *Businessman, Yachtsman*
89 Watkins Road, Dalkeith WA 6069, Australia
Bond, Christopher S (Kit) *Governor, Senator, MO*
308 E High St, #202, Jefferson City, MO 65101, USA
Bond, Edward *Writer*
Orchard Way, Great Wilbraham, Cambridge CB1 5KA, England
Bond, H Julian *Civil Rights Activist*
54435 41st Place NW, Washington, DC 20015, USA
Bond, J Max, Jr *Architect*
%Davis Broder Assoc, 100 E 42nd St, New York, NY 10017, USA
Bond, Samantha *Actress*
%Conway Van Gelder Robinson, 18-21 Jermyn St, London SW1Y 6NB, England
Bond, Steve *Actor*
14050 Marquesas Way, Marina del Rey, CA 90292, USA
Bond, Tommy (Butch) *Actor*
993 Delaware St, Imperial Beach, CA 91932, USA
Bond, Victoria A *Conductor, Composer*
%Roanoke Symphony, 541 Luck Ave SW, #200, Roanoke, VA 24016, USA
Bondar, Roberta L *Astronaut, Canada*
%Space Agency, PO Box 7014, Station V, Vanier ON K1L 8E2, Canada
Bondevik, Kjell Magne *Prime Minister, Norway*
%Statsministerens Kontor, Postboks 8001 Dep, 0030 Oslo, Norway
Bondi, Hermann *Applied Mathematician*
60 Mill Lane, Impington, Cambridgeshire CB4 4XN, England
Bonds, Barry L *Baseball Player*
%San Francisco Giants, Pacific Bell Park, 24 Mays Plz, San Francisco, CA 94103, USA
Bonds, Gary U S *Singer*
%Entity Communications, 875 Ave of Americas, #1908, New York, NY 10001, USA
Bonell, Carlos A *Concert Guitarist, Composer*
%Upbeat Mgmt, Sutton Business Centre, Wallington, Surrey SM6 7AH, England
Bonerz, Peter *Actor, Comedian, Director*
3637 Lowry Road, Los Angeles, CA 90027, USA
Bonet, Lisa *Actress*
5534 Encino Ave, #103, Encino, CA 91316, USA
Bonet, Pep *Architect*
C/Pujades 62, 08005 Barcelona, Spain
Bongo, Albert-Bernard Omar *President, Gabon*
%President's Office, Blvd de Independence, BP 546, Libreville, Gabon
Bonham Carter, Helena *Actress*
7 West Heath Ave, London NW11 7S, England

B

Bonham, Tracy *Singer, Songwriter*
%Artists Management Group, 207 Crabapple Dr, Baytown, TX 77520, USA
Bonilla, Roberto M A (Bobby) *Baseball Player*
390 Round Hill Road, Greenwich, CT 06831, USA
Bonin, Gordie *Auto Racing Driver*
12471 Sanford St, Los Angeles, CA 90066, USA
Bonington, Christian J S *Mountaineer*
Badger Hill, Nether Row, Hesket Newmarket, Wigton, Cumbria, England
Bonnefous, Jean-Pierre *Ballet Dancer, Choreographer*
%Indiana University, Ballet Dept, Music School, Bloomington, IN 47405, USA
Bonner, Frank *Actor*
%Stone Manners, 6500 Wilshire Blvd, #550, Los Angeles, CA 90048, USA
Bonner, John T *Biologist*
52 Patton Ave, #A, Princeton, NJ 08540, USA
Bonness, Rik *Football Player*
1650 Farnam St, Omaha, NE 68102, USA
Bonney, Barbara *Opera Singer*
Gunnarsbyn, 671 94 Edane, Sweden
Bono *Singer, Songwriter (U-2)*
%Regine Moylett, 145A Ladbroke Grove, London W10 6HJ, England
Bono, Chastity *Actress, Singer*
8968 Vista Grande, West Hollywood, CA 90069, USA
Bonoff, Karla *Singer, Pianist, Songwriter*
2122 E Valley Road, Santa Barbara, CA 93108, USA
Bonsall, Joseph S (Joe), Jr *Singer (Oak Ridge Boys)*
329 Rockland Road, Hendersonville, TN 37075, USA
Bontemps, Ronald (Ron) *Basketball Player*
133 S Illinois Ave, Morton, IL 61550, USA
Bonvicini, Joan *Basketball Coach*
%University of Arizona, Athletic Dept, McKale Memorial Center, Tucson, AZ 85721, USA
Bonynge, Richard A *Conductor*
Chalet Monet, Rte de Sonloup, 1833 Les Avants, Switzerland
Boo, Katherine *Journalist*
%Washington Post, Editorial Dept, 1150 15th St NW, Washington, DC 20071, USA
Boochever, Robert *Judge*
%US Court of Appeals, 125 S Grand Ave, Pasadena, CA 91105, USA
Bookwalter, J R *Movie Director*
PO Box 6573, Akron, OH 44312, USA
Boon, David C *Cricketer*
%Durham Cricket Club, Chester-le-Street, County Durham DH3 3QR, England
Boone, Bret R *Baseball Player*
5112 Isleworth Country Club Dr, Windermere, FL 34786, USA
Boone, Debby *Actress, Singer*
4334 Kester Ave, Sherman Oaks, CA 91403, USA
Boone, Pat *Actor, Singer*
904 N Beverly Dr, Beverly Hills, CA 90210, USA
Boone, Randy *Actor*
4150 Arch St, #223, Studio City, CA 91604, USA
Boone, Raymond O (Ray) *Baseball Player*
3728 Paseo Vista Famosa, Rancho Santa Fe, CA 92091, USA
Boone, Robert R (Bob) *Baseball Player, Manager*
18571 Villa Dr, Villa Park, CA 92861, USA
Boone, Ron *Basketball Player*
3877 Pheasant Ridge Road, Salt Lake City, UT 84109, USA
Boone, Steve *Bassist, Singer (Lovin' Spoonful)*
%Pipeline Artists Mgmt, 620 16th Ave S, Hopkins, MN 55343, USA
Boorman, John *Movie Director*
%Merlin Films, 16 Upper Pembroke St, Dublin 2, Ireland
Boorstin, Daniel J *Historian*
3541 Ordway St NW, Washington, DC 20016, USA
Boosler, Elayne *Actress, Comedienne*
%Siddons Assoc, 14930 Ventura Blvd, #205, Sherman Oaks, CA 91403, USA
Booth, Adrian *Actress*
3922 Glenridge Dr, Sherman Oaks, CA 91423, USA
Booth, Connie *Actress*
%Kate Feast, Primrose Hill Studios, Fitzroy Road, London NW1 8TR, England
Booth, George *Cartoonist*
PO Box 1539, Stony Brook, NY 11790, USA
Booth, James *Actor*
%Hillard/Elkins, 8306 Wilshire Blvd, #438, Beverly Hills, CA 90211, USA
Boothe, Powers *Actor*
23629 Long Valley Road, Hidden Hills, CA 91302, USA
Boothroyd, Betty *Government Official, England*
%House of Commons, Westminster, London SW1A 0AA, England
Boozer, Carlos *Basketball Player*
%Cleveland Cavaliers, Gund Arena, 1 Center Court, Cleveland, OH 44115, USA
Boozer, Robert (Bob) *Basketball Player*
100 S 19th St, Omaha, NE 68102, USA

Borcherds, Richard E *Mathematician*
%University of California, Mathematics Dept, Berkeley, CA 94720, USA
Bordaberry Arocena, Juan M *President, Uruguay*
Joaquin Suarez 2868, Montevideo, Uruguay
Borden, Amanda *Gymnast*
%Cincinnati Gymnastics Academy, 3536 Woodridge Blvd, Fairfield, OH 45014, USA
Borden, Lynn *Actress*
%Associated Artists, 6399 Wilshire Blvd, #211, Los Angeles, CA 90048, USA
Border, Allan R *Cricketer*
%Cricket Board, 90 Jolimont St, Jolimont VIC 3002, Australia
Boreanaz, David *Actor*
%Visionary Mgmt, 8265 Sunset Blvd, #104, West Hollywood, CA 90046, USA
Boren, David L *Governor, Senator, OK; Educator*
750 W Boyd, Norman, OK 73019, USA
Borg, Bjorn R *Tennis Player*
%International Mgmt Group, Pier House, Chiswick, London W4M 3NN, England
Borg, Kim *Opera Singer*
Osterbrogade 158, 2100 Copenhagen, Denmark
Borghi, Frank *Soccer Player*
4123 Poepping St, Saint Louis, MO 63123, USA
Borgman, James M (Jim) *Editorial Cartoonist*
%Cincinnati Enquirer, Editorial Dept, 617 Vine St, Cincinnati, OH 45202, USA
Borgnine, Ernest *Actor*
3055 Lake Glen Dr, Beverly Hills, CA 90210, USA
Boris, Ruthanna *Ballerina, Choreographer*
%Center for Dance, 555 Pierce St, #1033, Albany, CA 94706, USA
Bork, George *Football Player*
7316 Coventry Dr S, Spring Grove, IL 60081, USA
Bork, Robert H *Judge, Government Official*
6520 Ridge St, McLean, VA 22101, USA
Borkh, Inge *Opera Singer*
Haus Weitblick, 9405 Wienacht, Switzerland
Borlaug, Norman E *Nobel Peace Laureate*
PO Box 6-641, SP 06600, Mexico City DF, Mexico
Borlenghi, Matt *Actor*
%Paul Kohner, 9300 Wilshire Blvd, #555, Beverly Hills, CA 90212, USA
Borman, Frank *Astronaut, Businessman*
%Patlex Corp, PO Box 1139, Fairacres, NM 88033, USA
Borodina, Olga V *Opera Singer*
%Lies Askonas, 6 Henrietta St, London WC2E 8LA, England
Borofsky, Jonathan *Artist*
57 Market St, Venice, CA 90291, USA
Boron, Kathrin *Rowing Athlete*
%Potsdamer RG, An Der Pirschheide, 14471 Potsdam, Germany
Boros, Guy *Golfer*
2540 SE 8th St, Pompano Beach, FL 33062, USA
Boross, Peter *Prime Minister, Hungary*
Kossouth Lajos Ter 1-3, 1055 Budapest, Hungary
Borowiak, Tony *Singer (All-4-One)*
%MPI Talent, 9255 Sunset Blvd, #407, Los Angeles, CA 90069, USA
Borowy, Henry L (Hank) *Baseball Player*
57 Nina Court, Brick, NJ 08723, USA
Borrego, Jesse *Actor*
PO Box 785, Bellport, NY 11713, USA
Borst, Piet *Biochemist*
Meentweg 87, 1406 KE Bussum, Netherlands
Borten, Per *Prime Minister, Norway*
7095 Ler, Norway
Boryla, Vince *Basketball Player, Executive*
5577 S Emporia Circle, Englewood, CO 80111, USA
Borzov, Valeri F *Track Athlete*
%Sport & Youth Ministry, Esplanadna St 42, 252023 Kiev 23, Ukraine
Boschman, Ed *Religious Leader*
%Mennonite Brethren Churches General Conference, PO Box 347, Newton, KS 67114, USA
Bosco, Philip *Actor*
%Judy Schoen, 606 N Larchmont Blvd, #309, Los Angeles, CA 90004, USA
Bose, Amar G *Inventor (Audio Waveguide)*
%Bose Corp, Mountain, Framington, MA 01701, USA
Bose, Bimal K *Electrical Engineer*
215 Ski Mountain Road, Gatlinburg, TN 37738, USA
Bose, Eleanora *Model*
%I M G Models, 304 Park Ave S, #1200, New York, NY 10010, USA
Bose, Miguel *Singer, Songwriter, Actor*
%RLM Producciones, Puerto Santa Maria 65, 28043 Madrid, Spain
Boselli, Tony *Football Player*
6 Glendenning Lane, Houston, TX 77024, USA
Boskin, Michael J *Government Official*
%Stanford University, Hoover Institution, Stanford, CA 94305, USA

Bosley, Tom *Actor*
%Burton Moss, 8827 Beverly Blvd, #L, Los Angeles, CA 90048, USA

Bossard, Andre *Law Enforcement Official*
228 Rue de la Convention, 75015 Paris, France

Bosseler, Don J *Football Player*
7420 SW 133rd St, Miami, FL 33156, USA

Bossidy, Lawrence A (Larry) *Businessman*
%Honeywell Inc, Honeywell Plaza, Minneapolis, MN 55408, USA

Bosson, Barbara *Actress*
694 Amalfi Dr, Pacific Palisades, CA 90272, USA

Bossy, Michael (Mike) *Hockey Player*
136 Ducharme St, Rosemere QC J7A 4HB, Canada

Bostelle, Tom *Artist*
%Aeolian Palace Gallery, PO Box 8, Pocopson, PA 19366, USA

Bostic, Jeff *Football Player*
10701 Miller Road, Oakton, VA 22124, USA

Bostwick, Barry *Actor*
%Gersh Agency, 232 N Canon Dr, Beverly Hills, CA 90210, USA

Bostwick, Dunbar *Harness Racing Driver*
1623 Dewey Ave, Pompano Beach, FL 33060, USA

Boswell, David W (Dave) *Baseball Player*
309 Roxbury Court, Joppa, MD 21085, USA

Boswell, Thomas M *Sportswriter*
%Washington Post, Sports Dept, 1150 15th St NW, Washington, DC 20071, USA

Bosworth, Brian *Football Player, Actor*
%Artists Agency, 1180 S Beverly Dr, #301, Los Angeles, CA 90035, USA

Bosworth, Kate *Actress*
%United Talent Agency, 9560 Wilshire Blvd, #500, Beverly Hills, CA 90212, USA

Botehho, Joao *Movie Director*
%Assicuacai de Realizadores, Rua de Palmeira 7, R/C, 1200 Lisbon, Portugal

Botero, Fernando *Artist*
%Nohra Haime Gallery, 41 E 57th St, #600, New York, NY 10022, USA

Botha, Francois (Frans) *Boxer*
%White Buffalo, PO Box 3982, Clearwater, FL 33767, USA

Botha, Pieter W *President, South Africa*
Die Anker, Wilderness 6560, South Africa

Botha, Roelof F *Government Official, South Africa*
PO Box 16176, Pretoria North 0116, South Africa

Botham, Ian T *Cricketer*
%Ludorum Mgmt, 33 Tooley St, London SE1 2QF, England

Botsford, Beth *Swimmer*
405 Ivy Church Road, Timonium, MD 21093, USA

Botsford, Sara *Actress*
%Kordek Agency, 8490 W Sunset Blvd, #403, West Hollywood, CA 90069, USA

Bott, Raoul *Mathematician*
1 Richdale Ave, #9, Cambridge, MA 02140, USA

Botta, Mario *Architect*
Via Ciani 16, 6904 Lugano, Switzerland

Bottom, Joe *Swimmer*
PO Box 3840, Chico, CA 95927, USA

Bottomley, Virginia *Government Official, England*
%House of Commons, Westminster, London SW1A 0AA, England

Bottoms, Joseph *Actor*
%Sanford-Gross, 6715 Hollywood Blvd, #236, Los Angeles, CA 90028, USA

Bottoms, Sam *Actor*
4719 Willowcrest Ave, North Hollywood, CA 91602, USA

Bottoms, Timothy *Actor*
532 Hot Springs Road, Santa Barbara, CA 93108, USA

Boublil, Alain A *Lyricist*
%Cameron Mackintosh Ltd, 1 Bedford Square, London WC1B 3RA, England

Boucha, Henry *Hockey Player*
314 Minnesota St, Warroad, MN 56763, USA

Bouchard, Emile J (Butch) *Hockey Player*
%CSAS, PO Box 60036, RPO Glen Abbey, Oakville ON L6M 3H2, Canada

Boucher, Gaetan *Speed Skater*
%Center Sportif, 3850 Edgar, Saint Hubert QC J4T 368, Canada

Boucher, Pierre *Photographer*
L'Ermitage, 7 Ave Massoul, Faremountiers, 77120 Coulomiers, France

Boucher, Savannah *Actress*
%H W A Talent, 3500 W Olive Ave, #1400, Burbank, CA 91505, USA

Boudart, Michel *Chemical Engineer*
512 Gerona Road, Stanford, CA 94305, USA

Boudin, Michael *Judge*
%US Appeals Court, McCormack Federal Building, Boston, MA 02109, USA

Boulez, Pierre *Composer, Conductor*
%IRCAM, 1 Place Igor Stravinsky, 75004 Paris, France

Boulos, Frenchy *Soccer Player*
20 Elvin St, Staten Island, NY 10314, USA

Boulud, David *Chef*
%Daniel Restaurant, 60 E 65th St, New York, NY 10021, USA
Boulware, Peter *Football Player*
305 Leaning Tree Road, Columbia, SC 29223, USA
Bouquet, Carole *Actress, Model*
%Agents Associes Beaume, 201 Faubourg Saint Honore, 75008 Paris, France
Bourdain, Anthony *Chef*
%Food Network, 1180 Ave of Americas, #1200, New York, NY 10036, USA
Bourdeaux, Michael *Religious Leader*
%Keston College, Heathfield Road, Keston, Kent BR2 6BA, England
Bourgeois, Louise *Sculptor*
347 W 20th St, New York, NY 10011, USA
Bourgignon, Serge *Movie Director*
18 Rue de General-Malterre, 75016 Paris, France
Bourjaily, Vance *Writer*
Redbird Farm, RR 3, Iowa City, IA 52240, USA
Bourne, Shae-Lynn *Figure Skater*
%Connecticut Skating Center, 300 Alumni Road, Newington, CT 06111, USA
Bournissen, Chantal *Alpine Skier*
1983 Evolene, Switzerland
Bourque, Pierre *Horticulturist, Mayor*
%Hotel de Ville, 275 Rue Notre Dame Est, Montreal QC H2Y 1C6, Canada
Bourque, Raymond J (Ray) *Hockey Player*
78 Coppermine Road, Topsfield, MA 01983, USA
Boushka, Richard (Dick) *Basketball Player*
7676 E Polo Dr, #38, Wichita, KS 67206, USA
Bouteflika, Abdul Aziz *President, Algeria*
%President's Office, Al-Mouradia, Algiers, Algeria
Bouton, James A (Jim) *Baseball Player, Writer*
PO Box 188, North Edgemont, MA 01252, USA
Boutros-Ghali, Boutros *Secretary-General, United Nations*
%Inter'l Francophonie Org, 28 Rue de Bourgogne, 75007 Paris, France
Bouvet, Didier *Alpine Skier*
%Bouvet-Sports, 74360 Abondance, France
Bouvia, Gloria *Bowler*
685 NE 23rd Place, Gresham, OR 97030, USA
Bow Wow *Rap Artist, Actor*
%Premier Talent, 1790 Broadway, New York, NY 10019, USA
Bow, Chuck *Auto Racing Driver*
%National Assn of Stock Car Racing, 1801 Speedway Blvd, Daytona Beach, FL 32114, USA
Bowa, Lawrence R (Larry) *Baseball Player, Manager*
129 Upper Gulph Road, Radnor, PA 19087, USA
Bowden, Robert (Bobby) *Football Coach*
%Florida State University, Athletic Dept, Tallahassee, FL 32306, USA
Bowden, Terry *Football Coach, Sportscaster*
%ABC-TV, Sports Dept, 77 W 66th St, New York, NY 10023, USA
Bowden, Tommy *Football Coach*
%Clemson University, Athletic Dept, Clemson, SC 29364, USA
Bowdler, William G *Diplomat*
%State Department, 2201 C St NW, Washington, DC 20520, USA
Bowe, David *Actor*
%Karg/Weissenbach, 329 N Wetherly Dr, #101, Beverly Hills, CA 90211, USA
Bowe, Riddick L *Boxer*
714 Ahmer Dr, Fort Washington, MD 20744, USA
Bowe, Rosemarie *Actress*
321 Saint Pierre Road, Los Angeles, CA 90077, USA
Bowen, Michael *Actor*
%Diverse Talent Agency, 1875 Century Park East, #2250, Los Angeles, CA 90067, USA
Bowen, Otis R *Secretary, Health & Human Services*
PO Box 348, Bremen, IN 46506, USA
Bowen, William G *Foundation Executive, Educator*
%Andrew Mellon Foundation, 140 E 62nd St, New York, NY 10021, USA
Bower, Antoinette *Actress*
1529 N Beverly Glen Blvd, Los Angeles, CA 90077, USA
Bower, John W (Johnny) *Hockey Player*
3937 Parkgate Dr, Mississauga ON L5N 7B4, Canada
Bower, Robert W *Inventor (Semiconductor Insulated Gate)*
%University of California, Microelectronics Dept, Davis, CA 95616, USA
Bower, Rodney A *Labor Leader*
%Professional & Technical Engineers, 818 Roeder Road, Silver Spring, MD 20910, USA
Bowers, John *Labor Leader*
%International Longshoremen's Assn, 17 Battery Place, New York, NY 10004, USA
Bowers, John W *Religious Leader*
%Foursquare Gospel Int'l Church, 1100 Glendale Blvd, Los Angeles, CA 90026, USA
Bowersox, Kenneth D *Astronaut*
16907 Soaring Forest Dr, Houston, TX 77059, USA
Bowie, David *Singer, Actor*
%Outside, 180-182 Tottenham Court Road, London W1P 9LE, England

B

Bowie - Bracco

Bowie, Sam *Basketball Player*
901 The Curtilage, Lexington, KY 40502, USA
Bowker, Albert H *Educator*
1523 New Hampshire Ave NW, Washington, DC 20036, USA
Bowker, Judi *Actress*
%Howes & Prior, 66 Berkeley House, Hay Hill, London W1X 7LH, England
Bowles, Crandall C *Businessman*
%Springs Industries, 205 N White St, Fort Mill, SC 29715, USA
Bowles, Erskine B *Government Official*
6725 Old Providence Road, Charlotte, NC 28226, USA
Bowlin, Michael R *Businessman*
%Atlantic Richfield Co, 333 S Hope St, Los Angeles, CA 90071, USA
Bowman, Christopher *Figure Skater*
5653 Kester Ave, Van Nuys, CA 91411, USA
Bowman, Harry W *Businessman*
%Outboard Marine, PO Box 410, Waukegan, IL 60079, USA
Bowman, Pasco M, II *Judge*
%US Court of Appeals, US Courthouse, 811 Grand Ave, Kansas City, MO 64106, USA
Bowman, W Scott (Scotty) *Hockey Coach, Executive*
56 Halston Parkway, East Amherst, NY 14051, USA
Bownes, Hugh H *Judge*
%US Court of Appeals, Federal Courthouse, PO Box 311, Concord, NH 03302, USA
Bowyer, William *Artist*
12 Cleveland Ave, Chiswick, London W4 1SN, England
Boxberger, Loa *Bowler*
PO Box 708, Russell, KS 67665, USA
Boxleitner, Bruce *Actor*
23679 Calabasas Road, #181, Calabasas, CA 91302, USA
Boy George *Singer*
%Concorde Int'l Artists, 101 Shepherds Bush Road, London W6 9LP, England
Boyce, Kim *Singer*
200 Nathan Dr, Hollister, MO 65672, USA
Boycott, Geoffrey *Cricketer*
%Cricket Club, Headingley Cricket Ground, Leeds, Yorks LS6 3BY, England
Boyd, Alan S *Secretary, Transportation*
2922 Larranaga Dr, Lady Lake, FL 32162, USA
Boyd, Brandon *Singer, Percussionist (Incubus)*
%ArtistDirect, 10900 Wilshire Blvd, #1400, Los Angeles, CA 90024, USA
Boyd, Dennis (Oil Can) *Baseball Player*
1611 20th St, Meridian, MS 39301, USA
Boyd, Malcolm *Writer, Religious Leader*
%Saint Augustine-by-Sea Episcopal Church, 1227 4th St, Santa Monica, CA 90401, USA
Boyd, Richard A *Labor Leader*
%Fraternal Order of Police, 2100 Gardiner Lane, Louisville, KY 40205, USA
Boyd, Tanya *Actress*
%Amsel Eisenstadt Frazier, 5757 Wilshire Blvd, #510, Los Angeles, CA 90036, USA
Boyer, Cletis L (Clete) *Baseball Player*
2034 20th Avenue Parkway, Indian Rocks Beach, FL 33785, USA
Boyer, Herbert W *Biochemist, Inventor*
PO Box 7318, Rancho Santa Fe, CA 92067, USA
Boyer, Paul D *Nobel Chemistry Laureate*
1033 Somera Road, Los Angeles, CA 90077, USA
Boykin, William G *Army General*
%DepUndersecretary Intelligence, Defense Dept, Pentagon, Washington, DC 20301, USA
Boyle Clune, Charlotte *Swimmer*
50 Brown's Grove, Box 31, Scottsville, NY 14546, USA
Boyle, Danny *Movie Director*
%International Creative Mgmt, 76 Oxford St, London W1N 0AX, England
Boyle, Lara Flynn *Actress*
14617 Valley Vista Blvd, Sherman Oaks, CA 91403, USA
Boyle, Lisa *Model, Actress*
7336 Santa Monica Blvd, #776, West Hollywood, CA 90046, USA
Boyle, Peter *Actor*
130 E End Ave, New York, NY 10028, USA
Boyle, T Coraghessan *Writer*
%University of Southern California, English Dept, Los Angeles, CA 90089, USA
Boynton, Robert M *Psychologist*
376 Bellaire St, Del Mar, CA 92014, USA
Boynton, Sandra *Graphic Artist*
%Recycled Paper Products, 3636 N Broadway, Chicago, IL 60613, USA
Boysen, Sarah *Psychologist*
%Ohio State University, Psychology Dept, Columbus, OH 43210, USA
Bozanic, Josip Cardinal *Religious Leader*
%Zagreb Archdiocese, Kaptol 31, PP 553, 10001 Zagreb Hrvatska, Croatia
Brabham, John A (Jack) *Auto Racing Driver*
5 Ruxley Lane, Ewell, Surrey KT19 0JB, England
Bracco, Lorraine *Actress*
%Innovative Artists, 1505 10th St, Santa Monica, CA 90401, USA

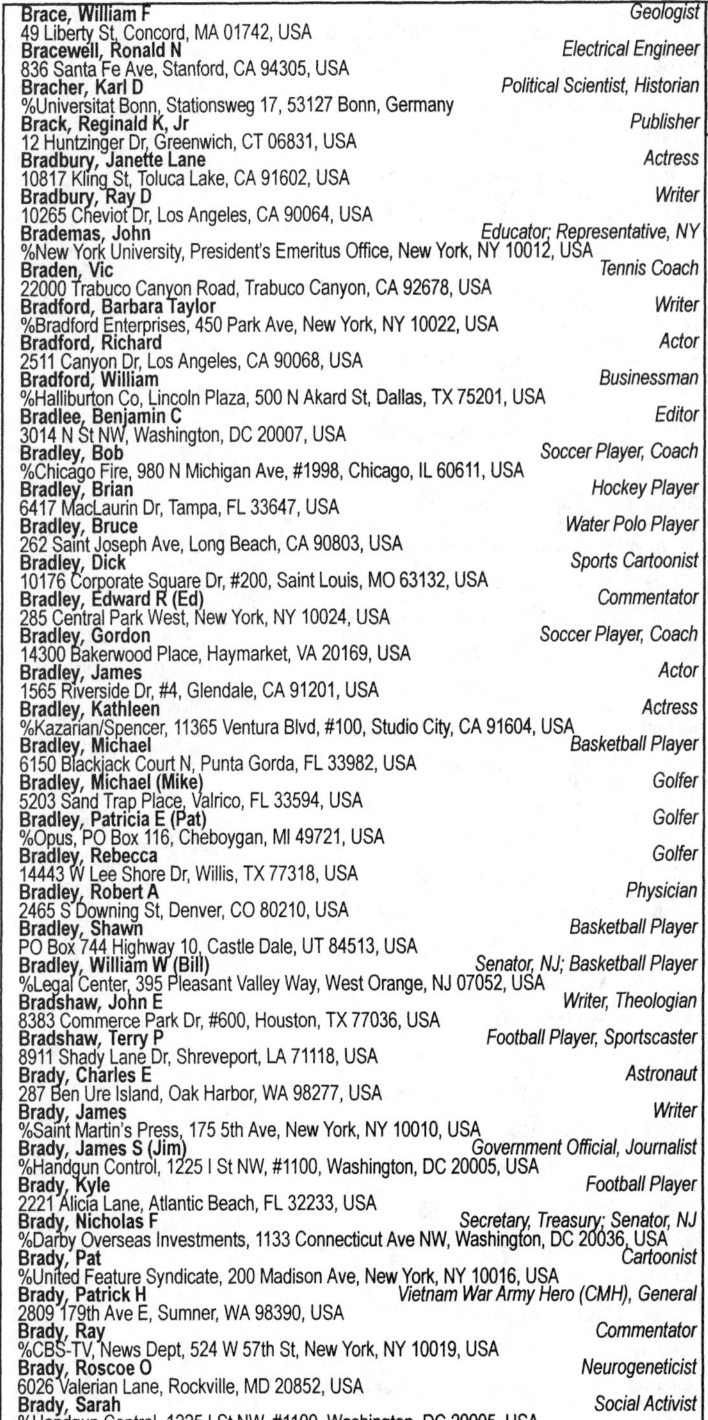

Brace, William F *Geologist*
49 Liberty St, Concord, MA 01742, USA
Bracewell, Ronald N *Electrical Engineer*
836 Santa Fe Ave, Stanford, CA 94305, USA
Bracher, Karl D *Political Scientist, Historian*
%Universitat Bonn, Stationsweg 17, 53127 Bonn, Germany
Brack, Reginald K, Jr *Publisher*
12 Huntzinger Dr, Greenwich, CT 06831, USA
Bradbury, Janette Lane *Actress*
10817 Kling St, Toluca Lake, CA 91602, USA
Bradbury, Ray D *Writer*
10265 Cheviot Dr, Los Angeles, CA 90064, USA
Brademas, John *Educator; Representative, NY*
%New York University, President's Emeritus Office, New York, NY 10012, USA
Braden, Vic *Tennis Coach*
22000 Trabuco Canyon Road, Trabuco Canyon, CA 92678, USA
Bradford, Barbara Taylor *Writer*
%Bradford Enterprises, 450 Park Ave, New York, NY 10022, USA
Bradford, Richard *Actor*
2511 Canyon Dr, Los Angeles, CA 90068, USA
Bradford, William *Businessman*
%Halliburton Co, Lincoln Plaza, 500 N Akard St, Dallas, TX 75201, USA
Bradlee, Benjamin C *Editor*
3014 N St NW, Washington, DC 20007, USA
Bradley, Bob *Soccer Player, Coach*
%Chicago Fire, 980 N Michigan Ave, #1998, Chicago, IL 60611, USA
Bradley, Brian *Hockey Player*
6417 MacLaurin Dr, Tampa, FL 33647, USA
Bradley, Bruce *Water Polo Player*
262 Saint Joseph Ave, Long Beach, CA 90803, USA
Bradley, Dick *Sports Cartoonist*
10176 Corporate Square Dr, #200, Saint Louis, MO 63132, USA
Bradley, Edward R (Ed) *Commentator*
285 Central Park West, New York, NY 10024, USA
Bradley, Gordon *Soccer Player, Coach*
14300 Bakerwood Place, Haymarket, VA 20169, USA
Bradley, James *Actor*
1565 Riverside Dr, #4, Glendale, CA 91201, USA
Bradley, Kathleen *Actress*
%Kazarian/Spencer, 11365 Ventura Blvd, #100, Studio City, CA 91604, USA
Bradley, Michael *Basketball Player*
6150 Blackjack Court N, Punta Gorda, FL 33982, USA
Bradley, Michael (Mike) *Golfer*
5203 Sand Trap Place, Valrico, FL 33594, USA
Bradley, Patricia E (Pat) *Golfer*
%Opus, PO Box 116, Cheboygan, MI 49721, USA
Bradley, Rebecca *Golfer*
14443 W Lee Shore Dr, Willis, TX 77318, USA
Bradley, Robert A *Physician*
2465 S Downing St, Denver, CO 80210, USA
Bradley, Shawn *Basketball Player*
PO Box 744 Highway 10, Castle Dale, UT 84513, USA
Bradley, William W (Bill) *Senator, NJ; Basketball Player*
%Legal Center, 395 Pleasant Valley Way, West Orange, NJ 07052, USA
Bradshaw, John E *Writer, Theologian*
8383 Commerce Park Dr, #600, Houston, TX 77036, USA
Bradshaw, Terry P *Football Player, Sportscaster*
8911 Shady Lane Dr, Shreveport, LA 71118, USA
Brady, Charles E *Astronaut*
287 Ben Ure Island, Oak Harbor, WA 98277, USA
Brady, James *Writer*
%Saint Martin's Press, 175 5th Ave, New York, NY 10010, USA
Brady, James S (Jim) *Government Official, Journalist*
%Handgun Control, 1225 I St NW, #1100, Washington, DC 20005, USA
Brady, Kyle *Football Player*
2221 Alicia Lane, Atlantic Beach, FL 32233, USA
Brady, Nicholas F *Secretary, Treasury; Senator, NJ*
%Darby Overseas Investments, 1133 Connecticut Ave NW, Washington, DC 20036, USA
Brady, Pat *Cartoonist*
%United Feature Syndicate, 200 Madison Ave, New York, NY 10016, USA
Brady, Patrick H *Vietnam War Army Hero (CMH), General*
2809 179th Ave E, Sumner, WA 98390, USA
Brady, Ray *Commentator*
%CBS-TV, News Dept, 524 W 57th St, New York, NY 10019, USA
Brady, Roscoe O *Neurogeneticist*
6026 Valerian Lane, Rockville, MD 20852, USA
Brady, Sarah *Social Activist*
%Handgun Control, 1225 I St NW, #1100, Washington, DC 20005, USA

B

Brady, Tom *Football Player*
%New England Patriots, Gillette Stadium, RR 1, 60 Washington, Foxboro, MA 02035, USA
Brady, Wayne *Actor, Comedian*
%Make It Up, 14622 Ventura Blvd, #1012, Sherman Oaks, CA 91403, USA
Braeden, Eric *Actor*
13723 Romany Dr, Pacific Palisades, CA 90272, USA
Braff, Zach *Actor*
%P M K Public Relations, 8500 Wilshire Blvd, #700, Beverly Hills, CA 90211, USA
Braga, Sonia *Actress*
41 River Terrace, #1403, New York, NY 10282, USA
Bragan, Robert R (Bobby) *Baseball Player*
7201 W Vickery Blvd, Benbrook, TX 76116, USA
Bragg, Billy *Singer*
%Sincere Mgmt, 6 Bravington Road, #6, London W9 3AH, England
Bragg, Darrell B *Nutritionist*
%University of British Columbia, Vancouver BC V6T 2AZ, Canada
Bragg, Donald G (Don) *Track Athlete*
90 State St, Penns Grove, NJ 08069, USA
Bragg, Melvyn *Writer*
12 Hampstead Hill Gardens, London NW3 2PL, England
Brahaney, Thomas F (Tom) *Football Player*
17 Winchester Court, Midland, TX 79705, USA
Brainin, Norbert *Concert Violinist*
19 Prowse Ave, Busbey Heath, Herts WD2 1JS, England
Bramall of Busfield, Edwin N W *Army Field Marshal, England*
%House of Lords, Westminster, London SW1A 0PW, England
Bramlett, Delaney *Singer, Guitarist (Delaney & Bonnie)*
PO Box 177, Sunland, CA 91041, USA
Branagh, Kenneth *Actor, Director*
%Marmont Mgmt, Langham House, 302/8 Regent St, London W1R 5AL, England
Branca, John G *Attorney*
%Ziffren Brittenham Branca, 1801 Century Park West, Los Angeles, CA 90067, USA
Branca, Ralph T J *Baseball Player*
%National Pension, 1025 Westchester, White Plains, NY 10604, USA
Branch, Clifford (Cliff) *Football Player, Coach*
2071 Stonefield Lane, Santa Rosa, CA 95403, USA
Branch, Michelle *Singer, Songwriter*
PO Box 20425, Sedona, AZ 86341, USA
Branch, William B *Writer*
53 Cortlandt Ave, New Rochelle, NY 10801, USA
Brand, Colette *Freestyle Aerials Skier*
Rigistr 24, 6340 Baar, Switzerland
Brand, Daniel (Dan) *Wrestler*
4321 Bridgeview Dr, Oakland, CA 94602, USA
Brand, Elton *Basketball Player*
%Los Angeles Clippers, Staples Center, 1111 S Figueroa St, Los Angeles, CA 90015, USA
Brand, Glen *Wrestler*
PO Box 6069, Omaha, NE 68106, USA
Brand, Myles *Educator*
%Indiana University, President's Office, Bloomington, IN 47405, USA
Brand, Oscar *Singer, Songwriter*
%Gypsy Hill Music, 141 Baker Hill Road, Great Neck, NY 11023, USA
Brand, Robert *Theater Lighting Designer*
505 W End Ave, New York, NY 10024, USA
Brand, Vance D *Astronaut*
%NASA Dryden Flight Center, PO Box 273, Edwards, CA 93523, USA
Brandauer, Klaus Maria *Actor*
%Novapool GmbH, Paul Lincke Ufer 42-43, 10999 Berlin, Germany
Brandenstein, Daniel C *Astronaut*
12802 Tri-City Beach Road, Baytown, TX 77520, USA
Brandi *Model*
%Next Model Mgmt, 23 Watts St, New York, NY 10013, USA
Brandis, Jonathan *Actor*
19250 Hamlin St, #5, Reseda, CA 91335, USA
Brando, Marlon *Actor*
%Brown Craft Co, 11940 San Vicente Blvd, Los Angeles, CA 90049, USA
Brandon, Barbara *Cartoonist (Where I'm Coming From)*
%Universal Press Syndicate, 4520 Main St, Kansas City, MO 64111, USA
Brandon, Clark *Actor*
%Jennings Assoc, 28035 Dorothy Dr, #210A, Agoura, CA 91301, USA
Brandon, John *Actor*
%Coast to Coast Talent, 3350 Barham Blvd, Los Angeles, CA 90068, USA
Brandon, Michael *Actor*
%Epstein-Wyckoff, 280 S Beverly Dr, #400, Beverly Hills, CA 90212, USA
Brands, Tom *Wrestler*
4494 Taft Ave SE, Iowa City, IA 52240, USA
Brands, X *Actor*
17171 Roscoe Blvd, #104, Northridge, CA 91325, USA

Brandt, Hank *Actor*
%Contemporary Artists, 610 Santa Monica Blvd, #202, Santa Monica, CA 90401, USA
Brandt, Jon *Singer, Bassist (Cheap Trick)*
%Monterey Peninsula Artists, 509 Hartnell St, Monterey, CA 93940, USA
Brandt, Paul *Singer*
%Creative Trust, 2105 Elliston Place, Nashville, TN 37203, USA
Brandt, Victor *Actor*
%H David Moss, 733 Seward St, #PH, Los Angeles, CA 90038, USA
Brandy *Singer, Actress*
22817 Ventura Blvd, #432, Woodland Hills, CA 91364, USA
Brandy, J C *Actress*
%Henderson/Hogan, 8285 W Sunset Blvd, #1, West Hollywood, CA 90046, USA
Brandywine, Marcia *Commentator*
743 Huntley Dr, Los Angeles, CA 90069, USA
Branigan, Laura *Singer, Songwriter*
%Evolution Talent, 1776 Broadway, #1500, New York, NY 10019, USA
Brannan, Charles F *Secretary, Agriculture*
3131 E Alameda Ave, Denver, CO 80209, USA
Brannon, Ronald *Religious Leader*
%Wesleyan Church, PO Box 50434, Indianapolis, IN 46250, USA
Branson, Richard *Businessman, Balloonist*
%Virgin Group, 120 Campden Hill Road, London W8 7AR, England
Brant, Tim *Sportscaster*
%ABC-TV, Sports Dept, 77 W 66th St, New York, NY 10023, USA
Brashear, Carl *Deep-Sea Diver Navy Hero*
804 Tenure Lane, Virginia Beach, VA 23462, USA
Braslow, Paul *Sculptor*
82 Neds Way, Bel Tiburon, CA 94920, USA
Brasseur, Claude *Actor*
%Artmedia, 20 Ave Rapp, 75007 Paris, France
Brathwaite, Edward *Writer*
%University of West Indies, History Dept, Mona, Kingston 7, Jamaica
Brathwaite, Nicholas *Prime Minister, Grenada*
%House of Representatives, Saint George's, Grenada
Bratkowski, Edmund R (Zeke) *Football Player, Coach*
224 Anchors Lake Dr N, Santa Rosa Beach, FL 32459, USA
Bratt, Benjamin *Actor*
11777 San Vicente Blvd, #700, Los Angeles, CA 90049, USA
Bratton, Creed *Guitarist (Grass Roots)*
%Thomas Cassidy, 11761 E Speedway Blvd, Tucson, AZ 85748, USA
Bratton, Joseph K *Army General*
1465 Goldrush Ave, Melbourne, FL 32940, USA
Bratton, William J *Law Enforcement Official*
%Los Angeles Police Dept, 150 S Los Angeles St, Los Angeles, CA 90012, USA
Bratz, Mike *Basketball Player*
7503 Tillman Hill Road, Colleyville, TX 76034, USA
Brauer, Arik *Artist*
%Academy of Fine Arts, Schillerplatz 3, Vienna 1010, Austria
Braugher, Andre *Actor*
361 Charlton Ave, South Orange, NJ 07079, USA
Brauman, John I *Chemist*
849 Tolman Dr, Palo Alto, CA 94305, USA
Braun, Allen *Neuroscientist*
%National Institute on Deafness, 9000 Rockville Pike, Bethesda, MD 20892, USA
Braun, Carl *Basketball Player, Coach*
5603 SE Foxcross Place, Stuart, FL 34997, USA
Braun, Lillian Jackson *Writer*
%Blanche Gregory Inc, 2 Tudor Place, New York, NY 10017, USA
Braun, Pinkas *Actor, Theater Director*
Unterdorf, 8261 Hemishofen/SH, Switzerland
Braun, Richard L *WW II Marine Corps Air Force Hero*
1912 Whittle Wood Road, Williamsburg, VA 23185, USA
Braun, Zev *Movie Producer*
%Zev Braun Pictures, 1438 N Gower St, #26, Los Angeles, CA 90028, USA
Braunwald, Eugene *Physician*
%Partners Healthcare, 800 Boylston St, Boston, MA 02199, USA
Braver, Rita *Commentator*
%CBS-TV, News Dept, 2020 M St NW, Washington, DC 20036, USA
Braverman, Bart *Actor*
%House of Representatives, 400 S Beverly Dr, #101, Beverly Hills, CA 90212, USA
Braxton, Anthony *Jazz Saxophonist, Composer*
%Berkeley Agency, 2608 9th St, Berkeley, CA 94710, USA
Braxton, Toni *Singer, Songwriter*
%Blackground, 10345 W Olympic Blvd, Los Angeles, CA 90064, USA
Braxton, Tyrone S *Football Player*
455 Kearney St, Denver, CO 80220, USA
Brayton, Tyler *Football Player*
%Oakland Raiders, 1220 Harbor Bay Parkway, Alameda, CA 94502, USA

B

Brazauskas, Algirdas *President, Lithuania*
Turniskiu 30, 2016 Vilnius, Lithuania
Brazelton, T Berry *Pediatrician*
23 Hawthorn St, Cambridge, MA 02138, USA
Brazil, Jeff *Journalist*
%Orlando Sentinel, Editorial Dept, 633 N Orange Ave, Orlando, FL 32801, USA
Brazil, John R *Educator*
%Bradley University, President's Office, Peoria, IL 61625, USA
Brazile, Robert L, Jr *Football Player*
263 Woodland Ave, Satsuma, AL 36572, USA
Brazile, Trevor *Rodeo Rider*
4609 US Highway 277 S, Anson, TX 79501, USA
Bready, Richard L *Businessman*
166 President Ave, Providence, RI 02906, USA
Bream, Julian A *Concert Guitarist*
%Hazard Chase, Richmond House, 16-20 Regent St, Cambridge CB2 1DB, England
Breathed, Berkeley *Cartoonist (Bloom County/Outland)*
%Washington Post Writers Group, 1150 15th St NW, Washington, DC 20071, USA
Brecheen, Harry D *Baseball Player*
1134 S Highschool St, Ada, OK 74820, USA
Breck, Peter *Actor*
%Artists Group, 10100 Santa Monica Blvd, #2490, Los Angeles, CA 90067, USA
Brecker, Michael *Jazz Saxophonist, Flutist, Pianist*
%International Music Network, 278 S Main St, #400, Gloucester, MA 01930, USA
Brecker, Randy *Jazz Trumpeter*
%Tropix International, 163 3rd Ave, #206, New York, NY 10003, USA
Breder, Charles M *Ichthyologist*
6275 Manasota Key Road, Englewood, FL 34223, USA
Bredesen, Espen *Ski Jumper*
Hellerud Gardsvei 18, 0671 Oslo, Norway
Breeden, Richard C *Government Official*
%Coopers & Lybrand, 1800 M St NW, Washington, DC 20036, USA
Breedlove, N Craig *Auto Racing Driver*
200 N Front St, Rio Vista, CA 94571, USA
Breen, Bobby *Singer, Actor*
10550 NW 71st Place, Tamarac, FL 33321, USA
Breen, Edward D *Businessman*
%Tyco International, 273 Corporate Dr, #100, Portsmouth, NH 03801, USA
Breen, George *Swimmer*
425 Pepper Mill Court, Sewell, NJ 08080, USA
Breen, John G *Businessman*
18800 N Park Blvd, Shaker Heights, OH 44122, USA
Breen, Patrick *Actor*
%Gersh Agency, 232 N Canon Dr, Beverly Hills, CA 90210, USA
Breen, Shelley *Singer (Point of Grace)*
%TBA Artists Mgmt, 300 10th Ave S, Nashville, TN 37203, USA
Breen, Stephen (Steve) *Editorial Cartoonist*
%San Diego Union-Telegram, PO Box 120191, San Diego, CA 92112, USA
Brees, Drew *Football Player*
%San Diego Chargers, 4020 Murphy Canyon Road, San Diego, CA 92123, USA
Bregman Recht, Tracey *Actress*
%Bell-Phillip Productions, 7800 Beverly Blvd, #3371, Los Angeles, CA 90036, USA
Bregman, Buddy *Movie Director, Producer*
11288 Ventura Blvd, #700, Studio City, CA 91604, USA
Bregman, Martin *Movie Producer*
%Bregman/Baer Productions, 641 Lexington Ave, New York, NY 10022, USA
Breidenbach, Warren *Surgeon*
%Jewish Hospital, Surgery Dept, 217 E Chestnut, Louisville, KY 40202, USA
Breitschwerdt, Werner *Businessman*
%Daimler-Benz AG, Mercedesstr 136, 70322 Stuttgart, Germany
Breland, Mark *Boxer*
5355 Carolina Highway, Denmark, SC 29042, USA
Bremner, Ewen *Actor*
%International Creative Mgmt, 76 Oxford St, London W1N 0AX, England
Brenan, Gerald *Writer*
Alhaurin El Grande, Malaga, Spain
Brendel, Alfred *Concert Pianist*
%Vanguard/Omega Classics, 27 W 72nd St, New York, NY 10023, USA
Brendel, Wolfgang *Opera Singer*
%Manuela Kursidem, Wasagasse 12/1/3, 1090 Vienna, Austria
Brenden, Hallgeir *Nordic Skier*
2417 Torberget, Norway
Brendon, Nicholas *Actor*
%Platform, 2666 N Beachwood Dr, Los Angeles, CA 90068, USA
Breneman, Curtis E *Chemist*
38 Carlyle Ave, Troy, NY 12180, USA
Brenly, Robert E (Bob) *Baseball Player, Manager*
9726 E Laurel Lane, Scottsdale, AZ 85260, USA

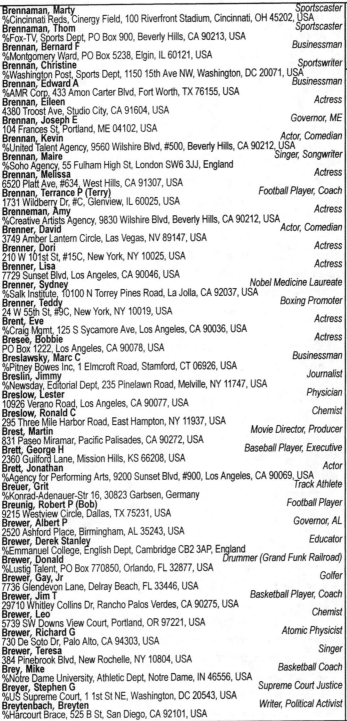

Brennaman, Marty *Sportscaster*
%Cincinnati Reds, Cinergy Field, 100 Riverfront Stadium, Cincinnati, OH 45202, USA
Brennaman, Thom *Sportscaster*
%Fox-TV, Sports Dept, PO Box 900, Beverly Hills, CA 90213, USA
Brennan, Bernard F *Businessman*
%Montgomery Ward, PO Box 5238, Elgin, IL 60121, USA
Brennan, Christine *Sportswriter*
%Washington Post, Sports Dept, 1150 15th Ave NW, Washington, DC 20071, USA
Brennan, Edward A *Businessman*
%AMR Corp, 433 Amon Carter Blvd, Fort Worth, TX 76155, USA
Brennan, Eileen *Actress*
4380 Troost Ave, Studio City, CA 91604, USA
Brennan, Joseph E *Governor, ME*
104 Frances St, Portland, ME 04102, USA
Brennan, Kevin *Actor, Comedian*
%United Talent Agency, 9560 Wilshire Blvd, #500, Beverly Hills, CA 90212, USA
Brennan, Maire *Singer, Songwriter*
%Soho Agency, 55 Fulham High St, London SW6 3JJ, England
Brennan, Melissa *Actress*
6520 Platt Ave, #634, West Hills, CA 91307, USA
Brennan, Terrance P (Terry) *Football Player, Coach*
1731 Wildberry Dr, #C, Glenview, IL 60025, USA
Brenneman, Amy *Actress*
%Creative Artists Agency, 9830 Wilshire Blvd, Beverly Hills, CA 90212, USA
Brenner, David *Actor, Comedian*
3749 Amber Lantern Circle, Las Vegas, NV 89147, USA
Brenner, Dori *Actress*
210 W 101st St, #15C, New York, NY 10025, USA
Brenner, Lisa *Actress*
7729 Sunset Blvd, Los Angeles, CA 90046, USA
Brenner, Sydney *Nobel Medicine Laureate*
%Salk Institute, 10100 N Torrey Pines Road, La Jolla, CA 92037, USA
Brenner, Teddy *Boxing Promoter*
24 W 55th St, #9C, New York, NY 10019, USA
Brent, Eve *Actress*
%Craig Mgmt, 125 S Sycamore Ave, Los Angeles, CA 90036, USA
Bresee, Bobbie *Actress*
PO Box 1222, Los Angeles, CA 90078, USA
Breslawsky, Marc C *Businessman*
%Pitney Bowes Inc, 1 Elmcroft Road, Stamford, CT 06926, USA
Breslin, Jimmy *Journalist*
%Newsday, Editorial Dept, 235 Pinelawn Road, Melville, NY 11747, USA
Breslow, Lester *Physician*
10926 Verano Road, Los Angeles, CA 90077, USA
Breslow, Ronald C *Chemist*
295 Three Mile Harbor Road, East Hampton, NY 11937, USA
Brest, Martin *Movie Director, Producer*
831 Paseo Miramar, Pacific Palisades, CA 90272, USA
Brett, George H *Baseball Player, Executive*
2360 Guilford Lane, Mission Hills, KS 66208, USA
Brett, Jonathan *Actor*
%Agency for Performing Arts, 9200 Sunset Blvd, #900, Los Angeles, CA 90069, USA
Breuer, Grit *Track Athlete*
%Konrad-Adenauer-Str 16, 30823 Garbsen, Germany
Breunig, Robert P (Bob) *Football Player*
9215 Westview Circle, Dallas, TX 75231, USA
Brewer, Albert P *Governor, AL*
2520 Ashford Place, Birmingham, AL 35243, USA
Brewer, Derek Stanley *Educator*
%Emmanuel College, English Dept, Cambridge CB2 3AP, England
Brewer, Donald *Drummer (Grand Funk Railroad)*
%Lustig Talent, PO Box 770850, Orlando, FL 32877, USA
Brewer, Gay, Jr *Golfer*
7736 Glendevon Lane, Delray Beach, FL 33446, USA
Brewer, Jim T *Basketball Player, Coach*
29710 Whitley Collins Dr, Rancho Palos Verdes, CA 90275, USA
Brewer, Leo *Chemist*
5739 SW Downs View Court, Portland, OR 97221, USA
Brewer, Richard G *Atomic Physicist*
730 De Soto Dr, Palo Alto, CA 94303, USA
Brewer, Teresa *Singer*
384 Pinebrook Blvd, New Rochelle, NY 10804, USA
Brey, Mike *Basketball Coach*
%Notre Dame University, Athletic Dept, Notre Dame, IN 46556, USA
Breyer, Stephen G *Supreme Court Justice*
%US Supreme Court, 1 1st St NE, Washington, DC 20543, USA
Breytenbach, Breyten *Writer, Political Activist*
%Harcourt Brace, 525 B St, San Diego, CA 92101, USA

B

Brezis, Haim *Mathematician*
18 Rue de la Glaciere, 75640 Paris Cedex 13, France
Brialy, Jean-Claude *Actor*
25 Quai Bourbon, 75004 Paris, France
Brian, Earl W *Publisher*
%United Press International, 1400 I St NW, Washington, DC 20005, USA
Brice, William J *Artist*
427 Beloit St, Los Angeles, CA 90049, USA
Brickel, James R *Air Force General, Hero*
4798 Hanging Moss Lane, Sarasota, FL 34238, USA
Brickell, Beth *Movie, Television Director*
PO Box 119, Paron, AR 72122, USA
Brickell, Edie *Singer (New Bohemians), Songwriter*
88 Central Park West, New York, NY 10023, USA
Bricker, Neal S *Physician*
4240 Piedmont Mesa Road, Claremont, CA 91711, USA
Brickhouse, Smith N *Religious Leader*
%Church of Christ, PO Box 472, Independence, MO 64051, USA
Bricklin, Daniel S *Computer Software Designer (VisiCalc)*
%Trellix Corp, 300 Bahr Ave, Concord, MA 01742, USA
Brickman, Jim *Pianist*
%Brickman Music, 11288 Ventura Blvd, #606, Studio City, CA 91604, USA
Brickman, Paul M *Movie Director*
4116 Holly Knoll Dr, Los Angeles, CA 90027, USA
Bricusse, Leslie *Composer, Lyricist*
8730 Sunset Blvd, #300W, Los Angeles, CA 90069, USA
Bridges, Alan J S *Movie Director*
2B High St, Shepperton, Middx TW7 9AW, England
Bridges, Alicia *Singer, Songwriter*
%Talent Consultants International, 1560 Broadway, #1308, New York, NY 10036, USA
Bridges, Angelica *Actress, Model*
7095 Hollywood Blvd, #771, Los Angeles, CA 90028, USA
Bridges, Beau *Actor*
5525 N Jed Smith Road, Hidden Hills, CA 91302, USA
Bridges, Bill *Basketball Player*
145 Bay St, #19, Santa Monica, CA 90405, USA
Bridges, Jeff *Actor*
985 Hot Springs Road, Montecito, CA 93108, USA
Bridges, Roy D, Jr *Astronaut, Air Force General*
750 N Atlantic Ave, #405, Cocoa Beach, FL 32931, USA
Bridges, Todd A *Actor*
2621 Oakwood Ave, Venice, CA 90291, USA
Bridgewater, Dee Dee *Jazz Singer*
%B H Hopper Mgmt, Elvirastr 25, 80636 Munich, Germany
Bridwell, Norman *Writer*
PO Box 869, Edgartown, MA 02539, USA
Brierley, Ronald A *Businessman*
%Guinness Peat Group, 21-26 Garlick Hill, London EC4V 2AU, England
Briers, Richard *Actor, Comedian*
%Hamilton Asper Mgmt, 24 Hanway St, London W1P 9DD, England
Brigati, Eddie *Singer, Songwriter (Rascals)*
%Dassinger Creative, 32 Ardsley Road, #201, Montclair, NJ 07042, USA
Briggs of Lewes, Asa *Historian*
Caprons, Keere St, Lewes, Sussex, England
Briggs, Edward S *Navy Admiral*
3648 Lago Sereno, Escondido, CA 92029, USA
Briggs, Raymond R *Writer, Illustrator, Cartoonist*
Weston, Underhill Lane, Westmeston near Hassocks, Sussex, England
Briggs, Robert W *Plant Biologist*
480 Hale St, Palo Alto, CA 94301, USA
Bright, Myron H *Judge*
655 1st Ave N, #340, Fargo, ND 58102, USA
Brightman, Sarah *Singer*
%Feinstein Mgmt, 420 Lexington Ave, #2150, New York, NY 10170, USA
Briles, Nelson K *Baseball Player*
78 Lakewood Road, Greensburg, PA 15601, USA
Brill, Charlie *Actor*
3635 Wrightwood Dr, Studio City, CA 91604, USA
Brill, Francesca *Actress*
%Kate Feast, Primrose Hill Studios, Fitzroy Road, London NW1 8TR, England
Brill, Steven *Editor, Publisher*
%American Lawyer Magazine, 600 3rd Ave, New York, NY 10016, USA
Brill, Steven *Movie Director, Writer*
%International Creative Mgmt, 8942 Wilshire Blvd, #219, Beverly Hills, CA 90211, USA
Brill, Winston J *Bacteriologist*
12529 237th Way NE, Redmond, WA 98053, USA
Brillstein, Bernie *Television Producer, Agent*
%Brillstein/Grey, 9150 Wilshire Blvd, #350, Beverly Hills, CA 90212, USA

Brimley, Wilford *Actor*
B7 Ranch, 10000 North, Lehi, UT 84043, USA
Brimmer, Andrew F *Government Official, Economist*
%Brimmer Co, 4400 MacArthur Blvd NW, Washington, DC 20007, USA
Brin, Sergey *Businessman, Computer Engineer*
%Google Inc, 2400 Bayshore Parkway, Mountain View, CA 94043, USA
Brinegar, Claude S *Secretary, Transportation; Businessman*
PO Box 4346, Stanford, CA 94309, USA
Bring, Murray H *Businessman*
%Altria Group, 120 Park Ave, New York, NY 10017, USA
Brink, Andre P *Writer*
%University of Cape Town, English Dept, Rondebosch 7700, South Africa
Brink, Frank, Jr *Biophysicist*
Pine Run, #E1, Ferry & Iron Hill Roads, Doylestown, PA 18901, USA
Brink, K Robert *Publisher*
%Town & Country Magazine, 1700 Broadway, New York, NY 10019, USA
Brink, R Alexander *Geneticist*
8301 Old Sauk Road, #326, Middleton, WI 53562, USA
Brinkley, Christie *Model, Actress*
%Ford Model Agency, 142 Greene St, #400, New York, NY 10012, USA
Brinkman, John A *Historian*
1321 E 56th St, #4, Chicago, IL 60637, USA
Brinkman, William F *Physicist*
20 Constitution Hill W, Princeton, NJ 08540, USA
Brinkmann, Robert S *Cinematographer*
%Spyros Skouras, 631 Wilshire Blvd, #2C, Santa Monica, CA 90401, USA
Brinster, Ralph L *Biologist*
%University of Pennsylvania, Veterinary Medicine School, Philadelphia, PA 19104, USA
Brion, John *Composer*
%Gorfaine/Schwartz, 13245 Riverside Dr, #450, Sherman Oaks, CA 91423, USA
Brisco, Jack *Wrestler*
19018 Blake Road, Odessa, FL 33556, USA
Brisco, Valerie *Track Athlete*
%USA Track & Field, 4341 Starlight Dr, Indianapolis, IN 46239, USA
Briscoe, Dolph, Jr *Governor, TX*
338 Pecan St, Uvalde, TX 78801, USA
Briscoe, Marlin *Football Player*
379 Newport Ave, #107, Long Beach, CA 90814, USA
Briscoe, Mary Beck *Judge*
%US Appeals Court, 4839 W 15th St, Lawrence, KS 66049, USA
Brisebois, Danielle *Actress, Singer*
%Haber Corp, 16830 Ventura Blvd, #501, Encino, CA 91436, USA
Brissie, Leland V (Lou) *Baseball Player*
1908 White Pine Dr, North Augusta, SC 29841, USA
Brister, Walter A (Bubby), III *Football Player*
139 Fontainbleau Dr, Mandeville, LA 70471, USA
Bristow, Allan M *Basketball Player, Coach, Executive*
PO Box 635, Gloucester Point, VA 23062, USA
Britain, Radie *Composer*
PO Box 17, Smithville, IN 47458, USA
Britt, Chris *Editorial Cartoonist*
%State Journal-Register, Editorial Dept, 1 Copley Plaza, Springfield, IL 62701, USA
Britt, Michael *Guitarist (Lonestar)*
%Borman Entertainment, 1222 16th Ave S, #23, Nashville, TN 37212, USA
Brittany, Morgan *Actress, Model*
3434 Cornell Road, Agoura Hills, CA 91301, USA
Britten, Roy J *Geneticist*
%Kerckhoff Marine Laboratory, 101 Dahlia Ave, Corona del Mar, CA 92625, USA
Brittenham, Harry *Attorney*
%Ziffren Brittenham Branca, 1801 Century Park West, Los Angeles, CA 90067, USA
Britton, Benjamin *Inventor (Lascaux Virtual Reality Cave)*
%University of Cincinnati, Fine Arts Dept, Cincinnati, OH 45221, USA
Britton, Tony *Actor*
%International Creative Mgmt, 76 Oxford St, London W1N 0AX, England
Britz, Jerilyn *Golfer*
415 E Lincoln St, #7, Luverne, MN 56156, USA
Brizan, George *Prime Minister, Grenada*
%Prime Minister's Office, Botanical Gardens, Saint George's, Grenada
Broadbent, Jim *Actor*
%International Creative Mgmt, 76 Oxford St, London W1N 0AX, England
Broadbent, John Edward *Government Official, Canada*
1386 Nicola, #30, Vancouver BC V6G 2G2, Canada
Broaddus, J Alfred, Jr *Financier*
%Federal Reserve Bank, PO Box 27622, Richmond, VA 23261, USA
Broadhead, James L *Businessman*
%FPL Group, 700 Universe Blvd, Juno Beach, FL 33408, USA
Brobeck, John R *Physiologist*
224 Vassar Ave, Swarthmore, PA 19081, USA

B

Broberg - Bronfman

Broberg, Gus *Basketball Player*
208 El Pueblo Way, Palm Beach, FL 33480, USA
Broches, Aron *Attorney*
44 Pond St, Wakefield, RI 02879, USA
Brochtrup, William (Bill) *Actor*
%S D B Partners, 1801 Ave of Stars, #902, Los Angeles, CA 90067, USA
Brock, Louis C (Lou) *Baseball Player*
61 Barkley Place, Saint Charles, MO 63301, USA
Brock, Stanley J (Stan) *Football Player*
2555 SW 81st Ave, Portland, OR 97225, USA
Brock, William E (Bill), III *Secretary of Labor; Senator, TN*
16 Revell St, Annapolis, MD 21401, USA
Brockert, Richard C *Labor Leader*
%United Telegraph Workers, 701 E Gude Dr, Rockville, MD 20850, USA
Brockington, John *Football Player*
%Equitable Insurance, 701 B St, #1500, San Diego, CA 92101, USA
Brockovich, Erin *Legal Activist, Writer*
5707 Corsa Ave, Westlake Village, CA 91362, USA
Brodbin, Kevin *Writer*
%Creative Artists Agency, 9830 Wilshire Blvd, Beverly Hills, CA 90212, USA
Broder, David S *Columnist*
4024 N 27th St, Arlington, VA 22207, USA
Broder, Samuel *Medical Administrator*
%IVAX Corp, 4400 Biscayne Blvd, Miami, FL 33137, USA
Broderick, Beth *Actress*
%Innovative Artists, 1505 10th St, Santa Monica, CA 90401, USA
Broderick, Matthew *Actor*
246 W 44th St, New York, NY 10036, USA
Brodeur, Martin (Marty) *Hockey Player*
40 Fox Run, North Caldwell, NJ 07006, USA
Brodie, H Keith H *Psychiatrist*
63 Beverly Dr, Durham, NC 27707, USA
Brodie, John R *Football Player, Sportscaster, Golfer*
49350 Avenida Fernando, La Quinta, CA 92253, USA
Brodie, Kevin *Actor*
20023 Lull St, Winnetka, CA 91306, USA
Brodsky, Julian A *Businessman*
%Comcast Corp, 1500 Market St, Philadelphia, PA 19102, USA
Brody, Adrien *Actor*
%Endeavor Talent Agency, 9701 Wilshire Blvd, #1000, Beverly Hills, CA 90212, USA
Brody, Jane E *Journalist*
%New York Times, Editorial Dept, 229 W 43rd St, New York, NY 10036, USA
Brody, Kenneth D *Financier*
%Export-Import Bank, 811 Vermont Ave NW, Washington, DC 20571, USA
Brody, Lane *Singer*
%Black Stallion Country Productions, PO Box 368, Tujunga, CA 91043, USA
Broecker, Wallace S *Geologist, Geochemist*
%Lamont-Doherty Earth Observatory, PO Box 1000, Palisades, NY 10964, USA
Broeg, Robert W (Bob) *Sportswriter*
60 Frontenac Estates Dr, Saint Louis, MO 63131, USA
Broelsch, Christopher E *Surgeon*
%University of Chicago, Medical Center, Surgery Dept, Box 259, Chicago, IL 60690, USA
Brogdon, Cindy *Basketball Player*
4932 Shawdowwood Parkway SE, Atlanta, GA 30339, USA
Broglio, Ernest G (Ernie) *Baseball Player*
2838 Via Carmen, San Jose, CA 95124, USA
Brokaw, Gary *Basketball Player, Coach, Executive*
1477 Langham Terrace, Lake Mary, FL 32746, USA
Brokaw, Thomas J (Tom) *Commentator*
941 Park Ave, #14C, New York, NY 10028, USA
Brolin, James *Actor*
%Metropolitan Talent Agency, 4526 Wilshire Blvd, Los Angeles, CA 90010, USA
Brolin, Josh *Actor*
450 N Rossmore Ave, #704, Los Angeles, CA 90004, USA
Bromfield, John *Actor*
PO Box 2655, Lake Havasu City, AZ 86405, USA
Bromley, D Allan *Government Official, Physicist*
35 Tokeneke Dr, North Haven, CT 06473, USA
Bron, Eleanor *Actress*
%Rebecca Blond, 69A King's Road, London SW3 4WX, England
Bronars, Edward J *Marine Corps General*
3354 Rose Lane, Falls Church, VA 22042, USA
Bronfman, Charles R *Businessman, Baseball Executive*
501 N Lake Way, Palm Beach, FL 33480, USA
Bronfman, Edgar M, Jr *Businessman*
%Seagram Co, 1430 Peel St, Montreal QC H3A 1S9, Canada
Bronfman, Edgar M, Sr *Businessman*
31122 Broad Beach Road, Malibu, CA 90265, USA

Bronfman, Yefin *Concert Pianist*
%I C M Artists, 40 W 57th St, New York, NY 10019, USA
Bronleewe, Matt *Guitarist (Jars of Clay)*
%Flood Bumstead McCready McCarthy, 1700 Hayes St, #304, Nashville, TN 37203, USA
Bronson, Oswald P, Sr *Educator*
%Bethune-Cookman College, President's Office, Daytona Beach, FL 32114, USA
Bronson, Po *Writer*
%Random House, 1745 Broadway, #B1, New York, NY 10019, USA
Brook, Jayne *Actress*
%Gersh Agency, 232 N Canon Dr, Beverly Hills, CA 90210, USA
Brook, Kelly *Model, Actress*
%M&S Mgmt, 13904 Fiji Way, #242, Marina del Rey, CA 90292, USA
Brook, Peter S P *Movie, Theater Director*
%CICT, 13 Blvd de Rochechouart, 75009 Paris, France
Brooke, Edward W, III *Senator, MA*
%O'Connor & Hannan, 1919 Pennsylvania Ave NW, #800, Washington, DC 20006, USA
Brooke, Jonatha *Singer (Story), Songwriter*
%Patrick Rains Assoc, 220 W 93rd St, #7B, New York, NY 10025, USA
Brooke-Taylor, Tim *Actor, Comedian*
%Jill Foster Ltd, 3 Lonsdale Road, London SW13 9ED, England
Brooker, Gary *Singer (Procul Harem), Songwriter*
5 Cranley Gardens, London SW7, England
Brookes, Harvey *Physicist*
%Harvard University, Aiken Computation Laboratory, Cambridge, MA 02138, USA
Brookes, Jacqueline *Actress*
%William Morris Agency, 151 El Camino Dr, Beverly Hills, CA 90212, USA
Brookes, Peter *Editorial Cartoonist*
%London Times, Editorial Dept, 1 Pennington St, London E98 1S5, England
Brookfield, Price *Basketball Player*
90 Fox Run Road, #HC57, Pinehurst, NC 28374, USA
Brookhart, Maurice S *Chemist*
%University of North Carolina, Chemistry Dept, Chapel Hill, NC 27514, USA
Brookins, Gary *Editorial Cartoonist*
%Richmond Newspapers, Editorial Dept, PO Box 85333, Richmond, VA 23293, USA
Brookner, Anita *Writer*
68 Elm Park Gardens, #6, London SW10 9PB, England
Brooks, Aaron *Football Player*
%LPS, PO Box 6282, Newport News, VA 23606, USA
Brooks, Albert *Actor, Director, Writer*
%Moress Nanas Enterprises, 14945 Ventura Blvd, #228, Sherman Oaks, CA 91403, USA
Brooks, Avery *Actor*
%Lynn Coles Productions, PO Box 4082, Oakland, CA 94614, USA
Brooks, Conrad *Actor*
PO Box 1192, Falling Waters, WV 25419, USA
Brooks, Danny *Singer (Dovells)*
%American Promotions, 2011 Ferry Ave, #U19, Camden, NJ 08104, USA
Brooks, Derrick *Football Player*
1713 Cedrus Lane, Pensacola, FL 32514, USA
Brooks, Donald M *Fashion, Theater Designer*
%Costume Guild, 13949 Ventura, #309, Sherman Oaks, CA 91423, USA
Brooks, Donnie *Singer*
%Al Lampkin Entertainment, 1817 W Verdugo Ave, Burbank, CA 91506, USA
Brooks, E R *Businessman*
%Central & South West Corp, 1616 Woodall Rogers Freeway, Dallas, TX 75202, USA
Brooks, Frederick P, Jr *Mathematician, Computer Scientist*
413 Granville Road, Chapel Hill, NC 27514, USA
Brooks, Garth *Singer, Songwriter*
%GB Mgmt, 1111 17th Ave S, Nashville, TN 37212, USA
Brooks, Geraldine *Writer*
%Viking Press, 375 Hudson St, New York, NY 10014, USA
Brooks, Harvey *Physicist*
46 Brewster St, #Y, Cambridge, MA 02138, USA
Brooks, Hubert (Hubie) *Baseball Player*
15001 Olive St, Hesperia, CA 92345, USA
Brooks, James *Football Player*
%Baltimore Ravens, Ravens Stadium, 11001 Russell St, Baltimore, MD 21230, USA
Brooks, James L *Movie Director, Producer, Writer*
833 Moraga Dr, #1, Los Angeles, CA 90049, USA
Brooks, Jason *Actor*
289 S Robertson Blvd, #424, Beverly Hills, CA 90211, USA
Brooks, John E *Educator*
%College of Holy Cross, President's Office, Worcester, MA 01610, USA
Brooks, Karen *Singer*
5408 Clear View Lane, Waterford, WI 53185, USA
Brooks, Kix *Singer (Brooks & Dunn), Songwriter*
%TBA Mgmt, 300 10th Ave S, Nashville, TN 37203, USA
Brooks, Lala *Singer (Crystals)*
%Superstars Unlimited, PO Box 371371, Las Vegas, NV 89137, USA

B

Brooks, Larry L, Sr *Football Player, Coach*
12721 NE 192nd Place, Kirkland, WA 98033, USA
Brooks, Mark *Golfer*
6417 Forest Highlands Dr, Fort Worth, TX 76132, USA
Brooks, Mel *Movie Director, Actor*
23868 Malibu Colony Road, Malibu, CA 90265, USA
Brooks, Meredith *Singer, Songwriter, Guitarist*
%Capitol Records, 1750 N Vine St, Los Angeles, CA 90028, USA
Brooks, Michael *Basketball Player*
495 Bethany St, San Diego, CA 92114, USA
Brooks, Michael *Football Player*
604 Spring Leaf Court, Greensboro, NC 27455, USA
Brooks, Nathan *Boxer*
3139 Albion Road, Cleveland, OH 44120, USA
Brooks, Randi *Actress, Model*
3205 Evergreen Point Road, Medina, WA 98039, USA
Brooks, Rich *Football Coach*
%University of Kentucky, Athletic Dept, Lexington, KY 40506, USA
Brooks, Richard *Actor*
333 Washington Blvd, #102, Marina del Rey, CA 90292, USA
Brooks, William (Bud) *Football Player*
302 Doubloon Circle, Hot Springs, AR 71913, USA
Brookshier, Thomas (Tom) *Sportscaster, Football Player*
1130 Riverview Lane, Conshohouken, PA 19428, USA
Brophy, Kevin *Actor*
15010 Hamlin St, Van Nuys, CA 91411, USA
Brophy, Theodore F *Businessman*
60 Arch St, Greenwich, CT 06830, USA
Brorby, Wade *Judge*
%US Court of Appeals, 2120 Capitol Ave, Cheyenne, WY 82001, USA
Broshears, Robert *Sculptor*
%Robert Broshears Studio, 8020 NW Holly Road, Bremerton, WA 98312, USA
Brosius, Scott D *Baseball Player*
3270 NW Westside Road, McMinnville, OR 97128, USA
Broski, David C *Educator*
%University of Illinois, President's Office, Chicago, IL 60607, USA
Brosky, Albert (Al) *Football Player*
2031 Yellow Daisy Court, Naperville, IL 60563, USA
Brosnan, Pierce *Actor*
24955 Pacific Coast Highway, #C-205, Malibu, CA 90265, USA
Brostek, Bern *Football Player*
%Saint Louis Rams, 901 N Broadway, Saint Louis, MO 63101, USA
Broten, Neal *Hockey Player*
N8216 690th St, Eagan, MN 55123, USA
Brothers, Joyce D *Psychologist*
%NBC Westwood One Radio Network, 524 W 57th St, New York, NY 10019, USA
Brotman, Jeffrey *Businessman*
%Costco Wholesale Corp, 999 Lake Dr, Issaquah, WA 98027, USA
Brough Clapp, A Louise *Tennis Player*
1808 Voluntary Road, Vista, CA 92084, USA
Brough, Randi *Actress*
11684 Ventura Blvd, #476, Studio City, CA 91604, USA
Broughton, Bruce *Composer*
%Air-Edel, 1416 N La Brea Ave, Los Angeles, CA 90028, USA
Broussard, Rebecca *Actress*
9911 W Pico Blvd, #PH A, Los Angeles, CA 90035, USA
Broussard, Steve *Football Player*
2028 Englewood Dr, Biloxi, MS 39532, USA
Brouwenstyn, Gerarda *Opera Singer*
3 Bachplein, Amsterdam, Netherlands
Browder, Felix E *Mathematician*
37 Quince Place, North Brunswick, NJ 08902, USA
Brown Heritage, Doris *Track Athlete*
%Seattle Pacific College, Athletic Dept, Seattle, WA 98119, USA
Brown, Aaron *Commentator*
%Cable News Network, News Dept, 1050 Techwood Dr NW, Atlanta, GA 30318, USA
Brown, Alison *Singer, Songwriter, Banjo Player*
%SRO Artists, 6629 University Ave, #206, Middleton, WI 53562, USA
Brown, Alton *Chef*
%Food Network, 1180 Ave of Americas, #1200, New York, NY 10036, USA
Brown, Amanda *Writer*
%EP Dutton, 375 Hudson St, New York, NY 10014, USA
Brown, Arthur E, Jr *Army General*
35 Fairway Winds Place, Hilton Head Island, SC 29928, USA
Brown, Ashley Nicole *Actress*
%Hervey/Grimes, PO Box 64249, Los Angeles, CA 90064, USA
Brown, Bailey *Judge*
%US Court of Appeals, Federal Building, 167 N Main St, Memphis, TN 38103, USA

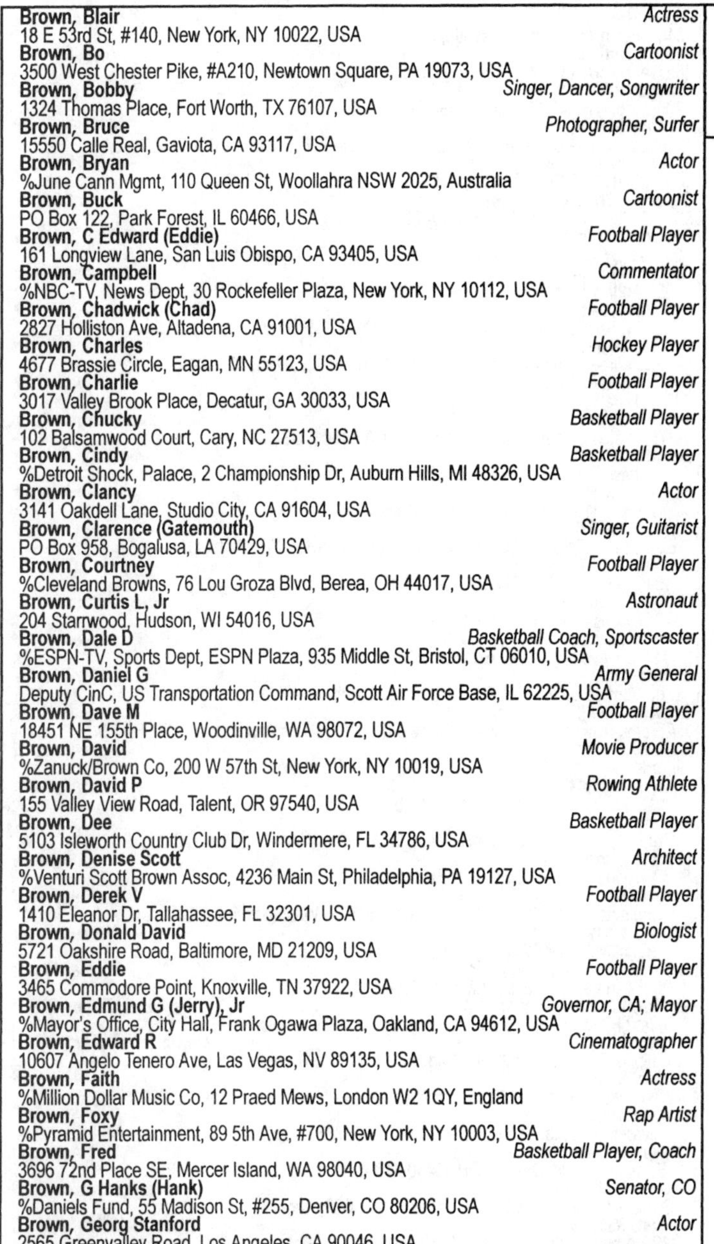

Brown, Blair *Actress*
18 E 53rd St, #140, New York, NY 10022, USA
Brown, Bo *Cartoonist*
3500 West Chester Pike, #A210, Newtown Square, PA 19073, USA
Brown, Bobby *Singer, Dancer, Songwriter*
1324 Thomas Place, Fort Worth, TX 76107, USA
Brown, Bruce *Photographer, Surfer*
15550 Calle Real, Gaviota, CA 93117, USA
Brown, Bryan *Actor*
%June Cann Mgmt, 110 Queen St, Woollahra NSW 2025, Australia
Brown, Buck *Cartoonist*
PO Box 122, Park Forest, IL 60466, USA
Brown, C Edward (Eddie) *Football Player*
161 Longview Lane, San Luis Obispo, CA 93405, USA
Brown, Campbell *Commentator*
%NBC-TV, News Dept, 30 Rockefeller Plaza, New York, NY 10112, USA
Brown, Chadwick (Chad) *Football Player*
2827 Holliston Ave, Altadena, CA 91001, USA
Brown, Charles *Hockey Player*
4677 Brassie Circle, Eagan, MN 55123, USA
Brown, Charlie *Football Player*
3017 Valley Brook Place, Decatur, GA 30033, USA
Brown, Chucky *Basketball Player*
102 Balsamwood Court, Cary, NC 27513, USA
Brown, Cindy *Basketball Player*
%Detroit Shock, Palace, 2 Championship Dr, Auburn Hills, MI 48326, USA
Brown, Clancy *Actor*
3141 Oakdell Lane, Studio City, CA 91604, USA
Brown, Clarence (Gatemouth) *Singer, Guitarist*
PO Box 958, Bogalusa, LA 70429, USA
Brown, Courtney *Football Player*
%Cleveland Browns, 76 Lou Groza Blvd, Berea, OH 44017, USA
Brown, Curtis L, Jr *Astronaut*
204 Starrwood, Hudson, WI 54016, USA
Brown, Dale D *Basketball Coach, Sportscaster*
%ESPN-TV, Sports Dept, ESPN Plaza, 935 Middle St, Bristol, CT 06010, USA
Brown, Daniel G *Army General*
Deputy CinC, US Transportation Command, Scott Air Force Base, IL 62225, USA
Brown, Dave M *Football Player*
18451 NE 155th Place, Woodinville, WA 98072, USA
Brown, David *Movie Producer*
%Zanuck/Brown Co, 200 W 57th St, New York, NY 10019, USA
Brown, David P *Rowing Athlete*
155 Valley View Road, Talent, OR 97540, USA
Brown, Dee *Basketball Player*
5103 Isleworth Country Club Dr, Windermere, FL 34786, USA
Brown, Denise Scott *Architect*
%Venturi Scott Brown Assoc, 4236 Main St, Philadelphia, PA 19127, USA
Brown, Derek V *Football Player*
1410 Eleanor Dr, Tallahassee, FL 32301, USA
Brown, Donald David *Biologist*
5721 Oakshire Road, Baltimore, MD 21209, USA
Brown, Eddie *Football Player*
3465 Commodore Point, Knoxville, TN 37922, USA
Brown, Edmund G (Jerry), Jr *Governor, CA; Mayor*
%Mayor's Office, City Hall, Frank Ogawa Plaza, Oakland, CA 94612, USA
Brown, Edward R *Cinematographer*
10607 Angelo Tenero Ave, Las Vegas, NV 89135, USA
Brown, Faith *Actress*
%Million Dollar Music Co, 12 Praed Mews, London W2 1QY, England
Brown, Foxy *Rap Artist*
%Pyramid Entertainment, 89 5th Ave, #700, New York, NY 10003, USA
Brown, Fred *Basketball Player, Coach*
3696 72nd Place SE, Mercer Island, WA 98040, USA
Brown, G Hanks (Hank) *Senator, CO*
%Daniels Fund, 55 Madison St, #255, Denver, CO 80206, USA
Brown, Georg Stanford *Actor*
2565 Greenvalley Road, Los Angeles, CA 90046, USA
Brown, George C, Jr *Football Player*
12517 Lakeshore Dr, Lakeside, CA 92040, USA
Brown, Harold *Secretary, Defense*
%Strategic/International Studies Center, 1800 K St NW, Washington, DC 20006, USA
Brown, Helen Gurley *Editor, Writer*
1 W 81st St, #22D, New York, NY 10024, USA
Brown, Henry *Actor*
1101 E Pike St, #300, Seattle, WA 98122, USA
Brown, Henry W *WW II Army Air Force Hero*
2389 Mount Vernon Dr, Sumter, SC 29154, USA

Brown, Herbert C *Nobel Chemistry Laureate*
1014 Lincoln Trail, West Lafayette, IN 47906, USA
Brown, Himan *Theater Director*
285 Central Park W, New York, NY 10024, USA
Brown, Hubie *Basketball Coach*
120 Foxridge Road NW, Atlanta, GA 30327, USA
Brown, Hyman *Civil Engineer*
%Colorado State University, Civil Engineering Dept, Fort Collins, CO 80523, USA
Brown, Iona *Concert Violinist, Conductor*
%I M G Artists, 3 Burlington Lane, Chiswick, London W4 2TH, England
Brown, J Cristopher (Cris) *Baseball Player*
5015 Brighton Ave, Los Angeles, CA 90062, USA
Brown, J Gordon *Government Official, England*
%House of Commons, Westminster, London SW1A 0AA, England
Brown, J Kevin *Baseball Player*
14023 Audrey Road, Beverly Hills, CA 90210, USA
Brown, James *Sportscaster*
%Fox-TV, Sports Dept, 205 W 67th St, New York, NY 10021, USA
Brown, James *Singer*
%James Brown Enterprises, PO Box 1051, Augusta, GA 30903, USA
Brown, James (Jim) *Actor*
20543 Tiara St, Woodland Hills, CA 91367, USA
Brown, James N (Jim) *Football Player, Actor*
11176 Huston St, #201, North Hollywood, CA 91601, USA
Brown, James R *Air Force General*
1591 Stowe Road, Reston, VA 20194, USA
Brown, Jay W, Jr *Financier*
%MBIA Inc, 113 King St, Armonk, NY 10504, USA
Brown, Jim Ed *Singer*
%Billy Deaton Talent, 5811 Still Hollow Road, Nashville, TN 37215, USA
Brown, Joe *Boxer*
1615 N Broad St, New Orleans, LA 70119, USA
Brown, John *Basketball Player*
1329 N Florissant Road, Saint Louis, MO 63135, USA
Brown, John Y, Jr *Governor, KY*
2601 Old Cave Hill Lane, Lexington, KY 40513, USA
Brown, Julie *Actress, Comedienne*
11288 Ventura Blvd, #728, Studio City, CA 91604, USA
Brown, Julie (Downtown) *Entertainer*
%Abrams-Rubaloff Lawrence, 8075 W 3rd St, #303, Los Angeles, CA 90048, USA
Brown, Junior *Singer, Guitarist*
%Force Inc, 1505 16th Ave S, Nashville, TN 37212, USA
Brown, Kedrick *Basketball Player*
%Boston Celtics, 151 Merrimac St, #1, Boston, MA 02114, USA
Brown, Kenneth J *Labor Leader*
%Graphic Communications Int'l Union, 1900 L St NW, Washington, DC 20036, USA
Brown, Kimberly J *Actress*
2069 Troon Dr, Henderson, NV 89074, USA
Brown, Kwame *Basketball Player*
%Washington Wizards, MCI Centre, 601 F St NW, Washington, DC 20004, USA
Brown, Larry *Hockey Player*
5781 Eucalyptus Dr, Garden Valley, CA 95633, USA
Brown, Lawrence (Larry), Jr *Football Player*
4390 Parliament Place, #A, Lanham, MD 20706, USA
Brown, Lawrence H (Larry) *Basketball Player, Coach*
%Detroit Pistons, Palace, 2 Championship Dr, Auburn Hills, MI 48326, USA
Brown, Lee P *Mayor, Government Official*
%Mayor's Office, City Hall, 901 Bagby St, #300, Houston, TX 77002, USA
Brown, Lester R *Ecologist*
%Worldwatch Institute, 1776 Massachusetts Ave NW, Washington, DC 20036, USA
Brown, Mack *Football Coach*
%University of Texas, Athletic Dept, Austin, TX 78712, USA
Brown, Mark N *Astronaut*
80 Earlsgate Road, Dayton, OH 45440, USA
Brown, Melanie *Singer (Spice Girls)*
%Spice Girls Ltd, 66-68 Bell St, London NW1 6SP, England
Brown, Michael S *Nobel Medicine Laureate*
5719 Redwood Lane, Dallas, TX 75209, USA
Brown, Mike *Football Executive*
%Cincinnati Bengals, 1 Paul Brown Stadium, Cincinnati, OH 45202, USA
Brown, Mike *Astronomer*
%California Institute of Technology, Astronomy Dept, Pasadena, CA 91125, USA
Brown, Napoleon (Nappy) *Singer*
1023 Moretz Ave, Charlotte, NC 28206, USA
Brown, Norman W *Businessman*
%Foote Cone Belding, 101 E Erie St, Chicago, IL 60611, USA
Brown, Olivia *Actress*
%David Shapira, 15821 Ventura Blvd, #235, Encino, CA 91436, USA

Brown, Owsley, II *Businessman*
%Brown-Forman Corp, 850 Dixie Highway, Louisville, KY 40210, USA
Brown, P J *Basketball Player*
903 Beverly Dr, Carthage, TX 75633, USA
Brown, Patrick *Biochemist*
%Stanford University, Medical School, Biochemistry Dept, Stanford, CA 94305, USA
Brown, Peter *Actor*
5328 Alhama Dr, Woodland Hills, CA 91364, USA
Brown, Phil *Actor*
23388 Mulholland Dr, #305, Woodland Hills, CA 91364, USA
Brown, Philip *Actor*
8721 Sunset Blvd, #200, Los Angeles, CA 90069, USA
Brown, R Hanbury *Astronomer*
%White Cottage, Penton Mewsey, Andover, Hants SP11 0RQ, England
Brown, Ray *Football Player*
%Detroit Lions, 222 Republic Dr, Allen Park, MI 48101, USA
Brown, Reb *Actor*
5454 Virgenes Road, Calabasas, CA 91302, USA
Brown, Reggie *Football Player*
2242 NW 93rd Terrace, Miami, FL 33147, USA
Brown, Richard E (Tex), III *Air Force General*
Deputy CofS for Personnel, HqUSAF, Pentagon, Washington, DC 20330, USA
Brown, Rita Mae *Writer, Social Activist*
%Wendy Weill Agency, 232 Madison Ave, New York, NY 10016, USA
Brown, Robert (Bobby) *Baseball Player, Executive*
4100 Clark Ave, Fort Worth, TX 76107, USA
Brown, Robert D *Businessman*
%Milacron Inc, 2090 Florence Ave, 2090 Florence Ave, Cincinnati, OH 45206, USA
Brown, Roger L *Football Player*
9 N Point Dr, Portsmouth, VA 23703, USA
Brown, Ron J *Football Player, Track Athlete*
3363 Milbury Ave, Baldwin Park, CA 91706, USA
Brown, Roosevelt, Jr *Football Player*
3 Hawk Dr, Columbus, NJ 08022, USA
Brown, Ruben *Football Player*
170 Fox Meadow Lane, Orchard Park, NY
Brown, Ruth *Singer*
%Rosebud Agency, PO Box 170429, San Francisco, CA 94117, USA
Brown, Sandra *Writer*
1306 W Abram St, Arlington, TX 76013, USA
Brown, Sara *Actress*
%Media Artists Group, 6300 Wilshire Blvd, #1470, Los Angeles, CA 90048, USA
Brown, Susan *Actress*
11931 Addison St, North Hollywood, CA 91607, USA
Brown, T Graham *Singer*
%Bobby Roberts, 909 Meadowlark Lane, Goodlettsville, TN 37072, USA
Brown, Theotis J *Football Player*
9604 W 121st Terrace, Overland Park, KS 66213, USA
Brown, Timothy D (Tim) *Football Player*
505 S Farrell Dr, #E28, Palm Springs, CA 92264, USA
Brown, Tom *Football Player*
679 Aldford Ave, Delta BC V3M 5P5, Canada
Brown, Tracy *Ballerina*
%Royal Ballet, Covent Garden, Bow St, London WC2E 9DD, England
Brown, Trisha *Choreographer, Dancer*
%Trisha Brown Dance Co, 211 W 61st St, New York, NY 10023, USA
Brown, Vincent B *Football Player*
1615 Thoreau Dr, Suwanee, GA 30024, USA
Brown, William D (Bill) *Football Player*
%Bromley Printing, 514 Northdale Blvd, Minneapolis, MN 55448, USA
Brown, William F (Willie) *Football Player, Coach*
27138 Lillegard Court, Tracy, CA 95304, USA
Browne, Chris *Cartoonist (Hagar the Horrible)*
%King Features Syndicate, 888 7th Ave, New York, NY 10106, USA
Browne, E John P *Businessman*
%BP Exploration Co, 1 Finsbury Circus, London EC2M 7BA, England
Browne, Gerald *Writer*
%Warner Books, 1271 6th Ave, New York, NY 10020, USA
Browne, Jackson *Singer, Songwriter*
%Donald Miller Mgmt, 12746 Kling St, Studio City, CA 91604, USA
Browne, Leslie *Ballerina, Actress*
2025 Broadway, #6F, New York, NY 10023, USA
Browne, Olin *Golfer*
%Larry Hayes, 1051 Runnymede Road, Dayton, OH 45419, USA
Browne, Roscoe Lee *Actor*
465 W 57th St, #1A, New York, NY 10019, USA
Browne, Secor D *Aviation Engineer, Government Official*
2101 L St NW, #207, Washington, DC 20037, USA

B

Browner - Brunell

Browner, Joey *Football Player*
PO Box 571, Pierz, MN 56364, USA
Browner, Keith *Football Player*
10200 Gandy Blvd, N, #620, Saint Petersburg, FL 33702, USA
Browner, Ross *Football Player*
%Ross Browner Enterprises, 1135 Flamingo Dr SW, Atlanta, GA 30311, USA
Browning, Dominique *Editor*
%Mirabella Magazine, Editorial Dept, 200 Madison Ave, New York, NY 10016, USA
Browning, Edmond L *Religious Leader*
5164 Imai Road, Hood River, OR 97031, USA
Browning, James R *Judge*
%US Court of Appeals, Court Building, 95 7th St, San Francisco, CA 94103, USA
Browning, Kurt *Figure Skater*
%Int'l Management Group, 175 Bloor St E, #400, Toronto ON M4W 3R8 Canada
Browning, Ricou *Actor*
5221 SW 196th Lane, Southwest Ranches, FL 33332, USA
Browning, Ryan *Actor*
%United Talent Agency, 9560 Wilshire Blvd, #500, Beverly Hills, CA 90212, USA
Browning, Thomas L (Tom) *Baseball Player*
3094 Friars St, Edgewood, KY 41017, USA
Brownlow, Kevin *Movie, Television Producer*
%Photoplay Productions, 21 Princes Road, London NW1, England
Brownmiller, Susan *Social Activist*
61 Jane St, New York, NY 10014, USA
Brownstein, Carrie *Singer, Guitarist (Sleater-Kinney)*
%Legends of 21st Century, 7 Trinity Row, Florence, MA 01062, USA
Brownstein, Michael L *Publisher*
%Ladies Home Journal, 125 Park Ave, New York, NY 10017, USA
Broyles, Frank F *Football Player, Coach, Sportscaster*
%University of Arkansas, Broyles Athletic Complex, Fayetteville, AR 72701, USA
Brubeck, David W (Dave) *Jazz Pianist*
221 Millstone Road, Wilton, CT 06897, USA
Brubeck, William H *Government Official*
7 Linden St, Cambridge, MA 02138, USA
Bruce, Aundray *Football Player*
1730 Wentworth Dr, Montgomery, AL 36106, USA
Bruce, Carol *Actress, Singer*
1055 N Kingsley Dr #AD-405, Los Angeles, CA 90029, USA
Bruce, Christopher *Choreographer*
%Rambert Dance Co, 94 Chiswick High Road, London W4 1SH, England
Bruce, Isaac I *Football Player*
373 NW 29th Ave, Fort Lauderdale, FL 33311, USA
Bruce, Jack *Singer (Cream), Bassist, Songwriter*
%International Creative Mgmt, 40 W 57th St, #1800, New York, NY 10019, USA
Bruce, Robert V *Historian*
3923 Westpark Court NW, Olympia, WA 98502, USA
Bruce, Thomas (Tom) *Swimmer*
122 Seaterrace Way, Aptos, CA 95003, USA
Bruckheimer, Jerry *Movie, Television Producer*
%Jerry Bruckheimer Films, 1631 10th St, Santa Monica, CA 90404, USA
Brudzinski, Robert L (Bob) *Football Player*
5466 W Sample Road, Margate, FL 33073, USA
Bruel, Patrick *Singer*
%Artmedia, 20 Ave Rapp, 75007 Paris, France
Brueland, Lowell K *WW II Army Air Force Hero*
118 Fairview Circle, Brewton,AL 36426, USA
Bruen, John D *Army General, Businessman*
6104 Greenlawn Court, Springfield, VA 22152, USA
Bruggink, Eric G *Judge*
%US Claims Court, 717 Madison Place NW, Washington, DC 20439, USA
Bruguera, Sergi *Tennis Player*
C'Escipion 42, 08023 Barcelona, Spain
Brumback, Charles T *Publisher*
1500 N Lake Shore Dr, Chicago, IL 60610, USA
Brumfield, Jacob D *Baseball Player*
43275 Tillman Dr, Hammond, LA 70403, USA
Brumm, Donald D (Don) *Football Player*
511 County Road 442, New Franklin, MO 65274, USA
Brummer, Renate *Astronaut, Germany*
%NOAA/FSL, 325 Broadway, Boulder, CO 80305, USA
Brunansky, Thomas A (Tom) *Baseball Player*
13411 Summit Circle, Poway, CA 92064, USA
Brundage, Howard D *Publisher*
RR 2 Box 332-47, Old Lyme, CT 06371, USA
Brundige, Bill *Football Player*
RR 2, Moneta, VA 24121, USA
Brunell, Mark *Football Player*
911 Ponte Vedra Blvd, Ponte Vedra, FL 32082, USA

Bruner, Jerome S *Psychologist*
200 Mercer St, New York, NY 10012, USA
Bruner, Michael L (Mike) *Swimmer*
1518 Hillview Dr, Los Altos, CA 94024, USA
Brunet, Andree Joly *Figure Skater*
2805 Boyne City Road, Boyne City, MI 49712, USA
Brunetti, Melvin T *Judge*
%US Court of Appeals, 40 W Liberty St, Reno, NV 89501, USA
Brunetti, Wayne H *Businessman*
%New Century Energies, 1225 17th St, Denver, CO 80202, USA
Bruni, Carla *Model, Singer, Songwriter*
%Marilyn Gauthier Agency, 4 Rue de la Paix, 75002 Paris, France
Brunner, J Terrance *Association Executive*
%Better Government Assn, 230 N Michigan Ave, Chicago, IL 60601, USA
Brunner, Jerome S *Psychologist, Educator*
200 Mercer St, New York, NY 10012, USA
Bruno, Chris *Actor*
%Stone Manners, 6500 Wilshire Blvd, #550, Los Angeles, CA 90048, USA
Bruno, Dylan *Actor*
%Gersh Agency, 232 N Canon Dr, Beverly Hills, CA 90210, USA
Bruno, Franklin R (Frank) *Boxer*
PO Box 2266, Brentwood, Essex CM15 0AQ, England
Bruschi, Tedy *Football Player*
21 Red Oak Road, North Attleboro, MA 02760, USA
Bruskin, Grisha *Artist*
236 W 26th St, #705, New York, NY 10001, USA
Bruson, Renato *Opera Singer*
%Columbia Artists Mgmt Inc, 165 W 57th St, New York, NY 10019, USA
Brustein, Robert S *Educator, Theater Producer, Critic*
%Harvard University, Loeb Drama Center, 64 Brattle St, Cambridge, MA 02138, USA
Bruton, John G *Prime Minister, Ireland*
Cornelstown, Dunboyne, County Meath, Ireland
Bry, Ellen *Actress*
%Media Artists Group, 6300 Wilshire Blvd, #1470, Los Angeles, CA 90048, USA
Bryan, Alan *Archaeologist*
%University of Alberta, Archaeology Dept, Edmonton AB T6G 2J8, Canada
Bryan, David *Keyboardist (Bon Jovi)*
%Bon Jovi Mgmt, 248 W 17th St, #501, New York, NY 10011, USA
Bryan, Donald S *WW II Army Air Force Hero*
702 Melba St, Adel, GA 31620, USA
Bryan, Dora *Actress*
11 Marine Parade, Brighton, Sussex, England
Bryan, Mark *Guitarist (Hootie & the Blowfish)*
%FishCo Mgmt, PO Box 5656, Columbia, SC 29250, USA
Bryan, Rick D *Football Player*
804 E South St, Coweta, OK 74429, USA
Bryan, Wright *Journalist*
3747 Peachtree Road NE, #516, Atlanta, GA 30319, USA
Bryan, Zachary Ty *Actor*
%Poz Entertainment, 2222 Foothill Blvd, #E285, La Canada, CA 91011, USA
Bryant Clark, Rosalyn *Track Athlete*
3901 Somerset Dr, Los Angeles, CA 90008, USA
Bryant, Anita *Singer, Social Activist*
%Blackwood Mgmt, PO Box 5331, Sevierville, TN 37864, USA
Bryant, Brad *Golfer*
2622 Northampton Ave, Orlando, FL 32828, USA
Bryant, Gay *Editor*
34 Horatio St, New York, NY 10014, USA
Bryant, Gyude *President, Liberia*
%President's Office, Executive Mansion, Capitol Hill, Monrovia, Liberia
Bryant, Joshua *Actor*
216 Paseo Del Pueblo Norte, #M, Taos, NM 87571, USA
Bryant, Kelvin *Football Player*
1803 Chiles Higgins Court, Greensboro, NC 27406, USA
Bryant, Kobe *Basketball Player*
PO Box 491787, Los Angeles, CA 90049, USA
Bryant, Mark *Basketball Player*
107 Kirkwood Court, Sugar Land, TX 77478, USA
Bryant, Ray *Jazz Pianist*
%Maxine Harvard Unlimited, 7942 W Bell Road, Glendale, AZ 85308, USA
Bryant, Todd *Actor*
9150 Wilshire Blvd, #175, Beverly Hills, CA 90212, USA
Bryant, W Cullen *Football Player*
6495 Timber Bluff Point, Colorado Springs, CO 80918, USA
Bryant, Waymond *Football Player*
2440 Covington Dr, Flower Mound, TX 75028, USA
Bryant, Wendell *Football Player*
%Arizona Cardinals, PO Box 888, Phoenix, AZ 85001, USA

B

Bryars - Buck

Bryars, R Gavin *Composer*
%Bolton-Quinn Ltd, 8 Pottery Lane, London W11 4LZ, England
Bryson, John E *Businessman*
%Edison International, 2244 Walnut Grove Ave, Rosemead, CA 91770, USA
Bryson, Peabo *Singer, Songwriter*
%Agency for Performing Arts, 9200 Sunset Blvd, #900, Los Angeles, CA 90069, USA
Bryson, William C *Judge*
%US Appeals Court, 717 Madison Place NW, Washington, DC 20439, USA
Brzeska, Magdalena *Rhythmic Gymnast*
%Vitesse Karcher GmbH, Porscestr 6, 70736 Fellbach, Germany
Brzezinski, Zbigniew *Government Official, Educator*
%Strategic/International Studies Center, 1800 K NW, Washington, DC 20006, USA
Buatta, Mario *Interior Designer*
120 E 80th St, New York, NY 10021, USA
Bubas, Vic *Basketball Player, Coach*
133 Robert E Lee Lane, Bluffton, SC 29909, USA
Bubka, Sergei N *Track Athlete*
%Andresj Kulikowski, Vasavagen 13, 171 39 Solna, Sweden
Bubna, P F *Religious Leader*
%Christian & Missionary Alliance, PO Box 3500, Colorado Springs, CO 80935, USA
Buccellati, Giorgio *Anthropologist*
%University of California, Near Eastern Languages Dept, Los Angeles, CA 90024, USA
Buccellato, Benedetta *Actress*
%Carol Levi Co, Via Giuseppe Pisanelli, 00196 Rome, Italy
Bucha, Paul W *Vietnam War Army Hero (CMH)*
601 N Salem Road, Ridgefield, CT 06877, USA
Buchanan, Edna *Journalist*
PO Box 403556, Miami Beach, FL 33140, USA
Buchanan, Ian *Actor, Model*
%Gold Marshak Liedtke, 3500 W Olive Ave, #1400, Burbank, CA 91505, USA
Buchanan, Isobel *Opera Singer*
%Marks Mgmt, 14 New Burlington St, London W1X 1FF, England
Buchanan, James M *Nobel Economics Laureate*
%George Mason University, Study of Public Choice Center, Fairfax, VA 22030, USA
Buchanan, Jensen *Actress*
%Paradigm Agency, 10100 Santa Monica Blvd, #2500, Los Angeles, CA 90067, USA
Buchanan, John M *Biochemist*
56 Meriam St, Lexington, MA 02420, USA
Buchanan, John M *Religious Leader*
%Presbyterian Church USA, 100 Witherspoon St, Louisville, KY 40202, USA
Buchanan, Ken *Boxer*
45 Marmion Road, Greenfaulds, Cumbernaul G67 4AN, Scotland
Buchanan, Larry *Movie Director*
4154 Via Andorra, #B, Santa Barbara, CA 93110, USA
Buchanan, Patrick J (Pat) *Commentator, Government Official*
8233 Old Courthouse Road, #200, Vienna, VA 22182, USA
Buchanan, Raymond L (Ray) *Football Player*
1010 Ridgewood Dr, Bolingbrook, IL 60440, USA
Buchanan, Robert S *Astronaut*
3 Lariat Lane, Rolling Hills, CA 90274, USA
Buchanon, Willie J *Football Player*
227 Cottingham Court, Oceanside, CA 92054, USA
Buchbinder, Rudolf *Concert Pianist*
%Columbia Artists Mgmt Inc, 165 W 57th St, New York, NY 10019, USA
Buchel, Marco *Alpine Skier*
Ramschwagweg 55, 9496 Balzers, Switzerland
Bucher, Lloyd M *Navy Hero, Captain of USS Pueblo*
16296 Rostrata Hill, Poway, CA 92064, USA
Buchheim, Lothar-Gunther *Writer*
Johann-Biersack-Str 23, 82340 Feldafing, Germany
Buchli, James F (Jim) *Astronaut*
1602 Fairoaks St, Seabrook, TX 77586, USA
Buchmann, Rainer *Auto Racing Executive*
%Project Indy, 434 E Main St, Brownsburg, IN 46112, USA
Buchwald, Art *Columnist*
4329 Hawthorne St NW, #W, Washington, DC 20016, USA
Buck, Craig *Volleyball Player*
PO Box 603, Goleta, CA 93116, USA
Buck, Detlev *Movie Director*
%Agentur Sigrid Narjes, Goethestr 17, 80336 Munich, Germany
Buck, Joe *Sportscaster*
%Fox-TV, Sports Dept, PO Box 900, Beverly Hills, CA 90213, USA
Buck, Mike E *Football Player*
321 Fox Den Court, Destin, FL 32541, USA
Buck, Peter *Guitarist (REM)*
%Rem/Athens Ltd, 170 College Ave, Athens, GA 30601, USA
Buck, Robert T, Jr *Museum Director*
%Brooklyn Museum, 200 Eastern Parkway, Brooklyn, NY 11238, USA

Buckbee, Ed *Space Scientist*
47 Revere Way, Huntsville, AL 35801, USA
Buckey, Jay C, Jr *Astronaut*
14 Valley Road, Hanover, NH 03755, USA
Buckingham, Gregory (Greg) *Swimmer*
338 Ridge Road, San Carlos, CA 94070, USA
Buckingham, Lindsey *Guitarist, Singer (Fleetwood Mac)*
%East End Mgmt, 8209 Melrose Ave, #200, Los Angeles, CA 90046, USA
Buckingham, Marcus *Writer*
%Simon & Schuster/Pocket/Summit, 1230 Ave of Americas, New York, NY 10020, USA
Buckland, Jonny *Guitarist (Coldplay)*
%Nettwerk Mgmt, 1650 W 2nd Ave, Vancouver BC V6J 4R3, Canada
Buckles, Bradley *Government, Law Enforcement Official*
%Alcohol Tobacco Firearms Agency, 650 Massachusetts NW, Washington, DC 20001, USA
Bucklew, Neil S *Educator*
%West Virginia University, President's Office, Morgantown, WV 26506, USA
Buckley, A J *Actor*
%Innovative Artists, 1505 10th St, Santa Monica, CA 90401, USA
Buckley, Betty *Actress, Singer, Director*
%Park Ave Talent, 404 Park Ave S, #1000, New York, NY 10016, USA
Buckley, Carol *Elephant Preservationist*
%Elephant Sanctuary, PO Box 393, Hohenwald, TN 38462, USA
Buckley, D Terrell *Football Player*
4215 Palmetto Trail, Weston, FL 33331, USA
Buckley, James L *Senator, NY; Judge*
4952 Sentinel Dr, #302, Bethesda, MD 20816, USA
Buckley, Marcus W *Football Player*
7100 Monterey Dr, Fort Worth, TX 76112, USA
Buckley, Richard E *Conductor*
310 W 55th St, #1K, New York, NY 10019, USA
Buckley, William F, Jr *Commentator, Editor*
215 Lexington Ave, New York, NY 10016, USA
Buckman, James E *Businessman*
%Cendant Corp, 9 W 57th St, New York, NY 10019, USA
Buckner, Pam *Bowler*
645 Utah St, Reno, NV 89506, USA
Buckner, William (Quinn) *Basketball Player, Coach*
1608 Dowling Dr, Irving, TX 75038, USA
Buckson, David P *Governor, DE*
110 N Main St, Camden Wyoming, DE 19934, USA
Bucyk, John P (Chief) *Hockey Player*
17 Boren Lane, Boxford, MA 01921, USA
Buczkowski, Bob *Football Player*
1205 Bowling Green Dr, Monroeville, PA 15146, USA
Budarin, Nikolai M *Cosmonaut*
%Potchta Kosmonavtov, Moskovskoi Oblasti, 141160 Syvisdny Goroduk, Russia
Budd Pieterse, Zola *Track Athlete*
General Delivery, Bloemfontein, South Africa
Budd, Frank *Track, Football Athlete*
138 Dorchester Road, Mount Laurel, NJ 08054, USA
Budd, Harold *Composer, Poet*
%Opal/Warner Bros Records, 6834 Camrose Dr, Los Angeles, CA 90068, USA
Budd, Julie *Actress, Singer*
%Julie Budd Productions, 163 Amsterdam Ave, #224, New York, NY 10023, USA
Budde, Brad E *Football Player*
34316 Via Fortuna, Capistrano Beach, CA 92624, USA
Budde, Ed *Football Player*
5121 W 159th Terrace, Stilwell, KS 66085, USA
Budig, Eugene A (Gene) *Baseball Executive, Educator*
%Baseball Commissioner's Office, 350 Park Ave, New York, NY 10022, USA
Budko, Walter *Basketball Player, Coach*
2525 Pot Spring Road, #L703, Lutherville Timon, MD 21093, USA
Budney, Albert J, Jr *Businessman*
%Niagara Mohawk Holdings, 300 Erie Blvd W, Syracuse, NY 13202, USA
Budnick, Neil G *Financier*
%MBIA Inc, 113 King St, Armonk, NY 10504, USA
Bueche, Wendell F *Businessman*
%IMC Global, 2100 Sanders Road, Northbrook, IL 60062, USA
Buechler, John Carl *Movie Director*
12031 Vose, #19-21, North Hollywood, CA 91605, USA
Buehler, Jud *Basketball Player*
1515 West Lane, Del Mar, CA 92014, USA
Buehrle, James *Baseball Player*
%Chicago White Sox, Comiskey Park, 333 W 35th St, Chicago, IL 60616, USA
Bueno, Maria E *Tennis Player*
Rua Consolagao 3414, #10, 1001 Edificio Augustus, Sao Paulo, Brazil
Buerger, Martin J *Mineralogist, Crystallographer*
Weston Road, Lincoln, MA 01773, USA

B

Buffa - Bumbry

Buffa, Dudley W *Writer*
%Henry Holt, 115 W 18th St, New York, NY 10011, USA
Buffenbarger, R Thomas *Labor Leader*
International Machinists Assn, 9000 Machinists Place, Upper Marlboro, MD 20772, USA
Buffett, Jimmy *Singer, Songwriter*
%Margaritaville, 424 Flemming St, #A, Key West, FL 33040, USA
Buffett, Warren E *Businessman*
%Berkshire Hathaway, 1440 Kiewit Plaza, Omaha, NE 68131, USA
Buffkins, Archie Lee *Performing Arts Administrator*
%Kennedy Center, Executive Suite, Washington, DC 20566, USA
Buffone, Douglas J (Doug) *Football Player*
%WSCR-Radio, Sports Dept, 4949 W Belmont, Chicago, IL 60641, USA
Bufi, Ylli *Prime Minister, Albania*
%Privatization Ministry, Keshilli i Ministrave, Tirana, Albania
Bufman, Zev *Theater Producer*
520 Brickell Key Dr, #612, Miami, FL 33131, USA
Buford, Damon J *Baseball Player*
15412 Valley Vista Blvd, Sherman Oaks, CA 91403, USA
Bugliosi, Vincent T *Attorney, Writer*
3699 Wilshire Blvd, #850, Los Angeles, CA 90010, USA
Bugner, Joe *Boxer*
22 Buckingham St, Surrey Hills NSW 2010, Australia
Buhari, Muhammadu *President, Nigeria; Army General*
%GRA, Daura, Katsina State, Nigeria
Buhner, Jay C *Baseball Player*
1420 NW Gilman Blvd, #2666, Issaquah, WA 98027, USA
Buhrmaster, Robert C *Businessman*
%Jostens Inc, 5501 Norman Center Dr, Minneapolis, MN 55437, USA
Bujold, Genevieve *Actress*
21642 Rambla Vista, Malibu, CA 90265, USA
Buktenica, Raymond *Actor*
%Special Artists Agency, 345 N Maple Dr, #302, Beverly Hills, CA 90210, USA
Bulaich, Norman B (Norm) *Football Player*
421 Lynndale Court, Hurst, TX 76054, USA
Bulatovic, Momir *President, Montenegro*
%Vlada Savezne Republike, Lenina 2, 11070 Belgrade, Serbia & Montenegro
Bulifant, Joyce *Actress*
%James/Levy/Jacobson, 3500 W Olive Ave, #1470, Burbank, CA 91505, USA
Bull, John S *Astronaut*
PO Box 1106, South Lake Tahoe, CA 96156, USA
Bull, Richard *Actor*
200 E Delaware Place, #20F, Chicago, IL 60611, USA
Bull, Ronald D (Ronnie) *Football Player*
15 Redspire Court, Bolingbrook, IL 60490, USA
Bullard, Louis E *Football Player*
3129 Friars Bridge Pass, Franklin, TN 37064, USA
Bullen, Voy M *Religious Leader*
%Church of God, 1207 Willow Brook, Huntsville, AL 35802, USA
Bullins, Ed *Writer*
425 Lafayette St, New York, NY 10003, USA
Bullitt, John C *Attorney, Government Official*
%Shearman Sterling, 53 Wall St, New York, NY 10005, USA
Bullmann, Maik *Wrestler*
%AC Bavaria Goldbach, Postfach 1112, 63769 Goldbach, Germany
Bulloch, Jeremy *Actor*
%Fett Photos, 10 Birchwood Rd, London SW17 9BQ, England
Bullock, Dona *Actress*
%Writers & Artists, 8383 Wilshire Blvd, #550, Beverly Hills, CA 90211, USA
Bullock, J R *Businessman*
%Laidlaw Inc, 3221 N Service Road, Burlington ON L7R 3Y8, Canada
Bullock, Jim J *Actor*
612 Lighthouse Ave, #220, Pacific Grove, CA 93950, USA
Bullock, Sandra *Actress*
%Fortis Films, 8581 Santa Monica Blvd, #1, West Hollywood, CA 90069, USA
Bullock, Theodore H *Biologist*
%University of California, Neurosciences Dept, La Jolla, CA 92093, USA
Bullock, Vicki *Basketball Player*
%Charlotte Sting, 100 Hive Dr, Charlotte, NC 28217, USA
Bulluck, Keith *Football Player*
641 Old Hickory Blvd, #301, Brentwood, TN 37027, USA
Bulriss, Mark P *Businessman*
%Great Lakes Chemical, 9025 River Road, #400, Indianapolis, IN 46240, USA
Bumbeck, David *Artist*
Drew Lane, RD 3, Middlebury, VT 05753, USA
Bumbry, Alonzo B (Al) *Baseball Player*
28 Tremblant Court, Lutherville, MO 21093, USA
Bumbry, Grace *Opera Singer*
%Opera et Concert, Maximilianstr 22, 80539 Munich, Germany

Bumpers, Dale L *Governor, Senator, AR*
7613 Honesty Way, Bethesda, MD 20817, USA
Bund, Karlheinz *Businessman*
Huyssenallee 82-84, 45128 Essen Ruhr, Germany
Bundchen, Gisele *Model*
%I M G Models, 304 Park Ave S, #1200, New York, NY 10010, USA
Bundy, Brooke *Actress*
833 N Martel Ave, Los Angeles, CA 90046, USA
Bunetta, Bill *Bowler*
1176 E San Bruno Ave, Fresno, CA 93710, USA
Bunker, Edward *Writer*
%Saint Martin's Press, 175 5th Ave, New York, NY 10010, USA
Bunker, Wallace E (Wally) *Baseball Player*
6149 Muskingum River Road, Lowell, OH 45744, USA
Bunkowsky-Scherbak, Barb *Golfer*
%Ladies Pro Golf Assn, 100 International Golf Dr, Daytona Beach, FL 32124, USA
Bunnell, Dewey *Singer, Guitarist (America)*
%Agency for Performing Arts, 9200 Sunset Blvd, #900, Los Angeles, CA 90069, USA
Bunnett, Joseph F *Chemist*
608 Arroyo Seca, Santa Cruz, CA 95060, USA
Bunning, James P D (Jim) *Senator, KY; Baseball Player*
4 Fairway Dr, Southgate, KY 41071, USA
Bunting, Eve *Writer*
%Harper Collins Publishers, 10 E 53rd St, New York, NY 10022, USA
Bunting, John *Football Player, Coach*
202 Oak Park Dr, Chapel Hill, NC 27517, USA
Bunton, Emma *Singer (Spice Girls)*
%Lee & Thompson, Green Garden House, 15 22nd St, London WC1M 5HE, England
Buoniconti, Nicholas A (Nick) *Football Player, Businessman*
445 Grand Bay Dr, #803, Key Biscayne, FL 33149, USA
Buono, Cara *Actress*
8675 W Washington Blvd, #203, Culver City, CA 90232, USA
Buraas, Hans-Petter *Alpine Skier*
%Norges Skiforbund, Postboks 3853, Ulleval Hageby, 0805 Oslo, Norway
Burba, Edwin H, Jr *Army General*
256 Montrose Dr, McDonough, GA 30253, USA
Burbank, Daniel C (Dan) *Astronaut*
3210 Water Elm Way, Houston, TX 77059, USA
Burbidge, E Margaret P *Astronomer*
%University of California, Astrophysics Center, 9500 Gilman, La Jolla, CA 92093, USA
Burbules, Peter G *Army General*
6321 Pasadena Point Blvd S, Gulfport, FL 33707, USA
Burch, Elliot *Thoroughbred Racing Trainer*
402 Corey Lane, Middletown, RI 02842, USA
Burchfiel, Burrell C *Geologist*
9 Robinson Park, Winchester, MA 01890, USA
Burchuladze, Paata *Opera Singer*
%Raab & Bohm, Plankengasse 7, 1010 Vienna, Austria
Burckhalter, Joseph H *Inventor (Florescent Dyes)*
705 Valley Brook Road, Wilmington, NC 28412, USA
Burd, Steven A *Businessman*
%Safeway Inc, 5918 Stoneridge Mall Road, Pleasanton, CA 94588, USA
Burden, William A M *Diplomat, Financier*
820 5th Ave, New York, NY 10021, USA
Burdette, S Lewis (Lew) *Baseball Player*
17709 Deer Isle Circle, Winter Garden, FL 34787, USA
Burditt, Joyce *Writer*
%Knopf, 201 E 50th St, New York, NY 10022, USA
Burdon, Eric *Singer (Animals); Songwriter*
%Variety Artists, 1924 Spring St, Paso Robles, CA 93446, USA
Bure, Pavel *Hockey Player*
12335 NW 10th Dr, #5, Coral Springs, FL 33071, USA
Bure, Valeri *Hockey Player*
10371 Golden Eagle Court, Plantation, FL 33324, USA
Burford, Anne M *Government Official*
3853 S Hudson St, Denver, CO 80237, USA
Burford, Christopher W (Chris) *Football Player*
1215 Broken Feather Court, Reno, NV 89511, USA
Burgee, John H *Architect*
Perelanda Farm, Skunks Misery Road, Millerton, NY 12546, USA
Burgess, Adrian *Mountaineer*
109 North St, Anderson, SC 29621, USA
Burgess, Don *Cinematographer*
%Gersh Agency, 232 N Canon Dr, Beverly Hills, CA 90210, USA
Burgess, Neil *Electrical Engineer*
201 E 5th St, #2200, Cincinnati, OH 45202, USA
Burgess, Robert K *Businessman*
%Pulte Corp, 33 Bloomfield Hills Parkway, Bloomfield Hills, MI 48304, USA

B

Burgess, Tony *Ecologist*
%US Geological Survey, 119 National Center, Reston, VA 22092, USA
Burgess, Warren D *Religious Leader*
%Reformed Church in America, 475 Riverside Dr, New York, NY 10115, USA
Burghardt, Raymond F *Diplomat*
%US Embassy, 7 Lang Ha St, Ba Dinh, Hanoi, Vietnam
Burghardt, Walter J *Theologian*
19 I St NW, Washington, DC 20001, USA
Burghoff, Gary *Actor*
%Scott Stander, 13701 Riverside Dr, #201, Sherman Oaks, CA 91423, USA
Burgi, Richard *Actor*
124 Sunset Terrace, Laguna Beach, CA 92651, USA
Burgin, C David *Editor*
%Oakland Tribune, Editorial Dept, 409 13th St, Oakland, CA 94612, USA
Burgon, Geoffrey *Composer*
%Chester Music 8-9 Firth St, London W1V 5TZ, England
Burham, Daniel *Businessman*
%Raytheon Co, 141 Spring St, Lexington, MA 02421, USA
Burham, James B *Financier*
%Mellon Bank, 1 Mellon Bank Center, #0400, Pittsburgh, PA 15258, USA
Burhoe, Ralph Wendell *Theologian*
Montgomery Place, 5550 S South Shore Dr, #715, Chicago, IL 60637, USA
Burke Hederman, Lynn *Swimmer*
26 White Oak Tree Road, Syosset, NY 11791, USA
Burke, Alfred *Actor*
%Jameson, 219 The Plaza, 535 Kings St, London SW10 0SZ, England
Burke, Bernard F *Physicist, Astrophysicist*
10 Bloomfield St, Lexington, MA 02421, USA
Burke, Billy *Actor*
%Writers & Artists, 8383 Wilshire Blvd, #550, Beverly Hills, CA 90211, USA
Burke, Brooke *Actress, Model*
%BLB Inc, 1880 Century Park E, #1600, Los Angeles, CA 90067, USA
Burke, Chris *Actor*
426 S Orange Grove Ave, Los Angeles, CA 90036, USA
Burke, Clement (Clem) *Drummer (Blondie)*
%Shore Fire Media, 32 Court St, #1600, Brooklyn, NY 11201, USA
Burke, David *Actor*
%Writers & Artists, 8383 Wilshire Blvd, #550, Beverly Hills, CA 90211, USA
Burke, Delta *Actress*
4270 Farmdale Ave, Studio City, CA 91604, USA
Burke, Jack, Sr *Golfer*
%Champions Golf Club, 13722 Champions Dr, Houston, TX 77069, USA
Burke, James *Commentator*
Henley House, Terrace Barnes, London SW13 0NP, England
Burke, James D *Museum Director*
%Saint Louis Art Museum, Forest Park, Saint Louis, MO 63110, USA
Burke, James E *Businessman*
%Johnson & Johnson, 317 George St, #200, New Brunswick, NJ 08901, USA
Burke, James Lee *Writer*
%Doubleday Press, 1540 Broadway, New York, NY 10036, USA
Burke, John F *Surgeon, Educator*
984 Memorial Dr, #503, Cambridge, MA 02138, USA
Burke, Joseph C *Educator*
%Rockefeller Institute, 411 State St, Albany, NY 12203, USA
Burke, Kathy *Actress*
%Stephen Hatton Mgmt, 83 Shepperton Road, London N1 3DF, England
Burke, Kelly H *Air Force General*
%Stafford Burke Hecker, 1006 Cameron St, Alexandria, VA 22314, USA
Burke, Patrick *Golfer*
24 Saint Georges Court, Coto de Caza, CA 92679, USA
Burke, Paul Timothy *Actor*
2217 Avenida Caballeros, Palm Springs, CA 92262, USA
Burke, Robert John *Actor*
%Gersh Agency, 232 N Canon Dr, Beverly Hills, CA 90210, USA
Burke, Solomon *Singer*
%Rodgers Redding, 1048 Tatnall St, Macon, GA 31201, USA
Burket, Harriet *Editor*
700 John Ringling Blvd, Sarasota, FL 34236, USA
Burkett, John D *Baseball Player*
104 Craydon Circle, Beaver, PA 15009, USA
Burkhalter, Edward A, Jr *Navy Admiral*
4128 Fort Washington Place, Alexandria, VA 22304, USA
Burkhardt, Francois *Architect*
3 Rue de Venise, 75004 Paris, France
Burkhardt, Lisa *Sportscaster*
%Madison Square Garden Network, 4 Pennsylvania Plaza, New York, NY 10001, USA
Burkholder, JoAnn *Medical Activist, Physician*
%North Carolina State University, Botany Dept, Raleigh, NC 27695, USA

Burkholder, Owen E *Religious Leader*
421 S 2nd St, #600, Elkhart, IN 46516, USA
Burki, Fred A *Labor Leader*
%United Retail Workers Union, 9865 W Roosevelt Road, Westchester, IL 60154, USA
Burkley, Dennis *Actor*
5145 Costello Ave, Sherman Oaks, CA 91423, USA
Burks, Arthur W *Applied Mathematician, Philosopher*
3445 Vintage Valley Road, Ann Arbor, MI 48105, USA
Burks, Ellis R *Baseball Player*
1427 Fitzroy St, Westlake, OH 44145, USA
Burleson, Richard P (Rick) *Baseball Player*
241 E Country Hills Dr, La Habra, CA 90631, USA
Burleson, Tom *Basketball Player*
PO Box 861, Newland, NC 28657, USA
Burlinson, Tom *Actor*
%June Cann Mgmt, 110 Queen St, Woollahra NSW 2025, Australia
Burnell, Jocelyn Bell *Astronomer*
%Bell Open University, Physics Dept, Milton Keynes MK7 6AA, England
Burner, David L *Businessman*
%B F Goodrich Co, 3 Coliseum Centre, 2550 W Tyvola Road, Charlotte, NC 28205, USA
Burnes, Karen *Commentator*
%CBS-TV, News Dept, 51 W 52nd St, New York, NY 10019, USA
Burnett, Carol *Actress, Comedienne*
%Kalola Productions, 270 N Canon Dr, #1186, Beverly Hills, CA 90210, USA
Burnett, Howard J *Educator*
%Washington & Jefferson College, President's Office, Washington, PA 15301, USA
Burnett, James E *Government Official*
%Transportation Safety Board, 800 Independence Ave SW, Washington, DC 20594, USA
Burnett, T-Bone *Singer, Songwriter, Music Producer*
%Immortal Ent Group, 1650 21st St, Santa Monica, CA 90404, USA
Burnette, Rocky *Singer*
1900 Ave of Stars, #2530, Los Angeles, CA 90067, USA
Burnette, Thomas N, Jr *Army General*
Deputy CinC, US Joint Forces Command, Norfolk, VA 23551, USA
Burning Spear *Singer*
13034 231st St, Springfield Gardens, NY 11413, USA
Burnley, James H, IV *Secretary, Transportation*
%Shaw Pittman Potts Trowbridge, 2300 N St NW, Washington, DC 20037, USA
Burns, Annie *Singer (Burns Sisters), Songwriter*
%Drake Assoc, 177 Woodland Ave, Westwood, NJ 07675, USA
Burns, Bob *Drummer (Lynyrd Skynyrd)*
%Vector Mgmt, 1607 17th Ave S, Nashville, TN 37212, USA
Burns, Christian *Singer, Guitarist (BBMak)*
%Day Time, Crown House, 225 Kensington High St, London W8 8SA, England
Burns, Edward *Movie Director, Actor*
451 Greenwich St, #200, New York, NY 10013, USA
Burns, Eric *Entertainer*
%Arts & Entertainment Revue Show, 402 E 76th St, New York, NY 10021, USA
Burns, Heather *Actress*
%Endeavor Talent Agency, 9701 Wilshire Blvd, #1000, Beverly Hills, CA 90212, USA
Burns, James MacGregor *Political Scientist, Historian*
High Mowing, Bee Hill Road, Williamstown, MA 01267, USA
Burns, Jeannie *Singer (Burns Sisters), Songwriter*
%Drake Assoc, 177 Woodland Ave, Westwood, NJ 07675, USA
Burns, Jere, II *Actor*
%Binder, 1465 Lindacrest Dr, Beverly Hills, CA 90210, USA
Burns, John F *Journalist*
%New York Times, Editorial Dept, 229 W 43rd St, New York, NY 10036, USA
Burns, Kenneth L (Ken) *Documentary Director*
%Florentine Films, Maple Grove Road, Walpole, NH 03608, USA
Burns, M Anthony *Businessman*
%Ryder System Inc, 3600 NW 82nd Ave, Miami, FL 33166, USA
Burns, Marie *Singer (Burns Sisters), Songwriter*
%Drake Assoc, 177 Woodland Ave, Westwood, NJ 07675, USA
Burns, Pat *Hockey Coach*
%New Jersey Devils, Continental Arena, 50 RR 120 N, East Rutherford, NJ 07073, USA
Burns, Robert H *Biochemist*
1015 University Bay Dr, Madison, WI 53705, USA
Burnside, R L *Guitarist*
%Billions Corp, 833 W Chicago Ave, #101, Chicago, IL 60622, USA
Burrell, Garland L, Jr *Judge*
%US District Court, 501 I St, Sacramento, CA 95814, USA
Burrell, Kenneth E (Kenny) *Jazz Guitarist, Composer*
%Tropix International, 163 3rd Ave, #143, New York, NY 10003, USA
Burrell, Leroy *Track Athlete*
%University of Houston, Athletic Dept, Houston, TX 77023, USA
Burrell, Scott *Basketball Player*
331 Evergreen Ave, Hamden, CT 06518, USA

Burress, Plaxico *Football Player*
%Pittsburgh Steelers, 3400 S Water St, Pittsburgh, PA 15203, USA
Burris, Jeffrey L (Jeff) *Football Player*
PO Box 5035, Zionsville, IN 46077, USA
Burris, Kurt (Buddy) *Football Player*
2617 Fairfield Dr, Norman, OK 73072, USA
Burris, Robert H *Biochemist*
6225 Mineral Point Road, #96, Madison, WI 53705, USA
Burrough, Kenneth O (Ken) *Football Player*
206 Sweetgum Dr, Haughton, LA 71037, USA
Burroughs, Jeffrey A (Jeff) *Baseball Player*
6155 Laguna Court, Long Beach, CA 90803, USA
Burrowes, Norma E *Opera Singer*
56 Rochester Road, London NW1 9JG, England
Burrows, Darren E *Actor*
%Writers & Artists, 8383 Wilshire Blvd, #550, Beverly Hills, CA 90211, USA
Burrows, Edwin G *Writer*
%Oxford University Press, 198 Madison Ave, New York, NY 10016, USA
Burrows, Eva *Religious Leader*
102 Domain Park, 193 Domain Road, South Yarra VIC 3141, Australia
Burrows, J Stuart *Opera Singer*
Nirvana, 35 Saint Fagans Dr, Saint Fagans, Cardiff CF5 6EF, Wales
Burrows, James E (Jim) *Television Director*
%Broder Kurland Webb Uffner, 9242 Beverly Blvd, #200, Beverly Hills, CA 90210, USA
Burrows, Saffron *Actress*
%Jonathan Altaras, 13 Shorts Gardens, London WC2H 9AT, England
Burrows, Stephen *Fashion Designer*
10 W 57th St, New York, NY 10019, USA
Burrus, William *Labor Leader*
%American Postal Workers Union, 1300 L St NW, Washington, DC 20005, USA
Bursch, Daniel W *Astronaut*
1119 Montecito Ave, Pacific Grove, CA 93950, USA
Burshnick, Anthony J *Air Force General*
7715 Carrleigh Parkway, Springfield, VA 22152, USA
Burstyn, Ellen *Actress*
%Matrix Movies, PO Box 217, Washington Springs Road, Palisades, NY 10964, USA
Burt, Adam *Hockey Player*
1508 Weiskopf Loop, Round Rock, TX 78664, USA
Burt, James M *WW II Army Hero (CMH)*
1621 Sherwood Road, Colony Park, Wyomissing, PA 19610, USA
Burt, Robert N *Businessman*
%FMC Corp, 200 E Randolph Dr, Chicago, IL 60601, USA
Burtnett, Wellington *Hockey Player*
1703 Pouliot Place, Wilmington, MA 01887, USA
Burton, Brandie *Golfer*
%Int'l Mgmt Group, 1 Erieview Plaza, 1360 E 9th St, #1300, Cleveland, OH 44114, USA
Burton, Gary *Jazz Vibist*
%Berklee College of Music, 1140 Boylston St, Boston, MA 02215, USA
Burton, Glenn W *Geneticist*
421 10th St W, Tifton, GA 31794, USA
Burton, Jake *Snowboard Skier*
%Burton Snowboards, 80 Industrial Parkway, Burlington, VT 05401, USA
Burton, Jeff *Auto Racing Driver*
15555 Huntersville Concord Road, Huntersville, NC 28078, USA
Burton, Kate *Actress, Singer*
%Gersh Agency, 232 N Canon Dr, Beverly Hills, CA 90210, USA
Burton, Lance *Illusionist*
%Monte Carlo Hotel, 3770 S Las Vegas Blvd, Las Vegas, NV 89109, USA
Burton, LeVar *Actor*
%Dolores Robinson, 9250 Wilshire Blvd, #220, Beverly Hills, CA 90212, USA
Burton, Nelson, Jr *Bowler*
9359 SW Eagles Landing, Stuart, FL 34997, USA
Burton, Norman *Actor*
3641 Meadville Dr, Sherman Oaks, CA 91403, USA
Burton, Robert G *Publisher*
%World Color Press, 101 Park Ave, New York, NY 10178, USA
Burton, Steve *Actor*
4814 Lemore Ave, Sherman Oaks, CA 91403, USA
Burton, Timothy W (Tim) *Movie Director*
1041 N Formosa Ave, #10, West Hollywood, CA 90046, USA
Burton, Ward *Auto Racing Driver*
PO Box 519, Halifax, VA 24558, USA
Burton, Willie *Basketball Player*
18900 Fleming St, Detroit, MI 48234, USA
Burum, Stephen H *Cinematographer*
%Mirisch Agency, 1801 Century Park E, #1801, Los Angeles, CA 90067, USA
Burwell, Carter *Composer*
%Creative Artists Agency, 9830 Wilshire Blvd, Beverly Hills, CA 90212, USA

Bury, Pol *Sculptor*
12 Vallee de la Taupe-Perdreauville, 78200 Mantes-La-Jolie, France
Busbee, George D *Governor, GA*
%King & Spalding, 191 Peachtree St NW, #4900, Atlanta, GA 30303, USA
Buscemi, Steve *Actor, Director*
%The Firm, 9100 Wilshire Blvd, #100W, Beverly Hills, CA 90210, USA
Busch, August A, III *Businessman, Baseball Executive*
%Anheuser-Busch Cos, 1 Busch Place, Saint Louis, MO 63118, USA
Busch, Frederick M *Writer*
RR 1 Box 31A, New Turnpike Road, Sherburne, NY 13460, USA
Buse, Don *Basketball Player*
7300 W State Road 64, Huntingburg, IN 47542, USA
Busemann, Frank *Track Athlete*
Borkumstr 13A, 45665 Recklinghausen, Germany
Buser, Martin *Dog Sled Racer*
PO Box 520997, Big Lake, AK 99652, USA
Busey, Gary *Actor*
18424 Coastline Dr, Malibu, CA 90265, USA
Busey, Jake *Actor*
%International Creative Mgmt, 8942 Wilshire Blvd, #219, Beverly Hills, CA 90211, USA
Busfield, Timothy *Actor*
2416 G St, #D, Sacramento, CA 95816, USA
Bush, Barbara P *Wife of US President*
9 W Oak Dr, Houston, TX 77056, USA
Bush, Dave *Keyboardist (Elastica)*
%CMO Mgmt, Ransomes Dock, 35-37 Parkgate Road, London SW11 4NP, England
Bush, George H W *President, USA*
9 W Oak Dr, Houston, TX 77056, USA
Bush, George H W, Jr *President, USA*
%White House, 1600 Pennsylvania Ave NW, Washington, DC 20500, USA
Bush, Jim *Track Coach*
5106 Bounty Lane, Culver City, CA 90230, USA
Bush, Kate *Singer, Songwriter*
PO Box 120, Welling, Kent DA16 3DS, England
Bush, Laura *Wife of US President*
%White House, 1600 Pennsylvania Ave NW, Washington, DC 20500, USA
Bush, Lesley L *Diver*
65 Birch Ave, Princeton, NJ 08542, USA
Bush, Richard E *WW II Marine Corps Hero (CMH)*
2200 Marshall Parkway, Waukegan, IL 60085, USA
Bush, Robert E *WW II Navy Hero (CMH)*
3148 Madrona Beach Road NW, Olympia, WA 98502, USA
Bush, Walter L *Hockey Executive*
5200 Malibu Dr, Minneapolis, MN 55436, USA
Bush, William Green *Actor*
%Gold Marshak Liedtke, 3500 W Olive Ave, #1400, Burbank, CA 91505, USA
Bushinsky, Joseph M (Jay) *Commentator*
Rehov Hatsafon 5, Savyon 56540, Israel
Bushland, Raymond C *Entomologist*
200 Concord Plaza Dr, San Antonio, TX 78216, USA
Bushnell, Bill *Theater Director*
2751 Pelham Place, Los Angeles, CA 90068, USA
Bushnell, Candace *Writer*
%Greater Talent Network, 437 5th Ave, New York, NY 10016, USA
Bushy, Ronald (Ron) *Drummer (Iron Butterfly)*
%Entertainment Services Int'l, 6400 Pleasant Park Dr, Chanhassen, MN 55317, USA
Busino, Orlando *Cartoonist (Mugsy)*
12 Shadblow Hill Road, Ridgefield, CT 06877, USA
Buss, Jerry H *Basketball Executive*
%Los Angeles Lakers, Staples Center, 1111 S Figueroa St, Los Angeles, CA 90015, USA
Bussard, Robert W *Physicist*
9705 Carroll Centre Road, #103, San Diego, CA 92126, USA
Bussell, Darcey A *Ballerina*
155 New King's Road, London SW6 4SJ, England
Bussey, Dexter M *Football Player*
2565 Bloomfield Crossing, Bloomfield Hills, MI 48304, USA
Busta Rhymes *Rap Artist, Actor*
%Violator Mgmt, 205 Lexington Ave, #400, New York, NY 10016, USA
Bustamante, Carlos *Molecular Scientist*
%University of California, Howard Hughes Medical Institute, Berkeley, CA 94720, USA
Buster, John E *Obstetrician*
%Harbor-UCLA Medical Center, PO Box 2910, Torrance, CA 90509, USA
Butala, Tony *Singer (Lettermen)*
PO Box 151, McKees Rocks, PA 15136, USA
Butcher, Clyde *Photographer*
52388 Tamiami Trail E, Chokoloskee, FL 34138, USA
Butcher, Susan H *Dog Sled Racer*
%Trail Breaker Kennel, 1 Eureka, Manley, AK 99756, USA

B

Butcher, Willard C — *Financier*
101 Park Ave, New York, NY 10178, USA

Buthelezi, Chief Mangosuthu G — *Chief Minister, KwaZulu/Natal*
%Home Affairs Ministry, Private Bag X741, Pretoria 0001, South Africa

Butkus, Richard J (Dick) — *Football Player, Actor*
21647 Rambla Vista, Malibu, CA 90265, USA

Butler, Bernard — *Guitarist (Suede)*
%Interceptor Enterprises, 98 White Lion St, London N1 9PF, England

Butler, Bill C — *Cinematographer*
1097 Aviation Blvd, Hermosa Beach, CA 90254, USA

Butler, Brett — *Actress, Comedienne*
%William Morris Agency, 151 El Camino Dr, Beverly Hills, CA 90212, USA

Butler, Brett M — *Baseball Player*
2286 Flowering Crab Dr E, Lafayette, IN 47905, USA

Butler, Caron — *Basketball Player*
%Miami Heat, American Airlines Arena, 601 Biscayne Blvd, Miami, FL 33132, USA

Butler, Conrad — *Actor*
%Paradigm Agency, 10100 Santa Monica Blvd, #2500, Los Angeles, CA 90067, USA

Butler, Dean — *Actor*
1310 Westholme Ave, Los Angeles, CA 90024, USA

Butler, Gary C — *Businessman*
%Automatic Data Processing, 1 ADP Blvd, Roseland, NJ 07068, USA

Butler, George L — *Air Force General*
%Peter Kiewit & Sons, 11122 William Plaza, Omaha, NE 68144, USA

Butler, Gerard — *Actor*
%Paradigm Agency, 10100 Santa Monica Blvd, #2500, Los Angeles, CA 90067, USA

Butler, Jerry (Iceman) — *Singer, Songwriter*
%Jerry Butler Productions, 164 Woodstone Dr, Buffalo Grove, IL 60089, USA

Butler, Jerry O — *Football Player*
2820 W Park Blvd, Shaker Heights, OH 44120, USA

Butler, Joe — *Drummer, Singer (Lovin'Spoonful)*
%Pipeline Artists Mgmt, 620 16th Ave S, Hopkins, MN 55343, USA

Butler, Kevin G — *Football Player*
262 Hawthorn Village Common, Vernon Hills, IL 60061, USA

Butler, LeRoy — *Football Player*
4119 Westloop Lane, Jacksonville, FL 32277, USA

Butler, Martin — *Composer*
%Princeton University, Music Dept, Princeton, NJ 08544, USA

Butler, Paul — *Astronomer*
%University of California, Astronomy Dept, Berkeley, CA 94720, USA

Butler, Robert — *Television Director*
650 Club View Dr, Los Angeles, CA 90024, USA

Butler, Robert N — *Gerontologist*
%Mount Sinai Medical Center, Geriatrics Dept, 1 Levy Plaza, New York, NY 10029, USA

Butler, Robert Olen — *Writer*
1009 Concord Road, #230, Tallahassee, FL 32308, USA

Butler, Samuel C — *Attorney*
%Cravath Swain Moore, 825 8th Ave, New York, NY 10019, USA

Butler, William E — *Businessman*
%Eaton Corp, Eaton Center, 1111 Superior Ave, Cleveland, OH 44114, USA

Butler, Yancy — *Actress*
%Writers & Artists, 8383 Wilshire Blvd, #550, Beverly Hills, CA 90211, USA

Butor, Michel — *Writer*
A L'Ecart, Lucinges, 74380 Bonne, France

Butsavage, Bernard — *Labor Leader*
%Molders & Allied Workers Union, 1225 E McMillan St, Cincinnati, OH 45206, USA

Butt, Yondani — *Conductor*
%Gurtman & Murtha, 450 Fashion Ave, #603, New York, NY 10123, USA

Butterfield, Alexander P — *Government Official*
3410 Brookwood Dr, Fairfax, VA 22030, USA

Butterfield, Jack A — *Hockey Executive*
55 Pineridge Dr, Westfield, MA 01085, USA

Buttle, Gregory E (Greg) — *Football Player*
5 Hollacher Dr, Northport, NY 11768, USA

Button, Richard T (Dick) — *Figure Skater, Television Producer*
%Candio Productions, 765 Park Ave, #6B, New York, NY 10021, USA

Buttons, Red — *Actor*
2142 Century Park Lane, #210, Los Angeles, CA 90067, USA

Butts, James — *Track Athlete*
16950 Belforest Dr, Carson, CA 90746, USA

Butz, David E (Dave) — *Football Player*
65 Oak Grove Dr, Belleville, IL 62221, USA

Butz, Earl — *Secretary, Agriculture*
2741 N Salisbury St, West Lafayette, IN 47906, USA

Butzer, Hans E — *Architect*
%University of Oklahoma, Architecture Division, Gould Hall, Norman, OK 73019, USA

Butzner, John D, Jr — *Judge*
%US Court of Appeals, PO Box 2188, Richmond, VA 23218, USA

Buxbaum, Richard M *Attorney, Educator*
%University of California, Boalt Hall, Berkeley, CA 94720, USA
Buzek, Jerzy *Prime Minister, Poland*
%Kancelaria Prezesa Ministrow, Al Ujazdowskie 1/3, 00-583 Warsaw, Poland
Buzzi, Ruth *Actress, Comedienne*
%Entertainment Alliance, PO Box 5734, Santa Rosa, CA 95402, USA
Byars, Betsy C *Writer*
401 Rudder Ridge, Seneca, SC 29678, USA
Byatt, Antonia Susan (A S) *Writer*
37 Rusholme Road, London SW15 3LF, England
Bychkov, Semyon *Conductor*
%Buffalo Symphony Orchestra, 71 Symphony Circle, Buffalo, NY 14201, USA
Bye, Karyn *Hockey Player*
335 Soo Line Road, Hudson, WI 54016, USA
Bye, Kermit E *Judge*
%US Court of Appeals, 657 2nd Ave N, Fargo ND 58102, USA
Byers, Nina *Physicist*
%University of California, Physics Dept, Los Angeles, CA 90024, USA
Byers, Walter *Athletic Association Executive*
PO Box 96, Saint Marys, KS 66536, USA
Bykovsky, Valeri F *Cosmonaut*
%Potchta Kosmonavtov, Moskovskoi Oblasti, 141160 Syvisdny Goroduk, Russia
Byner, Earnest A *Football Player*
850 Stembridge Road SE, Milledgeville, GA 31061, USA
Byner, John *Actor*
%American Mgmt, 19948 Mayall St, Chatsworth, CA 91311, USA
Bynes, Amanda *Actress, Comedienne*
%Tollin/Roberts, 10960 Ventura Blvd, Studio City, CA 91604, USA
Bynoe, Peter C B *Basketball Executive*
%Denver Nuggets, Pepsi Center, 1000 Chopper Circle, Denver, CO 80204, USA
Byrd, Benjamin F, Jr *Physician*
4220 Harding Pike, #380, Nashville, TN 37205, USA
Byrd, Donald *Jazz Trumpeter*
%DL Media, PO Box 2728, Bala Cynwyd, PA 19004, USA
Byrd, Eugene *Actor*
%Gersh Agency, 232 N Canon Dr, Beverly Hills, CA 90210, USA
Byrd, Gill A *Football Player*
510 E Glenbrook Dr, Pulaski, WI 54162, USA
Byrd, Harry F, Jr *Senator, VA*
%Rockingham Publishing Co, 2 N Kent St, Winchester, VA 22601, USA
Byrd, Tom *Actor*
%United Talent Agency, 14011 Ventura Blvd, #213, Sherman Oaks, CA 91423, USA
Byrd, Tracy *Singer*
%Carter & Co, 1114 17th Ave S, #103, Nashville, TN 37212, USA
Byrne, Brendan T *Governor, NJ*
6 Becker Farm Road, Roseland, NJ 07068, USA
Byrne, David *Singer (Talking Heads), Songwriter*
Maine Road, 48 Laight St, New York, NY 10013, USA
Byrne, Gabriel *Actor*
%Industry Entertainment, 955 Carillo Dr, #300, Los Angeles, CA 90048, USA
Byrne, Gerry *Publisher*
%Variety Inc, 5700 Wilshire Blvd, Los Angeles, CA 90036, USA
Byrne, John *Cartoonist (Superman)*
%DC Comics, 1700 Broadway, #700, New York, NY 10019, USA
Byrne, Josh *Actor*
%Hervey/Grimes, PO Box 64249, Los Angeles, CA 90064, USA
Byrne, Michael *Actor*
%Conway Van Gelder Robinson, 18-21 Jermyn St, London SW1Y 6NB, England
Byrne, Thomas J (Tommy) *Baseball Player*
1104 Chilmark Ave, Wake Forest, NC 27587, USA
Byrnes, Edd *Actor*
PO Box 1623, Beverly Hills, CA 90213, USA
Byrnes, Jim *Actor*
%Cannell Productions, 7083 Hollywood Blvd, Los Angeles, CA 90028, USA
Byrnes, Kevin P *Army General*
Assistant Vice Chief of Staff, HqUSA, Pentagon, Washington, DC 20310, USA
Byrom, Monty *Singer (Big House), Songwriter*
%Gurley Co, 1204B Cedar Lane, Nashville, TN 37212, USA
Byron, Don *Jazz Clarinetist*
%Hans Wendl Productions, 2220 California St, Berkeley, CA 94703, USA
Byron, Jeffrey *Actor*
%Shapiro-Lichtman, 8827 Beverly Blvd, Los Angeles, CA 90048, USA
Byrum, John W *Movie Director*
7435 Woodrow Wilson Dr, Los Angeles, CA 90046, USA
Bywater, William H *Labor Leader*
%International Electronic Workers, 1126 16th St NW, Washington, DC 20036, USA
Bzdelik, Jeff *Basketball Coach*
%Denver Nuggets, Pepsi Center, 1000 Chopper Circle, Denver, CO 80204, USA

C

Caan - Caldera Rodriguez

Caan, James *Actor*
PO Box 6646, Denver, CO 80206, USA
Caan, Scott *Actor*
%United Talent Agency, 9560 Wilshire Blvd, #500, Beverly Hills, CA 90212, USA
Caballe, Montserrat *Opera Singer*
%Opera Carlos Caballe, Via Augusta 59, 08006 Barcelona, Spain
Cabana, Robert D *Astronaut*
18315 Cape Bahamas Lane, Houston, TX 77058, USA
Cabibbo, Nicola *Physicist*
%ENEA, Viale Regina Margherita 125, 00198 Rome, Italy
Cabot, Louis W *Businessman*
%Brookings Institution, 1775 Massachusetts Ave NW, Washington, DC 20036, USA
Cabral, Sam A *Labor Leader*
%Police Associations International Union, 1421 Prince St, Alexandria, VA 22314, USA
Caccialanza, Lorenzo *Actor*
%Ambrosio/Mortimer, PO Box 16758, Beverly Hills, CA 90209, USA
Cacciavillan, Agnostino Cardinal *Religious Leader*
%Patrimony of Holy See, Palazzo Apostolico, 00120 Vatican City
Cacoyannis, Michael *Movie, Theatre Director*
15 Mouson St, Athens 117-41, Greece
Caddell, Patrick H *Statistician*
%Cambridge Research Inc, 1625 I St NW, Washington, DC 20006, USA
Cade, J Robert *Medical Researcher, Inventor (Gatorade)*
%University of Florida, Medical School, Physiology Dept, Gainesville, FL 32610, USA
Cadell, Ava *Actress, Model*
%Levin, 8484 Wilshire Blvd, #745, Beverly Hills, CA 90211, USA
Caesar, Shirley *Singer*
%Shirley Caesar Outreach Ministries, 3310 Croasdaile Dr, #902, Durham, NC 27705, USA
Caesar, Sid *Actor, Comedian*
1910 Loma Vista Dr, Beverly Hills, CA 90210, USA
Cafferata, Hector A, Jr *Korean War Marine Corps Hero (CMH)*
1807 Plum Lane, Venice, FL 34293, USA
Caffey, Charlotte *Guitarist (Go-Go's)*
4800 Bryn Mawr Road, Los Angeles, CA 90027, USA
Cafu *Soccer Player*
%AS Roma, Via di Trigoria Km 3.600, 00128 Rome, Italy
Cagatay, Mustafa *Prime Minister, Cyprus Federated State*
60 Cumhuriyet Caddesi, Kyrenia, Cyprus
Cage, Michael *Basketball Player*
%New Jersey Nets, 390 Murray Hill Parkway, East Rutherford, NJ 07073, USA
Cage, Nicolas *Actor*
%Creative Artists Agency, 9830 Wilshire Blvd, Beverly Hills, CA 90212, USA
Cagle, J Douglas *Businessman*
%Cagle's Inc, 2000 Hills Ave NW, Atlanta, GA 30318, USA
Cagle, Yvonne D *Astronaut*
10190 N Foothill Blvd, #F15, Cupertino, CA 95014, USA
Cahill, James *Actor*
31 Chambers St, #311, New York, NY 10007, USA
Cahill, John C *Businessman*
%Trans World Airlines, City Center, 515 N 6th St, Saint Louis, MO 63101, USA
Cahill, Teresa M *Opera, Concert Singer*
65 Leyland Road, London SE12 8DW, England
Cahill, Thomas *Writer*
%Doubleday Press, 1540 Broadway, New York, NY 10036, USA
Cahn, John W *Metallurgist*
6610 Pyle Road, Bethesda, MD 20817, USA
Cahouet, Frank V *Financier*
%Mellon Bank Corp, 1 Mellon Bank Center, 500 Grant St, Pittsburgh, PA 15219, USA
Cain, Carl *Basketball Player*
3045 Sun Valley Dr, Pickerington, OH 43147, USA
Cain, Dean *Actor*
%Sutton Barth Vennari, 145 S Fairfax Ave, #310, Los Angeles, CA 90036, USA
Caine, Michael *Actor*
%International Creative Mgmt, 76 Oxford St, London W1N 0AX, England
Caio, Francesco *Businessman*
%Ing C Olivetti Co, Via G Jervos 77, 10015 Ivrea/Truin, Italy
Calabresi, Guido *Judge*
%US Appeals Court, 157 Church St, New Haven, CT 06510, USA
Calabro, Thomas *Actor*
12400 Ventura Blvd, #369, Studio City, CA 91604, USA
Calatrava, Santiago *Architect, Engineer*
%Santiago Calatrava SA, Hoschgasse 5, 8008 Zurich, Switzerland
Calcevecchi, Mark *Golfer*
2785 Hawthorne Lane, West Palm Beach, FL 33409, USA
Caldeiro, Fernando (Frank) *Astronaut*
2211 Summer Reef Dr, League City, TX 77573, USA
Caldera Rodriguez, Rafael *President, Venezuela*
Ave Urdaneta 33-2, Apdo 2060, Caracas 1010, Venezuela

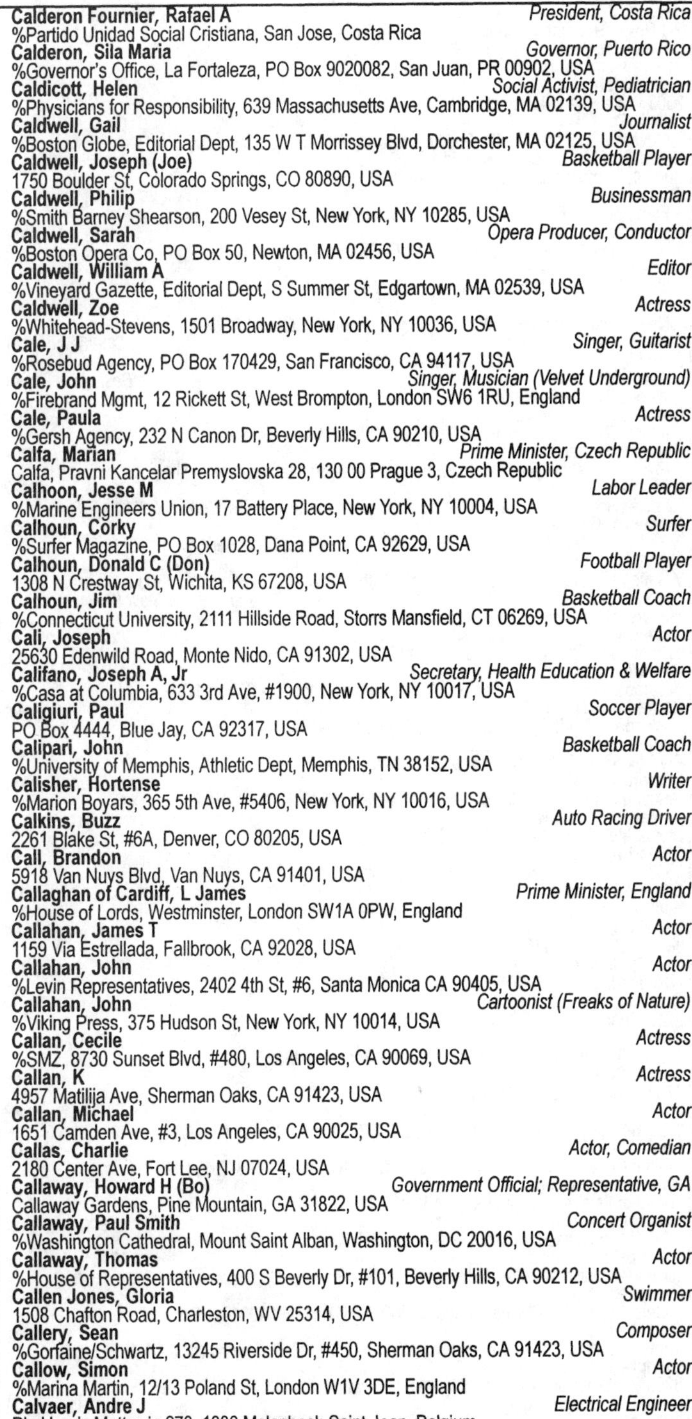

Calderon Fournier, Rafael A *President, Costa Rica*
%Partido Unidad Social Cristiana, San Jose, Costa Rica
Calderon, Sila Maria *Governor, Puerto Rico*
%Governor's Office, La Fortaleza, PO Box 9020082, San Juan, PR 00902, USA
Caldicott, Helen *Social Activist, Pediatrician*
%Physicians for Responsibility, 639 Massachusetts Ave, Cambridge, MA 02139, USA
Caldwell, Gail *Journalist*
%Boston Globe, Editorial Dept, 135 W T Morrissey Blvd, Dorchester, MA 02125, USA
Caldwell, Joseph (Joe) *Basketball Player*
1750 Boulder St, Colorado Springs, CO 80890, USA
Caldwell, Philip *Businessman*
%Smith Barney Shearson, 200 Vesey St, New York, NY 10285, USA
Caldwell, Sarah *Opera Producer, Conductor*
%Boston Opera Co, PO Box 50, Newton, MA 02456, USA
Caldwell, William A *Editor*
%Vineyard Gazette, Editorial Dept, S Summer St, Edgartown, MA 02539, USA
Caldwell, Zoe *Actress*
%Whitehead-Stevens, 1501 Broadway, New York, NY 10036, USA
Cale, J J *Singer, Guitarist*
%Rosebud Agency, PO Box 170429, San Francisco, CA 94117, USA
Cale, John *Singer, Musician (Velvet Underground)*
%Firebrand Mgmt, 12 Rickett St, West Brompton, London SW6 1RU, England
Cale, Paula *Actress*
%Gersh Agency, 232 N Canon Dr, Beverly Hills, CA 90210, USA
Calfa, Marian *Prime Minister, Czech Republic*
Calfa, Pravni Kancelar Premyslovska 28, 130 00 Prague 3, Czech Republic
Calhoon, Jesse M *Labor Leader*
%Marine Engineers Union, 17 Battery Place, New York, NY 10004, USA
Calhoun, Corky *Surfer*
%Surfer Magazine, PO Box 1028, Dana Point, CA 92629, USA
Calhoun, Donald C (Don) *Football Player*
1308 N Crestway St, Wichita, KS 67208, USA
Calhoun, Jim *Basketball Coach*
%Connecticut University, 2111 Hillside Road, Storrs Mansfield, CT 06269, USA
Cali, Joseph *Actor*
25630 Edenwild Road, Monte Nido, CA 91302, USA
Califano, Joseph A, Jr *Secretary, Health Education & Welfare*
%Casa at Columbia, 633 3rd Ave, #1900, New York, NY 10017, USA
Caligiuri, Paul *Soccer Player*
PO Box 4444, Blue Jay, CA 92317, USA
Calipari, John *Basketball Coach*
%University of Memphis, Athletic Dept, Memphis, TN 38152, USA
Calisher, Hortense *Writer*
%Marion Boyars, 365 5th Ave, #5406, New York, NY 10016, USA
Calkins, Buzz *Auto Racing Driver*
2261 Blake St, #6A, Denver, CO 80205, USA
Call, Brandon *Actor*
5918 Van Nuys Blvd, Van Nuys, CA 91401, USA
Callaghan of Cardiff, L James *Prime Minister, England*
%House of Lords, Westminster, London SW1A 0PW, England
Callahan, James T *Actor*
1159 Via Estrellada, Fallbrook, CA 92028, USA
Callahan, John *Actor*
%Levin Representatives, 2402 4th St, #6, Santa Monica CA 90405, USA
Callahan, John *Cartoonist (Freaks of Nature)*
%Viking Press, 375 Hudson St, New York, NY 10014, USA
Callan, Cecile *Actress*
%SMZ, 8730 Sunset Blvd, #480, Los Angeles, CA 90069, USA
Callan, K *Actress*
4957 Matilija Ave, Sherman Oaks, CA 91423, USA
Callan, Michael *Actor*
1651 Camden Ave, #3, Los Angeles, CA 90025, USA
Callas, Charlie *Actor, Comedian*
2180 Center Ave, Fort Lee, NJ 07024, USA
Callaway, Howard H (Bo) *Government Official; Representative, GA*
Callaway Gardens, Pine Mountain, GA 31822, USA
Callaway, Paul Smith *Concert Organist*
%Washington Cathedral, Mount Saint Alban, Washington, DC 20016, USA
Callaway, Thomas *Actor*
%House of Representatives, 400 S Beverly Dr, #101, Beverly Hills, CA 90212, USA
Callen Jones, Gloria *Swimmer*
1508 Chafton Road, Charleston, WV 25314, USA
Callery, Sean *Composer*
%Gorfaine/Schwartz, 13245 Riverside Dr, #450, Sherman Oaks, CA 91423, USA
Callow, Simon *Actor*
%Marina Martin, 12/13 Poland St, London W1V 3DE, England
Calvaer, Andre J *Electrical Engineer*
Blvd Louis Mettewie 270, 1080 Molenbeek-Saint-Jean, Belgium

C

Calvert - Campbell

Calvert, James F *Navy Admiral, Writer*
PO Box 479, Saint Michaels, MD 21663, USA
Calvet, Jacques *Financier*
31 Ave Victor Hugo, 75116 Paris, France
Calvin, John *Actor*
2503 Ware Road, Austin, TX 78741, USA
Calvo, Paul M *Governor, Guam*
%Governor's Office, Capitol Building, Agana, GU 96910, USA
Calvo-Sotelo Bustelo, Leopoldo *Prime Minister, Spain*
Buho 1, Somosaguas, Madrid, Spain
Cam'ron *Rap Artist*
%Famous Artists Agency, 250 W 57th St, New York, NY 10107, USA
Camacho, Hector (Macho) *Boxer*
8034 Solitaire Court, Orlando, FL 32836, USA
Camarda, Charles J *Astronaut*
2386 Sabal Park Lane, League City, TX 77573, USA
Cambre, Ronald C *Businessman*
%Newmont Mining, 9903 W Laurel Place, Littleton, CO 80127, USA
Cambria, John *Cinematogapher*
6910 Mayall St, North Hills, CA 91343, USA
Camby, Marcus *Basketball Player*
5 Woods End, Rye, NY 10580, USA
Camdessus, Michel J *Financier*
%International Monetary Fund, 700 19th St NW, Washington, DC 20431, USA
Camelia-Romer, Susanne *Premier, Netherland Antilles*
%Premier's Office, Fort Amsterdam 17, Willemstad, Netherlands Antilles
Cameron, Ann *Writer*
%Foster Books/Farrar Straus Giroux, 19 Union Square W, New York, NY 10003, USA
Cameron, Candance *Actress*
%Barbara Cameron Assoc, 8369 Sausalito Ave, #A, Canoga Park, CA 91304, USA
Cameron, Don R *Educator, Labor Leader*
%National Education Association, 1201 16th St NW, Washington, DC 20036, USA
Cameron, Duncan *Singer, Guitarist (Sawyer Brown)*
%Sawyer Brown Inc, 5200 Old Harding Road, Franklin, TN 37064, USA
Cameron, James *Movie Director, Producer*
%Lightstorm Entertainment, 919 Santa Monica Blvd, Santa Monica, CA 90401, USA
Cameron, Joanna *Actress*
%Cameron Productions, PO Box 1011, Pebble Beach, CA 93953, USA
Cameron, Kenneth D *Astronaut*
Austvagen 13, 42676 Vastra Frolunda, Sweden
Cameron, Kirk *Actor*
PO Box 8665, Calabasas, CA 91372, USA
Cameron, Matt *Drummer (Soundgarden)*
%Susan Silver Mgmt, 6523 California Ave SW, #348, Seattle, WA 98136, USA
Cameron, Michelle *Synchronized Swimmer*
Box 2 Site 1SS3, Calgary AL T3C 3N9, Canada
Cameron, Paul *Football Player*
3503 Terra Linda Lane, Fallbrook, CA 92028, USA
Camilleri, Andrea *Writer*
%Viking Press, 375 Hudson St, New York, NY 10014, USA
Camilleri, Louis C *Businessman*
%Altria Group, 120 Park Ave, New York, NY 10017, USA
Camilo, Michel *Jazz Pianist*
%Redondo Music, 590 W End Ave, #6, New York, NY 10024, USA
Caminiti, Kenneth G (Ken) *Baseball Player*
2210 Quarter Path, Richmond, TX 77469, USA
Caminito, Jerry *Auto Racing Driver*
%Blue Thunder Racing, PO Box 1486, Jackson, NJ 08527, USA
Camp, Colleen *Actress*
473 N Tigertail Road, Los Angeles, CA 90049, USA
Camp, John *Journalist*
%Saint Paul Pioneer Press, Editorial Dept, 345 Cedar St, Saint Paul, MN 55101, USA
Camp, Steve *Singer*
%Third Coast Artists, 2021 21st Ave S, #220, Nashville, TN 37212, USA
Campanella, Joseph *Actor*
4647 Arcola Ave, Toluca Lake, CA 91602, USA
Campaneris, B Dagoberto (Bert) *Baseball Player*
9797 N 105th Place, Scottsdale, AZ 85258, USA
Campbell, A Kim *Prime Minister, Canada*
%Harvard University, Kennedy School of Government, Cambridge, MA 02138, USA
Campbell, Alan *Actor*
%Gersh Agency, 41 Madison Ave, #3300, New York, NY 10010, USA
Campbell, Billy *Actor*
%International Creative Mgmt, 8942 Wilshire Blvd, #219, Beverly Hills, CA 90211, USA
Campbell, Bruce *Actor*
8205 Santa Monica Blvd, #1-87, West Hollywood, CA 90046, USA
Campbell, Carroll A, Jr *Governor, SC*
101 Constitution Ave, #708, Washington, DC 20001, USA

Campbell, Christian *Actor*
12533 Woodgreen, Los Angeles, CA 90066, USA
Campbell, Colin (Soupy) *Hockey Player, Coach*
%New York Rangers, Madison Square Garden, 2 Penn Plaza, New York, NY 10121, USA
Campbell, Earl C *Football Player*
2937 Thousand Oaks Dr, Austin, TX 78746, USA
Campbell, Elden *Basketball Player*
17252 Hawthorne Blvd, #493, Torrance, CA 90504, USA
Campbell, Gene *Hockey Player*
1554 Wilshire Dr NE, Rochester, MN 55906, USA
Campbell, Glen *Singer*
28 Biltmore Estates, Phoenix, AZ 85016, USA
Campbell, Isobel *Cellist (Belle & Sebastian)*
%Legends of 21st Century, 7 Trinity Row, Florence, MA 01062, USA
Campbell, John *Harness Racing Driver*
%John D Campbell Stable, 823 Allison Dr, River Vale, NJ 07675, USA
Campbell, Julia *Actress*
%Innovative Artists, 1505 10th St, Santa Monica, CA 90401, USA
Campbell, Keith H S *Biologist, Geneticist*
%Roslin Institute, Roslin Bio Centre, Midlothian EH25 9PS, Scotland
Campbell, L Arthur *Molecular Genticist*
%Rockefeller University, Medical Center, 1230 York Ave, New York, NY 10021, USA
Campbell, Lewis B *Businessman*
%Textron Inc, 40 Westminster St, Providence, RI 02903, USA
Campbell, Luther (Skywalker) *Singer (2 Live Crew)*
%Famous Artists Agency, 250 W 57th St, New York, NY 10107, USA
Campbell, Martin *Movie Director*
%International Creative Mgmt, 8942 Wilshire Blvd, #219, Beverly Hills, CA 90211, USA
Campbell, Milton (Milt) *Track Athlete, Football Player*
1132 Saint Marks Place, Plainfield, NJ 07062, USA
Campbell, Naomi *Model, Singer, Actress*
%Men/Women Model Inc, 199 Lafayette St, #700, New York, NY 10012, USA
Campbell, Nell *Actress*
246 W 14th St, New York, NY 10011, USA
Campbell, Neve *Actress*
12533 Woodgreen St, Los Angeles, CA 90066, USA
Campbell, Nicholas *Actor*
1206 N Orange Grove Ave, West Hollywood, CA 90046, USA
Campbell, Patrick J *Labor Leader*
%Carpenters & Joiners Union, 101 Constitution Ave NW, Washington, DC 20001, USA
Campbell, Robert *Architectural Critic*
54 Antrim St, Cambridge, MA 02139, USA
Campbell, Robert H *Businessman*
%Sunoco Inc, 10 Penn Center, 1801 Market St, Philadelphia, PA 19103, USA
Campbell, Tevin *Singer*
%Pyramid Entertainment, 89 5th Ave, #700, New York, NY 10003, USA
Campbell, Vivian *Guitarist (Def Leppard/Whitesnake)*
%Int'l Talent Booking, 27A Floral St, #300, London WC2E 9DQ, England
Campbell, William *Actor*
21502 Velicate St, Woodland Hills, CA 91364, USA
Campbell, William J *Air Force General*
3267 Alex Findlay Place, Sarasota, FL 34240, USA
Campbell-Martin, Tisha *Actress*
%Writers & Artists, 8383 Wilshire Blvd, #550, Beverly Hills, CA 90211, USA
Campese, David I *Rugby Player*
%D C Management Group, 870 Pacific Highway, #4, Gordon NSW 2072, Australia
Campion, Jane *Movie Director*
%Hilary Linstead, 500 Oxford St, Bondi Junction NSW 2022, Australia
Campo, Dave *Football Coach*
%Cleveland Browns, 76 Lou Groza Blvd, Berea, OH 44017, USA
Campos, Jorge *Soccer Player*
%Federacion de Futbol Assn, CP 06600, Col Juarez, Mexico City 6 DF, Mexico
Canadas, Esther *Model, Actress*
%Wilhelmina Models, 300 Park Ave S, #200, New York, NY 10010, USA
Canadeo, Anthony (Tony) *Football Player*
1769 Carriage Court, Green Bay, WI 54304, USA
Canary, David *Actor*
900 S Mansfield Ave, Los Angeles, CA 90036, USA
Candeloro, Philippe *Figure Skater*
Federation des Sports de Glace, 35 Rue Felicien David, 75016 Paris, France
Cane, Mark A *Oceanographer, Climatologist*
%Lamont Doherty Earth Observatory, Route 9W, Palisades, NY 10964, USA
Canella, Guido *Architect*
Via Revere 7, 20123 Milan, Italy
Canfield, Jack *Writer*
PO Box 30880, Santa Barbara, CA 93130, USA
Canfield, Mary Grace *Actress*
%Pierce & Shelly, 13775A Mono Way, #220, Sonora, CA 95370, USA

C

Canfield, Paul *Physicist*
%Iowa State University, Physics Dept, Ames, IA 50011, USA
Canfield, William N (Bill) *Editorial Cartoonist*
%Star Ledger, Editorial Dept, 1 Star Ledger Plaza, Newark, NJ 07102, USA
Canizales, Gaby *Boxer*
2205 Saint Maria Ave, Laredo, TX 78040, USA
Cannavale, Bobby *Actor*
251 W 95th St, #65, New York, NY 10025, USA
Cannell, Stephen J *Television Producer, Writer*
1220 Hillcrest, Pasadena, CA 91106, USA
Cannon, Dyan *Actress*
1100 Alta Loma Road, #808, West Hollywood, CA 90069, USA
Cannon, Freddy (Boom Boom) *Singer, Songwriter*
%Rick Levy Mgmt, 4250 A1A S, #D11, Saint Augustine, FL 32080, USA
Cannon, J D *Actor*
RR 2, Hudson, NY 12534, USA
Cannon, Joe *Soccer Player*
%Colorado Rapids, 555 17th St, #3350, Denver, CO 80202, USA
Cannon, Katherine *Actress*
1310 Westholme Ave, Los Angeles, CA 90024, USA
Cannon, William A (Billy) *Football Player*
176 Shirley Circle, Monterey, LA 71354, USA
Canova, Diana *Actress*
%Agency for Performing Arts, 9200 Sunset Blvd, #900, Los Angeles, CA 90069, USA
Canseco, Jose, Jr *Baseball Player*
5601 Collins Ave, #CU1, Miami Beach, FL 33140, USA
Cantaline, Anita *Bowler*
31455 Pinto Dr, Warren, MI 48093, USA
Cantalupo, James R *Businessman*
%McDonald's Corp, 1 McDonald's Plaza, 1 Kroc Dr, Oak Brook, IL 60523, USA
Cantey, Charlsie *Sportscaster*
%ABC-TV, Sports Dept, 77 W 66th St, New York, NY 10023, USA
Cantona, Eric *Soccer Player*
%French Federation de Football, 60 Bis Ave D'Ilena, 75783 Paris, France
Cantone, Vic *Editorial Cartoonist*
238 Blackpool Court, Ridge, NY 11961, USA
Cantoni, Giulio L *Biochemist*
6938 Blaisdell Road, Bethesda, MD 20817, USA
Cantrell, Blu *Singer*
%Family Tree Entertainment, 135 E 57th St, #2600, New York, NY 10022, USA
Cantrell, Lana *Singer*
300 E 71st St, New York, NY 10021, USA
Canup, Robin *Astronomer*
%Southwest Research Institute, 1050 Walnut St, #400, Boulder, CO 80302, USA
Capa, Cornell *Photographer*
275 5th Ave, New York, NY 10016, USA
Capalbo, Carmen C *Theater Producer, Director*
500 2nd Ave, New York, NY 10016, USA
Capasso, Federico *Physicist*
%Lucent Technologies, Bell Labs, 600 Mountain Ave, New Providence, NJ 07974, USA
Capecchi, Mario R *Biologist*
2529 E 1300 S, Salt Lake City, UT 84108, USA
Capek, Frantisek *Canoeing Athlete*
Michelangelova 4, 100 00 Prague 10, Czechoslovakia
Capellas, Michael *Businessman*
%MCI, 500 Clinton Center Dr, Clinton, MS 39056, USA
Capellino, Ally *Fashion Designer*
N1R, Metropolitan Wharf, Wapping Wall, London E1 9SS, England
Capers, Dom *Football Coach*
%Houston Texans, 4400 Post Oak Parkway, #1400, Houston, TX 77027, USA
Caperton, W Gaston, III *Governor, WV; Foundation Executive*
%College Board, President's Office, 45 Columbus Ave, New York, NY 10023, USA
Capilla Perez, Joaquin *Diver*
Torres de Mixcoac, Lomas de Plateros, Mexico City 19 DF, Mexico
Caplan, Arthur L *Bioethicist*
%University of Pennsylvania, Biomedical Ethics Center, Philadelphia, PA 19104, USA
Capobianco, Tito *Opera Director*
%Pittsburgh Opera Co, 711 Penn Ave, #800, Pittsburgh, PA 15222, USA
Capon, Edwin G *Religious Leader*
%Swedenborgian Church, 11 Highland Ave, Newtonville, MA 02460, USA
Caponi, Donna M *Golfer*
11 Bedford St, Burlington, MA 01803, USA
Cappelletti, Gino R M *Football Player*
19 Louis Dr, Wellesley, MA 02481, USA
Cappelletti, John R *Football Player*
28791 Brant Lane, Laguna Niguel, CA 92677, USA
Capps, Steve *Computer Software Designer*
%Microsoft Corp, 1 Microsoft Way, Redmond, WA 98052, USA

Capps, Thomas E *Businessman*
%Dominion Resources, 120 Tredegar St, Richmond, VA 23219, USA
Cappuccilli, Piero *Opera Singer*
%S A Gorlinsky, 33 Dover St, London W1X 4NJ, England
Capra, Frank, Jr *Movie Producer*
602 S Hudson, Los Angeles, CA 90005, USA
Capriati, Jennifer *Tennis Player*
5326 Foxhunt D, Wesley Chapel, FL 33543, USA
Caprice *Model, Singer, Songwriter*
%Mission Control, Business Center, Lower Road, London SE16 2XB, England
Caprio, Giuseppe Cardinal *Religious Leader*
Palazza del S Uffizio 1, 00193 Rome, Italy
Capshaw, Jessica *Actress*
%Endeavor Talent Agency, 9701 Wilshire Blvd, #1000, Beverly Hills, CA 90212, USA
Capshaw, Kate *Actress*
PO Box 869, Pacific Palisades, CA 90272, USA
Cara, Irene *Singer, Actress*
%Countdown Entertainment, 110 W 26th St, #300, New York, NY 10001, USA
Carafotes, Paul *Actor*
8033 Sunset Blvd, #3554, West Hollywood, CA 90046, USA
Carasco, Joe (King) *Singer*
%Texas Sounds, 2317 Pecan, Dickinson, TX 77539, USA
Caray, Skip *Sportscaster*
%Turner Broadcasting System, 1050 Techwood Dr NW, Atlanta, GA 30318, USA
Carazo Odio, Rodrigo *President, Costa Rica; Educator*
%University for Peace, Apdo 199, San Jose, Costa Rica
Carbajal, Michael *Boxer*
914 E Filmore St, Phoenix, AZ 85006, USA
Carbonell, Nestor *Actor*
%Rigberg Roberts Rugolo, 1180 S Beverly Dr, #601, Los Angeles, CA 90035, USA
Carbonneau, Guy *Hockey Player, Executive*
%Dallas Stars, StarCenter, 211 Cowboys Parkway, Irving, TX 75063, USA
Carcaterra, Lorenzo *Writer*
%William Morris Agency, 151 El Camino Dr, Beverly Hills, CA 90212, USA
Card, Andrew H, Jr *Secretary, Transportation*
%White House, 1600 Pennsylvania Ave NW, Washington, DC
Card, Michael *Banjoist, Pianist, Guitarist*
1143 Dora Whitley Road, Franklin, TN 37064, USA
Cardamone, Richard J *Judge*
%US Court of Appeals, 10 Broad St, Utica, NY 13501, USA
Cardellini, Linda *Actress*
%Gersh Agency, 232 N Canon Dr, Beverly Hills, CA 90210, USA
Carden, Joan M *Opera Singer*
%Jennifer Eddy, 596 Saint Kilda Road, #11, Melbourne 3004 VIC, Australia
Cardenal, Jose D *Baseball Player*
12 Country Club Dr, #UC, Prospect Heights, IL 60070, USA
Cardich, Augusto *Archaeologist*
%University of La Plata, Archaeology Dept, La Plata, Argentina
Cardiff, Jack *Cinematographer*
32 Woodland Rise, London N10, England
Cardin, Pierre *Fashion Designer*
59 Rue du Faubourg-Saint-Honore, 75008 Paris, France
Cardinal, Douglas J *Architect*
7011A Manchester Blvd, #315, Alexandria, VA 22310, USA
Cardinale, Claudia *Actress*
Via Flaminia Km 77, Prima Porta, 00188 Rome, Italy
Cardwell, Donald E (Don) *Baseball Player*
PO Box 454, Clemmons, NC 27012, USA
Carelli, Rick *Auto Racing Driver*
15764 W 63rd Ave, Golden, CO 80403, USA
Caretto-Brown, Patty *Swimmer*
16079 Mesquite Circle, Santa Ana, CA 92708, USA
Carew, Rodney C (Rod) *Baseball Player*
40 Tanglewood, Aliso Viejo, CA 92656, USA
Carey, Drew *Actor, Comedian*
%Messina Baker Entertainment, 955 Carillo Dr, #100, Los Angeles, CA 90048, USA
Carey, Duane G *Astronaut*
15706 Falmouth Dr, Houston, TX 77059, USA
Carey, Ezekiel *Singer (Flamingos)*
509 E Ridge Crest Blvd, #A, Ridge Crest, CA 93555, USA
Carey, Harry, Jr *Actor*
PO Box 1388, Goleta, CA 93116, USA
Carey, Hugh L *Governor, NY*
%WR Grace Co, 1114 Ave of Americas, New York, NY 10036, USA
Carey, Jim *Hockey Player*
4848 Hanging Moss Lane, Sarasota, FL 34238, USA
Carey, Mariah *Singer, Songwriter*
%Talent Entertainment Group, 9111 Wilshire Blvd, Beverly Hills, CA 90210, USA

C

Carey - Carlson

Carey, Peter *Writer*
%International Creative Mgmt, 40 W 57th St, #1800, New York, NY 10019, USA
Carey, Ron *Actor*
419 N Larchmont Ave, Los Angeles, CA 90004, USA
Cargo, David F *Governor, NM*
6422 Concordia Road NE, Albuquerque, NM 87111, USA
Carides, Gia *Actress*
%Robyn Gardiner Mgmt, 397 Riley St, Surrey Hills NSW 2010, Australia
Caridis, Miltiades *Conductor*
Himmelhofgasse 10, 1130 Vienna, Austria
Carillo, Mary *Sportscaster*
822 Boylston St, #203, Chestnut Hill, PA 02467, USA
Cariou, Len *Actor*
%Paradigm Agency, 10100 Santa Monica Blvd, #2500, Los Angeles, CA 90067, USA
Carl XVI Gustaf *King, Sweden*
Kungliga Slottet, Slottsbacken, 111 30 Stockholm, Sweden
Carlei, Carlo *Movie Director*
%Creative Artists Agency, 9830 Wilshire Blvd, Beverly Hills, CA 90212, USA
Carles Gordo, Ricardo M Cardinal *Religious Leader*
Carrer del Bisbe 5, 08002 Barcelona, Spain
Carlesimo, Pete J (P J) *Basketball Coach, Sportscaster*
%San Antonio Spurs, Alamodome, 1 SBC Center, San Antonio, TX 78219, USA
Carlestrom, John E *Astronomer*
%University of Chicago, Astronomy Dept, 5640 S Ellis Ave, Chicago, IL 60637, USA
Carlile, Forbes *Swimming Coach*
16 Cross St, Ryde NSW 2112, Australia
Carlin, George *Actor, Comedian*
%Carlin Productions, 11911 San Vicente Blvd, #348, Los Angeles, CA 90049, USA
Carlin, John W *Governor, KS*
18201 Allwood Terrace, Olney, MD 20832, USA
Carlin, Thomas R *Publisher*
%Saint Paul Pioneer Press, Publisher's Office, 345 Cedar, Saint Paul, MN 55101, USA
Carling, William D C *Rugby Player, Sportscaster*
%Insights Ltd, 22 Suffolk St, London SW1Y 4HG, England
Carlino, Lewis John *Movie Director, Writer*
991 Oakmont Dr, Los Angeles, CA 90049, USA
Carlisle, Belinda *Singer, Songwriter, Model*
%Firstars Mgmt, 14724 Ventura Blvd, #PH, Sherman Oaks, CA 91403, USA
Carlisle, Bob *Singer, Songwriter*
%Ray Ware Artist Mgmt, 251 2nd Ave, #5, Franklin, TN 37064, USA
Carlisle, James B *Governor General, Antigua & Barbuda*
%Governor General's Office, Government House, Saint John's, Antigua
Carlisle, Jodi *Actress, Comedienne*
%International Creative Mgmt, 8942 Wilshire Blvd, #219, Beverly Hills, CA 90211, USA
Carlisle, Kitty *Singer, Actress*
32 E 64th St, New York, NY 10021, USA
Carlisle, Mary *Actress*
517 N Rodeo Dr, Beverly Hills, CA 90210, USA
Carlisle, Rick *Basketball Player, Coach*
RR 4, Ogdensburg, NY 13669, USA
Carlos Moco, Marcolino Jose *Prime Minister, Angola*
%Movimento Popular de Libertacao de Angola, Luanda, Angola
Carlos, John *Track Athlete*
68640 Tortuga Road, Cathedral City, CA 92234, USA
Carlot, Maxime *Prime Minister, Vanuatu*
PO Box 698, Port Vila, Vanuatu
Carlson, Amy *Actress*
%Writers & Artists, 8383 Wilshire Blvd, #550, Beverly Hills, CA 90211, USA
Carlson, Arne H *Governor, MN*
22005 Iden Ave N, Forest Lake, MN 55025, USA
Carlson, Dudley L *Navy Admiral*
%Navy League, 2300 Wilson Blvd, Arlington, VA 22201, USA
Carlson, Jack W *Association Executive*
%American Assn of Retired Persons, 1901 K St NW, Washington, DC 20006, USA
Carlson, John A *Businessman*
%Cray Research, 655 Lone Oak Dr, #A, Eagan, MN 55121, USA
Carlson, K C *Cartoonist*
%DC Comics, 1700 Broadway, New York, NY 10019, USA
Carlson, Karen *Actress*
3700 Ventura Canyon Ave, Sherman Oaks, CA 91423, USA
Carlson, Katrina *Actress*
%Sara Bennett Agency, 1062 S Alfred St, Los Angeles, CA 90035, USA
Carlson, Paulette *Singer*
%Mark Sonder Music, Fisk Building, 250 W 57th St, #1830, New York, NY 10107, USA
Carlson, Tucker *Commentator*
PO Box 105366, Atlanta, GA 30348, USA
Carlson, Veronica *Actress*
7844 Kavanagh Court, Sarasota, FL 34240, USA

Carlsson, Arvid *Nobel Medicine Laureate*
%Gotheburg University, PO Box 100, 405 30, Gotheburg, Sweden
Carlsson, Ingvar G *Prime Minister, Sweden*
Riksdagen, 100 12 Stockholm, Sweden
Carlton, Carl *Singer*
%Randolph Enterprises, Oakland, Inkster, MI 48141, USA
Carlton, Paul K *Air Force General*
1716 Briescrest Dr, #702, Bryan, TX 77802, USA
Carlton, Steven N (Steve) *Baseball Player*
%GW Sports, 555 Camino Del Rio, #B2, Durango, CO 81301, USA
Carlton, Vanessa *Singer*
%Peter Malkin Mgmt, 410 Park Ave, #420, New York, NY 10022, USA
Carlucci, Dave *Singer (Danny & the Juniors)*
%Joe Terry Mgmt, PO Box 1017, Turnersville, NJ 08012, USA
Carlucci, Frank C, III *Secretary, Defense; Businessman*
%Carlyle Group, 1001 Pennsylvania Ave NW, Washington, DC 20004, USA
Carlyle, Joan H *Opera Singer*
Laundry Cottage, Hammer, North Wales SY13 4QX, England
Carlyle, Randy *Hockey Player, Coach*
%Washington Capitals, MCI Center, 601 F St NW, Washington, DC 20004, USA
Carlyle, Robert *Actor*
%International Creative Mgmt, 76 Oxford St, London W1N 0AX, England
Carman *Singer*
%Carman Ministries, PO Box 5093, Brentwood, TN 37024, USA
Carman, Gregory W *Judge; Representative, NY*
%US Court of International Trade, 1 Federal Plaza, New York, NY 10278, USA
Carmen, Eric *Singer, Songwriter*
%David Spero Mgmt, 1679 S Belvoir Blvd, South Euclid, OH 44121, USA
Carmen, Jeanne *Actress, Model*
%Brandon James, PO Box 11812, Newport Beach, CA 92658, USA
Carmen, Julie *Actress*
%Metropolitan Talent Agency, 4526 Wilshire Blvd, Los Angeles, CA 90010, USA
Carmichael, Ian *Actor*
%London Mgmt, 2-4 Noel St, London W1V 3RB, England
Carmichael, L Harold *Football Player*
38 Birch Lane, Glassboro, NJ 08028, USA
Carmona, Richard H *Government Official, Physician*
%Surgeon General's Office, 200 Independence Ave SW, Washington, DC 20201, USA
Carne, Jean *Singer*
%Walt Reeder Productions, PO Box 27641, Philadelphia, PA 19118, USA
Carne, Judy *Actress, Comedienne*
2 Horatio St, #10N, New York, NY 10014, USA
Carner, JoAnne *Golfer*
7641 Mackenzie Court, #314, Lake Worth, FL 33467, USA
Carnes, Kim *Singer, Songwriter*
1829 Tyne Blvd, Nashville, TN 37215, USA
Carnesale, Albert *Educator*
%University of California, Chancellor's Office, Los Angeles, CA 90024, USA
Carnevale, Bernard L (Ben) *Basketball Player, Coach*
5109 Dorset Mews, Williamsburg, VA 23188, USA
Carney, Art *Actor*
143 Kingfisher Lane, Westbrook, CT 06498, USA
Carney, John M *Football Player*
2950 Wishbone Way, Encinitas, CA 92024, USA
Carney, Thomas P *Army General*
9806 Kirktree Court, Fairfax, VA 22032, USA
Carns, Michael P C (Mike) *Air Force General*
966 Coral Dr, Pebble Beach, CA 93953, USA
Caro, Anthony A *Sculptor*
111 Frognal, Hampstead, London NW3, England
Caro, Robert A *Writer*
%Robert A Caro Assoc, 250 W 57th St, New York, NY 10107, USA
Caroline *Princess, Monaco*
Villa Le Clos Saint Pierre, Ave San-Martin, Monte Carlo, Monaco
Caroline, James C (J C) *Football Player*
2501 Stanford Dr, Champaign, IL 61820, USA
Caron, Leslie *Actress, Dancer*
6 Rue De Bellechaisse, 75007 Paris, France
Carothers, Robert L *Educator*
%University of Rhode Island, President's Office, Kingston, RI 02881, USA
Carothers, Veronica *Actress*
535 N Heatherstone Dr, Orange, CA 92869, USA
Carp, Daniel A (Dan) *Businessman*
%Eastman Kodak Co, 343 State St, Rochester, NY 14650, USA
Carpenter, Carleton *Actor*
RR 2, Chardavoyne Road, Warwick, NY 10990, USA
Carpenter, Charisma *Actress, Model*
%Irv Schechter, 9300 Wilshire Blvd, #410, Beverly Hills, CA 90212, USA

Carpenter, George *WW II Army Air Force Hero*
320 Walnut St, Paris, TN 38242, USA
Carpenter, John H *Movie Director*
%International Creative Mgmt, 8942 Wilshire Blvd, #219, Beverly Hills, CA 90211, USA
Carpenter, John M *Opera Singer*
%Maurel Enterprises, 225 W 34th St, #1012, New York, NY 10122, USA
Carpenter, Kip *Speedskater*
425 N Park Blvd, Brookfield, WI 53005, USA
Carpenter, Liz *Women's Activist*
116 Skyline Dr, Austin, TX 78746, USA
Carpenter, M Scott *Astronaut*
PO Box 3161, Vail, CO 81658, USA
Carpenter, Marj C *Religious Leader*
%Presbyterian Church USA, 100 Witherspoon St, Louisville, KY 40202, USA
Carpenter, Mary Chapin *Singer, Songwriter, Guitarist*
%AGF Entertainment, 30 W 21st St, #700, New York, NY 10010, USA
Carpenter, Richard *Pianist, Singer, Songwriter*
960 Country Valley Road, Westlake Village, CA 91362, USA
Carpenter, Russell P *Cinematographer*
%Gersh Agency, 232 N Canon Dr, Beverly Hills, CA 90210, USA
Carpenter, Teresa *Journalist*
%Village Voice, Editorial Dept, 36 Cooper Square, New York, NY 10003, USA
Carpenter, W M *Businessman*
%Bausch & Lomb, 1 Bausch & Lomb Place, Rochester, NY 14604, USA
Carpenter, William S (Bill), Jr *Army General, Hero, Football Player*
PO Box 4067, Whitefish, MT 59937, USA
Carpentier, Patrick *Auto Racing Driver*
%Team Players, 2015 Peel, #500, Montreal PQ H3A 1T8, Canada
Carr, Caleb *Writer*
%Don Buchwald, 6500 Wilshire Blvd, #2200, Los Angeles, CA 90048, USA
Carr, Catherine (Cathy) *Swimmer*
409 10th St, Davis, CA 95616, USA
Carr, Charmian *Actress, Singer*
%Arete Publishing Co, PO Box 127, Claremont, CA 91711, USA
Carr, David *Football Player*
%Houston Texans, 4400 Post Oak Parkway, #1400, Houston, TX 77027, USA
Carr, Gerald P (Jerry) *Astronaut*
%CAMUS Inc, PO Box 919, Huntsville, AR 72740, USA
Carr, Henry *Track Athlete, Football Player*
11642 Beaverland St, Detroit, MI 48239, USA
Carr, Jane *Actress*
6200 Mount Angelus Dr, Los Angeles, CA 90042, USA
Carr, Kenneth M *Navy Admiral*
2322 Fort Scott Dr, Arlington, VA 22202, USA
Carr, Kenny *Basketball Player*
24421 SW Valley View Dr, West Linn, OR 97068, USA
Carr, Lloyd *Football Coach*
%University of Michigan, Athletic Dept, Ann Arbor, MI 48109, USA
Carr, Michael L (M L) *Basketball Player, Coach, Executive*
%Boston Celtics, 151 Merrimac St, #1, Boston, MA 02114, USA
Carr, Paul *Actor*
%H David Moss, 733 Seward St, #PH, Los Angeles, CA 90038, USA
Carr, Roger D *Football Player*
107 Lark Lane, West Monroe, LA 71291, USA
Carr, Vikki *Singer*
3102 Iron Stone Lane, San Antonio, TX 78230, USA
Carrack, Paul *Singer, Songwriter*
%Firstars Mgmt, 14724 Ventura Blvd, #PH, Sherman Oaks, CA 91403, USA
Carradine, David *Actor*
628 S San Fernando Blvd, #C, Burbank, CA 91502, USA
Carradine, Ever *Actress*
%Three Arts Entertainment, 9460 Wilshire Blvd, #700, Beverly Hills, CA 90212, USA
Carradine, Keith *Actor, Singer, Songwriter*
PO Box 460, Placerville, CO 81430, USA
Carradine, Robert *Actor*
355 S Grand Ave, #4150, Los Angeles, CA 90071, USA
Carrasquel, Alfonso C (Chico) *Baseball Player*
4625 Wisconsin Ave, Berwyn,IL 60402, USA
Carrera, Barbara *Actress, Model*
%Chasin Agency, 8899 Beverly Blvd, #716, Los Angeles, CA 90048, USA
Carreras, Jose *Opera Singer*
%Fundacion Jose Carreras, Calle Muntaner 383, 08021 Barcelona, Spain
Carrere, Tia *Actress, Model*
836 N La Cienega Blvd, #204, West Hollywood, CA 90069, USA
Carretto, Joseph A, Jr *Astronaut*
4534 E 85th St, Tulsa, OK 74137, USA
Carrey, Jim *Actor, Comedian*
%Gold-Miller Mgmt, 9220 Sunset Blvd, #320, Los Angeles, CA 90069, USA

Carrier, George F *Mathematician*
7 Rice Spring Lane, Wayland, MA 01778, USA
Carrier, Mark A *Football Player*
7626 E Cholla Dr, Scottsdale, AZ 85260, USA
Carriere, Jean P J *Writer*
Les Broussanes, Domessargues, 30350 Ledignan, France
Carriere, Mathieu *Actor*
%Agentur Schafer, Friesenstr 53, 50670 Cologne, Germany
Carril, Pete *Basketball Coach*
%Sacramento Kings, Arco Arena, 1 Sports Parkway, Sacramento, CA 95834, USA
Carrillo, Elpidia *Actress*
%Bresler Kelly Assoc, 11500 W Olympic Blvd, #510, Los Angeles, CA 90064, USA
Carrington, Alan *Chemist*
46 Lakewood Road, Chandler's Ford, Hants SO53 1EX, England
Carrington, Debbie Lee *Actress*
%Jonis, 8147 Tunney Ave, Reseda, CA 91335, USA
Carrington, Peter A R *Government Official, England*
Manor House, Bledlow near Aylesbury, Bucks HP17 9PE, England
Carroll, Clay P *Baseball Player*
3040 Leisure Place, Sarasota, FL 34234, USA
Carroll, Diahann *Singer, Actress*
%William Morris Agency, 1325 Ave of Americas, New York, NY 10019, USA
Carroll, Earl (Speedo) *Singer (Cadillacs, Coasters)*
%PS #87, 180 W 78th St, New York, NY 10024, USA
Carroll, Earl W *Labor Official*
%United Garment Workers of America, PO Box 239, Hermitage, TN 37076, USA
Carroll, Joe Barry *Basketball Player*
%Denver Nuggets, Pepsi Center, 1000 Chopper Circle, Denver, CO 80204, USA
Carroll, John B *Psychologist*
2158 Penrose Lane, Fairbanks, AK 99709, USA
Carroll, John S *Editor*
%Los Angeles Times, Editorial Dept, 202 W 1st St, Los Angeles, CA 90012, USA
Carroll, Julian M *Governor, KY*
%Carroll Assoc, 25 Fountain Place, Frankfort, KY 40601, USA
Carroll, Kent J *Navy Admiral*
%Country Club of North Carolina, 1600 Morganton Road, #30X, Pinehurst, NC 28374, USA
Carroll, Lester (Les) *Cartoonist (Our Boarding House)*
1715 Ivyhill Loop N, Columbus, OH 43229, USA
Carroll, Pat *Actress*
14 Old Tavern Lane, Harwich Port, MA 02646, USA
Carroll, Pete *Football Coach*
%University of Southern California, Heritage Hall, Los Angeles, CA 90089, USA
Carroll, Phillip *Businessman*
%Fluor Corp, 3353 Michelson Dr, Irvine, CA 92612, USA
Carrot Top *Actor, Comedian*
%Carrot Top Inc, 420 Sylvan Dr, Winter Park, FL 32789, USA
Carruthers, Garrey E *Governor, NM*
5258 Redman Road, Las Cruces, NM 88011, USA
Carruthers, James H (Red) *Skier*
8 Malone Ave, Garnerville, NY 10923, USA
Carruthers, Kitty *Figure Skater*
22 E 71st St, New York, NY 10021, USA
Carruthers, Peter *Figure Skater*
22 E 71st St, New York, NY 10021, USA
Carry, Julius J, III *Actor*
4091 Farmdale Ave, Studio City, CA 91604, USA
Carsey, Marcia L P *Television Producer*
%Carsey-Warner Productions, 4024 Radford Ave, Building 3, Studio City, CA 91604, USA
Carson, Benjamin S *Neurosurgeon*
%Johns Hopkins University, Medical Center, Baltimore, MD 21218, USA
Carson, Carlos A *Football Player*
2621 SW Wintercreek Dr, Lees Summit, MO 64081, USA
Carson, David *Movie, Television Director*
10474 Santa Monica Blvd, Los Angeles, CA 90025, USA
Carson, Harold D (Harry) *Football Player*
732 Barrister Court, Franklin Lakes, NJ 07417, USA
Carson, James (Jimmy) *Hockey Player*
1154 Ridgeway Dr, Rochester, MI 48307, USA
Carson, Johnny *Entertainer*
6962 Wildlife Road, Malibu, CA 90265, USA
Carson, William H (Willie) *Thoroughbred Racing Jockey*
Minster House, Barnsley, Cirencester, Glos, England
Cartan, Henri P *Mathematician*
95 Blvd Jourdan, 75014 Paris, France
Carter, Aaron *Singer, Actor*
PO Box 5127, Bellingham, WA 98227, USA
Carter, Anthony *Football Player*
4314 Danielson Dr, Lake Worth, FL 33467, USA

C

Carter, Carlene *Singer, Songwriter*
%Warner Bros Records, 3300 Warner Blvd, Burbank, CA 91505, USA
Carter, Cheryl *Actress*
%CunninghamEscottDipene, 10635 Santa Monica Blvd, #130, Los Angeles, CA 90025, USA
Carter, Chris *Television Producer*
%Broder Kurland Webb Uffner, 9242 Beverly Blvd, #200, Beverly Hills, CA 90210, USA
Carter, Cris *Football Player*
1500 Mill Creek Dr, Desoto, TX 75115, USA
Carter, Deana *Singer, Songwriter*
PO Box 7877, Fredericksbrg, VA 22404, USA
Carter, Dixie *Actress*
9100 Hazen Dr, Beverly Hills, CA 90210, USA
Carter, Donald J (Don) *Bowler*
9895 SW 96th St, Miami, FL 33176, USA
Carter, Elliott C, Jr *Composer*
31 W 12th St, New York, NY 10011, USA
Carter, Frank *Labor Leader*
%Glass Molders Pottery Plastics Union, 608 E Baltimore Pike, Media, PA 19063, USA
Carter, Frederick J (Fred) *Basketball Player, Coach*
5070 Parkside Ave, #3500, Philadelphia, PA 19131, USA
Carter, Gary E *Baseball Player*
%Gary Carter Foundation, 560 Village Blvd, #260, West Palm Beach, FL 33409, USA
Carter, Jack *Actor, Comedian*
1023 Chevy Chase Dr, Beverly Hills, CA 90210, USA
Carter, James E (Jimmy), Jr *President, USA; Nobel Peace Laureate*
%Carter Center, 453 Freedom Parkway NE, Atlanta, GA 30307, USA
Carter, Jay *Singer (Crests)*
%Brothers Mgmt, 141 Dunbar Ave, Fords, NJ 08863, USA
Carter, Jim *Golfer*
12611 E Cortez Dr, Scottsdale. AZ 85259, USA
Carter, John *Singer (Flamingos)*
%Resort Attractions, 2375 E Tropicana Ave, #304, Las Vegas, NV 89119, USA
Carter, John Mack *Editor*
%Good Housekeeping Magazine, Editorial Dept, 959 8th Ave, New York, NY 10019, USA
Carter, LaVerne *Bowler*
4750 Madrigal Way, Las Vegas, NV 89122, USA
Carter, Lynda *Actress*
9200 Harrington Dr, Potomac, MD 20854, USA
Carter, Mel *Actor*
%Cape Entertainment, 1161 NW 76th Ave, Plantation, FL 33322, USA
Carter, Michael D *Football Player, Track Athlete*
901 Red Oak Creek Dr, Ovilla, TX 75154, USA
Carter, Nick *Singer (Backstreet Boys), Songwriter*
%The Firm, 9100 Wilshire Blvd, #100W, Beverly Hills, CA 90210, USA
Carter, Paula *Bowler*
9895 SW 96th St, Miami, FL 33176, USA
Carter, Powell F, Jr *Navy Admiral*
699 Fillmore St, Harpers Ferry, WV 25425, USA
Carter, Ronald L (Ron) *Jazz Bassist, Composer*
%Bridge Agency, 35 Clark St, #A5, Brooklyn, NY 11201, USA
Carter, Rosalynn S *Wife of US President*
%Carter Center, 451 Freedom Parkway NE, Atlanta, GA 30307, USA
Carter, Rubin (Hurricane) *Boxer*
%SCHR, 83 Poplar St NW, Atlanta, GA 30303, USA
Carter, Stephen L *Attorney, Educator, Writer*
%Yale University, Law School, New Haven, CT 06520, USA
Carter, Terry *Actor*
%CPA, 244 Madison Ave, #332, New York, NY 10016, USA
Carter, Thomas *Television Director*
140 N Tigertail Road, Los Angeles, CA 90049, USA
Carter, Vince *Basketball Player*
1978 Country Club Dr, Port Orange, FL 32128, USA
Carteri, Rosana *Opera Singer*
%Angel Records, 150 5th Ave, New York, NY 10011, USA
Carteris, Gabrielle *Actress*
%International Creative Mgmt, 8942 Wilshire Blvd, #219, Beverly Hills, CA 90211, USA
Carthy, Eliza *Singer, Fiddler, Songwriter*
%Agency Group Ltd, 1775 Broadway, #430, New York, NY 10019, USA
Cartier-Bresson, Henri *Photographer*
%Magnum Photos, 5 Passage Piver, 75011 Paris, France
Cartwright, Angela *Actress*
%Rubber Boots, 11333 Moorpark St, #433, Toluca Lake, CA 91602, USA
Cartwright, Bill *Basketball Player, Coach*
2222 Francisco Dr, #510, El Dorado Hills, CA 95762, USA
Cartwright, Lionel *Singer, Songwriter*
%Long Run Music, 21 Music Square E, Nashville, TN 37203, USA
Cartwright, Lynn *Actress*
%Don Gerler, 3349 Cahuenga Blvd W, #1, Los Angeles, CA 90068, USA

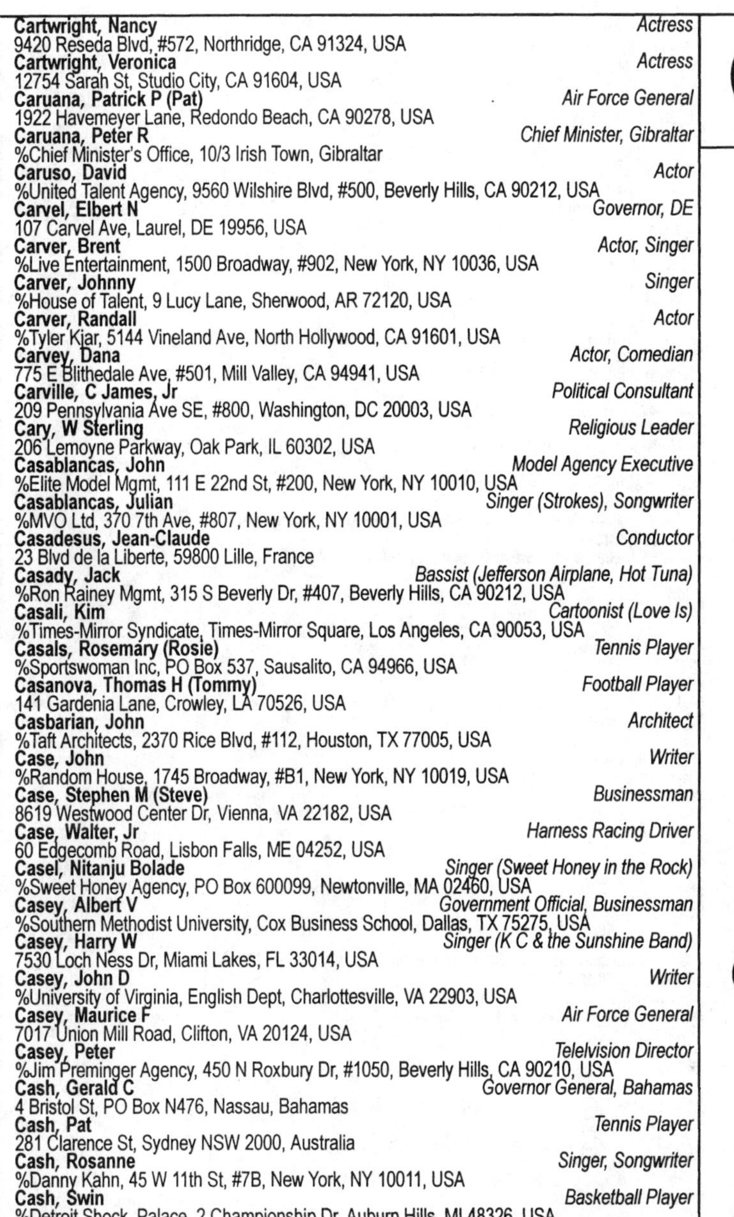

Cartwright, Nancy — *Actress*
9420 Reseda Blvd, #572, Northridge, CA 91324, USA

Cartwright, Veronica — *Actress*
12754 Sarah St, Studio City, CA 91604, USA

Caruana, Patrick P (Pat) — *Air Force General*
1922 Havemeyer Lane, Redondo Beach, CA 90278, USA

Caruana, Peter R — *Chief Minister, Gibraltar*
%Chief Minister's Office, 10/3 Irish Town, Gibraltar

Caruso, David — *Actor*
%United Talent Agency, 9560 Wilshire Blvd, #500, Beverly Hills, CA 90212, USA

Carvel, Elbert N — *Governor, DE*
107 Carvel Ave, Laurel, DE 19956, USA

Carver, Brent — *Actor, Singer*
%Live Entertainment, 1500 Broadway, #902, New York, NY 10036, USA

Carver, Johnny — *Singer*
%House of Talent, 9 Lucy Lane, Sherwood, AR 72120, USA

Carver, Randall — *Actor*
%Tyler Kjar, 5144 Vineland Ave, North Hollywood, CA 91601, USA

Carvey, Dana — *Actor, Comedian*
775 E Blithedale Ave, #501, Mill Valley, CA 94941, USA

Carville, C James, Jr — *Political Consultant*
209 Pennsylvania Ave SE, #800, Washington, DC 20003, USA

Cary, W Sterling — *Religious Leader*
206 Lemoyne Parkway, Oak Park, IL 60302, USA

Casablancas, John — *Model Agency Executive*
%Elite Model Mgmt, 111 E 22nd St, #200, New York, NY 10010, USA

Casablancas, Julian — *Singer (Strokes), Songwriter*
%MVO Ltd, 370 7th Ave, #807, New York, NY 10001, USA

Casadesus, Jean-Claude — *Conductor*
23 Blvd de la Liberte, 59800 Lille, France

Casady, Jack — *Bassist (Jefferson Airplane, Hot Tuna)*
%Ron Rainey Mgmt, 315 S Beverly Dr, #407, Beverly Hills, CA 90212, USA

Casali, Kim — *Cartoonist (Love Is)*
%Times-Mirror Syndicate, Times-Mirror Square, Los Angeles, CA 90053, USA

Casals, Rosemary (Rosie) — *Tennis Player*
%Sportswoman Inc, PO Box 537, Sausalito, CA 94966, USA

Casanova, Thomas H (Tommy) — *Football Player*
141 Gardenia Lane, Crowley, LA 70526, USA

Casbarian, John — *Architect*
%Taft Architects, 2370 Rice Blvd, #112, Houston, TX 77005, USA

Case, John — *Writer*
%Random House, 1745 Broadway, #B1, New York, NY 10019, USA

Case, Stephen M (Steve) — *Businessman*
8619 Westwood Center Dr, Vienna, VA 22182, USA

Case, Walter, Jr — *Harness Racing Driver*
60 Edgecomb Road, Lisbon Falls, ME 04252, USA

Casel, Nitanju Bolade — *Singer (Sweet Honey in the Rock)*
%Sweet Honey Agency, PO Box 600099, Newtonville, MA 02460, USA

Casey, Albert V — *Government Official, Businessman*
%Southern Methodist University, Cox Business School, Dallas, TX 75275, USA

Casey, Harry W — *Singer (K C & the Sunshine Band)*
7530 Loch Ness Dr, Miami Lakes, FL 33014, USA

Casey, John D — *Writer*
%University of Virginia, English Dept, Charlottesville, VA 22903, USA

Casey, Maurice F — *Air Force General*
7017 Union Mill Road, Clifton, VA 20124, USA

Casey, Peter — *Television Director*
%Jim Preminger Agency, 450 N Roxbury Dr, #1050, Beverly Hills, CA 90210, USA

Cash, Gerald C — *Governor General, Bahamas*
4 Bristol St, PO Box N476, Nassau, Bahamas

Cash, Pat — *Tennis Player*
281 Clarence St, Sydney NSW 2000, Australia

Cash, Rosanne — *Singer, Songwriter*
%Danny Kahn, 45 W 11th St, #7B, New York, NY 10011, USA

Cash, Swin — *Basketball Player*
%Detroit Shock, Palace, 2 Championship Dr, Auburn Hills, MI 48326, USA

Cashman, John, Jr — *Thoroughbred Racing Executive*
PO Box 11889, Lexington, KY 40578, USA

Cashman, Terry — *Singer (Buchanan Brothers)*
15 Engle St, Englewood, NJ 07631, USA

Cashman, Wayne J — *Hockey Player, Coach*
PO Box 280, Lowell, FL 32663, USA

Casida, John E — *Entomologist*
1570 La Vereda Road, Berkeley, CA 94708, USA

Casiraghi, Pierluigi — *Soccer Player*
%Lazio Roma, Via Novaro 32, 00197 Rome, Italy

Caslavska, Vera — *Gymnast*
SVS Sparta Prague, Korunovacni 29, Prague 7, Czech Republic

Casnoff, Phillip *Actor*
216 S Plymouth Blvd, Los Angeles, CA 90004, USA
Caspar, Donald L D *Biophysicist*
911 Gardenia Dr, Tallahassee, FL 32312, USA
Casper, David J (Dave) *Football Player*
1525 Alamo Way, Alamo, CA 94507, USA
Casper, John H *Astronaut*
4414 Village Corner Dr, Houston, TX 77059, USA
Casper, William E (Billy) *Golfer*
PO Box 210010, Chula Vista, CA 91921, USA
Caspersson, Tobjorn O *Biochemist, Cancer Specialist*
Emanuel Birkes Vag 2, 144 00 Ronninge, Sweden
Cass, Christopher *Actor*
%Halpern Assoc, PO Box 5597, Santa Monica, CA 90409, USA
Cassady, Howard (Hopalong) *Football Player*
539 Severn Ave, Tampa, FL 33606, USA
Cassavetes, Nick *Actor, Director*
22223 Buena Ventura St, Woodland Hills, CA 91364, USA
Cassel, Jean-Pierre *Actor*
%International Creative Mgmt, 76 Oxford St, London W1N 0AX, England
Cassel, Seymour *Actor*
%Innovative Artists, 1505 10th St, Santa Monica, CA 90401, USA
Cassel, Vincent *Actor*
%United Talent Agency, 9560 Wilshire Blvd, #500, Beverly Hills, CA 90212, USA
Cassell, Sam *Basketball Player*
6000 Reims Road, #3402, Houston, TX 77036, USA
Casseus, Gabriel *Actor*
%Metropolitan Talent Agency, 4526 Wilshire Blvd, Los Angeles, CA 90010, USA
Cassidy, Bruce *Hockey Player, Coach*
1810 Wilnella Dr SE, Grand Rapids, MI 49506, USA
Cassidy, David *Actor, Singer*
%MPI, 9255 Sunset Blvd, #407, Los Angeles, CA 90069, USA
Cassidy, Edward I Cardinal *Religious Leader*
%Council for Christian Unity, Piazza del S Uffizio 11, 00193 Rome, Italy
Cassidy, Joanna *Actress*
PO Box 74123, Los Angeles, CA 90004, USA
Cassidy, Patrick *Actor*
%Innovative Artists, 1505 10th St, Santa Monica, CA 90401, USA
Cassidy, Shaun *Actor, Singer*
19425 Shirley Court, Tarzana, CA 91356, USA
Cassini, Oleg L *Fashion Designer*
15 E 53rd St, New York, NY 10022, USA
Casson, Mel *Cartoonist (Redeye, Mixed Singles)*
%King Features Syndicate, 888 7th Ave, New York, NY 10106, USA
Cast, Tricia *Actress*
20 Georgette Road, Rolling Hills Estates, CA 90274, USA
Castaneda, Jorge A *Government Official, Mexico*
Anillo Periferico Sur 3180, #1120, Jardines del Pedregal, 01900 Mexico
Castel, Nico *Opera Singer*
%RPA Mgmt, 4 Adelaide Lane, Washingtonville, NY 10992, USA
Castellini, Clateo *Businessman*
%Becton Dickinson Co, 1 Becton Dr, Franklin Lakes, NJ 07417, USA
Castille, Jeremiah *Football Player*
210 Lorna Square, #160, Birmingham, AL 35216, USA
Castillo Lara, Rosalio Jose Cardinal *Religious Leader*
Palazzo del Governatorato, 00120 Vatican City
Castle, John *Actor*
%Larry Dalzell, 91 Regent St, London W1R 7TB, England
Castle, Michael N *Governor, Representative, DE*
300 S New St, Dover, DE 19904, USA
Castle, Nick C *Movie Director*
%Creative Artists Agency, 9830 Wilshire Blvd, Beverly Hills, CA 90212, USA
Castleman, Albert W, Jr *Chemist*
425 Hillcrest Ave, State College, PA 16803, USA
Castleman, E Riva *Museum Curator*
%Museum of Modern Art, 11 W 53rd St, New York, NY 10019, USA
Castrillon Hoyos, Dario Cardinal *Religious Leader*
%Arzobispado, Calle 33, N 21-18, Bucaramanga, Santander, Colombia
Castro Ruz, Fidel *President, Cuba*
%Palacio del Gobierno, Plaza de la Revolucion, Havana, Cuba
Castro Ruz, Raul *Prime Minister, Cuba; Army General*
%First Vice President's Office, Plaza de la Revolucion, Havana, Cuba
Castro, Emilio *Religious Leader*
%World Council of Churches, 475 Riverside Dr, New York, NY 10115, USA
Castro, Raul H *Governor, AZ; Diplomat*
429 W Crawford St, Nogales, AZ 85621, USA
Castroneves, Helio *Auto Racing Driver*
3138 Commodore Plaza, #307, Miami, FL 33133, USA

Catalano, Eduardo F *Architect*
44 Grozier Road, Cambridge, MA 02138, USA
Catalona, William J *Urologist*
%Washington University, Medical School, Urology Division, Saint Louis, MO 63110, USA
Catchings, Tamika *Basketball Player*
%Indiana Fever, Conseco Fieldhouse, 125 S Pennsylvania, Indianapolis, IN 46204, USA
Cates, Darlene *Actress*
13340 FM 740, Forney, TX 75126, USA
Cates, Gilbert *Movie, Television Director, Producer*
%Gilbert Cates Productions, 10920 Wilshire Blvd, #600, Los Angeles, CA 90024, USA
Cates, Phoebe *Actress*
1636 3rd Ave, #309, New York, NY 10128, USA
Cathcart, Patti *Singer (Tuck & Patti)*
%Windham Hill Records, PO Box 5501, Beverly Hills, CA 90209, USA
Catlett, Mary Jo *Actress*
4357 Farmdale Ave, North Hollywood, CA 91604, USA
Cato, Robert Milton *Prime Minister, Saint Vincent*
PO Box 138, Ratho Mill, Saint Vincent & Grenadines
Caton, Jack Joseph *Air Force General*
17230 Citronia St, Northridge, CA 91325, USA
Caton-Jones, Michael *Movie Director*
%William Morris Agency, 52/53 Poland Place, London W1F 7LX, England
Cattaneo, Peter *Movie Director*
%International Creative Mgmt, 76 Oxford St, London W1N 0AX, England
Cattell, Christine *Actress*
%Epstein-Wyckoff, 280 S Beverly Dr, #400, Beverly Hills, CA 90212, USA
Cattrall, Kim *Actress*
%Propaganda Films Mgmt, 1741 Ivar Ave, Los Angeles, CA 90028, USA
Caulfield, Emma *Actress*
%Metropolitan Talent Agency, 4526 Wilshire Blvd, Los Angeles, CA 90010, USA
Caulfield, Lore *Fashion Designer*
2228 Cotner Ave, Los Angeles, CA 90064, USA
Caulfield, Maxwell *Actor*
5252 Lennox Ave, Sherman Oaks, CA 91401, USA
Cauthen, Stephen M (Steve) *Thoroughbred Racing Jockey*
%Cauthen Ranch, RFD, Boone County, 167 S Main St, Walton, KY 41094, USA
Cavaiani, Jon R *Vietnam War Army Hero (CMH)*
10956 Green St, #230, Columbia, CA 95310, USA
Cavalera, Max *Singer, Guitrist*
%Variety Artists, 1924 Spring St, Paso Robles, CA 93446, USA
Cavaliere, Felix *Singer, Organist, Composer (Rascals)*
%Primo Productions, PO Box 253, Audubon, NJ 08106, USA
Cavalli, Roberto *Fashion Designer*
Via del Cantone 29, 50019 Osmannoro Sesto Florentino, Firenze, Italy
Cavanaugh, Christine *Actress*
%Allman, 342 S Cochran Ave, #30, Los Angeles, CA 90036, USA
Cavanaugh, Joe *Hockey Player*
25 Nathaniel Greene Dr, East Greenwich, RI 02818, USA
Cavanaugh, Matthew A (Matt) *Football Player*
6422 Cloister Gate Dr, Baltimore, MD 21212, USA
Cavanaugh, Page *Musician*
5442 Woodman Ave, Sherman Oaks, CA 91401, USA
Cavanuagh, Michael *Actor*
%Ambrosio/Mortimer, PO Box 16758, Beverly Hills, CA 90209, USA
Cavaretta, Philip J (Phil) *Baseball Player*
2200 Country Walk, Snellville, GA 30039, USA
Cavazos, Lauro F *Secretary, Education*
173 Annursnac Hill Road, Concord, MA 01742, USA
Cavazos, Lumi *Actress*
%Visionary Entertainment, 8265 W Sunset Blvd, #203, West Hollywood, CA 90046, USA
Cave, Nick *Singer, Songwriter*
%Billions Corp, 833 W Chicago Ave, #101, Chicago, IL 60622, USA
Cavett, Richard A (Dick) *Entertainer*
%Conversation Co, 697 Middle Neck Road, Great Neck, NY 11023, USA
Caviezel, Jim *Actor*
8929 Clifton Way, #103, Beverly Hills, CA 90211, USA
Cawley, Warren (Rex) *Track Athlete*
1655 San Rafael Dr, Corona, CA 92882, USA
Cazenove, Christopher *Actor*
32 Bolingbroke Grove, London SW11, England
Ce, Marco Cardinal *Religious Leader*
S Marco 318, 30124 Venice, Italy
Ceberano, Kate *Singer*
%Richard East Productions, Kildean Lane, Winchelsea VIC 3241, Australia
Ceccato, Aldo *Conductor*
Chaunt da Crusch, 7524 Zuoz, Switzerland
Cech, Thomas R *Nobel Chemistry Laureate*
PO Box 215, Boulder, CO 80309, USA

C

Cechmanek - Chadwick

Cechmanek, Roman *Hockey Player*
%Los Angeles Kings, Staples Center, 1111 S Figueroa St, Los Angeles, CA 90015, USA
Cedeno, Cesar E *Baseball Player*
2112 Marisol Loop, Kissimmee, FL 34743, USA
Cedras, Raoul *Army General, Haiti*
%Continental Riande Hotel, Panama City, Panama
Cedric the Entertainer *Comedian*
%Creative Artists Agency, 9830 Wilshire Blvd, Beverly Hills, CA 90212, USA
Ceglarski, Leonard (Len) *Hockey Player, Coach*
61 Lantern Lane, Duxbury, MA 02332, USA
Celant, Gerwano *Museum Curator*
%Solomon Guggenheim Museum, 1971 5th Ave, New York, NY 10128, USA
Cellucci, A Paul *Governor, MA; Diplomat*
%State Department, 2201 C St NW, Washington, DC 20520, USA
Celmins, Vija *Artist*
49 Crosby St, New York, NY 10012, USA
Cenac, Winston Francis *Prime Minister, Saint Lucia*
7 High St, Box 629, Castries, Saint Lucia
Cenker, Robert J *Astronaut*
%GORCA Inc, 155 Hickory Corner Road, East Windsor, NJ 08520, USA
Cennamo, Ralph *Labor Leader*
%Leather Plastics & Novelty Workers Union, 265 W 14th St, New York, NY 10011, USA
Cepeda, Orlando M *Baseball Player*
2305 Palmer Court, Fairfield, CA 94534, USA
Cerami, Anthony *Biochemist*
Ram Island Dr, Shelter Island, NY 11964, USA
Cerezo Arevalo, M Vinicio *President, Guatemala*
%Partido Democracia Cristiana, Avda Elena 20-66, Guatemala City, Guatemala
Cerf, Vinton G *Computer Scientist*
3614 Camelot Dr, Annandale, VA 22003, USA
Cerha, Friedrich *Composer, Conductor*
%Doblinger Music, Dorotheergasse 10, PO Box 882, 1011 Vienna, Austria
Cerjan, Paul G *Army General*
3524 Old Course Lane, Valrico, FL 33594, USA
Cernan, Eugene A *Astronaut*
5 Inwood Corner Road, Columbus, OH 43215, USA
Cerruti, Nino *Fashion Designer*
3 Place de la Madeleine, 75008 Paris, France
Cerv, Robert H (Bob) *Baseball Player*
3130 Williamsburg Dr, Lincoln, NE 68516, USA
Cervantes, Gary *Actor*
2240 Mardel Ave, Whittier, CA 90601, USA
Cervenka, Exene *Singer (X)*
%Performers of the World, 8901 Melrose Ave, #200, West Hollywood, CA 90069, USA
Cervi, Alfred N (Al) *Basketball Player*
177 Dunrovin Lane, Rochester, NY 14618, USA
Cervi, Valentina *Actress*
%Artmedia, 20 Ave Rapp, 75007 Paris, France
Cesarani, Sal *Fashion Designer*
%SJC Concepts, 40 E 80th St, New York, NY 10021, USA
Cetera, Peter *Singer, Bassist, Songwriter*
1880 Century Park East, #900, Los Angeles, CA 90067, USA
Cetlinski, Matthew (Matt) *Swimmer*
13121 SE 93rd Terrace Road, Summerfield, FL 34491, USA
Cey, Ronald C (Ron) *Baseball Player*
22714 Creole Road, Woodland Hills, CA 91364, USA
Chaber, Madelyn J *Attorney*
101 California St, San Francisco, CA 94111, USA
Chabert, Lacey *Actress*
%International Creative Mgmt, 8942 Wilshire Blvd, #219, Beverly Hills, CA 90211, USA
Chabon, Michael *Writer*
%Random House, 1745 Broadway, #B1, New York, NY 10019, USA
Chabraja, Nicholas D *Businessman*
%General Dynamics, 3190 Fairview Park Dr, Falls Church, VA 22042, USA
Chabrol, Claude *Movie Director, Producer*
%VMA, 40 Rue Francois 1er, 75008 Paris, France
Chacon, Alex Pineda *Soccer Player*
%Los Angeles Galaxy, 1010 Rose Bowl Dr, Pasadena, CA 91103, USA
Chacon, Bobby *Boxer*
%Main Street III Gym, Huntington Hotel, 752 S Main St, Los Angeles, CA 90014, USA
Chacurian, Chico *Soccer Player*
96 Stratford Road, Stratford, CT 06615, USA
Chadirji, Rifat Kamil *Architect*
28 Troy Court, Kensington High St, London W8, England
Chadli, Bendjedid *President, Algeria; Army Officer*
Palace Emir Abedelkader, Algiers, Algeria
Chadwick, J Leslie (Les) *Bassist (Gerry & the Pacemakers)*
%Barry Collins, 21A Cliftown Road, Southend-on-Sea, Essex SS1 1AB, England

Chadwick, June *Actress*
%Contemporary Artists, 610 Santa Monica Blvd, #202, Santa Monica, CA 90401, USA
Chadwick, William L (Bill) *Hockey Referee*
PO Box 501, Country Club Dr, Cutchogue, NY 11935, USA
Chafetz, Sidney *Artist*
%Ohio State University, Art Dept, Columbus, OH 43210, USA
Chaffee, Don *Movie Director*
7020 La Presa Dr, Los Angeles, CA 90068, USA
Chaffee, Susan (Suzy) *Alpine Skier*
5106 Woodwind Lane, Anaheim, CA 92807, USA
Chailly, Riccardo *Conductor*
Royal Concertgebrew, Jacob Obrechtstraat 51, 1071 KJ Amsterdam 41, Holland
Chakiris, George *Actor, Singer, Dancer*
7266 Clinton St, Los Angeles, CA 90036, USA
Chalayan, Hussein *Fashion Designer*
71 Endell Road, London WC2 9AJ, England
Chalfont, A G (Arthur) *Government Official, England*
%House of Lords, Westminster, London SW1A 0PW, England
Chalke, Sarah *Actress*
%Salt Spring, 8391 Beverly Blvd, #372, Los Angeles, CA 90048, USA
Chaloner, William G *Botanist*
20 Parke Road, London SW13 9NG, England
Chamberlain, John A *Sculptor*
%Ten Coconut Inc, 1315 10th St, Sarasota, FL 34236, USA
Chamberlain, Owen *Nobel Physics Laureate*
882 Santa Barbara Road, Berkeley, CA 94707, USA
Chamberlain, Richard *Actor*
2345 Makiki Heights Dr, Honolulu, HI 96822, USA
Chambers, Anne Cox *Businesswoman, Diplomat*
%Cox Enterprises, 1400 Lake Hearn Dr NE, Atlanta, GA 30319, USA
Chambers, Lester *Singer, Harmonicist (Chambers Brothers)*
%Lustig Talent, PO Box 770850, Orlando, FL 32877, USA
Chambers, Rebecca *Actress*
%Writers & Artists, 8383 Wilshire Blvd, #550, Beverly Hills, CA 90211, USA
Chambers, Tom *Basketball Player*
153 E 2550 N, Ogden, UT 84414, USA
Chambers, Wallace (Wally) *Football Player*
95 Meadle St, Mount Clemens, MI 48043, USA
Chambers, Willie *Singer, Guitarist (Chambers Brothers)*
%Noga Mgmt, PO Box 1428, Studio City, CA 91614, USA
Chambliss, C Christopher (Chris) *Baseball Player*
PO Box 440, Briarcliff Manor, NY 10510, USA
Chambon, Pierre H *Biochemist*
%Institut Genetique Moleculaire/Cellulaire, BP 163, 67404 Illkirch, France
Champion, Marge *Dancer, Actress*
484 W 43rd St, New York, NY 10036, USA
Champlin, Charles D *Movie Critic*
2169 Linda Flora Dr, Los Angeles, CA 90077, USA
Chan Sy *Premier, Kampuchea*
%Premier's Office, Phnom-Penh, People's Republic of Kampuchea
Chan, Ernie *Cartoonist (Conan the Barbarian)*
4131 Vale Ave, Oakland, CA 94619, USA
Chan, Jackie *Actor*
%Golden Harvest Studios, 145 Waterloo Road, Kowloon, Hong Kong, China
Chan, Julius *Prime Minister, Papua New Guinea*
PO Box 6030, Boroto, Papua New Guinea
Chance, Britton *Biophysicist, Yachtsman*
4014 Pine St, Philadelphia, PA 19104, USA
Chance, Larry *Singer (Earls)*
%Brothers Mgmt, 141 Dunbar Ave, Fords, NJ 08863, USA
Chance, W Dean *Baseball Player*
9505 W Smithville Western Road, Wooster, OH 44691, USA
Chancellor, Van *Basketball Coach*
%Houston Comets, 2 Greenway Plaza, #400, Houston, TX 77046, USA
Chandler, Christopher M (Chris) *Football Player*
2529 12th Ave W, Seattle, WA 98119, USA
Chandler, Colby H *Businessman*
%Ford Motor Co, American Road, Dearborn, MI 48121, USA
Chandler, Donald G (Don) *Football Player*
3248 E 93rd St, Tulsa, OK 74137, USA
Chandler, Gene *Singer*
%Entertainment Consultants, 164 Woodstone Dr, Buffalo Grove, IL 60089, USA
Chandler, Jeff *Boxer*
6242 Horner St, Philadelphia, PA 19144, USA
Chandler, Kyle *Actor*
%Brillstein/Grey, 9150 Wilshire Blvd, #350, Beverly Hills, CA 90212, USA
Chandler, Tyson *Basketball Player*
18903 Chickory Dr, Riverside, CA 92504, USA

C

Chandnois, Lynn *Football Player*
2048 Walden Court, Flint, MI 48532, USA
Chandrasekhar, Bhagwat S *Cricketer*
571 31st Cross, 4th Block, Jayanagar, Bangalore 56011, India
Chanel, Tally *Actress, Model*
%Don Gerler, 3349 Cahuenga Blvd W, #1, Los Angeles, CA 90068, USA
Chaney, Don *Basketball Player, Coach*
%New York Knicks, Madison Square Garden, 2 Penn Plaza, New York, NY 10121, USA
Chaney, John *Basketball Coach*
%Temple University, Athletic Dept, Philadelphia, PA 19122, USA
Chang Chun-hsiung *Prime Minister, Taiwan*
%Premier's Office, 1 Chunghsiao East Road, Section 1, Taipei, Taiwan
Chang, Jeannette *Publisher*
%Harper's Bazaar Magazine, 1700 Broadway, New York, NY 10019, USA
Chang, Michael *Tennis Player*
PO Box 6080, Mission Viejo, CA 92690, USA
Chang, Sarah *Concert Violinist*
%I C M Artists, 40 W 57th St, New York, NY 10019, USA
Chang-Diaz, Franklin R *Astronaut*
%NASA, Johnson Space Center, 2101 NASA Road, Houston, TX 77058, USA
Changeux, Jean-Pierre G *Molecular Biologist*
47 Rue du Four, 75006 Paris, France
Channing, Carol *Actress, Singer*
%William Morris Agency, 151 El Camino Dr, Beverly Hills, CA 90212, USA
Channing, Stockard *Actress*
%B & B Entertainment, 1640 S Sepulveda Blvd, #530, Los Angeles, CA 90025, USA
Chao, Elaine L *Secretary, Labor*
%Labor Department, 200 Constitution Ave NW, Washington, DC 20210, USA
Chao, Rosalind *Actress*
%Don Buchwald, 6500 Wilshire Blvd, #2200, Los Angeles, CA 90048, USA
Chapin, Dwight L *Publisher, Government Official*
%San Francisco Examiner, 110 5th St, San Francisco, CA 94103, USA
Chapin, Lauren *Actress*
11940 Reedy Creek Dr, #207, Orlando, FL 32836, USA
Chapin, Schuyler G *Opera Executive*
650 Park Ave, New York, NY 10021, USA
Chapin, Tom *Singer, Songwriter*
57 Piermont Place, Piermont, NY 10968, USA
Chaplin, Ben *Actor*
%London Mgmt, 2-4 Noel St, London W1V 3RB, England
Chaplin, Geraldine *Actress*
Manoir de Bau, Vevey, Switzerland
Chapman, Alvah H, Jr *Publisher*
Grove Harbour, 1690 S Bayshore Lane, #10A, Miami, FL 33133, USA
Chapman, Beth Nielsen *Singer, Songwriter*
%Sussman Assoc, 1222 16th Ave S, #300, Nashville, TN 37212, USA
Chapman, Gary *Songwriter*
%TBA Artist Mgmt, 300 10th Ave S, Nashville, TN 37203, USA
Chapman, Judith *Actress*
11670 Sunset Blvd, #312, Los Angeles, CA 90049, USA
Chapman, Lanei *Actress*
%Susan Smith, 121A N San Vicente Blvd, Beverly Hills, CA 90211, USA
Chapman, Marshall *Vocalist*
1906 South St, #704, Nashville, TN 37212, USA
Chapman, Max C, Jr *Financier*
%Nomura Securities, 2 World Financial Center, 200 Liberty St, New York, NY 10281, USA
Chapman, Michael J *Movie Director, Cinematographer*
501 S Beverly Dr, #300, Beverly Hills, CA 90212, USA
Chapman, Philip K *Astronaut*
416 Ives Terrace, Sunnyvale, CA 94087, USA
Chapman, Rex *Basketball Player*
2248 Terrace Woods Park, Lexington, KY 40513, USA
Chapman, Samuel B (Sam) *Football, Baseball Player*
11 Andrew Dr, #39, Tiburon, CA 94920, USA
Chapman, Steven Curtis *Singer, Guitarist, Songwriter*
%Creative Trust, 2105 Elliston Place, Nashville, TN 37203, USA
Chapman, Tracy *Singer, Songwriter*
%Gold Mountain, 3575 Cahuenga Blvd W, #450, Los Angeles, CA 90068, USA
Chapman, Wes *Ballet Dancer*
%American Ballet Theater, 890 Broadway, New York, NY 10003, USA
Chapot, Frank *Equestrian Rider*
1 Opie Road, Neshanic Station, NJ 08853, USA
Chappell, Crystal *Actress*
35 Chestnut Hill Place, Glen Ridge, NJ 07028, USA
Chappell, Gregory S (Greg) *Cricketer*
%S A Cricket Assn, Adelaide Oval, North Adelaide SA 5006, Australia
Chappelle, David *Actor, Comedian*
%Creative Artists Agency, 9830 Wilshire Blvd, Beverly Hills, CA 90212, USA

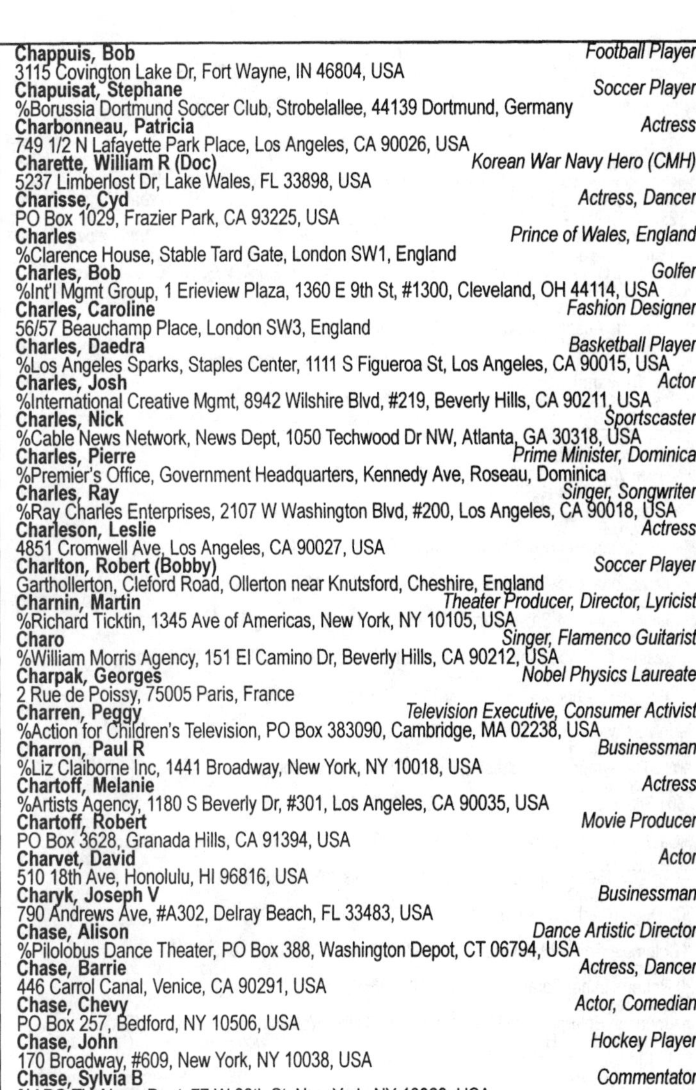

Chappuis, Bob — *Football Player*
3115 Covington Lake Dr, Fort Wayne, IN 46804, USA

Chapuisat, Stephane — *Soccer Player*
%Borussia Dortmund Soccer Club, Strobelallee, 44139 Dortmund, Germany

Charbonneau, Patricia — *Actress*
749 1/2 N Lafayette Park Place, Los Angeles, CA 90026, USA

Charette, William R (Doc) — *Korean War Navy Hero (CMH)*
5237 Limberlost Dr, Lake Wales, FL 33898, USA

Charisse, Cyd — *Actress, Dancer*
PO Box 1029, Frazier Park, CA 93225, USA

Charles — *Prince of Wales, England*
%Clarence House, Stable Tard Gate, London SW1, England

Charles, Bob — *Golfer*
%Int'l Mgmt Group, 1 Erieview Plaza, 1360 E 9th St, #1300, Cleveland, OH 44114, USA

Charles, Caroline — *Fashion Designer*
56/57 Beauchamp Place, London SW3, England

Charles, Daedra — *Basketball Player*
%Los Angeles Sparks, Staples Center, 1111 S Figueroa St, Los Angeles, CA 90015, USA

Charles, Josh — *Actor*
%International Creative Mgmt, 8942 Wilshire Blvd, #219, Beverly Hills, CA 90211, USA

Charles, Nick — *Sportscaster*
%Cable News Network, News Dept, 1050 Techwood Dr NW, Atlanta, GA 30318, USA

Charles, Pierre — *Prime Minister, Dominica*
%Premier's Office, Government Headquarters, Kennedy Ave, Roseau, Dominica

Charles, Ray — *Singer, Songwriter*
%Ray Charles Enterprises, 2107 W Washington Blvd, #200, Los Angeles, CA 90018, USA

Charleson, Leslie — *Actress*
4851 Cromwell Ave, Los Angeles, CA 90027, USA

Charlton, Robert (Bobby) — *Soccer Player*
Garthollerton, Cleford Road, Ollerton near Knutsford, Cheshire, England

Charnin, Martin — *Theater Producer, Director, Lyricist*
%Richard Ticktin, 1345 Ave of Americas, New York, NY 10105, USA

Charo — *Singer, Flamenco Guitarist*
%William Morris Agency, 151 El Camino Dr, Beverly Hills, CA 90212, USA

Charpak, Georges — *Nobel Physics Laureate*
2 Rue de Poissy, 75005 Paris, France

Charren, Peggy — *Television Executive, Consumer Activist*
%Action for Children's Television, PO Box 383090, Cambridge, MA 02238, USA

Charron, Paul R — *Businessman*
%Liz Claiborne Inc, 1441 Broadway, New York, NY 10018, USA

Chartoff, Melanie — *Actress*
%Artists Agency, 1180 S Beverly Dr, #301, Los Angeles, CA 90035, USA

Chartoff, Robert — *Movie Producer*
PO Box 3628, Granada Hills, CA 91394, USA

Charvet, David — *Actor*
510 18th Ave, Honolulu, HI 96816, USA

Charyk, Joseph V — *Businessman*
790 Andrews Ave, #A302, Delray Beach, FL 33483, USA

Chase, Alison — *Dance Artistic Director*
%Pilolobus Dance Theater, PO Box 388, Washington Depot, CT 06794, USA

Chase, Barrie — *Actress, Dancer*
446 Carrol Canal, Venice, CA 90291, USA

Chase, Chevy — *Actor, Comedian*
PO Box 257, Bedford, NY 10506, USA

Chase, John — *Hockey Player*
170 Broadway, #609, New York, NY 10038, USA

Chase, Sylvia B — *Commentator*
%ABC-TV, News Dept, 77 W 66th St, New York, NY 10023, USA

Chasez, Joshua Scott (J C) — *Singer ('N Sync)*
%Wright Entertainment, 7680 Universal Blvd, #500, Orlando, FL 32819, USA

Chast, Roz — *Cartoonist*
%New Yorker Magazine, Editorial Dept, 4 Times Square, New York, NY 10036, USA

Chastain, Brandi — *Soccer Player, Model*
1661 University Way, San Jose, CA 95126, USA

Chauvire, Yvette — *Ballerina*
21 Place du Commerce, 75015 Paris, France

Chaves, Richard — *Actor*
%Media Artists Group, 6300 Wilshire Blvd, #1470, Los Angeles, CA 90048, USA

Chavez Frias, Hugo R — *President, Venezuela*
%Palacio de Miraflores, Avenida Urdaneta, Caracas 1010, Venzuela

Chayanne — *Singer, Actress*
%Chaf Enterprises, 1717 N Bayshore Dr, #2146, Miami, FL 33132, USA

Chaykin, Maury — *Actor*
%Writers & Artists, 8383 Wilshire Blvd, #550, Beverly Hills, CA 90211, USA

Cheadle, Don — *Actor*
2454 Glyndon Ave, Venice, CA 90291, USA

Cheaney, Calbert N — *Basketball Player*
%Golden State Warriors, 1001 Broadway, Oakland, CA 94607, USA

C

Cheatham - Cherry

Cheatham, Maree *Actress*
%Yvette Schumer, 8787 Shoreham Dr, West Hollywood, CA 90069, USA
Checker, Chubby *Singer, Songwriter*
%Twisted Ent, 320 Fayette St, #200, Conshohocken, PA 19428, USA
Cheek, James E *Educator*
1201 S Benbow Road, Greensboro, NC 27406, USA
Cheek, Molly *Actress*
%Kazarian/Spencer, 11365 Ventura Blvd, #100, Studio City, CA 91604, USA
Cheeks, Maurice E (Mo) *Basketball Player, Coach*
7325 SW Childs Road, Portland, OR 97224, USA
Cheever, Eddie *Auto Racing Driver*
%Team Cheever, 8435 Georgetown Road, #600, Indianapolis, IN 46268, USA
Cheevers, Gerald M (Gerry) *Hockey Player, Coach; Sportscaster*
905 Lewis O'Gray Dr, Saugus, MA 01906, USA
Chekamauskas, Vitautas *Architect*
%State Arts Academy, Maironio 6, 2600 Vilnius, Lithuania
Chelberg, Robert D *Army General*
%Cubic Applications, Patch Community, Unit 30400, Box R65, APO, AE 09128, USA
Cheli, Giovanni Cardinal *Religious Leader*
%Pastoral Care of Migrants Council, Piazza Calisto 16, 00153 Rome, Italy
Cheli, Maurizio *Astronaut, Italy*
38 Via Ciro Santagata, Modena, Italy
Cheli-Merchez, Marianne *Astronaut*
132 Rue Van Allard, 1180 Bruxelles, Belgium
Chelios, Christos K (Chris) *Hockey Player*
790 Falmouth Dr, Bloomfield Hills, MI 48304, USA
Chellgren, Paul W *Businessman*
%Ashland Inc, PO Box 391, Covington, KY 41015, USA
Chen Kaige *Movie Director*
%International Creative Mgmt, 8942 Wilshire Blvd, #219, Beverly Hills, CA 90211, USA
Chen Lu *Figure Skater*
%Skating Assn, 54 Baishiqiao Road, Haidian District, Beijing 10044, China
Chen Shui-bian *President, Taiwan*
%President's Office, Chieshshou Hall, Chung-King Road, Taipei 100, Taiwan
Chen Xieyang *Conductor*
%Shanghai Symphony Orchestra, 105 Hunan Road, Shanghai 200031, China
Chen Yi *Composer*
%University of Missouri, Music Dept, Kansas City, MO 64110, USA
Chen Zuohuang *Conductor*
%Wichita Symphony Orchestra, Concert Hall, 225 W Douglas St, Wichita, KS 67202, USA
Chen, Joan *Actress, Director*
2601 Filbert St, San Francisco, CA 94123, USA
Chen, Joie *Commentator*
%Cable News Network, News Dept, 1050 Techwood Dr NW, Atlanta, GA 30318, USA
Chen, Julie *Commentator*
%CBS-TV, News Dept, 51 W 52nd St, New York, NY 10019, USA
Chen, Lincoln C *Nutritionist*
302 Dean Road, Brookline, MA
Chen, Robert *Concert Pianist*
%Columbia Artists Mgmt Inc, 165 W 57th St, New York, NY 10019, USA
Chenery, Penny *Thoroughbred Racing Owner*
20 Roberts Lane, Saratoga Springs, NY 12866, USA
Cheney, Lynne V *Government Official*
%American Enterprise Institute, 1150 17th St NW, Washington, DC 20036, USA
Cheney, Richard B *Vice President; Secretary, Defense*
6613 Madison Dr, McLean, VA 22101, USA
Chennault, Anna *Businesswoman, Writer*
%TAC International, Chennault Building, 1049 30th St NW, Washington, DC 20007, USA
Chenoweth, Kristin *Actress, Singer*
250 W 57th St, #2223, New York, NY 10019, USA
Cher *Actress, Singer*
%Goldman Grant Tani, 9100 Wilshire Blvd, #1000W, Beverly Hills, CA 90212, USA
Chereau, Patrice *Movie, Opera, Theater Director*
%Nanterre-Amandiers, 7 Ave Pablo Picasso, 9200 Nanterre, France
Cherestal, Jean-Marie *Prime Minister, Haiti*
%Prime Minister's Office, Palais Ministeres, Port-au-Prince, Haiti
Chermayeff, Peter *Architect*
15 E 26th St, New York, NY 10010, USA
Chernobrovkina, Tatyana A *Ballerina*
%Moscow Musical Theater, B Dimitrovka Str 17, Moscow 103009, Russia
Chernov, Vladimir K *Opera Singer*
%Columbia Artists Mgmt Inc, 165 W 57th St, New York, NY 10019, USA
Chernow, Ron *Writer*
63 Joralemon St, Brooklyn, NY 11201, USA
Cherrelle *Singer*
%Associated Booking Corp, 1995 Broadway, #501, New York, NY 10023, USA
Cherry, Don S *Hockey Player, Coach*
%Cherry's Grapevine, 1233 Queensway, Etobicoke ON M8Z 1S1, Canada

Cherry, Fred V *Vietnam War Air Force Hero*
720 Dale Dr, Silver Spring, MD 20910, USA
Cherry, Neneh *Singer*
PO Box 1622, London NW10 5TF, England
Chertoff, Michael *Attorney, Government Official*
%Justice Department, 10th St & Constitution Ave NW, Washington, DC 20530, USA
Chertok, Jack *Movie Producer*
515 Ocean Ave, #305, Santa Monica, CA 90402, USA
Chesney, Kenny *Singer*
PO Box 128558, Nashville, TN 37212, USA
Chester, Colby *Actor*
%Talent Group, 6300 Wilshire Blvd, #2100, Los Angeles, CA 90048, USA
Chester, Raymond T *Football Player*
4722 Grass Valley Road, Oakland, CA 94605, USA
Chestnut, Mary Boykin *Educator*
%Sweet Briar College, President's Office, Sweet Briar, VA 24595, USA
Chestnut, Morris *Actor*
%Talent Entertainment Group, 9111 Wilshire Blvd, Beverly Hills, CA 90210, USA
Chestnutt, Mark *Singer, Songwriter*
%Ladd Mgmt, 1106 16th Ave S, Nashville, TN 37212, USA
Chew, Geoffrey F *Physicist*
10 Maybeck Twin Dr, Berkeley, CA 94708, USA
Chi Haotian *General, China*
%National Defense Ministry, Jingshanqia Jie, Beijing, China
Chia, Sandro *Artist*
Castello Romitorio, Montalcino, Siena, Italy
Chiadel, Dana *Canoeing Athlete*
5302 Flanders Ave, Kensington, MD 20895, USA
Chiao, Leroy *Astronaut*
2108 Butler Dr, Friendswood, TX 77546, USA
Chiara, Maria *Opera Singer*
%Columbia Artists Mgmt Inc, 165 W 57th St, New York, NY 10019, USA
Chicago, Judy *Artist*
%ACA Contemporary, 41 E 57th St, New York, NY 10022, USA
Chihara, Charles S *Philosopher*
567 Cragmont Ave, Berkeley, CA 94708, USA
Chihara, Paul *Composer*
3815 W Olive Ave, #202, Burbank, CA 91505, USA
Chihuly, Dale P *Artist*
%Chihuly Inc, 1111 NW 50th St, Seattle, WA 98107, USA
Chiklis, Michael *Actor*
4310 Sutton Place, Sherman Oaks, CA 91403, USA
Child, Julia M *Food Expert, Writer*
300 Hot Springs Road, #I178, Santa Barbara, CA 93108, USA
Childers, Ernest *WW II Army Hero (CMH)*
13681 S 308th East Ave, Coweta, OK 74429, USA
Childress, Raymond C (Ray), Jr *Football Player*
639 Shady Hill St, Houston, TX 77056, USA
Childress, Richard (R C) *Auto Racing Executive*
%Childress Racing, PO Box 1189, Industrial Dr, Welcome, NC 27374, USA
Childs, Barton *Physician*
1019 Winding Way, Baltimore, MD 21210, USA
Childs, Billy *Jazz Pianist*
%Integrity Talent, PO Box 961, Burlington, MA 01803, USA
Childs, Brevard S *Theologian*
508 Amity Road, Bethany, CT 06524, USA
Childs, David M *Architect*
%Skidmore Owings Merrill, 14 Wall St, New York, NY 10005, USA
Childs, Toni *Singer, Songwriter*
%Geffen Records, 10900 Wilshire Blvd, #1000, Los Angeles, CA 90024, USA
Chiles, Henry G (Hank), Jr *Navy Admiral*
6436 Pima St, Alexandria, VA 22312, USA
Chiles, Linden *Actor*
2521 Topanga Skyline Dr, Topanga, CA 90290, USA
Chiles, Lois *Actress, Model*
%Ambrosio/Mortimer, PO Box 16758, Beverly Hills, CA 90209, USA
Chilstom, Ken *Test Pilot*
20 Selby Lane, Palm Beach Gardens, FL 33418, USA
Chilton, Alex *Singer, Guitarist (Box Tops)*
%Rick Levy Mgmt, 4250 A1AS, #D11, Saint Augustine, FL 32080, USA
Chilton, Kevin P *Astronaut*
71 Westover Ave SW, Bolling Air Force Base, DC 20336, USA
Chin, Tsai *Actress*
%Writers & Artists, 8383 Wilshire Blvd, #550, Beverly Hills, CA 90211, USA
Chinaglia, Giorgio *Soccer Player*
3-9-1 Via Quartara, 16148 Genoa, Italy
Chinlund, Nick *Actor*
%Writers & Artists, 8383 Wilshire Blvd, #550, Beverly Hills, CA 90211, USA

C

Chirac - Christian

Chirac, Jacques R *President, France*
%Palais de L'Elysee, 55-57 Faubourg Saint Honore, 75008 Paris, France
Chisholm, Melanie *Singer (Spice Girls)*
%Spice Girls Ltd, 66-68 Bell St, London NW1 6SP, England
Chisholm, Shirley A S *Representative, NY*
3344 Newbliss Circle, Ormond Beach, FL 32174, USA
Chisholm-Carrillo, Linda *Volleyball Player*
17213 Vose St, Van Nuys, CA 91406, USA
Chissano, Joaquim A *President, Mozambique*
%President's Office, Avda Julius Nyerere 2000, Maputo, Mozambique
Chitalada, Sot *Boxer*
%Home Express Co, 242/19 Moo 10, Sukhumvit Road, Cholburi 20210, Thailand
Chittister, Joan D *Social Psychologist*
%Saint Scholastica Priory, 335 E 9th St, Erie, PA 16503, USA
Chitwood, Joey, Jr *Stunt Car Driver*
863 Seddon Cove Way, Tampa, FL 33602, USA
Chivers, Warren *Skier*
%Vermont Academy, Saxtons River, WI 05154, USA
Chlumsky, Anna *Actress*
%David S Lee, 641 W Lake St, #402, Chicago, IL 60661, USA
Cho, Alfred Y *Electrical Engineer*
%AT&T Bell Lucent Laboratory, 600 Mountain Ave, New Providence, NJ 07974, USA
Cho, Catherine *Concert Violinist*
%Columbia Artists Mgmt Inc, 165 W 57th St, New York, NY 10019, USA
Cho, Fujio *Businessman*
%Toyota Motor Corp, 1 Toyotacho, Toyota City, Aicji Prefecture 471, Japan
Cho, Margaret *Actress, Comedienne*
%Gallin-Morey, 335 N Maple Dr, #351, Beverly Hills, CA 90210, USA
Cho, Paul *Evangelist*
%Full Gospel Central Church, Yoido Plaza, Seoul, South Korea
Choate, Jerry D *Businessman*
%Allstate Insurance, Allstate Plaza, 2775 Sanders Road, Northbrook, IL 60062, USA
Chodorow, Marvin *Physicist, Electrical Engineer*
81 Pearce Mitchell Place, Stanford, CA 94305, USA
Chojnowska-Liskiewicz, Krystyna *Yachtswoman*
Ul Norblina 29 m 50, 80 304 Gdansk-Oliwa, Poland
Chokachi, David *Actor*
11693 San Vicente Blvd, #216, Los Angeles, CA 90049, USA
Chomsky, A Noam *Linguist*
99 Gull Haven Lane, Wellfleet, MA 02667, USA
Chomsky, Marvin J *Television Director*
4707 Ocean Front Walk, Marina del Rey, CA 90292, USA
Chong, Rae Dawn *Actress*
PO Box 691600, Los Angeles, CA 90069, USA
Chong, Thomas (Tommy) *Actor, Comedian (Cheech & Chong)*
1625 Casale Road, Pacific Palisades, CA 90272, USA
Chopra, Deepak *Writer*
%Greater Talent Network, 437 5th Ave, New York, NY 10016, USA
Chorvat, Scarlett *Actress*
%Innovative Artists, 1505 10th St, Santa Monica, CA 90401, USA
Chorzempa, Daniel W *Concert Organist, Composer*
%Kunstleragentur Raab & Bohm, Plankengasse 7, 1010 Vienna, Austria
Choudhury, Sarita *Actress*
%William Morris Agency, 151 El Camino Dr, Beverly Hills, CA 90212, USA
Chouinard, Marie *Dancer, Choreographer*
%Compagnie Chouinard, 3981 Boul Saint-Laurent, Montreal PQ H2W 1Y5, Canada
Chow Yun-Fat *Actor*
PO Box 71288, Kowloon Central, Hong Kong, China
Chow, Amy *Gymnast*
%West Valley Gymnastics School, 1190 Dell Ave, #1, Campbell, CA 95008, USA
Choy, Herbert Y C *Judge*
%US Court of Appeals, 300 Ala Moana Blvd, #C328, Honolulu, HI 96850, USA
Chretien, J J Jean *Prime Minister, Canada*
%Prime Minister's Office, 24 Sussex Dr, Ottawa ON K1M 0MS, Canada
Chretien, Jean-Loup *Spatinaut, France; Air Force General*
%Astronautes Direction, 2 Place Maurice Quentin, 75029 Paris Cedex, France
Christensen, Erika *Actress*
521 Spoleto Dr, Pacific Palisades, CA 90272, USA
Christensen, Hayden *Actor*
PO Box 2459, San Rafael, CA 94912, USA
Christensen, Helena *Model*
%Select Model Mgmt, 43 King St, London WC2, England
Christensen, Kai *Architect*
100 Vester Voldgade, 1552 Copenhagen V, Denmark
Christensen, Todd J *Football Player, Sportscaster*
991 Sunburst Lane, Alpine, UT 84004, USA
Christian, Claudia *Actress*
%Zard Productions, 8491 Sunset Blvd, #140, West Hollywood, CA 90069, USA

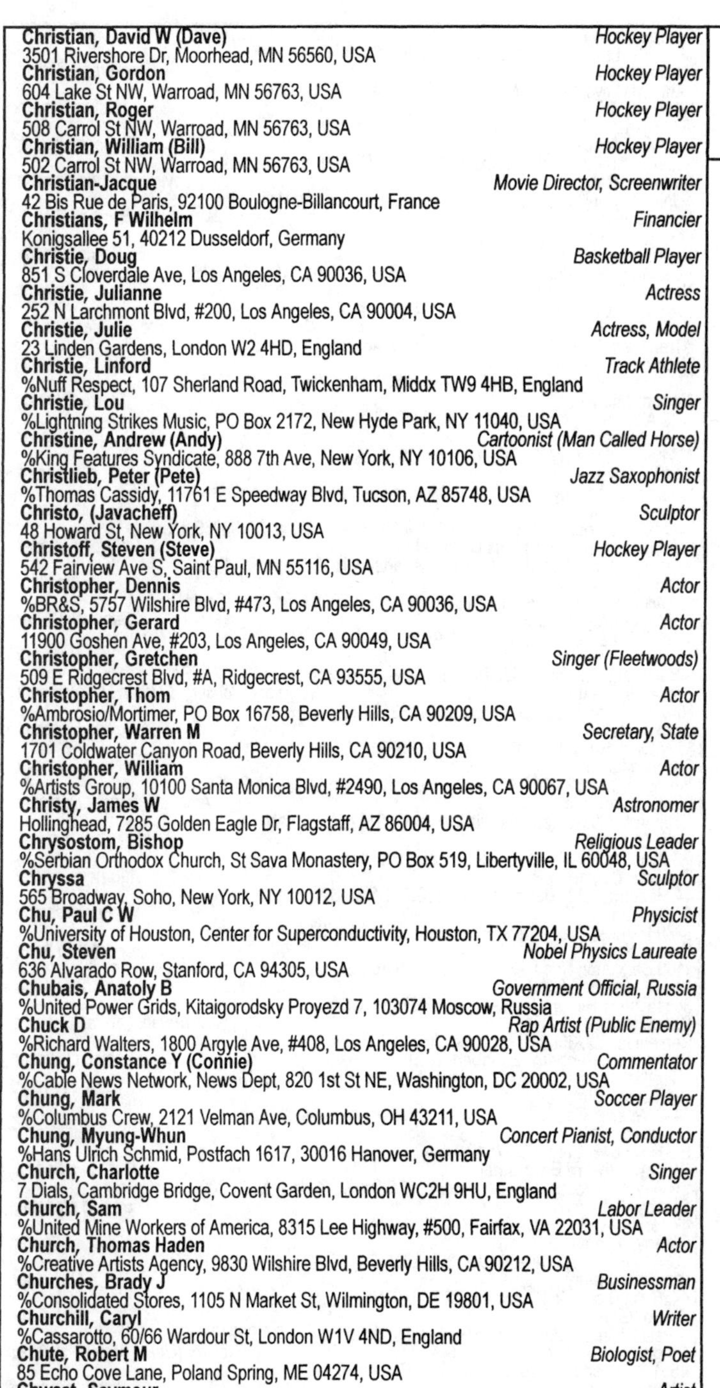

Christian, David W (Dave) *Hockey Player*
3501 Rivershore Dr, Moorhead, MN 56560, USA
Christian, Gordon *Hockey Player*
604 Lake St NW, Warroad, MN 56763, USA
Christian, Roger *Hockey Player*
508 Carrol St NW, Warroad, MN 56763, USA
Christian, William (Bill) *Hockey Player*
502 Carrol St NW, Warroad, MN 56763, USA
Christian-Jacque *Movie Director, Screenwriter*
42 Bis Rue de Paris, 92100 Boulogne-Billancourt, France
Christians, F Wilhelm *Financier*
Konigsallee 51, 40212 Dusseldorf, Germany
Christie, Doug *Basketball Player*
851 S Cloverdale Ave, Los Angeles, CA 90036, USA
Christie, Julianne *Actress*
252 N Larchmont Blvd, #200, Los Angeles, CA 90004, USA
Christie, Julie *Actress, Model*
23 Linden Gardens, London W2 4HD, England
Christie, Linford *Track Athlete*
%Nuff Respect, 107 Sherland Road, Twickenham, Middx TW9 4HB, England
Christie, Lou *Singer*
%Lightning Strikes Music, PO Box 2172, New Hyde Park, NY 11040, USA
Christine, Andrew (Andy) *Cartoonist (Man Called Horse)*
%King Features Syndicate, 888 7th Ave, New York, NY 10106, USA
Christlieb, Peter (Pete) *Jazz Saxophonist*
%Thomas Cassidy, 11761 E Speedway Blvd, Tucson, AZ 85748, USA
Christo, (Javacheff) *Sculptor*
48 Howard St, New York, NY 10013, USA
Christoff, Steven (Steve) *Hockey Player*
542 Fairview Ave S, Saint Paul, MN 55116, USA
Christopher, Dennis *Actor*
%BR&S, 5757 Wilshire Blvd, #473, Los Angeles, CA 90036, USA
Christopher, Gerard *Actor*
11900 Goshen Ave, #203, Los Angeles, CA 90049, USA
Christopher, Gretchen *Singer (Fleetwoods)*
509 E Ridgecrest Blvd, #A, Ridgecrest, CA 93555, USA
Christopher, Thom *Actor*
%Ambrosio/Mortimer, PO Box 16758, Beverly Hills, CA 90209, USA
Christopher, Warren M *Secretary, State*
1701 Coldwater Canyon Road, Beverly Hills, CA 90210, USA
Christopher, William *Actor*
%Artists Group, 10100 Santa Monica Blvd, #2490, Los Angeles, CA 90067, USA
Christy, James W *Astronomer*
Hollinghead, 7285 Golden Eagle Dr, Flagstaff, AZ 86004, USA
Chrysostom, Bishop *Religious Leader*
%Serbian Orthodox Church, St Sava Monastery, PO Box 519, Libertyville, IL 60048, USA
Chryssa *Sculptor*
565 Broadway, Soho, New York, NY 10012, USA
Chu, Paul C W *Physicist*
%University of Houston, Center for Superconductivity, Houston, TX 77204, USA
Chu, Steven *Nobel Physics Laureate*
636 Alvarado Row, Stanford, CA 94305, USA
Chubais, Anatoly B *Government Official, Russia*
%United Power Grids, Kitaigorodsky Proyezd 7, 103074 Moscow, Russia
Chuck D *Rap Artist (Public Enemy)*
%Richard Walters, 1800 Argyle Ave, #408, Los Angeles, CA 90028, USA
Chung, Constance Y (Connie) *Commentator*
%Cable News Network, News Dept, 820 1st St NE, Washington, DC 20002, USA
Chung, Mark *Soccer Player*
%Columbus Crew, 2121 Velman Ave, Columbus, OH 43211, USA
Chung, Myung-Whun *Concert Pianist, Conductor*
%Hans Ulrich Schmid, Postfach 1617, 30016 Hanover, Germany
Church, Charlotte *Singer*
7 Dials, Cambridge Bridge, Covent Garden, London WC2H 9HU, England
Church, Sam *Labor Leader*
%United Mine Workers of America, 8315 Lee Highway, #500, Fairfax, VA 22031, USA
Church, Thomas Haden *Actor*
%Creative Artists Agency, 9830 Wilshire Blvd, Beverly Hills, CA 90212, USA
Churches, Brady J *Businessman*
%Consolidated Stores, 1105 N Market St, Wilmington, DE 19801, USA
Churchill, Caryl *Writer*
%Cassarotto, 60/66 Wardour St, London W1V 4ND, England
Chute, Robert M *Biologist, Poet*
85 Echo Cove Lane, Poland Spring, ME 04274, USA
Chwast, Seymour *Artist*
%Push Pin Group, 18 E 16th St, #1700, New York, NY 10003, USA
Cialini, Julie *Model, Actress*
PO Box 55536, Valencia, CA 91385, USA

C

Ciampi - Clardy

Ciampi, Carlo A *President, Prime Minister, Italy*
%President's Office, Palazzo del Quirinale, 00187 Rome, Italy
Ciampi, Joe *Basketball Coach*
%Auburn University, Athletic Dept, Auburn, AL 36831, USA
Ciccarelli, Dino *Hockey Player*
1872 Clarence St, Sarnia ON N7X 1C7, Canada
Ciccolini, Aldo *Concert Pianist*
%Gerhild Baron Mgmt, Dornbacher Str 41/III/3, 1170 Vienna, Austria
Cicerone, Ralph J *Environmental Scientist*
%University of California, Earth Science Dept, Rowland Hall, Irvine, CA 92717, USA
Cichy, Joe J *Football Player*
9806 Island Road, Bismarck, ND 58503, USA
Cienfuegos, Mauricio *Soccer Player*
%Los Angeles Galaxy, 1010 Rose Bowl Dr, Pasadena, CA 91103, USA
Cilento, Diane *Actress*
Box 600, Spring Hill, Queensland 4004, Australia
Ciller, Tansu *Prime Minister, Turkey*
%True Path Party, Selanik Cod 40, Kizilay, Ankara, Turkey
Cimino, Leonardo *Actor*
%Michael Hartig Agency, 156 5th Ave, #820, New York, NY 10010, USA
Cimino, Michael *Movie Director*
9015 Alto Cedro, Beverly Hills, CA 90210, USA
Cink, Stewart *Golfer*
2741 NE 10th St, #705, Ocala, FL 34470, USA
Cioffi, Charles *Actor*
%Paradigm Agency, 10100 Santa Monica Blvd, #2500, Los Angeles, CA 90067, USA
Ciokey, Janna *Actress*
%J Michael Bloom, 9255 Sunset Blvd, #710, Los Angeles, CA 90069, USA
Cipriani Thorne, Juan Luis Cardinal *Religious Leader*
%Arzobispado, Plaza de Armas S/N, Apartado 1512, Lima 100, Peru
Cirici, Cristian *Architect*
%Cirici Arquitecte, Carrer de Pujades 63 2-N, 08005 Barcelona, Spain
Cirillo, Jeffrey H (Jeff) *Baseball Player*
8305 213th Dr NE, Redmond, WA 98053, USA
Cisneros, Evelyn *Ballerina*
%San Francisco Ballet, 455 Franklin St, San Francisco, CA 94102, USA
Cisneros, Henry G *Secretary, Housing & Urban Development*
2002 W Houston St, San Antonio, TX 78207, USA
Citro, Ralph *Boxing Historian*
32 N Black Horse Pike, Blackwood, NJ 08012, USA
Citron, Martin *Neurobiologist*
%Amgen Co, 152A 226 Amgen Center, Thousand Oaks, CA 91320, USA
Citterio, Antonio *Architect, Interior Designer*
%Antonio Citterio Partners, Via Cerva 4, 20122 Milan, Italy
Citti, Christine *Actress*
%Artmedia, 20 Ave Rapp, 75007 Paris, France
Civiletti, Benjamin R *Attorney General*
14 Meadow Road, Baltimore, MD 21212, USA
Cizik, Robert *Businessman*
8839 Harness Creek Lane, Houston, TX 77024, USA
Clabo, Neal *Football Player*
1100 Beaverton Road, Knoxville, TN 37919, USA
Clack, James T (Jim) *Football Player*
3631 Cherry Hill Dr, Greensboro, NC 27410, USA
Claes, Willy *Government Official, Belgium*
Berkenlaan 23, 3500 Hasselt, Belgium
Claiborne Ortenberg, Elisabeth (Liz) *Fashion Designer*
%Liz Claiborne Inc, 1441 Broadway, New York, NY 10018, USA
Claiborne, Chris *Football Player*
5440 Wessex Court, #210, Dearborn, MI 48126, USA
Clampett, Bobby *Golfer*
PO Box 5849, Cary, NC 27512, USA
Clancy, Edward B Cardinal *Religious Leader*
Sydney Archdiocese, Polding House, 276 Pitt St, Sydney NSW 2000, Australia
Clancy, Gil *Boxing Manager*
47 Morris Ave W, Malverne, NY 11565, USA
Clancy, Thomas J (Tom) *Writer*
1638 Lee Dr, Edgewater, MD 21037, USA
Clanton, Jimmy *Singer*
4425 Kingwood Dr, Kingwood, TX 77339, USA
Clapp, Gordon *Actor*
%Paul Kohner, 9300 Wilshire Blvd, #555, Beverly Hills, CA 90212, USA
Clapp, Nicholas R *Explorer (Ubar), Movie Producer*
1551 S Robertson Blvd, Los Angeles, CA 90035, USA
Clapton, Eric *Singer, Guitarist*
46 Kensington Court, London WE8 5DT, England
Clardy, Jon C *Chemist*
%Cornell University, Chemistry Dept, Ithaca, NY 14853, USA

Clark, Alan *Pianist (Dire Straits)*
%Damage Mgmt, 16 Lambton Place, London W11 2SH, England
Clark, Anthony *Actor, Comedian*
4933 W Craig Road, #268, Las Vegas, NV 89130, USA
Clark, Archie *Basketball Player*
Wayne County Building, 600 Randolph St, #323, Detroit, MI 48226, USA
Clark, Bob *Commentator*
%ABC-TV, News Dept, 5010 Creston St, Hyattsville, MD 20781, USA
Clark, Bryan *Actor*
%Epstein-Wyckoff, 280 S Beverly Dr, #400, Beverly Hills, CA 90212, USA
Clark, C Joseph (Joe) *Prime Minister, Canada*
707 7th Ave SW, #1300, Calgary AB T2P 3H6, Canada
Clark, Candy *Actress*
13935 Hatteras St, Van Nuys, CA 91401, USA
Clark, Carol Higgins *Writer*
300 E 56th St, New York, NY 10022, USA
Clark, Dallas *Football Player*
%Indianapolis Colts, 7001 W 56th St, Indianapolis, IN 46254, USA
Clark, Dwight E *Football Player, Executive*
98 Inglewood Lane, Atherton, CA 94027, USA
Clark, Earl *Diver*
1145 NE 126th St, #4, North Miami, FL 33161, USA
Clark, Eugenie *Zoologist*
1255 N Gulfstream Ave, #503, Sarasota, FL 34236, USA
Clark, Gene *Singer, Percussionist (Byrds)*
%Artists International Mgmt, 9850 Sandalfoot Road, #458, Boca Raton, FL 33428, USA
Clark, George W *Physicist*
%Massachusetts Institute of Technology, Physics Dept, Cambridge, MA 02139, USA
Clark, Guy *Singer, Songwriter*
%Keith Case Assoc, 1025 17th Ave S, #200, Nashville, TN 37212, USA
Clark, Helen *Prime Minister, New Zealand*
%Prime Minister's Office, Parliament Buildings, Wellington, New Zealand
Clark, Jack A *Baseball Player*
10800 E Cactus Road, #14, Scottsdale, AZ 85259, USA
Clark, James (Jim) *Businessman*
%Neoteris, 940 Stewart Dr, Sunnyvale, CA 94085, USA
Clark, Joe *Educator*
%Essex County Detention Center, 208 Essex Ave, Newark, NJ 07103, USA
Clark, Kelly *Snowboard Skier*
178 Route 100, PO Box 721, West Dover, VT 05356, USA
Clark, Kenneth B *Psychologist*
17 Pinecrest Dr, Hastings-on-Hudson, NY 10706, USA
Clark, Keon *Basketball Player*
%Utah Jazz, Delta Center, 301 W South Temple, Salt Lake City, UT 84101, USA
Clark, L Hill *Businessman*
%Crane Co, 100 Stamford Place, Stamford, CT 06902, USA
Clark, Marcia *Attorney*
%Bobby Bell, 4343 Lankershim Blvd, North Hollywood, CA 91602, USA
Clark, Mary Ellen *Diver*
213 Lauderdale Trail, Fort Lauderdale, FL 33312, USA
Clark, Mary Higgins *Writer*
Werimus Brook Road, Saddle River, NJ 07458, USA
Clark, Matt *Actor*
1199 Park Ave, #15D, New York, NY 10128, USA
Clark, Monte D *Football Player*
1482 Lochridge Road, Bloomfield Township, MI 48302, USA
Clark, Oliver *Actor*
%House of Representatives, 400 S Beverly Dr, #101, Beverly Hills, CA 90212, USA
Clark, Perry *Basketball Coach*
%Miami University, Athletic Dept, Coral Gables, FL 33124, USA
Clark, Peter B *Publisher*
7675 La Jolla Blvd, #203, La Jolla, CA 92037, USA
Clark, Petula *Singer, Actress*
15 Chemin Rieu Colign, Geneva, Switzerland
Clark, Richard A (Dick) *Entertainer, Television Producer*
%Dick Clark Enterprise, 3003 W Olive Ave, Burbank, CA 91505, USA
Clark, Richard C (Dick) *Senator, IA*
4424 Edmunds St NW, #1070, Washington, DC 20007, USA
Clark, Robert C *Artist*
34 Monterey Court, Manhattan Beach, CA 90266, USA
Clark, Roy *Singer, Guitarist*
%Roy Clark Productions, 3225 S Norwood Ave, Tulsa, OK 74135, USA
Clark, Stephen E (Steve) *Swimmer*
29 Martling Road, San Anselmo, CA 94960, USA
Clark, Susan *Actress*
13400 Riverside Dr, #308, Sherman Oaks, CA 91423, USA
Clark, Vernon E *Navy Admiral*
Chief of Naval Operations, HqUSN, Pentagon, Washington, DC 20350, USA

C

Clark, W G *Architect*
%Clark & Menefee Architects, 4048 E Main St, Charlottesville, VA 22902, USA
Clark, W Ramsey *Attorney General*
37 W 12th St, New York, NY 10011, USA
Clark, Wendel *Hockey Player*
%Toronto Maple Leafs, 40 Bay St, Toronto ON M5J 2K2, Canada
Clark, Wesley K (Wes) *Army General*
%Stephens Group, 111 Center St, Little Rock, AR 72201, USA
Clark, William N (Will), Jr *Baseball Player*
55 Tokalon Place, Metairie, LA 70001, USA
Clark, William P *Secretary, Interior*
4424 Edmunds St NW #1070, Washington, DC 20007, USA
Clarke, Allan *Singer, Musician (Hollies)*
Hill Farm, Hackleton, Northantshire NN7 2DH, England
Clarke, Angela *Actress*
7557 Mulholland Dr, Los Angeles, CA 90046, USA
Clarke, Arthur C *Writer, Underwater Explorer*
Leslie's House, 25 Barnes Place, Colombo 07, Sri Lanka
Clarke, Bob *Cartoonist*
7480 Rivershore Dr, Seaford, DE 19973, USA
Clarke, Brian Patrick *Actor*
333 N Kenwood St, #D, Burbank, CA 91505, USA
Clarke, Ellis E I *President, Trinidad & Tobago*
16 Frederick St, Port of Spain, Trinidad & Tobago
Clarke, Gilby *Guitarist (Guns n' Roses)*
%Sammy Boyd Entertainment, 212 Allen Ave, Allenhurst, NJ 07711, USA
Clarke, Gilmore D *Landscape Architect*
480 Park Ave, New York, NY 10022, USA
Clarke, John *Actor*
%Days of Our Lives Show, KNBC-TV, 3000 W Alameda Ave, Burbank, CA 91523, USA
Clarke, Kenneth H *Government Official, England*
%House of Commons, Westminster, London SW1A 0AA, England
Clarke, Lenny *Actor*
%Writers & Artists, 8383 Wilshire Blvd, #550, Beverly Hills, CA 90211, USA
Clarke, Martha *Dancer, Choreographer*
%Sheldon Soffer Mgmt, 130 W 56th St, New York, NY 10019, USA
Clarke, Melinda *Actress*
10600 Holman Ave, #1, Los Angeles, CA 90024, USA
Clarke, Michael *Drummer (Byrds)*
%Artists International Mgmt, 9850 Sandalfoot Blvd, #458, Boca Raton, FL 33428, USA
Clarke, Richard *Law Enforcement Official*
%National Security Council, 1600 Pennsylvania Ave NW, Washington, DC 20500, USA
Clarke, Robert *Actor*
4509 Laurel Canyon Blvd, #128, Valley Village, CA 91607, USA
Clarke, Robert E (Bobby) *Hockey Player, Executive*
1930 Glenwood Dr, Ocean City, NJ 08226, USA
Clarke, Robert L *Government Official*
%Bracewell & Patterson, 711 Louisiana St, #2900, Houston, TX 77002, USA
Clarke, Ronald (Ron) *Track Athlete*
1 Bay St, Brighton VIC 3186, Australia
Clarke, Sarah *Actress*
%William Morris Agency, 151 El Camino Dr, Beverly Hills, CA 90212, USA
Clarke, Stanley M *Jazz Bassist, Composer*
%Agency for Performing Arts, 9200 Sunset Blvd, #900, Los Angeles, CA 90069, USA
Clarke, Thomas E *Businessman*
%Nike Inc, 1 Bowerman Dr, Beaverton, OR 97005, USA
Clarkson, Adrienne *Governor General, Canada*
%Governor General's Office, 1 Sussex Dr, Ottawa ON K1A 0A2, Canada
Clarkson, Kelly *Singer*
%RCA Records, 8750 Wilshire Blvd, Beverly Hills, CA 90211, USA
Clarkson, Patricia *Actress*
%Gersh Agency, 232 N Canon Dr, Beverly Hills, CA 90210, USA
Clary, Robert *Actor*
1001 Sundial Lane, Beverly Hills, CA 90210, USA
Clatterbuck, Tamara *Actress*
%House of Representatives, 400 S Beverly Dr, #101, Beverly Hills, CA 90212, USA
Clatworthy, Robert *Sculptor*
Moelfre, Cynghordy, Landovery, Dyfed SA20 OUW Wales, England
Clausen, Raymond M (Mike), Jr *Vietnam War Marine Corps Hero (CMH)*
PO Box 991, Ponchatoula, LA 70454, USA
Clauser, Francis H *Aeronautical Engineer, Educator*
4072 Chevy Chase, Flintridge, CA 91011, USA
Clavel, Bernard *Writer*
Albin Michel, 22 Rue Huyghens, 75014 Paris, France
Clavier, Christian *Actor*
%Agents Associes Beaume, 201 Faubourg Saint Honore, 75008 Paris, France
Clawson, John *Basketball Player*
20 Velasco Court, Danville, CA 94526, USA

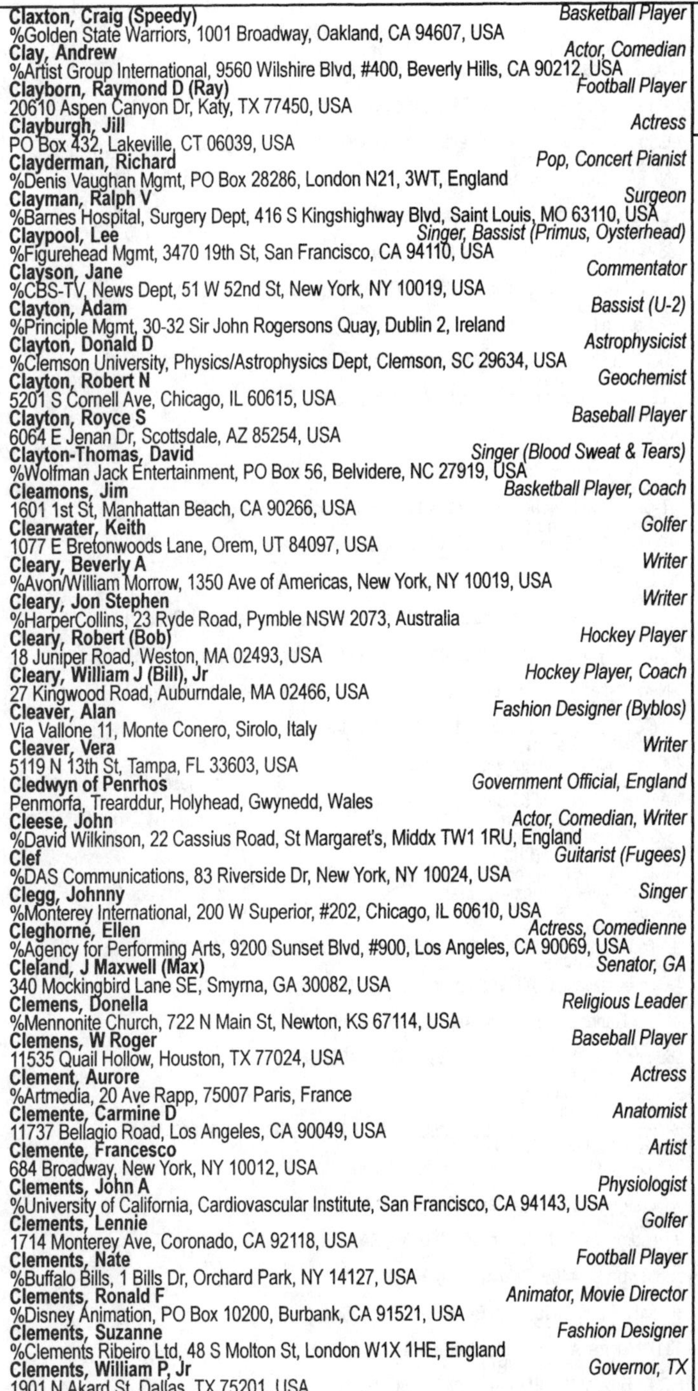

Claxton, Craig (Speedy) *Basketball Player*
%Golden State Warriors, 1001 Broadway, Oakland, CA 94607, USA
Clay, Andrew *Actor, Comedian*
%Artist Group International, 9560 Wilshire Blvd, #400, Beverly Hills, CA 90212, USA
Clayborn, Raymond D (Ray) *Football Player*
20610 Aspen Canyon Dr, Katy, TX 77450, USA
Clayburgh, Jill *Actress*
PO Box 432, Lakeville, CT 06039, USA
Clayderman, Richard *Pop, Concert Pianist*
%Denis Vaughan Mgmt, PO Box 28286, London N21, 3WT, England
Clayman, Ralph V *Surgeon*
%Barnes Hospital, Surgery Dept, 416 S Kingshighway Blvd, Saint Louis, MO 63110, USA
Claypool, Lee *Singer, Bassist (Primus, Oysterhead)*
%Figurehead Mgmt, 3470 19th St, San Francisco, CA 94110, USA
Clayson, Jane *Commentator*
%CBS-TV, News Dept, 51 W 52nd St, New York, NY 10019, USA
Clayton, Adam *Bassist (U-2)*
%Principle Mgmt, 30-32 Sir John Rogersons Quay, Dublin 2, Ireland
Clayton, Donald D *Astrophysicist*
%Clemson University, Physics/Astrophysics Dept, Clemson, SC 29634, USA
Clayton, Robert N *Geochemist*
5201 S Cornell Ave, Chicago, IL 60615, USA
Clayton, Royce S *Baseball Player*
6064 E Jenan Dr, Scottsdale, AZ 85254, USA
Clayton-Thomas, David *Singer (Blood Sweat & Tears)*
%Wolfman Jack Entertainment, PO Box 56, Belvidere, NC 27919, USA
Cleamons, Jim *Basketball Player, Coach*
1601 1st St, Manhattan Beach, CA 90266, USA
Clearwater, Keith *Golfer*
1077 E Bretonwoods Lane, Orem, UT 84097, USA
Cleary, Beverly A *Writer*
%Avon/William Morrow, 1350 Ave of Americas, New York, NY 10019, USA
Cleary, Jon Stephen *Writer*
%HarperCollins, 23 Ryde Road, Pymble NSW 2073, Australia
Cleary, Robert (Bob) *Hockey Player*
18 Juniper Road, Weston, MA 02493, USA
Cleary, William J (Bill), Jr *Hockey Player, Coach*
27 Kingwood Road, Auburndale, MA 02466, USA
Cleaver, Alan *Fashion Designer (Byblos)*
Via Vallone 11, Monte Conero, Sirolo, Italy
Cleaver, Vera *Writer*
5119 N 13th St, Tampa, FL 33603, USA
Cledwyn of Penrhos *Government Official, England*
Penmorfa, Trearddur, Holyhead, Gwynedd, Wales
Cleese, John *Actor, Comedian, Writer*
%David Wilkinson, 22 Cassius Road, St Margaret's, Middx TW1 1RU, England
Clef *Guitarist (Fugees)*
%DAS Communications, 83 Riverside Dr, New York, NY 10024, USA
Clegg, Johnny *Singer*
%Monterey International, 200 W Superior, #202, Chicago, IL 60610, USA
Cleghorne, Ellen *Actress, Comedienne*
%Agency for Performing Arts, 9200 Sunset Blvd, #900, Los Angeles, CA 90069, USA
Cleland, J Maxwell (Max) *Senator, GA*
340 Mockingbird Lane SE, Smyrna, GA 30082, USA
Clemens, Donella *Religious Leader*
%Mennonite Church, 722 N Main St, Newton, KS 67114, USA
Clemens, W Roger *Baseball Player*
11535 Quail Hollow, Houston, TX 77024, USA
Clement, Aurore *Actress*
%Artmedia, 20 Ave Rapp, 75007 Paris, France
Clemente, Carmine D *Anatomist*
11737 Bellagio Road, Los Angeles, CA 90049, USA
Clemente, Francesco *Artist*
684 Broadway, New York, NY 10012, USA
Clements, John A *Physiologist*
%University of California, Cardiovascular Institute, San Francisco, CA 94143, USA
Clements, Lennie *Golfer*
1714 Monterey Ave, Coronado, CA 92118, USA
Clements, Nate *Football Player*
%Buffalo Bills, 1 Bills Dr, Orchard Park, NY 14127, USA
Clements, Ronald F *Animator, Movie Director*
%Disney Animation, PO Box 10200, Burbank, CA 91521, USA
Clements, Suzanne *Fashion Designer*
%Clements Ribeiro Ltd, 48 S Molton St, London W1X 1HE, England
Clements, William P, Jr *Governor, TX*
1901 N Akard St, Dallas, TX 75201, USA
Clemons, Clarence *Saxophonist*
%Long Distance Enter, 568 E Woodbright Road, #234, Boynton Beach, FL 33435, USA

C

Clemons - Cloud

Clemons, Duane *Football Player*
10510 France Ave S, #203, Bloomington, MN 55431, USA
Clendenon, Donn A *Baseball Player*
2709 S Sandstone Circle, Sioux Falls, SD 57103, USA
Clennon, David *Actor*
2309 27th St, Santa Monica, CA 90405, USA
Clerico, Christian *Restauranteur*
%Lido-Normandie, 116 Bis Ave des Champs Elysees, 75008 Paris, France
Clervoy, Jean-Francois *Spatinaut, France*
%NASA, Johnson Space Flight Center, 2101 NASA Road 1, Houston, TX 77058, USA
Cleveland, Ashley *Singer, Songwriter*
%Street Level Artists, 106 N Buffalo St, #200, Warsaw, IN 46580, USA
Cleveland, J Harlan *Diplomat, Educator*
46891 Grissom St, Sterling, VA 20165, USA
Cleveland, Patience *Actress*
21321 Providencia St, Woodland Hills, CA 91364, USA
Cleveland, Paul M *Diplomat*
989 Saigon Road, McLean, VA 22102, USA
Clevenger, Raymond C, III *Judge*
%US Court of Appeals, 717 Madison Place NW, Washington, DC 20439, USA
Clexton, Edward W, Jr *Navy Admiral*
1000 Bobolink Dr, Virginia Beach, VA 23451, USA
Cliburn, Van *Concert Pianist*
PO Box 470219, Fort Worth, TX 76147, USA
Cliff, Jimmy *Singer, Songwriter*
51 Lady Musgrave Road, Kingston, Jamaica
Clifford, Linda *Singer*
%T-Best Talent Agency, 508 Honey Lake Court, Danville, CA 94506, USA
Clifford, M Richard (Rich) *Astronaut*
3700 Bay Area Blvd, Houston, TX 77058, USA
Clift, William B, III *Photographer*
PO Box 6035, Santa Fe, NM 87502, USA
Clijsters, Kim *Tennis Player*
%Assn of Tennis Professionals, 200 Tournament Road, Ponte Vedra Beach, FL 32082, USA
Cline, Martin J *Hematologist, Educator*
%University of California, Med Center, Hematology Dept, Los Angeles, CA 90024, USA
Cline, Richard *Cartoonist*
%New Yorker Magazine, Editorial Dept, 4 Times Square, New York, NY 10036, USA
Clinger, Debra *Actress*
1206 Chickasaw Dr, Brentwood, TN 37027, USA
Clinkscale, F Dextor *Football Player*
206 Michaux Dr, Greenville, SC 29605, USA
Clinton, George *Singer, Synthesizer Player, Songwriter*
%Available Mgmt, 6683 Sunset Blvd, Los Angeles, CA 90028, USA
Clinton, Hillary Rodham *Senator, NY; Wife of US President*
15 Old House Lane, Chappaqua, NY 10514, USA
Clinton, William J (Bill) *President, USA*
55 W 125th St, New York, NY 10027, USA
Clinton-Davis of Hackney, Stanley C *Government Official, England*
%House of Lords, Westminster, London SW1A 0PW, England
Cloepfil, Brad *Architect*
%Allied Works Architecture, 910 NW Hoyt St, #200, Portland, OR 97209, USA
Clohessy, Robert *Actor*
%Don Buchwald, 6500 Wilshire Blvd, #2200, Los Angeles, CA 90048, USA
Cloke, Kristen *Actress*
1450 S Robertson Blvd, Los Angeles, CA 90035, USA
Clokey, Art *Cartoonist (Gumby)*
359 Los Osos Valley Road, Los Osos, CA 93402, USA
Cloninger, Tony L *Baseball Player*
PO Box 1500, Denver, NC 28037, USA
Clooney, George *Actor*
%Creative Artists Agency, 9830 Wilshire Blvd, Beverly Hills, CA 90212, USA
Close, Charles T (Chuck) *Artist*
271 Central Park West, New York, NY 10024, USA
Close, Eric *Actor*
%Gersh Agency, 232 N Canon Dr, Beverly Hills, CA 90210, USA
Close, Glenn *Actress*
9 Desbrosses St, New York, NY 10013, USA
Closs, Bill *Basketball Player*
555 Byron St, #409, Palo Alto, CA 94301, USA
Clotet, Lluis *Architect*
%Studio PER, Caspe 151, Barcelona 08013, Spain
Clotworthy, Robert *Actor*
4317 Monroe Ave, Woodland Hills, CA 91364, USA
Clotworthy, Robert L (Bob) *Diver, Coach*
HC 74 Box 22313, El Prado, NM 87529, USA
Cloud, Jack M *Football Player*
805 Janice Dr, Annapolis, MD 21403, USA

Clough, Gerald W — *Educator*
%Georgia Institute of Technology, President's Office, Atlanta, GA 30332, USA

Clough, Ray W, Jr — *Structural Engineer*
PO Box 4625, Sunriver, OR 97707, USA

Clunie, Michelle — *Actress*
%Abrams Artists, 9200 Sunset Blvd, #1125, Los Angeles, CA 90069, USA

Clyne, Patricia — *Fashion Designer*
353 W 39th St, New York, NY 10018, USA

Coachman Davis, Alice — *Track Athlete*
811 Gibson St, Tuskegee, AL 36083, USA

Coase, Ronald H — *Nobel Economics Laureate*
%University of Chicago, Law School, 1111 E 60th St, Chicago, IL 60637, USA

Coates, Ben — *Football Player*
5940 Londonderry Court, Concord, NC 28027, USA

Coates, Kim — *Actor*
%Paradigm Agency, 10100 Santa Monica Blvd, #2500, Los Angeles, CA 90067, USA

Coates, Phyllis — *Actress*
PO Box 1969, Boyes Hot Springs, CA 95416, USA

Coats, Michael L — *Astronaut*
9128 E Star Hill Trail, Lone Tree, CO 80124, USA

Cobb, Geraldyn M (Jerrie) — *Astronaut*
1008 Beach Blvd, Sun City Center, FL 33573, USA

Cobb, Henry N — *Architect*
%Pei Cobb Freed Partners, 88 Pine St, New York, NY 10005, USA

Cobb, Julie — *Actress*
%S D B Partners, 1801 Ave of Stars, #902, Los Angeles, CA 90067, USA

Cobb, Keith Hamilton — *Actor*
%GVA Talent, 9229 Sunset Blvd, #320, Los Angeles, CA 90069, USA

Cobert, Bob — *Composer*
%B M I, 8730 Sunset Blvd, #300, Los Angeles, CA 90069, USA

Cobham, William C (Billy) — *Jazz Drummer, Composer*
%Joel Chriss, 300 Mercer St, #3J, New York, NY 10003, USA

Coblenz, Walter — *Movie Director, Producer*
4310 Cahuenga Blvd, #401, Toluca Lake, CA 91602, USA

Cobos, Jesus Lopez — *Conductor*
%Cincinnati Symphony, 1241 Elm St, Cincinnati, OH 45202, USA

Coburn, Cindy C — *Bowler*
%Ladies Professional Bowling Tour, 7200 Harrison Ave, #7171, Rockford, IL 61112, USA

Coburn, Doris — *Bowler*
130 Dalton Dr, Buffalo, NY 14223, USA

Coburn, John G — *Army General*
Commanding General, Army Material Command, Alexandria, VA 22333, USA

Cocanower, James S (Jaime) — *Baseball Player*
3620 Gresham Dr, Conway, AR 72034, USA

Cochereau, Pierre — *Concert Organist*
15 Bis des Ursins, 75004 Paris, France

Cochran, Anita L — *Astronomer*
%University of Texas, Astronomy Dept, Austin, TX 78712, USA

Cochran, Barbara Ann — *Skier*
213 Brown Hill W, El Prado, NM 87529, USA

Cochran, Hank — *Singer, Songwriter*
RR 2, Box 438, Hunters Lake, Hendersonville, TN 37075, USA

Cochran, John — *Commentator*
%ABC-TV, News Dept, 5010 Creston St, Hyattsville, MD 20781, USA

Cochran, John — *Football Player*
1249 Driftwood Dr, De Pere, WI 54115, USA

Cochran, Johnnie L, Jr — *Attorney*
4929 Wilshire Blvd, #1010, Los Angeles, CA 90010, USA

Cochran, Leslie H — *Educator*
%Youngstown State University, President's Office, Youngstown, OH 44555, USA

Cochran, Shannon — *Actress*
%Stubbs, 1450 S Robertson Blvd, Los Angeles, CA 90035, USA

Cochran, Tammy — *Singer, Songwriter*
%TBA Artists Mgmt, 300 10th Ave S, Nashville, TN 37203, USA

Cockburn, Bruce — *Singer, Songwriter, Guitarist*
%Agency Group Ltd, 1775 Broadway, #430, New York, NY 10019, USA

Cocker, Jarvis — *Singer (Pulp), Songwriter*
%Rough Trade Mgmt, 66 Golborne Road, London W10 5PS, England

Cocker, Joe — *Singer*
%Mag Dog Ranch, 4345 F Road, Crawford, CO 81415, USA

Cockerill, Franklin — *Microbiologist*
%Mayo Clinic, Microbiology Dept, 200 1st St SW, Rochester, MN 55905, USA

Cockey, Tim — *Writer*
%Hyperion Books, 114 5th Ave, New York, NY 10011, USA

Cockrell, Kenneth D — *Astronaut*
2030 Hillside Oak Lane, Houston, TX 77062, USA

Cockroft, Donald L (Don) — *Football Player*
2377 Thornhill Dr, Colorado Springs, CO 80920, USA

C

Code - Cohen

Code, Arthur D *Astronomer*
%University of Wisconsin, WUPPE Project, Astronomy Dept, Madison, WI 53706, USA
Codey, Lawrence R *Businessman*
%Public Service Enterprise, 80 Park Plaza, PO Box 1171, Newark, NJ 07101, USA
Codrescu, Andrei *Writer*
%Louisiana State University, English Dept, Baton Rouge, LA 70803, USA
Coduri, Camille *Actress*
%International Creative Mgmt, 76 Oxford St, London W1N 0AX, England
Coe, David Allan *Singer, Guitarist, Songwriter*
783 Rippling Creek, Nixa, MO 65714, USA
Coe, George *Actor*
%Bauman Assoc, 5750 Wilshire Blvd, #473, Los Angeles, CA 90036, USA
Coe, Sebastian N *Track Athlete*
Starswood, High Barn Road, Effingham, Surrey KT24 5PW, England
Coe, Sue *Artist*
%Galerie Saint Etienne, 24 W 57th St, New York, NY 10019, USA
Coe-Jones, Dawn *Golfer*
%Landmark Sports, 277 Richmond St W, Toronto ON M5V 1X1, Canada
Coelho, Susie *Actress*
1347 Rossmoyne Ave, Glendale, CA 91207, USA
Coen, Ethan *Movie Director, Writer*
%United Talent Agency, 9560 Wilshire Blvd, #500, Beverly Hills, CA 90212, USA
Coen, Joel *Movie Director, Writer*
%United Talent Agency, 9560 Wilshire Blvd, #500, Beverly Hills, CA 90212, USA
Coetzee, Gerrie *Boxer*
22 Sydney Road, Ravenswood, Boksburg 1460, South Africa
Coetzee, John M *Nobel Literature Laureate*
PO Box 92, Rondebosch, Cape Province 7700, South Africa
Coetzer, Amanda *Tennis Player*
%Octagon, 1751 Pinnacle Dr, #1500, McLean, VA 22102, USA
Cofer, J Michael (Mike) *Football Player*
4138 Brighton Lane, Southport, NC 28461, USA
Coffey, John L *Judge*
%US Court of Appeals, US Courthouse, 517 E Wisconsin Ave, Milwaukee, WI 53202, USA
Coffey, Junior L *Football Player*
17228 32nd Ave S, Seatac, WA 98188, USA
Coffey, Paul D *Hockey Player*
%Phoenix Coyotes, Alltel Ice Den, 9375 E Bell Road, Phoenix, AZ 85260, USA
Coffin, Edmund (Tad) *Equestrian Rider*
%General Delivery, Strafford, VT 05072, USA
Coffin, Fredrick *Actor*
%Susan Smith, 121A N San Vicente Blvd, Beverly Hills, CA 90211, USA
Coffin, William Sloane, Jr *Social Activist, Religious Leader*
%SANE/Freeze, 55 Van Dyke Ave, Hartford, CT 06106, USA
Coffman, Vance D *Businessman*
%Lockheed Martin Corp, 6801 Rockledge Dr, Bethesda, MD 20817, USA
Cogan, Kevin *Auto Racing Driver*
205 Rocky Point Road, Palos Verdes Estates, CA 90274, USA
Cogdill, Gail R *Football Player*
2013 SE Talton Ave, Vancouver, WA
Coghlan, Eamon *Track Athlete*
%Int'l Mgmt Group, 1 Erieview Plaza, 1360 E 9th St, #1300, Cleveland, OH 44114, USA
Coghlan, Frank (Junior), Jr *Actor*
28506 Ray Court, Saugus, CA 91350, USA
Cohan, Chris *Basketball Executive*
%Golden State Warriors, 1001 Broadway, Oakland, CA 94607, USA
Cohan, Robert P *Choreographer*
The Place, 17 Dukes Road, London WC1H 9AB, England
Coheleach, Guy J *Artist*
%Pandion Art, PO Box 96, Bernardsville, NJ 07924, USA
Cohen, Aaron *Space Administrator*
1310 Essex Green, College Station, TX 77845, USA
Cohen, Avishai *Jazz Bassist*
%Ron Moss Mgmt, 2635 Griffith Park Blvd, Los Angeles, CA 90039, USA
Cohen, Larry *Movie Director*
2111 Coldwater Canyon Dr, Beverly Hills, CA 90210, USA
Cohen, Leonard N *Writer, Singer, Songwriter*
121 Leslie St, North York ON M3C 2J9, Canada
Cohen, Marshall H *Astronomer*
%California Institute of Technology, Astronomy Dept, Pasadena, CA 91125, USA
Cohen, Marvin L *Physicist*
10 Forest Lane, Berkeley, CA 94708, USA
Cohen, Mary Ann *Judge*
%US Tax Court, 400 2nd St NW, Washington, DC 20217, USA
Cohen, Morris *Metallurgical Engineer*
491 Puritan Road, Swampscott, MA 01907, USA
Cohen, Paul J *Mathematician*
755 Santa Ynez St, Stanford, CA 94305, USA

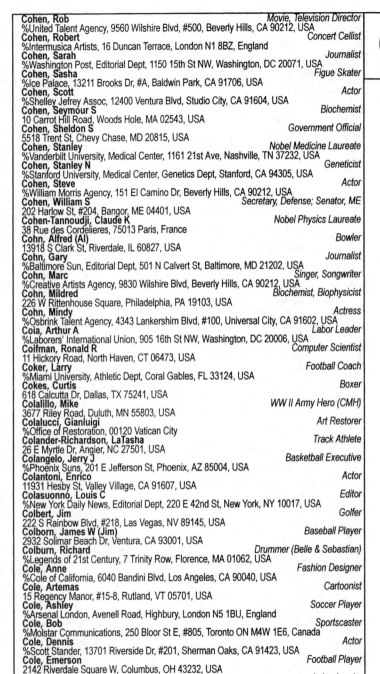

Cohen, Rob *Movie, Television Director*
%United Talent Agency, 9560 Wilshire Blvd, #500, Beverly Hills, CA 90212, USA
Cohen, Robert *Concert Cellist*
%Intermusica Artists, 16 Duncan Terrace, London N1 8BZ, England
Cohen, Sarah *Journalist*
%Washington Post, Editorial Dept, 1150 15th St NW, Washington, DC 20071, USA
Cohen, Sasha *Figue Skater*
%Ice Palace, 13211 Brooks Dr, #A, Baldwin Park, CA 91706, USA
Cohen, Scott *Actor*
%Shelley Jefrey Assoc, 12400 Ventura Blvd, Studio City, CA 91604, USA
Cohen, Seymour S *Biochemist*
10 Carrot Hill Road, Woods Hole, MA 02543, USA
Cohen, Sheldon S *Government Official*
5518 Trent St, Chevy Chase, MD 20815, USA
Cohen, Stanley *Nobel Medicine Laureate*
%Vanderbilt University, Medical Center, 1161 21st Ave, Nashville, TN 37232, USA
Cohen, Stanley N *Geneticist*
%Stanford University, Medical Center, Genetics Dept, Stanford, CA 94305, USA
Cohen, Steve *Actor*
%William Morris Agency, 151 El Camino Dr, Beverly Hills, CA 90212, USA
Cohen, William S *Secretary, Defense; Senator, ME*
202 Harlow St, #204, Bangor, ME 04401, USA
Cohen-Tannoudji, Claude K *Nobel Physics Laureate*
38 Rue des Cordelieres, 75013 Paris, France
Cohn, Alfred (Al) *Bowler*
13918 S Clark St, Riverdale, IL 60827, USA
Cohn, Gary *Journalist*
%Baltimore Sun, Editorial Dept, 501 N Calvert St, Baltimore, MD 21202, USA
Cohn, Marc *Singer, Songwriter*
%Creative Artists Agency, 9830 Wilshire Blvd, Beverly Hills, CA 90212, USA
Cohn, Mildred *Biochemist, Biophysicist*
226 W Rittenhouse Square, Philadelphia, PA 19103, USA
Cohn, Mindy *Actress*
%Osbrink Talent Agency, 4343 Lankershim Blvd, #100, Universal City, CA 91602, USA
Coia, Arthur A *Labor Leader*
%Laborers' International Union, 905 16th St NW, Washington, DC 20006, USA
Coifman, Ronald R *Computer Scientist*
11 Hickory Road, North Haven, CT 06473, USA
Coker, Larry *Football Coach*
%Miami University, Athletic Dept, Coral Gables, FL 33124, USA
Cokes, Curtis *Boxer*
618 Calcutta Dr, Dallas, TX 75241, USA
Colalillo, Mike *WW II Army Hero (CMH)*
3677 Riley Road, Duluth, MN 55803, USA
Colalucci, Gianluigi *Art Restorer*
%Office of Restoration, 00120 Vatican City
Colander-Richardson, LaTasha *Track Athlete*
26 E Myrtle Dr, Angier, NC 27501, USA
Colangelo, Jerry J *Basketball Executive*
%Phoenix Suns, 201 E Jefferson St, Phoenix, AZ 85004, USA
Colantoni, Enrico *Actor*
11931 Hesby St, Valley Village, CA 91607, USA
Colasuonno, Louis C *Editor*
%New York Daily News, Editorial Dept, 220 E 42nd St, New York, NY 10017, USA
Colbert, Jim *Golfer*
222 S Rainbow Blvd, #218, Las Vegas, NV 89145, USA
Colborn, James W (Jim) *Baseball Player*
2932 Solimar Beach Dr, Ventura, CA 93001, USA
Colburn, Richard *Drummer (Belle & Sebastian)*
%Legends of 21st Century, 7 Trinity Row, Florence, MA 01062, USA
Cole, Anne *Fashion Designer*
%Cole of California, 6040 Bandini Blvd, Los Angeles, CA 90040, USA
Cole, Artemas *Cartoonist*
15 Regency Manor, #15-8, Rutland, VT 05701, USA
Cole, Ashley *Soccer Player*
%Arsenal London, Avenell Road, Highbury, London N5 1BU, England
Cole, Bob *Sportscaster*
%Molstar Communications, 250 Bloor St E, #805, Toronto ON M4W 1E6, Canada
Cole, Dennis *Actor*
%Scott Stander, 13701 Riverside Dr, #201, Sherman Oaks, CA 91423, USA
Cole, Emerson *Football Player*
2142 Riverdale Square W, Columbus, OH 43232, USA
Cole, Eunice *Labor Leader*
%American Nurses Assn, 2420 Pershing Road, Kansas City, MO 64108, USA
Cole, Freddy *Singer*
%Producers Inc, 11806 N 56th St, Tampa, FL 33617, USA
Cole, Gary *Actor*
3855 Berry Dr, Studio City, CA 91604, USA

C

Cole - Coley

Cole, George *Actor*
%Joy Jameson Ltd, 2-19 The Plaza, 535 Kings Road, London SW10 0SZ, England
Cole, Holly *Singer*
%Alert Music, 41 Britain St, #305, Toronto ON M5A 1R7, Canada
Cole, John *Editorial Cartoonist*
%Durham Herald-Sun, 2828 Pickett Road, Durham, NC 27705, USA
Cole, Julie Dawn *Actress*
%Barry Burnett, 31 Coventry St, London W1V 8AS, England
Cole, Kimberly Lynn *Actress*
36 Longview Court, Montgomery, AL 36108, USA
Cole, Larry R *Football Player*
953 Harwood Terrace, Bedford, TX 76021, USA
Cole, Lloyd *Singer (Commotions), Songwriter*
%Agency Group Ltd, 1775 Broadway, #430, New York, NY 10019, USA
Cole, Lloyd *Singer/Guitarist*
%SuperVision Mgmt, 109B Regents Park Road, London NW1 8UR, England
Cole, Michael *Actor*
5121 Varna Ave, Sherman Oaks, CA 91423, USA
Cole, Natalie *Singer, Actress*
%Dan Cleary, 1801 Ave of Stars, #1105, Los Angeles, CA 90067, USA
Cole, Olivia *Actress*
%Century Artists, PO Box 59747, Santa Barbara, CA 93150, USA
Cole, Paula *Singer*
%Monterey Peninsula Artists, 509 Hartnell St, Monterey, CA 93940, USA
Cole, Robin *Football Player*
9 Brook Lane, Eighty Four, PA 15330, USA
Cole, Terry *Football Player*
743 Sanders St, Indianapolis, IN 46203, USA
Cole, Tina *Actress*
1540 Castec Dr, Sacramento, CA 95864, USA
Colella, Richard (Rick) *Swimmer*
217 19th Place, Kirkland, WA 98033, USA
Coleman, Catherine G (Cady) *Astronaut*
13619 Willow Heights Court, Houston, TX 77059, USA
Coleman, Cosey *Football Player*
11901 Northumberland Dr, Tampa, FL 33626, USA
Coleman, Cy *Composer*
447 E 57th St, New York, NY 10022, USA
Coleman, Dabney *Actor*
360 N Kenter Ave, Los Angeles, CA 90049, USA
Coleman, Daniel J *Publisher*
%Popular Mechanics Magazine, 224 W 57th St, New York, NY 10019, USA
Coleman, Derrick D *Basketball Player*
%Philadelphia 76ers, 1st Union Center, 3601 S Broad St, Philadelphia, PA 19148, USA
Coleman, Don E *Football Player*
424 McPherson Ave, Lansing, MI 48915, USA
Coleman, Gary *Actor*
4710 Don Miguel Dr, Los Angeles, CA 90008, USA
Coleman, George E *Jazz Saxophonist*
63 E 9th St, New York, NY 10003, USA
Coleman, Jack *Actor*
11333 Moorpark St, #156, Studio City, CA 91602, USA
Coleman, Jospeh H (Joe) *Baseball Player*
17851 Eagle View Lane, Cape Coral, FL 33909, USA
Coleman, Marco D *Football Player*
215 Straton Trace SW, Atlanta, GA 30331, USA
Coleman, Mary Sue *Educator*
%University of Michigan, President's Office, Ann Arbor, MI 48109, USA
Coleman, Ornette *Jazz Saxophonist, Composer*
%Monterey International, 200 W Superior, #202, Chicago, IL 60610, USA
Coleman, Sidney R *Physicist*
1 Richdale Ave, #12, Cambridge, MA 02140, USA
Coleman, Signy *Actress*
9200 Sunset Blvd, #625, Los Angeles, CA 90069, USA
Coleman, Vincent M (Vince) *Baseball Player*
1703 Flamm Road, Imperial, MO 63052, USA
Coleman, William T, Jr *Secretary, Transportation*
%O'Melveny & Myers, 555 13th St NW, #500, Washington, DC 20004, USA
Coles, Kim *Actress, Comedienne*
9000 Cynthia St, #403, West Hollywood, CA 90069, USA
Coles, Robert M *Psychiatrist*
%Harvard University Health Services, 75 Mount Auburn St, Cambridge, MA 02138, USA
Colescott, Warrington W *Artist*
RR 1, Hollandale, WI 53544, USA
Coley, Daryl *Clarinetist, Pianist*
%Daryl Coley Ministries, 417 E Regent St, Inglewood, CA 90301, USA
Coley, John Ford *Singer, Songwriter*
%Earthtone, 8306 Wilshire Blvd, #981, Beverly Hills, CA 90211, USA

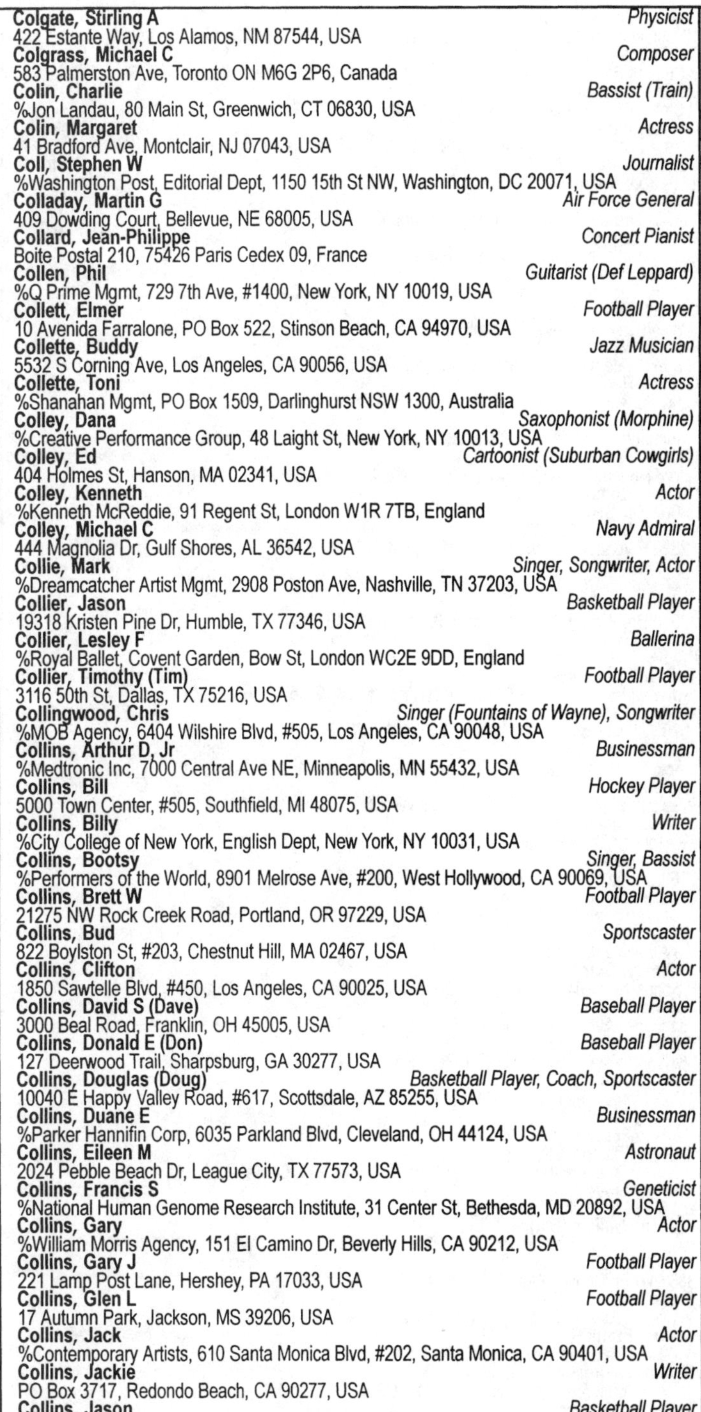

Colgate, Stirling A *Physicist*
422 Estante Way, Los Alamos, NM 87544, USA

Colgrass, Michael C *Composer*
583 Palmerston Ave, Toronto ON M6G 2P6, Canada

Colin, Charlie *Bassist (Train)*
%Jon Landau, 80 Main St, Greenwich, CT 06830, USA

Colin, Margaret *Actress*
41 Bradford Ave, Montclair, NJ 07043, USA

Coll, Stephen W *Journalist*
%Washington Post, Editorial Dept, 1150 15th St NW, Washington, DC 20071, USA

Colladay, Martin G *Air Force General*
409 Dowding Court, Bellevue, NE 68005, USA

Collard, Jean-Philippe *Concert Pianist*
Boite Postal 210, 75426 Paris Cedex 09, France

Collen, Phil *Guitarist (Def Leppard)*
%Q Prime Mgmt, 729 7th Ave, #1400, New York, NY 10019, USA

Collett, Elmer *Football Player*
10 Avenida Farralone, PO Box 522, Stinson Beach, CA 94970, USA

Collette, Buddy *Jazz Musician*
5532 S Corning Ave, Los Angeles, CA 90056, USA

Collette, Toni *Actress*
%Shanahan Mgmt, PO Box 1509, Darlinghurst NSW 1300, Australia

Colley, Dana *Saxophonist (Morphine)*
%Creative Performance Group, 48 Laight St, New York, NY 10013, USA

Colley, Ed *Cartoonist (Suburban Cowgirls)*
404 Holmes St, Hanson, MA 02341, USA

Colley, Kenneth *Actor*
%Kenneth McReddie, 91 Regent St, London W1R 7TB, England

Colley, Michael C *Navy Admiral*
444 Magnolia Dr, Gulf Shores, AL 36542, USA

Collie, Mark *Singer, Songwriter, Actor*
%Dreamcatcher Artist Mgmt, 2908 Poston Ave, Nashville, TN 37203, USA

Collier, Jason *Basketball Player*
19318 Kristen Pine Dr, Humble, TX 77346, USA

Collier, Lesley F *Ballerina*
%Royal Ballet, Covent Garden, Bow St, London WC2E 9DD, England

Collier, Timothy (Tim) *Football Player*
3116 50th St, Dallas, TX 75216, USA

Collingwood, Chris *Singer (Fountains of Wayne), Songwriter*
%MOB Agency, 6404 Wilshire Blvd, #505, Los Angeles, CA 90048, USA

Collins, Arthur D, Jr *Businessman*
%Medtronic Inc, 7000 Central Ave NE, Minneapolis, MN 55432, USA

Collins, Bill *Hockey Player*
5000 Town Center, #505, Southfield, MI 48075, USA

Collins, Billy *Writer*
%City College of New York, English Dept, New York, NY 10031, USA

Collins, Bootsy *Singer, Bassist*
%Performers of the World, 8901 Melrose Ave, #200, West Hollywood, CA 90069, USA

Collins, Brett W *Football Player*
21275 NW Rock Creek Road, Portland, OR 97229, USA

Collins, Bud *Sportscaster*
822 Boylston St, #203, Chestnut Hill, MA 02467, USA

Collins, Clifton *Actor*
1850 Sawtelle Blvd, #450, Los Angeles, CA 90025, USA

Collins, David S (Dave) *Baseball Player*
3000 Beal Road, Franklin, OH 45005, USA

Collins, Donald E (Don) *Baseball Player*
127 Deerwood Trail, Sharpsburg, GA 30277, USA

Collins, Douglas (Doug) *Basketball Player, Coach, Sportscaster*
10040 E Happy Valley Road, #617, Scottsdale, AZ 85255, USA

Collins, Duane E *Businessman*
%Parker Hannifin Corp, 6035 Parkland Blvd, Cleveland, OH 44124, USA

Collins, Eileen M *Astronaut*
2024 Pebble Beach Dr, League City, TX 77573, USA

Collins, Francis S *Geneticist*
%National Human Genome Research Institute, 31 Center St, Bethesda, MD 20892, USA

Collins, Gary *Actor*
%William Morris Agency, 151 El Camino Dr, Beverly Hills, CA 90212, USA

Collins, Gary J *Football Player*
221 Lamp Post Lane, Hershey, PA 17033, USA

Collins, Glen L *Football Player*
17 Autumn Park, Jackson, MS 39206, USA

Collins, Jack *Actor*
%Contemporary Artists, 610 Santa Monica Blvd, #202, Santa Monica, CA 90401, USA

Collins, Jackie *Writer*
PO Box 3717, Redondo Beach, CA 90277, USA

Collins, Jason *Basketball Player*
13120 Constable Ave, Granada Hills, CA 91344, USA

C

Collins, Joan *Actress*
16 Bulbecks Walk, S Woodham Ferrers, Chelmsford, Essex CM3 5ZN, England
Collins, John G *Financier*
%Summit Bancorp, Carnegie Center, PO Box 2066, Princeton, NJ 08543, USA
Collins, John W *Businessman*
%Clorox Co, 1221 Broadway, Oakland, CA 94612, USA
Collins, Judy *Singer, Songwriter*
%Stan Scotland Entertainment, 157 E 57th St, #18B, New York, NY 10022, USA
Collins, Kate *Actress*
1410 York Ave, #4D, New York, NY 10021, USA
Collins, Kerry *Football Player*
11403 Olde Saint Andrews Court, Charlotte, NC 28277, USA
Collins, Larry *Writer*
La Biche Niche, 83350 Ramatuelle, France
Collins, Martha Layne *Governor, KY; Educator*
%Saint Catherine College, President's Office, Saint Catherine, KY 40061, USA
Collins, Marva *Educator*
%Westside Preparatory School, 8035 S Honore St, Chicago, IL 60620, USA
Collins, Misha *Actor*
%S M S Talent, 8730 Sunset Blvd, #440, Los Angeles, CA 90069, USA
Collins, Patrick *Actor*
9200 Sunset Blvd, #702, Los Angeles, CA 90069, USA
Collins, Pauline *Actress*
%Michael Whitehall, 125 Gloucester Road, London SW7 4TE, England
Collins, Phil *Singer, Songwriter, Drummer*
Alfred House, 23-24 Cromwell Place, #300, London SW7 2LD, England
Collins, Roosevelt *Football Player*
3600 Holly St, Denison, TX 75020, USA
Collins, Samuel C *Mechanical Engineer, Cryogenist*
12322 Riverview Road, Fort Washington, MD 20744, USA
Collins, Shawn *Football Player*
2744 Preece St, San Diego, CA 92111, USA
Collins, Stephen *Actor*
12960 Brentwood Terrace, Los Angeles, CA 90049, USA
Collins, Terry L *Baseball Manager*
PO Box 508, Okemos, MI 48805, USA
Collins, Thomas H *Coast Guard Admiral*
Commandant, US Coast Guard, 2100 2nd St SW, Washington, DC 20593, USA
Collins, Todd F *Football Player*
1279 Collins Road, New Market, TN 37820, USA
Collinsworth, Cris *Football Player, Sportscaster*
%Fox-TV, Sports Dept, 205 W 67th St, New York, NY 10021, USA
Collison, Nick *Basketball Player*
%Seattle SuperSonics, 351 Elliott Ave W, #500, Seattle, WA 98119, USA
Collman, James P *Chemist*
794 Tolman Dr, Stanford, CA 94305, USA
Colman, Booth *Actor*
2160 Century Park E, #603, Los Angeles, CA 90067, USA
Colmes, Alan *Commentator*
%Conversation Co, 697 Middle Neck Road, Great Neck, NY 11023, USA
Colombo, Emilio *Prime Minister, Italy*
Via Aurelia 239, Rome, Italy
Colomby, Scott *Actor*
%Borinstein Oreck Bogart, 3172 Dona Susana Dr, Studio City, CA 91604, USA
Colone, Joe *Basketball Player*
534 Carter Ave, Woodbury, NJ 08096, USA
Colosi, Nicholas (Nick) *Baseball Umpire*
6817 54th Ave, Maspeth, NY 11378, USA
Colquitt, Jimmy *Football Player*
11722 Hardin Valley Road, Knoxville, TN 37932, USA
Colson, Charles W *Religious Leader, Watergate Figure*
%Prison Fellowship, PO Box 1550, Merrifield, VA 22116, USA
Colson, Elizabeth F *Anthropologist*
%University of California, Anthropology Dept, Berkeley, CA 94720, USA
Colson, Lloyd A *Baseball Player*
PO Box 128, Hollis, OK 73550, USA
Colson, William (Bill) *Editor*
%Sports Illustrated, Editorial Dept, Time-Life Building, New York, NY 10020, USA
Colt, Marshall *Actor*
333 Elm St, Denver, CO 80220, USA
Colter, Jessie *Singer*
1117 17th Ave S, Nashville, TN 37212, USA
Colton, Frank B *Inventor (Oral Contraceptive)*
6402 N 27th St, Phoenix, AZ 85016, USA
Colton, Lawrence R (Larry) *Baseball Player*
3027 NE 68th Ave, Portland, OR 97213, USA
Coltrane, Robbie *Actor*
%Inspirational Artists, PO Box 1AS, London W1A 1AS, England

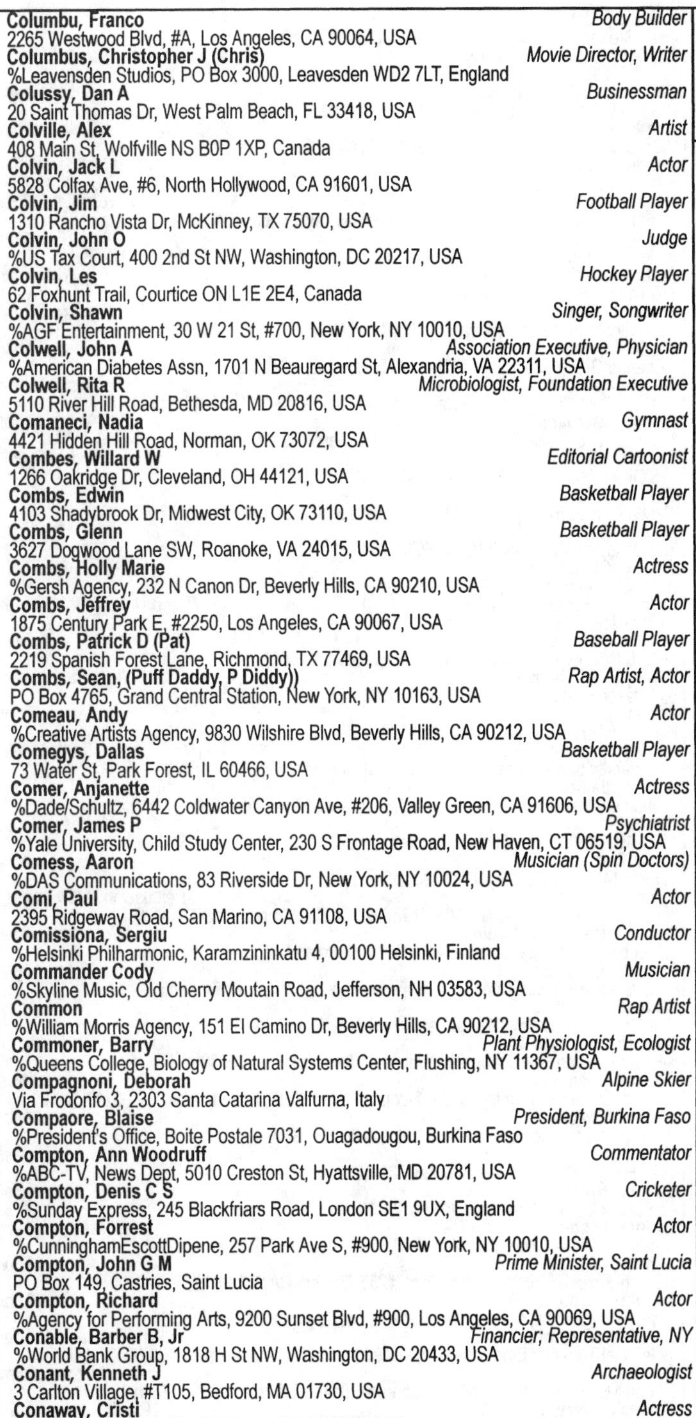

Columbu, Franco *Body Builder*
2265 Westwood Blvd, #A, Los Angeles, CA 90064, USA
Columbus, Christopher J (Chris) *Movie Director, Writer*
%Leavensden Studios, PO Box 3000, Leavesden WD2 7LT, England
Colussy, Dan A *Businessman*
20 Saint Thomas Dr, West Palm Beach, FL 33418, USA
Colville, Alex *Artist*
408 Main St, Wolfville NS B0P 1XP, Canada
Colvin, Jack L *Actor*
5828 Colfax Ave, #6, North Hollywood, CA 91601, USA
Colvin, Jim *Football Player*
1310 Rancho Vista Dr, McKinney, TX 75070, USA
Colvin, John O *Judge*
%US Tax Court, 400 2nd St NW, Washington, DC 20217, USA
Colvin, Les *Hockey Player*
62 Foxhunt Trail, Courtice ON L1E 2E4, Canada
Colvin, Shawn *Singer, Songwriter*
%AGF Entertainment, 30 W 21 St, #700, New York, NY 10010, USA
Colwell, John A *Association Executive, Physician*
%American Diabetes Assn, 1701 N Beauregard St, Alexandria, VA 22311, USA
Colwell, Rita R *Microbiologist, Foundation Executive*
5110 River Hill Road, Bethesda, MD 20816, USA
Comaneci, Nadia *Gymnast*
4421 Hidden Hill Road, Norman, OK 73072, USA
Combes, Willard W *Editorial Cartoonist*
1266 Oakridge Dr, Cleveland, OH 44121, USA
Combs, Edwin *Basketball Player*
4103 Shadybrook Dr, Midwest City, OK 73110, USA
Combs, Glenn *Basketball Player*
3627 Dogwood Lane SW, Roanoke, VA 24015, USA
Combs, Holly Marie *Actress*
%Gersh Agency, 232 N Canon Dr, Beverly Hills, CA 90210, USA
Combs, Jeffrey *Actor*
1875 Century Park E, #2250, Los Angeles, CA 90067, USA
Combs, Patrick D (Pat) *Baseball Player*
2219 Spanish Forest Lane, Richmond, TX 77469, USA
Combs, Sean, (Puff Daddy, P Diddy)) *Rap Artist, Actor*
PO Box 4765, Grand Central Station, New York, NY 10163, USA
Comeau, Andy *Actor*
%Creative Artists Agency, 9830 Wilshire Blvd, Beverly Hills, CA 90212, USA
Comegys, Dallas *Basketball Player*
73 Water St, Park Forest, IL 60466, USA
Comer, Anjanette *Actress*
%Dade/Schultz, 6442 Coldwater Canyon Ave, #206, Valley Green, CA 91606, USA
Comer, James P *Psychiatrist*
%Yale University, Child Study Center, 230 S Frontage Road, New Haven, CT 06519, USA
Comess, Aaron *Musician (Spin Doctors)*
%DAS Communications, 83 Riverside Dr, New York, NY 10024, USA
Comi, Paul *Actor*
2395 Ridgeway Road, San Marino, CA 91108, USA
Comissiona, Sergiu *Conductor*
%Helsinki Philharmonic, Karamzininkatu 4, 00100 Helsinki, Finland
Commander Cody *Musician*
%Skyline Music, Old Cherry Moutain Road, Jefferson, NH 03583, USA
Common *Rap Artist*
%William Morris Agency, 151 El Camino Dr, Beverly Hills, CA 90212, USA
Commoner, Barry *Plant Physiologist, Ecologist*
%Queens College, Biology of Natural Systems Center, Flushing, NY 11367, USA
Compagnoni, Deborah *Alpine Skier*
Via Frodonfo 3, 2303 Santa Catarina Valfurna, Italy
Compaore, Blaise *President, Burkina Faso*
%President's Office, Boite Postale 7031, Ouagadougou, Burkina Faso
Compton, Ann Woodruff *Commentator*
%ABC-TV, News Dept, 5010 Creston St, Hyattsville, MD 20781, USA
Compton, Denis C S *Cricketer*
%Sunday Express, 245 Blackfriars Road, London SE1 9UX, England
Compton, Forrest *Actor*
%CunninghamEscottDipene, 257 Park Ave S, #900, New York, NY 10010, USA
Compton, John G M *Prime Minister, Saint Lucia*
PO Box 149, Castries, Saint Lucia
Compton, Richard *Actor*
%Agency for Performing Arts, 9200 Sunset Blvd, #900, Los Angeles, CA 90069, USA
Conable, Barber B, Jr *Financier; Representative, NY*
%World Bank Group, 1818 H St NW, Washington, DC 20433, USA
Conant, Kenneth J *Archaeologist*
3 Carlton Village, #T105, Bedford, MA 01730, USA
Conaway, Cristi *Actress*
423 Westbourne Dr, West Hollywood, CA 90048, USA

C

Conaway - Connick

Conaway, Jeff *Actor*
4519 Greenbush Ave, Sherman Oaks, CA 91423, USA
Concannon, John J (Jack), Jr *Football Player*
11 Berlin St, Wollaston, MA 02170, USA
Concepion, David I (Davey) *Baseball Player*
Urb Los Caobos Botalon 5D, 5-Piso-Maracay, Venezuela
Condit, Philip M *Businessman*
%Boeing Co, PO Box 3707, Seattle, WA 98124, USA
Condon, Bill *Movie Director, Writer*
%Agency for Performing Arts, 9200 Sunset Blvd, #900, Los Angeles, CA 90069, USA
Condon, Paul *Law Enforcement Official*
Metropolitan Police, New Scotland Yard, Broadway, London SW1H 0BG, England
Condron, Christopher M *Financier*
%Mellon Financial Corp, Mellon Bank Center, 500 Grant St, Pittsburgh, PA 15258, USA
Cone Vanderbush, Carin *Swimmer*
116 Washington Road, #B, West Point, NY 10996, USA
Cone, David B *Baseball Player*
16 Hurlingham Dr, Greenwich, CT 06831, USA
Conforti, Gino *Actor*
%Orange Grove Group, 12178 Ventura Blvd, #205, Studio City, CA 91604, USA
Conger, Harry M *Businessman*
%Homestake Mining Co, 650 California St, San Francisco, CA 94108, USA
Conkey, Margaret *Archaeologist*
%University of California, Archaeological Research Facility, Berkeley, CA 94720, USA
Conlan, Shane P *Football Player*
428 Oliver Road, Sewickley, PA 15143, USA
Conlee, John *Singer*
%John Conlee Enterprises, 38 Music Square E, #117, Nashville, TN 37203, USA
Conley, Arthur *Singer*
630 Oakstone Dr, Roswell, GA 30075, USA
Conley, Clare D *Editor*
Hemlock Farms, Hawley, PA 18428, USA
Conley, D Eugene (Gene) *Baseball, Basketball Player*
2105 Grafton Ave, Clermont, FL 34711, USA
Conley, Darlene *Actress*
1840 S Beverly Glen Blvd, #501, Los Angeles, CA 90025, USA
Conley, Earl Thomas *Singer, Songwriter*
657 Baker Road, Smyrna, TN 37167, USA
Conley, Joe *Actor*
PO Box 6487, Thousand Oaks, CA 91359, USA
Conley, Michael (Mike) *Track Athlete*
%University of Arkansas, Athletic Dept, Fayetteville, AR 72701, USA
Conlon, James J *Conductor*
%Shuman Assoc, 120 W 58th St, #8D, New York, NY 10019, USA
Conn, Didi *Actress, Singer*
1901 Ave of Stars, #1450, Los Angeles, CA 90067, USA
Conn, Terri *Actress*
1268 E 14th St, Brooklyn, NY 11230, USA
Conneff, Kevin *Singer, Percussionist (Chieftains)*
%Macklam Feldman Mgmt, 1505 W 2nd Ave, #200, Vancouver BC V6H 3Y4, Canada
Connell, Desmond Cardinal *Religious Leader*
%Archbishop's House, Drumcondra, Dublin 9, Ireland
Connell, Elizabeth *Opera Singer*
%I M G Artists, 3 Burlington Lane, Chiswick, London W4 2TH, England
Connell, Evan S, Jr *Writer*
Fort Macy 13, 320 Artist Road, Santa Fe, NM 87501, USA
Connell, Thurman C *Financier*
%Federal Home Loan Bank, 907 Walnut St, Des Moines, IA 50309, USA
Connelly, Jennifer *Actress*
%International Creative Mgmt, 8942 Wilshire Blvd, #219, Beverly Hills, CA 90211, USA
Connelly, Michael *Writer*
%Little Brown, 3 Center Plaza, Boston, MA 02108, USA
Conner, Bart *Gymnast*
4421 Hidden Hill Road, Norman, OK 73072, USA
Conner, Bruce *Artist*
45 Sussex St, San Francisco, CA 94131, USA
Conner, Lester *Basketball Player*
45 Kings Way, #8, Waltham, MA 02451, USA
Connery, Jason *Actor*
%David Shapira, 15821 Ventura Blvd, #235, Encino, CA 91436, USA
Connery, Sean *Actor*
%Nancy Seltzer Assoc, 6220 Del Valle Dr, Los Angeles, CA 90048, USA
Connery, Vincent L *Labor Leader*
%National Treasury Employees Union, 1730 K St NW, Washington, DC 20006, USA
Connes, Alain *Mathematician*
%Leon Motchane l'HES, 35 Route Chartres, 91440 Bures-sur-Yvette, France
Connick, Harry, Jr *Pianist, Singer, Actor*
%Wilkins Mgmt, 323 Broadway, Cambridge, MA 02139, USA

Conniff, Cal *Skier*
157 Pleasantview Ave, Longmeadow, MA 01106, USA
Connolly, Billy *Actor*
%Tickety-Boo Ltd, Boathouse, Crabtree Lane, London SW6 6LU, England
Connolly, Olga Fikotova *Track Athlete*
4561 Montair Ave, #D10, Long Beach, CA 90808, USA
Connor, Chris *Singer*
%Maxine Harvard Unlimited, 7942 W Bell Road, #C5, Glendale, AZ 85308, USA
Connor, Christopher M *Businessman*
%Sherwin-Williams Co, 101 W Prospect Ave, Cleveland, OH 44115, USA
Connor, Joseph E *Government Official, Businessman*
%Under-Secretary General's Office, United Nations, UN Plaza, New York, NY 10021, USA
Connor, Kenneth *Actor*
%Peter Rogers Productions, Pinewood Films, Iver Heath SLO 0NH, England
Connor, Ralph *Chemist*
9866 Highwood Court, Sun City, AZ 85373, USA
Connor, Richard L *Publisher*
%Fort Worth Star-Telegram, 400 W 7th St, Fort Worth, TX 76102, USA
Connors, Carol *Songwriter*
1709 Ferrari Dr, Beverly Hills, CA 90210, USA
Connors, James S (Jimmy) *Tennis Player*
1962 E Valley Road, Santa Barbara, CA 93108, USA
Connors, Mike *Actor*
4810 Louise Ave, Encino, CA 91316, USA
Connway, Craig *Businessman*
%PeopleSoft Inc, 4460 Hacienda Dr, Pleasanton, CA 94588, USA
Conombo, Joseph I *Prime Minister, Upper Volta*
2003 Ave de la Liberte, BP 613, Dadoya, Ouagadougou, Burkina Faso
Conover, Lloyd H *Inventor (Tetracycline)*
27 Old Barry Road, Quaker Hill, CT 06375, USA
Conrad, David *Actor*
%Industry Entertainment, 955 Carillo Dr, #300, Los Angeles, CA 90048, USA
Conrad, Fred *Photographer*
%New York Times, Editorial Dept, 229 W 43rd St, New York, NY 10036, USA
Conrad, James A *Financier*
%Source One Mortgage, 27555 Farmington Road, Farmington Hills, MI 48334, USA
Conrad, Paul F *Editorial Cartoonist*
28649 Crestridge Road, Palos Verdes Estates, CA 90275, USA
Conrad, Robert *Actor*
PO Box 5237, Bear Valley, CA 95223, USA
Conradt, Jody *Basketball Coach*
9614 Leaning Rock Circle, Austin, TX 78730, USA
Conran, Jasper A T *Fashion Designer*
%Jasper Conran Ltd, 2 Munden St, London W14 0RH, England
Conran, Philip J *Vietnam War Air Force Hero*
4706 Calle Reina, Santa Barbara, CA 93110, USA
Conran, Terence O *Interior Designer*
22 Shad Thames, London SE1 2YU, England
Conroy, D Patrick (Pat) *Writer*
%Houghton Mifflin, 222 Berkeley St, #700, Boston, MA 02116, USA
Conroy, Frances *Actress*
%International Creative Mgmt, 8942 Wilshire Blvd, #219, Beverly Hills, CA 90211, USA
Conroy, Pat *Writer*
5053 Ocean Blvd, #134, Sarasota, FL 34242, USA
Consagra, Pietro *Sculptor*
Via Cassia 1162, Rome, Italy
Considine, John *Actor*
16 1/2 Red Coat Lane, Greenwich, CT 06830, USA
Considine, Tim *Actor*
3708 Mountain View Ave, Los Angeles, CA 90066, USA
Constable, George *Editor*
%Time-Life Books, Editorial Dept, Rockefeller Center, New York, NY 10020, USA
Constantine II *King, Greece*
4 Linnell Dr, Hampstead Way, London NW11, England
Constantine, Michael *Actor*
1604 Bern St, Reading, PA 19604, USA
Consuegra, Sandalio S C (Sandy) *Baseball Player*
3255 W Flagler St, #14, Miami, FL 33135, USA
Consuelos, Mark *Actor, Model*
646 Juniper Place, Franklin Lakes, NJ 07417, USA
Conte, John *Actor*
75600 Beryl Dr, Indian Wells, CA 92210, USA
Conte, Lansana *President, Guinea; Army General*
%President's Office, Conakry, Guinea
Conte, Lou *Choreographer*
%Hubbard Street Dance Co , 1147 W Jackson Blvd, Chicago, IL 60607, USA
Conti, Bill *Composer*
117 Fremont Place W, Los Angeles, CA 90005, USA

C

Conti - Cook

Conti, Tom *Actor*
%Chatto & Linnit, Prince of Wales, Coventry St, London W1V 7FE, England
Contino, Dick *Accordianist*
3355 Nahatan Way, Las Vegas, NV 89109, USA
Contner, James A *Cinematographer*
4146 Ventura Canyon Ave, Sherman Oaks, CA 91423, USA
Converse, Frank *Actor*
%Artists Group, 10100 Santa Monica Blvd, #2490, Los Angeles, CA 90067, USA
Converse-Roberts, William *Actor*
%Innovative Artists, 1505 10th St, Santa Monica, CA 90401, USA
Conway, Billy *Drummer (Morphine)*
%Creative Performance Group, 48 Laight St, New York, NY 10013, USA
Conway, Curtis L *Football Player*
250 Washington Road, Lake Forest, IL 60045, USA
Conway, Gary *Actor*
11240 Chimney Rock Road, Paso Robles, CA 93446, USA
Conway, James *Marine Corps General*
Commanding General, I Marine Expeditionary Force, Camp Pendleton, CA 92055, USA
Conway, James L *Movie Director*
%Creative Artists Agency, 9830 Wilshire Blvd, Beverly Hills, CA 90212, USA
Conway, Jill K *Historian*
65 Commonwealth Ave, #8B, Boston, MA 02116, USA
Conway, John Horton *Mathematician, Writer*
%Princeton University, Mathematics Dept, Fine Hall, Princeton, NJ 08544, USA
Conway, John W *Businessman*
%Crown Cork & Seal, 1 Crown Way, Philadelphia, PA 19154, USA
Conway, Kevin *Actor*
25 Century Park West, New York, NY 10023, USA
Conway, Tim *Actor, Comedian*
%Tim Conway Enterprises, PO Box 17047, Encino, CA 91416, USA
Conwell, Esther M *Physicist*
800 Phillips Road, Webster, NY 14580, USA
Conwell, Tommy *Guitarist*
%Brothers Mgmt, 141 Dunbar Ave, Fords, NJ 08863, USA
Coobar, Abdulmegid *Prime Minister, Libya*
Asadu El-Furat St 29, Garden City, Tripoli, Libya
Cooder, Ry *Singer, Guitarist, Composer*
326 Entrada Dr, Santa Monica, CA 90402, USA
Coody, Charles *Golfer*
%Int'l Mgmt Group, 1 Erieview Plaza, 1360 E 9th St, #1300, Cleveland, OH 44114, USA
Coogan, Keith *Actor*
1640 S Sepulveda Blvd, #218, Los Angeles, CA 90025, USA
Cook, Barbara *Singer, Actress*
%Abby Hoffer, 223 1/2 E 48th St, New York, NY 10017, USA
Cook, Beryl *Artist*
Coach House, 1A Camp Road, Clifton, Bristol BS8 3LW, England
Cook, Brian *Basketball Player*
%Los Angeles Lakers, Staples Center, 1111 S Figueroa St, Los Angeles, CA 90015, USA
Cook, Bruce *Writer*
502 N Plymouth Blvd, Los Angeles, CA 90004, USA
Cook, Carole *Actress, Comedienne*
8829 Ashcroft Ave, West Hollywood, CA 90048, USA
Cook, Donald G *Air Force General*
Commander, Air Education/Training Command, Randolph Air Force Base, TX 78155, USA
Cook, Jeffrey A (Jeff) *Singer, Guitarist (Alabama)*
PO Box 35967, Fort Payne, AL 35967, USA
Cook, John *Golfer*
1111 Tahquitz E, #203, Palm Springs, CA 92262, USA
Cook, Judy *Bowler*
%Ladies Professional Bowling Tour, 7200 Harrison Ave, #7171, Rockford, IL 61112, USA
Cook, Paul *Drummer (Sex Pistols)*
%Solo Agency, 55 Fulham High St, London SW6 3JJ, England
Cook, Paul M *Businessman*
%SRI International, 333 Ravenswood Ave, Menlo Park, CA 94025, USA
Cook, Peter F C *Architect*
54 Compayne Gardens, London NW6 3RY, England
Cook, Rachel Leigh *Actress*
%Moongate Mgmt, 4570 Van Nuys Blvd, #171, Sherman Oaks, CA 91403, USA
Cook, Robert *Opera Singer*
Quavers, 53 Friars Ave, Fiern Barnet, London N2O OXG, England
Cook, Robert F (Robin) *Government Official, England*
%House of Commons, Westminster, London SW1A 0AA, England
Cook, Robin *Writer*
4601 Gulf Shore Blvd, #P4, Naples, FL 34103, USA
Cook, Stanton R *Publisher*
224 Raleigh Road, Kenilworth, IL 60043, USA
Cook, Steve *Bowler*
1209 Devonshire Court, Roseville, CA 95661, USA

C

Cook, Thomas A *Writer*
%Bantam Books, 1540 Broadway, New York, NY 10036, USA
Cooke, A Alistair *Writer, Commentator*
Nassau Point, Cutchogue, NY 11935, USA
Cooke, Howard F H *Governor General, Jamaica*
King's House, Hope Road, Kingston 10, Jamaica
Cooke, Janis *Journalist*
%Washington Post, Editorial Dept, 1150 15th St NW, Washington, DC 20071, USA
Cooke, John P *Rower*
290 Old Branchville Road, Ridgefield, CT 06877, USA
Cooksey, Dave *Religious Leader*
%Brethren Church, 524 College Ave, Ashland, OH 44805, USA
Cooley, Denton A *Surgeon*
3014 Del Monte Dr, Houston, TX 77019, USA
Coolidge, Charles H *WW II Army Hero (CMH)*
1054 Balmoral Dr, Signal Mountain, TN 37377, USA
Coolidge, Charles H, Jr *Air Force General*
Vice CinC, Air Force Material Command, Wright-Patterson Air Force Base, OH 45433, USA
Coolidge, Harold J *Conservationist*
38 Standley St, Beverly, MA 01915, USA
Coolidge, Martha *Movie Director*
760 N La Cienega Blvd, Los Angeles, CA 90069, USA
Coolidge, Rita *Singer*
PO Box 571, Gwynedd Valley, PA 19437, USA
Coolio *Rap Artist, Actor*
%GLP Artists Marketing, Huetteldorferstrasse 259, Vienna 1140, Austria
Coombe, George W *Attorney*
%Graham & James, 1 Maritime Plaza, San Francisco, CA 94111, USA
Coombs, Philip H *Economist*
317 W Main St, Chester, CT 06412, USA
Coonce, Ricky *Drummer (Grass Roots)*
%Thomas Cassidy, 11761 E Speedway Blvd, Tucson, AZ 85748, USA
Cooney, Gerry *Boxer*
22501 Linden Blvd, Cambria Heights, NY 11411, USA
Cooney, Joan Ganz *Educator, Television Executive*
%Children's TV Workshop, 1 Lincoln Plaza, New York, NY 10023, USA
Coonts, Stephen *Writer*
8200 Crow Valley Lane, Las Vegas, NV 89113, USA
Cooper, Alexander *Architect*
%Cooper Robertson & Partners, 311 W 43rd St, New York, NY 10036, USA
Cooper, Alice *Singer, Songwriter*
4135 E Keim St, Paradise Valley, AZ 85253, USA
Cooper, Amy Levin *Editor*
60 Sutton Place S, #16C, New York, NY 10022, USA
Cooper, Anderson *Commentator*
%Cable News Network, News Dept, 1050 Techwood Dr NW, Atlanta, GA 30318, USA
Cooper, Bill *Football Player*
16056 Greenwood Road, Monte Sereno, CA 95030, USA
Cooper, Camille *Basketball Player*
%New York Liberty, Madison Square Garden, 2 Penn Plaza, New York, NY 10121, USA
Cooper, Cecil C *Baseball Player*
1431 Misty Bend Dr, Katy, TX 77494, USA
Cooper, Charles G *Marine Corps General*
3410 Barger Dr, Falls Church, VA 22044, USA
Cooper, Chris *Actor*
%P M K Public Relations, 8500 Wilshire Blvd, #700, Beverly Hills, CA 90211, USA
Cooper, Christin *Alpine Skier*
1001 E Hyman Ave, Aspen, CO 81611, USA
Cooper, Cortz *Religious Leader*
%Presbyterian Church in America, 1852 Century Place, Atlanta, GA 30345, USA
Cooper, Cynthia *Basketball Player, Coach*
3910 Chatfield Court, Sugar Land, TX 77479, USA
Cooper, Daniel L *Navy Admiral*
121 Leisure Court, Wyomissing, PA 19610, USA
Cooper, Hal *Television Director*
2651 Hutton Dr, Beverly Hills, CA 90210, USA
Cooper, Henry *Boxer*
16 Barley House, Hildenbroom Farm, Ridings Lane, Kent TN11 9JN, England
Cooper, Imogen *Concert Pianist*
%Van Walsum Mgmt, 4 Addison Bridge Place, London W14 8XP, England
Cooper, Jackie *Actor, Movie Director*
10430 Wilshire Blvd, #1603, Los Angeles, CA 90024, USA
Cooper, Jeanne *Actress*
8401 Edwin Dr, Los Angeles, CA 90046, USA
Cooper, Jilly *Writer*
%Desmond Elliott, 38 Bury St, London SW1Y 6AU, England
Cooper, Joel D *Thoracic Surgeon*
%Washington University, Medical School, Surgery Dept, Saint Louis, MO 63110, USA

Cooper, John M *Philosopher*
182 Western Way, Princeton, NJ 08540, USA

Cooper, L Gordon, Jr *Astronaut*
1338 Nathan Lane, Ventura, CA 93001, USA

Cooper, Leon N *Nobel Physics Laureate*
49 Intervale Road, Providence, RI 02906, USA

Cooper, Lester I *Television Producer*
45 Morningside Dr S, Westport, CT 06880, USA

Cooper, Marilyn *Actress*
%Gage Group, 315 W 57th St, #4H, New York, NY 10019, USA

Cooper, Matthew T *Marine Corps General*
9326 Fairfax St, Alexandria, VA 22309, USA

Cooper, Minor J *Biological Chemist*
1901 Austin Ave, Ann Arbor, MI 48104, USA

Cooper, Paula *Art Dealer*
%Paula Cooper Gallery, 534 W 21st St, New York, NY 10011, USA

Cooper, Stephen *Businessman*
%Enron Corp, 1400 Smith St, Houston, TX 77002, USA

Cooper, Wayne *Artist*
126 W 1025 S, Kouts, IN 46347, USA

Cooper, Wilma Lee *Singer, Guitarist*
%Charles Rapp Enterprises, 1650 Broadway, #1410, New York, NY 10019, USA

Coor, Lattie F *Educator*
%Arizona State University, President's Office, Tempe, AZ 85287, USA

Coors, William K *Businessman*
%Adolph Coors Co, 1221 Ford St, Golden, CO 80401, USA

Coover, Robert *Writer*
%Brown University, Linden Press, 49 George St, Providence, RI 02912, USA

Cope, Derrike *Auto Racing Driver*
%CLR Racing, 106C Motorsports Road, Mooresville, NC 28115, USA

Cope, Jonathan *Ballet Dancer*
%Royal Ballet, Covent Garden, Bow St, London WC2E 9DD, England

Cope, Julian *Singer, Songwriter*
%International Talent Group, 729 7th Ave, #1600, New York, NY 10019, USA

Copeland, Al *Boat Racing Driver, Businessman*
5001 Folse Dr, Metairie, LA 70006, USA

Copeland, Joan *Actress*
88 Central Park West, New York, NY 10023, USA

Copeland, Kenneth *Evangelist*
%Kenneth Copeland Ministries, PO Box 2908, Fort Worth, TX 76113, USA

Copeland, Stewart *Drummer (Police, Oysterhead), Composer*
181 N Saltair Ave, Los Angeles, CA 90049, USA

Copley, Helen K *Publisher*
%Copley Press, 7776 Ivanhoe Ave, La Jolla, CA 92037, USA

Copley, Teri *Actress, Model*
13351 Riverside Dr, #D513, Sherman Oaks, CA 91423, USA

Copp, D Harold *Physiologist*
4755 Belmont Ave, Vancouver BC V6T 1A8, Canada

Coppens, Yves *Palaeoanthropologist*
4 Rue du Pont-aux-Choux, 75003 Paris, France

Copperfield, David *Illusionist*
2000 West Loop S, #1300, Houston, TX 77027, USA

Copperwheat, Lee *Fashion Designer*
%Copperwheat Blundell, 14 Cheshire St, London E2 6EH, England

Copping, Allen A *Educator*
%Louisiana State University System, President's Office, Baton Rouge, LA 70808, USA

Coppola, Alicia *Actress*
%William Morris Agency, 151 El Camino Dr, Beverly Hills, CA 90212, USA

Coppola, Francis Ford *Movie Director*
%Zoetrope Studios, 916 Kearny St, San Francisco, CA 94133, USA

Coppola, Sofia *Actress, Director*
4078 Farmouth Dr, Los Angeles, CA 90027, USA

Cora, Jose M (Joey) *Baseball Player*
Calle 17, F12 Villa Nueva, Caguas, PR 00625, USA

Corabi, John *Singer (Motley Crue)*
%Union Entertainment Group, 31225 La Baya Dr, #213, Westlake Village, CA 91362, USA

Corbett, Gretchen *Actress*
%S D B Partners, 1801 Ave of Stars, #902, Los Angeles, CA 90067, USA

Corbett, Luke R *Businessman*
%Kerr-McGee Corp, Kerr-McGee Center, Oklahoma City, OK 73125, USA

Corbett, Michael *Actor*
2665 Charl Place, Los Angeles, CA 90046, USA

Corbett, Mike *Rock Climber*
PO Box 917, Yosemite National Park, CA 95389, USA

Corbett, Ronnie *Actor, Comedian*
%International Artistes, 235 Regent St, London W1R 8AX, England

Corbin, Barry *Actor*
2113 Greta Lane, Fort Worth, TX 76120, USA

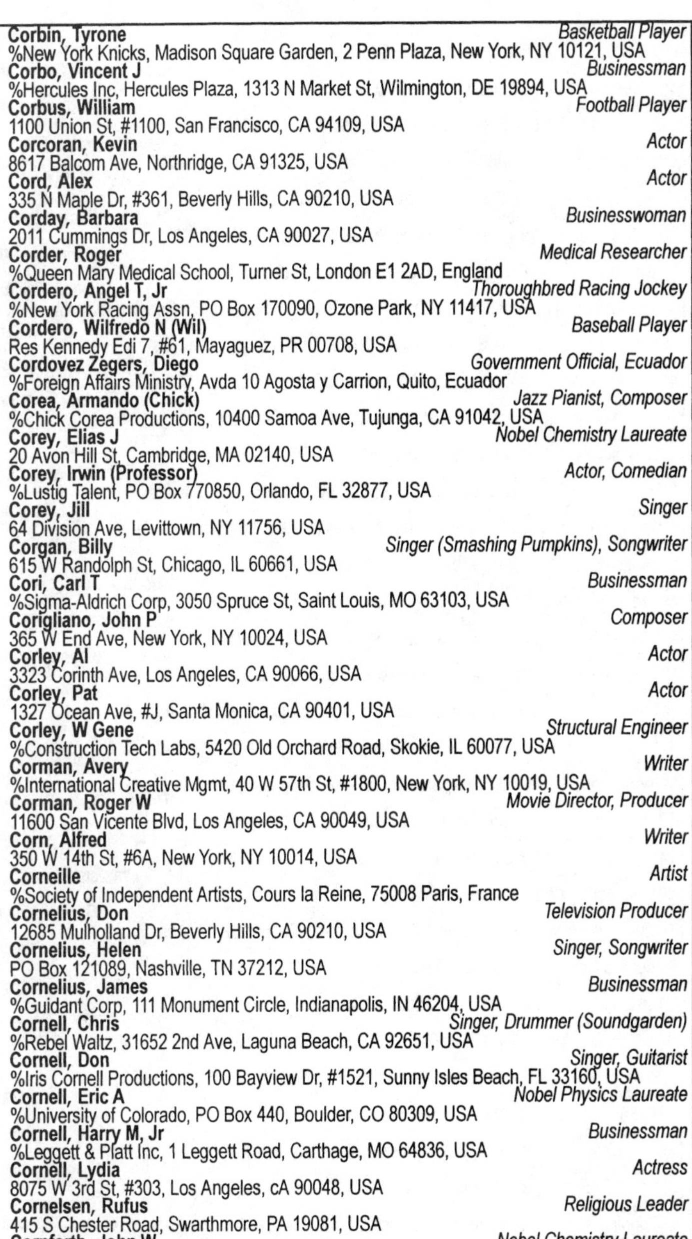

Corbin, Tyrone — *Basketball Player*
%New York Knicks, Madison Square Garden, 2 Penn Plaza, New York, NY 10121, USA

Corbo, Vincent J — *Businessman*
%Hercules Inc, Hercules Plaza, 1313 N Market St, Wilmington, DE 19894, USA

Corbus, William — *Football Player*
1100 Union St, #1100, San Francisco, CA 94109, USA

Corcoran, Kevin — *Actor*
8617 Balcom Ave, Northridge, CA 91325, USA

Cord, Alex — *Actor*
335 N Maple Dr, #361, Beverly Hills, CA 90210, USA

Corday, Barbara — *Businesswoman*
2011 Cummings Dr, Los Angeles, CA 90027, USA

Corder, Roger — *Medical Researcher*
%Queen Mary Medical School, Turner St, London E1 2AD, England

Cordero, Angel T, Jr — *Thoroughbred Racing Jockey*
%New York Racing Assn, PO Box 170090, Ozone Park, NY 11417, USA

Cordero, Wilfredo N (Wil) — *Baseball Player*
Res Kennedy Edi 7, #61, Mayaguez, PR 00708, USA

Cordovez Zegers, Diego — *Government Official, Ecuador*
%Foreign Affairs Ministry, Avda 10 Agosta y Carrion, Quito, Ecuador

Corea, Armando (Chick) — *Jazz Pianist, Composer*
%Chick Corea Productions, 10400 Samoa Ave, Tujunga, CA 91042, USA

Corey, Elias J — *Nobel Chemistry Laureate*
20 Avon Hill St, Cambridge, MA 02140, USA

Corey, Irwin (Professor) — *Actor, Comedian*
%Lustig Talent, PO Box 770850, Orlando, FL 32877, USA

Corey, Jill — *Singer*
64 Division Ave, Levittown, NY 11756, USA

Corgan, Billy — *Singer (Smashing Pumpkins), Songwriter*
615 W Randolph St, Chicago, IL 60661, USA

Cori, Carl T — *Businessman*
%Sigma-Aldrich Corp, 3050 Spruce St, Saint Louis, MO 63103, USA

Corigliano, John P — *Composer*
365 W End Ave, New York, NY 10024, USA

Corley, Al — *Actor*
3323 Corinth Ave, Los Angeles, CA 90066, USA

Corley, Pat — *Actor*
1327 Ocean Ave, #J, Santa Monica, CA 90401, USA

Corley, W Gene — *Structural Engineer*
%Construction Tech Labs, 5420 Old Orchard Road, Skokie, IL 60077, USA

Corman, Avery — *Writer*
%International Creative Mgmt, 40 W 57th St, #1800, New York, NY 10019, USA

Corman, Roger W — *Movie Director, Producer*
11600 San Vicente Blvd, Los Angeles, CA 90049, USA

Corn, Alfred — *Writer*
350 W 14th St, #6A, New York, NY 10014, USA

Corneille — *Artist*
%Society of Independent Artists, Cours la Reine, 75008 Paris, France

Cornelius, Don — *Television Producer*
12685 Mulholland Dr, Beverly Hills, CA 90210, USA

Cornelius, Helen — *Singer, Songwriter*
PO Box 121089, Nashville, TN 37212, USA

Cornelius, James — *Businessman*
%Guidant Corp, 111 Monument Circle, Indianapolis, IN 46204, USA

Cornell, Chris — *Singer, Drummer (Soundgarden)*
%Rebel Waltz, 31652 2nd Ave, Laguna Beach, CA 92651, USA

Cornell, Don — *Singer, Guitarist*
%Iris Cornell Productions, 100 Bayview Dr, #1521, Sunny Isles Beach, FL 33160, USA

Cornell, Eric A — *Nobel Physics Laureate*
%University of Colorado, PO Box 440, Boulder, CO 80309, USA

Cornell, Harry M, Jr — *Businessman*
%Leggett & Platt Inc, 1 Leggett Road, Carthage, MO 64836, USA

Cornell, Lydia — *Actress*
8075 W 3rd St, #303, Los Angeles, cA 90048, USA

Cornelsen, Rufus — *Religious Leader*
415 S Chester Road, Swarthmore, PA 19081, USA

Cornforth, John W — *Nobel Chemistry Laureate*
Saxon Down, Cuilfail, Lewes, East Sussex BN7 2BE, England

Cornish, Frank E — *Football Player*
305 Sheffield Dr, Southlake, TX 76092, USA

Cornish, Nick — *Actor*
%James Levy Jacobson Mgmt, 3500 W Olive Ave, #900, Burbank, CA 91505, USA

Cornog, Robert A — *Businessman*
%Snap-On Corp, 10801 Corporate Dr, Pleasant Prairie, WI 53158, USA

Cornthwaite, Robert — *Actor*
23388 Mulholland Dr, #12, Woodland Hills, CA 91364, USA

Cornwell, Johnny — *Guitarist (Dig)*
%Overland Productions, 156 W 56th St, #500, New York, NY 10019, USA

C

Cornwell - Coryell

Cornwell, Patricia D *Writer*
PO Box 5235, Greenwich, CT 06831, USA
Corr, Edwin G *Diplomat*
1617 Jenkins Ave, Norman, OK 73072, USA
Corrado, Fred *Businessman*
%Great A & P Tea Co, 2 Paragon Dr, Montvale, NJ 07645, USA
Corral, Frank *Football Player*
%Municipal Building, Graffiti Control, 3900 Main St, Riverside, CA 92522, USA
Correa, Charles M *Architect*
Sonmarg, Napean Sea Road, Bombay 40006, India
Correll, Alston D (Pete) *Businessman*
%Georgia-Pacific Corp, 133 Peachtree St NE, Atlanta, GA 30303, USA
Correnti, John D *Businessman*
%Nucor Corp, 2100 Rexford Road, Charlotte, NC 28211, USA
Corretja, Alex *Tennis Player*
%Assn of Tennis Professionals, 200 Tournament Road, Ponte Vedra Beach, FL 32082, USA
Corri, Adrienne *Actress*
%London Mgmt, 2-4 Noel St, London W1V 3RB, England
Corridon-Mortell, Marie *Swimmer*
13 Heritage Village, #A, Southbury, CT 06488, USA
Corrigan, E Gerald *Government Official, Financier*
%Goldman Sachs Co, 85 Broad St, New York, NY 10004, USA
Corrigan, Kevin *Actor*
%Innovative Artists, 1505 10th St, Santa Monica, CA 90401, USA
Corrigan, Patrick *Editorial Cartoonist*
%Toronto Star, Editorial Dept, 1 Yonge St, Toronto ON M5E 1E5, Canada
Corrigan, Robert A *Educator*
%San Francisco State University, President's Office, San Francisco, CA 94123, USA
Corrigan, Wilfred J *Businessman*
%LSI Logic, 1621 Barber Lane, Milpitas, CA 95035, USA
Corrigan-Maguire, Mairead *Nobel Peace Laureate*
%Peace People, 224 Lisburn Road, Belfast BT9 6GE, Northern Ireland
Corripio Ahumada, Ernesto Cardinal *Religious Leader*
Apolinar Nieto, 40 Col Tetlameyer, Mexico City 04730, Mexico
Corrs, Andrea *Singer (Corrs)*
%John Hughes, 6 Martello Terr, Sandycove, Dunlaoughaire, Dublin, Ireland
Corrs, Caroline *Singer (Corrs)*
%John Hughes, 6 Martello Terr, Sandycove, Dunlaoughaire, Dublin, Ireland
Corrs, Jim *Singer (Corrs)*
%John Hughes, 6 Martello Terr, Sandycove, Dunlaoughaire, Dublin, Ireland
Corrs, Sharon *Singer (Corrs)*
%John Hughes, 6 Martello Terr, Sandycove, Dunlaoughaire, Dublin, Ireland
Corsaro, Frank A *Theater, Opera Director*
33 Riverside Dr, New York, NY 10023, USA
Corso, John A *Cinematographer*
241 W 13th St, #21, New York, NY 10011, USA
Corson, Dale R *Physicist, Educator*
401 Savage Farm Dr, Ithaca, NY 14850, USA
Corson, Keith D *Businessman*
%Coachmen Industries, PO Box 3300, Elkhart, IN 46515, USA
Corson, Shayne *Hockey Player*
%Richard Curran, 411 Timber Lane, Devon, PA 19333, USA
Cort, Bud *Actor*
2149 Lyric Ave, Los Angeles, CA 90027, USA
Cortes, Joaquin *Flamenco Dancer, Choreographer*
%William Morris Agency, 151 El Camino Dr, Beverly Hills, CA 90212, USA
Cortes, Ron *Journalist*
%Philadelphia Inquirer, Editorial Dept, 400 N Broad St, Philadelphia, PA 19130, USA
Cortese, Dan *Actor*
28873 Via Venezia, Malibu, CA 90265, USA
Cortese, Joe *Actor*
2065 Coldwater Canyon Dr, Beverly Hills, CA 90210, USA
Cortese, Valentina *Actress*
Pretta S Erasmo 6, 20121 Milan, Italy
Cortez, Alfonso *Actor*
%CunninghamEscottDipene, 10635 Santa Monica Blvd, #130, Los Angeles, CA 90025, USA
Cortright, Edgar M, Jr *Aerospace Engineer*
9701 Calvin St, Northridge, CA 91324, USA
Corwin, Jeff *Actor*
%Jeff Corwin Experience, PO Box 2904, Toluca Lake, CA 91610, USA
Corwin, Norman *Writer*
%USC, 3551 Ironsdale Parkway, Los Angeles, CA 90089, USA
Coryatt, Quentin J *Football Player*
611 Cannon Lane, Sugar Land, TX 77479, USA
Coryell, Donald D (Don) *Football Coach*
PO Box 1576, Friday Harbor, WA 98250, USA
Coryell, Larry *Guitarist*
%Ted Kurland, 173 Brighton Ave, Boston, MA 02134, USA

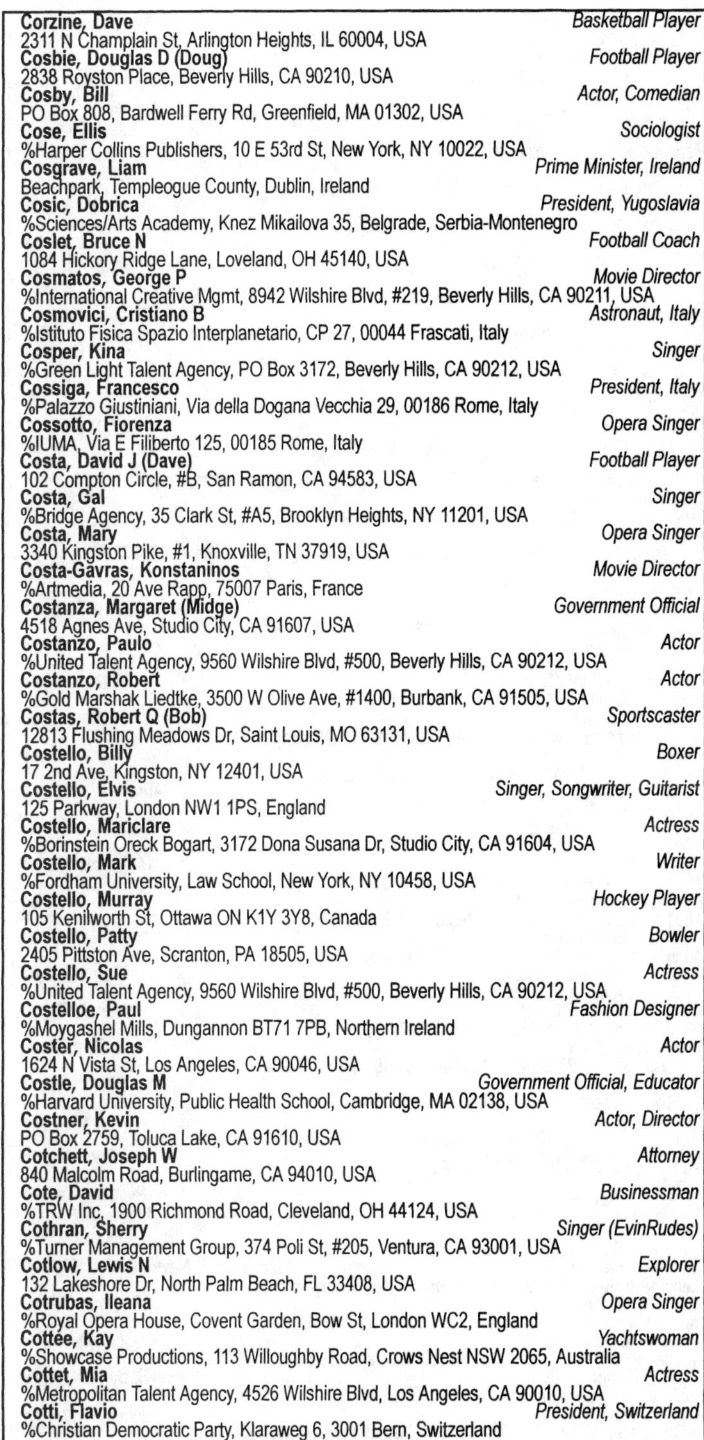

Corzine, Dave *Basketball Player*
2311 N Champlain St, Arlington Heights, IL 60004, USA
Cosbie, Douglas D (Doug) *Football Player*
2838 Royston Place, Beverly Hills, CA 90210, USA
Cosby, Bill *Actor, Comedian*
PO Box 808, Bardwell Ferry Rd, Greenfield, MA 01302, USA
Cose, Ellis *Sociologist*
%Harper Collins Publishers, 10 E 53rd St, New York, NY 10022, USA
Cosgrave, Liam *Prime Minister, Ireland*
Beachpark, Templeogue County, Dublin, Ireland
Cosic, Dobrica *President, Yugoslavia*
%Sciences/Arts Academy, Knez Mikailova 35, Belgrade, Serbia-Montenegro
Coslet, Bruce N *Football Coach*
1084 Hickory Ridge Lane, Loveland, OH 45140, USA
Cosmatos, George P *Movie Director*
%International Creative Mgmt, 8942 Wilshire Blvd, #219, Beverly Hills, CA 90211, USA
Cosmovici, Cristiano B *Astronaut, Italy*
%Istituto Fisica Spazio Interplanetario, CP 27, 00044 Frascati, Italy
Cosper, Kina *Singer*
%Green Light Talent Agency, PO Box 3172, Beverly Hills, CA 90212, USA
Cossiga, Francesco *President, Italy*
%Palazzo Giustiniani, Via della Dogana Vecchia 29, 00186 Rome, Italy
Cossotto, Fiorenza *Opera Singer*
%IUMA, Via E Filiberto 125, 00185 Rome, Italy
Costa, David J (Dave) *Football Player*
102 Compton Circle, #B, San Ramon, CA 94583, USA
Costa, Gal *Singer*
%Bridge Agency, 35 Clark St, #A5, Brooklyn Heights, NY 11201, USA
Costa, Mary *Opera Singer*
3340 Kingston Pike, #1, Knoxville, TN 37919, USA
Costa-Gavras, Konstaninos *Movie Director*
%Artmedia, 20 Ave Rapp, 75007 Paris, France
Costanza, Margaret (Midge) *Government Official*
4518 Agnes Ave, Studio City, CA 91607, USA
Costanzo, Paulo *Actor*
%United Talent Agency, 9560 Wilshire Blvd, #500, Beverly Hills, CA 90212, USA
Costanzo, Robert *Actor*
%Gold Marshak Liedtke, 3500 W Olive Ave, #1400, Burbank, CA 91505, USA
Costas, Robert Q (Bob) *Sportscaster*
12813 Flushing Meadows Dr, Saint Louis, MO 63131, USA
Costello, Billy *Boxer*
17 2nd Ave, Kingston, NY 12401, USA
Costello, Elvis *Singer, Songwriter, Guitarist*
125 Parkway, London NW1 1PS, England
Costello, Mariclare *Actress*
%Borinstein Oreck Bogart, 3172 Dona Susana Dr, Studio City, CA 91604, USA
Costello, Mark *Writer*
%Fordham University, Law School, New York, NY 10458, USA
Costello, Murray *Hockey Player*
105 Kenilworth St, Ottawa ON K1Y 3Y8, Canada
Costello, Patty *Bowler*
2405 Pittston Ave, Scranton, PA 18505, USA
Costello, Sue *Actress*
%United Talent Agency, 9560 Wilshire Blvd, #500, Beverly Hills, CA 90212, USA
Costelloe, Paul *Fashion Designer*
%Moygashel Mills, Dungannon BT71 7PB, Northern Ireland
Coster, Nicolas *Actor*
1624 N Vista St, Los Angeles, CA 90046, USA
Costle, Douglas M *Government Official, Educator*
%Harvard University, Public Health School, Cambridge, MA 02138, USA
Costner, Kevin *Actor, Director*
PO Box 2759, Toluca Lake, CA 91610, USA
Cotchett, Joseph W *Attorney*
840 Malcolm Road, Burlingame, CA 94010, USA
Cote, David *Businessman*
%TRW Inc, 1900 Richmond Road, Cleveland, OH 44124, USA
Cothran, Sherry *Singer (EvinRudes)*
%Turner Management Group, 374 Poli St, #205, Ventura, CA 93001, USA
Cotlow, Lewis N *Explorer*
132 Lakeshore Dr, North Palm Beach, FL 33408, USA
Cotrubas, Ileana *Opera Singer*
%Royal Opera House, Covent Garden, Bow St, London WC2, England
Cottee, Kay *Yachtswoman*
%Showcase Productions, 113 Willoughby Road, Crows Nest NSW 2065, Australia
Cottet, Mia *Actress*
%Metropolitan Talent Agency, 4526 Wilshire Blvd, Los Angeles, CA 90010, USA
Cotti, Flavio *President, Switzerland*
%Christian Democratic Party, Klaraweg 6, 3001 Bern, Switzerland

C

Cottier, George Cardinal *Religious Leader*
%Convento Santa Sabina, Piazza Pierro d'Illiria, 00193 Rome, Italy
Cottingham, Robert *Artist*
PO Box 604, Blackman Road, Newtown, CT 06470, USA
Cotton, Blaine *Actor*
%Jack Scagnetti Talent, 5118 Vineland Ave, #102, North Hollywood, CA 91601, USA
Cotton, Francis E (Fran) *Rugby Player*
Beechwood, Hulme Hall Road, Stockport, Cheshire SK8 6JZ, England
Cotton, Frank A *Chemist*
Twaycliffe Ranch, RR 2 Box 230, Bryan, TX 77808, USA
Cotton, James *Singer, Harmonica Player*
%James Cotton Mgmt, 235 W Eugene St, #G10, Chicago, IL 60614, USA
Cotton, Joseph F *Test Pilot*
20 Linda Vista Ave, Atherton, CA 94027, USA
Cotton, Josie *Singer*
2794 Hume Road, Malibu, CA 90265, USA
Cottrell, Ralph *Religious Leader*
%Baptist Missionary Assn, PO Box 1203, Van, TX 75790, USA
Couch, John N *Botanist*
1109 Carol Woods, Chapel Hill, NC 27514, USA
Couch, Tim *Football Player*
3083 Waterfall Way, Westlake, OH 44145, USA
Couffer, Jack *Cinematographer*
%Daniel Ostroff, 9200 W Sunset Blvd, #402, Los Angeles, CA 90069, USA
Coughlan, Marisa *Actress*
%International Creative Mgmt, 8942 Wilshire Blvd, #219, Beverly Hills, CA 90211, USA
Coughlin, Bernard J *Educator*
%Gonzaga University, Chancellor's Office, Spokane, WA 99258, USA
Coulier, David *Actor*
%International Creative Mgmt, 8942 Wilshire Blvd, #219, Beverly Hills, CA 90211, USA
Coulson, Catherine E *Actress*
1115 Terra Ave, Ashland, OR 97520, USA
Coulter, Brian *Guitarist (Blue October)*
%Ashley Talent, 2002 Hogback Road, #20, Ann Arbor, MI 48105, USA
Coulter, Catherine *Writer*
PO Box 17, Mill Valley, CA 94942, USA
Coulter, DeWitt E (Tex) *Football Player*
5001 Convict Hill Road, #503, Austin, TX 78749, USA
Coulter, Michael *Cinematographer*
35 Carlton Mansions, Randolph Ave, London W9 1NP, England
Coulter, Phil *Singer*
%57th Street Ltd, 24 Upper Mount St, Dublin, Ireland
Coulthard, David *Auto Racing Driver*
%Martin Brundle, Kings Lynn, Tottenhill, Norfolk PE32 0PX, England
Counsilman, James E (Doc) *Swimming Coach*
3602 William Court, Bloomington, IN 47401, USA
Counts, Mel *Basketball Player*
1581 Matheny Road, Gervais, OR 97026, USA
Couples, Fredrederick S (Fred) *Golfer*
1851 Alexander Bell Dr, #410, Reston, VA 20191, USA
Courant, Ernest D *Physicist*
40 W 72nd St, #4I, New York, NY 10023, USA
Couric, Katherine (Katie) *Commentator*
1100 Park Ave, #15A, New York, NY 10128, USA
Courier, James S (Jim), Jr *Tennis Player*
9533 Blandford Road, Orlando, FL 32827, USA
Cournoyer, Yvan S *Hockey Player*
%Brasserie 12, 625 32nd St, Lachine QC H8T 3G6, Canada
Courreges, Andre *Fashion Designer*
27 Rue Delabordere, 92 Neuilly-Sur-Seine, France
Courtenay, Tom *Actor*
%Jonathan Altaras, 13 Shorts Gardens, London WC2H 9AT, England
Courtney, Thomas W (Tom) *Track Athlete*
833 Wyndemere Way, Naples, FL 34105, USA
Cousin, Philip R *Religious Leader*
%Episcopal Church, District Headquarters, PO Box 2970, Jacksonville, FL 32203, USA
Cousineau, Tom *Football Player*
910 Eaton Ave, Akron, OH 44303, USA
Cousins, Ralph W *Navy Admiral, England*
Leconfield House, Curzon St, London W1Y 8JR, England
Cousins, Robin *Figure Skater*
%Billy Marsh, 174-8 N Gower St, London NW1 2NB, England
Cousteau, Jean-Michel *Oceanographer*
%Ocean Futures Society, 325 Chapala St, Santa Barbara, CA 93101, USA
Cousy, Robert J (Bob) *Basketball Player*
427 Salisbury St, Worcester, MA 01609, USA
Covay, Don *Singer, Songwriter*
%Rawstock, PO Box 110002, Cambria Heights, NY 11411, USA

Cover, Franklin *Actor*
%Sunset Lanai, 1422 N Sweetzer Ave, #402, Los Angeles, CA 90069, USA
Coverdale, David *Singer (Whitesnake/Deep Purple)*
%Agency for Performing Arts, 9200 Sunset Blvd, #900, Los Angeles, CA 90069, USA
Coverly, Dave *Editorial Cartoonist (Speed Bump)*
%Bloomington Herald-Times, Editorial Dept, 1900 S Walnut, Bloomington, IN 47401, USA
Covert, James (Jimbo) *Football Player*
450 Hunter Lane, Lake Forest, IL 60045, USA
Covey, Richard O *Astronaut*
1155 High Lake View, Colorado Springs, CO 80906, USA
Covey, Stephen R *Writer*
3507 N University Ave, #100, Provo, UT 84604, USA
Covic, Nebojsa *Prime Minister, Serbia*
%Prime Minister's Office, Nemanjina 11, 11000 Belgrade, Serbia
Covington, Warren *Orchestra Leader*
1627 Open Field Loop, Brandon, FL 33510, USA
Cowan, George A *Chemist*
%Santa Fe Institute, 1399 Hyde Park Road, Santa Fe, NM 87501, USA
Cowan, Ralph Wolfe *Artist*
243 29th St, West Palm Beach, FL 33407, USA
Cowart, Sam *Football Player*
PO Box 12431, Jacksonville, FL 32209, USA
Cowen, Robert E *Judge*
%US Court of Appeals, Judicial Complex, 402 E State St, Trenton, NJ 08608, USA
Cowen, Scott *Educator*
%Tulane University, President's Office, New Orleans, LA 70118, USA
Cowen, Wilson *Judge*
%US Court of Appeals, 717 Madison Place NW, Washington, DC 20439, USA
Cowen, Zelman *Attorney, Educator*
4 Treasury Place, East Melbourne VIC 3002, Australia
Cowens, David W (Dave) *Basketball Player, Coach*
746 Stonehill Run, Cincinnati, OH 45245, USA
Cowher, William L (Bill) *Football Player, Coach*
313 Olde Chapel Trail, Pittsburgh, PA 15238, USA
Cowhill, William J *Navy Admiral*
1336 Elsinore Ave, McLean, VA 22102, USA
Cowie, Lennox L *Astronomer*
%University of Hawaii, Astronomy Dept, 2600 Campus Road, Honolulu, HI 96822, USA
Cowper, Nicola *Actress*
%Brunskill Mgmt, 169 Queens Gate, #A8, London SW7 5EH, England
Cowper, Stephen C (Steve) *Governor, AK*
PO Box A, Juneau, AK 99811, USA
Cox Arquette, Courteney *Actress*
%Brillstein/Grey, 9150 Wilshire Blvd, #350, Beverly Hills, CA 90212, USA
Cox, Alex *Movie Director, Actor*
%United Talent Agency, 9560 Wilshire Blvd, #500, Beverly Hills, CA 90212, USA
Cox, Archibald *Attorney, Government Official*
78 Condon Point Road, Brookville, ME 04617, USA
Cox, Brian *Actor*
800 S Robertson Blvd, Los Angeles, CA 90035, USA
Cox, Bryan K *Football Player*
4484 4 Winds Lane, Northbrook, IL 60062, USA
Cox, Charles C *Government Official*
%Lexecon Inc, 332 S Michigan Ave, Chicago, IL 60604, USA
Cox, Christina *Actress*
%Rysher Entertainment, 3400 Riverside Dr, #600, Burbank, CA 91505, USA
Cox, Danny B *Baseball Player, Manager*
306 Feagin Mill Road, Warner Robins, GA 31088, USA
Cox, David R *Geneticist*
%Stanford University, Human Genome Center, Stanford, CA 94305, USA
Cox, Deborah *Singer, Songwriter*
%Evolution Talent, 1776 Broadway, #1500, New York, NY 10019, USA
Cox, Emmett R *Judge*
%US Court of Appeals, 113 St Joseph St, Mobile, AL 36602, USA
Cox, Frederick W (Fred) *Football Player*
401 E River St, Monticello, MN 55362, USA
Cox, G David *Religious Leader*
%Church of God, PO Box 2420, Anderson, IN 46018, USA
Cox, Harvey G, Jr *Educator, Theologian*
%Harvard University, Divinity School, Cambridge, MA 02140, USA
Cox, Jennifer Elise *Actress*
%Metropolitan Talent Agency, 4526 Wilshire Blvd, Los Angeles, CA 90010, USA
Cox, Johnny *Basketball Player, Coach*
849 N Main St, Hazard, KY 41701, USA
Cox, Lynne *Distance Swimmer*
%Advanced Sport Research, 4141 Ball Road, #142, Cypress, CA 90630, USA
Cox, Mark *Tennis Player*
Oaks, Astead Woods Road, Astead, Surrey KT21 2ER, England

C

Cox - Cramer

Cox, Nikki *Actress*
%United Talent Agency, 9560 Wilshire Blvd, #500, Beverly Hills, CA 90212, USA
Cox, Paul *Movie Director*
%Illumination Films, 1 Victoria Ave, Albert Park VIC 3208, Australia
Cox, Philip S *Architect*
%Cox Richardson Architects, 469 Kent St, Sydney NSW 2000, Australia
Cox, Ralph *Hockey Player*
%Massport, 1 Harborside Dr, #200S, East Boston, MA 02128, USA
Cox, Robert G *Financier*
%Summit Bancorp, PO Box 2066, Princeton, NJ 08543, USA
Cox, Robert J (Bobby) *Baseball Manager, Executive*
1572 Reids Ferry Way, Marietta, GA 30062, USA
Cox, Ronny *Actor*
13948 Magnolia Blvd, Sherman Oaks, CA 91423, USA
Cox, Stephen J *Artist*
154 Barnsbury Road, Islington, London N1 0ER, England
Cox, Warren J *Architect*
%Hartman Cox Architects, 1025 Thomas Jefferson St NW, Washington, DC 20007, USA
Coyne, Colleen *Hockey Player*
267 Lakeshore Dr N, East Falmouth, MA 02536, USA
Coyote, Peter *Actor*
774 Marin Dr, Mill Valley, CA 94941, USA
Cozier, Jimmy *Singer, Songwriter*
%J Records, 745 5th Ave, #600, New York, NY 10151, USA
Cozzarelli, Nicholas R *Biologist*
%University of California, Biology Dept, Berkeley, CA 94720, USA
Crable, Bob *Football Player*
564 Miami Trace, Loveland, OH 45140, USA
Craddock, Billy (Crash) *Singer, Songwriter*
3007 Old Martinsville Road, Greensboro, NC 27455, USA
Craft, Christine *Commentator*
%KRBK-TV, News Dept, 500 Media Place, Sacramento, CA 95815, USA
Cragg, Anthony D (Tony) *Sculptor*
Adolf-Vorwerk-Str 24, 42287 Wuppertal, Germany
Craggs, George *Soccer Player*
6223 6th Ave NW, Seattle, WA 98107, USA
Craig of Radley, David B *Air Force Marshal, England*
%House of Lords, Westminster, London SW1A 0PW, England
Craig, Daniel *Actor*
%International Creative Mgmt, 76 Oxford St, London W1N 0AX, England
Craig, Elijah *Actor*
%Agency for Performing Arts, 9200 Sunset Blvd, #900, Los Angeles, CA 90069, USA
Craig, James D (Jim) *Hockey Player*
15 Jyra Lane, North Easton, MA 02356, USA
Craig, Jenny *Nutritionist*
5770 Fleet St, Carlsbad, CA 92008, USA
Craig, Michael *Actor*
%Chatto & Linnit, Prince of Wales, Coventry St, London W1V 7FE, England
Craig, Richard *Inventor (Land-Mine Detector)*
%Pacific Northwest National Laboratory, 902 Battelle Blvd, Richland, WA 99352, USA
Craig, Roger L *Baseball Player, Manager*
PO Box 2174, Borrego Spings, CA 92004, USA
Craig, Roger T *Football Player*
271 Vista Verde Way, Portola Valley, CA 94028, USA
Craig, William *Government Official, England*
23 Annadale Ave, Belfast BT7 3JJ, Northern Ireland
Craig, William (Bill) *Swimmer*
PO Box 629, Newport Beach, CA 92661, USA
Craig, Yvonne *Actress*
%YC/MC Ltd, PO Box 827, Pacific Palisades, CA 90272, USA
Craighead, John J *Ecologist*
5125 Orchard Ave, Missoula, MT 59803, USA
Crain, Jeanne *Actress*
1029 Arbolado Road, Santa Barbara, CA 93103, USA
Crain, Keith E *Publisher*
%Crain Communications, 1400 Woodbridge Ave, Detroit, MI 48207, USA
Crain, Rance *Publisher*
%Crain Communications, 360 N Michigan Ave, Chicago, IL 60601, USA
Crain, William *Movie, Television Director*
%Contemporary Artists, 610 Santa Monica Blvd, #202, Santa Monica, CA 90401, USA
Crais, Robert *Writer*
12829 Landale St, Studio City, CA 91604, USA
Cram, Stephen (Steve) *Track Athlete*
%General Delivery, Jarrow, England
Cramer, Grant *Actor*
%Richard Sindell, 1910 Holmby Ave, #1, Los Angeles, CA 90025, USA
Cramer, Richard Ben *Journalist, Writer*
%Philadelphia Inquirer, Editorial Dept, 400 N Broad St, Philadelphia, PA 19130, USA

Crampton, Barbara *Actress*
%Stone Manners, 6500 Wilshire Blvd, #550, Los Angeles, CA 90048, USA
Crampton, Bruce *Golfer*
2404 A J Eagle Blvd, Annapolis, MD 21401, USA
Cramton, Roger C *Attorney, Educator*
49 Highgate Circle, Ithaca, NY 14850, USA
Crandall, Delmar W (Del) *Baseball Player*
1355 Clear Lake Place, Brea, CA 92821, USA
Crane, Horace R *Physicist*
66 Cavanaugh Lake Road, Chelsea, MI 48118, USA
Crane, Kenneth G *Movie Director*
6627 Linderhurst Ave, Los Angeles, CA 90048, USA
Crane, Tony *Actor*
%Abrams Artists, 9200 Sunset Blvd, #1125, Los Angeles, CA 90069, USA
Cranston, Toller *Figure Skater*
%Int'l Management Grp, 1 St Clair Ave E, #700, Toronto ON M4T 2V7, Canada
Cranz, Christl *Alpine Skier*
Steibis 61, 87534 Oberstaufen, Germany
Craven, Matt *Actor*
11445 Tongareva St, Malibu, CA 90265, USA
Craven, Ricky *Auto Racing Driver*
5918 Moray Court, Concord, NC 28027, USA
Craven, Wes *Movie Director*
2419 Solar Dr, Los Angeles, CA 90046, USA
Crawford, Bennie (Hank), Jr *Jazz Saxophonist, Pianist, Composer*
%Maxine Harvard, PM Box 51, #C5, 7942 Bell Road, Glendale, AZ 85308, USA
Crawford, Brad *Football Player*
RR 2, Winamac, IL 46996, USA
Crawford, Bryce L, Jr *Chemist*
3220 Lake Johanna Blvd, #58, Saint Paul, MN 55112, USA
Crawford, Christina *Writer*
7 Springs Farm, Sanders Road, Tensed, ID 83870, USA
Crawford, Cindy *Model, Actress*
%Wolf/Kasteller, 335 N Maple Dr, #351, Beverly Hills, CA 90210, USA
Crawford, Henry C (Shag) *Baseball Umpire*
1530 Virginia Ave, Havertown, PA 19083, USA
Crawford, Jamal *Basketball Player*
%Chicago Bulls, United Center, 1901 W Madison St, Chicago, IL 60612, USA
Crawford, Joan *Basketball Player*
4728 S Harvard Ave, #9, Tulsa, OK 74135, USA
Crawford, Johnny *Actor, Singer*
%Johnny Crawford Entertainment, PO Box 1851, Los Angeles, CA 90078, USA
Crawford, Michael *Actor, Singer*
%Night Ayrton, 10 Argyll St, London W1V 1AB, England
Crawford, Randy *Singer*
911 Park St SW, Grand Rapids, MI 49504, USA
Crawford, William J *WW II Army Hero (CMH)*
28520 County Road 14, Rocky Ford, CO 81067, USA
Cray, Robert *Singer, Guitarist*
%Rosebud Agency, PO Box 170429, San Francisco, CA 94117, USA
Creamer, Roger W *Sportswriter*
44 Fulling Ave, Tuckahoe, NY 10707, USA
Creamer, Timothy J *Astronaut*
5103 Carefree Dr, League City, TX 77573, USA
Crear, Mark *Track Athlete*
%Octagon, 1751 Pinnacle Dr, #1500, McLean, VA 22102, USA
Creech, Sharon *Writer*
%Harper Collins Publishers, 10 E 53rd St, New York, NY 10022, USA
Creech, Wilbur L *Air Force General*
20 Quail Run Road, Henderson, NV 89014, USA
Creeggan, Jim *Bassist (Barenaked Ladies)*
%Nettwerk Mgmt, 8730 Wilshire Blvd, #304, Beverly Hills, CA 90211, USA
Creekmur, Louis (Lou) *Football Player*
7521 SW 1st St, Plantation, FL 33317, USA
Creeley, Robert W *Writer*
PO Box 384, Waldoboro, ME 04572, USA
Creighton, David T, Sr *Hockey Player, Coach*
16113 E Course Dr, Tampa, FL 33624, USA
Creighton, Joanne V *Educator*
%Mount Holyoke College, President's Office, South Hadley, MA 01075, USA
Creighton, John D *Publisher*
%Toronto Sun, 333 King St E, Toronto ON M5A 3X5, Canada
Creighton, John O *Astronaut*
2111 SW 174th St, Burien, WA 98166, USA
Creme, Lol *Singer, Guitarist (Godley & Creme)*
Heronden Hall, Tenferden, Kent, England
Cremins, Bobby *Basketball Coach*
150 Bobby John Road, Atlanta, GA 30332, USA

Crenkovski, Branko *Prime Minister, Macedonia*
%Prime Minister's Office, Dame Grueva 6, 9100 Skopje, Macedonia
Crenshaw, Ben D *Golfer*
1800 Nueces St, Austin, TX 78701, USA
Crenshaw, Marshall *Singer, Songwriter*
%Rascoff/Zysblat, 110 W 57th St, #300, New York, NY 10019, USA
Crespin, Regine *Opera Singer*
%Musicaglotz, 3 Ave Frochet, 75009 Paris, France
Cresson, Edith *Prime Minister, France*
Mairie, 86018 Chatellerault Cedex, France
Cretier, Jean-Luc *Alpine Skier*
153 Ave du Marechal Lerelc, BP 20, 73700 Bourq Saint Maurice, France
Creutz, Edward C *Physicist*
PO Box 2757, Rancho Santa Fe, CA 92067, USA
Crewdson, John M *Journalist*
%Chicago Tribune, Editorial Dept, 435 N Michigan Ave, Chicago, IL 60611, USA
Crewe, Albert V *Physicist*
8 Summitt Dr, Chesterton, IN 46304, USA
Crews, David P *Psychobiologist*
%University of Texas, Zoology Dept, Austin, TX 78712, USA
Crews, Harry E *Writer*
%University of Florida, English Dept, Gainesville, FL 32611, USA
Crews, Phillip *Chemist*
%University of California, Chemistry Dept, Santa Cruz, CA 99504, USA
Crewson, Wendy *Actress*
438 Queen St E, Toronto ON M5A 1T4, Canada
Cribbins, Bernard *Actor*
Hamm Court, Weybridge, Surrey, England
Cribbs, Joe S *Football Player*
6131 Eagle Point Circle, Birmingham, AL 35242, USA
Crichton, J Michael *Writer, Movie Director*
7605 Santa Monica Blvd, #644, West Hollywood, CA 90046, USA
Crick, Francis H C *Nobel Medicine Laureate*
1792 Colgate Circle, La Jolla, CA 92037, USA
Crickhowell of Pont Esgob, Nicholas E *Government Leader, England*
4 Henning St, London SW11 3DR, England
Crider, Melissa *Actress*
%Paradigm Agency, 10100 Santa Monica Blvd, #2500, Los Angeles, CA 90067, USA
Crier, Catherine *Commentator*
%Cable News Network, News Dept, 1050 Techwood Dr NW, Atlanta, GA 30318, USA
Crile, Susan *Artist*
168 W 86th St, New York, NY 10024, USA
Crilley, Mark *Writer*
%Delacorte Press, 1540 Broadway, New York, NY 10036, USA
Crippen, Robert L *Astronaut*
691 E 3550 N, Ogden, UT 84414, USA
Criqui, Don *Sportscaster*
%CBS-TV, Sports Dept, 51 W 52nd St, New York, NY 10019, USA
Crisostomo, Manny *Photojournalist*
%Pacific Daily News, PO Box DN, Hagatna, GU 96932, USA
Crisp, Terry A *Hockey Player, Coach*
805 Cherry Laurel Court, Nashville, TN 37215, USA
Crispin, Anne C *Writer*
PO Box 522, Bryantown, MD 20617, USA
Criss, Peter *Singer, Drummer (Kiss)*
%McGhee Entertainment, 8730 Sunset Blvd, #195, West Hollywood, CA 90069, USA
Crist, George B *Marine Corps General*
%CBS-TV, News Dept, 51 W 52nd St, New York, NY 10019, USA
Crist, Judith *Journalist*
180 Riverside Dr, New York, NY 10024, USA
Cristal, Linda *Actress*
9129 Hazen Dr, Beverly Hills, CA 90210, USA
Cristofer, Michael *Writer*
%Richard Lovett, 9830 Wilshire Blvd, Beverly Hills, CA 90212, USA
Cristol, Stanley J *Chemist*
2918 3rd St, Boulder, CO 80304, USA
Critchfield, Charles L *Physicist*
PO Box 993, Los Alamos, NM 87544, USA
Critelli, Michael *Businessman*
%Pitney Bowes Inc, 1 Elmcroft Road, Stamford, CT 06926, USA
Crockett, Billy *Singer, Songwriter*
%Street Level Artists Agency, 106 N Buffalo St, #200, Warsaw, IN 46580, USA
Crockett, Gibson *Cartoonist*
4713 Great Oak Road, Rockville, MD 20853, USA
Croel, Mike *Football Player*
837 Traction Ave, Los Angeles, CA 90013, USA
Croft, Dwayne *Opera Singer*
%Columbia Artists Mgmt Inc, 165 W 57th St, New York, NY 10019, USA

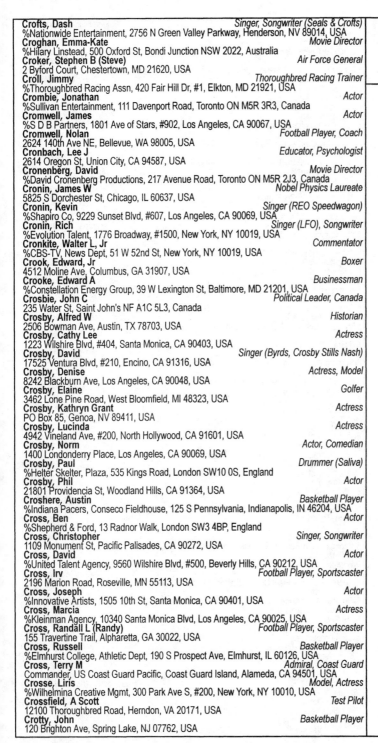

Crofts, Dash *Singer, Songwriter (Seals & Crofts)*
%Nationwide Entertainment, 2756 N Green Valley Parkway, Henderson, NV 89014, USA
Croghan, Emma-Kate *Movie Director*
%Hilary Linstead, 500 Oxford St, Bondi Junction NSW 2022, Australia
Croker, Stephen B (Steve) *Air Force General*
2 Byford Court, Chestertown, MD 21620, USA
Croll, Jimmy *Thoroughbred Racing Trainer*
%Thoroughbred Racing Assn, 420 Fair Hill Dr, #1, Elkton, MD 21921, USA
Crombie, Jonathan *Actor*
%Sullivan Entertainment, 111 Davenport Road, Toronto ON M5R 3R3, Canada
Cromwell, James *Actor*
%S D B Partners, 1801 Ave of Stars, #902, Los Angeles, CA 90067, USA
Cromwell, Nolan *Football Player, Coach*
2624 140th Ave NE, Bellevue, WA 98005, USA
Cronbach, Lee J *Educator, Psychologist*
2614 Oregon St, Union City, CA 94587, USA
Cronenberg, David *Movie Director*
%David Cronenberg Productions, 217 Avenue Road, Toronto ON M5R 2J3, Canada
Cronin, James W *Nobel Physics Laureate*
5825 S Dorchester St, Chicago, IL 60637, USA
Cronin, Kevin *Singer (REO Speedwagon)*
%Shapiro Co, 9229 Sunset Blvd, #607, Los Angeles, CA 90069, USA
Cronin, Rich *Singer (LFO), Songwriter*
%Evolution Talent, 1776 Broadway, #1500, New York, NY 10019, USA
Cronkite, Walter L, Jr *Commentator*
%CBS-TV, News Dept, 51 W 52nd St, New York, NY 10019, USA
Crook, Edward, Jr *Boxer*
4512 Moline Ave, Columbus, GA 31907, USA
Crooke, Edward A *Businessman*
%Constellation Energy Group, 39 W Lexington St, Baltimore, MD 21201, USA
Crosbie, John C *Political Leader, Canada*
235 Water St, Saint John's NF A1C 5L3, Canada
Crosby, Alfred W *Historian*
2506 Bowman Ave, Austin, TX 78703, USA
Crosby, Cathy Lee *Actress*
1223 Wilshire Blvd, #404, Santa Monica, CA 90403, USA
Crosby, David *Singer (Byrds, Crosby Stills Nash)*
17525 Ventura Blvd, #210, Encino, CA 91316, USA
Crosby, Denise *Actress, Model*
8242 Blackburn Ave, Los Angeles, CA 90048, USA
Crosby, Elaine *Golfer*
3462 Lone Pine Road, West Bloomfield, MI 48323, USA
Crosby, Kathryn Grant *Actress*
PO Box 85, Genoa, NV 89411, USA
Crosby, Lucinda *Actress*
4942 Vineland Ave, #200, North Hollywood, CA 91601, USA
Crosby, Norm *Actor, Comedian*
1400 Londonderry Place, Los Angeles, CA 90069, USA
Crosby, Paul *Drummer (Saliva)*
%Helter Skelter, Plaza, 535 Kings Road, London SW10 0S, England
Crosby, Phil *Actor*
21801 Providencia St, Woodland Hills, CA 91364, USA
Croshere, Austin *Basketball Player*
%Indiana Pacers, Conseco Fieldhouse, 125 S Pennsylvania, Indianapolis, IN 46204, USA
Cross, Ben *Actor*
%Shepherd & Ford, 13 Radnor Walk, London SW3 4BP, England
Cross, Christopher *Singer, Songwriter*
1109 Monument St, Pacific Palisades, CA 90272, USA
Cross, David *Actor*
%United Talent Agency, 9560 Wilshire Blvd, #500, Beverly Hills, CA 90212, USA
Cross, Irv *Football Player, Sportscaster*
2196 Marion Road, Roseville, MN 55113, USA
Cross, Joseph *Actor*
%Innovative Artists, 1505 10th St, Santa Monica, CA 90401, USA
Cross, Marcia *Actress*
%Kleinman Agency, 10340 Santa Monica Blvd, Los Angeles, CA 90025, USA
Cross, Randall L (Randy) *Football Player, Sportscaster*
155 Travertine Trail, Alpharetta, GA 30022, USA
Cross, Russell *Basketball Player*
%Elmhurst College, Athletic Dept, 190 S Prospect Ave, Elmhurst, IL 60126, USA
Cross, Terry M *Admiral, Coast Guard*
Commander, US Coast Guard Pacific, Coast Guard Island, Alameda, CA 94501, USA
Crosse, Liris *Model, Actress*
%Wilhelmina Creative Mgmt, 300 Park Ave S, #200, New York, NY 10010, USA
Crossfield, A Scott *Test Pilot*
12100 Thoroughbred Road, Herndon, VA 20171, USA
Crotty, John *Basketball Player*
120 Brighton Ave, Spring Lake, NJ 07762, USA

Crouch, Andrae *Singer, Pianist, Songwriter*
%Hervey Co, 300 Park Ave S, #300, New York, NY 10010, USA
Crouch, Eric *Football Player*
%ABC-TV, Sports Dept, 3240 S 10th St, Lincoln, NE 68502, USA
Crouch, Paul *Evangelist*
%Trinity Broadcasting Network, PO Box A, Santa Ana, CA 92711, USA
Crouch, Roger K *Astronaut*
Carriage Hill Dr, Laurel, MD 20707, USA
Crouch, Sandra *Drummer, Songwriter*
%Sparrow Communications Group, 101 Winners Circle, Brentwood, TN 37027, USA
Crouch, Stanley *Writer, Columnist*
%Georges Borchardt Agency, 136 E 57th St, New York, NY 10022, USA
Crouch, William T (Bill) *Photojournalist*
5660 Valley Oaks Court, Placerville, CA 95667, USA
Crouse, Lindsay *Actress*
15115 1/2 Sunset Blvd, #A, Pacific Palisades, CA 90272, USA
Crow, F Trammell *Businessman*
%Trammell Crow Co, Trammell Crow Center, 2001 Ross Ave, Dallas, TX 75201, USA
Crow, Harlan R *Businessman*
%Trammell Crow Co, Trammell Crow Center, 2001 Ross Ave, Dallas, TX 75201, USA
Crow, James F *Geneticist*
24 Glenway St, Madison, WI 53705, USA
Crow, John David *Football Player, Coach*
5004 Augusta Circle, College Station, TX 77845, USA
Crow, Lindon *Football Player*
6800 S Strand Ave, #481, Yuma, AZ 85364, USA
Crow, Martin D *Cricketer*
PO Box 109302, Newmarket, Auckland, New Zealand
Crow, Sheryl *Singer, Songwriter, Actress*
%Kathryn Schenker, 1776 Broadway, #1200, New York, NY 10019, USA
Crowe, Cameron *Movie Director, Writer*
%Creative Artists Agency, 9830 Wilshire Blvd, Beverly Hills, CA 90212, USA
Crowe, George D *Baseball, Basketball Player*
1544 Silas Tompkins Road, Long Eddy, NY 12760, USA
Crowe, Phil *Hockey Player*
PO Box 115, Willow Grove, PA 19090, USA
Crowe, Russell *Actor*
%Bedford/Pearce Mgmt, PO Box 271, Cammeray NSW 2062, Australia
Crowe, Tonya *Actress*
13030 Mindanao Way, #4, Marina del Rey, CA 90292, USA
Crowe, William J, Jr *Navy Admiral, Diplomat*
%Global Options, 1615 L St NW, #300, Washington, DC 20036, USA
Crowell, Craven H, Jr *Government Official*
%Tennessee Valley Authority, 400 W Summit Hill Dr, Knoxville, TN 37902, USA
Crowell, John C *Geologist*
300 Hot Springs Road, Montecito, CA 93108, USA
Crowell, Rodney J *Singer, Songwriter*
%Joe's Garage, 4405 Belmont Park Terrace, Nashville, TN 37215, USA
Crowley, Joseph N *Educator*
%University of Nevada, President's Office, Reno, NV 89557, USA
Crowley, Mart *Writer*
8955 Beverly Blvd, West Hollywood, CA 90048, USA
Crowley, Patricia *Actress*
%TMCE, 270 N Canon Dr, #1064, Beverly Hills, CA 90210, USA
Crown, David A *Criminologist*
3344 Twin Lakes Lane, Sanibel, FL 33957, USA
Crowson, Richard *Editorial Cartoonist*
%Wichita Eagle-Beacon, Editorial Dept, 825 E Douglas Ave, Wichita, KS 67202, USA
Crowton, Gary *Football Coach*
%Brigham Young University, Athletic Dept, Provo, UT 84602, USA
Crozier, Joseph R (Joe) *Hockey Player, Coach*
%Boston Bruins, 1 Fleet Center, Boston, MA 02114, USA
Crudup, Billy *Actor*
%Creative Artists Agency, 9830 Wilshire Blvd, Beverly Hills, CA 90212, USA
Cruikshank, Thomas H *Businessman*
5949 Sherry Lane, #1035, Dallas, TX 75225, USA
Cruise, Tom *Actor*
%Odin Productions, 253 26th St, #262, Santa Monica, CA 90402, USA
Crum, E Denzel (Denny) *Basketball Coach*
12038 Hunting Crest Dr, Prospect, KY 40059, USA
Crumb, George H *Composer*
240 Kirk Lane, Media, PA 19063, USA
Crumb, Robert (R) *Cartoonist (Keep on Truckin')*
20 Rue du Pont Vieux, 30610 Sauve, France
Crumley, James R, Jr *Religious Leader*
362 Little Creek Dr, Leesville, SC 29070, USA
Crutcher, Lawrence M *Publisher*
%Book-of-the-Month Club, Rockefeller Center, New York, NY 10020, USA

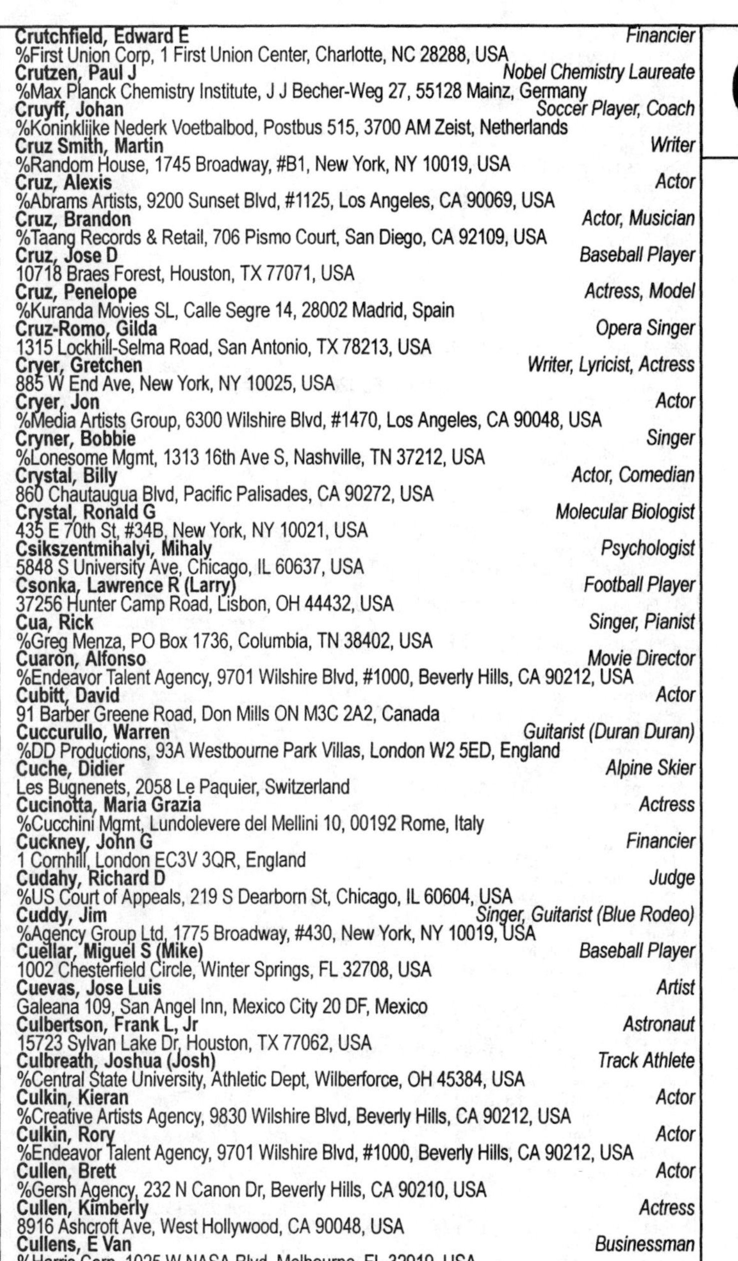
Crutchfield, Edward E *Financier*
%First Union Corp, 1 First Union Center, Charlotte, NC 28288, USA
Crutzen, Paul J *Nobel Chemistry Laureate*
%Max Planck Chemistry Institute, J J Becher-Weg 27, 55128 Mainz, Germany
Cruyff, Johan *Soccer Player, Coach*
%Koninklijke Nederk Voetbalbod, Postbus 515, 3700 AM Zeist, Netherlands
Cruz Smith, Martin *Writer*
%Random House, 1745 Broadway, #B1, New York, NY 10019, USA
Cruz, Alexis *Actor*
%Abrams Artists, 9200 Sunset Blvd, #1125, Los Angeles, CA 90069, USA
Cruz, Brandon *Actor, Musician*
%Taang Records & Retail, 706 Pismo Court, San Diego, CA 92109, USA
Cruz, Jose D *Baseball Player*
10718 Braes Forest, Houston, TX 77071, USA
Cruz, Penelope *Actress, Model*
%Kuranda Movies SL, Calle Segre 14, 28002 Madrid, Spain
Cruz-Romo, Gilda *Opera Singer*
1315 Lockhill-Selma Road, San Antonio, TX 78213, USA
Cryer, Gretchen *Writer, Lyricist, Actress*
885 W End Ave, New York, NY 10025, USA
Cryer, Jon *Actor*
%Media Artists Group, 6300 Wilshire Blvd, #1470, Los Angeles, CA 90048, USA
Cryner, Bobbie *Singer*
%Lonesome Mgmt, 1313 16th Ave S, Nashville, TN 37212, USA
Crystal, Billy *Actor, Comedian*
860 Chautaugua Blvd, Pacific Palisades, CA 90272, USA
Crystal, Ronald G *Molecular Biologist*
435 E 70th St, #34B, New York, NY 10021, USA
Csikszentmihalyi, Mihaly *Psychologist*
5848 S University Ave, Chicago, IL 60637, USA
Csonka, Lawrence R (Larry) *Football Player*
37256 Hunter Camp Road, Lisbon, OH 44432, USA
Cua, Rick *Singer, Pianist*
%Greg Menza, PO Box 1736, Columbia, TN 38402, USA
Cuaron, Alfonso *Movie Director*
%Endeavor Talent Agency, 9701 Wilshire Blvd, #1000, Beverly Hills, CA 90212, USA
Cubitt, David *Actor*
91 Barber Greene Road, Don Mills ON M3C 2A2, Canada
Cuccurullo, Warren *Guitarist (Duran Duran)*
%DD Productions, 93A Westbourne Park Villas, London W2 5ED, England
Cuche, Didier *Alpine Skier*
Les Bugnenets, 2058 Le Paquier, Switzerland
Cucinotta, Maria Grazia *Actress*
%Cucchini Mgmt, Lundolevere del Mellini 10, 00192 Rome, Italy
Cuckney, John G *Financier*
1 Cornhill, London EC3V 3QR, England
Cudahy, Richard D *Judge*
%US Court of Appeals, 219 S Dearborn St, Chicago, IL 60604, USA
Cuddy, Jim *Singer, Guitarist (Blue Rodeo)*
%Agency Group Ltd, 1775 Broadway, #430, New York, NY 10019, USA
Cuellar, Miguel S (Mike) *Baseball Player*
1002 Chesterfield Circle, Winter Springs, FL 32708, USA
Cuevas, Jose Luis *Artist*
Galeana 109, San Angel Inn, Mexico City 20 DF, Mexico
Culbertson, Frank L, Jr *Astronaut*
15723 Sylvan Lake Dr, Houston, TX 77062, USA
Culbreath, Joshua (Josh) *Track Athlete*
%Central State University, Athletic Dept, Wilberforce, OH 45384, USA
Culkin, Kieran *Actor*
%Creative Artists Agency, 9830 Wilshire Blvd, Beverly Hills, CA 90212, USA
Culkin, Rory *Actor*
%Endeavor Talent Agency, 9701 Wilshire Blvd, #1000, Beverly Hills, CA 90212, USA
Cullen, Brett *Actor*
%Gersh Agency, 232 N Canon Dr, Beverly Hills, CA 90210, USA
Cullen, Kimberly *Actress*
8916 Ashcroft Ave, West Hollywood, CA 90048, USA
Cullens, E Van *Businessman*
%Harris Corp, 1025 W NASA Blvd, Melbourne, FL 32919, USA
Culler, Glen *Computer Scientist*
%Culler Scientific Systems Corp, 100 Burns Place, Goleta, CA 93117, USA
Culligan, Joe *Private Investigator, Writer*
%Research Investigative Services, 650 NE 126th St, North Miami, FL 33161, USA
Cullinan, Edward H *Architect*
Wharf, 1 Baldwin Terrace, London N1 7RU, England
Cullum, John *Actor, Singer*
%Writers & Artists, 19 W 44th St, #1000, New York, NY 10036, USA
Cullum, Leo *Cartoonist*
2900 Valmere Dr, Malibu, CA 90265, USA

C

Cullum - Curb

Cullum, Mark E *Editorial Cartoonist*
5401 Forest Acres Dr, Nashville, TN 37220, USA
Culp, Curley *Football Player*
12405 Alameda Trace Circle, #1213, Austin, TX 78727, USA
Culp, Robert *Actor*
1324 N Spaulding Ave, Los Angeles, CA 90046, USA
Culp, Steven *Actor*
1680 Las Lunas St, Pasadena, CA 91106, USA
Culver, Curt S *Financier*
%MGIC Investment Corp, 250 E Kilbourn Ave, Milwaukee, WI 53202, USA
Culver, John C *Senator, IA*
5409 Spangler Ave, Bethesda, MD 20816, USA
Culver, Molly *Actress*
2658 Griffith Park Blvd, #284, Los Angeles, CA 90039, USA
Cumby, George E *Football Player*
22715 Leedstown Lane, Katy, TX 77449, USA
Cumming, Alan *Actor, Singer*
222 W 14th St, #2F, New York, NY 10011, USA
Cummings, Burton *Singer (Guess Who), Songwriter*
%Lustig Talent, PO Box 770850, Orlando, FL 32877, USA
Cummings, Constance *Actress*
68 Old Church St, London SW3 6EP, England
Cummings, Quinn *Actress*
%Pietragallo Agency, 398 Collins Dr, Pittsburgh, PA 15235, USA
Cummings, Ralph W *Agriculturist*
PO Box 1266, Clarksville, VA 23927, USA
Cummins, Gregory Scott *Actor*
%Schiowitz/Clay/Rose, 1680 N Vine St, #1016, Los Angeles, CA 90028, USA
Cummins, Peggy *Actress*
17 Brockley Road, Bexhill-on-Sea, Sussex TN39 4TT, England
Cundey, Dean R *Cinematographer*
344 Georgian Road, La Canada, CA 91011, USA
Cunniff, Jill *Singer, Bassist (Luscious Jackson)*
%Metropolitan Entertainment, 2 Penn Plaza, #2600, New York, NY 10121, USA
Cunningham, Bennie L *Football Player*
PO Box 1147, Clemson, SC 29633, USA
Cunningham, Bill *Bassist, Pianist (Box Tops)*
%Horizon Mgmt, PO Box 8770, Endwell, NY 13762, USA
Cunningham, Gunther *Football Player, Coach*
%Tennessee Titans, 460 Great Circle Road, Nashville, TN 37228, USA
Cunningham, Jeffrey M *Publisher*
%Forbes Magazine, 60 5th Ave, New York, NY 10011, USA
Cunningham, John *Actor*
%Gage Group, 14724 Ventura Blvd, #505, Sherman Oaks, CA 91403, USA
Cunningham, Liam *Actor*
%Marina Martin, 12/13 Poland St, London W1V 3DE, England
Cunningham, Merce *Dancer, Choreographer*
%Cunningham Dance Foundation, 55 Bethune St, New York, NY 10014, USA
Cunningham, Michael *Writer*
%Farrar Straus Giroux, 19 Union Square W, New York, NY 10003, USA
Cunningham, R Walter *Astronaut*
%AVD, PO Box 604, Glenn Dale, MD 20769, USA
Cunningham, Randall *Football Player*
2035 Helm Dr, Las Vegas, NV 89119, USA
Cunningham, Samuel L (Sam), Jr *Football Player*
5595 E 7th St, #238, Long Beach, CA 90804, USA
Cunningham, Sean S *Movie Director, Producer*
4420 Hayvenhurst Ave, Encino, CA 91436, USA
Cunningham, William J (Billy) *Basketball Player, Coach, Executive*
%Court Restaurant, 31 Front St, #33, Conshohocken, PA 19428, USA
Cuomo, Andrew M *Secretary, Housing & Urban Development*
787 7th Ave, New York, NY 10019, USA
Cuomo, Christopher *Commentator*
%ABC News, 147 Columbus Ave, New York, NY 10023, USA
Cuomo, Jerome J *Inventor (Read-Write Optical Storage)*
%IBM T J Watson Research Center, PO Box 218, Yorktown Heights, NY 10598, USA
Cuomo, Mario M *Governor, NY*
50 Sutton Place S, #11G, New York, NY 10022, USA
Cuomo, Rivers *Singer, Guitarist (Weezer), Songwriter*
%Atlas/Third World Entertainment, 9168 Sunset Blvd, Los Angeles, CA 90069, USA
Cuozzo, Gary S *Football Player*
4 Swimming River Road, Lincroft, NJ 07738, USA
Cupp, James N *WW II Marine Corps Air Force Hero*
7506 Todd Place, Manassas, VA 20109, USA
Cura, Jose *Opera Singer*
%Columbia Artists Mgmt Inc, 165 W 57th St, New York, NY 10019, USA
Curb, Michael (Mike) *Composer, Businessman*
3907 W Alameda Ave, #2, Burbank, CA 91505, USA

Curbeam, Robert L, Jr *Astronaut*
15806 Virginia Fern Way, Houston, TX 77059, USA
Cure, Armand *Basketball, Football Player*
6136 E Huntdale St, Long Beach, CA 90808, USA
Cureton, Thomas K *Swimming Executive*
501 E Washington, Urbana, IL 61801, USA
Curfman, Shannon *Singer*
%Monterey International, 200 W Superior, #202, Chicago, IL 60610, USA
Curl, Carolyn *Speed Skier, Mountain Bicyclist*
%Robert U Curl, 405 N Westridge Dr, Idaho Falls, ID 83402, USA
Curl, Robert F, Jr *Nobel Chemistry Laureate*
1824 Bolsover St, Houston, TX 77005, USA
Curlander, Paul J *Businessman*
%Lexmark International, 740 W New Circle Road, Lexington, KY 40550, USA
Curler, James *Businessman*
%Bemis Co, 222 S 9th St, Minneapolis, MN 55402, USA
Curley, Edwin M *Philosopher*
2645 Pin Oak Dr, Ann Arbor, MI 48103, USA
Curley, John J *Publisher*
%Gannett Co, 1100 Wilson Blvd, Arlington, VA 22209, USA
Curley, Thomas (Tom) *Publisher*
%Associated Press, 50 Rockefeller Plaza, New York, NY 10020, USA
Curley, Walter J P, Jr *Diplomat, Financier*
885 3rd Ave, #1200, New York, NY 10022, USA
Curnin, Thomas F *Attorney*
%Cahill Gordon Reindel, 80 Pine St, New York, NY 10005, USA
Curran, Charles E *Theologian*
%Southern Methodist University, Dallas Hall, Dallas, TX 75275, USA
Curran, Mike *Hockey Player*
7615 Lanewood Lane N, Maple Grove, MN 55311, USA
Curren, Kevin *Tennis Player*
5808 Back Court, Austin, TX 78731, USA
Currey, Francis S *WW II Army Hero (CMH)*
106 Catfish Landing Circle, Bonneau, SC 29431, USA
Currie, Cherie *Singer, Actress*
%Times Productions, 520 Washington Blvd, #199, Marina del Rey, CA 90292, USA
Currie, Daniel (Dan) *Football Player*
2801 Wynadotte St, #15, Las Vegas, NV 89102, USA
Currie, Louise *Actress*
1317 Delresto Dr, Beverly Hills, CA 90210, USA
Currie, Malcolm R *Businessman*
%Hughes Aircraft Co, PO Box 956, El Segundo, CA 90245, USA
Currie, Nancy J *Astronaut*
2390 Indigo Harbour Lane, League City, TX 77573, USA
Currie, Sondra *Actress*
3951 Longridge Ave, Sherman Oaks, CA 91423, USA
Curris, Constantine W *Educator*
%Clemson University, President's Office, Sikes Hall, Clemson, SC 29634, USA
Curry, Ann *Commentator*
%NBC-TV, News Dept, 30 Rockefeller Plaza, New York, NY 10112, USA
Curry, Bill *Football Player, Coach*
2730 Bowman Mill Road, Lexington, KY 40513, USA
Curry, Dell *Basketball Player*
8381 Providence Road, Charlotte, NC 28277, USA
Curry, Denise *Basketball Player, Coach*
%San Jose Lasers, 230 California St, #510, San Francisco, CA 94111, USA
Curry, Donald *Boxer*
6814 S Hulen St, #135, Fort Worth, TX 76133, USA
Curry, Eddy *Basketball Player*
%Chicago Bulls, United Center, 1901 W Madison St, Chicago, IL 60612, USA
Curry, Eric F *Football Player*
1050 E Piedmont Road, #E119, Marietta, GA 30062, USA
Curry, Tim *Singer, Actor*
%United Talent Agency, 9560 Wilshire Blvd, #500, Beverly Hills, CA 90212, USA
Curtin, David S *Journalist*
%Colorado Springs Gazette Telegraph, 30 S Prospect, Colorado Springs, CO 80903, USA
Curtin, David Y *Chemist*
2903 Rutherford Dr, Urbana, IL 61802, USA
Curtin, Jane T *Actress*
%International Creative Mgmt, 8942 Wilshire Blvd, #219, Beverly Hills, CA 90211, USA
Curtin, John J, Jr *Attorney*
%Bingham Dana Gould, 150 Federal St, #3500, Boston, MA 02110, USA
Curtin, Valerie *Actress*
%Writers & Artists, 8383 Wilshire Blvd, #550, Beverly Hills, CA 90211, USA
Curtis Cuneo, Ann E *Swimmer*
35 Golden Hinde Blvd, San Rafael, CA 94903, USA
Curtis, Cliff *Actor*
%R Bruce Ugly Agency, 218 Richmond Rd, Grey Lynn, Auckland 2, New Zealand

C

Curtis, Daniel M (Dan) *Movie Director*
143 S Rockingham Ave, Los Angeles, CA 90049, USA
Curtis, Isaac F *Football Player*
711 Clinton Springs Ave, Cincinnati, OH 45229, USA
Curtis, J Michael (Mike) *Football Player*
7917 Rivers Fall Dr, Potomac, MD 20854, USA
Curtis, Jamie Lee *Actress*
%Joan Cotler Books, 1325 Ave of Americas, New York, NY 10019, USA
Curtis, Kelly *Actress*
651 N Kikea Dr, Los Angeles, CA 90048, USA
Curtis, Kenneth M *Governor, ME; Diplomat*
%Curtis Thaxter, 1 Canal Plaza, Portland, ME 04112, USA
Curtis, Robin *Actress*
1147 Beverly Hill Dr, Cincinnati, OH 45208, USA
Curtis, Todd *Actor*
2046 14th St, #10, Santa Monica, CA 90405, USA
Curtis, Tony *Actor*
2598 Forest City Dr, Henderson, NV 89052, USA
Curtis-Hall, Vondie *Actor*
%The Firm, 9100 Wilshire Blvd, #100W, Beverly Hills, CA 90210, USA
Curtola, Bobby *Singer*
%ESP Productions, 720 Spadina Ave, #PH2, Toronto ON M5S 2T9, Canada
Cusack, Ann *Actress*
%Innovative Artists, 1505 10th St, Santa Monica, CA 90401, USA
Cusack, Joan *Actress, Comedienne*
%William Morris Agency, 151 El Camino Dr, Beverly Hills, CA 90212, USA
Cusack, John *Actor*
%Barnes Morris Klein Young, 1424 2nd St, #3, Santa Monica, CA 90401, USA
Cusack, Sinead *Actress*
%Markham & Froggatt, Julian House, 4 Windmill St, London W1P 1HF, England
Cushman, David W *Biochemist*
20 Lake Shore Dr, Princeton Junction, NJ 08550, USA
Cushman, Karen *Writer*
%Clarion Books, 215 Park Ave S, New York, NY 10003, USA
Cussler, Clive E *Writer*
13764 W 61st Circle, Arvada, CO 80004, USA
Custom *Singer*
%ArtistDirect, 10900 Wilshire Blvd, #1400, Los Angeles, CA 90024, USA
Cutcliffe, David *Football Coach*
%University of Mississippi, Athletic Dept, University, MS 38677, USA
Cuthbert, Elisha *Actress*
%Rozon Merder, 201 N Robertson Blvd, #F, Beverly Hills, CA 90211, USA
Cuthbeth, Elizabeth (Betty) *Track Athlete*
4/7 Karara Close, Hall's Head, Mandurah WA 6210, Australia
Cutler, Alexander M *Businessman*
%Eaton Corp, Eaton Center, 1111 Superior Ave, Cleveland, OH 44114, USA
Cutler, Bruce *Attorney*
41 Madison Ave, New York, NY 10010, USA
Cutler, Lloyd N *Government Official*
3115 O St NW, Washington, DC 20007, USA
Cutler, Walter L *Diplomat*
%Meridian International Center, 1630 Crescent Place NW, Washington, DC 20009, USA
Cutliffe, Molly *Actress*
%Hervey/Grimes, PO Box 64249, Los Angeles, CA 90064, USA
Cutrufello, Mary *Singer, Songwriter*
%Joe's Garage, 4405 Belmont Park Terrace, Nashville, TN 37215, USA
Cutter, Kiki *Alpine Skier*
PO Box 1317, Carbondale, CO 81623, USA
Cutter, Lise *Actress*
PO Box 2665, Sag Harbor, NY 11963, USA
Cutter, Slade D *Football Player*
6102 River Crescent Dr, Annapolis, MD 21401, USA
Cuviello, Peter M *Army General*
Director, Defense Information Systems Agency, Arlington, VA 22204, USA
Cypher, Jon *Actor*
498 Manzanita Ave, Ventura, CA 93001, USA
Cyr, Conrad K *Judge*
%US Court of Appeals, PO Box 635, Bangor, ME 04402, USA
Cyrus, Billy Ray *Singer, Songwriter*
%As Is Mgmt, 704 18th Ave S, Nashville, TN 37203, USA
Czapsky, Stefan *Cinematographer*
RR 3 Box 278, Unadilla, NY 13849, USA
Czrongursky, Jan *Prime Minister, Slovakia*
%Prime Minister's Office, Nam Slobody 1, 81370 Bratislava, Slovakia
Czyz, Bobby *Boxer*
110 Pennsylvania Ave, Flemington, NJ 08822, USA

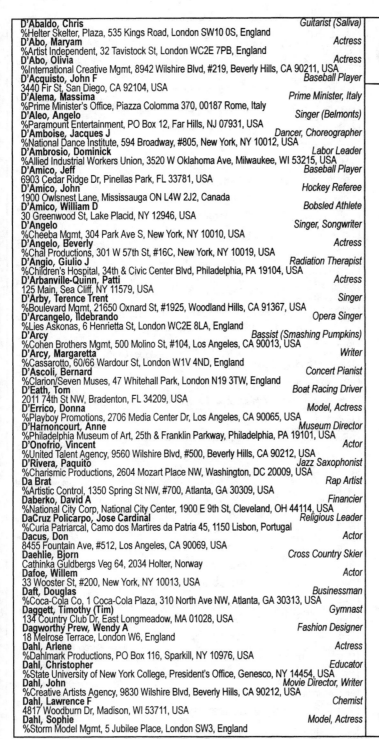

D'Abaldo, Chris *Guitarist (Saliva)*
%Helter Skelter, Plaza, 535 Kings Road, London SW10 0S, England
D'Abo, Maryam *Actress*
%Artist Independent, 32 Tavistock St, London WC2E 7PB, England
D'Abo, Olivia *Actress*
%International Creative Mgmt, 8942 Wilshire Blvd, #219, Beverly Hills, CA 90211, USA
D'Acquisto, John F *Baseball Player*
3440 Fir St, San Diego, CA 92104, USA
D'Alema, Massima *Prime Minister, Italy*
%Prime Minister's Office, Piazza Colomma 370, 00187 Rome, Italy
D'Aleo, Angelo *Singer (Belmonts)*
%Paramount Entertainment, PO Box 12, Far Hills, NJ 07931, USA
D'Amboise, Jacques J *Dancer, Choreographer*
%National Dance Institute, 594 Broadway, #805, New York, NY 10012, USA
D'Ambrosio, Dominick *Labor Leader*
%Allied Industrial Workers Union, 3520 W Oklahoma Ave, Milwaukee, WI 53215, USA
D'Amico, Jeff *Baseball Player*
6903 Cedar Ridge Dr, Pinellas Park, FL 33781, USA
D'Amico, John *Hockey Referee*
1900 Owlsnest Lane, Mississauga ON L4W 2J2, Canada
D'Amico, William D *Bobsled Athlete*
30 Greenwood St, Lake Placid, NY 12946, USA
D'Angelo *Singer, Songwriter*
%Cheeba Mgmt, 304 Park Ave S, New York, NY 10010, USA
D'Angelo, Beverly *Actress*
%Chal Productions, 301 W 57th St, #16C, New York, NY 10019, USA
D'Angio, Giulio J *Radiation Therapist*
%Children's Hospital, 34th & Civic Center Blvd, Philadelphia, PA 19104, USA
D'Arbanville-Quinn, Patti *Actress*
125 Main, Sea Cliff, NY 11579, USA
D'Arby, Terence Trent *Singer*
%Boulevard Mgmt, 21650 Oxnard St, #1925, Woodland Hills, CA 91367, USA
D'Arcangelo, Ildebrando *Opera Singer*
%Lies Askonas, 6 Henrietta St, London WC2E 8LA, England
D'Arcy *Bassist (Smashing Pumpkins)*
%Cohen Brothers Mgmt, 500 Molino St, #104, Los Angeles, CA 90013, USA
D'Arcy, Margaretta *Writer*
%Cassarotto, 60/66 Wardour St, London W1V 4ND, England
D'Ascoli, Bernard *Concert Pianist*
%Clarion/Seven Muses, 47 Whitehall Park, London N19 3TW, England
D'Eath, Tom *Boat Racing Driver*
2011 74th St NW, Bradenton, FL 34209, USA
D'Errico, Donna *Model, Actress*
%Playboy Promotions, 2706 Media Center Dr, Los Angeles, CA 90065, USA
D'Harnoncourt, Anne *Museum Director*
%Philadelphia Museum of Art, 25th & Franklin Parkway, Philadelphia, PA 19101, USA
D'Onofrio, Vincent *Actor*
%United Talent Agency, 9560 Wilshire Blvd, #500, Beverly Hills, CA 90212, USA
D'Rivera, Paquito *Jazz Saxophonist*
%Charismic Productions, 2604 Mozart Place NW, Washington, DC 20009, USA
Da Brat *Rap Artist*
%Artistic Control, 1350 Spring St NW, #700, Atlanta, GA 30309, USA
Daberko, David A *Financier*
%National City Corp, National City Center, 1900 E 9th St, Cleveland, OH 44114, USA
DaCruz Policarpo, Jose Cardinal *Religious Leader*
%Curia Patriarcal, Camo dos Martires da Patria 45, 1150 Lisbon, Portugal
Dacus, Don *Actor*
8455 Fountain Ave, #512, Los Angeles, CA 90069, USA
Daehlie, Bjorn *Cross Country Skier*
Cathinka Guldbergs Veg 64, 2034 Holter, Norway
Dafoe, Willem *Actor*
33 Wooster St, #200, New York, NY 10013, USA
Daft, Douglas *Businessman*
%Coca-Cola Co, 1 Coca-Cola Plaza, 310 North Ave NW, Atlanta, GA 30313, USA
Daggett, Timothy (Tim) *Gymnast*
134 Country Club Dr, East Longmeadow, MA 01028, USA
Dagworthy Prew, Wendy A *Fashion Designer*
18 Melrose Terrace, London W6, England
Dahl, Arlene *Actress*
%Dahlmark Productions, PO Box 116, Sparkill, NY 10976, USA
Dahl, Christopher *Educator*
%State University of New York College, President's Office, Genesco, NY 14454, USA
Dahl, John *Movie Director, Writer*
%Creative Artists Agency, 9830 Wilshire Blvd, Beverly Hills, CA 90212, USA
Dahl, Lawrence F *Chemist*
4817 Woodburn Dr, Madison, WI 53711, USA
Dahl, Sophie *Model, Actress*
%Storm Model Mgmt, 5 Jubilee Place, London SW3, England

D

Dahlberg, A William *Businessman*
%Southern Co, 270 Peachtree St NW, Atlanta, GA 30303, USA
Dahlberg, Kenneth H (Ken) *WW II Army Air Corps Hero*
19360 Walden Trail, Wayzata, MN 55391, USA
Dahlgren, Edward C *WW II Army Hero (CMH)*
PO Box 26, Mars Hill, ME 04758, USA
Dahm, Werner K *Space Scientist*
7605 Martha Dr SE, Huntsville, AL 35802, USA
Dai Ailian *Dancer, Choreographer*
Hua Qiao Gong Yu, #2-16, Hua Yuan Cun, Hai Dian, Beijing 100044, China
Daiches, David *Writer*
22 Belgrave Crescent, Edinburgh EH4 3AL, Scotland
Daigle, Alexander *Hockey Player*
3510 Rue Bordeaux, Trois-Rivieres-Quest QC G8Y 3P7, Canada
Daigneault, J J *Hockey Player*
%Minnesota Wild, XCel Energy Arena, 175 Kellogg Blvd W, Saint Paul, MN 55102, USA
Dailey, Janet *Writer*
HC 4, Box 2197, Branson, MO 65616, USA
Dailey, Peter H *Diplomat*
%State Department, 2201 C St NW, Washington, DC 20520, USA
Dailey, Quintin *Basketball Player*
22808 Hilton Head Dr, #28, Diamond Bar, CA 91765, USA
Daily, Bill *Actor*
1331 Park Ave SW, #802, Albuquerque, NM 87102, USA
Daily, E G *Singer, Songwriter, Actress*
%T-Best Talent Agency, 508 Honey Lake Court, Danville, CA 94506, USA
Daily, Gretchen *Ecologist*
%Stanford University, Ecology Dept, Stanford, CA 94305, USA
Daily, Parker *Religious Leader*
%Baptist Bible Fellowship International, PO Box 191, Springfield, MO 65801, USA
Dainton, Frederick S *Chemist*
Fieldside, Water Eaton Lane, Kidlington, Oxford OX5 2PR, England
Daio, Norberto J D C A *Prime Minister, Sao Tome & Principe*
%Prime Minister's Office, CP 38, Sao Tome, Sao Tome & Principe
Dajani, Nadia *Actress*
%Innovative Artists, 1505 10th St, Santa Monica, CA 90401, USA
Dalai Lama *Religious Leader; Nobel Peace Laureate*
Thekchen Choeling, McLeod Ganj 176219, Dharamsal, Himachal Pradesh, India
Daland, Peter *Diving Coach*
PO Box 2443, Aquebogue, NY 11931, USA
Dalbavie, Andre *Composer*
%Van Walsum Mgmt, 4 Addison Bridge Place, London W14 8XP, England
Dalberto, Michel *Concert Pianist*
13 Blvd Henri Plumhof, 1800 Vevey, Switzerland
Daldry, Stephen *Theater Director*
%Royal Court Theater, Sloane Square, London SW1, England
Dale, Bruce *Photographer*
%National Geographic Magazine, 1145 17th St NW, Washington, DC 20036, USA
Dale, Carroll W *Football Player*
%Clinch Valley College, Athletic Department, 1 College Ave, Wise, VA 24293, USA
Dale, Dick *Singer, Guitarist*
PO Box 1713, Twentynine Palms, CA 92277, USA
Dale, Jim *Actor*
%Mark Sendroff, 230 W 56th St, #63B, New York, NY 10019, USA
Dale, William B *Economist, Government Official*
6008 Landon Lane, Bethesda, MD 20817, USA
Dalembert, Samuel *Basketball Player*
%Philadelphia 76ers, 1st Union Center, 3601 S Broad St, Philadelphia, PA 19148, USA
Dales-Schuman, Stacey *Basketball Player*
%Washington Mystics, MCI Center, 601 F St NW, Washington, DC 20004, USA
Daley, Richard M *Mayor*
%Mayor's Office, City Hall, 121 N LaSalle St, Chicago, IL 60602, USA
Daley, Rosie *Chef, Writer*
%Harpo Productions, 110 N Carpenter St, Chicago, IL 60607, USA
Daley, William N (Bill) *Secretary, Commerce*
%SBC Communications, 175 E Houston, San Antonio, TX 78205, USA
Dalgarno, Alexander *Astronomer*
27 Robinson St, Cambridge, MA 02138, USA
Dalglish, Kenneth M (Kenny) *Soccer Player, Manager*
%FC Newcastle United, Saint James Park, Newcastle-on-Tyne NE1 4ST, England
Dalheimer, Patrick *Musician (Live)*
%Freedman & Smith, 350 W End Ave, #1, New York, NY 10024, USA
Dalhousie, Simon R *Government Official, England*
Brechin Castle, Brechin DD9 6SH, Scotland
Dali, Tracy *Actress, Model*
PO Box 69541, Los Angeles, CA 90069, USA
Dalis, Irene *Opera Singer*
1731 Cherry Grove Dr, San Jose, CA 95125, USA

Dall, Bobby *Bassist (Poison)*
%H K Mgmt, 9200 W Sunset Blvd, #530, Los Angeles, CA 90069, USA
Dalle, Beatrice *Actress*
%Artmedia, 20 Ave Rapp, 75007 Paris, France
Dallenbach, Wally *Auto Racing Executive*
5315 Stowe Lane, Harrisburg, NC 89134, USA
Dallesandro, Joe *Actor*
521 W Briar Place, #505, Chicago, IL 60657, USA
Dalrymple, Gary B *Geologist*
1847 NW Hillcrest Dr, Corvallis, OR 97330, USA
Dalton, Abby *Actress*
PO Box 100, Mammoth Lakes, CA 93546, USA
Dalton, Audrey *Actress*
2241 Labrusca, Mission Viejo, CA 92692, USA
Dalton, James E *Air Force General*
61 Misty Acres Road, Rolling Hills Estates, CA 90274, USA
Dalton, John H *Government Official*
3710 University Ave NW, Washington, DC 20016, USA
Dalton, Lacy J *Singer*
820 Cartwright Road, Reno, NV 89521, USA
Dalton, Nic *Musician (Lemonheads)*
%Agency Group Ltd, 1775 Broadway, #430, New York, NY 10019, USA
Dalton, Timothy *Actor*
%James Sharkey, 21 Golden Square, London W1R 3PA, England
Daltry, Roger *Singer (Who), Actor*
%Conway Van Gelder Robinson, 18-21 Jermyn St, London SW1Y 6NB, England
Daly, Cahal Brendan Cardinal *Religious Leader*
Ard Mhacha, 23 Rosetta Ave, Belfast BT7 3HG, Northern Ireland
Daly, Carson *Entertainer*
%William Morris Agency, 1325 Ave of Americas, New York, NY 10019, USA
Daly, Charles J (Chuck) *Basketball Coach*
18586 SE Village Circle, Tequesta, FL 33469, USA
Daly, John *Movie Producer*
%Hemdale, 7960 Beverly Blvd, Los Angeles, CA 90048, USA
Daly, John *Golfer*
%Cambridge Sports Int'l, 5335 Wisconsin Ave NW, #850, Washington, DC 20015, USA
Daly, Michael J *WW II Army Hero (CMH)*
155 Redding Road, Fairfield, CT 06824, USA
Daly, Timothy *Actor*
%Industry Entertainment, 955 Carillo Dr, #300, Los Angeles, CA 90048, USA
Daly, Tyne *Actress*
272 S Lasky Dr, #402, Beverly Hills, CA 90212, USA
Dam, Kenneth W *Government Official, Attorney*
%University of Chicago, Law School, 1111 E 60th St, Chicago, IL 60637, USA
Damadian, Raymond V *Inventor (Cancer Tissue Detector-MRI)*
%FONAR Corp, 110 Marcus Dr, Melville, NY 11747, USA
Damas, Bertila *Actress*
PO Box 17193, Beverly Hills, CA 90209, USA
Damasio, Antonio R *Neurologist*
%University of Iowa Hospital, Neurology Dept, Iowa City, IA 52242, USA
DaMatta, Cristiano *Auto Racing Driver*
%Newman-Haas Racing, 50 Tower Parkway, Lincolnshire, IL 60069, USA
Dame Edna *Actor, Comedian*
%PBJ Mgmt, 5 Soho Square, London W1V 5DE, England
Damian, Michael *Actor, Singer*
%Gold Marshak Liedtke, 3500 W Olive Ave, #1400, Burbank, CA 91505, USA
Damiani, Damiano *Movie Director*
Via Delle Terme Deciane 2, 00153 Rome, Italy
Dammerman, Dennis D *Businessman*
%General Electric Co, 3135 Easton Turnpike, Fairfield, CT 06828, USA
Damon, Johnny D *Baseball Player*
904 Main St, Windermere, FL 34786, USA
Damon, Mark *Actor*
2781 Benedict Canyon Dr, Beverly Hills, CA 90210, USA
Damon, Matt *Actor*
%P M K Public Relations, 8500 Wilshire Blvd, #700, Beverly Hills, CA 90211, USA
Damon, Stuart *Actor*
367 N Van Ness Ave, Los Angeles, CA 90004, USA
Damon, Una *Actress*
%Writers & Artists, 8383 Wilshire Blvd, #550, Beverly Hills, CA 90211, USA
Damone, Vic *Singer, Actor*
%International Ventures, 25864 Tournament Road, #L, Valencia, CA 91355, USA
Damphousse, Vincent *Hockey Player*
16780 Loma St, Los Gatos, CA 95032, USA
Dampier, Erick *Basketball Player*
2635 Sea View Parkway, Alameda, CA 94502, USA
Dampier, Louie *Basketball Player*
%Dampier Distributing, 2808 New Moody Lane, La Grange, KY 40031, USA

D

Dana, Bill *Actor, Comedian*
5965 Peacock Ridge, #563, Rancho Palos Verdes, CA 90275, USA
Dana, Justin *Actor*
13111 Ventura Blvd, #102, Studio City, CA 91604, USA
Dana, William (Bill) *Test Pilot*
21400 Grand Oaks Ave, Tehachapi, CA 93561, USA
Danby, Gordon T *Inventor (Magnetic Levitation Train)*
126 Sound Road, Wading River, NY 11792, USA
Dance, Charles *Actor*
7812 Forsythe St, Sunland, CA 91040, USA
Dancer, Stanley F *Harness Racing Driver*
1624 E Atlantic Blvd, Pompano Beach, FL 33060, USA
Dancy, John *Commentator*
%Harvard University, Kennedy Government School, Cambridge, MA 02138, USA
Dando, Evan *Singer (Lemonheads)*
%Agency Group Ltd, 1775 Broadway, #430, New York, NY 10019, USA
Dandridge, Bob *Basketball Player*
1708 Saint Denis Ave, Norfolk, VA 23509, USA
Dane, Alexandra *Actress*
%Rolf Kruger Mgmt, 205 Chudleigh Road, London SE4 1EG, England
Dane, Paul *Test Pilot*
12105 Ambassador Dr, #515, Colorado Springs, CO 80921, USA
Danelli, Dino *Drummer (Rascals)*
%Rascals, Cassidy, 11761 Speedway Blvd, Tucson, AZ 85748, USA
Danes, Claire *Actress*
%Industry Entertainment, 955 Carillo Dr, #300, Los Angeles, CA 90048, USA
Danforth, Douglas D *Businessman, Baseball Executive*
8720 Bay Colony Dr, #701, Naples, FL 34108, USA
Danforth, Fred *Artist*
PO Box 828, Middlebury, VT 05753, USA
Danforth, John C (Jack) *Senator, MO*
RR 1 Box 91, Newburg, MO 65550, USA
Dangerfield, Rodney *Actor, Comedian*
%Artist Group International, 9560 Wilshire Blvd, #400, Beverly Hills, CA 90212, USA
Daniel, Brittany *Actress*
%Handprint Entertainment, 1100 Glendon Ave, #1000, Los Angeles, CA 90024, USA
Daniel, Elizabeth A (Beth) *Golfer*
1350 Echo Dr, Jupiter, FL 33458, USA
Daniel, Jeffrey *Singer (Shalamar)*
%Green Light Talent Agency, PO Box 3172, Beverly Hills, CA 90212, USA
Daniel, Margaret Truman *Writer*
%Scott Meredith Literary Agency, 1675 Broadway, New York, NY 10019, USA
Daniel, Tony *Cartoonist*
%International Creative Mgmt, 8942 Wilshire Blvd, #219, Beverly Hills, CA 90211, USA
Danielpour, Richard *Composer*
%Sony Classics Records, 2100 Colorado Ave, Santa Monica, CA 90404, USA
Daniels, Antonio *Basketball Player*
%Seattle SuperSonics, 351 Elliott Ave W, #500, Seattle, WA 98119, USA
Daniels, Charlie *Singer, Songwriter*
%CDB Mgmt, 14410 Central Pike, Mount Joliet, TN 37122, USA
Daniels, Cheryl *Bowler*
6574 Crest Top Dr, West Bloomfield, MI 48322, USA
Daniels, Clemon (Bo) *Football Player*
1466 High St, Oakland, CA 94601, USA
Daniels, Jeff *Actor*
701 Glazier Road, Chelsea, MI 48118, USA
Daniels, Melvin (Mel) *Basketball Player*
19789 Centennial Road, Sheridan, IN 46069, USA
Daniels, William *Actor*
12805 Hortense St, Studio City, CA 91604, USA
Daniels, William B *Physicist*
283 Dallam Road, Newark, DE 19711, USA
Danielsen, Egil *Track Athlete*
Roreks Gate 9, 2300 Hamar, Norway
Danielson, Gary D *Football Player*
1686 Edinborough Dr, Rochester Hills, MI 48306, USA
Danielsson, Bengt F *Anthropologist*
Box 558, Papette, Tahiti
Daniloff, Nicholas *Journalist*
PO Box 892, Chester, VT 05143, USA
Danko, William D *Writer*
%Pocket Books, 1230 Ave of Americas, New York, NY 10020, USA
Dankworth, John P W *Jazz Saxophonist, Composer, Bandleader*
Old Rectory, Wavendon, Milton Kenyes MK17 8LT, England
Danneels, Godfried Cardinal *Religious Leader*
Aartsbisdom, Wollemarkt 15, 2800 Mechelen, Belgium
Danner, Blythe *Actress*
304 21st St, Santa Monica, CA 90402, USA

Danner, Christian *Auto Racing Executive*
%JAS Engineering, Viale Europa, 72 Strada Bn1, 20090 Cusago, Italy
Danning, Harry *Baseball Player*
212 Fox Chapel Court, Valparaiso, IN 46385, USA
Danning, Sybil *Actress, Model*
%Adventuress Production, 1438 N Gower St, Bldg 35, Los Angeles, CA 90028, USA
Dano, Linda *Actress*
%VSMP, 1010 Nautilus Lane, Mamaroneck, NY 10543, USA
Danson, Ted *Actor*
%Industry Entertainment, 955 Carillo Dr, #300, Los Angeles, CA 90048, USA
Dante, Joe *Movie Director*
2321 Holly Dr, Los Angeles, CA 90068, USA
Dante, Michael *Actor*
3349 Cahuenga Blvd W, #1, Los Angeles, CA 90068, USA
Dantine, Nikki *Actress*
707 N Palm Dr, Beverly Hills, CA 90210, USA
Dantley, Adrian D *Basketball Player, Coach*
1232 Via del Sol, San Dimas, CA 91773, USA
Danto, Arthur C *Philosopher*
%Columbia University, Philosophy Dept, New York, NY 10024, USA
Dantzig, George B *Computer Scientist*
821 Tolman Dr, Stanford, CA 94305, USA
Dantzig, Rudi Van *Choreographer*
Emma-Straat 27, Amsterdam, Netherlands
Danza, Tony *Actor*
25000 Malibu Road, Malibu, CA 90265, USA
Danzig, Frederick P *Editor*
%Advertising Age, Editorial Dept, 220 E 42nd St, New York, NY 10017, USA
Danziger, Jeff *Editorial Cartoonist*
RFD, Plainfield, VT 05667, USA
Daoud, Ignace Moussa I Cardinal *Religious Leader*
Palazzo del Bramante, Via della Conciliazione 34, 00193 Rome, Italy
Daphnis, Nassos *Artist*
362 W Broadway, New York, NY 10013, USA
Darabont, Frank *Movie Director, Writer*
%William Morris Agency, 151 El Camino Dr, Beverly Hills, CA 90212, USA
Darboven, Hanne *Artist*
Am Burgberg 26, 21079 Hamburg, Germany
Darby, Kim *Actress*
%Michael Slessinger, 8730 Sunset Blvd, #220W, Los Angeles, CA 90069, USA
Darc, Mireille *Actress*
%Agents Associes Beaume, 201 Faubourg Saint Honore, 75008 Paris, France
Dare, Yinka *Basketball Player*
PO Box 523, Redding Ridge, CT 06876, USA
Darehshori, Nader F *Publisher*
%Houghton Mifflin Co, 222 Berkeley St, Boston, MA 02116, USA
Dark, Alvin R *Baseball Player, Manager*
103 Cranberry Way, Easley, SC 29642, USA
Darling, Charles (Chuck) *Basketball Player*
8066 S Kramerie Way, Centennial, CO 80112, USA
Darling, Jennifer *Actress*
13351 Riverside Dr, #427, Sherman Oaks, CA 91423, USA
Darling, Joan *Actress*
PO Box 6700, Tesuque, NM 87574, USA
Darling, Ronald M (Ron) *Baseball Player*
19 Woodland St, Millbury, MA 01527, USA
Darmaatmadja, Julius Riyadi Cardinal *Religious Leader*
Keuskupan Agung, Jl Katedral 7, Jakarta 10710, Indonesia
Darman, Richard G *Government Official*
1137 Crest Lane, McLean, VA 22101, USA
Darnell, James E, Jr *Molecular Biologist*
%Rockefeller University, Medical Center, 1230 York Ave, New York, NY 10021, USA
Darnton, John *Journalist, Writer*
%New York Times, Editorial Dept, 229 W 43rd St, New York, NY 10036, USA
Darnton, Robert C *Historian*
6 McCosh Circle, Princeton, NJ 08540, USA
Darren, James *Singer, Actor*
PO Box 1088, Beverly Hills, CA 90213, USA
Darrieux, Danielle *Actress*
%Nicole Cann, 1 Rue Alfred de Vigny, 75008 Paris, France
Darrow, Henry *Actor*
980 Alta Vista Dr, Altadena, CA 91001, USA
Das, Alisha *Actress*
19583 Bowers Dr, Topanga, CA 90290, USA
Dascascos, Marc *Actor*
PO Box 1549, Studio City, CA 91614, USA
Dash, Leon D, Jr *Journalist*
%Washington Post, Editorial Dept, 1150 15th Ave NW, Washington, DC 20071, USA

D

Dash - Davidson

Dash, Samuel *Attorney, Watergate Committee Counsel*
110 Newlands St, Chevy Chase, MD 20815, USA
Dash, Sarah *Singer*
%Talent Consultants International, 1560 Broadway, #1308, New York, NY 10036, USA
Dash, Stacey *Actress*
519 E Palisade Ave, Englewood Cliffs, NJ 07632, USA
Dassin, Jules *Movie Director*
8 Melina Mercouri St, Athens 11521, Greece
Dassler, Uwe *Swimmer*
Stolze-Schrey-Str 6, 15745 Wilday, Germany
Dater, Judy L *Photographer*
2430 5th St, #J, Berkeley, CA 94710, USA
Daubechies, Ingrid C *Computer Mathematician*
%Princeton University, Mathematics Dept, Princeton, NJ 08544, USA
Dauben, William G *Chemist*
20 Eagle Hill, Kensington, CA 94707, USA
Daugherty, Bradley L (Brad) *Basketball Player*
1239 Cane Creek Road, Fletcher, NC 28732, USA
Daugherty, Michael *Composer*
%Argo London Records, 810 7th Ave, New York, NY 10019, USA
Daughtrey, Martha Craig *Judge*
%US Court of Appeals, 701 Broadway, Nashville, TN 37203, USA
Dauline, Marie *Singer (Zap Mama)*
%Todo Mundo, PO Box 652, Cooper Station, New York, NY 10276, USA
Daulton, Darren A *Baseball Player*
5 Meadow Lane, Arkansas City, KS 67005, USA
Dauplaise, Norman *Thoroughbred Racing Jockey*
29 W 36th St, #1000, New York, NY 10018, USA
Daurey, Dana *Actress*
%S M S Talent, 8730 Sunset Blvd, #440, Los Angeles, CA 90069, USA
Dausset, Jean B G *Nobel Medicine Laureate*
9 Rue de Villersexel, 75007 Paris, France
Davalos, Richard *Actor*
2311 Vista Gordo Dr, Los Angeles, CA 90026, USA
Davenport, A Nigel *Actor*
5 Ann's Close, Kinnerton St, London SW1, England
Davenport, Guy M, Jr *Writer*
621 Sayre Ave, Lexington, KY 40508, USA
Davenport, Lindsey *Tennis Player*
PO Box 10179, Newport Beach, CA 92658, USA
Davenport, Nigel *Actor*
%Green & Underwood, 2 Conduit St, London W1R 9TG, England
Davenport, Wilbur B, Jr *Electrical Engineer*
1120 Skyline Dr, Medford, OR 97504, USA
Davi, Robert *Actor*
10044 Calvin Ave, Northridge, CA 91324, USA
Daviau, Allen *Cinematographer*
2249 Bronson Hill Dr, Los Angeles, CA 90068, USA
Davich, Marty *Composer*
530 S Greenwood Lane, Pasadena, CA 91107, USA
David Mohato *Crown Prince, Lesotho*
%Royal Palace, PO Box 524, Maseru, Lesotho
David, Craig *Singer*
%Wildstar Atlantic Records, 1290 Ave of Americas, New York, NY 10104, USA
David, Edward E, Jr *Underwater Sound, Electrical Engineer*
%EED Inc, PO Box 435, Bedminster, NJ 07921, USA
David, George A L *Businessman*
%United Technologies Corp, United Technologies Building, Hartford, CT 06101, USA
David, Hal *Lyricist*
10430 Wilshire Blvd, Los Angeles, CA 90024, USA
David, John R *Internist*
%Harvard Public Health School, 665 Huntington Ave, Boston, MA 02115, USA
David, Keith *Actor, Singer*
1134 W 105th St, Los Angeles, CA 90044, USA
David, Larry *Writer, Actor*
%Endeavor Talent Agency, 9701 Wilshire Blvd, #1000, Beverly Hills, CA 90212, USA
David, Peter *Actor*
PO Box 239, Bayport, NY 11705, USA
Davidovich, Bella *Concert Pianist*
%Columbia Artists Mgmt Inc, 165 W 57th St, New York, NY 10019, USA
Davidovich, Lolita *Actress*
15200 Friends St, Pacific Palisades, CA 90272, USA
Davidovsky, Mario *Composer*
%Harvard University, Music Dept, Cambridge, MA 02138, USA
Davidson, Ben E *Football Player*
4737 Angels Point, La Mesa, CA 91941, USA
Davidson, Bruce O *Equestrian Rider*
RR 842, Unionville, PA 19375, USA

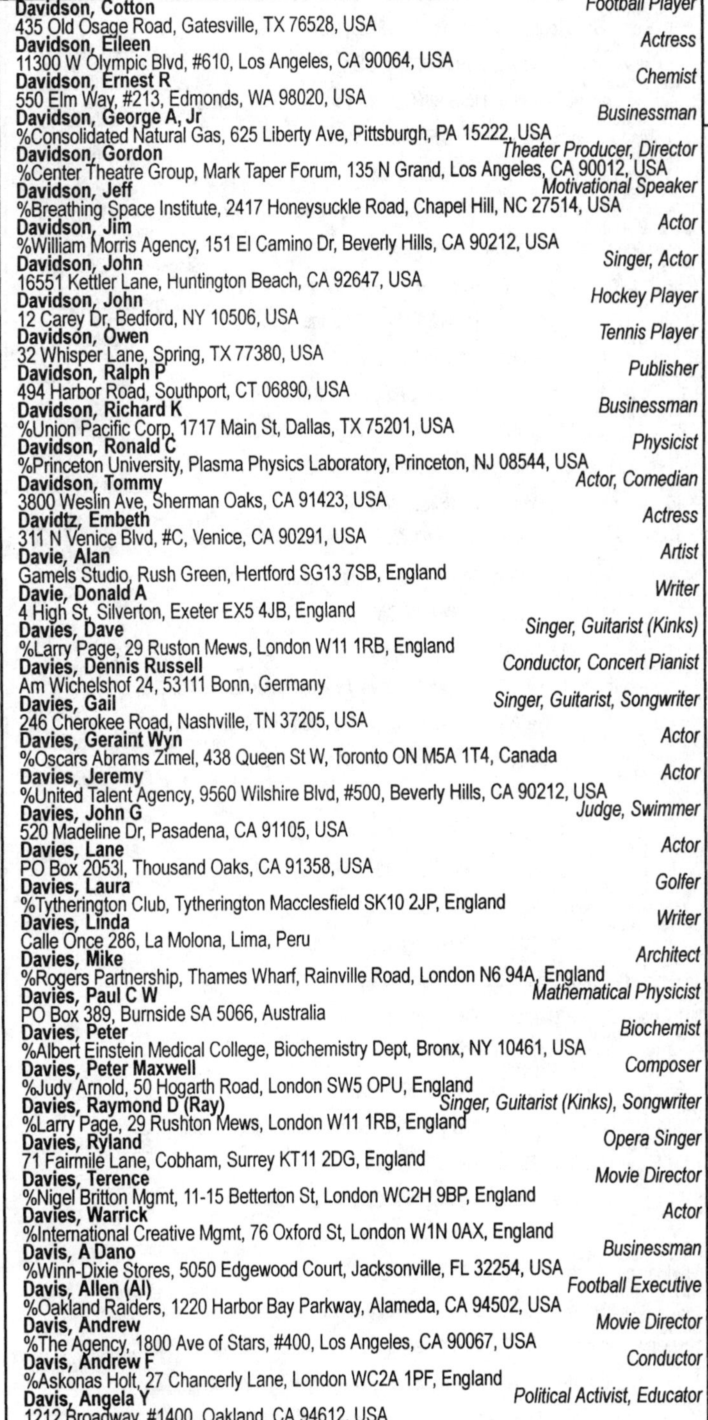

Davidson, Cotton *Football Player*
435 Old Osage Road, Gatesville, TX 76528, USA
Davidson, Eileen *Actress*
11300 W Olympic Blvd, #610, Los Angeles, CA 90064, USA
Davidson, Ernest R *Chemist*
550 Elm Way, #213, Edmonds, WA 98020, USA
Davidson, George A, Jr *Businessman*
%Consolidated Natural Gas, 625 Liberty Ave, Pittsburgh, PA 15222, USA
Davidson, Gordon *Theater Producer, Director*
%Center Theatre Group, Mark Taper Forum, 135 N Grand, Los Angeles, CA 90012, USA
Davidson, Jeff *Motivational Speaker*
%Breathing Space Institute, 2417 Honeysuckle Road, Chapel Hill, NC 27514, USA
Davidson, Jim *Actor*
%William Morris Agency, 151 El Camino Dr, Beverly Hills, CA 90212, USA
Davidson, John *Singer, Actor*
16551 Kettler Lane, Huntington Beach, CA 92647, USA
Davidson, John *Hockey Player*
12 Carey Dr, Bedford, NY 10506, USA
Davidson, Owen *Tennis Player*
32 Whisper Lane, Spring, TX 77380, USA
Davidson, Ralph P *Publisher*
494 Harbor Road, Southport, CT 06890, USA
Davidson, Richard K *Businessman*
%Union Pacific Corp, 1717 Main St, Dallas, TX 75201, USA
Davidson, Ronald C *Physicist*
%Princeton University, Plasma Physics Laboratory, Princeton, NJ 08544, USA
Davidson, Tommy *Actor, Comedian*
3800 Weslin Ave, Sherman Oaks, CA 91423, USA
Davidtz, Embeth *Actress*
311 N Venice Blvd, #C, Venice, CA 90291, USA
Davie, Alan *Artist*
Gamels Studio, Rush Green, Hertford SG13 7SB, England
Davie, Donald A *Writer*
4 High St, Silverton, Exeter EX5 4JB, England
Davies, Dave *Singer, Guitarist (Kinks)*
%Larry Page, 29 Ruston Mews, London W11 1RB, England
Davies, Dennis Russell *Conductor, Concert Pianist*
Am Wichelshof 24, 53111 Bonn, Germany
Davies, Gail *Singer, Guitarist, Songwriter*
246 Cherokee Road, Nashville, TN 37205, USA
Davies, Geraint Wyn *Actor*
%Oscars Abrams Zimel, 438 Queen St W, Toronto ON M5A 1T4, Canada
Davies, Jeremy *Actor*
%United Talent Agency, 9560 Wilshire Blvd, #500, Beverly Hills, CA 90212, USA
Davies, John G *Judge, Swimmer*
520 Madeline Dr, Pasadena, CA 91105, USA
Davies, Lane *Actor*
PO Box 2053l, Thousand Oaks, CA 91358, USA
Davies, Laura *Golfer*
%Tytherington Club, Tytherington Macclesfield SK10 2JP, England
Davies, Linda *Writer*
Calle Once 286, La Molona, Lima, Peru
Davies, Mike *Architect*
%Rogers Partnership, Thames Wharf, Rainville Road, London N6 94A, England
Davies, Paul C W *Mathematical Physicist*
PO Box 389, Burnside SA 5066, Australia
Davies, Peter *Biochemist*
%Albert Einstein Medical College, Biochemistry Dept, Bronx, NY 10461, USA
Davies, Peter Maxwell *Composer*
%Judy Arnold, 50 Hogarth Road, London SW5 OPU, England
Davies, Raymond D (Ray) *Singer, Guitarist (Kinks), Songwriter*
%Larry Page, 29 Rushton Mews, London W11 1RB, England
Davies, Ryland *Opera Singer*
71 Fairmile Lane, Cobham, Surrey KT11 2DG, England
Davies, Terence *Movie Director*
%Nigel Britton Mgmt, 11-15 Betterton St, London WC2H 9BP, England
Davies, Warrick *Actor*
%International Creative Mgmt, 76 Oxford St, London W1N 0AX, England
Davis, A Dano *Businessman*
%Winn-Dixie Stores, 5050 Edgewood Court, Jacksonville, FL 32254, USA
Davis, Allen (Al) *Football Executive*
%Oakland Raiders, 1220 Harbor Bay Parkway, Alameda, CA 94502, USA
Davis, Andrew *Movie Director*
%The Agency, 1800 Ave of Stars, #400, Los Angeles, CA 90067, USA
Davis, Andrew F *Conductor*
%Askonas Holt, 27 Chancerly Lane, London WC2A 1PF, England
Davis, Angela Y *Political Activist, Educator*
1212 Broadway, #1400, Oakland, CA 94612, USA

D

Davis, Ann B *Actress*
23315 Eagle Gap Road, San Antonio, TX 78255, USA
Davis, Anthony *Football Player*
9851 Oakwood Crest, Villa Park, CA 92861, USA
Davis, Anthony *Jazz Pianist, Composer*
%Andriolo Communications, 115 E 9th St, New York, NY 10003, USA
Davis, Antone *Football Player*
9034 Village Green Blvd, Clermont, FL 34711, USA
Davis, Antonio *Basketball Player*
625 Willow Glen Dr, El Paso, TX 79922, USA
Davis, Baron *Basketball Player*
%New Orleans Hornets, New Orleans Arena, 1501 Girod St, New Orleans, LA 70113, USA
Davis, Bennie L *Air Force General*
101 Golden Road, Georgetown, TX 78628, USA
Davis, Billy, Jr *Singer (Fifth Dimension)*
%Sterling/Winters, 10877 Wilshire Blvd, #15, Los Angeles, CA 90024, USA
Davis, Carl *Composer, Conductor*
99 Church Road, Barnes, London SW13 9HL, England
Davis, Charles T (Chili) *Baseball Player*
620 Juana Ave, San Leandro, CA 94577, USA
Davis, Clifton *Actor*
9200 Sunset Blvd, #900, Los Angeles, CA 90069, USA
Davis, Clive J *Businessman*
%RCA Records, 8750 Wilshire Blvd, Beverly Hills, CA 90211, USA
Davis, Colin R *Conductor*
%Alison Glaister, 39 Huntingdon St, London N1 1BP, England
Davis, Dale *Basketball Player*
7945 Beaumont, Indianapolis, IN 46250, USA
Davis, Danny *Singer, Musician (Nashville Brass)*
%Danny Davis Productions, PO Box 210317, Nashville, TN 37221, USA
Davis, David (Dave) *Bowler*
%DeStasio, 710 Shore Road, Spring Lake Heights, NJ 07762, USA
Davis, David Brion *Writer, Historian*
733 Lambert Road, Orange, CT 06477, USA
Davis, Don *Golfer*
15910 FM 529, #219, Houston, TX 77095, USA
Davis, Don H, Jr *Businessman*
%Rockwell International, 777 E Wisconsin Ave, #1400, Milwaukee, WI 53202, USA
Davis, Don S *Actor*
%Gold Marshak Liedtke, 3500 W Olive Ave, #1400, Burbank, CA 91505, USA
Davis, Elizabeth *Bassist (Seven Year Bitch)*
%Rave Booking, PO Box 310780, Jamaica, NY 11431, USA
Davis, Elliot M *Cinematographer*
1328 Arch St, Berkeley, CA 94708, USA
Davis, Emanuel *Basketball Player*
%Atlanta Hawks, 190 Marietta St SW, Atlanta, GA 30303, USA
Davis, Eric K *Baseball Player*
5616 Farmland Ave, Woodland Hills, CA 91367, USA
Davis, Eric W *Football Player*
4501 Old Course Dr, Charlotte, NC 28277, USA
Davis, Geena *Actress*
%Susan Geller, 1301 Belfast Dr, Los Angeles, CA 90069, USA
Davis, Glenn E *Baseball Player*
45 Cascade Road, Columbus, GA 31904, USA
Davis, Glenn H *Track Athlete*
801 Robinson Ave, Barberton, OH 44203, USA
Davis, Glenn W *Football Player*
6014 Varna Ave, Van Nuys, CA 91401, USA
Davis, H Thomas (Tommy) *Baseball Player*
9767 Whirlaway St, Alta Loma, CA 91737, USA
Davis, Hope *Actress*
%United Talent Agency, 9560 Wilshire Blvd, #500, Beverly Hills, CA 90212, USA
Davis, Hubert *Basketball Player*
7951 Glade Hill Court, Dallas, TX 75218, USA
Davis, James *Football Player*
5701 S Saint Andrews Place, Los Angeles, CA 90062, USA
Davis, James B *Air Force General*
3600 Wimber Blvd, Palm Harbor, FL 34685, USA
Davis, James O *Physician*
612 Maplewood Dr, Columbia, MO 65203, USA
Davis, James R (Jim) *Cartoonist (Garfield)*
5440 E County Road 450 N, Albany, IN 47320, USA
Davis, Jay *Golfer*
%Kevin Richardson, 1551 Forum Place, #300CF, West Palm Beach, FL 33401, USA
Davis, Jesse *Jazz Saxophonist*
%Concord Records, 100 N Crescent Dr, #275, Beverly Hills, CA 90210, USA
Davis, Jill A *Writer*
%Random House, 1745 Broadway, #B1, New York, NY 10019, USA

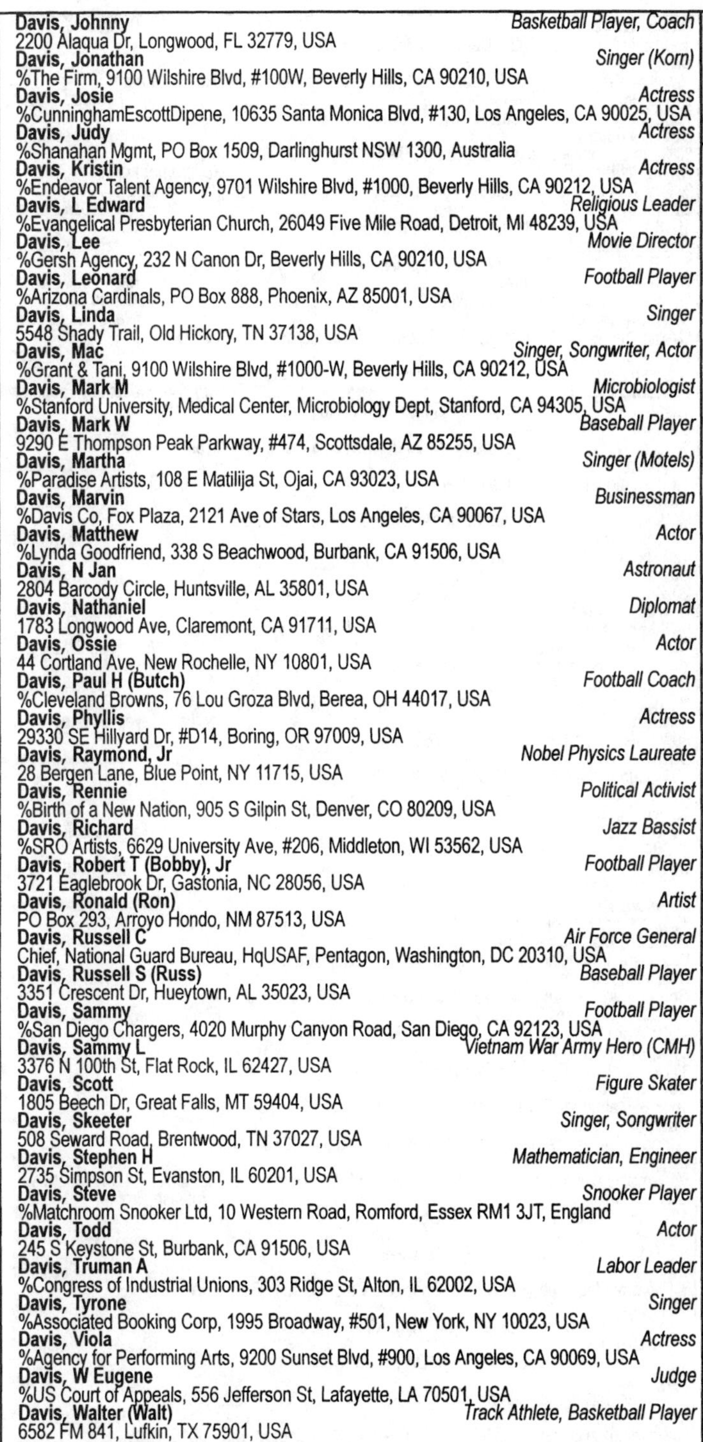

Davis, Johnny — *Basketball Player, Coach*
2200 Alaqua Dr, Longwood, FL 32779, USA

Davis, Jonathan — *Singer (Korn)*
%The Firm, 9100 Wilshire Blvd, #100W, Beverly Hills, CA 90210, USA

Davis, Josie — *Actress*
%CunninghamEscottDipene, 10635 Santa Monica Blvd, #130, Los Angeles, CA 90025, USA

Davis, Judy — *Actress*
%Shanahan Mgmt, PO Box 1509, Darlinghurst NSW 1300, Australia

Davis, Kristin — *Actress*
%Endeavor Talent Agency, 9701 Wilshire Blvd, #1000, Beverly Hills, CA 90212, USA

Davis, L Edward — *Religious Leader*
%Evangelical Presbyterian Church, 26049 Five Mile Road, Detroit, MI 48239, USA

Davis, Lee — *Movie Director*
%Gersh Agency, 232 N Canon Dr, Beverly Hills, CA 90210, USA

Davis, Leonard — *Football Player*
%Arizona Cardinals, PO Box 888, Phoenix, AZ 85001, USA

Davis, Linda — *Singer*
5548 Shady Trail, Old Hickory, TN 37138, USA

Davis, Mac — *Singer, Songwriter, Actor*
%Grant & Tani, 9100 Wilshire Blvd, #1000-W, Beverly Hills, CA 90212, USA

Davis, Mark M — *Microbiologist*
%Stanford University, Medical Center, Microbiology Dept, Stanford, CA 94305, USA

Davis, Mark W — *Baseball Player*
9290 E Thompson Peak Parkway, #474, Scottsdale, AZ 85255, USA

Davis, Martha — *Singer (Motels)*
%Paradise Artists, 108 E Matilija St, Ojai, CA 93023, USA

Davis, Marvin — *Businessman*
%Davis Co, Fox Plaza, 2121 Ave of Stars, Los Angeles, CA 90067, USA

Davis, Matthew — *Actor*
%Lynda Goodfriend, 338 S Beachwood, Burbank, CA 91506, USA

Davis, N Jan — *Astronaut*
2804 Barcody Circle, Huntsville, AL 35801, USA

Davis, Nathaniel — *Diplomat*
1783 Longwood Ave, Claremont, CA 91711, USA

Davis, Ossie — *Actor*
44 Cortland Ave, New Rochelle, NY 10801, USA

Davis, Paul H (Butch) — *Football Coach*
%Cleveland Browns, 76 Lou Groza Blvd, Berea, OH 44017, USA

Davis, Phyllis — *Actress*
29330 SE Hillyard Dr, #D14, Boring, OR 97009, USA

Davis, Raymond, Jr — *Nobel Physics Laureate*
28 Bergen Lane, Blue Point, NY 11715, USA

Davis, Rennie — *Political Activist*
%Birth of a New Nation, 905 S Gilpin St, Denver, CO 80209, USA

Davis, Richard — *Jazz Bassist*
%SRO Artists, 6629 University Ave, #206, Middleton, WI 53562, USA

Davis, Robert T (Bobby), Jr — *Football Player*
3721 Eaglebrook Dr, Gastonia, NC 28056, USA

Davis, Ronald (Ron) — *Artist*
PO Box 293, Arroyo Hondo, NM 87513, USA

Davis, Russell C — *Air Force General*
Chief, National Guard Bureau, HqUSAF, Pentagon, Washington, DC 20310, USA

Davis, Russell S (Russ) — *Baseball Player*
3351 Crescent Dr, Hueytown, AL 35023, USA

Davis, Sammy — *Football Player*
%San Diego Chargers, 4020 Murphy Canyon Road, San Diego, CA 92123, USA

Davis, Sammy L — *Vietnam War Army Hero (CMH)*
3376 N 100th St, Flat Rock, IL 62427, USA

Davis, Scott — *Figure Skater*
1805 Beech Dr, Great Falls, MT 59404, USA

Davis, Skeeter — *Singer, Songwriter*
508 Seward Road, Brentwood, TN 37027, USA

Davis, Stephen H — *Mathematician, Engineer*
2735 Simpson St, Evanston, IL 60201, USA

Davis, Steve — *Snooker Player*
%Matchroom Snooker Ltd, 10 Western Road, Romford, Essex RM1 3JT, England

Davis, Todd — *Actor*
245 S Keystone St, Burbank, CA 91506, USA

Davis, Truman A — *Labor Leader*
%Congress of Industrial Unions, 303 Ridge St, Alton, IL 62002, USA

Davis, Tyrone — *Singer*
%Associated Booking Corp, 1995 Broadway, #501, New York, NY 10023, USA

Davis, Viola — *Actress*
%Agency for Performing Arts, 9200 Sunset Blvd, #900, Los Angeles, CA 90069, USA

Davis, W Eugene — *Judge*
%US Court of Appeals, 556 Jefferson St, Lafayette, LA 70501, USA

Davis, Walter (Walt) — *Track Athlete, Basketball Player*
6582 FM 841, Lufkin, TX 75901, USA

D

Davis, Walter P *Basketball Player*
4500 S Monaco St, #1021, Denver, CO 80237, USA
Davis, Warwick *Actor*
%Willow Personal Mgmt, 63 Saint Martins Road, Walmer CT14 7RJ, England
Davis, William D (Willie) *Football Player*
7352 Vista Del Mar, Playa del Rey, CA 90293, USA
Davis, William E *Businessman*
%Niagara Mohawk Holdings, 300 Erie Blvd W, Syracuse, NY 13202, USA
Davis, William G *Government Official, Canada*
%Tory Tory DesLauriers, Aetna Tower, #3000, Toronto ON M5K 1N2, Canada
Davis, William H (Willie) *Baseball Player*
1916 W Victory Blvd, #6, Burbank, CA 91506, USA
Davis, William L *Businessman*
%R R Donnelley & Sons, 77 W Wacker Dr, Chicago, IL 60601, USA
Davis-Wrightsil, Clarissa *Basketball Player*
%Phoenix Mercury, American West Arena, 201 E Jefferson St, Phoenix, AZ 85004, USA
Davison, Beverly C *Religious Leader*
%American Baptist Churches, PO Box 851, Valley Forge, PA 19482, USA
Davison, Bruce *Actor*
%Gersh Agency, 232 N Canon Dr, Beverly Hills, CA 90210, USA
Davison, Fred C *Foundation Executive, Educator*
%National Science Foundation, PO Box 15577, Augusta, GA 30919, USA
Davison, Peter *Actor*
%Conway Van Gelder Robinson, 18-21 Jermyn St, London SW1Y 6NB, England
Davison, Sam *Religious Leader*
%International Baptist Bible Fellowship, 720 E Kearnet St, Springfield, MO 65803, USA
Dawber, Pam *Actress*
%Wings Inc, 2236 Encinitas Blvd, #A, Encinitas, CA 92024, USA
Dawes, Dominque *Gymnast*
129 Ritchie Ave, Silver Springs, MD 20910, USA
Dawes, Joseph *Cartoonist*
20 Church Court, Closter, NJ 07624, USA
Dawkins, Brian *Football Player*
%Philadelphia Eagles, 1 Novacare Way, Philadelphia, PA 19145, USA
Dawkins, C Richard *Biologist, Ethologist*
%Oxford University, Museum, Parks Road, Oxford OX1 3PW, England
Dawkins, Johnny *Basketball Player*
%Duke University, Cameron Indoor Stadium, Athletic Dept, Durham, NC 27708, USA
Dawkins, Peter M (Pete) *Football Player, Businessman*
80 W River Road, Rumson, NJ 07760, USA
Dawkins, Travis (Gookie) *Baseball Player*
501 Scurry Island Road, Chappells, SC 29037, USA
Dawley, Joseph W (Joe) *Artist*
13 Wholly St, Cranford, NJ 07016, USA
Dawsey, Lawrence *Football Player*
13704 Sun Court, Tampa, FL 33624, USA
Dawson, Andre N *Baseball Player*
6770 SW 101st St, Miami, FL 33156, USA
Dawson, Buck *Swimming Executive*
%Swimming Hall of Fame, 1 Hall of Fame Dr, Fort Lauderdale, FL 33316, USA
Dawson, Douglas A (Doug) *Football Player*
%Dawson Financial Services, 1175 Adkins Road, Houston, TX 77055, USA
Dawson, J Cutler, Jr *Navy Admiral*
Commander, Striking Fleet Atlantic/2nd Fleet, FPO, AE 09506, USA
Dawson, Leonard R (Lenny) *Football Player, Sportscaster*
5800 Ward Parkway, Kansas City, MO 64113, USA
Dawson, Richard *Actor*
1117 Angelo Dr, Beverly Hills, CA 90210, USA
Dawson, Rosario *Actress*
1635 N Cahuenga Blvd, #500, Los Angeles, CA 90028, USA
Dawson, Roxann *Actress*
%Innovative Artists, 1505 10th St, Santa Monica, CA 90401, USA
Day, Bill *Editorial Cartoonist*
%Memphis Commerical-Appeal, Editorial Dept, 495 Union Ave, Memphis, TN 38103, USA
Day, Chon *Cartoonist (Brother Sebastian)*
127 Main St, Ashaway, RI 02804, USA
Day, Doris *Singer, Actress*
PO Box 223163, Carmel, CA 93922, USA
Day, Gail *Publisher*
%Playboy Magazine, 680 N Lake Shore Dr, Chicago, IL 60611, USA
Day, Julian *Businessman*
%Kmart, 3100 W Big Beaver Road, Troy, MI 48084, USA
Day, Larraine *Actress*
10323 Lauriston Ave, Los Angeles, CA 90025, USA
Day, Laura *Writer*
%Harper Collins Publishers, 10 E 53rd St, New York, NY 10022, USA
Day, Mary *Ballet Executive*
%Washington Ballet, 3515 Wisconsin Ave NW, Washington, DC 20016, USA

Day, Matt *Actor*
%Robyn Gardiner Mgmt, 397 Riley St, Surrey Hills NSW 2010, Australia
Day, Peter R *Agricultural Scientist*
394 Franklin Road, New Brunswick, NJ 08902, USA
Day, Robert *Movie Director*
%Creative Artists Agency, 9830 Wilshire Blvd, Beverly Hills, CA 90212, USA
Day, Thomas B *Educator*
%San Diego State University, President's Office, San Diego, CA 92182, USA
Day-George, Lynda *Actress*
10310 Riverside Dr, #104, Toluca Lake, CA 91602, USA
Day-Lewis, Daniel *Actor*
%Julian Belfarge, 46 Albermarle St, London W1X 4PP, England
Dayne, Ron *Football Player*
%New York Giants, Giants Stadium, East Rutherford, NJ 07073, USA
Dayne, Taylor *Singer, Songwriter, Actress*
7933 Willow Glen Road, Los Angeles, CA 90046, USA
Days, Drews S, III *Government Official, Educator*
%Yale University, Law School, New Haven, CT 06520, USA
Dayton, June *Actress*
%Abrams Artists, 9200 Sunset Blvd, #1125, Los Angeles, CA 90069, USA
Deacon, John *Bassist (Queen)*
%The Mill, Mill Lane, 367 Windsor Highway, New Windsor, NY 12553, USA
Deacon, Richard *Sculptor*
%Lisson Gallery, 67 Lisson St, London NW1 5DA, England
Deacon, Terrence *Neuroanatomist*
%Harvard University, Neuroanatomy Dept, Cambridge, MA 02138, USA
Deadmarsh, Adam *Hockey Player*
PO Box 262, Metaline Falls, WA 99153, USA
DeAgostini, Doris *Skier*
6780 Airolo, Switzerland
Deakin, Paul *Drummer (Mavericks)*
%AristoMedia, 1620 16th Ave S, Nashville, TN 37212, USA
Deakins, Roger A *Cinematographer*
%International Creative Mgmt, 8942 Wilshire Blvd, #219, Beverly Hills, CA 90211, USA
Deal, Kim *Singer, Bassist (Breeders)*
%William Morris Agency, 151 El Camino Dr, Beverly Hills, CA 90212, USA
Deal, Lance *Track Athlete*
911 Elkay, Eugene, OR 97404, USA
Dean, Billy *Singer*
PO Box 870689, Stone Mountain, GA 30087, USA
Dean, Christopher *Ice Dancer*
124 Ladies Mile Road, Brighton, East Sussex BN1 8TE, England
Dean, Eddie *Singer, Actor*
32161 Sailview Lane, Westlake Village, CA 91361, USA
Dean, Ira *Singer (Trick Pony)*
%Creative Artists Agency, 9830 Wilshire Blvd, Beverly Hills, CA 90212, USA
Dean, Jimmy *Singer*
10151 Carver Road, Cincinnati, OH 45242, USA
Dean, John G *Diplomat*
29 Blvd Jules Sandeau, 75116 Paris, France
Dean, John W, III *Watergate Figure*
9496 Rembert Lane, Beverly Hills, CA 90210, USA
Dean, Laura *Choreographer, Composer*
%Dean Dance & Music Foundation, 552 Broadway, #400, New York, NY 10012, USA
Dean, Mark E *Inventor*
5901 Standing Rock Dr, Austin, TX 78730, USA
Dean, Stafford R *Opera Singer*
%I C M Artists, 40 W 57th St, New York, NY 10019, USA
Deane, William Patrick *Governor General, Australia*
%Government House, Canberra ACT 26000, Australia
DeAngelis, Beverly *Psychiatrist*
505 S Beverly Dr, #1017, Beverly Hills, CA 90212, USA
Dearden, James *Movie Director*
%International Creative Mgmt, 8942 Wilshire Blvd, #219, Beverly Hills, CA 90211, USA
Deardurff-Schmidt, Deena *Swimmer*
742 Murray Dr, El Cajon, CA 92020, USA
Dearie, Blossom *Singer, Songwriter, Pianist*
%F Sharp Productions, PO Box 2040, New York, NY 10101, USA
DeArmond, Frank *Astronaut*
3086 Ravencrest Circle, Prescott, AZ 86303, USA
Deas, Justin *Actor*
%Paradigm Agency, 10100 Santa Monica Blvd, #2500, Los Angeles, CA 90067, USA
Deavenport, Earnest, Jr *Businessman*
%Eastman Chemical Co, 100 N Eastman Road, Kingsport, TN 37660, USA
Deaver, Jeffrey *Writer*
%Pocket Star Books, 1230 Ave of Americas, New York, NY 10020, USA
Deaver, Michael K *Government Official*
%Deaver Assoc, 1025 Thomas Jefferson St NW, Washington, DC 20007, USA

D

DeBakey, Michael E *Surgeon*
%Baylor Medical Center, 1200 Moursand Ave, Houston, TX 77030, USA
DeBarge, Chico *Singer, Songwriter*
%International Creative Mgmt, 8942 Wilshire Blvd, #219, Beverly Hills, CA 90211, USA
DeBellevue, Charles B *Vietnam War Air Force Hero*
916 Huntsman Road, Edmond, OK 73003, USA
DeBenning, Burr *Actor*
4235 Kingfisher Road, Calabasas, CA 91302, USA
DeBerg, Steve *Football Player, Coach*
17920 Simms Road, Odessa, FL 33556, USA
DeBlanc, Jefferson J *WW II Marine Corps Hero (CMH)*
321 Saint Martin St, Saint Martinville, LA 70582, USA
DeBlasis, Celeste *Writer*
9 Kemper Campbell Ranch St, Victorville, CA 92392, USA
Debney, John *Composer*
%Kraft-Benjamin-Engel, 15233 Ventura Blvd, #200, Sherman Oaks, CA 91403, USA
DeBoer, Harm E *Businessman*
%Russell Corp, 755 Lee St, Alexander City, AL 35010, USA
DeBoer, Nicole *Actress*
3401 Lawrence Ave E, #577, Scarborough ON M1H 1B2, Canada
DeBoer, Rick *Actor*
%Pacific Artists, 510 W Hastings St, #1404, Vancouver BC V6B 1L8, Canada
DeBold, Adolfo J *Pathologist, Physiologist*
%Ottawa Civic Hospital, 1053 Carling Ave, Ottawa ON K1Y 4E9, Canada
DeBont, Jan *Cinematographer, Director*
1708 Berkeley St, Santa Monica, CA 90404, USA
DeBorba, Dorothy *Actress*
PO Box 2723, Livermore, CA 94551, USA
DeBorchgrave, Arnaud *Editor*
2141 Wyoming Ave NW, Washington, DC 20008, USA
DeBorda, Dorothy *Actress*
PO Box 2723, Livermore, CA 94551, USA
DeBranges, Louis *Mathematician*
%Purdue University, Mathematics Dept, West Lafayette, IN 47907, USA
Debre, Michel *Prime Minister, France*
20 Rue Jacob, 75006 Paris, France
Debreu, Gerard *Nobel Economics Laureate*
%University of California, Evans Hall, Economics Dept, Berkeley, CA 94720, USA
DeBrunhoff, Laurent *Writer, Illustrator (Babar)*
%Mary Ryan Gallery, 24 W 57th St, New York, NY 10019, USA
DeBurgh, Chris *Singer, Songwriter*
%Kenny Thomson Mgmt, 754 Fulham Road, London SW6 5SW, England
Deby, Idriss *President, Chad; Army General*
%President's Office, N'Djamena, Chad
DeCamilli, Pietro V *Biologist*
%Yale University, Medical School, Cell Biology Dept, New Haven, CT 06512, USA
DeCarava, Roy *Photographer*
81 Halsey St, Brooklyn, NY 11216, USA
DeCarlo, Yvonne *Actress*
1483 Golf Course Lane, Nipomo, CA 93444, USA
DeCasabianca, Camille *Actress*
%Artmedia, 20 Ave Rapp, 75007 Paris, France
DeCastella, F Robert *Track Athlete*
%Australian Institute of Sport, PO Box 176, Belconnen ACT 2616, Australia
DeCinces, Douglas V (Doug) *Baseball Player*
124 Riviera Way, Laguna Beach, CA 92651, USA
Decker, Franz-Paul *Conductor*
%Herbert Barrett, 266 W 37th St, #2000, New York, NY 10018, USA
Deckers, Daphne *Actress*
%Nagtzaan, Hoge Naardenweg 44, 1217 AG Hilversum, Netherlands
DeConcini, Dennis *Senator, AZ*
6014 Chesterbrook Road, McLean, VA 22101, USA
DeCosta, Sara *Hockey Player*
200 Cowesett Green Dr, Warwick, RI 02886, USA
DeCoster, Roger *Motorcycle Racing Rider*
%MC Sports, 1919 Torrance Blvd, Torrance, CA 90501, USA
Decter, Midge *Writer*
120 E 81st St, New York, NY 10028, USA
Dedeaux, Raoul M (Rod) *Baseball Coach*
1430 S Eastman Ave, Los Angeles, CA 90023, USA
Dedini, Eldon L *Cartoonist*
PO Box 1630, Monterey, CA 93942, USA
Dedkov, Anatoli I *Cosmonaut*
%Potchta Kosmonavtov, Moskovskoi Oblasti, 141160 Syvisdny Goroduk, Russia
DeDuve, Christian R *Nobel Medicine Laureate*
80 Central Park West, New York, NY 10023, USA
Dee, Donald (Don) *Basketball Player*
7924 N Pennsylvania Ave, Kansas City, MO 64118, USA

Dee, Frances *Actress*
RR 3 Box 375, Camarillo, CA 93010, USA
Dee, Joey *Singer*
%Horizon Mgmt, PO Box 8770, Endwell, NY 13762, USA
Dee, Ruby *Actress*
44 Cortland Ave, New Rochelle, NY 10801, USA
Dee, Sandra *Actress, Model*
18915 Nordhoff St, #5, Northridge, CA 91324, USA
Deeb, Gary *Television Critic*
%Chicago Sun-Times, Editorial Dept, 401 N Wabash Ave, Chicago, IL 60611, USA
Deedes of Aldington, William F *Government Official, England*
New Hayters, Aldington, Kent TN25 7DT, England
Deependra Bir Bikram Shah Dev *Crown Prince, Nepal*
%Narayanhiti Royal Palace, Durbag Marg, Kathmandu, Nepal
Deer, Ada E *Government Official*
2537 Mutchler Road, Fitchburg, WI 53711, USA
Deering, John *Editorial Cartoonist*
6701 Westover Dr, Little Rock, AR 72207, USA
Dees, Archie *Basketball Player*
4405 N Hillview Dr, Bloomington, IN 47408, USA
Dees, Bowen C *Science Administrator*
29059 Meadow Glen Way W, Escondido, CA 92026, USA
Dees, Morris S, Jr *Attorney, Civil Rights Activist*
%Southern Poverty Law Center, PO Box 548, Montgomery, AL 36101, USA
Dees, Rick *Entertainer, Singer*
%KIIS-Radio, 3400 W Riverside Dr, #800, Burbank, CA 91505, USA
DeFanti, Tom *Inventor (Cave Electronic Visualization)*
%University of Illinois, Electronic Visualization Lab, Chicago, IL 60607, USA
DeFerran, Gil *Auto Racing Driver*
524 Royal Plaza Dr, Fort Lauderdale, FL 33301, USA
DeFigueiredo, Rui J P *Computer Engineer*
%University of California, Intelligent Sensors/Systems Lab, Irvine, CA 92717, USA
DeFleur, Lois B *Educator*
%State University of New York, President's Office, Binghamton, NY 13902, USA
Deford, Frank *Sportswriter*
PO Box 1109, Greens Farms, CT 06838, USA
DeForest, Roy *Artist*
PO Box 47, Port Costa, CA 94569, USA
DeForrest, Jeff *Sportscaster*
5211 NE 14th Terrace, Fort Lauderdale, FL 33334, USA
DeFrancisco, Joseph E (Joe) *Army General*
7.34 Chars Lane, Springfield, VA 22153, USA
DeFranco, Buddy *Jazz Clarinetist*
22525 Coral Ave, Panama City, FL 32413, USA
DeFrank, Joe *Harness Racing Official*
29 Crescent Hollow Court, Ramsey, NJ 07446, USA
DeFrantz, Anita *Sports Executive*
%US Olympic Committee, 1 Olympia Plaza, Colorado Springs, CO 80909, USA
DeFreitas, Eric *Bowler*
175 W 12th St, New York, NY 10011, USA
Deganhardt, Johannes J Cardinal *Religious Leader*
Erzbischofliches Generalvikariat, Domplatz 3, 33098 Paderborn, Germany
DeGaspe, Philippe *Publisher*
%Canadian Living Magazine, 50 Holly St, Toronto ON M4S 3B3, Canada
DeGeneres, Ellen *Actress, Comedienne*
%Barnes Morris Klein Young, 1424 2nd St, #3, Santa Monica, CA 90401, USA
DeGennes, Pierre-Gilles *Nobel Physics Laureate*
11 Place Marcelin-Berthelot, 75005 Paris, France
DeGioia, John *Educator*
%Georgetown University, President's Office, Washington, DC 20057, USA
DeGiorgi, Salvatore Cardinal *Religious Leader*
%Curia Archivescovile, Corso Vittorio Emanuele 461, 90134 Palermo, Italy
DeGivenchy, Hubert T *Fashion Designer*
3 Ave George V, 75008 Paris, France
Degler, Carl N *Historian, Writer*
907 Mears Court, Stanford, CA 94305, USA
Degnan, John J *Businessman*
%Chubb Corp, 15 Mountain View Road, Warren, NJ 07059, USA
DeGrate, Tony *Football Player*
13007 Heineman Dr, #901, Austin, TX 78727, USA
DeHaan, Richard W *Religious Leader*
3000 Kraft Ave SE, Grand Rapids, MI 49512, USA
Dehaene, Jean-Luc *Prime Minister, Belgium*
Berkendallaan 52, 1800 Vilvoorde, Belgium
DeHaven, Gloria *Actress*
420 N Palm Dr, #304, Beverly Hills, CA 90210, USA
DeHaven, Robert M *WW II Army Air Corps Hero*
3716 Terrace View Dr, Encino, CA 91436, USA

D

DeHavilland - DeLaurentiis

DeHavilland, Olivia *Actress*
BP 156-16, 75764 Paris Cedex 16, France
Dehmelt, Hans G *Nobel Physics Laureate*
1600 43rd Ave E, Seattle, WA 98112, USA
Deighton, Leonard C (Len) *Writer*
Fairymount, Blackrock, Dundalk, County Louth, Ireland
Deisenhofer, Johann *Nobel Chemistry Laureate*
3860 Echo Brook Lane, Dallas, TX 75229, USA
Deitch, Donna *Movie Director*
%International Creative Mgmt, 8942 Wilshire Blvd, #219, Beverly Hills, CA 90211, USA
Deja, Andreas *Animator*
%Disney Animation, PO Box 10200, Lake Buena Vista, FL 32830, USA
DeJager, Cornelis *Astronomer*
Zonnenburg 1, 352 NL Utrecht, Netherlands
DeJohnette, Jack *Jazz Drummer, Composer*
Silver Hollow Road, Willow, NY 11201, USA
DeJong, Pierre *Geneticist*
%Lawrence Livermore Laboratory, 7000 East St, Livermore, CA 94550, USA
DeJordy, Denis E *Hockey Player*
472 Cherrin Des-Patriotes, Saint Charles QC J0L 2G0, Canada
DeKieweit, Cornelis W *Historian*
22 Berkeley St, Rochester, NY 14607, USA
Dekker, Desmond *Singer*
%Free World Music, 230 12th St, #117, Miami Beach, FL 33139, USA
DeKlerk, Albert *Concert Organist, Composer*
Crayenesterlaan 22, Haarlem, Netherlands
DeKlerk, Frederik W *Nobel Laureate; President, South Africa*
7 Eaton Square, London SW1, England
DeLaBilliere, Peter *Army General, England*
%Robert Fleming Holdings, 25 Copthall Ave, London EC2R 7DR, England
Delacote, Jacques *Conductor*
Dr Hilbert Maximilianstr 22, 80539 Munich, Germany
DeLaCruz, Rosie *Model*
%Wilhelmina Models, 300 Park Ave S, #200, New York, NY 10010, USA
DeLaFuente, Cristian *Actor*
%Stubbs Agency, 1450 S Robertson Blvd, Los Angeles, CA 90035, USA
DeLaFuente, Joel *Actor*
%LMRK, 130 W 42nd St, #1906, New York, NY 10036, USA
Delahoussaye, Ryan *Violinist (Blue October)*
%Ashley Talent, 2002 Hogback Road, #20, Ann Arbor, MI 48105, USA
DeLaHoya, Oscar *Boxer*
633 W 5th St, #6700, Los Angeles, CA 90071, USA
DeLamielleure, Joseph M (Joe) *Football Player*
7818 Ridgeloch Place, Charlotte, NC 28226, USA
DeLancie, John *Actor*
1313 Brunswick Ave, South Pasadena, CA 91030, USA
Delaney, F James (Jim) *Track Athlete*
PO Box 362, Sun Valley, ID 83353, USA
Delaney, Kim *Actress, Model*
%Gersh Agency, 232 N Canon Dr, Beverly Hills, CA 90210, USA
Delaney, Shelagh *Writer*
%Tess Sayle, 11 Jubilee Place, London SW3 3TE, England
Delano, Diane *Actress*
%Gold Marshak Liedtke, 3500 W Olive Ave, #1400, Burbank, CA 91505, USA
Delano, Robert B *Association Executive*
%American Farm Bureau Federation, 225 W Touhy Ave, Park Ridge, IL 60068, USA
Delany, Dana *Actress*
%Brillstein/Grey, 9150 Wilshire Blvd, #350, Beverly Hills, CA 90212, USA
Delany, Samuel R *Writer*
%Vintage Press, 1111 Rancho Conejo Blvd, Newbury Park, CA 91320, USA
DeLap, Tony *Artist*
225 Jasmine St, Corona del Mar, CA 92625, USA
DeLaPuente Raygada, Oscar *Prime Minister, Peru*
%Prime Minister's Office, Urb Corpac, Calle 1 Oeste S/N, Lima, Peru
DelArco, Jonathan *Actor*
%Michael Slessinger, 8730 Sunset Blvd, #220W, Los Angeles, CA 90069, USA
DeLaRocha, Zack *Singer (Rage Against the Machine)*
%GAS Entertainment, 8935 Lindblade St, Culver City, CA 90232, USA
DeLaRosa, Evelyn *Opera Singer*
%Dorothy Cone Artists, 150 W 55th St, New York, NY 10019, USA
DeLarrocha, Alicia *Concert Pianist*
Farmaceutic Carbonell, 46-48 Atic, Barcelona 34, Spain
Delasin, Dorothy *Golfer*
20 Longview Dr, Daly City, CA 94015, USA
DeLaTour, Frances *Actress*
%Kate Feast, Primrose Hill Studios, Fitzroy Road, London NW1 8TR, England
DeLaurentiis, Dino *Movie Producer*
Via Poutina Ku 23270, Rome, Italy

DeLeeuw, Ton *Composer*
Costeruslaan 4, Hilversum, Netherlands
Delehanty, Hugh *Editor*
%AARP Publications, Editorial Dept, 601 E St NW, Washington, DC 20049, USA
DeLeo, Dean *Guitarist (Stone Temple Pilots)*
%Q Prime, 729 7th Ave, #1600, New York, NY 10019, USA
DeLeo, Robert *Bassist (Stone Temple Pilots), Composer*
%Q Prime, 729 7th Ave, #1600, New York, NY 10019, USA
Delfino, Carlos Francisco *Basketball Player*
%Detroit Pistons, Palace, 2 Championship Dr, Auburn Hills, MI 48326, USA
Delfs, Andreas *Conductor*
%Saint Paul Chamber Orchestra, 408 Saint Peter St, Saint Paul, MN 55102, USA
Delgado, Carlos J *Baseball Player*
Borinquen Plaza, Apto Ramos #9, Aguadilla, PR 00603, USA
Delgado, Issac *Singer, Orchestra Leader*
%Ralph Mercado Mgmt, 568 Broadway, #806, New York, NY 10012, USA
Deligne, Pierre R *Mathematician*
%Institute for Advanced Study, Math School, Einstein Dr, Princeton, NJ 08540, USA
DeLillo, Don *Writer*
57 Rossmore Ave, Bronxville, NY 10708, USA
DeLint, Derek *Actor*
%Features Creative Mgmt, Entrepotdok 76A, 101 AD Amsterdam, Netherlands
DeLisle, Paul *Bassist (Smash Mouth)*
%Creative Artists Agency, 9830 Wilshire Blvd, Beverly Hills, CA 90212, USA
Delk, Joan *Golfer*
830 Forest Path Lane, Alpharetta, GA 30022, USA
Delk, Tony *Basketball Player*
5129 E Desert Jewel Dr, Paradise Valley, AZ 85253, USA
Dell, Michael S *Businessman*
%Dell Inc, 1 Dell Way, Round Rock, TX 78682, USA
DellaCasa-Debeljevic, Lisa *Opera Singer*
Schloss Gottlieben, Thurgau, Switzerland
DellaMalva, Joseph *Actor*
%William Morris Agency, 151 El Camino Dr, Beverly Hills, CA 90212, USA
Dellinger, Walter *Educator, Attorney*
%Duke University, Law School, Durham, NC 27706, USA
DelloJoio, Norman *Composer*
PO Box 154, East Hampton, NY 11937, USA
DelNegro, Vinny *Basketball Player*
7320 N 71st St, Paradise Valley, AZ 85253, USA
Delo, Ken *Actor*
161 Avondale Dr, #93-8, Branson, MO 65616, USA
DeLoach, Nikki *Singer (Innosense)*
%Evolution Talent, 1776 Broadway, #1500, New York, NY 10019, USA
Delock, Ivan M (Ike) *Baseball Player*
433 Cypress Way E, Naples, FL 34110, USA
Delon, Alain *Actor*
%Alain Delon Diffusion, 12 Rue Saint-Victor, 1206 Geneva, Switzerland
Delon, Anthony *Actor*
%Intertalent, 5 Rue Clement-Marot, 75008 Paris, France
DeLong, Keith A *Football Player*
915 Fairway Oaks Lane, Knoxville, TN 37922, USA
DeLong, Michael P *Marine Corps General*
Assistant Commander in Chief, HqUSMC, 2 Navy St, Washington, DC 20380, USA
DeLong, Steve C *Football Player*
4103 Dyanax St, Chesapeake, VA 23324, USA
DeLonge, Tom *Guitarist (Blink-182)*
750 W Bluff Dr, Encinitas, CA 92024, USA
DeLongis, Anthony *Actor*
PO Box 2445, Canyon Country, CA 91386, USA
Delora, Jennifer *Actress*
%Gilla Roos, 9744 Wilshire Blvd, #203, Beverly Hills, CA 90212, USA
DeLorean, John Z *Businessman*
PO Box 1092, Bedminster, NJ 07921, USA
DeLorenzo, Michael *Actor*
118 E Elk Ave, Glendale, CA 91204, USA
Deloria, Victor (Vine), Jr *Indian Rights Activist*
%University of Colorado, History Dept, PO Box 234, Boulder, CO 80309, USA
Delors, Jacques L J *Government Official, France*
19 Blvd de Bercy, 75012 Paris, France
DeLosAngeles, Victoria *Opera Singer*
Avenida de Pedralbes 57, 08034 Barcelona, Spain
Delp, Brad *Singer, Guitarist (Boston)*
%Agency for Performing Arts, 9200 Sunset Blvd, #900, Los Angeles, CA 90069, USA
DelPiero, Alessandro *Soccer Player*
%Juventus FC, Piazza Crimea 7, 10131 Turin, Italy
Delpino, Robert L *Football Player*
23276 Daisy Dr, Corona, CA 92883, USA

Delpy - Deming

Delpy, Julie *Actress*
%Endeavor Talent Agency, 9701 Wilshire Blvd, #1000, Beverly Hills, CA 90212, USA
DelRio, Jack *Football Player, Coach*
177 Archimedes Court, Baltimore, MD 21208, USA
Delson, Brad *Guitarist (Linkin Park)*
%Artist Group International, 9560 Wilshire Blvd, #400, Beverly Hills, CA 90212, USA
DelToro, Benicio *Actor*
%I F A Talent Agency, 8730 Sunset Blvd, #490, Los Angeles, CA 90069, USA
DelToro, Guillermo *Movie Director*
%Gersh Agency, 232 N Canon Dr, Beverly Hills, CA 90210, USA
DelTredici, David *Composer*
463 West St, #G121, New York, NY 10014, USA
DeLuca, Mike *Movie Producer*
%New Line Cinema, 716 N Robertson Blvd, Los Angeles, CA 90048, USA
DeLucas, Lawrence J *Astronaut*
909 19th St S, Birmingham, AL 35205, USA
DeLucchi, Michele *Architect*
Via Cenisio 40, 20154 Milan, Italy
DeLucia, Paco *Jazz Guitarist*
%International Music Network, 278 S Main St, #400, Gloucester, MA 01930, USA
Delugg, Milton *Musician*
2740 Claray Dr, Los Angeles, CA 90077, USA
DeLuise, Dom *Actor, Comedian*
1186 Corsica Dr, Pacific Palisades, CA 90272, USA
DeLuise, Michael *Actor*
1186 Corsica Dr, Pacific Palisades, CA 90272, USA
DeLuise, Peter *Actor*
%Premiere Artists Agency, 1875 Century Park E, #2250, Los Angeles, CA 90067, USA
Delvecchio, Alexander P (Alex) *Hockey Player*
1135 Maryland Blvd, Birmingham, MI 48009, USA
DeMaiziere, Lothar *Prime Minister, East Germany*
Am Kupfergraben 6/6A, 10117 Berlin, Germany
Demarchelier, Patrick *Photographer*
162 W 21st St, New York, NY 10011, USA
DeMarco, Guido *President, Malta*
%President's Office, Palace, Valletta, Malta
DeMarco, Jean *Sculptor*
Cervaro 03044, Prov-Frosinore, Italy
DeMarco, Tony *Boxer*
PO Box 53664, Indianapolis, IN 46253, USA
DeMarcus, Jay *Singer (Rascal Flatts)*
%LGB Media, 1228 Pineview Lane, Nashville, TN 37211, USA
Demarest, Arthur A *Archaeologist*
%Vanderbilt University, Anthropology Dept, Nashville, TN 37235, USA
Demars, Bruce *Navy Admiral*
41 Manters Point Road, Plymouth, MA 02360, USA
DeMatteo, Drea *Actor*
%Filthmart, 531 E 13th St, New York, NY 10009, USA
DeMatteo, Drea *Actress*
%Writers & Artists, 8383 Wilshire Blvd, #550, Beverly Hills, CA 90211, USA
DeMedeiros, Maria *Actress*
%William Morris Agency, 151 El Camino Dr, Beverly Hills, CA 90212, USA
DeMenezes, Fradique *President, Sao Tome & Principe*
%President's Office, Pargo do Povo, Sao Tome, Sao Tome & Principe
DeMent, Iris *Singer, Songwriter*
PO Box 28856, Gladstone, MO 64117, USA
DeMent, Jack *Chemist*
%Oregon Health Care Center, 11325 NE Weidler St, #44, Portland, OR 97220, USA
Dement, Kenneth *Football Player*
316 S Kingshighway St, Sikeston, MO 63801, USA
Dementieva, Elena *Tennis Player*
%Octagon, 1751 Pinnacle Dr, #1500, McLean, VA 22102, USA
DeMerchant, Paul *Religious Leader*
%Missionary Church, PO Box 9127, Fort Wayne, IN 46899, USA
Demetral, Chris *Actor*
%William Morris Agency, 151 El Camino Dr, Beverly Hills, CA 90212, USA
Demetriadis, Phokion *Editorial Cartoonist*
3rd September St 174, Athens, Greece
Demetrios *Religious Leader*
%Greek Orthodox Church, 89 E 79th St, #19, New York, NY 10021, USA
DeMeuron, Pierre *Architect, Pritzker Laureate*
%Herzog & De Meuron Architekten, Rheinschanze 6, 4056 Basel, Switzerland
DeMille, Nelson *Writer*
61 Hilton Ave, #23, Garden City, NY 11530, USA
Demin, Lev S *Cosmonaut*
%Potchta Kosmonavtov, Moskovskoi Oblasti, 141160 Syvisdny Goroduk, Russia
Deming, Peter *Cinematographer*
%Sandra Marsh Mgmt, 9150 Wilshire Blvd, #220, Beverly Hills, CA 90212, USA

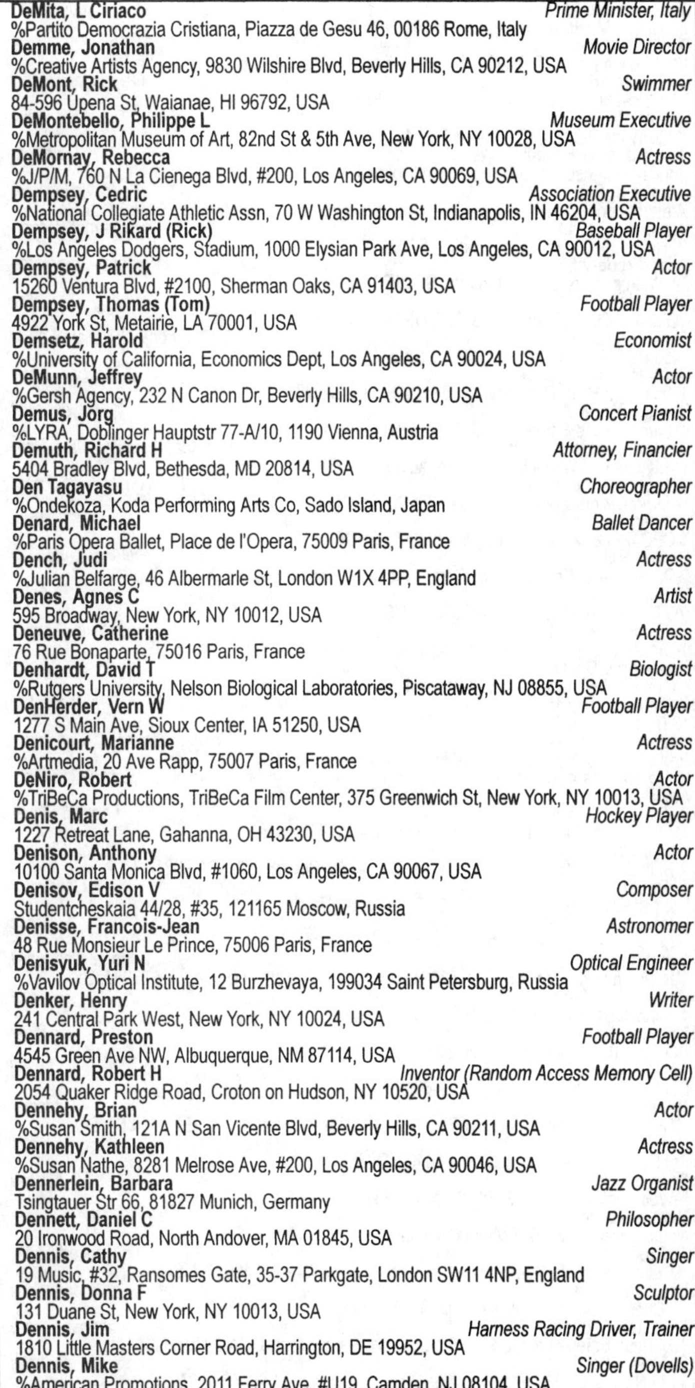

DeMita, L Ciriaco *Prime Minister, Italy*
%Partito Democrazia Cristiana, Piazza de Gesu 46, 00186 Rome, Italy
Demme, Jonathan *Movie Director*
%Creative Artists Agency, 9830 Wilshire Blvd, Beverly Hills, CA 90212, USA
DeMont, Rick *Swimmer*
84-596 Upena St, Waianae, HI 96792, USA
DeMontebello, Philippe L *Museum Executive*
%Metropolitan Museum of Art, 82nd St & 5th Ave, New York, NY 10028, USA
DeMornay, Rebecca *Actress*
%J/P/M, 760 N La Cienega Blvd, #200, Los Angeles, CA 90069, USA
Dempsey, Cedric *Association Executive*
%National Collegiate Athletic Assn, 70 W Washington St, Indianapolis, IN 46204, USA
Dempsey, J Rikard (Rick) *Baseball Player*
%Los Angeles Dodgers, Stadium, 1000 Elysian Park Ave, Los Angeles, CA 90012, USA
Dempsey, Patrick *Actor*
15260 Ventura Blvd, #2100, Sherman Oaks, CA 91403, USA
Dempsey, Thomas (Tom) *Football Player*
4922 York St, Metairie, LA 70001, USA
Demsetz, Harold *Economist*
%University of California, Economics Dept, Los Angeles, CA 90024, USA
DeMunn, Jeffrey *Actor*
%Gersh Agency, 232 N Canon Dr, Beverly Hills, CA 90210, USA
Demus, Jorg *Concert Pianist*
%LYRA, Doblinger Hauptstr 77-A/10, 1190 Vienna, Austria
Demuth, Richard H *Attorney, Financier*
5404 Bradley Blvd, Bethesda, MD 20814, USA
Den Tagayasu *Choreographer*
%Ondekoza, Koda Performing Arts Co, Sado Island, Japan
Denard, Michael *Ballet Dancer*
%Paris Opera Ballet, Place de l'Opera, 75009 Paris, France
Dench, Judi *Actress*
%Julian Belfarge, 46 Albermarle St, London W1X 4PP, England
Denes, Agnes C *Artist*
595 Broadway, New York, NY 10012, USA
Deneuve, Catherine *Actress*
76 Rue Bonaparte, 75016 Paris, France
Denhardt, David T *Biologist*
%Rutgers University, Nelson Biological Laboratories, Piscataway, NJ 08855, USA
DenHerder, Vern W *Football Player*
1277 S Main Ave, Sioux Center, IA 51250, USA
Denicourt, Marianne *Actress*
%Artmedia, 20 Ave Rapp, 75007 Paris, France
DeNiro, Robert *Actor*
%TriBeCa Productions, TriBeCa Film Center, 375 Greenwich St, New York, NY 10013, USA
Denis, Marc *Hockey Player*
1227 Retreat Lane, Gahanna, OH 43230, USA
Denison, Anthony *Actor*
10100 Santa Monica Blvd, #1060, Los Angeles, CA 90067, USA
Denisov, Edison V *Composer*
Studentcheskaia 44/28, #35, 121165 Moscow, Russia
Denisse, Francois-Jean *Astronomer*
48 Rue Monsieur Le Prince, 75006 Paris, France
Denisyuk, Yuri N *Optical Engineer*
%Vavilov Optical Institute, 12 Burzhevaya, 199034 Saint Petersburg, Russia
Denker, Henry *Writer*
241 Central Park West, New York, NY 10024, USA
Dennard, Preston *Football Player*
4545 Green Ave NW, Albuquerque, NM 87114, USA
Dennard, Robert H *Inventor (Random Access Memory Cell)*
2054 Quaker Ridge Road, Croton on Hudson, NY 10520, USA
Dennehy, Brian *Actor*
%Susan Smith, 121A N San Vicente Blvd, Beverly Hills, CA 90211, USA
Dennehy, Kathleen *Actress*
%Susan Nathe, 8281 Melrose Ave, #200, Los Angeles, CA 90046, USA
Dennerlein, Barbara *Jazz Organist*
Tsingtauer Str 66, 81827 Munich, Germany
Dennett, Daniel C *Philosopher*
20 Ironwood Road, North Andover, MA 01845, USA
Dennis, Cathy *Singer*
19 Music, #32, Ransomes Gate, 35-37 Parkgate, London SW11 4NP, England
Dennis, Donna F *Sculptor*
131 Duane St, New York, NY 10013, USA
Dennis, Jim *Harness Racing Driver, Trainer*
1810 Little Masters Corner Road, Harrington, DE 19952, USA
Dennis, Mike *Singer (Dovells)*
%American Promotions, 2011 Ferry Ave, #U19, Camden, NJ 08104, USA
Dennison, Rachel *Actress*
%Raymond Katz, 345 N Maple Dr, #205, Beverly Hills, CA 90210, USA

D

Denny, Floyd W, Jr *Pediatrician*
1 Carolina Meadows, #308, Chapel Hill, NC 27517, USA
Denny, John A *Baseball Player*
13430 E Camino la Cebadilla, Tucson, AZ 85749, USA
Denny, Martin *Composer, Pianist*
6770 Hawaii Kai Dr, #402, Honolulu, HI 96825, USA
Denny, Robyn *Artist*
20/30 Wilds Rents, #4B, London SE1 4QG, England
DenOuden, Wileminjntje (Willy) *Swimmer*
Goudsewagenstraat 23B, Rotterdam, Holland
Densham, Pen *Movie Director*
%International Creative Mgmt, 8942 Wilshire Blvd, #219, Beverly Hills, CA 90211, USA
Densmore, John *Drummer (Doors)*
49 Haldeman Road, Santa Monica, CA 90402, USA
Dent, Frederick B *Secretary, Commerce*
221 Montgomery St, Spartanburg, SC 29302, USA
Dent, Jim *Golfer*
PO Box 290656, Tampa, FL 33687, USA
Dent, Richard L *Football Player, Coach*
4453 RFD, Long Grove, IL 60047, USA
Dent, Russell E (Bucky) *Baseball Player*
8895 Indian River Run, Boynton Beach, FL 33437, USA
Denton, Derek A *Physiologist*
816 Irring Road, Toorak VIC 3142, Australia
Denton, Jeremiah A, Jr *Senator, AL; WW II Navy Hero*
11404 Queens Way, #B, Theodore, AL 36582, USA
Denton, Sandi (Pepa) *Rap Artist (Salt'N'Pepa)*
%Famous Artists Agency, 250 W 57th St, New York, NY 10107, USA
Denver, Bob *Actor*
%GFC, PO Box 269, Princeton, WV 24740, USA
DeOre, Bill *Editorial Cartoonist*
%Dallas News, Editorial Dept, Communications Center, Dallas, TX 75265, USA
DePaiva, James *Actor*
PO Box 11152, Greenwich, CT 06831, USA
DePalma, Brian R *Movie Director*
%Creative Artists Agency, 9830 Wilshire Blvd, Beverly Hills, CA 90212, USA
Depardieu, Gerard *Actor*
4 Place de la Chapelle, 75800 Bougival, France
Depardon, Raymond *Photographer*
18 Bis Rue Henri Barbusse, 75005 Paris, France
DePeyer, Gervase *Concert Clarinetist, Conductor*
Porto Vecchio 109, 1250 S Washington St, Alexandria, VA 22314, USA
DePortzamparc, Christian *Architect, Pritzker Laureate*
Architecte DPLG, 1 Rue de L'Aude, 75014 Paris, France
DePoyster, Jerry D *Football Player*
11111 Sceptre Ridge Terrace, Germantown, MD 20876, USA
Depp, Johnny *Actor, Director*
%United Talent Agency, 9560 Wilshire Blvd, #500, Beverly Hills, CA 90212, USA
DePreist, James A *Conductor*
Konsert AB, Kungsgatan 32, 111 35 Stockholm, Sweden
Dequenne, Emilie *Actress*
%Cineart, 36 Rue de Ponthieu, 75008 Paris, France
Der, Lambert *Editorial Cartoonist*
%Houston Post, Editorial Dept, 4888 Loop Central Dr, #390, Houston, TX 77081, USA
Derbyshire, Andrew G *Architect*
4 Sunnyfield, Hatfield, Herts AL9 5DX, England
Dercum, Max *Skier*
PO Box 189, Dillon, CO 80435, USA
Derek, Bo *Actress, Model*
PO Box 1940, Santa Ynez, CA 93460, USA
Deriso, Walter M, Jr *Financier*
%Synovus Financial Corp, 901 Front Ave, PO Box 120, Columbus, GA 31902, USA
Dern, Bruce *Actor*
PO Box 1581, Santa Monica, CA 90406, USA
Dern, Laura *Actress*
%Wolf/Kasteller, 335 N Maple Dr, #351, Beverly Hills, CA 90210, USA
Dernesch, Helga *Opera Singer*
Neutorgasse 2/22, 1013 Vienna, Austria
DeRosa, William *Concert Cellist*
%Columbia Artists Mgmt Inc, 165 W 57th St, New York, NY 10019, USA
DeRosier, David *Biophysicist*
27 Chesterfield Road, Newton, MA 02465, USA
Derosier, Michael *Drummer (Heart)*
%Borman Entertainment, 1250 6th St, #401, Santa Monica, CA 90401, USA
DeRossi, Portia *Actress*
1424 N Crescent Heights Blvd, #89, West Hollywood, CA 90046, USA
Derow, Peter A *Publisher*
PO Box 534, Bedford, NY 10506, USA

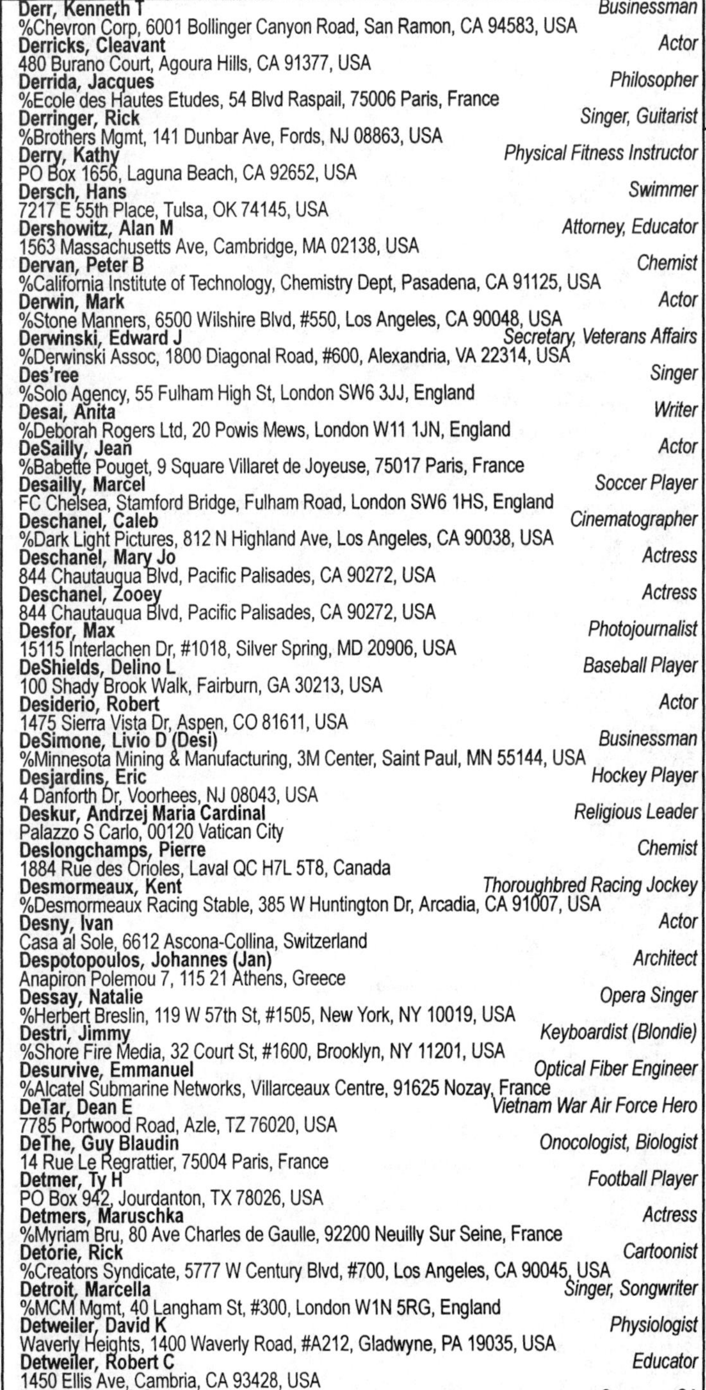

Derr, Kenneth T *Businessman*
%Chevron Corp, 6001 Bollinger Canyon Road, San Ramon, CA 94583, USA
Derricks, Cleavant *Actor*
480 Burano Court, Agoura Hills, CA 91377, USA
Derrida, Jacques *Philosopher*
%Ecole des Hautes Etudes, 54 Blvd Raspail, 75006 Paris, France
Derringer, Rick *Singer, Guitarist*
%Brothers Mgmt, 141 Dunbar Ave, Fords, NJ 08863, USA
Derry, Kathy *Physical Fitness Instructor*
PO Box 1656, Laguna Beach, CA 92652, USA
Dersch, Hans *Swimmer*
7217 E 55th Place, Tulsa, OK 74145, USA
Dershowitz, Alan M *Attorney, Educator*
1563 Massachusetts Ave, Cambridge, MA 02138, USA
Dervan, Peter B *Chemist*
%California Institute of Technology, Chemistry Dept, Pasadena, CA 91125, USA
Derwin, Mark *Actor*
%Stone Manners, 6500 Wilshire Blvd, #550, Los Angeles, CA 90048, USA
Derwinski, Edward J *Secretary, Veterans Affairs*
%Derwinski Assoc, 1800 Diagonal Road, #600, Alexandria, VA 22314, USA
Des'ree *Singer*
%Solo Agency, 55 Fulham High St, London SW6 3JJ, England
Desai, Anita *Writer*
%Deborah Rogers Ltd, 20 Powis Mews, London W11 1JN, England
DeSailly, Jean *Actor*
%Babette Pouget, 9 Square Villaret de Joyeuse, 75017 Paris, France
Desailly, Marcel *Soccer Player*
FC Chelsea, Stamford Bridge, Fulham Road, London SW6 1HS, England
Deschanel, Caleb *Cinematographer*
%Dark Light Pictures, 812 N Highland Ave, Los Angeles, CA 90038, USA
Deschanel, Mary Jo *Actress*
844 Chautauqua Blvd, Pacific Palisades, CA 90272, USA
Deschanel, Zooey *Actress*
844 Chautauqua Blvd, Pacific Palisades, CA 90272, USA
Desfor, Max *Photojournalist*
15115 Interlachen Dr, #1018, Silver Spring, MD 20906, USA
DeShields, Delino L *Baseball Player*
100 Shady Brook Walk, Fairburn, GA 30213, USA
Desiderio, Robert *Actor*
1475 Sierra Vista Dr, Aspen, CO 81611, USA
DeSimone, Livio D (Desi) *Businessman*
%Minnesota Mining & Manufacturing, 3M Center, Saint Paul, MN 55144, USA
Desjardins, Eric *Hockey Player*
4 Danforth Dr, Voorhees, NJ 08043, USA
Deskur, Andrzej Maria Cardinal *Religious Leader*
Palazzo S Carlo, 00120 Vatican City
Deslongchamps, Pierre *Chemist*
1884 Rue des Orioles, Laval QC H7L 5T8, Canada
Desmormeaux, Kent *Thoroughbred Racing Jockey*
%Desmormeaux Racing Stable, 385 W Huntington Dr, Arcadia, CA 91007, USA
Desny, Ivan *Actor*
Casa al Sole, 6612 Ascona-Collina, Switzerland
Despotopoulos, Johannes (Jan) *Architect*
Anapiron Polemou 7, 115 21 Athens, Greece
Dessay, Natalie *Opera Singer*
%Herbert Breslin, 119 W 57th St, #1505, New York, NY 10019, USA
Destri, Jimmy *Keyboardist (Blondie)*
%Shore Fire Media, 32 Court St, #1600, Brooklyn, NY 11201, USA
Desurvive, Emmanuel *Optical Fiber Engineer*
%Alcatel Submarine Networks, Villarceaux Centre, 91625 Nozay, France
DeTar, Dean E *Vietnam War Air Force Hero*
7785 Portwood Road, Azle, TZ 76020, USA
DeThe, Guy Blaudin *Onocologist, Biologist*
14 Rue Le Regrattier, 75004 Paris, France
Detmer, Ty H *Football Player*
PO Box 942, Jourdanton, TX 78026, USA
Detmers, Maruschka *Actress*
%Myriam Bru, 80 Ave Charles de Gaulle, 92200 Neuilly Sur Seine, France
Detorie, Rick *Cartoonist*
%Creators Syndicate, 5777 W Century Blvd, #700, Los Angeles, CA 90045, USA
Detroit, Marcella *Singer, Songwriter*
%MCM Mgmt, 40 Langham St, #300, London W1N 5RG, England
Detweiler, David K *Physiologist*
Waverly Heights, 1400 Waverly Road, #A212, Gladwyne, PA 19035, USA
Detweiler, Robert C *Educator*
1450 Ellis Ave, Cambria, CA 93428, USA
Deukmejian, C George *Governor, CA*
%Sidley & Austin, 555 W 5th St, Los Angeles, CA 90013, USA

D

Deutch, Howard *Movie Director*
%International Creative Mgmt, 8942 Wilshire Blvd, #219, Beverly Hills, CA 90211, USA
Deutch, John M *Government Official, Chemist*
51 Clifton St, Belmont, MA 02478, USA
Deutekom, Cristina *Opera Singer*
Lancasterdreef 41, Dronten 8251 TG, Holland
Deutsch, Patti *Actress*
%Yvette Bikoff, 1040 1st Ave, #1126, New York, NY 10022, USA
DeValeria, Dennis *Sportswriter*
213 Hillendale Road, Pittsburgh, PA 15237, USA
Devan Nair, Chengara Veetil *President, Singapore*
%Istana, Orchard Road, Singapore 0922, Singapore
Devane, William *Actor*
%Innovative Artists, 1505 10th St, Santa Monica, CA 90401, USA
DeVarona, Donna *Swimmer, Sportscaster*
%TWI, 420 W 45th St, #500, New York, NY 10036, USA
Devault, Calvin *Actor*
%Amsel Eisenstadt Frazier, 5757 Wilshire Blvd, #510, Los Angeles, CA 90036, USA
Dever, Barbara *Opera Singer*
%Wolf Artists Mgmt, 788 Columbus Ave, #15A, New York, NY 10025, USA
Deveraux, Jude *Writer*
%Pocket Books, 1230 Ave of Americas, New York, NY 10020, USA
Devers, Gail *Track Athlete*
%Kersee, 8519 Paul Jones Dr, Jacksonville, FL 32208, USA
DeVicenzo, Roberto *Golfer*
%Noni Lann, 5025 Veloz Ave, Tarzana, CA 91356, USA
Devicq, Paula *Actress, Model*
%William Morris Agency, 151 El Camino Dr, Beverly Hills, CA 90212, USA
DeVille, C C *Guitarist (Poison)*
%H K Mgmt, 9200 W Sunset Blvd, #530, Los Angeles, CA 90069, USA
Deville, Michel *Movie Director*
36 Rue Reinhardt, 92100 Boulogne, France
Devine, Harold *Boxer*
595 Wyckoff Ave, Wyckoff, NJ 07481, USA
Devine, Loretta *Actress*
3829 Crestway Place, Los Angeles, CA 90043, USA
DeVink, Lodewijk J R *Businessman*
%Warner-Lambert Co, 201 Tabor Road, Morris Plains, NJ 07950, USA
DeVita, Vincent T, Jr *Oncologist*
%Yale Comprehensive Cancer Center, 333 Cedar St, New Haven, CT 06510, USA
DeVito, Danny *Actor, Comedian, Director*
PO Box 491246, Los Angeles, CA 90049, USA
Devitt, John *Swimmer*
46 Beacon Ave, Beacon Hill NSW 2100, Australia
Devlin, Bruce *Golfer*
11429 E Mark Lane, Scottsdale, AZ 85262, USA
Devlin, Dean *Movie Director, Producer, Actor*
%Creative Artists Agency, 9830 Wilshire Blvd, Beverly Hills, CA 90212, USA
Devlin, Robert M *Businessman*
%American General Corp, 2929 Allen Parkway, Houston, TX 77019, USA
DeVries, William C *Surgeon*
%DeVries Assoc, 7 Snowmound Court, Rockville, MD 20850, USA
DeWaart, Edo *Conductor*
Essenlaan 68, Rotterdam 3016, Netherlands
Dewar, Jane E *Editor*
%Legion Magazine, 359 Kent St, #504, Ottawa ON K2P 0R6, Canada
Dewar, Susan *Cartoonist (Us & Them)*
%Universal Press Syndicate, 4520 Main St, Kansas City, MO 64111, USA
Dewey, Duane E *Korean War Marine Corps Hero (CMH)*
RR 1 Box 494, Irons, MI 49644, USA
DeWilde, Edy *Museum Director*
%Stedelijk Museum, Amsterdam, Netherlands
DeWinne, Frank *Cosmonaut*
%349 Squadron, Vliegbasis 10W TAC Kleine Brogel, 3990 Peer, Belgium
DeWitt, Bryce S *Physicist*
%University of Texas, Physics Dept, Austin, TX 78712, USA
DeWitt, Doug *Boxer*
2035 Central Ave, Yonkers, NY 10710, USA
DeWitt, Joyce *Actress*
PO Box 480033, Los Angeles, CA 90048, USA
Dewitt, Willie *Boxer*
605 N Water St, Burnet, TX 78611, USA
DeWitt-Morette, Cecile *Physicist*
2411 Vista Lane, Austin, TX 78703, USA
Dews, Peter B *Psychiatrist*
181 Upland Road, Newtonville, MA 02460, USA
Dexter, Mary *Movie Director*
%Hank Tani, 14542 Delaware Dr, Moorpark, CA 93021, USA

Dexter, Peter W *Writer*
%Sacramento Bee, Editorial Dept, 21st & Q Sts, Sacramento, CA 95852, USA
Dey, Susan *Actress*
1640 S Sepulveda Blvd, #530, Los Angeles, CA 90025, USA
DeYoung, Cliff *Actor*
481 Savona Way, Oak Park, CA 91377, USA
Dezhurov, Vladimir N *Cosmonaut*
%Potchta Kosmonavtov, Moskovskoi Oblasti, 141160 Syvisdny Goroduk, Russia
DeZonie, Hank *Basketball Player*
700 Lenox Ave, New York, NY 10039, USA
Dhabhara, Firdaus S *Neuroscientist*
%Rockefeller University, Neurology Dept, 1230 York Ave, New York, NY 10021, USA
Dharmasakti, Sanya *Prime Minister, Thailand*
15 Saukhumvit Road, Soi 41, Bangkok, Thailand
Dial, Leroy (Buddy) *Football Player*
115 Anna St, Tomball, TX 77375, USA
Diallo, Mmadou *Soccer Player*
%New England Revolution, CMGI Field, 1 Patriot Place, Foxboro, MA 02035, USA
Diamandis, Peter G *Publisher*
%Diamandis Communications, 1515 Broadway, New York, NY 10036, USA
Diamandopoulos, Peter *Educator*
530 E 76th St, #32G, New York, NY 10021, USA
Diamond, Abel J *Architect*
%Diamond Schmitz Co, 2 Berkeley St, #600, Toronto ON M5A 2W3, Canada
Diamond, David L *Composer*
249 Edgerton St, Rochester, NY 14607, USA
Diamond, Jared M *Biologist*
%University of California, Med School, Physiology Dept, Los Angeles, CA 90024, USA
Diamond, Marian C *Neuroanatomist*
2583 Virginia St, Berkeley, CA 94709, USA
Diamond, Michael (Mike D) *Rap Artist (Beastie Boys)*
%GAS Entertainment, 8935 Lindblade St, Culver City, CA 90232, USA
Diamond, Neil L *Singer, Songwriter*
10345 W Olympic Blvd, #200, Los Angeles, CA 90064, USA
Diamond, Reed *Actor*
%William Morris Agency, 151 El Camino Dr, Beverly Hills, CA 90212, USA
Diamond, Seymour *Physician*
%Diamond Headache Clinic, 467 W Deming Place, #500, Chicago, IL 60614, USA
Diamont, Anita *Writer*
%Charles Scribner's Sons, 866 3rd Ave, New York, NY 10022, USA
Diamont, Don *Actor*
%Craig Mgmt, 125 S Sycamore Ave, Los Angeles, CA 90036, USA
Dias, Ivan Cardinal *Religious Leader*
%Archbishop's House, 21 Nathalal Parekh Marg, Mumbai 400001, India
Diaw, Boris *Basketball Player*
%Atlanta Hawks, 190 Marietta St SW, Atlanta, GA 30303, USA
Diaz, Alex *Photojournalist*
%Associated Press, 50 Rockefeller Plaza, New York, NY 10020, USA
Diaz, Cameron *Actress, Model*
%The Firm, 9100 Wilshire Blvd, #100W, Beverly Hills, CA 90210, USA
Diaz, Manny *Mayor*
%Mayor's Office, 3500 Pan American Dr, Miami, FL 33133, USA
Diaz-Balart, Jose *Commentator*
%CBS-TV, News Dept, 51 W 52nd St, New York, NY 10019, USA
Diaz-Rahi, Yamila *Model*
%Next Model Mgmt, 23 Watts St, New York, NY 10013, USA
Dibela, Kingsford *Governor General, Papua New Guinea*
PO Box 113, Port Moresby, Papua New Guinea
DiBeligiojoso, Lodovico B *Architect*
%Studio Architetti BBPR, 2 Via Dei Chiostri, 20121 Milan, Italy
DiBiaggio, John A *Educator*
%Tufts University, President's Office, Medford, MA 02155, USA
DiBlasio, Raul *Singer*
%Estefan Enterprises, 420 Jefferson Ave, Miami Beach, FL 33139, USA
DiBona, Craig *Cinematographer*
333 E 66th St, #7O, New York, NY 10021, USA
DiCamillo, Gary T *Businessman*
1001 Saint Georges Road, Baltimore, MD 21210, USA
DiCaprio, Leonardo *Actor*
%P M K Public Relations, 8500 Wilshire Blvd, #700, Beverly Hills, CA 90211, USA
DiCenzo, George *Actor*
%Michael Hartig Agency, 156 5th Ave, #820, New York, NY 10010, USA
Dichter, Misha *Concert Pianist*
%Columbia Artists Mgmt Inc, 165 W 57th St, New York, NY 10019, USA
DiCillio, Tom *Movie Director*
%William Morris Agency, 151 El Camino Dr, Beverly Hills, CA 90212, USA
Dick, Andy *Actor, Comedian*
337 N Croft Ave, West Hollywood, CA 90048, USA

D

Dick, Douglas *Actor*
604 S Gretna Green Way, Los Angeles, CA 90049, USA
Dickau, Dan *Basketball Player*
%Atlanta Hawks, 190 Marietta St SW, Atlanta, GA 30303, USA
Dickens, Jimmy *Singer*
5010 W Concord Road, Brentwood, TN 37027, USA
Dickenson, Gary *Bowler*
501 Wade Martin Dr, Edmond, OK 73034, USA
Dickerson, Eric D *Football Player, Sportscaster*
26815 Mulholland Highway, Calabasas, CA 91302, USA
Dickerson, Sandra *Actress*
%Howes & Prior, Berkeley House, Hay Hill, London W1X 7LH, England
Dickey, Boh A *Businessman*
%SAFECO Corp, SAFECO Plaza, Seattle, WA 98185, USA
Dickey, C Lynn *Football Player*
6102 Mission Road, Fairway, KS 66205, USA
Dickinson, Angie *Actress*
1715 Carla Ridge, Beverly Hills, CA 90210, USA
Dickinson, Bruce *Singer (Iron Maiden)*
%Sanctuary Music Mgmt, 82 Bishops Bridge Road, London W2 6BB, England
Dickinson, Gary *Bowler*
501 Wade Martin Road, Edmond, OK 73034, USA
Dickinson, Peter *Writer*
%Mysterious Press, Warner Books, 1271 Ave of Americas, New York, NY 10020, USA
Dickinson, Steve *Cartoonist (Tar Pit)*
%King Features Syndicate, 888 7th Ave, New York, NY 10106, USA
Dickman, James B *Photojournalist*
1471 Peach Creek Dr, Splendora, TX 77372, USA
Dickson, Chris *Yachtsman*
%Int'l Mgmt Group, 1 Erieview Plaza, 1360 E 9th St, #1300, Cleveland, OH 44114, USA
Dickson, Clarence *Law Enforcement Official*
%Police Department, Metro Justice, 1351 NW 12th St, Miami, FL 33125, USA
Dickson, Jennifer *Artist, Photographer*
20 Osborne St, Ottawa ON K1S 4Z9, Canada
Dickson, Neil *Actor*
%International Creative Mgmt, 76 Oxford St, London W1N 0AX, England
Dicus, Charles (Chuck) *Football Player*
1500 E Clark St, Fayetteville, AR 72701, USA
Diddley, Bo *Singer, Guitarist*
PO Box 410, Archer, FL 32618, USA
Diddy, P *Rap Artist*
%Wright Entertainment Group, 7680 Universal Blvd, #500, Orlando, FL 32819, USA
Didion, Joan *Writer*
%Janklow & Nesbit, 445 Park Ave, #1300, New York, NY 10022, USA
Dido *Singer, Songwriter*
%Nettwerk Mgmt, 1650 W 2nd Ave, Vancouver BC V6J 4R3, Canada
Diebel, John C *Businessman*
%Meade Instruments Corp, 6001 Oak Canyon, Irvine, CA 92618, USA
Diebold, John *Businessman*
%Diebold Group, PO Box 515, Bedford Hills, NY 10507, USA
Diehl, Digby R *Journalist*
788 S Lake Ave, Pasadena, CA 91106, USA
Diehl, John *Actor*
13601 Ventura Blvd, #275, Sherman Oaks, CA 91423, USA
Diehl, William *Writer*
%William Morris Agency, 151 El Camino Dr, Beverly Hills, CA 90212, USA
Dieken, Doug H *Football Player*
209 Prospect Ave, Streator, IL 61364, USA
Diemecke, Enrique Arturo *Conductor*
%Herbert Barrett, 266 W 37th St, #2000, New York, NY 10018, USA
Diener, Theodor O *Plant Virologist*
PO Box 272, 11711 Battersea Dr, Beltsville, MD 20705, USA
Dierdof, Daniel L (Dan) *Football Player, Sportscaster*
13302 Buckland Hall Road, Saint Louis, MO 63131, USA
Dierker, Lawrence E (Larry) *Baseball Player, Manager*
8318 N Tahoe Dr, Houston, TX 77040, USA
Dierking, Connie *Basketball Player*
5665 Kugler Mill Road, Cincinnati, OH 45236, USA
Diesel, Vin *Movie Director, Actor*
%The Firm, 9100 Wilshire Blvd, #100W, Beverly Hills, CA 90210, USA
Dietrich, Dena *Actress*
%Peter Strain, 5724 W 3rd St, #302, Los Angeles, CA 90036, USA
Dietrich, William A (Bill) *Journalist*
%Seattle Times, Editorial Dept, 1120 John St, Seattle, WA 98109, USA
Diffie, Joe *Singer, Songwriter*
50 Music Square W, #300, Nashville, TN 37203, USA
Diffie, Whitfield *Inventor (Public Key Cryptology)*
%Sun Microsystems, 901 San Antonio Road, MS UMTV29-116, Palo Alto, CA 94303, USA

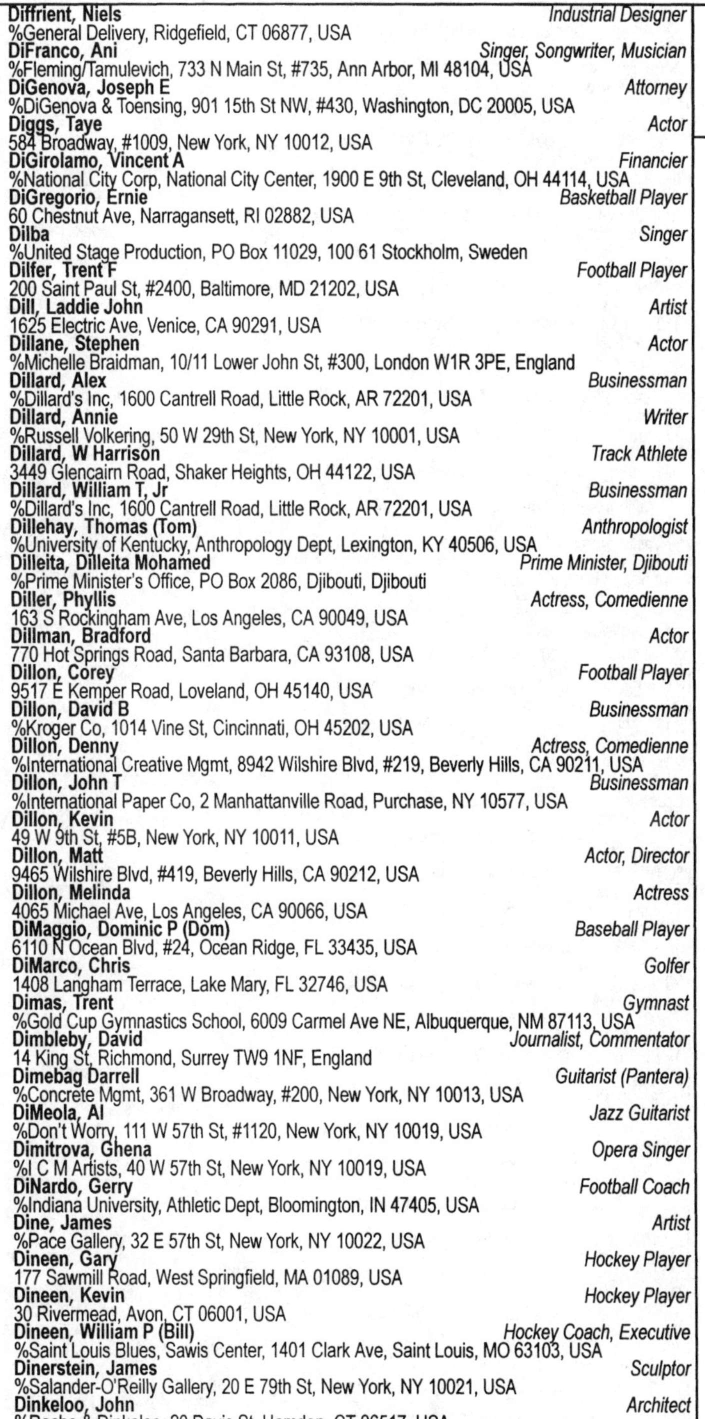

Diffrient, Niels *Industrial Designer*
%General Delivery, Ridgefield, CT 06877, USA
DiFranco, Ani *Singer, Songwriter, Musician*
%Fleming/Tamulevich, 733 N Main St, #735, Ann Arbor, MI 48104, USA
DiGenova, Joseph E *Attorney*
%DiGenova & Toensing, 901 15th St NW, #430, Washington, DC 20005, USA
Diggs, Taye *Actor*
584 Broadway, #1009, New York, NY 10012, USA
DiGirolamo, Vincent A *Financier*
%National City Corp, National City Center, 1900 E 9th St, Cleveland, OH 44114, USA
DiGregorio, Ernie *Basketball Player*
60 Chestnut Ave, Narragansett, RI 02882, USA
Dilba *Singer*
%United Stage Production, PO Box 11029, 100 61 Stockholm, Sweden
Dilfer, Trent F *Football Player*
200 Saint Paul St, #2400, Baltimore, MD 21202, USA
Dill, Laddie John *Artist*
1625 Electric Ave, Venice, CA 90291, USA
Dillane, Stephen *Actor*
%Michelle Braidman, 10/11 Lower John St, #300, London W1R 3PE, England
Dillard, Alex *Businessman*
%Dillard's Inc, 1600 Cantrell Road, Little Rock, AR 72201, USA
Dillard, Annie *Writer*
%Russell Volkering, 50 W 29th St, New York, NY 10001, USA
Dillard, W Harrison *Track Athlete*
3449 Glencairn Road, Shaker Heights, OH 44122, USA
Dillard, William T, Jr *Businessman*
%Dillard's Inc, 1600 Cantrell Road, Little Rock, AR 72201, USA
Dillehay, Thomas (Tom) *Anthropologist*
%University of Kentucky, Anthropology Dept, Lexington, KY 40506, USA
Dilleita, Dilleita Mohamed *Prime Minister, Djibouti*
%Prime Minister's Office, PO Box 2086, Djibouti, Djibouti
Diller, Phyllis *Actress, Comedienne*
163 S Rockingham Ave, Los Angeles, CA 90049, USA
Dillman, Bradford *Actor*
770 Hot Springs Road, Santa Barbara, CA 93108, USA
Dillon, Corey *Football Player*
9517 E Kemper Road, Loveland, OH 45140, USA
Dillon, David B *Businessman*
%Kroger Co, 1014 Vine St, Cincinnati, OH 45202, USA
Dillon, Denny *Actress, Comedienne*
%International Creative Mgmt, 8942 Wilshire Blvd, #219, Beverly Hills, CA 90211, USA
Dillon, John T *Businessman*
%International Paper Co, 2 Manhattanville Road, Purchase, NY 10577, USA
Dillon, Kevin *Actor*
49 W 9th St, #5B, New York, NY 10011, USA
Dillon, Matt *Actor, Director*
9465 Wilshire Blvd, #419, Beverly Hills, CA 90212, USA
Dillon, Melinda *Actress*
4065 Michael Ave, Los Angeles, CA 90066, USA
DiMaggio, Dominic P (Dom) *Baseball Player*
6110 N Ocean Blvd, #24, Ocean Ridge, FL 33435, USA
DiMarco, Chris *Golfer*
1408 Langham Terrace, Lake Mary, FL 32746, USA
Dimas, Trent *Gymnast*
%Gold Cup Gymnastics School, 6009 Carmel Ave NE, Albuquerque, NM 87113, USA
Dimbleby, David *Journalist, Commentator*
14 King St, Richmond, Surrey TW9 1NF, England
Dimebag Darrell *Guitarist (Pantera)*
%Concrete Mgmt, 361 W Broadway, #200, New York, NY 10013, USA
DiMeola, Al *Jazz Guitarist*
%Don't Worry, 111 W 57th St, #1120, New York, NY 10019, USA
Dimitrova, Ghena *Opera Singer*
%I C M Artists, 40 W 57th St, New York, NY 10019, USA
DiNardo, Gerry *Football Coach*
%Indiana University, Athletic Dept, Bloomington, IN 47405, USA
Dine, James *Artist*
%Pace Gallery, 32 E 57th St, New York, NY 10022, USA
Dineen, Gary *Hockey Player*
177 Sawmill Road, West Springfield, MA 01089, USA
Dineen, Kevin *Hockey Player*
30 Rivermead, Avon, CT 06001, USA
Dineen, William P (Bill) *Hockey Coach, Executive*
%Saint Louis Blues, Sawis Center, 1401 Clark Ave, Saint Louis, MO 63103, USA
Dinerstein, James *Sculptor*
%Salander-O'Reilly Gallery, 20 E 79th St, New York, NY 10021, USA
Dinkeloo, John *Architect*
%Roche & Dinkeloo, 20 Davis St, Hamden, CT 06517, USA

D

Dinnigan, Collette *Fashion Designer*
22-24 Hutchinson St, Surry Hills, Sydney NSW 2010, Australia
Dion *Singer*
%Fox Entertainment, 1650 Broadway, #503, New York, NY 10019, USA
Dion, Celine *Singer*
4 Place Laval, #500, Laval QC H7N 5Y3, Canada
Dion, Colleen *Actress*
%Abrams Artists, 9200 Sunset Blvd, #1125, Los Angeles, CA 90069, USA
Dionisi, Stefano *Actor*
%Carol Levi Co, Via Giuseppe Pisanelli, 00196 Rome, Italy
Dionne, Joseph L *Businessman, Publisher*
%McGraw-Hill Inc, 1221 Ave of Americas, New York, NY 10020, USA
Dionne, Marcel E *Hockey Player*
%Dionne Enterprises, 9930 Keller Road, Clarence Center, NY 14032, USA
Diop, DeSagana *Basketball Player*
%Cleveland Cavaliers, Gund Arena, 1 Center Court, Cleveland, OH 44115, USA
Diop, Majhemout *President, Senegal*
210 HCM, Guediawaye, Dakar, Senegal
Diorio, Nick *Soccer Player*
273 Clark St, Lemoyne, PA 17043, USA
DiPasquale, James *Composer*
%Gorfaine/Schwartz, 13245 Riverside Dr, #450, Sherman Oaks, CA 91423, USA
DiPietro, Rick *Hockey Player*
63 Loring Road, Winthrop, MA 02152, USA
DiPreta, Tony *Cartoonist (Rex Morgan MD/Joe Palooka)*
%North American Syndicate, 235 E 45th St, New York, NY 10017, USA
DiPrete, Edward D *Governor, RI*
555 Wilbur Ave, Cranston, RI 02921, USA
Dirda, Michael *Journalist*
%Washington Post, Editorial Dept, 1150 15th St NW, Washington, DC 20071, USA
Dirie, Waris *Model, Human Rights Activist*
%London Mgmt, 2-4 Noel St, London W1V 3RB, England
Discala, Jamie-Lynn *Actress, Singer*
%Writers & Artists, 8383 Wilshire Blvd, #550, Beverly Hills, CA 90211, USA
Disch, Thomas M *Writer*
%Karpfinger Agency, 357 W 20th St, New York, NY 10011, USA
Dischinger, Terry *Basketball Player*
1259 Lake Garden Court, Lake Oswego, OR 97034, USA
Dishman, Cris E *Football Player*
5453 W Venus Way, Chandler, AZ 85226, USA
Dishy, Bob *Actor*
20 E 9th St, New York, NY 10003, USA
Disl, Ursula *Biathlete, Cross-Country Skier*
Krumme Gasse 10A, 83324 Ruhpolding, Germany
Disl, Uschi *Biathlete*
Unterer Plattenberg 6, 92696 Flossenberg, Germany
Disney, Anthea *Editor*
%News America Publishing Group, 211 Ave of Americas, New York, NY 10036, USA
Disney, Roy E *Businessman*
%Walt Disney Co, 500 S Buena Vista St, Burbank, CA 91521, USA
Disney, William *Speed Skater*
1610 Kirk Dr, Lake Havasu City, AZ 86404, USA
Distel, Sacha *Singer, Songwriter*
20 Rue de Fosses-Saint-Jacques, 75005 Paris, France
DiSuvero, Mark *Sculptor*
PO Box 2218, Astoria, NY 11102, USA
Ditka, Michael K (Mike) *Football Player, Coach*
161 E Chicago Ave, #39F, Chicago, IL 60611, USA
Ditmar, Arthur J (Art) *Baseball Player*
6687 Wisteria Dr, Myrtle Beach, SC 29588, USA
Dittmer, Andreas *Canoeing Athlete*
Fischerbank 5, 17033 Neubrandenburg, Germany
Dittmer, Edward C *Space Scientist*
702 Old Mescalero Road, Tularosa, NM 88352, USA
Dityatin, Aleksandr N *Gymnast*
Nevski Prosp 18, #25, Saint Petersburg, Russia
Ditz, Nancy *Track Athlete*
524 Moore Road, Woodside, CA 94062, USA
Diulio, Albert J *Educator*
%Marquette University, President's Office, Milwaukee, WI 53233, USA
Divac, Vlade *Basketball Player*
17535 Camino de Yatasto, Pacific Palisades, CA 90272, USA
Divine, Gary W *Labor Leader*
%National Federation of Federal Employees, 1016 16th St, Washington, DC 20038, USA
Diwakar, R R *Writer*
%Sri Arvind Krupa, 233 Sadashiv Nagar, Bangalore 560006, Karnataka, India
Dix, Drew D *Vietnam War Army Hero (CMH)*
1829 S Pueblo Blvd, Pueblo, CO 81005, USA

D

Dixon - Dobslow

Dixon, Alan J *Senator, IL*
7606 Foley Dr, Belleville, IL 62223, USA
Dixon, Becky *Sportscaster*
%ABC-TV, Sports Dept, 77 W 66th St, New York, NY 10023, USA
Dixon, Craig *Track Athlete*
10630 Wellworth Ave, Los Angeles, CA 90024, USA
Dixon, D Jeremy *Architect*
41 Shelton St, London WC2H 9HJ, England
Dixon, Donna *Actress*
%Edrick/Rich Mgmt, 8955 Norma Place, Los Angeles, CA 90069, USA
Dixon, Floyd *Singer, Pianist*
%Folklore Prod, 1671 Appian Way, Santa Monica, CA 90401, USA
Dixon, Frank J *Pathologist, Immunologist*
2355 Avenida de la Playa, La Jolla, CA 92037, USA
Dixon, Hanford *Football Player*
30166 Lake Road, Bay Village, OH 44140, USA
Dixon, Ivan *Actor, Director*
27350 Barkes Way, Tehachapi, CA 93561, USA
Dixon, Juan *Basketball Player*
%Washington Wizards, MCI Centre, 601 F St NW, Washington, DC 20004, USA
Dixon, Randolph C (Randy) *Football Player*
9910 Summerlakes Dr, Carmel, IN 46032, USA
Dixon, Robert J *Air Force General*
29342 Ridgeview Terrace, Boerne, TX 78015, USA
Dixon, Rodney (Rod) *Track Athlete*
22 Entrican Ave, Remuera, Auckland 5, New Zealand
Dixon, Tamecka *Basketball Player*
%Los Angeles Sparks, Staples Center, 1111 S Figueroa St, Los Angeles, CA 90015, USA
Dixon, Thomas F *Aerospace Engineer*
1761 Cuba Island Lane, Hayes, VA 23072, USA
DJ Premier *Rap Artist (Gang Starr)*
%William Morris Agency, 151 El Camino Dr, Beverly Hills, CA 90212, USA
Djerassi, Carl *Inventor (Oral Contraceptive)*
2325 Bear Gulch Road, Redwood City, CA 94062, USA
Djerassi, Isaac *Physician*
2034 Delancey Place, Philadelphia, PA 19103, USA
Djoussouf, Abbass *Prime Minister, Comoros*
%Prime Minister's Office, BP 421, Moroni, Comoros
Djukanovic, Milo *President, Yugoslavia*
%Executive Council, Bul Lenjina 2, 11075 Novi Belgrad, Serbia & Montenegro
Dlamini, Barnabas S *Prime Minister, Swaziland*
%Prime Minister's Office, PO Box 395, Mbabane, Swaziland
Dmitriev, Artur *Figure Skater*
%Russian Skating Federation, Luchneksaia Nab 8, Moscow 119871, Russia
DMX *Rap Artist (Ruff Ryders), Actor*
%Famous Artists Agency, 250 W 57th St, New York, NY 10107, USA
Do Amaral, Diogo F *Government Official, Portugal*
Ave Fontes Pereira de Melo 35, #13A, 1050 Lisbon, Portugal
Do Muoi *Party Chairman, Vietnam*
%Chairman's Office, Council of Ministers, Hanoi, Vietnam
Do Nascimento, Alexandre Cardinal *Religious Leader*
%Arcebispado, CP 87, 1230C Luanda, Angola
Doan, Charles A *Physician*
4935 Oletangy Blvd, Columbus, OH 43214, USA
Doar, John *Attorney*
9 E 63rd St, New York, NY 10021, USA
Dobbin, Edmund J *Educator*
%Villanova University, President's Office, Villanova, PA 19085, USA
Dobbins, Herb *Football Player*
10 Keating Point, Saint Albert AB T6N 5N8, Canada
Dobbs, Lou *Commentator*
%Cable News Network, News Dept, 820 1st St NE, Washington, DC 20002, USA
Dobbs, Mattiwilda *Opera Singer*
1101 S Arlington Ridge Road, Arlington, VA 22202, USA
Dobek, Michelle *Golfer*
292 Chicopee St, Chicopee, MA 01013, USA
Dobelle, William *Inventor (Artificial Vision System)*
%Dobelle Institute, 1 Lincoln Place, New York, NY 10023, USA
Dobkin, David *Movie Director*
%H S I Productions, 3630 Eastham Dr, Culver City, CA 90232, USA
Dobkins, Carl, Jr *Singer*
7640 Cheviot Road, #212, Cincinnati, OH 45247, USA
Dobler, Conrad F *Football Player*
12600 Fairway Road, Shawnee Mission, KS 66209, USA
Dobler, David *Religious Leader*
%Presbyterian Church USA, 100 Witherspoon St, Louisville, KY 40202, USA
Dobslow, Bill *Singer (Rivieras)*
945 Handlebar Road, Mishawaka, IN 46544, USA

D

Dobson - Dold

Dobson, James C — *Religious Leader*
%Focus on the Family, 8605 Explorer Dr, Colorado Springs, CO 80920, USA
Dobson, Kevin — *Actor*
%Side Action, 685 Miramonte Dr, Santa Barbara, CA 93109, USA
Dobson, Peter — *Actor*
1351 N Crescent Heights Blvd, #318, West Hollywood, CA 90046, USA
Dockson, Robert R — *Financier*
1301 Collingwood Place, Los Angeles, CA 90069, USA
Dockstader, Frederick J — *Museum Director*
165 W 66th St, New York, NY 10023, USA
Doctorow, Edgar Lawrence (E L) — *Writer*
333 E 57th St, #11B, New York, NY 10022, USA
Doda, Carol — *Exotic Dancer, Actress*
PO Box 387, Fremont, CA 94537, USA
Dodd, Deryl — *Singer, Songwriter*
%823 Mgmt, PO Box 186, Waring, TX 78074, USA
Dodd, Maurice — *Cartoonist (Perishers)*
%Daily Mirror, Editorial Dept, 1 Canada Square, London E14 5AP, England
Dodd, Michael T (Mike) — *Volleyball Player*
1017 Manhattan Ave, Manhattan Beach, CA 90266, USA
Dodd, Patty D — *Volleyball Player*
1017 Manhattan Ave, Manhattan Beach, CA 90266, USA
Dodge, Brooks — *Skier*
PO Box C, Jackson, NH 03846, USA
Dodge, Geoffrey — *Publisher*
%Money Magazine, Time-Life Building, New York, NY 10020, USA
Doenges, Bessie R — *Writer*
%Russell & Volkening, 50 W 29th St, New York, NY 10001, USA
Doerr, Robert P (Bobby) — *Baseball Player*
33705 Illamo-Agness Road, Agness, OR 97406, USA
Doerre-Heinig, Katrin — *Track Athlete*
Westring 53, 6471 Erbach, Germany
Dogg, Nate — *Singer*
%Elektra Records, 75 Rockefeller Plaza, New York, NY 10019, USA
Doherty, Dennis (Denny) — *Singer (Mamas & Papas)*
1262 Contour Dr, Mississaugua ON L5H 1B2, Canada
Doherty, Peter C — *Nobel Medicine Laureate*
172 Kimbrough Place, #506, Memphis, TN 38104, USA
Doherty, Shannen — *Actress*
%United Talent Agency, 9560 Wilshire Blvd, #500, Beverly Hills, CA 90212, USA
Dohm, Gaby — *Actress*
%Omnis Agentur, Wiedenmayerstr 11, 80538 Munich, Germany
Dohrmann, Angela — *Actress*
%Innovative Artists, 1505 10th St, Santa Monica, CA 90401, USA
Dohrmann, George — *Journalist*
%Saint Paul Pioneer Press, Editorial Dept, 345 Cedar St, Saint Paul, MN 55101, USA
Doi, Takako — *Government Official, Japan*
%Daini Giinkaikan, 2-1-2 Nagatacho, Chiyodaku, Tokyo, Japan
Doi, Takao — *Astronaut, Japan*
%NASDA, Tsukuba Space Ctr, 2-1-1 Sengen, Tukubashi, Ibaraki 305, Japan
Doig, Ivan — *Writer*
%Charles Scribner's Sons, 866 3rd Ave, New York, NY 10022, USA
Dokes, Michael — *Boxer*
5151 Collins Ave, #522, Miami Beach, FL 33140, USA
Dokken, Don — *Guitarist*
%Agency for Performing Arts, 9200 Sunset Blvd, #900, Los Angeles, CA 90069, USA
Doktor, Martin — *Canoeing Athlete*
%Canoe Prosport Sezemice, Slunecni 627, Sezemice 533 04, Czech Republic
Dolan, Don — *Actor*
14228 Emelita St, Van Nuys, CA 91401, USA
Dolan, Ellen — *Actress*
%Don Buchwald, 10 E 44th St, New York, NY 10017, USA
Dolan, Louise A — *Physicist*
%University of North Carolina, Physics Dept, Chapel Hill, NC 27599, USA
Dolan, Michael P — *Government Official*
%Internal Revenue Service, 1111 Constitution Ave NW, Washington, DC 20224, USA
Dolby, David C — *Vietnam War Army Hero (CMH)*
PO Box 218, Pekiomen Ave, Oaks, PA 19456, USA
Dolby, Ray M — *Inventor, Sound Engineer*
%Dolby Laboratories, 100 Potrero Ave, San Francisco, CA 94103, USA
Dolby, Thomas — *Singer, Songwriter*
%International Talent Group, 729 7th Ave, #1600, New York, NY 10019, USA
Dolce, Domenico — *Fashion Designer*
%Dolce & Gabbana, Via Santa Cecilia 7, 20122 Milan, Italy
Dolci, Danilo — *Writer, Social Worker*
%Centro Iniziative Studi, Largo Scalia 5, Partinico/Palermo, Sicily, Italy
Dold, R Bruce — *Journalist*
501 N Park Road, #HSE, La Grange Park, IL 60526, USA

Dole, Elizabeth H *Secretary, Transportation; Labor*
1035 N Maple Dr, Russell, KS 67665, USA
Dole, Robert J *Senator, KS*
1035 N Maple Dr, Russell, KS 67665, USA
Dole, Vincent P *Medical Researcher*
%Rockefeller University, 1230 York Ave, New York, NY 10021, USA
Doleac, Michael *Basketball Player*
7372 Comstock Circle, Salt Lake City, UT 84121, USA
Doleman, Christopher J (Chris) *Football Player*
1025 Leadenhall St, Alpharetta, GA 30022, USA
Dolenz, Ami *Actress*
1860 Bel Air Road, Los Angeles, CA 90077, USA
Dolenz, Micky *Actor, Singer, Drummer (Monkees)*
22 Baymare Road, Bell Canyon, CA 91307, USA
Doll, W Richard S *Epidemiologist*
12 Rawlinson Road, Oxford OX2 6UE, England
Dollar, Linda *Volleyball Coach*
%Southwest Missouri State University, Athletic Dept, Springfield, MO 65804, USA
Dollard, Christopher Edward *Actor*
%Gold Marshak Liedtke, 3500 W Olive Ave, #1400, Burbank, CA 91505, USA
Dollens, Ronald *Businessman*
%Guidant Corp, 111 Monument Circle, Indianapolis, IN 46204, USA
Dollfus, Audouin *Astronomer, Physicist*
77 Rue Albert Perdreaux, 92370 Chaville, France
Dolmayan, John *Drummer (System of a Down)*
%Velvet Hammer, 9911 W Pico Blvd, #350, Los Angeles, CA 90035, USA
Dologuele, Anicet Georges *Prime Minister, Central African Republic*
%Prime Minister's Office, Bangui, Central African Republic
Domar, Evsey D *Economist*
264 Heath's Bridge Road, Concord, MA 01742, USA
Dombasle, Arielle *Actress*
%Agence Intertalent, 5 Rue Clement Marot, 75008 Paris, France
Dombrowski, James M (Jim) *Football Player*
220 Evangeline Dr, Mandeville, LA 70471, USA
Domi, Tim *Hockey Player*
46 Florence St, Ottawa ON K2P 0W7, Canada
Dominczyk, Dagmara *Actress*
%Gersh Agency, 232 N Canon Dr, Beverly Hills, CA 90210, USA
Domingo, Placido *Opera Singer*
Zaungergasse 1-3, Tur 16, 1030 Vienna, Austria
Dominguez Fernandez, Adolfo *Fashion Designer*
Polingono Industrial Calle 4, 32901 San Ciprian de Vinas, Ourense, Spain
Dominis, John *Photographer*
16 Jackson St, East Hampton, NY 11937, USA
Domino, Antoine (Fats) *Singer, Pianist*
5515 Marais St, New Orleans, LA 70117, USA
Dominy, Charles E (Chuck) *Army General*
300 Fox Mill Road, Oakton, VA 22124, USA
Domnanovich, Joseph (Joe) *Football Player*
3101 Lorna Road, #1112, Birmingham, AL 35216, USA
Domres, Martin F (Marty) *Football Player*
24 Mansel Dr, Reistertown, MD 21136, USA
Donahue, Archie G *WW II Marine Air Force Hero*
2402 Lazy Lake Dr, Harlingen, TX 78550, USA
Donahue, Elinor *Actress*
78533 Sunrise Mountain View, Palm Desert, CA 92211, USA
Donahue, Heather *Actress*
%Rigberg Roberts Rugolo, 1180 S Beverly Dr, #601, Los Angeles, CA 90035, USA
Donahue, Kenneth *Museum Director*
245 S Westgate Ave, Los Angeles, CA 90049, USA
Donahue, Phil *Entertainer*
244 Madison Ave, #707, New York, NY 10016, USA
Donahue, Terry *Football Coach, Sportscaster*
9130 Woolley St, Temple City, CA 91780, USA
Donahue, Thomas M *Atmospheric Scientist*
1781 Arlington Blvd, Ann Arbor, MI 48104, USA
Donahue, Thomas R *Labor Leader*
%American Federation of Labor, 815 16th St NW, Washington, DC 20006, USA
Donald, David Herbert *Writer*
41 Lincoln Road, PO Box 158, Lincoln, MA 01773, USA
Donaldson, James *Basketball Player*
2843 34th Ave W, Seattle, WA 98199, USA
Donaldson, Raymond C (Ray) *Football Player*
3520 W 86th St, Indianapolis, IN 46268, USA
Donaldson, Roger *Movie Director*
%Creative Artists Agency, 9830 Wilshire Blvd, Beverly Hills, CA 90212, USA
Donaldson, Samuel A (Sam) *Commentator*
1125 Crest Lane, McLean, VA 22101, USA

D

Donaldson, Simon K *Mathematician*
%Bristol University, Mathematics Dept, Bristol BS8 1TH, England
Donaldson, William H *Financier, Government Official*
%Securities & Exchange Commission, 450 5th St NW, Washington, DC 20549, USA
Donan, Holland R *Football Player*
5918 Almaden Dr, Naples, FL 34119, USA
Donat, Peter *Actor*
PO Box 441, Wolfville NS B0P 1X0, Canada
Donath, Helen *Opera Singer*
Bergstr 5, 30900 Wedemark, Germany
Done, Kenneth S (Ken) *Graphic Artist*
28 Hopetoun Ave, Mosman NSW 2088, Australia
Donegan, Dan *Guitarist (Disturbed)*
%Mitch Schneider Organization, 14724 Ventura Blvd, #410, Sherman Oaks, CA 91403, USA
Donelly, Tanya *Singer, Songwriter*
%Helter Skelter, Plaza, 535 Kings Road, London SW10 0S, England
Donen, Stanley *Movie Director*
30 W 63rd St, #25, New York, NY 10023, USA
Doniger, Wendy *Theologian, Historian*
1319 E 55th St, Chicago, IL 60615, USA
Donlan, Yolande *Actress*
11 Mellina Place, London NW8, England
Donleavy, James Patrick (J P) *Writer*
Levington Park, Mullingar, County Westmeath, Ireland
Donlon, Roger H C *Vietnam War Army Hero (CMH)*
2101 Wilson Ave, Leavenworth, KS 66048, USA
Donnan, Jim *Football Coach*
%University of Georgia, Athletic Dept, Athens, GA 30602, USA
Donnellan, Declan *Theater, Opera Director*
%Cheek by Jowl Theatre Co, Aveline St, London SW11 5DQ, England
Donnelley, James R *Businessman*
%R R Donnelley & Sons, 77 W Wacker Dr, Chicago, IL 60601, USA
Donnelly, Brendan *Baseball Player*
%Anaheim Angels, Edison Field, 2000 Gene Autry Way, Anaheim, CA 92806, USA
Donnelly, Russell J *Physicist*
2175 Olive St, Eugene, OR 97405, USA
Donner, Clive *Movie Director*
20 Thames Reach, 80 Rainville Road, London W6 9HS, England
Donner, Jorn J *Movie Director*
Pohjoisranta 12, 00170 Helsinki 17, Finland
Donner, Richard D *Movie Director*
1444 Forest Knoll, Los Angeles, CA 90069, USA
Donner, Robert *Actor*
3828 Glenridge Dr, Sherman Oaks, CA 91423, USA
Donohoe, Amanda *Actress*
%Markham & Froggatt, Julian House, 4 Windmill St, London W1P 1HF, England
Donohoe, Peter *Concert Pianist*
82 Hampton Lane, Solihull, West Midlands B91 2RS, England
Donohue, Timothy *Businessman*
%Nextel Communications, 2001 Edmund Halley Dr, Reston, VA 20191, USA
Donoso, Jose *Writer*
Calceite, Province of Teruel, Spain
Donovan *Singer, Songwriter*
PO Box 1119, London SW9 9JW, England
Donovan, Alan B *Educator*
%State University of New York College, President's Office, Oneonta, NY 13820, USA
Donovan, Anne *Basketball Player, Coach*
3638 Cordwood Lane, Indianapolis, IN 46214, USA
Donovan, Arthur J (Art), Jr *Football Player*
%Valley Country Club, 1512 Jeffers Road, Baltimore, MD 21204, USA
Donovan, Brian *Journalist*
%Newsday, Editorial Dept, 235 Pinelawn Road, Melville, NY 11747, USA
Donovan, Elisa *Actress*
%Talent Group, 6300 Wilshire Blvd, #2100, Los Angeles, CA 90048, USA
Donovan, Francis R (Frank) *Navy Admiral*
9216 Dellwood Dr, Vienna, VA 22180, USA
Donovan, Jason S *Singer, Actor*
%Richard East Productions, PO Box 342, South Yarra VIC 3141, Australia
Donovan, Landon *Soccer Player*
%San Jose Earthquakes, 3550 Stevens Creek Blvd, #200, San Jose, CA 95117, USA
Donovan, Martin *Actor*
%Paradigm Agency, 10100 Santa Monica Blvd, #2500, Los Angeles, CA 90067, USA
Donovan, Raymond J *Secretary, Labor*
1600 Paterson Park Road, Secaucusm NJ 07094, USA
Donovan, Tate *Actor*
8033 W Sunset Blvd, #831, West Hollywood, CA 90046, USA
Doob, Joseph L *Mathematician*
101 W Windsor Road, #1104, Urbana, IL 61802, USA

Doody, Alison *Actress*
%Julian Belfarge, 46 Albermarle St, London W1X 4PP, England
Doohan, James *Actor*
%DoFame, PO Box 2800, Redmond, WA 98073, USA
Dooley, Paul *Actor*
%Innovative Artists, 1505 10th St, Santa Monica, CA 90401, USA
Dooley, Thomas *Soccer Player*
28391 Daroca, Mission Viejo, CA 92692, USA
Dooley, Vincent J (Vince) *Football Player, Coach, Administrator*
%University of Georgia, Athletic Dept, PO Box 1472, Athens, GA 30603, USA
Dooling, Keyon *Basketball Player*
%Los Angeles Clippers, Staples Center, 1111 S Figueroa St, Los Angeles, CA 90015, USA
Doran, Walter F *Navy Admiral*
Chairman, Joint Chiefs of Staff, Pentagon, Washington, DC 20318, USA
Dore, Andre *Hockey Player*
73 Betsys Lane, Kingston ON K7M 7B6, Canada
Dore, Patricia *Actress*
%Cineart, 36 Rue de Ponthieu, 75008 Paris, France
Dore, Ronald Philip *Educator*
157 Surrenden Road, Brighton, East Sussex BN1 6ZA, England
Dorensky, Sergey L *Concert Pianist*
Bryusov Per 8/10, #75, Moscow 103009, Russia
Dorff, Stephen *Actor*
%Endeavor Talent Agency, 9701 Wilshire Blvd, #1000, Beverly Hills, CA 90212, USA
Dorfman, Ariel *Writer*
%Duke University, International Studies Center, 2122 Campus Dr, Durham, NC 27706, USA
Dorfman, Dan *Columnist, Commentator*
%CBS-TV, News Dept, 51 W 52nd St, New York, NY 10019, USA
Dorfmeister, Michaela *Alpine Skier*
Quellensteig, 2763 Neusiedl, Austria
Dorin, Francoise A R *Writer, Actress*
%Artmedia, 20 Ave Rapp, 75007 Paris, France
Dorio, Gabriella *Track Athlete*
%Federation of Light Athletics, Viale Tiaiano 70, 00196 Rome, Italy
Dority, Douglas H *Labor Leader*
%United Food & Commercial Workers Union, 1775 K St NW, Washington, DC 20006, USA
Dorman, David *Businessman*
%American Telephone & Telegraph Corp, 32 Ave of Americas, New York, NY 10013, USA
Dorman, Gerald D *Physician*
2365 Village Lane, Orient, NY 11957, USA
Dorman, Lee *Bassist (Iron Butterfly)*
%Entertainment Services Int'l, 6400 Pleasant Park Dr, Chanhassen, MN 55317, USA
Dorn, Michael *Actor*
115 N Orange Dr, Los Angeles, CA 90036, USA
Dorney, Keith R *Football Player*
2450 Blucher Valley Road, Sebastopol, CA 95472, USA
Doronina, Tatyana *Actress*
%Gorky Arts Theater, 22 Tverskoi Blvd, 119146 Moscow, Russia
Dorough, Howie *Singer (Backstreet Boys)*
%Mitch Schneider Organization, 14724 Ventura Blvd, #410, Sherman Oaks, CA 91403, USA
Dorrell, Karl *Football Coach*
%University of California, Athletic Dept, Los Angeles, CA 90024, USA
Dorroh, Jefferson D *WW II Marine Corps Air Force Hero*
24603 12th Ave S, Des Moines, WA 98198, USA
Dorsen, Norman *Attorney*
%New York University, Law School, 40 Washington Square S, New York, NY 10012, USA
Dorsett, Anthony D (Tony) *Football Player*
%D A Chemical, 2415 Midway Road, #105, Carrollton, TX 75006, USA
Dorsey, Ken *Football Player*
%San Francisco 49ers, 4949 Centennial Blvd, Santa Clara, CA 95054, USA
Dos Santos, Alexandre J M Cardinal *Religious Leader*
Paco Arquiepiscopal, Avenida Eduardo Mondlane 1448, CP Maputo, Mozambique
Dos Santos, Jose Eduardo *President, Angola*
%President's Office, Palacio do Povo, Luanda, Angola
Doshi, Balkkrishna V *Architect*
Sangath, Thaltej Road, Almedabad 380 054, India
Doss, Desmond T *WW II Army Medical Corps Hero (CMH)*
4600 Highway 157, Lookout Mountain, Rising Fawn, GA 30738, USA
Dotrice, Roy *Actor*
%Lord, 6 Meadow Lane, Leasingham, Sleaford, Lincolnshire NG34 8LL, England
Dotson, Richard E (Rich) *Baseball Player*
7 Colonel Watson Dr, New Richmond, OH 45157, USA
Dotson, Santana *Football Player*
11002 Greenbay St, Houston, TX 77024, USA
Dotter, Bobby *Auto/Truck Racing Driver*
%MPH Racing, 118 Stutt Road, Mooresville, NC 28117, USA
Doty, Paul M *Biochemist*
4 Kirland Place, Cambridge, MA 02138, USA

Douaihy, Saliba *Artist*
Vining Road, Windham, NY 12496, USA
Doucet, Michael *Singer, Fiddler (BeauSoleil)*
%Rosebud Agency, PO Box 170429, San Francisco, CA 94117, USA
Doucett, Linda *Actress, Model*
%Michael Slessinger, 8730 Sunset Blvd, #220W, Los Angeles, CA 90069, USA
Dougan, Angel Serafin Seriche *Prime Minister, Equatorial Guinea*
%Prime Minister's Office, Malabo, Equatorial Guinea
Dougherty, Dennis A *Chemist*
1817 Bushnell Ave, South Pasadena, CA 91030, USA
Dougherty, Ed *Golfer*
448 SW Fairway Vista, Port Saint Lucie, FL 34986, USA
Dougherty, James J *Labor Leader*
%Plasters' & Cement Masons' Int'l, 14405 Laurel Place, Laurel, MD 20707, USA
Dougherty, William A, Jr *Navy Admiral*
1505 Colonial Court, Arlington, VA 22209, USA
Douglas, Anslem *Composer, Entertainer*
%JW Records, 2833 Church Ave, Brooklyn, NY 11226, USA
Douglas, Barry *Concert Pianist*
%I C M Artists, 40 W 57th St, New York, NY 10019, USA
Douglas, Carol *Singer*
%Famous Artists Agency, 250 W 57th St, New York, NY 10107, USA
Douglas, Cathleen *Lawyer, Conservationist*
815 Connecticut Ave NW, Washington, DC 20006, USA
Douglas, Denzil L *Prime Minister, Saint Kitts & Nevis*
%Premier's Office, Government Building, Basseterre, Saint Kitts & Nevis
Douglas, Donna *Actress*
PO Box 1511, Huntington Beach, CA 92647, USA
Douglas, Hugh *Football Player*
%Jacksonville Jaguars, 1 AllTel Stadium Place, Jacksonville, FL 32202, USA
Douglas, Illeana *Actress*
%Baumgarten Agency, 1041 N Formosa Ave, #200, West Hollywood, CA 90046, USA
Douglas, James (Buster) *Boxer*
PO Box 342, Johnstown, OH 43031, USA
Douglas, Jerry *Actor*
17336 Rancho St, Encino, CA 91316, USA
Douglas, Kirk *Actor*
805 N Rexford Dr, Beverly Hills, CA 90210, USA
Douglas, Leon *Basketball Player*
PO Box 58, Leighton, AL 35646, USA
Douglas, Michael K *Actor, Director, Producer*
%William Morris Agency, 151 El Camino Dr, Beverly Hills, CA 90212, USA
Douglas, Sarah *Actress*
%Craig Mgmt, 125 S Sycamore Ave, Los Angeles, CA 90036, USA
Douglas, Sherman *Basketball Player*
%New Jersey Nets, 390 Murray Hill Parkway, East Rutherford, NJ 07073, USA
Douglass, Dale *Golfer*
100 Coulter Place, Castle Rock, CO 80108, USA
Douglass, Michael R (Mike) *Football Player*
1725 Porterfield Place, El Cajon, CA 92019, USA
Douglass, Robyn *Actress*
1301 S Federal St, Chicago, IL 60605, USA
Dourda, Abu Zaid Umar *Prime Minister, Libya*
%Prime Minister's Office, Bab el Aziziya Barracks, Tripoli, Libya
Dourdan, Gary *Actor*
%GMA, 10100 Santa Monica Blvd, #2500, Los Angeles, CA 90067, USA
Dourif, Brad *Actor*
%Innovative Artists, 1505 10th St, Santa Monica, CA 90401, USA
Dove, Rita F *Writer*
1757 Lambs Road, Charlottesville, VA 22901, USA
Dove, Robert (Bob) *Football Player*
6 Neff Dr, Canfield, OH 44406, USA
Dove, Ronnie *Singer*
%Ken Keene Artists, PO Box 1875, Gretna, LA 70054, USA
Dow, Peggy *Actress*
2121 S Yorktown Ave, Tulsa, OK 74114, USA
Dow, Tony *Actor*
%Diamond Artists, 215 N Barrington Ave, Los Angeles, CA 90049, USA
Dowd, Maureen *Columnist*
%New York Times, Editorial Dept, 229 W 43rd St, New York, NY 10036, USA
Dowdle, Walter R *Microbiologist*
1708 Mason Mill Road, Atlanta, GA 30329, USA
Dowdy, Steven *Medical Researcher*
%Howard Hughes Medical Institute, Washington University, Saint Louis, MO 63110, USA
Dowell, Anthony J *Ballet Dancer*
%Royal Ballet, Covent Garden, Bow St, London WC2E 9DD, England
Dower, John W *Writer*
%Massachusetts Institute of Technology, History Dept, Cambridge, MA 02139, USA

Dowle, David *Drummer (Whitesnake)*
%Int'l Talent Booking, 27A Floral St, #300, London WC2E 9DQ, England
Dowler, Boyd H *Football Player*
%Carr Assoc, 2303 S Lila Lane, Tampa, FL 33629, USA
Dowling, Doris *Actress*
9026 Elevado Ave, Los Angeles, CA 90069, USA
Dowling, John E *Biologist, Neurobiologist*
135 Charles St, Boston, MA 02114, USA
Dowling, Robert J *Editor, Publisher*
%Hollywood Reporter, 5055 Wilshire Blvd, Los Angeles, CA 90036, USA
Dowling, Vincent *Theater Director, Writer*
322 East River Road, Huntington, MA 01050, USA
Down, Lesley-Anne *Actress*
%Artists Group, 10100 Santa Monica Blvd, #2490, Los Angeles, CA 90067, USA
Down, Sarah *Cartoonist (Betsey's Buddies)*
%Playboy Magazine, Reader Services, 680 N Lake Shore Dr, Chicago, IL 60611, USA
Downes, Edward *Conductor*
%Royal Opera House, Covent Garden, London WC2E 9DD, England
Downey, Robert J *Movie Director*
55 W 900 S, Salt Lake City, UT 84101, USA
Downey, Robert, Jr *Actor*
1 Christopher St, #15F, New York, NY 10014, USA
Downey, Roma *Actress*
55 W 900 St, Salt Lake City, UT 84101, USA
Downie, Gordon *Singer (Tragically Hip)*
%Management Trust, 219 Dufferin St, #309B, Toronto ON M5K 3J1, Canada
Downie, Leonard, Jr *Editor*
%Washington Post, Editorial Dept, 1150 15th St NW, Washington, DC 20071, USA
Downing, Alphonso E (Al) *Baseball Player*
25399 Old Road, #108, Newhall, CA 91381, USA
Downing, Big Al *Singer/Pianist*
%Tessier-Marsh Talent, 2825 Blue Book Dr, Nashville, TN 37214, USA
Downing, Brian J *Baseball Player*
8095 County Road 135, Celina, TX 75009, USA
Downing, George *Surfer*
%Get Wet!, 3021 Waialee Ave, Honolulu, HI 96816, USA
Downing, Kathryn *Publisher*
%Mypotential.com, 2821 Main St, Santa Monica, CA 90405, USA
Downing, Walt *Football Player*
1141 Durham Circle NW, Massillon, OH 44646, USA
Downing, Wayne A *General, Army*
11200 N Pawnee Road, Peoria, IL 61615, USA
Downs, Hugh M *Commentator*
%Arizona State University, Human Communications Dept, Tempe, AZ 85287, USA
Dowson, Philip M *Architect*
%Royal Academy of the Arts, Piccadilly, London W1V 0DS, England
Doyle, Chris *Cinematographer*
10866 Wilshire Blvd, #1000, Los Angeles, CA 90024, USA
Doyle, James H, Jr *Navy Admiral*
5121 Baltan Road, Bethesda, MD 20816, USA
Doyle, Patrick *Composer*
%Air-Edel, 18 Rodmarton St, London W1H 3FW, England
Doyle, Roddy *Writer*
%Secker & Warburg, 38A West Road, Bromsgrove, Worc B60 2NQ, England
Doyle-Murray, Brian *Actor, Comedian*
555 W 57th St, #1230, New York, NY 10019, USA
Dozier, James L *Army General*
2150 Channel Way, North Fort Myers, FL 33917, USA
Dozier, Lamont *Singer, Songwriter*
%McMullen Co, 433 N Camden Dr, #400, Beverly Hills, CA 90210, USA
Dr Demento *Entertainer*
6102 Pimenta Ave, Lakewood, CA 90712, USA
Dr Dre *Rap Artist*
%Richard Walters, 1800 Argyle Ave, #408, Los Angeles, CA 90028, USA
Dr John *Jazz Pianist, Singer, Songwriter*
%Impact Artists, 121 W 27th St, #1001, New York, NY 10001, USA
Drabble, Margaret *Writer*
%P F D, Drury House, 34-43 Russell St, London WC2B 5HA, England
Drabek, Douglas D (Doug) *Baseball Player*
15 Ivy Pond Place, The Woodlands, TX 77381, USA
Drabinsky, Garth H *Theater Producer*
%Livent Inc, 165 Avenue Road, #600, Toronto ON M5R 3S4, Canada
Drabowsky, Myron W (Moe) *Baseball Player*
4741 Oak Run Dr, Sarasota, FL 34243, USA
Draffen, Willis *Singer (Bloodstone)*
16103 Vista Del Mar Dr, Houston, TX 77083, USA
Draglia, Stacy *Track Athlete*
1112 E Monte Cristo Ave, Phoenix, AZ 85022, USA

D

Drago, Billy *Actor*
3800 Barham Blvd, #303, Los Angeles, CA 90068, USA
Drago, Richard A (Dick) *Baseball Player*
12626 Castle Hill Dr, Tampa, FL 33624, USA
Dragon, Daryl *Musician (Captain & Tennille)*
7123 Franktown Road, Carson City, NV 89704, USA
Dragoti, Stan *Movie Director*
1800 Ave of Stars, #430, Los Angeles, CA 90067, USA
Dragojevic, Srdjan *Movie Director, Writer*
%William Morris Agency, 151 El Camino Dr, Beverly Hills, CA 90212, USA
Drai, Victor *Movie Producer*
10527 Bellagio Road, Beverly Hills, CA 90210, USA
Draiman, Dave *Singer (Disturbed)*
%Mitch Schneider Organization, 14724 Ventura Blvd, #410, Sherman Oaks, CA 91403, USA
Drake, Betsy *Actress*
10850 Wilshire Blvd, #575, Los Angeles, CA 90024, USA
Drake, Dallas *Hockey Player*
11472 E Cedar Bay Trail, Traverse City, MI 49684, USA
Drake, Frank D *Astronomer*
%University of California, Lick Observatory, Santa Cruz, CA 9064, USA
Drake, Jeremy *Astronomer*
%Harvard-Smithsonian Center for Astrophysics, Cambridge, MA 02138, USA
Drake, Judith *Actress*
%20th Century Artists, 4605 Lankershim Blvd, #305, North Hollywood, CA 91602, USA
Drake, Juel D *Labor Leader*
%Iron Workers Union, 1750 New York Ave NW, Washington, DC 20006, USA
Drake, Larry *Actor*
15260 Ventura Blvd, #2100, Sherman Oaks, CA 91403, USA
Draper, E Lynn, Jr *Businessman*
%American Electric Power, 1 Riverside Plaza, Columbus, OH 43215, USA
Draper, Polly *Actress*
1324 N Orange Grove, West Hollywood, CA 90046, USA
Draper, William H, III *Financier*
91 Tallwood Court, Atherton, CA 94027, USA
Drasner, Fred *Publisher*
%New York Daily News, 220 E 42nd St, New York, NY 10017, USA
Dratch, Rachel *Actress, Comedienne*
%Michael Mann Talent, 617 S Olive St, #311, Los Angeles, CA 90014, USA
Dravecky, David F (Dave) *Baseball Player*
%Outreach of Hope, 13840 Gleneagle Dr, Colorado Springs, CO 80921, USA
Draves, Victoria (Vickie) *Diver*
23842 Shady Tree Circle, Laguna Niguel, CA 92677, USA
Drayton, Charlie *Drummer (B-52's)*
%Direct Management Group, 947 N La Cienega Blvd, #2, Los Angeles, CA 90069, USA
Dre *Rap Artist*
%Family Tree Entertainment, 135 E 57th St, #2600, New York, NY 10022, USA
Drechsler, Heike *Track Athlete*
%LAC Chemnitz, Reichenhainer Str 154, 09125 Chemnitz, Germany
Dreesen, Tom *Actor, Comedian*
14538 Benefit St, #301, Sherman Oaks, CA 91403, USA
Dreifuss, Ruth *President, Switzerland*
%Federal Chancellery, Bundeshaus-W, Bundesgasse, 3033 Berne, Switzerland
Drell, Persis *Physicist*
%Stanford University, Linear Accelerator Center, Stanford, CA 94305, USA
Drell, Sidney D *Physicist*
570 Alvarado Row, Stanford, CA 94305, USA
Drescher, Fran *Actress*
%International Creative Mgmt, 8942 Wilshire Blvd, #219, Beverly Hills, CA 90211, USA
Dreschler, David *Football Player*
1135 Arabian Farms Road, Clover, SC 29710, USA
Dresselhaus, Mildred S *Physicist, Electrical Engineer*
%Energy Department, 1000 Independence Ave SW, Washington, DC 20585, USA
Drew, B Alvin *Astronaut*
2814 Lighthouse Dr, Houston, TX 77058, USA
Drew, David Jonathan (J D) *Baseball Player*
%Saint Louis Cardinals, Busch Stadium, 250 Stadium Plaza, Saint Louis, MO 63102, USA
Drew, Dennis *Keyboardist (10000 Maniacs)*
%Agency for Performing Arts, 9200 Sunset Blvd, #900, Los Angeles, CA 90069, USA
Drew, Elizabeth H *Publisher*
%Avon/William Morrow, 1350 Ave of Americas, New York, NY 10019, USA
Drew, Griffin *Actress, Model*
PO Box 16753, Beverly Hills, CA 90209, USA
Drew, Larry *Basketball Player*
4942 Densmore Ave, Encino, CA 91436, USA
Drew, Urban *WW II Army Air Corps Hero*
451 Neptune Ave, Encinitas, CA 92024, USA
Drexler, Clyde *Basketball Player, Coach*
%Dade/Schultz, 6442 Coldwater Canyon Ave, #206, North Hollywood, CA 91606, USA

Dreyfus, George *Composer*
3 Grace St, Camberwell VIC 3124, Australia
Dreyfus, Lee S *Governor, WI*
3159 Madison St, Waukesha, WI 53188, USA
Dreyfuss, Richard S *Actor*
PO Box 10459, Burbank, CA 91510, USA
Drickamer, Harry G *Chemical Engineer*
304 E Pennsylvania Ave, Urbana, IL 61801, USA
Driedger, Florence G *Social Agency Executive*
3833 Montaigne St, Regina SK S4S 3J6, Canada
Driessen, Daniel (Dan) *Baseball Player*
97 William Hilton Parkway, Hilton Head, SC 29926, USA
Drinan, Robert F *Educator, Representative, MA*
%Georgetown University, 1507 Isherwood St NE, #1, Washington, DC 20002, USA
Drinfeld, Vladimir *Mathematician*
%Steklov Mathematics Institute, 42 Vavilova, 117966 ESP-1 Moscow, Russia
Driver, Bruce *Hockey Player*
21A Crest Terrace, Montville, NJ 07045, USA
Driver, Minnie *Actress*
%Lou Coulson, 37 Berwick St, London W1V 3RF, England
Driver, William J *Government Official*
215 W Columbia St, Falls Church, VA 22046, USA
Drnovsek, Janez *Prime Minister, Slovenia*
%Prime Minister's Office, Gregorcicova St 20, 61000 Ljublijana, Slovenia
Droge, Pete *Singer, Songwriter*
1423 34th Ave, Seattle, WA 98122, USA
Dropo, Walter (Walt) *Baseball Player*
65 E India Row, Boston, MA 02110, USA
Drosdick, John G *Businessman*
%Sunoco Inc, 10 Penn Center, 1801 Market St, Philadelphia, PA 19103, USA
Drozdova, Margarita S *Ballerina*
%Stanislavsky Musical Theater, Pushkinskaya Str 17, Moscow, Russia
Drucker, Eugene *Violinist (Emerson String Quartet)*
%I M G Artists, 3 Burlington Lane, Chiswick, London W4 2TH, England
Drucker, Mort *Cartoonist (Ort)*
%Famous Artists Agency, 250 W 57th St, New York, NY 10107, USA
Drucker, Peter F *Educator, Management Consultant, Writer*
636 Wellesley Dr, Claremont, CA 91711, USA
Druk, Mirchea *Prime Minister, Moldova*
Str 31 August 123, #7, 277012 Kishinev, Moldova
Druker, Brian J *Ococologist, Hematologist*
%Oregon Health Science University, Cancer Research Center, Portland, OR 97201, USA
Drummond, Alice *Actress*
351 E 50th St, New York, NY 10003, USA
Drummond, Jonathan (Jon) *Track Athlete*
113 Cascade Lake St, Las Vegas, NV 89148, USA
Drummond, Roscoe *Columnist*
6637 MacLean Dr, Olde Dominion Square, McLean, VA 22101, USA
Drury, Chris *Hockey Player*
57 W Oak Hills Dr, Castle Rock, CO 80108, USA
Drury, James *Actor*
12126 Osage Park Dr, Houston, TX 77065, USA
Drury, Ted *Hockey Player*
64 Glenwood Ave, Point Lookout, NY 11569, USA
Drut, Guy J *Track Athlete*
Mairie, 77120 Coulommiers, France
Dryburgh, Stuart *Cinematographer*
%Sandra Marsh Mgmt, 9150 Wilshire Blvd, #220, Beverly Hills, CA 90212, USA
Dryden, Kenneth W (Ken) *Hockey Player*
58 Poplar Plains Road, Toronto ON M4V 2M8, Canada
Dryer, J Frederick (Fred) *Football Player, Actor*
4117 Radford Ave, Studio City, CA 91604, USA
Dryke, Matthew (Matt) *Marksman*
4702 Davis Ave S, #2B102, Renton, WA 98055, USA
Drysdale, Cliff *Tennis Player, Sportscaster*
%Landfall, 1801 Eastwood Road, #F, Wilmington, NC 28403, USA
Duany, Andres *Architect*
%Duany & Plater-Zyberk Architects, 1023 SW 25th Ave, Miami, FL 33135, USA
Dubbels, Britta *Model*
%Ford Model Agency, 142 Greene St, #400, New York, NY 10012, USA
Dubbie, Curtis *Religious Leader*
%Church of Brethren, 1451 Dundee Ave, Elgin, IL 60120, USA
Dube, Joseph (Joe) *Weightlifter*
8821 Eaton Ave, Jacksonville, FL 32211, USA
Dubia, John A *Army General*
1154 N Pitt St, Alexandria, VA 22314, USA
Dubinbaum, Gail *Opera Singer*
%Metropolitan Opera Assn, Lincoln Center Plaza, New York, NY 10023, USA

D

Dubinin, Yuri V *Government Official, Russia*
Gazprom RAO, Nametkina Str 16, Moscow 117884, Russia
DuBois, Ja'Net *Actress*
8306 Wilshire Blvd, #189, Beverly Hills, CA 90211, USA
DuBois, Marta *Actress*
%Three Moons Entertainment, 5441 E Beverly Blvd, #G, Los Angeles, CA 90022, USA
DuBose, G Thomas *Labor Leader*
%United Transportation Union, 14600 Detroit Ave, Cleveland, OH 44107, USA
Dubus, Andre, III *Writer*
%Penguin Group, 375 Hudson St, New York, NY 10014, USA
Dubzinski, Walt *Football Player*
158 Lovewell St, Gardner, MA 01440, USA
Ducasse, Alain *Chef*
%Louis XV Restaurant, Hotel de Paris, Monte Carlo, Monaco
Duchesnay, Isabelle *Ice Dancer*
Im Steinach 30, 87561 Oberstdorf, Germany
Duchesnay, Paul *Figure Skater*
%Bundesleistungszentrum, Rossbichstr 2-6, 87561 Oberstdorf, Germany
Duchin, Peter *Jazz Pianist, Band Leader*
%Peter Duchin Orchestra, 60 E 42nd St, #1625, New York, NY 10165, USA
Duchovny, David *Actor*
%Creative Artists Agency, 9830 Wilshire Blvd, Beverly Hills, CA 90212, USA
DuCille, Michel *Photojournalist*
9571 Pine Meadow Lane, Burke, VA 22015, USA
Ducsmal, Agnieszka *Conductor*
%Polish Radio Orchestra, Al Marchinkowskiego 3, 61-745 Pozna, Poland
Dudek, Joseph A (Joe) *Football Player*
17 Adams Dr, Hudson, NH 03051, USA
Duden, H Richard (Dick), Jr *Football Player*
900 Bestgate Road, Annapolis, MD 21401, USA
Duderstadt, James J *Government Official, Educator*
%National Science Foundation, 1800 G St NW, Washington, DC 20006, USA
Dudikoff, Michael *Actor*
4341 Birch St, #201, Newport Beach, CA 92660, USA
Dudley, Chris *Basketball Player*
1150 Fairway Road, Lake Oswego, OR 97034, USA
Dudley, Jaquelin *Microbiologist*
%University of Texas, Microbiology Dept, Austin, TX 78712, USA
Dudley, Rick *Hockey Player, Coach, Executive*
921 NW 118th Lane, Coral Springs, FL 33071, USA
Dudley, Rickey *Football Player*
23968 Cottage Trail, Olmsted Falls, OH 44138, USA
Dudley, William M (Bill) *Football Player*
303 Barkley Court, Lynchburg, VA 24503, USA
Duenkel Fuldner, Virginia *Swimmer*
2132 NE 17th Terrace, #500, Wilton Manors, FL 33305, USA
Duerson, David R (Dave) *Football Player*
2605 Kelly Lane, Highland Park, IL 60035, USA
Dufay, Rick *Guitarist (Aerosmith)*
%H K Mgmt, 9200 W Sunset Blvd, #530, Los Angeles, CA 90069, USA
Duff, John B *Educator*
%Columbia College, President's Office, Chicago, IL 60605, USA
Duff, John E *Sculptor*
7 Doyers St, New York, NY 10013, USA
Duff, T Richard (Dick) *Hockey Player*
4-7 Elmwood Ave S, Mississauga ON L5G 3J6, Canada
Duffield, David *Businessman*
%PeopleSoft Inc, 4460 Hacienda Dr, Pleasanton, CA 94588, USA
Duffner, Mark *Football Coach*
%University of Maryland, Athletic Dept, College Park, MD 20740, USA
Duffy, Brian *Astronaut*
2260 Marsh Harbor Ave, Merritt Island, FL 32952, USA
Duffy, Brian *Editorial Cartoonist*
%Des Moines Register, Editorial Dept, PO Box 957, Des Moines, IA 50304, USA
Duffy, J C *Cartoonist (Fusco Brothers)*
%Universal Press Syndicate, 4520 Main St, Kansas City, MO 64111, USA
Duffy, James *Businessman*
%Saint Paul Companies, 385 Washington St, Saint Paul, MN 55102, USA
Duffy, John *Composer*
%Meet the Composer, 2112 Broadway, New York, NY 10023, USA
Duffy, Julia *Actress*
%Lacey, 5699 Kanan Road, #285, Agoura, CA 91301, USA
Duffy, Karen *Actress, Model*
%Ford Model Agency, 142 Greene St, #400, New York, NY 10012, USA
Duffy, Keith *Singer (Boyzone)*
%Carol Assoc-War Mgmt, Bushy Park Road, 57 Meadowgate, Dublin, Ireland
Duffy, Patrick *Actor*
PO Box 1, Eagle Point, OR 97524, USA

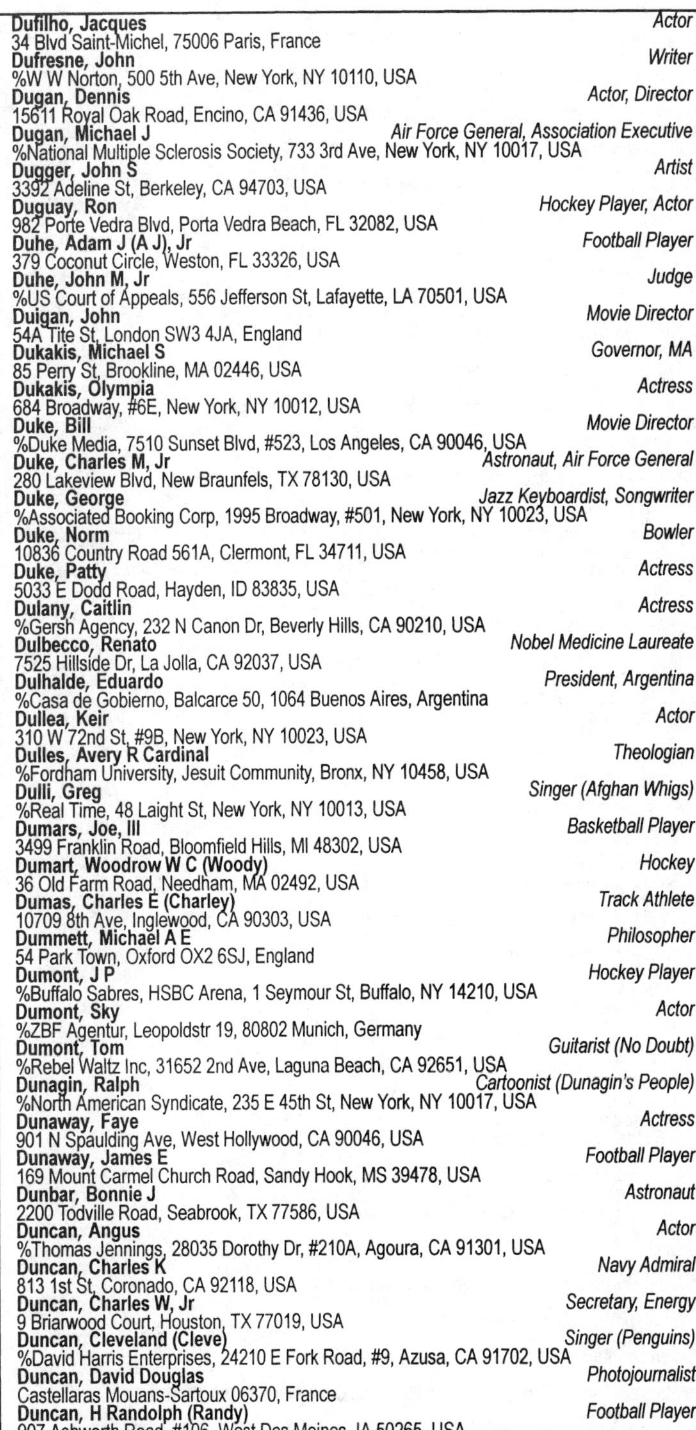

Dufilho, Jacques *Actor*
34 Blvd Saint-Michel, 75006 Paris, France

Dufresne, John *Writer*
%W W Norton, 500 5th Ave, New York, NY 10110, USA

Dugan, Dennis *Actor, Director*
15611 Royal Oak Road, Encino, CA 91436, USA

Dugan, Michael J *Air Force General, Association Executive*
%National Multiple Sclerosis Society, 733 3rd Ave, New York, NY 10017, USA

Dugger, John S *Artist*
3392 Adeline St, Berkeley, CA 94703, USA

Duguay, Ron *Hockey Player, Actor*
982 Porte Vedra Blvd, Porta Vedra Beach, FL 32082, USA

Duhe, Adam J (A J), Jr *Football Player*
379 Coconut Circle, Weston, FL 33326, USA

Duhe, John M, Jr *Judge*
%US Court of Appeals, 556 Jefferson St, Lafayette, LA 70501, USA

Duigan, John *Movie Director*
54A Tite St, London SW3 4JA, England

Dukakis, Michael S *Governor, MA*
85 Perry St, Brookline, MA 02446, USA

Dukakis, Olympia *Actress*
684 Broadway, #6E, New York, NY 10012, USA

Duke, Bill *Movie Director*
%Duke Media, 7510 Sunset Blvd, #523, Los Angeles, CA 90046, USA

Duke, Charles M, Jr *Astronaut, Air Force General*
280 Lakeview Blvd, New Braunfels, TX 78130, USA

Duke, George *Jazz Keyboardist, Songwriter*
%Associated Booking Corp, 1995 Broadway, #501, New York, NY 10023, USA

Duke, Norm *Bowler*
10836 Country Road 561A, Clermont, FL 34711, USA

Duke, Patty *Actress*
5033 E Dodd Road, Hayden, ID 83835, USA

Dulany, Caitlin *Actress*
%Gersh Agency, 232 N Canon Dr, Beverly Hills, CA 90210, USA

Dulbecco, Renato *Nobel Medicine Laureate*
7525 Hillside Dr, La Jolla, CA 92037, USA

Dulhalde, Eduardo *President, Argentina*
%Casa de Gobierno, Balcarce 50, 1064 Buenos Aires, Argentina

Dullea, Keir *Actor*
310 W 72nd St, #9B, New York, NY 10023, USA

Dulles, Avery R Cardinal *Theologian*
%Fordham University, Jesuit Community, Bronx, NY 10458, USA

Dulli, Greg *Singer (Afghan Whigs)*
%Real Time, 48 Laight St, New York, NY 10013, USA

Dumars, Joe, III *Basketball Player*
3499 Franklin Road, Bloomfield Hills, MI 48302, USA

Dumart, Woodrow W C (Woody) *Hockey*
36 Old Farm Road, Needham, MA 02492, USA

Dumas, Charles E (Charley) *Track Athlete*
10709 8th Ave, Inglewood, CA 90303, USA

Dummett, Michael A E *Philosopher*
54 Park Town, Oxford OX2 6SJ, England

Dumont, J P *Hockey Player*
%Buffalo Sabres, HSBC Arena, 1 Seymour St, Buffalo, NY 14210, USA

Dumont, Sky *Actor*
%ZBF Agentur, Leopoldstr 19, 80802 Munich, Germany

Dumont, Tom *Guitarist (No Doubt)*
%Rebel Waltz Inc, 31652 2nd Ave, Laguna Beach, CA 92651, USA

Dunagin, Ralph *Cartoonist (Dunagin's People)*
%North American Syndicate, 235 E 45th St, New York, NY 10017, USA

Dunaway, Faye *Actress*
901 N Spaulding Ave, West Hollywood, CA 90046, USA

Dunaway, James E *Football Player*
169 Mount Carmel Church Road, Sandy Hook, MS 39478, USA

Dunbar, Bonnie J *Astronaut*
2200 Todville Road, Seabrook, TX 77586, USA

Duncan, Angus *Actor*
%Thomas Jennings, 28035 Dorothy Dr, #210A, Agoura, CA 91301, USA

Duncan, Charles K *Navy Admiral*
813 1st St, Coronado, CA 92118, USA

Duncan, Charles W, Jr *Secretary, Energy*
9 Briarwood Court, Houston, TX 77019, USA

Duncan, Cleveland (Cleve) *Singer (Penguins)*
%David Harris Enterprises, 24210 E Fork Road, #9, Azusa, CA 91702, USA

Duncan, David Douglas *Photojournalist*
Castellaras Mouans-Sartoux 06370, France

Duncan, H Randolph (Randy) *Football Player*
907 Ashworth Road, #106, West Des Moines, IA 50265, USA

D

Duncan - Dunn

Duncan, Lindsay — *Actress*
%Ken McReddie, 91 Regent St, London W1R 7TB, England
Duncan, Mariano — *Baseball Player*
Ingenio Angelina #137, San Pedro de Macoris, Dominican Republic
Duncan, Michael Clark — *Actor*
%Dolores Robinson, 9250 Wilshire Blvd, #220, Beverly Hills, CA 90212, USA
Duncan, Robert — *Astrophysicist*
%University of Texas, Astronomy Dept, Austin, TX 78712, USA
Duncan, Sandy — *Actress*
%Litke/Gale Madden, 1640 S Sepulveda Blvd, #530, Los Angeles, CA 90025, USA
Duncan, Tim — *Basketball Player*
%San Antonio Spurs, Alamodome, 1 SBC Center, San Antonio, TX 78219, USA
Dundee, Angelo — *Boxing Manager*
1487 Camellia Circle, Weston, FL 33326, USA
Dunderstadt, James — *Educator*
%University of Michigan, President's Office, Ann Arbor, MI 48109, USA
Dungy, Tony — *Football Coach*
16604 Villalenda de Avila, Tampa, FL 33613, USA
Dunham, Archie W — *Businessman*
%ConocoPhillips Inc, 600 N Dairy Ashford, Houston, TX 77079, USA
Dunham, Chip — *Cartoonist (Overboard)*
%Universal Press Syndicate, 4520 Main St, Kansas City, MO 64111, USA
Dunham, Duane R — *Businessman*
%Bethlehem Steel Corp, 1170 8th Ave, Bethlehem, PA 18016, USA
Dunham, John L — *Businessman*
%May Department Stores, 611 Olive St, Saint Louis, MO 63101, USA
Dunham, Katherine — *Dancer, Choreographer*
%Children's Workshop, 532 N 10th St, East Saint Louis, IL 62201, USA
Dunham, Michael (Mike) — *Hockey Player*
277 Gloucester Court, Matawan, NJ 07747, USA
Dunham, Russell E — *WW II Army Hero (CMH)*
31405 Sunderland Road, Jerseyville, IL 62052, USA
Dunitz, Jack D — *Chemist*
Obere Heslibachstr 77, 8700 Kusnacht, Switzerland
Dunkle, Nancy — *Basketball Player*
%University of California, Campus Police, Berkeley, CA 94720, USA
Dunlap, Alexander W — *Astronaut*
721 Parkside Dr, Woodstock, GA 30188, USA
Dunlap, Carla — *Bodybuilder*
%Diamond, 732 Irvington Ave, Maplewood, NJ 07040, USA
Dunlap, Robert H — *WW II Marine Corps Hero (CMH)*
PO Box 584, Monmouth, IL 61462, USA
Dunleavy, Mary — *Opera Singer*
%Columbia Artists Mgmt Inc, 165 W 57th St, New York, NY 10019, USA
Dunleavy, Michael J (Mike) — *Basketball Player, Coach*
555 S Barrington Ave, Los Angeles, CA 90049, USA
Dunleavy, Mike — *Basketball Player*
%Golden State Warriors, 1001 Broadway, Oakland, CA 94607, USA
Dunlop, Andy — *Guitarist (Travis)*
%Wildlife Entertainment, 21 Heathmans Road, London SW6 4TJ, England
Dunn, Adam — *Baseball Player*
%Cincinnati Reds, Cinergy Field, 100 Riverfront Stadium, Cincinnati, OH 45202, USA
Dunn, Andrew W — *Cinematographer*
525 Broadway, #250, Santa Monica, CA 90401, USA
Dunn, Gregory — *Publisher*
%Redbook Magazine, 224 W 57th St, New York, NY 10019, USA
Dunn, Halbert L — *Statistician*
3637 Edelmar Terrace, Silver Spring, MD 20906, USA
Dunn, Holly — *Singer, Songwriter*
PO Box 1258, Gallatin, TN 37066, USA
Dunn, Kevin — *Actor*
321 E Grandview Ave, Sierra Madre, CA 91024, USA
Dunn, Martin — *Editor*
%New York Daily News, Editorial Dept, 220 E 42nd St, New York, NY 10017, USA
Dunn, Mignon — *Opera Singer*
%Warden Assoc, 5626 Deer Run Road, Doylestown, PA 18901, USA
Dunn, Mike — *Drag Racing Driver*
%Circle A Racing, RR 24 Box 537A, Keeney Lane, York, PA 17406, USA
Dunn, Nora — *Actress, Comedienne*
%Innovative Artists, 1505 10th St, Santa Monica, CA 90401, USA
Dunn, Patricia (Tricia) — *Hockey Player*
5 Twinbrook Dr, Derry, NH 03038, USA
Dunn, Ronnie — *Singer (Brooks & Dunn), Songwriter*
%TBA Mgmt, 300 10th Ave S, Nashville, TN 37203, USA
Dunn, Stephen — *Writer*
%Stockton State College, Humanities/Fine Arts Dept, Pomona, NJ 08240, USA
Dunn, Stephen L — *Religious Leader*
%Churches of God General Conference, 7176 Glenmeadow Dr, Frederick, MD 21703, USA

Dunn, Susan *Opera Singer*
1212 Lancaster, Champaign, IL 61821, USA
Dunn, T R *Basketball Player*
1014 19th St SW, Birmingham, AL 35211, USA
Dunn, Tricia *Hockey Player*
5 Twinbrook Dr, Derry, NH 03038, USA
Dunn, Warrick *Football Player*
9823 Bay Island Dr, Tampa, FL 33615, USA
Dunne, Dominick *Writer*
155 E 49th St, New York, NY 10017, USA
Dunne, Griffin *Actor, Director*
445 Park Ave, #701, New York, NY 10022, USA
Dunne, John Gregory *Writer*
%Janklow & Nesbit, 445 Park Ave, #1300, New York, NY 10022, USA
Dunne, Robin *Actor*
%United Talent Agency, 9560 Wilshire Blvd, #500, Beverly Hills, CA 90212, USA
Dunne, Roisin *Guitarist (Seven Year Bitch)*
%Rave Booking, PO Box 310780, Jamaica, NY 11431, USA
Dunnigan, Frank J *Publisher*
1500 Palisade Ave, Fort Lee, NJ 07024, USA
Dunnigan, T Kevin *Businessman*
%Thomas & Betts Corp, 8155 Thomas & Betts Blvd, Memphis,TN 38125, USA
Dunning, Debbe *Actress, Model*
PO Box 2748, Toluca Lake, CA 91610, USA
Dunning, John *Writer*
%Pocket Books, 1230 Ave of Americas, New York, NY 10020, USA
Dunphy, Marv *Volleyball Coach*
33370 Decker School Road, Malibu, CA 90265, USA
Dunphy, T J Dermot *Businessman*
%Sealed Air Corp, Park 80 Plaza E, Saddle Park, NJ 07663, USA
Dunsmore, Barrie *Commentator*
%ABC-TV, News Dept, 5010 Creston St, Hyattsville, MD 20781, USA
Dunst, Kirsten *Actress*
8916 Ashcroft Ave, West Hollywood, CA 90048, USA
Dunston, Shawon D *Baseball Player*
594 Louisiana Ave, #3, Brooklyn, NY 11239, USA
Dunton, Gary C *Financier*
%MBIA Inc, 113 King St, Armonk, NY 10504, USA
Dunwoody, Richard *Thoroughbred Racing Jockey*
14 Saint Maur Road, Fulham, London SW6 4DP, England
DuPlessis, Christian *Opera Singer*
%Performing Arts, 1 Hinde St, London W1M 5RH, England
Dupont, Jacques *Minister of State, Monaco*
%Minister of State's Office, Boite Postale 522, 98015 Monaco-Cedex, Monaco
DuPont, Pierre S, IV *Governor, DE*
%Richards Layton Finger, 1 Rodney Square, PO Box 551, Wilmington, DE 19899, USA
DuPree, Billy Joe *Football Player*
PO Box 720334, Dallas, TX 75372, USA
Dupree, Donald (Don) *Bobsled Athlete*
3 Center St, Saranac Lake, NY 12983, USA
Dupree, Marcus *Football Player*
%Bossier City Battle Wings, 2000 Century Tel Dr, Bossier City, LA 71112, USA
DuPrez, John *Composer*
%Air-Edel, 1416 N La Brea Ave, Los Angeles, CA 90028, USA
Duque, Pedro *Astronaut, Spain*
1103 Virginia St, South Houston, TX 77587, USA
Durack, David T *Physician*
1700 Woodstock Road, Durham, NC 27705, USA
Duran, Roberto *Boxer*
Nuevo Reperto El Carmen, Panama
Durand, Kevin *Actor*
%Stubbs Agency, 1450 S Robertson Blvd, Los Angeles, CA 90035, USA
Durang, Christopher *Writer*
%Helen Merrill Agency, 337 W 22nd St, New York, NY 10011, USA
Durant, Graham J *Inventor (Antiulcer Compound)*
%Cambridge NeuroScience, 333 Boston Providence Turnpike, Norwood, MA 02062, USA
Durante, Viviana P *Ballerina*
20 Bristol Gardens, Little Venice, London W9, England
Durbin, Deanna *Actress, Singer*
BP 3315, 75123 Paris Cedex 03, France
Durbin, Mike *Bowler*
%Professional Bowlers Assn, 719 2nd Ave, #701, Seattle, WA 98104, USA
Duren, Rinold G (Ryne) *Baseball Player*
5629 Struthers Court, Winter Haven, FL 33884, USA
Durham, Hugh *Basketball Coach*
%Jacksonville University, Athletic Dept, Jacksonville, FL 32211, USA
Durham, Ray (Sugar Ray) *Baseball Player*
1815 Lake Dr, Charlotte, NC 28214, USA

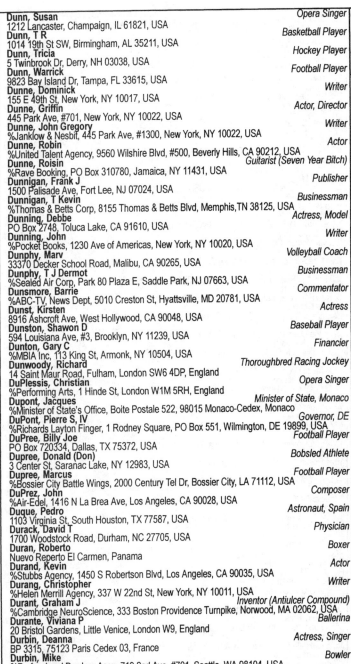

Duritz - Dwork

Duritz, Adam *Singer (Counting Crowes), Lyricist*
%Direct Mgmt, 947 N La Cienega Blvd, #G, Los Angeles, CA 90069, USA
Durkin, Clare *Model*
%Ford Model Agency, 142 Greene St, #400, New York, NY 10012, USA
Durkin, John A *Senator, NH*
60 Lenz St, Manchester, NH 03102, USA
Durning, Charles *Actor*
10590 Wilshire Blvd, #506, Los Angeles, CA 90024, USA
Durr Browning, Francoise *Tennis Player*
195 Rue de Lourmel, 75015 Paris, France
Durrance, Samuel T *Astronaut, Astronomer*
770 Kerry Downs Circle, Melbourne, FL 32940, USA
Durrant, Devin *Basketball Player*
1716 W 1825 N, Provo, UT 84604, USA
Durst, Will *Actor, Comedian*
%Entertainment Alliance, PO Box 5734, Santa Rosa, CA 95402, USA
Dusay, Debra *Actress*
%Susan Nathe, 8281 Melrose Ave, #200, Los Angeles, CA 90046, USA
Dusay, Marj *Actress*
320 W 66th St, New York, NY 10023, USA
Dusenberry, Ann *Actress*
1615 San Leandro Lane, Montecito, CA 93108, USA
Dushku, Eliza *Actress*
%The Firm, 9100 Wilshire Blvd, #100W, Beverly Hills, CA 90210, USA
Dussault, Jean H *Endocrinologist*
%Laval Medical Center, 2705 Blvd Laurier, Sainte Foy PQ G1V 4G2, Canada
Dussault, Nancy *Actress, Singer*
12211 Iredell St, North Hollywood, CA 91604, USA
Dutch, Deborah *Actress*
850 N Kings Road, PO Box 100, West Hollywood, CA 90069, USA
Dutilleux, Henri *Composer*
12 Rue Saint Louis-en-l'Isle, 75004 Paris, France
Dutoit, Charles E *Conductor*
%Montreal Symphony, 85 Sainte Catherine St W, Montreal QC H2X 3P4, Canada
Dutt, Hank *Concert Violist (Kronos Quartet)*
%Kronos Quartet, 1235 9th Ave, San Francisco, CA 94122, USA
Dutton, Charles S *Actor*
10061 Riverside Dr, #821, Toluca Lake, CA 91602, USA
Dutton, John O *Football Player*
5706 Moss Creek Trail, Dallas, TX 75252, USA
Dutton, Lawrence *Violist (Emerson String Quartet)*
%I M G Artists, 3 Burlington Lane, Chiswick, London W4 2TH, England
Dutton, Simon *Actor*
%Marmont Mgmt, Langham House, 302/8 Regent St, London W1R 5AL, England
Duva, Lou *Boxing Promoter*
%Main Events, 811 Totowa Road, #100, Totowa, NJ 07512, USA
Duval, David *Golfer*
135 Professional Dr, #4, Ponte Vedra, FL 32082, USA
Duval, Helen *Bowler*
1624 Posen Ave, Berkeley, CA 94707, USA
Duval, Juliette *Actress*
%Cineart, 36 Rue de Ponthieu, 75008 Paris, France
DuVall, Clea *Actress*
%Innovative Artists, 1505 10th St, Santa Monica, CA 90401, USA
Duvall, Jed *Commentator*
%ABC-TV, News Dept, 5010 Creston St, Hyattsville, MD 20781, USA
Duvall, Robert *Actor*
%William Morris Agency, 151 El Camino Dr, Beverly Hills, CA 90212, USA
Duvall, Sammy *Water Skier*
PO Box 871, Windermere, FL 34786, USA
Duvall-Hero, Camille *Water Skier*
PO Box 871, Windermere, FL 34786, USA
Duvignaud, Jean *Writer*
28 Rue Saint-Leonard, 1700 La Rochelle, France
Duvillard, Henri *Alpine Skier*
Le Mont d'Arbois, 74120 Megere, France
Duwelius, Rick *Volleyball Player*
345 W Juniper St, #5, San Diego, CA 92101, USA
Duwez, Pol E *Applied Physicist*
1535 Oakdale St, Pasadena, CA 91106, USA
Dvorovenko, Irina *Ballerina*
%American Ballet Theatre, 890 Broadway, New York, NY 10003, USA
Dvorsky, Peter *Opera Singer*
Bradianska Ulica 11, SK-811 08, Bratislava, Slovakia
Dwight, Edward, Jr *Astronaut*
4022 Montview Blvd, Denver, CO 80207, USA
Dwork, Melvin *Interior Designer*
%Melvin Dwork Inc, 196 Ave of Americas, New York, NY 10013, USA

Dworkin, Andrea *Writer*
%Elaine Markson, 44 Greenwich Ave, New York, NY 10011, USA

Dworkin, Martin *Microbiologist*
2123 Hoyt Ave W, Saint Paul, MN 55108, USA

Dworkins, Lenny *Cartoonist (Buck Rogers)*
2906 Wilmette Ave, Wilmette, IL 60091, USA

Dworsky, Daniel L (Dan) *Football Player, Architect*
9225 Nightingale Dr, Los Angeles, CA 90069, USA

Dwyer, Karyn *Actress*
%Oscars Abrams Zimel, 438 Queen St E, Toronto ON M5A 1T4, Canada

Dychtwald, Ken *Psychologist*
%Age Wave Inc, 1900 Powell St, Emeryville, CA 94608, USA

Dydek, Malforzata (Margo) *Basketball Player*
%San Antonio Silver Stars, 1 SBC Center, San Antonio, TX 78219, USA

Dye, Cameron *Actor*
13035 Woodbridge St, Studio City, CA 91604, USA

Dye, Ian *Composer*
%Gorfaine/Schwartz, 13245 Riverside Dr, #450, Sherman Oaks, CA 91423, USA

Dye, John *Actor*
%William Morris Agency, 151 El Camino Dr, Beverly Hills, CA 90212, USA

Dye, Lee *Golf Course Architect*
%Dye Designs, 5500 E Yale Ave, Denver, CO 80222, USA

Dye, Nancy Schrom *Educator*
%Oberlin College, President's Office, Oberlin, OH 44074, USA

Dyer, David W *Judge*
%US Court of Appeals, 300 NE 1st Ave, Miami, FL 33132, USA

Dyer, Hector *Track Athlete*
1620 E Chapman, #214, Fullerton, CA 92831, USA

Dyer, Joseph W, Jr *Navy Admiral*
Commander, Naval Air Systems Command, Patuxent River, MD 20670, USA

Dyer, Wayne W *Psychologist, Writer*
Shore Club, Tower House C, 1905 N Atlantic Blvd, Fort Lauderdale, FL 33305, USA

Dyk, Timothy B *Judge*
%US Court of Appeals, 717 Madison Place NW, Washington, DC 20439, USA

Dyke, Charles W *Army General, Association Executive*
%International Technical/Trade Assoc, 1330 Connecticut NW, Washington, DC 20036, USA

Dykes Bower, John *Concert Organist*
4-Z Artillery Mansions, Westminster, London SW1, England

Dykinga, Jack *Photojournalist*
2865 N Tomas Road, Tucson, AZ 85745, USA

Dykstra, John *Artist, Animator, Cinematographer*
15060 Encanto Dr, Sherman Oaks, CA 91403, USA

Dykstra, Leonard K (Lenny) *Baseball Player*
2672 Ladbrook Way, Thousand Oaks, CA 91361, USA

Dylan, Bob *Singer, Songwriter*
%Elliot Mintz, 2934 Beverly Glen Circle, #412, Los Angeles, CA 90077, USA

Dylan, Jakob *Singer (Wallflowers)*
%H K Mgmt, 9200 W Sunset Blvd, #530, Los Angeles, CA 90069, USA

Dymally, Mervyn M *Representative, CA*
%Dymally International Group, 9111 S La Cienega Blvd, Compton, CA 90220, USA

Dysart, Richard *Actor*
654 Copeland Court, Santa Monica, CA 90405, USA

Dyson, Esther *Businesswoman, Writer*
%Edventure Holdings, 104 5th Ave, #2000, New York, NY 10011, USA

Dyson, Freeman J *Physicist, Writer*
105 Battle Road Circle, Princeton, NJ 08540, USA

Dyson, Michael Eric *Writer*
%DePaul University, English Dept, Chicago, IL 60604, USA

Dystel, Oscar *Publisher*
Springs, Purchase Hills Dr, Purchase, NY 10577, USA

Dzau, Victor *Medical Researcher*
%Stanford University Hospital, Cardiovascular Medicine Div, Stanford, CA 94305, USA

Dzeliwe *Queen Regent, Swaziland*
%Royal Palace, Mbabane, Swaziland

Dzhanibekov, Vladimir A *Cosmonaut, Air Force General*
%Potchta Kosmonavtov, Moskovskoi Oblasti, 141160 Syvisdny Goroduk, Russia

Dzundza, George *Actor*
PO Box 573250, Tarzana, CA 91357, USA

Dzurinda, Mikulas *Prime Minister, Slovakia*
%Prime Minister's Office, Nam Slobody 1, 81370 Bratislava 1, Slovakia

Eade, George J *Air Force General*
1131 Sunnyside Dr, Healdsburg, CA 95448, USA
Eads, George *Actor*
%Shelter Entertainment, 9255 Sunset Blvd, #1010, Los Angeles, CA 90069, USA
Eads, Ora W *Religious Leader*
%Christian Congregation, 804 W Hemlock St, La Follette, TN 37766, USA
Eagle, Ian *Sportscaster*
%CBS-TV, Sports Dept, 51 W 52nd St, New York, NY 10019, USA
Eagleburger, Lawrence S *Secretary, State*
1450 Owensville Road, Charlottesville, VA 22901, USA
Eaglen, Jane *Opera Singer*
%Columbia Artists Mgmt Inc, 165 W 57th St, New York, NY 10019, USA
Eagleson, Alan *Labor Leader, Hockey Executive*
37 Maitland St, Toronto ON M4Y 1C8, Canada
Eagleton, Thomas F *Senator, MO*
1 Firstar Center, Saint Louis, MO 63101, USA
Eagling, Wayne J *Ballet Dancer, Choreographer*
Postbus 16486, 1001 RN Amsterdam, Netherlands
Eakes, Bobbie *Actress, Singer*
27400 Pacific Coast Highway, #2, Malibu, CA 90265, USA
Eakin, Richard R *Educator*
%East Carolina University, Chancellor's Office, Greenville, NC 27858, USA
Eakin, Thomas C *Businessman*
2729 Shelley Road, Shaker Heights, OH 44122, USA
Eakins, Dallas *Hockey Player*
751 New Romaine, Peterborough ON K9L 2G4, Canada
Eakins, James (Jim) *Basketball Player*
2575 E 9600th St S, Sandy, UT 84092, USA
Eanes, Antonio dos Santos R *President, Portugal; Army General*
%Partido Renovador Democratico, Travessa do Falo 9, 1200 Lisbon, Portugal
Earl, Anthony S *Governor, WI*
2810 Arbor Dr, #B, Madison, WI 53711, USA
Earl, Robin D *Football Player*
9 Middlebury Lane, Lincolnshire, IL 60069, USA
Earl, Roger *Drummer (Foghat)*
%Lustig Talent, PO Box 770850, Orlando, FL 32877, USA
Earle, Ed *Basketball Player*
1940 Burton Lane, Park Ridge, IL 60068, USA
Earle, Stacey *Singer*
%Grassroots Media, 800 18th Ave S, #B, Nashville, TN 37203, USA
Earle, Steve *Singer, Songwriter, Guitarist*
%Dan Gillis Mgmt, 1223 17th Ave S, Nashville, TN 37212, USA
Earle, Sylvia Alice *Oceanographer*
12812 Skyline Blvd, Oakland, CA 94619, USA
Earley, Anthony F, Jr *Businessman*
%Detroit Edison, 2000 2nd Ave, Detroit, MI 48226, USA
Earley, Michael M *Businessman*
%Triton Group, 550 W C St, San Diego, CA 92101, USA
Early, Gerald L *Writer*
%Washington University, English Dept, Saint Louis, MO 63130, USA
Earnhardt, Kerry *Auto Racing Driver*
%FitzBradshaw Racing, 129 Bevan Dr, Mooresville, NC 28115, USA
Earnhardt, R Dale, Jr *Auto Racing Driver*
1675 Coddle Creek Highway, Mooresville, NC 28115, USA
Easley, Bill *Jazz Saxophonist, Clarinetist, Flutist*
%Hot Jazz Mgmt, 328 W 43rd St, #4FW, New York, NY 10036, USA
Easmon, Ricky *Football Player*
6605 N Riviera Manor St, #A4, Tampa, FL 33604, USA
Eason, Tony *Football Player*
851 Cocos Dr, San Marcos, CA 92078, USA
East, Clyde B *WW II Army Air Force Hero*
6643 Maplegrove St, Oak Park, CA 91377, USA
Easterbrook, Frank H *Judge*
%US Court of Appeals, 111 N Canal St, Building 6, Chicago, IL 60606, USA
Easterbrook, Leslie *Actress, Singer*
5218 Bellingham Ave, Valley Village, CA 91607, USA
Easterling, Ray *Football Player*
2533 Pocoshock Blvd, Richmond, VA 23235, USA
Easterly, David E *Businessman*
%Cox Enterprises, 1400 Lake Hearn Dr NE, Atlanta, GA 30319, USA
Eastham, Richard *Actor, Singer*
211 S Spalding Dr, Beverly Hills, CA 90212, USA
Eastman, Dean E *Physicist*
281 Bloomingbank Road, Riverside, IL 60546, USA
Eastman, John *Attorney*
%Eastman & Eastman, 39 W 54th St, New York, NY 10019, USA
Eastman, Kevin *Cartoonist (Ninja Turtles)*
%Teenage Mutant Ninja Turtles, PO Box 417, Haydenville, MA 01039, USA

Eastman, Madeline *Singer*
%Prince/SF Productions, 1450 Southgate Ave, #206, Daly City, CA 94015, USA
Eastman, Marilyn *Actress*
%Hardman-Eastman Studios, 138 Hawthorne St, Pittsburgh, PA 15218, USA
Easton, Michael *Actor*
2810 Baseline Trail, Los Angeles, CA 90068, USA
Easton, Millard E (Bill) *Track Coach*
1704 NW Weatherstone Dr, Blue Springs, MO 64015, USA
Easton, Robert *Actor*
%Paul Kohner, 9300 Wilshire Blvd, #555, Beverly Hills, CA 90212, USA
Easton, Sheena *Singer*
%Emmis Mgmt, 18136 Califa St, Tarzana, CA 91356, USA
Eastwick-Field, Elizabeth *Architect*
Low Farm, Low Road, Denham, Eye, Suffolk IP21 5ET, England
Eastwood, Alison *Model, Actress*
2334 Benedict Canyon, Beverly Hills, CA 90210, USA
Eastwood, Bob *Golfer*
3826 Falmouth Court, Stockton, CA 95219, USA
Eastwood, Clint *Actor, Director*
Hogs Breath Inn, Carlos St, PO Box 4366, Carmel, CA 93921, USA
Easum, Donald B *Diplomat*
801 W End Ave, #3A, New York, NY 10025, USA
Eaton, Dan L *Hematologist*
%Genentech Inc, 460 Point San Bruno Blvd, South San Francisco, CA 94080, USA
Eaton, Don (Babtunde) *Rap Artist, Drummer (Last Poets)*
%Agency Group Ltd, 370 City Road, London EC1V 2QA, England
Eaton, John C *Composer*
4585 N Hartstrait Road, Bloomington, IN 47404, USA
Eaton, Mark E *Basketball Player*
PO Box 982108, Park City, UT 84098, USA
Eaton, Meredith *Actress*
%Susan Smith, 121A N San Vicente Blvd, Beverly Hills, CA 90211, USA
Eaton, Shirley *Actress*
%Guild House, Upper Saint Martin's Lane, London WC2H PEG, England
Ebadi, Shirin *Nobel Peace Laureate*
%University of Tehran, Enghelab Ave & 16 Azar St, Tehran, Iran
Ebashi, Setsuro *Biophysicist, Pharmacologist*
17-503 Nahaizumi Myodaiji, Okazaki 444, Japan
Ebb, Fred *Lyricist, Librettist*
%San Remo Apts, 146 Central Park West, #14D, New York, NY 10023, USA
Ebel, David M *Judge*
%US Court of Appeals, US Courthouse, 1929 Stout St, Denver, CO 80294, USA
Eben, Petr *Composer*
Hamsikova 19, 150 00 Prague 5, Czech Republic
Eber, Lorenz *Inventor (Mechanical Cable Drum Lift)*
2 Byron Close, Laguna Niguel, CA 92677, USA
Eberhart, Ralph E (Ed) *Air Force General*
Commander, US Northern Command, Peterson Air Force Base, CO 80914, USA
Eberhart, Richard G *Writer*
80 Lyme Road, #32, Hanover, NH 03755, USA
Eberharter, Stefan *Alpine Skier*
Dorfstr 21, 6272 Stumm, Austria
Eberle, Markus *Alpine Skier*
Unterwestweg 27, 87567 Riezlern, Germany
Eberle, William D *Government Official, Businessman*
13 Garland Road, Concord, MA 01742, USA
Ebershoff, David *Writer*
%Viking Press, 375 Hudson St, New York, NY 10014, USA
Ebersol, Dick *Businessman*
174 West St, #54, Litchfield, CT 06759, USA
Ebersole, Christine *Actress, Singer*
%Agency for Performing Arts, 9200 Sunset Blvd, #900, Los Angeles, CA 90069, USA
Ebert, Peter *Opera Director*
Col di Mura, 06010 Lippiano, Italy
Ebert, Robert D *Physician*
16 Brewster Road, Wayland, MA 01778, USA
Ebert, Roger J *Movie Critic*
%Ebert at the Movies, 630 N McClurg Court, Chicago, IL 60611, USA
Ebi, Ndudi *Basketball Player*
%Minnesota Timberwolves, Target Center, 600 1st Ave N, Minneapolis, MN 55403, USA
Ebsen, Bonnie *Actress*
PO Box 356, Agoura, CA 91376, USA
Eccleston, Christopher *Actor*
%Hamilton Asper Mgmt, 24 Hanway St, London W1T 1UH, England
Ecclestone, Bernie *Auto Racing Executive*
%Formula One Ltd, 6 Prince's Gate, London SW7 1QJ, England
Ecclestone, Timothy J (Tim) *Hockey Player*
10095 Fairway Village Dr, Roswell, GA 30076, USA

E

Ecevit - Edmunds

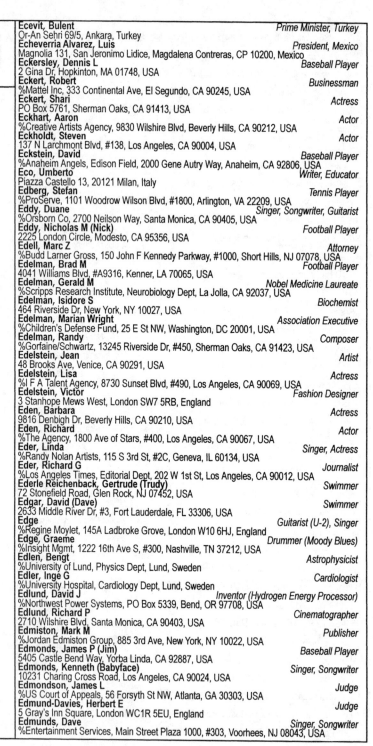

Ecevit, Bulent *Prime Minister, Turkey*
Or-An Sehri 69/5, Ankara, Turkey
Echeverria Alvarez, Luis *President, Mexico*
Magnolia 131, San Jeronimo Lidice, Magdalena Contreras, CP 10200, Mexico
Eckersley, Dennis L *Baseball Player*
2 Gina Dr, Hopkinton, MA 01748, USA
Eckert, Robert *Businessman*
%Mattel Inc, 333 Continental Ave, El Segundo, CA 90245, USA
Eckert, Shari *Actress*
PO Box 5761, Sherman Oaks, CA 91413, USA
Eckhart, Aaron *Actor*
%Creative Artists Agency, 9830 Wilshire Blvd, Beverly Hills, CA 90212, USA
Eckholdt, Steven *Actor*
137 N Larchmont Blvd, #138, Los Angeles, CA 90004, USA
Eckstein, David *Baseball Player*
%Anaheim Angels, Edison Field, 2000 Gene Autry Way, Anaheim, CA 92806, USA
Eco, Umberto *Writer, Educator*
Piazza Castello 13, 20121 Milan, Italy
Edberg, Stefan *Tennis Player*
%ProServe, 1101 Woodrow Wilson Blvd, #1800, Arlington, VA 22209, USA
Eddy, Duane *Singer, Songwriter, Guitarist*
%Orsborn Co, 2700 Neilson Way, Santa Monica, CA 90405, USA
Eddy, Nicholas M (Nick) *Football Player*
2225 London Circle, Modesto, CA 95356, USA
Edell, Marc Z *Attorney*
%Budd Larner Gross, 150 John F Kennedy Parkway, #1000, Short Hills, NJ 07078, USA
Edelman, Brad M *Football Player*
4041 Williams Blvd, #A9316, Kenner, LA 70065, USA
Edelman, Gerald M *Nobel Medicine Laureate*
%Scripps Research Institute, Neurobiology Dept, La Jolla, CA 92037, USA
Edelman, Isidore S *Biochemist*
464 Riverside Dr, New York, NY 10027, USA
Edelman, Marian Wright *Association Executive*
%Children's Defense Fund, 25 E St NW, Washington, DC 20001, USA
Edelman, Randy *Composer*
%Gorfaine/Schwartz, 13245 Riverside Dr, #450, Sherman Oaks, CA 91423, USA
Edelstein, Jean *Artist*
48 Brooks Ave, Venice, CA 90291, USA
Edelstein, Lisa *Actress*
%I F A Talent Agency, 8730 Sunset Blvd, #490, Los Angeles, CA 90069, USA
Edelstein, Victor *Fashion Designer*
3 Stanhope Mews West, London SW7 5RB, England
Eden, Barbara *Actress*
9816 Denbigh Dr, Beverly Hills, CA 90210, USA
Eden, Richard *Actor*
%The Agency, 1800 Ave of Stars, #400, Los Angeles, CA 90067, USA
Eder, Linda *Singer, Actress*
%Randy Nolan Artists, 115 S 3rd St, #2C, Geneva, IL 60134, USA
Eder, Richard G *Journalist*
%Los Angeles Times, Editorial Dept, 202 W 1st St, Los Angeles, CA 90012, USA
Ederle Reichenback, Gertrude (Trudy) *Swimmer*
72 Stonefield Road, Glen Rock, NJ 07452, USA
Edgar, David (Dave) *Swimmer*
2633 Middle River Dr, #3, Fort Lauderdale, FL 33306, USA
Edge *Guitarist (U-2), Singer*
%Regine Moylet, 145A Ladbroke Grove, London W10 6HJ, England
Edge, Graeme *Drummer (Moody Blues)*
%Insight Mgmt, 1222 16th Ave S, #300, Nashville, TN 37212, USA
Edlen, Bengt *Astrophysicist*
%University of Lund, Physics Dept, Lund, Sweden
Edler, Inge G *Cardiologist*
%University Hospital, Cardiology Dept, Lund, Sweden
Edlund, David J *Inventor (Hydrogen Energy Processor)*
%Northwest Power Systems, PO Box 5339, Bend, OR 97708, USA
Edlund, Richard P *Cinematographer*
2710 Wilshire Blvd, Santa Monica, CA 90403, USA
Edmiston, Mark M *Publisher*
%Jordan Edmiston Group, 885 3rd Ave, New York, NY 10022, USA
Edmonds, James P (Jim) *Baseball Player*
5405 Castle Bend Way, Yorba Linda, CA 92887, USA
Edmonds, Kenneth (Babyface) *Singer, Songwriter*
10231 Charing Cross Road, Los Angeles, CA 90024, USA
Edmondson, James L *Judge*
%US Court of Appeals, 56 Forsyth St NW, Atlanta, GA 30303, USA
Edmund-Davies, Herbert E *Judge*
5 Gray's Inn Square, London WC1R 5EU, England
Edmunds, Dave *Singer, Songwriter*
%Entertainment Services, Main Street Plaza 1000, #303, Voorhees, NJ 08043, USA

E

Edney, Leon A (Bud) 1037 Encino Row, Coronado, CA 92118, USA	*Navy Admiral*
Edney, Tyus 1800 S Floyd Court, La Habra, CA 90631, USA	*Basketball Player*
Edson, Hilary 400 S Beverly Road, #216, Beverly Hills, CA 90212, USA	*Actress*
Eduardo dos Santos, Jose %President's Office, Palacio do Povo, Luanda, Angola	*President, Angola*
Edward %Bagshot, Bagshot Park, Surrey GU19 5PN, England	*Prince, England*
Edward, John %Berkley Publishing Group, 375 Hudson St, New York, NY 10014, USA	*Psychic*
Edwards, Anthony %United Talent Agency, 9560 Wilshire Blvd, #500, Beverly Hills, CA 90212, USA	*Actor*
Edwards, Antonio 716 2nd St NW, Moultrie, GA 31768, USA	*Football Player*
Edwards, Barbara %Hansen, 7767 Hollywood Blvd, #202, Los Angeles, CA 90046, USA	*Model, Actress*
Edwards, Blue %Miami Heat, American Airlines Arena, 601 Biscayne Blvd, Miami, FL 33132, USA	*Basketball Player*
Edwards, Carl %Roush Racing, 122 Knob Hill Road, Mooresville, NC 28117, USA	*Truck Racing Driver*
Edwards, Charles C Keeney Park, 10666 N Torrey Pines Road, La Jolla, CA 92037, USA	*Physician*
Edwards, Charles C, Jr %Des Moines Register & Tribune, 715 Locust St, Des Moines, IA 50309, USA	*Publisher*
Edwards, Dennis %Green Light Talent Agency, PO Box 3172, Beverly Hills, CA 90212, USA	*Singer (Temptations)*
Edwards, Don 435 Meredith Anne Court, #102, Raleigh, NC 27606, USA	*Hockey Player*
Edwards, Don %Scott O'Malley Assoc, 433 S Cuchamas St, Colorado Springs, CO 80903, USA	*Singer*
Edwards, Earl 1534 W Saint Thomas Dr, Gilbert, AZ 85233, USA	*Football Player*
Edwards, Eric 3404 SW Water Ave, Portland, OR 97239, USA	*Cinematographer*
Edwards, Gareth 211 West Road, Nottage, Porthcawl, Mid-Clamorgan CF36 3RT, Wales	*Rugby Player*
Edwards, Harry %University of California, Sociology Dept, Berkeley, CA 94720, USA	*Educator, Social Activist*
Edwards, Harry T %US Court of Appeals, 333 Constitution Ave NW, Washington, DC 20001, USA	*Judge*
Edwards, Herman L 1627 Highland St, Seaside, CA 93955, USA	*Football Player, Coach*
Edwards, James 3890 Lakeland Lane, Bloomfield Township, MI 48302, USA	*Basketball Player*
Edwards, James B 100 Venning St, Mount Pleasant, SC 29464, USA	*Secretary, Energy; Governor, SC*
Edwards, Jay 121 N Washington St, #506, Marion, IN 46952, USA	*Basketball Player*
Edwards, Jennifer 4123 Saint Clair, Studio City, CA 91604, USA	*Actress*
Edwards, Jesse E 1565 Edgcumbe Road, Saint Paul, MN 55116, USA	*Cardiac Pathologist*
Edwards, Joe F, Jr %Enron Broadband Services, PO Box 1188, Houston, TX 77251, USA	*Astronaut*
Edwards, Joel 280 Benson Lane, Coppell, TX 75019, USA	*Golfer*
Edwards, John %Buddy Allen Mgmt, 3750 Hudson Manor Terrace, #3AE, Bronx, NY 10463, USA	*Singer (Spinners)*
Edwards, Jonathan %MTC, 10 Kendall Place, London W1H 3AH, England	*Track Athlete*
Edwards, Jonathan %Northern Lights, 437 Live Oak Loop NE, Albuquerque, NM 87122, USA	*Singer, Songwriter*
Edwards, Lena F 821 Woodland Dr, Lakewood, NJ 08701, USA	*Physician*
Edwards, Luke %Savage Agency, 6212 Banner Ave, Los Angeles, CA 90038, USA	*Actor*
Edwards, R LaVell %Brigham Young University, Athletic Dept, Provo, UT 84602, USA	*Football Player, Coach*
Edwards, Ralph 6922 Hollywood Blvd, #415, Los Angeles, CA 90028, USA	*Entertainer*
Edwards, Robert 931 Knight Road, Tennille, GA 31089, USA	*Football Player*
Edwards, Robert A (Bob) %National Public Radio, News Dept, 635 Massachusetts NW, Washington, DC 20001, USA	*Commentator*
Edwards, Robert G Duck End Farm, Dry Drayton, Cambridge CB3 8DB, England	*Physiologist*

Edwards, Robert J *Editor*
Williamscot House, near Banbury, Oxon OX17 1AE, England
Edwards, Sian *Conductor*
70 Twisden Road, London NW5 1DN, England
Edwards, Stacy *Actress*
%Paradigm Agency, 10100 Santa Monica Blvd, #2500, Los Angeles, CA 90067, USA
Edwards, Stephanie *Actress*
8075 W 3rd St, #303, Los Angeles, CA 90048, USA
Edwards, Steve *Composer*
3980 Royal Oak Place, Encino, CA 91436, USA
Edwards, Teresa *Basketball Player, Coach*
291 Union Grove Church Road SE, Calhoun, GA 30701, USA
Edwards, Tommy Lee *Cartoonist*
%DC Comics, 1700 Broadway, New York, NY 10019, USA
Edwards, Tonya *Basketball Player*
%Phoenix Mercury, American West Arena, 201 E Jefferson St, Phoenix, AZ 85004, USA
Edwards, W Blake *Movie Director, Producer*
%Blake Edwards Entertainment, 9336 W Washington Blvd, Culver City, CA 90232, USA
Egan, Edward M Cardinal *Religious Leader*
%Archdiocese of New York, 1011 1st St, New York, NY 10022, USA
Egan, Jennifer *Writer*
%Doubleday Press, 1540 Broadway, New York, NY 10036, USA
Egan, John (Johnny) *Basketball Player, Coach*
2124 Nantucket Dr, #B, Houston, TX 77057, USA
Egan, John L *Businessman*
130 Wilton Road, London SW1V 1LQ, England
Egan, Peter *Actor*
%James Sharkey, 21 Golden Square, London W1R 3PA, England
Egan, Richard J *Businessman*
%ECM Corp, 35 Parkwood Dr, Hopkinton, MA 01748, USA
Egan, Susan *Actress, Singer, Dancer*
%Himber Entertainment, 211 S Beverly Dr, #208, Beverly Hills, CA 90212, USA
Egdahl, Richard H *Surgeon*
333 Commonwealth Ave, #23, Boston, MA 02115, USA
Ege, Julie *Actress*
%Guild House, Upper Saint Martins, London WC2H 9EG, England
Egerszegi, Krisztina *Swimmer*
%Budapest Spartacus, Koer Utca 1/A, 1103 Budapest, Hungary
Eggar, Samantha *Actress*
15430 Mulholland Dr, Los Angeles, CA 90077, USA
Eggby, David *Cinematographer*
4324 Promenade Way, #109, Marina del Rey, CA 90292, USA
Eggers, Dave *Writer*
%Simon & Schuster 1230 Ave of Americas, New York, NY 10020, USA
Eggert, Nicole *Actress*
11360 Brill Dr, Studio City, CA 91604, USA
Eggert, Robert J *Economist*
%Eggert Economic Enterprises, PO Box 4313, Sedona, AZ 86340, USA
Eggleston, William *Photographer, Artist*
%Robert Miller Gallery, 526 W 26th St, #10A, New York, NY 10001, USA
Eggleton, Arthur C *Government Official, Canada*
%National Defense Ministry, 101 Colonel By Dr, Ottawa ON K1A 0K2, Canada
Egoyan, Atom *Movie Director*
%Ego Film Artists, 80 Niagara St, Toronto ON M5V 1C5, Canada
Ehle, Jennifer *Actress*
134 W 70th St, #4, New York, NY 10023, USA
Ehlers, Beth *Actress*
%Gage Group, 14724 Ventura Blvd, #505, Sherman Oaks, CA 91403, USA
Ehlers, Walter D *WW II Army Hero (CMH)*
8382 Valley View, Buena Park, CA 90620, USA
Ehrenreich, Barbara *Women's Activist, Writer*
%Farrar Straus Giroux, 19 Union Square W, New York, NY 10003, USA
Ehrlich, Paul R *Population Biologist*
%Stanford University, Biological Sciences Dept, Stanford, CA 94305, USA
Ehrlich, S Paul, Jr *Physician*
1132 Seaspray Ave, Delray Beach, FL 33483, USA
Eichelberger, Charles B *Army General*
%California Microwave, 124 Sweetwater Oaks, Peachtree City, GA 30269, USA
Eichhorn, Lisa *Actress*
1919 W 44th St, #1000, New York, NY 10036, USA
Eigen, Manfred *Nobel Chemistry Laureate*
Georg-Dehio-Weg 4, 37075 Gottingen, Germany
Eigsti, Roger H *Businessman*
%SAFECO Corp, SAFECO Plaza, Seattle, WA 98185, USA
Eikenberry, Jill *Actress*
197 Oakdale Ave, Mill Valley, CA 94941, USA
Eikenes, Adele *Opera Singer*
%Van Walsum Mgmt, 4 Addison Bridge Place, London W14 8XP, England

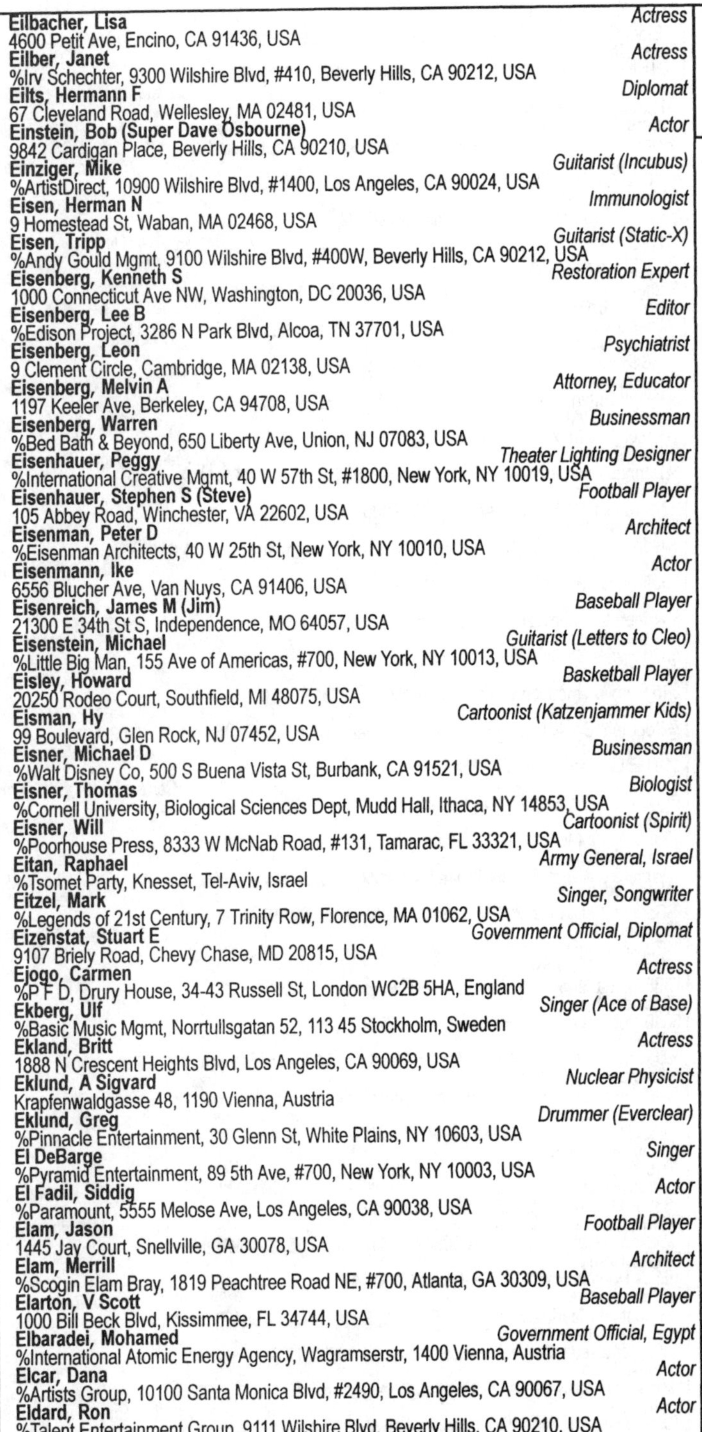

Eilbacher, Lisa *Actress*
4600 Petit Ave, Encino, CA 91436, USA
Eilber, Janet *Actress*
%Irv Schechter, 9300 Wilshire Blvd, #410, Beverly Hills, CA 90212, USA
Eilts, Hermann F *Diplomat*
67 Cleveland Road, Wellesley, MA 02481, USA
Einstein, Bob (Super Dave Osbourne) *Actor*
9842 Cardigan Place, Beverly Hills, CA 90210, USA
Einziger, Mike *Guitarist (Incubus)*
%ArtistDirect, 10900 Wilshire Blvd, #1400, Los Angeles, CA 90024, USA
Eisen, Herman N *Immunologist*
9 Homestead St, Waban, MA 02468, USA
Eisen, Tripp *Guitarist (Static-X)*
%Andy Gould Mgmt, 9100 Wilshire Blvd, #400W, Beverly Hills, CA 90212, USA
Eisenberg, Kenneth S *Restoration Expert*
1000 Connecticut Ave NW, Washington, DC 20036, USA
Eisenberg, Lee B *Editor*
%Edison Project, 3286 N Park Blvd, Alcoa, TN 37701, USA
Eisenberg, Leon *Psychiatrist*
9 Clement Circle, Cambridge, MA 02138, USA
Eisenberg, Melvin A *Attorney, Educator*
1197 Keeler Ave, Berkeley, CA 94708, USA
Eisenberg, Warren *Businessman*
%Bed Bath & Beyond, 650 Liberty Ave, Union, NJ 07083, USA
Eisenhauer, Peggy *Theater Lighting Designer*
%International Creative Mgmt, 40 W 57th St, #1800, New York, NY 10019, USA
Eisenhauer, Stephen S (Steve) *Football Player*
105 Abbey Road, Winchester, VA 22602, USA
Eisenman, Peter D *Architect*
%Eisenman Architects, 40 W 25th St, New York, NY 10010, USA
Eisenmann, Ike *Actor*
6556 Blucher Ave, Van Nuys, CA 91406, USA
Eisenreich, James M (Jim) *Baseball Player*
21300 E 34th St S, Independence, MO 64057, USA
Eisenstein, Michael *Guitarist (Letters to Cleo)*
%Little Big Man, 155 Ave of Americas, #700, New York, NY 10013, USA
Eisley, Howard *Basketball Player*
20250 Rodeo Court, Southfield, MI 48075, USA
Eisman, Hy *Cartoonist (Katzenjammer Kids)*
99 Boulevard, Glen Rock, NJ 07452, USA
Eisner, Michael D *Businessman*
%Walt Disney Co, 500 S Buena Vista St, Burbank, CA 91521, USA
Eisner, Thomas *Biologist*
%Cornell University, Biological Sciences Dept, Mudd Hall, Ithaca, NY 14853, USA
Eisner, Will *Cartoonist (Spirit)*
%Poorhouse Press, 8333 W McNab Road, #131, Tamarac, FL 33321, USA
Eitan, Raphael *Army General, Israel*
%Tsomet Party, Knesset, Tel-Aviv, Israel
Eitzel, Mark *Singer, Songwriter*
%Legends of 21st Century, 7 Trinity Row, Florence, MA 01062, USA
Eizenstat, Stuart E *Government Official, Diplomat*
9107 Briely Road, Chevy Chase, MD 20815, USA
Ejogo, Carmen *Actress*
%P F D, Drury House, 34-43 Russell St, London WC2B 5HA, England
Ekberg, Ulf *Singer (Ace of Base)*
%Basic Music Mgmt, Norrtullsgatan 52, 113 45 Stockholm, Sweden
Ekland, Britt *Actress*
1888 N Crescent Heights Blvd, Los Angeles, CA 90069, USA
Eklund, A Sigvard *Nuclear Physicist*
Krapfenwaldgasse 48, 1190 Vienna, Austria
Eklund, Greg *Drummer (Everclear)*
%Pinnacle Entertainment, 30 Glenn St, White Plains, NY 10603, USA
El DeBarge *Singer*
%Pyramid Entertainment, 89 5th Ave, #700, New York, NY 10003, USA
El Fadil, Siddig *Actor*
%Paramount, 5555 Melose Ave, Los Angeles, CA 90038, USA
Elam, Jason *Football Player*
1445 Jay Court, Snellville, GA 30078, USA
Elam, Merrill *Architect*
%Scogin Elam Bray, 1819 Peachtree Road NE, #700, Atlanta, GA 30309, USA
Elarton, V Scott *Baseball Player*
1000 Bill Beck Blvd, Kissimmee, FL 34744, USA
Elbaradei, Mohamed *Government Official, Egypt*
%International Atomic Energy Agency, Wagramserstr, 1400 Vienna, Austria
Elcar, Dana *Actor*
%Artists Group, 10100 Santa Monica Blvd, #2490, Los Angeles, CA 90067, USA
Eldard, Ron *Actor*
%Talent Entertainment Group, 9111 Wilshire Blvd, Beverly Hills, CA 90210, USA

Elder, Lee E *Golfer*
%Elder Group, 4737 N Ocean Dr, #220, Lauderdale by the Sea, FL 33308, USA

Elder, Mark P *Conductor*
%National Opera, London Coliseum, London WC2N 4ES, England

Elder, Will *Cartoonist (Little Annie Fanny)*
311 Jutland Dr, #A, Monroe Township, NJ 08831, USA

Elders, M Jocelyn *Government Official, Pediatrician*
%University of Arkansas Medical School, Pediatrics Dept, Little Rock, AR 72205, USA

Eldredge, Allison *Concert Cellist*
%I C M Artists, 40 W 57th St, New York, NY 10019, USA

Eldredge, Todd *Figure Skater*
888 Denison Court, Bloomfield Hills, MI 48302, USA

Electra, Carmen *Actress, Singer, Model*
%United Talent Agency, 9560 Wilshire Blvd, #500, Beverly Hills, CA 90212, USA

Elegant, Robert S *Writer*
Manor House, Middle Green near Langley, Bucks SL3 6BS, England

Eleniak, Erika *Model, Actress*
%Deloitte/Touche, 2029 Century Park E, #1300, Los Angeles, CA 90067, USA

Elfman, Danny *Singer, Composer*
3236 Primera Ave, Los Angeles, CA 90068, USA

Elfman, Jenna *Actress, Model*
%Talent Entertainment Group, 9111 Wilshire Blvd, Beverly Hills, CA 90210, USA

Elgart, Larry J *Orchestra Leader*
2065 Gulf of Mexico Dr, Longboat Key, FL 34228, USA

Elias, Eliane *Jazz Pianist, Singer, Composer*
%Bennett Morgan, 1282 RR 376, Wappingers Falls, NY 12590, USA

Elias, Hector *Actor*
28 N Mansfield Ave, Los Angeles, CA 90038, USA

Elias, Jonathan *Composer*
%Gorfaine/Schwartz, 13245 Riverside Dr, #450, Sherman Oaks, CA 91423, USA

Elias, Patrick *Hockey Player*
1005 Smith Manor Blvd, #98, West Orange, NJ 07052, USA

Elias, Rosalind *Opera Singer*
%Robert Lombardo, Harkness Plaza, 61 W 62nd St, #6F, New York, NY 10023, USA

Eliason, Donald *Basketball, Football Player*
5690 Fisher St, Saint Paul, MN 55110, USA

Eliel, Ernest L *Chemist*
345 Carolina Meadows Villa, Chapel Hill, NC 27517, USA

Eliff, Tom *Religious Leader*
%Southern Baptist Convention, 901 Commerce St, #750, Nashville, TN 37203, USA

Elinson, Jack *Sociomedical Scientist*
1181 E Laurelton Parkway, Teaneck, NJ 07666, USA

Eliot, Jan *Cartoonist (Stone Soup)*
PO Box 50032, Eugene, OR 97405, USA

Elise, Christine *Actress*
10390 Santa Monica Blvd, #300, Los Angeles, CA 90025, USA

Elise, Kimberly *Actress*
%Writers & Artists, 8383 Wilshire Blvd, #550, Beverly Hills, CA 90211, USA

Elisha, Walter Y *Businessman*
%Springs Industries, 205 N White St, Fort Mill, SC 29715, USA

Elizabeth II *Queen, England*
%Buckingham Palace, London SW1A 1AA, England

Elizabeth, Shannon *Actress, Model*
7336 Santa Monica Blvd, #690, West Hollywood, CA 90046, USA

Elizondo, Hector *Actor*
5040 Noble Ave, Sherman Oaks, CA 91403, USA

Elk, Jim *Actor*
%Dade/Schultz, 6442 Coldwater Canyon Ave, #206, Valley Green, CA 91606, USA

Elkes, Joel *Psychiatrist*
%University of Louisville, Psychiatry/Behavioral Sci Dept, Louisville, KY 40292, USA

Elkind, Mortimer M *Biophysicist*
16925 Hierba Dr, San Diego, CA 92128, USA

Elkington, Steve *Golfer*
7010 Kelsey Rae Court, Houston, TX 77069, USA

Elkins, Hillard *Theater Producer*
1335 N Doheny Dr, Los Angeles, CA 90069, USA

Elkins, Lawrence C (Larry) *Football Player*
%Saline Water Corp, PO Box 60889, Al Riyadh 11555, Saudi Arabia

Ellard, Henry A *Football Player*
161 W Portland Ave, Fresno, CA 93711, USA

Ellena, Jack *Football Player*
%Mountain Meadow Ranch, PO Box 610, Susanville, CA 96130, USA

Ellenstein, Robert *Actor*
5215 Sepulveda Blvd, #23F, Culver City, CA 90230, USA

Ellenthal, Ira *Publisher*
%New York Daily News, 220 E 42nd St, New York, NY 10017, USA

Eller, Carl *Football Player, Executive*
1035 Washburn Ave N, Minneapolis, MN 55411, USA

Ellerbee, Linda *Commentator*
%Lucky Duck Productions, 96 Morton St, #600, New York, NY 10014, USA
Elliman, Donald M, Jr *Publisher*
%Sports Illustrated Magazine, Rockefeller Center, New York, NY 10020, USA
Elliman, Yvonne *Singer*
%Talent Consultants International, 1560 Broadway, #1308, New York, NY 10036, USA
Ellin, Doug *Movie Director*
%Creative Artists Agency, 9830 Wilshire Blvd, Beverly Hills, CA 90212, USA
Elling, Kurt *Singer*
%Open Door Mgmt, 15327 Sunset Blvd, #365, Pacific Palisades, CA 90272, USA
Elliott, Alecia *Singer, Actress*
PO Box 3075, Muscle Shoals, AL 35662, USA
Elliott, Alison *Actress*
2 Ironsides, #18, Marina del Rey, CA 90292, USA
Elliott, Chalmers (Bump) *Football Player, Coach*
%University of Iowa, Athletic Dept, Iowa City, IA 52242, USA
Elliott, Chris *Actor, Comedian*
9000 Sunset Blvd, #1200, Los Angeles, CA 90069, USA
Elliott, David James *Actor*
%United Talent Agency, 9560 Wilshire Blvd, #500, Beverly Hills, CA 90212, USA
Elliott, Dennis *Drummer (Foreigner)*
%Hard to Handle Mgmt, 16501 Ventura Blvd, #602, Encino, CA 91436, USA
Elliott, Gordon *Chef*
%Food Network, 1180 Ave of Americas, #1200, New York, NY 10036, USA
Elliott, Herbert (Herb) *Track Athlete*
%Athletics Australia, 431 St Kilda Rd, #22, Melbourne VIC 3004, Australia
Elliott, Jack *Singer, Songwriter, Guitarist*
%Day, 300 W 55th St, New York, NY 10019, USA
Elliott, Joe *Singer (Def Leppard)*
%Q Prime Inc, 729 7th Ave, #1400, New York, NY 10019, USA
Elliott, John *Football Player*
PO Box 340, Warren, TX 77664, USA
Elliott, John (Jumbo) *Football Player*
%New York Jets, 1000 Fulton Ave, Hempstead, NY 11550, USA
Elliott, Michael *Organic Chemist*
45 Larkfield, Ewhurst, Cranleigh, Surrey GU6 7QU, England
Elliott, Missy Misdemeanor *Singer, Songwriter*
%Violator Mgmt, 205 Lexington Ave, #500, New York, NY 10016, USA
Elliott, Osborn *Journalist*
31 E 72nd St, #6B, New York, NY 10021, USA
Elliott, Paul H *Cinematographer*
%Sandra Marsh Mgmt, 9150 Wilshire Blvd, #220, Beverly Hills, CA 90212, USA
Elliott, Peggy Gordon *Educator*
929 Harvey Dunn St, Brookings, SD 57006, USA
Elliott, Peter R (Pete) *Football Player, Coach*
3003 Dunbarton Ave NW, Canton, OH 44708, USA
Elliott, R Keith *Businessman*
%Hercules Inc, Hercules Plaza, 1313 N Market St, Wilmington, DE 19894, USA
Elliott, Ralph E *WW II Navy Air Force Hero*
5150 Damascus Road S, Jacksonville, FL 32207, USA
Elliott, Sam *Actor*
33050 Pacific Coast Highway, Malibu, CA 90265, USA
Elliott, Sean M *Basketball Player*
%San Antonio Spurs, Alamodome, 1 SBC Center, San Antonio, TX 78219, USA
Elliott, Stephen *Movie Director*
PO Box 452, Paddington NSW 2021, Australia
Elliott, William C (Wild Bill) *Auto Racing Driver*
PO Box 665, Dawsonville, GA 30534, USA
Ellis, Albert *Clinical Psychologist*
%Institute for Rational-Emotional Therapy, 45 E 65th St, New York, NY 10021, USA
Ellis, Alton *Singer*
27 McConnell House, Deeley Road, London SW8, England
Ellis, Aunjanue *Actress*
%Creative Artists Agency, 9830 Wilshire Blvd, Beverly Hills, CA 90212, USA
Ellis, Bret Easton *Writer*
%International Creative Mgmt, 40 W 57th St, #1800, New York, NY 10019, USA
Ellis, Caroline *Actress*
8060 Saint Clair Ave, North Hollywood, CA 91605, USA
Ellis, Clarence J, Jr *Football Player*
3140 Robinwood Trail, Decatur, GA 30034, USA
Ellis, Cliff *Basketball Coach*
%Auburn University, Athletic Dept, Auburn, AL 36831, USA
Ellis, Dale *Basketball Player*
18110 SE 41st Place, Bellevue, WA 98008, USA
Ellis, Dock P *Baseball Player*
121 E 139th St, Los Angeles, CA 90061, USA
Ellis, Don *Bowler*
34 Crestwood Circle, Sugar Land, TX 77478, USA

Ellis - Elton

Ellis, Elmer *Historian*
3300 New Haven Ave, #223, Columbia, MO 65201, USA
Ellis, James R *Army General*
4213 Swann Ave, Tampa, FL 33609, USA
Ellis, Janet *Actress*
%Arlington Entertainments, 1/3 Charlotte St, London W1P 1HD, England
Ellis, Jimmy *Boxer*
5218 Saint Gabriel Lane, Louisville, KY 40291, USA
Ellis, Joseph J *Writer*
%Mount Holyoke College, History Dept, South Hadley, MA 01075, USA
Ellis, Kathleen (Kathy) *Swimmer*
3024 Woodshore Court, Carmel, IN 46033, USA
Ellis, LaPhonso *Basketball Player*
7041 Old Cutler Road, Coral Gables, FL 33143, USA
Ellis, Larry R *Army General*
Deputy Chief of Staff Operations/Plans, HqUSA, Pentagon, Washington, DC 20310, USA
Ellis, Leroy *Basketball Player, Coach*
4633 Marine Ave, #239, Lawndale, CA 90260, USA
Ellis, Luther *Football Player*
527 Riverside Ave, Mancos, CO 81328, USA
Ellis, M Herbert (Herb) *Jazz Guitarist*
%Producers Inc, 11806 N 56th St, Tampa, FL 33617, USA
Ellis, Maurice (Bo) *Basketball Player*
516 N 14th St, Milwaukee, WI 53233, USA
Ellis, Osian G *Concert Harpist*
90 Chandos Ave, London N20 9DZ, England
Ellis, Patrick (H J) *Educator*
%Catholic University, President's Office, Washington, DC 20064, USA
Ellis, Romallis *Boxer*
2062 San Marco Dr, Ellenwood, GA 30294, USA
Ellis, Ronald J E (Ron) *Hockey Player*
B C E Place, 30 Yonge St, Toronto ON M5E 1X8, Canada
Ellis, Samuel J (Sam) *Baseball Player*
12511 Forest Highlands Dr, Dade City, FL 33525, USA
Ellis, Scott *Theater Director*
420 Central Park West, #5B, New York, NY 10025, USA
Ellis, Shaun *Football Player*
%New York Jets, 1000 Fulton Ave, Hempstead, NY 11550, USA
Ellis, Terry *Singer (En Vogue)*
%East West Records, 75 Rockefeller Plaza, #1200, New York, NY 10019, USA
Ellison, Harlan J *Writer*
%Kilimajaro Group, PO Box 55548, Sherman Oaks, CA 91413, USA
Ellison, Lawrence J *Businessman*
%Oracle Systems, 500 Oracle Parkway, Redwood City, CA 94065, USA
Ellison, Pervis *Basketball Player*
36 Bishop Terrace, Waltham, MA 02452, USA
Ellison, William H (Willie) *Football Player*
3503 Mosley Court, Houston, TX 77004, USA
Elliss, Luther *Football Player*
2521 Plum Creek Court, Oakland, MI 48363, USA
Ellroy, James *Writer*
%Sobel Weber Assoc, 146 E 19th St, New York, NY 10003, USA
Ellsberg, Daniel *Political Activist*
90 Norwood Ave, Kensington, CA 94707, USA
Ellsworth, Frank L *Educator*
254 La Mirada Road, Pasadena, CA 91105, USA
Ellsworth, Richard C (Dick) *Baseball Player*
1099 W Morris Ave, Fresno, CA 93711, USA
Ellwood, Paul M, Jr *Physician*
%Jackson Hole Group, PO Box 270, Bondurant, WY 82922, USA
Elmore, Len *Basketball Player*
7118 Deer Valley Road, Highland, MD 20777, USA
Elrod, Jack *Cartoonist (Mark Trail)*
7240 Hunter's Branch Dr NE, Atlanta, GA 30328, USA
Els, Ernie *Golfer*
46 Chapman Road, Klippoortjie 1401, South Africa
Elsna, Hebe *Writer*
%Curtis Brown, 162/168 Regent St, London W1R 5TB, England
Elson, Karen *Model*
%Ford Models Agence, 9 Rue Scribe, 75009 Paris, France
Elster, Kevin D *Baseball Player*
5801 Marshall Dr, Huntington Beach, CA 92649, USA
Elswit, Richard (Rik) *Singer, Guitarist (Dr Hook)*
%Artists Int'l Mgmt, 9850 Sandalwood Blvd, #458, Boca Raton, FL 33428, USA
Elsworth, Michael *Actor*
%Sharon Power, PO Box 1243, Wellington, New Zealand
Elton, Ben *Actor, Comedian*
%Phil McIntyre Mgmt, 35 Soho Square, London W1V 5DG, England

Elvin, Violetta *Ballerina*
Marina di Equa, 80066 Seiano, Bay of Naples, Italy
Elvira, (Cassandra Peterson) *Actress*
%Queen B Productions, PO Box 38246, Los Angeles, CA 90038, USA
Elway, John A *Football Player*
10531 E Arapahoe Road, Centennial, CO 80112, USA
Elwes, Cary *Actor*
%Three Arts Entertainment, 9460 Wilshire Blvd, #700, Beverly Hills, CA 90212, USA
Ely, Alexandre *Soccer Player*
5526 N 2nd St, Philadelphia, PA 19120, USA
Ely, Jack *Singer, Guitarist (Kingsmen)*
%Jeff Hubbard Productions, PO Box 53664, Indianapolis, IN 46253, USA
Ely, Joe *Singer, Songwriter*
%Fitzgerald-Hartley, 34 N Palm St, #100, Ventura, CA 93001, USA
Ely, Melvin *Basketball Player*
%Los Angeles Clippers, Staples Center, 1111 S Figueroa St, Los Angeles, CA 90015, USA
Eman, J H A (Henny) *Prime Minister, Aruba*
%Prime Minister's Office, Oranjestad, Aruba
Emanuel, Alphonsia *Actress*
%Marina Martin, 12/13 Poland St, London W1V 3DE, England
Emanuel, Elizabeth F *Fashion Designer*
42A Warrington Crescent, Maida Vale, London W9 1EP, England
Emanuel, Frank *Football Player*
16614 E Course Dr, Tampa, FL 33624, USA
Emanuel, Rahm *Journalist, Government Official*
%White House, 1600 Pennsylvania Ave NW, Washington, DC 20500, USA
Embach, Carsten *Bobsled Athlete*
%BSR Rennsteig e V, Grafenrodaer Str 2, 98559 Oberhof, Germany
Emberg, Kelly *Actress, Model*
2835 McConnell Dr, Los Angeles, CA 90064, USA
Embry, Ethan *Actor*
%Kelly Bush, 3859 Cardiff Ave, #200, Culver City, CA 90232, USA
Embry, Wayne *Basketball Player, Executive*
130 W Juniper Lane, Moreland Hills, OH 44022, USA
Emburey, John E *Cricketer*
%Northantshire Cricket Club, Wantage Road, Northampton NN1 4TJ, England
Emerson, Alice F *Educator*
%Andrew Mellon Foundation, 140 E 62nd St, New York, NY 10021, USA
Emerson, David F *Navy Admiral*
1777 Chelwood Circle, Charleston, SC 29407, USA
Emerson, Douglas *Actor*
1450 Belfast Dr, Los Angeles, CA 90069, USA
Emerson, J Martin *Labor Leader*
%American Federation of Musicians, 1501 Broadway, New York, NY 10036, USA
Emerson, Keith *Musician (Emerson Lake & Palmer)*
%Columbia Artists Mgmt Inc, 165 W 57th St, New York, NY 10019, USA
Emerson, Roy *Tennis Player*
Private Bag 6060, Richmond South VIC 3121, Australia
Emert, George H *Educator*
%Utah State University, President's Office, Logan, UT 84322, USA
Emery, John *Bobsled Athlete*
2001 Union St, San Francisco, CA 94123, USA
Emery, Kenneth O *Oceanographer*
35 Horseshoe Lane, North Falmouth, MA 02556, USA
Emery, Lin *Sculptor*
7820 Dominican St, New Orleans, LA 70118, USA
Emery, Oren D *Religious Leader*
%Wesleyan International, 6060 Castleway West Dr, Indianapolis, IN 46250, USA
Emery, Ralph *Entertainer*
PO Box 23470, Nashville, TN 37202, USA
Emery, Victor *Bobsled Athlete*
61 Walton St, London SW 3J, England
Emick, Jarrod *Actor*
%Gersh Agency, 232 N Canon Dr, Beverly Hills, CA 90210, USA
Emilio *Singer*
%Refugee Mgmt, 209 10th Ave S, #347 Cummins Station, Nashville, TN 37203, USA
Eminem *Rap Artist, Actor*
%United Talent Agency, 9560 Wilshire Blvd, #500, Beverly Hills, CA 90212, USA
Emmanuel *Singer*
%Sendyk Leonard, 532 Colorado Ave, Santa Monica, CA 90401, USA
Emme *Model*
%Ford Model Agency, 142 Greene St, #400, New York, NY 10012, USA
Emmerich, Noah *Actor*
%William Morris Agency, 151 El Camino Dr, Beverly Hills, CA 90212, USA
Emmerich, Roland *Movie Director, Producer*
6073 Senalda Road, Los Angeles, CA 90068, USA
Emmert, Mark *Educator*
%Louisiana State University, President's Office, Baton Rouge, LA 70803, USA

E

Emmerton - English

Emmerton, Bill *Track Athlete*
615 Ocean Ave, Santa Monica, CA 90402, USA
Emmett, John C *Inventor (Antiulcer Compound)*
Oak House, Hatfield Broad Oak, Bishop's Stortford, Herts CM22 7HG, England
Emmons, Howard W *Mechanical Engineer*
1010 Waltham St, #443B, Lexington, MA 02421, USA
Emmott, Bill *Editor*
%Economist Magazine, 25 Saint James's St, London SW1A 1HG, England
Emory, Sonny *Drummer (Earth Wind & Fire)*
%Great Scott Productions, 137 N Wetherly Dr, #403, Los Angeles, CA 90048, USA
Emtman, Steven C (Steve) *Football Player*
19601 S Cheney Spangle Road, Cheney, WA 99004, USA
Enberg, Dick *Sportscaster*
1275 Virginia Way, La Jolla, CA 92037, USA
Endelman, Stephen *Composer*
%Gorfaine/Schwartz, 13245 Riverside Dr, #450, Sherman Oaks, CA 91423, USA
Ender Grummt, Kornelia *Swimmer*
%DSV, Postfach 420140, 34070 Kassel, Germany
Enevoldsen, Einar *Test Pilot*
9651 Lewis Ave, California City, CA 93505, USA
Engel, Albert E *Geologist*
%University of California, Scripps Institute, Geology Dept, La Jolla, CA 92093, USA
Engel, Albert J *Judge*
%US Court of Appeals, 110 Michigan Ave NW, Grand Rapids, MI 49503, USA
Engel, Georgia *Actress*
10820 Camarillo St, #3, North Hollywood, CA 91602, USA
Engelbart, Douglas C *Computer Scientist (Mouse Inventor)*
89 Catalpa Dr, Menlo Park, CA 94027, USA
Engelberger, Joseph F *Robotics Engineer*
%Transition Research Corp, 15 Durant Ave, Bethel, CT 06801, USA
Engelhard, David H *Religious Leader*
%Christian Reformed Church, 2850 Kalamazoo Ave SE, Grand Rapids, MI 49560, USA
Engelhardt, Thomas A (Tom) *Editorial Cartoonist*
%Saint Louis Post-Dispatch, Editorial Dept, 900 N Tucker, Saint Louis, MO 63101, USA
Engen, Corey *Skier*
506 N 40 W, Lindon, UT 84042, USA
Engen, D Travis *Businessman*
%ITT Industries, 4 W Red Oak Lane, White Plains, NY 10604, USA
Engerman, Stanley L *Economist, Historian*
181 Warrington Dr, Rochester, NY 14618, USA
Engholm, Bjorn *Government Official, Germany*
Jurgen-Wallenwever-Str 9, 23566 Lubeck, Germany
Engibous, Thomas J *Businessman*
%Texas Instruments, 8505 Forest Lane, PO Box 660199, Dallas, TX 75266, USA
England, Anthony W *Astronaut, Geophysicist*
7949 Ridgeway Court, Dexter, MI 48130, USA
England, Gordon R *Secretary, Navy*
%Homeland Security Department, Washington, DC 20528, USA
England, Richard *Architect*
26/1 Merchants St, Valletta, Malta
England, Tyler *Singer*
%Buddy Lee, 38 Music Square E, #300, Nashville, TN 37203, USA
Englander, Harold R *Dental Researcher*
11502 Whisper Bluff St, San Antonio, TX 78230, USA
Engle, Joe H *Astronaut, Air Force General*
3280 Cedar Heights Dr, Colorado Springs, CO 80904, USA
Engle, Robert F *Nobel Economics Laureate*
%New York University, Stern Business School, New York, NY 10012, USA
Englehart, Robert W (Bob), Jr *Editorial Cartoonist*
%Hartford Courant, Editorial Dept, 280 Broad St, Hartford, CT 06105, USA
English, Alexander (Alex) *Basketball Player*
596 Rimer Pond Road, Blythewood, SC 29016, USA
English, Diane *Writer*
%Shukovsky-English Ent, 4024 Radford Ave, Studio City, CA 91604, USA
English, Edmond J *Businessman*
%TJX Companies, 770 Cochituate Road, Framingham, MA 01701, USA
English, Floyd L *Businessman*
%Andrew Corp, 10500 W 153rd St, Orland Park, IL 60462, USA
English, James F, Jr *Educator*
31 Potter St, Groton, CT 06340, USA
English, Joseph T *Psychiatrist*
%Saint Vincent's Hospital, 203 W 12th St, New York, NY 10011, USA
English, L Douglas (Doug) *Football Player*
4306 Benedict Lane, Austin, TX 78746, USA
English, Michael *Singer*
%Trifecta Entertainment, 209 10th Ave S, #302, Nashville, TN 37203, USA
English, Paul *Actor*
%Wurzel Talent Mgmt, 19528 Ventura Blvd, #501, Tarzana, CA 91356, USA

Englund, Robert *Actor*
1616 Santa Cruz St, Laguna Beach, CA 92651, USA
Engstrom, Ted W *Association Executive*
%World Vision, 919 W Huntington Dr, Arcadia, CA 91007, USA
Engvall, Bill *Actor, Comedian*
%Four Points Entertainment, 8380 Melrose Ave, #310, Los Angeles, CA 90069, USA
Enis, Curtis *Football Player*
305 SE Deerfield Road, Union City, OH 45390, USA
Enke-Kania, Karin *Speed Skater*
Tolstoistr 3, 01326 Dresden, Germany
Enkhbayar, Nambaryn *Prime Minister, Mongolia*
%Prime Minister's Office, Great Hural, Ulan Bator 12, Mongolia
Enn, Hans *Alpine Skier*
Hinterglemm 400, 5754 Saalbach, Austria
Ennis, Ralph *Singer, Guitarist*
2 Kirklake Bank, Formby, Liverpool L37 2Y5, England
Ennis, Ray *Singer, Guitarist*
2 Kirklake Bank, Formby, Liverpool L37 2Y5, England
Eno, Brian *Composer, Musician*
%Opal Music, 3 Pembridge Mews, London W11 3EQ, England
Enrico, Roger A *Businessman*
%PepsiCo Inc, 700 Anderson Hill Road, Purchase, NY 10577, USA
Ensher, Jason R *Physicist*
%University of Colorado, Physics Dept, Boulder, CO 80309, USA
Ensign, Michael *Actor*
%Abrams Artists, 9200 Sunset Blvd, #1125, Los Angeles, CA 90069, USA
Entner, Warren *Singer, Guitarist (Grass Roots)*
%Thomas Cassidy, 11761 E Speedway Blvd, Tucson, AZ 85748, USA
Entremont, Philippe *Conductor, Concert Pianist*
10 Rue de Castuglione, 75001 Paris, France
Enya *Singer, Composer*
Ayesha Castle, County Dublin, Ireland
Enzensberger, Hans M *Writer*
Lindenstr 29, 60325 Frankfurt am Maim, Germany
Eotvos, Peter *Composer, Conductor*
Naardeweg 56, 1261 BV Blaircum, Netherlands
Ephron, Nora *Writer, Movie Director*
390 W End Ave, New York, NY 10024, USA
Epic *Rap Artist (Crazy Town)*
%Wyze Mgmt, 34 Maple St, London W1 5GD, England
Epperson-Doumani, Brenda *Actress*
%Kazarian/Spencer, 11365 Ventura Blvd, #100, Studio City, CA 91604, USA
Eppinger, Dale L *Vietnam War Air Force Hero*
101 Windy Hollow St, Victoria, TX 77904, USA
Epple, Maria *Alpine Skier*
Gunzesried 3, 87544 Blaicach, Germany
Epple-Beck, Irene *Alpine Skier*
Aufmberg 235, 87637 Seeg, Germany
Epps, Omar *Actor*
%Endeavor Talent Agency, 9701 Wilshire Blvd, #1000, Beverly Hills, CA 90212, USA
Epstein, Daniel M *Writer*
843 W University Parkway, Baltimore, MD 21210, USA
Epstein, David *Composer, Conductor*
%Thea Dispeker Artists, 59 E 54th St, New York, NY 10022, USA
Epstein, Gabriel *Architect*
3 Rue Mazet, 75006 Paris, France
Epstein, Jason *Editor*
%Random House, 1745 Broadway, #B1, New York, NY 10019, USA
Epstein, Joseph *Writer, Educator*
522 Church St, #6B, Evanston, IL 60201, USA
Erb, Donald J *Composer*
4073 Bluestone Road, Cleveland, OH 44121, USA
Erb, Richard D *Government Official*
%International Monetary Fund, 700 19th St NW, Washington, DC 20431, USA
Erbakan, Necmettin *Prime Minister, Turkey*
%National Salvation Party, Balgat, Ankara, Turkey
Erbe, Kathryn *Actress*
%LMR, 1964 Westwood, #400, Los Angeles, CA 90025, USA
Erburu, Robert F *Publisher, Businessman*
1518 Blue Jay Way, Los Angeles, CA 90069, USA
Erdman, Paul E *Writer*
1817 Lytton Springs Road, Healdsburg, CA 95448, USA
Erdman, Richard *Actor*
5655 Greenbush Ave, Van Nuys, CA 91401, USA
Erdmann, Susi-Lisa *Bobsled Athlete*
Karwendelstr 8A, 81369 Munich, Germany
Erdo, Peter Cardinal *Religious Leader*
%Mindszenty Hercegprimas Ter 2, 2501 Esztergom Magyarirszay, Hungary

Erdogan, Recep Tayyip *Prime Minister, Turkey*
%Premier's Office, Eski Basbakanlik Binasi, Bakanliklar, Ankara, Turkey

Erdrich, K Louise *Writer*
%Rambar & Curtis, 19 W 44th St, New York, NY 10036, USA

Ergen, Charles W *Businessman*
%EchoStar Communications Corp, 5701 S Santa Fe Dr, Littleton, CO 80120, USA

Erhardt, Warren R *Publisher*
455 Wakefield Dr, Metuchen, NJ 08840, USA

Eric B *Rap Artist (Eric B & Rakim)*
%Rush Artists, 1600 Varick St, New York, NY 10013, USA

Erickson, Arthur C *Architect*
%Arthur Erickson Architects, 1672 W 1st Ave, Vancouver BC V6J 1G1, Canada

Erickson, Craig *Football Player*
420 N Country Club Dr, Lake Worth, FL 33462, USA

Erickson, Dennis *Football Coach*
%San Francisco 49ers, 4949 Centennial Blvd, Santa Clara, CA 95054, USA

Erickson, Ethan *Actor*
%Gold Marshak Liedtke, 3500 W Olive Ave, #1400, Burbank, CA 91505, USA

Erickson, Keith *Basketball, Volleyball Player*
333 23rd St, Santa Monica, CA 90402, USA

Erickson, Robert *Composer*
%University of California, Music Dept, La Jolla, CA 92093, USA

Erickson, Scott G *Baseball Player*
1183 Corral Ave, Sunnyvale, CA 94086, USA

Erickson, Steve *Writer*
%Poseidon Press, 1230 Ave of Americas, New York, NY 10020, USA

Ericson, John *Actor*
7 Avenida Vista Grande, #310, Santa Fe, NM 87508, USA

Eriksen, Stein *Skier*
7700 Stein Way, Park City, UT 84060, USA

Erikson, Duke *Bassist, Keyboardist (Garbage)*
%Borman Entertainment, 1250 6th St, #401, Santa Monica, CA 90401, USA

Erikson, Raymond L *Medical Researcher*
%Harvard University, Medical School, 25 Shattuck St, Boston, MA 02115, USA

Erixon, Jan *Hockey Player*
PO Box 90111, Arlington, TX 76004, USA

Erlandson, Eric *Guitarist (Hole), Songwriter*
%Artist Group International, 9560 Wilshire Blvd, #400, Beverly Hills, CA 90212, USA

Erman, John *Movie Director*
%Creative Artists Agency, 9830 Wilshire Blvd, Beverly Hills, CA 90212, USA

Ermey, R Lee *Actor*
4348 W Ave N3, Palmdale, CA 93551, USA

Erni, Hans *Artist*
6045 Meggen, Lucerne, Switzerland

Ernst, Mark A *Businessman*
%H & R Block Inc, 4400 Main St, Kansas City, MO 64111, USA

Ernst, Richard R *Nobel Chemistry Laureate*
Kurlistr 24, 8404 Winterthur, Switzerland

Errazuriz Ossa, Francisco J Cardinal *Religious Leader*
Casilla 30D, Erasmo Escala 1894, Santiago, Chile

Erskine, Carl D *Baseball Player*
4031 Fallbrook Lane, Anderson, IN 46011, USA

Erskine, Peter *Jazz Drummer*
1727 Hill St, Santa Monica, CA 90405, USA

Erskine, Ralph *Architect*
Box 156, Gustav III's Vag, 170 11 Drottningholm, Sweden

Erstad, Darin C *Baseball Player*
141 Estancia, Irvine, CA 92602, USA

Ertl, Martina *Alpine Skier*
Erthofe 17, 83661 Lenggries, Germany

Eruzione, Michael (Mike) *Hockey Player*
274 Bowdoin St, Winthrop, MA 02152, USA

Erving, Julius W (Dr J) *Basketball Player*
400 E Colonial Dr, #1607, Orlando, FL 32803, USA

Ervolino, Frank *Labor Leader*
%Laundry & Dry Cleaning Union, 107 Delaware Ave, Buffalo, NY 14202, USA

Erwin, Bill *Actor*
12324 Moorpark St, Studio City, CA 91604, USA

Erwitt, Elliott R *Photographer*
88 Central Park West, New York, NY 10023, USA

Erxleban, Russell A *Football Player*
144 World of Tennis Square, Lakeway, TX 78738, USA

Esaki, Leo *Nobel Physics Laureate*
2484 Uenomuro, Tsukuba Ibaraki 305, Japan

Escalante, Jaime A *Educator*
%Hiram Johnson High School, 6879 14th Ave, Sacramento, CA 95820, USA

Eschbach, Jesse E *Judge*
%US Court of Appeals, US Courthouse, 701 Clematis St, West Palm Beach, FL 33401, USA

Eschenbach, Christoph *Conductor, Concert Pianist*
Maspalomas, Monte Leon 760625, Gran Canaria, Spain
Eschenmoser, Albert J *Chemist*
Bergstra 9, 8700 Kusnacht ZH, Switzerland
Eschert, Jurgen *Canoeing Athlete*
Tornowstr 8, 1447 Potsdam, Germany
Esiason, Norman J (Boomer) *Football Player, Sportscaster*
25 Heights Road, Plandome, NY 11030, USA
Esler-Smith, Frank *Keyboardist (Air Supply)*
%Agency for Performing Arts, 9200 Sunset Blvd, #900, Los Angeles, CA 90069, USA
Esmond, Carl *Actor*
576 N Tigertail Road, Los Angeles, CA 90049, USA
Esperian, Kallen R *Opera Singer*
514 Lindseywood Cove, Memphis, TN 38117, USA
Esposito, Anthony J (Tony) *Hockey Player, Executive*
418 55th Ave, Saint Petersburg Beach, FL 33706, USA
Esposito, Frank *Bowling Executive*
200 N State Route 17, Paramus, NJ 07652, USA
Esposito, Jennifer *Actress*
648 Broadway, #912, New York, NY 10012, USA
Esposito, Laura *Actress*
%Gersh Agency, 232 N Canon Dr, Beverly Hills, CA 90210, USA
Esposito, Philip A (Phil) *Hockey Player, Executive*
4807 Tea Rose Court, Lutz, FL 33558, USA
Espy, A Michael (Mike) *Secretary, Agriculture*
154 Deertrail Lane, Madison, MS 39110, USA
Esquivel, Laura *Writer*
%Creative Artists Agency, 9830 Wilshire Blvd, Beverly Hills, CA 90212, USA
Esquivel, Manuel *Prime Minister, Belize*
%United Democratic Party, 19 King St, PO Box 1143, Belize City, Belize
Essensa, Bob *Hockey Player, Coach*
%Boston Bruins, 1 Fleet Center, Boston, MA 02114, USA
Essex, David *Singer, Actor, Composer*
%London Mgmt, 2-4 Noel St, London W1V 3RB, England
Essex, Myron E *Microbiologist*
%Harvard School of Public Health, 665 Huntington Ave, Boston, MA 02115, USA
Essian, James S (Jim) *Baseball Manager*
134 Eckford Dr, Troy, MI 48085, USA
Esslinger, Hartmut *Industrial Designer*
%FrogDesign, 1327 Chesapeake Terrace, Sunnyvale, CA 94089, USA
Esswood, Paul L V *Opera Singer*
Jasmine Cottage, 42 Ferring Lane, Ferring, West Sussex BN12 6QT, England
Esteban, Manuel A *Educator*
%California State University, President's Office, Chico, CA 95929, USA
Estefan, Emilio *Musician, Producer*
%Estefan Enterprises, 420 Jefferson Ave, Miami Beach, FL 33139, USA
Estefan, Gloria *Singer, Songwriter*
%Estefan Enterprises, 420 Jefferson Ave, Miami Beach, FL 33139, USA
Estern, Neil *Sculptor*
82 Remsen St, Brooklyn, NY 11201, USA
Estes, A Shawn *Baseball Player*
%Tim Estes, 974 Casey St, Gardnerville, NY 89460, USA
Estes, Bob *Golfer*
4408 Long Champ Dr, #21, Austin, TX 78746, USA
Estes, Clarissa Pinkola *Psychologist, Writer*
%Knopf Publishers, 201 E 50th St, New York, NY 10022, USA
Estes, Ellen *Water Polo Player*
%Stanford University, Athletic Dept, Stanford, CA 94305, USA
Estes, Howell M, Jr *Air Force General, Businessman*
7603 Shadywood Road, Bethesda, MD 20817, USA
Estes, James *Cartoonist*
1103 Callahan St, Amarillo, TX 79106, USA
Estes, Robert *Actor*
910 Idaho Ave, Santa Monica, CA 90403, USA
Estes, Simon L *Opera Singer*
Hochstr 43, 8706 Feldmeilen, Switzerland
Estes, Will *Actor*
%Kelman & Arletta, 7813 Sunset Blvd, Los Angeles, CA 90046, USA
Estes, William K *Psychologist*
2714 E Pine Lane, Bloomington, IN 47401, USA
Esteve-Coll, Elizabeth *Museum Curator*
27 Ursula St, London SW11 3DW, England
Estevez, Emilio *Actor, Director*
PO Box 6448, Malibu, CA 90264, USA
Estevez, Luis *Fashion Designer*
122 E 7th St, Los Angeles, CA 90014, USA
Estevez, Ramon *Actor*
837 Ocean Ave, #101, Santa Monica, CA 90403, USA

Estevez - Evans

Estevez, Renee *Actress*
%Michael Mann Talent, 617 S Olive St, #311, Los Angeles, CA 90014, USA
Esthero *Singer*
%ArtistDirect, 10900 Wilshire Blvd, #1400, Los Angeles, CA 90024, USA
Estleman, Loren Daniel *Writer*
5552 Walsh Road, Whitmore Lake, MI 48189, USA
Estrada, Charle L (Chuck) *Baseball Player*
2225 Exposition Dr, #14, San Luis Obispo, CA 93401, USA
Estrada, Erik *Actor*
3768 Eureka Dr, North Hollywood, CA 91604, USA
Estrada, Erik-Michael *Singer (O-Town)*
%Trans Continetal Records, 7380 Sand Lake Road, #350, Orlando, FL 32819, USA
Estrich, Susan R *Attorney*
9255 Doheny Road, #802, West Hollywood, CA 90069, USA
Eszterhas, Joseph A *Writer*
%Rogers & Cowan, 6340 Breckenridge Run, Rex, GA 30273, USA
Etaix, Pierre *Movie Director, Actor*
Cirque Fratellini, 2 Rue de la Cloture, 75019 Paris, France
Etchegaray, Roger Cardinal *Religious Leader*
Piazza San Calisto, 00120 Vatican City
Etcheverry, Marco *Soccer Player*
%DC United, 14120 Newbrook Dr, Chantilly, VA 20151, USA
Etcheverry, Michel *Actor*
47 Rue du Borrego, 75020 Paris, France
Etheridge, Melissa L *Singer, Songwriter, Guitarist*
%W F Leopold Mgmt, 4425 Riverside Dr, #102, Burbank, CA 91505, USA
Ethridge, Mark F, III *Editor*
5516 Gorham Dr, Charlotte, NC 28226, USA
Etienne-Martin *Sculptor*
7 Rue du Pot de Fer, 75005 Paris, France
Etrog, Sorel *Artist*
PO Box 67034, 23 Yonge St, Toronto ON M4P 1E0, Canada
Etsel, Edward (Ed) *Marksman*
%University of Virginia, Athletic Dept, Charlottesville, VA 22906, USA
Etsou-Nzabi-Bamungwabi, Frederic *Religious Leader (Cardinal)*
%Archdiocese of Kinshasa, BP 8431, Kinshasa 1, Congo Democratic Republic
Etzel, Gregory A M *Vietnam War Air Force Hero*
7822 Wonder St, Citrus Heights, CA 95610, USA
Etzioni, Amitai W *Sociologist*
7110 Arran Place, Bethesda, MD 20817, USA
Etzwiler, Donnell D *Pediatrician*
7611 Bush Lake Dr, Minneapolis, MN 55438, USA
Eubank, Chris *Boxer*
9 Upper Dr, Hove, East Sussex BN3 6GR, England
Eubanks, Bob *Television Host*
3617 Roblar Ave, Santa Ynez, CA 93460, USA
Eubanks, Kevin *Jazz Guitarist*
%Ted Kurland, 173 Brighton Ave, Boston, MA 02134, USA
Eure, Wesley *Actor*
%Irv Schechter, 9300 Wilshire Blvd, #410, Beverly Hills, CA 90212, USA
Evangelista, Linda *Model*
655 Madison Ave, #2300, New York, NY 10021, USA
Evanovich, Janet *Writer*
PO Box 5487, Hanover, NH 03755, USA
Evans, Andrea *Actress*
%ARL, 8075 W 3rd St, #303, Los Angeles, CA 90048, USA
Evans, Anthony H *Educator*
%California State University, President's Office, San Bernardino, CA 92407, USA
Evans, Bill *Jazz Saxophonist, Keyboardist*
%Dept of Field Mgmt, 1501 Broadway, #1304, New York, NY 10036, USA
Evans, Bob O *Electrical Engineer, Computer Scientist*
170 Robin Road, Hillsborough, CA 94010, USA
Evans, Daniel J *Governor, Senator, WA; Educator*
%Daniel J Evans Assoc, 1111 3rd Ave, #3400, Seattle, WA 98101, USA
Evans, Darrell W *Baseball Player*
354 Provencal Road, Grosse Pointe, MI 48236, USA
Evans, Dick *Bowling Writer*
121 Morning Dove Court, Daytona Beach, FL 32119, USA
Evans, Donald L *Secretary, Commerce*
%Commerce Department, 14th St & Constitution Ave NW, Washington, DC 20230, USA
Evans, Dwayne *Track Athlete*
PO Box 91291, Phoenix, AZ 85066, USA
Evans, Edward P *Publisher*
712 5th Ave, #4900, New York, NY 10019, USA
Evans, Evans *Actress*
3114 Abington Dr, Beverly Hills, CA 90210, USA
Evans, Faith *Singer, Songwriter*
%J L Entertainment, 18653 Ventura Blvd, #340, Tarzana, CA 91356, USA

Evans, George *Cartoonist (Anna & Corrigan)*
%King Features Syndicate, 888 7th Ave, New York, NY 10106, USA
Evans, Glen *Molecular Biologist*
%Salk Institute, 10100 N Torrey Pines Road, La Jolla, CA 92037, USA
Evans, Greg *Cartoonist (Luann)*
216 Country Garden Lane, San Marcos, CA 92069, USA
Evans, Harold J *Plant Physiologist*
17320 Holy Names Dr, #C105, Lake Oswego, OR 97034, USA
Evans, Harold M *Editor*
%Random House, 1745 Broadway, #B1, New York, NY 10019, USA
Evans, J Handel *Educator*
%San Jose State University, President's Office, San Jose, CA 95192, USA
Evans, J Thomas *Wrestler*
607 S Fir Court, Broken Arrow, OK 74012, USA
Evans, James B (Jim) *Baseball Umpire*
1801 Rogge Lane, Austin, TX 78723, USA
Evans, Janet *Swimmer*
8 Barneburg, Dove Canyon, CA 92679, USA
Evans, John *Businessman*
%Alcan Aluminium, 1188 Sherbrooke St W, Montreal PC H3A 3G2, Canada
Evans, John B *Publisher*
%Murdoch Magazines, 755 2nd Ave, New York, NY 10017, USA
Evans, John E *Businessman*
%Allied Group, 701 5th Ave, Des Moines, IA 50391, USA
Evans, John R *Foundation Executive*
%Rockefeller Foundation, 1133 Ave of Americas, New York, NY 10036, USA
Evans, John V *Governor, ID*
%D L Evans Bank, 397 N Overland, Burley, ID 83318, USA
Evans, Lee *Actor*
%GAT Productions, 17 Brickwood Road, Croydon, Surrey CR0 6UL, England
Evans, Lee E *Track Athlete*
2650 College Place, Fullerton, CA 92831, USA
Evans, Linda *Actress*
PO Box 29, Rainier, WA 98576, USA
Evans, Lynn *Singer (Chordettes)*
%Richard Paul Assoc, 16207 Mott, Macomb Township, MI 48044, USA
Evans, Marsha Johnson *Association Executive, Navy Admiral*
%American Red Cross, 431 18th St NW, Washington, DC 20006, USA
Evans, Martin J *Geneticist*
Castle Rise 41, Rumney, Cardiff CF3 9BB, Wales
Evans, Mary Beth *Actress*
PO Box 50105, Pasadena, CA 91115, USA
Evans, Michael (Mike) *Actor*
12530 Collins St, North Hollywood, CA 91607, USA
Evans, Nicholas (Nick) *Writer*
%Delacorte Press, 1540 Broadway, New York, NY 10036, USA
Evans, Norm E *Football Player*
4143 Via Marina, Marina Del Rey, CA 90292, USA
Evans, Raymond R (Ray) *Football Player, Basketball Player*
8449 Somerset Dr, Prairie Village, KS 66207, USA
Evans, Richard *Sports Executive*
%Madison Square Garden, 4 Pennsylvania Plaza, New York, NY 10001, USA
Evans, Richard Paul *Writer*
%Simon & Schuster, 1230 Ave of Americas, New York, NY 10020, USA
Evans, Rob *Basketball Coach*
%Arizona State University, Athletic Dept, Tempe, AZ 85287, USA
Evans, Robert C *Mountaineer*
Ardincaple, Capel Curig, Betws-y-Coed, Northern Wales, Wales
Evans, Robert J (Bob) *Movie Producer*
%Robert Evans Productions, Paramount Pictures, 5555 Melrose, Los Angeles, 90038, USA
Evans, Robert S *Businessman*
%Crane Co, 100 Stamford Plaza, Stamford, CT 06902, USA
Evans, Ronald M *Geneticist*
%Salk Institute, 10100 N Torrey Pines Road, La Jolla, CA 92037, USA
Evans, Sara *Singer, Songwriter*
%William Morris Agency, 2100 W End Ave, #1000, Nashville, TN 37203, USA
Evans, Troy *Actor*
PO Box 834, Lakeside, MT 59922, USA
Evans, Walker *Truck/Off-Road Racing Driver*
%Walker Evans Racing, PO Box 2469, Riverside, CA 92516, USA
Evashevski, Forest *Football Coach*
5820 Clubhouse Dr, Vero Beach, FL 32967, USA
Evdokimova, Eva *Ballerina*
%Gregori Productions, PO Box 1586, New York, NY 10150, USA
Eve *Rap Artist (Ruff Ryders)*
%Creative Artists Agency, 9830 Wilshire Blvd, Beverly Hills, CA 90212, USA
Eve, Trevor J *Actor*
%International Creative Mgmt, 76 Oxford St, London W1N 0AX, England

Everest - Ezra

Everest, Frank K (Pete), Jr *Test Pilot, Air Force General*
12440 E Barbary Coast Road, Tucson, AZ 85749, USA
Everett, Carl E *Baseball Player*
%Chicago White Sox, Comiskey Park, 333 W 35th St, Chicago, IL 60616, USA
Everett, Chad *Actor*
5472 Island Forest Place, Westlake Village, CA 91362, USA
Everett, Danny *Track Athlete*
%Santa Monica Track Club, 1801 Ocean Park Ave, #112, Santa Monica, CA 90405, USA
Everett, James S (Jim) *Football Player*
31741 Contijo Way, Coto de Caza, CA 92679, USA
Everett, Rupert *Actor*
%International Creative Mgmt, 76 Oxford St, London W1N 0AX, England
Everett, Thomas G *Football Player*
5639 Bent Creek Trail, Dallas, TX 75252, USA
Everhard, Nancy *Actress*
%Kazarian/Spencer, 11365 Ventura Blvd, #100, Studio City, CA 91604, USA
Everhart, Angie *Model, Actress*
%Karin, 524 Broadway, #404, New York, NY 10012, USA
Everly, Donald (Don) *Singer (Everly Brothers)*
10414 Camarillo St, Toluca Lake, CA 91602, USA
Everly, Phil *Singer (Everly Brothers)*
10414 Camarillo St, Toluca Lake, CA 91602, USA
Evers, Charles *Civil Rights Activist*
1018 Pecan Park Dr, Jackson, MS 39209, USA
Evers, Jason *Actor*
232 N Crescent Dr, #101, Beverly Hills, CA 90210, USA
Evers-Williams, Myrlie *Association Executive*
15 SW Colorado Ave, #310, Bend, OR 97702, USA
Eversley, Frederick J *Sculptor*
1110 W Albert Kinney Blvd, Venice, CA 90291, USA
Everson, Corinna (Cory) *Body Builder*
23705 Van Owen St, West Hills, CA 91307, USA
Everson, Mark *Government Official*
%Internal Revenue Service, 1111 Constitution Ave NW, Washington, DC 20224, USA
Evert, Christine M (Chris) *Tennis Player*
6181 Hollow Lane, Delray Beach, FL 33484, USA
Evert, Ray F *Botanist*
810 Woodward Dr, Madison, WI 53704, USA
Evora, Cesaria *Singer*
%Monterey International, 200 W Superior, #202, Chicago, IL 60610, USA
Evren, Kenan *President, Turkey; Army General*
Beyaz Ev Sokak 21, Armutalan, Marmaris, Turkey
Evron, Ephraim *Government Official, Israel*
%Ministry of Foreign Affairs, Tel-Aviv, Israel
Ewald, Elwyn *Religious Leader*
%Free Lutheran Congregations, 12015 Manchester Road, Saint Louis, MO 63131, USA
Ewald, Reinhold *Cosmonaut, Germany*
%DLR Astronauterburo WT/AN, Linder Hohe, 51140 Cologne, Germany
Ewing, Barbara *Actress*
%Scott Marshall, 44 Perryn Road, London W3 7NA, England
Ewing, Maria L *Opera Singer*
33 Bramerton St, London SW3, England
Ewing, Patrick A *Basketball Player*
37 Summit St, Englewood Cliffs, NJ 07632, USA
Eyadema, E Gnassingbe *President, Togo; Army General*
%President's Office, Palais Presidentiel, Ave de la Marina, Lome, Togo
Eyes, Raymond *Publisher*
%McCall's Magazine, 375 Lexington Ave, New York, NY 10017, USA
Eyharts, Leopold *Spatinaut, France*
49 Rue Desnouttes, 75015 Paris, France
Eyler, John *Businessman*
%Toys 'R' Us Inc, 461 From Road, Paramus, NJ 07652, USA
Eyre, Richard *Movie, Theater, Television Director*
%Judy Daish, 2 Saint Charles Place, London W10 6EG, England
Eysenck, Hans J *Psychologist*
10 Dorchester Dr, London SE24, England
Eyskens, Mark *Government Official, Belgium*
Graaf de Grunnelaan, 3001 Heverlee, Belgium
Eytchison, Ronald M *Navy Admiral*
11 Prentice Lane, Signal Mountain, TN 37377, USA
Ezra, Derek *Government Official, Businessman*
2 Salisbury Road, Wimbledon, London SW19 4EZ, England

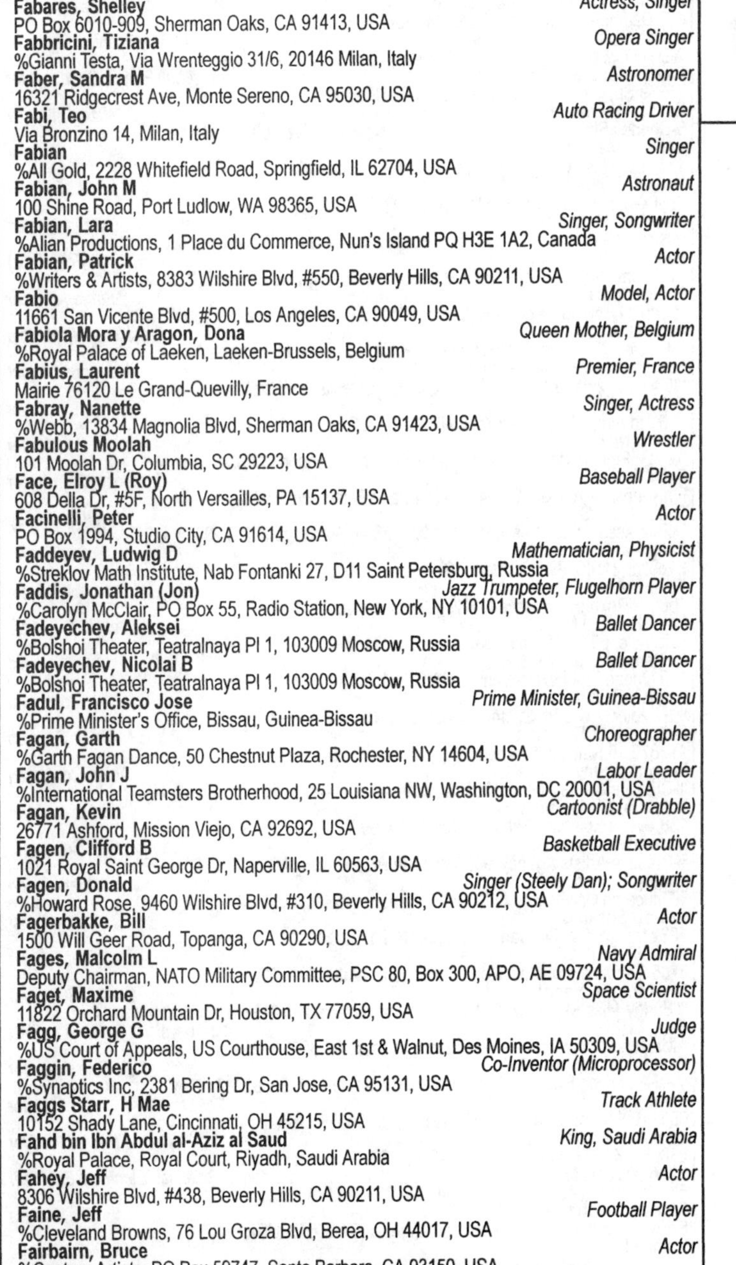

Fabares, Shelley — *Actress, Singer*
PO Box 6010-909, Sherman Oaks, CA 91413, USA
Fabbricini, Tiziana — *Opera Singer*
%Gianni Testa, Via Wrenteggio 31/6, 20146 Milan, Italy
Faber, Sandra M — *Astronomer*
16321 Ridgecrest Ave, Monte Sereno, CA 95030, USA
Fabi, Teo — *Auto Racing Driver*
Via Bronzino 14, Milan, Italy
Fabian — *Singer*
%All Gold, 2228 Whitefield Road, Springfield, IL 62704, USA
Fabian, John M — *Astronaut*
100 Shine Road, Port Ludlow, WA 98365, USA
Fabian, Lara — *Singer, Songwriter*
%Alian Productions, 1 Place du Commerce, Nun's Island PQ H3E 1A2, Canada
Fabian, Patrick — *Actor*
%Writers & Artists, 8383 Wilshire Blvd, #550, Beverly Hills, CA 90211, USA
Fabio — *Model, Actor*
11661 San Vicente Blvd, #500, Los Angeles, CA 90049, USA
Fabiola Mora y Aragon, Dona — *Queen Mother, Belgium*
%Royal Palace of Laeken, Laeken-Brussels, Belgium
Fabius, Laurent — *Premier, France*
Mairie 76120 Le Grand-Quevilly, France
Fabray, Nanette — *Singer, Actress*
%Webb, 13834 Magnolia Blvd, Sherman Oaks, CA 91423, USA
Fabulous Moolah — *Wrestler*
101 Moolah Dr, Columbia, SC 29223, USA
Face, Elroy L (Roy) — *Baseball Player*
608 Della Dr, #5F, North Versailles, PA 15137, USA
Facinelli, Peter — *Actor*
PO Box 1994, Studio City, CA 91614, USA
Faddeyev, Ludwig D — *Mathematician, Physicist*
%Streklov Math Institute, Nab Fontanki 27, D11 Saint Petersburg, Russia
Faddis, Jonathan (Jon) — *Jazz Trumpeter, Flugelhorn Player*
%Carolyn McClair, PO Box 55, Radio Station, New York, NY 10101, USA
Fadeyechev, Aleksei — *Ballet Dancer*
%Bolshoi Theater, Teatralnaya Pl 1, 103009 Moscow, Russia
Fadeyechev, Nicolai B — *Ballet Dancer*
%Bolshoi Theater, Teatralnaya Pl 1, 103009 Moscow, Russia
Fadul, Francisco Jose — *Prime Minister, Guinea-Bissau*
%Prime Minister's Office, Bissau, Guinea-Bissau
Fagan, Garth — *Choreographer*
%Garth Fagan Dance, 50 Chestnut Plaza, Rochester, NY 14604, USA
Fagan, John J — *Labor Leader*
%International Teamsters Brotherhood, 25 Louisiana NW, Washington, DC 20001, USA
Fagan, Kevin — *Cartoonist (Drabble)*
26771 Ashford, Mission Viejo, CA 92692, USA
Fagen, Clifford B — *Basketball Executive*
1021 Royal Saint George Dr, Naperville, IL 60563, USA
Fagen, Donald — *Singer (Steely Dan); Songwriter*
%Howard Rose, 9460 Wilshire Blvd, #310, Beverly Hills, CA 90212, USA
Fagerbakke, Bill — *Actor*
1500 Will Geer Road, Topanga, CA 90290, USA
Fages, Malcolm L — *Navy Admiral*
Deputy Chairman, NATO Military Committee, PSC 80, Box 300, APO, AE 09724, USA
Faget, Maxime — *Space Scientist*
11822 Orchard Mountain Dr, Houston, TX 77059, USA
Fagg, George G — *Judge*
%US Court of Appeals, US Courthouse, East 1st & Walnut, Des Moines, IA 50309, USA
Faggin, Federico — *Co-Inventor (Microprocessor)*
%Synaptics Inc, 2381 Bering Dr, San Jose, CA 95131, USA
Faggs Starr, H Mae — *Track Athlete*
10152 Shady Lane, Cincinnati, OH 45215, USA
Fahd bin Ibn Abdul al-Aziz al Saud — *King, Saudi Arabia*
%Royal Palace, Royal Court, Riyadh, Saudi Arabia
Fahey, Jeff — *Actor*
8306 Wilshire Blvd, #438, Beverly Hills, CA 90211, USA
Faine, Jeff — *Football Player*
%Cleveland Browns, 76 Lou Groza Blvd, Berea, OH 44017, USA
Fairbairn, Bruce — *Actor*
%Century Artists, PO Box 59747, Santa Barbara, CA 93150, USA
Fairchild, Barbara — *Singer, Songwriter*
%Blackwood Mgmt, PO Box 5331, Sevierville, TN 37864, USA
Fairchild, John B — *Publisher*
Chalet Bianchina, Talstr GR, 7250 Klosters, Switzerland
Fairchild, Morgan — *Actress*
%Bartels Co, PO Box 57593, Sherman Oaks, CA 91413, USA
Fairchild, Thomas E — *Judge*
%US Court of Appeals, 111 N Canal St, Building 6, Chicago, IL 60606, USA

F

Faircloth - Fargas

Faircloth, D McLauchlin (Lauch) *Senator, NC*
813 Beamon St, Clinton, NC 28328, USA
Faircloth, Michael *Fashion Designer*
%Lilly Dodson, 33 Highland Park Village, Dallas, TX 75205, USA
Fairly, Ronald R (Ron) *Baseball Player, Sportscaster*
75369 Spyglass Dr, Indian Wells, CA 92210, USA
Fairstein, Linda *Writer, Attorney*
%Charles Scribner's Sons, 866 3rd Ave, New York, NY 10022, USA
Faison, Matthew *Actor*
13701 E Kagel Canyon Road, Sylmar, CA 91342, USA
Faison, William E (Earl) *Football Player*
7886 Mission Vista Dr, San Diego, CA 92120, USA
Faithfull, Marianne *Singer, Songwriter, Actress*
%Susan Dewsnap, 235 Footscray Road, New Eltham, London SE9 2EL, England
Fakir, Abdul (Duke) *Singer (Four Tops)*
%William Morris Agency, 151 El Camino Dr, Beverly Hills, CA 90212, USA
Falana, Lola *Singer, Dancer*
%Capital Entertainment, 217 Seaton Place NE, Washington, DC 20002, USA
Falcam, Leo A *President, Micronesia*
%President's Office, Palikir, Kolonia, Pohnpei FM 96941, Micronesia
Falcao, Jose Freire Cardinal *Religious Leader*
QL 12-CJ12, Lote 1, Lago Sul, 71630-325 Brasilia DF, Brazil
Falco, Edie *Actor*
733 3rd Ave, #1900, New York, NY 10017, USA
Faldo, Nicholas A (Nick) *Golfer*
%IMG, Pier House, Strand on Green, Chiswick, London W4 3NN, England
Falik, Yuri A *Composer, Conductor*
Finlyandsky Prospekt 1, #54, 194044 Saint Petersburg, Russia
Falk, David B *Sports Attorney*
%Falk Assoc, 5335 Wisconsin Ave NW, #850, Washington, DC 20015, USA
Falk, Paul *Figure Skater*
Sybelstr 21, 40239 Dusseldorf, Germany
Falk, Peter *Actor*
1004 N Roxbury Dr, Beverly Hills, CA 90210, USA
Falk, Randall M *Religious Leader*
%Temple, 5015 Harding Road, Nashville, TN 37205, USA
Falkenstein, Claire *Artist*
719 Ocean Front Walk, Venice, CA 90291, USA
Fallaci, Oriana *Journalist*
%Rizzoli, 31 W 57th St, #400, New York, NY 10019, USA
Falldin, N O Thorbjorn *Prime Minister, Sweden*
As, 870 16 Ramvik, Sweden
Fallon, Jimmy *Actor, Comedian*
%Creative Artists Agency, 9830 Wilshire Blvd, Beverly Hills, CA 90212, USA
Faloona, Christopher J *Cinematographer*
138 Via La Soledad, Redondo Beach, CA 90277, USA
Faltermayer, Harold *Composer*
%Creative Artists Agency, 9830 Wilshire Blvd, Beverly Hills, CA 90212, USA
Faltings, Gerd *Mathematician*
%Princeton University, Mathematics Dept, Princeton, NJ 08544, USA
Faludi, Susan C *Journalist*
1032 Irving St, #204, San Francisco, CA 94122, USA
Falwell, Jerry L *Religious Leader*
3765 Candlers Mountain Road, Lynchburg, VA 24502, USA
Fambrough, Henry *Singer (Spinners)*
%Buddy Allen Mgmt, 3750 Hudson Manor Terrace, #3AG, Bronx, NY 10463, USA
Fang Lizhi *Astrophysicist, Political Activist*
%University of Arizona, Physics Dept, Tucson, AZ 85721, USA
Fangio, Juan Manuel, II *Auto Racing Driver*
%All-American Racers, 2334 S Broadway, Santa Ana, CA 92707, USA
Fann, Al *Actor*
6051 Hollywood Blvd, #207, Hollywood, CA 90028, USA
Fanning, Michael L (Mike) *Football Player*
28808 S 4190 Road, Inola, OK 74036, USA
Fano, Robert M *Computer Scientist, Electrical Engineer*
51 Woodland Way, North Chatham, MA 02650, USA
Faracy, Stephanie *Actress*
8765 Lookout Mountain Road, Los Angeles, CA 90046, USA
Faragalli, Lindy *Bowler*
113 N 5th Ave, Manville, NJ 08835, USA
Farar, Hassan Abshir *Prime Minister, Somalia*
%Prime Minister's Office, People's Palace, Mogadishy, Somalia
Farentino, James *Actor*
1340 Londonderry Place, Los Angeles, CA 90069, USA
Fares, Muhammad Ahmed Al *Cosmonaut, Syria*
PO Box 1272, Aleppo, Syria
Fargas, Antonio *Actor*
%H David Moss, 733 Seward St, #PH, Los Angeles, CA 90038, USA

Fargis, Joe *Equestrian Rider*
PO Box 2168, Middlebury, CA 20118, USA
Fargo, Donna *Singer*
PO Box 210877, Nashville, TN 37221, USA
Fargo, Thomas B *Navy Admiral*
Commander, Pacific Fleet, Camp H M Smith, Honolulu, HI 96861, USA
Farina, David *Religious Leader*
%Christian Church of North America, 41 Sherbrooke Road, Trenton, NJ 08638, USA
Farina, Dennis *Actor*
217 Edgewood Ave, Clearwater, FL 33755, USA
Farina, Johnny *Guitarist (Santo & Johnny)*
%Bellrose Music, 308 E 6th St, #13, New York, NY 10003, USA
Faris, Anna *Actress*
%Raw Talent, 9615 Brighton Way, #300, Beverly Hills, CA 90210, USA
Farish, William S *Diplomat*
%US Embassy, Grosvenor Square, 55 Upper Brook St, London W1A 2LQ, England
Farkas, Bertalan *Cosmonaut, Hungary*
A Magyar Koztarsasag, Kutato Urhajosa, Pf 25, 1885 Budapest, Hungary
Farkas, Ferenc *Composer*
Nagyatai Utca 12, 1026 Budapest, Hungary
Farley, Carole *Opera, Concert Singer*
270 Riverside Dr, New York, NY 10025, USA
Farmer, John, Jr *Governor, NJ*
%Attorney General's Office, Hughes Justice Complex, Trenton, NJ 08625, USA
Farmer, Mike *Basketball Player, Coach*
308 W McDonald Ave, Richmond, CA 94801, USA
Farmer, Mimsy *Actress*
%Cineart, 36 Rue de Ponthieu, 75008 Paris, France
Farmer, Phillip W *Businessman*
%Harris Corp, 1025 W NASA Blvd, Melbourne, FL 32919, USA
Farner, Mark *Singer, Guitarist*
%Bobby Roberts, PO Box 1547, Goodlettsville, TN 37070, USA
Farnham, John P *Singer*
%TalentWorks, 663 Victoria St, Abbottsford VIC 3067, Australia
Farquhar, Marilyn G *Cell Biologist, Pathologist*
12894 Via Latina, Del Mar, CA 92014, USA
Farr, Bruce *Marine Architect*
%Bruce Farr Assoc, 613 3rd St, Annapolis, MD 21403, USA
Farr, Felicia *Actress*
1143 Tower Road, Beverly Hills, CA 90210, USA
Farr, Jaime *Actor*
51 Ranchero Road, Bell Canyon, CA 91307, USA
Farr, Melvin (Mel), Sr *Football Player*
4525 Lakeview Court, Bloomfield Hills, MI 48301, USA
Farrakhan, Louis *Religious Leader*
%Nation of Islam, 734 W 79th St, Chicago, IL 60620, USA
Farrar, Frank L *Governor, SD*
203 9th Ave, Britton, SD 57430, USA
Farrel, Franklin *Hockey Player*
89 Notch Hill Road, #223, North Branford, CT 06471, USA
Farreley, Alexander *Governor, VI*
%Governor's Office, Government Offices, Charlotte Amalie, VI 00801, USA
Farrell, Colin *Actor*
10 Herbert Lane, Dublin 2, Ireland
Farrell, Mike *Actor*
14011 Ventura Blvd, Sherman Oaks, CA 91423, USA
Farrell, Perry *Singer (Jane's Addiction)*
%H K Mgmt, 9200 W Sunset Blvd, #530, Los Angeles, CA 90069, USA
Farrell, Sean *Football Player*
7 Legends Circle, Melville, NY 11747, USA
Farrell, Sharon *Actress*
369 S Doheny Dr, Beverly Hills, CA 90211, USA
Farrell, Shea *Actor*
%Artists Agency, 1180 S Beverly Dr, #301, Los Angeles, CA 90035, USA
Farrell, Suzanne *Ballet Dancer*
%Kennedy Center for Performing Arts, Education Dept, Washington, DC 20566, USA
Farrell, Terence (Terry) *Architect*
17 Hatton St, London NW8 8PL, England
Farrell, Terry *Actress*
%Don Buchwald, 6500 Wilshire Blvd, #2200, Los Angeles, CA 90048, USA
Farrelly, Bobby *Movie Director*
%Creative Artists Agency, 9830 Wilshire Blvd, Beverly Hills, CA 90212, USA
Farrelly, Peter *Movie Director*
%Creative Artists Agency, 9830 Wilshire Blvd, Beverly Hills, CA 90212, USA
Farrimond, Richard A *Astronaut, England*
%Metra Marconi Center, Gunnels Wood Rd, Stevenage, Herts SG1 2AS, England
Farrington, Robert G (Bob) *Harness Racing Driver*
201 Lake Hinsdale Dr, #211, Willowbrook, IL 60527, USA

Farris, Dionne *Singer*
%Creative Artists Agency, 9830 Wilshire Blvd, Beverly Hills, CA 90212, USA
Farris, Jerome *Judge*
%US Court of Appeals, US Courthouse, 1010 5th Ave, Seattle, WA 98104, USA
Farris, Joseph *Cartoonist*
68 Sunburst Circle, Fairport, NY 14450, USA
Farriss, Andrew *Keyboardist (INXS)*
8 Hayes St, #1, Neutral Bay 20891 NSW, Australia
Farriss, Jon *Drummer, Singer (INXS)*
8 Hayes St, #1, Neutral Bay 20891 NSW, Australia
Farriss, Tim *Guitarist (INXS)*
8 Hayes St, #1, Neutral Bay 20891 NSW, Australia
Farrow, Mia V *Actress*
124 Henry Sanford Road, Bridgewater, CT 06752, USA
Fasman, Gerald D *Biochemist*
69 Kingswood Road, Newton, MA 02166, USA
Fass, Horst *Photojournalist*
12 Norwich St, London EC4A, England
Fassbaender, Brigitte *Opera Singer*
Am Theater, 38100 Braunschweig, Germany
Fassell, Jim *Football Coach*
%New York Giants, Giants Stadium, East Rutherford, NJ 07073, USA
Fast, Darrell *Religious Leader*
%Mennonite Church General Conference, PO Box 347, Newton, KS 67114, USA
Fast, Larry *Composer, Musician*
%Polydor Records, 70 Universal City Plaza, Universal City, CA 91608, USA
Fat Joe *Rap Artist, Actor*
%Famous Artists Agency, 250 W 57th St, New York, NY 10107, USA
Fatone, Joey, Jr *Singer ('N Sync)*
%Wright Entertainment, 7680 Universal Blvd, #500, Orlando, FL 32819, USA
Fauci, Anthony S *Immunologist*
3012 43rd St NW, Washington, DC 20016, USA
Faucon, Bernard *Photographer*
6 Rue Barbanegre, 75019 Paris, France
Faulk, Marshall *Football Player*
6430 Clayton Road, #305, Saint Louis, MO 63117, USA
Faulkner, Eric *Guitarist (Bay City Rollers)*
27 Preston Grange, Preston Pans E, Lothian, Scotland
Faure, Maurice H *Government Official, France*
28 Blvd Raspail, 75007 Paris, France
Faustino, David *Actor*
%Artists Agency, 1180 S Beverly Dr, #301, Los Angeles, CA 90035, USA
Fauza, Dario *Surgeon*
%Harvard Medical School, 25 Shattuck St, Boston, MA 02115, USA
Favier, Jean-Jacques *Spatinaut, France*
%Technologies Avances, 17 Ave des Martys, 38054 Grenoble Cedex, France
Favre, Brett L *Football Player*
3071 Gothic Court, Green Bay, WI 54313, USA
Favreau, Jon *Actor, Writer*
%United Talent Agency, 9560 Wilshire Blvd, #500, Beverly Hills, CA 90212, USA
Fawcett, Don W *Anatomist*
1224 Lincoln Road, Missoula, MT 59802, USA
Fawcett, Farrah *Actress, Model*
10580 Wilshire Blvd, #14NE, Los Angeles, CA 90024, USA
Faxon, Brad *Golfer*
77 Rumstick Road, Barrington, RI 02806, USA
Fay, Martin *Fiddler (Chieftains)*
%Macklam Feldman Mgmt, 1505 W 2nd Ave, #200, Vancouver BC V6H 3Y4, Canada
Fay, Peter T *Judge*
%US Court of Appeals, 99 NE 4th St, Miami, FL 33132, USA
Fayed, Mohamed al- *Businessman*
Craven Cottage, Stevenage Road, Fulham, London SW6 6HH, England
Fazio, Tom *Golf Course Architect*
%Fazio Golf Course Designers, 401 N Main St, #400, Hendersonville, NV 28792, USA
Fearon, Douglas T *Immunologist*
%Wellcome Trust Immunology Unit, Hills Road, Cambridge CB2 2SP, England
Feaster, Allison *Basketball Player*
%Charlotte Sting, 100 Hive Dr, Charlotte, NC 28217, USA
Federko, Bernie *Hockey Player*
2219 Devonsbrook Dr, Chesterfield, MO 63005, USA
Federman, Raymond *Writer*
12428 Avenida Consentido, San Diego, CA 92128, USA
Fedewa, Tim *Auto Racing Driver*
1737 Onondaga Road, Holt, MI 48842, USA
Fedorov, Sergei *Hockey Player*
1966 Tiverton Road, Bloomfield Hills, MI 48304, USA
Fedoseyev, Vladimir I *Conductor*
%Moscow House of Recording, Kachalova 24, 121069 Moscow, Russia

Fedotov, Maxim V *Concert Violinist*
Tolbukhin Str 8, Kop 1, #6, 121596 Moscow, Russia
Fee, Melinda *Actress*
145 S Fairfax Ave, #310, Los Angeles, CA 90036, USA
Fegley, Richard *Photographer*
%Playboy Magazine, Reader Services, 680 N Lake Shore Dr, Chicago, IL 60611, USA
Feher, George *Physicist*
%University of California, Physics Dept, 9500 Gilman Dr, La Jolla, CA 92093, USA
Fehr, Brendan *Actor*
%Look Mgmt, 1529 W 6th Ave, #110, Vancouver BC V5J 1R1, Canada
Fehr, Donald M *Labor Leader*
%Major League Baseball Players Assn, 805 3rd Ave, New York, NY 10022, USA
Fehr, Oded *Actor*
%I F A Talent Agency, 8730 Sunset Blvd, #490, Los Angeles, CA 90069, USA
Fehr, Rick *Golfer*
2731 223rd Ave NE, Sammamish, WA 98074, USA
Fehr, Steve *Bowler*
6216 Highcedar Court, Cincinnati, OH 45233, USA
Fehrenbach, Charles M *Astronomer*
Les Magnanarelles, 84160 Lourmarin, France
Feiffer, Jules *Cartoonist*
325 W End Ave, #12A, New York, NY 10023, USA
Feigenbaum, Armand V *Businessman, Systems Engineer*
%General Systems, 23 South St, #250, Pittsfield, MA 01201, USA
Feigenbaum, Edward A *Computer Scientist*
1017 Cathcart Way, Stanford, CA 94305, USA
Feilden, Bernard M *Architect*
Stiffkey Old Hall, Wells-next-to-the-Sea, Norfolk NR23 1QJ, England
Feinberg, Wilfred *Judge*
%US Court of Appeals, US Courthouse, Foley Square, New York, NY 10007, USA
Feinstein, A Richard *Physician*
1760 2nd Ave, #32C, New York, NY 10128, USA
Feinstein, Alan *Actor*
%Badgley Connor Talent, 9229 Sunset Blvd, #311, Los Angeles, CA 90069, USA
Feinstein, John *Sportswriter, Commentator*
22 Tuthill Dr, Shelter Island, NY 11964, USA
Feinstein, Michael *Singer, Pianist*
4647 Kingswell Ave, #110, Los Angeles, CA 90027, USA
Felber, Dean *Bassist (Hootie & the Blowfish)*
%FishCo Mgmt, PO Box 5456, Columbia, SC 29250, USA
Felch, William C *Physician*
8545 Carmel Valley Road, Carmel, CA 93923, USA
Feld, Eliot *Dancer, Choreographer*
%Feld Ballet, 890 Broadway, #800, New York, NY 10003, USA
Feldenkrais, Moshe *Psychologist*
University of Tel-Aviv, Psychology Dept, Tel-Aviv, Israel
Felder, Don *Singer, Guitarist (Eagles)*
PO Box 6051, Malibu, CA 90264, USA
Felder, Raoul Lionel *Attorney*
437 Madison Ave, New York, NY 10022, USA
Feldman, Bella *Artist*
12 Summit Lane, Berkeley, CA 94708, USA
Feldman, Corey *Actor*
%Baker/Winokur/Ryder, 9100 Wilshire Blvd, #600, Beverly Hills, CA 90212, USA
Feldman, Jerome M *Physician*
2744 Sevier St, Durham, NC 27705, USA
Feldman, Michelle *Bowler*
%Gary Feldman, PO Box 713, Skaneateles, NY 13152, USA
Feldman, Myer *Government Official*
%Ginsberg Feldman Bress, 1250 Connecticut Ave NW, Washington, DC 20036, USA
Feldman, Sandra (Sandy) *Labor Leader*
%American Federation of Teachers, 555 New Jersey Ave NW, Washington, DC 20001, USA
Feldmann, Marc *Rheumatologist*
%Charing Cross Hospital, Saint Dunstan's Road, London W6 8RP, England
Feldon, Barbara *Actress, Model*
14 E 74th St, New York, NY 10021, USA
Feldshuh, Tovah S *Actress*
322 Central Park W, #11B, New York, NY 10025, USA
Feldstein, Martin S *Government Official, Economist*
147 Clifton St, Belmont, MA 02478, USA
Felici, Angelo Cardinal *Religious Leader*
Piazza della Citta Leonina 9, 00193 Rome, Italy
Feliciano, Jose *Singer, Guitarist*
%World Entertainment Assoc, 297101 Kinderkamack Road, #128, Oradell, NJ 07649, USA
Felipe *Crown Prince, Spain*
%Palacio de la Zarzuela, 28080 Madrid, Spain
Felke, Petra *Track Athlete*
%SC Motor Jena, Wollnitzevstr 42, 07749 Jena, Germany

F

Felker - Ferguson

Felker, Clay *Editor*
322 E 57th St, New York, NY 10022, USA
Feller, Robert W A (Bob) *Baseball Player*
PO Box 157, Gates Mills, OH 44040, USA
Fellowes, Julian *Actor*
%International Creative Mgmt, 76 Oxford St, London W1N 0AX, England
Fellows, Edith *Actress*
2016 1/2 N Vista del Mar, Los Angeles, CA 90068, USA
Felsenstein, Lee *Inventor (Portable Computer)*
2490 Greer Road, Palo Alto, CA 94303, USA
Felton, Dennis *Basketball Coach*
%University of Georgia, Athletic Dept, Athens, GA 30602, USA
Felton, John *Singer (Diamonds)*
%GMS, PO Box 1031, Montrose, CA 91021, USA
Felts, Narvel *Singer, Songwriter*
2005 Narvel Felts Way, Malden, MO 63863, USA
Feltsman, Vladimir *Concert Pianist*
%Columbia Artists Mgmt Inc, 165 W 57th St, New York, NY 10019, USA
Fencik, J Gary *Football Player*
1134 W Schubert Ave, Chicago, IL 60614, USA
Fender, Freddy *Singer, Songwriter, Guitarist*
6438 Revolution Dr, Corpus Christi, TX 78413, USA
Fenech, Edwige *Actress*
%Carol Levi Co, Via Giuseppe Pisanelli, 00196 Rome, Italy
Fenech, Jeff *Boxer*
PO Box 21, Hardys Bay, NSW 2257, Australia
Fenech-Adami, Edward *Prime Minister, Malta*
176 Main St, Birkikara, Malta
Feng Ying *Ballerina*
%Central Ballet of China, 3 Taiping St, Beijing 100050, China
Feng-HsiungHsu *Computer Engineer*
%IBM T J Watson Research Center, PO Box 218, Yorktown Heights, NY 10598, USA
Fenimore, Robert D (Bob) *Football Player*
1214 Fairway Dr, Stillwater, OK 74074, USA
Fenn, John B *Nobel Chemistry Laureate*
4909 Cary Street Road, Richmond, VA 23226, USA
Fenn, Sherilyn *Actress*
16501 Ventura Blvd, #304, Encino, CA 91436, USA
Fenton, James *Writer*
%P F D, Drury House, 34-43 Russell St, London WC2B 5HA, England
Feoktistov, Konstantin P *Cosmonaut*
%Potchta Kosmonavtov, Moskovskoi Oblasti, 141160 Syvisdny Goroduk, Russia
Feranec, Peter *Conductor*
%Artists Mgmt Zurich, Rutistra 52, 8044 Zurich-Gockhausen, Sweden
Feraud, Gianfranco *Fashion Designer*
25 Rue Saint Honore, 75001 Paris, France
Ferdinand, Marie *Basketball Player*
%San Antonio Silver Stars, 1 SBC Center, San Antonio, TX 78219, USA
Ferentz, Kirk *Football Coach*
%University of Iowa, Athletic Dept, Iowa City, IA 52242, USA
Fergason, James L (Jim) *Inventor (Thermal Imaging Device)*
145 Garland Dr, Menlo Park, CA 94025, USA
Fergus, Keith *Golfer*
%Advantage International, 1751 Pinnacle Dr, #1500, McLean, VA 22102, USA
Fergus-Thompson, Gordo *Concert Pianist*
150 Audley Road, Hendon, London NW4 3EG, England
Ferguson Cullum, Cathy *Swimmer*
21861 Oceanview Lane, Huntington Beach, CA 92646, USA
Ferguson, Alexander C (Alex) *Soccer Player, Manager*
%Manchester United FC, Old Trafford, Manchester M16 0RA, England
Ferguson, Charles A *Editor*
1448 Joseph St, New Orleans, LA 70115, USA
Ferguson, Christopher J *Astronaut*
16111 Park Center Way, Houston, TX 77059, USA
Ferguson, Clarence C, Jr *Diplomat, Attorney*
%Harvard University, Law School, Cambridge, MA 02138, USA
Ferguson, Craig *Actor, Comedian*
%Creative Artists Agency, 9830 Wilshire Blvd, Beverly Hills, CA 90212, USA
Ferguson, Frederick E *Vietnam War Army Hero (CMH)*
106 E Stellar Parkway, Chandler, AZ 85226, USA
Ferguson, James (Jim) *Water Polo Player*
26931 Whitehouse Road, Santa Clarita, CA 91351, USA
Ferguson, James L *Businessman*
%General Foods Corp, 800 Westchester Ave, Rye Brook, NY 10573, USA
Ferguson, Jay *Actor*
560 N St SW, #304, Washington, DC 20024, USA
Ferguson, Joe C, Jr *Football Player, Coach*
10457 Ervin McGarrah Road, Lowell, AR 72745, USA

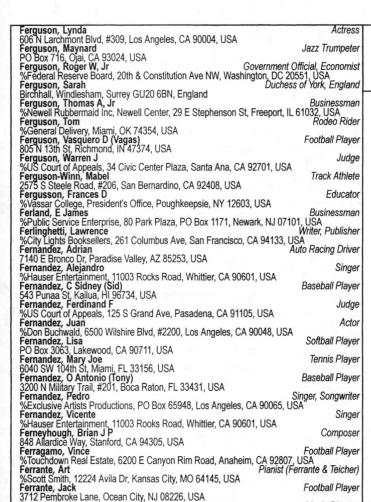

Ferguson, Lynda *Actress*
606 N Larchmont Blvd, #309, Los Angeles, CA 90004, USA
Ferguson, Maynard *Jazz Trumpeter*
PO Box 716, Ojai, CA 93024, USA
Ferguson, Roger W, Jr *Government Official, Economist*
%Federal Reserve Board, 20th & Constitution Ave NW, Washington, DC 20551, USA
Ferguson, Sarah *Duchess of York, England*
Birchhall, Windlesham, Surrey GU20 6BN, England
Ferguson, Thomas A, Jr *Businessman*
%Newell Rubbermaid Inc, Newell Center, 29 E Stephenson St, Freeport, IL 61032, USA
Ferguson, Tom *Rodeo Rider*
%General Delivery, Miami, OK 74354, USA
Ferguson, Vasquero D (Vagas) *Football Player*
805 N 13th St, Richmond, IN 47374, USA
Ferguson, Warren J *Judge*
%US Court of Appeals, 34 Civic Center Plaza, Santa Ana, CA 92701, USA
Ferguson-Winn, Mabel *Track Athlete*
2575 S Steele Road, #206, San Bernardino, CA 92408, USA
Fergusson, Frances D *Educator*
%Vassar College, President's Office, Poughkeepsie, NY 12603, USA
Ferland, E James *Businessman*
%Public Service Enterprise, 80 Park Plaza, PO Box 1171, Newark, NJ 07101, USA
Ferlinghetti, Lawrence *Writer, Publisher*
%City Lights Booksellers, 261 Columbus Ave, San Francisco, CA 94133, USA
Fernandez, Adrian *Auto Racing Driver*
7140 E Bronco Dr, Paradise Valley, AZ 85253, USA
Fernandez, Alejandro *Singer*
%Hauser Entertainment, 11003 Rocks Road, Whittier, CA 90601, USA
Fernandez, C Sidney (Sid) *Baseball Player*
543 Punaa St, Kailua, HI 96734, USA
Fernandez, Ferdinand F *Judge*
%US Court of Appeals, 125 S Grand Ave, Pasadena, CA 91105, USA
Fernandez, Juan *Actor*
%Don Buchwald, 6500 Wilshire Blvd, #2200, Los Angeles, CA 90048, USA
Fernandez, Lisa *Softball Player*
PO Box 3063, Lakewood, CA 90711, USA
Fernandez, Mary Joe *Tennis Player*
6040 SW 104th St, Miami, FL 33156, USA
Fernandez, O Antonio (Tony) *Baseball Player*
3200 N Military Trail, #201, Boca Raton, FL 33431, USA
Fernandez, Pedro *Singer, Songwriter*
%Exclusive Artists Productions, PO Box 65948, Los Angeles, CA 90065, USA
Fernandez, Vicente *Singer*
%Hauser Entertainment, 11003 Rooks Road, Whittier, CA 90601, USA
Ferneyhough, Brian J P *Composer*
848 Allardice Way, Stanford, CA 94305, USA
Ferragamo, Vince *Football Player*
%Touchdown Real Estate, 6200 E Canyon Rim Road, Anaheim, CA 92807, USA
Ferrante, Art *Pianist (Ferrante & Teicher)*
%Scott Smith, 12224 Avila Dr, Kansas City, MO 64145, USA
Ferrante, Jack *Football Player*
3712 Pembroke Lane, Ocean City, NJ 08226, USA
Ferrara, Abel *Movie Director*
%International Creative Mgmt, 8942 Wilshire Blvd, #219, Beverly Hills, CA 90211, USA
Ferrara, Adam *Actor*
%Conversation Co, 697 Middle Neck Road, Great Neck, NY 11023, USA
Ferrare, Cristina *Model, Entertainer*
10727 Wilshire Blvd, #1602, Los Angeles, CA 90024, USA
Ferrari, Gianantonio *Businessman*
%Honeywell Inc, Honeywell Plaza, Minneapolis, MN 55408, USA
Ferrari, Michael R, Jr *Educator*
570 Greenway Dr, Lake Forest, IL 60045, USA
Ferrari, Tina *Dancer, Wrestler*
2901 S Las Vegas Blvd, Las Vegas, NV 89109, USA
Ferraro, Dave *Bowler*
672 E Chester St, Kingston, NY 12401, USA
Ferraro, Geraldine A *Representative, NY*
575 Park Ave, New York, NY 10021, USA
Ferratti, Rebecca *Model, Actress*
10061 Riverside Dr, #721, Toluca Lake, CA 91602, USA
Ferrazzi, Ferruccio *Artist*
Piazza delle Muse, Via G G Porro 27, 00197 Rome, Italy
Ferrazzi, Pierpaolo *Canoeing Athlete*
%EuroGrafica, Via del Progresso, 36035 Marano Vicenza, Italy
Ferre, Gianfranco *Fashion Designer*
Villa Della Spiga 19/A, 20121 Milan, Italy
Ferreira, Wayne *Tennis Player*
%Int'l Mgmt Group, 1 Erieview Plaza, 1360 E 9th St, #1300, Cleveland, OH 44114, USA

Ferrell Edmonson, Barbara A *Track Athlete*
%University of Nevada, Athletic Dept, Las Vegas, NV 89154, USA
Ferrell, Conchata *Actress*
1335 N Seward St, Los Angeles, CA 90028, USA
Ferrell, Rachelle *Singer*
%Vida Music Group, 19800 Cornerstone Square, #415, Ashburn, VA 20147, USA
Ferrell, Tyra *Actress*
%Gersh Agency, 232 N Canon Dr, Beverly Hills, CA 90210, USA
Ferrell, Will *Actor, Comedian*
%MSI, 237 W 35th St, #400, New York, NY 10001, USA
Ferrer, Danay *Singer (Innosense)*
%Evolution Talent, 1776 Broadway, #1500, New York, NY 10019, USA
Ferrer, Mel *Actor*
6590 Camino Caretta, Carpinteria, CA 93013, USA
Ferrer, Miguel *Actor*
1007 Maybrook Dr, Beverly Hills, CA 90210, USA
Ferreras, Francisco (Pipin) *Free Diver*
7548 W Treasure Dr, North Bay Village, FL 33141, USA
Ferrero, Louis P *Businessman*
PO Box 675744, Rancho Santa Fe, CA 92067, USA
Ferrigno, Lou *Actor, Bodybuilder*
%Craig Mgmt, 125 S Sycamore Ave, Los Angeles, CA 90036, USA
Ferrin, Arnie *Basketball Player*
910 Donner Way, #301, Salt Lake City, UT 84108, USA
Ferris, John *Swimmer*
1961 Klamath River Dr, Rancho Cordova, CA 95670, USA
Ferriss, David M (Boo) *Baseball Player*
510 Robinson Dr, Cleveland, MS 38732, USA
Ferritor, Daniel E *Educator*
%University of Arkansas, Chancellor's Office, Fayetteville, AR 72701, USA
Ferron *Singer, Songwriter*
%JR Productions, 4930 Paradise Dr, Tiburon, CA 94920, USA
Ferry, Bryan *Singer, Songwriter*
%IE Mgmt, 59-A Chesson Road, London W14 9QS, England
Ferry, Daniel J W (Danny) *Basketball Player*
%San Antonio Spurs, Alamodome, 1 SBC Center, San Antonio, TX 78219, USA
Ferry, David R *Writer*
%Wellesley College, English Dept, Wellesley, MA 02181, USA
Ferry, John D *Chemist*
6175 Mineral Point Road, Madison, WI 53705, USA
Ferry, Robert (Bob) *Basketball Player*
2129 Beach Haven Road, Annapolis, MD 21401, USA
Fersht, Alan R *Organic Chemist*
2 Barrow Close, Cambridge CB2 2AT, England
Fesperman, John E *Businessman*
%J C Penney Co, 6501 Legacy Dr, Plano, TX 75024, USA
Festinger, Leon *Psychologist*
37 W 12th St, New York, NY 10011, USA
Fetisov, Viacheslav (Slava) *Hockey Player*
65 Avon Dr, Essex Fells, NJ 07021, USA
Fetter, Trevor *Businessman*
%Tenet Healthcare Corp, 3820 State St, Santa Barbara, CA 93105, USA
Fetterhoff, Robert *Religious Leader*
%Fellowship of Grace Brethern, PO Box 386, Winona Lake, IN 46590, USA
Fettig, Jeff M *Businessman*
%Whirlpool Corp, 2000 N State St, RR 63, Benton Harbor, MI 49022, USA
Fetting, Rainer *Artist*
Hasenheide 61, 1000 Berlin 61, Germany
Fettman, Martin J *Astronaut, Veterinarian*
5468 Tiller Court, Fort Collins, CO 80528, USA
Feuer, Cy *Theater, Movie Producer*
%Feuer & Martin, 630 Park Ave, New York, NY 10021, USA
Feuerstein, Mark *Actor*
%Innovative Artists, 1505 10th St, Santa Monica, CA 90401, USA
Feulner, Edwin J, Jr *Foundation Executive*
%Heritage Foundation, 214 Massachusetts Ave NE, Washington, DC 20002, USA
Feustel, Andrew J *Astronaut*
4003 Elm Crest Trail, Houston, TX 77059, USA
Fewx, Gene *Sculptor*
666 15th St NE, Salem, OR 97301, USA
Fey *Singer*
%RAC, Paseo Palmas 1005, #1, Chapultapec Lomas, Mexico City 11000, Mexico
Fey, Michael *Cartoonist (Committed)*
%United Feature Syndicate, 200 Madison Ave, New York, NY 10016, USA
Fforde, Jasper *Writer*
%Viking Press, 375 Hudson St, New York, NY 10014, USA
Fichter, Rick T *Cinematographer*
7 Kramer Place, San Francisco, CA 94133, USA

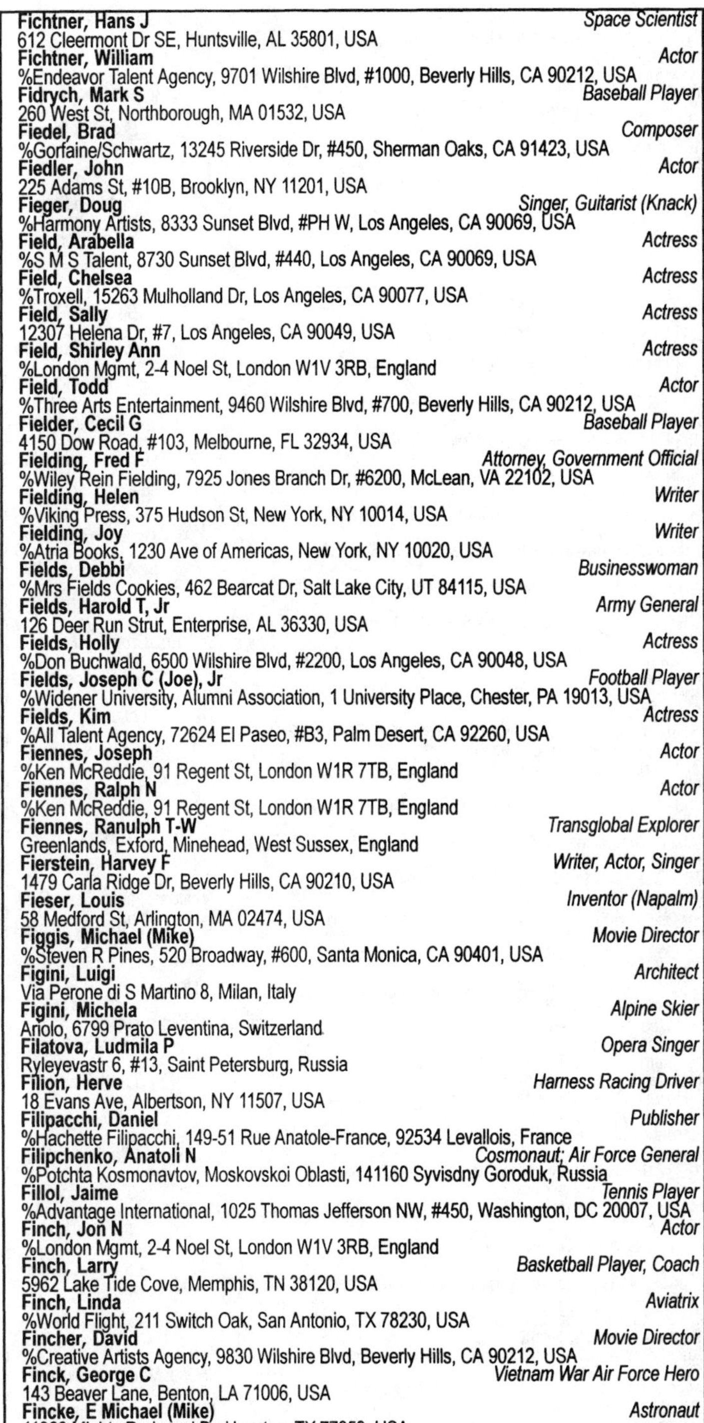

Fichtner, Hans J *Space Scientist*
612 Cleermont Dr SE, Huntsville, AL 35801, USA
Fichtner, William *Actor*
%Endeavor Talent Agency, 9701 Wilshire Blvd, #1000, Beverly Hills, CA 90212, USA
Fidrych, Mark S *Baseball Player*
260 West St, Northborough, MA 01532, USA
Fiedel, Brad *Composer*
%Gorfaine/Schwartz, 13245 Riverside Dr, #450, Sherman Oaks, CA 91423, USA
Fiedler, John *Actor*
225 Adams St, #10B, Brooklyn, NY 11201, USA
Fieger, Doug *Singer, Guitarist (Knack)*
%Harmony Artists, 8333 Sunset Blvd, #PH W, Los Angeles, CA 90069, USA
Field, Arabella *Actress*
%S M S Talent, 8730 Sunset Blvd, #440, Los Angeles, CA 90069, USA
Field, Chelsea *Actress*
%Troxell, 15263 Mulholland Dr, Los Angeles, CA 90077, USA
Field, Sally *Actress*
12307 Helena Dr, #7, Los Angeles, CA 90049, USA
Field, Shirley Ann *Actress*
%London Mgmt, 2-4 Noel St, London W1V 3RB, England
Field, Todd *Actor*
%Three Arts Entertainment, 9460 Wilshire Blvd, #700, Beverly Hills, CA 90212, USA
Fielder, Cecil G *Baseball Player*
4150 Dow Road, #103, Melbourne, FL 32934, USA
Fielding, Fred F *Attorney, Government Official*
%Wiley Rein Fielding, 7925 Jones Branch Dr, #6200, McLean, VA 22102, USA
Fielding, Helen *Writer*
%Viking Press, 375 Hudson St, New York, NY 10014, USA
Fielding, Joy *Writer*
%Atria Books, 1230 Ave of Americas, New York, NY 10020, USA
Fields, Debbi *Businesswoman*
%Mrs Fields Cookies, 462 Bearcat Dr, Salt Lake City, UT 84115, USA
Fields, Harold T, Jr *Army General*
126 Deer Run Strut, Enterprise, AL 36330, USA
Fields, Holly *Actress*
%Don Buchwald, 6500 Wilshire Blvd, #2200, Los Angeles, CA 90048, USA
Fields, Joseph C (Joe), Jr *Football Player*
%Widener University, Alumni Association, 1 University Place, Chester, PA 19013, USA
Fields, Kim *Actress*
%All Talent Agency, 72624 El Paseo, #B3, Palm Desert, CA 92260, USA
Fiennes, Joseph *Actor*
%Ken McReddie, 91 Regent St, London W1R 7TB, England
Fiennes, Ralph N *Actor*
%Ken McReddie, 91 Regent St, London W1R 7TB, England
Fiennes, Ranulph T-W *Transglobal Explorer*
Greenlands, Exford, Minehead, West Sussex, England
Fierstein, Harvey F *Writer, Actor, Singer*
1479 Carla Ridge Dr, Beverly Hills, CA 90210, USA
Fieser, Louis *Inventor (Napalm)*
58 Medford St, Arlington, MA 02474, USA
Figgis, Michael (Mike) *Movie Director*
%Steven R Pines, 520 Broadway, #600, Santa Monica, CA 90401, USA
Figini, Luigi *Architect*
Via Perone di S Martino 8, Milan, Italy
Figini, Michela *Alpine Skier*
Ariolo, 6799 Prato Leventina, Switzerland
Filatova, Ludmila P *Opera Singer*
Ryleyevastr 6, #13, Saint Petersburg, Russia
Filion, Herve *Harness Racing Driver*
18 Evans Ave, Albertson, NY 11507, USA
Filipacchi, Daniel *Publisher*
%Hachette Filipacchi, 149-51 Rue Anatole-France, 92534 Levallois, France
Filipchenko, Anatoli N *Cosmonaut; Air Force General*
%Potchta Kosmonavtov, Moskovskoi Oblasti, 141160 Syvisdny Goroduk, Russia
Fillol, Jaime *Tennis Player*
%Advantage International, 1025 Thomas Jefferson NW, #450, Washington, DC 20007, USA
Finch, Jon N *Actor*
%London Mgmt, 2-4 Noel St, London W1V 3RB, England
Finch, Larry *Basketball Player, Coach*
5962 Lake Tide Cove, Memphis, TN 38120, USA
Finch, Linda *Aviatrix*
%World Flight, 211 Switch Oak, San Antonio, TX 78230, USA
Fincher, David *Movie Director*
%Creative Artists Agency, 9830 Wilshire Blvd, Beverly Hills, CA 90212, USA
Finck, George C *Vietnam War Air Force Hero*
143 Beaver Lane, Benton, LA 71006, USA
Fincke, E Michael (Mike) *Astronaut*
11923 Mighty Redwood Dr, Houston, TX 77059, USA

F

Finckel, David *Cellist (Emerson String Quartet)*
%I M G Artists, 3 Burlington Lane, Chiswick, London W4 2TH, England
Finder, Joseph *Writer*
%Avon William Morrow, 1350 Ave of Americas, New York, NY 10019, USA
Findlay, Conn F *Rowing Athlete, Yachtsman*
1920 Oak Knoll, Belmont, CA 94002, USA
Fingers, Roland G (Rollie) *Baseball Player*
10675 Fairfield Ave, Las Vegas, NV 89123, USA
Finkel, Fyvush *Actor*
155 E 50th St, #6E, New York, NY 10022, USA
Finkel, Henry (Hank) *Basketball Player*
2 Pocahontas Way, Lynnfield, MA 01940, USA
Finkel, Shelly *Boxing Promoter*
310 Madison Ave, #804, New York, NY 10017, USA
Finlay, Frank *Actor*
%Ken McReddie, 91 Regent St, London W1R 7TB, England
Finley, Charles E (Chuck) *Baseball Player*
22 Old Course Dr, Newport Beach, CA 92660, USA
Finley, David *Astronaut, Astronomer*
1642 Milvia St, #3S, Berkeley, CA 94709, USA
Finley, Gerard H *Opera Singer*
%I M G Artists, 3 Burlington Lane, Chiswick, London W4 2TH, England
Finley, John L *Astronaut*
1894 Woodchase Glen Dr, Cordova, TN 38016, USA
Finley, Karen *Conceptual Artist*
%Creative Time, 307 7th Ave, #1904, New York, NY 10001, USA
Finley, Michael *Basketball Player*
%Dallas Mavericks, 2909 Taylor St, Dallas, TX 75226, USA
Finn, John W *WW II Navy Hero (CMH)*
36585 Old Highway 80, Pine Valley, CA 91962, USA
Finn, Neil *Singer, Songwriter*
%William Morris Agency, 151 El Camino Dr, Beverly Hills, CA 90212, USA
Finn, Patrick *Actor*
%Brillstein/Grey, 9150 Wilshire Blvd, #350, Beverly Hills, CA 90212, USA
Finn, Tim *Singer (Split Enz/Crowded House)*
%Grant Thomas Mgmt, 98 Surrey St, Darlinghurst NSW 2010, Australia
Finn, Veronica *Singer (Innosense)*
%Evolution Talent, 1776 Broadway, #1500, New York, NY 10019, USA
Finn, William *Composer, Lyricist*
%New York University, Music Dept, New York, NY 10012, USA
Finneran Rittenhouse, Sharon *Swimmer*
212 Harbor Dr, Santa Cruz, CA 95062, USA
Finneran, John G *Navy Admiral*
2904 N Leisure World Blvd, #404, Silver Spring, MD 20906, USA
Finney, Albert *Actor*
%Michael Simkins, 45/51 Whitfield St, London W1P 6AA, England
Finney, Allison *Golfer*
78160 Desert Mountain Circle, Indio, CA 92201, USA
Finney, Tom *Soccer Player, Executive*
%Preston North End FC, Deepdale, Sir Finney Way, Preston PR1 6RU, England
Finnie, Linda A *Concert Singer*
16 Golf Course, Girvan, Ayrshire KA26 9HW, England
Finsterwald, Dow *Golfer*
%Broadmoor Golf Club, 1 Lake Circle, Colorado Springs, CO 80906, USA
Fiorentino, Linda *Actress*
%United Talent Agency, 9560 Wilshire Blvd, #500, Beverly Hills, CA 90212, USA
Fiorillo, Elisbetta *Opera Singer*
%Columbia Artists Mgmt Inc, 165 W 57th St, New York, NY 10019, USA
Fiorina, Carleton S (Carly) *Businesswoman*
%Hewlett-Packard Co, 19111 Pruneridge Ave, Cupertino, CA 95014, USA
Fireman, Paul B *Businessman*
%Reebok International, 1895 J W Foster Blvd, Canton, MA 02021, USA
Fires, Earlie S *Thoroughbred Racing Jockey*
16337 Rivervale Lane, Rivervale, AR 72377, USA
Firestone, Roy *Sportscaster*
%Seizen/Wallach Productions, 257 S Rodeo Dr, Beverly Hills, CA 90212, USA
First, Neal L *Geneticist*
9437 W Garnette Dr, Sun City, AZ 85373, USA
Firth, Colin *Actor*
%International Creative Mgmt, 76 Oxford St, London W1N 0AX, England
Firth, Peter *Actor*
%Markham & Froggatt, Julian House, 4 Windmill St, London W1P 1HF, England
Fischer Schmidt, Birgit *Canoeing Athlete*
Kuckuckswald 11, 14532 Kleinmachnow, Germany
Fischer, Edmond H *Nobel Medicine Laureate*
5540 N Windermere Road, Seattle, WA 98105, USA
Fischer, Ernst Otto *Nobel Chemistry Laureate*
Sohnckestr 16, 81479 Munich, Germany

Fischer, Ivan 1 Andrassy Utca 27, 1061 Budapest, Hungary	*Conductor*
Fischer, Lisa %Alive Enterprises, 3264 S Kihei Road, Kihei, HI 96753, USA	*Singer*
Fischer, Patrick (Pat) PO Box 4289, Leesburg, VA 20177, USA	*Football Player*
Fischer, Stanley 181 E 65th St, #23A, New York, NY 10021, USA	*Economist*
Fischer, Sven Schillerhoehe 7, 98574 Schmalkalden, Germany	*Biathlete*
Fischer, William A (Moose) 1790 Pinnacle Ridge Lane, Colorado Springs, CO 80919, USA	*Football Player*
Fischer-Dieskau, Dietrich Lindenallee 22, 12587 Berlin, Germany	*Opera, Concert Singer; Conductor*
Fischetti, Vincent %Rockefeller University, Medical Center, 1230 York Ave, New York, NY 10021, USA	*Microbiologist*
Fish, Ginger %Mitch Schneider Organization, 14724 Ventura Blvd, #410, Sherman Oaks, CA 91403, USA	*Drummer (Marilyn Manson)*
Fish, Howard M 1223 Capilano Dr, Shreveport, LA 71106, USA	*Air Force General*
Fishburne, Laurence %Landmark Entertainment, 4116 W Magnolia Blvd, #101, Burbank, CA 91505, USA	*Actor*
Fisher, Anna L 1912 Elmen St, Houston, TX 77019, USA	*Astronaut*
Fisher, Bernard 5636 Aylesboro Ave, Pittsburgh, PA 15217, USA	*Surgeon*
Fisher, Bernard F 4200 W King Road, Kuna, ID 83634, USA	*Vietnam War Air Force Hero (CMH)*
Fisher, Carrie 1700 Coldwater Canyon Road, Beverly Hills, CA 90210, USA	*Actress, Writer*
Fisher, Derek %Los Angeles Lakers, Staples Center, 1111 S Figueroa St, Los Angeles, CA 90015, USA	*Basketball Player*
Fisher, Eddie 1000 North Point St, #1802, San Francisco, CA 94109, USA	*Singer, Actor*
Fisher, Eddie G 408 Cardinal Circle S, Altus, OK 73521, USA	*Baseball Player*
Fisher, Elder A (Bud) 7551 Brackenwood Circle N, Indianapolis, IN 46260, USA	*Bowling Executive*
Fisher, Evan %GEMS, PO Box 1031, Montrose, CA 91021, USA	*Singer (Diamonds)*
Fisher, Frances %I F A Talent Agency, 8730 Sunset Blvd, #490, Los Angeles, CA 90069, USA	*Actress*
Fisher, Jeff %Tennessee Titans, 460 Great Circle Road, Nashville, TN 37228, USA	*Football Coach*
Fisher, Joely %Krost-Chapin, 9000 W Sunset Blvd, #711, West Hollywood, CA 90069, USA	*Actress*
Fisher, Jules E %Jules Fisher Enterprises, 126 5th Ave, New York, NY 10011, USA	*Theater Lighting Designer*
Fisher, Mary %Charles Scribner's Sons, 866 3rd Ave, New York, NY 10022, USA	*AIDS Activist*
Fisher, Matthew 39 Croham Road, South Croydon CR2 7HD, England	*Organist (Procul Harum)*
Fisher, Raymond C %US Court of Appeals, 125 S Grand Ave, Pasadena, CA 91105, USA	*Judge*
Fisher, Red %Montreal Gazette, 250 Saint Antoine W, Montreal QC H2Y 3R7, Canada	*Sportswriter*
Fisher, Roger %Borman Entertainment, 1250 6th St, #401, Santa Monica, CA 90401, USA	*Guitarist (Heart)*
Fisher, Sarah PO Box 533189, Indianapolis, IN 46253, USA	*Auto Racing Driver*
Fisher, Steve %San Diego State University, Athletic Dept, San Diego, CA 92182, USA	*Basketball Coach*
Fisher, Thomas L %Nicor Inc, 1844 Ferry Road, Naperville, IL 60563, USA	*Businessman*
Fisher, William F 1119 Woodbank Dr, Seabrook, TX 77586, USA	*Astronaut*
Fishman, Jerald G %Analog Devices Inc, 1 Technology Way, Norwood, MA 02062, USA	*Businessman*
Fishman, Jon %Dionysian Productions, 431 Pine St, Burlington, VT 05401, USA	*Drummer (Phish)*
Fishman, Michael 1530 Bainum Dr, Topanga, CA 90290, USA	*Actor*
Fisk, Carlton E 16612 S Catawba Road, Horner Glenn, IL 60441, USA	*Baseball Player*
Fisk, Pliny, III %Maximum Potential Building Systems Center, 8604 FM 969, Austin, TX 78724, USA	*Architect, Environmentalist*
Fiske, Robert B, Jr 19 Juniper Road, Darien, CT 06820, USA	*Attorney*

Fister, Bruce L *Air Force General*
9001 S Jimson Weed Way, Highlands Ranch, CO 80126, USA
Fitch, Val L *Nobel Physics Laureate*
292 Hartley Ave, Princeton, NJ 08540, USA
Fites, Donald V *Businessman*
%Caterpillar Inc, 100 NE Adams St, Peoria, IL 61629, USA
Fitt of Bell's Hill, Gerard *Government Official, England*
%Irish Club, 82 Eaton Square, London SW1, England
Fittipaldi, Christian *Auto Racing Driver*
282 Alphaville Barueri, 064500 San Paulo, Brazil
Fittipaldi, Emerson *Auto Racing Driver*
735 Crandon Blvd, #503, Miami, FL 33149, USA
Fitz, Raymond L *Educator*
%University of Dayton, President's Office, Dayton, OH 45469, USA
Fitzgerald Mosley, Benita *Track Athlete*
%Women in Cable/Telecommunications, 14555 Avion Parkway, Chantilly, VA 20151, USA
Fitzgerald, A Ernest *Government Efficiency Advocate*
%Air Force Management Systems, Pentagon, Washington, DC 20330, USA
FitzGerald, Frances *Writer*
%Simon & Schuster, 1230 Ave of Americas, New York, NY 10020, USA
FitzGerald, Garret *Prime Minister, Ireland*
30 Palmerston Road, Dublin 6, Ireland
Fitzgerald, Geraldine *Actress*
%Lip Service, 4 Kingly St, London W1R 3RB, England
FitzGerald, Helen *Actress*
%Paul Kohner, 9300 Wilshire Blvd, #555, Beverly Hills, CA 90212, USA
Fitzgerald, Jack *Actor*
%William Kerwin Agency, 1605 N Cahuenga, #202, Los Angeles, CA 90028, USA
Fitzgerald, James F *Basketball Executive*
%Golden State Warriors, 1001 Broadway, Oakland, CA 94607, USA
FitzGerald, Niall W A *Businessman*
%Unilever NV, Weena 455, 3000 DK Rotterdam, Netherlands
Fitzgerald, Tara *Actress*
%Caroline Dawson, 19 Sydney Mews, London SW3 6HL, England
Fitzmaurice, David J *Labor Leader*
%Electrical Radio & Machinists Union, 11256 156th St NW, Washington, DC 20005, USA
Fitzmaurice, Michael J *Vietnam War Army Hero (CMH)*
PO Box 178, Hartford, SD 57033, USA
Fitzpatrick, Leo *Actor*
9350 Wilshire Blvd, #328, Beverly Hills, CA 90212, USA
Fitzsimmons, Lowell (Cotton) *Basketball Coach, Executive*
%Phoenix Suns, 201 E Jefferson St, Phoenix, AZ 85004, USA
Fitzsimonds, Roger L *Financier*
%Firstar Corp, 777 E Wisconsin Ave, Milwaukee, WI 53202, USA
Fitzwater, Marlin *Government Official*
851 Cedar Dr, Deale, MD 20751, USA
Fix, Oliver *Canoeing Athlete*
Ringstr 6, 86391 Stadtbergen, Germany
Fixman, Marshall *Chemist*
%Colorado State University, Chemistry Dept, Fort Collins, CO 80523, USA
Fizer, Marcus *Basketball Player*
%Chicago Bulls, United Center, 1901 W Madison St, Chicago, IL 60612, USA
Fjeldstad, Oivin *Conductor*
Damfaret 59, Bryn-Oslo 6, Norway
Flach, Ken *Tennis Player, Coach*
%Vanderbilt University, Athletic Dept, Nashville, TN 37240, USA
Flach, Thomas *Yachtsman*
Johanna-Resch-Str 13, 12439 Berlin, Germany
Flack, Roberta *Singer, Songwriter*
234 5th Ave, #504, New York, NY 10001, USA
Flade, H Klaus-Dietrich *Cosmonaut, Germany*
%Airbus Industries, 1 Rond Point M Bellonte, 31707 Blagnac Cedex, France
Flagg, Fannie *Actress, Comedienne*
1569 Miramar Lane, Santa Barbara, CA 93108, USA
Flaherty, John T *Baseball Player*
43981 Needmore Court, Ashburn, VA 20147, USA
Flaherty, Stephen *Composer*
%William Morris Agency, 151 El Camino Dr, Beverly Hills, CA 90212, USA
Flaim, Eric *Speedskater*
116 Bellvue Ave, Rutland, VT 05701, USA
Flaman, Ferdinand C (Fernie) *Hockey Player*
29 Church St, Westwood, MA 02090, USA
Flanagan, Barry *Sculptor*
5E Fawe St, London E14 6PD, England
Flanagan, Ed *Football Player*
10981 Clayton St, Northglenn, CO 80233, USA
Flanagan, Edward M, Jr *Army General*
Parade Rest, 12 Oyster Catcher Road, Beaufort, SC 29907, USA

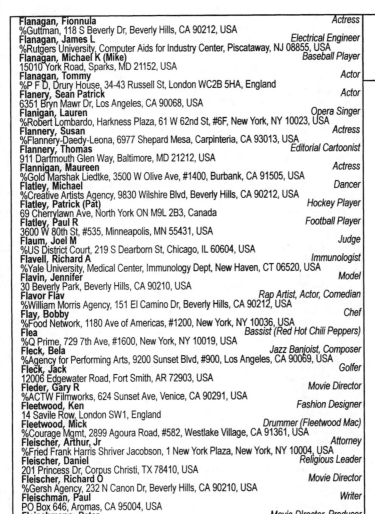

Flanagan, Fionnula *Actress*
%Guttman, 118 S Beverly Dr, Beverly Hills, CA 90212, USA
Flanagan, James L *Electrical Engineer*
%Rutgers University, Computer Aids for Industry Center, Piscataway, NJ 08855, USA
Flanagan, Michael K (Mike) *Baseball Player*
15010 York Road, Sparks, MD 21152, USA
Flanagan, Tommy *Actor*
%P F D, Drury House, 34-43 Russell St, London WC2B 5HA, England
Flanery, Sean Patrick *Actor*
6351 Bryn Mawr Dr, Los Angeles, CA 90068, USA
Flanigan, Lauren *Opera Singer*
%Robert Lombardo, Harkness Plaza, 61 W 62nd St, #6F, New York, NY 10023, USA
Flannery, Susan *Actress*
%Flannery-Daedy-Leona, 6977 Shepard Mesa, Carpinteria, CA 93013, USA
Flannery, Thomas *Editorial Cartoonist*
911 Dartmouth Glen Way, Baltimore, MD 21212, USA
Flannigan, Maureen *Actress*
%Gold Marshak Liedtke, 3500 W Olive Ave, #1400, Burbank, CA 91505, USA
Flatley, Michael *Dancer*
%Creative Artists Agency, 9830 Wilshire Blvd, Beverly Hills, CA 90212, USA
Flatley, Patrick (Pat) *Hockey Player*
69 Cherrylawn Ave, North York ON M9L 2B3, Canada
Flatley, Paul R *Football Player*
3600 W 80th St, #535, Minneapolis, MN 55431, USA
Flaum, Joel M *Judge*
%US District Court, 219 S Dearborn St, Chicago, IL 60604, USA
Flavell, Richard A *Immunologist*
%Yale University, Medical Center, Immunology Dept, New Haven, CT 06520, USA
Flavin, Jennifer *Model*
30 Beverly Park, Beverly Hills, CA 90210, USA
Flavor Flav *Rap Artist, Actor, Comedian*
%William Morris Agency, 151 El Camino Dr, Beverly Hills, CA 90212, USA
Flay, Bobby *Chef*
%Food Network, 1180 Ave of Americas, #1200, New York, NY 10036, USA
Flea *Bassist (Red Hot Chili Peppers)*
%Q Prime, 729 7th Ave, #1600, New York, NY 10019, USA
Fleck, Bela *Jazz Banjoist, Composer*
%Agency for Performing Arts, 9200 Sunset Blvd, #900, Los Angeles, CA 90069, USA
Fleck, Jack *Golfer*
12006 Edgewater Road, Fort Smith, AR 72903, USA
Fleder, Gary R *Movie Director*
%ACTW Filmworks, 624 Sunset Ave, Venice, CA 90291, USA
Fleetwood, Ken *Fashion Designer*
14 Savile Row, London SW1, England
Fleetwood, Mick *Drummer (Fleetwood Mac)*
%Courage Mgmt, 2899 Agoura Road, #582, Westlake Village, CA 91361, USA
Fleischer, Arthur, Jr *Attorney*
%Fried Frank Harris Shriver Jacobson, 1 New York Plaza, New York, NY 10004, USA
Fleischer, Daniel *Religious Leader*
201 Princess Dr, Corpus Christi, TX 78410, USA
Fleischer, Richard O *Movie Director*
%Gersh Agency, 232 N Canon Dr, Beverly Hills, CA 90210, USA
Fleischman, Paul *Writer*
PO Box 646, Aromas, CA 95004, USA
Fleischmann, Peter *Movie DIrector, Producer*
%Filmzentrum Babelsberg, August-Bebel-Str 26-53, 14482 Potsdam, Germany
Fleisher, Bruce *Golfer*
207 Grand Pointe Dr, West Palm Beach, FL 33418, USA
Fleisher, Leon *Concert Pianist, Conductor*
20 Merrymount Road, Baltimore, MD 21210, USA
Fleming Jenkins, Peggy *Figure Skater*
16387 Aztec Ridge Dr, Los Gatos, CA 95030, USA
Fleming, James P *Vietnam War Air Force Hero (CMH)*
PO Box 703, Longview, WA 98632, USA
Fleming, Mac A *Labor Leader*
%Maintenance of Ways Brotherhood, 26555 Evergreen Road, Southfield, MI 48076, USA
Fleming, Marvin (Marv) *Football Player*
909 Howard St, Marina del Rey, CA 90292, USA
Fleming, Peter E, Jr *Attorney*
%Curtis Mallet-Prevost Colt Mosle, 101 Park Ave, New York, NY 10178, USA
Fleming, Reginald S (Reggie) *Hockey Player*
1605 E Central Road, #406A, Arlington Heights, IL 60005, USA
Fleming, Renee *Opera Singer*
%M L Falcone, 155 W 68th St, #1104, New York, NY 10023, USA
Fleming, Rhonda *Actress*
10281 Century Woods Dr, Los Angeles, CA 90067, USA
Fleming, Richard C D *City Planner*
%Greater Denver Chamber of Commerce, 1445 Market St, Denver, CO 80202, USA

F

Fleming - Floria

Fleming, Scott *Government Official*
2750 Shasta Road, Berkeley, CA 94708, USA
Fleming, Vern *Basketball Player*
10713 Brixton Lane, Fishers, IN 46038, USA
Fleming, Wendell H *Mathematician*
9 Dolly Dr, Bristol, RI 02809, USA
Flemming, John *Artist*
1409 Cambronne St, New Orleans, LA 70118, USA
Flemming, William N (Bill) *Sportscaster*
%ABC-TV, Sports Dept, 77 W 66th St, New York, NY 10023, USA
Flemyng, Gordon *Movie Director*
1 Albert Road, Wilmslow, Cheshire SK9 5HT, England
Flemyng, Jason *Actor*
%Conway Van Gelder Robinson, 18-21 Jermyn St, London SW1Y 6NB, England
Flemyng, Robert *Actor*
4 Netherbourne Road, London SW4, England
Flessel, Craig *Cartoonist (Sandman)*
40 Camino Alto, #2306, Mill Valley, CA 94941, USA
Fletcher, Andy *Synthesizer Musician (Depeche Mode)*
%Reach Media, 295 Greenwich St, #109, New York, NY 10007, USA
Fletcher, Arthur A *Government Official*
%Commission on Civil Rights, 1121 Vermont Ave NW, Washington, DC 20005, USA
Fletcher, Betty Binns *Judge*
%US Court of Appeals, US Courthouse, 1010 5th Ave, Seattle, WA 98104, USA
Fletcher, Brendan *Actor*
%Seven Summits Mgmt, 8447 Wilshire Blvd, #200, Beverly Hills, CA 90211, USA
Fletcher, Charles M *Physician, Research Scientist*
2 Coastguard Cottages, Newtown PO30 4PA, England
Fletcher, Colin *Backpacker, Writer*
%Brandt & Brandt, 1501 Broadway, New York, NY 10036, USA
Fletcher, Diane *Actress*
%Ken McReddie, 91 Regent St, London W1R 7TB, England
Fletcher, Guy *Keyboardist (Dire Straits)*
%Damage Mgmt, 16 Lambton Place, London W11 2SH, England
Fletcher, Jamar *Football Player*
%Miami Dolphins, 7500 SW 30th St, Davie, FL 33314, USA
Fletcher, Louise *Actress*
1520 Camden Ave, #105, Los Angeles, CA 90025, USA
Fletcher, Martin *Commentator*
%NBC-TV, News Dept, 4001 Nebraska Ave NW, Washington, DC 20016, USA
Fletcher, Scott B *Baseball Player*
300 Birkdale Dr, Fayetteville, GA 30215, USA
Fletcher, William A *Judge*
%US Court of Appeals, Court Building, 95 7th St, San Francisco, CA 94103, USA
Fleury, Theoren *Hockey Player*
%Chicago Blackhawks, United Center, 1901 W Madison St, Chicago, IL 60612, USA
Flick, Bob *Fiddle Player (Brothers Four)*
%Bob Flick Productions, 300 Vine, #14, Seattle, WA 98121, USA
Flicker, John *Association Executive*
%National Audubon Society, President's Office, 700 Broadway, New York, NY 10003, USA
Flindt, Flemming O *Ballet Dancer, Choreographer*
Christiansholms Parkv 24, 2930 Klampenborg, Denmark
Flint, Keith *Dancer, Singer (Prodigy)*
%Midi Mgmt, Jenkins Lane, Great Hallinsbury, Essex CM22 7QL, England
Flockhart, Calista *Actress*
%Talent Mgmt, 9100 Wilshire Blvd, #725E, Beverly Hills, CA 90212, USA
Flom, Joseph H *Attorney*
%Skadden Arps Slate Meagher Flom, 4 Times Square, New York, NY 10036, USA
Flood, Ann *Actress*
15 E 91st St, New York, NY 10128, USA
Flor, Claus Peter *Conductor*
%Intermusica Artists, 16 Duncan Terrace, London N1 8BZ, England
Florance, Sheila *Actress*
%Melbourne Artists, 643 Saint Kikla Road, Melbourne VIC 3004, Australia
Florek, Dann *Actor*
145 W 45th St, #1204, New York, NY 10036, USA
Floren, Myron *Accordionist*
26 Georgeff Road, Rolling Hills, CA 90274, USA
Flores Facusse, Carlos *President, Honduras*
%Casa Presidencial, Blvd Juan Pablo II, Tegucigalpa, Honduras
Flores, Francisco *President, El Salvador*
%President's Office, Casa Presidencial, San Salvador, El Salvador
Flores, Patrick F *Religious Leader*
%Archbishop's Residence, 2600 Woodlawn Ave, San Antonio, TX 78228, USA
Flores, Thomas R (Tom) *Football Player, Coach, Executive*
77741 Cove Point Circle, Indian Wells, CA 92210, USA
Floria, Holly *Actress*
%Epstein-Wyckoff, 280 S Beverly Dr, #400, Beverly Hills, CA 90212, USA

Florio, James J (Jim) *Governor, NJ*
%Mudge Rose Guthrie, Corporate Center 2, 1673 E 16th St, #16, Brooklyn, NY 11229, USA
Florio, Steven T *Publisher*
%Conde Nast Publications, Publisher's Office, 4 Times Square, New York, NY 10036, USA
Florio, Thomas A *Publisher*
%New Yorker Magazine, Publisher's Office, 4 Times Square, New York, NY 10036, USA
Flory, Med *Actor*
6044 Ensign Ave, North Hollywood, CA 91606, USA
Flournoy, Craig *Journalist*
%Dallas News, Editorial Dept, Communications Center, Dallas, TX 75265, USA
Flower, Joseph R *Religious Leader*
%Assemblies of God, 1445 N Boonville Ave, Springfield, MO 65802, USA
Flowers of Queen's Gate, Brian H *Physicist*
53 Athenaeum Road, London N20 9AL, England
Flowers, Charles (Charlie) *Football Player*
6170 Mount Brook Way NW, Atlanta, GA 30342, USA
Floyd, C Clifford (Cliff) *Baseball Player*
3804 Edgewater Dr, Hazel Crest, IL 60429, USA
Floyd, Carlisle *Composer*
4491 Yoakum Blvd, Houston, TX 77006, USA
Floyd, Eddie *Singer, Songwriter*
%Jason West, Gables House, Saddlebow Kings Lynn PE34 3AR, England
Floyd, Eric (Sleepy) *Basketball Player*
22136 Westheimer Parkway, #201, Katy, TX 77450, USA
Floyd, George *Football Player*
8621 Heritage Dr, Florence, KY 41042, USA
Floyd, Heather *Singer (Point of Grace)*
%TBA Artists Mgmt, 300 10th Ave S, Nashville, TN 37203, USA
Floyd, Marlene *Golfer*
%Marlene Floyd Golf School, 5350 Club House Lane, Hope Mills, NC 28348, USA
Floyd, Raymond (Ray) *Golfer*
PO Box 2163, Palm Beach, FL 33480, USA
Floyd, Tim *Basketball Coach*
%New Orleans Hornets, New Orleans Arena, 1501 Girod St, New Orleans, LA 70113, USA
Fluckey, Eugene B *WW II Navy Hero (CMH); Admiral*
1016 Sandpiper Lane, Annapolis, MD 21403, USA
Fluegel, Darlanne *Actress*
%Shelter Entertainment, 9255 Sunset Blvd, #1010, Los Angeles, CA 90069, USA
Fluno, Jere D *Businessman*
%W W Grainger Inc, 5500 W Howard St, Skokie, IL 60077, USA
Flutie, Doug *Football Player*
%Provident Financial Mgmt, 10345 W Olympic Blvd, Los Angeles, CA 90064, USA
Flynn, Barbara *Actress*
%Markham & Froggatt, Julian House, 4 Windmill St, London W1P 1HF, England
Flynn, Colleen *Actress*
%LGM, 10390 Santa Monica Blvd, #300, Los Angeles, CA 90025, USA
Flynn, George W *Chemist*
382 Summit Ave, Leonia, NJ 07605, USA
Flynn, Raymond L *Mayor, Diplomat*
%Catholic Alliance, Via CatholiCity, PO Box 1872, Chesapeake, VA 23327, USA
Flynt, Larry *Publisher*
%Hustler Magazine, 9171 Wilshire Blvd, #300, Beverly Hills, CA 90210, USA
Fo, Dario *Nobel Literature Laureate*
%Pietro Sciotto, Via Alessandria 4, 20144 Milan, Italy
Foale, C Michael (Mike) *Astronaut*
2101 Todville Road, #11, Seabrook, TX 77586, USA
Foch, Nina *Actress*
PO Box 1884, Beverly Hills, CA 90213, USA
Fodor, Eugene N *Concert Violinist*
22314 N Turkey Creek Road, Morrison, CO 80465, USA
Foege, William H *Public Health Official*
10610 SW Cowan Road, Vashon, WA 98070, USA
Foeger, Luggi *Skier*
%Christopher Foeger, 230 S Balsamina Way, Portola Valley, CA 94028, USA
Foer, Jonathan Safran *Writer*
%Houghton Mifflin, 222 Berkeley St, #700, Boston, MA 02116, USA
Fogel, Robert W *Nobel Economics Laureate*
5321 S University Ave, Chicago, IL 60615, USA
Fogelberg, Dan *Singer, Songwriter*
%H K Mgmt, 9200 W Sunset Blvd, #530, Los Angeles, CA 90069, USA
Fogerty, John *Singer, Songwriter*
4570 Van Nuys Blvd, #3517, Sherman Oaks, CA 91403, USA
Fogleman, Ronald R (Ron) *Air Force General*
406 Snowshoe Lane, Durango, CO 81301, USA
Fogler, Eddie *Basketball Coach*
%University of South Carolina, Athletic Dept, Columbia, SC 53233, USA
Foglesong, Robert H (Doc) *Air Force General*
Vice Chief of Staff, HqUSAF, Pentagon, Washington, DC 20330, USA

F

Fokin - Forbes

Fokin, Vitold P — *Prime Minister, Ukraine*
%Cabinet of Ministers, Government Building, Kiev, Ukraine
Foldberg, Henry C (Hank) — *Football Player*
1204 S 12th St, Rogers, AR 72756, USA
Folds, Ben — *Singer, Pianist, Songwriter*
%CEC, 1123 Broadway, #317, New York, NY 10010, USA
Foley, Dave — *Actor*
%Baker/Winokur/Ryder, 9100 Wilshire Blvd, #600, Beverly Hills, CA 90212, USA
Foley, Maurice B — *Judge*
%US Tax Court, 400 2nd St NW, Washington, DC 20217, USA
Foley, Robert F — *Vietnam War Army Hero (CMH), General*
110 Wilkerson Dr, Marion, AL 36756, USA
Foley, Scott — *Actor*
%Handprint Entertainment, 1100 Glendon Ave, #1000, Los Angeles, CA 90024, USA
Foley, Sylvester R, Jr — *Navy Admiral*
50 Apple Hill Dr, Tewksbury, MA 01876, USA
Foley, Thomas S — *Representative, WA; Speaker; Diplomat*
PO Box 1047, Medical Lake, WA 99022, USA
Foley, Tim J — *Football Player*
2851 Old Clifton Road, Springfield, OH 45502, USA
Folger, Franklin — *Cartoonist*
%King Features Syndicate, 888 7th Ave, New York, NY 10106, USA
Folkenberg, Robert S — *Religious Leader*
%Seventh-Day Adventists, 12501 Old Columbia Pike, Silver Spring, MD 20904, USA
Folkman, M Judah — *Surgeon*
18 Chatham Circle, Brookline, MA 02446, USA
Follesdal, Dagfinn K — *Philosopher*
Staverhagen 7, 1312 Slepemdem, Norway
Follett, Ken — *Writer*
Box 4, Knebworth SG3 6UT, England
Follows, Megan — *Actress*
%Susan Smith, 121A N San Vicente Blvd, Beverly Hills, CA 90211, USA
Folon, Jean-Michel — *Artist*
Burcy, 77890 Beaumont-du-Gatinais, France
Folsom, James E (Jim), Jr — *Governor, AL*
1482 Orchard Dr NE, Cullman, AL 35055, USA
Folsome, Claire — *Microbiologist*
%University of Hawaii, Microbiology Dept, 2600 Campus Road, Honolulu, HI 96822, USA
Fonda, Bridget — *Actress*
%United Talent Agency, 9560 Wilshire Blvd, #500, Beverly Hills, CA 90212, USA
Fonda, Jane — *Actress*
%Fonda Inc, PO Box 5840, Atlanta, GA 31107, USA
Fonda, Peter — *Actor*
21 Foothills Dr, Bozeman, MT 59718, USA
Fondren, Debra Jo — *Model, Actress*
PO Box 4351-856, Los Angeles, CA 90078, USA
Foner, Eric — *Historian*
606 W 116th St, New York, NY 10027, USA
Fong, Hiram L — *Senator, HI*
1102 Alewa Dr, Honolulu, HI 96817, USA
Fontaine, Joan — *Actress*
PO Box 222600, Carmel, CA 93922, USA
Fontaine, Lucien — *Thoroughbred Racing Jockey*
1226 NW 11th Way, Pompano Beach, FL 33071, USA
Fontaine, Maurice A — *Physiologist*
25 Rue Pierre Nicole, 75005 Paris, France
Fontana, Isabeli — *Model*
%Women Model Mgmt, 107 Greene St, #200, New York, NY 10012, USA
Fontana, Wayne — *Singer*
%Brian Gannon Mgmt, PO Box 106, Rochdale OL16 4HW, England
Fontes, Wayne H — *Football Player, Coach*
2043 Harbour Watch Circle, Tarpon Springs, FL 34689, USA
Fonville, Charles — *Track Athlete*
1845 Wintergreen Court, Ann Arbor, MI 48103, USA
Foot, Michael M — *Government Official, England*
308 Gray's Inn Road, London WC1X 8DY, England
Foote, Adam — *Hockey Player*
11 Mountain Laurel Dr, Littleton, CO 80127, USA
Foote, Dan — *Editorial Cartoonist*
%Dallas Times Herald, Editorial Dept, Herald Square, Dallas, TX 75202, USA
Foote, Horton — *Writer*
95 Horatio St, #322, New York, NY 10014, USA
Foote, Shelby — *Writer*
542 East Parkway S, Memphis, TN 38104, USA
Foray, June — *Actress*
22745 Erwin St, Woodland Hills, CA 91367, USA
Forbes, Bryan — *Movie Director, Writer*
Bookshop, Virginia Water, Surrey, England

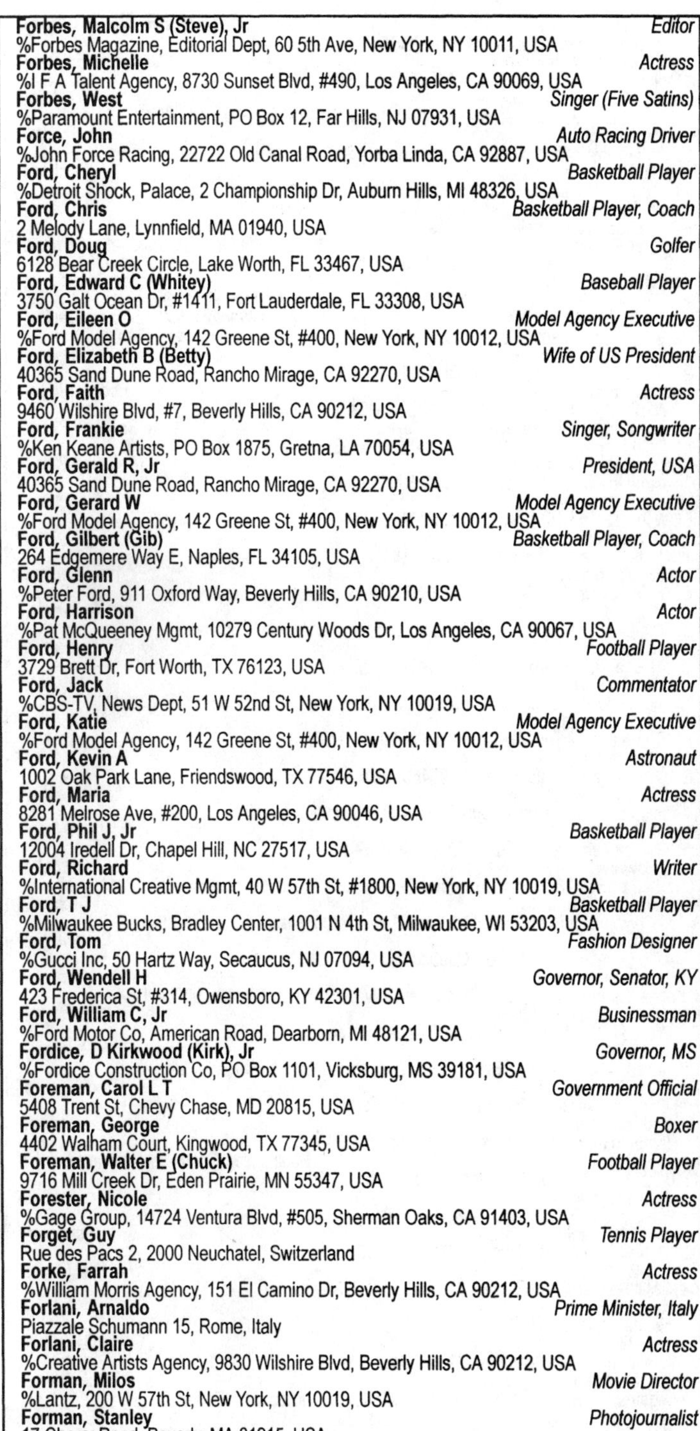

Forbes, Malcolm S (Steve), Jr *Editor*
%Forbes Magazine, Editorial Dept, 60 5th Ave, New York, NY 10011, USA
Forbes, Michelle *Actress*
%I F A Talent Agency, 8730 Sunset Blvd, #490, Los Angeles, CA 90069, USA
Forbes, West *Singer (Five Satins)*
%Paramount Entertainment, PO Box 12, Far Hills, NJ 07931, USA
Force, John *Auto Racing Driver*
%John Force Racing, 22722 Old Canal Road, Yorba Linda, CA 92887, USA
Ford, Cheryl *Basketball Player*
%Detroit Shock, Palace, 2 Championship Dr, Auburn Hills, MI 48326, USA
Ford, Chris *Basketball Player, Coach*
2 Melody Lane, Lynnfield, MA 01940, USA
Ford, Doug *Golfer*
6128 Bear Creek Circle, Lake Worth, FL 33467, USA
Ford, Edward C (Whitey) *Baseball Player*
3750 Galt Ocean Dr, #1411, Fort Lauderdale, FL 33308, USA
Ford, Eileen O *Model Agency Executive*
%Ford Model Agency, 142 Greene St, #400, New York, NY 10012, USA
Ford, Elizabeth B (Betty) *Wife of US President*
40365 Sand Dune Road, Rancho Mirage, CA 92270, USA
Ford, Faith *Actress*
9460 Wilshire Blvd, #7, Beverly Hills, CA 90212, USA
Ford, Frankie *Singer, Songwriter*
%Ken Keane Artists, PO Box 1875, Gretna, LA 70054, USA
Ford, Gerald R, Jr *President, USA*
40365 Sand Dune Road, Rancho Mirage, CA 92270, USA
Ford, Gerard W *Model Agency Executive*
%Ford Model Agency, 142 Greene St, #400, New York, NY 10012, USA
Ford, Gilbert (Gib) *Basketball Player, Coach*
264 Edgemere Way E, Naples, FL 34105, USA
Ford, Glenn *Actor*
%Peter Ford, 911 Oxford Way, Beverly Hills, CA 90210, USA
Ford, Harrison *Actor*
%Pat McQueeney Mgmt, 10279 Century Woods Dr, Los Angeles, CA 90067, USA
Ford, Henry *Football Player*
3729 Brett Dr, Fort Worth, TX 76123, USA
Ford, Jack *Commentator*
%CBS-TV, News Dept, 51 W 52nd St, New York, NY 10019, USA
Ford, Katie *Model Agency Executive*
%Ford Model Agency, 142 Greene St, #400, New York, NY 10012, USA
Ford, Kevin A *Astronaut*
1002 Oak Park Lane, Friendswood, TX 77546, USA
Ford, Maria *Actress*
8281 Melrose Ave, #200, Los Angeles, CA 90046, USA
Ford, Phil J, Jr *Basketball Player*
12004 Iredell Dr, Chapel Hill, NC 27517, USA
Ford, Richard *Writer*
%International Creative Mgmt, 40 W 57th St, #1800, New York, NY 10019, USA
Ford, T J *Basketball Player*
%Milwaukee Bucks, Bradley Center, 1001 N 4th St, Milwaukee, WI 53203, USA
Ford, Tom *Fashion Designer*
%Gucci Inc, 50 Hartz Way, Secaucus, NJ 07094, USA
Ford, Wendell H *Governor, Senator, KY*
423 Frederica St, #314, Owensboro, KY 42301, USA
Ford, William C, Jr *Businessman*
%Ford Motor Co, American Road, Dearborn, MI 48121, USA
Fordice, D Kirkwood (Kirk), Jr *Governor, MS*
%Fordice Construction Co, PO Box 1101, Vicksburg, MS 39181, USA
Foreman, Carol L T *Government Official*
5408 Trent St, Chevy Chase, MD 20815, USA
Foreman, George *Boxer*
4402 Walham Court, Kingwood, TX 77345, USA
Foreman, Walter E (Chuck) *Football Player*
9716 Mill Creek Dr, Eden Prairie, MN 55347, USA
Forester, Nicole *Actress*
%Gage Group, 14724 Ventura Blvd, #505, Sherman Oaks, CA 91403, USA
Forget, Guy *Tennis Player*
Rue des Pacs 2, 2000 Neuchatel, Switzerland
Forke, Farrah *Actress*
%William Morris Agency, 151 El Camino Dr, Beverly Hills, CA 90212, USA
Forlani, Arnaldo *Prime Minister, Italy*
Piazzale Schumann 15, Rome, Italy
Forlani, Claire *Actress*
%Creative Artists Agency, 9830 Wilshire Blvd, Beverly Hills, CA 90212, USA
Forman, Milos *Movie Director*
%Lantz, 200 W 57th St, New York, NY 10019, USA
Forman, Stanley *Photojournalist*
17 Cherry Road, Beverly, MA 01915, USA

F

Forman - Foster

Forman, Tom *Cartoonist (Motley's Crew)*
10544 James Road, Celina, TX 75009, USA
Forney, G David, Jr *Computer Scientist*
6 Coolidge Hill Road, Cambridge, MA 02138, USA
Foronjy, Richard *Actor*
%House of Representatives, 400 S Beverly Dr, #101, Beverly Hills, CA 90212, USA
Forrest, Frederic *Actor*
11300 W Olympic Blvd, #610, Los Angeles, CA 90064, USA
Forrest, Sally *Actress*
1125 Angelo Dr, Beverly Hills, CA 90210, USA
Forrest, Steve *Actor*
1605 Michael Lane, Pacific Palisades, CA 90272, USA
Forrestal, Robert P *Financier, Government Official*
3949 Vermont Road NE, Atlanta, GA 30319, USA
Forrester, James *Medical Researcher*
%Cedars-Sinai Medical Center, 8700 Beverly Blvd, West Hollywood, CA 90048, USA
Forrester, Jay W *Inventor (Digital Storage Device)*
%Massachusetts Institute of Technology, Management School, Cambridge, MA 02139, USA
Forrester, Patrick G *Astronaut*
3923 Park Circle Way, Houston, TX 77059, USA
Forsberg, Peter *Hockey Player*
475 W 12th Ave, #16C, Denver, CO 80204, USA
Forsch, Kenneth R (Ken) *Baseball Player*
881 S Country Glen Way, Anaheim, CA 92808, USA
Forsch, Robert H (Bob) *Baseball Player*
9 Westmeade Court, Chesterfield, MO 63005, USA
Forslund, Constance *Actress*
165 W 46th St, #1109, New York, NY 10036, USA
Forster, Robert *Actor*
1115 Pine St, Santa Monica, CA 90405, USA
Forster, William H *Army General*
10245 Fairfax Dr, Fort Belvoir, VA 22060, USA
Forsyth, Bill *Movie Director*
%P F D, Drury House, 34-43 Russell St, London WC2B 5HA, England
Forsyth, Bruce *Actor, Comedian*
Kent House, Upper Ground, London SE1, England
Forsyth, Frederick *Writer*
%Trans World Publishers, 61-63 Oxbridge Rd, Ealing, London W5 5SA, England
Forsyth, Rosemary *Actress*
1591 Benedict Canyon, Beverly Hills, CA 90210, USA
Forsythe, John *Actor*
3849 Roblar Ave, Santa Ynez, CA 93460, USA
Forsythe, William *Choreographer*
%Frankfurt Ballet, Untermainanlage 11, 60311 Frankfurt, Germany
Forsythe, William *Actor*
7532 Melba Ave, Canoga Park, CA 91304, USA
Fort, Edward B *Educator*
%North Carolina A&T State University, Chancellor's Office, Greensboro, NC 27411, USA
Fort-Brescia, Bernardo *Architect*
%Arquitectonica International, 550 Brickell Ave, #200, Miami, FL 33131, USA
Fortier, Claude *Physiologist*
1014 De Grenoble, Sainte-Foy, Quebec QC G1V 2Z9, Canada
Fortier, Laurie *Actress*
%Kritzer Entertainment, 12200 W Olympic Blvd, #400, Los Angeles, 90064, USA
Fortunato, Joseph F (Joe) *Football Player*
PO Box 934, Natchez, MS 39121, USA
Fortune, Jimmy *Singer (Statler Brothers)*
%American Major Talent, 8747 Highway 304, Hernando, MS 38632, USA
Fosbury, Richard D (Dick) *Track Athlete*
708 Canyon Run Blvd, Ketchum, ID 83340, USA
Foss, John W, II *Army General*
16 Hampton Key, Williamsburg, VA 23185, USA
Foss, Lukas *Composer, Conductor, Concert Pianist*
1140 5th Ave #4B, New York, NY 10128, USA
Fossey, Brigitte *Actress*
18 Rue Troyon, 75017 Paris, France
Fossum, Michael E *Astronaut*
822 Rolling Run Court, Houston, TX 77062, USA
Foster, Barry *Football Player*
4604 Mill Springs Court, Colleyville, TX 76034, USA
Foster, Ben *Actor*
%Gold Marshak Liedtke, 3500 W Olive Ave, #1400, Burbank, CA 91505, USA
Foster, Bill *Basketball Coach*
%Virginia Polytechnic Institute, Athletic Dept, Blacksburg, VA 24061, USA
Foster, Brendan *Track Athlete*
Whitegates, 31 Meadowfield Road, Stocksfield, Northumberland, England
Foster, Coy *Balloonist*
5486 Glen Lakes Dr, Dallas, TX 75231, USA

Foster, David *Songwriter, Musician*
3469 Cross Creek Road, Malibu, CA 90265, USA
Foster, George A *Baseball Player*
%Pro-Concepts, 2046 Treasure Coast Plaza, #341, Vero Beach, FL 32960, USA
Foster, Jodie *Actress, Director*
%P M K Public Relations, 8500 Wilshire Blvd, #700, Beverly Hills, CA 90211, USA
Foster, Lawrence T *Conductor*
%International Creative Mgmt, 40 W 57th St, #1800, New York, NY 10019, USA
Foster, Lisa Raines *Actress*
%Diamond Artists, 215 N Barrington Ave, Los Angeles, CA 90049, USA
Foster, Meg *Actress*
%Judy Schoen, 606 N Larchmont Blvd, #309, Los Angeles, CA 90004, USA
Foster, Norman R *Architect*
%Foster Assoc, Riverside 3, 22 Hester Road, London SW11 4AN, England
Foster, Radney *Singer, Songwriter*
PO Box 121452, Nashville, TN 37212, USA
Foster, Robert W (Bob) *Boxer*
913 Valencia Dr NE, Albuquerque, NM 87108, USA
Foster, Roy A *Football Player*
11522 W State Road 84, #267, Davie, FL 33325, USA
Foster, Susannah *Actress, Singer*
11255 W Morrison St, #F, North Hollywood, CA 91601, USA
Foster, William E (Bill) *Basketball Coach*
152 Hollywood Dr, Coppell, TX 75019, USA
Foudy, Judy (Julie) *Soccer Player, Model*
%US Soccer Federation, 1801 S Prairie Ave, Chicago, IL 60616, USA
Fountain, Peter D (Pete), Jr *Jazz Clarinetist*
%Paradise Artists, 108 E Matilija St, Ojai, CA 93023, USA
Fouts, Daniel F (Dan) *Football Player, Sportscaster*
%ABC-TV, Sports Dept, 77 W 66th St, New York, NY 10023, USA
Fowler, E Michael C *Architect*
Branches, Giffords Road, RD 3, Blenheim, New Zealand
Fowler, J Arthur (Art) *Baseball Player*
3046 E Main Street Extension, Spartanburg, SC 29307, USA
Fowler, Peggy Y *Businesswoman*
%Portland General Electric, 121 SW Salmon St, Portland, OR 97204, USA
Fowler, W Wyche, Jr *Senator, GA; Diplomat*
701 A St NE, Washington, DC 20002, USA
Fowles, John R *Writer*
%Sheil Kand Assoc, 43 Dougherty St, London WC1N 2LF, England
Fox, Bernard *Actor*
6601 Burnet Ave, Van Nuys, CA 91405, USA
Fox, Edward *Actor*
25 Maida Ave, London W2, England
Fox, James *Actor*
%International Creative Mgmt, 76 Oxford St, London W1N 0AX, England
Fox, John *Football Coach*
%Carolina Panthers, Ericsson Stadium, 800 S Mint St, Charlotte, NC 28202, USA
Fox, Jorja *Actress*
%Flick East-West, 9057 Nemo St, #A, West Hollywood, CA 90069, USA
Fox, Marye Anne *Organic Chemist*
1903 Hillsborough St, Raleigh, NC 27607, USA
Fox, Maurice S *Molecular Biologist*
983 Memorial Dr, #401, Cambridge, MA 02138, USA
Fox, Michael J *Actor*
%Creative Artists Agency, 9830 Wilshire Blvd, Beverly Hills, CA 90212, USA
Fox, Rick *Basketball Player, Actor*
%Healthsouth Training Center, 555 N Nash St, El Segundo, CA 90245, USA
Fox, Samantha *Singer, Model*
%Session Connection, 110-112 Disraeli Road, London SW15 2DX, England
Fox, Sheldon *Architect*
%Kohn Pedersen Fox Assoc, 111 W 57th St, New York, NY 10019, USA
Fox, Tim *Football Player*
10 Longmeadow Dr, Westwood, MA 02090, USA
Fox, Vicente *President, Mexico*
%Palacio Nacional, Patio de Honor, 2 Piso, Mexico City DF 06067, Mexico
Fox, Vivica A *Actress*
PO Box 3538, Granada Hills, CA 91394, USA
Fox, Wesley L *Vietnam War Marine Corps Hero (CMH)*
855 Deercraft Dr, Blacksburg, VA 24060, USA
Foxworth, Robert *Actor*
9763 Donington Place, Beverly Hills, CA 90210, USA
Foxworthy, Jeff *Actor, Comedian*
%Four Points Entertainment, 8380 Melrose Ave, #310, Los Angeles, CA 90069, USA
Foxx, Jamie *Actor, Comedian*
%Nationwide Entertainment, 2756 N Green Valley Parkway, Henderson, NV 89014, USA
Foy, Eddie, III *Actor*
3003 W Olive Ave, Burbank, CA 91505, USA

Foyt, Anthony J (A J), Jr *Auto Racing Driver*
19480 Stokes Road, Waller, TX 77484, USA
Fradon, Dana *Cartoonist*
2 Brushy Hill Road, Newtown, CT 06470, USA
Fradon, Ramona *Cartoonist (Brenda Starr)*
%Tribune Media Services, 435 N Michigan Ave, #1500, Chicago, IL 60611, USA
Fraiture, Nikolai *Bassist (Strokes)*
%MVO Ltd, 370 7th Ave, #807, New York, NY 10001, USA
Fraker, William A *Cinematographer*
337 Lorraine Blvd, Los Angeles, CA 90020, USA
Frakes, Jonathan *Actor, Director*
10990 Wilshire Blvd, #1600, Los Angeles, CA 90024, USA
Fralic, William (Bill) *Football Player*
%Fralic Insurance, 1145 Sanctuary Parkway, #150, Alpharetta, GA 30004, USA
Frampton, Peter *Singer, Guitarist, Songwriter*
1016 17th Ave S, #1, Nashville, TN 37212, USA
Franca, Celia *Ballerina, Choreographer*
157 King St E, Toronto ON M5C 1G9, Canada
France, Brian *Auto Racing Executive*
%National Assn of Stock Car Racing, 1801 Speedway Blvd, Daytona Beach, FL 32114, USA
France, F Douglas (Doug), Jr *Football Player*
25993 Atherton Ave, Laguna Hills, CA 92653, USA
Franchione, Dennis *Football Coach*
%Texas A&M University, Athletic Dept, College Station, TX 77843, USA
Franchitti, Dario *Auto Racing Driver*
7615 Zionsville Road, Indianapolis, IN 46268, USA
Franciosa, Anthony (Tony) *Actor*
567 N Tigertail Road, Los Angeles, CA 90049, USA
Francis, Anne *Actress*
PO Box 5608, Santa Barbara, CA 93150, USA
Francis, Bob *Hockey Player, Coach*
7510 E Monterra Way, Scottsdale, AZ 85262, USA
Francis, Clarence (Bevo) *Basketball Player*
18340 Steubenville Pike Road, Salineville, OH 43945, USA
Francis, Connie *Singer, Actress*
6413 NW 102nd Terrace, Parkland, FL 33076, USA
Francis, Emile P *Hockey Coach, Executive*
7220 Crystal Lake Dr, West Palm Beach, FL 33411, USA
Francis, Freddie *Cinematographer*
12 Ashley Dr, Jersey Road, Osterly, Middx TW7 5QA, England
Francis, Genie *Actress*
10990 Wilshire Blvd, #1600, Los Angeles, CA 90024, USA
Francis, James *Football Player*
2903 Main St, La Marque, TX 77568, USA
Francis, Richard S (Dick) *Writer*
PO Box 30866, Seven Mile Beach, Grand Cayman, West Indies
Francis, Ron *Hockey Player*
12312 Birchfalls Dr, Raleigh, NC 27614, USA
Francis, Steve *Basketball Player*
%Houston Rockets, Toyota Center, 2 E Greenway Plaza, Houston, TX 77046, USA
Francis, William (Bill) *Keyboardist, Singer*
%Artists International, 9850 Sandalwood Blvd, #458, Boca Raton, FL 33428, USA
Francisco, George J *Labor Leader*
%Fireman & Oilers Union, 1100 Circle 75 Parkway, Atlanta, GA 30339, USA
Franck, George H (Sonny) *Football Player*
2714 29th Ave, Rock Island, IL 61201, USA
Franco, James *Actor*
%International Creative Mgmt, 8942 Wilshire Blvd, #219, Beverly Hills, CA 90211, USA
Franco, John A *Baseball Player*
111 Helena Road, Staten Island, NY 10304, USA
Franco, Julio C *Baseball Player*
651 NE 23rd Court, Pompano Beach, FL 33064, USA
Francois-Poncet, Jean A *Financier; Government Official, France*
6 Blvd Suchet, 75116 Paris, France
Francona, John P (Tito) *Baseball Player*
1109 Penn Ave, New Brighton, PA 15066, USA
Francona, Terry J *Baseball Manager*
958 Hunt Dr, Yardley, PA 19067, USA
Frank, Anthony M *Government Official, Financier*
%Independent Bancorp, 3800 N Central, Phoenix, AZ 85012, USA
Frank, Charles *Actor*
%S D B Partners, 1801 Ave of Stars, #902, Los Angeles, CA 90067, USA
Frank, Claude *Concert Pianist*
%Columbia Artists Mgmt Inc, 165 W 57th St, New York, NY 10019, USA
Frank, Diana *Actress*
%The Agency, 1800 Ave of Stars, #400, Los Angeles, CA 90067, USA
Frank, Gary *Actor*
1401 S Bentley Ave, #202, Los Angeles, CA 90025, USA

F

Frank, Howard *Businessman*
%Carnival Corp, 3655 NW 87th Ave, Miami, FL 33178, USA
Frank, Jerome D *Psychiatrist, Educator*
818 W 40th St, #K, Baltimore, MD 21211, USA
Frank, Joanna *Actress*
1274 Capri Dr, Pacific Palisades, CA 90272, USA
Frank, Joe *Entertainer*
%KCRW-FM, 1900 Pico Blvd, Santa Monica, CA 90405, USA
Frank, Larry *Auto Racing Driver*
%Larry Frank Auto Body Works, 832 Fork Shoals Road, Greenville, SC 29605, USA
Frank, Louis A *Astronomer*
%Univesity of Iowa, Astronomy Dept, Iowa City, IA 52242, USA
Frank, Neil L *Meteorologist*
%National Hurricane Center, 1320 S Dixie Highway, Coral Gables, FL 33146, USA
Frank, Phil *Cartoonist (Farley)*
500 Turley St, Sausalito, CA 94965, USA
Frankel, Felice *Artist, Photographer*
%Massachusetts Institute of Technology, Edgerton Center, Cambridge, MA 02139, USA
Frankel, Max *Editor*
%New York Times, Editorial Dept, 229 W 43rd St, New York, NY 10036, USA
Franken, Al *Actor, Comedian, Writer*
%Special Artists, 345 N Maple Dr, #302, Beverly Hills, CA 90210, USA
Franken, Steve *Actor*
%Acme Talent, 4727 Wilshire Blvd, #333, Los Angeles, CA 90010, USA
Frankenthaler, Helen *Artist*
19 Contentment Island Road, Darien, CT 06820, USA
Frankl, Peter *Concert Pianist*
5 Gresham Gardens, London NW11 8NX, England
Franklin, Allen *Businessman*
%Southern Co, 270 Peachtree St NW, Atlanta, CA 30303, USA
Franklin, Anthony R (Tony) *Football Player*
117 Shady Trail St, San Antonio, TX 78232, USA
Franklin, Aretha *Singer*
8450 Linwood St, Detroit, MI 48206, USA
Franklin, Barbara Hackman *Secretary, Commerce*
1875 Perkins St, Bristol, CT 06010, USA
Franklin, Bonnie *Actress*
175 E 72nd St, #20A, New York, NY 10021, USA
Franklin, Carl M *Movie Director*
%Broder Kurland Webb Uffner, 9242 Beverly Blvd, #200, Beverly Hills, CA 90210, USA
Franklin, Diane *Actress*
%Third Hill Entertainment, 195 S Beverly Dr, #400, Beverly Hills, CA 90212, USA
Franklin, Don *Actor*
%Paradigm Agency, 10100 Santa Monica Blvd, #2500, Los Angeles, CA 90067, USA
Franklin, Howard *Movie Director, Writer*
%Creative Artists Agency, 9830 Wilshire Blvd, Beverly Hills, CA 90212, USA
Franklin, John *Actor*
%Gilla Roos, 9744 Wilshire Blvd, #203, Beverly Hills, CA 90212, USA
Franklin, John Hope *Historian, Judge*
208 Pineview Road, Durham, NC 27707, USA
Franklin, Jon D *Journalist*
9650 Strickland Road, Raleigh, NC 27615, USA
Franklin, Kirk *Singer, Songwriter*
%Covenant Agency, 1011 4th St, #315, Santa Monica, CA 90403, USA
Franklin, Melissa *Physicist*
%Harvard University, Physics Dept, Cambridge, MA 02138, USA
Franklin, Robert *Businessman*
%Placer Dome Inc, 1600-1055 Dunsmuir St, Vancouver BC V7X 1P1, Canada
Franklin, Ryan *Baseball Player*
PO Box 321, Shawnee, OK 74802, USA
Franklin, Shirley *Mayor*
%Mayor's Office, City Hall, 55 Trinity Ave S, Atlanta, GA 30303, USA
Franklin, William *Bowling Executive*
920 La Sombra Dr, San Marcos, CA 92069, USA
Franklyn, Sabina *Actress*
%CCA Mgmt, 4 Court Lodge, 48 Sloane Square, London SW1W 8AT, England
Franks, Frederick M, Jr *Army General*
6364 Brampton Court, Alexandria, VA 22304, USA
Franks, Michael *Singer, Songwriter, Guitarist*
%Agency for Performing Arts, 9200 Sunset Blvd, #900, Los Angeles, CA 90069, USA
Franks, Tommy R (Tom) *Army General*
%Washington Speakers Bureau, 1660 Prince St, Arlington, VA 22014, USA
Frankston, Robert M (Bob) *Computer Software Designer (VisiCalc)*
%Slate Corp, 15035 N 73rd St, Scottsdale, AZ 85260, USA
Fransioli, Thomas A *Artist*
55 Dodges Row, Wenham, MA 01984, USA
Franti, Michael *Singer (Spearhead)*
%William Morris Agency, 151 El Camino Dr, Beverly Hills, CA 90212, USA

F

Frantz - Frears

Frantz, Adrienne *Actress*
%Acme Talent, 4727 Wilshire Blvd, #333, Los Angeles, CA 90010, USA
Frantz, Chris *Drummer (Talking Heads, Tom Tom Club)*
%Premier Talent, 3 E 54th St, #1100, New York, NY 10022, USA
Franz, Arthur *Actor*
1736 Talon Ave, Henderson, NV 89074, USA
Franz, Dennis *Actor*
2300 Century Hill, #75, Los Angeles, CA 90067, USA
Franz, Frederick W *Religious Leader*
%Jehovah's Witnesses, 25 Columbia Heights, Brooklyn, NY 11201, USA
Franz, Judy R *Physicist*
%American Physical Society, 1 Physics Eclipse, College Park, MD 20740, USA
Franz, Rodney T (Rod) *Football Player*
1448 Engberg Court, Carmichael, CA 95608, USA
Franzen, Jonathan *Writer*
%Farrar Straus Giroux, 19 Union Square W, New York, NY 10003, USA
Franzen, Ulrich J *Architect*
975 Park Ave, New York, NY 10028, USA
Frasca, Robert J *Architect*
%Zimmer Gunsul Frasca, 320 SW Oak St, #500, Portland, OR 97204, USA
Frasconi, Antonio *Artist*
26 Dock Road, Norwalk, CT 06854, USA
Fraser Ware, Dawn *Swimmer*
403 Darling St, Balmain NSW 2041, Australia
Fraser, Antonia *Writer*
%Curtis Brown, Haymarket House, 28/29 Haymarket, London SW1Y 4SP, England
Fraser, Brad *Writer*
%Great North Artists Mgmt, 350 Dupont Ave, Toronto ON M5R 1V9, Canada
Fraser, Brendan *Actor*
2118 Wilshire Blvd, #513, Santa Monica, CA 90403, USA
Fraser, Douglas *Labor Leader*
%United Auto Workers, 8000 E Jefferson Ave, Detroit, MI 48214, USA
Fraser, Elisabeth *Singer (Cocteau Twins)*
%Int'l Talent Booking, 27A Floral St, #300, London WC2E 9DQ, England
Fraser, George MacDonald *Writer*
%Curtis Brown, 28/29 Haymarket, London SW1Y 4SP, England
Fraser, Honor *Model*
%Select Model Mgmt, Archer House, 43 King St, London WC2E 8RJ, England
Fraser, Hugh *Actor*
%Jonathan Altaras, 13 Shorts Gardens, London WC2H 9AT, England
Fraser, Ian E *WW II British Navy Hero (VC)*
Innisfallen, 47 Warren Dr, Wallasey, Merseyside, England
Fraser, Malcolm *Prime Minister, Australia*
Thurulgoona, Redhill VIC 3937, Australia
Fraser, Neale *Tennis Player*
21 Bolton Ave, Hampton VIC 3188, Australia
Frashilla, Fran *Basketball Coach*
%New Mexico University, Athletic Dept, Albuquerque, NM 87131, USA
Fratello, Michael R (Mike) *Basketball Coach, Sportcaster*
%NBC-TV, Sports Dept, 30 Rockefeller Plaza, New York, NY 10112, USA
Fratianne, Linda S *Figure Skater*
15691 Borgas Court, Moorpark, CA 93021, USA
Fraumeni, Joseph F, Jr *Cancer Researcher*
%National Cancer Institute, Cancer Etiology Division, Bethesda, MD 20892, USA
Frayn, Michael *Writer*
%Greene & Heaton, 37A Goldhawk Road, London W12 8QQ, England
Frazer, Liz *Actress*
%Peter Charlesworth, 68 Old Brompton Road, #200, London SW7 3LQ, England
Frazetta, Frank *Artist*
%Frazetta Art Museum, 82 S Courtland St, East Stroudsburg, PA 18301, USA
Frazier, Charles *Writer*
%Atlantic Monthly Press, 841 Broadway, New York, NY 10003, USA
Frazier, Dallas *Singer, Songwriter*
RR 5 Box 133, Longhollow Pike, Gallatin, TN 37066, USA
Frazier, Herman *Track Athlete*
1777 Ala Moana Blvd, Honolulu, HI 96815, USA
Frazier, Ian *Writer*
%Farrar Straus Giroux, 19 Union Square W, New York, NY 10003, USA
Frazier, Joseph (Smokin' Joe) *Boxer*
2917 N Broad St, Philadelphia, PA 19132, USA
Frazier, Mavis *Boxer*
2917 N Broad St, Philadelphia, PA 19132, USA
Frazier, Owsley B *Businessman*
%Brown-Forman Corp, 850 Dixie Highway, Louisville, KY 40210, USA
Frazier, Walter (Clyde), II *Basketball Player*
%WFAN-AM, 3412 36th St, Long Island City, NY 11106, USA
Frears, Stephen A *Movie Director*
93 Talbot Road, London W2, England

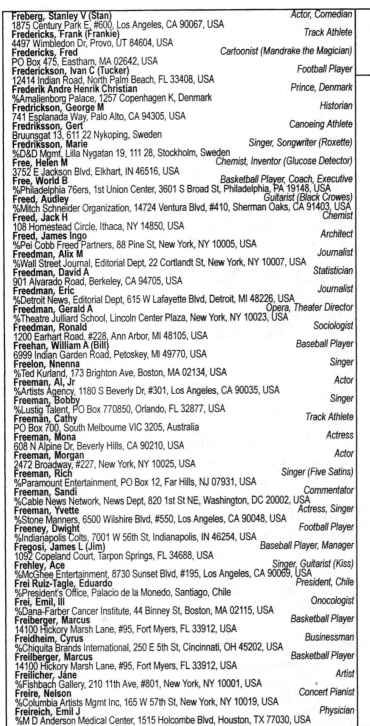

Freberg, Stanley V (Stan) *Actor, Comedian*
1875 Century Park E, #600, Los Angeles, CA 90067, USA
Fredericks, Frank (Frankie) *Track Athlete*
4497 Wimbledon Dr, Provo, UT 84604, USA
Fredericks, Fred *Cartoonist (Mandrake the Magician)*
PO Box 475, Eastham, MA 02642, USA
Frederickson, Ivan C (Tucker) *Football Player*
12414 Indian Road, North Palm Beach, FL 33408, USA
Frederik Andre Henrik Christian *Prince, Denmark*
%Amalienborg Palace, 1257 Copenhagen K, Denmark
Fredrickson, George M *Historian*
741 Esplanada Way, Palo Alto, CA 94305, USA
Fredriksson, Gert *Canoeing Athlete*
Bruunsgat 13, 611 22 Nykoping, Sweden
Fredriksson, Marie *Singer, Songwriter (Roxette)*
%D&D Mgmt, Lilla Nygatan 19, 111 28, Stockholm, Sweden
Free, Helen M *Chemist, Inventor (Glucose Detector)*
3752 E Jackson Blvd, Elkhart, IN 46516, USA
Free, World B *Basketball Player, Coach, Executive*
%Philadelphia 76ers, 1st Union Center, 3601 S Broad St, Philadelphia, PA 19148, USA
Freed, Audley *Guitarist (Black Crowes)*
%Mitch Schneider Organization, 14724 Ventura Blvd, #410, Sherman Oaks, CA 91403, USA
Freed, Jack H *Chemist*
108 Homestead Circle, Ithaca, NY 14850, USA
Freed, James Ingo *Architect*
%Pei Cobb Freed Partners, 88 Pine St, New York, NY 10005, USA
Freedman, Alix M *Journalist*
%Wall Street Journal, Editorial Dept, 22 Cortlandt St, New York, NY 10007, USA
Freedman, David A *Statistician*
901 Alvarado Road, Berkeley, CA 94705, USA
Freedman, Eric *Journalist*
%Detroit News, Editorial Dept, 615 W Lafayette Blvd, Detroit, MI 48226, USA
Freedman, Gerald A *Opera, Theater Director*
%Theatre Julliard School, Lincoln Center Plaza, New York, NY 10023, USA
Freedman, Ronald *Sociologist*
1200 Earhart Road, #228, Ann Arbor, MI 48105, USA
Freehan, William A (Bill) *Baseball Player*
6999 Indian Garden Road, Petoskey, MI 49770, USA
Freelon, Nnenna *Singer*
%Ted Kurland, 173 Brighton Ave, Boston, MA 02134, USA
Freeman, Al, Jr *Actor*
%Artists Agency, 1180 S Beverly Dr, #301, Los Angeles, CA 90035, USA
Freeman, Bobby *Singer*
%Lustig Talent, PO Box 770850, Orlando, FL 32877, USA
Freeman, Cathy *Track Athlete*
PO Box 700, South Melbourne VIC 3205, Australia
Freeman, Mona *Actress*
608 N Alpine Dr, Beverly Hills, CA 90210, USA
Freeman, Morgan *Actor*
2472 Broadway, #227, New York, NY 10025, USA
Freeman, Rich *Singer (Five Satins)*
%Paramount Entertainment, PO Box 12, Far Hills, NJ 07931, USA
Freeman, Sandi *Commentator*
%Cable News Network, News Dept, 820 1st St NE, Washington, DC 20002, USA
Freeman, Yvette *Actress, Singer*
%Stone Manners, 6500 Wilshire Blvd, #550, Los Angeles, CA 90048, USA
Freeney, Dwight *Football Player*
%Indianapolis Colts, 7001 W 56th St, Indianapolis, IN 46254, USA
Fregosi, James L (Jim) *Baseball Player, Manager*
1092 Copeland Court, Tarpon Springs, FL 34688, USA
Frehley, Ace *Singer, Guitarist (Kiss)*
%McGhee Entertainment, 8730 Sunset Blvd, #195, Los Angeles, CA 90069, USA
Frei Ruiz-Tagle, Eduardo *President, Chile*
%President's Office, Palacio de la Monedo, Santiago, Chile
Frei, Emil, III *Onocologist*
%Dana-Farber Cancer Institute, 44 Binney St, Boston, MA 02115, USA
Freiberger, Marcus *Basketball Player*
14100 Hickory Marsh Lane, #95, Fort Myers, FL 33912, USA
Freidheim, Cyrus *Businessman*
%Chiquita Brands International, 250 E 5th St, Cincinnati, OH 45202, USA
Freilberger, Marcus *Basketball Player*
14100 Hickory Marsh Lane, #95, Fort Myers, FL 33912, USA
Freilicher, Jane *Artist*
%Fishbach Gallery, 210 11th Ave, #801, New York, NY 10001, USA
Freire, Nelson *Concert Pianist*
%Columbia Artists Mgmt Inc, 165 W 57th St, New York, NY 10019, USA
Freireich, Emil J *Physician*
%M D Anderson Medical Center, 1515 Holcombe Blvd, Houston, TX 77030, USA

Freis, Edward D *Physician*
4515 Willard Ave, Chevy Chase, MD 20815, USA
Frelich, Phyllis *Actress*
%Artists Group, 10100 Santa Monica Blvd, #2490, Los Angeles, CA 90067, USA
French, Dawn *Actress, Comedienne*
%P F D, Drury House, 34-43 Russell St, London WC2B 5HA, England
French, Leigh *Actress*
1850 N Vista St, Los Angeles, CA 90046, USA
French, Marilyn *Writer*
%Charlotte Sheedy Agency, 65 Bleecker St, #1200, New York, NY 10012, USA
French, Niki *Singer*
%Mega Artists Mgmt, PO Box 89, 1135 ZJ Edam, Netherlands
French, Paige *Actress*
%Gersh Agency, 232 N Canon Dr, Beverly Hills, CA 90210, USA
French, Rufus *Football Player*
%Green Bay Packers, PO Box 10628, Green Bay, WI 54307, USA
Freni, Mirella *Opera Singer*
%John Coast Mgmt, 31 Sinclair Road, London W14 0NS, England
Frenkiel, Richard H *Systems Engineer, Inventor*
%Rutgers University, WINLAB, PO Box 909, Piscataway, NJ 08855, USA
Frentzen, Heinz-Harald *Auto Racing Driver*
%Formula One Ltd, Silverstone Circuit, Northamptonshire NN12 8TN, England
Frerotte, Gus *Football Player*
1360 Herschel Ave, Cincinnati, OH 45208, USA
Fresco, Paolo *Businessman*
%Fiat SpA, Corso Marconi 10/20, 10125 Turin, Italy
Fresh, Doug E *Rap Artist*
%Agency Group Ltd, 1775 Broadway, #430, New York, NY 10019, USA
Fresno Larrain, Juan Cardinal *Religious Leader*
Erasmo Escala 1822, Santiago 30D, Chile
Freud, Bella *Fashion Designer*
48 Rawstorne St, London EC1V 7ND, England
Freud, Lucian *Artist*
%Rawstron-Derrick, 90 Fetter Lane, London EC4A 1EQ, England
Freund, Lambert B *Mechanical Engineer*
3 Palisade Lane, Barrington, RI 02806, USA
Frewer, Matt *Actor*
%International Creative Mgmt, 8942 Wilshire Blvd, #219, Beverly Hills, CA 90211, USA
Frey, Donald N *Industrial Engineer, Businessman*
2758 Sheridan Road, Evanston, IL 60201, USA
Frey, Glenn *Singer (Eagles), Songwriter, Actor*
5020 Brent Knoll Lane, Suwanee, GA 30024, USA
Frey, James G (Jim) *Baseball Manager*
12101 Tullamore Court, #406, Timonium, MD 21093, USA
Freyndlikh, Alisa B *Actress*
Rubinstein Str 11, #7, Saint Petersburg 191002, Russia
Freytag, Arny *Photographer*
22735 MacFarlane Dr, Woodland Hills, CA 91364, USA
Frick, Gottlob *Opera Singer*
Eichelberg-Haus Waldfrieden, 75248 Olbronn-Durrn, Germany
Frick, Stephen N *Astronaut*
4322 Towering Oak Court, Houston, TX 77059, USA
Fricke, Janie *Singer*
%Janie Fricke Concerts, PO Box 798, Lancaster, TX 75146, USA
Fricker, Brenda *Actress*
%Meyer & Eden, 34 Kingly Court, London W1R 5LE, England
Frid, Jonathan *Actor*
PO Box 2429, New York, NY 10108, USA
Friday, Elbert W, Jr *Government Official*
%US National Weather Service, 1125 East-West Highway, Silver Spring, MD 20910, USA
Friday, Nancy *Writer*
%Harper Collins Publishers, 10 E 53rd St, New York, NY 10022, USA
Fridovich, Irwin *Biochemist*
3517 Courtland Dr, Durham, NC 27707, USA
Fridriksson, Fridrik T *Movie Director*
Bjarkargata 8, 101 Reykjavik, Iceland
Fried, Charles *Government Official, Educator*
%Harvard University, Law School, Cambridge, MA 02138, USA
Friedan, Betty *Writer, Social Activist*
2022 Columbia Road NW, #414, Washington, DC 20009, USA
Friedel, Jacques *Physicist*
2 Rue Jean-Francois Gerbillon, 75006 Paris, France
Friedgen, Ralph *Football Coach*
%University of Maryland, Athletic Dept, College Park, MD 20742, USA
Friedkin, William *Movie Director*
10451 Bellagio Road, Los Angeles, CA 90077, USA
Friedlander, Lee *Artist, Photographer*
44 S Mountain Road, New City, NY 10956, USA

Friedman, Daniel M — *Judge*
%US Court of Appeals, 717 Madison Place NW, Washington, DC 20439, USA

Friedman, Emanuel A — *Medical Educator, Obstetrician*
%Beth-Israel Hospital, 330 Brookline Ave, Boston, MA 02215, USA

Friedman, Jeffrey — *Molecular Geneticist*
%Rockefeller University, Hughes Medical Institute, New York, NY 10021, USA

Friedman, Jerome I — *Nobel Physics Laureate*
75 Greenough St, Brookline, MA 02445, USA

Friedman, Lawrence M — *Attorney, Educator*
724 Frenchmans Road, Palo Alto, CA 94305, USA

Friedman, Milton — *Nobel Economics Laureate*
%Stanford University, Hoover Institution, Stanford, CA 94305, USA

Friedman, Peter — *Actor, Singer*
%J Michael Bloom, 233 Park Ave S, #1000, New York, NY 10003, USA

Friedman, Philip — *Writer*
%Ivy Books/Random House Inc, 1745 Broadway, #B1, New York, NY 10019, USA

Friedman, Stephen — *Government Official, Financier*
%White House, 1600 Pennsylvania Ave NW, Washington, DC 20500, USA

Friedman, Thomas L — *Journalist*
%New York Times, Editorial Dept, 229 W 43rd St, New York, NY 10036, USA

Friedman, Tom — *Artist*
%Artists on the Corner, 802 DeMun, Clayton, MO 63105, USA

Friedman, Yona — *Architect*
33 Blvd Garibaldi, 75015 Paris, France

Friedmann, Phil — *Bassist (Dig)*
%Overland Productions, 156 W 56th St, #500, New York, NY 10019, USA

Friel, Brian — *Writer*
Drumaweir House, Greencastle, County Donegal, Ireland

Friels, Colin — *Actor*
129 Brooke St, Woollomooloo, Sydney NSW 2011, Australia

Friend, Lionel — *Conductor*
136 Rosendale Road, London SE21 8LG, England

Friend, Patricia A — *Labor Leader*
1275 K St NW, #5, Washington, DC 20005, USA

Friend, Richard H — *Chemist*
%Cavendish Laboratory, Chemistry Dept, Cambridge, England

Friend, Robert B (Bob) — *Baseball Player*
4 Salem Circle, Pittsburgh, PA 15238, USA

Fries, Donald B — *Publisher*
%Life Magazine, Time-Life Building, New York, NY 10020, USA

Friesen, David — *Jazz Bassist*
%Thomas Cassidy, 11761 E Speedway Blvd, Tucson, AZ 85748, USA

Friesinger, Anni — *Speedskater*
%WIGE Media AG, Geibelweg 24, 70736 Fellbach, Germany

Friesz, John — *Football Player*
19116 NE 48th St, Redmond, WA 98074, USA

Frimout, Dirk D — *Astronaut, Belgium*
%D-1/Nieuwe Ontwikkelingen, Bd E Jacqmainlaan 151, 1210 Brussels, Belgium

Frischmann, Justine — *Singer (Elastica)*
%CMO Mgmt, Ransomes Dock, 357-37 Parkgate Road, London SW11 4NP, England

Frishberg, David L — *Jazz Singer, Pianist, Composer*
%Irvin Arthur Assoc, PO Box 1358, New York, NY 10028, USA

Fritsch, Ted, Jr — *Football Player*
5014 Odins Way, Marietta, GA 30068, USA

Fritz, Harold A — *Vietnam War Army Hero (CMH)*
1017 W Scottwood Dr, Peoria, IL 61615, USA

Fritz, Nikki — *Actress*
PO Box 57764, Sherman Oaks, CA 91413, USA

Frizzell, David — *Singer*
4694 E Robertson Road, Cross Plains, TN 37049, USA

Frizzell, John — *Composer*
%B M I, 8730 Sunset Blvd, #300, Los Angeles, CA 90069, USA

Froemming, Bruce N — *Baseball Umpire*
702 W Haddonstone Place, Thiensville, WI 53092, USA

Froese, Bob — *Hockey Player*
5140 Strickler Road, Clarence, NY 14031, USA

Frohnmayer, David B (Dave) — *Educator*
%University of Oregon, President's Office, Eugene, OR 97403, USA

Frohnmayer, John E — *Government Official*
14080 Lone Bear Road, Bozeman, MT 59715, USA

Froines, John — *Social Activist, Educator*
%University of California, Public Health School, Los Angeles, CA 90024, USA

Fromherz, Peter — *Biophysicist*
%Max Planck Biochemistry Institute, Biophysics Dept, Martinsried, Germany

Fromm, Fritz — *Handball Player*
An der Bismarckschule 64, 30173 Hannover, Germany

Frommelt, Paul — *Alpine Skier*
%Liechtenstein Ski Federation, Vaduz, Liechtenstein

F

Frondel - Fuente

Frondel, Clifford *Mineralogist*
299 Cambridge St, #413, Winchester, MA 01890, USA
Fronius, Hans *Artist*
Guggenberggasse 18, 2380 Perchtoldadorf bei Vienna, Austria
Frontiere, Georgia *Football Executive*
%Saint Louis Rams, 901 N Broadway, Saint Louis, MO 63101, USA
Froom, Mitchell *Keyboardist (Latin Playboys)*
%Gary Stamler Mgmt, 3055 Overland Ave, #200, Los Angeles, CA 90034, USA
Frosch, Robert A *Government Official, Space Executive*
1 Heritage Hills Dr, #42A, Somers, NY 10589, USA
Frost, Craig *Keyboardist (Grand Funk Railroad)*
%Lustig Talent, PO Box 770850, Orlando, FL 32877, USA
Frost, David *Golfer*
%Professional Golfer's Assn, PO Box 109601, Palm Beach Gardens, FL 33410, USA
Frost, David P *Entertainer*
13355 Noel Road, #1600, Dallas, TX 75240, USA
Frost, Lindsay *Actress*
%Broder Kurland Webb Uffner, 9242 Beverly Blvd, #200, Beverly Hills, CA 90210, USA
Frost, Mark *Writer*
%Mark Frost Productions, PO Box 1723, North Hollywood, CA 91614, USA
Frost, Sadie *Actress*
%Julian Belfarge, 46 Albermarle St, London W1X 4PP, England
Fruedek, Jacques *Physicist*
2 Rue Jean-Francois Gerbillion, 70006 Paris, France
Fruh, Eugen *Artist*
Romergasse 9, 8001 Zurich, Switzerland
Fruhbeck de Burgos, Rafael *Conductor*
Avenida dek Mediterraneo 21, 28007 Madrid, Spain
Frusciante, John *Guitarist (Red Hot Chili Peppers)*
10345 Olympic Blvd, #200, Los Angeles, CA 90064, USA
Frutig, Ed *Football Player*
8343 Sego Court, Vero Beach, FL 32963, USA
Fruton, Joseph S *Biochemist*
123 York St, New Haven, CT 06511, USA
Fry Irvin, Shirley *Tennis Player*
1970 Asylum Ave, West Hartford, CT 06117, USA
Fry, Arthur L *Inventor (Post-Its)*
%Minnesota Mining & Manufacturing, 3M Center, Bldg 230-2S, Saint Paul, MN 55144, USA
Fry, Christopher *Writer*
Toft, East Dean near Chichester, Sussex, England
Fry, Michael *Cartoonist (Committed/Over the Hedge)*
%United Feature Syndicate, 200 Madison Ave, New York, NY 10016, USA
Fry, Scott A *Navy Admiral*
Director, Joint Staff Operations, Pentagon, Washington, DC 20318, USA
Fry, Stephen J *Actor, Comedian, Writer*
%Lorraine Hamilton Asper, 76 Oxford St, London W1N 0AT, England
Fry, Thornton C *Mathematician*
500 Mohawk Dr, Boulder, CO 80303, USA
Fryar, Irving D *Football Player, Sportscaster*
51 Applegate Road, Jobstown, NJ 08041, USA
Frye, Soliel Moon *Actress*
PO Box 3743, Glendale, CA 91221, USA
Fryling, Victor J *Businessman*
%CMS Energy, Fairlane Plaza South, 330 Town Center Dr, Dearborn, MI 48126, USA
Fryman, D Travis *Baseball Player*
2600 Highway 196, Molino, FL 32577, USA
Fryman, Woodrow T (Woodie) *Baseball Player*
RR 1 Box 21, Ewing, KY 41039, USA
Ftorek, Robert B (Robbie) *Hockey Player, Coach*
79 Sunset Point Road, Wolfeboro, NH 03894, USA
Fu Mingxia *Diver*
%General Physical Culture Bureau, 9 Tiyuguan Road, Beijing, China
Fuchs, Ann Sutherland *Publisher*
%Vogue Magazine, 350 Madison Ave, New York, NY 10017, USA
Fuchs, Joseph L *Publisher*
%Mademoiselle Magazine, 350 Madison Ave, New York, NY 10017, USA
Fuchs, Michael J *Television Executive*
%Home Box Office, 1100 Ave of Americas, New York, NY 10036, USA
Fuchs, Victor R *Economist*
796 Cedro Way, Stanford, CA 94305, USA
Fuchsberger, Joachim *Actor*
Hubertusstr 62, 82031 Grunwald, Germany
Fudge, Alan *Actor*
355 S Rexford Dr, Beverly Hills, CA 90212, USA
Fuente, David I *Businessman*
%Office Depot Inc, 2200 Old Germantown Road, Delray Beach, FL 33445, USA
Fuente, Luis *Ballet Dancer*
98 Rue Lepic, 75018 Paris, France

Fuentealba, Victor W *Labor Leader*
4501 Arabia Ave, Baltimore, MD 21214, USA
Fuentes, Carlos *Writer*
%Harvard University, Latin American Studies Dept, Cambridge, MA 02138, USA
Fuentes, Daisy *Entertainer, Model*
%Vin DiBona, 12233 W Olympic Blvd, #170, Los Angeles, CA 90064, USA
Fuentes, Julio M *Judge*
%US Court of Appeals, US Courthouse, 50 Walnut St, Newark, NJ 07102, USA
Fugard, Athol H *Writer*
PO Box 5090, Walmer, Port Elizabeth 6065, South Africa
Fugate, Judith *Ballerina*
%New York City Ballet, Lincoln Center Plaza, New York, NY 10023, USA
Fugelsang, John *Actor, Comedian*
%William Morris Agency, 151 El Camino Dr, Beverly Hills, CA 90212, USA
Fugett, Jean *Football Player*
4801 Westparkway, Baltimore, MD 21229, USA
Fugger, Edward *Reproductive Biologist*
305 Island View Dr, Penhook, VA 24137, USA
Fugit, Patrick *Actor*
%Gersh Agency, 232 N Canon Dr, Beverly Hills, CA 90210, USA
Fuglesang, Christer *Astronaut*
108 Englewood St, Bellaire, TX 77401, USA
Fuhr, Grant *Hockey Player*
80 Oswald Dr, Spruce Grove AB T7X 3A1, Canada 63103, USA
Fujita, Hiroyuki *Microbiotics Engineer*
1-9-14 Senkawa, Toshimaku, Tokyo 171, Japan
Fujita, Yoshio *Astronomer*
6-21-7 Renkoji, Tamashi 206, Japan
Fukuto, Maru *Television Director*
%Jim Preminger Agency, 450 N Roxbury Dr, #1050, Beverly Hills, CA 90210, USA
Fukuyama, Francis *Social Scientist*
%George Mason University, Public Policy Dept, Fairfax, VA 22030, USA
Fuld, Richard S, Jr *Financier*
%Lehman Bros, 745 7th Ave, New York, NY 10019, USA
Fulford, Carlton W, Jr *Marine Corps General*
Deputy CinC, US European Command Stuttgart-Vaihingen Germany, APO, AE 09128, USA
Fulghum, Robert *Religious Leader, Writer*
%Random House, 1745 Broadway, #B1, New York, NY 10019, USA
Fulks, Robbie *Singer, Songwriter*
%Mongrel Music, 743 Center Blvd, Fairfax, CA 94930, USA
Fuller, Bob B *Writer*
37 Langton Way, London 5E3, England
Fuller, Bonnie *Editor*
%Glamour Magazine, Editorial Dept, 350 Madison Ave, New York, NY 10017, USA
Fuller, Charles *Writer*
%William Morris Agency, 1325 Ave of Americas, New York, NY 10019, USA
Fuller, Curtis D *Jazz Trombonist*
%Denon Records, 135 W 50th St, #1915, New York, NY 10020, USA
Fuller, Delores *Actress, Songwriter*
3628 Ottawa Circle, Las Vegas, NV 89109, USA
Fuller, Jack W *Editor, Publisher*
%Chicago Tribune, Editorial Dept, 435 N Michigan, Chicago, IL 60611, USA
Fuller, Kathryn S *Association Official*
%World Wildlife Fund, 1250 24th St NW, Washington, DC 20037, USA
Fuller, Linda *Association Executive, Social Activist*
%Habitat for Humanity, 121 Habitat St, Americus, GA 31709, USA
Fuller, Mark *Sculptor*
%Wet Design, 90 Universal City Plaza, Universal City, CA 91608, USA
Fuller, Marvin D *Army General*
6799 Patton Dr, Fort Hood, TX 76544, USA
Fuller, Millard *Association Executive, Social Activist*
%Habitat for Humanity, 121 Habitat St, Americus, GA 31709, USA
Fuller, Penny *Actress*
12428 Hesby St, North Hollywood, CA 91607, USA
Fuller, Robert (Bob) *Actor*
5012 Auckland Ave, North Hollywood, CA 91601, USA
Fuller, Todd *Basketball Player*
%Miami Heat, American Airlines Arena, 601 Biscayne Blvd, Miami, FL 33132, USA
Fuller, William H, Jr *Football Player*
1424 Blue Heron Road, Virginia Beach, VA 23454, USA
Fullerton, C Gordon *Astronaut, Test Pilot*
44046 28th St W, Bldg 4800D, Lancaster, CA 93536, USA
Fullerton, Fiona *Actress*
%London Mgmt, 2-4 Noel St, London W1V 3RB, England
Fullerton, Larry *Inventor (Low Power Pulses for Messages)*
%Time Domain, 6700 Odyssey Dr NW, Huntsville, AL 35806, USA
Fullmer, Gene *Boxer*
9250 S 2200 West, West Jordan, UT 84088, USA

F

Fulmer - Fylstra

Fulmer, Phillip *Football Coach*
%University of Tennessee, Athletic Dept, Knoxville, TN 37996, USA
Fulton, Eileen *Actress, Singer*
%"As the World Turns" Show, CBS-TV, 524 W 57nd St, New York, NY 10019, USA
Fulton, Fitzhugh, Jr *Test Pilot*
1023 E Ave J, #5, Lancaster, CA 93535, USA
Fulton, Robert D *Governor, IA*
141 Hillcrest Road, Waterloo, IA 50701, USA
Funaki, Kazuyoshi *Ski Jumper*
2-52-203 Kotori 4JO, Nishiku Sapporoshi, Hokkaido 063-08, Japan
Funderburk, Leonard J *Vietnam War Air Force Hero*
2311 Lathan Road, Monroe, NC 28112, USA
Funicello, Annette *Actress, Singer*
16102 Sandy Lane, Encino, CA 91436, USA
Funk, Eric *Composer*
PO Box 1073, Helena, MT 59624, USA
Funk, Fred *Golfer*
24711 Harbour View Dr, Ponte Vedra, FL 32082, USA
Funke, Alex *Cinematographer*
1176 Fiske St, Pacific Palisades, CA 90272, USA
Fuqua, Antoine *Movie Director*
%International Creative Mgmt, 8942 Wilshire Blvd, #219, Beverly Hills, CA 90211, USA
Furchgott, Robert F *Nobel Medicine Laureate*
%State University of New York, Health Science Center, Brooklyn, NY 11203, USA
Furey, John *Actor*
%House of Representatives, 400 S Beverly Dr, #101, Beverly Hills, CA 90212, USA
Furgler, Kurt *President, Switzerland*
Dufourstr 34, 9000 Saint-Gall, Switzerland
Furlan, Mira *Actress*
6410 Blarney Stone Court, Springfield, VA 22152, USA
Furlanetto, Ferruccio *Opera Singer*
%Metropolitan Opera Assn, Lincoln Center Plaza, New York, NY 10023, USA
Furlong, Edward *Actor*
10573 W Pico Blvd, #853, Los Angeles, CA 90064, USA
Furniss, Bruce *Swimmer*
655 S Westford St, Anaheim, CA 92807, USA
Furno, Carlo Cardinal *Religious Leader*
Piazza Della Citta Leonina, 00193 Rome, Italy
Furst, Janos K *Conductor*
%I M G Artists, 3 Burlington Lane, Chiswick, London W4 2TH, England
Furst, Stephen *Actor, Comedian*
%Gold Marshak Liedtke, 3500 W Olive Ave, #1400, Burbank, CA 91505, USA
Furstenfeld, Jeremy *Drummer (Blue October)*
%Ashley Talent, 2002 Hogback Road, #20, Ann Arbor, MI 48105, USA
Furstenfeld, Justin *Singer, Guitarist (Blue October)*
%Ashley Talent, 2002 Hogback Road, #20, Ann Arbor, MI 48105, USA
Furtado, Nelly *Singer, Singwriter*
%Chris Smith Mgmt, 193 King St E, #302, Toronto ON M5A 1J5, Canada
Furth, George *Actor, Playwright*
%Bresler Kelly Assoc, 11500 W Olympic Blvd, #510, Los Angeles, CA 90064, USA
Furuhashi, Hironshin *Swimmer*
3-9-11 Nozawa, Setagayaku, Tokyo, Japan
Furukawa, Masaru *Swimmer*
5-5-12 Shinohara Honmachi, Nadaku, Kobe, Japan
Furukawa, Satoshi *Astronaut*
%NASDA, Tsukuba Space Center, 2-1-1 Sengen, Tukuhashi, Ibaraka 305, Japan
Furuseth, Ole Christian *Alpine Skier*
John Colletts Alle 74, 0854 Oslo, Norway
Furyk, Jim *Golfer*
29 Loggerhead Lane, Ponte Vedra, FL 32082, USA
Fusina, Chuck A *Football Player*
1548 King James St, Pittsburgh, PA 15237, USA
Futey, Bohdan A *Judge*
%US Claims Court, 717 Madison Place NW, Washington, DC 20439, USA
Futral, Elizabeth *Opera Singer*
%Neil Funkhouser Mgmt, 105 Arden St, #5G, New York, NY 10040, USA
Futrell, Mary H *Labor Leader*
%George Washington University, Education School, Washington, DC 20052, USA
Futter, Ellen V *Educator, Museum Executive*
%American Natural History Museum, Park Ave West & 79th St, New York, NY 10034, USA
Futterman, Dan *Actor*
%Gersh Agency, 232 N Canon Dr, Beverly Hills, CA 90210, USA
Fuzz *Bassist (Disturbed)*
%Mitch Schneider Organization, 14724 Ventura Blvd, #410, Sherman Oaks, CA 91403, USA
Fylstra, Daniel *Computer Software Designer*
%Visicorp, 2895 Zanken Road, San Jose, CA 95134, USA

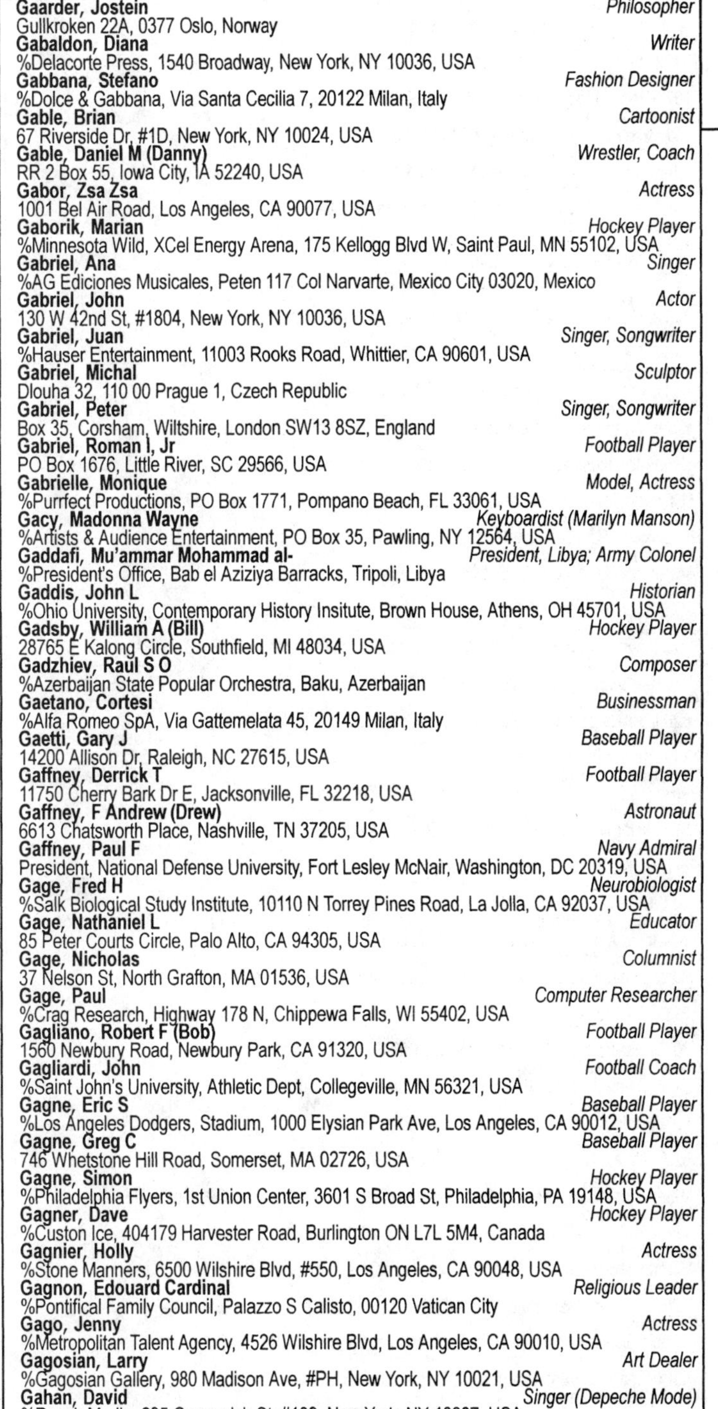

Gaarder, Jostein Gullkroken 22A, 0377 Oslo, Norway	*Philosopher*
Gabaldon, Diana %Delacorte Press, 1540 Broadway, New York, NY 10036, USA	*Writer*
Gabbana, Stefano %Dolce & Gabbana, Via Santa Cecilia 7, 20122 Milan, Italy	*Fashion Designer*
Gable, Brian 67 Riverside Dr, #1D, New York, NY 10024, USA	*Cartoonist*
Gable, Daniel M (Danny) RR 2 Box 55, Iowa City, IA 52240, USA	*Wrestler, Coach*
Gabor, Zsa Zsa 1001 Bel Air Road, Los Angeles, CA 90077, USA	*Actress*
Gaborik, Marian %Minnesota Wild, XCel Energy Arena, 175 Kellogg Blvd W, Saint Paul, MN 55102, USA	*Hockey Player*
Gabriel, Ana %AG Ediciones Musicales, Peten 117 Col Narvarte, Mexico City 03020, Mexico	*Singer*
Gabriel, John 130 W 42nd St, #1804, New York, NY 10036, USA	*Actor*
Gabriel, Juan %Hauser Entertainment, 11003 Rooks Road, Whittier, CA 90601, USA	*Singer, Songwriter*
Gabriel, Michal Dlouha 32, 110 00 Prague 1, Czech Republic	*Sculptor*
Gabriel, Peter Box 35, Corsham, Wiltshire, London SW13 8SZ, England	*Singer, Songwriter*
Gabriel, Roman I, Jr PO Box 1676, Little River, SC 29566, USA	*Football Player*
Gabrielle, Monique %Purrfect Productions, PO Box 1771, Pompano Beach, FL 33061, USA	*Model, Actress*
Gacy, Madonna Wayne %Artists & Audience Entertainment, PO Box 35, Pawling, NY 12564, USA	*Keyboardist (Marilyn Manson)*
Gaddafi, Mu'ammar Mohammad al- %President's Office, Bab el Aziziya Barracks, Tripoli, Libya	*President, Libya; Army Colonel*
Gaddis, John L %Ohio University, Contemporary History Insitute, Brown House, Athens, OH 45701, USA	*Historian*
Gadsby, William A (Bill) 28765 E Kalong Circle, Southfield, MI 48034, USA	*Hockey Player*
Gadzhiev, Raul S O %Azerbaijan State Popular Orchestra, Baku, Azerbaijan	*Composer*
Gaetano, Cortesi %Alfa Romeo SpA, Via Gattemelata 45, 20149 Milan, Italy	*Businessman*
Gaetti, Gary J 14200 Allison Dr, Raleigh, NC 27615, USA	*Baseball Player*
Gaffney, Derrick T 11750 Cherry Bark Dr E, Jacksonville, FL 32218, USA	*Football Player*
Gaffney, F Andrew (Drew) 6613 Chatsworth Place, Nashville, TN 37205, USA	*Astronaut*
Gaffney, Paul F President, National Defense University, Fort Lesley McNair, Washington, DC 20319, USA	*Navy Admiral*
Gage, Fred H %Salk Biological Study Institute, 10110 N Torrey Pines Road, La Jolla, CA 92037, USA	*Neurobiologist*
Gage, Nathaniel L 85 Peter Courts Circle, Palo Alto, CA 94305, USA	*Educator*
Gage, Nicholas 37 Nelson St, North Grafton, MA 01536, USA	*Columnist*
Gage, Paul %Crag Research, Highway 178 N, Chippewa Falls, WI 55402, USA	*Computer Researcher*
Gagliano, Robert F (Bob) 1560 Newbury Road, Newbury Park, CA 91320, USA	*Football Player*
Gagliardi, John %Saint John's University, Athletic Dept, Collegeville, MN 56321, USA	*Football Coach*
Gagne, Eric S %Los Angeles Dodgers, Stadium, 1000 Elysian Park Ave, Los Angeles, CA 90012, USA	*Baseball Player*
Gagne, Greg C 746 Whetstone Hill Road, Somerset, MA 02726, USA	*Baseball Player*
Gagne, Simon %Philadelphia Flyers, 1st Union Center, 3601 S Broad St, Philadelphia, PA 19148, USA	*Hockey Player*
Gagner, Dave %Custon Ice, 404179 Harvester Road, Burlington ON L7L 5M4, Canada	*Hockey Player*
Gagnier, Holly %Stone Manners, 6500 Wilshire Blvd, #550, Los Angeles, CA 90048, USA	*Actress*
Gagnon, Edouard Cardinal %Pontifical Family Council, Palazzo S Calisto, 00120 Vatican City	*Religious Leader*
Gago, Jenny %Metropolitan Talent Agency, 4526 Wilshire Blvd, Los Angeles, CA 90010, USA	*Actress*
Gagosian, Larry %Gagosian Gallery, 980 Madison Ave, #PH, New York, NY 10021, USA	*Art Dealer*
Gahan, David %Reach Media, 295 Greenwich St, #109, New York, NY 10007, USA	*Singer (Depeche Mode)*

G

Gaidar - Gallagher

Gaidar, Yegor T *Prime Minister, Russia*
Gazetny Per 5, Moscow 111024, Russia
Gail, Max *Actor*
28198 Rey de Copas Lane, Malibu, CA 90265, USA
Gailey, T Chandler (Chan) *Football Player, Coach*
3497 Paces Valley Road NW, Atlanta, GA 30327, USA
Gaillard, Bob *Basketball Coach*
50 Bonnie Brae Dr, Novato, CA 94949, USA
Gaillard, Charles *Businessman*
%General Mills Inc, 1 General Mills Blvd, PO Box 1113, Minneapolis, MN 55440, USA
Gaillard, Mary Katharine *Physicist*
%University of California, Physics Dept, Berkeley, CA 94720, USA
Gain, Robert (Bob) *Football Player*
11 Nokomis Dr, Eastlake, OH 44095, USA
Gaines, Ambrose (Rowdy), IV *Swimmer*
6800 Hawaii Kai Dr, Honolulu, HI 96825, USA
Gaines, Boyd *Actor, Singer*
%Duva/Flack, 200 W 57th St, #1407, New York, NY 10019, USA
Gaines, Clarence E (Big House) *Basketball Coach*
2015 E End Blvd, Winston Salem, NC 27101, USA
Gaines, Ernest J *Writer*
128 Buena Vista Blvd, Lafayette, LA 70503, USA
Gaines, James R *Editor, Publisher*
%Time Warner Inc, Time Magazine, Rockefeller Center, New York, NY 10020, USA
Gaines, Reese *Basketball Player*
%Orlando Magic, Waterhouse Center, 8701 Maitland Summit Blvd, Orlando, FL 32810, USA
Gaines, William C *Journalist*
%Chicago Tribune, Editorial Dept, 435 N Michigan Ave, Chicago, IL 60611, USA
Gainey, Robert M (Bob) *Hockey Player, Coach, Executive*
PO Box 829, Coppell, TX 75019, USA
Gainsbourg, Charlotte *Actress*
%Artmedia, 20 Ave Rapp, 75007 Paris, France
Gaither, Bill *Gospel Singer, Songwriter*
%Gaither Music Co, PO Box 737, Alexandria, IN 46001, USA
Gajarsa, Arthur J *Judge*
%US Court of Appeals, 717 Madison Place NW, Washington, DC 20439, USA
Gajdusek, D Carleton *Nobel Medicine Laureate*
%Human Virology Institute, 725 W Lombard St, #N460, Baltimore, MD 21201, USA
Galambos, Robert *Neuroscientist*
8826 La Jolla Scenic Dr, La Jolla, CA 92037, USA
Galanos, James *Fashion Designer*
1316 Sunset Plaza Dr, Los Angeles, CA 90069, USA
Galarraga, Andres J P *Baseball Player*
Barrio Nuevo Chapellin, Clejon Soledad #5, Caracas, Venezuela
Galati, Frank J *Theater, Opera Director*
1144 Michigan Ave, Evanston, IL 60202, USA
Galbraith, Clint *Harness Racing Driver*
PO Box 902, Edwardsville, IL 62025, USA
Galbraith, Evan G *Diplomat, Financier*
133 E 64th St, New York, NY 10021, USA
Galbraith, J Kenneth *Government Official, Economist*
30 Francis Ave, Cambridge, MA 02138, USA
Galdikas, Birute M F *Anthropologist*
%Orangutan Foundation International, 822 Wellesley Ave, Los Angeles, CA 90049, USA
Gale, Joseph H *Judge*
%US Tax Court, 400 2nd St NW, Washington, DC 20217, USA
Gale, Robert P *Medical Researcher*
980 Bluegrass Lane, Los Angeles, CA 90049, USA
Galella, Ronald E (Ron) *Photographer*
%Ron Galella Ltd, 12 Nelson Lane, Montville, NJ 07045, USA
Galer, Robert E *WW II Marine Corps Hero (CMH), General*
3131 Maple Ave, #6D, Dallas, TX 75201, USA
Galigher, Ed *Football Player*
862 E Angela St, Pleasanton, CA 94566, USA
Galik, Denise *Actress*
%Badgley Connor Talent, 9229 Sunset Blvd, #311, Los Angeles, CA 90069, USA
Galindo, Rudy *Figure Skater*
1115 E Haley St, Santa Barbara, CA 93103, USA
Gall, Hugues *Opera Executive*
%Grand Theatre de Geneva, 11 Blvd du Theatre, Geneva 1211, Switzerland
Gall, Joseph G *Biologist*
107 Bellemore Road, Baltimore, MD 21210, USA
Gallacher, Kevin *Soccer Player*
%Blackburn Rovers, Ewood Park, Blackburn, Lancashire BB2 4JF, England
Gallagher *Illusionist*
14984 Roan Court, Wellington, FL 33414, USA
Gallagher, Brian *Association Executive*
%United Way of America, 701 N Fairfax Ave, Alexandria, VA 22314, USA

Gallagher, Bronagh *Actor*
%Marmont Mgmt, Langham House, 302/8 Regent St, London W1R 5AL, England
Gallagher, Helen *Singer, Actress*
260 W End Ave, New York, NY 10023, USA
Gallagher, Jim, Jr *Golfer*
PO Box 507, Greenwood, MS 38935, USA
Gallagher, John *Religious Leader*
%Advent Christian Church, PO Box 551, Presque Isle, ME 04769, USA
Gallagher, Liam *Singer (Oasis)*
%Ignition Mgmt, 54 Linhope St, London NW1 6HL, England
Gallagher, Megan *Actress*
%Don Buchwald, 6500 Wilshire Blvd, #2200, Los Angeles, CA 90048, USA
Gallagher, Noel *Singer, Guitarist (Oasis), Songwriter*
%Ignition Mgmt, 54 Linhope St, London NW1 6HL, England
Gallagher, Peter *Actor*
2124 Broadway, #131, New York, NY 10023, USA
Gallagher-Smith, Jackie *Golfer*
%Int'l Golf Partners, 3300 PGA Blvd, #909, West Palm Beach, FL 33410, USA
Gallant, Mavis *Writer*
14 Rue Jean Ferrandi, 75006 Paris, France
Gallardo, Camilio *Actor*
%Innovative Artists, 1505 10th St, Santa Monica, CA 90401, USA
Gallatin, Harry J *Basketball Player, Coach*
2010 Madison Ave, Edwardsville, IL 62025, USA
Gallego, Gina *Actress*
%The Agency, 1800 Ave of Stars, #400, Los Angeles, CA 90067, USA
Gallegos, Gilbert G *Labor Leader*
%Fraternal Order of Police, 1410 Donaldson Pike, Nashville, TN 37217, USA
Galles, John *Association Executive*
%National Small Business United, 1156 15th St NW, #1100, Washington, DC 20005, USA
Galliano, John C *Fashion Designer*
%House of Dior, 60 Rue D'Avron, 75020 Paris, France
Gallico, Gregory, III *Surgeon, Inventor (Synthetic Skin)*
%Massachusetts General Hospital, 275 Cambridge St, Boston, MA 02114, USA
Gallison, Joe *Actor*
PO Box 10187, Wilmington, NC 28404, USA
Gallo, Ernest *Businessman*
%E&J Gallo Winery, 600 Yosemite Blvd, Modesto, CA 95354, USA
Gallo, Frank *Sculptor*
%University of Illinois, Art Dept, Urbana, IL 61801, USA
Gallo, Robert C *Research Scientist*
%University of Maryland, Study of Viruses Institute, Baltimore, MD 21228, USA
Gallo, Vincent *Actor, Director*
432 La Guardia Place, #600, New York, NY 10012, USA
Gallo, William V (Bill) *Sports Cartoonist, Boxer*
1 Mayflower Dr, Yonkers, NY 10710, USA
Galloway, Don *Actor*
2501 Colorado Ave, #350, Santa Monica, CA 90404, USA
Galloway, Jean *Religious Leader*
%Volunteers of America, 1660 Duke St, Alexandria, VA 22314, USA
Galloway, Joey *Football Player*
507 Lilly Court, Irving, TX 75063, USA
Gallup, George H, II *Statistician, Pollster*
Great Road, Princeton, NJ 08540, USA
Galotti, Donna *Publisher*
%Ladies Home Journal, 100 Park Ave, New York, NY 10017, USA
Galotti, Ronald A *Publisher*
%Conde Nast Publications, Publisher's Office, 4 Times Square, New York, NY 10036, USA
Galston, Arthur W *Biologist*
307 Manley Heights Road, Orange, CT 06477, USA
Galvin, James *Writer*
%University of Iowa, Writers' Workshop, Iowa City, IA 52242, USA
Galvin, John R *Army General*
2714 Jodeco Circle, Jonesboro, GA 30236, USA
Galway, James *Concert Flutist*
Benseholzstr 11, 6045 Meggan, Switzerland
Gam, Rita *Actress*
180 W 58th St, #8B, New York, NY 10019, USA
Gam, Stefan *Auto Racing Executive*
%Indy Regency Racing, 5811 W 73rd St, Indianapolis, IN 46278, USA
Gamache, Joey *Boxer*
66 Oak St, Lewiston, ME 04240, USA
Gambee, Dave *Basketball Player*
PO Box 3070, Portland, OR 97208, USA
Gamble, Ed *Editorial Cartoonist*
%Florida Times-Union, Editorial Dept, 1 Riverside Ave, Jacksonville, FL 32202, USA
Gamble, Kenny (Ken) *Football Player*
194 Haverford St, Hamden, CT 06517, USA

Gamble, Kevin *Basketball Player*
41 Forest Ridge, Springfield, IL 62707, USA
Gamble, Mason *Actor*
%United Talent Agency, 9560 Wilshire Blvd, #500, Beverly Hills, CA 90212, USA
Gambon, Michael J *Actor*
%International Creative Mgmt, 40 W 57th St, #1800, New York, NY 10019, USA
Gambrell, David H *Senator, GA*
3205 Arden Road NW, Atlanta, GA 30305, USA
Gambril, Don *Swimming Coach*
2 Old North River Point, Tuscaloosa, AL 35406, USA
Gambucci, Andre *Hockey Player, Coach*
660 Southpointe Court, Colorado Springs, CO 80906, USA
Gammon, James *Actor*
414 N Sycamore Ave, #3, Los Angeles, CA 90036, USA
Gammons, Peter *Sportswriter*
%Boston Globe, Editorial Dept, PO Box 2378, Boston, MA 02107, USA
Ganassi, Chip *Auto Racing Driver, Owner*
%Chip Ganassi Racing, 11901 W Baseline Road, Avondale, AZ 85323, USA
Ganassi, Sonia *Opera Singer*
%Columbia Artists Mgmt Inc, 165 W 57th St, New York, NY 10019, USA
Gandhi, Sonia *Government Official, India*
%All India Congress Party, 24 Akbar Road, New Delhi 110011, India
Gandler, Markus *Cross Country Skier*
Sinwell 22, 6370 Kitzbuhel, Austria
Gandolfini, James *Actor*
838 Greenwich St, New York, NY 10014, USA
Gandy, Wayne L *Football Player*
130 Sand Pine Lane, Davenport, FL 33837, USA
Ganellin, C Robin *Inventor (Antiulcer Compound)*
%University College, Chemistry Dept, 20 Gordon, London WC1H OAJ, England
Gangel, Jamie *Commentator*
%NBC-TV, News Dept, 30 Rockefeller Plaza, New York, NY 10112, USA
Gannon, Richard J (Rich) *Football Player*
%Oakland Raiders, 1220 Harbor Bay Parkway, Alameda, CA 94502, USA
Gansler, Bob *Soccer Coach*
%Kansas City Wizards, 2 Arrowhead Dr, Kansas City, MO 64129, USA
Ganson, Arthur *Sculptor*
%Massachusetts Institute of Technology, Compton Gallery, Cambridge, MA 02139, USA
Gant, Harry *Auto Racing Driver*
RR 3 Box 587, Taylorsville, NC 28681, USA
Gant, Ronald E (Ron) *Baseball Player*
2005 Kings Cross Road, Alpharetta, GA 30022, USA
Gantin, Bernardin Cardinal *Religious Leader*
%Congregation for Bishops, Piazza Pio XII 10, 00193 Rome, Italy
Gantos, Jack *Writer*
%Farrar Straus Giroux, 19 Union Square W, New York, NY 10003, USA
Ganz, Bruno *Actor*
%Mgmt Erna Baumbauer, Keplerstr 2, 81679 Munich, Germany
Ganzel, Teresa *Actress*
%Irv Schechter, 9300 Wilshire Blvd, #410, Beverly Hills, CA 90212, USA
Gao Xingjian *Nobel Literature Laureate*
%Chinese University of Hong Kong Press, Shatin, Hong Kong, China
Gao, Xiang *Concert Violinist*
%Columbia Artists Mgmt Inc, 165 W 57th St, New York, NY 10019, USA
Garabedian, Paul R *Mathematician*
110 Bleecker St, New York, NY 10012, USA
Garagiola, Joe *Sportscaster, Baseball Player*
7433 E Tuckey Lane, Scottsdale, AZ 85250, USA
Garan, Ronald J, Jr *Astronaut*
2002 Sea Cove Court, Houston, TX 77058, USA
Garas, Kaz *Actor*
10145 N Buchanan Ave, Portland, OR 97203, USA
Garavito, R Michael *Biochemist*
%Michigan State University, Biochemisty Dept, East Lansing, MI 48824, USA
Garber, H Eugene (Gene) *Baseball Player*
771 Stonemill Dr, Elizabethtown, PA 17022, USA
Garber, Terri *Actress*
%Metropolitan Talent Agency, 4526 Wilshire Blvd, Los Angeles, CA 90010, USA
Garber, Victor *Actor*
%Gersh Agency, 232 N Canon Dr, Beverly Hills, CA 90210, USA
Garci, Jose Luis *Movie Director*
%Direccion General del Libro, Paseo de la Castellana 109, Madrid 16, Spain
Garcia Marquez, Gabriel *Nobel Literature Laureate*
Fuego 144, Pedregal de San Angel, Mexico City DF, Mexico
Garcia, Andy *Actor*
4343 Forman Ave, Toluca Lake, CA 91602, USA
Garcia, David (Dave) *Baseball Player*
15420 Olde Highway 80, #19, El Cajon, CA 92021, USA

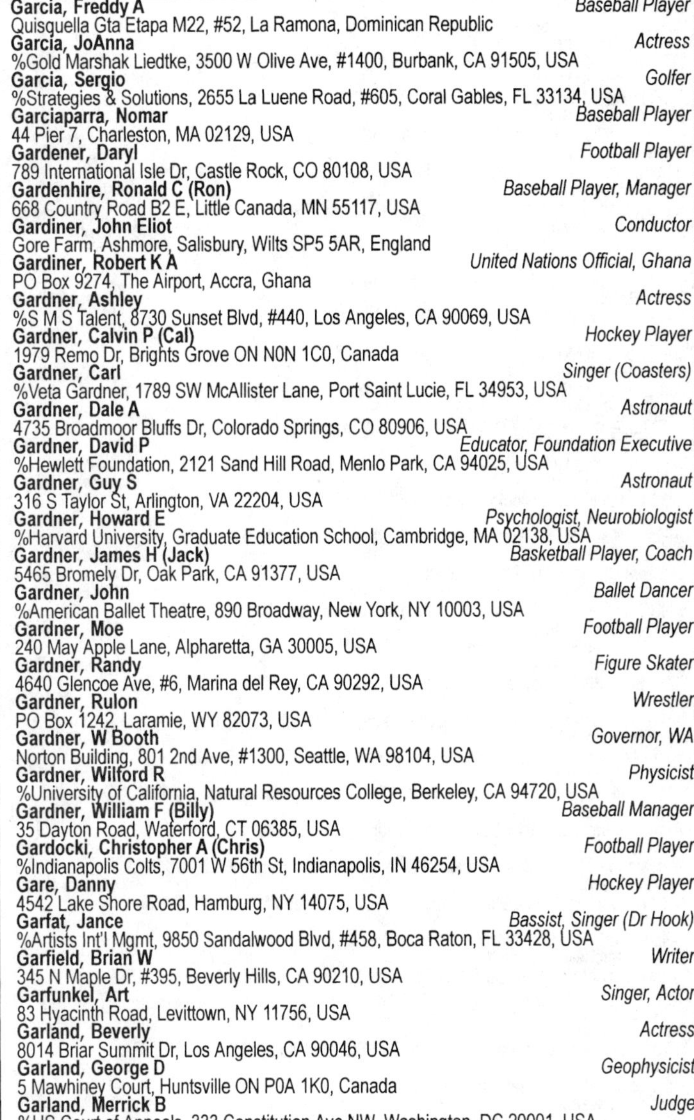

Garcia, Freddy A *Baseball Player*
Quisquella Gta Etapa M22, #52, La Ramona, Dominican Republic
Garcia, JoAnna *Actress*
%Gold Marshak Liedtke, 3500 W Olive Ave, #1400, Burbank, CA 91505, USA
Garcia, Sergio *Golfer*
%Strategies & Solutions, 2655 La Luene Road, #605, Coral Gables, FL 33134, USA
Garciaparra, Nomar *Baseball Player*
44 Pier 7, Charleston, MA 02129, USA
Gardener, Daryl *Football Player*
789 International Isle Dr, Castle Rock, CO 80108, USA
Gardenhire, Ronald C (Ron) *Baseball Player, Manager*
668 Country Road B2 E, Little Canada, MN 55117, USA
Gardiner, John Eliot *Conductor*
Gore Farm, Ashmore, Salisbury, Wilts SP5 5AR, England
Gardiner, Robert K A *United Nations Official, Ghana*
PO Box 9274, The Airport, Accra, Ghana
Gardner, Ashley *Actress*
%S M S Talent, 8730 Sunset Blvd, #440, Los Angeles, CA 90069, USA
Gardner, Calvin P (Cal) *Hockey Player*
1979 Remo Dr, Brights Grove ON N0N 1C0, Canada
Gardner, Carl *Singer (Coasters)*
%Veta Gardner, 1789 SW McAllister Lane, Port Saint Lucie, FL 34953, USA
Gardner, Dale A *Astronaut*
4735 Broadmoor Bluffs Dr, Colorado Springs, CO 80906, USA
Gardner, David P *Educator, Foundation Executive*
%Hewlett Foundation, 2121 Sand Hill Road, Menlo Park, CA 94025, USA
Gardner, Guy S *Astronaut*
316 S Taylor St, Arlington, VA 22204, USA
Gardner, Howard E *Psychologist, Neurobiologist*
%Harvard University, Graduate Education School, Cambridge, MA 02138, USA
Gardner, James H (Jack) *Basketball Player, Coach*
5465 Bromely Dr, Oak Park, CA 91377, USA
Gardner, John *Ballet Dancer*
%American Ballet Theatre, 890 Broadway, New York, NY 10003, USA
Gardner, Moe *Football Player*
240 May Apple Lane, Alpharetta, GA 30005, USA
Gardner, Randy *Figure Skater*
4640 Glencoe Ave, #6, Marina del Rey, CA 90292, USA
Gardner, Rulon *Wrestler*
PO Box 1242, Laramie, WY 82073, USA
Gardner, W Booth *Governor, WA*
Norton Building, 801 2nd Ave, #1300, Seattle, WA 98104, USA
Gardner, Wilford R *Physicist*
%University of California, Natural Resources College, Berkeley, CA 94720, USA
Gardner, William F (Billy) *Baseball Manager*
35 Dayton Road, Waterford, CT 06385, USA
Gardocki, Christopher A (Chris) *Football Player*
%Indianapolis Colts, 7001 W 56th St, Indianapolis, IN 46254, USA
Gare, Danny *Hockey Player*
4542 Lake Shore Road, Hamburg, NY 14075, USA
Garfat, Jance *Bassist, Singer (Dr Hook)*
%Artists Int'l Mgmt, 9850 Sandalwood Blvd, #458, Boca Raton, FL 33428, USA
Garfield, Brian W *Writer*
345 N Maple Dr, #395, Beverly Hills, CA 90210, USA
Garfunkel, Art *Singer, Actor*
83 Hyacinth Road, Levittown, NY 11756, USA
Garland, Beverly *Actress*
8014 Briar Summit Dr, Los Angeles, CA 90046, USA
Garland, George D *Geophysicist*
5 Mawhiney Court, Huntsville ON P0A 1K0, Canada
Garland, Merrick B *Judge*
%US Court of Appeals, 333 Constitution Ave NW, Washington, DC 20001, USA
Garlick, Scott *Soccer Player*
%Colorado Rapids, 555 17th St, #3350, Denver, CO 80202, USA
Garlits, Donald G (Big Daddy) *Drag Racing Driver*
%Garlits Racing Museum, 13700 SW 16th Ave, Ocala, FL 34473, USA
Garmaker, Dick *Basketball Player*
5824 E 111th St, Tulsa, OK 74137, USA
Garmann, Greg *Actor*
8383 Wilshire Blvd, #550, Beverly Hills, CA 90211, USA
Garn, E Jacob (Jake) *Senator, UT; Astronaut*
1626 Yale Ave, Salt Lake City, UT 84105, USA
Garn, Stanley M *Anthropologist*
1200 Earhart Road, #223, Ann Arbor, MI 48105, USA
Garneau, Marc *Astronaut, Canada*
%Space Agency, 6767 Route de Aeroport, Sainte-Hubert QC J3Y 8Y9, Canada
Garner, Charlie *Football Player*
%Oakland Raiders, 1220 Harbor Bay Parkway, Alameda, CA 94502, USA

G

Garner - Garth

Garner, James *Actor*
33 Oakmont Dr, Los Angeles, CA 90049, USA
Garner, Jennifer *Actress*
%Three Arts Entertainment, 9460 Wilshire Blvd, #700, Beverly Hills, CA 90212, USA
Garner, Philip M (Phil) *Baseball Player, Manager*
7503 Prairie Oak Trail, Humble, TX 77346, USA
Garner, Wendell R *Psychologist*
PO Box 650, Branford, CT 06405, USA
Garner, William S *Editorial Cartoonist*
%Memphis Commercial Appeal, Editorial Dept, 495 Union Ave, Memphis, TN 38103, USA
Garnett, Kevin *Basketball Player*
%Minnesota Timberwolves, Target Center, 600 1st Ave N, Minneapolis, MN 55403, USA
Garofalo, Janeane *Actress, Comedienne*
%Messina-Baker Entertainment, 955 Carillo Dr 100, Los Angeles, CA 90048, USA
Garouste, Gerard *Artist*
La Mesangere, 27810 Marcilly-sur-Eure, France
Garr, Ralph A *Baseball Player*
7819 Chaseway Dr, Missouri City, TX 77489, USA
Garr, Teri *Actress*
8686 Lookout Mountain Dr, Los Angeles, CA 90046, USA
Garrahy, J Joseph *Governor, RI*
988 Centerville Road, Warwick, RI 02886, USA
Garrard, Rose *Artist*
105 Carpenters Road, #21, London E18, England
Garrels, Robert M *Geologist*
%South Florida University, Marine Science Dept, Saint Petersburg, FL 33701, USA
Garrett, Betty *Actress, Singer*
3231 Oakdell Road, Studio City, CA 91604, USA
Garrett, Brad *Actor, Comedian*
%Raw Talent, 9615 Brighton Way, #300, Beverly Hills, CA 90210, USA
Garrett, Carl *Football Player*
314 Teal St, Pittsburg, TX 75686, USA
Garrett, Cynthia *Entertainer*
%NBC-TV, News Dept, 30 Rockefeller Plaza, New York, NY 10112, USA
Garrett, George P, Jr *Writer*
1845 Wayside Place, Charlottesville, VA 22903, USA
Garrett, H Lawrence, III *Government Official*
RR 1 Box 136-18, Boyce, VA 22620, USA
Garrett, Jeremy *Actor*
%Sterling/Winters, 10877 Wilshire Blvd, #15, Los Angeles, CA 90024, USA
Garrett, Kathleen *Actress*
%The Agency, 1800 Ave of Stars, #400, Los Angeles, CA 90067, USA
Garrett, Kenneth *Photographer*
%National Geographic Magazine, 1145 17th St NW, Washington, DC 20036, USA
Garrett, Kenny *Jazz Saxophonist*
%Von Productions, 1915 Cullen Ave, Austin, TX 78757, USA
Garrett, Leif *Actor, Singer*
%Artists Int'l Mgmt, 9850 Sandalfoot Blvd, #458, Boca Raton, FL 33428, USA
Garrett, Lesley *Opera Singer*
%PV Productions, Park Offices, 121 Dora Road, London SW19 7JT, England
Garrett, Lila *Movie Director*
1245 Laurel Way, Beverly Hills, CA 90210, USA
Garrett, Michael L (Mike) *Football Player, Sports Administrator*
%University of Southern California, Heritage Hall, Los Angeles, CA 90089, USA
Garrett, Pat *Singer, Songwriter*
%Patrick Sickafus, PO Box 84, Strausstown, PA 19559, USA
Garrett, Wilbur E *Editor*
%National Geographic Magazine, 17th & M Sts, Washington, DC 20036, USA
Garrett, William E *Photographer*
209 Seneca Road, Great Falls, VA 22066, USA
Garriott, Owen K *Astronaut*
111 Lost Tree Dr SW, Huntsville, AL 35824, USA
Garrison, David *Actor*
630 Estrada Redona, Santa Fe, NM 87501, USA
Garrison, John *Hockey Player*
Old Concord Road, Lincoln, MA 01773, USA
Garrison, Walt *Football Player*
187 E Hickory Hill Road, Argyle, TX 76226, USA
Garrison-Jackson, Zina *Tennis Player*
1701 Hermann Dr, #705, Houston, TX 77004, USA
Garrity, Freddie *Singer*
16 Ascot Close, Congleton, Cheshire CW1Z 1LL, England
Garrum, Larry *Hockey Player*
987 Pleasant St, Framingham, MA 01701, USA
Garson, Willie *Actor*
%Writers & Artists, 8383 Wilshire Blvd, #550, Beverly Hills, CA 90211, USA
Garth, Jennie *Actress*
PO Box 1944, Studio City, CA 91614, USA

G

Garth, Leonard I *Judge*
%US Court of Appeals, US Courthouse, 50 Walnut St, Newark, NJ 07102, USA
Gartner, Michael G *Businessman, Publisher, Editor*
366 W 11th St, New York, NY 10014, USA
Gartner, Mike *Hockey Player*
%NHL Players' Association, 2400-777 Bay St, Toronto ON M5G 2C8, Canada
Garver, Cathy *Actress*
550 Mountain Home Road, Woodside, CA 94062, USA
Garver, Kathy *Actress*
%April Cheeseman, 620 Country Club Lane, Coronado, CA 92118, USA
Garver, Ned F *Baseball Player*
1121 Town Line Road, #164, Bryan, OH 43506, USA
Garvey, Steven P (Steve) *Baseball Player*
11718 Barrington Court, #6, Los Angeles, CA 90049, USA
Garwin, Richard L *Physicist*
16 Ridgecrest E, Scarsdale, NY 10583, USA
Garwood, Julie *Writer*
%Pocket Books, 1230 Ave of Americas, New York, NY 10020, USA
Garwood, William L (Will) *Judge*
%US Court of Appeals, 903 San Jacinto Blvd, Austin, TX 78701, USA
Gary, Cleveland E *Football Player*
1446 SW 169th Ave, Indiantown, FL 37956, USA
Gary, Lorraine *Actress*
1158 Tower Dr, Beverly Hills, CA 90210, USA
Garza, David *Singer*
%Partisan Arts, PO Box 5085, Larkspur, CA 94977, USA
Garza, Emilio M *Judge*
%US Court of Appeals, US Courthouse, 8200 I-10 W, San Antonio, TX 78230, USA
Gascoigne, Paul J *Soccer Player*
%Arran Gardner, Holborn Hall, 10 Grays Inn Road, London WC1X 8BY, England
Gascoine, Jill *Actress*
%Marina Martin, 12/13 Poland St, London W1V 3DE, England
Gash, Samuel L (Sam) *Football Player*
53 Michael Anthony Lane, Depew, NY 14043, USA
Gaspari, Rich *Body Builder*
PO Box 29, Milltown, NJ 08850, USA
Gass, William H *Philosopher, Writer*
6304 Westminster Place, Saint Louis, MO 63130, USA
Gassiyev, Nikolai T *Opera Singer*
%Mariinsky Theater, Teartalnaya Pl 1, Saint Petersburg, Russia
Gast, Leon *Movie Director*
%William Morris Agency, 151 El Camino Dr, Beverly Hills, CA 90212, USA
Gastineau, Marcus D (Mark) *Football Player*
1717 S Dorsey Lane, Tempe, AZ 85281, USA
Gaston, Clarence E (Cito) *Baseball Player, Manager*
2 Blyth Dale Road, Toronto ON M4N 3M2, Canada
Gately, Stephen *Singer (Boyzone)*
%Carol Assoc-War Mgmt, Bushy Park Road, 57 Meadowbanl, Dublin, Ireland
Gates, Daryl F *Law Enforcement Official*
24962 Sea Crest Dr, Dana Point, CA 92629, USA
Gates, David *Singer, Keyboardist (Bread), Songwriter*
%Paradise Artists, 108 E Matilija St, Ojai, CA 93023, USA
Gates, Henry Lewis, Jr *Educator*
%Harvard University, Afro-American Studies Dept, Cambridge, MA 02138, USA
Gates, Robert M *Government Official, Educator*
%Texas A&M University, President's Office, College Station, TX 77843, USA
Gates, William H, III *Computer Software Designer, Businessman*
%Microsoft Corp, 1 Microsoft Way, Redmond, WA 98052, USA
Gatlin, Larry W *Singer, Songwriter (Gatlin Brothers)*
%McLachlan-Scruggs, 2821 Bransford Ave, Nashville, TN 37204, USA
Gatski, Frank *Football Player*
PO Box 677, Grafton, WV 26354, USA
Gatti, Arturo *Boxer*
3208 Bergen Line Ave, Union City, NJ 07087, USA
Gatti, Jennifer *Actress*
%S D B Partners, 1801 Ave of Stars, #902, Los Angeles, CA 90067, USA
Gatting, Michael W *Cricketer*
%Middlesex Cricket Club, Saint John's Wood Road, London NW8 8QN, England
Gauci, Miriam *Opera Singer*
%Kunstleragentur Raab & Bohm, Plankengasse 7, 1010 Vienna, Austria
Gaudiani, Claire L *Educator*
53 Neptune Dr, Groton, CT 06340, USA
Gaul, Gilbert M *Journalist*
%Philadelphia Inquirer, Editorial Dept, 400 N Broad St, Philadelphia, PA 19130, USA
Gault, William Campbell *Writer*
481 Mountain Dr, Santa Barbara, CA 93103, USA
Gault, Willie J *Football Player*
PO Box 10759, Marina del Rey, CA 90295, USA

G

Gaultier, Jean-Paul *Fashion Designer*
%Jean-Paul Gaultier SA, 70 Galerie Vivienne, 75002 Paris, France
Gauthier, Daniel *Circus Executive*
%Cirque du Soleil, 8400 2nd Ave, Montreal QC H1Z 4M6, Canada
Gautier, Dick *Actor*
11333 Moorpark St, #59, North Hollywood, CA 91602, USA
Gava, Cassandra *Actress*
1745 Camino Palmero St, #210, Los Angeles, CA 90046, USA
Gavaskar, Sunil M *Cricketer*
40 Sir Bhalchandra Road, #A, Dadar, Bombay 400014, India
Gavin, John *Actor, Diplomat*
10263 Century Woods Dr, Los Angeles, CA 90067, USA
Gaviria Trujillo, Cesar *President, Colombia*
%Organization of American States, 17th & Constitution NW, Washington, DC 20006, USA
Gavitt, Dave *Basketball Executive*
%Boston Celtics, 151 Merrimac St, #1, Boston, MA 02114, USA
Gavrilov, Andrei V *Concert Pianist*
%Konzertdirektion Schlote, Danreitergasse 4, 5020 Salzburg, Austria
Gay, Gerald H (Jerry) *Photojournalist*
PO Box 938, Blaine, WA 98231, USA
Gay, Peter J *Historian*
760 W End Ave, #15A, New York, NY 10025, USA
Gaydukov, Sergei N *Cosmonaut*
%Potchta Kosmonavtov, Moskovskoi Oblasti, 141160 Syvisdny Goroduk, Russia
Gayheart, Rebecca *Actress, Model*
%BTA Mgmt, 853 7th Ave, #9A, New York, NY 10019, USA
Gayle, Crystal *Singer*
%Gayle Enterprises, 51 Music Square E, Nashville, TN 37203, USA
Gaylor, Noel *Navy Admiral*
2111 Mason Hill Dr, Alexandria, VA 22306, USA
Gaylord, Mitchell J (Mitch) *Gymnast, Actor*
1593 Little Lake Dr, Park City, UT 84098, USA
Gaynes, George *Actor*
3344 Campanil Dr, Santa Barbara, CA 93109, USA
Gaynor, Gloria *Singer*
%Cliffside Music, PO Box 7172, Warren, NJ 07059, USA
Gaynor, Mitzi *Actress, Dancer, Singer*
610 N Arden Dr, Beverly Hills, CA 90210, USA
Gayoom, Maumoon Abdul *President, Maldives*
%Presidential Palace, Orchid Magu, Male 20-05, Maldives
Gayson, Eunice *Actress*
%Spotlight, 7 Leicester Place, London WC2H 7BP, England
Gazit, Doron *Artist*
%Air Dimensional Inc, 14141 Covello St, Building 1, Van Nuys, CA 91405, USA
Gazzara, Ben *Actor*
%Stone Manners, 6500 Wilshire Blvd, #550, Los Angeles, CA 90048, USA
Gbagbo, Laurent *President, Ivory Coast*
%President's Office, Boulevard Clozel, Abidijan, Ivory Coast
Gearan, Mark *Government Official, Educator*
%Hobart & William Smith College, President's Office, Geneva, NY 14456, USA
Gearhart, John *Neurologist, Biologist*
%Johns Hopkins University, Medical Center, Baltimore, MD 21218, USA
Geary, Anthony (Tony) *Actor*
7010 Pacific View Dr, Los Angeles, CA 90068, USA
Geary, Cynthia *Actress*
%Baumgarten/Prophet, 1041 N Formosa Ave, #200, West Hollywood, CA 90046, USA
Gebo, Daniel *Paleontolgist*
%Northern Illinois University, Paleontology Dept, De Kalb, IL 60115, USA
Gebrselassie, Haile *Track Athlete*
%Ethiopian Athletic Federation, PO Box 3241, Addis Ababa, Ethiopia
Gedda, Nicolai *Opera Singer*
Valhavagen 128, 114 41 Stockholm, Sweden
Geddes, Jane *Golfer*
1139 Abbeys Way, Tampa, FL 33602, USA
Gedrick, Jason *Actor*
%I F A Talent Agency, 8730 Sunset Blvd, #490, Los Angeles, CA 90069, USA
Gee, E Gordon *Educator*
%Vanderbilt University, Chancellor's Office, Nashville, TN 37240, USA
Gee, James D *Religious Leader*
%Pentecostal Church of God, 4901 Pennsylvania, Joplin, MO 64804, USA
Gee, Prunella *Actress*
%Michael Ladkin Mgmt, 1 Duchess St, #1, London W1N 3DE, England
Geer, Dennis *Financier*
%Federal Deposit Insurance, 550 17th St NW, Washington, DC 20429, USA
Geer, Ellen *Actress*
21418 W Entrada Road, Topanga, CA 90290, USA
Geertz, Clifford J *Anthropologist*
%Institute for Advanced Study, Social Science Dept, Princeton, NJ 08540, USA

Geeson, Judy *Actress*
%MLR Ltd, 200 Fulham Road, London SW10 9PN, England
Geffen, David *Movie Producer, Businessman*
%DreamWorks SKG, 100 Universal City Plaza, Universal City, CA 91608, USA
Gehring, Frederick W *Mathematician*
2139 Melrose Ave, Ann Arbor, MI 48104, USA
Gehring, Walter J *Geneticist*
Hochfeldstr 32, 4106 Therwil, Switzerland
Gehry, Frank O *Architect, Pritzker Laureate*
%Gehry Partners, 12541 Beatrice St, Los Angeles, CA 90066, USA
Geiberger, Al *Golfer*
%Professional Golfer's Assn, PO Box 109601, Palm Beach Gardens, FL 33410, USA
Geiberger, Brent *Golfer*
%Cross Consulting, 5 Cathy Place, Menlo Park, CA 94025, USA
Geiduschek, E Peter *Biologist*
%University of California, Biology Dept, 9500 Gilman Dr, La Jolla, CA 92093, USA
Geier, Philip H, Jr *Businessman*
%Interpublic Group, 1271 Ave of Americas, New York, NY 10020, USA
Geiger, Ken *Photojournalist*
%Dallas Morning News, Communications Center, Dallas, TX 75265, USA
Geiger, Matt *Basketball Player*
5317 Boardwalk St, Holiday, FL 34690, USA
Geingob, Hage G *Prime Minister, Namibia*
%Prime Minister's Office, Private Bag 13338, Windhoek 9000, Namibia
Geismar, Thomas H *Architect*
%Cambridge Seven Assoc, 1050 Massachusetts Ave, Cambridge, MA 02138, USA
Geiss, Johannes *Physicist*
%University of Berne, Physics Instit, Sidlerstr 5, 3012 Berne, Switzerland
Geithner, Timothy *Financier*
%Federal Reserve Bank, 33 Liberty St, New York, NY 10045, USA
Gelb, Leslie H *Educator*
%Council on Foreign Relations, 58 E 68th St, New York, NY 10021, USA
Gelb, Richard L *Businessman*
%Bristol-Myers Squibb, 345 Park Ave, New York, NY 10154, USA
Gelbart, Larry *Movie, Television Producer; Writer*
807 N Alpine Dr, Beverly Hills, CA 90210, USA
Geldof, Bob *Singer*
14 Clifford St, Bond St House, London W1X 2JD, England
Gelfand, Izrael M *Mathematician*
118 N 5th Ave, Highland Park, NJ 08904, USA
Gelfant, Alan *Actor*
%Peter Strain, 5724 W 3rd St, #302, Los Angeles, CA 90036, USA
Gelinas, Gratien *Actor, Writer*
316 Girouard St, #207, Oka QC J0N 1E0, Canada
Gell-Mann, Murray *Nobel Physics Laureate*
%Santa Fe Institute, 1399 Hyde Park Road, Santa Fe, NM 87501, USA
Gellar, Sarah Michelle *Actress*
%International Creative Mgmt, 8942 Wilshire Blvd, #219, Beverly Hills, CA 90211, USA
Geller, Margaret J *Astronomer*
%Harvard University, Astronomy Dept, 60 Garden St, Cambridge, MA 02138, USA
Gelman, Larry *Actor*
5121 Greenbush Ave, Sherman Oaks, CA 91423, USA
Gemar, Charles D *Astronaut*
7660 N 159th St Court E, Benton, KS 67017, USA
Gems, Pam *Writer*
%Cassarotto, 60/66 Wardour St, London W1V 4ND, England
Genaux, Vivica *Opera Singer*
%Robert Lombardo, Harkness Plaza, 61 W 62nd St, #6F, New York, NY 10023, USA
Gendron, George *Editor*
%Inc Magazine, Editorial Dept, 77 N Washington St, Boston, MA 02114, USA
Genovese, Eugene D *Historian*
1487 Sheridan Walk NE, Atlanta, GA 30324, USA
Genscher, Hans-Dietrich *Government Official, Germany*
Am Kottenforst 16, 5307 Wachtberg 3, Germany
Gensler, M Arthur, Jr *Architect*
%Gensler & Assoc Architects, 550 Kearny St, San Francisco, CA 94108, USA
Gent, Peter *Writer*
208 Center St, South Haven, MI 49090, USA
Gentry, Alvin *Basketball Coach, Executive*
%New Orleans Hornets, New Orleans Arena, 1501 Girod St, New Orleans, LA 70113, USA
Gentry, Bobbie *Singer*
269 S Beverly Dr, #368, Beverly Hills, CA 90212, USA
Gentry, Teddy W *Singer, Guitarist (Alabama)*
PO Box 529, Fort Payne, AL 35968, USA
Gentry, Troy *Singer (Montgomery Gentry)*
%Hallmark Direction, 15 Music Square W, Nashville, TN 37203, USA
Genzel, Carrie *Actress*
%Pakula/King, 9229 Sunset Blvd, #315, Los Angeles, CA 90069, USA

G

Genzmer, Harald *Composer*
Eisensteinstr 10, 81679 Munich, Germany
Geoffrin, Bernard (Boom Boom) *Hockey Player*
4431 Dobbs Ferry Crossing Dr, Marietta, GA 30068, USA
Geoffrion, Scott *Pro Stock Racing Driver*
592 Explorer St, #B, Brea, CA 92821, USA
George, Eddie *Football Player*
4708 Stuart Glen Dr, Nashville, TN 37215, USA
George, Edward A J *Financier*
%Bank of England, Threadneedle St, London EC2R 8AH, England
George, Elizabeth *Writer*
%William Morris Agency, 151 El Camino Dr, Beverly Hills, CA 90212, USA
George, Eric *Actor*
%Lasher McManus Robinson, 1964 Westwood Blvd, #400, Los Angeles, CA 90025, USA
George, Francis E Cardinal *Religious Leader*
%Chicago Archidiocese, 1555 N State Parkway, Chicago, IL 60610, USA
George, Jeffrey S (Jeff) *Football Player*
1980 Schwier Court, Indianapolis, IN 46229, USA
George, Melissa *Actress*
%The Firm, 9100 Wilshire Blvd, #100W, Beverly Hills, CA 90210, USA
George, Phyllis *Television Host, Beauty Queen*
%Miss America Organization, 2 Miss America Way, #1000, Atlantic City, NJ 08401, USA
George, Susan *Actress*
%McKorkindale & Holton, 1-2 Langham Place, London W1A 3DD, England
George, Tony *Auto Racing Executive*
%Indianapolis Motor Speedway, 4790 W 16th St, Indianapolis, IN 46222, USA
George, William W *Businessman*
%Medtronic Inc, 7000 Central Ave NE, Minneapolis, MN 55432, USA
Georgel, Pierre *Museum Official*
24 Rue Richer, 76009 Paris, France
Georgi, Howard *Physicist*
%Harvard University, Physics Dept, Lyman Laboratory, Cambridge, MA 02138, USA
Georgian, Theodore J *Religious Leader*
%Orthodox Presbyterian Church, PO Box P, Willow Grove, PA 19090, USA
Georgievski, Ljubisa (Ljupco) *Prime Minister, Macedonia*
%Prime Minister's Office, Dame Grueva 6, 91000 Skopje, Macedonia
Georgije, Bishop *Religious Leader*
%Serbian Orthodox Church, Sava Monastery, PO Box 519, Libertyville, IL 60048, USA
Geraci, Sonny *Singer (Outsiders, Climax)*
%Mars Talent, 27 L'Ambiance Court, Bardonia, NY 10954, USA
Gerard, Gil *Actor*
23679 Calabasas Road, #325, Calabasas, CA 91302, USA
Gerard, Jean Shevlin *Diplomat*
%American Embassy, 22 Blvd Emannanuel Servais, 2535 Luxembourg
Gerardo *Rap Artist*
%Tapestry Artists, 17337 Ventura Blvd, #208, Encino, CA 91316, USA
Gerber, H Joseph *Businessman*
%Gerber Scientific Inc, 83 Gerber Road W, South Windsor, CT 06074, USA
Gerber, Joel *Judge*
%US Tax Court, 400 2nd St NW, Washington, DC 20217, USA
Gerberding, Julie *Government Official, Physician*
%Centers for Disease Control, 1600 Clifton Road NE, Atlanta, GA 30329, USA
Gere, Richard *Actor*
14 E 4th St, #509, New York, NY 10012, USA
Gerela, Roy *Football Player*
PO Box 30001, Las Cruces, NM 88003, USA
Gerety, Tom, Jr *Educator*
%Amherst College, President's Office, Amherst, MA 01002, USA
Gerg, Hilde *Alpine Skier*
Brauneck Tolzer Hutte, 83661 Lenggries, Germany
Gerg-Leitner, Michaela *Alpine Skier*
Jachenauer Str 26, 83661 Lenggries, Germany
Gergen, David R *Editor*
31 Ash St, Cambridge, MA 02138, USA
Gergiev, Valery A *Conductor*
%Kunstleragentur Raab & Bohm, Plankengasse 7, 1010 Vienna, Austria
Gerhardt, Alben *Concert Cellist*
%Columbia Artists Mgmt Inc, 165 W 57th St, New York, NY 10019, USA
Gerlach, Gary *Publisher*
%Des Moines Register & Tribune, 715 Locust St, Des Moines, IA 50309, USA
Germain, Paul M *Mechanical Engineer*
3 Ave de Xhampaubert, 75015 Paris, France
German, Aleksei G *Movie Director*
Marsovo Pole 7, #37, Saint Petersburg 191041, Russia
German, William *Editor*
%San Francisco Chronicle, Editorial Dept, 901 Mission, San Francisco, CA 94103, USA
Germane, Geoffrey J *Mechanical Engineer*
%Brigham Young University, Mechanical Engineering Dept, Provo, UT 84602, USA

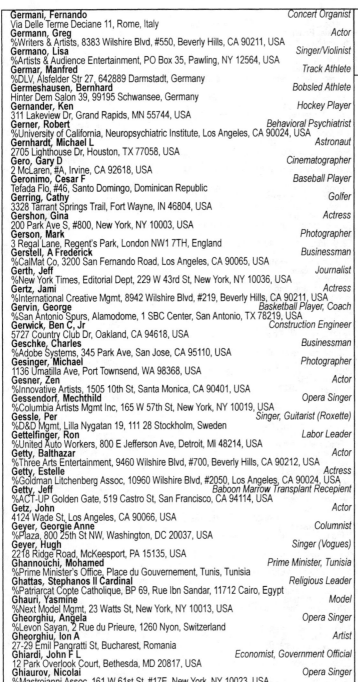

Germani, Fernando *Concert Organist*
Via Delle Terme Deciane 11, Rome, Italy
Germann, Greg *Actor*
%Writers & Artists, 8383 Wilshire Blvd, #550, Beverly Hills, CA 90211, USA
Germano, Lisa *Singer/Violinist*
%Artists & Audience Entertainment, PO Box 35, Pawling, NY 12564, USA
Germar, Manfred *Track Athlete*
%DLV, Alsfelder Str 27, 642889 Darmstadt, Germany
Germeshausen, Bernhard *Bobsled Athlete*
Hinter Dem Salon 39, 99195 Schwansee, Germany
Gernander, Ken *Hockey Player*
311 Lakeview Dr, Grand Rapids, MN 55744, USA
Gerner, Robert *Behavioral Psychiatrist*
%University of California, Neuropsychiatric Institute, Los Angeles, CA 90024, USA
Gernhardt, Michael L *Astronaut*
2705 Lighthouse Dr, Houston, TX 77058, USA
Gero, Gary D *Cinematographer*
2 McLaren, #A, Irvine, CA 92618, USA
Geronimo, Cesar F *Baseball Player*
Tefada Flo, #46, Santo Domingo, Dominican Republic
Gerring, Cathy *Golfer*
3328 Tarrant Springs Trail, Fort Wayne, IN 46804, USA
Gershon, Gina *Actress*
200 Park Ave S, #800, New York, NY 10003, USA
Gerson, Mark *Photographer*
3 Regal Lane, Regent's Park, London NW1 7TH, England
Gerstell, A Frederick *Businessman*
%CalMat Co, 3200 San Fernando Road, Los Angeles, CA 90065, USA
Gerth, Jeff *Journalist*
%New York Times, Editorial Dept, 229 W 43rd St, New York, NY 10036, USA
Gertz, Jami *Actress*
%International Creative Mgmt, 8942 Wilshire Blvd, #219, Beverly Hills, CA 90211, USA
Gervin, George *Basketball Player, Coach*
%San Antonio Spurs, Alamodome, 1 SBC Center, San Antonio, TX 78219, USA
Gerwick, Ben C, Jr *Construction Engineer*
5727 Country Club Dr, Oakland, CA 94618, USA
Geschke, Charles *Businessman*
%Adobe Systems, 345 Park Ave, San Jose, CA 95110, USA
Gesinger, Michael *Photographer*
1136 Umatilla Ave, Port Townsend, WA 98368, USA
Gesner, Zen *Actor*
%Innovative Artists, 1505 10th St, Santa Monica, CA 90401, USA
Gessendorf, Mechthild *Opera Singer*
%Columbia Artists Mgmt Inc, 165 W 57th St, New York, NY 10019, USA
Gessle, Per *Singer, Guitarist (Roxette)*
%D&D Mgmt, Lilla Nygatan 19, 111 28 Stockholm, Sweden
Gettelfinger, Ron *Labor Leader*
%United Auto Workers, 800 E Jefferson Ave, Detroit, MI 48214, USA
Getty, Balthazar *Actor*
%Three Arts Entertainment, 9460 Wilshire Blvd, #700, Beverly Hills, CA 90212, USA
Getty, Estelle *Actress*
%Goldman Litchenberg Assoc, 10960 Wilshire Blvd, #2050, Los Angeles, CA 90024, USA
Getty, Jeff *Baboon Marrow Transplant Recepient*
%ACT-UP Golden Gate, 519 Castro St, San Francisco, CA 94114, USA
Getz, John *Actor*
4124 Wade St, Los Angeles, CA 90066, USA
Geyer, Georgie Anne *Columnist*
%Plaza, 800 25th St NW, Washington, DC 20037, USA
Geyer, Hugh *Singer (Vogues)*
2218 Ridge Road, McKeesport, PA 15135, USA
Ghannouchi, Mohamed *Prime Minister, Tunisia*
%Prime Minister's Office, Place du Gouvernement, Tunis, Tunisia
Ghattas, Stephanos II Cardinal *Religious Leader*
%Patriarcat Copte Catholique, BP 69, Rue Ibn Sandar, 11712 Cairo, Egypt
Ghauri, Yasmine *Model*
%Next Model Mgmt, 23 Watts St, New York, NY 10013, USA
Gheorghiu, Angela *Opera Singer*
%Levon Sayan, 2 Rue du Prieure, 1260 Nyon, Switzerland
Gheorghiu, Ion A *Artist*
27-29 Emil Pangratti St, Bucharest, Romania
Ghiardi, John F L *Economist, Government Official*
12 Park Overlook Court, Bethesda, MD 20817, USA
Ghiaurov, Nicolai *Opera Singer*
%Mastroianni Assoc, 161 W 61st St, #17E, New York, NY 10023, USA
Ghiglia, Oscar A *Concert Guitarist*
Helfembergstr 14, 4059 Basel, Switzerland
Ghiorso, Albert *Chemist*
%Lawrence Berkeley Laboratory, 1 Cyclotron Road, Berkeley, CA 94720, USA

G

Ghiuselev - Gibbs

Ghiuselev, Nicola *Opera Singer*
Villa della Pisana 370/B-2, 00163 Rome, Italy
Ghizikis, Phaidon *President, Greece; Army General*
25 Kountouriotou, 151 21 Pefki, Greece
Ghosh, Gautam *Movie Director*
28/1-A Gariahat Road, Block 5, #50, Calcutta 700029, India
Ghostface Killa *Rap Artist (Wu-Tang Clan)*
%Famous Artists Agency, 250 W 57th St, New York, NY 10107, USA
Ghostley, Alice *Actress*
3800 Reklaw Dr, Studio City, CA 91604, USA
Ghouri, Yasmeen *Model*
%Next Model Mgmt, 23 Watts St, New York, NY 10013, USA
Giacconi, Riccardo *Nobel Physics Laureate*
%Associated Universities Inc, 1440 16th St NW, #730, Washington, DC 20036, USA
Giacomin, Edward (Ed) *Hockey Player*
3427 S Bloomington Dr W, Saint George, UT 84790, USA
Giaever, Ivar *Nobel Physics Laureate*
2080 Van Antwerp Road, Schenectady, NY 12309, USA
Giamatti, Paul *Actor*
%Endeavor Talent Agency, 9701 Wilshire Blvd, #1000, Beverly Hills, CA 90212, USA
Giambastiani, Edmund P, Jr *Navy Admiral*
Deputy CNO for Resources/Warfare Requirements, HqUSN, Washington, DC 20350, USA
Giambi, Jason G *Baseball Player*
1034 E Belmont Abbey Lane, Claremont, CA 91711, USA
Giambra, Joey *Boxer*
7950 W Flamingo Road, #1188, Las Vegas, NV 89147, USA
Gianelli, John *Basketball Player*
PO Box 1097, Pinecrest, CA 95364, USA
Giannini, Giancarlo *Actor*
Via Salaria 292, 00199 Rome, Italy
Giannulli, Mossimo *Fashion Designer*
%Mossimo Supply, 2450 White Road, #200, Irvine, CA 92614, USA
Gianulias, Nicole (Nikki) *Bowler*
%Ladies Professional Bowling Tour, 7200 Harrison Ave, #7171, Rockford, IL 61112, USA
Giardello, Joey *Boxer*
1214 Severn Ave, Cherry Hill, NJ 08002, USA
Gibara, Samir *Businessman*
%Goodyear Tire & Rubber, 1144 E Market St, Akron, OH 44316, USA
Gibb, Barry *Singer (Bee Gees), Songwriter*
20505 US 19 N, #12-290, Clearwater, FL 33764, USA
Gibb, Cynthia *Actress*
1139 S Hill St, #177, Los Angeles, CA 90015, USA
Gibb, Robin *Singer (Bee Gees), Songwriter*
%Middle Ear, 1801 Bay Road, Miami Beach, FL 33139, USA
Gibberd, Frederick *Architect*
House, Marsh Lane, Old Harlow, Essex CM17 0NA, England
Gibbons, Beth *Singer (Portishead), Songwriter*
%Fruit, Saga Centre, 326 Kensal Road, London W10 5BZ, England
Gibbons, Billy *Singer, Guitarist (ZZ Top)*
%Lone Wolf Mgmt, PO Box 16390, Austin, TX 78761, USA
Gibbons, James F *Electrical Engineer*
320 Tennyson Ave, Palo Alto, CA 94301, USA
Gibbons, John D *Prime Minister, Bermuda*
Leeward, 5 Leeside Dr, Pembroke HM 05, Bermuda
Gibbons, Leeza *Entertainer*
PO Box 4321, Los Angeles, CA 90078, USA
Gibbs, Georgia *Singer*
%Frank Gervasi, 965 5th Ave, New York, NY 10021, USA
Gibbs, H Jarrell *Businessman*
%Texas Utilities Co, Energy Plaza, 1601 Bryan St, Dallas, TX 75201, USA
Gibbs, Jerry D (Jake) *Football, Baseball Player*
223 Saint Andres Circle, Oxford, MS 38655, USA
Gibbs, Joe J *Football Coach, Auto Racing Executive*
%Joe Gibbs Racing, 13415 Reese Blvd W, Huntersville, NC 28078, USA
Gibbs, L Richard *Cricketer*
276 Republic Park, Peter's Hall EBD, Guyana
Gibbs, Lawrence B *Government Official*
%Miller & Chevalier, 655 15th St NW, #900, Washington, DC 20005, USA
Gibbs, Marla *Actress, Singer*
3500 W Manchester Blvd, #267, Inglewood, CA 90305, USA
Gibbs, Martin *Biologist*
32 Slocum Road, Lexington, MA 02421, USA
Gibbs, Patt *Labor Leader*
%Flight Attendants Assn, 1275 K St NW, #500, Washington, DC 20005, USA
Gibbs, Roland C *Army Field Marshal, England*
Patney Rectory, Devizes, Wilts SN10 3QZ, England
Gibbs, Terri *Singer, Songwriter*
312 Crawford Mill Lane, Grovetown, GA 30813, USA

Gibbs, Terry *Jazz Vibist, Drummer*
%Thomas Cassidy, 11761 E Speedway Blvd, Tucson, AZ 85748, USA
Gibbs, Timothy *Actor*
PO Box 8764, Calabasas, CA 91372, USA
Giblett, Eloise R *Hematologist*
6533 53rd St NE, Seattle, WA 98115, USA
Gibran, Kahlil *Sculptor*
160 W Canton St, Boston, MA 02118, USA
Gibson, Brian *Movie Director*
%William Morris Agency, 52/53 Poland Place, London W1F 7LX, England
Gibson, Charles *Movie Director*
%Gersh Agency, 232 N Canon Dr, Beverly Hills, CA 90210, USA
Gibson, Charles D *Commentator*
%ABC-TV, News Dept, 77 W 66th St, New York, NY 10023, USA
Gibson, Deborah *Singer, Actress*
%GMI Entertainment, 666 5th Ave, #302, New York, NY 10103, USA
Gibson, Derrick *Football Player*
%Oakland Raiders, 1220 Harbor Bay Parkway, Alameda, CA 94502, USA
Gibson, Don *Singer, Guitarist, Songwriter*
PO Box 50474, Nashville, TN 37205, USA
Gibson, Edward G *Astronaut*
%Aviation Managment Services, 1658 S Litchfield Road, Goodyear, AZ 85338, USA
Gibson, Everett K, Jr *Geologist*
1015 Trowbridge Dr, Houston, TX 77062, USA
Gibson, Henry *Actor*
26740 Latigo Shore Dr, Malibu, CA 90265, USA
Gibson, Kirk H *Baseball, Football Player*
%Detroit Tigers, Comerica Park, 2100 Woodward Ave, Detroit, MI 48201, USA
Gibson, Mel *Actor, Director*
%Creative Artists Agency, 9830 Wilshire Blvd, Beverly Hills, CA 90212, USA
Gibson, Quentin H *Biochemist*
3 Woods End Road, Etna, NH 03750, USA
Gibson, Ralph H *Photographer*
331 W Broadway, New York, NY 10013, USA
Gibson, Reginald W *Judge*
%US Claims Court, 717 Madison Place NW, Washington, DC 20439, USA
Gibson, Robert (Bob) *Baseball Player*
215 Bellevue Blvd S, Bellevue, NE 68005, USA
Gibson, Robert L (Hoot) *Astronaut*
1709 Shagbark Trail, Murfreesboro, TN 37130, USA
Gibson, Thomas *Actor*
%Alliance Talent, 9171 Wilshire Blvd, #441, Beverly Hills, CA 90210, USA
Gibson, William *Writer, Photographer*
%Berkley Publishing Group, 375 Hudson St, New York, NY 10014, USA
Gidada, Negasso *President, Ethiopia*
%President's Office, PO Box 5707, Addis Ababa, Ethiopia
Gideon, Raynold *Actor, Writer*
3524 Multiview Dr, Los Angeles, CA 90068, USA
Gidley, Pamela *Actress*
650 Hernando Dr, Marco Island, FL 34145, USA
Gidzenko, Yuri P *Cosmonaut*
%Potchta Kosmonavtov, Moskovskoi Oblasti, 141160 Syvisdny Goroduk, Russia
Gielen, Michael A *Conductor, Composer*
%Hans Ulrich Schmid, Postfach 1617, 30016 Hanover, Germany
Giella, Joseph *Cartoonist (Mary Worth)*
191 Morris Dr, East Meadow, NY 11554, USA
Gierer, Vincent A, Jr *Businessman*
%UST Inc, 100 W Putnam Ave, Greenwich, CT 06830, USA
Gierowski, Stefan *Artist*
Ul Gagarina 15 m 97, 00-753 Warsaw, Poland
Gifford, Frank N *Football Player, Sportscaster*
108 Cedar Cliff Road, Riverside, CT 06878, USA
Gifford, Gloria *Actress*
%Schiowitz/Clay/Rose, 1680 N Vine St, #1016, Los Angeles, CA 90028, USA
Gifford, Kathie Lee *Entertainer*
108 Cedar Cliff Road, Riverside, CT 06878, USA
Gift, Roland *Singer (Fine Young Cannibals), Actor*
%Primary Talent Int'l, 2-12 Petonville Road, London N1 9PL, England
Gigli, Romeo *Fashion Designer*
37 W 57th St, #900, New York, NY 10019, USA
Gigot, Paul *Journalist*
%Wall Street Journal, Editorial Dept, 200 Liberty St, New York, NY 10281, USA
Giguere, Russ *Singer, Guitarist (Association)*
%Variety Artists, 1924 Spring St, Paso Robles, CA 93446, USA
Giheno, John *President, Papua New Guinea*
%Prime Minister's Office, Marera Hau, Port Moresby, Papua New Guinea
Gil, Ariadna *Actress*
%Cineart, 36 Rue de Ponthieu, 75008 Paris, France

G

Gil - Gill

Gil, Gilberto *Singer, Songwriter*
%BPR, 36 Como St, Ramford, Essex RM7 7DR, England
Gil, R Benjamin (Benji) *Baseball Player*
417 Marshall Road, Southlake, TX 76092, USA
Gilbert, Bradley (Brad) *Tennis Player*
%ProServe, 1101 Woodrow Wilson Blvd, #1800, Arlington, VA 22209, USA
Gilbert, Chris *Football Player*
%Greenbriar Mgmt, 4422 FM 1960 Road W, Houston, TX 77068, USA
Gilbert, David *Cartoonist (Buckles)*
%King Features Syndicate, 888 7th Ave, New York, NY 10106, USA
Gilbert, Felix *Historian*
918 Bluffwood Dr, Iowa City, IA 52245, USA
Gilbert, Greg *Hockey Player, Coach*
303 Main St, Worcester, MA 01608, USA
Gilbert, J Freeman *Geophysicist*
780 Kalamath Dr, Del Mar, CA 92014, USA
Gilbert, Kenneth A *Concert Harpsichordist*
23 Cloitre Notre-Dame, 28000 Chartres, France
Gilbert, Lawrence I *Biologist*
1105 Phils Creek Road, Chapel Hill, NC 27516, USA
Gilbert, Lewis *Movie Director, Producer*
19 Blvd de Suisse, Monte Carlo, Monaco
Gilbert, Martin J *Historian*
%Merton College, Oxford OX1 4JD, England
Gilbert, Melissa *Actress*
25717 Mulholland Highway, Calabasas, CA 91302, USA
Gilbert, Peter *Movie Director*
%Innovative Artists, 1505 10th St, Santa Monica, CA 90401, USA
Gilbert, Richard W *Publisher*
%Des Moines Register & Tribune, 715 Locust St, Des Moines, IA 50309, USA
Gilbert, Rodrique G (Rod) *Hockey Player*
344 Pacific Ave, Cedarhurst, NY 11516, USA
Gilbert, Ronnie *Singer*
%Donna Korones Mgmt, PO Box 8388, Berkeley, CA 94707, USA
Gilbert, S J, Sr *Religious Leader*
%Baptist Convention of America, 6717 Centennial Blvd, Nashville, TN 37209, USA
Gilbert, Sara *Actress*
16254 High Valley Dr, Encino, CA 91346, USA
Gilbert, Sean *Football Player*
7912 Baltusrol Lane, Charlotte, NC 28210, USA
Gilbert, Simon *Drummer (Suede)*
%Interceptor Enterprises, 98 White Lion St, London N1 9PF, England
Gilbert, Walter *Nobel Chemistry Laureate*
15 Gray Gardens W, Cambridge, MA 02138, USA
Gilberto, Astrud *Singer*
%Absolute Artists, 530 Howard Ave, #200, San Francisco, CA 94105, USA
Gilberto, Bebel *Singer*
%Miracle Prestige, 1 Water Lane, Camden Town, London NW1 8NZ, England
Gilbertson, Keith *Football Coach*
%University of Washington, Athletic Dept, Seattle, WA 98195, USA
Gilbride, Kevin *Football Player, Coach*
%Pittsburgh Steelers, 3400 S Water St, Pittsburgh, PA 15203, USA
Gilchrist, Brent *Hockey Player*
204 Olive Branch Road, Nashville, TN 37205, USA
Gilchrist, Cookie *Football Player*
PO Box 5109, Wilmington, DE 19808, USA
Gilchrist, Paul R *Religious Leader*
%Presbyterian Church in America, 1862 Century Place, Atlanta, GA 30345, USA
Gilder, Bob *Golfer*
1977 NW Bonney Dr, Corvallis, OR 97330, USA
Gilder, George F *Writer, Economist*
Main Road, Tyringham, MA 01264, USA
Giles, Brian J *Baseball Player*
444 Graves Ave, El Cajon, CA 92020, USA
Giles, Jimmie *Football Player*
10429 Greenmont Dr, Tampa, FL 33626, USA
Giles, Nancy *Actress*
12047 178th St, Jamaica, NY 11434, USA
Giletti, Alain *Figure Skater*
103 Place de L'Eglise, 74400 Chamonix, France
Gilfry, Rodney *Opera Singer*
%Columbia Artists Mgmt Inc, 165 W 57th St, New York, NY 10019, USA
Gilgorov, Kiro *President, Macedonia*
%President's Office, Skopje, Macedonia
Gill, George N *Publisher*
%Louisville Courier-Journal & Times, 525 W Broadway, Louisville, KY 40202, USA
Gill, Janis *Singer (Sweethearts of the Rodeo)*
%Monty Hitchcock Mgmt, 5101 Overton Road, Nashville, TN 37220, USA

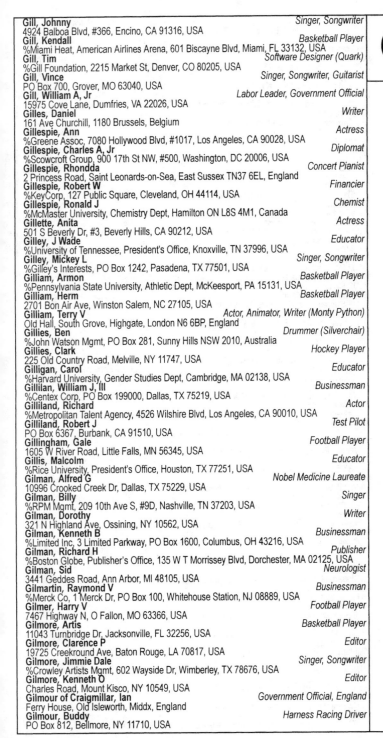

Gill, Johnny *Singer, Songwriter*
4924 Balboa Blvd, #366, Encino, CA 91316, USA
Gill, Kendall *Basketball Player*
%Miami Heat, American Airlines Arena, 601 Biscayne Blvd, Miami, FL 33132, USA
Gill, Tim *Software Designer (Quark)*
%Gill Foundation, 2215 Market St, Denver, CO 80205, USA
Gill, Vince *Singer, Songwriter, Guitarist*
PO Box 700, Grover, MO 63040, USA
Gill, William A, Jr *Labor Leader, Government Official*
15975 Cove Lane, Dumfries, VA 22026, USA
Gilles, Daniel *Writer*
161 Ave Churchill, 1180 Brussels, Belgium
Gillespie, Ann *Actress*
%Greene Assoc, 7080 Hollywood Blvd, #1017, Los Angeles, CA 90028, USA
Gillespie, Charles A, Jr *Diplomat*
%Scowcroft Group, 900 17th St NW, #500, Washington, DC 20006, USA
Gillespie, Rhondda *Concert Pianist*
2 Princess Road, Saint Leonards-on-Sea, East Sussex TN37 6EL, England
Gillespie, Robert W *Financier*
%KeyCorp, 127 Public Square, Cleveland, OH 44114, USA
Gillespie, Ronald J *Chemist*
%McMaster University, Chemistry Dept, Hamilton ON L8S 4M1, Canada
Gillette, Anita *Actress*
501 S Beverly Dr, #3, Beverly Hills, CA 90212, USA
Gilley, J Wade *Educator*
%University of Tennessee, President's Office, Knoxville, TN 37996, USA
Gilley, Mickey L *Singer, Songwriter*
%Gilley's Interests, PO Box 1242, Pasadena, TX 77501, USA
Gilliam, Armon *Basketball Player*
%Pennsylvania State University, Athletic Dept, McKeesport, PA 15131, USA
Gilliam, Herm *Basketball Player*
2701 Bon Air Ave, Winston Salem, NC 27105, USA
Gilliam, Terry V *Actor, Animator, Writer (Monty Python)*
Old Hall, South Grove, Highgate, London N6 6BP, England
Gillies, Ben *Drummer (Silverchair)*
%John Watson Mgmt, PO Box 281, Sunny Hills NSW 2010, Australia
Gillies, Clark *Hockey Player*
225 Old Country Road, Melville, NY 11747, USA
Gilligan, Carol *Educator*
%Harvard University, Gender Studies Dept, Cambridge, MA 02138, USA
Gillilan, William J, III *Businessman*
%Centex Corp, PO Box 199000, Dallas, TX 75219, USA
Gilliland, Richard *Actor*
%Metropolitan Talent Agency, 4526 Wilshire Blvd, Los Angeles, CA 90010, USA
Gilliland, Robert J *Test Pilot*
PO Box 6367, Burbank, CA 91510, USA
Gillingham, Gale *Football Player*
1605 W River Road, Little Falls, MN 56345, USA
Gillis, Malcolm *Educator*
%Rice University, President's Office, Houston, TX 77251, USA
Gilman, Alfred G *Nobel Medicine Laureate*
10996 Crooked Creek Dr, Dallas, TX 75229, USA
Gilman, Billy *Singer*
%RPM Mgmt, 209 10th Ave S, #9D, Nashville, TN 37203, USA
Gilman, Dorothy *Writer*
321 N Highland Ave, Ossining, NY 10562, USA
Gilman, Kenneth B *Businessman*
%Limited Inc, 3 Limited Parkway, PO Box 1600, Columbus, OH 43216, USA
Gilman, Richard H *Publisher*
%Boston Globe, Publisher's Office, 135 W T Morrissey Blvd, Dorchester, MA 02125, USA
Gilman, Sid *Neurologist*
3441 Geddes Road, Ann Arbor, MI 48105, USA
Gilmartin, Raymond V *Businessman*
%Merck Co, 1 Merck Dr, PO Box 100, Whitehouse Station, NJ 08889, USA
Gilmer, Harry V *Football Player*
7467 Highway N, O Fallon, MO 63366, USA
Gilmore, Artis *Basketball Player*
11043 Turnbridge Dr, Jacksonville, FL 32256, USA
Gilmore, Clarence P *Editor*
19725 Creekround Ave, Baton Rouge, LA 70817, USA
Gilmore, Jimmie Dale *Singer, Songwriter*
%Crowley Artists Mgmt, 602 Wayside Dr, Wimberley, TX 78676, USA
Gilmore, Kenneth O *Editor*
Charles Road, Mount Kisco, NY 10549, USA
Gilmour of Craigmillar, Ian *Government Official, England*
Ferry House, Old Isleworth, Middx, England
Gilmour, Buddy *Harness Racing Driver*
PO Box 812, Bellmore, NY 11710, USA

G

Gilmour, David *Singer, Guitarist (Pink Floyd)*
PO Box 62, Heathfield, East Sussex TN21 8ZE, England
Gilmour, Doug *Hockey Player*
%Octagon, 1751 Pinnacle Dr, #1500, McLean, VA 22102, USA
Gilpin, Peri *Actress*
%William Morris Agency, 151 El Camino Dr, Beverly Hills, CA 90212, USA
Gilroy, Frank D *Writer*
6 Mangin Road, Monroe, NY 10950, USA
Gilyard, Clarence, Jr *Actor*
24040 Camino del Avion, #A239, Monarch Bay, CA 92629, USA
Gimbel, Norman *Songwriter*
PO Box 50013, Santa Barbara, CA 93150, USA
Gimbrone, Michael A, Jr *Pathologist*
%Brigham & Women's Hospital, Vascular Pathology Dept, Boston, MA 02115, USA
Gimeno, Andres *Tennis Player*
Paseo de la Bonanova 38, Barcelona 6, Spain
Gina G *Singer*
%What Mgmt, PO Box 1463, Culver City, CA 90232, USA
Ging, Jack *Actor*
48701 San Pedro St, La Quinta, CA 92253, USA
Gingerich, Philip D *Paleontologist*
%University of Michigan, Paleontolgy Dept, Ann Arbor, MI 48109, USA
Gingrich, Newton L (Newt) *Representative, GA; Speaker*
700 New Hampshire Ave NW, Washington, DC 20037, USA
Ginibre, Jean-Louis *Editor*
%Hachette Filipacchi, 1633 Broadway, New York, NY 10019, USA
Ginn, William H, Jr *Air Force General*
1002 Priscilla Lane, Alexandria, VA 22308, USA
Ginsburg, Douglas H *Judge*
%US Court of Appeals, 333 Constitution Ave NW, Washington, DC 20001, USA
Ginsburg, Ruth Bader *Supreme Court Justice*
%US Supreme Court, 1 1st St NE, Washington, DC 20543, USA
Ginty, Robert *Actor*
%Introvision, 1011 N Fuller Ave, West Hollywood, CA 90046, USA
Ginuwine *Singer*
%International Creative Mgmt, 8942 Wilshire Blvd, #219, Beverly Hills, CA 90211, USA
Ginzburg, Vitaly L *Nobel Physics Laureate*
%Lebedev Physical Institute, Leninsky Prospect 53, 117924 Moscow, Russia
Ginzton, Edward L *Electrical Engineer, Businessman*
%Varian Assoc, 3100 Hansen Way, Palo Alto, CA 94304, USA
Giola, Dana *Government Official, Writer*
%National Endowment for Arts, 1100 Pennsylvania Ave NW, Washington, DC 20506, USA
Giordano, Michele Cardinal *Religious Leader*
%Arcivescovado di Napoli, Largo Donnaregina 22, 80138 Naples, Italy
Giovanni, Joseph *Architect*
%Giovanni Assoc, 140 E 40th St, New York, NY 10016, USA
Giovanni, Nikki E *Writer*
%Virginia Polytechnic Institute, English Dept, Blacksburg, VA 24061, USA
Giradelli, Marc *Alpine Skier*
9413 Oberegg-Sulzbach, Switzerland
Giraldi, Robert N (Bob) *Movie Director*
%Giraldi Suarez, 581 Ave of Americas, New York, NY 10011, USA
Girardi, Joseph E (Joe) *Baseball Player*
1845 Saint James Court N, Lake Forest, IL 60045, USA
Girardot, Annie S *Actress*
%Artmedia, 20 Ave Rapp, 75007 Paris, France
Giraudeau, Bernard *Actor*
%Cineart, 36 Rue de Ponthieu, 75008 Paris, France
Giri, Tulsi *Prime Minister, Nepal*
Jawakpurdham, District Dhanuka, Nepal
Girone, Remo *Actor*
%Cineart, 36 Rue de Ponthieu, 75008 Paris, France
Giroux, Robert *Publisher*
%Farrar Straus Giroux, 19 Union Square W, New York, NY 10003, USA
Giscard d'Estaing, Valery *President, France*
199 Blvd Saint-Germain, 75007 Paris, France
Gish, Annabeth *Actress*
2104 E Main St, #841, Ventura, CA 93001, USA
Gismonti, Egberto *Jazz Guitarist, Composer*
%International Music Network, 278 S Main St, #400, Gloucester, MA 01930, USA
Gitlin, Todd *Historian*
%New York University, Culture & Communications Dept, New York, NY 10012, USA
Giuffre, James P (Jimmy) *Jazz Clarinetist, Saxophonist*
%Legacy Records, 550 Madison Ave, #1700, New York, NY 10022, USA
Giuliani, Rudolph W *Mayor*
%Giuliani Partners, 5 Times Square, New York, NY 10036, USA
Giuliano, Louis J *Businessman*
%ITT Industries, 4 W Red Oak Lane, White Plains, NY 10604, USA

Giuliano, Tom *Singer (Happenings)*
6929 N Hayden Road, Scottsdale, AZ 85250, USA
Giulini, Carlo Maria *Conductor*
%Francesco Giulini, Via Bonnet 7, 20121 Milan, Italy
Giuranna, Bruno *Concert Violist*
Via Bembo 96, 31011 Asolo TV, Italy
Giusti, David J (Dave) *Baseball Player*
524 Clair Dr, Pittsburgh, PA 15241, USA
Givens, Jack *Basketball Player, Executive*
1536 Frazier Ave, Orlando, FL 32811, USA
Givens, Robin *Actress*
%Innovative Artists, 1505 10th St, Santa Monica, CA 90401, USA
Givins, Ernest P, Jr *Football Player*
1447 Manor Way S, Saint Petersburg, FL 33705, USA
Gizzi, Claudio *Composer*
%SIAE, Viaile dell Letteratura 30, 00100 Rome, Italy
Glamack, George *Basketball Player*
50 Pleasant Way, Rochester, NY 14622, USA
Glance, Harvey *Track Athlete*
2408 Old Creek Road, Montgomery, AL 36117, USA
Glanville, Jerry *Football Coach, Sportscaster*
%CBS-TV, Sports Dept, 51 W 52nd St, New York, NY 10019, USA
Glasbergen, Randy *Cartoonist (Better Half)*
%King Features Syndicate, 888 7th Ave, New York, NY 10106, USA
Glaser, Donald A *Nobel Physics Laureate*
%University of California, Molecular Biology Laboratory, Berkeley, CA 94720, USA
Glaser, Gabrielle (Gabby) *Singer, Guitarist (Luscious Jackson)*
%Metropolitan Entertainment, 2 Penn Plaza, #2600, New York, NY 10121, USA
Glaser, Jim *Singer*
%Joe Taylor Artist Agency, 2802 Columbine Place, Nashville, TN 37204, USA
Glaser, Milton *Graphic Artist*
%Milton Glaser Assoc, 207 E 32nd St, New York, NY 10016, USA
Glaser, Paul Michael *Actor, Movie Director*
1221 Ocean Ave, #1601, Santa Monica, CA 90401, USA
Glaser, Robert *Psychologist*
%University of Pittsburgh, Psychology Dept, Pittsburgh, PA 15260, USA
Glaser, Robert J *Foundation Executive*
555 Byron St, #305, Palo Alto, CA 94301, USA
Glasgow, W Victor (Vic) *Basketball Player*
6312 King Dr, Bartlesville, OK 74006, USA
Glashow, Sheldon Lee *Nobel Physics Laureate*
30 Prescott St, Brookline, MA 02446, USA
Glaspie, April *Diplomat*
%State Department, 2201 C St NW, Washington, DC 20520, USA
Glass, David D *Businessman*
%Wal-Mart Stores, 702 SW 8th St, Bentonville, AK 72712, USA
Glass, H Bentley *Biologist*
PO Box 65, East Setauket, NY 11733, USA
Glass, Philip *Composer*
%IPA, 584 Broadway, #108, New York, NY 10012, USA
Glass, Ron *Actor*
2485 Wild Oak Dr, Los Angeles, CA 90068, USA
Glass, William S (Bill) *Football Player*
%Bill Glass Ministries, PO Box 761101, Dallas, TX 75376, USA
Glasser, Ira S *Attorney, Legal Activist*
%American Civil Liberties Union, 132 W 43rd St, New York, NY 10036, USA
Glasser, Isabel *Actress*
%Paul Kohner, 9300 Wilshire Blvd, #555, Beverly Hills, CA 90212, USA
Glasser, William *Psychiatrist*
11633 San Vicente Blvd, Los Angeles, CA 90049, USA
Glatter, Lesli L *Movie Director*
%United Talent Agency, 9560 Wilshire Blvd, #500, Beverly Hills, CA 90212, USA
Glaus, Troy E *Baseball Player*
PO Box 4445, Carlsbad, CA 92018, USA
Glavin, Denis Joseph *Labor Leader*
%Electrical Radio & Machine Workers Union, 11 E 1st St, New York, NY 10003, USA
Glavine, Thomas M (Tom) *Baseball Player*
8925 Old Southwick Pass, Alpharetta, GA 30022, USA
Glazer, Jay *Sportscaster*
%CBS-TV, Sports Dept, 51 W 52nd St, New York, NY 10019, USA
Glazer, Nathan *Sociologist*
12 Scott St, Cambridge, MA 02138, USA
Glazkov, Yuri N *Cosmonaut; Air Force General*
%Potchta Kosmonavtov, Moskovskoi Oblasti, 141160 Syvisdny Goroduk, Russia
Glazunov, Ilya S *Artist*
%Razhviz Academy, Kamergersky Per 2, Moscow 103009, Russia
Gleason, Andrew M *Mathematician*
110 Larchwood Dr, Cambridge, MA 02138, USA

Gleason, Joanna *Actress*
%United Talent Agency, 9560 Wilshire Blvd, #500, Beverly Hills, CA 90212, USA
Gleason, Paul *Actor*
%Stone Manners, 6500 Wilshire Blvd, #550, Los Angeles, CA 90048, USA
Glemp, Jozef Cardinal *Religious Leader*
Sekretariat Prymasa, Kolski, Ul Miodowa 17, 00 246 Warsaw, Poland
Glen, John *Movie Director*
%Spyros Skouras, 1015 Gayley Ave, #300, Los Angeles, CA 90024, USA
Glenn, John H, Jr *Senator, OH; Astronaut*
%Ohio State University, Stillman Hall, 1947 College Road, Columbus, OH 43210, USA
Glenn, Scott *Actor*
126 E De Vargas St, #1902, Santa Fe, NM 87501, USA
Glenn, Terry *Football Player*
%Dallas Cowboys, 1 Cowboys Parkway, Irving, TX 75063, USA
Glenn, Wayne E *Labor Leader*
%United Paperworkers Int'l Union, 3340 Perimeter Hill Dr, Nashville, TN 37211, USA
Glennan, Robert E, Jr *Educator*
%Emporia State University, President's Office, Emporia, KS 66801, USA
Glennie, Evelyn E A *Concert Percussionist*
PO Box 6, Sawtry, Huntingdon, Cambs PE17 5WE, England
Glennie-Smith, Nick *Composer*
%Vangelos Mgmt, 15233 Ventura Blvd, #200, Sherman Oaks, CA 91403, USA
Gless, Sharon *Actress*
%Rosenzweig Productions, PO Box 48005, Los Angeles, CA 90048, USA
Glick, Frederick (Freddie) *Football Player*
4226 Antlers Court, Fort Collins, CO 80526, USA
Glickman, Daniel R *Secretary, Agriculture*
%Harvard University, Kennedy Government School, Cambridge, MA 02138, USA
Glidden, Bob *Auto Racing Driver*
PO Box 183, Whiteland, IN 46184, USA
Glidden, Robert *Educator*
%Ohio University, President's Office, Athens, OH 45701, USA
Glidewell, Iain *Judge*
Rough Heys Farm, Macclesfield, Cheshire SK11 9PF, England
Glimcher, Arnold O (Arne) *Art Dealer*
%Pace Gallery, 32 E 57th St, New York, NY 10022, USA
Glimm, James G *Mathematician*
%State University of New York, Applied Math Dept, Stony Brook, NY 11794, USA
Glitman, Maynard W *Diplomat*
PO Box 438, Jeffersonville, VT 05464, USA
Glitter, Gary *Singer, Songwriter*
%Jef Hanlon Mgmt, 1 York St, London W1H 1PZ, England
Globus, Yoram *Movie Producer*
%Pathe International, 8670 Wilshire Blvd, Beverly Hills, CA 90211, USA
Glossop, Peter *Opera Singer*
End Cottage, 7 Gate Close, Hawkchurch near Axminster, Devon, England
Glover, Bloc *Motorcycle Racing Rider*
%American Motorcycle Assn, 13515 Yarmouth Dr, Pickerington, OH 43147, USA
Glover, Brian *Actor*
%DeWolfe, Manfield House, 376/378 Strand, London WC2R OLR, England
Glover, Bruce *Actor*
11449 Woodbine St, Los Angeles, CA 90066, USA
Glover, Crispin *Actor*
3573 Carnation Ave, Los Angeles, CA 90026, USA
Glover, Danny *Actor*
PO Box 170069, San Francisco, CA 94117, USA
Glover, Jane A *Conductor*
%Kaylor Mgmt, 130 W 57th St, #8G, New York, NY 10019, USA
Glover, John *Actor*
130 W 42nd St, #2400, New York, NY 10036, USA
Glover, Kevin B *Football Player*
11553 Manor Stone Lane, Columbia, MD 21044, USA
Glover, La'Roi *Football Player*
841 49th St, San Diego, CA 92102, USA
Glover, Richard E (Rich) *Football Player*
4636 Nogal Canyon Road, Las Cruces, NM 88011, USA
Glowacki, Janusz *Writer*
845 W End Ave, #4B, New York, NY 10025, USA
Gluck, Carol *Historian*
440 Riverside Dr, New York, NY 10027, USA
Gluck, Louise E *Writer*
%Williams College, English Dept, Williamstown, MA 02167, USA
Glushchenko, Fedor I *Conductor*
1st Pryadilnaya Str 11, #5, 105037 Moscow, Russia
Glynn, Carlin *Actress*
1165 5th Ave, New York, NY 10029, USA
Glynn, Ian M *Physiologist*
Daylesford, Conduit Head Road, Cambridge CB3 0EY, England

Glynn, Robert D, Jr *Businessman*
%PG&E Corp, Spear Tower, 1 Market St, San Francisco, CA 94105, USA
Gminski, Mike *Basketball Player, Sportscaster*
1309 Canterbury Hill Circle, Charlotte, NC 28211, USA
Gnedovsky, Yuri P *Architect*
%Union of Architects, Granatny Per 22, Moscow 103001, Russia
Goad, Jim *Journalist, Writer*
%Simon & Schuster Books, 1230 Ave of Americas, New York, NY 10020, USA
Goalby, Bob *Golfer*
5950 Town Hall Road, Belleville, IL 62223, USA
Godard, Jean-Luc *Movie Director*
15 Rue du Nord, 1180 Roulle, Switzerland
Godbold, John C *Judge*
%US Court of Appeals, PO Box 1589, Montgomery, AL 36102, USA
Goddard, John *Explorer*
4224 Beulah Dr, La Canada, CA 91011, USA
Goddard, Mark *Actor*
PO Box 778, Middleboro, MA 02346, USA
Goddard, Samuel P (Sam), Jr *Governor, AZ*
4724 E Camelback Canyon Dr, Phoenix, AZ 85018, USA
Godfrey, Paul V *Publisher*
%Toronto Sun, 333 King St E, Toronto ON M5A 3X5, Canada
Godfrey, Randall *Football Player*
512 Cason St, Valdosta, GA 31601, USA
Godley, Georgina *Fashion Designer*
42 Bassett Road, London W10 6UL, England
Godley, Kevin *Singer, Drummer (Godley & Creme)*
Heronden Hall, Tenterden, Kent, England
Godmanis, Ivars *Ministers Council Chairman, Latvia*
Palasta St 1, 1954 Riga, Latvia
Godreche, Judith *Actress*
%William Morris Agency, 151 El Camino Dr, Beverly Hills, CA 90212, USA
Godwin, Fay S *Photographer*
%Fay Godwin Network, 3-4 Kirby St, London E4N 8TS, England
Godwin, Gail K *Writer*
PO Box 946, Woodstock, NY 12498, USA
Godwin, Linda M *Astronaut, Physicist*
16923 Cottonwood Way, Houston, TX 77059, USA
Godynyuk, Alexander *Hockey Player*
%VIP Sports International, 110 E 59th St, New York, NY 10022, USA
Goebel, Timothy *Figure Skater*
%Healthsouth Training Center, 555 N Nash St, El Segundo, CA 90245, USA
Goehr, P Alexander *Composer*
%University of Cambridge, Music Faculty, 11 West Road, Cambridge, England
Goellner, Marc-Kevin *Tennis Athlete*
%Blau-Weiss Neuss, Tennishall Jahnstrasse, 41464 Neuss, Germany
Goelz, Dave (Gonzo) *Puppeteer*
%Jim Henson Productions, 117 E 69th St, New York, NY 10021, USA
Goen, Bob *Entertainer*
21767 Plainwood Dr, Woodland Hills, CA 91364, USA
Goerke, Glenn A *Educator*
%University of Houston, President's Office, Houston, TX 77204, USA
Goestenkors, Gail *Basketball Coach*
%Duke University, Athletic Dept, Durham, NC 27708, USA
Goestschi, Renate *Alpine Skier*
Schwarzenbach 3, 8742 Obdach, Austria
Goetz, Eric *Yacht Builder*
%Eric Goetz Marine & Technology, 15 Broad Common Road, Bristol, RI 02809, USA
Goffin, Gerry *Lyricist*
9171 Hazen Dr, Beverly Hills, CA 90210, USA
Gogolak, Charles P (Charlie) *Football Player*
47 Village Ave, #211, Dedham, MA 02026, USA
Gogolak, Peter (Pete) *Football Player*
%R R Donnelley Financial, 75 Park Ave, #300, New York, NY 10007, USA
Goh Chok Tong *Prime Minister, Singapore*
%Prime Minister's Office, Istana Annexe, Singapore 0923, Singapore
Goh, Rex *Guitarist (Air Supply)*
%Agency for Performing Arts, 9200 Sunset Blvd, #900, Los Angeles, CA 90069, USA
Goheen, Robert F *Educator, Diplomat*
1 Orchard Circle, Princeton, NJ 08540, USA
Goings, E V *Businessman*
%Tupperware Corp, PO Box 2353, Orlando, FL 32802, USA
Goitschel-Beranger, Marielle *Alpine Skier*
Val Thorens, 73440 Saint-Martin de Belleville, France
Gola, Thomas J (Tom) *Basketball Player*
40 Governors Court, West Palm Beach, FL 33418, USA
Gold, Andrew *Singer, Songwriter*
%Store, 22207 Summit Vue Dr, Woodland Hills, CA 91367, USA

G

Gold - Goldreich

Gold, Brandy *Actress*
%Gold Marshak Liedtke, 3500 W Olive Ave, #1400, Burbank, CA 91505, USA
Gold, Elon *Actor, Comedian*
%United Talent Agency, 9560 Wilshire Blvd, #500, Beverly Hills, CA 90212, USA
Gold, Herbert *Writer*
1051 Broadway, #A, San Francisco, CA 94133, USA
Gold, Jack *Movie Director*
24 Wood Vale, London N1O 3DP, England
Gold, Joe *Bodybuilder*
%World Gym, 2210 Main St, Santa Monica, CA 90405, USA
Gold, Thomas *Astronomer, Physicist*
7 Pleasant Grove Lane, Ithaca, NY 14850, USA
Gold, Tracey *Actress*
3500 W Olive Ave, #1190, Burbank, CA 91505, USA
Goldberg, Adam *Actor*
%Innovative Artists, 1505 10th St, Santa Monica, CA 90401, USA
Goldberg, Bernard R *Commentator*
%CBS-TV, News Dept, 51 W 52nd St, New York, NY 10019, USA
Goldberg, Bill *Wrestler, Football Player*
167 New Hope Road, Dawsonville, GA 30534, USA
Goldberg, Edward D *Geochemist*
750 Val Sereno Dr, Encinitas, CA 92024, USA
Goldberg, Eric *Animator*
%Walt Disney Studios, Animation Dept, 500 S Buena Vista St, Burbank, CA 91521, USA
Goldberg, Leonard *Movie, Television Producer*
%Spectradyne Inc, 1198 Commerce Dr, Richardson, TX 75081, USA
Goldberg, Luella G *Educator*
7019 Tupa Dr, Minneapolis, MN 55439, USA
Goldberg, Marshall (Biggie) *Football Player*
180 E Pearson St, #4202, Chicago, IL 60611, USA
Goldberg, Michael *Artist*
222 Bowery Place, New York, NY 10012, USA
Goldberg, Richard W *Judge*
%US International Trade Court, 1 Federal Plaza, New York, NY 10278, USA
Goldberg, Stan *Cartoonist (Archie)*
8 White Birch Lane, Scarsdale, NY 10583, USA
Goldberg, Whoopi *Actress, Comedienne*
%Bragman/Nyman/Cafarelli, 9171 Wilshire Blvd, #300, Beverly Hills, CA 90210, USA
Goldberger, Andreas *Ski Jumper*
Bleckenwegen 4, 4924 Waldzell, Austria
Goldberger, Marvin L *Physicist, Educator*
621 Mira Monte, La Jolla, CA 92037, USA
Goldberger, Paul J *Journalist, Architecture Critic*
%New York Times, Editorial Dept, 229 W 43rd St, New York, NY 10036, USA
Goldblatt, Stephen L *Cinematographer*
%Spyros Skouras, 631 Wilshire Blvd, #2C, Santa Monica, CA 90401, USA
Goldblum, Jeff *Actor*
%Industry Entertainment, 955 Carillo Dr, #300, Los Angeles, CA 90048, USA
Golden, Arthur *Writer*
%Vintage Press, 1111 Rancho Conejo Blvd, Newbury Park, CA 91320, USA
Golden, Harry *Bowling Executive*
%Professional Bowlers Assn, 719 2nd Ave, #701, Seattle, WA 98104, USA
Golden, Michael *Businessman*
%New York Times Co, 229 W 43rd St, New York, NY 10036, USA
Golden, William Lee *Singer (Oak Ridge Boys); Songwriter*
329 Rockland Road, Hendersonville, TN 37075, USA
Goldenthal, Elliot *Composer*
%Gorfaine/Schwartz, 13245 Riverside Dr, #450, Sherman Oaks, CA 91423, USA
Goldhaber, Maurice *Physicist*
91 S Gillette Ave, Bayport, NY 11705, USA
Goldin, Claudia D *Economist*
%Harvard University, Economics Dept, Cambridge, MA 02138, USA
Goldin, Judah *Educator*
3300 Darby Road, Haverford, PA 19041, USA
Goldin, Nan *Photographer*
334 Bowry, New York, NY 10012, USA
Goldin, Ricky Paull *Actor*
365 W 52nd St, #LE, New York, NY 10019, USA
Goldin, Ricky Paull *Actor*
%Metropolitan Talent Agency, 4526 Wilshire Blvd, Los Angeles, CA 90010, USA
Goldman, Bo *Writer*
%Creative Artists Agency, 9830 Wilshire Blvd, Beverly Hills, CA 90212, USA
Goldman, Matt *Entertainer (Blue Man Group)*
%Blue Man Group, Luxor Hotel, 3900 Las Vegas Blvd S, Las Vegas, NV 89119, USA
Goldman, William *Writer*
%Janklow & Nesbit, 445 Park Ave, #1300, New York, NY 10022, USA
Goldreich, Peter M *Astronomer*
471 S Catalina Ave, Pasadena, CA 91106, USA

Goldsboro, Bobby *Singer, Songwriter*
%La Rana Productions, PO Box 4979, Ocala, FL 34478, USA
Goldschmidt, Neil E *Secretary, Transportation; Governor, OR*
222 SW Columbia St, Portland, OR 97201, USA
Goldsmith, Barbara *Writer*
%Janklow Nesbit Assocs, 445 Park Ave, #1300, New York, NY 10022, USA
Goldsmith, Jerry *Composer, Conductor*
%Savitsky Sain Geibelson, 1901 Ave of Stars, #1450, Los Angeles, CA 90067, USA
Goldsmith, Judy *Social Activist*
%National Organization for Women, 425 13th St NW, Washington, DC 20002, USA
Goldsmith, Olivia *Writer*
%Metropolitan Talent Agency, 4526 Wilshire Blvd, Los Angeles, CA 90010, USA
Goldsmith, Stephen *Mayor*
%Governor's Office, State House, Indianapolis, IN 46204, USA
Goldstein, Allan L *Biochemist, Immunologist*
800 25th St NW, #1005, Washington, DC 20037, USA
Goldstein, Avram *Pharmacologist*
735 Dolores St, Stanford, CA 94305, USA
Goldstein, Joseph L *Nobel Medicine Laureate*
3831 Turtle Creek Blvd, #22B, Dallas, TX 75219, USA
Goldstein, Michael *Businessman*
%Toys R Us Inc, 461 From Road, Paramus, NJ 07652, USA
Goldstein, Murray *Physician, Association Executive*
%United Cerebral Palsey Foundation, 1660 L St NW, #700, Washington, DC 20036, USA
Goldstine, Herman H *Mathematician, Computer Scientist*
56 Pasture Lane, Bryn Mawr, PA 19010, USA
Goldstone, Jeffrey *Physicist*
77 Massachusetts Ave, #6-313, Cambridge, MA 02139, USA
Goldstone, Richard J *Judge*
%Constitutional Court, Private Bag X32, Braamfontein 2017, South Africa
Goldstone, Steven F *Businessman*
%Nabisco Group Holdings, 1301 Ave of Americas, New York, NY 10019, USA
Goldsworthy, Andrew C (Andy) *Artist, Photographer*
%Hue-Williams Fine Art, 21 Cork St, London W1X 1HB, England
Goldthwait, Bob (Bobcat) *Actor, Comedian*
10061 Riverside Dr, #760, Toluca Lake, CA 91602, USA
Goldwasser, Eugene *Biochemist*
5656 S Dorchester Ave, Chicago, IL 60637, USA
Goldwyn, Samuel J, Jr *Movie Producer*
%Samuel Goldwyn Co, 9570 W Pico Blvd, #400, Los Angeles, CA 90035, USA
Goldwyn, Tony *Actor, Director*
%Creative Artists Agency, 9830 Wilshire Blvd, Beverly Hills, CA 90212, USA
Golembiewski, Billy *Bowler*
4966 N Wise Road, Coleman, MI 48618, USA
Golic, Robert P (Bob) *Football Player, Sportscaster*
1817 6th St, Manhattan Beach, CA 90266, USA
Golimowski, David A *Astronomer*
515 Holden Road, Towson, MD 21286, USA
Golino, Valeria *Actress*
%Creative Artists Agency, 9830 Wilshire Blvd, Beverly Hills, CA 90212, USA
Golisano, B Thomas *Businessman*
%Paychex Inc, 911 Panorama Trail S, Rochester, NY 14625, USA
Golonka, Arlene *Actress*
%Silver/Kass/Massetti, 8730 Sunset Blvd, #480, Los Angeles, CA 90069, USA
Golson, Benny *Jazz Saxophonist, Composer*
%Abby Hoffer, 223 1/2 E 48th St, New York, NY 10017, USA
Golub, Leon A *Artist*
530 LaGuardia Place, New York, NY 10012, USA
Gomez, Andres *Tennis Player*
%ProServe, 1101 Woodrow Wilson Blvd, #1800, Arlington, VA 22209, USA
Gomez, Edgar (Eddie) *Jazz Bassist*
%Integrity Talent, PO Box 961, Burlington, MA 01803, USA
Gomez, Jill *Opera Singer*
16 Milton Park, London N6 5QA, England
Gomez, Rick *Actor*
%United Talent Agency, 9560 Wilshire Blvd, #500, Beverly Hills, CA 90212, USA
Gomez, Ruben C *Baseball Player*
N43 Calle Luisa E, Toa Baja, PR 00949, USA
Gomez, Scott *Hockey Player*
1812 Toklat St, Anchorage, AK 99508, USA
Gomory, Ralph E *Mathematician, Foundation Executive*
%Alfred P Sloan Foundation, President's Office, 630 5th Ave, New York, NY 10111, USA
Gompf, Thomas (Tom) *Diver*
2716 Barret Ave, Plant City, FL 33566, USA
Goncalves, Vascos dos Santos *Prime Minister, Portugal; Army General*
Ave Estados Unidos da America 86, 5 Esq, 1700 Lisbon, Portugal
Gonchar, Sergei *Hockey Player*
%Int'l Management Group, 801 6th St SW, #235, Calgary AB T2P 3V8, Canada

G

Gong Li - Goodlin

Gong Li *Actress, Model*
%Xi'an Film Studio, Xi'an City, Shaanxi Province, China
Gonick, Larry *Cartoonist*
247 Missouri St, San Francisco, CA 94107, USA
Gonnenwein, Wolfgang *Conductor*
%Opera et Concert, Maximilianstr 22, 80539 Munich, Germany
Gonshaw, Francesca *Actress*
%Greg Mellard, 12 D'Arblay St, #200, London W1V 3FP, England
Gonsoulin, Austin (Goose) *Football Player*
5966 Reeves Dr, Silsbee, TX 77656, USA
Gonzales, Alberto *Judge, Government Official*
%White House, 1600 Pennsylvania Ave NW, Washington, DC 20500, USA
Gonzales, Carlos *Cinematographer*
1549 1/2 N Commonwealth Ave, Los Angeles, CA 90027, USA
Gonzalez Macchi, Luis *President, Paraguay*
%Palacio de Gobierno, Ave Marisol Lopez, Asuncion, Paraguay
Gonzalez Marquez, Felipe *Prime Minister, Spain*
%Fundacion Socialismo XXI, Gobelas 31, 28023 Madrid, Spain
Gonzalez Martin, Marcelo Cardinal *Religious Leader*
Arco de Palacio 1, 45002 Toledo, Spain
Gonzalez Zumarraga, Antonio J Cardinal *Religious Leader*
%Arzobispado, Apartado 17-01-00106, Called Chile 1140, Quito, Ecuador
Gonzalez, Alexander S (Alex) *Baseball Player*
8620 SW 102nd Ave, Miami, FL 33173, USA
Gonzalez, Arthur *Judge*
%US Bankruptcy Court, 1 Bowling Greeen, New York, NY 10004, USA
Gonzalez, Hector *Religious Leader*
%Baptist Churches USA, PO Box 851, Valley Forge, PA 19482, USA
Gonzalez, Juan A *Baseball Player*
Ext Catoni A9, Vega Baja, PR 00693, USA
Gonzalez, Luis E *Baseball Player*
6026 E Jenan Dr, Scottsdale, AZ 85254, USA
Gonzalez, Raul *Soccer Player*
%Real Madrid FC, Avda Concha Espina 1, 28036 Madrid, Spain
Gonzalez, Tony *Football Player*
%Kansas City Chiefs, 1 Arrowhead Dr, Kansas City, KS 64129, USA
Good, Hugh W *Religious Leader*
%Primitive Advent Christian Church, 273 Frame Road, Elkview, WV 25071, USA
Good, Melanie *Actress*
11288 Ventura Blvd, #175, Studio City, CA 91604, USA
Good, Michael T *Astronaut*
2617 Broussard Court, Seabrook, TX 77586, USA
Goodacre Connick, Jill *Model*
%Harry Connick, Wilkins Mgmt, 323 Broadway, Cambridge, MA 02139, USA
Goodacre, Glenna *Sculptor*
%National Academy Museum, 1083 5th Ave, New York, NY 10128, USA
Goodall, Caroline *Actress*
%P F D, Drury House, 34-43 Russell St, London WC2B 5HA, England
Goodall, V Jane *Ethologist, Primatologist*
%Jane Goodall Institute, PO Box 14890, Silver Spring, MD 20911, USA
Goode, David R *Businessman*
%Norfolk Southern Corp, 3 Commercial Place, Norfolk, VA 23510, USA
Goode, Joe *Artist*
1645 Electric Ave, Venice, CA 90291, USA
Goode, Richard S *Concert Pianist*
%Frank Salomon, 201 W 54th St, #1C, New York, NY 10019, USA
Goodell, Brian S *Swimmer*
27040 S Ridge Dr, Mission Viejo, CA 92692, USA
Gooden, Drew *Basketball Player*
%Orlando Magic, Waterhouse Center, 8701 Maitland Summit Blvd, Orlando, FL 32810, USA
Gooden, Dwight E *Baseball Player*
8380 Golden Prairie Dr, Tampa, FL 33647, USA
Goodenough, Ward H *Antropologist*
3300 Darby Road, #5306, Haverford, PA 19041, USA
Goodeve, Charles P *Physical Chemist*
38 Middleway, London NW11, England
Goodeve, Grant *Actor*
21416 NE 68th Court, Redmond, WA 98053, USA
Goodfellow, Peter N *Geneticist*
%Cancer Research Fund, Lincoln Inn Fields, London WC2A 3PX, England
Goodfriend, Lynda *Actress*
338 S Beachwood Dr, Burbank, CA 91506, USA
Gooding, Cuba, Jr *Actor*
%Creative Artists Agency, 9830 Wilshire Blvd, Beverly Hills, CA 90212, USA
Gooding, Cuba, Sr *Singer (Main Ingredient)*
%Winston Collection, 630 9th Ave, #908, New York, NY 10036, USA
Goodlin, Chalmers *Test Pilot*
7620 Red River Road, West Palm Beach, FL 33411, USA

G

Goodman, Alfred *Composer*
Bodenstedtstr 31, 81241 Munich, Germany
Goodman, Allegra *Writer*
%Dial Press, 375 Hudson St, New York, NY 10014, USA
Goodman, Corey S *Neurobiologist*
Howard Hughes Medical Institute, Molecular/Cell Biology Dept, Berkeley, CA 94720, USA
Goodman, Dody *Actress, Comedienne*
%Scott Stander, 13701 Riverside Dr, #201, Sherman Oaks, CA 91423, USA
Goodman, Ellen H *Columnist*
%Boston Globe, Editorial Dept, 135 W T Morrissey Blvd, Dorchester, MA 02125, USA
Goodman, John *Actor*
619 Amalfi Dr, Pacific Palisades, CA 90272, USA
Goodman, Joseph W *Electrical Engineer*
570 University Terrace, Los Altos, CA 94022, USA
Goodman, Oscar *Attorney*
520 S 4th St, Las Vegas, NV 89101, USA
Goodnoff, Irvin *Cinematographer*
29997 Mulholland Highway, Agoura Hills, CA 91301, USA
Goodpaster, Andrew J *Army General, Educator*
6200 Oregon Ave NW, #345, Washington, DC 20015, USA
Goodreault, Gene J *Football Player*
95 Colby St, Bradford, MA 01835, USA
Goodrich, Gail C, Jr *Basketball Player*
270 Oceano Dr, Los Angeles, CA 90049, USA
Goodson, James A *WW II Army Air Corps Hero*
37 Carolina Trail, Marshfield, MA 02050, USA
Goodwin, Doris Kearns *Historian, Commentator*
1649 Monument Lane, Concord, MA 01742, USA
Goodwin, Michael *Actor*
8271 Melrose Ave, #110, Los Angeles, CA 90046, USA
Goody, Joan E *Architect*
%Goody Clancy Assoc, 334 Boylston St, Boston, MA 02116, USA
Goodyear, Scott *Auto Racing Driver*
%Scott Goodyear Racing, PO Box 589, Carmel, IN 46082, USA
Goolagong Cawley, Evonne F *Tennis Player*
Private Bag 6060, Richmond SV 3121, Australia
Goorjian, Michael *Actor*
%Evolution Entertainment, 7722 Sunset Blvd, Los Angeles, CA 90046, USA
Goosen, Don *Boxing Promoter, Manager*
6320 Van Nuys Blvd, Van Nuys, CA 91401, USA
Gorbachev, Mikhail S *Nobel Peace Laureate; Gen Sec, USSR*
Leningradsky Prospekt 49, 125468 Moscow, Russia
Gorbachev, Yuri *Artist*
%Adrienne Editions, 377 Geary St, San Francisco, CA 94102, USA
Gorbatko, Viktor V *Cosmonaut; Air Force General*
%Potchta Kosmonavtov, Moskovskoi Oblasti, 141160 Syvisdny Goroduk, Russia
Gorchakova, Galina *Opera Singer*
%Askonas Holt Ltd, 27 Chancery Lane, London WC2A 1PF, England
Gordeeva, Ekaterina *Figure Skater*
%International Skating Center, PO Box 577, Simsbury, CT 06070, USA
Gordeyev, Vyacheslav M *Ballet Dancer, Choreographer*
Tverskaya Str 9, #78, Moscow 103009, Russia
Gordimer, Nadine *Nobel Literature Laureate*
7 Frere Road, Parktown, Johannesburg 2193, South Africa
Gordon, Barry *Actor, Singer*
1912 Kaweah Dr, Pasadena, CA 91105, USA
Gordon, Bert I *Movie Director*
9640 Arby Dr, Beverly Hills, CA 90210, USA
Gordon, Bridgette *Basketball Player*
421 E Chelsea St, Deland, FL 32724, USA
Gordon, Bruce *Actor*
231 Tano Road, #C, Santa Fe, NM 87506, USA
Gordon, David *Choreographer*
47 Great Jones St, #2, New York, NY 10012, USA
Gordon, Don *Actor*
%Acme Talent, 4727 Wilshire Blvd, #333, Los Angeles, CA 90010, USA
Gordon, Ed *Commentator*
%NBC-TV, News Dept, 30 Rockefeller Plaza, New York, NY 10112, USA
Gordon, Hannah Taylor *Actress*
%Hutton Mgmt, 4 Old Manor Close, Askett, Buckinghamshire HP27 9NA, England
Gordon, Harold P *Businessman*
%Hasbro Inc, 1027 Newport Ave, Pawtucket, RI 02861, USA
Gordon, Jeff *Auto Racing Driver*
1730 S Federal Highway, Delray Beach, FL 33483, USA
Gordon, Lancaster *Basketball Player*
2022 Murray Ave, #1, Louisville, KY 40205, USA
Gordon, Lawrence *Businessman*
%Largo Entertainment, 20th Century Fox, 10201 W Pico Blvd, Los Angeles, CA 90064, USA

G

Gordon - Gorrell

Gordon, Lincoln *Economist, Diplomat*
3069 University Terrace NW, Washington, DC 20016, USA
Gordon, Mark *Actor*
%Fifi Oscard Agency, 24 W 40th St, #1700, New York, NY 10018, USA
Gordon, Mary C *Writer*
%Viking Penguin Press, 375 Hudson St, New York, NY 10014, USA
Gordon, Mike *Bassist (Phish)*
%Dionysian Productions, 431 Pine St, Burlington, VT 05401, USA
Gordon, Milton A *Educator*
%California State University, President's Office, Fullerton, CA 99264, USA
Gordon, Mita *Governor General, Belize*
Belize House, Belnopan, Belize
Gordon, Nathan G *WW II Navy Hero (CMH)*
606 Green St, Morrilton, AZ 72110, USA
Gordon, Nina *Singer, Songwriter*
%Q Prime, 729 7th Ave, #1600, New York, NY 10019, USA
Gordon, Pamela *Prime Minister, Bermuda*
%United Bermuda Party, Burrows Bldg, Hamilton HM CX, Bermuda
Gordon, Richard F, Jr *Astronaut*
65 Woodside Dr, Prescott, AZ 86305, USA
Gordon, Robby *Auto, Truck Racing Driver*
201 Rollings Hills Road, Mooresville, NC 28117, USA
Gordon, William E *Radio Physicist*
%Rice University, Space Physics Dept, PO Box 1892, Houston, TX 77251, USA
Gordon-Levitt, Joseph *Actor*
%Gersh Agency, 232 N Canon Dr, Beverly Hills, CA 90210, USA
Gordy, John *Football Player*
40 Calle Fresno, San Clemente, CA 92672, USA
Gordy, Walter *Physicist*
2521 Perkins Road, Durham, NC 27705, USA
Gore, Albert A, Jr *Vice President*
312 Lynnwood Blvd, Nashville, TN 37205, USA
Gore, Lesley *Singer, Songwriter, Actress*
%World Entertainment Assoc, 297101 Kinderkamack Road, #128, Oradell, NJ 07649, USA
Gore, Martin *Synthesizer Musician (Depeche Mode)*
%Reach Media, 295 Greenwich St, #109, New York, NY 10007, USA
Gorecki, Henryk M *Composer*
Ul HA Gornika 4 m 1, 40-133 Katowice, Poland
Goren, Shlomo *Religious Leader, Army General*
Chief Rabbinate, Hechal Shlomo, Jerusalem, Israel
Gorenstein, Mark B *Conductor*
Rublevskoye Shosse 28, #25, 121609 Moscow, Russia
Goretta, Claude *Movie Director*
10 Tour de Boel, 1204 Geneva, Switzerland
Gorham, Christopher *Actor*
%S M S Talent, 8730 Sunset Blvd, #440, Los Angeles, CA 90069, USA
Gorham, Eville *Botanist*
1933 E River Terrace, Minneapolis, MN 55414, USA
Gorie, Dominic L *Astronaut*
16522 Craighurst Dr, Houston, TX 77059, USA
Goring, Robert T (Butch) *Hockey Player*
245 W 5th Ave, #108, Anchorage, AK 99501, USA
Goris, Eva *Actress*
%International Creative Mgmt, 8942 Wilshire Blvd, #219, Beverly Hills, CA 90211, USA
Gorlin, Alexander *Architect*
%Alexander Gorlin Architect, 137 Varick St, New York, NY 10013, USA
Gorman, Joseph T *Businessman*
%TRW Inc, 1900 Richmond Road, Cleveland, OH 44124, USA
Gorman, Paul F, Jr *Army General*
9175 Batesville Road, Afton, VA 22920, USA
Gorman, R C *Artist*
PO Box 1258, El Prado, NM 87529, USA
Gorman, Steve *Drummer (Black Crowes)*
%Mitch Schneider Organization, 14724 Ventura Blvd, #410, Sherman Oaks, CA 91403, USA
Gorman, Tom *Tennis Player*
%ProServe, 1101 Woodrow Wilson Blvd, #1800, Arlington, VA 22209, USA
Gorme, Eydie *Singer*
944 Pinehurst Dr, Las Vegas, NV 89109, USA
Gormley, Antony *Sculptor*
13 South Villas, London NW1 9BS, England
Gorney, Karen Lynn *Actress*
%Karen Company, PO Box 23-1060, New York, NY 10023, USA
Gorouuch, Edward Lee *Educator*
%University of Alaska, President's Office, Anchorage, AK 99508, USA
Gorrell, Bob *Editorial Cartoonist*
%Creators Syndicate, 5777 W Century Blvd, #700, Los Angeles, CA 90045, USA
Gorrell, Fred *Balloonist*
501 E Port au Prince Lane, Phoenix, AZ 85022, USA

Gorshin, Frank *Actor, Comedian*
%Scott Stander, 13701 Riverside Dr, #201, Sherman Oaks, CA 91423, USA
Gorter, Cornelis J *Physicist*
Klobeniersburgwal 29, Amsterdam, Netherlands
Gortman, Shaunzinski *Basketball Player*
%Charlotte Sting, 100 Hive Dr, Charlotte, NC 28217, USA
Gosdin, Vern *Singer, Songwriter*
%Rising Star, 1415 River Landing Way, Woodstock, GA 30188, USA
Goslin, Thomas B, Jr *Air Force General*
Deputy CinC, US Strategic Command, Offutt Air Force Base, NE 68113, USA
Gosling, James *Computer Software Designer (Java)*
%Sun Microsystems, 2550 Garcia Ave, Mountain View, CA 94043, USA
Gosling, Ryan *Actor*
%The Firm, 9100 Wilshire Blvd, #100W, Beverly Hills, CA 90210, USA
Goss, Robert F *Labor Leader*
%Oil Chemical & Atomic International, 1636 Champa St, Denver, CO 80202, USA
Gossage, Richard M (Goose) *Baseball Player*
35 Marland Dr, Colorado Springs, CO 80906, USA
Gossard, Stone *Guitarist (Pearl Jam)*
%Annie Ohayon Media Relations, 525 Broadway, #600, New York, NY 10012, USA
Gosselaar, Mark-Paul *Actor*
30853 Romero Canyon Road, Castaic, CA 91384, USA
Gosselin, Mario *Hockey Player*
3225 NE 16th St, Pompano Beach, FL 33062, USA
Gossett, D Bruce *Football Player*
6109 Puerto Dr, Rancho Murieta, CA 95683, USA
Gossett, Louis, Jr *Actor*
%Writers & Artists, 8383 Wilshire Blvd, #550, Beverly Hills, CA 90211, USA
Gossett, Robert *Actor*
8306 Wilshire Blvd, #438, Beverly Hills, CA 90211, USA
Gossick Crockatt, Sue *Diver*
13768 Christian Barrett Dr, Moorpark, CA 93021, USA
Gott, Karel *Singer*
Nad Bertramkou 18, 160 00 Prague, Czech Republic
Gottfried, Brian *Tennis Player*
129 Teal Pointe Lane, Ponte Vedra Beach, FL 32082, USA
Gottfried, Gilbert *Actor, Comedian*
%William Morris Agency, 151 El Camino Dr, Beverly Hills, CA 90212, USA
Gottlieb, Michael *Movie Director*
2436 Washington Ave, Santa Monica, CA 90403, USA
Gottlieb, Robert A *Editor, Publisher*
237 E 48th St, New York, NY 10017, USA
Gougeon, Donni *Keyboardist (Association)*
%Variety Artists, 1924 Spring St, Paso Robles, CA 93446, USA
Gough, Michael *Actor*
Torleigh Green Lane, Ashmore, Salisbury, Wilts SP5 5AQ, England
Gough, Tommy *Singer (Crests)*
%Brothers Mgmt, 141 Dunbar Ave, Fords, NJ 08863, USA
Gould Innes, Shane *Swimmer*
207 Kent St, Level 18, Sydney 2000 NSW, Australia
Gould, Elizabeth *Neurosurgeon*
%Princeton University, Medical Center, Neurosciences Dept, Princeton, NJ 08544, USA
Gould, Elliott *Actor*
21250 Califa St, #201, Woodland Hills, CA 91367, USA
Gould, Gordon *Inventor (Optical-Pump Laser Amplifier)*
105 Buckeye Court, Sterling, VA 20164, USA
Gould, Harold *Actor*
603 Ocean Ave, #4E, Santa Monica, CA 90402, USA
Gould, Laurence M *Geologist*
201 E Rudasill Road, Tucson, AZ 85704, USA
Gould, Ronald M *Judge*
%US Court of Appeals, US Courthouse, 1010 5th Ave, Seattle, WA 98104, USA
Goulet, Michel *Hockey Player*
817 Fairchild Dr, Highlands Ranch, CO 80126, USA
Goulet, Robert *Singer, Actor*
3110 Monte Rosa Ave, Las Vegas, NV 89120, USA
Gourley, Roark *Artist*
%Roark Gourley Art Gallery, 33151 Paso Dr, South Laguna Beach, CA 92677, USA
Gowan, James *Architect*
2 Linden Gardens, London W2 4ES, England
Gowdy, Curt *Sportscaster*
28 Graham St, Leominster, MA 01453, USA
Gower, David I *Cricketer*
%David Gower Promotions, 6 George St, Nottingham NG1 3BE, England
Gowers, W Timothy *Mathematician*
%Cambridge University, 16 Mill Lane, Cambridge CB2 1SB, England
Gowon, Yakub *President, Nigeria; Army General*
%National Oil/Chemical Marketing Co, 38-39 Marina, 2052 Lagos, Nigeria

G

Gowrie, Earl of *Government Official, England*
%Government Securities, Stag Place, London SW1E 5DS, England
Goycoechea, Sergio *Soccer Player*
%Argentine Football Assn, Via Monte 1366-76, 1053 Buenos Aires, Argentina
Goyette, J G Philippe (Phil) *Hockey Player*
815 38-E Ave, Lachine QC H8T 2C4, Canada
Grabe, Ronald J *Astronaut*
13302 E Country Shadows Road, Chandler, AZ 85249, USA
Graber, Bill *Track Athlete*
PO Box 5019, Upland, CA 91785, USA
Graber, Susan P *Judge*
%US Court of Appeals, Pioneer Courthouse, 555 SW Yamhill St, Portland, OR 97204, USA
Grabois, Neil R *Educator*
%Colgate University, President's Office, Hamilton, NY 13346, USA
Grabowski, James S (Jim) *Football Player*
1523 W Withorn Lane, Palatine, IL 60067, USA
Grace, April *Actress*
%Liberman/Zerman, 252 N Larchmont, #200, Los Angeles, CA 90004, USA
Grace, Bud *Cartoonist (Ernie, Piranha Club)*
PO Box 66, Oakton, VA 22124, USA
Gracen, Elizabeth *Actress, Beauty Queen*
%Metropolitan Talent Agency, 4526 Wilshire Blvd, Los Angeles, CA 90010, USA
Gracey, James S *Coast Guard Admiral, Businessman*
1 Westin Center, 2445 M St NW, #260, Washington, DC 20037, USA
Grach, Eduard D *Concert Violinist*
1st Smolensky Per 9, #98, 113324 Moscow, Russia
Grachev, Pavel S *Army Marshal, Russia*
Ovchinnikovskaya Nab 18/1, 113324 Moscow, Russia
Gracheva, Nadezhda A *Ballerina*
1st Truzhennikov Per 17, #49, 119121 Moscow, Russia
Gracie, Charlie *Singer, Guitarist*
%Jeff Hubbard Productions, PO Box 53664, Indianapolis, IN 46253, USA
Grad, Harold *Mathematician*
248 Overlook Road, New Rochelle, NY 10804, USA
Gradishar, Randy C *Football Player*
6441 S Southwood Dr, Centennial, CO 80121, USA
Grady, Don *Actor, Songwriter*
4444 Lankershim Blvd, #207, North Hollywood, CA 91602, USA
Grady, James T *Labor Leader*
%International Teamsters Brotherhood, 25 Louisiana Ave NW, Washington, DC 20001, USA
Grady, Wayne *Golfer*
%Advantage International, 1751 Pinnacle Dr, #1500, McLean, VA 22102, USA
Graeber, Clark *Tennis Player*
411 Harbor Road, Fairfield, CT 06431, USA
Graells, Francisco (Pancho) *Editorial Cartoonist*
%Le Monde, Editorial Dept, 21 Bis Rue Claude Bernard, 75005 Paris, France
Graf, Hans *Conductor*
%Houston Symphony, Jesse Jones Hall, 615 Louisiana St, Houston, TX 77002, USA
Graf, Stefanie M (Steffi) *Tennis Player*
8921 Andre Dr, Las Vegas, NV 89148, USA
Graff, Ilene *Actress*
11455 Sunshine Terrace, Studio City, CA 91604, USA
Graff, Randy *Actress*
%Peter Strawn Assoc, 1501 Broadway, #2900, New York, NY 10036, USA
Graffin, Guillaume *Ballet Dancer*
%American Ballet Theatre, 890 Broadway, New York, NY 10003, USA
Graffman, Gary *Concert Pianist*
%Curtis Institute of Music, 1726 Locust St, Philadelphia, PA 19103, USA
Grafstein, Bernice *Neurologist, Physiologist*
%Weill Medical College, Physiology Dept, 1300 York Ave, New York, NY 10021, USA
Grafton, Sue *Writer*
PO Box 41446, Santa Barbara, CA 93140, USA
Graham, Alex *Cartoonist (Fred Basset)*
%Tribune Media Services, 435 N Michigan Ave, #1500, Chicago, IL 60611, USA
Graham, Bruce J *Architect*
%Graham & Graham, PO Box 8589, Hobe Sound, FL 33475, USA
Graham, Charles P *Army General*
134 Warbler Way, Georgetown, TX 78628, USA
Graham, Daniel *Football Player*
%New England Patriots, Gillette Stadium, RR 1, 60 Washington, Foxboro, MA 02035, USA
Graham, David *Golfer*
PO Box 4997, Whitefish, MT 59937, USA
Graham, Dirk *Hockey Player, Coach*
7238 E Tyndall St, Mesa, AZ 85207, USA
Graham, Donald E *Publisher*
%Washington Post Co, 1150 15th St NW, Washington, DC 20071, USA
Graham, Franklin *Religious Leader*
%Samaritan's Purse, PO Box 3000, Boone, NC 28607, USA

Graham, Gerrit %S M S Talent, 8730 Sunset Blvd, #440, Los Angeles, CA 90069, USA	*Actor*
Graham, Glen %Shapiro Co, 9229 Sunset Blvd, #607, Los Angeles, CA 90069, USA	*Drummer (Blind Melon)*
Graham, Heather %Creative Artists Agency, 9830 Wilshire Blvd, Beverly Hills, CA 90212, USA	*Actress*
Graham, John R %University of California, Astronomy Dept, Berkeley, CA 94720, USA	*Astronomer*
Graham, Jorie General Delivery, West Tisbury, MA 02575, USA	*Writer*
Graham, Larry %Groove Entertainment, 1005 N Alfred St, #2, West Hollywood, CA 90069, USA	*Guitarist (Sly & Family Stone), Singer*
Graham, Lauren %Writers & Artists, 8383 Wilshire Blvd, #550, Beverly Hills, CA 90211, USA	*Actress*
Graham, Linda 4147 E Seneca Ave, Des Moines, IA 50317, USA	*Bowler*
Graham, Loren R 7 Francis Ave, Cambridge, MA 02138, USA	*Historian*
Graham, Lou 85 Concord Park W, Nashville, TN 37205, USA	*Golfer*
Graham, Mikey %JC Music, 84A Strand on the Green, London W43 PU, England	*Singer (Boyzone)*
Graham, Otto E, Jr 2216 Riviera Dr, Sarasota, FL 34232, USA	*Football Player, Coach*
Graham, Robert 35 Market St, Venice, CA 90291, USA	*Sculptor*
Graham, Susan %Columbia Artists Mgmt Inc, 165 W 57th St, New York, NY 10019, USA	*Opera Singer*
Graham, William B 40 Devonshire Lane, Kenilworth, IL 60043, USA	*Businessman*
Graham, William F (Billy) PO Box 937, Montreat, NC 28757, USA	*Evangelist*
Graham, William R %Xsirius Inc, 1110 N Glebe Road, #620, Arlington, VA 22201, USA	*Government Official*
Graham-Smith, Francis Old School House, Henbury, Macclesfield, Cheshire SK11 9PH, England	*Astronomer*
Grahn, Nancy Lee 4910 Agnes Ave, North Hollywood, CA 91607, USA	*Actress*
Grainger, David W %WW Grainger Inc, 100 Grainger Parkway, Lake Forest, IL 60045, USA	*Businessman*
Gralish, Tom 203 E Cottage Ave, Haddonfield, NJ 08033, USA	*Photojournalist*
Gralla, Lawrence %Gralla Publications, 1515 Broadway, New York, NY 10036, USA	*Publisher*
Gralla, Milton %Gralla Publications, 1515 Broadway, New York, NY 10036, USA	*Publisher*
Gramatica, Martin PO Box 2291, Labelle, FL 33975, USA	*Football Player*
Gramlich, Edward M %Federal Reserve Board, 20th & Constitution Aves NW, Washington, DC 20551, USA	*Economist, Government Official*
Gramm, Lou %Hard to Handle Mgmt, 16501 Ventura Blvd, #602, Encino, CA 91436, USA	*Singer (Foreigner)*
Gramm, W Philip (Phil) %UBS Warburg, 299 Park Ave, New York, NY 10171, USA	*Senator, TX*
Gramm, Wendy L %Commodity Futures Trading Commission, 2033 K St NW, Washington, DC 20006, USA	*Government Official*
Grammer, Kathy %Artists Agency, 1180 S Beverly Dr, #301, Los Angeles, CA 90035, USA	*Actress*
Grammer, Kelsey %Grammnet Inc, Paramount Studios, 5555 Melrose Ave, Los Angeles, CA 90038, USA	*Actor*
Granatelli, Andy 1469 Edgecliff Lane, Montecito, CA 93108, USA	*Auto Racing Executive*
Granato, Catherine (Cammi) 13454 Wood Duck Dr, Plainfield, IL 60544, USA	*Hockey Player*
Granato, Tony 11657 E Berry Dr, Englewood, CO 80111, USA	*Hockey Player, Coach*
Grandin, Temple 2918 Silver Plume Dr, #C3, Fort Collins, CO 80526, USA	*Animal Scientist*
Grandmaster Mele-Mel %Groove Entertainment, 1005 N Alfred St, #2, West Hollywood, CA 90069, USA	*Rap Artist*
Grandmont, Jean-Michel 55 Blvd de Charonne, Les Doukas 23, 75011 Paris, France	*Economist*
GrandPre, Mary %Scholastic Press, 555 Broadway, New York, NY 10012, USA	*Illustrator*
Grandy, Fred 9417 Spruce Tree Circle, Bethesda, MD 20814, USA	*Actor; Representative, IA*
Grandy, John %White's, Saint James's St, London SW1, England	*Air Force Marshal, England*

G

Granger - Graves

Granger, Clive W J *Nobel Economics Laureate*
%University of California, Economics Dept, 9500 Gilman Dr, La Jolla, CA 92093, USA
Granger, David *Bobsled Athlete*
%Ingalls & Snyder, 61 Broadway, #3100, New York, NY 10006, USA
Granger, Farley *Actor*
%Dakota Hotel, 1 W 72nd St, #25D, New York, NY 10023, USA
Grannis, Paul D *Physicist*
%Fermi Nat Accelerator Lab, CDF Collaboration, PO Box 500, Batavia, IL 60510, USA
Grant, Amy *Singer, Songwriter*
Riverston Farm, Moran Road, Franklin, TN 37064, USA
Grant, Boyd *Basketball Coach*
%Colorado State University, Athletic Dept, Fort Collins, CO 80523, USA
Grant, Brian *Basketball Player*
145 Solano Prado, Coral Gables, FL 33156, USA
Grant, Charles *Actor*
%Media Artists Group, 6300 Wilshire Blvd, #1470, Los Angeles, CA 90048, USA
Grant, Deborah *Actress*
%Larry Dalzall, 17 Broad Court, #12, London WC2B 5QN, England
Grant, Edmond (Eddy) *Singer, Songwriter*
%Consolidated Ale, PO Box 87, Tarporley CW6 9FN, England
Grant, Faye *Actress*
%B & B Entertainment, 1640 S Sepulveda Blvd, #530, Los Angeles, CA 90025, USA
Grant, Gogi *Singer*
10323 Alamo Ave, #202, Los Angeles, CA 90064, USA
Grant, Harold P (Bud) *Football, Basketball Player, Coach*
8134 Oakmere Road, Bloomington, MN 55438, USA
Grant, Horace *Basketball Player*
719 N Eucalyptus Ave, #258, Inglewood, CA 90302, USA
Grant, Hugh *Actor*
Redcliffe Road, #36, London SW10 JNJ, England
Grant, Hugh, Jr *Harness Racing Executive*
414 E 75th St, #4, Gainesville, FL 32604, USA
Grant, James T (Mudcat) *Baseball Player*
1020 S Dunsmuir Ave, Los Angeles, CA 90019, USA
Grant, Jennifer *Actress*
%Karg/Weissenbach, 329 N Wetherly Dr, #101, Beverly Hills, CA 90211, USA
Grant, Lee *Actress, Director*
%Artists Group, 10100 Santa Monica Blvd, #2490, Los Angeles, CA 90067, USA
Grant, Mickie *Actress*
250 W 94th St, #6G, New York, NY 10025, USA
Grant, Paul *Basketball Player*
%Milwaukee Bucks, Bradley Center, 1001 N 4th St, Milwaukee, WI 53203, USA
Grant, Richard E *Actor*
%International Creative Mgmt, 76 Oxford St, London W1N 0AX, England
Grant, Robert M *Educator*
RR 1 Box 1423, Berlin, NH 03570, USA
Grant, Rodney A *Actor*
%Omar, 526 N Larchmont Blvd, Los Angeles, CA 90004, USA
Grant, Tom *Jazz Musician*
%Brad Simon Organization, 122 E 57th St, #300, New York, NY 10022, USA
Grant, Toni *Radio Psychologist*
610 S Ardmore Ave, Los Angeles, CA 90005, USA
Granville, Joseph *Financier, Writer*
%Granville Market Letter, 2525 Market St, Kansas City, MO 64108, USA
Grass, Gunter *Nobel Literature Laureate*
Sekretariat, Glockengiesserstr 21, 23552 Lubeck, Germany
Grassle, Karen *Actress*
PO Box 913, Pacific Palisades, CA 90272, USA
Grasso, Richard A *Financier*
%New York Stock Exchange, 11 Wall St, New York, NY 10005, USA
Grau, Shirley Ann *Writer*
12 Nassau Dr, Metairie, LA 70005, USA
Grausman, Phillip *Sculptor*
21 Barnes Road, Washington, CT 06793, USA
Gravel, Maurice R (Mike) *Senator, AK*
1600 N Oak St, #1412, Arlington, VA 22209, USA
Graveline, Duane E *Astronaut*
494 Pleasant St, Island Pond, VT 05846, USA
Graves, Adam *Hockey Player*
574 Lis Crescent, Windsor ON N9G 2M5, Canada
Graves, Denyce *Opera Singer*
%Columbia Artists Mgmt Inc, 165 W 57th St, New York, NY 10019, USA
Graves, Earl G *Publisher*
%Black-Enterprise Magazine, 130 5th Ave, New York, NY 10011, USA
Graves, Ernest, Jr *Army General*
2328 S Nash St, Arlington, VA 22202, USA
Graves, Harold N, Jr *Journalist, Government Official*
4816 Grantham Ave, Chevy Chase, MD 20815, USA

Graves, Michael — *Architect*
341 Nassau St, Princeton, NJ 08540, USA

Graves, Peter — *Actor*
660 E Channel Road, Santa Monica, CA 90402, USA

Graves, Peter — *Actor*
%International Creative Mgmt, 76 Oxford St, London W1N 0AX, England

Graves, Ray — *Football Coach*
4230 Hartwood Lane, Tampa, FL 33624, USA

Graves, Richard G — *Army General*
3107 Iron Stone Lane, San Antonio, TX 78230, USA

Graves, Rupert — *Actor*
%P F D, Drury House, 34-43 Russell St, London WC2B 5HA, England

Gravitte, Beau — *Actor*
%Paradigm Agency, 10100 Santa Monica Blvd, #2500, Los Angeles, CA 90067, USA

Gray, Alasdair J — *Writer*
%McAlpine, 2 Marchmont Terrace, Glasgow G12 9LT, Scotland

Gray, Alfred M, Jr — *Marine Corps General*
6317 Chaucer View Circle, Alexandria, VA 22304, USA

Gray, Billy — *Actor*
19612 Grandview Dr, Topanga Canyon, CA 90290, USA

Gray, C Boyden — *Government Official*
%Wilmer Cutler Pickering, 2445 M St NW, Washington, DC 20037, USA

Gray, Coleen — *Actress*
2337 Roscomare Road, #2-112, Los Angeles, CA 90077, USA

Gray, D'Wayne — *Marine Corps General*
3423 Barger Dr, Falls Church, VA 22044, USA

Gray, David — *Singer, Songwriter*
%Helter Skelter, Plaza, 535 Kings Road, London SW10 0S, England

Gray, Dobie — *Singer*
2211 Elliott Ave, Nashville, TN 37204, USA

Gray, Doug — *Singer (Marshall Tucker Band)*
%Ron Rainey Mgmt, 315 S Beverly Dr, #407, Beverly Hills, CA 90212, USA

Gray, Dulcie — *Actress*
%Barry Burnett, 31 Coventry St, London W1V 8AS, England

Gray, Ed — *Basketball Player*
%Houston Rockets, Toyota Center, 2 E Greenway Plaza, Houston, TX 77046, USA

Gray, Erin — *Actress, Model*
10921 Alta View Dr, Studio City, CA 91604, USA

Gray, F Gary — *Movie Director*
%H S I Productions, 3630 Eastham Dr, Culver City, CA 90232, USA

Gray, Fred, Sr — *Attorney*
1005 Lakeshore Dr, Tuskegee, AL 36083, USA

Gray, George W — *Organic Chemist*
Juniper House, Furzehill, Wimborne, Dorset BH21 4HD, England

Gray, Harry B — *Chemist*
1415 E California Blvd, Pasadena, CA 91106, USA

Gray, James — *Movie Director, Writer*
%United Talent Agency, 9560 Wilshire Blvd, #500, Beverly Hills, CA 90212, USA

Gray, Jerry — *Football Player*
27 Birdsong Parkway, Orchard Park, NY 14127, USA

Gray, John — *Writer*
%Relationship Speakers Network, PO Box 12695, Scottsdale, AZ 85267, USA

Gray, Ken — *Football Player*
356 Camoa Pajama Lane, Kingsland, TX 78639, USA

Gray, L Patrick, III — *Law Enforcement Official*
PO Box 1591, New London, CT 06320, USA

Gray, Linda — *Actress*
PO Box 5064, Sherman Oaks, CA 91413, USA

Gray, Macy — *Singer, Songwriter*
%H K Mgmt, 9200 W Sunset Blvd, #530, Los Angeles, CA 90069, USA

Gray, Mel — *Football Player*
2415 S Perryville Road, Rockford, IL 61108, USA

Gray, Simon J H — *Writer*
%Judy Daish, 2 Saint Charles Place, London W10 6EG, England

Gray, Spalding — *Performance Artist, Writer*
22 Wooster St, New York, NY 10013, USA

Gray, Theordore G (Ted) — *Baseball Player*
2917 S Ocean Blvd, #1005, Highland Beach, FL 33487, USA

Gray, William H, III — *Association Leader; Representative, PA*
%United Negro College Fund, 500 E 62nd St, New York, NY 10021, USA

Graybiel, Ann M — *Anatomist*
%Massachusetts Institute of Technology, Cognitive Sci Dept, Cambridge, MA 02139, USA

Graysmith, Robert — *Editorial Cartoonist*
%San Francisco Chronicle, 901 Mission St, San Francisco, CA 94103, USA

Grayson, C Jackson, Jr — *Government Official, Educator*
123 N Post Oak Lane, Houston, TX 77024, USA

Grayson, Kathryn — *Singer, Actress*
%Ruth Webb, 10580 Des Moines Ave, Northridge, CA 91326, USA

G

Grazia, Eugene *Hockey Player*
2421 NE 49th St, Fort Lauderdale, FL 33308, USA
Graziani, Ariel *Soccer Player*
%San Jose Earthquakes, 3550 Stevens Creek Blvd, #200, San Jose, CA 95117, USA
Grazzola, Kenneth E *Publisher*
%Aviation Week Magazine, 1221 Ave of Americas, New York, NY 10020, USA
Greatbatch, Wilson *Inventor (Cardiac Pacemaker)*
10000 Wehrle Dr, Clarence, NY 14031, USA
Grebenshchikov, Boris *Singer, Guitarist (Akvarium)*
2 Marata St, #3, 191025 Saint Petersburg, Russia
Grechko, Georgi M *Cosmonaut*
%Potchta Kosmonavtov, Moskovskoi Oblasti, 141160 Syvisdny Goroduk, Russia
Greco, Buddy *Singer, Pianist*
%Zane Mgmt, 1301 Yarmouth Road, Wynnewood, PA 19096, USA
Greco, Emilio *Sculptor*
Viale Cortina d'Ampezzo 132, 00135 Rome, Italy
Greco, Juliette *Actress, Singer*
%Maurice Maraouani, 37 Rue Marbeuf, 75008 Paris, France
Greeley, Andrew M (Andy) *Writer, Sociologist*
6030 S Ellis Ave, Chicago, IL 60637, USA
Green, A C *Basketball Player*
201 E Jefferson St, Phoenix, AZ 85004, USA
Green, Ahman *Football Player*
%Green Bay Packers, PO Box 10628, Green Bay, WI 54307, USA
Green, Al *Singer, Songwriter*
PO Box 456, Millington, TN 38083, USA
Green, B Eric *Football Player*
13131 Luntz Point Lane, Windermere, FL 34786, USA
Green, Barry *Auto Racing Executive*
%Team Green, 7615 Zionsville Road, Indianapolis, IN 46268, USA
Green, Benny *Jazz Pianist*
%Jazz Tree, 211 Thompson St, #1D, New York, NY 10012, USA
Green, Brian Austin *Actor*
11333 Moorpark St, #27, Studio City, CA 91602, USA
Green, Darrell *Football Player*
PO Box 30003, Alexandria, VA 22310, USA
Green, David *Movie Director*
%International Creative Mgmt, 76 Oxford St, London W1N 0AX, England
Green, David E *Chemist*
5339 Brody Dr, Madison, WI 53705, USA
Green, David T *Inventor (Surgical Instruments)*
%US Surgical Corp, 150 Glover Ave, Norwalk, CT 06850, USA
Green, Debbie *Volleyball Player*
239 5th St, Seal Beach, CA 90740, USA
Green, Dennis *Football Coach*
%FLW Outdoors, Pax-TV, 601 Clearwater Park Road, West Palm Beach, FL 33401, USA
Green, G Dallas *Baseball Player, Manager, Executive*
548 S Guernsey Road, West Grove, PA 19390, USA
Green, Gary F *Football Player*
16330 Walnut Creek Dr, San Antonio, TX 78247, USA
Green, Gerald *Writer*
88 Arrowhead Trail, New Canaan, CT 06840, USA
Green, Guy M *Cinematographer, Director*
%Gersh Agency, 232 N Canon Dr, Beverly Hills, CA 90210, USA
Green, Hamilton *Prime Minister, Guyana*
Plot D Lodge, Georgetown, Guyana
Green, Howard *Cellular Physiologist*
%Harvard Medical School, Physiology & Biophysics Dept, Boston, MA 02115, USA
Green, Hubert *Golfer*
PO Box 142, Bay Point, Panama City, FL 32402, USA
Green, Jeff *Auto Racing Driver*
%Continental, 5909 Peachtree Dunwoody Road NE, Atlanta, GA 30328, USA
Green, John M (Johnny) *Basketball Player*
9 Susan Lane, Dix Hills, NY 11746, USA
Green, John N (Jack), Jr *Cinematographer*
516 Esplanade, #E, Redondo Beach, CA 90277, USA
Green, Kate *Writer*
%Bantam/Delacorte/Dell/Doubleday Press, 1540 Broadway, New York, NY 10036, USA
Green, Ken *Golfer*
2875 Antietam Lane, West Palm Beach, FL 33409, USA
Green, Leonard I *Businessman*
%Rite Aid Corp, 30 Hunter Lane, Camp Hill, PA 17011, USA
Green, Lucinda *Equestrian Rider*
Appleshaw House, Andover, Hants, England
Green, Mark J *Activist, Attorney, Writer*
%Democracy Project, 530 E 90th St, #6K, New York, NY 10128, USA
Green, Maurice Spurgeon *Editor*
Hermitage, Twyford House, Hants, England

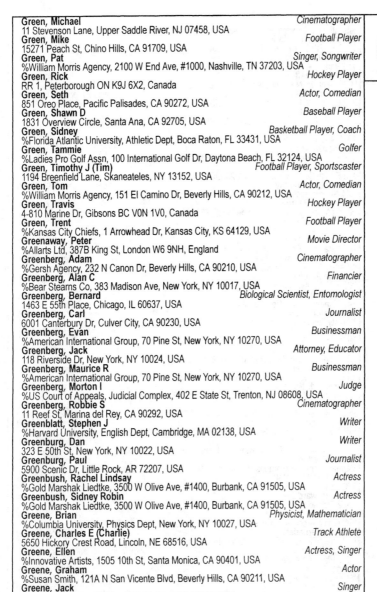

Green, Michael *Cinematographer*
11 Stevenson Lane, Upper Saddle River, NJ 07458, USA
Green, Mike *Football Player*
15271 Peach St, Chino Hills, CA 91709, USA
Green, Pat *Singer, Songwriter*
%William Morris Agency, 2100 W End Ave, #1000, Nashville, TN 37203, USA
Green, Rick *Hockey Player*
RR 1, Peterborough ON K9J 6X2, Canada
Green, Seth *Actor, Comedian*
851 Oreo Place, Pacific Palisades, CA 90272, USA
Green, Shawn D *Baseball Player*
1831 Overview Circle, Santa Ana, CA 92705, USA
Green, Sidney *Basketball Player, Coach*
%Florida Atlantic University, Athletic Dept, Boca Raton, FL 33431, USA
Green, Tammie *Golfer*
%Ladies Pro Golf Assn, 100 International Golf Dr, Daytona Beach, FL 32124, USA
Green, Timothy J (Tim) *Football Player, Sportscaster*
1194 Breenfield Lane, Skaneateles, NY 13152, USA
Green, Tom *Actor, Comedian*
%William Morris Agency, 151 El Camino Dr, Beverly Hills, CA 90212, USA
Green, Travis *Hockey Player*
4-810 Marine Dr, Gibsons BC V0N 1V0, Canada
Green, Trent *Football Player*
%Kansas City Chiefs, 1 Arrowhead Dr, Kansas City, KS 64129, USA
Greenaway, Peter *Movie Director*
%Allarts Ltd, 387B King St, London W6 9NH, England
Greenberg, Adam *Cinematographer*
%Gersh Agency, 232 N Canon Dr, Beverly Hills, CA 90210, USA
Greenberg, Alan C *Financier*
%Bear Stearns Co, 383 Madison Ave, New York, NY 10017, USA
Greenberg, Bernard *Biological Scientist, Entomologist*
1463 E 55th Place, Chicago, IL 60637, USA
Greenberg, Carl *Journalist*
6001 Canterbury Dr, Culver City, CA 90230, USA
Greenberg, Evan *Businessman*
%American International Group, 70 Pine St, New York, NY 10270, USA
Greenberg, Jack *Attorney, Educator*
118 Riverside Dr, New York, NY 10024, USA
Greenberg, Maurice R *Businessman*
%American International Group, 70 Pine St, New York, NY 10270, USA
Greenberg, Morton I *Judge*
%US Court of Appeals, Judicial Complex, 402 E State St, Trenton, NJ 08608, USA
Greenberg, Robbie S *Cinematographer*
11 Reef St, Marina del Rey, CA 90292, USA
Greenblatt, Stephen J *Writer*
%Harvard University, English Dept, Cambridge, MA 02138, USA
Greenburg, Dan *Writer*
323 E 50th St, New York, NY 10022, USA
Greenburg, Paul *Journalist*
5900 Scenic Dr, Little Rock, AR 72207, USA
Greenbush, Rachel Lindsay *Actress*
%Gold Marshak Liedtke, 3500 W Olive Ave, #1400, Burbank, CA 91505, USA
Greenbush, Sidney Robin *Actress*
%Gold Marshak Liedtke, 3500 W Olive Ave, #1400, Burbank, CA 91505, USA
Greene, Brian *Physicist, Mathematician*
%Columbia University, Physics Dept, New York, NY 10027, USA
Greene, Charles E (Charlie) *Track Athlete*
5650 Hickory Crest Road, Lincoln, NE 68516, USA
Greene, Ellen *Actress, Singer*
%Innovative Artists, 1505 10th St, Santa Monica, CA 90401, USA
Greene, Graham *Actor*
%Susan Smith, 121A N San Vicente Blvd, Beverly Hills, CA 90211, USA
Greene, Jack *Singer*
%Ace Productions, PO Box 428, Portland, TN 37148, USA
Greene, Jack P *Historian*
1974 Division Road, East Greenwich, RI 02818, USA
Greene, Joseph E (Mean Joe) *Football Player, Coach*
3380 S Horizon Place, Chandler, AZ 85248, USA
Greene, Leonard M *Inventor (Airplane Stall Warning Device)*
6 Hickory Road, Scarsdale, NY 10583, USA
Greene, Maurice *Track Athlete*
%HSI Sports Mgmt, 2600 Michelson Dr, #680, Irvine, CA 92612, USA
Greene, Michele *Actress, Singer*
PO Box 29117, Los Angeles, CA 90029, USA
Greene, Robert B (Bob), Jr *Columnist*
%Chicago Tribune, Editorial Dept, 435 N Michigan Ave, Chicago, IL 60611, USA
Greene, Shecky *Actor, Comedian*
1642 S La Verne Way, Palm Springs, CA 92264, USA

Greene, Tony *Football Player*
%Southeast Recyling, 9001 Brookville Road, Silver Spring, MD 20910, USA
Greene-Mercier, Marie Z *Sculptor*
1232 E 57th St, Chicago, IL 60637, USA
Greenfield, James L *Journalist*
470 Park Ave, #9A, New York, NY 10022, USA
Greenfield, Jeff *Commentator*
%Cable News Network, News Dept, 820 1st St NE, Washington, DC 20002, USA
Greengard, Paul *Nobel Medicine Laureate*
362 E 69th St, New York, NY 10021, USA
Greenhouse, Linda *Journalist*
%New York Times, Editorial Dept, 229 W 43rd St, New York, NY 10036, USA
Greenlee, David *Actor*
1811 N Whitley Ave, #800, Los Angeles, CA 90028, USA
Greenspan, Alan *Financier, Government Official*
%Federal Reserve Board, 20th St & Constitution Ave NW, Washington, DC 20551, USA
Greenspan, Bud *Producer, Director*
118 E 57th St, New York, NY 10022, USA
Greenspoon, Jimmy *Organist (Three Dog Night)*
%McKenzie Accountancy, 5171 Caliente St, #134, Las Vegas, NV 89119, USA
Greenville, Georgina *Model*
%Next Model Mgmt, 188 Rue de Rivoli, 75001 Paris, France
Greenwald, Milton *Paleontologist*
%University of California, Museum of Paleontology, Berkeley, CA 94720, USA
Greenwalt, T Jack *Medical Administrator*
2444 Madison Road, #1501, Cincinnati, OH 45208, USA
Greenwell, Michael L (Mike) *Baseball Player*
%Family Fun Park, 35 NE Pine Island Road, Cape Coral, FL 33909, USA
Greenwich, Ellie *Singer*
203 SW 3rd Ave, Gainesville, FL 32601, USA
Greenwood, Bruce *Actor*
1465 Lindacrest Dr, Beverly Hills, CA 90210, USA
Greenwood, Colin *Bassist (Radiohead)*
%Nasty Little Man, 72 Spring St, #1100, New York, NY 10012, USA
Greenwood, Jonny *Guitarist (Radiohead)*
%Nasty Little Man, 72 Spring St, #1100, New York, NY 10012, USA
Greenwood, L C H (L C) *Football Player*
329 S Dallas Ave, Pittsburgh, PA 15208, USA
Greenwood, Lee *Singer, Songwriter*
%Lee Greenwood Inc, 1025 16th Ave S, #301, Nashville, TN 37212, USA
Greenwood, Norman *Chemist*
%University of Leeds, Chemistry Dept, Leeds LS2 9JT, England
Greer, Dabbs *Actor*
284 S Madison Ave, #102, Pasadena, CA 91101, USA
Greer, David S *Internist*
%Brown University, PO Box G, Providence, RI 02912, USA
Greer, Germaine *Writer, Feminist*
%Atkin & Stone, 29 Fernshaw Road, London SW10 0TG, England
Greer, Gordon G *Editor*
%Better Homes & Gardens Magazine, 1716 Locust St, Des Moines, IA 50309, USA
Greer, Harold E (Hal) *Basketball Player*
7900 E Princess Dr, #1021, Scottsdale, AZ 85255, USA
Greer, Howard E *Navy Admiral*
8539 Prestwick Dr, La Jolla, CA 92037, USA
Greer, Judy *Actress*
%Creative Artists Agency, 9830 Wilshire Blvd, Beverly Hills, CA 90212, USA
Greevy, Bernadette *Concert Singer*
Melrose, 672 Howth Road, Dublin 5, Ireland
Gregg, A Forrest *Football Player, Coach, Administrator*
2985 Plaza Azul, Santa Fe, NM 87507, USA
Gregg, Clark *Actor*
%United Talent Agency, 9560 Wilshire Blvd, #500, Beverly Hills, CA 90212, USA
Gregg, Eric E *Baseball Umpire*
34 S Merion Ave, Bryn Mawr, PA 19010, USA
Gregg, Ricky Lynn *Singer*
%ER Rimes Mgmt, 1103 Bell Grimes Lane, Nashville, TN 37207, USA
Gregg, Stephen R *WW II Army Hero (CMH)*
130 Lexington Ave, Bayonne, NJ 07002, USA
Gregorian, Vartan *Educator*
%Carnegie Corp, President's Office, 437 Madison Ave, New York, NY 10022, USA
Gregorio, Rose *Actress*
%Don Buchwald, 6500 Wilshire Blvd, #2200, Los Angeles, CA 90048, USA
Gregorios, Metropolitan Paulos M *Religious Leader*
%Orthodox Seminary, PO Box 98, Kottayam, Kerala 686001, India
Gregory, Bettina L *Commentator*
%ABC-TV, News Dept, 5010 Creston St, Hyattsville, MD 20781, USA
Gregory, Cynthia *Ballet Dancer*
%American Ballet Theatre, 890 Broadway, New York, NY 10003, USA

G

Gregory, Dick *Actor, Comedian, Social Activist*
%Dick Gregory Health Enterprises, PO Box 3270, Plymouth, MA 02361, USA
Gregory, Frederick D *Astronaut*
506 Tulip Road, Annapolis, MD 21403, USA
Gregory, Jack, Jr *Football Player*
30098 Chapel Grove Road, Okolona, MS 38860, USA
Gregory, Kathy *Cartoonist*
%Playboy Magazine, Reader Services, 680 N Lake Shore Dr, Chicago, IL 60611, USA
Gregory, Mary *Actress*
%Lovell Assoc, 7095 Hollywood Blvd, #1006, Los Angeles, CA 90028, USA
Gregory, Nick *Actor*
%Writers & Artists, 8383 Wilshire Blvd, #550, Beverly Hills, CA 90211, USA
Gregory, Richard *Religious Leader*
%Independent Fundamental Churches, 2684 Meadow Ridge, Byron Center, MI 49315, USA
Gregory, Stephen *Actor*
%Carey, 64 Thornton Ave, London W4 1QQ, England
Gregory, William G *Astronaut*
2027 E Freeport Lane, Gilbert, AZ 85234, USA
Gregory, William H *Editor*
%Aviation Week Magazine, 1221 Ave of Americas, New York, NY 10020, USA
Gregory, Wilton D *Religious Leader*
%Illinois Diocese, Chancery Office, 222 S 3rd St, Belleville, IL 62220, USA
Gregson Wagner, Natasha *Actress*
%Writers & Artists, 8383 Wilshire Blvd, #550, Beverly Hills, CA 90211, USA
Gregson, Wallace C *Marine Corps General*
Commanding General, III Expeditionary Force Okinawa, FPO, AP 96602, USA
Gregson-Williams, Harry *Composer*
%Gorfaine/Schwartz, 13245 Riverside Dr, #450, Sherman Oaks, CA 91423, USA
Grehl, Michael *Editor*
%Memphis Commercial Appeal, Editorial Dept, 495 Union Ave, Memphis, TN 38103, USA
Greif, Michael *Theater Director*
%La Jolla Playhouse, PO Box 12039, La Jolla, CA 92039, USA
Greiner, William R *Educator*
%State University of New York, President's Office, Buffalo, NY 14221, USA
Greist, Kim *Actress*
%Innovative Artists, 1505 10th St, Santa Monica, CA 90401, USA
Grenier, Adrian *Actor*
1610 Broadway, Santa Monica, CA 90404, USA
Grentz, Theresa Shank *Basketball Coach*
%University of Illinois, Athletic Dept, Champaign, IL 61820, USA
Gretzky, Wayne D *Hockey Player*
%Goldman Grant Tani, 9100 Wilshire Blvd, #1000W, Beverly Hills, CA 90212, USA
Grevey, Kevin *Basketball Player*
528 River Bend Road, Great Falls, VA 22066, USA
Grey, Beryl E *Ballerina*
Fernhill, Priory Road, Forest Row, East Sussex RH18 5JE, England
Grey, Jennifer *Actress*
%Jason Weinberg Mgmt, 122 E 25th St, #124, New York, NY 10010, USA
Grey, Joel *Actor*
%Park Ave Talent Network, 404 Park Ave S, #1000, New York, NY 10016, USA
Grey, Virginia *Actress*
15101 Magnolia Blvd, #54, Sherman Oaks, CA 91403, USA
Grich, Robert A (Bobby) *Baseball Player*
31 Madison Lane, Coto de Caza, CA 92679, USA
Grieco, Richard *Actor*
%CR&G Enterprises, 95 Public Square, #304, Watertown, NY 13601, USA
Grieder, William *Journalist*
%Simon & Schuster, 1230 Ave of Americas, New York, NY 10020, USA
Griem, Helmut *Actor*
%Mgmt Erna Baumbauer, Keplerstr 2, 81679 Munich, Germany
Grier, David Alan *Actor, Comedian*
%Endeavor Talent Agency, 9701 Wilshire Blvd, #1000, Beverly Hills, CA 90212, USA
Grier, Herbert E *Electrical Engineer*
9648 Blackgold Road, La Jolla, CA 92037, USA
Grier, Pam *Actress*
PO Box 370958, Denver, CO 80237, USA
Grier, Roosevelt (Rosey) *Football Player, Actor*
1250 4th St, #600, Santa Monica, CA 90401, USA
Griese, Brian *Football Player*
%Miami Dolphins, 7500 SW 30th St, Davie, FL 33314, USA
Griese, Robert A (Bob) *Football Player, Sportscaster*
3195 Ponce de Leon Blvd, #412, Coral Gables, FL 33134, USA
Griesemer, John N *Government Official*
RR 2 Box 204B, Springfield, MO 65802, USA
Grieve, Pierson M *Businessman*
%Ecolab Inc, Ecolab Center, 370 Wabasha St N, Saint Paul, MN 55102, USA
Griffey, G Kenneth (Ken) *Baseball Player*
24606 SE Old Black Nugget Road, Issaquah, WA 98029, USA

G

Griffey - Grimm

Griffey, G Kenneth (Ken), Jr *Baseball Player*
9935 Lake Louise Dr, Windemere, FL 34786, USA
Griffin, Adrian *Basketball Player*
%Dallas Mavericks, 2909 Taylor St, Dallas, TX 75226, USA
Griffin, Archie M *Football Player*
6845 Temperance Point Place, Westerville, OH 43082, USA
Griffin, Donald R *Biologist*
Brookhaven, 1010 Waltham St, #A212, Lexington, MA 02421, USA
Griffin, Eddie *Actor, Comedian*
%Brillstein/Grey, 9150 Wilshire Blvd, #350, Beverly Hills, CA 90212, USA
Griffin, Eddie *Basketball Player*
%Houston Rockets, Toyota Center, 2 E Greenway Plaza, Houston, TX 77046, USA
Griffin, Eric *Boxer*
PO Box 964, Jasper, TN 37347, USA
Griffin, James Bennett *Anthropologist*
5023 Wyandot Court, Bethesda, MD 20816, USA
Griffin, Johnny *Jazz Saxophonist*
%Joel Chriss, 300 Mercer St, #3J, New York, NY 10003, USA
Griffin, Kathy *Actress*
%United Talent Agency, 9560 Wilshire Blvd, #500, Beverly Hills, CA 90212, USA
Griffin, Merv E *Entertainer*
%Merv Griffin Enterprises, 9860 Wilshire Blvd, Beverly Hills, CA 90210, USA
Griffin, Patty *Singer, Songwriter, Guitarist*
%Monterey Peninsula Artists, 509 Hartnell St, Monterey, CA 93940, USA
Griffin, Robert P *Senator, MI; Judge*
%Michigan Supreme Court, PO Box 30052, Lansing, MI 48909, USA
Griffin, Thomas N, Jr *Army General*
9749 S Park Circle, Fairfax Station, VA 22039, USA
Griffith, Alan R *Financier*
%Bank of New York, 1 Wall St, New York, NY 10286, USA
Griffith, Andy *Actor, Singer*
%Sony Records, 2100 Colorado Ave, Santa Monica, CA 90404, USA
Griffith, Bill *Cartoonist (Zippy the Pinhead)*
%Pinhead Productions, PO Box 88, Hadlyme, CT 06439, USA
Griffith, Darrell *Basketball Player*
1300 Leighton Circle, Louisville, KY 40222, USA
Griffith, Emile A *Boxer*
150 Washington St, #6J, Hempstead, NY 11550, USA
Griffith, James *Businessman*
%Timken Co, 1835 Dueber Ave SW, Canton, OH 44706, USA
Griffith, Melanie *Actress, Model*
%Elliot Mintz, 2934 Beverly Glen Circle, #412, Los Angeles, CA 90077, USA
Griffith, Nanci *Singer, Songwriter*
%Gold Mountain, 2 Music Circle S, #212, Nashville, TN 37203, USA
Griffith, Robert *Football Player*
%Cleveland Browns, 76 Lou Groza Blvd, Berea, OH 44017, USA
Griffith, Thomas Ian *Actor*
%Endeavor Talent Agency, 9701 Wilshire Blvd, #1000, Beverly Hills, CA 90212, USA
Griffith, Tom W *Labor Leader*
%Rural Letter Carriers Assn, 1448 Duke St, #100, Alexandria, VA 22314, USA
Griffith, Yolanda *Basketball Player*
%Sacramento Monarchs, Arco Arena, 1 Sports Parkway, Sacramento, CA 95834, USA
Griffiths, Phillip A *Mathematician*
%Advanced Study Institute, Director's Office, Olden Lane, Princeton, NJ 08540, USA
Griffiths, Rachel *Actress*
%United Talent Agency, 9560 Wilshire Blvd, #500, Beverly Hills, CA 90212, USA
Griggs, Andy *Singer*
PO Box 120835, Nashville, TN 37212, USA
Grijalva, Victor E *Businessman*
%Schlumberger Ltd, 277 Park Ave, New York, NY 10172, USA
Grill, Rob *Singer, Bassist (Grass Roots)*
%Paradise Artists, 108 E Matilija St, Ojai, CA 93023, USA
Grim, Robert (Bob) *Football Player*
18 NW Saginaw Ave, Bend, OR 97701, USA
Grimaud, Helene *Concert Pianist*
%I C M Artists, 40 W 57th St, New York, NY 10019, USA
Grimes, Martha *Writer*
115 D St SE, #G-6, Washington, DC 20003, USA
Grimes, Scott *Actor*
12019 Moccasin Court, Orlando, FL 32828, USA
Grimes, Tammy *Actress, Singer*
%Don Buchwald, 10 E 44th St, New York, NY 10017, USA
Griminelli, Andrea *Concert Flutist*
%Columbia Artists Mgmt Inc, 165 W 57th St, New York, NY 10019, USA
Grimm, Russ *Football Player, Coach*
12177 Hickory Knoll Place, Fairfax, VA 22033, USA
Grimm, Tim *Actor*
%Abrams Artists, 9200 Sunset Blvd, #1125, Los Angeles, CA 90069, USA

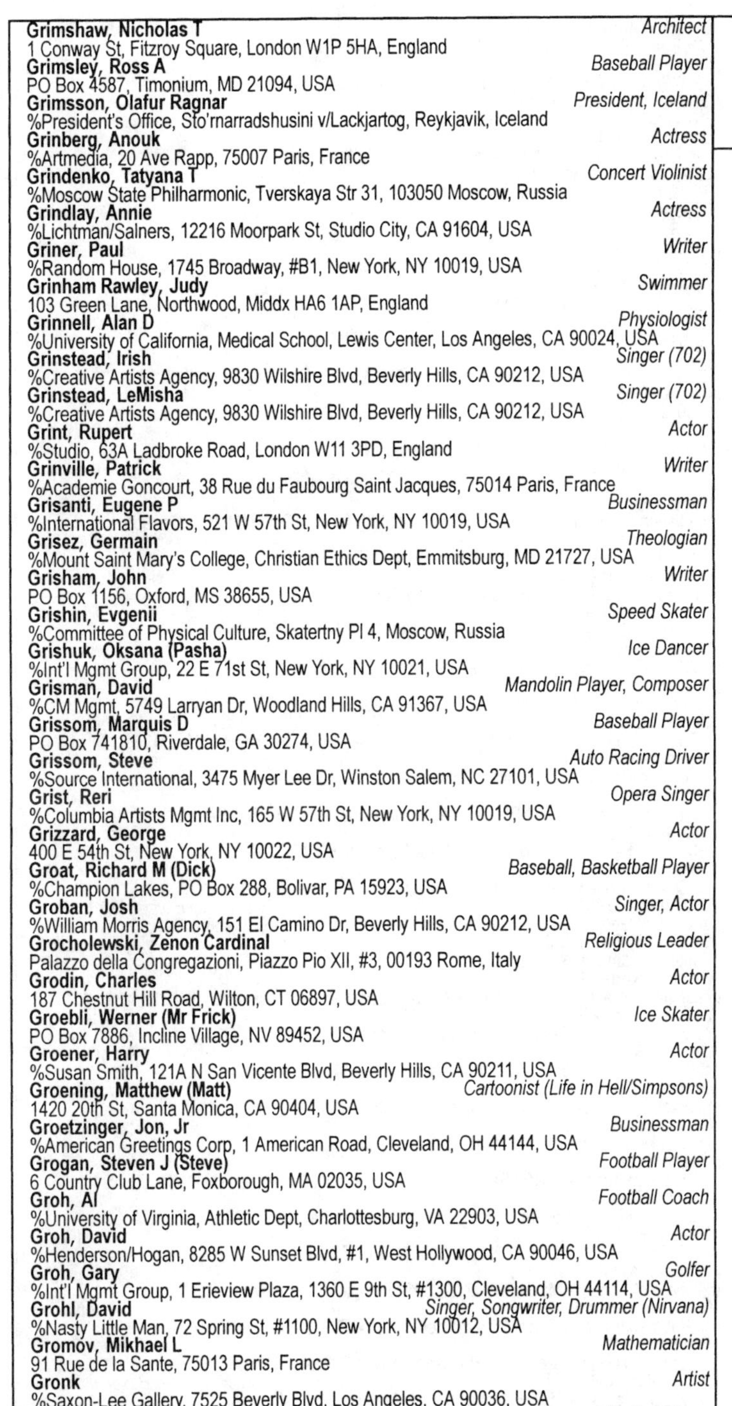

Grimshaw, Nicholas T *Architect*
1 Conway St, Fitzroy Square, London W1P 5HA, England
Grimsley, Ross A *Baseball Player*
PO Box 4587, Timonium, MD 21094, USA
Grimsson, Olafur Ragnar *President, Iceland*
%President's Office, Sto'rnarradshusini v/Lackjartog, Reykjavik, Iceland
Grinberg, Anouk *Actress*
%Artmedia, 20 Ave Rapp, 75007 Paris, France
Grindenko, Tatyana T *Concert Violinist*
%Moscow State Philharmonic, Tverskaya Str 31, 103050 Moscow, Russia
Grindlay, Annie *Actress*
%Lichtman/Salners, 12216 Moorpark St, Studio City, CA 91604, USA
Griner, Paul *Writer*
%Random House, 1745 Broadway, #B1, New York, NY 10019, USA
Grinham Rawley, Judy *Swimmer*
103 Green Lane, Northwood, Middx HA6 1AP, England
Grinnell, Alan D *Physiologist*
%University of California, Medical School, Lewis Center, Los Angeles, CA 90024, USA
Grinstead, Irish *Singer (702)*
%Creative Artists Agency, 9830 Wilshire Blvd, Beverly Hills, CA 90212, USA
Grinstead, LeMisha *Singer (702)*
%Creative Artists Agency, 9830 Wilshire Blvd, Beverly Hills, CA 90212, USA
Grint, Rupert *Actor*
%Studio, 63A Ladbroke Road, London W11 3PD, England
Grinville, Patrick *Writer*
%Academie Goncourt, 38 Rue du Faubourg Saint Jacques, 75014 Paris, France
Grisanti, Eugene P *Businessman*
%International Flavors, 521 W 57th St, New York, NY 10019, USA
Grisez, Germain *Theologian*
%Mount Saint Mary's College, Christian Ethics Dept, Emmitsburg, MD 21727, USA
Grisham, John *Writer*
PO Box 1156, Oxford, MS 38655, USA
Grishin, Evgenii *Speed Skater*
%Committee of Physical Culture, Skatertny Pl 4, Moscow, Russia
Grishuk, Oksana (Pasha) *Ice Dancer*
%Int'l Mgmt Group, 22 E 71st St, New York, NY 10021, USA
Grisman, David *Mandolin Player, Composer*
%CM Mgmt, 5749 Larryan Dr, Woodland Hills, CA 91367, USA
Grissom, Marquis D *Baseball Player*
PO Box 741810, Riverdale, GA 30274, USA
Grissom, Steve *Auto Racing Driver*
%Source International, 3475 Myer Lee Dr, Winston Salem, NC 27101, USA
Grist, Reri *Opera Singer*
%Columbia Artists Mgmt Inc, 165 W 57th St, New York, NY 10019, USA
Grizzard, George *Actor*
400 E 54th St, New York, NY 10022, USA
Groat, Richard M (Dick) *Baseball, Basketball Player*
%Champion Lakes, PO Box 288, Bolivar, PA 15923, USA
Groban, Josh *Singer, Actor*
%William Morris Agency, 151 El Camino Dr, Beverly Hills, CA 90212, USA
Grocholewski, Zenon Cardinal *Religious Leader*
Palazzo della Congregazioni, Piazzo Pio XII, #3, 00193 Rome, Italy
Grodin, Charles *Actor*
187 Chestnut Hill Road, Wilton, CT 06897, USA
Groebli, Werner (Mr Frick) *Ice Skater*
PO Box 7886, Incline Village, NV 89452, USA
Groener, Harry *Actor*
%Susan Smith, 121A N San Vicente Blvd, Beverly Hills, CA 90211, USA
Groening, Matthew (Matt) *Cartoonist (Life in Hell/Simpsons)*
1420 20th St, Santa Monica, CA 90404, USA
Groetzinger, Jon, Jr *Businessman*
%American Greetings Corp, 1 American Road, Cleveland, OH 44144, USA
Grogan, Steven J (Steve) *Football Player*
6 Country Club Lane, Foxborough, MA 02035, USA
Groh, Al *Football Coach*
%University of Virginia, Athletic Dept, Charlottesburg, VA 22903, USA
Groh, David *Actor*
%Henderson/Hogan, 8285 W Sunset Blvd, #1, West Hollywood, CA 90046, USA
Groh, Gary *Golfer*
%Int'l Mgmt Group, 1 Erieview Plaza, 1360 E 9th St, #1300, Cleveland, OH 44114, USA
Grohl, David *Singer, Songwriter, Drummer (Nirvana)*
%Nasty Little Man, 72 Spring St, #1100, New York, NY 10012, USA
Gromov, Mikhael L *Mathematician*
91 Rue de la Sante, 75013 Paris, France
Gronk *Artist*
%Saxon-Lee Gallery, 7525 Beverly Blvd, Los Angeles, CA 90036, USA
Gronman, Tuomas *Hockey Player*
%Pittsburgh Penguins, Mellon Arena, 66 Mario Lemieux Place, Pittsburgh, PA 15219, USA

G

Groom, Jerome P (Jerry) *Football Player*
625 Beach Road, #201, Sarasota, FL 34242, USA
Groom, Sam *Actor*
8730 Sunset Blvd, #440, Los Angeles, CA 90069, USA
Grooms, Charles R (Red) *Artist*
85 Walker St, New York, NY 10013, USA
Gropp, Louis Oliver *Editor*
140 Riverside Dr, #6G, New York, NY 10024, USA
Gros Louis, Kenneth R R *Educator*
%Indiana University, President's Office, Bloomington, IN 47405, USA
Gros, Francois *Biochemist*
102 Rue de la Tour, 75116 Paris, France
Grosbard, Ulu *Movie Director*
29 W 10th St, New York, NY 10011, USA
Gross, Charles G *Psychologist*
45 Woodside Lane, Princeton, NJ 08540, USA
Gross, Henry *Guitarist (Sha-Na-Na)*
%Zelda Mgmt, PO Box 150163, Nashville, TN 37215, USA
Gross, Jordan *Football Player*
%Carolina Panthers, Ericsson Stadium, 800 S Mint St, Charlotte, NC 28202, USA
Gross, Mary *Actress, Comedienne*
9100 Sunset Blvd, #300, Los Angeles, CA 90069, USA
Gross, Michael *Swimmer*
Paul-Ehrlich-Str 6, 60596 Frankfurt/Main, Germany
Gross, Michael *Actor*
4431 Woodleigh Lane, La Canada Flintridge, CA 91011, USA
Gross, Paul *Actor*
%Alliance Communications, 121 Bloor E, #1400, Toronto ON M4M 3M5, Canada
Gross, Ricco *Biathlete*
Waldbahnstr 34A, 83324 Ruhpolding, Germany
Gross, Robert (Bob) *Basketball Player*
13466 SE Red Rose Lane, Portland, OR 97236, USA
Gross, Robert A *Physicist*
14 Sunnyside Way, New Rochelle, NY 10804, USA
Gross, Terry R *Commentator*
%WHYY-Radio, News Dept, Independence Mall W, Philadelphia, PA 19104, USA
Grosscup, Lee *Football Player*
330 Westline Dr, #B227, Alameda, CA 94501, USA
Grossfeld, Stanley *Photojournalist*
%Boston Globe, Editorial Dept, 135 W T Morrissey Blvd, Dorchester, MA 02125, USA
Grossman, Allen R *Writer*
100 W University Parkway, #8A, Baltimore, MD 21210, USA
Grossman, Judith *Writer*
%Warren Wilson College, English Dept, Swannanoa, NC 28778, USA
Grossman, Rex *Football Player*
%Chicago Bears, 1000 Football Dr, Lake Forest, IL 60045, USA
Grossman, Robert *Illustrator*
19 Crosby St, New York, NY 10013, USA
Grosvenor, Gilbert M *Foundation Executive, Publisher*
%National Geographic Society, 17th & M NW, Washington, DC 20036, USA
Grotenfelt, Georg E J *Architect*
Kapteeninkatu 20D, 00140 Helsinki, Finland
Grouch, Roger K *Astronaut*
%Life/Microgravity Sciences Office, NASA Headquarters, Washington, DC 20546, USA
Grove, Andrew S *Businessman*
%Intel Corp, 2200 Mission College Blvd, Santa Clara, CA 95054, USA
Groves, Richard H *Army General*
400 Madison St, #1302, Alexandria, VA 22314, USA
Growney, Robert L *Businessman*
%Motorola Inc, 1303 E Schaumburg, IL 60196, USA
Groza, Louis R (Lou) *Football Player*
287 Parkway Dr, Berea, OH 44017, USA
Grubbs, Gary *Actor*
%Paradigm Agency, 10100 Santa Monica Blvd, #2500, Los Angeles, CA 90067, USA
Grubbs, Robert H *Chemist*
%California Institute of Technology, Chemistry Dept, Pasadena, CA 91125, USA
Gruber, Kelly W *Baseball Player*
3300 Bee Cave Road, #650-227, Austin, TX 78746, USA
Gruberova, Edita *Opera Singer*
%Opera et Concert, Maximilianstr 22, 80539 Munich, Germany
Grubman, Allen J *Attorney*
%Grubman Indursky Schindler Goldstein, 152 W 57th St, New York, NY 10019, USA
Gruden, Jon *Football Coach*
%Tampa Bay Buccaneers, 1 W Buccaneer Place, Tampa, FL 33607, USA
Grudzielanek, Mark J *Baseball Player*
%Tom Grudzielanek, 550 E Mona Dr, Oak Creek, WI 53154, USA
Gruenberg, Erich *Concert Violinist*
80 Northway, Hampstead Garden Suburb, London NW11 6PA, England

Gruffudd, Ioan *Actor*
%Hamilton Hodell, 24 Hanway St, London W1T 1UH, England
Grum, Clifford J *Businessman*
%Temple-Inland Inc, 303 S Temple Dr, Diboll, TX 75941, USA
Grumman, Cornelia *Journalist*
%Chicago Tribune, Editorial Dept, 435 N Michigan Ave, Chicago, IL 60611, USA
Grummer, Elisabeth *Opera Singer*
Am Schlachtensee 104, 14163 Berlin, Germany
Grunberg, Greg *Actor*
%Greene Assoc, 7080 Hollywood Blvd, #1017, Los Angeles, CA 90028, USA
Grunberg-Manago, Marianne *Biochemist*
80 Boulevard Pasteur, 75015 Paris, France
Grundfest, Joseph A *Government Official*
%Stanford University, Law School, Stanford, CA 94305, USA
Grundhofer, Jerry A *Financier*
%Firstar Corp, 777 E Wisconsin Ave, Milwaukee, WI 53202, USA
Grundhofer, John F *Financier*
%US Bancorp, US Bank Place, 601 2nd Ave S, Minneapolis, MN 55402, USA
Grundy, Hugh *Drummer (Zombies)*
%Lustig Talent, PO Box 770850, Orlando, FL 32877, USA
Grune, George V *Publisher, Foundation Executive*
PO Box 2348, Ponte Vedra Beach, FL 32004, USA
Grunfeld, Ernie *Basketball Player, Executive*
1950 W Dean Road, Milwaukee, WI 53217, USA
Grunsfeld, John M *Astronaut*
4202 Lake Grove Dr, Seabrook, TX 77586, USA
Grunwald, Henry A *Editor, Diplomat*
654 Madison Ave, #1605, New York, NY 10021, USA
Grushin, Pyotr D *Aviation Engineer*
%Academy of Sciences, 14 Lenisky Prospekt, Moscow, Russia
Grusin, Dave *Composer, Pianist*
%Monterey International, 200 W Superior, #202, Chicago, IL 60610, USA
Grutman, N Roy *Attorney*
%Grutman Miller Greenspoon Hendler, 505 Park Ave, New York, NY 10022, USA
Guadagnino, Kathy Baker *Golfer*
%Int'l Mgmt Group, 1 Erieview Plaza, 1360 E 9th St, #1300, Cleveland, OH 44114, USA
Guardado, Edward A (Eddie) *Baseball Player*
10715 Plumas Way, Tustin, CA 92782, USA
Guardino, Harry *Actor*
2949 E Via Vaquero Road, Palm Springs, CA 92262, USA
Guare, John *Writer*
%R Andrew Boose, 1 Dag Hammarskjold Plaza, New York, NY 10017, USA
Guarrera, Frank *Concert, Opera Singer*
4514 Latona Ave NE, Seattle, WA 98105, USA
Gubaidulina, Sofia A *Composer*
2D Pugachevskaya 8, Korp 5, #130, 107061 Moscow, Russia
Gubarev, Aleksei A *Cosmonaut; Air Force General*
%Potchta Kosmonavtov, Moskovskoi Oblasti, 141160 Syvisdny Goroduk, Russia
Guber, Peter *Movie Producer*
%Mandaly Entertainment, 10202 W Washington Blvd, #1070, Culver City, CA 90232, USA
Gubert, Walter A *Financier*
%J P Morgan Chase, 270 Park Ave, New York, NY 10017, USA
Guccione, Robert (Bob) *Publisher*
11 Penn Plaza, #1200, New York, NY 10001, USA
Guckel, Henry *Microbiotics Engineer*
%University of Wisconsin, Engineering Dept, Madison, WI 53706, USA
Guelleh, Ismail Omar *President, Djibouti*
%President's Office, 8-10 Ahmed Nessim St, Djibouti, Djibouti
Guennel, Joe *Soccer*
835 Front Range Road, Littleton, CO 80120, USA
Guenther, Johnny *Bowler*
23826 115th Place W, Woodway, WA 98020, USA
Guerard, Michel E *Chef*
Les Pres d'Eugenie, 40320 Eugenie les Bains, France
Guerin, Bill *Hockey Player*
39 W Colonial Road, Wibraham, MA 01905, USA
Guerin, Richie *Basketball Player*
1355 Bear Island Dr, West Palm Beach, FL 33409, USA
Guerra, Saverio *Actor*
%Writers & Artists, 8383 Wilshire Blvd, #550, Beverly Hills, CA 90211, USA
Guerrero Coles, Lisa *Sportscaster, Actress*
%ABC-TV, Sports Dept, 77 W 66th St, New York, NY 10023, USA
Guerrero, Julen *Soccer Player*
%AC Bilbao, Alameda Mazarredo 23, 48009 Bilbao, Spain
Guerrero, Pedro *Baseball Player*
4004 Saint Andrews Dr SE, Rio Rancho, NM 87124, USA
Guerrero, Roberto *Auto Racing Driver*
31642 Via Cervantes, San Juan Capistrano, CA 92675, USA

G

Guerrero, Vladimir *Baseball Player*
%Montreal Expos, Olympic Stadium, Montreal QC H1V 3N7, Canada
Guest, Christopher H *Movie Director, Actor*
%Creative Artists Agency, 9830 Wilshire Blvd, Beverly Hills, CA 90212, USA
Guest, Cornelia *Model*
1419 Donhill Dr, Beverly Hills, CA 90210, USA
Guest, Douglas *Concert Organist*
Gables, Minchinhampton, Gloscester GL6 9JE, England
Guest, Lance *Actor*
%Badgley Connor Talent, 9229 Sunset Blvd, #311, Los Angeles, CA 90069, USA
Guetary, Francois *Actor*
%Cineart, 36 Rue de Ponthieu, 75008 Paris, France
Guffey, John W, Jr *Businessman*
%Coltec Industries, 2550 W Tyvola Road, Charlotte, NC 28217, USA
Gugelmin, Mauricio *Auto Racing Driver*
%PacWest Racing Group, PO Box 1607, Bellevue, WA 98009, USA
Guggenheim, Alan *Inventor (Hydrogen Energy Processor)*
%Northwest Power Systems, PO Box 5339, Bend, OR 97708, USA
Gugino, Carla *Actress*
%Three Arts Entertainment, 9460 Wilshire Blvd, #700, Beverly Hills, CA 90212, USA
Guglielmi, Ralph *Football Player*
8501 White Pass Court, Potomac, MD 20854, USA
Gugliotta, Tom *Basketball Player*
27 W Sierra Vista Dr, Phoenix, AZ 85013, USA
Guice, Jackson *Cartoonist*
%DC Comics, 1700 Broadway, New York, NY 10019, USA
Guida, Lou *Harness Racing Breeder*
4800 N Highway A1A, #505, Vero Beach, FL 32963, USA
Guidelli, Giovanni *Actor*
%Carol Levi Co, Via Giuseppe Pisanelli, 00196 Rome, Italy
Guidoni, Umberto *Astronaut*
15010 Cobre Valley Dr, Houston, TX 77062, USA
Guidry, N T *Aeronautical Engineer*
23971 Coral Springs Lane, Tehachapi, CA 93561, USA
Guidry, Ronald A (Ron) *Baseball Player*
PO Box 278, Scott, LA 70583, USA
Guilbert, Ann *Actress*
550 Erskine Dr, Pacific Palisades, CA 90272, USA
Guilfoyle, Paul *Actor*
%S M S Talent, 8730 Sunset Blvd, #440, Los Angeles, CA 90069, USA
Guillaume, Robert *Actor*
4709 Noeline Ave, Encino, CA 91436, USA
Guillem, Sylvie *Ballerina*
%Royal Ballet, Covent Garden, Bow St, London WC2E 9DD, England
Guillemin, Roger C L *Nobel Medicine Laureate*
7316 Encelia Ave, La Jolla, CA 92037, USA
Guillen, Oswaldo J (Ozzie) *Baseball Player, Manager*
21218 Saint Andrews Blvd, #305, Boca Raton, FL 33433, USA
Guillerman, John *Movie Director*
309 S Rockingham Ave, Los Angeles, CA 90049, USA
Guillo, Dominque *Actor*
%Cineart, 36 Rue de Ponthieu, 75008 Paris, France
Guindon, Richard G *Cartoonist (Guindon)*
321 W Lafayette Blvd, Detroit, MI 48226, USA
Guinee, Tim *Actor*
%Lighthouse, 409 N Camden Dr, #202, Beverly Hills, CA 90210, USA
Guinier, Lani *Attorney, Educator*
%University of Pennsylvania, Law School, 3400 Chestnut, Philadelphia, PA 19104, USA
Guisewite, Cathy L *Cartoonist (Cathy)*
4039 Camilla Ave, Studio City, CA 91604, USA
Gujral, Inder Kumar *Prime Minister, India*
5 Janpath, New Delhi 11011, India
Gulager, Clu *Actor*
%Clu Gulager Acting, 320 Wilshire Blvd, Santa Monica, CA 90401, USA
Gulbinowicx, Henryk Roman Cardinal *Religious Leader*
%Metropolita Wroclawski, Ul Katedraina 11, 50-328 Wroclaw, Poland
Guleghina, Maria *Opera Singer*
%Askonas Holt Ltd, 27 Chancery Lane, London WC2A 1PF, England
Gullett, Donald E (Don) *Baseball Player*
RR 1 Box 615N, South Shore, KY 41175, USA
Gulli, Franco *Concert Violinist*
%Columbia Artists Mgmt Inc, 165 W 57th St, New York, NY 10019, USA
Gullickson, William L (Bill) *Baseball Player*
3 Banchory Court, Palm Beach Gardens, FL 33418, USA
Gullit, Ruud *Soccer Player*
%FC Chelsea, Stamford Bridge, Fulham Road, London SW6 1HS, England
Gulliver, Harold *Editor*
%Atlanta Constitution, Editorial Dept, 72 Marieta St NW, Atlanta, GA 30303, USA

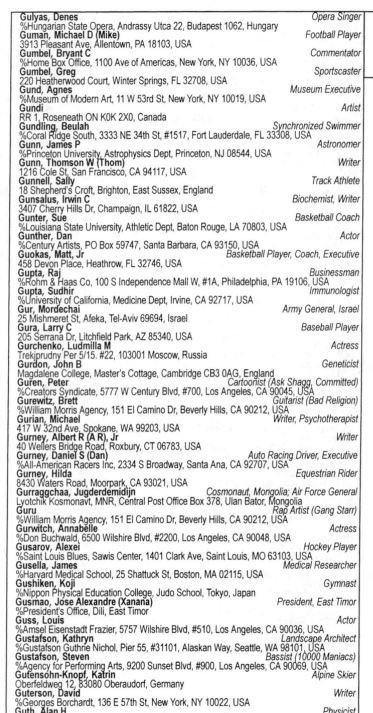

Gulyas, Denes *Opera Singer*
%Hungarian State Opera, Andrassy Utca 22, Budapest 1062, Hungary
Guman, Michael D (Mike) *Football Player*
3913 Pleasant Ave, Allentown, PA 18103, USA
Gumbel, Bryant C *Commentator*
%Home Box Office, 1100 Ave of Americas, New York, NY 10036, USA
Gumbel, Greg *Sportscaster*
220 Heatherwood Court, Winter Springs, FL 32708, USA
Gund, Agnes *Museum Executive*
%Museum of Modern Art, 11 W 53rd St, New York, NY 10019, USA
Gundi *Artist*
RR 1, Roseneath ON K0K 2X0, Canada
Gundling, Beulah *Synchronized Swimmer*
%Coral Ridge South, 3333 NE 34th St, #1517, Fort Lauderdale, FL 33308, USA
Gunn, James P *Astronomer*
%Princeton University, Astrophysics Dept, Princeton, NJ 08544, USA
Gunn, Thomson W (Thom) *Writer*
1216 Cole St, San Francisco, CA 94117, USA
Gunnell, Sally *Track Athlete*
18 Shepherd's Croft, Brighton, East Sussex, England
Gunsalus, Irwin C *Biochemist, Writer*
3407 Cherry Hills Dr, Champaign, IL 61822, USA
Gunter, Sue *Basketball Coach*
%Louisiana State University, Athletic Dept, Baton Rouge, LA 70803, USA
Gunther, Dan *Actor*
%Century Artists, PO Box 59747, Santa Barbara, CA 93150, USA
Guokas, Matt, Jr *Basketball Player, Coach, Executive*
458 Devon Place, Heathrow, FL 32746, USA
Gupta, Raj *Businessman*
%Rohm & Haas Co, 100 S Independence Mall W, #1A, Philadelphia, PA 19106, USA
Gupta, Sudhir *Immunologist*
%University of California, Medicine Dept, Irvine, CA 92717, USA
Gur, Mordechai *Army General, Israel*
25 Mishmeret St, Afeka, Tel-Aviv 69694, Israel
Gura, Larry C *Baseball Player*
205 Serrana Dr, Litchfield Park, AZ 85340, USA
Gurchenko, Ludmilla M *Actress*
Trekjprudny Per 5/15. #22, 103001 Moscow, Russia
Gurdon, John B *Geneticist*
Magdalene College, Master's Cottage, Cambridge CB3 0AG, England
Guren, Peter *Cartoonist (Ask Shagg, Committed)*
%Creators Syndicate, 5777 W Century Blvd, #700, Los Angeles, CA 90045, USA
Gurewitz, Brett *Guitarist (Bad Religion)*
%William Morris Agency, 151 El Camino Dr, Beverly Hills, CA 90212, USA
Gurian, Michael *Writer, Psychotherapist*
417 W 32nd Ave, Spokane, WA 99203, USA
Gurney, Albert R (A R), Jr *Writer*
40 Wellers Bridge Road, Roxbury, CT 06783, USA
Gurney, Daniel S (Dan) *Auto Racing Driver, Executive*
%All-American Racers Inc, 2334 S Broadway, Santa Ana, CA 92707, USA
Gurney, Hilda *Equestrian Rider*
8430 Waters Road, Moorpark, CA 93021, USA
Gurraggchaa, Jugderdemidijn *Cosmonaut, Mongolia; Air Force General*
Lyotchik Kosmonavt, MNR, Central Post Office Box 378, Ulan Bator, Mongolia
Guru *Rap Artist (Gang Starr)*
%William Morris Agency, 151 El Camino Dr, Beverly Hills, CA 90212, USA
Gurwitch, Annabelle *Actress*
%Don Buchwald, 6500 Wilshire Blvd, #2200, Los Angeles, CA 90048, USA
Gusarov, Alexei *Hockey Player*
%Saint Louis Blues, Sawis Center, 1401 Clark Ave, Saint Louis, MO 63103, USA
Gusella, James *Medical Researcher*
%Harvard Medical School, 25 Shattuck St, Boston, MA 02115, USA
Gushiken, Koji *Gymnast*
%Nippon Physical Education College, Judo School, Tokyo, Japan
Gusmao, Jose Alexandre (Xanana) *President, East Timor*
%President's Office, Dili, East Timor
Guss, Louis *Actor*
%Amsel Eisenstadt Frazier, 5757 Wilshire Blvd, #510, Los Angeles, CA 90036, USA
Gustafson, Kathryn *Landscape Architect*
%Gustafson Guthrie Nichol, Pier 55, #31101, Alaskan Way, Seattle, WA 98101, USA
Gustafson, Steven *Bassist (10000 Maniacs)*
%Agency for Performing Arts, 9200 Sunset Blvd, #900, Los Angeles, CA 90069, USA
Gutensohn-Knopf, Katrin *Alpine Skier*
Oberfeldweg 12, 83080 Oberaudorf, Germany
Guterson, David *Writer*
%Georges Borchardt, 136 E 57th St, New York, NY 10022, USA
Guth, Alan H *Physicist*
%Massachusetts Institute of Technology, Physics Dept, Cambridge, MA 02139, USA

G

Guthe, Manfred *Cinematographer*
122 Collier St, Toronto ON M4W 1M3, Canada
Guthman, Edwin O *Editor*
%Philadelphia Inquirer, Editorial Dept, 400 N Broad St, Philadelphia, PA 19130, USA
Guthrie, Arlo *Singer, Songwriter*
The Farm, Washington, MA 01223, USA
Guthrie, Janet *Auto Racing Driver*
PO Box 505, Aspen, CO 81612, USA
Guthrie, Jennifer *Actress*
%Don Buchwald, 6500 Wilshire Blvd, #2200, Los Angeles, CA 90048, USA
Gutierrez, Carlos M *Businessman*
%Kellogg Co, 1 Kellogg Square, PO Box 3599, Battle Creek, MI 49016, USA
Gutierrez, Gerald A *Theater Director*
%International Creative Mgmt, 40 W 57th St, #1800, New York, NY 10019, USA
Gutierrez, Gustavo *Theologian*
%Instituto Bartolome Las Casas-Rimac, Apartado 3090, Lima 100, Peru
Gutierrez, Horacio *Concert Pianist*
%I C M Artists, 40 W 57th St, New York, NY 10019, USA
Gutierrez, Lucio *President, Ecuador*
%Palacio de Gobierno, Garcia Moreno 1043, Quito, Ecuador
Gutierrez, Sidney M *Astronaut*
324 Sarah Lane NW, Albuquerque, NM 87114, USA
Gutman, Natalia G *Concert Cellist*
%Askonas Holt Ltd, 27 Chancery Lane, London WC2A 1PF, England
Gutman, Roy W *Journalist*
13132 Curved Iron Road, Herndon, VA 20171, USA
Gutsche, Torsten *Canoeing Athlete*
Hans-Marchwitza-Ring 51, 14473 Potsdam, Germany
Guttenberg, Steve *Actor*
15237 Sunset Blvd, #48, Pacific Palisades, CA 90272, USA
Guy, Buddy *Singer, Guitarist*
%Monterey International, 200 W Superior, #202, Chicago, IL 60610, USA
Guy, Francois-Frederic *Concert Pianist*
%Van Walsum Mgmt, 4 Addison Bridge Place, London W14 8XP, England
Guy, Jasmine *Actress*
%Pantich, 21243 Ventura Blvd, #101, Woodland Hills, CA 91364, USA
Guy, W Ray *Football Player*
1389 Wrightsboro Road NW, Thomson, GA 30824, USA
Guy, William L *Governor, ND*
5210 12th St S, #105, Fargo, ND 58104, USA
Guyer, David B *Foundation Executive*
%Save the Children Foundation, 514 2nd St, Owyhee, NV 89832, USA
Guynn, Jack *Government Official, Financier*
%Federal Reserve Bank, 1000 Peachtree St NE, Atlanta, GA 30309, USA
Guyon, John C *Educator*
%Southern Illinois University, President's Office, Carbondale, IL 62901, USA
Guzman, Luis *Actor*
%Gersh Agency, 232 N Canon Dr, Beverly Hills, CA 90210, USA
Guzy, Carol *Photojournalist*
2145 Fort Scott Dr, Arlington, VA 22202, USA
Gwathmey, Charles *Architect*
%Gwathmey Siegel Architects, 475 10th Ave, New York, NY 10018, USA
Gwinn, Mary Ann *Journalist*
%Seattle Times, Editorial Dept, 1120 John St, Seattle, WA 98109, USA
Gwynn, Anthony K (Tony) *Baseball Player, Coach*
15643 Boulder Ridge Lane, Poway, CA 92064, USA
Gwynn, Darrell *Auto Racing Driver*
4850 SW 52nd St, Davie, FL 33314, USA
Gwynne, A Patrick *Architect*
Homewood, Esher, Surrey KT10 9JL, England
Gyanendra *King, Nepal*
%Royal Palace, Narayanhiti, Durbag Marg, Kathmandu, Nepal
Gyll, J Soren *Businessman*
%Volvo AB, 405 08 Goteborg, Sweden
Gyllenhaal, Jake *Actor*
%Creative Artists Agency, 9830 Wilshire Blvd, Beverly Hills, CA 90212, USA
Gyllenhaal, Maggie *Actress*
%Creative Artists Agency, 9830 Wilshire Blvd, Beverly Hills, CA 90212, USA
Gyllenhammar, Pehr G *Businessman*
CHU PLC, Saint Helen's, 1 Undershaft, London EC3P 3DQ, England
GZA *Rap Artist (Wu-Tang Clan)*
%Agency Group Ltd, 1775 Broadway, #430, New York, NY 10019, USA

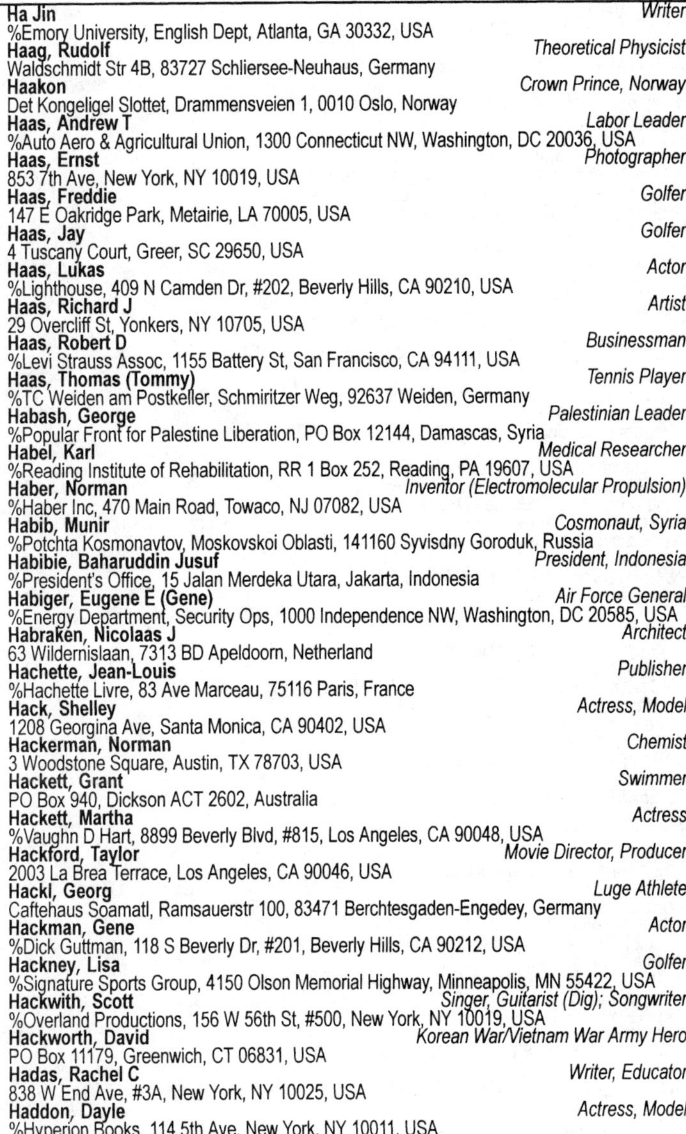

Ha Jin *Writer*
%Emory University, English Dept, Atlanta, GA 30332, USA

Haag, Rudolf *Theoretical Physicist*
Waldschmidt Str 4B, 83727 Schliersee-Neuhaus, Germany

Haakon *Crown Prince, Norway*
Det Kongeligel Slottet, Drammensveien 1, 0010 Oslo, Norway

Haas, Andrew T *Labor Leader*
%Auto Aero & Agricultural Union, 1300 Connecticut NW, Washington, DC 20036, USA

Haas, Ernst *Photographer*
853 7th Ave, New York, NY 10019, USA

Haas, Freddie *Golfer*
147 E Oakridge Park, Metairie, LA 70005, USA

Haas, Jay *Golfer*
4 Tuscany Court, Greer, SC 29650, USA

Haas, Lukas *Actor*
%Lighthouse, 409 N Camden Dr, #202, Beverly Hills, CA 90210, USA

Haas, Richard J *Artist*
29 Overcliff St, Yonkers, NY 10705, USA

Haas, Robert D *Businessman*
%Levi Strauss Assoc, 1155 Battery St, San Francisco, CA 94111, USA

Haas, Thomas (Tommy) *Tennis Player*
%TC Weiden am Postkeller, Schmiritzer Weg, 92637 Weiden, Germany

Habash, George *Palestinian Leader*
%Popular Front for Palestine Liberation, PO Box 12144, Damascas, Syria

Habel, Karl *Medical Researcher*
%Reading Institute of Rehabilitation, RR 1 Box 252, Reading, PA 19607, USA

Haber, Norman *Inventor (Electromolecular Propulsion)*
%Haber Inc, 470 Main Road, Towaco, NJ 07082, USA

Habib, Munir *Cosmonaut, Syria*
%Potchta Kosmonavtov, Moskovskoi Oblasti, 141160 Syvisdny Goroduk, Russia

Habibie, Baharuddin Jusuf *President, Indonesia*
%President's Office, 15 Jalan Merdeka Utara, Jakarta, Indonesia

Habiger, Eugene E (Gene) *Air Force General*
%Energy Department, Security Ops, 1000 Independence NW, Washington, DC 20585, USA

Habraken, Nicolaas J *Architect*
63 Wildernislaan, 7313 BD Apeldoorn, Netherland

Hachette, Jean-Louis *Publisher*
%Hachette Livre, 83 Ave Marceau, 75116 Paris, France

Hack, Shelley *Actress, Model*
1208 Georgina Ave, Santa Monica, CA 90402, USA

Hackerman, Norman *Chemist*
3 Woodstone Square, Austin, TX 78703, USA

Hackett, Grant *Swimmer*
PO Box 940, Dickson ACT 2602, Australia

Hackett, Martha *Actress*
%Vaughn D Hart, 8899 Beverly Blvd, #815, Los Angeles, CA 90048, USA

Hackford, Taylor *Movie Director, Producer*
2003 La Brea Terrace, Los Angeles, CA 90046, USA

Hackl, Georg *Luge Athlete*
Caftehaus Soamatl, Ramsauerstr 100, 83471 Berchtesgaden-Engedey, Germany

Hackman, Gene *Actor*
%Dick Guttman, 118 S Beverly Dr, #201, Beverly Hills, CA 90212, USA

Hackney, Lisa *Golfer*
%Signature Sports Group, 4150 Olson Memorial Highway, Minneapolis, MN 55422, USA

Hackwith, Scott *Singer, Guitarist (Dig); Songwriter*
%Overland Productions, 156 W 56th St, #500, New York, NY 10019, USA

Hackworth, David *Korean War/Vietnam War Army Hero*
PO Box 11179, Greenwich, CT 06831, USA

Hadas, Rachel C *Writer, Educator*
838 W End Ave, #3A, New York, NY 10025, USA

Haddon, Dayle *Actress, Model*
%Hyperion Books, 114 5th Ave, New York, NY 10011, USA

Haddon, Lawrence *Actor*
14950 Sutton St, Sherman Oaks, CA 91403, USA

Haden, Charles E (Charlie) *Jazz Bassist, Composer*
%Merlin Co, 17609 Ventura Blvd, #212, Encino, CA 91316, USA

Haden, Patrick C (Pat) *Football Player, Sportscaster*
1525 Wilson Ave, San Marino, CA 91108, USA

Hadfield, Chris A *Astronaut, Canada*
638 Shorewood Dr, Kemah, TX 77565, USA

Hadid, Zaha *Architect*
%Studio 9, 10 Bowling Green Lane, London WC1R 0BD, England

Hadl, John W *Football Player*
%Kansas University, Allen Field House, Lawrence, KS 66045, USA

Hadlee, Richard J *Cricketer*
PO Box 29186, Christchurch, New Zealand

Hadley, Brett *Actor*
5070 Woodley Ave, Encino, CA 91436, USA

Hadley - Haig

Hadley, Jerry *Opera Singer*
%George M Martynuk, 352 7th Ave, New York, NY 10001, USA
Hadley, Tony *Singer (Spandau Ballet)*
%Mission Control, Business Center, Lower Road, London SE16 2XB, England
Haebler, Ingrid *Concert Pianist*
%Ibbs & Tillett, 420-452 Edgware Road, London W2 1EG, England
Haegg, Gunder *Track Athlete*
%Swedish Olympic Committee, Idrottens Hus, 123 87 Farsta, Sweden
Haenchen, Hartmut *Conductor*
%Organisation Int'l Artistique, 16 Ave F D Roosevelt, 75008 Paris, France
Haendel, Ida *Concert Violinist*
%Harold Holt, 31 Sinclair Road, London W14 0NS, England
Hafer, Fred D *Businessman*
%GPU Inc, 300 Madison Ave, Morristown, NJ 07960, USA
Hafner, Dudley H *Foundation Executive*
140 Estrada Maya, Santa Fe, NM 87506, USA
Hafstein, Johann *Prime Minister, Iceland*
Sjalfstaedisflokkurinn, Laufasvegi 46, Reykjavik, Iceland
Hagan, Clifford O (Cliff) *Basketball Player, Coach*
3637 Castlegate West Wynd, Lexington, KY 40502, USA
Hagan, Molly *Actress*
210 S Arnaz Dr, #3, Beverly Hills, CA 90211, USA
Hagar, Sammy *Singer, Songwriter, Guitarist*
%Rogers & Cowan, 6340 Breckenridge Run, Rex, GA 30273, USA
Hagee, Michael W *Marine Corps General*
Commandant, HqUSMC, 2 Navy Annex, Washington, DC 20380, USA
Hagegard, Hakan *Opera Singer*
Gunnarsbyn, 670 30 Edane, Sweden
Hagemeister, Charles C *Vietnam War Army Hero (CMH)*
1908 Canterbury Court, Leavenworth, KS 66048, USA
Hagen, Kevin *Actor*
PO Box 1862, Grants Pass, OR 97528, USA
Hagen, Nina *Singer*
%Performers of the World, 8901 Melrose Ave, #200, West Hollywood, CA 90069, USA
Hagen, Uta T *Actress*
27 Washington Square N, New York, NY 10011, USA
Hager, Robert *Commentator*
%NBC-TV, News Dept, 4001 Nebraska Ave NW, Washington, DC 20016, USA
Hagerty, Julie *Actress*
%The Firm, 9100 Wilshire Blvd, #100W, Beverly Hills, CA 90210, USA
Haggard, Merle *Singer, Songwriter*
235 Murrell Meadows Dr, #72, Sevierville, TN 37876, USA
Hagge, Marlene Bauer *Golfer*
PO Box 570, La Quinta, CA 92253, USA
Haggerty, Dan *Actor*
404 E 1st St, #1287, Long Beach, CA 90802, USA
Haggerty, H B *Actor*
%First Artists, 1631 N Bristol St, #B20, Santa Ana, CA 92706, USA
Haggerty, Tim *Cartoonist (Ground Zero)*
%United Feature Syndicate, 200 Madison Ave, New York, NY 10016, USA
Hagler, Marvin *Boxer*
%Peter Devener, 75 Presidential Dr, #4, Quincy, MA 02169, USA
Hagman, Larry *Actor*
9950 Sulphur Mountain Road, Ojai, CA 93023, USA
Hagn, Johanna *Judo Athlete*
%ASG Elsdorf, Behrgasse 6, 50198 Elsdorf, Germany
Hague, William *Government Official, England*
%House of Commons, Westminster, London SW1A 0AA, England
Hahn, Beatrice H *Microbiologist*
%University of Alabama, Medical School, Microbiology Dept, Birmingham, AL 35294, USA
Hahn, Erwin L *Physicist*
69 Stevenson Ave, Berkeley, CA 94708, USA
Hahn, Frank H *Economist*
16 Adams Road, Cambridge CB3 9AD, England
Hahn, Hilary *Concert Violinist*
%Hans Ulrich Schmid, Postfach 1617, 30016 Hanover, Germany
Hahn, James *Mayor*
%Mayor's Office, City Hall, 200 N Spring St, Los Angeles, CA 90012, USA
Hahn, Jessica *Model, Actress*
6345 Balboa Blvd, #375, Encino, CA 91316, USA
Hahn, Joseph *DJ (Linkin Park)*
%Artist Group International, 9560 Wilshire Blvd, #400, Beverly Hills, CA 90212, USA
Haid, Charles *Actor*
4376 Forman Ave, Toluca Lake, CA 91602, USA
Haider, Jorg *Government Official, Austria*
%Freedom Party, Karntnerstr 28, 1010 Vienna, Austria
Haig, Alexander M, Jr *Secretary, State; Army General*
685 Island Dr, Palm Beach, FL 33480, USA

Haignere, Jean-Pierre *Spatinaut, France*
%CNES, 2 Place Maurice Quentin, 75039 Paris Cedeux, France
Hailey, Arthur *Writer*
Lyford Cay, PO Box N7776, Nassau, Bahamas
Hailey, Leisha *Singer (Murmurs), Songwriter*
%Evolution Talent, 1776 Broadway, #1500, New York, NY 10019, USA
Hailston, Earl B *Marine Corps General*
Commanding General, Marine Corps Forces Pacific, Camp H M Smith, HI 96861, USA
Haim, Corey *Actor*
%David Shapira, 15821 Ventura Blvd, #235, Encino, CA 91436, USA
Haimovitz, Matt *Concert Cellist*
%Columbia Artists Mgmt Inc, 165 W 57th St, New York, NY 10019, USA
Haines, Connie *Singer*
880 Mandalay Ave, #3-109, Clearwater, FL 33767, USA
Haines, George *Swimming Coach*
1033 Tioga Court, Lincoln, CA 95648, USA
Haines, Lee M *Religious Leader*
%Wesleyan Church, PO Box 50434, Indianapolis, IN 46250, USA
Haines, Randa *Movie Director*
1429 Avon Park Terrace, Los Angeles, CA 90026, USA
Hairi, Gisue *Architect*
%Hairi & Hairi, 18 E 12th St, New York, NY 10003, USA
Hairi, Mojgan *Architect*
%Hairi & Hairi, 18 E 12th St, New York, NY 10003, USA
Haise, Fred W, Jr *Astronaut, Test Pilot*
9038 N Point Dr, Baytown, TX 77520, USA
Haislip, Marcus *Basketball Player*
%Milwaukee Bucks, Bradley Center, 1001 N 4th St, Milwaukee, WI 53203, USA
Haitink, Bernard J H *Conductor*
%Harold Holt, 31 Sinclair Road, London W14 0NS, England
Haje, Khrystyne *Actress*
PO Box 8750, Universal City, CA 91618, USA
Hajek, Andreas *Rowing Athlete*
Weissbundenweg 18, Halle/Saale 06128, Germany
Hajiro, Barney *WW II Army Hero (CMH)*
94-535 Awamoi St, Waipahu, HI 96797, USA
Hakkinen, Mikka *Auto Racing Driver*
%McLaren International, Albert Dr, Woking, Surrey GU21 5JY, England
Halas, John *Animator*
%Educational Film Center, 5-7 Kean St, London WC2B 4AT, England
Halavalu Mata'aho *Queen, Tonga*
%Royal Palace, PO Box 6, Nuku'alofa, Tonga
Halberstam, David *Writer*
%William Morrow, 1350 Ave of Americas, New York, NY 10019, USA
Halbreich, Kathy *Museum Director*
%Walker Art Center, 725 Vineland Place, Minneapolis, MN 55403, USA
Haldeman, Charles (Ed) *Financier*
%Putnam Investments, 1 Post Office Square, Boston, MA 02109, USA
Haldorson, Burdette (Burdie) *Basketball Player*
2422 Zane Place, Colorado Springs, CO 80909, USA
Hale, Alan *Astronomer*
%Southwest Space Research Institute, 15 E Spur Road, Cloudcraft, NM 88317, USA
Hale, Barbara *Actress*
PO Box 6061-261, Sherman Oaks, CA 91413, USA
Hale, Georgina *Actress*
74A Saint John's Wood, High St, London NW8, England
Hale, Monte *Actor, Singer*
11732 Moorpark St, #B, Studio City, CA 91604, USA
Haley, Charles L *Football Player*
1502 Estates Way, Carrollton, TX 75006, USA
Halffter, Cristobal J *Composer, Conductor*
%Jurgen Erlebach, Grillparserstr 24, 22085 Hamburg, Germany
Halford, Rob *Singer (Judas Priest)*
%International Creative Mgmt, 40 W 57th St, #1800, New York, NY 10019, USA
Halfvarson, Eric *Opera Singer*
%Munro Artist Mgmt, 786 Dartmouth St, South Dartmouth, MA 02748, USA
Hall Greff, Kaye *Swimmer*
906 3rd St, Mukilteo, WA 98275, USA
Hall, Anthony Michael *Actor, Comedian*
%International Creative Mgmt, 8942 Wilshire Blvd, #219, Beverly Hills, CA 90211, USA
Hall, Arsenio *Entertainer*
%Endeavor Talent Agency, 9701 Wilshire Blvd, #1000, Beverly Hills, CA 90212, USA
Hall, Bridget *Model*
%I M G Models, 304 Park Ave S, #1200, New York, NY 10010, USA
Hall, Charles *Inventor (Waterbed)*
%Basic Designs, 5815 Bennett Valley Road, Santa Rosa, CA 95404, USA
Hall, Cynthia Holcomb *Judge*
%US Court of Appeals, 125 S Grand Ave, Pasadena, CA 91105, USA

Hall, Daryl *Singer (Hall & Oates), Songwriter*
%Creative Artists Agency, 9830 Wilshire Blvd, Beverly Hills, CA 90212, USA
Hall, Deidre *Actress*
11041 Santa Monica Blvd, PO Box 715, Los Angeles, CA 90078, USA
Hall, Delores *Singer, Actress*
%Agency for Performing Arts, 485 Madison Ave, New York, NY 10022, USA
Hall, Donald *Writer*
%Eagle Point Farm, Wilmot, NH 03287, USA
Hall, Donald J *Businessman*
%Hallmark Cards, 2501 McGee St, Kansas City, MO 64108, USA
Hall, Edward T *Anthropologist, Writer*
8 Calle Jacinta, Santa Fe, NM 87508, USA
Hall, Ervin (Erv) *Track Athlete*
%Citicorp Mortgage, 670 Mason Ridge Center Dr, Saint Louis, MO 63141, USA
Hall, Galen *Football Coach*
%University of Florida, Athletic Dept, Gainesville, FL 32611, USA
Hall, Gary *Swimmer*
2501 N 32nd St, Phoenix, AZ 85008, USA
Hall, Glenn H *Hockey Player*
%CSAS, PO Box 60036, RPO Glen Abbey, Oakville ON L6M 3H2, Canada
Hall, James E (Jim) *Auto Racing Driver, Executive*
RR 7 Box 640, Midland, TX 79706, USA
Hall, James S (Jim) *Jazz Guitarist*
%Jazz Tree, 211 Thompson St, #LD, New York, NY 10012, USA
Hall, Jerry *Model, Actress*
471-473 Kings Road, London SW10 0LU, England
Hall, Jerry *Geneticist*
%George Washington University, Med Center, 2300 I St NW, Washington, DC 20037, USA
Hall, Joe B *Basketball Coach*
%Central Bank & Trust Co, 300 W Vine St, Lexington, KY 40507, USA
Hall, Kevan *Fashion Designer*
%Kevan Hall Studio, 756 S Spring St, #11E, Los Angeles, CA 90014, USA
Hall, L Parker *Football Player*
4712 Cole Road, Memphis, TN 38117, USA
Hall, Lani *Singer*
31930 Pacific Coast Highway, Malibu, CA 90265, USA
Hall, Lloyd M, Jr *Religious Leader*
%Congregation Christian Church Assn, PO Box 1620, Oak Creek, MI 53154, USA
Hall, Peter R F *Theater, Opera, Movie Director*
%Peter Hall Co, 18 Exeter St, London WC2E 7DU, England
Hall, Philip Baker *Actor*
%Writers & Artists, 8383 Wilshire Blvd, #550, Beverly Hills, CA 90211, USA
Hall, Regina *Actress*
100 N Clark Dr, #205, West Hollywood, CA 90048, USA
Hall, Robert N *Inventor*
2315 Gurenson Lane, Niskayuna, NY 12309, USA
Hall, Samuel (Sam) *Diver*
5759 Wilcke Way, Dayton, OH 45459, USA
Hall, Sonny *Labor Leader*
%Transport Workers Union, 80 W End Ave, New York, NY 10023, USA
Hall, Tom T *Singer, Songwriter*
%Tom T Hall Enterprises, PO Box 1246, Franklin, TN 37065, USA
Hall, William, Sr *Bowler*
5108 N 126th Ave, Omaha, NE 68164, USA
Halla, Brian L *Businessman*
%National Semiconductor, 2900 Semiconductor Dr, Santa Clara, CA 95051, USA
Halladay, H Leroy (Roy) *Baseball Player*
4537 Rutledge Dr, Palm Harbor, FL 34685, USA
Haller, Gordon *Triathlete*
20514 E Caley Dr, Centennial, CO 80016, USA
Hallet, Jim *Golfer*
232 Shell Bluff Court, Ponte Vedra, FL 32082, USA
Hallier, Lori *Actress*
%Epstein-Wyckoff, 280 S Beverly Dr, #400, Beverly Hills, CA 90212, USA
Hallinan, Joseph T *Journalist*
%Random House, 1745 Broadway, #B1, New York, NY 10019, USA
Halliwell, Geri *Singer (Spice Girls)*
%Andy Stephens, 60A Highgate High St, London N6 5HX, England
Hallman, Tom, Jr *Journalist*
%Portland Oregonian, Editorial Dept, 1320 SW Broadway, Portland, OR 97201, USA
Hallstrom, Holly *Model, Entertainer*
5757 Wilshire Blvd, #206, Los Angeles, CA 90036, USA
Hallstrom, Lasse *Movie Director*
%United Talent Agency, 9560 Wilshire Blvd, #500, Beverly Hills, CA 90212, USA
Hallyday, Johnny *Singer, Actor*
%CC Productions, 6 Rue Deubigny, 75017 Paris, France
Halonen Tarja, Kaarina *President, Finland*
%Presidential Palace, Pohjoisesplandi 1, 00170 Helsinki 17, Finland

Halperin, Bertrand I *Physicist*
%Harvard University, Physics Dept, Cambridge, MA 02138, USA
Halpern, Daniel *Writer*
9 Mercer St, Princeton, NJ 08540, USA
Halpern, Jack *Chemist*
5801 S Dorchester Ave, #4A, Chicago, IL 60637, USA
Halpern, James S *Judge*
%US Tax Court, 400 2nd St NW, Washington, DC 20217, USA
Halprin, Lawrence *Landscape Architect, Planner*
1160 Battery St, #50, San Francisco, CA 94111, USA
Halsell, James D, Jr *Astronaut*
1617 Stoney Lake Dr, Friendswood, TX 77546, USA
Ham, Jack R *Football Player*
%Ham Enterprises, 540 Lindergh Dr, Moon Township, PA 15108, USA
Ham, Kenneth T *Astronaut*
904 W Viejo Dr, Friendswood, TX 77546, USA
Hamao, Stephen Fumio Cardinal *Religious Leader*
%Pastoral Care of Migrants, Piazza S Calisto 16, 00120 Vatican City
Hamari, Julia *Opera Singer*
Max Brod-Weg 14, 70437 Stuttgart, Germany
Hambro, Leonid *Concert Pianist*
%California Institute of Arts, Music Dept, Valencia, CA 91355, USA
Hamburger, Michael P L *Writer*
%John Johnson, 45/47 Clerkenwell Green, London EC1R 0HT, England
Hamed, Nihad *Religious Leader*
%Islamic Assn in US/Canada, 25351 Five Mile Road, Redford Township, MI 48239, USA
Hamed, Prince Naseem *Boxer*
26 Newman Road, Wincobank, Sheffield S9 1LP, England
Hamel, Michael A *Astronaut*
HQ AFSPC/DR, 150 Vandenburg St, #1105, Colorado Springs, CO 80914, USA
Hamel, Veronica *Actress, Model*
10102 Empyrean Way, #304, Los Angeles, CA 90067, USA
Hamel, William *Religious Leader*
%Evangelical Free Church, 901 E 78th St, Minneapolis, MN 55420, USA
Hamill, Dorothy S *Figure Skater*
%Int'l Mgmt Group, 1 Erieview Plaza, 1360 E 9th St, #1300, Cleveland, OH 44114, USA
Hamill, Mark *Actor*
1101 Holly Spring Lane, Grand Blanc, MI 48439, USA
Hamill, W Pete *Writer, Editor*
8 Whiskey Hill Road, Wallkill, NY 12589, USA
Hamilton, Allan G (Al) *Hockey Player*
2452 115th St, Edmonton AB T6J 3S1, Canada
Hamilton, Ashley *Actor*
9255 Doheny Rd, #2302, Los Angeles, CA 90069, USA
Hamilton, Bobby, Jr *Auto Racing Driver*
%Motorsports Decisions, 1435 W Morehead St, #190, Charlotte, NC 28208, USA
Hamilton, David *Photographer*
41 Blvd du Montparnasse, 75006 Paris, France
Hamilton, Forestorn (Chico) *Jazz Drummer*
%Chico Hamilton Productions, 321 E 45th St, #PH A, New York, NY 10017, USA
Hamilton, George *Actor*
%Agency for Performing Arts, 9200 Sunset Blvd, #900, Los Angeles, CA 90069, USA
Hamilton, George H *Museum Director*
121 Gale Road, Williamstown, MA 01267, USA
Hamilton, George, IV *Singer, Songwriter, Guitarist*
%Blade Agency, 203 SW 3rd Ave, Gainesville, FL 32601, USA
Hamilton, Guy *Movie Director*
%London Mgmt, 2-4 Noel St, London W1V 3RB, England
Hamilton, Josh *Actor*
%William Morris Agency, 151 El Camino Dr, Beverly Hills, CA 90212, USA
Hamilton, Lee H *Representative, IN*
%Wilson Int'l Scholars Center, 1300 Pennsylvania Ave NW, Washington, DC 20004, USA
Hamilton, Leonard *Basketball Coach*
%Florida State University, Athletic Dept, Tallahassee, FL 32306, USA
Hamilton, Linda *Actress*
%Edrick/Rich Mgmt, 8955 Norma Place, Los Angeles, CA 90069, USA
Hamilton, Lisa Gay *Actress*
%Writers & Artists, 8383 Wilshire Blvd, #550, Beverly Hills, CA 90211, USA
Hamilton, Michael *Artist*
2012 N 19th St, Boise, ID 83702, USA
Hamilton, Richard *Artist*
Northend Farm, Northend, Oxon RG9 6LQ, England
Hamilton, Richard *Basketball Player*
%Detroit Pistons, Palace, 2 Championship Dr, Auburn Hills, MI 48326, USA
Hamilton, Scott S *Figure Skater*
%Berkeley Agency, 2608 9th St, Berkeley, CA 94710, USA
Hamilton, Suzanna *Actress*
%Julian Belfarge, 46 Albermarle St, London W1X 4PP, England

Hamilton, Tom *Bassist (Aerosmith)*
PO Box 67039, Newton, MA 02167, USA
Hamilton, William *Cartoonist, Writer*
17 E 95th St, #3F, New York, NY 10128, USA
Hamlin, Harry *Actor*
PO Box 25578, Los Angeles, CA 90025, USA
Hamlisch, Marvin *Composer, Conductor*
970 Park Ave, #501, New York, NY 10028, USA
Hamm, Mia *Soccer Player, Model*
%US Soccer Federation, 1801 S Prairie Ave, Chicago, IL 60616, USA
Hamm, Nick *Movie Director*
%International Creative Mgmt, 8942 Wilshire Blvd, #219, Beverly Hills, CA 90211, USA
Hammer *Rap Artist*
%Terrie Williams Agency, 1500 Broadway Front, #7, New York, NY 10036, USA
Hammer, Victor S *Cinematographer*
PO Box 10788, Marina del Rey, CA 90295, USA
Hammes, Gordon G *Chemist*
11 Staley Place, Durham, NC 27705, USA
Hammett, Kirk *Guitarist (Metallica)*
2505 Divisadero St, San Francisco, CA 94115, USA
Hammon, Becky *Basketball Player*
%New York Liberty, Madison Square Garden, 2 Penn Plaza, New York, NY 10121, USA
Hammond, Albert, Jr *Guitarist (Strokes)*
%MVO Ltd, 370 7th Ave, #807, New York, NY 10001, USA
Hammond, Caleb D, Jr *Publisher, Cartographer*
61 Woodland Road, Maplewood, NJ 07040, USA
Hammond, Darrell *Actor, Comedian*
%International Creative Mgmt, 8942 Wilshire Blvd, #219, Beverly Hills, CA 90211, USA
Hammond, Fred *Singer*
%Face to Face, 21421 Hilltop St Blvd 20, Southfield, MI 48034, USA
Hammond, James T *Religious Leader*
%Pentecostal Free Will Baptist Church, PO Box 1568, Dunn, NC 28335, USA
Hammond, Jay S *Governor, AK*
Lake Charles Lodge, Port Alsworth, AK 99652, USA
Hammond, Joan H *Opera Singer*
Private Bag 101, Geelong Mail Center VIC 3221, Australia
Hammond, John *Singer, Guitarist*
%Rosebud Agency, PO Box 170429, San Francisco, CA 94117, USA
Hammond, L Blaine, Jr *Astronaut*
%Gulfstream Aircraft, 4150 E Donald Douglas Dr, #926, Long Beach, CA 90808, USA
Hammond, Robert D *Army General*
PO Box 222032, Carmel, CA 93922, USA
Hammond, Tom *Sportscaster*
%NBC-TV, Sports Dept, 30 Rockefeller Plaza, New York, NY 10112, USA
Hammons, Roger *Religious Leader*
%Primitive Advent Christian Church, 273 Frame Road, Elkview, WV 25071, USA
Hamnett, Katharine *Fashion Designer*
%Katharine Hamnett Ltd, 202 New North Road, London N1, England
Hampel, Olaf *Bobsled Athlete*
Pommenweg 2, 33689 Bielefeld, Germany
Hampshire, Susan *Actress*
%Chatto & Linnit, Prince of Wales, Coventry St, London W1V 7FE, England
Hampson, Thomas *Opera Singer*
Starkfriedgasse 53, 1180 Vienna, Austria
Hampton, Christopher J *Writer*
2 Kensington Park Gardens, London W11, England
Hampton, Daniel O (Dan) *Football Player*
8641 Oak Park Ave, Burbank, IL 60459, USA
Hampton, James *Actor*
102 Forest Hill Dr, Roanoke, TX 76262, USA
Hampton, Locksley (Slide) *Jazz Trombonist*
%Charismic Productions, 2604 Mozart Place NW, Washington, DC 20009, USA
Hampton, Michael W (Mike) *Baseball Player*
%YSA, 2001 Blake St, Denver, CO 80205, USA
Hampton, Millard *Track Athlete*
201 W Mission St, San Jose, CA 95110, USA
Hampton, Ralph C, Jr *Religious Leader*
%Free Will Baptist Bible College, 3606 W End Ave, Nashville, TN 37205, USA
Hamrlik, Roman *Hockey Player*
%New York Islanders, Nassau Coliseum, Hempstead Turnpike, Uniondale, NY 11553, USA
Hamzah *Crown Prince, Jordan*
%Crown Prince's Office, Royal Palace, Amman, Jordan
Han Suyin *Writer*
37 Montoie, 1007 Lausanne, Switzerland
Hanafusa, Hidesaburo *Microbiologist*
%Rockefeller University, 1230 York Ave, New York, NY 10021, USA
Hanauer, Chip *Boat Racing Driver*
%Hanauer Enterprises, 2702 NE 88th St, Seattle, WA 98115, USA

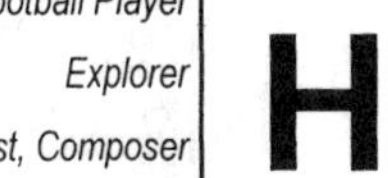

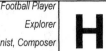

Hanburger, Christian (Chris), Jr — *Football Player*
708 Winter Hill Dr, Apex, NC 27502, USA

Hanbury-Tenison, Robin — *Explorer*
%Maidenwell, Cardinham, Bodmin, Cornwall PL3O 4DW, England

Hancock, Herbert J (Herbie) — *Jazz Pianist, Composer*
%DL Media, PO Box 2728, Bala Cynwyd, PA 19004, USA

Hancock, John D — *Movie Director*
7355 N Fail Road, La Porte, IN 46350, USA

Hand, Jon T — *Football Player*
13013 Broad St, Carmel, IN 46032, USA

Handelsman, J B — *Cartoonist*
%New Yorker Magazine, Editorial Dept, 4 Times Square, New York, NY 10036, USA

Handelsman, Walt — *Editorial Cartoonist*
%Newsday, Editorial Dept, 235 Pinelawn Road, Melville, NY 11747, USA

Handford, Martin — *Cartoonist (Where's Waldo)*
%Walker Books, 87 Vauxhall Walk, London SE11 5HU, England

Handke, Peter — *Writer*
%Farrar Straus Giroux, 19 Union Square W, New York, NY 10003, USA

Handler, Evan — *Actor*
%Liberman/Zerman, 252 N Larchmont, #200, Los Angeles, CA 90004, USA

Handlin, Oscar — *Historian*
18 Agassiz St, Cambridge, MA 02140, USA

Hands, Terence — *Theater Director*
Clwyd Theater Cymru, Mold, Flintshire, North Wales

Hands, William A (Bill) — *Baseball Player*
PO Box 334, Orient, NY 11957, USA

Handy, John — *Jazz Saxophonist*
%Integrity Talent, PO Box 961, Burlington, MA 01803, USA

Handy, John W — *Air Force General*
Commander-in-Chief, Transportation Command, Scott Air Force Base, IL 62225, USA

Haney, Lee — *Body Builder*
%Lee Haney Enterprises, 105 Trail Point Circle, Fairburn, GA 30213, USA

Hankinson, Tim — *Soccer Coach*
%Columbus Crew, 2121 Velman Ave, Columbus, OH 43211, USA

Hanks, Colin — *Actor*
%Creative Artists Agency, 9830 Wilshire Blvd, Beverly Hills, CA 90212, USA

Hanks, Merton E — *Football Player*
855 E Davisburg Road, Holly, MI 48442, USA

Hanks, Tom — *Actor*
%P M K Public Relations, 8500 Wilshire Blvd, #700, Beverly Hills, CA 90211, USA

Hanley, Charles — *Journalist*
%Associated Press, 50 Rockefeller Plaza, New York, NY 10020, USA

Hanley, Frank — *Labor Leader*
%Int'l Union of Operating Engineers, 1125 17th St NW, Washington, DC 20036, USA

Hanley, Jenny — *Actress*
%MGA, Southbank House, Black Prince Road, London SE1 7SJ, England

Hanley, Kay — *Singer (Letters to Cleo)*
%Little Big Man, 155 Ave of Americas, #700, New York, NY 10013, USA

Hanley, Richard — *Swimmer*
E266 Lake Road, Ironwood, MI 49938, USA

Hanlon, Edward, Jr — *Marine Corps General*
Commanding General, Marine Combat Development Command, Quantico, VA 22134, USA

Hanna, Jerome — *Singer (Jive Five)*
%Paramount Entertainment, PO Box 12, Far Hills, NJ 07931, USA

Hannah, Bob — *Motorcycle Racing Rider*
%American Motorcycle Assn, 13515 Yarmouth Dr, Pickerington, OH 43147, USA

Hannah, Bob — *Baseball Coach*
%University of Delaware, Athletic Dept, Newark, DE 19716, USA

Hannah, Charles A (Charley) — *Football Player*
PO Box 2671, Lutz, FL 33548, USA

Hannah, Daryl — *Actress*
%Chuck Binder, 1465 Lindacrest Dr, Beverly Hills, CA 90210, USA

Hannah, John — *Actor*
%William Morris Agency, 52/53 Poland Place, London W1F 7LX, England

Hannah, John A — *Football Player*
26 Bartletts Beach, Amesbury, MA 01913, USA

Hannah, Wayne — *Religious Leader*
%Fellowship of Grace Brethren Churches, PO Box 386, Winona Lake, IN 46590, USA

Hannawald, Sven — *Ski Jumper*
%WH Sport Int'l GmbH, Im Sabel 4, 54294 Trier, Germany

Hannigan, Alyson — *Actress*
%Innovative Artists, 1505 10th St, Santa Monica, CA 90401, USA

Hannity, Sean — *Commentator*
%Fox-TV, News Dept, 205 E 67th St, New York, NY 10021, USA

Hannula, Dick — *Swimming Coach*
1021 Westley Dr, Tacoma, WA 98465, USA

Hanratty, Terrance R (Terry) — *Football Player*
22 Hunters Creek Lane, New Canaan, CT 06840, USA

Hans-Adam II — *Prince, Liechtenstein*
%Schloss Vaduz, 9490 Vaduz, Liechtenstein

Hansen, Alfred G — *Air Force General, Businessman*
%Lockheed Aero Systems, 86 S Cobb Dr, Marietta, GA 30063, USA

Hansen, Clifford P — *Governor, Senator, WY*
PO Box 448, Jackson, WY 83001, USA

Hansen, Frederick M (Fred) — *Track Athlete*
201 Vanderpool Lane, #12, Houston, TX 77024, USA

Hansen, Gale — *Actress*
721 SE 29th Ave, Portland, OR 97214, USA

Hansen, Gunnar — *Actor*
PO Box 368, North East Harbor, ME 04662, USA

Hansen, James E — *Meteorologist, Physicist*
%Goddard Institute for Space Studies, 2880 Broadway, New York, NY 10025, USA

Hansen, Patti — *Model*
Redlands, W Wittering, Chichester, Sussex, England

Hanson, Carl T — *Navy Admiral*
900 Birdseye Road, Orient, NY 11967, USA

Hanson, Curtis — *Movie Director, Screenwriter*
%United Talent Agency, 9560 Wilshire Blvd, #500, Beverly Hills, CA 90212, USA

Hanson, Isaac — *Singer, Guitarist (Hanson); Songwriter*
1045 W 78th St, Tulsa, OK 74132, USA

Hanson, Jason D — *Football Player*
3165 Midvale Dr, Rochester Hills, MI 48309, USA

Hanson, Taylor — *Singer, Keyboardist (Hanson); Songwriter*
1045 W 78th St, Tulsa, OK 74132, USA

Hanson, Zachary — *Singer, Drummer (Hanson); Songwriter*
1045 W 78th St, Tulsa, OK 74132, USA

Hanss, Ted — *Computer Scientist*
%Information Technology Intergration Center, 3025 Boardwalk, Ann Arbor, MI 48108, USA

Hanzlik, Bill — *Basketball Player, Coach*
5701 Green Oaks Dr, Greenwood Village, CO 80121, USA

Harad, George J — *Businessman*
%Boise Cascade Corp, 1111 W Jefferson St, Boise, ID 83728, USA

Harada, Masahiko (Fighting) — *Boxer*
2-21-5 Azabu-Juban, Minatoku, Tokyo 106, Japan

Harald V — *King, Norway*
Det Kongelige Slott, Drammensveien 1, 0010 Oslo, Norway

Harbaugh, Gregory J — *Astronaut*
2434 Hollingsworth Hill Ave, Lakeland, FL 33803, USA

Harbaugh, James J (Jim) — *Football Player*
7051 Broadway Terrace, Oakland, CA 94611, USA

Harbison, John H — *Composer*
479 Franklin St, Cambridge, MA 02139, USA

Hard, Darlene R — *Tennis Player*
22924 Erwin St, Woodland Hills, CA 91367, USA

Hardaway, Anfernee (Penny) — *Basketball Player*
PO Box 2132, Farmington Hills, MI 48333, USA

Hardaway, Timothy D (Tim) — *Basketball Player*
10050 SW 62nd Ave, Miami, FL 33156, USA

Harden, Marcia Gay — *Actress*
1358 Woodbrook Lane, Southlake, TX 76092, USA

Hardenberger, Hahan — *Concert Trumpeter*
%Columbia Artists Mgmt Inc, 165 W 57th St, New York, NY 10019, USA

Hardin, Clifford M — *Secretary, Agriculture*
10 Roan Lane, Saint Louis, MO 63124, USA

Hardin, Melora — *Actress*
3256 Hilloak Dr, Los Angeles, CA 90068, USA

Hardin, Ty — *Actor*
PO Box 1821, Gig Harbor, WA 98335, USA

Harding, John Wesley — *Singer, Songwriter*
%Sincere Mgmt, 6 Bravington Road, #6, London W9 3AH, England

Harding, Tonya M — *Figure Skater, Actress*
PO Box 6132, Vancouver, WA 98668, USA

Hardis, Stephen R — *Businessman*
%Eaton Corp, Eaton Center, 1111 Superior Ave, Cleveland, OH 44114, USA

Hardison, Kadeem — *Actor*
19743 Valleyview Dr, Topanga, CA 90290, USA

Hardisty, Huntington — *Navy Admiral*
%Lexington Institute, 1600 Wilson Blvd, #900, Arlington,VA 22209, USA

Hardnett, Charles (Charlie) — *Basketball Player, Coach*
1906 Swainsboro Dr, Louisville, KY 40218, USA

Hardt, Michael — *Educator*
%Duke University, English Dept, Durham, NC 27708, USA

Hardwick, Elizabeth — *Writer*
15 W 67th St, New York, NY 10023, USA

Hardwick, William B (Billy) — *Bowler*
10266 Waterford Road, Collierville, TN 38017, USA

Hardy, Bruce A — *Football Player*
5150 SW 20th St, Plantation, FL 33317, USA
Hardy, Carroll — *Football, Baseball Player*
27875 E Whitewood Dr, Steamboat Springs, CO 80487, USA
Hardy, Hagood — *Vibrist, Composer*
%SOCAN, 41 Valleybrook Dr, Don Mills ON M3B 2S6, Canada
Hardy, Hugh — *Architect*
%Hardy Holzman Pfeiffer, 902 Broadway, New York, NY 10010, USA
Hardy, Kevin — *Football Player*
2118 College St, Jacksonville, FL 32204, USA
Hardy, Robert — *Actor*
%Chatto & Linnit, Prince of Wales, Coventry St, London W1V 7FE, England
Hare, David — *Writer*
95 Linden Gardens, London WC2, England
Harewood, Dorian — *Actor*
2 Bearwood Dr, Toronto ON M9A 4G4, Canada
Harewood, Nancy — *Actress*
%Metropolitan Talent Agency, 4526 Wilshire Blvd, Los Angeles, CA 90010, USA
Hargis, Billy James — *Religious Leader*
Rose of Sharon Farm, Neosho, MO 64850, USA
Hargitay, Mariska — *Actress*
305 W Broadway, #115, New York, NY 10013, USA
Hargrove, D Michael (Mike) — *Baseball Player, Manager*
3925 Ramblewood Dr, Richfield, OH 44286, USA
Harker, Al — *Soccer*
620 Wigard Ave, Philadelphia, PA 19128, USA
Harket, Morten — *Singer (A-Ha)*
%Bandana Mgmt, 11 Elvaston Place, #300, London SW7 5QC, England
Harkness, Ned — *Hockey Coach*
12 Fowler Ave, Glens Falls, NY 12801, USA
Harlan, Jack R — *Plant Geneticist*
%University of Illinois, Agronomy Dept, Urbana, IL 61801, USA
Harlan, Kevin — *Sportscaster*
%CBS-TV, Sports Dept, 51 W 52nd St, New York, NY 10019, USA
Harley, Steve — *Singer*
%Work Hard, 19D Pinfold Road, London SW16 2SL, England
Harlin, Renny — *Movie Director, Producer*
%Midnight Sun Pictures, 8800 Sunset Blvd, #400, Los Angeles, CA 90069, USA
Harlow, Bill — *Writer*
%Charles Scribner's Sons, 866 3rd Ave, New York, NY 10022, USA
Harlow, Shalom — *Model*
38 Stephen Ave, Courtice ON L1E 1Z1, Canada
Harman, Denham — *Biochemist*
9817 Harney Parkway S, Omaha, NE 68114, USA
Harmon, Joy — *Actress*
9901 Poole Ave, Sunland, CA 91040, USA
Harmon, Kelly — *Actress, Model*
13224 Old Oak Lane, Los Angeles, CA 90049, USA
Harmon, Mark — *Actor*
%Wings Inc, 2236 Encinitas Blvd, #A, Encinitas, CA 92024, USA
Harmon, Merle — *Sportscaster*
424 E Lamar Blvd, #210, Arlington, TX 76011, USA
Harmon, Ronnie K — *Football Player*
13022 218th St, Laurelton, NY 11413, USA
Harmon-Sehorn, Angie — *Actress*
%Creative Artists Agency, 9830 Wilshire Blvd, Beverly Hills, CA 90212, USA
Harms, Alfred G, Jr — *Navy Admiral*
Chief, Education/Training, Naval Air Station, Pensacola, FL 32508, USA
Harms, Joni — *Singer, Songwriter*
%David Skepner/Buckskin Co, PO Box 158488, Nashville, TN 37215, USA
Harnell, Joe — *Composer, Conductor*
41616 Weslin Ave, Sherman Oaks, CA 91423, USA
Harner, Levi — *Harness Racing Driver*
RR 1, Millville, PA 17846, USA
Harness, William E — *Opera Singer*
PO Box 328, Washougal, WA 98671, USA
Harney, Paul — *Golfer*
72 Club Valley Dr, East Falmouth, MA 02536, USA
Harnick, Sheldon M — *Lyricist*
%Deutsch & Blasband, 800 3rd Ave, New York, NY 10022, USA
Harnisch, Peter T (Pete) — *Baseball Player*
2 Cornfield Lane, Commack, NY 11725, USA
Harnoncourt, Nikolaus — *Conductor*
38 Piaristangasse, 1080 Vienna, Austria
Harnos, Christine — *Actress*
%Gersh Agency, 232 N Canon Dr, Beverly Hills, CA 90210, USA
Harnoy, Ofra — *Concert Cellist*
437 Spadina Road, PO Box 23046, Toronto ON M5P 2W0, Canada

H

Harout - Harris

Harout, Magda *Actress*
13452 Vose St, Van Nuys, CA 91405, USA
Harper, Alvin C *Football Player*
1304 Split Rock Lane, Fort Washington, MD 20744, USA
Harper, Ben *Singer, Guitarist, Songwriter*
%Nasty Little Man, 15 Maiden Lane, #800, New York, NY 10038, USA
Harper, Chandler *Golfer*
4412 Gannon Road, Portsmouth, VA 23703, USA
Harper, Charles M *Businessman*
6625 State St, Omaha, NE 68152, USA
Harper, Derek *Basketball Player*
2214 Highpoint Circle, Carrollton, TX 75007, USA
Harper, Donald D W (Don) *Diver*
1765 Lynnhaven Dr, Columbus, OH 43221, USA
Harper, Edward J *Composer*
7 Morningside Park, Edinburgh EH10 5HD, Scotland
Harper, Heather M *Opera Singer*
20 Milverton Road, London NW6 7AS, England
Harper, Jessica *Actress, Singer*
15430 Brownwood Place, Los Angeles, CA 90077, USA
Harper, Ron *Basketball Player*
8934 Brecksville Road, #417, Cleveland, OH 44141, USA
Harper, Ron *Actor*
13317 Ventura Blvd, #1, Sherman Oaks, CA 91423, USA
Harper, Tess *Actress*
2271 Betty Lane, Beverly Hills, CA 90210, USA
Harper, Valerie *Actress*
%David Shapira, 15821 Ventura Blvd, #235, Encino, CA 91436, USA
Harper, Willie M *Football Player*
777 Hollenbeck Ave, #7G, Sunnyvale, CA 94087, USA
Harrah, Colbert D (Toby) *Baseball Player, Manager*
316 Leewood Circle, Azle, TX 76020, USA
Harrah, Dennis W *Football Player*
1509 Oak Ave, Panama City, FL 32405, USA
Harrell, James A *Geologist*
%University of Toledo, Geology Dept, Toledo, OH 43606, USA
Harrell, Lynn M *Concert Cellist, Conductor*
%I M G Artists, 420 W 45th St, New York, NY 10036, USA
Harrell, Tom *Jazz Trumpeter, Flugelhorn Player*
%Joel Chriss, 300 Mercer St, #3J, New York, NY 10003, USA
Harrelson, Brett *Actor*
%Agency for Performing Arts, 9200 Sunset Blvd, #900, Los Angeles, CA 90069, USA
Harrelson, Derrell M (Bud) *Baseball Player, Manager*
357 Ridgefield Road, Hauppauge, NY 11788, USA
Harrelson, Kenneth S (Ken) *Baseball Player*
90006 Shawn Park Place, Orlando, FL 32819, USA
Harrelson, Woody *Actor*
%Creative Artists Agency, 9830 Wilshire Blvd, Beverly Hills, CA 90212, USA
Harrick, Jim *Basketball Coach*
%Denver Nuggets, Pepsi Center, 1000 Chopper Circle, Denver, CO 80204, USA
Harring, Laura Elena *Actress, Beauty Queen*
12335 Santa Monica Blvd, #302, Los Angeles, CA 90025, USA
Harrington, Curtis *Movie Director*
6288 Vine Way, Los Angeles, CA 90068, USA
Harrington, David *Concert Violinist (Kronos Quartet)*
%Kronos Quartet, 1235 9th Ave, San Francisco, CA 94122, USA
Harrington, Donald J *Educator*
%Saint John's University, President's Office, Jamaica, NY 11439, USA
Harrington, Joey *Football Player*
%Detroit Lions, 222 Republic Dr, Allen Park, MI 48101, USA
Harrington, John *Hockey Player, Coach*
%Saint Johns University, Athletic Dept, PO Box 7277, Collegeville, MN 56321, USA
Harrington, Pat, Jr *Actor*
730 Marzella Ave, Los Angeles, CA 90049, USA
Harrington, Robert *Auto Racing Driver*
2609 Woodshade Ave, Kannapolis, NC 28127, USA
Harris, Barbara C *Religious Leader, Social Activist*
%Episcopal Diocese of Massachusetts, 138 Tremont St, Boston, MA 02111, USA
Harris, Barry *Jazz Pianist*
%Brad Simon Organization, 122 E 57th St, #300, New York, NY 10022, USA
Harris, Bernard A, Jr *Astronaut*
3411 Erin Knoll Court, Houston, TX 77059, USA
Harris, Cliff *Football Player*
722 Kentwood Dr, Rockwall, TX 75032, USA
Harris, Damian *Movie Director*
%International Creative Mgmt, 8942 Wilshire Blvd, #219, Beverly Hills, CA 90211, USA
Harris, Danielle *Actress*
%Gold Marshak Liedtke, 3500 W Olive Ave, #1400, Burbank, CA 91505, USA

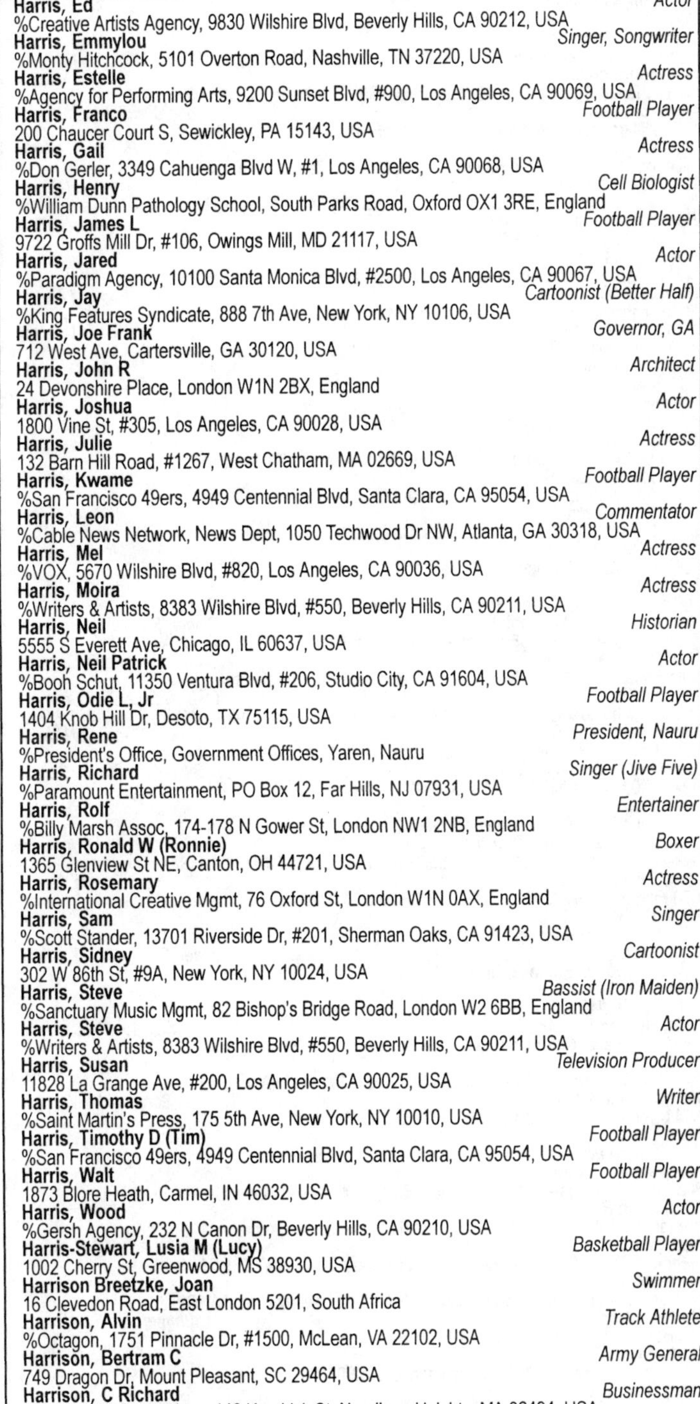

Harris, Ed *Actor*
%Creative Artists Agency, 9830 Wilshire Blvd, Beverly Hills, CA 90212, USA
Harris, Emmylou *Singer, Songwriter*
%Monty Hitchcock, 5101 Overton Road, Nashville, TN 37220, USA
Harris, Estelle *Actress*
%Agency for Performing Arts, 9200 Sunset Blvd, #900, Los Angeles, CA 90069, USA
Harris, Franco *Football Player*
200 Chaucer Court S, Sewickley, PA 15143, USA
Harris, Gail *Actress*
%Don Gerler, 3349 Cahuenga Blvd W, #1, Los Angeles, CA 90068, USA
Harris, Henry *Cell Biologist*
%William Dunn Pathology School, South Parks Road, Oxford OX1 3RE, England
Harris, James L *Football Player*
9722 Groffs Mill Dr, #106, Owings Mill, MD 21117, USA
Harris, Jared *Actor*
%Paradigm Agency, 10100 Santa Monica Blvd, #2500, Los Angeles, CA 90067, USA
Harris, Jay *Cartoonist (Better Half)*
%King Features Syndicate, 888 7th Ave, New York, NY 10106, USA
Harris, Joe Frank *Governor, GA*
712 West Ave, Cartersville, GA 30120, USA
Harris, John R *Architect*
24 Devonshire Place, London W1N 2BX, England
Harris, Joshua *Actor*
1800 Vine St, #305, Los Angeles, CA 90028, USA
Harris, Julie *Actress*
132 Barn Hill Road, #1267, West Chatham, MA 02669, USA
Harris, Kwame *Football Player*
%San Francisco 49ers, 4949 Centennial Blvd, Santa Clara, CA 95054, USA
Harris, Leon *Commentator*
%Cable News Network, News Dept, 1050 Techwood Dr NW, Atlanta, GA 30318, USA
Harris, Mel *Actress*
%VOX, 5670 Wilshire Blvd, #820, Los Angeles, CA 90036, USA
Harris, Moira *Actress*
%Writers & Artists, 8383 Wilshire Blvd, #550, Beverly Hills, CA 90211, USA
Harris, Neil *Historian*
5555 S Everett Ave, Chicago, IL 60637, USA
Harris, Neil Patrick *Actor*
%Booh Schut, 11350 Ventura Blvd, #206, Studio City, CA 91604, USA
Harris, Odie L, Jr *Football Player*
1404 Knob Hill Dr, Desoto, TX 75115, USA
Harris, Rene *President, Nauru*
%President's Office, Government Offices, Yaren, Nauru
Harris, Richard *Singer (Jive Five)*
%Paramount Entertainment, PO Box 12, Far Hills, NJ 07931, USA
Harris, Rolf *Entertainer*
%Billy Marsh Assoc, 174-178 N Gower St, London NW1 2NB, England
Harris, Ronald W (Ronnie) *Boxer*
1365 Glenview St NE, Canton, OH 44721, USA
Harris, Rosemary *Actress*
%International Creative Mgmt, 76 Oxford St, London W1N 0AX, England
Harris, Sam *Singer*
%Scott Stander, 13701 Riverside Dr, #201, Sherman Oaks, CA 91423, USA
Harris, Sidney *Cartoonist*
302 W 86th St, #9A, New York, NY 10024, USA
Harris, Steve *Bassist (Iron Maiden)*
%Sanctuary Music Mgmt, 82 Bishop's Bridge Road, London W2 6BB, England
Harris, Steve *Actor*
%Writers & Artists, 8383 Wilshire Blvd, #550, Beverly Hills, CA 90211, USA
Harris, Susan *Television Producer*
11828 La Grange Ave, #200, Los Angeles, CA 90025, USA
Harris, Thomas *Writer*
%Saint Martin's Press, 175 5th Ave, New York, NY 10010, USA
Harris, Timothy D (Tim) *Football Player*
%San Francisco 49ers, 4949 Centennial Blvd, Santa Clara, CA 95054, USA
Harris, Walt *Football Player*
1873 Blore Heath, Carmel, IN 46032, USA
Harris, Wood *Actor*
%Gersh Agency, 232 N Canon Dr, Beverly Hills, CA 90210, USA
Harris-Stewart, Lusia M (Lucy) *Basketball Player*
1002 Cherry St, Greenwood, MS 38930, USA
Harrison Breetzke, Joan *Swimmer*
16 Clevedon Road, East London 5201, South Africa
Harrison, Alvin *Track Athlete*
%Octagon, 1751 Pinnacle Dr, #1500, McLean, VA 22102, USA
Harrison, Bertram C *Army General*
749 Dragon Dr, Mount Pleasant, SC 29464, USA
Harrison, C Richard *Businessman*
%Parametric Technology, 140 Kendrick St, Needham Heights, MA 02494, USA

Harrison, Granville *Football Player*
200 S High St, Franklin, VA 23851, USA
Harrison, Gregory *Actor*
%Metropolitan Talent Agency, 4526 Wilshire Blvd, Los Angeles, CA 90010, USA
Harrison, Jenilee *Actress*
%DDK Talent Agency, 3800 Barham Blvd, #303, Los Angeles, CA 90068, USA
Harrison, Jerry *Keyboardist (Talking Heads)*
%Sire/Warner Bros Records, 3300 Warner Blvd, Burbank, CA 91505, USA
Harrison, Jim *Writer*
%Longstreet Press, 2974 Hardman Court NE, Atlanta, GA 30305, USA
Harrison, Kathryn *Writer*
%Random House, 1745 Broadway, #B1, New York, NY 10019, USA
Harrison, Linda *Actress*
211A N Main St, Berlin, MD 21811, USA
Harrison, Mark *Editor*
%The Gazette, 250 Saint Antoine St W, Montreal QC H2Y 3R7, Canada
Harrison, Marvin *Football Player*
5519 Nighthawk Dr, Indianapolis, IN 46254, USA
Harrison, Matthew *Movie Director*
%Rigberg Roberts Rugolo, 1180 S Beverly Dr, #601, Los Angeles, CA 90035, USA
Harrison, Nolan *Football Player*
20245 Augusta Dr, Olympia Fields, IL 60461, USA
Harrison, Tony *Writer*
%Gordon Dickinson, 2 Crescent Grove, London SW4 7AH, England
Harrison, William B, Jr *Financier*
%Chase Manhattan Corp, 270 Park Ave, New York, NY 10017, USA
Harrison, William H *Army General*
7302 Amber Lane SW, Tacoma, WA 98498, USA
Harrold, Kathryn *Actress*
9255 Sunset Blvd, #901, Los Angeles, CA 90069, USA
Harron, Mary *Movie Director*
%William Morris Agency, 151 El Camino Dr, Beverly Hills, CA 90212, USA
Harry *Prince, England*
%Clarence House, Stable Yard Gate, London SW1, England
Harry, Deborah A (Debbie) *Singer, Songwriter, Actress*
%T-Best Talent Agency, 508 Honey Lake Court, Danville, CA 94506, USA
Harryhausen, Ray F *Movie Director*
2 Ilchester Place, West Kensington, London W14 8AA, England
Harsch, Eddie *Keyboardist (Black Crowes)*
%Mitch Schneider Organization, 14724 Ventura Blvd, #410, Sherman Oaks, CA 91403, USA
Harshman, John E (Jack) *Baseball Player*
2003 Bayview Heights Dr, #12, San Diego, CA 92105, USA
Harshman, Marvel K (Marv) *Basketball Player, Coach*
19221 90th Place NE, Bothell, WA 98011, USA
Hart, Bob *Bowler*
5740 Laurel Oak Dr, Suwanee, GA 30024, USA
Hart, Dolores (Mother Dolores) *Actress*
%Regina Laudis Abbey, 275 Flanders Road, Bethlehem, CT 06751, USA
Hart, Doris *Tennis Player*
600 Biltmore Way, #306, Coral Gables, FL 33134, USA
Hart, Dudley *Golfer*
10401 Golden Eagle Court, Plantation, FL 33324, USA
Hart, Freddie *Singer, Songwriter, Guitarist*
317 N Kenwood, Burbank, CA 91505, USA
Hart, Gary W *Senator, CO*
950 17th St, #1800, Denver, CO 80202, USA
Hart, Herbert L A *Solicitor, Philosopher*
11 Manor Place, Oxford, England
Hart, Ian *Actor*
%P F D, Drury House, 34-43 Russell St, London WC2B 5HA, England
Hart, James W (Jim) *Football Player, Sports Administrator*
3141 Dominica Way, Naples, FL 34119, USA
Hart, John *Actor*
35109 Highway 79, #134, Warner Springs, CA 92086, USA
Hart, John L (Johnny) *Cartoonist (BC, Wizard of Id)*
%Creators Syndicate, 5777 W Century Blvd, #700, Los Angeles, CA 90045, USA
Hart, John R *Commentator*
%International Creative Mgmt, 40 W 57th St, #1800, New York, NY 10019, USA
Hart, Mary *Entertainer*
%Brokaw Co, 9255 Sunset Blvd, #804, Los Angeles, CA 90069, USA
Hart, Melissa Joan *Actress*
%United Talent Agency, 9560 Wilshire Blvd, #500, Beverly Hills, CA 90212, USA
Hart, Mickey *Drummer (Grateful Dead)*
PO Box 1073, San Rafael, CA 94915, USA
Hart, Parker T *Diplomat*
4705 Berkeley Terrace NW, Washington, DC 20007, USA
Hart, Roxanne *Actress*
%Agency for Performing Arts, 9200 Sunset Blvd, #900, Los Angeles, CA 90069, USA

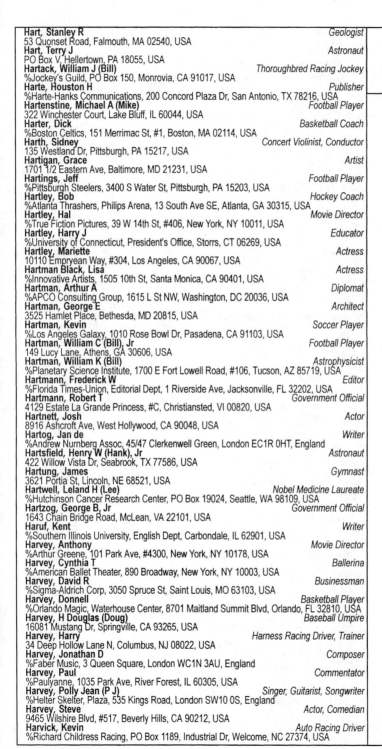

Hart, Stanley R 53 Quonset Road, Falmouth, MA 02540, USA	*Geologist*
Hart, Terry J PO Box V, Hellertown, PA 18055, USA	*Astronaut*
Hartack, William J (Bill) %Jockey's Guild, PO Box 150, Monrovia, CA 91017, USA	*Thoroughbred Racing Jockey*
Harte, Houston H %Harte-Hanks Communications, 200 Concord Plaza Dr, San Antonio, TX 78216, USA	*Publisher*
Hartenstine, Michael A (Mike) 322 Winchester Court, Lake Bluff, IL 60044, USA	*Football Player*
Harter, Dick %Boston Celtics, 151 Merrimac St, #1, Boston, MA 02114, USA	*Basketball Coach*
Harth, Sidney 135 Westland Dr, Pittsburgh, PA 15217, USA	*Concert Violinist, Conductor*
Hartigan, Grace 1701 1/2 Eastern Ave, Baltimore, MD 21231, USA	*Artist*
Hartings, Jeff %Pittsburgh Steelers, 3400 S Water St, Pittsburgh, PA 15203, USA	*Football Player*
Hartley, Bob %Atlanta Thrashers, Philips Arena, 13 South Ave SE, Atlanta, GA 30315, USA	*Hockey Coach*
Hartley, Hal %True Fiction Pictures, 39 W 14th St, #406, New York, NY 10011, USA	*Movie Director*
Hartley, Harry J %University of Connecticut, President's Office, Storrs, CT 06269, USA	*Educator*
Hartley, Mariette 10110 Empryean Way, #304, Los Angeles, CA 90067, USA	*Actress*
Hartman Black, Lisa %Innovative Artists, 1505 10th St, Santa Monica, CA 90401, USA	*Actress*
Hartman, Arthur A %APCO Consulting Group, 1615 L St NW, Washington, DC 20036, USA	*Diplomat*
Hartman, George E 3525 Hamlet Place, Bethesda, MD 20815, USA	*Architect*
Hartman, Kevin %Los Angeles Galaxy, 1010 Rose Bowl Dr, Pasadena, CA 91103, USA	*Soccer Player*
Hartman, William C (Bill), Jr 149 Lucy Lane, Athens, GA 30606, USA	*Football Player*
Hartman, William K (Bill) %Planetary Science Institute, 1700 E Fort Lowell Road, #106, Tucson, AZ 85719, USA	*Astrophysicist*
Hartmann, Frederick W %Florida Times-Union, Editorial Dept, 1 Riverside Ave, Jacksonville, FL 32202, USA	*Editor*
Hartmann, Robert T 4129 Estate La Grande Princess, #C, Christiansted, VI 00820, USA	*Government Official*
Hartnett, Josh 8916 Ashcroft Ave, West Hollywood, CA 90048, USA	*Actor*
Hartog, Jan de %Andrew Nurnberg Assoc, 45/47 Clerkenwell Green, London EC1R 0HT, England	*Writer*
Hartsfield, Henry W (Hank), Jr 422 Willow Vista Dr, Seabrook, TX 77586, USA	*Astronaut*
Hartung, James 3621 Portia St, Lincoln, NE 68521, USA	*Gymnast*
Hartwell, Leland H (Lee) %Hutchinson Cancer Research Center, PO Box 19024, Seattle, WA 98109, USA	*Nobel Medicine Laureate*
Hartzog, George B, Jr 1643 Chain Bridge Road, McLean, VA 22101, USA	*Government Official*
Haruf, Kent %Southern Illinois University, English Dept, Carbondale, IL 62901, USA	*Writer*
Harvey, Anthony %Arthur Greene, 101 Park Ave, #4300, New York, NY 10178, USA	*Movie Director*
Harvey, Cynthia T %American Ballet Theater, 890 Broadway, New York, NY 10003, USA	*Ballerina*
Harvey, David R %Sigma-Aldrich Corp, 3050 Spruce St, Saint Louis, MO 63103, USA	*Businessman*
Harvey, Donnell %Orlando Magic, Waterhouse Center, 8701 Maitland Summit Blvd, Orlando, FL 32810, USA	*Basketball Player*
Harvey, H Douglas (Doug) 16081 Mustang Dr, Springville, CA 93265, USA	*Baseball Umpire*
Harvey, Harry 34 Deep Hollow Lane N, Columbus, NJ 08022, USA	*Harness Racing Driver, Trainer*
Harvey, Jonathan D %Faber Music, 3 Queen Square, London WC1N 3AU, England	*Composer*
Harvey, Paul %Paulyanne, 1035 Park Ave, River Forest, IL 60305, USA	*Commentator*
Harvey, Polly Jean (P J) %Helter Skelter, Plaza, 535 Kings Road, London SW10 0S, England	*Singer, Guitarist, Songwriter*
Harvey, Steve 9465 Wilshire Blvd, #517, Beverly Hills, CA 90212, USA	*Actor, Comedian*
Harvick, Kevin %Richard Childress Racing, PO Box 1189, Industrial Dr, Welcome, NC 27374, USA	*Auto Racing Driver*

H

Harwell - Hatcher

Harwell, Steve *Singer (Smash Mouth)*
%Creative Artists Agency, 9830 Wilshire Blvd, Beverly Hills, CA 90212, USA
Harwell, W Earnest (Ernie) *Sportscaster*
141 Fernery Road, #A6, Lakeland, FL 33809, USA
Hary, Armin *Track Athlete*
Scholss, 86911 Diessen/Ammersee, Germany
Hase, Dagmar *Swimmer*
Niederndodeleber Str 14, 29110 Magdeburg, Germany
Haselkorn, Robert *Virologist*
5834 S Stony Island Ave, Chicago, IL 60637, USA
Haseltine, Dan *Singer (Jars of Clay)*
%Flood Bumstead McCready McCarthy, 1700 Hayes St, #304, Nashville, TN 37203, USA
Haseltine, William A *Molecular Biologist*
%Human Genome Sciences, 9410 Key West Ave, Rockville, MD 20850, USA
Hasen, Irvin H *Cartoonist (Goldbergs, Dondi)*
68 E 79th St, New York, NY 10021, USA
Hashimoto, Ryutaro *Prime Minister, Japan*
%Liberal Democratic Party, 1-11-23 Nagatocho, Chiyodaku, Tokyo 100, Japan
Haskell, Peter *Actor*
19924 Acre St, Northridge, CA 91324, USA
Haskins, Clem *Basketball Player, Coach*
2632 Roberts Road, Campbellsville, KY 42718, USA
Haskins, Dennis *Actor*
345 N Maple Dr, #302, Beverly Hills, CA 90210, USA
Haskins, Don *Basketball Coach*
%Chicago Bulls, United Center, 1901 W Madison St, Chicago, IL 60612, USA
Haskins, Michael D *Navy Admiral*
Inspector General, HqUSN, Pentagon, Washington, DC 20350, USA
Haskins, Samuel J (Sam) *Photographer*
PO Box 59, Wimbledon, London SW19, England
Hasler, Otmar *Prime Minister, Liechtenstein*
%Premier's Office, Regierungsgebaude, 9490 Vaduz, Liechtenstein
Haslett, James D (Jim) *Football Player, Coach*
PO Box 190, Destrehan, LA 70047, USA
Hasluck, Paul M C *Government Official, Australia*
2 Adams Road, Dalkeith WA 6009, Australia
Hass, Robert *Writer*
%University of California, English Dept, Berkeley, CA 94720, USA
Hassan Ibn Talal *Crown Prince, Jordan*
%Deputy King's Office, Royal Palace, Amman, Jordan
Hassan, Fred *Businessman*
%Schering-Plough Corp, 1 Giralda Farms, Madison, NJ 07940, USA
Hassel, Gerald L *Financier*
%Bank of New York, 1 Wall St, New York, NY 10286, USA
Hasselbeck, Donald W (Don) *Football Player*
38 Noon Hill Ave, Norfolk, VA 02056, USA
Hasselhoff, David *Actor, Singer*
5180 Louise Ave, Encino, CA 91316, USA
Hasselmo, Nils *Educator*
%Assn of American Universities, 1200 New York Ave, #1200, Washington, DC 20005, USA
Hassenfeld, Alan G *Businessman*
%Hasbro Inc, 1027 Newport Ave, Pawtucket, RI 02861, USA
Hassett, Marilyn *Actress*
8905 Rosewood Ave, West Hollywood, CA 90048, USA
Hasson, Maurice *Concert Violinist*
18 West Heath Court, North End Road, London NW11, England
Hast, Adele *Editor*
%Newberry Library, 60 W Walton St, Chicago, IL 60610, USA
Hastings, Barry G *Financier*
%Northern Trust Corp, 50 S La Salle St, Chicago, IL 60603, USA
Hastings, Don *Actor*
524 W 57th St, #5330, New York, NY 10019, USA
Haston, Kirk *Basketball Player*
382 E Mill St, Henderson, TN 38340, USA
Hatch, Harold A *Marine Corps General*
8655 White Beach Way, Vienna, VA 22182, USA
Hatch, Henry J *Army General*
2715 Silkwood Court, Oakton, VA 22124, USA
Hatch, Monroe W, Jr *Air Force General*
8210 Thomas Ashleigh Lane, Clifton, VA 20124, USA
Hatch, Richard *Actor*
10977 Bluffside Dr, #1403, Studio City, CA 91604, USA
Hatchell, Sylvia *Basketball Coach*
%University of North Carolina, Athletic Dept, Chapel Hill, NC 27515, USA
Hatcher, Kevin *Hockey Player*
1225 S Water St, Marine City, MI 48039, USA
Hatcher, R Dale *Football Player*
906 White Plains Road, Gaffney, SC 29340, USA

Hatcher, Teri *Actress*
%Jorgensen & Rogers, 10100 Santa Monica Blvd, #410, Los Angeles, CA 90067, USA
Hatchett, Joseph W *Judge*
%US Court of Appeals, 810 Lewis State Bank Building, Tallahassee, FL 32302, USA
Hatfield, Juliana *Singer, Songwriter*
%Fort Apache Mgmt, 1 Camp St, Cambridge, MA 02140, USA
Hatfield, Mark O *Governor, Senator, OR*
17400 Holy Names Dr, #E306, Lake Oswego, OR 97034, USA
Hathaway, Anne *Actress*
%William Morris Agency, 151 El Camino Dr, Beverly Hills, CA 90212, USA
Hathaway, William D *Senator, ME*
%Federal Maritime Commission, 800 N Capitol St NW, Washington, DC 20002, USA
Hatori, Miho *Singer (Cibo Matto)*
%Billions Corp, 833 W Chicago Ave, #101, Chicago, IL 60622, USA
Hatosy, Shawn *Actor*
853 7th Ave, #9A, New York, NY 10019, USA
Hatsopoulos, George N *Businessman, Mechanical Engineer*
%Thermo Electron Corp, 81 Wyman St, PO Box 9046, Waltham, MA 02454, USA
Hatten, Tom *Actor*
1759 Sunset Plaza Dr, Los Angeles, CA 90069, USA
Hattersley, Roy S G *Government Official, England*
%House of Lords, Westminster, London SW1A 0PW, England
Hattestad, Stine Lise *Moguls Skier*
Sundlia 1B, 1315 Nesoya, Norway
Hatton, Vernon *Basketball Player*
PO Box 8405, Lexington, KY 40533, USA
Hau, Lene Vestergaard *Physicist*
%Harvard University, Applied Physics Dept, Cambridge, MA 02138, USA
Hauck, Frederick H (Rick) *Astronaut*
7918 Turncrest Dr, Potomac, MD 20854, USA
Hauer, Rutger *Actor*
1601 Cloverfield Blvd, #5000N, Santa Monica, CA 90404, USA
Hauerwas, Stanley *Theologian*
%Duke University, Divinity School, Durham, NC 27706, USA
Haughey, Charles J *Prime Minister, Ireland*
Abbeville, Kinsakey, Malahide County Dublin, Ireland
Hauk, A Andrew *Judge, Skier*
%US Court House, 312 N Spring St, Los Angeles, CA 90012, USA
Hauptman, Herbert A *Nobel Chemistry Laureate*
121 Woodbury Dr, Buffalo, NY 14226, USA
Haus, Hermann A *Electrical Engineer, Computer Scientist*
38 Jeffrey Terrace, Lexington, MA 02420, USA
Hauser, Cole *Actor*
2133 Holly Dr, Los Angeles, CA 90068, USA
Hauser, Erich *Sculptor*
Saline 36, 78628 Rottweil, Germany
Hauser, Tim *Singer (Manhattan Transfer)*
3855 Lankershim Blvd, #214, North Hollywood, CA 91604, USA
Hauser, Wings *Actor*
9450 Chivers Ave, Sun Valley, CA 91352, USA
Hausman, Jerry A *Economist*
%Massachusetts Institute of Technology, Economics Dept, Cambridge, MA 02139, USA
Hauss, Lenard M (Len) *Football Player*
PO Box 1808, Reidsville, GA 30453, USA
Havel, Vaclav *President, Czech Republic; Writer*
%Kancelar Prezidenta Republiky, Hradecek, 119 08 Prague 1, Czech Republic
Havelange, Jean M F G (Joao) *Soccer Executive*
Ave Rio Branco 89B, Conj 602 Centro, 20040-004 Rio de Janiero, Brazil
Havelid, Niclas *Hockey Player*
%Anaheim Mighty Ducks, 2000 E Gene Autry Way, Anaheim, CA 92806, USA
Havens, Frank B *Canoeing Athlete*
PO Box 55, Harborton, VA 23389, USA
Havens, Richie *Singer, Songwriter, Guitarist*
%Drake, 177 Woodland Ave, Westwood, NJ 07675, USA
Haver, June *Actress*
485 Halvern Dr, Los Angeles, CA 90049, USA
Havers, Nigel *Actor*
%Michael Whitehall, 125 Gloucester Road, London SW7 4TE, England
Havlat, Martin *Hockey Player*
%Ottawa Senators, 1000 Palladium Dr, Kanata ON K2V 1A4, Canada
Havlish, Jean *Bowler*
1277 Kent St, Saint Paul, MN 55117, USA
Havoc, June *Actress*
405 Old Long Ridge Road, Stamford, CT 06903, USA
Hawerchuk, Dale *Hockey Player*
%Grand Farms, 95404 7th Line EHS, RR 5, Orangeville ON L9W 2Z2, Canada
Hawk, John D *WW II Army Hero (CMH)*
3243 Solie Ave, Bremerton, WA 98310, USA

Hawk - Hayden

Hawk, Tony *Skateboarding Athlete, Actor*
31878 Del Obispo, #118-602, San Juan Capistrano, CA 92675, USA
Hawke, Ethan *Actor*
%Three Arts Entertainment, 9460 Wilshire Blvd, #700, Beverly Hills, CA 90212, USA
Hawke, Robert J L *Prime Minister, Australia*
GPO Box 36, Sydney NSW 2001, Australia
Hawkes, Christopher *Archaeologist*
19 Walton St, Oxford OX1 2HQ, England
Hawking, Stephen W *Theoretical Physicist*
%University of Cambridge, Applied Math Dept, Cambridge CB3 9EW, England
Hawkins, Arthur R *WW II Navy Air Force Hero*
28496 Perdido Pass Dr, Orange Beach, AL 36561, USA
Hawkins, Barbara *Singer (Dixie Cups)*
%Superstars Unlimited, PO Box 371371, Las Vegas, NV 89137, USA
Hawkins, Benjamin C (Ben) *Football Player*
104 Deforest St, Roslindale, MA 02131, USA
Hawkins, Cornelius L (Connie) *Basketball Player, Executive*
%Phoenix Suns, 201 E Jefferson St, Phoenix, AZ 85004, USA
Hawkins, Dale *Singer, Songwriter, Guitarist*
4618 John F Kennedy Blvd, #107, North Little Rock, AR 72116, USA
Hawkins, Edwin *Vocal Group Leader*
%PAZ Entertainment, 2041 Locust St, Philadelphia, PA 19103, USA
Hawkins, Frank *Football Player*
2300 Alta Dr, Las Vegas, NV 89107, USA
Hawkins, Hersey R, Jr *Basketball Player*
%New Orleans Hornets, New Orleans Arena, 1501 Girod St, New Orleans, LA 70113, USA
Hawkins, M Andrew (Andy) *Baseball Player*
RR 1, Dawson, TX 76639, USA
Hawkins, Michael Daly *Judge*
%US Court of Appeals, 230 N 1st St, Phoenix, AZ 85025, USA
Hawkins, Paula *Senator, FL*
1214 Park Ave N, Winter Park, FL 32789, USA
Hawkins, Ronnie *Singer*
%Agency Group Ltd, 59 Berkeley St, Toronto ON M5A 2W5, Canada
Hawkins, Rosa *Singer (Dixie Cups)*
%Superstars Unlimited, PO Box 371371, Las Vegas, NV 89137, USA
Hawkins, Sophie B *Singer, Songwriter*
%Trumpet Swan Productions, 520 Washington Blvd, #337, Marina del Rey, CA 90292, USA
Hawkins, Tommy *Basketball Player*
1745 Manzanita Park Ave, Malibu, CA 90265, USA
Hawkins, Willis M *Space Scientist*
%Marshall Institute, 1625 K St NW, #1050, Washington, DC 20006, USA
Hawkinson, Tim *Artist*
%Ace Gallery, 5514 Wilshire Blvd, Los Angeles, CA 90036, USA
Hawks, Steve *Artist*
%Hadley House, 1101 Hampshire Road S, Bloomington, MN 55438, USA
Hawlata, Franz *Opera Singer*
%I M G Artists, 3 Burlington Lane, Chiswick, London W4 2TH, England
Hawley, Frank *Auto Racing Driver*
%Frank Hawley Drag Racing School, County Road 225, Gainesville, FL 32609, USA
Hawley, Sandy *Thoroughbred Racing Jockey*
9625 Merrill Road, Silverwood, MI 48760, USA
Hawley, Steven A *Astronaut*
3929 Walnut Pond Dr, Houston, TX 77059, USA
Hawn, Goldie *Actress*
%International Creative Mgmt, 8942 Wilshire Blvd, #219, Beverly Hills, CA 90211, USA
Haworth, Jill *Actress*
300 E 51st St, New York, NY 10022, USA
Hawpe, David V *Editor*
%Louisville Courier-Journal, Editorial Dept, 525 Broadway, Louisville, KY 40202, USA
Hawthorne, William R *Thermodynamics Engineer*
%Churchill College, Engineering School, Cambridge CB3 0DS, England
Hax, Carolyn *Columnist*
%Washington Post, Editorial Dept, 1150 15th St NW, Washington, DC 20071, USA
Hay, Colin *Singer (Men at Work)*
%TPA, PO Box 125, Round Corner NSW 2158, Australia
Hayaishi, Osamu *Biochemist*
1-29 Izumigawacho, Shimogamo Sakyoku, Kyoto 606-0807, Japan
Hayashi, Izuo *Engineer*
%OptoElectrics Research Lab, 5-5 Tohkodai, Tsukuba, Ibaraki 300-26, Japan
Hayashi, Shizuya *WW II Army Hero (CMH)*
1331 Hoowai St, Pearl City, HI 96782, USA
Haydee, Marcia *Ballerina*
%Stuttgart Ballet, Oberer Schlossgarten 6, 70173 Stuttgart, Germany
Hayden, Frederick *Microbiologist*
%University of Virginia, Med Ctr, Microbiology Dept, Charlottesville, VA 22903, USA
Hayden, J Michael (Mike) *Governor, KS*
5809 Sagamore Court, Lawrence, KS 66047, USA

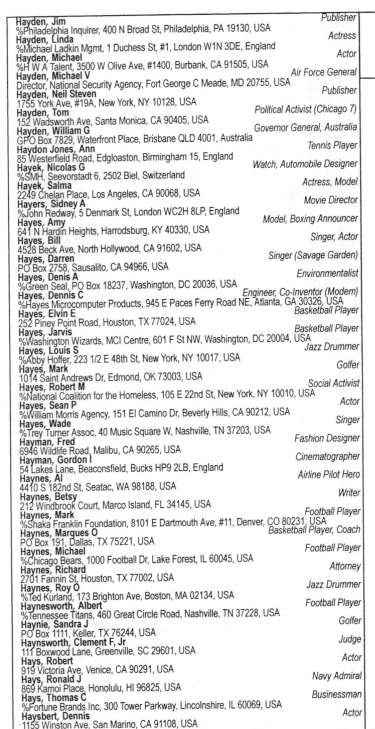

Hayden, Jim *Publisher*
%Philadelphia Inquirer, 400 N Broad St, Philadelphia, PA 19130, USA
Hayden, Linda *Actress*
%Michael Ladkin Mgmt, 1 Duchess St, #1, London W1N 3DE, England
Hayden, Michael *Actor*
%H W A Talent, 3500 W Olive Ave, #1400, Burbank, CA 91505, USA
Hayden, Michael V *Air Force General*
Director, National Security Agency, Fort George C Meade, MD 20755, USA
Hayden, Neil Steven *Publisher*
1755 York Ave, #19A, New York, NY 10128, USA
Hayden, Tom *Political Activist (Chicago 7)*
152 Wadsworth Ave, Santa Monica, CA 90405, USA
Hayden, William G *Governor General, Australia*
GPO Box 7829, Waterfront Place, Brisbane QLD 4001, Australia
Haydon Jones, Ann *Tennis Player*
85 Westerfield Road, Edgloaston, Birmingham 15, England
Hayek, Nicolas G *Watch, Automobile Designer*
%SMH, Seevorstadt 6, 2502 Biel, Switzerland
Hayek, Salma *Actress, Model*
2249 Chelan Place, Los Angeles, CA 90068, USA
Hayers, Sidney A *Movie Director*
%John Redway, 5 Denmark St, London WC2H 8LP, England
Hayes, Amy *Model, Boxing Announcer*
641 N Hardin Heights, Harrodsburg, KY 40330, USA
Hayes, Bill *Singer, Actor*
4528 Beck Ave, North Hollywood, CA 91602, USA
Hayes, Darren *Singer (Savage Garden)*
PO Box 2758, Sausalito, CA 94966, USA
Hayes, Denis A *Environmentalist*
%Green Seal, PO Box 18237, Washington, DC 20036, USA
Hayes, Dennis C *Engineer, Co-Inventor (Modem)*
%Hayes Microcomputer Products, 945 E Paces Ferry Road NE, Atlanta, GA 30326, USA
Hayes, Elvin E *Basketball Player*
252 Piney Point Road, Houston, TX 77024, USA
Hayes, Jarvis *Basketball Player*
%Washington Wizards, MCI Centre, 601 F St NW, Washington, DC 20004, USA
Hayes, Louis S *Jazz Drummer*
%Abby Hoffer, 223 1/2 E 48th St, New York, NY 10017, USA
Hayes, Mark *Golfer*
1014 Saint Andrews Dr, Edmond, OK 73003, USA
Hayes, Robert M *Social Activist*
%National Coalition for the Homeless, 105 E 22nd St, New York, NY 10010, USA
Hayes, Sean P *Actor*
%William Morris Agency, 151 El Camino Dr, Beverly Hills, CA 90212, USA
Hayes, Wade *Singer*
%Trey Turner Assoc, 40 Music Square W, Nashville, TN 37203, USA
Hayman, Fred *Fashion Designer*
6946 Wildlife Road, Malibu, CA 90265, USA
Hayman, Gordon I *Cinematographer*
54 Lakes Lane, Beaconsfield, Bucks HP9 2LB, England
Haynes, Al *Airline Pilot Hero*
4410 S 182nd St, Seatac, WA 98188, USA
Haynes, Betsy *Writer*
212 Windbrook Court, Marco Island, FL 34145, USA
Haynes, Mark *Football Player*
%Shaka Franklin Foundation, 8101 E Dartmouth Ave, #11, Denver, CO 80231, USA
Haynes, Marques O *Basketball Player, Coach*
PO Box 191, Dallas, TX 75221, USA
Haynes, Michael *Football Player*
%Chicago Bears, 1000 Football Dr, Lake Forest, IL 60045, USA
Haynes, Richard *Attorney*
2701 Fannin St, Houston, TX 77002, USA
Haynes, Roy O *Jazz Drummer*
%Ted Kurland, 173 Brighton Ave, Boston, MA 02134, USA
Haynesworth, Albert *Football Player*
%Tennessee Titans, 460 Great Circle Road, Nashville, TN 37228, USA
Haynie, Sandra J *Golfer*
PO Box 1111, Keller, TX 76244, USA
Haynsworth, Clement F, Jr *Judge*
111 Boxwood Lane, Greenville, SC 29601, USA
Hays, Robert *Actor*
919 Victoria Ave, Venice, CA 90291, USA
Hays, Ronald J *Navy Admiral*
869 Kamoi Place, Honolulu, HI 96825, USA
Hays, Thomas C *Businessman*
%Fortune Brands Inc, 300 Tower Parkway, Lincolnshire, IL 60069, USA
Haysbert, Dennis *Actor*
1155 Winston Ave, San Marino, CA 91108, USA

Hayward, Charles E *Publisher*
%Little Brown Co, Time-Life Building, Rockefeller Center, New York, NY 10020, USA
Hayward, Justin *Singer, Guitarist (Moody Blues)*
%Bright Music, PO Box 4536, Henley-on-Thames, Berkshire RG9 3YD, England
Hayward, Thomas B *Navy Admiral*
2200 Ross Ave, #3800, Dallas, TX 75201, USA
Haywood, Spencer *Basketball Player*
46866 Mornington Road, Canton, MI 48188, USA
Hazard, Geoffrey C, Jr *Attorney, Educator*
200 W Willow Grove Ave, Philadelphia, PA 19118, USA
Haziza, Shlomi *Artist*
%H Studio, 8640 Tamarack Ave, Sun Valley, CA 91352, USA
Hazzard, Shirley *Writer*
200 E 66th St, New York, NY 10021, USA
Head, Anthony Stewart *Actor*
710 Ocean Park Blvd, #3, Santa Monica, CA 90405, USA
Head, James W *Space Scientist*
%Brown University, Geological Sciences Dept, Providence, RI 02912, USA
Headden, Susan M *Journalist*
%Indianapolis Star, Editorial Dept, 307 N Pennsylvania, Indianapolis, IN 46204, USA
Headley, Heather *Singer, Actress*
%Paradigm Agency, 10100 Santa Monica Blvd, #2500, Los Angeles, CA 90067, USA
Headly, Glenne *Actress*
7929 Hollywood Blvd, Los Angeles, CA 90046, USA
Heald, Anthony *Actor*
%Endeavor Talent Agency, 9701 Wilshire Blvd, #1000, Beverly Hills, CA 90212, USA
Healey, Denis W *Government Official, England*
Pingles Place, Alfriston, East Sussex BN26 5TT, England
Healey, John G *Association Executive*
%Amnesty International USA, 322 8th Ave, New York, NY 10001, USA
Healy, Cornelius T *Labor Leader*
%Plate Die Engravers Union, 228 S Swarthmore Ave, Ridley Park, PA 19078, USA
Healy, Fran *Singer (Travis)*
%Wildlife Entertainment, 21 Heathmans Road, London SW6 4TJ, England
Healy, Jane E *Journalist*
%Orlando Sentinel, Editorial Dept, 633 N Orange Ave, Orlando, FL 32801, USA
Healy, Mary *Actress*
8641 Robinson Ridge Dr, Las Vegas, NV 89117, USA
Healy, Patricia *Actress*
%Shelter Entertainment, 9255 Sunset Blvd, #1010, Los Angeles, CA 90069, USA
Heaney, Gerald W *Judge*
%US Court of Appeals, Federal Building, Duluth, MN 55802, USA
Heaney, Seamus J *Nobel Literature Laureate*
191 Strand Road, Dublin 4, Ireland
Heard, G Alexander *Educator, Political Scientist*
2100 Golf Club Lane, Nashville, TN 37215, USA
Heard, John *Actor*
853 7th Ave, #9A, New York, NY 10019, USA
Hearn, George *Actor, Singer*
211 S Beverly Dr, #211, Beverly Hills, CA 90212, USA
Hearn, J Woodrow *Religious Leader*
%United Methodist Church, PO Box 320, Nashville, TN 37202, USA
Hearn, Kevin *Musician (Barenaked Ladies)*
%Nettwerk Mgmt, 8730 Wilshire Blvd, #304, Beverly Hills, CA 90211, USA
Hearn, Thomas K, Jr *Educator*
%Wake Forest University, President's Office, Winston Salem, NC 27109, USA
Hearne, Bill *Singer, Guitarist*
%Class Act Entertainment, PO Box 160236, Nashville, TN 37216, USA
Hearns, Thomas (Tommy) *Boxer*
3165 Castle Canyon Ave, Henderson, NV 89052, USA
Hearst, G Garrison *Football Player*
3753 Augusta Road, Lincolnton, GA 30817, USA
Hearst, Rick *Actor*
%Stone Manners, 6500 Wilshire Blvd, #550, Los Angeles, CA 90048, USA
Heath, Albert (Tootie) *Jazz Drummer (Modern Jazz Quarter)*
%Ted Kurland, 173 Brighton Ave, Boston, MA 02134, USA
Heath, Edward R G *Prime Minister, England*
%House of Commons, Westminster, London SW1A 0AA, England
Heath, James E (Jimmy) *Jazz Saxophonist, Composer*
%Ted Kurland, 173 Brighton Ave, Boston, MA 02134, USA
Heath, Percy *Jazz Bassist (Modern Jazz Quartet)*
%Atlantic Records, 1290 Ave of Americas, New York, NY 10104, USA
Heathcock, Clayton H *Chemist*
5235 Alhambra Valley Road, Martinez, CA 94553, USA
Heathcote, Jud *Basketball Coach*
5418 S Quail Ridge Circle, Spokane, WA 99223, USA
Heaton, Patricia *Actress*
%United Talent Agency, 9560 Wilshire Blvd, #500, Beverly Hills, CA 90212, USA

Heavy D *Rap Artist*
%Soul On Soul, PO Box 1009, Pelham, NY 10803, USA
Hebert, Johnny *Auto Racing Driver*
%Team Lotus, Kettering Hamm Hall, Wymondham, Norfolk NR18 7HW, England
Heche, Anne *Actress*
%Huvane Baum Halls, 8500 Wilshire Blvd, #700, Beverly Hills, CA 90211, USA
Hecht, Anthony E *Writer*
4256 Nebraska Ave NW, Washington, DC 20016, USA
Hecht, Duvall *Rower*
2910 W Garry Ave, Santa Ana, CA 92704, USA
Hecht, Gina *Actress*
5930 Foothill Dr, Los Angeles, CA 90068, USA
Heckerling, Amy *Movie Director, Producer*
1330 Schuyler Road, Beverly Hills, CA 90210, USA
Heckler, Margaret M *Secretary, Health & Human Services*
1401 N Oak St, Arlington, VA 22209, USA
Heckman, James J *Nobel Economics Laureate*
4807 S Greenwood Ave, Chicago, IL 60615, USA
Hedaya, Dan *Actor*
%Gersh Agency, 232 N Canon Dr, Beverly Hills, CA 90210, USA
Hedeman, Richard (Tuff) *Rodeo Bull Rider*
PO Box 224, Morgan Mill, TX 76465, USA
Hedford, Eric *Singer, Drummer (Dandy Warhols)*
%Monqui Mgmt, PO Box 5908, Portland, OR 97228, USA
Hedges, Peter *Movie Director, Writer*
%Hyperion Books, 114 5th Ave, New York, NY 10011, USA
Hedican, Bret *Hockey Player*
2500 E Las Olas Blvd, #502, Fort Lauderdale, FL 33301, USA
Hedison, David *Actor*
PO Box 1470, Beverly Hills, CA 90213, USA
Hedren, Tippi *Actress*
6867 Soledad Canyon Road, Acton, CA 93510, USA
Hedrick, Joan D *Writer*
%Trinity College, Women's Studies Program, 300 Summit St, Hartford, CT 06106, USA
Heeger, Alan J *Nobel Chemistry Laureate*
1042 Las Alturas Road, Santa Barbara, CA 93103, USA
Heeschen, David S *Radio Astronomer*
702 Copa D'Oro, Marathon, FL 33050, USA
Heeter, Carrie *Inventor (Sign-Language Software)*
%Michigan State University, Communication Technology Lab, East Lansing, MI 48824, USA
Hefner, Christie A *Publisher*
%Playboy Enterprises, 680 N Lake Shore Dr, Chicago, IL 60611, USA
Hefner, Hugh M *Publisher, Editor*
10236 Charing Cross Road, Los Angeles, CA 90024, USA
Heft, Robert (Bob) *Flag Designer*
PO Box 20404, Saginaw, MI 48602, USA
Hefti, Neal *Composer*
%Encino Music, 9454 Wilshire Blvd, #405, Beverly Hills, CA 90212, USA
Heggtveit, Ann Hamilton *Alpine Skier*
%General Delivery, Grand Isle, VT 05458, USA
Hegyes, Robert *Actor*
2404 Pacific Ave, Venice, CA 90291, USA
Heiden, Elizabeth L (Beth) *Speedskater*
PO Box 110, Dollar Bay, MI 49922, USA
Heiden, Eric A *Speedskater, Cyclist*
240 Sandburg Dr, Sacramento, CA 95819, USA
Heigl, Jennifer *Actress*
%Writers & Artists, 8383 Wilshire Blvd, #550, Beverly Hills, CA 90211, USA
Heigl, Katherine *Actress, Model*
8436 W 3rd St, #650, Los Angeles, CA 90048, USA
Heilbroner, Robert L *Economist*
435 E 57th St, New York, NY 10022, USA
Heilmeier, George H *Inventor (Liquid Crystal Display)*
%Telecordia Technologies, 445 South St, Morristown, NJ 07960, USA
Heimbold, Charles A, Jr *Businessman*
%Bristol-Myers Squibb, 345 Park Ave, New York, NY 10154, USA
Heimel, Cynthia *Writer*
%Simon & Schuster, 1230 Ave of Americas, New York, NY 10020, USA
Heimlich, Henry J *Physician*
17 Elmhurst St, Cincinnati, OH 45208, USA
Heine, Jutta *Track Athlete*
Blaue Muhle, 57614 Burglahr, Germany
Heinle, Amelia *Actress*
%Gallin Morey, 335 N Maple Dr, #351, Beverly Hills, CA 90210, USA
Heinsohn, Thomas W (Tom) *Basketball Player, Coach*
PO Box 422, Newton Upper Falls, MA 02464, USA
Heinz, W C *Sportswriter*
1150 Nichols Hill Road, Dorset, VT 05251, USA

Heinzer, Franz *Alpine Skier*
Lauenen, 6432 Rickenbach/Schwyz, Switzerland
Heiss Jenkins, Carol *Figure Skater*
3183 Regency Place, Westlake, OH 44145, USA
Hejduk, Milan *Hockey Player*
3155 Rockbridge Dr, Littleton, CO 80129, USA
Held, Archie *Sculptor*
%A New Leaf Garden, 1286 Gilman St, Berkeley, CA 94706, USA
Held, Franklin (Bud) *Track Athlete*
13367 Caminito Mar Villa, Del Mar, CA 92014, USA
Held, Richard M *Psychologist*
%Massachusetts Institute of Technology, Psychology Dept, Cambridge, MA 02139, USA
Helfand, David *Astronomer*
%Columbia University, Astronomer Dept, New York, NY 10027, USA
Helfer, Ricki Tigert *Financier*
%Federal Deposit Insurance, 550 17th St NW, Washington, DC 20429, USA
Helgeland, Brian *Movie Director*
%United Talent Agency, 9560 Wilshire Blvd, #500, Beverly Hills, CA 90212, USA
Helgenberger, Marg *Actress*
%International Creative Mgmt, 8942 Wilshire Blvd, #219, Beverly Hills, CA 90211, USA
Hellawell, Keith *Law Enforcment Official*
%Government Offices, Great George St, London SW1A 2AL, England
Heller, Daniel M *Attorney*
Israel Discount Bank Building, 14 NE 1st Ave, Miami, FL 33132, USA
Heller, Jane *Writer*
208 S Spalding Dr, Beverly Hills, CA 90212, USA
Heller, Jeffrey M *Businessman*
%Electronic Data Systems, 5400 Legacy Dr, Plano, TX 75024, USA
Heller, John H *Research Scientist*
74 Horseshoe Road, Wilton, CT 06897, USA
Hellerman, Fred *Singer (Weavers), Songwriter*
83 Goodhill Road, Weston, CT 06883, USA
Hellickson, Russell (Russ) *Wrestler*
6893 Lauren Place, Columbus, OH 43235, USA
Helling, Ricky A (Rick) *Baseball Player*
2706 Henry, Irving, TX 75062, USA
Helliwell, Robert A *Radio Scientist*
2240 Page Mill Road, Palo Alto, CA 94304, USA
Hellman, Martin E *Inventor (Public Key Cryptology)*
855 Serra St, Stanford, CA 94305, USA
Hellman, Monte *Movie Director*
8588 Appian Way, Los Angeles, CA 90046, USA
Hellmann, Martina *Track Athlete*
Neue Leipziger Str 14, 04205 Leipzig, Germany
Hellmuth, George F *Architect*
10111 Ingleside Dr, Saint Louis, MO 63124, USA
Hellstrand, Kristoffer *Microbiologist*
%Goteborg University, Virology Dept, Goteborg 405 30, Sweden
Hellyer, Paul T *Government Official, Canada*
65 Harbour Square, #506, Toronto ON M5J 2L4, Canada
Helm, Levon *Singer, Drummer (Band); Actor*
160 Plochman Lane, Woodstock, NY 12498, USA
Helmberger, Don V *Seismologist*
%California Institute of Technology, Seismology Dept, Pasadena, CA 91125, USA
Helmerich, Hans C *Businessman*
%Helmerich & Payne Inc, Utica & 21st St, Tulsa, OK 74114, USA
Helmerich, Walter H, III *Businessman*
%Helmerich & Payne Inc, Utica & 21st St, Tulsa, OK 74114, USA
Helmerson, Frans *Concert Cellist*
%Columbia Artists Mgmt Inc, 165 W 57th St, New York, NY 10019, USA
Helmond, Katherine *Actress*
14170 Montecito Place, Victorville, CA 92392, USA
Helmreich, Ernst J M *Physiological Chemist*
%University of Wurzburg Biozentrum, Am Hubland, 97074 Wurzburg, Germany
Helms, L S *Financier*
%KeyCorp, 127 Public Square, Cleveland, OH 44114, USA
Helms, Susan J *Astronaut*
%NASA, Johnson Space Center, 2101 NASA Road, Houston, TX 77058, USA
Helmsley, Leona M *Businesswoman*
36 Central Park South, New York, NY 10019, USA
Helnwein, Gottfried *Artist*
Auf der Burg 2, 56659 Burgbrol, Germany
Heloise, (Cruse Evans) *Journalist*
PO Box 795000, San Antonio, TX 78279, USA
Helpern, Joan G *Fashion Designer*
%Joan & David Helpern Inc, 46 W 55th St, #200, New York, NY 10019, USA
Heltau, Michael *Actor, Singer*
Sulzweg 11, 1190 Vienna, Austria

Helton, Bill D *Businessman*
%New Century Energies, 1225 17th St, Denver, CO 80202, USA
Helton, Todd L *Baseball Player*
1 White Pelican Circle, Denver, CO 80241, USA
Helvin, Marie *Model*
%IMG Models, 23 Eyot Gardens, London W6 9TN, England
Helwig, David G *Writer*
Belfast Prince Edward Island C0A 1A0, Canada
Hemenway, Robert E *Educator*
%University of Kansas, President's Office, Lawrence, KS 66045, USA
Hemingway, Gerardine *Fashion Designer*
%Red or Dead Ltd, Courtney Road, Bldg 201, Wembley, Middx HA9 7PP, England
Hemingway, Mariel *Model, Actress*
PO Box 2249, Ketchum, ID 83340, USA
Hemingway, Wayne *Fashion Designer*
%Red or Dead Ltd, Courtney Road, Bldg 201, Wembley, Middx HA9 7PP, England
Hemmer, Bill *Commentator*
%Cable News Network, News Dept, 1050 Techwood Dr NW, Atlanta, GA 30318, USA
Hemmi, Heini *Alpine Skier*
Chalet Bel-Lia, 7077 Valbella, Switzerland
Hemmings, David L E *Actor*
%Michael Whitehall, 125 Gloucester Road, London SW7 4TE, England
Hempel, Amy *Writer*
%Charles Scribner's Sons, 866 3rd Ave, New York, NY 10022, USA
Hemphill, Joel *Singer*
%Harper Agency, PO Box 144, Goodlettsville, TN 37070, USA
Hemphill, Labreeska *Singer*
%Harper Agency, PO Box 144, Goodlettsville, TN 37070, USA
Hempstone, Smith, Jr *Columnist, Diplomat*
7611 Fairfax Road, Bethesda, MD 20814, USA
Hemsley, Sherman *Actor*
%Kenny Johnston, PO Box 5344, Sherman Oaks, CA 91413, USA
Hemsley, Stephen J *Businessman*
%United HealthCare Corp, Opus Center, 9900 Bren Road E, Minnetonka, MN 55343, USA
Hencken, John F *Swimmer*
10532 Tujunga Canyon Blvd, Tujunga, CA 91042, USA
Henderson, Alan *Basketball Player*
%Atlanta Hawks, 190 Marietta St SW, Atlanta, GA 30303, USA
Henderson, Billy *Singer (Spinners)*
%Buddy Allen Mgmt, 3750 Hudson Manor Terrace, #3AG, Bronx, NY 10463, USA
Henderson, Bruce *Singer, Songwriter*
%Fitch Thomas Mgmt, 75 E End Ave, #4C, New York, NY 10028, USA
Henderson, Chris *Soccer Player*
%Columbus Crew, 2121 Velman Ave, Columbus, OH 43211, USA
Henderson, David L (Dave) *Baseball Player*
6004 142nd Court SE, Bellevue, WA 98006, USA
Henderson, Donald A *Epidemologist, Educator*
3802 Greenway, Baltimore, MD 21218, USA
Henderson, Florence *Actress, Singer*
%Cliff Ayers Enterprises, PO Box 17059, Nashville, TN 37217, USA
Henderson, Gordon *Fashion Designer*
%World Hong Kong, 80 W 40th St, New York, NY 10018, USA
Henderson, James A *Businessman*
%Cummins Engine Co, PO Box 3005, 500 Jackson St, Columbus, IN 47201, USA
Henderson, John *Football Player*
%Jacksonville Jaguars, 1 AllTel Stadium Place, Jacksonville, FL 32202, USA
Henderson, Karen LeCraft *Judge*
%US Court of Appeals, 333 Constitution Ave NW, Washington, DC 20001, USA
Henderson, Lyle (Skitch) *Pianist, Conductor, Composer*
Hunt Hill Farm, 44 Upland Road, New Milford, CT 06776, USA
Henderson, Mike *Singer, Guitarist, Songwriter*
%Press Network, PO Box 90528, Nashville, TN 37209, USA
Henderson, Paul, III *Journalist*
%Seattle Times, Editorial Dept, 1120 John St, Seattle, WA 98109, USA
Henderson, Richard *Molecular Biologist*
%MRC Molecular Biology Laboratory, Hills Road, Cambridge CB2 2QH, England
Henderson, Rickey H *Baseball Player*
10561 Englewood Dr, Oakland, CA 94605, USA
Henderson, Shirley *Actress*
%Hamilton Hodell, 24 Hanway St, London W1T 1UH, England
Henderson, Thomas (Tom) *Basketball Player*
14003 Piney Run Court, Houston, TX 77066, USA
Hendricks, Barbara *Opera Singer*
%I M G Artists, 420 W 45th St, New York, NY 10036, USA
Hendricks, Jon *Singer*
%Virginia Wicks, 2737 Edwin Place, Los Angeles, CA 90046, USA
Hendricks, Theodore P (Ted) *Football Player*
1232 W Weston Dr, Arlington Heights, IL 60004, USA

H

Hendrix - Henricks

Hendrix, Elaine *Actress*
%Rigberg Roberts Rugolo, 1180 S Beverly Dr, #601, Los Angeles, CA 90035, USA
Hendrix, John W *Army General*
Commanding General, Army Forces Command, Fort McPherson, GA 30330, USA
Hendry, Gloria *Actress*
%H David Moss, 733 Seward St, #PH, Los Angeles, CA 90038, USA
Hendryx, Nona *Drummer (Eagles)*
%Black Rock, 6201 Sunset Blvd, #329, Hollywood, CA 90028, USA
Henenlotter, Frank *Movie Director*
81 Bedford St, #6E, New York, NY 10014, USA
Henke, Nolan *Golfer*
19662 Lost Creek Dr, Fort Myers, FL 33912, USA
Henkel, Andrea *Biathlete*
%TKW Sport-Promotion, Lerchenstr 39, 87700 Memmingen, Germany
Henkel, Heike *Track Athlete*
Tannenbergstr 57, 51373 Leverkusen, Germany
Henkel, Herbert L *Businessman*
%Ingersoll-Rand Co, 200 Chestnut Ridge Road, Woodcliff Lake, NJ 07677, USA
Henkin, Louis *Attorney, Educator*
460 Riverside Dr, New York, NY 10027, USA
Henle, Gertrude *Virologist*
533 Ott Road, Bala Cynwyd, PA 19004, USA
Henley, Beth *Writer*
%William Morris Agency, 1325 Ave of Americas, New York, NY 10019, USA
Henley, Don *Singer (Eagles), Songwriter*
%H K Mgmt, 9200 W Sunset Blvd, #530, Los Angeles, CA 90069, USA
Henley, Edward T *Labor Leader*
%Hotel & Restaurant Employees Union, 1219 28th St NW, Washington, DC 20007, USA
Henley, Elizabeth B (Beth) *Writer*
%William Morris Agency, 1325 Ave of Americas, New York, NY 10019, USA
Henley, J Smith *Judge*
%US Court of Appeals, 200 Federal Building, Harrison, AR 72601, USA
Henley, Larry *Composer*
%Creative Directions, PO Box 335, Brentwood, TN 37024, USA
Henley, Virginia *Writer*
%Penguin Putnam Press, 375 Hudson St, New York, NY 10014, USA
Henman, Graham *Movie Director*
%Agency for Performing Arts, 9200 Sunset Blvd, #900, Los Angeles, CA 90069, USA
Henn, Mark *Animator (Little Mermaid)*
%Walt Disney Animation, PO Box 10200, Lake Buena Vista, FL 32830, USA
Henn, Walter *Architect*
Ramsachleite 13, 82418 Murnau, Germany
Henneman, Brian *Singer (Bottle Rockets)*
%Hard Head Productions, 180 Varick St, #800, New York, NY 10014, USA
Hennen, Thomas J *Astronaut*
522 Villa Dr, Seabrook, TX 77586, USA
Henner, Marilu *Actress*
2101 Castilian Dr, Los Angeles, CA 90068, USA
Hennessey, Tom *Bowler*
157 Forest Brook Lane, Saint Louis, MO 63146, USA
Hennessy, Jill *Actress, Model*
%Creative Artists Agency, 9830 Wilshire Blvd, Beverly Hills, CA 90212, USA
Hennessy, John *Educator*
%Stanford University, President's Office, Stanford, CA 94305, USA
Hennessy, John B *Archaeologist*
497 Old Windsor Road, Kellyville NSW 2153, Australia
Henney, Jane *Government Official*
%Food & Drug Administration, 5600 Fishers Lane, Rockville, MD 20852, USA
Henning, Anne *Speed Skater*
5001 W Portland Dr, Littleton, CO 80128, USA
Henning, Harold *Golfer*
PO Box 9161, Jupiter, FL 33468, USA
Henning, John F, Jr *Publisher*
%Sunset Magazine, 80 Willow Road, Menlo Park, CA 94025, USA
Henning, Linda *Actress*
843 N Sycamore Ave, Los Angeles, CA 90038, USA
Henning, Lorne E *Hockey Player, Coach*
59 Bankside Dr, Centerport, NY 11721, USA
Henning-Walker, Anne *Speed Skater*
5001 W Portland Dr, Littleton, CO 80128, USA
Hennings, Chad W *Football Player*
6101 Bay Valley Court, Flower Mound, TX 75022, USA
Henrich, Dieter *Philosopher*
Gerlichstr 7A, 81245 Munich, Germany
Henrich, Thomas D (Tommy) *Baseball Player*
3801 Woodbine Ave, Dayton, OH 45420, USA
Henricks, Jon N *Swimmer*
254 Laurel Ave, Des Plaines, IL 60016, USA

H

Henricks, Terence T (Tom) *Astronaut*
%Timken Aerospace, PO Box 547, Keene, NH 03431, USA
Henrik *Prince, Denmark*
%Amalienborg Palace, 1257 Copenhagen K, Denmark
Henriksen, Lance *Actor*
%Innovative Artists, 1505 10th St, Santa Monica, CA 90401, USA
Henriquez, Ron *Actor*
PO Box 38027, Los Angeles, CA 90038, USA
Henry, Buck *Actor, Writer*
117 E 57th St, New York, NY 10022, USA
Henry, Carl F H *Theologian*
1141 Hus Dr, #206, Watertown, WI 53098, USA
Henry, Clarence (Frogman) *Singer, Songwriter*
3309 Lawrence St, New Orleans, LA 70114, USA
Henry, Geoffrey A *Prime Minister, Cook Islands*
PO Box 281, Rarotonga, Cook Islands
Henry, Gloria *Actress*
849 N Harper Ave, Los Angeles, CA 90046, USA
Henry, Gregg *Actor*
8956 Appian Way, Los Angeles, CA 90046, USA
Henry, Joe *Singer, Songwriter*
%Monterey Peninsula Artists, 509 Hartnell St, Monterey, CA 93940, USA
Henry, Joseph L *Dentist*
60 Marinita Ave, San Rafael, CA 94901, USA
Henry, Justin *Actor*
%Artists Agency, 1180 S Beverly Dr, #301, Los Angeles, CA 90035, USA
Henry, Lenny *Actor, Comedian*
%PBJ Management Ltd, 7 Soho St, London W1D 3DQ, England
Henry, Pierre *Composer*
32 Rue Toul, 75012 Paris, France
Henry, Robert H *Judge*
%US Court of Appeals, PO Box 1767, Oklahoma City, OK 73101, USA
Henry, William H, Jr *Publisher*
%Time-Life Books, Rockefeller Center, New York, NY 10020, USA
Hensel, Witold *Archaeologist*
Ul Marszalkowska 84/92M, 109 00-514 Warsaw, Poland
Hensilwood, Christopher *Anthropologist*
%Iziko Museum, 25 Queen Victoria St, Cape Town, South Africa
Hensley, Kirby J *Religious Leader*
%Universal Life Church, 601 3rd St, Modesto, CA 95351, USA
Hensley, Pamela *Actress*
9526 Dalegrove Dr, Beverly Hills, CA 90210, USA
Henson, John *Actor, Comedian*
PO Box 48972, Los Angeles, CA 90048, USA
Henson, Lisa *Movie Producer*
%Columbia Pictures, 3400 Riverside Dr, Burbank, CA 91505, USA
Henson, Lou *Basketball Coach*
%New Mexico State University, Athletic Dept, Las Cruces, NM 88033, USA
Henstridge, Natasha *Actress, Model*
345 N Maple Dr, #397, Beverly Hills, CA 90210, USA
Hentgen, Patrick G (Pat) *Baseball Player*
14451 Knightsbridge Dr, Shelby Township, MI 48315, USA
Hentoff, Nathan I (Nat) *Jazz Critic*
%Village Voice, Editorial Dept, 36 Cooper Square, New York, NY 10003, USA
Hentrich, Helmut *Architect*
Dusseldorfer Str 67, 40545 Dusseldorf-Oberkassel, Germany
Henze, Hans Werner *Composer, Conductor*
Weihergarten 1-5, 55116 Mainz, Germany
Heppel, Leon A *Biochemist*
%Cornell University, Biochemistry Dept, Ithaca, NY 14850, USA
Heppner, Ben *Opera Singer*
%Columbia Artists Mgmt Inc, 165 W 57th St, New York, NY 10019, USA
Herbert of Hemingford, D Nicholas *Publisher*
Old Rectory, Hemingford Abbots, Huntington Cambs PE18 9AN, England
Herbert, Bob *Columnist*
%New York Times, Editorial Dept, 229 W 43rd St, New York, NY 10036, USA
Herbert, Don (Mr Wizard) *Educator*
%"Mr Wizard's World" Show, PO Box 83, Canoga Park, CA 91305, USA
Herbert, Michael K *Editor*
990 Grove St, Evanston, IL 60201, USA
Herbert, Raymond E (Ray) *Baseball Player*
9360 Taylors Turn, Stanwood, AL 35901, USA
Herbert, Walter W (Wally) *Explorer*
Rowan Cottage, Catlodge, Laggan, Inverness-shire PH20 1AH, England
Herbig, George H *Astronomer*
%University of Hawaii, Astronomy Institute, 2680 Woodlawn Dr, Honolulu, HI 96822, USA
Herbig, Gunther *Conductor*
%Toronto Symphony, 60 Simcoe St, #C116, Toronto ON MJ5 2H5, Canada

Herbst, William *Astronomer*
%Wesleyan University, Astronomy Dept, Middletown, CT 06459, USA
Herczegh, Gezar G *Judge*
%Int'l Court of Justice, Carnegieplein 2, 2517 KJ Hague, Netherlands
Herd, Richard *Actor*
PO Box 56297, Sherman Oaks, CA 91413, USA
Herda, Frank A *Vietnam War Army Hero (CMH)*
PO Box 34239, Cleveland, OH 44134, USA
Herek, Stephen R *Movie Director*
%Endeavor Talent Agency, 9701 Wilshire Blvd, #1000, Beverly Hills, CA 90212, USA
Herincx, Raimund *Opera Singer*
Monks' Vineyard, Larkbarrow, Shepton Mallet, Somerset BA4 4NR, England
Herman, David J *Businessman*
%Adam Opel AG, Bahnhofplatz 1, 65429 Russelsheim, Germany
Herman, George E *Commentator*
4500 Q Lane NW, Washington, DC 20007, USA
Herman, Jerry *Composer, Lyricist*
1196 Cabrillo Dr, Beverly Hills, CA 90210, USA
Herman, Pee Wee (Paul Reubens) *Actor, Comedian*
PO Box 29373, Los Angeles, CA 90029, USA
Hermann, Allen M *Physicist*
2704 Lookout View Dr, Golden, CO 80401, USA
Hermannsson, Steingrimur *Prime Minister, Iceland*
Mavanes 19, 210 Gardaba, Iceland
Hermanson, Dustin M *Baseball Player*
9002 E Rimrock Dr, Scottsdale, AZ 85255, USA
Hermaszewski, Miroslav *Cosmonaut, Poland; Air Force General*
Ul Czeczota 25, 02-650 Warsaw, Poland
Hermlin, Stephan *Writer*
Hermann-Hesse-Str 39, 13156 Berlin, Germany
Hermon, John C *Law Enforcement Official*
Warren Road, Donaghadee, County Down, Northern Ireland
Herms, George *Sculptor*
%Jack Rutberg Fine Arts, 357 N La Brea Ave, Los Angeles, CA 90036, USA
Hernandez Colon, Rafael *Govenor, PR*
PO Box 5788, Puerta de Tierra, San Juan, PR 00906, USA
Hernandez, Genaro *Boxer*
24442 Ferrocarril, Mission Viejo, CA 92691, USA
Hernandez, Guillermo (Willie) *Baseball Player*
PO Box 125, Bo Espina, Calle C Buzon, Aguada, PR 00602, USA
Hernandez, Jay *Actor*
%United Talent Agency, 9560 Wilshire Blvd, #500, Beverly Hills, CA 90212, USA
Hernandez, Jose A *Baseball Player*
22 Calle Sur, Vega Alta, PR 00692, USA
Hernandez, Keith *Baseball Player*
255 E 49th St, #28D, New York, NY 10017, USA
Hernandez, Robert J *Businessman*
%USX Corp, 600 Grant St, Pittsburgh, PA 15219, USA
Hernandez, Rodolfo P *Korean War Army Hero (CMH)*
5328 Bluewater Place, College Lakes, Fayetteville, NC 28311, USA
Herndon, Mark J *Singer, Drummer (Alabama)*
RR 1 Box 239A, Mentone, AL 35984, USA
Herndon, Ty *Singer*
PO Box 121858, Nashville, TN 37212, USA
Herr, John C *Immunologist*
%University of Virginia, Med Center, Immunology Dept, Charlottesville, VA 22903, USA
Herr, Thomas M (Tommy) *Baseball Player*
1077 Olde Forge Crossing, Lancaster, PA 17601, USA
Herranz Casado, Julian Cardinal *Religious Leader*
%Legislative Texts Curia, Piazza Pio XII, #10, 00193 Rome, Italy
Herrera, Carolina *Fashion Designer*
%Carolina Herrera Ltd, 501 Fashion Ave, #1700, New York, NY 10018, USA
Herrera, Efren *Football Player*
2437 E Parkside Ave, Orange, CA 92867, USA
Herrera, Pamela *Ballerina*
%American Ballet Theatre, 890 Broadway, New York, NY 10003, USA
Herrera, Silvestre S *WW II Army Hero (CMH)*
7222 W Windsor Blvd, Glendale, AZ 85303, USA
Herres, Robert T *Air Force General, Businessman*
%United Services Automobile Assn, USAA Building, San Antonio, TX 78288, USA
Herring, Lynn *Actress*
37900 Road 800, Raymond, CA 93653, USA
Herring, Vincent *Jazz Saxophonist, Composer*
%Fat City Artists, 1906 Chet Atkins Place, #502, Nashville, TN 37212, USA
Herrington, John B *Astronaut*
16411 Clearcrest Dr, Houston, TX 77059, USA
Herrington, John S *Secretary, Energy; Businessman*
%Harcourt Brace, 525 B St, San Diego, CA 92101, USA

Herrmann, Edward *Actor*
220 E 23rd St, #400, New York, NY 10010, USA
Herrmann, Mark *Football Player*
8525 Tidewater Dr W, Indianapolis, IN 46236, USA
Herron, Cindy *Singer (En Vogue)*
%East West Records, 75 Rockefeller Plaza, #1200, New York, NY 10019, USA
Herron, Denis *Hockey Player*
12841 Marsh Point Way, West Palm Beach, FL 33418, USA
Herron, Robert J *Architect*
%Herron Assoc, 28-30 Rivington St, London EC2A 3DU, England
Herron, Tim *Golfer*
3630 Archer Lane N, Plymouth, MN 55446, USA
Hersch, Fred *Jazz Pianist*
%SRO Artists, PO Box 9532, Madison, WI 53715, USA
Hersch, Michael *Composer*
%21C Music Publishing, 30 W 63rd St, #15S, New York, NY 10023, USA
Herschler, E David *Artist*
PO Box 5859, Santa Barbara, CA 93150, USA
Hersh, Kristin *Singer, Songwriter*
%Throwing Mgmt, PO Box 248, Batesville, VA 22924, USA
Hersh, Seymour M *Writer, Journalist*
1211 Connecticut Ave NW, Washington, DC 20036, USA
Hershey, Barbara *Actress*
%Talent Entertainment Group, 9111 Wilshire Blvd, Beverly Hills, CA 90210, USA
Hershey, Erin *Actress*
PO Box 16212, Irvine, CA 92623, USA
Hershiser, Orel L Q *Baseball Player, Sportscaster*
6230 Stefani Dr, Dallas, TX 75225, USA
Herta, Bryan *Auto Racing Driver*
5449 Briardale Lane, Dublin, OH 43016, USA
Hertz, C Hellmuth *Physicist*
%Lund Institute of Technology, Physics School, Lund, Sweden
Hertzberg, Arthur *Religious Leader*
83 Glenwood Road, Englewood, NJ 07631, USA
Hertzberg, Daniel *Journalist*
%Wall Street Journal, Editorial Dept, 200 Liberty St, New York, NY 10281, USA
Hertzberg, Sidney (Sonny) *Basketball Player*
535 Hazel Dr, Woodmere, NY 11598, USA
Hertzberger, Herman *Architect*
%Architectourstudio, Box 74665, 1070 BR Amsterdam, Netherlands
Hervey, Jason *Actor*
2049 Century Park E, #2500, Los Angeles, CA 90067, USA
Herzenberg, Caroline Littlejohn *Physicist*
1700 E 56th St, #2707, Chicago, IL 60637, USA
Herzfeld, John M *Movie Director*
%Industry Entertainment, 955 Carillo Dr, #300, Los Angeles, CA 90048, USA
Herzigova, Eva *Model*
%Men/Women Model Inc, 199 Lafayette St, #700, New York, NY 10012, USA
Herzog, Arthur, III *Writer*
4 E 81st St, New York, NY 10028, USA
Herzog, Dorrel N E (Whitey) *Baseball Player, Manager, Executive*
9426 Sappington Estates Dr, Saint Louis, MO 63127, USA
Herzog, Jacques *Architect, Pritzker Laureate*
%Herzog & De Meuron Architekten, Rheinschanze 6, 4056 Basel, Switzerland
Herzog, Maurice *Mountaineer*
84 Chemin De La Tournette, 74400 Chamoinix-Mont-Blanc, France
Herzog, Roman *President, Germany*
Schloss Bellevue, Spreeweg 1, 10557 Berlin, Germany
Herzog, Werner *Movie Director*
%Herzog Film Productions, Turkenstr 91, 80799 Munich, Germany
Hesburgh, Theodore M *Educator*
%University of Notre Dame, 1301 Hesburgh Library, Notre Dame, IN 46556, USA
Heseltine, Michael R D *Government Official, England*
Thenford House, near Banbury, Oxon OX17 2BX, England
Hess, Erika *Alpine Skier*
Aeschi, 6388 Gratenort, Switzerland
Hess, John B *Businessman*
%Amerada Hess Corp, 1185 Ave of Americas, New York, NY 10036, USA
Hesseman, Howard *Actor*
7146 La Presa Dr, Los Angeles, CA 90068, USA
Hessler, Curtis A *Publisher*
%Times-Mirror Co, Times-Mirror Square, Los Angeles, CA 90053, USA
Hessler, Gordon *Movie Director*
8910 Holly Place, Los Angeles, CA 90046, USA
Hessler, Robert R *Oceanographer*
%Scripps Institute of Oceanography, Biodiversity Dept, La Jolla, CA 92037, USA
Hester, Jessie L *Football Player*
12813 Pine Acre Court, Wellington, FL 33414, USA

Hester, Paul V *Air Force General*
Commander, Special Operations Command, Hurlbut Field, FL 32544, USA
Heston, Charlton *Actor*
2859 Coldwater Canyon, Beverly Hills, CA 90210, USA
Hetfield, James *Singer, Guitarist (Metallica)*
2020 Union St, San Francisco, CA 94123, USA
Hetherington, Eileen M *Psychologist*
%University of Virginia, Psychology Dept, Gilmer Hall, Charlottesville, VA
Hetrick, Jennifer *Actress*
%Borinstein Oreck Bogart, 3172 Dona Susana, Studio City, CA 91604, USA
Hettich, Arthur M *Editor*
606 Shore Acres Dr, Mamaroneck, NY 10543, USA
Hetzel, Fred *Basketball Player*
218 Cornwall St NW, Leesburg, VA 20176, USA
Heuga, Jimmie *Skier*
111 Rawhide, PO Box 686, Avon, CO 81620, USA
Hewett, Howard *Singer*
%GHR Entertainment, 6014 N Pointe Place, Woodland Hills, CA 91367, USA
Hewish, Anthony *Nobel Physics Laureate*
Pryor's Cottage, Kingston, Cambridge CB3 7NQ, England
Hewitt, Angela *Concert Pianist*
%Cramer/Marder Artists, 3436 Springhill Road, Lafayette, CA 94549, USA
Hewitt, Bob *Tennis Player*
822 Boylston St, #203, Chestnut Hill, MA 02467, USA
Hewitt, Christopher *Actor*
154 E 66th St, New York, NY 10021, USA
Hewitt, Don S *Television Producer*
%CBS-TV, News Dept, 51 W 52nd St, New York, NY 10019, USA
Hewitt, Jennifer Love *Actress, Singer*
8436 W 3rd St, #650, Los Angeles, CA 90048, USA
Hewitt, Lleyton *Tennis Player*
PO Box 1235, North Sydney NSW 2059, Australia
Hewitt, Martin *Actor*
1147 Horn Ave, #3, Los Angeles, CA 90069, USA
Hewitt, Paul *Basketball Coach*
%Georgia Institute of Technology, Athletic Dept, Atlanta, GA 30332, USA
Hewitt, Peter *Movie Director*
%Creative Artists Agency, 9830 Wilshire Blvd, Beverly Hills, CA 90212, USA
Hewlett, Howard *Singer (Shalamar)*
%Green Light Talent Agency, PO Box 3172, Beverly Hills, CA 90212, USA
Hewson, John *Government Official, Australia*
%ABN Amro Australia, 10 Spring St, #14, Sydney NSW 2000, Australia
Hextall, Dennis H *Hockey Player*
2631 Harvest Hills Dr, Brighton, MI 48114, USA
Hextall, Ronald (Ron) *Hockey Player*
%Philadelphia Flyers, 1st Union Center, 3601 S Broad St, Philadelphia, PA 19148, USA
Hey, John D *Economist, Statistician*
%University of York, Economics Dept, Heslington, York YO1 5DD, England
Hey, Virginia *Actress*
%Anthony Williams Mgmt, 50 Oxford St, Paddington NSW 2021, Australia
Heyliger, Vic *Hockey Coach*
2122 Hercules Dr, Colorado Springs, CO 80906, USA
Heyman, Arthur B (Art) *Basketball Player*
321 Lincoln Ave, Rockville Centre, NY 11570, USA
Heyman, Richard *Geneticist*
%Ligand Pharmaceuticals, 9393 Town Center Dr, #100, San Diego, CA 92121, USA
Heywood, Anne *Actress*
9966 Liebe Dr, Beverly Hills, CA 90210, USA
Hiassen, Carl *Writer*
%Knopf Publishers, 201 E 50th St, New York, NY 10022, USA
Hiatt, Andrew *Molecular Biologist*
%Scripps Research Foundation, 10666 N Torrey Pines Road, La Jolla, CA 92037, USA
Hiatt, John *Singer, Guitarist, Songwriter*
%Metropolitan Entertainment, 363 US Highway 46, #300F, Fairfield, NJ 07004, USA
Hibbert, Edward *Actor*
%Gage Group, 14724 Ventura Blvd, #505, Sherman Oaks, CA 91403, USA
Hick, Graeme A *Cricketer*
%Worcestershire County Cricket Club, New Road, Worcester, England
Hick, John H *Theologian*
144 Oak Tree Lane, Selly Oak, Birmingham B29 6HU, England
Hickam, Homer H, Jr *Writer*
9532 Hemlok Dr SE, Huntsville, AL 35803, USA
Hickcox, Charles B (Charlie) *Swimmer*
8315 Redfield Road, Scottsdale, AZ 85260, USA
Hicke, William A (Bill) *Hockey Player*
61 Dogwood Place, Regina SK S4S 5A1, Canada
Hickel, Walter J *Secretary, Interior; Governor, AK*
1905 Loussac Dr, Anchorage, AK 99517, USA

Hickerson, R Gene *Football Player*
4471 Nagle Road, Avon, CO 44011, USA
Hickey, James A Cardinal *Religious Leader*
%Archdiocesan Pastoral Center, 5002 Eastern Ave, Washington, DC 20017, USA
Hickey, Maurice *Publisher*
%Denver Post, 650 15th St, Denver, CO 80202, USA
Hickey, Thomas J *Air Force General*
2127 Bobbyber Dr, Vienna, VA 22182, USA
Hickey, William V *Businessman*
%Sealed Air Corp, Park 80 E, Saddle Brook, NJ 07663, USA
Hickland, Catherine *Actress*
255 W 84th St, #2A, New York, NY 10024, USA
Hickman, Darryl *Actor*
171 Hermosillo Road, Santa Barbara, CA 93108, USA
Hickman, Dwayne *Actor*
PO Box 17226, Encino, CA 91416, USA
Hickman, Fred *Sportscaster*
%Cable News Network, Sports Dept, 1050 Techwood Dr NW, Atlanta, GA 30318, USA
Hickman, Sara *Singer, Songwriter*
%Valdenn, 13801 RR 12, #202, Wimberley, TX 78676, USA
Hickox, Richard S *Conductor*
35 Ellington St, London N7 8PN, England
Hicks, Catherine *Actress*
%Gersh Agency, 232 N Canon Dr, Beverly Hills, CA 90210, USA
Hicks, Dan *Sportscaster*
%NBC-TV, Sports Dept, 30 Rockefeller Plaza, New York, NY 10112, USA
Hicks, Dan *Singer*
%Leslie Wiener, PO Box 245, Sausalito, CA 94966, USA
Hicks, John *Jazz Pianist*
%John Penny Enterprises, 484 Lexington St, Waltham, MA 02452, USA
Hicks, John C, Jr *Football Player*
3287 Green Cook Road, Johnstown, OH 43031, USA
Hicks, Scott *Movie Director*
PO Box 824, Kent Town 5071, South Africa
Hidalgo, David *Singer, Songwriter (Los Lobos)*
%Gold Mountain, 3575 Cahuenga Blvd W, #450, Los Angeles, CA 90068, USA
Hidalgo, John *Government Official*
%Mays Valentine Davenport Moore, 1899 L St NW, Washington, DC 20036, USA
Hide, Herbie *Boxer*
%Matchroom, 10 Western Road, Romford, Essex RM1 3JT, England
Hide, Raymond *Geophysicist*
%University of Oxford, Jesus College, Oxford OX1 3DW, England
Hieb, Richard J *Astronaut*
%Allied Signal Tech Services, 7515 Mission Dr, Lanham Seabrook, MD 20706, USA
Hiebert, Erwin N *Historian*
40 Payson Road, Belmont, MA 02478, USA
Hier, Marvin *Religious Leader, Social Activist*
%Simon Wiesenthal Holocaust Center, 9766 W Pico Blvd, Los Angeles, CA 90035, USA
Hieronymus, Clara W *Journalist*
50 Spring St, Savannah, TN 38372, USA
Higdon, Bruce *Cartoonist*
210 Canvasback Court, Murfreesboro, TN 37130, USA
Higginbotham, Joan E *Astronaut*
1409 Mija Lane, Seabrook, TX 77586, USA
Higginbotham, Patrick E *Judge*
%US Court of Appeals, US Courthouse, 1100 Commerce St, Dallas, TX 75242, USA
Higgins, Bertie *Singer, Songwriter*
5775 Peachtree Dunwoody, Atlanta, GA 30342, USA
Higgins, Chester, Jr *Photographer*
%New York Times, Editorial Dept, 229 W 43rd St, New York, NY 10036, USA
Higgins, J Kenneth *Test Pilot*
%Boeing Commercial Airplane Group, PO Box 3707, Seattle, WA 98124, USA
Higgins, Jack *Editorial Cartoonist*
59 Waverly Ave, Clarendon Hills, IL 60514, USA
Higgins, Jack *Writer*
September Tide, Mont de la Roque, Jersey, Channel Islands, England
Higgins, Joel *Actor*
3 Devon Road, Westport, CT 06880, USA
Higgins, John *Swimmer, Swimming Coach*
40 Williams Dr, Annapolis, MD 21401, USA
Higgins, Michael *Actor*
%Michael Hartig Agency, 156 5th Ave, #820, New York, NY 10010, USA
Higgins, Robert *Businessman*
%Fleet Boston Corp, 1 Federal St, Boston, MA 02110, USA
Higgins, Rosalyn *Judge*
%International Court of Justice, Peace Palace, 2517 KJ Hague, Netherlands
Higginson, John *Pathologist*
16 Sundew Road, Savannah, GA 31411, USA

H

Higham, Scott *Journalist*
%Washington Post, Editorial Dept, 1150 15th St NW, Washington, DC 20071, USA
Hightower, John B *Museum Director*
101 Museum Parkway, Newport News, VA 23606, USA
Hightower, Rosella *Ballet, Dance Choreographer*
Villa Piege Luiere, Parc Fiorentina, Ave Vallauris, 06400 Cannes, France
Hijuelos, Oscar *Writer*
%Hofstra University, English Dept, 10000 Fulton Ave, Hempstead, NY 11550, USA
Hilario, Maybyner (Nene) *Basketball Player*
%Denver Nuggets, Pepsi Center, 1000 Chopper Circle, Denver, CO 80204, USA
Hilbe, Alfred J *Head of Government, Liechtenstein*
9494 Schaan, Garsill 11, Liechtenstein
Hildebrand, John G *Neurobiologist*
629 N Olsen Ave, Tucson, AZ 85719, USA
Hildebrandt, Greg *Cartoonist (Terry & the Pirates)*
%Dark Horse, 10956 SE Main St, Milwaukie, OR 97222, USA
Hildegarde *Singer*
230 E 48th St, New York, NY 10017, USA
Hildreth, Eugene A *Physician*
5285 Sweitzer Road, Mohnton, PA 19540, USA
Hilfiger, Tommy *Fashion Designer*
%Tommy Hilfiger USA, 485 5th Ave, New York, NY 10017, USA
Hilgenberg, Jay W *Football Player*
1296 Kimmer Court, Lake Forest, IL 60045, USA
Hilger, Rusty *Football Player*
1145 SW 78th Terrace, Oklahoma City, OK 73139, USA
Hill Smith, Marilyn *Opera Singer*
%Music International, 13 Ardilaun Road, Highbury, London N5 2QR, England
Hill, A Derek *Artist*
%National Art Collections Fund, 20 John Islip St, London SW1, England
Hill, Andrew (Drew) *Football Player*
37 Westgate Park Lane, Newnan, GA 30263, USA
Hill, Anita *Educator*
600 3rd Ave, #200, New York, NY 10016, USA
Hill, Arthur *Actor*
2220 Ave of Stars, #605, Los Angeles, CA 90067, USA
Hill, Bernard *Actor*
%Julian Belfarge, 46 Albermarle St, London W1X 4PP, England
Hill, Brendan *Drummer (Blues Traveler)*
%ArtistDirect, 10900 Wilshire Blvd, #1400, Los Angeles, CA 90024, USA
Hill, Calvin *Football Player, Executive*
10300 Walker Lake Dr, Great Falls, VA 22066, USA
Hill, Damon G D *Auto Racing Driver*
PO Box 100, Nelson, Lanscashire BB9 8AQ, England
Hill, Dan *Singer, Songwriter*
%Paquin Entertainment, 1067 Sherwin Road, Winnipeg MB R3H 0TB, Canada
Hill, Daniel W (Dan) *Football Player*
171 Montrose Dr, Dunbarton, Durham, NC 27707, USA
Hill, Dave *Golfer*
%Eddie Elias Enterprises, PO Box 5118, Akron, OH 44334, USA
Hill, David L (Tex) *WW II Army Air Corps Hero*
317 Elizabeth Road, San Antonio, TX 78209, USA
Hill, Draper *Editorial Cartoonist*
368 Washington Road, Grosse Pointe Woods, MI 48230, USA
Hill, Dusty *Singer, Bassist (ZZ Top)*
%Lone Wolf Mgmt, PO Box 163690, Austin, TX 78716, USA
Hill, Faith *Singer*
620 Eddy St, #21, San Francisco, CA 94109, USA
Hill, Gary *Artist*
%Cornish College of the Arts Galleries, 1000 Lenora St, Seattle, WA 98121, USA
Hill, Geoffrey W *Writer*
%Boston University, University Professors, 745 Commonwealth St, Boston, MA 02215, USA
Hill, Grant *Basketball Player*
9113 Southern Breeze Dr, Orlando, FL 32836, USA
Hill, Greg L *Football Player*
301 N Joe Wilson Road, #1726, Cedar Hill, TX 75104, USA
Hill, Harlon *Football Player*
400 Country Road 388, Killen, AL 35645, USA
Hill, Jack *Movie Director, Producer*
1445 N Fairfax Ave, #105, West Hollywood, CA 90046, USA
Hill, James C *Judge*
%US Court of Appeals, 56 Forsyth St NW, Atlanta, GA 30303, USA
Hill, James T *Army General*
Commanding General, Army Forces Command, Fort McPherson, GA 30330, USA
Hill, Jessie *Singer, Pianist*
1210 Caffin Ave, New Orleans, LA 70117, USA
Hill, Jim *Sportscaster*
%ABC-TV, Sports Dept, 77 W 66th St, New York, NY 10023, USA

H

Hill, Julia Butterfly *Environmental Activist*
%Circle of Life Foundation, PO Box 3764, Oakland, CA 94609, USA
Hill, Kent A *Football Player*
630 Hawthorne Place, Fayetteville, GA 30214, USA
Hill, Kim *Singer*
%Ambassador Artist Agency, PO Box 50358, Nashville, TN 37205, USA
Hill, Lauryn *Singer, Actress*
%Columbia Records, 2100 Colorado Ave, Santa Monica, CA 90404, USA
Hill, Pat *Football Coach*
%California State University, Athletic Dept, Fresno, CA 93740, USA
Hill, Phil *Auto Racing Driver*
PO Box 3008, Santa Monica, CA 90408, USA
Hill, Ron *Track Athlete*
PO Box 11, Hyde, Cheshire SK14 1RD, England
Hill, Sean *Hockey Player*
12441 Bagleaf Church Road, Raleigh, NC 27614, USA
Hill, Steven *Actor*
18 Jill Lane, Monsey, NY 10952, USA
Hill, Susan E *Writer*
Longmoor Farmhouse, Ebrington, Chipping Campden, Glos GL55 6NW, England
Hill, Terence *Actor*
3 Los Pinos Road, Santa Fe, NM 87507, USA
Hill, Terrell L *Biophysicist, Chemist*
3400 Paul Sweet Road, #C220, Santa Cruz, CA 95065, USA
Hill, Thomas (Tom) *Track Athlete*
428 Elmcrest Dr, Norman, OK 73071, USA
Hill, Virgil *Boxer*
1618 Santa Gertrudis Loop, Bismarck, ND 58503, USA
Hill, Virgil L, Jr *Navy Admiral*
1000 Glendevon Court, Ambler, PA 19002, USA
Hill, Walter *Movie Director*
836 Greenway Dr, Beverly Hills, CA 90210, USA
Hill-Norton, Peter J *Navy Admiral, England*
Cass Cottage, Hyde, Fordingbridge, Hampshire, England
Hillaby, John *Writer*
%Constable Co, Lanchesters, 102 Fulham Palace Road, London W6 9ER, England
Hillaker, Harry *Aeronautical Engineer*
1802 Palace Dr, Grand Prairie, TX 75050, USA
Hillary, Edmund P *Mountaineer, Explorer*
278A Remuera Road, Auckland SE2, New Zealand
Hille, Bertil *Physiologist*
10630 Lakeside Ave NE, Seattle, WA 98125, USA
Hille, Einar *Mathematician*
8862 La Jolla Scenic Dr N, La Jolla, CA 92037, USA
Hillebrecht, Rudolf F H *Architect*
Gneiststr 7, 30169 Hanover, Germany
Hillel, Shlomo *Government Official, Israel*
14 Gelber St, Jerusalem 96755, Israel
Hilleman, Maurice R *Virologist*
%Merck Therapeutic Research Institute, WP53C 350, West Point, PA 19118, USA
Hillen, Bobby *Auto Racing Driver*
%Donlavey Racing, 5011 Midlothian Turnpike, Richmond, VA 23225, USA
Hillenbrand, Daniel A *Businessman*
%Hillenbrand Industries, 700 State RR 46 E, Batesville, IN 47006, USA
Hillenbrand, Laura *Writer*
%Random House, 1745 Broadway, #B1, New York, NY 10019, USA
Hillenbrand, Martin J *Diplomat*
%University of Georgia, International Trade/Security Center, Athens, GA 30602, USA
Hillenbrand, Shea *Baseball Player*
16208 E Via De Palmas, Gilbert, AZ 85297, USA
Hiller, Arthur *Movie Director*
1218 Benedict Canyon, Beverly Hills, CA 90210, USA
Hiller, Susan *Artist*
83 Loudoun Road, London NW8 0DL, England
Hillerman, John *Actor*
1110 Bade St, Houston, TX 77055, USA
Hillerman, Tony *Writer*
1632 Francisca Road NW, Albuquerque, NM 87107, USA
Hillery, Patrick J *President, Ireland*
Grasmere, Greenfield Road, Sutton, Dublin 13, Ireland
Hilliard, Ike *Football Player*
%New York Giants, Giants Stadium, East Rutherford, NJ 07073, USA
Hillier, James *Inventor (Electron Lens Corrector)*
22 Arreton Road, #CR31, Princeton, NJ 08540, USA
Hillier, Steve *Keyboardist (Dubstar)*
%Primary Talent Int'l, 2-12 Petonville Road, London N1 9PL, England
Hillis, W Daniel (Danny) *Computer Scientist*
%Applied Minds, 1209 Grand Central Ave, Glendale, CA 91201, USA

Hillman, Chris *Singer, Bassist (Byrds), Songwriter*
%McMullen Co, 433 N Camden Dr, #400, Beverly Hills, CA 90210, USA
Hills, Carla A *Secretary, Housing & Urban Development*
3125 Chain Bridge Road NW, Washington, DC 20016, USA
Hills, Roderick M *Businessman, Government Official*
%Mudge Rose Guthrie Alexander Ferdon, 1200 19th St NW, Washington, DC 20036, USA
Hilmers, David C *Astronaut*
18502 Point Lookout Dr, Houston, TX 77058, USA
Hilmes, Jerome B *Army General*
4900 Windsor Park, Sarasota, FL 34235, USA
Hilton, Barron *Businessman*
%Hilton Hotels Corp, 9336 Civic Center Dr, Beverly Hills, CA 90210, USA
Hilton, Janet *Concert Clarinetist*
Holly House, E Downs Road, Bowdon, Altrincham, Cheshire WA14 2LH, England
Hiltzik, Michael A *Journalist*
%Los Angeles Times, Editorial Dept, 202 W 1st St, Los Angeles, CA 90012, USA
Himmelfarb, Gertrude *Historian*
2510 Virginia Ave NW, Washington, DC 20037, USA
Hinckley, Gordon B *Religious Leader*
%Church of Latter Day Saints, 50 E North Temple, Salt Lake City, UT 84150, USA
Hindle, Art *Actor*
3005 Main St, Santa Monica, CA 90405, USA
Hinds, Ciaran *Actor*
%Larry Dalzell, 91 Regent St, London W1R 7TB, England
Hinds, Samuel A A *Prime Minister, Guyana*
%Prime Minister's Office, Public Buildings, Georgetown, Guyana
Hinds, William E *Cartoonist (Tank McNamara)*
1301 Spring Oaks Circle, Houston, TX 77055, USA
Hine, Maynard K *Dentist*
1121 W Michigan St, Indianapolis, IN 46202, USA
Hine, Patrick *Air Force Marshal, England*
%Lloyd's Bank, Cox's & Kings, 7 Pall Mall, London SW1 5NA, England
Hiner, Glen H *Businessman*
%Owens-Corning, 1 Owens Corning Parkway, Toledo, OH 43659, USA
Hines, Deni *Singer*
%Peter Rix Mgmt, 49 Hume St, #200, Crows Nest NSW 2065, Australia
Hingis, Martina *Tennis Player*
30165 Fairway Dr, Wesley Chapel, FL 33543, USA
Hingle, Pat *Actor*
PO Box 2228, Carolina Beach, NC 28428, USA
Hingorani, Narain G *Electrical Engineer*
1286 Lexington Lane, Lake Zurich, IL 60047, USA
Hingsen, Jurgen *Track Athlete*
655 Circle Dr, Santa Barbara, CA 93108, USA
Hinners, Noel *Government Official*
7 Greyswood Court, Rockville, MD 20854, USA
Hino, Kazuyoshi *Fashion Designer*
%Hino & Malee Inc, 3701 N Ravenswood Ave, Chicago, IL 60613, USA
Hinojosa, Ricardo H *Judge*
%US District Court, PO Box 5007, McAllen, TX 78502, USA
Hinojosa, Tish *Singer, Songwriter*
PO Box 3304, Austin, TX 78764, USA
Hinrich, Kurt *Basketball Player*
%Chicago Bulls, United Center, 1901 W Madison St, Chicago, IL 60612, USA
Hinske, Eric *Baseball Player*
%Toronto Blue Jays, Skydome, 1 Blue Jay Way, Toronto ON M5V 1J1, Canada
Hinson, Larry *Golfer*
3179 Highway 32 E, Douglas, GA 31533, USA
Hinson, Roy *Basketball Player*
4272 State Highway 27, Monmouth Junction, NJ 08852, USA
Hinterseer, Ernst *Skier*
Hahnenkammstr, 6370 Kitzbuhel, Austria
Hintikka, Jaakko J *Philosopher*
%University of Helsinki, PO Box 24, 00014 Helsinki, Finland
Hinton of Bankside, Christopher *Government Official, England; Engineer*
Tiverton Lodge, Dulwich Common, London SG2 7EW, England
Hinton, Christopher J (Chris) *Football Player*
5136 Falcon Chase Lane, Atlanta, GA 30342, USA
Hinton, Darby *Actor*
1267 Bel Air Road, Los Angeles, CA 90077, USA
Hinton, Eddie *Football Player*
12109 Poulson Dr, Houston, TX 77031, USA
Hinton, Sam *Singer, Songwriter*
9420 La Jolla Shores Dr, La Jolla, CA 92037, USA
Hinton, Susan Eloise (S E) *Writer*
%Delacorte Press, 1540 Broadway, New York, NY 10036, USA
Hintz, Donald C *Businessman*
%Entergy Corp, 10055 Grogans Mill Road, #5A, The Woodlands, TX 77380, USA

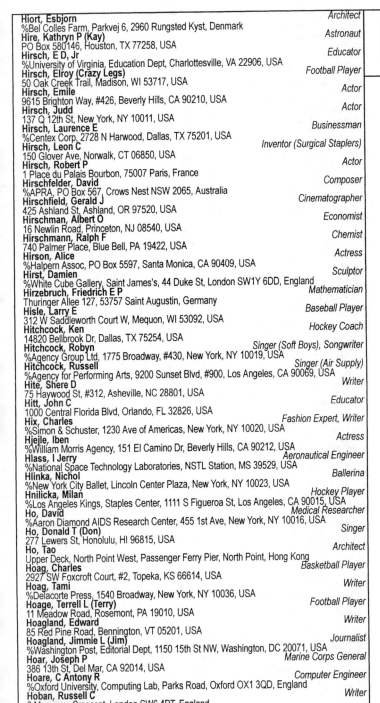

Hiort, Esbjorn *Architect*
%Bel Colles Farm, Parkvej 6, 2960 Rungsted Kyst, Denmark
Hire, Kathryn P (Kay) *Astronaut*
PO Box 580146, Houston, TX 77258, USA
Hirsch, E D, Jr *Educator*
%University of Virginia, Education Dept, Charlottesville, VA 22906, USA
Hirsch, Elroy (Crazy Legs) *Football Player*
50 Oak Creek Trail, Madison, WI 53717, USA
Hirsch, Emile *Actor*
9615 Brighton Way, #426, Beverly Hills, CA 90210, USA
Hirsch, Judd *Actor*
137 Q 12th St, New York, NY 10011, USA
Hirsch, Laurence E *Businessman*
%Centex Corp, 2728 N Harwood, Dallas, TX 75201, USA
Hirsch, Leon C *Inventor (Surgical Staplers)*
150 Glover Ave, Norwalk, CT 06850, USA
Hirsch, Robert P *Actor*
1 Place du Palais Bourbon, 75007 Paris, France
Hirschfelder, David *Composer*
%APRA, PO Box 567, Crows Nest NSW 2065, Australia
Hirschfield, Gerald J *Cinematographer*
425 Ashland St, Ashland, OR 97520, USA
Hirschman, Albert O *Economist*
16 Newlin Road, Princeton, NJ 08540, USA
Hirschmann, Ralph F *Chemist*
740 Palmer Place, Blue Bell, PA 19422, USA
Hirson, Alice *Actress*
%Halpern Assoc, PO Box 5597, Santa Monica, CA 90409, USA
Hirst, Damien *Sculptor*
%White Cube Gallery, Saint James's, 44 Duke St, London SW1Y 6DD, England
Hirzebruch, Friedrich E P *Mathematician*
Thuringer Allee 127, 53757 Saint Augustin, Germany
Hisle, Larry E *Baseball Player*
312 W Saddleworth Court W, Mequon, WI 53092, USA
Hitchcock, Ken *Hockey Coach*
14820 Bellbrook Dr, Dallas, TX 75254, USA
Hitchcock, Robyn *Singer (Soft Boys), Songwriter*
%Agency Group Ltd, 1775 Broadway, #430, New York, NY 10019, USA
Hitchcock, Russell *Singer (Air Supply)*
%Agency for Performing Arts, 9200 Sunset Blvd, #900, Los Angeles, CA 90069, USA
Hite, Shere D *Writer*
75 Haywood St, #312, Asheville, NC 28801, USA
Hitt, John C *Educator*
1000 Central Florida Blvd, Orlando, FL 32826, USA
Hix, Charles *Fashion Expert, Writer*
%Simon & Schuster, 1230 Ave of Americas, New York, NY 10020, USA
Hjejle, Iben *Actress*
%William Morris Agency, 151 El Camino Dr, Beverly Hills, CA 90212, USA
Hlass, I Jerry *Aeronautical Engineer*
%National Space Technology Laboratories, NSTL Station, MS 39529, USA
Hlinka, Nichol *Ballerina*
%New York City Ballet, Lincoln Center Plaza, New York, NY 10023, USA
Hnilicka, Milan *Hockey Player*
%Los Angeles Kings, Staples Center, 1111 S Figueroa St, Los Angeles, CA 90015, USA
Ho, David *Medical Researcher*
%Aaron Diamond AIDS Research Center, 455 1st Ave, New York, NY 10016, USA
Ho, Donald T (Don) *Singer*
277 Lewers St, Honolulu, HI 96815, USA
Ho, Tao *Architect*
Upper Deck, North Point West, Passenger Ferry Pier, North Point, Hong Kong
Hoag, Charles *Basketball Player*
2927 SW Foxcroft Court, #2, Topeka, KS 66614, USA
Hoag, Tami *Writer*
%Delacorte Press, 1540 Broadway, New York, NY 10036, USA
Hoage, Terrell L (Terry) *Football Player*
11 Meadow Road, Rosemont, PA 19010, USA
Hoagland, Edward *Writer*
85 Red Pine Road, Bennington, VT 05201, USA
Hoagland, Jimmie L (Jim) *Journalist*
%Washington Post, Editorial Dept, 1150 15th St NW, Washington, DC 20071, USA
Hoar, Joseph P *Marine Corps General*
386 13th St, Del Mar, CA 92014, USA
Hoare, C Antony R *Computer Engineer*
%Oxford University, Computing Lab, Parks Road, Oxford OX1 3QD, England
Hoban, Russell C *Writer*
6 Musgrave Crescent, London SW6 4PT, England
Hobaugh, Charles O *Astronaut*
%NASA, Johnson Space Center, 2101 NASA Road, Houston, TX 77058, USA

Hobault, John *Space Scientist*
51 Winster Fax, Williamsburg, VA 23185, USA
Hobbs, Franklin (Fritz) *Rower*
151 E 79th St, New York, NY 10021, USA
Hoch, Danny *Performance Artist*
%Columbia Artists Mgmt Inc, 165 W 57th St, New York, NY 10019, USA
Hoch, Scott *Golfer*
9239 Cypress Cove Dr, Orlando, FL 32819, USA
Hochhuth, Rolf *Writer*
PO Box 661, 4002 Basel, Switzerland
Hochwald, Bari *Actress*
%Herb Tannen, 10801 National Blvd, #101, Los Angeles, CA 90064, USA
Hock, Dee Ward *Businessman*
%Visa International, 900 Metro Center Blvd, Foster City, CA 94404, USA
Hocke, Stefan *Ski Jumper*
%Sportgymnasium, Am Harzwald 3, 98558 Oberhof, Germany
Hockenberry, John *Commentator*
%ABC-TV, News Dept, 77 W 66th St, New York, NY 10023, USA
Hockney, David *Artist*
7508 Santa Monica Blvd, West Hollywood, CA 90046, USA
Hodder, Kane *Actor*
3701 Senda Calma, Calabasas, CA 91302, USA
Hodder, Kenneth *Religious Leader*
%Salvation Army, 615 Slaters Lane, Alexandria, VA 22314, USA
Hoddinott, Alun *Composer*
64 Gowerton Road, Three Crosses, Swansea SA4 3PX, Wales
Hoddle, Glenn *Soccer Player, Manager*
%Football Assn, 16 Lancaster Gate, London W2 3LW, England
Hodel, Donald P *Secretary, Energy; Labor*
%CCA, 499 S Capitol St SW, Washington, DC 20003, USA
Hodge, Charles E (Charlie) *Hockey Player*
21356 86A Crescent, Langley BC V1M 2A2, Canada
Hodge, Daniel A (Dan) *Wrestler*
General Delivery, Perry, OK 73077, USA
Hodge, Kenneth R (Ken), Sr *Hockey Player*
1115 Main St, Lynnfield, MA 01940, USA
Hodge, Patricia *Actress*
%International Creative Mgmt, 76 Oxford St, London W1N 0AX, England
Hodge, Stephanie *Actress*
%Gersh Agency, 232 N Canon Dr, Beverly Hills, CA 90210, USA
Hodges, Bill *Basketball Coach*
%Georgia College, Athletic Dept, Milledgeville, GA 31061, USA
Hodges, Mike *Movie Director*
Wesley Farm, Durweston, Blanford Forum, Dorset DT11 0QG, England
Hodgkin, Howard *Artist*
%Anthony D'Offay Gallery, 9/24 Dering St, London W1R 9AA, England
Hodgson, James D *Secretary, Labor*
10132 Hillgrove Dr, Beverly Hills, CA 90210, USA
Hodler, Marc *Ski Executive*
%Int'l Ski Federation, Worbstr 210, 3073 Gumligen B Bern, Switzerland
Hodo, David *Singer (Village People)*
8255 Sunset Blvd, West Hollywood, CA 90046, USA
Hoeft, William F (Billy) *Baseball Player*
%Canadian Lakes, 9965 Lost Canyon Dr, Stanwood, MI 49346, USA
Hoenig, Michael *Composer*
%Gorfaine/Schwartz, 13245 Riverside Dr, #450, Sherman Oaks, CA 91423, USA
Hoenig, Thomas M *Financier, Government Official*
615 W Meyer Blvd, Kansas City, MO 64113, USA
Hoest, Bunny *Cartoonist (Lockhorns)*
%William Hoest Enterprises, 27 Watch Way, Lloyd Neck, Huntington, NY 11743, USA
Hoff, Marcian E (Ted), Jr *Inventor (Microprocessor)*
12226 Colina Dr, Los Altos Hills, CA 94024, USA
Hoff, Philip H *Governor, VT*
%Hoff Wilson Powell Lang, PO Box 567, Burlington, VT 05402, USA
Hoff, Sydney (Syd) *Writer, Cartoonist (Laugh It Off)*
PO Box 2463, Miami Beach, FL 33140, USA
Hoffa, James P *Labor Leader*
2593 Hounds Chase Dr, Troy, MI 48098, USA
Hoffman, Alice *Writer*
3 Hurlbut St, Cambridge, MA 02138, USA
Hoffman, Basil *Actor*
26 Aller Court, Glendale, CA 91206, USA
Hoffman, Darleane C *Nuclear Physicist*
%Lawrence Berkeley Laboratory, 1 Cyclotron Road, Berkeley, CA 94720, USA
Hoffman, Dustin L *Actor*
%Punch Productions, 11661 San Vicente Blvd, #222, Los Angeles, CA 90049, USA
Hoffman, Glenn E *Baseball Manager*
201 S Old Bridge Road, Anaheim, CA 92808, USA

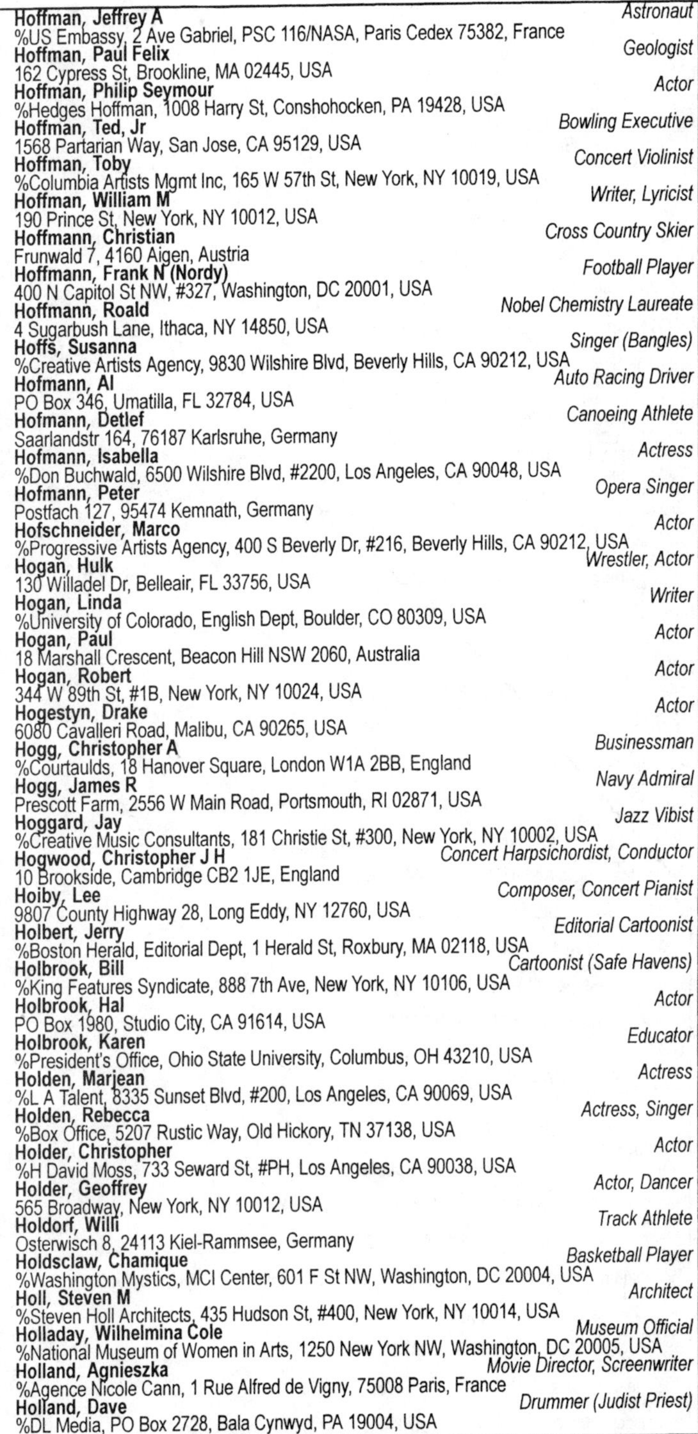

Hoffman, Jeffrey A *Astronaut*
%US Embassy, 2 Ave Gabriel, PSC 116/NASA, Paris Cedex 75382, France
Hoffman, Paul Felix *Geologist*
162 Cypress St, Brookline, MA 02445, USA
Hoffman, Philip Seymour *Actor*
%Hedges Hoffman, 1008 Harry St, Conshohocken, PA 19428, USA
Hoffman, Ted, Jr *Bowling Executive*
1568 Partarian Way, San Jose, CA 95129, USA
Hoffman, Toby *Concert Violinist*
%Columbia Artists Mgmt Inc, 165 W 57th St, New York, NY 10019, USA
Hoffman, William M *Writer, Lyricist*
190 Prince St, New York, NY 10012, USA
Hoffmann, Christian *Cross Country Skier*
Frunwald 7, 4160 Aigen, Austria
Hoffmann, Frank N (Nordy) *Football Player*
400 N Capitol St NW, #327, Washington, DC 20001, USA
Hoffmann, Roald *Nobel Chemistry Laureate*
4 Sugarbush Lane, Ithaca, NY 14850, USA
Hoffs, Susanna *Singer (Bangles)*
%Creative Artists Agency, 9830 Wilshire Blvd, Beverly Hills, CA 90212, USA
Hofmann, Al *Auto Racing Driver*
PO Box 346, Umatilla, FL 32784, USA
Hofmann, Detlef *Canoeing Athlete*
Saarlandstr 164, 76187 Karlsruhe, Germany
Hofmann, Isabella *Actress*
%Don Buchwald, 6500 Wilshire Blvd, #2200, Los Angeles, CA 90048, USA
Hofmann, Peter *Opera Singer*
Postfach 127, 95474 Kemnath, Germany
Hofschneider, Marco *Actor*
%Progressive Artists Agency, 400 S Beverly Dr, #216, Beverly Hills, CA 90212, USA
Hogan, Hulk *Wrestler, Actor*
130 Willadel Dr, Belleair, FL 33756, USA
Hogan, Linda *Writer*
%University of Colorado, English Dept, Boulder, CO 80309, USA
Hogan, Paul *Actor*
18 Marshall Crescent, Beacon Hill NSW 2060, Australia
Hogan, Robert *Actor*
344 W 89th St, #1B, New York, NY 10024, USA
Hogestyn, Drake *Actor*
6080 Cavalleri Road, Malibu, CA 90265, USA
Hogg, Christopher A *Businessman*
%Courtaulds, 18 Hanover Square, London W1A 2BB, England
Hogg, James R *Navy Admiral*
Prescott Farm, 2556 W Main Road, Portsmouth, RI 02871, USA
Hoggard, Jay *Jazz Vibist*
%Creative Music Consultants, 181 Christie St, #300, New York, NY 10002, USA
Hogwood, Christopher J H *Concert Harpsichordist, Conductor*
10 Brookside, Cambridge CB2 1JE, England
Hoiby, Lee *Composer, Concert Pianist*
9807 County Highway 28, Long Eddy, NY 12760, USA
Holbert, Jerry *Editorial Cartoonist*
%Boston Herald, Editorial Dept, 1 Herald St, Roxbury, MA 02118, USA
Holbrook, Bill *Cartoonist (Safe Havens)*
%King Features Syndicate, 888 7th Ave, New York, NY 10106, USA
Holbrook, Hal *Actor*
PO Box 1980, Studio City, CA 91614, USA
Holbrook, Karen *Educator*
%President's Office, Ohio State University, Columbus, OH 43210, USA
Holden, Marjean *Actress*
%L A Talent, 8335 Sunset Blvd, #200, Los Angeles, CA 90069, USA
Holden, Rebecca *Actress, Singer*
%Box Office, 5207 Rustic Way, Old Hickory, TN 37138, USA
Holder, Christopher *Actor*
%H David Moss, 733 Seward St, #PH, Los Angeles, CA 90038, USA
Holder, Geoffrey *Actor, Dancer*
565 Broadway, New York, NY 10012, USA
Holdorf, Willi *Track Athlete*
Osterwisch 8, 24113 Kiel-Rammsee, Germany
Holdsclaw, Chamique *Basketball Player*
%Washington Mystics, MCI Center, 601 F St NW, Washington, DC 20004, USA
Holl, Steven M *Architect*
%Steven Holl Architects, 435 Hudson St, #400, New York, NY 10014, USA
Holladay, Wilhelmina Cole *Museum Official*
%National Museum of Women in Arts, 1250 New York NW, Washington, DC 20005, USA
Holland, Agnieszka *Movie Director, Screenwriter*
%Agence Nicole Cann, 1 Rue Alfred de Vigny, 75008 Paris, France
Holland, Dave *Drummer (Judist Priest)*
%DL Media, PO Box 2728, Bala Cynwyd, PA 19004, USA

H

Holland, Dexter *Singer (Offspring)*
%Rebel Waltz, 31652 2nd Ave, Laguna Beach, CA 92651, USA
Holland, Heinrich D *Geologist*
14 Rangely Road, Winchester, MA 01890, USA
Holland, John R *Religious Leader*
%Foursquare Gospel Int'l Church, 1910 W Sunset Blvd, Los Angeles, CA 90026, USA
Holland, Juliam M (Jools) *Pianist*
%One Fifteen, Gallery, 28 Wood Wharf, Horseferry, London SE10 9BT, England
Holland, Paul *Bassist (Association)*
%Variety Artists, 1924 Spring St, Paso Robles, CA 93446, USA
Holland, Tom *Artist*
8957 Norma Place, Los Angeles, CA 90069, USA
Holland, Willard R, Jr *Businessman*
%FirstEnergy Corp, 76 S Main St, Akron, OH 44308, USA
Hollander, John *Writer*
%Yale University, English Dept, New Haven, CT 06520, USA
Hollander, Lorin *Concert Pianist*
%I C M Artists, 40 W 57th St, New York, NY 10019, USA
Hollander, Nicole *Cartoonist (Sylvia)*
%Sylvia Syndicate, 1440 N Dayton St, Chicago, IL 60622, USA
Hollander, Zander *Sportswriter*
1018 N Carolina Ave SE, Washington, DC 20003, USA
Hollandsworth, Todd M *Baseball Player*
4020 Ghiotti Court, Pleasanton, CA 94588, USA
Holldobler, Berthold K *Writer, Biologist, Zoologist*
%University of Wurzburg, Zoologie II, Am Nubland, 97074 Wurzburg, Germany
Hollein, Hans *Architect, Pritzker Laureate*
Eiskellerstr 1, 40213 Dusseldorf, Germany
Hollerer, Walter F *Writer*
Heerstr 99, 14055 Berlin, Germany
Holliday, Charles O *Businessman*
%E I DuPont de Nemours, 1007 Market St, Wilmington, DE 19801, USA
Holliday, Fred *Actor*
4610 Forman Ave, Toluca Lake, CA 91602, USA
Holliday, Jennifer *Singer, Actress*
%Evolution Talent, 1776 Broadway, #1500, New York, NY 10019, USA
Holliday, Polly D *Actress, Singer*
201 E 17th St, #23H, New York, NY 10003, USA
Holliger, Heinz *Concert Oboist, Composer*
%Konzertgellschaft, Hochstr 51, 4002 Basel, Switzerland
Holliman, Earl *Actor*
PO Box 1969, Studio City, CA 91614, USA
Hollings, Michael R *Religious Leader*
Saint Mary of Angels, Moorhouse Road, Bayswater, London W2 5DJ, England
Hollins, Lionel *Basketball Player, Coach*
7594 Tagg Dr, Germantown, TN 38138, USA
Hollister, Dave *Singer*
%Creative Artists Agency, 9830 Wilshire Blvd, Beverly Hills, CA 90212, USA
Holloway, Brian *Football Player*
742 New York Route 43, Stephentown, NY 12168, USA
Holloway, James L, III *Navy Admiral*
4800 Fillmore Ave, #1058, Alexandria, VA 22311, USA
Holloway, Ken *Singer*
%World Class/Berry Mgmt, 1848 Tyne Blvd, Nashville, TN 37215, USA
Holloway, Loleatta *Singer*
%Atlantic Entertainment Group, 2922 Atlantic Ave, #200, Atlantic City, NJ 08401, USA
Holloway, Robin G *Composer*
%Gonville & Caius College, Music Dept, Cambridge CB2 1TA, England
Holloway, William J, Jr *Judge*
%US Court of Appeals, PO Box 1767, Oklahoma City, OK 73101, USA
Holly, Lauren *Actress*
%The Firm, 9100 Wilshire Blvd, #100W, Beverly Hills, CA 90210, USA
Hollyday, Christopher *Jazz Saxophonist*
%Ted Kurland, 173 Brighton Ave, Boston, MA 02134, USA
Holm Whalen, Eleanor *Swimmer, Actress*
1800 NE 114th St, #1503, North Miami, FL 33181, USA
Holm, Celeste *Actress*
88 Central Park West, New York, NY 10023, USA
Holm, Ian *Actor*
%Markham & Froggatt, Julian House, 4 Windmill St, London W1P 1HF, England
Holm, Jeanne M *Air Force General*
2707 Thyme Dr, Edgewater, MD 21037, USA
Holm, Joan *Bowler*
5829 N Magnolia Ave, Chicago, IL 60660, USA
Holm, Richard H *Chemist*
483 Pleasant St, #10, Belmont, MA 02478, USA
Holman, C Ray *Businessman*
%Mallinckrodt Inc, 675 McDonnell Blvd, Saint Louis, MO 63134, USA

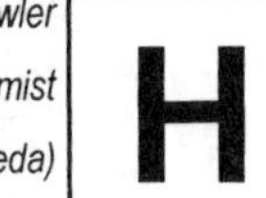

Holman - Holway

Holman, Marshall *Bowler*
1610 Thrasher Lane, Medford, OR 97504, USA
Holman, Ralph T *Biochemist*
1403 2nd Ave SW, Austin, MN 55912, USA
Holmberg, Mark *Bassist (Komeda)*
%MOB Agency, 6404 Wilshire Blvd, #505, Los Angeles, CA 90048, USA
Holmes, A M *Writer*
%Columbia University, English Dept, New York, NY 10027, USA
Holmes, Clint *Singer*
%Conversation Co, 697 Middle Neck Road, Great Neck, NY 11023, USA
Holmes, D Brainerd *Space Engineer, Businessman*
%Bay Colony Corp Center, 950 Winter St, #4350, Waltham, MA 02451, USA
Holmes, Ernie *Football Player*
PO Box 299, Wiergate, TX 75977, USA
Holmes, Jennifer *Actress*
PO Box 6303, Carmel, CA 93921, USA
Holmes, Katie *Actress*
17430 Miranda St, Encino, CA 91316, USA
Holmes, Larry *Boxer*
91 Larry Holmes Dr, #200, Easton, PA 18042, USA
Holmes, Priest *Football Player*
%Kansas City Chiefs, 1 Arrowhead Dr, Kansas City, KS 64129, USA
Holmes, Rupert *Singer, Songwriter*
%Mars Talent, 27 L'Ambiance Court, Bardonia, NY 10954, USA
Holmes, Thomas F (Tommy) *Baseball Player*
1 Pine Dr, Woodbury, NY 11797, USA
Holmgren, Janet L *Educator*
%Mills College, President's Office, Oakland, CA 94613, USA
Holmgren, Michael G (Mike) *Football Coach*
%Seattle Seahawks, 11220 NE 53rd St, Kirkland, WA 98033, USA
Holmgren, Paul H *Hockey Player, Coach*
724 Southwick Circle, Somerdale, NJ 08083, USA
Holmquest, Donald L *Astronaut*
229 Princeton Road, Menlo Park, CA 94025, USA
Holmstrom, Carl *Skier*
1703 E 3rd St, #101, Duluth, MN 55812, USA
Holmstrom, Peter *Guitarist (Dandy Warhols)*
%Monqui Mgmt, PO Box 5908, Portland, OR 97228, USA
Holovak, Michael J (Mike) *Football Player, Coach, Executive*
3432 Highlands Bridge Road, Sarasota, FL 34235, USA
Holroyd, Michael *Writer*
85 Saint Marks Road, London W10 6JS England
Holst, Per *Movie Producer*
%Per Holst Film A/S, Rentemestervej 69A, 2400 Copenhagen NV, Denmark
Holt, David Lee *Guitarist (Mavericks)*
%AristoMedia, 1620 16th Ave S, Nashville, TN 37212, USA
Holt, Glenn L *Labor Leader*
PO Box 4055, Kokomo, IN 46904, USA
Holt, Lester *Commentator*
%NBC-TV, News Dept, 30 Rockefeller Plaza, New York, NY 10112, USA
Holt, Sandrine *Actress*
%Somers Teitelbaum David, 8840 Wilshire Blvd, #200, Beverly Hills, CA 90211, USA
Holtermann, E Louis, Jr *Publisher*
%Glamour Magazine, 350 Madison Ave, New York, NY 10017, USA
Holton, A Linwood, Jr *Governor, VA*
3883 Black Stump Road, Weems, VA 22576, USA
Holton, Gerald *Physicist*
64 Francis Ave, Cambridge, MA 02138, USA
Holton, Michael *Basketball Player, Coach*
10657 SW Adele Dr, Portland, OR 97225, USA
Holtz, Louis L (Lou) *Football Coach*
1300 Rosewood Dr, Columbia, SC 29208, USA
Holtzman, Elizabeth (Liz) *Representative, NY*
2 Park Ave, #2100, New York, NY 10016, USA
Holtzman, Jerome *Sportswriter*
1225 Forest Ave, Evanston, IL 60202, USA
Holtzman, Kenneth D (Ken) *Baseball Player*
256 Waterside Dr, Grover, MO 63040, USA
Holtzman, Wayne H *Psychologist*
3300 Foothill Dr, Austin, TX 78731, USA
Holub, E J *Football Player*
2311 S County Road 1120, Midland, TX 79706, USA
Holum, Dianne *Speedskater*
1344 McIntosh Ave, Broomfield, CO 80020, USA
Holum, Kristin *Speedskater*
10596 Steele St, Northglenn, CO 80233, USA
Holway, Jerome F *Cinematographer*
448 Spruce Dr, Exton, PA 19341, USA

Holyfield, Evander *Boxer*
794 Evander Holyfield Highway, Fairburn, GA 30213, USA
Holzer, Helmut *Space Scientist*
2103 Greenwood Place SW, Huntsville, AL 35802, USA
Holzer, Jenny *Artist*
80 Hewitts Road, Hoosick Falls, NY 12090, USA
Holzman, Malcolm *Architect*
%Hardy Holzman Pfeiffer, 902 Broadway, New York, NY 10010, USA
Homes, A M *Writer*
%Charles Scribner's Sons, 866 3rd Ave, New York, NY 10022, USA
Homfeld, Conrad *Equestrian Rider*
%Sandron, 11744 Marblestone Court, Wellington, FL 33414, USA
Honda, Yuka *Singer (Cibo Matto)*
%Billions Corp, 833 W Chicago Ave, #101, Chicago, IL 60622, USA
Honderich, Beland H *Publisher*
%Toronto Star, 1 Yonge St, Toronto ON M5E 1E6, Canada
Honderich, John H *Editor*
%Toronto Star, Editorial Dept, 1 Yonge St, Toronto ON M5E 1E6, Canada
Honegger, Fritz *President, Switzerland*
Schloss-Str 29, 8803 Ruschlikon, Switzerland
Honeycutt, Frederick W (Rick) *Baseball Player*
207 Forrest Road, Fort Oglethorpe, GA 30742, USA
Honeycutt, Van B *Businessman*
%Computer Sciences Corp, 2100 E Grand Ave, El Segundo, CA 90245, USA
Honeyghan, Lloyd *Boxer*
50 Barnfield Wood Road, Park Langley, Beckenham, Kent, England
Hong Song Nam *Prime Minister, North Korea*
%Premier's Office, Pyongynag, North Korea
Hong, James *Actor*
8235 Sunset Blvd, #202, West Hollywood, CA 90046, USA
Honig, Edwin *Writer*
229 Medway St, #305, Providence, RI 02906, USA
Honore, Jean Cardinal *Religious Leader*
%Archeveche, BP 1117, 27 Rue Jules-Simon, 37011 Tours Cedex, France
Hood, Kenneth *Religious Leader*
5799 Bloomfield Ave, Verona, NJ 07044, USA
Hood, Leroy E *Inventor (DNA Sequencer), Geneticist*
1441 N 34th St, Seattle, WA 98103, USA
Hood, Robert *Editor*
%Boys Life Magazine, Editorial Dept, 1325 Walnut Hill Lane, Irving, TX 75038, USA
Hood, Robin *Golfer*
6705 Shoal Creek Dr, Arlington, TX 76001, USA
Hooker, Charles R *Artist*
28 Whippingham Road, Brighton, Sussex BN2 3PG, England
Hooks, Bell *Writer*
291 W 12th St, New York, NY 10014, USA
Hooks, Benjamin L *Civil Rights Activist*
200 Wagner Place, #407-8, Memphis, TN 38103, USA
Hooks, Kevin *Movie Director*
%International Creative Mgmt, 8942 Wilshire Blvd, #219, Beverly Hills, CA 90211, USA
Hooks, Robert *Actor*
145 N Valley St, Burbank, CA 91505, USA
Hookstratten, Edward G *Attorney*
%Ed Hookstratten Mgmt, 9536 Wilshire Blvd, #500, Beverly Hills, CA 90212, USA
Hooper, C Darrow *Track Athlete*
10909 Strait Lane, Dallas, TX 75229, USA
Hooper, Kay *Writer*
%Bantam Books, 1540 Broadway, New York, NY 10036, USA
Hooton, Burt C *Baseball Player*
3619 Granby Court, San Antonio, TX 78217, USA
Hoover, Dick *Bowler*
112 Melody Dr, Copley, OH 44321, USA
Hoover, Robert A (Bob) *Test Pilot*
%Bob Hoover Airshows, 1100 E Imperial Ave, El Segundo, CA 90245, USA
Hope, Alec D *Writer*
PO Box 7949, Alice Springs NT 0871, Australia
Hope, Leslie *Actress*
%Kritzer, 12200 W Olympic Blvd, #400, Los Angeles, CA 90064, USA
Hope, Maurice *Boxer*
582 Kingsland Road, London E8, England
Hopkins, Anthony *Actor*
%Global Business Mgmt, 15250 Ventura Blvd, #710, Sherman Oaks, CA 91403, USA
Hopkins, Antony *Composer, Writer*
Woodyard Cottage, Ashridge, Berkhamsted, Herts HP4 1PS, England
Hopkins, Bo *Actor*
6628 Ethel Ave, North Hollywood, CA 91606, USA
Hopkins, Godfrey T *Photographer*
Wilmington Cottage, Wilmington Road, Seaford, E Sussex BN25 2EH, England

Hopkins, Jan *Commentator*
%Cable News Network, News Dept, 1050 Techwood Dr NW, Atlanta, GA 30318, USA
Hopkins, Josh *Actor*
%Gersh Agency, 232 N Canon Dr, Beverly Hills, CA 90210, USA
Hopkins, Kaitlin *Actress*
19528 Ventura Blvd, #559, Tarzana, CA 91356, USA
Hopkins, Linda *Singer*
2055 N Ivar St, #PH 21, Los Angeles, CA 90068, USA
Hopkins, Michael J *Architect*
27 Broadley Terrace, London NW1 6LG, England
Hopkins, Stephen J *Movie Director*
%International Creative Mgmt, 8942 Wilshire Blvd, #219, Beverly Hills, CA 90211, USA
Hopkins, Sy *Singer (Five Satins)*
%Paramount Entertainment, PO Box 12, Far Hills, NJ 07931, USA
Hopkins, Telma *Actress, Singer*
4122 Don Luis Dr, Los Angeles, CA 90008, USA
Hoppe, Fred *Sculptor*
7401 NW 105th St, Malcolm, NE 68402, USA
Hoppe, Wolfgang *Bobsled Athlete*
Dieterstedter Str 11, 99510 Apolda, Germany
Hopper, Dennis *Actor, Director*
330 Indiana Ave, Venice, CA 90291, USA
Hopper, John D, Jr *Air Force General*
Commander, Air Education/Training Command, Randolph Air Force Base, TX 78155, USA
Hoppus, Mark *Bassist (Blink-182)*
%Creative Artists Agency, 9830 Wilshire Blvd, Beverly Hills, CA 90212, USA
Hopson, Dennis *Basketball Player*
5608 Brickstone Place, Hilliard, OH 43026, USA
Horan, Michael W (Mike) *Football Player*
5440 Lakeshore Dr, Littleton, CO 80123, USA
Horecker, Bernard L *Biochemist*
16517 Cypress Villa Lane, Fort Myers, FL 33908, USA
Horgan, Patrick *Actor*
201 E 89th St, New York, NY 10128, USA
Horinek, Ramon A *Vietnam War Air Force Hero*
181 National Blvd, Universal City, TX 78148, USA
Horlock, John H *Mechanical Engineer, Educator*
2 The Avenue, Ampthill, Bedford MK45 2NR, England
Horn, Gyula *Prime Minister, Hungary*
%Parliament, Kossuth Lajos Ter 1/3, 1055 Budapest, Hungary
Horn, Marian Blank *Judge*
%US Claims Court, 717 Madison Place NW, Washington, DC 20439, USA
Horn, Paul J *Jazz Flutist, Saxophonist*
4601 Leyns Road, Victoria BC V8N 3A1, Canada
Horn, Shirley *Singer*
1007 Towne Lane, Charlottesville, VA 22901, USA
Hornaday, Ron *Auto Racing Driver*
PO Box 229, Mooresville, NC 28115, USA
Hornburg, Hal M *Air Force General*
Commander, Air Combat Command, Langley Air Force Base, VA 23665, USA
Hornby, Nick *Writer*
%Cassarotto, 60/66 Wardour St, London W1V 4ND, England
Horne, Donald R *Writer*
53 Grosvenor St, Woollahra, Sydney NSW 2025, Australia
Horne, Jimmy Bo *Singer, Dancer*
%Talent Consultants International, 1560 Broadway, #1308, New York, NY 10036, USA
Horne, John R *Businessman*
%Navistar International, PO Box 1488, Warrenville, IL 60555, USA
Horne, Lena *Singer, Actress*
%Volney Apartments, 23 E 74th St, New York, NY 10021, USA
Horne, Marilyn *Opera Singer*
%Columbia Artists Mgmt Inc, 165 W 57th St, New York, NY 10019, USA
Horne, Steve *Auto Racing Executive*
%Tasman Motor Sports Group, 4192 Weaver Court, Hilliard, OH 43026, USA
Horneber, Petra *Markswoman*
Ringstr 77, 85402 Kranzberg, Germany
Horner, Charles A *Air Force General*
2824 Jack Nicklaus Way, Shalimar, FL 32579, USA
Horner, Freeman V *WW II Army Hero (CMH)*
1501 Doubletree Dr, Columbus, GA 31904, USA
Horner, George R (Red) *Hockey Player*
CSAS, PO Box 60036, RPO Glen Abbey, Oakville ON L6M 3H2, Canada
Horner, James *Composer*
13245 Riverside Dr, #450, Sherman Oaks, CA 91423, USA
Horner, John R (Jack) *Palentologist*
70 Cougar Dr, Bozeman, MT 59718, USA
Horner, Martina S *Educator, Businesswoman*
%TIAA-CREF, 730 3rd Ave, New York, NY 10017, USA

Hornig - Hou

Hornig, Donald F *Chemist*
1 Little Pond Cove Road, Little Compton, RI 02837, USA
Hornsby, Bruce *Singer, Pianist*
PO Box 3545, Williamsburg, VA 23187, USA
Hornung, Paul V *Football Player*
3700 Kernen Court, Louisville, KY 40241, USA
Horovitz, Adam (King Ad-Rock) *Rap Artist (Beastie Boys)*
%GAS Entertainment, 8935 Lindblade St, Culver City, CA 90232, USA
Horovitz, Israel A *Writer*
146 W 11th St, New York, NY 10011, USA
Horovitz, Joseph *Composer*
%Royal College of Music, Prince Consort Road, London SW7 2BS, England
Horowitz, David C *Commentator*
4267 Marina City Dr, #810, Marina del Rey, CA 90292, USA
Horowitz, Jerome P *Medical Researcher*
%Michigan Cancer Foundation, 110 E Warren Ave, Detroit, MI 48201, USA
Horowitz, Norman H *Biologist*
2495 Brighton Road, Pasadena, CA 91104, USA
Horowitz, Paul *Physician*
111 Chilton St, Cambridge, MA 02138, USA
Horowitz, Sari *Journalist*
%Washington Post, Editorial Dept, 1150 15th St NW, Washington, DC 20071, USA
Horowitz, Scott J *Astronaut*
16819 Whitewater Falls Court, Houston, TX 77059, USA
Horrocks, Jane *Actress, Singer*
%P F D, Drury House, 34-43 Russell St, London WC2B 5HA, England
Horry, Robert *Basketball Player*
9 E Rivercrest Dr, Houston, TX 77042, USA
Horsey, David *Editorial Cartoonist*
%King Features Syndicate, 888 7th Ave, New York, NY 10106, USA
Horsford, Anna Maria *Actress*
PO Box 48082, Los Angeles, CA 90048, USA
Horsley, Lee A *Actor*
9350 E Caley Ave, #200, Englewood, CO 80111, USA
Horsley, Richard D *Financier*
%Regions Financial Corp, 417 20th St N, Birmingham, AL 35203, USA
Horton, Ethan S *Football Player*
%WFNZ-Radio, PO Box 30247, Charlotte, NC 28230, USA
Horton, Frank E *Educator*
288 River Ranch Circle, Bayfield, CO 81122, USA
Horton, Peter *Actor*
409 Santa Monica Blvd, #PH, Santa Monica, CA 90401, USA
Horton, Robert *Actor*
5317 Andasol Ave, Encino, CA 91316, USA
Horton, William W (Willie) *Baseball Player*
%Reid, 15124 Warwick, Detroit, MI 48223, USA
Horvath, Bronco J *Hockey Player*
27 Oliver St, South Yarmouth, MA 02664, USA
Horvitz, H Robert *Nobel Medicine Laureate*
%Massachusetts Institute of Technology, Biology Dept, Cambridge, MA 02139, USA
Horwitz, Tony *Journalist*
%Wall Street Journal, Editorial Dept, 200 Liberty St, New York, NY 10281, USA
Hosket, William (Bill) *Basketball Player*
7461 Worthington Galena Road, Worthington, OH 43085, USA
Hoskins, Bob *Actor*
%Cassarotto, 60/66 Wardour St, London W1V 4ND, England
Hosmer, Bradley C (Brad) *Air Force General*
PO Box 1128, Cedar Crest, NM 87008, USA
Hossein, Robert *Actor, Theater Director*
%Ghislaine de Wing, 10 Rue du Docteur Roux, 75015 Paris, France
Hostak, Al *Boxer*
11501 161st Ave SE, Renton, WA 98059, USA
Hostetler, David L *Sculptor*
PO Box 989, Athens, OH 45701, USA
Hostetter, G Richard *Religious Leader*
%Presbyterian Church in America, 1852 Century Place, Atlanta, GA 30345, USA
Hotani, Hirokazu *Microbiotics Engineer*
%Teikyo University, Biosciences Dept, Toyosatodai, Utsunomiya 320, Japan
Hotchkiss, Rob *Guitarist (Train)*
%Jon Landau, 80 Mason St, Greenwich, CT 06830, USA
Hotchkiss, Rollin D *Bacterial Physiologist*
2-4 Rolling Hills, Lenox, MA 01240, USA
Hottelet, Richard C *Commentator*
120 Chestnut Hill Road, Wilton, CT 06897, USA
Hotter, Hans *Opera Singer*
%Bayerische Staatsoper, Portiastr 8, 81545 Munich, Germany
Hou, Ya-Ming *Biologist*
%Massachusetts Institute of Technology, Biology Dept, Cambridge, MA 02139, USA

Houbregs, Robert J (Bob) *Basketball Player*
6042 Troon Lane SE, Olympia, WA 98501, USA
Houcke, Sara *Circus Animal Trainer*
%Feld Enterprises, 1313 17th St E, Palmetto, FL 34221, USA
Hough, Charles O (Charlie) *Baseball Player*
2266 Shade Tree Circle, Brea, CA 92821, USA
Hough, John *Movie Director*
%Associated International Mgmt, 5 Denmark St, London WC2H 8LP, England
Hough, Joseph C, Jr *Educator*
%Union Theological Seminary, President's Office, New York, NY 10027, USA
Hough, Stephen A G *Concert Pianist*
%Harrison/Parrott, 12 Penzance Place, London W11 4PA England
Houghton of Sowerby, Douglas *Government Official, England*
110 Marsham Court, London SW1, England
Houghton, Charles N *Theater Director*
11 E 9th St, New York, NY 10003, USA
Houghton, James R *Businessman*
Field, 36 Spencer Hill Road, Corning, NY 14830, USA
Houghton, John *Physicist*
%Rutherford Appleton Laboratory, Chilton, Didcot Oxon OX11 0QX, England
Houghton, Katherine *Actress*
345 E 68th St, #11J, New York, NY 10021, USA
Hougland, William (Bill) *Basketball Player*
PO Box 2629, Edwards, CO 81632, USA
Houk, Ralph G *Baseball Manager*
3000 Plantation Road, Winter Haven, FL 33884, USA
Houle, Rejean *Hockey Player*
7941 Boul Lasalle, Lasalle QC H8P 3R1, Canada
Hounsfield, Godfrey N *Nobel Medicine Laureate*
15 Crane Park Road, Whitton, Twickenham, Middx TW2 6DF, England
Hounsou, Djimon *Actor, Model*
%Brillstein/Grey, 9150 Wilshire Blvd, #350, Beverly Hills, CA 90212, USA
House, David (Dave) *Businessman*
%Nortel Networks Corp, 8200 Dixie Road, Brampton ON L6T 5P6, Canada
House, H Franklin (Frank) *Baseball Player*
875 Calellmium Way, Birmingham, AL 35242, USA
House, Karen Eliot *Journalist*
58 Cleveland Lane, Princeton, NJ 08540, USA
Houseley, Phil *Hockey Player*
%Chicago Blackhawks, United Center, 1901 W Madison St, Chicago, IL 60612, USA
Houser, Jerry *Actor*
8325 Skyline Dr, Los Angeles, CA 90046, USA
Housner, George W *Civil Engineer, Seismologist*
%California Institute of Technology, Engineering Dept, Pasadena, CA 91125, USA
Houston, Allan *Basketball Player*
%New York Knicks, Madison Square Garden, 2 Penn Plaza, New York, NY 10121, USA
Houston, Byron *Basketball Player*
1732 Lionsgate Circle, Bethany, OK 73008, USA
Houston, Cissy *Singer*
2160 N Central Road, Fort Lee, NJ 07024, USA
Houston, Edwin A *Businessman*
%Ryder System Inc, 3600 NW 82nd Ave, Miami, FL 33166, USA
Houston, James A *Writer*
24 Main St, Stonington, CT 06378, USA
Houston, Kenneth R (Ken) *Football Player*
3603 Forest Village Dr, Kingwood, TX 77339, USA
Houston, Penelope *Singer*
%Absolute Artists, 8490 W Sunset Blvd, #403, West Hollywood, CA 90069, USA
Houston, Russell *Artist*
General Delivery, Eagar, AZ 85925, USA
Houston, Thelma *Singer*
4296 Mount Vernon Dr, Los Angeles, CA 90008, USA
Houston, Wade *Basketball Coach*
%University of Tennessee, Athletic Dept, Knoxville, TN 37901, USA
Houston, Whitney *Singer*
%Nippy Inc, 60 Park Place, Newark, NJ 07102, USA
Houthakker, Hendrik S *Economist*
1 Ivy Pointe Way, Hanover, NH 03755, USA
Hovan, Chris *Football Player*
%Minnesota Vikings, 9520 Viking Dr, Eden Prairie, MN 55344, USA
Hove, Andrew C, Jr *Financier*
%Federal Deposit Insurance, 550 17th St NW, Washington, DC 20429, USA
Hovind, David J *Businessman*
%PACCAR Inc, 777 106th Ave NE, Bellevue, WA 98004, USA
Hoving, Thomas *Museum Director, Editor*
%Hoving Assoc, 150 E 73rd St, New York NY 10021, USA
Hovland, Tim *Volleyball Player*
%Assn of Volleyball Pros, 330 Washington Blvd, #400, Marina del Rey, CA 90292, USA

H

Hovsepian - Howe

Hovsepian, Vatche *Religious Leader*
%Armenian Church of America West, 1201 N Vine St, Los Angeles, CA 90038, USA
Howard, Adina *Singer*
%International Creative Mgmt, 40 W 57th St, #1800, New York, NY 10019, USA
Howard, Alan M *Actor*
%Julian Belfarge, 46 Albermarle St, London W1X 4PP, England
Howard, Ann *Opera Singer*
%Stafford Law Assoc, 6 Barham Close, Weybridge, Surrey KT13 9PR, England
Howard, Arliss *Actor, Director*
%William Morris Agency, 151 El Camino Dr, Beverly Hills, CA 90212, USA
Howard, Barbara *Actress*
%Artists Group, 10100 Santa Monica Blvd, #2490, Los Angeles, CA 90067, USA
Howard, Clint *Actor*
4286 Clybourn Ave, Burbank, CA 91505, USA
Howard, Desmond K *Football Player*
7459 Winding Way, Tampa, FL 33625, USA
Howard, Frank O *Baseball Player*
20784 Iris Dr, Sterling, VA 20165, USA
Howard, George *Bowler*
8415 Brookwood Dr, Portage, MI 49024, USA
Howard, George *Jazz Saxophonist*
%David Rubinson, PO Box 411197, San Francisco, CA 94141, USA
Howard, Greg *Cartoonist (Sally Forth)*
3403 W 28th St, Minneapolis, MN 55416, USA
Howard, Harry N *Historian*
6508 Greentree Road, Bradley Hills Grove, Bethesda, MD 20817, USA
Howard, Hobie *Singer (Sawyer Brown)*
%Sawyer Brown Inc, 5200 Old Harding Road, Franklin, TN 37064, USA
Howard, James J, III *Businessman*
%Northern States Power, 414 Nicollett Mall, Minneapolis, MN 55401, USA
Howard, James Newton *Composer*
%Gorfaine/Schwartz, 13245 Riverside Dr, #450, Sherman Oaks, CA 91423, USA
Howard, Jan *Singer*
%Tessier-Marsh Talent, 2825 Blue Brick Dr, Nashville, TN 37214, USA
Howard, Jeffrey R *Judge*
US Court of Appeals, US Courthouse, 55 Pleasant St, Concord, NH 03301, USA
Howard, John W *Prime Minister, Australia*
%Prime Minister's Office, Parliament House, Canbera ACT 2600, Australia
Howard, Josh *Basketball Player*
%Dallas Mavericks, 2909 Taylor St, Dallas, TX 75226, USA
Howard, Ken *Actor*
%Ken Howard Productions, 59 E 54th St, #22, New York, NY 10022, USA
Howard, Michael *Government Official, England*
%House of Commons, Westminster, London SW1A 0AA, England
Howard, Miki *Singer*
%GHR Entertainment, 6014 N Pointe Place, Woodland Hills, CA 91367, USA
Howard, Rance *Actor*
4286 Clybourn Ave, Burbank, CA 91505, USA
Howard, Rebecca Lynn *Singer*
%William Morris Agency, 2100 W End Ave, #1000, Nashville, TN 37203, USA
Howard, Richard *Writer*
23 Waverly Place, #5X, New York, NY 10003, USA
Howard, Ron *Actor, Director*
%Bloom DeKom Hergott, 150 S Rodeo Dr, Beverly Hills, CA 90212, USA
Howard, Sherri *Track Athlete*
14059 Bridle Ridge Road, Sylmar, CA 91342, USA
Howard, Susan *Actress*
PO Box 1456, Boerne, TX 78006, USA
Howard, Traylor *Actress*
%United Talent Agency, 9560 Wilshire Blvd, #500, Beverly Hills, CA 90212, USA
Howard, William W, Jr *Association Executive*
%National Wildlife Federation, 11100 Wildlife Center Dr, Reston, VA 20190, USA
Howarth, Elgar *Composer*
27 Cromwell Ave, London N6 5HN, England
Howarth, Judith *Opera Singer*
%Lies Askonas, 6 Henrietta St, London WC2E 8LA, England
Howarth, Roger *Actor*
%K&H, 1212 Ave of Americas, #3, New York, NY 10036, USA
Howarth, Thomas *Architect*
%University of Toronto, 230 College St, Toronto ON M5S 1R1, Canada
Howatch, Susan *Writer*
%Aitken & Stone, 29 Fernshaw Road, London SW10 0TG, England
Howe of Aberavon, R E Geoffrey *Government Official, England*
%Barclays Bank, Cavendish Square Branch, 4 Vere St, London W1, England
Howe, Arthur *Journalist*
%Philadelphia Inquirer, Editorial Dept, 400 N Broad St, Philadelphia, PA 19130, USA
Howe, Arthur H (Art), Jr *Baseball Player, Manager*
711 Kahldon Court, Houston, TX 77079, USA

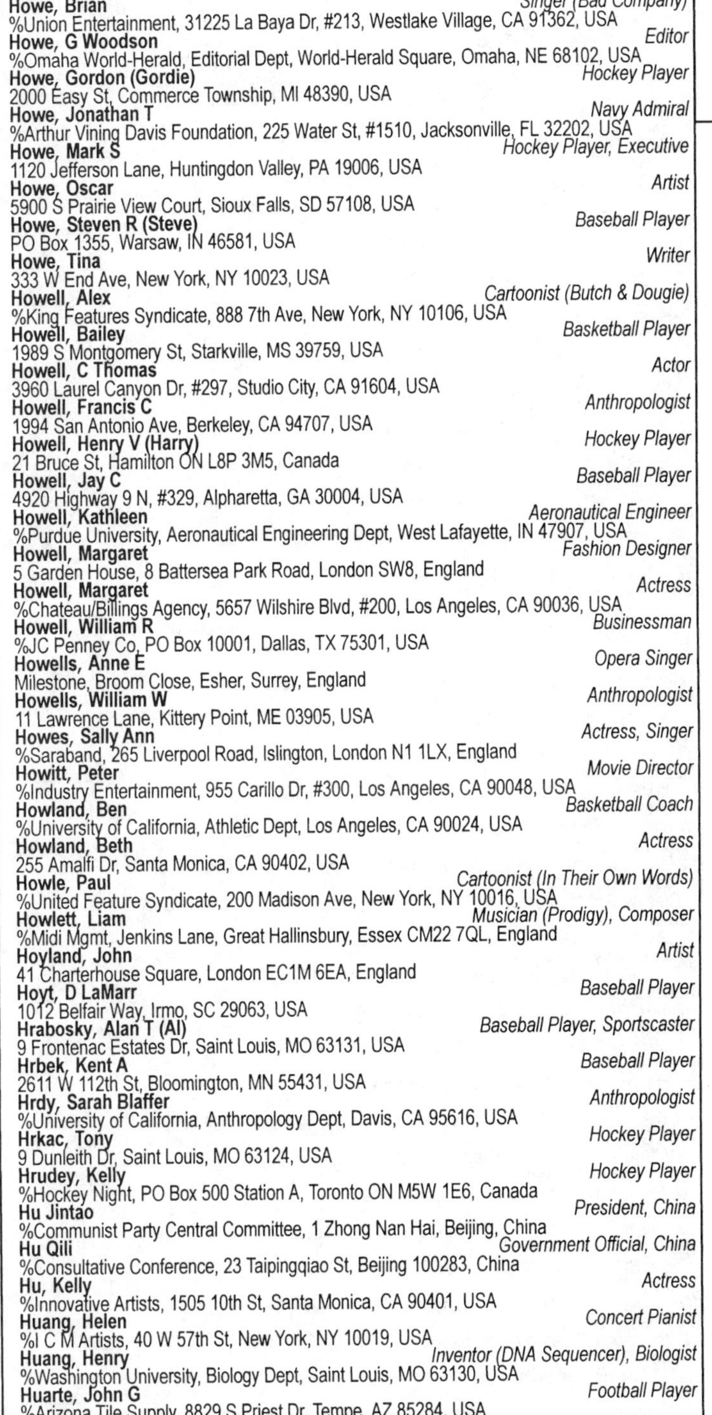

Howe, Brian *Singer (Bad Company)*
%Union Entertainment, 31225 La Baya Dr, #213, Westlake Village, CA 91362, USA
Howe, G Woodson *Editor*
%Omaha World-Herald, Editorial Dept, World-Herald Square, Omaha, NE 68102, USA
Howe, Gordon (Gordie) *Hockey Player*
2000 Easy St, Commerce Township, MI 48390, USA
Howe, Jonathan T *Navy Admiral*
%Arthur Vining Davis Foundation, 225 Water St, #1510, Jacksonville, FL 32202, USA
Howe, Mark S *Hockey Player, Executive*
1120 Jefferson Lane, Huntingdon Valley, PA 19006, USA
Howe, Oscar *Artist*
5900 S Prairie View Court, Sioux Falls, SD 57108, USA
Howe, Steven R (Steve) *Baseball Player*
PO Box 1355, Warsaw, IN 46581, USA
Howe, Tina *Writer*
333 W End Ave, New York, NY 10023, USA
Howell, Alex *Cartoonist (Butch & Dougie)*
%King Features Syndicate, 888 7th Ave, New York, NY 10106, USA
Howell, Bailey *Basketball Player*
1989 S Montgomery St, Starkville, MS 39759, USA
Howell, C Thomas *Actor*
3960 Laurel Canyon Dr, #297, Studio City, CA 91604, USA
Howell, Francis C *Anthropologist*
1994 San Antonio Ave, Berkeley, CA 94707, USA
Howell, Henry V (Harry) *Hockey Player*
21 Bruce St, Hamilton ON L8P 3M5, Canada
Howell, Jay C *Baseball Player*
4920 Highway 9 N, #329, Alpharetta, GA 30004, USA
Howell, Kathleen *Aeronautical Engineer*
%Purdue University, Aeronautical Engineering Dept, West Lafayette, IN 47907, USA
Howell, Margaret *Fashion Designer*
5 Garden House, 8 Battersea Park Road, London SW8, England
Howell, Margaret *Actress*
%Chateau/Billings Agency, 5657 Wilshire Blvd, #200, Los Angeles, CA 90036, USA
Howell, William R *Businessman*
%JC Penney Co, PO Box 10001, Dallas, TX 75301, USA
Howells, Anne E *Opera Singer*
Milestone, Broom Close, Esher, Surrey, England
Howells, William W *Anthropologist*
11 Lawrence Lane, Kittery Point, ME 03905, USA
Howes, Sally Ann *Actress, Singer*
%Saraband, 265 Liverpool Road, Islington, London N1 1LX, England
Howitt, Peter *Movie Director*
%Industry Entertainment, 955 Carillo Dr, #300, Los Angeles, CA 90048, USA
Howland, Ben *Basketball Coach*
%University of California, Athletic Dept, Los Angeles, CA 90024, USA
Howland, Beth *Actress*
255 Amalfi Dr, Santa Monica, CA 90402, USA
Howle, Paul *Cartoonist (In Their Own Words)*
%United Feature Syndicate, 200 Madison Ave, New York, NY 10016, USA
Howlett, Liam *Musician (Prodigy), Composer*
%Midi Mgmt, Jenkins Lane, Great Hallinsbury, Essex CM22 7QL, England
Hoyland, John *Artist*
41 Charterhouse Square, London EC1M 6EA, England
Hoyt, D LaMarr *Baseball Player*
1012 Belfair Way, Irmo, SC 29063, USA
Hrabosky, Alan T (Al) *Baseball Player, Sportscaster*
9 Frontenac Estates Dr, Saint Louis, MO 63131, USA
Hrbek, Kent A *Baseball Player*
2611 W 112th St, Bloomington, MN 55431, USA
Hrdy, Sarah Blaffer *Anthropologist*
%University of California, Anthropology Dept, Davis, CA 95616, USA
Hrkac, Tony *Hockey Player*
9 Dunleith Dr, Saint Louis, MO 63124, USA
Hrudey, Kelly *Hockey Player*
%Hockey Night, PO Box 500 Station A, Toronto ON M5W 1E6, Canada
Hu Jintao *President, China*
%Communist Party Central Committee, 1 Zhong Nan Hai, Beijing, China
Hu Qili *Government Official, China*
%Consultative Conference, 23 Taipingqiao St, Beijing 100283, China
Hu, Kelly *Actress*
%Innovative Artists, 1505 10th St, Santa Monica, CA 90401, USA
Huang, Helen *Concert Pianist*
%I C M Artists, 40 W 57th St, New York, NY 10019, USA
Huang, Henry *Inventor (DNA Sequencer), Biologist*
%Washington University, Biology Dept, Saint Louis, MO 63130, USA
Huarte, John G *Football Player*
%Arizona Tile Supply, 8829 S Priest Dr, Tempe, AZ 85284, USA

H

Hub *Bassist (Roots)*
%William Morris Agency, 1325 Ave of Americas, New York, NY 10019, USA
Hubbard, Frederick D (Freddie) *Jazz Trumpeter, Composer*
%Thomas Cassidy, 11761 E Speedway Blvd, Tucson, AZ 85748, USA
Hubbard, Gregg (Hobie) *Singer, Keyboardist (Sawyer Brown)*
%Sawyer Brown Inc, 5200 Old Harding Road, Franklin, TN 37064, USA
Hubbard, John *Artist*
Chilcombe House, Chilcombe near Bridport, Dorset, England
Hubbard, Marvin R (Marv) *Football Player*
5804 Dawn View Court, Castro Valley, CA 94552, USA
Hubbard, Philip (Phil) *Basketball Player, Coach*
%Washington Wizards, MCI Centre, 601 F St NW, Washington, DC 20004, USA
Hubel, David H *Nobel Medicine Laureate*
98 Collins Road, Waban, MA 02468, USA
Hubenthal, Karl *Editorial Cartoonist*
5536 Via La Mesa, #A, Laguna Hills, CA 92653, USA
Huber, Anke *Tennis Player*
Dieselstr 10, 76689 Karlsdorf-Neuthard, Germany
Huber, Robert *Nobel Chemistry Laureate*
%Planck Biochemie Institut, Am Klopferspitz, 82152 Martinsried, Germany
Hubley, Season *Actress*
31 Mansfield Ave, Essex Junction, VT 05452, USA
Huchra, John P *Astronomer*
%Harvard University, Astronomy Dept, Cambridge, MA 02138, USA
Huckabee, Cooper *Actor*
1800 El Cerrito Place, #34, Los Angeles, CA 90068, USA
Hucknall, Mick *Singer*
%So What Arts, Lock Keeper's Cottage, Manchester M3 4QL, England
Huckstep, Ronald L *Orthopedic Surgeon*
108 Sugarloaf Crescent, Castlecrag, Syndey NSW 2068, Australia
Huddleston, David *Actor*
9200 Sunset Blvd, #612, Los Angeles, CA 90069, USA
Hudecek, Vaclav *Concert Violinist*
Londynska 25, 120 00 Prague 2, Czech Republic
Hudner, Thomas J, Jr *Korean War Navy Hero (CMH)*
31 Allen Farm Lane, Concord, MA 01742, USA
Hudson, C B, Jr *Businessman*
%Torchmark Corp, 2001 3rd Ave S, Birmingham, AL 35233, USA
Hudson, Clifford G *Financier*
%Securities Investor Protection, 805 15th St NW, Washington, DC 20005, USA
Hudson, Ernie *Actor*
5711 Hoback Glen Road, Hidden Hills, CA 91302, USA
Hudson, Garth *Organist (Band)*
%Skyline Music, 32 Clayton St, Portland, ME 04103, USA
Hudson, Hugh *Movie Director*
%Jenks & Partners, 37 W 28th St, #7, New York, NY 10001, USA
Hudson, James *Psychiatrist*
%Harvard Medical School, Psychiatry Dept, 25 Shattuck St, Boston, MA 02115, USA
Hudson, Kate *Actress*
%Creative Artists Agency, 9830 Wilshire Blvd, Beverly Hills, CA 90212, USA
Hudson, Lou *Basketball Player*
1589 Little Kate Road, Park City, UT 84060, USA
Hudson, Ray *Soccer Player, Coach*
%DC United, 14120 Newbrook Dr, Chantilly, VA 20151, USA
Hudson, Sally *Skier*
PO Box 2343, Olympic Valley, CA 96146, USA
Hudson, Timothy A (Tim) *Baseball Player*
705 Watson Canyon Court, #202, San Ramon, CA 94583, USA
Huertas, Jon *Actor*
%Cirrincione Assoc, 300 W 5th St, New York, NY 10019, USA
Huff, Brent *Actor*
%Artists Group, 10100 Santa Monica Blvd, #2490, Los Angeles, CA 90067, USA
Huff, Gary E *Football Player*
5648 Braveheart Way, Tallahassee, FL 32317, USA
Huff, Kenneth W (Ken) *Football Player*
105 Blackford Court, Durham, NC 27712, USA
Huff, Robert L (Sam) *Football Player*
%Middleburg Broadcasting Network, 8 N Jay St, Middleburg, VA 20118, USA
Huffington, Arianna S *Writer*
3299 K St NW, #402, Washington, DC 20007, USA
Huffins, Chris *Track Athlete*
%Georgia Institute of Technology, Athletic Dept, Atlanta, GA 30332, USA
Huffman, Felicity *Actress*
%International Creative Mgmt, 8942 Wilshire Blvd, #219, Beverly Hills, CA 90211, USA
Hufsey, Billy *Actor*
15415 Muskingam, Brook Park, OH 44142, USA
Hufstedler, Shirley M *Secretary, Education*
720 Iverness Dr, La Canada-Flintridge, CA 91011, USA

Hug, Procter R, Jr *Judge*
%US Court of Appeals, 400 S Virginia St, Reno, NV 89501, USA

Huggins, Bob *Basketball Coach*
207 Beecher Hall, Cincinnati, OH 45221, USA

Hughes, Albert *Movie Director*
%Creative Artists Agency, 9830 Wilshire Blvd, Beverly Hills, CA 90212, USA

Hughes, Allen *Movie Director*
%Creative Artists Agency, 9830 Wilshire Blvd, Beverly Hills, CA 90212, USA

Hughes, Barnard *Actor*
1244 11th St, #A, Santa Monica, CA 90401, USA

Hughes, Edward Z *Publisher*
%American Heritage Magazine, Forbes Building, 60 5th Ave, New York, NY 10011, USA

Hughes, Finola *Actress*
%Metropolitan Talent Agency, 4526 Wilshire Blvd, Los Angeles, CA 90010, USA

Hughes, Gene *Singer (Casinos)*
%Lustig Talent, PO Box 770850, Orlando, FL 32877, USA

Hughes, H Richard *Architect*
47 Chiswick Quay, London W4 3UR, England

Hughes, Harold R (Harry) *Governor, MD*
%Patton Boggs Blow, 2550 M St NW, #500, Washington, DC 20037, USA

Hughes, John *Hockey Player*
73 Lowell St, Somerville, MA 02143, USA

Hughes, John W *Movie Director, Screenwriter*
%Hughes Entertainment, 1 Westminster Place, Lake Forest, IL 60045, USA

Hughes, Karen *Government Official*
%White House, 1600 Pennsylvania Ave NW, Washington, DC 20500, USA

Hughes, Kathleen *Actress*
8818 Rising Glen Place, Los Angeles, CA 90069, USA

Hughes, Keith W *Financier*
%Associates First Capital, 250 E John Carpenter Freeway, Irving, TX 75062, USA

Hughes, Larry *Basketball Player*
%Washington Wizards, MCI Centre, 601 F St NW, Washington, DC 20004, USA

Hughes, Mervyn G *Cricketer*
%Australian Cricket Board, 90 Jollimant St, Melbourne VIC 3002, Australia

Hughes, Miko *Actor*
%Jamieson Assoc, 53 Sunrise Road, Superior, MT 59872, USA

Hughes, Richard H (Dick) *Baseball Player*
PO Box 598, Stephens, AR 71764, USA

Hughes, Robert S F *Art Critic*
143 Prince St, New York, NY 10012, USA

Hughes, Sarah *Figure Skater*
%John Hughes, 12 Channel Dr, Great Neck, NY 11024, USA

Hughes, Thomas J, Jr *Navy Admiral*
400 Mar Vista Dr, #4, Monterey, CA 93940, USA

Hughes, Tyrone C *Football Player*
7340 Crestmont Road, New Orleans, LA 70126, USA

Hughes, Wendy *Actress*
129 Bourke St, Woolloomooloo, Sydney NSW 2011, Australia

Hughes-Fulford, Millie *Astronaut*
%Veterans Affairs Dept, Medical Center, 4150 Clement St, San Francisco, CA 94121, USA

Hughley, D L *Actor, Comedian*
%Creative Artists Agency, 9830 Wilshire Blvd, Beverly Hills, CA 90212, USA

Hugstedt, Petter *Ski Jumper*
3600 Kongsberg, Norway

Huguenin, G Richard *Inventor (Portable Gun Detector Camera)*
%Millitech Corp, South Deerfield, MA 01373, USA

Huisgen, Rolf *Chemist*
Kaulbachstr 10, 80539 Munich, Germany

Huizenga, H Wayne *Businessman*
%Huizenga Holdings, 200 S Andrews Ave, Fort Lauderdale, FL 33301, USA

Huizenga, John R *Nuclear Chemist*
43 McMichael Dr, Pinehurst, NC 28374, USA

Hulce, Tom *Actor*
2305 Stanley Hills Dr, Los Angeles, CA 90046, USA

Hull, Brett A *Hockey Player*
3520 Eben Way, Stillwater, MN 55082, USA

Hull, Dennis W *Hockey Player*
%Rose City Dodge, 435 West Side, Welland ON L3B 5X1, Canada

Hull, Don *Olympics Official*
%US Olympic Committee, 1 Olympia Plaza, Colorado Springs, CO 80909, USA

Hull, J Kent *Football Player*
RR 1 Box 574B, Greenwood, MS 38930, USA

Hull, James D *Coast Guard Admiral*
Commander, US Coast Guard Atlantic, 4131 Crawford St, Portsmouth, VA 23704, USA

Hull, Robert M (Bobby) *Hockey Player*
48 Huntington Chase Dr, Asheville, NC 28805, USA

Hull, Roger H *Educator*
%Union College, Chancellor's Office, Schenectady, NY 12308, USA

Hullar, Theodore L *Educator*
3 Lowell Place, Ithaca, NY 14850, USA
Hulme, Denis *Auto Racing Driver*
Cl-6, RDTE Puke, Bay of Plenny, New Zealand
Hulme, Etta *Editorial Cartoonist*
%Fort Worth Star-Telegram, Editorial Dept, 400 W 7th St, Fort Worth, TX 76102, USA
Hulme, Keri *Writer*
%Hodder & Stoughton, 338 Euston Road, London NW1 3BH, England
Hulse, Russell A *Nobel Physics Laureate*
PO Box 451, Princeton, NJ 08543, USA
Humann, L Phillip *Financier*
%SunTrust Banks, 303 Peachtree St NE, Atlanta, GA 30308, USA
Humayan, Mark S *Ophthalmologist*
%Johns Hopkins University, Wilmer Ophthalmology Institute, Baltimore, MD 21218, USA
Humbert, John O *Religious Leader*
%Christian Church Disciples of Christ, 130 E Washington, Indianapolis, IN 46204, USA
Hume, A Britton (Brit) *Commentator*
3100 N St NW, #9, Washington, DC 20007, USA
Hume, John *Nobel Peace Laureate*
5 Bayview Terrace, Derry BT48 7EE, Northern Ireland
Hume, Stephen *Editor*
%Vancouver Sun, 2250 Granville St, Vancouver BC V6H 3G2, Canada
Humes, Edward *Journalist*
%Simon & Schuster, 1230 Ave of Americas, New York, NY 10020, USA
Humes, John P *Diplomat*
Forest Mill Road, Mill Neck, NY 11765, USA
Humes, Mary-Margaret *Actress, Model*
%Stone Manners, 6500 Wilshire Blvd, #550, Los Angeles, CA 90048, USA
Hummes, Claudio Hummes Cardinal *Religious Leader*
Avenida Higienopolis 890, CP 1670, 01238-908 Sao Paulo, Brazil
Humperdinck, Engelbert *Singer*
14724 Ventura Blvd, #507, Sherman Oaks, CA 91403, USA
Humphrey, Gordon J *Senator, NH*
78 Garvin Hill Road, Chichester, NH 03258, USA
Humphrey, Jackie *Track Athlete*
616 Powder Horn Road, Richmond, KY 40475, USA
Humphrey, Ryan *Basketball Player*
%Memphis Grizzlies, 175 Toyota Plaza, #150, Memphis, TN 38103, USA
Humphries, Jay *Basketball Player*
PO Box 1810, Parker, CO 80134, USA
Humphries, Stan *Football Player*
%Northeast Louisiana Univ, Alumni Assn, 700 University Ave, Monroe, LA 71209, USA
Humphry, Derek *Social Activist*
%ERGO, 24828 Norris Lane, Junction City, OR 97448, USA
Hun Sen *Prime Minister, Cambodia*
%Prime Minister's Office, Supreme National Council, Phnom Penh, Cambodia
Hundley, Randy (C Randolph) *Baseball Player*
122 E Forest Lane, Palatine, IL 60067, USA
Hundley, Rod (Hot Rod) *Basketball Player, Sportscaster*
1860 E Siggard Dr, Salt Lake City, UT 84106, USA
Hundt, Reed E *Government Official*
6416 Brookside Dr, Bethesda, MD 20815, USA
Hung, Sammo *Actor*
PO Box 1566, Los Angeles, CA 90078, USA
Hunger, Daniela *Swimmer*
%SV Preussen, Hansastr 190, 13088 Berlin, Germany
Huniford, James *Interior Designer, Architect*
%Sills Hunifor Assoc, 30 E 67th St, New York, NY 10021, USA
Hunkapiller, Michael *Inventor (DNA Sequencer), Biochemist*
%Applied Biosystems, 850 Lincoln Centre Dr, Foster City, CA 94404, USA
Hunley, Leann *Actress*
%Susan Smith, 121A N San Vicente Blvd, Beverly Hills, CA 90211, USA
Hunley, Ricky C *Football Player*
9617 Stonemasters Dr, Loveland, OH 45140, USA
Hunnicutt, Gayle *Actress*
174 Regents Park Road, London NW1, England
Hunt, Bonnie *Actress, Director*
%International Creative Mgmt, 8942 Wilshire Blvd, #219, Beverly Hills, CA 90211, USA
Hunt, Bryan *Artist*
31 Great Jones St, New York, NY 10012, USA
Hunt, Helen *Actress*
%Creative Artists Agency, 9830 Wilshire Blvd, Beverly Hills, CA 90212, USA
Hunt, Jimmy *Actor*
2279 Lansdale Court, Simi Valley, CA 93065, USA
Hunt, John R *Religious Leader*
%Evangelical Covenant Church, 5101 N Francisco Ave, Chicago, IL 60625, USA
Hunt, Lamar *Football, Tennis, Soccer Executive*
Thanksgiving Tower, 1601 Elm St, #2800, Dallas, TX 75201, USA

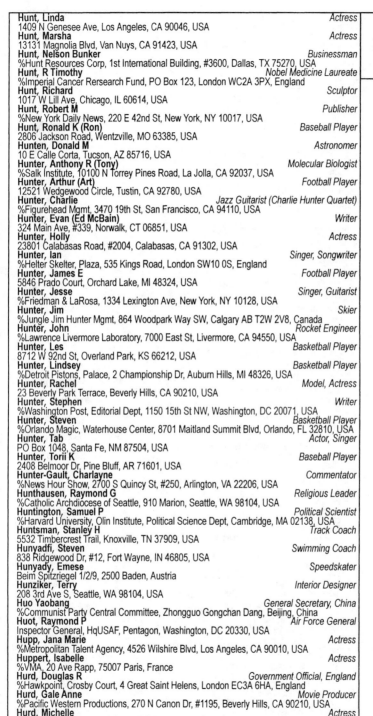

Hunt, Linda *Actress*
1409 N Genesee Ave, Los Angeles, CA 90046, USA
Hunt, Marsha *Actress*
13131 Magnolia Blvd, Van Nuys, CA 91423, USA
Hunt, Nelson Bunker *Businessman*
%Hunt Resources Corp, 1st International Building, #3600, Dallas, TX 75270, USA
Hunt, R Timothy *Nobel Medicine Laureate*
%Imperial Cancer Rersearch Fund, PO Box 123, London WC2A 3PX, England
Hunt, Richard *Sculptor*
1017 W Lill Ave, Chicago, IL 60614, USA
Hunt, Robert M *Publisher*
%New York Daily News, 220 E 42nd St, New York, NY 10017, USA
Hunt, Ronald K (Ron) *Baseball Player*
2806 Jackson Road, Wentzville, MO 63385, USA
Hunten, Donald M *Astronomer*
10 E Calle Corta, Tucson, AZ 85716, USA
Hunter, Anthony R (Tony) *Molecular Biologist*
%Salk Institute, 10100 N Torrey Pines Road, La Jolla, CA 92037, USA
Hunter, Arthur (Art) *Football Player*
12521 Wedgewood Circle, Tustin, CA 92780, USA
Hunter, Charlie *Jazz Guitarist (Charlie Hunter Quartet)*
%Figurehead Mgmt, 3470 19th St, San Francisco, CA 94110, USA
Hunter, Evan (Ed McBain) *Writer*
324 Main Ave, #339, Norwalk, CT 06851, USA
Hunter, Holly *Actress*
23801 Calabasas Road, #2004, Calabasas, CA 91302, USA
Hunter, Ian *Singer, Songwriter*
%Helter Skelter, Plaza, 535 Kings Road, London SW10 0S, England
Hunter, James E *Football Player*
5846 Prado Court, Orchard Lake, MI 48324, USA
Hunter, Jesse *Singer, Guitarist*
%Friedman & LaRosa, 1334 Lexington Ave, New York, NY 10128, USA
Hunter, Jim *Skier*
%Jungle Jim Hunter Mgmt, 864 Woodpark Way SW, Calgary AB T2W 2V8, Canada
Hunter, John *Rocket Engineer*
%Lawrence Livermore Laboratory, 7000 East St, Livermore, CA 94550, USA
Hunter, Les *Basketball Player*
8712 W 92nd St, Overland Park, KS 66212, USA
Hunter, Lindsey *Basketball Player*
%Detroit Pistons, Palace, 2 Championship Dr, Auburn Hills, MI 48326, USA
Hunter, Rachel *Model, Actress*
23 Beverly Park Terrace, Beverly Hills, CA 90210, USA
Hunter, Stephen *Writer*
%Washington Post, Editorial Dept, 1150 15th St NW, Washington, DC 20071, USA
Hunter, Steven *Basketball Player*
%Orlando Magic, Waterhouse Center, 8701 Maitland Summit Blvd, Orlando, FL 32810, USA
Hunter, Tab *Actor, Singer*
PO Box 1048, Santa Fe, NM 87504, USA
Hunter, Torii K *Baseball Player*
2408 Belmoor Dr, Pine Bluff, AR 71601, USA
Hunter-Gault, Charlayne *Commentator*
%News Hour Show, 2700 S Quincy St, #250, Arlington, VA 22206, USA
Hunthausen, Raymond G *Religious Leader*
%Catholic Archdiocese of Seattle, 910 Marion, Seattle, WA 98104, USA
Huntington, Samuel P *Political Scientist*
%Harvard University, Olin Institute, Political Science Dept, Cambridge, MA 02138, USA
Huntsman, Stanley H *Track Coach*
5532 Timbercrest Trail, Knoxville, TN 37909, USA
Hunyadfi, Steven *Swimming Coach*
838 Ridgewood Dr, #12, Fort Wayne, IN 46805, USA
Hunyady, Emese *Speedskater*
Beim Spitzriegel 1/2/9, 2500 Baden, Austria
Hunziker, Terry *Interior Designer*
208 3rd Ave S, Seattle, WA 98104, USA
Huo Yaobang *General Secretary, China*
%Communist Party Central Committee, Zhongguo Gongchan Dang, Beijing, China
Huot, Raymond P *Air Force General*
Inspector General, HqUSAF, Pentagon, Washington, DC 20330, USA
Hupp, Jana Marie *Actress*
%Metropolitan Talent Agency, 4526 Wilshire Blvd, Los Angeles, CA 90010, USA
Huppert, Isabelle *Actress*
%VMA, 20 Ave Rapp, 75007 Paris, France
Hurd, Douglas R *Government Official, England*
%Hawkpoint, Crosby Court, 4 Great Saint Helens, London EC3A 6HA, England
Hurd, Gale Anne *Movie Producer*
%Pacific Western Productions, 270 N Canon Dr, #1195, Beverly Hills, CA 90210, USA
Hurd, Michelle *Actress*
%William Morris Agency, 151 El Camino Dr, Beverly Hills, CA 90212, USA

H

Hurdle, Clinton M (Clint) *Baseball Player, Manager*
9068 Sturbridge Place, Littleton, CO 80129, USA
Hurford, Peter J *Concert Organist*
Broom House, Saint Bernard's Road, Saint Albans, Herts AL3 5RA, England
Hurley, Alfred F *Historian*
%University of North Texas, President's Office, Denton, TX 76203, USA
Hurley, Bobby *Basketball Player*
6 Orchard Lane, Colts Neck, NJ 07722, USA
Hurley, Denis E *Religious Leader*
%Emanuel Catholic Cathedral, Cathedral Road, Durban 4001, South Africa
Hurley, Douglas G *Astronaut*
700 Thornwood Dr, Friendswood, TX 77546, USA
Hurley, Elizabeth *Model, Actress*
36 Redcliff Road, London SW10 9NJ, England
Hurn, David *Photographer*
Prospect Cottage, Tintern, Gwent, Wales
Hurnik, Ilja *Concert Pianist, Composer*
Narodni Trida 35, 11000 Prague 1, Czech Republic
Hurst, Bruce V *Baseball Player*
1080 N Riata St, Gilbert, AZ 85234, USA
Hurst, Michael *Actor*
%Bruce Ugly Agency, 218 Richmond Road, Grey Lynn, Auckland 2, New Zealand
Hurst, Ryan *Actor*
%Endeavor Talent Agency, 9701 Wilshire Blvd, #1000, Beverly Hills, CA 90212, USA
Hurt, Frank *Labor Leader*
%Bakery Confectionery Tobacco Union, 10401 Connecticut, Kensington, MD 20895, USA
Hurt, John *Actor*
%Julian Belfarge, 46 Albermarle St, London W1X 4PP, England
Hurt, Mary Beth *Actress*
1619 Broadway, #900, New York, NY 10019, USA
Hurt, William *Actor*
%Wolf/Kasteller, 335 N Maple Dr, #351, Beverly Hills, CA 90210, USA
Hurtado Larrea, Oswaldo *President, Ecuador*
Suecia 277 y Av Los Shyris, Quito, Ecuador
Hurvich, Leo M *Psychologist*
%University of Pennsylvania, Psychology Dept, Philadelphia, PA 19104, USA
Hurwicz, Leonid *Economist*
3318 Edmund Blvd, Minneapolis, MN 55406, USA
Hurwitz, Emanuel H *Concert Violinist*
25 Dollis Ave, London N3 1DA, England
Hurwitz, Jerard *Molecular Biologist*
%Memorial Sloan Kettering Cancer Center, 1275 York Ave, New York, NY 10021, USA
Husa, Karel J *Composer, Conductor*
1 Bellwood Lane, Ithaca, NY 14850, USA
Husar, Lubomyr Cardinal *Religious Leader*
Ploscha Sviatoho Jura 5, 290000 Lviv, Ukraine
Husbands, Clifford *Governor General, Barbados*
%Governor General's Office, Bay St, Saint Michael, Bridgetown, Barbados
Huselius, Kristian *Hockey Player*
%Florida Panthers, 1 Panthers Parkway, Sunrise, FL 33323, USA
Husen, Torsten *Educator*
%Int'l Educational Institute, Armfeltsgatan 10, 115 34 Stockholm, Sweden
Huseynov, Surat *Prime Minister, Azerbaijan*
%Prime Minister's Office, Baku, Azerbaijan
Husky, Ferlin *Singer, Songwriter*
%Richard Davis Mgmt, 1030 N Woodland Dr, Kansas City, MO 64118, USA
Husted, Dave *Bowler*
8880 SE Manfield Court, Clackamas, OR 97015, USA
Husted, Wayne D *Glass Artist*
%Keep Homestead Museum, Ely Road, Monson, MA 01057, USA
Huston, Anjelica *Actress, Director*
57 Windward Ave, Venice, CA 90291, USA
Huston, Daniel (Danny) *Movie Director*
%William Morris Agency, 151 El Camino Dr, Beverly Hills, CA 90212, USA
Huston, John *Golfer*
307 Lakeview Dr, Tarpon Springs, FL 34689, USA
Hutcherson, Robert (Bobby) *Jazz Vibist*
%Abby Hoffer, 223 1/2 E 48th St, New York, NY 10017, USA
Hutchins, Mel *Basketball Player*
1211 S Pacific St, #B, Oceanside, CA 92054, USA
Hutchins, Will *Actor*
PO Box 371, Glen Head, NY 11545, USA
Hutchinson, Barbara *Labor Leader*
%American Federation of Labor, 815 15th St NW, Washington, DC 20005, USA
Hutchinson, Frederick E *Educator*
%University of Maine, President's Office, Orono, ME 04469, USA
Hutchinson, J Maxwell *Architect*
Cavendish Mansions, #61, Clerkenwell Road, London EC1R 5DH, England

Hutchison, Clyde A, Jr *Chemist*
%University of Chicago, Searle Laboratory, Chemistry Dept, Chicago, IL 60637, USA
Hutchison, Doug *Actor*
%United Talent Agency, 9560 Wilshire Blvd, #500, Beverly Hills, CA 90212, USA
Huth, Edward J *Editor, Physician*
1124 Morris Ave, Bryn Mawr, PA 19010, USA
Hutt, Peter B *Attorney*
%Covington & Burling, 1201 Pennsylvania Ave NW, Washington, DC 20004, USA
Hutton, Betty *Actress, Singer*
%Edward Arrendardo, 1024 S Golden West, Arcadia, CA 91007, USA
Hutton, Danny *Singer (Three Dog Night)*
2437 Horseshoe Canyon Road, Los Angeles, CA 90046, USA
Hutton, Lauren *Model, Actress*
382 Lafayette St, #6, New York, NY 10003, USA
Hutton, Ralph *Swimmer*
%Vancouver Police Department, 312 Main St, Vancouver BC, Canada
Hutton, Timothy *Actor*
%Creative Artists Agency, 9830 Wilshire Blvd, Beverly Hills, CA 90212, USA
Huxley, Andrew F *Nobel Medicine Laureate*
Manor Field, 1 Vicarage Dr, Grantchester, Cambridge CB3 9NG, England
Huxley, Hugh E *Biologist*
349 Nashawtuc Road, Concord, MA 01742, USA
Huxley, Laura *Therapist, Writer*
6233 Mulholland Dr, Los Angeles, CA 90068, USA
Huxtable, Ada Louise *Architectural Critic*
969 Park Ave, New York, NY 10028, USA
Huyck, Willard *Movie Director*
39 Oakmont Dr, Los Angeles, CA 90049, USA
Hvorostovsky, Dmitri *Opera Singer*
%Lies Askonas, 6 Henrietta St, London WC2E 8LA, England
Hwang, David Henry *Writer*
70 W 36th St, #501, New York, NY 10018, USA
Hyams, Joseph I (Joe), Jr *Writer*
10375 Wilshire Blvd, #4D, Los Angeles, CA 90024, USA
Hyams, Peter *Movie Director*
PO Box 10, Basking Ridge, NJ 07920, USA
Hyatt, Joel Z *Attorney, Businessman*
%Hyatt Legal Services, 1215 Superior Ave E, Cleveland, OH 44114, USA
Hybl, William J *Sports Official*
%US Olympic Committee, 1 Olympia Plaza, Colorado Springs, CO 80909, USA
Hyde, Christopher *Writer*
%Onyx Penguin Putnam, 375 Hudson St, New York, NY 10014, USA
Hyde, Jonathan *Actor*
%William Morris Agency, 52/53 Poland Place, London W1F 7LX, England
Hyde-White, Alex *Actor*
%Borinstein Oreck Bogart, 3172 Dona Susana Dr, Studio City, CA 91604, USA
Hyland, Brian *Singer*
%Stone Buffalo, PO Box 101, Helendale, CA 92342, USA
Hylton, Thomas J *Journalist*
%Pottstown Mercury, Editorial Dept, Hanover & King Sts, Pottstown, PA 19464, USA
Hyman, Earle *Actor*
%Manhattan Towers, 484 W 43rd St, #33E, New York, NY 10036, USA
Hyman, Misty *Swimmer*
3826 E Lupine Ave, Phoenix, AZ 85028, USA
Hyman, Richard R (Dick) *Jazz Pianist, Composer*
%Abby Hoffer, 223 1/2 E 48th St, New York, NY 10017, USA
Hynd, Ronald *Ballet Dancer, Choreographer*
Fern Cottage, Up Somerton, Bury Saint Edmonds, Suffolk IP29 4ND, England
Hynde, Chrissie *Singer, Guitarist, Songwriter*
%Premier Talent, 3 E 54th St, #1100, New York, NY 10022, USA
Hynes, Garry *Theater Director*
%Druid Theater Co, Chapel Lane, Galway, Ireland
Hynes, Samuel *Writer*
130 Moore St, Princeton, NJ 08540, USA
Hynes, Tyler *Actor*
201 Laurier Ave E, #202, Ottawa ON K1N 6P1, Canada
Hyser, Joyce *Actress*
%Artists Agency, 1180 S Beverly Dr, #301, Los Angeles, CA 90035, USA
Hysong, Nick *Track Athlete*
2822 E Cholla St, Phoenix, AZ 85028, USA
Hytner, Nicholas R *Theater, Film Director*
%National Theatre, South Bank, London SE1 9PX, England

I

Iacocca - Ilgauskas

Iacocca, Lido A (Lee) *Businessman*
%EV Global Motors, 10900 Wilshire Blvd, #520, Los Angeles, CA 90024, USA
Iaconio, Frank *Auto Racing Driver*
250 US Highway 206, Flanders, NJ 07836, USA
Iafrate, Al A *Hockey Player*
27480 Five Mile Road, Livonia, MI 48154, USA
Iakovos, Primate Archbishop *Religious Leader*
31 Park Dr, South Rye, NY 10021, USA
Ian, Janis *Singer, Songwriter*
%Senior Mgmt, 56 Lindsley Ave, Nashville, TN 37210, USA
Ibbetson, Arthur *Cinematographer*
%Tanglewood, Chalfont Lane, Chorlry Wood, Herts, England
Ibers, James A *Chemist*
2657 Orrington Ave, Evanston, IL 60201, USA
Ibiam, Francis A *Religious Leader*
Ganymede, Unwana, PO Box 240, Afikpo, Imo State, Nigeria
Ibn Salman Ibn 'Abd Al-'Aziz Al-Saud *Cosmonaut*
PO Box 18368, Riyadh 11415, Saudi Arabia
Ibrahim, Abdullah (Dollar Brand) *Jazz Pianist, Composer*
%Brad Simon Organization, 122 E 57th St, #300, New York, NY 10022, USA
Ibrahim, Barre Mainassara *Head of State, Niger; Army Officer*
%Head of State's Office, Presidential Palace, Niamey, Niger
Ibuka, Yaeko *Social Worker*
%Fukusei Byoin, Leprosarium, Mount Fuji, Japan
Icahn, Carl C *Businessman*
%Icahn Co, 100 S Bedford Road, Mount Kisco, NY 10549, USA
Ice Cube *Rap Artist, Actor, Director*
5420 Lindley Ave, #4, Encino, CA 91316, USA
Ice T *Rap Artist, Actor*
%Coast II Coast, 3350 Wilshire Blvd, #1200, Los Angeles, CA 90010, USA
Ichaso, Leon *Movie Director*
%Creative Artists Agency, 9830 Wilshire Blvd, Beverly Hills, CA 90212, USA
Ickx, Jacky *Auto Racing Driver*
171 Chaussee de la Hulpe, 1170 Brussels, Belgium
Idle, Eric *Actor, Comedian (Monty Python)*
%Mayday Mgmt, 68A Delancey St, Camden Town, London NW1 7RY, England
Idol, Billy *Singer, Songwriter*
%East End Mgmt, 8209 Melrose Ave, #200, Los Angeles, CA 90046, USA
Ifans, Rhys *Actor*
%Endeavor Talent Agency, 9701 Wilshire Blvd, #1000, Beverly Hills, CA 90212, USA
Ifukube, Akira *Composer*
7-13-1 Nishishimbashi, Minatoku, Tokyo 105, Japan
Iger, Robert A *Businessman*
%Walt Disney Co, 500 S Buena Vista St, Burbank, CA 91521, USA
Iginla, Jarome *Hockey Player*
%Newport Mgmt, 601-201 City Centre Dr, Mississauga ON L58 2T4, Canada
Iglesias, Enrique *Singer*
%Fernan Martinez, 601 Brickell Key Dr, Miami, FL 33131, USA
Iglesias, Enrique V *Financier; Government Official, Uruguay*
%Inter-American Development Bank, 1300 New York Ave NW, Washington, DC 20577, USA
Iglesias, Julio *Singer*
1177 Kane Concourse, Bay Harbor Islands, FL 33154, USA
Iglesias, Julio, Jr *Singer, Songwriter*
%Creative Artists Agency, 9830 Wilshire Blvd, Beverly Hills, CA 90212, USA
Ignarro, Louis J *Nobel Medicine Laureate*
%University of California, Medical School, 10833 LeConte, Los Angeles, CA 90095, USA
Ignatius Zakka I Iwas, Patriarch *Religious Leader*
%Syrian Orthodox Patriarchate, Bab Toma, PB 22260, Damascus, Syria
Ignatius, Paul R *Government Official*
3650 Fordham Road, Washington, DC 20016, USA
Iha, James *Guitarist (Smashing Pumpkins)*
1245 W Glenlake, Chicago, IL 60660, USA
Ihnatowicz, Zbigniew *Architect*
Ul Mokotowska 31 M 15, 00-560 Warsaw, Poland
Ike, Reverend *Evangelist*
4140 Broadway, New York, NY 10033, USA
Ikeda, Daisaku *Religious Leader, Philosopher*
%Soka Gakkai, 32 Shinanomachi, Shinjuku, Tokyo 160-8583, Japan
Ikenberry, Stanley O *Educator*
%American Council on Education, 1 Dupont Circle NW, Washington, DC 20036, USA
Ikola, Willard *Hockey Player, Coach*
5697 Green Circle Drive, #316, Minnetonka, MN 55343, USA
Iley, Barbara *Actress*
%Paradigm Agency, 10100 Santa Monica Blvd, #2500, Los Angeles, CA 90067, USA
Ilg, Raymond P *Navy Admiral*
5504 Teak Court, Alexandria, VA 22309, USA
Ilgauskas, Zydrunas *Basketball Player*
%Cleveland Cavaliers, Gund Arena, 1 Center Court, Cleveland, OH 44115, USA

I

Iliescu, Ion *President, Romania*
%President's Office, Calea Victoriei 59-53, Bucharest, Romania
Ilitch, Michael *Hockey Executive, Baseball Executive*
%Detroit Red Wings, Joe Louis Arena, 600 Civic Center Dr, Detroit, MI 48226, USA
Illmann, Margaret *Ballerina*
%National Ballet of Canada, 157 E King St, Toronto ON M5C 1G9, Canada
Illsley, John *Bassist (Dire Straits)*
%Damage Mgmt, 16 Lambton Place, London W11 2SH, England
Iloilo, Ratu Josefa *President, Fiji*
%President's Office, PO Box 2513, Suva, Viti Levu, Fiji
Ilyenko, Yuriy G *Cinematograper*
9 Michail Koyzybinksy Str, #22, 252030 Kiev, Ukraine
Imai, Kenji *Architect*
4-12-28 Kitazawa, Setagayaku, Tokyo, Japan
Imamura, Shohei *Movie Director*
%Toei Co, 3-2-17 Ginza, Chuoku, Tokyo 104, Japan
Iman *Model, Actress*
%Essex House, 160 Central Park S, New York, NY 10019, USA
Imbert, Bertrand S M *Explorer, Engineer*
50 Rue de Turenne, 75003 Paris, France
Imbert, Peter M *Law Enforcement Official*
%Lieutenancy Office, City Hall, Victoria St, London S1E 6QP, England
Imbrie, Andrew W *Composer*
2625 Rose St, Berkeley, CA 94708, USA
Imbruglia, Natalie *Singer, Songwriter, Actress*
%Russells, Regency House, 1-4 Warwick St, London W1R 6LJ, England
Imhoff, Darrall *Basketball Player*
3637 Sterling Wood Dr, Eugene, OR 97408, USA
Imhoff, Gary *Actor*
%Samantha Group, 300 S Raymond Ave, Pasadena, CA 91105, USA
Imle, John F, Jr *Businessman*
%Unocal Corp, 2141 Rosecrans Ave, El Segundo, CA 90245, USA
Immelt, Jeffrey (Jeff) *Businessman*
%General Electric Co, 3135 Easton Turnpike, Fairfield, CT 06828, USA
Immerfall, Daniel (Dan) *Speedskater*
5421 Trempeleau Trail, Madison, WI 53705, USA
Imperioli, Michael *Actor*
3141 Baisley Ave, Bronx, NY 10465, USA
Imran Khan Niazi *Cricketer*
%Shankat Khanum Memorial Trust, 29 Shah Jamal, Lahore 546000, Pakistan
Imus, Don *Entertainer*
%WFAN-Radio, 3412 36th St, Astoria, NY 11106, USA
Inamori, Kazuo *Businessman*
%KDDI Corp, 3-22 Nishi-Shinjuku, Shinjuku, Tokyo 163-8003, Japan
Inbal, Eliahu *Conductor*
%Hessischer Rundfunk, Bertramstr 8, 60320 Frankfurt/Main, Germany
Incandella, Sal *Auto Racing Executive*
%Indy Racing Regency, 5811 W 73rd St, Indianapolis, IN 46278, USA
Incaviglia, Peter J (Pete) *Baseball Player*
PO Box 526, Pebble Beach, CA 93953, USA
India.Arie *Singer, Guitar, Songwriter*
%Helter Skelter, Plaza, 535 Kings Road, London SW10 0S, England
Indiana, Robert *Artist*
%Press Box 464, Vinalhaven, ME 04863, USA
Infante, Lindy *Football Coach*
6780 A1AS, Saint Augustine, FL 32080, USA
Infill, O Urcille, Jr *Religious Leader*
%African Methodist Church, PO Box 19039 Philadelphia, PA 19138, USA
Ing Huot *Government Official, Cambodia*
%Foreign Affairs Ministry, Phnom Penh, Cambodia
Inge, Peter A *Army Field Marshal, England*
%House of Lords, Westminster, London SW1A 0PW, England
Ingels, Marty *Actor, Comedian*
16400 Ventura Blvd, Encino, CA 91436, USA
Ingersoll, Ralph, II *Publisher*
%Ingersoll Publications, PO Box 1869, Lakeville, CT 06039, USA
Inghram, Mark G *Physicist*
13837 W Casa Linda Dr, Sun City West, AZ 85375, USA
Ingle, Doug *Singer, Keyboardist (Iron Butterfly)*
%Entertainment Services Int'l, 6400 Pleasant Park Dr, Chanhassen, MN 55317, USA
Ingle, John *Actor*
%Artists Group, 10100 Santa Monica Blvd, #2490, Los Angeles, CA 90067, USA
Ingle, Robert D *Editor*
%San Jose Mercury News, Editorial Dept, 750 Ridder Park Dr, San Jose, CA 95131, USA
Ingman, Einar H, Jr *Korean War Army Hero (CMH)*
W4053 N Silver Lake Road, Irma, WI 54442, USA
Ingraham, Hubert A *Prime Minister, Bahamas*
%Prime Minister's Office, Whitfield Center, Box CB10980, Nassau, Bahamas

I

Ingram - Irvan

Ingram, A John *Surgeon*
4940 Sullivan Woods Cove, Memphis, TN 38117, USA

Ingram, James *Singer, Songwriter*
867 S Muirfield Road, Los Angeles, CA 90005, USA

Ingram, Lonnie *Microbiologist*
%University of Florida, Microbiology/Cell Science Dept, Gainesville, FL 32611, USA

Ingram, Vernon M *Biochemist*
%Massachusetts Institute of Technology, Biochemistry Dept, Cambridge, MA 02139, USA

Ingrao, Pietro *Government Official, Italy*
%Centro Studie Iniziative Per La Reforma, Via Della Vite 13, Rome, Italy

Ingrassia, Paul J *Journalist*
111 Division Ave, New Providence, NJ 07974, USA

Inkeles, Alex *Sociologist*
1001 Hamilton Ave, Palo Alto, CA 94301, USA

Inkster, Juli Simpson *Golfer*
23140 Mora Glen Dr, Los Altos Hills, CA 94024, USA

Inman, Bobby Ray *Navy Admiral, Government Official*
701 Brazos St, #500, Austin, TX 78701, USA

Inman, Jerry *Football Player*
PO Box 1113, Battle Ground, WA 98604, USA

Inman, John *Actor*
%AMG Ltd, 8 King St, London WC2E 8HN, England

Inman, John *Golfer*
2210 Chase St, Durham, NC 27707, USA

Innauer, Anton (Toni) *Ski Jumper, Coach*
Steinbruckstr 8/II, 6024 Innsbruck, Austria

Innaurato, Albert F *Writer*
325 W 22nd St, New York, NY 10011, USA

Innes, Laura *Actress*
%Paradigm Agency, 10100 Santa Monica Blvd, #2500, Los Angeles, CA 90067, USA

Innis, Roy E A *Civil Rights Activist*
817 Broadway, New York, NY 10003, USA

Innocenti, Antonio Cardinal *Religious Leader*
Piazza della Citta Lemonina 9, 00193 Rome, Italy

Inogradov, Pavel *Cosmonaut*
%Potchta Kosmonavtov, Moskovskoi Oblasti, 141160 Syvisdny Goroduk, Russia

Inoue, Shinya *Biologist, Photographer*
%Marine Biological Laboratory, 167 Water St, Woods Hole, MA 02543, USA

Inoue, Yuichi *Artist*
Ohkamiyashiki, 2475-2 Kurami, Samakawamachi 253-01, Kozagun, Kam, Japan

Inouye, Daniel K *Senator, HI; WW II Army Hero (CMH)*
300 Ala Moana Blvd, #7-212, Honolulu, HI 96850, USA

Inouye, Lisa *Actress*
%Media Artists Group, 6300 Wilshire Blvd, #1470, Los Angeles, CA 90048, USA

Insko, Delmer M (Del) *Harness Racing Driver*
2360 Fischer Road, South Beloit, IL 61080, USA

Insley, Will *Artist*
231 Bowery, New York, NY 10002, USA

Insolia, Anthony *Editor*
%Newsday, Editorial Dept, 235 Pinelawn, Melville, NY 11747, USA

Inspectah Deck *Rap Artist (Wu-Tang Clan)*
%Famous Artists Agency, 250 W 57th St, New York, NY 10107, USA

Ionatana, Ionatana *Prime Minister, Tuvalu*
%Prime Minister's Office, Vaiaku, Funafuti, Tuvalu

Ioss, Walter *Photographer*
152 De Forrest Road, Montauk, NY 11954, USA

Irani, Ray R *Businessman*
%Occidental Petroleum, 10889 Wilshire Blvd, Los Angeles, CA 90024, USA

Irbe, Arturs *Hockey Player*
10733 Trego Trail, Raleigh, NC 27614, USA

Iredale, Randle W *Architect*
1151 W 8th Ave, Vancouver BC V6H 1C5, Canada

Ireland, Kathy *Model, Actress*
%Sterling/Winters, 10877 Wilshire Blvd, #15, Los Angeles, CA 90024, USA

Ireland, Patricia *Association Executive*
%Katz Kutter Haigler Assoc, 801 Pennsylvania Ave NW, #750, Washington, DC 20004, USA

Iris, Donnie *Singer, Songwriter*
807 Darlington Road, Beaver Falls, PA 15010, USA

Irizarry, Vincent *Actor*
%David Shapira, 15821 Ventura Blvd, #235, Encino, CA 91436, USA

Irobe, Yoshiaki *Financier*
26-6-6 Saginomiya, Nakanoku, Tokyo, Japan

Irons, Jeremy *Actor*
%Hutton Mgmt, 4 Old Manor Close, Askett, Buckinghamshire HP27 9NA, England

Irrera, Dom *Actor, Comedian*
%Irvin Arthur Assoc, PO Box 1358, New York, NY 10028, USA

Irvan, Ernie *Auto Racing Driver*
626 El Cardinal Lane, Mooresville, NC 28115, USA

Irvin, John *Movie Director*
6 Lower Common South, London SW15 1BP, England
Irvin, LeRoy, Jr *Football Player*
2905 Ruby Dr, #C, Fullerton, CA 92831, USA
Irvin, Michael J *Football Player*
1221 Brickell Ave, #900, Miami, FL 33131, USA
Irvin, Monford M (Monte) *Baseball Player*
11 Douglas Court S, Homosassa, FL 34446, USA
Irvine, Eddie *Auto Racing Driver*
%Ferrari SpA, Casella Postale 589, 41100 Modena, Italy
Irving, Amy *Actress*
%Rigberg Roberts Rugolo, 1180 S Beverly Dr, #601, Los Angeles, CA 90035, USA
Irving, John W *Writer*
%Turnbull Agency, PO Box 757, Dorset, VT 05251, USA
Irving, Paul H *Attorney*
%Manatt Phelps Phillips, 11355 W Olympic Blvd, Los Angeles, CA 90064, USA
Irving, Stu *Hockey Player*
93 Hart St, Beverly Farms, MA 01915, USA
Irwin, Bill *Entertainer, Clown*
20 1st Ave, Nyack, NY 10960, USA
Irwin, Hale S *Golfer*
10726 Manchester Road, #212, Saint Louis, MO 63122, USA
Irwin, Malcolm R *Biologist*
4720 Regent St, Madison, WI 53705, USA
Irwin, Mark *Cinematographer*
1522 Olive St, Santa Barbara, CA 93101, USA
Irwin, Paul G *Association Executive*
%Humane Society of the United States, 2100 L St NW, Washington, DC 20037, USA
Irwin, Robert W *Artist*
%Pace Gallery, 32 E 57th St, New York, NY 10022, USA
Irwin, Steve *Actor, Zookeeper*
%Australian Zoo, Goasshouse Mountains Route, Beerwah QLD, Australia
Irwin-Mellencamp, Elaine *Model*
%John Cougar Mellencamp, 5072 W Stevens Road, Nashville, IN 47448, USA
Isaacks, Levie C *Cinematographer*
6634 Sunnyslope Ave, Van Nuys, CA 91401, USA
Isaacs, Jason *Actor*
%Paradigm Agency, 10100 Santa Monica Blvd, #2500, Los Angeles, CA 90067, USA
Isaacs, Jeremy I *Opera Director*
%Royal Opera House, Covent Garden, Bow St, London WC2 7Q4, England
Isaacs, John (Speed) *Basketball Player*
1412 Crotona Ave, Bronx, NY 10456, USA
Isaacs, Susan *Writer*
%Harper Collins Publishers, 10 E 53rd St, New York, NY 10022, USA
Isaacson, Julius *Labor Leader*
%Novelty & Production Workers Union, 1815 Franklin Ave, Valley Stream, NY 11581, USA
Isaacson, Walter S *Journalist*
%Simon & Schuste, 1230 Ave of Americas, New York, NY 10020, USA
Isaak, Chris *Singer, Songwriter, Actor*
PO Box 547, Larkspur, CA 94977, USA
Isaak, Russell *Businessman*
%CPI Corp, 1706 Washington Ave, Saint Louis, MO 63103, USA
Isacksen, Peter *Actor*
4635 Placidia Ave, Toluca Lake, CA 91602, USA
Isaksson, Irma Sara *Singer, Songwriter*
%United Stage Artists, PO Box 11029, 100 61, Stockholm, Sweden
Isard, Walter *Regional Economist*
3218 Garrett Road, Drexel Hill, PA 19026, USA
Isbin, Sharon *Concert Guitarist*
%Columbia Artists Mgmt Inc, 165 W 57th St, New York, NY 10019, USA
Iscove, Robert (Rob) *Movie, Television Director*
16045 Royal Oak Road, Encino, CA 91436, USA
Isenburger, Eric *Artist*
140 E 56th St, New York, NY 10022, USA
Isham, Mark *Composer*
%Ron Moss Mgmt, 2635 Griffith Park Blvd, Los Angeles, CA 90039, USA
Ishibashi, Kanichiro *Businessman*
1 Nagasakacho, Azabu, Minatoku, Tokyo, Japan
Ishida, Jim *Actor*
871 N Vail Ave, Montebello, CA 90640, USA
Ishiguro, Kazuo *Writer*
%Rogers Coleridge White, 20 Powis Mews, London W11 1JN, England
Ishihara, Shintaro *Government Official, Japan*
Sanno Grand Building, #606, 2-14-2 Nagatocho, Chiyodaku, Tokyo, Japan
Ishii, Kazuhiro *Architect*
4-14-27 Akasaka, Minatoku, Tokyo 107, Japan
Ishikawa, Sigeru *Economist*
19-8-4 Chome Kugayama, Suginamiku, Tokyo 168-0082, Japan

I

Ishimaru - Izzo

Ishimaru, Akira *Electrical Engineer*
2913 165th Place NE, Bellevue, WA 98008, USA
Ishizaka, Kimishige *Allergist*
%Allergy/Immunology Institute, 11149 N Torrey Pines Road, La Jolla, CA 92037, USA
Ishizaka, Teruko *Allergist*
%Good Samaritan Hospital, 5601 Loch Raven Blvd, Baltimore, MD 21239, USA
Iskander, Fazil A *Writer*
Krasnoarmeiskaya Str 23, #104, 125319 Moscow, Russia
Isley, Ronald (Ron) *Singer (Isley Brothers)*
%Ron Weisner Mgmt, PO Box 261640, Encino, CA 91426, USA
Ismail, Ahmed Sultan *Mechanical Engineer*
43 Ahmed Abdel Aziz St, Dokki, Cairo, Egypt
Ismail, Raghib R (Rocket) *Football Player*
7423 Marigold Dr, Irving, TX 75063, USA
Ison, Christopher J *Journalist*
%Minneapolis-Saint Paul Star Tribune, 425 Portland Ave, Minneapolis, MN 55488, USA
Isozaki, Arata *Architect*
%Arata Assoc, 6-17-9 Akasaka, Minatoku, Tokyo 107, Japan
Israel, Werner *Physicist*
5189 Polson Terrace, Victoria BC V8Y 2C5, Canada
Isringhausen, Jason D *Baseball Player*
207 E Center St, Brighton, IL 62012, USA
Issel, Daniel P (Dan) *Basketball Player, Coach, Executive*
10163 E Fair Circle, Englewood, CO 80111, USA
Isselbacher, Kurt J *Physician*
20 Nobscot Road, Newton Center, MA 02459, USA
Isserlis, Steven *Concert Cellist*
%Harrison/Parrott, 12 Penzance Place, London W11 4PA England
Ito, Lance *Judge*
%Los Angeles Superior Court, 210 W Temple St, Los Angeles, CA 90012, USA
Ito, Masayoshi *Government Official, Japan*
1-28-3 Chitose-Dai, Setagayaku, Tokyo 157, Japan
Ito, Midori *Figure Skater*
%Skating Federation, Kryshi Taaikukan 1-1-1, Shibuyaku, Tokyo 10, Japan
Ito, Robert *Actor*
843 N Sycamore Ave, Los Angeles, CA 90038, USA
Itzin, Gregory *Actor*
%Borinstein Oreck Bogart, 3172 Dona Susana Dr, Studio City, CA 91604, USA
Ivanchenkov, Aleksandr S *Cosmonaut*
%Potchta Kosmonavtov, Moskovskoi Oblasti, 141160 Syvisdny Goroduk, Russia
Ivanisevic, Goran *Tennis Player*
Alijnoviceva 28, 58000 Split, Serbia & Montenegro
Ivanov, Igor S *Government Official, Russia*
%Foreign Affairs Ministry, Smolenskaya-Sennaya 32/34, Moscow, Russia
Ivers, Eileen *Fiddle Player*
%Sony Records, 2100 Colorado Ave, Santa Monica, CA 90404, USA
Iverson, Allen *Basketball Player*
PO Box 901, Conshohocken, PA 19428, USA
Ivery, Eddie Lee *Football Player*
49 Rocky Ford Road, Atlanta, GA 30317, USA
Ives, J Atwood *Businessman*
%Eastern Enterprises, 201 Rivermoor St, West Roxbury, MA 02132, USA
Ivey, Dana *Actress*
%Paradigm Agency, 10100 Santa Monica Blvd, #2500, Los Angeles, CA 90067, USA
Ivey, James B (Jim) *Editorial Cartoonist*
5840 Dahlia Dr, #7, Orlando, FL 32807, USA
Ivey, Judith *Actress*
53 W 87th St, #2, New York, NY 10024, USA
Ivins, Marsha S *Astronaut*
2811 Timber Briar Circle, Houston, TX 77059, USA
Ivins, Molly *Commentator, Columnist*
%CBS-TV, News Dept, 51 W 52nd St, New York, NY 10019, USA
Ivory, Horace O *Football Player*
5321 Diaz Ave, Fort Worth, TX 76107, USA
Ivory, James F *Movie Director, Producer*
18 Patroon St, Claverack, NY 12513, USA
Ivosev, Aleksandra *Markswoman*
Sluzbeni put Zavoda 5, Careva Cuprija, 11030 Belgrad, Serbia & Montenegro
Iwago, Mitsuaki *Photographer*
Edelhof Daichi Building, #2F, 8 Honsio-cho, Shinjukaku, Tokyo 160, Japan
Iwerks, Donald W *Businessman*
%Iwerks Entertainment, 4520 W Valerio St, Burbank, CA 91505, USA
Iyanaga, Shokichi *Mathematician*
12-4 Otsuka 6-Chome, Bunkyoku, Tokyo 112-0012, Japan
Izzard, Eddie *Actor, Comedian*
%Mitch Schneider Organization, 14724 Ventura Blvd, #410, Sherman Oaks, CA 91403, USA
Izzo, Tom *Basketball Coach*
%Michigan State University, Athletic Dept, East Lansing, MI 48824, USA

Ja Rule *Rap Artist, Actor*
%Violator Mgmt, 205 Lexington Ave, #400, New York, NY 10016, USA
Jablonski, Henryk *President, Poland*
Ul Filtrowa 61 m 4, 02-056 Warsaw, Poland
Jacke, Christopher L (Chris) *Football Player*
%Arizona Cardinals, PO Box 888, Phoenix, AZ 85001, USA
Jackee *Actress*
8649 Metz Place, Los Angeles, CA 90069, USA
Jacklin, Tony *Golfer, Sportscaster*
1175 51st St W, Bradenton, FL 34209, USA
Jackman, Hugh *Actor*
%Endeavor Talent Agency, 9701 Wilshire Blvd, #1000, Beverly Hills, CA 90212, USA
Jackson, Alan *Singer, Songwriter*
%Force Inc, 1505 16th Ave S, Nashville, TN 37212, USA
Jackson, Alvin N (Al) *Baseball Player*
3321 SE Morningside Blvd, Port Saint Lucie, FL 34952, USA
Jackson, Anne *Actress*
90 Riverside Dr, New York, NY 10024, USA
Jackson, Arthur J *WW II Marine Corps Hero (CMH)*
1290 E Spring Court, Boise, ID 83712, USA
Jackson, Bobby *Basketball Player*
%Sacramento Kings, Arco Arena, 1 Sports Parkway, Sacramento, CA 95834, USA
Jackson, Chuck *Singer*
%Universal Attractions, 225 W 57th St, #500, New York, NY 10019, USA
Jackson, Danny L *Baseball Player*
%Philadelphia Phillies, Veterans Stadium, 3501 S Broad, Philadelphia, PA 19148, USA
Jackson, Daryl S *Architect*
161 Hotham St, East Melbourne VIC 3002, Australia
Jackson, Deanna *Basketball Player*
%Cleveland Rockers, Gund Arena, 1 Center Court, Cleveland, OH 44115, USA
Jackson, Doris *Singer (Shirelles)*
%Nationwide Entertainment, 2756 N Green Valley Parkway, Henderson, NV 89014, USA
Jackson, Eddie *Bowler*
3961 Glenmore Ave, Cincinnati, OH 45211, USA
Jackson, Francis A *Concert Organist, Composer*
Nether Garth, East Acklam, Malton North Yorkshire YO17 9RG, England
Jackson, Freddie *Singer, Songwriter*
%Associated Booking Corp, 1995 Broadway, #501, New York, NY 10023, USA
Jackson, Glenda *Actress*
%Crouch Assoc, 9-15 Neal St, London WC2H 9PF, England
Jackson, Harold *Football Player, Coach*
6144 Flight Ave, Los Angeles, CA 90056, USA
Jackson, Harold *Journalist*
%Birmingham News, Editorial Dept, 2200 N 4th Ave N, Birmingham, AL 35203, USA
Jackson, Harry A *Artist*
PO Box 2836, Cody, WY 82414, USA
Jackson, Huson *Architect*
%Sert Jackson Assoc, 442 Marrett Road, #101, Lexington, MA 02421, USA
Jackson, James A (Jim) *Basketball Player*
17827 Windflower Way, Dallas, TX 75252, USA
Jackson, Janet *Singer, Dancer, Actress*
%United Talent Agency, 9560 Wilshire Blvd, #500, Beverly Hills, CA 90212, USA
Jackson, Jeremy *Actor*
%Mary Grady Agency, 221 E Walnut St, #130, Pasadena, CA 91101, USA
Jackson, Jermaine *Singer, Songwriter, Guitarist*
4641 Hayvenhurst Dr, Encino, CA 91436, USA
Jackson, Jermaine *Basketball Player*
%Atlanta Hawks, 190 Marietta St SW, Atlanta, GA 30303, USA
Jackson, Jesse L *Evangelist, Civil Rights Activist*
400 T St NW, Washington, DC 20001, USA
Jackson, Joe *Singer, Songwriter*
%Primary Talent Int'l, 2-12 Pentonville Road, London N1 9PL, England
Jackson, Joe M *Vietnam War Air Force Hero (CMH)*
25320 38th Ave S, Kent, WA 98032, USA
Jackson, John David *Boxer*
1022 S State St, Tacoma, WA 98405, USA
Jackson, Jonathan *Actor*
1815 Butler Ave, #120, Los Angeles, CA 90025, USA
Jackson, Joshua *Actor*
%Johansmeier, 326 Columbus Ave, #5G, New York, NY 10023, USA
Jackson, Kate *Actress*
1628 Marlay Dr, Los Angeles, CA 90069, USA
Jackson, Keith J *Football Player*
1801 Champlin Dr, #1707, Little Rock, AR 72223, USA
Jackson, Keith M *Sportscaster*
%ABC-TV, Sports Dept, 77 W 66th St, New York, NY 10023, USA
Jackson, Kevin *Wrestler*
7215 Montarbor Dr, Colorado Springs, CO 80918, USA

J

Jackson - Jacob

Jackson, Larry R *Labor Leader*
%Grain Millers Federation, 4949 Olson Memorial Parkway, Minneapolis, MN 55422, USA
Jackson, LaToya *Singer, Model*
14126 Rosecrans Ave, Santa Fe Springs, CA 90670, USA
Jackson, Lauren *Basketball Player*
%Seattle Storm, Key Arena, 351 Elliott Ave W, #500, Seattle, WA 98119, USA
Jackson, Lucious (Luke) *Basketball Player*
4580 Cartwright St, Beaumont, TX 77707, USA
Jackson, Mark A *Basketball Player*
628 Main St, Windsor, CO 80550, USA
Jackson, Mary *Actress*
2055 Grace Ave, Los Angeles, CA 90068, USA
Jackson, Mary Ann *Actress*
1242 Alessandro Dr, Newbury Park, CA 91320, USA
Jackson, Michael J *Singer, Songwriter, Actor*
5225 Figueroa Mountain Road, Los Olivos, CA 93441, USA
Jackson, Mick *Movie Director*
1349 Berea Place, Pacific Palisades, CA 90272, USA
Jackson, Millie *Singer, Songwriter*
%Associated Booking Corp, 1995 Broadway, #501, New York, NY 10023, USA
Jackson, Monte C *Football Player*
7646 Westbrook Ave, San Diego, CA 92139, USA
Jackson, Pervis *Singer (Spinners)*
%Buddy Allen Mgmt, 3750 Hudson Manor Terrace, #3AG, Bronx, NY 10463, USA
Jackson, Peter *Movie Director*
%Wing Nut Films, PO Box 15208, Miramar, Wellington, New Zealand
Jackson, Philip *Actor*
%Markham & Froggatt, Julian House, 4 Windmill St, London W1P 1HF, England
Jackson, Philip D (Phil) *Basketball Player, Coach*
%Los Angeles Lakers, Staples Center, 1111 S Figueroa St, Los Angeles, CA 90015, USA
Jackson, R Graham *Architect*
%Calhoun Tungate Jackson Dill Architects, 6200 Savoy Dr, Houston, TX 77036, USA
Jackson, Randy *Singer*
%Big J Productions, PO Box 24455, New Orleans, LA 70184, USA
Jackson, Rebbie *Singer, Songwriter*
4641 Hayvenhurst Dr, Encino, CA 91436, USA
Jackson, Reginald M (Reggie) *Baseball Player*
305 Amador Ave, Seaside, CA 93955, USA
Jackson, Richard A *Religious Leader*
%North Phoenix Baptist Church, 5757 N Central Ave, Phoenix, AZ 85012, USA
Jackson, Richard S (Richie) *Football Player*
%All Pro Inc, 6000 Kingston Court, New Orleans, LA 70131, USA
Jackson, Rickey A *Football Player*
325 S Barfield Highway, Pahokee, FL 33476, USA
Jackson, Ronald Shannon *Jazz Drummer*
%Worldwide Jazz, 1128 Broadway, #425, New York, NY 10010, USA
Jackson, Samuel L *Actor*
%P M K Public Relations, 8500 Wilshire Blvd, #700, Beverly Hills, CA 90211, USA
Jackson, Sherry *Actress*
4933 Encino Ave, Encino, CA 91316, USA
Jackson, Shirley Ann *Theoretical Physicist, Educator*
%Rensselaer Polytechnic Institute, President's Office, Troy, NY 12180, USA
Jackson, Stonewall *Singer, Songwriter*
6007 Cloverland Dr, Brentwood, TN 37027, USA
Jackson, Stoney *Actor*
3151 Cahuenga Blvd W, #310, Los Angeles, CA 90068, USA
Jackson, Thomas (Tom) *Football Player, Sportscaster*
%ESPN-TV, Sports Dept, ESPN Plaza, 935 Middle St, Bristol, CT 06010, USA
Jackson, Thomas Penfield *Judge*
%US District Court, 333 Constitution Ave NW, Washington, DC 20001, USA
Jackson, Tito *Singer*
4301 Willow Glen St, Calabasas, CA 91302, USA
Jackson, Trina *Swimmer*
8727 Hunters Creek Dr S, Jacksonville, FL 32256, USA
Jackson, Victoria *Actress, Comedienne*
14631 Belgowan Road, #2-5, Hialeah, FL 33016, USA
Jackson, Vincent E (Bo) *Football, Baseball Player*
PO Box 158, Mobile, AL 36601, USA
Jackson, Wanda *Singer*
%Wanda Jackson Enterprises, 8200 S Pennsylvania Ave, Oklahoma City, OK 73159, USA
Jacob, Francois *Nobel Medicine Laureate*
15 Rue de Conde, 75006 Paris, France
Jacob, Irene *Actress*
%Nicole Cann, 1 Rue Alfred de Vigny, 75008 Paris, France
Jacob, John E *Civil Rights Activist*
%National Urban League, 120 Wall St, #700, New York, NY 10005, USA
Jacob, Katerina *Actress*
%Agentur Doris Mattes, Merzstr 14, 81679 Munich, Germany

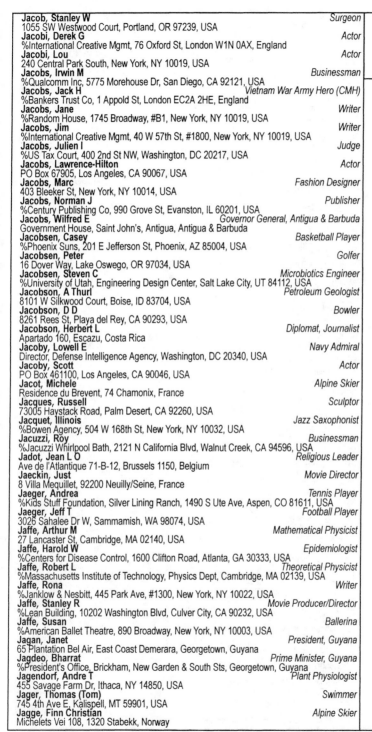

Jacob, Stanley W — *Surgeon*
1055 SW Westwood Court, Portland, OR 97239, USA
Jacobi, Derek G — *Actor*
%International Creative Mgmt, 76 Oxford St, London W1N 0AX, England
Jacobi, Lou — *Actor*
240 Central Park South, New York, NY 10019, USA
Jacobs, Irwin M — *Businessman*
%Qualcomm Inc, 5775 Morehouse Dr, San Diego, CA 92121, USA
Jacobs, Jack H — *Vietnam War Army Hero (CMH)*
%Bankers Trust Co, 1 Appold St, London EC2A 2HE, England
Jacobs, Jane — *Writer*
%Random House, 1745 Broadway, #B1, New York, NY 10019, USA
Jacobs, Jim — *Writer*
%International Creative Mgmt, 40 W 57th St, #1800, New York, NY 10019, USA
Jacobs, Julien I — *Judge*
%US Tax Court, 400 2nd St NW, Washington, DC 20217, USA
Jacobs, Lawrence-Hilton — *Actor*
PO Box 67905, Los Angeles, CA 90067, USA
Jacobs, Marc — *Fashion Designer*
403 Bleeker St, New York, NY 10014, USA
Jacobs, Norman J — *Publisher*
%Century Publishing Co, 990 Grove St, Evanston, IL 60201, USA
Jacobs, Wilfred E — *Governor General, Antigua & Barbuda*
Government House, Saint John's, Antigua, Antigua & Barbuda
Jacobsen, Casey — *Basketball Player*
%Phoenix Suns, 201 E Jefferson St, Phoenix, AZ 85004, USA
Jacobsen, Peter — *Golfer*
16 Dover Way, Lake Oswego, OR 97034, USA
Jacobsen, Steven C — *Microbiotics Engineer*
%University of Utah, Engineering Design Center, Salt Lake City, UT 84112, USA
Jacobson, A Thurl — *Petroleum Geologist*
8101 W Silkwood Court, Boise, ID 83704, USA
Jacobson, D D — *Bowler*
8261 Rees St, Playa del Rey, CA 90293, USA
Jacobson, Herbert L — *Diplomat, Journalist*
Apartado 160, Escazu, Costa Rica
Jacoby, Lowell E — *Navy Admiral*
Director, Defense Intelligence Agency, Washington, DC 20340, USA
Jacoby, Scott — *Actor*
PO Box 461100, Los Angeles, CA 90046, USA
Jacot, Michele — *Alpine Skier*
Residence du Brevent, 74 Chamonix, France
Jacques, Russell — *Sculptor*
73005 Haystack Road, Palm Desert, CA 92260, USA
Jacquet, Illinois — *Jazz Saxophonist*
%Bowen Agency, 504 W 168th St, New York, NY 10032, USA
Jacuzzi, Roy — *Businessman*
%Jacuzzi Whirlpool Bath, 2121 N California Blvd, Walnut Creek, CA 94596, USA
Jadot, Jean L O — *Religious Leader*
Ave de l'Atlantique 71-B-12, Brussels 1150, Belgium
Jaeckin, Just — *Movie Director*
8 Villa Mequillet, 92200 Neuilly/Seine, France
Jaeger, Andrea — *Tennis Player*
%Kids Stuff Foundation, Silver Lining Ranch, 1490 S Ute Ave, Aspen, CO 81611, USA
Jaeger, Jeff T — *Football Player*
3026 Sahalee Dr W, Sammamish, WA 98074, USA
Jaffe, Arthur M — *Mathematical Physicist*
27 Lancaster St, Cambridge, MA 02140, USA
Jaffe, Harold W — *Epidemiologist*
%Centers for Disease Control, 1600 Clifton Road, Atlanta, GA 30333, USA
Jaffe, Robert L — *Theoretical Physicist*
%Massachusetts Institute of Technology, Physics Dept, Cambridge, MA 02139, USA
Jaffe, Rona — *Writer*
%Janklow & Nesbitt, 445 Park Ave, #1300, New York, NY 10022, USA
Jaffe, Stanley R — *Movie Producer/Director*
%Lean Building, 10202 Washington Blvd, Culver City, CA 90232, USA
Jaffe, Susan — *Ballerina*
%American Ballet Theatre, 890 Broadway, New York, NY 10003, USA
Jagan, Janet — *President, Guyana*
65 Plantation Bel Air, East Coast Demerara, Georgetown, Guyana
Jagdeo, Bharrat — *Prime Minister, Guyana*
%President's Office, Brickham, New Garden & South Sts, Georgetown, Guyana
Jagendorf, Andre T — *Plant Physiologist*
455 Savage Farm Dr, Ithaca, NY 14850, USA
Jager, Thomas (Tom) — *Swimmer*
745 4th Ave E, Kalispell, MT 59901, USA
Jagge, Finn Christian — *Alpine Skier*
Michelets Vei 108, 1320 Stabekk, Norway

Jagger, Bianca *Actress, Model*
530 Park Ave, #18D, New York, NY 10021, USA
Jagger, Mick *Singer, Harmonicist (Rolling Stones)*
%Marathon Music, 5 Church Row, Wandsworth Plain, London SW18 1ES, England
Jagland, Thorbjoern *Prime Minister, Norway*
%Stortinget, Karl Johans Gate 22, 0026 Oslo, Norway
Jaglom, Henry *Movie Director*
9165 W Sunset Blvd, #300, Los Angeles, CA 90069, USA
Jagr, Jaromir *Hockey Player*
2548 Appletree Dr, Pittsburgh, PA 15241, USA
Jahan, Marine *Actress, Dancer*
%Media Artists Group, 6300 Wilshire Blvd, #1470, Los Angeles, CA 90048, USA
Jaheim *Singer*
%Diane Mill, 100 Evergreen Point, #402, East Orange, NJ 07018, USA
Jahn, Helmut *Architect*
%Murphy/Jahn, 35 E Wacker Dr, Chicago, IL 60601, USA
Jahn, Robert G *Aeronautical Engineer*
%Princeton University, Aerospace Sciences Dept, Princeton, NJ 08544, USA
Jahn, Sigmund *Cosmonaut, East Germany; General*
Fontanestr 35, 15344 Strausberg, Germany
Jai *Singer, Songwriter*
%Evolution Talent, 1776 Broadway, #1500, New York, NY 10019, USA
Jaidah, Ali Mohammed *Government Official, Qatar*
%Qatar Petroleum Corp, PO Box 3212, Doha, Qatar
Jakel, Bernd *Yachtsman*
Salvador-Allende-Str 48, 12559 Berlin, Germany
Jakes, John *Writer*
34 Brams Point Road, Hilton Head Island, SC 29926, USA
Jakes, T D *Religious Leader*
%Potter's House, 6777 W Kiest Blvd, Dallas, TX 75211, USA
Jaki, Stanley L *Physicist, Theologian*
PO Box 167, Princeton, NJ 08542, USA
Jakobs, Marco *Bobsled Athlete*
Oststr 1B, 59427 Unna, Germany
Jakobson, Maggie *Actress*
%Writers & Artists, 8383 Wilshire Blvd, #550, Beverly Hills, CA 90211, USA
Jakobson, Max *Journalist; Government Official, Finland*
Rahapajankatu 3B 17, 00160 Helsinki 16, Finland
Jakosits, Michael *Marksman*
Karlsbergstr 140, 66424 Homburg/Saar, Germany
Jakub, Lisa *Actress*
%Metropolitan Talent Agency, 4526 Wilshire Blvd, Los Angeles, CA 90010, USA
Jamail, Joseph D, Jr *Attorney*
%Jamail & Kolius, 500 Dallas St, #3434, Houston, TX 77002, USA
Jamal, Ahmad *Jazz Pianist*
%Brad Simon Organization, 122 E 57th St, #300, New York, NY 10022, USA
Jamali, Mir Zafarullah Khan *Prime Minister, Pakistan*
%Prime Minister's Office, Old State Bank Building, Islamabad, Pakistan
Jambor, Agi *Concert Pianist*
1616 Bolton St, Baltimore, MD 21217, USA
James of Holland Park, Phyllis D *Writer*
%Elaine Green Ltd, 37A Goldhawk Road, London W12 SQQ, England
James, Anthony *Actor*
%C N A Assoc, 1925 Century Park East, #750, Los Angeles, CA 90067, USA
James, Charmayne *Rodeo Rider*
%Gold Buckle Ranch, 2100 N Highway 360, #1207, Grand Prairie, TX 75050, USA
James, Cheryl (Salt) *Rap Artist (Salt'N'Pepa)*
%Famous Artists Agency, 250 W 57th St, New York, NY 10107, USA
James, Clifton *Actor*
500 W 43rd St, #25D, New York, NY 10036, USA
James, Clive V L *Broadcaster, Journalist*
%P F D, Drury House, 34-43 Russell St, London WC2B 5HA, England
James, Craig *Football Player*
12714 W FM 455, Celina, TX 75009, USA
James, D Clayton *Historian*
106 Wagon Wheel Trail, Moneta, VA 24121, USA
James, Don *Football Coach*
7047 Chanticleer Ave SE, Snoqualmie, WA 98065, USA
James, Donald M *Businessman*
%Vulcan Materials Co, 1200 Urban Center Dr, Birmingham, AL 35242, USA
James, Edgerrin *Football Player*
709 Hendry St, Immokalee, FL 34142, USA
James, Etta *Singer*
16409 Sally Lane, Riverside, CA 92504, USA
James, Forrest H (Fob), Jr *Governor, AL*
39 Alabama Road, Lehigh Acres, FL 33936, USA
James, G Larry *Track Athlete*
%Stockton State College, Athletic Dept, Pomona, NJ 08240, USA

James, Geraldine *Actress*
%Julian Belfarge, 46 Albermarle St, London W1X 4PP, England
James, Jesse *Actor*
%Coast to Coast Talent, 3350 Barham Blvd, Los Angeles, CA 90068, USA
James, John *Actor*
PO Box 9, Cambridge, NY 12816, USA
James, Joni *Singer*
PO Box 7027, Westchester, IL 60154, USA
James, Kate *Model*
%Men/Women Model Inc, 199 Lafayette St, New York, NY 10012, USA
James, Kevin *Illusionist, Actor*
1471 E Mosherville Road, Jonesville, MI 49250, USA
James, Larry D *Astronaut*
%AFELM, USS Space Command, Peterson Air Force Base, CP 80914, USA
James, LeBron *Basketball Player*
%GAP Communications, 5000 Euclid Ave, #400, Cleveland, OH 44103, USA
James, P D *Writer*
%Elaine Greene Ltd, 37A Goldhawk Road, London W12 8QQ, England
James, Rick *Singer, Songwriter*
%Richard Walters, 1800 Argyle Ave, #408, Los Angeles, CA 90028, USA
James, Robert (Bob) *Jazz Keyboardist, Composer*
%Monterey International, 200 W Superior, #202, Chicago, IL 60610, USA
James, Sheila *Actress*
3201 Pearl St, Santa Monica, CA 90405, USA
James, Sheryl *Journalist*
%Saint Petersburg Times, Editorial Dept, 490 1st Ave, Saint Petersburg, FL 33701, USA
James, Sonny *Singer, Guitarist, Songwriter*
%McFadden Artists, 818 18th Ave S, Nashville, TN 37203, USA
James, Stanislaus A *Governor General, Saint Lucia*
Government House, Morue, Castries, Saint Lucia
James, Tommy *Singer (Shondells)*
%Aura Entertainment, PO Box 4354, Clifton, NJ 07012, USA
James-Rodman, Charmayne *Rodeo Rider*
%General Delivery, Clayton, NM 88415, USA
Jameson, Elizabeth M (Betty) *Golfer*
514 SW 20th St, Boynton Beach, FL 33426, USA
Jamieson, John K *Businessman*
10313 Stanley Circle, Minneapolis, MN 55437, USA
Jamison, Antawn *Basketball Player*
%Dallas Mavericks, 2909 Taylor St, Dallas, TX 75226, USA
Jamison, Jayne *Publisher*
%Redbook Magazine, 224 W 57th St, New York, NY 10019, USA
Jamison, Judith *Dancer, Choreographer*
%Alvin Ailey American Dance Foundation, 211 W 61st St, #300, New York, NY 10023, USA
Jammeh, Yahya A J J *Head of State, Gambia; Army Officer*
%President's Office, State House, Banjul, Gambia
Jammer, Quentin *Football Player*
%San Diego Chargers, 4020 Murphy Canyon Road, San Diego, CA 92123, USA
Jance, J A *Writer*
%Avon/William Morrow, 1350 Ave of Americas, New York, NY 10019, USA
Jancso, Miklos *Movie Director*
Solyom Laszlo Utca 17, 1022 Budapest II, Hungary
Janda, Krystyna *Actress*
%Teatr Powszechny, Ul Zamoyskiego 20, Warsaw, Poland
Jane, Thomas *Actor*
%Kelly Bush, 3859 Cardiff Ave, #200, Culver City, CA 90232, USA
Janeway, Elizabeth H *Writer*
350 E 79th St, New York, NY 10021, USA
Janeway, Michael C *Editor*
%Northwestern University, Fisk Hall, Evanston, IL 60201, USA
Janeway, Richard *Physician*
PO Box 188, Blowing Rock, NC 28605, USA
Janikowski, Sebastian *Football Player*
%Oakland Raiders, 1220 Harbor Bay Parkway, Alameda, CA 94502, USA
Janis, Byron *Concert Pianist*
%Columbia Artists Mgmt Inc, 165 W 57th St, New York, NY 10019, USA
Janis, Conrad *Actor, Jazz Trombonist*
1434 N Genesee Ave, Los Angeles, CA 90046, USA
Janitz, John A *Businessman*
%Textron Inc, 40 Westminster St, Providence, RI 02903, USA
Jankowska-Cieslak, Jadwiga *Actress*
%Film Polski, Ul Mazewiecka 6/8, 00-950 Warsaw, Poland
Jankowski, Gene F *Television Executive*
%American Film Institute, 901 15th St NW, #700, Washington, DC 20005, USA
Jannazzo, Izzy *Boxer*
6924 62nd Ave, Flushing, NY 11379, USA
Janney, Allison *Actress*
%Paradigm Agency, 10100 Santa Monica Blvd, #2500, Los Angeles, CA 90067, USA

J

Janney, Craig H *Hockey Player*
3 Overhill Road, Enfield, CT 06082, USA
Janov, Arthur *Psychologist, Psychotherapist*
1205 Abbot Kinney Blvd, Venice, CA 90291, USA
Janowitz, Gundula *Opera Singer*
3072 Kasten 75, Austria
Janowitz, Tama *Writer*
%Doubleday Press, 1540 Broadway, New York, NY 10036, USA
Janowski, Marek *Conductor*
%I M G Artists, 3 Burlington Lane, Chiswick, London W4 2TH, England
Jansch, Heather *Artist*
Knowle, Rundlerohy, Newton Abbot, Devon TQ12 2PJ, England
Jansen, Daniel E (Dan) *Speedskater*
PO Box 567, Greendale, WI 53129, USA
Jansen, Lawrence J (Larry) *Baseball Player*
3207 NW Highway 27, Forest Grove, OR 97116, USA
Jansen, Raymond A *Publisher*
%Newsday Inc, 235 Pinelawn Road, Melville, NY 11747, USA
Jansons, Mariss *Conductor*
%I M G Artists, 3 Burlington Lane, Chiswick, London W4 2TH, England
Janssen, Daniel *Businessman*
%Solvay & Cie, 33 Rue du Prince Albert, 1050 Brussels, Belgium
Janssen, Famke *Actress, Model*
%Creative Artists Agency, 9830 Wilshire Blvd, Beverly Hills, CA 90212, USA
Jantz, Richard *Antropologist*
%University of Tennessee, Anthropology Dept, Knoxville, TN 37996, USA
January, Don *Golfer*
14316 Hughes Lane, Dallas, TX 75254, USA
January, Lois *Actress*
PO Box 1233, Beverly Hills, CA 90213, USA
Jany, Alexandre (Alex) *Swimmer*
104 Blvd Livon, 13007 Marseille, France
Janzen, Daniel H *Biologist*
%University of Pennsylvania, Biology Dept, Philadelphia, PA 19104, USA
Janzen, Edmund *Religious Leader*
%General Conference of Mennonite Brethren, 8000 W 21st St, Wichita, KS 67205, USA
Janzen, Lee *Golfer*
9088 Point Cypress Dr, Orlando, FL 32836, USA
Jardine, Alan C (Al) *Singer, Guitarist (Beach Boys)*
PO Box 36, Big Sur, CA 93920, USA
Jarman, Claude, Jr *Actor*
11 Dos Encinas, Orinda, CA 94563, USA
Jarmusch, Jim *Movie Director*
%Exoskeleton Inc, 208 E 6th St, New York, NY 10003, USA
Jarre, Maurice A *Composer*
27011 Sea Vista Dr, Malibu, CA 90265, USA
Jarreau, Al *Singer*
%Patrick Rains, 29161 Grayfox St, Malibu, CA 90265, USA
Jarrett, Dale *Auto Racing Driver*
1510 46th Ave NE, Hickory, NC 28601, USA
Jarrett, Keith *Jazz Pianist, Composer*
%Stephen Cloud, PO Box 4774, Santa Barbara, CA 93140, USA
Jarrett, Ned M *Auto Racing Driver*
%Ned Jarrett Enterprises, RR 1 Box 160, Newton, NC 28658, USA
Jarrett, Will *Editor*
%Dallas Times Herald, Editorial Dept, Herald Square, Dallas, TX 75202, USA
Jarriel, Thomas E (Tom) *Commentator*
%ABC-TV, News Dept, 77 W 66th St, New York, NY 10023, USA
Jarrott, Charles *Movie Director*
4314 Marina City Dr, #418, Marina del Rey, CA 90292, USA
Jarryd, Anders *Tennis Player*
Maaneskoldsgatan 37, 531 00 Lidkoping, Sweden
Jaru the Damaja *Rap Artist*
%William Morris Agency, 1325 Ave of Americas, New York, NY 10019, USA
Jaruzelski, Wojciech *President, Poland; Army General*
%Biuro Bylego, Al Jerozolimskie 91, 02-001 Warsaw, Poland
Jarvi, Neeme *Conductor*
PO Box 305, Sea Bright, NJ 07760, USA
Jarvi, Paavo *Conductor*
%Cincinnati Symphony, Music Hall, 1241 Elm St, Cincinnati, OH 45202, USA
Jarvis, Doug *Hockey Player*
812 Crane Dr, Coppell, TX 75019, USA
Jason, David *Actor, Comedian*
%Richard Stone, 2 Henrietta St, London WC2E 8PS, England
Jason, Sybil *Actress*
PO Box 40024, Studio City, CA 91614, USA
Jasrai, Puntsagiin *Prime Minister, Mongolia*
%Prime Minister's Office, Ulan Bator, Mongolia

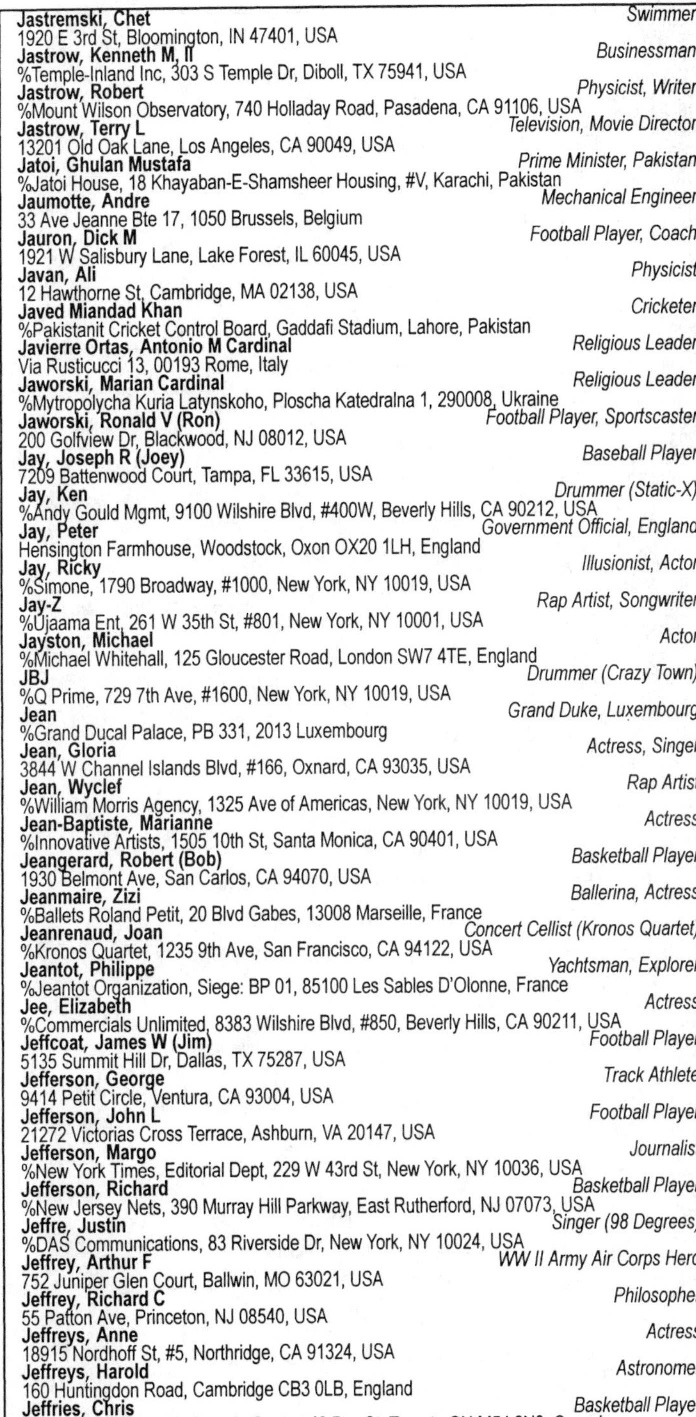

Jastremski, Chet — *Swimmer*
1920 E 3rd St, Bloomington, IN 47401, USA

Jastrow, Kenneth M, II — *Businessman*
%Temple-Inland Inc, 303 S Temple Dr, Diboll, TX 75941, USA

Jastrow, Robert — *Physicist, Writer*
%Mount Wilson Observatory, 740 Holladay Road, Pasadena, CA 91106, USA

Jastrow, Terry L — *Television, Movie Director*
13201 Old Oak Lane, Los Angeles, CA 90049, USA

Jatoi, Ghulan Mustafa — *Prime Minister, Pakistan*
%Jatoi House, 18 Khayaban-E-Shamsheer Housing, #V, Karachi, Pakistan

Jaumotte, Andre — *Mechanical Engineer*
33 Ave Jeanne Bte 17, 1050 Brussels, Belgium

Jauron, Dick M — *Football Player, Coach*
1921 W Salisbury Lane, Lake Forest, IL 60045, USA

Javan, Ali — *Physicist*
12 Hawthorne St, Cambridge, MA 02138, USA

Javed Miandad Khan — *Cricketer*
%Pakistanit Cricket Control Board, Gaddafi Stadium, Lahore, Pakistan

Javierre Ortas, Antonio M Cardinal — *Religious Leader*
Via Rusticucci 13, 00193 Rome, Italy

Jaworski, Marian Cardinal — *Religious Leader*
%Mytropolycha Kuria Latynskoho, Ploscha Katedralna 1, 290008, Ukraine

Jaworski, Ronald V (Ron) — *Football Player, Sportscaster*
200 Golfview Dr, Blackwood, NJ 08012, USA

Jay, Joseph R (Joey) — *Baseball Player*
7209 Battenwood Court, Tampa, FL 33615, USA

Jay, Ken — *Drummer (Static-X)*
%Andy Gould Mgmt, 9100 Wilshire Blvd, #400W, Beverly Hills, CA 90212, USA

Jay, Peter — *Government Official, England*
Hensington Farmhouse, Woodstock, Oxon OX20 1LH, England

Jay, Ricky — *Illusionist, Actor*
%Simone, 1790 Broadway, #1000, New York, NY 10019, USA

Jay-Z — *Rap Artist, Songwriter*
%Ujaama Ent, 261 W 35th St, #801, New York, NY 10001, USA

Jayston, Michael — *Actor*
%Michael Whitehall, 125 Gloucester Road, London SW7 4TE, England

JBJ — *Drummer (Crazy Town)*
%Q Prime, 729 7th Ave, #1600, New York, NY 10019, USA

Jean — *Grand Duke, Luxembourg*
%Grand Ducal Palace, PB 331, 2013 Luxembourg

Jean, Gloria — *Actress, Singer*
3844 W Channel Islands Blvd, #166, Oxnard, CA 93035, USA

Jean, Wyclef — *Rap Artist*
%William Morris Agency, 1325 Ave of Americas, New York, NY 10019, USA

Jean-Baptiste, Marianne — *Actress*
%Innovative Artists, 1505 10th St, Santa Monica, CA 90401, USA

Jeangerard, Robert (Bob) — *Basketball Player*
1930 Belmont Ave, San Carlos, CA 94070, USA

Jeanmaire, Zizi — *Ballerina, Actress*
%Ballets Roland Petit, 20 Blvd Gabes, 13008 Marseille, France

Jeanrenaud, Joan — *Concert Cellist (Kronos Quartet)*
%Kronos Quartet, 1235 9th Ave, San Francisco, CA 94122, USA

Jeantot, Philippe — *Yachtsman, Explorer*
%Jeantot Organization, Siege: BP 01, 85100 Les Sables D'Olonne, France

Jee, Elizabeth — *Actress*
%Commercials Unlimited, 8383 Wilshire Blvd, #850, Beverly Hills, CA 90211, USA

Jeffcoat, James W (Jim) — *Football Player*
5135 Summit Hill Dr, Dallas, TX 75287, USA

Jefferson, George — *Track Athlete*
9414 Petit Circle, Ventura, CA 93004, USA

Jefferson, John L — *Football Player*
21272 Victorias Cross Terrace, Ashburn, VA 20147, USA

Jefferson, Margo — *Journalist*
%New York Times, Editorial Dept, 229 W 43rd St, New York, NY 10036, USA

Jefferson, Richard — *Basketball Player*
%New Jersey Nets, 390 Murray Hill Parkway, East Rutherford, NJ 07073, USA

Jeffre, Justin — *Singer (98 Degrees)*
%DAS Communications, 83 Riverside Dr, New York, NY 10024, USA

Jeffrey, Arthur F — *WW II Army Air Corps Hero*
752 Juniper Glen Court, Ballwin, MO 63021, USA

Jeffrey, Richard C — *Philosopher*
55 Patton Ave, Princeton, NJ 08540, USA

Jeffreys, Anne — *Actress*
18915 Nordhoff St, #5, Northridge, CA 91324, USA

Jeffreys, Harold — *Astronomer*
160 Huntingdon Road, Cambridge CB3 0LB, England

Jeffries, Chris — *Basketball Player*
%Toronto Raptors, Air Canada Center, 40 Bay St, Toronto ON M5J 2N8, Canada

Jeffries, Herb *Singer, Actor*
%Flaming-O Productions, 44489 Town Center Way, Palm Desert, CA 92260, USA
Jeffries, Jared *Basketball Player*
%Washington Wizards, MCI Centre, 601 F St NW, Washington, DC 20004, USA
Jeffries, John T *Astronomer*
1652 E Camino Cielo, Tucson, AZ 85718, USA
Jeffries, Lionel *Actor, Director*
%International Creative Mgmt, 76 Oxford St, London W1N 0AX, England
Jellicoe, George P J R *Government Official, England*
Tidcombe Manor, Tidcombe near Marlborough, Wilts SN8 3SL, England
Jemison, Mae C *Astronaut*
%Dartmouth College, Environmental Studies Dept, Hanover, NH 03755, USA
Jemison, Theodore J *Religious Leader*
%National Baptist Convention USA, 1620 White's Creek Pike, Nashville, TN 37207, USA
Jencks, William P *Biochemist*
11 Revere St, Lexington, MA 02420, USA
Jenes, Theodore G, Jr *Army General*
809 169th Place SW, Lynnwood, WA 98037, USA
Jenifer, Franklyn G *Educator*
%University of Texas at Dallas, President's Office, Richardson, TX 75083, USA
Jenkin of Roding, Patrick F *Government Official, England*
703 Howard House, Dolphin Square, London SW1V 3PQ, England
Jenkins, Alfred *Football Player*
2993 Cascade Road SW, Atlanta, GA 30311, USA
Jenkins, Alfred le Sesne *Diplomat*
Stalsama High Knob, PO Box 586, Front Royal, VA 22630, USA
Jenkins, Bill (Grumpy) *Drag Racing Driver*
%Jenkins Competition, 153 Pennsylvania Ave, Malvern, PA 19355, USA
Jenkins, Daniel *Actor*
%S M S Talent, 8730 Sunset Blvd, #440, Los Angeles, CA 90069, USA
Jenkins, David W *Figure Skater*
5947 S Atlanta Ave, Tulsa, OK 74105, USA
Jenkins, Don J *Vietnam War Army Hero (CMH)*
3783 Bowling Green Road, Morgantown, KY 42261, USA
Jenkins, Ferguson A (Fergie), Jr *Baseball Player*
PO Box 1202, Guthrie, OK 73044, USA
Jenkins, George *Stage Designer, Movie Art Director*
740 Kingman Ave, Santa Monica, CA 90402, USA
Jenkins, Hayes Alan *Figure Skater*
3183 Regency Place, Westlake, OH 44145, USA
Jenkins, Jackie (Butch) *Actor*
PO Box 541G, Fairview, NC 28730, USA
Jenkins, Jerry B *Writer*
%Tyndale House Publishers, 351 Executive Dr, PO Box 80, Wheaton, IL 60189, USA
Jenkins, Kris *Football Player*
%Carolina Panthers, Ericsson Stadium, 800 S Mint St, Charlotte, NC 28202, USA
Jenkins, Loren *Journalist*
%Washington Post, Editorial Dept, 1150 15th St NW, Washington, DC 20071, USA
Jenkins, Paul *Artist*
%Imago Terrae, PO Box 6833, Yorkville Station, New York, NY 10128, USA
Jenkins, Stephan *Singer (Third Eye Blind)*
%Eric Godtland Mgmt, 5715 Claremont Ave, #C, Oakland, CA 94618, USA
Jenner, Bruce *Track Athlete, Actor*
2345 Elbury Court, Thousand Oaks, CA 91361, USA
Jennings, David T (Dave) *Football Player*
1 Briarcliff Road, Upper Saddle River, NJ 07458, USA
Jennings, Delbert O *Vietnam War Army Hero (CMH)*
3701 25th Way SE, Olympia, WA 98501, USA
Jennings, Jason *Baseball Player*
%Colorado Rockies, Coors Field, 2001 Blake St, Denver, CO 80205, USA
Jennings, Lynn *Track Athlete*
17 Cushing Road, Newmarket, NH 03857, USA
Jennings, Paul C *Civil Engineer*
640 S Grand Ave, Pasadena, CA 91105, USA
Jennings, Peter C *Commentator*
%ABC-TV, News Dept, 47 W 66th St, New York, NY 10023, USA
Jennings, Robert Y *Judge*
61 Bridle Way, Grantchester, Cambridge CB3 9NY, England
Jennings, Will *Songwriter*
%Gorfaine/Schwartz, 13245 Riverside Dr, #450, Sherman Oaks, CA 91423, USA
Jenrette, Richard H *Businessman*
67 E 93rd St, New York, NY 10128, USA
Jens, Salome *Actress*
%Richard Sindell, 1910 Holmby Ave, #1, Los Angeles, CA 90025, USA
Jens, Walter *Writer*
Sonnenstr 5, 72076 Tubingen, Germany
Jensen, Arthur R *Educational Psychologist*
30 Canyon View Dr, Orinda, CA 94563, USA

Jensen, Elwood V *Biochemist*
%Karolinska Institute, Medical Nutrition Dept, 141 86 Huddinge, Sweden
Jensen, James *Geologist*
%Brigham Young University, Geology Dept, Provo, UT 84602, USA
Jensen, James W, Jr *Cinematographer*
28853 Garnet Hill Court, Agoura Hills, CA 91301, USA
Jensen, Karen *Actress*
9363 Wilshire Blvd, #212, Beverly Hills, CA 90210, USA
Jepsen, Roger W *Senator, IA*
3542 Pennyroyal Road, Port Charlotte, FL 33953, USA
Jeremiah, David E *Navy Admiral*
2898 Melanie Lane, Oakton, VA 22124, USA
Jerkens, H Allen *Thoroughbred Racing Trainer*
9509 242nd St, Floral Park, NY 11001, USA
Jernberg, Sixten *Nordic Skier*
Fritidsby 780, 7806 Lima, Sweden
Jernigan, Tamara E (Tammy) *Astronaut*
4268 Brindisi Place, Pleasanton, CA 94566, USA
Jerusalem, Siegfried *Opera Singer*
Sudring 9, 90542 Eckental, Germany
Jessee, Michael A *Financier*
%Federal Home Loan Bank, 1 Financial Center, Boston, MA 02111, USA
Jet Li *Actor*
%International Creative Mgmt, 8942 Wilshire Blvd, #219, Beverly Hills, CA 90211, USA
Jeter, Derek S *Baseball Player*
%New York Yankees, Yankee Stadium, 161st St & River Ave, Bronx, NY 10451, USA
Jeter, Gary M *Football Player*
32725 Shadowbrook Dr, Solon, OH 44139, USA
Jeter, Robert D (Bob) *Football Player*
7147 S Paxton Ave, Chicago, IL 60649, USA
Jett, Brent W *Astronaut*
1120 Texas St, #4C, Houston, TX 77002, USA
Jett, Joan *Singer, Songwriter*
%Jet Lagg, Blackheart Records, 636 Broadway, #1218, New York, NY 10012, USA
Jeunet, Jean-Pierre *Movie Director*
%International Creative Mgmt, 8942 Wilshire Blvd, #219, Beverly Hills, CA 90211, USA
Jevanord, Oystein *Drummer (A-Ha)*
%Bandana Mgmt, 11 Elvaston Place, #300, London SW7 5QC, England
Jewel *Singer, Songwriter, Actress*
PO Box 1388, Brea, CA 92822, USA
Jewison, Norman F *Movie Director, Producer*
%Yorktown Productions, 3000 W Olympic Blvd, #1314, Santa Monica, CA 90404, USA
Jhabvala, Ruth Prawer *Writer*
400 E 52nd St, New York, NY 10022, USA
Jia, Li *Hematologist*
%Duke University, Medical Center, Hematology Dept, Durham, NC 27708, USA
Jiang Tiefeng *Artist*
%Fingerhut Gallery, 690 Bridgeway, Sausalito, CA 94965, USA
Jiang Zemin *President, China*
%Central Military Committee, Zhonganahai, Beijing, China
Jiang, Tian *Concert Pianist*
%Columbia Artists Mgmt Inc, 165 W 57th St, New York, NY 10019, USA
Jiles, Pamela (Pam) *Track Athlete*
2623 Wisteria St, New Orleans, LA 70122, USA
Jillian, Ann *Actress*
PO Box 57739, Sherman Oaks, CA 91413, USA
Jimenez, Carlos *Architect*
%Jimenez Architectural Design Studio, 1116 Willard St, Houston, TX 77006, USA
Jimenez, Flaco *Accordianist*
%DeLeon Artists, 4031 Panama Court, Piedmont, CA 94611, USA
Jimenez, Nicario *Artist*
5531 Teak Wood Dr NW, Naples, FL 34119, USA
Jiminez, Joe *Golfer*
29243 Enchanted Glen, Boerne, TX 78015, USA
Jirsa, Ron *Basketball Coach*
%University of Georgia, Athletic Dept, Athens, GA 30613, USA
Jiscke, Martin C *Educator*
%Iowa State University, President's Office, Ames, IA 50011, USA
Joanou, Phil *Movie Director*
%Creative Artists Agency, 9830 Wilshire Blvd, Beverly Hills, CA 90212, USA
Job, Brian *Swimmer*
PO Box 70427, Sunnyvale, CA 94086, USA
Jobs, Steven P *Businessman, Computer Developer*
%Apple Computer, 1 Infinite Loop, Cupertino, CA 95014, USA
Joe, William (Billy) *Football Player*
%Florida A&M University, Athletic Dept, Tallahassee, FL 32307, USA
Joel, Billy *Singer, Songwriter*
PO Box 5060, East Hampton, NY 11937, USA

J

Joel - Johnson

Joel, Richard M *Educator*
%Yeshiva University, President's Office, 500 W 185th St, New York, NY 10033, USA
Joey Z *Guitarist (Stereo Mud)*
%Agency Group Ltd, 1775 Broadway, #430, New York, NY 10019, USA
Joffe, Roland V *Movie Director, Producer*
%Nomad, 10351 Santa Monica Blvd, #402, Los Angeles, CA 90025, USA
Jofre, Eder *Boxer*
Alamo de Ministero Rocha, Azevedo 373, C Cesar 21-15, Sao Paulo, Brazil
Johannsson, Kristjan *Opera Singer*
%Herbert Breslin, 119 W 57th St, #1505, New York, NY 10019, USA
Johanos, Donald *Conductor*
%Honolulu Symphony, 650 Iwilei Road, #202, Honolulu, HI 96817, USA
Johansen, David *Singer*
%Agency Group Ltd, 1775 Broadway, #430, New York, NY 10019, USA
Johansen, John M *Architect*
%Johansen & Bhavnani, 821 Broadway, New York, NY 10003, USA
Johanson, Donald C *Anthropologist*
%Arizona State University, Human Origins Institute, Tempe, AZ 85287, USA
Johansson, Paul *Actor*
%Gilbertson & Kincaid Mgmt, 1330 4th St, Santa Monica, CA 90401, USA
Johansson, Scarlett *Actress*
7135 Hollywood Blvd, #804, Los Angeles, CA 90046, USA
John Paul II *Religious Leader*
Palazzo Apostolico, 00120 Vatican City
John, Caspar *Navy Admiral, England*
Trethewey, Mousehole, Penzance, Cornwall, England
John, David D *Museum Official, Explorer*
7 Cyncoed Ave, Cardiff CF2 6ST, Wales
John, Elton *Singer, Songwriter*
%John Reid, Singes House, 32 Galena Road, London W6 0LT, England
John, Thomas E (Tommy) *Baseball Player*
6202 Seton House Lane, Charlotte, NC 28277, USA
John-Roger *Religious Leader*
%John Roger Foundation, 2101 Wilshire Blvd, Santa Monica, CA 90403, USA
Johncock, Gordon *Auto Racing Driver*
931 Bedtelyon Road, West Branch, MI 48661, USA
Johns, Daniel *Guitarist (Silverchair)*
%John Watson Mgmt, PO Box 281, Sunny Hills NSW 2010, Australia
Johns, Glynis *Actress*
10701 Wilshire Blvd, #2201, Los Angeles, CA 90024, USA
Johns, Jasper *Artist*
97 Low Road, #642, Sharon, CT 06069, USA
Johns, Lori *Drag Racing Driver*
4418 Congressional Dr, Corpus Christi, TX 78413, USA
Johnson Jerald, Penny *Actress*
%Susan Smith, 121A N San Vicente Blvd, Beverly Hills, CA 90211, USA
Johnson Pucci, Gail *Synchronized Swimmer*
2132 Ward Dr, Walnut Creek, CA 94596, USA
Johnson, Addison *Cartoonist (Bringing Up Father)*
%King Features Syndicate, 888 7th Ave, New York, NY 10106, USA
Johnson, Allen *Track Athlete*
%Octagon, 1751 Pinnacle Dr, #1500, McLean, VA 22102, USA
Johnson, Amy Jo *Actress*
3940 Laurel Canyon Blvd, #463, Studio City, CA 91604, USA
Johnson, Anne-Marie *Actress*
2522 Silver Lake Terrace, Los Angeles, CA 90039, USA
Johnson, Arte *Actor, Comedian*
2725 Bottlebrush Dr, Los Angeles, CA 90077, USA
Johnson, Ashley *Actress*
%Untitled Entertainment, 8436 W 3rd St, #650, Los Angeles, CA 90048, USA
Johnson, Benjamin S (Ben), Jr *Track Athlete*
%Ed Futerman, 2 Saint Clair Ave E, #1500, Toronto ON M4T 2R1, Canada
Johnson, Betsey L *Fashion Designer*
%Betsey Johnson Co, 127 E 9th St, #703, Los Angeles, CA 90015, USA
Johnson, Beverly *Model, Actress*
2711 Angelo Dr, Los Angeles, CA 90077, USA
Johnson, Brad *Model, Actor*
%Bresler Kelly Assoc, 11500 W Olympic Blvd, #510, Los Angeles, CA 90064, USA
Johnson, Brad *Football Player*
%Tampa Bay Buccaneers, 1 W Buccaneer Place, Tampa, FL 33607, USA
Johnson, Brian *Singer (AC/DC)*
11 Leominster Road, Morden, Surrey SA4 6HN, England
Johnson, Brooks *Track Coach*
%Stanford University, Athletic Dept, Stanford, CA 94305, USA
Johnson, Butch *Football Player*
9719 S Red Oakes Dr, Highlands Ranch, CO 80126, USA
Johnson, Carolyn Dawn *Singer, Songwriter*
%RPM Mgmt, 209 10th Ave S, #229, Nashville, TN 37203, USA

Johnson, Charles E — *Baseball Player*
12301 NW 7th St, Plantation, FL 33325, USA

Johnson, Charles L (Charley) — *Football Player*
PO Box 1312, Mesilla, NM 88046, USA

Johnson, Charles R — *Writer*
%University of Washington, English Dept, Seattle, WA 98105, USA

Johnson, Chris — *Golfer*
%W K Shearman Co, 7925 N Oracle Road, #388, Tucson, AZ 85704, USA

Johnson, Claude (Juan) — *Singer (Don & Juan)*
%Mars Talent, 27 L'Ambiance Court, Bardonia, NY 10954, USA

Johnson, Claudia A (Lady Bird) — *Wife of US President*
LBJ Ranch, Stonewall, TX 78671, USA

Johnson, Courtney — *Water Polo Player*
8472 W Granite Dr, Granite Bay, CA 95746, USA

Johnson, Darrell D — *Baseball Player, Manager*
65 Willotta Dr, Suisun City, CA 94534, USA

Johnson, Dave — *Labor Leader*
%United Garment Workers, 4207 Lebanon Road, Hermitage, TN 37076, USA

Johnson, David A (Davey) — *Baseball Player, Manager*
1064 Howell Branch Road, Winter Park, FL 32789, USA

Johnson, David Cay — *Journalist*
%New York Times, Editorial Dept, 229 W 43rd St, New York, NY 10036, USA

Johnson, David G — *Economist*
1700 E 56th St, #1306, Chicago, IL 60637, USA

Johnson, David W — *Businessman*
%Campbell Soup Co, 1 Campbell Place, Camden, NJ 08103, USA

Johnson, Dennis W — *Basketball Player*
15003 Chuparosa St, Victorville, CA 92394, USA

Johnson, DerMarr — *Basketball Player*
%Phoenix Suns, 201 E Jefferson St, Phoenix, AZ 85004, USA

Johnson, Don — *Actor*
%William Morris Agency, 151 El Camino Dr, Beverly Hills, CA 90212, USA

Johnson, Dwayne — *Actor, Wrestler*
2045 S Barrington Ave, #A, Los Angeles, CA 90025, USA

Johnson, Earl — *Bowler*
3625 Woody Lane, Minnetonka, MN 55305, USA

Johnson, Earvin (Magic), Jr — *Basketball Player, Coach*
%Magic Johnson Ent, 9100 Wilshire Blvd, #700E Tower, Beverly Hills, CA 90212, USA

Johnson, Edward (Eddie) — *Basketball Player*
6133 N 61st Place, Paradise Valley, AZ 85253, USA

Johnson, Emma — *Concert Clarinetist*
%Columbia Artists Mgmt Inc, 165 W 57th St, New York, NY 10019, USA

Johnson, Ernie, Jr — *Sportscaster*
%TNT-TV, Sports Department, 1050 Techwood Dr, Atlanta, GA 30318, USA

Johnson, Ervin — *Basketball Player*
%Minnesota Timberwolves, Target Center, 600 1st Ave N, Minneapolis, MN 55403, USA

Johnson, Frank — *Basketball Player, Coach*
10929 Pebble Run Dr, Silver Spring, MD 20902, USA

Johnson, Gary L — *Football Player*
450 Oliver Road, Haughton, LA 71037, USA

Johnson, Georgann — *Actress*
218 Glenroy Place, Los Angeles, CA 90049, USA

Johnson, Gregory C — *Astronaut*
1002 Applewood Dr, Friendswood, TX 77546, USA

Johnson, Hansford T — *Air Force General*
%USAA Capital Corp, 9800 Fredericksburg Road, San Antonio, TX 78284, USA

Johnson, Harold — *Boxer*
6101 Morris St, Philadelphia, PA 19144, USA

Johnson, Haynes B — *Journalist*
%George Washington University, Communications Studies Ctr, Washington, DC 20052, USA

Johnson, I Birger — *Electrical Engineer*
1508 Barclay Place, Niskayuna, NY 12309, USA

Johnson, Ian — *Journalist*
%Wall Street Journal, Editorial Dept, 200 Liberty St, New York, NY 10281, USA

Johnson, J Bradley (Brad) — *Football Player*
PO Box 732, Black Mountain, NC 28711, USA

Johnson, J Seward — *Sculptor*
%Sculpture Foundation, 2525 Michigan Ave, #A6, Santa Monica, CA 90404, USA

Johnson, James A — *Financier*
%Federal National Mortgage Assn, 3900 Wisconsin Ave NW, Washington, DC 20016, USA

Johnson, James E (Johnnie) — *WW II Air Force Hero, England*
Stables, Hargate Hall, Buxton, Derbyshire SK17 8TA, England

Johnson, Jannette — *Skier*
PO Box 901, Sun Valley, ID 83353, USA

Johnson, Jenna — *Swimmer, Coach*
%University of Tennessee, Athletic Dept, PO Box 15016, Knoxville, TN 37901, USA

Johnson, Jerome L — *Navy Admiral*
%Navy-Marine Corps Relief Society, 801 N Randolph St, Arlington, VA 22203, USA

Johnson, Jimmie — *Auto Racing Driver*
%Jimmie Johnson Racing, PO Box 4283, Mooresville, NC 28117, USA

Johnson, Jimmy — *Football Player*
656 Amaranth Blvd, Mill Valley, CA 94941, USA

Johnson, Jimmy — *Cartoonist (Arlo & Janis)*
%United Feature Syndicate, 200 Madison Ave, New York, NY 10016, USA

Johnson, Joe — *Basketball Player*
%Phoenix Suns, 201 E Jefferson St, Phoenix, AZ 85004, USA

Johnson, Johari — *Actress*
%H W A Talent, 3500 W Olive Ave, #1400, Burbank, CA 91505, USA

Johnson, John H — *Publisher*
%Johnson Publishing Co, 1750 Pennsylvania Ave NW, Washington, DC 20006, USA

Johnson, Johnnie — *Singer, Pianist, Songwriter*
%Talent Source, 1560 Broadway, #1308, New York, NY 10036, USA

Johnson, Johnnie, Jr — *Football Player*
PO Box 114, La Grange, TX 78945, USA

Johnson, Joseph E, III — *Physician*
%Philadelphian, 2401 Pennsylvania Ave, #15C44, Philadelphia, PA 19130, USA

Johnson, Junior — *Auto Racing Driver, Executive*
1100 Glen Oaks Dr, Hamptonville, NC 27020, USA

Johnson, Keith — *Labor Leader*
%Woodworkers of America Union, 1622 N Lombard St, Portland, OR 97217, USA

Johnson, Kermit — *Football Player*
3259 Lincoln Ave, Altadena, CA 91001, USA

Johnson, Kevin — *Basketball Player, Sportscaster*
%NBC-TV, Sports Dept, 30 Rockefeller Plaza, New York, NY 10112, USA

Johnson, Keyshawn — *Football Player*
%Reign, 180 N Robertson Blvd, Beverly Hills, CA 90211, USA

Johnson, Lamont — *Movie Director*
935 Mesa Road, Monterey, CA 93940, USA

Johnson, Larry — *Football Player*
%Kansas City Chiefs, 1 Arrowhead Dr, Kansas City, KS 64129, USA

Johnson, Larry D — *Basketball Player*
310 N Kings Dr, Charlotte, NC 28204, USA

Johnson, Laurie — *Composer*
Priority House, Camp Hill, Stanmore, Middx HA7 3JQ, England

Johnson, Lynn-Holly — *Actress*
%Cavaleri, 178 S Victory Blvd, #205, Burbank, CA 91502, USA

Johnson, Manuel H, Jr — *Economist, Government Official*
%Johnson Smick Int'l, 2099 Pennsylvania Ave NW, #950, Washington, 20006, USA

Johnson, Mark — *Boxer*
1204 Howison Place SW, Washington, DC 20024, USA

Johnson, Mark E — *Hockey Player, Coach*
5901 Hempstead Road, Madison, WI 53711, USA

Johnson, Marvin — *Boxer*
5452 Turfway Circle, Indianapolis, IN 46228, USA

Johnson, Marvin M — *Chemical Engineer*
4413 Woodland Road, Bartlesville, OK 74006, USA

Johnson, Michael D — *Track Athlete*
%Gold Medal Mgmt, 1750 14th St, Boulder, CO 80302, USA

Johnson, Michelle — *Actress, Model*
%Agency for Performing Arts, 9200 Sunset Blvd, #900, Los Angeles, CA 90069, USA

Johnson, Neil — *Basketball Player*
821 Plymouth Lane, Virginia Beach, VA 23451, USA

Johnson, Norm — *Football Player*
400 Peachtree Industrial Blvd, #1615, Suwanee, GA 30024, USA

Johnson, Norman — *Singer (Jive Five)*
%Paramount Entertainment, PO Box 12, Far Hills, NJ 07931, USA

Johnson, Ora J — *Religious Leader*
%General Assn of General Baptists, 100 Stinson Dr, Poplar Bluff, MO 63901, USA

Johnson, Paul — *Hockey Player*
1719 Yale Ave, Burley, ID 83318, USA

Johnson, Paul B — *Historian*
Coach House, Over Stowey near Bridgewater, Somerset TA5 1HA, England

Johnson, Philip C — *Architect, Pritzker Laureate*
%John Burgee Architects, 4 Columbus Circle, New York, NY 10013, USA

Johnson, R E — *Labor Leader*
%Train Dispatchers Assn, 1370 Ontario St, #1040, Cleveland, OH 44113, USA

Johnson, Rafer L — *Track Athlete, Actor*
4217 Woodcliff Road, Sherman Oaks, CA 91403, USA

Johnson, Randall D (Randy) — *Baseball Player*
%Arizona Diamondbacks, Bank One Ballpark, 401 E Jefferson, Phoenix, AZ 85004, USA

Johnson, Richard K — *Actor*
%Conway Van Gelder Robinson, 18-21 Jermyn St, London SW1Y 6NB, England

Johnson, Rob — *Football Player*
26635 Aracena Dr, Mission Viejo, CA 92691, USA

Johnson, Robert D (Bob) — *Football Player*
2 Ault Lane, Cincinnati, OH 45246, USA

Johnson, Robert L *Businessman, Basketball Executive*
%Black Entertainment TV, 1900 W Place NE, Washington, DC 20018, USA
Johnson, Ronald A (Ron) *Football Player*
226 Summit Ave, Summit, NJ 07901, USA
Johnson, Roy *Labor Leader*
%Roofers & Waterproofers Union, 1125 17th St NW, Washington, DC 20036, USA
Johnson, Russell *Actor*
%Professor's Place, PO Box 11198, Bainbridge Island, WA 98110, USA
Johnson, Samuel C *Businessman*
%SC Johnson & Son, 1525 Howe St, Racine, WI 53403, USA
Johnson, Shannon *Basketball Player*
%Connecticut Sun, Mohegan Sun Arena, Uncasville, CT 06382, USA
Johnson, Shelly W *Cinematographer*
970 Jimeno Road, Santa Barbara, CA 93103, USA
Johnson, Sonia *Women's/Religious Activist*
3318 2nd St S, Arlington, VA 22204, USA
Johnson, Spencer *Writer*
%G P Putnam's Sons, 375 Hudson St, New York, NY 10014, USA
Johnson, Thomas C (Tom) *Hockey Player*
16 Spartina Place, West Falmouth, MA 02574, USA
Johnson, Tim *Football Player*
%Washington Redskins, 21300 Redskin Park Dr, Ashburn, VA 20147, USA
Johnson, Torrence V *Astronomer*
%Jet Propulsion Laboratory, 4800 Oak Grove Dr, Pasadena, CA 91109, USA
Johnson, Van *Actor*
%Studio Artists, 305 W 52nd St, #1H, New York, NY 10019, USA
Johnson, Vaughan M *Football Player*
%New Orleans Saints, 5800 Airline Highway, Metairie, LA 70003, USA
Johnson, Vinnie *Basketball Player*
5236 Elmsgate Dr, Orchard Lake, MI 48324, USA
Johnson, Virginia *Ballerina*
133 W 71st St, New York, NY 10023, USA
Johnson, Virginia E *Sex Therapist, Psychologist*
%Johnson Assoc, 800 Holland Road, Ballwin, MO 63021, USA
Johnson, Warren *Auto Racing Driver*
PO Box 1357, Buford, GA 30515, USA
Johnson, Warren C *Chemist*
946 Bellclair Road SE, Grand Rapids, MI 49506, USA
Johnson, Wendy *Auto Racing Driver*
126 Red Brook Lane, Mooresville, NC 28117, USA
Johnson, William A (Billy White Shoes) *Football Player*
3701 Whitney Place, Duluth, GA 30096, USA
Johnson, William B *Businessman*
%Ritz-Carlton Hotels, 4445 Willard Ave, #800, Chevy Chase, MD 20815, USA
Johnson, William R *Businessman*
%H J Heinz Co, PO Box 57, Pittsburgh, PA 15230, USA
Johnston McKay, Mary H *Astronaut*
%University of Tennessee, Space Institute, Tullahoma, TN 37388, USA
Johnston, Alastair *Sports Agent*
%International Mgmt Group, 75490 Fairway Dr, Indian Wells, CA 92210, USA
Johnston, Allen H *Religious Leader*
%Bishop's House, 3 Wymer Terrace, PO Box 21, Hamilton, New Zealand
Johnston, Bruce *Singer (Beach Boys)*
%International Creative Mgmt, 8942 Wilshire Blvd, #219, Beverly Hills, CA 90211, USA
Johnston, Daryl (Moose) *Football Player*
5520 Roland Dr, Plano, TX 75093, USA
Johnston, Freedy *Singer, Songwriter*
%Morebarn Music, 30 Hilcrest Ave, Morristown, NJ 07960, USA
Johnston, Gerald A *Businessman*
%McDonnell Douglas Corp, PO Box 516, Saint Louis, MO 63166, USA
Johnston, Gerald E *Businessman*
%Clorox Co, 1221 Broadway, Oakland, CA 94612, USA
Johnston, Harold S *Chemist*
285 Franklin St, Harrisonburg, VA 22801, USA
Johnston, J Bennett, Jr *Senator, LA*
%Johnston Assoc, 2099 Pennsylvania Ave NW, #1000, Washington, DC 20006, USA
Johnston, John Dennis *Actor*
%S D B Partners, 1801 Ave of Stars, #902, Los Angeles, CA 90067, USA
Johnston, Kristen *Actress*
%Creative Artists Agency, 9830 Wilshire Blvd, Beverly Hills, CA 90212, USA
Johnston, Lynn *Cartoonist (For Better or For Worse)*
%Universal Press Syndicate, 4520 Main St, Kansas City, MO 64111, USA
Johnston, Rex D *Football, Baseball Player*
11372 Weatherby Road, Los Alamitos, CA 90720, USA
Johnston, S K, Jr *Businessman*
%Coca-Cola Enterprises, 2500 Windy Ridge Parkway, Atlanta, GA 30339, USA
Johnston-Forbes, Cathy *Golfer*
%Ladies Pro Golf Assn, 100 International Golf Dr, Daytona Beach, FL 32124, USA

Johnstone, John W, Jr *Businessman*
467 Carter St, New Canaan, CT 06840, USA
Joiner, Charles (Charlie), Jr *Football Player, Coach*
2254 Moore St, San Diego, CA 92110, USA
Jolas, Betsy M *Composer*
%Nat Superieur Musique Conservatoire, 209 Ave Jaures, 75019 Paris, France
Joli, France *Singer*
%Brothers Mgmt, 141 Dunbar Ave, Fords, NJ 08863, USA
Joliceur, David *Rap Artist (DeLaSoul)*
%Famous Artists Agency, 250 W 57th St, New York, NY 10107, USA
Jolie, Angelina *Actress, Model*
%Industry Entertainment, 955 Carillo Dr, #300, Los Angeles, CA 90048, USA
Joliot, Pierre A *Biologist*
16 Rue de la Glaciere, 75013 Paris, France
Jolly, Allison *Yachtswoman*
1275 Seville Lane NE, Saint Petersburg, FL 33704, USA
Jolly, E Grady *Judge*
%US Court of Appeals, Eastland Courthouse, 245 E Capitol St, Jackson, MS 39201, USA
Joltz, Joachim *Electrical Engineer*
AM Forsthof 16, 42119 Wuppertal, Germany
Jon B *Singer, Songwriter*
%Devour Mgmt, 6399 Wilshire Blvd, #426, Los Angeles, CA 90048, USA
Jones, Alex S *Journalist*
1 Waterhouse St, #61, Cambridge, MA 02138, USA
Jones, Allen *Artist*
41 Charterhouse Square, London EC1M 6EA, England
Jones, Antonia *Actress*
%Buzz Halliday, 8899 Beverly Blvd, #620, Los Angeles, CA 90048, USA
Jones, Arthur *Inventor (Nautilus Exercise Machine)*
%MedX, 1155 NE 77th St, Ocala, FL 34479, USA
Jones, Asjha *Basketball Player*
%Washington Mystics, MCI Center, 601 F St NW, Washington, DC 20004, USA
Jones, Ben J *Prime Minister, Grenada*
Victoria St, Greenville, Saint Andrew's, Grenada
Jones, Bertram H (Bert) *Football Player*
%Mid-States Wood Preservers, PO Box 248, Simsboro, LA 71275, USA
Jones, Bill T *Choreographer*
%Bill T Jones/Arnie Zane Dance Co, 853 Broadway, #1706, New York, NY 10003, USA
Jones, Booker T *Singer, Organist (Booker T & the MG's)*
%Rosebud Agency, PO Box 170429, San Francisco, CA 94117, USA
Jones, Brent M *Football Player, Sportscaster*
5483 Blackhawk Dr, Danville, CA 94506, USA
Jones, Bryn Terfel *Opera Singer*
%Harlequin Agency, 203 Fidlas Road, Cardiff CF4 5NA, Wales
Jones, Carnetta *Actress*
%CunninghamEscottDipene, 10635 Santa Monica Blvd, #130, Los Angeles, CA 90025, USA
Jones, Charles W *Labor Leader*
%Brotherhood of Boilermakers, 753 S 8th Ave, Kansas City, KS 66105, USA
Jones, Charlie *Sportscaster*
8080 El Paseo Grande, La Jolla, CA 92037, USA
Jones, Cherry *Actress*
%William Morris Agency, 151 El Camino Dr, Beverly Hills, CA 90212, USA
Jones, Claude Earl *Actor*
%Henderson/Hogan, 8285 W Sunset Blvd, #1, West Hollywood, CA 90046, USA
Jones, Cobi *Soccer Player*
501 N Edinburgh Ave, Los Angeles, CA 90048, USA
Jones, Courtney J L *Figure Skating Executive*
%National Skating Assn, 15-27 Gee St, London EC1V 3RE, England
Jones, Darryl *Bassist (Rolling Stones)*
%Rascoff/Zysblat, 110 W 57th St, #300, New York, NY 10019, USA
Jones, David (Davy) *Singer, Guitarist (Monkees)*
%Paradise Artists, 108 E Matilija St, Ojai, CA 93023, USA
Jones, David (Deacon) *Football Player, Executive*
715 S Canyon Mist Lane, Anaheim, CA 92808, USA
Jones, David A *Businessman*
%Humana Corp, 500 W Main St, Louisville, KY 40202, USA
Jones, Davy *Auto Racing Driver*
%TRW Racing, 2000 Jaguar Dr, Valparaiso, IN 46383, USA
Jones, Dean *Actor, Singer*
PO Box 570276, Tarzana, CA 91357, USA
Jones, Denise *Singer (Point of Grace)*
%TBA Artists Mgmt, 300 10th Ave S, Nashville, TN 37203, USA
Jones, E Edward *Religious Leader*
%Baptist Convention of America, 777 S R L Thornton Freeway, Dallas, TX 75203, USA
Jones, E Fay *Architect*
%Fay Jones/Maurice Jennings Architects, 619 W Dickson, Fayetteville, AR 72701, USA
Jones, Eddie *Basketball Player*
3400 Paddock Road, Weston, FL 33331, USA

Jones, Edith H *Judge*
%US Court of Appeals, US Courthouse, 515 Rusk Ave, Houston, TX 77002, USA
Jones, Elvin R *Jazz Drummer, Bandleader*
%DL Media, PO Box 2728, Bala Cynwyd, PA 19004, USA
Jones, Gemma *Actress*
%Conway Van Gelder Robinson, 18-21 Jermyn St, London SW1Y 6NB, England
Jones, George *Singer, Songwriter*
%George Jones Enterprises, 500 Wilson Pike Circle, #200, Brentwood, TN 37027, USA
Jones, Grace *Model, Actress, Singer*
%Denis Vaughan Mgmt, PO Box 28286, London N21 3WT, England
Jones, Greg *Skier*
PO Box 500, Tahoe City, CA 96145, USA
Jones, Gwyneth *Opera Singer*
PO Box 556, 8037 Zurich, Switzerland
Jones, Hayes W *Track Athlete*
1040 James K Blvd, Pontiac, MI 48341, USA
Jones, Henry (Hank) *Jazz Pianist*
%Joel Chriss, 300 Mercer St, #3J, New York, NY 10003, USA
Jones, Homer C *Football Player*
408 S Texas St, Pittsburg, TX 75686, USA
Jones, Howard *Singer, Songwriter*
%FML, 33 Alexander Road, Aylesbury HP20 2NR, England
Jones, Jack *Singer*
75-825 Osage Trail, Indian Wells, CA 92210, USA
Jones, James Earl *Actor*
226 W 46th St, New York, NY 10036, USA
Jones, James L (Jack) *Labor Leader*
74 Ruskin Park House, Champion Hill, London SE5, England
Jones, James L, Jr *Marine Corps General*
Supreme Allied Commander, Supreme Headquarters, APO, AE 09705, USA
Jones, Jamie *Singer (All-4-One)*
%MPI Talent, 9255 Sunset Blvd, #407, Los Angeles, CA 90069, USA
Jones, Janet *Actress*
9100 Wilshire Blvd, #1000W, Beverly Hills, CA 90212, USA
Jones, Jeffrey *Actor*
7336 Santa Monica Blvd, #691, West Hollywood, CA 90046, USA
Jones, Jennifer *Actress*
22400 Pacific Coast Highway, Malibu, CA 90265, USA
Jones, Jenny *Entertainer, Comedienne*
600 Plum Tree Road, Barrington, IL 60010, USA
Jones, Jerrauld C (Jerry) *Football Executive*
%Dallas Cowboys, 1 Cowboys Parkway, Irving, TX 75063, USA
Jones, John Paul *Bassist, Keyboardist (Led Zepplin)*
%Opium Arts, 49 Portland Road, London W11 4LJ, England
Jones, June S, III *Football Player, Coach*
%University of Hawaii, Athletic Dept, 2600 Campus Road, Honolulu, HI 96822, USA
Jones, Kelly *Singer, Guitarist (Stereophonics)*
%Marsupial Mgmt, Home Farm, Welfor, Newbury, Berkshire RG20 8HR, England
Jones, L Q *Actor*
2144 1/2 N Cahuenga Blvd, Los Angeles, CA 90068, USA
Jones, Larry W (Chipper) *Baseball Player*
63 W Wieuca Road NE, #2, Atlanta, GA 30342, USA
Jones, Leilani *Actress*
%Writers & Artists, 8383 Wilshire Blvd, #550, Beverly Hills, CA 90211, USA
Jones, LeRoi, (Imamu Amiri Baraka) *Writer*
%State University of New York, Afro American Studies Dept, Stony Brook, NY 11794, USA
Jones, Lou *Track Athlete*
14 Winyah Terrace, New Rochelle, NY 10801, USA
Jones, Marcia Mae *Actress*
4541 Hazeltine, #4, Sherman Oaks, CA 91423, USA
Jones, Marilyn *Actress*
%Kaplan-Stahler Agency, 8383 Wilshire Blvd, #923, Beverly Hills, CA 90211, USA
Jones, Marion *Track Athlete*
PO Box 3065, Cary, NC 27519, USA
Jones, Marvin M *Football Player*
8891 NW 193rd St, Miami, FL 33157, USA
Jones, Maxine *Singer (En Vogue)*
%East West Records, 75 Rockefeller Plaza, #1200, New York, NY 10019, USA
Jones, Merlakia *Basketball Player*
%Cleveland Rockers, Gund Arena, 1 Center Court, Cleveland, OH 44115, USA
Jones, Mick *Guitarist (Clash, Foreigner)*
%Hard to Handle Mgmt, 16501 Ventura Blvd, #602, Encino, CA 91436, USA
Jones, Mickey *Actor, Musician*
%Lichtman/Salners, 12216 Moorpark St, Studio City, CA 91604, USA
Jones, Nathaniel R *Judge*
%US Court of Appeals, US Courthouse, 425 Walnut St, Cincinnati, OH 45202, USA
Jones, Norah *Jazz Singer, Pianist*
%Macklam Feldman Mgmt, 1505 W 2nd Ave, #200, Vancouver BC V6H 3YA, Canada

J

Jones - Jones

Jones, Orlando *Actor*
%Creative Artists Agency, 9830 Wilshire Blvd, Beverly Hills, CA 90212, USA
Jones, P J *Auto Racing Driver*
%Patrick Racing, 8431 Georgetown Road, Indianapolis, IN 46268, USA
Jones, Parnelli *Auto Racing Driver, Executive*
20550 Earl St, Torrance, CA 90503, USA
Jones, Quincy D, Jr *Composer, Conductor*
%Quincy Jones Productions, 3800 Barham Blvd, #503, Los Angeles, CA 90068, USA
Jones, Randall L (Randy) *Baseball Player*
2638 Cranston Dr, Escondido, CA 92025, USA
Jones, Rebinhak *Actress*
%Writers & Artists, 8383 Wilshire Blvd, #550, Beverly Hills, CA 90211, USA
Jones, Renee *Actress*
256 S Robertson, #700, Beverly Hills, CA 90211, USA
Jones, Richard T *Actor*
%Endeavor Talent Agency, 9701 Wilshire Blvd, #1000, Beverly Hills, CA 90212, USA
Jones, Rickie Lee *Singer, Songwriter*
476 Broome St, #6A, New York, NY 10013, USA
Jones, Robert (K C) *Basketball Player, Coach*
6734 Cortez Place NW, Bremerton, WA 98311, USA
Jones, Rosie *Golfer*
4895 High Point Road, Atlanta, GA 30342, USA
Jones, Roy, Jr *Boxer*
%Square Ring, 200 W LaRue St, Pensacola, FL 32501, USA
Jones, Rulon K *Football Player*
3985 N 3775 E, Eden, UT 84310, USA
Jones, Sam J *Actor*
%Artists Group, 10100 Santa Monica Blvd, #2490, Los Angeles, CA 90067, USA
Jones, Samuel (Sam) *Basketball Player*
15417 Tierra Dr, Silver Spring, MD 20906, USA
Jones, Shirley *Actress, Singer*
4531 Noeline Way, Encino, CA 91436, USA
Jones, Simon *Actor*
%Innovative Artists, 1505 10th St, Santa Monica, CA 90401, USA
Jones, Star *Commentator*
%William Morris Agency, 151 El Camino Dr, Beverly Hills, CA 90212, USA
Jones, Stephen *Attorney*
%Jones & Wyatt, PO Box 472, Enid, OK 73702, USA
Jones, Stephen J M *Fashion Designer*
36 Great Queen St, London WC1E 6BT, England
Jones, Steve *Golfer*
3150 Graf St, #5, Bozeman, MT 59715, USA
Jones, Steve *Guitarist (Sex Pistols)*
%Solo Agency, 55 Fulham High St, London SW6 3JJ, England
Jones, Steve *Basketball Player*
2871 NE Alameda St, Portland, OR 97212, USA
Jones, Steven *Physicist*
%Brigham Young University, Physics Dept, Provo, UT 84602, USA
Jones, Taylor *Cartoonist*
%Times-Mirror Syndicate, Times-Mirror Square, Los Angeles, CA 90053, USA
Jones, Terry *Animator, Director (Monty Python)*
%Python Pictures, 34 Thistlewaite Road, London E5 QQQ, England
Jones, Terry *Singer (Point of Grace)*
%TBA Artists Mgmt, 300 10th Ave S, Nashville, TN 37203, USA
Jones, Thomas D *Astronaut*
3105 Windsong Dr, Oakton, VA 22124, USA
Jones, Thomas V *Businessman*
1050 Moraga Dr, Los Angeles, CA 90049, USA
Jones, Todd B G *Baseball Player*
4205 Mays Bend Road, Pell City, AL 35128, USA
Jones, Tom *Singer*
13976 Aubrey Road, Beverly Hills, CA 90210, USA
Jones, Tommy Lee *Actor*
%Michael Black Mgmt, 5750 Wilshire Blvd, #640, Los Angeles, CA 90036, USA
Jones, Trevor *Composer*
46 Ave Road, Highgate, London N6 5DR, England
Jones, Vaughan F R *Mathematician*
%University of California, Mathematics Dept, Berkeley, CA 94720, USA
Jones, Wali *Basketball Player*
PO Box 3642, Winter Haven, FL 33885, USA
Jones, Wallace (Wah-Wah) *Basketball Player*
512 Chinoe Road, Lexington, KY 40502, USA
Jones, Walter *Football Player*
RR 1 Box 128, Carrolton, AL 35447, USA
Jones, Walter Emanuel *Actor*
%K & K Entertainment, 1498 W Sunset Blvd, Los Angeles, CA 90026, USA
Jones, Wayne *Actor, Comedian*
%Smooth Man Productions, 206 Belmont Dr, Palatka, FL 32177, USA

Jones, Wesley *Architect*
%Holt Hinshaw Jones, 320 Florida St, San Francisco, CA 94110, USA
Jones, William A (Dub) *Football Player*
904 Glendale Dr, Ruston, LA 71270, USA
Jong, Erica M *Writer*
PO Box 1434, New York, NY 10021, USA
Jonrowe, Dee Dee *Dog Sled Racer*
PO Box 272, Willow, AK 99688, USA
Jonsen, Albert R *Physician*
%University of Washington, Med School, Medical Ethics Dept, Seattle, WA 98195, USA
Jonsson, Jorgen *Hockey Player*
%Anaheim Mighty Ducks, 2000 E Gene Autry Way, Anaheim, CA 92806, USA
Jonsson, Kenny *Hockey Player*
37 Midway Ave, Locust Valley, NY 11560, USA
Jonze, Spike *Movie Director, Actor*
1741 Ivar Ave, Los Angeles, CA 90028, USA
Joop, Wolfgang *Fashion Designer*
%Joop!, Harvestehuder Weg 22, 20149 Hamburg, Germany
Joos, Gustaaf Cardinal *Religious Leader*
%Dioceseof Ghent, Bisdomplein 1, 9000 Ghent, Belgium
Joost, Edwin D (Eddie) *Baseball Player*
303 Belhaven Circle, Santa Rosa, CA 95409, USA
Joosten, Kathryn *Actress*
%Schiowitz/Clay/Rose, 1680 N Vine St, #1016, Los Angeles, CA 90028, USA
Jopling, T Michael *Government Official, England*
Ainderby Hall, Thirsk, North Yorks YO7 4HZ, England
Jordan, Charles M *Automobile Designer*
PO Box 8330, Rancho Santa Fe, CA 92067, USA
Jordan, Don *Boxer*
5100 2nd Ave, Los Angeles, CA 90043, USA
Jordan, Don D *Businessman*
%Reliant Energy, 1111 Louisiana Ave, Houston, TX 77002, USA
Jordan, Eddie *Basketball Player, Coach*
%Washington Wizards, MCI Centre, 601 F St NW, Washington, DC 20004, USA
Jordan, Glenn *Movie Director*
9401 Wilshire Blvd, #700, Beverly Hills, CA 90212, USA
Jordan, I King *Educator*
%Gallaudet University, President's Office, 800 Florida NW, Washington, DC 20001, USA
Jordan, Kathy *Tennis Player*
114 Walter Hays Dr, Palo Alto, CA 94303, USA
Jordan, Larry R *Army General*
Deputy Commander in Chief, US Army Europe/7th Army, APO, AE 09014, USA
Jordan, Lee Roy *Football Player*
7710 Caruth Blvd, Dallas, TX 75225, USA
Jordan, Mary *Journalist*
%Washington Post, Editorial Dept, 1150 15th St NW, Washington, DC 20071, USA
Jordan, Michael J *Basketball Player*
676 N Michigan Ave, #2940, Chicago, IL 60611, USA
Jordan, Montell *Singer*
%Mitch Schneider Organization, 14724 Ventura Blvd, #410, Sherman Oaks, CA 91403, USA
Jordan, Neil P *Movie Director*
6 Sorrento Terrace, Dalkey, County Dublin, Ireland
Jordan, Payton *Track Coach*
3775 Modoc Road, #264, Santa Barbara, CA 93105, USA
Jordan, Stanley *Jazz Guitarist*
%SJ Productions, 16845 N 29th Ave, #2000, Phoenix, AZ 85053, USA
Jordan, Steve *Football Player*
581 W San Marcos Dr, Chandler, AZ 85225, USA
Jordan, Vernon E, Jr *Civil Rights Activist*
%Lazard Freres, 30 Rockefeller Plaza, #400, New York, NY 10112, USA
Jorgensen, Anker *Prime Minister, Denmark*
Borgbjergvej 1, 2450 SV Copenhagen, Denmark
Jorgenson, Dale W *Economist*
1010 Memorial Dr, #14C, Cambridge, MA 02138, USA
Jorginho *Soccer Player*
Rua Levi Carreiro 420, Barra de Tijuca, Brazil
Jorndt, L Daniel *Businessman*
%Walgreen Co, 200 Wilmot Road, Deerfield, IL 60015, USA
Jose, Jose *Singer*
%Fanny Schatz Mgmt, Melchor Ocampo 309, Mexico City DF CP 11590, Mexico
Josefowicz, Leila *Concert Violinist*
%I M G Artists, 420 W 45th St, New York, NY 10036, USA
Joseph, Curtis *Hockey Player*
%Newport Sports Mgmt, 601-201 City Centre, Mississauga ON L5B 2T4, Canada
Joseph, Daryl J *Astronaut*
1657 Luika Place, Campbell, CA 95008, USA
Joseph, Joseph E, III *Physician*
%University of Michigan, Taubman Center, Ann Arbor, MI 48109, USA

Joseph, Stephen *Physician*
%New York City Health Department, 125 Worth St, New York, NY 10013, USA
Joseph, William *Football Player*
%New York Giants, Giants Stadium, East Rutherford, NJ 07073, USA
Josephine Charlotte *Princess, Luxembourg*
Grand Ducal Palace, Luxembourg, Luxembourg
Josephs, Wilfred *Composer*
4 Grand Union Walk, Kentish Town Rd, Camden Town, London NW1 9LP, England
Josephson, Brian D *Nobel Physics Laureate*
%Cavendish Laboratory, Madingley Road, Cambridge CB3 0HE, England
Josephson, Erland *Actor*
%Royal Dramatic Theater, Nybroplan, Box 5037, 102 41 Stockholm, Sweden
Josephson, Karen *Synchronized Swimmer*
1923 Junction Dr, Concord, CA 94518, USA
Josephson, Lester (Josey) *Football Player*
5388 N Genematas Dr, Tucson, AZ 85704, USA
Josephson, Sarah *Synchronized Swimmer*
1923 Junction Dr, Concord, CA 94518, USA
Jospin, Lionel R *Prime Minister, France*
%Haute-Garonne Conseil, Place Saint Etienne, 31090 Toulouse Cedex, France
Joubert, Beverly *Photographer*
%National Geographic Magazine, 17th & M Sts NW, Washington, DC 20036, USA
Joubert, Dereck *Photographer*
%National Geographic Magazine, 17th & M Sts NW, Washington, DC 20036, USA
Joulwan, George A *Army General*
1348 S 19th St, Arlington, VA 22202, USA
Jourdain, Michel, Jr *Auto Racing Driver*
%Team Rahal, 4601 Lyman Dr, Hilliard, OH 43026, USA
Jourdan, Louis *Actor*
1139 Maybrook Dr, Beverly Hills, CA 90210, USA
Jovanovich, Peter W *Publisher*
%MacMillan, 1177 Ave of Americas, #1965, New York, NY 10036, USA
Jovanovski, Ed *Hockey Player*
2382 NW 49th Lane, Boca Raton, FL 33431, USA
Jovovich, Milla *Actress, Model, Singer*
%The Firm, 9100 Wilshire Blvd, #100W, Beverly Hills, CA 90210, USA
Joyce, Andrea *Sportscaster, Commentator*
%Arts & Entertainment, 235 E 45th St, New York, NY 10017, USA
Joyce, Elaine *Actress*
10745 Chalon Road, Los Angeles, CA 90077, USA
Joyce, Joan *Softball Player, Golfer*
22856 Marbella Circle, Boca Raton, FL 33433, USA
Joyce, John T *Labor Leader*
%Bricklayers & Allied Craftsmen, 815 15th St NW, Washington, DC 20005, USA
Joyce, Tom *Sculptor*
21 Likely Road, Santa Fe, NM 87508, USA
Joyce, William *Artist, Writer*
3302 Centenary Blvd, Shreveport, LA 71104, USA
Joyce, William H *Businessman*
%Union Carbide, 39 Old Ridgebury Road, Danbury, CT 06810, USA
Joyner, Alrederick (Al) *Track Athlete*
%JJK Assoc, PO Box 69047, Saint Louis, MO 63169, USA
Joyner, Michelle *Actress*
%Paradigm Agency, 10100 Santa Monica Blvd, #2500, Los Angeles, CA 90067, USA
Joyner, Wallace K (Wally) *Baseball Player*
856 Hawks Rest Dr, Mapleton, UT 84664, USA
Joyner-Kersee, Jacqueline (Jackie) *Track Athlete*
%JJK Assoc, PO Box 69047, Saint Louis, MO 63169, USA
Jozwiak, Brian J *Football Player, Coach*
51 Rohor Ave, Buckhannon, WV 26201, USA
Ju Ming *Sculptor*
28 Lane 460, Chih Shan Road, Section 2, Taipei, Taiwan
Ju-Ju *Rap Artist (Beatnuts)*
%Agency Group Ltd, 1775 Broadway, #430, New York, NY 10019, USA
Juan Carlos I *King, Spain*
%Palacio de la Zarzuela, 28671 Madrid, Spain
Juanes *Singer*
%William Morris Agency, 151 El Camino Dr, Beverly Hills, CA 90212, USA
Juantorena Danger, Alberto *Track Athlete*
%National Institute for Sports, Sports City, Havana, Cuba
Juby, Marcus L *Religious Leader*
%Reformed Church of Latter-Day Saints, 801 W 23rd St, Independence, MO 64055, USA
Juckes, Gordon W *Hockey Executive*
1475 Avenue B, Big Pine Key, FL 33043, USA
Judd, Ashley *Actress*
PO Box 1569, Franklin, TN 37065, USA
Judd, Bob *Writer*
%Harper Collins Publishers, 10 E 53rd St, New York, NY 10022, USA

Judd, Howard L *Obstetrician*
%University of California, Medical Center, Ob-Gyn Dept, Los Angeles, CA 90024, USA
Judd, Jackie *Commentator*
%ABC-TV, News Dept, 77 W 66th St, New York, NY 10023, USA
Judd, Naomi *Singer (Judds), Songwriter*
%Wynonna Inc, PO Box 1207, Franklin, TN 37065, USA
Judd, Wynonna *Singer (Judds)*
%William Morris Agency, 151 El Camino Dr, Beverly Hills, CA 90212, USA
Judge, George *Economist*
%University of California, Economics Dept, Berkeley, CA 94720, USA
Judge, Mike *Animator (Beavis & Butt-Head)*
%Three Arts Entertainment, 9460 Wilshire Blvd, #700, Beverly Hills, CA 90212, USA
Judkins, Jeff *Basketball Player, Coach*
3471 S 3570 E, Salt Lake City, UT 84109, USA
Jugnauth, Anerood *Prime Minister, Mauritius*
La Caverne 1, Vacoas, Mauritius
Juhl, Finn *Furniture Designer*
%Kratvaenget 15, 2920 Chartottenlund, Denmark
Julavits, Heidi *Writer*
%G P Putnam's Sons, 375 Hudson St, New York, NY 10014, USA
Julesz, Bela *Psychologist*
%Rutgers University, Vision Research Laboratory, New Brunswick, NJ 08903, USA
Julian, Alexander, II *Fashion Designer*
%Alexander Julian Inc, PO Box 60, Georgetown, CT 06829, USA
Julian, Janet *Actress*
%Borinstein Oreck Bogart, 3172 Dona Susana Dr, Studio City, CA 91604, USA
Juliana *Queen, Netherlands*
%Soestdijk Palace, Amsterdamsestraatweg 1, 3744 AA Baarn, Netherlands
Julien, Max *Actor*
3580 Avenida del Sol, Studio City, CA 91604, USA
Julius, DeAnne *Economist*
%Bank of England, Threadneedle St, London EC2R 8AH, England
Jumper, John P *Air Force General*
Chief of Staff, HqUSAF, Pentagon, Washington, DC 20330, USA
Junck, Mary *Publisher*
%Baltimore Sun, 501 N Calvert St, Baltimore, MD 21202, USA
Juncker, Jean-Claude *Prime Minister, Luxembourg*
Hotel de Bourgogne, 4 Rue de la Congregation, 2910 Luxembourg
Jung, Ernst *Writer*
88515 Lagenensligen/Wiltlingen, Germany
Jung, Richard *Neurologist*
Waldhofstr 42, 71691 Freiburg, Germany
Junger, Gil *Movie Director*
%Creative Artists Agency, 9830 Wilshire Blvd, Beverly Hills, CA 90212, USA
Junger, Sebastian *Writer*
%United Talent Agency, 9560 Wilshire Blvd, #500, Beverly Hills, CA 90212, USA
Junior, Ester J (E J) *Football Player*
1001 NW 78th Terrace, Plantation, FL 33322, USA
Junqueira, Bruno *Auto Racing Driver*
2127 Brickell Ave, #3105, Miami, FL 33129, USA
Juppe, Alain M *Prime Minister, France*
Mairie, Place Pey-Berland, 33077 Bordeaux Cedex, France
Jur, Jeffrey *Cinematographer*
10615 Northvale Road, Los Angeles, CA 90064, USA
Juran, Joseph M *Engineer, Management Consultant*
%Juran Institute, 11 River Road, Wilton, CT 06897, USA
Jurasik, Peter *Actor*
969 1/2 Manzanita St, Los Angeles, CA 90029, USA
Jurgensen, Christian A (Sonny), III *Football Player*
PO Box 53, Mount Vernon, VA 22121, USA
Jurgensen, Karen *Editor*
%USA Today, Editorial Dept, 1000 Wilson Blvd, Arlington, VA 22229, USA
Jurich, Tom *Football Player*
%Northern Arizona University, Athletic Dept, Flagstaff, AZ 86011, USA
Juriga, Jim *Football Player*
3001 Easton Place, Saint Charles, IL 60175, USA
Jurinac, Sena *Opera Singer*
%State Opera House, Opernring 2, 1010 Vienna, Austria
Just, Walter *Publisher*
%Milwaukee Journal, 333 W State St, Milwaukee, WI 53203, USA
Just, Ward S *Writer*
36 Ave Junot, Paris, France
Justice, David C *Baseball Player*
15260 Ventura Blvd, #2100, Sherman Oaks, CA 91403, USA
Justice, Donald R *Writer*
338 Rocky Shore Dr, Iowa City, IA 52246, USA
Justman, Seth *Singer, Keyboardist (J Geils Band)*
%Nick Ben-Meir, 652 N Doheny Dr, Los Angeles, CA 90069, USA

K

Kaake, Jeff *Actor*
2533 N Carson St, #3105, Carson City, NV 89706, USA
Kaas, Carmen *Model*
%Men/Women Model Inc, 199 Lafayette St, #700, New York, NY 10012, USA
Kaas, Jon H *Psychologist*
%Vanderbilt University, Psychology Dept, Nashville, TN 37240, USA
Kaas, Patricia *Singer*
%Talent Sorcier, 3 Rue des Petites-Ecuries, 75010 Paris, France
Kaat, James L (Jim) *Baseball Player*
PO Box 1130, Port Salerno, FL 34992, USA
Kabakov, Ilya *Artist*
%Gladstone Gallery, 525 W 52nd St, New York, NY 10019, USA
Kabbah, Ahmad Tejan *President, Sierra Leone*
%President's Office, State House, Independence Ave, Freetown, Sierra Leone
Kabila, Joseph *President, Congo; Army General*
%President's Office, Mont Ngaliema, Kinshasa, Congo Democratic Republic
Kabua, Imata *President, Marshall Islands*
%President's Office, Cabinet Building, PO Box 2, Majuro, Marshall Islands
Kaci *Singer*
%Curb Records, 47 Music Square East, Nashville, TN 37203, USA
Kaczmarek, Jane *Actress*
5761 Valley Oak Dr, Los Angeles, CA 90068, USA
Kadanoff, Leo P *Physicist*
5421 S Cornell Ave, Chicago, IL 60615, USA
Kadare, Ismael *Writer*
63 Blvd Saint-Michel, 75005 Paris, France
Kadenyuk, Leonid K *Cosmonaut*
%Potchta Kosmonavtov, Moskovskoi Oblasti, 141160 Syvisdny Goroduk, Russia
Kadish, Michael S (Mike) *Football Player*
7941 Sudbury Lane SE, Ada, MI 49301, USA
Kadish, Ronald T (Ron) *Air Force General*
Director, Missile Defense Agency, Washington, DC 20301, USA
Kadison, Joshua *Singer, Songwriter, Pianist*
%Nick Bode, 1265 Electric Ave, Venice, CA 90291, USA
Kaestle, Carl F *Historian*
35 Charlesfield St, Providence, RI 02906, USA
Kafelnikov, Yevgeny A *Tennis Player*
%Int'l Mgmt Group, 26 Riverside Dr, Rumson, NJ 07760, USA
Kagan, Daryn *Commentator*
%Cable News Network, News Dept, 1050 Techwood Dr NW, Atlanta, GA 30318, USA
Kagan, Henri Boris *Chemist*
%Universite Paris-Sud, Institut de Chimie Moleculaire, 91405 Orsay, France
Kagan, Jeremy Paul *Movie Director*
2024 N Curson Ave, Los Angeles, CA 90046, USA
Kagen, David *Actor*
6457 Firmament Ave, Van Nuys, CA 91406, USA
Kagge, Erling *Polar Skier*
Munkedamsveien 86, 0270 Oslo, Norway
Kahane, Jeffrey *Concert Pianist, Conductor*
%I M G Artists, 420 W 45th St, New York, NY 10036, USA
Kahin, Brian *Educator*
%Harvard University, Information Infrastructure Project, Cambridge, MA 02138, USA
Kahlil, Aisha *Singer (Sweet Honey in the Rock)*
%Sweet Honey Agency, PO Box 600099, Newtonville, MA 02460, USA
Kahn, Alfred E *Government Official, Economist*
308 N Cayuga St, Ithaca, NY 14850, USA
Kahn, David R *Publisher*
%New Yorker Magazine, Publisher's Office, 4 Times Square, New York, NY 10036, USA
Kahn, Robert E *Computer Scientist*
909 Lynton Place, McLean, VA 22102, USA
Kahn, Roger *Writer*
280 Marcotte Road, Kingston, NY 12401, USA
Kahneman, Daniel *Nobel Economics Laureate*
41 Adams Dr, Princeton, NJ 08540, USA
Kaifu, Toshiki *Prime Minister, Japan*
%House of Representatives, Diet, Tokyo 100, Japan
Kain, Karin A *Ballet Dancer*
%National Ballet of Canada, 470 Queens Quay, Toronto ON M5V 3K4, Canada
Kaiser, A Dale *Biochemist*
832 Santa Fe Ave, Stanford, CA 94305, USA
Kaiser, George B *Financier*
%Bank of Oklahoma, Bank of Oklahoma Tower, PO Box 2300, Tulsa, OK 74102, USA
Kaiser, Michael *Concert Executive*
%Kennedy Center for Performing Arts, Washington, DC 20011, USA
Kaiser, Natasha *Track Athlete*
2601 Hickman Road, Des Moines, IA 50310, USA
Kaiserman, William *Fashion Designer*
29 W 56th St, New York, NY 10019, USA

Kaji, Gautam S — *Financier*
%World Bank Group, 1818 H St NW, Washington, DC 20433, USA

Kakhidze, Djansug I — *Conductor*
Leselidze St 18, 380005 Tbilisi, Georgia

Kakutani, Michiko — *Journalist*
%New York Times, Editorial Dept, 229 W 43rd St, New York, NY 10036, USA

Kalafat, Ed — *Basketball Player*
1814 Pinehurst Ave, Saint Paul, MN 55116, USA

Kalam, A P J Abdul — *President, India*
%President's Office, Bharat Ka, Rashtrapti Bhavan, New Delhi 110004, India

Kalangis, Ike — *Financier*
%Boatmen's Sunwest, 303 Roma Ave NW, Albuquerque, NM 87102, USA

Kalas, Harry — *Sportscaster*
%Philadelphia Phillies, Veterans Stadium, 3501 S Broad, Philadelphia, PA 19148, USA

Kalashnikov, Mikhail T — *Weapon Designer (AK-47), Army General*
%A O Izhmash, 426006 Izhevsk, Udmurtia Republic, Russia

Kalb, Marvin — *Commentator, Educator*
%Harvard University, Shorenstein Center, 79 J F Kennedy St, Cambridge, MA 02138, USA

Kalber, Floyd — *Commentator*
%NBC-TV, News Dept, 30 Rockefeller Plaza, New York, NY 10112, USA

Kalem, Toni — *Actress*
%House of Representatives, 400 S Beverly Dr, #101, Beverly Hills, CA 90212, USA

Kalember, Patricia — *Actress*
%Innovative Artists, 1505 10th St, Santa Monica, CA 90401, USA

Kalen, Herbert D — *Vietnam War Air Force Hero*
General Delivery, Angel Fire, NM 87710, USA

Kaleri, Aleksandr Y — *Cosmonaut*
141 160 Svyosdny Gorodok, Moskovskoi Oblasti, Potchta Kosmonavtor, Russia

Kalichstein, Joseph — *Concert Pianist*
%I C M Artists, 40 W 57th St, New York, NY 10019, USA

Kalikow, Peter S — *Publisher*
%H J Kalikow Co, 101 Park Ave, New York, NY 10178, USA

Kalina, Mike — *Chef*
%Travelin' Gourmet Show, PBS-TV, 1320 Braddock Place, Alexandria, VA 22314, USA

Kalina, Richard — *Artist*
44 King St, New York, NY 10014, USA

Kaline, Albert W (Al) — *Baseball Player*
%Detroit Tigers, Comerica Park, 2100 Woodward Ave, Detroit, MI 48201, USA

Kalis, Todd A — *Football Player*
172 Woodhaven Dr, Mars, PA 16046, USA

Kalish, Martin — *Labor Leader*
%School Administrators Federation, 853 Broadway, New York, NY 10003, USA

Kalish, Robert P — *Financier*
%Government National Mortgage Assn, 451 7th St SW, Washington, DC 20410, USA

Kalitta, Connie — *Auto Racing Driver*
%American International Airways, 804 Willow Run Airport, Ypsilanti, MI 48198, USA

Kallaugher, Kevin (Kall) — *Editorial Cartoonist*
%Baltimore Sun, Editorial Dept, 501 N Calvert St, Baltimore, MD 21202, USA

Kallen, Kitty — *Singer*
35 Winthrop Place, Englewood, NJ 07631, USA

Kallir, Lilian — *Concert Pianist*
%Columbia Artists Mgmt Inc, 165 W 57th St, New York, NY 10019, USA

Kallmann, Gerhard M — *Architect*
%Kallmann McKinnell Wood, 939 Boylston St, Boston, MA 02115, USA

Kalman, Rudolf E — *Mathematician*
%ETH Zentrum, 8092 Zurich, Switzerland

Kalpokas, Donald — *Prime Minister, Vanuatu*
%Prime Minister's Office, PO Box 110, Port Vila, Vanuta

Kalule, Ayub — *Boxer*
%Palle, Skjulet, Bagsvaert 12, Copenhagen 2880, Denmark

Kalyagin, Aleksander A — *Actor*
1905 Goda Str 3, #91, Moscow 123100, Russia

Kamal Gray — *Keyboardist (Roots)*
%William Morris Agency, 1325 Ave of Americas, New York, NY 10019, USA

Kamali, Norma — *Fashion Designer*
%OMO Norma Kamali, 11 W 56th St, New York, NY 10019, USA

Kamarck, Martin A — *Financier*
%Export-Import Bank, 811 Vermont Ave NW, Washington, DC 20571, USA

Kamb, Alexander — *Geneticist*
202 Katahdin Dr, Lexington, MA 02421, USA

Kamel, Stanley — *Actor*
%Irv Schechter, 9300 Wilshire Blvd, #410, Beverly Hills, CA 90212, USA

Kamen, Dean — *Inventor (Portable Dialysis Machine)*
15 W Wind Dr, Bedford, NH 03110, USA

Kamen, Michael — *Composer, Conductor*
%B M I, 8730 Sunset Blvd, #300, Los Angeles, CA 90069, USA

Kamensky, Valeri — *Hockey Player*
4 Bermuda Lake Dr, West Palm Beach, FL 33418, USA

K

Kamin, Blair *Archietctural Critic*
%Chicago Tribune, Editorial Dept, 435 N Michigan Ave, Chicago, IL 60611, USA
Kaminir, Lisa *Actress*
%Ellis Talent Group, 14241 N Maple Dr, #207, Sherman Oaks, CA 01423, USA
Kaminski, Janusz Z *Cinematographer*
23801 Calabasas Road, #2004, Calabasas, CA 91302, USA
Kaminski, Marek *Explorer*
Ul Dickmana 14/15, 80-339 Gdansk, Poland
Kaminsky, Arthur C *Sports Attorney*
%Athletes & Artists, 888 7th Ave, #3700, New York, NY 10106, USA
Kaminsky, Walter *Chemist*
%Hamburg University, Martin-Luther-King Platz 6, 20146 Hamburg, Germany
Kamisar, Yale *Attorney, Educator*
2910 Daleview Dr, Ann Arbor, MI 48105, USA
Kamm, Henry *Journalist*
%New York Times, Editorial Dept, 229 W 43rd St, New York, NY 10036, USA
Kammen, Michael G *Historian*
%Cornell University, History Dept, McGraw Hall, Ithaca, NY 14853, USA
Kamoze, Ini *Singer*
%Famous Artists Agency, 250 W 57th St, New York, NY 10107, USA
Kampelman, Max M *Government Official, Diplomat*
3154 Highland Place NW, Washington, DC 20008, USA
Kamu, Okko T *Conductor*
Calle Mozart 7, Rancho Domingo, 29369 Benalmedina Pueblo, Spain
Kan, Yuet Wai *Geneticist*
20 Yerba Buena Ave, San Francisco, CA 94127, USA
Kanaan, Tony *Auto Racing Driver*
%Mo Nunn Racing, 2920 Fortune Circle W, #E, Indianapolis, IN 46241, USA
Kanakaredes, Melina *Actress*
%Gersh Agency, 232 N Canon Dr, Beverly Hills, CA 90210, USA
Kanal, Tony *Bassist, Songwriter (No Doubt)*
%Rebel Waltz Inc, 31652 2nd Ave, Laguna Beach, CA 92651, USA
Kanaly, Steve *Actor*
4663 Grand Ave, Ojai, CA 93023, USA
Kanamori, Hiroo *Geophysicist*
%California Institute of Technology, Geophysics Dept, Pasadena, CA 91125, USA
Kananin, Roman G *Architect*
%Joint-Stock Mosprojekt, 13/14 1 Brestkaya Str, 125190 Moscow, Russia
Kancheli, Giya A (Georgy) *Composer*
Tovstonogov Str 6, 380064 Tbilisi, Georgia
Kandel, Eric R *Nobel Medicine Laureate*
9 Sigma Place, Bronx, NY 10471, USA
Kander, John H *Composer*
%B M I, 8730 Sunset Blvd, #300, Los Angeles, CA 90069, USA
Kane Elson, Marion *Synchronized Swimmer*
4669 Badger Road, Santa Rosa, CA 95409, USA
Kane, Carol *Actress*
%Slater, PO Box 8002, Universal City, CA 91618, USA
Kane, Christian *Actor*
%Blue Train Entertainment, 9333 Wilshire Blvd, G Level, Beverly Hills, CA 90210, USA
Kane, John C *Businessman*
%Cardinal Health, 7000 Cardinal Place, Dublin, OH 43017, USA
Kane, Kelly *Actress*
%D H Talent, 1800 N Highland Ave, #300, Los Angeles, CA 90028, USA
Kane, Nick *Singer (Mavericks)*
%AstroMedia, 1620 16th Ave S, Nashville, TN 37212, USA
Kanell, Danny *Football Player*
5340 NE 33rd Ave, Fort Lauderdale, FL 33308, USA
Kanew, Jeffrey R *Movie Director*
%Gersh Agency, 232 N Canon Dr, Beverly Hills, CA 90210, USA
Kang, Dong-Suk *Concert Violinist*
%Clarion/Seven Muses, 47 Whitehall Park, London N19 3TW, England
Kanievska, Marek *Movie Director*
%International Creative Mgmt, 8942 Wilshire Blvd, #219, Beverly Hills, CA 90211, USA
Kanin, Fay *Writer*
653 Palisades Beach Road, Santa Monica, CA 90402, USA
Kann Valar, Paula *Alpine Skier*
34 Hubertus Ring, Franconia, NH 03580, USA
Kann, Peter R *Businessman, Publisher, Journalist*
%Dow Jones Co, 200 Liberty St, New York, NY 10281, USA
Kanne, Michael S *Judge*
%US Court of Appeals, PO Box 1340, Lafayette, IN 47902, USA
Kannenberg, Bernd *Track Athlete*
Sportschule, 87527 Sonthofen/Allgau, Germany
Kanovitz, Howard *Artist*
361 N Sea Mecox Road, Southampton, NY 11968, USA
Kanter, Hal *Movie, TV Producer; Screenwriter*
%Hecox Horn Wheeler, 4730 Woodman Ave, Sherman Oaks, CA 91423, USA

Kantner, Paul *Guitarist (Jefferson Airplane, Starship)*
%Ron Rainey Mgmt, 315 S Beverly Dr, #407, Beverly Hills, CA 90212, USA
Kantor, Michael (Mickey) *Secretary, Commerce*
4436 Edmunds St NW, Washington, DC 20007, USA
Kantrowitz, Adrian *Heart Surgeon*
70 Gallogly Road, Lake Angelus, MI 48326, USA
Kantrowitz, Arthur R *Physicist*
4 Downing Road, Hanover, NH 03755, USA
Kao, Archie *Actor*
%Gold Marshak Liedtke, 3500 W Olive Ave, #1400, Burbank, CA 91505, USA
Kao, Charles K *Electrical Engineer*
%Transtech Services, 3 Gloucester Road, Wanchai, Hong Kong, China
Kapanen, Sami *Hockey Player*
104 Royal Pine Court, Cary, NC 27511, USA
Kapioitas, John *Businessman*
%ITT Sheraton Corp, 1111 Westchester Ave, West Harrison, NY 10604, USA
Kaplan, Gabe *Actor, Comedian*
9551 Hidden Valley Road, Beverly Hills, CA 90210, USA
Kaplan, Jonathan S *Movie Director*
4323 Ben Ave, Studio City, CA 91604, USA
Kaplan, Justin *Writer*
PO Box 219, Truro, MA 02666, USA
Kaplan, Marvin *Actor*
PO Box 1522, Burbank, CA 91507, USA
Kaplan, Nathan O *Biochemist*
8587 La Jolla Scenic Dr, La Jolla, CA 92037, USA
Kaplow, Herbert E *Commentator*
211 N Van Buren St, Falls Church, VA 22046, USA
Kapoor, Anish *Sculptor*
33 Coleherne Road, London SW10, England
Kapoor, Shashi *Actor*
%Film Valas, Janki Kutir, Juhu Church Road, Bombay 400049, India
Kapor, Mitchell D *Computer Programmer*
%Open Source Application Foundation, 177 Post St, #900, San Francisco, CA 94108, USA
Kapp, Joseph (Joe) *Football Player, Coach*
233 Edelen Ave, Los Gatos, CA 95030, USA
Kaprisky, Valerie *Actress*
%Artmedia, 20 Ave Rapp, 75007 Paris, France
Kapture, Mitzi *Actress*
%Bradley-Kapture, 3605 Sandy Plains Road, #240-116, Marietta, GA 30066, USA
Karageorghis, Vassos *Archaeologist*
%Foundation Anastasios Leventis, 28 Sofoulis St, Nicosia, Cyprus
Karamanov, Alemdar S *Composer*
Voykova Str 2, #4, Simferopol, Crimea, Ukraine
Karan, Donna *Fashion Designer*
%Donna Karan Co, 361 Newbury St, Boston, MA 02115, USA
Karathanasis, Sotirios K *Medical Researcher*
%Harvard Medical School, 25 Shattuck St, Boston, MA 02115, USA
Karatz, Bruce E *Businessman*
%Kaufman & Broad Home, 10990 Wilshire Blvd, Los Angeles, CA 90024, USA
Karelskaya, Rimma K *Ballerina*
%Bolshoi Theater, Teatralnaya Pl 1, 103009 Moscow, Russia
Karieva, Bernara *Ballerina*
%Navoi Opera Theater, 28 M K Otaturk St, 700029 Tashkent, Uzbekistan
Karim-Lamrani, Mohammed *Prime Minister, Morocco*
Rue du Mont Saint Michel, Anfa Superieur, Casablanca 21300, Morocco
Karimov, Islam M *President, Uzbekistan*
%President's Office, Uzbekistansky Prosp 45, Tashkent, Uzbekistan
Karin, Anna *Actress*
%Greene Assoc, 7080 Hollywood Blvd, #1017, Los Angeles, CA 90028, USA
Karina, Anna *Actress*
%Artmedia, 20 Ave Rapp, 75007 Paris, France
Kariya, Paul *Hockey Player*
2493 Aquasanta, Tustin, CA 92782, USA
Karl, George *Basketball Coach*
10936 N Port Washington Road, Mequon, WI 53092, USA
Karle, Isabella *Chemist*
6304 Lakeview Dr, Falls Church, VA 22041, USA
Karle, Jerome *Nobel Chemistry Laureate*
6304 Lakeview Dr, Falls Church, VA 22041, USA
Karlen, John *Actor*
PO Box 1195, Santa Monica, CA 90406, USA
Karlin, Samuel *Mathematician*
%Stanford University, Mathematics Dept, Stanford, CA 94305, USA
Karling, John S *Mycologist*
1219 Tuckahoe Lane, West Lafayette, IN 47906, USA
Karlsson, Lena *Singer (Komeda)*
%MOB Agency, 6404 Wilshire Blvd, #807, Los Angeles, CA 90048, USA

Karlstad, Geir *Speedskater*
Hamarveien 5A, 1472 Fjellhamar, Norway
Karlzen, Mary *Singer, Songwriter*
%Little Big Man, 155 Ave of Americas, #700, New York, NY 10013, USA
Karmanos, Peter, Jr *Businessman, Hockey Executive*
%Compuware Corp, 1 Campus Martius, Detroit, MI 48226, USA
Karmazin, Mel *Businessman*
%Viacom Inc, 1515 Broadway, New York, NY 10036, USA
Karmi, Ram *Architect*
%Karmi Architects, 17 Kaplan St, Tel Aviv 64734, Israel
Karmi-Melamede, Ada *Architect*
%Karmi Architects, 17 Kaplan St, Tel Aviv 64734, Israel
Karn, Richard *Actor*
%Special Artists Agency, 345 N Maple Dr, #302, Beverly Hills, CA 90210, USA
Karnes, David K *Senator, NE*
%Kutak Rock, Omaha Building, 1650 Farnam St, Omaha, NE 68102, USA
Karnow, Stanley *Historian*
10850 Spring Knolls Dr, Potomac, MD 20854, USA
Karolyi, Bela *Gymnastics Coach*
478 Forest Service 200 Road, Huntsville, TX 77340, USA
Karon, Jan *Writer*
7060 Esmont Farm, Esmont, VA 22937, USA
Karp, Richard M *Computer Scientist, Engineer*
%University of Washington, Computer Science Dept, Seattle, WA 98195, USA
Karpati, Gyorgy *Water Polo Player*
II Liva Utca 1, 1025 Budapest, Hungary
Karpatkin, Rhoda H *Publisher*
%Consumer Reports Magazine, 101 Truman Ave, Yonkers, NY 10703, USA
Karplus, Martin *Chemist*
%Harvard University, Chemistry Dept, Cambridge, MA 02138, USA
Karpov, Anatoly *Chess Player*
%International Peace Fund, Prechistenka 10, Moscow, Russia
Karr, Mary *Writer*
%Syracuse University, English Dept, Syracuse, NY 13244, USA
Karras, Alexander G (Alex) *Football Player, Actor*
7943 Woodrow Wilson Dr, Los Angeles, CA 90046, USA
Karrass, Chester L *Writer*
1633 Stanford St, Santa Monica, CA 90404, USA
Karros, Eric P *Baseball Player*
6212 Madra Ave, San Diego, CA 92120, USA
Kartheiser, Vincent *Actor*
%Douglas Mgmt, 515 N Robertson Blvd, West Hollywood, CA 90048, USA
Karusseit, Ursula *Actress*
%Volksbuhne, Rasa Luxemburg Platz, 10178 Berlin, Germany
Karzai, Hamid *Prime Minister, Afghanistan*
%Prime Minister's Office, Shar Rahi Sedarat, Kabul, Afghanistan
Kasaks, Sally Frame *Businesswoman*
%AnnTaylor Stores, 142 W 57th St, New York, NY 10019, USA
Kasarova, Vesselina *Opera Singer*
%Columbia Artists Mgmt Inc, 165 W 57th St, New York, NY 10019, USA
Kasatkina, Natalya K *Ballerina, Choreographer*
Saint Karietny Riad, H 5/10, B 37, 103006 Moscow, Russia
Kasatonov, Alexei *Hockey Player*
153 Eagle Rock Way, Montclair, NJ 07042, USA
Kasay, John *Football Player*
12707 NE 101st Place, Kirkland, WA 98033, USA
Kasdan, Lawrence E *Movie Director, Writer*
%Creative Artists Agency, 9830 Wilshire Blvd, Beverly Hills, CA 90212, USA
Kasem, Casey *Entertainer, Actor*
138 N Mapleton Dr, Los Angeles, CA 90077, USA
Kasem, Jean *Actress*
138 N Mapleton Dr, Los Angeles, CA 90077, USA
Kaser, Helmut A *Soccer Executive*
Hitzigweg 11, 8032 Zurich, Switzerland
Kasha, Al *Composer, Lyricist*
458 N Oakhurst Dr, #102, Beverly Hills, CA 90210, USA
Kashkashian, Kim *Concert Violist*
%Musicians Corporate Mgmt, PO Box 589, Millbrook, NY 12545, USA
Kaskey, Raymond J *Sculptor*
%Portlandia Productions, PO Box 25658, Portland, OR 97298, USA
Kason, Corinne *Actress*
%Lovell Assoc, 7095 Hollywood Blvd, #1006, Los Angeles, CA 90028, USA
Kasparaitis, Darius *Hockey Player*
48 Steers Ave, Northport, NY 11768, USA
Kasparov, Garri K *Chess Player*
%Russian Chess Federation, Luzhnetskaya 8, 119270 Moscow, Russia
Kasper, Steve *Hockey Player, Coach*
156 Lancaster Road, North Andover, MA 01845, USA

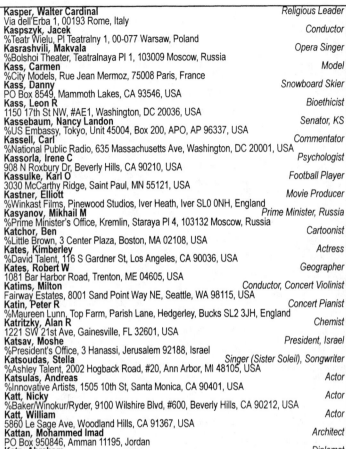

Kasper, Walter Cardinal *Religious Leader*
Via dell'Erba 1, 00193 Rome, Italy
Kaspszyk, Jacek *Conductor*
%Teatr Wielu, Pl Teatralny 1, 00-077 Warsaw, Poland
Kasrashvili, Makvala *Opera Singer*
%Bolshoi Theater, Teatralnaya Pl 1, 103009 Moscow, Russia
Kass, Carmen *Model*
%City Models, Rue Jean Mermoz, 75008 Paris, France
Kass, Danny *Snowboard Skier*
PO Box 8549, Mammoth Lakes, CA 93546, USA
Kass, Leon R *Bioethicist*
1150 17th St NW, #AE1, Washington, DC 20036, USA
Kassebaum, Nancy Landon *Senator, KS*
%US Embassy, Tokyo, Unit 45004, Box 200, APO, AP 96337, USA
Kassell, Carl *Commentator*
%National Public Radio, 635 Massachusetts Ave, Washington, DC 20001, USA
Kassorla, Irene C *Psychologist*
908 N Roxbury Dr, Beverly Hills, CA 90210, USA
Kassulke, Karl O *Football Player*
3030 McCarthy Ridge, Saint Paul, MN 55121, USA
Kastner, Elliott *Movie Producer*
%Winkast Films, Pinewood Studios, Iver Heath, Iver SL0 0NH, England
Kasyanov, Mikhail M *Prime Minister, Russia*
%Prime Minister's Office, Kremlin, Staraya Pl 4, 103132 Moscow, Russia
Katchor, Ben *Cartoonist*
%Little Brown, 3 Center Plaza, Boston, MA 02108, USA
Kates, Kimberley *Actress*
%David Talent, 116 S Gardner St, Los Angeles, CA 90036, USA
Kates, Robert W *Geographer*
1081 Bar Harbor Road, Trenton, ME 04605, USA
Katims, Milton *Conductor, Concert Violinist*
Fairway Estates, 8001 Sand Point Way NE, Seattle, WA 98115, USA
Katin, Peter R *Concert Pianist*
%Maureen Lunn, Top Farm, Parish Lane, Hedgerley, Bucks SL2 3JH, England
Katritzky, Alan R *Chemist*
1221 SW 21st Ave, Gainesville, FL 32601, USA
Katsav, Moshe *President, Israel*
%President's Office, 3 Hanassi, Jerusalem 92188, Israel
Katsoudas, Stella *Singer (Sister Soleil), Songwriter*
%Ashley Talent, 2002 Hogback Road, #20, Ann Arbor, MI 48105, USA
Katsulas, Andreas *Actor*
%Innovative Artists, 1505 10th St, Santa Monica, CA 90401, USA
Katt, Nicky *Actor*
%Baker/Winokur/Ryder, 9100 Wilshire Blvd, #600, Beverly Hills, CA 90212, USA
Katt, William *Actor*
5860 Le Sage Ave, Woodland Hills, CA 91367, USA
Kattan, Mohammed Imad *Architect*
PO Box 950846, Amman 11195, Jordan
Katz, Abraham *Diplomat*
%US Council for International Business, 1212 Ave of Americas, New York, NY 10036, USA
Katz, Alex *Artist*
435 W Broadway, New York, NY 10012, USA
Katz, Donald L *Petroleum Engineer*
2011 Washtenaw Ave, Ann Arbor, MI 48104, USA
Katz, Douglas J (Doug) *Navy Admiral*
1530 Gordon Cove Dr, Annapolis, MD 21403, USA
Katz, Harold *Basketball Executive*
%Philadelphia 76ers, 1st Union Center, 3601 S Broad St, Philadelphia, PA 19148, USA
Katz, Hilda *Artist*
915 W End Ave, #5D, New York, NY 10025, USA
Katz, Jonathan *Actor, Comedian, Animator*
%Creative Artists Agency, 9830 Wilshire Blvd, Beverly Hills, CA 90212, USA
Katz, Michael *Pediatrician*
1 Griggs Lane, Chappaqua, NY 10514, USA
Katz, Omri *Actor*
%JH Productions, 23679 Calabasas Road, #333, Calabasas, CA 91302, USA
Katz, Samuel L *Pediatrician*
1917 Wildcat Creek Road, Chapel Hill, NC 27516, USA
Katz, Simon *Guitarist (Jamiroquai)*
%Searles, Chapel, 26A Munster St, London SW6 4EN, England
Katz, Stephen M *Cinematographer*
8581 Santa Monica Blvd, PO Box 453, West Hollywood, CA 90069, USA
Katz, Tonnie L *Editor*
%Orange County Register, Editorial Dept, 625 N Grand Ave, Santa Ana, CA 92701, USA
Katz, Vera *Mayor*
%Mayor's Office, City Hall, 1221 SW 4th Ave, #340, Portland, OR 97204, USA
Katzenbach, John *Writer*
%Knopf/Ballatine/Fawcett Publishers, 201 E 50th St, New York, NY 10022, USA

K

Katzenbach, Nicholas deB *Attorney General*
33 Greenhouse Dr, Princeton, NJ 08540, USA
Katzenberg, Jeffrey *Businessman*
%DreamWorks SKG, 100 Universal City Plaza, Universal City, CA 91608, USA
Katzenmoyer, Andy *Football Player*
859 W Main St, Westerville, OH 43081, USA
Katzir, Ephraim *President, Israel*
%Weizmann Institute of Science, PO Box 26, Rehovot, Israel
Katzur, Klaus *Swimmer*
Robert-Siewart-Str 76, 0912 Chemnitz, Germany
Kaufman, Dan S *Hematologist*
%University of Wisconsin, Medical School, Hematology Dept, Madison, WI 53706, USA
Kaufman, Henry *Financier*
%Henry Kaufman Co, 65 E 55th St, New York, NY 10022, USA
Kaufman, Napoleon *Football Player*
72 Incline Green Lane, Alamo, CA 94507, USA
Kaufmann, Bob (Ajax) *Basketball Player*
1677 Rivermist Dr SW, Lilburn, GA 30047, USA
Kaukonen, Jorma *Guitarist (Jefferson Airplane/Hot Tuna)*
%Agency Group Ltd, 1775 Broadway, #430, New York, NY 10019, USA
Kavanaugh, Kenneth W (Ken) *Football Player*
4907 Palm Aire Dr, Sarasota, FL 34243, USA
Kavandi, Janet L *Astronaut*
3907 Park Circle Way, Houston, TX 77059, USA
Kavner, Julie *Actress*
25154 Malibu Road, #2, Malibu, CA 90265, USA
Kawakubo, Rei *Fashion Designer*
%Comme des Garcons, 5-11-5 Minamiaoyama, Minatoku, Tokyo, Japan
Kawalerowicz, Jersy *Movie Director, Writer*
Ul Marconich 5 m 21, 02-954 Warsaw, Poland
Kawawa, Rashidi M *Prime Minister, Tanzania*
%Ministry of Defense, Dar es Salaam, Tanzania
Kay, Alan C *Computer Software (Object Oriented)*
%Viewpoints Research Institute, 1209 Grand Capital Ave, Glendale, CA 91201, USA
Kay, Dianne *Actress*
1559 Palisades Dr, Pacific Palisades, CA 90272, USA
Kay, Jason (Jay) *Singer (Jamiroquai)*
%Searles, Chapel, 26A Munster St, London SW6 4 EN, England
Kay, John *Singer, Guitarist (Steppenwolf)*
%Elite Management Corp, 2211 Norfolk St, #760, Houston, TX 77098, USA
Kaye, Judy *Actress, Singer*
%Bret Adams, 448 W 44th St, New York, NY 10036, USA
Kaye, Tony *Keyboardist (Yes)*
%Sun Artists, 9 Hillgate St, London W8 7SP, England
Kaysen, Carl *Economist*
41 Holden St, Cambridge, MA 02138, USA
Kayser, Elmer L *Historian*
2921 34th St NW, Washington, DC 20008, USA
Kazan, Lainie *Singer, Actress*
9903 Santa Monica Blvd, #283, Beverly Hills, CA 90212, USA
Kazankina, Tatyana *Track Athlete*
Hoshimina St, 111211 Saint Petersburg, Russia
Kazarnovskaya, Lubov Y *Opera Singer*
Hohenbergstr 50, 1120 Vienna, Austria
Kazmaier, Richard W (Dick), Jr *Football Player*
24 Dockside Lane, Box 29, Key Largo, FL 33037, USA
Keach, James *Actor*
%Metropolitan Talent Agency, 4526 Wilshire Blvd, Los Angeles, CA 90010, USA
Keach, Stacy *Actor*
27525 Winding Way, Malibu, CA 90265, USA
Keady, Gene *Basketball Coach*
%Purdue University, Mackey Arena, West Lafayette, IN 47907, USA
Kean, Thomas H *Governor, NJ; Educator*
%Drew University, President's Office, 36 Madison Ave, Madison, NJ 07940, USA
Keanan, Staci *Actress*
%Metropolitan Talent Agency, 4526 Wilshire Blvd, Los Angeles, CA 90010, USA
Keane, Bil *Cartoonist (Family Circus)*
5815 E Joshua Tree Lane, Paradise Valley, AZ 85253, USA
Keane, Glen *Animator*
%Walt Disney Studios, Animation Dept, 500 S Buena Vista St, Burbank, CA 91521, USA
Keane, John M (Jack) *Army General*
Vice Chief of Staff, HqUSA, Pentagon, Washington, DC 20310, USA
Keane, Kerrie *Actress*
%S D B Partners, 1801 Ave of Stars, #902, Los Angeles, CA 90067, USA
Keane, Sean *Fiddler (Chieftains)*
%Macklam Feldman Mgmt, 1505 W 2nd Ave, #200, Vancouver BC V6H 3Y4, Canada
Kear, David *Geologist*
34 W End, Ohope, New Zealand

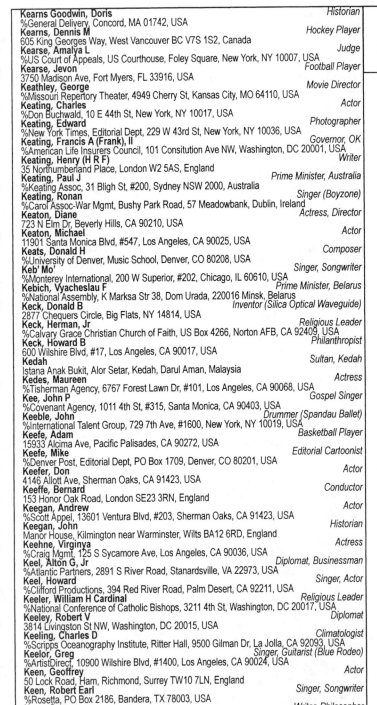

Kearns Goodwin, Doris *Historian*
%General Delivery, Concord, MA 01742, USA
Kearns, Dennis M *Hockey Player*
605 King Georges Way, West Vancouver BC V7S 1S2, Canada
Kearse, Amalya L *Judge*
%US Court of Appeals, US Courthouse, Foley Square, New York, NY 10007, USA
Kearse, Jevon *Football Player*
3750 Madison Ave, Fort Myers, FL 33916, USA
Keathley, George *Movie Director*
%Missouri Repertory Theater, 4949 Cherry St, Kansas City, MO 64110, USA
Keating, Charles *Actor*
%Don Buchwald, 10 E 44th St, New York, NY 10017, USA
Keating, Edward *Photographer*
%New York Times, Editorial Dept, 229 W 43rd St, New York, NY 10036, USA
Keating, Francis A (Frank), II *Governor, OK*
%American Life Insurers Council, 101 Consitution Ave NW, Washington, DC 20001, USA
Keating, Henry (H R F) *Writer*
35 Northumberland Place, London W2 5AS, England
Keating, Paul J *Prime Minister, Australia*
%Keating Assoc, 31 Bligh St, #200, Sydney NSW 2000, Australia
Keating, Ronan *Singer (Boyzone)*
%Carol Assoc-War Mgmt, Bushy Park Road, 57 Meadowbank, Dublin, Ireland
Keaton, Diane *Actress, Director*
723 N Elm Dr, Beverly Hills, CA 90210, USA
Keaton, Michael *Actor*
11901 Santa Monica Blvd, #547, Los Angeles, CA 90025, USA
Keats, Donald H *Composer*
%University of Denver, Music School, Denver, CO 80208, USA
Keb' Mo' *Singer, Songwriter*
%Monterey International, 200 W Superior, #202, Chicago, IL 60610, USA
Kebich, Vyacheslau F *Prime Minister, Belarus*
%National Assembly, K Marksa Str 38, Dom Urada, 220016 Minsk, Belarus
Keck, Donald B *Inventor (Silica Optical Waveguide)*
2877 Chequers Circle, Big Flats, NY 14814, USA
Keck, Herman, Jr *Religious Leader*
%Calvary Grace Christian Church of Faith, US Box 4266, Norton AFB, CA 92409, USA
Keck, Howard B *Philanthropist*
600 Wilshire Blvd, #17, Los Angeles, CA 90017, USA
Kedah *Sultan, Kedah*
Istana Anak Bukit, Alor Setar, Kedah, Darul Aman, Malaysia
Kedes, Maureen *Actress*
%Tisherman Agency, 6767 Forest Lawn Dr, #101, Los Angeles, CA 90068, USA
Kee, John P *Gospel Singer*
%Covenant Agency, 1011 4th St, #315, Santa Monica, CA 90403, USA
Keeble, John *Drummer (Spandau Ballet)*
%International Talent Group, 729 7th Ave, #1600, New York, NY 10019, USA
Keefe, Adam *Basketball Player*
15933 Alcima Ave, Pacific Palisades, CA 90272, USA
Keefe, Mike *Editorial Cartoonist*
%Denver Post, Editorial Dept, PO Box 1709, Denver, CO 80201, USA
Keefer, Don *Actor*
4146 Allott Ave, Sherman Oaks, CA 91423, USA
Keeffe, Bernard *Conductor*
153 Honor Oak Road, London SE23 3RN, England
Keegan, Andrew *Actor*
%Scott Appel, 13601 Ventura Blvd, #203, Sherman Oaks, CA 91423, USA
Keegan, John *Historian*
Manor House, Kilmington near Warminster, Wilts BA12 6RD, England
Keehne, Virginya *Actress*
%Craig Mgmt, 125 S Sycamore Ave, Los Angeles, CA 90036, USA
Keel, Alton G, Jr *Diplomat, Businessman*
%Atlantic Partners, 2891 S River Road, Stanardsville, VA 22973, USA
Keel, Howard *Singer, Actor*
%Clifford Productions, 394 Red River Road, Palm Desert, CA 92211, USA
Keeler, William H Cardinal *Religious Leader*
%National Conference of Catholic Bishops, 3211 4th St, Washington, DC 20017, USA
Keeley, Robert V *Diplomat*
3814 Livingston St NW, Washington, DC 20015, USA
Keeling, Charles D *Climatologist*
%Scripps Oceanography Institute, Ritter Hall, 9500 Gilman Dr, La Jolla, CA 92093, USA
Keelor, Greg *Singer, Guitarist (Blue Rodeo)*
%ArtistDirect, 10900 Wilshire Blvd, #1400, Los Angeles, CA 90024, USA
Keen, Geoffrey *Actor*
50 Lock Road, Ham, Richmond, Surrey TW10 7LN, England
Keen, Robert Earl *Singer, Songwriter*
%Rosetta, PO Box 2186, Bandera, TX 78003, USA
Keen, Sam *Writer, Philosopher*
16331 Norrbom Road, Sonoma, CA 95476, USA

Keenan, Joseph D *Labor Leader*
2727 29th St NW, Washington, DC 20008, USA

Keenan, Maynard James *Singer (Tool, Perfect Circle)*
%Spivak Entertainment, 11845 W Olympic Blvd, #1125, Los Angeles, CA 90064, USA

Keenan, Mike *Hockey Coach, Executive*
550 NE 21st Ave, #13, Deerfield Beach, FL 33441, USA

Keene, Donald L *Language Educator*
%Columbia University, Language Dept, Kent Hall, New York, NY 10027, USA

Keene, Tommy *Singer, Songwriter*
%Black Park Mgmt, PO Box 107, Sunbury, NC 27979, USA

Keener, Catherine *Actress*
%More/Medavoy, 7920 W Sunset Blvd, #400, Los Angeles, CA 90046, USA

Keenlyside, Simon *Opera Singer*
%Columbia Artists Mgmt Inc, 165 W 57th St, New York, NY 10019, USA

Keeny, Spurgeon M, Jr *Association Executive*
3600 Albemarle St NW, Washington, DC 20008, USA

Keeshan, Bob *Actor (Captain Kangaroo)*
%Robert Keeshan Assoc, 40 W 57th St, #1600, New York, NY 10019, USA

Keezer, Geoff *Jazz Pianist*
%DL Media, PO Box 2728, Bala Cynwyd, PA 19004, USA

Kegel, Oliver *Canoeing Athlete*
Am Bogen 23, 13589 Berlin, Germany

Kehoe, Rick *Hockey Player, Coach*
1027 Highland Dr, Cincinnati, OH 45211, USA

Keightley, David N *Historian*
%University of California, History Dept, Berkeley, CA 94720, USA

Keillor, Garrison E *Writer, Commentator*
%A Prairie Home Companion, 611 Frontenac Place, Saint Paul, MN 55104, USA

Keim, Jenny *Diver*
%R O'Brien, Swimming Hall of Fame, 1 Hall of Fame Dr, Fort Lauderdale, FL 33316, USA

Keita, Ibrahaim Boubakar *Prime Minister, Mali*
%Prime Minister's Office, BP 97, Bamako, Mali

Keita, Salif *Singer, Composer*
%International Music Network, 278 S Main St, #400, Gloucester, MA 01930, USA

Keitel, Harvey *Actor*
25 N Moore St, #2A, New York, NY 10013, USA

Keith, David *Actor*
%Writers & Artists, 8383 Wilshire Blvd, #550, Beverly Hills, CA 90211, USA

Keith, Louis *Physician*
333 E Superior St, #476, Chicago, IL 60611, USA

Keith, Penelope *Actress*
66 Berkeley House, Hay Hill, London SW3, England

Keith, Toby *Singer*
%TKO Artist Mgmt, 1107 17th Ave S, Nashville, TN 37212, USA

Kekalainen, Jarmo *Hockey Player*
145 Hillcrest Road, Needham, MA 02492, USA

Kelcher, Louie J *Football Player*
10204 Carlotta Cove, Austin, TX 78733, USA

Keleti, Agnes *Gynmast*
%Wingate Institute for Physical Education & Sport, Matanya 42902, Israel

Kell, George C *Baseball Player*
PO Box 158, Swifton, AR 72471, USA

Kellaway, Roger *Composer, Jazz Pianist*
%Pat Phillips Mgmt, 520 E 81st St, #PH C, New York, NY 10028, USA

Kelleher, Herbert D *Businessman*
144 Thelma Dr, San Antonio, TX 78212, USA

Keller, Bill *Journalist*
%New York Times, Editorial Dept, 229 W 43rd St, New York, NY 10036, USA

Keller, Erhard *Speedskater*
Sudliche Munchneustr 6A, 82031 Grunwald, Germany

Keller, Jason *Auto Racing Driver*
%Progressive Motorsports, 177 Knob Hill Road, Mooresville, NC 28117, USA

Keller, John *Basketball Player*
2100 24th St, Great Bend, KS 67530, USA

Keller, Joseph B *Mathematician*
820 Sonoma Terrace, Stanford, CA 94305, USA

Keller, Leonard B *Vietnam War Army Hero (CMH)*
6350 Majzun Road, Milton, FL 32570, USA

Keller, Marthe *Actress*
%Lemonstr 9, 81679 Munich, Germany

Keller, Mary Page *Actress*
%William Morris Agency, 151 El Camino Dr, Beverly Hills, CA 90212, USA

Keller, Thomas *Chef*
%French Laundry, 6540 Washington St, Yountville, CA 94599, USA

Kellerman, Faye *Writer*
%Karpfinger Agency, 357 W 20th St, New York, NY 10011, USA

Kellerman, Jonathan S *Writer*
%Karpfinger Agency, 357 W 20th St, New York, NY 10011, USA

Kellerman, Sally — *Actress*
7944 Woodrow Wilson Dr, Los Angeles, CA 90046, USA
Kelley, Allen (Al) — *Basketball Player*
5900 Longleaf Dr, Lawrence, KS 66049, USA
Kelley, David E — *Television Producer, Writer*
%David Kelley Productions, 10201 W Pico Blvd, Los Angeles, CA 90064, USA
Kelley, Dean — *Basketball Player*
5900 Longleaf Dr, Lawrence, KS 66049, USA
Kelley, Donald R — *Historian*
45 Jefferson Ave, New Brunswick, NJ 08901, USA
Kelley, Earl A — *Basketball Player*
21430 Windemere Lane, Tremont, IL 61566, USA
Kelley, Gaynor N — *Businessman*
%Perkin-Elmer Corp, 710 Bridgeport Ave, Shelton, CT 06484, USA
Kelley, Harold H — *Psychologist*
21634 Rambla Vista St, Malibu, CA 90265, USA
Kelley, John A (Marathon) — *Track Athlete*
136 Cedar Hill Road, East Dennis, MA 02641, USA
Kelley, Kitty — *Writer*
1228 Eton Court NW, Washington, DC 20007, USA
Kelley, Mike — *Sculptor*
2472 Eastman Ave, #35-36, Ventura, CA 93003, USA
Kelley, Paul X — *Marine Corps General*
1600 N Oak St, #1619, Arlington, VA 22209, USA
Kelley, Rich — *Basketball Player*
314 Raymundo Dr, Woodside, CA 94062, USA
Kelley, Sheila — *Actress*
537 N June St, Los Angeles, CA 90004, USA
Kelley, Steve — *Editorial Cartoonist*
%San Diego Union, Editorial Dept, 350 Camino de la Reina, San Diego, CA 92108, USA
Kelley, Thomas G — *Vietnam War Navy Hero (CMH)*
693 E 8th St, Boston, MA 02127, USA
Kelley, William G — *Businessman*
%Consolidated Stores, 1105 N Market St, Wilmington, DE 19801, USA
Kellogg, Allan J, Jr — *Vietnam War Marine Corps Air Hero (CMH)*
250 Ilihau St, Kailua, HI 96734, USA
Kellogg, Clark — *Basketball Player, Sportscaster*
5423 Medallion Dr E, Westerville, OH 43082, USA
Kellogg, William S — *Businessman*
%Kohl's Corp, N56W17000 Ridgewood Dr, Menomonee Falls, WI 53051, USA
Kelly, Annesse — *Bowler*
2912 Cape Verde Lane, Las Vegas, NV 89128, USA
Kelly, Daniel Hugh — *Actor*
%Innovative Artists, 1505 10th St, Santa Monica, CA 90401, USA
Kelly, Donald P — *Businessman*
%DP Kelly Assoc, 701 Harger Road, #190, Oak Brook, IL 60523, USA
Kelly, Eamon M — *Educator*
3122 Octavia St, New Orleans, LA 70125, USA
Kelly, Ellsworth — *Artist*
PO Box 170B, Chatham, NY 12037, USA
Kelly, J Thomas (Tom) — *Baseball Player, Manager*
1643 Carrie St, Maplewood, MN 55119, USA
Kelly, James E (Jim) — *Football Player*
44 Hillsboro Dr, Orchard Park, NY 14127, USA
Kelly, James M (Jim) — *Astronaut*
14634 Graywood Groove Lane, Houston, TX 77062, USA
Kelly, John — *Singer (Kelly Family)*
%EMI America Records, 6920 Sunset Blvd, Los Angeles, CA 90028, USA
Kelly, John H — *Diplomat*
%International Equity Partners, 1808 Overlake Dr SE, #D, Conyers, GA 30013, USA
Kelly, Leonard P (Red) — *Hockey Player*
30 Dunvegan, Toronto ON M4V 2P6, Canada
Kelly, Leroy — *Football Player*
115 Eastbrook Lane, Willingboro, NJ 08046, USA
Kelly, Mark E — *Astronaut*
2121 Barrington Dr, League City, TX 77573, USA
Kelly, Moira — *Actress*
2329 Rodeo Dr, Austin, TX 78727, USA
Kelly, Paul — *Singer, Songwriter*
%Robert Barnham Mgmt, 432 Tyagarah Road, Myocum NSW 2038, Australia
Kelly, R — *Rap Artist, Singer, Songwriter*
%Creative Artists Agency, 9830 Wilshire Blvd, Beverly Hills, CA 90212, USA
Kelly, Raymond — *Law Enforcement Official*
%Police Commissioner's Office, 1 Police Plaza, New York, NY 10038, USA
Kelly, Scott J — *Astronaut*
2121 Barrington Dr, League City, TX 77573, USA
Kelly, Thomas J, III — *Photojournalist*
PO Box 2208, Sanatoga Branch, Pottstown, PA 19464, USA

K

Kelly - Kenne

Kelly, Thomas J, Jr *Molecular Biologist*
%Memorial Sloan Kettering Cancer Center, 1275 York Ave, New York, NY 10021, USA
Kelman, Arthur *Plant Pathologist*
1406 Springmoor Circle, Raleigh, NC 27615, USA
Kelman, Charles D *Ophthalmologist*
%Eye Center, 220 Madison Ave, New York, NY 10016, USA
Kelman, James *Writer*
%Weidenfeld-Nicolson, Upper Saint Martin's Lane, London WC2H 9EA, England
Kelsey, Frances O *Pharmacologist*
%Federal Drug Administration, 5600 Fishers Lane, Rockville, MD 20852, USA
Kelsey, Linda *Actress*
400 S Beverly Dr, #101, Beverly Hills, CA 90212, USA
Kelso, Frank B, II *Navy Admiral*
7794 Turlock Road, Springfield, VA 22153, USA
Kemal, Yashar *Writer*
PK 14 Basinkoy, Istanbul, Turkey
Kemmer, Ed *Actor*
11 Riverside Dr, #17PE, New York, NY 10023, USA
Kemp, Gary *Guitarist (Spandau Ballet)*
%International Talent Group, 729 7th Ave, #1600, New York, NY 10019, USA
Kemp, Jeremy *Actor*
%Marina Martin, 12/13 Poland St, London W1V 3DE, England
Kemp, John F (Jack) *Secretary, Housing & Urban Development*
7904 Greentree Road, Bethesda, MD 20817, USA
Kemp, Martin *Bassist (Spandau Ballet)*
%Mission Control, Business Center, Lower Road, London SE16 2XB, England
Kemp, Shawn T *Basketball Player*
1700 E 13th St, #12T, Cleveland, OH 44114, USA
Kemp, Steve F *Baseball Player*
4208 City Lights Dr, Aliso Viego, CA 92656, USA
Kemper, David W, II *Financier*
%Commerce Bancshares, 1000 Walnut St, Kansas City, MO 64106, USA
Kemper, Randolph E (Randy) *Fashion Designer*
%Randy Kemper Corp, 530 Fashion Ave, #1400, New York, NY 10018, USA
Kemper, Victor J *Cinematographer*
%Gersh Agency, 232 N Canon Dr, Beverly Hills, CA 90210, USA
Kempf, Cecil J *Navy Admiral*
831 Olive Ave, Coronado, CA 92118, USA
Kempner, Walter *Nutritionist*
1505 Virginia Ave, Durham, NC 27705, USA
Kendal, Felicity *Actress*
%Chatto & Linnit, Prince of Wales, Coventry St, London W1V 7FE, England
Kendall, A Bruce *Yachtsman*
6 Pedersen Place, Bucklands Beach, Auckland, New Zealand
Kendall, Barbara *Yachtswoman*
%Kendall Distributing, 82B Great South Road, Auckland, New Zealand
Kendall, Donald M *Businessman*
%PepsiCo Inc, Anderson Hill Road, Purchase, NY 10577, USA
Kendall, Jason *Baseball Player*
612 John St, Manhattan Beach, CA 90266, USA
Kendall, Jeannie *Singer (Kendalls)*
%Joe Taylor Artist Agency, 2802 Columbine Place, Nashville, TN 37204, USA
Kendall, Pete *Football Player*
%Arizona Cardinals, PO Box 888, Phoenix, AZ 85001, USA
Kendall, Tom *Auto Racing Driver*
%International Motor Sports Assn, 1394 Broadway Ave, Braselton, GA 30517, USA
Kendler, Bob *Handball, Raquetball Player*
%US Handball Assn, 4101 Dempster St, Skokie, IL 60076, USA
Kendrick, Rodney *Singer, Jazz Pianist, Composer*
%Carolyn McClair, 410 W 53rd St, #128C, New York, NY 10019, USA
Keneally, Thomas M *Writer*
24 Serpentine, Bilgola Beach NSW 2107, Australia
Kenilorea, Peter *Prime Minister, Solomon Islands*
Kalala House, PO Box 535, Honiara, Guadacanal, Solomon Islands
Kenn, Michael L (Mike) *Football Player*
360 Bardolier, Alpharetta, GA 30022, USA
Kenna, E Douglas (Doug) *Businessman, Football Player*
11450 Turtle Beach Road, North Palm Beach, FL 33408, USA
Kenna, Edward *WW II Australian Army Hero (VC)*
121 Coleraine Road, Hamilton VIC 3300, Australia
Kennan, Brian *Drummer (Chambers Brothers)*
%Lustig Talent, PO Box 770850, Orlando, FL 32877, USA
Kennan, George F *Diplomat, Writer*
%Institute for Advanced Study, Olden Lane, Princeton, NJ 08540, USA
Kennard, William (Bill) *Government Official*
%Carlyle Group, 1001 Pennsylvania Ave NW, Washington, DC 20004, USA
Kenne, Leslie F *Air Force General*
Deputy CofS for Warfighting Integration, HqUSA, Pentagon, Washington, DC 20310, USA

Kennedy, Alan D *Businessman*
%Tupperware Corp, PO Box 2353, Orlando, FL 32802, USA
Kennedy, Anthony M *Supreme Court Justice*
%US Supreme Court, 1 1st St NE, Washington, DC 20543, USA
Kennedy, Claudia J *Army General*
%William Morris Agency, 151 El Camino Dr, Beverly Hills, CA 90212, USA
Kennedy, Cornelia G *Judge*
%US Court of Appeals, US Courthouse, 231 W Lafayette Blvd, Detroit, MI 48226, USA
Kennedy, Cortez *Football Player*
3005 122nd Place NE, Bellevue, WA 98005, USA
Kennedy, D James *Religious Leader*
%Coral Ridge Presbyterian Church, 5554 N Federal Hwy, Fort Lauderdale, FL 33308, USA
Kennedy, David M *Secretary, Treasury*
3838 Ruth Dr, Salt Lake City, UT 84124, USA
Kennedy, David M *Historian*
%Stanford University, History Dept, Stanford, CA 94305, USA
Kennedy, Donald *Educator*
%Stanford University, International Studies Institute, Stanford, CA 94305, USA
Kennedy, Forbes T *Hockey Player*
9 Birchwood St, Charlottetown PE C1A 5B4, Canada
Kennedy, George *Actor*
1617 N Dunsmuir Way, Eagle, ID 83616, USA
Kennedy, James C *Businessman*
%Cox Enterprises, 1400 Lake Hearn Dr NE, Atlanta, GA 30319, USA
Kennedy, Jamie *Actor*
%The Firm, 9100 Wilshire Blvd, #100W, Beverly Hills, CA 90210, USA
Kennedy, Jimmy *Football Player*
%Saint Louis Rams, 901 N Broadway, Saint Louis, MO 63101, USA
Kennedy, Joey D (Joe), Jr *Journalist*
1635 11th Place S, Birmingham, AL 35205, USA
Kennedy, John Milton *Actor*
5711 Reseda Blvd, #204, Tarzana, CA 91356, USA
Kennedy, Kathleen *Movie Producer*
%Kennedy-Marshall Co, 650 N Bronson Ave, #100, Los Angeles, CA 90004, USA
Kennedy, Lee *Businessman*
%Equifax Inc, 1550 Peachtree St NE, Atlanta, GA 30309, USA
Kennedy, Leon Isaac *Actor*
859 N Hollywood Way, #384, Burbank, CA 91505, USA
Kennedy, Mimi *Actress*
%Agency for Performing Arts, 9200 Sunset Blvd, #900, Los Angeles, CA 90069, USA
Kennedy, Nigel *Concert Violinist*
%Russells, Regency House, 1-4 Warwick St, London W1R 5WB, England
Kennedy, Paul M *Historian*
409 Humphrey St, New Haven, CT 06511, USA
Kennedy, Randall L *Attorney, Educator*
%Harvard University, Law School, Cambridge, MA 02138, USA
Kennedy, Ray F *Businessman*
%Masco Corp, 21001 Van Born Road, Taylor, MI 48180, USA
Kennedy, T Lincoln *Football Player*
3917 Spring Garden Place, #1, Spring Valley, CA 91977, USA
Kennedy, Terrence E (Terry) *Baseball Player*
PO Box 6670, Chandler, AZ 85246, USA
Kennedy, Theodore S (Teeder) *Hockey Player*
22 Lakeside Place W, Port Colborne ON L3K 6B1, Canada
Kennedy, William J *Writer*
%New York State Writers Institute, Washington Ave, Albany, NY 12222, USA
Kennedy, X Joseph (X J) *Writer*
22 Revere St, Lexington, MA 02420, USA
Kennedy-Powell, Kathleen *Judge*
%Los Angeles Municipal Court, 110 N Grand Ave, Los Angeles, CA 90012, USA
Kenner, Kevin *Concert Pianist*
%Columbia Artists Mgmt Inc, 165 W 57th St, New York, NY 10019, USA
Kennerly, David Hume *Photojournalist*
1015 18th St, Santa Monica, CA 90403, USA
Kenney, Stephen F (Steve) *Football Player*
1105 Silver Oaks Court, Raleigh, NC 27614, USA
Kennibrew, Dee Dee *Singer (Crystals)*
%Superstars Unlimited, PO Box 371371, Las Vegas, NV 89137, USA
Kennison, Eddie *Football Player*
%Kansas City Chiefs, 1 Arrowhead Dr, Kansas City, KS 64129, USA
Kenny G *Saxophonist*
%Turner Management Group, 374 Poli St, #205, Ventura, CA 93001, USA
Kenny, Shirley Strum *Educator*
%State University of New York, President's Office, Stony Brook, NY 11794, USA
Kenny, Yvonne *Opera Singer*
%I M G Artists, 3 Burlington Lane, Chiswick, London W4 2TH, England
Kenseth, Matt *Auto Racing Driver*
111 Stonewall Beach Lane, Mooresville, NC 28117, USA

K

Kensit, Patsy *Actress, Singer*
14 Lambton Place, Nottinghill, London W11 2SH, England
Kent, (Edward G N P Patrick) *Duke, Great Britain*
York House, Saint James's Place, London SW1, England
Kent, Allegra *Ballerina*
%New York City Ballet, Lincoln Center Plaza, New York, NY 10023, USA
Kent, Arthur *Commentator*
2184 Torringford St, Torrington, CT 06790, USA
Kent, Jean *Actress*
%London Mgmt, 2-4 Noel St, London W1V 3RB, England
Kent, Jeffrey A (Jeff) *Baseball Player*
%Houston Astros, Astros Field, 501 Crawford St, Houston, TX 77002, USA
Kent, Jonathan *Theater Director*
%International Creative Mgmt, 76 Oxford St, London W1N 0AX, England
Kent, Julie *Ballerina*
%American Ballet Theatre, 890 Broadway, New York, NY 10003, USA
Kent, Peter *Geologist*
43 Trinity Court, Gray's Inn Road, London WC1, England
Kentner, Louis P *Concert Pianist*
1 Mallord St, London SW3, England
Kenty, Hilmer *Boxer*
%Escot Boxing, 19260 Bretton Dr, Detroit, MI 48223, USA
Kenyon, Mel *Auto Racing Driver*
2645 S 25th West, Lebanon, IN 46052, USA
Kenzle, Leila *Actress*
%William Morris Agency, 151 El Camino Dr, Beverly Hills, CA 90212, USA
Kenzo *Fashion Designer*
3 Place des Victories, 75001 Paris, France
Keobouphan, Sisavat *Prime Minister, Laos*
%Premier's Office, Vientiane, Laos
Keogh, James *Government Official*
Byram Dr, Belle Haven, Greenwich, CT 06830, USA
Keohane, Nannerl O *Educator*
%Duke University, President's Office, Durham, NC 27706, USA
Keon, David M (Dave) *Hockey Player*
115 Brackenwood Road, Palm Beach Gardens, FL 33418, USA
Keough, Donald R *Financier*
200 Galleria Parkway, #970, Atlanta, GA 30339, USA
Keough, Harry J *Soccer Player, Coach*
7325 Rainor Court, Saint Louis, MO 63116, USA
Keough, Lainey *Fashion Designer*
42 Dawson St, Dublin 2, Ireland
Kercheval, Ken *Actor*
PO Box 4844, Louisville, KY 40204, USA
Kerekou, Mathieu A *President, Benin; Army General*
%President's Office, Boite Postale 2020, Cotonou, Benin
Keresztes, K Sandor *Architect*
Fo Utca 44/50, 1011 Budapest, Hungary
Kerkorian, Kirk *Businessman*
%MGM/UA Communications, 2500 Broadway St, Santa Monica, CA 90404, USA
Kern, Geof *Photographer*
1355 Conant St, Dallas, TX 75207, USA
Kern, Rex W *Football Player*
2816 Avenida de Autlan, Camarillo, CA 93010, USA
Kerns, David V, Jr *Microbiotics Engineer*
%Vanderbilt University, Electrical Engineering Dept, Nashville, TN 37235, USA
Kerns, Joanna *Actress*
PO Box 49216, Los Angeles, CA 90049, USA
Kerr, Clark *Educator*
8300 Buckingham Dr, El Cerrito, CA 94530, USA
Kerr, Deborah *Actress*
Wyhergut, Klosters, 7250 Grisons, Switzerland
Kerr, Donald M, Jr *Physicist*
%Science Applications International, 1241 Cave St, La Jolla, CA 92037, USA
Kerr, Graham *Food Expert, Writer*
%Kerr Corp, 1020 N Sunset Dr, Camano Island, WA 98282, USA
Kerr, John G *Actor*
2975 Monterey Road, San Marino, CA 91108, USA
Kerr, John G (Red) *Basketball Player, Coach, Sportscaster*
8700 W Bryn Mawr Ave, #600SO, Chicago, IL 60631, USA
Kerr, Judy *Actress*
4139 Tujunga Ave, Studio City, CA 91604, USA
Kerr, Pat *Fashion Designer*
%Pat Kerr Inc, 200 Wagner Place, Memphis, TN 38103, USA
Kerr, Philip *Writer*
%AP Watts Agents, 20 John St, London WC1N 2DR, England
Kerr, Steve *Basketball Player*
789 Grandview, San Antonio, TX 78209, USA

K

Kerr, Tim *Hockey Player, Coach*
%Power Play Realty, 2528 Dune Dr, Avalon, NJ 08202, USA
Kerr, William T *Businessman*
%Meredith Corp, 1716 Locust St, Des Moines, IA 50309, USA
Kerrey, J Robert (Bob) *Governor, Senator, NE;Vietnam Hero (CMH)*
%New School University, President's Office, 66 W 12th St, New York, NY 10011, USA
Kerrick, Donald L *Army General*
Deputy Assistant, National Security Agency, Fort George C Meade, MD 20755, USA
Kerrigan, Joseph T (Joe) *Baseball Player, Manager*
450 Forest Lane, North Wales, PA 19454, USA
Kerrigan, Nancy *Figure Skater*
11 Cedar Ave, Stoneham, MA 02180, USA
Kersey, Jerome *Basketball Player*
%Portland Trail Blazers, Rose Garden, 1 Center Court St, Portland, OR 97227, USA
Kersh, David *Singer*
%Mark Hybner Entertainment, PO Box 223, Shiner, TX 77984, USA
Kershaw, Doug *Singer, Fiddler*
RR 1, Box 34285, Weld County Road 47, Eaton, CO 80615, USA
Kershaw, Sammy *Singer*
%Go Tell Mgmt, 4773 Lickton Park, Whites Creek, TN 37189, USA
Kershner, Irvin *Movie Director*
%Somers Teitelbaum David, 8840 Wilshire Blvd, #200, Beverly Hills, CA 90211, USA
Kertesz, Imre *Nobel Literature Laureate*
%Northwestern University Press, 625 Colfax St, Evanston, IL 60208, USA
Kerwin, Brian *Actor*
%Paradigm Agency, 200 W 57th St, #900, New York, NY 10019, USA
Kerwin, Joseph P *Astronaut*
1802 Royal Fern Court, Houston, TX 77062, USA
Kerwin, Lance *Actor*
PO Box 101, Temecula, CA 92593, USA
Kerwin, Larkin *Physicist*
2166 Bourboniere Park, Sillery QC G1T 1B4, Canada
Kesner, Jillian *Actress*
%William Carroll Agency, 11360 Brill Dr, Studio City, CA 91604, USA
Kessel, Barney *Jazz Guitarist, Composer*
4445 North Ave, San Diego, CA 92116, USA
Kessinger, Donald E (Don) *Baseball Player*
2200 Longspur Point, Oxford, MS 38655, USA
Kessler, David A *Physician, Government Official*
%University of California, Med School, Dean's Office, San Francisco, CA 94143, USA
Kessler, Robert (Bob) *Basketball Player*
14 Twin Pines Road, Hilton Head, SC 29928, USA
Kessler, Ron *Writer*
%William Morris Agency, 151 El Camino Dr, Beverly Hills, CA 90212, USA
Kestner, Boyd *Actor*
%Mirisch Agency, 1801 Century Park E, #1801, Los Angeles, CA 90067, USA
Ketchum, Hal *Singer, Songwriter*
602 Wayside Dr, Wimberley, TX 78676, USA
Ketchum, Howard *Color Engineer*
3800 Washington Road, West Palm Beach, FL 33405, USA
Ketterle, Wolfgang *Nobel Physics Laureate*
25 Bellingham Dr, Brookline, MA 02446, USA
Kettle, Roger *Cartoonist*
%King Features Syndicate, 888 7th Ave, New York, NY 10106, USA
Keves, Gyorgy *Architect*
Keves es Epitesztarsai Rt, Melinda Utca 21, 1121 Budapest, Hungary
Key, James E (Jimmy) *Baseball Player*
30 June Road, North Salem, NY 10560, USA
Key, Ted *Cartoonist (Hazel)*
1694 Glenhardie Road, Wayne, PA 19087, USA
Keyes, Daniel *Writer*
222 NW 69th St, Boca Raton, FL 33487, USA
Keyes, Evelyn *Actress*
999 N Doheny Dr, #509, Los Angeles, CA 90069, USA
Keyes, Leroy *Football Player*
6156 Pleasant Ave, Pennsauken, NJ 08110, USA
Keyes, Robert W *Physicist, Engineer*
%IBM Research Division, PO Box 218, Yorktown Heights, NY 10598, USA
Keyfitz, Nathan *Statistician*
61 Mill Road, North Hampton, NH 03862, USA
Keys, Alicia *Singer, Songwriter, Pianist*
%MBK Ent, 156 W 56th St, #400, New York, NY 10019, USA
Keys, Ronald E *Air Force General*
Commander in Chief, Allied Forces South Europe, Box 1 PSC 813, FPO, AE 09620, USA
Keyser, F Ray, Jr *Governor, VT*
64 Warner Ave, Proctor, VT 05765, USA
Keyser, Richard L *Businessman*
%WW Grainger Inc, 100 Grainger Parkway, Lake Forest, IL 60045, USA

Khabibulin, Nikolai *Hockey Player*
11424 E Palomino Road, Scottsdale, AZ 85259, USA
Khajag Barsamian *Religious Leader*
%Armenian Church of America, Eastern Diocese, 630 2nd Ave, New York, NY 10016, USA
Khaled *Singer*
%Firstars Mgmt, 14724 Ventura Blvd, #PH, Sherman Oaks, CA 91403, USA
Khali, Simbi *Actress*
%Innovative Artists, 1505 10th St, Santa Monica, CA 90401, USA
Khalifa al-Thani, Hamad Bin *Prime Minister, Qatar; Prince*
%Royal Palace, PO Box 923, Doha, Qatar
Khalifa, Sheikh Hamad bin Isa al- *Emir, Bahrain*
%Rifa's Palace, Manama, Bahrain
Khalifa, Sheikh Khalifa bin Sulman, al- *Prime Minister, Bahrain*
%Prime Minister's Office, Government House, Manama, Bahrain
Khalil, Mustafa *Prime Minister, Egypt*
9A El Maahad El Swisry St, Zamalek, Cairo, Egypt
Khamenei, Hojatolislam Sayyed Ali *President, Iran*
%Religious Leader's Office, Teheran, Iran
Khamtai Siphandon *Prime Minister, Laos; Army General*
%Prime Minister's Office, Council of Ministers, Vientiane, Laos
Khan, Ali Akbar *Sarod Player, Composer*
%Gregory DiGiovine Mgmt, 121 Jordan St, San Rafael, CA 94901, USA
Khan, Amjad Ali *Sarod Player, Composer*
3 Sadhna Enclave, Panchsheel Park, New Delhi 110 017, India
Khan, Chaka *Singer, Actress*
%Earthsong, 12431 Oxnard St, #B, North Hollywood, CA 91606, USA
Khan, Gulam Ishaq *President, Pakistan*
3B University Town, Jamrud Road, Peshawar, Pakistan
Khan, Inamullah *Religious Leader*
%Muslim Congress, D26, Block 8, Gulshan-E-Iqbal, Karachi 75300, Pakistan
Khan, Niazi Imran *Cricketer*
%Shankat Khanum Memorial Trust, 29 Shah Jamal, Lahore 546000, Pakistan
Khanh, Emanuelle *Fashion Designer*
%Emanuelle Khanh International, 45 Ave Victor Hugo, 75116 Paris, France
Khanzadian, Vahan *Opera Singer*
3604 Broadway, #2N, New York, NY 10031, USA
Khariton, Yuli B *Physicist*
%Nuclear Energy Center, Arsamas 16, Nizhy Novgorog Region, Russia
Khashoggi, Adnan M *Businessman*
La Baraka, Marbella, Spain
Khatami, Mohammad *President, Iran*
%President's Office, Dr Ali Shariati Ave, Teheran, Iran
Khavin, Vladimir Y *Architect*
%Glavmosarchitectura, Mayakovsky Square 1, 103001 Moscow, Russia
Khayat, Edward (Eddie) *Football Player, Coach*
7813 Haydenberry Cove, Nashville, TN 37221, USA
Khayat, Robert *Educator*
%University of Mississippi, Chancellor's Office, University, MS 38677, USA
Kheel, Theodore W *Labor Mediator*
280 Park Ave, New York, NY 10017, USA
Khokhlov, Boris *Ballet Dancer*
Myaskovsky St 11-13, #102, 121019 Moscow, Russia
Khondji, Darius *Cinematographer*
%International Creative Mgmt, 8942 Wilshire Blvd, #219, Beverly Hills, CA 90211, USA
Khorana, Har Gobind *Nobel Medicine Laureate*
39 Amherst Road, Belmont, MA 02478, USA
Khouna, Sheikh El Afia Quid Mohamed *Prime Minister, Mauritania*
%Prime Minister's Office, Nouakchott, Mauritania
Khouri, Callie *Movie Director*
%International Creative Mgmt, 8942 Wilshire Blvd, #219, Beverly Hills, CA 90211, USA
Khrennikov, Tikhon N *Composer*
Plotnikov Per 10/28, #19, 121200 Moscow, Russia
Khush, Gurdev S *Agricultural Researcher*
%Int'l Rice Research Insitute, PO Box 933, 1099 Manila, Phillippines
Khvorostovsky, Dimitri A *Opera Singer*
%Elen Victorova, Mosfilmovskaya 26, #5, Moscow, Russia
Kiarostami, Abbas *Movie Director*
%Zeitgeist Films, 247 Centre St, #200, New York, NY 10013, USA
Kibaki, Mwai *President, Kenya*
%President's Office, Harambee House, Harambee Ave, Nairobi, Kenya
Kibrick, Anne *Medical Educator*
130 Seminary Ave, #312, Auburndale, MA 02466, USA
Kid Creole *Singer*
%Ron Rainey Mgmt, 315 S Beverly Dr, #407, Beverly Hills, CA 90212, USA
Kid Rock *Musician*
%Pinnacle Entertainment, 30 Glenn St, White Plains, NY 10603, USA
Kidd, Jason *Basketball Player*
7535 E Gainey, #191, Scottsdale, AZ 85258, USA

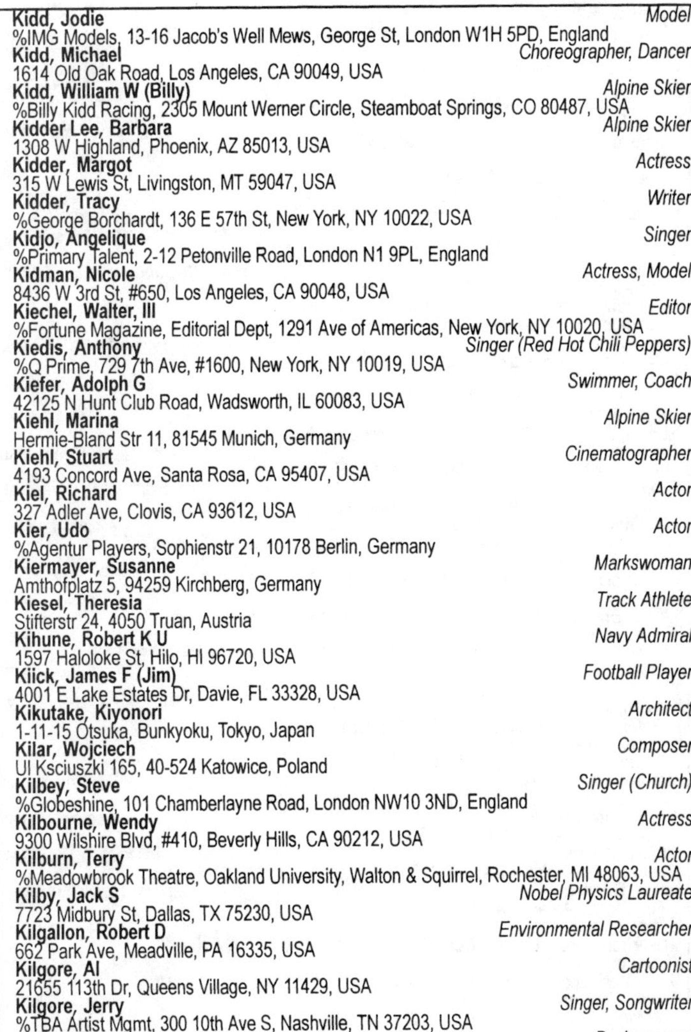

Kidd, Jodie *Model*
%IMG Models, 13-16 Jacob's Well Mews, George St, London W1H 5PD, England

Kidd, Michael *Choreographer, Dancer*
1614 Old Oak Road, Los Angeles, CA 90049, USA

Kidd, William W (Billy) *Alpine Skier*
%Billy Kidd Racing, 2305 Mount Werner Circle, Steamboat Springs, CO 80487, USA

Kidder Lee, Barbara *Alpine Skier*
1308 W Highland, Phoenix, AZ 85013, USA

Kidder, Margot *Actress*
315 W Lewis St, Livingston, MT 59047, USA

Kidder, Tracy *Writer*
%George Borchardt, 136 E 57th St, New York, NY 10022, USA

Kidjo, Angelique *Singer*
%Primary Talent, 2-12 Petonville Road, London N1 9PL, England

Kidman, Nicole *Actress, Model*
8436 W 3rd St, #650, Los Angeles, CA 90048, USA

Kiechel, Walter, III *Editor*
%Fortune Magazine, Editorial Dept, 1291 Ave of Americas, New York, NY 10020, USA

Kiedis, Anthony *Singer (Red Hot Chili Peppers)*
%Q Prime, 729 7th Ave, #1600, New York, NY 10019, USA

Kiefer, Adolph G *Swimmer, Coach*
42125 N Hunt Club Road, Wadsworth, IL 60083, USA

Kiehl, Marina *Alpine Skier*
Hermie-Bland Str 11, 81545 Munich, Germany

Kiehl, Stuart *Cinematographer*
4193 Concord Ave, Santa Rosa, CA 95407, USA

Kiel, Richard *Actor*
327 Adler Ave, Clovis, CA 93612, USA

Kier, Udo *Actor*
%Agentur Players, Sophienstr 21, 10178 Berlin, Germany

Kiermayer, Susanne *Markswoman*
Amthofplatz 5, 94259 Kirchberg, Germany

Kiesel, Theresia *Track Athlete*
Stifterstr 24, 4050 Truan, Austria

Kihune, Robert K U *Navy Admiral*
1597 Haloloke St, Hilo, HI 96720, USA

Kiick, James F (Jim) *Football Player*
4001 E Lake Estates Dr, Davie, FL 33328, USA

Kikutake, Kiyonori *Architect*
1-11-15 Otsuka, Bunkyoku, Tokyo, Japan

Kilar, Wojciech *Composer*
Ul Ksciuszki 165, 40-524 Katowice, Poland

Kilbey, Steve *Singer (Church)*
%Globeshine, 101 Chamberlayne Road, London NW10 3ND, England

Kilbourne, Wendy *Actress*
9300 Wilshire Blvd, #410, Beverly Hills, CA 90212, USA

Kilburn, Terry *Actor*
%Meadowbrook Theatre, Oakland University, Walton & Squirrel, Rochester, MI 48063, USA

Kilby, Jack S *Nobel Physics Laureate*
7723 Midbury St, Dallas, TX 75230, USA

Kilgallon, Robert D *Environmental Researcher*
662 Park Ave, Meadville, PA 16335, USA

Kilgore, Al *Cartoonist*
21655 113th Dr, Queens Village, NY 11429, USA

Kilgore, Jerry *Singer, Songwriter*
%TBA Artist Mgmt, 300 10th Ave S, Nashville, TN 37203, USA

Kilian, Thomas J *Businessman*
%Conseco Inc, PO Box 1957, Carmel, IN 46082, USA

Kilius, Marika *Figure Skater*
Postfach 201151, 63271 Dreieich, Germany

Killebrew, Harmon C *Baseball Player*
PO Box 14550, Scottsdale, AZ 85267, USA

Killinger, Kerry K *Financier*
%Washington Mutual Inc, 1201 3rd Ave, Seattle, WA 98101, USA

Killip, Christopher D *Photographer*
%Harvard University, Visual Studies Dept, 24 Quincy St, Cambridge, MA 02138, USA

Killy, Jean-Claude *Alpine Skier*
Villa Les Oiseaux 13 Chemin Bellefontaine, 1223 Cologny-GE, Switzerland

Kilmer, Val *Actor*
%William Morris Agency, 151 El Camino Dr, Beverly Hills, CA 90212, USA

Kilmer, William O (Billy) *Football Player*
1853 Monte Carlo Way, #36, Coral Springs, FL 33071, USA

Kilmore, Chris *DJ (Incubus)*
%ArtistDirect, 10900 Wilshire Blvd, #1400, Los Angeles, CA 90024, USA

Kilner, Kevin *Actor*
%Innovative Artists, 1505 10th St, Santa Monica, CA 90401, USA

Kilpatrick, James J, Jr *Columnist*
White Walnut Hill, Woodville, VA 22749, USA

K

Kilpatrick - Kinder

Kilpatrick, Kwame *Mayor*
%Mayor's Office, City-County Building, 2 Woodward Ave, Detroit, MI 48226, USA
Kilpatrick, Lincoln *Actor*
1710 Garth Ave, Los Angeles, CA 90035, USA
Kilrain, Susan L *Astronaut*
PO Box 420201, Roosevelt Roads, PR 00742, USA
Kilrea, Brian *Hockey Player, Coach*
2192 Saunderson Dr, Ottawa ON K1G 2G4, Canada
Kilts, James M *Businessman*
%Gillette Co, Prudential Tower Building, Boston, MA 02199, USA
Kilzer, Louis C (Lon) *Journalist*
%Minneapolis-Saint Paul Star-Tribune, 425 Portland Ave, Minneapolis, MN 55488, USA
Kim Jong Il *President, North Korea; Army Marshal*
%President's Office, Central Committee, Pyongyang, North Korea
Kim Jong Pil *Prime Minister, South Korea; General*
%Prime Minister's Office, 77 Sejong-no, Chongnoku, Seoul, South Korea
Kim Young Sam *President, South Korea*
Sangdo-dong 7-6, Tongjakku, Seoul, South Korea
Kim, Byung-Hyun *Baseball Player*
2037 N Chestnut, Mesa, AZ 85213, USA
Kim, Jacqueline *Actress*
%Innovative Artists, 1505 10th St, Santa Monica, CA 90401, USA
Kim, Jaegwon *Philosopher*
%Brown University, Philosophy Dept, Providence, RI 02912, USA
Kim, Nelli V *Gymnast*
2480 Cobblehill, #A, Alocove, Woodbury, MN 55125, USA
Kim, Peter S *Biochemist, Geneticist*
%Whitehead Institute, 9 Cambridge Center, Cambridge, MA 02142, USA
Kim, Stephan Sou-hwan Cardinal *Religious Leader*
Archbishop's House, 2 Ka 1 Myong Dong, Chungku, Seoul 100, South Korea
Kim, Young Uck *Concert Violinist*
%Columbia Artists Mgmt Inc, 165 W 57th St, New York, NY 10019, USA
Kimball, Bobby *Singer (Toto)*
%World Entertainment Assoc, 297101 Kinderkamack Road, #128, Oradell, NJ 07649, USA
Kimball, Christopher *Chef*
%Public Broadcasting System, 1320 Braddock Place, Alexandria, VA 22314, USA
Kimball, Dick *Diver, Diving Coach*
1540 Waltham Dr, Ann Arbor, MI 48103, USA
Kimball, Warren F *Historian*
2540 Otter Lane, Johns Island, SC 29455, USA
Kimble, Warren *Artist*
RR 3 Box 1038, Brandon, VT 05733, USA
Kimbrough, Charles *Actor, Singer*
255 Amalfi Dr, Santa Monica, CA 90402, USA
Kimbrough, John A *Football Player*
801 N Ave L, Haskell, TX 79521, USA
Kimery, James L *Association Executive*
%Veterans of Foreign Wars, 405 W 34th St, Kansas City, MO 64111, USA
Kimm, Bruce E *Baseball Player, Manager*
3168 121st St, Amana, IA 52203, USA
Kimmelman, Michael *Art Critic*
%New York Times, Editorial Dept, 229 W 43rd St, New York, NY 10036, USA
Kimmins, Kenneth *Actor*
%J Michael Bloom, 9255 Sunset Blvd, #710, Los Angeles, CA 90069, USA
Kimura, Doreen *Psychologist*
211 Madison Ave, Toronto ON M5R 2S6, Canada
Kimura, Kazuo *Industrial Designer*
%Japan Design Foundation, 2-2 Cenba Chuo, Higashiku, Osaka 541, Japan
Kimura, Motoo *Geneticist, Biologist*
%Institute of Genetics, Yata 1, 111, Mishima, Shizuokaken 411, Japan
Kinard, Terry *Football Player*
19 English St, Sumter, SC 29150, USA
Kincaid, Aron *Actor*
%Coast to Coast Talent, 3350 Barham Blvd, Los Angeles, CA 90068, USA
Kincaid, Jamaica *Writer*
College Road, North Bennington, VT 05257, USA
Kinchen, Todd W *Football Player*
1010 S Acadian Thruway, Building F, Baton Rouge, LA 70806, USA
Kinchla, Chan *Guitarist (Blues Traveler)*
%ArtistDirect, 10900 Wilshire Blvd, #1400, Los Angeles, CA 90024, USA
Kincses, Veronika *Opera Singer*
%Hungarian State Opera, Andrassy Utca 22, 1061 Budapest, Hungary
Kind, Richard *Actor*
144 W 82nd St, New York, NY 10024, USA
Kind, Roslyn *Actress, Singer*
%Scott Stander, 13701 Riverside Dr, #201, Sherman Oaks, CA 91423, USA
Kinder, Melvyn *Psychologist*
1951 San Ysidro Dr, Beverly Hills, CA 90210, USA

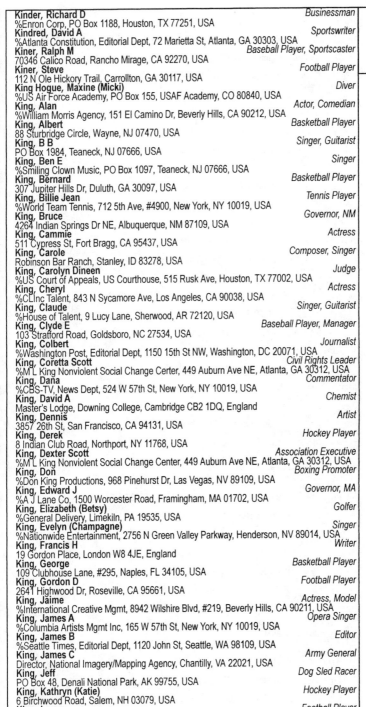

Kinder, Richard D — *Businessman*
%Enron Corp, PO Box 1188, Houston, TX 77251, USA

Kindred, David A — *Sportswriter*
%Atlanta Constitution, Editorial Dept, 72 Marietta St, Atlanta, GA 30303, USA

Kiner, Ralph M — *Baseball Player, Sportscaster*
70346 Calico Road, Rancho Mirage, CA 92270, USA

Kiner, Steve — *Football Player*
112 N Ole Hickory Trail, Carrollton, GA 30117, USA

King Hogue, Maxine (Micki) — *Diver*
%US Air Force Academy, PO Box 155, USAF Academy, CO 80840, USA

King, Alan — *Actor, Comedian*
%William Morris Agency, 151 El Camino Dr, Beverly Hills, CA 90212, USA

King, Albert — *Basketball Player*
88 Sturbridge Circle, Wayne, NJ 07470, USA

King, B B — *Singer, Guitarist*
PO Box 1984, Teaneck, NJ 07666, USA

King, Ben E — *Singer*
%Smiling Clown Music, PO Box 1097, Teaneck, NJ 07666, USA

King, Bernard — *Basketball Player*
307 Jupiter Hills Dr, Duluth, GA 30097, USA

King, Billie Jean — *Tennis Player*
%World Team Tennis, 712 5th Ave, #4900, New York, NY 10019, USA

King, Bruce — *Governor, NM*
4264 Indian Springs Dr NE, Albuquerque, NM 87109, USA

King, Cammie — *Actress*
511 Cypress St, Fort Bragg, CA 95437, USA

King, Carole — *Composer, Singer*
Robinson Bar Ranch, Stanley, ID 83278, USA

King, Carolyn Dineen — *Judge*
%US Court of Appeals, US Courthouse, 515 Rusk Ave, Houston, TX 77002, USA

King, Cheryl — *Actress*
%CLInc Talent, 843 N Sycamore Ave, Los Angeles, CA 90038, USA

King, Claude — *Singer, Guitarist*
%House of Talent, 9 Lucy Lane, Sherwood, AR 72120, USA

King, Clyde E — *Baseball Player, Manager*
103 Strafford Road, Goldsboro, NC 27534, USA

King, Colbert — *Journalist*
%Washington Post, Editorial Dept, 1150 15th St NW, Washington, DC 20071, USA

King, Coretta Scott — *Civil Rights Leader*
%M L King Nonviolent Social Change Certer, 449 Auburn Ave NE, Atlanta, GA 30312, USA

King, Dana — *Commentator*
%CBS-TV, News Dept, 524 W 57th St, New York, NY 10019, USA

King, David A — *Chemist*
Master's Lodge, Downing College, Cambridge CB2 1DQ, England

King, Dennis — *Artist*
3857 26th St, San Francisco, CA 94131, USA

King, Derek — *Hockey Player*
8 Indian Club Road, Northport, NY 11768, USA

King, Dexter Scott — *Association Executive*
%M L King Nonviolent Social Change Center, 449 Auburn Ave NE, Atlanta, GA 30312, USA

King, Don — *Boxing Promoter*
%Don King Productions, 968 Pinehurst Dr, Las Vegas, NV 89109, USA

King, Edward J — *Governor, MA*
%A J Lane Co, 1500 Worcester Road, Framingham, MA 01702, USA

King, Elizabeth (Betsy) — *Golfer*
%General Delivery, Limekiln, PA 19535, USA

King, Evelyn (Champagne) — *Singer*
%Nationwide Entertainment, 2756 N Green Valley Parkway, Henderson, NV 89014, USA

King, Francis H — *Writer*
19 Gordon Place, London W8 4JE, England

King, George — *Basketball Player*
109 Clubhouse Lane, #295, Naples, FL 34105, USA

King, Gordon D — *Football Player*
2641 Highwood Dr, Roseville, CA 95661, USA

King, Jaime — *Actress, Model*
%International Creative Mgmt, 8942 Wilshire Blvd, #219, Beverly Hills, CA 90211, USA

King, James A — *Opera Singer*
%Columbia Artists Mgmt Inc, 165 W 57th St, New York, NY 10019, USA

King, James B — *Editor*
%Seattle Times, Editorial Dept, 1120 John St, Seattle, WA 98109, USA

King, James C — *Army General*
Director, National Imagery/Mapping Agency, Chantilly, VA 22021, USA

King, Jeff — *Dog Sled Racer*
PO Box 48, Denali National Park, AK 99755, USA

King, Kathryn (Katie) — *Hockey Player*
6 Birchwood Road, Salem, NH 03079, USA

King, Lamar — *Football Player*
1453 Browning Dr, Essex, MD 21221, USA

K

King - Kinney

King, Larry *Commentator, Columnist*
13607 Hatteras St, Van Nuys, CA 91401, USA
King, Martin Luther, III *Civil Rights Activist*
%Southern Christian Leadership, 591 Edgewood Ave SE, #A, Atlanta, GA 30312, USA
King, Mary-Claire *Geneticist*
%University of Washington, Medical School, Genetics Dept, Seattle, WA 98195, USA
King, Mervyn A *Economist*
%Bank of England, Threadneedle St, London EC2R 8AH, England
King, Michael *Businessman*
%King World Productions, 12400 Wilshire Blvd, Los Angeles, CA 90025, USA
King, Morgana *Singer, Actress*
%Subrena Artists, 330 W 56th St, #18M, New York, NY 10019, USA
King, Perry *Actor*
3647 Wrightwood Dr, Studio City, CA 91604, USA
King, Phillip *Sculptor*
%Bernard Jackson Gallery, 14A Clifford St, London W1X 1RF, England
King, R Stacey *Basketball Player*
5340 Prairie Crossing, Long Grove, IL 60047, USA
King, Regina *Actress*
%Gersh Agency, 232 N Canon Dr, Beverly Hills, CA 90210, USA
King, Richard L *Businessman*
%Albertson's Inc, 250 Parkcenter Blvd, Boise, ID 83726, USA
King, Roger *Businessman*
%King World Productions, 12400 Wilshire Blvd, Los Angeles, CA 90025, USA
King, Stephen E *Writer*
%Juliann Eugley, 49 Florida Ave, Bangor, ME 04401, USA
King, Thea *Concert Clarinetist*
16 Milverton Road, London NW6 7AS, England
King, Thomas J (Tom) *Government Official, England*
%House of Commons, Westminster, London SW1A 0AA, England
King, W David *Hockey Coach*
%Calgary Flames, PO Box 1540, Station M, Calgary AB T2P 3B9, Canada
King, William (Bill) *Trumpeter (Commodores)*
%Management Assoc, 1920 Benson Ave, Saint Paul, MN 55116, USA
King, Woodie, Jr *Theater Producer*
417 Convent Ave, New York, NY 10031, USA
King, Zalman *Movie Director*
308 Alta Ave, Santa Monica, CA 90402, USA
Kingdom, Roger *Track Athlete*
146 S Fairmont St, #1, Pittsburgh, PA 15206, USA
Kinglsey, Ben *Actor*
%International Creative Mgmt, 76 Oxford St, London W1N 0AX, England
Kings Norton, (Harold R Cox) *Engineer, Scientist*
Westcote House, Chipping Campden, Glos, England
Kingsley, Ben *Actor*
New Penworth House, Stratford upon Avon, Warwickshire 0V3 7QX, England
Kingsolver, Barbara E *Writer*
PO Box 31870, Tucson, AZ 85751, USA
Kingston, Alex *Actress*
3400 Floyd Terrace, Los Angeles, CA 90068, USA
Kingston, Maxine Hong *Writer*
%University of California, English Dept, Berkeley, CA 94720, USA
Kinkade, Thomas *Artist*
%Media Arts Group, 900 Lightpost Way, Morgan Hill, CA 95037, USA
Kinkel, Klaus *Government Official, Germany*
%Auswartigen Amt, Adenauerallee 101, 53113 Bonn, Germany
Kinley, Heather *Singer (Kinleys)*
%Epic Records, 1211 S Highland Ave, Los Angeles, CA 90019, USA
Kinley, Jennifer *Singer (Kinleys)*
%Epic Records, 1211 S Highland Ave, Los Angeles, CA 90019, USA
Kinmont Boothe, Jill *Alpine Skier*
310 Sunland Dr, RR 1 Box 11, Bishop, CA 93514, USA
Kinmont, Kathleen *Actress*
9929 Sunset Blvd, #310, Los Angeles, CA 90069, USA
Kinnan, Timothy A *Air Force General*
US Military Representaive, NATO, Blvd Leopold III, 1110 Brussels, Belgium
Kinnear, Greg *Actor, Comedian*
2280 Mandeville Canyon Road, Los Angeles, CA 90049, USA
Kinnear, James W, III *Businessman*
%Ten Standard Forum, PO Box 120, Stamford, CT 06904, USA
Kinnell, Galway *Writer*
110 Bleecker St, #6D, New York, NY 10012, USA
Kinney, Dallas *Photojournalist*
484 Egret Circle, Sebastian, FL 32976, USA
Kinney, Kathy *Actress*
10061 Riverside Dr, #777, Toluca Lake, CA 91602, USA
Kinney, Terry *Actor*
%Gersh Agency, 232 N Canon Dr, Beverly Hills, CA 90210, USA

Kinnock, Neil G *Government Official, England*
%European Communities Commission, 200 Rue de Loi, 1049 Brussels, Belgium
Kinsella, John P *Swimmer*
PO Box 3067, Sumas, WA 98295, USA
Kinsella, Thomas *Writer*
Killalane, Laragh, County Wicklow, Ireland
Kinsella, William Patrick (W P) *Writer*
1952-152A St, #216, Surrey BC V4A 9T2, Canada
Kinser, Steve *Auto Racing Driver*
%King Racing, PO Box 2115, Allen, TX 75013, USA
Kinsey, James L *Chemist*
%Rice University, Natural Sciences School, Houston, TX 77005, USA
Kinshofer-Guthlein, Christa *Alpine Skier*
Munchnerstr 44, 83026 Rosenheim, Germany
Kinski, Nastassja *Actress, Model*
1000 Bel Air Place, Los Angeles, CA 90077, USA
Kinsley, Michael E *Editor, Commentator*
14150 NE 20th St, #527, Bellevue, WA 98007, USA
Kinsman, T James (Jim) *Vietnam War Army Hero (CMH)*
111 Howe Road E, Winlock, WA 98596, USA
Kintner, William R *Political Scientist*
%Foreign Policy Research Institute, 3508 Market St, Philadelphia, PA 19104, USA
Kiper, Mel, Jr *Sportscaster*
%ESPN-TV, Sports Dept, ESPN Plaza, 935 Middle St, Bristol, CT 06010, USA
Kipketer, Wilson *Track Athlete*
Atletik Forbund, Idraettens Hus, Brondby Stadion 20, 2605 Brondby, Denmark
Kiplinger, Austin H *Publisher*
Montevideo, 1680 River Road, Poolesville, MD 20837, USA
Kiraly, Charles F (Karch) *Volleyball Player, Coach*
%Assn of Volleyball Pros, 330 Washington Blvd, #400, Marina del Rey, CA 90292, USA
Kirby, Bruce *Actor*
629 N Orlando Ave, #3, West Hollywood, CA 90048, USA
Kirby, Durwood *Writer*
PO Box 3454, Fort Myers, FL 33918, USA
Kirby, Ronald H *Architect*
PO Box 337, Melville, 2109 Johannesburg, South Africa
Kirchbach, Gunar *Canoeing Athlete*
Georgi-Dobrowolski-Str 10, 15517 Furstenwalde, Germany
Kirchhoff, Ulrich *Equestrian Rider*
Hoven 258, 48720 Rosendahl, Germany
Kirchner, Leon *Composer, Concert Pianist, Conductor*
%Harvard University, Music Dept, Cambridge, MA 02138, USA
Kirchner, Mark *Biathlete*
Hauptstr 74A, 98749 Scheibe-Alsbach, Germany
Kirchner, Nestor *President, Argentina*
%Casa de Gobierno, Balcarce 50, 1064 Buenos Aires, Argentina
Kirchschlager, Angelika *Opera Singer*
%Mastrioanni Assoc, 161 W 61st St, #17E, New York, NY 10023, USA
Kirgo, George *Actor, Writer*
178 N Carmelina Ave, Los Angeles, CA 90049, USA
Kirilenko, Andrei *Basketball Player*
%Utah Jazz, Delta Center, 301 W South Temple, Salt Lake City, UT 84101, USA
Kirk, Claude R, Jr *Governor, FL*
%Kirk Co, 1180 Gator Trail, West Palm Beach, FL 33409, USA
Kirk, Phyllis *Actress*
321 S Beverly Dr, #M, Beverly Hills, CA 90212, USA
Kirk, Rahsaan Roland *Jazz Musician*
%Atlantic Records, 9229 Sunset Blvd, #900, Los Angeles, CA 90069, USA
Kirk, Thomas B *Physicist*
%Brookhaven National Laboratory, Physics Dept, 2 Center St, Upton, NY 11973, USA
Kirk, Walton (Walt), Jr *Basketball Player*
2355 Coventry Parkway, #B202, Dubuque, IA 52001, USA
Kirkby, Emma *Concert Singer*
%Consort of Music, 54A Leamington Road Villas, London W11 1HT, England
Kirkeby, Per *Artist*
%Margarete Roeder Gallery, 545 Broadway, New York, NY 10012, USA
Kirkland, Gelsey *Ballerina*
500 Mount Tailac Court, Roseville, CA 95747, USA
Kirkland, Mike *Banjo Player (Brothers Four)*
%Bob Flick Productions, 300 Vine, #14, Seattle, WA 98121, USA
Kirkland, Sally *Actress*
11300 W Olympic Blvd, #610, Los Angeles, CA 90064, USA
Kirkman, Rick *Cartoonist (Baby Blues)*
%King Features Syndicate, 888 7th Ave, New York, NY 10106, USA
Kirkpatrick, Chris *Singer ('N Sync)*
%Wright Entertainment, 7680 Universal Blvd, #500, Orlando, FL 32819, USA
Kirkpatrick, Jeane D J *Government Official*
%American Enterprise Institute, 1150 17th St NW, Washington, DC 20036, USA

Kirkpatrick, Maggie *Actress*
%Shanahan Mgmt, PO Box 1509, Darlinghurst NSW 1300, Australia
Kirkpatrick, Ralph *Concert Harpsichordist*
Old Quarry, Guilford, CT 06437, USA
Kirkup, James *Writer*
%British Monomarks, BM-Box 2780, London WC1V 6XX, England
Kirrane, John (Jack) *Hockey Player*
3 Centre St, Brookline, MA 02446, USA
Kirsch, Stan *Actor*
%Kritzer, 12200 W Olympic Blvd, #400, Los Angeles, CA 90064, USA
Kirschner, Carl *Educator*
%Rutgers State University College, President's Office, New Brunswick, NJ 08093, USA
Kirschstein, Ruth L *Physician*
%National Institutes of Health, 9000 Rockville Pike, Bethesda, MD 20892, USA
Kirshbaum, Laurence J *Publisher*
%Warner Books, Time-Life Building, Rockefeller Center, New York, NY 10020, USA
Kirshbaum, Ralph *Concert Cellist*
%Columbia Artists Mgmt Inc, 165 W 57th St, New York, NY 10019, USA
Kirszenstein Szewinska, Irena *Track Athlete*
Ul Bagno 5 m 80, 00-112 Warsaw, Poland
Kisabaka, Lisa *Track Athlete*
Franz-Hitze-Str 22, 51372 Leverkusen, Germany
Kiser, Terry *Actor*
%Innovative Artists, 1505 10th St, Santa Monica, CA 90401, USA
Kishlansky, Mark A *Historian*
%Harvard University, History Dept, Cambridge, MA 02138, USA
Kisio, Kelly *Hockey Player*
Birch Cliff, Bentley AB T0C 0J0, Canada
Kisner, Jacob *Writer*
245 Park Ave S, #PH F, New York, NY 10003, USA
Kison, Bruce E *Baseball Player*
1403 Riverside Circle, Bradenton, FL 33529, USA
Kissin, Evgeni I *Concert Pianist*
%Harold Holt, 31 Sinclair Road, London W14 0NS, England
Kissinger, Henry A *Secretary, State; Nobel Peace Laureate*
350 Park Ave, New York, NY 10022, USA
Kissling, Conny *Freestyle Skier*
Hubel, 3254 Messen, Switzerland
Kistler, Darci *Ballerina*
%New York City Ballet, Lincoln Center Plaza, New York, NY 10023, USA
Kitaen, Tawny *Actress*
650 Town Center Dr, #1000, Costa Mesa, CA 92626, USA
Kitaj, R B *Artist*
%Marlborough Fine Art, 6 Albemarle St, London W1, England
Kitano, Takeshi *Actor, Director*
%Office Kitano, 5-4-14 Akasaka Minataku, 107-0052 Tokyo, Japan
Kitaro *Musician, Composer*
%GLP, Huetteldorferstra 259, Vienna 1140, Austria
Kitayenko, Dmitri G *Conductor*
Chalet Kalimor, 1652 Botterens, Switzerland
Kitbunchu, M Michai Cardinal *Religious Leader*
122 Soi Naaksuwan, Thanon Nonsi, Yannawa, Bangkok 10120, Thailand
Kite, Greg *Basketball Player*
3060 Seigneury Dr, Windermere, FL 34786, USA
Kite, Thomas O (Tom), Jr *Golfer*
%Pros Inc, 7100 Forest Ave, #201, Richmond, VA 23226, USA
Kitna, John *Football Player*
11317 Madera Circle SW, Lakewood, WA 98499, USA
Kitt, A J *Alpine Skier*
2437 Franklin Ave, Louisville, CO 80027, USA
Kitt, Eartha M *Singer, Actress*
PO Box 36, Scarsdale, NY 10583, USA
Kittel, Charles *Physicist*
%University of California, Physics Dept, Berkeley, CA 94720, USA
Kittinger, Joseph W (Joe), Jr *Parachutist, Balloonist*
608 Mariner Way, Altamonte Springs, FL 32701, USA
Kittle, Ronald D (Ron) *Baseball Player*
68 Ridge Ave, Greendale, IN 47025, USA
Kittles, Kerry *Basketball Player*
%New Jersey Nets, 390 Murray Hill Parkway, East Rutherford, NJ 07073, USA
Kitzhaber, John A *Governor, OR*
%Oregon Health & Science University, Evidence Based Policy, Portland, OR 97201, USA
Kiyosaki, Robert T *Writer*
%Cashflow Technologies, 4330 N Civic Center Plaza, Scottsdale, AZ 85251, USA
Kizer, Carolyn A *Writer*
%University of Arizona, English Dept, Tucson, AZ 85721, USA
Kizim, Leonid D *Cosmonaut; Air Force General*
%Mojaysky Military School, Russian Space Forces, Saint Petersburg, Russia

Kjer, Bodil *Actress*
Vestre Pavilion, Frydenlund, Frydenlunds Alle 19, 2950 Vedbaek, Denmark
Kjus, Lasse *Alpine Skier*
Rugdeveien 2C, 1404 Siggerud, Norway
Klabunde, Charles S *Artist*
68 W 3rd St, New York, NY 10012, USA
Klammer, Franz *Alpine Skier*
Mooswald 22, 9712 Friesach/Ktn, Austria
Klaplisch, Cedric *Movie Director*
%Cineart, 36 Rue de Ponthieu, 75008 Paris, France
Klares, John *Bowler*
1760 N Decatur Blvd, #10, Las Vegas, NV 89108, USA
Klas, Eri *Conductor*
Nurme 54, 0016 Tallinn, Estonia
Klausing, Chuck *Football Coach*
2115 Lazor St, Indiana, PA 15701, USA
Klausner, Richard D *Cell Biologist*
%National Cancer Institute, 31 Center Dr, Bethesda, MD 20892, USA
Klavan, Andrew *Writer*
%Dell Publishing, 1540 Broadway, New York, NY 10036, USA
Klaw, Spencer *Editor*
280 Cream Hill Road, West Cornwall, CT 06796, USA
Klebe, Giselher *Composer*
Bruchstr 16, 32756 Detmold, Germany
Klecko, Joseph E (Joe) *Football Player*
105 Stella Lane, Aston, PA 19014, USA
Klees, Christian *Marksman*
%Eutiner Sportschutzen, Schutzenweg 26, 23701 Eutin, Germany
Kleiber, Carlos *Conductor*
Max-Joseph-Platz 2, 80539 Munich, Germany
Kleihues, Josef P *Architect*
Schlickweg 4, 14129 Berlin, Germany
Klein, Alex *Concert Oboist*
%Columbia Artists Mgmt Inc, 165 W 57th St, New York, NY 10019, USA
Klein, Calvin R *Fashion Designer*
%Calvin Klein Industries, 205 W 39th St, New York, NY 10018, USA
Klein, Chris *Actor*
%William Morris Agency, 151 El Camino Dr, Beverly Hills, CA 90212, USA
Klein, Danny *Bassist (J Geils Band)*
%Nick Ben-Meir, 652 N Doheny Dr, Los Angeles, CA 90069, USA
Klein, David *Geneticist*
%National Child Health Institute, 9000 Rockville Pike, Bethesda, MD 20892, USA
Klein, Emilee *Golfer*
%Int'l Mgmt Group, 1 Erieview Plaza, 1360 E 9th St, #1300, Cleveland, OH 44114, USA
Klein, George *Tumor Biologist*
Kottlavagen 10, 181 61 Lidingo, Sweden
Klein, Herbert G *Publisher, Government Official*
%Copley Press, 350 Camino de Reina, San Diego, CA 92108, USA
Klein, Jess *Singer, Songwriter*
%Drake Assoc, 177 Woodland Ave, Westwood, NJ 07675, USA
Klein, Joe *Journalist, Writer*
%Newsweek Magazine, Editorial Dept, 251 W 57th St, New York, NY 10019, USA
Klein, Joel *Attorney, Government Official, Educator*
%NY City Schools, Chancellor's Office, 110 Livingston St, Brooklyn, NY 11201, USA
Klein, Lawrence R *Nobel Economics Laureate*
101 Cheswold Lane, #4C, Haverford, PA 19041, USA
Klein, Lester A *Urologist*
%Scripps Clinic, Urology Dept, 10666 N Torrey Pines Road, La Jolla, CA 92037, USA
Klein, Robert *Entertainer*
67 Ridgecrest Road, Briarcliff Manor, NY 10510, USA
Klein, Robert O (Bob) *Football Player*
15933 Alcima Ave, Pacific Palisades, CA 90272, USA
Kleine, Joseph (Joe) *Basketball Player*
4819 Stony Ford Dr, Dallas, TX 75287, USA
Kleinert, Harold E *Microsurgeon*
225 Abraham Flexner Way, Louisville, KY 40202, USA
Kleinfeld, Andrew J *Judge*
%US Court of Appeals, Courthouse Square, 250 Cushman St, Fairbanks, AK 99701, USA
Kleinman, Arthur M *Anthropologist, Psychiatrist*
%Harvard University, Anthropology Dept, Cambridge, MA 02138, USA
Kleinrock, Leonard *Computer Scientist*
318 N Rockingham Ave, Los Angeles, CA 90049, USA
Kleinsmith, Bruce *Cartoonist*
PO Box 325, Aromas, CA 95004, USA
Kleiser, Randal *Movie Director*
3050 Runyan Canyon Road, Los Angeles, CA 90046, USA
Klemmer, John *Jazz Saxophonist*
%Boardman, 10548 Clearwood Court, Los Angeles, CA 90077, USA

Klemperer, William *Chemist*
53 Shattuck Road, Watertown, MA 02472, USA
Klemt, Becky *Attorney*
%Pence & MacMillan, PO Box 1285, Laramie, WY 82073, USA
Kleppe, Thomas S *Secretary, Interior*
7100 Darby Road, Bethesda, MD 20817, USA
Klesko, Ryan A *Baseball Player*
9219 Nickles Blvd, Boynton Beach, FL 33436, USA
Klesla, Rotislav *Hockey Player*
%Columbus Blue Jackets, Arena, 200 W Nationwide Blvd, Columbus, OH 43215, USA
Klestil, Thomas *President, Austria*
Prasidentschaftskanzlei, Hofburg, 1010 Vienna, Austria
Klett, Peter *Guitarist (Candlebox)*
11410 NE 124th St, #627, Kirkland, WA 98034, USA
Kliesmet, Robert B *Labor Leader*
%Union of Police Assns, 815 16th St NW, #307, Washington, DC 20006, USA
Kliks, Rudolf R *Architect*
%Russian Chamber of Commerce, Ul Kuibysheva 6, Moscow, Russia
Klim, Michael *Swimmer*
177 Bridge Road, Richmond VIC 3121, Australia
Klima, Petr *Hockey Player*
5002 Avenue Avignon, Lutz, FL 33558, USA
Klimke, Reiner *Equestrian Rider*
Krumme Str 3, 48143 Munster, Germany
Klimuk, Pyotr I *Cosmonaut, Air Force General*
%Potchta Kosmonavtov, Moskovskoi Oblasti, 141160 Syvisdny Goroduk, Russia
Kline, Kevin D *Actor*
1636 3rd Ave, #309, New York, NY 10128, USA
Klingensmith, Michael J *Publisher*
%Entertainment Weekly Magazine, Rockefeller Center, New York, NY 10020, USA
Klinger, Georgette *Beauty Consultant*
131 S Rodeo Dr, #102, Beverly Hills, CA 90212, USA
Klingler, David *Football Player*
11215 Valley Spring Dr, Houston, TX 77043, USA
Klinsmann, Jurgen *Soccer Player*
3419 Via Lido, #600, Newport Beach, CA 92663, USA
Klippstein, John C (Johnny) *Baseball Player*
12500 Elmwood Court, Huntley, IL 60142, USA
Klitschko, Wladimir *Boxer*
Am Stradtrand 2, 22047 Hamburg, Germany
Klotz, H Louis (Red) *Basketball Player, Coach*
114 S Osbourne Ave, Margate City, NJ 08402, USA
Klotz, Irving M *Chemist, Biochemist*
1500 Sheridan Road, #7D, Wilmette, IL 60091, USA
Klous, Patricia *Actress*
2539 Benedict Canyon Dr, Beverly Hills, CA 90210, USA
Kluer, Duane *Basketball Player, Coach*
252 Francis Avenue Court, Terre Haute, IN 47804, USA
Klug, Aaron *Nobel Chemistry Laureate*
70 Cavendish Ave, Cambridge CB1 40T, England
Kluge, John W *Businessman*
%Metromedia Co, 1 Meadowlands Plaza, #300, East Rutherford, NJ 07073, USA
Kluger, Richard *Writer*
%William Morris Agency, 151 El Camino Dr, Beverly Hills, CA 90212, USA
Klugh, Earl *Jazz Guitarist*
%International Creative Mgmt, 8942 Wilshire Blvd, #219, Beverly Hills, CA 90211, USA
Klugman, Jack *Actor*
22548 W Pacific Coast Highway, #110, Malibu, CA 90265, USA
Klum, Heidi *Model, Actress*
%Elite Model Mgmt, 111 E 22nd St, #200, New York, NY 10010, USA
Klyszewski, Waclaw *Architect*
Ul Gornoslaska 16 m 15A, 00-432 Warsaw, Poland
Knape Lindberg, Ulrike *Diver*
Drostvagen 7, 691 33 Karlskoga, Sweden
Knapp, Charles B *Educator*
%Aspen Institute, 1333 New Hampshire Ave NW, Washington, DC 20036, USA
Knapp, Cleon T *Publisher*
%Talewood Corp, 10100 Santa Monica Blvd, #2000, Los Angeles, CA 90067, USA
Knapp, Jennifer *Singer*
%Creative Artists Agency, 9830 Wilshire Blvd, Beverly Hills, CA 90212, USA
Knapp, John W *Educator, Army General*
%Virginia Military Institute, Superintendent's Office, Lexington, VA 24450, USA
Knapp, Stefan *Artist*
Sandhills, Godalming, Surrey, England
Knappenberger, Alton W *WW II Army Hero (CMH)*
PO Box 364, Main St, Schwenksville, PA 19473, USA
Knaus, William *Physician, Medical Activist*
%George Washington University, Medical Center, Washington, DC 20052, USA

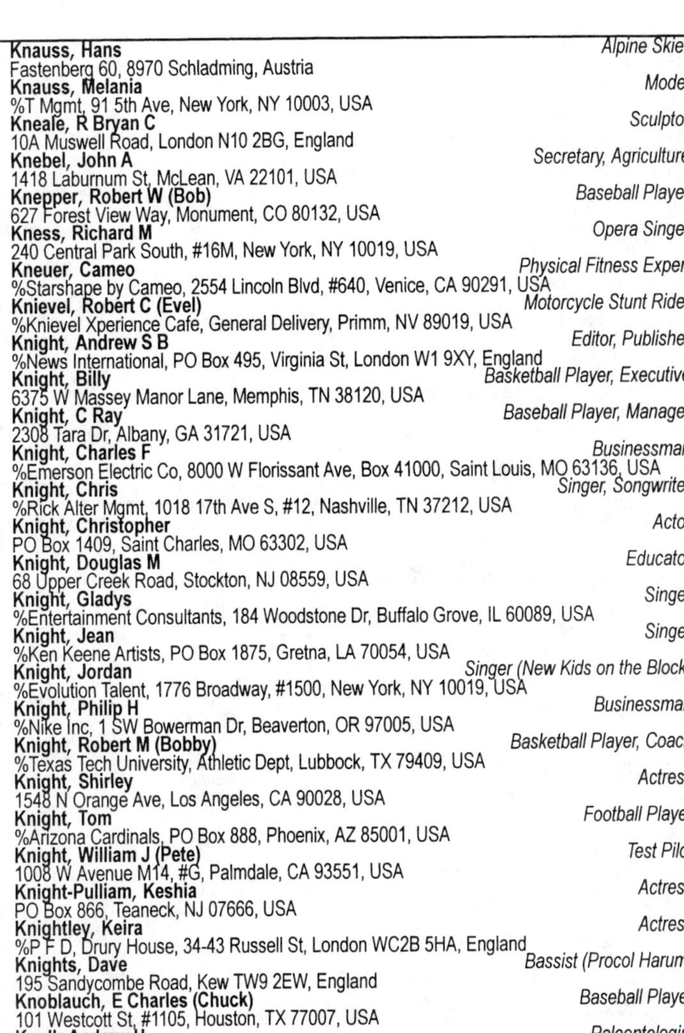

Knauss, Hans *Alpine Skier*
Fastenberg 60, 8970 Schladming, Austria
Knauss, Melania *Model*
%T Mgmt, 91 5th Ave, New York, NY 10003, USA
Kneale, R Bryan C *Sculptor*
10A Muswell Road, London N10 2BG, England
Knebel, John A *Secretary, Agriculture*
1418 Laburnum St, McLean, VA 22101, USA
Knepper, Robert W (Bob) *Baseball Player*
627 Forest View Way, Monument, CO 80132, USA
Kness, Richard M *Opera Singer*
240 Central Park South, #16M, New York, NY 10019, USA
Kneuer, Cameo *Physical Fitness Expert*
%Starshape by Cameo, 2554 Lincoln Blvd, #640, Venice, CA 90291, USA
Knievel, Robert C (Evel) *Motorcycle Stunt Rider*
%Knievel Xperience Cafe, General Delivery, Primm, NV 89019, USA
Knight, Andrew S B *Editor, Publisher*
%News International, PO Box 495, Virginia St, London W1 9XY, England
Knight, Billy *Basketball Player, Executive*
6375 W Massey Manor Lane, Memphis, TN 38120, USA
Knight, C Ray *Baseball Player, Manager*
2308 Tara Dr, Albany, GA 31721, USA
Knight, Charles F *Businessman*
%Emerson Electric Co, 8000 W Florissant Ave, Box 41000, Saint Louis, MO 63136, USA
Knight, Chris *Singer, Songwriter*
%Rick Alter Mgmt, 1018 17th Ave S, #12, Nashville, TN 37212, USA
Knight, Christopher *Actor*
PO Box 1409, Saint Charles, MO 63302, USA
Knight, Douglas M *Educator*
68 Upper Creek Road, Stockton, NJ 08559, USA
Knight, Gladys *Singer*
%Entertainment Consultants, 184 Woodstone Dr, Buffalo Grove, IL 60089, USA
Knight, Jean *Singer*
%Ken Keene Artists, PO Box 1875, Gretna, LA 70054, USA
Knight, Jordan *Singer (New Kids on the Block)*
%Evolution Talent, 1776 Broadway, #1500, New York, NY 10019, USA
Knight, Philip H *Businessman*
%Nike Inc, 1 SW Bowerman Dr, Beaverton, OR 97005, USA
Knight, Robert M (Bobby) *Basketball Player, Coach*
%Texas Tech University, Athletic Dept, Lubbock, TX 79409, USA
Knight, Shirley *Actress*
1548 N Orange Ave, Los Angeles, CA 90028, USA
Knight, Tom *Football Player*
%Arizona Cardinals, PO Box 888, Phoenix, AZ 85001, USA
Knight, William J (Pete) *Test Pilot*
1008 W Avenue M14, #G, Palmdale, CA 93551, USA
Knight-Pulliam, Keshia *Actress*
PO Box 866, Teaneck, NJ 07666, USA
Knightley, Keira *Actress*
%P F D, Drury House, 34-43 Russell St, London WC2B 5HA, England
Knights, Dave *Bassist (Procol Harum)*
195 Sandycombe Road, Kew TW9 2EW, England
Knoblauch, E Charles (Chuck) *Baseball Player*
101 Westcott St, #1105, Houston, TX 77007, USA
Knoll, Andrew H *Paleontologist*
%Harvard University, Botanical Museum, 26 Oxford St, Cambridge, MA 02138, USA
Knoll, Jozsef *Pharmacologist*
%Semmelweis Medical University, Pharmacology Dept, 1089 Budapest, Hungary
Knopf, Sascha *Actress, Model*
%Gold Marshak Liedtke, 3500 W Olive Ave, #1400, Burbank, CA 91505, USA
Knopfler, David *Guitarist (Dire Straits)*
%Damage Mgmt, 16 Lambton Place, London W11 2SH, England
Knopfler, Mark *Singer, Guitarist (Dire Straits)*
%Paul Crockford Mgmt, 37 Ruston Mews, London W11 1RB, England
Knopoff, Leon *Geophysicist*
%University of California, Geophysics Institute, Los Angeles, CA 90024, USA
Knostman, Richard (Dick) *Basketball Player*
3960 Schooner Ridge, Alpharetta, GA 30005, USA
Knotts, Don *Actor, Comedian*
%Scott Stander, 13701 Riverside Dr, #201, Sherman Oaks, CA 91423, USA
Knowles, Beyonce *Singer (Destiny's Child), Actress*
%Music World, PO Box 53208, Houston, TX 77052, USA
Knowles, Jeremy R *Chemist*
67 Francis Ave, Cambridge, MA 02138, USA
Knowles, William S *Nobel Chemistry Laureate*
PO Box 71, Kelly, WY 83011, USA
Knowlton, Steve R *Skier*
%Palmer Yeager Assoc, 6600 E Hampden Ave, #210, Denver, CO 80224, USA

K

Knowlton, William A *Army General*
4520 4th Road North, Arlington, VA 22203, USA
Knox-Johnston, Robin *Yachtsman*
26 Sefton St, Putney, London SW15, England
Knoxville, Johnny *Actor*
%Handprint Entertainment, 1100 Glendon Ave, #1000, Los Angeles, CA 90024, USA
Knudsen, Arthur G *Skier*
5111 Wright Ave, #104, Racine, WI 53406, USA
Knudsen, Keith *Drummer, Singer (Doobie Brothers)*
%Monterey Peninsula Artists, 509 Hartnell St, Monterey, CA 93940, USA
Knudson, Alfred G, Jr *Geneticist*
%Institute for Cancer Research, 7701 Burholme Ave, Philadelphia, PA 19111, USA
Knudson, Thomas J *Journalist*
%Sacramento Bee, Editorial Dept, 21st & Q Sts, Sacramento, CA 95852, USA
Knussen, S Oliver *Conductor, Composer*
%Harrison/Parrott, 12 Penzance Place, London W11 4PA England
Knuth, Donald E *Computer Scientist*
%Stanford University, Computer Sciences Dept, Gates Building, Stanford, CA 94305, USA
Knutson, Ronald *Religious Leader*
%Free Lutheran Congregations Assn, 402 W 11th St, Canton, SD 57013, USA
Kobashigawa, Yeiki *WW II Army Hero (CMH)*
85-120 Mill St, Waianae, HI 96793, USA
Kober, Jeff *Actor*
4544 Ethel Ave, Studio City, CA 91604, USA
Koblik, Steven *Museum Executive, Educator*
%Huntington Library & Art Gallery, 1151 Oxford Road, San Marino, CA 91108, USA
Koch, Desmond (Des) *Track Athlete, Football Player*
23296 Gilmore St, Canoga Park, CA 91307, USA
Koch, Ed *Artist*
1211 NW Ogden Ave, Bend, OR 97701, USA
Koch, Edward I *Mayor*
%Robinson Silverman Pearce, 1290 Ave of Americas, New York, NY 10104, USA
Koch, Gregory M (Greg) *Football Player*
4412 Darsey St, Bellaire, TX 77401, USA
Koch, James V *Educator*
%Old Dominion University, President's Office, Norfolk, VA 23529, USA
Koch, William (Bill) *Nordic Skier*
PO Box 115, Ashland, OR 97520, USA
Koch, William I (Bill) *Yachtsman, Businessman*
%Oxbow Corp, 1601 Forum Place, West Palm Beach, FL 33401, USA
Kocharian, Robert *President, Prime Minister, Armenia*
%President's Office, Marshal Bagramian Prosp 19, 375010 Yerevan, Armenia
Kocherga, Anatoli I *Opera Singer*
Gogolevskaya 37/2/47, 254053 Kiev, Russia
Kochi, Jay K *Chemist*
4372 Faculty Lane, Houston, TX 77004, USA
Kocsis, Zoltan *Concert Pianist, Composer*
Narcisa Utca 29, 1126 Budapest, Hungary
Kodes, Jan *Tennis Player*
Na Berance 18, 160 00 Prague 6/Dejvioe, Czech Republic
Kodjoe, Boris *Model, Actor*
9100 Wilshire Blvd, #503E, Beverly Hills, CA 90212, USA
Koehler, Horst *Financier*
%International Monetary Fund, 700 19th St NW, Washington, DC 20431, USA
Koelle, George B *Pharmacologist*
3300 Darby Road, #3310, Haverford, PA 19041, USA
Koen, Karleen *Writer*
%Random House, 1745 Broadway, #B1, New York, NY 10019, USA
Koenekamp, Fred *Cinematographer*
9756 Shoshine Ave, Northridge, CA 91325, USA
Koenig, Pierre *Architect*
12221 Dorothy St, Los Angeles, CA 90049, USA
Koenig, Walter *Actor*
PO Box 4395, North Hollywood, CA 91617, USA
Koepp, David *Movie Director, Writer*
%Hofflund-Polone, 9465 Wilshire Blvd, #820, Beverly Hills, CA 90212, USA
Koester, Helmut H K E *Theologian*
12 Flintlock Road, Lexington, MA 02420, USA
Koetter, Dirk *Football Coach*
%Arizona State University, Athletic Dept, Tempe, AZ 85287, USA
Kogan, Pavel L *Concert Violinist, Conductor*
Bryusov Per 8/10, 103009 Moscow, Russia
Kogan, Theo *Singer (Lunachicks), Actress*
%Wilhelmina Creative Mgmt, 300 Park Ave S, #200, New York, NY 10010, USA
Kohde-Kilsch, Claudia *Tennis Player*
Elsa-Brandstrom-Str 22, 66119 Saarbrucken, Germany
Kohl, Helmut *Chancellor, Germany*
%CDU/CSU, Maurerstr 85, 10117 Berlin, Germany

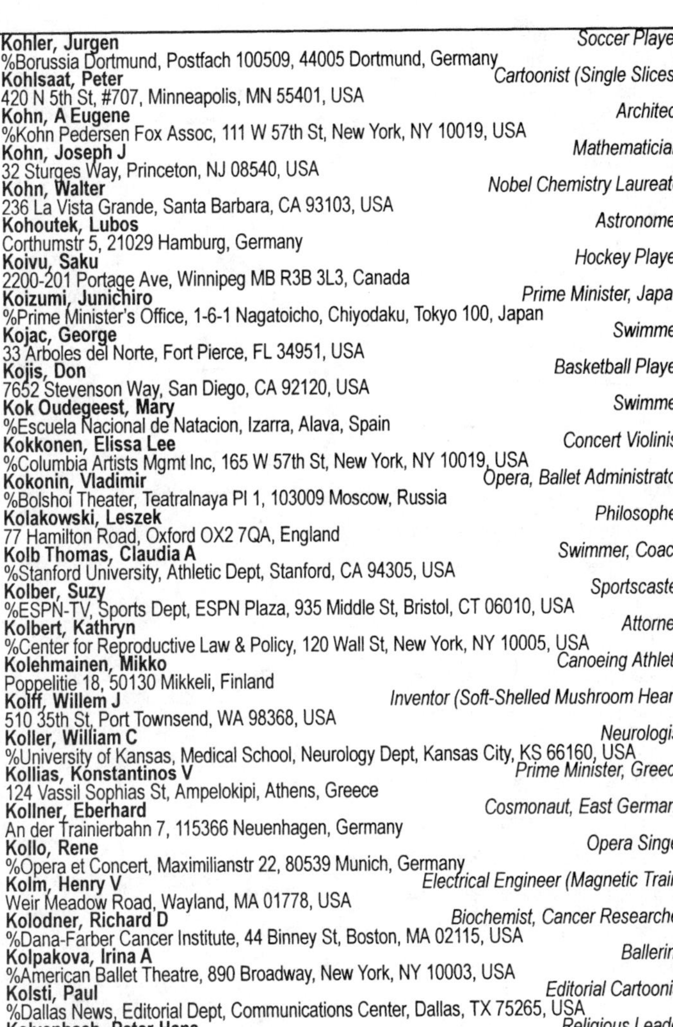

Kohler, Jurgen — *Soccer Player*
%Borussia Dortmund, Postfach 100509, 44005 Dortmund, Germany

Kohlsaat, Peter — *Cartoonist (Single Slices)*
420 N 5th St, #707, Minneapolis, MN 55401, USA

Kohn, A Eugene — *Architect*
%Kohn Pedersen Fox Assoc, 111 W 57th St, New York, NY 10019, USA

Kohn, Joseph J — *Mathematician*
32 Sturges Way, Princeton, NJ 08540, USA

Kohn, Walter — *Nobel Chemistry Laureate*
236 La Vista Grande, Santa Barbara, CA 93103, USA

Kohoutek, Lubos — *Astronomer*
Corthumstr 5, 21029 Hamburg, Germany

Koivu, Saku — *Hockey Player*
2200-201 Portage Ave, Winnipeg MB R3B 3L3, Canada

Koizumi, Junichiro — *Prime Minister, Japan*
%Prime Minister's Office, 1-6-1 Nagatoicho, Chiyodaku, Tokyo 100, Japan

Kojac, George — *Swimmer*
33 Arboles del Norte, Fort Pierce, FL 34951, USA

Kojis, Don — *Basketball Player*
7652 Stevenson Way, San Diego, CA 92120, USA

Kok Oudegeest, Mary — *Swimmer*
%Escuela Nacional de Natacion, Izarra, Alava, Spain

Kokkonen, Elissa Lee — *Concert Violinist*
%Columbia Artists Mgmt Inc, 165 W 57th St, New York, NY 10019, USA

Kokonin, Vladimir — *Opera, Ballet Administrator*
%Bolshoi Theater, Teatralnaya Pl 1, 103009 Moscow, Russia

Kolakowski, Leszek — *Philosopher*
77 Hamilton Road, Oxford OX2 7QA, England

Kolb Thomas, Claudia A — *Swimmer, Coach*
%Stanford University, Athletic Dept, Stanford, CA 94305, USA

Kolber, Suzy — *Sportscaster*
%ESPN-TV, Sports Dept, ESPN Plaza, 935 Middle St, Bristol, CT 06010, USA

Kolbert, Kathryn — *Attorney*
%Center for Reproductive Law & Policy, 120 Wall St, New York, NY 10005, USA

Kolehmainen, Mikko — *Canoeing Athlete*
Poppelitie 18, 50130 Mikkeli, Finland

Kolff, Willem J — *Inventor (Soft-Shelled Mushroom Heart)*
510 35th St, Port Townsend, WA 98368, USA

Koller, William C — *Neurologist*
%University of Kansas, Medical School, Neurology Dept, Kansas City, KS 66160, USA

Kollias, Konstantinos V — *Prime Minister, Greece*
124 Vassil Sophias St, Ampelokipi, Athens, Greece

Kollner, Eberhard — *Cosmonaut, East Germany*
An der Trainierbahn 7, 115366 Neuenhagen, Germany

Kollo, Rene — *Opera Singer*
%Opera et Concert, Maximilianstr 22, 80539 Munich, Germany

Kolm, Henry V — *Electrical Engineer (Magnetic Train)*
Weir Meadow Road, Wayland, MA 01778, USA

Kolodner, Richard D — *Biochemist, Cancer Researcher*
%Dana-Farber Cancer Institute, 44 Binney St, Boston, MA 02115, USA

Kolpakova, Irina A — *Ballerina*
%American Ballet Theatre, 890 Broadway, New York, NY 10003, USA

Kolsti, Paul — *Editorial Cartoonist*
%Dallas News, Editorial Dept, Communications Center, Dallas, TX 75265, USA

Kolvenbach, Peter-Hans — *Religious Leader*
Borgo Santo Spirito 5, CP 6139, 00195 Rome, Italy

Kolzig, Olaf — *Hockey Player*
10931 E Bahia Dr, Scottsdale, AZ 85255, USA

Komal — *Queen, Nepal*
%Royal Palace, Narayanhiti, Durbag Marg, Kathmandu, Nepal

Komarkova, Vera — *Mountaineer*
%University of Colorado, INSTAAR, Boulder, CO 80302, USA

Komenich, Kim — *Photojournalist*
111 Cornelia Ave, Mill Valley, CA 94941, USA

Kominsky, Cheryl — *Bowler*
%Ladies Professional Bowling Tour, 7200 Harrison Ave, #7171, Rockford, IL 61112, USA

Komleva, Gabriela T — *Ballerina*
Fontanka River 116, #34, 198005 Saint Petersburg, Russia

Komlos, Peter — *Concert Violinist*
Torokvesz Utca 94, 1025 Budapest, Hungary

Komunyakaa, Yusef — *Writer*
526 N Washington St, Bloomington, IN 47408, USA

Konare, Alpha Oumar — *President, Mali*
%President's Office, BP 1463, Bamako, Mali

Koncak, Jon — *Basketball Player*
2575 Red House Road, Jackson, WY 83001, USA

Koncar, Mark — *Football Player*
447 N Alpine Blvd, Alpine, UT 84004, USA

K

Konchalovsky - Kord

Konchalovsky, Andrei *Movie Director*
%Creative Artists Agency, 9830 Wilshire Blvd, Beverly Hills, CA 90212, USA
Kondakova, Elena V *Cosmonaut*
%Scientific Industrial Assn, Ulica Lenina 4A, 141070 Kaliningrad, Russia
Kondratiyeva, Maria V *Ballerina*
%Bolshoi Theater, Teatralnaya Pl 1, 103009 Moscow, Russia
Konerko, Paul *Baseball Player*
%Chicago White Sox, Comiskey Park, 333 W 35th St, Chicago, IL 60616, USA
Konig, Franz Cardinal *Religious Leader*
Wollzeile 2, 1010 Vienna, Austria
Konik, George *Hockey Player*
1027 Savannah Road, Eagan, MN 55123, USA
Konitz, Lee *Jazz Saxophonist*
%Bennett Morgan, 1282 RR 376, Wappingers Falls, NY 12590, USA
Kononenko, Oleg D *Cosmonaut*
%Potchta Kosmonavtov, Moskovskoi Oblasti, 141160 Syvisdny Goroduk, Russia
Konrad, John H *Astronaut*
%Hughes Space-Communications Group, PO Box 92919, Los Angeles, CA 90009, USA
Konstantinidis, Aris *Architect*
4 Vasilissis Sofias Blvd, 106 74 Athens, Greece
Konstantinov, Vladimir *Hockey Player*
15 Windsor Place, Essex Fells, NJ 07021, USA
Konyukhov, Fedor F *Explorer*
%Tourism/Sports Union, Studeniy Proyezd 7, 129282 Moscow, Russia
Koolhaas, Rem *Architect*
%Metropolitan Architecture, Heer Bokelweg 149, 3032 Rotterdam, Netherlands
Koolman, Olindo *Governor, Aruba*
%Governor's Office, Oranjestad, Aruba
Koons, Jeff *Artist*
600 Broadway, New York, NY 10012, USA
Koontz, Dean R *Writer*
PO Box 9529, Newport Beach, CA 92658, USA
Koop, C Everett *Physician, Pediatrician*
3 Ivy Pointe Way, Hanover, NH 03755, USA
Kooper, Al *Singer, Guitarist*
%Legacy Records, 550 Madison Ave, #1700, New York, NY 10022, USA
Koopman, A Ton G M *Conductor, Concert Keyboardist*
Meerweg 23, 1405 BC Bussu, Netherlands
Koopmans-Kint, Cor *Swimmer*
Pacific Sands C'Van Park, Nambucca Heads NSW 2448, Australia
Koosman, Jerry M *Baseball Player*
2483 State Road 35, Osceola, WI 54020, USA
Kopell, Bernie *Actor*
19413 Olivos Dr, Tarzana, CA 91356, USA
Kopelson, Arnold *Movie Producer*
901 N Roxbury Dr, Beverly Hills, CA 90210, USA
Kopervas, Gary *Cartoonist (Out on a Limb)*
%King Features Syndicate, 888 7th Ave, New York, NY 10106, USA
Kopins, Karen *Actress*
%Sutton Barth Vennari, 145 S Fairfax Ave, #310, Los Angeles, CA 90036, USA
Kopit, Arthur *Writer*
240 W 98th St, #11B, New York, NY 10025, USA
Koplan, Jeffrey *Medical Administrator*
%Emory University, Academic Health Affairs Dept, Atlanta, GA 30322, USA
Kopp, Wendy *Association Executive*
%Teach for America Foundation, 315 W 36th St, #6, New York, NY 10018, USA
Koppel, Ted *Commentator*
11910 Glen Mill Road, Potomac, MD 20854, USA
Koppelman, Chaim *Artist*
498 Broome St, New York, NY 10013, USA
Kopper, Hilmar *Financier*
%Deutsche Bank AG, Taunusanlage 12, 60325 Frankfurt/Main, Germany
Koppes, Peter *Guitarist (Church)*
%Globeshine, 101 Chamberlayne Road, London NW10 3ND, England
Kopple, Barbara J *Movie Director*
%Cabin Creek Films, 155 Ave of Americas, New York, NY 10013, USA
Kopra, Timothy L *Astronaut*
2518 Lakeside Dr, Seabrook, TX 77586, USA
Koprowski, Hilary *Microbiologist*
334 Fairhill Road, Wynnewood, PA 19096, USA
Koptchak, Sergei *Opera Singer*
%Robert Lombardo, Harkness Plaza, 61 W 62nd St, #6F, New York, NY 10023, USA
Koralek, Paul G *Architect*
7 Chalcot Road, #1, London NW1 8LH, England
Korbut, Olga V *Gymnast*
8250 N Via Paseo Del Norte, #E106, Scottsdale, AZ 85258, USA
Kord, Kazimierz *Conductor*
%Filharmonia Narodowa, Ul Jasna 5, 00-950, Warsaw, Poland

Korda, Michael V *Writer*
%Simon & Schuster/Pocket/Summit, 1230 Ave of Americas, New York, NY 10020, USA
Korda, Petr *Tennis Player*
4909 61st Ave Dr W, Bradenton, FL 34210, USA
Korec, Jan Chryzostom Cardinal *Religious Leader*
Biskupstvo Nitra, PP 46A, 95050 Nitra, Slovakia
Koren, Edward B *Cartoonist*
%New Yorker Magazine, Editorial Dept, 4 Times Square, New York, NY 10036, USA
Korf, Mia *Actress*
%Paradigm Agency, 10100 Santa Monica Blvd, #2500, Los Angeles, CA 90067, USA
Korjus, Tapio *Track Athlete*
%General Delivery, Lapua, Finland
Korman, Harvey *Actor, Comedian*
1136 Stradella Road, Los Angeles, CA 90077, USA
Korman, Maxime Carlot *Prime Minister, Vanuatu*
%Prime Minister's Office, PO Box 110, Port Vila, Vanuatu
Kormann, Peter *Gymnast, Coach*
%US Olympic Committee, 1 Olympia Plaza, Colorado Springs, CO 80909, USA
Kornberg, Arthur *Nobel Medicine Laureate*
365 Golden Oak Dr, Portola Valley, CA 94028, USA
Kornheiser, Tony *Sportswriter, Sportscaster*
%Washington Post, Editorial Dept, 1150 15th St NW, Washington, DC 20071, USA
Korowi, Wiwa *Governor General, Papua New Guinea*
Government House, Konedobu, Box 79, Port Moresby, Boroko, Papua New Guinea
Korpan, Richard *Businessman*
%Florida Progress Corp, 100 Central Ave, Saint Petersburg, FL 33701, USA
Kors, Michael *Fashion Designer*
550 Fashion Ave, #700, New York, NY 10018, USA
Korsantiya, Alexander *Concert Pianist*
%Columbia Artists Mgmt Inc, 165 W 57th St, New York, NY 10019, USA
Korvald, Lars *Prime Minister, Norway*
Vinkelgaten 6, 3050 Mjondalen, Norway
Korzun, Valery G *Cosmonaut*
%Potchta Kosmonavtov, Moskovskoi Oblasti, 141160 Syvisdny Goroduk, Russia
Kosar, Bernie J, Jr *Football Player*
2672 Riviera Manor, Weston, FL 33332, USA
Koshalek, Richard *Museum Director*
%Museum of Contemporary Art, 250 S Grand Ave, Los Angeles, CA 90012, USA
Koshiba, Masatoshi *Nobel Physics Laureate*
%University of Tokyo, 7-3-1 Hongo, Nunkyoku, Tokyo 113-8654, Japan
Koshiro, Matsumoto, IV *Kabuki Actor, Dancer*
%Kabukiza Theatre, 12-15-4 Ginza, Chuoku, Tokyo 104, Japan
Koshland, Daniel E, Jr *Biochemist*
3991 Happy Valley Road, Lafayette, CA 94549, USA
Koslow, Lauren *Actress*
%Michael Bruno, 13756 Cheltenham Dr, Sherman Oaks, CA 91423, USA
Kosner, Edward A *Editor*
%Esquire Magazine, Editorial Dept, 1790 Broadway, #1300, New York, NY 10019, USA
Koss, Johann Olav *Speedskater*
Dagaliveien 21, 0387 Oslo, Norway
Koss, John C *Inventor*
%Koss Corp, 4129 N Port Washington Ave, Milwaukee, WI 53212, USA
Kostadinova, Stefka *Track Athlete*
Rue Anghel Kantchev 4, 1000 Sofia, Bulgaria
Kostelic, Janica *Alpine Skier*
%Ski Association, Trg Sportova 11, 1000 Zagreb, Croatia
Koster, Steven J *Cinematographer*
26881 Goya Circle, Mission Viejo, CA 92691, USA
Kostner, Isolde *Alpine Skier*
General Delivery, Hortisei BZ, Italy
Kosuth, Joseph *Artist*
591 Broadway, New York, NY 10012, USA
Kotcheff, W Theodore (Ted) *Movie Director*
%Ted Kotcheff Productions, 13451 Firth Dr, Beverly Hills, CA 90210, USA
Koterba, Jeff *Sports, Editorial Cartoonist*
%Omaha World Herald, Editorial Dept, 14th & Dodge St, Wichita, Omaha, NE 68102, USA
Kotite, Richard E (Rich) *Football Player, Coach*
241 Fanning St, Staten Island, NY 10314, USA
Kotlarek, Gene *Ski Jumper*
4910 Walking Horse Point, Colorado Springs, CO 80917, USA
Kotlarek, George *Skier*
330 N Arlington Ave, #512, Duluth, MN 55811, USA
Kotlayakov, Vladimir M *Geographer, Glacierologist*
%Geography Institute, Staromonetny per 29, 109017 Moscow, Russia
Kotsonis, Ieronymous *Religious Leader*
%Archdiocese of Athens, Hatzichristou 8, Athens 402, Greece 53212, USA
Kottke, Leo *Singer, Songwriter, Guitarist*
%Chuck Morris Entertainment, 1658 York St, Denver, CO 80206, USA

K

Kotto, Yaphet F — *Actor*
%Artists Group, 10100 Santa Monica Blvd, #2490, Los Angeles, CA 90067, USA

Kotulak, Ronald — *Editor*
%Chicago Tribune, Editorial Dept, 435 N Michigan Ave, Chicago, IL 60611, USA

Kotz, John — *Basketball Player*
PO Box 7900, Madison, WI 53707, USA

Kotzky, Alex S — *Cartoonist (Apartment 3-G)*
20317 56th Ave, Oakland Gardens, NY 11364, USA

Kouchner, Bernard — *Physician*
%L'Action d'Humanitaire, 8 Ave de Segur, 75350 Paris, France

Koudelka, Josef — *Photographer*
%Magnum Photos, Moreland Bldgs, 23 Old St, London EC1V 9HL, England

Koufax, Sanford (Sandy) — *Baseball Player*
106 Amy Ann Lane, Vero Beach, FL 32963, USA

Kournikova, Anna — *Tennis Player*
300 S Pointe Dr, #PH 3, Miami Beach, FL 33139, USA

Kovacevich, Richard M — *Financier*
%Wells Fargo Co, 420 Montgomery St, San Francisco, CA 94163, USA

Kovacevich, Stephen — *Concert Pianist, Conductor*
%Van Walsum Mgmt, 4 Addison Bridge Place, London W14 8XP, England

Kovach, Bill — *Editor, Foundation Executive*
%Harvard University, Nieman Fellows Program, Cambridge, MA 02138, USA

Kovacic, Ernst — *Concert Violinist*
%Ingpen & Williams, 14 Kensington Court, London W8 5DN, England

Kovacic-Ciro, Zdravko — *Water Polo Player*
JP Kamova 57, 51000 Rijeka, Serbia & Montenegro

Kovacs, Andras — *Movie Director*
Magyar Jakobinusok Ter 2/3, 1122 Budapest, Hungary

Kovacs, Denes — *Concert Violinist*
Iranyi Utca 12, Budapest V, Hungary

Kovacs, Laszlo — *Cinematographer*
%Feinstein & Berson, 16255 Ventura Blvd, #625, Encino, CA 91436, USA

Kovalchuk, Ilya — *Hockey Player*
%SFX Sports, 220 W 42nd St, New York, NY 10036, USA

Kovalenko, Alexei — *Hockey Player*
1 Trimont Lane, #2000A, Pittsburgh, PA 15211, USA

Kovalenok, Vladimir S — *Cosmonaut, Air Force General*
3 Ap 22, Hovanskaya St, 129515 Moscow, Russia

Kovalev, Alexei — *Hockey Player*
4 Kassel Court, Mamaroneck, NY 10543, USA

Kovalevsky, Jean — *Astronomer*
Villa La Padovane, 8 Rue Saint Michel, Saint-Antoine, 06130 Grasse, France

Kove, Martin — *Actor*
11595 Huston St, North Hollywood, CA 91601, USA

Kowal, Charles T — *Astronomer*
%Space Telescope Science Institute, Homewood Campus, Baltimore, MD 21218, USA

Kowalczyk, Ed — *Singer, Guitarist (Live)*
%Freedman & Smith, 350 W End Ave, #1, New York, NY 10024, USA

Kowalczyk, Jozef — *Religious Leader*
%Nuncjatura Apostolska, Al J Ch Szucha 12, #163, 00-582 Warsaw, Poland

Kowalski, Ted — *Singer (Diamonds)*
%GEMS, PO Box 1031, Montrose, CA 91021, USA

Koy, Ernest M (Ernie) — *Football Player*
7 E Hacienda, Bellville, TX 77418, USA

Koz, Dave — *Jazz Saxophonist, Flutist*
5850 W 3rd St, #307, Los Angeles, CA 90036, USA

Kozak, Harley Jane — *Actress*
21336 Colina Dr, Topanga, CA 90290, USA

Kozakov, Mikhail M — *Actor, Director*
%Mayakovsky Theater, B Nikitskaya Str 17, 103009 Moscow, Russia

Kozeev, Konstantin — *Cosmonaut*
%Potchta Kosmonavtov, Moskovskoi Oblasti, 141160 Syvisdny Goroduk, Russia

Kozena, Magdalena — *Opera Singer*
Narodni Divadlo, Dvorakova 11, 60000 Brno, Czech Republic

Kozinski, Alex — *Judge*
%US Court of Appeals, 125 S Grand Ave, Pasadena, CA 91105, USA

Kozlova, Valentina — *Ballerina*
%New York City Ballet, Lincoln Center Plaza, New York, NY 10023, USA

Kozlowiecki, Adam Cardinal — *Religious Leader*
PO Box 50003, 15101 Ridgeway, Zambia

Kozlowski, Linda — *Actress*
18 Marshall Crescent, Beacon Hill NSW 2060, Australia

Kozol, Jonathan — *Writer*
PO Box 145, Byfield, MA 01922, USA

Kraatz, Victor — *Figure Skater*
%Connecticut Skating Center, 300 Alumni Road, Newington, CT 06111, USA

Krabbe, Jeroen — *Actor*
Van Eeghaustraat 107, 1071 EZ Amsterdam, Netherlands

Krabbe-Zimmermann, Katrin *Track Athlete*
Dorfstr 9, 17091 Pinnow, Germany
Krackow, Jurgen *Businessman*
Schumannstr 100, 40237 Dusseldorf, Germany
Kraemer, Harry J *Businessman*
%Baxter International, 1 Baxter Parkway, Deerfield, IL 60015, USA
Kraft, Christopher C (Chris), Jr *Space Administrator*
14919 Village Elm St, Houston, TX 77062, USA
Kraft, Craig A *Artist*
931 R St NW, Washington, DC 20001, USA
Kraft, Greg *Golfer*
14820 Rue de Bayonne, #302, Clearwater, FL 33762, USA
Kraft, Leo A *Composer*
9 Dunster Road, Great Neck, NY 11021, USA
Kraft, Robert *Composer*
4722 Noeline Ave, Encino, CA 91436, USA
Kraft, Robert P *Astrophysicist*
%University of California, Lick Observatory, Santa Cruz, CA 95064, USA
Krainev, Vladimir V *Concert Pianist*
%Staatliche Hochschule fur Musik, Walderseestr 100, Hanover, Germany
Krajicek, Richard *Tennis Player*
%Octagon, 1751 Pinnacle Dr, #1500, McLean, VA 22102, USA
Krakowski, Jane *Actress, Singer*
%Borinstein Oreck Bogart, 3172 Dona Susana Dr, Studio City, CA 91604, USA
Krall, Diana *Singer, Pianist*
%Macklam Feldman Mgmt, 1505 W 2nd Ave, #200, Vancouver BC V6H 3Y4, Canada
Kramarsky, David *Movie Director*
1336 Havenhurst Dr, West Hollywood, CA 90046, USA
Kramer, Billy J *Singer*
%Mars Talent, 27 L'Ambiance Court, Bardonia, NY 10954, USA
Kramer, Clare *Actress*
%Propaganda Films Mgmt, 1741 Ivar Ave, Los Angeles, CA 90028, USA
Kramer, Gerald L (Jerry) *Football Player*
11768 Chinden Blvd, Boise, ID 83714, USA
Kramer, Joel R *Editor*
%Minneapolis Star Tribune, 425 Portland Ave, Minneapolis, MN 55488, USA
Kramer, Joey *Drummer (Aerosmith)*
282 Pudding Hill Road, Marshfield, MA 02050, USA
Kramer, John A (Jack) *Tennis Player, Executive*
231 Glenroy Place, Los Angeles, CA 90049, USA
Kramer, Larry *Social Activist, Writer*
%Gay Men's Health Crisis, 119 W 24th St, New York, NY 10011, USA
Kramer, Ronald J (Ron) *Football Player*
%Ron Kramer Industries, PO Box 473, Fenton, MI 48430, USA
Kramer, Stepfanie *Actress*
8455 Beverly Blvd, #505, Los Angeles, CA 90048, USA
Kramer, Thomas (Tommy) *Football Player*
6381 Stable Farm, San Antonio, TX 78249, USA
Kramer, W Erik *Football Player*
3150 Fallen Oaks Court, Rochester Hills, MI 48309, USA
Kramer, Wayne *Jazz Guitarist (Was Not Was, MC5)*
%Performers of the World, 8901 Melrose Ave, #200, West Hollywood, CA 90069, USA
Kramnik, Vladimir *Chess Player*
%Russian Chess Federation, Luchnetskaya 8, 119270 Moscow, Russia
Krantz, Judith T *Writer*
166 Groverton Place, Los Angeles, CA 90077, USA
Kranz, Eugene (Gene) *Space Scientist*
1108 Shady Oak Lane, Dickinson, TX 77539, USA
Krapek, Karl *Businessman*
%United Technologies Corp, United Technologies Building, Hartford, CT 06101, USA
Krasniqi, Luan *Boxer*
Oschleweg 10, 78628 Rottweil, Germany
Krasnoff, Eric *Businessman*
%Pall Corp, 2200 Northern Blvd, Greenvale, NY 11548, USA
Krasny, Yuri *Artist*
%Sloane Gallery, Oxford Office Building, 1612 17th St, Denver, CO 80202, USA
Kratochvilova, Jarmila *Track Athlete*
Goleuv Jenikov, 582 82, Czech Republic
Kratzert, Bill *Golfer*
7470 Founders Way, Ponte Vedra, FL 32082, USA
Krause, Chester L *Publisher*
%Krause Publications, 700 E State St, Iola, WI 54990, USA
Krause, Dieter *Canoeing Athlete*
Karl-Marx-Allee 21, 1017 Berlin, Germany
Krause, Paul J *Football Player*
18099 Judicial Way N, Lakeville, MN 55044, USA
Krause, Peter *Actor*
%The Firm, 9100 Wilshire Blvd, #100W, Beverly Hills, CA 90210, USA

K

Krause, Richard M *Immunologist*
4000 Cathedral Ave NW, #413B, Washington, DC 20016, USA
Kraushaar, Silke *Luge Athlete*
Friedr-Ludwig-Jahn-Str 34, 02692 Sonneberg, Germany
Kraushaar, William L *Physicist*
27 Stoney Creek Road, Scarborough, ME 04074, USA
Krauss, Alison *Singer, Fiddler*
%Keith Case Assoc, 1025 17th Ave S, #200, Nashville, TN 37212, USA
Krauss, Lawrence M *Physicist*
%Case Western Reserve University, Physics Dept, Cleveland, OH 44106, USA
Krausse, Stefan *Luge Athlete*
Karl-Zink-Str 2, 96883 Ilmenau, Germany
Krauthammer, Charles *Columnist*
%Washington Post Writers Group, 1150 15th St NW, Washington, DC 20071, USA
Kravchuk, Igor *Hockey Player*
%Florida Panthers, 1 Panthers Parkway, Sunrise, FL 33323, USA
Kravitch, Phyllis A *Judge*
%US Court of Appeals, 56 Forsyth St NW, Atlanta, GA 30303, USA
Kravitz, Lenny *Singer, Songwriter, Guitarist*
14681 Harrison St, Miami, FL 33176, USA
Krayer, Otto H *Pharmacologist*
4140 E Cooper St, Tucson, AZ 85711, USA
Krayzelburg, Lenny *Swimmer*
%Octagon, 1751 Pinnacle Dr, #1500, McLean, VA 22102, USA
Krayzie Bone *Rap Artist (Bone Thugs-N-Harmony)*
%Creative Artists Agency, 9830 Wilshire Blvd, Beverly Hills, CA 90212, USA
Krebbs, John *Auto Racing Driver*
Diamond Ridge, 3232 Amoruso Way, Roseville, CA 95747, USA
Krebs, Edwin G *Nobel Medicine Laureate*
1819 41st Ave E, Seattle, WA 98112, USA
Krebs, Robert D *Businessman*
%Burlington North/Santa Fe, 2650 Lou Menk Dr, Fort Worth, TX 76131, USA
Krebs, Susan *Actress*
4704 Tobias Ave, Sherman Oaks, CA 91403, USA
Kredel, Elmar Maria *Religious Leader*
Obere Karolinenstra 5, 96033 Bamber, Germany
Kregel, Kevin R *Astronaut*
858 Shadwell Dr, Houston, TX 77062, USA
Kreis, Jason *Soccer Player*
%Dallas Burn, 14800 Quorum Dr, #300, Dallas, TX 75254, USA
Krementz, Jill *Photographer*
620 Sagaponack Main St, Southampton, NY 11968, USA
Kremer, Andrea *Sportscaster*
%ESPN-TV, Sports Dept, ESPN Plaza, 935 Middle St, Bristol, CT 06010, USA
Kremer, Gidon *Concert Violinist*
%I C M Artists, 40 W 57th St, New York, NY 10019, USA
Krens, Thomas *Museum Administrator*
%Solomon R Guggenheim Museum, 1071 5th Ave, New York, NY 10128, USA
Krentz, Jayne Ann (Amanda Quick) *Writer*
%Axelrod Agency, 66 Church St, Lenox, MA 01240, USA
Krenz, Jan *Conductor, Composer*
%Filharmonia Narodowa, Ul Jasna 5, Warsaw, Poland
Kreps, David M *Economist*
%Stanford University, Graduate Business School, Stanford, CA 94305, USA
Kreps, Juanita M *Secretary, Commerce*
1407 W Pettigrew St, Durham, NC 27705, USA
Kresa, Kent *Businessman*
%Northrop Grumman Corp, 1840 Century Park East, Los Angeles, CA 90067, USA
Kreskin *Illusionist*
444 2nd St, Pitcairn, PA 15140, USA
Kretchmer, Arthur *Editor*
%Playboy Magazine, Editorial Dept, 680 N Lake Shore Dr, Chicago, IL 60611, USA
Kreuk, Kristin *Actress*
%Pacific Artists Mgmt, 1404-510 W Hastings, Vancouver BC V6B 1L8, Canada
Kreutzmann, Bill *Drummer (Grateful Dead)*
PO Box 1073, San Rafael, CA 94915, USA
Kreviazuk, Chantal *Singer, Pianist, Songwriter*
%Macklam Feldman Mgmt, 1505 W 2nd Ave, #200, Vancouver BC V6H 3Y4, Canada
Kriangsak Chomanan *Prime Minister, Thailand; Army General*
%National Assembly, Bangkok, Thailand
Krickstein, Aaron *Tennis Player*
7559 Fairmont Court, Boca Raton, FL 33496, USA
Krieg, Arthur M *Immunologist*
%University of Iowa, Medical College, Immunology Dept, Iowa City, IA 52242, USA
Krieg, David M (Dave) *Football Player*
2439 E Desert Willow Dr, Phoenix, AZ 85048, USA
Krieger, Robbie *Guitarist (Doors), Songwriter*
3011 Ledgewood Dr, Los Angeles, CA 90068, USA

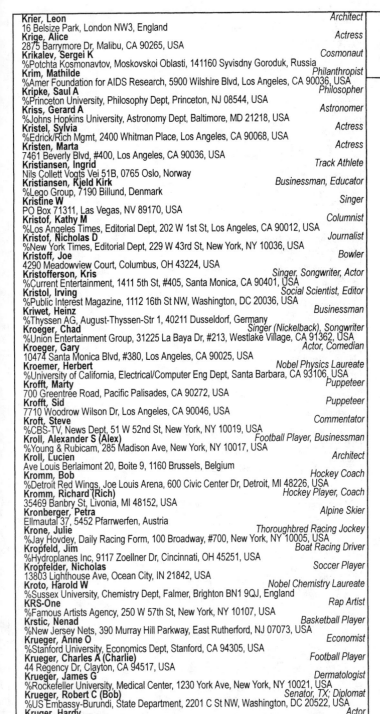

Krier, Leon *Architect*
16 Belsize Park, London NW3, England
Krige, Alice *Actress*
2875 Barrymore Dr, Malibu, CA 90265, USA
Krikalev, Sergei K *Cosmonaut*
%Potchta Kosmonavtov, Moskovskoi Oblasti, 141160 Syvisdny Goroduk, Russia
Krim, Mathilde *Philanthropist*
%Amer Foundation for AIDS Research, 5900 Wilshire Blvd, Los Angeles, CA 90036, USA
Kripke, Saul A *Philosopher*
%Princeton University, Philosophy Dept, Princeton, NJ 08544, USA
Kriss, Gerard A *Astronomer*
%Johns Hopkins University, Astronomy Dept, Baltimore, MD 21218, USA
Kristel, Sylvia *Actress*
%Edrick/Rich Mgmt, 2400 Whitman Place, Los Angeles, CA 90068, USA
Kristen, Marta *Actress*
7461 Beverly Blvd, #400, Los Angeles, CA 90036, USA
Kristiansen, Ingrid *Track Athlete*
Nils Collett Vogts Vei 51B, 0765 Oslo, Norway
Kristiansen, Kjeld Kirk *Businessman, Educator*
%Lego Group, 7190 Billund, Denmark
Kristine W *Singer*
PO Box 71311, Las Vegas, NV 89170, USA
Kristof, Kathy M *Columnist*
%Los Angeles Times, Editorial Dept, 202 W 1st St, Los Angeles, CA 90012, USA
Kristof, Nicholas D *Journalist*
%New York Times, Editorial Dept, 229 W 43rd St, New York, NY 10036, USA
Kristoff, Joe *Bowler*
4290 Meadowview Court, Columbus, OH 43224, USA
Kristofferson, Kris *Singer, Songwriter, Actor*
%Current Entertainment, 1411 5th St, #405, Santa Monica, CA 90401, USA
Kristol, Irving *Social Scientist, Editor*
%Public Interest Magazine, 1112 16th St NW, Washington, DC 20036, USA
Kriwet, Heinz *Businessman*
%Thyssen AG, August-Thyssen-Str 1, 40211 Dusseldorf, Germany
Kroeger, Chad *Singer (Nickelback), Songwriter*
%Union Entertainment Group, 31225 La Baya Dr, #213, Westlake Village, CA 91362, USA
Kroeger, Gary *Actor, Comedian*
10474 Santa Monica Blvd, #380, Los Angeles, CA 90025, USA
Kroemer, Herbert *Nobel Physics Laureate*
%University of California, Electrical/Computer Eng Dept, Santa Barbara, CA 93106, USA
Krofft, Marty *Puppeteer*
700 Greentree Road, Pacific Palisades, CA 90272, USA
Krofft, Sid *Puppeteer*
7710 Woodrow Wilson Dr, Los Angeles, CA 90046, USA
Kroft, Steve *Commentator*
%CBS-TV, News Dept, 51 W 52nd St, New York, NY 10019, USA
Kroll, Alexander S (Alex) *Football Player, Businessman*
%Young & Rubicam, 285 Madison Ave, New York, NY 10017, USA
Kroll, Lucien *Architect*
Ave Louis Berlaimont 20, Boite 9, 1160 Brussels, Belgium
Kromm, Bob *Hockey Coach*
%Detroit Red Wings, Joe Louis Arena, 600 Civic Center Dr, Detroit, MI 48226, USA
Kromm, Richard (Rich) *Hockey Player, Coach*
35469 Banbry St, Livonia, MI 48152, USA
Kronberger, Petra *Alpine Skier*
Ellmautal 37, 5452 Pfarrwerfen, Austria
Krone, Julie *Thoroughbred Racing Jockey*
%Jay Hovdey, Daily Racing Form, 100 Broadway, #700, New York, NY 10005, USA
Kropfeld, Jim *Boat Racing Driver*
%Hydroplanes Inc, 9117 Zoellner Dr, Cincinnati, OH 45251, USA
Kropfelder, Nicholas *Soccer Player*
13803 Lighthouse Ave, Ocean City, IN 21842, USA
Kroto, Harold W *Nobel Chemistry Laureate*
%Sussex University, Chemistry Dept, Falmer, Brighton BN1 9QJ, England
KRS-One *Rap Artist*
%Famous Artists Agency, 250 W 57th St, New York, NY 10107, USA
Krstic, Nenad *Basketball Player*
%New Jersey Nets, 390 Murray Hill Parkway, East Rutherford, NJ 07073, USA
Krueger, Anne O *Economist*
%Stanford University, Economics Dept, Stanford, CA 94305, USA
Krueger, Charles A (Charlie) *Football Player*
44 Regency Dr, Clayton, CA 94517, USA
Krueger, James G *Dermatologist*
%Rockefeller University, Medical Center, 1230 York Ave, New York, NY 10021, USA
Krueger, Robert C (Bob) *Senator, TX; Diplomat*
%US Embassy-Burundi, State Department, 2201 C St NW, Washington, DC 20522, USA
Kruger, Hardy *Actor*
%L Von dem Knesebeck, Maximilianstr 23, 80539 Munich, Germany

K

Kruger - Kuhn

Kruger, Pit *Actor*
Geleitstr 10, 60599 Frankfurt/Main, Germany
Krugman, Paul R *Economist*
70 Lambert Dr, Princeton, NJ 08540, USA
Krulwich, Robert *Commentator*
%CBS-TV, News Dept, 524 W 57th St, New York, NY 10019, USA
Krumholtz, David *Actor*
8809 Appian Way, Los Angeles, CA 90046, USA
Krumrie, Tim *Football Player*
%Cincinnati Bengals, 1 Paul Brown Stadium, Cincinnati, OH 45202, USA
Kruse, Earl J *Labor Leader*
%Roofers/Waterproofers/Allied Workers, 1125 17th St NW, Washington, DC 20036, USA
Kruse, Martin *Religious Leader*
Prinz-Friedrrich-Leopold-Str 14, 14219 Berlin, Germany
Kruskal, Martin D *Mathematician*
60 Littlebrook Road N, Princeton, NJ 08540, USA
Krypreos, Nick *Hockey Player*
9209 Copenhaven Dr, Potomac, MD 20854, USA
Krzyzewski, Michael W (Mike) *Basketball Coach*
%Duke University, Cameron Indoor Stadium, Athletic Dept, Durham, NC 27706, USA
Kuban, Bob *Singer, Drummer*
17626 Lasiandra Dr, Chesterfield, MO 63005, USA
Kubasov, Valeri N *Cosmonaut*
%Potchta Kosmonavtov, Moskovskoi Oblasti, 141160 Syvisdny Goroduk, Russia
Kubek, Anthony C (Tony) *Baseball Player, Sportscaster*
W6129 Pilgrim St, Appleton, WI 54914, USA
Kubiak, Gary *Football Player, Coach*
4330 Preserve Parkway S, Littleton, CO 80121, USA
Kubler-Ross, Elisabeth *Psychiatrist, Writer*
PO Box 6168, Scottsdale, AZ 85261, USA
Kucan, Milan *President, Slovenia*
%President's Office, Erjavcera 17, 61000 Ljubljana, Slovenia
Kucera, Frantisek *Hockey Player*
%Pittsburgh Penguins, Mellon Arena, 66 Mario Lemieux Place, Pittsburgh, PA 15219, USA
Kuchma, Leonid D *President, Ukraine*
%President's Office, Bankova Str 11, 252011 Kiev, Ukraine
Kucinich, Dennis J *Representative, OH; Mayor*
14518 Drake Road, Cleveland, OH 44136, USA
Kuczynski, Betty *Bowler*
4515 Prescott Ave, Lyons, IL 60534, USA
Kud *Singer (Mudvayne)*
%Agency Group Ltd, 1775 Broadway, #430, New York, NY 10019, USA
Kudelka, James A *Ballet Choreographer, Dancer*
%National Ballet of Canada, 470 Queens Quay W, Toronto ON M5V 3K4, Canada
Kudelski, Bob *Hockey Player*
64 Diamond Basin Road, Cody, WY 82414, USA
Kuder, Mary *Artist*
%Kuder Art Studio, 539 Navahopi Road, Sedona, AZ 86336, USA
Kudrna, Julius *Canoeing Athlete*
Sekaninova 36, 120 00 Prague 2, Czech Republic
Kudrow, Lisa *Actress*
PO Box 691900, Los Angeles, CA 90069, USA
Kuebler, David *Opera Singer*
%Haydn Rawstron, 36 Station Road, London SE20 7BQ, England
Kuechenberg, Robert J (Bob) *Football Player*
2519 SW 30th Terrace, Fort Lauderdale, FL 33312, USA
Kuehn, Enrico *Bobsled Athlete*
%BSD, An der Schiessstatte 4, 83471 Berchtesgaden, Germany
Kuehne, Kelli *Golfer*
%Gaylord Sports Mgmt, 14646 N Kierland Blvd, #230, Scottsdale, AZ 85254, USA
Kuerten, Gustavo *Tennis Player*
%Octagon, 1751 Pinnacle Dr, #1500, McLean, VA 22102, USA
Kufeldt, James *Businessman*
%Winn-Dixie Stores, 5050 Edgewood Court, Jacksonville, FL 32254, USA
Kufuor, John Agyekum *President, Ghana*
%Chairman's Office, Castle, PO Box 1627, Accra, Ghana
Kuhaulua, Jesse *Sumo Wrestler*
%Azumazeki Stable, 4-6-4 Higashi Komagata, Ryogoku, Tokyo, Japan
Kuhlman, Ron *Actor*
5738 Willis Ave, Van Nuys, CA 91411, USA
Kuhlmann, Kathleen M *Opera Singer*
%Int'l Management Group, G Paris, 54 Ave Marceau, 75008 Paris, France
Kuhlmann-Wilsdorf, Doris *Physicist*
%University of Virginia, Materials Science Dept, Charlottesville, VA 22901, USA
Kuhn, Gustav *Conductor*
6343 Ere, Austria
Kuhn, Stephen L (Steve) *Jazz Pianist, Composer*
%Berkeley Agency, 2608 9th St, Berkeley, CA 94710, USA

Kukoc, Toni *Basketball Player*
1850 Hybernia Dr, Highland Park, IL 60035, USA
Kuleshov, Valery *Concert Pianist*
%Musicians Corporate Mgmt, PO Box 589, Millbrook, NY 12545, USA
Kulich, Vladimir *Actor*
1007 Montana Ave, #363, Santa Monica, CA 90403, USA
Kulikov, Viktor G *Army Marshal, Russia*
%Ministry of Defense, Myasnitskaya Str 37, 10100 Moscow, Russia
Kulka, Konstanty A *Concert Violinist*
%Filharmonia Narodowa, Ul Jasna 5, 00-007 Warsaw, Poland
Kulkarni, Shrinivas R *Astronomer*
%California Institute of Technology, Astronomy Dept, Pasadena, CA 91125, USA
Kumanyika, Shiriki K *Nutritionist*
%University of Illinois, Nutrition/Dietetics Dept, Chicago, IL 60607, USA
Kumar, Sanjay *Businessman*
%Computer Associates Int'l, 1 Computer Associates Plaza, Islandia, NY 11749, USA
Kumaratunga, Chandrika B *President, Sri Lanka*
%President's Office, Republic Square, Sri Jayewardenepura Kotte, Sri Lanka
Kumbernuss, Astrid *Track Athlete*
%Neubrandenburg Jahnstadion, Schwedenstr 25, 17033 Neubrandenburg, Germany
Kumin, Maxine W *Writer*
Joppa Road, Warner, NH 03278, USA
Kummer, Glenn F *Businessman*
%Fleetwood Enterprises, 3125 Myers St, Riverside, CA 92503, USA
Kump, Ernest J *Architect*
Villa Boecklin, Jupiterstr 15, 8032 Zurich, Switzerland
Kundera, Milan *Writer*
%Gallimard, 5 Rue Sebastien-Bottin, 75007 Paris, France
Kundla, John A *Basketball Player, Coach*
4519 Zenith Ave N, Minneapolis, MN 55422, USA
Kunes, Ellen *Editor*
%Oprah Magazine, 224 W 57th St, #900, New York, NY 10019, USA
Kung, Hans *Theologian*
Waldhauserstr 23, 72076 Tubingen, Germany
Kung, Patrick C *Pharmacologist*
%T Cell Sciences, 119 4th Ave, Needham, MA 02494, USA
Kunitz, Stanley J *Writer*
37 W 12th St, New York, NY 10011, USA
Kunkel, Louis M *Pediatrician*
%Children's Hospital, 300 Longwood Ave, Boston, MA 02115, USA
Kunkle, John F *Religious Leader*
%Evangelical Methodist Church, 3000 W Kellogg Dr, Wichita, KS 67213, USA
Kunnert, Kevin *Basketball Player*
8286 SW Qilderland Court, Tigard, OR 97224, USA
Kunz, George J *Football Player*
8215 S Bermuda Road, Las Vegas, NV 89123, USA
Kunzel, Erich, Jr *Conductor*
%TRM Mgmt, 825 S Lazelle St, Columbus, OH 43206, USA
Kupchak, Mitchell (Mitch) *Basketball Player*
156 N Gunston Dr, Los Angeles, CA 90049, USA
Kupcinet, Irv *Columnist*
%Chicago Sun-Times, Editorial Dept, 401 N Wabash Ave, Chicago, IL 60611, USA
Kupcinet, Kari *Actress*
1931 W Roscoe St, Chicago, IL 60657, USA
Kupfer, Carl *Ophthalmologist*
%National Eye Institute, 9000 Rockville Pike, Bethesda, MD 20892, USA
Kupfer, Harry *Opera Director*
%Komische Oper, Behrenstr 55-57, 10117 Berlin, Germany
Kupferberg, Sabine *Ballerina*
%Dans Theater 3, Scheldoldoekshaven 60, 2511 EN Gravenhage, Netherlands
Kupp, Jacob (Jake) *Football Player*
4801 Snowmountain Road, Yakima, WA 98908, USA
Kupper, William P, Jr *Publisher*
%Business Week, 1221 Ave of Americas, New York, NY 10020, USA
Kuranari, Tadashi *Government Official, Japan*
2-18-12 Daita, Setangayaku, Tokyo 155, Japan
Kurant, Willy *Cinematographer*
%Lyons Sheldon Agency, 800 S Robertson Blvd, #6, Los Angeles, CA 90035, USA
Kuras, Ellen M *Cinematographer*
54 Summit St, Nyack, NY 10960, USA
Kurasov, Georgy *Artist*
4/2 Inzenernaja St, Saint Petersburg 191011, Russia
Kureishi, Hanif *Writer*
81 Comeragh Road, London W14 9HS, England
Kurkova, Karolina *Model*
%DNA Model Mgmt, 520 Broadway, New York, NY 10012, USA
Kurland, Robert A (Bob) *Basketball Player*
1024 Kings Crown Dr, Sanibel, FL 33957, USA

K

Kurokawa - Kyo

Kurokawa, Kisho *Architect*
Aoyama Building, #11F, 1-2-3 Kita Aoyama, Minatoku, Tokyo, Japan
Kurrat, Klaus-Dieter *Track Athlete*
Am Hochwald 30, 28460, 1453 Klemmachow, Germany
Kurri, Jarri *Hockey Player*
%Colorado Avalanche, Pepsi Center, 1000 Chopper Circle, Denver, CO 80204, USA
Kurtag, Gyorgy *Composer*
Lihego V3, 2621 Veroce, Hungary
Kurtenbach, Orland J *Hockey Player*
119-15500 Rosemary Heights Crescent, Surrey BC V3S 0K1, Canada
Kurth, Wallace (Wally) *Actor, Singer*
2143 N Valley Dr, Manhattan Beach, CA 90266, USA
Kurtz, Swoosie *Actress*
320 Central Park West, New York, NY 10025, USA
Kurtzberg, Joanne *Physician*
%Duke University, Medical Center, Durham, NC 27708, USA
Kurtze, Andrew *Businessman*
%Sprint PCS Group, PO Box 11315, Kansas City, MO 64112, USA
Kurupt *Rap Artist*
%William Morris Agency, 151 El Camino Dr, Beverly Hills, CA 90212, USA
Kurzweil, Raymond *Inventor (Computer-Generated Voice)*
%Kurzweil Applied Intelligence, 411 Waverly Oaks Road, Waltham, MA 02452, USA
Kusama, Karyn *Movie Director*
%Endeavor Talent Agency, 9701 Wilshire Blvd, #1000, Beverly Hills, CA 90212, USA
Kusatsu, Clyde *Actor*
%Paradigm Agency, 10100 Santa Monica Blvd, #2500, Los Angeles, CA 90067, USA
Kuschak, Metropolitan Andrei *Religious Leader*
%Ukranian Orthodox Church in America, 3 Davenport Ave, New Rochelle, NY 10805, USA
Kushner, Robert E *Artist*
%DC Moore Gallery, 724 5th Ave, New York, NY 10019, USA
Kushner, Tony *Writer*
%Joyce Ketay Agency, 1501 Broadway, #1910, New York, NY 10036, USA
Kuske, Kevin *Bobsled Athlete*
%BSD, An der Schiessstatte 4, 83471 Berchtesgaden, Germany
Kuter, Kay E *Actor*
6207 Satsuma Ave, North Hollywood, CA 91606, USA
Kuti, Fela *Singer*
%Rosebud Agency, PO Box 170429, San Francisco, CA 94117, USA
Kutner, Malcolm J (Mal) *Football Player*
6502 Ashmore Lane, Tyler, TX 75703, USA
Kuttner, Stephan G *Historian*
2270 Le Conte Ave, #601, Berkeley, CA 94709, USA
Kutyna, Donald J *Army General, Businessman*
4818 Kenyon Court, Colorado Springs, CO 80917, USA
Kuykendall, John W *Educator*
%Davidson College, President's Office, Davidson, NC 28036, USA
Kuznetsoff, Alexei *Concert Pianist*
%Columbia Artists Mgmt Inc, 165 W 57th St, New York, NY 10019, USA
Kuzyk, Mimi *Actress*
%Artists Agency, 1180 S Beverly Dr, #301, Los Angeles, CA 90035, USA
Kwalick, Thaddeus J (Ted) *Football Player*
755 Purdue Court, Santa Clara, CA 95051, USA
Kwan, Jennie *Actress*
%Innovative Artists, 1505 10th St, Santa Monica, CA 90401, USA
Kwan, Michelle *Figure Skater*
%Ice Skating Castle, 27307 Highway 189, Blue Jay, CA 92317, USA
Kwan, Nancy *Actress*
%Contemporary Artists, 610 Santa Monica Blvd, #202, Santa Monica, CA 90401, USA
Kwasniewski, Aleksander *President, Poland*
%Kancelaria Prezydenta RP, Ul Wiejska 4/8, 00-902 Warsaw, Poland
Kwoh, Yik San *Electrical Engineer*
%Memorial Medical Center, PO Box 1428, Long Beach, CA 90801, USA
Kwolek, Stephanie L *Inventor (Kevlar)*
312 Spalding Road, Wilmington, DE 19803, USA
Kwouk, Burt *Actor*
%London Mgmt, 2-4 Noel St, London W1V 3RB, England
Kyle, David L *Businessman*
%ONEOK Inc, 100 W 5th St, PO Box 871, Tulsa, OK 74102, USA
Kylian, Jiri *Ballet Dancer*
%Dance Theatre, Scheldeldoekshaven 60, 2511 EN Gravenhage, Netherlands
Kyo, Machiko *Actress*
Olimpia Copu, 6-35 Jingumae, Shibuyaku, Tokyo, Japan

L'Engle, Madeleine *Writer*
924 W End Ave, New York, NY 10025, USA
L, (Lauryn Hill) *Rap Artist (Fugees)*
%Writers & Artists, 8383 Wilshire Blvd, #550, Beverly Hills, CA 90211, USA
Laatasi, Kamuta *Prime Minister, Tuvalu*
%Prime Minister's Office, Vaiaku, Funafuti, Tuvalu
Labaff, Ernie *Labor Leader*
%Aluminum Brick Glass Workers Union, 3362 Hollenberg, Bridgeton, MO 63044, USA
LaBeef, Sleepy *Singer*
14469 E Highway 264, Lowell, AR 72745, USA
LaBelle, Patti *Singer*
%Direct Management, 947 N La Cienega Blvd, #G, Los Angeles, CA 90069, USA
Labeque, Katia *Concert Pianist*
%Columbia Artists Mgmt Inc, 165 W 57th St, New York, NY 10019, USA
Labeque, Marielle *Concert Pianist*
%Columbia Artists Mgmt Inc, 165 W 57th St, New York, NY 10019, USA
Labeyrie, Antoine *Astronomer*
%Haute-Provence Observatoire, Saint-Michel Observatoire, France
Labine, Clement W (Clem) *Baseball Player*
311 N Grove Isle Circle, #311, Vero Beach, FL 32962, USA
Labis, Attilo *Ballet Dancer, Choreographer*
%Opera de Paris, 120 Rue Lyon, 75012 Paris, France
Labonte, Bobby *Auto Racing Driver*
403 Interstate Dr, Archdale, NC 27263, USA
Labonte, Terry *Auto Racing Driver*
%Melanie Trader, 5740 Hopewell Church Road, Trinity, NC 27370, USA
Laborde, Alden J *Businessman*
63 Oriole St, New Orleans, LA 70124, USA
Labre, Yvon *Hockey Player*
PO Box 3994, Crofton, MD 21114, USA
LaBute, Neil *Movie Director, Writer*
%Sanford Gross, 6715 Hollywood Blvd, #236, Los Angeles, CA 90028, USA
Labyorteaux, Matthew *Actor*
167 W 72nd St, #3F, New York, NY 10023, USA
Labyorteaux, Patrick *Actor*
8447 Wilshire Blvd, #206, Beverly Hills, CA 90211, USA
Lach, Elmer J *Hockey Player*
89 Bayview Ave, Pointe Claire QC M9S 5C4, Canada
Lachance, Michel (Mike) *Harness Racing Driver*
183 Sweetmans Lane, Englishtown, NJ 07726, USA
LaChapelle, David *Photographer*
%Simon & Schuster/Pocket/Summit, 1230 Ave of Americas, New York, NY 10020, USA
LaChappelle, Sean P *Football Player*
8724 Lodestone Circle, Elk Grove, CA 95624, USA
Lachemann, Marcel E *Baseball Player, Manager*
PO Box 587, Penryn, CA 95663, USA
Lachemann, Rene G *Baseball Player, Manager*
7500 E Boulders Parkway, #68, Scottsdale, AZ 85262, USA
Lachey, Drew *Singer (98 Degrees)*
%DAS Communications, 83 Riverside Dr, New York, NY 10024, USA
Lachey, James M (Jim) *Football Player*
1445 Roxbury Road, Columbus, OH 43212, USA
Lachey, Nick *Singer (98 Degrees)*
%DAS Communications, 83 Riverside Dr, New York, NY 10024, USA
Lachhiman Gurung *WW II Nepal Army Hero (VC)*
Village Dahakhani, Village Development, Conmelle, Ward 4, Chitwan, Nepal
Lackey, Brad *Motorcycle Racing Rider*
%Badco, 35 Monument Plaza, Pleasant Hill, CA 94523, USA
Laclavere, Georges *Geophysicist*
53 Ave de Breteuil, 70075 Paris, France
Laclotte, Michel R *Museum Director*
10 Bis Rue du Pre-aux-Clerc, 75007 Paris, France
Lacombe, Henri *Oceanographer*
20 Bis Ave de Lattre de Tassigny, 92340 Bourg-la-Reine, France
Lacoste, Catherine *Golfer*
Calle B6, #4, El Soto de la Moraleja Alcobendas, Madrid, Spain
Lacroix, Andre J *Hockey Player*
6770 Oakwood Dr, Oakland, CA 94611, USA
Lacroix, Christian M M *Fashion Designer*
73 Rue du Faubourg Saint Honore, 75008 Paris, France
Lacy, Alan *Businessman*
%Sears Roebuck Co, 3333 Beverly Blvd, Hoffman Estates, IL 60179, USA
Lacy, Steven M (Steve) *Jazz Saxophonist, Composer*
%Ted Kurland, 173 Brighton Ave, Boston, MA 02134, USA
Ladd, Alan W, Jr *Movie Producer*
1005 Benedict Canyon Dr, Beverly Hills, CA 90210, USA
Ladd, Cheryl *Actress*
%International Creative Mgmt, 8942 Wilshire Blvd, #219, Beverly Hills, CA 90211, USA

Ladd, David *Actor*
9212 Hazen Dr, Beverly Hills, CA 90210, USA
Ladd, Diane *Actress*
3860 Grand Ave, Ojai, CA 93023, USA
Ladd, Margaret *Actress*
444 21st St, Santa Monica, CA 90402, USA
Laderman, Ezra *Composer*
%Yale University, Music School, New Haven, CT 06520, USA
Ladewig, Marion *Bowler*
%Ladies Professional Bowling Tour, 7200 Harrison Ave, #7171, Rockford, IL 61112, USA
Laettner, Christian D *Basketball Player*
1225 Church Road, Angola, NY 14006, USA
Laffer, Arthur B *Economist*
24255 Pacific Coast Highway, Malibu, CA 90263, USA
Lafforgue, Laurent *Mathematician*
%IHES, Mathematics Dept, 91440 Bures-sur-Yvette, France
Lafleur, Guy D *Hockey Player*
14 Place du Molin, L'Ile-Bizard QC H9E 1N2, Canada
Lafley, Alan G *Businessman*
%Procter & Gamble Co, 1 Procter & Gamble Plaza, Cincinnati, OH 45202, USA
Lafontaine, Oskar *Government Official, Germany*
%Landtag Saarland, Postfach 101833, 66018 Saarbrucken, Germany
LaFontaine, Patrick (Pat) *Hockey Player*
3 Beach Dr, Lloyd Harbor, NY 11743, USA
LaFrentz, Raef *Basketball Player*
1100 La Paloma Court, Southlake, TX 76092, USA
LaGarde, Tom *Basketball Player*
135 Rivington St, New York, NY 10002, USA
Lagasse, Emeril *Chef*
829 Saint Charles Ave, New Orlean, LA 70130, USA
Lagattuta, Bill *Commentator*
%CBS-TV, News Dept, 7800 Beverly Blvd, Los Angeles, CA 90036, USA
Lagerberg, Bengt *Drummer (Cardigans)*
%Motor SE, Gotabergs Gatan 2, 400 14 Gothenburg, Sweden
Lagerfeld, Karl *Fashion Designer*
14 Blvd de la Madeleine, 75008 Paris, France
Lagerfelt, Caroline *Actress*
8730 Sunset Blvd, #480, Los Angeles, CA 90069, USA
Laghi, Pio Cardinal *Religious Leader*
%Catholic Education Congregation, Piazza Pio XII 3, 00193 Rome, Italy
Lagos, Richard *President, Chile*
%President's Office, Palacio de la Monedo, Santiago, Chile
Laguna, Frederica de *Anthropologist*
Quadrangle, 3300 Darby Road, #1310, Haverford, PA 19041, USA
Laguna, Ismael *Boxer*
%Panama Zona 6, Entrega General, Panama
LaHaie, Dick *Auto Racing Driver*
%Dick LaHaie Racing, 14155 Wood Road, Lansing, MI 48906, USA
LaHaye, Tim *Writer*
%Tyndale House Publishers, 351 Executive Dr, PO Box 80, Wheaton, IL 60189, USA
Lahiri, Jhumpa *Writer*
%Houghton Mifflin, 222 Berkeley St, #700, Boston, MA 02116, USA
Lahoud, Emile *President, Lebanon; General*
%Presidential Palace, Baabda, Beirut, Lebanon
Lahti, Christine *Actress, Director*
237 S Burlingame Ave, Los Angeles, CA 90049, USA
Lai, Francis *Composer*
23 Rue Franklin, 75016 Paris, France
Laimbeer, Bill *Basketball Player*
4310 S Bay Dr, Orchard Lake, MI 48323, USA
Laine, Cleo *Singer*
%Acker's Int'l Jazz, 53 Cambridge Mansions, London SW11 4RX, England
Laine, Frankie *Singer, Songwriter*
352 San Gorgonio St, San Diego, CA 92106, USA
Laingen, L Bruce *Diplomat*
5627 Old Chester Road, Bethesda, MD 20814, USA
Laird, Melvin R *Secretary, Defense; Businessman*
1730 Rhode Island Ave NW, #406, Washington, DC 20036, USA
Laird, Peter *Cartoonist (Ninja Turtles)*
%Teenage Mutant Ninja Turtles, PO Box 417, Haydenville, MA 01039, USA
Laird, Ronald (Ron) *Track Athlete*
4706 Diane Dr, Ashtabula, OH 44004, USA
Laithwaite, Eric R *Electrical Engineer*
%Imperial College, Electrical Engineering Dept, London SW7 2BT, England
Laitman, Jeffrey *Anatomist*
%Mount Sinai Medical Center, Anatomy Dept, 1 Levy Place, New York, NY 10029, USA
LaJoie, Randy *Auto Racing Driver*
%Phoenix Racing, 195 Jones Road, Spartanburg, SC 29307, USA

Lake, Carnell A *Football Player*
%Baltimore Ravens, Ravens Stadium, 11001 Russell St, Baltimore, MD 21230, USA
Lake, Greg *Guitarist/Bassist (Emerson Lake Palmer)*
%Asia, 9 Hillgate St, London W8 7SP, England
Lake, James A *Molecular Biologist*
%University of California, Molecular Biology Institute, Los Angeles, CA 90024, USA
Lake, Oliver E *Jazz Saxophonist, Synthesizer Player*
%DL Media, PO Box 2728, Bala Cynwyd, PA 19004, USA
Lake, Ricki *Actress*
%Gersh Agency, 232 N Canon Dr, Beverly Hills, CA 90210, USA
Laker, Frederick A *Businessman*
Princess Tower, West Sunrise, Box F207, Freeport, Grand Bahamas, Bahamas
Laker, Jim *Cricketer*
Oak End, 9 Portinscale Road, Putney, London SW15, England
Lakes, Gary *Opera Singer*
%I C M Artists, 40 W 57th St, New York, NY 10019, USA
Lakner, Yehoshua *Composer*
Postfach 7851, 6000 Lucerne 7, Switzerland
Lakoue, Enoch Devant *Prime Minister, Central African Republic*
%Prime Minister's Office, Bangui, Central African Republic
LaLanne, Jack *Physical Fitness Expert*
430 Quitana Road, Morro Bay, CA 93442, USA
Laliberte, Guy *Circus Executive*
%Cirque du Soleil, 8400 2nd Ave, Montreal QC H1Z 4M6, Canada
Laliberte-Bourque, Andree *Museum Director*
%Musee du Quebec, 1 Ave Wolfe-Montcalm, Quebec QC G1R 5H3, Canada
Lalli, Frank *Editor*
%Money Magazine, Editorial Dept, Rockefeller Center, New York, NY 10020, USA
Lalonde, Larry *Guitarist (Primus)*
%Figurehead Mgmt, 3470 19th St, San Francisco, CA 94110, USA
Lamar, Dwight (Bo) *Basketball Player*
103 Claire St, Lafayette, LA 70507, USA
Lamas, Lorenzo *Actor*
2149 E Live Oak Dr, Los Angeles, CA 90068, USA
Lamb, Allan J *Cricketer*
%Lamb Assoc, 4 Saint Giles St, #400, Northampton NN1 1JB, England
Lamb, Dennis *Diplomat*
19 Rue de Franqueville, 75016 Paris, France
Lamb, Willis E, Jr *Nobel Physics Laureate*
315 Red Rock Dr, Sedona, AZ 86351, USA
Lambert, Christophe *Actor*
9 Ave Trempley, C/Lui, 1209 Geneva, Switzerland
Lambert, John H (Jack) *Football Player*
RR 2 Box 101A, Worthington, PA 16262, USA
Lambert, Mary M *Movie Director*
%International Creative Mgmt, 8942 Wilshire Blvd, #219, Beverly Hills, CA 90211, USA
Lambert, Phyllis *Architect*
%Centre d'Architecture, 1920 Rue Baile, Montreal QC H3H 2S6, Canada
Lambert, Sheila *Basketball Player*
%Charlotte Sting, 100 Hive Dr, Charlotte, NC 28217, USA
Lambrecht, Dietrich R *Electrical Engineer*
Rathenaustr 11, 45470 Mulheim an der Ruhr, Germany
Lambro, Phillip *Composer, Pianist*
%Trigram Music, 1888 Century Park East, #10, Los Angeles, CA 90067, USA
Lambsdorff, Otto *Government Official, West Germany*
Strasschensweg 7, 53113 Bon, Germany
Lamm, Richard D *Governor, CO*
%University of Denver, Public Policy Center, Denver, CO 80208, USA
Lamm, Robert *Singer, Keyboardist (Chicago)*
%Air Tight Mgmt, 115 West Road, Winchester Center, CT 06098, USA
Lammers, Esmee *Movie Director, Writer*
%Features Creative Mgmt, Entrepotdok 76A, 101 AD Amsterdam, Netherlands
Lamonica, Darryl P *Football Player*
%Mad Bomber Fishing Lures, 8796 N 6th St, Fresno, CA 93720, USA
Lamonica, Roberto de *Artist*
Rua Anibal de Mendanca 180, AP 202, Rio de Janeiro ZC-37 RJ, Brazil
Lamont, Gene W *Baseball Player, Manager*
5194 Siesta Woods Dr, Sarasota, FL 34242, USA
Lamont, Norman S H *Government Official, England*
%Balli Group PLC, 5 Stanhope Gate, London W1Y 5LA, England
Lamontagne, Donald A *Air Force General*
Commander, Air University, Maxwell Air Force Base, AL 36112, USA
LaMotta, Jake *Boxer*
400 E 57th St, New York, NY 10022, USA
LaMotta, Vikki *Model*
PO Box 152, Deerfield Beach, FL 33443, USA
Lamp, Jeff *Basketball Player*
4971 Credit River Dr, Savage, MN 55378, USA

L

Lamparski, Richard *Writer*
216 N Milpas St, #G, Santa Barbara, CA 93103, USA
Lampert, Zohra *Actress*
%Don Buchwald, 6500 Wilshire Blvd, #2200, Los Angeles, CA 90048, USA
Lampley, Jim *Sportscaster*
PO Box 763, Rancho Santa Fe, CA 92067, USA
Lampton, Michael *Astronaut*
%University of California, Space Science Laboratory, Berkeley, CA 94720, USA
Lance, Dirk *Bassist (Incubus)*
%ArtistDirect, 10900 Wilshire Blvd, #1400, Los Angeles, CA 90024, USA
Landau, Irvin *Editor*
%Consumer Reports Magazine, Editorial Dept, 101 Truman Ave, Yonkers, NY 10703, USA
Landau, Jacob *Artist*
2 Pine Dr, Roosevelt, NJ 08555, USA
Landau, Martin *Actor*
PO Box 10959, Beverly Hills, CA 90213, USA
Landau, Saul *Writer*
%Institute for Policy Studies, 1601 Connecticut Ave NW, Washington, DC 20009, USA
Lander, Benjamin *Educator*
%American University, President's Office, Washington, DC 20016, USA
Lander, David L *Actor*
5819 Saint Laurent Dr, Agoura Hills, CA 91301, USA
Landers, Andy *Basketball Coach*
%University of Georgia, Athletic Dept, Athens, GA 30602, USA
Landers, Audrey *Actress, Singer*
4048 Las Palmas Dr, Sarasota, FL 34238, USA
Landers, Judy *Actress*
%Media Artists Group, 6300 Wilshire Blvd, #1470, Los Angeles, CA 90048, USA
Landes, David S *Historian*
24 Highland St, Cambridge, MA 02138, USA
Landesberg, Steve *Actor*
%Mucci & Lagnese Inc, 6300 Wilshire Blvd, #1190, Los Angeles, CA 90048, USA
Landis, John D *Movie Director*
1168 San Ysidro Dr, Beverly Hills, CA 90210, USA
Lando, Joe *Actor*
%Rip Ortella, 70 Sabra Ave, Oak Park, CA 91377, USA
Landon, Howard C R *Writer*
Chateau de Foncoussieres, 81800 Rabastens, Tarn, France
Landrieu, Moon *Secretary, Housing & Urban Development*
4301 S Prieur St, New Orleans, LA 70125, USA
Landry, Ali *Model, Beauty Queen, Actress*
%United Talent Agency, 9560 Wilshire Blvd, #500, Beverly Hills, CA 90212, USA
Landry, Gregory P (Greg) *Football Player, Coach*
133 Melanie Lane, Troy, MI 48098, USA
Landsburg, Valerie *Actress*
22745 Chamera Lane, Topanga Canyon, CA 90290, USA
Landy, Bernard *Government Official, Canada*
%Gouvement du Quebec, 885 Grand Allee Est, Quebec QC GLA 1A2, Canada
Lane of St Ippollitts, Geoffrey D *Judge*
%Royal Courts of Justice, Strand, London WC2A 2LL, England
Lane, Abbe *Singer, Actress*
444 N Faring Road, Los Angeles, CA 90077, USA
Lane, Cristy *Singer*
PO Box 654, Madison, TN 37116, USA
Lane, Diane *Actress*
%Gary Cohen, 9100 Wilshire Blvd, #305E, Beverly Hills, CA 90212, USA
Lane, John R (Jack) *Museum Curator*
%San Francisco Museum of Modern Art, 151 3rd St, San Francisco, CA 94103, USA
Lane, Kenneth Jay *Fashion Designer*
%Kenneth Jay Lane Inc, 20 W 37th St, New York, NY 10018, USA
Lane, Lawrence W, Jr *Publisher, Diplomat*
3000 Sandhill Road, #215, Menlo Park, CA 94025, USA
Lane, MacArthur *Football Player*
3238 Knowland Ave, Oakland, CA 94619, USA
Lane, Malcolm D *Biological Chemist*
5607 Roxbuy Place, Baltimore, MD 21209, USA
Lane, Melvin B *Publisher*
99 Tallwood Court, Menlo Park, CA 94027, USA
Lane, Mike *Editorial Cartoonist*
%Baltimore Sun, Editorial Dept, 501 N Calvert St, Baltimore, MD 21202, USA
Lane, Nathan *Actor, Singer*
%Creative Artists Agency, 9830 Wilshire Blvd, Beverly Hills, CA 90212, USA
Lanegan, Mark *Singer (Screaming Trees)*
%Helter Skelter, Plaza, 535 Kings Road, London SW10 0S, England
Laneuville, Eric *Actor*
5138 W Slauson Ave, Los Angeles, CA 90056, USA
Laney, James T *Educator, Diplomat*
2015 Grand Prix Dr NE, Atlanta, GA 30345, USA

Lang, Belinda *Actress*
%Ken McReddie, 91 Regent St, London W1R 7TB, England
Lang, Ed *Photographer*
%Elysium Growth Press, 16255 Ventura Blvd, #515, Encino, CA 91436, USA
Lang, George C *Vietnam War Army Hero (CMH)*
3786 Clark St, Seaford, NY 11783, USA
Lang, Helmut *Fashion Designer*
%Michele Morgan, 184 Rue Saint-Maur, 75010 Paris, France
Lang, Jack *Government Official, France*
Mairie, 41000 Blois, France
Lang, Jack *Sportswriter*
%Baseball Writers' Assn, 36 Brookfield Road, Northport, NY 11768, USA
Lang, Jonny *Singer, Guitarist*
%Blue Sky Artists, 761 Washington Ave N, Minneapolis, MN 55401, USA
Lang, June *Actress*
12756 Kahlenberg Lane, North Hollywood, CA 91607, USA
lang, k d *Singer, Actress*
8062 Woodrow Wilson Dr, Los Angeles, CA 90046, USA
Lang, Katherine Kelly *Actress, Model*
%Agency for Performing Arts, 9200 Sunset Blvd, #900, Los Angeles, CA 90069, USA
Lang, Pearl *Dancer, Choreographer*
382 Central Park West, New York, NY 10025, USA
Lang, Robert *Hockey Player*
PO Box 663, Diablo, CA 94528, USA
Langbo, Arnold G *Businessman*
%Kellogg Co, 1 Kellogg Square, PO Box 3599, Battle Creek, MI 49016, USA
Langdon, Harry *Photographer*
PO Box 16816, Beverly Hills, CA 90209, USA
Langdon, Sue Ane *Actress*
24115 Long Valley Road, Hidden Hills, CA 91302, USA
Lange, Andre *Bobsled Athlete*
%BSD, An der Schiessstatte 4, 83471 Berchtesgaden, Germany
Lange, Andrew *Astronomer*
%University of California, Astronomy Dept, Berkeley, CA 94720, USA
Lange, David R *Prime Minister, New Zealand*
14 Ambury Road, Mangere Bridge, Auckland, New Zealand
Lange, Hope *Actress*
10601 Wilshire Blvd, #301, Los Angeles, CA 90024, USA
Lange, Ted *Actor*
6950 McLennan Ave, Van Nuys, CA 91406, USA
Lange, Thomas *Rowing Athlete*
%Ratzeburger Ruderclub, Domhof 57, 23909 Ratzburg, Germany
Langella, Frank *Actor*
108 Sunlit Dr W, Santa Fe, NM 87508, USA
Langen, Christoph *Bobsled Athlete*
BC Unterhaching, Ottobrunner Str 16, 82008 Unterhaching, Germany
Langencamp, Heather *Actress*
156 F St SE, Washington, DC 20003, USA
Langer, A J *Actress*
%Gersh Agency, 232 N Canon Dr, Beverly Hills, CA 90210, USA
Langer, Alois A *Inventor (Implantable Defibrillator)*
111 Saddlebrook Dr, Harrison City, PA 15636, USA
Langer, Bernhard *Golfer*
1120 SW 21st Lane, Boca Raton, FL 33486, USA
Langer, James J (Jim) *Football Player*
14280 Wolfram St NW, Ramsey, MN 55303, USA
Langer, James S *Physicist*
1130 Las Canoas Lane, Santa Barbara, CA 93105, USA
Langer, Robert S *Chemical Engineer, Inventor*
%Massachusetts Institute of Technolgy, Engineering Dept, Cambridge, MA 02139, USA
Langevin, Dave *Hockey Player*
2224 Copperfield Dr, Saint Paul, MN 55120, USA
Langford, Frances *Singer, Actress*
PO Box 96, Jensen Beach, FL 34958, USA
Langford, John *Aeronautical Engineer*
%Aurora Flight Sciences, 9950 Wakeman Dr, Manassas, VA 20110, USA
Langham, C Antonio *Football Player*
PO Box 232, Town Creek, AL 35672, USA
Langham, Michael *Theater Director*
%Julliard School, Drama Division, 144 W 66th St, New York, NY 10023, USA
Langham, Wallace *Actor*
10264 Rochester Ave, Los Angeles, CA 90024, USA
Langkow, Daymond *Hockey Player*
7940 E Quill Lane, Scottsdale, AZ 85255, USA
Langley, H Desmond A *Governor General, Bermuda; Army General*
%Governor's Office, 11 Langton Hill, Pembroke, Hamilton HM 13, Bermuda
Langley, Roger *Skier*
Broad St, Barre, MA 01005, USA

Langlois, Albert, Jr *Hockey Player*
2473 Crest View Dr, Los Angeles, CA 90046, USA
Langlois, Lisa *Actress*
%House of Representatives, 400 S Beverly Dr, #101, Beverly Hills, CA 90212, USA
Langlois, Paul *Guitarist (Tragically Hip)*
%Management Trust, 219 Dufferin St, #309B, Toronto ON M5K 3J1, Canada
Langston, J William *Neurologist*
%Parkinson's Foundation, 2444 Moorpark Ave, San Jose, CA 95128, USA
Langston, Mark E *Baseball Player*
2511 N Skytop Court, Orange, CA 92867, USA
Langston, Murray *Actor, Comedian*
%Entertainment Alliance, PO Box 4734, Santa Rosa, CA 95402, USA
Langton, Brooke *Actress*
%Rigberg Roberts Rugolo, 1180 S Beverly Dr, #601, Los Angeles, CA 90035, USA
Langway, Rod C *Hockey Player*
3613 Brook Road, Richmond, VA 23227, USA
Lanier, H Max *Baseball Player*
11250 SW Rio Vista Dr, Dunnellon, FL 31630, USA
Lanier, Harold C (Hal) *Baseball Manager*
19380 SW 90th Lane Road, Dunnellon, FL 34432, USA
Lanier, Jaron *Computer Engineer (Virtual Reality)*
%Advanced Network Services, 200 Business Park Dr, Armonk, NY 10504, USA
Lanier, Robert J (Bob), Jr *Basketball Player, Coach*
%National Basketball Assn, TeamUp Program, 645 5th Ave, New York, NY 10022, USA
Lanier, Willie E *Football Player*
2911 E Brigstock Road, Midlothian, VA 23113, USA
Lanin, Lester *Orchestra Leader*
%Ted Schmidt Assoc, 901 Winding River Road, Vero Beach, FL 32963, USA
Lanker, Brian *Photojournalist*
1993 Kimberly Dr, Eugene, OR 97405, USA
Lankford, Kim *Actress*
%House of Representatives, 400 S Beverly Dr, #101, Beverly Hills, CA 90212, USA
Lanois, Daniel *Singer, Songwriter*
%Feinstein Mgmt, 410 Lexington Ave, #2150, New York, NY 10017, USA
Lansbury, Angela *Actress, Singer*
635 N Bonhill Road, Los Angeles, CA 90049, USA
Lansbury, David *Actor*
%Don Buchwald, 6500 Wilshire Blvd, #2200, Los Angeles, CA 90048, USA
Lansdowne, J Fenwick *Artist*
941 Victoria Ave, Victoria BC V8S 4N6, Canada
Lansing, Sherry L *Movie Producer*
10451 Bellagio Road, Los Angeles, CA 90077, USA
Lanvin, Bernard *Fashion Designer*
22 Rue du Faubourg Saint Honore, 70008 Paris, France
Lanz, David *Pianist*
%Siddons Assoc, 14930 Ventura Blvd, #205, Sherman Oaks, CA 91403, USA
Laoretti, Larry *Golfer*
10567 Whooping Crane Way, Palm City, FL 34990, USA
LaPaglia, Anthony *Actor*
%International Creative Mgmt, 8942 Wilshire Blvd, #219, Beverly Hills, CA 90211, USA
Lapaine, Daniel *Actor*
%Envision Entertainment, 409 Santa Monica Blvd, Santa Monica, CA 90401, USA
Laperriere, J Jacques H *Hockey Player, Coach*
1983 Nice Chomedey Estate, Laval QC H7S 1G5, Canada
Lapham, Lewis H *Editor*
%Harper's Magazine, Editorial Dept, 666 Broadway, New York, NY 10012, USA
Lapidus, Alan *Architect*
%Lapidus Assoc, 43 W 61st St, New York, NY 10023, USA
Lapidus, Edmond (Ted) *Fashion Designer*
66 Blvd Maurice-Barres, 92200 Neuilly-sur-Seine, France
Lapierre, Dominique *Historian*
Les Bignoles, 83350 Ramatuelle, France
Lapine, James E *Writer, Theater Director*
85 Mill River Road, South Salem, NY 10590, USA
LaPlaca, Alison *Actress*
1614 N Argyle Ave, Hollywood, CA 90028, USA
LaPlanche, Rosemary *Actress, Beauty Queen*
13914 Hartsook St, Sherman Oaks, CA 91423, USA
LaPlante, Lynda *Writer*
%Random House, 1745 Broadway, #B1, New York, NY 10019, USA
Lapli, John *Governor General, Solomon Islands*
%Governor General's House, Box 252, Honiara, Guadacanal, Solomon Islands
LaPorte, Danny *Motorcycle Racing Rider*
949 Via Del Monte, Palos Verdes Estates, CA 90274, USA
Laposata, Joseph S *Army General*
%Battle Monuments Commission, 20 Massachusetts, Washington, DC 20314, USA
Lapotaire, Jane *Actress*
92 Oxford Gardens, #C, London W10, England

Lappalainen, Markku *Bassist (Hoobastank)*
%Island Def Jam Records, 8920 Sunset Blvd, #200, Los Angeles, CA 90069, USA
Lappas, Steve *Basketball Coach*
%Villanova University, Athletic Dept, Villanova, PA 19085, USA
Laprade, Edgar *Hockey Player*
12 Shuniah St, Thunder Bay ON P7A 2Y8, Canada
LaPraed, Ronald (Ron) *Bassist, Trumpeter (Commodores)*
%Management Assoc, 1920 Benson Ave, Saint Paul, MN 55116, USA
Laquer, Walter *Historian*
%Georgetown University, Strategic Studies, 1800 K St NW, Washington, DC 20006, USA
Lara, Brian C *Cricketer*
%West Indies Cricket Club, PO Box 616, Saint John's, Antigua
Laragh, John H *Physician, Educator*
435 E 70th St, New York, NY 10021, USA
Laraki, Azeddine *Prime Minister, Morocco*
%Islamic Conference, Kilo 6, Mecca Road, Jeddah 21411, Saudi Arabia
Larch, John *Actor*
4506 Varna Ave, Sherman Oaks, CA 91423, USA
Lardner, George, Jr *Journalist*
%Washington Post, Editorial Dept, 1150 15th St NW, Washington, DC 20071, USA
Lardy, Henry A *Biochemist*
1829 Thorstrand Road, Madison, WI 53705, USA
Laredo, Jaime *Concert Violinist*
%Harold Holt, 31 Sinclair Road, London W14 0NS, England
Laredo, Ruth *Concert Pianist*
%I C M Artists, 40 W 57th St, New York, NY 10019, USA
Largent, Steve M *Football Player; Representative, OK*
6150 S Louisville Ave, Tulsa, OK 74136, USA
Larionov, Igor *Hockey Player*
%Detroit Red Wings, Joe Louis Arena, 600 Civic Center Dr, Detroit, MI 48226, USA
Larkin, Barry L *Baseball Player*
3348 Brinton Trail, Cincinnati, OH 45241, USA
Larkin, Patty *Singer, Songwriter*
%SRO Artists, 6629 University Ave, #206, Middleton, WI 53562, USA
Larmore, Jennifer *Opera Singer*
%I C M Artists, 40 W 57th St, New York, NY 10019, USA
Larner, Stevan *Cinematographer*
1209 Ballard Canyon Road, Solvang, CA 93463, USA
Laro, David *Judge*
%US Tax Court, 400 2nd St NW, Washington, DC 20217, USA
LaRoche, Philippe *Freestyle Aerials Skier*
%Club de Ski Acrobatique, Lac Beauport QC G0A 20Q, Canada
LaRocque, Gene R *Government Official, Navy Admiral*
5015 Macomb St NW, Washington, DC 20016, USA
Laroque, Michele *Actress*
%Artmedia, 20 Ave Rapp, 75007 Paris, France
LaRosa, Julius *Singer*
67 Sycamore Lane, Irvington, NY 10533, USA
Larose, Claude D *Hockey Player*
5060 NW 54th St, Coconut Creek, FL 33073, USA
LaRouche, Lyndon H, Jr *Political Activist*
18520 Round Top Lane, Round Hill, VA 20141, USA
Larouche, Pierre *Hockey Player*
112 Vanderbilt Dr, Pittsburgh, PA 15243, USA
Larroquette, John *Actor*
%Port Street Films, 15332 Antioch St, PO Box 318, Pacific Palisades, CA 90272, USA
Larry, Wendy *Basketball Coach*
%Old Dominion University, Athletic Dept, Norfolk, VA 23529, USA
Larsen, Art *Tennis Player*
203 Lorraine Blvd, San Leandro, CA 94577, USA
Larsen, Bruce *Editor*
%Vancouver Sun, 2250 Granville St, Vancouver BC V6H 3G2, Canada
Larsen, Don J *Baseball Player*
PO Box 2863, Hayden Lake, ID 83835, USA
Larsen, Gary L *Football Player*
4612 141st Court SE, Bellevue, WA 98006, USA
Larsen, Libby *Composer*
2205 Kenwood Parkway, Minneapolis, MN 55405, USA
Larsen, Paul E *Religious Leader*
%Evangelical Convenant Church, 5101 N Francisco Ave, Chicago, IL 60625, USA
Larsen, Ralph S *Businessman*
%Johnson & Johnson, 1 Johnson & Johnson Plaza, New Brunswick, NJ 08933, USA
Larson, April U *Religious Leader*
%Evangelical Lutheran Church, PO Box 4900, Rochester, MN 55903, USA
Larson, Charles R (Chuck) *Navy Admiral*
591 Coover Road, Annapolis, MD 21401, USA
Larson, Eric *Publisher*
%TV Guide Magazine, 100 Matsonford Road, Radnor, PA 19080, USA

Larson, Erik *Writer*
%Crown Publishers, 225 Park Ave S, New York, NY 10003, USA
Larson, Gary *Cartoonist (Far Side)*
%Universal Press Syndicate, 4520 Main St, Kansas City, MO 64111, USA
Larson, Jack *Actor*
449 N Skyewiay Road, Los Angeles, CA 90049, USA
Larson, Jill *Actress*
%Innovative Artists, 1505 10th St, Santa Monica, CA 90401, USA
Larson, Lance *Swimmer*
41 Balboa Coves, Newport Beach, CA 92663, USA
Larson, Peter N *Businessman*
%Brunswick Corp, 1 N Field Court, Lake Forest, IL 60045, USA
Larson, Wolf *Actor*
10600 Holman Ave, #1, Los Angeles, CA 90024, USA
LaRue Callahan, Eva *Actress*
11661 San Vicente Blvd, #307, Los Angeles, CA 90049, USA
LaRue, Florence *Singer (Fifth Dimension), Actress*
%Sterling/Winters, 10877 Wilshire Blvd, #15, Los Angeles, CA 90024, USA
LaRusso, Rudy *Basketball Player*
%Los Angeles Lakers, Staples Center, 1111 S Figueroa St, Los Angeles, CA 90015, USA
Lary, Frank S *Baseball Player*
11813 Baseball Dr, Northport, AL 35475, USA
Lary, R Yale *Football Player*
6366 Lansdale Road, Fort Worth, TX 76116, USA
LaSala, James *Labor Leader*
%Amalgamated Transit Union, 5025 Wisconsin Ave NW, Washington, DC 20016, USA
LaSalle, Denise *Singer*
%CAI Entertainment Agency, PO Box 9267, Jackson, MS 39286, USA
LaSalle, Eriq *Actor, Director*
PO Box 2369, Beverly Hills, CA 90213, USA
LaScola, Judith *Artist*
%Compositions Gallery, 317 Sutter St, San Francisco, CA 94108, USA
Lash, Bill *Skier*
17438 Bothell Way NE, #C305, Bothell, WA 98011, USA
Lasker, Dee Dee *Golfer*
1665 Chamisal Court, Carlsbad, CA 92009, USA
Lasorda, Thomas C (Tommy) *Baseball Player, Manager, Executive*
1473 W Maxzim Ave, Fullerton, CA 92833, USA
Lassally, Walter *Cinematographer*
6 Ladbroke Gardens, London W11 2PT, England
Lassaw, Ibram *Sculptor*
PO Box 487, East Hampton, NY 11937, USA
Lasser, Louise *Actress, Comedienne*
200 E 71st St, #20C, New York, NY 10021, USA
Lasseter, John *Movie Director, Animator*
%Pixar, 1200 Park Ave, Emeryville, CA 94608, USA
Lassez, Sarah *Actress*
%Innovative Artists, 1505 10th St, Santa Monica, CA 90401, USA
Lassiter, Amanda *Basketball Player*
%Seattle Storm, Key Arena, 351 Elliott Ave W, #500, Seattle, WA 98119, USA
Last, James *Orchestra Leader*
Schone Aussicht 16, 22085 Hamburg, Germany
Laster, Danny B *Animal Research Scientist*
%Hruska Meat Animal Research Center, PO Box 166, Clay Center, NE 68933, USA
Laszlo, Andrew *Cinematographer*
15838 Magnolia Blvd, Encino, CA 91436, USA
Lateef, Yusef *Jazz Saxophonist, Flutist, Composer*
%Rhino Records, 10635 Santa Monica Blvd, Los Angeles, CA 90025, USA
Latham, David *Astronomer*
%Harvard University, Astronomy Dept, Cambridge, MA 02138, USA
Latham, Louise *Actress*
2125 Piedras Dr, Santa Barbara, CA 93108, USA
Lathan, Sanaa *Actress*
%Brookside Artist Mgmt, 250 W 57th St, #2303, New York, NY 10107, USA
Lathiere, Bernard *Businessman*
%Airbus-Industrie, 5 Ave de Villiers, 75017 Paris, France
Lathon, Lamar L *Football Player*
14803 Via del Norte, Houston, TX 77083, USA
Latimore *Singer*
%Rodgers Redding, 1048 Tatnall St, Macon, GA 31201, USA
LaTourette, John E *Educator*
218 S Deerview Circle, Prescott, AZ 86303, USA
Lattimore, Kenny *Singer*
%Rhythm Jazz Entertainment Group, 4465 Don Milagro Dr, Los Angeles, CA 90008, USA
Lattisaw, Stacy *Singer*
%Walter Reeder Productions, PO Box 27641, Philadelphia, PA 19118, USA
Lattner, John J (Johnny) *Football Player*
1700 Riverwoods Dr, #503, Melrose Park, IL 60160, USA

Lauda, Andreas-Nikolaus (Niki) *Auto Racing Driver*
San Costa de Baix, Santa Eulalia, Ibiza, Spain
Lauder, Estee *Businesswoman*
%Estee Lauder Companies, 767 5th Ave, New York, NY 10153, USA
Lauder, Leonard A *Businessman*
%Estee Lauder Companies, 767 5th Ave, New York, NY 10153, USA
Lauderdale, Jim *Singer, Songwriter*
%Press Network, 1035 16th Ave S, #200, Nashville, TN 37212, USA
Lauer, Andrew *Actor*
3018 3rd St, Santa Monica, CA 90405, USA
Lauer, Martin *Track Athlete*
Hardstr 41, 77886 Lauf, Germany
Lauer, Matt *Commentator*
%NBC-TV, News Dept, 30 Rockefeller Plaza, New York, NY 10112, USA
Lauer, Tod R *Astronomer*
6471 N Tierra de Las Catalina, Tucson, AZ 85718, USA
Laughlin, John *Actor*
%Laughlin Enterprises, 13116 Albers St, Sherman Oaks, CA 91401, USA
Laughlin, Robert B *Nobel Physics Laureate*
%Stanford University, Physics Dept, Stanford, CA 94305, USA
Laughlin, Thomas R (Tom) *Actor, Director*
PO Box 840, Moorpark, CA 93020, USA
Laukkanen, Janne *Hockey Player*
%Tampa Bay Lightning, Ice Palace, 401 Channelside Dr, Tampa, FL 33602, USA
Lauper, Cyndi *Singer, Songwriter*
%William Morris Agency, 1325 Ave of Americas, New York, NY 10019, USA
Laurance, Dale *Businessman*
%Occidental Petroleum, 10889 Wilshire Blvd, Los Angeles, CA 90024, USA
Laurance, Matthew *Actor*
1951 Hillcrest Road, Los Angeles, CA 90068, USA
Laure, Carole *Singer, Actress*
%Cineart, 36 Rue de Ponthieu, 75008 Paris, France
Lauren, Ralph *Fashion Designer*
%Polo Ralph Lauren Corp, 650 Madison Ave, #C1, New York, NY 10022, USA
Lauren, Tammy *Actress*
%Gage Group, 14724 Ventura Blvd, #505, Sherman Oaks, CA 91403, USA
Laurents, Arthur *Writer*
PO Box 582, Quogue, NY 11959, USA
Lauria, Dan *Actor*
3960 Carpenter Ave, #5, Studio City, CA 91604, USA
Lauricella, Francis E (Hank) *Football Player*
1200 S Clearview Parkway, #1166, Harahan, LA 70123, USA
Lauridsen, Morten *Composer, Musician*
%University of Southern California, Music Dept, Los Angeles, CA 90089, USA
Laurie, Greg *Religious Leader*
%Harvest Christian Fellowship Church, 6115 Arlington Ave, Riverside, CA 92504, USA
Laurie, Hugh *Actor, Comedian, Writer*
%Gersh Agency, 232 N Canon Dr, Beverly Hills, CA 90210, USA
Laurie, Piper *Actress*
2118 Wilshire Blvd, #931, Santa Monica, CA 90403, USA
Lauter, Ed *Actor*
9165 Sunset Blvd, #202, Los Angeles, CA 90069, USA
Lauterbur, Paul C *Nobel Medicine Laureate*
2702 Holcomb Dr, Urbana, IL 61802, USA
Lautner, Georges C *Movie Director*
9 Chemin des Basses Ribes, 06130 Grasse, France
Lave, Lester B *Economist*
1008 Devonshire Road, Pittsburgh, PA 15213, USA
Laveikin, Aleksandr I *Cosmonaut*
%Potchta Kosmonavtov, Moskovskoi Oblasti, 141160 Syvisdny Goroduk, Russia
Lavelli, Dante B J *Football Player*
23273 Pheasant Lane, #11, Cleveland, OH 44145, USA
Laventhol, Henry L (Hank) *Artist*
445 Heritage Hills, #F, Somers, NY 10589, USA
Laver, Rodney G (Rod) *Tennis Player*
PO Box 4798, Hilton Head Island, SC 29938, USA
Lavery, Sean *Ballet Dancer*
%New York City Ballet, Lincoln Center Plaza, New York, NY 10023, USA
Lavi, Daliah *Actress*
Dahlienweg 2, 58313 Herdecke, Germany
Lavigne, Avril *Singer, Songwriter*
%Arista Records, 888 7th Ave, #3800, New York, NY 10106, USA
Lavin, Bernice E *Businesswoman*
%Alberto-Culver, 2525 Armitage Ave, Melrose Park, IL 60160, USA
Lavin, Leonard H *Businessman*
%Alberto-Culver, 2525 Armitage Ave, Melrose Park, IL 60160, USA
Lavin, Linda *Actress, Singer*
321 N Front St, Wilmington, NC 28401, USA

Laviolette, Peter *Hockey Player, Coach*
233 Huntington Bay Road, Halesite, NY 11743, USA
Lavrosky, Mikhail L *Ballet Dancer*
Voznesesenky Per 16/4, #7, 103009 Moscow, Russia
Lavrov, Kyrill Y *Actor*
Michurinskaya 1, #36, 197046 Saint Petersburg, Russia
Law, Bernard F Cardinal *Religious Leader*
%Archdiocese of Boston, 2121 Commonwealth Ave, Brighton, MA 02135, USA
Law, John Phillip *Actor*
1339 Miller Dr, Los Angeles, CA 90069, USA
Law, Jude *Actor*
%Julian Belfarge, 46 Albermarle St, London W1X 4PP, England
Law, Vernon S *Baseball Player*
1718 N 1050 West, Provo, UT 84604, USA
Lawless, Lucy *Actress*
PO Box 90409, Auckland, New Zealand
Lawless, Robert W *Educator*
%University of Tulsa, President's Office, Tulsa, OK 74104, USA
Lawn, John C *Law Enforcement Official*
%New York Yankees, Yankee Stadium, 161st St & River Ave, Bronx, NY 10451, USA
Lawrence Braxton, Janice *Basketball Player*
%Cleveland Rockers, Gund Arena, 1 Center Court, Cleveland, OH 44115, USA
Lawrence, Andrea Meade *Skier*
PO Box 43, Mammoth Lakes, CA 93546, USA
Lawrence, Carol *Actress, Singer*
12337 Ridge Circle, Los Angeles, CA 90049, USA
Lawrence, Cynthia *Opera Singer*
%Herbert Breslin, 119 W 57th St, #1505, New York, NY 10019, USA
Lawrence, David, Jr *Publisher*
%Miami Herald, 1 Herald Plaza, Miami, FL 33132, USA
Lawrence, Francis L *Educator*
%Rutgers University, President's Office, New Brunswick, NJ 08903, USA
Lawrence, Henry *Football Player*
2110 2nd Ave E, Palmetto, FL 34221, USA
Lawrence, James (Loz) *Guitarist (Strawberry Blondes)*
PO Box 33, Pontypool, Gwent NP4 6YU, England
Lawrence, Jerome *Writer*
PO Box 2770, Malibu, CA 90265, USA
Lawrence, Joseph *Actor*
%William Morris Agency, 151 El Camino Dr, Beverly Hills, CA 90212, USA
Lawrence, Marc *Actor*
2200 N Vista Grande Ave, Palm Springs, CA 92262, USA
Lawrence, Martin *Actor, Comedian*
%The Firm, 9100 Wilshire Blvd, #100W, Beverly Hills, CA 90210, USA
Lawrence, Matthew *Actor*
%William Morris Agency, 151 El Camino Dr, Beverly Hills, CA 90212, USA
Lawrence, Richard D *Army General*
7301 Valburn Dr, Austin, TX 78731, USA
Lawrence, Robert S *Physician*
Highfield House, 4000 N Charles St, #1112, Baltimore, MD 21218, USA
Lawrence, Sharon *Actress*
PO Box 462048, Los Angeles, CA 90046, USA
Lawrence, Steve *Singer*
944 Pinehurst Dr, Las Vegas, NV 89109, USA
Lawrence, Tracy *Singer, Songwriter*
%Holley, 3415 W End Ave, #101D, Nashville, TN 37203, USA
Lawrence, Vicki *Actress, Singer*
6000 Lido Ave, Long Beach, CA 90803, USA
Lawrence, Wendy B *Astronaut*
%National Reconnaissance Office, 14675 Lee Road, Chantilly, VA 20151, USA
Lawrence, William P *Navy Admiral*
303 Kyle Road, Crownsville, MD 21032, USA
Laws, Ronnie *Jazz Saxophonist*
%Pyramid Entertainment, 89 5th Ave, #700, New York, NY 10003, USA
Lawson of Blaby, Nigel *Government Official, England*
32 Sutherland Walk, London SE17, England
Lawson, Leigh *Actress*
%P F D, Drury House, 34-43 Russell St, London WC2B 5HA, England
Lawson, Nigella *Chef, Writer*
%E! Television, 5750 Wilshire Blvd, Los Angeles, CA 90036, USA
Lawson, Richard *Actor*
8840 Wilshire Blvd, #200, Beverly Hills, CA 90211, USA
Lawson, Richard L *Air Force General*
6910 Clifton Road, Clifton, VA 20124, USA
Lawton, Mary *Cartoonist (Nowhere to Hide)*
%Chronicle Features, 901 Mission St, San Francisco, CA 94103, USA
Lawton, Matthew (Matt) *Baseball Player*
27264 Highway 67, Saucier, MS 39574, USA

Lawton, Robert B *Educator*
%Loyola Marymount University, President's Office, Los Angeles, CA 90045, USA
Lawwill, Theodore *Ophthalmologist*
7609 Tallwood Road, Prospect, KY 40059, USA
Lax, John *Hockey Player*
3 Greendale Lane, Harwich, MA 02645, USA
Lax, Melvin *Physicist*
12 High St, Summit, NJ 07901, USA
Lax, Peter D *Mathematician*
251 Mercer St, New York, NY 10012, USA
Laxalt, Paul D *Governor, Senator, NV*
801 Pennsylvania Ave NW, #750, Washington, DC 20004, USA
Lay, Donald P *Judge*
%US Court of Appeals, 316 Robert St N, Saint Paul, MN 55101, USA
Layzie Bone *Rap Artist (Bone Thugs-N-Harmony)*
%Creative Artists Agency, 9830 Wilshire Blvd, Beverly Hills, CA 90212, USA
Lazar, Laurence *Religious Leader*
%Romanian Orthodox Episcopate, 2522 Grey Tower Road, Jackson, MI 49201, USA
Lazarev, Alexander N *Conductor*
%Christopher Tennant Artists, 39 Tadema Road, #2, London SW10 0PY, England
Lazarus, Mell *Cartoonist (Miss Peach, Momma)*
%Creators Syndicate, 5777 W Century Blvd, #700, Los Angeles, CA 90045, USA
Lazarus, Shelly *Businesswoman*
%Ogilvy & Mather Worldwide, 309 W 49th St, New York, NY 10019, USA
Lazear, Edward P *Economist*
277 Old Spanish Trail, Portola Valley, CA 94028, USA
Lazenby, George *Actor*
PO Box 55306, Sherman Oaks, CA 91413, USA
Lazier, Buddy *Auto Racing Driver*
%Performance Marketing, 1545 W 4th Ave, Vancouver BC V6U 1L6, Canada
Lazuktin, Alexander I *Cosmonaut*
%Potchta Kosmonavtov, Moskovskoi Oblasti, 141160 Syvisdny Goroduk, Russia
Lazure, Gabrielle *Actress*
%Cineart, 36 Rue de Ponthieu, 75008 Paris, France
Le Duc Anh *President, Vietnam; Army General*
%President's Office, Hoang Hoa Tham, Hanoi, Vietnam
Lea, Charles W (Charlie) *Baseball Player, Manager*
521 Old Collierville Arlin Road, Collierville, TN 38017, USA
Leach, Henry C *Navy Admiral, England*
Wonston Lea, Winchester, Hants SO21 3LS, England
Leach, Penelope *Child Psychologist*
3 Tanza Lane, London NW3 2UA, England
Leach, Robin *Television Producer, Entertainer*
1 Dag Hammarskjold Plaza, #2100, New York, NY 10017, USA
Leach, Rosemary *Actress*
%Felix de Wolfe, 51 Maida Vale, London W9 1SD, England
Leach, Sheryl *Animator (Barney)*
%Lyons Group, 300 E Bethany Road, Allen, TX 75002, USA
Leachman, Cloris *Actress*
410 S Barrington Ave, #307, Los Angeles, CA 90049, USA
Leader, George M *Governor, PA*
%Country Meadows, 830 Cherry Dr, Hershey, PA 17033, USA
Leader, Tom *Architect*
1212 Nelson St, Albany, CA 94706, USA
Leadon, Bernie *Singer, Guitarist (Eagles)*
%Joe's Garage, 4405 Belmont Park Terrace, Nashville, TN 37215, USA
Leaf, Alexander *Physician*
5 Sussex Road, Winchester, MA 01890, USA
Leahy, Patrick J (Pat) *Football Player*
717 Chamblee Lane, Saint Louis, MO 63141, USA
Leakey, Meave G *Paleontologist*
PO Box 24926, Nairobi, Kenya
Leakey, Richard E F *Paleonotolgist*
PO Box 24926, Nairobi, Kenya
Leaks, Roosevelt, Jr *Football Player*
%Roosevelt Leaks Properties, 8907 N Plaza Court, Austin, TX 78753, USA
Leal, Sharon *Actress, Singer*
%Meridian Artists Agency, 8265 W Sunset Blvd, #100, West Hollywood, CA 90046, USA
Lear, Evelyn *Opera Singer*
414 Sailboat Circle, Weston, FL 33326, USA
Lear, Norman M *Television Producer, Director*
100 N Crescent Dr, #250, Beverly Hills, CA 90210, USA
Learned, Michael *Actress*
1600 N Beverly Dr, Beverly Hills, CA 90210, USA
Leary, Denis *Actor, Comedian*
%Entertainment Tavel, 9171 Wilshire Blvd, #406, Beverly Hills, CA 90210, USA
Leatherdale, Douglas W *Businessman*
%Saint Paul Companies, 385 Washington St, Saint Paul, MN 55102, USA

L

Leaud - Ledley

Leaud, Jean-Pierre *Actor*
%Artmedia, 20 Ave Rapp, 75007 Paris, France
Leavitt, Michael O *Government Official, Governor, UT*
%Environmental Protection Agency, 401 M St SW, Washington, DC 20460, USA
Leavitt, Phil *Singer (Diamonds)*
%GEMS, PO Box 1031, Montrose, CA 91021, USA
Leavy, Edward *Judge*
%US Court of Appeals, 555 SW Yamhill St, Portland, OR 97204, USA
Lebadang *Artist*
%Circle Gallery, 303 E Wacker Dr, Chicago, IL 60601, USA
LeBaron, Edward W (Eddie), Jr *Football Player*
7524 Pineridge Lane, Fair Oaks, CA 95628, USA
LeBeau, C Richard (Dick) *Football Player, Coach*
10405 Stone Court, Cincinnati, OH 45242, USA
LeBeauf, Sabrina *Actress*
735 Kappock St, #6F, Bronx, NY 10463, USA
Lebedev, Valentin V *Cosmonaut*
%Potchta Kosmonavtov, Moskovskoi Oblasti, 141160 Syvisdny Goroduk, Russia
LeBel, B Harper *Football Player*
3379 Scadlock Lane, Sherman Oaks, CA 91403, USA
LeBel, Robert (Bob) *Hockey Executive*
25 Rue Saint Pierre, Cite de Chambly QC J3L 1L7, Canada
LeBlanc, Matt *Actor*
%United Talent Agency, 9560 Wilshire Blvd, #500, Beverly Hills, CA 90212, USA
LeBlanc, Sherri *Ballerina*
%New York City Ballet, Lincoln Center Plaza, New York, NY 10023, USA
LeBoeuf, Raymond W *Businessman*
%PPG Industries, 1 PPG Place, Pittsburgh, PA 15272, USA
LeBon, Simon *Singer, Songwriter (Duran Duran)*
%DD Productions, 93A Westbourne Park Villas, London W2 5ED, England
Lebovitz, Hall *Sportswriter*
2380 Edgerton Road, Cleveland, OH 44118, USA
Lebowitz, Fran *Writer*
%Random House, 1745 Broadway, #B1, New York, NY 10019, USA
Lebowitz, Joel L *Mathematician*
%Rutgers University, Mathematics Dept, New Brunswick, NJ 08903, USA
Leboyer, Frederick *Physician*
%Georges Borchardt, 136 E 57th St, New York, NY 10022, USA
LeBrock, Kelly *Actress, Model*
%Bartels Co, PO Box 57593, Sherman Oaks, CA 91413, USA
LeBrun, Christopher M *Artist*
%Marlborough Fine Art, 6 Albermarle St, London W1X 4BY, England
LeCarre, John *Writer*
9 Gainsborough Gardens, London NW3 1BJ, England
Lecavalier, Vincent *Hockey Player*
843 Seddon Cove Way, Port Huron, MI 48060, USA
Lechter, Sharon L *Writer*
%Cashflow Technologies, 4330 N Civic Center Plaza, Scottsdale, AZ 85251, USA
LeClair, James M (Jim) *Football Player*
43 4th Ave NE, Mayville, ND 58257, USA
LeClair, John *Hockey Player*
715 Dodds Lane, Gladwyne, PA 19035, USA
LeClerc, Jean *Actor*
19 W 44th St, #1500, New York, NY 10036, USA
LeClezio, Jean-Marie *Writer*
%Editions Gallimard, 5 Rue Sebastien-Bottin, 75007 Paris, France
Lecomte, Benoit *Swimmer*
%Cross Atlantic Swimming Challenge, 3005 S Lamar, #D109-353, Austin, TX 78704, USA
Leconte, Henri *Tennis Player*
%IMG, Pier House, Strand-on-Green, Chiswick, London W4 3NN, England
Leconte, Patrice *Movie Director*
%William Morris Agency, 151 El Camino Dr, Beverly Hills, CA 90212, USA
Leder, Mimi *Movie Director*
%Creative Artists Agency, 9830 Wilshire Blvd, Beverly Hills, CA 90212, USA
Leder, Philip *Geneticist*
%Howard Hughes Med Institute, 4000 Jones Bridge Road, Chevy Chase, MD 20815, USA
Lederberg, Joshua *Nobel Medicine Laureate*
%Rockefeller University, President's Office, 1230 York Ave, New York, NY 10021, USA
Lederer, Jerome *Aerospace Engineer*
468 Calle Cadiz, #D, Laguna Beach, CA 92653, USA
Lederman, Leon M *Nobel Physics Laureate*
3101 S Dearborn St, Chicago, IL 60616, USA
Ledford, Frank F, Jr *Army General, Physician*
%Southwest Biomed Research Foundation, PO Box 760549, San Antonio, TX 78245, USA
Ledger, Heath *Actor*
%John La Violette, 150 S Rodeo Dr, #300, Beverly Hills, CA 90212, USA
Ledley, Robert S *Inventor (Diagnostic X-Ray Systems)*
17000 Melbourne Dr, Laurel, MD 20707, USA

L

LeDoux, Chris *Singer, Songwriter, Rodeo Rider*
PO Box 253, Sumner, IA 50674, USA
Ledoyen, Virginie *Actress, Model*
80 Ave Gen Charles de Gaulle, 92200 Neuilly, France
Lee Kuan Yew *Prime Minister, Singapore*
Senior Minister's Office, Istana Annexe, Istana, Singapore 0923, Singapore
Lee, Alexondra *Actress*
%Writers & Artists, 8383 Wilshire Blvd, #550, Beverly Hills, CA 90211, USA
Lee, Ang *Movie Director*
417 Canal St, #410, New York, NY 10013, USA
Lee, Anna *Actress*
%TMCE, 270 N Canon Dr, #1064, Beverly Hills, CA 90210, USA
Lee, Anthonia W (Amp) *Football Player*
990 Brickyard Road, Chipley, FL 32428, USA
Lee, Bertram M *Basketball Executive*
%Denver Nuggets, Pepsi Center, 1000 Chopper Circle, Denver, CO 80204, USA
Lee, Beverly *Singer (Shirelles)*
%Bevi Corp, PO Box 100, Clifton, NJ 07015, USA
Lee, Brenda *Singer*
%Brenda Lee Productions, 2175 Carson St, Nashville, TN 37211, USA
Lee, Butch *Basketball Player*
1322 Teller Ave, Bronx, NY 10456, USA
Lee, Catherine J *Artist*
2625 Harkness St, Sacramento, CA 95818, USA
Lee, Chang-Rae *Writer*
%International Creative Mgmt, 40 W 57th St, #1800, New York, NY 10019, USA
Lee, Charles R *Businessman*
%GTE Corp, 1255 Corporate Dr, Irving, TX 75038, USA
Lee, Christopher F C *Actor*
5 Sandown House, Wheat Field Terrace, London W4, England
Lee, Daniel *Concert Cellist*
%Columbia Artists Mgmt Inc, 165 W 57th St, New York, NY 10019, USA
Lee, David *Television Director, Writer*
%Jim Preminger Agency, 450 N Roxbury Dr, #1050, Beverly Hills, CA 90210, USA
Lee, David H *Astronomer, Writer*
%Plenum Publishing Group, 233 Spring St, New York, NY 10013, USA
Lee, David L *Businessman*
%Global Crossing Ltd, Wessex House, 45 Reid St, Hamilton HM 12, Bermuda
Lee, David M *Nobel Physics Laureate*
%Cornell University, Physics Dept, Clark Hall, Ithaca, NY 14853, USA
Lee, Dickey *Singer*
%Mars Talent, 27 L'Ambiance Court, Bardonia, NY 10954, USA
Lee, Eunice *Concert Violinist*
%Columbia Artists Mgmt Inc, 165 W 57th St, New York, NY 10019, USA
Lee, Geddy *Singer, Bassist (Rush)*
%Macklam Feldman Mgmt, 1505 W 2nd Ave, #200, Vancouver BC V6H 3Y4, Canada
Lee, Gordon (Porky) *Actor*
%Dick Strand, 800 W 65th St, #103, Richfield, MN 55423, USA
Lee, Grandma *Actress, Comedienne*
%Lee Strong, 626 Staffordshire Dr, Jacksonville, FL 32225, USA
Lee, H Douglas *Educator*
%Stetson University, President's Office, Deland, FL 32720, USA
Lee, Harper *Writer*
%McIntosh & Otis, 353 Lexington Ave, #1500, New York, NY 10016, USA
Lee, Howard V *Vietnam War Marine Corps Hero (CMH)*
529 King Arthur Dr, Virginia Beach, VA 23464, USA
Lee, Jared B *Cartoonist*
%Jared B Lee Studio, 2942 Hamilton Road, Lebanon, OH 45036, USA
Lee, Jason *Actor*
PO Box 1083, Pearl City, HI 96782, USA
Lee, Jason Scott *Actor*
%United Talent Agency, 9560 Wilshire Blvd, #500, Beverly Hills, CA 90212, USA
Lee, Jeanette *Billards Player*
1427 W 86th St, #183, Indianapolis, IN 46260, USA
Lee, Joe *Businessman*
%Darden Restaurants, 5900 Lake Ellenor Dr, Orlando, FL 32809, USA
Lee, Johnny *Singer, Songwriter*
%WIFT Mgmt, 2317 Pecan, Dickinson,TX 77539, USA
Lee, Jong-Wook *Government Official*
%World Health Organization, Ave Appia, 1211 Geneva, Switzerland
Lee, Jonna *Actress*
8721 Sunset Blvd, #103, Los Angeles, CA 90069, USA
Lee, Keith *Basketball Player*
3617 Clearbrook St, Memphis, TN 38118, USA
Lee, Mark C *Astronaut*
6833 Phil Lewis Way, Middleton, WI 53562, USA
Lee, Michelle *Actress*
830 Birchwood Dr, Los Angeles, CA 90024, USA

L	
	Lee, Raphael C *Surgeon* %Massachusetts Institute Technology, Engineering Dept, Cambridge, MA 02139, USA
	Lee, Ron *Basketball Player* 35788 Woodridge Court, Farmington, MI 48335, USA
	Lee, Ruta *Actress* 2623 Laurel Canyon Road, Los Angeles, CA 90046, USA
	Lee, Samuel (Sammy) *Diver, Coach* 16537 Harbour Lane, Huntington Beach, CA 92649, USA
	Lee, Sheryl *Actress* %William Morris Agency, 151 El Camino Dr, Beverly Hills, CA 90212, USA
	Lee, Spike *Movie Director* %Forty Acres & A Mule Filmworks, 124 DeKalb Ave, #2, Brooklyn, NY 11217, USA
	Lee, Stan *Publisher, Cartoonist* %Marvel Entertainment, 1440 S Sepulveda Blvd, #114, Los Angeles, CA 90025, USA
	Lee, Tommy *Drummer, Singer (Motley Crue)* %Eagle Cove, 922 Masselin Ave, Los Angeles, CA 90036, USA
	Lee, Tsung-Dao *Nobel Physics Laureate* 25 Claremont Ave, New York, NY 10027, USA
	Lee, Vernon R *Religious Leader* %Wyatt Baptist Church, 4621 W Hillsboro St, El Dorado, AR 71730, USA
	Lee, William F (Bill) *Baseball Player* 305 Common View Dr, Craftsbury, VT 05826, USA
	Lee, Yuan T *Nobel Chemistry Laureate* Academy Sinica, Nankang, Taipei 11529, Taiwan
	Leech, Richard *Opera Singer* %Thea Dispeker Artists, 59 E 54th St, New York, NY 10022, USA
	Leek, Sybil *Self-Acclaimed Witch* %Prentice-Hall, RR 9W, Englewood Cliffs, NJ 07632, USA
	Leen, Bill *Bassist (Gin Blossoms)* %William Morris Agency, 2100 W End Ave, #1000, Nashville, TN 37203, USA
	Leese, Howard *Guitarist (Heart)* 219 1st Ave N, #333, Seattle, WA 98109, USA
	Leestma, David C *Astronaut* 4314 Lake Grove Dr, Seabrook, TX 77586, USA
	Leetch, Brian J *Hockey Player* 225 W 83rd St, New York,NY 10024, USA
	Leeves, Jane *Actress* %United Talent Agency, 9560 Wilshire Blvd, #500, Beverly Hills, CA 90212, USA
	Lefebvre, James K (Jim) *Baseball Manager* 10160 E Whispering Wind Dr, Scottsdale, AZ 85255, USA
	Leftwich, Byron *Football Player* %Jacksonville Jaguars, 1 AllTel Stadium Place, Jacksonville, FL 32202, USA
	Legace, Jean-Guy *Hockey Player* 126 Casa Grande Lane, Santa Rosa Beach, FL 32459, USA
	LeGault, Lance *Actor* 16105-8H Victory Blvd, #382, Van Nuys, CA 91406, USA
	Leggett, Anthony J *Nobel Physics Laureate* 607 W Pennsylvania Ave, Urbana, IL 61801, USA
	Legien, Waldemar *Judo Athlete* Ul Grottgera 10, 41-902 Bytom, Poland
	Legorreta Vilchis, Ricardo *Architect* %Palacio de Versalles, #285A, C Lomas Reforma, Mexico City 11020, Mexico
	Legrand, Michel *Composer, Conductor, Concert Pianist* %F Sharp Productions, PO Box 2040, New York, NY 10101, USA
	Legris, Manuel C *Ballet Dancer* %National Theater of Paris Opera, 8 Rue Scribe, 75009 Paris, France
	LeGros, James *Actor* %I F A Talent Agency, 8730 Sunset Blvd, #490, Los Angeles, CA 90069, USA
	LeGuin, Ursula K *Writer* 3321 NW Thurman St, Portland, OR 97210, USA
	Leguizano, John *Actor* %I D Public Relations, 8409 Santa Monica Blvd, West Hollywood, CA 90069, USA
	Lehane, Dennis *Writer* 1412 Jackson Road, Kerrville, TX 78028, USA
	Lehman, I Robert *Biochemist* 895 Cedro Way, Palo Alto, CA 94305, USA
	Lehman, Jeffrey *Educator* %Cornell University, President's Office, Ithaca, NY 14853, USA
	Lehman, Tom *Golfer* 9820 E Thompson Peak Parkway, #704, Scottsdale, AZ 85255, USA
	Lehmann, Edie *Actress* 24844 Malibu Road, Malibu, CA 90265, USA
	Lehmann, Erich L *Statistician* %Research Statistics Group, Education Testing Service, Princeton, NJ 08541, USA
	Lehmann, Karl Cardinal *Religious Leader* Bischofliches Ordinariat, PF 1560, Bischofsplatz 2, 55116 Mainz, Germany
	Lehmann, Michael *Movie Director* %Creative Artists Agency, 9830 Wilshire Blvd, Beverly Hills, CA 90212, USA
Lee - Lehmann	

Lehmberg, Stanford E *Historian*
1005 Calle Largo, Santa Fe, NM 87501, USA
Lehn, Jean-Marie P *Nobel Chemistry Laureate*
%Louis Pasteur Universite, 4 Rue Blaise Pascal, 67008 Strasbourg, France
Lehninger, Albert L *Biochemist*
15020 Tanyard Road, Sparks, MD 21152, USA
Lehrer, James C (Jim) *Commentator, Writer*
%News Hour Show, 2700 S Quincy St, #250, Arlington, VA 22206, USA
Lehrer, Robert I *Molecular Biologist*
%University of California, Med Center, Hematology Dept, Los Angeles, CA 90024, USA
Lehrer, Thomas A (Tom) *Pianist, Comedian*
%University of California, Cowell College, Santa Cruz, CA 95064, USA
Lehtinen, Dexter *Attorney, Government Official*
%US Attorney's Office, Justice Dept, 155 S Miami Ave, Miami, FL 33130, USA
Lehtinen, Jere *Hockey Player*
569 Indian Rock Dr, Coppell, TX 75019, USA
Leibel, Rudolph *Obesity Researcher*
464 Riverside Dr, #95, New York, NY 10027, USA
Leiber, Jerry *Lyricist*
%Leiber & Stoller Ent, 9000 W Sunset Blvd, West Hollywood, CA 90069, USA
Leibman, Ron *Actor*
27 W 87th St, #2, New York, NY 10024, USA
Leibovitz, Annie *Photographer*
547 W 26th St, New York, NY 10001, USA
Leibovitz, Mitchell G *Businessman*
%Pep Boys-Manny Moe & Jack, 3111 W Allegheny Ave, Philadelphia, PA 19132, USA
Leifer, Carol *Actress, Comedienne*
%Brillstein/Grey, 9150 Wilshire Blvd, #350, Beverly Hills, CA 90212, USA
Leiferkus, Sergei P *Opera Singer*
5 The Paddocks, Abberbury Road, Iffley, Oxford OX4 4ET, England
Leifheit, Sylvia *Model*
%Agentur Reed, Treppendorfer Weg 13, 12527 Berlin, Germany
Leigh, Danni *Singer*
%Shipley Biddy Entertainment, 1400 South St, Nashville, TN 37212, USA
Leigh, Janet *Actress*
1625 Summitridge Dr, Beverly Hills, CA 90210, USA
Leigh, Jennifer Jason *Actress*
%Edrick/Rich Mgmt, 2400 Whitman Place, Los Angeles, CA 90068, USA
Leigh, Mike *Movie, Theater Director*
%Thin Man Films, 9 Greek St, Soho, London W1D 4DQ, England
Leigh, Mitch *Composer*
29 W 57th St, #1000, New York, NY 10019, USA
Leigh, Regina *Singer (Regina Regina)*
%Bobby Roberts, 909 Meadowlark Lane, Goodlettsville, TN 37072, USA
Leija, James (Jesse) *Boxer*
9735 Richey Otis Way, San Antonio, TX 78223, USA
Leimkuehler, Paul *Amputee Skier, Businessman*
351 Darbys Run, Bay Village, OH 44140, USA
Leisure, David *Actor*
26358 Woodlark Lane, Valencia, CA 91355, USA
Leiter, Alois T (Al) *Baseball Player*
2660 Riviera Manor, Weston, FL 33332, USA
Leith, Emmett N *Electrical Engineer*
51325 Murray Hill Dr, Canton, MI 48187, USA
Leitner, Patric-Fritz *Luge Athlete*
%BSD, An der Schiessstatte 4, 83471 Berchtesgaden, Germany
Leitzel, Joan *Educator*
%University of Nebraska, President's Office, Lincoln, NE 68588, USA
Lekang, Anton *Ski Jumper*
47 Pratt St, Winsted, CT 06098, USA
Lelong, Pierre J *Mathematician*
9 Place de Rungis, 75013 Paris, France
Lelouch, Claude *Movie Director*
15 Ave Hoche, 75008 Paris, France
Lelyveld, Joseph *Editor*
%New York Times, Editorial Dept, 229 W 43rd St, New York, NY 10036, USA
Lem, Stanislaw *Writer*
Ul Narwik 66, 30-437 Cracow, Poland
Lemaire, Jacques G *Hockey Player, Coach*
6667 Avenue B, Sarasota, FL 34231, USA
LeMat, Paul *Actor*
1100 N Alta Loma Road, #805, West Hollywood, CA 90069, USA
LeMay-Doan, Michelle *Speedskater*
%Landmark Sport Group, 277 Richmond St W, Toronto ON M5V 1X1, Canada
Lembeck, Michael *Television Director, Actor*
23852 Pacific Coast Highway, #355, Malibu, CA 90265, USA
Lemelson, Jerome H *Inventor (Industrial Warehouse Systems)*
48 Parkside Dr, Princeton, NJ 08540, USA

LeMesurier, John *Actor*
56 Barron's Keep, London W14, England
Lemieux, Claude *Hockey Player*
6008 N Saguaro Place, Paradise Valley, AZ 85253, USA
Lemieux, Jocelyn *Hockey Player*
1123 Sandhurst Court, Buffalo Grove, IL 60089, USA
Lemieux, Joseph H *Businessman*
%Owens-Illinois Inc, 1 Sea Gate, Toledo, OH 43666, USA
LeMieux, Kathryn *Cartoonist (Six Chix)*
%King Features Syndicate, 888 7th Ave, New York, NY 10106, USA
Lemieux, Mario *Hockey Player*
630 Academy St, Sewickley, PA 15143, USA
Lemieux, Raymond U *Chemist*
7602 119th St, Edmonton AB T6G 1W3, Canada
Lemke, Mark A *Baseball Player*
3 Olena Dr, Whitesboro, NY 13492, USA
Lemmon, Chris *Actor*
80 Murray St, South Glastonbury, CT 06073, USA
Lemmons, Kasi *Movie Director, Writer*
8605 Appian Way, Los Angeles, CA 90046, USA
Lemon, Chester E (Chet) *Baseball Player*
PO Box 951436, Lake Mary, FL 32795, USA
Lemon, Peter C *Vietnam War Army Hero (CMH)*
6245 Viewfield Heights, Colorado Springs, CO 80919, USA
Lemos, Richie *Boxer*
18658 Klum Place, Rowland Heights, CA 91748, USA
Lemper, Ute *Singer, Actress, Dancer*
%Les Visiteurs du Soir, 40 Rue de la Folie Regnault, 75011 Paris, France
Lenahan, Edward P *Publisher*
%Fortune Magazine, Rockefeller Center, New York, NY 10020, USA
Lenard, Michael B *Sports Executive*
%US Olympic Committee, 1 Olympia Plaza, Colorado Springs, CO 80909, USA
Lenard, Voshon *Basketball Player*
%Denver Nuggets, Pepsi Center, 1000 Chopper Circle, Denver, CO 80204, USA
Lendl, Ivan *Tennis Player*
400 5 1/2 Mile Road, Goshen, CT 06756, USA
Lenfant, Claude J M *Physician*
PO Box 83027, Gaithersburg, MD 20883, USA
Lenihan, Brian J *Government Official, Ireland*
24 Park View, Castleknock, County Dublin, Ireland
Lenk, Maria *Swimmer*
Rua Cupertino Durao 16, Leblon, Rio de Janeiro 22441, Brazil
Lenk, Thomas *Sculptor*
Gemeinde Braunsbach, 7176 Schloss Tierberg, Germany
Lennie, Angus *Actor*
%Jean Drysdale, 15 Pembroke Gardens, London W8, England
Lennon, Diane *Singer (Lennon Sisters)*
1984 State Highway 165, Branson, MO 65616, USA
Lennon, Janet *Singer (Lennon Sisters)*
1984 State Highway 165, Branson, MO 65616, USA
Lennon, Julian *Singer, Songwriter*
30 Ives St, London SW3 2ND, England
Lennon, Kathy *Singer (Lennon Sisters)*
Overlook Dr, #10, Branson, MO 65616, USA
Lennon, Peggy *Singer (Lennon Sisters)*
1984 State Highway 165, Branson, MO 65616, USA
Lennon, Richard G *Religious Leader*
%Archdiocese of Boston, 2121 Commonwealth Ave, Boston, MA 02135, USA
Lennon, Sean *Singer*
%Dakota Hotel, 1 W 72nd St, New York, NY 10023, USA
Lennox, Annie *Singer (Eurythmics), Songwriter*
%Nineteen Music Mgmt, 35-37 Parkgate Road, London SW11 4NP, England
Lennox, William, Jr *Army General, Educator*
Superintendent, US Military Academy, West Point, NY 10996, USA
Leno, Jay *Actor, Comedian*
%Big Dog Productions, PO Box 7885, Burbank, CA 91510, USA
Lenoir, William B *Astronaut*
%Space Flight & Station Office, NASA Hq, Code M/S, Washington, DC 20546, USA
Lenska, Rula *Model, Actress*
%David Daley Assoc, 586A Kings Road, London SW6 2DX, England
Lenz, Kay *Actress*
5916 Filaree Heights, Malibu, CA 90265, USA
Lenz, Kim *Singer, Songwriter*
%Mark Pucia Media, 5000 Oak Bluff Court, Atlanta, GA 30350, USA
Lenz, Rick *Actor*
12955 Calvert St, Van Nuys, CA 91401, USA
Lenzi, Mark *Diver*
117 Bay Meadow Lane, Benson, NC 27504, USA

Leo, Melissa *Actress*
%Agency for Performing Arts, 9200 Sunset Blvd, #900, Los Angeles, CA 90069, USA
Leon, Valerie *Actress*
%Essanay Ltd, 2 Conduit St, London W1R 9TG, England
Leonard, Bob (Slick) *Basketball Player, Coach*
1241 Hillcrest Dr, Carmel, IN 46033, USA
Leonard, Dennis P *Baseball Player*
4102 SW Evergreen Lane, Blue Springs, MO 64015, USA
Leonard, Elmore *Writer*
2192 Yarmouth Road, Bloomfield Village, MI 48301, USA
Leonard, Hugh *Writer*
6 Rossaun, Pilot View, Dalkey, County Dublin, Ireland
Leonard, Joanne *Photographer*
%University of Michigan, Art Dept, Ann Arbor, MI 48109, USA
Leonard, Joe *Motorcycle Racing Rider, Auto Driver*
%Motorsports Hall of Fame, PO Box 194, Novi, MI 48376, USA
Leonard, Justin *Golfer*
3304 Dartmouth Ave, Dallas, TX 75205, USA
Leonard, Ray C (Sugar Ray) *Boxer*
4401 East West Highway, #206B, Bethesda, MD 20814, USA
Leonard, Robert Sean *Actor*
14 Bergen Ave, Waldwick, NJ 07463, USA
Leonard, Wayne *Businessman*
%Entergy Corp, 10055 Grogans Mill Road, #5A, The Woodlands, TX 77380, USA
Leonetti, John R *Cinematographer*
5251 Genesta Ave, Encino, CA 91316, USA
Leonetti, Matthew F *Cinematographer*
1362 Bella Oceana Vista, Pacific Palisades, CA 90272, USA
Leong, Page *Actress*
%C N A Assoc, 1925 Century Park East, #750, Los Angeles, CA 90067, USA
Leonhart, William *Diplomat*
2618 30th St NW, Washington, DC 20008, USA
Leoni, Tea *Actress*
PO Box 10459, Burbank, CA 91510, USA
Leonov, Aleksei A *Cosmonaut, Air Force General*
%Alfa Capital, Acad Sakharov Prospect 12, 107078 Moscow, Russia
Leonskaja, Elisabeth *Concert Pianist*
%Columbia Artists Mgmt Inc, 165 W 57th St, New York, NY 10019, USA
Leopold, Luna B *Hydraulic Engineer*
PO Box 1040, Pinedale, WY 82941, USA
LePelley, Guernsey *Editorial Cartoonist*
35 Saint Germain St, Boston, MA 02115, USA
LePichon, Xavier *Geologist*
%Ecole Normale Superieure, 24 Rue Lhomond, 75005 Paris Cedex 05, France
Leppard, Raymond J *Conductor*
%Indianapolis Symphony, 32 E Washington St, #600, Indianapolis, IN 46204, USA
Lerach, William (Bill) *Attorney*
%Milberg Weiss Hynes Lerach, 1600 W Broadway, #1800, San Diego, CA 92101, USA
Lerner, Michael *Actor*
%Innovative Artists, 1505 10th St, Santa Monica, CA 90401, USA
LeRoux, Francois *Opera Singer*
%I M G Artists, 3 Burlington Lane, Chiswick, London W4 2TH, England
LeRoy, Gloria *Actress*
%Shelly & Pierce, 13775A Mono Way, #220, Sonora, CA 95370, USA
Lesar, David *Businessman*
%Halliburton Co, Lincoln Plaza, 500 N Akard St, Dallas, TX 75201, USA
Lesco, Lisa *Actress*
1224 N Crescent Heights Blvd, #6, West Hollywood, CA 90046, USA
Lesh, Phil *Bassist (Grateful Dead)*
PO Box 1073, San Rafael, CA 94915, USA
LeShana, David C *Educator*
5737 Charles Circle, Lake Oswego, OR 97035, USA
Leslie, Fred W *Astronaut*
2513 Clifton Dr SE, Huntsville, AL 35803, USA
Leslie, Joan *Actress*
2228 N Catalina St, Los Angeles, CA 90027, USA
Leslie, Lisa *Basketball Player, Model*
5200 Shenandoah Ave, Los Angeles, CA 90056, USA
Lessard, Stefan *Bassist (Dave Matthews Band), Songwriter*
%Red Light Mgmt, 3302 Loban Place, Charlottesville, VA 22903, USA
Lesser, Len *Actor*
934 N Evergreen St, Burbank, CA 91505, USA
Lessing, Doris M *Writer*
11 Kingscroft Road, #3, London NW2 3QE, England
Lester of Herne Hill, Anthony P *Attorney*
%Blackstone Chambers, Blackstone House, Temple, London EC4Y 9BW, England
Lester, Darrell G *Football Player*
3103 Meadow Oaks Dr, Temple, TX 76502, USA

L

Lester - Levingston

Lester, Ketty — *Actress, Singer*
5931 Comey Ave, Los Angeles, CA 90034, USA

Lester, Mark — *Actor*
%Carlton Clinic, 1 Carlton St, Cheltenham, Glou GLS2 6AG, England

Lester, Mark L — *Movie Director*
17268 Camino Yatasto, Pacific Palisades, CA 90272, USA

Lester, Richard (Dick) — *Movie Director*
River Lane, Petersham, Surrey, England

Letarte, Pierre — *Cinematographer*
551 W Pinacle, Abercorn QC J0E 1B0, Canada

Letbetter, R Steve — *Businessman*
%Reliant Energy, 1111 Louisiana, Houston, TX 77002, USA

Letlow, W R (Russ) — *Football Player*
1876 Thelma Dr, San Luis Obispo, CA 93405, USA

Leto, Jared — *Actor*
%United Talent Agency, 9560 Wilshire Blvd, #500, Beverly Hills, CA 90212, USA

Letsie III — *King, Lesotho*
%Royal Palace, PO Box 524, Maseru, Lesotho

Lett, Leon — *Football Player*
4959 Cape Coral Dr, Dallas, TX 75287, USA

Letterman, David — *Entertainer, Comedian*
%Worldwide Pants, 1697 Broadway, New York, NY 10019, USA

Letts, Billie — *Writer*
%Warner Books, 1271 Ave of Americas, New York, NY 10020, USA

LeVay, Simon — *Neuroscientist*
970 Palm Ave, West Hollywood, CA 90069, USA

Levene, Ben — *Artist*
%Royal Academy of Arts, Piccadilly, London W1V 2LP, England

Levens, Dorsey — *Football Player*
224 Primrose Ave, Syracuse, NY 13205, USA

Leveque, Michel — *Minister of State, Monaco*
%Minister of State's Office, BP 522, 98015 Monaco Cedex, Monaco

Levert, Eddie — *Singer (O'Jays)*
%Associated Booking Corp, 1995 Broadway, #501, New York, NY 10023, USA

Levert, Gerald — *Singer, Songwriter*
%Associated Booking Corp, 1995 Broadway, #501, New York, NY 10023, USA

Levi, Wayne — *Golfer*
17 Ironwood Road, New Hartford, NY 13413, USA

Levi, Yoel — *Conductor*
%Askonas Holt Ltd, 27 Chancery Lane, London WC2A 1PF, England

Levi-Montalcini, Rita — *Nobel Medicine Laureate*
%Cell Biology Institute, Piazzale Aldo Moro 7, 00185 Rome, Italy

Levi-Strauss, Claude — *Anthropologist*
2 Rue des Marronniers, 75016 Paris, France

LeVias, Jerry — *Football Player*
3322 Chris Dr, Houston, TX 77063, USA

Levin, Drake — *Guitarist (Paul Revere & the Raiders)*
%Paradise Artists, 108 E Matilija St, Ojai, CA 93023, USA

Levin, Ira — *Writer*
1172 Park Ave, New York, NY 10128, USA

Levin, Richard C — *Educator*
%Yale University, President's Office, New Haven, CT 06520, USA

Levine, Arnold — *Molecular Biologist, Educator*
%Rockefeller University, President's Office, 1230 York Ave, New York, NY 10021, USA

Levine, David — *Artist, Caricaturist*
161 Henry St, Brooklyn, NY 11201, USA

Levine, Ellen R — *Editor*
%Good Housekeeping Magazine, 959 8th Ave, New York, NY 10019, USA

Levine, Irving R — *Commentator*
%Lynn University, International Studies/Economics Dept, Boca Raton, FL 33431, USA

Levine, Jack — *Artist*
68 Morton St, New York, NY 10014, USA

Levine, James — *Conductor*
%Boston Symphony Orchestra, 301 Massachusetts Ave, Boston, MA 02115, USA

Levine, Philip — *Writer*
4549 N Van Ness Blvd, Fresno, CA 93704, USA

Levine, Rachmiel — *Endocrinologist*
614 Walnut St, Newton, MA 02460, USA

Levine, S Robert — *Businessman*
%Cabletron Systems, PO Box 5005, Rochester, NH 03866, USA

Levine, Seymour — *Psychobiologist*
1512 Notre Dame Dr, Davis, CA 95616, USA

Levine, Sol — *Sociologist*
30 Powell St, Brookline, MA 02446, USA

Levine, Ted — *Actor*
%Innovative Artists, 1505 10th St, Santa Monica, CA 90401, USA

Levingston, Cliff — *Basketball Player*
%Denver Nuggets, Pepsi Center, 1000 Chopper Circle, Denver, CO 80204, USA

Levingstone, Ken *Government Official, England*
%House of Commons, Westminster, London SW1A 0AA, England
Levinson, Barry L *Movie Director*
%United Talent Agency, 9560 Wilshire Blvd, #500, Beverly Hills, CA 90212, USA
Levinson, Sanford V *Attorney, Educator*
3410 Windsor Road, Austin, TX 78703, USA
Levinthal, Cyrus *Biologist*
%Columbia University, Biological Sciences Dept, New York, NY 10027, USA
Levitas, Andrew *Actor*
%Metropolitan Talent Agency, 4526 Wilshire Blvd, Los Angeles, CA 90010, USA
Levitt, Arthur, Jr *Government Official, Financier*
%Carlyle Group, 1001 Pennsylvania Ave NW, Washington, DC 20004, USA
Levitt, George *Chemist*
82 Via Del Corso, Palm Beach Gardens, FL 33418, USA
Levitt, Joseph Gordon *Actor*
%Gersh Agency, 232 N Canon Dr, Beverly Hills, CA 90210, USA
LeVox, Gary *Singer (Rascal Flatts)*
%LGB Media, 1228 Pineview Lane, Nashville, TN 37211, USA
Levy, Clifford J *Journalist*
%New York Times, Editorial Dept, 229 W 43rd St, New York, NY 10036, USA
Levy, David *Government Official, Israel*
%New Way Party, Knesset, Kiryat Ben Gurion, 91950 Jerusalem, Israel
Levy, David H *Astronomer*
%Mount Palomar Observatory, Palomar Mountain, Mount Palomar, CA 92060, USA
Levy, Eugene *Actor, Director*
7481 Beverly Blvd, #301, Los Angeles, CA 90036, USA
Levy, Kenneth *Businessman*
%KLA-Tencor Corp, 160 Rio Robles, San Jose, CA 95134, USA
Levy, Leonard W *Historian*
1025 Timberline Terrace, Ashland, OR 97520, USA
Levy, Marvin David *Composer*
%Sheldon Sofer Mgmt, 130 W 56th St, New York, NY 10019, USA
Levy, Michael R *Publisher*
%Texas Monthly Magazine, PO Box 1569, Austin, TX 78767, USA
Levy, Peter *Cinematographer*
%International Creative Mgmt, 8942 Wilshire Blvd, #219, Beverly Hills, CA 90211, USA
LeWinter, Nancy Nadler *Publisher*
%Esquire Magazine, 1790 Broadway, 1300, New York, NY 10019, USA
Lewis, Al (Grandpa) *Actor*
PO Box 277, New York, NY 10044, USA
Lewis, Albert R *Football Player*
3532 Macedonia Road, Centreville, MS 39631, USA
Lewis, Allen *Government Official, Saint Lucia*
Beaver Lodge, Morn, PO Box 1076, Castries, Saint Lucia, West Indies
Lewis, Andrew L (Drew) *Secretary, Transportation; Businessman*
PO Box 70, Lederach, PA 19450, USA
Lewis, Anthony *Columnist*
%New York Times, Editorial Dept, 2 Faneuil Hall, Boston, MA 02109, USA
Lewis, Barbara *Singer*
%Hello Stranger Productions, PO Box 300488, Fern Park, FL 32730, USA
Lewis, Bernard *Historian*
%Princeton University, Near Eastern Studies Dept, Princeton, NJ 08544, USA
Lewis, Bill *Football Coach*
%Georgia Institute of Technology, Athletic Dept, Atlanta, GA 30332, USA
Lewis, Bobby *Singer*
%Lustig Talent, PO Box 770850, Orlando, FL 32877, USA
Lewis, Charlotte *Basketball Player*
2814 N Sheridan Road, Peoria, IL 61604, USA
Lewis, Clea *Actress*
1659 S Highland Ave, Los Angeles, CA 90019, USA
Lewis, Crystal *Singer*
%Proper Mgmt, PO Box 150867, Nashville, TN 37215, USA
Lewis, Cynthia R *Publisher*
%Harper's Bazaar, 1770 Broadway, New York, NY 10019, USA
Lewis, D D *Football Player*
%PCS Sales, 1624 Northcrest Dr, Plano, TX 75075, USA
Lewis, Damione *Football Player*
%Saint Louis Rams, 901 N Broadway, Saint Louis, MO 63101, USA
Lewis, Darren *Football Player*
641 Seabeach Road, Dallas, TX 75232, USA
Lewis, Dave *Hockey Player, Coach*
22583 Heatherbridge Lane, Northville, MN 48167, USA
Lewis, David Levering *Writer*
%Rutgers University, History Dept, East Rutherford, NJ 08903, USA
Lewis, David R *Football Player*
2363 Gallant Fox Court, Reston, VA 20191, USA
Lewis, Dawnn *Actress*
PO Box 56718, Sherman Oaks, CA 91413, USA

Lewis, Edward B *Nobel Medicine Laureate*
805 Winthrop Road, San Marino, CA 91108, USA
Lewis, F Carlton (Carl) *Track Athlete*
9777 Harwin, #307, Houston, TX 77036, USA
Lewis, Gary *Singer (Gary Lewis & the Playboys)*
701 Balin Court, Nashville, TN 37221, USA
Lewis, Geoffrey *Actor*
%William Morris Agency, 151 El Camino Dr, Beverly Hills, CA 90212, USA
Lewis, Grady *Basketball Player*
8926 W Topeka Dr, Peoria, IL 61615, USA
Lewis, Huey *Singer, Actor*
%Bob Brown Mgmt, PO Box 779, Mill Valley, CA 94942, USA
Lewis, Jamal *Football Player*
%Baltimore Ravens, Ravens Stadium, 11001 Russell St, Baltimore, MD 21230, USA
Lewis, Jermaine *Football Player*
%Octagon, 1751 Pinnacle Dr, #1500, McLean, VA 22102, USA
Lewis, Jerry *Actor, Comedian, Director*
1701 Waldman Ave, Las Vegas, NV 89102, USA
Lewis, Jerry Lee *Singer, Pianist, Composer*
%JKL Enterprises, PO Box 384, Nesbit, MS 38651, USA
Lewis, Juliette *Actress*
8995 Elevado, Los Angeles, CA 90069, USA
Lewis, Kenneth D *Financier*
%Bank of America Corp, 100 N Tryon St, Charlotte, NC 28255, USA
Lewis, Lennox *Boxer*
%Panix Promotions, 99 Middlesex St, London E1 7DA, England
Lewis, Marvin *Football Coach*
%Cincinnati Bengals, 1 Paul Brown Stadium, Cincinnati, OH 45202, USA
Lewis, Mary (Christianni Brand) *Writer*
88 Maida Vale, London W9, England
Lewis, Michael *Writer*
%W W Norton, 500 5th Ave, New York, NY 10110, USA
Lewis, Mo *Football Player*
89 The Glen, Glen Head, NY 11545, USA
Lewis, Monica *Singer*
%Lang, 1100 Alta Loma Road, #16A, Los Angeles, CA 90069, USA
Lewis, Peter B *Businessman*
%Progressive Corp, 6300 Wilson Mills Road, Cleveland, OH 44143, USA
Lewis, Ramsey *Jazz Pianist, Composer*
%Bennett Morgan, 1282 RR 376, Wappingers Falls, NY 12590, USA
Lewis, Rashard *Basketball Player*
%Seattle SuperSonics, 351 Elliott Ave W, #500, Seattle, WA 98119, USA
Lewis, Ray *Football Player*
1421 Connestee Road, Lakeland, FL 33805, USA
Lewis, Richard *Actor, Comedian*
8001 Hemet Place, Los Angeles, CA 90046, USA
Lewis, Russell T *Businessman, Publisher*
%New York Times Co, 229 W 43rd St, New York, NY 10036, USA
Lewis, Vaughan A *Prime Minister, Saint Lucia*
%United Workers Party, 1 Riverside Road, Castries, Saint Lucia
Lewis, Vicki *Actress, Comedienne*
%Special Artists Agency, 345 N Maple Dr, #302, Beverly Hills, CA 90210, USA
Lewis, Victor *Jazz Drummer*
%Joanne Klein, 130 W 28th St, New York, NY 10001, USA
Lewiston, Denis C *Cinematographer*
13700 Tahiti Way, #24, Marina del Rey, CA 90292, USA
Lewit-Nirenberg, Julie *Publisher*
%Mademoiselle Magazine, 350 Madison Ave, New York, NY 10017, USA
LeWitt, Sol *Artist*
20 Pratt St, Chester, CT 06412, USA
Lewitzky, Bella *Dancer, Choreographer*
2587 E Washington Blvd, #215, Pasadena, CA 91107, USA
Leygue, Louis Georges *Sculptor*
6 Rue de Docteur Blanche, 75016 Paris, France
Leyland, James R (Jim) *Baseball Manager*
261 Tech Road, Pittsburgh, PA 15205, USA
Leyritz, James J (Jim) *Baseball Player*
495 Vinegarten Dr, Cincinnati, OH 45255, USA
Leyton, John *Actor, Singer*
53 Keyes House, Dolphin Square, London SW1V 3NA, England
Leyva, Nicholas T (Nick) *Baseball Manager*
1098 Tilghman Road, Chesterbrook, PA 19087, USA
Li Keyu *Fashion Designer*
21 Gong-Jian Hutong, Di An-Men, Beijing 100009, China
Li Lanqing *Government Official, China*
%Communist Party Central Committee, Zhong Nan Hai, Beijing, China
Li Peng *Premier, China*
%Communist Party Central Committee, Zhong Nan Hai, Beijing, China

Li, Frederick *Molecular Biologist*
%Dana-Farber Cancer Institute, 44 Binney St, Boston, MA 02115, USA
Li, Jet *Actor*
%Current Ent, 366 Adelaide St, #437, Toronto ON M5A 3X9, Canada
Liacouras, Peter J *Educator*
%Temple University, President's Office, Philadelphia, PA 19122, USA
Liaklev, Reidar *Speedskater*
2770 Jaren, Norway
Libano Christo, Carlos A *Social Activist, Writer*
Rua Atibaia 420, 01235-010 Sao Paulo, Brazil
Libertini, Richard *Actor*
2313 McKinley Ave, Venice, CA 90291, USA
Libeskind, Daniel *Architect*
%Studio Daniel Libeskund, Windscheidstr 18, 10627 Berlin, Germany
Libutti, Frank *Marine Corps General, Police Official*
%New York City Deputy Commissioner's Office, 1 Police Plaza, New York, NY 10038, USA
Licad, Cecile *Concert Pianist*
%Columbia Artists Mgmt Inc, 165 W 57th St, New York, NY 10019, USA
Lichfield, Earl of *Photographer*
%Lichfield Studios, 133 Oxford Gardens, London W10 6NE, England
Licht, Jeremy *Actor*
4355 Clybourn Ave, Toluca Lake, CA 91602, USA
Licht, Louis *Environmental Scientist*
%Ecoltree, 3017 Valley View Lane NE, North Liberty, IA 52317, USA
Lichtenberg, Byron K *Astronaut*
5701 Impala South Road, Athens, TX 75752, USA
Lichtenberger, H W *Businessman*
%Praxair Inc, 39 Old Ridgebury Road, Danbury, CT 06810, USA
Lichtenstein, Harvey *Music Executive*
%Brooklyn Academy of Music, 30 Lafayette Ave, Brooklyn, NY 11217, USA
Lick, Dennis A *Football Player*
6140 S Knox Ave, Chicago, IL 60629, USA
Lidback, Jenny *Golfer*
%Ladies Pro Golf Assn, 100 International Golf Dr, Daytona Beach, FL 32124, USA
Liddy, Edward M *Businessman*
%Allstate Corp, Allstate Plaza, 2775 Sanders Road, Northbrook, IL 60062, USA
Liddy, G Gordon *Watergate Figure, Actor*
9112 Riverside Dr, Fort Washington, MD 20744, USA
Lidov, Arthur *Artist*
Pleasant Ridge Road, Poughquag, NY 12570, USA
Lidstrom, Nicklas *Hockey Player*
21174 Dundee Dr, Novi, MI 48375, USA
Lieber, Jonathan R (Jon) *Baseball Player*
310 Main St, Springville, AL 35146, USA
Lieber, Larry *Cartoonist (Amazing Spider-Man)*
%King Features Syndicate, 888 7th Ave, New York, NY 10106, USA
Lieberman, William S *Museum Curator*
%Metropolitan Museum of Art, 5th Ave & 82nd St, New York, NY 10028, USA
Lieberman-Cline, Nancy *Basketball Player*
6616 Dupper Court, Dallas, TX 75252, USA
Liebert, Ottmar *Guitarist*
%Jones & O'Malley, 10123 Camarillo St, Toluca Lake, CA 91602, USA
Lieberthal, Michael S (Mike) *Baseball Player*
1740 Larkfield Ave, Westlake Village, CA 91362, USA
Liebeskind, John *Brain Surgeon, Psychologist*
%University of California Medical Center, Surgery Dept, Los Angeles, CA 90024, USA
Liebman, David *Jazz Saxophonist*
2206 Brislin Road, Stroudsberg, PA 18360, USA
Liefeld, Rob *Cartoonist (Youngblood)*
%Image Comics, 1071 N Batavia St, #A, Orange, CA 92867, USA
Lien Chan *Prime Minister, Taiwan*
%Prime Minister's Office, 1 Chunghsiano East Road, Sec 1, Taipei, Taiwan
Lien, Jennifer *Actress*
1700 Varilla Dr, West Covina, CA 91792, USA
Lienhard, William (Bill) *Basketball Player*
1320 Lawrence Ave, Lawrence, KS 66049, USA
Liepa, Andris *Ballet Dancer*
Bryusov Per 17, #12, 103009 Moscow, Russia
Liepa, Ilsa *Ballerina*
Bryusov Per 17, #12, 103009 Moscow, Russia
Liepmann, Hans W *Aeronautical Engineer, Physicist*
55 Haverstock Road, La Canada-Flintridge, CA 91011, USA
Lietzke, Bruce *Golfer*
5716 Arcady Place, Plano, TX 75093, USA
Lifeson, Alex *Guitarist (Rush)*
%Macklam Feldman Mgmt, 1505 W 2nd Ave, #200, Vancouver BC V6H 3Y4, Canada
Lifvendahl, Harold R *Publisher*
%Orlando Sentinel, 633 N Orange Ave, Orlando, FL 32801, USA

Ligeti, Gyorgy S *Composer*
Himmelhofgasse 34, 1130 Vienna, Austria
Light, Judith *Actress*
1888 Century Park East, #500, Los Angeles, CA 90067, USA
Lightfoot, Gordon *Singer, Songwriter*
%That's Entertainment, 1711 Lawrence Road, #101, Franklin, TN 37069, USA
Lightner, Candy *Social Activist*
22653 Pacific Coast Highway, #I289, Malibu, CA 90265, USA
Ligouri, James A *Educator*
%Iona College, President's Office, New Rochelle, NY 10801, USA
Likens, Gene E *Ecologist, Biologist*
%Ecosystem Studies Institute, PO Box AB, Millbrook, NY 12545, USA
Likins, Peter W *Educator*
%Lehigh University, President's Office, Bethlehem, PA 18015, USA
Lil' Cease *Rap Artist*
%Famous Artists Agency, 250 W 57th St, New York, NY 10107, USA
Lil' Kim *Rap Artist*
%Entertainment Artists, 2409 21st Ave S, #100, Nashville, TN 37212, USA
Lilienfeld, Abraham M *Epidemiologist*
3203 Old Post Dr, Pikesville, MD 21208, USA
Lill, John R *Concert Pianist*
%Harold Holt, 31 Sinclair Road, London W14 0NS, England
Lillard, Bill *Bowler*
5418 Imogene St, Houston, TX 77096, USA
Lillard, Matthew *Actor*
%William Morris Agency, 151 El Camino Dr, Beverly Hills, CA 90212, USA
Lillee, Dennis K *Cricketer*
%Swan Sport, PO Box 158, Byron Bay NSW 2481, Australia
Lilley, James R *Diplomat*
2801 New Mexico Ave NW, #407, Washington, DC 20007, USA
Lillis, Charles M *Businessman*
%MediaOne Group, 188 Iverness Dr W, Englewood, CO 80112, USA
Lilly, Robert L (Bob) *Football Player*
104 Aster Circle, Georgetown, TX 78628, USA
Lima, Jose *Baseball Player*
Carr Janico Km 12 1/2, #61, Santiago, Dominican Republic
Lima, Luis *Opera Singer*
1950 Redondela Dr, Rancho Palos Verdes, CA 90275, USA
Limbaugh, Rush *Entertainer*
PO Box 2182, Palm Beach, FL 33480, USA
Lime, Yvonne *Actress*
%Fedderson, 6135 E McDonald Dr, Paradise Valley, AZ 85253, USA
Lin Ching-Hsia *Actress*
%Taiwan Cinema-Drama Assn, 196 Chunghua Road, 10/F, Sec 1 Taipei, Taiwan
Lin, Bridget *Actress*
8 Fei Ngo Shan Road, Kowloon, Hong Kong, China
Lin, Cho-Liang *Concert Violinist*
%Julliard School, 60 Lincoln Center Plaza, New York, NY 10023, USA
Lin, Maya Ying *Sculptor, Architect*
%Sidney Janis Gallery, 120 E 75th St, #6A, New York, NY 10021, USA
Lin, Tsung-Yi *Psychiatrist*
6287 MacDonald St, Vancouver BC V6N 1E7, Canada
Lin, Tung Yen *Civil Engineer*
825 Battery St, San Francisco, CA 94111, USA
Lincoln, Abbey *Singer, Songwriter*
645 W End Ave, New York, NY 10025, USA
Lincoln, Keith P *Football Player*
770 SE Ridgeview Court, Pullman, WA 99163, USA
Lind, Don L *Astronaut*
51 N 376 E, Smithfield, UT 84335, USA
Lind, Joan *Rowing Athlete*
240 Euclid Ave, Long Beach, CA 90803, USA
Lind, Juha *Hockey Player*
%Montreal Canadiens, 1260 de la Gauchetiere W, Montreal QC H3B 5E8, Canada
Lind, Marshall L *Educator*
%University of Alaska Southeast, Chancellor's Office, Juneau, AK 99801, USA
Lindahl, George, III *Businessman*
%Union Pacific Resources, PO Box 1330, Houston, TX 77251, USA
Lindbeck, Assar *Economist*
50 Ostermalmsgatan, 114 26 Stockholm, Sweden
Lindelind, Liv *Model*
PO Box 1029, Frazier Park, CA 93225, USA
Linden, Hal *Actor*
%Studio 54, 254 W 54th St, New York, NY 10019, USA
Lindenlaub, Karl W *Cinematographer*
3021 Nichols Canyon Road, Los Angeles, CA 90046, USA
Lindenmann, Tony *Bowler*
35096 Jefferson Ave, #216, Harrison Township, MI 48045, USA

Linder, Kate *Actress*
9111 Wonderland Ave, Los Angeles, CA 90046, USA
Lindes, Hal *Guitarist (Dire Straits)*
%Damage Mgmt, 16 Lambton Place, London W11 2SH, England
Lindh, Hilary *Alpine Skier*
PO Box 33036, Juneau, AK 99803, USA
Lindig, Bill M *Businessman*
%Sysco Corp, 1390 Enclave Parkway, Houston, TX 77077, USA
Lindley, John W *Cinematographer*
15332 Antioch St, PO Box 351, Pacific Palisades, CA 90272, USA
Lindner, William G *Labor Leader*
%Transport Workers Union, 80 W End Ave, New York, NY 10023, USA
Lindon, Vincent *Actor*
%Artmedia, 20 Ave Rapp, 75007 Paris, France
Lindquist, Susan L *Biologist*
%Whitehead Institute, 9 Cambridge Circle, Cambridge, MA 02142, USA
Lindros, Eric *Hockey Player*
411 Glencairn Ave, Toronto ON M5N 1V4, Canada
Lindroth, Eric *Water Polo Player*
13151 Dufresne Place, San Diego, CA 92129, USA
Lindsay, Jack *Writer*
56 Maids Causeway, Cambridge, England
Lindsay, Mark *Singer, Songwriter*
%Mars Talent, 27 L'Ambiance Court, Bardonia, NY 10954, USA
Lindsay, R B Theodore (Ted) *Hockey Player*
2598 Invitational Dr, Oakland, MI 48363, USA
Lindsay, Robert *Actor, Singer*
%Felix de Wolfe, 1 Robert St, Adelphi, London WC2N 6BH, England
Lindsay, Robert V *Financier*
PO Box 1454, Millbrook, NY 12545, USA
Lindsey, George (Goober) *Actor, Singer*
PO Box 12089, Nashville, TN 37212, USA
Lindsey, Johanna *Writer*
%Avon/William Morrow, 1350 Ave of Americas, New York, NY 10019, USA
Lindsey, Steven W *Astronaut*
14702 Dawn Vale Dr, Houston, TX 77062, USA
Lindsley, Blake *Actress*
%Gold Marshak Liedtke, 3500 W Olive Ave, #1400, Burbank, CA 91505, USA
Lindsley, Donald B *Psychologist, Physiologist*
517 11th St, Santa Monica, CA 90402, USA
Lindstrand, Per *Balloonist*
%Thunder & Colt, Maesbury Road, Oswestry, Shropshire SY10 8HA, England
Lindstrom, Jack *Cartoonist (Executive Suite)*
%United Feature Syndicate, 200 Madison Ave, New York, NY 10016, USA
Lindstrom, Jon *Actor*
%Artists Group, 10100 Santa Monica Blvd, #2490, Los Angeles, CA 90067, USA
Lindvall, Angela *Model, Actress*
%I M G Models, 304 Park Ave S, #1200, New York, NY 10010, USA
Lindvall, Olle *Neurologist*
%University of Lund, Medical Cell Research Dept, 233 62 Lund, Sweden
Lindwall, Raymond R *Cricketer*
3 Wentworth Court, Endeavour St, Mt Ommaney, Brisbane 4074 QLD, Australia
Lineker, Gary W *Soccer Player*
%Markee UK, 6 Saint George St, Nottingham NG1 3BE, England
Linenger, Jerry M *Astronaut*
550 S Stoney Point Road, Suttons Bay, MI 49682, USA
Liney, John *Cartoonist (Henry)*
%King Features Syndicate, 888 7th Ave, New York, NY 10106, USA
Ling *Model*
%I M G Models, 304 Park Ave S, #1200, New York, NY 10010, USA
Ling, Bai *Actress*
%Agency for Performing Arts, 9200 Sunset Blvd, #900, Los Angeles, CA 90069, USA
Ling, Lisa *Commentator*
%William Morris Agency, 1325 Ave of Americas, New York, NY 10019, USA
Ling, Sergei S *Prime Minister, Belarus*
%Prime Minister's Office, Pl Nezavisimosti, 220010 Minsk, Belarus
Link, Arthur A *Governor, ND*
2201 Grimsrud Dr, Bismarck, ND 58501, USA
Linke, Paul *Actor*
%Zealous Artists, 139 S Beverly Dr, #225, Beverly Hills, CA 90212, USA
Linkert, Lo *Cartoonist (Peter Panic)*
%Singer Media Corp, 23411 Summerfield, #16E, Aliso Viejo, CA 92656, USA
Linklater, Richard *Movie Director, Writer*
%Creative Artists Agency, 9830 Wilshire Blvd, Beverly Hills, CA 90212, USA
Linkletter, Art *Entertainer*
1100 Bel Air Road, Los Angeles, CA 90077, USA
Linkletter, John A *Editor*
%Popular Mechanics Magazine, Editorial Dept, 224 W 57th St, New York, NY 10019, USA

L

Linn - Lister

Linn, Richard *Judge*
%US Court of Appeals, 717 Madison Place NW, Washington, DC 20439, USA

Linn, Teri Ann *Actress*
%Sutton Barth Vennari, 145 S Fairfax Ave, #310, Los Angeles, CA 90036, USA

Linn-Baker, Mark *Actor*
27702 Fairweather St, Canyon Country, CA 91351, USA

Linnehan, Richard M *Astronaut*
16802 Hartwood Way, Houston, TX 77058, USA

Linney, Laura *Actress*
%The Firm, 9100 Wilshire Blvd, #100W, Beverly Hills, CA 90210, USA

Linowitz, Sol M *Diplomat*
2230 California St NW, #4B, Washington, DC 20008, USA

Linseman, Ken *Hockey Player*
1070 Ocean Blvd, Hampton, NH 03842, USA

Linson, Art *Movie Director, Producer*
%Art Linson Productions, Warner Bros, 4000 Warner Blvd, Burbank, CA 91522, USA

Linteris, Gregory T *Astronaut*
%US Commerce Dept, Fire Science Division, Gaithersburg, MD 20899, USA

Linville, Joanne *Actress*
345 N Maple Dr, #302, Beverly Hills, CA 90210, USA

Linz, Alex D *Actor*
%Innovative Artists, 1505 10th St, Santa Monica, CA 90401, USA

Lioeanjie, Rene *Labor Leader*
%National Maritime Union, 1150 17th St NW, Washington, DC 20036, USA

Lionetti, Donald M *Army General*
7648 San Remo Place, Orlando, FL 32835, USA

Lions, Jacques-Louis *Mathematician*
7 Rue Paul Barruel, 75015 Paris, France

Lions, Pierre-Louis *Mathematician*
%Paris University, Place Marechal Lattre-de-Tessigny, 75775 Paris, France

Liotta, Ray *Actor*
16829 Monte Hermosa Dr, Pacific Palisades, CA 90272, USA

Lipa, Elisabeta *Rowing Athlete*
Str Reconstructiei 1, #78, Bucharest, Romania

Lipinski, Ann Marie *Journalist*
%Chicago Tribune, Editorial Dept, 435 N Michigan Ave, Chicago, IL 60611, USA

Lipinski, Tara *Figure Skater, Actress*
PO Box 1487, Sugar Land, TX 77487, USA

Lipovsek, Marjana *Opera Singer*
%Artists Mgmt Zurich, Rutistr 52, 8044 Zurich-Gockhausen, Switzerland

Lippard, Stephen J *Chemist*
975 Memorial Dr, #602, Cambridge, MA 02138, USA

Lippincott, Philip E *Businessman*
%Campbell Soup Co, Campbell Place, Camden, NJ 08103, USA

Lipponen Paavo, Tapio *Prime Minister, Finland*
%Premier's Office, Snellmaninkatu 1, 00170, Helsinki, Finland

Lipps, Louis *Football Player*
276 Annex Dr, Reserve, LA 70084, USA

Lipscomb, William N, Jr *Nobel Chemistry Laureate*
142 Garden St, Cambridge, MA 02138, USA

Lipset, Seymour M *Sociologist*
900 N Stafford St, #2131, Arlington, VA 22203, USA

Lipsett, Mortimer B *Physician*
%National Institutes of Health, 9000 Rockville Pike, Bethesda, MD 20892, USA

Lipshutz, Bruce H *Organic Chemist*
%University of California, Chemistry Dept, Santa Barbara, CA 93106, USA

Lipson, D Herbert *Publisher*
%Philadelphia Magazine, 1500 Walnut St, Philadelphia, PA 19102, USA

Lipton, Martin *Attorney*
%Wachtell Lipton Rosen Katz, 51 W 52nd St, New York, NY 10019, USA

Lipton, Peggy *Actress*
%Innovative Artists, 1505 10th St, Santa Monica, CA 90401, USA

Liquori, Martin (Marty) *Track Athlete, Sportscaster*
2915 NW 58th Blvd, Gainesville, FL 32606, USA

Lisa Lisa *Singer (Lisa Lisa & Cult Jam)*
%Talent Consultants International, 1560 Broadway, #1308, New York, NY 10036, USA

Lisi, Virna *Actress*
Via di Filomarino 4, Rome, Italy

Lisitsa, Valentina *Concert Pianist*
%Columbia Artists Mgmt Inc, 165 W 57th St, New York, NY 10019, USA

Liskov, Barbara H *Computer Engineer*
%Massachusetts Institute of Technology, Computer Sci Lab, Cambridge, MA 02139, USA

Lissner, Stephane *Opera Director*
%Theatre du Chatelet, 2 Rue Eduouard Colonne, 75001 Paris, France

List, Robert F *Governor, NV*
1660 Catalpa Lane, Reno, NV 89511, USA

Lister, Alton *Basketball Player*
233 Hudson Bay, Alameda, CA 94502, USA

Listowel, Earl of (William F Hare) *Government Official, England*
10 Downshire Hill, London NW3, England
Lithgow, John *Actor*
1319 Warnall Ave, Los Angeles, CA 90024, USA
Littell, Robert *Writer*
%Penguin Books, 375 Hudson St, New York, NY 10014, USA
Littenberg, Barbara *Architect*
%Peterson/Littenberg Architecture, 13 E 66th St, New York, NY 10021, USA
Litterell, Brian *Singer (Backstreet Boys)*
%The Firm, 9100 Wilshire Blvd, #100W, Beverly Hills, CA 90210, USA
Little Anthony, (Gordine) *Singer*
%Mars Talent, 27 L'Ambiance Court, Bardonia, NY 10954, USA
Little Milton *Singer, Guitarist*
%Camil Productions, 6606 Solitary Ave, Las Vegas, NV 89110, USA
Little Richard *Singer*
%Hyatt Sunset Hotel, 8401 W Sunset Blvd, Los Angeles, CA 90069, USA
Little Steven *Singer*
%Premier Talent, 3 E 54th St, #1100, New York, NY 10022, USA
Little, Carole *Fashion Designer*
%Carole Little Inc, PO Box 77917, Los Angeles, CA 90007, USA
Little, Chad *Auto Racing Driver*
5400 Little Parkway, Sherrills Ford, NC 28673, USA
Little, Charles L *Labor Leader*
%United Transportation Union, 14600 Detroit Ave, Cleveland, OH 44107, USA
Little, David L *Football Player*
4237 Nandina St, Lake Wales, FL 33898, USA
Little, Dwight H *Movie Director*
%Creative Artists Agency, 9830 Wilshire Blvd, Beverly Hills, CA 90212, USA
Little, Floyd D *Football Player*
%Pacific Coast Ford, 33207 Pacific Highway S, Federal Way, WA 98003, USA
Little, Larry C *Football Player, Coach*
14761 SW 169th Lane, Miami, FL 33187, USA
Little, Rich *Actor, Comedian*
%Rich Little Enterprises, 21550 Oxnard St, #630, Woodland Hills, CA 91367, USA
Little, Robert A *Chef*
49 Firth St, London W1V 5TE, England
Little, Sally *Golfer*
%Endicott Assoc, PO Box 10850, Palm Desert, CA 92255, USA
Little, Tasmin E *Concert Violinist*
%Harold Holt, 31 Sinclair Road, London W14 0NS, England
Little, Tawny Godin *Entertainer, Beauty Queen*
17941 Sky Park Circle, #F, Irvine, CA 92614, USA
Little, W Grady *Baseball Manager*
1 Glen Abbey Trail, Pinehurst, NC 28374, USA
Littler, Gene *Golfer*
PO Box 1949, Rancho Santa Fe, CA 92067, USA
Littles, Gene *Basketball Coach*
%Denver Nuggets, Pepsi Center, 1000 Chopper Circle, Denver, CO 80204, USA
Littleton, Harvey K *Sculptor*
RR 1 Box 843, Spruce Pine, NC 28777, USA
Litton, Andrew *Conductor*
%IMG Artists, Media House, 3 Burlington Lane, London W4 2TH, England
Litton, Drew *Editorial Cartoonist*
%Rocky Mountain News, Editorial Dept, 400 W Colfax Ave, Denver, CO 80204, USA
Littrell, Gary L *Vietnam War Army Hero (CMH)*
4302 Belle Vista Dr, Saint Petersburg Beach, FL 33706, USA
Liu, Lucy *Actress*
%Innovative Artists, 1505 10th St, Santa Monica, CA 90401, USA
Liut, Mike *Hockey Player*
945 Wellsley Court, Bloomfield Hills, MI 48304, USA
Livage, Jacques *Chemist*
%College de France, 11 Place M Berthelot, 75231 Paris Cedex 05, France
Lively, Eric *Actor*
%Gersh Agency, 232 N Canon Dr, Beverly Hills, CA 90210, USA
Lively, Penelope M *Writer*
Duck End, Great Rollright, Chipping, Northern Oxfordshire OX7 5SB, England
Lively, Robyn *Actress*
%William Morris Agency, 151 El Camino Dr, Beverly Hills, CA 90212, USA
Livermore, Ann *Businesswoman*
%Hewlett-Packard Co, 300 Hanover St, Palo Alto, CA 94304, USA
Livingston, Barry *Actor*
11310 Blix St, North Hollywood, CA 91602, USA
Livingston, James E *Vietnam Marine Corps Hero (CMH), General*
3609 Red Oak Court, New Orleans, LA 70131, USA
Livingston, Robert L, Jr *Representative, LA*
%Livingston Group, 499 S Capitol St SW, #600, Washington, DC 20003, USA
Livingston, Ron *Actor*
%Rigberg Roberts Rugolo, 1180 S Beverly Dr, #601, Los Angeles, CA 90035, USA

Livingston, Stanley *Actor*
PO Box 1782, Studio City, CA 91614, USA
Lizer, Kari *Actress*
15260 Ventura Blvd, #1040, Sherman Oaks, CA 91403, USA
LL Cool J *Rap Artist, Actor*
405 Park Ave, #1500, New York, NY 10022, USA
Llamosa, Carlos *Soccer Player*
%New England Revolution, CMGI Field, 1 Patriot Place, Foxboro, MA 02035, USA
Llewellyn, John A *Astronaut*
%University of South Florida, 4202 E Fowler Ave, Tampa, FL 33620, USA
Lloyd Webber, Andrew *Composer*
%Really Useful Group, 19/22 Tower St, London WC2H 9NS, England
Lloyd Webber, Julian *Concert Cellist*
%I M G Artists, 3 Burlington Lane, Chiswick, London W4 2TH, England
Lloyd, Charles *Jazz Saxophonist, Composer*
%Joel Chriss, 300 Mercer St, #3J, New York, NY 10003, USA
Lloyd, Christopher *Actor*
%Managemint, PO Box 491246, Los Angeles, CA 90049, USA
Lloyd, Clive H *Cricketer*
%Harefield, Harefield Dr, Wilmslow, Cheshire SK9 1NJ, England
Lloyd, Earl *Basketball Player, Coach*
PO Box 1976, Crossville, TN 38558, USA
Lloyd, Emily *Actress*
%Malcolm Sheddon Mgmt, 1 Charlotte Square, London W1P 1DH, England
Lloyd, Geoffrey E R *Philosopher*
2 Prospect Row, Cambridge CB1 1DU, England
Lloyd, Georgina *Writer*
%Bantam Books, 1540 Broadway, New York, NY 10036, USA
Lloyd, Jake *Actor*
%Osbrink Talent, 4343 Lankershim Blvd, #100, North Hollywood, CA 91602, USA
Lloyd, Kathleen *Actress*
%House of Representatives, 400 S Beverly Dr, #101, Beverly Hills, CA 90212, USA
Lloyd, Madison *Actress*
%Osbrink Talent, 4343 Lankershim Blvd, #100, North Hollywood, CA 91602, USA
Lloyd, Norman *Actor*
1813 Old Ranch Road, Los Angeles, CA 90049, USA
Lloyd, Robert A *Opera Singer*
67B Fortis Green, London SE1 9HL, England
Lloyd, Sabrina *Actress*
%Paradigm Agency, 10100 Santa Monica Blvd, #2500, Los Angeles, CA 90067, USA
Lloyd, Sue *Actress*
%Barry Burnett, 31 Coventry St, London W1V 8AS, England
Lloyd, Walt *Cinematographer*
22287 Mulholland Highway, #393, Calabasas, CA 91302, USA
Lo, Ismael *Singer*
%Mad Minute Music, 5-7 Rue Paul Bert, 93400 Saint Ouen, France
Loach, Kenneth (Ken) *Movie Director*
%Parallax Pictures, 7 Denmark St, London WC2H 8LS, England
Loaiza, Esteban A *Baseball Player*
779 Florida St, Imperial Beach, CA 91932, USA
Lobel, Anita *Writer*
%Greenwillow Books/William Morrow, 1350 Ave of Americas, New York, NY 10019, USA
LoBianco, Tony *Actor*
327 Central Park W, #16B, New York, NY 10025, USA
Lobkowicz, Nicholas *Philosopher*
%Katholische Universitat, 85071 Eichstatt, Germany
Lobo, Rebecca *Basketball Player*
216 Klaus Anderson Road, Southwick, MA 01077, USA
Local, Ivars Godmanis *Prime Minister, Latvia*
Brivibus Bluv 36, PDP Riga 226170, Latvia
Locatelli, Paul L *Educator*
%Santa Clara University, President's Office, Santa Clara, CA 95053, USA
Locher, Richard (Dick) *Editorial Cartoonist*
%Chicago Tribune, Editorial Dept, 435 N Michigan Ave, Chicago, IL 60611, USA
Lochhead, Kenneth C *Artist*
35 Wilton Crescent, Ottawa ON K1S 2T4, Canada
Lochner, Philip R, Jr *Government Official, Businessman*
%Time Warner Inc, 75 Rockefeller Plaza, New York, NY 10019, USA
Lockbaum, Gordie *Football Player*
35 Brookshire Road, Worcester, MA 01609, USA
Locke, Philip *Actor*
%Conway Van Gelder Robinson, 18-21 Jermyn St, London SW1Y 6NB, England
Locke, Sondra *Actress*
7465 Hillside Ave, Los Angeles, CA 90046, USA
Lockhart, Anne *Actress*
191 Upper Lake Road, Lake Sherwood, CA 91361, USA
Lockhart, Eugene *Football Player*
2215 High Country Dr, Carrollton, TX 75007, USA

Lockhart, James *Conductor*
105 Woodcock Hill, Harrow, Middx HA3 0JJ, England
Lockhart, June *Actress*
12850 Marlboro St, Los Angeles, CA 90049, USA
Lockhart, Keith *Conductor*
%Boston Pops Orchestra, Symphony Hall, 301 Massachusetts Ave, Boston, MA 02115, USA
Lockhart, Paul S *Astronaut*
3142 Pleasant Cove Court, Houston, TX 77059, USA
Lockington, David *Conductor*
%Cramer/Marder Artists, 3436 Springhill Road, Lafayette, CA 94549, USA
Locklear, Heather *Actress*
%United Talent Agency, 9560 Wilshire Blvd, #500, Beverly Hills, CA 90212, USA
Lockman, Carroll W (Whitey) *Baseball Player*
8234 N 75th St, Scottsdale, AZ 85258, USA
Lockwood, Gary *Actor*
1065 E Loma Alta Dr, Altadena, CA 91001, USA
Locorriere, Dennis *Singer, Guitarist (Dr Hook)*
%Artists Interntional Mgmt, 9850 Sandalwood Blvd, #458, Boca Raton, FL 33428, USA
Lodge, David John *Writer*
%University of Birmingham, English Dept, Birmingham B15 2TT, England
Lodish, Harvey F *Biologist*
195 Fisher Ave, Brookline, MA 02445, USA
Loe, Harald A *Dentist*
%National Dental Research Institute, 9000 Rockville Pike, Bethesda, MD 20892, USA
Loeb, Jerome T *Businessman*
%May Department Stores, 611 Olive St, Saint Louis, MO 63101, USA
Loeb, John L, Jr *Diplomat, Financier*
1 Rockefeller Plaza, #2500, New York, NY 10020, USA
Loeb, Lisa *Singer, Songwriter*
1028 3rd Ave, #A, New York, NY 10021, USA
Loeb, Marshall R *Editor*
31 Montrose Road, Scarsdale, NY 10583, USA
Loengard, John *Photographer*
20 W 86th St, New York, NY 10024, USA
Loewen, James W *Historian*
%Catholic University, History Dept, Washington, DC 20064, USA
Lofgren, Nils *Singer, Songwriter, Guitarist*
%Vision Music, 8012 Old Georgetown Road, Bethesda, MD 20814, USA
Lofton, Fred C *Religious Leader*
%Progressive National Baptist Convention, 601 50th St NE, Washington, DC 20019, USA
Lofton, James D *Football Player*
15487 Mesquite Tree Trail, Poway, CA 92064, USA
Lofton, Kenneth (Kenny) *Baseball Player*
PO Box 68473, Tucson, AZ 85737, USA
Logan, Don *Publisher*
%Time Inc, Time-Life Building, Rockefeller Center, New York, NY 10020, USA
Logan, Jack *Singer*
%William Morris Agency, 1325 Ave of Americas, New York, NY 10019, USA
Logan, James K *Judge*
%US Court of Appeals, PO Box 790, 1 Patrons Plaza, Olathe, KS 66061, USA
Logan, Jerry *Football Player*
112 Guinevere Court, Weatherford, TX 76086, USA
Logan, John (Johnny) *Baseball Player*
6115 W Cleveland Ave, Milwaukee, WI 53219, USA
Logan, Melissa *Singer (Chicks in Speed)*
%K Records, 924 Jefferson St SE, #101, Olympia, WA 98501, USA
Logan, Rayford W *Historian*
3001 Veazey Terrace NW, Washington, DC 20008, USA
Loges, Stephan *Opera Singer*
%Van Walsum Mgmt, 4 Addison Bridge Place, London W14 8XP, England
Loggia, Robert *Actor*
544 Bellagio Terrace, Los Angeles, CA 90049, USA
Loggins, Kenny *Singer, Songwriter*
670 Oak Springs Lane, Santa Barbara, CA 93108, USA
Logue, Donal *Actor*
%Lasher McManus Robinson, 1964 Westwood Blvd, #400, Los Angeles, CA 90025, USA
Loh, John M (Mike) *Air Force General*
125 Captain Graves, Williamsburg, VA 23185, USA
Lohan, Sinead *Singer, Songwriter*
%Pat Egan Sound, Merchant's Court, 24 Merchant's Quay, Dublin, Ireland
Lohman, Alison *Actress*
%United Talent Agency, 9560 Wilshire Blvd, #500, Beverly Hills, CA 90212, USA
Lohr, Bob *Golfer*
8225 Breeze Cove Lane, Orlando, FL 32819, USA
Loiola, Jose *Volleyball Player*
3521 Maple Dr, Manhattan Beach, CA 90266, USA
Loisel, John S *WW II Army Air Corps Hero*
2504 Overcreek Dr, Richardson, TX 75080, USA

Lokoloko, Tore *Governor General, Papua New Guinea*
PO Box 5622, Port Moresby, Papua New Guinea
Lolich, Michael S (Mickey) *Baseball Player*
6252 Robin Hill, Washington, MI 48094, USA
Lollobrigida, Gina *Actress*
Via Appia Antica 223, 00178 Rome, Italy
Lom, Herbert *Actor*
%London Mgmt, 2-4 Noel St, London W1V 3RB, England
Lomax, Neil V *Football Player*
6191 SW Wilhelm Road, Tualatin, OR 97062, USA
Lombard, Karina *Actress, Model*
%Metropolitan Talent Agency, 4526 Wilshire Blvd, Los Angeles, CA 90010, USA
Lombard, Louise *Actress*
%P F D, Drury House, 34-43 Russell St, London WC2B 5HA, England
Lombardi, John V *Educator*
%University of Florida, President's Office, Gainesville, FL 32611, USA
Lombardo, John *Guitarist (10,000 Maniacs, John & Mary)*
%Agency for Performing Arts, 9200 Sunset Blvd, #900, Los Angeles, CA 90069, USA
Lombreglio, Ralph *Writer*
%Doubleday Press, 1540 Broadway, New York, NY 10036, USA
Lonborg, James R (Jim) *Baseball Player*
498 First Parish Road, Scituate, MA 02066, USA
Lonchakov, Yuri V *Cosmonaut*
%Potchta Kosmonavtov, Moskovskoi Oblasti, 141160 Syvisdny Goroduk, Russia
London, Irving M *Physician*
%Harvard-MIT Health Sciences, 77 Massachusetts Ave, Cambridge, MA 02139, USA
London, Jason *Actor*
%Industry Entertainment, 955 Carillo Dr, #300, Los Angeles, CA 90048, USA
London, Jeremy *Actor*
%Gersh Agency, 232 N Canon Dr, Beverly Hills, CA 90210, USA
London, Jonathan *Writer*
%Chronicle Books, 85 2nd St, San Francisco, CA 94105, USA
London, Lisa *Actress, Model*
8949 Sunset Blvd, #201, Los Angeles, CA 90069, USA
London, Rick *Cartoonist*
503 W Main Ave, #B, Lumberton, MS 39455, USA
Lone, John *Actor*
%Levine Thall Plotkin, 1740 Broadway, New York, NY 10019, USA
Long, Anthony A *Educator*
1088 Telvin St, Albany, CA 94706, USA
Long, Charles F (Chuck), II *Football Player*
2425 N MacArthur Blvd, Oklahoma City, OK 73127, USA
Long, Dale W *Publisher*
%Working Woman Magazine, 342 Madison Ave, New York, NY 10173, USA
Long, Dallas *Track Athlete*
1337 Galaxy Dr, Newport Beach, CA 92660, USA
Long, David L *Publisher*
%Sports Illustrated Magazine, Rockefeller Center, New York, NY 10020, USA
Long, Dennis (Denny) *Soccer Official*
RR 5, Poplar Bluff, MO 63901, USA
Long, Elizabeth Valk *Publisher*
%Time Magazine, Rockefeller Center, New York, NY 10020, USA
Long, Grant *Basketball Player*
3257 Belmont Glen Dr, Marietta, GA 30067, USA
Long, Howie *Football Player, Sportscaster, Actor*
%International Creative Mgmt, 8942 Wilshire Blvd, #219, Beverly Hills, CA 90211, USA
Long, Joan D *Movie Producer*
La Burrage Place, Lindfield 2070 NSW, Australia
Long, Nia *Actress*
%Hansen Jacobsen, 450 N Roxbury Dr, #800, Beverly Hills, CA 90210, USA
Long, Richard *Sculptor*
Old School, Lower Failand, Bristol BS8 3SL, England
Long, Rien *Football Player*
%Tennessee Titans, 460 Great Circle Road, Nashville, TN 37228, USA
Long, Robert *Paleontologist*
%University of California, Paleontology Museum, Berkeley, CA 94720, USA
Long, Robert M *Businessman*
%Longs Drug Stores, 141 N Civic Dr, Walnut Creek, CA 94596, USA
Long, Sharon R *Molecular Geneticist*
%Stanford University, Biological Sciences Dept, Stanford, CA 94305, USA
Long, Shelley *Actress*
15237 Sunset Blvd, Pacific Palisades, CA 90272, USA
Long, William Ivey *Costume Designer*
%International Creative Mgmt, 40 W 57th St, #1800, New York, NY 10019, USA
Longet, Claudine *Actress*
%Ronald D Austin, 6000 E Hopkins, Aspen, CO 81611, USA
Longfield, William H *Businessman*
%CR Bard Inc, 730 Central Ave, New Providence, NJ 07974, USA

Longley, Luc *Basketball Player*
%New York Knicks, Madison Square Garden, 2 Penn Plaza, New York, NY 10121, USA
Longmuir, Alan *Bassist (Bay City Rollers)*
27 Preston Grange, Preston Pans E, Lothian, Scotland
Longmuir, Derek *Drummer (Bay City Rollers)*
27 Preston Grange, Preston Pans E, Lothian, Scotland
Longo, Lenny *Singer (Box Tops)*
%Texas Sounds, PO Box 1644, Dickinson, TX 77539, USA
Longo, Robert *Artist*
%Longo Studio, 224 Center St, New York, NY 10013, USA
Longuet-Higgins, H Christopher *Chemist*
%Sussex University, Exper Psych Lab, Falmer, Brighton BN1 9QG, England
Lonneke *Model*
%Pauline's Talent Corp, 379 W Broadway, #502, New York, NY 10012, USA
Lonsbrough Porter, Anita *Swimmer*
6 Rivendell Gardens, Tettendall, Wolverhampton WV6 8SY, England
Lonsdale, Gordon C *Cinematographer*
532 W 740 N, Orem, UT 84057, USA
Look, Dean Z *Baseball, Football Player*
4708 Okemos Road, Okemos, MI 48864, USA
Lookinland, Mike *Actor*
PO Box 9968, Salt Lake Cty, UT 84109, USA
Looney, Donald L (Don) *Football Player*
PO Box 3103, Midland, TX 79702, USA
Looney, Shelley *Hockey Player*
31 Beaman Lane, North Falmouth, MA 02556, USA
Looney, William R, III *Air Force General*
Commander, Electronic Systems Center, Hanscom Air Force Base, MA 01731, USA
Loose, John W *Businessman*
%Corning Corp, Houghton Park, Corning, NY 14831, USA
Lopardo, Frank *Opera Singer*
7 Suzanne B Court, Massapequa, NY 11758, USA
Lopert, Tanya *Actress*
%Cineart, 36 Rue de Ponthieu, 75008 Paris, France
Lopes, David E (Davey) *Baseball Player, Manager*
17762 Vineyard Lane, Poway, CA 92064, USA
Lopez Arellano, Oswaldo *President, Honduras; Air Force General*
Servico Aereo de Honduras, Apdo 129, Tegucigalpa DC, Honduras
Lopez Rodriguez, Nicolas de J Cardinal *Religious Leader*
%Archdiocese of Santo Domingo, Santo Domingo, AP 186, Dominican Republic
Lopez Trujillo, Alfonso Cardinal *Religious Leader*
Arzobispado, Calle 57, N 48-28 , Medellin, Colombia
Lopez, Alfonso R (Al) *Baseball Player, Manager*
3601 Beach Dr, Tampa, FL 33629, USA
Lopez, Danny (Little Red) *Boxer*
16531 Aquamarine Court, Chino Hills, CA 91709, USA
Lopez, George *Actor, Comedian*
%Harvey Elkin Mgmt, 6515 Sunset Blvd, #305, Los Angeles, CA 90028, USA
Lopez, Israel (Cachao) *Mambo Musician*
%Estefan Enterprises, 6205 SW 40th St, Miami, FL 33155, USA
Lopez, Jennifer *Actress, Singer*
%Endeavor Talent Agency, 9701 Wilshire Blvd, #1000, Beverly Hills, CA 90212, USA
Lopez, Jose M *WW II Army Hero (CMH)*
1347 Lockhill Selma Road, San Antonio, TX 78213, USA
Lopez, Lourdes *Ballerina*
%New York City Ballet, Lincoln Center Plaza, New York, NY 10023, USA
Lopez, Mario *Actor*
%Metropolitan Talent Agency, 4526 Wilshire Blvd, Los Angeles, CA 90010, USA
Lopez, Nancy *Golfer*
2308 Tara Dr, Albany, GA 31721, USA
Lopez, Priscilla *Actress*
%Writers & Artists, 19 W 44th St, #1000, New York, NY 10036, USA
Lopez, Raul *Basketball Player*
%Utah Jazz, Delta Center, 301 W South Temple, Salt Lake City, UT 84101, USA
Lopez, Robert S *Historian*
41 Richmond Ave, New Haven, CT 06515, USA
Lopez, Rodrigo *Baseball Player*
%Baltimore Orioles, Oriole Park, 333 W Camden St, Baltimore, MD 21201, USA
Lopez, Trini *Singer, Actor, Orchestra Leader*
1139 Abrigo Road, Palm Springs, CA 92262, USA
Lopez-Alegria, Michael E *Astronaut*
1919 Tangle Press Court, Houston, TX 77062, USA
Lopez-Cobos, Jesus *Conductor*
%Terry Harrison Mgmt, 1 Clarendon Court, Charlbury, Oxon OX7 3PS, England
Lopez-Garcia, Antonio *Artist*
%Marlborough Fine Art, 6 Albermarle St, London W1, England
Loquasto, Santo *Lighting, Costume Designer*
%Paradigm Agency, 10100 Santa Monica Blvd, #2500, Los Angeles, CA 90067, USA

L

Lorch - Louis-Dreyfus

Lorch, George A *Businessman*
%Armstrong World, 313 W Liberty St, Lancaster, PA 17603, USA
Lord, Albert L *Businessman*
%SLM Holding Corp, 11600 Sallie Mae Dr, Reston, VA 20193, USA
Lord, Lance W *Air Force General*
Commander, US Space Command, Peterson Air Force Base, CO 80914, USA
Lord, M G *Editorial Cartoonist*
%Newsday, Editorial Dept, 235 Pinelawn Road, Melville, NY 11747, USA
Lord, Marjorie *Actress*
1110 Maytor Place, Beverly Hills, CA 90210, USA
Lord, Peter *Animator/Movie Director*
%Aardman Animations, Gas Ferry Road, Bristol BS1 6UN, England
Lord, Winston *Diplomat*
740 Park Ave, New York, NY 10021, USA
Loren, Sophia *Actress*
La Concordia Ranch, 1151 Hidden Valley Road, Thousand Oaks, CA 91361, USA
Lorentz, Jim *Hockey Player*
2555 Staley Road, Grand Island, NY 14072, USA
Lorenz, Edward N *Meteorogist, Geophysicist*
%Massachusetts Institute of Technology, Earth Sciences Dept, Cambridge, MA 02139, USA
Lorenz, Lee *Cartoonist*
PO Box 131, Easton, CT 06612, USA
Lorenzen, Fred *Auto Racing Driver*
906 Burr Oak Court, Oak Brook, IL 60523, USA
Lorenzoni, Andrea *Astronaut, Italy*
Via B Vergine del Carmelo 168, 00144 Rome, Italy
Loria, Christopher (Gus) *Astronaut*
102 Sea Mist Dr, League City, TX 77573, USA
Loring, Gloria *Singer, Actress*
PO Box 1243, Cedar Glen, CA 92321, USA
Loring, John R *Artist*
403 W 46th St, New York, NY 10036, USA
Loring, Lynn *Actress*
1232 Sunset Plaza Dr, Los Angeles, CA 90069, USA
Loriod, Yvonne *Concert Pianist*
%Bureau de Concerts, 7 Rue de Richepanse, 75008 Paris, France
Lorius, Claude *Glaciologist*
%Glaciologies Laboratoire, Rue Moliere, 38402 Saint-Martin d'Heres, France
Lorscheider, Aloisio Cardinal *Religious Leader*
Guna Metropolitana, CP 05, Tone Basilica, 12570-000 Aparecida SP, Brazil
Lortie, Louis *Concert Pianist*
%Cramer/Marder Artists, 3436 Springhill Road, Lafayette, CA 94549, USA
Los, Marinus *Chemist*
%American Cyanamid Corp, 4201 Quakerbridge Road, Princeton Junction, NJ 08550, USA
Loscutoff, James (Jim) *Basketball Player, Coach*
166 Jenkins Road, Andover, MA 01810, USA
Lott, Felicity A *Opera Singer*
%Kunstleragentur Raab & Bohm, Plankengasse 7, 1010 Vienna, Austria
Lott, Ronald M (Ronnie) *Football Player, Sportscaster*
%Fox-TV, Sports Dept, PO Box 900, Beverly Hills, CA 90213, USA
Lotz, Anne Graham *Religious Leader*
%AnGel Ministries, 3246 Lewis Farm Road, Raleigh, NC 27607, USA
Lotz, Dick *Golfer*
6052 Southerness Dr, El Dorado Hills, CA 95762, USA
Loucks, Vernon R, Jr *Businessman*
%Baxter International, 1 Baxter Parkway, Deerfield, IL 60015, USA
Loudon, Dorothy *Actress*
101 Central Park West, New York, NY 10023, USA
Loudon, Rodney *Theoretical Physicist*
3 Gaston St, East Bergholt, Colchester, Essex CO7 6SD, England
Louganis, Gregory E (Greg) *Diver*
PO Box 4130, Malibu, CA 90264, USA
Loughery, Kevin *Basketball Player, Coach, Executive*
4474 Club Dr NE, Atlanta, GA 30319, USA
Loughlin, Lori *Actress, Singer*
%Miller/Boyette, 10202 W Washington Blvd, Culver City, CA 90232, USA
Loughlin, Mary Anne *Commentator*
%WTBS-TV, News Dept, 1050 Techwood Dr NW, Atlanta, GA 30318, USA
Loughran, James *Conductor*
34 Cleveden Dr, Glasgow G12 0RX, Scotland
Louis Jin Luxian *Religions Leader*
Shesshan Catholic Seminary, Beijing, China
Louis, Murray *Dancer, Choreographer*
%Nikolais/Louis Foundation, 375 W Broadway, New York, NY 10012, USA
Louis-Dreyfus, Julia *Actress*
131 S Rodeo Dr, #300, Beverly Hills, CA 90212, USA
Louis-Dreyfus, Robert L M *Businessman*
%Adidas AG, Adi Dassler Str 2, 91702 Herzogenaurach, Germany

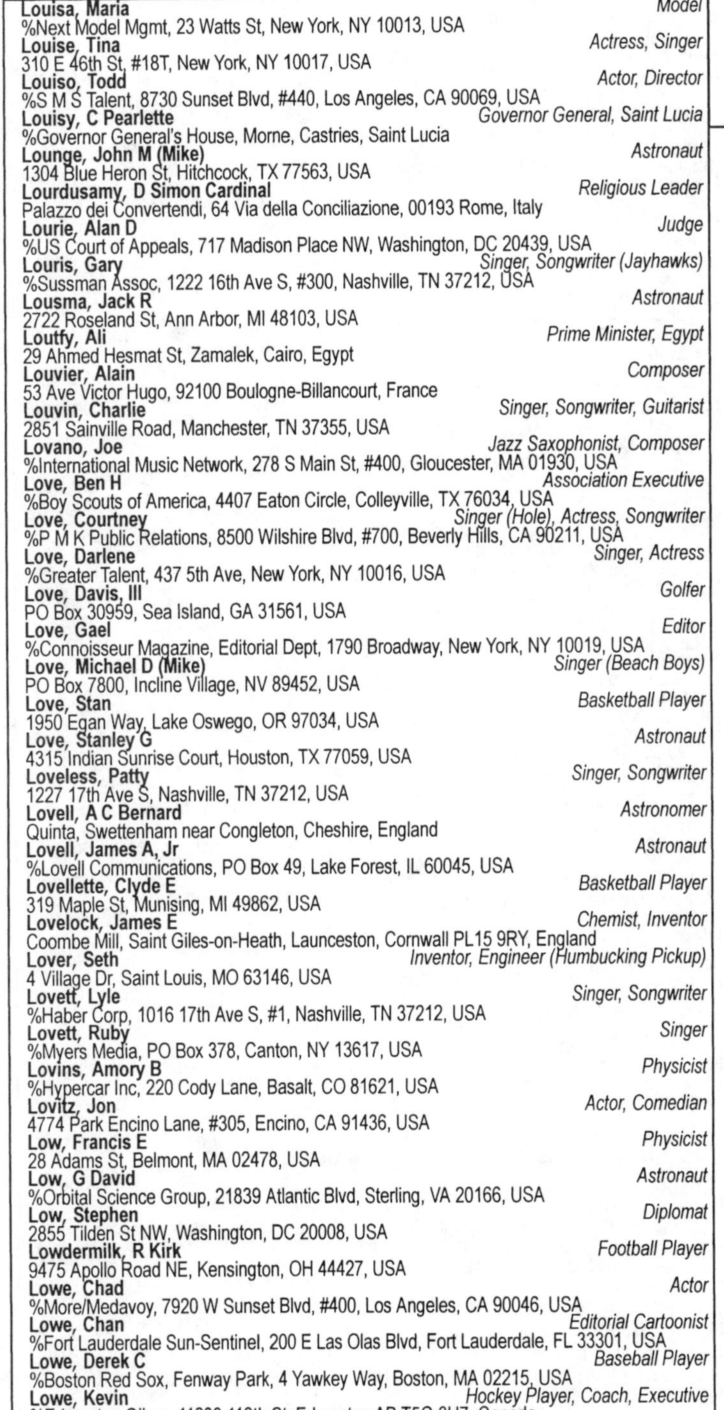

Louisa, Maria *Model*
%Next Model Mgmt, 23 Watts St, New York, NY 10013, USA
Louise, Tina *Actress, Singer*
310 E 46th St, #18T, New York, NY 10017, USA
Louiso, Todd *Actor, Director*
%S M S Talent, 8730 Sunset Blvd, #440, Los Angeles, CA 90069, USA
Louisy, C Pearlette *Governor General, Saint Lucia*
%Governor General's House, Morne, Castries, Saint Lucia
Lounge, John M (Mike) *Astronaut*
1304 Blue Heron St, Hitchcock, TX 77563, USA
Lourdusamy, D Simon Cardinal *Religious Leader*
Palazzo dei Convertendi, 64 Via della Conciliazione, 00193 Rome, Italy
Lourie, Alan D *Judge*
%US Court of Appeals, 717 Madison Place NW, Washington, DC 20439, USA
Louris, Gary *Singer, Songwriter (Jayhawks)*
%Sussman Assoc, 1222 16th Ave S, #300, Nashville, TN 37212, USA
Lousma, Jack R *Astronaut*
2722 Roseland St, Ann Arbor, MI 48103, USA
Loutfy, Ali *Prime Minister, Egypt*
29 Ahmed Hesmat St, Zamalek, Cairo, Egypt
Louvier, Alain *Composer*
53 Ave Victor Hugo, 92100 Boulogne-Billancourt, France
Louvin, Charlie *Singer, Songwriter, Guitarist*
2851 Sainville Road, Manchester, TN 37355, USA
Lovano, Joe *Jazz Saxophonist, Composer*
%International Music Network, 278 S Main St, #400, Gloucester, MA 01930, USA
Love, Ben H *Association Executive*
%Boy Scouts of America, 4407 Eaton Circle, Colleyville, TX 76034, USA
Love, Courtney *Singer (Hole), Actress, Songwriter*
%P M K Public Relations, 8500 Wilshire Blvd, #700, Beverly Hills, CA 90211, USA
Love, Darlene *Singer, Actress*
%Greater Talent, 437 5th Ave, New York, NY 10016, USA
Love, Davis, III *Golfer*
PO Box 30959, Sea Island, GA 31561, USA
Love, Gael *Editor*
%Connoisseur Magazine, Editorial Dept, 1790 Broadway, New York, NY 10019, USA
Love, Michael D (Mike) *Singer (Beach Boys)*
PO Box 7800, Incline Village, NV 89452, USA
Love, Stan *Basketball Player*
1950 Egan Way, Lake Oswego, OR 97034, USA
Love, Stanley G *Astronaut*
4315 Indian Sunrise Court, Houston, TX 77059, USA
Loveless, Patty *Singer, Songwriter*
1227 17th Ave S, Nashville, TN 37212, USA
Lovell, A C Bernard *Astronomer*
Quinta, Swettenham near Congleton, Cheshire, England
Lovell, James A, Jr *Astronaut*
%Lovell Communications, PO Box 49, Lake Forest, IL 60045, USA
Lovellette, Clyde E *Basketball Player*
319 Maple St, Munising, MI 49862, USA
Lovelock, James E *Chemist, Inventor*
Coombe Mill, Saint Giles-on-Heath, Launceston, Cornwall PL15 9RY, England
Lover, Seth *Inventor, Engineer (Humbucking Pickup)*
4 Village Dr, Saint Louis, MO 63146, USA
Lovett, Lyle *Singer, Songwriter*
%Haber Corp, 1016 17th Ave S, #1, Nashville, TN 37212, USA
Lovett, Ruby *Singer*
%Myers Media, PO Box 378, Canton, NY 13617, USA
Lovins, Amory B *Physicist*
%Hypercar Inc, 220 Cody Lane, Basalt, CO 81621, USA
Lovitz, Jon *Actor, Comedian*
4774 Park Encino Lane, #305, Encino, CA 91436, USA
Low, Francis E *Physicist*
28 Adams St, Belmont, MA 02478, USA
Low, G David *Astronaut*
%Orbital Science Group, 21839 Atlantic Blvd, Sterling, VA 20166, USA
Low, Stephen *Diplomat*
2855 Tilden St NW, Washington, DC 20008, USA
Lowdermilk, R Kirk *Football Player*
9475 Apollo Road NE, Kensington, OH 44427, USA
Lowe, Chad *Actor*
%More/Medavoy, 7920 W Sunset Blvd, #400, Los Angeles, CA 90046, USA
Lowe, Chan *Editorial Cartoonist*
%Fort Lauderdale Sun-Sentinel, 200 E Las Olas Blvd, Fort Lauderdale, FL 33301, USA
Lowe, Derek C *Baseball Player*
%Boston Red Sox, Fenway Park, 4 Yawkey Way, Boston, MA 02215, USA
Lowe, Kevin *Hockey Player, Coach, Executive*
%Edmonton Oilers, 11230 110th St, Edmonton AB T5G 3H7, Canada

L

Lowe - Lucas

Lowe, Nick *Singer, Songwriter, Guitarist*
%MVO Ltd, 307 7th Ave, #807, New York, NY 10001, USA
Lowe, Rob *Actor*
270 N Canon Dr, #1072, Beverly Hills, CA 90210, USA
Lowe, Sidney *Basketball Player, Coach*
2631 Wallingford Road, Winston Salem, NC 27101, USA
Lowe, Woodrow *Football Player, Coach*
282 Grande View Parkway, Maylene, AL 35114, USA
Lowell, Carey *Actress, Model*
%International Creative Mgmt, 8942 Wilshire Blvd, #219, Beverly Hills, CA 90211, USA
Lowell, Charlie *Keyboardist (Jars of Clay)*
%Flood Bumstead McCready McCarthy, 1700 Hayes St, #304, Nashville, TN 37203, USA
Lowell, Elizabeth *Writer*
%Avon Books, 1350 Ave of Americas, New York, NY 10019, USA
Lowell, Michael A (Mike) *Baseball Player*
620 Santurce Ave, Coral Gables, FL 33143, USA
Lowenstein, Louis *Attorney, Educator*
5 Oak Lane, Larchmont, NY 10538, USA
Lowery, Corey *Bassist (Stereo Mud)*
%Agency Group Ltd, 1775 Broadway, #430, New York, NY 10019, USA
Lowman, Frank A *Financier*
%Federal Home Loan Bank, 2 Townsite Plaza, Topeka, KS 66603, USA
Lown, Bernard *Cardiologist*
%Lown Cardiovascular Group, 21 Longwood Ave, Brookline, MA 02446, USA
Lowry, Lois *Writer*
205 Brattle St, Cambridge, MA 02138, USA
Loy, Frank E *Environmentalist*
%Marshall German Fund, 11 Dupont Circle NW, Washington, DC 20036, USA
Loy, James M *Coast Guard Admiral, Government Official*
%Transportation Security Administration, 400 7th St SW, Washington, DC 20590, USA
Lozano Barragan, Javier Cardinal *Religious Leader*
%Health Care Workers Assistance, Via Conciliazione 3, 00193 Rome, Italy
Lozano, Conrad *Singer (Los Lobos)*
%Gold Mountain, 3575 Cahuenga Blvd W, #450, Los Angeles, CA 90068, USA
Lozano, Ignacio E, Jr *Editor*
%La Opinion, 411 W 5th St, Los Angeles, CA 90013, USA
Lozano, Silvia *Choreographer*
%Ballet Folklorico, 31 Esq Con Riva Palacio, Mexico City DF, Mexico
Lu Qihui *Sculptor*
100-301, 398 Xin-Pei Road, Xin-Zuan, Shanghai, China
Lu, Edward T (Ed) *Astronaut*
18222 Bal Harbour Dr, Houston, TX 77058, USA
Lubanski, Ed *Bowler*
5326 Christi Dr, Warren, MI 48091, USA
Lubbers, Ruud F M *Prime Minister, Netherlands*
Lambertweg 4, Rotterdam RA 3062, Netherlands
Lubchenco, Jane *Marine Biologist, Zoologist*
%Oregon State University, Marine Biology Dept, Corvallis, OR 97331, USA
Lubezki, Emmanuel *Cinematographer*
%Broder Kurland Webb Uffner, 9242 Beverly Blvd, #200, Beverly Hills, CA 90210, USA
Lubich Silvia, Chiara *Evangelist*
%Focolare Movement, 306 Via di Frascati, 00040 Rocca di Papa RM, Italy
Lubich, Bronko *Wrestler*
3146 Whitemarsh Circle, Dallas, TX 75234, USA
Lubin, Steven *Concert Pianist*
%State University of New York, School of Arts, Purchase, NY 10577, USA
Lubotsky, Mark *Concert Violinist*
Overtoom 329 III, 1054 JM Amsterdam, Netherlands
Lubovitch, Lar *Dancer, Choreographer*
%Lar Lubovitch Dance Co, 229 W 42nd St, #8, New York, NY 10036, USA
Lubs, Herbert A *Geneticist*
5133 SW 71st Place, Miami, FL 33155, USA
Lubys, Bronislovas *Prime Minister, Lithuania*
%Prime Minister's Office, Tuo-Vaizganto 2, Vilnius, Lithuania
Luc, Tone *Rap Artist, Actor*
%Headline Talent, 1650 Broadway, #508, New York, NY 10019, USA
Lucas, Aubrey K *Educator*
%University of Southern Mississippi, President's Office, Hattiesburg, MS 39406, USA
Lucas, Cornel *Photographer*
57 Addison Road, London W148JJ, England
Lucas, Craig *Lyricist, Writer*
%William Morris Agency, 1325 Ave of Americas, New York, NY 10019, USA
Lucas, George *Movie Director, Producer*
%LucasFilm, PO Box 2009, San Rafael, CA 94912, USA
Lucas, Jacklyn H (Jack) *WW II Marine Corps Hero (CMH)*
75 Elks Lake Road, Hattiesburg, MS 39401, USA
Lucas, Jerry R *Basketball Player*
3904 Lori Dr, #A1, Erlanger, KY 41018, USA

Lucas, Josh *Actor*
%International Creative Mgmt, 8942 Wilshire Blvd, #219, Beverly Hills, CA 90211, USA

Lucas, Maurice *Basketball Player, Coach*
5691 Bonita Road, Lake Oswego, OR 97035, USA

Lucas, Richard J (Richie) *Football Player*
1269 Estate Dr, West Chester, PA 19380, USA

Lucas, Robert E, Jr *Nobel Economics Laureate*
5448 S East View Park, #3, Chicago, IL 60615, USA

Lucas, William *Government Official*
%Justice Department, Constitution & 10th NW, Washington, DC 20530, USA

Lucchesini, Andrea *Concert Pianist*
%Arts Manangement Group, 1133 Broadway, #1025, New York, NY 10010, USA

Lucci, Susan *Actress*
16 Carteret Place, Garden City, NY 11530, USA

Lucci, Vince, Sr *Bowler*
1182 Queens Way, West Chester, PA 19382, USA

Luce, Henry, III *Publisher*
Mill Hill Road, Mill Neck, NY 11765, USA

Luce, R Duncan *Psychologist*
20 Whitman Court, Irvine, CA 92612, USA

Luce, Richard N *Governor, Gibraltar*
%Governor's Office, Convent, Gibraltar

Luce, William (Bill) *Writer*
PO Box 370, Depoe Bay, OR 97341, USA

Lucebert *Artist, Writer*
Boendermakerhof 10, 1861 TB Bergen N-H, Netherlands

Lucero, Carlos *Judge*
%US Court of Appeals, 1929 Stout St, Denver, CO 80294, USA

Luchko, Klara S *Actress*
Kotelmicheskaya Nab 1/15 Korp B, #308, 109240 Moscow, Russia

Lucid, Shannon W *Astronaut, Biophysicist*
1622 Gunwale Road, Houston, TX 77062, USA

Lucien, Jon *Singer*
%Maxine Harvard, 7942 W Bell Road, Glendale, AZ 85308, USA

Luck, Frank *Biathlete*
Lerchenweg 9, 98587 Springstille, Germany

Luckinbill, Lawrence *Actor*
PO Box 636, Cross River, NY 10518, USA

Luckovich, Mike *Editorial Cartoonist*
%Atlanta Constitution, Editorial Dept, 72 Marietta St, Atlanta, GA 30303, USA

Lucky Dube *Singer*
%Fast Lane Int'l, 4856 Haygood Road, #200, Virginia Beach, VA 23455, USA

Lucky, Robert W *Electrical Engineer*
48 Gillespie Ave, Fair Haven, NJ 07704, USA

Luczo, Stephen J *Businessman*
%Seagate Technology, 920 Disc Dr, Scotts Valley, CA 95066, USA

Luder, Owen H *Architect*
%Communication in Construction, 2 Smith Square, London SW1P 3H5, England

Ludes, John T *Businessman*
%Fortune Brands Inc, 300 Tower Parkway, Lincolnshire, IL 60069, USA

Luding-Rothenburger, Christa *Speedskater, Cyclist*
%Dresdener Eisspot-Club, Pieschener Allee 1, 01067 Dresden, Germany

Ludwig, Christa *Opera Singer*
%Calliopie, 162 Chemin du Santon, 06250 Mougins, France

Ludwig, George H *Physicist*
215 Aspen Trail, Winchester, VA 22602, USA

Ludwig, Ken *Writer*
%Steptoe & Johnson, 4603 Harrison St, Chevy Chase, MD 20815, USA

Luft, Lorna *Actress, Singer*
%Golden Goldberg, 9100 Wilshire Blvd, #455, Beverly Hills, CA 90212, USA

Lugbill, Jon *Canoeing Athlete*
%American Canoe Assn, 7432 Alban Station Blvd, #B232, Springfield, VA 22150, USA

Luhrmann, Baz *Movie Director*
%Hilary Linstead, 500 Oxford St, Bondi Junction NSW 2022, Australia

Lujack, John C (Johnny) *Football Player*
3700 N Harrison St, Davenport, IA 52806, USA

Lujan, Manuel, Jr *Secretary, Interior*
%Manuel Lujan Agencies, PO Box 3727, Albuquerque, NM 87190, USA

Lukas, D Wayne *Thoroughbred Racing Trainer*
5242 Katella Ave, #103, Los Alamitos, CA 90720, USA

Lukashenko, Aleksandr *President, Belarus*
%President's Office, JK Marks St 38, 220016 Minsk, Belarus

Lukather, Steve *Guitarist (Toto)*
%Fitzgerald-Hartley, 34 N Palm St, Ventura, CA 93001, USA

Luke *Rap Artist*
%Richard Walters, 1800 Argyle Ave, #408, Los Angeles, CA 90028, USA

Luke, Derek *Actor*
651 N Kilkea Dr, Los Angeles, CA 90048, USA

L

Luke, John A, Jr *Businessman*
%Westvaco Corp, 299 Park Ave, New York, NY 10171, USA
Lukens, Max L *Businessman*
%Baker Hughes Inc, 3900 Essex Lane, Houston, TX 77027, USA
Lukin, Matt *Bassist (Mudhoney)*
%Legends of 21st Century, 7 Trinity Row, Florence, MA 01062, USA
Lukkarinen, Marjut *Cross Country Skier*
%Lohja Ski Team, Lohja, Finland
Lula da Silva, Luis Ignacio *President, Brazil*
%Palacio do Planalto, Praca dos 3 Poderas, 70 150 Brasilia DF, Brazil
Lulu *Singer, Actress*
%CIA, 101 Shepherds Bush, Concorde House, London W6 7LP, England
Lumbly, Carl *Actor*
8721 Sunset Blvd, #205, Los Angeles, CA 90069, USA
Lumet, Sidney *Movie Director*
%Amjen Entertainment, 259 W 54th St, New York, NY 10019, USA
Lumley, Joanna *Actress*
%International Creative Mgmt, 76 Oxford St, London W1N 0AX, England
Lumley, John L *Physicist*
743 Snyder Hill Road, Ithaca, NY 14850, USA
Lumme, Jyrki *Hockey Player*
%Toronto Maple Leafs, 40 Bay St, Toronto ON M5J 2K2, Canada
Lumpp, Raymond (Ray) *Basketball Player*
21 Hewlett Dr, East Williston, NY 11596, USA
Lumsden, David J *Conductor, Concert Organist*
Melton House, Soham, Cambridgeshire, England
Luna, Barbara *Actress*
18026 Rodarte Way, Encino, CA 91316, USA
Luna, Denise *Rodeo Rider, Model*
PO Box 2462, Burleson, TX 76097, USA
Lund, Deanna *Actress*
545 Howard Dr, Salem, VA 24153, USA
Lundberg, Anders *Physiologist*
%Goteberg University, Physiology Dept, Box 33031, 40 033 Goteborg, Sweden
Lundberg, Fred Borre *Nordic Combined Skier*
Skogbrynet 11, 9250 Bardu, Norway
Lunden, Joan *Commentator*
%Tekepictures Productions, 1271 Ave of Americas, #4332, New York, NY 10020, USA
Lundgren, Dolph *Actor*
%William Morris Agency, 151 El Camino Dr, Beverly Hills, CA 90212, USA
Lundgren, Terry *Businessman*
%Federated Department Stores, 151 W 34th St, New York, NY 10001, USA
Lundquist, Gus *Test Pilot*
100 Holley Ridge Road, Aiken, SC 29803, USA
Lundquist, Steve *Swimmer*
PO Box 1545, Stockbridge, GA 30281, USA
Lundquist, Verne *Sportscaster*
%NBC-TV, Sports Dept, 30 Rockefeller Plaza, New York, NY 10112, USA
Lundy, Carmen *Singer*
%Abby Hoffer, 223 1/2 E 48th St, New York, NY 10017, USA
Lundy, Jessica *Actress*
280 S Beverly Dr, #400, Beverly Hills, CA 90212, USA
Lundy, Victor A *Architect*
%Victor A Lundy Assoc, 701 Mulberry Lane, Bellaire, TX 77401, USA
Luner, Jaime *Actress*
%Martin Hurwitz, 427 N Canon Dr, #215, Beverly Hills, CA 90210, USA
Lunghi, Cherie *Actress*
%Marion Rosenberg, PO Box 69826, West Hollywood, CA 90069, USA
Lunka, Zoltan *Boxer*
Weinheimer Str 2, 69198 Schriesheim, Germany
Lunn, Bob *Golfer*
PO Box 1495, Woodbridge, CA 95258, USA
Lunney, Glenn *Space Scientist*
%United Space Alliance, 1150 Gemini Dr, Houston, TX 77058, USA
Lupberger, Edwin A *Businessman*
%Entergy Corp, 10055 Grogans Mill Road, # 5A, The Woodlands, TX 77380, USA
Lupica, Mike *Sportswriter*
55 Runningbrook Lane, New Canaan, CT 06840, USA
Lupo, Benedetto *Concert Pianist*
%Gerhild Baron Mgmt, Dornbacher Str 41/III/3, 1170 Vienna, Austria
LuPone, Patti *Singer, Actress*
%International Creative Mgmt, 40 W 57th St, #1800, New York, NY 10019, USA
Lupu, Radu *Concert Pianist*
%Terry Harrison Mgmt, 3 Clarendon Court, Charlbury, Oxon 0X7 3PS, England
Lupus, Peter *Actor*
2401 S 24th St, #110, Phoenix, AZ 85034, USA
Lurie, Alison *Writer*
%Cornell University, English Dept, Ithaca, NY 14850, USA

Lurie, Ranan R *Editorial Cartoonist*
%Cartoonnews International, PO Box 698, Greenwich, CT 06836, USA
Lusis, Janis *Track Athlete*
Vesetas 8-3, 1013 Riga, Latvia
Lustiger, Jean-Marie Cardinal *Religious Leader*
Maison Dioceine, 8 Rue de la Ville-l'Eveque, 75008 Paris, France
Lusztig, George *Mathematician*
106 Grant Ave, Newton, MA 02459, USA
Lutcher, Nellie *Singer*
%Alan Eichler, 6064 Selma Ave, Los Angeles, CA 90028, USA
Lutes, Eric *Actor*
%Artists Group, 10100 Santa Monica Blvd, #2490, Los Angeles, CA 90067, USA
Luttig, J Michael *Judge*
%US Appeals Court, 200 S Washington St, Alexandria, VA 22314, USA
Lutz, Bob *Tennis Player*
101 Via Ensueno, San Clemente, CA 92672, USA
Lutz, Joleen *Actress*
%H David Moss, 733 Seward St, #PH, Los Angeles, CA 90038, USA
Lutz, Robert A *Businessman*
3600 Green Court, #720, Ann Arbor, MI 48105, USA
LuValle, James *Track Athlete*
1174 Los Altos Ave, #160, Los Altos, CA 94022, USA
Luxon, Benjamin M *Opera Singer*
%Mazet, Relubbus Lane, Saint Hilary, Penzance, Cornwall TR20 9DS, England
Luyendyk, Arie *Auto Racing Driver*
12494 N 116th St, Scottsdale, AZ 85259, USA
Luyties, Ricci *Volleyball Player*
%Assn of Volleyball Pros, 330 Washington Blvd, #400, Marina del Rey, CA 90292, USA
Luzhkov, Yuri M *Mayor*
%Government of Moscow, Tverskaya Str 13, 103032 Moscow, Russia
Luzi, Mario *Writer*
Via Bella Riva 20, 50136 Florence, Italy
Luzinski, Gregory M (Greg) *Baseball Player*
25680 Streamlet Court, Bonita Springs, FL 34135, USA
Lyakhov, Vladimir A *Cosmonaut*
%Potchta Kosmonavtov, Moskovskoi Oblasti, 141160 Syvisdny Goroduk, Russia
Lydon, James (Jimmy) *Actor*
3538 Lomacitas Lane, Bonita, CA 91902, USA
Lydon, John (Johnny Rotten) *Singer, Musician (Sex Pistols)*
31962 Pacific Coast Highway, Malibu, CA 90265, USA
Lydon, Malcolm *Astronaut*
1429 Jaudon Road, Dover, FL 33527, USA
Lyght, Todd W *Football Player*
2185 Lindsey Court, Tustin, CA 92782, USA
Lyle, Kami *Singer, Trumpeter, Songwriter*
%DS Mgmt, 2814 12th Ave S, #202, Nashville, TN 37204, USA
Lyle, Sandy *Golfer*
%Advantage International, 1025 Thomas Jefferson NW, #450, Washington, DC 20007, USA
Lyles, Lester L (Les) *Air Force General*
Commander, Air Material Command, Wright-Patterson Air Force Base, OH 45433, USA
Lyman, Richard W *Foundation Executive, Educator*
%Stanford University, Education School, Stanford, CA 94305, USA
Lympany, Moura *Concert Pianist*
%Transart, 8 Bristol Gardens, London W9 2JG, England
Lyn, Dawn *Actress*
PO Box 1527, Avalon, CA 90704, USA
Lynch, Allen J *Vietnam War Army Hero (CMH)*
438 Belle Plaine Ave, Gurnee, IL 60031, USA
Lynch, Dan *Editorial Cartoonist*
%Fort Wayne Journal-Gazette, Editorial Dept, 600 W Main St, Fort Wayne, IN 46802, USA
Lynch, David K *Movie Director*
PO Box 93624, Los Angeles, CA 90093, USA
Lynch, Edele *Singer (B*Witched)*
%Clintons, 55 Drury Lane, Covent Garden, London WC2B 5SQ, England
Lynch, James E (Jim) *Football Player*
1717 W 91st Place, Kansas City, MO 64114, USA
Lynch, Jennifer *Actress*
1894 El Cerrito Place, Los Angeles, CA 90068, USA
Lynch, John *Football Player*
%Tampa Bay Buccaneers, 1 W Buccaneer Place, Tampa, FL 33607, USA
Lynch, Keavy *Singer (B*Witched)*
%Clintons, 55 Drury Lane, Covent Garden, London WC2B 5SQ, England
Lynch, Kelly *Model, Actress*
2648 Mandeville Canyon Road, Los Angeles, CA 90049, USA
Lynch, Peter S *Financier*
27 State St, Boston, MA 02109, USA
Lynch, Richard *Actor*
%Richard Sindell, 1910 Holmby Ave, #1, Los Angeles, CA 90025, USA

L

Lynch - Lyubshin

Lynch, Richard (Dick) *Football Player*
203 Manor Road, Douglaston, NY 11363, USA
Lynch, Sandra L *Judge*
%US Appeals Court, McCormack Federal Building, Boston, MA 02109, USA
Lynch, Shane *Singer (Boyzone)*
%Carol Assoc-War Mgmt, Bushy Park Road, 57 Meadowbank, Dublin, Ireland
Lynch, Thomas C *Navy Admiral*
1236 Denbigh Lane, Radnor, PA 19087, USA
Lynden-Bell, Donald *Astronomer*
%Institute of Astronomy, Madingley Road, Cambridge CB3 0HA, England
Lyndon, Frank *Singer (Belmonts)*
%Paramount Entertainment, PO Box 12, Far Hills, NJ 07931, USA
Lynds, Roger *Astronomer*
%Kitt Peak National Observatory, Tucson, AZ 85726, USA
Lyne, Adrian *Movie Director*
9876 Beverly Grove Dr, Beverly Hills, CA 90210, USA
Lyngstad, Anni-Frida *Singer (ABBA), Songwriter*
%Mono Music, Sodra Brobaeken 41A, 111 49 Stockholm, Sweden
Lynley, Carol *Actress*
%Don Gerler, 3349 Cahuenga Blvd W, #1, Los Angeles, CA 90068, USA
Lynn Salomon, Janet *Figure Skater*
4215 Marsh Ave, Rockford, IL 61114, USA
Lynn, Cheryl *Singer, Actress*
PO Box 667, Smithtown, NY 11787, USA
Lynn, Frederic M (Fred) *Baseball Player*
7336 El Fuerte St, Carlsbad, CA 92009, USA
Lynn, Greg *Architect*
%University of California, Architecture School, Los Angeles, CA 90024, USA
Lynn, James T *Secretary, Housing & Urban Development*
6 Sunset Cay Road, Key Largo, FL 33037, USA
Lynn, Jonathan *Movie Director*
%Hofflund/Polone, 9465 Wilshire Blvd, #820, Beverly Hills, CA 90212, USA
Lynn, Loretta *Singer, Songwriter*
%Loretta Lynn Enterprises, PO Box 120369, Nashville, TN 37212, USA
Lynn, Meredith Scott *Actress*
%Rigberg Roberts Rugolo, 1180 S Beverly Dr, #601, Los Angeles, CA 90035, USA
Lynn, Vera *Actress, Singer*
Ditchling, Sussex, England
Lynne, Gillian *Dance Director, Choreographer*
%Lean-2 Productions, 18 Rutland St, Knightsbridge, London SW7 1EF, England
Lynne, Gloria *Singer*
%Subrena Artists, 330 W 56th St, #18M, New York, NY 10019, USA
Lynne, Jeff *Singer, Songwriter*
PO Box 5850, Santa Barbara, CA 93150, USA
Lynne, Shelby *Singer, Songwriter*
%High Road, 751 Bridgeway, #300, Sausalito, CA 94965, USA
Lyon, Lisa *Body Builder, Actress*
%Jungle Gym, PO Box 585, Santa Monica, CA 90406, USA
Lyon, Sue *Actress*
1244 N Havenhurst Dr, West Hollywood, CA 90046, USA
Lyon, William *Air Force General, Businessman*
%William Lyon Co, 4490 Von Karman Ave, Newport Beach, CA 92660, USA
Lyonne, Natasha *Actress*
5255 Collins Ave, Miami, FL 33140, USA
Lyons, James A, Jr *Navy Admiral*
9481 Piney Mountain Road, Warrenton, VA 20186, USA
Lyons, Mitchell W (Mitch) *Football Player*
7355 Decosta Dr NE, Rockford, MI 49341, USA
Lyons, Robert F *Actor*
1801 Ave of Stars, #1250, Los Angeles, CA 90067, USA
Lyons, Steve *Commentator*
%Fox-TV, Sports Dept, 205 W 67th St, New York, NY 10021, USA
Lysiak, Tom *Hockey Player*
13064 Highway 278 E, Social Circle, GA 30025, USA
Lyst, John H *Editor*
%Indianapolis Star, Editorial Dept, 307 N Pennsylvania, Indianapolis, IN 46204, USA
Lyubimov, Alexey B *Concert Pianist*
Klimentovskiy Per 9, #12, Moscow, Russia
Lyubimov, Yuri P *Theater Director, Actor*
%Tanganka Theater, Chkalova Str 76, Moscow, Russia
Lyubshin, Stanislav A *Actor*
Vernadskogo Prosp 123, #171, 117571 Moscow, Russia

M'Bow, Amadou-Mahtar *Government Official, Senegal*
BP 5276, Dakar-Fann, Senegal
Ma, Yo-Yo *Concert Cellist*
%Askonas Holt Ltd, 27 Chancery Lane, London WC2A 1PF, England
Maas, William T (Bill) *Football Player*
PO Box 2175, Lees Summit, MO 64063, USA
Maathai, Wangari *Social Activist, Environmentalist*
%Green Belt Movement, PO Box 67545, Nairobi, Kenya
Maazel, Lorin V *Conductor, Concert Violinist*
%New York Philharmonic, Avery Fisher Hall, 10 Lincoln Center, New York, NY 10023, USA
Mabe, Manabu *Artist*
Rua das Canjeranas 321, Jabaquara, Sao Paulo SP, Brazil
Mabus, Raymond E, Jr *Governor, MS*
PO Box 200, Jackson, MS 39205, USA
Mac, Bernie *Actor, Comedian*
%Associated Booking Corp, 1995 Broadway, #501, New York, NY 10023, USA
MacAfee, Kenneth A (Ken) *Football Player*
8 Deerfield Dr, Medfield, MA 02052, USA
Macapagal-Arroyo, Gloria *President, Philippines*
%Malacanang Palace, JP Laurel St, Metro Manila 100, Philippines
MacArthur, James *Actor*
74092 Covered Wagon Trail, Palm Desert, CA 92260, USA
Macauley, Edward C (Easy Ed) *Basketball Player*
13277 Barrett Chase Circle, Ballwin, MO 63021, USA
MacAvoy, Paul W *Economist*
6 Mechanic St, Woodstock, VT 05091, USA
Macchio, Ralph *Actor*
451 Deerpark Ave, Dix Hills, NY 11746, USA
MacCorkindale, Simon *Actor*
%James Sharkey, 21 Golden Square, London W1R 3PA, England
MacCormack, Jean F *Educator*
%University of Massachusetts, President's Office, Boston, MA 02125, USA
MacCready, Paul B *Aeronautical Engineer*
%AeroVironment Inc, 222 E Huntington Dr, Monrovia, CA 91016, USA
MacDermot, Galt *Composer*
%MacDermot Assoc, 12 Silver Lake Road, Staten Island, NY 10301, USA
MacDiarmid, Alan G *Nobel Chemistry Laureate*
635 Drexel Ave, Drexel Hill, PA 19026, USA
MacDonald, C Parker *Hockey Player*
3 Miller Road, Northford, CT 06472, USA
MacDonald, Charles *WW II Army Air Corps Hero*
RR 5 Box C77, Definiak Springs, FL 32433, USA
Macdonald, Norm *Actor, Comedian*
%Endeavor Talent Agency, 9701 Wilshire Blvd, #1000, Beverly Hills, CA 90212, USA
MacDowell, Andie *Model, Actress*
939 8th Ave, #400, New York, NY 10019, USA
MacFadyen, Angus *Actor*
%International Creative Mgmt, 8942 Wilshire Blvd, #219, Beverly Hills, CA 90211, USA
MacGowan, Shane *Singer, Guitarist (Pogues)*
%Free Trade Agency, Chapel Place, Rivington St, London EC2A 3DQ, England
MacGraw, Ali *Actress*
%Agency for Performing Arts, 9200 Sunset Blvd, #900, Los Angeles, CA 90069, USA
MacGregor, Ian K *Government Official, England*
Castleton House, Lochgilphead, Argyll, Scotland
MacGregor, Joanna C *Concert Pianist*
%Columbia Artists Mgmt Inc, 165 W 57th St, New York, NY 10019, USA
Macha, Kenneth H (Ken) *Baseball Player, Manager*
6934 Berkshire Dr, Export, PA 15632, USA
Macharski, Franciszak Cardinal *Religious Leader*
%Metropolita Krakowski, Ul Franciszkanska 3, 31-004 Krakow, Poland
Machlis, Gail *Cartoonist (Quality Time)*
%Chronicle Features, 150 4th St, #695, San Francisco, CA 94103, USA
Machover, Tod *Composer*
%Massachusetts Institute of Technology, Media Laboratory, Cambridge, MA 02139, USA
Macht, Gabriel *Actor*
%Three Arts Entertainment, 9460 Wilshire Blvd, #700, Beverly Hills, CA 90212, USA
Macht, Stephen *Actor*
248 S Rodeo Dr, Beverly Hills, CA 90212, USA
MacInnis, Allan (Al) *Hockey Player*
710 Hamptons Lane, Chesterfield, MO 63017, USA
MacIntosh, Craig *Cartoonist (Sally Forth)*
3403 W 28th St, Minneapolis, MN 55416, USA
Macionis, John *Swimmer*
25 Washington Lane, #607, Wyncote, PA 19095, USA
Mack, John E *Psychiatrist*
%Harvard Medical School, 25 Shattuck St, Boston, MA 02115, USA
Mack, Lonnie *Singer, Guitarist*
%Concerted Efforts, 59 Parsons St, West Newton, MA 02465, USA

M

Mack - Maddy

Mack, Thomas I (Tom) *Football Player*
%Palo Verde Nuclear Generating Plant, Palo Verde, AZ 85343, USA
Macke, Richard C *Navy Admiral*
1887 Alaweo St, Honolulu, HI 96821, USA
MacKenzie, John L *Movie Director*
%International Creative Mgmt, 8942 Wilshire Blvd, #219, Beverly Hills, CA 90211, USA
Mackerras, A Charles M *Conductor*
10 Hamilton Terrace, London NW8 9UG, England
Mackey, John *Football Player*
1198 Pacific Coast Highway, #D506, Seal Beach, CA 90740, USA
Mackey, Rick *Dog Sled Racer*
5938 Four Mile Road, Nenana, AK 99760, USA
Mackie, Robert G (Bob) *Fashion Designer*
%Bob Mackie Ltd, 530 Fashion Ave, New York, NY 10018, USA
MacKinnon, Roderick *Nobel Chemistry Laureate*
545 W End Ave, New York, NY 10024, USA
Mackintosh, Cameron A *Theater Producer*
%Cameron Mackintosh Ltd, 1 Bedford Square, London WC1B 3RA, England
Macknowski, Stephen *Canoeing Athlete*
462 Kimball Ave, Yonkers, NY 10704, USA
MacLachlan, Kyle *Actor*
%Industry Entertainment, 955 Carillo Dr, #300, Los Angeles, CA 90048, USA
MacLaine, Shirley *Actress*
25200 Malibu Road, #4, Malibu, CA 90265, USA
MacLane, Saunders *Mathematician*
42 Circle Dr, Chesterton, IN 46304, USA
MacLean, Doug *Hockey Coach*
330 Tucker Dr, Worthington, OH 43085, USA
MacLean, Steven G *Astronaut, Canada*
%Astronaut Program, 6767 Rt de l'Aeroport, Saint-Hubert QC J3Y 8Y9, Canada
MacLeod, Gavin *Actor*
1877 Michael Lane, Pacific Palisades, CA 90272, USA
MacLeod, John *Basketball Coach*
4610 E Fanfol Dr, Phoenix, AZ 85028, USA
MacMillan, Shannon *Soccer Player*
%Portland University, Athletic Dept, Portland, OR 97203, USA
MacMurray, William *Electrical Engineer*
200 Deer Run Road, Schaghticoke, NY 12154, USA
Macnee, Patrick *Actor*
PO Box 1853, Rancho Mirage, CA 92270, USA
MacNeil, Cornell H *Opera Singer*
%Columbia Artists Mgmt Inc, 165 W 57th St, New York, NY 10019, USA
MacNichol, Peter *Actor*
%International Creative Mgmt, 8942 Wilshire Blvd, #219, Beverly Hills, CA 90211, USA
Macomber, George B H *Skier*
1 Design Center Place, #600, Boston, MA 02210, USA
MacPhail, Leland S (Lee), Jr *Baseball Executive*
1421 Meadow Ridge, Redding, CT 06896, USA
MacPherson, Duncan I *Editorial Cartoonist*
%Toronto Star, Editorial Dept, 1 Yonge St, Toronto ON M5E 1E6, Canada
Macpherson, Elle *Model*
%Artist Mgmt Assn, 118 Lake Dr, Bethlehem, CT 06751, USA
Macpherson, Wendy *Bowler*
PO Box 93433, Henderson, NV 89009, USA
MacQuitty, Jonathan *Inventor (Immunodeficient Mouse)*
%Abingworth Mgmt Inc, 2465 E Bayshore Road, #348, Palo Alto, CA 94303, USA
MacRae, Sheila *Actress, Singer*
666 W End Ave, #10H, New York, NY 10025, USA
MacTavish, Craig *Hockey Player, Coach*
3 Quail Hollow Court, Voorhees, NJ 08043, USA
Macy, Geoffrey W *Astronomer*
%University of California, Integrative Planetary Science Ctr, Berkeley, CA 94720, USA
Macy, William H *Actor*
%Writers & Artists, 8383 Wilshire Blvd, #550, Beverly Hills, CA 90211, USA
Madden, D S *Religious Leader*
%American Baptist Assn, 4605 N State Line, Texarkana, TX 75503, USA
Madden, Dave *Actor*
9921 Belville Road, Miami, FL 33157, USA
Madden, David *Writer*
%Louisiana State University, US Civil War Center, Baton Rouge, LA 70803, USA
Madden, John E *Football Player, Coach, Sportscaster*
5955 Coronado Blvd, Pleasanton, CA 94588, USA
Madden, John P *Movie Director*
%William Morris Agency, 52/53 Poland Place, London W1F 7LX, England
Maddux, Gregory A (Greg) *Baseball Player*
4132 S Rainbow Blvd, Las Vegas, NV 89103, USA
Maddy, Penelope Jo *Philosopher*
%University of California, Philosophy Dept, Irvine, CA 92717, USA

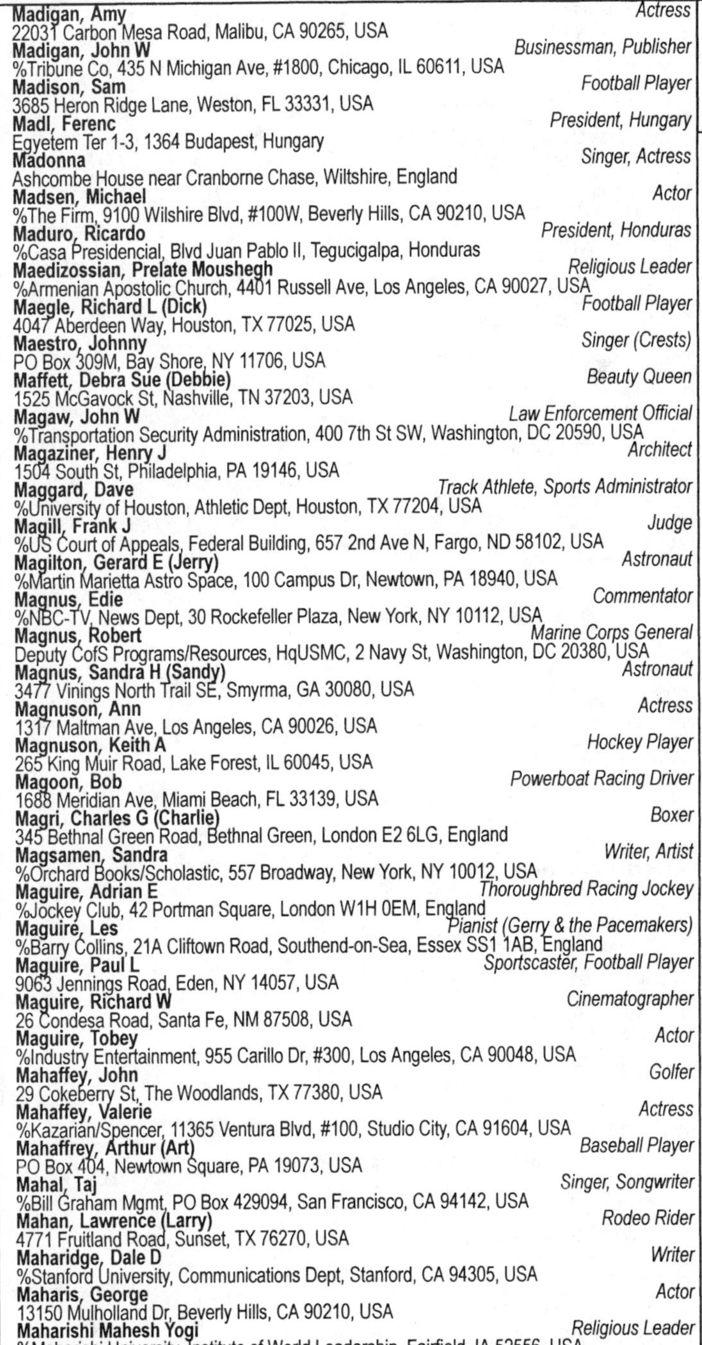

Madigan, Amy *Actress*
22031 Carbon Mesa Road, Malibu, CA 90265, USA

Madigan, John W *Businessman, Publisher*
%Tribune Co, 435 N Michigan Ave, #1800, Chicago, IL 60611, USA

Madison, Sam *Football Player*
3685 Heron Ridge Lane, Weston, FL 33331, USA

Madl, Ferenc *President, Hungary*
Egyetem Ter 1-3, 1364 Budapest, Hungary

Madonna *Singer, Actress*
Ashcombe House near Cranborne Chase, Wiltshire, England

Madsen, Michael *Actor*
%The Firm, 9100 Wilshire Blvd, #100W, Beverly Hills, CA 90210, USA

Maduro, Ricardo *President, Honduras*
%Casa Presidencial, Blvd Juan Pablo II, Tegucigalpa, Honduras

Maedizossian, Prelate Moushegh *Religious Leader*
%Armenian Apostolic Church, 4401 Russell Ave, Los Angeles, CA 90027, USA

Maegle, Richard L (Dick) *Football Player*
4047 Aberdeen Way, Houston, TX 77025, USA

Maestro, Johnny *Singer (Crests)*
PO Box 309M, Bay Shore, NY 11706, USA

Maffett, Debra Sue (Debbie) *Beauty Queen*
1525 McGavock St, Nashville, TN 37203, USA

Magaw, John W *Law Enforcement Official*
%Transportation Security Administration, 400 7th St SW, Washington, DC 20590, USA

Magaziner, Henry J *Architect*
1504 South St, Philadelphia, PA 19146, USA

Maggard, Dave *Track Athlete, Sports Administrator*
%University of Houston, Athletic Dept, Houston, TX 77204, USA

Magill, Frank J *Judge*
%US Court of Appeals, Federal Building, 657 2nd Ave N, Fargo, ND 58102, USA

Magilton, Gerard E (Jerry) *Astronaut*
%Martin Marietta Astro Space, 100 Campus Dr, Newtown, PA 18940, USA

Magnus, Edie *Commentator*
%NBC-TV, News Dept, 30 Rockefeller Plaza, New York, NY 10112, USA

Magnus, Robert *Marine Corps General*
Deputy CofS Programs/Resources, HqUSMC, 2 Navy St, Washington, DC 20380, USA

Magnus, Sandra H (Sandy) *Astronaut*
3477 Vinings North Trail SE, Smyrma, GA 30080, USA

Magnuson, Ann *Actress*
1317 Maltman Ave, Los Angeles, CA 90026, USA

Magnuson, Keith A *Hockey Player*
265 King Muir Road, Lake Forest, IL 60045, USA

Magoon, Bob *Powerboat Racing Driver*
1688 Meridian Ave, Miami Beach, FL 33139, USA

Magri, Charles G (Charlie) *Boxer*
345 Bethnal Green Road, Bethnal Green, London E2 6LG, England

Magsamen, Sandra *Writer, Artist*
%Orchard Books/Scholastic, 557 Broadway, New York, NY 10012, USA

Maguire, Adrian E *Thoroughbred Racing Jockey*
%Jockey Club, 42 Portman Square, London W1H 0EM, England

Maguire, Les *Pianist (Gerry & the Pacemakers)*
%Barry Collins, 21A Cliftown Road, Southend-on-Sea, Essex SS1 1AB, England

Maguire, Paul L *Sportscaster, Football Player*
9063 Jennings Road, Eden, NY 14057, USA

Maguire, Richard W *Cinematographer*
26 Condesa Road, Santa Fe, NM 87508, USA

Maguire, Tobey *Actor*
%Industry Entertainment, 955 Carillo Dr, #300, Los Angeles, CA 90048, USA

Mahaffey, John *Golfer*
29 Cokeberry St, The Woodlands, TX 77380, USA

Mahaffey, Valerie *Actress*
%Kazarian/Spencer, 11365 Ventura Blvd, #100, Studio City, CA 91604, USA

Mahaffrey, Arthur (Art) *Baseball Player*
PO Box 404, Newtown Square, PA 19073, USA

Mahal, Taj *Singer, Songwriter*
%Bill Graham Mgmt, PO Box 429094, San Francisco, CA 94142, USA

Mahan, Lawrence (Larry) *Rodeo Rider*
4771 Fruitland Road, Sunset, TX 76270, USA

Maharidge, Dale D *Writer*
%Stanford University, Communications Dept, Stanford, CA 94305, USA

Maharis, George *Actor*
13150 Mulholland Dr, Beverly Hills, CA 90210, USA

Maharishi Mahesh Yogi *Religious Leader*
%Maharishi University, Institute of World Leadership, Fairfield, IA 52556, USA

Maher, Bill *Commentator, Comedian*
%Agency for Performing Arts, 9200 Sunset Blvd, #900, Los Angeles, CA 90069, USA

Mahfouz, Naguib *Nobel Literature Laureate*
172 Nile St, Cairo, Egypt

Mahoney, J Daniel *Judge*
%US Court of Appeals, 40 Foley Square, New York, NY 10007, USA
Mahoney, John *Actor*
%International Creative Mgmt, 8942 Wilshire Blvd, #219, Beverly Hills, CA 90211, USA
Mahoney, Roger *Cartoonist (Millie)*
%King Features Syndicate, 888 7th Ave, New York, NY 10106, USA
Mahony, Roger Cardinal *Religious Leader*
%Archdiocese of Los Angeles, 3424 Wilshire Blvd, Los Angeles, CA 90010, USA
Mahovlich, Francis W (Frank) *Hockey Player*
2-954 Ave Road, Toronto ON M5P 2K8, Canada
Mahre, Phillip (Phil) *Alpine Skier*
70 Roza View Dr, Yakima, WA 98901, USA
Mahre, Steve *Alpine Skier*
100 McCormick Road, Yakima, WA 98908, USA
Maida, Adam J Cardinal *Religious Leader*
%Archdiocese of Detroit, 1234 Washington Blvd, Detroit, MI 48226, USA
Maiden-Naccarato, Jeanne *Bowler*
1 N Stadium Way, #4, Tacoma, WA 98403, USA
Maier, Hermann *Alpine Skier*
Reitdorf 116, 5542 Flachau, Austria
Maier, Pauline R *Historian*
60 Larchwood Dr, Cambridge, MA 02138, USA
Maier, Sepp *Soccer Player*
Parkstr 62, 84405 Anzing, Germany
Mailer, Norman K (Norm) *Writer*
625 Commerical St, Provincetown, MA 02657, USA
Maillard, Carol *Singer (Sweet Honey in the Rock)*
%Sweet Honey Agency, PO Box 600099, Newtonville, MA 02460, USA
Maiman, Theodore H (Ted) *Inventor (Ruby Laser Systems)*
15A Alberni St, Vancouver BC V6G 3N7, Canada
Maines, Natalie *Singer (Dixie Chicks)*
%Senior Mgmt, 56 Lindsey Ave, Nashville, TN 37210, USA
Maisel, Jay *Photographer*
190 Bowery, New York, NY 10012, USA
Maisky, Mischa M *Concert Cellist*
%Columbia Artists Mgmt Inc, 165 W 57th St, New York, NY 10019, USA
Maisonneuve, Brian *Soccer Player*
%Columbus Crew, 2121 Velman Ave, Columbus, OH 43211, USA
Maitland, Beth *Actress*
%Epstein-Wyckoff, 280 S Beverly Dr, #400, Beverly Hills, CA 90212, USA
Majdarzavyn Ganzorig *Cosmonaut, Mongolia*
%Academy of Sciences, Peace Ave 54B, Ulan Bator 51, Mongolia
Majerus, Rick *Basketball Coach*
%University of Utah, Athletic Dept, Huntsman Center, Salt Lake City, UT 84112, USA
Majoli, Iva *Tennis Player*
27 Framingham Lane, Pittsford, NY 14534, USA
Major, Clarence L *Writer*
%University of California, English Dept, Voorhies Hall, Davis, CA 95616, USA
Major, John *Prime Minister, England*
8 Stukley Road, Huntingdon, Cambs, England
Majors, John T (Johnny) *Football Player, Coach*
4215 Bigelow Blvd, Pittsburgh, PA 15213, USA
Majors, Lee *Actor*
PO Box 3457, Beverly Hills, CA 90212, USA
Makarov, Sergei *Hockey Player*
%Professional Sports Services, 4072 Teale Ave, San Jose, CA 95117, USA
Makarova, Natalia R *Ballerina*
%Herbert Breslin, 119 W 57th St, #1505, New York, NY 10019, USA
Makeba, Miriam *Singer*
%Sadiane Corp, 60 E 42nd St, #1201, New York, NY 10165, USA
Makhalina, Yulia *Ballerina*
%Kirov Ballet Theater, 1 Pl Iskusstr, 190000 Saint Petersburg, Russia
Maki, Fumihiko *Architect, Pritzker Laureate*
5-16-22 Higashi-Gotanda, Shinagawaku, Tokyo, Japan
Makk, Karoly *Movie Director*
Hankoczy Jeno Utca 15, 1022 Budapest, Hungary
Mako *Actor*
6477 Pepper Tree Lane, Somis, CA 93066, USA
Mako, C Gene *Tennis Player*
430 S Burnside Ave, #MC, Los Angeles, CA 90036, USA
Maksimova, Yekaterina S *Ballerina*
%Bolshoi Theater, Teatralnaya Pl 1, 103009 Moscow, Russia
Maksymiuk, Jerzy *Conductor*
Hoza 5A m 13, 00-528 Warsaw, Poland
Maktoum, Sheikh Maktoum bin Rashid al- *Prime Minister, United Arab Emirates*
%Royal Palace, PO Box 899, Abu Dubai, United Arab Emirates
Malakhov, Vladimir *Hockey Player*
31 Mary Court, Melville, NY 11747, USA

Malakian, Daron *Singer, Guitarist (System of a Down)*
%Velvet Hammer, 9911 W Pico Blvd, #350, Los Angeles, CA 90035, USA
Malandrino, Catherine *Fashion Designer*
468 Bromme St, New York, NY 10013, USA
Malandro, Kristina *Actress*
2518 Cardigan Court, Los Angeles, CA 90077, USA
Malcolm, George J *Concert Harpsichordist*
99 Wimbledon Hill Road, London SW19 4BE, England
Malden, Karl *Actor*
1845 Mandeville Canyon Road, Los Angeles, CA 90049, USA
Maldini, Paolo *Soccer Player, Coach*
%AC Milan, Via Turati 3, 20221 Milan, Italy
Malee, Chompoo *Fashion Designer*
%Hino & Malee Inc, 3701 N Ravenswood Ave, Chicago, IL 60613, USA
Maleeva, Katerina *Tennis Player*
Mladostr 1, #45, NH 14, Sofia 1174, Bulgaria
Maleeva-Fragniere, Manuela *Tennis Player*
Bourg-Dessous 28, 1814 La Tour de Peitz, Switzerland
Malenchenko, Yuri I *Cosmonaut*
%Potchta Kosmonavtov, Moskovskoi Oblasti, 141160 Syvisdny Goroduk, Russia
Malerba, Franco E *Astronaut*
Via Cantore 10, 16149 Genova, Italy
Malfitano, Catherine *Opera Singer*
%Columbia Artists Mgmt Inc, 165 W 57th St, New York, NY 10019, USA
Malice *Rap Artist (Clipse)*
%Star Trak/Arista Records, 888 7th Ave, #3800, New York, NY 10106, USA
Malick, Wendie *Actress, Model*
%Innovative Artists, 1505 10th St, Santa Monica, CA 90401, USA
Malicky, Neal *Educator*
%Baldwin-Wallace College, President's Office, Berea, OH 44017, USA
Malielegaoi, Tuila'epa Sa'ilele *Prime Minister, Samoa*
%Prime Minister's Office, PO Box L1861, Vailima, Apia, Samoa
Malik, Art *Actor*
18 Sydney Mews, London SW3 6HL, England
Malinin, Mike *Drummer (Goo Goo Dolls)*
%Atlas/Third Rail Entertainment, 9200 W Sunset Blvd, West Hollywood, CA 90069, USA
Malinvaud, Edmond *Economist*
42 Ave de Saxe, 75007 Paris, France
Maliponte, Adrianna *Opera Singer*
%Gorlinsky Promotions, 35 Darer, London W1, England
Malkan, Matthew A *Astronomer*
%University of Arizona, Steward Observatory, Tucson, AZ 85721, USA
Malkhov, Vladimir *Ballet Dancer*
%American Ballet Theatre, 890 Broadway, New York, NY 10003, USA
Malkin, Peter Z *Law Enforcement Official*
135 W 74th St, #2R, New York, NY 10023, USA
Malkovich, John *Actor*
PO Box 5106, Westport, CT 06881, USA
Mallary, Robert *Sculptor*
PO Box 97, Conway, MA 01341, USA
Mallea, Eduardo *Writer*
Posadas 1120, Buenos Aires, Argentina
Mallet, W George *Governor General, Saint Lucia*
%Governor General's House, Morne, Castries, Saint Lucia
Mallette, Alfred J *Army General*
681 Lambeth Dr, Evans, GA 30809, USA
Malley, Kenneth C *Navy Admiral*
136 Riverside Road, Edgewater, MD 21037, USA
Mallick, Don *Test Pilot*
42045 N Tilton Dr, Quartz Hill, CA 93536, USA
Mallon, Meg *Golfer*
%Pro's Inc, 7100 Forest Ave, #201, Richmond, VA 23226, USA
Mallory, Carole *Actress*
2300 5th Ave, New York, NY 10037, USA
Mallory, Glynn C, Jr *Army General*
19221 Heather Forest, San Antonio, TX 78258, USA
Malloy, Edward A *Educator*
%University of Notre Dame, President's Office, Notre Dame, IN 46556, USA
Malo, Raul *Singer (Mavericks), Songwriter*
%AristoMedia, 1620 16th Ave S, Nashville, TN 37212, USA
Maloff, Sam *Furniture Designer*
PO Box 51, Alta Loma, CA 91701, USA
Malone, Arthur L (Art) *Football Player*
1619 E Carmen St, Tempe, AZ 85283, USA
Malone, Beverly L *Labor Leader*
%American Nurses Assn, 800 Maryland Ave SW, Washington, DC 20002, USA
Malone, Brendan *Basketball Coach*
%Indiana Pacers, Conseco Fieldhouse, 125 S Pennsylvania, Indianapolis, IN 46204, USA

Malone, Dorothy *Actress*
PO Box 7287, Dallas, TX 75209, USA
Malone, James W *Religious Leader*
%Catholic Bishops Conference, 1312 Massachusetts Ave NW, Washington, DC 20005, USA
Malone, Jeff *Basketball Player*
364 Lee Road, #504, Phenix City, AL 36870, USA
Malone, Jena *Actress*
459 Columbus Ave, #514, New York, NY 10024, USA
Malone, Karl *Basketball Player*
%Los Angeles Lakers, Staples Center, 1111 S Figueroa St, Los Angeles, CA 90015, USA
Malone, Mark *Football Player*
7069 Clubview Dr, Bridgefield, PA 15017, USA
Malone, Michael P *Educator*
%Montana State University, President's Office, Bozeman, MT 59717, USA
Malone, Nancy *Actress*
4604 Ledge Ave, Toluca Lake, CA 91602, USA
Malone, Wallace D, Jr *Financier*
%SouthTrust Corp, 420 20th St N, Birmingham, AL 35203, USA
Maloney, Dan *Hockey Player, Coach*
%Sutton Group Incentive Realty, 241 Minet's Point Road, Barrie ON L4N 4C4,
Maloney, Dave *Hockey Player*
1 Vista Ave, Old Greenwich, CT 06870, USA
Maloney, Don *Hockey Player*
29 Waters Edge, Rye, NY 10580, USA
Maloney, James W (Jim) *Baseball Player*
7027 N Teilman Ave, #102, Fresno, CA 93711, USA
Maloney, William R *Marine Corps General*
%Navy Mutual Aid Assn, Henderson Hall, 29 Carpenter Road, Arlington, VA 22204, USA
Malouf, David G J *Writer*
%Mobbs, 35 Sutherland Crescent, Darling Point, Sydney NSW 2027, Australia
Maloy, Robert *Educator, Librarian*
PO Box 524, Washington, DC 20044, USA
Maltbie, Roger *Golfer*
179 Longmeadow Dr, Los Gatos, CA 95032, USA
Maltby, Richard E, Jr *Lyricist, Theater Director*
1111 Park Ave, #4D, New York, NY 10128, USA
Maltin, Leonard *Movie, Television Critic*
10424 Whipple St, Toluca Lake, CA 91602, USA
Maltzan, Michael *Architect*
2801 Hyperion Ave, Los Angeles, CA 90027, USA
Malyshev, Yuri V *Cosmonaut*
%Potchta Kosmonavtov, Moskovskoi Oblasti, 141160 Syvisdny Goroduk, Russia
Malzone, Frank J *Baseball Player*
16 Aletha Road, Needham, MA 02492, USA
Mamadou, Tandja *President, Niger*
%President's Office, State House, Niamey, Niger
Mamby, Saoul *Boxer*
20 E Mosholu Parkway S, #17, Bronx, NY 10468, USA
Mamet, David A *Writer, Director*
2 Northfield Plaza, Northfield, IL 60093, USA
Mami, Cheb *Singer*
%Firstars Mgmt, 14724 Ventura Blvd, #PH, Sherman Oaks, CA 91403, USA
Mamo, Anthony J *President, Malta*
%Casa Arkati, Constitution St, Mosta, Malta
Mamohato *Queen Regent, Lesotho*
%Royal Palace, PO Box 524, Maseru, Lesotho
Mamula, Mike *Football Player*
2909 Pleasant Ave, Hamburg, NY 14075, USA
Manakov, Gennadi M *Cosmonaut*
%Potchta Kosmonavtov, Moskovskoi Oblasti, 141160 Syvisdny Goroduk, Russia
Manarov, Musa C *Cosmonaut*
Khovanskeya 3, 129515 Moscow, Russia
Manasseh, Leonard S *Architect*
6 Bacon's Lane, Highgate, London N6 6BL, England
Manatt, Charles T *Political Leader*
%Manatt Phelps Phillips, Trident Center, 11355 W Olympic, Los Angeles, CA 90064, USA
Mancha, Vaughn H *Football Player*
1308 High Road, Tallahassee, FL 32304, USA
Mancham, James R M *President, Seychelles*
%Lloyd's Bank, 81 Edgware Road, London W2 2HY, England
Manchester, Melissa *Singer, Songwriter*
5440 Corbin Ave, Tarzana, CA 91356, USA
Manchester, William *Writer*
PO Box 329, Wesleyan Station, Middletown, CT 06457, USA
Manchevski, Milcho *Movie Director*
%International Creative Mgmt, 8942 Wilshire Blvd, #219, Beverly Hills, CA 90211, USA
Mancina, Mark *Composer*
%Gorfaine/Schwartz, 13245 Riverside Dr, #450, Sherman Oaks, CA 91423, USA

Mancini, Ray (Boom Boom) *Boxer, Actor*
12524 Indianapolis St, Los Angeles, CA 90066, USA
Mancuso, Frank G *Businessman*
377 S Mapleton Dr, Los Angeles, CA 90024, USA
Mancuso, Nick *Actor*
%Agency for Performing Arts, 9200 Sunset Blvd, #900, Los Angeles, CA 90069, USA
Mandabach, Caryn *Television Producer*
%Carsey-Warner Productions, 4024 Radford Ave, Building 3, Studio City, CA 91604, USA
Mandan, Robert *Actor*
100 N Clark Dr, #205, West Hollywood, CA 90048, USA
Mandarich, Tony *Football Player*
%Indianapolis Colts, 7001 W 56th St, Indianapolis, IN 46254, USA
Mandel, Harvey *Guitarist*
%David Gross, PO Box 338, Mill Valley, CA 94942, USA
Mandel, Howie *Actor*
23456 Malibu Colony Road, Malibu, CA 90265, USA
Mandel, Johnny *Composer*
2401 Main St, Santa Monica, CA 90405, USA
Mandel, Robert C *Movie Director*
%International Creative Mgmt, 8942 Wilshire Blvd, #219, Beverly Hills, CA 90211, USA
Mandela, N Winnie Madikizela- *Social Activist*
Orlando West, Soweto, Johannesburg, South Africa
Mandela, Nelson R *President, South Africa; Nobel Laureate*
Private Bag X70000, Houghton 2041, South Africa
Mandelbrot, Benoit B *Mathematician*
%Yale University, Mathematics Dept, New Haven, CT 06520, USA
Mandich, Jim *Football Player*
16101 Aberdeen Way, Miami Lakes, FL 33014, USA
Mandle, E Roger *Museum Director*
%Rhode Island School of Design, President's Office, Providence, RI 02903, USA
Mandler, George *Psychologist*
1406 La Jolla Knoll, La Jolla, CA 92037, USA
Mandler, Jean M *Psychologist*
1406 La Jolla Knoll, La Jolla, CA 92037, USA
Mandlikova, Hana *Tennis Player*
%Octagon, 1751 Pinnacle Dr, #1500, McLean, VA 22102, USA
Mandrell, Barbara *Singer, Actress*
PO Box 100, Whites Creek, TN 37189, USA
Mandrell, Erline *Singer*
544 Nashville Pike, #244, Gallatin, TN 37066, USA
Mandrell, Louise *Singer*
%Mandrell Inc, 1101 Hunters Lane, Ashland City, TN 37015, USA
Mandylor, Costas *Actor*
6100 Wilshire Blvd, #1170, Los Angeles, CA 90048, USA
Mandylor, Louis *Actor*
%Stone Manners, 6500 Wilshire Blvd, #550, Los Angeles, CA 90048, USA
Manekshaw, Sam H F J *Army Field Marshal, India*
Stavka Springfield, Coonor, Nilgiris, South India, India
Manery, Randy *Hockey Player*
6587 Garrett Road, Buford, GA 30518, USA
Manetti, Larry *Actor*
%Epstein-Wyckoff, 280 S Beverly Dr, #400, Beverly Hills, CA 90212, USA
Mangelsdorf, David *Geneticist*
%Salk Institute, 10100 N Torrey Pines Road, La Jolla, CA 92037, USA
Mangelsdorf, Paul C *Geneticist*
510 Caswell Road, Chapel Hill, NC 27514, USA
Mangione, Chuck *Jazz Trumpeter, Composer*
%Gates Music, 23 W 73rd St, #915, New York, NY 10023, USA
Mangold, James *Movie Director*
%Susan Smith, 121A N San Vicente Blvd, Beverly Hills, CA 90211, USA
Mangold, Sylvia P *Artist*
1 Bull Road, Washingtonville, NY 10992, USA
Manh, Nong Duc *General Secretary, Vietnam*
%General's Secretary Office, Hoang Hoa Tham St, Hanoi, Vietnam
Manheim, Camryn *Actor*
%Gersh Agency, 232 N Canon Dr, Beverly Hills, CA 90210, USA
Maniatis, Thomas P *Genetics Engineer, Molecular Biolgist*
%Harvard University, Biochemistry Dept, 7 Divinity St, Cambridge, MA 02138, USA
Manilow, Barry *Singer, Songwriter*
%Bragman/Nyman/Cafarelli, 9171 Wilshire Blvd, #300, Beverly Hills, CA 90210, USA
Manion, Daniel A *Judge*
US Court of Appeals, 204 S Main St, South Bend, IN 46601, USA
Mankiller, Wilma P *Social Activist*
%Cherokee Nation, PO Box 948, Tahlequah, OK 74465, USA
Mankiw, N Gregory *Government Official*
%Council of Economic Advisers, Old Executive Office Bldg, Washington, DC 20500, USA
Mankoff, Robert *Cartoonist*
%New Yorker Magazine, Editorial Dept, 4 Times Square, New York, NY 10036, USA

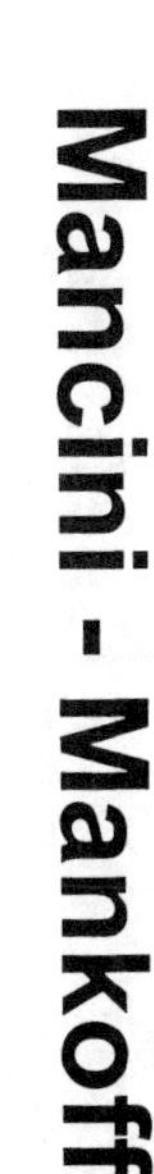

M

Manley, Elizabeth *Figure Skater*
%Marco Enterprises, 74830 Velie Dr, #A, Palm Desert, CA 92260, USA
Mann, Abby *Writer*
%Writers & Artists, 8383 Wilshire Blvd, #550, Beverly Hills, CA 90211, USA
Mann, Aimee *Singer ('Til Tuesday); Songwriter*
%Michael Hausman Mgmt, 511 Ave of Americas, #197, New York, NY 10011, USA
Mann, Barry *Composer*
1010 Laurel Way, Beverly Hills, CA 90210, USA
Mann, Carol A *Golfer*
6 Cape Chestnut Dr, The Woodlands, TX 77381, USA
Mann, David W *Religious Leader*
10550 S 200 W, Columbia City, IN 46725, USA
Mann, Delbert *Movie Director, Producer*
%Caroline Productions, 556 S Ogden Dr, Los Angeles, CA 90036, USA
Mann, Dick *Motorcycle Racing Rider*
%American Motorcycle Assn, 13515 Yarmouth Dr, Pickerington, OH 43147, USA
Mann, Gabriel *Actor*
%United Talent Agency, 9560 Wilshire Blvd, #500, Beverly Hills, CA 90212, USA
Mann, H Thompson *Swimmer*
49 Water St, Newburyport, MA 01950, USA
Mann, Johnny *Composer, Conductor*
78516 Gorman Lane, Indio, CA 92203, USA
Mann, Marvin L *Businessman*
%Lexmark International, 740 W New Circle Road, Lexington, KY 40550, USA
Mann, Michael K *Television Producer, Director*
13746 Sunset Blvd, Pacific Palisades, CA 90272, USA
Mann, Robert *Football Player*
1979 Orleans St, #252, Detroit, MI 48207, USA
Mann, Robert W *Biomedical Engineer*
5 Pelham Road, Lexington, MA 02421, USA
Mann, Shelley I *Swimmer*
1301 S Scott St, #638S, Arlington, VA 22204, USA
Mann, Terrence V *Actor*
111 W 96th St, #1, New York, NY 10025, USA
Manning Mims, Madeline *Track Athlete*
7477 E 48th St, #83-4, Tulsa, OK 74145, USA
Manning, E Archie, III *Football Player, Sportscaster*
%WWL-TV, Sports Dept, 1024 N Rampart St, New Orleans, LA 70116, USA
Manning, Irene *Actress*
3165 La Mesa Dr, San Carlos, CA 94070, USA
Manning, Jane *Opera Singer*
2 Wilton Square, London N1, England
Manning, Peyton *Football Player*
1420 1st St, New Orleans, LA 70130, USA
Manning, Richard E (Rick) *Baseball Player*
12151 New Market, Chesterland, OH 44026, USA
Manning, Robert J *Editor*
191 Commonwealth Ave, Boston, MA 02116, USA
Manning, Taryn *Singer (Boomkat), Actress*
%Platform, 2666 N Beachwood Dr, Los Angeles, CA 90068, USA
Manoff, Dinah *Actress*
%Innovative Artists, 1505 10th St, Santa Monica, CA 90401, USA
Manoogian, Richard A *Businessman*
%Masco Corp, 21001 Van Born Road, Taylor, MI 48180, USA
Mansell, Kevin *Businessman*
%Kohl's Corp, N56W17000 Ridgewood Dr, Menomonee Falls, WI 53051, USA
Mansell, Nigel *Auto Racing Driver*
%Nigel Mansell Racing, Brands Hatch, Longfield, Kent DA3 8NG, England
Manser, Michael J *Architect*
Morton House, Chiswick Mall, London W4 2PS, England
Mansfield, Peter *Nobel Medicine Laureate*
%Nottingham University, Physics Dept, Nottingham NG7 2RD, England
Mansholt, Sicco L *Government Official, Netherlands*
Oosteinde 18, 8351 HB Wapserveen, Netherlands
Manske, Edgar J *Football Player*
5046 Montezuma St, Los Angeles, CA 90042, USA
Manson, Dave *Hockey Player*
%Dallas Stars, StarCenter, 211 Cowboys Parkway, Irving, TX 75063, USA
Manson, Marilyn *Singer (Marilyn Manson)*
25935 Detroit Road, Westlake, OH 44145, USA
Manson, Shirley *Singer (Garbage)*
%Borman Entertainment, 1250 6th St, #401, Santa Monica, CA 90401, USA
Mansouri, Lotfi *Opera Director*
%San Francisco Opera House, 301 Van Ness Ave, San Francisco, CA 94102, USA
Mantee, Paul *Actor*
%Flick East-West, 9057 Nemo St, #A, West Hollywood, CA 90069, USA
Mantegna, Joe *Actor*
PO Box 7304, #103, North Hollywood, CA 91603, USA

Mantel, Hillary M *Writer*
%AM Heath, 79 Saint Martin's Lane, London WC2N 4AA, England
Mantello, Joe *Theater Director*
%Writers & Artists, 19 W 44th St, #1000, New York, NY 10036, USA
Mantha, Moe *Hockey Player*
1538 Scio Ridge Road, Ann Arbor, MI 48103, USA
Mantilla, Felix *Baseball Player*
6973 N Tacoma St, Milwaukee, WI 53224, USA
Mantooth, Randolph *Actor*
2830 Lambert Dr, Los Angeles, CA 90068, USA
Manuel, Charles F (Chuck) *Baseball Player, Manager*
2931 Plantation Road, Winter Haven, FL 33884, USA
Manuel, Jerry *Baseball Player, Manager*
1111 Fawn Creek Lane, Orland Park, IL 60467, USA
Manuel, Robert *Actor*
La Maison du Buisson, 22-26 Rue Jules Regnier, 78370 Plaisir, France
Manuelidis, Laura *Neuropathologist*
%Yale University, Medical School, Neuropathology Dept, New Haven, CT 06520, USA
Manwaring, Kurt D *Baseball Player*
20 Prospect Ridge, Horseheads, NY 14845, USA
Manz, Wolfgang *Concert Pianist*
Pasteuralle 55, 30655 Hanover, Germany
Manzanero, Armando *Singer*
%Pro Art, Paz Soldan 170, Of 903, San Isidro, Lima 27, Peru
Manzarek, Ray *Keyboardist (Doors)*
%Goldman & Knell, 1801 Century Park E, #2160, Los Angeles, CA 90067, USA
Manzi, Catello *Harness Racing Driver*
1 Hickory Lane, Freehold, NJ 07728, USA
Manzoni, Giacomo *Composer*
Viale Papiniano 31, 20123 Milan, Italy
Mapother, William *Actor*
%Creative Artists Agency, 9830 Wilshire Blvd, Beverly Hills, CA 90212, USA
Mara, Adele *Actress, Dancer*
1928 Mandeville Canyon Road, Los Angeles, CA 90049, USA
Mara, Ratu Sir Kamisese K T *President, Fiji*
11 Battery Road, Suva, Fiji
Mara, Wellington T *Football Executive*
16 Park Dr S, Rye, NY 10580, USA
Maramorosch, Karl *Entomologist*
1050 George St, New Brunswick, NJ 08901, USA
Maraniss, David *Journalist*
%Washington Post, Editorial Dept, 1150 15th St NW, Washington, DC 20071, USA
Maratos-Flier, Elfetheria *Geneticist*
%Joslin Diabetes Center, 1 Joslin Place, Boston, MA 02215, USA
Marber, Patrick *Writer*
%Judy Daish, 2 Saint Charles Place, London W10 6EG, England
Marbury, Stephon *Basketball Player*
%Phoenix Suns, 201 E Jefferson St, Phoenix, AZ 85004, USA
Marbut, Robert G *Publisher*
%Argyle Communications, 100 NE Loop, #1400, San Antonio, TX 78216, USA
Marc, Alessandra *Opera Singer*
%Columbia Artists Mgmt Inc, 165 W 57th St, New York, NY 10019, USA
Marceau, Marcel *Actor, Mime*
%Compagne de Mime, 32 Rue de Londres, 75009 Paris, France
Marceau, Sophie *Actress*
%Artmedia, 20 Ave Rapp, 75007 Paris, France
March, Jane *Actress, Model*
%Storm Model Mgmt, 5 Jubilee Place, #100, London SW3 3TD, England
March, Little Peggy *Singer*
%Cape Entertainment, 1161 NW 76th Ave, Plantation, FL 33322, USA
Marchetti, Gino J *Football Player*
324 Devon Way, West Chester, PA 19380, USA
Marchetti, Leo V *Labor Leader*
%Fraternal Order of Police, 5613 Belair Road, Baltimore, MD 21206, USA
Marchisano, Francesco Cardinal *Religious Leader*
%Cancelleria Apostolica Palazzo, Piazza Cancelleria 1, 00186 Rome, Italy
Marchuk, Guri I *Applied Mathematician*
%Numerical Mathematics Institute, Gubkin Str 8, 117333 Moscow, Russia
Marchuk, Yevhen K *Prime Minister, Ukraine*
Verkovna Rada, M Hrushevskoho Str 5, 252008 Kiev, Ukraine
Marcikjc, Ivan *Physicist, Inventor (Unbreakable Codes)*
%Geneva University, 24 Rue du General Dufour, 1211 Geneva 4, Switzerland
Marcil, Vanessa *Actress*
11110 Ohio Ave, #104, Los Angeles, CA 90025, USA
Marcinkevicius, Iustinas M *Writer*
Mildos Str 33, #6, 232055 Vilnius, Lithuania
Marcis, Dave *Auto Racing Driver*
71 Beadle Road, Arden, NC 28704, USA

M

Marcol - Marie

Marcol, Czeslaw C (Chester) *Football Player*
PO Box 466, Dollar Bay, MI 49922, USA
Marcos *Guitarist (POD)*
%East West America Records, 75 Rockefeller Plaza, New York, NY 10019, USA
Marcotte, Don *Hockey Player*
12 Cote St, Amesbury, MA 01913, USA
Marcovicci, Andrea *Actress, Singer*
%Donald Smith Promotions, 1640 E 48th St, #14U, New York, NY 10017, USA
Marcus, Bernard *Businessman*
%Home Depot Inc, 2455 Paces Ferry Road SE, Atlanta, GA 30339, USA
Marcus, Ken *Photographer*
6916 Melrose Ave, Los Angeles, CA 90038, USA
Marcus, Rudolph A *Nobel Chemistry Laureate*
331 S Hill Ave, Pasadena, CA 91106, USA
Marcus, Ruth B *Philosopher*
311 Saint Roman St, New Haven, CT 06511, USA
Marcus, Trula M *Actress*
%The Agency, 1800 Ave of Stars, #400, Los Angeles, CA 90067, USA
Marcy, Geoffrey *Astronomer*
%San Francisco State University, Astronomy Dept, San Francisco, CA 94132, USA
Mardall, Cyril L *Architect*
5 Boyne Terrace Mews, London W11 3LR, England
Marden, Brice *Artist*
6 Saint Lukes Place, New York, NY 10014, USA
Mardones, Benny *Singer*
%Tony Cee, PO Box 410, Utica, NY 13503, USA
Mare, Olindo *Football Player*
2961 W Lake Circle, Davie, FL 33328, USA
Maree, Sydney *Track Athlete*
2 Braxton Road, Bryn Mawr, PA 19010, USA
Maren, Elizabeth *Actress*
3126 Oakcrest Dr, Los Angeles, CA 90068, USA
Margal, Albert M *Prime Minister, Sierra Leone*
8 Hornsey Rise Gardens, London N19, England
Margalit, Israela *Concert Pianist*
%Columbia Artists Mgmt Inc, 165 W 57th St, New York, NY 10019, USA
Margeot, Jean Cardinal *Religious Leader*
Bonne Terre, Vacoas, Mauritius
Margison, Richard *Opera Singer*
%George Martynuk, 352 7th Ave, New York, NY 10001, USA
Margo, Philip *Singer, Pianist, Drummer (Tokens)*
%American Mgmt, 19948 Mayall St, Chatsworth, CA 91311, USA
Margoliash, Emmanuel *Biochemist*
353 Madison Ave, Glencoe, IL 60022, USA
Margolin, Phillip *Writer*
%Harper Collins Publishers, 10 E 53rd St, New York, NY 10022, USA
Margolin, Stuart *Actor*
%Three Owl Productions, Box 478, Ganges BC V0S 1E0, Canada
Margolis, Cindy *Model, Actress*
32215 Sheridan, Garden City, MI 48135, USA
Margolis, Lawrence S *Judge*
%US Claims Court, 717 Madison Place NW, Washington, DC 20439, USA
Margon, Bruce H *Astronomer*
%University of Washington, Astronomy Dept, PO Box 351580, Seattle, WA 98195, USA
Margoyles, Miriam *Actress*
%P F D, Drury House, 34-43 Russell St, London WC2B 5HA, England
Margrave, John L *Chemist*
4511 Vrone, Bellaire, TX 77401, USA
Margrethe II *Queen, Denmark*
%Amalienborg Palace, 1257 Copenhagen K, Denmark
Margulies, Donald *Writer*
%Yale University, English Dept, New Haven, CT 06520, USA
Margulies, James H (Jimmy) *Editorial Cartoonist*
%Hackensack Record, Editorial Dept, 150 River St, Hackensack, NJ 07601, USA
Margulies, Julianna *Actress*
%The Firm, 9100 Wilshire Blvd, #100W, Beverly Hills, CA 90210, USA
Margulis, Lynn *Biologist, Botanist*
2 Cummington St, Boston, MA 02215, USA
Mariam, Mengistu Haile *President, Ethiopia; Army Officer*
PO Box 1536, Gunhill Enclave, Harare, Zimbabwe
Mariategui, Sandro *Prime Minister, Peru*
Ave Ramirez Gaston 375, Miraflores, Lima, Peru
Marichal, Juan A S *Baseball Player*
9458 Doral Blvd, Miami, FL 33178, USA
Marie *Princess, Liechtenstein*
%Schloss Vaduz, 9490 Vaduz, Liechtenstein
Marie, Aurelius J B L *President, Dominica*
Zicack, Portsmouth, Dominica

Marie, Lisa *Model, Actress*
1041 N Formosa Ave, #10, West Hollywood, CA 90046, USA
Marie, Teena *Singer*
1000 Laguna Road, Pasadena, CA 91105, USA
Marimow, William K *Journalist*
1025 Winding Way, Baltimore, MD 21210, USA
Marin, Jack *Basketball Player*
3909 Regent Road, Durham, NC 27707, USA
Marin, Maguy *Choreographer*
%Compagnie Maguy Marin, Place Salvador Allende, 94000 Creteil, France
Marin, Richard A (Cheech) *Actor, Comedian (Cheech & Chong)*
%Joseph Mannis, 9150 Wilshire Blvd, #209, Beverly Hills, CA 90212, USA
Marinaro, Edward F (Ed) *Actor, Football Player*
%Innovative Artists, 1505 10th St, Santa Monica, CA 90401, USA
Marino, Daniel C (Dan), Jr *Football Player*
300 SW 1st Ave, Fort Lauderdale, FL 33301, USA
Marino, Ken *Actor*
%I F A Talent Agency, 8730 Sunset Blvd, #490, Los Angeles, CA 90069, USA
Mario, Ernest *Businessman, Pharmacist*
%ALZA Corp, 1950 Charleston Road, Mountain View, CA 94043, USA
Marion, Brock E *Football Player*
13825 Luray Road, SW Ranches, FL 33330, USA
Marion, Martin W (Marty) *Baseball Player*
8 Forcee Lane, Saint Louis, MO 63124, USA
Marion, Shawn *Basketball Player*
%Phoenix Suns, 201 E Jefferson St, Phoenix, AZ 85004, USA
Mariotti, Ray *Editor*
%Austin American-Statesman, Editorial Dept, 166 E Riverside, Austin, TX 78704, USA
Marisol *Sculptor*
%Marlborough Gallery, 40 W 57th St, New York, NY 10019, USA
Mariucci, Steve *Football Coach*
%Detroit Lions, 222 Republic Dr, Allen Park, MI 48101, USA
Mark, Hans M *Government Official, Physicist, Educator*
1715 Scenic Dr, Austin, TX 78703, USA
Mark, Mary Ellen *Photographer*
143 Price St, New York, NY 10012, USA
Mark, Reuben *Businessman*
%Colgate-Palmolive Co, 300 Park Ave, New York, NY 10022, USA
Mark, Robert *Law Enforcement Official*
Esher, Surrey KT10 8LU, England
Markaryants, Vladimir S *Government Official, Armenia*
%Council of Ministers, Yerevan, Armenia
Marken, William R *Editor*
%Sunset Magazine, Editorial Dept, 80 Willow Road, Menlo Park, CA 94025, USA
Marker, Laurie *Animal Activist, Biologist*
%Cheetah Conservation Fund, PO Box 1380, Ojai, CA 93024, USA
Marker, Steve *Guitarist (Garbage)*
%Borman Entertainment, 1250 6th St, #401, Santa Monica, CA 90401, USA
Markey, Lucille P *Thoroughbred Racing Breeder*
18 La Gorce Circle Lane, La Gorce Island, Miami Beach, FL 33141, USA
Markham, Monte *Actor*
PO Box 607, Malibu, CA 90265, USA
Markle, C Wilson *Film Engineer*
%Colorization Inc, 26 Soho St, Toronto ON M5T 1Z7, Canada
Markle, Peter F *Movie Director*
7510 W Sunset Blvd, #509, Los Angeles, CA 90046, USA
Markova, Alicia *Ballerina*
%Barclays Bank, PO Box 4599, London SW3 1KE, England
Markowitz, Barry *Cinematographer*
225 W 83rd St, #20G, New York, NY 10024, USA
Markowitz, Harry M *Nobel Economics Laureate*
1010 Turquoise St, #245, San Diego, CA 92109, USA
Markowitz, Michael *Artist*
%23rd Street Gallery, 3747 23rd St, San Francisco, CA 94114, USA
Markowitz, Robert *Movie Director, Producer*
11521 Amanda Dr, Studio City, CA 91604, USA
Marks, Albert J *Beauty Pageant Executive*
%Miss American Pageant, 1325 Broadway, Atlantic City, NJ 08401, USA
Marks, Bruce *Ballet Dancer, Artistic Director*
%Boston Ballet Co, 19 Clarendon St, Boston, MA 02116, USA
Marks, Paul A *Oncologist, Cell Biologist*
25680 Military Road, Watertown, NY 13601, USA
Markstein, Gary *Editorial Cartoonist*
%Milwaukee Journal, Editorial Dept, 333 W State St, Milwaukee, WI 53203, USA
Markwart, Nevin *Hockey Player*
210 Cushing Hill Road, Hanover, MA 02339, USA
Marlette, Douglas N (Doug) *Editorial Cartoonist*
PO Box 32188, Charlotte, NC 28232, USA

M

Marley, Ziggy *Singer, Songwriter*
Jack's Hill, Kingston, Jamaica
Marlin, Sterling *Auto Racing Driver*
995 Mahon Road, Columbia, TN 38401, USA
Marm, Walter J, Jr *Vietnam War Army Hero (CMH)*
PO Box 2017, Fremont, NC 27830, USA
Marnie, Larry *Football Coach*
%Arizona State University, Athletic Dept, Tempe, AZ 85287, USA
Marohn, William D *Businessman*
%Whirlpool Corp, 2000 N State St, RR 63, Benton Harbor, MI 49022, USA
Maroney, Daniel V, Jr *Labor Leader*
%Amalgamated Transit Union, 5025 Wisconsin Ave NW, Washington, DC 20016, USA
Maroney, Kelli *Actress*
%Peter Strain, 5724 W 3rd St, #302, Los Angeles, CA 90036, USA
Marotte, J Gilles *Hockey Player*
1759 Notre Dameo, Victoriaville QC G6A 7M4, Canada
Marriner, Neville *Conductor*
%Academy Saint Martin in Fields, Raine St, London E1 9RG, England
Marriott, J Willard, Jr *Businessman*
%Marriott International, 10400 Fernwood Road, Bethesda, MD 20817, USA
Marriott, Richard E *Businessman*
%Host Marriott Corp, 10400 Fernwood Road, Bethesda, MD 20817, USA
Marro, Anthony J *Editor*
%Newsday, Editorial Dept, 235 Pinelawn Road, Melville, NY 11747, USA
Marron, Donald B *Financier*
%UBS PaineWebber, 1285 6th Ave, New York, NY 10019, USA
Mars, Kenneth *Actor*
%International Creative Mgmt, 8942 Wilshire Blvd, #219, Beverly Hills, CA 90211, USA
Marsalis, Branford *Jazz Saxophonist, Composer*
%Wilkins Mgmt, 323 Broadway, Cambridge, MA 02139, USA
Marsalis, Ellis *Jazz Pianist*
%Management Ark, 116 Village Blvd, #200, Princeton, NJ 08540, USA
Marsalis, Wynton *Jazz Trumpeter, Composer*
%Management Ark, 116 Village Blvd, #200, Princeton, NJ 08540, USA
Marschall, Marita *Actress*
%Agentur Alexander, Lamontstr 9, 81679 Munich, Germany
Marsden, Bernie *Guitarist (Whitesnake)*
%Int'l Talent Booking, 27A Floral St, #300, London WC2E 9DQ, England
Marsden, Freddie *Drummer (Gerry & Pacemakers)*
%Barry Collins, 21A Cliftown Road, Southend-on-Sea, Essex SS1 1AB, England
Marsden, Gerard (Gerry) *Singer, Guitarist (Gerry & Pacemakers)*
%Barry Collins, 21A Cliftown Road, Southend-on-Sea, Essex SS1 1AB, England
Marsden, James *Actor*
881 Alma Real Dr, #308, Pacific Palisades, CA 90272, USA
Marsden, Roy *Actor*
%London Mgmt, 2-4 Noel St, London W1V 3RB, England
Marsh of Mannington, Richard W *Government Official, England*
%House of Lords, Westminster, London SW1A 0PW, England
Marsh, Brad *Hockey Player*
%Ottawa Senators, 1000 Palladium Dr, Kanata ON K2V 1A4, Canada
Marsh, Graham *Golfer*
%PGA Tour, 112 PGA Tour Blvd, Ponte Vedra Beach, FL 32082, USA
Marsh, Henry *Track Athlete*
%General Delivery, Bountiful, UT 84010, USA
Marsh, Jean *Actress*
52 Shaftesbury Ave, London W1V 7DE, England
Marsh, Linda *Actress*
170 W End Ave, 22P, New York, NY 10023, USA
Marsh, Marian *Actress*
PO Box 1, Palm Desert, CA 92261, USA
Marsh, Michael (Mike) *Track Athlete*
2425 Holly Hall St, #152, Houston, TX 77054, USA
Marsh, Miles L *Businessman*
%Fort James Corp, 1919 S Broadway, Green Bay, WI 54304, USA
Marsh, Robert T *Air Force General, Businessman*
6659 Avignon Blvd, Falls Church, VA 22043, USA
Marshall of Knightsbridge, Colin M *Businessman*
%British Airways, Heathrow Airport, Hounslow, Middx TW6 2JA, England
Marshall, Albert L (Bert) *Hockey Player*
9603 166th Street Court E, Puyallup, WA 98375, USA
Marshall, Amanda *Singer*
%Macklam Feldman Mgmt, 1505 W 2nd Ave, #200, Vancouver BC V6H 3Y4, Canada
Marshall, Barry J *Medical Researcher*
%Queen Elizabeth II Med Center, Nedlands WA 6009, Australia
Marshall, Brian *Bassist (Creed)*
%Agency Group, 1776 Broadway, #430, New York, NY 10019, USA
Marshall, Carolyn M *Religious Leader*
%United Methodist Church, 204 N Newlin St, Veedersburg, IN 47987, USA

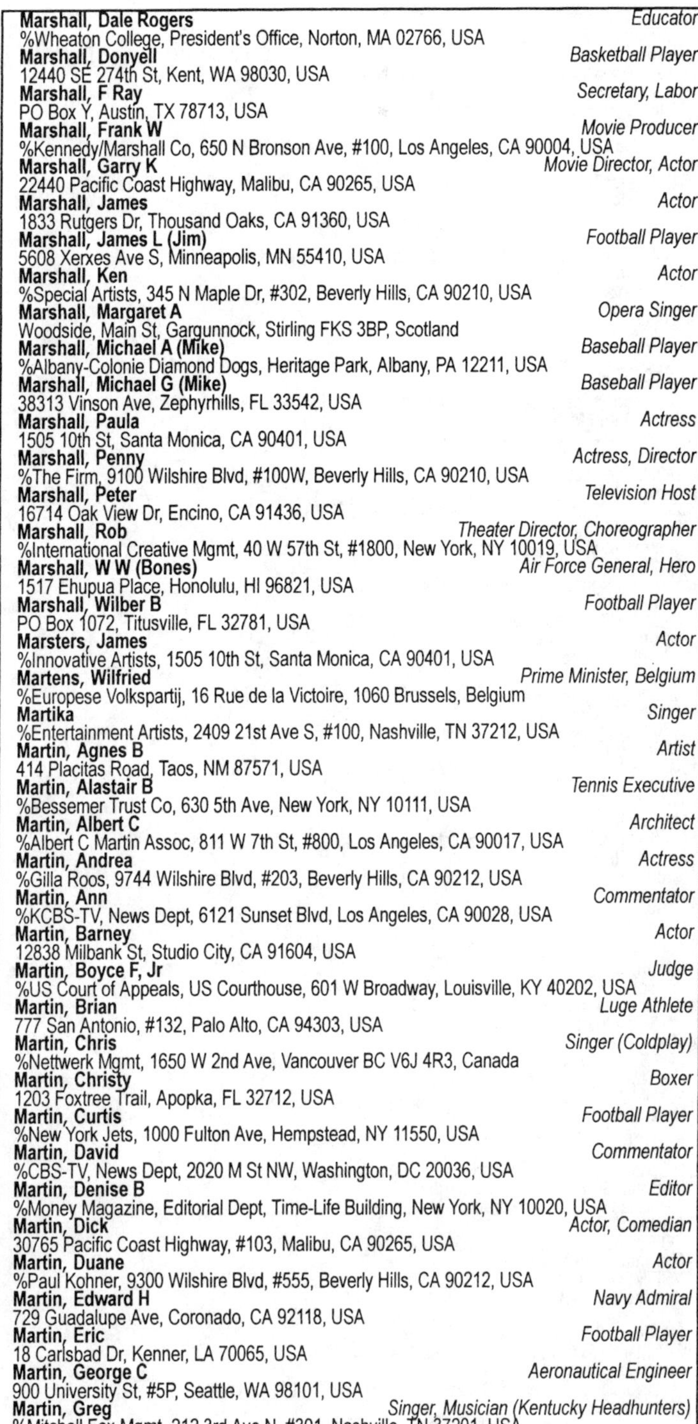
Marshall, Dale Rogers *Educator*
%Wheaton College, President's Office, Norton, MA 02766, USA
Marshall, Donyell *Basketball Player*
12440 SE 274th St, Kent, WA 98030, USA
Marshall, F Ray *Secretary, Labor*
PO Box Y, Austin, TX 78713, USA
Marshall, Frank W *Movie Producer*
%Kennedy/Marshall Co, 650 N Bronson Ave, #100, Los Angeles, CA 90004, USA
Marshall, Garry K *Movie Director, Actor*
22440 Pacific Coast Highway, Malibu, CA 90265, USA
Marshall, James *Actor*
1833 Rutgers Dr, Thousand Oaks, CA 91360, USA
Marshall, James L (Jim) *Football Player*
5608 Xerxes Ave S, Minneapolis, MN 55410, USA
Marshall, Ken *Actor*
%Special Artists, 345 N Maple Dr, #302, Beverly Hills, CA 90210, USA
Marshall, Margaret A *Opera Singer*
Woodside, Main St, Gargunnock, Stirling FKS 3BP, Scotland
Marshall, Michael A (Mike) *Baseball Player*
%Albany-Colonie Diamond Dogs, Heritage Park, Albany, PA 12211, USA
Marshall, Michael G (Mike) *Baseball Player*
38313 Vinson Ave, Zephyrhills, FL 33542, USA
Marshall, Paula *Actress*
1505 10th St, Santa Monica, CA 90401, USA
Marshall, Penny *Actress, Director*
%The Firm, 9100 Wilshire Blvd, #100W, Beverly Hills, CA 90210, USA
Marshall, Peter *Television Host*
16714 Oak View Dr, Encino, CA 91436, USA
Marshall, Rob *Theater Director, Choreographer*
%International Creative Mgmt, 40 W 57th St, #1800, New York, NY 10019, USA
Marshall, W W (Bones) *Air Force General, Hero*
1517 Ehupua Place, Honolulu, HI 96821, USA
Marshall, Wilber B *Football Player*
PO Box 1072, Titusville, FL 32781, USA
Marsters, James *Actor*
%Innovative Artists, 1505 10th St, Santa Monica, CA 90401, USA
Martens, Wilfried *Prime Minister, Belgium*
%Europese Volkspartij, 16 Rue de la Victoire, 1060 Brussels, Belgium
Martika *Singer*
%Entertainment Artists, 2409 21st Ave S, #100, Nashville, TN 37212, USA
Martin, Agnes B *Artist*
414 Placitas Road, Taos, NM 87571, USA
Martin, Alastair B *Tennis Executive*
%Bessemer Trust Co, 630 5th Ave, New York, NY 10111, USA
Martin, Albert C *Architect*
%Albert C Martin Assoc, 811 W 7th St, #800, Los Angeles, CA 90017, USA
Martin, Andrea *Actress*
%Gilla Roos, 9744 Wilshire Blvd, #203, Beverly Hills, CA 90212, USA
Martin, Ann *Commentator*
%KCBS-TV, News Dept, 6121 Sunset Blvd, Los Angeles, CA 90028, USA
Martin, Barney *Actor*
12838 Milbank St, Studio City, CA 91604, USA
Martin, Boyce F, Jr *Judge*
%US Court of Appeals, US Courthouse, 601 W Broadway, Louisville, KY 40202, USA
Martin, Brian *Luge Athlete*
777 San Antonio, #132, Palo Alto, CA 94303, USA
Martin, Chris *Singer (Coldplay)*
%Nettwerk Mgmt, 1650 W 2nd Ave, Vancouver BC V6J 4R3, Canada
Martin, Christy *Boxer*
1203 Foxtree Trail, Apopka, FL 32712, USA
Martin, Curtis *Football Player*
%New York Jets, 1000 Fulton Ave, Hempstead, NY 11550, USA
Martin, David *Commentator*
%CBS-TV, News Dept, 2020 M St NW, Washington, DC 20036, USA
Martin, Denise B *Editor*
%Money Magazine, Editorial Dept, Time-Life Building, New York, NY 10020, USA
Martin, Dick *Actor, Comedian*
30765 Pacific Coast Highway, #103, Malibu, CA 90265, USA
Martin, Duane *Actor*
%Paul Kohner, 9300 Wilshire Blvd, #555, Beverly Hills, CA 90212, USA
Martin, Edward H *Navy Admiral*
729 Guadalupe Ave, Coronado, CA 92118, USA
Martin, Eric *Football Player*
18 Carlsbad Dr, Kenner, LA 70065, USA
Martin, George C *Aeronautical Engineer*
900 University St, #5P, Seattle, WA 98101, USA
Martin, Greg *Singer, Musician (Kentucky Headhunters)*
%Mitchell Fox Mgmt, 212 3rd Ave N, #301, Nashville, TN 37201, USA

M

Martin - Martinez

Martin, Gregory S *Air Force General*
Commander, US Air Forces Europe, Ramstein Air Base, APO, AE 09094, USA
Martin, Henry R *Cartoonist (Good News Bad News)*
1382 Newtown Langhorne Road, #G206, Newtown, PA 18940, USA
Martin, Jacques *Hockey Coach*
%Ottawa Senators, 1000 Palladium Dr, Kanata ON K2V 1A4, Canada
Martin, James G *Governor, NC*
%Carolina Medical Center, PO Box 32861, Charlotte, NC 28232, USA
Martin, Jesse L *Actor*
%Endeavor Talent Agency, 9701 Wilshire Blvd, #1000, Beverly Hills, CA 90212, USA
Martin, Joe *Cartoonist (Mister Boffo)*
%King Features Syndicate, 888 7th Ave, New York, NY 10106, USA
Martin, John H *Educator*
%JHM Corp, 3930 RCA Blvd, #3240, Palm Beach Gardens, FL 33410, USA
Martin, Judith (Miss Manners) *Journalist*
1651 Harvard St NW, Washington, DC 20009, USA
Martin, Kellie *Actress*
5918 Van Nuys Blvd, Van Nuys, CA 91401, USA
Martin, Kenyon *Basketball Player*
%New Jersey Nets, 390 Murray Hill Parkway, East Rutherford, NJ 07073, USA
Martin, LeRoy *Law Enforcement Official*
%Chicago Police Dept, Superintendent's Office, Chicago, IL 60602, USA
Martin, Lynn M *Secretary, Labor*
171 Willabay Dr, Williams Bay, WI 53191, USA
Martin, Marilyn *Singer*
%422 Mgmt, 1808 W End Ave, #1100, Nashville, TN 37203, USA
Martin, Mark *Auto Racing Driver*
1648 Taylor Road, #606, Port Orange, FL 32128, USA
Martin, Marsha P *Financier*
%Farm Credit Administration, 1501 Farm Credit Dr, McLean, VA 22102, USA
Martin, Millicent *Actress, Singer*
%London Mgmt, 2-4 Noel St, London W1V 3RB, England
Martin, Nan *Actress*
33604 Pacific Coast Highway, Malibu, CA 90265, USA
Martin, Pamela Sue *Actress*
%Shelly & Pierce, 13775A Mono Way, #220, Sonora, CA 95370, USA
Martin, Paul *Government Official, Canada*
%Finance Department, 140 O'Connor St, Ottawa ON K1A 0G5, Canada
Martin, Preston *Government Official, Financier*
1130 N Lake Shore Dr, #4E, Chicago, IL 60611, USA
Martin, R Bruce *Chemist*
%University of Virginia, Chemistry Dept, Charlottesville, VA 22903, USA
Martin, Ray *Billiards Player*
11-05 Cadmus Place, Fair Lawn, NJ 07410, USA
Martin, Ricky *Actor, Singer*
%Angelo Medino Entertainment, 1406 Georgetti St, Santurce, PR 00909, USA
Martin, Ronald D *Editor*
%Atlanta Journal-Constitution, Editorial Dept, 72 Marietta, Atlanta, GA 30303, USA
Martin, Sandy *Actress*
%C N A Assoc, 1925 Century Park East, #750, Los Angeles, CA 90067, USA
Martin, Slater N *Basketball Player*
4119 Placid St, Houston, TX 77022, USA
Martin, Steve *Actor, Comedian*
PO Box 929, Beverly Hills, CA 90213, USA
Martin, Sylvia Wene *Bowler*
3875 Cambridge St, #1003, Las Vegas, NV 89119, USA
Martin, Todd *Tennis Player*
24586 Harbour View Dr, Ponte Vedra Beach, FL 32082, USA
Martin, Tony *Singer, Actor*
10724 Wilshire Blvd, #1406, Los Angeles, CA 90024, USA
Martindale, Wink *Entertainer, Singer*
5744 Newcastle Lane, Calabasas, CA 91302, USA
Martinelli, Elsa *Actress*
%Consul Cinemat, Viale Parioli 5944, 00197 Rome, Italy
Martinez Somalo, Eduardo Cardinal *Religious Leader*
%Palazzo delle Congregazioni, Piazza Pio XII 3, 00193 Rome, Italy
Martinez, A *Actor*
PO Box 6387, Malibu, CA 90264, USA
Martinez, Ana Maria *Opera Singer*
%JF Mastroianni, 161 W 61st St, #17E, New York, NY 10023, USA
Martinez, Conchita *Tennis Player*
511 Westminster Dr, Cardiff-by-the-Sea, CA 92007, USA
Martinez, Constantino (Tino) *Baseball Player*
324 Blanca Ave, Tampa, FL 33606, USA
Martinez, Daniel J *Artist*
%University of California, Studio Art Dept, Irvine, CA 92717, USA
Martinez, Edgar *Baseball Player*
Bo Maguayo Buzon 1295RR, Dorado, PR 00646, USA

Martinez, J Dennis *Baseball Player*
9400 SW 63rd Court, Miami, FL 33156, USA
Martinez, Mel *Secretary, Housing & Urban Development*
%Housing & Urban Development Department, 451 7th SW, Washington, DC 20410, USA
Martinez, Olivier *Actor*
%Artmedia, 20 Ave Rapp, 75007 Paris, France
Martinez, Pedro A *Baseball Player*
186 Fairmont Ave, Hyde Park, MA 02136, USA
Martinez, Ramon J *Baseball Player*
3029 Birkdale Dr, Weston, FL 33332, USA
Martinez, Robert (Bob) *Government Official; Governor, FL*
4647 W San Jose St, Tampa, FL 33629, USA
Martini, Carlo Maria Cardinal *Religious Leader*
Palazzo Arcivescovile, Piazza Fontana 2, 20122 Milan, Italy
Martini, Steve *Writer*
%G P Putnam's Sons, 375 Hudson St, New York, NY 10014, USA
Martino, Al *Singer, Actor*
927 N Rexford Dr, Beverly Hills, CA 90210, USA
Martino, Donald J *Composer*
%Harvard University, Music Dept, Cambridge, MA 02138, USA
Martino, Frank D *Labor Leader*
%Chemical Workers Union, 1655 W Market St, Akron, OH 44313, USA
Martino, Pat *Jazz Guitarist, Composer*
2318 S 16th St, Philadelphia, PA 19145, USA
Martino, Renato R Cardinal *Religious Leader*
%Justice & Peace Curia, Piazzo S Calisto 16, 00120 Vatican City
Martins, Joao Carlos *Concert Pianist*
%Musicians Corporate Mgmt, PO Box 589, Millbrook, NY 12545, USA
Martins, Peter *Ballet Dancer, Artistic Director*
%New York City Ballet, Lincoln Center Plaza, New York, NY 10023, USA
Martinson, Leslie H *Movie Director*
2288 Coldwater Canyon Dr, Beverly Hills, CA 90210, USA
Marton, Eva *Opera Singer*
%Opera et Concert, Maximilianstr 22, 80539 Munich, Germany
Marty, Martin E *Theologian*
239 Scottswood Road, Riverside, IL 60546, USA
Martz, Mike *Football Coach*
%Saint Louis Rams, 901 N Broadway, Saint Louis, MO 63101, USA
Martzke, Rudy *Sportswriter*
%USA Today, Editorial Dept, 1000 Wilson Blvd, Arlington, VA 22209, USA
Marusin, Yury M *Opera Singer*
%Mariinsky Theater, Teatralnaya Pl 1, Saint Petersburg, Russia
Marx, Gilda *Fashion Designer*
%Gilda Marx Industries, 11755 Exposition Blvd, Los Angeles, CA 90064, USA
Marx, Gyorgy *Physicist*
Fehervari Utca 119, 1119 Budapest, Hungary
Marx, Jeffrey A *Journalist*
%Lexington Herald-Leader, Editorial Dept, Main & Midland, Lexington, KY 40507, USA
Marx, Richard *Singer, Songwriter*
%Principal Artists, 9777 Wilshire Blvd, #1018, Beverly Hills, CA 90212, USA
Maryland, Russell *Football Player*
1330 Eagle Bend, Southlake, TX 76092, USA
Marzich, Andy *Bowler*
1421 Cravens Ave, #318, Torrance, CA 90501, USA
Marzio, Peter C *Museum Director*
%Houston Museum of Fine Arts, 1001 Bissonnet, PO Box 6826, Houston, TX 77265, USA
Marzoli, Andrea *Geologist*
%Berkeley Geochronolgy Center, 2455 Ridge Road, Berkeley, CA 94709, USA
Masak, Ron *Actor*
5440 Shirley Ave, Tarzana, CA 91356, USA
Masakayan, Liz *Volleyball Player*
2864 Palomino Circle, La Jolla, CA 92037, USA
Masako *Crown Princess, Japan*
%Imperial Palace, 1-1 Chiyoda-ku, Tokyo, Japan
Mase *Rap Artist*
%International Creative Mgmt, 8942 Wilshire Blvd, #219, Beverly Hills, CA 90211, USA
Masefield, J Thorold *Governor, Bermuda*
%Government House, 11 Langton Hill, Pembroke HM13, Bermuda
Masekela, Hugh R *Jazz Trumpeter*
%Performers of the World, 8901 Melrose Ave, #200, West Hollywood, CA 90069, USA
Mashburn, Jamal *Basketball Player*
5529 Saint Andrews Court, Plano, TX 75093, USA
Mashburn, Jesse *Track Athlete*
8520 S Pennsylvania Ave, Oklahoma City, OK 73159, USA
Mashkov, Vladimir L *Actor*
%Oleg Tabakov Theater, Chaokygina Str 12A, Moscow, Russia
Masiello, Tony *Mayor*
%Mayor's Office, City Hall, 65 Niagara Square, Buffalo, NY 14202, USA

M

Masire, Q Ketumile J *President, Botswana*
PO Box 70, Gaborone, Botswana
Maske, Henry *Boxer*
%Sauerland Promotion, Hochstadenstr 1-3, 50674 Cologne, Germany
Maslansky, Paul *Movie Producer, Director*
%Henry Bamberger, 10866 Wilshire Blvd, #1000, Los Angeles, CA 90024, USA
Masloff, Sophie *Mayor*
%Mayor's Office, City-County Building, 414 Grant St, Pittsburgh, PA 15219, USA
Mason of Barnsley, Roy *Government Official, England*
12 Victoria Ave, Barnsley, South Yorks S7O 2BH, England
Mason, Anthony *Basketball Player*
7818 Sawyer Brown Road, Nashville, TN 37221, USA
Mason, B John *Meteorologist*
64 Christchurch Road, East Sheen, London SW14, England
Mason, Birny, Jr *Chemical Engineer*
6 Island Dr, Rye, NY 10580, USA
Mason, Bobbie Ann *Writer*
PO Box 518, Lawrenceburg, KY 40342, USA
Mason, Brent *Singer*
%Mercury Records, 54 Music Square E, #300, Nashville, TN 37203, USA
Mason, Dave *Singer, Songwriter*
11205 McPherson Way, Ventura, CA 93001, USA
Mason, Desmond *Basketball Player*
%Milwaukee Bucks, Bradley Center, 1001 N 4th St, Milwaukee, WI 53203, USA
Mason, Glen *Football Coach*
%University of Minnesota, Athletic Dept, Minneapolis, MN 55455, USA
Mason, Jackie *Actor, Comedian*
%World According to Me, 146 W 57th St, #68D, New York, NY 10019, USA
Mason, Larry B *Vietnam War Air Force Hero*
826 Cinebar Road, Cinebar, WA 98533, USA
Mason, Marlyn *Actress, Singer*
27 Glen Oak Court, Medford, OR 97504, USA
Mason, Marsha *Actress*
528 Don Gaspar Ave, Santa Fe, NM 87505, USA
Mason, Mila *Singer*
PO Box 24392, Louisville, KY 40224, USA
Mason, Monica *Ballerina*
%Royal Opera House, Convent Garden, Bow St, London WC2, England
Mason, Nick *Drummer (Pink Floyd)*
%Agency Group, 370 City Road, London EC1V 2QA, England
Mason, Ron *Hockey Coach*
%Michigan State University, Athletic Dept, East Lansing, MI 48224, USA
Mason, Stephen *Singer (Beta Band), Songwriter*
%Evolution Talent, 1776 Broadway, #1500, New York, NY 10019, USA
Mason, Stephen *Guitarist (Jars of Clay)*
%Flood Bumstead McCready McCarthy, 1700 Hayes St, #304, Nashville, TN 37203, USA
Mason, Steve *Guitarist (Gene)*
%Agency Group Ltd, 370 City Road, London EC1V 2QA, England
Mason, Thomas C (Tommy) *Football Player*
920 Heather Ave, La Habra, CA 90631, USA
Mason, Tom *Actor*
870 Heights Place, Oyster Bay, NY 11771, USA
Mason, Vince *Rap Artist (DeLaSoul)*
%Famous Artists Agency, 250 W 57th St, New York, NY 10107, USA
Masri, Tahir Nashat *Prime Minister, Jordan*
PO Box 5550, Amman, Jordan
Mass, Jochen *Auto Racing Driver*
RTL-Sportredaktion, 50570 Cologne, Germany
Massengale, Don *Golfer*
715 W Davis St, Conroe, TX 77301, USA
Massevitch, Alla G *Astronomer*
6 Pushkurev Per, #4, 103045 Moscow, Russia
Massey, Anna *Actress*
%Markham & Froggatt, Julian House, 4 Windmill St, London W1P 1HF, England
Massey, Debbie *Golfer*
PO Box 116, Cheboygan, MI 49721, USA
Massey, Vincent *Biochemist*
%University of Michigan, Biochemistry Dept, Ann Arbor, MI 48109, USA
Massey, Walter E *Educator, Physicist*
%Morehouse College, President's Office, 830 Westview Dr SW, Atlanta, GA 30314, USA
Massie, Robert K *Writer*
52 W Clinton Ave, Irvington, NY 10533, USA
Massimino, Michael J *Astronaut*
15814 Elk Park Lane, Houston, TX 77062, USA
Massimino, Rollie *Basketball Coach*
18578 SE Ferland Court, Jupiter, FL 33469, USA
Mast, Rick *Auto Racing Driver*
390 E Midland Trail, Lexington, VA 24450, USA

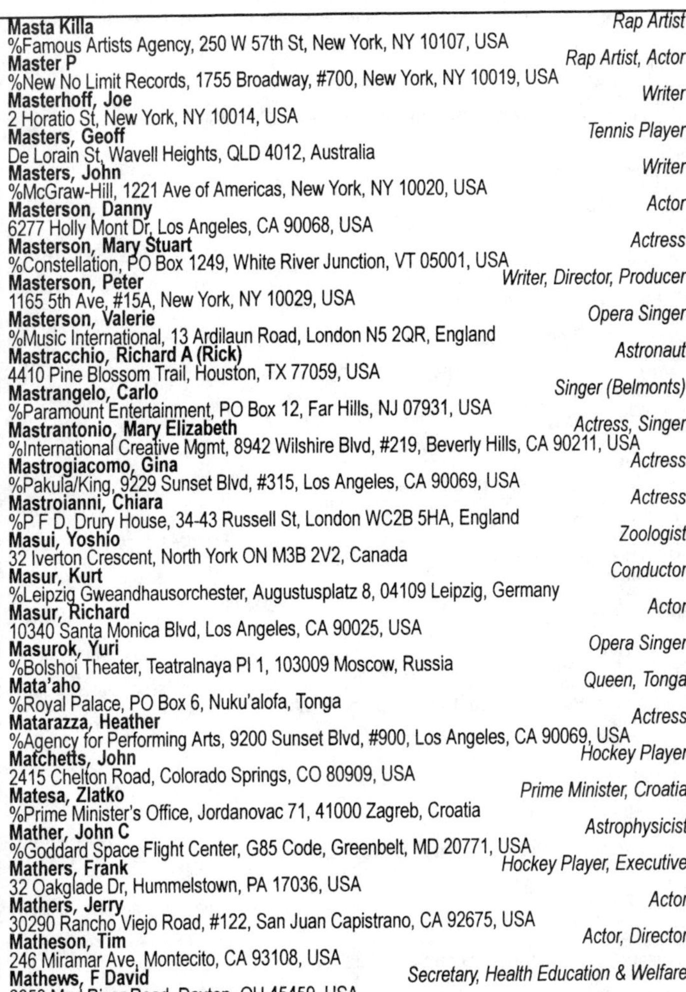

Masta Killa — *Rap Artist*
%Famous Artists Agency, 250 W 57th St, New York, NY 10107, USA

Master P — *Rap Artist, Actor*
%New No Limit Records, 1755 Broadway, #700, New York, NY 10019, USA

Masterhoff, Joe — *Writer*
2 Horatio St, New York, NY 10014, USA

Masters, Geoff — *Tennis Player*
De Lorain St, Wavell Heights, QLD 4012, Australia

Masters, John — *Writer*
%McGraw-Hill, 1221 Ave of Americas, New York, NY 10020, USA

Masterson, Danny — *Actor*
6277 Holly Mont Dr, Los Angeles, CA 90068, USA

Masterson, Mary Stuart — *Actress*
%Constellation, PO Box 1249, White River Junction, VT 05001, USA

Masterson, Peter — *Writer, Director, Producer*
1165 5th Ave, #15A, New York, NY 10029, USA

Masterson, Valerie — *Opera Singer*
%Music International, 13 Ardilaun Road, London N5 2QR, England

Mastracchio, Richard A (Rick) — *Astronaut*
4410 Pine Blossom Trail, Houston, TX 77059, USA

Mastrangelo, Carlo — *Singer (Belmonts)*
%Paramount Entertainment, PO Box 12, Far Hills, NJ 07931, USA

Mastrantonio, Mary Elizabeth — *Actress, Singer*
%International Creative Mgmt, 8942 Wilshire Blvd, #219, Beverly Hills, CA 90211, USA

Mastrogiacomo, Gina — *Actress*
%Pakula/King, 9229 Sunset Blvd, #315, Los Angeles, CA 90069, USA

Mastroianni, Chiara — *Actress*
%P F D, Drury House, 34-43 Russell St, London WC2B 5HA, England

Masui, Yoshio — *Zoologist*
32 Iverton Crescent, North York ON M3B 2V2, Canada

Masur, Kurt — *Conductor*
%Leipzig Gweandhausorchester, Augustusplatz 8, 04109 Leipzig, Germany

Masur, Richard — *Actor*
10340 Santa Monica Blvd, Los Angeles, CA 90025, USA

Masurok, Yuri — *Opera Singer*
%Bolshoi Theater, Teatralnaya Pl 1, 103009 Moscow, Russia

Mata'aho — *Queen, Tonga*
%Royal Palace, PO Box 6, Nuku'alofa, Tonga

Matarazza, Heather — *Actress*
%Agency for Performing Arts, 9200 Sunset Blvd, #900, Los Angeles, CA 90069, USA

Matchetts, John — *Hockey Player*
2415 Chelton Road, Colorado Springs, CO 80909, USA

Matesa, Zlatko — *Prime Minister, Croatia*
%Prime Minister's Office, Jordanovac 71, 41000 Zagreb, Croatia

Mather, John C — *Astrophysicist*
%Goddard Space Flight Center, G85 Code, Greenbelt, MD 20771, USA

Mathers, Frank — *Hockey Player, Executive*
32 Oakglade Dr, Hummelstown, PA 17036, USA

Mathers, Jerry — *Actor*
30290 Rancho Viejo Road, #122, San Juan Capistrano, CA 92675, USA

Matheson, Tim — *Actor, Director*
246 Miramar Ave, Montecito, CA 93108, USA

Mathews, F David — *Secretary, Health Education & Welfare*
6050 Mad River Road, Dayton, OH 45459, USA

Mathews, Francine — *Writer*
%Doubleday Press, 1540 Broadway, New York, NY 10036, USA

Mathews, Harlan — *Senator, TN*
420 Hunt Club Road, Nashville, TN 37221, USA

Mathews, Kerwin — *Actor*
67 Buena Vista Terrace, #A, San Francisco, CA 94117, USA

Mathias, Buster, Jr — *Boxer*
4409 Carol Ave SW, Wyoming, MI 49509, USA

Mathias, Charles McC, Jr — *Senator, MD; Financier*
3808 Leland St, Chevy Chase, MD 20815, USA

Mathias, Robert B (Bob) — *Track Athlete; Representative, CA*
7469 E Pine Ave, Fresno, CA 93727, USA

Mathias, William — *Composer*
Y Graigwen Cadnant Road, Menai Bridge, Anglesey, Gwynedd LL59 5NG, Wales

Mathieu, Georges V A — *Artist*
125 Ave de Makakoff, 75116 Paris, France

Mathieu, Philip — *Concert Guitarist*
%Lindy S Martin Mgmt, 5 Lob Lolly Court, Executive Suite, Pinehurst, NC 28374, USA

Mathilde — *Crown Princess, Belgium*
%Koninklijk Palace, Rue de Brederode, 1000 Brussels, Belgium

Mathis, Clint — *Soccer Player*
%New York/New Jersey MetroStars, 1 Harmon Plaza, #300, Secaucus, NJ 07094, USA

Mathis, Edith — *Opera Singer*
%Ingpen & Williams, 14 Kensington Court, London W8 5DN, England

Mathis, Johnny — *Singer*
%Rojon Productions, 1612 W Olive Ave, #305, Burbank, CA 91506, USA
Mathis, Samantha — *Actress*
7536 Sunnywood Lane, Los Angeles, CA 90046, USA
Mathis, Terance — *Football Player*
%Pittsburgh Steelers, 3400 S Water St, Pittsburgh, PA 15203, USA
Mathis-Eddy, Darlene — *Writer*
1409 W Cardinal St, Muncie, IN 47303, USA
Mathison, Melissa — *Writer*
655 MacCulloch Dr, Los Angeles, CA 90049, USA
Matlin, Marlee — *Actress*
10340 Santa Monica Blvd, Los Angeles, CA 90025, USA
Matlock, Glen — *Bassist (Sex Pistols)*
%Solo Agency, 55 Fulham High St, London SW6 3JJ, England
Matlock, Jack F, Jr — *Diplomat*
940 Princeton Kingston Road, Princeton, NJ 08540, USA
Matola, Sharon — *Zoo Director, Conservationist*
%Belize Zoo & Tropical Education Center, PO Box 1787, Belize City, Belize
Matorin, Vladimir A — *Opera Singer*
Ulansky Per 21, Korp 1, #53, 103045 Moscow, Russia
Matricaria, Ronald — *Businessman*
%Saint Jude Medical Inc, 1 Lillehei Plaza, Saint Paul, MN 55117, USA
Matsch, Richard P — *Judge*
%US District Court, 1929 Stout St, Denver, CO 80294, USA
Matsik, George A — *Businessman*
%Ball Corp, 10 Longs Peak Dr, Broomfield, CO 80021, USA
Matson, J Randel (Randy) — *Track Athlete*
1002 Park Place, College Station, TX 77840, USA
Matson, Oliver G (Ollie) — *Football Player, Track Athlete*
1319 S Hudson Ave, Los Angeles, CA 90019, USA
Matsuda, Seiko — *Singer, Actress*
%Propaganda Films Mgmt, 1741 Ivar Ave, Los Angeles, CA 90028, USA
Matsui, Keiko — *Pianist*
%Ted Kurland, 173 Brighton Ave, Boston, MA 02134, USA
Matsui, Kosei — *Pottery Maker*
Ibaraki-ken, Kasama-shi, Kasama 350, Japan
Matsumoto, Shigeharu — *Writer, Association Executive*
%International House of Japan, 11-16 Roppongi, Minatuku, Tokyo, Japan
Matsushita, Hiro — *Auto Racing Driver*
14772 Ridgeboro Place, Tustin, CA 92780, USA
Matt, Mike — *Rodeo Rider*
111 S 24th St W, #9125, Billings, MT 59102, USA
Matta del Meskin — *Religious Leader*
Deir el Makarios Monastery, Cairo, Egypt
Matte, Thomas R (Tom) — *Football Player*
11309 Old Carriage Road, Glen Arm, MD 21057, USA
Mattea, Kathy — *Singer*
%TBA Artists Mgmt, 300 10th Ave S, Nashville, TN 37203, USA
Mattei, Frank — *Singer (Danny & the Juniors)*
%Joe Taylor Mgmt, PO Box 1017, Turnersville, NJ 08012, USA
Mattes, Eva — *Actress*
%Agentur Carola Studlar, Neurieder Str, #1C, 92152 Planegg, Germany
Mattesich, Rudi — *Skier*
%General Delivery, Troy, VT 05868, USA
Matthes, Roland — *Swimmer*
Luitpoldstr 35A, 97828 Marktheidenfeld, Germany
Matthes, Ulrich — *Actor*
Kuno-Fischer-Str 14, 14057 Berlin, Germany
Matthews, Bruce R — *Football Player*
6423 Oilfield Road, Sugar Land, TX 77479, USA
Matthews, Cerys — *Singer (Catatonia)*
%MRM Productions, 5 Kirby St, London EC1N 8TS, England
Matthews, Dakin — *Actor*
%Henderson/Hogan, 8285 W Sunset Blvd, #1, West Hollywood, CA 90046, USA
Matthews, Dave — *Singer, Guitarist (Dave Matthews Band)*
%Red Light Mgmt, 3302 Lobban Place, Charlottesville, VA 22903, USA
Matthews, DeLane — *Actress*
%Don Buchwald, 6500 Wilshire Blvd, #2200, Los Angeles, CA 90048, USA
Matthews, Gary N — *Baseball Player*
1542 W Jackson Blvd, Chicago, IL 60607, USA
Matthews, Ian — *Singer, Guitarist*
%Geoffrey Blumenauer, 11846 Balboa Blvd, #204, Granada Hills, CA 91344, USA
Matthews, Keith — *Astronomer*
%California Institute of Technology, Astronomy Dept, Pasadena, CA 91125, USA
Matthews, Pat Stanley — *Actress*
210 Stanton, Walla Walla, WA 99362, USA
Matthews, Robert C O — *Economist*
%Clare College, Cambridge CB2 1TL, England

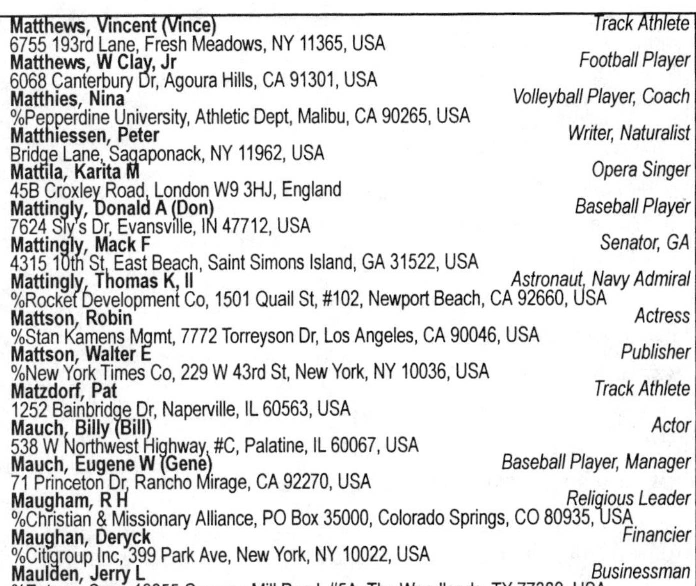

Matthews, Vincent (Vince) — *Track Athlete*
6755 193rd Lane, Fresh Meadows, NY 11365, USA

Matthews, W Clay, Jr — *Football Player*
6068 Canterbury Dr, Agoura Hills, CA 91301, USA

Matthies, Nina — *Volleyball Player, Coach*
%Pepperdine University, Athletic Dept, Malibu, CA 90265, USA

Matthiessen, Peter — *Writer, Naturalist*
Bridge Lane, Sagaponack, NY 11962, USA

Mattila, Karita M — *Opera Singer*
45B Croxley Road, London W9 3HJ, England

Mattingly, Donald A (Don) — *Baseball Player*
7624 Sly's Dr, Evansville, IN 47712, USA

Mattingly, Mack F — *Senator, GA*
4315 10th St, East Beach, Saint Simons Island, GA 31522, USA

Mattingly, Thomas K, II — *Astronaut, Navy Admiral*
%Rocket Development Co, 1501 Quail St, #102, Newport Beach, CA 92660, USA

Mattson, Robin — *Actress*
%Stan Kamens Mgmt, 7772 Torreyson Dr, Los Angeles, CA 90046, USA

Mattson, Walter E — *Publisher*
%New York Times Co, 229 W 43rd St, New York, NY 10036, USA

Matzdorf, Pat — *Track Athlete*
1252 Bainbridge Dr, Naperville, IL 60563, USA

Mauch, Billy (Bill) — *Actor*
538 W Northwest Highway, #C, Palatine, IL 60067, USA

Mauch, Eugene W (Gene) — *Baseball Player, Manager*
71 Princeton Dr, Rancho Mirage, CA 92270, USA

Maugham, R H — *Religious Leader*
%Christian & Missionary Alliance, PO Box 35000, Colorado Springs, CO 80935, USA

Maughan, Deryck — *Financier*
%Citigroup Inc, 399 Park Ave, New York, NY 10022, USA

Maulden, Jerry L — *Businessman*
%Entergy Corp, 10055 Grogans Mill Road, #5A, The Woodlands, TX 77380, USA

Maulnier, Thierry — *Writer*
3 Rue Yves-Carriou, 92430 Marnes-la-Coquette, France

Maumenee, Alfred E — *Ophthalmologist*
1700 Hillside Road, Stevenson, MD 21153, USA

Maupin, Armistead J, Jr — *Writer*
584 Castro St, #528, San Francisco, CA 94114, USA

Maura, Carmen — *Actress*
%GRPC SL, Calle Fuencarral 17, 28004 Madrid, Spain

Maurer, Gilbert C — *Publisher*
%Hearst Corp, 250 W 55th St, New York, NY 10019, USA

Maurer, Robert D — *Inventor (Silica Optical Waveguide)*
2572 W 28th Ave, Eugene, OR 97405, USA

Mauriac, Claude — *Writer*
24 Quai de Bethune, 75004 Paris, France

Maurice, Paul — *Hockey Coach*
205 Calm Winds Court, Cary, NC 27513, USA

Mauriello, Tammy — *Boxer*
1148 E 81st St, Brooklyn, NY 11236, USA

Maurin, Laurence — *Skier, Conservationist*
PO Box 1980, West Bend, WI 53095, USA

Mauroy, Pierre — *Prime Minister, France*
17-19 Rue Voltaire, 59800 Lille, France

Maurstad, Toralv — *Theater Director, Actor*
%Nationaltheatret, Stortingsgt 15, Oslo 1, Norway

Mauz, Henry H (Hank), Jr — *Navy Admiral*
1608 Viscaine Road, Pebble Beach, CA 93953, USA

Mawae, Kevin J — *Football Player*
11220 NE 53rd St, Kirkland, WA 98033, USA

Mawby, Russell G — *Foundation Executive*
%WK Kellogg Foundation, 1 Michigan Ave E, Battle Creek, MI 49017, USA

Max, Peter — *Artist*
118 Riverside Dr, New York, NY 10024, USA

Maximova, Ekaterina — *Ballerina*
%Bolshoi Theater, Teatralnaya Pl 1, 103009 Moscow, Russia

Maxson, Robert — *Educator*
%California State University, President's Office, Long Beach, CA 90840, USA

Maxwell — *Singer*
%Violator Mgmt, 205 Lexington Ave, #400, New York, NY 10016, USA

Maxwell, Arthur E — *Oceanographer*
8115 Two Coves Dr, Austin, TX 78730, USA

Maxwell, Cedric (Cornbread) — *Basketball Player*
%WEEI Sports Radio, 116 Huntington Ave, Boston, MA 02116, USA

Maxwell, Frank — *Labor Leader*
%Federation of TV-Radio Artists, 260 Madison Ave, New York, NY 10016, USA

Maxwell, Ian — *Publisher*
Eaton Terrace, London SW1, England

Maxwell, Kevin F H *Publisher*
Hill Burn, Hailey near Wallingford, Oxford OX10 6AD, England
Maxwell, Lois *Actress*
%International Creative Mgmt, 76 Oxford St, London W1N 0AX, England
Maxwell, Robert D *WW II Army Hero (CMH)*
1001 SE 15th St, #44, Bend, OR 97702, USA
Maxwell, Ronald F (Ron) *Movie Director, Writer*
5531 Bonneville Road, Hidden Hills, CA 91302, USA
May, Arthur *Architect*
%Kohn Pedersen Fox Assoc, 111 W 57th St, New York, NY 10019, USA
May, Billy *Trumpeter, Conductor, Composer*
31351 Via Santa Maria, San Juan Capistrano, CA 92675, USA
May, Brian *Guitarist (Queen), Songwriter*
Old Bakehouse, 16A High St, Barnes, London SW13, England
May, Deborah *Actress*
%Artists Agency, 1180 S Beverly Dr, #301, Los Angeles, CA 90035, USA
May, Don *Basketball Player*
1128 Colwick Dr, Dayton, OH 45420, USA
May, Elaine *Actress, Comedienne, Movie Director*
%William Morris Agency, 151 El Camino Dr, Beverly Hills, CA 90212, USA
May, Joe *Dog Sled Racer*
General Delivery, Thorne Bay, AK 99919, USA
May, Lee A *Baseball Player*
5593 Hill & Dale Dr, Cincinnati, OH 45213, USA
May, Mark E *Football Player, Sportscaster*
%Mark May Salisbury Ford, 1902 N Salisbury Blvd, Salisbury, MD 21801, USA
May, Mathilda *Actress*
%Artmedia, 20 Ave Rapp, 75007 Paris, France
May, Misty *Volleyball Player*
%Assn of Volleyball Pros, 330 Washington Blvd, #400, Marina del Rey, CA 90292, USA
May, Scott G *Basketball Player*
2001 E Hillside Dr, Bloomington, IN 47401, USA
May, Torsten *Boxer*
%Sauerland Promotion, Hans-Bockler-Str 163, 50354 Hurth, Germany
Mayaki, Ibrahim Hassane *Prime Minister, Niger*
%Prime Minister's Office, State House, Niamey, Niger
Mayall, John *Singer, Keyboardist, Composer*
%Monterey International, 200 W Superior, #202, Chicago, IL 60610, USA
Mayall, Rik *Actor, Comedian*
%Brunskill Mgmt, 169 Queen's Gate, London SW7 5HE, England
Mayasich, John E *Hockey Player*
2250 Riverwood Place, Saint Paul, MN 55104, USA
Mayberry, John C *Baseball Player*
11115 W 121st Terrace, Overland Park, KS 66213, USA
Maydan, Dan *Businessman*
%Applied Materials, 3050 Bowers Ave, Santa Clara, CA 95054, USA
Mayer, Christian *Alpine Skier*
Siedlerweg 18, 9584 Finkelstein, Austria
Mayer, Gene *Tennis Player*
115 South St, Glen Dale, MD 20769, USA
Mayer, H Robert *Judge*
%US Court of Appeals, 717 Madison Place NW, Washington, DC 20439, USA
Mayer, John *Singer, Songwriter*
%Columbia Records, 2100 Colorado Ave, Santa Monica, CA 90404, USA
Mayer, Joseph E *Chemical Physicist*
2345 Via Siena, La Jolla, CA 92037, USA
Mayer, Martin J *Navy Admiral*
Deputy CinC, Joint Forces Command, 116 Lake View Parkway, Suffolk, VA 23435, USA
Mayer, P Augustin Cardinal *Religious Leader*
Ecclesia Dei, 00120 Vatican City
Mayer, Travis *Freestyle Skier*
37050 Williams St, Steamboat Springs, CO 80487, USA
Mayes, Rueben *Football Player*
610 SE Edge Knoll Dr, Pullman, WA 99163, USA
Mayfair, Billy *Golfer*
7666 E Campo Bello Dr, Scottsdale, AZ 85255, USA
Mayfield, Jeremy *Auto Racing Driver*
%Everham Motorsports, 320 Aviation Dr, Statesville, NC 28677, USA
Mayhew, Patrick B B *Government Official, England*
%House of Lords, Westminster, London SW1A 0PW, England
Mayle, Peter *Writer*
%Knopf Publishers, 201 E 50th St, New York, NY 10022, USA
Maynard, Andrew *Boxer*
%Mike Trainer, 3922 Fairmont Ave, Bethesda, MD 20814, USA
Maynard, Donald R (Don) *Football Player*
6545 Butterfield Dr, El Paso, TX 79932, USA
Maynard, Mimi *Actress*
%Badgley Connor Talent, 9229 Sunset Blvd, #311, Los Angeles, CA 90069, USA

Mayne, D Roger *Photographer*
Colway Manor, Colway Lane, Lyme Regis, Dorset DT7 3HD, England
Mayne, Kenny *Sportscaster*
%ESPN-TV, Sports Dept, ESPN Plaza, 935 Middle St, Bristol, CT 06010, USA
Mayne, Thomas *Architect*
%Morphosis Architects, 2041 Colorado Ave, Santa Monica, CA 90404, USA
Mayne, William *Writer*
%Harold Ober Assoc, 425 Madison Ave, New York, NY 10017, USA
Mayo, Virginia *Actress*
109 E Avenida de las Aboles, Thousand Oaks, CA 91360, USA
Mayor Zaragoza, Federico *Government Official, Spain*
%UNESCO, 7 Place de Fonteroy, 75352 Paris, France
Mayor, Michel *Astronomer*
%University of Geneva, Geneva Observatory, Geneva, Switzerland
Mayotte, Timothy S (Tim) *Tennis Player*
%SFX Sports Group, 2665 S Bayshore Dr, #602, Miami, FL 33133, USA
Mayr, Ernst *Biologist, Zoologist*
207 Badger Terrace, Bedford, MA 01730, USA
Mayron, Melanie *Actress, Director*
1435 N Ogden Dr, Los Angeles, CA 90046, USA
Mays, Lowry *Businessman*
%Clear Channel Communications, 200 Concord Plaza, San Antonio, TX 78216, USA
Mays, Lyle *Jazz Pianist*
%Ted Kurland, 173 Brighton Ave, Boston, MA 02134, USA
Mays, Mark P *Businessman*
%Clear Channel Communications, 200 Concord Plaza, San Antonio, TX 78216, USA
Mays, Willie H *Baseball Player*
51 Mount Vernon Lane, Atherton, CA 94027, USA
Mayweather, Floyd, Jr *Boxer*
4720 Laguna Vista St, Las Vegas, NV 89147, USA
Mazach, John J *Navy Admiral*
5423 Grist Mills Woods Road, Alexandria, VA 22309, USA
Mazar, Debi *Actress*
%United Talent Agency, 9560 Wilshire Blvd, #500, Beverly Hills, CA 90212, USA
Mazer, Bill *Sportscaster*
140 Kent Dr, Berkeley Heights, NJ 07922, USA
Mazeroski, William S (Bill) *Baseball Player*
RR 6 Box 130, Greensburg, PA 15601, USA
Mazor, Stanley (Stan) *Inventor (Microprocessor)*
%FTI/Teklicon, 3031 Tisch Way, San Jose, CA 95128, USA
Mazowiecki, Tadeusz *Prime Minister, Poland*
Sejm RP, Ul Qiejska 4/6/8, 00-902 Warsaw, Poland
Mazur, Jay J *Labor Leader*
%Industrial Textile Employees Needletrades, 1710 Broadway, New York, NY 10019, USA
Mazurok, Yuri A *Opera Singer*
%Boshoi State Theater, Teatralnaya Pl 1, 103009 Moscow, Russia
Mazursky, Paul *Movie Director*
614 26th St, Santa Monica, CA 90402, USA
Mazza, Valeria *Model*
%Riccardo Ga, 8/10 Via Revere, 20123 Milan, Italy
Mazzie, Marin *Actress, Singer*
%J Michael Bloom, 233 Park Ave S, #1000, New York, NY 10003, USA
Mazzo, Kay *Ballerina*
%American Ballet School, 144 W 66th St, New York, NY 10023, USA
Mazzola, Anthony T *Editor*
%Town & Country Magazine, Editorial Dept, 1790 Broadway, New York, NY 10019, USA
Mba, Casimir Oye *Prime Minister, Gabon*
%Prime Minister's Office, Boite Postale 546, Libreville, Gabon
Mbasogo, Teodoro Obiang Nguema *President, Equatorial Guinea*
%President's Office, Malabo, Equatorial Guinea
Mbeki, Thabo *President, South Africa*
%President's Office, Union Buildings, Pretoria 0001, South Africa
McAdoo, Robert A (Bob) *Basketball Player, Coach*
16710 SW 82nd Ave, Village of Palmetto Bay, FL 33157, USA
McAfee, George A *Football Player*
2600 Croasdaile Farm Parkway, #D105, Durham, NC 27705, USA
McAleese, Mary P *President, Ireland*
%President's Office, Baile Athe Cliath 8, Dublin, Ireland
McAlpine, Donald M *Cinematographer*
377 Placer Creek Lane, Henderson, NV 89014, USA
McArdle, Andrea *Actress, Singer*
%Edd Kalehoff, 14 Shady Glen Court, New Rochelle, NY 10805, USA
McArthur, Alex *Actor*
10435 Wheatland Ave, Sunland, CA 91040, USA
McArthur, William S (Bill), Jr *Astronaut*
14503 Sycamore Lake Road, Houston, TX 77062, USA
McAuliffe, Dennis P *Army General*
9076 Belvoir Woods Parkway, Fort Belvoir, VA 22060, USA

McBain, Diane *Actress*
13317 Ventura Blvd, #1, Sherman Oaks, CA 91423, USA
McBain, Ed *Writer*
324 Main Ave, PO Box 339, Norwalk, CT 06856, USA
McBride, Chi *Actor*
%United Talent Agency, 9560 Wilshire Blvd, #500, Beverly Hills, CA 90212, USA
McBride, Jon A *Astronaut*
%Image Development Group, 1018 Kanawha Blvd, #901, Charleston, WV 25301, USA
McBride, Martina *Singer*
%Bruce Allen Talent, 406-68 Water St, Vancouver BC V6B 1A4, Canada
McBride, Patricia *Ballerina*
%Sharon Wagner Artists, 150 W End Ave, New York, NY 10023, USA
McBroom, Amanda *Singer, Songwriter*
167 Fairview Road, Ojai, CA 93023, USA
McCabe, Frank *Basketball Player*
6202 N Fairlane Dr, Peoria, IL 61614, USA
McCabe, Patrick *Writer*
%Picador, Macmillan Books, 25 Eckceston Place, London SW1W 9NF, England
McCabe, Zia *Singer, Guitarist (Dandy Warhols)*
%Mongui Mgmt, PO Box 5908, Portland, OR 97228, USA
McCafferty, Donald F (Don), Jr *Football Coach*
167 E Shore Road, Halesite, NY 11743, USA
McCaffrey, Barry R *Army General*
506 Crown View Dr, Alexandria, VA 22314, USA
McCallister, Lon *Actor*
PO Box 6030, Stateline, NV 89449, USA
McCallum, David *Actor*
%Hilary Gagan, Caprice House, 3 New Burlington St, London W1X 1FE, England
McCallum, Napoleon A *Football Player*
314 Doe Run Circle, Henderson, NV 89012, USA
McCambridge, Mercedes *Actress*
156 5th Ave, #820, New York, NY 10010, USA
McCandless, Bruce, II *Astronaut*
210932 Pleasant Park Dr, Conifer, CO 80433, USA
McCann, Les *Jazz Singer, Pianist, Composer*
%DeLeon Artists, 4031 Panama Court, Piedmont, CA 94611, USA
McCann, Terrence (Terry) *Wrestler*
PO Box 9052, Mission Viejo, CA 92690, USA
McCarrick, Theodore E Cardinal *Religious Leader*
%Archdiocesan Pastoral Center, 5001 Eastern Ave, Washington, DC 20017, USA
McCarron, Christopher (Chris) *Thoroughbred Racing Jockey*
%Dun Roamin, 318 N Terrace View Dr, Monrovia, CA 91016, USA
McCarron, Douglas J *Labor Leader*
%Carperters/Joiners Brotherhood, 101 Connecticut Ave NW, Washington, DC 20001, USA
McCartan, Jack *Hockey Player*
8818 Logan Ave S, Bloomington, MN 55431, USA
McCarthy, Andrew *Actor*
4708 Vesper Ave, Sherman Oaks, CA 91403, USA
McCarthy, Cormac *Writer*
1101 N Mesa, El Paso, TX 79002, USA
McCarthy, Dennis M *Marine Corps General*
Commander, Forces Reserve, HqUSMC, 2 Navy St, Washington, DC 20380, USA
McCarthy, Eugene J *Senator, MN*
%Harcout Brace Jovanovich, 1666 Connecticut Ave NW, #300, Washington, DC 20009, USA
McCarthy, Jenny *Model, Actress*
8424A Santa Monica Blvd, #504, Los Angeles, CA 90069, USA
McCarthy, Kevin *Actor*
14854 Sutton St, Sherman Oaks, CA 91403, USA
McCartney, Paul *Singer (Beatles), Songwriter*
%MPL Communications Ltd, 1 Soho Square, London W1V 6BQ, England
McCartney, Stella *Fashion Designer*
13 Rue Turbigo, 75002 Paris, France
McCarty, Maclyn *Bacteriologist, Immunologist*
%Rockefeller University, 66th St & York Ave, New York, NY 10021, USA
McCarver, J Timothy (Tim) *Baseball Player, Sportscaster*
118 County Line Road, Bryn Mawr, PA 19010, USA
McCary, Michael *Singer (Boyz II Men)*
%Southpaw Entertainment, 10675 Santa Monica Blvd, Los Angeles, CA 90025, USA
McCauley, Barry *Opera Singer*
598 Ridgewood Road, Oradell, NJ 07649, USA
McCauley, Donald F (Don), Jr *Football Player*
36 Taylor Road, Halesite, NY 11743, USA
McCauley, William F *Navy Admiral*
670 Margarita Ave, Coronado, CA 92118, USA
McCay, Peggy *Actress*
2714 Carmar Dr, Los Angeles, CA 90046, USA
McClain, Katrina *Basketball Player*
155 Standing Oak Place, Fairburn, GA 30213, USA

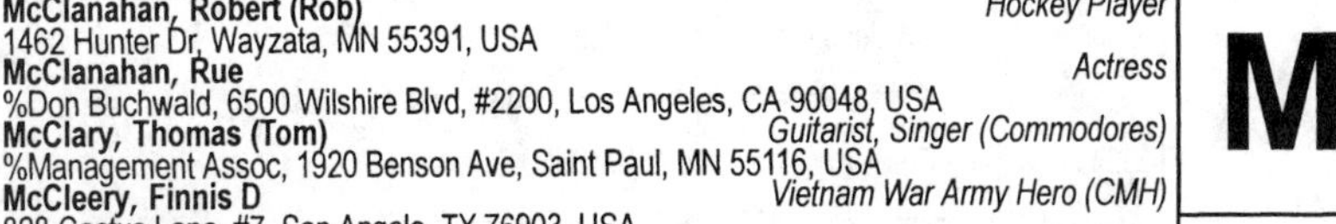

McClanahan, Robert (Rob) *Hockey Player*
1462 Hunter Dr, Wayzata, MN 55391, USA
McClanahan, Rue *Actress*
%Don Buchwald, 6500 Wilshire Blvd, #2200, Los Angeles, CA 90048, USA
McClary, Thomas (Tom) *Guitarist, Singer (Commodores)*
%Management Assoc, 1920 Benson Ave, Saint Paul, MN 55116, USA
McCleery, Finnis D *Vietnam War Army Hero (CMH)*
828 Cactus Lane, #7, San Angelo, TX 76903, USA
McClellan, Scott *Government Official*
%White House, 1600 Pennsylvania Ave NW, Washington, DC 20500, USA
McClenathan, Cory *Auto Racing Driver*
%MBNA Motorsports, 1198 Knollwood Circle, Anaheim, CA 92801, USA
McClinton, Delbert *Singer, Songwriter*
%Harriet Sternberg Mgmt, 4530 Gloria Ave, Encino, CA 91436, USA
McCloskey, Paul N (Pete), Jr *Representative, CA*
305 Grant Ave, Palo Alto, CA 94306, USA
McClure, James A *Senator, ID*
9440 W Pebble Brook Lane, Boise, ID 83714, USA
McClurg, Edie *Actress*
3306 Wonderview Plaza, Los Angeles, CA 90068, USA
McClurg, Robert (Bob) *WW II Marine Corps Air Force Hero*
1646 New Seneca Turnpike, Skaneateles, NY 13152, USA
McClurkin, Donnie *Singer*
%Sierra Mgmt, 107 Hemlock Court, Hendonsonville, TN 37205, USA
McColl, Hugh L, Jr *Financier*
%Bank of America Corp, 100 N Tryon St, Charlotte, NC 28255, USA
McColl, William F (Bill), Jr *Football Player*
5166 Chelsea St, La Jolla, CA 92037, USA
McColm, Matt *Actor*
10061 Riverside Dr, #722, Toluca Lake, CA 91602, USA
McComb, Heather *Actress*
%Raw Talent, 9615 Brighton Way, #300, Beverly Hills, CA 90210, USA
McConaughey, Matthew *Actor*
%The Firm, 9100 Wilshire Blvd, #100W, Beverly Hills, CA 90210, USA
McConnell-Serio, Suzie *Basketball Player*
1324 Chartwell Dr, Upper Saint Clair, PA 15241, USA
McCoo, Marilyn *Singer (Fifth Dimension), Actress*
2639 Lavery Court, #5, Newbury Park, CA 91320, USA
McCook, John *Actor*
10245 Briarwood, Los Angeles, CA 90077, USA
McCool, Richard M, Jr *WW II Navy Hero (CMH)*
PO Box 11347, Bainbridge Island, WA 98110, USA
McCord, Darris *Football Player*
6160 W Surrey Road, Bloomfield Hills, MI 48301, USA
McCord, Joe Milton *Biochemist*
%University of Colorado, Waring Institute, 4200 E 9th Ave, Denver, CO 80262, USA
McCord, Kent *Actor*
1738 N Orange Grove Ave, Los Angeles, CA 90046, USA
McCorkindale, Douglas *Businessman*
%Gannett Co, 1100 Wilson Blvd, Arlington, VA 22209, USA
McCormack, Catherine *Actress*
120 Riverside Dr, #7G, New York, NY 10024, USA
McCormack, Eric *Actor*
%Endeavor Talent Agency, 9701 Wilshire Blvd, #1000, Beverly Hills, CA 90212, USA
McCormack, Mary *Actress*
PO Box 67335, Los Angeles, CA 90067, USA
McCormack, Michael J (Mike) *Football Player, Coach, Executive*
%Seattle Seahawks, 11220 NE 53rd St, Kirkland, WA 98033, USA
McCormack, Patty *Actress, Model*
4360 Tujunga Ave, Studio City, CA 91604, USA
McCormack, Will *Actor*
%United Talent Agency, 9560 Wilshire Blvd, #500, Beverly Hills, CA 90212, USA
McCormick, Maureen *Actress, Singer*
32118 Beach Lake Lane, Westlake Village, CA 91361, USA
McCormick, Michael F (Mike) *Baseball Player*
1600 Morganton Road, #U9, Pinehurst, NC 28374, USA
McCormick, Patricia J (Pat) *Diver*
92 Riversea Road, Seal Beach, CA 90740, USA
McCorvey, Norma *Litigant (Jane Roe vs Wade)*
%Roe No More Ministry, PO Box 550626, Dallas, TX 75355, USA
McCourt, Frank *Writer*
%Charles Scribner's Sons, 866 3rd Ave, New York, NY 10022, USA
McCoury, Del *Singer*
%RS Entertainment, 329 Rockland Road, Hendersonville, TN 37075, USA
McCovey, Willie L *Baseball Player*
PO Box 620342, Woodside, CA 94062, USA
McCowen, Alec *Actor*
%Conway Van Gelder Robinson, 18-21 Jermyn St, London SW1Y 6NB, England

M

McCoy, John B *Financier*
%Corillian, 3400 NW John Olsen Place, Hillsboro, OR 97124, USA
McCoy, Matt *Actor*
%Artists Agency, 1180 S Beverly Dr, #301, Los Angeles, CA 90035, USA
McCracken, Paul W *Economist, Government Official*
2564 Hawthorne Road, Ann Arbor, MI 48104, USA
McCrane, Paul *Actor*
%VOX, 5670 Wilshire Blvd, #820, Los Angeles, CA 90036, USA
McCray, Nikki *Basketball Player*
288 S Center St, #6, Collierville, TN 38017, USA
McCrea, John *Singer (Cake), Songwriter*
%Absolute Artists, 8490 W Sunset Blvd, #403, West Hollywood, CA 90069, USA
McCready, Mike *Guitarist (Pearl Jam)*
%Annie Ohayon Media Relations, 525 Broadway, #600, New York, NY 10012, USA
McCready, Mindy *Singer*
%Creative Artists Agency, 3310 W End Ave, #500, Nashville, TN 37203, USA
McCrimmon, Brad *Hockey Player*
%Atlanta Thrashers, Philips Arena, 13 South Ave SE, Atlanta, GA 30315, USA
McCrory, Milton (Milt) *Boxer*
%Escot Boxing Enterprises, 19244 Bretton Dr, Detroit, MI 48223, USA
McCulley, Michael J *Astronaut*
1112 Tall Pines Dr, Friendswood, TX 77546, USA
McCulloch, Ed *Auto Racing Driver*
1397 Cherry Tree Road, Avon, IN 46123, USA
McCullough, Colleen *Writer*
PO Box 333, Norfolk Island NSW 2899, Australia
McCullough, David *Writer*
%Janklow & Nesbit Assoc, 445 Park Ave, #1300, New York, NY 10022, USA
McCullough, Earl *Football Player, Track Athlete*
2108 Santa Fe Ave, Long Beach, CA 90810, USA
McCullough, Julie *Model, Actress*
8033 Sunset Blvd, #353, West Hollywood, CA 90046, USA
McCullough, Wayne *Boxer*
601 Hermosa Canyon Dr, Las Vegas, NV 89145, USA
McCumber, Mark *Golfer, Sportscaster*
53 Ponte Vedra Blvd, Ponte Vedra Beach, FL 32082, USA
McCurry, Mike *Government Leader, Journalist*
%Cable News Network, News Dept, 1050 Techwood Dr NW, Atlanta, GA 30318, USA
McCutcheon, Martine *Actress, Singer*
%P F D, Drury House, 34-43 Russell St, London WC2B 5HA, England
McDaniel Singleton, Mildred *Track Athlete*
211 W Poppy Field Dr, Altadena, CA 91001, USA
McDaniel, James *Actor*
%Innovative Artists, 1505 10th St, Santa Monica, CA 90401, USA
McDaniel, Lyndall D (Lindy) *Baseball Player*
RR 2 Box 355, Hollis, OK 73550, USA
McDaniels, Darryl (Darryl M) *Rap Artist (Run-DMC)*
%Entertainment Artists, 2409 21st Ave S, #100, Nashville, TN 37212, USA
McDermott, Dylan *Actor*
201 S Rockingham Ave, Los Angeles, CA 90049, USA
McDermott, R Terrance (Terry) *Speed Skater*
5078 Chainbridge, Bloomfield Hills, MI 48304, USA
McDiarmid, Ian *Actor*
Wood Lane, London W12 7RJ, England
McDivitt, James A (Jim) *Astronaut, Air Force General*
3530 E Calle Puerta den Acero, Tucson, AZ 85718, USA
McDonagh, Martin *Writer*
%Creative Artists Agency, 9830 Wilshire Blvd, Beverly Hills, CA 90212, USA
McDonald, Audra *Actress, Singer*
%Gersh Agency, 232 N Canon Dr, Beverly Hills, CA 90210, USA
McDonald, Country Joe *Singer, Guitarist*
PO Box 7054, Berkeley, CA 94707, USA
McDonald, David L *Navy Admiral*
PO Box 45214, Jacksonville, FL 32232, USA
McDonald, Gregory C *Writer*
%Arthur Greene, 101 Park Ave, New York, NY 10178, USA
McDonald, Jiggs *Sportscaster*
5272 NW 106th Dr, Coral Springs, FL 33076, USA
McDonald, Lanny *Hockey Player, Executive*
%CHA, 2424 University NW, Calgary AB T2N 3Y9, Canada
McDonald, Michael *Singer, Songwriter*
%Lippin Group, 369 Lexington Ave, #1100, New York, NY 10017, USA
McDonald, Richie *Singer (Lonestar)*
PO Box 128648, Nashville, TN 37212, USA
McDonald, Thomas F (Tommy) *Football Player*
537 W Valley Forge Road, King of Prussia, PA 19406, USA
McDonell, R Terry *Editor*
%US Weekly, Editorial Dept, 1290 Ave of Americas, New York, NY 10104, USA

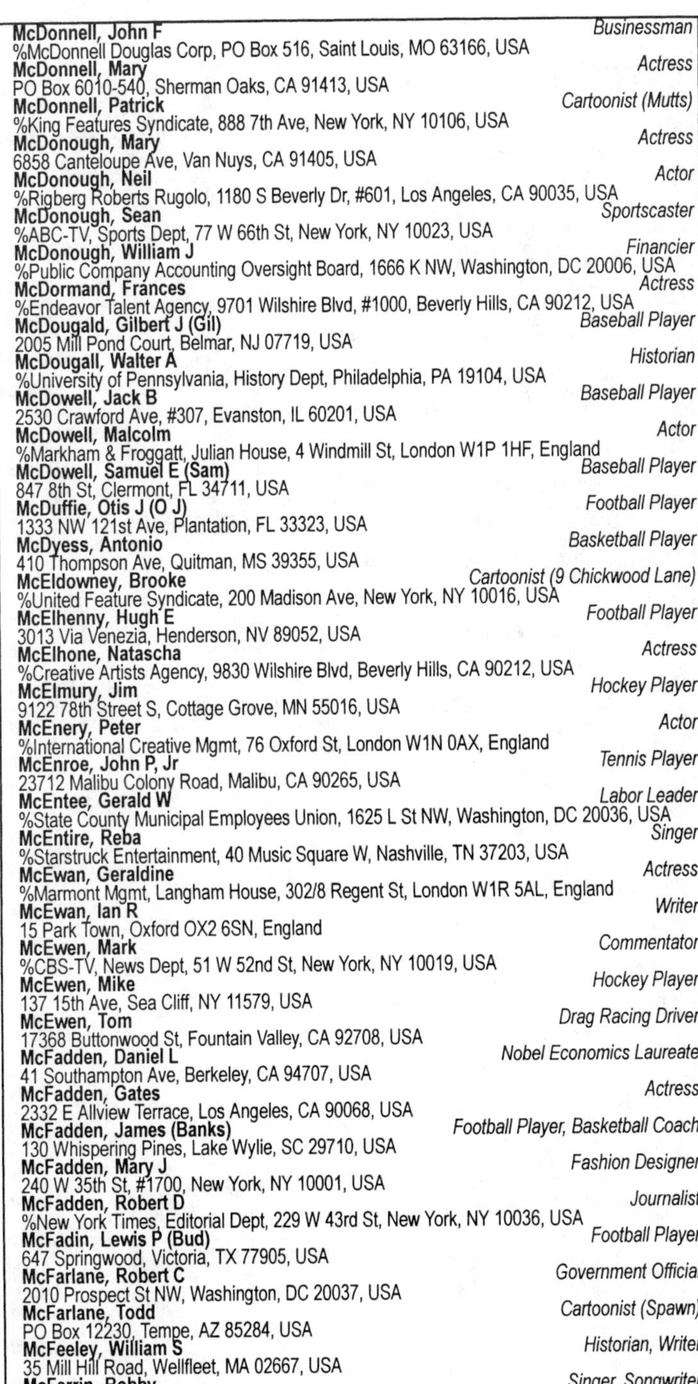

McDonnell, John F *Businessman*
%McDonnell Douglas Corp, PO Box 516, Saint Louis, MO 63166, USA
McDonnell, Mary *Actress*
PO Box 6010-540, Sherman Oaks, CA 91413, USA
McDonnell, Patrick *Cartoonist (Mutts)*
%King Features Syndicate, 888 7th Ave, New York, NY 10106, USA
McDonough, Mary *Actress*
6858 Canteloupe Ave, Van Nuys, CA 91405, USA
McDonough, Neil *Actor*
%Rigberg Roberts Rugolo, 1180 S Beverly Dr, #601, Los Angeles, CA 90035, USA
McDonough, Sean *Sportscaster*
%ABC-TV, Sports Dept, 77 W 66th St, New York, NY 10023, USA
McDonough, William J *Financier*
%Public Company Accounting Oversight Board, 1666 K NW, Washington, DC 20006, USA
McDormand, Frances *Actress*
%Endeavor Talent Agency, 9701 Wilshire Blvd, #1000, Beverly Hills, CA 90212, USA
McDougald, Gilbert J (Gil) *Baseball Player*
2005 Mill Pond Court, Belmar, NJ 07719, USA
McDougall, Walter A *Historian*
%University of Pennsylvania, History Dept, Philadelphia, PA 19104, USA
McDowell, Jack B *Baseball Player*
2530 Crawford Ave, #307, Evanston, IL 60201, USA
McDowell, Malcolm *Actor*
%Markham & Froggatt, Julian House, 4 Windmill St, London W1P 1HF, England
McDowell, Samuel E (Sam) *Baseball Player*
847 8th St, Clermont, FL 34711, USA
McDuffie, Otis J (O J) *Football Player*
1333 NW 121st Ave, Plantation, FL 33323, USA
McDyess, Antonio *Basketball Player*
410 Thompson Ave, Quitman, MS 39355, USA
McEldowney, Brooke *Cartoonist (9 Chickwood Lane)*
%United Feature Syndicate, 200 Madison Ave, New York, NY 10016, USA
McElhenny, Hugh E *Football Player*
3013 Via Venezia, Henderson, NV 89052, USA
McElhone, Natascha *Actress*
%Creative Artists Agency, 9830 Wilshire Blvd, Beverly Hills, CA 90212, USA
McElmury, Jim *Hockey Player*
9122 78th Street S, Cottage Grove, MN 55016, USA
McEnery, Peter *Actor*
%International Creative Mgmt, 76 Oxford St, London W1N 0AX, England
McEnroe, John P, Jr *Tennis Player*
23712 Malibu Colony Road, Malibu, CA 90265, USA
McEntee, Gerald W *Labor Leader*
%State County Municipal Employees Union, 1625 L St NW, Washington, DC 20036, USA
McEntire, Reba *Singer*
%Starstruck Entertainment, 40 Music Square W, Nashville, TN 37203, USA
McEwan, Geraldine *Actress*
%Marmont Mgmt, Langham House, 302/8 Regent St, London W1R 5AL, England
McEwan, Ian R *Writer*
15 Park Town, Oxford OX2 6SN, England
McEwen, Mark *Commentator*
%CBS-TV, News Dept, 51 W 52nd St, New York, NY 10019, USA
McEwen, Mike *Hockey Player*
137 15th Ave, Sea Cliff, NY 11579, USA
McEwen, Tom *Drag Racing Driver*
17368 Buttonwood St, Fountain Valley, CA 92708, USA
McFadden, Daniel L *Nobel Economics Laureate*
41 Southampton Ave, Berkeley, CA 94707, USA
McFadden, Gates *Actress*
2332 E Allview Terrace, Los Angeles, CA 90068, USA
McFadden, James (Banks) *Football Player, Basketball Coach*
130 Whispering Pines, Lake Wylie, SC 29710, USA
McFadden, Mary J *Fashion Designer*
240 W 35th St, #1700, New York, NY 10001, USA
McFadden, Robert D *Journalist*
%New York Times, Editorial Dept, 229 W 43rd St, New York, NY 10036, USA
McFadin, Lewis P (Bud) *Football Player*
647 Springwood, Victoria, TX 77905, USA
McFarlane, Robert C *Government Official*
2010 Prospect St NW, Washington, DC 20037, USA
McFarlane, Todd *Cartoonist (Spawn)*
PO Box 12230, Tempe, AZ 85284, USA
McFeeley, William S *Historian, Writer*
35 Mill Hill Road, Wellfleet, MA 02667, USA
McFerrin, Bobby *Singer, Songwriter*
%Original Artists, 826 Broadway, #400, New York, NY 10003, USA
McGahee, Willis *Football Player*
%Buffalo Bills, 1 Bills Dr, Orchard Park, NY 14127, USA

M

McGahern, John *Writer*
%Faber & Faber, 3 Queen Square, London WC1N 3AU, England
McGann, Michelle *Golfer*
1200 Singer Dr, Riviera Beach, FL 33404, USA
McGann, Paul *Actor*
%Marina Martin, 12/13 Poland St, London W1V 3DE, England
McGarity, Vernon *WW II Army Hero (CMH)*
6901 Andrews Road, Bartlett, TN 38135, USA
McGarry, Steve *Cartoonist (Pop Culture)*
%United Feature Syndicate, 200 Madison Ave, New York, NY 10016, USA
McGavin, Darren *Actor*
PO Box 2939, Beverly Hills, CA 90213, USA
McGeady, Sister Mary Rose *Social Activist*
%Covenant House, 460 W 41st St, New York, NY 10036, USA
McGee, Michael B (Mike) *Football Player*
%University of South Carolina, Athletic Dept, Columbia, SC 29208, USA
McGee, Pamela (Pam) *Basketball Player*
%Los Angeles Sparks, Staples Center, 1111 S Figueroa St, Los Angeles, CA 90015, USA
McGee, Willie D *Baseball Player*
2081 Lupine Road, Hercules, CA 94547, USA
McGegan, Nicholas *Conductor*
%Schwalbe Partners, 170 E 61st St, #5N, New York, NY 10021, USA
McGill, Billy *Basketball Player*
5129 W 58th Place, Los Angeles, CA 90056, USA
McGill, Bruce *Actor*
3920 East Blvd, Los Angeles, CA 90066, USA
McGillis, Kelly *Actress*
%Kelly's Caribbean Bar & Grill, 303 Whitehead St, Key West, FL 33040, USA
McGinest, Willie *Football Player*
2001 Marina Dr, #211, Quincy, MA 02171, USA
McGinley, John C *Actor*
%Innovative Artists, 1505 10th St, Santa Monica, CA 90401, USA
McGinley, Ted *Actor*
14951 Alva Dr, Pacific Palisades, CA 90272, USA
McGinn, Bernard J *Theologian*
5702 Kenwood Ave, Chicago, IL 60637, USA
McGinnis, Dave *Football Coach*
%Arizona Cardinals, PO Box 888, Phoenix, AZ 85001, USA
McGinnis, George *Basketball Player*
11245 Marlin Road, Indianapolis, IN 46239, USA
McGinnis, Joe *Writer*
%Janklow & Nesbit, 445 Park Ave, #1300, New York, NY 10022, USA
McGinty, John J, III *Vietnam War Marine Corps Hero (CMH)*
51 Barbara Lane, Hudson, NH 03051, USA
McGirt, James (Buddy) *Boxer*
195 Suffolk Ave, Brentwood, NY 11717, USA
McGlockin, Jon *Basketball Player*
5281 State Road, #83, Heartland, WI 53029, USA
McGlockton, Chester *Football Player*
6930 S Perth St, Aurora, CO 80016, USA
McGlynn, Dick *Hockey Player*
17 Butternut Ave, Peabody, MA 01960, USA
McGlynn, Pat *Guitarist (Bay City Rollers)*
27 Preston Grange, Preston Pans E, Lothian, Scotland
McGoohan, Patrick *Actor*
523 Chapala Dr, Pacific Palisades, CA 90272, USA
McGoon, Dwight C *Surgeon*
211 2nd St NW, #2016, Rochester, MN 55901, USA
McGovern, Elizabeth *Actress*
17319 Magnolia Blvd, Encino, CA 91316, USA
McGovern, George S *Senator, SD*
%FAO, Via delle Terme di Carachkka, 00100 Rome, Italy
McGovern, Maureen *Singer*
%Agency for Performing Arts, 9200 Sunset Blvd, #900, Los Angeles, CA 90069, USA
McGowan, Charles E *Religious Leader*
%Presbyterian Church in America, 1852 Century Place, Atlanta, GA 30345, USA
McGowan, Rose *Actress*
%Fulton & Meyer, 17530 Ventura Blvd, #201, Encino, CA 91316, USA
McGrady, Tracy *Basketball Player*
9209 Charles Limpus Road, Orlando, FL 32836, USA
McGrath, Eugene R *Businessman*
%Consolidated Edison, 4 Irving Place, New York, NY 10003, USA
McGrath, James *Geneticist*
%Yale University, Genetics Dept, New Haven, CT 06520, USA
McGrath, Jeremy *Motorcycle Racing Rider*
%American Motorcycle Assn, 13515 Yarmouth Dr, Pickerington, OH 43147, USA
McGrath, Mark *Singer (Sugar Ray)*
%Pinnacle Ent, 30 Glenn St, White Plains, NY 10603, USA

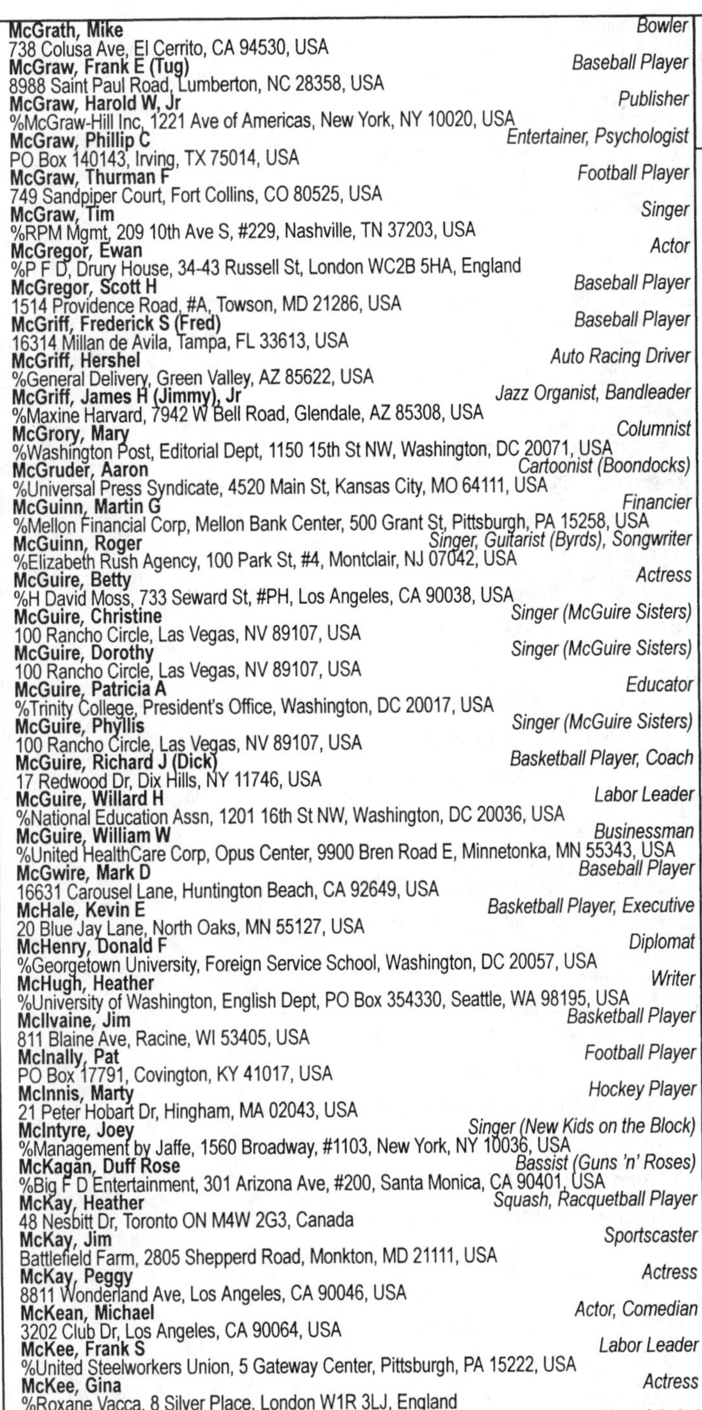

McGrath, Mike *Bowler*
738 Colusa Ave, El Cerrito, CA 94530, USA
McGraw, Frank E (Tug) *Baseball Player*
8988 Saint Paul Road, Lumberton, NC 28358, USA
McGraw, Harold W, Jr *Publisher*
%McGraw-Hill Inc, 1221 Ave of Americas, New York, NY 10020, USA
McGraw, Phillip C *Entertainer, Psychologist*
PO Box 140143, Irving, TX 75014, USA
McGraw, Thurman F *Football Player*
749 Sandpiper Court, Fort Collins, CO 80525, USA
McGraw, Tim *Singer*
%RPM Mgmt, 209 10th Ave S, #229, Nashville, TN 37203, USA
McGregor, Ewan *Actor*
%P F D, Drury House, 34-43 Russell St, London WC2B 5HA, England
McGregor, Scott H *Baseball Player*
1514 Providence Road, #A, Towson, MD 21286, USA
McGriff, Frederick S (Fred) *Baseball Player*
16314 Millan de Avila, Tampa, FL 33613, USA
McGriff, Hershel *Auto Racing Driver*
%General Delivery, Green Valley, AZ 85622, USA
McGriff, James H (Jimmy), Jr *Jazz Organist, Bandleader*
%Maxine Harvard, 7942 W Bell Road, Glendale, AZ 85308, USA
McGrory, Mary *Columnist*
%Washington Post, Editorial Dept, 1150 15th St NW, Washington, DC 20071, USA
McGruder, Aaron *Cartoonist (Boondocks)*
%Universal Press Syndicate, 4520 Main St, Kansas City, MO 64111, USA
McGuinn, Martin G *Financier*
%Mellon Financial Corp, Mellon Bank Center, 500 Grant St, Pittsburgh, PA 15258, USA
McGuinn, Roger *Singer, Guitarist (Byrds), Songwriter*
%Elizabeth Rush Agency, 100 Park St, #4, Montclair, NJ 07042, USA
McGuire, Betty *Actress*
%H David Moss, 733 Seward St, #PH, Los Angeles, CA 90038, USA
McGuire, Christine *Singer (McGuire Sisters)*
100 Rancho Circle, Las Vegas, NV 89107, USA
McGuire, Dorothy *Singer (McGuire Sisters)*
100 Rancho Circle, Las Vegas, NV 89107, USA
McGuire, Patricia A *Educator*
%Trinity College, President's Office, Washington, DC 20017, USA
McGuire, Phyllis *Singer (McGuire Sisters)*
100 Rancho Circle, Las Vegas, NV 89107, USA
McGuire, Richard J (Dick) *Basketball Player, Coach*
17 Redwood Dr, Dix Hills, NY 11746, USA
McGuire, Willard H *Labor Leader*
%National Education Assn, 1201 16th St NW, Washington, DC 20036, USA
McGuire, William W *Businessman*
%United HealthCare Corp, Opus Center, 9900 Bren Road E, Minnetonka, MN 55343, USA
McGwire, Mark D *Baseball Player*
16631 Carousel Lane, Huntington Beach, CA 92649, USA
McHale, Kevin E *Basketball Player, Executive*
20 Blue Jay Lane, North Oaks, MN 55127, USA
McHenry, Donald F *Diplomat*
%Georgetown University, Foreign Service School, Washington, DC 20057, USA
McHugh, Heather *Writer*
%University of Washington, English Dept, PO Box 354330, Seattle, WA 98195, USA
McIlvaine, Jim *Basketball Player*
811 Blaine Ave, Racine, WI 53405, USA
McInally, Pat *Football Player*
PO Box 17791, Covington, KY 41017, USA
McInnis, Marty *Hockey Player*
21 Peter Hobart Dr, Hingham, MA 02043, USA
McIntyre, Joey *Singer (New Kids on the Block)*
%Management by Jaffe, 1560 Broadway, #1103, New York, NY 10036, USA
McKagan, Duff Rose *Bassist (Guns 'n' Roses)*
%Big F D Entertainment, 301 Arizona Ave, #200, Santa Monica, CA 90401, USA
McKay, Heather *Squash, Racquetball Player*
48 Nesbitt Dr, Toronto ON M4W 2G3, Canada
McKay, Jim *Sportscaster*
Battlefield Farm, 2805 Shepperd Road, Monkton, MD 21111, USA
McKay, Peggy *Actress*
8811 Wonderland Ave, Los Angeles, CA 90046, USA
McKean, Michael *Actor, Comedian*
3202 Club Dr, Los Angeles, CA 90064, USA
McKee, Frank S *Labor Leader*
%United Steelworkers Union, 5 Gateway Center, Pittsburgh, PA 15222, USA
McKee, Gina *Actress*
%Roxane Vacca, 8 Silver Place, London W1R 3LJ, England
McKee, Kinnaird R *Navy Admiral*
7101 Bay Front Dr, #608, Annapolis, MD 21403, USA

McKee, Maria *Singer*
%Geffen Records, 10900 Wilshire Blvd, #1000, Los Angeles, CA 90024, USA
McKee, Theodore A *Judge*
%US Appeals Court, US Courthouse, 601 Market St, Philadelphia, PA 19106, USA
McKee, Todd *Actor*
611 N Flores St, #2, West Hollywood, CA 90048, USA
McKeever, Marlin *Football Player*
4000 E 2nd St, Long Beach, CA 90803, USA
McKellar, Danica *Actress*
10635 Santa Monica Blvd, #130, Los Angeles, CA 90025, USA
McKellen, Ian *Actor*
25 Earl's Terrace, London W8, England
McKenna, David (Dave) *Jazz Pianist*
%Thomas Cassidy, 11761 E Speedway Blvd, Tucson, AZ 85748, USA
McKenna, T P *Actor*
28 Claverley Grove, London N3 2DH, England
McKenna, Virginia *Actress*
8 Buckfast Court, Runcorn, Cheshire WA7 1QJ, England
McKenney, Donald H (Don) *Hockey Player*
16 Edgewater Dr, Norton, MA 02766, USA
McKennitt, Lorena *Singer, Songwriter*
%Quinlan Road, PO Box 933, Stratford ON N5A 7M3, Canada
McKennon, Keith R *Businessman*
6079 N Paradise View Dr, Paradise Valley, AZ 85253, USA
McKenzie, Andrew *Labor Leader*
%Leather Goods Plastics Novelty Union, 265 W 14th St, New York, NY 10011, USA
McKenzie, Kevin *Ballet Dancer*
%American Ballet Theatre, 890 Broadway, New York, NY 10003, USA
McKenzie, Reginald (Reggie) *Football Player*
3174 Outing Court, Green Bay, WI 54313, USA
McKenzie, Vashti *Religious Leader*
%Payne Memorial Church, 1714 Madison Ave, #16, Baltimore, MD 21217, USA
McKeon, Doug *Actor*
818 6th St, #202, Santa Monica, CA 90403, USA
McKeon, John A (Jack) *Baseball Player, Manager*
13453 Luna Dr, Redding, CA 96003, USA
McKeon, Matt *Soccer Player*
%Kansas City Wizards, 2 Arrowhead Dr, Kansas City, MO 64129, USA
McKeon, Nancy *Actress*
PO Box 6778, Burbank, CA 91510, USA
McKeown, Bob *Commentator*
%CBS-TV, News Dept, 51 W 52nd St, New York, NY 10019, USA
McKeown, Leslie (Les) *Singer (Bay City Rollers)*
%Brian Gannon Mgmt, PO Box 106, Rochdale OL16 4HW, England
McKeown, M Margaret *Judge*
%US Court of Appeals, US Courthouse, 1010 5th Ave, Seattle, WA 98104, USA
McKernan, John R, Jr *Governor, ME*
77 Sanderson Road, Cumberland Foreside, ME 04110, USA
McKiernan, David *Army General*
Commanding General, 3rd Army, Fort McPherson, GA 30330, USA
McKinley, John *Rower*
952 Bloomfield Village, Auburn Hills, MI 48326, USA
McKinney, Kurt *Actor*
5003 Tilden Ave, #206, Sherman Oaks, CA 91423, USA
McKinney, Richard (Rick) *Archery Athlete*
7659 Kavooras Dr, Sacramento, CA 95831, USA
McKinney, Tamara *Alpine Skier*
4935 Parkers Mill Road, Lexington, KY 40513, USA
McKinnie, Bryant *Football Player*
%Minnesota Vikings, 9520 Viking Dr, Eden Prairie, MN 55344, USA
McKinnon, Bruce *Editorial Cartoonist*
%Halifax Herald, Editorial Dept, PO Box 610, Halifax NS B3J 2T2, Canada
McKinnon, Dan *Hockey Player*
610 E River Dr, Warroad, MN 56763, USA
McKissock, Gary S *Marine Corps General*
Deputy CofS for Installations/Logistics, HqUSMC, 2 Navy St, Washington, 20380, USA
McKnight, Brian *Singer, Songwriter*
%William Morris Agency, 151 El Camino Dr, Beverly Hills, CA 90212, USA
McKnight, Clarence E, Jr *Army General*
1624 Linway Park Dr, McLean, VA 22101, USA
McKnight, Steven L *Molecular Biologist*
3717 Euclid Ave, Dallas, TX 75205, USA
McKuen, Rod *Writer, Singer, Songwiter*
PO Box 2783, Los Angeles, CA 90078, USA
McKusick, Victor A *Geneticist*
221 Morthway, Baltimore, MD 21218, USA
McLachlan, Sarah *Singer, Songwriter*
%Nettwerk Mgmt, 1650 W 2nd Ave, Vancouver BC V6J 4R3, Canada

McLafferty, Fred W *Chemist*
103 Needham Place, Ithaca, NY 14850, USA
McLaglen, Andrew V *Movie Director*
%Stanmore Productions, PO Box 1056, Friday Harbor, WA 98250, USA
McLain, Dennis D (Denny) *Baseball Player*
276 Redmaple Lane, Brighton, MI 48116, USA
McLane, James P (Jimmy), Jr *Swimmer*
85 Pinckney St, Boston, MA 02114, USA
McLaughlin, Ann Dore *Secretary, Labor*
%Urban Institute of Washington, 2100 M St NW, Washington, DC 20037, USA
McLaughlin, John *Singer, Songwriter, Guitarist*
%International Music Network, 278 S Main St, #400, Gloucester, MA 01930, USA
McLaughlin, John J *Commentator*
%Oliver Productions, 1211 Connecticut Ave NW, Washington, DC 20036, USA
McLaughlin, Mike *Auto Racing Driver*
%Joe Gibbs Racing, 13415 Reese Blvd W, Huntersville, NC 28078, USA
McLean, A J *Singer (Backstreet Boys), Actor*
%The Firm, 9100 Wilshire Blvd, #100W, Beverly Hills, CA 90210, USA
McLean, Barney *Skier*
11745 W 66th Place, #D, Arvada, CO 80004, USA
McLean, Don *Singer, Songwriter*
PO Box 102, Castine, ME 04421, USA
McLean, John L (Jackie), Jr *Jazz Saxophonist, Composer*
261 Ridgefield St, Hartford, CT 06112, USA
McLemore, LaMonte *Singer (Fifth Dimension)*
%Sterling/Winters, 10877 Wilshire Blvd, #15, Los Angeles, CA 90024, USA
McLerie, Allyn Ann *Actress, Dancer*
3344 Campanil Dr, Santa Barbara, CA 93109, USA
McLish, Rachel *Actress, Bodybuilder*
PO Box 1690, Rancho Mirage, CA 92270, USA
McMahon, Ed *Entertainer*
1200 Crest Court, Beverly Hills, CA 90210, USA
McMahon, James R (Jim) *Football Player*
34 Bridlewood Road, Northbrook, IL 60062, USA
McMahon, Vincent K *Wrestling Executive, Promoter*
47 Hurtingham Dr, Greenwich, CT 06831, USA
McMenamin, Mark *Geologist*
%Mount Holyoke College, Geology Dept, South Hadley, MA 01075, USA
McMichael, Steve D *Football Player*
4250 N Marine Dr, #1027, Chicago, IL 60613, USA
McMichen, Robert S *Labor Leader*
%International Typographical Union, PO Box 157, Colorado Springs, CO 80901, USA
McMillan, Nate *Basketball Player, Coach*
2520 39th Ave E, Seattle, WA 98112, USA
McMillan, Terry *Writer*
PO Box 2408, Danville, CA 94526, USA
McMillan, William (Bill) *Marksman*
1930 Sandstone Vista, Encinitas, CA 92024, USA
McMillen, C Thomas (Tom) *Basketball Player; Representative, MD*
1167 Jeffrey Dr, Crofton, MD 21114, USA
McMonagle, Donald R *Astronaut*
46 SW Riverway Blvd, Palm City, FL 34990, USA
McMullen, Curtis T *Mathematician*
%Harvard University, Science Center, Cambridge, MA 02138, USA
McMullin, Ernan V *Philosopher*
PO Box 1066, Notre Dame, IN 46556, USA
McMurray, W Grant *Religious Leader*
%Reorganized Church of Latter Day Saints, PO Box 1059, Independence, MO 64051, USA
McMurtry, James *Singer, Songwriter*
%High Road, 751 Bridgeway, #300, Sausalito, CA 94965, USA
McMurtry, Larry *Writer*
PO Box 552, Archer City, TX 76351, USA
McNabb, Donovan *Football Player*
100 Springdale Road A-3, #270, Cherry Hill, NJ 08003, USA
McNair, Barbara *Singer*
%Thomas Cassidy, 11761 E Speedway Blvd, Tucson, AZ 85748, USA
McNair, Robert E *Governor, SC*
RR 2 Box 310, Columbia, SC 29212, USA
McNair, Steve *Football Player*
%Tennessee Titans, 460 Great Circle Road, Nashville, TN 37228, USA
McNally, Stephen (Ste) *Singer, Guitarist (BBMak)*
%Day Time, Crown House, 225 Kensington High St, London W8 8SA, England
McNally, Terrence *Writer, Actor*
%William Morris Agency, 1325 Ave of Americas, New York, NY 10019, USA
McNamara, Brian *Actor*
11730 National Blvd, #19, Los Angeles, CA 90064, USA
McNamara, Eileen *Journalist*
%Boston Globe, Editorial Dept, 135 W T Morrissey Blvd, Dorchester, MA 02125, USA

M

McNamara - McWherter

McNamara, John F *Baseball Player, Manager*
1206 Beech Hill Road, Brentwood, TN 37027, USA
McNamara, Julianne L *Gymnast, Actress*
%Barry Axelrod, 2236 Encinitas Blvd, #A, Encinitas, CA 92024, USA
McNamara, Robert S *Secretary, Defense*
700 New Hampshire Ave NW, #101, Washington, DC 20037, USA
McNamara, William *Actor*
199 Maple Ave, Victor, NY 14564, USA
McNaughton, Robert F, Jr *Computer Scientist*
2511 15th St, Troy, NY 12180, USA
McNealy, Scott G *Businessman*
%Sun Microsystems, 901 San Antonio Road, Palo Alto, CA 94303, USA
McNeil, Frederick A (Fred) *Football Player*
9667 W Olympic Blvd, #5, Beverly Hills, CA 90212, USA
McNeil, Freeman *Football Player*
%A+ Technology Solutions, 4177 Merrick Road, Massapequa, NY 11758, USA
McNeil, Kate *Actress*
1743 N Dillon St, Los Angeles, CA 90026, USA
McNeil, Lori *Tennis Player*
%Int'l Mgmt Group, 1 Erieview Plaza, 1360 E 9th St, #1300, Cleveland, OH 44114, USA
McNeill, Robert Duncan *Actor*
%Susan Smith, 121A N San Vicente Blvd, Beverly Hills, CA 90211, USA
McNeill, W Donald (Don) *Tennis Player*
2165 15th Ave, Vero Beach, FL 32960, USA
McNerney, David H *Vietnam War Army Hero (CMH)*
20322 New Moon Trail, Crosby, TX 77532, USA
McNichol, Kristy *Actress*
12001 Ventura Blvd, #201, Studio City, CA 91604, USA
McPartland, Marian M *Jazz Pianist*
%Abby Hoffer, 223 1/2 E 48th St, New York, NY 10017, USA
McPeak, Holly *Volleyball Player*
%Women's Pro Volleyball Assn, 840 Apollo St, #204, El Segundo, CA 90245, USA
McPeak, Merrill A (Tony) *Air Force General*
17360 Grandview Court, Lake Oswego, OR 97034, USA
McPhee, John A *Writer*
475 Drake's Corner Road, Princeton, NJ 08540, USA
McPherson, Don *Football Player*
360 Huntington Ave, Boston, MA 02115, USA
McPherson, Harry C, Jr *Government Official*
10213 Montgomery Ave, Kensington, MD 20895, USA
McPherson, James M *Historian*
15 Randall Road, Princeton, NJ 08540, USA
McPherson, John *Cartoonist (Close to Home)*
%Universal Press Syndicate, 4520 Main St, Kansas City, MO 64111, USA
McPherson, M Peter *Educator*
%Michigan State University, President's Office, East Lansing, MI 48824, USA
McPherson, Rolf K *Religious Leader*
%Church of Foursquare Gospel, 1100 Glendale Blvd, Los Angeles, CA 90026, USA
McQuagg, Sam *Auto Racing Driver*
8886 Hamilton Road, Midland, GA 31820, USA
McQueen, Alexander *Fashion Designer*
%House of Givenchy, 3 Ave Saint George, 75008 Paris, France
McQueen, Chad *Actor*
8306 Wilshire Blvd, #438, Beverly Hills, CA 90211, USA
McRae, Harold O (Hal) *Baseball Player, Manager*
2431 Landing Circle, Bradenton, FL 34209, USA
McRaney, Gerald *Actor*
1012 Royal St, New Orleans, LA 70116, USA
McShane, Ian *Actor*
%International Creative Mgmt, 76 Oxford St, London W1N 0AX, England
McShann, James C (Jay) *Jazz Pianist*
%Ozark Talent, 718 Schwarz Road, Lawrence, KS 66049, USA
McTeer, Janet *Actress*
%Propaganda Films Mgmt, 1741 Ivar Ave, Los Angeles, CA 90028, USA
McTeer, Robert D, Jr *Financier, Government Official*
%Federal Reserve Bank, 2200 N Pearl St, Dallas, TX 75201, USA
McTiernan, John *Movie Director*
%The Firm, 9100 Wilshire Blvd, #100W, Beverly Hills, CA 90210, USA
McVicar, Daniel *Actor*
1704 Oak St S, Santa Monica, CA 90405, USA
McVie, Christine *Singer (Fleetwood Mac), Songwriter*
406 Poplar Dr, Wilmette, IL 60091, USA
McVie, John *Bassist (Fleetwood Mac), Songwriter*
%Boulevard Mgmt, 21650 Oxnard St, #1925, Woodland Hills, CA 91367, USA
McVie, Tom *Hockey Coach*
%Boston Bruins, 1 Fleet Center, Boston, MA 02114, USA
McWherter, Ned R *Governor, TN*
321 Linden St, Dresden, TN 38225, USA

McWhirter, Jillian — *Actress*
PO Box 6308, Beverly Hills, CA 90212, USA

McWilliams, Brian — *Labor Leader*
%Longshoremen/Warehousemen Union, 1188 Franklin St, San Francisco, CA 94109, USA

McWilliams, Caroline — *Actress*
%Premiere Artists Agency, 1875 Century Park E, #2250, Los Angeles, CA 90067, USA

McWilliams, David — *Football Coach, Administrator*
%University of Texas, Athletic Dept, Austin, TX 78712, USA

McWilliams, Fleming — *Singer*
%Michael Dixon Mgmt, 119 Pebble Creek Road, Franklin, TN 37064, USA

Mead, Shepherd — *Writer*
53 Rivermead Court, London SW6 3RY, England

Meade, Carl J — *Astronaut*
5711 Bienveneda Terrace, Palmdale, CA 93551, USA

Meadows, Jayne — *Actress*
16185 Woodvale Road, Encino, CA 91436, USA

Meadows, Stephen — *Actor*
1760 Courtney Ave, Los Angeles, CA 90046, USA

Meadows, Tim — *Actor, Comedian*
%Brillstein/Grey, 9150 Wilshire Blvd, #350, Beverly Hills, CA 90212, USA

Meagher, Mary T — *Swimmer*
404 Vanderwall, Peachtree City, GA 30269, USA

Meaney, Colm — *Actor*
11921 Laurel Hills Road, Studio City, CA 91604, USA

Meaney, Kevin — *Actor, Comedian*
28 Beech Lane, Tarrytown, NY 10591, USA

Means, Natrone J — *Football Player*
862 Kings Crossing Dr, Concord, NC 28027, USA

Means, Russell — *Indian Activist*
444 Crazy Horse Dr, Porcupine, SD 57772, USA

Meara, Anne — *Actress, Comedienne*
118 Riverside Dr, #5A, New York, NY 10024, USA

Mears, Casey — *Auto Racing Driver*
%Chip Ganassi Racing, 600 E Laburnum Ave, Richmond, VA 23222, USA

Mears, Gary — *Singer (Casuals)*
12170 Country Road 215, Tyler, TX 75707, USA

Mears, Rick — *Auto Racing Driver*
1536 NW Buttonbush Circle, Palm City, FL 34990, USA

Mears, Roger, Sr — *Truck Racing Driver*
PO Box 520, Terrell, NC 28682, USA

Mears, Walter R — *Journalist*
%Associated Press, Editorial Dept, 2021 K St NW, Washington, DC 20006, USA

Meat Loaf — *Singer, Actor*
%Solo Agency, 252-260 Regent St, #100, London W1B 3BX, England

Mecham, Evan — *Governor, AZ*
%Mecham Pontiac-AMC-Renault, 4510 W Glendale Ave, Glendale, AZ 85301, USA

Mechem, Charles S, Jr — *Golf Executive, Businessman*
%United States Show, 1 Eastwood Dr, Cincinnati, OH 45227, USA

Meciar, Vladimir — *Prime Minister, Slovakia*
Urad Vlady SR, Nam Slobody 1, 81370 Bratislava, Slovakia

Mecir, Miloslav — *Tennis Player*
Julova 1, 83101 Bratislava, Czech Republic

Medak, Peter — *Movie Director*
1355 N Laurel Ave, #9, West Hollywood, CA 90046, USA

Meddick, Jim — *Cartoonist (Robot Man)*
%United Feature Syndicate, 200 Madison Ave, New York, NY 10016, USA

Medgyessy, Peter — *Prime Minister, Hungary*
%Prime Minister's Office, Kossuth Lajos Ter 1-3, 1055 Budapest, Hungary

Medina Estevez, Jorge Arturo Cardinal — *Religious Leader*
%Congregation for Divine Worship, 00120 Vatican City

Medina, Patricia — *Actress*
10787 Wilshire Blvd, #1503, Los Angeles, CA 90024, USA

Medley, Bill — *Singer (Righteous Brothers)*
%Barry Rillera, 9841 Hot Springs Dr, Huntington Beach, CA 92646, USA

Medoff, Mark H — *Writer*
PO Box 3072, Las Cruces, NM 88003, USA

Medress, Henry — *Singer, Pianist, Bassist (Tokens)*
%Brothers Mgmt, 141 Dunbar Ave, Fords, NJ 08863, USA

Medved, Aleksandr V — *Wrestler*
%Central Soviet Sports Federation, Skatertny p 4, Moscow, Russia

Medvedev, Andrei — *Tennis Player*
6352 Ellmau/Tirol, Austria

Medvedev, Zhores A — *Biologist*
4 Osborn Gardens, London NW7 1DY, England

Medwin, Michael — *Actor*
%International Creative Mgmt, 76 Oxford St, London W1N 0AX, England

Meehl, Paul E — *Psychologist*
1544 E River Terrace, Minneapolis, MN 55414, USA

M

Meeker - Melvin

Meeker, Howie *Hockey Player, Sportscaster*
979 Dickenson Way, Parksville BC V9P 1Z7, Canada
Meese, Edwin, III *Attorney General*
1075 Springhill Road, McLean, VA 22102, USA
Meggett, David L (Dave) *Football Player*
8 Brisbane Dr, Charleston, SC 29407, USA
Mehl, Lance A *Football Player*
44920 Kacsmar Estates Dr, Saint Clairsville, OH 43950, USA
Mehrabian, Robert *Educator*
%Carnegie Mellon University, President's Office, Pittsburgh, PA 15213, USA
Mehringer, David M *Astronomer*
%University of Illinois, Astronomy Dept, Champaign, IL 61820, USA
Mehta, Shailesh J *Businessman*
%Providian Financial Corp, 201 Mission St, San Francisco, CA 94105, USA
Mehta, Ved *Writer*
139 E 79th St, New York, NY 10021, USA
Mehta, Zubin *Conductor*
%Israel Philharmonic, 1 Huberman St, 61112 Tel Aviv, Israel
Meier, Richard A *Architect, Pritzker Laureate*
%Richard Meier Partners, 475 10th Ave, New York, NY 10018, USA
Meier, Waltraud *Opera Singer*
%Festspielhugel 3, 95445 Bayreuth, Germany
Meiselas, Susan *Photographer*
256 Mott St, New York, NY 10012, USA
Meisner, Joachim Cardinal *Religious Leader*
%Archbishop's Diocese, Marzellenstr 32, 50668 Cologne, Germany
Meisner, Randy *Bassist, Singer (Eagles/Poco)*
3706 Eureka Dr, Studio City, CA 91604, USA
Meja *Singer (Legacy of Sound)*
%Basic Music Mgmt, Norrtullsgatan 51, 113 45 Stockholm, Sweden
Mejdani, Rexhep *President, Albania*
%President's Office, Keshilli i Ministrave, Tirana, Albania
Mejia, Hipolito *President, Dominican Republic*
%Palacio Nacional, Calle Moises Garcia, Santo Domingo, Dominican Republic
Mejia, Jorge Maria Cardinal *Religious Leader*
Biblioteca Apostolica Vaticina, 00120 Vatican CIty
Mejia, Paul R *Ballet Dancer, Choreographer*
%Fort Worth Ballet, 6848 Green Oaks Road, Fort Worth, TX 76116, USA
Mekka, Eddie *Actor*
%Cosden Morgan, 129 W Wilson St, #202, Costa Mesa, CA 92627, USA
Melanie *Singer, Songwriter*
53 Baymont St, #5, Clearwater Beach, FL 33767, USA
Melato, Mariangela *Actress*
%Carol Levi Co, Via Giuseppe Pisanelli, 00196 Rome, Italy
Melcher, John *Senator, MT*
230 Maryland Ave NE, #B, Washington, DC 20002, USA
Melchionni, Bill *Basketball Player*
115 Whitehall Blvd, Garden City, NY 11530, USA
Melchior, Ib *Writer*
8228 Marymount Lane, Los Angeles, CA 90069, USA
Melendez, Bill *Animator*
%Bill Melendez Productions, 13400 Riverside Dr, #201, Sherman Oaks, CA 91423, USA
Melinda *Illusionist*
%M Entertainment, 120 E Flamingo Road, Las Vegas, NV 89109, USA
Mellencamp, John *Singer, Songwriter*
PO Box 6777, Bloomington, IN 47407, USA
Melles, Carl *Conductor*
Grunbergstr 4, 1130 Vienna, Austria
Mello, Tamara *Actress*
%Abrams Artists, 9200 Sunset Blvd, #1125, Los Angeles, CA 90069, USA
Mellor, John W *Economist*
%John Mellor Assoc, 801 Pennsylvania Ave NW, #PH18, Washington, DC 20004, USA
Melnick, Bruce E *Astronaut*
%Boeing Aerospace, PO Box 21233, Kennedy Space Center, FL 32815, USA
Melnick, Daniel *Movie, Television Producer*
1123 Sunset Hills Dr, Los Angeles, CA 90069, USA
Meloni, Christopher *Actor*
%Gersh Agency, 232 N Canon Dr, Beverly Hills, CA 90210, USA
Melrose, Barry J *Hockey Player, Coach*
%ESPN-TV, Sports Dept, ESPN Plaza, 935 Middle St, Bristol, CT 06010, USA
Melroy, Pamela A *Astronaut*
3910 Valley Green Court, Houston, TX 77059, USA
Melton, Sid *Actor*
PO Box 57933, Sherman Oaks, CA 91413, USA
Melvin, Allan *Actor*
271 N Bowling Green Way, Los Angeles, CA 90049, USA
Melvin, Murray *Actor*
%Joy Jameson, Plaza, 535 Kings Road, London SW10 0SZ, England

Melzack, Ronald *Psychologist*
51 Banstead Road, Montreal QC H4X 1P1, Canada
Menand, Louis *Writer, Historian*
%New Yorker Magazine, Editorial Dept, 4 Times Square, New York, NY 10036, USA
Menchu Tum, Rigoberta *Nobel Peace Laureate*
%UN Working Group on Indigenous Populations, UN Plaza, New York, NY 10017, USA
Mendes, Eva *Actress*
%Industry Entertainment, 955 Carillo Dr, #300, Los Angeles, CA 90048, USA
Mendes, Sam *Theater, Movie Director*
%Donmar Warehouse, 41 Earlham St, London WC2H 9LD, England
Mendes, Sergio *Pianist*
PO Box 118, Los Angeles, CA 90053, USA
Menges, Chris *Cinematographer, Director*
%Harmony Pictures, 420 S Beverly Dr, #1-100, Beverly Hills, CA 90212, USA
Menichetti, Roberto *Fashion Designer*
3 Loc Monteleto, Gubbio, Italy
Menken, Alan *Composer*
%Shukat Co, 670 W End Ave, #8D, New York, NY 10025, USA
Mennea, Pietro *Track Athlete*
Via Cassia 1041, 00189 Rome, Italy
Menon, Mambillikalathil G K *Physicist*
C-63 Tarang Apts, Mother Dairy Road, Patparganj, Delhi 110092, India
Menotti, Gian-Carlo *Composer*
Yester House, Gifford Haddington, East Lothian EH41 4JF, Scotland
Menshov, Vladimir V *Actor, Director*
3D Tverskaya-Yamskaya 52, #29, 125047 Moscow, Russia
Menzel, Jiri *Movie, Theater Director*
%Studio 89, Kratky Film Jindrisska 34, 112 07 Prague 1, Czech Republic
Menzies, Heather *Actress*
PO Box 1645, Park City, UT 84060, USA
Menzies, Peter G, Jr *Cinematographer*
903 Tahoe Blvd, #802, Incline Village, NV 89451, USA
Meola, Eric *Photographer*
535 Greenwich St, New York, NY 10013, USA
Meola, Tony *Soccer Player*
488 Forest St, Kearny, NJ 07032, USA
Merbold, Ulf *Astronaut, Germany*
Am Sonnenhang 4, 53721 Siegburg, Germany
Mercante, Arthur *Boxing Referee*
135 Wickham Road, Garden City, NY 11530, USA
Mercer, Marian *Actress, Singer*
5250 Colodny Dr, #13, Agoura Hills, CA 91301, USA
Mercer, Ron *Basketball Player*
%San Antonio Spurs, Alamodome, 1 SBC Center, San Antonio, TX 78219, USA
Merchant, Ismail N *Movie Producer*
%Merchant-Ivory Productions, 46 Lexington St, London W1P 3LH, England
Merchant, Natalie *Singer, Songwriter*
%Fort Apache, 51 the Square, Bellows Falls, VT 05101, USA
Mercurio, Nicole *Actress*
%Innovative Artists, 1505 10th St, Santa Monica, CA 90401, USA
Mercurio, Paul *Actor, Singer*
%Beyond Films, 53-55 Brisbane St, Sunnyhills, Sydney NSW 2010, Australia
Meredith, J Don *Football Player, Sportscaster*
PO Box 597, Santa Fe, NM 87504, USA
Meredith, James H *Civil Rights Activist*
929 Meadowbrook Road, Jackson, MS 39206, USA
Meredith, Richard *Hockey Player*
6520 Ridgeview Dr, Edina, MN 55439, USA
Meredith, William *Writer*
%Connecticut College, PO Box 1498, New London, CT 06320, USA
Meri, Lennart *President, Estonia*
%President's Office, 39 Weizenberg St, 0100 Tallinn, Estonia
Meriweather, Joe C *Basketball Player*
5316 NW 64th Terrace, Kansas City, MO 64151, USA
Meriwether, Lee *Actress, Beauty Queen*
12139 Jeanette Place, Granada Hills, CA 91344, USA
Merkerson, S Epatha *Actress*
%Alliance Talent, 9171 Wilshire Blvd, #441, Beverly Hills, CA 90210, USA
Merle, Carole *Alpine Skier*
Chalet La Calette, 04400 Super-Sauze, France
Merletti, Lewis C *Law Enforcement Official*
%Cleveland Browns, 76 Lou Groza Blvd, Berea, OH 44017, USA
Merlin, Jan *Actor*
347 N California St, Burbank, CA 91505, USA
Merlyn-Rees, Merlyn *Government Official, England*
%House of Lords, Westminster, London SW1A 0PW, England
Mero, Rena (Sable) *Wrestler, Model, Actress*
PO Box 469, Geneva, FL 32732, USA

M

Merovich, Pete *Soccer*
945 Spruce St, Pittsburgh, PA 15234, USA
Merow, James F *Judge*
%US Claims Court, 717 Madison Place NW, Washington, DC 20439, USA
Merrifield, R Bruce *Nobel Chemistry Laureate*
43 Mezzine Dr, Cresskill, NJ 07626, USA
Merrill, Catherine *Artist*
%Old Church Pottery, 1456 Florida St, San Francisco, CA 94110, USA
Merrill, Dina *Actress*
%Sue Siegel, 405 E 54th St, #12A, New York, NY 10022, USA
Merrill, Edward W *Chemical Engineer*
90 Somerset St, Belmont, MA 02478, USA
Merrill, John O *Architect*
101 Gardner Place, Colorado Springs, CO 80906, USA
Merrill, Robert *Opera Singer*
%Robert Merrill Assoc, 79 Oxford Road, New Rochelle, NY 10804, USA
Merrill, Stephen E (Steve) *Governor, NH*
562 S Main, Farmington, NH 03855, USA
Merriman, Ryan *Actor*
%Jamieson, PO Box 70025, Houston, TX 77270, USA
Merritt, Gilbert S *Judge*
%US Court of Appeals, US Courthouse, 701 Broadway, Nashville, TN 37203, USA
Merritt, Jack N *Army General*
%US Army Assn, 2425 Wilson Blvd, Arlington, VA 22201, USA
Merritt, James J (Jim) *Baseball Player*
833 Sandwagon Circle, Hemet, CA 92544, USA
Merrow, Susan *Association Executive*
%Sierra Club, 85 2nd St, #200, San Francisco, CA 94105, USA
Merson, Michael *Government Official*
%World Health Organization, Ave Appia, 1211 Geneva 27, Switzerland
Merten, Lauri *Golfer*
105 Foulk Road, Wilmington, DE 19803, USA
Mertens, Alan *Auto Racing Executive*
%PacWest Racing Group, 150 Gasoline Alley Road, Indianapolis, IN 46222, USA
Merton, Robert C *Nobel Economics Laureate*
%Harvard University, Business School, Boston, MA 02163, USA
Mertz, Edwin T *Biochemist*
1504 Via Della Scala, Henderson, NV 89052, USA
Mertz, Francis J *Educator*
%Farleigh Dickinson University, President's Office, Teaneck, NJ 07666, USA
Merwin, John D *Governor, VI*
PO Box 2213, New London, NH 03257, USA
Merwin, William Stanley *Writer*
%Farleigh Dickinson University Press, 285 Madison Ave, Madison, NJ 07940, USA
Merz, Suzanne (Sue) *Hockey Player*
5 Douglas Dr, Greenwich, CT 06831, USA
Mesa, Carlos *President, Bolivia*
%President's Office, Palacio de Gobierno, Plaza Murilla, La Paz, Bolivia
Meschery, Tom *Basketball Player*
PO Box 1297, Truckee, CA 96160, USA
Mesic, Stipe *President, Croatia*
%Presidential Palace, Pantovcak 241, Zagreb 10000, Croatia
Meskill, Thomas J *Governor, CT, Judge*
218 Stony Mill Lane, East Berlin, CT 06023, USA
Messenger, Melinda *Model*
%Arcadia Mgmt, 2-3 Golden Square, London W1R 3AD, England
Messer, Thomas M *Museum Director*
1105 Park Ave, New York, NY 10128, USA
Messerschmid, Ernst *Astronaut, Germany*
%Universitat Stuttgart, Pfaffenwaldring 31, 70569 Stuttgart, Germany
Messerschmidt, J Alexander (Andy) *Baseball Player*
200 Lagunita Dr, Soquel, CA 95073, USA
Messick, Dale *Cartoonist (Brenda Starr)*
%Tribune Media Services, 435 N Michigan Ave, #1500, Chicago, IL 60611, USA
Messier, Mark D *Hockey Player*
205 W 57th St, New York, NY 10019, USA
Messina, Jim *Singer, Songwriter*
%Entertainment Artists, 2409 21st Ave S, #100, Nashville, TN 37212, USA
Messina, Jo Dee *Singer, Songwriter*
PO Box 8031, Hermitage, TN 37076, USA
Messing, Debra *Actress*
%Gersh Agency, 232 N Canon Dr, Beverly Hills, CA 90210, USA
Messner, Heinrich (Heini) *Alpine Skier*
Huebenweg 11, 6150 Steinach, Austria
Messner, Reinhold *Explorer, Mountaineer*
Schloss Juval, 39020 Kastelbell/Tschars, Italy
Metcalf, Eric Q *Football Player*
7465 S 114th St, Seattle, WA 98178, USA

Metcalf, Joseph, III *Navy Admiral*
4658 Charleston Terrace NW, Washington, DC 20007, USA
Metcalf, Laurie *Actress*
109 E 950 S, Victor, ID 83455, USA
Metcalf, Shelby *Basketball Coach*
%Texas A&M University, Athletic Dept, College Station, TX 77843, USA
Metcalf, Terrance R (Terry) *Football Player*
5112 S Fountain St, Seattle, WA 98178, USA
Metcalfe, Robert M *Computer Scientist*
%Polaris Venture Partners, 1000 Winter St, #3350, Waltham, MA 02451, USA
Metheny, Patrick B (Pat) *Jazz Guitarist, Composer*
%Ted Kurland, 173 Brighton Ave, Boston, MA 02134, USA
Method Man *Rap Artist (Wu-Tang Clan)*
%International Creative Mgmt, 8942 Wilshire Blvd, #219, Beverly Hills, CA 90211, USA
Metrano, Art *Actor*
131 N Croft Ave, #402, Los Angeles, CA 90048, USA
Mette-Marit *Princess, Norway*
%Det Kongelige, Slottet, Drammensvein 1, 0010 Oslo, Norway
Metzenbaum, Howard M *Senator, OH*
%Consumer Federation of America, 1424 16th St NW, Washington, DC 20036, USA
Mey, Uwe-Jens *Speedskater*
Vulkanstr 22, 10367 Berlin, Germany
Meyer Reyes, Deborah E (Debbie) *Swimmer*
4840 Marconi Ave, Carmichael, CA 95608, USA
Meyer, Breckin *Actor*
%Brillstein/Grey, 9150 Wilshire Blvd, #350, Beverly Hills, CA 90212, USA
Meyer, Daniel J *Businessman*
%Milacron Inc, 2090 Florence Ave, Cincinnati, OH 45206, USA
Meyer, Dina *Actress*
2804 6th St, Santa Monica, CA 90405, USA
Meyer, Edward C *Army General*
1101 S Arlington Ridge Road, #1116, Arlington, VA 22202, USA
Meyer, Jerome J *Businessman*
%Tektronix Inc, 26600 Southwest Parkway, Wilsonville, OR 97070, USA
Meyer, Laurence H *Economist, Government Official*
%Federal Reserve Board, 20th & Constitution NW, Washington, DC 20551, USA
Meyer, Nicholas *Movie Director*
%Creative Artists Agency, 9830 Wilshire Blvd, Beverly Hills, CA 90212, USA
Meyer, Raymond J (Ray) *Basketball Coach*
2518 Cedar Glen Dr, Arlington Heights, IL 60005, USA
Meyer, Robert K *Philosopher, Logician*
3 Rawlings Place, Fadden ACT 2904, Australia
Meyer, Russ *Movie Producer, Photographer*
3121 Arrowhead Dr, Los Angeles, CA 90068, USA
Meyerowitz, Elliot M *Biologist*
%California Institute of Technology, Biology Dept, Pasadena, CA 91125, USA
Meyerowitz, Joel *Photographer*
817 W End Ave, New York, NY 10025, USA
Meyerriecks, Jeffrey *Concert Guitarist*
%Lindy Martin Mgmt, 5 Lob Lolly Court, Pinehurst, NC 28374, USA
Meyers Drysdale, Ann E *Basketball Player, Sportscaster*
6621 Doral Dr, Huntington Beach, CA 92648, USA
Meyers, Ari *Actress*
17 E 96th St, #7B, New York, NY 10128, USA
Meyers, Augie *Organist*
%Encore Talent, 2137 Zercher Road, San Antonio, TX 78209, USA
Meyers, Nancy *Movie Director*
%William Morris Agency, 151 El Camino Dr, Beverly Hills, CA 90212, USA
Meyerson, Martin *Educator*
2016 Spruce St, Philadelphia, PA 19103, USA
Meyfarth, Ulrike Nasse- *Track Athlete*
Buschweg 53, 51519 Odenthal, Germany
Mezentseva, Galina *Ballerina*
%Kirov Ballet Theatre, 1 Ploshchad Iskusstr, Saint Petersburg, Russia
Mezlekia, Nega *Writer*
%Picador USA Books, 175 5th Ave, New York, NY 10010, USA
Mfume, Kweisi *Association Executive*
%NAACP, President's Office, 4805 Mount Hope Dr, Baltimore, MD 21215, USA
Miceli, Justine *Actress*
%Don Buchwald, 6500 Wilshire Blvd, #2200, Los Angeles, CA 90048, USA
Michael *King, Romania*
Villa Serena, 77 Chemin Louis-Degallier, 1290 Versoix-Geneva, Switzerland
Michael, Alum E *Government Official, Wales*
%National Assembly for Wales, Cardiff Bay, Cardiff CF99 1NA, Wales
Michael, Archbishop *Religious Leader*
%Antiochian Orthodox Christian Church, 358 Mountain Road, Englewood, NJ 07631, USA
Michael, Eugene R (Gene) *Baseball Manager, Executive*
49 Union Ave, Upper Saddle River, NJ 07458, USA

Michael, Gary G — *Businessman*
%Albertson's Inc, 250 E Parkcenter Blvd, Boise, ID 83706, USA
Michael, George — *Singer, Songwriter*
2 Elgin Mews, London W9 1NN, England
Michael, Ralph — *Actor*
%Rolf Kruger, 121 Gloucester Place, London W1H 3PJ, England
Michaels, Alan R (Al) — *Sportscaster*
%ABC-TV, Sports Dept, 77 W 66th St, New York, NY 10023, USA
Michaels, Brett — *Singer (Poison)*
%H K Mgmt, 9200 W Sunset Blvd, #530, Los Angeles, CA 90069, USA
Michaels, Fern — *Writer*
9 David Court, Edison, NJ 08820, USA
Michaels, Lorne — *Television Producer, Screenwriter*
%Broadway Video, 1619 Broadway, #900, New York, NY 10019, USA
Michaels, Louis A (Lou) — *Football Player*
69 Grace St, Swoyersville, PA 18704, USA
Michaels, Walter (Walt) — *Football Player, Coach*
282 Michaels Road, Shickshinny, PA 18655, USA
Michaelsen, Kari — *Actress*
%Kazarian/Spencer, 11365 Ventura Blvd, #100, Studio City, CA 91604, USA
Michaleczewski, Dariusz — *Boxer*
%Universum Box-Promotion, Am Stadtrand 27, 22047 Hamburg, Germany
Michals, Duane — *Photographer*
109 E 19th St, New York, NY 10003, USA
Micheel, Shaun — *Golfer*
%Professional Golfer's Assn, PO Box 109601, Palm Beach Gardens, FL 33410, USA
Michel, F Curtis — *Astronaut*
2101 University Blvd, Houston, TX 77030, USA
Michel, Hartmut — *Nobel Chemistry Laureate*
%Max-Planck Institut, Heinrich-Hoffmann-Str 7, 60528 Frankfort, Germany
Michel, Jean-Louis — *Underwater Scientist*
%IFREMER, Center de Toulon, 83500 La Seyne dur Mer, Toulon, France
Michel, Paul R — *Judge*
%US Court of Appeals, 717 Madison Place NW, Washington, DC 20439, USA
Michele, Michael — *Actress*
%Gersh Agency, 232 N Canon Dr, Beverly Hills, CA 90210, USA
Micheler, Elisabeth — *Canoeing Athlete*
Gruntenstr 45, 86163 Augsburg, Germany
Michell, Keith — *Actor*
%Chatto & Linnit, Prince of Wales, Coventry St, London W1V 7FE, England
Michell, Roger — *Movie Director*
%Duncan Heath, Paramount House, 162 Wardour, London W1V 3AT, England
Michels, John J — *Football Player*
10720 Nesbitt Ave S, Bloomington, MN 55437, USA
Michels, Rinus — *Soccer Coach*
Hotel Breitenbacher Hof, H-Heine-Allee 36, 40213 Dusseldorf, Germany
Michie, Donald — *Computer Scientist*
6 Inveralmond Grove, Cramond, Edinburgh EH4 6RA, Scotland
Michiko — *Empress, Japan*
Imperial Palace, 1-1 Chiyoda-ku, Tokyo 100, Japan
Mickal, Abe — *Football Player, Physician*
774 Topaz St, New Orleans, LA 70124, USA
Mickelson, Phil — *Golfer*
%Gaylord Sports Mgmt, 14646 N Kierland Blvd, #230, Scottsdale, AZ 85254, USA
Middendorf, J William, II — *Secretary, Navy; Diplomat*
565 W Main Road, Little Compton, RI 02837, USA
Middendorf, Tracy — *Actress*
PO Box 480410, Los Angeles, CA 90048, USA
Midkiff, Dale — *Actor*
11541 Morrison St, North Hollywood, CA 91601, USA
Midler, Bette — *Singer, Actress*
%Sussman Assoc, 1222 16th Ave S, #300, Nashville, TN 37212, USA
Midori — *Concert Violinist*
%Midori Foundation, 850 7th Ave, #705, New York, NY, 10019, USA
Miechur, Thomas F — *Labor Leader*
%Cement & Allied Workers Union, 2500 Brickdale, Elk Grove Village, IL 60007, USA
Mieczko, A J — *Hockey Player*
295 Central Park W, #9G, New York, NY 10024, USA
Mientkiewicz, Douglas (Doug) — *Baseball Player*
13560 SW 67th Circle, Miami, FL 33156, USA
Mieto, Juha — *Nordic Skier*
%General Delivery, Mieto, Finland
Migenes, Julia — *Opera Singer*
%Artists Group, 10100 Santa Monica Blvd, #2490, Los Angeles, CA 90067, USA
Mignola, Mike — *Cartoonist (Hellboy)*
%Dark Horse Publishing, 10956 SE Main St, Portland, OR 97216, USA
Miguel, Luis — *Singer*
%William Morris Agency, 1325 Ave of Americas, New York, NY 10019, USA

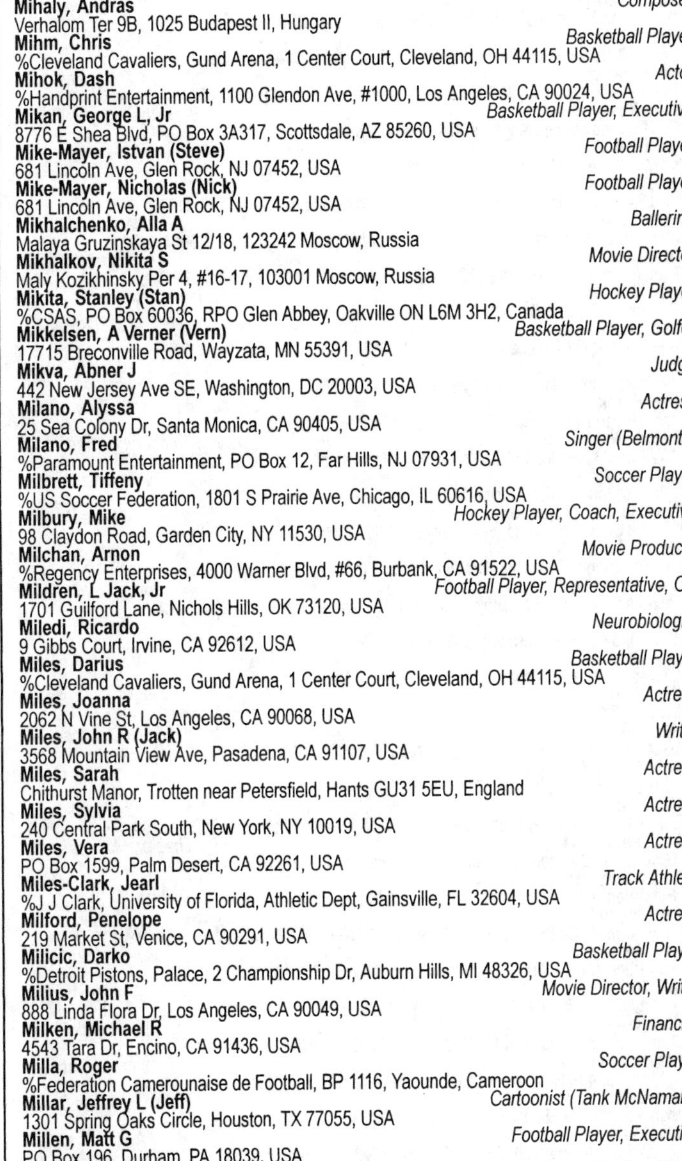

Mihaly, Andras *Composer*
Verhalom Ter 9B, 1025 Budapest II, Hungary
Mihm, Chris *Basketball Player*
%Cleveland Cavaliers, Gund Arena, 1 Center Court, Cleveland, OH 44115, USA
Mihok, Dash *Actor*
%Handprint Entertainment, 1100 Glendon Ave, #1000, Los Angeles, CA 90024, USA
Mikan, George L, Jr *Basketball Player, Executive*
8776 E Shea Blvd, PO Box 3A317, Scottsdale, AZ 85260, USA
Mike-Mayer, Istvan (Steve) *Football Player*
681 Lincoln Ave, Glen Rock, NJ 07452, USA
Mike-Mayer, Nicholas (Nick) *Football Player*
681 Lincoln Ave, Glen Rock, NJ 07452, USA
Mikhalchenko, Alla A *Ballerina*
Malaya Gruzinskaya St 12/18, 123242 Moscow, Russia
Mikhalkov, Nikita S *Movie Director*
Maly Kozikhinsky Per 4, #16-17, 103001 Moscow, Russia
Mikita, Stanley (Stan) *Hockey Player*
%CSAS, PO Box 60036, RPO Glen Abbey, Oakville ON L6M 3H2, Canada
Mikkelsen, A Verner (Vern) *Basketball Player, Golfer*
17715 Breconville Road, Wayzata, MN 55391, USA
Mikva, Abner J *Judge*
442 New Jersey Ave SE, Washington, DC 20003, USA
Milano, Alyssa *Actress*
25 Sea Colony Dr, Santa Monica, CA 90405, USA
Milano, Fred *Singer (Belmonts)*
%Paramount Entertainment, PO Box 12, Far Hills, NJ 07931, USA
Milbrett, Tiffeny *Soccer Player*
%US Soccer Federation, 1801 S Prairie Ave, Chicago, IL 60616, USA
Milbury, Mike *Hockey Player, Coach, Executive*
98 Claydon Road, Garden City, NY 11530, USA
Milchan, Arnon *Movie Producer*
%Regency Enterprises, 4000 Warner Blvd, #66, Burbank, CA 91522, USA
Mildren, L Jack, Jr *Football Player, Representative, OK*
1701 Guilford Lane, Nichols Hills, OK 73120, USA
Miledi, Ricardo *Neurobiologist*
9 Gibbs Court, Irvine, CA 92612, USA
Miles, Darius *Basketball Player*
%Cleveland Cavaliers, Gund Arena, 1 Center Court, Cleveland, OH 44115, USA
Miles, Joanna *Actress*
2062 N Vine St, Los Angeles, CA 90068, USA
Miles, John R (Jack) *Writer*
3568 Mountain View Ave, Pasadena, CA 91107, USA
Miles, Sarah *Actress*
Chithurst Manor, Trotten near Petersfield, Hants GU31 5EU, England
Miles, Sylvia *Actress*
240 Central Park South, New York, NY 10019, USA
Miles, Vera *Actress*
PO Box 1599, Palm Desert, CA 92261, USA
Miles-Clark, Jearl *Track Athlete*
%J J Clark, University of Florida, Athletic Dept, Gainsville, FL 32604, USA
Milford, Penelope *Actress*
219 Market St, Venice, CA 90291, USA
Milicic, Darko *Basketball Player*
%Detroit Pistons, Palace, 2 Championship Dr, Auburn Hills, MI 48326, USA
Milius, John F *Movie Director, Writer*
888 Linda Flora Dr, Los Angeles, CA 90049, USA
Milken, Michael R *Financier*
4543 Tara Dr, Encino, CA 91436, USA
Milla, Roger *Soccer Player*
%Federation Camerounaise de Football, BP 1116, Yaounde, Cameroon
Millar, Jeffrey L (Jeff) *Cartoonist (Tank McNamara)*
1301 Spring Oaks Circle, Houston, TX 77055, USA
Millen, Matt G *Football Player, Executive*
PO Box 196, Durham, PA 18039, USA
Miller, Aaron *Hockey Player*
1501 10th St, Manhattan Beach, CA 90266, USA
Miller, Alan *Journalist*
%Los Angeles Times, Editorial Dept, 202 W 1st St, Los Angeles, CA 90012, USA
Miller, Alice *Golfer*
%Ladies Pro Golf Assn, 100 International Golf Dr, Daytona Beach, FL 32124, USA
Miller, Ann *Actress, Dancer*
618 N Alta Dr, Beverly Hills, CA 90210, USA
Miller, Arthur *Writer*
RR 1 Box 320, Tophet Road, Roxbury, CT 06783, USA
Miller, Bode *Alpine Skier*
63 Eastern Valley Road, Franconia, NH 03580, USA
Miller, Brad *Basketball Player*
%Sacramento Kings, Arco Arena, 1 Sports Parkway, Sacramento, CA 95834, USA

Miller, C Arden *Pediatrician*
350 Carolina Meadows Villa, Chapel Hill, NC 27517, USA
Miller, C Ray *Religious Leader*
%United Brethren in Christ, 302 Lake St, Huntington, IN 46750, USA
Miller, Charles D *Businessman*
%Avery Dennison Corp, 150 N Orange Grove Blvd, Pasadena, CA 91103, USA
Miller, Cheryl D *Basketball Player, Coach*
3206 Ellington Dr, Los Angeles, CA 90068, USA
Miller, Christa *Actress*
%K&H, 1212 Ave of Americas, #3, New York, NY 10036, USA
Miller, Christine Cook *Judge*
%US Claims Court, 717 Madison Place NW, Washington, DC 20439, USA
Miller, Coco *Basketball Player*
%Washington Mystics, MCI Center, 601 F St NW, Washington, DC 20004, USA
Miller, Dan *Singer (O-Town)*
%Trans Continental Records, 7380 Sand Lake Road, #350, Orlando, FL 32819, USA
Miller, David *Cartoonist (Dave)*
167 Tremont St, Rehoboth, MA 02769, USA
Miller, Dennis *Actor, Comedian*
814 N Mansfield Ave, Los Angeles, CA 90038, USA
Miller, Denny *Actor*
9612 Gavin Stone Ave, Las Vegas, NV 89145, USA
Miller, Frank *Cartoonist (Sin City, Dark Knight)*
%Dark House Publishing, 10956 SE Main St, Milwaukie, OR 97222, USA
Miller, G William *Secretary, Treasury; Businessman*
%G William Miller Co, 1215 19th St NW, Washington, DC 20036, USA
Miller, George D *Air Force General*
20 Phillips Pond South, Natick, MA 01760, USA
Miller, George T (Kennedy) *Movie Director*
30 Orwell St, King's Cross, Sydney NSW 2011, Australia
Miller, J Ronald *Religious Leader*
%Int'l Community Churches Council, 21116 Washington Parkway, Frankfort, Il 60423, USA
Miller, James C, III *Government Official*
%Citizens for Sound Economy, 1250 H St NW, Washington, DC 20005, USA
Miller, Jamir *Football Player*
331 Grenadine Way, Hercules, CA 94547, USA
Miller, Jeremy *Actor*
5255 Vesper Ave, Sherman Oaks, CA 91411, USA
Miller, Jody *Singer*
PO Box 413, Blanchard, OK 73010, USA
Miller, John *Commentator*
%ABC-TV, News Dept, 77 W 66th St, New York, NY 10023, USA
Miller, John L (Johnny) *Golfer*
1621 Ripley Run, Wellington, FL 33414, USA
Miller, Jon *Sportscaster*
%ESPN-TV, Sports Dept, ESPN Plaza, 935 Middle St, Bristol, CT 06010, USA
Miller, Jonathan W *Theater, Movie Director*
63 Gloucester Crescent, London NW1, England
Miller, Jonny Lee *Actor*
%I F A Talent Agency, 8730 Sunset Blvd, #490, Los Angeles, CA 90069, USA
Miller, Joyce D *Labor Leader*
%Amalgamated Clothing & Textile Workers, 1710 Broadway, #3, New York, NY 10019, USA
Miller, Julie *Singer, Songwriter*
%Mark Pucci Media, 5000 Oak Bluff Court, Atlanta, GA 30350, USA
Miller, Keith H *Governor, AK*
3605 Arctic Blvd, #1001, Anchorage, AK 99503, USA
Miller, Kelly *Basketball Player*
%Charlotte Sting, 100 Hive Dr, Charlotte, NC 28217, USA
Miller, Kristen *Actress*
%Lighthouse, 409 N Camden Dr, #202, Beverly Hills, CA 90210, USA
Miller, Lajos *Opera Singer*
Balogh Adam Utca 28, 1026 Budapest, Hungary
Miller, Larry *Actor, Comedian*
%Spivak Entertainment, 11845 W Olympic Blvd, #1125, Los Angeles, CA 90064, USA
Miller, Larry H *Basketball Executive, Softball Player*
%Utah Jazz, Delta Center, 301 W South Temple, Salt Lake City, UT 84101, USA
Miller, Lawrence (Larry) *Basketball Player*
1300 Paddock Dr, Raleigh, NC 27609, USA
Miller, Lennox *Track Athlete*
1213 N Lake Ave, Pasadena, CA 91104, USA
Miller, Lenore *Labor Leader*
%Retail/Wholesale/Department Store Union, 30 E 29th St, New York, NY 10016, USA
Miller, Mark *Singer (Sawyer Brown)*
%Sawyer Brown Inc, 5200 Old Harding Road, Franklin, TN 37064, USA
Miller, Marvin J *Labor Leader*
211 E 70th St, New York, NY 10021, USA
Miller, Mike *Basketball Player*
%Memphis Grizzlies, 175 Toyota Plaza, #150, Memphis, TN 38103, USA

Miller, Mildred *Opera Singer*
PO Box 110108, Pittsburgh, PA 15232, USA
Miller, Mitch *Conductor, Orchestra Leader*
345 W 58th St, New York, NY 10019, USA
Miller, Mulgrew *Jazz Pianist*
3725 Farmersville Road, Easton, PA 18045, USA
Miller, Nate *Boxer*
1214 Allengrove St, Philadelphia, PA 19124, USA
Miller, Nicole J *Fashion Designer*
780 Madison Ave, New York, NY 10021, USA
Miller, Oliver *Basketball Player*
2912 S Meadow Dr, Fort Worth, TX 76133, USA
Miller, Penelope Ann *Actress*
%United Talent Agency, 9560 Wilshire Blvd, #500, Beverly Hills, CA 90212, USA
Miller, Peter North *Businessman*
Dawson House, 5 Jewry St, London EC3N 2EX, England
Miller, Raymond R (Ray) *Baseball Player, Manager*
PO Box 41, New Athens, OH 43981, USA
Miller, Reginald W (Reggie) *Basketball Player*
14301 E 113th St, Fortville, IN 46040, USA
Miller, Robert Ellis *Movie Director*
1901 Ave of Stars, #1040, Los Angeles, CA 90067, USA
Miller, Shannon *Gymnast*
221 Magill Dr, Grafton, MA 01519, USA
Miller, Steve *Singer, Songwriter, Band Leader*
PO Box 12680, Seattle, WA 98111, USA
Miller, Stuart L (Stu) *Baseball Player*
3701 Ocaso Court, Cameron Park, CA 95682, USA
Miller, Tangi *Actress*
%Gersh Agency, 232 N Canon Dr, Beverly Hills, CA 90210, USA
Miller, Warren *Photographer*
505 Pier Ave, Hermosa Beach, CA 90254, USA
Miller, Wiley *Cartoonist (Non Sequitur/Us & Them)*
345 Canon Dr, Santa Barbara, CA 93105, USA
Millett, Kate *Feminist Leader, Writer*
20 Old Overlook Road, Poughkeepsie, NY 12603, USA
Millett, Lewis L *Korean War Army Hero (CMH)*
%Korean War Memorial, Patriotic Hall, 1816 Figueroa, #700, Los Angeles, CA 90015, USA
Millhauser, Steven *Writer*
235 Caroline St, Saratoga Springs, NY 12866, USA
Millman, Irving *Inventor (Hepatitis B Tests, Vaccine)*
310 Windsor Circle, Cherry Hill, NJ 08002, USA
Millo, Aprile E *Opera Singer*
%Columbia Artists Mgmt Inc, 165 W 57th St, New York, NY 10019, USA
Milloy, Lawyer *Football Player*
%Buffalo Bills, 1 Bills Dr, Orchard Park, NY 14127, USA
Mills, Alley *Actress*
444 Carol Canal, Venice, CA 90291, USA
Mills, Chris *Basketball Player*
%Boston Celtics, 151 Merrimac St, #1, Boston, MA 02114, USA
Mills, Curtis *Track Athlete*
328 Lake St, Lufkin, TX 75904, USA
Mills, Donna *Actress*
253 26th St, #259, Santa Monica, CA 90402, USA
Mills, Erie *Opera Singer*
%John J Miller, 801 W 181st St, #20, New York, NY 10033, USA
Mills, Frank *Pianist, Composer*
%Rocklands Talent, PO Box 1282, Peterborough ON K9L 7H5, Canada
Mills, Hayley *Actress, Singer*
81 High St, Hampton, Middx, England
Mills, John *Actor*
Hill House, Denham Village, Buckinghamshire, England
Mills, Juliet *Actress*
%Waters & Nicolosi, 1501 Broadway, New York, NY 10036, USA
Mills, Mike *Bassist (REM)*
%REM/Athens Ltd, PO Box 8032, Athens, GA 30603, USA
Mills, Samuel D (Sam), Jr *Football Player*
%Carolina Panthers, Ericsson Stadium, 800 S Mint St, Charlotte, NC 28202, USA
Mills, Stephanie *Singer, Actress*
%Associated Booking Corp, 1995 Broadway, #501, New York, NY 10023, USA
Mills, Terry *Basketball Player*
%Indiana Pacers, Conseco Fieldhouse, 125 S Pennsylvania, Indianapolis, IN 46204, USA
Mills, William M (Billy) *Track Athlete*
7760 Winding Way, Fair Oaks, CA 95628, USA
Milner, Martin *Actor*
3106 Azahar St, Carlsbad, CA 92009, USA
Milnes, Sherrill E *Opera Singer*
%Herbert Barrett, 266 W 37th St, #2000, New York, NY 10018, USA

M

Milnor, John W *Mathematician*
3 Laurel Lane, Setauket, NY 11733, USA
Milongo, Andre *Prime Minister, Congo*
%Union for Democracy & Republic, Brazzaville, Congo Republic
Milosz, Czeslaw *Nobel Literature Laureate*
%University of California, Slavic Languages Dept, Berkeley, CA 94720, USA
Milsap, Ronnie *Singer, Songwriter*
%Ronnie Milsap Enterprises, PO Box 40665, Nashville, TN 37204, USA
Milsome, Doug *Cinematographer*
%Smith/Gosnell/Nicholson, PO Box 1156, Studio City, CA 91614, USA
Milton, DeLisha *Basketball Player*
%Los Angeles Sparks, Staples Center, 1111 S Figueroa St, Los Angeles, CA 90015, USA
Mimieux, Yvette *Actress*
%Sterling/Winters, 10877 Wilshire Blvd, #15, Los Angeles, CA 90024, USA
Mimoun, Alain *Track Athlete*
27 Ave Edouard-Jenner, 94500 Champigny-sur-Marne, France
Min, Gao *Diver*
%Olympic Committee, 9 Tiyuguan Road, Beijing, China
Mindel, Lee F *Architect*
%Shelton Mindel Assoc, 216 W 18th St, New York, NY 10011, USA
Minehan, Cathy E *Financier, Government Official*
%Federal Reserve Bank, 600 Atlantic Ave, Boston, MA 02210, USA
Miner, Jan *Actress*
PO Box 293, Southbury, CT 06488, USA
Miner, Roger J *Judge*
%US Court of Appeals, 445 Broadway, #414, Albany, NY 12207, USA
Miner, Steve *Movie, Television Director*
1137 2nd St, #103, Santa Monica, CA 90403, USA
Mineta, Norman Y *Secretary, Commerce, Transportation*
%Transportation Department, 400 7th St SW, Washington, DC 20590, USA
Ming Tsai *Chef*
%Food Network, 1180 Ave of Americas, #1200, New York, NY 10036, USA
Ming-Na Wen *Actress*
9903 Santa Monica Blvd, #575, Beverly Hills, CA 90212, USA
Minghella, Anthony *Movie Director*
%Judy Daish, 2 Saint Charles Place, London W10 6EG, England
Minh Tran *Dancer, Choreographer*
2014 NE 47th Ave, Portland, OR 97213, USA
Minisi, Anthony S (Skip) *Football Player*
300 Continental Lane, Paoli, PA 19301, USA
Minkoff, Rob *Movie Director*
%Creative Artists Agency, 9830 Wilshire Blvd, Beverly Hills, CA 90212, USA
Minnelli, Liza *Actress, Singer*
160 Central Park Square, New York, NY 10019, USA
Minnifield, Frank *Football Player*
4809 Chaffey Lane, Lexington, KY 40515, USA
Minogue, Kylie *Singer, Actress*
%Terry Blamey Mgmt, 329 Montague St, Albert Park VIC 3206, Australia
Minor, Ronald R *Religious Leader*
%Pentecostal Church of God, 4901 Pennsylvania, Joplin, MO 64804, USA
Minoso, Saturino O A A (Minnie) *Baseball Player, Coach*
324 W 35th St, Chicago, IL 60616, USA
Minow, Newton N *Government Official*
179 E Lake Shore Dr, #15W, Chicago, IL 60611, USA
Minsky, Marvin L *Computer Scientist*
%Massachusetts Institute of Technology, Computer Sci Dept, Cambridge, MA 02139, USA
Minter, Kristin *Actress*
%Baumgarten, 1041 N Formosa Ave, #200, West Hollywood, CA 90046, USA
Mintoff, Dominic *Prime Minister, Malta*
Olives, Xintill St, Tarxien, Malta
Minton, Yvonne F *Opera Singer*
%Ingpen & Williams, 26 Wadham Road, London SW15 2LR, England
Mintz, Shlomo *Concert Violinist, Conductor*
%I C M Artists, 40 W 57th St, New York, NY 10019, USA
Miou-Miou *Actress*
%VMA, 20 Ave Rapp, 75007 Paris, France
Mir, Isabelle *Alpine Skier*
65170 Saint-Lary, France
Mira, George *Football Player*
19225 SW 128th Court, Miami, FL 33177, USA
Mirabella, Grace *Editor, Publisher*
%Mirabella Magazine, 200 Madison Ave, New York, NY 10016, USA
Miricioiu, Nelly *Opera Singer*
53 Midhurst Ave, Muswell Hill, London N10, England
Mirikitani, Janice *Writer*
%Glide Memorial United Methodist Church, 330 Ellis St, San Francisco, CA 94102, USA
Mirisch, Walter M *Movie Producer*
647 Warner Ave, Los Angeles, CA 90024, USA

Mirkerevic, Dragen *Prime Minister, Bosnia-Herzegovia*
%Premier's Office, Vojvode Putnkia 3, 71000 Sarajevo, Bosnia & Herzegovina
Mironov, Boris *Hockey Player*
%New York Rangers, Madison Square Garden, 2 Penn Plaza, New York, NY 10121, USA
Mironov, Dmitri *Hockey Player*
%Anaheim Mighty Ducks, 2000 E Gene Autry Way, Anaheim, CA 92806, USA
Mironov, Yevgeniy V *Actor*
%Oleg Tabajiv Theater, Chaokygina Str 12A, Moscow, Russia
Mirren, Helen *Actress*
%Ken McReddie, 91 Regent St, London W1R 7TB, England
Mirrlees, James A *Nobel Economics Laureate*
%Trinity College, Economics Dept, Cambridge CB2 1TQ, England
Mirzoev, Akbar *Prime Minister, Tajikistan*
%Prime Minister's Office, Dushaube, Tajikistan
Mischka, James *Fashion Designer*
%Badgley Mischka, 525 Fashion Ave, New York, NY 10018, USA
Misersky, Antje *Biathlete*
Grenzgraben 3A, 98714 Stutzerbach, Germany
Mitchell, Andrea *Commentator*
2710 Chain Bridge Road NW, Washington, DC 20016, USA
Mitchell, Betsy *Swimmer*
%Laurel High School, Athletic Dept, 1 Lyman Circle, Cleveland, OH 44122, USA
Mitchell, Brian *Actor*
5307B Wilkinson Ave, #20, Valley Village, CA 91607, USA
Mitchell, Brian K *Football Player*
%New York Giants, Giants Stadium, East Rutherford, NJ 07073, USA
Mitchell, Brian Stokes *Actor, Singer*
243 W 98th St, #5C, New York, NY 10025, USA
Mitchell, Darryl *Actor*
%William Morris Agency, 151 El Camino Dr, Beverly Hills, CA 90212, USA
Mitchell, Edgar D *Astronaut*
PO Box 540037, Greenacres, FL 33454, USA
Mitchell, Elizabeth *Actress*
%Paradigm Agency, 10100 Santa Monica Blvd, #2500, Los Angeles, CA 90067, USA
Mitchell, George J *Senator, ME*
%Piper Rudnick, 1251 Ave of Americas, New York, NY 10020, USA
Mitchell, Harris A *WW II Navy Air Force Hero*
2701 Dees St, San Marcos, TX 78666, USA
Mitchell, James *Actor*
320 W 66th St, New York, NY 10023, USA
Mitchell, James Fitzallen *Premier, Saint Vincent & Grenadines*
%Premier's Office, Kingstown, Saint Vincent, Saint Vincent & Grenadines
Mitchell, Joni *Singer, Songwriter*
624 Funchal Road, Los Angeles, CA 90077, USA
Mitchell, Keith C *Prime Minister, Grenada*
%Prime Minister's Office, Botanical Gardens, Saint George's, Grenada
Mitchell, Leona *Opera Singer*
%Columbia Artists Mgmt Inc, 165 W 57th St, New York, NY 10019, USA
Mitchell, Lydell D *Football Player*
702 Reservoir St, Baltimore, MD 21217, USA
Mitchell, Mike *Basketball Player*
1510 Crescent Way, San Antonio, TX 78258, USA
Mitchell, Radha *Actress*
%William Morris Agency, 151 El Camino Dr, Beverly Hills, CA 90212, USA
Mitchell, Roscoe E, Jr *Jazz Reeds Player, Composer*
%SRO Artists, 6629 University Ave, #206, Middleton, WI 53562, USA
Mitchell, Sasha *Actor*
%Flick East-West, 9057 Nemo St, #A, West Hollywood, CA 90069, USA
Mitchell, Shareen *Actress*
%J Michael Bloom, 9255 Sunset Blvd, #710, Los Angeles, CA 90069, USA
Mitchell, Stump *Football Player, Coach*
%Seattle Seahawks, 11220 NE 53rd St, Kirkland, WA 98033, USA
Mitchelson, Marvin *Attorney*
2500 Apollo Dr, Los Angeles, CA 90046, USA
Mitchison, N Avrion *Zoologist, Anatomist*
14 Belitha Villas, London N1 1PD, England
Mitchum, Carrie *Actress*
%Camden ITG Talent, 1501 Main St, #204, Venice, CA 90291, USA
Mitsotakis, Constantine *Prime Minister, Greece*
1 Aravantinou St, 106 74 Athens, Greece
Mittermaier-Neureuther, Rosi *Alpine Skier*
Winkelmoosalm, 83242 Reit Im Winkel, Germany
Mittermayer, Tatjana *Freestyle Moguls Skier*
Bucha 2A, 83661 Lenggries, Germany
Mivelaz, Betty *Bowler*
6671 Shadygrove St, Tujunga, CA 91042, USA
Mix, Ronald J (Ron) *Football Player*
2317 Caminto Recodo, San Diego, CA 92107, USA

M

Mix, Steve *Basketball Player*
25743 Willowbend Road, Newtown, PA 18940, USA
Mixon, J Wayne *Governor, FL*
2219 Demeron Road, Tallahassee, FL 32308, USA
Miyamura, Hiroshi H *Korean War Army Hero (CMH)*
659 Kaimalino St, Kailua, HI 96734, USA
Miyazawa, Kiichi *Prime Minister, Japan*
6-34-1 Jingu-Mae, Shibuyaku, Tokyo 150, Japan
Miyori, Kim *Actress*
%Susan Smith, 121A N San Vicente Blvd, Beverly Hills, CA 90211, USA
Mize, John D *Vietnam War Air Force Hero*
112 Sunset Dr, Belmond, IA 50421, USA
Mize, Larry *Golfer*
106 Graystone Court, Columbus, GA 31904, USA
Mize, Ola L *Korean War Army Hero (CMH)*
211 Hartwood Dr, Gadsden, AL 35901, USA
Mizerak, Steve *Billiards Player*
140 Alfred St, Edison, NJ 08820, USA
Mizerock, John J *Baseball Player, Manager*
PO Box 580, Punxsutawney, PA 15767, USA
Mizrahi, Isaac *Fashion Designer*
876 Centennial Ave, Piscataway, NJ 08854, USA
Mkapa, Benjamin William *President, Tanzania*
%President's Office, State House, PO Box 9120, Dar es Salaam, Tanzania
Mlkvy, Bill *Basketball Player*
586 Linton Hill Road, Newtown, PA 18940, USA
Mnouchkine, Ariane *Theater Director*
%Theatre du Soleil, Cartoucherie, 75012 Paris, France
Moats, David *Journalist*
%Rutland Herald, Editorial Dept, PO Box 668, Rutland, VT 05702, USA
Mobley, Mary Ann *Actress, Beauty Queen*
2751 Hutton Dr, Beverly Hills, CA 90210, USA
Moceanu, Dominique *Gymnast*
%Brown's Gymnastics Metro, 4676 McLeod Road, Orlando, FL 32811, USA
Mochrie Pepper, Dorothy (Dottie) *Golfer*
15 Blazing Star Trail, Landrum, SC 29356, USA
Mocumbi, Pascoal *Prime Minister, Mozambique*
%Prime Minister's Office, Avenida Julius Nyerere 1780, Maputo, Mozambique
Modano, Mike *Hockey Player*
200 Crescent Court, #S600, Dallas, TX 75201, USA
Modell, Frank *Cartoonist*
115 Three Mile Course, Guilford, CT 06437, USA
Modine, Matthew *Actor*
9696 Culver Blvd, #203, Culver City, CA 90232, USA
Modrow, Hans *Prime Minister, East Germany*
Frankfurter Tor 6, 10243 Berlin, Germany
Modrzejewski, Robert J *Vietnam War Marine Corps Hero (CMH)*
4725 Oporto Court, San Diego, CA 92124, USA
Modzelewski, Richard B (Dick) *Football Player*
1 Pier Pointe, New Bern, NC 28562, USA
Moe, Douglas E (Doug) *Basketball Player, Coach*
13 Arnold Palmer, San Antonio, TX 78257, USA
Moe, Thomas S (Tommy) *Alpine Skier*
1556 Hidden Lane, Anchorage, AK 99501, USA
Moe-Humphreys, Karen *Swimmer*
505 Augusta Dr, Moraga, CA 94556, USA
Moeller, Dennis *Inventor*
25 Cobble Ridge Dr, Chapel Hill, NC 27516, USA
Moellering, John H *Army General*
50130 Manly, Chapel Hill, NC 27517, USA
Moffat, Donald *Actor*
%William Morris Agency, 151 El Camino Dr, Beverly Hills, CA 90212, USA
Moffatt, Henry K *Mathematical Physicist*
6 Banhams Close, Cambridge CB4 1HX, England
Moffett, D W *Actor*
%Three Arts Entertainment, 9460 Wilshire Blvd, #700, Beverly Hills, CA 90212, USA
Moffo, Anna *Opera Singer*
%Columbia Artists Mgmt Inc, 165 W 57th St, New York, NY 10019, USA
Mofford, Rose *Governor, AZ*
330 W Maryland Ave, #104, Phoenix, AZ 85013, USA
Mogae, Festus G *President, Botswana*
%President's Office, State House, Private Bag 001, Gaborone, Botswana
Mogenburg, Dietmar *Track Athlete*
Alter Garfen 34, 51371 Leverkusen, Germany
Mogilny, Alexander *Hockey Player*
%Int'l Management Group, 801 6th St SW, #235, Calgary AB T2P 3V8, Canada
Mohacsi, Mary *Bowler*
15445 Sunset St, Livonia, MI 48154, USA

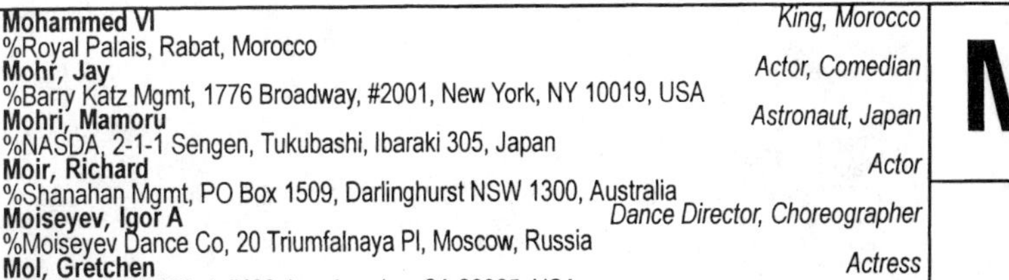

Mohammed VI — *King, Morocco*
%Royal Palais, Rabat, Morocco

Mohr, Jay — *Actor, Comedian*
%Barry Katz Mgmt, 1776 Broadway, #2001, New York, NY 10019, USA

Mohri, Mamoru — *Astronaut, Japan*
%NASDA, 2-1-1 Sengen, Tukubashi, Ibaraki 305, Japan

Moir, Richard — *Actor*
%Shanahan Mgmt, PO Box 1509, Darlinghurst NSW 1300, Australia

Moiseyev, Igor A — *Dance Director, Choreographer*
%Moiseyev Dance Co, 20 Triumfalnaya Pl, Moscow, Russia

Mol, Gretchen — *Actress*
1964 Westwood Blvd, #400, Los Angeles, CA 90025, USA

Molina, Alfred — *Actor*
%Hyler Mgmt, 25 Sea Colony Dr, Santa Monica, CA 90405, USA

Molina, Mario J — *Nobel Chemistry Laureate*
8 Clematis Road, Lexington, MA 02421, USA

Molinaro, Al — *Actor*
1530 Arboles Dr, Glendale, CA 91207, USA

Molitor, Paul L — *Baseball Player, Coach*
34 Kirby Puckett Place, Minneapolis, MN 55415, USA

Moll, John L — *Electronics Engineer*
4111 Old Trace Road, Palo Alto, CA 94306, USA

Moll, Kurt — *Opera Singer*
Voigtelstr 22, 50933 Cologne, Germany

Moll, Richard — *Actor*
1119 Amalfi Dr, Pacific Palisades, CA 90272, USA

Moller, Paul — *Inventor (Sky Car), Engineer*
%Moller International, 1222 Research Park Dr, Davis, CA 95616, USA

Moller-Gladisch, Silke — *Track Athlete*
Lange Str 6, 18055 Rostock, Germany

Mollo-Christensen, Erik L — *Oceanographer*
10 Barberry Road, Lexington, MA

Molloy, Bryan B — *Inventor (Prozac)*
7948 Beaumont Green Place, Indianapolis, IN 46250, USA

Molne, Marc Forne — *Head of Government, Andorra*
%President's Office, Casa de la Valle, Andorra la Vella, Andorra

Moloney, Paddy — *Singer (Chieftains)*
%Macklam Feldman Mgmt, 1505 W 2nd Ave, #200, Vancouver BC V6H 3Y4, Canada

Molyneux, Juan Pablo — *Architect*
%J P Molyneux Studio, 29 E 69th St, New York, NY 10021, USA

Mom Rajawong Sirikit Kitiyarara — *Queen, Thailand*
%Royal Residence, Chirtalad a Villa, Bangkok, Thailand

Momaday, N Scott — *Writer*
%University of Arizona, English Dept, Tucson, AZ 85721, USA

Monacelli, Amieto — *Bowler*
%Professional Bowlers Assn, 719 2nd Ave, #701, Seattle, WA 98104, USA

Monaghan, Dominic — *Actor*
%P F D, Drury House, 34-43 Russell St, London WC2B 5HA, England

Monahan, Pat — *Singer (Train)*
%Jon Landau, 80 Mason St, Greenwich, CT 06830, USA

Monbouquette, William C (Bill) — *Baseball Player*
46 Doonan St, Medford, MA 02155, USA

Moncrief, Sidney — *Basketball Player*
4304 Carter Lane, Little Rock, AR 72223, USA

Mondale, Walter F — *Vice President; Senator, MN*
50 S 6th St, #1500, Minneapolis, MN 55402, USA

Mondavi, Robert G — *Businessman*
%Robert Mondavi Winery, 7801 St Helena Highway, Oakville, CA 94562, USA

Monduzzi, Dino Cardinal — *Religious Leader*
Via Monfe della Farina 64, 00186 Rome, Italy

Moneo, J Rafael — *Architect, Pritzker Laureate*
Calle Mino 5, Madrid 28002, Spain

Money, Eddie — *Singer*
%International Creative Mgmt, 40 W 57th St, #1800, New York, NY 10019, USA

Money, Ken — *Astronaut, Canada*
%DCIEM, 1133 Sheppard Ave W, #2000, Downsview ON M3M 3B9, Canada

Monheit, Jane — *Singer, Songwriter*
%N-Coded Music/Warlock Records, 126 5th Ave, #200, New York, NY 10011, USA

Monica — *Singer*
%Rowdy/Arista Records, 8750 Wilshire Blvd, #300, Beverly Hills, CA 90211, USA

Monicelli, Mario — *Movie Director*
Via del Babuino 135, 00137 Rome, Italy

Monk, Arthur (Art) — *Football Player, Sportscaster*
8251 Greensboro Dr, McLean, VA 22102, USA

Monk, Debra — *Actress*
%Gage Group, 315 W 57th St, #4H, New York, NY 10019, USA

Monk, Meredith J — *Choreographer, Composer*
%House Foundation for Arts, 131 Varick St, New York, NY 10013, USA

M

Monkhouse, Bob *Actor*
%Peter Prichard, Regent House, 235 Regent St, London W1R 8AX, England
Monroe, A L (Mike) *Labor Leader*
%International Brotherhood of Painters, 1750 New York NW, Washington, DC 20006, USA
Monroe, Earl (Pearl) *Basketball Player*
31 Meadowview Lane, Oneonta, NY 13620, USA
Montagnier, Luc *Medical Researcher*
%Institut Pasteur, 25 Rue du Docteur Roux, 75015 Paris Cedux 15, France
Montague, Diana *Opera Singer*
91 Saint Martin's Lane, London WC2, England
Montalban, Ricardo *Actor*
1423 Oriole Dr, Los Angeles, CA 90069, USA
Montana, Claude *Fashion Designer*
131 Rue Saint-Denis, 75001 Paris, France
Montana, Joseph C (Joe), Jr *Football Player*
3455 State Hwy 128, Calistoga, CA 94515, USA
Montazeri, Ayatollah Hussein Ali *Religious Leader*
%Madresseh Faizieh, Qom, Iran
Monteiro, Antonio M *President, Cape Verde*
%President's Office, Cia de la Republica, Sao Tiago, Praia, Cape Verde
Montermini, Andrea *Auto Racing Driver*
434 E Main St, Brownsburg, IN 46112, USA
Monteveecchi, Liliane *Singer*
%Buzz Halliday, 8899 Beverly Blvd, #620, Los Angeles, CA 90048, USA
Montez, Chris *Singer*
%Arsisanian Assoc, 6671 Sunset Blvd, #1502, Los Angeles, CA 90028, USA
Montgomerie, Colin S *Golfer*
%Int'l Mgmt Group, Pier House, Strand-on-the-Green, London W4 3NN, England
Montgomery, Anne *Sportscaster*
%ESPN-TV, Sports Dept, ESPN Plaza, 935 Middle St, Bristol, CT 06010, USA
Montgomery, Belinda *Actress*
%Epstein-Wyckoff, 280 S Beverly Dr, #400, Beverly Hills, CA 90212, USA
Montgomery, Clifford E (Cliff) *Football Player*
362 I U Willets Road, Roslyn Heights, NY 11577, USA
Montgomery, Eddie *Singer (Montgomery Gentry)*
%Hallmark Direction, 15 Music Square W, Nashville, TN 37203, USA
Montgomery, James P (Jim) *Swimmer, Coach*
3141 Westminster Ave, Dallas, TX 75205, USA
Montgomery, John Michael *Singer*
PO Box 128229, Nashville, TN 37212, USA
Montgomery, Melba *Singer*
%Joe Taylor Artist Agency, 2802 Columbine Place, Nashville, TN 37204, USA
Montgomery, Poppy *Actress*
%Mindel/Donigan, 9057 Nemo St, #C, West Hollywood, CA 90069, USA
Montgomery, Wilbert N *Football Player*
950 Mid Point Dr, O Fallon, MO 63366, USA
Montminy, Marc R *Neurochemist*
%Salk Institute, 10100 N Torrey Pines Road, La Jolla, CA 92037, USA
Montoya, Juan *Auto Racing Driver*
%Williams Grand Prix, Grove, Wontage, Oxfordshire OX12 0D0, England
Montsho Este *Soul/Rap Artist (Arrested Development)*
%William Morris Agency, 1325 Ave of Americas, New York, NY 10019, USA
Montvidas, Edgaras *Opera Singer*
%Van Walsum Mgmt, 4 Addison Bridge Place, London W14 8XP, England
Moody, Lynne *Actress*
8708 Skyline Dr, Los Angeles, CA 90046, USA
Moody, Orville *Golfer*
%Int'l Mgmt Group, 1 Erieview Plaza, 1360 E 9th St, #1300, Cleveland, OH 44114, USA
Moody, Ron *Actor*
%Eric Glass, 28 Berkeley Square, London W1X 6HD, England
Moog, Andy *Hockey Player*
530 Rolling Hills Road, Coppell, TX 75019, USA
Moomaw, Donn D *Football Player*
3124 Corda Dr, Los Angeles, CA 90049, USA
Moon, H Warren *Football Player*
PO Box 22388, Houston, TX 77227, USA
Moon, Sun Myung *Religious Leader*
%Unification Church, 4 W 43rd St, New York, NY 10036, USA
Moon, Wallace W (Wally) *Baseball Player*
702 Ellen Lee Court, Bryan, TX 77802, USA
Moonves, Leslie *Television Producer*
%CBS-TV, 51 W 52nd St, New York, NY 10019, USA
Moore, Abra *Singer*
%Haber Corp, 16830 Ventura Blvd, #501, Encino, CA 91436, USA
Moore, Arch A, Jr *Governor, WV*
507 Jefferson Ave, Glen Dale, WV 26038, USA
Moore, Arthur *Labor Leader*
%Sheet Metal Workers Int'l Assn, 1750 New York Ave NW, Washington, DC 20006, USA

Moore, Benjamin *Artist*
3123 39th Place S, Seattle, WA 98144, USA
Moore, Billie *Basketball Coach*
2247 Meadow Lane, Fullerton, CA 92831, USA
Moore, Bud *Auto Racing Driver*
4 Duck Lane, Isle of Palms, SC 29451, USA
Moore, Calvin C *Mathematician*
1408 Eagle Pointe Court, Lafayette, CA 94549, USA
Moore, Chante *Singer, Songwriter*
%Artistic Control, 1350 Spring St NW, #700, Atlanta, GA 30309, USA
Moore, Charles, Jr *Track Athlete*
2018 Hillyer Place NW, Washington, DC 20009, USA
Moore, Constance *Actress, Singer*
4729 Libbit Ave, Encino, CA 91436, USA
Moore, Demi *Actress*
%Creative Artists Agency, 9830 Wilshire Blvd, Beverly Hills, CA 90212, USA
Moore, Derland P *Football Player*
925 Dove Park Road, Covington, LA 70433, USA
Moore, Dick *Cartoonist (Our Gang)*
%Dick Moore Assoc, 1560 Broadway, New York, NY 10036, USA
Moore, Herman J *Football Player*
265 Mount Hermon Circle, Danville, VA 24540, USA
Moore, James E, Jr *Army General*
18940 Joaquin Court, Salinas, CA 93908, USA
Moore, John W *Educator*
%Indiana State University, President's Office, Terre Haute, IN 47809, USA
Moore, Julianne *Actress*
%Talent Entertainment Group, 9111 Wilshire Blvd, Beverly Hills, CA 90210, USA
Moore, Leonard E (Lenny) *Football Player*
8815 Stonehaven Road, Randallstown, MD 21133, USA
Moore, LeRoi *Saxophonist (Dave Matthews Band)*
%Red Light Mgmt, 3302 Lobban Place, Charlottesville, VA 22903, USA
Moore, Lorrie *Writer*
%University of Wisconsin, English Dept, Madison, WI 53706, USA
Moore, Mandy *Singer, Actress*
PO Box 6079, Bellingham, WA 98227, USA
Moore, Mary Tyler *Actress*
%MTM, 1133 Ave of Americas, New York, NY 10022, USA
Moore, Melba *Singer, Actress*
%Artist Services Inc, 1017 O St NW, #B, Washington, DC 20001, USA
Moore, Melissa Anne *Actress*
PO Box 55, Versailles, KY 40383, USA
Moore, Michael *Movie Director*
%Creative Artists Agency, 9830 Wilshire Blvd, Beverly Hills, CA 90212, USA
Moore, Michael (Mike) *Attorney*
%Attorney General's Office, PO Box 220, Jackson, MS 39205, USA
Moore, Michael K (Mike) *Prime Minister, New Zealand*
%World Trade Organization, 154 Rue Lausanne, 1211 Geneva 21, Switzerland
Moore, Patrick *Astronomer, Writer*
Farthings, 39 West St, Selsey, Sussex PO20 9AAD, England
Moore, Ralph *Jazz Saxophonist*
%Denon Records, 135 W 50th St, #1915, New York, NY 10020, USA
Moore, Richard W (Dickie) *Hockey Player*
4955 Clemin Saint Francois, Saint Laurent QC H4S 1P3, Canada
Moore, Roger *Actor*
%London Mgmt, 2-4 Noel St, London W1V 3RB, England
Moore, Sam *Singer (Sam & Dave)*
%I'ma Da Wife Enterprises, 7119 E Shea Blvd, #109-436, Scottsdale, AZ 85254, USA
Moore, Shemar *Actor*
4424 Moorpark Way, #1, Toluca Lake, CA 91602, USA
Moore, Tamara *Basketball Player*
%Phoenix Mercury, American West Arena, 201 E Jefferson St, Phoenix, AZ 85004, USA
Moore, Thomas *Writer*
%Harper/Collins Publishers, 10 E 53rd St, New York, NY 10022, USA
Moore, Zeke *Football Player*
3422 Prudence Court, Houston, TX 77045, USA
Moore-Watkins, Pauline *Actress*
4077 SW Sunset Dr, #202, Lake Oswego, OR 97035, USA
Moorer, Allison *Singer, Songwriter, Actress*
%TKO Artist Mgmt, 1107 17th Ave S, Nashville, TN 37212, USA
Moorer, Michael *Boxer*
5000 Town Center, #2203, Southfield, MI 48075, USA
Moorer, Thomas H *Navy Admiral, Businessman*
9707 Old Georgetown Road, Bethesda, MD 20814, USA
Moorse, Kiki *Singer (Chicks on Speed)*
%K Records, 924 Jefferson St SE, #101, Olympia, WA 98501, USA
Mora Gramunt, Gabriel *Architect*
Passtage Sant Felip, 12 Bis, 08006 Barcelona, Spain

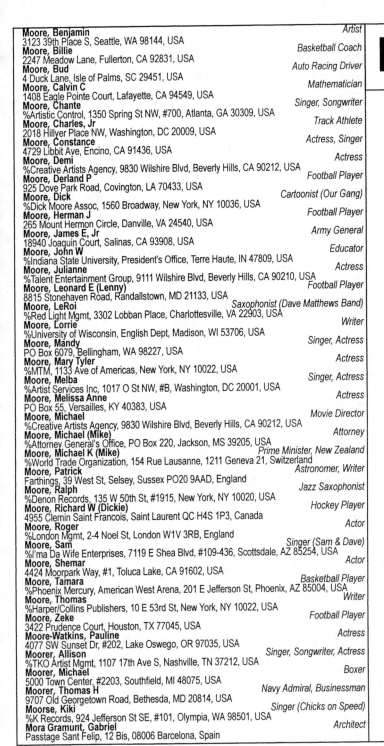

M

Mora - Morgan

Mora, Gene *Cartoonist (Graffiti)*
%United Feature Syndicate, 200 Madison Ave, New York, NY 10016, USA
Mora, Philippe *Movie Director*
%Altman Co, 9255 Sunset Blvd, #901, Los Angeles, CA 90069, USA
Morabito, Rocky *Photojournalist*
3036 Gilmore St, Jacksonville, FL 32205, USA
Morahan, Christopher T *Movie, Theater Director*
Highcombe, Devil's Punchbowl, Thursley, Godalming, Surrey GU8 6NS, England
Morales, Esai *Actor*
7527 Woodrow Wilson Dr, Los Angeles, CA 90046, USA
Morales, P Pablo *Swimmer*
%University of Nebraska, Athletic Dept, Lincoln, NE 68588, USA
Moran, Erin *Actress*
PO Box 3261, Quartz Hill, CA 93586, USA
Moran, John *Religious Leader*
%Missionary Church, PO Box 9127, Fort Wayne, IN 46899, USA
Moran, Julie *Sportscaster, Entertainer*
%Creative Artists Agency, 9830 Wilshire Blvd, Beverly Hills, CA 90212, USA
Moran, Richard J (Rich) *Football Player*
7252 Mimosa Dr, Carlsbad, CA 92009, USA
Moranis, Rick *Actor*
101 Central Park West, #12B, New York, NY 10023, USA
Morath, Max *Singer*
%Producers Inc, 11806 N 56th St, Tampa, FL 33617, USA
Morauta, Mekere *Prime Minister, Papua New Guinea*
%Premier's Office, Marea Haus, Waigani, Port Moresby, Papua New Guinea
Morawetz, Cathleen S *Mathematician*
3298 Monteith Ave, Cincinnati, OH 45208, USA
Morceli, Noureddine *Track Athlete*
%Youth & Sports Ministry, 3 Rue Mohamed Belouizdad, Algiers, Algeria
Morcott, Southwood J *Businessman*
%Dana Corp, PO Box 1000, Toledo, OH 43697, USA
Mordillo, Guillermo *Cartoonist*
%Haye Top Present, Oberweg 8, 82008 Unterhacing, Germany
Mordkovitch, Lydia *Concert Violinist*
25B Belsize Ave, London NW3 3BL, England
More, Camilla *Actress*
%Sharon Kemp, 477 S Robertson Blvd, #204, Beverly Hills, CA 90211, USA
Moreau, Jeanne *Actress*
%Agence Intertalent, 5 Rue Clement Marot, 75008 Paris, France
Moreira, Airto *Jazz Percussionist*
%A Train Mgmt, PO Box 29242, Oakland, CA 94604, USA
Morello, Tom *Guitarist (Rage Against the Machine)*
%GAS Entertainment, 8935 Lindblade St, Culver City, CA 90232, USA
Moreno, Jaime *Soccer Player*
%New York/New Jersey MetroStars, 1 Harmon Plaza, #300, Secaucus, NJ 07094, USA
Moreno, Rita *Actress, Singer*
%Leonard Gordon, 160 Gravatt Dr, Berkeley, CA 94705, USA
Moreno, Roberto *Auto Racing Driver*
252 Montclaire Circle, Weston, FL 33326, USA
Moretti, Fabrizio *Drummer (Strokes)*
%MVO Ltd, 370 7th Ave, #807, New York, NY 10001, USA
Morey, Bill *Actor*
%Kazarian/Spencer, 11365 Ventura Blvd, #100, Studio City, CA 91604, USA
Morgan, Barbara R *Astronaut*
15602 River Maple Lane, Houston, TX 77062, USA
Morgan, Debbi *Actress*
%Mitchell K Stubbs, 8675 Washington Blvd, #203, Culver City, CA 90232, USA
Morgan, Donald M *Cinematographer*
15826 Mayall St, North Hills, CA 91343, USA
Morgan, Gil *Golfer*
PO Box 806, Edmond, OK 73083, USA
Morgan, Harry *Actor*
13172 Boca de Canon Lane, Los Angeles, CA 90049, USA
Morgan, James C *Businessman*
%Applied Materials, 3050 Bowers Ave, Santa Clara, CA 95054, USA
Morgan, James N *Economist*
1217 Bydding Road, Ann Arbor, MI 48103, USA
Morgan, Jane *Singer*
27740 Pacific Coast Highway, Malibu, CA 90265, USA
Morgan, Jaye P *Singer, Actress*
1185 La Grange Ave, Newbury Park, CA 91320, USA
Morgan, Joseph L (Joe) *Baseball Player*
3523 Country Club Place, Danville, CA 94506, USA
Morgan, Joseph M (Joe) *Baseball Player, Manager*
15 Oak Hill Dr, Walpole, MA 02081, USA
Morgan, Kim *Actress*
%Artists Group, 10100 Santa Monica Blvd, #2490, Los Angeles, CA 90067, USA

Morgan, Lewis R *Judge*
%US Court of Appeals, 25 Elmtree Dr, Sharpsburg, GA 30277, USA
Morgan, Lorrie *Singer*
%Martin Assoc, 1207 17th Ave S, #101, Nashville, TN 37212, USA
Morgan, Marabel *Writer*
%Total Woman Inc, 1300 NW 167th St, Miami, FL 33169, USA
Morgan, Michael *Geneticist*
%Wellcome Trust, 183 Euston Road, London NW1 2BE, England
Morgan, Michele *Actress, Singer*
5 Rue Jacques Dulud, 92200 Neuilly-sur-Seine, France
Morgan, Mike *Cartoonist (For Heaven's Sake)*
%Creators Syndicate, 5777 W Century Blvd, #700, Los Angeles, CA 90045, USA
Morgan, Robert B *Senator, NC*
PO Box 377, Lillington, NC 27546, USA
Morgan, Robert K *WW II Army Air Corps Hero*
%Morgan Productions, 175 Lakeshore Dr, Asheville, NC 28804, USA
Morgan, Robin E *Editor, Writer*
%Ms Magazine, Editorial Dept, 230 Park Ave, New York, NY 10169, USA
Morgan, Shelly Taylor *Actress*
%Pakula/King, 9229 Sunset Blvd, #315, Los Angeles, CA 90069, USA
Morgan, Tracy *Actor, Comedian*
%William Morris Agency, 151 El Camino Dr, Beverly Hills, CA 90212, USA
Morgan, Trevor *Actor*
%Gilbertson-Kinkaid, 43 Navy St, #300, Venice, CA 90291, USA
Morgan, William N *Architect*
%William Morgan Architects, 220 E Forsyth St, Jacksonville, FL 32202, USA
Morganna *Entertainer, Model*
PO Box 20281, Columbus, OH 43220, USA
Morgenson, Gretchen *Journalist*
%New York Times, Editorial Dept, 229 W 43rd St, New York, NY 10036, USA
Morgenthau, Robert M *Attorney*
1085 Park Ave, New York, NY 10128, USA
Morgenweck, Henry C *Baseball Umpire*
33 Bogert St, Teaneck, NJ 07666, USA
Morgridge, John P *Businessman*
%Cisco Systems, 170 W Tasan Dr, San Jose, CA 95134, USA
Mori, Hanae *Fashion Designer*
%Hanae Mori Haute Couture, 17-19 Ave Montaigne, 75008 Paris, France
Mori, Yoshiro *Prime Minister, Japan*
%Prime Minister's Office, 1-6-1 Nagatoicho, Chiyodaku, Tokyo 100, Japan
Moriarty, Michael *Actor*
200 W 58th St, #3B, New York, NY 10019, USA
Moriarty, Phillip (Phil) *Swimming Coach*
12 Vista de Laguna, Fort Pierce, FL 34951, USA
Moriarty-Gentile, Cathy *Actress*
15300 Ventura Blvd, #315, Sherman Oaks, CA 91403, USA
Morin, Jim *Editorial Cartoonist*
%Miami Herald, Editorial Dept, Herald Plaza, Miami, FL 33101, USA
Morin, Lee M E *Astronaut*
10 Marys Creek Lane, Friendswood, TX 77546, USA
Morin, Milt *Football Player*
45 N Maple St, #B, Hadley, MA 01035, USA
Morishima, Michio *Economist*
31 Greenway, Hutton Mount, Brentwood, Essex CM13 2NP, England
Morison, Patricia *Actress, Singer*
%Craig Mgmt, 125 S Sycamore Ave, Los Angeles, CA 90036, USA
Morissette, Alanis *Singer, Songwriter*
%Atlas/Third Rail Entertainment, 9200 W Sunset Blvd, West Hollywod, CA 90069, USA
Morita, Pat (Noriyuki) *Actor*
6399 Wilshire Blvd, #444, Los Angeles, CA 90048, USA
Moriyama, Raymond *Architect*
32 Davenport Road, Toronto ON M5R 1H3, Canada
Morkis, Dorothy *Equestrian Rider*
17 Farm St, Dover, MA 02030, USA
Morley, Lawrence W *Geophysicist*
90 Hemlock St, Saint Thomas ON N5R 1X9, Canada
Moroder, Giorgio *Composer*
1880 Century Park East, #900, Los Angeles, CA 90067, USA
Morozov, Akexei *Hockey Player*
%Pittsburgh Penguins, Mellon Arena, 66 Mario Lemieux Place, Pittsburgh, PA 15219, USA
Morozov, Vladimir M *Opera Singer*
%Kirov Opera, Mariinsky Theater, Reatralnaya 1, Saint Petersburg, Russia
Morrall, Earl E *Football Player*
2751 68th St SW, Naples, FL 34105, USA
Morrell, David *Writer*
%Warner Books, 1271 6th Ave, New York, NY 10020, USA
Morrey, Charles B, Jr *Mathematician*
210 Yale Ave, Kensington, CA 94708, USA

M

Morrice, Norman A *Ballet Choreographer*
%Royal Ballet, Covent Garden, Bow St, London WC2E 9DD, England
Morricone, Ennio *Composer*
Viaile della Letterature, #30, 00144 Rome, Italy
Morris Wingerter, Pam *Synchronized Swimmer*
PO Box 14381, New Bern, NC 28561, USA
Morris, Betty *Bowler*
225 Lemming Dr, Reno, NV 89523, USA
Morris, Byron (Bam) *Football Player*
251 NE 4th St, Cooper, TX 75432, USA
Morris, Desmond J *Writer, Zoologist*
%Jonathan Cape Ltd, 20 Vauxhall Bridge Road, London SW1V 2SA, England
Morris, Edmund *Writer, Educator*
222 Central Park S, #14A, New York, NY 10019, USA
Morris, Errol *Movie Director*
%Endeavor Talent Agency, 9701 Wilshire Blvd, #1000, Beverly Hills, CA 90212, USA
Morris, Eugene (Mercury) *Football Player*
7000 SW 73rd Court, Miami, FL 33143, USA
Morris, Garrett *Actor, Singer*
%Stone Manners, 6500 Wilshire Blvd, #550, Los Angeles, CA 90048, USA
Morris, Gary *Singer*
%Gurley Co, 1204B Cedar Lane, Nashville, TN 37212, USA
Morris, George A *Football Player*
720 Fair Oaks Manor NW, Atlanta, GA 30327, USA
Morris, Howard *Actor, Comedian, Director*
742 N Sycamore Ave, Los Angeles, CA 90038, USA
Morris, James P *Opera Singer*
%Colbert Artists, 111 W 57th St, New York, NY 10019, USA
Morris, Jan *Writer*
Trefan Morys, Llanystumdwy, Criccieth, Gwymedd, Wales
Morris, Jason *Judo Athlete*
16 Gail St, Chelmsford, MA 01824, USA
Morris, Jenny *Singer*
%Artist & Event Mgmt, PO Box 537, Randwick NSW 2031, Australia
Morris, John S (Jack) *Baseball Player*
PO Box 2112, West Yellowstone, MT 59758, USA
Morris, Keith *Singer (Black Flag, Circle Jerks)*
%International Creative Mgmt, 8942 Wilshire Blvd, #219, Beverly Hills, CA 90211, USA
Morris, Larry *Sculptor*
105 N Union St, #4, Alexandria, VA 22314, USA
Morris, Lawrence C (Larry) *Football Player*
4737 Upper Berkshire Road, Flowery Branch, GA 30542, USA
Morris, Mark W *Choreographer*
%Mark Morris Dance Group, 3 Lafayette Ave, #504, Brooklyn, NY 11217, USA
Morris, Matthew C (Matt) *Baseball Player*
%Saint Louis Cardinals, Busch Stadium, 250 Stadium Plaza, Saint Louis, MO 63102, USA
Morris, Nathan *Singer (Boyz II Men)*
%Southpaw Entertainment, 10675 Santa Monica Blvd, Los Angeles, CA 90025, USA
Morris, Norval *Attorney, Criminologist*
1207 E 50th St, Chicago, IL 60615, USA
Morris, Oswald (Ossie) *Cinematographer*
Holbrook, Church St, Fontmell Magna, Shaftesbury SP7 0NY, England
Morris, Phil *Actor*
704 Strand, Manhattan Beach, CA 90266, USA
Morris, Robert *Sculptor*
%Hunter College, Art Dept, New York, NY 10021, USA
Morris, Ronald (Ron) *Track Athlete*
330 S Reese Place, Burbank, CA 91506, USA
Morris, Wayna *Singer (Boyz II Men)*
%Southpaw Entertainment, 10675 Santa Monica Blvd, Los Angeles, CA 90025, USA
Morrison, Ian (Scotty) *Hockey Executive*
Kennisis Lake, RR 1 PO Box 314, Haliburton ON K0M 1S0, Canada
Morrison, Mark *Singer*
%Atlantic Records, 1290 Ave of Americas, New York, NY 10104, USA
Morrison, Philip *Astronomer, Physicist*
11 Bowden St, Cambridge, MA 02138, USA
Morrison, Robert S (Bob) *Businessman*
%Quaker Oats Co, Quaker Tower, PO Box 049001, Chicago, IL 60604, USA
Morrison, Shelley *Actress*
1209 S Alfred St, Los Angeles, CA 90035, USA
Morrison, Toni *Nobel Literature Laureate*
185 Nassau St, Princeton, NJ 08542, USA
Morrison, Van *Singer, Guitarist, Songwriter*
#8 Glenthorne, 115A Glenthorne, Hammersmith, London W6 OLJ, England
Morrissey *Singer, Songwriter*
%MVO Ltd, 307 7th Ave, #807, New York, NY 10001, USA
Morrissey, Bill *Singer, Songwriter*
%Sage Productions, 1437 Firebird Way, Sunnyvale, CA 94087, USA

Morrone, Joe *Soccer Coach*
%University of Connecticut, Athletic Dept, Storrs Mansfield, CT 06269, USA
Morrow, Bobby Joe *Track Athlete*
PO Box 9, Beeville, TX 78104, USA
Morrow, Bruce (Cousin Brucie) *Entertainer*
%CBS Radio Network, 51 W 52nd St, New York, NY 10019, USA
Morrow, Kenneth (Ken) *Hockey Player*
39 Crystal Dr, Warwick, RI 02889, USA
Morrow, Rob *Actor*
%Hofflund/Polone, 9465 Wilshire Blvd, #820, Beverly Hills, CA 90212, USA
Morse, Barry *Actor*
71 Charles St E, #506, Toronto ON M4Y 2T3, Canada
Morse, David *Actor*
%Yvette Bikoff, 1040 1st Ave, #1126, New York, NY 10022, USA
Morse, David *Guitarist (Air Supply)*
%Agency for Performing Arts, 9200 Sunset Blvd, #900, Los Angeles, CA 90069, USA
Morse, David E *Publisher*
%Christian Science Monitor, Publisher's Office, 1 Norway St, Boston, MA 02115, USA
Morse, Robert *Actor*
13830 Davana Terrace, Sherman Oaks, CA 91423, USA
Mortensen, Chris *Sportscaster*
%ESPN-TV, Sports Dept, ESPN Plaza, 935 Middle St, Bristol, CT 06010, USA
Mortensen, Viggo *Actor*
5417 Skyview Dr, #D, Agoura Hills, CA 91301, USA
Mortier, Gerard *Opera Director*
%Salzburg Festpiele, Hofstallgasse 1, 5020 Salzburg, Austria
Mortimer Barrett, Angela *Tennis Player*
Oaks, Coombe Hill, Beverly Lane, Kingston-on-Thames, Surrey, England
Mortimer, Emily *Actress*
%Kelly Bush, 3859 Cardiff Ave, #200, Culver City, CA 90232, USA
Mortimer, John C *Writer*
Turville Heath Cottage, Henley-on-Thames, Oxon, England
Morton, Bruce A *Commentator*
%Cable News Network, News Dept, 820 1st St NE, Washington, DC 20002, USA
Morton, Joe *Actor*
%Judy Schoen, 606 N Larchmont Blvd, #309, Los Angeles, CA 90004, USA
Morton, Johnnie J *Football Player*
2911 Oakwood Lane, Torrance, CA 90505, USA
Morton, L Craig *Football Player*
500 S Eliseo Dr, #22, Greenbrae, CA 94904, USA
Morton, R Alastair *Businessman*
Senator House, 85 Queen St, London EC4V 4DP, England
Morton, Samantha *Actress*
%Conway Van Gelder Robinson, 18-21 Jermyn St, London SW1Y 6NB, England
Morukov, Boris V *Cosmonaut*
%Potchta Kosmonavtov, Moskovskoi Oblasti, 141160 Syvisdny Goroduk, Russia
Mos Def *Rap Artist, Actor*
%Kathryn Schenker, 1776 Broadway, #1200, New York, NY 10019, USA
Mosbacher, Robert A *Secretary, Commerce*
%Mosbacher Energy Co, 712 Main St, #2200, Houston, TX 77002, USA
Moschen, Michael *Juggler*
PO Box 178, Cornwall Bridge, CT 06754, USA
Moscoso Rodriguez, Mireya E *President, Panama*
%Palacio Presidencial, Valija 50, Panama City 1, Panama
Mosebar, Donald H (Don) *Football Player*
1713 Walnut Ave, Manhattan Beach, CA 90266, USA
Mosel, Tad *Writer*
149 East Side Dr, PO Box 249, Concord, NH 03302, USA
Moseley, Jonny *Freestyle Moguls Skier*
167 Trinidad Dr, Tiburon, CA 94920, USA
Moser, Donald B (Don) *Editor*
%Smithsonian Magazine, Editorial Dept, 900 Jefferson SW, Washington, DC 20560, USA
Moser, Thomas *Opera Singer*
%Lies Askonas, 6 Henrietta St, London WC2E 8LA, England
Moser-Proll, Annemarie *Alpine Skier*
%Moser Cafe-Bar #92, 5602 Kleinarl 115, Austria
Moses, Edwin C *Track Athlete*
%Robinson-Humphrey, 3333 Peachtree Road NE, Atlanta, GA 30326, USA
Moses, Rick *Actor, Singer*
%Calder Agency, 19919 Redwing St, Woodland Hills, CA 91364, USA
Moses, Robert (Bob) *Educator, Social Activist*
99 Bishop Allen Dr, Cambridge, MA 02139, USA
Moses, Yolanda T *Educator*
%City College of New York, President's Office, New York, NY 10031, USA
Mosher, Gregry D *Theater Director, Producer*
%Lincoln Center Theater, 150 W 165th St, New York, NY 10023, USA
Moshinsky, Elijah *Opera Director*
28 Kidbrooke Groove, London SE3 0LG, England

Mosimann, Anton *Chef*
%Mosimann's, 11B W Halkin St, London SW1X 8JL, England
Mosisili, Pakalitha *Prime Minister, Lesotho*
%Chairman's Office, Military Council, PO Box 527, Maseru 100, Lesotho
Moskow, Michael *Financier, Government Official*
%Federal Reserve Bank, 230 S LaSalle St, Chicago, IL 60604, USA
Moskowitz, Robert *Artist*
81 Leonard St, New York, NY 10013, USA
Mosley, J Brooke *Religious Leader*
1604 Foulkeways, Gwynedd, PA 19436, USA
Mosley, Max R *Auto Racing Executive*
%Int'l Automobile Fed, 2 Chemin Blandonnet, 1215 Geneva, Switzerland
Mosley, Roger E *Actor*
4470 W Sunset Blvd, #107-342, Los Angeles, CA 90027, USA
Mosley, Walter *Writer*
37 Carmine St, #275, New York, NY 10014, USA
Mosoke, Kintu *Prime Minister, Uganda*
%Prime Minister's Office, PO Box 341, Kampala, Uganda
Moss, Carrie-Ann *Actress*
%United Talent Agency, 9560 Wilshire Blvd, #500, Beverly Hills, CA 90212, USA
Moss, Cynthia *Elephant Conservationist*
%African Wildlife Foundation, Mara Road, PO Box 48177, Nairobi, Kenya
Moss, Elisabeth *Actress*
%United Talent Agency, 9560 Wilshire Blvd, #500, Beverly Hills, CA 90212, USA
Moss, Elza *Religious Leader*
%Primitive Advent Christian Church, 273 Frame Road, Elkview, WV 25071, USA
Moss, Eric Owen *Architect*
8557 Higuera St, Culver City, CA 90232, USA
Moss, Geoffrey *Cartoonist, Illustrator*
315 E 68th St, New York, NY 10021, USA
Moss, Kate *Model*
%Women Model Mgmt, 107 Greene St, #200, New York, NY 10012, USA
Moss, Randy *Football Player*
%Minnesota Vikings, 9520 Viking Dr, Eden Prairie, MN 55344, USA
Moss, Ronn *Actor*
2401 Nottingham Ave, Los Angeles, CA 90027, USA
Moss, Santana *Football Player*
%New York Jets, 1000 Fulton Ave, Hempstead, NY 11550, USA
Moss, Stirling *Auto Racing Driver*
%Stirling Moss Ltd, 46 Shephard St, Mayfair, London W1Y 8JN, England
Mossbauer, Rudolf L *Nobel Physics Laureate*
Stumpflingstr 6A, 82031 Grunwald, Germany
Mossi, Donald L (Don) *Baseball Player*
23250 Canyon Lane, Caldwell, ID 83607, USA
Most, Don *Actor*
6643 Buttonwood Ave, Agoura, CA 91301, USA
Mostert, Dutch *Artist*
93696 Mallard Lane, North Bend, OR 97459, USA
Mostow, George D *Mathematician*
25 Beechwood Road, Woodbridge, CT 06525, USA
Mostow, Jonathan *Movie Director*
%Creative Artists Agency, 9830 Wilshire Blvd, Beverly Hills, CA 90212, USA
Mota, Manuel R (Manny) *Baseball Player, Coach*
1506 Canada Blvd, #3, Glendale, CA 91208, USA
Mota, Rosa *Track Athlete*
R Teatro 194 4 Esq, 4100 Porto, Portugal
Mote, Bobby *Rodeo Rider*
20840 NW Kachina Ave, Redmond, OR 97756, USA
Motion, Andrew *Writer*
%University of East Anglia, English Dept, Norwich NR4 7TJ, England
Motley, Constance Baker *Judge*
%US District Court, US Courthouse, Foley Square, New York, NY 10007, USA
Motley, Isolde *Editor*
%Life Magazine, Editorial Dept, Time-Life Building, New York, NY 10020, USA
Mott, Stewart R *Political Activist*
515 Madison Ave, New York, NY 10022, USA
Motta, Dick *Basketball Coach*
PO Box 4, Fish Haven, ID 83287, USA
Mottelson, Ben R *Nobel Physics Laureate*
Nordita, Blegdamsvej 17, 2100 Copenhagen 0, Denmark
Motz, Diana Gribbon *Judge*
%US Appeals Court, 101 W Lombard St, Baltimore, MD 21201, USA
Motzfeldt, Jonathan *Prime Minister, Greenland*
%Greenland Home Rule Government, PO Box 1015, 3900 Nuuk, Greenland
Mouawad, Jerry *Theater Director*
%Imago Theater, 17 SE 8th Ave, Portland, OR 97214, USA
Moulds, Eric *Football Player*
5295 Briefcliff Dr, Hamburg, NY 14075, USA

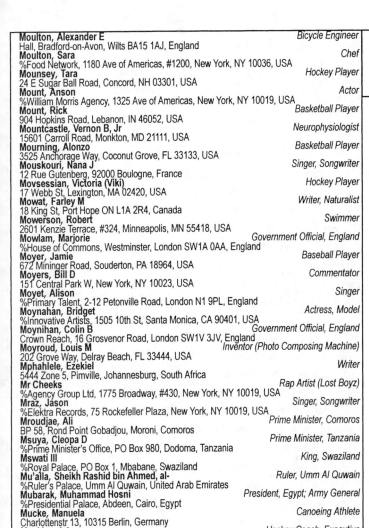

Moulton, Alexander E *Bicycle Engineer*
Hall, Bradford-on-Avon, Wilts BA15 1AJ, England
Moulton, Sara *Chef*
%Food Network, 1180 Ave of Americas, #1200, New York, NY 10036, USA
Mounsey, Tara *Hockey Player*
24 E Sugar Ball Road, Concord, NH 03301, USA
Mount, Anson *Actor*
%William Morris Agency, 1325 Ave of Americas, New York, NY 10019, USA
Mount, Rick *Basketball Player*
904 Hopkins Road, Lebanon, IN 46052, USA
Mountcastle, Vernon B, Jr *Neurophysiologist*
15601 Carroll Road, Monkton, MD 21111, USA
Mourning, Alonzo *Basketball Player*
3525 Anchorage Way, Coconut Grove, FL 33133, USA
Mouskouri, Nana J *Singer, Songwriter*
12 Rue Gutenberg, 92000 Boulogne, France
Movsessian, Victoria (Viki) *Hockey Player*
17 Webb St, Lexington, MA 02420, USA
Mowat, Farley M *Writer, Naturalist*
18 King St, Port Hope ON L1A 2R4, Canada
Mowerson, Robert *Swimmer*
2601 Kenzie Terrace, #324, Minneapolis, MN 55418, USA
Mowlam, Marjorie *Government Official, England*
%House of Commons, Westminster, London SW1A 0AA, England
Moyer, Jamie *Baseball Player*
672 Mininger Road, Souderton, PA 18964, USA
Moyers, Bill D *Commentator*
151 Central Park W, New York, NY 10023, USA
Moyet, Alison *Singer*
%Primary Talent, 2-12 Petonville Road, London N1 9PL, England
Moynahan, Bridget *Actress, Model*
%Innovative Artists, 1505 10th St, Santa Monica, CA 90401, USA
Moynihan, Colin B *Government Official, England*
Crown Reach, 16 Grosvenor Road, London SW1V 3JV, England
Moyroud, Louis M *Inventor (Photo Composing Machine)*
202 Grove Way, Delray Beach, FL 33444, USA
Mphahlele, Ezekiel *Writer*
5444 Zone 5, Pimville, Johannesburg, South Africa
Mr Cheeks *Rap Artist (Lost Boyz)*
%Agency Group Ltd, 1775 Broadway, #430, New York, NY 10019, USA
Mraz, Jason *Singer, Songwriter*
%Elektra Records, 75 Rockefeller Plaza, New York, NY 10019, USA
Mroudjae, Ali *Prime Minister, Comoros*
BP 58, Rond Point Gobadjou, Moroni, Comoros
Msuya, Cleopa D *Prime Minister, Tanzania*
%Prime Minister's Office, PO Box 980, Dodoma, Tanzania
Mswati III *King, Swaziland*
%Royal Palace, PO Box 1, Mbabane, Swaziland
Mu'alla, Sheikh Rashid bin Ahmed, al- *Ruler, Umm Al Quwain*
%Ruler's Palace, Umm Al Quwain, United Arab Emirates
Mubarak, Muhammad Hosni *President, Egypt; Army General*
%Presidential Palace, Abdeen, Cairo, Egypt
Mucke, Manuela *Canoeing Athlete*
Charlottenstr 13, 10315 Berlin, Germany
Muckler, John *Hockey Coach, Executive*
%Ottawa Senators, 1000 Palladium Dr, Kanata ON K2V 1A4, Canada
Mudd, Roger H *Commentator*
7167 Old Dominion Dr, McLean, VA 22101, USA
Mudra, Darrell *Football Coach*
424 Tiger Hammock Road, Crawfordville, FL 32327, USA
Mueller, George E *Electrical Engineer, Missile Scientist*
%Kistler Aerospace Corp, 3760 Carillon Point, Kirkland, WA 98033, USA
Mueller, Gerd *Soccer Player*
Neuestr 21, 81479 Munich, Germany
Mueller, Leah Poulos *Speedskater*
11455 N Mulberry Dr, Mequon, WI 53092, USA
Mueller, Lisel *Writer*
%LSU Press, PO Box 25053, Baton Rouge, LA 70894, USA
Mueller, Robert *Law Enforcement Official*
%Federal Bureau of Investigation, 9th & Pennsylvania NW, Washington, DC 20535, USA
Mueller-Stahl, Armin *Actor*
Gartenweg 31, 23730 Sierksdorf, Germany
Muench, David *Photographer*
PO Box 30500, Santa Barbara, CA 93130, USA
Mugabe, Robert G *President, Zimbabwe*
%President's Office, Munhumutapa Bldg, Samora Machel Ave, Harare, Zimbabwe
Mugler, Thierry *Fashion Designer*
4-6 Rue Aux Ours, 75003 Paris, France

Muhammad, Wallace D *Religious Leader*
%American Muslim Mission, 7351 S Stony Island Blvd, Chicago, IL 60649, USA
Muir DeGraad, Karen *Swimmer*
%Applebosch State Hospital, Ozwatini, Natal, South Africa
Mukai, Chiaki Naito- *Astronaut, Japan*
15836 Seahorse Dr, #253, Houston, TX 77062, USA
Mukherjee, Bharati *Writer*
130 Rivoli St, San Francisco, CA 94117, USA
Mulari, Tarja *Speed Skier*
%Motion Oy, Vanhan Mankkaantie 33, 02180 Espoo, Finland
Mulcahy, Anne *Businesswoman*
%Xerox Corp, 800 Long Ridge Road, Stamford, CT 06902, USA
Mulcahy, J Patrick *Businessman*
%Ralston Purina Co, Checkerboard Square, Saint Louis, MO 63164, USA
Muldaur, Diana *Actress*
20 Cummings Way, Edgertown, MA 02539, USA
Muldaur, Maria *Singer, Songwriter*
%Piedmont Talent, PO Box 680006, Charlotte, NC 28216, USA
Mulder, Karen *Model*
%Metropolitan Modeling Agency, 220 5th Ave, New York, NY 10001, USA
Mulder, Mark *Baseball Player*
33196 N 74th Way, Scottsdale, AZ 85262, USA
Muldoon, Patrick *Actor, Model*
11030 Ventura Blvd, #3, Studio City, CA 91604, USA
Muldoon, Paul B *Writer*
%Princeton University, Creative Writing Progam, Princeton, NJ 08544, USA
Muldowney, Dominic J *Composer*
%Royal National Theater, Music Dept, South Bank, London SE1 1PX, England
Muldowney, Shirley *Auto Racing Driver*
79559 North Ave, Armada, MI 48005, USA
Mulgrew, Kate *Actress*
%Marie Ambrosino Mgmt, 10351 Santa Monica Blvd, #220, Los Angeles, CA 90025, USA
Mulhern, Matt *Actor*
%Gold Marshak Liedtke, 3500 W Olive Ave, #1400, Burbank, CA 91505, USA
Mulhern, Sinead *Opera Singer*
%Van Walsum Mgmt, 4 Addison Bridge Place, London W14 8XP, England
Mulkey, Chris *Actor*
%Paradigm Agency, 10100 Santa Monica Blvd, #2500, Los Angeles, CA 90067, USA
Mulkey-Robertson, Kim *Basketball Player, Coach*
%Baylor University, Athletic Dept, Waco, TX 76798, USA
Mull, Martin *Actor*
338 S Chadbourne Ave, Los Angeles, CA 90049, USA
Mullally, Megan *Actress, Singer*
%Baker/Winokur/Ryder, 9100 Wilshire Blvd, #600, Beverly Hills, CA 90212, USA
Mullane, Richard M (Mike) *Astronaut*
1301 Las Lomas Road NE, Albuquerque, NM 87106, USA
Mullavey, Greg *Actor*
1818 Thayer Ave, #303, Los Angeles, CA 90025, USA
Mullen, Joseph P (Joey) *Hockey Player*
126 Fieldgate Dr, Pittsburgh, PA 15241, USA
Mullen, Larry, Jr *Drummer (U-2)*
%Principle Mgmt, 30-32 Sir John Rogerson Quay, Dublin 2, Ireland
Muller, Egon *Motorcycle Racing Rider*
Dorfstr 17, 24247 Rodenbek/Kiel, Germany
Muller, Jorg *Auto Racing Driver*
%Insert Motorsport, Fassoldshof 1, 95336 Mainleus, Germany
Muller, K Alex *Nobel Physics Laureate*
%IBM Research Laboratory, Saumerstr 4, 8803 Ruschlikon, Switzerland
Muller, Kirk *Hockey Player*
4577 Belfort Ave, Dallas, TX 75205, USA
Muller, Lillian *Model, Actress*
PO Box 20029-414, Encino, CA 91416, USA
Muller, Marcia *Writer*
%Mysterious Press, Warner Books, 1271 6th Ave, New York, NY 10020, USA
Muller, Peter *Alpine Skier*
Haldenstr 18, 8134 Adliswil, Switzerland
Muller, Robby *Cinematographer*
%Smith/Gosnell/Nicholson, PO Box 1156, Studio City, CA 91614, USA
Mulligan, Robert P *Movie Director*
%JV Broffman, 5150 Wilshire Blvd, #505, Los Angeles, CA 90036, USA
Mulliken, William (Bill) *Swimmer*
4216 N Keeler Ave, Chicago, IL 60641, USA
Mullin, Christopher P (Chris) *Basketball Player*
116 Laurelwood Dr, Danville, CA 94506, USA
Mullin, Leo F *Businessman*
%Delta Air Lines, Hartsfield International Airport, Atlanta, GA 30320, USA
Mullins, Jeffrey (Jeff) *Basketball Player, Coach*
8866 N Sea Oaks Way, #202, Vero Beach, FL 32963, USA

Mullins, Shawn *Singer, Songwriter*
%High Road, 751 Bridgeway, #300, Sausalito, CA 94965, USA
Mullis, Kary B *Nobel Chemistry Laureate*
%Vyrex, 2519 Avenida de la Palaya, La Jolla, CA 92037, USA
Mullova, Viktoria Y *Concert Violinist*
%Askonas Holt Ltd, 27 Chancery Lane, London WC2A 1PF, England
Mulloy, Gardner *Tennis Player*
800 NW 9th Ave, Miami, FL 33136, USA
Mulroney, Dermot *Actor*
5200 Linwood Dr, Los Angeles, CA 90027, USA
Mulroney, M Brian *Prime Minister, Canada*
47 Forden Crescent, Westmount QC H3Y 2Y5, Canada
Muluzi, Bakili *President, Malawi*
%President's Office, Private Bag 301, Capitol City, Lilongwe 3, Malawi
Mulva, James J *Businessman*
%Conoco/Phillips Inc, 600 N Daisy Ashford, Houston, TX 77029, USA
Mumba, Samantha *Singer, Actress*
%Polydor Records, 1 Sussex Place, London W6 9XT, England
Mumy, Billy *Actor*
11333 Moorpark St, PO Box 433, Studio City, CA 91602, USA
Muna, Solomon Tandeng *Prime Minister, Western Cameroon*
PO Box 15, Mbengwi, Mono Division, North West Province, Cameroon
Munchak, Michael A (Mike) *Football Player*
9155 Saddlebow Dr, Brentwood, TN 37027, USA
Muncie, Harry V (Chuck) *Football Player*
%Chuck Muncie Youth Foundation, 3334 Woodview Court, Lafayette, CA 94549, USA
Mundell, Robert A *Nobel Economics Laureate*
35 Claremont Ave, New York, NY 10027, USA
Mundy, Carl E, Jr *Marine Corps General*
9308 Ludgate Dr, Alexandria, VA 22309, USA
Munitz, Barry A *Educator*
%California State University System, 400 Golden Shore St, Long Beach, CA 90802, USA
Munk, Walter H *Geophysicist*
9530 La Jolla Shores Dr, La Jolla, CA 92037, USA
Munoz, M Anthony *Football Player, Sportscaster*
6529 Irwin Simpson Road, Mason, OH 45040, USA
Munro, Alice *Writer*
PO Box 1133, Clinton ON N0M 1L0, Canada
Munro, Caroline *Actress*
PO Box 2589, London W1A 3NQ, England
Munro, J Richard *Publisher*
%Time Warner Inc, Rockefeller Plaza, New York, NY 10020, USA
Munro, Lochlyn *Actor*
%International Creative Mgmt, 8942 Wilshire Blvd, #219, Beverly Hills, CA 90211, USA
Munsel, Patrice *Opera Singer*
PO Box 472, Schroon Lake, NY 12870, USA
Muntyan, Mikhail *Opera Singer*
16 N Iorga Str, #13, 277012 Chisnau, Moldova
Murad, Ferid *Nobel Medicine Laureate*
2121 W Holcombe Blvd, Houston, TX 77030, USA
Muradov, Sakhat A *Head of Government, Turkmenistan*
%Turkmenistan Mejlis, 17 Gogol St, 744017 Ashkhabad, Turkmenistan
Murakami, Masanori *Baseball Player*
1-4-15-1506 Nisho Ohi Shinagawaku, Tokyo 140-0015, Japan
Muraliyev, Amangeldy *Prime Minister, Kyrgyzstan*
%Prime Minister's Office, Ul Perromayskaya 57, Bishkek, Kyrgyzstan
Muratova, Kira G *Movie Director*
Proletarsjy Blvd 14B, #15, 270015 Odessa, Russia
Murayama, Makio *Biochemist*
5010 Benton Ave, Bethesda, MD 20814, USA
Murayama, Tomiichi *Prime Minister, Japan*
3-2-2 Chiyomachi, Oita, Oita 870, Japan
Murcer, Bobby R *Baseball Player*
4323 NW 63rd St, #100, Oklahoma City, OK 73116, USA
Murchison, Ira *Track Athlete*
10113 S Sangamon St, Chicago, IL 60643, USA
Murdoch, K Rupert *Publisher*
%News America Publishing, 1211 Ave of Americas, New York, NY 10036, USA
Murdoch, Murray *Hockey Player*
190 Dessa Dr, Hamden, CT 06517, USA
Murdoch, Robert J (Bob) *Hockey Player, Coach*
410 11th Ave S, Cranbrook BC V1C 2P9, Canada
Murdoch, Stuart *Singer, Songwriter (Belle & Sebastian)*
%Legends of 21st Century, 7 Trinity Row, Florence, MA 01062, USA
Murdock, David H *Businessman*
10900 Wilshire Blvd, #1600, Los Angeles, CA 90024, USA
Murdock, George *Actor*
5733 Sunfield Ave, Lakewood, CA 90712, USA

M

Murdock, George P *Anthropologist*
Wynnewood Plaza, #107, Wynnewood, PA 19096, USA
Murdock, Shirley *Singer*
%Millennium Entertainment Group, 1315 5th Ave N, Nashville, TN 37208, USA
Muresan, Gheorghe *Basketball Player, Actor*
%New Jersey Nets, 390 Murray Hill Parkway, East Rutherford, NJ 07073, USA
Muris, Timothy *Government Official*
%Federal Trade Commission, Pennsylvania Ave & 6th St NW, Washington, DC 20580, USA
Murphey, Michael Martin *Singer, Songwriter*
%Wildfire Productions, PO Box 450, Rancho de Taos, NM 87557, USA
Murphy, Ben *Actor*
2690 Rambla Pacifico St, Malibu, CA 90265, USA
Murphy, Bob *Sportscaster*
1401 Bonnie Lane, Bayside, NY 11360, USA
Murphy, Bob *Golfer*
%Eddie Elias Enterprises, PO Box 5118, Akron, OH 44334, USA
Murphy, Brittany *Actress*
2545 Verbena Dr, Los Angeles, CA 90068, USA
Murphy, Calvin J *Basketball Player, Executive*
43 Sterling St, Sugar Land, TX 77479, USA
Murphy, Carolyn *Model*
%I M G Models, 304 Park Ave S, #1200, New York, NY 10010, USA
Murphy, Caryle M *Journalist*
%Washington Post, Editorial Dept, 1150 15th St NW, Washington, DC 20071, USA
Murphy, Dale B *Baseball Player*
%Church Securities Corp, 605 Claremont Ave, Decatur, GA 30030, USA
Murphy, David Lee *Singer*
%D Mgmt, 1102 18th Ave S, Nashville, TN 37212, USA
Murphy, Donna *Actress, Singer*
%Gerson Saines, 250 W 57th St, #2303, New York, NY 10107, USA
Murphy, Eddie *Actor, Comedian*
1081 Wallace Ridge, Beverly Hills, CA 90210, USA
Murphy, Erin *Actress*
%James/Levy/Jacobson, 3500 W Olive Ave, #1470, Burbank, CA 91505, USA
Murphy, John Cullen *Cartoonist (Prince Valiant)*
14 Mead Ave, Cos Cob, CT 06807, USA
Murphy, Lawrence T (Larry) *Hockey Player*
927 S Bates St, Birmingham, MI 48009, USA
Murphy, Mark H *Football Player*
736 Michigan Ave, Evanston, IL 60202, USA
Murphy, Michael R *Judge*
%US Court of Appeals, Federal Building, 125 S State St, Salt Lake City, UT 84138, USA
Murphy, Mike *Hockey Player, Coach*
17072 Oak View Dr, Encino, CA 91436, USA
Murphy, Raymond D *Korean War Marine Corps Hero (CMH)*
4677 Sutton St NW, Albuquerque, NM 87114, USA
Murphy, Reg *Editor, Publisher*
%National Geographic Society, 1145 17th St NW, Washington, DC 20036, USA
Murphy, Rosemary *Actress*
220 E 73rd St, New York, NY 10021, USA
Murphy, Terry *Entertainer*
%Sherry Ingram, 3575 Cahuenga Blvd W, #600, Los Angeles, CA 90068, USA
Murphy, Thomas (Tom) *Writer*
4 Garville Road, Dublin 6, Ireland
Murphy, Thomas S *Businessman*
%Capital Cities/ABC, 77 W 66th St, New York, NY 10023, USA
Murphy-O'Connor, Cormac Cardinal *Religious Leader*
%Archbishop's House, Ambrosden Ave, London SW1P 1QJ, England
Murray of Epping Forest, Lionel (Len) *Labor Leader*
29 Crescent, Loughton, Essex 1G10 4PY, England
Murray, Andy *Hockey Coach*
%Los Angeles Kings, Staples Center, 1111 S Figueroa St, Los Angeles, CA 90015, USA
Murray, Anne *Singer*
%Bruce Allen Talent, 406-68 Water St, Vancouver BC V6B 1A4, Canada
Murray, Anne *Opera Singer*
%Helge Rudolf Augstein, Sebastianplatz 3, 80331 Munich, Germany
Murray, Bill *Actor, Comedian*
%Creative Artists Agency, 9830 Wilshire Blvd, Beverly Hills, CA 90212, USA
Murray, Brian Doyle *Actor*
%Abrams Artists, 9200 Sunset Blvd, #1125, Los Angeles, CA 90069, USA
Murray, Bruce C *Planetary Scientist, Geologist*
%Jet Propulsion Laboratory, 4800 Oak Grove Dr, Pasadena, CA 91109, USA
Murray, Bryan C *Hockey Coach, Executive*
2215 NE 32nd Ave, Fort Lauderdale, FL 33305, USA
Murray, Charles A *Social Scientist*
%American Enterprise Institute, 1150 17th St NW, Washington, DC 20036, USA
Murray, Charles P, Jr *WW II Army Hero (CMH)*
5906 Northridge Road, Columbia, SC 29206, USA

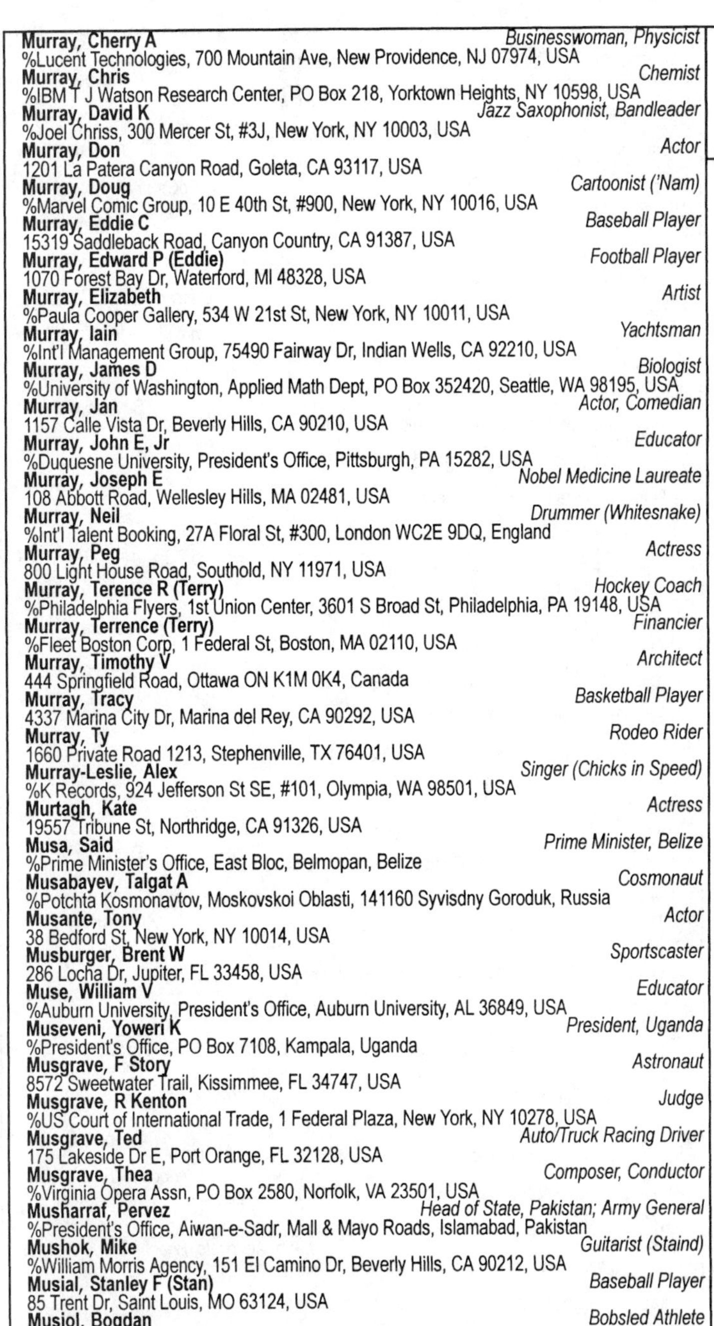

Murray, Cherry A *Businesswoman, Physicist*
%Lucent Technologies, 700 Mountain Ave, New Providence, NJ 07974, USA
Murray, Chris *Chemist*
%IBM T J Watson Research Center, PO Box 218, Yorktown Heights, NY 10598, USA
Murray, David K *Jazz Saxophonist, Bandleader*
%Joel Chriss, 300 Mercer St, #3J, New York, NY 10003, USA
Murray, Don *Actor*
1201 La Patera Canyon Road, Goleta, CA 93117, USA
Murray, Doug *Cartoonist ('Nam)*
%Marvel Comic Group, 10 E 40th St, #900, New York, NY 10016, USA
Murray, Eddie C *Baseball Player*
15319 Saddleback Road, Canyon Country, CA 91387, USA
Murray, Edward P (Eddie) *Football Player*
1070 Forest Bay Dr, Waterford, MI 48328, USA
Murray, Elizabeth *Artist*
%Paula Cooper Gallery, 534 W 21st St, New York, NY 10011, USA
Murray, Iain *Yachtsman*
%Int'l Management Group, 75490 Fairway Dr, Indian Wells, CA 92210, USA
Murray, James D *Biologist*
%University of Washington, Applied Math Dept, PO Box 352420, Seattle, WA 98195, USA
Murray, Jan *Actor, Comedian*
1157 Calle Vista Dr, Beverly Hills, CA 90210, USA
Murray, John E, Jr *Educator*
%Duquesne University, President's Office, Pittsburgh, PA 15282, USA
Murray, Joseph E *Nobel Medicine Laureate*
108 Abbott Road, Wellesley Hills, MA 02481, USA
Murray, Neil *Drummer (Whitesnake)*
%Int'l Talent Booking, 27A Floral St, #300, London WC2E 9DQ, England
Murray, Peg *Actress*
800 Light House Road, Southold, NY 11971, USA
Murray, Terence R (Terry) *Hockey Coach*
%Philadelphia Flyers, 1st Union Center, 3601 S Broad St, Philadelphia, PA 19148, USA
Murray, Terrence (Terry) *Financier*
%Fleet Boston Corp, 1 Federal St, Boston, MA 02110, USA
Murray, Timothy V *Architect*
444 Springfield Road, Ottawa ON K1M 0K4, Canada
Murray, Tracy *Basketball Player*
4337 Marina City Dr, Marina del Rey, CA 90292, USA
Murray, Ty *Rodeo Rider*
1660 Private Road 1213, Stephenville, TX 76401, USA
Murray-Leslie, Alex *Singer (Chicks in Speed)*
%K Records, 924 Jefferson St SE, #101, Olympia, WA 98501, USA
Murtagh, Kate *Actress*
19557 Tribune St, Northridge, CA 91326, USA
Musa, Said *Prime Minister, Belize*
%Prime Minister's Office, East Bloc, Belmopan, Belize
Musabayev, Talgat A *Cosmonaut*
%Potchta Kosmonavtov, Moskovskoi Oblasti, 141160 Syvisdny Goroduk, Russia
Musante, Tony *Actor*
38 Bedford St, New York, NY 10014, USA
Musburger, Brent W *Sportscaster*
286 Locha Dr, Jupiter, FL 33458, USA
Muse, William V *Educator*
%Auburn University, President's Office, Auburn University, AL 36849, USA
Museveni, Yoweri K *President, Uganda*
%President's Office, PO Box 7108, Kampala, Uganda
Musgrave, F Story *Astronaut*
8572 Sweetwater Trail, Kissimmee, FL 34747, USA
Musgrave, R Kenton *Judge*
%US Court of International Trade, 1 Federal Plaza, New York, NY 10278, USA
Musgrave, Ted *Auto/Truck Racing Driver*
175 Lakeside Dr E, Port Orange, FL 32128, USA
Musgrave, Thea *Composer, Conductor*
%Virginia Opera Assn, PO Box 2580, Norfolk, VA 23501, USA
Musharraf, Pervez *Head of State, Pakistan; Army General*
%President's Office, Aiwan-e-Sadr, Mall & Mayo Roads, Islamabad, Pakistan
Mushok, Mike *Guitarist (Staind)*
%William Morris Agency, 151 El Camino Dr, Beverly Hills, CA 90212, USA
Musial, Stanley F (Stan) *Baseball Player*
85 Trent Dr, Saint Louis, MO 63124, USA
Musiol, Bogdan *Bobsled Athlete*
%Fitness-Studio, Talstr 50, 98544 Zella-Mehlis, Germany
Musiq *Singer*
%Def Soul Records, 825 8th Ave, #2700, New York, NY 10019, USA
Musker, John *Animator, Movie Director*
%Walt Disney Productions, 500 S Buena Vista St, Burbank, CA 91521, USA
Musonge, Peter Mafani *Prime Minister, Cameroon*
%Prime Minister's Office, BP 1057, Yaounde, Cameroon

M

Mussa - Mystikal

Mussa, Michael *Economist*
%International Monetary Fund, 700 19th St NW, Washington, DC 20431, USA
Musselman, Eric *Basketball Coach*
%Golden State Warriors, 1001 Broadway, Oakland, CA 94607, USA
Mussina, Michael C (Mike) *Baseball Player*
%Ashton Group, 5 Shawan Road, #2, Hunt Valley, MD 21030, USA
Musso, Johnny *Football Player*
242 E 3rd St, Hinsdale, IL 60521, USA
Mussolini, Alessandra *Government Official, Italy*
%Italian Social Movement (MSI), Chamber of Deputies, 00100 Rome, Italy
Muster, Thomas *Tennis Player*
370 Felter Ave, Hewlett, NY 11557, USA
Mustin, Henry C *Navy Admiral*
2347 S Rolfe St, Arlington, VA 22202, USA
Mustonen, Olli *Concert Pianist, Composer*
%Shuman Assoc, 120 W 58th St, #8D, New York, NY 10019, USA
Mutalov, Abdulkhashim M *Prime Minister, Uzbekistan*
%Government House, 700008 Tashkent, Uzbekistan
Muteba II, Ronald Muwenda *King, Uganda*
%Royal Palace, Kampala, Uganda
Muth, Rene *Basketball Coach*
%Pennsylvania State University, Athletic Dept, University Park, PA 16802, USA
Muti, Ornella *Actress*
33 Via Porta de Pinta, 24100 Bergamo, Italy
Muti, Riccardo *Conductor*
Via Corti Alle Mura 25, 48100 Ravenna, Italy
Mutombo, Dikembe *Basketball Player*
1300 Valley Road, Villanova, PA 19085, USA
Mutter, Anne-Sophie *Concert Violinist*
Effnerstr 48, 81925 Munich, Germany
Muzorewa, Abel T *Religious Leader*
PO Box 353, Borrowdale, Harare, Zimbabwe
Mwanawasa, Levy P *President, Zambia*
%President's Office, State House, PO Box 135, Lusaka, Zambia
Mwinyi, Ali Hassam *President, Tanzania*
%President's Office, State House, PO Box 9120, Dar es Salaam, Tanzania
Mya *Singer*
PO Box 569, Glenn Dale, MD 20769, USA
Mydans, Carl *Photographer*
212 Hommocks Road, Larchmont, NY 10538, USA
Myers Tikalsky, Linda *Skier*
RR 5 Box 265T, Santa Fe, NM 87506, USA
Myers, A Maurice *Businessman*
%Waste Management Inc, 1001 Fannin St, Houston, TX 77002, USA
Myers, Anne M *Religious Leader*
%Church of the Brethren, 1451 Dundee Ave, Elgin, IL 60120, USA
Myers, Barton *Architect*
%Barton Myers Assoc, 9348 Civic Center Dr, Beverly Hills, CA 90210, USA
Myers, Danny *Auto Racing Driver*
%Childress Racing, PO Box 1189, Industrial Dr, Welcome, NC 27374, USA
Myers, Jack D *Physician*
%University of Pittsburgh, 1291 Scaife Hall, Pittsburgh, PA 15261, USA
Myers, Lisa *Commentator*
%NBC-TV, News Dept, 4001 Nebraska Ave NW, Washington, DC 20016, USA
Myers, Margaret J (Dee Dee) *Government Official*
%Equal Time Show, CBS-TV, 1233 20th St NW, #302, Washington, DC 20036, USA
Myers, Mike *Actor, Comedian*
%Creative Artists Agency, 9830 Wilshire Blvd, Beverly Hills, CA 90212, USA
Myers, Reginald R *Korean War Marine Corps Hero (CMH)*
PO Box 803, Annandale, VA 22003, USA
Myers, Richard B (Dick) *Air Force General*
Chairman, Joint Chiefs of Staff, Pentagon, Washington, DC 20318, USA
Myers, Russell *Cartoonist (Broom Hilda)*
%Tribune Media Services, 435 N Michigan Ave, #1500, Chicago, IL 60611, USA
Myers, Terry-Jo *Golfer*
%Ladies Pro Golf Assn, 100 International Golf Dr, Daytona Beach, FL 32124, USA
Myerson, Bess *Consumer Advocate, Beauty Queen, Actress*
3 E 71st St, #9A, New York, NY 10021, USA
Myles, Alannah *Singer*
%Miracle Prestige, 1 Water Lane, Camden Town, London NW1 8N2, England
Myrick, Daniel *Movie Director*
%Artisan Entertainment, 2700 Colorado Ave, Santa Monica, CA 90404, USA
Mystikal *Rap Artist*
%International Creative Mgmt, 8942 Wilshire Blvd, #219, Beverly Hills, CA 90211, USA

N'Dour, Youssou *Singer*
%Konzertagentur Berthold Seliger, Nonnengasse 15, 36037 Fulda, Germany
Naber, John P *Swimmer*
PO Box 50107, Pasadena, CA 91115, USA
Nabers, Drayton, Jr *Businessman*
%Protective Life Corp, 2801 Highway 280 S, Birmingham, AL 35223, USA
Nabokov, Evgeni *Hockey Player*
%San Jose Sharks, San Jose Arena, 525 W Santa Clara St, San Jose, CA 95113, USA
Nabors, Jim *Actor, Singer*
PO Box 10364, Honolulu, HI 96816, USA
Nabors, Richard *Football Player*
1625 Brighton Court, Beaumont, TX 77706, USA
Naccarato, Vin *Singer (Capris)*
%Paramount Entertainment, PO Box 12, Far Hills, NJ 07931, USA
Nachamkin, Boris *Basketball Player*
350 E 62nd St, #5J, New York, NY 10021, USA
Nachbar, Bostjan *Basketball Player*
%Houston Rockets, Toyota Center, 2 E Greenway Plaza, Houston, TX 77046, USA
Nachmansohn, David *Biochemist*
560 Riverside Dr, New York, NY 10027, USA
Nadeau, Jerry *Auto Racing Driver*
565 Pitts School Road, Concord, NC 28027, USA
Nader, Michael *Actor*
28 E 10th St, New York, NY 10003, USA
Nader, Ralph *Consumer Activist*
1600 20th St NW, Washington, DC 20009, USA
Naehring, Timothy J (Tim) *Baseball Player*
7300 Pinehurst Dr, Cincinnati, OH 45244, USA
Nafziger, Dana A *Football Player*
251 El Dorado Way, Pismo Beach, CA 93449, USA
Nagakura, Saburo *Chemist*
2-7-13 Higashicho, Kichijoji, Musashino, Tokyo 1800002, Japan
Nagano, Kent G *Conductor*
%Van Walsum Mgmt, 4 Addison Bridge Place, London W14 8XP, England
Nagashima, Shigeo *Baseball Player, Manager*
3-29-19 Denenchofu, Ohtaku, Tokyo 145, Japan
Nagel, Sidney R *Physicist*
4919 S Blackstone Ave, Chicago, IL 60615, USA
Nagel, Steven R *Astronaut*
16923 Cottonwood Way, Houston, TX 77059, USA
Nagel, Thomas *Philosopher*
%New York University, Law School, 40 Washington Square S, New York, NY 10012, USA
Nagy, Stanislaw Cardinal *Religious Leader*
%Priests of Sacred Heart, Via Casale S Piov 20, 00165 Rome, Italy
Nahan, Stu *Sportscaster*
11274 Canton Dr, Studio City, CA 91604, USA
Naharin, Ohad *Choreographer*
%Dance Theater, Scheldeldoekshaven 60, 2511 EN Gravenhage, Netherlands
Nahyan, Sheikh Zayed bin Sultan al- *Ruler, Abu Dhabi*
%President's Office, Manhal Palace, Abu Dhabi, United Arab Emirates
Naifeh, Steven W *Writer*
335 Sumter St SE, Aiken, SC 29801, USA
Naipaul, V S *Nobel Literature Laureate*
%Aitken & Stone Ltd, 29 Fernshaw Road, London SW10 0TG, England
Nair, Mira *Movie Director*
%International Creative Mgmt, 8942 Wilshire Blvd, #219, Beverly Hills, CA 90211, USA
Naisbitt, John *Writer*
Spittelauer Platz 5A3A, 1090 Vienna, Austria
Naish, Bronwen *Concert Double Bass Player*
Moelfre, Xwm Pennant, Garndolbenmaen, Gwunedd, North Wales LL5 9AX, Wales
Najarian, John S *Surgeon*
%University of Minnesota, Health Center, Surgery Dept, Minneapolis, MN 55455, USA
Najee *Jazz Saxophonist*
%Associated Booking Corp, 1995 Broadway, #501, New York, NY 10023, USA
Najimy, Kathy *Actress*
3366 Wrightwood Dr, Studio City, CA 91604, USA
Nakajiim, Tadashi *Astronomer*
%California Institute of Technology, Astronomy Dept, Pasadena, CA 91125, USA
Nakama, Keo *Swimmer*
1344 9th Ave, Honolulu, HI 96816, USA
Nakano, Shinji *Auto Racing Driver*
%Fernandez Racing, 6950 Guion Circle W, #E, Indianapolis, IN 46268, USA
Nakasone, Yasuhiro *Prime Minister, Japan*
3-22-7 Kamikitazawa, Setagayaku, Tokyo, Japan
Nalder, Eric C *Journalist*
%Seattle Times, Editorial Dept, 1120 John St, Seattle, WA 98109, USA
Nall, N Anita *Swimmer*
PO Box 872505, Tempe, AZ 85287, USA

N

Namaliu, Rabbie L *Prime Minister, Papua New Guinea*
PO Box 6655, National Capital District, Boroko, Papua New Guinea
Namath, Joseph W (Joe) *Football Player, Actor*
%William Morris Agency, 151 El Camino Dr, Beverly Hills, CA 90212, USA
Nambu, Yoichiro *Physicist*
5535 University Ave, Chicago, IL 60637, USA
Namesnik, Eric *Swimmer*
114 Hickory St, Butler, PA 16001, USA
Nance, John J *Writer*
4512 8th Ave, West Tacoma, WA 98466, USA
Nance, Todd *Drummer (Widespread Panic)*
%Brown Cat Inc, 400 Foundry St, Athens, GA 30601, USA
Nanne, Louis V (Lou) *Hockey Player, Executive*
6982 Tupa Dr, Edina, MN 55439, USA
Nannini, Alessandro *Auto Racing Driver*
Via del Paradiso 4, 53100 Siena, Italy
Nanoski, John (Jukey) *Soccer Player*
RR 1, Herkimer, NY 11350, USA
Nantz, Jim *Sportscaster*
%CBS-TV, Sports Dept, 51 W 52nd St, New York, NY 10019, USA
Napier, Charles *Actor*
Star Route Box 60H, Caliente, CA 93518, USA
Napier, John *Theater Designer*
%MLR, Douglas House, 16-18 Douglas St, London SW1P 4PB, England
Napier, Wilfrid F Cardinal *Religious Leader*
%Archbishop's House, 154 Gordon Road, Greyville 4023, South Africa
Napoles, Jose *Boxer*
Cerrada De Tizapan 9-303 Ediciov, Codigo Postel 06080 Mexico City, Mexico
Narasimha Rao, P V *Prime Minister, India*
Vangara Post, Karimnagar District, Andhra Pradesh, India
Narayanan, Kocheril Raman *President, India*
81 Lodhi Estate, New Delhi 11003, India
Narducci, Tim *Singer, Guitarist (Systematic)*
%Artist Group International, 9560 Wilshire Blvd, #400, Beverly Hills, CA 90212, USA
Narita, Hiro *Cinematographer*
2262 Magnolia Ave, Petaluma, CA 94952, USA
Narizzano, Silvio (Cas) *Movie Director*
%Al Parker, 55 Park Lane, London W1Y 3DD, England
Narleski, Raymond E (Ray) *Baseball Player*
1183 Chews Landing Road, Laurel Springs, NJ 08021, USA
Narron, Jerry A *Baseball Player, Manager*
206 Friendswood Dr, Goldsboro, NC 27530, USA
Naruhito *Crown Prince, Japan*
%Imperial Palace, 1-1 Chiyoda, Chiyoda-ku, Tokyo, Japan
Narvekar, Prabhakar R *Financier*
%International Monetary Fund, 700 19th St NW, Washington, DC 20431, USA
Narz, Jack *Television Host*
1906 Beverly Place, Beverly Hills, CA 90210, USA
Nasciemento, Milton *Singer, Songwriter*
%Tribo Producoes, Av A Lombardi 800, Rio de Janeiro 22.640-000, Brazil
Nash, Charles F (Cotton) *Basketball, Baseball Player*
600 Summershade Circle, Lexington, KY 40502, USA
Nash, David *Sculptor*
Capel Rhiw, Blanau, Ffestiniog, Gwynedd Wales LL41 3NT, Wales
Nash, Graham W *Singer, Songwriter (Crosby Stills Nash)*
PO Box 838, Hanalei, HI 96714, USA
Nash, John F, Jr *Nobel Economics Laureate*
%Princeton University, Economics Department, Fine Hall, Princeton, NJ 08544, USA
Nash, Johnny *Singer, Songwriter*
%Legacy Records, 550 Madison Ave, #1700, New York, NY 10022, USA
Nash, Leigh *Singer (Sixpence)*
%William Morris Agency, 151 El Camino Dr, Beverly Hills, CA 90212, USA
Nash, Noreen *Actress*
4990 Puesta del Sol, Malibu, CA 90265, USA
Nash, Steve *Basketball Player*
3607 Cole Ave, #162, Dallas, TX 75204, USA
Naslund, Markus *Hockey Player*
%Mike Gillis Assoc, 154 Earl St, Kingston ON K7L 2H2, Canada
Naslund, Mats *Hockey Player*
6963 Pregassona, Switzerland
Naslund, Ron *Hockey Player*
2600 Cheyenne Circle, Minnetonka, MN 55305, USA
Nasr, Seyyed Hossein *Theologian*
%George Washington University, Gelman Library, Washington, DC 20052, USA
Nasser, Jacques A *Businessman*
%One Equity Partners, 1st National Plaza, Chicago, IL 60607, USA
Nastase, Ilie *Tennis Player*
Calea Plevnei 14, Bucarest, Hungary

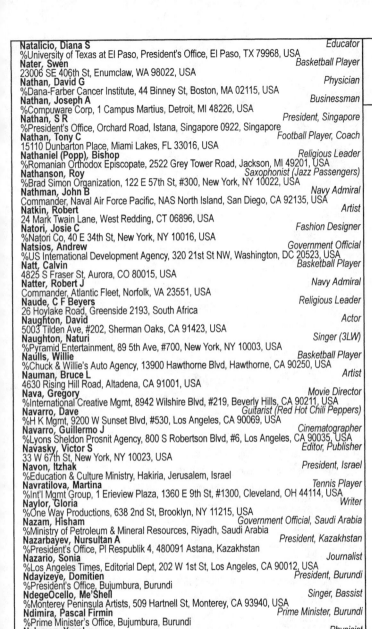

Natalicio, Diana S — *Educator*
%University of Texas at El Paso, President's Office, El Paso, TX 79968, USA

Nater, Swen — *Basketball Player*
23006 SE 406th St, Enumclaw, WA 98022, USA

Nathan, David G — *Physician*
%Dana-Farber Cancer Institute, 44 Binney St, Boston, MA 02115, USA

Nathan, Joseph A — *Businessman*
%Compuware Corp, 1 Campus Martius, Detroit, MI 48226, USA

Nathan, S R — *President, Singapore*
%President's Office, Orchard Road, Istana, Singapore 0922, Singapore

Nathan, Tony C — *Football Player, Coach*
15110 Dunbarton Place, Miami Lakes, FL 33016, USA

Nathaniel (Popp), Bishop — *Religious Leader*
%Romanian Orthodox Episcopate, 2522 Grey Tower Road, Jackson, MI 49201, USA

Nathanson, Roy — *Saxophonist (Jazz Passengers)*
%Brad Simon Organization, 122 E 57th St, #300, New York, NY 10022, USA

Nathman, John B — *Navy Admiral*
Commander, Naval Air Force Pacific, NAS North Island, San Diego, CA 92135, USA

Natkin, Robert — *Artist*
24 Mark Twain Lane, West Redding, CT 06896, USA

Natori, Josie C — *Fashion Designer*
%Natori Co, 40 E 34th St, New York, NY 10016, USA

Natsios, Andrew — *Government Official*
%US International Development Agency, 320 21st St NW, Washington, DC 20523, USA

Natt, Calvin — *Basketball Player*
4825 S Fraser St, Aurora, CO 80015, USA

Natter, Robert J — *Navy Admiral*
Commander, Atlantic Fleet, Norfolk, VA 23551, USA

Naude, C F Beyers — *Religious Leader*
26 Hoylake Road, Greenside 2193, South Africa

Naughton, David — *Actor*
5003 Tilden Ave, #202, Sherman Oaks, CA 91423, USA

Naughton, Naturi — *Singer (3LW)*
%Pyramid Entertainment, 89 5th Ave, #700, New York, NY 10003, USA

Naulls, Willie — *Basketball Player*
%Chuck & Willie's Auto Agency, 13900 Hawthorne Blvd, Hawthorne, CA 90250, USA

Nauman, Bruce L — *Artist*
4630 Rising Hill Road, Altadena, CA 91001, USA

Nava, Gregory — *Movie Director*
%International Creative Mgmt, 8942 Wilshire Blvd, #219, Beverly Hills, CA 90211, USA

Navarro, Dave — *Guitarist (Red Hot Chili Peppers)*
%H K Mgmt, 9200 W Sunset Blvd, #530, Los Angeles, CA 90069, USA

Navarro, Guillermo J — *Cinematographer*
%Lyons Sheldon Prosnit Agency, 800 S Robertson Blvd, #6, Los Angeles, CA 90035, USA

Navasky, Victor S — *Editor, Publisher*
33 W 67th St, New York, NY 10023, USA

Navon, Itzhak — *President, Israel*
%Education & Culture Ministry, Hakiria, Jerusalem, Israel

Navratilova, Martina — *Tennis Player*
%Int'l Mgmt Group, 1 Erieview Plaza, 1360 E 9th St, #1300, Cleveland, OH 44114, USA

Naylor, Gloria — *Writer*
%One Way Productions, 638 2nd St, Brooklyn, NY 11215, USA

Nazam, Hisham — *Government Official, Saudi Arabia*
%Ministry of Petroleum & Mineral Resources, Riyadh, Saudi Arabia

Nazarbayev, Nursultan A — *President, Kazakhstan*
%President's Office, Pl Respublik 4, 480091 Astana, Kazakhstan

Nazario, Sonia — *Journalist*
%Los Angeles Times, Editorial Dept, 202 W 1st St, Los Angeles, CA 90012, USA

Ndayizeye, Domitien — *President, Burundi*
%President's Office, Bujumbura, Burundi

NdegeOcello, Me'Shell — *Singer, Bassist*
%Monterey Peninsula Artists, 509 Hartnell St, Monterey, CA 93940, USA

Ndimira, Pascal Firmin — *Prime Minister, Burundi*
%Prime Minister's Office, Bujumbura, Burundi

Ne'eman, Yuval — *Physicist*
%Tel-Aviv University, Physics/Astronomy Dept, Tel-Aviv 69978, Israel

Neagle, Dennis E (Denny) — *Baseball Player*
945 Waugh Chapel Road, Gambrills, MD 21054, USA

Neal, Dylan — *Actor*
%Pakula/King, 9229 Sunset Blvd, #315, Los Angeles, CA 90069, USA

Neal, Edwin — *Actor*
501 W Powell Lane, Austin, TX 78753, USA

Neal, Elise — *Actress*
3626 Oakfield Dr, Sherman Oaks, CA 91423, USA

Neal, Fred (Curly) — *Basketball Player*
PO Box 915415, Longwood, FL 32791, USA

Neal, James — *Basketball Player*
803 Medora Dr, Greer, SC 29650, USA

Neal, James F *Attorney*
%Neal & Harwell, 3rd National Bank Building, #800, Nashville, TN 37219, USA
Neal, Lloyd *Basketball Player*
8640 SE Causey Ave, Portland, OR 97266, USA
Neal, Patricia *Actress*
45 E End Ave, #4C, New York, NY 10028, USA
Neal, Philip M *Businessman*
%Avery Dennison Corp, 150 N Orange Grove Blvd, Pasadena, CA 91103, USA
Neal, T Daniel (Dan) *Football Player*
5329 Briercliff Dr, Hamburg, NY 14075, USA
Neale, Gary L *Businessman*
%Northern Indiana Service, 801 E 86th Ave, Merrillville, IN 46410, USA
Nealon, Kevin *Actor, Comedian*
%Agency for Performing Arts, 9200 Sunset Blvd, #900, Los Angeles, CA 90069, USA
Nealy, Eddie *Basketball Player*
702 Lightstone Dr, San Antonio, TX 78258, USA
Neame, Christopher *Actor*
%Borinstein Oreck Bogart, 3172 Dona Susana Dr, Studio City, CA 91604, USA
Neame, Ronald *Movie Director*
%Kimridge Corp, 2317 Kimridge Ave, Beverly Hills, CA 90210, USA
Near, Holly *Singer, Songwriter, Actress*
PO Box 236, Ukiah, CA 95482, USA
Neary, Martin G J *Concert Organist, Conductor*
2 Little Cloister, Westminster Abbey, London SW1P 3PL, England
Nebel, Dorothy Hoyt *Skier*
5340 Balfor Dr, Virginia Beach, VA 23464, USA
Neblett, Carol *Opera Singer*
%Sardos Artists, 180 W End Ave, New York, NY 10023, USA
Nebout, Claire *Actress*
%Artmedia, 20 Ave Rapp, 75007 Paris, France
Nechaev, Victor *Hockey Player*
6820 La Presa Dr, San Gabriel, CA 91775, USA
Ned, Derrick *Football Player*
430 Charles St, Eunice, LA 70535, USA
Nederlander, James M *Theater Producer*
%Nederlander Organization, 810 7th Ave, New York, NY 10019, USA
Nedomansky, Vaclav *Hockey Player*
57 Crest Verde Lane, Rolling Hills Estates, CA 90274, USA
Nedorost, Vaclav *Hockey Player*
%Florida Panthers, 1 Panthers Parkway, Sunrise, FL 33323, USA
Nedved, Petr *Hockey Player*
%New York Rangers, Madison Square Garden, 2 Penn Plaza, New York, NY 10121, USA
Needham, Connie *Actress*
19721 Castlebar Dr, Rowland Heights, CA 91748, USA
Needham, Hal *Movie Director*
%Laura Lizer Assoc, PO Box 46609, Los Angeles, CA 90046, USA
Needham, James J *Businessman*
97 Coopers Farm Road, #1, Southampton, NY 11968, USA
Needham, Tracey *Actress*
%Badgley Connor Talent, 9229 Sunset Blvd, #311, Los Angeles, CA 90069, USA
Needleman, Jacob *Philosopher*
841 Wawona Ave, Oakland, CA 94610, USA
Neely, Cam *Hockey Player*
76 Davison Dr, Lincoln, MA 01773, USA
Neely, Mark E, Jr *Historian*
%Oxford University Press, 198 Madison Ave, New York, NY 10016, USA
Neely, Ralph E *Football Player*
6943 Sperry St, Dallas, TX 75214, USA
Neeson, Liam *Actor*
%International Creative Mgmt, 40 W 57th St, #1800, New York, NY 10019, USA
Nef, John U *Historian*
2726 N St NW, Washington, DC 20007, USA
Nef, Sonja *Alpine Skier*
Halten 345, 9035 Grub, Switzerland
Neff, Francine I *Government Official*
1509 Sagebrush Trail SE, Albuquerque, NM 87123, USA
Neff, William D *Psychologist*
2080 Hideaway Court, Morris, IL 60450, USA
Negishi, Takashi *Economist*
2-10-5-301 Motoazabu, Minatoku, Tokyo 106, Japan
Negoesco, Stephen *Soccer Coach*
%University of San Francisco, Athletic Dept, San Francisco, CA 94117, USA
Negri Sembilan, Yang Di-Pertuan Besar *Ruler, Malaysia*
%Yang Di-Pertuan Agong's Residence, Serembam, Malaysia
Negron, Chuck *Singer (Three Dog Night)*
%Mitch Schneider Organization, 14724 Ventura Blvd, #410, Sherman Oaks, CA 91403, USA
Negroponte, John D *Diplomat*
%US Permanent Mission, United Nations, 799 UN Plaza, New York, NY 10017, USA

Negroponte, Nicholas *Computer Engineer*
69 Mount Vernon St, Boston, MA 02108, USA
Nehamas, Alexander *Philosopher*
%Princeton University, Philosophy Dept, Princeton, NJ 08544, USA
Nehemiah, Renaldo *Track Athlete*
1751 Pinnacle Dr, #1500, McLean, VA 22102, USA
Neher, Erwin *Nobel Medicine Laureate*
Domane 11, 37120 Bovenden, Germany
Nehmer, Meinhard *Bobsled Athlete*
Varnkevitz, 18556 Altenkirchen, Germany
Neid, Silvia *Soccer Player*
Betramstr 18, 60320 Frankfurt/Main, Germany
Neidich, Charles *Conductor, Concert Clarinetist*
%Colbert Artists, 111 W 57th St, New York, NY 10019, USA
Neighbors, William (Billy) *Football Player*
1904 Chippendale Dr SE, Huntsville, AL 35801, USA
Neil, Andrew F *Editor*
%Glenburn Enterprises, PO Box 584, London SW7 3QY, England
Neil, Hildegarde *Actress*
%Vernon Conway, 5 Spring St, London W2 3RA, England
Neil, Vince *Singer (Motley Crue)*
%Ashley Talent, 2002 Hogback Road, #20, Ann Arbor, MI 48105, USA
Neill, Mary Gardner *Museum Director*
%Seattle Art Museum, Volunteer Park, Seattle, WA 98112, USA
Neill, Rolfe *Publisher*
%Charlotte News-Observer, 600 S Tryon St, Charlotte, NC 28202, USA
Neill, Sam *Actor*
%Shanahan Mgmt, PO Box 1509, Darlinghurst NSW 1300, Australia
Neilson-Bell, Sandra *Swimmer*
3101 Mistyglen Circle, Austin, TX 78746, USA
Neiman, LeRoy *Artist*
1 W 67th St, New York, NY 10023, USA
Neinas, Charles M (Chuck) *Football Executive*
5344 Westridge Dr, Boulder, CO 80301, USA
Neizvestny, Ernst I *Artist*
81 Grand St, New York, NY 10013, USA
Nelissen, Roelof J *Financier, Government Official*
PO Box 552, 1250 AN Laren, Netherlands
Nelligan, Kate *Actress*
%Innovative Artists, 1505 10th St, Santa Monica, CA 90401, USA
Nellis, William J *Physicist*
%Lawrence Livermore Laboratory, 7000 East St, Livermore, CA 94550, USA
Nelly *Rap Artist (Saint Lunatics)*
%International Creative Mgmt, 40 W 57th St, #1800, New York, NY 10019, USA
Nelms, Michael (Mike) *Football Player*
%Champion Chevrolet, 10411 James Monroe Highway, Culpeper VA 22701, USA
Nelson, Barry *Actor*
120 W 58th St, #2B, New York, NY 10019, USA
Nelson, Cailin *Astrophysicist*
%Lawrence Livermore Laboratory, 7000 East Ave, Livermore, CA 94550, USA
Nelson, Cordner *Track Executive*
%USA Track & Field, 4341 Starlight Dr, Indianapolis, IN 46239, USA
Nelson, Craig Richard *Actor*
%Borinstein Oreck Bogart, 3172 Dona Susana Dr, Studio City, CA 91604, USA
Nelson, Craig T *Actor*
%Entertainment Tavel, 9171 Wilshire Blvd, #406, Beverly Hills, CA 90210, USA
Nelson, Cynthia (Cindy) *Alpine Skier*
PO Box 1699, 0171 Larkspur Lane, Vail, CO 81658, USA
Nelson, Daniel R *Financier*
%West One Bancorp, 101 S Capitol Blvd, Boise, ID 83702, USA
Nelson, Darrin *Football Player*
215 Marianne Court, Mountain View, CA 94040, USA
Nelson, David A *Judge*
%US Court of Appeals, Courthouse Building, 425 Walnut St, Cincinnati, OH 45202, USA
Nelson, David O *Actor, Television Director*
124 Sidney Bay Dr, Newport Beach, CA 92657, USA
Nelson, Deborah *Journalist*
%Seattle Times, Editorial Dept, 1120 John St, Seattle, WA 98109, USA
Nelson, Donald A (Nellie) *Basketball Player, Coach, Executive*
%Dallas Mavericks, 2909 Taylor St, Dallas, TX 75226, USA
Nelson, Dorothy W *Judge*
%US Court of Appeals, 125 S Grand Ave, Pasadena, CA 91105, USA
Nelson, Ed *Actor*
1038 Marina Dr, Slidell, LA 70458, USA
Nelson, Edmund *Football Player*
1160 Billings Dr, Pittsburgh, PA 15241, USA
Nelson, Gaylord A *Governor, Senator, WI; Environmentalist*
3611 Calvend Lane, Kensington, MD 20895, USA

N

Nelson, George D *Astronaut*
%AAAS Project, 1200 New York Ave NW, #100, Washington, DC 20005, USA
Nelson, Glen D *Businessman*
%Medtronic Inc, 7000 Central Ave NE, Minneapolis, MN 55432, USA
Nelson, J Byron, Jr *Golfer*
Fairway Ranch, RR 2 Box 5, Litsey Road, Roanoke, TX 76262, USA
Nelson, James E *Religious Leader*
%Baha'i Faith, 536 Sheridan Road, Wilmette, IL 60091, USA
Nelson, Jim *Editor*
%Gentlemen's Quarterly Magazine, 350 Madison Avenue, New York, NY 10017, USA
Nelson, John Allen *Actor*
4960 Fulton Ave, Sherman Oaks, CA 91423, USA
Nelson, John R *Theologian*
1111 Hermann Dr, #19A, Houston, TX 77004, USA
Nelson, John W *Conductor*
%Astrid Schoerke, Monckebergallee 41, 30453 Hannover, Germany
Nelson, Judd *Actor*
409 N Camden Dr, #202, Beverly Hills, CA 90210, USA
Nelson, Judith *Opera, Concert Singer*
2600 Buena Vista Way, Berkeley, CA 94708, USA
Nelson, Kent C *Businessman*
%United Parcel Service, 55 Glenlake Parkway NE, Atlanta, GA 30328, USA
Nelson, Larry *Golfer*
421 Oakmont Circle, Marietta, GA 30067, USA
Nelson, Liza *Writer*
%G P Putnam's Sons, 375 Hudson St, New York, NY 10014, USA
Nelson, Lori *Actress*
13263 Ventura Blvd, #4, Studio City, CA 91604, USA
Nelson, Marilyn Carlson *Businesswoman*
%Carlson Companies, Carlson Parkway, PO Box 59159, Minneapolis, MN 55459, USA
Nelson, Ralph A *Nutritionist*
%Carle Foundation Hospital, 611 W Park St, Urbana, IL 61801, USA
Nelson, Steven L (Steve) *Football Player, Coach*
42 Noon Hill Ave, Box 132, Norfolk, MA 02056, USA
Nelson, Thomas G *Judge*
%US Court of Appeals, 550 W Fort St, Boise, ID 83724, USA
Nelson, Tracy *Actress*
13451 Galewood Dr, Sherman Oaks, CA 91423, USA
Nelson, William (Bill) *Senator, FL; Astronaut*
%Florida Insurance Dept, 200 E Gaines St, Tallahassee, FL 32399, USA
Nelson, Willie *Singer, Songwriter*
%Pedernails Studio, RR 1 Briarcliff TT, Spicewood, TX 78669, USA
Nemchinov, Sergei *Hockey Player*
53 Walker Ave, Rye, NY 10580, USA
Nemec, Corin *Actor*
859 N Hollywood Way, #104, Burbank, CA 91505, USA
Nemecek, Bohumil *Boxer*
V Zahradkach 30, 400 00 Usti Nad Labem, Czech Republic
Nemechek, Joe *Auto Racing Driver*
530 Mount Moriah Church Road, China Grove, NC 28023, USA
Nemelka, Richard *Basketball Player*
1949 Sunridge Dr, Sandy, UT 84093, USA
Nemeth, Miklos *Prime Minister, Hungary*
%European Reconstruction Bank, 1 Exchange Square, London EC2A 2EH, England
Nemov, Alexei *Gymnast*
%Gymnastics Federation, Lujnetskaya Nabereynaya 8, 119270 Moscow, Russia
Nenneman, Richard A *Editor*
PO Box 992, East Brunswick, NJ 08816, USA
Nepote, Jean *Law Enforcement Official*
26 Rue Armengaud, 92210 Saint-Cloud, Hauts-de-Seine, France
Nerem, Robert M *Mechanical Engineer*
2950 Waverly Court, Atlanta, GA 30339, USA
Nerette, Joseph *President, Haiti; Judge*
%Supreme Court, Chief Justice's Office, Port-au-Prince, Haiti
Neri Vela, Rodolfo *Astronaut, Mexico*
Playa Copacabana 131, Col Marte, Mexico City DF 08830, Mexico
Neri, Manuel *Artist*
%Greg Kucera Gallery, 212 3rd Ave S, Seattle, WA 98104, USA
Nerlove, Marc L *Economist*
%University of Maryland, Agricultural/Resource Economics, College Park, MD 20742, USA
Nero, Peter *Pianist, Conductor*
202 Hidden Acres Lane, Media, PA 19063, USA
Nerud, John *Thoroughbred Racing Executive*
19 Pound Hollow Road, Glen Head, NY 11545, USA
Nesher, Avi *Movie Director*
%Gersh Agency, 232 N Canon Dr, Beverly Hills, CA 90210, USA
Nesmith, Michael (Mike) *Singer, Guitarist (Monkees)*
%Videoranch, 8 Harris Court, #C1, Monterey, CA 93940, USA

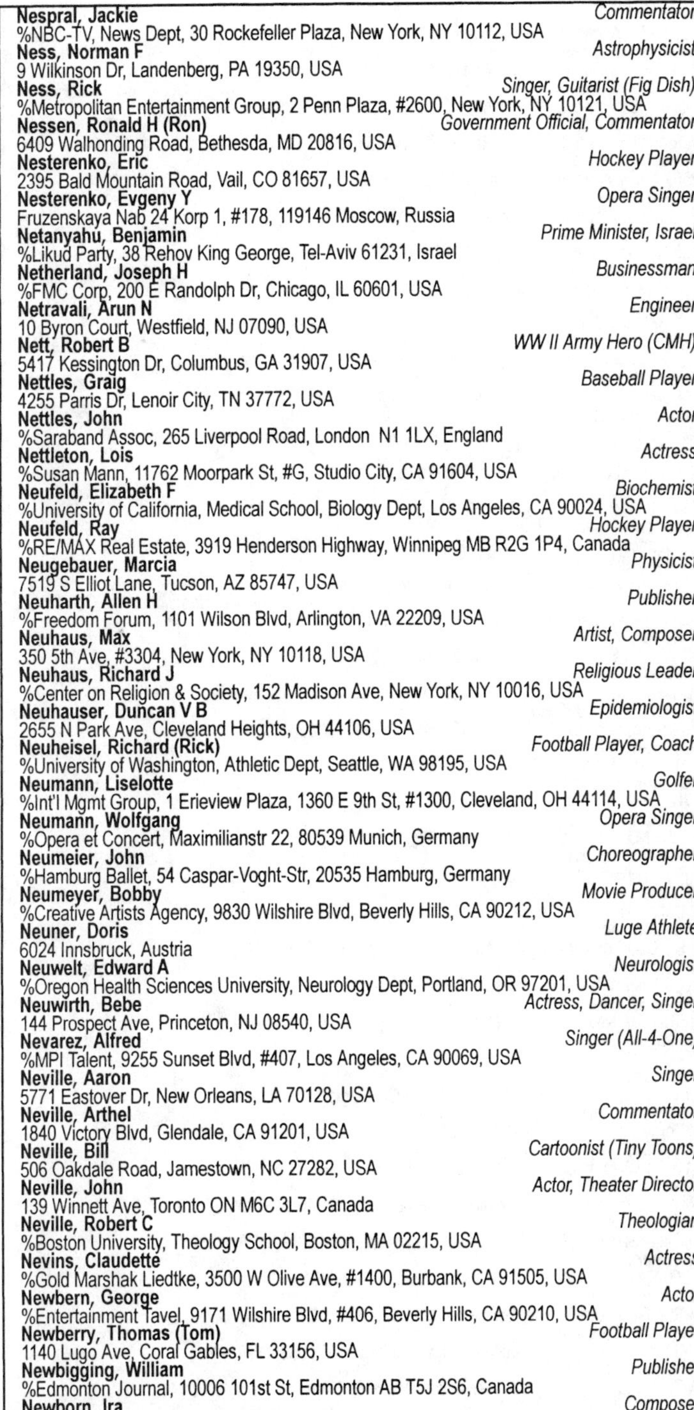

Nespral, Jackie — *Commentator*
%NBC-TV, News Dept, 30 Rockefeller Plaza, New York, NY 10112, USA

Ness, Norman F — *Astrophysicist*
9 Wilkinson Dr, Landenberg, PA 19350, USA

Ness, Rick — *Singer, Guitarist (Fig Dish)*
%Metropolitan Entertainment Group, 2 Penn Plaza, #2600, New York, NY 10121, USA

Nessen, Ronald H (Ron) — *Government Official, Commentator*
6409 Walhonding Road, Bethesda, MD 20816, USA

Nesterenko, Eric — *Hockey Player*
2395 Bald Mountain Road, Vail, CO 81657, USA

Nesterenko, Evgeny Y — *Opera Singer*
Fruzenskaya Nab 24 Korp 1, #178, 119146 Moscow, Russia

Netanyahu, Benjamin — *Prime Minister, Israel*
%Likud Party, 38 Rehov King George, Tel-Aviv 61231, Israel

Netherland, Joseph H — *Businessman*
%FMC Corp, 200 E Randolph Dr, Chicago, IL 60601, USA

Netravali, Arun N — *Engineer*
10 Byron Court, Westfield, NJ 07090, USA

Nett, Robert B — *WW II Army Hero (CMH)*
5417 Kessington Dr, Columbus, GA 31907, USA

Nettles, Graig — *Baseball Player*
4255 Parris Dr, Lenoir City, TN 37772, USA

Nettles, John — *Actor*
%Saraband Assoc, 265 Liverpool Road, London N1 1LX, England

Nettleton, Lois — *Actress*
%Susan Mann, 11762 Moorpark St, #G, Studio City, CA 91604, USA

Neufeld, Elizabeth F — *Biochemist*
%University of California, Medical School, Biology Dept, Los Angeles, CA 90024, USA

Neufeld, Ray — *Hockey Player*
%RE/MAX Real Estate, 3919 Henderson Highway, Winnipeg MB R2G 1P4, Canada

Neugebauer, Marcia — *Physicist*
7519 S Elliot Lane, Tucson, AZ 85747, USA

Neuharth, Allen H — *Publisher*
%Freedom Forum, 1101 Wilson Blvd, Arlington, VA 22209, USA

Neuhaus, Max — *Artist, Composer*
350 5th Ave, #3304, New York, NY 10118, USA

Neuhaus, Richard J — *Religious Leader*
%Center on Religion & Society, 152 Madison Ave, New York, NY 10016, USA

Neuhauser, Duncan V B — *Epidemiologist*
2655 N Park Ave, Cleveland Heights, OH 44106, USA

Neuheisel, Richard (Rick) — *Football Player, Coach*
%University of Washington, Athletic Dept, Seattle, WA 98195, USA

Neumann, Liselotte — *Golfer*
%Int'l Mgmt Group, 1 Erieview Plaza, 1360 E 9th St, #1300, Cleveland, OH 44114, USA

Neumann, Wolfgang — *Opera Singer*
%Opera et Concert, Maximilianstr 22, 80539 Munich, Germany

Neumeier, John — *Choreographer*
%Hamburg Ballet, 54 Caspar-Voght-Str, 20535 Hamburg, Germany

Neumeyer, Bobby — *Movie Producer*
%Creative Artists Agency, 9830 Wilshire Blvd, Beverly Hills, CA 90212, USA

Neuner, Doris — *Luge Athlete*
6024 Innsbruck, Austria

Neuwelt, Edward A — *Neurologist*
%Oregon Health Sciences University, Neurology Dept, Portland, OR 97201, USA

Neuwirth, Bebe — *Actress, Dancer, Singer*
144 Prospect Ave, Princeton, NJ 08540, USA

Nevarez, Alfred — *Singer (All-4-One)*
%MPI Talent, 9255 Sunset Blvd, #407, Los Angeles, CA 90069, USA

Neville, Aaron — *Singer*
5771 Eastover Dr, New Orleans, LA 70128, USA

Neville, Arthel — *Commentator*
1840 Victory Blvd, Glendale, CA 91201, USA

Neville, Bill — *Cartoonist (Tiny Toons)*
506 Oakdale Road, Jamestown, NC 27282, USA

Neville, John — *Actor, Theater Director*
139 Winnett Ave, Toronto ON M6C 3L7, Canada

Neville, Robert C — *Theologian*
%Boston University, Theology School, Boston, MA 02215, USA

Nevins, Claudette — *Actress*
%Gold Marshak Liedtke, 3500 W Olive Ave, #1400, Burbank, CA 91505, USA

Newbern, George — *Actor*
%Entertainment Tavel, 9171 Wilshire Blvd, #406, Beverly Hills, CA 90210, USA

Newberry, Thomas (Tom) — *Football Player*
1140 Lugo Ave, Coral Gables, FL 33156, USA

Newbigging, William — *Publisher*
%Edmonton Journal, 10006 101st St, Edmonton AB T5J 2S6, Canada

Newborn, Ira — *Composer*
%Vangelos Mgmt, 15233 Ventura Blvd, #200, Sherman Oaks, CA 91403, USA

Newcomb, Gerry *Artist*
7029 17th Ave NW, Seattle, WA 98117, USA
Newcomb, Jonathan *Publisher*
35 Pierrepont St, Brooklyn, NY 11201, USA
Newcombe, Donald (Don) *Baseball Player*
%Paralysis Project, PO Box 627, Glendale, CA 91209, USA
Newcombe, John D *Tennis Player*
%John Newcombe's Tennis Ranch, PO Box 310469, New Braunfels, TX 78131, USA
Newell, Homer E *Physicist*
2567 Nicky Lane, Alexandria, VA 22311, USA
Newell, Mike *Movie Director*
%Dogstar, 76 Oxford St, London W1N 0AX, England
Newell, Norman D *Paleontologist, Geologist*
135 Knapp Terrace, Leonia, NJ 07605, USA
Newell, Peter F (Pete) *Basketball Coach*
16078 Via Viajera, Rancho Santa Fe, CA 92091, USA
Newfield, Heidi *Singer (Trick Pony)*
%Creative Artists Agency, 9830 Wilshire Blvd, Beverly Hills, CA 90212, USA
Newgard, Christopher *Biochemist*
%Southwestern Medical Center, Biochemistry Dept, Dallas, TX 75237, USA
Newhart, Bob *Actor, Comedian*
420 Amapola Lane, Los Angeles, CA 90077, USA
Newhouse, Donald E *Publisher*
%Advance Publications, 950 W Fingerboard Road, Staten Island, NY 10305, USA
Newhouse, Frederick (Fred) *Track Athlete*
3003 Pine Lake Trail, Houston, TX 77068, USA
Newhouse, Robert F *Football Player*
6847 Truxton Dr, Dallas, TX 75231, USA
Newhouse, Samuel I, Jr *Publisher*
%Advance Publications, 950 W Fingerboard Road, Staten Island, NY 10305, USA
Newlin, Mike *Basketball Player*
1414 Horseshoe Dr, Sugar Land, TX 77478, USA
Newman, Anthony *Concert Harpsichordist, Conductor*
%I C M Artists, 40 W 57th St, New York, NY 10019, USA
Newman, Arnold *Photographer*
33 W 67th St, New York, NY 10023, USA
Newman, David *Composer*
%Agency for Performing Arts, 9200 Sunset Blvd, #900, Los Angeles, CA 90069, USA
Newman, David (Fathead) *Jazz Saxophonist*
%Maxine Harvard, 7942 W Bell Road, Glendale, AZ 85308, USA
Newman, Edward K (Ed) *Football Player*
10100 SW 140th St, Miami, FL 33176, USA
Newman, Edwin H *Commentator*
870 United Nations Plaza, #18D, New York, NY 10017, USA
Newman, James H *Astronaut*
18583 Martinique Dr, Houston, TX 77058, USA
Newman, Jimmy C *Singer, Songwriter*
RR 2, Christiana, TN 37037, USA
Newman, Johnny *Basketball Player*
%Dallas Mavericks, 2909 Taylor St, Dallas, TX 75226, USA
Newman, Jon O *Judge*
%US Court of Appeals, 450 Main St, Hartford, CT 06103, USA
Newman, Joseph M *Movie Director*
10900 Winnetka Ave, Chatsworth, CA 91311, USA
Newman, Kevin *Commentator*
%ABC-TV, News Dept, 77 W 66th St, New York, NY 10023, USA
Newman, Laraine *Actress, Comedienne*
10480 Ashton Ave, Los Angeles, CA 90024, USA
Newman, Nanette *Actress*
Seven Pines, Wentworth, Surrey GU25 4QP, England
Newman, Oscar *Architect, Urban Planner*
%Community Design Analysis Institute, 66 Clover Dr, Great Neck, NY 11021, USA
Newman, Paul *Actor*
1120 5th Ave, #1C, New York, NY 10128, USA
Newman, Pauline *Judge*
%US Court of Appeals, 717 Madison Place NW, Washington, DC 20439, USA
Newman, Phyllis *Actress, Singer*
%Gage Group, 315 W 57th St, #4H, New York, NY 10019, USA
Newman, Randy *Singer, Songwriter, Composer*
1610 San Remo Dr, Pacific Palisades, CA 90272, USA
Newman, Ryan *Auto Racing Driver*
%Tom Roberts PR, 123 Woodview Dr, Statesville, NC 28625, USA
Newman, Terence *Football Player*
%Dallas Cowboys, 1 Cowboys Parkway, Irving, TX 75063, USA
Newman, Thomas *Composer*
%Gorfaine/Schwartz, 13245 Riverside Dr, #450, Sherman Oaks, CA 91423, USA
Newman, Thomas *Actor*
%Badgley Connor Talent, 9229 Sunset Blvd, #311, Los Angeles, CA 90069, USA

N

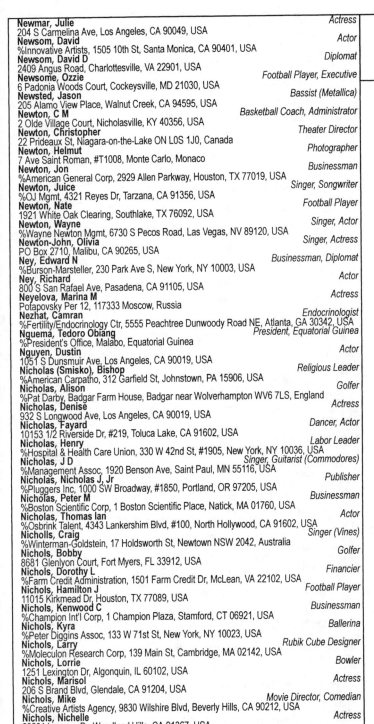

Newmar, Julie *Actress*
204 S Carmelina Ave, Los Angeles, CA 90049, USA
Newsom, David *Actor*
%Innovative Artists, 1505 10th St, Santa Monica, CA 90401, USA
Newsom, David D *Diplomat*
2409 Angus Road, Charlottesville, VA 22901, USA
Newsome, Ozzie *Football Player, Executive*
6 Padonia Woods Court, Cockeysville, MD 21030, USA
Newsted, Jason *Bassist (Metallica)*
205 Alamo View Place, Walnut Creek, CA 94595, USA
Newton, C M *Basketball Coach, Administrator*
2 Olde Village Court, Nicholasville, KY 40356, USA
Newton, Christopher *Theater Director*
22 Prideaux St, Niagara-on-the-Lake ON L0S 1J0, Canada
Newton, Helmut *Photographer*
7 Ave Saint Roman, #T1008, Monte Carlo, Monaco
Newton, Jon *Businessman*
%American General Corp, 2929 Allen Parkway, Houston, TX 77019, USA
Newton, Juice *Singer, Songwriter*
%OJ Mgmt, 4321 Reyes Dr, Tarzana, CA 91356, USA
Newton, Nate *Football Player*
1921 White Oak Clearing, Southlake, TX 76092, USA
Newton, Wayne *Singer, Actor*
%Wayne Newton Mgmt, 6730 S Pecos Road, Las Vegas, NV 89120, USA
Newton-John, Olivia *Singer, Actress*
PO Box 2710, Malibu, CA 90265, USA
Ney, Edward N *Businessman, Diplomat*
%Burson-Marsteller, 230 Park Ave S, New York, NY 10003, USA
Ney, Richard *Actor*
800 S San Rafael Ave, Pasadena, CA 91105, USA
Neyelova, Marina M *Actress*
Potapovsky Per 12, 117333 Moscow, Russia
Nezhat, Camran *Endocrinologist*
%Fertility/Endocrinology Ctr, 5555 Peachtree Dunwoody Road NE, Atlanta, GA 30342, USA
Nguema, Tedoro Obiang *President, Equatorial Guinea*
%President's Office, Malabo, Equatorial Guinea
Nguyen, Dustin *Actor*
1051 S Dunsmuir Ave, Los Angeles, CA 90019, USA
Nicholas (Smisko), Bishop *Religious Leader*
%American Carpatho, 312 Garfield St, Johnstown, PA 15906, USA
Nicholas, Alison *Golfer*
%Pat Darby, Badgar Farm House, Badgar near Wolverhampton WV6 7LS, England
Nicholas, Denise *Actress*
932 S Longwood Ave, Los Angeles, CA 90019, USA
Nicholas, Fayard *Dancer, Actor*
10153 1/2 Riverside Dr, #219, Toluca Lake, CA 91602, USA
Nicholas, Henry *Labor Leader*
%Hospital & Health Care Union, 330 W 42nd St, #1905, New York, NY 10036, USA
Nicholas, J D *Singer, Guitarist (Commodores)*
%Management Assoc, 1920 Benson Ave, Saint Paul, MN 55116, USA
Nicholas, Nicholas J, Jr *Publisher*
%Pluggers Inc, 1000 SW Broadway, #1850, Portland, OR 97205, USA
Nicholas, Peter M *Businessman*
%Boston Scientific Corp, 1 Boston Scientific Place, Natick, MA 01760, USA
Nicholas, Thomas Ian *Actor*
%Osbrink Talent, 4343 Lankershim Blvd, #100, North Hollywood, CA 91602, USA
Nicholls, Craig *Singer (Vines)*
%Winterman-Goldstein, 17 Holdsworth St, Newtown NSW 2042, Australia
Nichols, Bobby *Golfer*
8681 Glenlyon Court, Fort Myers, FL 33912, USA
Nichols, Dorothy L *Financier*
%Farm Credit Administration, 1501 Farm Credit Dr, McLean, VA 22102, USA
Nichols, Hamilton J *Football Player*
11015 Kirkmead Dr, Houston, TX 77089, USA
Nichols, Kenwood C *Businessman*
%Champion Int'l Corp, 1 Champion Plaza, Stamford, CT 06921, USA
Nichols, Kyra *Ballerina*
%Peter Diggins Assoc, 133 W 71st St, New York, NY 10023, USA
Nichols, Larry *Rubik Cube Designer*
%Moleculon Research Corp, 139 Main St, Cambridge, MA 02142, USA
Nichols, Lorrie *Bowler*
1251 Lexington Dr, Algonquin, IL 60102, USA
Nichols, Marisol *Actress*
206 S Brand Blvd, Glendale, CA 91204, USA
Nichols, Mike *Movie Director, Comedian*
%Creative Artists Agency, 9830 Wilshire Blvd, Beverly Hills, CA 90212, USA
Nichols, Nichelle *Actress*
23281 Leonora Dr, Woodland Hills, CA 91367, USA

N

Nichols - Nieuwendyk

Nichols, Peter R *Writer*
%Alan Brodie, 211 Piccadilly, London W1V 9LD, England
Nichols, Stephen *Actor*
11664 National Blvd, #116, Los Angeles, CA 90064, USA
Nicholson, Jack *Actor*
%Bresler Kelly Assoc, 11500 W Olympic Blvd, #510, Los Angeles, CA 90064, USA
Nicholson, Jim *Diplomat*
%US Embassy, Via delle Terme de Clare 26, 00162 Rome, Italy
Nicholson, Julianne *Actress*
939 8th Ave, #609, New York, NY 10019, USA
Nickerson, Donald A, Jr *Religious Leader*
%Episcopal Church, 815 2nd Ave, New York, NY 10017, USA
Nickerson, Hardy O *Football Player*
3319 Deer Hollow Dr, Danville, CA 94506, USA
Nicklaus, Jack W *Golfer*
%Golden Bear International, 11760 US Highway 1, North Palm Beach, FL 33408, USA
Nicks, John A W *Figure Skating Coach*
%Ice Capades Chalet, 13211 Brooks Dr, #A, Baldwin Park, CA 91706, USA
Nicks, Regina *Singer (Regina Regina)*
%Bobby Roberts, 909 Meadowlark Lane, Goodlettsville, TN 37072, USA
Nicks, Stevie *Singer, Songwriter*
%H K Mgmt, 9200 W Sunset Blvd, #530, Los Angeles, CA 90069, USA
Nickson, Julia *Actress*
%Elkins Entertainment, 8306 Wilshire Blvd, #438, Beverly Hills, CA 90211, USA
Nicol, Steve *Soccer Coach*
%New England Revolution, CMGI Field, 1 Patriot Place, Foxboro, MA 02035, USA
Nicolaou, Kyriacos Costa *Chemist*
%Scripps Research Institute, 10550 N Torrey Pines Road, La Jolla, CA 92037, USA
Nicolet, Aurele *Concert Flutist*
%Hans Ulrich Schmid, Postfach 1617, 30016 Hanover, Germany
Nicollier, Claude *Astronaut, Switzerland*
18710 Martinique Dr, Houston, TX 77058, USA
Nicolson, Nigel *Writer*
Sissinghurst Castle, Kent, England
Nicora, Attilio Cardinal *Religious Leader*
%Patrimony of Apostolic See, Palazzo Apostolico, 00120 Vatican City
Nidetch, Jean *Businesswoman*
%Weight Watchers International, 3860 Crenshaw Blvd, Los Angeles, CA 90008, USA
Nieberg, Lars *Equestrian Rider*
Gestit Waldershausen, 35315 Homberg, Germany
Nieder, William H (Bill) *Track Athlete*
PO Box 310, Mountain Ranch, CA 95246, USA
Niederhoffer, Victor *Squash Player*
%Niederhoffer Cross Zeckhauser, 757 3rd Ave, New York, NY 10017, USA
Niedermayer, Scott *Hockey Player*
32 Prospect Ave, Montclair, NJ 07042, USA
Niedernhuber, Barbara *Luge Athlete*
Schwarzeckstr 58, 83486 Ramsau, Germany
Niehaus, Dave *Sportscaster*
%Seattle Mariners, Safeco Field, PO Box 4100, Seattle, WA 98194, USA
Niehaus, Lennie *Composer*
%Robert Light Agency, 6404 Wilshire Blvd, #1225, Los Angeles, CA 90048, USA
Niekro, Joseph F (Joe) *Baseball Player*
2707 Fairway Dr S, Plant City, FL 33566, USA
Niekro, Philip H (Phil) *Baseball Player*
%Atlanta Braves, Turner Field, 755 Hank Aaron Dr, Atlanta, GA 30315, USA
Nielsen, Brigitte *Actress, Model*
%Bartels Co, PO Box 57593, Sherman Oaks, CA 91413, USA
Nielsen, Connie *Actress*
%Lasher McManus Robinson, 1964 Westwood Blvd, #400, Los Angeles, CA 90025, USA
Nielsen, Gifford *Football Player*
10 Sarahs Cove, Sugar Land, TX 77479, USA
Nielsen, Leslie *Actor*
1622 Viewmont Dr, Los Angeles, CA 90069, USA
Nielsen, Rick *Singer, Guitarist (Cheap Trick)*
%Monterey Peninsula Artists, 509 Hartnell St, Monterey, CA 93940, USA
Niemann-Stirnemann, Gunda *Speedskater*
Postfach 503, 99010 Erfurt, Germany
Niemeyer, Paul V *Judge*
%US Court of Appeals, 101 W Lombard St, Baltimore, MD 21201, USA
Niemi, Lisa *Actress*
%Flick East-West, 9057 Nemo St, #A, West Hollywood, CA 90069, USA
Nieminen, Toni *Ski Jumper*
%Landen Kanava 99, Vesijarvenkatu 74, 15140 Lahti, Finland
Nierman, Leonardo *Artist*
Amsterdam 43 PH, Mexico City 11 DF, Mexico
Nieuwendyk, Joe *Hockey Player*
1493 Taughannock Blvd, Ithaca, NY 14850, USA

N

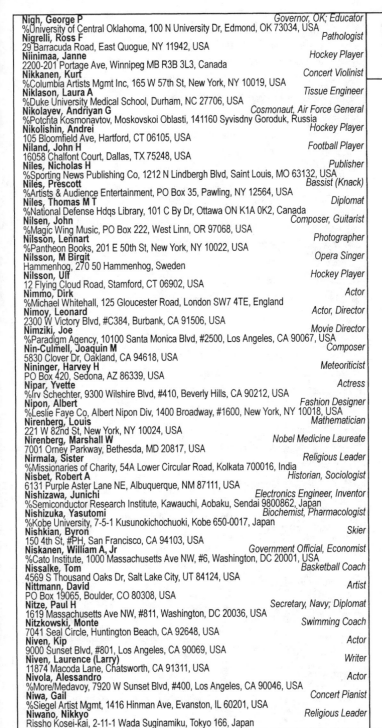

Nigh, George P *Governor, OK; Educator*
%University of Central Oklahoma, 100 N University Dr, Edmond, OK 73034, USA
Nigrelli, Ross F *Pathologist*
29 Barracuda Road, East Quogue, NY 11942, USA
Niinimaa, Janne *Hockey Player*
2200-201 Portage Ave, Winnipeg MB R3B 3L3, Canada
Nikkanen, Kurt *Concert Violinist*
%Columbia Artists Mgmt Inc, 165 W 57th St, New York, NY 10019, USA
Niklason, Laura A *Tissue Engineer*
%Duke University Medical School, Durham, NC 27706, USA
Nikolayev, Andriyan G *Cosmonaut, Air Force General*
%Potchta Kosmonavtov, Moskovskoi Oblasti, 141160 Syvisdny Goroduk, Russia
Nikolishin, Andrei *Hockey Player*
105 Bloomfield Ave, Hartford, CT 06105, USA
Niland, John H *Football Player*
16058 Chalfont Court, Dallas, TX 75248, USA
Niles, Nicholas H *Publisher*
%Sporting News Publishing Co, 1212 N Lindbergh Blvd, Saint Louis, MO 63132, USA
Niles, Prescott *Bassist (Knack)*
%Artists & Audience Entertainment, PO Box 35, Pawling, NY 12564, USA
Niles, Thomas M T *Diplomat*
%National Defense Hdqs Library, 101 C By Dr, Ottawa ON K1A 0K2, Canada
Nilsen, John *Composer, Guitarist*
%Magic Wing Music, PO Box 222, West Linn, OR 97068, USA
Nilsson, Lennart *Photographer*
%Pantheon Books, 201 E 50th St, New York, NY 10022, USA
Nilsson, M Birgit *Opera Singer*
Hammenhog, 270 50 Hammenhog, Sweden
Nilsson, Ulf *Hockey Player*
12 Flying Cloud Road, Stamford, CT 06902, USA
Nimmo, Dirk *Actor*
%Michael Whitehall, 125 Gloucester Road, London SW7 4TE, England
Nimoy, Leonard *Actor, Director*
2300 W Victory Blvd, #C384, Burbank, CA 91506, USA
Nimziki, Joe *Movie Director*
%Paradigm Agency, 10100 Santa Monica Blvd, #2500, Los Angeles, CA 90067, USA
Nin-Culmell, Joaquin M *Composer*
5830 Clover Dr, Oakland, CA 94618, USA
Nininger, Harvey H *Meteoriticist*
PO Box 420, Sedona, AZ 86339, USA
Nipar, Yvette *Actress*
%Irv Schechter, 9300 Wilshire Blvd, #410, Beverly Hills, CA 90212, USA
Nipon, Albert *Fashion Designer*
%Leslie Faye Co, Albert Nipon Div, 1400 Broadway, #1600, New York, NY 10018, USA
Nirenberg, Louis *Mathematician*
221 W 82nd St, New York, NY 10024, USA
Nirenberg, Marshall W *Nobel Medicine Laureate*
7001 Orney Parkway, Bethesda, MD 20817, USA
Nirmala, Sister *Religious Leader*
%Missionaries of Charity, 54A Lower Circular Road, Kolkata 700016, India
Nisbet, Robert A *Historian, Sociologist*
6131 Purple Aster Lane NE, Albuquerque, NM 87111, USA
Nishizawa, Junichi *Electronics Engineer, Inventor*
%Semiconductor Research Institute, Kawauchi, Aobaku, Sendai 9800862, Japan
Nishizuka, Yasutomi *Biochemist, Pharmacologist*
%Kobe University, 7-5-1 Kusunokichochuoki, Kobe 650-0017, Japan
Nishkian, Byron *Skier*
150 4th St, #PH, San Francisco, CA 94103, USA
Niskanen, William A, Jr *Government Official, Economist*
%Cato Institute, 1000 Massachusetts Ave NW, #6, Washington, DC 20001, USA
Nissalke, Tom *Basketball Coach*
4569 S Thousand Oaks Dr, Salt Lake City, UT 84124, USA
Nittmann, David *Artist*
PO Box 19065, Boulder, CO 80308, USA
Nitze, Paul H *Secretary, Navy; Diplomat*
1619 Massachusetts Ave NW, #811, Washington, DC 20036, USA
Nitzkowski, Monte *Swimming Coach*
7041 Seal Circle, Huntington Beach, CA 92648, USA
Niven, Kip *Actor*
9000 Sunset Blvd, #801, Los Angeles, CA 90069, USA
Niven, Laurence (Larry) *Writer*
11874 Macoda Lane, Chatsworth, CA 91311, USA
Nivola, Alessandro *Actor*
%More/Medavoy, 7920 W Sunset Blvd, #400, Los Angeles, CA 90046, USA
Niwa, Gail *Concert Pianist*
%Siegel Artist Mgmt, 1416 Hinman Ave, Evanston, IL 60201, USA
Niwano, Nikkyo *Religious Leader*
Rissho Kosei-kai, 2-11-1 Wada Suginamiku, Tokyo 166, Japan

N

Nixon, Agnes E *Television Producer, Writer*
774 Conestoga Road, Bryn Mawr, PA 19010, USA
Nixon, Cynthia *Actress*
%William Morris Agency, 1325 Ave of Americas, New York, NY 10019, USA
Nixon, Gary *Motorcycle Racing Rider*
%Gary Nixon Enterprises, 2408 Carroll Mill Road, Phoenix, MD 21131, USA
Nixon, Marni *Singer, Actress*
%Agency for Performing Arts, 9200 Sunset Blvd, #900, Los Angeles, CA 90069, USA
Niyazov, Saparmurad *President, Turkmenistan*
%President's Office, Karl Marx Str 24, 744017 Ashkabad, Turkmenistan
Noah, John *Hockey Player*
3315 Prairiewood Dr W, Fargo, ND 58103, USA
Noah, Max W *Army General*
820 Arcturus-on-Potomac, Alexandria, VA 22308, USA
Noah, Yannick *Tennis Player, Coach*
20 Rue Billancourt, 92100 Boulogne, France
Noakes, Michael *Artist*
146 Hamilton Terrace, Saint John's Wood, London NW8 9UX, England
Nobilo, Frank *Golfer*
%Int'l Mgmt Group, 1 Erieview Plaza, 1360 E 9th St, #1300, Cleveland, OH 44114, USA
Nobis, Thomas H (Tommy), Jr *Football Player, Executive*
40 S Battery Place NE, Atlanta, GA 30342, USA
Noble, Adrian K *Theater Director*
%Royal Shakespeare Co, Barbican Theater, London EC2Y 8BQ, England
Noble, Brian D *Football Player*
2912 Nikki Lee Court, Green Bay, WI 54313, USA
Noble, Chelsea *Actress*
PO Box 8665, Calabasas, CA 91372, USA
Noble, James *Actor*
113 Ledgebrook Dr, Norwalk, CT 06854, USA
Noble, John *Actor*
%A A Williams Mgmt, PO Box 1397, Darlinghurst NSW 1300, Australia
Noblitt, Niles L *Businessman*
%Biomet Inc, Airport Industrial Park, PO Box 587, Warsaw, IN 46581, USA
Noboa, Gustavo *President, Ecuador*
%Palacio de Gobierno, Garcia Moreno 1043, Quito, Ecuador
Nodell, Mart *Cartoonist (Green Lantern)*
117 Lake Irene Dr, West Palm Beach, FL 33411, USA
Noe, Vergilius Cardinal *Religious Leader*
Piazza della Citta Leonina 1, 00193 Rome, Italy
Noel, Monique *Model, Actress*
PO Box 232058, Encinitas, CA 92023, USA
Noel, Philip W *Governor, RI*
345 Channel View, #105, Warwick, RI 02889, USA
Nofziger, Lyn *Government Official*
2000 Pennsylvania Ave NW, #365, Washington, DC 20006, USA
Noguchi, Soichi *Astronaut*
%NASA, Johnson Space Center, 2101 NASA Road, Houston, TX 77058, USA
Noguchi, Thomas T *Pathologist*
1110 Avoca Ave, Pasadena, CA 91105, USA
Nogulich, Natalija *Actress*
11841 Kiowa Ave, #7, Los Angeles, CA 90049, USA
Noiret, Philippe *Actor*
104 Rue des Sablons, 78750 Mareil-Marly, France
Nojima, Minoru *Concert Pianist*
%John Gingrich Mgmt, PO Box 515, New York, NY 10023, USA
Nokes, Matthew D (Matt) *Baseball Player*
13553 Poway Road, #181, Poway, CA 92064, USA
Nolan, Christopher *Writer*
158 Vernon Ave, Clontanf, Dublin 3, Ireland
Nolan, Deanna *Basketball Player*
%Detroit Shock, Palace, 2 Championship Dr, Auburn Hills, MI 48326, USA
Nolan, Kathleen (Kathy) *Actress*
250 W 57th St, #703, New York, NY 10107, USA
Nolan, Owen *Hockey Player*
5729 La Seyne Place, San Jose, CA 95138, USA
Nolan, Richard C (Dick) *Football Player, Coach*
4 Gentry Court, Trophy Club, TX 76262, USA
Nolan, Ted *Hockey Player, Coach*
269 Queen St E, Sault Sainte Marie ON P6A 1Y9, Canada
Nolan, Thomas B *Geologist*
2219 California St NW, Washington, DC 20008, USA
Noland, Kenneth C *Artist*
183 Park St, North Bennington, VT 05257, USA
Nolin, Gena Lee *Actress*
6230 Wilshire Blvd, #171, Los Angeles, CA 90048, USA
Noll, Charles H (Chuck) *Football Player, Coach*
201 Grant St, Sewickley, PA 15143, USA

Nolte, Claudia *Government Official, Germany*
Mulgarten 28, 98693 Ilmenau, Germany
Nolte, Nick *Actor*
%Kingsgate Films, 6153 Bonsall Dr, Malibu, CA 90265, USA
Nolting, Paul F *Religious Leader*
%Church of Lutheran Confession, 620 E 50th St, Loveland, CO 80538, USA
Nomura, Masayasu *Molecular Biologist*
74 Whitman Court, Irvine, CA 92612, USA
Nool, Erki *Track Athlete*
Regati 1, Tallinn 119871, Estonia
Noonan, Danny *Football Player*
%Dallas Cowboys, 1 Cowboys Parkway, Irving, TX 75063, USA
Noonan, John T, Jr *Judge*
%US Court of Appeals, Court Building, 95 7th St, San Francisco, CA 94103, USA
Noonan, Patrick F *Association Executive, Conservationist*
11901 Glen Mills Road, Potomac, MD 20854, USA
Noonan, Peggy *Writer*
%Reagan Books, 10 E 53rd St, New York, NY 10022, USA
Noonan, Robert W, Jr *Army General*
Deputy Chief of Staff for Intelligence, HqUSA, Pentagon, Washington, DC 20310, USA
Noonan, Timothy J *Businessman*
%Rite Aid Corp, 30 Hunter Lane, Camp Hill, PA 17011, USA
Noone, Kathleen *Actress*
130 W 42nd St, #1804, New York, NY 10036, USA
Noone, Peter *Singer, Actor*
9265 Robin Lane, Los Angeles, CA 90069, USA
Noor Al-Hussein *Queen Mother, Jordan*
%Royal Palace, Amman, Jordan
Nordenberg, Mark A *Educator*
%University of Pittsburgh, President's Office, Pittsburgh, PA 15261, USA
Nordenstrom, Bjorn *Cancer Radiologist*
%Karolinska Institute, Radiology Dept, Stockholm, Sweden
Nordheim, Arne *Composer*
Wergelandsveien 2, 0167 Oslo, Norway
Nordlander, Mattias *Guitarist (Komeda)*
%MOB Agency, 6404 Wilshire Blvd, #505, Los Angeles, CA 90048, USA
Nordli, Odvar *Prime Minister, Norway*
Snarveien 4, 2312 Ottestad, Norway
Nordsieck, Kenneth H *Astronaut*
%University of Wisconsin, Space Astronomy Laboratory, Madison, WI 53706, USA
Noren, Irving A (Irv) *Baseball, Basketball Player*
3154 Camino Crest Dr, Oceanside, CA 92056, USA
Noren, Lars *Writer*
Ostermalmsgatan 33, 11426 Stockholm, Sweden
Norgard, Erik C *Football Player*
60 Harbor View Dr, Sugar Land, TX 77479, USA
Noriega, Carlos I *Astronaut*
13710 Shadow Falls Court, Houston, TX 77059, USA
Norlander, John *Basketball Player*
801 9th St N, #102, Virginia, MN 55792, USA
Norman, Chris *Singer*
%Denis Vaughan Mgmt, PO Box 28286, London N21 3WT, England
Norman, Edie Jo *Bowler*
3544 Mariner Blvd, Spring Hill, FL 34609, USA
Norman, Gregory J (Greg) *Golfer*
%Great White Shark Enterprises, 501 N Highway A1A, Jupiter, FL 33477, USA
Norman, Jessye *Concert Singer*
L'Orchidee, PO Box South, Crugers, NY 10521, USA
Norman, Ken *Basketball Player*
19020 Kelzie Ave, Homewood, IL 60430, USA
Norman, Marsha *Writer*
%Abrams, 275 7th Ave, #2600, New York, NY 10001, USA
Norman, Michael *Astrophysicist*
%University of California, Astronomy Dept, La Jolla, CA 90293, USA
Norman, Monty *Composer*
%PRS, 29/33 Berners St, London W1P 4AA, England
Norman, Steve *Guitarist, Saxophonist (Spandau Ballet)*
%International Talent Group, 729 7th Ave, #1600, New York, NY 10019, USA
Norodom Sihanouk, Prince Samdech Preah *King, Cambodia*
%Khemarindra Palace, Phnom Penh, Cambodia
Norrington, Roger A C *Conductor*
%Camerata Academica Salzburg, Bergstr 22, 5020 Salzburg, Austria
Norris, Alan E *Judge*
%US Court of Appeals, US Courthouse, 85 Marconi Blvd, Columbus, OH 43215, USA
Norris, Chuck *Actor*
%Amadea Film Productions, 4024 Radford Ave, #320, Studio City, CA 91604, USA
Norris, David Owen *Concert Pianist*
Aughton Rise, Collingbourne, Kingston Wilts SN8 3SA, England

Norris, James R, Jr *Chemist*
%University of Chicago, Chemistry Dept, 5735 S Ellis Ave, Chicago, IL 60637, USA
Norris, Michael K (Mike) *Baseball Player*
407 Perkins St, #105B, Oakland, CA 94610, USA
Norris, Michele *Commentator*
%ABC-TV, News Dept, 5010 Creston St, Hyattsville, MD 20781, USA
Norris, Paul J *Businessman*
%WR Grace Co, 7500 Grace Dr, Columbia, MD 21044, USA
Norris, Terry *Boxer*
%Don King Productions, 968 Pinehurst Dr, Las Vegas, NV 89109, USA
Norris, William A *Judge*
%US Court of Appeals, 312 N Spring St, Los Angeles, CA 90012, USA
Norstrom, Mattias *Hockey Player*
2513 Laurel Ave, Manhattan Beach, CA 90266, USA
North, Andy *Golfer*
3289 High Point Road, Madison, WI 53719, USA
North, Chandra *Model*
%Women Model Mgmt, 107 Greene St, #200, New York, NY 10012, USA
North, Douglass C *Nobel Economics Laureate*
7569 Homestead Road, Benzonia, MI 49616, USA
North, Jay *Actor*
290 NE 1st Ave, Lake Butler, FL 32054, USA
North, Oliver L *Government Official, Marine Officer*
22570 Markley Circle, #240, Dulles, VA 20166, USA
North, Sheree *Actress*
%Bessie Agency, 812 21st St, #C, Santa Monica, CA 90403, USA
Northam, Jeremy *Actor*
%Kelly Bush, 3859 Cardiff Ave, #200, Culver City, CA 90232, USA
Northcutt, Dennis *Football Player*
%Cleveland Browns, 76 Lou Groza Blvd, Berea, OH 44017, USA
Northrip, Richard A *Labor Leader*
%Cement & Allied Workers Union, 2500 Brickdale, Elk Grove Village, IL 60007, USA
Northrop, Wayne *Actor*
37900 Road 800, Raymond, CA 93653, USA
Northrup, James T (Jim) *Baseball Player*
29508 Southfield Road, Southfield, MI 48076, USA
Northway, Douglas (Doug) *Swimmer*
3239 E 3rd St, Tucson, AZ 85716, USA
Norton, Edward *Actor*
%The Firm, 9100 Wilshire Blvd, #100W, Beverly Hills, CA 90210, USA
Norton, Gale *Secretary, Interior*
%Interior Department, 1849 C St NW, Washington, DC 20240, USA
Norton, Gerard Ross (Toys) *WW II Rhodesian Army Hero (VC)*
Box 112, PO Banket, Zimbabwe
Norton, James J *Labor Leader*
%Graphic Communications International, 1900 L St NW, Washington, DC 20036, USA
Norton, Jeff *Hockey Player*
1701 E Las Olas Blvd, #1, Fort Lauderdale, FL 33301, USA
Norton, Kenneth H (Ken) *Boxer, Actor*
29 Gavina, Dana Point, CA 92629, USA
Norton, Peter *Computer Software Designer*
225 Arizona Ave, #200W, Santa Monica, CA 90401, USA
Norton, Virginia *Bowler*
11706 Mindanao St, Cypress, CA 90630, USA
Norville, Deborah *Commentator*
PO Box 426, Mill Neck, NY 11765, USA
Norwood, Scott *Football Player*
14529 Picket Oaks Road, Centreville, VA 20121, USA
Nossal, Gustav J V *Immunologist, Pathologist*
46 Fellows St, Kew VIC 3101, Australia
Nosseck, Noel *Movie Director*
1435 San Ysidro Dr, Beverly Hills, CA 90210, USA
Notaro, Phyllis *Bowler*
20284 Brant Angola Road, Angola, NY 14006, USA
Notebaert, Richard *Businessman*
%Quest Communications, 1801 California St, Denver, CO 80202, USA
Noth, Christopher *Actor*
%United Talent Agency, 9560 Wilshire Blvd, #500, Beverly Hills, CA 90212, USA
Notkins, Abner L *Virologist*
%National Institute of Dental Research, 9000 Rockville Pike, Bethesda, MD 20892, USA
Noto, Lucio A *Businessman*
%Mobil Corp, 3225 Gallows Road, Fairfax, VA 22037, USA
Nott, John W F *Government Official, England*
%Hillsdown Holdings PLC, 32 Hampstead High St, London NW3 1QD, England
Nottebohm, Andreas *Artist*
Mentzstr 44, Mulheim An Der Ruhr, Germany
Nouhak Phoumsavanh *President, Laos*
%President's Office, Presidential House, Vientiane, Laos

Nouri, Michael *Actor*
%Burnstein, 15304 W Sunset Blvd, #208, Pacific Palisades, CA 90272, USA
Nouvel, Jean *Architect*
%Architectures Jean Nouvel, 10 Cite d'Angouleme, 75011 Paris, France
Novack, K J *Businessman*
%America Online, 22000 AOL Way, Dulles, VA 20166, USA
Novak Popper, Ilona *Swimmer*
Il Orso Utca 23, Budapest, Hungary
Novak, David C *Businessman*
%Tricon Global Restaurants, 1441 Gardiner Lane, Louisville, KY 40213, USA
Novak, John R *Inventor (Air Cleaning Radiator)*
%Engelhard Corp, Automotive Emissions Systems, 101 Wood Ave, Iselin, NJ 08830, USA
Novak, Kim *Actress*
5611 Valley View Lane, Klamath Falls, OR 97601, USA
Novak, Michael *Theologian*
%American Enterprise Institute, 1150 17th St NW, Washington, DC 20036, USA
Novak, Robert D S *Columnist, Commentator*
1750 Pennsylvania Ave NW, #1312, Washington, DC 20006, USA
Novarina, Maurice P J *Architect*
52 Rue Raynouard, 75116 Paris, France
Novelli, William *Association Executive*
%American Association of Retired Persons, 601 E St NW, Washington, DC 20049, USA
Novello, Antonia C *Medical Administrator*
2700 Virginia Ave NW, #501, Washington, DC 20037, USA
Novello, Don (Fr Guido Sarducci) *Actor, Comedian*
%Elizabeth Rush Agency, 100 Park St, #4, Montclair, NJ 07042, USA
Noveskey, Matt *Bassist (Blue October)*
%Ashley Talent, 2002 Hogback Road, #20, Ann Arbor, MI 48105, USA
Novosel, Michael J *Vietnam War Army Hero (CMH)*
202 Oakwood Dr, Enterprise, AL 36330, USA
Novotna, Jana *Tennis Player*
7834 Montvale Way, McLean, VA 22102, USA
Novotny, Dave *Bassist (Saliva)*
%Helter Skelter, Plaza, 535 Kings Road, London SW10 0S, England
Nowak, Lisa M *Astronaut*
17123 Parsley Hawthorne Court, Houston, TX 77059, USA
Nowell, Peter C *Pathologist, Biologist*
345 Mount Alverno Road, Media, PA 19063, USA
Nowra, Louis *Writer*
Level 18, Plaza 11, 500 Oxford St, Bondi Junction NSW 2011, Australia
Noyce, Phillip *Movie Director*
%Cresswell, 163 Brougham St, Woolloomooloo, Sydney 2011, Australia
Noyd, R Allen *Religious Leader*
%General Council, Christian Church, 1294 Rutledge Road, Transfer, PA 16154, USA
Noyes, Albert, Jr *Chemist*
5102 Fairview Dr, Austin, TX 78731, USA
Noyori, Ryoji *Nobel Chemistry Laureate*
135-417 Shinden, Umemoricho, Nisshin, Aichi 470-0132, Japan
Nozieres, Philippe P G F *Physicist*
15 Route d Saint Nizier, 38180 Seyssins, France
Nsengiyremeye, Dismas *Prime Minister, Rwanda*
%Prime Minister's Office, Kigali, Rwanda
Nsibanbi, Apolo *Prime Minister, Uganda*
%Premier's Office, International Conference Center, Kampala, Uganda
Ntombi *Queen, Swaziland*
%Royal Residence, PO Box 1, Lobamba, Swaziland
Ntoutoume, Jean-Francois *Prime Minister, Gabon*
%Prime Minister's Office, BP 546, Libreville, Gabon
Nuami, Sheikh Humaid bin Rashid, an- *Ruler, Ajman*
%Royal Palace, PO Box 1, Ajman, United Arab Emirates
Nucci, Danny *Actor*
%Gold Marshak Liedtke, 3500 W Olive Ave, #1400, Burbank, CA 91505, USA
Nucci, Leo *Opera Singer*
%I C M Artists, 40 W 57th St, New York, NY 10019, USA
Nugent, Nelle *Theater Producer*
%Foxboro Entertainment, 133 E 58th St, #301, New York, NY 10022, USA
Nugent, Ted *Singer, Guitarist*
%Madhouse Mgmt, PO Box 130109, Ann Arbor, MI 48113, USA
Nujoma, Sam S *President, Namibia*
%President's Office, State House, Mugabe Ave, 9000 Windhoek, Namibia
Numan, Gary *Singer, Songwriter*
86 Staines Road, Wraysbury, N Staines, Middlesex TW19 5A, England
Numminen, Teppo *Hockey Player*
3422 E Palo Verde Dr, Paradise Valley, AZ 85253, USA
Nunez, Miguel Angel, Jr *Actor*
%Abrams Artists, 9200 Sunset Blvd, #1125, Los Angeles, CA 90069, USA
Nunez, Victor *Movie Director*
%Paul Kohner, 9300 Wilshire Blvd, #555, Beverly Hills, CA 90212, USA

N

Nunley, Frank — *Football Player*
24632 Olive Tree Lane, Los Altos Hills, CA 94024, USA
Nunn, Louie B — *Governor, KY*
1501 Wellesley Dr, Lexington, KY 40513, USA
Nunn, Michael — *Boxer*
3517 W 47th St, #4, Davenport, IA 52806, USA
Nunn, Samuel A (Sam) — *Senator, GA*
75 14th St NE, #4810, Atlanta, GA 30309, USA
Nunn, Teri — *Singer (Berlin)*
%MOB Agency, 6404 Wilshire Blvd, #505, Los Angeles, CA 90048, USA
Nunn, Trevor R — *Theater Director*
%Royal National Theater, South Bank, London SE1 9PX, England
Nurmi, Maila (Vampira) — *Actress*
4310 1/? Gateway Ave, Los Angeles, CA 90029, USA
Nurse, Paul M — *Nobel Medicine Laureate*
%Clare Hall Laboratories, Cell Cycle Control Lab, Herts EN6 3LD, England
Nussbaum, Danny — *Actor*
%Conway Van Gelder Robinson, 18-21 Jermyn St, London SW1Y 6NB, England
Nussbaum, Karen — *Labor Activist*
%9-5 National Working Women Assn, 231 W Wisconsin, #900, Milwaukee, WI 53203, USA
Nussbaum, Martha C — *Philosopher*
%University of Chicago, Law School, 111 E 60th St, Chicago, IL 60637, USA
Nusslein-Volhard, Christiane — *Nobel Medicine Laureate*
%Max Planck Biology Institute, Spenmannstr 35/III, 72076 Tubingen, Germany
Nutt, Jim — *Artist*
1035 Greenwood Ave, Wilmette, IL 60091, USA
Nutter, Alice — *Singer (Chumbawamba)*
%Doug Smith Assoc, PO Box 1151, London W3 8ZJ, England
Nutter, David — *Movie, Television Director*
%Shapiro-Lichtman, 8827 Beverly Blvd, Los Angeles, CA 90048, USA
Nutting, Wallace H — *Army General*
PO Box 96, Biddeford Pool, ME 04006, USA
Nutzle, Futzie — *Artist, Cartoonist*
PO Box 325, Aromas, CA 95004, USA
Nuwer, Hank — *Writer, Journalist*
%Franklin College, Journalism Dept, 501 E Monroe St, Franklin, IN 46131, USA
Nuxhall, Joseph H (Joe) — *Baseball Player*
5706 Lindenwood Lane, Fairfield, OH 45014, USA
Nuyen, France — *Actress*
PO Box 18437, Beverly Hills, CA 90209, USA
Nuzorewa, Abel Tendekayi — *Prime Minister, Zimbabwe*
%United African National Council, 40 Charter Road, Harare, Zimbabwe
Nyad, Diana — *Swimmer, Sportscaster*
%Uptown Racquet Club, 151 E 86th St, New York, NY 10028, USA
Nyberg, Frederik — *Alpine Skier*
Kaptensgatan 2C, 832 00 Froson, Sweden
Nyberg, Karen L — *Astronaut*
2518 Lakeside Landing, Seabrook, TX 77586, USA
Nye, Carrie — *Actress*
%Paradigm Agency, 200 W 57th St, #900, New York, NY 10019, USA
Nye, Erle — *Businessman*
%Texas Utilities Co, Energy Plaza, 1601 Bryan St, Dallas, TX 75201, USA
Nye, Louis — *Actor, Comedian*
1241 Corsica Dr, Pacific Palisades, CA 90272, USA
Nye, Robert — *Writer*
Thornfield, Kingsland, Ballinghassig, County Cork, Ireland
Nyers, Rezso — *Secretary General, Hungary*
Ozgida Utca 22/A, 1025 Budapest, Hungary
Nygaard, Richard L — *Judge*
%US Court of Appeals, 1st National Bank Building, 717 State St, Erie, PA 16501, USA
Nykvist, Sven V — *Cinematographer*
Strandpromenaden 4, Saltjso-Duvnas 131 50, Sweden
Nyland, William L — *Marine Corps General*
Deputy CofS Aviation, HqUSMC, 2 Navy St, Washington, DC 20380, USA
Nyman, Michael L — *Composer, Pianist*
%Michael Nyman Ltd, PO Box 430, High Wycombe HP13 5QT, England
Nystrom, Bob — *Hockey Player*
475 Berry Hill Road, Oyster Bay, NY 11771, USA
Nystrom, Joakim — *Tennis Player*
Torsgatan 194, 931 00 Skellefteaa, Sweden

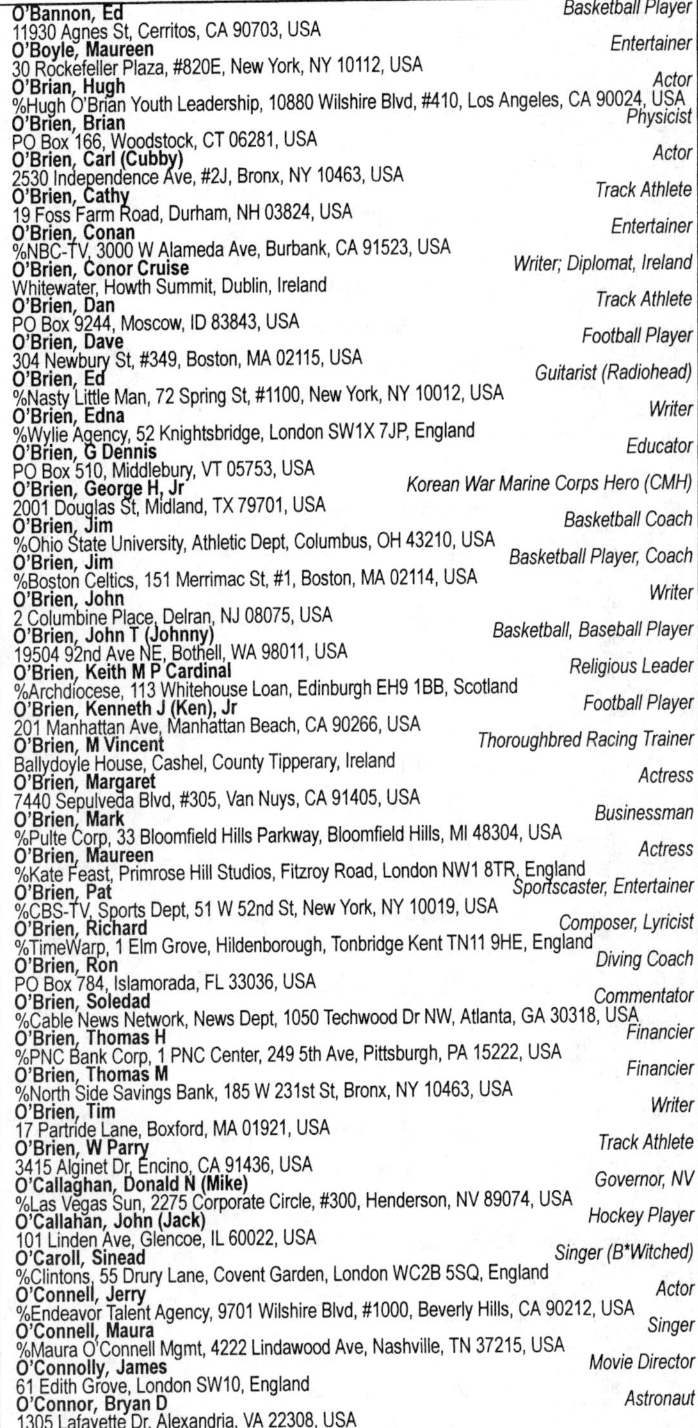

O'Bannon, Ed — *Basketball Player*
11930 Agnes St, Cerritos, CA 90703, USA

O'Boyle, Maureen — *Entertainer*
30 Rockefeller Plaza, #820E, New York, NY 10112, USA

O'Brian, Hugh — *Actor*
%Hugh O'Brian Youth Leadership, 10880 Wilshire Blvd, #410, Los Angeles, CA 90024, USA

O'Brien, Brian — *Physicist*
PO Box 166, Woodstock, CT 06281, USA

O'Brien, Carl (Cubby) — *Actor*
2530 Independence Ave, #2J, Bronx, NY 10463, USA

O'Brien, Cathy — *Track Athlete*
19 Foss Farm Road, Durham, NH 03824, USA

O'Brien, Conan — *Entertainer*
%NBC-TV, 3000 W Alameda Ave, Burbank, CA 91523, USA

O'Brien, Conor Cruise — *Writer; Diplomat, Ireland*
Whitewater, Howth Summit, Dublin, Ireland

O'Brien, Dan — *Track Athlete*
PO Box 9244, Moscow, ID 83843, USA

O'Brien, Dave — *Football Player*
304 Newbury St, #349, Boston, MA 02115, USA

O'Brien, Ed — *Guitarist (Radiohead)*
%Nasty Little Man, 72 Spring St, #1100, New York, NY 10012, USA

O'Brien, Edna — *Writer*
%Wylie Agency, 52 Knightsbridge, London SW1X 7JP, England

O'Brien, G Dennis — *Educator*
PO Box 510, Middlebury, VT 05753, USA

O'Brien, George H, Jr — *Korean War Marine Corps Hero (CMH)*
2001 Douglas St, Midland, TX 79701, USA

O'Brien, Jim — *Basketball Coach*
%Ohio State University, Athletic Dept, Columbus, OH 43210, USA

O'Brien, Jim — *Basketball Player, Coach*
%Boston Celtics, 151 Merrimac St, #1, Boston, MA 02114, USA

O'Brien, John — *Writer*
2 Columbine Place, Delran, NJ 08075, USA

O'Brien, John T (Johnny) — *Basketball, Baseball Player*
19504 92nd Ave NE, Bothell, WA 98011, USA

O'Brien, Keith M P Cardinal — *Religious Leader*
%Archdiocese, 113 Whitehouse Loan, Edinburgh EH9 1BB, Scotland

O'Brien, Kenneth J (Ken), Jr — *Football Player*
201 Manhattan Ave, Manhattan Beach, CA 90266, USA

O'Brien, M Vincent — *Thoroughbred Racing Trainer*
Ballydoyle House, Cashel, County Tipperary, Ireland

O'Brien, Margaret — *Actress*
7440 Sepulveda Blvd, #305, Van Nuys, CA 91405, USA

O'Brien, Mark — *Businessman*
%Pulte Corp, 33 Bloomfield Hills Parkway, Bloomfield Hills, MI 48304, USA

O'Brien, Maureen — *Actress*
%Kate Feast, Primrose Hill Studios, Fitzroy Road, London NW1 8TR, England

O'Brien, Pat — *Sportscaster, Entertainer*
%CBS-TV, Sports Dept, 51 W 52nd St, New York, NY 10019, USA

O'Brien, Richard — *Composer, Lyricist*
%TimeWarp, 1 Elm Grove, Hildenborough, Tonbridge Kent TN11 9HE, England

O'Brien, Ron — *Diving Coach*
PO Box 784, Islamorada, FL 33036, USA

O'Brien, Soledad — *Commentator*
%Cable News Network, News Dept, 1050 Techwood Dr NW, Atlanta, GA 30318, USA

O'Brien, Thomas H — *Financier*
%PNC Bank Corp, 1 PNC Center, 249 5th Ave, Pittsburgh, PA 15222, USA

O'Brien, Thomas M — *Financier*
%North Side Savings Bank, 185 W 231st St, Bronx, NY 10463, USA

O'Brien, Tim — *Writer*
17 Partride Lane, Boxford, MA 01921, USA

O'Brien, W Parry — *Track Athlete*
3415 Alginet Dr, Encino, CA 91436, USA

O'Callaghan, Donald N (Mike) — *Governor, NV*
%Las Vegas Sun, 2275 Corporate Circle, #300, Henderson, NV 89074, USA

O'Callahan, John (Jack) — *Hockey Player*
101 Linden Ave, Glencoe, IL 60022, USA

O'Caroll, Sinead — *Singer (B*Witched)*
%Clintons, 55 Drury Lane, Covent Garden, London WC2B 5SQ, England

O'Connell, Jerry — *Actor*
%Endeavor Talent Agency, 9701 Wilshire Blvd, #1000, Beverly Hills, CA 90212, USA

O'Connell, Maura — *Singer*
%Maura O'Connell Mgmt, 4222 Lindawood Ave, Nashville, TN 37215, USA

O'Connolly, James — *Movie Director*
61 Edith Grove, London SW10, England

O'Connor, Bryan D — *Astronaut*
1305 Lafayette Dr, Alexandria, VA 22308, USA

O

O'Connor - O'Keefe

O'Connor, Edmund F *Army General*
1169 Ironsides Ave, Melbourne, FL 32940, USA
O'Connor, Frances *Actress*
%Robyn Gardiner Mgmt, 397 Riley St, Surrey Hills NSW 2010, Australia
O'Connor, Gavin *Movie Director*
%United Talent Agency, 9560 Wilshire Blvd, #500, Beverly Hills, CA 90212, USA
O'Connor, Glynnis *Actress*
%Bill Treusch, 853 7th Ave, #9A, New York, NY 10019, USA
O'Connor, J Dennis *Educator*
%Smithsonian Institution, Provost's Office, Washington, DC 20560, USA
O'Connor, Mark *Fiddle Player, Violinist*
%CM Mgmt, 5749 Larryan Dr, Woodland Hills, CA 91367, USA
O'Connor, Martin J *Religious Leader*
Palazzo San Carlo, 00120 Vatican City
O'Connor, Maryanne *Basketball Player*
60 Romanock Place, Fairfield, CT 06825, USA
O'Connor, Patrick D (Pat) *Movie Director*
%International Creative Mgmt, 76 Oxford St, London W1N 0AX, England
O'Connor, Sandra Day *Supreme Court Justice*
%US Supreme Court, 1 1st St NE, Washington, DC 20543, USA
O'Connor, Sinead *Singer, Songwriter*
%Free Trade Agency, Chapel Place, Rivington St, London EC21 3DQ, England
O'Connor, Thom *Artist*
Moss Road, Voorheesville, NY 12186, USA
O'Connor, Tim *Actor*
PO Box 458, Nevada City, CA 95959, USA
O'Day, Alan *Singer, Songwriter*
%Talent Consultants International, 1560 Broadway, #1308, New York, NY 10036, USA
O'Day, Anita *Singer*
%Richard Barz, 21 Cobble Creek Dr, Tannersville, PA 18372, USA
O'Day, George *Yachtsman*
6 Turtle Lane, Dover, MA 02030, USA
O'Donnell, Annie *Actress*
%Capital Artists, 6404 Wilshire Blvd, #950, Los Angeles, CA 90048, USA
O'Donnell, Charles (Chuck) *Bowler*
7354 Forest Haven E, Saint Louis, MO 63123, USA
O'Donnell, Chris *Actor*
%Creative Artists Agency, 9830 Wilshire Blvd, Beverly Hills, CA 90212, USA
O'Donnell, John J *Labor Leader*
%Air Line Pilots Assn, 1625 Massachusetts Ave NW, Washington, DC 20036, USA
O'Donnell, Mark *Writer*
202 Riverside Dr, #8E, New York, NY 10025, USA
O'Donnell, Neil K *Football Player*
PO Box 403, New Vernon, NJ 07976, USA
O'Donnell, Rosie *Actress*
%Bernie Young Agency, 9800 Topanga Canyon Blvd, #D, Chatsworth, CA 91311, USA
O'Donnell, William (Bill) *Harness Racing Driver*
569 Penn Estate, East Stroudsburg, PA 18301, USA
O'Driscoll, Martha *Actress*
22 Indian Creek Island Road, Indian Creek Village, FL 33154, USA
O'Grady, Gail *Actress*
%Agency for Performing Arts, 9200 Sunset Blvd, #900, Los Angeles, CA 90069, USA
O'Grady, Sean *Boxer*
%Adoreable Promotions, PO Box 9, Bay City, MI 48707, USA
O'Hara, Catherine *Actress, Comedienne*
%Brillstein/Grey, 9150 Wilshire Blvd, #350, Beverly Hills, CA 90212, USA
O'Hara, Jenny *Actress*
8663 Wonderland Ave, Los Angeles, CA 90046, USA
O'Hara, Maureen *Actress*
PO Box 1400, Christeansted, Kingshill, VI 00851, USA
O'Hara, Terrence J *Movie Director*
%Armstrong/Hirsch, 1888 Century Park East, #1800, Los Angeles, CA 90067, USA
O'Hare, Michael *Actor*
%E/W, 280 S Beverly Dr, #400, Beverly Hills, CA 90212, USA
O'Herlihy, Daniel *Actor*
%Fifi Oscard, 110 W 40th St, #1500, New York, NY 10018, USA
O'Horgan, Thomas F (Tom) *Composer, Director*
%Carl Goldstein, 9951 Seacrest Circle, #201, Boynton Beach, FL 33437, USA
O'Hurley, John *Actor*
11661 San Vicente Blvd, #307, Los Angeles, CA 90049, USA
O'Keefe, Jeremiah J, Sr *WW II Marine Corps Air Force Hero*
PO Box 430, Ocean Springs, MS 39566, USA
O'Keefe, Jodie Lyn *Actress*
%J Michael Bloom, 9255 Sunset Blvd, #710, Los Angeles, CA 90069, USA
O'Keefe, Michael *Actor*
5850 W 3rd St, #144, Los Angeles, CA 90036, USA
O'Keefe, Miles *Actor*
%Irv Schechter, 9300 Wilshire Blvd, #410, Beverly Hills, CA 90212, USA

O'Keefe, Sean *Government Official*
%National Aviation/Space Administration, 300 E St SW, Washington, DC 20024, USA
O'Koren, Mike *Basketball Player*
%Washington Wizards, MCI Centre, 601 F St NW, Washington, DC 20004, USA
O'Leary, Brian T *Astronaut*
1993 S Kihei Road, #21200, Kihei, HI 96753, USA
O'Leary, Hazel R *Secretary, Energy*
%Energy Department, 1000 Independence Ave SW, Washington, DC 20585, USA
O'Leary, John *Actor*
%Gage Group, 14724 Ventura Blvd, #505, Sherman Oaks, CA 91403, USA
O'Leary, Michael *Actor*
38 Prospect Ave, Montclair, NJ 07042, USA
O'Leary, William *Actor*
%House of Representatives, 400 S Beverly Dr, #101, Beverly Hills, CA 90212, USA
O'Loughlin, Gerald S *Actor*
23388 Mulholland Dr, #204, Woodland Hills, CA 91364, USA
O'Malley, Peter *Baseball Executive*
326 S Hudson Ave, Los Angeles, CA 90020, USA
O'Malley, Robert E *Vietnam War Marine Corps Hero (CMH)*
PO Box 775, Goldthwaite, TX 76844, USA
O'Malley, Sean Patrick *Religious Leader*
%Archdiocese of Boston, 2121 Commonwealth Ave, Brighton, MA 02135, USA
O'Malley, Susan *Basketball Executive*
%Washington Wizards, MCI Centre, 601 F St NW, Washington, DC 20004, USA
O'Malley, Thomas D *Businessman*
%Tosco Corp, 1700 E Putnam Ave, #500, Old Greenwich, CT 06870, USA
O'Mara, Kate *Actress*
%Michael Ladkin Mgmt, 1 Duchess St, #1, London W1N 3DE, England
O'Mara, Mark *Harness Racing Driver, Trainer*
6882 NW 65th Terrace, Parkland, FL 33067, USA
O'Meara, Mark *Golfer*
6312 Deacon Circle, Windermere, FL 34786, USA
O'Neal, Alexander *Singer, Songwriter*
%Green Light Talent Agency, PO Box 3172, Beverly Hills, CA 90212, USA
O'Neal, E Stanley *Businessman*
%Merrill Lynch Co, World Financial Center, 2 Vesey St, New York, NY 10007, USA
O'Neal, Griffin *Actor*
14209 Riverside Dr, Van Nuys, CA 91423, USA
O'Neal, Jamie *Singer, Songwriter*
%Fitzgerald Hartley, 1908 Wedgewood Ave, Nashville, TN 37212, USA
O'Neal, Jermaine *Basketball Player*
%Indiana Pacers, Conseco Fieldhouse, 125 S Pennsylvania, Indianapolis, IN 46204, USA
O'Neal, Leslie C *Football Player*
5617 Adobe Falls Road, #A, San Diego, CA 92120, USA
O'Neal, Ryan *Actor*
21368 Pacific Coast Highway, Malibu, CA 90265, USA
O'Neal, Shaquille R *Basketball Player*
3110 Main St, #225, Santa Monica, CA 90405, USA
O'Neal, Stan *Financier*
%Merrill Lynch Co, World Financial Center, 2 Vesey St, New York, NY 10007, USA
O'Neal, Tatum *Actress*
%El Dorado Apartments, 300 Central Park West, #16G, New York, NY 10024, USA
O'Neil, John B (Buck) *Baseball Player, Coach*
3049 E 32nd St, Kansas City, MO 64128, USA
O'Neil, Lawrence *Movie Director*
%International Creative Mgmt, 8942 Wilshire Blvd, #219, Beverly Hills, CA 90211, USA
O'Neil, Tricia *Actress*
%David Shapira, 15821 Ventura Blvd, #235, Encino, CA 91436, USA
O'Neill of Bengarve, O Sylvia *Philosopher*
%Newham College, Cambridge CB3 9DF, England
O'Neill, Brian *Hockey Executive*
2600-1800 McGill College Ave, Montreal QC H3A 3J6, Canada
O'Neill, Ed *Actor*
2607 Grand Canal, Venice, CA 90291, USA
O'Neill, Eugene F *Communications Engineer*
17 Dellwood Court, Middletown, NJ 07748, USA
O'Neill, Jennifer *Actress, Model*
7500 W Lake Mead Blvd, #492, Las Vegas, NV 89128, USA
O'Neill, Kevin *Basketball Coach*
%Toronto Raptors, Air Canada Center, 40 Bay St, Toronto ON M5J 2N8, Canada
O'Neill, Michael J *Editor*
23 Cayuga Road, Scarsdale, NY 10583, USA
O'Neill, Paul A *Baseball Player*
7785 Hartford Hill Lane, Cincinnati, OH 45242, USA
O'Neill, Paul H *Secretary, Treasury*
3 Von Lent Place, Pittsburgh, PA 15232, USA
O'Neill, Susan (Susie) *Swimmer*
207 Kent St, #1800, Sydney NSW 2000, Australia

O'Neill, William A *Governor, CT*
PO Box 360, East Hampton, CT 06424, USA
O'Quinn, John M *Attorney*
%O'Quinn Kerensky McAnich, 2300 Lyric Center, 440 Louisiana, Houston, TX 77002, USA
O'Quinn, Terry *Actor*
%Innovative Artists, 1505 10th St, Santa Monica, CA 90401, USA
O'Ree, William E (Willie) *Hockey Player*
7961 Anders Circle, La Mesa, CA 91942, USA
O'Reilly, Anthony J F *Businessman, Publisher*
%HJ Heinz Co, PO Box 57, Pittsburgh, PA 15230, USA
O'Reilly, Bill *Commentator*
%Fox-TV, News Dept, 205 E 67th St, New York, NY 10021, USA
O'Reilly, Cyril *Actor*
%Stone Manners, 6500 Wilshire Blvd, #550, Los Angeles, CA 90048, USA
O'Reilly, Terry *Hockey Player, Coach*
PO Box 5544, Salisbury, MA 01952, USA
O'Riordan, Dolores *Singer (Cranberries)*
%Sendyk Leonard, 532 Colorado Ave, Santa Monica, CA 90401, USA
O'Rourke, Charles C *Football Player*
220 Bedford St, #A7, Bridgewater, MA 02324, USA
O'Scannlain, Diarmuid F *Judge*
%US Court of Appeals, Pioneer Courthouse, 555 SW Yamhill St, Portland, OR 97204, USA
O'Shea, Kevin *Basketball Player, Coach*
87 Aquauista Way, San Francisco, CA 94131, USA
O'Shea, Milo *Actor*
%Bancroft Hotel, 40 W 72nd St, #17A, New York, NY 10023, USA
O'Sullivan, Gilbert *Singer*
%Park Promotions, PO Box 651, Park Road, Oxford OX2 9RB, England
O'Sullivan, Peter *Editor*
%Houston Post, Editorial Dept, 4747 Southwest Freeway, Houston, TX 77027, USA
O'Sullivan, Richard *Actor*
%Al Mitchell, 5 Anglers Lane, Kentish Town, London NW5 3DG, England
O'Sullivan, Shawn *Boxer*
231 Donlea Dr, Toronto ON M4F 2N3, Canada
O'Sullivan, Sonia *Track Athlete*
%Kim McDonald, 201 High St, Hampton Hill, Middx TW12 1NL, England
O'Toole, Annette *Actress*
11936 Gorham Ave, #106, Los Angeles, CA 90049, USA
O'Toole, S Peter *Actor*
%Stephen Kenis, Royalty House, 72-74 Dean St, London W1D 3SG, England
Oakes, James L *Judge*
%US Court of Appeals, PO Box 696, Brattleboro, VT 05302, USA
Oakley, Charles *Basketball Player*
%Washington Wizards, MCI Centre, 601 F St NW, Washington, DC 20004, USA
Oates, Adam R *Hockey Player*
1480 S County Road, Osterville, MA 02655, USA
Oates, Bart S *Football Player, Sportscaster*
1 Silverbrook Dr, Morristown, NJ 07960, USA
Oates, John *Singer (Hall & Oates), Songwriter*
%Creative Artists Agency, 9830 Wilshire Blvd, Beverly Hills, CA 90212, USA
Oates, John L (Johnny) *Baseball Player, Manager*
20222 Eagle Cove Court, Petersburg, VA 23803, USA
Oates, Joyce Carol *Writer*
%John Hawkins, 71 W 23rd St, #1600, New York, NY 10010, USA
Obando Bravo, Miguel Cardinal *Religious Leader*
Arzobispado, Apartado 3050, Managua, Nicaragua
Obasanjo, Olusegun *President, Nigeria; Army General*
%President's Office, State House, Ribadu Road, Ikoyi, Lagos, Nigeria
Obato, Gyo *Architect*
%Hellmuth Obato Kassabaum, 1 Metropolitan Square, #600, Saint Louis, MO 63102, USA
Obee, Duncan *Football Player*
4488 283rd St, Toledo, OH 43611, USA
Obeid, Atef *Prime Minister, Egypt*
%Prime Minister's Office, PO Box 191, 1 Majlis El-Shaab St, Cairo, Egypt
Obeidat, Ahmad Abdul-Majeed *Prime Minister, Jordan*
%Law & Arbitration Center, PO Box 926544, Amman, Jordan
Oberg, Margo *Surfer*
RR 1 Box 73, Koloa, Kaui HI 96756, USA
Oberlin, David W *Government Official*
800 Independence Ave SW, #814, Washington, DC 20591, USA
Obote, A Milton *President, Uganda*
%Uganda People's Congress, PO Box 1951, Kampala, Uganda
Obradors, Jacqueline *Actress*
%Writers & Artists, 8383 Wilshire Blvd, #550, Beverly Hills, CA 90211, USA
Obradovich, James R (Jim) *Football Player*
437 7th Place, Manhattan Beach, CA 90266, USA
Obraztsova, Elena V *Opera Singer*
%Bolshoi Theater, Teatralnaya Pl 1, 103009 Moscow, Russia

Obregon, Ana *Actress*
%Paul Kohner, 9300 Wilshire Blvd, #555, Beverly Hills, CA 90212, USA

Ocampo Uria, Adriana C *Geologist, Planetary Scientist*
%National Aeronautics/Space Administration, 300 E St SW, Washington, DC 20546, USA

Ocasek, Ric *Singer (Cars), Songwriter*
%Elektra Records, 75 Rockefeller Plaza, New York, NY 10019, USA

Ocean, Billy *Singer, Songwriter*
%Laura Jay Enterprises, 32 Willesden Lane, London NW6 7ST, England

Ochirbat, Punsalmaagiyn *President, Mongolia*
%Tengeriin Tsag Co, Olympic St 14, Ulan Bator, Mongolia

Ochman, Wieslaw *Opera Singer*
Ul Miaczynska 46B, 02-637 Warsaw, Poland

Ochoa, Ellen *Astronaut*
11810 Mighty Redwood Dr, Houston, TX 77059, USA

Ockels, Wubbo *Astronaut, Netherlands*
%ESTEC, Postbus 299, 2200 AG Noordwijk, Netherlands

ODB *Rap Artist (Wu-Tang Clan)*
%Famous Artists Agency, 250 W 57th St, New York, NY 10107, USA

Oddsson, David *Prime Minister, Iceland*
%Prime Minister's Office, Stjo'rnaaroshusio, 150 Reykjavik, Iceland

Odelein, Selmar *Hockey Player*
Farm, Quill Lake SK S0A 3E0, Canada

Odell, Bob H *Football Player, Coach*
340 Beth Ellen Dr, Lewisburg, PA 17837, USA

Oden, Derrick *Football Player*
1805 S Barkley Dr, Mobile, AL 36606, USA

Odenkirk, Bob *Actor*
%Endeavor Talent Agency, 9701 Wilshire Blvd, #1000, Beverly Hills, CA 90212, USA

Odermatt, Robert A *Architect*
140 Camino Don Miguel, Orinda, CA 94563, USA

Odetta *Singer*
%Douglas Yeager Productions, 300 W 55th St, New York, NY 10019, USA

Odjig, Daphne *Artist*
102 Foresbrook Place, Penticton BC V2A 7N4, Canada

Odom, John Lee (Blue Moon) *Baseball Player*
10343 Slater Ave, #204, Fountain Valley, CA 92708, USA

Odom, Lamar *Basketball Player*
%Miami Heat, American Airlines Arena, 601 Biscayne Blvd, Miami, FL 33132, USA

Odom, William E *Army General*
5112 38th St NW, Washington, DC 20016, USA

Odomes, Nathaniel B (Nate) *Football Player*
900 Quail Creek Dr, Columbus, GA 31907, USA

Odoms, Riley M *Football Player*
834 1/2 Staffordshire Road, Stafford, TX 77477, USA

Oduber, Nelson O *Prime Minister, Aruba*
%Movimenti Electoral di Pueblo, Cumana 84, Oranjestad, Aruba

Oe, Kenzaburo *Nobel Literature Laureate*
585 Seijo-Machi, Setagayaku, Tokyo, Japan

Oedekerk, Steve *Movie Director*
%William Morris Agency, 151 El Camino Dr, Beverly Hills, CA 90212, USA

Oefelein, William A *Astronaut*
1205 Hawkhill Dr, Friendswood, TX 77546, USA

Oenish, Dean *Physician*
%Preventive Medical Research Institute, 900 Bridgeway, #2, Sausalito, CA 94965, USA

Oerter, Alfred A (Al) *Track Athlete*
4745 Estero Blvd, #501, Fort Myers Beach, FL 33931, USA

Oetiker, Phil *Cinematographer*
422 10th St, Brooklyn, NY 11215, USA

Oettinger, Anthony G *Mathematician*
65 Elizabeth Road, Belmont, MA 02478, USA

Offerdahl, John A *Football Player*
2749 NE 37th Dr, Fort Lauderdale, FL 33308, USA

Offerman, Jose A *Baseball Player*
Ed 81, Urb Anscaono Moscoso, San Pedro de Marcos, Dominican Republic

Ogato, Sadako *Government Official, Japan*
%United Nations Office for Refugees, CP 2500, 1211 Geneva 2, Switzerland

Ogden, Jonathan (Jon) *Football Player*
%Baltimore Ravens, Ravens Stadium, 11001 Russell St, Baltimore, MD 21230, USA

Ogi, Adolf *President, Switzerland*
Bundesjause-Nord, Kochergasse 10, 3003 Berne, Switzerland

Ogier, Bulle *Actress*
%Artmedia, 20 Ave Rapp, 75007 Paris, France

Ogilvie, Kelvin K *Chemist, Educator*
PO Box 307, Canning NS B0P 1X0, Canada

Ogilvie, Lana *Model*
%Company Models, 17 Little West 12th St, #333, New York, NY 10014, USA

Ogilvy, Ian *Actor*
%Julian Belfarge, 46 Albermarle St, London W1X 4PP, England

O

Ogle - Olbermann

Ogle, Brett — *Golfer*
%Advantage International, 1751 Pinnacle Dr, #1500, McLean, VA 22102, USA

Oglesby, Alfred L — *Football Player*
111 Pendelton Place Circle, Sugar Land, TX 77479, USA

Oglivie, Benjamin A (Ben) — *Baseball Player*
1012 E Sandpiper Dr, Tempe, AZ 85283, USA

Ogrin, David — *Golfer*
37300 Golf Club Trail, Magnolia, TX 77355, USA

Ogrodnick, John — *Hockey Player*
37034 Aldgate Court, Farmington Hills, MI 48335, USA

Oh, Sadaharu — *Baseball Player*
%Fukuoka Dome Daiei Hawks, 6F 2-2-2 Jigyohama, Chuo-Ku Fukouka 810, Japan

Oh, Soon-Teck — *Actor*
128 N Kenwood St, #1, Burbank, CA 91505, USA

Ohl, Don — *Basketball Player*
2 E Lockhaven Court, Edwardsville, IL 62025, USA

Ohlsson, Garrick — *Concert Pianist*
%International Creative Mgmt, 8942 Wilshire Blvd, #219, Beverly Hills, CA 90211, USA

Ohlund, Mattias — *Hockey Player*
%Vancouver Canucks, 800 Griffiths Way, Vancouver BC V6B 6G1, Canada

Ohman, Jack — *Editorial Cartoonist (Mixed Media)*
%Portland Oregonian, Editorial Dept, 1320 SW Broadway, Portland, OR 97201, USA

Ohno, Apolo Anton — *Speed Skater*
%US Speedskating, PO Box 450639, Westlake, OH 44145, USA

Ohtani, Monshu Koshin — *Religious Leader*
Horikawa-Dori, Hanayachosagaru, Shimogyoku, Kyoto 600, Japan

Ohyama, Heiichiro — *Conductor*
6305 Via Cabrera, La Jolla, CA 92037, USA

Oimeon, Casper — *Skier*
540 S Mountain Ave, Ashland, OR 97520, USA

Oistrakh, Igor D — *Concert Violinist*
Novolesnaya Str 3, Korp 2, #10, Moscow, Russia

Oiter, Bailey — *President, Micronesia*
%President's Office, Palikia, Pohnepei FM, 96941 Kolonia, Micronesia

Ojukwu, Chukwuemeka O — *President, Biafra; Army General*
Villaska Lodge, 29 Queen's Dr, Ikoyi, Lagos State, Nigeria

Oka, Takeshi — *Chemist*
1463 E Park Place, Chicago, IL 60637, USA

Okabe, Nororki — *Engineer, Architect*
%Kansai Airport, 1 Banchi Senshu-Kuko Kita, Izumisanoshi, Osaka 549, Japan

Okamoto, Ayako — *Golfer*
22627 Ladeene Ave, Torrance, CA 90505, USA

Okamura, Arthur — *Artist*
210 Kale St, Bolinas, CA 94924, USA

Okhotnikoff, Nikolai P — *Opera Singer*
Canal Griboedova 109, #13, 190068 Saint Petersburg, Russia

Okogie, Anthony Olubunmi Cardinal — *Religious Leader*
%Archdiocese, PO Box 8, 19 Catholic Mission St, Lagos, Nigeria

Okolowicz, Jeff — *Guitarist (Chesterfield Kings)*
%Living Eye Productions, PO Box 12956, Rochester, NY 14612, USA

Okolowicz, Ted — *Guitarist (Chesterfield Kings)*
%Living Eye Productions, PO Box 12956, Rochester, NY 14612, USA

Okoye, Christian E — *Football Player*
10082 Big Pine Dr, Alta Loma, CA 91737, USA

Okubo, Susumu — *Physicist*
1209 East Ave, Rochester, NY 14607, USA

Okuda, Hiroshi — *Businessman*
%Toyota Motor Corp, 1 Toyotacho, Toyota City, Aichi Prefecture 471, Japan

Okumura, Tomohiro — *Concert Violinist*
%Jecklin Assoc, 2717 Nichols Lane, Davenport, IA 52803, USA

Okun, Daniel A — *Environmental Engineer*
204 Carol Woods, 750 Weaver Dairy Road, Chapel Hill, NC 27514, USA

Olafsson, Olafur J — *Publisher*
%Sony Electronics Publishing USA, 9 W 57th St, New York, NY 10019, USA

Olah, George A — *Nobel Chemistry Laureate*
2252 Gloaming Way, Beverly Hills, CA 90210, USA

Olander, Ed — *WW II Marine Corps Air Force Hero*
61 Fox Farms Road, Florence, MA 01062, USA

Olander, Jimmy — *Guitarist (Diamond Rio)*
%Dreamcatcher Artists Mgmt, 2908 Poston Ave, Nashville, TN 37203, USA

Olandt, Ken — *Actor*
%Gold Marshak Liedtke, 3500 W Olive Ave, #1400, Burbank, CA 91505, USA

Olazabel, Jose Maria — *Golfer*
%Sergio Gomez, Apartado 26, 20080 San Sebastian, Spain

Olberding, Mark — *Basketball Player*
4131 Cliff Oaks St, San Antonio, TX 78229, USA

Olbermann, Keith — *Sportscaster*
%Cable News Network, Sports Dept, 1050 Techwood Dr NW, Atlanta, GA 30318, USA

Olbrychski, Daniel — *Actor*
%Teatr Polski, Ul Karasia 2, 00-327 Warsaw, Poland

Olczyk, Ed — *Hockey Player, Coach*
%Pittsburgh Penguins, Mellon Arena, 66 Mario Lemieux Place, Pittsburgh, PA 15219, USA

Old, Lloyd J — *Cancer Biologist*
%Ludwig Institute of Cancer Research, 1345 Ave of Americas, New York, NY 10105, USA

Oldenburg, Claes T — *Sculptor*
556 Broome St, New York, NY 10013, USA

Oldenburg, Richard E — *Museum Director*
447 E 57th St, New York, NY 10022, USA

Oldendorf, William — *Physician*
%University of California, Medical Center, Neurology Dept, Los Angeles, CA 90024, USA

Older, Charles (Chuck) — *WW II Army Air Corps Hero*
930 Thayer Ave, Los Angeles, CA 90024, USA

Olderman, Murray — *Sportswriter*
832 Inverness Dr, Rancho Mirage, CA 92270, USA

Oldfield, Bruce — *Fashion Designer*
27 Beauchamp Place, London SW3, England

Oldfield, Mike — *Singer, Songwriter*
%Management Works, Singes House, 32 Galena Road, London W6 OLT, England

Oldfield, Sally — *Singer*
%Global Artists Mgmt, Willy-Brandt-Str 39, 50374 Erftstadt, Germany

Oldham, D Ray — *Football Player*
1096 Harbor Landing Dr, Soddy Daisy, TN 37379, USA

Oldham, John — *Basketball Player, Coach*
2127 Sycamore Dr, Bowling Green, KY 42104, USA

Oldham, Todd — *Fashion Designer*
120 Wooster St, New York, NY 10012, USA

Oldman, Gary — *Actor, Director*
%William Morris Agency, 151 El Camino Dr, Beverly Hills, CA 90212, USA

Olds, Robin — *WW II Air Force Hero, Football Player*
PO Box 1478, Steamboat Springs, CO 80477, USA

Olds, Walter (Wally) — *Hockey Player*
37296 Pincherry Road, Cohasset, MN 55721, USA

Oleksy, Jozef — *Prime Minister, Poland*
Ul Wiktorii Wiedenskiej 5 M 4, 02-954 Warsaw, Poland

Olerud, John G — *Baseball Player*
1310 180th Ave NE, Bellevue, WA 98008, USA

Olevsky, Julian — *Concert Violinist*
68 Blue Hills Road, Amherst, MA 01002, USA

Oleynik, Larisa — *Actress*
%Savage Agency, 6212 Banner Ave, Los Angeles, CA 90038, USA

Olin, Ken — *Actor*
%Endeavor Talent Agency, 9701 Wilshire Blvd, #1000, Beverly Hills, CA 90212, USA

Olin, Lena — *Actress*
%Industry Entertainment, 955 Carillo Dr, #300, Los Angeles, CA 90048, USA

Oliphant, Patrick B — *Editorial Cartoonist*
%Universal Press Syndicate, 4520 Main St, Kansas City, MO 64111, USA

Oliphant, Randall — *Businessman*
%Barrick Gold Corp, 200 Bay St, Toronto ON M5J 2J3, Canada

Olitski, Jules — *Artist*
PO Box 440, Marlboro, VT 05344, USA

Oliva, L Jay — *Educator*
%New York University, President's Office, New York, NY 10012, USA

Oliva, Pedro (Tony) — *Baseball Player*
PO Box 13448, Minneapolis, MN 55414, USA

Oliva, Sergio — *Body Builder*
%Oliva's Gym, 7383 Rogers Ave, Chicago, IL 60626, USA

Olivares, Ruben — *Boxer*
%Geno Productions, PO Box 113, Montebello, CA 90640, USA

Olivas, John D — *Astronaut*
2618 Sunset Blvd, Houston, TX 77005, USA

Oliveira, Elmar — *Concert Violinist*
%Cramer/Marder Artists, 3436 Springhill Road, Lafayette, CA 94549, USA

Oliveira, Nathan J — *Artist*
785 Santa Maria Ave, Palo Alto, CA 94305, USA

Oliver, Albert (Al) — *Baseball Player*
PO Box 1466, Portsmouth, OH 45662, USA

Oliver, Christian — *Actor*
7211 Mulholland Dr, Los Angeles, CA 90068, USA

Oliver, Covey T — *Attorney, Diplomat*
Ingleton-on-Miles, RR 1 Box 194, Easton, MD 21601, USA

Oliver, Daniel — *Government Official*
%Heritage Foundation, 214 Massachusetts Ave NW, Washington, DC 20002, USA

Oliver, Dean — *Rodeo All-Around Rider, Calf Roper*
21386 Notus Road, Greenleaf, ID 83626, USA

Oliver, Jamie — *Chef*
15 Brambles, Bishops Storford, Herts CM23 4PX, England

O

Oliver, Mary *Writer*
%Molly Malone Cook Agency, PO Box U, Sweet Briar, VA 24595, USA
Oliver, Murray C *Hockey Player*
5505 McGuire Road, Minneapolis, MN 55439, USA
Oliver, Pam *Sportscaster*
%Fox-TV, Sports Dept, 205 W 67th St, New York, NY 10021, USA
Olivo, Joey *Boxer*
9628 Poinciana St, Pico Rivera, CA 90660, USA
Olivor, Jane *Singer*
%Ed Keane, 32 Saint Edwards Road, Boston, MA 02128, USA
Olkewicz, Walter *Actor*
%Gold Marshak Liedtke, 3500 W Olive Ave, #1400, Burbank, CA 91505, USA
Olmedo, Alex *Tennis Player*
5067 Woodley Ave, Encino, CA 91436, USA
Olmos, Edward James *Actor*
%Olmos Productions, 18034 Ventura Blvd, #228, Encino, CA 91316, USA
Olney, Claude W *Educator*
%Olney 'A' Seminars, PO Box 686, Scottsdale, AZ 85252, USA
Olowokandi, Michael *Basketball Player*
%Minnesota Timberwolves, Target Center, 600 1st Ave N, Minneapolis, MN 55403, USA
Olsen, Ashley *Actress*
%Reach Media, 295 Greenwich St, #109, New York, NY 10007, USA
Olsen, David A *Financier*
%Marsh & McLennan Co, 1166 Ave of Americas, New York, NY 10036, USA
Olsen, Kenneth H *Inventor (Magnetic Core Memory)*
111 Powder Mill Road, Maynard, MA 01754, USA
Olsen, Mary Kate *Actress*
%Reach Media, 295 Greenwich St, #109, New York, NY 10007, USA
Olsen, Merlin J *Football Player, Actor, Sportscaster*
11755 Wilshire Blvd, #2320, Los Angeles, CA 90025, USA
Olsen, Olaf *Archaeologist*
Strevelsjovedvej 2, Alro, 8300 Oder, Denmark
Olsen, Paul E *Geologist*
%Columbia University, Lamont-Doherty Geological Laboratory, New York, NY 10027, USA
Olsen, Robert C, Jr *Coast Guard Admiral, Educator*
Superintendent's Office, US Coast Guard Academy, New London, CT 06320, USA
Olsen, Stanford *Opera Singer*
%Columbia Artists Mgmt Inc, 165 W 57th St, New York, NY 10019, USA
Olshwanger, Ron *Photojournalist*
1447 Meadowside Dr, Saint Louis, MO 63146, USA
Olson, Allen I *Governor, ND*
9435 Libby Lane, Eden Prairie, MN 55347, USA
Olson, James *Actor*
250 W 57th St, #803, New York, NY 10107, USA
Olson, Lisa *Sportswriter*
%New York Daily News, Editorial Dept, 220 E 42nd St, New York, NY 10017, USA
Olson, Mancur *Economist*
4316 Claggett Pine Way, University Park, MD 20782, USA
Olson, Mark *Singer, Songwriter (Jayhawks)*
%Sussman Assoc, 1222 16th Ave S, #300, Nashville, TN 37212, USA
Olson, Mark *Government Official, Economist*
%Federal Reserve Board, 20th St & Constitution Ave, Washington, DC 20551, USA
Olson, Nancy *Actress*
945 N Alpine Dr, Beverly Hills, CA 90210, USA
Olson, R Lute *Basketball Coach*
%University of Arizona, McKale Memorial Center, Tucson, AZ 85721, USA
Olson, Richard E *Businessman*
%Champion Int'l Corp, 1 Champion Plaza, Stamford, CT 06921, USA
Olson, Weldon *Hockey Player*
2623 Goldenrod Lane, Findlay, OH 45840, USA
Olszewski, Jan F *Prime Minister, Poland*
Biuro Poselskie, Al Ujazdowskie 13, 00-567 Warsaw, Poland
Omar, Chamassi Said *Prime Minister, Comoros*
%Prime Minister's Office, BP 421, Moroni, Comoros
Omidyar, Pierre *Businessman*
%eBay, 2145 Hamilton Ave, San Jose, CA 95125, USA
Onanian, Edward *Religious Leader*
%Diocese of Armenian Church, 630 2nd Ave, New York, NY 10016, USA
Ondaatje, Michael *Writer*
%Glendon College, English Dept, 2275 Bayview, Toronto ON M4N 3M6, Canada
Ondetti, Miguel A *Biochemist*
79 Hemlock Circle, Princeton, NJ 08540, USA
Ondricek, Miroslav *Cinematographer*
Nad Pomnikem 1, 15200 Prague 5 Smichow, Czech Republic
Onkotz, Dennis H *Football Player*
270 Walker Dr, State College, PA 16801, USA
Ono, Yoko *Filmmaker, Artist*
%Studio One, 1 W 52nd St, New York, NY 10019, USA

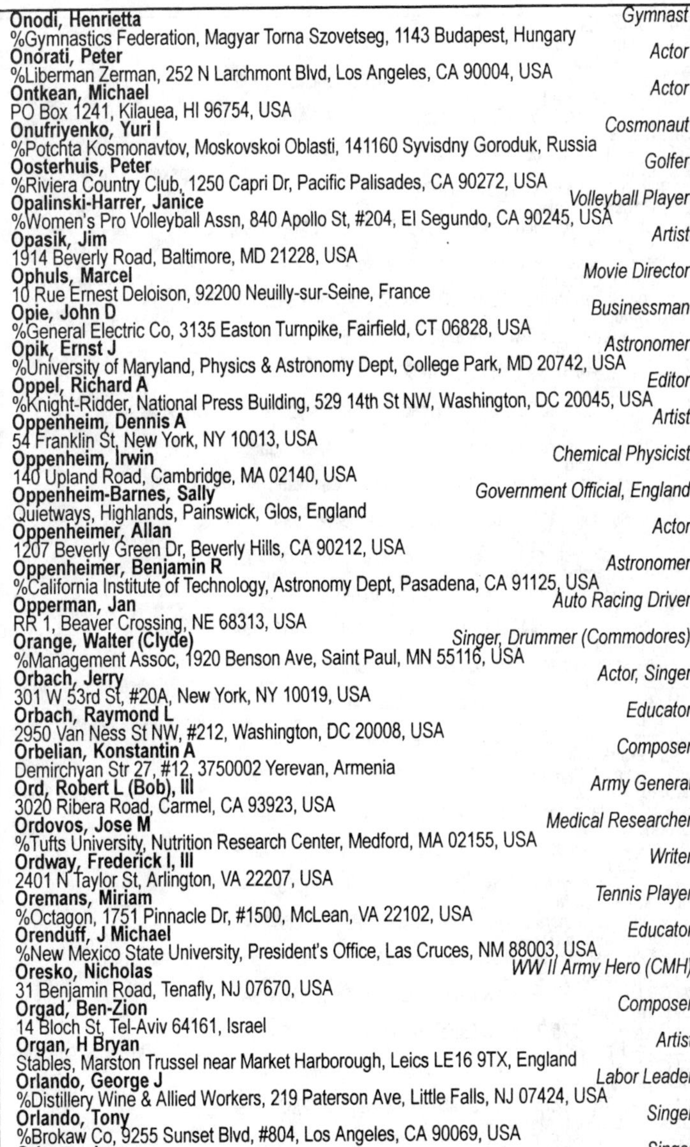

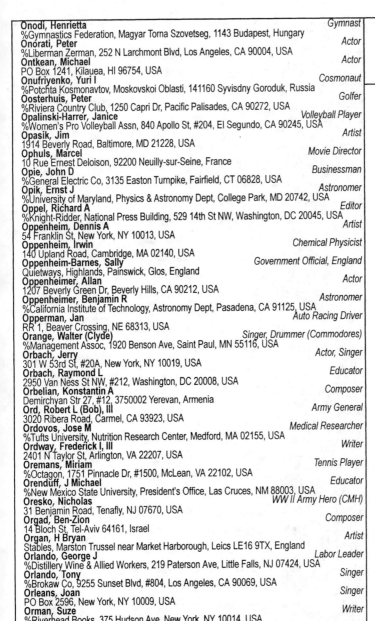

Onodi, Henrietta *Gymnast*
%Gymnastics Federation, Magyar Torna Szovetseg, 1143 Budapest, Hungary

Onorati, Peter *Actor*
%Liberman Zerman, 252 N Larchmont Blvd, Los Angeles, CA 90004, USA

Ontkean, Michael *Actor*
PO Box 1241, Kilauea, HI 96754, USA

Onufriyenko, Yuri I *Cosmonaut*
%Potchta Kosmonavtov, Moskovskoi Oblasti, 141160 Syvisdny Goroduk, Russia

Oosterhuis, Peter *Golfer*
%Riviera Country Club, 1250 Capri Dr, Pacific Palisades, CA 90272, USA

Opalinski-Harrer, Janice *Volleyball Player*
%Women's Pro Volleyball Assn, 840 Apollo St, #204, El Segundo, CA 90245, USA

Opasik, Jim *Artist*
1914 Beverly Road, Baltimore, MD 21228, USA

Ophuls, Marcel *Movie Director*
10 Rue Ernest Deloison, 92200 Neuilly-sur-Seine, France

Opie, John D *Businessman*
%General Electric Co, 3135 Easton Turnpike, Fairfield, CT 06828, USA

Opik, Ernst J *Astronomer*
%University of Maryland, Physics & Astronomy Dept, College Park, MD 20742, USA

Oppel, Richard A *Editor*
%Knight-Ridder, National Press Building, 529 14th St NW, Washington, DC 20045, USA

Oppenheim, Dennis A *Artist*
54 Franklin St, New York, NY 10013, USA

Oppenheim, Irwin *Chemical Physicist*
140 Upland Road, Cambridge, MA 02140, USA

Oppenheim-Barnes, Sally *Government Official, England*
Quietways, Highlands, Painswick, Glos, England

Oppenheimer, Allan *Actor*
1207 Beverly Green Dr, Beverly Hills, CA 90212, USA

Oppenheimer, Benjamin R *Astronomer*
%California Institute of Technology, Astronomy Dept, Pasadena, CA 91125, USA

Opperman, Jan *Auto Racing Driver*
RR 1, Beaver Crossing, NE 68313, USA

Orange, Walter (Clyde) *Singer, Drummer (Commodores)*
%Management Assoc, 1920 Benson Ave, Saint Paul, MN 55116, USA

Orbach, Jerry *Actor, Singer*
301 W 53rd St, #20A, New York, NY 10019, USA

Orbach, Raymond L *Educator*
2950 Van Ness St NW, #212, Washington, DC 20008, USA

Orbelian, Konstantin A *Composer*
Demirchyan Str 27, #12, 3750002 Yerevan, Armenia

Ord, Robert L (Bob), III *Army General*
3020 Ribera Road, Carmel, CA 93923, USA

Ordovos, Jose M *Medical Researcher*
%Tufts University, Nutrition Research Center, Medford, MA 02155, USA

Ordway, Frederick I, III *Writer*
2401 N Taylor St, Arlington, VA 22207, USA

Oremans, Miriam *Tennis Player*
%Octagon, 1751 Pinnacle Dr, #1500, McLean, VA 22102, USA

Orenduff, J Michael *Educator*
%New Mexico State University, President's Office, Las Cruces, NM 88003, USA

Oresko, Nicholas *WW II Army Hero (CMH)*
31 Benjamin Road, Tenafly, NJ 07670, USA

Orgad, Ben-Zion *Composer*
14 Bloch St, Tel-Aviv 64161, Israel

Organ, H Bryan *Artist*
Stables, Marston Trussel near Market Harborough, Leics LE16 9TX, England

Orlando, George J *Labor Leader*
%Distillery Wine & Allied Workers, 219 Paterson Ave, Little Falls, NJ 07424, USA

Orlando, Tony *Singer*
%Brokaw Co, 9255 Sunset Blvd, #804, Los Angeles, CA 90069, USA

Orleans, Joan *Singer*
PO Box 2596, New York, NY 10009, USA

Orman, Suze *Writer*
%Riverhead Books, 375 Hudson Ave, New York, NY 10014, USA

Orme, Stanley *Government Official, England*
8 Northwood Grove, Sale, Cheshire M33 3DZ, England

Ormond, Julia *Actress*
%Endeavor Talent Agency, 9701 Wilshire Blvd, #1000, Beverly Hills, CA 90212, USA

Ormond, Paul *Businessman*
%Manor Care Inc, 333 N Summit St, Toledo, OH 43604, USA

Ornish, Dean *Cardiologist, Writer*
%Preventive Medicine Research Institute, 900 Bridgeway, #2, Sausalito, CA 94965, USA

Ornstein, Donald S *Mathematician*
857 Tolman Dr, Stanford, CA 94305, USA

Orr, David A *Businessman*
Home Farm House, Shackleford, Godalming, Surrey GU8 6AH, England

O

Orr - Oscar Scheid

Orr, James E (Jim), Jr *Football Player*
3104 Glynn Ave, Brunswick, GA 31520, USA
Orr, James F, III *Businessman*
%UNUMProvident Corp, 2211 Congress St, Portland, ME 04122, USA
Orr, John (Johnny) *Basketball Coach, Administrator*
5736 Gallery Court, West Des Moines, IA 50266, USA
Orr, Kay S *Governor, NE*
1425 H St, Lincoln, NE 68508, USA
Orr, Louis *Basketball Player, Coach*
14 Powell Dr, West Orange, NJ 07052, USA
Orr, Robert G (Bobby) *Hockey Player*
%Woolf Assoc, 101 Huntington Ave, #2575, Boston, MA 02199, USA
Orr, Terrence S *Ballet Dancer*
%American Ballet Theatre, 890 Broadway, New York, NY 10003, USA
Orr-Cahall, Christina *Museum Director*
%Norton Gallery of Art, 1451 S Olive Ave, West Palm Beach, FL 33401, USA
Orr-Ewing, Hamish *Businessman*
Fox Mill, Purton near Swindon, Wilts SN5 9EF, England
Orrall, Robert Ellis *Singer*
3 E 54th St, #1400, New York, NY 10022, USA
Orrico, Stacie *Gospel Singer*
%Forefront Records, 230 Franklin Road, Building 2A, Franklin, TN 37064, USA
Orser, Brian *Figure Skater*
1600 James Naismith Dr, Gloucester ON L1B 5N4, Canada
Orsin, Raymond *Cartoonist*
%Cleveland Plain Dealer, 1801 Superior Ave E, Cleveland, OH 44114, USA
Orsini, Myrna J *Sculptor*
%Orsini Studios, 4411 N 7th St, Tacoma, WA 98406, USA
Ortega Saavedra, Daniel *President, Nicaragua*
%Frente Sandinista de Liberacion National, Managua, Nicaragua
Ortega y Alamino, Jaime Cardinal *Religious Leader*
Apartado 594, Calle Habana 152, Havana 10100, Cuba
Ortenberg, Arthur *Businessman*
%Liz Claiborne Inc, 1441 Broadway, New York, NY 10018, USA
Ortiz, Carlos *Boxer*
2050 Seward Ave, #3C, Bronx, NY 10473, USA
Ortiz, Cristina *Concert Pianist*
%Harrison/Parrott, 12 Penzance Place, London W11 4PA England
Ortiz, Domingo *Percussionist (Widespread Panic)*
%Brown Cat Inc, 400 Foundry St, Athens, GA 30601, USA
Ortiz, Frank V, Jr *Diplomat*
663 Garcia St, Santa Fe, NM 87505, USA
Ortlieb, Patrick *Alpine Skier*
%Hotel Montana, Oberlech, 6764 Lech, Austria
Ortner, Bev *Bowler*
PO Box 493, Odebolt, IA 51458, USA
Orton, Beth *Singer*
%LBM, 155 Ave of Americas, #700, New York, NY 10013, USA
Orvick, George M *Religious Leader*
%Evangelical Lutheran Synod, 6 Browns Court, Mankato, MN 56001, USA
Osborn, David V (Dave) *Football Player*
18067 Judicial Way N, Lakeville, MN 55044, USA
Osborn, Kassidy *Singer (SheDaisy)*
%LGB Media, 1228 Pineview Lane, Nashville, TN 37211, USA
Osborn, Kelsi *Singer (SheDaisy)*
%LGB Media, 1228 Pineview Lane, Nashville, TN 37211, USA
Osborn, Kristyn *Singer (SheDaisy), Songwriter*
%LGB Media, 1228 Pineview Lane, Nashville, TN 37211, USA
Osborn, William A *Financier*
%Northern Trust Corp, 50 S LaSalle St, Chicago, IL 60675, USA
Osborne DuPont, Margaret *Tennis Player*
415 Camino Real, El Paso, TX 79922, USA
Osborne, Burl *Editor, Publisher*
%Dallas Morning News, Editorial Dept, Communications Center, Dallas, TX 75265, USA
Osborne, James A *Religious Leader*
%Salvation Army, 799 Bloomfield Ave, Verona, NJ 07044, USA
Osborne, Jeffrey *Singer, Songwriter*
%Entertainment Artists, 2409 21st Ave S, #100, Nashville, TN 37212, USA
Osborne, Joan *Singer, Songwriter*
%DAS Communications, 83 Riverside Dr, New York, NY 10024, USA
Osborne, Mary Pope *Writer*
%Random House, 1745 Broadway, #B1, New York, NY 10019, USA
Osbourne, Ozzy *Singer, Songwriter*
66 Malibu Colony Road, Malibu, CA 90265, USA
Osby, Greg *Jazz Saxophonist*
%Bridge Agency, 35 Clark St, #A5, Brooklyn Heights, NY 11201, USA
Oscar Scheid, Eusebio Cardinal *Religious Leader*
%Archdiocese, Rua Benjamin Constant 23/502, 20241 Rio de Janeiro, Brazil

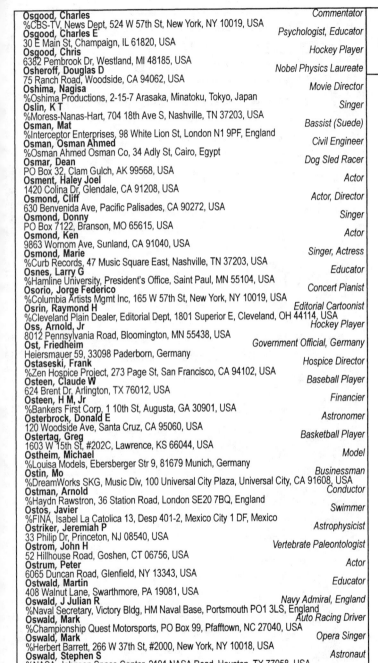

Osgood, Charles *Commentator*
%CBS-TV, News Dept, 524 W 57th St, New York, NY 10019, USA
Osgood, Charles E *Psychologist, Educator*
30 E Main St, Champaign, IL 61820, USA
Osgood, Chris *Hockey Player*
6382 Pembrook Dr, Westland, MI 48185, USA
Osheroff, Douglas D *Nobel Physics Laureate*
75 Ranch Road, Woodside, CA 94062, USA
Oshima, Nagisa *Movie Director*
%Oshima Productions, 2-15-7 Arasaka, Minatoku, Tokyo, Japan
Oslin, K T *Singer*
%Moress-Nanas-Hart, 704 18th Ave S, Nashville, TN 37203, USA
Osman, Mat *Bassist (Suede)*
%Interceptor Enterprises, 98 White Lion St, London N1 9PF, England
Osman, Osman Ahmed *Civil Engineer*
%Osman Ahmed Osman Co, 34 Adly St, Cairo, Egypt
Osmar, Dean *Dog Sled Racer*
PO Box 32, Clam Gulch, AK 99568, USA
Osment, Haley Joel *Actor*
1420 Colina Dr, Glendale, CA 91208, USA
Osmond, Cliff *Actor, Director*
630 Benvenida Ave, Pacific Palisades, CA 90272, USA
Osmond, Donny *Singer*
PO Box 7122, Branson, MO 65615, USA
Osmond, Ken *Actor*
9863 Wornom Ave, Sunland, CA 91040, USA
Osmond, Marie *Singer, Actress*
%Curb Records, 47 Music Square East, Nashville, TN 37203, USA
Osnes, Larry G *Educator*
%Hamline University, President's Office, Saint Paul, MN 55104, USA
Osorio, Jorge Federico *Concert Pianist*
%Columbia Artists Mgmt Inc, 165 W 57th St, New York, NY 10019, USA
Osrin, Raymond H *Editorial Cartoonist*
%Cleveland Plain Dealer, Editorial Dept, 1801 Superior E, Cleveland, OH 44114, USA
Oss, Arnold, Jr *Hockey Player*
8012 Pennsylvania Road, Bloomington, MN 55438, USA
Ost, Friedheim *Government Official, Germany*
Heiersmauer 59, 33098 Paderborn, Germany
Ostaseski, Frank *Hospice Director*
%Zen Hospice Project, 273 Page St, San Francisco, CA 94102, USA
Osteen, Claude W *Baseball Player*
624 Brent Dr, Arlington, TX 76012, USA
Osteen, H M, Jr *Financier*
%Bankers First Corp, 1 10th St, Augusta, GA 30901, USA
Osterbrock, Donald E *Astronomer*
120 Woodside Ave, Santa Cruz, CA 95060, USA
Ostertag, Greg *Basketball Player*
1603 W 15th St, #202C, Lawrence, KS 66044, USA
Ostheim, Michael *Model*
%Louisa Models, Ebersberger Str 9, 81679 Munich, Germany
Ostin, Mo *Businessman*
%DreamWorks SKG, Music Div, 100 Universal City Plaza, Universal City, CA 91608, USA
Ostman, Arnold *Conductor*
%Haydn Rawstron, 36 Station Road, London SE20 7BQ, England
Ostos, Javier *Swimmer*
%FINA, Isabel La Catolica 13, Desp 401-2, Mexico City 1 DF, Mexico
Ostriker, Jeremiah P *Astrophysicist*
33 Philip Dr, Princeton, NJ 08540, USA
Ostrom, John H *Vertebrate Paleontologist*
52 Hillhouse Road, Goshen, CT 06756, USA
Ostrum, Peter *Actor*
6065 Duncan Road, Glenfield, NY 13343, USA
Ostwald, Martin *Educator*
408 Walnut Lane, Swarthmore, PA 19081, USA
Oswald, J Julian R *Navy Admiral, England*
%Naval Secretary, Victory Bldg, HM Naval Base, Portsmouth PO1 3LS, England
Oswald, Mark *Auto Racing Driver*
%Championship Quest Motorsports, PO Box 99, Pfafftown, NC 27040, USA
Oswald, Mark *Opera Singer*
%Herbert Barrett, 266 W 37th St, #2000, New York, NY 10018, USA
Oswald, Stephen S *Astronaut*
%NASA, Johnson Space Center, 2101 NASA Road, Houston, TX 77058, USA
Oswalt, Roy *Baseball Player*
RR 1 Box 156AA, Weir, MS 39772, USA
Oszajca, John *Singer*
%Interscope Records, 2220 Colorado Ave, Santa Monica, CA 90404, USA
Otaka, Tadaaki *Conductor*
%Harold Holt, 31 Sinclair Road, London W14 0NS, England

O

Otellini, Paul *Businessman*
%Intel Corp, 2200 Mission College Blvd, Santa Clara, CA 95054, USA
Oteri, Cheri *Actress, Comedienne*
%Endeavor Talent Agency, 9701 Wilshire Blvd, #1000, Beverly Hills, CA 90212, USA
Othenin-Girard, Dominque *Movie Director*
327 Church Lane, Los Angeles, CA 90049, USA
Otis, Amos J *Baseball Player*
568 Preakness Stakes St, Henderson, NV 89015, USA
Otis, Carre *Actress, Model*
%Goldman/Knell Agency, 1801 Century Park E, #2160, Los Angeles, CA 90067, USA
Otis, Glenn K *Army General*
3401 RR 9, Lake Shore Road, Peru, NY 12972, USA
Otis, James L (Jim) *Football Player*
14795 Greenleaf Valley Dr, Chesterfield, MO 63017, USA
Otis, Johnny *Singer, Guitarist, Songwriter*
7105 Baker Lane, Sebastopol, CA 95472, USA
Otman Assed, Mohamed *Prime Minister, Libya*
Villa Rissani, Route Oued Akrach, Souissi, Rabat, Morocco
Otstott, Charles P *Army General*
6152 Pohick Station Dr, Fairfax Station, VA 22039, USA
Ottey-Page, Merlene *Track Athlete*
%Jamaican Olympic Committee, PO Box 544, Kingston 10, Jamaica
Otto, A T, Jr *Labor Leader*
%Railroad Yardmasters Union, 1411 Peterson Ave, #201, Park Ridge, IL 60068, USA
Otto, August J (Gus) *Football Player*
8 Cool Meadows Dr, Ballwin, MO 63011, USA
Otto, Frei *Architect*
Berghalde 19, 7250 Leonberg, 71229 Warmbroun, Germany
Otto, James E (Jim) *Football Player*
00 Estates Dr, Auburn, CA 95602, USA
Otto, Joel *Hockey Player*
77 Sunset Way SE, Calgary AB T2X 3C1, Canada
Otto, Kristin *Swimmer*
%ZDF Sportedaktion, Postfach 4040, 55100 Mainz, Germany
Otto, Michael *Businessman*
%Spiegel Inc, 3500 Lacey Road, Downers Grove, IL 60515, USA
Otto, Miranda *Actress*
%Shanahan Mgmt, PO Box 1509, Darlinghurst NSW 1300, Australia
Otto, Sylke *Luge Athlete*
%BSD, An der Schiessstatte 4, 83471 Berchtesgaden, Germany
Otwell, Ralph M *Editor*
2750 Hurd Ave, Evanston, IL 60201, USA
Ouaido, Nassour Guelengdoussia *Prime Minister, Chad*
%Prime Minister's Office, N'Djamena, Chad
Ouattara, Alassane D *Prime Minister, Ivory Coast; Financier*
%International Monetary Fund, 700 19th St NW, #12-300H, Washington, DC 20431, USA
Ouchi, William G *Educator*
%University of California, Graduate Management School, Los Angeles, CA 90024, USA
Ouedraogo, Gerard Kango *Prime Minister, Burkina Faso*
01 BP 347, Ouagadougou, Burkina Faso
Ouedraogo, Idrissa *Movie Director*
%FEPACI, 01 BP 2524, Ouagadougou, Burkina Faso
Ouedraogo, Kdre Desire *Prime Minister, Burkina Faso*
%Prime Minister's Office, Parliament Building, Ouagadougou, Burkina Faso
Ouellet, Joseph G N Cardinal *Religious Leader*
%Archdiocese, 34 Rue de l'Eveche E, CP 730, Rimouski QC G5L 7C7, Canada
Ourisson, Guy *Chemist*
10 Rue Geiler, 67000 Strasbourg, France
Ousland, Borge *Trans Polar Skier*
Axel Huitfeldts V5, 1170 Oslo, Norway
Outlar, Jesse *Sportswriter*
116 Loblolly Circle, Peachtree City, GA 30269, USA
Outlaw, Charles (Bo) *Basketball Player*
14815 River Mill, San Antonio, TX 78216, USA
Outlaw, Travis *Basketball Player*
%Portland Trail Blazers, Rose Garden, 1 Center Court St, Portland, OR 97227, USA
Outman, Tim *Sculptor*
57101 N Bank Road, McKenzie Bridge, OR 97413, USA
Ovchinikov, Vladimir P *Concert Pianist*
%Manygate, 13 Cotswold Mews, 30 Battersea Square, London SW11 3RA, England
Overall, Park *Actress*
33150 Drill Road, Santa Clarita, CA 91390, USA
Overbeek, Jan T G *Physical Chemist*
Zweerslaan 35, 3723 HN Bilthoven, Netherlands
Overgard, Robert M *Religious Leader*
%Church of Lutheran Brethren, PO Box 655, Fergus Falls, MN 56538, USA
Overgard, William *Cartoonist (Rudy)*
%United Feature Syndicate, 200 Madison Ave, New York, NY 10016, USA

Overhauser, Albert W *Physicist*
236 Pawnee Dr, West Lafayette, IN 47906, USA
Overman, Larry E *Chemist*
%University of California, Chemistry Dept, Irvine, CA 92717, USA
Overmyer, Eric *Writer*
%Yale University, English Dept, New Haven, CT 06520, USA
Overstreet, Paul *Singer, Songwriter*
%White Horse Enterprises, 475 Annex Ave, Nashville, TN 37209, USA
Overstreet, Tommy *Singer, Songwriter*
PO Box 455, Brentwood, TN 37024, USA
Ovitz, Michael S *Businessman*
457 N Rockingham Ave, Los Angeles, CA 90049, USA
Ovshinsky, Stanford R *Ovionics Engineer, Inventor*
%Energy Conversion Devices, 2956 Waterview Dr, Rochester Hills, MI 48309, USA
Owen, Clive *Actor*
%International Creative Mgmt, 8942 Wilshire Blvd, #219, Beverly Hills, CA 90211, USA
Owen, David A L *Government Official, England*
78 Narrow St, Limehouse, London E14 8BP, England
Owen, Edwyn (Bob) *Hockey Player*
3630 SW Stratford Road, Topeka, KS 66604, USA
Owen, Henry *Diplomat*
%Brookings Institute, 1775 Massachusetts Ave NW, Washington, DC 20036, USA
Owen, Randy Y *Singer, Guitarist (Alabama)*
PO Box 529, Fort Payne, AL 35968, USA
Owen, Ray D *Biologist*
1583 Rose Villa St, Pasadena, CA 91106, USA
Owens, Buck *Singer, Songwriter*
%Buck Owens Productions, 3223 Sillect Ave, Bakersfield, CA 93308, USA
Owens, Burgess *Football Player*
1430 Telegraph Road, West Chester, PA 19380, USA
Owens, Charles W (Tinker) *Football Player*
4512 Hunters Hill Circle, Norman, OK 73072, USA
Owens, Cotton *Auto Racing Driver*
7605 White Ave, Spartanburg, SC 29303, USA
Owens, Gary *Entertainer*
17856 Via Vallarta, Encino, CA 91316, USA
Owens, James D (Jim) *Football Player, Coach*
PO Box 1749, Bigfork, MT 59911, USA
Owens, Rawleigh C (R C) *Football Player*
1533 Brook Dale Way, Manteca, CA 95336, USA
Owens, Steve *Football Player*
812 Cedarbrook Dr, Norman, OK 73072, USA
Owens, Terrell *Football Player*
105 Emerson St, Alexander City, AL 35010, USA
Owens, William A *Navy Admiral*
510 Lake St S, #B302, Kirkland, WA 98033, USA
Owsley, Douglas *Anthropologist*
%Smithsonian Institute, 17th & M Sts NW, Washington, DC 20036, USA
Oxenberg, Catherine *Actress*
9461 Charleville Blvd, #380, Beverly Hills, CA 90212, USA
Oyakawa, Yoshinobu (Yoshi) *Swimmer*
4171 Hutchinson Road, Cincinnati, OH 45248, USA
Oz, Amos *Writer*
Ben Gurion University, PO Box 653, 84195 Beer-Sheva, Israel
Oz, Frank R *Puppeteer, Movie Director*
%Henson Co, PO Box 20726, New York, NY 10023, USA
Ozaki, Masashi *Golfer*
%Bridgestone Sports, 14230 Lochridge Blvd, #G, Covington, GA 30014, USA
Ozaki, Satoshi *Physicist*
%Brookhaven National Lab, Heavy Ion Collider, 2 Center St, Upton, NY 11973, USA
Ozark, Daniel L (Danny) *Baseball Executive*
PO Box 6666, Vero Beach, FL 32961, USA
Ozawa, Ichiro *Government Official, Japan*
Daiichi Giia Kaikan, Nagatacho, Chiyodaku, Tokyo 100, Japan
Ozawa, Seiji *Conductor*
%Columbia Artists Mgmt Inc, 165 W 57th St, New York, NY 10019, USA
Ozbek, Rifat *Fashion Designer*
%Ozbek Ltd, 18 Haunch of Venison Yard, London W1Y 1AF, England
Ozick, Cynthia *Writer*
%Knopf Publishers, 201 E 50th St, New York, NY 10022, USA
Ozio, David *Bowler*
5915 Ventura Lane, Beaumont, TX 77706, USA
Ozolinsh, Sandis *Hockey Player*
%Anaheim Mighty Ducks, 2000 E Gene Autry Way, Anaheim, CA 92806, USA
Ozzie, Raymond (Ray) *Computer Software Designer*
33 Harbor St, Manchester-by-the Sea, MA 01944, USA

P

Paar - Page

Paar, Jack *Entertainer*
9 Chateau Ridge Dr, Greenwich, CT 06831, USA
Paavola, Rodney *Hockey Player*
General Delivery, Hancock, MI 49930, USA
Pace, Darrell O *Archery Athlete*
4394 Princeton Road, Hamilton, OH 45011, USA
Pace, Judy *Actress*
4139 Cloverdale Ave, Los Angeles, CA 90008, USA
Pace, Orlando *Football Player*
4203 Windham Place S, Sandusky, OH 44870, USA
Pace, Peter *Marine Corps General*
Vice Chairman, Joint Chiefs of Staff, Pentagon, Washington, DC 20318, USA
Pacheco, Abel *President, Costa Rica*
%Casa Presidencial, Apdo 520-2010, San Jose 1000, Costa Rica
Pacheco, Ferdie *Sportscaster*
4151 Gate Lane, Miami, FL 33137, USA
Pacino, Al *Actor*
%Chal Productions, 301 W 57th St, #16C, New York, NY 10019, USA
Packard, Kelly *Actress, Model*
2520 30th Dr, Astoria, NY 11102, USA
Packer, A William (Billy) *Sportscaster*
165 Tescue Dr, Advance, NC 27006, USA
Packwood, Robert W (Bob) *Senator, OR*
%Sunrise Research, 2201 Wisconsin Ave NW, Washington, DC 20007, USA
Pacula, Joanna *Actress*
%Chuck Binder, 1465 Lindacrest Dr, Beverly Hills, CA 90210, USA
Padalka, Gennadi I *Cosmonaut*
%Potchta Kosmonavtov, Moskovskoi Oblasti, 141160 Syvisdny Goroduk, Russia
Paddock, John *Hockey Player, Coach, Executive*
1315 Penn Ave, Hershey, PA 17033, USA
Padilla, Douglas (Doug) *Track Athlete*
182 N 555 W, Orem, UT 84057, USA
Padma-Nathan, Harin *Urologist*
1245 16th St, #312, Santa Monica, CA 90404, USA
Paez, Jorge (Maromero) *Boxer*
233 Paulin Ave, Calexico, CA 92231, USA
Paez, Richard A *Judge*
%US Appellate Court, Court Building, 125 S Grand Ave, Pasadena, CA 91105, USA
Pafko, Andrew (Andy) *Baseball Player*
1420 Blackhawk Dr, Mount Prospect, IL 60056, USA
Paganelli, Robert P *Diplomat*
331 S Main St, Albion, NY 14411, USA
Pagano, Lindsay *Singer*
%Azoff Music, 1100 Glendon Ave, #2000, Los Angeles, CA 90024, USA
Page, Alan C *Football Player, Judge*
PO Box 581254, Minneapolis, MN 55458, USA
Page, Anita *Actress*
14840 Valerio St, Van Nuys, CA 91405, USA
Page, Ashley *Ballet Dancer, Choreographer*
%Royal Ballet, Covent Garden, Bow St, London WC2E 9DD, England
Page, Bettie *Model*
%JL Swanson, PO Box 56176, Chicago, IL 60656, USA
Page, Corey *Actor*
%Agency for Performing Arts, 9200 Sunset Blvd, #900, Los Angeles, CA 90069, USA
Page, David C *Geneticist*
%Whitehead Institute, 9 Cambridge Center, Cambridge, MA 02142, USA
Page, Erika *Actress*
%Progressive Artists Agency, 400 S Beverly Dr, #216, Beverly Hills, CA 90212, USA
Page, Genevieve *Actress*
52 Rue de Vaugirard, 75006 Paris, France
Page, Greg *Boxer*
%Don King Promotions, 968 Pinehurst Dr, Las Vegas, NV 89109, USA
Page, Harrison *Actor*
%S D B Partners, 1801 Ave of Stars, #902, Los Angeles, CA 90067, USA
Page, Jimmy *Singer (Yardbirds/Led Zeppelin)*
%Trinifold Mgmt, 12 Oval Road, London NW1 7DH, England
Page, Larry *Businessman, Computer Scientist*
%Google Inc, 2400 Bayshore Parkway, Mountain View, CA 94043, USA
Page, Michael *Equestrian Rider*
PO Box 229, North Salem, NY 10560, USA
Page, Oscar C *Educator*
%Austin College, President's Office, Sherman, TX 75090, USA
Page, Patti *Singer, Actress*
404 Loma Larga Dr, Solana Beach, CA 92075, USA
Page, Pierre *Hockey Coach, Executive*
%Anaheim Mighty Ducks, 2000 E Gene Autry Way, Anaheim, CA 92806, USA
Page, Steven *Singer, Guitarist (Barenaked Ladies)*
%Nettwerk Mgmt, 8730 Wilshire Blvd, #304, Beverly Hills, CA 90211, USA

Page, Tim *Journalist*
%Washington Post, Editorial Dept, 1150 15th St NW, Washington, DC 20071, USA
Paget, Debra *Actress*
411 Kari Court, Houston, TX 77024, USA
Pagett, Nicola *Actress*
22 Victoria Road, Mortlake, London SW14, England
Paglia, Camille *Writer, Educator*
%University of the Arts, Humanities Dept, 320 S Broad St, Philadelphia, PA 19102, USA
Pagliarulo, Michael T (Mike) *Baseball Player*
11 Fieldstone Dr, Winchester, MA 01890, USA
Pagonis, William G *Army General*
25190 N Pawnee Road, Barrington, IL 60010, USA
Pahang *Sultan, Malaysia*
%Istana Abu Bakar, Pekan, Pahang, Malaysia
Paich, David *Singer, Keyboardist (Toto)*
%Fitzgerald-Hartley, 34 N Palm St, Ventura, CA 93001, USA
Paige, Elaine *Singer, Actress*
DeWalden Court, 85 New Cavendish St, London W1M 7RA, England
Paige, Janis *Actress*
1700 Rising Glen Road, Los Angeles, CA 90069, USA
Paige, Jennifer *Singer, Songwriter*
%Evolution Talent, 1776 Broadway, #1500, New York, NY 10019, USA
Paige, Mitchell *WW II Marine Corps Hero (CMH)*
PO Box 2358, Palm Desert, CA 92261, USA
Paige, Rod *Secretary, Education*
%Education Department, 400 Maryland Ave SW, Washington, DC 20202, USA
Paik, Kun Woo *Concert Pianist*
%Worldwide Artists, 12 Rosebery, Thornton Heath, Surrey CR7 8PT, England
Paik, Nam June *Video Artist*
%Galerie Bonino, 48 Great Jones St, New York, NY 10012, USA
Pailes, William A *Astronaut*
105 LCR 409B, Mexia, TX 76667, USA
Paine, John *Guitarist (Brothers Four)*
%Bob Flick Productions, 300 Vine, #14, Seattle, WA 98121, USA
Painter, John Mark *Musician (Fleming & John)*
%Michael Dixon Mgmt, 119 Pebblecreek Road, Franklin, TN 37064, USA
Paisley, Brad *Singer*
PO Box 121113, Nashville, TN 37212, USA
Paisley, Ian R K *Political Leader, Northern Ireland*
%Parsonage, 17 Cyprus Ave, Belfast BT5 5NT, Northern Ireland
Pak, Charles *Medical Researcher*
%University of Texas, Health Sciences Center, Dallas, TX 75235, USA
Pak, Se Ri *Golfer*
%Steven Sung Yong Kil, 5817 Bent Pine Dr, #210, Orlando, FL 32822, USA
Pake, George E *Physicist*
13851 E Langtree Lane, Tucson, AZ 85747, USA
Pakledinaz, Martin *Costume Designer*
%Gersh Agency, 232 N Canon Dr, Beverly Hills, CA 90210, USA
Paksas, Rolandus *Prime Minister, Lithuania*
%President's Office, Gediminas 53, Vilnius 232026, Lithuania
Palade, George E *Nobel Medicine Laureate*
%University of California, Cellular & Molecular Division, La Jolla, CA 92093, USA
Palance, Jack *Actor*
%Martin Hurwitz, 427 N Canon Dr, #215, Beverly Hills, CA 90210, USA
Palastra, Joseph T, Jr *Army General*
RR 1 Box 267, Myrtle, MO 65778, USA
Palau, Luis *Evangelist*
1500 NW 167th Place, Beaverton, OR 97006, USA
Palazzari, Doug *Hockey Player*
4370 Dynasty Dr, Colorado Springs, CO 80918, USA
Palazzi, Lou *Football Player*
1521 W Gibson St, Scranton, PA 18504, USA
Palermo, Stephen M (Steve) *Baseball Umpire*
7921 W 118th St, Overland Park, KS 66210, USA
Paley, Albert R *Sculptor*
%Paley Studio, 25 N Washington St, Rochester, NY 14614, USA
Paley, Grace *Writer*
PO Box 620, Thetford Hill, VT 05074, USA
Palias, Cecile *Actress*
%P F D, Drury House, 34-43 Russell St, London WC2B 5HA, England
Palillo, Ron *Actor*
%Spotlight, 322 Bowling Green, New York, NY 10274, USA
Palin, Michael E *Actor, Writer (Monty Python)*
%Gumby Corp, 68A Delancey St, Camden Town, London NW1 7RY, England
Pall, Olga *Skier*
Fahrenweg 28, 6060 Absam, Austria
Palladino, Eric *Actor*
341 N Van Ness Ave, Los Angeles, CA 90004, USA

P

Palladino, Vincent — *Labor Leader*
%National Assn of Postal Supervisors, 1727 King St, Alexandria, VA 22314, USA
Palm, Siegfried — *Concert Cellist*
%Gerhild Baron Mgmt, Dornbacher Str 41/III/3, 1170 Vienna, Austria
Palmeiro, Rafael C — *Baseball Player*
5216 Reims Court, Colleyville, TX 76034, USA
Palmer, Arnold D — *Golfer*
9000 Bay Hill Blvd, Orlando, FL 32819, USA
Palmer, Betsy — *Actress*
8756 Wonderland Ave, Los Angeles, CA 90046, USA
Palmer, C R — *Businessman*
%Rowan Companies, Transco Tower, 2800 Post Oak Blvd, Houston, TX 77056, USA
Palmer, Carl — *Drummer (Emerson Lake & Palmer)*
%Asia, 9 Hillgate St, London W8 7SP, England
Palmer, Carson — *Football Player*
%Cincinnati Bengals, 1 Paul Brown Stadium, Cincinnati, OH 45202, USA
Palmer, Dave R — *Army General, Educator*
4531 Blue Ridge Dr, Belton, TX 76513, USA
Palmer, Dean W — *Baseball Player*
6420 Thomasville Road, Tallahassee, FL 32312, USA
Palmer, Geoffrey — *Actor*
%Marmont Mgmt, Langham House, 302/8 Regent St, London W1R 5AL, England
Palmer, Geoffrey W R — *Prime Minister, New Zealand*
63 Roxburgh St, Mount Victoria, Wellington, New Zealand
Palmer, James A (Jim) — *Baseball Player, Sportscaster*
201 W Padonia Road, #600, Timonium, MD 21093, USA
Palmer, Peter — *Actor*
216 Kingsway Dr, Temple Terrace, FL 33617, USA
Palmer, Reginald Oswald — *Governor General, Grenada*
Government House, Saint George's, Grenada
Palmer, Sandra — *Golfer*
%Ladies Pro Golf Assn, 100 International Golf Dr, Daytona Beach, FL 32124, USA
Palmer, William R — *Publisher*
%Detroit News, 615 W Lafayette Blvd, Detroit, MI 48226, USA
Palmieri, Eddie — *Jazz Pianist, Singer*
%Berkeley Agency, 2608 9th St, #301, Berkeley, CA 94710, USA
Palmieri, Paul — *Religious Leader*
%Church of Jesus Christ, 6th & Lincoln Sts, Monongahela, PA 15063, USA
Palminteri, Chazz — *Actor*
375 Greenwich St, New York, NY 10013, USA
Palmisano, Samuel J — *Businessman*
%IBM Corp, 1 N Castle Dr, Armonk, NY 10504, USA
Palms, John M — *Educator*
%University of South Carolina, President's Office, Columbia, SC 29208, USA
Palomino, Carlos — *Boxer*
14242 Burbank Blvd, #8, Sherman Oaks, CA 91401, USA
Paltrow, Gwyneth — *Actress*
%Creative Artists Agency, 9830 Wilshire Blvd, Beverly Hills, CA 90212, USA
Palumba, Joe — *Football Player*
927 Old Garth Road, Charlottesville, VA 22901, USA
Pamuk, Orhan — *Writer*
%Farrar Straus Giroux, 19 Union Square W, New York, NY 10003, USA
Pan Hong — *Actress*
%Omei Film Studio, Tonghui Menwai, Chengdu City, Sichuan Province, China
Panafieu, Bernard L A Cardinal — *Religious Leader*
%Archdiocese, 14 Place du Colonel-Edon, 13284 Marseille Cedex 07, France
Panday, Basdeo — *Prime Minister, Trinidad & Tobago*
%Premier's Office, Eric Williams Plaza, Port of Spain, Trinidad & Tobago
Panetta, Leon E — *Government Official; Representative, NY*
15 Panetta Road, Carmel Valley, CA 93924, USA
Panhofer, Walter — *Concert Pianist*
Erdbergstr 35/9, 1030 Vienna, Austria
Panic, Milan — *Prime Minister, Yugoslavia; Businessman*
1050 Arden Road, Pasadena, CA 91106, USA
Panichas, George A — *Writer*
PO Box AB, College Park, MD 20741, USA
Panish, Morton B — *Physical Chemist*
9 Persimmon Way, Springfield, NJ 07081, USA
Pankey, Irv — *Football Player*
348 Walker St, Aberdeen, MD 21001, USA
Pankin, Stuart — *Actor*
1288 Bienevenda Ave, Pacific Palisades, CA 90272, USA
Pankow, James — *Trumpeter (Chicago)*
3874 Puerco Canyon Road, Malibu, CA 90265, USA
Pankow, John — *Actor*
%Gersh Agency, 232 N Canon Dr, Beverly Hills, CA 90210, USA
Panni, Marcello — *Conductor, Composer*
3 Piazza Borghese, 00186 Rome, Italy

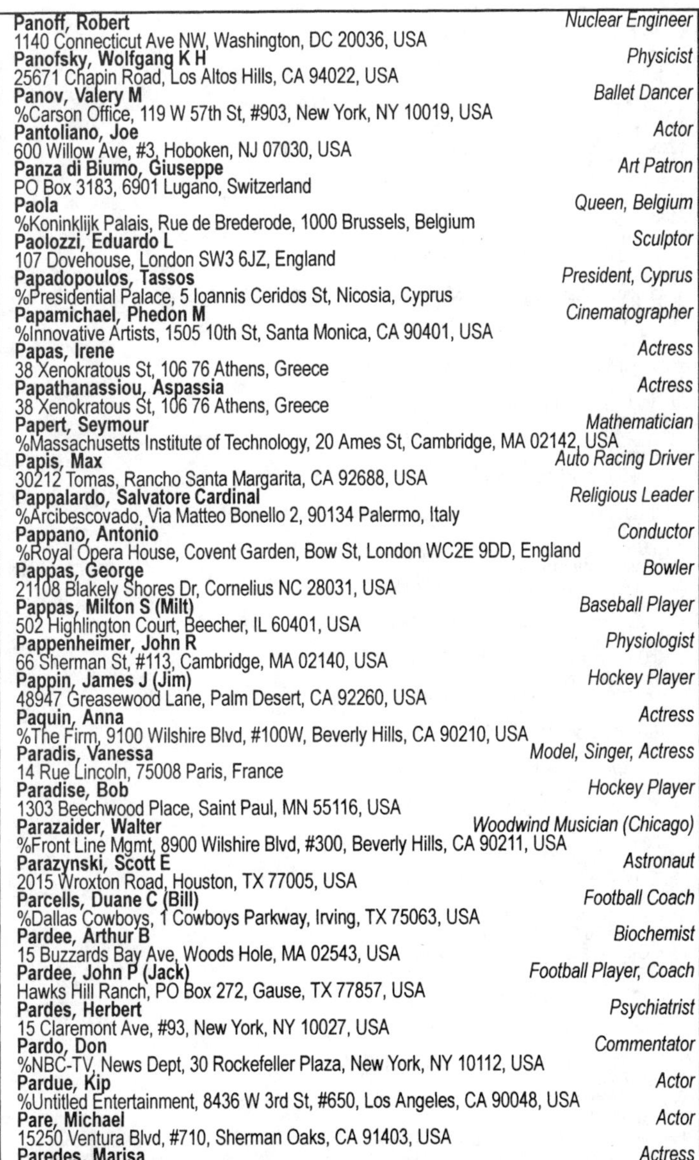

Panoff, Robert *Nuclear Engineer*
1140 Connecticut Ave NW, Washington, DC 20036, USA
Panofsky, Wolfgang K H *Physicist*
25671 Chapin Road, Los Altos Hills, CA 94022, USA
Panov, Valery M *Ballet Dancer*
%Carson Office, 119 W 57th St, #903, New York, NY 10019, USA
Pantoliano, Joe *Actor*
600 Willow Ave, #3, Hoboken, NJ 07030, USA
Panza di Biumo, Giuseppe *Art Patron*
PO Box 3183, 6901 Lugano, Switzerland
Paola *Queen, Belgium*
%Koninklijk Palais, Rue de Brederode, 1000 Brussels, Belgium
Paolozzi, Eduardo L *Sculptor*
107 Dovehouse, London SW3 6JZ, England
Papadopoulos, Tassos *President, Cyprus*
%Presidential Palace, 5 Ioannis Ceridos St, Nicosia, Cyprus
Papamichael, Phedon M *Cinematographer*
%Innovative Artists, 1505 10th St, Santa Monica, CA 90401, USA
Papas, Irene *Actress*
38 Xenokratous St, 106 76 Athens, Greece
Papathanassiou, Aspassia *Actress*
38 Xenokratous St, 106 76 Athens, Greece
Papert, Seymour *Mathematician*
%Massachusetts Institute of Technology, 20 Ames St, Cambridge, MA 02142, USA
Papis, Max *Auto Racing Driver*
30212 Tomas, Rancho Santa Margarita, CA 92688, USA
Pappalardo, Salvatore Cardinal *Religious Leader*
%Arcibescovado, Via Matteo Bonello 2, 90134 Palermo, Italy
Pappano, Antonio *Conductor*
%Royal Opera House, Covent Garden, Bow St, London WC2E 9DD, England
Pappas, George *Bowler*
21108 Blakely Shores Dr, Cornelius NC 28031, USA
Pappas, Milton S (Milt) *Baseball Player*
502 Highlington Court, Beecher, IL 60401, USA
Pappenheimer, John R *Physiologist*
66 Sherman St, #113, Cambridge, MA 02140, USA
Pappin, James J (Jim) *Hockey Player*
48947 Greasewood Lane, Palm Desert, CA 92260, USA
Paquin, Anna *Actress*
%The Firm, 9100 Wilshire Blvd, #100W, Beverly Hills, CA 90210, USA
Paradis, Vanessa *Model, Singer, Actress*
14 Rue Lincoln, 75008 Paris, France
Paradise, Bob *Hockey Player*
1303 Beechwood Place, Saint Paul, MN 55116, USA
Parazaider, Walter *Woodwind Musician (Chicago)*
%Front Line Mgmt, 8900 Wilshire Blvd, #300, Beverly Hills, CA 90211, USA
Parazynski, Scott E *Astronaut*
2015 Wroxton Road, Houston, TX 77005, USA
Parcells, Duane C (Bill) *Football Coach*
%Dallas Cowboys, 1 Cowboys Parkway, Irving, TX 75063, USA
Pardee, Arthur B *Biochemist*
15 Buzzards Bay Ave, Woods Hole, MA 02543, USA
Pardee, John P (Jack) *Football Player, Coach*
Hawks Hill Ranch, PO Box 272, Gause, TX 77857, USA
Pardes, Herbert *Psychiatrist*
15 Claremont Ave, #93, New York, NY 10027, USA
Pardo, Don *Commentator*
%NBC-TV, News Dept, 30 Rockefeller Plaza, New York, NY 10112, USA
Pardue, Kip *Actor*
%Untitled Entertainment, 8436 W 3rd St, #650, Los Angeles, CA 90048, USA
Pare, Michael *Actor*
15250 Ventura Blvd, #710, Sherman Oaks, CA 91403, USA
Paredes, Marisa *Actress*
%Alsira Maroto Garcia, Gran Via 63, #3 Izda, 28013 Madrid, Spain
Parent, Bernard M (Bernie) *Hockey Player*
535 Route 38, Cherry Hill, NJ 08002, USA
Parent, Monique *Actress, Model*
PO Box 3458, Ventura, CA 93006, USA
Paret, Peter *Historian, Writer*
%Institute for Advanced Studies, Historical Studies School, Princeton, NJ 08540, USA
Paretsky, Sara N *Writer*
1504 E 53rd St, #302, Chicago, IL 60615, USA
Parfit, Derek A *Philosopher*
%All Souls College, Philosophy Dept, Oxford OX1 4AL, England
Parillaud, Anne *Actress*
%Artmedia, 20 Ave Rapp, 75007 Paris, France
Parilli, Vito (Babe) *Football Player, Coach*
8060 E Girard Ave, #218, Denver, CO 80231, USA

P

Paris - Parker

Paris, Johnny *Saxophonist*
%Atila Records, 195 Hannum Ave, Rossford, OH 43460, USA
Paris, Mica *Singer*
%Richard Walters, 1800 Argyle Ave, #408, Los Angeles, CA 90028, USA
Paris, Twila *Singer, Songwriter*
%Proper Mgmt, PO Box 150867, Nashville, TN 37215, USA
Parise, Louis *Labor Leader*
%National Maritime Union, 1125 15th St NW, Washington, DC 20005, USA
Parise, Ronald A *Astronaut*
15419 Good Hope Road, Silver Spring, MD 20905, USA
Parish, Robert L *Basketball Player*
20 Stonybrook Road, #1, Framingham, MA 01702, USA
Parizeau, Jacques *Political Leader, Canada*
88 S Grand Alle Est, Quebec PQ G1A 1A2, Canada
Park, Alyssa *Concert Violinist*
%Columbia Artists Mgmt Inc, 165 W 57th St, New York, NY 10019, USA
Park, Chan Ho *Baseball Player*
2400 Hollister Terrace, Glendale, CA 91206, USA
Park, Charles R *Physiologist*
5325 Stanford Dr, Nashville, TN 37215, USA
Park, D Bradford (Brad) *Hockey Player, Coach*
20 Stanley Road, Lynnfield, MA 01940, USA
Park, Grace *Golfer*
%Gaylord Sports Mgmt, 14646 N Kierland Blvd, #230, Scottsdale, AZ 85254, USA
Park, Merle F *Ballerina*
%Royal Ballet School, 144 Talgarth Road, London W14 9DE, England
Park, Nicholas W (Nick) *Animator, Director*
%Aardvark Animation, Gas Ferry Road, Bristol B51 6UN, England
Park, Steve *Auto Racing Driver*
1675 Coddle Creek Highway, Mooresville, NC 28115, USA
Parkening, Christopher *Concert Guitarist*
%I M G Artists, 420 W 45th St, New York, NY 10036, USA
Parker, Alan W *Movie Director*
%Parker Film Co, Pinewood Studios, Iver Heath, Bucks SL0 0NH, England
Parker, Andrea *Actress*
6250 Canoga Ave, Woodland Hills, CA 91367, USA
Parker, Anthony *Basketball Player*
%Orlando Magic, Waterhouse Center, 8701 Maitland Summit Blvd, Orlando, FL 32810, USA
Parker, Bob *Skier*
408 Camino Don Miguel, Santa Fe, NM 87505, USA
Parker, Brant J *Cartoonist (Wizard of Id)*
901 Glenwood Blvd, Waynesboro, VA 22980, USA
Parker, Bruce C *Botanist*
841 Hutcheson Dr, Blacksburg, VA 24060, USA
Parker, Caryl Mack *Singer*
%Scream Marketing, PO Box 120053, Nashville, TN 37212, USA
Parker, Clarence M (Ace) *Football Player*
210 Snead's Fairway, Portsmouth, VA 23701, USA
Parker, Corey *Actor*
%Gersh Agency, 232 N Canon Dr, Beverly Hills, CA 90210, USA
Parker, David G (Dave) *Baseball Player*
4036 Oak Tree Court, Loveland, OH 45140, USA
Parker, Denise *Archery Athlete*
4601 Wallace Lane, Salt Lake City, UT 84117, USA
Parker, Eleanor *Actress*
2195 La Paz Way, Palm Springs, CA 92264, USA
Parker, Eugene N *Physicist*
1323 Evergreen Road, Homewood, IL 60430, USA
Parker, Fess *Actor, Singer*
%Fess Parker Winery, PO Box 908, Los Olivos, CA 93441, USA
Parker, Franklin *Writer*
%Western Carolina University, Education & Psychology Dept, Cullowhee, NC 28723, USA
Parker, George M *Labor Leader*
%Glass Workers Union, 1440 S Byrne Road, Toledo, OH 43614, USA
Parker, Graham *Singer, Guitarist*
%Performers of the World, 8901 Melrose Ave, #200, West Hollywood, CA 90069, USA
Parker, Jack D (Jackie) *Football Player*
10623 65 Ave NW, Edmonton AB T6H 1V5, Canada
Parker, James T (Jim) *Football Player*
1902 Cedar Circle Dr, Catonsville, MD 21228, USA
Parker, Jameson *Actor*
%Stone Manners, 6500 Wilshire Blvd, #550, Los Angeles, CA 90048, USA
Parker, Lara *Actress*
PO Box 1254, Topanga, CA 90290, USA
Parker, Maceo *Jazz Saxophonist*
%Central Entertainment Services, 123 Harvard Ave, Staten Island, NY 10301, USA
Parker, Mary-Louise *Actress*
%William Morris Agency, 1325 Ave of Americas, New York, NY 10019, USA

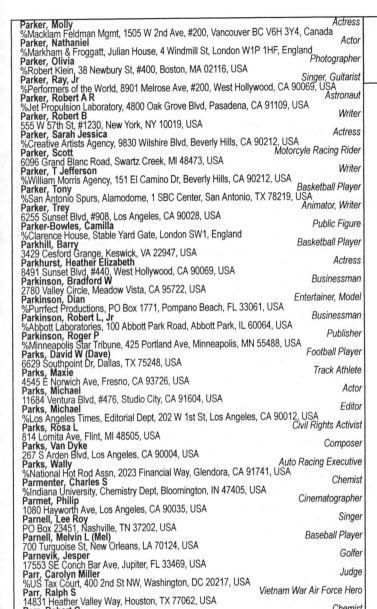

Parker, Molly *Actress*
%Macklam Feldman Mgmt, 1505 W 2nd Ave, #200, Vancouver BC V6H 3Y4, Canada

Parker, Nathaniel *Actor*
%Markham & Froggatt, Julian House, 4 Windmill St, London W1P 1HF, England

Parker, Olivia *Photographer*
%Robert Klein, 38 Newbury St, #400, Boston, MA 02116, USA

Parker, Ray, Jr *Singer, Guitarist*
%Performers of the World, 8901 Melrose Ave, #200, West Hollywood, CA 90069, USA

Parker, Robert A R *Astronaut*
%Jet Propulsion Laboratory, 4800 Oak Grove Blvd, Pasadena, CA 91109, USA

Parker, Robert B *Writer*
555 W 57th St, #1230, New York, NY 10019, USA

Parker, Sarah Jessica *Actress*
%Creative Artists Agency, 9830 Wilshire Blvd, Beverly Hills, CA 90212, USA

Parker, Scott *Motorcyle Racing Rider*
6096 Grand Blanc Road, Swartz Creek, MI 48473, USA

Parker, T Jefferson *Writer*
%William Morris Agency, 151 El Camino Dr, Beverly Hills, CA 90212, USA

Parker, Tony *Basketball Player*
%San Antonio Spurs, Alamodome, 1 SBC Center, San Antonio, TX 78219, USA

Parker, Trey *Animator, Writer*
6255 Sunset Blvd, #908, Los Angeles, CA 90028, USA

Parker-Bowles, Camilla *Public Figure*
%Clarence House, Stable Yard Gate, London SW1, England

Parkhill, Barry *Basketball Player*
3429 Cesford Grange, Keswick, VA 22947, USA

Parkhurst, Heather Elizabeth *Actress*
8491 Sunset Blvd, #440, West Hollywood, CA 90069, USA

Parkinson, Bradford W *Businessman*
2780 Valley Circle, Meadow Vista, CA 95722, USA

Parkinson, Dian *Entertainer, Model*
%Purrfect Productions, PO Box 1771, Pompano Beach, FL 33061, USA

Parkinson, Robert L, Jr *Businessman*
%Abbott Laboratories, 100 Abbott Park Road, Abbott Park, IL 60064, USA

Parkinson, Roger P *Publisher*
%Minneapolis Star Tribune, 425 Portland Ave, Minneapolis, MN 55488, USA

Parks, David W (Dave) *Football Player*
6629 Southpoint Dr, Dallas, TX 75248, USA

Parks, Maxie *Track Athlete*
4545 E Norwich Ave, Fresno, CA 93726, USA

Parks, Michael *Actor*
11684 Ventura Blvd, #476, Studio City, CA 91604, USA

Parks, Michael *Editor*
%Los Angeles Times, Editorial Dept, 202 W 1st St, Los Angeles, CA 90012, USA

Parks, Rosa L *Civil Rights Activist*
814 Lomita Ave, Flint, MI 48505, USA

Parks, Van Dyke *Composer*
267 S Arden Blvd, Los Angeles, CA 90004, USA

Parks, Wally *Auto Racing Executive*
%National Hot Rod Assn, 2023 Financial Way, Glendora, CA 91741, USA

Parmenter, Charles S *Chemist*
%Indiana University, Chemistry Dept, Bloomington, IN 47405, USA

Parmet, Philip *Cinematographer*
1080 Hayworth Ave, Los Angeles, CA 90035, USA

Parnell, Lee Roy *Singer*
PO Box 23451, Nashville, TN 37202, USA

Parnell, Melvin L (Mel) *Baseball Player*
700 Turquoise St, New Orleans, LA 70124, USA

Parnevik, Jesper *Golfer*
17553 SE Conch Bar Ave, Jupiter, FL 33469, USA

Parr, Carolyn Miller *Judge*
%US Tax Court, 400 2nd St NW, Washington, DC 20217, USA

Parr, Ralph S *Vietnam War Air Force Hero*
14831 Heather Valley Way, Houston, TX 77062, USA

Parr, Robert G *Chemist*
701 Kenmore Road, Chapel Hill, NC 27514, USA

Parra, Derek *Speedskater*
%US Speedskating, PO Box 450639, Westlake, OH 44145, USA

Parrett, William *Businessman*
%Deloitte Touche Tohmatsu, 433 Country Club Road, New Canaan, CT 06840, USA

Parris, Fred *Singer (Five Satins)*
%Paramount Entertainment, PO Box 12, Far Hills, NJ 07931, USA

Parrish, Bernard J (Bernie) *Football Player*
1633 NE 18th Place, Gainesville, FL 32609, USA

Parrish, Lance M *Baseball Player*
5141 Via Samuel, Yorba Linda, CA 92886, USA

Parrish, Larry A *Baseball Player, Manager*
234 Green Haven Lane W, Dundee, FL 33838, USA

P

Parros - Pasquin

Parros, Peter *Actor*
PO Box 241, Boonton, NJ 07005, USA
Parrott, Andrew *Conductor*
%Jonathan Wentworth, 10 Fiske Place, #530, Mount Vernon, NY 10550, USA
Parry, Craig *Golfer*
%Int'l Mgmt Group, 1 Erieview Plaza, 1360 E 9th St, #1300, Cleveland, OH 44114, USA
Parry, Robert T *Financier*
2 Ellis Court, Lafayette, CA 94549, USA
Parseghian, Ara R *Football Coach, Sportscaster*
51767 Oakbridge Court, Granger, IN 46539, USA
Parseghian, Gregory *Businessman*
%Federal Home Loan Mortgage, 8200 Jones Branch Dr, McLean, VA 22102, USA
Parshall, George W *Chemist*
2504 Delaware Ave, Wilmington, DE 19806, USA
Parsky, Gerald L *Attorney*
%Aurora Capital Partners, 1800 Century Park East, Los Angeles, CA 90067, USA
Parsons, Alan *Musician*
%Agency Group Ltd, 1775 Broadway, #430, New York, NY 10019, USA
Parsons, Benny *Auto Racing Driver*
2049 Country Club Dr, Port Orange, FL 32128, USA
Parsons, David *Choreographer*
%Parsons Dance Foundation, 476 Broadway, New York, NY 10013, USA
Parsons, Estelle *Actress*
924 W End Ave, #T5, New York, NY 10025, USA
Parsons, John T *Inventor (Machine Numerical Control)*
1456 Brigadoon Court, Traverse City, MI 49686, USA
Parsons, Karyn *Actress*
10351 Santa Monica Blvd, #211, Los Angeles, CA 90025, USA
Parsons, Nicholas *Actor*
%Susan Shaper, 174/178 N Gower St, London NW1 2NB, England
Parsons, Phil *Auto Racing Driver*
18801 WIndy Point Dr, Cornelius, NC 28031, USA
Parsons, Richard D *Businessman, Financier*
%Time Warner Inc, 75 Rockefeller Plaza, New York, NY 10019, USA
Part, Arvo *Composer*
%Universal Editions, Warwick House, 9 Warrick St, London W1R 5RA, England
Partee, Barbara H *Educator*
50 Hobart Lane, Amherst, MA 01002, USA
Parton, Dolly *Singer, Actress, Songwriter*
RR 1, Brentwood, TN 37027, USA
Parton, Stella *Singer*
PO Box 120871, Nashville, TN 37212, USA
Partridge, John A *Architect*
20 Old Pye St, Westminster, London SW1, England
Parvanov, Georgi *President, Bulgaria*
%President's Office, 2 Dondukov Blvd, 1123 Sofia, Bulgaria
Pasanella, Giovanni *Architect*
%Pasanella & Klein, 330 W 42nd St, New York, NY 10036, USA
Pasanella, Marco *Furniture Designer*
%Pasanella Co, 45 W 18th St, New York, NY 10011, USA
Pasarell, Charles *Tennis Player*
78200 Miles Ave, Indian Wells, CA 92210, USA
Paschall, Jim *Auto Racing Driver*
RR 2 Box 450, Denton, NC 27239, USA
Paschke, Melanie *Track Athlete*
Asseweg 2, 38124 Braunschweig, Germany
Pasco, Richard *Actor*
%Michael Whitehall, 125 Gloucester Road, London SW7 4TE, England
Pascoal, Hermeto *Jazz Musician*
%Brasil Universo Prod, RVN Vitor Guisard 209, Rio de Janerio 21832, Brazil
Pascual, Camilo A *Baseball Player*
7741 SW 32nd St, Miami, FL 33155, USA
Pascual, Luis *Theater Director*
%Theatre de l'Europe, 1 Place Paul Claudel, 75006 Paris, France
Pascual, Mercedes *Ecologist, Evolutionary Biologist*
%University of Michigan, Ecology & Biology Dept, Ann Arbor, MI 48109, USA
Pasdar, Adrian *Actor*
%International Creative Mgmt, 8942 Wilshire Blvd, #219, Beverly Hills, CA 90211, USA
Pasillas, Jose *Drummer (Incubus)*
%ArtistDirect, 10900 Wilshire Blvd, #1400, Los Angeles, CA 90024, USA
Paskai, Laszlo Cardinal *Religious Leader*
Uri Utca 62, 1014 Budapest, Hungary
Pasmore, E J Victor *Artist*
Dar Gamri, Gudja, Malta
Pasqualoni, Paul *Football Coach*
%Syracuse University, Athletic Dept, Syracuse, NY 13244, USA
Pasquin, John R *Movie, Television Director, Producer*
%Creative Artists Agency, 9830 Wilshire Blvd, Beverly Hills, CA 90212, USA

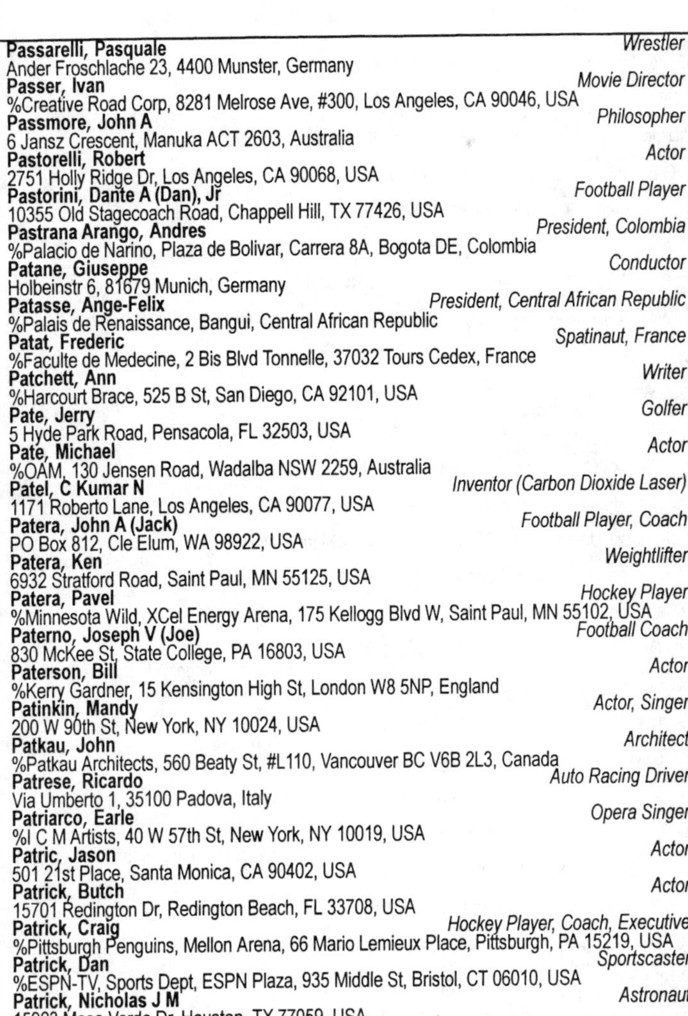

Passarelli, Pasquale *Wrestler*
Ander Froschlache 23, 4400 Munster, Germany

Passer, Ivan *Movie Director*
%Creative Road Corp, 8281 Melrose Ave, #300, Los Angeles, CA 90046, USA

Passmore, John A *Philosopher*
6 Jansz Crescent, Manuka ACT 2603, Australia

Pastorelli, Robert *Actor*
2751 Holly Ridge Dr, Los Angeles, CA 90068, USA

Pastorini, Dante A (Dan), Jr *Football Player*
10355 Old Stagecoach Road, Chappell Hill, TX 77426, USA

Pastrana Arango, Andres *President, Colombia*
%Palacio de Narino, Plaza de Bolivar, Carrera 8A, Bogota DE, Colombia

Patane, Giuseppe *Conductor*
Holbeinstr 6, 81679 Munich, Germany

Patasse, Ange-Felix *President, Central African Republic*
%Palais de Renaissance, Bangui, Central African Republic

Patat, Frederic *Spatinaut, France*
%Faculte de Medecine, 2 Bis Blvd Tonnelle, 37032 Tours Cedex, France

Patchett, Ann *Writer*
%Harcourt Brace, 525 B St, San Diego, CA 92101, USA

Pate, Jerry *Golfer*
5 Hyde Park Road, Pensacola, FL 32503, USA

Pate, Michael *Actor*
%OAM, 130 Jensen Road, Wadalba NSW 2259, Australia

Patel, C Kumar N *Inventor (Carbon Dioxide Laser)*
1171 Roberto Lane, Los Angeles, CA 90077, USA

Patera, John A (Jack) *Football Player, Coach*
PO Box 812, Cle Elum, WA 98922, USA

Patera, Ken *Weightlifter*
6932 Stratford Road, Saint Paul, MN 55125, USA

Patera, Pavel *Hockey Player*
%Minnesota Wild, XCel Energy Arena, 175 Kellogg Blvd W, Saint Paul, MN 55102, USA

Paterno, Joseph V (Joe) *Football Coach*
830 McKee St, State College, PA 16803, USA

Paterson, Bill *Actor*
%Kerry Gardner, 15 Kensington High St, London W8 5NP, England

Patinkin, Mandy *Actor, Singer*
200 W 90th St, New York, NY 10024, USA

Patkau, John *Architect*
%Patkau Architects, 560 Beaty St, #L110, Vancouver BC V6B 2L3, Canada

Patrese, Ricardo *Auto Racing Driver*
Via Umberto 1, 35100 Padova, Italy

Patriarco, Earle *Opera Singer*
%I C M Artists, 40 W 57th St, New York, NY 10019, USA

Patric, Jason *Actor*
501 21st Place, Santa Monica, CA 90402, USA

Patrick, Butch *Actor*
15701 Redington Dr, Redington Beach, FL 33708, USA

Patrick, Craig *Hockey Player, Coach, Executive*
%Pittsburgh Penguins, Mellon Arena, 66 Mario Lemieux Place, Pittsburgh, PA 15219, USA

Patrick, Dan *Sportscaster*
%ESPN-TV, Sports Dept, ESPN Plaza, 935 Middle St, Bristol, CT 06010, USA

Patrick, Nicholas J M *Astronaut*
15923 Mesa Verde Dr, Houston, TX 77059, USA

Patrick, Pat *Auto Racing Executive*
%Patrick Racing, 8431 Green Town Road, #400, Indianapolis, IN 46234, USA

Patrick, Robert *Actor*
2700 La Cuesta Dr, Los Angeles, CA 90046, USA

Patrick, Ruth *Educator*
%Academy of Natural Sciences, 19th & Parkway, Philadelphia, PA 19103, USA

Patrick, Thomas M *Businessman*
%Peoples Energy Corp, 130 E Randolph Dr, Chicago, IL 60601, USA

Patten, Christopher F *Governor General, Hong Kong*
%Coutts Co, Campbells Office, 440 Strand, London WC2R 0QS, England

Patterson, Elvis V *Football Player*
3939 Alberta St, Houston, TX 77021, USA

Patterson, Floyd *Boxer*
PO Box 336, Springtown Road, New Paltz, NY 12561, USA

Patterson, Francine G (Penny) *Animal Psychologist (Koko Trainer)*
%Gorilla Foundation, PO Box 620-640, Woodside, CA 94062, USA

Patterson, Gary *Cartoonist*
%Patterson International, 25208 Malibu Road, Malibu, CA 90265, USA

Patterson, James *Writer, Businessman*
%J Walter Thompson, 466 Lexington Ave, New York, NY 10017, USA

Patterson, John M *Governor, AL*
%Court of Judiciary, PO Box 30155, Montgomery, AL 36103, USA

Patterson, Katerine *Writer*
70 Wildersburg Common, Barre, VT 05641, USA

Patterson, Lorna *Actress*
23852 Pacific Coast Highway, #355, Malibu, CA 90265, USA
Patterson, Michael *Financier*
%JP Morgan Chase, 270 Park Ave, New York, NY 10017, USA
Patterson, Percival J *Prime Minister, Jamaica*
%Prime Minister's Office, 1 Devon Road, PO Box 272, Kingston 6, Jamaica
Patterson, Richard North *Writer*
PO Box 183, West Tisbury, MA 02575, USA
Patterson, Robert M *Vietnam War Army Air Hero (CMH)*
907 Ironwood Dr, Henderson, KY 42420, USA
Patti, Sandi *Singer, Pianist*
%Anderson Group, 2200 Madison Square, Anderson, IN 46011, USA
Pattillo, Linda *Commentator*
%Cable News Network, News Dept, 820 1st St NE, Washington, DC 20002, USA
Patton, Antoine (Big Boi) *Rap Artist*
%William Morris Agency, 1325 Ave of Americas, New York, NY 10019, USA
Patton, Melvin (Mel) *Track Athlete*
2312 Via Del Aguagate, Fallbrook, CA 92028, USA
Patton, Will *Actor*
520 Washington Blvd, #903, Marina del Rey, CA 90292, USA
Patty, J Edward (Budge) *Tennis Player*
La Marne, 14 Ave de Jurigoz, 1006 Lausanne, Switzerland
Patulski, Walter G (Walt) *Football Player*
4899 Abbottsbury Lane, Syracuse, NY 13215, USA
Patz, Arnall *Ophthalmologist*
%Johns Hopkins Hospital, Wilmer Eye Institute, 600 N Wolfe, Baltimore, MD 21287, USA
Patzaichin, Ivan *Canoeing Athlete*
SC Sportiv, Unirea Tricolor, Soseaua Stefan Cel Mare 9, Bucharest, Romania
Patzakis, Michele *Opera Singer*
%Kunstleragentur Raab & Bohm, Plankengasse 7, 1010 Vienna, Austria
Pauk, Gyorgy *Concert Violinist*
27 Armitage Road, London NW11, England
Paul, Adrian *Actor*
PO Box 4593, North Hollywood, CA 91617, USA
Paul, Alan *Musician, Singer (Manhattan Transfer)*
%Columbia/CBS Records, 1801 Century Park West, Los Angeles, CA 90067, USA
Paul, Alexandra *Actress*
%Innovative Artists, 1505 10th St, Santa Monica, CA 90401, USA
Paul, Billy *Singer*
8215 Winthrop St, Philadelphia, PA 19136, USA
Paul, Christi *Commentator*
%Cable News Network, News Dept, 1050 Techwood Dr NW, Atlanta, GA 30318, USA
Paul, Henry *Singer (BlackHawk)*
%Vector Mgmt, 1607 17th Ave S, Nashville, TN 37212, USA
Paul, Les *Guitarist, Inventor (Recording Methods)*
78 Deerhaven Road, Mahwah, NJ 07430, USA
Paul, Robert *Figure Skater*
10675 Rochester Ave, Los Angeles, CA 90024, USA
Paul, Vinnie *Drummer (Pantera)*
%Concrete Mgmt, 361 W Broadway, #200, New York, NY 10013, USA
Paul, Wolfgang *Soccer Player*
Postfach 1324, 59939 Olsberg-Bigge, Germany
Paula, Alejandro F (Jandi) *Prime Minister, Netherlands Antilles*
%Premier's Office, Fort Amsterdam 17, Willemstad, Netherlands Antilles
Pauley, Jane *Commentator*
271 Central Park West, #10E, New York, NY 10024, USA
Pauls, Raymond *Jazz Pianist, Composer*
Veidenbaum Str 41/43, #26, 226001 Riga, Latvia
Paulsen, Albert *Actor*
%H David Moss, 733 Seward St, #PH, Los Angeles, CA 90038, USA
Paulson, Dennis *Golfer*
1721 Aryana Dr, Encinitas, CA 92024, USA
Paulson, Richard L *Businessman*
%Potlatch Corp, 601 W Riverside Ave, Spokane, WA 99201, USA
Paulson, Sarah *Actress*
10390 Santa Monica Blvd, #300, Los Angeles, CA 90025, USA
Paultz, Billy *Basketball Player*
7049 Spout Springs Road, Flowery Branch, GA 30542, USA
Paup, Bryce E *Football Player*
1112 Moraine Way, Green Bay, WI 54303, USA
Paupua, Tomasi *Governor-General, Tuvalu*
%Governor General's Office, Government House, Vaiaku, Funafuti, Tuvalu
Pavan, Marisa *Actress*
4 Allee des Brouillards, 75018 Paris, France
Pavarotti, Luciano *Opera Singer*
Stradelho Nava u 8, 41199 Modena, Italy
Pavin, Corey *Golfer*
6505 Aladdin Dr, Orlando, FL 32818, USA

Pavletic, Vlatko *President, Croatia*
%Presidential Palace, Pantovcak 241, Zagreb 10000, Croatia
Pavlovic, Aleksandar *Basketball Player*
%Utah Jazz, Delta Center, 301 W South Temple, Salt Lake City, UT 84101, USA
Pawelczyk, James A (Jim) *Astronaut*
%NASA, Johnson Space Center, 2101 NASA Road, Houston, TX 77058, USA
Paxon, L William (Bill) *Representative, NY*
%Akin Gump Strauss Hauer Feld, 1333 New Hampshire NW, Washington, DC 20036, USA
Paxson, Jim *Basketball Player, Executive*
%Cleveland Cavaliers, Gund Arena, 1 Center Court, Cleveland, OH 44115, USA
Paxson, John *Basketball Player, Executive*
125 Boardman Court, Lake Bluff, IL 60044, USA
Paxton, Bill *Actor*
742 La Gracia, Santa Maria, CA 93455, USA
Paxton, John *Editor*
%Saint Martin's Press, 175 5th Ave, New York, NY 10010, USA
Paxton, Tom *Singer, Songwriter*
%Fleming Tamulevich Assoc, 733 N Main St, Ann Arbor, MI 48104, USA
Payette, Julie *Astronaut, Canada*
%Space Agency, Rockliffe Base, Ottawa ON K1A 1A1, Canada
Paymer, David *Actor*
327 19th St, Santa Monica, CA 90402, USA
Payne, Anthony E *Composer*
2 Wilton Square, London N1 3DL, England
Payne, David N *Optical Fiber Engineer*
%Southampton University, Highfield, Southampton SO17 1BJ, England
Payne, Dougie *Bassist (Travis)*
%Wildlife Entertainment, 21 Heathmans Road, London SW6 4TJ, England
Payne, Freda *Singer*
%Ira Okun Entertainment, 708 Palisades Dr, Pacific Palisades, CA 90272, USA
Payne, Harry C *Educator*
%Williams College, President's Office, Williamstown, MA 01267, USA
Payne, Henry *Editorial Cartoonist*
%Detroit News, Editorial Dept, 615 W Lafayette, Detroit, MI 48226, USA
Payne, Keith *Vietnam War Australian Army Hero (VC)*
2 Saint Bee's Ave, Bucasia QLD 4740, Australia
Payne, Ladell *Educator*
%Randolph-Macon College, President's Office, Ashland, VA 23005, USA
Payne, Roger S *Biologist, Conservationist*
191 Western Road, Lincoln, MA 01773, USA
Pays, Amanda *Actress*
11075 Santa Monica Blvd, #150, Los Angeles, CA 90025, USA
Payton, Benjamin F *Educator*
%Tuskegee Institute, President's Office, Tuskegee, AL 36088, USA
Payton, Gary *Basketball Player*
14003 SE 43rd St, Bellevue, WA 98006, USA
Payton, Gary E *Astronaut*
10140 Community Lane, Fairfax Station, VA 22039, USA
Payton, Melvin *Basketball Player*
17310 River Ave, Noblesville, IN 46060, USA
Payton, Nicholas *Jazz Trumpeter*
%Management Ark, 116 Village Blvd, #200, Princeton, NJ 08540, USA
Pazienza, Vinny *Boxer*
65 Waterman Ave, Cranston, RI 02910, USA
Peace, Terry *Actor*
PO Box 74, Allison Park, PA 15101, USA
Peacock, Andrew S *Government Official, Australia*
30 Monomeath Ave, Canterbury VIC 3126, Australia
Peacocke, Arthur R *Templeton Laureate, Biochemist*
%Society of Ordained Scientists, St Mark's Rectory, 11 Summer, Augusta, ME 04330, USA
Peake, James B *Army General*
Surgeon General, US Army, 5109 Leesburg Pike, Falls Church, VA 22041, USA
Peaker, E J *Actress*
4935 Densmore Ave, Encino, CA 91436, USA
Peaks, Clarence *Football Player*
%Creekside Apartments, 2500 Knights Road, #3-2, Bensalem, PA 19020, USA
Pearce, Guy *Actor*
%Shanahan Mgmt, PO Box 1509, Darlinghurst NSW 1300, Australia
Pearce, Jacqueline *Actress*
%Rhubarb Personal Mgmt, 6 Langley St, #41, London WC2H 9JA, England
Pearce, Richard I *Movie Director*
%Bauer Co, 9465 Wilshire Blvd, Beverly Hills, CA 90212, USA
Pearlstein, Philip *Artist*
361 W 36th St, New York, NY 10018, USA
Pearlstine, Norman *Editor*
%Time Warner Inc, Magazines Division, Rockefeller Plaza, New York, NY 10020, USA
Pears, David F *Philosopher*
7 Sandford Road, Littlemore, Oxford OX4 4PU, England

P	
Pearson, Andrall E	*Businessman*
%Tricon Global Restaurants, 1441 Gardiner Lane, Louisville, KY 40213, USA	
Pearson, David G	*Auto Racing Driver*
290 Burnett Road, Spartanburg, SC 29316, USA	
Pearson, Drew	*Football Player*
3721 Mount Vernon Way, Plano, TX 75025, USA	
Pearson, Larry	*Auto Racing Driver*
PO Box 1788, Kernersville, NC 27285, USA	
Pearson, Louis O	*Sculptor*
768 Delano Ave, #2D, San Francisco, CA 94112, USA	
Pearson, Mike	*Football Player*
%Jacksonville Jaguars, 1 AllTel Stadium Place, Jacksonville, FL 32202, USA	
Pearson, Preston J	*Football Player*
%Pro Style Assoc, 9104 Moss Farm Lane, Dallas, TX 75243, USA	
Pearson, Ralph G	*Chemist*
715 Grove Lane, Santa Barbara, CA 93105, USA	
Peart, Neal	*Drummer (Rush)*
%Macklam Feldman Mgmt, 1505 W 2nd Ave, #200, Vancouver BC V6H 3Y4, Canada	
Pease, Patsy	*Actress*
15432 Hartland St, Van Nuys, CA 91406, USA	
Pease, Rendel S	*Physicist*
Poplars, West Isley, Newbury, Berks RG16 OAW, England	
Peay, Francis	*Football Player, Coach*
123 Reynolds, Columbia, MO 65211, USA	
Peca, Michael (Mike)	*Hockey Player*
46 Golden Pheasant Dr, Getzville, NY 14068, USA	
Pechstein, Claudia	*Speedskater*
Allee der Kosmonauten 99, 12681 Berlin, Germany	
Peck, Carolyn	*Basketball Player, Coach*
%University of Florida, Athletic Dept, Gainesville, FL 32611, USA	
Peck, J Eddie	*Actor*
%David Shapira, 15821 Ventura Blvd, #235, Encino, CA 91436, USA	
Peck, M Scott	*Psychiatrist, Writer*
RR 1, New Preston Marble Bliss Road, Washington Depot, CT 06793, USA	
Peck, Ralph B	*Civil Engineer*
1101 Warm Sands Dr SE, Albuquerque, NM 87123, USA	
Peck, Richard	*Writer*
%Bantam Books, 1540 Broadway, New York, NY 10036, USA	
Peck, Richard E	*Educator*
96 Homesteads Road, Placitas, NM 87043, USA	
Peck, Tom	*Auto Racing Driver*
197 Water Tank Lane, McConnellsburg, PA 17233, USA	
Pecker, David J	*Publisher*
%National Enquirer, 1000 American Media Way, Boca Raton, FL 33464, USA	
Pecker, Jean-Claude	*Astronomer*
Pusat-Tasek, Les Corbeaux, 85350 L'Ile d'Yeu, France	
Peddle, Chuck	*Computer Designer*
PO Box 91346, Mission Hill, CA 91345, USA	
Pedersen, Richard F	*Diplomat*
PO Box 104, Haines Falls, NY 12436, USA	
Pedersen, William	*Architect*
%Kohn Pedersen Fox Assoc, 111 W 57th St, New York, NY 10019, USA	
Pederson, Donald O	*Electrical Engineer*
1436 Via Loma, Walnut Creek, CA 94598, USA	
Pedregon, Cruz	*Auto Racing Driver*
%McDonald's Racing, PO Box 52, Moorpark, CA 93020, USA	
Pedroni, Simone	*Concert Pianist*
%Columbia Artists Mgmt Inc, 165 W 57th St, New York, NY 10019, USA	
Peebles, Ann	*Singer*
%Bullseye Blues, 1 Camp St, Cambridge, MA 02140, USA	
Peebles, P James E	*Physicist, Educator*
24 Markham Road, Princeton, NJ 08540, USA	
Peek, Dan	*Singer, Guitarist (America)*
%Agency for Performing Arts, 9200 Sunset Blvd, #900, Los Angeles, CA 90069, USA	
Peeples, Lewis	*Singer (Five Satins)*
%Paramount Entertainment, PO Box 12, Far Hills, NJ 07931, USA	
Peeples, Nia	*Actress, Singer*
PO Box 21833, Waco, TX 76702, USA	
Peerce, Larry	*Movie Director*
225 W 34th St, #1012, New York, NY 10122, USA	
Peet, Amanada	*Actress*
%P M K Public Relations, 8500 Wilshire Blvd, #700, Beverly Hills, CA 90211, USA	
Peete, Calvin	*Golfer*
128 Garden Gate Dr, Ponte Vedra Beach, FL 32082, USA	
Peete, Rodney	*Football Player*
11964 Crest Place, Beverly Hills, CA 90210, USA	
Peeters, Pete	*Hockey Player*
%Farm, Namao AB T0A 2N0, Canada	

Pei, Ieoh Ming (I M) *Architect, Pritzker Laureate*
%Pei Cobb Freed Partners, 88 Pine St, New York, NY 10005, USA
Peirce, Kimberly *Movie Director*
%United Talent Agency, 9560 Wilshire Blvd, #500, Beverly Hills, CA 90212, USA
Pekarkova, Iva *Writer*
%Farrar Straus Giroux, 19 Union Square W, New York, NY 10003, USA
Peladeau, Pierre *Editor*
%Quebecor Inc, 612 Saint Jacques St, Montreal QC H3C 4M8, Canada
Peldon, Ashley *Actress*
%Bartels Co, PO Box 57593, Sherman Oaks, CA 91413, USA
Pele *Soccer Player*
Rua Riachuelo 121-3, Andar-Fones 34-1633/35 Santos SP, Brazil
Pelecanos, George P *Writer*
%Little Brown, 3 Center Plaza, Boston, MA 02108, USA
Pelen, Perrine *Alpine Skier*
31 Ave de l'Eygala, 38700 Corens Mont Fleury, France
Pelikan, Jaroslav J *Historian, Writer*
156 Chestnut Lane, Hamden, CT 06518, USA
Pelikan, Lisa *Actress*
%House of Representatives, 400 S Beverly Dr, #101, Beverly Hills, CA 90212, USA
Pelka, Valentine *Actor*
%Conway Van Gelder Robinson, 18-21 Jermyn St, London SW1Y 6NB, England
Pell, Claiborne De B *Senator, RI*
3425 Prospect St NW, Washington, DC 20007, USA
Pell, George Cardinal *Religious Leader*
%Archdiocese, Polding Centre, 133 Liverpool St, Sydney NSW 2000, Australia
Pellegrini, Bob F *Football Player*
5124 Haven Ave, Ocean City, NJ 08226, USA
Pellegrini, Margaret *Actress*
5018 N 61st Ave, Glendale, AZ 85301, USA
Pellegrino, Edmund D *Physician*
5610 Wisconsin Ave, Chevy Chase, MD 20815, USA
Pelletreau, Robert H, Jr *Diplomat*
%State Department, 2201 C St NW, Washington, DC 20520, USA
Pelli, Cesar A *Architect*
%Cesar Pelli Assoc, 1056 Chapel St, New Haven, CT 06510, USA
Pellington, William A *Football Player*
6 Chapel Court, Lutherville Timonium, MD 21093, USA
Peltason, Jack W *Educator*
18 Whistler Court, Irvine, CA 92612, USA
Peltonen, Ville *Hockey Player*
%Nashville Predators, 501 Broadway, Nashville, TN 37203, USA
Peluce, Meeno *Actor*
PO Box 3743, Glendale, CA 91221, USA
Peluso, Lisa *Actress*
%Shauna Sickenger, PO Box 301, Ramona, CA 92065, USA
Pelzer, Dave *Writer*
%D-Esprit, PO Box 1846, Rancho Mirage, CA 92270, USA
Pena, Alejandro *Baseball Player*
12635 Etris Road, Roswell, GA 30075, USA
Pena, Antonio F (Tony) *Baseball Player, Manager*
Comp Hab 30 Demarzo Man #1, Ed 14, Santiago, Dominican Republic
Pena, Elizabeth *Actress*
PO Box 904, Topanga, CA 90290, USA
Pena, Federico F *Secretary, Transportation, Energy*
362 Detroit St, #A, Denver, CO 80206, USA
Pena, Paco *Concert Guitarist, Composer*
%Grosvenor Gardens House, 35-7 Grosvenor Gardens, London SW1W 0BS, England
Pender, Melvin (Mel) *Track Athlete*
2330 Goodwood Blvd SE, Smyrna, GA 30080, USA
Penderecki, Krzysztof *Composer, Conductor*
Ul Cisowa 22, 30-229 Cracow, Poland
Pendergrass, Henry P *Physician, Educator*
%Vanderbilt University, Medical School, 1621 21st Ave S, Nashville, TN 37212, USA
Pendergrass, Teddy *Singer, Songwriter*
1505 Flat Rock Road, Narberth, PA 19072, USA
Penders, Tom *Basketball Coach*
%George Washington University, Athletic Dept, Washington, DC 20052, USA
Pendleton, Moses *Dancer, Choreographer*
%Momix, PO Box 35, Washington, CT 06794, USA
Penghlis, Thaao *Actor*
3107 Barbara Court, Los Angeles, CA 90068, USA
Pengily, Kirk *Guitarist, Saxophonist, Singer (INXS)*
8 Hayes St, #1, Neutral Bay 20891 NSW, Australia
Pengo, Polycarp Cardinal *Religious Leader*
PO Box 167, Dar-es-Salaam, Tanzania
Penicheiro, Ticha *Basketball Player*
%Sacramento Monarchs, Arco Arena, 1 Sports Parkway, Sacramento, CA 95834, USA

P

Penick - Peralta

Penick, Trevor *Singer (O-Town)*
%Trans Continental Records, 7380 Sand Lake Road, #350, Orlando, FL 32819, USA
Peniston, CeCe *Singer*
250 W 57th St, #821, New York, NY 10107, USA
Penky, Joseph F *Chemical Engineer*
%Purdue University, Chemical Engineering Dept, West Lafayette, IN 47907, USA
Penn, (Jillette) *Comedian, Illusionist (Penn & Teller)*
%William Morris Agency, 151 El Camino Dr, Beverly Hills, CA 90212, USA
Penn, Arthur H *Movie Director*
%William Morris Agency, 151 El Camino Dr, Beverly Hills, CA 90212, USA
Penn, Christopher *Actor*
6728 Zumirez Dr, Malibu, CA 90265, USA
Penn, Irving *Photographer*
%Irving Penn Studio, 89 5th Ave, New York, NY 10003, USA
Penn, Michael *Singer, Songwriter*
%H K Mgmt, 9200 W Sunset Blvd, #530, Los Angeles, CA 90069, USA
Penn, Sean *Actor, Director*
%P M K Public Relations, 8500 Wilshire Blvd, #700, Beverly Hills, CA 90211, USA
Pennacchio, Len A *Geneticist*
%Stanford University, Human Genome Center, Stanford, CA 94305, USA
Pennario, Leonard *Concert Pianist*
%Columbia Artists Mgmt Inc, 165 W 57th St, New York, NY 10019, USA
Pennebaker, Ed *Artist*
428 County Road 9351, Green Forest, AR 72638, USA
Penner, Jonathan *Actor*
%Banner Entertainment, 8265 W Sunset Blvd, #200, West Hollywood, CA 90046, USA
Penner, Stanford S *Aeronautical Engineer*
5912 Avenida Chamnez, La Jolla, CA 92037, USA
Pennington, Chad *Football Player*
%New York Jets, 1000 Fulton Ave, Hempstead, NY 11550, USA
Pennington, Janice *Model, Actress*
PO Box 11402, Beverly Hills, CA 90213, USA
Pennington, Michael *Actor*
%Marmont Mgmt, Langham House, 302/8 Regent St, London W1R 5AL, England
Pennock of Norton, Raymond *Businessman*
%Morgan Grenfell Group, 23 Great Winchester St, London EC2P 2AX, England
Pennock, Chris *Actor*
25150 1/2 Malibu Road, Malibu, CA 90265, USA
Penny, Joe *Actor*
10453 Sarah St, Toluca Lake, CA 91602, USA
Penny, Roger P *Businessman*
%Bethlehem Steel, 1170 8th Ave, Bethlehem, PA 18016, USA
Penny, Sydney *Actress*
%Baker/Winokur/Ryder, 9100 Wilshire Blvd, #600, Beverly Hills, CA 90212, USA
Penrose, Craig R *Football Player*
1609 Camino Way, Woodland, CA 95695, USA
Penske, Roger S *Auto Racing Driver, Builder*
%Penske Racing, 163 Rolling Hills Road, Mooresville, NC 28117, USA
Pentland, Alex P *Computer Scientist*
%Massachusetts Institute of Technology, Media Laboratory, Cambridge, MA 02139, USA
Penzias, Arno A *Nobel Physics Laureate*
%AT&T Bell Laboratories, 600 Mountain Ave, New Providence, NJ 07974, USA
Peoples, John *Physicist*
%Fermi Nat Acceleration Lab, CDF Collaboration, PO Box 500, Batavia, IL 60510, USA
Peoples, Woodrow (Woody) *Football Player*
1810 Eufaula Ave, Birmingham, AL 35208, USA
Pep, Willie *Boxer*
130 Hartford Ave, Wethersfield, CT 06109, USA
Pepitone, Joseph A (Joe) *Baseball Player*
32 Lois Lane, Farmingdale, NY 11735, USA
Peplinski, Jim *Hockey Player*
%Peplinski Auto Leasing, 212 Meridian Road NE, Calgary AB T2A 2N6, Canada
Pepper, Barry *Actor*
%Paul Kohner, 9300 Wilshire Blvd, #555, Beverly Hills, CA 90212, USA
Pepper, Gene *Football Player*
159 Cedar Mill Court, Saint Charles, MO 63304, USA
Peppers, Julius *Football Player*
%Carolina Panthers, Ericsson Stadium, 800 S Mint St, Charlotte, NC 28202, USA
Peppler, Mary Jo *Volleyball Player*
%Coast Volleyball Club, 11526 Sorrento Valley Road, San Diego, CA 92121, USA
Perabo, Piper *Actress*
648 Broadway, #1002, New York, NY 10012, USA
Perahia, Murray *Concert Pianist*
%I M G Artists, 420 W 45th St, New York, NY 10036, USA
Perak, Sultan of *Ruler, Malaysia*
%Sultan's Palace, Istana Bukit Serene, Kuala Lumpur, Malaysia
Peralta, Ricardo *Astronaut, Mexico*
%Ingeneria Instituto, Ciudad Universitaria, 04510 Mexico City DF, Mexico

Percival, Lance %PVA, 2 High St, Westbury-on-Trim, Bristol BS9 3DU, England	*Actor*
Percival, Troy E 28920 Greick Dr, Moreno Valley, CA 92555, USA	*Baseball Player*
Percy, Charles H 1691 34th St NW, Washington, DC 20007, USA	*Senator, IL*
Perdue, Franklin P (Frank) %Perdue Farms, PO Box 1656, Horsham, PA 19044, USA	*Businessman*
Perdue, Will 3332 SE Salmon St, Portland, OR 97214, USA	*Basketball Player*
Perec, Marie-Jose %Federacion d'Athletisme, 10 Rue du Fg Poissonniere, 75480 Paris Cedex 10	*Track Athlete*
Pereira, Aristides M PO Box 172, Praia, Cape Verde	*President, Cape Verde*
Perek, Lubos %Astronomical Institute, Budecska 6, Prague 2, Czech Republic	*Astronomer*
Perelman, Ronald O %Revlon Group, 625 Madison Ave, New York, NY 10022, USA	*Businessman*
Perenyi, Miklos Erdoalja Utca 1/B, 1037 Budapest, Hungary	*Concert Violinist*
Peres, Shimon Amot Law House, 8 Shaul Hamelech Blvd, Tel Aviv 64733, Israel	*Nobel Peace Laureate; Premier, Israel*
Peretokin, Mark %Bolshoi Theater, Teatralnaya Pl 1, 103009 Moscow, Russia	*Ballet Dancer*
Perez de Cuellar, Javier Avenida A Miro Quesada, 1071 Lima, Peru	*Secretary General, United Nations*
Perez Esquivel, Adolfo %Servicio Paz y Justicia, Piedras 730, 1070 Buenos Aires, Argentina	*Nobel Peace Laureate*
Perez Fernandez, Pedro %PSOE, Ferraz 68 y 70, 28008 Madrid, Spain	*Government Official, Spain*
Perez, Atanasio R (Tony) 1717 N Bayshore Dr, #2735, Miami, FL 33132, USA	*Baseball Player, Manager*
Perez, Chris %Big FD Entertainment, 301 Arizona Ave, #200, Santa Monica, CA 90401, USA	*Guitarist, Band Leader*
Perez, Hugo 22018 Newbridge Dr, Lake Forest, CA 92630, USA	*Soccer Player*
Perez, Luiz (Louie) %Gold Mountain, 3575 Cahuenga Blvd W, #450, Los Angeles, CA 90068, USA	*Guitarist, Singer (Los Lobos)*
Perez, Odalis A %Los Angeles Dodgers, Stadium, 1000 Elysian Park Ave, Los Angeles, CA 90012, USA	*Baseball Player*
Perez, Pascual %Salvador, Cucurulo #105, Santiago, Dominican Republic	*Baseball Player*
Perez, Rosie 1990 S Bundy Dr, #600, Los Angeles, CA 90025, USA	*Actress*
Perez, Scott %DC Comics, 1700 Broadway, New York, NY 10019, USA	*Cartoonist*
Perez, Timothy Paul %Badgley Connor Talent, 9229 Sunset Blvd, #311, Los Angeles, CA 90069, USA	*Actor*
Perez, Vincent %Artmedia, 20 Ave Rapp, 75007 Paris, France	*Actor*
Perick, Christof %Kaylor Mgmt, 130 W 57th St, #8G, New York, NY 10019, USA	*Conductor*
Perkins, David D 345 Vine St, Menlo Park, CA 94025, USA	*Biologist, Geneticist*
Perkins, Edward J %State Department, 2201 C St NW, Washington, DC 20520, USA	*Diplomat*
Perkins, Elizabeth %Brillstein/Grey, 9150 Wilshire Blvd, #350, Beverly Hills, CA 90212, USA	*Actress*
Perkins, John M 1655 Saint Charles St, Jackson, MS 39209, USA	*Social Activist*
Perkins, Kendrick %Boston Celtics, 151 Merrimac St, #1, Boston, MA 02114, USA	*Basketball Player*
Perkins, Lawrence B, Jr %Perkins Eastman Partners, 437 5th Ave, New York, NY 10016, USA	*Architect*
Perkins, Lucian 3103 17th St NW, Washington, DC 20010, USA	*Photojournalist*
Perkins, Millie 2511 Canyon Dr, Los Angeles, CA 90068, USA	*Actress*
Perkins, Tex %Slack/Polydor Records, 70 Universal City Plaza, Universal City, CA 91608, USA	*Singer*
Perkins, W Ray 57 Honors Lane, Hattiesburg, MS 39402, USA	*Football Player, Coach*
Perkoff, Gerald T 1300 Torrey Pines Dr, Columbia, MO 65203, USA	*Physician*
Perl, Frank J 5020 Biloxi Ave, North Hollywood, CA 91601, USA	*Cinematographer*
Perl, Martin L 3737 El Centro Ave, Palo Alto, CA 94306, USA	*Nobel Physics Laureate*

P

Perle, George *Composer*
%Queens College, Music Dept, Flushing, NY 11367, USA
Perley, James *Labor Leader*
%American Assn of University Professors, 1012 14th St NW, Washington, DC 20005, USA
Perlich, Max *Actor*
%Innovative Artists, 1505 10th St, Santa Monica, CA 90401, USA
Perlman, Itzhak *Concert Violinist, Conductor*
%I M G Artists, 420 W 45th St, New York, NY 10036, USA
Perlman, Lawrence *Businessman*
%Ceridian Corp, 3311 E Old Shakopee Road, Minneapolis, MN 55425, USA
Perlman, Rhea *Actress*
PO Box 491246, Los Angeles, CA 90049, USA
Perlman, Ron *Actor*
%Kritzer Entertainment, 12200 W Olympic Blvd, #400, Los Angeles, CA 90064, USA
Perls, Tom *Geriatician*
2 Harrington Lane, Weston, MA 02493, USA
Perner, Wolfgang *Biathlete*
Schildlehen 29, 8972 Ramsau-D, Austria
Pernice, Tom, Jr *Golfer*
%Gaylord Sports Mgmt, 14646 N Kierland Blvd, #230, Scottsdale, AZ 85254, USA
Pero, Perry R *Financier*
%Northern Trust Corp, 50 S La Salle St, Chicago, IL 60675, USA
Peron, Isabelita Martinez de *President, Argentina*
Moreto 3, Los Jeronimos, 28014 Madrid, Spain
Perot, H Ross *Businessman*
%Perot Group, Lakeside Square, 12377 Merit Dr, #1700, Dallas, TX 75251, USA
Perot, Henry Ross, Jr *Aviator*
%Perot Group, Lakeside Square, 12377 Merit Dr, #1700, Dallas, TX 75251, USA
Perranoski, Ronald P (Ron) *Baseball Player*
3805 Indian River Dr, Vero Beach, FL 32963, USA
Perrault, Dominique *Architect*
%Perrault Architecte, 26 Rue Brunneseau, 75629 Paris Cedex 13, France
Perreau, Gigi *Actress*
5841 Cantaloupe Ave, Van Nuys, CA 91401, USA
Perreault, Gilbert (Gil) *Hockey Player*
4 Rue de la Serenite, Victoriaville QC G6P 6S2, Canada
Perrella, James E *Businessman*
%Ingersoll-Rand Co, 200 Chestnut Ridge Road, Woodcliff Lake, NJ 07677, USA
Perrier, Mireille *Actress*
%Cineart, 36 Rue de Ponthieu, 75008 Paris, France
Perrin, Philippe *Astronaut*
11923 Mighty Redwood Dr, Houston, TX 77059, USA
Perrine, Valerie *Actress*
%Bret Adams, 440 W 44th St, New York, NY 10036, USA
Perrineau, Harry, Jr *Actor*
%Creative Artists Agency, 9830 Wilshire Blvd, Beverly Hills, CA 90212, USA
Perron, Jean *Hockey Coach*
5 Thomas Mellon Circle, San Francisco, CA 94134, USA
Perry, Anne *Writer*
Tyrn Vawr, Seafield, Portmahomack, Rosshire IV20 1RE, Scotland
Perry, Barry W *Businessman*
%Engelhard Corp, 101 Wood Ave, Iselin, NJ 08830, USA
Perry, Charles O *Sculptor*
20 Shorehaven Road, Norwalk, CT 06855, USA
Perry, Chris *Golfer*
%Clayton Hoskins, 1161 Gamblier Road, Mount Vernon, OH 43050, USA
Perry, Felton *Actor*
PO Box 931359, Los Angeles, CA 90093, USA
Perry, Fletcher (Joe) *Football Player*
1644 E Chicago St, Chandler, AZ 85225, USA
Perry, Gaylord J *Baseball Player*
PO Box 489, Spruce Pine, NC 28777, USA
Perry, Gerald *Football Player*
2940 Dell Dr, Columbia, SC 29209, USA
Perry, James E (Jim) *Baseball Player*
2608 S Ridgeview Way, Sioux Falls, SD 57105, USA
Perry, Joe *Guitarist (Aerosmith), Songwriter*
PO Box 2665, Duxbury, MA 02331, USA
Perry, John Bennett *Actor*
%Judy Schoen, 606 N Larchmont Blvd, #309, Los Angeles, CA 90004, USA
Perry, John R *Philosopher*
%Stanford University, Language & Information Study Center, Stanford, CA 94305, USA
Perry, Kenny *Golfer*
418 Quail Ridge Road, Franklin, KY 42134, USA
Perry, Linda *Singer (Four Non Blondes), Songwriter*
%Premier Talent, 3 E 54th St, #1100, New York, NY 10022, USA
Perry, Matthew *Actor*
%Creative Artists Agency, 9830 Wilshire Blvd, Beverly Hills, CA 90212, USA

Perry, Michael Dean *Football Player*
19125 Peninsula Point Road, Cornelius, NC 28031, USA

Perry, Nickolas *Movie Director, Writer*
%William Morris Agency, 151 El Camino Dr, Beverly Hills, CA 90212, USA

Perry, Robert P *Molecular Biologist*
1808 Bustleton Pike, Churchville, PA 18966, USA

Perry, Roger *Actor*
3800 Barham Blvd, #303, Los Angeles, CA 90068, USA

Perry, Ruth *Prime Minister, Liberia*
%Prime Minister's Office, Capitol Hill, Monrovia, Liberia

Perry, Steve *Singer (Journey)*
3905 Peartree Place, Calabasas, CA 91302, USA

Perry, Troy D *Religious Leader*
%Metropolitan Churches Fellowship, 5300 Santa Monica Blvd, Los Angeles, CA 90029, USA

Perry, William (Refrigerator) *Football Player*
1463 Edgefield Highway, Aiken, SC 29801, USA

Perry, William J *Secretary, Defense*
11210 Hooper Lane, Los Altos Hills, CA 94024, USA

Perry, Yvonne *Actress*
%As World Turns Show, CBS-TV, 524 W 57th St, New York, NY 10019, USA

Persoff, Nehemiah *Actor*
5670 Moonstone Beach Dr, Cambria, CA 93428, USA

Person, Chuck *Basketball Player*
%Cleveland Cavaliers, Gund Arena, 1 Center Court, Cleveland, OH 44115, USA

Person, Wesley *Basketball Player*
8961 Golf Walk Circle S, Memphis, TN 38125, USA

Persson, Goeran *Prime Minister, Sweden*
%Statsradsberedningen, Rosenbad 4, 103 33 Stockholm, Sweden

Persson, Nina *Singer (Cardigans)*
%Motor SE, Gotabergs Gatan 2, 400 14 Gothenburg, Sweden

Pesce, P J *Movie Director, Writer*
%Writers & Artists, 8383 Wilshire Blvd, #550, Beverly Hills, CA 90211, USA

Pesci, Joe *Actor*
%Falu Productions, PO Box 6, Lavallette, NJ 08735, USA

Pescia, Lisa *Actress*
%Epstein-Wyckoff, 280 S Beverly Dr, #400, Beverly Hills, CA 90212, USA

Pescow, Donna *Actress*
8267 Paseo Canyon Dr, Malibu, CA 90265, USA

Pesek, Libor *Conductor*
%IMG Artists, Media House, 3 Burlington Lane, London W4 2TH, England

Pesky, John M (Johnny) *Baseball Player*
2201 Edison Ave, Fort Myers, FL 33901, USA

Pestka, Sidney *Molecular Geneticist*
%Robert Wood Johnson Medical School, 675 Hoes Lane, Piscataway, NJ 08854, USA

Peter, Edward C, II *Army General*
4521 Lake Dr, Lees Summit, MO 64064, USA

Peter, Valentine J *Religious Leader, Educator*
%Father Flanagan's Boys Home, Boys Town, NE 68010, USA

Peterdi, Gabor *Artist*
108 Highland Ave, Norwalk, CT 06853, USA

Peterman, Donald W *Cinematograher*
%Gersh Agency, 232 N Canon Dr, Beverly Hills, CA 90210, USA

Peters, Anthony L (Tony) *Football Player*
2402 Boston St, Muskogee, OK 74401, USA

Peters, Barbara *Movie Director*
1118 Magnolia Blvd, North Hollywood, CA 91601, USA

Peters, Bernadette *Singer, Actress*
%MCA Records, 70 Universal City Plaza, Universal City, CA 91608, USA

Peters, Bob *Hockey Coach*
%Bemidji State University, Athletic Dept, Bemidji, MN 56601, USA

Peters, Brock *Actor*
1420 Rising Glen Road, Los Angeles, CA 90069, USA

Peters, Charles G, Jr *Editor*
%Washington Monthly, 1611 Connecticut Ave NW, Washington, DC 20009, USA

Peters, Dan *Drummer (Mudhoney)*
%Legends of 21st Century, 7 Trinity Row, Florence, MA 01062, USA

Peters, Elizabeth *Writer*
%Avon Books, 1350 Ave of Americas, New York, NY 10019, USA

Peters, Emmitt *Dog Sled Racer*
General Delivery, Ruby, AK 99768, USA

Peters, Floyd *Football Player, Coach*
9222 Hyland Creek Road, Bloomington, MN 55437, USA

Peters, Gary C *Baseball Player*
7121 N Serenoa Dr, Sarasota, FL 34241, USA

Peters, Gretchen *Singer, Songwriter*
%Purple Crayon Mgmt, PO Box 358, Hendersonville, TN 37077, USA

Peters, Jon *Movie Producer*
9941 Tower Lane, Beverly Hills, CA 90210, USA

P

Peters, Maria Liberia *Prime Minister, Netherlands Antilles*
%Prime Minister's Office, Fort Amsterdam, Willemstad, Netherlands Antilles
Peters, Mary *Track Athlete*
Willowtree Cottage, River Road, Dunmurray, Belfast, Northern Ireland
Peters, Mike *Editorial Cartoonist (Grimmy)*
PO Box 957, Bradenton, FL 34206, USA
Peters, Roberta *Opera Singer, Actress*
19356 Cedar Glen Dr, Boca Raton, FL 33434, USA
Peters, Tom *Writer, Management Consultant*
%Tom Peters Group, 555 Hamilton Ave, Palo Alto, CA 94301, USA
Petersdorf, Robert G *Physician*
8001 Sand Point Way NE, #C71, Seattle, WA 98115, USA
Petersen, Byron *Liver Disease Researcher*
%University of Pittsburgh, Medical Center, Pittsburgh, PA 15260, USA
Petersen, Jan *Government Official, Norway*
%Utenriksdepatementet, Postboks 8114 Dep, 0032 Oslo, Norway
Petersen, Niels Helveg *Government Official, Denmark*
Drosselvej 72, 2000 Frederiksberg, Denmark
Petersen, Paul *Actor, Singer*
%A Minor Consideration, 14530 Denker Ave, Gardena, CA 90247, USA
Petersen, Raymond J *Publisher*
%Hearst Corp, 250 W 55th St, New York, NY 10019, USA
Petersen, Robert E *Publisher*
%Petersen Publishing Co, 6420 Wilshire Blvd, #100, Los Angeles, CA 90048, USA
Petersen, William L *Actor*
%United Talent Agency, 9560 Wilshire Blvd, #500, Beverly Hills, CA 90212, USA
Petersen, Wolfgang *Movie Director*
%Creative Artists Agency, 9830 Wilshire Blvd, Beverly Hills, CA 90212, USA
Peterson, Bruce *Test Pilot*
23792 Marguerite Parkway, #120, Mission Viejo, CA 92692, USA
Peterson, Buzz *Basketball Coach*
%University of Tennessee, Athletic Dept, Knoxville, TN 37996, USA
Peterson, David C *Photojournalist*
4805 Pinehurst Court, Pleasant Hill, IA 50327, USA
Peterson, Debbi *Drummer (Bangles)*
%Creative Artists Agency, 9830 Wilshire Blvd, Beverly Hills, CA 90212, USA
Peterson, Donald H *Astronaut*
%Aerospace Operations Consultants, 427 Pebblebrook Dr, Seabrook, TX 77586, USA
Peterson, Elly *Women's Activist*
1515 M St NW, Washington, DC 20005, USA
Peterson, Forrest J *Test Pilot*
17 Collins Meadow Dr, Georgetown, SC 29440, USA
Peterson, Fred I (Fritz) *Baseball Player*
PO Box 802, Dubuque, IA 52004, USA
Peterson, John *Wrestler*
457 19th Ave, Comstock, WI 54826, USA
Peterson, Lars *Surgeon*
%Sahlgrenska University Hospital, Surgery Dept, 413 45 Goteborg, Sweden
Peterson, Michael *Singer*
Falcon/Goodman Mgmt, 1103 17th Ave S, Nashville, TN 37212, USA
Peterson, Morris *Basketball Player*
%Toronto Raptors, Air Canada Center, 40 Bay St, Toronto ON M5J 2N8, Canada
Peterson, Oscar E *Jazz Pianist, Composer*
%Regal Recordings, 2421 Hammond Road, Mississauga ON L5K 1T3, Canada
Peterson, Paul E *Political Scientist*
5 Midland Road, Wellesley, MA 02482, USA
Peterson, Peter G *Financier, Secretary of Commerce*
%Blackstone Group, 345 Park Ave, New York, NY 10154, USA
Peterson, Ray *Singer*
%Lustig Talent, PO Box 770850, Orlando, FL 32877, USA
Peterson, Rudolph A *Financier*
86 Sea View Ave, Piedmont, CA 94611, USA
Peterson, Russell W *Governor, DE*
11 E Mozart Dr, Wilmington, DE 19807, USA
Peterson, Steven *Architect*
%Peterson/Littenberg Architecture, 131 E 66th St, New York, NY 10021, USA
Peterson, Todd *Football Player*
3249 Chatham Road NW, Atlanta, GA 30305, USA
Peterson, Vicki *Guitarist (Bangles)*
%Creative Artists Agency, 9830 Wilshire Blvd, Beverly Hills, CA 90212, USA
Peterson, Walter R *Governor, NH; Educator*
PO Box 3100, Peterborough, NH 03458, USA
Peterson, William L *Actor*
%United Talent Agency, 9560 Wilshire Blvd, #500, Beverly Hills, CA 90212, USA
Petherbridge, Edward *Actor*
%Jonathan Altaras, 13 Shorts Gardens, London WC2H 9AT, England
Petit, Philippe *High Wire Walker*
%Cathedral of Saint John the Devine, 1047 Amsterdam Ave, New York, NY 10025, USA

Petit, Roland *Ballet Dancer, Choreographer*
20 Blvd Gabes, 13008 Marseilles, France
Petke, Mike *Soccer Player*
%DC United, 14120 Newbrook Dr, Chantilly, VA 20151, USA
Peto, Richard *Epidemiologist*
%Radcliffe Infirmary, Harkness Building, Oxford ON OX2 6HE, England
Petra, Yvon *Tennis Player*
Residence du Prieure, 78100 Saint Germain en Laye, France
Petrenko, Viktor *Figure Skater*
%International Skating Center, PO Box 577, Simsbury, CT 06070, USA
Petri, Michala *Concert Recorder Player*
Nordskraenten 3, 2980 Kokkedal, Denmark
Petri, Nina *Actress*
%Agentur Carola Studlar, Agnesstr 47, 80798 Munich, Germany
Petrie, Daniel M, Jr *Movie Director*
%Richland/Wunsch/Hohman Agency, 9220 Sunset Blvd, #311, Los Angeles, CA 90069, USA
Petrie, Daniel M, Sr *Movie, Theater Director*
13201 Haney Place, Los Angeles, CA 90049, USA
Petrie, Geoff *Basketball Player, Executive*
%Sacramento Kings, Arco Arena, 1 Sports Parkway, Sacramento, CA 95834, USA
Petrocelli, Americo P (Rico) *Baseball Player*
37 Green Heron Lane, Nashua, NH 03062, USA
Petrocelli, Daniel *Attorney*
%Mitchell Silverberg Krupp, 11377 W Olympic Blvd, Los Angeles, CA 90064, USA
Petrone, Rocco A *Missile Engineer*
1329 Granvia Altamira, Palos Verdes Estates, CA 90274, USA
Petrone, Shana *Singer*
%Creative Artists Agency, 3310 W End Ave, #500, Nashville, TN 37203, USA
Petroni, Michael *Movie Director*
%United Talent Agency, 9560 Wilshire Blvd, #500, Beverly Hills, CA 90212, USA
Petronio, Stephen *Dancer, Choreographer*
95 Saint Marks Place, New York, NY 10009, USA
Petroske, John *Hockey Player*
PO Box 366, Side Lake, MN 55781, USA
Petrov, Andrei P *Composer*
Petrovskaya Str 42, #75, 197046 Saint Petersburg, Russia
Petrov, Nikolai A *Concert Pianist*
Kutuzovsky Prosp 26, #23, 121165 Moscow, Russia
Petrovics, Emil *Composer*
Attila Utca 29, 1013 Budapest, Hungary
Petrovsky, Daniel J *Army General*
Commanding General, UN Command Korea, APO, AE 96343, USA
Petry, Daniel J (Dan) *Baseball Player*
1808 Cartlen Dr, Placentia, CA 92870, USA
Petsko, Gregory A *Chemist, Biochemist*
8 Jason Road, Belmont, MA 02478, USA
Pett, Joel *Editorial Cartoonist*
%Lexington Herald-Leader, 1010 New Circle Road NW, Lexington, KY 40511, USA
Pettengill, Gordon H *Planetary Physicist*
%Massachusetts Institute of Technology, Space Research Ctr, Cambridge, MA 02139, USA
Petterson, Donald K *Diplomat*
American Embassy Khartoum, #63900, APO, AE 09829, USA
Pettet, Joanna *Actress*
%Paradigm Agency, 10100 Santa Monica Blvd, #2500, Los Angeles, CA 90067, USA
Pettibon, Raymond *Artist*
%Michael Kohn Gallery, 920 Colorado Ave, Santa Monica, CA 90401, USA
Pettibon, Richard A (Richie) *Football Player*
9628 Percussion Way, Vienna, VA 22182, USA
Pettigrew, Antonio *Track Athlete*
%Saint Augustine's College, Athletic Dept, Raleigh, NC 27610, USA
Pettigrew, L Eudora *Educator*
%State University of New York, President's Office, Old Westbury, NY 11568, USA
Pettijohn, Francis J *Geologist*
11630 Glen Arm Road, #V51, Glen Arm, MD 21057, USA
Pettit, Donald R *Astronaut*
2014 Country Ridge Dr, Houston, TX 77062, USA
Pettit, Robert L (Bob), Jr *Basketball Player*
7 Garden Lane, New Orleans, LA 70124, USA
Pettite, Andrew E (Andy) *Baseball Player*
2310 W Lawther Dr, Deer Park, TX 77536, USA
Petty, Kyle *Auto Racing Driver*
135 Longfield Dr, Mooresville, NC 28115, USA
Petty, Lori *Actress*
4001 W Alameda Ave, #301, Burbank, CA 91505, USA
Petty, Richard L *Auto Racing Driver*
%Petty Enterprises, 311 Branson Mill Road, Randleman, NC 27317, USA
Petty, Tom *Singer, Guitarist, Songwriter*
%East End Mgmt, 8209 Melrose Ave, #200, Los Angeles, CA 90046, USA

P

Peyroux, Madeline *Singer, Songwriter*
%Bumstead Productions, PO Box 158, Station E, Toronto ON M6H 4E2, Canada
Peyser, Penny *Actress*
%Epstein-Wyckoff, 280 S Beverly Dr, #400, Beverly Hills, CA 90212, USA
Peyton of Yeovil, John W W *Government Official, England*
Old Malt House, Hinton Saint George, Somerset TA17 8SE, England
Pezzano, Chuck *Bowling Writer*
27 Mountainside Terrace, Clifton, NJ 07013, USA
Pfaff, Judy *Artist*
%Holly Solomon Gallery, 175 E 79th St, #2B, New York, NY 10021, USA
Pfann, George R *Football Player, Coach*
120 Warwick Place, Ithaca, NY 14850, USA
Pfeiffer, Dedee *Actress, Model*
%Baker/Winokur/Ryder, 9100 Wilshire Blvd, #600, Beverly Hills, CA 90212, USA
Pfeiffer, Doug *Ski Instructor, Editor*
PO Box 1806, Big Bear Lake, CA 92315, USA
Pfeiffer, Michelle *Actress*
3737 W Magnolia Blvd, #300, Burbank, CA 91505, USA
Pfeiffer, Norman *Architect*
%Hardy Holzman Pfeiffer, 811 W 7th St, Los Angeles, CA 90017, USA
Pflug, Jo Ann *Actress*
2865 Lenox Road NE, #509, Atlanta, GA 30324, USA
Pfund, Randy *Basketball Coach, Executive*
%Miami Heat, American Airlines Arena, 601 Biscayne Blvd, Miami, FL 33132, USA
Phair, Liz *Singer, Songwriter, Actress*
315 23rd St, #A, Manhattan Beach, CA 90266, USA
Pham Dinh Tung, Paul J Cardinal *Religious Leader*
%Archdiocese, Toa Tong Giam Muc, 40 Pho Nha Chung, Hanoi, Vietnam
Pham Minh Man, Jean-Baptiste Cardinal *Religious Leader*
%Toa Tonggiam Muc, 180 Nguyen Dink Chieu, Thanh-Pho Ho Chi Minh, Vietnam
Pham Tuan *Cosmonaut, Vietnam*
4C-1000-Soc Son, Hanoi, Vietnam
Phan Van Khai *Prime Minister, Vietnam*
%Prime Minister's Office, Hoang Hoa Thum St, Hanoi, Vietnam
Phantog *Mountaineer*
%Wuxi Sports & Physical Culture Commission, Jiagnsu, China
Phelan, Jim *Basketball Player, Coach*
16579 Old Emmitsburg Road, Emmitsburg, MD 21727, USA
Phelps, Ashton, Jr *Publisher*
%New Orleans Times-Picayune, 3800 Howard Ave, New Orleans, LA 70125, USA
Phelps, Doug *Singer, Musician (Kentucky Headhunters)*
%Mitchell Fox Mgmt, 212 3rd Ave N, #301, Nashville, TN 37201, USA
Phelps, Edmund S *Economist*
45 E 89th St, New York, NY 10128, USA
Phelps, James *Actor*
%JOP Project, PO Box 9765, Coldfield, Sutton B75 5XB, England
Phelps, Jaycie *Gymnast*
%Cincinnati Gymnastics Academy, 3635 Woodridge Blvd, Fairfield, OH 45014, USA
Phelps, Kelly Joe *Singer, Guitarist*
%Fleming/Tamulevich Assoc, 733 N Main St, #35, Ann Arbor, MI 48104, USA
Phelps, Michael *Swimmer*
%Octagon, 1751 Pinnacle Dr, #1500, McLean, VA 22102, USA
Phelps, Michael E *Neuroscientist*
16720 Huerta Road, Encino, CA 91436, USA
Phelps, Richard F (Digger) *Basketball Coach*
%ESPN-TV, Sports Dept, ESPN Plaza, 935 Middle St, Bristol, CT 06010, USA
Phifer, Mekhi *Actor*
%William Morris Agency, 1325 Ave of Americas, New York, NY 10019, USA
Phifer, Roman Z *Football Player*
1764 S Garth Ave, Los Angeles, CA 90035, USA
Philaret, Patriarch *Religious Leader*
10 Osvobozdeniya St, 22004 Minsk, Belarus
Philbin, Regis *Entertainer*
101 W 67th St, #51A, New York, NY 10023, USA
Philip *Prince, England; Duke of Edinburgh*
%Buckingham Palace, London SW1A 1AA, England
Philip, Primate *Religious Leader*
%Antiochian Orthodox Christian Church, 358 Mountain Road, Englewood, NJ 07631, USA
Philipp, Stephanie *Model*
%Agentur Margit de la Berg, 82057 Icking-Isartal, Germany
Philippe *Crown Prince, Belgium*
%Koninklijk Palais, Rue de Brederode, 1000 Brussels, Belgium
Philippoussis, Mark *Tennis Player*
%Octagon, 1751 Pinnacle Dr, #1500, McLean, VA 22102, USA
Philips, Chuck *Journalist*
%Los Angeles Times, Editorial Dept, 202 W 1st St, Los Angeles, CA 90012, USA
Phillippe, Ryan *Actor*
%Paradigm Agency, 10100 Santa Monica Blvd, #2500, Los Angeles, CA 90067, USA

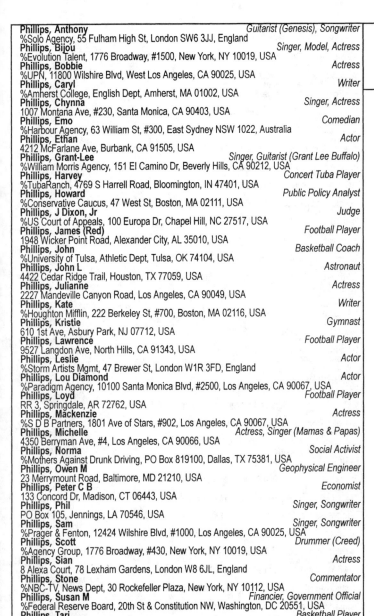

Phillips, Anthony *Guitarist (Genesis), Songwriter*
%Solo Agency, 55 Fulham High St, London SW6 3JJ, England
Phillips, Bijou *Singer, Model, Actress*
%Evolution Talent, 1776 Broadway, #1500, New York, NY 10019, USA
Phillips, Bobbie *Actress*
%UPN, 11800 Wilshire Blvd, West Los Angeles, CA 90025, USA
Phillips, Caryl *Writer*
%Amherst College, English Dept, Amherst, MA 01002, USA
Phillips, Chynna *Singer, Actress*
1007 Montana Ave, #230, Santa Monica, CA 90403, USA
Phillips, Emo *Comedian*
%Harbour Agency, 63 William St, #300, East Sydney NSW 1022, Australia
Phillips, Ethan *Actor*
4212 McFarlane Ave, Burbank, CA 91505, USA
Phillips, Grant-Lee *Singer, Guitarist (Grant Lee Buffalo)*
%William Morris Agency, 151 El Camino Dr, Beverly Hills, CA 90212, USA
Phillips, Harvey *Concert Tuba Player*
%TubaRanch, 4769 S Harrell Road, Bloomington, IN 47401, USA
Phillips, Howard *Public Policy Analyst*
%Conservative Caucus, 47 West St, Boston, MA 02111, USA
Phillips, J Dixon, Jr *Judge*
%US Court of Appeals, 100 Europa Dr, Chapel Hill, NC 27517, USA
Phillips, James (Red) *Football Player*
1948 Wicker Point Road, Alexander City, AL 35010, USA
Phillips, John *Basketball Coach*
%University of Tulsa, Athletic Dept, Tulsa, OK 74104, USA
Phillips, John L *Astronaut*
4422 Cedar Ridge Trail, Houston, TX 77059, USA
Phillips, Julianne *Actress*
2227 Mandeville Canyon Road, Los Angeles, CA 90049, USA
Phillips, Kate *Writer*
%Houghton Mifflin, 222 Berkeley St, #700, Boston, MA 02116, USA
Phillips, Kristie *Gymnast*
610 1st Ave, Asbury Park, NJ 07712, USA
Phillips, Lawrence *Football Player*
9527 Langdon Ave, North Hills, CA 91343, USA
Phillips, Leslie *Actor*
%Storm Artists Mgmt, 47 Brewer St, London W1R 3FD, England
Phillips, Lou Diamond *Actor*
%Paradigm Agency, 10100 Santa Monica Blvd, #2500, Los Angeles, CA 90067, USA
Phillips, Loyd *Football Player*
RR 3, Springdale, AR 72762, USA
Phillips, Mackenzie *Actress*
%S D B Partners, 1801 Ave of Stars, #902, Los Angeles, CA 90067, USA
Phillips, Michelle *Actress, Singer (Mamas & Papas)*
4350 Berryman Ave, #4, Los Angeles, CA 90066, USA
Phillips, Norma *Social Activist*
%Mothers Against Drunk Driving, PO Box 819100, Dallas, TX 75381, USA
Phillips, Owen M *Geophysical Engineer*
23 Merrymount Road, Baltimore, MD 21210, USA
Phillips, Peter C B *Economist*
133 Concord Dr, Madison, CT 06443, USA
Phillips, Phil *Singer, Songwriter*
PO Box 105, Jennings, LA 70546, USA
Phillips, Sam *Singer, Songwriter*
%Prager & Fenton, 12424 Wilshire Blvd, #1000, Los Angeles, CA 90025, USA
Phillips, Scott *Drummer (Creed)*
%Agency Group, 1776 Broadway, #430, New York, NY 10019, USA
Phillips, Sian *Actress*
8 Alexa Court, 78 Lexham Gardens, London W8 6JL, England
Phillips, Stone *Commentator*
%NBC-TV, News Dept, 30 Rockefeller Plaza, New York, NY 10112, USA
Phillips, Susan M *Financier, Government Official*
%Federal Reserve Board, 20th St & Constitution NW, Washington, DC 20551, USA
Phillips, Tari *Basketball Player*
%New York Liberty, Madison Square Garden, 2 Penn Plaza, New York, NY 10121, USA
Phillips, Warren H *Publisher*
%Bridge Works Publications, PO Box 1798, Bridgehampton, NY 11932, USA
Phillips, Wendy *Actress*
1642 Westwood Blvd, #300, Los Angeles, CA 90024, USA
Phillips, William D *Nobel Physics Laureate*
13409 Chestnut Oak Dr, Gaithersburg, MD 20878, USA
Phipps, Michael E (Mike) *Football Player*
2748 NE 26th St, Lighthouse Point, FL 33064, USA
Phoebus, Thomas H (Tom) *Baseball Player*
2822 SW Lakemont Place, Palm City, FL 34990, USA
Phoenix, Joaquin *Actor*
%Endeavor Talent Agency, 9701 Wilshire Blvd, #1000, Beverly Hills, CA 90212, USA

P

Pianalto - Pierce

Pianalto, Sandra *Financier*
%Federal Reserve Bank, 1455 E 6th St, Cleveland, OH 44114, USA
Piano, Renzo *Architect, Pritzker Laureate*
%Renzo Piano Building Workshop, Via Rubens 29, 16158 Genoa, Italy
Piatkowski, Eric *Basketball Player*
%Houston Rockets, Toyota Center, 2 E Greenway Plaza, Houston, TX 77046, USA
Piazza, Michale J (Mike) *Baseball Player*
PO Box 864, Valley Forge, PA 19482, USA
Picardo, Robert *Actor*
%Don Buchwald, 6500 Wilshire Blvd, #2200, Los Angeles, CA 90048, USA
Picasso, Paloma *Jewelry Designer, Actress*
%Quintana Ron Ltd, 291A Brompton Road, London SW3 2DY, England
Piccard, Bertrand *Balloonist*
%Media Impact, Rue de Lausanne 42, 1201 Geneva, Switzerland
Piccard, Jacques E J *Underwater Scientist*
Place d'Armes, 1096 Cully, Switzerland
Piccoli, Camille *Actress*
%Cineart, 36 Rue de Ponthieu, 75008 Paris, France
Piccoli, Michel *Actor*
11 Rue des Lions Saint Paul, 75004 Paris, France
Piccone, Robin *Fashion Designer*
%Piccone Apparel Corp, 1424 Washington Blvd, Venice, CA 90291, USA
Picerni, Paul *Actor*
PO Box 572257, Tarzana, CA 91357, USA
Pichler, Joseph A *Businessman*
%Kroger Co, 1014 Vine St, Cincinnati, OH 45202, USA
Pick, Amelie *Actress*
%Artmedia, 20 Ave Rapp, 75007 Paris, France
Pickard, Nancy *Writer*
2502 W 71st Terrace, Prairie Village, KS 66208, USA
Pickel, Bill *Football Player*
9 Autumn Ridge Road, South Salem, NY 10590, USA
Pickens, Carl M *Football Player*
623 Terrace Ave, Murphy, NC 28906, USA
Pickens, Jo Ann *Opera Singer*
%Norman McCann Artists, 56 Lawrie Park Gardens, London SE26 6XJ, England
Pickens, T Boone, Jr *Businessman*
1 Woodstone St, Amarillo, TX 79106, USA
Pickering, Byron *Artist*
6919 NE Highland Dr, Lincoln City, OR 97367, USA
Pickering, Jeff *Cartoonist (Spats)*
%King Features Syndicate, 888 7th Ave, New York, NY 10106, USA
Pickering, Thomas R *Diplomat, Businessman*
%Boeing Corp, PO Box 3707, Seattle, WA 98124, USA
Pickering, William H *Physicist, Educator*
294 Saint Katherine Dr, Flintridge, CA 91011, USA
Pickett, Bobby (Boris) *Singer*
4015 1/2 Alla Road, Los Angeles, CA 90066, USA
Pickett, Cindy *Actress*
662 N Van Ness Ave, #305, Los Angeles, CA 90004, USA
Pickett, Ryan *Football Player*
%Saint Louis Rams, 901 N Broadway, Saint Louis, MO 63101, USA
Pickett, Wilson *Singer*
%Talent Source, 1560 Broadway, #1308, New York, NY 10036, USA
Pickitt, John L *Air Force General*
38 Sunrise Point Road, Lake Wylie, SC 29710, USA
Pickler, John M *Army General*
Director, Army Staff, HqUSA, Pentagon, Washington, DC 20310, USA
Pickles, Christina *Actress*
137 S Westgate Ave, Los Angeles, CA 90049, USA
Pictor, Bruce *Drummer (Association)*
%Variety Artists, 1924 Spring St, Paso Robles, CA 93446, USA
Pidgeon, Rebecca *Actress*
%Julian Belfarge, 46 Albermarle St, London W1X 4PP, England
Piech, Ferdinand *Businessman*
%Volkswagenwerk AG, Braunschweiger Str 63, 38179 Schwulper, Germany
Piel, Gerard *Editor, Publisher*
%Scientific American Magazine, 415 Madison Ave, New York, NY 10017, USA
Piel, Jonathan *Editor*
%Scientific American Magazine, 415 Madison Ave, New York, NY 10017, USA
Pienaar, Jacobus F *Rugby Player*
%Rugby Football Union, PO Box 99, Newlands 7725, South Africa
Piene, Otto *Sculptor*
383 Old Ayer Road, Groton, MA 01450, USA
Pierce, Chester M *Psychiatrist*
17 Prince St, Jamaica Plain, MA 02130, USA
Pierce, David Hyde *Actor*
4724 Cromwell, Los Angeles, CA 90027, USA

Pierce, Jill *Actress*
%Extreme Team Productions, 15941 S Harlem, #319, Tinley Park, IL 60477, USA
Pierce, Jonathan *Singer*
%Muse Assoc, 330 Franklin Road, #135-8, Brentwood, TN 37027, USA
Pierce, Lincoln *Cartoonist (Big Nate)*
%United Feature Syndicate, 200 Madison Ave, New York, NY 10016, USA
Pierce, Mary *Tennis Player*
6023 26th St W, #113, Bradenton, FL 34207, USA
Pierce, Paul *Basketball Player*
%Boston Celtics, 151 Merrimac St, #1, Boston, MA 02114, USA
Pierce, Stack *Actor*
%Haeggstrom Office, 11288 Ventura Blvd, #620, Studio City, CA 91604, USA
Pierce, W William (Billy) *Baseball Player*
1321 Baileys Crossing Dr, Lemont, IL 60439, USA
Pierce, Wendell *Actor*
%Writers & Artists, 8383 Wilshire Blvd, #550, Beverly Hills, CA 90211, USA
Pierce-Roberts, Tony *Cinematographer*
1 Princes Gardens, London W5 1SD, England
Piercy, Marge *Writer*
PO Box 1473, Wellfleet, MA 02667, USA
Pierpoint, Eric *Actor*
2199 Topanga Skyline Dr, Topanga, CA 90290, USA
Pierpoint, Robert *Commentator*
%CBS-TV, News Dept, 2020 M St NW, Washington, DC 20036, USA
Pierre of Normandy, Abbe *Religious Leader, Social Activist*
La Halte d'Emmaus, 76690 Esteville, France
Pierre, Andrew J *Political Scientist*
%Carnegie Endowment for Peace, 1779 Massachusetts NW, Washington, DC 20036, USA
Piersall, James A (Jimmy) *Baseball Player*
12462 N 72nd Place, Scottsdale, AZ 85260, USA
Pierson, Frank R *Movie, Television Director, Writer*
1223 Amalfi Dr, Pacific Palisades, CA 90272, USA
Pierson, Kate *Singer (B-52's)*
%Direct Management Group, 947 N La Cienega Blvd, #2, Los Angeles, CA 90069, USA
Pierson, Markus *Sculptor*
%OutWest, 7216 Washington St NE, #A, Albuquerque, NM 87109, USA
Pierzynski, Anthony J (A J) *Baseball Player*
5209 Pleasure Island Road, Orlando, FL 32809, USA
Pietrangeli, Nicola *Tennis Player*
Via Eustachio Manfredi 15, Rome, Italy
Pietrangelo, Frank *Hockey Player*
11 Buttonwood Lane, Avon, CT 06001, USA
Pietrus, Mickael *Basketball Player*
%Golden State Warriors, 1001 Broadway, Oakland, CA 94607, USA
Pietruski, John M, Jr *Businessman*
27 Paddock Lane, Colts Neck, NJ 07722, USA
Pietrzykowski, Zbigniew *Boxer*
Ul Gomicza 5, Bielsko-Blata 43-409, Poland
Pietz, Amy *Actress*
%Geddes Agency, 8430 Santa Monica Blvd, #200, West Hollywood, CA 90069, USA
Piggott, Lester K *Thoroughbred Racing Jockey*
Beech Tree House, Tostock, Bury Saint Edmonds, Suffolk 1P30 9NY, England
Pigott, Mark C *Businessman*
%PACCAR Inc, 777 106th Ave NE, Bellevue, WA 98004, USA
Pigott-Smith, Tim *Actor*
%P F D, Drury House, 34-43 Russell St, London WC2B 5HA, England
Pihos, Peter L (Pete) *Football Player*
2755 Winslow Lane, Winston Salem, NC 27103, USA
Pikaizen, Viktor A *Concert Violinist*
Chekhova Str 31/22, #37, Moscow, Russia
Pike, Gary *Singer (Lettermen)*
10031 Benares Place, Sun Valley, CA 91352, USA
Pike, Jim *Singer (Lettermen)*
%MPI Talent Agency, 9255 Sunset Blvd, #407, Los Angeles, CA 90069, USA
Pilarczyk, Daniel E *Religious Leader*
100 E 8th St, Cincinnati, OH 45202, USA
Pileggi, Mitch *Actor*
26893 Bouquet Canyon Road, #C237, Santa Clarita, CA 91350, USA
Pileggi, Nicholas *Writer*
%Creative Artists Agency, 9830 Wilshire Blvd, Beverly Hills, CA 90212, USA
Pilic, Nicki *Tennis Player*
%DTB, Otto-Fleck-Schneise 8, 60528 Frankfurt/Maim, Germany
Pilkis, Simon J *Physiologist, Biophysicist*
%State University of New York, Health Sciences Center, Stony Brook, NY 11794, USA
Pilla, Anthony M *Religious Leader*
%Catholic Bishops National Conference, 3211 4th St, Washington, DC 20017, USA
Pilliod, Charles J, Jr *Diplomat, Businessman*
494 Saint Andrews Dr, Akron, OH 44303, USA

P

Pillow, Ray *Singer*
%Joe Taylor Artist Agency, 2802 Columbine Place, Nashville, TN 37204, USA
Pillsbury, Edmund P *Museum Director*
3601 Potomac Ave, Fort Worth, TX 76107, USA
Pilote, Pierre P *Hockey Player*
25 Mary Jane, Elmwood ON L0L 2PO, Canada
Pilson, Neal H *Television Producer*
%CBS-TV, Sports Dept, 51 W 52nd St, New York, NY 10019, USA
Pimenta, Simon Ignatius Cardinal *Religious Leader*
%Archbishop's House, 21 Nathalal Parekh Marg, Bombay 400 039, India
Pincay, Laffit, Jr *Thoroughbred Racing Jockey*
5200 Los Grandes Way, Los Angeles, CA 90027, USA
Pinchot, Bronson *Actor*
10061 Riverside Dr, Toluca Lake, CA 91602, USA
Pinckney, Ed *Basketball Player*
6 Coconut Lane, Miami, FL 33149, USA
Pinckney, Sandra *Chef*
%Food Network, 1180 Ave of Americas, #1200, New York, NY 10036, USA
Pinder, Michael (Mike) *Keyboardist (Moody Blues)*
%Moody Blues, 53-55 High St, Cobham, Surrey KT11 3DP, England
Pine, Courtney *Jazz Saxophonist*
%Elizabeth Rush Agency, 100 Park St, #4, Montclair, NJ 07042, USA
Pine, Robert *Actor*
4212 Ben Ave, Studio City, CA 91604, USA
Pineau-Valencienne, Didier *Businessman*
%Schneider, 64/70 J Baptiste Clement, 92646 Boulogne-Billancourt, France
Pinera, Mike *Singer, Guitarist*
18407 Chase St, Northridge, CA 91325, USA
Pines, Alexander *Chemist*
%University of California, Chemistry Dept, Hildebrand Hall, Berkeley, CA 94720, USA
Ping Lu, Kun *Biochemist*
%Beth Israel Deaconess Medical Center, 3300 Brookline Ave, Boston, MA 02215, USA
Pingel, John S *Football Player*
80 Celestial Way, #203, Juno Beach, FL 33408, USA
Pinger, Mark *Swimmer*
5201 Orduna Dr, #6, Coral Gables, FL 33146, USA
Piniella, Louis V (Lou) *Baseball Player, Manager*
1005 Taray De Avila, Tampa, FL 33613, USA
Pink *Singer*
%Lindsey Scott, 8899 Beverly Blvd, #, Los Angeles, CA 90048, USA
Pinkel, Donald P *Pediatrician*
275 Marlene Dr, San Luis Obispo, CA 93405, USA
Pinkel, Gary *Football Coach*
%University of Missouri, Athletic Dept, Columbia, MO 64211, USA
Pinkett Smith, Jada *Actress*
%Endeavor Talent Agency, 9701 Wilshire Blvd, #1000, Beverly Hills, CA 90212, USA
Pinkett, Allen *Football Player*
1849 Portsmouth St, Houston, TX 77098, USA
Pinkham, Daniel R, Jr *Composer*
150 Chilton St, Cambridge, MA 02138, USA
Pinkins, Tonya *Actress*
%Innovative Artists, 1505 10th St, Santa Monica, CA 90401, USA
Pinkney, Bill *Singer (Drifters)*
%Superstars Unlimited, PO Box 371371, Las Vegas, NV 89137, USA
Pinnock, Trevor *Conductor, Concert Harpsichordist*
35 Gloucester Crescent, London NW1 7DL, England
Pinos, Carmen *Architect*
Av Diagonal 490, #3/2, 08006 Barcelona, Spain
Pinsky, Robert N *Writer*
%Boston University, Creative Writing Dept, 236 Bay State Road, Boston, MA 02215, USA
Pinson, Julie *Actress*
13576 Cheltenham Dr, Sherman Oaks, CA 91423, USA
Pintasilgo, Maria de Lourdes *Prime Minister, Portugal*
Alameda Santo Antonio dos Capuchos 4-5, 1150 Lisbon, Portugal
Pintauro, Danny *Actor*
%FHL, 10667 Adamsong Ave, Las Vegas, NV 89135, USA
Pinter, Harold *Writer*
%Judy Daish, 2 Saint Charles Place, London W10 6EG, England
Pintilie, Lucian *Theater, Movie Director*
44 Mihail Kogalniceanu Blvd, Bucharest, Romania
Pintscher, Matthias *Composer*
%Van Walsum Mgmt, 4 Addison Bridge Place, London W14 8XP, England
Piovanelli, Silvano Cardinal *Religious Leader*
Piazzi S Giovanni 3, 50129 Florence, Italy
Piper, Jacki *Actress*
%Langford Assoc, 17 Westfields Ave, Barnes, London SW13 0AT, England
Piper, Roddy *Wrestler, Actor*
18645 SW Farmington Road, #312, Aloha, OR 97007, USA

Pipes, R Byron *Educator*
PO Box 1147, Hudson, OH 44236, USA
Pippard, A Brian *Physicist*
30 Porson Road, Cambridge CB2 2EU, England
Pippen, Scottie *Basketball Player*
%Chicago Bulls, United Center, 1901 W Madison St, Chicago, IL 60612, USA
Pippig, Uta *Track Athlete*
4279 Niblick Dr, Longmont, CO 80503, USA
Piquet, Nelson *Auto Racing Driver*
%Autodromo, SEN/CDPM, Rua da Gasolina #01, 7007-400 Brasilia DF, Brazil
Piraro, Dan *Cartoonist (Bizarro)*
%United Feature Syndicate, 200 Madison Ave, New York, NY 10016, USA
Pirelli, Leopoldo *Businessman*
Via Gaetano Negri 10, 20123 Milan, Italy
Pires de Miranda, Pedro *Government Official, Portugal*
Avenida da India 10, 1300 Lisbon, Portugal
Pires, Mary Joao *Concert Pianist*
%Columbia Artists Mgmt Inc, 165 W 57th St, New York, NY 10019, USA
Pires, Pedro V R *Prime Minister, Cape Verde; Army General*
%PAICV, CP 22, Praia, Santiago, Cape Verde
Pirner, Dave *Singer (Soul Asylum), Songwriter*
%Monterey Peninsula Artists, 509 Hartnell St, Monterey, CA 93940, USA
Piro, Stephanie *Cartoonist (Six Chix)*
PO Box 605, Hampton, NH 03843, USA
Pischetsrider, Bernd *Businessman*
%Bayerishe Motoren Werke, Petuelring 130, 80788 Munich, Germany
Piscopo, Joe *Actor, Comedian*
PO Box 258, Bernardsville, NJ 07924, USA
Pisier, Marie-France *Actress*
%Gaumont International, 30 Ave Charles de Gaulle, 92200 Neuilly, France
Pister, Karl S *Educator*
%University of California, Chancellor's Office, Santa Cruz, CA 95064, USA
Pistone, Tom *Auto Racing Driver*
4405 Woodwind St, Charlotte, NC 28213, USA
Pitel, Piyush *Businessman*
%Cabletron Systems, 35 Industrial Way, Rochester, NY 14614, USA
Pithart, Petr *Government Official, Czech Republic*
%Senate, Vakdstejnske Nam 4, 118 11 Prague, Czech Republic
Pitillo, Maria *Actress*
%William Morris Agency, 151 El Camino Dr, Beverly Hills, CA 90212, USA
Pitino, Richard (Rick) *Basketball Coach*
%University of Louisville, Crawford Gym, Louisville, KY 40292, USA
Pitman, Jennifer S *Thoroughbred Racing Trainer*
Weathercock House, Upper Lambourn, Hungerford, Berks RG17 8QT, England
Pitney, Gene *Singer, Songwriter*
6201 39th Ave, Kenosha, WI 53142, USA
Pitou Zimmerman, Penny *Alpine Skier*
560 Sanborn Road, Sanbornton, NH 03269, USA
Pitt, Brad *Actor*
%Brillstein/Grey, 9150 Wilshire Blvd, #350, Beverly Hills, CA 90212, USA
Pitt, Eugene *Singer (Jive Five)*
%Paramount Entertainment, PO Box 12, Far Hills, NJ 07931, USA
Pitt, Ingrid *Actress*
%Langford, 17 Westfields Ave, London SW13 0AT, England
Pitt, Michael *Actor*
%United Talent Agency, 9560 Wilshire Blvd, #500, Beverly Hills, CA 90212, USA
Pittenger, Mark F *Medical Reseacher*
%Osiris Therapeutics, 2001 Aliceanna St, Baltimore, MD 21231, USA
Pittman, Charles *Basketball Player*
16286 N 29th Dr, Phoenix, AZ 85053, USA
Pittman, James A, Jr *Endocrinologist*
5 Ridge Dr, Birmingham, AL 35213, USA
Pittman, R F *Publisher*
%Tampa Tribune, 202 S Parker St, Tampa, FL 33606, USA
Pittman, Richard A *Vietnam War Marine Corps Hero (CMH)*
5380 Dehesa Road, El Cajon, CA 92019, USA
Pitts, Robert (R C) *Basketball Player*
12655 E Milburn Ave, Baton Rouge, LA 70815, USA
Pitts, Ron *Sportscaster*
%Fox-TV, Sports Dept, 205 W 67th St, New York, NY 10021, USA
Pitts, Tyrone S *Religious Leader*
%Progressive National Baptist Convention, 601 50th St NE, Washington, DC 20019, USA
Piven, Jeremy *Actor*
150 S Rodeo Dr, #300, Beverly Hills, CA 90212, USA
Piza, Arthur Luiz de *Artist*
16 Rue Dauphine, 75006 Paris, France
Pizarro, Artur *Concert Pianist*
%Musicians Corporate Mgmt, PO Box 589, Millbrook, NY 12545, USA

P

Place, Mary Kay *Actress*
2739 Motor Ave, Los Angeles, CA 90064, USA
Plachta, Leonard E *Educator*
%Central Michigan University, President's Office, Mount Pleasant, MI 48859, USA
Plager, Robert B (Bob) *Hockey Player, Coach, Executive*
362 Branchport Dr, Chesterfield, MO 63017, USA
Plager, S Jay *Judge*
%US Court of Appeals, 7171 Madison Place NW, Washington, DC 20439, USA
Plain, Belva *Writer*
%Houghton Mifflin, 215 Park Ave S, New York, NY 10003, USA
Plainic, Zoran *Basketball Player*
%New Jersey Nets, 390 Murray Hill Parkway, East Rutherford, NJ 07073, USA
Plakson, Suzie *Actress*
302 N La Brea Ave, #363, Los Angeles, CA 90036, USA
Plana, Tony *Actor*
%Metropolitan Talent Agency, 4526 Wilshire Blvd, Los Angeles, CA 90010, USA
Planchon, Roger *Theater Director, Writer*
%Teatre National Populaire, 8 Pl Lazare Goujon, 69627 Villeurbanne, France
Planinc, Milka *Prime Minister, Yugoslavia*
%Fed Exec Council, Bul Lenjina 2, 11075 Novi Belgrad, Serbia-Montenegro
Plank, Raymond *Businessman*
%Apache Corp, 2000 Post Oak Blvd, Houston, TX 77056, USA
Plano, Richard J *Physicist*
PO Box 5306, Somerset, NJ 08875, USA
Plant, Robert *Singer, Songwriter*
%Trinifold Mgmt, 12 Oval Road, London NW1 7DH, England
Plante, Bruce *Editorial Cartoonist*
%Chattanooga Times, Editorial Dept, 100 E 11th St, #400, Chattanooga, TN 37402, USA
Plante, William M *Commentator*
%CBS-TV, News Dept, 2020 M St NW, Washington, DC 20036, USA
Plantu *Editorial Cartoonist*
%Le Monde, Editorial Dept, 21 Bis Rue Claude Bernard, 75005 Paris, France
Plaskett, Thomas G *Businessman*
5215 N O'Connor Blvd, #1070, Irving, TX 75039, USA
Plater-Zyberk, Elizabeth M *Architect*
%Duany & Plater-Zyberk Architects, 1023 SW 25th Ave, Miami, FL 33135, USA
Platini, Michel *Soccer Player*
%World Cup Organization, 17-21 Ave Gen Mangin, 75024 Paris Cedex, France
Platon, Nicolas *Archaeologist*
Leof Alexandras 126, 11471 Athens, Greece
Platov, Yevgeni *Ice Dancer*
%Connecticut Skating Center, 300 Alumni Road, Newington, CT 06111, USA
Platt, Kenneth A *Physician*
11435 Quivas Way, Westminster, CO 80234, USA
Platt, Lewis E (Lew) *Businessman*
%Hewlett-Packard Co, 3000 Hanover St, Palo Alto, CA 94304, USA
Platt, Nicholas *Diplomat*
131 E 69th St, New York, NY 10021, USA
Platt, Oliver *Actor*
%Three Arts Entertainment, 9460 Wilshire Blvd, #700, Beverly Hills, CA 90212, USA
Plavinsky, Dmitri P *Artist*
Arbat Str 51, Kotp 2, #97, 121002 Moscow, Russia
Player, Gary J *Golfer*
3930 RCA Blvd, #3001, Palm Beach Gardens, FL 33410, USA
Playten, Alice *Actress*
33 5th Ave, New York, NY 10003, USA
Pleau, Lawrence W (Larry) *Hockey Player, Coach*
650 Spyglass Summit Dr, Chesterfield, MO 63017, USA
Pleshette, John *Actor*
2643 Creston Dr, Los Angeles, CA 90068, USA
Pleshette, Suzanne *Actress*
10375 Wilshire Blvd, #5B, Los Angeles, CA 90024, USA
Pletcher, Eldon *Editorial Cartoonist*
210 Canberra Court, Slidell, LA 70458, USA
Pletnev, Mikhail V *Conductor, Concert Pianist*
Starpkonyushenny Per 33, #16, Moscow, Russia
Plimpton, Calvin H *Physician*
%Downstate Medical Center, 450 Clarkson Ave, Brooklyn, NY 11203, USA
Plimpton, Martha *Actress*
502 Park Ave, #15G, New York, NY 10022, USA
Plisetskaya, Maiya M *Ballerina*
Tverskaya 25/9, #31, 103050 Moscow, Russia
Pliska, Paul *Opera Singer*
%George M Martynuk, 352 7th Ave, New York, NY 10001, USA
Plotkin, Stanley A *Virologist*
3940 Delancey St, Philadelphia, PA 19104, USA
Plott, Charles R *Economist*
881 El Campo Dr, Pasadena, CA 91107, USA

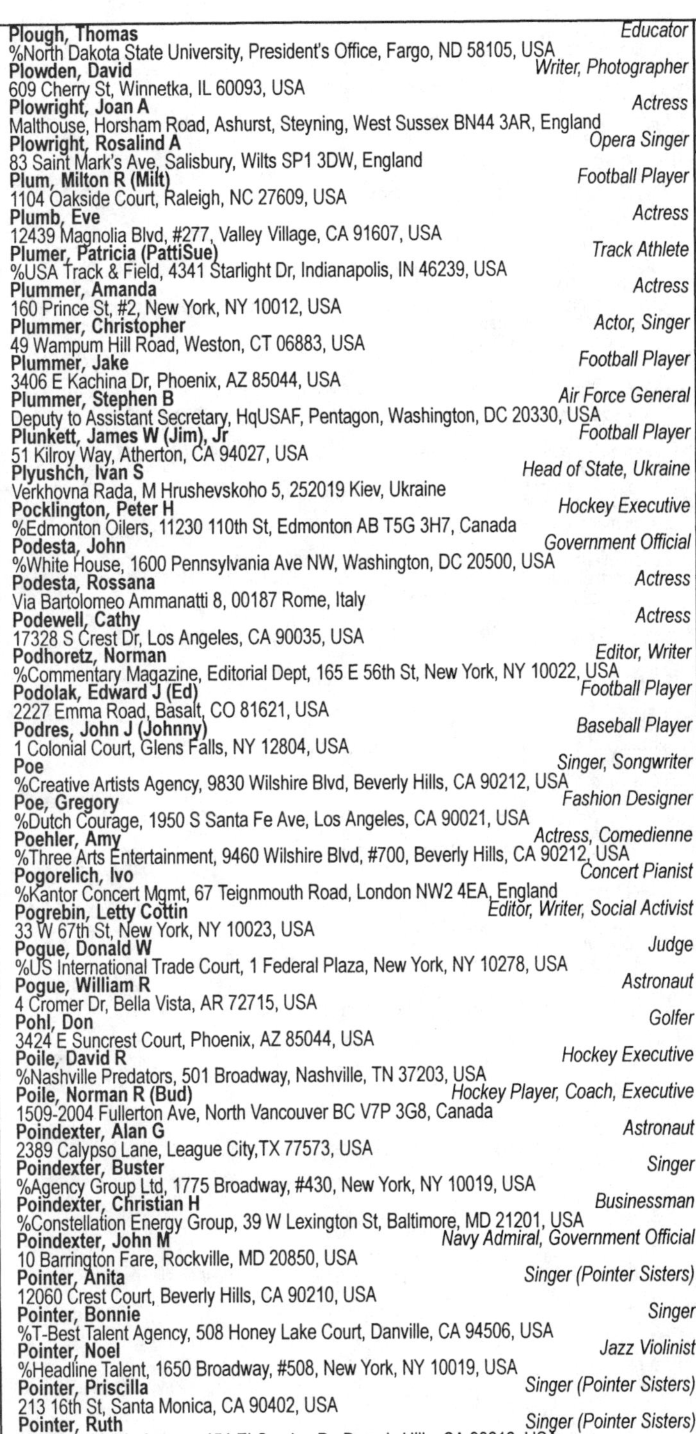

Plough, Thomas *Educator*
%North Dakota State University, President's Office, Fargo, ND 58105, USA

Plowden, David *Writer, Photographer*
609 Cherry St, Winnetka, IL 60093, USA

Plowright, Joan A *Actress*
Malthouse, Horsham Road, Ashurst, Steyning, West Sussex BN44 3AR, England

Plowright, Rosalind A *Opera Singer*
83 Saint Mark's Ave, Salisbury, Wilts SP1 3DW, England

Plum, Milton R (Milt) *Football Player*
1104 Oakside Court, Raleigh, NC 27609, USA

Plumb, Eve *Actress*
12439 Magnolia Blvd, #277, Valley Village, CA 91607, USA

Plumer, Patricia (PattiSue) *Track Athlete*
%USA Track & Field, 4341 Starlight Dr, Indianapolis, IN 46239, USA

Plummer, Amanda *Actress*
160 Prince St, #2, New York, NY 10012, USA

Plummer, Christopher *Actor, Singer*
49 Wampum Hill Road, Weston, CT 06883, USA

Plummer, Jake *Football Player*
3406 E Kachina Dr, Phoenix, AZ 85044, USA

Plummer, Stephen B *Air Force General*
Deputy to Assistant Secretary, HqUSAF, Pentagon, Washington, DC 20330, USA

Plunkett, James W (Jim), Jr *Football Player*
51 Kilroy Way, Atherton, CA 94027, USA

Plyushch, Ivan S *Head of State, Ukraine*
Verkhovna Rada, M Hrushevskoho 5, 252019 Kiev, Ukraine

Pocklington, Peter H *Hockey Executive*
%Edmonton Oilers, 11230 110th St, Edmonton AB T5G 3H7, Canada

Podesta, John *Government Official*
%White House, 1600 Pennsylvania Ave NW, Washington, DC 20500, USA

Podesta, Rossana *Actress*
Via Bartolomeo Ammanatti 8, 00187 Rome, Italy

Podewell, Cathy *Actress*
17328 S Crest Dr, Los Angeles, CA 90035, USA

Podhoretz, Norman *Editor, Writer*
%Commentary Magazine, Editorial Dept, 165 E 56th St, New York, NY 10022, USA

Podolak, Edward J (Ed) *Football Player*
2227 Emma Road, Basalt, CO 81621, USA

Podres, John J (Johnny) *Baseball Player*
1 Colonial Court, Glens Falls, NY 12804, USA

Poe *Singer, Songwriter*
%Creative Artists Agency, 9830 Wilshire Blvd, Beverly Hills, CA 90212, USA

Poe, Gregory *Fashion Designer*
%Dutch Courage, 1950 S Santa Fe Ave, Los Angeles, CA 90021, USA

Poehler, Amy *Actress, Comedienne*
%Three Arts Entertainment, 9460 Wilshire Blvd, #700, Beverly Hills, CA 90212, USA

Pogorelich, Ivo *Concert Pianist*
%Kantor Concert Mgmt, 67 Teignmouth Road, London NW2 4EA, England

Pogrebin, Letty Cottin *Editor, Writer, Social Activist*
33 W 67th St, New York, NY 10023, USA

Pogue, Donald W *Judge*
%US International Trade Court, 1 Federal Plaza, New York, NY 10278, USA

Pogue, William R *Astronaut*
4 Cromer Dr, Bella Vista, AR 72715, USA

Pohl, Don *Golfer*
3424 E Suncrest Court, Phoenix, AZ 85044, USA

Poile, David R *Hockey Executive*
%Nashville Predators, 501 Broadway, Nashville, TN 37203, USA

Poile, Norman R (Bud) *Hockey Player, Coach, Executive*
1509-2004 Fullerton Ave, North Vancouver BC V7P 3G8, Canada

Poindexter, Alan G *Astronaut*
2389 Calypso Lane, League City,TX 77573, USA

Poindexter, Buster *Singer*
%Agency Group Ltd, 1775 Broadway, #430, New York, NY 10019, USA

Poindexter, Christian H *Businessman*
%Constellation Energy Group, 39 W Lexington St, Baltimore, MD 21201, USA

Poindexter, John M *Navy Admiral, Government Official*
10 Barrington Fare, Rockville, MD 20850, USA

Pointer, Anita *Singer (Pointer Sisters)*
12060 Crest Court, Beverly Hills, CA 90210, USA

Pointer, Bonnie *Singer*
%T-Best Talent Agency, 508 Honey Lake Court, Danville, CA 94506, USA

Pointer, Noel *Jazz Violinist*
%Headline Talent, 1650 Broadway, #508, New York, NY 10019, USA

Pointer, Priscilla *Singer (Pointer Sisters)*
213 16th St, Santa Monica, CA 90402, USA

Pointer, Ruth *Singer (Pointer Sisters)*
%William Morris Agency, 151 El Camino Dr, Beverly Hills, CA 90212, USA

Poitier, Sidney *Actor*
%Creative Artists Agency, 9830 Wilshire Blvd, Beverly Hills, CA 90212, USA
Polamalu, Troy *Football Player*
%Pittsburgh Steelers, 3400 S Water St, Pittsburgh, PA 15203, USA
Polanski, Roman *Movie Director*
%Agents Associes Beaume, 201 Faubourg Saint Honore, 75008 Paris, France
Polansky, Mark *Astronaut*
2010 Hillside Oak Lane, Houston, TX 77062, USA
Polanyi, John C *Nobel Chemistry Laureate*
142 Collier St, Toronto ON M4W 1M3, Canada
Polchinski, Joseph G *Physicist*
%University of California, Physics Institute, Santa Barbara, CA 93106, USA
Poledouris, Basil *Composer*
%Kraft-Benjamin-Engel, 15233 Ventura Blvd, #200, Sherman Oaks, CA 91403, USA
Poleshchuk, Alexander F *Cosmonaut*
%Potchta Kosmonavtov, Moskovskoi Oblasti, 141160 Syvisdny Goroduk, Russia
Poletto, Severino Cardinal *Religious Leader*
Via Arcivescovado 12, 10121 Torino, Italy
Polgar, Laszlo *Opera Singer*
Abel Jeno Utca 12, 1113 Budapest, Hungary
Polic, Henry, II *Actor*
%Sutton Barth Vennari, 145 S Fairfax Ave, #310, Los Angeles, CA 90036, USA
Polish, Michael *Movie Director*
%Endeavor Talent Agency, 9701 Wilshire Blvd, #1000, Beverly Hills, CA 90212, USA
Politz, Henry A *Judge*
%US Court of Appeals, 500 Fannin St, Shreveport, LA 71101, USA
Polk, Steven R *Air Force General*
Vice Commander, Pacific Air Forces, Hickam Air Force Base, HI 96853, USA
Polke, Sigmar *Artist*
%Michael Werner, 4 E 77th St, #200, New York, NY 10021, USA
Polkinghorne, John C *Theologian, Physicist*
%Queen's College, Cambridge University, Cambridge CB3 9ET, England
Poll, Martin H *Movie Producer*
%Martin Poll Productions, 8961 Sunset Blvd, #E, Los Angeles, CA 90069, USA
Polla, Dennis L *Microbiotics Engineer*
%University of Minnesota, Electrical Engineering Dept, Minneapolis, MN 55455, USA
Pollack, Andrea *Swimmer*
%SSV, Postfach 420140, 34070 Kassel, Germany
Pollack, Daniel *Concert Pianist*
%University of Southern California, Music Dept, Los Angeles, CA 90089, USA
Pollack, Jim *Actor*
%Ericka Wain, 1418 N Highland Ave, #102, Los Angeles, CA 90028, USA
Pollack, Joseph *Labor Leader*
%Insurance Workers Union, 1017 12th St NW, Washington, DC 20005, USA
Pollack, Kevin *Actor*
%International Creative Mgmt, 8942 Wilshire Blvd, #219, Beverly Hills, CA 90211, USA
Pollack, Sam *Hockey Executive*
6811 Monkland Ave, Montreal QC H4B 1J2, Canada
Pollack, Sydney *Movie Director, Actor*
%The Firm, 9100 Wilshire Blvd, #100W, Beverly Hills, CA 90210, USA
Pollak, Cheryl A *Actress*
%Kritzer, 12200 W Olympic Blvd, #400, Los Angeles, CA 90064, USA
Pollak, Kevin *Actor, Comedian*
12021 Wilshire Blvd, Los Angeles, CA 90025, USA
Pollak, Lisa *Journalist*
%Baltimore Sun, Editorial Dept, 501 N Calvert St, Baltimore, MD 21202, USA
Pollan, Tracy *Actress*
%Baker/Winokur/Ryder, 9100 Wilshire Blvd, #600, Beverly Hills, CA 90212, USA
Pollard, Michael J *Actor*
520 S Burnside Ave, #12A, Los Angeles, CA 90036, USA
Pollard, Scott *Basketball Player*
%Indiana Pacers, Conseco Fieldhouse, 125 S Pennsylvania, Indianapolis, IN 46204, USA
Pollen, Arabella R H *Fashion Designer*
Canham Mews, #8, Canham Road, London W3 7SR, England
Polley, Eugene J *Inventor (Flash-Matic Remote Control)*
202 W Berkshire Ave, Lombard, IL 60148, USA
Polley, Sarah *Actress*
10 Mary St, #308, Toronto ON M4Y 1P9, Canada
Pollin, Abe *Basketball, Hockey Executive*
%Centre Group, Capital Centre, 1 Truman Dr, Landover, MD 20785, USA
Pollini, Maurizio *Concert Pianist*
%RESIA, Via Manzoni 31, 20120 Milan, Italy
Pollock, Alex J *Businessman*
%Federal Home Loan Bank, 111 E Wacker Dr, Chicago, IL 60601, USA
Pollock, Michael P *Navy Admiral, England*
Ivy House, Churchstoke, Montgomery, Powys SY15 6DU, Wales
Poloujadoff, Michel E *Electrical Engineer*
8 Rue Roches, 77760 Buthiers, France

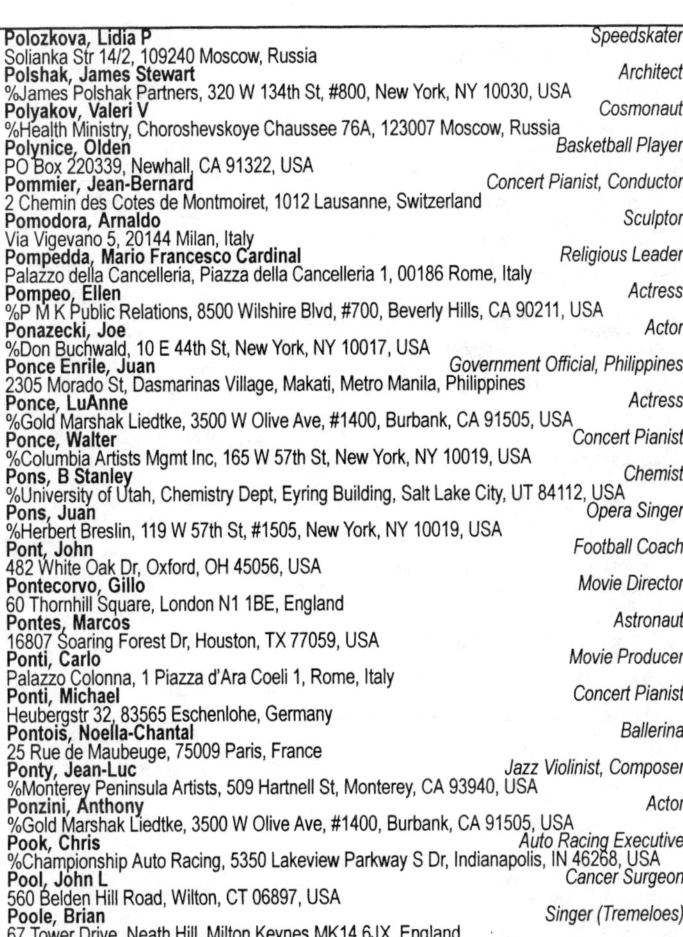

Polozkova, Lidia P *Speedskater*
Solianka Str 14/2, 109240 Moscow, Russia
Polshak, James Stewart *Architect*
%James Polshak Partners, 320 W 134th St, #800, New York, NY 10030, USA
Polyakov, Valeri V *Cosmonaut*
%Health Ministry, Choroshevskoye Chaussee 76A, 123007 Moscow, Russia
Polynice, Olden *Basketball Player*
PO Box 220339, Newhall, CA 91322, USA
Pommier, Jean-Bernard *Concert Pianist, Conductor*
2 Chemin des Cotes de Montmoiret, 1012 Lausanne, Switzerland
Pomodora, Arnaldo *Sculptor*
Via Vigevano 5, 20144 Milan, Italy
Pompedda, Mario Francesco Cardinal *Religious Leader*
Palazzo della Cancelleria, Piazza della Cancelleria 1, 00186 Rome, Italy
Pompeo, Ellen *Actress*
%P M K Public Relations, 8500 Wilshire Blvd, #700, Beverly Hills, CA 90211, USA
Ponazecki, Joe *Actor*
%Don Buchwald, 10 E 44th St, New York, NY 10017, USA
Ponce Enrile, Juan *Government Official, Philippines*
2305 Morado St, Dasmarinas Village, Makati, Metro Manila, Philippines
Ponce, LuAnne *Actress*
%Gold Marshak Liedtke, 3500 W Olive Ave, #1400, Burbank, CA 91505, USA
Ponce, Walter *Concert Pianist*
%Columbia Artists Mgmt Inc, 165 W 57th St, New York, NY 10019, USA
Pons, B Stanley *Chemist*
%University of Utah, Chemistry Dept, Eyring Building, Salt Lake City, UT 84112, USA
Pons, Juan *Opera Singer*
%Herbert Breslin, 119 W 57th St, #1505, New York, NY 10019, USA
Pont, John *Football Coach*
482 White Oak Dr, Oxford, OH 45056, USA
Pontecorvo, Gillo *Movie Director*
60 Thornhill Square, London N1 1BE, England
Pontes, Marcos *Astronaut*
16807 Soaring Forest Dr, Houston, TX 77059, USA
Ponti, Carlo *Movie Producer*
Palazzo Colonna, 1 Piazza d'Ara Coeli 1, Rome, Italy
Ponti, Michael *Concert Pianist*
Heubergstr 32, 83565 Eschenlohe, Germany
Pontois, Noella-Chantal *Ballerina*
25 Rue de Maubeuge, 75009 Paris, France
Ponty, Jean-Luc *Jazz Violinist, Composer*
%Monterey Peninsula Artists, 509 Hartnell St, Monterey, CA 93940, USA
Ponzini, Anthony *Actor*
%Gold Marshak Liedtke, 3500 W Olive Ave, #1400, Burbank, CA 91505, USA
Pook, Chris *Auto Racing Executive*
%Championship Auto Racing, 5350 Lakeview Parkway S Dr, Indianapolis, IN 46268, USA
Pool, John L *Cancer Surgeon*
560 Belden Hill Road, Wilton, CT 06897, USA
Poole, Brian *Singer (Tremeloes)*
67 Tower Drive, Neath Hill, Milton Keynes MK14 6JX, England
Poole, David J *Artist*
Trinity Flint Barn, Weston Lane, Petersfield Hants GU32 3NN, England
Poole, G Barney *Football Player*
213 E Railroad Ave, Gloster, MS 39638, USA
Poole, William *Government Official, Economist*
%Federal Reserve Bank, 411 Locust St, Saint Louis, MO 63102, USA
Pooley, Don *Golfer*
5251 N Camino Sumo, Tucson, AZ 85718, USA
Poons, Larry *Artist*
PO Box 115, Islamorada, FL 33036, USA
Pop, Iggy *Singer, Songwriter, Actor*
%MVO Ltd, 307 7th Ave, #807, New York, NY 10001, USA
Pope, Carly *Actress*
%Handprint Entertainment, 1100 Glendon Ave, #1000, Los Angeles, CA 90024, USA
Pope, Clarence C, Jr *Religious Leader*
%Fort Worth Episcopal Church Diocese, 6300 Ridlea Place, Fort Worth, TX 76116, USA
Pope, Eddie *Soccer Player*
%New York/New Jersey MetroStars, 1 Harmon Plaza, #300, Secaucus, NJ 07094, USA
Pope, Edwin *Sportswriter*
%Miami Herald, Editorial Dept, 1 Herald Plaza, Miami, FL 33132, USA
Pope, Everett P *WW II Marine Corps Hero (CMH)*
16 Osprey Village Dr, Fernandina, FL 32034, USA
Pope, Marquez P *Football Player*
PO Box 470487, San Francisco, CA 94147, USA
Pope, Odeon *Jazz Trumpeter, Bandleader*
%Brad Simon Organization, 122 E 57th St, #300, New York, NY 10022, USA
Popiel, Poul P *Hockey Player*
2501 Peppermill Ridge Dr, Chesterfield, MO 63005, USA

P

Pople, John A *Nobel Chemistry Laureate*
770 S Palm Ave, #1103, Sarasota, FL 34236, USA
Popoff, A Jay *Singer (Lit)*
%Sepetys Entertainment, 1223 Wilshire Blvd, #804, Santa Monica, CA 90403, USA
Popoff, Frank P *Businessman*
%Dow Chemical, 2030 Dow Center, Midland, MI 48674, USA
Popov, Aleksandr *Swimmer*
%Swimming Assn, Sports House, Maitland Road, #7, Hackett 2602, Australia
Popov, Leonid I *Cosmonaut*
%Potchta Kosmonavtov, Moskovskoi Oblasti, 141160 Syvisdny Goroduk, Russia
Popovac, Gwynn *Artist*
17270 Robin Ridge, Sonora, CA 95370, USA
Popovich, Gregg *Basketball Executive, Coach*
%San Antonio Spurs, Alamodome, 1 SBC Center, San Antonio, TX 78219, USA
Popovich, Pavel R *Cosmonaut, Air Force General*
%AIUS-Agroressurs, VNIZ, Bolshevitskij Per 11, 101000 Moscow, Russia
Popp, Nathaniel *Religious Leader*
%Romanian Orthodox Episcopate, PO Box 309, Grass Lake, MI 49240, USA
Popper, John *Harmonica Player (Blues Traveler)*
%ArtistDirect, 10900 Wilshire Blvd, #1400, Los Angeles, CA 90024, USA
Porcaro, Steve *Composer*
13596 Contour Dr, Sherman Oaks, CA 91423, USA
Porcaro, Steve *Singer, Keyboardist (Toto)*
%Fitzgerald-Hartley, 34 N Palm St, Ventura, CA 93001, USA
Porcher, Robert *Football Player*
160 Grosvenor Dr, Rochester Hills, MI 48307, USA
Porfilio, John C *Judge*
%US Court of Appeals, 1919 Stout St, Denver, CO 80294, USA
Porizkova, Paulina *Model, Actress*
%First Artists Assoc, 18 E 53 St, #1400, New York, NY 10022, USA
Porretta, Matthew *Actor*
%Damage Mgmt, 10 Southwick Mews, London W2, England
Portale, Carl *Publisher*
%Elle Magazine, Hachette Filipacchi, 1633 Broadway, New York, NY 10019, USA
Porter, Billy *Singer*
%William Morris Agency, 151 El Camino Dr, Beverly Hills, CA 90212, USA
Porter, David H *Educator*
%Skidmore College, President's Office, Saratoga Springs, NY 12866, USA
Porter, Howard *Basketball Player*
1034 Iglehart Ave, Saint Paul, MN 55104, USA
Porter, Jody *Singer (Fountains of Wayne), Guitarist*
%MOB Agency, 6404 Wilshire Blvd, #505, Los Angeles, CA 90048, USA
Porter, Joey *Football Player*
1118 Virginia St, Bakersfield, CA 93305, USA
Porter, Terry *Basketball Player, Coach*
%Milwaukee Bucks, Bradley Center, 1001 N 4th St, Milwaukee, WI 53203, USA
Portes, Richard D *Economist*
%Economic Policy Centre, 90-98 Goswell Road, London EC1V 7RR, England
Portillo, Alfonso *President, Guatemala*
%President's Office, Palacio Nacional, Guatemala City, Guatemala
Portillo, Michael D X *Government Official, England*
%House of Commons, Westminster, London SW1A 0AA, England
Portis, Charles *Writer*
7417 Kingwood Road, Little Rock, AR 72207, USA
Portisch, Lajos *Chess Player*
%Chess Federation, Nephadsereg Utca 10, 1055 Budapest, Hungary
Portland, Rene *Basketball Coach*
%Pennsylvania State University, Greenberg Complex, University Park, PA 16802, USA
Portman, John C, Jr *Architect*
%Charles Portman Assoc, 225 Peachtree St NE, #200, Atlanta, GA 30303, USA
Portman, Natalie *Actress*
%The Firm, 9100 Wilshire Blvd, #100W, Beverly Hills, CA 90210, USA
Portman, Rachel *Composer*
%PRS, 29/33 Berners St, London W1P 4AA, England
Porto, James *Photographer*
601 W 26th St, #1321, New York, NY 10001, USA
Portwich, Ramona *Canoeing Athlete*
KC Limmer, Stockhardtweg 3, 30453 Hanover, Germany
Posada, Jorge R *Baseball Player*
Calle Ronda, Rio Piedras, PR 00926, USA
Poses, Frederic M *Businessman*
%AlliedSignal Inc, PO Box 4000, Morristown, NJ 07962, USA
Posey, Parker *Actress*
1216 N 6th Ave, Laurel, MS 39440, USA
Posner, Richard A *Judge*
%US Court of Appeals, 219 S Dearborn St, Chicago, IL 60604, USA
Posokhin, Mikhail M *Architect*
Mosproyekt-2, 2 Brestskaya Str 5, 123056 Moscow, Russia

Post, Avery D *Religious Leader*
39 Boothman Lane, Randolph, NH 03593, USA
Post, Glen F, III *Businessman*
%Centurytel Inc, 100 Century Park Dr, Monroe, LA 71203, USA
Post, Markie *Actress*
10153 1/2 Riverside Dr, #333, Toluca Lake, CA 91602, USA
Post, Mike *Composer*
%Mike Post Productions, 1007 W Olive Ave, Burbank, CA 91506, USA
Post, Sandra *Golfer*
%Ladies Pro Golf Assn, 100 International Golf Dr, Daytona Beach, FL 32124, USA
Post, Ted *Movie Director*
%Norman Blumenthal, 11030 Santa Monica Blvd, Los Angeles, CA 90025, USA
Post, William *Businessman*
%Pinnacle West Capital, 400 E Van Buren St, PO Box 52132, Phoenix, AZ 85072, USA
Poster, Steve *Cinematographer*
%Smith/Gosnell/Nicholson, PO Box 1156, Studio City, CA 91614, USA
Postlethwaite, Pete *Actor*
%Markham & Froggatt, Julian House, 4 Windmill St, London W1P 1HF, England
Postlewait, Kathy *Golfer*
%A Thomason, 4355 Cobb Parkway, #R, Atlanta, GA 30339, USA
Postman, Marc *Astronomer*
3303 Lightfoot Dr, Pikesville, MD 21208, USA
Poston, Tom *Actor*
1 N Venice Blvd, #106, Venice, CA 90291, USA
Potente, Franka *Actress*
%Presseburo Sohela Emani, Etterschlager Str 60, 82237 Steinebach, Germany
Poti, Tom *Hockey Player*
103 Alvarado Ave, Worcester, MA 01604, USA
Potrykus, Ingo *Plant Scientist*
%Eidgenossische Tech Hochshule, Plant Sci Dept, 8093 Zurich, Switzerland
Potter, Chris *Actor*
565 Orwell St, Missigauga ON L5A 2W4, Canada
Potter, Chris *Saxophonist*
%Joel Chriss, 300 Mercer St, #3J, New York, NY 10003, USA
Potter, Cynthia (Cindy) *Diver, Sportscaster*
1188 Ragley Hall Road NE, Atlanta, GA 30319, USA
Potter, Dan M *Religious Leader*
21 Forest Dr, Albany, NY 12205, USA
Potter, Huntington *Medical Researcher*
%Harvard Medical School, 25 Shattuck St, Boston, MA 02115, USA
Potter, John *Government Official*
%US Postal Service, 475 L'Enfant Plaza SW, Washington, DC 20260, USA
Potter, Nelson *Businessman*
%Fleetwood Enterprises, 3125 Myers St, Riverside, CA 92503, USA
Potter, Philip A *Religious Leader*
3A York Castle Ave, Kingston 6, Jamaica
Pottinger, Stanley *Writer*
%William Morris Agency, 151 El Camino Dr, Beverly Hills, CA 90212, USA
Pottios, Myron J (Mike) *Football Player*
71569 Sahara Road, Rancho Mirage, CA 92270, USA
Pottruck, David S *Financier*
%Charles Schwab Co, 101 Montgomery St, San Francisco, CA 94104, USA
Potts, Annie *Actress*
PO Box 29400, Los Angeles, CA 90029, USA
Potts, Cliff *Actor*
PO Box 131, Topanga, CA 90290, USA
Potts, Erwin *Businessman*
%McClatchy Newspapers, 2100 "Q" St, Sacramento, CA 95816, USA
Potvin, Denis *Hockey Player*
6820 NW 101st Terrace, Parkland, FL 33076, USA
Potvin, Felix *Hockey Player*
%Boston Bruins, 1 Fleet Center, Boston, MA 02114, USA
Potvin, Jean R *Hockey Player*
24 Longwood Dr, Huntington Station, NY 11746, USA
Pouget, Ely *Actress*
%Writers & Artists, 8383 Wilshire Blvd, #550, Beverly Hills, CA 90211, USA
Poulin, Dave *Hockey Player, Coach*
16771 Orchard Ridge Court, Granger, IN 46530, USA
Pound, Richard W D *Olympics Official*
87 Arlington Ave, Westmount QC H3Y 2W5, Canada
Pound, Robert V *Physicist*
87 Pinehurst Road, Belmont, MA 02478, USA
Pounder, C C H *Actress*
%Susan Smith, 121A N San Vicente Blvd, Beverly Hills, CA 90211, USA
Poundstone, Paula *Actress, Comedienne*
1223 Broadway, #162, Santa Monica, CA 90404, USA
Poupard, Paul Cardinal *Religious Leader*
%Pontificium Consilium Pro Dialogo, 00120 Vatican City

P

Pousette - Pratiwi Sudarmono

Pousette, Lena *Actress*
%Atkins Assoc, 8040 Ventura Canyon Ave, Panorama City, CA 91402, USA
Poussaint, Alvin F *Psychiatrist, Educator*
%Judge Baker Guidance Center, 295 Longwood Ave, Boston, MA 02115, USA
Povich, Maury R *Commentator, Entertainer*
%Maury Povich Show, 1515 Broadway, #33-88, New York, NY 10036, USA
Powell, A J Philip *Architect*
16 Little Boltons, London SW10, England
Powell, Arthur (Art) *Football Player*
25221 Via Lido, Laguna Niguel, CA 92677, USA
Powell, Billy *Keyboardist (Lynyrd Skynyrd)*
%Vector Mgmt, 1607 17th Ave S, Nashville, TN 37212, USA
Powell, Brittney *Actress, Model*
%Amsel Eisenstadt Frazier, 5757 Wilshire Blvd, #510, Los Angeles, CA 90036, USA
Powell, Cecil *Test Pilot*
939 Bobcat Blvd NE, Albuquerque, NM 87122, USA
Powell, Clifton *Actor*
%Abrams Artists, 9200 Sunset Blvd, #1125, Los Angeles, CA 90069, USA
Powell, Colin L *Army General, Secretary of State*
1317 Ballantrae Farm Dr, McLean, VA 22101, USA
Powell, D Duane, Jr *Cartoonist*
215 S McDowell St, Raleigh, NC 27601, USA
Powell, Earl A (Rusty), III *Museum Executive*
%National Gallery of Art, Constitution Ave & 4th St NW, Washington, DC 20565, USA
Powell, James R *Inventor (Magnetic Levitation Train)*
%Plus Ultra Technologies, 25 E Loop Road, Stony Brook, NY 11790, USA
Powell, Jane *Singer, Actress*
62 Cedar Road, Wilton, CT 06897, USA
Powell, Jesse *Pop Singer*
%Pyramid Entertainment, 89 5th Ave, #700, New York, NY 10003, USA
Powell, John *Composer*
%Kraft-Benjamin-Engel, 15233 Ventura Blvd, #200, Sherman Oaks, CA 91403, USA
Powell, John G *Track Athlete*
%John Powell Assoc, 10445 Mary Ave, Cupertino, CA 95014, USA
Powell, John W (Boog) *Baseball Player*
%Boog's Barbeque, 333 W Camden St, Baltimore, MD 21201, USA
Powell, Joseph L (Jody) *Government Official, Journalist*
%Powell Tate, 700 13th St NW, #1000, Washington, DC 20005, USA
Powell, Marvin *Football Player*
5441 8th Ave, Los Angeles, CA 90043, USA
Powell, Michael (Mike) *Track Athlete*
%Team Powell, PO Box 8000-354, Alta Loma, CA 91701, USA
Powell, Michael K *Government Official*
%Federal Communications Commission, 1919 M St NW, Washington, DC 20036, USA
Powell, Monroe *Singer (Platters)*
%Personality Presents, 880 E Sahara Ave, #101, Las Vegas, NV 89104, USA
Powell, Robert *Actor*
10 Pond Place, London W12 7RJ, England
Powell, Sandy *Costume Designer*
%London Mgmt, 2-4 Noel St, London W1V 3RB, England
Powell, Susan *Actress*
6333 Bryn Mawr Dr, Los Angeles, CA 90068, USA
Power, J D (Dave) *Businessman*
%J D Power Associates, 2625 Townsgate Road, Westlake Village, CA 91361, USA
Powers, Alexandra *Actress*
%United Talent Agency, 9560 Wilshire Blvd, #500, Beverly Hills, CA 90212, USA
Powers, James B *Religious Leader*
%American Baptist Assn, 4605 N State Line, Texarkana, TX 75503, USA
Powers, Mala *Actress*
10543 Valley Spring Lane, Toluca Lake, CA 91602, USA
Powers, Ross *Snowboard Skier*
PO Box 283, South Londonderry, VT 05155, USA
Powers, Stefanie *Actress*
PO Box 67981, Los Angeles, CA 90067, USA
Powter, Susan *Physical Fitness Instructor, Writer*
%Stop the Insanity, 6250 Ridgewood Road, Saint Cloud, MN 56395, USA
Pozsgay, Imre *Government Official, Hungary*
%Parliament Buildings, Kossuth Lajos Ter 1, 1055 Budapest, Hungary
Prance, Ghillean T *Botanist*
%Kew Royal Botanic Gardens, Richmond, Surrey TW9 3AE, England
Pras *Rap Artist (Fugees)*
%DAS Communications, 83 Riverside Dr, New York, NY 10024, USA
Pratchett, Terry *Writer*
%Colin Smythe, PO Box 6, Gerrards Cross, Bucks SL9 8XA, England
Prather, Joan *Actress*
31647 Sea Level Dr, Malibu, CA 90265, USA
Pratiwi Sudarmono *Astronaut, Indonesia*
Jalan Pegangsaan, Timur 16, Jakarta, Indonesia

Pratt, Awadagin *Concert Pianist*
%Cramer/Marder Artists, 3436 Springhill Road, Lafayette, CA 94549, USA
Pratt, Roger *Cinematographer*
10 Nightingale Lane, Hornsey, London N8 7QU, England
Preate, Ernest D, Jr *Attorney, Government Official*
%Attorney General's Office, 4th & Walnut, Harrisburg, PA 17120, USA
Precourt, Charles J *Astronaut*
7015 Little Redwood Dr, Pasadena, TX 77505, USA
Predock, Antoine *Architect*
%Antoine Predock Architect, 300 12th St, Northwest Albuquerque, NM 87102, USA
Preer, John R, Jr *Biologist*
1414 E Maxwell Lane, Bloomington, IN 47401, USA
Pregerson, Harry *Judge*
%US Court of Appeals, 21800 Oxnard St, Woodland Hills, CA 91367, USA
Pregulman, Merv *Football Player*
44 S Crest Road, Chattanooga, TN 37404, USA
Prejean, Sister Helen *Social Activist, Writer*
%Vintage Books, 201 E 50th St, New York, NY 10022, USA
Preki *Soccer Player*
%Kansas City Wizards, 2 Arrowhead Dr, Kansas City, MO 64129, USA
Prentice, Dean S *Hockey Player*
13-220 Salisbury Ave, Cambridge ON N1S 1K5, Canada
Prentiss, Paula *Actress, Comedienne*
719 Foothill Road, Beverly Hills, CA 90210, USA
Prescott, John L *Government Official, England*
365 Saltshouse Road, Sutton-on-Hull, North Humberside, England
Presle, Micheline *Actress*
6 Rue Antoine Dubois, 75006 Paris, France
Presley, Lisa-Marie *Actress, Singer*
12614 Promontory Road, Los Angeles, CA 90049, USA
Presley, Priscilla *Actress*
1167 Summit Dr, Beverly Hills, CA 90210, USA
Presley, Richard *Guitarist (Breeders)*
%William Morris Agency, 151 El Camino Dr, Beverly Hills, CA 90212, USA
Presnell, Glenn E *Football Player, Coach*
510 Happy Hollow, Ironton, OH 45638, USA
Presnell, Harve *Actor, Singer*
%Abrams Artists, 9200 Sunset Blvd, #1125, Los Angeles, CA 90069, USA
Press, Bill *Commentator*
%Cable News Network, News Dept, 1050 Techwood Dr NW, Atlanta, GA 30318, USA
Press, Frank *Geophysicist*
2500 Virginia Ave, #616, Washington, DC 20037, USA
Pressey, Paul *Basketball Player, Coach*
8415 N Indian Creek Parkway, Milwaukee, WI 53217, USA
Pressler, H Paul *Attorney, Judge*
3711 San Felipe St, #9J, Houston, TX 77027, USA
Pressler, Larry L *Senator, SD*
2812 Davis Ave, Alexandria, VA 22302, USA
Pressler, Menahem M J *Concert Pianist*
%Melvin Kaplan, 115 College St, Burlington, VT 05401, USA
Pressley, Robert *Auto/Truck Racing Driver*
6 Forestdale Dr, Asheville, NC 28803, USA
Pressly, Jaime *Actress, Model*
8265 Sunset Blvd, #101, West Hollywood, CA 90046, USA
Pressman, Edward R *Movie Producer*
%Edward Pressman Films, 130 El Camino Dr, Beverly Hills, CA 90212, USA
Pressman, Lawrence *Actor*
15033 Encanto Dr, Sherman Oaks, CA 91403, USA
Pressman, Michael *Movie, Television Director*
%William Morris Agency, 151 El Camino Dr, Beverly Hills, CA 90212, USA
Preston, Billy *Singer, Songwriter, Keyboardist*
%Celebresearch, 7119 E Shea Blvd, #109-436, Scottsdale, AZ 85254, USA
Preston, J A *Actor*
%Paradigm Agency, 10100 Santa Monica Blvd, #2500, Los Angeles, CA 90067, USA
Preston, Johnny *Singer*
%Ken Keene Artists, PO Box 1875, Gretna, LA 70054, USA
Preston, Kelly *Actress, Model*
15821 Ventura Blvd, #460, Encino, CA 91436, USA
Preston, Mike *Actor*
%House of Representatives, 400 S Beverly Dr, #101, Beverly Hills, CA 90212, USA
Preston, Simon J *Concert Organist, Choirmaster*
Little Hardwick, Langton Green, Tunbridge Wells, Kent TN3 OEY, England
Pretre, Georges *Conductor*
Chateau de Vaudricourt, A Naves, Par Castres 81100, France
Preus, David W *Religious Leader*
2481 Como Ave, Saint Paul, MN 55108, USA
Previn, Andre G *Conductor, Composer, Jazz Pianist*
180 W 80th St, #206, New York, NY 10024, USA

P

Previn - Priestley

Previn, Dory *Singer, Songwriter*
2533 Zorada Dr, Los Angeles, CA 90046, USA
Previte, Richard *Businessman*
%Advanced Micro Devices, 1 AMD Place, PO Box 3453, Sunnyvale, CA 94088, USA
Prevost, Josette *Actress*
%Tisherman Agency, 6767 Forest Lawn Dr, #101, Los Angeles, CA 90068, USA
Prew, William A *Swimmer, Businessman*
30600 Telegraph Road, #3110, Bingham Farms, MI 48025, USA
Pribilinec, Jozef *Track Athlete*
Moyzesova 75, 966 22 Lutila, Slovakia
Price, Alan *Singer, Organist (Animals), Songwriter*
%Crowell Mgmt, 4/5 High St, Huntingdon, Cambs PE18 6TE, England
Price, Antony *Fashion Designer*
468 Kings Road, London SW1, England
Price, Charles H, II *Diplomat, Businessman*
1 W Armour Blvd, #300, Kansas City, MO 64111, USA
Price, Frank *Movie Executive*
%Price Entertainment, 2425 Olympic Blvd, Santa Monica, CA 90404, USA
Price, Frederick K C *Religious Leader*
%Crenshaw Christian Church, 7901 S Vermont Ave, Los Angeles, CA 90044, USA
Price, George C *Prime Minister, Belize*
%House of Representatives, Belmopan, Belize
Price, Hillary *Cartoonist (Rhymes with Orange)*
221 Pine St, #4G3, Florence, MA 01062, USA
Price, James G *Physician, Columnist*
12205 Mohawk Road, Leawood, KS 66209, USA
Price, Kelly *Singer*
%JL Ent, 18653 Ventura Blvd, #340, Tarzana, CA 91356, USA
Price, Larry C *Photojournalist*
1020 S Josephine St, Denver, CO 80209, USA
Price, Lindsay *Actress*
3033 Vista Crest, Los Angeles, CA 90068, USA
Price, Lloyd *Singer, Pianist, Songwriter*
95 Horseshoe Hill Road, Pound Ridge, MY 10576, USA
Price, M V Leontyne *Opera Singer*
9 Van Dam St, New York, NY 10013, USA
Price, Marc *Actor*
8444 Magnolia Dr, Los Angeles, CA 90046, USA
Price, Margaret B *Opera Singer*
%Ulf Tornqvist , Sankt Eriksgatan 100, 113 31 Stockholm, Sweden
Price, Nick *Golfer*
300 S Beach Road, Hobe Sound, FL 33455, USA
Price, Noel *Hockey Player*
21 Windeyer Crescent, Kanata ON K2K 2P6, Canada
Price, Paul B *Physicist*
1056 Overlook Road, Berkeley, CA 94708, USA
Price, Ray *Singer*
%Original Artists Agency, 1031 E Battlefield Road, Springfield, MO 65807, USA
Price, Reynolds *Writer*
PO Box 99014, Durham, NC 27708, USA
Price, Richard *Writer*
%Greater Talent Network, 437 5th Ave, New York, NY 10016, USA
Price, Rod *Guitarist (Foghat)*
%Lustig Talent, PO Box 770850, Orlando, FL 32877, USA
Price, S H *Publisher*
%Newsweek Inc, 251 W 57th St, New York, NY 10019, USA
Price, W Mark *Basketball Player*
%Georgia Institute of Technology, Athletic Dept, Atlanta, GA 30332, USA
Price, Willard D *Explorer*
814 Via Alhambra, #N, Laguna Hills, CA 92653, USA
Prichard, Peter S *Editor*
%USA Today, Editorial Dept, 1000 Wilson Blvd, Arlington, VA 22209, USA
Priddy, Nancy *Actress*
11223 Sunshine Terrace, Studio City, CA 91604, USA
Pride, Charlie *Singer*
%Cecca Productions, 3198 Royal Lane, #200, Dallas, TX 75229, USA
Pride, Lynn *Basketball Player*
%Minnesota Lynx, Target Center, 600 1st Ave N, Minneapolis, MN 55403, USA
Priesand, Sally J *Religious Leader*
10 Wedgewood Circle, Eatontown, NJ 07724, USA
Priest, Maxi *Singer*
%Virgin Records, 150 5th Ave, New York, NY 10011, USA
Priest, Pat *Actress*
146 Huckleberry Lane, Buhl, ID 83316, USA
Priest, Steve *Singer, Bassist (Sweet)*
%DCM International, 296 Nether St, Finchley, London N3 1RJ, England
Priestley, Jason *Actor*
%United Talent Agency, 9560 Wilshire Blvd, #500, Beverly Hills, CA 90212, USA

Primack, Joel R *Astronomer*
%University of California, Astronomy Dept, Santa Cruz, CA 95064, USA
Primatesta, Raul Francisco Cardinal *Religious Leader*
Arzobispado, Ave H Irigoyen 98, 5000 Cordoba, Argentina
Primeau, Keith *Hockey Player*
2 Danforth Dr, Voorhees, NJ 08043, USA
Primis, Lance R *Publisher*
%New York Times Co, 229 W 43rd St, New York, NY 10036, USA
Primrose, Neil *Drummer (Travis)*
%Wildlife Entertainment, 21 Heathmans Road, London SW6 4TJ, England
Prince *Singer, Songwriter*
%Paisley Park Enterprises, 7801 Audubon Road, Chanhassen, MN 55317, USA
Prince, Charles (Chuck) *Financier*
%Citigroup Inc, 399 Park Ave, New York, NY 10022, USA
Prince, Faith *Actress, Singer*
%Innovative Artists, 1505 10th St, Santa Monica, CA 90401, USA
Prince, Gregory S, Jr *Educator*
%Hampshire College, President's Office, Amherst, MA 01002, USA
Prince, Harold S (Hal) *Theater Producer, Director*
%Harold Prince Organization, 10 Rockefeller Plaza, #1009, New York, NY 10020, USA
Prince, Larry L *Businessman*
%Genuine Parts Co, 2999 Circle 75 Parkway, Atlanta, GA 30339, USA
Prince, Tayshaun *Basketball Player*
%Detroit Pistons, Palace, 2 Championship Dr, Auburn Hills, MI 48326, USA
Principal, Victoria *Actress*
120 S Spalding Dr, #205, Beverly Hills, CA 90212, USA
Principi, Anthony *Secretary, Veteran Affairs*
%Veteran Affairs Department, 810 Vermont Ave NW, Washington, DC 20420, USA
Prine, Andrew *Actor*
3364 Longridge Ave, Sherman Oaks, CA 91423, USA
Prine, John *Singer, Songwriter*
%Al Bunetta Mgmt, 33 Music Square W, #102B, Nashville, TN 37203, USA
Pringle, Joan *Actress*
%Gold Marshak Liedtke, 3500 W Olive Ave, #1400, Burbank, CA 91505, USA
Prinosil, David *Tennis Athlete*
%TC Wolfsberg, Am Schanzl 3, 92224 Amberg, Germany
Prinze, Freddie, Jr *Actor*
4348 Ledge Ave, Toluca Lake, CA 91602, USA
Prinzi, Frank *Cinematographer*
571 W 113th St, #24, New York, NY 10025, USA
Prior of Brampton, James M L *Government Official, England*
36 Morpeth Mansions, London SW1, England
Prior, Anthony *Football Player*
12738 Longhorne Dr, Corona, CA 92880, USA
Prior, Maddy *Singer*
%Park Promotions, PO Box 651, Park Road, Oxford OX2 9RB, England
Prior, Mark *Baseball Player*
3256 Casa Bonita Dr, Bonita, CA 91902, USA
Priory, Richard B *Businessman*
%Duke Energy Co, 526 S Church St, Charlotte, NC 28202, USA
Pritchard, Barry *Singer, Guitarist (Fortunes)*
%Lustig Talent, PO Box 770850, Orlando, FL 32877, USA
Pritchard, David E *Physicist*
%Massachusetts Institute of Technology, Physics Dept, Cambridge, MA 02139, USA
Pritchard, Ron *Football Player*
690 E Park Ave, Gilbert, AZ 85234, USA
Pritchett, James *Actor*
53 W 74th St, New York, NY 10023, USA
Pritchett, Matt *Cartoonist (Matt)*
%London Daily Telegraph, 181 Marsh Wall, London E14 9SR, England
Pritkin, Roland I *Eye Surgeon*
4128 Grove Ave, Stickney, IL 60402, USA
Pritzker, Robert A *Businessman*
%Marmon Group, 225 W Washington St, Chicago, IL 60606, USA
Prix, Wolf *Architect*
%Coop Himmelblau, 3526 Beethoven St, Los Angeles, CA 90066, USA
Probert, Bob *Hockey Player*
2109 N Seminary Ave, Chicago, IL 60614, USA
Prochazka, Martin *Hockey Player*
%Toronto Maple Leafs, 40 Bay St, Toronto ON M5J 2K2, Canada
Prochnow, Jurgen *Actor*
Lamontstr 98, 81679 Munich, Germany
Prock, Markus *Luge Athlete*
6142 Mieders, Austria
Procter, Emily *Actress*
%Innovative Artists, 1505 10th St, Santa Monica, CA 90401, USA
Proctor, Charles N *Skier*
100 Lockwood Lane, #238, Scotts Valley, CA 95066, USA

P

Prodi, Romano *Prime Minister, Italy*
%European Communities Commission, 200 Rue de la Loi, Brussels, Belgium
Professor Griff *Rap Artist (Public Enemy)*
%William Morris Agency, 151 El Camino Dr, Beverly Hills, CA 90212, USA
Profumo, John D *Government Official, England*
28 Commercial St, London E1 6LS, England
Pronger, Chris *Hockey Player*
10454 Ladue Road, Saint Louis, MO 63141, USA
Pronovost, R Marcel *Hockey Player*
4620 Dali Court, Windsor ON N9G 2M8, Canada
Prophet, Billy *Singer (Jive Five)*
%Paramount Entertainment, PO Box 12, Far Hills, NJ 07931, USA
Prophet, Elizabeth Clare *Religious Leader*
%Church Universal & Triumphant, Box A, Livingston, MT 59047, USA
Propp, Brian *Hockey Player*
5023 Church Road, Mount Laurel, NJ 08054, USA
Props, Rene *Actress*
%Agency for Performing Arts, 9200 Sunset Blvd, #900, Los Angeles, CA 90069, USA
Prosky, Robert *Actor*
309 9th St, Washington, DC 20003, USA
Prospal, Vaclav *Hockey Player*
%Tampa Bay Lightning, Ice Palace, 401 Channelside Dr, Tampa, FL 33602, USA
Prosser, C Ladd *Physiologist*
101 W Windsor Road, #2106, Urbana, IL 61802, USA
Prosser, James *Singer*
%Refugee Mgmt, 209 10th Ave S, #347, Cummins Station, Nashville, TN 37203, USA
Prosser, Robert *Religious Leader*
%Cumberland Presbyterian Church, 1978 Union Ave, Memphis, TN 38104, USA
Prost, Alain M P *Auto Racing Driver*
%Prost-Grand-Prix, 7 Ave Eugene Freyssinet, 78286 Guyancourt, France
Prost, Sharon *Judge*
%US Court of Appeals, 717 Madison Place NW, Washington, DC 20439, USA
Protopopov, Oleg *Figure Skater*
Chalet Hubel, 3818 Grindelwald, Switzerland
Proulx, E Annie *Writer*
PO Box 230, Centennial, WY 82055, USA
Prout, Brian *Singer, Drummer (Diamond Rio)*
%Dreamcatcher Artists Mgmt, 2908 Poston Ave, Nashville, TN 37203, USA
Provenza, Paul *Actor*
%Patterson Assoc, 8271 Melrose Ave, #201, Los Angeles, CA 90046, USA
Provine, Dorothy *Actress*
8832 Ferncliff NE, Bainbridge Island, WA 98110, USA
Prowse, David *Actor*
%Spotlight, 7 Leicester Place, London WC2H 7BP, England
Proyas, Alex *Movie Director*
%International Creative Mgmt, 8942 Wilshire Blvd, #219, Beverly Hills, CA 90211, USA
Prudden, Bonnie *Physical Fitness Expert*
PO Box 65240, Tucson, AZ 85728, USA
Prudhomme, Don *Auto Racing Driver*
1232 Distribution Way, Vista, CA 92081, USA
Prudhomme, Paul *Chef*
2424 Chartres, New Orleans, LA 70117, USA
Pruett, Jeanne *Singer, Songwriter*
%Joe Taylor Artist Agency, 2802 Columbine Place, Nashville, TN 37204, USA
Pruett, Scott *Auto Racing Driver*
%Arciero-Wells Racing, 30212 Tomas, Rancho Santa Margarita, CA 92688, USA
Pruitt, Basil A, Jr *Burn Surgeon*
%US Army Institute of Surgical Research, Fort Sam Houston, TX 78234, USA
Pruitt, Gregory D (Greg) *Football Player*
13851 Larchmere Blvd, Cleveland, OH 44120, USA
Pruitt, Michael (Mike) *Football Player*
472 S Mumaugh Road, Lima, OH 45804, USA
Prunariu, Dumitru D *Cosmonaut, Romania*
Str Sf Spiridon 12, #4, 70231 Bucharest, Romania
Prunskiene, Kazimiera *Council of Ministers Chairman, Lithuania*
%Lithuanian-European Institute, Vilnius St 45-13, 2001 Vilnius, Lithuania
Prusiner, Stanley B *Nobel Medicine Laureate*
%University of California, Biochemistry Dept, San Francisco, CA 94143, USA
Pryce, Jonathan *Actor, Singer*
%Julian Belfarge, 46 Albermarle St, London W1X 4PP, England
Pryce, Trevor *Football Player*
%Denver Broncos, 13655 E Broncos Parkway, Englewood, CO 80112, USA
Pryor, David H *Senator, Governor, AR*
2209 Julie Ann Lane, Paragould, AR 72450, USA
Pryor, Hubert *Editor, Publisher*
3560 S Ocean Blvd, #607, Palm Beach, FL 33480, USA
Pryor, Nicholas *Actor*
%S D B Partners, 1801 Ave of Stars, #902, Los Angeles, CA 90067, USA

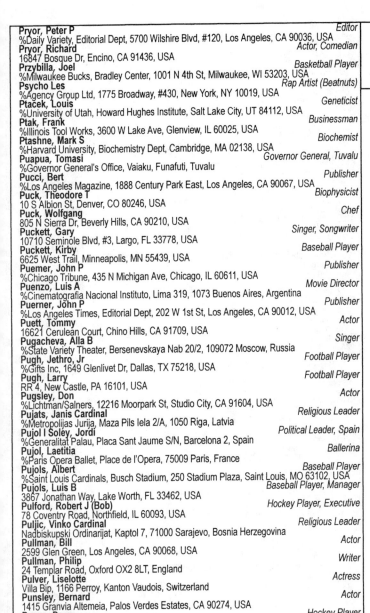

Pryor, Peter P — *Editor*
%Daily Variety, Editorial Dept, 5700 Wilshire Blvd, #120, Los Angeles, CA 90036, USA

Pryor, Richard — *Actor, Comedian*
16847 Bosque Dr, Encino, CA 91436, USA

Przybilla, Joel — *Basketball Player*
%Milwaukee Bucks, Bradley Center, 1001 N 4th St, Milwaukee, WI 53203, USA

Psycho Les — *Rap Artist (Beatnuts)*
%Agency Group Ltd, 1775 Broadway, #430, New York, NY 10019, USA

Ptacek, Louis — *Geneticist*
%University of Utah, Howard Hughes Institute, Salt Lake City, UT 84112, USA

Ptak, Frank — *Businessman*
%Illinois Tool Works, 3600 W Lake Ave, Glenview, IL 60025, USA

Ptashne, Mark S — *Biochemist*
%Harvard University, Biochemistry Dept, Cambridge, MA 02138, USA

Puapua, Tomasi — *Governor General, Tuvalu*
%Governor General's Office, Vaiaku, Funafuti, Tuvalu

Pucci, Bert — *Publisher*
%Los Angeles Magazine, 1888 Century Park East, Los Angeles, CA 90067, USA

Puck, Theodore T — *Biophysicist*
10 S Albion St, Denver, CO 80246, USA

Puck, Wolfgang — *Chef*
805 N Sierra Dr, Beverly Hills, CA 90210, USA

Puckett, Gary — *Singer, Songwriter*
10710 Seminole Blvd, #3, Largo, FL 33778, USA

Puckett, Kirby — *Baseball Player*
6625 West Trail, Minneapolis, MN 55439, USA

Puemer, John P — *Publisher*
%Chicago Tribune, 435 N Michigan Ave, Chicago, IL 60611, USA

Puenzo, Luis A — *Movie Director*
%Cinematografia Nacional Instituto, Lima 319, 1073 Buenos Aires, Argentina

Puerner, John P — *Publisher*
%Los Angeles Times, Editorial Dept, 202 W 1st St, Los Angeles, CA 90012, USA

Puett, Tommy — *Actor*
16621 Cerulean Court, Chino Hills, CA 91709, USA

Pugacheva, Alla B — *Singer*
%State Variety Theater, Bersenevskaya Nab 20/2, 109072 Moscow, Russia

Pugh, Jethro, Jr — *Football Player*
%Gifts Inc, 1649 Glenlivet Dr, Dallas, TX 75218, USA

Pugh, Larry — *Football Player*
RR 4, New Castle, PA 16101, USA

Pugsley, Don — *Actor*
%Lichtman/Salners, 12216 Moorpark St, Studio City, CA 91604, USA

Pujats, Janis Cardinal — *Religious Leader*
%Metropolijas Jurija, Maza Pils Iela 2/A, 1050 Riga, Latvia

Pujol I Soley, Jordi — *Political Leader, Spain*
%Generalitat Palau, Placa Sant Jaume S/N, Barcelona 2, Spain

Pujol, Laetitia — *Ballerina*
%Paris Opera Ballet, Place de l'Opera, 75009 Paris, France

Pujols, Albert — *Baseball Player*
%Saint Louis Cardinals, Busch Stadium, 250 Stadium Plaza, Saint Louis, MO 63102, USA

Pujols, Luis B — *Baseball Player, Manager*
3867 Jonathan Way, Lake Worth, FL 33462, USA

Pulford, Robert J (Bob) — *Hockey Player, Executive*
78 Coventry Road, Northfield, IL 60093, USA

Puljic, Vinko Cardinal — *Religious Leader*
Nadbiskupski Ordinarijat, Kaptol 7, 71000 Sarajevo, Bosnia Herzegovina

Pullman, Bill — *Actor*
2599 Glen Green, Los Angeles, CA 90068, USA

Pullman, Philip — *Writer*
24 Templar Road, Oxford OX2 8LT, England

Pulver, Liselotte — *Actress*
Villa Bip, 1166 Perroy, Kanton Vaudois, Switzerland

Punsley, Bernard — *Actor*
1415 Granvia Altemeia, Palos Verdes Estates, CA 90274, USA

Puppa, Daren — *Hockey Player*
4526 Cheval Blvd, Lutz, FL 33558, USA

Purcell, James N — *Government Official*
6 Chateau-Banquet, 1202 Geneva, Switzerland

Purcell, Lee — *Actress*
11101 Provence Lane, Tujunga, CA 91042, USA

Purcell, Patrick B — *Publisher*
%Boston Herald, 1 Herald St, Boston, MA 02118, USA

Purcell, Philip J — *Financier*
%Morgan Stanley Co, 1585 Broadway, New York, NY 10036, USA

Purcell, Sarah — *Actress*
6525 Esplanade St, Playa del Rey, CA 90293, USA

Purcell, William — *Astrophysicist*
%Northwestern University, Astrophysics Dept, Evanston, IL 60208, USA

P

Purdee, Nathan *Actor*
56 W 66th St, New York, NY 10023, USA
Purdom, Edmund *Actor*
Via Isonzo 42/C, 00198 Rome, Italy
Purdy, Alfred *Writer*
%Harbour Publishing, PO Box 219, Madeira Park BC V0N 2H0, Canada
Purdy, James *Writer*
236 Henry St, Brooklyn, NY 11201, USA
Purefoy, James *Actor*
%International Creative Mgmt, 76 Oxford St, London W1N 0AX, England
Purim, Flora *Singer*
%A Train Mgmt, PO Box 29242, Oakland, CA 94604, USA
Purkey, Robert T (Bob) *Baseball Player*
5767 Kings School Road, Bethel Park, PA 15102, USA
Purl, Linda *Actress*
612 Lighthouse Ave, #220, Pacific Grove, CA 93950, USA
Purpura, Dominick P *Neuroscientist*
%Albert Einstein College of Medicine, 1300 Morris Park Ave, Bronx, NY 10461, USA
Purves, William *Financier*
87 Chester Square, London SW1W 9HT, England
Purvis, Jeff *Auto Racing Driver*
4106 Roberta Road, Concord, NC 28027, USA
Puryear, Martin *Sculptor*
%Nancy Drysdale Gallery, 700 New Hampshire Ave NW, #917, Washington, DC 20037, USA
Pusha T *Rap Artist (Clipse)*
%Star Trax/Arista Records, 888 7th Ave, #3800, New York, NY 10106, USA
Pushelberg, Glenn *Interior Designer*
%Yabu Pushelberg, 55 Booth Ave, Toronto ON M4M 2M3, Canada
Putch, John *Actor*
3972 Sunswept Dr, Studio City, CA 91604, USA
Putilin, Nikolai G *Opera Singer*
%Mariinsky Theater, Teatralnaya Square 1, 190000 Saint Petersburg, Russia
Putin, Vladimir V *President, Russia*
%President's Office, Kremlin, Staraya Pl 4, 103132 Moscow, Russia
Putnam, Ashley *Opera Singer*
%Maurice Mayer, 201 W 54th St, #1C, New York, NY 10019, USA
Putnam, Duane *Football Player*
1545 Magnolia Ave, Ontario, CA 91762, USA
Putnam, Hilary W *Philosopher*
116 Winchester Road, Arlington, MA 02474, USA
Putterman, Seth J *Physicist*
%University of California, Physics Dept, Los Angeles, CA 90024, USA
Puttnam, David T *Movie Producer*
%Enigma Productions, 29A Tufton St, London SW1P 3QL, England
Puyana, Rafael *Concert Harpsichordist*
88 Rue de Grenelle, 75007 Paris, France
Pyavko, Vladislav I *Opera Singer*
Bryusov Per 2/14, #27, 103009 Moscow, Russia
Pye, William B *Sculptor*
43 Hambalt Road, Clapham, London SW4 9EQ, England
Pyle, Andy *Bassist (Kinks)*
%Larry Page, 29 Ruston Mews, London W11 1RB, England
Pyle, Michael J (Mike) *Football Player*
2436 Saranac Court, Glenview, IL 60025, USA
Pyle, Missy *Actress*
%Paradigm Agency, 10100 Santa Monica Blvd, #2500, Los Angeles, CA 90067, USA
Pym of Sandy, Francis L *Government Official, England*
Everton Park, Sandy, Beds SG19 2DE, England
Pynchon, Thomas *Writer*
%Henry Holt, 115 W 18th St, New York, NY 10011, USA
Pyne, Natasha *Actress*
%Kate Feast, Primrose Hill Studios, Fitzroy Road, London NW1 8TR, England
Pyne, Stephen J *Historian, Writer*
%Arizona State University, History Dept, Tempe, AZ 85287, USA
Pyott, David E I *Buisnessman*
%Allergan Inc, 2525 Dupont St, Irvine, CA 92612, USA

Q

Qabas ibn Sa'id al Sa'id *Sultan, Oman*
%Royal Palace, PO Box 252, Muscat, Oman
Qarase, Laisenia *Prime Minister, Fiji*
%Prime Minister's Office, 6 Berkeley Crescent, Suva, Viti Levu, Fiji
Qasimi, Sheikh Saqr bin Muhammad al- *Ruler, Ras Al Khaimah*
%Ruler's Palace, Ras Al Khaimah, United Arab Emirates
Qasimi, Sheikh Sultan bin Muhammad al- *Ruler, Sharjah*
%Ruler's Palace, Sharjah, United Arab Emirates
Quaid, Dennis *Actor*
11718 Barrington Court, #508, Los Angeles, CA 90049, USA
Quaid, Randy *Actor*
%Mirisch, 1801 Century Park East, #1801, Los Angeles, CA 90067, USA
Quaife, Pete *Bassist (Kinks)*
%Larry Page, 29 Ruston Mews, London W11 1RB, England
Qualls, D J *Actor*
%Talent Group, 561 W Pike St, #100A, Lawrenceville, GA 30045, USA
Quandt, Richard E *Economist*
162 Springdale Road, Princeton, NJ 08540, USA
Quann, Megan *Swimmer*
%Thomas Quann, 8421 Woodland Ave E, Puyallup, WA 98371, USA
Quant, Mary *Fashion Designer*
%Mary Quant Ltd, 3 Ives St, London SW3 2NE, England
Quaresma, Rhonda Lee *Bodybuilder*
PO Box 22033, Kingston ON K7M 8S5, Canada
Quarrie, Donald (Don) *Track Athlete*
%Jamaican Amateur Athletic Assn, PO Box 272, Kingston 5, Jamaica
Quarry, Mike *Boxer*
12728 Oxford Dr, La Mirada, CA 90638, USA
Quarry, Robert *Actor*
11032 Moorpark St, #A3, North Hollywood, CA 91602, USA
Quasha, Alan G *Businessman*
%Hanover Direct Inc, 1509 Harbor Blvd, Weehawken, NJ 07086, USA
Quate, Calvin F *Electrical Engineer*
340 Princeton Road, Menlo Park, CA 94025, USA
Quatro, Suzi *Singer, Songwriter, Actress*
%Jive, 4 Pasteur Courtyard, Whittle Road, Corby, Norths NN17 5DX, England
Quayle, Anna *Actress*
%CDA, 47 Courtfield Road, London SW7 4DB, England
Quayle, J Danforth (Dan) *Vice President*
5395 Emerson Way, Indianapolis, IN 46226, USA
Queen Ida *Singer, Accordianist*
%Traditional Arts Services, 16045 36th Ave NE, Lake Forest Park, WA 98155, USA
Queen Latifah *Rap Artist, Actress*
%Flavor Unit Mgmt, 155 Morgan St, Jersey City, NJ 07302, USA
Queffelec, Anne *Concert Pianist*
15 Ave Corneille, 78600 Maisons-Laffitte, France
Queler, Eve *Conductor*
%Opera Orchestra of New York, 239 W 72nd St, #2R, New York, NY 10023, USA
Quellmalz, Udo *Judo Athlete*
Friedhofstr 10, 85049 Omgolstadt, Germany
Queloz, Didier *Astronomer*
%University of Geneva, Geneva Observatory, Geneva, Switzerland
Quenard, Nathalie *Actress*
%Cineart, 36 Rue de Ponthieu, 75008 Paris, France
Quenneville, Joel *Hockey Player, Coach*
13039 Starbuck Road, Saint Louis, MO 63141, USA
Questlove *Rap Artist (Roots)*
%Motown Records, 6255 Sunset Blvd, Los Angeles, CA 90028, USA
Questrom, Allen I *Businessman*
%J C Penney Co, 6501 Legacy Dr, Plano, TX 75024, USA
Quezada Toruno, Rodolfo Cardinal *Religious Leader*
%Archdiocese, 7A Avenida 6-21, Zona 1, 01001 Guatemala City, Guatemala
Quick, Clarence E *Singer (Del Vikings), Songwriter*
376 Quincy St, Brooklyn, NY 11216, USA
Quick, Diana *Actress*
39 Seymour Walk, London SW10, England
Quick, Michael A (Mike) *Football Player*
13 Slab Branch Road, Marlton, NJ 08053, USA
Quick, Richard *Swimming Coach*
%Stanford University, Athletic Dept, Stanford, CA 94305, USA
Quie, Albert H (Al) *Governor, MN*
4209 Christy Lane, Hopkins, MN 55345, USA
Quigley, Austin E *Educator*
%Columbia College, President's Office, New York, NY 10027, USA
Quigley, Dana *Golfer*
%Crestwood Country Club, 90 Wheeler St, Rehoboth, MA 02769, USA
Quigley, Linnea *Actress*
2608-1 N Ocean Blvd, #126, Pompano Beach, FL 33062, USA

Q

Quigley, Philip J (Phil) *Businessman*
%Pacific Telesis Group, 130 Kearny St, San Francisco, CA 94108, USA
Quik, D J *Rap Artist*
%International Creative Mgmt, 8942 Wilshire Blvd, #219, Beverly Hills, CA 90211, USA
Quill, Leonard W *Financier*
%Wilmington Trust Corp, Rodney Square N, 1100 N Market St, Wilmington, DE 19801, USA
Quill, Timothy E *Social Activist, Litigant, Internist*
%University of Rochester, Medical & Dentistry School, Rochester, NY 14642, USA
Quillan, Frederick (Fred) *Football Player*
2924 Bailey Lane, Eugene, OR 97401, USA
Quindlen, Anna M *Columnist*
%Random House, 1745 Broadway, #B1, New York, NY 10019, USA
Quinlan, Kathleen *Actress*
PO Box 861, Rockaway, OR 97136, USA
Quinlan, William D (Bill) *Football Player*
393 Mount Vernon St, Lawrence, MA 01843, USA
Quinn, Aidan *Actor*
%Bumble Wald, 8383 Wilshire Blvd, #323, Beverly Hills, CA 90211, USA
Quinn, Aileen *Actress*
400 Madison Ave, #20, New York, NY 10017, USA
Quinn, Brian *Soccer Player, Coach*
%San Jose Earthquakes, 3550 Stevens Creek Blvd, #200, San Jose, CA 95117, USA
Quinn, Carmel *Singer*
%Jane Mathers Mgmt, 230 W Summit Ave, #1, Haddonfield, NJ 08033, USA
Quinn, Colin *Actor, Comedian*
%William Morris Agency, 151 El Camino Dr, Beverly Hills, CA 90212, USA
Quinn, Colleen *Actress*
%Bauman Assoc, 5750 Wilshire Blvd, #473, Los Angeles, CA 90036, USA
Quinn, Danny *Actor*
%Don Buchwald, 6500 Wilshire Blvd, #2200, Los Angeles, CA 90048, USA
Quinn, David W *Businessman*
%Centex Corp, 2728 N Harwood, Dallas, TX 75201, USA
Quinn, DeClan *Cinematographer*
22 Cherry Ave, Cornwall on Hudson, NY 12520, USA
Quinn, Ed *Actor*
%Endeavor Talent Agency, 9701 Wilshire Blvd, #1000, Beverly Hills, CA 90212, USA
Quinn, Francesco *Actor*
3910 Woodcliff Road, Sherman Oaks, CA 91403, USA
Quinn, J B Patrick (Pat) *Hockey Player, Coach, Executive*
%Toronto Maple Leafs, 40 Bay St, Toronto ON M5J 2K2, Canada
Quinn, Jane Bryant *Columnist*
%Newsweek Magazine, Editorial Dept, 251 W 57th St, New York, NY 10019, USA
Quinn, Jim *Body Builder*
675 S Sierra Ave, #32, Solana Beach, CA 92075, USA
Quinn, John A *Chemical Engineer*
275 E Wynnewood Road, Merion Station, PA 19066, USA
Quinn, John C *Editor*
365 S Atlantic Ave, Cocoa Beach, FL 32931, USA
Quinn, Martha *Actress, Model*
%Panacea Entertainment, 12020 Chandler Blvd, #300, North Hollywood, CA 91607, USA
Quinn, Sally *Journalist*
3014 N St NW, Washington, DC 20007, USA
Quinn, William F *Governor, HI*
4340 Pahoa Ave, #13C, Honolulu, HI 96816, USA
Quintal, Stephane *Hockey Player*
1356A La Fontaine, Montreal QC H2L 1T5, Canada
Quintana, Chela *Golfer*
%Ladies Pro Golf Assn, 100 International Golf Dr, Daytona Beach, FL 32124, USA
Quiones, John *Commentator*
%ABC-TV, News Dept, 77 W 66th St, New York, NY 10023, USA
Quiring, Frederic *Actor*
%Cineart, 36 Rue de Ponthieu, 75008 Paris, France
Quirk, James P (Jamie) *Baseball Player*
12500 Aberdeen Road, Leawood, KS 66209, USA
Quirk, Michael J *WW II Army Air Corps Hero*
1700 Kit Lane, Navarre, FL 32566, USA
Quiroga, Elena *Writer*
%Agencia Balcells, Diagonal 580, 08021 Barcelona, Spain
Quiroga, Jorge (Tuto) *President, Bolivia*
%President's Office, Palacio de Gobierno, Plaza Murilla, La Paz, Bolivia
Quist, Janet *Model*
13446 Poway Road, #239, Poway, CA 92064, USA
Quivar, Florence *Opera Singer*
%Columbia Artists Mgmt Inc, 165 W 57th St, New York, NY 10019, USA
Quivers, Robin *Entertainer*
350 E 79th St, #16H, New York, NY 10021, USA
Qureia, Ahmed *Prime Minister, Palastine*
%Prime Minister's Office, Gaza City, Gaza Strip, Palestine, Israel

Raabe, Max *Opera Singer*
%Klimperkasten, Thuyring 63, 12101 Berlin, Germany
Raaum, Gustav *Skier*
PO Box 700, Mercer Island, WA 98040, USA
Rabe, Pamela *Actress*
%Shanahan Mgmt, PO Box 1509, Darlinghurst NSW 1300, Australia
Rabin, Trevor *Composer*
%Kraft-Benjamin-Engel, 15233 Ventura Blvd, #200, Sherman Oaks, CA 91403, USA
Rabinovitch, Benton S *Chemist*
12530 42nd Ave NE, Seattle, WA 98125, USA
Rabinow, Jacob *Electrical Engineer, Inventor*
6920 Selkirk Dr, Bethesda, MD 20817, USA
Rabinowitz, Dorothy *Journalist*
%Wall Street Journal, Editorial Dept, 200 Liberty St, New York, NY 10281, USA
Rabinowitz, Harry *Conductor, Composer*
11 Mead Road, Cranleigh, Surrey GU6 7BG, England
Rabinowitz, Jesse C *Biochemist*
%University of California, Molecular & Cell Biology Dept, Berkeley, CA 94720, USA
Rabkin, Mitchell T *Physician*
%Beth Israel Deaconess Medical Center, 330 Brookline Ave, Boston, MA 02215, USA
Raby, Stuart *Physicist*
%Ohio State University, Physics Dept, Columbus, OH 43210, USA
Racan, Ivica *Prime Minister, Croatia*
%Prime Minister's Office, Jordanovac 71, 41000 Zagreb, Croatia
Racette, Patricia *Opera Singer*
%Columbia Artists Mgmt Inc, 165 W 57th St, New York, NY 10019, USA
Rachins, Alan *Actor*
1274 Capri Dr, Pacific Palisades, CA 90272, USA
Rachlin, Julian *Concert Violinist*
%Columbia Artists Mgmt Inc, 165 W 57th St, New York, NY 10019, USA
Racicot, Marc F *Governor, MT*
901 15th St S, #201, Arlington, VA 22202, USA
Racimo, Victoria *Actress*
%Marion Rosenberg, PO Box 69826, West Hollywood, CA 90069, USA
Radatz, Richard R (Dick) *Baseball Player*
17 Hilltop Lane, #1, South Easton, MA 02375, USA
Radcliffe, Daniel *Actor*
%HP Prod, Leavesden Studios, PO Box 3000, Leavesden, Her W2D 7LT, England
Rademacher, Ingo *Actor*
%S D B Partners, 1801 Ave of Stars, #902, Los Angeles, CA 90067, USA
Rademacher, T Peter (Pete) *Boxer*
5585 River Styx Road, Medina, OH 44256, USA
Rader, Dotson C *Writer*
%Parade Magazine, Editorial Dept, 750 3rd Ave, New York, NY 10017, USA
Rader, Douglas L (Doug) *Baseball Player, Manager*
1822 Sullins Way, Houston, TX 77058, USA
Rader, Randall R *Judge*
%US Appeals Court, 717 Madison Place NW, Washington, DC 20439, USA
Radford, Mark *Basketball Player*
3423 NE 22nd Ave, Portland, OR 97212, USA
Radford, Michael *Movie Director*
3B Rickering Mews, London W2 5AD, England
Radigan, Terry *Singer, Songwriter*
%Frank Callari Corp, 6039 Robin Hill Road, Nashville, TN 37205, USA
Radisic, Zivko *Co-President, Bosnia-Herzegovina*
%President's Office, Marsala Titz 7, 71000 Sarajevo, Bosnia & Herzegovina
Radke, Brad W *Baseball Player*
%Richard Radke, 3107 Emerson, Tampa, FL 33629, USA
Radko, Christopher *Artist*
PO Box 536, Elmsford, NY 10523, USA
Radmanovic, Vladimir *Basketball Player*
%Seattle SuperSonics, 351 Elliott Ave W, #500, Seattle, WA 98119, USA
Radner, Roy *Economist*
30711 Overlook Run, Buena Vista, CO 81211, USA
Radojevic, Danilo *Ballet Dancer*
%American Ballet Theatre, 890 Broadway, New York, NY 10003, USA
Raduege, Harry D, Jr *Air Force General*
Director, Defense Information Systems Agency, Arlington, VA 22204, USA
Radwanski, George *Editor*
%Toronto Star, Editorial Dept, 1 Yonge St, Toronto ON M5E 1E6, Canada
Rae, Cassidy *Actress*
24708 Riverchase Dr, #B-213, Valencia, CA 91355, USA
Rae, Charlotte *Actress*
10790 Wilshire Blvd, #903, Los Angeles, CA 90024, USA
Rae, Robert K (Bob) *Political Leader, Canada*
%Goodman Phillips Vineberg, 250 Yonge St, Toronto ON M5B 2M6, Canada
Raekwon *Rap Artist (Wu-Tang Clan)*
%Famous Artists Agency, 250 W 57th St, New York, NY 10107, USA

R

Rafalski - Rakhmonov

Rafalski, Brian *Hockey Player*
%New Jersey Devils, Continental Arena, 50 RR 120 N, East Rutherford, NJ 07073, USA
Rafelson, Bob *Movie Director*
1543 Dog Team Road, New Haven, VT 05472, USA
Raffarin, Jean-Pierre *Prime Minister, France*
%Premier's Office, Hotel Matignon, 57 Rue de Varenne, 75700 Paris, France
Rafferty, Frances *Actress*
22141 Burbank Blvd, #4, Woodland Hills, CA 91367, USA
Rafferty, Thomas M (Tom) *Football Player*
1107 Travis Court, Southlake, TX 76092, USA
Raffi *Singer*
%Agency for Performing Arts, 9200 Sunset Blvd, #900, Los Angeles, CA 90069, USA
Raffin, Deborah *Actress*
301 N Canon Dr, #214, Beverly Hills, CA 90210, USA
Rafikov, Mars Z *Cosmonaut*
Ul M Gorkova 59, KV 44, 480 002 Almaty, Kazakhstan
Rafsanjani, Hojatoleslam H *President, Iran*
%Expediency Council of Islamic Order, Majilis, Teheran, Iran
Rafter, Patrick *Tennis Player*
PO Box 1235, North Sydney NSW 2059, Australia
Raftery, S Frank *Labor Leader*
%Painters & Allied Trades Union, 1750 New York Ave NW, Washington, DC 20006, USA
Ragin, Derek Lee *Opera Singer*
%Colbert Artists, 111 W 57th St, New York, NY 10019, USA
Ragin, John S *Actor*
5706 Briarcliff Road, Los Angeles, CA 90068, USA
Ragsdale, William *Actor*
%Innovative Artists, 1505 10th St, Santa Monica, CA 90401, USA
Rahal, Robert W (Bobby) *Auto Racing Driver, Owner*
5 New Albany Farms Road, New Albany, OH 43054, USA
Rahlves, Daron *Alpine Skier*
PO Box 333, Truckee, CA 96160, USA
Rahman Khan, Ataur *Prime Minister, Bangladesh*
%Bangladesh Jatiya League, 500A Dhanmondi R/A, Road 7, Dhaka, Bangladesh
Rahzel *Vocal Percussionist (Roots)*
%Agency Group Ltd, 1775 Broadway, #430, New York, NY 10019, USA
Raichle, Marcus E *Neurologist, Radiologist*
%Washington University, Medical School, Neurology Dept, Saint Louis, MO 63130, USA
Railsback, Steve *Actor*
11684 Ventura Blvd, #581, Studio City, CA 91604, USA
Raimi, Sam *Movie Director, Actor*
8381 Hollywood Blvd, #680, Los Angeles, CA 90069, USA
Raimond, Jean-Bernard *Government Official, France*
Servier SA, 22 Rue Garnier, 92200 Neuilly-sur-Seine, France
Raimondi, Ruggero *Opera Singer*
%M Gromof, 140 Bis Rue Lecourbe, 75015 Paris, France
Raine, Craig A *Writer*
%New College, English Dept, Oxford OX1 3BN, England
Rainer, Luise *Actress*
54 Eaton Square, London SW1, England
Raines, Franklin D *Government Official, Financier*
%Federal National Mortgage Assn, 3900 Wisconsin Ave NW, Washington, DC 20016, USA
Raines, Timothy (Tim) *Baseball Player*
310 Saddleworth Place, Lake Mary, FL 32746, USA
Rainey, Ford *Actor*
3821 Carbon Canyon Road, Malibu, CA 90265, USA
Rainey, Matt *Photojournalist*
%Star-Ledger, Editorial Dept, 1 Star-Ledger Plaza, Newark, NJ 07102, USA
Rainey, Wayne *Motorcycle Racing Rider*
1660 Akron Peninsula Road, #201, Akron, OH 44313, USA
Rainier III *Prince, Monaco*
%Palais de Monaco, Boite Postale 518, 98015 Monte Carlo Cedex, Monaco
Rainwater, G L *Businessman*
%Ameren Corp, 1901 Chouteau Ave, Saint Louis, MO 63103, USA
Rainwater, Gregg *Actor*
PO Box 291836, Los Angeles, CA 90029, USA
Rainwater, Keech *Drummer (Lonestar)*
%Borman Entertainment, 1222 16th Ave S, #23, Nashville, TN 37212, USA
Rainwater, Marvin *Singer*
36968 295th St, Aitkin, MN 56431, USA
Raitt, Bonnie L *Singer, Songwriter*
3575 Cahuenga Blvd W, #590, Los Angeles, CA 90068, USA
Raitt, John *Singer, Actor*
1164 Napoli Dr, Pacific Palisades, CA 90272, USA
Rajna, Thomas *Concert Pianist, Composer*
10 Wyndover Road, Claremont, Cape 7700, South Africa
Rakhmonov, Emomali *President, Tajikistan*
%President's Office, Supreme Soviet, Dushanbe, Tajikistan

Raki, Laya *Actress*
%Atkins Assoc, 8040 Ventura Canyon Ave, Panorama City, CA 91402, USA

Rakim *Rap Artist (Eric B & Rakim)*
%Padell Nadell Fine Wineberger, 156 W 56th St, #400, New York, NY 10019, USA

Rakotomavo, Pascal *Prime Minister, Madagascar*
%Prime Minister's Office, Mahazoarivo, Antananarivo, Madagascar

Rakowski, Mieczyslaw F *Prime Minister, Poland*
Miesiecznik Dzis, Ul Poznanska 3, 00-680 Warsaw, Poland

Raksin, David *Composer, Conductor*
6519 Aldea Ave, Van Nuys, CA 91406, USA

Rales, Steven M *Businessman*
%Danaher Corp, 1250 24th St NW, Washington, DC 20037, USA

Rall, Gunther *WW II Air Force Hero*
Schmalschlagerstr 17, 83435 Bad Reichenhall, Germany

Rall, J Edward *Physician*
3947 Baltimore St, Kensington, MD 20895, USA

Rall, Ted *Editorial Cartoonist*
%Chronicle Features, 901 Mission St, San Francisco, CA 94103, USA

Rallis, George J *Prime Minister, Greece*
4 Kanari St, 106 71 Athens, Greece

Ralph, Michael *Actor*
%Abrams-Rubaloff Lawrence, 8075 W 3rd St, #303, Los Angeles, CA 90048, USA

Ralph, Richard P *Governor, Falkland Islands*
%Governor's Office, Government House, Stanley, Falkland Islands

Ralph, Sheryl Lee *Actress, Singer*
938 S Longwood Ave, Los Angeles, CA 90019, USA

Ralston, Dennis *Tennis Player*
2005 San Vicente Dr, Concord, CA 94519, USA

Ralston, John R *Football Player, Coach*
5958 Dry Oak Dr, San Jose, CA 95120, USA

Ralston, Steve *Soccer Player*
%New England Revolution, CMGI Field, 1 Patriot Place, Foxboro, MA 02035, USA

Ram, C Venkata *Physician*
%Texas Southwestern Medical Center, 5323 Harry Hines Blvd, Dallas, TX 75390, USA

Rama IX *King, Thailand*
%Chitralada Villa, Bangkok, Thailand

Rama Rau, Santha *Writer*
496 Leedsville Road, Amenia, NY 12501, USA

Ramage, Rob *Hockey Player*
16127 Wilson Manor Dr, Chesterfield, MO 63005, USA

Ramahatra, Victor *Prime Minister, Madagascar; Army Officer*
PO Box 6004, Antanarivo 101, Madagascar

Ramaphosa, M Cyril *Government Official, South Africa*
%New Africa Investments, PO Box 782922, Sandton 2146, South Africa

Rambahadur Limbu *Vietnam War Borneo Army Hero (VC)*
Box 420, Bandar Seri Begawan, Negara Brunei Darussalam, Brunei

Rambert, Charles J J *Architect*
179 Rue de Courcelles, 75017 Paris, France

Rambis, Kurt *Basketball Player, Coach*
20 Chatham, Manhattan Beach, CA 90266, USA

Rambo, David L *Religious Leader*
%Christian & Missionary Alliance, PO Box 35000, Colorado Springs, CO 80935, USA

Rambo, John *Track Athlete*
1847 Myrtle Ave, Long Beach, CA 90806, USA

Rambola, Tony *Guitarist (Godsmack)*
%William Morris Agency, 151 El Camino Dr, Beverly Hills, CA 90212, USA

Ramey, Samuel E *Opera Singer*
320 Central Park West, New York, NY 10025, USA

Ramgoolam, Navinchandra *Prime Minister, Mauritius*
85 Sir Seewiisagur Ramgoolam St, Port Louis, Mauritius

Ramgoolam, Seewosagur *Prime Minister, Mauritius*
85 Desforges St, Port Louis, Mauritius

Ramirez Vazquez, Pedro *Architect*
Ave de la Fuentes 170, Mexico City 01900 DF, Mexico

Ramirez, Manuel A (Manny) *Baseball Player*
29315 Regency Circle, Westlake, OK 44145, USA

Ramirez, Michael P (Mike) *Editorial Cartoonist*
%Los Angeles Times, Editorial Dept, 202 W 1st St, Los Angeles, CA 90012, USA

Ramirez, Pedro J *Editor*
%El Mundo, Calle Pradillo 42, 28002 Madrid, Spain

Ramirez, Raul *Tennis Player*
Avenida Ruiz, 65 Sur Ensenada, Baja California, Mexico

Ramirez, Twiggy *Bassist (Marilyn Manson)*
%Mitch Schneider Organization, 14724 Ventura Blvd, #410, Sherman Oaks, CA 91403, USA

Ramis, Harold A *Actor, Movie Director*
160 Euclid Ave, Glencoe, IL 60022, USA

Ramo, Simon *Businessman*
9200 Sunset Blvd, #401, West Hollywood, CA 90069, USA

Ramon, Haim *Government Official, Israel*
%Knesset, Jerusalem 91010, Israel
Ramos, Del *Singer (Association)*
%Variety Artists, 1924 Spring St, Paso Robles, CA 93446, USA
Ramos, Hilario (Larry), Jr *Singer, Guitarist (Association)*
%Variety Artists, 1924 Spring St, Paso Robles, CA 93446, USA
Ramos, Mando *Boxer*
1252 W Park Western Dr, #91, San Pedro, CA 90732, USA
Ramos, Mel *Artist*
5941 Ocean View Dr, Oakland, CA 94618, USA
Ramos, Monica *Singer*
%MNW Records Group, PO Box 535, 183 25 Taby, Sweden
Ramos, Tab *Soccer Player*
%William Morris Agency, 151 El Camino Dr, Beverly Hills, CA 90212, USA
Ramos-Horta, Jose *Nobel Peace Laureate*
Rua Sao Lazoro 16, #1, 1150 Lisbon, Portugal
Rampling, Charlotte *Actress*
1 Ave Emile Augier, 78290 Croissy-sur-Seine, France
Ramsay, Craig *Hockey Player, Coach*
9701 NW 58th Court, Parkland, FL 33076, USA
Ramsay, John T (Jack) *Basketball Coach, Executive*
444 Ridgeway Road, Lake Oswego, OR 97034, USA
Ramsay, Wayne *Hockey Player*
%General Delivery, Oak River MB R0K 1T0, Canada
Ramsey, Frank V, Jr *Basketball Player, Coach*
363 Buckner Ridge Lane, Madisonville, KY 42431, USA
Ramsey, Garrard S (Buster) *Football Player*
4102 Highway 411S, Maryville, TN 37801, USA
Ramsey, Mary *Singer (10000 Maniacs)*
%Agency for Performing Arts, 9200 Sunset Blvd, #900, Los Angeles, CA 90069, USA
Ramsey, Michael (Mike) *Hockey Player*
445 W 79th St, Chanhassen, MN 55317, USA
Ramsey, Norman F, Jr *Nobel Physics Laureate*
24 Monmouth Court, Brookline, MA 02446, USA
Ramsey, Ray *Football, Basketball Player*
1612 Sequoia Dr, Chatham, IL 62629, USA
Ramsey, William (Bill) *Singer, Songwriter*
Elbchaussee 118, 22763 Hamburg, Germany
Ramsey, William E *Navy Admiral*
825 Bayshore Dr, Pensacola, FL 32507, USA
Ran, Shulamit *Composer*
%University of Chicago, Music Dept, 5845 S Ellis Ave, Chicago, IL 60637, USA
Rand Reese, Mary *Track Athlete*
6650 Los Gatos, Atascadero, CA 93422, USA
Rand, Marvin *Photographer*
%Marvin Rand Assoc, 1310 Abbot Kinney Blvd, Venice, CA 90291, USA
Rand, Robert W *Neurosurgeon, Educator*
%Good Samaritan Hospital, Neurosciences Institute, Los Angeles, CA 90017, USA
Randall, Carolyn D *Judge*
%US Court of Appeals, 515 Rusk St, Houston, TX 77002, USA
Randall, Claire *Religious Leader*
10015 W Royal Oak Road, #120, Sun City, AZ 85351, USA
Randall, Frankie *Boxer*
355 Fish Hatchery Road, #02, Morristown, TN 37813, USA
Randall, Jon *Singer*
%Joe's Garage, 4405 Belmont Park Terrace, Nashville, TN 37215, USA
Randall, Josh *Actor*
%I F A Talent Agency, 8730 Sunset Blvd, #490, Los Angeles, CA 90069, USA
Randall, Rebel *Actress*
%Women United Int'l, 32969 Shifting Sands Trail, Cathedral City, CA 92234, USA
Randall, Tony *Actor*
%Beresford, 1 W 81st St, #6D, New York, NY 10024, USA
Randi, James *Illusionist*
12000 NW 8th St, Plantation, FL 33325, USA
Randle, John *Football Player*
PO Box 489, Harrisonburg, VA 22803, USA
Randle, Theresa *Actress*
350 S Catalina St, #307, Los Angeles, CA 90020, USA
Randle, Ulmo (Sonny) *Football Player*
2361 Meadow Court, Harrisonburg, VA 22801, USA
Randolph, A Raymond *Judge*
%US Court of Appeals, 333 Constitution NW, Washington, DC 20001, USA
Randolph, Boots *Jazz Saxophonist*
541 Richmar Dr, Nashville, TN 37211, USA
Randolph, Carl *Bassist (Reveille)*
%David Levin Mgmt, 200 W 57th St, #308, New York, NY 10019, USA
Randolph, Jackson H *Businessman*
%Cinergy Corp, 139 E 4th St, Cincinnati, OH 45202, USA

Randolph, John *Actor*
1850 N Whitney Place, Los Angeles, CA 90028, USA
Randolph, Judson G *Pediatric Surgeon*
111 Michigan Ave NW, Washington, DC 20010, USA
Randolph, Willie L *Baseball Player*
648 Juniper Place, Franklin Lakes, NJ 07417, USA
Randolph, Zach *Basketball Player*
%Portland Trail Blazers, Rose Garden, 1 Center Court St, Portland, OR 97227, USA
Randrup, Michael *Test Pilot*
10 Fairlawn Road, Lythamst, Annes, Lancashire FY8 5PT, England
Rands, Bernard *Composer*
%Harvard University, Music Dept, Cambridge, MA 02138, USA
Ranford, William (Bill) *Hockey Player*
%Coquitlam Express, 633 Poirier St, Coquitlam BC V3J 6B1, Canada
Ranger Doug *Singer (Riders in the Sky), Songwriter*
%New Frontier Mgmt, 1921 Broadway, Nashville, TN 37203, USA
Rania *Queen, Jordan*
%Royal Palace, Amman, Jordan
Ranis, Gustav *Economist*
7 Mulberry Road, Woodbridge, CT 06525, USA
Ranki, Dezso *Concert Pianist*
OrdogoromLejto 11/B, 1112 Budapest, Hungary
Rankin, Alfred M, Jr *Businessman*
%NACCO Industries, 5875 Landerbrook Dr, Mayfield Heights, OH 44124, USA
Rankin, Judy *Golfer*
2715 Racquet Club Dr, Midland, TX 79705, USA
Rankin, Kenny *Singer, Songwriter, Guitarist*
%Absolute Artists, 530 Howard St, #200, San Francisco, CA 94105, USA
Rankine, Terry *Architect*
%Cambridge Seven Assoc, 1050 Massachusetts Ave, Cambridge, MA 02138, USA
Ranks, Shabba *Singer*
%Epic Records, 550 Madison Ave, #2500, New York, NY 10022, USA
Ranney, Helen M *Physician*
6229 La Jolla Mesa Dr, La Jolla, CA 92037, USA
Ransdell, Gary *Educator*
%Western Kentucky University, President's Office, Bowling Green, KY 42101, USA
Ransey, Kelvin *Basketball Player*
3195 Monterey Dr, Tupelo, MS 38801, USA
Rao, C N Ramachandra *Chemist*
JNC President's House, Indian Science Institute, Bangalor 560012, India
Rao, Calyampudi R *Statistician, Mathematician*
826 W Aaron Dr, State College, PA 16803, USA
Rao, P V Narasimha *Prime Minister, India*
Lok Sabha, New Delhi, India
Rapaport, Michael *Actor*
%Innovative Artists, 1505 10th St, Santa Monica, CA 90401, USA
Raper, Kenneth B *Bacteriologist*
602 N Segoe Road, Madison, WI 53705, USA
Raphael *Singer, Actor*
%Kaduri Agency, 16125 NE 18th Ave, North Miami Beach, FL 33162, USA
Raphael, Fredric M *Writer*
Largadelle, Saint Lauraent la Vallee, 24170 Belves, France
Raphael, Sally Jessy *Entertainer*
249 Quaker Hill Road, Pawling, NY 12564, USA
Rappeneau, Jean-Paul *Movie Director*
24 Rue Henri Barbusse, 75005 Paris, France
Rapping 4-Tay *Rap Artist*
%Richard Walters, 1800 Argyle Ave, #408, Los Angeles, CA 90028, USA
Rappuoli, Rino *Medical Researcher*
%Sclavo Research Center, Via Fiorentina 1, 53100, Siena, Italy
Rapson, Ralph *Architect*
1 Seymour Ave, Minneapolis, MN 55414, USA
Rarick, Cindy *Golfer*
%Ladies Pro Golf Assn, 100 International Golf Dr, Daytona Beach, FL 32124, USA
Rasa Don *Soul/Rap Artist (Arrested Development)*
%William Morris Agency, 1325 Ave of Americas, New York, NY 10019, USA
Rasche, David *Actor*
687 Grove Lane, Santa Barbara, CA 93105, USA
Rascon, Alfred V *Vietnam War Army Hero (CMH)*
10397 Derby Dr, Laurel, MD 20723, USA
Rash, Steve *Movie Director*
%Broder Kurland Webb Uffner, 9242 Beverly Blvd, #200, Beverly Hills, CA 90210, USA
Rashad, Ahmad *Football Player, Sportscaster*
%NBA Ent, 450 Harmon Meadow Blvd, Secaucus, NJ 07094, USA
Rashad, Phylicia *Actress*
25 Magnolia Ave, Mount Vernon, NY 10553, USA
Rasheeda *Rap Artist*
%International Creative Mgmt, 8942 Wilshire Blvd, #219, Beverly Hills, CA 90211, USA

R

Rashid, Karim *Furniture Designer*
357 W 17th St, New York, NY 10011, USA
Raskin, Alex *Journalist*
%Los Angeles Times, Editorial Dept, 202 W 1st St, Los Angeles, CA 90012, USA
Raskin, David *Composer*
%Robert Light, 6404 Wilshire Blvd, Los Angeles, CA 90048, USA
Rasmussen, Anders Fogh *Prime Minister, Denmark*
Prins Jorgens Gard 11, 1218 Copenhagen K, Denmark
Rasmussen, Poul Nyrup *Prime Minister, Denmark*
Allegade 6A, 2000 Frederiksberg, Denmark
Raspberry, Larry *Singer (Gentrys)*
%Craig Nowag Attractions, 6037 Haddington Place, Memphis, TN 38119, USA
Raspberry, William J *Journalist*
%Washington Post, Editorial Dept, 1150 15th St NW, Washington, DC 20071, USA
Ratchford, Jeremy *Actor*
%Paradigm Agency, 10100 Santa Monica Blvd, #2500, Los Angeles, CA 90067, USA
Ratcliffe, John A *Radio Astronomer*
193 Huntingdon Road, Cambridge CB3 0DL, England
Ratelle, J G Y Jean *Hockey Player*
1200 Salem St, #111, Lynnfield, MA 01940, USA
Rather, Dan *Commentator*
%CBS-TV, News Dept, 51 W 52nd St, New York, NY 10019, USA
Rathke, Henrich K M H *Religious Leader*
Schleifmuhlenweg 11, 19061 Schwering, Germany
Rathmann, George B *Businessman*
%ICOS Corp, 22021 20th Ave SE, Bothell, WA 98021, USA
Rathmann, Jim *Auto Racing Driver*
14 Marina Isles Blvd, #14G, Indian Harbor Beach, FL 32937, USA
Ratleff, Ed *Basketball Player*
4202 Paseo de Oro, Cypress, CA 90630, USA
Ratliff, Theo *Basketball Player*
%Atlanta Hawks, 190 Marietta St SW, Atlanta, GA 30303, USA
Ratner, Brett *Movie Director*
%William Morris Agency, 151 El Camino Dr, Beverly Hills, CA 90212, USA
Ratner, Helmer *Movie Director*
%Creative Artists Agency, 9830 Wilshire Blvd, Beverly Hills, CA 90212, USA
Ratner, Mark A *Chemist*
615 Greenleaf Ave, Glencoe, IL 60022, USA
Ratnoff, Oscar D *Physician*
1801 Chestnut Hills Dr, Cleveland, OH 44106, USA
Ratser, Dmitri *Concert Pianist*
%Naxim Gershunoff, 1401 NE 9th St, #38, Fort Lauderdale, FL 33304, USA
Ratsiraka, Didier *President, Madagascar; Navy Admiral*
%President's Office, Iavoloha, Antananarivo, Madagascar
Ratterman, George *Football Player*
6745 S Cook St, Centennial, CO 80122, USA
Rattle, Simon D *Conductor*
%Frank Salomon, 201 W 54th St, #1C, New York, NY 10019, USA
Ratushinskaya, Irina B *Writer*
%Vargius Publishing House, Kuzakova Str 18, 107005 Moscow, Russia
Ratzenberger, John *Actor*
%Shelter Entertainment, 9255 Sunset Blvd, #1010, Los Angeles, CA 90069, USA
Ratzinger, Joseph A Cardinal *Religious Leader*
Palazzo del S Uffizio II, 00193 Rome, Italy
Rau, Johannes *President, Germany*
Haroldstr 2, 47057 Dusseldorf, Germany
Rauch, John (Johnny) *Football Player, Coach*
30 Tads Trail, Oldsmar, FL 34677, USA
Raup, David M *Paleontologist*
RR 1 Box 168Y, Washington Island, WI 54246, USA
Rauschenberg, Robert *Artist*
381 Lafayette St, New York, NY 10003, USA
Rautio, Nina *Opera Singer*
%Herbert Breslin, 119 W 57th St, #1505, New York, NY 10019, USA
Ravalec, Blanche *Actress*
%Babette Pouget, 6 Square Villaret de Joyeuse, 75017 Paris, France
Ravalomanana, Marc *President, Madagascar*
%President's Office, Iavoloha, Antananarivo, Madagascar
Raven *Wrestler*
3665 Wintershill Dr, Atlanta, GA 30380, USA
Raven, Eddy *Singer, Songwriter, Guitarist*
%Great American Talent, PO Box 2476, Hendersonvlle, TN 37077, USA
Raven, Peter H *Botanist*
%Missouri Botanical Garden, PO Box 299, Saint Louis, MO 63166, USA
Raven, Robert D *Attorney*
%Morrison & Foerster, 345 California St, #3500, San Francisco, CA 94104, USA
Raver, Kim *Actress*
853 7th St, #9A, New York, NY 10019, USA

Ravitch, Diane S *Historian*
%New York University, Press Building, Washington Place, New York, NY 10003, USA
Ravony, Francisque *Prime Minister, Madagascar*
%Union des Forces Vivas Democratiques, Antananarivo, Madagascar
Rawlins, V Lane *Educator*
%Washington State University, President's Office, Pullman, WA 99164, USA
Rawlinson of Ewell, Peter A G *Government Official, England*
Wardour Castle, Tisbury, Wilts SP3 6RH, England
Rawls, Elizabeth E (Betsy) *Golfer*
501 Country Club Dr, Wilmington, DE 19803, USA
Rawls, Lou *Singer, Actor*
8428 E Preserve Way, Scottsdale, AZ 85262, USA
Rawls, Sam *Cartoonist (Pops Place)*
%King Features Syndicate, 888 7th Ave, New York, NY 10106, USA
Ray, Alexa *Actress*
%The Agency, 1800 Ave of Stars, #400, Los Angeles, CA 90067, USA
Ray, Amy *Singer (Indigo Girls), Songwriter*
%Russell Carter Artist Mgmt, 315 W Ponce de Leon Ave, #756, Decatur, GA 30030, USA
Ray, Edward J *Educator*
%Oregon State University, President's Office, Corvallis, OR 97331, USA
Ray, Gene Anthony *Actor*
PO Box 135, Massapequa Park, NY 11762, USA
Ray, Jeanne *Writer*
%Harmony Books, 201 E 50th St, New York, NY 10022, USA
Ray, Jimmy *Singer*
%Nineteen Music/Mgmt, 35-37 Parkgate Road, London SW11 4NP, England
Ray, Marguerite *Actress*
1329 N Vista St, #106, Los Angeles, CA 90046, USA
Ray, Rachel *Chef*
%Food Network, 1180 Ave of Americas, #1200, New York, NY 10036, USA
Ray, Robert D *Governor, IA*
%Blue Cross/Blue Shield of Iowa, 636 Grand Ave, Des Moines, IA 50309, USA
Ray, Ronald E *Vietnam War Army Hero (CMH)*
4324 Belle Vista Dr, Saint Petersburg Beach, FL 33706, USA
Raybon, Marty *Singer*
%Hallmark Direction, 15 Music Square W, Nashville, TN 37203, USA
Raye, Collin *Singer*
%Scott Dean Mgmt, 612 Humboldt St, Reno, NV 89509, USA
Rayl, Jim *Basketball Player*
201 West Boulevard, Kokomo, IN 46902, USA
Raymo, Maureen *Geologist*
%Boston University, Geology Dept, Boston, MA 02215, USA
Raymond, Guy *Actor*
550 Erskine Dr, Pacific Palisades, CA 90272, USA
Raymond, Kenneth N *Chemist*
%University of California, Chemistry Dept, Berkeley, CA 94720, USA
Raymond, Lee R *Businessman*
%Exxon Corp, 5959 Las Colinas Blvd, Irving, TX 75039, USA
Raymond, Lisa *Tennis Player*
%Octagon, 1751 Pinnacle Dr, #1500, McLean, VA 22102, USA
Raymond, Paula *Actress*
PO Box 86, Beverly Hills, CA 90213, USA
Raymond, Ralph *Softball Coach*
%USA Softball, 1 Olympia Plaza, Colorado Springs, CO 80909, USA
Raz, Kavi *Actor*
%Dale Garrick, 8831 Sunset Blvd, #402, Los Angeles, CA 90069, USA
Raza, S Atiq *Businessman*
%Advanced Micro Devices, 1 AMD Place, Sunnyvale, CA 94085, USA
Razafindratandra, Armand Gaetan Cardinal *Religious Leader*
Archeveche, Andohalo, 101 Antananarivo, Madagascar
Razanamasy, Guy *Prime Minister, Madagascar*
%Prime Minister's Office, Mahazoarivo, Antananarivo, Madagascar
Razborov, A A *Mathematician*
%Princeton University, Mathematics Dept, Princeton, NJ 08540, USA
Re, Giovanni Battisti Cardinal *Religious Leader*
Palazzo delle Congregazioni, Piazza Pio XII, #10, 00193 Rome, Italy
Rea, Chris *Singer, Guitarist*
%Real Life, 122 Holland Park Ave, London W11 4UA, England
Rea, Peggy *Actress*
10231 Riverside Dr, #201, Toluca Lake, CA 91602, USA
Rea, Stephen *Actor*
861 Sutherland Ave, London W9, England
Read, James *Actor*
3713 Hitchcock Ranch Road, Santa Barbara, CA 93105, USA
Read, Richard *Journalist*
%Portland Oregonian, Editorial Dept, 1320 SW Broadway, Portland, OR 97201, USA
Read, Sister Joel *Educator*
%Alverno College, President's Office, PO Box 343922, Milwaukee, WI 53234, USA

R

Readdy, William F (Bill) *Astronaut*
%NASA, Johnson Space Center, 2101 NASA Road, Houston, TX 77058, USA
Reagan, Nancy D *Wife of US President, Actress*
10880 Wilshire Blvd, #870, Los Angeles, CA 90024, USA
Reagan, Ronald W *President, USA; Governor, CA; Actor*
10880 Wilshire Blvd, #870, Los Angeles, CA 90024, USA
Reagon, Bernice Johnson *Singer (Sweet Honey in the Rock)*
%American University, History Dept, Washington, DC 20016, USA
Reality, Maxim *Singer, Emcee (Prodigy)*
%Midi Mgmt, Jenkins Lane, Great Hallinsbury, Essex CM22 7QL, England
Reardon, Jeffrey J (Jeff) *Baseball Player*
5 Marlwood Lane, Palm Beach Gardens, FL 33418, USA
Reardon, Kenneth J (Ken) *Hockey Player*
568 Ave Grosvenor, Westmount QC H3Y 2S7, Canada
Reason, Rex *Actor*
%Roadside Productions, 20105 Rhapsody Road, Walnut Creek, CA 91789, USA
Reasons, Gary P *Football Player*
16303 Perry Pass Court, Spring, TX 77379, USA
Reaves, Stephanie *Motorcycle Racing Rider*
PO Box 55, Bar Mills, ME 04004, USA
Rebhorn, James *Actor*
145 W 45th St, #1204, New York, NY 10036, USA
Recchi, Mark *Hockey Player*
%Philadelphia Flyers, 1st Union Center, 3601 S Broad St, Philadelphia, PA 19148, USA
Rechichar, Albert (Bert) *Football Player*
141 W McClain Road, Belle Vernon, PA 15012, USA
Rechin, Bill *Cartoonist (Crock)*
%North American Syndicate, 235 E 45th St, New York, NY 10017, USA
Reckell, Peter *Actor*
PO Box 2704-462, Huntington Beach, CA 92647, USA
Rector, Jeff *Actor*
10748 Aqua Vista St, North Hollywood, CA 91602, USA
Redbone, Leon *Singer*
%Red Shark Inc, 2169 Aquetong Road, New Hope, PA 18938, USA
Reddy, D Raj *Computer Scientist*
%Robotics Institute, Carnegie-Mellon University, Pittsburgh, PA 15213, USA
Reddy, Helen *Singer*
%Helen Reddy Inc, 2029 Century Park E, #600, Los Angeles, CA 90067, USA
Redeker, Quinn *Actor*
8075 3rd Ave, #303, Los Angeles, CA 90048, USA
Redfield, James *Writer*
%Warner Books, 1271 6th Ave, New York, NY 10020, USA
Redford, Robert *Actor, Movie Director*
RR 3 Box 837, Provo, UT 84604, USA
Redgrave, Corin *Actor*
%Kate Feast, Primrose Hill Studios, Fitzroy Road, London NW1 8TR, England
Redgrave, Jemma *Actress*
%Conway Van Gelder Robinson, 18-21 Jermyn St, London SW1Y 6NB, England
Redgrave, Lynn *Actress*
%P F D, Drury House, 34-43 Russell St, London WC2B 5HA, England
Redgrave, Vanessa *Actress*
%Gavin Barker Assoc, 2D Wimpole St, London W1G 0EB, England
Reding, Juli *Actress*
PO Box 1806, Beverly Hills, CA 90213, USA
Redman *Rap Artist*
%International Creative Mgmt, 8942 Wilshire Blvd, #219, Beverly Hills, CA 90211, USA
Redman, Dewey *Jazz Reeds Player, Composer*
%Joel Chriss, 300 Mercer St, #3J, New York, NY 10003, USA
Redman, Joshua *Jazz Saxophonist, Composer*
%Wilkins Mgmt, 323 Broadway, Cambridge, MA 02139, USA
Redman, Joyce *Actress*
%P F D, Drury House, 34-43 Russell St, London WC2B 5HA, England
Redman, Michele *Golfer*
%Ladies Pro Golf Assn, 100 International Golf Dr, Daytona Beach, FL 32124, USA
Redman, Richard C (Rick) *Football Player*
153 Prospect St, Seattle, WA 98109, USA
Redmond, Markus *Actor*
%Writers & Artists, 8383 Wilshire Blvd, #550, Beverly Hills, CA 90211, USA
Redmond, Michael E (Mickey) *Hockey Player*
30699 Harlincin Court, Franklin, MI 48025, USA
Redpath, Jean *Singer*
Sunny Knowe, Promenade, Leven, Fife, Scotland
Redstone, Sumner M *Businessman*
%Viacom Inc, 1515 Broadway, New York, NY 10036, USA
Redwine, Jarvis J *Football Player*
2707 W 79th St, Inglewood, CA 90305, USA
Reece, Beasley *Football Player, Sportscaster*
717 S Columbus Blvd, #821, Philadelphia, PA 19147, USA

Reece, Daniel (Danny) *Football Player*
24610 S Avalon Blvd, Wilmington, CA 90744, USA
Reece, Gabrielle (Gabby) *Volleyball Player, Model*
PO Box 2246, Malibu, CA 90265, USA
Reece, Thomas L *Businessman*
%Dover Corp, 280 Park Ave, New York, NY 10017, USA
Reed, Andre D *Football Player*
PO Box 9383, Rancho Santa Fe, CA 92067, USA
Reed, Brandy *Basketball Player*
%Phoenix Mercury, American West Arena, 201 E Jefferson St, Phoenix, AZ 85004, USA
Reed, Brian *Guitarist (EvinRudes), Songwriter*
%Turner Management Group, 374 Poli St, #205, Ventura, CA 93001, USA
Reed, Eric *Jazz Pianist*
%Joel Chriss, 300 Mercer St, #3J, New York, NY 10003, USA
Reed, Herb *Singer (Platters)*
%Platters Mgmt, 990 Massachusetts Ave, Arlington, MA 02476, USA
Reed, Ishmael S *Writer*
1446 6th St, #C, Berkeley, CA 94710, USA
Reed, Jerry *Singer, Songwriter, Actor*
%Jerry Lee Enterprises, PO Box 3586, Brentwood, TN 37024, USA
Reed, John H *Governor, ME; Diplomat*
410 O St SW, Washington, DC 20024, USA
Reed, John S *Financier*
%Citigroup Inc, 399 Park Ave, New York, NY 10022, USA
Reed, Johnny *Singer (Orioles)*
%Jackson Artists, 7251 Lowell Dr, #200, Overland Park, KS 66204, USA
Reed, Lou *Singer (Velvet Undergound), Songwriter*
%Three Artist Mgmt, 2550 Laurel Pass, Los Angeles, CA 90046, USA
Reed, Mark A *Physicist*
%Yale University, Electrical Engineering Dept, PO Box 2157, New Haven, CT 06520, USA
Reed, Pamela *Actress*
%Innovative Artists, 1505 10th St, Santa Monica, CA 90401, USA
Reed, Ralph *Religious Leader*
1801 Sarah Dr, #L, Chesapeake, VA 23320, USA
Reed, Rex *Movie Critic*
%Dakota Hotel, 1 W 72nd St, #86, New York, NY 10023, USA
Reed, Richard A (Rick) *Baseball Player*
2205 Jefferson Ave, Huntington, WV 25704, USA
Reed, Richard J *Meteorologist*
%University of Washington, Atmospheric Sciences Dept, Seattle, WA 98195, USA
Reed, Ronald L (Ron) *Basketball, Baseball Player*
2613 Cliffview Dr, Lilburn, GA 30047, USA
Reed, Shanna *Actress*
1327 Brinkley Ave, Los Angeles, CA 90049, USA
Reed, Thomas C *Government Official*
%Quaker Hill Development Corp, PO Box 2240, Healdsburg, CA 95448, USA
Reed, Willis, Jr *Basketball Player, Coach, Executive*
28-2419 W 3rd St, South Orange, NJ 07079, USA
Reeds, Mark *Hockey Player*
7823 Cardinal Ridge Court, Saint Louis, MO 63119, USA
Reedus, Norman *Actor, Model*
527 Hudson St, New York, NY 10014, USA
Rees, Andrew *Opera Singer*
%Van Walsum Mgmt, 4 Addison Bridge Place, London W14 8XP, England
Rees, Angharad *Actress*
%James Sharkey, 21 Golden Square, London W1R 3PA, England
Rees, Clifford H (Ted), Jr *Air Force General*
1620 Mayflower Court, #B414, Winter Park, FL 32792, USA
Rees, Eberhard *Physicist*
69 Revere Way, Huntsville, AL 35801, USA
Rees, John *Bassist (Men at Work)*
%TPA, PO Box 124, Round Corner NSW 2158, Australia
Rees, Martin J *Astronomer*
%King's College, Astronomy Institute, Cambridge CB2 1ST, England
Rees, Mina *Mathematician*
301 E 66th St, New York, NY 10021, USA
Rees, Norma S *Educator*
%California State University, President's Office, Hayward, CA 94542, USA
Rees, Roger *Actor*
%Innovative Artists, 1505 10th St, Santa Monica, CA 90401, USA
Rees-Mogg of Hinton Blewett, William *Publisher*
3 Smith Square, London SW1, England
Reese, Della *Singer, Actress*
55 W 900 S, Salt Lake City, UT 84101, USA
Reese, Eddie *Swimming Coach*
%University of Texas, Athletic Dept, Austin, TX 78712, USA
Reese, Miranda *Ballerina*
%New York City Ballet, Lincoln Center Plaza, New York, NY 10023, USA

R

Reeve, Christopher — *Actor, Activist*
500 Morris Ave, Springfield, NJ 07081, USA
Reeves, Bryant — *Basketball Player*
%Memphis Grizzlies, 175 Toyota Plaza, #150, Memphis, TN 38103, USA
Reeves, Daniel E (Dan) — *Football Player, Coach*
%Atlanta Falcons, 4400 Falcon Parkway, Flowery Branch, GA 30542, USA
Reeves, Del — *Singer, Songwriter*
%Billy Deaton Talent, 5811 Still Hollow Road, Nashville, TN 37215, USA
Reeves, Dianne — *Singer*
PO Box 66, Englishtown, NJ 07726, USA
Reeves, Keanu — *Actor*
%Three Arts Entertainment, 9460 Wilshire Blvd, #700, Beverly Hills, CA 90212, USA
Reeves, Martha — *Singer (Martha & the Vandellas)*
%Mars Talent, 27 L'Ambiance Court, Bardonia, NY 10954, USA
Reeves, Perrey — *Actress*
%Prophet, 1640 S Sepulveda Blvd, #218, Los Angeles, CA 90025, USA
Reeves, Richard — *Columnist*
%Universal Press Syndicate, 4520 Main St, Kansas City, MO 64111, USA
Reeves, Saskia — *Actress*
%Markham & Froggatt, Julian House, 4 Windmill St, London W1P 1HF, England
Reeves, Scott — *Actor*
6520 Platt Ave, #634, West Hills, CA 91307, USA
Regalbuto, Joe — *Actor*
724 24th St, Santa Monica, CA 90402, USA
Regan, Brian — *Actor, Comedian*
%Conversation Co, 697 Middle Neck Road, Great Neck, NY 11023, USA
Regan, Gerald A — *Government Official, Canada*
PO Box 828, Station B, Ottawa ON K1P 5P9, Canada
Regan, Judith — *Writer, Talk Show Host*
%New Enterprises, 1211 Ave of Americas, New York, NY 10036, USA
Regan, Larry — *Hockey Player*
4A-260 Metcalfe St, Ottawa ON K2P 1R6, Canada
Regan, Philip R (Phil) — *Baseball Player, Manager*
1375 108th St, Byron Center, MI 49315, USA
Regazzoni, Clay — *Auto Racing Driver*
Via Monzoni 13, 6900 Lugano, Switzerland
Regehr, Duncan — *Actor*
2501 Main St, Santa Monica, CA 90405, USA
Reggiani, Serge — *Singer, Actor*
%Charley Marouani, 4 Ave Hoche, 75008 Paris, France
Reggio, Godfrey — *Movie Director*
%Regional Education Institute, PO Box 2404, Santa Fe, NM 87504, USA
Regine — *Restauranteur*
502 Park Ave, New York, NY 10022, USA
Regis, John — *Track Athlete*
67 Fairby Road, London SE12, England
Regnier, Charles — *Actor, Theater Director*
Neherstr 7, 81675 Munich, Germany
Rehm, Daniel R, Jr — *WW II Navy Air Force Hero*
1043 Del Norte St, Houston, TX 77018, USA
Rehm, Jack D — *Publisher*
19 Neponset Ave, #9A, Old Saybrook, CT 06475, USA
Rehnquist, William H — *Supreme Court Chief Justice*
2329 N Glebe Road, Arlington, VA 22207, USA
Rehr, Frank — *Cartoonist (Ferd'nand)*
%United Feature Syndicate, 200 Madison Ave, New York, NY 10016, USA
Reich, Charles A — *Attorney, Educator*
%Crown Publishers, 225 Park Ave S, New York, NY 10003, USA
Reich, Frank M — *Football Player*
8820 Covey Rise Court, Charlotte, NC 28226, USA
Reich, John — *Theater Director*
724 Bohemia Parkway, Sayville, NY 11782, USA
Reich, Robert B — *Secretary, Labor*
4 Mercer Circle, Cambridge, MA 02138, USA
Reich, Steve M — *Composer*
%Nonesuch Records, 75 Rockefeller Plaza, New York, NY 10019, USA
Reichel, Robert — *Hockey Player*
%Toronto Maple Leafs, 40 Bay St, Toronto ON M5J 2K2, Canada
Reichert, Jack F — *Businessman, Bowling Executive*
580 Douglas Dr, Lake Forest, IL 60045, USA
Reichert, Tanja — *Actress*
%Pacific Artists, 1404-510 W Hastings St, Vancouver BC V6B 1L8, Canada
Reichl, Ruth M — *Editor, Columnist*
%Gourmet Magazine, Editorial Dept, 4 Times Square, New York, NY 10036, USA
Reichman, Fred — *Artist*
1235 Stanyan St, San Francisco, CA 94117, USA
Reichs, Kathy — *Writer*
%Charles Scribner's Sons, 866 3rd Ave, New York, NY 10022, USA

Reid, Andy *Football Coach*
%Philadelphia Eagles, 1 Novacare Way, Philadelphia, PA 19145, USA
Reid, Antonio (L A) *Songwriter*
%Kear Music, Carter Turner Co, 9229 W Sunset Blvd, West Hollywood, CA 90069, USA
Reid, Daphne Maxwell *Actress*
10520 Wilshire Blvd, #1507, Los Angeles, CA 90024, USA
Reid, Don S *Singer (Statler Brothers), Songwriter*
%American Major Talent, 8747 Highway 304, Hernando, MS 38632, USA
Reid, Frances *Actress*
235 Oceano Dr, Los Angeles, CA 90049, USA
Reid, Harold W *Singer (Statler Brothers), Songwriter*
%American Major Talent, 8747 Highway 304, Hernando, MS 38632, USA
Reid, J R *Basketball Player*
121 Cemetary St, Chester, SC 29706, USA
Reid, Michael B (Mike) *Football Player, Composer*
825 Overton Lane, Nashville, TN 37220, USA
Reid, Norman R *Museum Executive*
50 Brabourne Rise, Park Langley, Beckenham, Kent, England
Reid, Ogden R *Journalist, Diplomat*
Ophir Hill, Purchase, NY 10577, USA
Reid, Robert *Basketball Player, Coach*
%Washington Wizards, MCI Centre, 601 F St NW, Washington, DC 20004, USA
Reid, Robert *Skier*
%Dixfield Health Care Center, Dixfield, ME 04224, USA
Reid, Stephen E (Steve) *Football Player, Physician*
800 S River Road, #1017, Des Plaines, IL 60016, USA
Reid, Tara *Actress*
124 W 60th St, #39D, New York, NY 10023, USA
Reid, Terry *Singer*
%Blumenauer, PO Box 343, Burbank, CA 91503, USA
Reid, Tim *Actor, Director*
1 New Millennium Dr, Petersburg, VA 23805, USA
Reidy, Carolyn K *Publisher*
%Simon & Schuster, 1230 Ave of Americas, New York, NY 10020, USA
Reifsnyder, Robert H (Bob) *Football Player*
681 Ocean Parkway, Berlin, MD 21811, USA
Reightler, Kenneth S, Jr *Astronaut*
1602 Honeysuckle Ridge Court, Annapolis, MD 21401, USA
Reilly, Charles Nelson *Actor*
2341 Gloaming Way, Beverly Hills, CA 90210, USA
Reilly, James F, II *Astronaut*
15903 Lake Lodge Dr, Houston, TX 77062, USA
Reilly, John *Actor*
335 N Maple Dr, #3360, Beverly Hills, CA 90210, USA
Reilly, John C *Actor*
%United Talent Agency, 9560 Wilshire Blvd, #500, Beverly Hills, CA 90212, USA
Reilly, William K *Government Official*
%Stanford University, International Studies Institute, Stanford, CA 94305, USA
Reimer, Dennis J (Denny) *Army General*
MIPT, PO Box 889, Oklahoma City, OK 73101, USA
Reimer, Roland *Religious Leader*
%Mennonite Brethren Churches Conference, 8000 W 21st St N, Wichita, KS 67205, USA
Reineck, Thomas *Canoeing Athlete*
Graf-Bernadotte-Str 4, 45133 Essen, Germany
Reinemund, Steven S *Businessman*
%PepsiCo Inc, 700 Anderson Hill Road, Purchase, NY 10577, USA
Reiner, Carl *Actor, Writer, Director*
714 N Rodeo Dr, Beverly Hills, CA 90210, USA
Reiner, John *Cartoonist (Howard Huge)*
%Parade Magazine, Editorial Dept, 750 3rd Ave, New York, NY 10017, USA
Reiner, Rob *Actor, Director*
%Castle Rock Pictures, 335 N Maple Dr, #135, Beverly Hills, CA 90210, USA
Reinhard, Robert R (Bob) *Football Player*
37230 NW Soap Creek Road, Corvallis, OR 97330, USA
Reinhardt, John E *Diplomat*
4200 Massachusetts Ave NW, #702, Washington, DC 20016, USA
Reinhardt, Stephen R *Judge*
%US Court of Appeals, 312 N Spring St, Los Angeles, CA 90012, USA
Reinharz, Jehuda *Educator*
%Brandeis University, President's Office, Waltham, MA 02254, USA
Reinhold, Judge *Actor, Director*
%Paradigm Agency, 10100 Santa Monica Blvd, #2500, Los Angeles, CA 90067, USA
Reinking, Ann *Actress, Dancer, Choreographer, Director*
%International Creative Mgmt, 40 W 57th St, #1800, New York, NY 10019, USA
Reiser, Jerry *Architect*
28 S Washington Ave, Dobbs Ferry, NY 10522, USA
Reiser, Paul *Actor*
%Creative Artists Agency, 9830 Wilshire Blvd, Beverly Hills, CA 90212, USA

R

Reisman, Garrett E *Astronaut*
1715 Hedgecroft Dr, Seabrook, TX 77586, USA
Reiss, Howard *Chemist*
16656 Oldham St, Encino, CA 91436, USA
Reiter, Mario *Alpine Skier*
Hauselweg 5, 6830 Rankweil, Austria
Reiter, Thomas *Astronaut, Germany*
%Europe Astronaut Center, Linder Hohe, Box 906096, 51127 Cologne, Germany
Reitman, Ivan *Movie Director, Producer*
900 Cold Springs Road, Montecito, CA 93108, USA
Reitz, Bruce *Surgeon*
%Johns Hopkins Hospital, 600 N Wolfe St, Baltimore, MD 21287, USA
Reklow, Jesse *Cartoonist (Submit Your Dream)*
2415 College Ave, #20, Berkeley, CA 94704, USA
Relman, Arnold S *Editor, Physician*
%New England Journal of Medicine, 860 Winter St, #2, Waltham, MA 02451, USA
Relph, Michael *Movie Producer*
71 Maltings, Westgate, Chichester, West Sussex PO19 3DN, England
Remar, James *Actor*
409 N Camden Dr, #202, Beverly Hills, CA 90210, USA
Remedios, Alberto T *Opera Singer*
21 Lanhill Road, London W9 2BS, England
Remek, Vladimir *Cosmonaut, Czech Republic*
Veletrzni 17, Prague 7 17000, Czech Republic
Remigino, Lindy *Track Athlete*
22 Paris Lane, Newington, CT 06111, USA
Remington, Deborah W *Artist*
309 W Broadway, New York, NY 10013, USA
Remini, Leah *Actress*
%Gold Marshak Liedtke, 3500 W Olive Ave, #1400, Burbank, CA 91505, USA
Remnick, David J *Writer, Editor*
257 W 86th St, #11A, New York, NY 10024, USA
Rempt, Rodney *Navy Admiral, Educator*
Superintendent, US Naval Academy, Annapolis, MD 21402, USA
Remy, Gerald P (Jerry) *Baseball Player*
33 Viles St, Weston, MA 02493, USA
Renaud, Line *Singer*
5 Rue de Bois de Boulogne, 75016 Paris, France
Renault, Dennis *Editorial Cartoonist*
%Sacramento Bee, Editorial Dept, 21st & Q Sts, Sacramento, CA 95852, USA
Renbourn, John *Guitarist*
%Folklore Inc, 1671 Appian Way, Santa Monica, CA 90401, USA
Rendell of Barbergh, Ruth B *Writer*
Nussteads, Polstead, Suffolk, Colchester CO6 5DN, England
Rendell, Marjorie O *Judge*
%US Court of Appeals, US Courthouse, 601 Market St, Philadelphia, PA 19106, USA
Rene, France-Albert *President, Seychelles*
%President's Office, State House, Victoria, Mahe, Seychelles
Reneau, Daniel D *Educator*
%Louisiana Tech University, President's Office, Ruston, LA 71272, USA
Renfrew of Kaimsthorn, Andrew C *Archaeologist*
%McDonald Archaeological Institute, Downing St, Cambridge CB2 3ER, England
Renfro, Brad *Actor*
%Writers & Artists, 8383 Wilshire Blvd, #550, Beverly Hills, CA 90211, USA
Renfro, Melvin L (Mel) *Football Player*
6060 N Central Expressway, #560, Dallas, TX 75206, USA
Renger, Annemarie *Government Official, Germany*
%Bundestag, Bundeshaus, Platz der Republik 1, 11011 Berlin, Germany
Renick, Jesse (Cab) *Basketball Player, Coach*
2656 SE Washington Blvd, Bartlesville, OK 74006, USA
Renier, Jeremie *Actor*
%Artmedia, 20 Ave Rapp, 75007 Paris, France
Renk, Silke *Track Athlete*
Erhard-Hubner-Str 13, 06132 Halle/S, Germany
Renko, Steven (Steve) *Baseball Player*
PO Box 3566, West Palm Beach, FL 33402, USA
Renna, Eugene A *Businessman*
%Mobil Corp, 3225 Gallows Road, Fairfax, VA 22037, USA
Renne, Paul *Geologist*
%Berkeley Geochronology Center, 2445 Ridge Road, Berkeley, CA 94709, USA
Rennebohm, J Fred *Religious Leader*
%Congregational Christian Churches Assn, PO Box 1620, Oak Creek, MI 53154, USA
Rennert, Gunther *Opera Director*
Holbeinstr 58, 12203 Berlin, Germany
Rennert, Laurence H (Dutch) *Baseball Umpire*
306 N Lark St, Oshkosh, WI 54902, USA
Rennert, Wolfgang *Conductor*
Holbeinstr 58, 12203 Berlin, Germany

Renney, Tom *Hockey Coach*
%New York Rangers, Madison Square Garden, 2 Penn Plaza, New York, NY 10121, USA
Reno, Janet *Attorney General*
11200 N Kendall Dr, Miami, FL 33176, USA
Reno, Jean *Actor*
%CBC M C1 Besson, 11 Rue de la Croix Boissee, 79154 Mennecy, France
Reno, William H *Army General*
2706 S Ives St, Arlington, VA 22202, USA
Renoth, Heidi *Snowboard Skier*
Lercheckerweg 23, 83471 Berchtesgaden, Germany
Rense, Paige *Editor*
%Architectural Digest, Editorial Dept, 5900 Wilshire Blvd, Los Angeles, CA 90036, USA
Renteria, Edgar *Baseball Player*
1408 N West Shore Blvd, #512, Tampa, FL 33607, USA
Rentmeester, Co *Photographer*
PO Box 1562, West Hampton Beach, NY 11978, USA
Renton of Mount Harry, R Timothy *Government Official, England*
%House of Lords, Westminster, London SW1A 0PW, England
Rentzel, T Lance *Football Player*
%Trust Data Corp, 159 Almanden Blvd, #500, San Jose, CA 95113, USA
Rentzepis, Peter M *Chemist*
%University of California, Chemistry Dept, Irvine, CA 92717, USA
Renvall, Johan *Ballet Dancer*
%American Ballet Theatre, 890 Broadway, New York, NY 10003, USA
Renyi, Thomas A *Financier*
%Bank of New York, 1 Wall St, New York, NY 10286, USA
Repin, Vadim V *Concert Violinist*
Eckholdtweg 2A, 23566 Lubeck, Germany
Rerych, Stephen (Steve) *Swimmer*
445 Baltimore Ave, Asheville, NC 28801, USA
Resch, Alexander *Luge Athlete*
%BSD, An der Schiessstatte 4, 83471 Berchtesgaden, Germany
Rescher, Nicholas *Philosopher*
5818 Aylesboro Ave, Pittsburgh, PA 15217, USA
Rescigno, Nicola *Conductor*
%Robert Lombardo, 61 W 62nd St, #6F, New York, NY 10023, USA
Resin, Dan *Actor*
%Don Buchwald, 6500 Wilshire Blvd, #2200, Los Angeles, CA 90048, USA
Resnais, Alain *Movie Director*
70 Rue des Plantes, 75014 Paris, France
Resnick, Milton *Artist*
87 Eldridge St, New York, NY 10002, USA
Resnik, Regina *Opera Singer*
%American Guild of Musical Arts, 1430 Broadway, New York, NY 10018, USA
Ressler, Glenn E *Football Player*
1524 Woodcreek Dr, Mechanicsburg, PA 17055, USA
Restani, Jane A *Judge*
%US Court of International Trade, 1 Federal Plaza, New York, NY 10278, USA
Restani, Kevin *Basketball Player*
16 Lyndhurst Dr, San Francisco, CA 94132, USA
Reswick, James B *Engineer*
1834 Calf Mountain Road, Crozet, VA 22932, USA
Retore, Guy *Theater Director*
%Theatre de l'Est Parisien, 159 Ave Gambetta, 75020 Paris, France
Retton, Mary Lou *Gymnast*
114 White Ave, Fairmont, WV 26554, USA
Retzer, Otto W *Movie Director*
Justinus-Kerner-Str 10, 80686 Munich, Germany
Retzlaff, Palmer (Pete) *Football Player*
669 New Road, Gilbertsville, PA 19525, USA
Reuben, David R *Psychiatrist, Writer*
%Scott Meredith, 1675 Broadway, New York, NY 10019, USA
Reuben, Gloria *Actress*
%William Morris Agency, 151 El Camino Dr, Beverly Hills, CA 90212, USA
Reubens, Paul *Comedian, Actor*
PO Box 29373, Los Angeles, CA 90029, USA
Reuschel, Ricky E (Rick) *Baseball Player*
PO Box 143, Renfrew, PA 16053, USA
Reuss, Jerry *Baseball Player*
350 SW 1st St, Des Moines, IA 50309, USA
Reusser, Ken L *WW II Marine Corps Air Force Hero*
17345 SW Reusser Court, Aloha, OR 97007, USA
Reuter, Edzard *Businessman*
%Daimler-Benz AG, Postfach 800230, 70546 Stuttgart, Germany
Reutersward, Carl Fredrik *Artist*
6 Rue Montolieu, 1030 Bussigny/Lausanne, Switzerland
Revel, Jean-Francois *Writer*
55 Quai de Bourbon, 75004 Paris, France

R

Revell - Rhoads

Revell, Graeme *Composer*
%APRA, PO Box 567, Crow's Nest NSW 2065, Australia
Revere, Paul *Pianist (Paul Revere & the Raiders)*
%Paradise Artists, 108 E Matilija St, Ojai, CA 93023, USA
Reverho, Christine *Actress*
%Artmedia, 20 Ave Rapp, 75007 Paris, France
Revill, Clive *Actor*
15029 Encanto Dr, Sherman Oaks, CA 91403, USA
Rex *Bassist (Pantera)*
%Concrete Mgmt, 361 W Broadway, #200, New York, NY 10013, USA
Rey, Reynaldo *Actor, Comedian, Writer*
%Starwil Talent, 433 N Camden Dr, #400, Beverly Hills, CA 90210, USA
Reynolds Booth, Nancy *Skier*
3197 Padaro Lane, Carpinteria, CA 93013, USA
Reynolds, Alastair *Writer*
%P F D, Drury House, 34-43 Russell St, London WC2B 5HA, England
Reynolds, Albert *Prime Minister, Ireland*
Mount Carmel House, Dublin Road, Longford, Ireland
Reynolds, Anna *Opera Singer*
Peesten 9, 95359 Kasendorf, Germany
Reynolds, Burt *Actor*
PO Box 3288, Tequesta, FL 33469, USA
Reynolds, David S *Historian*
16 Linden Lane, Old Westbury, NY 11568, USA
Reynolds, Dean *Commentator*
%ABC-TV, News Dept, 5010 Creston St, Hyattsville, MD 20781, USA
Reynolds, Debbie *Actress, Singer*
1700 Coldwater Canyon Dr, Beverly Hills, CA 90210, USA
Reynolds, Gene *Actor, Television Producer*
2034 Castillian Dr, Los Angeles, CA 90068, USA
Reynolds, Glenn F *Inventor (Proscar Drug)*
242 Edgewood Ave, Westfield, NJ 07090, USA
Reynolds, Harry (Butch) *Track Athlete*
%Advantage International, 1025 Thomas Jefferson NW, #450, Washington, DC 20007, USA
Reynolds, J Guy *Navy Admiral*
1605 Fox Hunt Court, Alexandria, VA 22307, USA
Reynolds, Jamal *Football Player*
%Green Bay Packers, PO Box 10628, Green Bay, WI 54307, USA
Reynolds, James *Actor*
1925 Hanscom Dr, South Pasadena, CA 91030, USA
Reynolds, Jerry O *Basketball Coach, Executive*
%Sacramento Kings, Arco Arena, 1 Sports Parkway, Sacramento, CA 95834, USA
Reynolds, John H *Physicist, Educator*
%University of California, Physics Dept, Berkeley, CA 94720, USA
Reynolds, R Shane *Baseball Player*
23 Beacon Hill, Sugar Land, TX 77479, USA
Reynolds, Randolph N *Businessman*
%Reynolds Metals Co, 6601 Broad St, PO Box 27003, Richmond, VA 23261, USA
Reynolds, Richard V *Air Force General*
Commander, Aeronautical Systems, Wright-Patterson Air Force Base, OH 45433, USA
Reynolds, Robert *Bassist (Mavericks, Swag)*
%AristoMedia, 1620 16th Ave S, Nashville, TN 37212, USA
Reynolds, Ryan *Actor*
%Endeavor Talent Agency, 9701 Wilshire Blvd, #1000, Beverly Hills, CA 90212, USA
Reynolds, Sheldon *Guitarist (Earth Wind & Fire)*
%Great Scott Productions, 137 N Wetherly Dr, #403, Los Angeles, CA 90048, USA
Reynolds, Thomas A, Jr *Attorney*
%Winston & Strawn, 1 First National Plaza, 45 W Wacker Dr, Chicago, IL 60601, USA
Reynolds, W Ann *Educator*
%City University of New York, Chancellor's Office, New York, NY 10021, USA
Reza, Yasmina *Writer, Actresss, Comedienne*
%Marta Andras, 14 Rue des Sablons, 75116 Paris, France
Reznor, Trent *Singer (Nine Inch Nails)*
%Artists & Audience Entertainment, PO Box 35, Pawling, NY 12564, USA
Rhames, Ving *Actor*
1158 26th St, #549, Santa Monica, CA 90403, USA
Rhea, Caroline *Actress, Comedienne*
%Hofflund/Polone, 9465 Wilshire Blvd, #820, Beverly Hills, CA 90212, USA
Rheaume, Manon *Hockey Player*
%University of Minnesota, Athletic Dept, Duluth, MN 55812, USA
Rhines, Peter B *Oceanographer*
5753 61st Ave NE, Seattle, WA 98105, USA
Rhoades, Barbara *Actress*
90 Old Redding Road, Weston, CT 06883, USA
Rhoads, George *Sculptor*
1478 Mecklenburg Road, Ithaca, NY 14850, USA
Rhoads, James B *Archivist*
1300 Fox Run Trail, Platte City, MO 64079, USA

Rhoden, Richard A (Rick) *Baseball Player*
8009 Whisper Lake Lane E, Ponte Vedra, FL 32082, USA

Rhodes, Cynthia *Actress, Dancer*
15260 Ventura Blvd, #2100, Sherman Oaks, CA 91403, USA

Rhodes, Donnelly *Actor*
%Gold Marshak Liedtke, 3500 W Olive Ave, #1400, Burbank, CA 91505, USA

Rhodes, Frank H T *Geologist, Educator*
%Cornell University, Geology Dept, Snee Hall, Ithaca, NY 14853, USA

Rhodes, Nick *Keyboardist (Duran Duran)*
%DD Productions, 93A Westbourne Park Villas, London W2 5ED, England

Rhodes, Philip *Drummer (Gin Blossoms, Pharaohs)*
%William Morris Agency, 2100 W End Ave, #1000, Nashville, TN 37203, USA

Rhodes, Ray *Football Player, Coach*
25812 NE 4th Place, Sammamish, WA 98074, USA

Rhodes, Richard L *Writer*
%Janklow & Nesbit, 445 Park Ave, #1300, New York, NY 10022, USA

Rhodes, Tom *Actor, Comedian*
%William Morris Agency, 151 El Camino Dr, Beverly Hills, CA 90212, USA

Rhodes, Zandra *Fashion Designer*
79-85 Bermondsey St, London SE1 3XF, England

Rhome, Gerald B (Jerry) *Football Player, Coach*
3883 Morning Meadow Lane, Buford, GA 30519, USA

Rhone, Earnest C (Ernie) *Football Player*
6102 Sleepy Hollow Ave, Texarkana, TX 75503, USA

Rhue, Madlyn *Actress*
23388 Mulholland Dr, Woodland Hills, CA 91364, USA

Rhys, Paul *Actor*
%Gersh Agency, 232 N Canon Dr, Beverly Hills, CA 90210, USA

Rhys-Davies, John *Actor*
3428 Oak Glen Dr, Los Angeles, CA 90068, USA

Rhys-Meyers, Jonathan *Actor*
Velvets Town House, Buttevont, County Cork, Ireland

Ri Jong Ok *Premier, North Korea*
%Vice President's Office, Pyongyang, North Korea

Ribas Reig, Oscar *Head of Government, Andorra*
%Governmental Offices, Andorra la Vella, Andorra

Ribbs, Willy T *Auto Racing Driver*
2343 Ribbs Lane, San Jose, CA 95116, USA

Ribeau, Sidney A *Educator*
%Bowling Green State University, President's Office, Bowling Green, OH 43403, USA

Ribeiro, Alfonso *Actor*
19122 Halstead St, Northridge, CA 91324, USA

Ribeiro, Andre *Auto Racing Driver*
%Tasman Motor Sports Group, 4192 Weaver Court, Hilliard, OH 43026, USA

Ribeiro, Ignacio *Fashion Designer*
%Clements Ribeiro Ltd, 48 S Molton St, London W1X 1HE, England

Ribisi, Giovanni *Actor*
%William Morris Agency, 151 El Camino Dr, Beverly Hills, CA 90212, USA

Ribisi, Marissa *Actress*
4121 Wilshire Blvd, #415, Los Angeles, CA 90010, USA

Ricci, Christina *Actress*
%International Creative Mgmt, 8942 Wilshire Blvd, #219, Beverly Hills, CA 90211, USA

Ricci, Ruggiero *Concert Violinist*
2930 E Delhi Road, Ann Arbor, MI 48103, USA

Ricciarelli, Katia *Opera Singer*
Via Magellana 2, 20097 Corsica, Italy

Rice, Anne *Writer*
1239 1st St, New Orleans, LA 70130, USA

Rice, Condoleezza *Government Official*
%National Security Council, 1600 Pennsylvania Ave NW, Washington, DC 20500, USA

Rice, Gene D *Religious Leader*
%Church of God, PO Box 2430, Cleveland, TN 37320, USA

Rice, Gigi *Actress*
14951 Alva Dr, Pacific Palisades, CA 90272, USA

Rice, James E (Jim) *Baseball Player*
35 Bobby Jones Dr, Andover, MA 01810, USA

Rice, James R *Geophysicist*
%Harvard University, Applied Science Division, Cambridge, MA 02138, USA

Rice, Jerry L *Football Player*
222 S Central Ave, #1008, Clayton, MO 63105, USA

Rice, Norman B *Mayor*
%Mayor's Office, Municipal Building, 600 4th Ave, Seattle, WA 98104, USA

Rice, Simeon *Football Player*
2777 E Camelback Road, #300, Phoenix, AZ 85016, USA

Rice, Stuart A *Chemist*
5517 S Kimbark Ave, Chicago, IL 60637, USA

Rice, Thomas M *Theoretical Physicist*
%Theoretische Physik, ETH-Honggerberg, 8093 Zurich, Switzerland

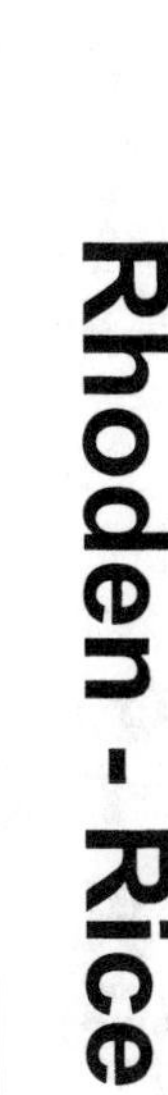

R

Rice, Timothy M B (Tim) *Lyricist*
Chilterns, France-Hill Dr, Camberley, Surrey GU153-30A, England
Rich, Adam *Actor*
4814 Lemona Ave, Sherman Oaks, CA 91403, USA
Rich, Adrienne *Writer*
%Stanford University, English Dept, Stanford, CA 94305, USA
Rich, Alexander *Molecular Biologist*
2 Walnut Ave, Cambridge, MA 02140, USA
Rich, Allan *Actor*
225 E 57th St, New York, NY 10022, USA
Rich, Christopher *Actor*
%Bresler Kelly Assoc, 11500 W Olympic Blvd, #510, Los Angeles, CA 90064, USA
Rich, Clayton *Physician*
%University of Oklahoma, Health Services Center, Oklahoma City, OK 73190, USA
Rich, Frank H *Drama Critic, Columnist*
%New York Times, Editorial Dept, 229 W 43rd St, New York, NY 10036, USA
Rich, Lee *Businessman*
%Lee Rich Productions, Warner, 75 Rockefeller Plaza, New York, NY 10019, USA
Rich, Tony *Singer, Keyboardist*
%Prestige, 220 E 23rd St, #303, New York, NY 10010, USA
Richard, Cliff *Singer*
Harley House, Portsmouth Road, Box 46C, Esher, Surrey KT10 9AA, England
Richard, Henri *Hockey Player*
905-4300 Place de Cageux, Ile Paton Laval QC H7W 4Z3, Canada
Richard, Ivor S *Government Official, England*
11 South Square, Gray's Inn, London WC1R 5EU, England
Richard, James Rodney (J R) *Baseball Player*
5134 Bungalow Lane, Houston, TX 77048, USA
Richard, Oliver G, III *Businessman*
%Columbia Energy Group, 200 Civic Center Dr, Columbus, OH 43215, USA
Richards, Ariana *Actress*
%Don Buchwald, 6500 Wilshire Blvd, #2200, Los Angeles, CA 90048, USA
Richards, D Ann W *Governor, TX*
98 San Jacinto Blvd, #1440, Austin, TX 78701, USA
Richards, Denise *Actress*
%Gersh Agency, 232 N Canon Dr, Beverly Hills, CA 90210, USA
Richards, Frederic M *Biochemist*
69 Andrews Road, Guilford, CT 06437, USA
Richards, I Vivian A (Viv) *Cricketer*
%West Indian Cricket Board, PO Box 616, Saint John's, Antigua & Barbuda
Richards, J August *Actor*
PO Box 99, China Spring, TX 76633, USA
Richards, J R *Singer (Dishwalla)*
%William Morris Agency, 1325 Ave of Americas, New York, NY 10019, USA
Richards, Keith *Singer (Rolling Stones), Songwriter*
Redlands, West Wittering near Chichester, Sussex, England
Richards, Kim *Actress*
10326 Orton Ave, Los Angeles, CA 90064, USA
Richards, Lloyd G *Theatre Director*
18 W 95th St, New York, NY 10025, USA
Richards, Mark *Surfer*
755 Hunter St, Newcastle NSW 2302, Australia
Richards, Michael *Actor*
%Entertainment Tavel, 9171 Wilshire Blvd, #406, Beverly Hills, CA 90210, USA
Richards, Paul G *Theoretical Seismologist*
%Lamont-Doherty Geological Observatory, Palisades, NY 10964, USA
Richards, Paul W *Astronaut*
%NASA, Johnson Space Center, 2101 NASA Road, Houston, TX 77058, USA
Richards, Renee *Tennis Player*
1604 Union St, San Francisco, CA 94123, USA
Richards, Rex E *Chemist*
13 Woodstock Close, Oxford OX2 8DB, England
Richards, Richard N *Astronaut*
%NASA, Johnson Space Center, 2101 NASA Road, Houston, TX 77058, USA
Richards, Robert E (Bob) *Track Athlete*
1616 Estates Dr, Waco, TX 76712, USA
Richards, Stephanie *Actress*
%H David Moss, 733 Seward St, #PH, Los Angeles, CA 90038, USA
Richardson of Lee, John S *Physician*
Windcutter, Lee, North Devon EX34 8LW, England
Richardson, Ashley *Model*
%Ford Model Agency, 142 Greene St, #400, New York, NY 10012, USA
Richardson, Cheryl *Actress*
8900 Amestoy Ave, Northridge, CA 91325, USA
Richardson, Dan *Drummer (Stereo Mud)*
%Agency Group Ltd, 1775 Broadway, #430, New York, NY 10019, USA
Richardson, Donna *Physical Fitness Expert*
%Anchor Bay Entertainment, 500 Kirts Blvd, Troy, MI 48084, USA

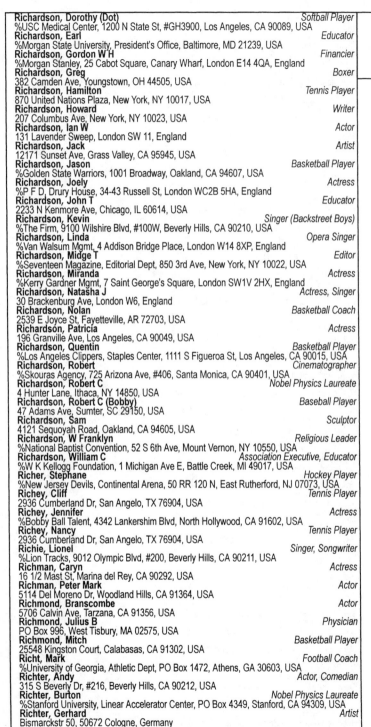

Richardson, Dorothy (Dot) *Softball Player*
%USC Medical Center, 1200 N State St, #GH3900, Los Angeles, CA 90089, USA
Richardson, Earl *Educator*
%Morgan State University, President's Office, Baltimore, MD 21239, USA
Richardson, Gordon W H *Financier*
%Morgan Stanley, 25 Cabot Square, Canary Wharf, London E14 4QA, England
Richardson, Greg *Boxer*
382 Camden Ave, Youngstown, OH 44505, USA
Richardson, Hamilton *Tennis Player*
870 United Nations Plaza, New York, NY 10017, USA
Richardson, Howard *Writer*
207 Columbus Ave, New York, NY 10023, USA
Richardson, Ian W *Actor*
131 Lavender Sweep, London SW 11, England
Richardson, Jack *Artist*
12171 Sunset Ave, Grass Valley, CA 95945, USA
Richardson, Jason *Basketball Player*
%Golden State Warriors, 1001 Broadway, Oakland, CA 94607, USA
Richardson, Joely *Actress*
%P F D, Drury House, 34-43 Russell St, London WC2B 5HA, England
Richardson, John T *Educator*
2233 N Kenmore Ave, Chicago, IL 60614, USA
Richardson, Kevin *Singer (Backstreet Boys)*
%The Firm, 9100 Wilshire Blvd, #100W, Beverly Hills, CA 90210, USA
Richardson, Linda *Opera Singer*
%Van Walsum Mgmt, 4 Addison Bridge Place, London W14 8XP, England
Richardson, Midge T *Editor*
%Seventeen Magazine, Editorial Dept, 850 3rd Ave, New York, NY 10022, USA
Richardson, Miranda *Actress*
%Kerry Gardner Mgmt, 7 Saint George's Square, London SW1V 2HX, England
Richardson, Natasha J *Actress, Singer*
30 Brackenburg Ave, London W6, England
Richardson, Nolan *Basketball Coach*
2539 E Joyce St, Fayetteville, AR 72703, USA
Richardson, Patricia *Actress*
196 Granville Ave, Los Angeles, CA 90049, USA
Richardson, Quentin *Basketball Player*
%Los Angeles Clippers, Staples Center, 1111 S Figueroa St, Los Angeles, CA 90015, USA
Richardson, Robert *Cinematographer*
%Skouras Agency, 725 Arizona Ave, #406, Santa Monica, CA 90401, USA
Richardson, Robert C *Nobel Physics Laureate*
4 Hunter Lane, Ithaca, NY 14850, USA
Richardson, Robert C (Bobby) *Baseball Player*
47 Adams Ave, Sumter, SC 29150, USA
Richardson, Sam *Sculptor*
4121 Sequoyah Road, Oakland, CA 94605, USA
Richardson, W Franklyn *Religious Leader*
%National Baptist Convention, 52 S 6th Ave, Mount Vernon, NY 10550, USA
Richardson, William C *Association Executive, Educator*
%W K Kellogg Foundation, 1 Michigan Ave E, Battle Creek, MI 49017, USA
Richer, Stephane *Hockey Player*
%New Jersey Devils, Continental Arena, 50 RR 120 N, East Rutherford, NJ 07073, USA
Richey, Cliff *Tennis Player*
2936 Cumberland Dr, San Angelo, TX 76904, USA
Richey, Jennifer *Actress*
%Bobby Ball Talent, 4342 Lankershim Blvd, North Hollywood, CA 91602, USA
Richey, Nancy *Tennis Player*
2936 Cumberland Dr, San Angelo, TX 76904, USA
Richie, Lionel *Singer, Songwriter*
%Lion Tracks, 9012 Olympic Blvd, #200, Beverly Hills, CA 90211, USA
Richman, Caryn *Actress*
16 1/2 Mast St, Marina del Rey, CA 90292, USA
Richman, Peter Mark *Actor*
5114 Del Moreno Dr, Woodland Hills, CA 91364, USA
Richmond, Branscombe *Actor*
5706 Calvin Ave, Tarzana, CA 91356, USA
Richmond, Julius B *Physician*
PO Box 996, West Tisbury, MA 02575, USA
Richmond, Mitch *Basketball Player*
25548 Kingston Court, Calabasas, CA 91302, USA
Richt, Mark *Football Coach*
%University of Georgia, Athletic Dept, PO Box 1472, Athens, GA 30603, USA
Richter, Andy *Actor, Comedian*
315 S Beverly Dr, #216, Beverly Hills, CA 90212, USA
Richter, Burton *Nobel Physics Laureate*
%Stanford University, Linear Accelerator Center, PO Box 4349, Stanford, CA 94309, USA
Richter, Gerhard *Artist*
Bismarckstr 50, 50672 Cologne, Germany

R

Richter - Riessen

Richter, James A (Jim) *Football Player*
8620 Bournemouth Dr, Raleigh, NC 27615, USA
Richter, Jason James *Actor*
%United Talent Agency, 9560 Wilshire Blvd, #500, Beverly Hills, CA 90212, USA
Richter, Leslie A (Les) *Football Player*
1405 Via Vallarta, Riverside, CA 92506, USA
Richter, Michael T (Mike) *Hockey Player*
314 Mount Holly Road, Katonah, NY 10536, USA
Richter, Pat V *Football Player, Administrator*
45 Cambridge Road, Madison, WI 53704, USA
Richwine, Maria *Actress*
%Abrams-Rubaloff Lawrence, 8075 W 3rd St, #303, Los Angeles, CA 90048, USA
Ricker, Robert S *Religious Leader*
%Baptist Conference, 2002 Arlington Heights Road, Arlington Heights, IL 60005, USA
Rickles, Don *Actor, Comedian*
10249 Century Woods Dr, Los Angeles, CA 90067, USA
Rickman, Alan *Actor*
%Creative Artists Agency, 9830 Wilshire Blvd, Beverly Hills, CA 90212, USA
Ricoeur, Paul *Philosopher*
18 Rue Henri Marrou, 92290 Chatenay Malabry, France
Ridder, Eric *Publisher*
Piping Rock Road, Locust Valley, NY 11560, USA
Ridder, P Anthony *Businessman, Publisher*
%Knight-Ridder Inc, 50 W San Fernando St, San Jose, CA 95113, USA
Riddick, Frank A, Jr *Physician*
1923 Octavia St, New Orleans, LA 70115, USA
Riddick, Steven (Steve) *Track Athlete*
7601 Crittenden, #F2, Philadelphia, PA 19118, USA
Riddiford, Lynn M *Zoologist*
16324 51st Ave SE, Bothell, WA 98012, USA
Riddles, Libby *Dog Sled Racer*
PO Box 15253, Fritz Creek, AK 99603, USA
Ride, Sally K *Astronaut*
%California Space Institute, PO Box 0221, 9500 Gilman Dr, La Jolla, CA 92093, USA
Rider, Isaiah (J R) *Basketball Player*
PO Box 121R, Montchanin, DE 19710, USA
Ridge, Thomas J (Tom) *Secretary, Home Security; Governor, PA*
%Homeland Security Department, Washington, DC 20528, USA
Ridgeley, Andrew *Singer, Guitarist (Wham)*
8800 Sunset Blvd, #401, Los Angeles, CA 90069, USA
Ridgeway, Frank *Cartoonist (Mr Abernathy)*
%King Features Syndicate, 888 7th Ave, New York, NY 10106, USA
Ridgley, Bob *Actor*
%20th Century Artists, 4605 Lankershim Blvd, #305, North Hollywood, CA 91602, USA
Ridgway, Brunilde S *Archaeologist*
%Bryn Mawr College, Archaeology Dept, Bryn Mawr, PA 19010, USA
Ridker, Paul *Cardiologist*
%Brigham & Women's Hospital, 75 Francis St, Boston, MA 02115, USA
Ridley, John *Writer*
%Endeavor Talent Agency, 9701 Wilshire Blvd, #1000, Beverly Hills, CA 90212, USA
Ridnour, Luke *Basketball Player*
%Seattle SuperSonics, 351 Elliott Ave W, #500, Seattle, WA 98119, USA
Riedel, Deborah *Opera Singer*
%Columbia Artists Mgmt Inc, 165 W 57th St, New York, NY 10019, USA
Riedel, Lars *Track Athlete*
%LAC Chemnitz, Reichenhainer Str 154, 09125 Chemnitz, Germany
Riedlbauch, Vaclav *Composer*
Revolucni 6, 110 00 Prague 1, Czech Republic
Rieger, Max *Alpine Skier*
Innsbrucker Str 12, 82481 Mittenwald, Germany
Riegert, Peter *Actor*
%Innovative Artists, 1505 10th St, Santa Monica, CA 90401, USA
Riegle, Donald W, Jr *Senator, MI*
352 S Saginaw St, Flint, MI 48502, USA
Riegle, Gene *Harness Racing Driver, Trainer*
1162 Fort Jefferson Ave, Greenville, OH 45331, USA
Riehle, Richard *Actor*
%Abrams Artists, 9200 Sunset Blvd, #1125, Los Angeles, CA 90069, USA
Rienstra, John *Football Player*
1374 Top of the Rock Way, Monument, CO 80132, USA
Riepe, James S *Businessman*
%T Rowe Price Assoc, 100 E Pratt St, Baltimore, MD 21202, USA
Ries, Christopher D *Artist*
Keelersburg Road, Tunkhannock, PA 18657, USA
Riess, Adam *Astrophysicist*
%Space Telescope Science Institute, 3700 San Martin Dr, Baltimore, MD 21218, USA
Riessen, Marty *Tennis Player*
PO Box 5444, Santa Barbara, CA 93150, USA

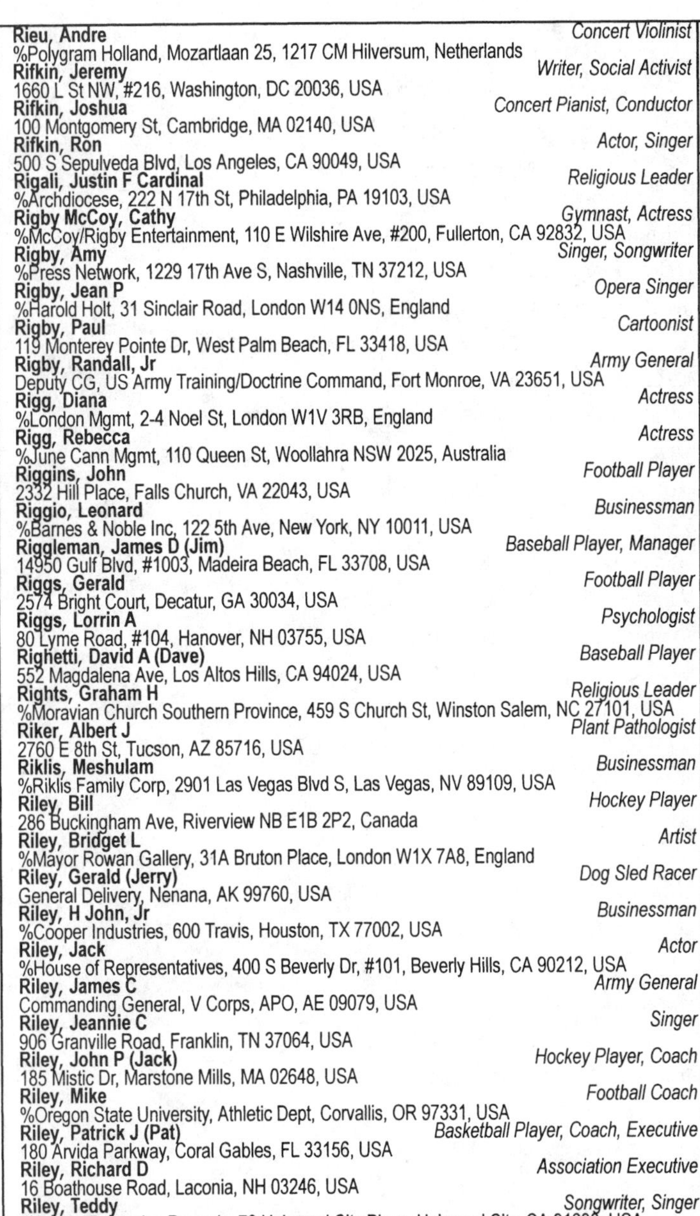

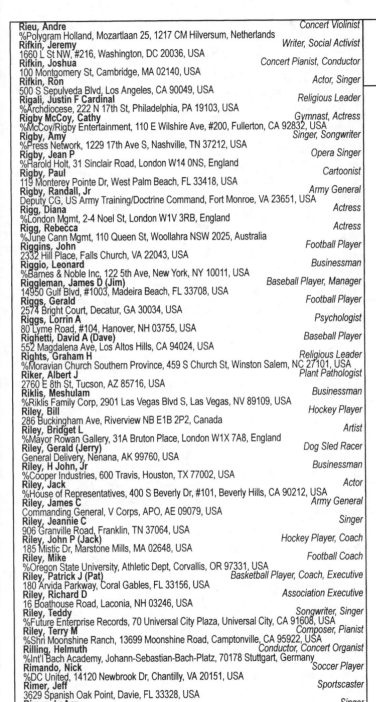

Rieu, Andre *Concert Violinist*
%Polygram Holland, Mozartlaan 25, 1217 CM Hilversum, Netherlands
Rifkin, Jeremy *Writer, Social Activist*
1660 L St NW, #216, Washington, DC 20036, USA
Rifkin, Joshua *Concert Pianist, Conductor*
100 Montgomery St, Cambridge, MA 02140, USA
Rifkin, Ron *Actor, Singer*
500 S Sepulveda Blvd, Los Angeles, CA 90049, USA
Rigali, Justin F Cardinal *Religious Leader*
%Archdiocese, 222 N 17th St, Philadelphia, PA 19103, USA
Rigby McCoy, Cathy *Gymnast, Actress*
%McCoy/Rigby Entertainment, 110 E Wilshire Ave, #200, Fullerton, CA 92832, USA
Rigby, Amy *Singer, Songwriter*
%Press Network, 1229 17th Ave S, Nashville, TN 37212, USA
Rigby, Jean P *Opera Singer*
%Harold Holt, 31 Sinclair Road, London W14 0NS, England
Rigby, Paul *Cartoonist*
119 Monterey Pointe Dr, West Palm Beach, FL 33418, USA
Rigby, Randall, Jr *Army General*
Deputy CG, US Army Training/Doctrine Command, Fort Monroe, VA 23651, USA
Rigg, Diana *Actress*
%London Mgmt, 2-4 Noel St, London W1V 3RB, England
Rigg, Rebecca *Actress*
%June Cann Mgmt, 110 Queen St, Woollahra NSW 2025, Australia
Riggins, John *Football Player*
2332 Hill Place, Falls Church, VA 22043, USA
Riggio, Leonard *Businessman*
%Barnes & Noble Inc, 122 5th Ave, New York, NY 10011, USA
Riggleman, James D (Jim) *Baseball Player, Manager*
14950 Gulf Blvd, #1003, Madeira Beach, FL 33708, USA
Riggs, Gerald *Football Player*
2574 Bright Court, Decatur, GA 30034, USA
Riggs, Lorrin A *Psychologist*
80 Lyme Road, #104, Hanover, NH 03755, USA
Righetti, David A (Dave) *Baseball Player*
552 Magdalena Ave, Los Altos Hills, CA 94024, USA
Rights, Graham H *Religious Leader*
%Moravian Church Southern Province, 459 S Church St, Winston Salem, NC 27101, USA
Riker, Albert J *Plant Pathologist*
2760 E 8th St, Tucson, AZ 85716, USA
Riklis, Meshulam *Businessman*
%Riklis Family Corp, 2901 Las Vegas Blvd S, Las Vegas, NV 89109, USA
Riley, Bill *Hockey Player*
286 Buckingham Ave, Riverview NB E1B 2P2, Canada
Riley, Bridget L *Artist*
%Mayor Rowan Gallery, 31A Bruton Place, London W1X 7A8, England
Riley, Gerald (Jerry) *Dog Sled Racer*
General Delivery, Nenana, AK 99760, USA
Riley, H John, Jr *Businessman*
%Cooper Industries, 600 Travis, Houston, TX 77002, USA
Riley, Jack *Actor*
%House of Representatives, 400 S Beverly Dr, #101, Beverly Hills, CA 90212, USA
Riley, James C *Army General*
Commanding General, V Corps, APO, AE 09079, USA
Riley, Jeannie C *Singer*
906 Granville Road, Franklin, TN 37064, USA
Riley, John P (Jack) *Hockey Player, Coach*
185 Mistic Dr, Marstone Mills, MA 02648, USA
Riley, Mike *Football Coach*
%Oregon State University, Athletic Dept, Corvallis, OR 97331, USA
Riley, Patrick J (Pat) *Basketball Player, Coach, Executive*
180 Arvida Parkway, Coral Gables, FL 33156, USA
Riley, Richard D *Association Executive*
16 Boathouse Road, Laconia, NH 03246, USA
Riley, Teddy *Songwriter, Singer*
%Future Enterprise Records, 70 Universal City Plaza, Universal City, CA 91608, USA
Riley, Terry M *Composer, Pianist*
%Shri Moonshine Ranch, 13699 Moonshine Road, Camptonville, CA 95922, USA
Rilling, Helmuth *Conductor, Concert Organist*
%Int'l Bach Academy, Johann-Sebastian-Bach-Platz, 70178 Stuttgart, Germany
Rimando, Nick *Soccer Player*
%DC United, 14120 Newbrook Dr, Chantilly, VA 20151, USA
Rimer, Jeff *Sportscaster*
3629 Spanish Oak Point, Davie, FL 33328, USA
Rimes, LeAnn *Singer*
193 Carronbridge Way, Franklin, TN 37067, USA
Rimington, Stella *Government Official, England*
PO Box 1604, London SW1P 1XB, England

Rimmel, James E *Religious Leader*
%Evangelical Presbyterian Church, 26049 Five Mile Road, Detroit, MI 48239, USA
Rinaldi, Kathy *Tennis Player*
%Advantage International, 1025 Thomas Jefferson NW, #450, Washington, DC 20007, USA
Rinaldo, Benjamin *Skier*
%Ski World, 3680 Buena Park Dr, North Hollywood, CA 91604, USA
Rinearson, Peter M *Journalist*
%Seattle Times, Editorial Dept, 1120 John St, Seattle, WA 98109, USA
Rinehart, Kenneth *Chemist*
%University of Illinois, Chemistry Dept, Urbana, IL 61801, USA
Rines, Robert H *Inventor*
17 Ripley Road, Belmont, MA 02478, USA
Ringadoo, Veerasamy *President, Mauritius*
Corner of Farquhar & Sir Celicourt Antelme Sts, Quatre-Bornes, Mauritius
Ringer, Jennifer *Ballerina*
%New York City Ballet, Lincoln Center Plaza, New York, NY 10023, USA
Ringer, Robert J *Writer, Publisher*
%Stratford Press, 1880 Century Park East, Los Angeles, CA 90067, USA
Ringo, James S (Jim) *Football Player*
408 Montross Court, Chesapeake, VA 23323, USA
Ringwald, Molly *Actress*
%Writers & Artists, 19 W 44th St, #1000, New York, NY 10036, USA
Rinna, Lisa *Actress*
%B & B Entertainment, 1640 S Sepulveda Blvd, #530, Los Angeles, CA 90025, USA
Rintzler, Marius A *Opera Singer*
Friedingstr 18, 40625 Dusseldorf, Germany
Riordan, Mike *Basketball Player*
%Riordan's Saloon, 26 Market Place, Annapolis, MD 21401, USA
Riordan, Richard J *Mayor*
141 N Bristol Ave, Los Angeles, CA 90049, USA
Rios Montt, Efrain *President, Guatemala; Army General*
6A Avenida A 3-18 Zona 1, Guatamela City, Guatemala
Rios, Alberto *Writer*
%Arizona State University, English Dept, Tempe, AZ 85287, USA
Rios, Marcelo *Tennis Player*
%Int'l Mgmt Group, Via Augusta 200, #400, 08021 Barcelona, Spain
Ripa, Kelly *Actress*
646 Juniper Place, Franklin Lakes, NJ 07417, USA
Ripert, Eric *Chef*
%Le Bernardin, 787 7th Ave, New York, NY 10019, USA
Ripken, Calvin E (Cal), Jr *Baseball Player*
10801 Tony Dr, #A, Lutherville, MD 21093, USA
Ripley, Alexandra *Writer*
24 Ripley St, Newport News, VA 23603, USA
Ripley, Alice *Actress, Singer*
%Douglas Gorman Rothacker Wilhelm, 1501 Broadway, #703, New York, NY 10036, USA
Rippey, Rodney Allan *Actor*
3941 Veselich Ave, #4-251, Los Angeles, CA 90039, USA
Ripple, Kenneth F *Judge*
%US Court of Appeals, 204 S Main St, South Bend, IN 46601, USA
Ris, Hans *Zoologist*
5542 Riverview Dr, Waunakee, WI 53597, USA
Risebrough, Doug *Hockey Player, Coach, Executive*
5809 Schaefer Road, Edina, MN 55436, USA
Risen, Arnold (Arnie) *Basketball Player*
3217 Bremerton Road, Pepper Pike, OH 44124, USA
Risien, Cody L *Football Player*
209 Spanish Oak Trail, Dripping Springs, TX 78620, USA
Risk, Thomas N *Financier*
10 Belford Place, Edinburgh EH4 3DH, Scotland
Ristorucci, Lisa *Actress*
%Progressive Artists Agency, 400 S Beverly Dr, #216, Beverly Hills, CA 90212, USA
Ritcher, James A (Jim) *Football Player*
8620 Bournemouth Dr, Raleigh, NC 27615, USA
Ritchie, Daniel L *Educator, Television Executive*
%University of Denver, Chancellor's Office, Denver, CO 80208, USA
Ritchie, Guy *Movie Director*
%SKA Films, 1 Horse & Dolphin Yard, London W1V 7LG, England
Ritchie, Ian *Architect*
110 Three Colt St, London E14 8A2, England
Ritchie, Jim *Sculptor*
%Adelson Galleries, Mark Hotel, 25 E 77th St, New York, NY 10021, USA
Ritchie, John H *Architect*
Mount, Heswall, Wirral L60 4RD, England
Ritenour, Lee *Jazz Guitarist, Singer, Composer*
11808 Dorothy St, #108, Los Angeles, CA 90049, USA
Ritger, Dick *Bowler*
804 Valley View Dr, River Falls, WI 54022, USA

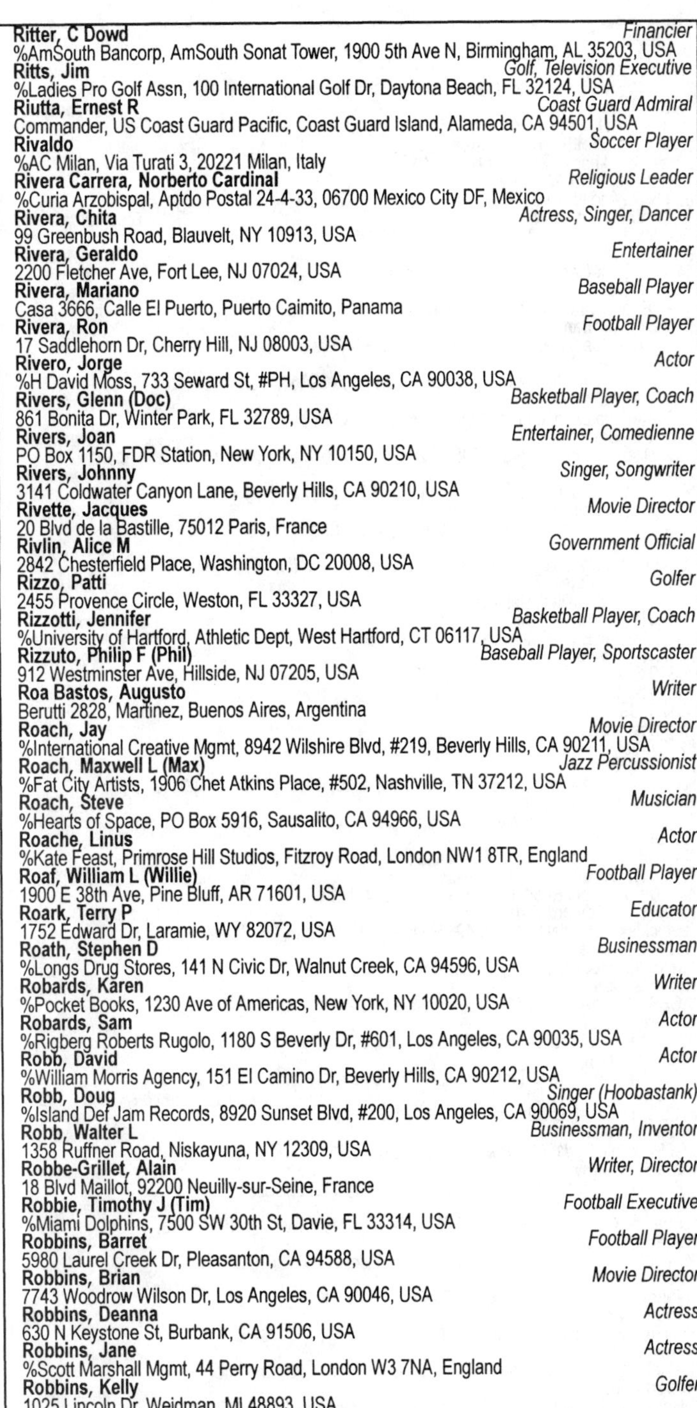

Ritter, C Dowd *Financier*
%AmSouth Bancorp, AmSouth Sonat Tower, 1900 5th Ave N, Birmingham, AL 35203, USA
Ritts, Jim *Golf, Television Executive*
%Ladies Pro Golf Assn, 100 International Golf Dr, Daytona Beach, FL 32124, USA
Riutta, Ernest R *Coast Guard Admiral*
Commander, US Coast Guard Pacific, Coast Guard Island, Alameda, CA 94501, USA
Rivaldo *Soccer Player*
%AC Milan, Via Turati 3, 20221 Milan, Italy
Rivera Carrera, Norberto Cardinal *Religious Leader*
%Curia Arzobispal, Aptdo Postal 24-4-33, 06700 Mexico City DF, Mexico
Rivera, Chita *Actress, Singer, Dancer*
99 Greenbush Road, Blauvelt, NY 10913, USA
Rivera, Geraldo *Entertainer*
2200 Fletcher Ave, Fort Lee, NJ 07024, USA
Rivera, Mariano *Baseball Player*
Casa 3666, Calle El Puerto, Puerto Caimito, Panama
Rivera, Ron *Football Player*
17 Saddlehorn Dr, Cherry Hill, NJ 08003, USA
Rivero, Jorge *Actor*
%H David Moss, 733 Seward St, #PH, Los Angeles, CA 90038, USA
Rivers, Glenn (Doc) *Basketball Player, Coach*
861 Bonita Dr, Winter Park, FL 32789, USA
Rivers, Joan *Entertainer, Comedienne*
PO Box 1150, FDR Station, New York, NY 10150, USA
Rivers, Johnny *Singer, Songwriter*
3141 Coldwater Canyon Lane, Beverly Hills, CA 90210, USA
Rivette, Jacques *Movie Director*
20 Blvd de la Bastille, 75012 Paris, France
Rivlin, Alice M *Government Official*
2842 Chesterfield Place, Washington, DC 20008, USA
Rizzo, Patti *Golfer*
2455 Provence Circle, Weston, FL 33327, USA
Rizzotti, Jennifer *Basketball Player, Coach*
%University of Hartford, Athletic Dept, West Hartford, CT 06117, USA
Rizzuto, Philip F (Phil) *Baseball Player, Sportscaster*
912 Westminster Ave, Hillside, NJ 07205, USA
Roa Bastos, Augusto *Writer*
Berutti 2828, Martinez, Buenos Aires, Argentina
Roach, Jay *Movie Director*
%International Creative Mgmt, 8942 Wilshire Blvd, #219, Beverly Hills, CA 90211, USA
Roach, Maxwell L (Max) *Jazz Percussionist*
%Fat City Artists, 1906 Chet Atkins Place, #502, Nashville, TN 37212, USA
Roach, Steve *Musician*
%Hearts of Space, PO Box 5916, Sausalito, CA 94966, USA
Roache, Linus *Actor*
%Kate Feast, Primrose Hill Studios, Fitzroy Road, London NW1 8TR, England
Roaf, William L (Willie) *Football Player*
1900 E 38th Ave, Pine Bluff, AR 71601, USA
Roark, Terry P *Educator*
1752 Edward Dr, Laramie, WY 82072, USA
Roath, Stephen D *Businessman*
%Longs Drug Stores, 141 N Civic Dr, Walnut Creek, CA 94596, USA
Robards, Karen *Writer*
%Pocket Books, 1230 Ave of Americas, New York, NY 10020, USA
Robards, Sam *Actor*
%Rigberg Roberts Rugolo, 1180 S Beverly Dr, #601, Los Angeles, CA 90035, USA
Robb, David *Actor*
%William Morris Agency, 151 El Camino Dr, Beverly Hills, CA 90212, USA
Robb, Doug *Singer (Hoobastank)*
%Island Def Jam Records, 8920 Sunset Blvd, #200, Los Angeles, CA 90069, USA
Robb, Walter L *Businessman, Inventor*
1358 Ruffner Road, Niskayuna, NY 12309, USA
Robbe-Grillet, Alain *Writer, Director*
18 Blvd Maillot, 92200 Neuilly-sur-Seine, France
Robbie, Timothy J (Tim) *Football Executive*
%Miami Dolphins, 7500 SW 30th St, Davie, FL 33314, USA
Robbins, Barret *Football Player*
5980 Laurel Creek Dr, Pleasanton, CA 94588, USA
Robbins, Brian *Movie Director*
7743 Woodrow Wilson Dr, Los Angeles, CA 90046, USA
Robbins, Deanna *Actress*
630 N Keystone St, Burbank, CA 91506, USA
Robbins, Jane *Actress*
%Scott Marshall Mgmt, 44 Perry Road, London W3 7NA, England
Robbins, Kelly *Golfer*
1025 Lincoln Dr, Weidman, MI 48893, USA
Robbins, Tim *Actor, Director*
%International Creative Mgmt, 40 W 57th St, #1800, New York, NY 10019, USA

R

Robbins, Tom *Writer*
PO Box 338, La Conner, WA 98257, USA
Robbins, Tony *Writer*
%Jennifer Martinez, 9888 Carrole Center, San Diego, CA 92126, USA
Robelot, Jane *Commentator*
%CBS-TV, News Dept, 51 W 52nd St, New York, NY 10019, USA
Robens of Woldingham, Alfred *Government Official, England; Educator*
2 Laleham Abbey, Staines, Middx TW18 1SZ, England
Roberson, Irvin (Bo) *Track Athlete*
820 N Raymond Ave, #47, Pasadena, CA 91103, USA
Roberson, James W *Cinematographer*
PO Box 121013, Big Bear Lake, CA 92315, USA
Robert, Jacques F *Attorney*
14 Villa Saint-Georges, 92160 Antony, France
Robert, Rene *Hockey Player*
4020 Rue Savard, Troie Rivieres QC G8Y 4B8, Canada
Roberts, Bernard *Concert Pianist*
Uwchlaw'r Coed, Llanbedr, Gwynedd LL45 2NA, Wales
Roberts, Bert C, Jr *Businessman*
%MCI WorldCom Inc, 500 Clinton Dr, Clinton, MS 39056, USA
Roberts, Beverly *Actress*
30912 Ariana Lane, Laguna Niguel, CA 92677, USA
Roberts, Brad *Singer (Crash Test Dummies)*
%Macklam Feldman Mgmt, 1505 W 2nd Ave, #200, Vancouver BC V6H 3Y4, Canada
Roberts, Brian L *Businessman*
%Storer Communications, 1500 Market St, Philadelphia, PA 19102, USA
Roberts, Bruce *Singer, Songwriter*
%Gorfaine/Schwartz, 13245 Riverside Dr, #450, Sherman Oaks, CA 91423, USA
Roberts, Cecil *Labor Leader*
%United Mine Workers, 8315 Lee Highway, #500, Fairfax, VA 22031, USA
Roberts, Chalmers M *Journalist*
6699 MacArthur Blvd, Bethesda, MD 20816, USA
Roberts, Corrine (Cokie) *Commentator*
5315 Bradley Blvd, Bethesda, MD 20814, USA
Roberts, David (Dave) *Track Athlete*
14310 SW 73rd Ave, Archer, FL 32618, USA
Roberts, Dee *Artist*
2012 N 19th St, Boise, ID 83702, USA
Roberts, Doris *Actress*
6225 Quebec Dr, Los Angeles, CA 90068, USA
Roberts, Eric *Actor*
%United Talent Agency, 9560 Wilshire Blvd, #500, Beverly Hills, CA 90212, USA
Roberts, Eugene L, Jr *Editor*
%New York Times, Editorial Dept, 229 W 43rd St, New York, NY 10036, USA
Roberts, Gary *Hockey Player*
%Wooden Sticks, PO Box 848 Station Main, Uxbridge PM L9P 1N2, Canada
Roberts, Gordon R *Vietnam War Army Hero (CMH)*
445 Ward-Koebel Road, Oregonia, OH 45054, USA
Roberts, H Edward (Ed) *Computer Designer*
%Bleckley Memorial Hospital, 408 Peacock St, Cochran, GA 31014, USA
Roberts, James A (Jim) *Hockey Player, Coach*
137 Ridgecrest Dr, Chesterfield, MO 63017, USA
Roberts, John *Commentator*
%CBS-TV, News Dept, 51 W 52nd St, New York, NY 10019, USA
Roberts, John *Movie Director*
%International Creative Mgmt, 76 Oxford St, London W1N 0AX, England
Roberts, John D *Chemist*
%California Institute of Technology, Chemistry Dept, Pasadena, CA 91125, USA
Roberts, John D (J D) *Football Player, Coach*
6708 Trevi Court, Oklahoma City, OK 73116, USA
Roberts, Julia *Actress*
386 Park Ave S, #1000, New York, NY 10016, USA
Roberts, Kenny *Motorcycle Racing Rider*
%KR Marketing, 419 Medina Road, Medina, OH 44256, USA
Roberts, Kevin *Businessman*
%Saatchi & Saatchi Worldwide, 375 Hudson St, New York, NY 10014, USA
Roberts, Lawrence G *Computer Scientist*
%Caspian Networks, 170 Baytech Dr, San Jose, CA 95134, USA
Roberts, Leonard *Businessman*
%Tandy Corp, 100 Throckmorton St, Fort Worth, TX 76102, USA
Roberts, Loren *Golfer*
3311 Tournament Dr S, Memphis, TN 38125, USA
Roberts, M Brigitte *Writer*
%Atkin & Stone, 29 Fernshaw Road, London SW10 0TG, England
Roberts, Marcus *Jazz Pianist*
%Columbia Artists Mgmt Inc, 165 W 57th St, New York, NY 10019, USA
Roberts, Michele *Writer*
%Henry Holt, 115 W 18th St, New York, NY 10011, USA

Roberts, Nora — *Writer*
19239 Burnside Bridge Road, Keedysville, MD 21756, USA
Roberts, Oral — *Evangelist*
%Oral Roberts University, 7777 S Lewis Ave, Tulsa, OK 74171, USA
Roberts, Paul H — *Mathematician*
PO Box 951567, Los Angeles, CA 90095, USA
Roberts, Pernell — *Actor*
20395 Seaboard Road, Malibu, CA 90265, USA
Roberts, R Michael — *Animal Scientist*
2213 Hominy Branch Court, Columbia, MO 65201, USA
Roberts, Ralph J — *Businessman*
%Comcast Corp, 1500 Market St, Philadelphia, PA 19102, USA
Roberts, Richard J — *Nobel Medicine Laureate*
%New England Biolabs, 32 Tozer Road, Beverly, MA 01915, USA
Roberts, Richard L — *Educator*
%Oral Roberts University, President's Office, 7777 S Lewis Ave, Tulsa, OK 74171, USA
Roberts, Robin — *Sportscaster*
%ESPN-TV, Sports Dept, ESPN Plaza, 935 Middle St, Bristol, CT 06010, USA
Roberts, Robin E — *Baseball Player*
504 Terrace Hill Road, Temple Terrace, FL 33617, USA
Roberts, Stanley — *Basketball Player*
1192 Congaree Road, Hopkins, SC 29061, USA
Roberts, Tanya — *Actress*
8410 Allenwood Road, Los Angeles, CA 90046, USA
Roberts, Tony — *Actor*
970 Park Ave, #8N, New York, NY 10028, USA
Roberts, Trish — *Basketball Player*
218 Carver Dr, Monroe, GA 30655, USA
Roberts, Xavier — *Businessman, Doll Designer*
PO Box 1438, Cleveland, GA 30528, USA
Robertson, Alvin C — *Basketball Player*
3 Birnam Oaks, San Antonio, TX 78248, USA
Robertson, Belinda — *Fashion Designer*
%BR Cashmere, 22 Palmerston Place, Edinburgh EH12 5AL, Scotland
Robertson, Cliff — *Actor*
325 Dunemere Dr, La Jolla, CA 92037, USA
Robertson, Dale — *Actor*
PO Box 850707, Yukon, OK 73085, USA
Robertson, Davis — *Dancer*
%Joffrey Ballet, 70 E Lake St, #1300, Chicago, IL 60601, USA
Robertson, DeWayne — *Football Player*
%New York Jets, 1000 Fulton Ave, Hempstead, NY 11550, USA
Robertson, Ed — *Guitarist (Barenaked Ladies), Songwriter*
%Nettwerk Mgmt, 8730 Wilshire Blvd, #304, Beverly Hills, CA 90211, USA
Robertson, Georgina — *Model*
%Compagny, 270 Lafayette, #1400, New York, NY 10012, USA
Robertson, Isiah — *Football Player*
1115 N Florida St, Covington, LA 70433, USA
Robertson, Jenny — *Actress*
%Shelter Entertainment, 9255 Sunset Blvd, #1010, Los Angeles, CA 90069, USA
Robertson, Kathleen — *Actress*
%Three Arts Entertainment, 9460 Wilshire Blvd, #700, Beverly Hills, CA 90212, USA
Robertson, Kimmy — *Actress*
%Commercials Unlimited, 8383 Wilshire Blvd, #850, Beverly Hills, CA 90211, USA
Robertson, Leslie E — *Structural Engineer*
%Robertson Fowler Assoc, 211 E 46th St, New York, NY 10017, USA
Robertson, M G (Pat) — *Evangelist*
%Christian Broadcast Network, 100 Centerville Turnpike, Virginia Beach, VA 23463, USA
Robertson, Marcus A — *Football Player*
3218 Cypress Point, Missouri City, TX 77459, USA
Robertson, Oscar P — *Basketball Player*
621 Tusculum Ave, Cincinnati, OH 45226, USA
Robertson, Robbie — *Singer, Guitarist (Band); Songwriter*
323 14th St, Santa Monica, CA 90402, USA
Robes, Ernest C (Bill) — *Ski Jumper*
3 Mile Road, Etna, NH 03750, USA
Robie, Carl — *Swimmer*
2525 Sunnybrook Dr, Sarasota, FL 34239, USA
Robinowitz, Joseph R — *Editor, Publisher*
%TV Guide Magazine, Editorial Dept, 100 Matsonford Road, Radnor, PA 19080, USA
Robins, Lee N — *Social Scientist*
%Washington University, Medical School, Psychiatry Dept, Saint Louis, MO 63110, USA
Robinson of Woolwich, John — *Religious Leader*
%Trinity College, Cambridge CB2 1TQ, England
Robinson, Andrew — *Actor*
2671 Byron Place, Los Angeles, CA 90046, USA
Robinson, Ann — *Actress*
1357 Elysian Park Dr, Los Angeles, CA 90026, USA

R

Robinson - Robisch

Robinson, Anne *Entertainer*
19 Victoria Grove, London W8 5RW, England
Robinson, Arthur H *Cartographer*
7707 N Brookline Dr, #302, Madison, WI 53719, USA
Robinson, Brooks C *Baseball Player*
9210 Baltimore National Pike, Ellicot, MD 21042, USA
Robinson, Bumper *Actor*
1551 Majesty St, Upland, CA 91784, USA
Robinson, Chip *Auto Racing Driver*
3034 Lake Forest Dr, Augusta, GA 30909, USA
Robinson, Chris *Actor*
3800 Barham Blvd, #303, Los Angeles, CA 90068, USA
Robinson, Chris *Singer (Black Crowes)*
%Mitch Schneider Organization, 14724 Ventura Blvd, #410, Sherman Oaks, CA 91403, USA
Robinson, Clarence (Arnie) *Track Athlete*
2904 Ocean View Blvd, San Diego, CA 92113, USA
Robinson, Cliff *Basketball Player*
57 Fire Flicker Place, The Woodlands, TX 77381, USA
Robinson, Clifford *Basketball Player*
PO Box 3357, San Ramon, CA 94583, USA
Robinson, David W *Basketball Player*
1 Admirals Way, San Antonio, TX 78257, USA
Robinson, Dawn *Singer (En Vogue, Lucy Pearl)*
%William Morris Agency, 151 El Camino Dr, Beverly Hills, CA 90212, USA
Robinson, Dwight P *Financier*
%Government National Mortgage Assn, 451 7th St SW, Washington, DC 20410, USA
Robinson, Edward G (Eddie) *Football Coach*
PO Box 331, Grambling, LA 71245, USA
Robinson, Emily Erwin *Singer (Dixie Chicks)*
%Senior Mgmt, 56 Lindsey Ave, Nashville, TN 37210, USA
Robinson, Eugene *Football Player*
%Atlanta Falcons, 4400 Falcon Parkway, Flowery Branch, GA 30542, USA
Robinson, Flynn *Basketball Player*
11875 Manor Dr, #1, Hawthorne, CA 90250, USA
Robinson, Frank *Baseball Player, Manager*
15557 Aqua Verde Dr, Los Angeles, CA 90077, USA
Robinson, Glenn *Basketball Player*
%Philadelphia 76ers, 1st Union Center, 3601 S Broad St, Philadelphia, PA 19148, USA
Robinson, Janice *Singer (Livin' Joy)*
%Flavor Unit Entertainment, 155 Morgan St, Jersey City, NJ 07302, USA
Robinson, Jay *Actor*
13757 Milbank Ave, Sherman Oaks, CA 91423, USA
Robinson, John A *Football Coach*
45 Anthem Creek Circle, Henderson, NV 89052, USA
Robinson, Johnny N *Football Player*
3209 S Grand St, Monroe, LA 71202, USA
Robinson, Kenneth *Government Official, England*
12 Grove Terrace, London NW5, England
Robinson, Koren *Football Player*
12 Henry Ave, Belmont, NC 28012, USA
Robinson, Larry *Hockey Player, Coach*
3211 Stevenson St, Plant City, FL 33566, USA
Robinson, Laura *Actress*
%Henderson/Hogan, 8285 W Sunset Blvd, #1, West Hollywood, CA 90046, USA
Robinson, Mary *President, Ireland*
'Aras an Uachtarain, Phoenix Park, Dublin 8, Ireland
Robinson, Patrick *Fashion Designer*
%Ann Klein Co, 11 W 42nd St, #2300, New York, NY 10036, USA
Robinson, Phil Alden *Movie Director*
%Creative Artists Agency, 9830 Wilshire Blvd, Beverly Hills, CA 90212, USA
Robinson, Rich *Guitarist (Black Crowes)*
%Mitch Schneider Organization, 14724 Ventura Blvd, #410, Sherman Oaks, CA 91403, USA
Robinson, Richard D (Dave) *Football Player*
406 S Rose Blvd, Akron, OH 44320, USA
Robinson, Rumeal *Basketball Player*
%Detroit Pistons, Palace, 2 Championship Dr, Auburn Hills, MI 48326, USA
Robinson, Shawna *Auto/Truck Racing Driver*
%Performance One, 545C Pitts School Road NW, Concord, NC 28027, USA
Robinson, Smokey *Singer, Songwriter*
%Mitch Schneider Organization, 14724 Ventura Blvd, #410, Sherman Oaks, CA 91403, USA
Robinson, Stephen K *Astronaut*
2405 Airline Dr, Friendswood, TX 77546, USA
Robinson, V Gene *Religious Leader*
%Saint Paul's Church, 21 Centre St, Concord, NH 03301, USA
Robinson-Peete, Holly *Actress*
11964 Crest Place, Beverly Hills, CA 90210, USA
Robisch, Dave *Basketball Player*
1401 Guemes Court, Springfield, IL 62702, USA

Robison, Bruce *Singer, Songwriter*
%Artist Envoy Agency, 1016 16th Ave S, #101, Nashville, TN 37212, USA
Robison, Charlie *Singer, Songwriter*
%Steve Hoiberg Organization, 2021 21st Ave S, #120, Nashville, TN 37212, USA
Robison, Paula *Concert Flutist*
%Matthew Sprizzo, 477 Durant Ave, Staten Island, NY 10308, USA
Robitaille, Luc *Hockey Player*
13801 Ventura Blvd, Sherman Oaks, CA 91423, USA
Robles, Marisa *Concert Harpist*
38 Luttrell Ave, London SW15 6PE, England
Roboz, Zsuzsi *Artist*
6 Bryanston Court, George St, London W1H 7HA, England
Robson, Bryan *Soccer Player*
%Middlesbrough FC, Riverside Stadium, Midds, Cleveland TS3 6RS, England
Robuchon, Joel *Chef*
%Societe de Gestion Culinaire, 67 Blvd du Gen M Valin, 75015 Paris, France
Robustelli, Andrew R (Andy) *Football Player*
30 Spring St, Stamford, CT 06901, USA
Robyn *Singer*
%Lifeline, 73C Saint Charles Square, London W10 6EJ, England
Rocard, Michel L L *Prime Minister, France*
Hotel de Ville, 63 Rue M Berteaux, 78700 Conflans-Sainte-Honorine, France
Rocca, Constantino *Golfer*
%Golf Products International, 5719 Lake Lindero Dr, Agoura Hills, CA 91301, USA
Rocca, Peter *Swimmer*
534 Hazel Ave, San Bruno, CA 94066, USA
Rocco, Alex *Actor*
PO Box 302, Carpinteria, CA 93014, USA
Rocco, Rinaldo *Actor*
%Carol Levi Co, Via Giuseppe Pisanelli, 00196 Rome, Italy
Rocha, Ephraim (Red) *Basketball Player, Coach*
3045 NW Roosevelt Dr, Corvallis, OR 97330, USA
Rochberg, George *Composer*
3500 West Chester Pike, #CH118, Newtown Square, PA 19073, USA
Roche, Anthony D (Tony) *Tennis Player*
5 Kapiti St, Saint Ives NSW 2075, Australia
Roche, E Kevin *Architect, Pritzker Laureate*
%Roche Dinkeloo Assoc, 20 Davis St, Hamden, CT 06517, USA
Roche, Eugene *Actor*
9911 W Pico Blvd, #PH A, Los Angeles, CA 90035, USA
Roche, George A *Financier*
%T Rowe Price Assoc, 100 E Pratt St, Baltimore, MD 21202, USA
Roche, James G *Secretary, Air Force*
%Air Force Department, Secretary's Office, Pentagon, Washington, DC 20310, USA
Roche, John *Basketball Player*
6401 E 6th Ave, Denver, CO 80220, USA
Rochefort, Jean *Actress*
Le Chene Rogneaux, 078125 Grosvre, France
Rochon, Lela *Actress*
%Gersh Agency, 232 N Canon Dr, Beverly Hills, CA 90210, USA
Rock *Wrestler, Actor*
%World Wrestling Entertainment, Titan Towers, 1241 E Main St, Stamford, CT 06902, USA
Rock, Angela *Volleyball Player*
4134 Lymer Dr, San Diego, CA 92116, USA
Rock, Chris *Actor, Comedian*
%ML Management Assoc, 1740 Broadway, #1500, New York, NY 10019, USA
Rockburne, Dorothea G *Artist*
140 Grand St, New York, NY 10013, USA
Rockefeller, David *Financier*
1 Chase Manhattan Plaza, New York, NY 10005, USA
Rockefeller, Laurance S *Foundation Executive*
%Rockefeller Bros Fund, 30 Rockefeller Plaza, #5600, New York, NY 10112, USA
Rocker, John *Baseball Player*
1425 Old Forsyth Road, Macon, GA 31210, USA
Rockett, Rikki *Drummer (Poison)*
%H K Mgmt, 9200 W Sunset Blvd, #530, Los Angeles, CA 90069, USA
Rockwell, Martha *Skier, Coach*
%Dartmouth College, PO Box 9, Hanover, NH 03755, USA
Rockwell, Sam *Actor*
9 Desbrosses St, #200, New York, NY 10013, USA
Rockwood, Marcia *Editor*
%Reader's Digest, Editorial Dept, PO Box 100, Pleasantville, NY 10572, USA
Rodd, Marcia *Actress*
11738 Moorpark St, #C, Studio City, CA 91604, USA
Roddam, Franc *Movie Director*
%William Morris Agency, 52/53 Poland Place, London W1F 7LX, England
Roddick, Andy *Tennis Player*
1499 Las Casas Road, Boca Raton, FL 33486, USA

R

Rodenheiser, Richard (Dick) *Hockey Player*
186 State St, Framingham, MA 01702, USA
Rodgers of Quarry Bank, William T *Government Official, England*
48 Patshull Road, London NW3 2LD, England
Rodgers, Anton *Actor*
%Michael Whitehall, 125 Gloucester Road, London SW7 4TE, England
Rodgers, Franklin C (Pepper) *Football Player, Coach*
%Washington Redskins, 21300 Redskin Park Dr, Ashburn, VA 20147, USA
Rodgers, Jimmie *Singer, Songwriter*
PO Box 685, Forsyth, MO 65653, USA
Rodgers, Joan *Opera Singer*
113 Sotheby Road, London N5 2UT, England
Rodgers, Joe M *Diplomat*
%JMR Investments, Vanderbilt Plaza, 2100 W End Ave, Nashville, TN 37203, USA
Rodgers, John *Geologist*
%Yale University, Geology Dept, New Haven, CT 06520, USA
Rodgers, Paul *Singer (Bad Company), Songwriter*
%Work Hard PR, 19D Pinhold Road, London SW16 5GD, England
Rodgers, Robert L (Buck) *Baseball Player, Manager*
5181 West Knoll Dr, Yorba Linda, CA 92886, USA
Rodgers, William H (Bill) *Track Athlete*
372 Chestnut Hill Ave, Boston, MA 02135, USA
Rodin, Judith S *Psychiatrist, Educator*
%University of Pennsylvania, President's Office, Philadelphia, PA 19104, USA
Roditi, Claudio *Trumpeter*
%Carolyn McClair PR, PO Box 55, Radio Station, New York, NY 10101, USA
Rodl, Henrik *Basketball Player*
%ALBA Berlin, Olympischer Platz 4, 14053 Berlin, Germany
Rodman, Dennis *Basketball Player, Actor*
PO Box 5670, Orange, CA 92863, USA
Rodnina, Irina *Figure Skater*
13243 Fiji Way, #G, Marina del Rey, CA 90292, USA
Rodrigue, George *Journalist*
PO Box 51227, Lafayette, LA 70505, USA
Rodrigue, George *Artist*
721 Royal St, New Orleans, LA 70116, USA
Rodrigues, Charlie *Cartoonist (Charlie)*
%Tribune Media Services, 435 N Michigan Ave, #1500, Chicago, IL 60611, USA
Rodriguez Madariaga, Oscar A Cardinal *Religious Leader*
Arzobispado, Apartado 106, 3A y 2A Ave 1113, Tegucigalpa, Honduras
Rodriguez, Adam *Actor*
%International Creative Mgmt, 8942 Wilshire Blvd, #219, Beverly Hills, CA 90211, USA
Rodriguez, Alexander E (Alex) *Baseball Player*
%Texas Rangers, 1000 Ballpark Way, Arlington, TX 76011, USA
Rodriguez, Arturo S *Labor Leader*
%United Farm Workers, 29700 Woodford Tehachapi Road, Keene, CA 93531, USA
Rodriguez, Beatriz *Ballerina*
8215 Britton Ave, Flushing, NY 11373, USA
Rodriguez, Ivan (Pudge) *Baseball Player*
1000 Ballpark Way, #306, Arlington, TX 76011, USA
Rodriguez, Jennifer *Speedskater*
PO Box 450639, Westlake, OH 44145, USA
Rodriguez, Johnny *Singer, Songwriter*
PO Box 190514, Saint Louis, MO 63119, USA
Rodriguez, Joseph C *Korean War Army Hero (CMH)*
1736 Tommy Aaron Dr, El Paso, TX 79936, USA
Rodriguez, Juan (Chi Chi) *Golfer*
%Eddie Elias Enterprises, 3916 Clock Pointe Trail, #101, Stow, OH 44224, USA
Rodriguez, Larry *Religious Leader*
%Metropolitan Churches Fellowship, 5300 Santa Monica Blvd, Los Angeles, CA 90029, USA
Rodriguez, Michelle *Actress*
%William Morris Agency, 151 El Camino Dr, Beverly Hills, CA 90212, USA
Rodriguez, Paul *Actor, Comedian*
%Paul Rodriguez Productions, PO Box 1327, Beverly Hills, CA 90213, USA
Rodriguez, Raul *Float Designer*
%Fiesta Floats, 9362 Lower Azusa Road, Temple City, CA 91780, USA
Rodriguez, Rich *Football Coach*
%West Virginia University, Athletic Dept, Morgantown, WV 26506, USA
Rodriguez, Rita M *Financier*
%Export-Import Bank, 811 Vermont Ave NW, Washington, DC 20571, USA
Rodriguez, Robert *Movie Director*
%International Creative Mgmt, 8942 Wilshire Blvd, #219, Beverly Hills, CA 90211, USA
Roe, Elwin C (Preacher) *Baseball Player*
204 Wildwood Terrace, West Plains, MO 65775, USA
Roe, John H *Businessman*
%Bemis Co, Northstar Center, 222 S 9th St, Minneapolis, MN 55402, USA
Roe, Marty *Singer, Guitarist (Diamond Rio)*
%Dreamcatcher Artists Mgmt, 2908 Poston Ave, Nashville, TN 37203, USA

Roe, Tommy *Singer, Songwriter*
%American Mgmt, 19948 Mayall St, Chatsworth, CA 91311, USA
Roebuck, Edward J (Ed) *Baseball Player*
3434 Warwood Road, Lakewood, CA 90712, USA
Roeder, Kenneth D *Physiologist*
454 Monument St, Concord, MA 01742, USA
Roeder, Robert G *Biochemist*
504 E 63rd St, #36P, New York, NY 10021, USA
Roeg, Nicolas J *Movie Director*
2 Oxford & Cambridge Mansions, Old Marylebone Road, London NW1, England
Roehm, Carolyne J *Fashion Designer*
%Carolyn Roehm Inc, 257 W 39th St, #400, New York, NY 10018, USA
Roel, Charlotte *Singer, Songwriter*
%World Wide Mgmt, 11 Koebmagergade, DK 1150, Copenhagen, Denmark
Roelofs, Wendell L *Biochemist, Entomologist*
4 Crescence Dr, Geneva, NY 14456, USA
Roemer, John E *Economist*
%University of California, Economics Dept, Davis, CA 95616, USA
Roenick, Jeremy *Hockey Player*
229 Saint Anthonys Dr, Moorestown, NJ 08057, USA
Roenicke, Gary S *Baseball Player*
14152 Greenwood Court, Nevada City, CA 95959, USA
Roenicke, Ronald J (Ron) *Baseball Player*
2212 Avenida Las Ramblas, Chino Hills, CA 91709, USA
Roesky, Herbert W *Chemist*
%University of Gotingen, Inorganic Chem Dept, 37077 Gottingen, Germany
Rogallo, Francis *Inventor (Hang Glider)*
91 Osprey Lane, Kitty Hawk, NC 27949, USA
Roge, Pascal *Concert Pianist*
17 Ave des Cavaliers, 1224 Geneva, Switzerland
Rogel, Steven R *Businessman*
%Weyerhaeuser Co, 3363 32nd Ave S, Tacoma, WA 98023, USA
Roger of Taize, Brother *Religious Leader, Templeton Laureate*
Taize Community, 71250 Cluny, France
Rogers, Bernard W *Army General*
1467 Hampton Ridge Dr, McLean, VA 22101, USA
Rogers, Bill *Golfer*
710 Patterson Ave, San Antonio, TX 78209, USA
Rogers, Charles *Football Player*
%Detroit Lions, 222 Republic Dr, Allen Park, MI 48101, USA
Rogers, Erik *Singer (Stereo Mud)*
%Agency Group Ltd, 1775 Broadway, #430, New York, NY 10019, USA
Rogers, George W, Jr *Football Player*
1007 Lofty Pine Dr, Columbia, SC 29212, USA
Rogers, Greg *Writer*
PO Box 3787, Mcalester, OK 74502, USA
Rogers, James E *Businessman*
%Cinergy Corp, 139 E 4th St, Cincinnati, OH 45202, USA
Rogers, Jane A *Actress*
1485 S Beverly Dr, #8, Los Angeles, CA 90035, USA
Rogers, Judith W *Judge*
%US Appeals Court, 333 Constitution NW, Washington, DC 20001, USA
Rogers, June Scobee *Writer*
%Challenger Center, 1250 N Pitt St, Alexandria, VA 22314, USA
Rogers, Kenny *Singer, Songwriter, Actor*
PO Box 967, Durant, FL 33530, USA
Rogers, Lynn L *Wildlife Biologist, Ecologist*
145 W Conan St, Ely, MN 55731, USA
Rogers, Melody *Actress*
2051 Nicols Canyon Road, Los Angeles, CA 90046, USA
Rogers, Mimi *Actress*
8409 Santa Monica Blvd, West Hollywood, CA 90069, USA
Rogers, Paul *Government Official*
%Hogan & Hartson, 555 13th St NW, #1200, Washington, DC 20004, USA
Rogers, Paul *Actor*
9 Hillside Gardens, Highgate, London N6 5SU, England
Rogers, Ray *Labor Leader*
%Corporate Campaign Inc, 80 8th Ave, New York, NY 10011, USA
Rogers, Richard G *Architect*
%Rogers Partnership, Thames Wharf, Rainville Road, London W6 9HA, England
Rogers, Rob *Editorial Cartoonist*
%Pittsburgh Post-Gazette, Editorial Dept, 23 Blvd Allies, Pittsburgh, PA 15230, USA
Rogers, Rodney *Basketball Player*
%New Jersey Nets, 390 Murray Hill Parkway, East Rutherford, NJ 07073, USA
Rogers, Rosemary *Writer*
%Avon Books, 959 8th Ave, New York, NY 10019, USA
Rogers, Rutherford D *Librarian*
1111 S Lakemont Ave, #605, Winter Park, FL 32792, USA

R

Rogers, Stephen D (Steve) *Baseball Player*
3746 S Madison Ave, Tulsa, OK 74105, USA
Rogers, Suzanne *Actress*
11266 Canton Dr, Studio City, CA 91604, USA
Rogers, Tristan *Actor*
%Don Buchwald, 6500 Wilshire Blvd, #2200, Los Angeles, CA 90048, USA
Rogers, Wayne *Actor*
11828 La Grange Ave, Los Angeles, CA 90025, USA
Rogerson, Kate *Golfer*
%Debra Oberg, 42 Nelson St, Harrington Park, NJ 07640, USA
Rogge, Jacques *Sports Official*
%Int'l Olympic Committee, Chateau de Vidy, 1007 Lausanne, Switzerland
Rogin, Gilbert L *Editor*
21 W 10th St, #5A, New York, NY 10011, USA
Rogoff, Ilan *Concert Pianist*
Apdo 1098, 07080 Palma de Mallorca, Spain
Roh Moo-hyun *President, South Korea*
%President's Office, Chong Wa Dae, 1 Sejong-no, Seoul, South Korea
Rohde, Bruce *Businessman*
%ConAgra Inc, 1 ConAgra Dr, Omaha, NE 68102, USA
Rohde, David *Journalist*
%Christian Science Monitor, Editorial Dept, 1 Norway St, Boston, MA 02115, USA
Rohlander, Uta *Track Athlete*
Liebigstr 9, 06237 Leuna, Germany
Rohm, Elisabeth *Actress*
%Brillstein/Grey, 9150 Wilshire Blvd, #350, Beverly Hills, CA 90212, USA
Rohmer, Eric *Movie Director*
%Films du Losange, 22 Ave Pierre-de-Serbie, 75116 Paris, France
Rohner, Georges *Artist*
%Galerie Framond, 3 Rue des Saints Peres, 75006 Paris, France
Rohr, James E *Financier*
%PNC Bank Corp, 1 PNC Plaza, 249 5th Ave, Pittsburgh, PA 15222, USA
Rohrer, Heinrich *Nobel Physics Laureate*
%IBM Research Laboratory, Saumerstr 4, 8803 Ruschlikon, Switzerland
Roizman, Bernard *Virologist*
5555 S Everett Ave, Chicago, IL 60637, USA
Roizman, Owen *Cinematographer*
17533 Magnolia Blvd, Encino, CA 91316, USA
Rojas, Nydia *Singer*
%Silverlight Entertainment, 9171 Wilshire Blvd, #426, Beverly Hills, CA 90210, USA
Rojas, Octavio R (Cookie) *Baseball Player, Manager*
19195 Mystic Pointe Dr, #Loop 2, Aventura, FL 33180, USA
Rojcewicz, Susan (Sue) *Basketball Player*
48 Elena Circle, San Rafael, CA 94903, USA
Roker, Al *Entertainer*
%CNBC-TV, 2200 Fletcher Ave, Fort Lee, NJ 07024, USA
Rokke, Ervin J *Air Force General*
79 W Church St, Bethlehem, PA 18018, USA
Roland, Ed *Singer (Collective Soul), Songwriter*
%Spivak Entertainment, 11845 W Olympic Blvd, #1125, Los Angeles, CA 90064, USA
Roland, Johnny E *Football Player, Coach*
8701 S Hardy Dr, Tempe, AZ 85284, USA
Rolandi, Gianna *Opera Singer*
%Columbia Artists Mgmt Inc, 165 W 57th St, New York, NY 10019, USA
Rolen, Scott B *Baseball Player*
638 Dundee Lane, Holmes Beach, FL 34217, USA
Roles-Williams, Barbara *Figure Skater*
3790 Leisure Lane, Las Vegas, NV 89103, USA
Rolfe Johnson, Anthony *Opera Singer*
%I C M Artists, 40 W 57th St, New York, NY 10019, USA
Rollin, Betty *Writer, Commentator*
%NS Bienstack Inc, 1740 Broadway, New York, NY 10019, USA
Rollins, Henry *Singer, Songwriter*
%Three Artists Mgmt, 14260 Ventura Blvd, #201, Sherman Oaks, CA 91423, USA
Rollins, Henry *Actor*
7615 Hollywood Blvd, Los Angeles, CA 90046, USA
Rollins, James (Jimmy) *Baseball Player*
%Philadelphia Phillies, Veterans Stadium, 3501 S Broad, Philadelphia, PA 19148, USA
Rollins, Kenneth (Kenny) *Basketball Player*
Gardens, 220 Hibiscus Way, Parrish, FL 34219, USA
Rollins, Theodore W (Sonny) *Jazz Saxophonist, Composer*
RR 9G, Germantown, NY 12526, USA
Rollins, Wayne (Tree) *Basketball Player, Coach*
2107 Westover Reserve Blvd, Windermere, FL 34786, USA
Roloson, Dwayne *Hockey Player*
%Minnesota Wild, XCel Energy Arena, 175 Kellogg Blvd W, Saint Paul, MN 55102, USA
Rolston, Holmes III *Philosopher, Theologian*
%Colorado State University, Philosophy Dept, Fort Collins, CO 80523, USA

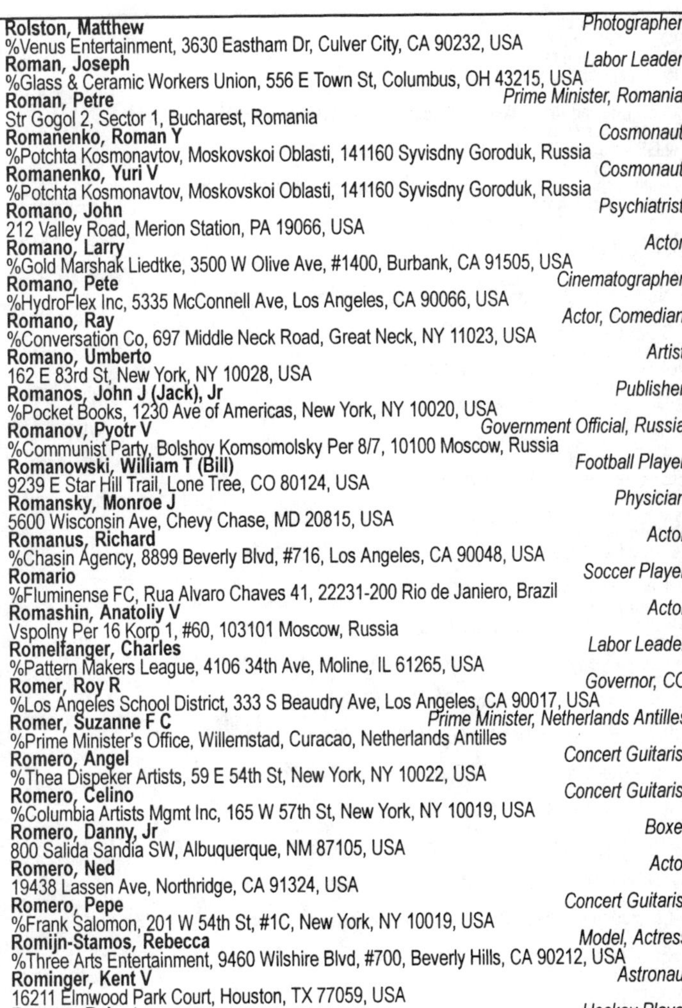

Rolston, Matthew *Photographer*
%Venus Entertainment, 3630 Eastham Dr, Culver City, CA 90232, USA
Roman, Joseph *Labor Leader*
%Glass & Ceramic Workers Union, 556 E Town St, Columbus, OH 43215, USA
Roman, Petre *Prime Minister, Romania*
Str Gogol 2, Sector 1, Bucharest, Romania
Romanenko, Roman Y *Cosmonaut*
%Potchta Kosmonavtov, Moskovskoi Oblasti, 141160 Syvisdny Goroduk, Russia
Romanenko, Yuri V *Cosmonaut*
%Potchta Kosmonavtov, Moskovskoi Oblasti, 141160 Syvisdny Goroduk, Russia
Romano, John *Psychiatrist*
212 Valley Road, Merion Station, PA 19066, USA
Romano, Larry *Actor*
%Gold Marshak Liedtke, 3500 W Olive Ave, #1400, Burbank, CA 91505, USA
Romano, Pete *Cinematographer*
%HydroFlex Inc, 5335 McConnell Ave, Los Angeles, CA 90066, USA
Romano, Ray *Actor, Comedian*
%Conversation Co, 697 Middle Neck Road, Great Neck, NY 11023, USA
Romano, Umberto *Artist*
162 E 83rd St, New York, NY 10028, USA
Romanos, John J (Jack), Jr *Publisher*
%Pocket Books, 1230 Ave of Americas, New York, NY 10020, USA
Romanov, Pyotr V *Government Official, Russia*
%Communist Party, Bolshoy Komsomolsky Per 8/7, 10100 Moscow, Russia
Romanowski, William T (Bill) *Football Player*
9239 E Star Hill Trail, Lone Tree, CO 80124, USA
Romansky, Monroe J *Physician*
5600 Wisconsin Ave, Chevy Chase, MD 20815, USA
Romanus, Richard *Actor*
%Chasin Agency, 8899 Beverly Blvd, #716, Los Angeles, CA 90048, USA
Romario *Soccer Player*
%Fluminense FC, Rua Alvaro Chaves 41, 22231-200 Rio de Janiero, Brazil
Romashin, Anatoliy V *Actor*
Vspolny Per 16 Korp 1, #60, 103101 Moscow, Russia
Romelfanger, Charles *Labor Leader*
%Pattern Makers League, 4106 34th Ave, Moline, IL 61265, USA
Romer, Roy R *Governor, CO*
%Los Angeles School District, 333 S Beaudry Ave, Los Angeles, CA 90017, USA
Romer, Suzanne F C *Prime Minister, Netherlands Antilles*
%Prime Minister's Office, Willemstad, Curacao, Netherlands Antilles
Romero, Angel *Concert Guitarist*
%Thea Dispeker Artists, 59 E 54th St, New York, NY 10022, USA
Romero, Celino *Concert Guitarist*
%Columbia Artists Mgmt Inc, 165 W 57th St, New York, NY 10019, USA
Romero, Danny, Jr *Boxer*
800 Salida Sandia SW, Albuquerque, NM 87105, USA
Romero, Ned *Actor*
19438 Lassen Ave, Northridge, CA 91324, USA
Romero, Pepe *Concert Guitarist*
%Frank Salomon, 201 W 54th St, #1C, New York, NY 10019, USA
Romijn-Stamos, Rebecca *Model, Actress*
%Three Arts Entertainment, 9460 Wilshire Blvd, #700, Beverly Hills, CA 90212, USA
Rominger, Kent V *Astronaut*
16211 Elmwood Park Court, Houston, TX 77059, USA
Rompre, Robert *Hockey Player*
316 W Maple Ave, Beaver Dam, WI 53916, USA
Ronaldo *Soccer Player*
%Real Madrid FC, Avda Concha Espina 1, 28036 Madrid, Spain
Ronan, William J *Railway Engineer*
525 S Flagler Dr, West Palm Beach, FL 33401, USA
Roney, Paul H *Judge*
%US Court of Appeals, 100 1st Ave S, Saint Petersburg, FL 33701, USA
Ronney, Paul D *Astronaut*
613 Ranchito Road, Monrovia, CA 91016, USA
Ronning, Cliff *Hockey Player*
316 Newton Dr, RR 3, Penticton BC V2A 8Z5, Canada
Ronningen, Jon *Wrestler*
Mellomasveien 132, 1414 Trollasen, Norway
Rono, Peter *Track Athlete*
%Mount Saint Mary's College, Athletic Dept, Emmitsburg, MD 21727, USA
Ronstadt, Linda *Singer*
%Krost-Chapin, 9000 W Sunset Blvd, #711, West Hollywood, CA 90069, USA
Roocroft, Amanda *Opera Singer*
%Ingpen & Williams, 26 Wadham Road, London SW15 2LR, England
Rook, Susan *Commentator*
%Cable News Network, News Dept, 1050 Techwood Dr NW, Atlanta, GA 30318, USA
Rooker, Michael *Actor*
275 S Beverly Dr, #215, Beverly Hills, CA 90212, USA

R

Rooney, Andrew A (Andy) *Commentator*
PO Box 48, Rensselaervle, NY 12147, USA
Rooney, Daniel M *Football Executive*
940 N Lincoln Ave, Pittsburgh, PA 15233, USA
Rooney, Jim *Soccer Player*
%New England Revolution, CMGI Field, 1 Patriot Place, Foxboro, MA 02035, USA
Rooney, Joe Don *Singer (Rascal Flatts)*
%LGB Media, 1228 Pineview Lane, Nashville, TN 37211, USA
Rooney, Mickey *Actor*
%Ruth Webb, 10580 Des Moines Ave, Northridge, CA 91326, USA
Rooney, Patrick W *Businessman*
%Cooper Tire & Rubber Co, Lima & Western Aves, Findlay, OH 45840, USA
Roots, Melvin H *Labor Leader*
%Plasters & Cement Workers Union, 1125 17th St NW, Washington, DC 20036, USA
Roper, Dee Dee (Spinderella) *Rap Artist (Salt'N'Pepa)*
%Next Plateau Records, 1650 Broadway, #1103, New York, NY 10019, USA
Rorem, Ned *Composer, Writer*
PO Box 764, Nantucket, MA 02554, USA
Rorty, Richard M *Philosopher*
402 Peacock Dr, Charlottesville, VA 22903, USA
Rosa, John *Air Force General, Educator*
Superintendent, US Air Force Academy, Colorado Springs, CO 80840, USA
Rosado, Eduardo *Opera Singer*
Calle 3, Ave Cupules 112A, Col G Giberes, Menda, Yucatan 97070, Mexico
Rosand, David *Art Historian*
560 Riverside Dr, New York, NY 10027, USA
Rosas, Cesar *Singer, Songwriter (Los Lobos)*
%Monterey International, 200 W Superior, #202, Chicago, IL 60610, USA
Rosato, Genesia *Ballerina*
%Royal Ballet, Covent Garden, Bow St, London WC2E 9DD, England
Rosberg, Keke *Auto Racing Driver*
7 Rue Gabian, 9800 Monte Carlo, Monaco
Rosburg, Bob *Golfer*
49425 Avenida Club La Quinta, La Quinta, CA 92253, USA
Roschkov, Victor *Editorial Cartoonist*
%Toronto Star, Editorial Dept, 1 Yonge St, Toronto ON M5E 1E5, Canada 90068, USA
Rose Marie *Actress*
6916 Chisholm Ave, Van Nuys, CA 91406, USA
Rose, Axl *Singer (Guns'n'Roses), Songwriter*
5055 Latigo Canyo Road, Malibu, CA 90265, USA
Rose, Charles (Charlie) *Commentator*
%Rose Communications, 499 Park Ave, #1500, New York, NY 10022, USA
Rose, Clarence *Golfer*
405 Walnut Creek Dr, Goldsboro, NC 27534, USA
Rose, Cristine *Actress*
%Paradigm Agency, 10100 Santa Monica Blvd, #2500, Los Angeles, CA 90067, USA
Rose, H Michael *Army General, England*
%Coldstream Guards, Wellington Barracks, London SW1E 6HQ, England
Rose, Jalen *Basketball Player*
%Chicago Bulls, United Center, 1901 W Madison St, Chicago, IL 60612, USA
Rose, Jamie *Actress*
%Gold Marshak Liedtke, 3500 W Olive Ave, #1400, Burbank, CA 91505, USA
Rose, Matthew *Businessman*
%Burlington North/Santa Fe, 2650 Lou Menk Dr, Fort Worth, TX 76131, USA
Rose, Murray *Swimmer*
77 Berry, Level 3, North Sydney NSW 2060, Australia
Rose, Peter E (Pete) *Baseball Player, Manager*
8144 W Glades Road, Boca Raton, FL 33434, USA
Rose, Peter H *Businessman*
%Krytek Corp, 2 Centennial Dr, Peabody, MA 01960, USA
Rose, Richard *Political Scientist*
Bennochy, 1 E Abercromby St, Helensburgh, Dunbartonshire G84 7SP, Scotland
Rose, Sherrie *Actress, Model*
1758 Laurel Canyon Blvd, Los Angeles, CA 90046, USA
Roseanne *Actress, Comedienne*
5 Crest Road, Rolling Hills, CA 90274, USA
Roseau, Maurice E D *Mechanical Engineer*
144 Bis Ave du General Leclerc, 92330 Sceaux, France
Roselle, David P *Educator*
47 Kent Way, Newark, DE 19711, USA
Rosellini, Albert D *Governor, WA*
5936 6th Ave S, Seattle, WA 98108, USA
Roseman, Saul *Biochemist*
8206 Cranwood Court, Baltimore, MD 21208, USA
Rosen, Albert (Al) *Conductor*
%Corbett Arts Mgmt, 2101 California St, #2, San Francisco, CA 94115, USA
Rosen, Albert L (Al) *Baseball Player, Executive*
15 Mayfair Dr, Rancho Mirage, CA 92270, USA

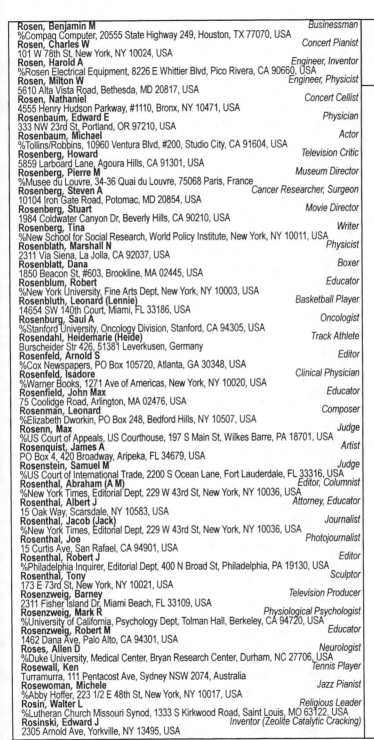

Rosen, Benjamin M *Businessman*
%Compaq Computer, 20555 State Highway 249, Houston, TX 77070, USA
Rosen, Charles W *Concert Pianist*
101 W 78th St, New York, NY 10024, USA
Rosen, Harold A *Engineer, Inventor*
%Rosen Electrical Equipment, 8226 E Whittier Blvd, Pico Rivera, CA 90660, USA
Rosen, Milton W *Engineer, Physicist*
5610 Alta Vista Road, Bethesda, MD 20817, USA
Rosen, Nathaniel *Concert Cellist*
4555 Henry Hudson Parkway, #1110, Bronx, NY 10471, USA
Rosenbaum, Edward E *Physician*
333 NW 23rd St, Portland, OR 97210, USA
Rosenbaum, Michael *Actor*
%Tollins/Robbins, 10960 Ventura Blvd, #200, Studio City, CA 91604, USA
Rosenberg, Howard *Television Critic*
5859 Larboard Lane, Agoura Hills, CA 91301, USA
Rosenberg, Pierre M *Museum Director*
%Musee du Louvre, 34-36 Quai du Louvre, 75068 Paris, France
Rosenberg, Steven A *Cancer Researcher, Surgeon*
10104 Iron Gate Road, Potomac, MD 20854, USA
Rosenberg, Stuart *Movie Director*
1984 Coldwater Canyon Dr, Beverly Hills, CA 90210, USA
Rosenberg, Tina *Writer*
%New School for Social Research, World Policy Institute, New York, NY 10011, USA
Rosenblath, Marshall N *Physicist*
2311 Via Siena, La Jolla, CA 92037, USA
Rosenblatt, Dana *Boxer*
1850 Beacon St, #603, Brookline, MA 02445, USA
Rosenblum, Robert *Educator*
%New York University, Fine Arts Dept, New York, NY 10003, USA
Rosenbluth, Leonard (Lennie) *Basketball Player*
14654 SW 140th Court, Miami, FL 33186, USA
Rosenburg, Saul A *Oncologist*
%Stanford University, Oncology Division, Stanford, CA 94305, USA
Rosendahl, Heidemarie (Heide) *Track Athlete*
Burscheider Str 426, 51381 Leverkusen, Germany
Rosenfeld, Arnold S *Editor*
%Cox Newspapers, PO Box 105720, Atlanta, GA 30348, USA
Rosenfeld, Isadore *Clinical Physician*
%Warner Books, 1271 Ave of Americas, New York, NY 10020, USA
Rosenfield, John Max *Educator*
75 Coolidge Road, Arlington, MA 02476, USA
Rosenman, Leonard *Composer*
%Elizabeth Dworkin, PO Box 248, Bedford Hills, NY 10507, USA
Rosenn, Max *Judge*
%US Court of Appeals, US Courthouse, 197 S Main St, Wilkes Barre, PA 18701, USA
Rosenquist, James A *Artist*
PO Box 4, 420 Broadway, Aripeka, FL 34679, USA
Rosenstein, Samuel M *Judge*
%US Court of International Trade, 2200 S Ocean Lane, Fort Lauderdale, FL 33316, USA
Rosenthal, Abraham (A M) *Editor, Columnist*
%New York Times, Editorial Dept, 229 W 43rd St, New York, NY 10036, USA
Rosenthal, Albert J *Attorney, Educator*
15 Oak Way, Scarsdale, NY 10583, USA
Rosenthal, Jacob (Jack) *Journalist*
%New York Times, Editorial Dept, 229 W 43rd St, New York, NY 10036, USA
Rosenthal, Joe *Photojournalist*
15 Curtis Ave, San Rafael, CA 94901, USA
Rosenthal, Robert J *Editor*
%Philadelphia Inquirer, Editorial Dept, 400 N Broad St, Philadelphia, PA 19130, USA
Rosenthal, Tony *Sculptor*
173 E 73rd St, New York, NY 10021, USA
Rosenzweig, Barney *Television Producer*
2311 Fisher Island Dr, Miami Beach, FL 33109, USA
Rosenzweig, Mark R *Physiological Psychologist*
%University of California, Psychology Dept, Tolman Hall, Berkeley, CA 94720, USA
Rosenzweig, Robert M *Educator*
1462 Dana Ave, Palo Alto, CA 94301, USA
Roses, Allen D *Neurologist*
%Duke University, Medical Center, Bryan Research Center, Durham, NC 27706, USA
Rosewall, Ken *Tennis Player*
Turramurra, 111 Pentacost Ave, Sydney NSW 2074, Australia
Rosewoman, Michele *Jazz Pianist*
%Abby Hoffer, 223 1/2 E 48th St, New York, NY 10017, USA
Rosin, Walter L *Religious Leader*
%Lutheran Church Missouri Synod, 1333 S Kirkwood Road, Saint Louis, MO 63122, USA
Rosinski, Edward J *Inventor (Zeolite Catalytic Cracking)*
2305 Arnold Ave, Yorkville, NY 13495, USA

R

Roskill of Newtown - Rosskopf

Roskill of Newtown, Eustace W *Judge*
New Court, Temple, London EC4, England
Rosner, Robert *Astrophysicist*
4950 S Greenwood Ave, Chicago, IL 60615, USA
Rosnes, Renee *Jazz Pianist*
%Integrity Talent, PO Box 961, Burlington, MA 01803, USA
Ross Fairbanks, Anne *Swimmer*
10 Grandview Ave, Troy, NY 12180, USA
Ross, Al *Cartoonist*
2185 Bolton St, Bronx, NY 10462, USA
Ross, Annie *Actress*
%Virginia Wicks Entertainment, 2737 Edwin Place, Los Angeles, CA 90046, USA
Ross, Ben *Movie Director*
%United Talent Agency, 9560 Wilshire Blvd, #500, Beverly Hills, CA 90212, USA
Ross, Betsy *Sportscaster*
%ESPN-TV, Sports Dept, ESPN Plaza, 935 Middle St, Bristol, CT 06010, USA
Ross, Charlotte *Actress*
%Abrams Artists, 9200 Sunset Blvd, #1125, Los Angeles, CA 90069, USA
Ross, David A *Museum Director*
%Whitney Museum of American Art, 945 Madison Ave, New York, NY 10021, USA
Ross, Diana *Singer, Actress*
PO Box 11059, Glenville Station, Greenwich, CT 06831, USA
Ross, Don *Body Builder*
PO Box 981, Venice, CA 90294, USA
Ross, Donald R *Judge*
%US Court of Appeals, Federal Building, PO Box 307, Omaha, NE 68101, USA
Ross, Douglas T *Computer Scientist*
%Softech Inc, 2 Highwood Dr, #200, Tewksbury, MA 01876, USA
Ross, Gary *Movie Director*
%Creative Artists Agency, 9830 Wilshire Blvd, Beverly Hills, CA 90212, USA
Ross, Ian M *Electrical Engineer*
5 Blackpoint Road, Horsehoe, Rumson, NJ 07760, USA
Ross, Jerry L *Astronaut*
%NASA, Johnson Space Center, 2101 NASA Road, Houston, TX 77058, USA
Ross, Jimmy D *Army General*
4981 Maple Glen Road, Lake Forest, FL 32771, USA
Ross, John *Chemist*
738 Mayfield Ave, Palo Alto, CA 94305, USA
Ross, Karie *Sportscaster*
%ESPN-TV, Sports Dept, ESPN Plaza, 935 Middle St, Bristol, CT 06010, USA
Ross, Katherine *Actress*
33050 Pacific Coast Highway, Malibu, CA 90265, USA
Ross, Marion *Actress*
21755 Ventura Blvd, PO Box 144, Woodland Hills, CA 91365, USA
Ross, Robert *Foundation Executive*
%Muscular Dystrophy Assn, 3300 E Sunrise Dr, Tucson, AZ 85718, USA
Rossdale, Gavin *Singer, Songwriter (Bush)*
%Reach Media, 295 Greenwich St, #109, New York, NY 10007, USA
Rosse, James N *Publisher*
%Freedom Newspapers Inc, PO Box 19549, Irvine, CA 92623, USA
Rossellini, Isabella *Model, Actress*
%Viyella, 57 Broadwick St, London W1F 9OS, England
Rossen, Carol *Actress*
15450 Longbow Dr, Sherman Oaks, CA 91403, USA
Rosser, James M *Educator*
%California State University, President's Office, Los Angeles, CA 90032, USA
Rosser, Ronald E *WW II Army Hero (CMH)*
36 James St, Roseville, OH 43777, USA
Rosset, Barnet L, Jr *Publisher, Editor*
%Rosset Co, 61 4th Ave, New York, NY 10003, USA
Rosset, Marc *Tennis Player*
%Michel Rosset, Rue Albert Gos 16, 1206 Geneva, Switzerland
Rossi, Leo *Actor*
%Richard Sindell, 1910 Holmby Ave, #1, Los Angeles, CA 90025, USA
Rossi, Opilio Cardinal *Religious Leader*
Via Della Scrofa 70, 00186 Rome, Italy
Rossi, Paolo *Soccer Player*
%Juventus FC Turin, Piazza Crimea 7, 10131 Turin, Italy
Rossilli, Paul *Actor*
%Kaman, 12831 Mulholland Dr, Beverly Hills, CA 90210, USA
Rossington, Gary *Guitarist (Lynyrd Skynyrd)*
%Vector Mgmt, 1607 17th Ave S, Nashville, TN 37212, USA
Rossini, Bianca *Actress*
%Arlene Thornton, 12001 Ventura Blvd, #201, Studio City, CA 91604, USA
Rossiter, Martin *Singer, Pianist (Gene)*
%Agency Group Ltd, 370 City Road, London EC1V 2QA, England
Rosskopf, Joerg *Table Tennis Player*
%Tischtennisbund, Otto-Fleck-Schneise 12A, 60528 Frankfurt/Maim, Germany

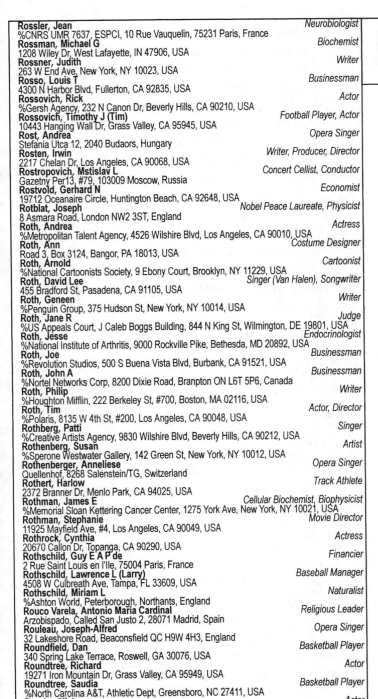

Rossler, Jean *Neurobiologist*
%CNRS UMR 7637, ESPCI, 10 Rue Vauquelin, 75231 Paris, France
Rossman, Michael G *Biochemist*
1208 Wiley Dr, West Lafayette, IN 47906, USA
Rossner, Judith *Writer*
263 W End Ave, New York, NY 10023, USA
Rosso, Louis T *Businessman*
4300 N Harbor Blvd, Fullerton, CA 92835, USA
Rossovich, Rick *Actor*
%Gersh Agency, 232 N Canon Dr, Beverly Hills, CA 90210, USA
Rossovich, Timothy J (Tim) *Football Player, Actor*
10443 Hanging Wall Dr, Grass Valley, CA 95945, USA
Rost, Andrea *Opera Singer*
Stefania Utca 12, 2040 Budaors, Hungary
Rosten, Irwin *Writer, Producer, Director*
2217 Chelan Dr, Los Angeles, CA 90068, USA
Rostropovich, Mstislav L *Concert Cellist, Conductor*
Gazetny Per13, #79, 103009 Moscow, Russia
Rostvold, Gerhard N *Economist*
19712 Oceanaire Circle, Huntington Beach, CA 92648, USA
Rotblat, Joseph *Nobel Peace Laureate, Physicist*
8 Asmara Road, London NW2 3ST, England
Roth, Andrea *Actress*
%Metropolitan Talent Agency, 4526 Wilshire Blvd, Los Angeles, CA 90010, USA
Roth, Ann *Costume Designer*
Road 3, Box 3124, Bangor, PA 18013, USA
Roth, Arnold *Cartoonist*
%National Cartoonists Society, 9 Ebony Court, Brooklyn, NY 11229, USA
Roth, David Lee *Singer (Van Halen), Songwriter*
455 Bradford St, Pasadena, CA 91105, USA
Roth, Geneen *Writer*
%Penguin Group, 375 Hudson St, New York, NY 10014, USA
Roth, Jane R *Judge*
%US Appeals Court, J Caleb Boggs Building, 844 N King St, Wilmington, DE 19801, USA
Roth, Jesse *Endocrinologist*
%National Institute of Arthritis, 9000 Rockville Pike, Bethesda, MD 20892, USA
Roth, Joe *Businessman*
%Revolution Studios, 500 S Buena Vista Blvd, Burbank, CA 91521, USA
Roth, John A *Businessman*
%Nortel Networks Corp, 8200 Dixie Road, Branpton ON L6T 5P6, Canada
Roth, Philip *Writer*
%Houghton Mifflin, 222 Berkeley St, #700, Boston, MA 02116, USA
Roth, Tim *Actor, Director*
%Polaris, 8135 W 4th St, #200, Los Angeles, CA 90048, USA
Rothberg, Patti *Singer*
%Creative Artists Agency, 9830 Wilshire Blvd, Beverly Hills, CA 90212, USA
Rothenberg, Susan *Artist*
%Sperone Westwater Gallery, 142 Green St, New York, NY 10012, USA
Rothenberger, Anneliese *Opera Singer*
Quellenhof, 8268 Salenstein/TG, Switzerland
Rothert, Harlow *Track Athlete*
2372 Branner Dr, Menlo Park, CA 94025, USA
Rothman, James E *Cellular Biochemist, Biophysicist*
%Memorial Sloan Kettering Cancer Center, 1275 York Ave, New York, NY 10021, USA
Rothman, Stephanie *Movie Director*
11925 Mayfield Ave, #4, Los Angeles, CA 90049, USA
Rothrock, Cynthia *Actress*
20670 Callon Dr, Topanga, CA 90290, USA
Rothschild, Guy E A P de *Financier*
2 Rue Saint Louis en l'Ile, 75004 Paris, France
Rothschild, Lawrence L (Larry) *Baseball Manager*
4508 W Culbreath Ave, Tampa, FL 33609, USA
Rothschild, Miriam L *Naturalist*
%Ashton World, Peterborough, Northants, England
Rouco Varela, Antonio Maria Cardinal *Religious Leader*
Arzobispado, Called San Justo 2, 28071 Madrid, Spain
Rouleau, Joseph-Alfred *Opera Singer*
32 Lakeshore Road, Beaconsfield QC H9W 4H3, England
Roundfield, Dan *Basketball Player*
340 Spring Lake Terrace, Roswell, GA 30076, USA
Roundtree, Richard *Actor*
19271 Iron Mountain Dr, Grass Valley, CA 95949, USA
Roundtree, Saudia *Basketball Player*
%North Carolina A&T, Athletic Dept, Greensboro, NC 27411, USA
Rourke, Mickey *Actor*
%International Creative Mgmt, 8942 Wilshire Blvd, #219, Beverly Hills, CA 90211, USA
Rouse, Christopher *Composer*
%University of Rochester, Eastman Music School, 26 Gibbs St, Rochester, NY 14604, USA

R

Rouse, Irving *Anthropologist*
12 Ridgewood Terrace, North Haven, CT 06473, USA
Rouse, Jeffrey (Jeff) *Swimmer*
302 Gerber Dr, Fredericksburg, VA 22408, USA
Rouse, Mitch *Actor*
%Three Arts Entertainment, 9460 Wilshire Blvd, #700, Beverly Hills, CA 90212, USA
Roush, Jack *Auto Racing Executive*
%Roush Racing, 122 Knob Hill Road, Mooresville, NC 28115, USA
Rousselot, Philippe *Cinematographer*
%Gersh Agency, 232 N Canon Dr, Beverly Hills, CA 90210, USA
Rousset, Christophe *Concert Harpsichordist*
%Trawick Artists, 1926 Broadway, New York, NY 10023, USA
Routledge, Alison *Actress*
%Marmont Mgmt, Langham House, 302/8 Regent St, London W1R 5AL, England
Routledge, Patricia *Actress*
%Marmont Mgmt, Langham House, 302/8 Regent St, London W1R 5AL, England
Roux, Albert H *Chef*
%Le Gavroche, 43 Upper Brook St, London W1Y 1PF, England
Roux, Jean-Louis *Theater Director, Actor*
4145 Blueridge Crescent, #2, Montreal QC H3H 1S7, Canada
Roux, Michel A *Chef*
%Waterside Inn, Ferry Road, Bray, Berks SL6 2AT, England
Rove, Karl *Government Official*
%White House, 1600 Pennsylvania Ave NW, Washington, DC
Rowan, Kelly *Actress*
9028 W Sunset Blvd, #PH 1, Los Angeles, CA 90069, USA
Rowden, William H *Navy Admiral*
55 Pinewood Court, Lancaster, VA 22503, USA
Rowe, Brad *Actor*
1327 Brinkley Ave, Los Angeles, CA 90049, USA
Rowe, Jack *Writer*
%Pocket Books, 1230 Ave of Americas, New York, NY 10020, USA
Rowe, John W *Businessman*
%Unicom Corp, 10 S Dearborn St, Chicago, IL 60603, USA
Rowe, John W *Businessman*
%Aetna Inc, 151 Farmington Ave, Hartford, CT 06156, USA
Rowe, Misty *Actress*
2193 River Road, Egg Harbor Cay, NJ 08215, USA
Rowe, Sandra M *Editor*
%Portland Oregonian, Editorial Dept, 1320 SW Broadway, Portland, OR 97201, USA
Rowell, Victoria *Actress*
195 S Beverly Dr, #400, Beverly Hills, CA 90212, USA
Rowland, Betty *Exotic Dancer*
125 N Barrington Ave, #103, Los Angeles, CA 90049, USA
Rowland, F Sherwood *Nobel Chemistry Laureate*
4807 Dorchester Road, Corona del Mar, CA 92625, USA
Rowland, J David *Businessman*
%National Westminster Bank, 41 Lothbury, London EC2P 2BP, England
Rowland, James A *Air Force Marshal, Australia*
17 Pindari Ave, Mosman NSW 2088, Australia
Rowland, John W *Labor Leader*
%Amalgamated Transit Union, 5025 Wisconsin Ave NW, Washington, DC 20016, USA
Rowland, Kelly *Singer (Destiny's Child)*
%Creative Artists Agency, 9830 Wilshire Blvd, Beverly Hills, CA 90212, USA
Rowland, Landon H *Businessman*
%Kansas City Southern, PO Box 219335, Kansas City, MO 64121, USA
Rowland, Rodney *Actor, Model*
%Booh Schut, 11350 Ventura Blvd, #206, Studio City, CA 91604, USA
Rowlands, Gena *Actress*
7917 Woodrow Wilson Dr, Los Angeles, CA 90046, USA
Rowley, Cynthia *Fashion Designer*
498 Fashion Ave, New York, NY 10018, USA
Rowley, Janet D *Physician*
5310 S University Ave, Chicago, IL 60615, USA
Rowling, J K (Jo) *Writer*
%Levine/Scolastic Press, 555 Broadway, New York, NY 10012, USA
Rowlinson, John S *Chemist*
12 Pullens Field, Headington OX3 0BU, England
Rowny, Edward L *Army General*
2700 Calvert St NW, #813, Washington, DC 20008, USA
Roy *Animal Illusionist (Siegfried & Roy)*
%Beyond Belief, 1639 N Valley Dr, Las Vegas, NV 89108, USA
Roy, Arundhati *Writer*
%Random House, 1745 Broadway, #B1, New York, NY 10019, USA
Roy, James D *Financier*
%Federal Home Loan Bank, 601 Grant St, Pittsburgh, PA 15219, USA
Roy, Patrick *Hockey Player*
5340 S Race Court, Greenwood Village, CO 80121, USA

Royal, Billy Joe *Singer, Songwriter*
304 Somerset Way, Newport, NC 28570, USA
Royal, Darrell K *Football Player, Coach*
3752 Crestone Dr, Loveland, CO 80537, USA
Royo Sanchez, Aristides *President, Panama*
%Morgan & Morgan, PO Box 1824, Panama City 1, Panama
Royster, Jeron K (Jerry) *Baseball Player, Manager*
1 Brewers Way, Milwaukee, WI 53214, USA
Rozanov, Evgeny G *Architect*
%Int'l Architecture Academy, Bolshara Dmitrovka 24, 103284 Moscow, Russia
Rozhdestvensky, Gennady N *Conductor*
%Victor Hochhauser Ltd, 4 Oak Hill Way, London NW3, England
Rozhdestvensky, Valery I *Cosmonaut*
%Potchta Kosmonavtov, Moskovskoi Oblasti, 141160 Syvisdny Goroduk, Russia
Rozier, Clifford *Basketball Player*
%Toronto Raptors, Air Canada Center, 40 Bay St, Toronto ON M5J 2N8, Canada
Rozier, Mike *Football Player*
9 Hidden Hollow Lane, Sicklerville, NJ 08081, USA
Rubalcaba, Gonzalo *Jazz Pianist*
%Eardrums Music, 5930 NW 201st St, Miami, FL 33105, USA
Rubbia, Carlo *Nobel Physics Laureate*
%CERN, Particle Physics Laboratory, 1211 Geneva 23, Switzerland
Ruben, Joseph P (Joe) *Movie Director*
250 W 57th St, #1905, New York, NY 10107, USA
Rubenstein, Ann *Commentator*
%NBC-TV, News Dept, 30 Rockefeller Plaza, New York, NY 10112, USA
Rubenstein, Edward *Physician*
%Stanford University, Medical School, Surgery Dept, Stanford, CA 94305, USA
Rubiano Saenz, Pedro Cardinal *Religious Leader*
Arzubispado, Carrera 7A N 10-20, Santafe de Bogota DC 1, Colombia
Rubik, Erno *Inventor (Rubik Cube)*
Rubik Studio, Varosmajor Utca 74, 1122 Budapest, Hungary
Rubin, Amy *Actress*
%Hervey/Grimes, PO Box 64249, Los Angeles, CA 90064, USA
Rubin, Benjamin A *Inventor (Bifurcated Needle)*
1329 173rd St, Hazel Crest, IL 60429, USA
Rubin, Chandra *Tennis Player*
708 S Saint Antoine St, Lafayette, LA 70501, USA
Rubin, Ellis *Attorney*
4141 NE 2nd Ave, #203A, Miami, FL 33137, USA
Rubin, Harry *Biologist*
%University of California, Molecular Biology Dept, Berkeley, CA 94720, USA
Rubin, Leigh *Cartoonist*
%Creators Syndicate, 5777 W Century Blvd, #700, Los Angeles, CA 90045, USA
Rubin, Louis D, Jr *Writer*
702 Ginghoul Road, Chapel Hill, NC 27514, USA
Rubin, Robert *Medical Researcher*
%Massachusetts General Hospital, 32 Fruit St, Boston, MA 02114, USA
Rubin, Robert E *Secretary, Treasury; Financier*
%Citigroup Inc, 399 Park Ave, New York, NY 10022, USA
Rubin, Stephen E *Publisher*
%Doubleday Co, 1540 Broadway, New York, NY 10036, USA
Rubin, Theodore I *Psychiatrist*
219 E 62nd St, New York, NY 10021, USA
Rubin, Vanessa *Singer*
%Joel Chriss, 300 Mercer St, #3J, New York, NY 10003, USA
Rubin, Vera C *Astronomer*
%Carnegie Institution, 5241 Broad Branch Road NW, Washington, DC 20015, USA
Rubin, William *Museum Curator*
%Museum of Modern Art, 11 W 53rd St, New York, NY 10019, USA
Rubin-Vega, Daphne *Actress*
300 Park Ave S, #300, New York, NY 10010, USA
Rubinek, Saul *Actor*
%Gersh Agency, 232 N Canon Dr, Beverly Hills, CA 90210, USA
Rubini, Cesare *Water Polo Player, Basketball Coach*
%Federazione Italian Pallacanestro, Via Fogliano 15, 00199 Rome, Italy
Rubino, Frank A *Attorney*
2601 S Bayshore Dr, Miami, FL 33133, USA
Rubinoff, Ira *Biologist*
%Smithsonian Tropical Research Institute, Unit 0848, APO, AA 34002, USA
Rubinstein, John *Actor*
4417 Leydon Ave, Woodland Hills, CA 91364, USA
Rubinstein, Zelda *Actress*
%The Agency, 1800 Ave of Stars, #400, Los Angeles, CA 90067, USA
Ruccolo, Richard *Actor*
%ER Talent, 301 W 53rd St, #4K, New York, NY 10019, USA
Ruch, Charles *Educator*
%Boise State University, President's Office, Boise, ID 83725, USA

R

Rucinsky, Martin *Hockey Player*
%New York Rangers, Madison Square Garden, 2 Penn Plaza, New York, NY 10121, USA
Ruck, Alan *Actor*
%Innovative Artists, 1505 10th St, Santa Monica, CA 90401, USA
Ruckelshaus, William D *Businessman, Government Official*
PO Box 76, Medina, WA 98039, USA
Ruckenstein, Eli *Chemical Engineer*
94 North Dr, Buffalo, NY 14226, USA
Rucker, Anja *Track Athlete*
%TUS Jena, Wollnitzer Str 42, 07749 Jena, Germany
Rucker, Darius *Singer (Hootie & the Blowfish)*
%FishCo Mgmt, PO Box 5656, Columbia, SC 29250, USA
Rucker, Reginald J (Reggie) *Football Player*
3128 Richmond Road, Beachwood, OH 44122, USA
Rudbottom, Roy R, Jr *Diplomat*
7831 Park Lane, #213A, Dallas, TX 75225, USA
Rudd, Paul *Actor*
9465 Wilshire Blvd, #517, Beverly Hills, CA 90212, USA
Rudd, Ricky *Auto Racing Driver*
124 Summerville Dr, Mooresville, NC 28115, USA
Ruddle, Francis H *Biologist, Geneticist*
%Yale University, Biology Dept, New Haven, CT 06511, USA
Ruddock, Donovan (Razor) *Boxer*
7379 NW 34th St, Lauderhill, FL 33319, USA
Rudel, Julius *Conductor*
101 Central Park West, #11A, New York, NY 10023, USA
Rudenstine, Neil L *Educator*
41 Armour Road, Princeton, NJ 08540, USA
Ruder, David S *Government Official, Educator*
%Baker & McKenzie, 1 Prudential Plaza, 130 E Randolph Dr, Chicago, IL 60601, USA
Rudi, Joseph O (Joe) *Baseball Player*
17667 Deer Park Loop, Baker City, OR 97814, USA
Rudie, Evelyn *Actress*
%Santa Monica Playhouse, 7514 Hollywood Blvd, Los Angeles, CA 90046, USA
Rudin, Scott *Movie, Theater Producer*
%Scott Rudin Productions, 120 W 45th St, New York, NY 10036, USA
Rudman, Warren B *Senator, NH*
327 10th St SE, Washington, DC 20003, USA
Rudner, Rita *Actress, Comedienne*
2877 Paradise Road, #1605, Las Vegas, NV 89109, USA
Rudnick, Paul *Writer*
%Creative Artists Agency, 9830 Wilshire Blvd, Beverly Hills, CA 90212, USA
Rudoff, Sheldon *Religious Leader*
%Union of Orthodox Jewish Congregations, 333 7th Ave, New York, NY 10001, USA
Rudolph, Alan S *Movie Director*
%International Creative Mgmt, 8942 Wilshire Blvd, #219, Beverly Hills, CA 90211, USA
Rudolph, Donald E *WW II Army Hero (CMH)*
33799 Shamrock Dr, Bovey, MN 55709, USA
Rudolph, Frederick *Historian*
234 Ide Road, Williamstown, MA 01267, USA
Rudometkin, John *Basketball Player*
6181 Wise Road, Newcastle, CA 95658, USA
Rudzinski, Witold *Composer*
Ul Narbutta 50 m 6, 02-541 Warsaw, Poland
Rue, Sara *Actress, Comedienne*
%Innovative Artists, 1505 10th St, Santa Monica, CA 90401, USA
Ruehe, Volker *Government Official, Germany*
%Bundesministerium Der Verteidigung, Hardthoehe, 53125 Bonn, Germany
Ruehl, Mercedes *Actress*
%United Talent Agency, 9560 Wilshire Blvd, #500, Beverly Hills, CA 90212, USA
Ruelas, Gabriel (Gabe) *Boxer*
1242 S Tremaine Ave, Los Angeles, CA 90019, USA
Ruelle, David P *Mathematician*
1 Ave Charles-Comar, 91440 Bures-sur-Yvette, France
Ruether, Rosemary R *Theologian*
530 Mayflower Road, Claremont, CA 91711, USA
Ruettgers, Ken *Football Player*
69550 Deer Ridge Road, Sisters, OR 97759, USA
Ruettgers, Michael C *Businessman*
%ECM Corp, 35 Parkwood Dr, Hopkinton, MA 01748, USA
Ruff, Howard J *Fiscal Analyst, Writer*
PO Box 441, Orem, UT 84059, USA
Ruff, Lindy *Hockey Player, Coach*
4980 Shadow Rock Lane, Clarence, NY 14031, USA
Ruffalo, Mark *Actor*
%William Morris Agency, 151 El Camino Dr, Beverly Hills, CA 90212, USA
Ruffini, Attilio *Government Official, Italy*
Camera dei Deputati, Via della Missione 10, 00187 Rome, Italy

R

Ruge, John A *Cartoonist*
240 Bronxville Road, #B4, Bronxville, NY 10708, USA
Rugers, Martin *Astronomer*
%University of Washington, Astronomy Dept, Seattle, WA 98195, USA
Ruggiero, Angela *Hockey Player*
421 Old Military Road, Lake Placid, NY 12946, USA
Ruhsam, John W *WW II Marine Corps Air Force Hero*
1010 American Eagle Blvd, #346, Sun City Center, FL 33573, USA
Ruini, Camillo Cardinal *Religious Leader*
Vicar of Rome, 00120 Vatican City
Ruiz Garcia, Samuel *Religious Leader*
%San Cristobal Diocese, 20 de Noviembre 1, San Cristobal de Casas, Mexico
Ruiz, Alejandro R *WW II Army Hero (CMH)*
PO Box 536, Visalia, CA 93279, USA
Ruiz, Hilton *Jazz Pianist*
%Joel Chriss, 300 Mercer St, #3J, New York, NY 10003, USA
Ruiz-Anchia, Juan *Cinematographer*
%Gersh Agency, 232 N Canon Dr, Beverly Hills, CA 90210, USA
Rukeyser, Louis R *Commentator*
586 Round Hill Road, Greenwich, CT 06831, USA
Rukeyser, William S *Publisher*
1509 Rudder Lane, Knoxville, TN 37919, USA
Ruklick, Joe *Basketball Player*
1300 Central St, Evanston, IL 60201, USA
Ruland, Jeff *Basketball Player, Coach*
%Iona College, Athletic Dept, New Rochelle, NY 10801, USA
Rule, Ann *Writer*
PO Box 98846, Seattle, WA 98198, USA
Rullo, Jerry *Basketball Player*
1517 S Myrtlewood St, Philadelphia, PA 19146, USA
Rummenigge, Karl-Heinz *Soccer Player*
Eichleite 4, 80231 Grunwald, Germany
Rumsfeld, Donald H *Secretary, Defense; Businessman*
%Defense Department, Pentagon, Washington, DC 20301, USA
Runco, Mario, Jr *Astronaut*
207 Lakeshore Dr, Seabrook, TX 77586, USA
Rundgren, Todd *Singer, Songwriter*
%Panacea Entertainment, 2705 Glendower Road, Los Angeles, CA 90027, USA
Runge, Jeffrey *Government Official*
%Nat'l Highway Traffic Safety Administration, 400 7th SW, Washington, DC 20590, USA
Runnells, Thomas W (Tom) *Baseball Player, Manager*
4322 Todd Dr, Sylvania, OH 43560, USA
Runyan, Joe *Dog Sled Racer*
314 1/2 Parks Highway, Nenana, AK 99704, USA
Runyon, Edwin *Religious Leader*
%General Baptists Assn, 100 Stinson Dr, Poplar Bluff, MO 63901, USA
Runyon, Jennifer *Actress*
5922 SW Amberwood Ave, Corvallis, OR 97333, USA
RuPaul *Entertainer*
%Evolution Talent, 1776 Broadway, #1500, New York, NY 10019, USA
Ruppel, Adam *Guitarist (Systematic)*
%Artist Group International, 9560 Wilshire Blvd, #400, Beverly Hills, CA 90212, USA
Rusch, Kristine Kathryn *Writer*
PO Box 479, Lincoln City, OR 97367, USA
Ruscha, Edward *Artist*
1024 3/4 N Western Ave, Los Angeles, CA 90029, USA
Ruse, Michael *Philosopher*
651 E 6th Ave, Tallahassee, FL 32303, USA
Rusedski, Greg *Tennis Player*
%SFX Sports Group, 2665 S Bayshore Dr, #602, Miami, FL 33133, USA
Rush, Barbara *Actress*
%House of Representatives, 400 S Beverly Dr, #101, Beverly Hills, CA 90212, USA
Rush, Geoffrey *Actor*
%Shanahan Mgmt, PO Box 1509, Darlinghurst NSW 1300, Australia
Rush, Kareem *Basketball Player*
%Los Angeles Lakers, Staples Center, 1111 S Figueroa St, Los Angeles, CA 90015, USA
Rush, Merrilee *Singer, Songwriter*
%MGW Advertising, 408 NE 40th, Seattle, WA 98105, USA
Rush, Otis *Singer, Guitarist*
%Concerted Efforts, 59 Parsons St, West Newton, MA 02465, USA
Rush, Richard W *Movie Director, Producer*
821 Stradella Road, Los Angeles, CA 90077, USA
Rush, Robert J (Bob) *Football Player*
8201 Scruggs Drive, Germantown, TN 38138, USA
Rush, Robert R (Bob) *Baseball Player*
4330 S Eastern Ave, #135, Las Vegas, NV 89119, USA
Rushdie, A Salman *Writer*
%Wylie Agency, 42 Knightsbridge, London SW1X 7JR, England

R

Rushe - Russo

Rushe, Eric *Concert Horn Player*
%Columbia Artists Mgmt Inc, 165 W 57th St, New York, NY 10019, USA
Rushing, Brad *Cinematographer*
10865 Walnut Dr, Sunland, CA 91040, USA
Rushlow, Tim *Singer (Little Texas)*
%Collinsworth Bright, 50 Music Square W, #702, Nashville, TN 37203, USA
Ruskin, Joseph *Actor*
13840 Kittridge St, Van Nuys, CA 91405, USA
Russ, Tim *Actor*
%Stone Manners, 6500 Wilshire Blvd, #550, Los Angeles, CA 90048, USA
Russ, William *Actor*
894 Camino Colibri, Calabasas, CA 91302, USA
Russell, Andy *Football Player*
CNN Tower, 625 Liberty Ave, Pittsburgh, PA 15222, USA
Russell, Anna *Actress, Comedienne*
%Arthur Shafman, 163 Amsterdam Ave, #121, New York, NY 10023, USA
Russell, Betsy *Actress*
PO Box 1759, La Jolla, CA 92038, USA
Russell, Brenda *Singer, Songwriter, Keyboardist*
%Turner Management Group, 374 Poli St, #205, Ventura, CA 93001, USA
Russell, Bryon *Basketball Player*
%Los Angeles Lakers, Staples Center, 1111 S Figueroa St, Los Angeles, CA 90015, USA
Russell, C Andrew (Andy) *Football Player*
%National Waste Industries, 625 Liberty Ave, Pittsburgh, PA 15222, USA
Russell, Campy *Basketball Player*
66 Earlmoor Blvd, Pontiac, MI 48341, USA
Russell, Cazzie L *Basketball Player*
%Savannah College of Art & Design, Athletic Dept, Savannah, GA 31402, USA
Russell, Charles O (Chuck) *Movie Director*
%William Morris Agency, 151 El Camino Dr, Beverly Hills, CA 90212, USA
Russell, Darrell *Football Player*
535 Ocean Ave, #4A, Santa Monica, CA 90402, USA
Russell, David O *Movie Director*
%United Talent Agency, 9560 Wilshire Blvd, #500, Beverly Hills, CA 90212, USA
Russell, George A *Jazz Drummer, Pianist, Composer*
%Joel Chriss, 300 Mercer St, #3J, New York, NY 10003, USA
Russell, Graham *Singer (Air Supply)*
%Air Supply, PO Box 25909, Los Angeles, CA 90025, USA
Russell, Jane *Actress, Model*
2430 Ridgemark Dr, Santa Maria, CA 93455, USA
Russell, Ken *Movie Director*
16 Salisbury Place, London W1H 1FH, England
Russell, Keri *Actress*
520 Salerno Dr, Pacific Palisades, CA 90272, USA
Russell, Kimberly *Actress*
14622 Ventura Blvd, Sherman Oaks, CA 91403, USA
Russell, Kurt *Actor*
229 E Gainsborough Road, Thousand Oaks, CA 91360, USA
Russell, Leon *Singer, Songwriter*
%Paradise Artists, 108 E Matilija St, Ojai, CA 93023, USA
Russell, Liane B *Geneticist*
130 Tabor Road, Oak Ridge, TN 37830, USA
Russell, Mark *Actor, Comedian*
4417 Canterbury Dr, Mayville, NY 14757, USA
Russell, Nipsy *Actor, Comedian*
353 W 57th St, New York, NY 10019, USA
Russell, Theresa *Actress*
PO Box 16018, Beverly Hills, CA 90209, USA
Russell, Tom *Singer*
%Valdenn Agency, 13801 RR 12, #202, Wimberley, TX 78676, USA
Russell, William E (Bill) *Baseball Player, Manager*
1641 Santa Rosa Ave, Glendale, CA 91208, USA
Russell, William F (Bill) *Basketball Player, Coach*
PO Box 1200, Mercer Island, WA 98040, USA
Russell, Willy *Writer*
%Willie Russell Ltd, 43 Canning St, London L87 NN, England
Russert, Timothy J (Tim) *Commentator*
%Meet the Press Show, NBC-TV, 4001 Nebraska Ave NW, Washington, DC 20016, USA
Russi, Bernhard *Alpine Skier*
Postfach 107, 5620 Bremgarten, Switzerland
Russo, Daniel *Actor*
%Artmedia, 20 Ave Rapp, 75007 Paris, France
Russo, Gianni *Actor*
%Sanders Agency, 9014 Melrose Ave, West Hollywood, CA 90069, USA
Russo, James *Actor*
%Gold Marshak Liedtke, 3500 W Olive Ave, #1400, Burbank, CA 91505, USA
Russo, John *Writer*
216 Euclid Ave, Irwin, PA 15045, USA

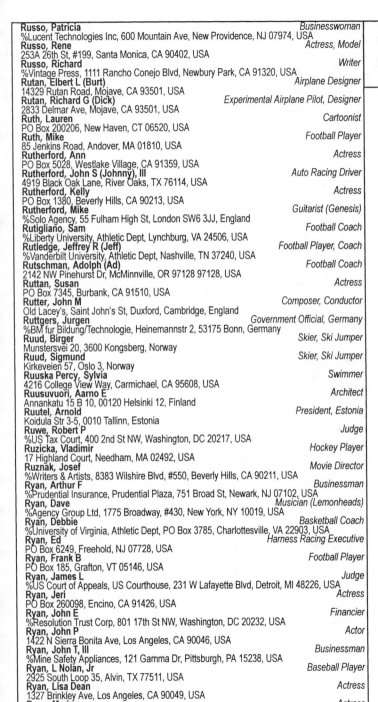

Russo, Patricia *Businesswoman*
%Lucent Technologies Inc, 600 Mountain Ave, New Providence, NJ 07974, USA
Russo, Rene *Actress, Model*
253A 26th St, #199, Santa Monica, CA 90402, USA
Russo, Richard *Writer*
%Vintage Press, 1111 Rancho Conejo Blvd, Newbury Park, CA 91320, USA
Rutan, Elbert L (Burt) *Airplane Designer*
14329 Rutan Road, Mojave, CA 93501, USA
Rutan, Richard G (Dick) *Experimental Airplane Pilot, Designer*
2833 Delmar Ave, Mojave, CA 93501, USA
Ruth, Lauren *Cartoonist*
PO Box 200206, New Haven, CT 06520, USA
Ruth, Mike *Football Player*
85 Jenkins Road, Andover, MA 01810, USA
Rutherford, Ann *Actress*
PO Box 5028, Westlake Village, CA 91359, USA
Rutherford, John S (Johnny), III *Auto Racing Driver*
4919 Black Oak Lane, River Oaks, TX 76114, USA
Rutherford, Kelly *Actress*
PO Box 1380, Beverly Hills, CA 90213, USA
Rutherford, Mike *Guitarist (Genesis)*
%Solo Agency, 55 Fulham High St, London SW6 3JJ, England
Rutigliano, Sam *Football Coach*
%Liberty University, Athletic Dept, Lynchburg, VA 24506, USA
Rutledge, Jeffrey R (Jeff) *Football Player, Coach*
%Vanderbilt University, Athletic Dept, Nashville, TN 37240, USA
Rutschman, Adolph (Ad) *Football Coach*
2142 NW Pinehurst Dr, McMinnville, OR 97128 97128, USA
Ruttan, Susan *Actress*
PO Box 7345, Burbank, CA 91510, USA
Rutter, John M *Composer, Conductor*
Old Lacey's, Saint John's St, Duxford, Cambridge, England
Ruttgers, Jurgen *Government Official, Germany*
%BM fur Bildung/Technologie, Heinemannstr 2, 53175 Bonn, Germany
Ruud, Birger *Skier, Ski Jumper*
Munstersvei 20, 3600 Kongsberg, Norway
Ruud, Sigmund *Skier, Ski Jumper*
Kirkeveien 57, Oslo 3, Norway
Ruuska Percy, Sylvia *Swimmer*
4216 College View Way, Carmichael, CA 95608, USA
Ruusuvuori, Aarno E *Architect*
Annankatu 15 B 10, 00120 Helsinki 12, Finland
Ruutel, Arnold *President, Estonia*
Koidula Str 3-5, 0010 Tallinn, Estonia
Ruwe, Robert P *Judge*
%US Tax Court, 400 2nd St NW, Washington, DC 20217, USA
Ruzicka, Vladimir *Hockey Player*
17 Highland Court, Needham, MA 02492, USA
Ruznak, Josef *Movie Director*
%Writers & Artists, 8383 Wilshire Blvd, #550, Beverly Hills, CA 90211, USA
Ryan, Arthur F *Businessman*
%Prudential Insurance, Prudential Plaza, 751 Broad St, Newark, NJ 07102, USA
Ryan, Dave *Musician (Lemonheads)*
%Agency Group Ltd, 1775 Broadway, #430, New York, NY 10019, USA
Ryan, Debbie *Basketball Coach*
%University of Virginia, Athletic Dept, PO Box 3785, Charlottesville, VA 22903, USA
Ryan, Ed *Harness Racing Executive*
PO Box 6249, Freehold, NJ 07728, USA
Ryan, Frank B *Football Player*
PO Box 185, Grafton, VT 05146, USA
Ryan, James L *Judge*
%US Court of Appeals, US Courthouse, 231 W Lafayette Blvd, Detroit, MI 48226, USA
Ryan, Jeri *Actress*
PO Box 260098, Encino, CA 91426, USA
Ryan, John E *Financier*
%Resolution Trust Corp, 801 17th St NW, Washington, DC 20232, USA
Ryan, John P *Actor*
1422 N Sierra Bonita Ave, Los Angeles, CA 90046, USA
Ryan, John T, III *Businessman*
%Mine Safety Appliances, 121 Gamma Dr, Pittsburgh, PA 15238, USA
Ryan, L Nolan, Jr *Baseball Player*
2925 South Loop 35, Alvin, TX 77511, USA
Ryan, Lisa Dean *Actress*
1327 Brinkley Ave, Los Angeles, CA 90049, USA
Ryan, Marisa *Actress*
%Stubbs Agency, 1450 S Robertson Blvd, Los Angeles, CA 90035, USA
Ryan, Meg *Actress*
11718 Barrington Court, #508, Los Angeles, CA 90049, USA

R

Ryan - Rzeznik

Ryan, Mitchell — *Actor*
30355 Mulholland Dr, Cornell, CA 91301, USA
Ryan, Norbert R, Jr — *Navy Admiral*
Chief of Naval Personnel, 2 Navy St, Washington, DC 20370, USA
Ryan, Patrick G — *Businessman*
%Aon Corp, 200 E Randolph St, Chicago, IL 60601, USA
Ryan, Peggy — *Actress*
1821 E Oakley Blvd, Las Vegas, NV 89104, USA
Ryan, Terry — *Writer*
%Simon & Schuster, 1230 Ave of Americas, New York, NY 10020, USA
Ryan, Thomas M — *Businessman*
%CVS Corp, 1 CVS Dr, Woonsocket, RI 02895, USA
Ryan, Tim — *Sportscaster*
%NBC-TV, Sports Dept, 30 Rockefeller Plaza, New York, NY 10112, USA
Ryan, Tim — *Actor*
%SAA, 335 N Maple Dr, #360, Beverly Hills, CA 90210, USA
Ryan, Tim E — *Football Player*
6089 Blacklock Court, San Jose, CA 95123, USA
Ryan, Timothy T (Tim) — *Football Player*
4901 Sugar Creek Dr, Evansville, IN 47715, USA
Ryan, Tom K — *Cartoonist (Tumbleweeds)*
%North American Syndicate, 235 E 45th St, New York, NY 10017, USA
Ryazanov, Eldar A — *Movie Director*
%Bolshoi Tishinski Per 12, #70, 123557 Moscow, Russia
Rybczynski, Witold — *Writer*
%Charles Scribner's Sons, 866 3rd Ave, New York, NY 10022, USA
Rybkin, Ivan — *Government Official, Russia*
%National Security Council, 4 Staraya Ploschad, 103073 Moscow, Russia
Rybska, Agnieszka — *Singer, Musician (Rasputina)*
%RPM Music Productions, 130 W 57th St, #9D, New York, NY 10019, USA
Rydell, Bobby — *Singer, Actor*
917 Bryn Mawr Ave, Narberth, PA 19072, USA
Rydell, Christopher — *Actor*
911 N Sweetzer, #C, Los Angeles, CA 90069, USA
Rydell, Mark — *Movie Director*
%Concourse Productions, 3110 Main St, #220, Santa Monica, CA 90405, USA
Ryder, Mitch — *Singer*
%Entertainment Services Int'l, 6400 Pleasant Park Dr, Chanhassen, MN 55317, USA
Ryder, Thomas O — *Publisher*
%Reader's Digest Assn, PO Box 100, Pleasantville, NY 10572, USA
Ryder, Winona — *Actress*
721 N Fairview St, Burbank, CA 91505, USA
Rydze, Richard — *Diver*
125 7th St, Pittsburgh, PA 15222, USA
Rykiel, Sonia F — *Fashion Designer*
175 Blvd Saint Germain, 75006 Paris, France
Ryknow — *Bassist (Mudvayne)*
%Agency Group Ltd, 1775 Broadway, #430, New York, NY 10019, USA
Rylance, Mark — *Theater Director, Actor*
%Shakespeare's Globe, Southwark, London SE1, England
Ryman, Robert T — *Artist*
17 W 16th St, New York, NY 10011, USA
Rymer, Pamela Ann — *Judge*
%US Court of Appeals, 125 S Grand Ave, Pasadena, CA 91105, USA
Rynkiewicz, Mariusz — *Glass Sculptor*
12401 Alexander Road, Everett, WA 98204, USA
Rypdal, Terje — *Musician*
%PJP as, Utragata 16, 5700 Voss, Norway
Rypien, Mark R — *Football Player*
5855 W Riverside Dr, Post Falls, ID 83854, USA
Ryumin, Valery V — *Cosmonaut*
%Potchta Kosmonavtov, Moskovskoi Oblasti, 141160 Syvisdny Goroduk, Russia
Ryun, James R (Jim) — *Track Athlete; Representative, KS*
PO Box 62B, Lawrence, KS 66044, USA
Ryzhkov, Nikolai I — *Premier, USSR*
%State Duma, Okhotny Ryad 1, 103009 Moscow, Russia
RZA — *Rap Artist (Wu-Tang Clan)*
%Famous Artists Agency, 250 W 57th St, New York, NY 10107, USA
Rzeznik, Johnny — *Singer, Guitarist (Goo Goo Dolls)*
%Atlas/Third Rail Entertainment, 9200 W Sunset Blvd, West Hollywood, CA 90069, USA

Saadiq, Raphael *Singer (Tony Toni Tone, Lucy Pearl)*
%Family Tree Entertainment, 135 E 57th St, #2600, New York, NY 10022, USA

Saar, Bettye *Artist*
8074 Willow Glen Road, Los Angeles, CA 90046, USA

Saari, Roy A *Swimmer*
PO Box 7086, Mammoth Lakes, CA 93546, USA

Saatchi, Charles *Businessman*
36 Golden Square, London W1R 4EE, England

Saatchi, Maurice *Businessman*
36 Golden Square, London W1R 4EE, England

Sabah, Sheikh Jaber al-Ahmad al-Jabar al *Emir, Kuwait*
%Sief Palace, Amiry Diwan, Kuwait City, Kuwait

Sabah, Sheikh Saad al-Abdullah al-Salem *Crown Prince & Prime Minister, Kuwait*
%Prime Minister's Office, PO Box 4, Safat, 13001 Kuwait City, Kuwait

Saban, Louis H (Lou) *Football Player, Coach*
177 Lake Laurel Dr, Dahlonega, GA 30533, USA

Sabates, Felix *Auto Racing Executive*
%Sabco Racing, PO Box 560579, Charlotte, NC 28258, USA

Sabathia, C C *Baseball Player*
%Cleveland Indians, Jacobs Field, 2401 Ontario St, Cleveland, OH 44115, USA

Sabatini, Gabriela *Tennis Player*
35/35 Grosvenor St, London W1K 4QX, England

Sabatino, Michael *Actor*
13538 Valleyheart Dr, Sherman Oaks, CA 91423, USA

Sabato, Antonio, Jr *Actor, Model*
28035 Dorothy Dr, #210A, Agoura, CA 91301, USA

Sabato, Ernesto *Writer*
Severino Langeri 3135, Santos Lugares, Argentina

Sabbah, Michel *Religious Leader*
%Latin Patriarch Office, PO Box 14152, Jerusalem, Israel

Sabelle *Singer, Songwriter*
%Sarmast Entertainment, 241 W 36th St, #2R, New York, NY 10018, USA

Saberhagen, Bret W *Baseball Player*
5535 Amber Circle, Calabasas, CA 91302, USA

Sabiston, David C, Jr *Surgeon*
1528 Pinecrest Road, Durham, NC 27705, USA

Sabo, Christopher A (Chris) *Baseball Player*
7455 Stonemeadow Lane, Cincinnati, OH 45242, USA

Sacco, Michael *Labor Leader*
%Seafarers International Union, 5201 Auth Way, Suitland, MO 20746, USA

Sachar, Louis *Writer*
%Foster Books/Farrar Straus Giroux, 19 Union Square W, New York, NY 10003, USA

Sachenbacher, Evi *Cross Country Skier*
%WSV Reit im Winkl, Rthausplatz 1, 83242 Reit im Winkl, Germany

Sachs, Andrew *Actor*
%Richard Stone, 2 Henrietta St, London WC2E 8PS, England

Sachs, Gloria *Fashion Designer*
117 E 57th St, New York, NY 10022, USA

Sachs, Jeffrey D *Economist*
%Harvard University, International Development Institute, Cambridge, MA 02138, USA

Sachs, Richard *Surgeon*
6 Saint Ronan Terrace, New Haven, CT 06511, USA

Sachs, William *Movie Director*
3739 Montuso Place, Encino, CA 91436, USA

Sack, Kevin *Journalist*
%Los Angeles Times, Editorial Dept, 202 W 1st St, Los Angeles, CA 90012, USA

Sack, Steve *Cartoonist (Professor Doodle's)*
%Minneapolis Star-Tribune, 425 Portland Ave, Minneapolis, MN 55488, USA

Sacks, Greg *Auto Racing Driver*
6092 Sabal Creek Blvd, Port Orange, FL 32128, USA

Sacks, Jonathan H *Religious Leader*
735 High Road, London N12 0US, England

Sacks, Oliver W *Physician, Neurologist, Writer*
2 Horatio St, #3G, New York, NY 10014, USA

Sadat, Jehan El- *Social Activist*
%University of Maryland, Int'l Development Center, College Park, MD 20742, USA

Saddler, Donald E *Choreographer, Dancer*
%Coleman-Rosenberg Agency, 210 E 58th St, New York, NY 10022, USA

Sade *Singer, Songwriter*
1 Red Place, London W1Y 3RE, England

Sadecki, Raymond M (Ray) *Baseball Player*
4237 E Clovis Ave, Mesa, AZ 85206, USA

Sadik, Nafis *Government Official, Pakistan*
%United Nations Population Fund, 220 E 42nd St, New York, NY 10017, USA

Sadler, Elliott *Auto Racing Driver*
PO Box 871, Emporia, VA 23847, USA

Sadoulet, Bernard *Astronomer*
2824 Forest Ave, Berkeley, CA 94705, USA

S

Safdie - Sainz

Safdie, Moshe *Architect*
100 Rev Nazareno Properzi Way, Somerville, MA 02143, USA
Safer, Morley *Commentator*
%CBS-TV, News Dept, 51 W 52nd St, New York, NY 10019, USA
Saffiotti, Umberto *Pathologist*
5114 Wissioming Road, Bethesda, MD 20816, USA
Saffman, Philip G *Mathematician*
%California Institute of Technology, Firestone Hall, Pasadena, CA 91125, USA
Safin, Marat *Tennis Player*
%TC Weiden am Postkeller, Schirmitzer Weg, 92637 Weiden, Germany
Safina, Alessandro *Opera Singer*
%Interscope Records, 2220 Colorado Ave, Santa Monica, CA 90404, USA
Safina, Carl *Marine Biologist*
%Living Oceans Program, Audubon Society, 100 W Main St, East Islip, NY 11730, USA
Safire, William *Journalist, Writer*
6200 Elmwood Road, Chevy Chase, MD 20815, USA
Safuto, Dominick (Randy) *Singer (Randy & the Rainbows)*
PO Box 656507, Fresh Meadows, NY 11365, USA
Safuto, Frank *Singer (Randy & the Rainbows)*
PO Box 656507, Fresh Meadows, NY 11365, USA
Sagal, Jean *Actress*
%Progressive Artists Agency, 400 S Beverly Dr, #216, Beverly Hills, CA 90212, USA
Sagal, Katey *Actress*
7095 Hollywood Blvd, #792, Los Angeles, CA 90028, USA
Sagan, Francoise *Writer*
%Equemauville, 14600 Honfleur, France
Sagdeev, Roald Z *Physicist*
%Space Research Institute, Profsoyuznaya 84/32, 11780 Moscow B485, Russia
Sage, William *Actor*
%Gersh Agency, 232 N Canon Dr, Beverly Hills, CA 90210, USA
Sagebrecht, Marianne *Actress*
Kaulbachstr 61, Ruckgeb, 80539 Munich, Germany
Sagemiller, Melissa *Actress*
%Abrams Artists, 9200 Sunset Blvd, #1125, Los Angeles, CA 90069, USA
Sager, Carole Bayer *Singer, Songwriter*
10761 Bellagio Road, Los Angeles, CA 90077, USA
Sager, Craig *Sportscaster*
3064 Spring Hill Road, Smyrna, GA 30080, USA
Saget, Bob *Actor*
PO Box 4333, Los Angeles, CA 90078, USA
Saglio, Laura *Actress*
%Cineart, 36 Rue de Ponthieu, 75008 Paris, France
Sagona, Katie *Actress*
%Wilhelmina Creative Mgmt, 300 Park Ave S, #200, New York, NY 10010, USA
Sahagun, Elena *Actress*
%Artists Agency, 1180 S Beverly Dr, #301, Los Angeles, CA 90035, USA
Sahgal, Nayantara *Writer*
181B Rajpur Road, Dehra Dun, 248009 Uttar Pradesh, India
Sahl, Mort *Actor, Comedian*
1441 3rd Ave, #12-C, New York, NY 10028, USA
Sahm, Hans-Werner *Artist*
Zur Wasserburg 7, Bidingen, Schwab, Germany
Sailer, Anton (Toni) *Alpine Skier*
%Gundhabing 19, 6370 Kitzbuhl, Austria
Sailors, Kenny (Ken) *Basketball Player*
1614 Shoestring Road, Gooding, ID 83330, USA
Saimes, George *Football Player, Executive*
2307 Beechmoor Dr NW, North Canton, OH 44720, USA
Sain, John F (Johnny) *Baseball Player*
2S707 Ave Latour, Oak Brook, IL 60523, USA
Sainsbury of Preston Candover, John D *Businessman*
%J Sainsbury PLC, Stamford House, Stamford St, London SE1 9LL, England
Sainsbury of Turville, David J *Businessman*
4 Charterhouse Mews, Charterhouse Square, London EC1M 6BB, England
Saint James, Susan *Actress*
174 West St, #54, Litchfield, CT 06759, USA
Saint Laurent, Yves *Fashion Designer*
7 Rue Leonce Reynaud, 75116 Paris, France
Saint, Crosbie E *Army General*
1116 N Pitt St, Alexandria, VA 22314, USA
Saint, Eva Marie *Actress*
10590 Wilshire Blvd, #408, Los Angeles, CA 90024, USA
Saint-Subber, Arnold *Theater Producer*
116 E 64th St, New York, NY 10021, USA
Sainte-Marie, Buffy *Singer, Songwriter*
%Paquin Entertainment, 395 Notre Dame Ave, Winnipeg MB R3B 1R2, Canada
Sainz, Salvador *Actor, Director*
Ave Prat de la Riba 43, 43201 Reus (Tarragona), Spain

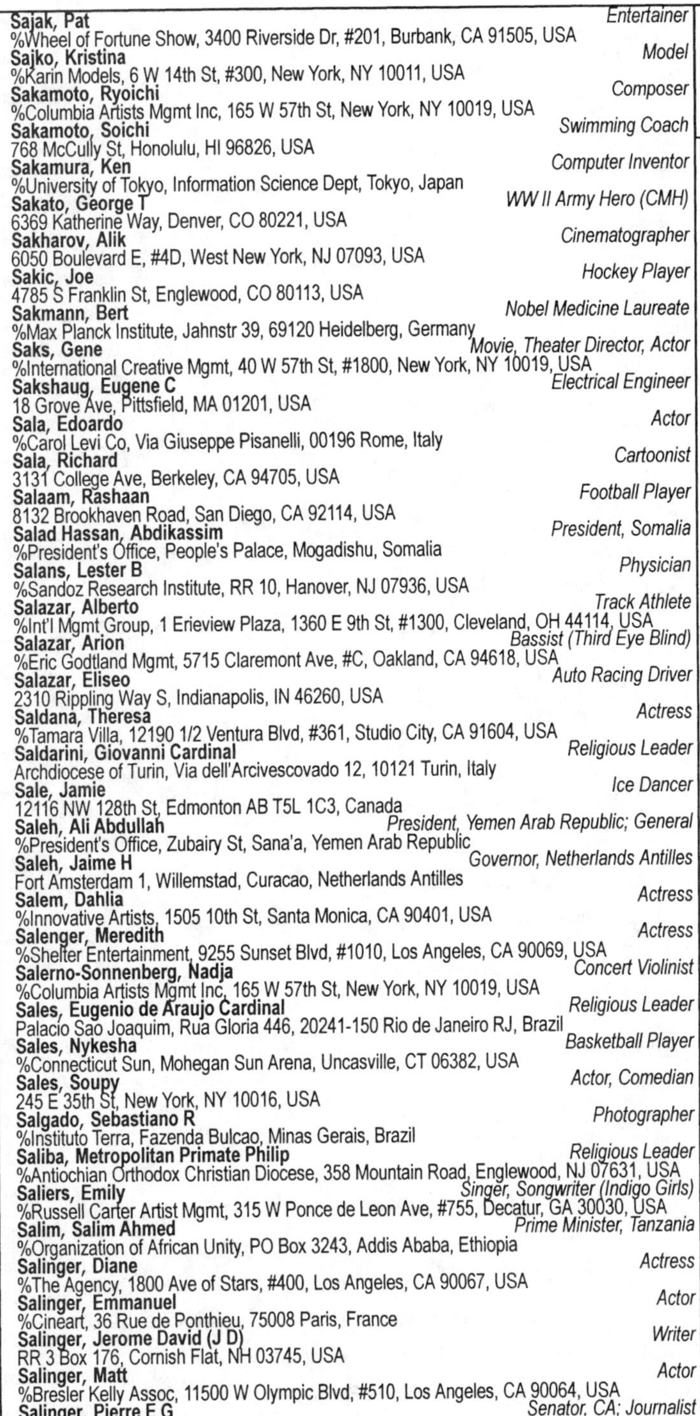

Sajak, Pat *Entertainer*
%Wheel of Fortune Show, 3400 Riverside Dr, #201, Burbank, CA 91505, USA
Sajko, Kristina *Model*
%Karin Models, 6 W 14th St, #300, New York, NY 10011, USA
Sakamoto, Ryoichi *Composer*
%Columbia Artists Mgmt Inc, 165 W 57th St, New York, NY 10019, USA
Sakamoto, Soichi *Swimming Coach*
768 McCully St, Honolulu, HI 96826, USA
Sakamura, Ken *Computer Inventor*
%University of Tokyo, Information Science Dept, Tokyo, Japan
Sakato, George T *WW II Army Hero (CMH)*
6369 Katherine Way, Denver, CO 80221, USA
Sakharov, Alik *Cinematographer*
6050 Boulevard E, #4D, West New York, NJ 07093, USA
Sakic, Joe *Hockey Player*
4785 S Franklin St, Englewood, CO 80113, USA
Sakmann, Bert *Nobel Medicine Laureate*
%Max Planck Institute, Jahnstr 39, 69120 Heidelberg, Germany
Saks, Gene *Movie, Theater Director, Actor*
%International Creative Mgmt, 40 W 57th St, #1800, New York, NY 10019, USA
Sakshaug, Eugene C *Electrical Engineer*
18 Grove Ave, Pittsfield, MA 01201, USA
Sala, Edoardo *Actor*
%Carol Levi Co, Via Giuseppe Pisanelli, 00196 Rome, Italy
Sala, Richard *Cartoonist*
3131 College Ave, Berkeley, CA 94705, USA
Salaam, Rashaan *Football Player*
8132 Brookhaven Road, San Diego, CA 92114, USA
Salad Hassan, Abdikassim *President, Somalia*
%President's Office, People's Palace, Mogadishu, Somalia
Salans, Lester B *Physician*
%Sandoz Research Institute, RR 10, Hanover, NJ 07936, USA
Salazar, Alberto *Track Athlete*
%Int'l Mgmt Group, 1 Erieview Plaza, 1360 E 9th St, #1300, Cleveland, OH 44114, USA
Salazar, Arion *Bassist (Third Eye Blind)*
%Eric Godtland Mgmt, 5715 Claremont Ave, #C, Oakland, CA 94618, USA
Salazar, Eliseo *Auto Racing Driver*
2310 Rippling Way S, Indianapolis, IN 46260, USA
Saldana, Theresa *Actress*
%Tamara Villa, 12190 1/2 Ventura Blvd, #361, Studio City, CA 91604, USA
Saldarini, Giovanni Cardinal *Religious Leader*
Archdiocese of Turin, Via dell'Arcivescovado 12, 10121 Turin, Italy
Sale, Jamie *Ice Dancer*
12116 NW 128th St, Edmonton AB T5L 1C3, Canada
Saleh, Ali Abdullah *President, Yemen Arab Republic; General*
%President's Office, Zubairy St, Sana'a, Yemen Arab Republic
Saleh, Jaime H *Governor, Netherlands Antilles*
Fort Amsterdam 1, Willemstad, Curacao, Netherlands Antilles
Salem, Dahlia *Actress*
%Innovative Artists, 1505 10th St, Santa Monica, CA 90401, USA
Salenger, Meredith *Actress*
%Shelter Entertainment, 9255 Sunset Blvd, #1010, Los Angeles, CA 90069, USA
Salerno-Sonnenberg, Nadja *Concert Violinist*
%Columbia Artists Mgmt Inc, 165 W 57th St, New York, NY 10019, USA
Sales, Eugenio de Araujo Cardinal *Religious Leader*
Palacio Sao Joaquim, Rua Gloria 446, 20241-150 Rio de Janeiro RJ, Brazil
Sales, Nykesha *Basketball Player*
%Connecticut Sun, Mohegan Sun Arena, Uncasville, CT 06382, USA
Sales, Soupy *Actor, Comedian*
245 E 35th St, New York, NY 10016, USA
Salgado, Sebastiano R *Photographer*
%Instituto Terra, Fazenda Bulcao, Minas Gerais, Brazil
Saliba, Metropolitan Primate Philip *Religious Leader*
%Antiochian Orthodox Christian Diocese, 358 Mountain Road, Englewood, NJ 07631, USA
Saliers, Emily *Singer, Songwriter (Indigo Girls)*
%Russell Carter Artist Mgmt, 315 W Ponce de Leon Ave, #755, Decatur, GA 30030, USA
Salim, Salim Ahmed *Prime Minister, Tanzania*
%Organization of African Unity, PO Box 3243, Addis Ababa, Ethiopia
Salinger, Diane *Actress*
%The Agency, 1800 Ave of Stars, #400, Los Angeles, CA 90067, USA
Salinger, Emmanuel *Actor*
%Cineart, 36 Rue de Ponthieu, 75008 Paris, France
Salinger, Jerome David (J D) *Writer*
RR 3 Box 176, Cornish Flat, NH 03745, USA
Salinger, Matt *Actor*
%Bresler Kelly Assoc, 11500 W Olympic Blvd, #510, Los Angeles, CA 90064, USA
Salinger, Pierre E G *Senator, CA; Journalist*
La Bastiderose, 99 Cherin des Croupieres, 84250 Le Thor, France

S

Salkind - Sampson

Salkind, Ilya *Movie Producer*
%Pinewood Studios, Iverheath, Iver, Bucks SL0 0NH, England
Salle, David *Artist*
%Larry Gagosian Gallery, 980 Madison Ave, #PH, New York, NY 10021, USA
Sallinen, Aulis H *Composer*
Runnebergìnkatu 37A, 00100 Helsinki 10, Finland
Sallis, Peter *Actor*
%Jonathan Altaras, 13 Shorts Gardens, London WC2H 9AT, England
Salminen, Matti *Opera Singer*
%Mariedi Anders Artists, 535 El Camino del Mar, San Francisco, CA 94121, USA
Salming, Borje *Hockey Player*
%Borje Salming Assoc, Box 45438, 104 31 Stockholm, Sweden
Salmon, Colin *Actor*
%Markham & Froggatt, Julian House, 4 Windmill St, London W1P 1HF, England
Salmon, Timothy J (Tim) *Baseball Player*
24767 Masters Cup Way, Valencia, CA 91355, USA
Salmons, John *Basketball Player*
%Philadelphia 76ers, 1st Union Center, 3601 S Broad St, Philadelphia, PA 19148, USA
Salmons, Steve *Volleyball Player*
1717 N El Dorado Ave, Ontario, CA 91764, USA
Salo, Mika *Auto Racing Driver*
%TWI Formula One, Leafield, Whitney, Oxon OX8 5PF, England
Salome, Jens *Actress*
%Badgley Connor Talent, 9229 Sunset Blvd, #311, Los Angeles, CA 90069, USA
Salomon, Mikael *Cinematographer*
PO Box 2230, Los Angeles, CA 90078, USA
Salomon, Sandy *Actress*
%Cineart, 36 Rue de Ponthieu, 75008 Paris, France
Salonen, Esa-Pekka *Conductor, Composer*
%Los Angeles Philharmonic, Music Center, 135 N Grand Ave, Los Angeles, CA 90012, USA
Salonga, Lea *Singer, Actress*
%Writers & Artists, 8383 Wilshire Blvd, #550, Beverly Hills, CA 90211, USA
Salopek, Paul *Journalist*
%Chicago Tribune, Editorial Dept, 435 N Michigan Ave, Chicago, IL 60611, USA
Salpeter, Edwin E *Physicist*
116 Westbourne Lane, Ithaca, NY 14850, USA
Salt, Jennifer *Actress*
9045 Elevado St, West Hollywood, CA 90069, USA
Saltpeter, Edwin E *Meteorologist*
%Cornell University, Physical Sciences Dept, Ithaca, NJ 14853, USA
Saltykov, Aleksey A *Movie Director*
%Institute Mosfilmosvsky Per 4A #104, 119285 Moscow, Russia
Saltykov, Boris G *Economist; Government Official, Russia*
Bryusov Per 11, 103009 Moscow, Russia
Salvay, Bennett *Composer*
%Gorfaine/Schwartz, 13245 Riverside Dr, #450, Sherman Oaks, CA 91423, USA
Salvino, Carmen *Bowler*
65 Stevens Dr, Schaumburg, IL 60173, USA
Salzman, Marc *Writer*
%Knopf Publishers, 201 E 50th St, New York, NY 10022, USA
Sam the Sham *Singer*
6123 Old Brunswick Road, Arlington, TN 38002, USA
Samaranch Torello, Juan Antonio *International Olympics Official*
Avenida Pau Casals 24, 08021 Barcelona 6, Spain
Samaras, Lucas *Sculptor, Photographer*
%Pace Gallery, 32 E 57th St, New York, NY 10022, USA
Sambora, Richie *Singer, Songwriter (Bon Jovi)*
4970 Summit View Dr, Westlake Village, CA 91362, USA
Samios, Nicholas P *Science Administrator, Physicist*
%Brookhaven National Laboratory, Director's Office, 2 Center St, Upton, NY 11973, USA
Samms, Emma *Actress*
2934 1/2 N Beverly Glen Circle, #417, Los Angeles, CA 90077, USA
Samoilova, Tatiana Y *Actress*
Spiridonyevsky Per 8/11, 103104 Moscow, Russia
Samotsvetov, Anatoly *Hockey Player*
%Nashville Predators, 501 Broadway, Nashville, TN 37203, USA
Sampaio, Jorge *President, Portugal*
%President's Office, Palacio de Belem, 1300 Lisbon, Portugal
Sample, Joe *Jazz Pianist*
%Patrick Rains Assoc, 220 W 93rd St, #7B, New York, NY 10025, USA
Sample, Steven B *Educator*
%University of Southern California, President's Office, Los Angeles, CA 90089, USA
Sampson, Kelvin *Basketball Coach*
%University of Oklahoma, Lloyd Noble Complex, Norman, OK 73019, USA
Sampson, Ralph L, Jr *Basketball Player, Coach*
10831 W Broad St, Glen Allen, VA 23060, USA
Sampson, Robert *Actor*
%20th Century Artists, 4605 Lankershim Blvd, #305, North Hollywood, CA 91602, USA

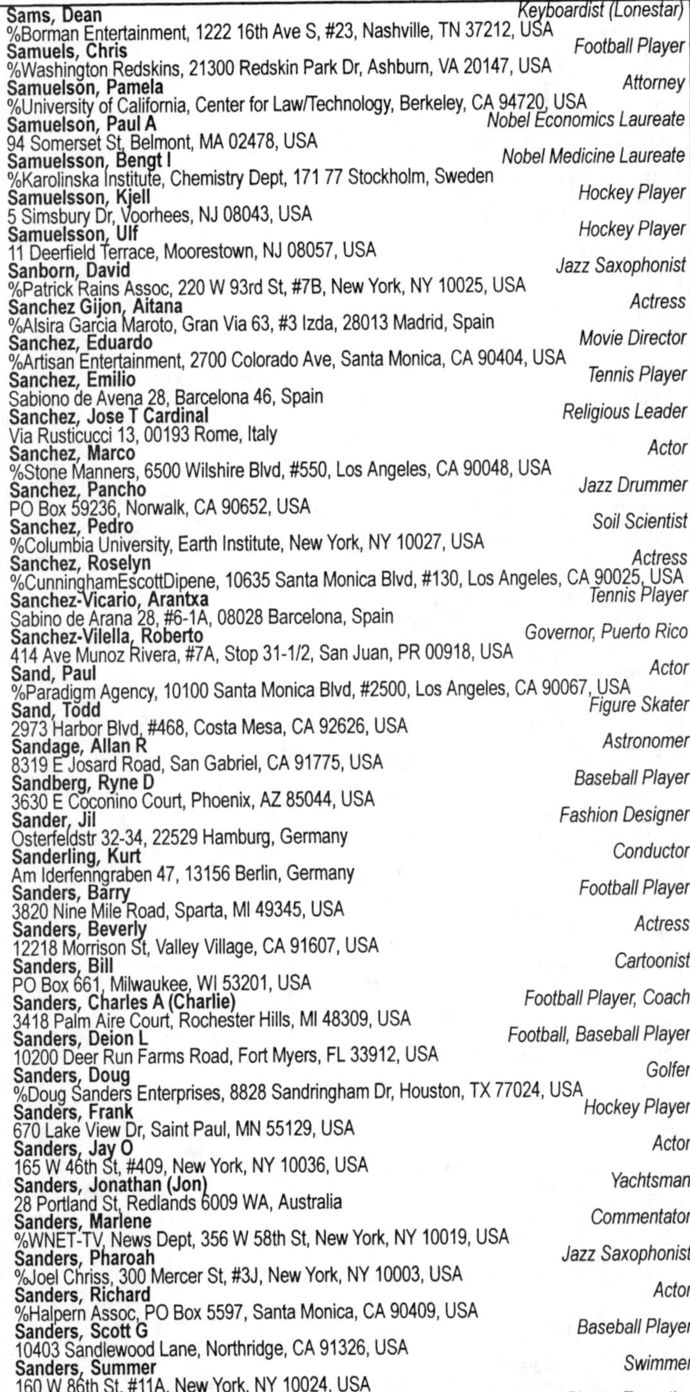

Sams, Dean *Keyboardist (Lonestar)*
%Borman Entertainment, 1222 16th Ave S, #23, Nashville, TN 37212, USA
Samuels, Chris *Football Player*
%Washington Redskins, 21300 Redskin Park Dr, Ashburn, VA 20147, USA
Samuelson, Pamela *Attorney*
%University of California, Center for Law/Technology, Berkeley, CA 94720, USA
Samuelson, Paul A *Nobel Economics Laureate*
94 Somerset St, Belmont, MA 02478, USA
Samuelsson, Bengt I *Nobel Medicine Laureate*
%Karolinska Institute, Chemistry Dept, 171 77 Stockholm, Sweden
Samuelsson, Kjell *Hockey Player*
5 Simsbury Dr, Voorhees, NJ 08043, USA
Samuelsson, Ulf *Hockey Player*
11 Deerfield Terrace, Moorestown, NJ 08057, USA
Sanborn, David *Jazz Saxophonist*
%Patrick Rains Assoc, 220 W 93rd St, #7B, New York, NY 10025, USA
Sanchez Gijon, Aitana *Actress*
%Alsira Garcia Maroto, Gran Via 63, #3 Izda, 28013 Madrid, Spain
Sanchez, Eduardo *Movie Director*
%Artisan Entertainment, 2700 Colorado Ave, Santa Monica, CA 90404, USA
Sanchez, Emilio *Tennis Player*
Sabiono de Avena 28, Barcelona 46, Spain
Sanchez, Jose T Cardinal *Religious Leader*
Via Rusticucci 13, 00193 Rome, Italy
Sanchez, Marco *Actor*
%Stone Manners, 6500 Wilshire Blvd, #550, Los Angeles, CA 90048, USA
Sanchez, Pancho *Jazz Drummer*
PO Box 59236, Norwalk, CA 90652, USA
Sanchez, Pedro *Soil Scientist*
%Columbia University, Earth Institute, New York, NY 10027, USA
Sanchez, Roselyn *Actress*
%CunninghamEscottDipene, 10635 Santa Monica Blvd, #130, Los Angeles, CA 90025, USA
Sanchez-Vicario, Arantxa *Tennis Player*
Sabino de Arana 28, #6-1A, 08028 Barcelona, Spain
Sanchez-Vilella, Roberto *Governor, Puerto Rico*
414 Ave Munoz Rivera, #7A, Stop 31-1/2, San Juan, PR 00918, USA
Sand, Paul *Actor*
%Paradigm Agency, 10100 Santa Monica Blvd, #2500, Los Angeles, CA 90067, USA
Sand, Todd *Figure Skater*
2973 Harbor Blvd, #468, Costa Mesa, CA 92626, USA
Sandage, Allan R *Astronomer*
8319 E Josard Road, San Gabriel, CA 91775, USA
Sandberg, Ryne D *Baseball Player*
3630 E Coconino Court, Phoenix, AZ 85044, USA
Sander, Jil *Fashion Designer*
Osterfeldstr 32-34, 22529 Hamburg, Germany
Sanderling, Kurt *Conductor*
Am Iderfenngraben 47, 13156 Berlin, Germany
Sanders, Barry *Football Player*
3820 Nine Mile Road, Sparta, MI 49345, USA
Sanders, Beverly *Actress*
12218 Morrison St, Valley Village, CA 91607, USA
Sanders, Bill *Cartoonist*
PO Box 661, Milwaukee, WI 53201, USA
Sanders, Charles A (Charlie) *Football Player, Coach*
3418 Palm Aire Court, Rochester Hills, MI 48309, USA
Sanders, Deion L *Football, Baseball Player*
10200 Deer Run Farms Road, Fort Myers, FL 33912, USA
Sanders, Doug *Golfer*
%Doug Sanders Enterprises, 8828 Sandringham Dr, Houston, TX 77024, USA
Sanders, Frank *Hockey Player*
670 Lake View Dr, Saint Paul, MN 55129, USA
Sanders, Jay O *Actor*
165 W 46th St, #409, New York, NY 10036, USA
Sanders, Jonathan (Jon) *Yachtsman*
28 Portland St, Redlands 6009 WA, Australia
Sanders, Marlene *Commentator*
%WNET-TV, News Dept, 356 W 58th St, New York, NY 10019, USA
Sanders, Pharoah *Jazz Saxophonist*
%Joel Chriss, 300 Mercer St, #3J, New York, NY 10003, USA
Sanders, Richard *Actor*
%Halpern Assoc, PO Box 5597, Santa Monica, CA 90409, USA
Sanders, Scott G *Baseball Player*
10403 Sandlewood Lane, Northridge, CA 91326, USA
Sanders, Summer *Swimmer*
160 W 86th St, #11A, New York, NY 10024, USA
Sanders, Thomas (Satch) *Basketball Player, Executive*
114 Fenway, Boston, MA 02115, USA

Sanders, W J (Jerry), III *Businessman*
%Advanced Micro Devices, 1 AMD Place, PO Box 3453, Sunnyvale, CA 94088, USA
Sanderson, Cael *Wrestler*
%Steve Sanderson, 1380 Valley Hills Blvd, Heber City, UT 84032, USA
Sanderson, Derek M *Hockey Player*
267 Manning St, Needham, MA 02492, USA
Sanderson, Geoff *Hockey Player*
1988 Berkshire Road, Upper Arlington, OH 43221, USA
Sanderson, Peter *Artist*
1105 Shell Gate Plaza, Alameda, CA 94501, USA
Sanderson, Theresa (Tessa) *Track Athlete*
%Tee-Dee Promotion, Atlas Center, Oxgate Lane, London NW2 7HU, England
Sanderson, William *Actor*
4251 W Sarah St, Burbank, CA 91505, USA
Sandeson, William S *Editorial Cartoonist*
119 W Sherwood Terrace, Fort Wayne, IN 46807, USA
Sandford, John *Writer*
%G P Putnam's Sons, 375 Hudson St, New York, NY 10014, USA
Sandiford, L Erskine *Prime Minister, Barbados*
Hillvista, Porters, Saint James, Barbados
Sandin, Bill *Inventor (Cave Electronic Visualization)*
%University of Illinois, Electronic Visualization Lab, Chicago, IL 60607, USA
Sandler, Adam *Actor, Comedian*
%Brillstein/Grey, 9150 Wilshire Blvd, #350, Beverly Hills, CA 90212, USA
Sandler, Herbert M *Financier*
%Golden West Financial, 1901 Harrison St, Oakland, CA 94612, USA
Sandler, Marion O *Financier*
%Golden West Financial, 1901 Harrison St, Oakland, CA 94612, USA
Sandlund, Debra *Actress*
%Innovative Artists, 1505 10th St, Santa Monica, CA 90401, USA
Sandor, Gyorgy *Concert Pianist*
%Jack Brennan, 500 E 85th St, #31, New York, NY 10028, USA
Sandoval Iniguez, Juan Cardinal *Religious Leader*
Morelos 244, 45500 San Pedro Tlaquepaque Jal, Mexico
Sandoval, Arturo *Jazz Trumpeter*
PO Box 660335, Miami Springs, FL 33266, USA
Sandoval, Hope *Singer (Mazzy Star)*
%Rough Trade Mgmt, 66 Golbarne Road, London W10 5PS, England
Sandoval, Miguel *Actor*
%Paradigm Agency, 10100 Santa Monica Blvd, #2500, Los Angeles, CA 90067, USA
Sandoval, Sonny *Singer (POD)*
%East West America Records, 75 Rockefeller Plaza, New York, NY 10019, USA
Sandre, Didier *Actor*
%Agents Associes Beaume, 201 Faubourg Saint Honore, 75008 Paris, France
Sandrelli, Stefania *Actress*
%TNA, Viale Parioli 41, 00197 Rome, Italy
Sandrich, Jay H *Television Director*
610 N Maple Dr, Beverly Hills, CA 90210, USA
Sands, Julian *Actor*
1287 Ozeta Terrace, Los Angeles, CA 90069, USA
Sands, Tommy *Singer, Actor*
225 N Evergreen St, #301, Burbank, CA 91505, USA
Sandstrom, Sven *Financier*
%World Bank Group, 1818 H St NW, Washington, DC 20433, USA
Sandstrom, Tomas *Hockey Player*
156 Iron Run Road, Bethel Park, PA 15102, USA
Sandusky, Alexander B (Alex) *Football Player*
636 Oakland Hills Dr, #2A, Arnold, MD 21012, USA
Sandy B *Singer*
%Atlantic Entertainment Group, 2922 Atlantic Ave, #200, Atlantic City, NJ 08401, USA
Sandy, Gary *Actor*
PO Box 818, Cynthiana, KY 41031, USA
Sanford, Isabel *Actress*
2501 Colorado Ave, #350, Santa Monica, CA 90404, USA
Sanford, Lucius M *Football Player*
1350 Allegheny St SW, Atlanta, GA 30310, USA
Sanford, Richard M (Rick) *Football Player*
335 Lemonts Road, Chapin, SC 29036, USA
Sanger, David J *Concert Organist*
%Old Wesleyan Chapel, Embleton Near Cockermouth, Cumbria CA13 9YA, England
Sanger, Frederick *Nobel Chemistry Laureate*
Far Leys, Fen Lane, Swaffham Bulbeck, Cambridge CB5 0NJ, England
Sanger, Stephen W *Businessman*
%General Mills Inc, 1 General Mills Blvd, PO Box 1113, Minneapolis, MN 55440, USA
SanGiacomo, Laura *Actress*
%Rigberg Roberts Rugolo, 1180 S Beverly Dr, #601, Los Angeles, CA 90035, USA
Sangster, Jimmy *Writer*
1590 Lindercrest Dr, Beverly Hills, CA 90210, USA

Sangueli, Andrei *Prime Minister, Moldova*
%Parliament House, Prosp 105, 277073 Kishineau, Moldova
Sanguinetti Cairolo, Julio Maria *President, Uruguay*
%Partido Colorado, Andres Martinez Trueba 1271, Montevideo, Uruguay
Sanha, Malam Bacai *President, Guinea-Bissau*
%President's Office, Bissau, Guinea-Bissau
SanJuan, Olga *Actress*
%O'Brien, 12100 Sunset Blvd, #2, Los Angeles, CA 90049, USA
Sano, Roya A *Religious Leader*
%United Methodist Church, PO Box 320, Nashville, TN 37202, USA
Sansom, Bruce *Ballet Dancer*
%Royal Ballet, Covent Garden, Bow St, London WC2E 9DD, England
Sansom, Chip *Cartoonist (Born Loser)*
204 Long Beach Road, Centerville, MA 02632, USA
Sant, Alfred *Prime Minister, Malta*
%National Labor Center, Mills End Road, Hanrum, Malta
Santa Rosa, Gilberto *Singer*
%Universal Attractions, 225 W 57th St, #500, New York, NY 10019, USA
Santana, Carlos *Guitarist, Singer, Songwriter*
%Santana Mgmt, 121 Jordan St, San Rafael, CA 94901, USA
Santana, Manuel *Tennis Player*
%International Tennis Hall of Fame, 194 Bellevue Ave, Newport, RI 02840, USA
Santer, Jacques *Premier, Luxembourg*
69 Rue J P Huberty, 1742 Luxembourg
Santiago, Benito R *Baseball Player*
12503 NW 23rd St, Pembroke Pines, FL 33028, USA
Santiago-Hudson, Ruben *Actor*
%Gersh Agency, 232 N Canon Dr, Beverly Hills, CA 90210, USA
Santo, Ronald E (Ron) *Baseball Player*
1721 Meadow Lane, Bannockburn, IL 60015, USA
Santoni, Reni *Actor*
%Henderson/Hogan, 8285 W Sunset Blvd, #1, West Hollywood, CA 90046, USA
Santorini, Paul E *Physicist, Engineer*
PO Box 49, Athens, Greece
Santos de Oliveira, Alessandra *Basketball Player*
%Washington Mystics, MCI Center, 601 F St NW, Washington, DC 20004, USA
Santos, Joe *Actor*
1444 Queens Dr, Los Angeles, CA 90069, USA
Sanz, Alejandro *Singer, Songwriter*
%RLM Intl, 800 Ocean Dr, #19, Miami Beach, FL 33139, USA
Saper, Clifford *Neurologist*
%Beth Israel Hospital, Neurology Dept, 330 Brookline Ave, Boston, MA 02215, USA
Sapienza, Al *Actor*
PO Box 691240, West Hollywood, CA 90069, USA
Sapp, Warren *Football Player*
16609 Villalenda de Avila, Tampa, FL 33613, USA
Sara, Mia *Actress*
2311 Alto Oak Dr, Los Angeles, CA 90068, USA
Sarachan, Dave *Soccer Coach*
%Chicago Fire, 980 N Michigan Ave, #1998, Chicago, IL 60611, USA
Sarafanov, Gennadi V *Cosmonaut*
%Potchta Kosmonavtov, Moskovskoi Oblasti, 141160 Syvisdny Goroduk, Russia
Saraiva Martins, Jose Cardinal *Religious Leader*
Via Pancrazio Pfeiffer 10, 00193 Rome, Italy
Saralegui, Cristina *Commentator*
%William Morris Agency, 151 El Camino Dr, Beverly Hills, CA 90212, USA
Saramago, Jose *Writer*
Los Topes 3, 35572 Tias/Lansarote, Canaries, Spain
Sarandon, Chris *Actor*
9540 Hidden Valley Road, Beverly Hills, CA 90210, USA
Sarandon, Susan *Actress*
%International Creative Mgmt, 40 W 57th St, #1800, New York, NY 10019, USA
Saraste, Jukka-Pekka *Conductor*
%Van Walsum Mgmt, 4 Addison Bridge Place, London W14 8XP, England
Sardi, Vincent, Jr *Restauranteur*
%Sardi's Restaurant, 234 W 44th St, New York, NY 10036, USA
Sarfati, Alain *Architect*
28 Rue Barbet du Jouy, 75007 Paris, France
Sargent, Ben *Editorial Cartoonist*
%Austin American-Statesman, 166 E Riverside Dr, Austin, TX 78704, USA
Sargent, John T *Publisher*
Halsey Lane, Watermill, NY 11976, USA
Sargent, Joseph D *Movie Producer, Director*
27432 Latigo Bay View Dr, Malibu, CA 90265, USA
Sargent, Ronald L *Businessman*
%Staples Inc, PO Box 9265, Framingham, MA 01701, USA
Sargent, Wallace *Astronomer*
400 S Berkeley Ave, Pasadena, CA 91107, USA

Sargeson, Alan M *Inorganic Chemist*
%National University, Chemistry Dept, Canberra ACT 0200, Australia
Sarkisian, Alex *Football Player*
1604 E 142nd St, East Chicago, IN 46312, USA
Sarna, Craig *Hockey Player*
1375 Brown Road S, Wayzata, MN 55391, USA
Sarne, Tanya *Fashion Designer*
Ghost, Chapel, 263 Kensal Road, London W10 5DB, England
Sarner, Craig *Hockey Player*
1375 Brown Road S, Wayzata, MN 55391, USA
Sarni, Vincent A *Baseball Executive*
%Pittsburgh Pirates, PNC Park, 115 Federal St, Pittsburgh, PA 15212, USA
Sarnoff, William *Publisher*
%Warner Publishing Inc, 1325 Ave of Americas, New York, NY 10019, USA
Sarosi, Imre *Swimming Coach*
1033 Bp Harrer Dal Utca 4, Hungary
Sarrazin, Michael *Actor*
9696 Culver Blvd, #203, Culver City, CA 90232, USA
Sarsgaard, Peter *Actor*
%Creative Artists Agency, 9830 Wilshire Blvd, Beverly Hills, CA 90212, USA
Sartzetakis, Christos *President, Greece*
%Presidential Palace, 7 Vas Georgiou B, Odos Zalokosta 10, Athens, Greece
Sasaki, Kazuhiro *Baseball Player*
%Seattle Mariners, Safeco Field, PO Box 4100, Seattle, WA 98194, USA
Sassano, C E *Businessman*
%Bausch & Lomb, 1 Bausch & Lomb Place, Rochester, NY 14604, USA
Sasselov, Dimitar *Astronomer*
%Harvard-Smithsonian Astrophysics Center, 60 Garden St, Cambridge, MA 02138, USA
Sasser, Clarence E *Vietnam War Army Hero (CMH)*
13414 FM 521, Rosharon, TX 77583, USA
Sasso, Will *Actor, Comedian*
%InnerAct Entertainment, 141 S Barrington Ave, #E, Los Angeles, CA 90049, USA
Sasson, Debra *Opera Singer*
Erlenhaupstr 10, 64625 Bensheim, Germany
Sassoon, Beverly *Model*
1511 SE 2nd St, Fort Lauderdale, FL 33301, USA
Sassoon, David *Fashion Designer*
%Bellville Sassoon, 18 Culford Gardens, London SW3 2ST, England
Sassoon, Vidal *Hair Stylist*
1163 Calle Vista Dr, Beverly Hills, CA 90210, USA
Sassou-Nguesso, Denis *President, Congo People's Republic*
%President's Office, Brazzaville, Congo Republic
Satanowski, Robert *Conductor*
Ul Madalinskiego 50/52 m 1, 02-581 Warsaw, Poland
Satcher, David *Medical Executive, Government Leader*
%Kaiser Family Foundation, 2400 Sand Hill Road, Menlo Park, CA 94025, USA
Satcher, Leslie *Singer, Songwriter*
%Warner Bros Records, 3300 Warner Blvd, Burbank, CA 91505, USA
Sather, Glen C *Hockey Player, Coach, Executive*
505 Buffalo St, Banff AB T0L 0C0, Canada
Sato, Kazuo *Economist*
300 E 71st St, #15H, New York, NY 10021, USA
Satra, Sonia *Actress*
%Innovative Artists, 1505 10th St, Santa Monica, CA 90401, USA
Satre, Philip G *Businessman*
%Harrah's Entertainment, 1023 Cherry Road, Memphis, TN 38117, USA
Satriani, Joe *Singer, Guitarist*
%Bill Graham Mgmt, 360 17th St, Oakland, CA 94612, USA
Satterfield, Paul *Actor*
PO Box 6945, Beverly Hills, CA 90212, USA
Saturno, William *Archaelolgist*
%University of New Hampshire, Archaelogy Dept, Durham, NH 03824, USA
Saubert, Jean M *Alpine Skier*
147 Harbor Heights Blvd, Bigfork, MT 59911, USA
Saud, Prince Sultan Bin Abdulaziz al *Government Official, Saudi Arabia*
%Defense Ministry, PO Box 26731, Airport Road, Riyadh 11165, Saudi Arabia
Saudek, Jan *Photographer*
Blodkova 6, 130 00 Prague 3, Czech Republic
Sauer, George H, Jr *Football Player*
2608 E 8th St, #201, Sioux Falls, SD 57103, USA
Sauer, Louis *Architect*
3472 Marlowe St, Montreal QC H4A 3L7, Canada
Sauer, Richard J *Educator, Association Executive*
%National 4-H Council, 7100 Connecticut Ave, Bethesda, MD 20815, USA
Sauerlander, Willibald P W *Art Historian*
%Zentralinstitut fyr Kunstgeschichte, Meiserstr 10, 80333 Munich, Germany
Saul, April *Journalist*
%Philadelphia Inquirer, Editorial Dept, 400 N Broad St, Philadelphia, PA 19130, USA

Saul, John W, III *Writer*
%The Firm, 9100 Wilshire Blvd, #100W, Beverly Hills, CA 90210, USA
Saul, Ralph S *Businessman*
805 Oxford Crest, Villanova, PA 19085, USA
Saul, Richard R (Rich) *Football Player*
127 G St, Newport Beach, CA 92661, USA
Saul, Stephanie *Journalist*
%Newsday, Editorial Dept, 235 Pinelawn Road, Melville, NY 11747, USA
Sauls, Don *Religious Leader*
%Pentecostal Free Will Baptist Church, PO Box 1568, Dunn, NC 28335, USA
Saunders, Cicely *Hospice Movement Founder*
%Saint Christopher's Hospice, 51 Lawreie Park Road, Sydenham 6DZ, England
Saunders, George *Writer*
%Random House, 1745 Broadway, #B1, New York, NY 10019, USA
Saunders, George L, Jr *Attorney*
179 E Lake Shore Dr, Chicago, IL 60611, USA
Saunders, Jennifer *Actress*
%P F D, Drury House, 34-43 Russell St, London WC2B 5HA, England
Saunders, John *Cartoonist (Mary Worth)*
%King Features Syndicate, 888 7th Ave, New York, NY 10106, USA
Saunders, John *Sportscaster*
%ESPN-TV, Sports Dept, ESPN Plaza, 935 Middle St, Bristol, CT 06010, USA
Saunders, John R *Auto Racing Executive*
%Watkins Glen Speedway, PO Box 500F, Watkins Glen, NY 14891, USA
Saunders, Lori *Actress*
110 S Carmelina Ave, Los Angeles, CA 90049, USA
Saunders, Phil (Flip) *Basketball Coach*
%Minnesota Timberwolves, Target Center, 600 1st Ave N, Minneapolis, MN 55403, USA
Saunders, Townsend *Wrestler*
733 Chantilly Dr, Sierra Vista, AZ 85635, USA
Saura, Carlos *Movie Director*
%Antonio Duran, Calle Arturo Soria 52, #Edif 2, 1-5A, 28027 Madrid, Spain
Sauve, Robert (Bob) *Hockey Player*
%Jandec Inc, 803-3080 Boul le Carrefour, Laval QC H7T 2R5, Canada
Savage, Ann *Actress*
1541 N Hayworth Ave, #203, Los Angeles, CA 90046, USA
Savage, Ben *Actor*
%International Creative Mgmt, 8942 Wilshire Blvd, #219, Beverly Hills, CA 90211, USA
Savage, Chantay *Singer*
%Famous Artists Agency, 250 W 57th St, New York, NY 10107, USA
Savage, Fred *Actor*
%Banner Entertainment, 8265 W Sunset Blvd, #200, West Hollywood, CA 90046, USA
Savage, John *Actor*
5584 Bonneville Road, Hidden Hills, CA 91302, USA
Savage, Randy (Macho Man) *Wrestler*
7650 Bayshore Dr, #10038, Treasure Island, FL 33706, USA
Savage, Rick *Bassist (Def Leppard)*
%Q Prime Mgmt, 729 7th Ave, #1400, New York, NY 10019, USA
Savant, Doug *Actor*
1015 E Angeleno Ave, Burbank, CA 91501, USA
Savard, Denis *Hockey Player*
%Chicago Blackhawks, United Center, 1901 W Madison St, Chicago, IL 60612, USA
Savard, Serge A *Hockey Player, Executive*
1790 Ch du Golf, RR 1, Saint Bruno QC J3V 4P6, Canada
Savary, Jerome *Theater Director*
%Theatre National de Chaillot, 1 Place du Trocadero, 75116 Paris, France
Savchenko, Arkadiy M *Opera Singer*
8-358 Storozhovskaya Str, 220002 Minsk, Belarus
Saveleva, Lyudmila M *Actress*
Tverskaya Str 19, #76, 103050 Moscow, Russia
Savidge, Jennifer *Actress*
2705 Glenower Ave, Los Angeles, CA 90027, USA
Saville, Curtis *Long Distance Rower, Explorer*
RFD Box 44, West Charleston, VT 05872, USA
Saville, Kathleen *Long Distance Rower, Explorer*
RFD Box 44, West Charleston, VT 05872, USA
Savinykh, Viktor P *Cosmonaut*
%Moscow State University, Gorochovskii 4, 103064 Moscow, Russia
Savitskaya, Svetlana Y *Cosmonaut*
%Russian Association, Khovanskaya Str 3, 129515 Moscow, Russia
Savitsky, George M *Football Player*
350 E Seabright Road, Ocean City, NJ 08226, USA
Savitt, Richard (Dick) *Tennis Player*
19 E 80th St, New York, NY 10021, USA
Savoy, Guy *Chef*
101 Blvd Pereire, 75017 Paris, France
Savvina, Iya S *Actress*
%Bolshaya Grunzinskaya St 12, #43, 123242 Moscow, Russia

Saw Maung *Prime Minister, Myanmar; Army General*
%Prime Minister's Office, Yangon, Myanmar
Sawa, Devon *Actor*
7201 Melrose Ave, #202, Los Angeles, CA 90046, USA
Sawalha, Julia *Actress*
%P F D, Drury House, 34-43 Russell St, London WC2B 5HA, England
Sawallisch, Wolfgang *Conductor, Concert Pianist*
Hinterm Bichl 2, 83224 Grassau, Germany
Sawyer, Amos *President, Liberia*
%President's Office, Executive Mansion, PO Box 9001, Monrovia, Liberia
Sawyer, Charles H *Anatomist*
466 Tuallitan Road, Los Angeles, CA 90049, USA
Sawyer, Diane *Commentator*
147 Columbus Ave, #300, New York, NY 10023, USA
Sawyer, Elton *Auto Racing Driver*
%Lysol, 400 Odell School Road, Concord, NC 28027, USA
Sawyer, Forrest *Commentator*
%NBC-TV, News Dept, 30 Rockefeller Plaza, New York, NY 10112, USA
Sawyer, James L *Labor Leader*
%Leather Workers Union, 11 Peabody Square, Peabody, MA 01960, USA
Sawyer, Paul *Auto Racing Executive*
%Richmond International Raceway, PO Box 9257, Richmond, VA 23227, USA
Sawyer, Robert E *Religious Leader*
%Moravian Church Southern Province, 459 S Church St, Winston Salem, NC 27101, USA
Sax, Stephen L (Steve) *Baseball Player*
201 Wesley Court, Roseville, CA 95661, USA
Saxbe, William H *Attorney General; Senator, OH*
4600 N Ocean Blvd, #200, Boynton Beach, FL 33435, USA
Saxe, Adrian *Artist*
4835 N Figueroa St, Los Angeles, CA 90042, USA
Saxon, David S *Physicist*
1008 Hilts Ave, Los Angeles, CA 90024, USA
Saxon, James E *Football Player*
RR 3 Box 34X, Beaufort, SC 29906, USA
Saxon, John *Actor*
2432 Banyan Dr, Los Angeles, CA 90049, USA
Saxton, James E (Jimmy) *Football Player*
1 Mulberry Lane, Austin, TX 78746, USA
Saxton, Johnny *Boxer*
Crystal Palms, 1710 4th Ave N, Lake Worth, FL 33460, USA
Saxton, Shirley Childress *Singer (Sweet Honey in the Rock)*
%Sweet Honey Agency, PO Box 600099, Newtonville, MA 02460, USA
Sayed, Mostafa Amr El *Chemist*
579 Westover Dr NW, Atlanta, GA 30305, USA
Sayer, Leo *Singer, Songwriter*
%Mission Control, Business Center, Lower Road, London SE16 2XB, England
Sayers, E Roger *Educator*
%University of Alabama, President's Office, Tuscaloosa, AL 35487, USA
Sayers, Gale E *Football Player*
1313 N Ritchie Court, #407, Chicago, IL 60610, USA
Saykally, Richard J *Chemist*
%University of California, Chemistry Dept, Latimer Hall, Berkeley, CA 94720, USA
Sayles, John T *Movie Director*
130 W 25th St, #12A, New York, NY 10001, USA
Scaasi, Arnold *Fashion Designer*
16 E 52nd St, New York, NY 10022, USA
Scacchi, Greta *Actress*
%P F D, Drury House, 34-43 Russell St, London WC2B 5HA, England
Scaduto, Al *Cartoonist (They'll Do It Everytime)*
250 Chapel St, Milford, CT 06460, USA
Scaggs, William R (Boz) *Singer, Songwriter*
%H K Mgmt, 9200 W Sunset Blvd, #530, Los Angeles, CA 90069, USA
Scales, Dwight *Football Player*
6112 Roosevelt Circle NW, Huntsville, AL 35810, USA
Scales, Prunella M *Actress*
%Conway Van Gelder Robinson, 18-21 Jermyn St, London SW1Y 6NB, England
Scalia, Antonin *Supreme Court Justice*
%US Supreme Court, 1 1st St NE, Washington, DC 20543, USA
Scalia, Jack *Actor*
16260 Ventura Blvd, Encino, CA 91436, USA
Scallions, Bret *Singer/Guitarist (Fuel)*
%Media Five Entertainment, 3005 Brodhead Road, #170, Bethlehem, PA 18020, USA
Scalzo, Tony *Singer, Bassist (Fastball)*
%Russell Carter Artists, 315 Ponce de Leon Blvd, #755, Decatur, GA 30030, USA
Scaminace, Joseph M *Businessman*
%Sherwin-Williams Co, 101 W Prospect Ave, Cleveland, OH 44115, USA
Scancarelli, Jim *Cartoonist (Gasoline Alley)*
%Mark J Cohen, PO Box 1892, Santa Rosa, CA 95402, USA

Scandiuzzi, Roberto *Opera Singer*
%Opera et Concert, Maximilianstr 22, 80539 Munich, Germany
Scanga, Italo *Artist*
7127 Olivetas, La Jolla, CA 92037, USA
Scanlan, Hugh P S *Labor Leader*
23 Seven Stones Dr, Broadstairs, Kent, England
Scarabelli, Michele *Actress*
9157 Sunset Blvd, #215, Los Angeles, CA 90069, USA
Scarbath, John C (Jack) *Football Player*
736 Calvert Road, Rising Sun, MD 21911, USA
Scarbrough, W Carl *Labor Leader*
%Furniture Workers Union, 1910 Airlane Dr, Nashville, TN 37210, USA
Scardelletti, Robert A *Labor Leader*
%Transportation Communications Union, 3 Research Place, Rockville, MD 20850, USA
Scardino, Albert J *Journalist*
19 Empire House, Thurloe Place, London SW7 2RU, England
Scarf, Herbert E *Economist*
88 Blake Road, Hamden, CT 06517, USA
Scarfe, Gerald A *Cartoonist*
10 Cheyne Walk, London SW3, England
Scargill, Arthur *Labor Leader*
%National Union of Mineworkers, 2 Huddersfield Road, Barnsley, England
Scarwid, Diana *Actress*
PO Box 3614, Savannah, GA 31414, USA
Scates, Al *Volleyball Coach*
8433 Apple Hill Court, Las Vegas, NV 89128, USA
Scattini, Monica *Actress*
%Carol Levi Co, Via Giuseppe Pisanelli, 00196 Rome, Italy
Scavullo, Francesco *Photographer*
140 E 72nd St, #7B, New York, NY 10021, USA
Schaal, Richard *Actor*
612 Gulf Blvd, #9, Indian Rocks Beach, FL 33785, USA
Schaal, Wendy *Actress*
%Gage Group, 14724 Ventura Blvd, #505, Sherman Oaks, CA 91403, USA
Schacher, Mel *Bassist (Grand Funk Railroad)*
%Lustig Talent, PO Box 770850, Orlando, FL 32877, USA
Schachman, Howard K *Molecular Biochemist*
%University of California, Molecular Biology Dept, Berkeley, CA 94720, USA
Schacht, Henry B *Businessman*
%Lucent Technologies Inc, 600 Mountain Ave, New Providence, NJ 07974, USA
Schachter, Norm *Football Referee*
7716 Westlawn Ave, Los Angeles, CA 90045, USA
Schacter-Shalomi, Zalman *Religious Leader*
%Spiritual Eldering Institute, 970 Aurora Ave, Boulder, CO 80302, USA
Schadler, Jay *Commentator*
%ABC-TV, News Dept, 77 W 66th St, New York, NY 10023, USA
Schadt, James P *Publisher*
%Reader's Digest Assn, Reader's Digest Road, Pleasantville, NY 10570, USA
Schaech, Jonathan *Actor*
9055 Hollywood Hills Road, Los Angeles, CA 90046, USA
Schaefer, Ernst J *Medical Researcher*
%Tufts University, Nutrition Research Center, Medford, MA 02155, USA
Schaefer, George A, Jr *Financier*
%Fifth Third Bancorp, 38 Fountain Square Plaza, Cincinnati, OH 45263, USA
Schaefer, Henry F, III *Chemist*
%University of Georgia, Computational Quantum Chemistry Center, Athens, GA 30602, USA
Schaefer, Molly *Publisher*
%Town & Country Magazine, 1700 Broadway, New York, NY 10019, USA
Schaefer, Roberto *Cinematographer*
%Innovative Artists, 1505 10th St, Santa Monica, CA 90401, USA
Schaefer, William D *Governor, MD*
7184 Springhouse Lane, Baltimore, MD 21226, USA
Schaeffer, Eric *Actor, Director*
%Writers & Artists, 8383 Wilshire Blvd, #550, Beverly Hills, CA 90211, USA
Schaeffer, Leonard *Businessman*
%WellPoint Health Networks, 1 Wellpoint Way, Westlake Village, CA 91362, USA
Schaetzel, John R *Writer*
2 Bay Tree Lane, Bethesda, MD 20816, USA
Schaffel, Lewis *Basketball Executive*
%Miami Heat, American Airlines Arena, 601 Biscayne Blvd, Miami, FL 33132, USA
Schaffer, Eric *Concert Executive*
%Kennedy Center for Performing Arts, Washington, DC 20011, USA
Schaffer, Peter L *Writer*
%McNaughton-Lowe Representation, 200 Fulham Road, London SW10, England
Schafrath, Dick *Football Player*
3040 Shad Dr E, Mansfield, OH 44903, USA
Schall, Alvin A *Judge*
%US Appeals Court, 717 Madison Place NW, Washington, DC 20439, USA

S

Schaller - Schellhase

Schaller, George B *Zoologist*
90 Sentry Hill Road, Roxbury, CT 06783, USA
Schaller, Willie *Soccer Player*
3283 S Indiana St, Lakewood, CO 80228, USA
Schallert, William *Actor*
14920 Ramos Place, Pacific Palisades, CA 90272, USA
Schally, Andrew V *Nobel Medicine Laureate*
5025 Kawanee Ave, Metairie, LA 70006, USA
Schama, Simon M *Historian, Writer*
%Minda de Gunzburg European Studies Center, Adolphus Hall, Cambridge, MA 02138, USA
Schanberg, Sydney H *Journalist*
164 W 79th St, #12D, New York, NY 10024, USA
Schank, Roger C *Computer Scientist, Psychologist*
%Northwestern University, Learning Sciences Institute, Evanston, IL 60201, USA
Schanz, Heidi *Actress*
%Gersh Agency, 232 N Canon Dr, Beverly Hills, CA 90210, USA
Schapp, Dick *Sportscaster*
%ESPN-TV, Sports Dept, ESPN Plaza, 935 Middle St, Bristol, CT 06010, USA
Scharansky, Natan *Social Activist, Computer Scientist*
%Trade & Industry Ministry, 30 Rehov Agron, Jerusalem 91002, Israel
Scharer, Erich *Bobsled Athlete*
Grutstrasse 63, 8074 Herrliberg, Switzerland
Scharping, Rudolf *Government Official, Germany*
Wilhelmstr 5, 56112 Lahnstein, Germany
Schatz, Albert *Microbiologist*
%Rutgers University, Research/Endowment Foundation, New Brunswick, NJ 08903, USA
Schatz, Gottfried *Biochemist*
%Basle University, Klingelbergstr 70 4056 Basle, Switzerland
Schatz, Howard *Photographer*
435 W Broadway, #2, New York, NY 10012, USA
Schatzberg, Jerry N *Movie Director*
%International Creative Mgmt, 8942 Wilshire Blvd, #219, Beverly Hills, CA 90211, USA
Schatzman, Evry *Astrophysicist*
11 Rue de l'Eglise, Dompierre, 60420 Maignelay-Montigny, France
Schaudt, Martin *Equestrian Athlete*
Gerhardstr 10/2, 72461 Albstadt, Germany
Schaufuss, Peter *Ballet Dancer, Director*
%Papoutsis Representation, 18 Sundial Ave, London SE25 4BX, England
Schayes, Adolph (Dolph) *Basketball Player*
PO Box 156, DeWitt, NY 13214, USA
Schayes, Danny *Basketball Player*
PO Box 665, Windermere, FL 34786, USA
Scheck, Barry *Attorney, Educator*
%Yeshiva University, Law School, 55 5th Ave, New York, NY 10003, USA
Scheckter, Jody D *Auto Racing Driver*
39 Ave Princess Grace, Monte Carlo, Monaco
Schedeen, Anne *Actress*
%Metropolitan Talent Agency, 4526 Wilshire Blvd, Los Angeles, CA 90010, USA
Scheffczyk, Leo Cardinal *Religious Leader*
PD Comboni 2, Rome, Italy
Scheffer, Victor B *Zoologist*
14806 SE 54th St, Bellevue, WA 98006, USA
Scheffler, Israel *Philosopher*
%Harvard University, Larsen Hall, Cambridge, MA 02138, USA
Scheibel, Arnold B *Psychiatrist*
16231 Morrison St, Encino, CA 91436, USA
Scheider, Roy *Actor*
PO Box 364, Sagaponack, NY 11962, USA
Schein, Philip S *Physician*
6212 Robinwood Road, Bethesda, MD 20817, USA
Schekman, Randy W *Medical Researcher*
%Howard Hughes Institute, 4000 Jones Bridge Road, Chevy Chase, MD 20815, USA
Schell, Catherine *Actress*
Postfach 800504, 51005 Cologne, Germany
Schell, Jonathan *Journalist*
%Newsday, Editorial Dept, 235 Pinelawn Road, Melville, NY 11747, USA
Schell, Jozef S *Geneticist*
%College de France, 11 Pl Marcelin-Berthelot, 75231 Paris Cedex 05, France
Schell, Maria *Actress*
9451 Preitenegg, Austria
Schell, Maximilian *Actor*
2869 Royston Place, Beverly Hills, CA 90210, USA
Schellenbach, Kate *Drummer (Luscious Jackson)*
%Metropolitan Entertainment, 2 Penn Plaza, #2600, New York, NY 10121, USA
Schellenberg, August *Actor*
%Gold Marshak Liedtke, 3500 W Olive Ave, #1400, Burbank, CA 91505, USA
Schellhase, Dave *Basketball Player*
31139 Wrencrest Dr, Zephyrhills, FL 33543, USA

Schelling, Gunther F K *Civil Engineer*
%Graz University, Rechbauerstr 12, 8010 Graz, Austria
Schelling, Thomas C *Economist*
%University of Maryland, Economics Dept, College Park, MD 20742, USA
Schellman, John A *Chemist*
65 W 30th Ave, #508, Eugene, OR 97405, USA
Schelmerding, Kirk *Auto Racing Mechanic*
%Childress Racing, PO Box 1189, Industrial Dr, Welcome, NC 27374, USA
Schemansky, Norbert *Weightlifter*
24826 New York St, Dearborn, MI 48124, USA
Schembechler, Glenn E (Bo), Jr *Football Player, Coach*
1904 Boulder Dr, Ann Arbor, MI 48104, USA
Schenk, Franziska *Speedskater*
%DESG, Menzinger Str 68, 80992 Munich, Germany
Schenkel, Chris *Sportscaster*
7101 N Kalorama Road, Leesburg, IN 46538, USA
Schenkenberg, Markus *Model, Actor*
%Wilhelmina Models, 300 Park Ave S, #200, New York, NY 10010, USA
Schenkkan, Robert F *Writer*
%Dramatist Guild, 1501 Broadway, #701, New York, NY 10036, USA
Schenkman, Eric *Musician (Spin Doctors)*
%DAS Communications, 84 Riverside Dr, New York, NY 10024, USA
Schepisi, Frederic A *Movie Director*
%Film House, 159 Eastern Road, South Melbourne, VIC 3205, Australia
Scheraga, Harold A *Chemist*
212 Homestead Terrace, Ithaca, NY 14850, USA
Scherbo, Vitali *Gymnast*
8308 Aqua Spray Ave, Las Vegas, NV 89128, USA
Scherrer, Jean-Louis *Fashion Designer*
51 Ave du Montaigne, 75008 Paris, France
Scherrer, Tom *Golfer*
%Gaylord Sports Mgmt, 14646 N Kierland Blvd, #230, Scottsdale, AZ 85254, USA
Scheuer, Paul J *Chemist*
3271 Melemele Place, Honolulu, HI 96822, USA
Schevill, James *Writer*
1309 Oxford St, Berkeley, CA 94709, USA
Schiavelli, Vincent *Actor*
450 N Rossmore Ave, #206, Los Angeles, CA 90004, USA
Schiavo, Mary *Government Official, Social Activist*
%Ohio State University, Public Policy Dept, Columbus, OH 43210, USA
Schickel, Richard *Writer, Movie Critic*
9051 Dicks St, Los Angeles, CA 90069, USA
Schickele, Peter *Composer, Comedian*
%International Creative Mgmt, 40 W 57th St, #1800, New York, NY 10019, USA
Schiebold, Hans *Artist*
13705 SW 118th Court, Tigard, OR 97223, USA
Schieffer, Bob *Commentator*
%CBS-TV, News Dept, 51 W 52nd St, New York, NY 10019, USA
Schiff, Andras *Concert Pianist*
%Shirley Kirshbaum, 711 W End Ave, #5KN, New York, NY 10025, USA
Schiff, Heinrich *Concert Cellist, Conductor*
%Astrid Schoerke, Monckegergallee 41, 30453 Hannover, Germany
Schiff, John J, Jr *Financier*
%Cincinnati Financial Corp, 6200 S Gilmore Road, Fairfield, OH 45014, USA
Schiff, Mark *Actor, Comedian*
%Gail Stocker Presents, 1025 N Kings Road, #113, Los Angeles, CA 90069, USA
Schiff, Richard *Actor*
537 N June St, Los Angeles, CA 90004, USA
Schiffer, Claudia *Model*
Aussenwall 94, 47495 Rheinberg, Germany
Schiffer, Menahem M *Mathematician*
6404 Ruffin Road, Chevy Chase, MD 20815, USA
Schiffman, Michael *Actor*
%Harvest Mgmt, 132 W 80th St, #3F, New York, NY 10024, USA
Schiffrin, Andre *Publisher*
%New Press, 201 E 50th St, New York, NY 10022, USA
Schifrin, Lalo *Composer*
710 N Hillcrest Road, Beverly Hills, CA 90210, USA
Schillebeeckx, Edward *Theologian*
%Crossroad Publishing Co, 575 Lexington Ave, New York, NY 10022, USA
Schiller, Harvey W *Sports Executive*
%Turner Sports, 1050 Techwood Dr NW, Atlanta, GA 30318, USA
Schiller, Lawrence J *Television Director, Writer*
5430 Oakdale Ave, Woodland Hills, CA 91364, USA
Schilling, Curtis M (Curt) *Baseball Player*
105 Blackshire Road, Kennet Square, PA 19348, USA
Schimberg, Henry R *Businessman*
%Coca-Cola Enterprises, 2500 Windy Ridge Parkway, Atlanta, GA 30339, USA

S

Schimberni - Schmidt

Schimberni, Mario *Businessman*
%Armando Curcio Editore SpA, Via IV Novembre, 00187 Rome, Italy
Schimmel, Paul R *Biochemist*
%Scripps Research Institute, 10550 N Torrey Pines Road, La Jolla, CA 92037, USA
Schindelholz, Lorenz *Bobsled Athlete*
Hardstr 184, 4715 Herbetswil, Switzerland
Schinkel, Kenneth (Ken) *Hockey Player*
19927 Beaulieu Court, Fort Myers, FL 33908, USA
Schipper, Ron *Football Coach*
2406 Orchard Ave, Holland, MI 49424, USA
Schirra, Walter M, Jr *Astronaut*
PO Box 73, 16834 Via de Santa Fe, Rancho Santa Fe, CA 92067, USA
Schisgal, Murray J *Writer*
%International Creative Mgmt, 40 W 57th St, #1800, New York, NY 10019, USA
Schissler, Les *Bowler*
3060 E Bridge St, #20, Brighton, CO 80601, USA
Schlafly, Phyllis S *Women's Activist*
68 Fairmount Ave, Alton, IL 62002, USA
Schlag, Edward W *Chemist*
Osterwaldstr 91, 80805 Munich, Germany
Schlatter, Charlie *Actor*
638 Lindero Canyon Road, #322, Oak Park, CA 91377, USA
Schleeh, Russ *Test Pilot*
21634 Paseo Maravia, Mission Viejo, CA 92692, USA
Schlegel, Hans W *Astronaut, Germany*
DLR Astronautenburo, Linder Hohe, Postfach 906058, 51140 Cologne, Germany
Schlegel, John P *Educator*
%University of San Francisco, President's Office, San Francisco, CA 94117, USA
Schlein, Dov C *Financier*
%Republic New York Corp, 452 5th Ave, New York, NY 10018, USA
Schlesinger, Adam *Singer (Fountains of Wayne), Songwriter*
%MOB Agency, 6404 Wilshire Blvd, #505, Los Angeles, CA 90048, USA
Schlesinger, Arthur M, Jr *Historian*
455 E 51st St, New York, NY 10022, USA
Schlesinger, James R *Secretary, Defense & Energy*
%Georgetown University, 1800 K St NW, #400, Washington, DC 20006, USA
Schlessinger, Laura *Radio Psychologist, Physiologist*
25065 Ashley Ridge Road, Hidden Hills, CA 91302, USA
Schleyer, Paul Von R *Chemist*
%Friedrich-Alexander-Universitat, Henkestr 41, 91469 Erlangen, Germany
Schlichtmann, Jan *Attorney*
359 Hale St, Beverly Farms, MA 01915, USA
Schlondorff, Volker O *Movie Director*
%Studio Babelsberg, Postfach 900361, 14439 Potsdam, Germany
Schloredt, Robert S (Bob) *Football Player*
%Nestle-Beich, 1827 N 167th St, Shoreline, WA 98133, USA
Schlossberg, Katie *Actress*
%Talent Group, 6300 Wilshire Blvd, #2100, Los Angeles, CA 90048, USA
Schlueter, Dale *Basketball Player*
15555 SW Harcourt Terrace, Portland, OR 97224, USA
Schluter, Poul H *Prime Minister, Denmark*
Frederiksberg Allee 66, 1820 Frederiksberg C, Denmark
Schmeichel, Peter *Soccer Player*
%Aston Villa, Villa Park, Trinity Road, Brimingham B6 6HE, England
Schmeling, Maximilian (Max) *Boxer*
Sonnenweg 1, 21279 Hollenstedt, Germany
Schmemann, Serge *Journalist*
%New York Times, Editorial Dept, 229 W 43rd St, New York, NY 10036, USA
Schmid, Harald *Track Athlete*
Schulstr 11, 63594 Hasselroth, Germany
Schmid, Rudi *Internist*
211 Woodland Road, Kentfield, CA 94904, USA
Schmid, Sigi *Soccer Coach*
%Los Angeles Galaxy, 1010 Rose Bowl Dr, Pasadena, CA 91103, USA
Schmidgall, Jennifer *Hockey Player*
3850 Xenium Court N, Minneapolis, MN 55441, USA
Schmidly, David J *Educator*
%Texas Tech University, President's Office, Lubbock, TX 79409, USA
Schmidt, Andreas *Opera Singer*
Fossredder 51, 22359 Hamburg, Germany
Schmidt, Benno C, Jr *Educator*
%Edison Project, 375 Park Ave, New York, NY 10152, USA
Schmidt, Eric E *Businessman, Computer Engineer*
%Google Inc, 2400 Bayshore Parkway, Mountain View, CA 94043, USA
Schmidt, Helmut *Chancellor, West Germany*
Neuberger Weg 80, 22419 Hamburg, Germany
Schmidt, Jason D *Baseball Player*
35 View Ridge Circle, Longview, WA 98632, USA

Schmidt, Joseph P (Joe) *Football Player*
226 Norcliff Dr, Bloomfield Hills, MI 48302, USA
Schmidt, Kathryn (Kate) *Track Athlete*
1008 Dexter St, Los Angeles, CA 90042, USA
Schmidt, Maarten *Astronomer*
%California Institute of Technology, Astronomy Dept, Pasadena, CA 91125, USA
Schmidt, Michael J (Mike) *Baseball Player*
373 Eagle Dr, Jupiter, FL 33477, USA
Schmidt, Milton C (Milt) *Hockey Player*
10 Longwood Dr, #376, Westwood, MA 02090, USA
Schmidt, Ole *Conductor, Composer*
Puggaardsgade 17, 1573 Copenhagen, Denmark
Schmidt, Richard *Surgeon*
%University of Pennsylvania Hospital, 3400 Spruce St, Philadelphia, PA 19104, USA
Schmidt, William (Bill) *Track Athlete*
1809 Devonwood Court, Knoxville, TN 37922, USA
Schmidt, Wolfgang *Track Athlete*
Birkheckenstr 116B, 70599 Stuttgart, Germany
Schmidt, Wolfgang *Opera Singer*
%Kunstleragentur Raab & Bohm, Plankengasse 7, 1010 Vienna, Austria
Schmidt-Nielsen, Knut *Physiologist*
%Duke University, Zoology Dept, Durham, NC 27706, USA
Schmidtmer, Christiane *Model, Actress*
Postfach 120617, 69067 Heidelberg, Germany
Schmiege, Marilyn *Opera Singer*
%Opera et Concert, Maximilianstr 22, 80539 Munich, Germany
Schmiegel, Klaus K *Inventor (Prozac)*
4507 Stoughton Dr, Indianapolis, IN 46226, USA
Schmit, Timothy B *Singer, Bassist (Eagles)*
%William Morris Agency, 1325 Ave of Americas, New York, NY 10019, USA
Schmitt, Harrison H (Jack) *Senator, NM; Astronaut*
PO Box 90730, Albuquerque, NM 87199, USA
Schmitt, Martin *Ski Jumper*
Muhleschweg 4, 78052 VA-Tannehim, Germany
Schmitz, John A (Johnny) *Baseball Player*
526 W Union Ave, Wausau, WI 54401, USA
Schmoeller, David *Movie Director*
3910 Woodhill Ave, Las Vegas, NV 89121, USA
Schnabel, Julian *Artist, Movie Director*
%Pace Gallery, 32 E 57th St, New York 10022, USA
Schnackenberg, Roy L *Artist*
1919 N Orchard St, Chicago, IL 60614, USA
Schnarre, Monika *Model, Actress*
%Alex Stevens, 137 N Larchmont, #259, Los Angeles, CA 90004, USA
Schnebli, Dolf *Architect*
Sudstr 45, 8008 Zurich, Switzerland
Schneer, Charles *Movie Producer*
8 Ilchester Place, London W14 8AA, England
Schneider, Andrew *Journalist*
%Pittsburgh Press, Editorial Dept, 34 Blvd of Allies, Pittsburgh, PA 15230, USA
Schneider, Bernd *Auto Racing*
%Team AMG Mercedes, Daimlerstr 1, 71563 Affalterbach, Germany
Schneider, Fred *Singer, Songwriter (B-52s)*
%Direct Management Group, 947 N La Cienega Blvd, #2, Los Angeles, CA 90069, USA
Schneider, Howie *Cartoonist (Eek & Meek)*
%United Feature Syndicate, 200 Madison Ave, New York, NY 10016, USA
Schneider, John *Actor, Singer*
30169 Alexander Dr, Cathedral Cty, CA 92234, USA
Schneider, Mathieu *Hockey Player*
1311 6th St, Manhattan Beach, CA 90266, USA
Schneider, Rob *Actor, Comedian*
%Borinstein Oreck Bogart, 3172 Dona Susana Dr, Studio City, CA 91604, USA
Schneider, Vreni *Alpine Skier*
Dorf, 8767 Elm, Switzerland
Schneider, William (Buzz) *Hockey Player*
5656 Turtle Lake Road, Shoreview, MN 55126, USA
Schneider, William G *Physical Chemist*
%National Research Council, 65 Whitemarl Dr, #2, Ottawa ON K1L 8J9, Canada
Schneiderman, David A *Publisher, Editor*
%Village Voice, President's Office, 36 Cooper Square, New York, NY 10003, USA
Schnellbacher, Otto O *Football, Basketball Player*
2010 SW Bowman Court, Topeka, KS 66604, USA
Schnelldorfer, Manfred *Figure Skater*
Seydlitzstr 55, 80993 Munich, Germany
Schnellenberger, Howard *Football Coach*
5109 N Ocean Blvd, #G, Ocean Ridge, FL 33435, USA
Schnittker, Richard (Dick) *Basketball Player*
2303 E Las Granadas, Green Valley, AZ 85614, USA

S

Schochet - Schowalter

Schochet, Bob *Cartoonist*
6 Sunset Road, Highland Mills, NY 10930, USA
Schock, Gina *Singer, Drummer (Go-Go's)*
PO Box 4398, North Hollywood, CA 91617, USA
Schockemohle, Alwin *Equestrian Rider*
Munsterlandstr 51, 49439 Muhlen, Germany
Schoelen, Jill *Actress*
%Gold Marshak Liedtke, 3500 W Olive Ave, #1400, Burbank, CA 91505, USA
Schoen, Max H *Dentist*
5818 S Sherbourne Dr, Los Angeles, CA 90056, USA
Schoenbaechler, Andreas *Freestyle Aerials Skier*
Muhlrutistr 2, 8910 Affoltern a A, Switzerland
Schoenborn, Christoph Cardinal *Religious Leader*
Wollzeile 2, 1010 Vienna, Austria
Schoenfeld, Gerald *Theater Producer*
%Shubert Organization Inc, 225 W 44th St, New York, NY 10036, USA
Schoenfeld, Jim *Hockey Player, Coach*
11745 E Cortez Dr, Scottsdale, AZ 85259, USA
Schoenfield, Al *Swimming Executive*
2731 Pecho Road, Los Osos, CA 93402, USA
Schoenfield, Dana *Swimmer*
7734 Lakeview Trail, Orange, CA 92869, USA
Schoffer, Nicolas *Sculptor*
Villa Des Arts, 15 Rue Hegesippe-Moreau, 75018 Paris, France
Schofield, Annabel *Actress*
%Special Artists Agency, 345 N Maple Dr, #302, Beverly Hills, CA 90210, USA
Scholder, Fritz *Artist*
118 Cattletrack Road, Scottsdale, AZ 85251, USA
Scholes, Clarke *Swimmer*
1360 Somerset Ave, Grosse Pointe Woods, MI 48230, USA
Scholes, Myron S *Nobel Economics Laureate*
%Stanford University, Graduate Business School, Stanford, CA 94305, USA
Schollander, Donald A (Don) *Swimmer*
3576 Lakeview Blvd, Lake Oswego, OR 97035, USA
Scholten, Jim *Singer, Bassist (Sawyer Brown)*
%Sawyer Brown Inc, 5200 Old Harding Road, Franklin, TN 37064, USA
Scholz, Rupert *Government Official, Germany*
Postfach 1328, 5300 Bonn 1, Germany
Scholz, Tom *Guitarist (Boston)*
%Agency for Performing Arts, 9200 Sunset Blvd, #900, Los Angeles, CA 90069, USA
Schomberg, A Thomas *Sculptor*
4923 S Snowberry Lane, Evergreen, CO 80439, USA
Schon, Jan Hendrik *Inventor (Molecule Transistor)*
%Lucent Technology Bell Laboratory, 600 Mountain Ave, New Providence, NJ 07974, USA
Schon, Kyra *Actress*
930 N Sheridan Ave, Pittsburgh, PA 15206, USA
Schon, Neal *Guitarist (Journey)*
%Artists & Audience Entertainment, PO Box 35, Pawling, NY 12564, USA
Schonberg, Claude-Michel *Composer*
%Stephen Tenenbaum, 605 3rd Ave, New York, NY 10158, USA
Schonhuber, Franz *Commentator*
%Europaburo, Fraunhoferstr 23, 80469 Munich, Germany
Schoofs, Mark *Journalist*
%Village Voice, Editorial Dept, 32 Cooper Square, New York, NY 10003, USA
Schoolnik, Gary *Microbiologist*
%Stanford University, Medical School, Microbiology Dept, Stanford, CA 94305, USA
Schools, Dave *Bassist (Widespread Panic)*
%Brown Cat Inc, 400 Foundry St, Athens, GA 30601, USA
Schoomaker, Peter J (Pete) *Army General*
Chief of Staff, HqUSA, Pentagon, Washington, DC 20310, USA
Schopf, J William *Paleobiologist*
%University of California, Study of Evolution Center, Los Angeles, CA 90024, USA
Schorer, Jane *Journalist*
%Des Moines Register, Editorial Dept, PO Box 957, Des Moines, IA 50304, USA
Schorr, Bill *Cartoonist (Phoebe's Place)*
%United Feature Syndicate, 200 Madison Ave, New York, NY 10016, USA
Schorr, Daniel L *Journalist, Writer*
3113 Woodley Road, Washington, DC 20008, USA
Schorske, Carl E *Historian, Writer*
106 Winant Road, Princeton, NJ 08540, USA
Schotte, Jan P Cardinal *Religious Leader*
Sinodo dei Vescovi, 00120 Vatican City
Schottenheimer, Martin E (Marty) *Football Coach, Sportscaster*
%San Diego Chargers, 4020 Murphy Canyon Road, San Diego, CA 92123, USA
Schou, Mogens *Psychiatrist*
%Aarhus University, Institute of Psychiatry, Aarhus, Denmark
Schowalter, Edward R, Jr *Korean War Army Hero (CMH)*
913 Bibb Ave, #312, Auburn, AL 36830, USA

Schrader, Ken *Auto, Truck Racing Driver*
PO Box 325, East Flat Rock, NC 28726, USA
Schrader, Paul J *Movie Director, Writer*
9696 Culver Blvd, #203, Culver City, CA 90232, USA
Schramm, David *Actor*
3521 Berry Dr, Studio City, CA 91604, USA
Schranz, Karl *Alpine Skier*
Hotel Garni, 6580 Saint Anton, Austria
Schreiber, Liev *Actor*
%William Morris Agency, 151 El Camino Dr, Beverly Hills, CA 90212, USA
Schreiber, Martin J *Governor, WI*
2700 S Shore Dr, #B, Milwaukee, WI 53207, USA
Schreier, Peter *Opera Singer, Conductor*
Calberlastr 13, 01326 Dresden, Germany
Schrempf, Detlef *Basketball Player*
4025 94th Ave NE, Bellevue, WA 98004, USA
Schrempp, Jurgen E *Businessman*
%Daimler-Chrysler AG, Plieningerstra, 70546 Stuttgart, Germany
Schreyer, Edward R *Governor General, Canada*
250 Wellington Crescent, #401, Winnipeg MB R3M 0B3, Canada
Schrieffer, John R *Nobel Physics Laureate*
%Florida State University, 1800 E Paul Dirac Dr, Tallahassee, FL 32310, USA
Schrier, Eric W *Editor*
%Reader's Digest, Editorial Dept, PO Box 100, Pleasantville, NY 10572, USA
Schriesheim, Alan *Applied Chemist*
1440 N Lake Shore Dr, #31AC, Chicago, IL 60610, USA
Schriever, Bernard A *Air Force General*
2300 M St NW, #900, Washington, DC 20037, USA
Schrimshaw, Nevin S *Nutritionist*
Sandwich Notch Farm, Thornton, NH 03223, USA
Schrock, Richard R *Chemist*
%Massachusetts Institute of Technology, Chemistry Dept, Cambridge, MA 02139, USA
Schroder, Ernst A *Actor*
Podere Montalto, Castellina In Chianti, 53011 Siena, Italy
Schroder, Rick *Actor*
%International Creative Mgmt, 8942 Wilshire Blvd, #219, Beverly Hills, CA 90211, USA
Schroeder, Barbet G *Movie Director, Producer*
8033 W Sunset Blvd, #51, West Hollywood, CA 90046, USA
Schroeder, Frederick R (Ted), Jr *Tennis Player*
1010 W Muirlands Dr, La Jolla, CA 92037, USA
Schroeder, Gerhard *Chancellor, Germany*
%Bundeskanzlerant, Willy-Brandt-Str 1, 10557 Berlin, Germany
Schroeder, Jim *Bowler*
3 Greenhaven Terrace, Tonawanda, NY 14150, USA
Schroeder, John H *Educator*
%University of Wisconsin, Chancellor's Office, Milwaukee, WI 53211, USA
Schroeder, Kenneth L *Businessman*
%KLA-Tencor Corp, 160 Rio Robles, San Jose, CA 95134, USA
Schroeder, Manfred R *Physicist*
Rieswartenweg 8, 37073 Gottingen, Germany
Schroeder, Mary M *Judge*
%US Court of Appeals, 230 N 1st Ave, Phoenix, AZ 85025, USA
Schroeder, Patricia S *Representative, CO*
%William Morris Agency, 151 El Camino Dr, Beverly Hills, CA 90212, USA
Schroeder, Paul W *Writer*
%University of Illinois, History Dept, 810 S Wright St, Urbana, IL 61801, USA
Schroeder, Steven A *Foundation Executive, Physician*
10 Paseo Mirasol, Bel Tiburon, CA 94920, USA
Schroeder, Terry *Water Polo Player, Coach*
4901 Lewis Road, Agoura Hills, CA 91301, USA
Schrom, Kenneth M (Ken) *Baseball Player*
4733 Rosinante Road, El Paso, TX 79922, USA
Schruefer, John J *Physician*
%Georgetown University Hospital, Ob-Gyn Dept, Washington, DC 20007, USA
Schuba, Beatrice (Trixi) *Figure Skater*
Giorgengasse 2/1/8, Vienna 1190, Austria
Schubert, Mark *Swimming Coach*
PO Box 479, Surfside, CA 90743, USA
Schubert, Richard F *Association Executive*
6615 Madison McLean Dr, McLean, VA 22101, USA
Schuck, Anett *Canoeing Athlete*
Defoestry 6A, 04159 Leipzig, Germany
Schuck, John *Actor*
1501 Broadway, #703, New York, NY 10036, USA
Schueler, Jon R *Artist*
40 W 22nd St, New York, NY 10010, USA
Schuenke, Donald J *Businessman*
%Nortel Networks Corp, 8200 Dixie Road, Brampton ON L6T 5P6, Canada

S

Schuessel - Schussler Fiorenza

Schuessel, Wolfgang *Chancellor, Austria*
%Chancellor's Office, Ballhausplatz 2, 1014, Vienna, Austria
Schuessler, Jack *Businesssman*
%Wendy's International, 4288 W Dublin-Granville Road, Dublin, OH 43017, USA
Schuh, Harry F *Football Player*
2309 Massey Road, Memphis, TN 38119, USA
Schul, Robert (Bob) *Track Athlete*
320 Wisteria Dr, Dayton, OH 45419, USA
Schulberg, Budd *Writer*
Brookside, PO Box 707, Westhampton Beach, NY 11978, USA
Schuler, Carolyn *Swimmer*
26552 Via del Sol, Mission Viejo, CA 92691, USA
Schulhofer, Scotty *Thoroughbred Racing Trainer*
PO Box 1581, Waynesville, NC 28786, USA
Schull, Rebecca *Actress*
%Writers & Artists, 8383 Wilshire Blvd, #550, Beverly Hills, CA 90211, USA
Schuller, Grete *Sculptor*
8 Barstow Road, #7G, Great Neck, NY 11021, USA
Schuller, Gunther *Composer, Conductor*
%Margun Music, 167 Dudley Road, Newton Center, MA 02459, USA
Schuller, Robert H *Evangelist*
%Crystal Cathedral Ministries, 12141 Lewis St, Garden Grove, CA 92840, USA
Schult, Jurgen *Track Athlete*
Drosselweg 6, 19069 Leuna, Germany
Schultz, Axel *Boxer*
%Axel Schulz Mgmt, Kloetzrstr 15, 01587 Riesa, Germany
Schultz, Dave *Hockey Player*
329 Oxford Place, Macungie, PA 18062, USA
Schultz, Dave *Auto Racing Driver*
2365 Lazy River Lane, Fort Myers, FL 33905, USA
Schultz, Dean *Financier*
%Federal Home Loan Bank, 1079 Hutchinson Road, Walnut Creek, CA 94598, USA
Schultz, Dwight *Actor*
%Borinstein Oreck Bogart, 3172 Dona Susana Dr, Studio City, CA 91604, USA
Schultz, Frederick H *%Government Official*
PO Box 1200, Jacksonville, FL 32201, USA
Schultz, Howard *Businessman*
%Starbucks Corp, 2401 Utah Ave S, Seattle, WA 98134, USA
Schultz, Howard H (Howie) *Basketball, Baseball Player*
1333 McKusick Road Lane W, Stillwater, MN 55082, USA
Schultz, Michael A *Movie Director*
%Chrystalite Productions, PO Box 1940, Santa Monica, CA 90406, USA
Schultz, Peter C *Inventor (Silica Optical Waveguide)*
%Heraeus Amersil Inc, 3473 Satellite Blvd, #300, Duluth, GA 30096, USA
Schultz, Peter G *Chemist*
%Salk Research Institute, 10550 N Torrey Pine Road, La Jolla, CA 92037, USA
Schultz, Richard D *Association Executive*
%US Olympic Committee, 1 Olympia Plaza, Colorado Springs, CO 80909, USA
Schultze, Charles L *Government Official*
%Brookings Institute, 1775 Massachusetts Ave NW, Washington, DC 20036, USA
Schulz, William *Editor*
%Reader's Digest, Editorial Dept, PO Box 100, Pleasantville, NY 10572, USA
Schulze, Matt *Actor*
%Gersh Agency, 232 N Canon Dr, Beverly Hills, CA 90210, USA
Schulze, Richard M *Businessman*
%Best Buy Co, 7601 Penn Ave S, Minneapolis, MN 55423, USA
Schumacher, Joel *Movie Director*
%Greenfield & Selvaggi, 11766 Wilshire Blvd, #1610, Los Angeles, CA 90025, USA
Schumacher, Kelly *Basketball Player*
%Indiana Fever, Conseco Fieldhouse, 125 S Pennsylvania, Indianapolis, IN 46204, USA
Schumacher, Michael *Auto Racing Driver*
Via Ascari 55-57, 40153 Maranello, Italy
Schumacher, Ralf *Auto Racing Driver*
%Weber Mgmt, Transkestr 11, 70597 Stuttgart, Germany
Schuman, Allan L *Businessman*
%Ecolab Inc, Ecolab Center, 370 Wabasha St N, Saint Paul, MN 55102, USA
Schuman, Tom *Keyboardist (Spyro Gyro)*
%Crosseyed Bear Productions, 926 Haverstraw Road, Suffern, NY 10901, USA
Schumann, Jochen *Yachtsman*
Birkenstr 88, 48336 Penzberg, Germany
Schumann, Ralf *Marksman*
Steomach 22, 97640 Stockheim, Germany
Schurmann, Petra *Swimmer*
Max-Emanuel-Str 7, 82319 Starnberg, Germany
Schurr, Harry W *Vietnam War Air Force Hero*
1178 Davis Dr, Fairborn, OH 45324, USA
Schussler Fiorenza, Elisabeth *Writer, Theologian*
%Notre Dame University, Theology Dept, Notre Dame, IN 46556, USA

Schuster, Rudolf *President, Slovakia*
%President's Office, Nam Slobody 1, 91370 Bratislava, Slovakia
Schutz, Klaus *Mayor, Berlin; Government Official*
9 Konstanzerstr, 10707 Berlin, Germany
Schutz, Stephen *Graphic Artist*
%Blue Mountain Arts Inc, PO Box 4549, Boulder, CO 80306, USA
Schutz, Susan Polis *Writer*
%Blue Mountain Arts Inc, PO Box 4549, Boulder, CO 80306, USA
Schutze, Jim *Writer, Journalist*
%Avon Books, 1350 Ave of Americas, New York, NY 10019, USA
Schuur, Diane *Singer*
%Paul Canter Enterprises, 33042 Ocean Ridge, Dana Point, CA 92629, USA
Schwab, Charles R *Financier*
%Charles Schwab Co, 101 Montgomery St, San Francisco, CA 94104, USA
Schwab, John J *Psychiatrist*
6217 Innes Trace Road, Louisville, KY 40222, USA
Schwarthoff, Florian *Track Athlete*
Fischweiher 51, 64646 Heppenheim, Germany
Schwartsman, John *Cinematographer*
%Mirisch Agency, 1801 Century Park E, #1801, Los Angeles, CA 90067, USA
Schwartz, Jacob T *Computer Scientist*
%New York University, Courant Math Sciences Institute, New York, NY 10012, USA
Schwartz, Lloyd *Journalist*
27 Pennsylvania Ave, Somerville, MA 02145, USA
Schwartz, Maxime *Medical Administrator*
%Institut Pasteur, 25-28 Rue du Docteur-Roux, 75724 Paris Cedex 15, France
Schwartz, Melvin *Nobel Physics Laureate*
PO Box 5068, Ketchum, ID 83340, USA
Schwartz, Neil J *Actor*
3044 Pearl Harbor Dr, Las Vegas, NV 89117, USA
Schwartz, Norton A *Air Force General*
Commander, 11th Air Force, Elmendorf Air Force Base, AK 99506, USA
Schwartz, Stephen L *Composer, Lyricist, Singer*
%Chaplin Entertainment, 545 8th Ave, #14, New York, NY 10018, USA
Schwartz, Thomas A *Army General*
Commander, United Nations Command/US Forces Korea, APO, AP 96205, USA
Schwartz, Tony *Communications Specialist*
455 W 56th St, New York, NY 10019, USA
Schwarz, Gerard R *Conductor*
%New York Chamber Symphony, 1395 Lexington Ave, New York, NY 10128, USA
Schwarz, Hanna *Opera Singer*
%Opera et Concert, Maximilianstr 22, 80539 Munich, Germany
Schwarz, John H *Physicist*
%California Institute of Technology, Physics Dept, Pasadena, CA 91125, USA
Schwarz-Schilling, Christian *Government Official, Germany*
%Post-Telecomm Ministry, Heinrich-von-Stephanstr 1, 53175 Bonn, Germany
Schwarzbein, Diana *Physician, Writer*
%Health Communications, 3201 SW 15th St, Deerfield Beach, FL 33442, USA
Schwarzenegger, Arnold A *Body Builder, Actor; Governor, CA*
14209 W Sunset Blvd, Pacific Palisades, CA 90272, USA
Schwarzkopf, H Norman *Army General*
%Black Summit, 400 N Ashley Dr, #3050, Tampa, FL 33602, USA
Schwebel, Stephen M *Judge*
PO Box 356, Woodstock, VT 05091, USA
Schweickart, Russell L *Astronaut*
PO Box 381, Sea Ranch, CA 95497, USA
Schweig, Eric *Actor*
%Prime Talent, PO Box 5163, Vancouver BC V6B 1M4, Canada
Schweiger, Til *Actor*
%Agentur Players, Sophienstr 21, 10178 Berlin, Germany
Schweiker, Richard S *Secretary, Health & Human Services*
8890 Windy Ridge Way, McLean, VA 22102, USA
Schweikert, J E *Religious Leader*
%Old Roman Catholic Church, 4200 N Kedvale Ave, Chicago, IL 60641, USA
Schweikher, Paul *Architect*
3222 E Missouri Ave, Phoenix, AZ 85018, USA
Schwertsik, Kurt *Composer*
%Doblinger Music, Dorotheerhgasse 10, 1011 Vienna, Austria
Schwery, Henri Cardinal *Religious Leader*
%Bishoporic of Sion, CP 2068, 1950 Sion 2, Switzerland
Schwimmer, David *Actor*
%Talent Entertainment Group, 9111 Wilshire Blvd, Beverly Hills, CA 90210, USA
Schwinden, Ted *Governor, MT*
401 N Fee St, Helena, MT 59601, USA
Schwitters, Roy F *Physicist*
1718 Cromwell Hill, Austin, TX 78703, USA
Schygulla, Hanna *Actress*
%ZBF Agentur, Leopoldstr 19, 80802 Munich, Germany

S

Scialfa - Scott

Scialfa, Patty *Singer (E Street Band)*
1224 Benedict Canyon, Beverly Hills, CA 90210, USA
Sciarra, John M *Football Player*
4420 Woodleigh Lane, La Canada Flintridge, CA 91011, USA
Sciorra, Anabella *Actress*
%Writers & Artists, 8383 Wilshire Blvd, #550, Beverly Hills, CA 90211, USA
Scioscia, Michael L (Mike) *Baseball Player, Manager*
1915 Falling Star Ave, Westlake Village, CA 91362, USA
Scirica, Anthony J *Judge*
%US Court of Appeals, US Courthouse, 601 Market St, Philadelphia, PA 19106, USA
Scofield, Dino *Actor*
3330 Barham Blvd, #103, Los Angeles, CA 90068, USA
Scofield, John *Jazz Electric Guitarist*
%Ted Kurland, 173 Brighton Ave, Boston, MA 02134, USA
Scofield, Paul *Actor*
Gables, Balcombe, Sussex RH17 6ND, England
Scofield, Richard M (Dick) *Air Force General*
3661 Grandview Circle, Shingle Springs, CA 95682, USA
Scoggins, Matt *Swimmer*
4900 Calhoun Canyon Loop, Austin, TX 78735, USA
Scoggins, Tracy *Actress*
%Jorgensen & Rogers, 10100 Santa Monica Blvd, #410, Los Angeles, CA 90067, USA
Scogin, Mack *Architect*
%Scogin Elam Bray, 1819 Peachtree Road NE, #700, Atlanta, GA 30309, USA
Scola, Angelo Cardinal *Religious Leader*
%Archdiocese, S Marco 320/A, 30124 Venezia, Italy
Scola, Ettore *Movie Director*
Via Bertoloni 1/E, 00197 Rome, Italy
Scolari, Peter *Actor*
%Artists Agency, 1180 S Beverly Dr, #301, Los Angeles, CA 90035, USA
Scolnick, Edward M *Geneticist, Virologist*
811 Wickfield Road, Wynnewood, PA 19096, USA
Score, Herbert J (Herb) *Baseball Player, Sportscaster*
12700 Lake Ave, Lakewood, OH 44107, USA
Scorpio *Rap Artist*
%Famous Artists Agency, 250 W 57th St, New York, NY 10107, USA
Scorsese, Martin *Movie Director*
445 Park Ave, #700, New York, NY 10022, USA
Scorupco, Izabella *Actress, Singer, Model*
Vuorimiehenkatu 20, 00150 Helsinki, Finland
Scott Brown, Denise *Architect*
%Venturi Scott Brown Assoc, 4236 Main St, Philadelphia, PA 19127, USA
Scott Thomas, Kristin *Actress*
%P M K Public Relations, 8500 Wilshire Blvd, #700, Beverly Hills, CA 90211, USA
Scott, Adam *Actor*
%Metropolitan Talent Agency, 4526 Wilshire Blvd, Los Angeles, CA 90010, USA
Scott, Andy *Guitarist (Sweet)*
%DCM International, 296 Nether St, Finchley, London N3 1RJ, England
Scott, Byron *Basketball Player, Coach*
405 Murray Hill Parkway, East Rutherford, NJ 07073, USA
Scott, Campbell *Actor*
3211 Retreat Court, Malibu, CA 90265, USA
Scott, Charles (Charlie) *Basketball Player*
300 Chastain Manor Dr, Norcross, GA 30071, USA
Scott, Clarence *Football Player*
216 Sisson Ave NE, Atlanta, GA 30317, USA
Scott, Clyde L (Smackover) *Football Player, Track Athlete*
12840 Rivercrest Dr, Little Rock, AR 72212, USA
Scott, David R *Astronaut*
%Merces, VC Johnson, 30 Hackamore Lane, #1, Bell Canyon, CA 91307, USA
Scott, Deborah L *Costume Designer*
%Gersh Agency, 232 N Canon Dr, Beverly Hills, CA 90210, USA
Scott, Debralee *Actress*
1180 S Beverly Dr, #608, Beverly Hills, CA 90212, USA
Scott, Dennis *Basketball Player*
5425 Palm Lake Circle, Orlando, FL 32819, USA
Scott, Donovan *Actor*
%Talent Group, 6300 Wilshire Blvd, #2100, Los Angeles, CA 90048, USA
Scott, Dougray *Actor*
%P F D, Drury House, 34-43 Russell St, London WC2B 5HA, England
Scott, Freddie *Singer*
%Headline Talent, 1650 Broadway, #508, New York, NY 10019, USA
Scott, Freddie L *Football Player*
29209 Northwestern Highway, #694, Southfield, MI 48034, USA
Scott, George *Baseball Player*
1216 Fair Park Blvd, Harlingen, TX 78550, USA
Scott, Gloria Dean Randle *Educator*
%Bennett College, President's Office, Greensboro, NC 27401, USA

Scott, Gordon *Actor*
116 Santa Monica Blvd, Santa Monica, CA 90401, USA
Scott, H Lee, Jr *Businessman*
%Wal-Mart Stores, 702 SW 8th St, Bentonville, AR 72712, USA
Scott, Irene F *Judge*
%US Tax Court, 400 2nd St NW, Washington, DC 20217, USA
Scott, Jack *Singer, Songwriter*
34039 Coachwood Dr, Sterling Heights, MI 48312, USA
Scott, Jacob E (Jake), Jr *Football Player*
PO Box 857, Hanalei, HI 96714, USA
Scott, Jacqueline *Actress*
%Lichtman/Salners, 12216 Moorpark St, Studio City, CA 91604, USA
Scott, Jane *Jazz Critic*
%Cleveland Plain Dealer, 1801 Superior Ave, Cleveland, OH 44114, USA
Scott, Jean Bruce *Actress*
144 N Westerly Dr, Los Angeles, CA 90048, USA
Scott, Jerry *Cartoonist (Baby Blues)*
%Creators Syndicate, 5777 W Century Blvd, #700, Los Angeles, CA 90045, USA
Scott, Jill *Singer, Songwriter*
%Rhythm Jazz Entertainment, 4465 Don Milagro Dr, Los Angeles, CA 90008, USA
Scott, Jimmy *Singer*
%J's Way Jazz, 175 Prospect St, #20D, East Orange, NJ 07017, USA
Scott, Josey *Singer (Saliva)*
%Helter Skelter, Plaza, 535 Kings Road, London SW10 0S, England
Scott, Kathryn Leigh *Actress*
3236 Bennett Dr, Los Angeles, CA 90068, USA
Scott, Klea *Actress*
%Talent Entertainment Group, 9111 Wilshire Blvd, Beverly Hills, CA 90210, USA
Scott, Larry *Body Builder*
PO Box 162, Bountiful, UT 84011, USA
Scott, Lary R *Businessman*
%Carolina Freight Corp, PO Box 1000, Cherryville, NC 28021, USA
Scott, Lizabeth *Actress*
8277 Hollywood Blvd, Los Angeles, CA 90069, USA
Scott, Melody Thomas *Actress*
12068 Crest Court, Beverly Hills, CA 90210, USA
Scott, Michael W (Mike) *Baseball Player*
28355 Chat Dr, Laguna Niguel, CA 92677, USA
Scott, Paul *Writer*
33 Drumsheugh Gardens, Edinburgh, Scotland
Scott, Pippa *Actress*
10850 Wilshire Blvd, #250, Los Angeles, CA 90024, USA
Scott, Ray *Basketball Player, Coach*
%Colonial Life Insurance, 33200 Schoolcraft Road, Livonia, MI 48150, USA
Scott, Richard U (Dick) *Football Player*
3369 Upland Court, Adamstown, MD 21710, USA
Scott, Ridley *Movie Director*
%Scott Free, 42/44 Beak St, London W1R 3DA, England
Scott, Robert L, Jr *WW II Army Air Corps Hero, Writer*
96 Ridgecrest Place, Warner Robins, GA 31088, USA
Scott, Robert W *Governor, NC; Educator*
%North Carolina Community College System, 200 W Jones St, Raleigh, NC 27603, USA
Scott, Shelby *Labor Leader*
%American Federation of TV/Radio Artists, 260 Madison Ave, New York, NY 10016, USA
Scott, Stephen *Jazz Pianist*
%Bridge Agency, 35 Clark St, #A5, Brooklyn Heights, NY 11201, USA
Scott, Steven M (Steve) *Track Athlete*
4106 La Portalada Dr, Carlsbad, CA 92008, USA
Scott, Thomas C (Tom) *Football Player*
3259 Kirkwood Court, Keswick, VA 22947, USA
Scott, Tom *Jazz Saxophonist*
%Performers of the World, 8901 Melrose Ave, #200, West Hollywood, CA 90069, USA
Scott, Tom Everett *Actor*
%United Talent Agency, 9560 Wilshire Blvd, #500, Beverly Hills, CA 90212, USA
Scott, Tony *Movie Director*
%Totem Productions, 8009 Santa Monica Blvd, West Hollywood, CA 90046, USA
Scott, W Richard *Sociologist*
940 Lathrop Place, Stanford, CA 94305, USA
Scott, Willard H, Jr *Entertainer*
%NBC-TV, News Dept, 30 Rockefeller Plaza, New York, NY 10112, USA
Scott, Willard W, Jr *Army General, Educator*
9115 McNair Dr, Alexandria, VA 22309, USA
Scott, Winston E *Astronaut*
PO Box 1192, Cape Canaveral, FL 32920, USA
Scott-Brown, Denise *Architect*
%Venturi Scott Brown Assoc, 4236 Main St, Philadelphia, PA 19127, USA
Scott-Heron, Gil *Singer, Songwriter*
PO Box 31, Malverne, NY 11565, USA

S

Scotto - Seau

Scotto, Renata *Opera Singer*
%Robert Lombardo, Harkness Plaza, 61 W 62nd St, #6F, New York, NY 10023, USA
Scottoline, Lisa *Writer*
%Harper Collins Publishers, 10 E 53rd St, New York, NY 10022, USA
Scoular, Angela *Actress*
%Daly Gagan, 60 Old Brompton Road, London SW7 3LQ, England
Scowcroft, Brent *Air Force General, Government Official*
350 Park Ave, #2600, New York, NY 10022, USA
Scranton, Nancy *Golfer*
%Int'l Mgmt Group, 1 Erieview Plaza, 1360 E 9th St, #1300, Cleveland, OH 44114, USA
Scranton, William W *Governor, PA; Ambassador to UN*
PO Box 116, Dalton, PA 18414, USA
Scratch *Rap Artist*
%William Morris Agency, 1325 Ave of Americas, New York, NY 10019, USA
Scribner, Rick *Auto Racing Driver*
8904 Amerigo Ave, Orangevale, CA 95662, USA
Scrimm, Angus *Actor*
PO Box 5193, North Hollywood, CA 91616, USA
Scrimshaw, Nevin S *Nutritionist*
Sandwich Mountain Farm, PO Box 330, Campton, NH 03223, USA
Scripps, Charles E *Publisher*
10 Grandin Lane, Cincinnati, OH 45208, USA
Scruggs, Earl *Singer, Banjoist, Songwriter*
774 Elysian Road, Nashville, TN 37204, USA
Scudamore, Peter *Steeplechase Racing Jockey*
Mucky Cottage, Grangehill, Naunton, Cheltenham, Glos GL54 3AY, England
Scully, Sean P *Artist*
%Timothy Taylor Gallery, 1 Bruton Place, London W1X 7AB, England
Scully, Vincent E (Vin) *Sportscaster*
%Los Angeles Dodgers, Stadium, 1000 Elysian Park Ave, Los Angeles, CA 90012, USA
Scully-Power, Paul D *Astronaut*
%Civil Aviation Safety Authority, Box 2005, Canberra ACT 2600, Australia
Sculthorpe, Peter J *Composer*
91 Holdsworth St, Woollahra, NSW 2025, Australia
Scutt, Der *Architect*
%Der Scutt Architect, 44 W 28th St, New York, NY 10001, USA
Seabra, Verissimo Correia *President, Guinea-Bissau; General*
%President's Office, Bissau, Guinea-Bissau
Seaga, Edward P G *Prime Minister, Jamaica*
24-26 Grenada Crescent, New Kingston, Kingston 5, Jamaica
Seagal, Steven *Actor*
3288 Foxridge Dr, Jasper, IN 47546, USA
Seagrave, Jocelyn *Actress*
%David Shapira, 15821 Ventura Blvd, #235, Encino, CA 91436, USA
Seagraves, Ralph *Auto Racing Driver*
RR 10 Box 413, Winston Salem, NC 27127, USA
Seagren, Robert L (Bob) *Track Athlete, Actor*
21902 Velicata St, Woodland Hills, CA 91364, USA
Seagrove, Jenny *Actress*
%Marmont Mgmt, Langham House, 302/8 Regent St, London W1R 5AL, England
Seal *Singer, Songwriter*
%Atlas/Third Rail Entertainment, 9200 W Sunset Blvd, West Hollywood, CA 90069, USA
Seale, Bobby *Political Activist (Black Panthers)*
%Cafe Society, 302 W Chelton Ave, Philadelphia, PA 19144, USA
Seale, John C *Cinematographer*
%Mirisch Agency, 1801 Century Park E, Los Angeles, CA 90067, USA
Seals, Dan *Singer, Songwriter*
%Morningstar Productions, 153 Sanders Ferry Road, Hendersonville, TN 37075, USA
Seals, Son *Singer*
%Bad Axe Entertainment, 14514 San Francisco, Posen, IL 60469, USA
Seaman, Christopher *Conductor*
25 Westfield Dr, Glasgow G52 2SG, Scotland
Seaman, David *Soccer Player*
%Arsenal London, Avenell Road, Highbury, London N5 1BU, England
Seamans, Robert C, Jr *Aeronautical Engineer*
Sea Meadow, 675 Hale St, Beverly Farms, MA 01915, USA
Searcy, Leon *Football Player*
3841 Biggin Church Road, Jacksonville, FL 32224, USA
Searfoss, Richard A *Astronaut*
24480 Silver Creek Way, Tehachapi, CA 93561, USA
Searle, Ronald *Cartoonist, Animator*
%Elaine McMahon Agency, PO Box 1062, Bayonne, NJ 07002, USA
Sears, Paul B *Ecologist*
17 Las Milpas, Taos, NM 87571, USA
Sears, Victor W (Vic) *Football Player*
2501 Webb Chapel Extension 9105, Dallas, TX 75220, USA
Seau, Tiana (Junior), Jr *Football Player*
1904 Via Casa Alta, La Jolla, CA 92037, USA

Seaver, G Thomas (Tom) *Baseball Player*
1761 Diamond Mountain Road, Calistoga, CA 94515, USA
Seavey, David *Editorial Cartoonist*
%USA Today, Editorial Dept, 1000 Wilson Blvd, Arlington, VA 22209, USA
Seawell, William T *Businessman*
21 Westridge Dr, Pine Bluff, AR 71603, USA
Sebastian, Cuthbert *Governor General, Saint Kitts & Nevis*
%Governor General's House, Basseterre, Saint Kitts & Nevis
Sebastian, John *Singer, Songwriter*
%Lustig Talent, PO Box 770850, Orlando, FL 32877, USA
Sebastiani, Sergio Cardinal *Religious Leader*
Palazzo delle Congregazioni, Lardo del Colonnato 3, 00193 Rome, Italy
Sebestyen, Marta *Singer (Muzsik)*
%Konzertagentur Berthold Seliger, Nonnengasse 15, 36037 Fulda, Germany
Sebold, Alice *Writer*
%Little Brown, 3 Center Plaza, Boston, MA 02108, USA
Secada, Jon *Singer, Songwriter*
PO Box 145247, Coral Gables, FL 33114, USA
Seck, Idrissa *Prime Minister, Senegal*
%Prime Minister's Office, Ave Leopold Sedar Senghor, Dakar, Senegal
Secor, Kyle *Actor*
%Brillstein/Grey, 9150 Wilshire Blvd, #350, Beverly Hills, CA 90212, USA
Secord, John *Singer*
%Making Texas Music, Old Putnam Bank Building, PO Box 1013, Putnam, TX 76469, USA
Secord, Richard V *Army General*
%Computerized Thermal Imaging, 1719 W 2800 S, Ogden, UT 84401, USA
Seda, Jon *Actor*
%Epstein-Wyckoff, 280 S Beverly Dr, #400, Beverly Hills, CA 90212, USA
Sedaka, Neil *Singer, Songwriter*
%Sedaka Music, 201 E 66th St, #3N, New York, NY 10021, USA
Sedaris, David *Writer*
%Doubleday Press, 1540 Broadway, New York, NY 10036, USA
Seddon, Margaret Rhea *Astronaut*
1709 Shagbark Trail, Murfreesboro, TN 37130, USA
Sedelmaier, J Josef (Joe) *Movie, Television Director; Animator*
%Sedelmaier Film Productions, 858 W Armitage Ave, #267, Chicago, IL 60614, USA
Sedgman, Frank A *Tennis Player*
26 Bolton Ave, Hampton VIC 3188, Australia
Sedgwick, Kyra *Actress*
PO Box 668, Sharon, CT 06069, USA
Sedney, Jules *Prime Minister, Suriname*
Maystreet 24, Paramaribo, Suriname
Sedykh, Yuri G *Track Athlete*
%Russian Light Athletics Federation, Luzhnetskaya Nab 8, Moscow, Russia
See, Carolyn *Writer*
17339 Tramonto Dr, #303, Pacific Palisades, CA 90272, USA
Seear, Beatrice N S *Government Official, England*
189B Kennington Road, London SE11 6ST, England
Seeger, Pete *Singer, Songwriter, Guitarist*
PO Box 431, Dutchess Junction, Beacon, NY 12508, USA
Seeler, Uwe *Soccer Player*
%HSV, Rothenbaumchaussee 125, 20149 Hamburg, Germany
Seeling, Angelle *Motorcycle Racing Rider*
%Star Performance Suzuki Racing Team, PO Box 1241, Americus, GA 31709, USA
Seely, Jeannie *Singer, Songwriter*
%Tessier-Marsh Talent, 2825 Blue Book Dr, Nashville, TN 37214, USA
Sega, Ronald M *Astronaut, Electrical Engineer*
711 Slaters Lane, #B, Alexandria, VA 22314, USA
Segal, Erich *Writer*
%Wolfson College, English School, Oxford OX2 6UD, England
Segal, Fred *Fashion Designer*
%Fred Segal Jeans, 8100 Melrose Ave, Los Angeles, CA 90046, USA
Segal, George *Actor*
515 N Robertson Blvd, West Hollywood, CA 90048, USA
Segal, Peter *Movie Director*
%William Morris Agency, 151 El Camino Dr, Beverly Hills, CA 90212, USA
Segel, Jason *Actor*
%United Talent Agency, 9560 Wilshire Blvd, #500, Beverly Hills, CA 90212, USA
Seger, Bob *Singer, Songwriter*
%Capitol Records, 1750 N Vine St, Los Angeles, CA 90028, USA
Seger, Shea *Singer*
%Helter Skelter, Plaza, 535 Kings Road, London SW10 0S, England
Segerstam, Leif S *Composer, Conductor*
%Garvey & Ivor, 59 Lansdowne Place, Hove BN3 1FL, England
Segui, Diego P *Baseball Player*
7520 King St, #J, Shawnee Mission, KS 66214, USA
Segura, Francisco (Pancho) *Tennis Player*
%Rancho La Costa Hotel & Spa, 7690 Camino Real, Carlsbad, CA 92009, USA

S

Seguso - Selmon

Seguso, Robert *Tennis Player*
%Advantage International, 1025 Thomas Jefferson NW, #450, Washington, DC 20007, USA
Seibou, Ali *President, Niger; Army General*
%Chairman's Office, National Orientation Higher Council, Niamey, Niger
Seidel, Martie *Singer (Dixie Chicks)*
%Senior Mgmt, 56 Lindsey Ave, Nashville, TN 37210, USA
Seidelman, Susan *Movie Director*
%Michael Shedler, 225 W 34th St, #1012, New York, NY 10122, USA
Seidman, L William *Government Official, Businessman*
1025 Connecticut Ave NW, #800, Washington, DC 20036, USA
Seifert, George G *Football Coach, Sportscaster*
1908 Bay Flat Road, Bodega Bay, CA 94923, USA
Seigenthaler, John L *Publisher*
%Tennessean, 1100 Broadway, Nashville, TN 37203, USA
Seigner, Emmanuelle *Actress*
%Artmedia, 20 Ave Rapp, 75007 Paris, France
Seigner, Mathilde *Actress*
%Artmedia, 20 Ave Rapp, 75007 Paris, France
Seignoret, Clarence H A *President, Dominica*
24 Cork St, Roseau, Dominica
Seikaly, Rony *Basketball Player*
27 E Dilido Dr, Miami Beach, FL 33139, USA
Seilacher, Adolf *Geologist, Geophysicist*
%Yale University, Geology/Geophysics Laboratory, New Haven, CT 06520, USA
Seinfeld, Jerry *Actor, Comedian*
211 Central Park W, New York, NY 10024, USA
Seinfeld, John H *Chemical Engineer*
363 Patrician Way, Pasadena, CA 91105, USA
Seiple, Larry *Football Player*
1361 W Golfview Dr, Pembroke Pines, FL 33026, USA
Seiwald, Robert J *Inventor (Fluorescent Dye)*
59 Burnside Ave, San Francisco, CA 94131, USA
Seixas, E Victor (Vic), Jr *Tennis Player*
8 Harbor Point Dr, #207, Mill Valley, CA 94941, USA
Seizinger, Katja *Alpine Skier*
Rudolf-Epp-Str 48, 69412 Eberbach, Germany
Sela, Michael *Immunologist, Chemist*
%Weizmann Science Institute, Immunology Dept, Rehovot 76100, Israel
Selanne, Teemu *Hockey Player*
31731 Madre Selva Lane, Trabuco Canyon, CA 92679, USA
Selby, David *Actor*
%International Creative Mgmt, 8942 Wilshire Blvd, #219, Beverly Hills, CA 90211, USA
Seldin, Donald W *Physician*
%Texas Southwestern Medical Center, 5323 Harry Hines Blvd, Dallas, TX 75390, USA
Seldon, Bruce *Boxer*
%Don King Productions, 968 Pinehurst Dr, Las Vegas, NV 89109, USA
Sele, Aaron H *Baseball Player*
5760 NE Gunderson Road, Poulsbo, WA 98370, USA
Seles, Monica *Tennis Player*
2895 Dick Wilson Dr, Sarasota, FL 34240, USA
Seley, Jason *Sculptor*
%Cornell University, Art Dept, Ithaca, NY 14853, USA
Self, Bill *Basketball Coach*
%University of Kansas, Athletic Dept, Allen Fieldhouse, Lawrence, KS 66045, USA
Selig, Allan H (Bud) *Baseball Executive*
%Baseball Commissioner's Office, 245 Park Ave, #3100, New York, NY 10167, USA
Seligman, Martin E P *Psychologist*
%University of Pennsylvania, Psychology Dept, Philadelphia, PA 19104, USA
Selkirk, George N *Government Official, England*
Rose Lawn Coppice, Wimborne, Dorset, England
Sellars, Peter *Theater Director*
%Creative Artists Agency, 9830 Wilshire Blvd, Beverly Hills, CA 90212, USA
Selleca, Connie *Actress*
15050 Ventura Blvd, #916, Sherman Oaks, CA 91403, USA
Selleck, Tom *Actor*
2899 Agoura Road, #560, Westlake Village, CA 91361, USA
Seller, Peg *Sychronized Swimmer, Coach*
72 Monkswood Crescent, Newmarket ON L3Y 2K1, Canada
Sellers, Franklin *Religious Leader*
%Reformed Episcopal Church, 2001 Frederick Road, Baltimore, MD 21228, USA
Sellers, Piers J *Astronaut*
16011 Craighurst Dr, Houston, TX 77059, USA
Sellers, Ron F *Football Player*
4109 Hickory Dr, Palm Beach Gardens, FL 33418, USA
Selmon, Dewey W *Football Player*
2725 S Berry Road, Norman, OK 73072, USA
Selmon, Lee Roy *Football Player*
15350 Amberly Dr, #624, Tampa, FL 33647, USA

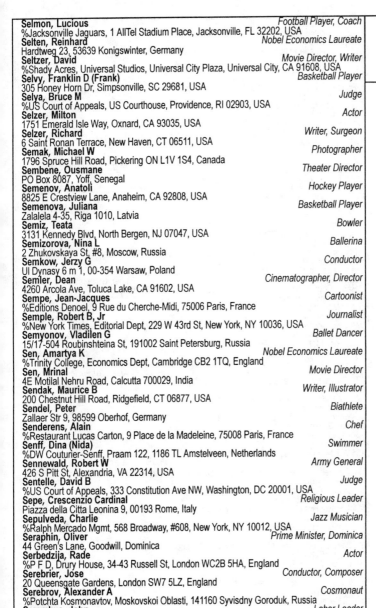

Selmon, Lucious *Football Player, Coach*
%Jacksonville Jaguars, 1 AllTel Stadium Place, Jacksonville, FL 32202, USA
Selten, Reinhard *Nobel Economics Laureate*
Hardtweg 23, 53639 Konigswinter, Germany
Seltzer, David *Movie Director, Writer*
%Shady Acres, Universal Studios, Universal City Plaza, Universal City, CA 91608, USA
Selvy, Franklin D (Frank) *Basketball Player*
305 Honey Horn Dr, Simpsonville, SC 29681, USA
Selya, Bruce M *Judge*
%US Court of Appeals, US Courthouse, Providence, RI 02903, USA
Selzer, Milton *Actor*
1751 Emerald Isle Way, Oxnard, CA 93035, USA
Selzer, Richard *Writer, Surgeon*
6 Saint Ronan Terrace, New Haven, CT 06511, USA
Semak, Michael W *Photographer*
1796 Spruce Hill Road, Pickering ON L1V 1S4, Canada
Sembene, Ousmane *Theater Director*
PO Box 8087, Yoff, Senegal
Semenov, Anatoli *Hockey Player*
8825 E Crestview Lane, Anaheim, CA 92808, USA
Semenova, Juliana *Basketball Player*
Zalalela 4-35, Riga 1010, Latvia
Semiz, Teata *Bowler*
3131 Kennedy Blvd, North Bergen, NJ 07047, USA
Semizorova, Nina L *Ballerina*
2 Zhukovskaya St, #8, Moscow, Russia
Semkow, Jerzy G *Conductor*
Ul Dynasy 6 m 1, 00-354 Warsaw, Poland
Semler, Dean *Cinematographer, Director*
4260 Arcola Ave, Toluca Lake, CA 91602, USA
Sempe, Jean-Jacques *Cartoonist*
%Editions Denoel, 9 Rue du Cherche-Midi, 75006 Paris, France
Semple, Robert B, Jr *Journalist*
%New York Times, Editorial Dept, 229 W 43rd St, New York, NY 10036, USA
Semyonov, Vladilen G *Ballet Dancer*
15/17-504 Roubinshteina St, 191002 Saint Petersburg, Russia
Sen, Amartya K *Nobel Economics Laureate*
%Trinity College, Economics Dept, Cambridge CB2 1TQ, England
Sen, Mrinal *Movie Director*
4E Motilal Nehru Road, Calcutta 700029, India
Sendak, Maurice B *Writer, Illustrator*
200 Chestnut Hill Road, Ridgefield, CT 06877, USA
Sendel, Peter *Biathlete*
Zallaer Str 9, 98599 Oberhof, Germany
Senderens, Alain *Chef*
%Restaurant Lucas Carton, 9 Place de la Madeleine, 75008 Paris, France
Senff, Dina (Nida) *Swimmer*
%DW Couturier-Senff, Praam 122, 1186 TL Amstelveen, Netherlands
Sennewald, Robert W *Army General*
426 S Pitt St, Alexandria, VA 22314, USA
Sentelle, David B *Judge*
%US Court of Appeals, 333 Constitution Ave NW, Washington, DC 20001, USA
Sepe, Crescenzio Cardinal *Religious Leader*
Piazza della Citta Leonina 9, 00193 Rome, Italy
Sepulveda, Charlie *Jazz Musician*
%Ralph Mercado Mgmt, 568 Broadway, #608, New York, NY 10012, USA
Seraphin, Oliver *Prime Minister, Dominica*
44 Green's Lane, Goodwill, Dominica
Serbedzija, Rade *Actor*
%P F D, Drury House, 34-43 Russell St, London WC2B 5HA, England
Serebrier, Jose *Conductor, Composer*
20 Queensgate Gardens, London SW7 5LZ, England
Serebrov, Alexander A *Cosmonaut*
%Potchta Kosmonavtov, Moskovskoi Oblasti, 141160 Syvisdny Goroduk, Russia
Serembus, John *Labor Leader*
%Upholsterers Union, 25 N 4th St, Philadelphia, PA 19106, USA
Seresin, Michael *Cinematographer*
59 North Wharf Road, London W2 1LA, England
Serkin, Peter A *Concert Pianist*
%Manne Music College, 150 W 85th St, New York, NY 10024, USA
Serlemitsos, Peter J *Astronomer*
%BBXRT Project, Goddard Space Flight Center, Greenbelt, MD 20771, USA
Serna, Assumpta *Actress*
8306 Wilshire Blvd, #438, Beverly Hills, CA 90211, USA
Serna, Diego *Soccer Player*
%Los Angeles Galaxy, 1010 Rose Bowl Dr, Pasadena, CA 91103, USA
Serna, Pepe *Actor*
127 Ruby Ave, Newport Beach, CA 92662, USA

S

Serota - Sfar

Serota, Nicholas A *Museum Director*
%Tate Gallery, Millbank, London SW1P 4RG, England
Serra, Eduardo *Cinematographer*
4324 Promenade Way, #109, Marina del Rey, CA 90292, USA
Serra, Richard *Sculptor*
173 Duane St, New York, NY 10013, USA
Serrano, Juan *Concert Guitarist*
%Prince/SF Productions, 1450 Southgate Ave, #206, Daly City, CA 94015, USA
Serre, Jean-Pierre *Mathematician*
6 Ave de Montespan, 75116 Paris, France
Serreau, Coline *Movie Director*
%Artmedia, 20 Ave Rapp, 75007 Paris, France
Servan-Schreiber, Jean-Claude *Journalist*
147 Bis Rue d'Alesia, 75014 Paris, France
SerVass, Cory J *Editor*
%Saturday Evening Post Magazine, 1100 Waterway Blvd, Indianapolis, IN 46202, USA
Sessions, William S *Law Enforcement Official, Judge*
112 E Pecan, #2900, San Antonio, TX 78205, USA
Sessler, Gerhard M *Inventor (Telephone Microphone)*
Fichtenstra 30B, 64285 Darmstadt, Germany
Seter, Mordecai *Composer*
1 Karny St, Ramat Aviv, Tel-Aviv, Israel
Seth, Oliver *Judge*
%US Court of Appeals, PO Box 1, Santa Fe, NM 87504, USA
Seth, Vikram *Writer*
%Phoenix House, Orion House, 5 Upper St, London WC2H 9EA, England
Sethna, Homi N *Engineer*
Old Yacht Club, Chatrapati Shrivaji Maharaj, Bombay 400 038, India
Setzer, Brian *Singer, Guitarist, Band Leader*
%Haber Corp, 16830 Ventura Blvd, #501, Encino, CA 91436, USA
Setziol, LeRoy I (Roy) *Sculptor*
30450 Moriah Lane, Sheridan, OR 97378, USA
Sevastyanov, Vitayi I *Cosmonaut*
%Potchta Kosmonavtov, Moskovskoi Oblasti, 141160 Syvisdny Goroduk, Russia
Severeid, Suzanne *Model, Actress*
PO Box 4171, Malibu, CA 90264, USA
Severin, G Timothy (Tim) *Explorer*
Inchy Bridge, Timoleague, County Cork, Ireland
Severinsen, Carl H (Doc) *Jazz Trumpeter, Conductor*
4275 White Pine Lane, Santa Ynez, CA 93460, USA
Sevigny, Chloe *Actress*
%Brillstein/Grey, 9150 Wilshire Blvd, #350, Beverly Hills, CA 90212, USA
Seward, George C *Attorney*
%Seward & Kissel, 1 Battery Park Plaza, New York, NY 10004, USA
Sewell, George *Actor*
%Peter Charlesworth, 68 Old Brompton Road, London SW7 3LQ, England
Sewell, Harley *Football Player*
104 W Lily Lane, Arlington, TX 76010, USA
Sewell, Rufus *Actor*
%Julian Belfarge, 46 Albermarle St, London W1X 4PP, England
Seweryn, Andrzej *Actor*
%Comedie Francaise, Place Colette, 75001 Paris, France
Seydoux, Geraldine *Molecular Biologist, Geneticist*
%Johns Hopkins University, Molecular Biology Dept, Baltimore, MD 21218, USA
Seyferth, Dietmar *Chemist*
%Massachusetts Institute of Technology, Chemistry Dept, Cambridge, MA 02139, USA
Seyler, Athene *Actress*
Coach House, 26 Upper Mall, Hammersmith, London W8, England
Seymour, Caroline *Actress*
%Langford Assoc, 17 Westfields Ave, London SW13 0AT, England
Seymour, Carolyn *Actress*
%Chasin Agency, 8899 Beverly Blvd, #716, Los Angeles, CA 90048, USA
Seymour, Jane *Actress*
23852 Pacific Coast Highway, #337, Malibu, CA 90265, USA
Seymour, John *Senator, CA*
46393 Blackhawk Dr, Indian Wells, CA 92210, USA
Seymour, Lynn *Ballerina*
%Artistes in Action, 16 Balderton St, London W1Y 1TF, England
Seymour, Paul C *Football Player*
4188 Shoals Dr, Okemos, MI 48864, USA
Seymour, Stephanie *Model*
5415 Oberlin Dr, San Diego, CA 92121, USA
Seymour, Stephanie K *Judge*
%US Court of Appeals, US Courthouse, 333 W 4th St, Tulsa, OK 74103, USA
Sezer, Ahmet Necdet *President, Turkey*
%President's Office, Cumhurbaskanlgl Kosku, Cankaya, Ankara, Turkey
Sfar, Rachid *Prime Minister, Tunisia*
278 Ave de Tervuren, 1150 Brussels, Belgium

Sfeir, Nasrallah Pierre Cardinal *Religious Leader*
Patriarcat Maronite, Bkerke, Lebanon
Sgouros, Dimitris *Concert Pianist*
Tompazi 28 Str, Piraeus 18537, Greece
Shackelford, Ted *Actor*
12305 Valley Heart Dr, Studio City, CA 91604, USA
Shackouls, Bobby S *Businessman*
%Burlington Resources, 5051 Westheimer, Houston, TX 77056, USA
Shadyac, Tom *Movie Director*
%United Talent Agency, 9560 Wilshire Blvd, #500, Beverly Hills, CA 90212, USA
Shafer, R Donald *Religious Leader*
%Brethren in Christ Church, PO Box 290, Grantham, PA 17027, USA
Shaffer, David H *Publisher*
%MacMillan, 1177 Ave of Americas, #1965, New York, NY 10036, USA
Shaffer, Peter L *Writer*
%Lantz, 888 7th Ave, #2500, New York, NY 10106, USA
Shagan, Steve *Writer*
285 W Via Lola, Palm Springs, CA 92262, USA
Shagari, Alhaji Shehu Usman Aliu *President, Nigeria*
22 Shehu Crescent, PO Box 162, Adarawa, Sokoto State, Nigeria
Shaggy *Singer*
%Artist Group International, 9560 Wilshire Blvd, #400, Beverly Hills, CA 90212, USA
Shah, Idries *Writer*
%AP Watt Ltd, 26/28 Bedford Row, London WC1R 4HL, England
Shahmatova, Larissa *Concert Violinist*
%Julliard Music School, Lincoln Center Plaza, New York, NY 10023, USA
Shaiman, Marc *Composer*
8476 Brier Dr, West Hollywood, CA 90046, USA
Shakespeare, Frank J, Jr *Television Executive, Diplomat*
303 Coast Blvd, La Jolla, CA 92037, USA
Shakira *Singer*
%Sony Music, Cl 94 A 11 A-50, Bogota DF, Colombia
Shalala, Donna E *Secretary, Health & Human Services*
%University of Miami, President's Office, Coral Gables, FL 33124, USA
Shales, Thomas W *Journalist*
%Washington Post, Editorial Dept, 1150 15th St NW, Washington, DC 20071, USA
Shalhoub, Tony *Actor*
%United Talent Agency, 9560 Wilshire Blvd, #500, Beverly Hills, CA 90212, USA
Shalikashvili, John M (Shali) *Army General*
55 Chapman Loop, Steilacoom, WA 98388, USA
Shalit, Gene *Movie Critic*
%NBC-TV, News Dept, 30 Rockefeller Plaza, New York, NY 10112, USA
Shamir, Yitzhak *Prime Minister, Israel*
Beit Amot Mishpat, 8 Shaul Hamelech Blvd, Tel Aviv 64733, Israel
Shan Kuo-Hsi, Paul Cardinal *Religious Leader*
%Bishop's House, 125 Szu-Wie 3rd Road, Kaohsiung 80203, Taiwan
Shanahan, Brendan *Hockey Player*
473 Puritan Ave, Birmingham, MI 48009, USA
Shanahan, Mike *Football Coach*
%Denver Broncos, 13655 E Broncos Parkway, Englewood, CO 80112, USA
Shand, Remy *Singer, Songwriter*
%Universal Records, 2550 Victoria Park, Toronto ON M2J 4A2, Canada
Shandling, Garry *Actor, Comedian*
%Endeavor Talent Agency, 9701 Wilshire Blvd, #1000, Beverly Hills, CA 90212, USA
Shandrowsky, Alex *Labor Leader*
%Marine Engineer Beneficial Assn, 444 N Capitol St NW, Washington, DC 20001, USA
Shane, Bob *Singer (Kingston Trio)*
9410 S 46th St, Phoenix, AZ 85044, USA
Shange, Ntozake *Writer*
%Saint Martin's Press, 175 5th Ave, New York, NY 10010, USA
Shanice *Singer*
%Richard Walters, 1800 Argyle Ave, #408, Los Angeles, CA 90028, USA
Shank, Clarence E (Bud) *Jazz Saxophonist, Flutist*
PO Box 70128, Tucson, AZ 85737, USA
Shank, Roger C *Computer Scientist*
%Northwestern University, Learning Sciences Institute, Evanston, IL 60201, USA
Shankar, Ravi *Concert Sitar Player, Composer*
17 Warden Court, Gowalia Tank Road, Bombay 36, India
Shannon *Singer*
%Big Mgmt, 226 5th Ave, New York, NY 10001, USA
Shannon, Elizabeth *Actress*
%International Creative Mgmt, 8942 Wilshire Blvd, #219, Beverly Hills, CA 90211, USA
Shannon, Mem *Singer, Guitarist, Songwriter*
%Miasma Mgmt, PO Box 27037, Los Angeles, CA 90027, USA
Shannon, Molly *Actress, Comedienne*
%Innovative Artists, 1505 10th St, Santa Monica, CA 90401, USA
Shantz, Robert C (Bobby) *Baseball Player*
152 E Mount Pleasant Ave, Ambler, PA 19002, USA

Shapiro, Debbie *Actress*
%Agency for Performing Arts, 9200 Sunset Blvd, #900, Los Angeles, CA 90069, USA
Shapiro, Harold T *Educator*
10 Campbelton Circle, Princeton, NJ 08540, USA
Shapiro, Joel E *Artist*
%Pace Gallery, 32 E 57th St, New York, NY 10022, USA
Shapiro, Maurice M *Astrophysicist*
5809 Nicholson Lane, #801, Rockville, MD 20852, USA
Shapiro, Robert B *Businessman*
%Monsanto Co, 800 N Lindbergh Blvd, Saint Louis, MO 63167, USA
Shapiro, Robert L *Attorney*
1421 Ambassador St, #206, Los Angeles, CA 90035, USA
Sharif, Omar *Actor*
BP 41, 78380 Bougival, Yvelines, France
Sharipov, Salizhan S *Cosmonaut*
%Potchta Kosmonavtov, Moskovskoi Oblasti, 141160 Syvisdny Goroduk, Russia
Sharma, Barbara *Actress*
PO Box 29125, Los Angeles, CA 90029, USA
Sharma, Rakesh *Cosmonaut, India*
%Hindustan Aeronautics, Bangalore 560037, India
Sharman, Helen *Cosmonaut*
12 Stratton Court, Adelade Road, Surbiton, Surrey, England
Sharman, Jim *Movie Director*
%M&L, 49 Daringhurst St, Kings Cross NSW 2100, Australia
Sharman, William W (Bill) *Basketball Player, Coach, Executive*
7510 W 81st St, Playa del Rey, CA 90293, USA
Sharon, Ariel *President, Israel; Army General*
%President's Office, 3 Hanassi, Jerusalem 92188, Israel
Sharp, Dee Dee *Singer*
%Cape Entertainment, 1161 NW 76th Ave, Plantation, FL 33322, USA
Sharp, Kevin *Singer*
%Rising Star, 1415 River Landing Way, Woodstock, GA 30188, USA
Sharp, Linda K *Basketball Coach*
%Phoenix Mercury, American West Arena, 201 E Jefferson St, Phoenix, AZ 85004, USA
Sharp, Marsha *Basketball Coach*
%Texas Tech University, Athletic Dept, Lubbock, TX 79409, USA
Sharp, Mitchell W *Government Official, Canada*
33 Monkland Ave, Ottawa ON K1S 1Y8, Canada
Sharp, Phillip A *Nobel Medicine Laureate*
36 Fairmont Ave, Newton, MA 02458, USA
Sharpe, Luis E, Jr *Football Player*
12641 S 34th Place, Phoenix, AZ 85044, USA
Sharpe, Rochelle P *Journalist*
94 Dudley St, #2, Brookline, MA 02445, USA
Sharpe, Shannon *Football Player*
204 Jay St, Glennville, GA 30427, USA
Sharpe, Sterling *Football Player, Sportscaster*
%ESPN-TV, Sports Dept, ESPN Plaza, 935 Middle St, Bristol, CT 06010, USA
Sharpe, Thomas R (Tom) *Writer*
38 Tunwells Lane, Great Shelford, Cambridge CB2 5LJ, England
Sharpe, William F *Nobel Economics Laureate*
532 Orange Ave, Los Altos, CA 94022, USA
Sharper, Jamie *Football Player*
10707 Bluebill Dr, Glen Allen, VA 23060, USA
Sharpless, K Barry *Nobel Chemistry Laureate*
%Scripps Research Institute, 10650 Torrey Pines Road, La Jolla, CA 92037, USA
Sharpton, Al *Religious Leader, Social Activist*
1941 Madison Ave, #2, New York, NY 10035, USA
Sharqi, Sheikh Hamad bin Muhammad al- *Ruler, Fujairah*
%Royal Palace, Emiri Court, PO Box 1, Fujairah, United Arab Emirates
Shatalov, Valdimir A *Cosmonaut*
%Potchta Kosmonavtov, Moskovskoi Oblasti, 141160 Syvisdny Goroduk, Russia
Shatner, Melanie *Actress*
%Henderson/Hogan, 8285 W Sunset Blvd, #1, West Hollywood, CA 90046, USA
Shatner, William *Actor*
%William Shatner Connection, 7059 Atoll Ave, North Hollywood, CA 91605, USA
Shattuck, Kim *Singer, Guitarist (Muffs)*
%International Creative Mgmt, 40 W 57th St, #1800, New York, NY 10019, USA
Shaud, Grant *Actor*
8738 Appian Way, Los Angeles, CA 90046, USA
Shaud, John A *Air Force General, Association Executive*
%Air Force Aid Society, 1745 Jefferson Davis Highway, #202, Arlington, VA 22202, USA
Shaughnessy, Charles *Actor*
534 15th St, Santa Monica, CA 90402, USA
Shavelson, Melville *Producer, Writer*
%William Morris Agency, 151 El Camino Dr, Beverly Hills, CA 90212, USA
Shaver, Billy Joe *Singer, Songwriter*
435 N Martell Ave, Los Angeles, CA 90036, USA

Shaver, Helen — *Actress*
%Innovative Artists, 1505 10th St, Santa Monica, CA 90401, USA

Shavers, Ernie — *Boxer*
30 Doreen Ave Moretown Wirral, Merseyside CH46 6DN, England

Shaw, Artie — *Jazz Clarinetist*
2127 W Palos Court, Newbury Park, CA 91320, USA

Shaw, Bernard — *Commentator*
7526 Heatherton Lane, Potomac, MD 20854, USA

Shaw, Brewster H, Jr — *Astronaut*
4123 University Blvd, Houston, TX 77005, USA

Shaw, Brian — *Basketball Player*
540 Brickell Key Dr, #1513, Miami, FL 33131, USA

Shaw, David L — *Journalist*
%Los Angeles Times, Editorial Dept, 202 W 1st St, Los Angeles, CA 90012, USA

Shaw, Fiona — *Actress*
%International Creative Mgmt, 76 Oxford St, London W1N 0AX, England

Shaw, John H — *Geophysicist*
%Harvard University, Geophysics Dept, Cambridge, MA 02138, USA

Shaw, Robert J (Bob) — *Baseball Player*
2225 US Highway 1, #208, Tequesta, FL 33469, USA

Shaw, Run Run — *Movie Producer*
Shaw House, Lot 220 Clear Water Bay Road, Kowloon, Hong Kong, China

Shaw, Scott — *Photojournalist*
20771 Lake Road, Cleveland, OH 44116, USA

Shaw, Timothy A (Tim) — *Swimmer, Water Polo Player*
5315 River Ave, Newport Beach, CA 92663, USA

Shaw, Tommy — *Singer, Guitarist (Styx); Songwriter*
%Alliance Artists, 1225 Northmeadow Parkway, #100, Roswell, GA 30076, USA

Shaw, Vernon — *President, Dominica*
%President's Office, Morne Bruce, Victoria St, Roseau, Dominica

Shaw, Victoria — *Singer, Songwriter*
PO Box 120512, Nashville, TN 37212, USA

Shaw, Vinessa — *Actress*
%Industry Entertainment, 955 Carillo Dr, #300, Los Angeles, CA 90048, USA

Shaw, William L (Billy) — *Football Player*
3427 Old Rothell Road, Toccoa, GA 30577, USA

Shawn, Wallace — *Actor, Writer*
%Gersh Agency, 232 N Canon Dr, Beverly Hills, CA 90210, USA

Shaye, Lin — *Actress*
%Paul Kohner, 9300 Wilshire Blvd, #555, Beverly Hills, CA 90212, USA

Shea, John — *Actor*
%Mutant X, 40 Carl Hall Road, Toronto ON M3K 2B8, Canada

Shea, Katt — *Actress*
%International Creative Mgmt, 8942 Wilshire Blvd, #219, Beverly Hills, CA 90211, USA

Shear, Jules — *Singer, Songwriter*
%Concerted Efforts, 59 Parsons St, West Newton, MA 02465, USA

Shear, Rhonda — *Actress, Comedienne, Model*
9297 Burton Way, #6, Beverly Hills, CA 90210, USA

Shearer, Alan — *Soccer Player*
%Newcastle United FC, Saint James Park, Newcastle-Tyne NE1 4ST, England

Shearer, Harry — *Actor, Comedian*
1900 W Pico Blvd, Santa Monica, CA 90405, USA

Shearer, Moira — *Ballerina, Actress*
%Rogers Coleridge White, 2 Powis Mews, London W11 1JN, England

Shearer, Peter M — *Geophysicist*
%Scripps Oceanography Institute, Geophysics Dept, La Jolla, CA 92093, USA

Shearer, S Bradford (Brad) — *Football Player*
1909 Lakeshore Dr, #B, Austin, TX 78746, USA

Shearing, George A — *Jazz Pianist, Composer*
350 5th Ave, #6215, New York, NY 10118, USA

Sheed, Wilfrid J J — *Writer*
%General Delivery, Sag Harbor, NY 11963, USA

Sheedy, Ally — *Actress*
%Don Buchwald, 6500 Wilshire Blvd, #2200, Los Angeles, CA 90048, USA

Sheehan, Doug — *Actor*
%Innovative Artists, 1505 10th St, Santa Monica, CA 90401, USA

Sheehan, Neil — *Journalist*
4505 Klingle St NW, Washington, DC 20016, USA

Sheehan, Patricia A (Patty) — *Golfer*
2300 Skyline Blvd, Reno, NV 89509, USA

Sheehan, Susan — *Writer*
4505 Klingle St NW, Washington, DC 20016, USA

Sheehy, Gail H — *Writer*
300 E 57th St, #18D, New York, NY 10022, USA

Sheehy, Timothy (Tim) — *Hockey Player*
4 Boswell Lane, Southborough, MA 01772, USA

Sheen, Charles — *Actor*
%Jeffrey Ballard, 4814 Lemara Ave, Sherman Oaks, CA 91403, USA

Sheen, Martin *Actor*
29351 Bluewater Road, Malibu, CA 90265, USA
Sheets, Ben *Baseball Player*
11234 George Lambert Road, Saint Amant, LA 70774, USA
Sheffer, Craig *Actor*
5699 Kanan Dr, #275, Agoura, CA 91301, USA
Sheffield, Gary A *Baseball Player*
2247 Queensborough Lane, Los Angeles, CA 90077, USA
Sheffield, John M (Johnny) *Actor*
834 1st Ave, Chula Vista, CA 91911, USA
Sheffield, William J (Bill) *Governor, AK*
PO Box 91476, Anchorage, AK 99509, USA
Sheik, Duncan *Singer, Songwriter*
%Nonesuch Records, 75 Rockefeller Plaza, New York, NY 10019, USA
Sheila E *Singer, Drummer*
%Groove Ent, 1005 N Alfred St, #2, West Hollywood, CA 90069, USA
Sheindlin, Judy (Judge) *Entertainer, Judge*
PO Box 949, Los Angeles, CA 90078, USA
Sheiner, David S *Actor*
1827 Veteran Ave, #19, Los Angeles, CA 90025, USA
Sheinkman, Jack *Labor Leader*
%Amalgamated Clothing & Textile Workers, 1710 Broadway, #3, New York, NY 10019, USA
Shelby, Carroll *Auto Racing Driver, Executive*
19020 Anelo Ave, Gardena, CA 90248, USA
Shelby, Mark *Jazz Bassist, Composer*
%Thomas Cassidy, 11761 E Speedway Blvd, Tucson, AZ 85748, USA
Sheldon, Sidney *Writer*
10250 W Sunset Blvd, Los Angeles, CA 90077, USA
Shell, Arthur (Art) *Football Player, Coach*
7090 Island Queen Court, Sparks, NV 89436, USA
Shell, Donnie *Football Player*
2945 Shandon Road, Rock Hill, SC 29730, USA
Shelley, Barbara *Actress*
%Ken McReddie, 91 Regent St, London W1R 7TB, England
Shelley, Carole *Actress*
333 W 56th St, New York, NY 10019, USA
Shelley, Howard G *Concert Pianist, Conductor*
38 Cholmeley Park, London N6 5ER, England
Shelton, Abigail *Actress*
%Dale Garrick, 8831 Sunset Blvd, #402, Los Angeles, CA 90069, USA
Shelton, Deborah *Actress*
2265 Westwood Blvd, #251, Los Angeles, CA 90064, USA
Shelton, Lonnie *Basketball Player*
860 S 8th Ave, Kingsburg, CA 93631, USA
Shelton, Ricky Van *Singer, Songwriter*
%Michael Campbell Assoc, PO Box 120356, Nashville, TN 37212, USA
Shelton, Ronald W *Movie Director*
15200 Friends St, Pacific Palisades, CA 90272, USA
Shenandoh, Joanne *Singer, Songwriter*
%Oneida Nation Territory, PO Box 450, Oneida, NY 13421, USA
Shepard, Elizabeth *Actress*
%London Mgmt, 2-4 Noel St, London W1V 3RB, England
Shepard, Jean *Singer*
%Billy Deaton Talent, 5811 Still Hollow Road, Nashville, TN 37215, USA
Shepard, Roger N *Psychologist*
5775 Montclair Ave, Marysville, CA 95901, USA
Shepard, Samuel K (Sam) *Writer, Actor*
1801 Martha St, Encino, CA 91316, USA
Shepard, Vonda *Singer, Songwriter*
%William Morris Agency, 151 El Camino Dr, Beverly Hills, CA 90212, USA
Shepherd, Ben *Bassist (Soundgarden)*
%Susan Silver Mgmt, 6523 California Ave SW, #348, Seattle, WA 98136, USA
Shepherd, Cybill *Model, Actress*
PO Box 261503, Encino, CA 91426, USA
Shepherd, Elizabeth *Actress*
%London Mgmt, 2-4 Noel St, London W1V 3RB, England
Shepherd, Morgan *Auto/Truck Racing Driver*
57 Rhody Creek Loop, Stuart, VA 24171, USA
Shepherd, Sherrie *Cartoonist (Francie)*
%United Feature Syndicate, 200 Madison Ave, New York, NY 10016, USA
Shepherd, William M *Astronaut*
18623 Prince William Lane, Houston, TX 77058, USA
Sheppard, Jonathan *Steeplechase Racing Trainer*
287 Lamborn Town Road, West Grove, PA 19390, USA
Sheppard, Mike *Football Coach*
%University of New Mexico, Athletic Dept, Albuquerque, NM 87131, USA
Sheppard, T G *Singer*
%RJ Kaltenbach Mgmt, 35W741 Valley View Road, Dundee, IL 60118, USA

Shepperd, Alfred J *Businessman*
Court Mead, 6 Guildown Ave, Guildford, Surrey GU2 5HB, England
Sher, Antony *Actor*
%Conway Van Gelder Robinson, 18-21 Jermyn St, London SW1Y 6NB, England
Shera, Mark *Actor*
PO Box 15717, Beverly Hills, CA 90209, USA
Sherbedgia, Rade *Actor*
%Innovative Artists, 1505 10th St, Santa Monica, CA 90401, USA
Sherffius, John *Editorial Cartoonist*
%Saint Louis Post Dispatch, Editorial Dept, 900 N Tucker, Saint Louis, MO 63101, USA
Sheridan, Bonnie Bramlett *Singer (Delaney & Bonnie), Actress*
18011 Martha St, Encino, CA 91316, USA
Sheridan, Dinah *Actress*
%International Creative Mgmt, 76 Oxford St, London W1N 0AX, England
Sheridan, Jamey *Actor*
%Sames/Rollnick Assoc, 250 W 57th St, New York, NY 10107, USA
Sheridan, Jim *Movie Director, Producer*
%Creative Artists Agency, 9830 Wilshire Blvd, Beverly Hills, CA 90212, USA
Sheridan, Nicolette *Actress*
%Gersh Agency, 232 N Canon Dr, Beverly Hills, CA 90210, USA
Sheridan, Tony *Singer*
%Gems, PO Box 1031, Montrose, CA 91021, USA
Sherlock, Nancy J *Astronaut*
%NASA, Johnson Space Center, 2101 NASA Road, Houston, TX 77058, USA
Sherman, Alex (Allie) *Football Player, Coach*
%New York Off Track Betting Corp, 1501 Broadway, #1000, New York, NY 10036, USA
Sherman, Bobby *Singer, Actor*
1870 Sunset Plaza Dr, Los Angeles, CA 90069, USA
Sherman, Cindy *Photographer*
%Metro Pictures, 519 W 24th St, New York, NY 10011, USA
Sherman, Edgar A *Football Coach*
681 Nancy Lane, Newark, OH 43055, USA
Sherman, Mike *Football Coach*
%Green Bay Packers, PO Box 10628, Green Bay, WI 54307, USA
Sherman, Richard M *Composer, Lyricist*
PO Box 17740, Beverly Hills, CA 90209, USA
Sherman, Vincent *Movie Director*
6355 Sycamore Meadows Dr, Malibu, CA 90265, USA
Sherrard, Michael W (Mike) *Football Player*
30130 Cuthbert Road, Malibu, CA 90265, USA
Sherrill, Jackie W *Football Coach*
%Mississippi State University, Athletic Dept, Mississippi State, MS 39762, USA
Sherrin, Edward G (Ned) *Television Director*
4 Cornwall Mansions, Ashburnham Road, London SW10 0PE, England
Sherry, Lawrence (Larry) *Baseball Player*
27181 Arena Lane, Mission Viejo, CA 92691, USA
Sherry, Paul H *Religious Leader*
%United Church of Christ, 700 Prospect Ave, Cleveland, OH 44115, USA
Shesol, Jeff *Cartoonist (Thatch)*
%Creators Syndicate, 5777 W Century Blvd, #700, Los Angeles, CA 90045, USA
Shevardnadze, Eduard A *President, Georgia*
%President's Office, Rustaveli Prosp 29, Tbilsi 380008, Georgia
Shicoff, Neil *Opera Singer*
%Opera et Concert, Maximilianstr 22, 80539 Munich, Germany
Shields, Brooke *Model, Actress*
%Christa Inc, 10061 Riverside Dr, #1013, Toluca Lake, CA 91602, USA
Shields, Perry *Judge*
%US Tax Court, 400 2nd St NW, Washington, DC 20217, USA
Shields, Robert *Mime (Shields & Yarnell)*
%Robert Shields Designs, PO Box 10024, Sedona, AZ 86339, USA
Shields, Will H *Football Player*
%Kansas City Chiefs, 1 Arrowhead Dr, Kansas City, KS 64129, USA
Shifty Shellshock *Rap Artist, Lyricist (Crazy Town)*
%Q Prime, 729 7th Ave, #1600, New York, NY 10019, USA
Shigeta, James *Actor*
10635 Santa Monica Blvd, #130, Los Angeles, CA 90025, USA
Shikler, Aaron *Artist*
44 W 77th St, New York, NY 10024, USA
Shiley Newhouse, Jean *Track Athlete*
11000 Sunnybrae Ave, Chatsworth, CA 91311, USA
Shilton, Peter *Soccer Player*
Hubbards Cottage, Bentley Lane, Maxstoke near Coleshill B46 2QR, England
Shima, Masatoshi *Electronics Engineer*
%Shima Co, 260 Tsurumaki, Omika Haramachishi, Fukushima 975-0049, Japan
Shimell, William *Opera Singer*
%I M G Artists, 3 Burlington Lane, Chiswick, London W4 2TH, England
Shimerman, Armin *Actor*
%Innovative Artists, 1505 10th St, Santa Monica, CA 90401, USA

S

Shimkus - Shorthill

Shimkus, Joanna *Actress*
%Creative Artists Agency, 9830 Wilshire Blvd, Beverly Hills, CA 90212, USA
Shimono, Sab *Actor*
12711 Ventura Blvd, #440, Studio City, CA 91604, USA
Shine, Michael (Mike) *Track Athlete*
508 Royal Road, State College, PA 16801, USA
Shinefield, Henry R *Pediatrician*
2240 Hyde St, #2, San Francisco, CA 94109, USA
Shinnick, Donald (Don) *Football Player*
3721 Northampton Lane, Modesto, CA 95356, USA
Shinoda, Mike *Singer (Linkin Park)*
%Artist Group International, 9560 Wilshire Blvd, #400, Beverly Hills, CA 90212, USA
Shipler, David K *Journalist*
4005 Thornapple St, Bethesda, MD 20815, USA
Shipley, Walter V *Financier*
%Chase Manhattan Corp, 270 Park Ave, New York, NY 10017, USA
Shipman, Claire *Commentator*
%ABC-TV, News Dept, 77 W 66th St, New York, NY 10023, USA
Shipp, E R *Columnist*
%New York Daily News, Editorial Dept, 220 E 42nd St, New York, NY 10017, USA
Shipp, Jerry *Basketball Player*
PO Box 370, Kingston, OK 73439, USA
Shipp, John Wesley *Actor*
1219 Sunset Plaza Dr, West Hollywood, CA 90069, USA
Shirakawa, Hideki *Nobel Chemistry Laureate*
%University of Tsukuba, Chemistry Dept, Sakura-Mura, Ibaraki 305, Japan
Shirayanagi, Peter Seiichi Cardinal *Religious Leader*
%Archbishop's House, 3-16-15 Sekiguchi, Bunkyoku, Tokyo 112, Japan
Shire, David L *Composer*
19 Ludlow Ave, Palisades, NY 10964, USA
Shire, Talia *Actress, Director*
10730 Bellagio Road, Los Angeles, CA 90077, USA
Shirley, George I *Opera Singer*
%University of Michigan, Music School, Ann Arbor, MI 48109, USA
Shirley, J Dallas *Basketball Referee*
5324 Pommel Dr, Mount Airy, MD 21771, USA
Shirley-Quirk, John S *Opera Singer*
6062 Red Clover Lane, Clarksville, MD 21029, USA
Shobert, Bubba *Motorcycle Racing Rider*
8905 153rd St, Wolfforth, TX 79382, USA
Shocked, Michelle *Singer*
%Siddons Assoc, 584 N Larchmont Blvd, Los Angeles, CA 90004, USA
Shockley, Jeremy *Football Player*
%New York Giants, Giants Stadium, East Rutherford, NJ 07073, USA
Shockley, William *Actor*
6345 Balboa Blvd, #375, Encino, CA 91316, USA
Shoecraft, John A *Balloonist*
%Shoecraft Contracting Co, 7430 E Stetson Dr, Scottsdale, AZ 85251, USA
Shoemaker, Carolyn S *Geologist, Astronomer*
%Lowell Observatory, 1400 W Mars Hill Road, Flagstaff, AZ 86001, USA
Shoemaker, Robert M *Army General*
PO Box 768, Belton, TX 76513, USA
Shofner, Delbert M (Del) *Football Player*
1665 Del Mar Ave, San Marino, CA 91108, USA
Shofner, James (Jim) *Football Player*
9620 Champions Dr, Granbury, TX 76049, USA
Shoji, Dave *Volleyball Coach*
%University of Hawaii, Athletic Dept, Hilo, HI 96720, USA
Shonekan, Ernest A O *President, Nigeria*
12 Alexander Ave, Ikoyi, Lagos, Nigeria
Shonin, Georgi S *Cosmonaut, Air Force General*
%Potchta Kosmonavtov, Moskovskoi Oblasti, 141160 Syvisdny Goroduk, Russia
Shore, Howard *Composer*
%Gorfaine/Schwartz, 13245 Riverside Dr, #450, Sherman Oaks, CA 91423, USA
Shore, Pauly *Actor, Comedian*
8491 W Sunset Blvd, #700, West Hollywood, CA 90069, USA
Short, Bobby *Singer, Actor, Pianist*
444 E 57th St, #9E, New York, NY 10022, USA
Short, Martin *Actor, Comedian, Singer*
%J/P/M, 760 N La Cienega Blvd, #200, Los Angeles, CA 90069, USA
Short, Thomas C *Labor Leader*
%Theatrical Stage Employees Alliance, 1515 Broadway, New York, NY 10036, USA
Shorter, Frank *Track Athlete*
558 Utica Court, Boulder, CO 80304, USA
Shorter, Wayne *Jazz Saxophonist, Composer*
%International Music Network, 278 S Main St, #400, Gloucester, MA 01930, USA
Shorthill, Richard W *Engineer*
%University of Utah, Mechanical Engineering Dept, Salt Lake City, UT 84112, USA

Shostakovich, Maxim D *Conductor, Concert Pianist*
PO Box 273, Jordanville, NY 13361, USA
Shou, Robin *Actor*
%Paradigm Agency, 10100 Santa Monica Blvd, #2500, Los Angeles, CA 90067, USA
Show, Grant *Actor*
937 S Tremaine Ave, Los Angeles, CA 90019, USA
Showalter, William N (Buck), III *Baseball Manager*
3839 W Madura Road, Gulf Breeze, FL 32563, USA
Shower, Kathy *Model, Actress*
Provenca 23 1-1, Barcelona, Spain
Shreve, Susan R *Writer*
3319 Newark St NW, Washington DC 20008, USA
Shribman, David M *Journalist*
%Boston Globe, Editorial Dept, 1130 Connecticut Ave NW, Washington, DC 20036, USA
Shrimpton, Jean *Model, Actress*
Abbey Hotel, Penzance, Cornwall, England
Shriner, Kin *Actor*
%Don Buchwald, 6500 Wilshire Blvd, #2200, Los Angeles, CA 90048, USA
Shriner, Wil *Entertainer*
5313 Quakertown Ave, Woodland Hills, CA 91364, USA
Shriver, Eunice Kennedy *Association Executive*
9109 Harrington Dr, Potomac, MD 20854, USA
Shriver, Loren J *Astronaut*
108 Charleston St, Friendswood, TX 77546, USA
Shriver, Maria *Commentator*
3110 Main St, #300, Santa Monica, CA 90405, USA
Shriver, Pamela H (Pam) *Tennis Player*
509 S Gretna Green Way, Los Angeles, CA 90049, USA
Shriver, R Sargent, Jr *Government Official, Diplomat*
%Special Olympics Int'l, 1325 G St NW, #500, Washington, DC 20005, USA
Shrontz, Frank A *Businessman*
2949 81st Place, #P, Mercer Island, WA 98040, USA
Shrowder, Lisa *Auto Racing Driver*
1650 E Golf Road, Schaumburg, IL 60196, USA
Shroyer, Sonny *Actor*
12725 Ventura Blvd, #F, Studio City, CA 91604, USA
Shtalenkov, Mikhail *Hockey Player*
501 Broadway, Nashville, TN 37203, USA
Shtokolov, Boris T *Opera Singer*
%Mariinsky Theater, Teatralnaya Pl 1, Saint Petersburg, Russia
Shue, Andrew *Actor*
%Do Something, 423 W 55th St, #800, New York, NY 10019, USA
Shue, Elisabeth *Actress*
%Creative Artists Agency, 9830 Wilshire Blvd, Beverly Hills, CA 90212, USA
Shue, Gene *Basketball Coach, Executive*
4338 Redwood Ave, #B303, Marina del Rey, CA 90292, USA
Shugart, Alan F *Inventor (Computer Disc Drive)*
%Seagate Technologies, 920 Disc Dr, Scotts Valley, CA 95066, USA
Shula, David D (Dave) *Football Coach*
10805 Indian Trail, Cooper City, FL 33328, USA
Shula, Donald F (Don) *Football Player, Coach*
16 Indian Creek Island Road, Indian Creek Village, FL 33154, USA
Shula, Mike *Football Player, Coach*
7518 Spinnaker Ave NE, Tuscaloosa, AL 35406, USA
Shuler, Ellie G (Buck), Jr *Air Force General*
32 Willow Way W, Alexander City, AL 35010, USA
Shuler, Mickey C *Football Player*
332 Belle Vista Dr, Marysville, PA 17053, USA
Shultz, George P *Secretary, State, Treasury & Labor*
776 Dolores St, Stanford, CA 94305, USA
Shumate, John *Basketball Player, Coach*
306 E Calle de Arco S, Tempe, AZ 85284, USA
Shumway, Norman E *Heart Surgeon*
%Stanford University, Medical Center, 300 Pasteur Dr, Palo Alto, CA 94304, USA
Shutt, Steve *Hockey Player, Coach*
%Cimco Refrigeration, 65 Villiers, Toronto ON M5A 3S1, Canada
Shuttleworth, Mark *Astronaut*
%HBD Venture Capital, PO Box 1159, Durbanville 7551, South Africa
Shyamalan, M Night *Movie Director*
%United Talent Agency, 9560 Wilshire Blvd, #500, Beverly Hills, CA 90212, USA
Siani, Michael J (Mike) *Football Player*
748 Conifer Court, Myrtle Beach, SC 29572, USA
Sibbett, Jane *Actress*
2144 Nichols Canyon Road, Los Angeles, CA 90046, USA
Siberry, Jane *Singer, Songwriter*
%Sheeba, 238 Davenport Road, #291, Toronto ON M5R 1J6, Canada
Sibley, Antoinette *Ballerina*
%Royal Dancing Academy, 36 Battersea Square, London SW11 3LT, England

Sidgmore, John *Businessman*
%WorldCom, 500 Clinton Center Dr, Clinton, MS 39056, USA
Sidime, Lamine *Prime Minister, Guinea*
%Prime Minister's Office, Conakry, Guinea
Sidlin, Murry *Conductor*
%Catholic University, Music School, Washington, DC 20064, USA
Siebert, Wilfred C (Sonny) *Baseball Player*
2555 Brush Creek, Saint Louis, MO 63129, USA
Siegal, Jay *Singer, Guitarist (Tokens)*
%Brothers Mgmt, 141 Dunbar Ave, Fords, NJ 08863, USA
Siegbahn, Kai M B *Nobel Physics Laureate*
%University of Uppsala, Physics Institute, Box 530, 75 121 Uppsala, Sweden
Siegel, Barry *Journalist*
%Los Angeles Times, Editorial Dept, 202 W 1st St, Los Angeles, CA 90012, USA
Siegel, Herbert J *Businessman*
%Chris-Craft Industries, 767 5th Ave, New York, NY 10153, USA
Siegel, Janis *Singer (Manhattan Transfer)*
%International Creative Mgmt, 40 W 57th St, #1800, New York, NY 10019, USA
Siegel, L Pendleton *Businessman*
%Potlatch Corp, 601 W Riverside Ave, Spokane, WA 99201, USA
Siegfried *Animal Illusionist (Siegfried & Roy)*
%Beyond Belief, 1639 N Valley Dr, Las Vegas, NV 89108, USA
Siegfried, Larry *Basketball Player*
4178 Covert Road, Perrysville, OH 44864, USA
Siemaszko, Casey *Actor*
%Gersh Agency, 232 N Canon Dr, Beverly Hills, CA 90210, USA
Siemon, Jeffrey G (Jeff) *Football Player*
5401 Londonderry Road, Edina, MN 55436, USA
Siepi, Cesare *Opera Singer*
12095 Brookfield Club Dr, Roswell, GA 30075, USA
Siering, Lauri *Swimmer*
3829 Rotterdam Ave, Modesto, CA 95356, USA
Sierra, Gregory *Actor*
8050 Selma Ave, Los Angeles, CA 90046, USA
Sierra, Ruben A *Baseball Player*
1500 Copeland Road, Arlington, TX 76011, USA
Sievers, Roy E *Baseball Player*
11505 Bellefontaine Road, Saint Louis, MO 63138, USA
Sifford, Charlie *Golfer*
PO Box 43128, Highland Heights, OH 44143, USA
Sific, Mokdad *Prime Minister, Algeria*
%Prime Minister's Office, Government Palais, Al-Moradia, Algiers, Algeria
Sigel, Jay *Golfer*
1284 Farm Road, Berwyn, PA 19312, USA
Sigel, Tom *Cinematographer*
%International Creative Mgmt, 8942 Wilshire Blvd, #219, Beverly Hills, CA 90211, USA
Siilasvuo, Ensio *Army General, Finland*
Castrenikatu 6A17, 00530 Helsinki 53, Finland
Sikahema, Vai *Football Player*
28 Abington Road, Mount Laurel, NJ 08054, USA
Sikes, Cynthia *Actress*
250 Delfern Dr, Los Angeles, CA 90077, USA
Sikharulidze, Anton *Figure Skater*
%Ice House Skating Rink, 111 Midtown Bridge Approach, Hackensack, NJ 07601, USA
Sikking, James B *Actor*
258 S Carmelina Ave, Los Angeles, CA 90049, USA
Sikma, Jack *Basketball Player*
8005 SE 28th St, Mercer Island, WA 98040, USA
Silas, Paul *Basketball Player, Coach*
14 Colony Lane, Cleveland, OH 44108, USA
Silatolu, Ratu Timoci *Prime Minister, Fiji*
%Prime Minister's Office, 6 Berkeley Crescent, Suva, Viti Levu, Fiji
Silberman, Laurence H *Judge, Diplomat*
%US Court of Appeals, 3rd & Constitution NW, Washington, DC 20001, USA
Silberstein, Diane Wichard *Publisher*
%New Yorker Magazine, Publisher's Office, 4 Times Square, New York, NY 10036, USA
Silbey, Robert J *Chemist*
%Massachusetts Institute of Technology, Chemistry Dept, Cambridge, MA 02139, USA
Silja, Anja *Opera Singer*
%Colbert Artists, 111 W 57th St, New York, NY 10019, USA
Silk *Rap Artist*
%Creative Artists Agency, 9830 Wilshire Blvd, Beverly Hills, CA 90212, USA
Silk, David (Dave) *Hockey Player*
4 Glen Ridge Terrace, Norwell, MA 02061, USA
Silk, George *Photographer*
27 Owenoke Park, Westport, CT 06880, USA
Silla, Felix *Actor*
8927 Snowden Ave, Arleta, CA 91331, USA

Sillas, Karen *Actress*
PO Box 725, Wading River, NY 11792, USA
Silliman, Michael B (Mike) *Basketball Player*
6602 Deep Creek Dr, Prospect, KY 40059, USA
Sillitoe, Alan *Writer*
14 Ladbroke Terrace, London W11 3PG, England
Sills, Beverly *Opera Singer, Director*
Rural Farm Delivery, Lambert's Cove Road, Vinegard Haven, MA 02568, USA
Sills, Stephen *Architect, Interior Designer*
%Sills Huniford Assoc, 30 E 67th St, New York, NY 10021, USA
Silva, Henry *Actor*
8747 Clifton Way, #305, Beverly Hills, CA 90211, USA
Silva, Jackie *Volleyball Player*
%Marcia Esposito, PO Box 931416, Los Angeles, CA 90093, USA
Silver, Casey *Businessman*
%Universal Pictures, Universal City Plaza, Universal City, CA 91608, USA
Silver, Horace *Jazz Pianist, Composer*
%Bridge Agency, 35 Clark St, #A5, Brooklyn, NY 11201, USA
Silver, Joan Macklin *Movie Director*
%Silverfilm Productions, 510 Park Ave, #9B, New York, NY 10022, USA
Silver, Joel *Movie Producer*
%Creative Artists Agency, 9830 Wilshire Blvd, Beverly Hills, CA 90212, USA
Silver, Ron *Actor*
6116 Tyndall Ave, Bronx, NY 10471, USA
Silverman, Barry G *Judge*
%US Court of Appeals, 230 N 1st St, Phoenix, AZ 85025, USA
Silverman, Henry R *Businessman*
%Cendant Corp, 9 W 57th St, New York, NY 10019, USA
Silverman, Jonathan *Actor*
2255 Mountain Oak Dr, Los Angeles, CA 90068, USA
Silverman, Kenneth E *Writer, Educator*
%New York University, English Dept, 19 University Place, New York, NY 10003, USA
Silvers, Robert *Artist*
%Henry Holt, 115 W 18th St, New York, NY 10011, USA
Silverstein, Elliott *Movie Director*
%Gersh Agency, 232 N Canon Dr, Beverly Hills, CA 90210, USA
Silverstein, Joseph H *Conductor, Concert Violinist*
%Utah Symphony Orchestra, 123 W South Temple, Salt Lake City, UT 84101, USA
Silverstone, Alicia *Actress*
PO Box 1847, Burlingame, CA 94011, USA
Silvestri, Alan A *Composer*
%Gorfaine/Schwartz, 13245 Riverside Dr, #450, Sherman Oaks, CA 91423, USA
Silvestrini, Achille Cardinal *Religious Leader*
%Oriental Churches Congregation, Via Conciliazione 34, 00193 Rome, Italy
Silvia *Queen, Sweden*
Kungliga Slottet, Stottsbacken, 111 30 Stockholm, Sweden
Silvstedt, Victoria *Model, Actress*
%Andy Gould Mgmt, 8484 Wilshire Blvd, #425, Beverly Hills, CA 90211, USA
Sim, Gerald *Actor*
%Associated International Mgmt, 5 Denmark St, London WC2H 8LP, England
Simanek, Robert E *Korean War Marine Corps Hero (CMH)*
25194 Westmoreland Dr, Farmington Hills, MI 48336, USA
Sime, David W (Dave) *Track Athlete, Physician*
240 Harbor Dr, Key Biscayne, FL 33149, USA
Simeon II *King, Bulgaria; Prime Minister*
%Prime Minister's Office, 1 Dondukov Blvd, 1000 Sofia, Bulgaria
Simeoni, Sara *Track Athlete*
Via Castello Rivoli Veronese, 37010 Verona, Italy
Simic, Charles *Writer*
PO Box 192, Strafford, NH 03884, USA
Simitis, Costas *Prime Minister, Greece*
%Premier's Office, Leoferos Vassilssis Sophia 15, 106 74 Athens, Greece
Simmer, Charlie *Hockey Player*
17635 N 52nd Place, Scottsdale, AZ 85254, USA
Simmonds, Kennedy A *Prime Minister, Saint Kitts & Nevis*
PO Box 167, Earle Morne Development, Basseterre, Saint Kitts & Nevis
Simmons, Curtis T (Curt) *Baseball Player*
200 Park Road, Ambler, PA 19002, USA
Simmons, Floyd (Chunk) *Track Athlete*
2330 Pembroke Ave, #8, Charlotte, NC 28207, USA
Simmons, Gene *Singer, Bassist (Kiss)*
%McGhee Entertainment, 8730 Sunset Blvd, #195, Los Angeles, CA 90069, USA
Simmons, Jaason *Actor*
%Gilbertson & Kincaid Mgmt, 1330 4th St, Santa Monica, CA 90401, USA
Simmons, Jean *Actress*
636 Adelaide Place, Santa Monica, CA 90402, USA
Simmons, John E *Basketball, Baseball Player*
9 Lee Dr, Farmingdale, NY 11735, USA

S

Simmons - Simpson

Simmons, Joseph — *Rap Artist (Run-DMC)*
%Entertainment Artists, 2409 21st Ave S, #100, Nashville, TN 37212, USA
Simmons, Lionel J — *Basketball Player*
108 Wellesley Court, Mount Laurel, NJ 08054, USA
Simmons, Richard — *Physical Fitness Instructor*
9306 Civic Center Dr, Beverly Hills, CA 90210, USA
Simmons, Richard D — *Publisher*
%Int'l Herald Tribune, 181 Ave Charles de Gaulle, 92521 Neuilly, France
Simmons, Ruth — *Educator*
%Brown University, President's Office, Providence, RI 02912, USA
Simmons, Ted L — *Baseball Player*
PO Box 26, Chesterfield, MO 63006, USA
Simms, Larry — *Actor*
1043 Keeho Marina, Honolulu, HI 96819, USA
Simms, Philip (Phil) — *Football Player, Sportscaster*
%David Fishof Productions, 252 W 71st St, New York, NY 10023, USA
Simollardes, Drew — *Singer (Reveille)*
%David Levin Mgmt, 200 W 57th St, #308, New York, NY 10019, USA
Simon, Bob — *Commentator*
%CBS-TV, News Dept, 2020 M St NW, Washington, DC 20036, USA
Simon, Carly — *Singer, Songwriter*
%C Winston Simone Mgmt, 1790 Broadway, 1000, New York, NY 10019, USA
Simon, Claude — *Nobel Literature Laureate*
Place Vieille, Salses, 66600 Rivesaltes, France
Simon, Dick — *Auto Racing Executive*
%Dick Simon Racing, 701 S Girls School Road, Indianapolis, IN 46231, USA
Simon, George W — *Astronaut*
PO Box 62, Sunspot, NM 88349, USA
Simon, John I — *Movie, Drama Critic*
%New York Magazine, Editorial Dept, 444 Madison Ave, New York, NY 10022, USA
Simon, Josette — *Actress*
%Conway Van Gelder Robinson, 18-21 Jermyn St, London SW1Y 6NB, England
Simon, Neil — *Writer*
10745 Chalon Road, Los Angeles, CA 90077, USA
Simon, Paul — *Singer, Songwriter*
%Michael Tannen, 36 E 61st St, New York, NY 10021, USA
Simon, Paul M — *Senator, IL*
%Southern Illinois University, Public Policy Institute, Carbondale, IL 62901, USA
Simon, Scott — *Commentator*
%NBC-TV, News Dept, 30 Rockefeller Plaza, New York, NY 10112, USA
Simon, Simone — *Actress*
5 Rue de Tilsitt, 75008 Paris, France
Simonini, Edward (Ed) — *Football Player*
6617 E 113th St S, Bixby, OK 74008, USA
Simonis, Adrianus J Cardinal — *Religious Leader*
Aartsbisdom, BP 14019, Maliebaan, 3508 SB Utrecht, Netherlands
Simonon, Paul — *Bassist (Clash)*
%Premier Talent, 3 E 54th St, #1100, New York, NY 10022, USA
Simonov, Yuriy I — *Conductor*
%Moscow Conservatory, Gertsema St 13, Moscow, Russia
Simonsen, Renee — *Model, Actress*
%Ford Model Agency, 142 Greene St, #400, New York, NY 10012, USA
Simpson, Alan — *Educator*
Yellow Gate Farm, Little Compton, RI 02837, USA
Simpson, Alan K — *Senator, WY*
1201 Sunshine Ave, PO Box 270, Cody, WY 82414, USA
Simpson, Carole — *Commentator*
%ABC-TV, News Dept, 77 W 66th St, New York, NY 10023, USA
Simpson, Charles R — *Judge*
%US Tax Court, 400 2nd St NW, Washington, DC 20217, USA
Simpson, Geoffrey — *Cinematographer*
PO Box 3194, Bellevue Hills NSW 2023, Australia
Simpson, Jessica — *Singer*
%Hoffman Entertainment, 20 W 55th St, #1100, New York, NY 10019, USA
Simpson, Jimmi — *Actor*
%Agency for Performing Arts, 485 Madison Ave, New York, NY 10022, USA
Simpson, John F, Sr — *Harness Racing Driver*
Mount Morris Star Route, Waynesburg, PA 15370, USA
Simpson, Juliene Brazinski — *Basketball Player*
PO Box 1267, Stroudsburg, PA 18360, USA
Simpson, Louis A M — *Writer*
PO Box 119, Setauket, NY 11733, USA
Simpson, Orenthal James (O J) — *Football Player, Actor, Sportscaster*
9450 SW 112th St, Miami, FL 33176, USA
Simpson, Ralph — *Basketball Player*
5189 Fraser St, Denver, CO 80239, USA
Simpson, Scott — *Golfer*
15778 Paseo Hermosa, Poway, CA 92064, USA

Simpson, Suzi *Model, Actress*
24338 El Toro Road, #E315, Laguna Woods, CA 92653, USA
Simpson, Valerie *Singer (Ashford & Simpson), Songwriter*
%Associated Booking Corp, 1995 Broadway, #501, New York, NY 10023, USA
Simpson, Wayne K *Baseball Player*
330 E Collamer Dr, Carson, CA 90746, USA
Sims, Billy R *Football Player*
PO Box 3147, Coppell, TX 75019, USA
Sims, Kenneth W *Football Player*
PO Box 236, Kosse, TX 76653, USA
Sin, Jaime L Cardinal *Religious Leader*
121 Arzobispo St, Entramuros, PO Box 132, 10099 Manila, Philippines
Sinatra, Frank, Jr *Singer, Actor*
%Jack Grenier Productions, 32630 Concord Dr, Madison Heights, MI 48071, USA
Sinatra, Nancy *Singer, Actress*
7215 Williams Road, Lansing, MI 48911, USA
Sinbad *Actor, Comedian*
%Creative Artists Agency, 9830 Wilshire Blvd, Beverly Hills, CA 90212, USA
Sinclair, Clive M *Inventor (Pocket Calculator)*
%Sinclair Research, 7 York Central, 70 York Way, London N1 9AG, England
Sindelar, Joey *Golfer*
%PGA Tour, 112 PGA Tour Blvd, Ponte Vedra Beach, FL 32082, USA
Sinden, Donald A *Actor*
Rats Castle, Isle of Oxney, Kent TN30 7HX, England
Sinden, Harry *Hockey Player, Coach, Executive*
9 Olde Village Dr, Winchester, MA 01890, USA
Sinfelt, John H *Chemist*
%Exxon Research & Engineering, Clinton Township, RR 22E, Annandale, NJ 08801, USA
Singer, Isadore M *Mathematician*
%Massachusetts Institute of Technology, Mathematics Dept, Cambridge, MA 02139, USA
Singer, Lori *Actress*
%Chuck Binder, 1465 Lindacrest Dr, Beverly Hills, CA 90210, USA
Singer, Marc *Actor*
11218 Canton Dr, Studio City, CA 91604, USA
Singer, Maxine F *Educator, Molecular Biochemist*
5410 39th St NW, Washington, DC 20015, USA
Singer, William R (Bill) *Baseball Player*
1119 Mallard Marsh Dr, Osprey, FL 34229, USA
Singh, Tjinder *Singer (Cornershop)*
%Legends of 21st Century, 7 Trinity Row, Florence, MA 01062, USA
Singh, Vijay *Golfer*
%Int'l Mgmt Group, 1 Erieview Plaza, 1360 E 9th St, #1300, Cleveland, OH 44114, USA
Singh, Vishwanath Pratap *Prime Minister, India*
1 Teen Murti Marg, New Delhi 110001, India
Singletary, Michael (Mike) *Football Player*
8 Dipping Pond Court, Lutherville Timon, MD 21093, USA
Singleton, Chris *Football Player*
1461 W Hawk Way, Chandler, AZ 85248, USA
Singleton, John D *Movie Director*
PO Box 92547, Pasadena, CA 91109, USA
Singleton, Kenneth W (Kenny) *Baseball Player*
10 Sparks Farm Road, Sparks, MD 21152, USA
Singleton, Penny *Actress*
15245 La Maida St, #101, Sherman Oaks, CA 91403, USA
Sinise, Gary *Actor*
PO Box 6704, Malibu, CA 90264, USA
Sinner, George A *Governor, ND*
101 3rd St N, Moorhead, MN 56560, USA
Sinowatz, Fred *Chancellor, Austria*
Loewelstr 18, 1010 Vienna, Austria
Sinyavskaya, Tamara I *Opera Singer*
%Kunstleragentur Raab & Bohm, Plankengasse 7, 1010 Vienna, Austria
Siouxsie Sioux *Singer (Siouxsie & the Banshees)*
%Helter Skelter, Plaza, 535 Kings Road, London SW10 0S, England
Sipchen, Bob *Journalist*
%Los Angeles Times, Editorial Dept, 202 W 1st St, Los Angeles, CA 90012, USA
Sipe, Brian W *Football Player*
1630 Luneta Dr, Del Mar, CA 92014, USA
Siphandon, Khamtay *President, Laos; Army General*
%President's Office, Vientiane, Laos
Sir Mix-A-Lot *Rap Artist*
%Richard Walters, 1800 Argyle Ave, #408, Los Angeles, CA 90028, USA
Siren, Heikki *Architect*
Tiirasaarentie 35, 00200 Helsinki, Finland
Siren, Katri A H *Architect*
Tiirasaarentie 35, 00200 Helsinki, Finland
Sirico, Tony *Actor*
%Writers & Artists, 8383 Wilshire Blvd, #550, Beverly Hills, CA 90211, USA

Sirikit *Queen, Thailand*
%Chritrada Villa, Bangkok, Thailand
Sirtis, Marina *Actress*
%Metropolitan Talent Agency, 4526 Wilshire Blvd, Los Angeles, CA 90010, USA
Sisemore, Jerald G (Jerry) *Football Player*
1730 Whipporwill Trail, Leander, TX 78641, USA
Sisqo *Singer (Dru Hill)*
%Evolution Talent, 1776 Broadway, #1500, New York, NY 10019, USA
Sissons, Kimber *Actress*
412 Arnaz Dr, #204, Los Angeles, CA 90048, USA
Sister Max *Fashion Designer*
%Mount Everest Centre for Buddhist Studies, Katmandu, Nepal
Sisti, Sebastian D (Sibby) *Baseball Player*
38 Clifford Heights, Amherst, NY 14226, USA
Sisto, Jeremy *Actor*
%Bymel/O'Neil Mgmt, 1724 N Vine St, Los Angeles, CA 90028, USA
Sistrunk, Otis *Football Player*
PO Box 372, Dupont, WA 98327, USA
Sitkovetsky, Dmitry *Concert Violinist, Conductor*
%Columbia Artists Mgmt Inc, 165 W 57th St, New York, NY 10019, USA
Sittler, Darryl G *Hockey Player*
84 Buttonwood Court, East Amherst, NY 14051, USA
Sixx, Nikki *Singer, Bassist, Drummer (Motley Crue)*
936 Vista Ridge Lane, Westlake Village, CA 91362, USA
Siza, Alvaro *Architect, Pritzker Laureate*
%Oporto University, Architecture School, Oporto, Portugal
Sizemore, Tom *Actor*
%United Talent Agency, 9560 Wilshire Blvd, #500, Beverly Hills, CA 90212, USA
Sizer, Theodore R *Educator*
%Brown University, Essential Schools Coalition, Providence, RI 02912, USA
Sizova, Alla I *Ballerina*
%Universal Ballet School, 4301 Harewood Road NE, Washington, DC 20017, USA
Sjoberg, Patrik *Track Athlete*
Hokegatan 17, 416 66 Goteberg, Sweden
Sjoman, Vilgot *Movie Director*
Banergatan 53, 115 22 Stockholm, Sweden
Skaggs, Ricky *Singer, Guitarist*
380 Forest Retreat, Hendersonville, TN 37075, USA
Skah, Khalid *Track Athlete*
Boite Postale 2577, Fez, Morocco
Skarsgard, J Stellan *Actor*
Hogersgatan 40, 118 26 Stockholm, Sweden
Skele, Andris *Prime Minister, Latvia*
%Prime Minister's Office, Brivibus Bulv 36, Riga 226170 PDP, Latvia
Skelton, Byron G *Judge*
%US Court of Appeals, 717 Madison Ave NW, Washington, DC 20439, USA
Skelton, Richard K (Rich), Jr *Rodeo Rider*
1139 County Road 312, Llano, TX 78643, USA
Skerritt, Tom *Actor*
%United Talent Agency, 9560 Wilshire Blvd, #500, Beverly Hills, CA 90212, USA
Skibbie, Lawrence F *Army General*
2309 S Queen St, Arlington, VA 22202, USA
Skinner, Jimmy *Hockey Coach*
2860 Askin Ave, Windsor ON N9E 3H9, Canada
Skinner, Joel P *Baseball Player, Manager*
24310 Lake Road, Cleveland, OH 44140, USA
Skinner, Jonty *Swimmer, Coach*
%University of Alabama, Athletic Dept, Tuscaloosa, AL 35487, USA
Skinner, Mike *Auto, Truck Racing Driver*
%Lisa Shealy, 218 Sease Hill Road, Lexington, SC 29073, USA
Skinner, Robert R (Bob) *Baseball Player*
1576 Diamond St, San Diego, CA 92109, USA
Skinner, Samuel K *Secretary, Transportation; Businessman*
%Commonwealth Edison, 1 First National Plaza, PO Box 767, Chicago, IL 60690, USA
Skinner, Val *Golfer*
%Debbie Massey, PO Box 116, Cheboygan, MI 49721, USA
Skjelbreid, Ann-Elen *Biathlete*
5640 Eikelandsosen, Norway
Skjvorecky, Josef *Writer*
%Erindale College, English Dept, Toronto ON M5S 1A5, Canada
Skolimowski, Jerzy *Movie Director, Actor*
%Film Polski, Ul Mazowiecka 6/8, 00-048 Warsaw, Poland
Skoog, Meyer (Whitey) *Basketball Player, Coach*
35689 398th Lane, Saint Peter, MN 56082, USA
Skopil, Otto R, Jr *Judge*
%US Court of Appeals, Pioneer Courthouse, 555 SW Yamhill St, Portland, OR 97204, USA
Skorich, Nicholas L *Football Player, Coach*
8 Briarwood Court, Columbus, NJ 08022, USA

Skou, Jens C *Nobel Chemistry Laureate*
Rislundvej 9, Risskov 8240, Denmark
Skovhus, Bo *Opera Singer*
%Balmer & Dixon Mgmt, Granitweg 2, 8006 Zurich, Switzerland
Skowron, William J (Moose) *Baseball Player*
1118 Beachcomber Dr, Schaumburg, IL 60193, USA
Skrebneski, Victor *Photographer*
1350 N LaSalle Dr, Chicago, IL 60610, USA
Skrowaczewski, Stanislaw *Conductor, Composer*
%Minnesota Symphony, 1111 Nicollet Mall, Minneapolis, MN 55403, USA
Skvorecky, Josef V *Writer*
487 Sackville St, Montreal ON M4X 1T6, Canada
Sky, Alison *Architect*
%Site, 65 Bleecker St, New York, NY 10012, USA
Sky, Jennifer *Actress*
12533 Woodgreen, Los Angeles, CA 90066, USA
Skye, Ione *Actress*
8794 Lookout Mountain Ave, Los Angeles, CA 90046, USA
Skyrms, Brian *Philosopher*
%University of California, Philosophy Dept, Irvine, CA 92717, USA
Slade, Bernard N *Writer*
345 N Saltair Ave, Los Angeles, CA 90049, USA
Slade, Chris *Drummer (AC/DC)*
11 Leominster Road, Morden, Surrey SA4 6HN, England
Slade, Mark *Actor*
38 Joppa Road, Worcester, MA 01602, USA
Slaney, Mary Decker *Track Athlete*
2923 Flintlock St, Eugene, OR 97408, USA
Slash *Singer, Guitarist (Guns n' Roses)*
801 N Roxbury Dr, Beverly Hills, CA 90210, USA
Slater, Christian *Actor*
%International Creative Mgmt, 8942 Wilshire Blvd, #219, Beverly Hills, CA 90211, USA
Slater, Helen *Actress*
1327 Brinkley Ave, Los Angeles, CA 90049, USA
Slatkin, Leonard E *Conductor*
%Washington National Symphony, Kennedy Center, Washington, DC 20011, USA
Slaton, Tony *Football Player*
122 E Childs Ave, Merced, CA 95340, USA
Slattvik, Simon *Nordic Combined Athlete*
Bankgata 22, 2600 Lillehammer, Norway
Slaughter, John B *Educator*
%Occidental College, President's Office, Los Angeles, CA 90041, USA
Slaughter, Karin *Writer*
%Harper Collins Publishers, 10 E 53rd St, New York, NY 10022, USA
Slavin, Randall *Actor*
%Gold Marshak Liedtke, 3500 W Olive Ave, #1400, Burbank, CA 91505, USA
Slavitt, David R *Writer*
35 West St, #5, Cambridge, MA 02139, USA
Slay, Brandon *Wrestler*
6155 Lehman Dr, Colorado Springs, CO 80918, USA
Sledge, Percy *Singer*
PO Box 220082, Great Neck, NY 11022, USA
Slegr, Jiri *Hockey Player*
%Vancouver Canucks, 800 Griffiths Way, Vancouver BC V6B 6G1, Canada
Slezak, Erika *Actress*
%International Creative Mgmt, 40 W 57th St, #1800, New York, NY 10019, USA
Slichter, Charles P *Physicist*
61 Chestnut Court, Champaign, IL 61822, USA
Slick, Grace *Singer (Jefferson Airplane), Songwriter*
%Bill Thompson Mgmt, 2051 3rd St, San Francisco, CA 94107, USA
Sloan, Gerald E (Jerry) *Basketball Player, Coach*
300 S Washington St, McLeansboro, IL 62859, USA
Sloan, Norm L, Jr *Basketball Player, Coach*
%University of Florida, Athletic Dept, Gainesville, FL 32611, USA
Sloan, Robert B, Jr *Educator*
%Baylor University, President's Office, Waco, TX 76798, USA
Sloan, Stephen C (Steve) *Football Player, Coach, Administrator*
%University of Central Florida, Athletic Dept, Orlando, FL 32816, USA
Sloane, Carol *Singer*
%Magi Productions, 705 Centre St, #300, Boston, MA 02130, USA
Sloane, Lindsay *Actress*
%Abrams Artists, 9200 Sunset Blvd, #1125, Los Angeles, CA 90069, USA
Slobodyanik, Alexander *Concert Pianist*
%Columbia Artists Mgmt Inc, 165 W 57th St, New York, NY 10019, USA
Slonimsky, Sergey M *Composer*
9 Kanal Griboedova, #97, Saint Petersburg, Russia
Slotnick, Bernard *Publisher*
%DC Comics Group, 355 Lexington Ave, New York, NY 10017, USA

S

Slotnick - Smith

Slotnick, Joey *Actor*
%Gersh Agency, 232 N Canon Dr, Beverly Hills, CA 90210, USA
Sloviter, Dolores K *Judge*
%US Court of Appeals, US Courthouse, 601 Market St, Philadelphia, PA 19106, USA
Sloyan, James *Actor*
920 Kagawa St, Pacific Palisades, CA 90272, USA
Sluman, Jeff *Golfer*
808 McKinley Lane, Hinsdale, IL 60521, USA
Smagorinsky, Joseph *Meteorologist*
72 Gabriel Court, Hillsborough, NJ 08844, USA
Smale, Stephen *Mathematician*
68 Highgate Road, Kensington, CA 94707, USA
Small, Marya *Actress*
%CL Inc, 843 N Sycamore Ave, Los Angeles, CA 90038, USA
Small, William N *Navy Admiral*
1605 Bluecher Court, Virginia Beach, VA 23454, USA
Smalley, Richard E *Nobel Chemistry Laureate*
1816 Bolsolver St, Houston, TX 77005, USA
Smalley, Roy F, Jr *Baseball Player*
6319 Timber Trail, Edina, MN 55439, USA
Smallwood, Dwana *Dancer*
%Alvin Ailey American Dance Foundation, 211 W 61st St, #300, New York, NY 10023, USA
Smallwood, Richard *Singer*
%Sierra Mgmt, 1035 Bates Court, Hendersonville, TN 37075, USA
Smart, Amy *Actress*
%Endeavor Talent Agency, 9701 Wilshire Blvd, #1000, Beverly Hills, CA 90212, USA
Smart, Jean *Actress*
17351 Rancho St, Encino, CA 91316, USA
Smart, Keith *Basketball Player, Coach*
5306 Asterwood Dr, Dublin, CA 94568, USA
Smathers, George A *Senator, FL*
Alfred I du Pont Building, 169 E Flagler St, Miami, FL 33131, USA
Smeal, Eleanor C *Women's Activist*
900 N Stafford St, #1217, Arlington, VA 22203, USA
Smedley, Geoffrey *Sculptor*
RR 3, Gambier Island, Gibsons, BC V0N 1V0, Canada
Smehlik, Richard *Hockey Player*
8824 Hearthstone Dr, East Amherst, NY 14051, USA
Smerlas, Frederick C (Fred) *Football Player*
400 Main St, Waltham, MA 02452, USA
Smiley, Jane G *Writer*
316 Mid Valley Center, #273, Carmel, CA 93923, USA
Smirnoff, Yakov *Actor, Comedian*
%Comrade Entertainment, 3750 W 76 Country Blvd, Branson, MO 65616, USA
Smith Court, Margaret *Tennis Player*
21 Lewanna Way, City Beach, Perth WA 6010, Australia
Smith Osborne, Madolyn *Actress*
%United Talent Agency, 9560 Wilshire Blvd, #500, Beverly Hills, CA 90212, USA
Smith, Adrian *Guitarist (Iron Maiden)*
%Chipster Entertainment, 1976 E High St, #101, Pottstown, PA 19464, USA
Smith, Adrian *Basketball Player*
2829 Saddleback Dr, Cincinnati, OH 45244, USA
Smith, Alexis *Artist*
1907 Lincoln Blvd, Venice, CA 90291, USA
Smith, Allison *Actress*
%Innovative Artists, 1505 10th St, Santa Monica, CA 90401, USA
Smith, Amber *Model, Actress*
%Shelter Entertainment, 9255 Sunset Blvd, #1010, Los Angeles, CA 90069, USA
Smith, Andrea *Artist*
%Lahaina Gallery, 728 Front St, Lahaina, HI 96761, USA
Smith, Ann *Tennis Player*
2 Rivers Edge Road, Hull, MA 02045, USA
Smith, Anna Deavere *Actress*
%Creative Artists Agency, 9830 Wilshire Blvd, Beverly Hills, CA 90212, USA
Smith, Anna Nicole *Model, Actress*
330 Washington Blvd, #609, Marina del Rey, CA 90292, USA
Smith, Arthur K, Jr *Educator*
5346 Mcculloch Circle, Houston, TX 77056, USA
Smith, Beau *Cartoonist*
Flying Fist Ranch, PO Box 706, Ceredo, WV 25507, USA
Smith, Ben *Hockey Coach*
47 Norwood Heights, Gloucester, MA 01930, USA
Smith, Ben *Cartoonist (Ratz)*
%King Features Syndicate, 888 7th Ave, New York, NY 10106, USA
Smith, Bennett W *Religious Leader*
%Progressive National Baptist Convention, 601 50th St NE, Washington, DC 20019, USA
Smith, Billy *Hockey Player*
8356 Quail Meadow Way, West Palm Beach, FL 33412, USA

Smith, Billy Ray, Jr *Football Player*
14755 Caminito Porta Delgada, Del Mar, CA 92014, USA
Smith, Bob *Golfer*
%Signature Sports Group, 4150 Olson Memorial Highway, Minneapolis, MN 55422, USA
Smith, Brooke *Actress*
1860 N Fuller Ave, #104, Los Angeles, CA 90046, USA
Smith, Bruce B *Football Player*
20473 Tappahannock Place, Sterling, VA 20165, USA
Smith, C Reginald (Reggie) *Baseball Player*
22239 1/2 Erwin St, Woodland Hills, CA 91367, USA
Smith, Calvin *Track Athlete*
16703 Sheffield Park Dr, Lutz, FL 33549, USA
Smith, Carl R *Air Force General*
2345 S Queen St, Arlington, VA 22202, USA
Smith, Chad *Drummer (Red Hot Chili Peppers)*
%Q Prime, 729 7th Ave, #1600, New York, NY 10019, USA
Smith, Charles A (Bubba) *Football Player, Actor*
6085 Adobe Summit Ave, Las Vegas, NV 89110, USA
Smith, Charles Martin *Actor, Director*
980 Cedarcliff Court, Westlake Village, CA 91362, USA
Smith, Clinton J (Clint) *Hockey Player*
501-1919 Bellview Ave, West Vancouver BC V7V 1B7, Canada
Smith, Connie *Singer*
%Gurley Co, 1204B Cedar Lane, Nashville, TN 37212, USA
Smith, Cotter *Actor*
15332 Antioch St, #800, Pacific Palisades, CA 90272, USA
Smith, D Brooks *Judge*
%US Court of Appeals, Penn Traffic Bldg, 319 Washington St, Johnstown, PA 15901, USA
Smith, Darden *Singer, Songwriter*
%AGF Entertainment, 30 W 21st St, #700, New York, NY 10010, USA
Smith, Dean E *Basketball Coach*
%University of North Carolina, PO Box 2126, Chapel Hill, NC 27515, USA
Smith, Dick *Diving Coach*
5810 N 59th Ave, Glendale, AZ 85301, USA
Smith, Elmore *Basketball Player*
33065 Cedar Road, Mayfield Heights, OH 44124, USA
Smith, Emil L *Biochemist, Biophysicist*
%University of California, Medical School, Los Angeles, CA 90024, USA
Smith, Emmitt J, III *Football Player*
15001 Winnwood, Road, Dallas, TX 75254, USA
Smith, F Dean *Track Athlete*
PO Box 71, Breckenridge, TX 76424, USA
Smith, Frederick W *Businessman*
%FDX Corp, 942 S Shady Grove Road, Memphis, TN 38120, USA
Smith, G Elaine *Religious Leader*
%American Baptist Churches USA, PO Box 851, Valley Forge, PA 19482, USA
Smith, Gary *Hockey Player*
Villa Cortina, 4451 Albert St, #102, Burnaby BC V5C 2G4, Canada
Smith, George *Cartoonist (Smith Family)*
%Universal Press Syndicate, 4520 Main St, Kansas City, MO 64111, USA
Smith, Gregory *Actor*
4570 Van Nuys Blvd, #171, Sherman Oaks, CA 91403, USA
Smith, Gregory White *Writer*
129 1st Ave SW, Aiken, SC 29801, USA
Smith, Hamilton O *Nobel Medicine Laureate*
13607 Hanover Road, Reisterstown, MD 21136, USA
Smith, Harry *Commentator*
%CBS-TV, News Dept, 51 W 52nd St, New York, NY 10019, USA
Smith, Harry *Bowler*
580 E Cuyahoga Falls Ave, Akron, OH 44310, USA
Smith, Harry E (Blackjack) *Football Player, Coach*
805 Leawood Terrace, Columbia, MO 65203, USA
Smith, Hedrick L *Journalist*
4204 Rosemary St, Chevy Chase, MD 20815, USA
Smith, Hulett C *Governor, WV*
2105 Harper Road, Beckley, WV 25801, USA
Smith, Ian D *Prime Minister, Rhodesia*
Gwenoro Farm, Selukwe, Zimbabwe
Smith, Ivor *Architect*
Station Officer's House, Prawle Point, Kingsbridge, Devon TQ7 2BX, England
Smith, Jackie L *Football Player*
1566 Walpole Dr, Chesterfield, MO 63017, USA
Smith, Jaclyn *Actress*
10398 Sunset Blvd, #1200, Los Angeles, CA 90077, USA
Smith, James (Bonecrusher) *Boxer*
355 Keith Hills Road, Lillington, NC 27546, USA
Smith, Jennifer M *Premier, Bermuda*
%Premier's Office, Cabinet Building, 105 Front St, Hamilton HM 12, Bermuda

S

Smith - Smith

Smith, Jerry E *Judge*
%US Court of Appeals, 515 Rusk Ave, Houston, TX 77002, USA
Smith, Jim Ray *Football Player*
7049 Cliffbrook Dr, Dallas, TX 75254, USA
Smith, Jimmy O *Jazz Organist*
2761 Lacy Lane, Sacramento, CA 95821, USA
Smith, Joe *Basketball Player*
7639 Leafwood Dr, Norfolk, VA 23518, USA
Smith, John F (Jack), Jr *Businessman*
%General Motors Corp, 100 Renaissance Center, Detroit, MI 48243, USA
Smith, John L *Football Coach*
%Michigan State University, Daugherty Field House, East Lansing, MI 48824, USA
Smith, John W *Wrestler, Coach*
5315 S Sangre Road, Stillwater, OK 74074, USA
Smith, Josh *Palentologist*
%University of Pennsylvania, 240 S 33rd St, Philadelphia, PA 19104, USA
Smith, Justin *Football Player*
%Cincinnati Bengals, 1 Paul Brown Stadium, Cincinnati, OH 45202, USA
Smith, Kathy *Physical Fitness Instructor*
PO Box 491433, Los Angeles, CA 90049, USA
Smith, Katie *Basketball Player*
%Minnesota Lynx, Target Center, 600 1st Ave N, Minneapolis, MN 55403, USA
Smith, Ken *Landscape Architect*
80 Warren St, #28, New York, NY 10007, USA
Smith, Kerr *Actor*
%Sharp Assoc, 8721 Sunset Blvd, Los Angeles, CA 90069, USA
Smith, Kevin *Movie Director, Writer*
%View Askew Productions, 69 Broad St, #B, Red Bank, NJ 07701, USA
Smith, Kurtwood *Actor*
1146 N Central Ave, #521, Glendale, CA 91202, USA
Smith, Lane *Actor*
%Paradigm Agency, 10100 Santa Monica Blvd, #2500, Los Angeles, CA 90067, USA
Smith, Larry *Basketball Player*
4118 Waterview Court, Missouri City, TX 77459, USA
Smith, Lee A *Baseball Player*
2124 Highway 507, Castor, LA 71016, USA
Smith, Lois *Actress*
%Abrams Artists, 420 Madison Ave, #1400, New York, NY 10017, USA
Smith, Lonnie Liston, Jr *Jazz Keyboardist*
%Associated Booking Corp, 1995 Broadway, #501, New York, NY 10023, USA
Smith, Loren A *Judge*
%US Claims Court, 717 Madison Place NW, Washington, DC 20439, USA
Smith, Louise *Auto Racing Driver*
12 Carlton Ave, Greenville, SC 29611, USA
Smith, M Elizabeth (Liz) *Columnist*
160 E 38th St, New York, NY 10016, USA
Smith, Madeline *Actress*
%Joan Gray, Sunbury Island, Sunbury on Thames, Middx, England
Smith, Maggie *Actress*
%International Creative Mgmt, 76 Oxford St, London W1N 0AX, England
Smith, Marilynn *Golfer*
2503 Bluebonnet Dr, Richardson, TX 75082, USA
Smith, Martha *Actress, Model*
9690 Heather Road, Beverly Hills, CA 90210, USA
Smith, Marvin (Smitty) *Jazz Drummer*
%Joel Chriss, 300 Mercer St, #3J, New York, NY 10003, USA
Smith, Melanie *Actress*
%Innovative Artists, 1505 10th St, Santa Monica, CA 90401, USA
Smith, Michael W *Singer, Songwriter*
%GET Mgmt, 25 Music Square W, Nashville, TN 37203, USA
Smith, Mike *Editorial Cartoonist*
%Las Vegas Sun, Editorial Dept, 2275 Corporate Circle Dr, Henderson, NV 89074, USA
Smith, Moishe *Artist*
%Utah State University, Art Dept, Logan, UT 84322, USA
Smith, Nicholas *Actor*
%Michelle Braidman, 10/11 Lower John St, London W1R 3PE, England
Smith, O Guinn *Track Athlete*
2164 Hyde St, #306, San Francisco, CA 94109, USA
Smith, Orlando (Tubby) *Basketball Coach*
%University of Kentucky, Athletic Dept, Lexington, KY 40536, USA
Smith, Osborne E (Ozzie) *Baseball Player, Sportscaster*
PO Box 164, Saint Albans, MO 63073, USA
Smith, Patti *Singer, Songwriter*
%High Road, 751 Bridgeway, #300, Sausalito, CA 94965, USA
Smith, R Jackson *Diver*
122 Palmers Hill Road, #3101, Stamford, CT 06902, USA
Smith, Randy *Basketball Player*
1542 Amherst Ave, Buffalo, NY 14214, USA

Smith, Ray E *Religious Leader*
%Open Bible Standard Churches, 2020 Bell Ave, Des Moines, IA 50315, USA
Smith, Raymond W *Financier, Businessman*
%Rothschild North America, 1251 Ave of Americas, New York, NY 10020, USA
Smith, Rex *Actor*
16986 Encino Hills Dr, Encino, CA 91436, USA
Smith, Richard M *Editor*
%Newsweek Magazine, Editorial Dept, 251 W 57th St, New York, NY 10019, USA
Smith, Robert Gray (Graysmith) *Editorial Cartoonist*
%San Francisco Chronicle, 901 Mission St, San Francisco, CA 94103, USA
Smith, Robert Lee *Singer (Tams)*
%Speer Entertainment Services, PO Box 49612, Atlanta, GA 30359, USA
Smith, Robert S *Football Player*
5668 Harrison Ave, Maple Heights, OH 44137, USA
Smith, Robyn *Thoroughbred Racing Jockey*
1155 San Ysidro Dr, Beverly Hills, CA 90210, USA
Smith, Rod *Football Player*
821 W 4th St, Charlotte, NC 28202, USA
Smith, Roger *Actor*
2707 Benedict Canyon Dr, Beverly Hills, CA 90210, USA
Smith, Rolland *Commentator*
%CBS-TV, News Dept, 524 W 57th St, New York, NY 10019, USA
Smith, Ronnie Ray *Track Athlete*
752 W Athens Blvd, Los Angeles, CA 90044, USA
Smith, Royce *Football Player*
404 S College St, Claxton, GA 30417, USA
Smith, Russell *Singer (Amazing Rhythm Aces)*
%LC Media, PO Box 965, Antioch, TN 37011, USA
Smith, Sammi *Singer*
RR 4 Box 362, Bristow, OK 74010, USA
Smith, Shawnee *Actress*
%Diverse Talent, 1875 Century Park E, #2250, Los Angeles, CA 90067, USA
Smith, Sinjin *Volleyball Player*
%Assn of Volleyball Pros, 330 Washington Blvd, #400, Marina del Rey, CA 90292, USA
Smith, Stanley R (Stan) *Tennis Player*
%ProServe, 1101 Woodrow Wilson Blvd, #1800, Arlington, VA 22209, USA
Smith, Steven D (Steve) *Basketball Player*
24 Champions Trail, San Antonio, TX 78258, USA
Smith, Steven L *Astronaut*
15726 Lake Lodge Dr, Houston, TX 77062, USA
Smith, Taran *Actor*
%Full Circle Mgmt, 12665 Kling St, North Hollywood, CA 91604, USA
Smith, Tasha *Actress*
%Writers & Artists, 8383 Wilshire Blvd, #550, Beverly Hills, CA 90211, USA
Smith, Tommie *Track Athlete, Football Player*
13338 Lilac St, Chino, CA 91710, USA
Smith, Vernon L *Nobel Economics Laureate*
3830 9th St N, # PH 1E, Arlington, VA 22203, USA
Smith, Walter H F *Oceanographer, Cartologist*
%Nat'l Oceanic/Atmospheric Administration, Commerce Dept, Washington, DC 20230, USA
Smith, Wilbur *Writer*
%Charles Pick Consultancy, 3 Bryanston Place, #3, London W1H 7FN, England
Smith, Will *Actor, Singer, Rap Artist*
%Handprint Entertainment, 1100 Glendon Ave, #1000, Los Angeles, CA 90024, USA
Smith, William *Actor*
3202 Anacapa St, Santa Barbara, CA 93105, USA
Smith, William (Bill), Jr *Swimmer*
46-049 Alii Anela Place, #1726, Kaneohe, HI 96744, USA
Smith, William D *Navy Admiral*
7025 Fairway Oaks, Fayetteville, PA 17222, USA
Smith, William Jay *Writer*
62 Luther Shaw Road, RR 1 Box 151, Cummington, MA 01026, USA
Smith, William R, Jr *Attorney*
1 Harbour Place, PO Box 3239, Tampa, FL 33601, USA
Smith, William Y *Army General*
6541 Brooks Place, Falls Church, VA 22044, USA
Smith, Willie *Football Player*
%Baltimore Ravens, Ravens Stadium, 11001 Russell St, Baltimore, MD 21230, USA
Smith, Yeardley *Actress*
%Bresler Kelly Assoc, 11500 W Olympic Blvd, #510, Los Angeles, CA 90064, USA
Smith, Zadie *Writer*
%Random House, 1745 Broadway, #B1, New York, NY 10019, USA
Smithies, Oliver *Geneticist*
318 Umstead Dr, Chapel Hill, NC 27516, USA
Smitrovich, Bill *Actor*
5075 Amestoy Ave, Encino, CA 91316, USA
Smits, Jimmy *Actor*
%El Sendero, PO Box 49922, Barrington Station, Los Angeles, CA 90049, USA

S

Smogolski - Snow

Smogolski, Henry R *Financier*
%Northwestern Savings & Loan, 2300 N Western Ave, Chicago, IL 60647, USA
Smolan, Rick *Photographer*
%Workman Publishers, 708 Broadway, New York, NY 10003, USA
Smolinski, Mark *Football Player*
3300 Country Club Road, Petoskey, MI 49770, USA
Smolka, James W *Test Pilot*
PO Box 2123, Lancaster, CA 93539, USA
Smoltz, John A *Baseball Player*
5950 State Bridge Road, #H303, Duluth, GA 30097, USA
Smoot, George F, III *Astrophysicist*
%Lawrence Berkeley Laboratory, 1 Cyclotron Blvd, Berkeley, CA 94720, USA
Smothers, Dick *Actor, Comedian (Smothers Brothers)*
6442 Coldwater Canyon Ave, #107B, North Hollywood, CA 91606, USA
Smothers, Tom *Actor, Comedian (Smothers Brothers)*
6442 Coldwater Canyon Ave, #107B, North Hollywood, CA 91606, USA
Smuin, Michael *Ballet Dancer, Choreographer*
%Smuin Ballets, 1314 34th Ave, San Francisco, CA 94122, USA
Smylie, Robert E *Governor, ID*
1436 Lewis St, Boise, ID 83712, USA
Smyth, Charles P *Physical Chemist*
245 Prospect Ave, Princeton, NJ 08540, USA
Smyth, Joe *Singer, Drummer (Sawyer Brown)*
%Sawyer Brown Inc, 5200 Old Harding Road, Franklin, TN 37064, USA
Smyth, Patty *Singer, Songwriter*
23712 Malibu Colony Road, Malibu, CA 90265, USA
Smyth, Randy *Yachtsman*
17136 Bluewater Lane, Huntington Beach, CA 92649, USA
Smyth, Ryan *Hockey Player*
%Newport Sports, 601-201 City Centre Dr, Mississauga ON L5B 2T4, Canada
Snead, Jesse Caryle (J C) *Golfer*
PO Box 782170, Wichita, KS 67278, USA
Snead, Norman B (Norm) *Football Player*
3951 Gulf Shore Blvd, #303, Naples, FL 34103, USA
Snead, W T, Sr *Religious Leader*
%Baptist Convention Missionary, 1404 E Firestone Blvd, Los Angeles, CA 90001, USA
Sneed, Floyd *Drummer (Three Dog Night)*
%McKenzie Accountancy, 5171 Caliente St, #134, Las Vegas, NV 89119, USA
Sneed, Joseph T *Judge*
%US Court of Appeals, Court Building, 95 7th St, San Francisco, CA 94103, USA
Sneider, Richard L *Diplomat*
211 Central Park West, New York, NY 10024, USA
Snell, Esmond E *Biochemist*
970 Aurora Ave, #A202, Boulder, CO 80302, USA
Snell, Matthews (Matt) *Football Player*
%Snell Construction, 175 Clendenny Ave, Jersey City, NJ 07304, USA
Snell, Peter *Track Athlete*
6452 Dunston Lane, Dallas, TX 75214, USA
Sneva, Tom *Auto Racing Driver*
3301 E Valley Vista Lane, Paradise Valley, AZ 85253, USA
Snider, Dee *Singer (Twisted Sister)*
%Pooch, 9511 Weldon Circle, #316, Fort Lauderdale, FL 33321, USA
Snider, Edwin D (Duke) *Baseball Player*
3037 Lakemont Dr, Fallbrook, CA 92028, USA
Snider, R Michael *Medical Researcher*
%Pfizer Pharmaceuticals, Eastern Point Road, Groton, CT 06340, USA
Snider, Todd *Singer, Songwriter*
%Al Bunneta Mgmt, 33 Music Square W, #102B, Nashville, TN 37203, USA
Snipes, Wesley *Actor*
%Nadashingha, PO Box 490, New York, NY 10014, USA
Snodgrass, William D *Writer*
3061 Hughes Road, Erieville, NY 13061, USA
Snodgress, Carrie *Actress*
3025 Surry St, Los Angeles, CA 90027, USA
Snoop Doggy Dogg *Rap Artist*
%Firstars Mgmt, 14724 Ventura Blvd, #PH, Sherman Oaks, CA 91403, USA
Snow *Rap Artist, Songwriter*
%Hype Music, 2076 Sherobee Road, #510, Mississauga ON L5A 4C4, Canada
Snow, Eric *Basketball Player*
%Philadelphia 76ers, 1st Union Center, 3601 S Broad St, Philadelphia, PA 19148, USA
Snow, Jack T *Football Player*
205 Los Lomas, Palm Desert, CA 92260, USA
Snow, Jack T (J T) *Baseball Player*
351 Fairfax Ave, San Mateo, CA 94402, USA
Snow, John W *Secretary, Treasury*
%Treasury Department, 1500 Pennsylvania Ave NW, Washington, DC 20220, USA
Snow, Mark *Composer*
%Gorfaine/Schwartz, 13245 Riverside Dr, #450, Sherman Oaks, CA 91423, USA

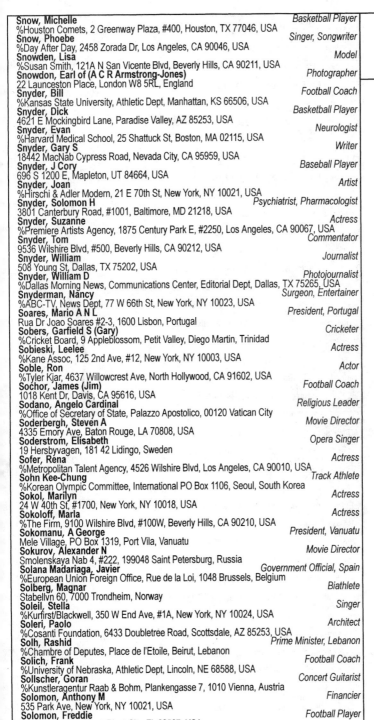

Snow, Michelle *Basketball Player*
%Houston Comets, 2 Greenway Plaza, #400, Houston, TX 77046, USA
Snow, Phoebe *Singer, Songwriter*
%Day After Day, 2458 Zorada Dr, Los Angeles, CA 90046, USA
Snowden, Lisa *Model*
%Susan Smith, 121A N San Vicente Blvd, Beverly Hills, CA 90211, USA
Snowdon, Earl of (A C R Armstrong-Jones) *Photographer*
22 Launceston Place, London W8 5RL, England
Snyder, Bill *Football Coach*
%Kansas State University, Athletic Dept, Manhattan, KS 66506, USA
Snyder, Dick *Basketball Player*
4621 E Mockingbird Lane, Paradise Valley, AZ 85253, USA
Snyder, Evan *Neurologist*
%Harvard Medical School, 25 Shattuck St, Boston, MA 02115, USA
Snyder, Gary S *Writer*
18442 MacNab Cypress Road, Nevada City, CA 95959, USA
Snyder, J Cory *Baseball Player*
696 S 1200 E, Mapleton, UT 84664, USA
Snyder, Joan *Artist*
%Hirschi & Adler Modern, 21 E 70th St, New York, NY 10021, USA
Snyder, Solomon H *Psychiatrist, Pharmacologist*
3801 Canterbury Road, #1001, Baltimore, MD 21218, USA
Snyder, Suzanne *Actress*
%Premiere Artists Agency, 1875 Century Park E, #2250, Los Angeles, CA 90067, USA
Snyder, Tom *Commentator*
9536 Wilshire Blvd, #500, Beverly Hills, CA 90212, USA
Snyder, William *Journalist*
508 Young St, Dallas, TX 75202, USA
Snyder, William D *Photojournalist*
%Dallas Morning News, Communications Center, Editorial Dept, Dallas, TX 75265, USA
Snyderman, Nancy *Surgeon, Entertainer*
%ABC-TV, News Dept, 77 W 66th St, New York, NY 10023, USA
Soares, Mario A N L *President, Portugal*
Rua Dr Joao Soares #2-3, 1600 Lisbon, Portugal
Sobers, Garfield S (Gary) *Cricketer*
%Cricket Board, 9 Appleblossom, Petit Valley, Diego Martin, Trinidad
Sobieski, Leelee *Actress*
%Kane Assoc, 125 2nd Ave, #12, New York, NY 10003, USA
Soble, Ron *Actor*
%Tyler Kjar, 4637 Willowcrest Ave, North Hollywood, CA 91602, USA
Sochor, James (Jim) *Football Coach*
1018 Kent Dr, Davis, CA 95616, USA
Sodano, Angelo Cardinal *Religious Leader*
%Office of Secretary of State, Palazzo Apostolico, 00120 Vatican City
Soderbergh, Steven A *Movie Director*
4335 Emory Ave, Baton Rouge, LA 70808, USA
Soderstrom, Elisabeth *Opera Singer*
19 Hersbyvagen, 181 42 Lidingo, Sweden
Sofer, Rena *Actress*
%Metropolitan Talent Agency, 4526 Wilshire Blvd, Los Angeles, CA 90010, USA
Sohn Kee-Chung *Track Athlete*
%Korean Olympic Committee, International PO Box 1106, Seoul, South Korea
Sokol, Marilyn *Actress*
24 W 40th St, #1700, New York, NY 10018, USA
Sokoloff, Marla *Actress*
%The Firm, 9100 Wilshire Blvd, #100W, Beverly Hills, CA 90210, USA
Sokomanu, A George *President, Vanuatu*
Mele Village, PO Box 1319, Port Vila, Vanuatu
Sokurov, Alexander N *Movie Director*
Smolenskaya Nab 4, #222, 199048 Saint Petersburg, Russia
Solana Madariaga, Javier *Government Official, Spain*
%European Union Foreign Office, Rue de la Loi, 1048 Brussels, Belgium
Solberg, Magnar *Biathlete*
Stabellvn 60, 7000 Trondheim, Norway
Soleil, Stella *Singer*
%Kurfirst/Blackwell, 350 W End Ave, #1A, New York, NY 10024, USA
Soleri, Paolo *Architect*
%Cosanti Foundation, 6433 Doubletree Road, Scottsdale, AZ 85253, USA
Solh, Rashid *Prime Minister, Lebanon*
%Chambre of Deputes, Place de l'Etoile, Beirut, Lebanon
Solich, Frank *Football Coach*
%University of Nebraska, Athletic Dept, Lincoln, NE 68588, USA
Sollscher, Goran *Concert Guitarist*
%Kunstleragentur Raab & Bohm, Plankengasse 7, 1010 Vienna, Austria
Solomon, Anthony M *Financier*
535 Park Ave, New York, NY 10021, USA
Solomon, Freddie *Football Player*
803 Turtle River Court, Plant City, FL 33567, USA

S

Solomon - Sorenstam

Solomon, Harold *Tennis Player*
%Int'l Mgmt Group, 1 Erieview Plaza, 1360 E 9th St, #1300, Cleveland, OH 44114, USA
Solomon, Richard H *Political Scientist, Diplomat*
%US Institute for Peace, 1200 17th St NW, #200, Washington, DC 20036, USA
Solomon, Susan *Atmospheric Chemist*
%National Oceanic & Atmospheric Admin, 325 Broadway, Boulder, CO 80305, USA
Solomon, Yonty *Concert Pianist*
56 Canonbury Park N, London N1 2JT, England
Solondz, Todd *Movie Director, Writer*
%Industry Entertainment, 955 Carillo Dr, #300, Los Angeles, CA 90048, USA
Soloviyev, Vladimir A *Cosmonaut*
Khovanskaya Ul D 3, Kv 28, 129515 Moscow, Russia
Solovyev, Anatoli Y *Cosmonaut*
%Potchta Kosmonavtov, Moskovskoi Oblasti, 141160 Syvisdny Goroduk, Russia
Solovyev, Sergei A *Movie Director, Writer*
Akademika Pilyugina Str 8, Korp 1, #330, 11393 Moscow, Russia
Solow, Robert M *Nobel Economics Laureate*
528 Lewis Wharf, Boston, MA 02110, USA
Soltau, Gordon (Gordy) *Football Player*
1290 Sharon Park Dr, Menlo Park, CA 94025, USA
Solzhenitsyn, Aleksandr I *Nobel Literature Laureate*
%Farrar Straus Giroux, 19 Union Square W, New York, NY 10003, USA
Somare, Michael T *Prime Minister, Papua New Guinea*
%Assembly House, Karan, Murik Lakes, East Sepik, Papua New Guinea
Somers, Brett *Actress*
4 Willow Wall, Westport, CT 06880, USA
Somers, Gwen *Actress, Model*
%Alice Fries Agency, 1927 Vista Del Mar Ave, Los Angeles, CA 90068, USA
Somers, Suzanne *Actress*
%William Morris Agency, 151 El Camino Dr, Beverly Hills, CA 90212, USA
Sommars, Julie *Actress*
%S D B Partners, 1801 Ave of Stars, #902, Los Angeles, CA 90067, USA
Sommaruga, Cornelio *Association Executive*
%International Red Cross, 19 Ave de la Paix, 1202 Genoa, Switzerland
Sommer, Elke *Actress*
Atzelsberger Str 46, 91080 Marloffstein, Germany
Sommers, Joanie *Singer*
%Xentel, 900 SE 3rd Ave, #201, Fort Lauderdale, FL 33316, USA
Somogyi, Jozsef *Sculptor*
Marton Utca 3/5, 1038 Budapest, Hungary
Somorjai, Gabor A *Chemist*
665 San Luis Road, Berkeley, CA 94707, USA
Sondheim, Stephen J *Composer, Lyricist*
300 Park Ave, #1700, New York, NY 10022, USA
Songaila, Antoinette *Astronomer*
%University of Hawaii, Astronomy Dept, Honolulu, HI 96822, USA
Sonja *Queen, Norway*
Det Kongelige Slott, Drammensveien 1, 0010 Oslo, Norway
Sonnenfeld, Barry *Movie Director*
%Endeavor Talent Agency, 9701 Wilshire Blvd, #1000, Beverly Hills, CA 90212, USA
Sonnenschein, Hugo F *Educator*
%University of Chicago, President's Office, Chicago, IL 60637, USA
Sonnier, Jo-El *Singer*
%Entertainment Artists, 2409 21st Ave S, #100, Nashville, TN 37212, USA
Sonsini, Larry W *Attorney*
%Wilson Sonsini Goodrich Rosati, 650 Page Mill Road, Palo Alto, CA 94304, USA
Sontag, Susan *Writer*
470 W 24th St, New York, NY 10011, USA
Sophia *Queen, Spain*
%Palacio de la Zarzuela, 28071 Madrid, Spain
Soraya *Singer*
%Firstars Mgmt, 14724 Ventura Blvd, #PH, Sherman Oaks, CA 91403, USA
Sorbo, Kevin *Actor*
%Gold-Miller Mgmt, 9220 Sunset Blvd, #320, Los Angeles, CA 90069, USA
Sorel, Edward *Artist*
156 Franklin St, New York, NY 10013, USA
Sorel, Jean *Actor*
%Cineart, 36 Rue de Ponthieu, 75008 Paris, France
Sorel, Louise *Actress*
10808 Lindbrook Dr, Los Angeles, CA 90024, USA
Sorel, Nancy *Actress*
%Paul Kohner, 9300 Wilshire Blvd, #555, Beverly Hills, CA 90212, USA
Sorensen, Jacki F *Physical Fitness Expert*
%Jacki's Inc, 129 1/2 N Woodland Blvd, #5, Deland, FL 32720, USA
Sorenson, Richard K *WW II Marine Corps Hero (CMH)*
3393 Skyline Blvd, Reno, NV 89509, USA
Sorenstam, Annika *Golfer*
%Int'l Mgmt Group, 1 Erieview Plaza, 1360 E 9th St, #1300, Cleveland, OH 44114, USA

Soriano, Alfonso G *Baseball Player*
%New York Yankees, Yankee Stadium, 161st St & River Ave, Bronx, NY 10451, USA
Soriano, Edward *Army General*
Vice Commander, I Corps/Fort Lewis, Fort Lewis, WA 98433, USA
Sorkin, Arleen *Actress*
623 S Beverly Glen Blvd, Los Angeles, CA 90024, USA
Sorlie, Donald M *Test Pilot*
14612 44th Ave NW, Gig Harbor, WA 98332, USA
Sorokin, Peter P *Physicist*
5 Ashwood Road, South Salem, NY 10590, USA
Soros, George *Financier*
%Soros Fund Mgmt, 888 7th Ave, #3300, New York, NY 10106, USA
Sorsa, T Kalevi *Prime Minister, Finland*
Hakaniemenranta 16D, 00530 Helsinki, Finland
Sorvino, Mira *Actress*
200 Park Ave S, #800, New York, NY 10003, USA
Sorvino, Paul *Actor*
110 E 87th St, New York, NY 10128, USA
Sosa, Mercedes *Singer, Songwriter*
%Blue Moon Art Mgmt, 270 Ave of Americas, New York, NY 10014, USA
Sosa, Samuel (Sammy) *Baseball Player*
505 N Lake Shore Dr, #5500, Chicago, IL 60611, USA
Sossamon, Shannyn *Actress*
550 N Larchmont Blvd, #201, Los Angeles, CA 90004, USA
Sotin, Hans *Opera Singer*
Schulheide 10, 21227 Bendestorf, Germany
Sotkilava, Zurab L *Opera Singer*
%Bolshoi Theater, Teatralnaya Pl 1, 103009 Moscow, Russia
Soto, Jock *Ballet Dancer*
%New York City Ballet, Lincoln Center Plaza, New York, NY 10023, USA
Soto, Mario M *Baseball Player*
Joachs-Lachaustegui #42, Sur-Bani, Dominican Republic
Soto, Talisa *Actress, Model*
%Flick East-West, 9057 Nemo St, #A, West Hollywood, CA 90069, USA
Sotomayor Sanabria, Javier *Track Athlete*
%Int'l Mgmt Group, 1 Erieview Plaza, 1360 E 9th St, #1300, Cleveland, OH 44114, USA
Sottsass, Ettore, Jr *Industrial Designer*
Via Manzoni 14, 20121 Milan, Italy
Souchak, Mike *Golfer*
79 Pelican Place, Belleair, FL 33756, USA
Soul, David *Actor, Singer*
%Innovative Artists, 1505 10th St, Santa Monica, CA 90401, USA
Soulages, Pierre *Artist*
18 Rue des Trois-Portes, 75005 Paris, France
Sousa, Mauricio de *Cartoonist (Monica)*
%Mauricio de Sousa Producoes, Rua do Curtume 745, Sao Paulo SP, Brazil
Soutar, Dave *Bowler*
6910 Chickasaw Falls Ave, Bradenton, FL 34203, USA
Soutar, Judy *Bowler*
3914 102nd Place N, Clearwater, FL 33762, USA
Soutendijk, Renee *Actress*
%Marion Rosenberg, PO Box 69826, West Hollywood, CA 90069, USA
Souter, David H *Supreme Court Justice*
%US Supreme Court, 1 1st St NE, Washington, DC 20543, USA
South, Joe *Singer, Songwriter, Guitarist*
3051 Claremont Road NE, Atlanta, GA 30329, USA
South, Leonard J *Cinematographer*
6208 Orion Ave, Van Nuys, CA 91411, USA
Souther, J D *Singer, Songwriter*
8263 Hollywood Blvd, Los Angeles, CA 90069, USA
Southern, Silas (Eddie) *Track Athlete*
1045 Rosewood Dr, Desoto, TX 75115, USA
Souza, Francis N *Artist*
148 W 67th St, New York, NY 10023, USA
Souzay, Gerard M *Opera Singer*
26 Rue Freycinet, 75116 Paris, France
Sowell, Arnold (Arnie) *Track Athlete*
1647 Waterstone Lane, #1, Charlotte, NC 28262, USA
Soyinka, Wole *Nobel Literature Laureate*
%University of Nevada, Creative Writing Dept, Las Vegas, NV 89154, USA
Soyster, Harry E *Army General*
4706 Duncan Dr, Annandale, VA 22003, USA
Spacek, Jaroslav *Hockey Player*
%Columbus Blue Jackets, Arena, 200 W Nationwide Blvd, Columbus, OH 43215, USA
Spacek, Sissy *Actress*
Beau Val Farm, Box 22, #640, Cobham, VA 22929, USA
Spacey, Kevin *Actor*
120 W 45th St, #3600, New York, NY 10036, USA

S

Spade - Spence

Spade, David *Actor, Comedian*
%International Creative Mgmt, 8942 Wilshire Blvd, #219, Beverly Hills, CA 90211, USA
Spader, James *Actor*
9530 Heather Road, Beverly Hills, CA 90210, USA
Spahn, Warren E *Baseball Player*
RR 2, Hartshorne, OK 74547, USA
Spahr, Charles E *Businessman*
800 Beach Road, Vero Beach, FL 32963, USA
Spain, Douglas *Actor*
%Innovative Artists, 1505 10th St, Santa Monica, CA 90401, USA
Spall, Timothy *Actor*
%Markham & Froggatt, Julian House, 4 Windmill St, London W1P 1HF, England
Spanarkel, Jim *Basketball Player*
436 Edgewood Place, Rutherford, NJ 07070, USA
Spano, Joe *Actor*
%EC Assoc, 10315 Woodley Ave, #110, Granada Hills, CA 91344, USA
Spano, Robert *Conductor*
%Atlanta Symphony, 1293 Peachtree St NE, Atlanta, GA 30309, USA
Spano, Vincent *Actor*
%More/Medavoy, 7920 W Sunset Blvd, #400, Los Angeles, CA 90046, USA
Spark, Muriel S *Writer*
%David Higham, 5-8 Lower John St, Golden Square, London W1R 4H4, England
Sparks, Dana *Actress*
%VOX, 5670 Wilshire Blvd, #820, Los Angeles, CA 90036, USA
Sparks, Hal *Actor, Singer, Comedian*
%Writers & Artists, 8383 Wilshire Blvd, #550, Beverly Hills, CA 90211, USA
Sparks, Nicholas *Writer*
%Warner Books, 1271 Ave of Americas, New York, NY 10020, USA
Sparlis, Alexander (Al) *Football Player*
13206 Mindanao Way, Marina del Rey, CA 90292, USA
Sparv, Camilla *Actress*
957 Cole Ave, Los Angeles, CA 90038, USA
Spassky, Boris V *Chess Player*
%State Committee for Sports, Skatertny Pereulok 4, Moscow, Russia
Speakman-Pitt, William *Korean War South African Army Hero (VC)*
%Victoria Cross Assn, Old Admiralty Building, London SW1A 2BL, England
Spear, Laurinda H *Architect*
%Arquitectonica International, 550 Brickell Ave, #200, Miami, FL 33131, USA
Spears, Billie Jo *Singer*
PO Box 23470, Nashville, TN 37202, USA
Spears, Britney *Singer, Actress*
%Rudolph & Beer, 432 Park Ave S, New York, NY 10016, USA
Spears, William D *Football Player*
63 Waterbridge Place, Ponte Vedra Beach, FL 32082, USA
Spector, Phil *Businessman, Songwriter*
686 S Arroyo Parkway, #175, Pasadena, CA 91105, USA
Spector, Ronnie *Singer*
%Absolute Artists, 8490 W Sunset Blvd, #403, West Hollywood, CA 90069, USA
Speech *Rap Artist (Arrested Development)*
%William Morris Agency, 1325 Ave of Americas, New York, NY 10019, USA
Speed, Lake *Auto Racing Driver*
4027 Old Salisbury Road, Kannapolis, NC 28083, USA
Speedman, Scott *Actor*
%Endeavor Talent Agency, 9701 Wilshire Blvd, #1000, Beverly Hills, CA 90212, USA
Speier, Chris E *Baseball Player*
6240 N 30th Place, Phoeniz, AZ 85016, USA
Speiser, Jerry *Drummer (Men At Work)*
%TPA, PO Box 124, Round Corner NSW, Australia
Spelling, Aaron *Television Producer*
%Aaron Spelling Productions, 5700 Wilshire Blvd, #575, Los Angeles, CA 90036, USA
Spelling, Randy *Actor*
%Aaron Spelling Productions, 5700 Wilshire Blvd, #575, Los Angeles, CA 90036, USA
Spelling, Tori *Actress*
594 N Mapleton Dr, Los Angeles, CA 90024, USA
Spellman, Alonzo R *Football Player*
1300 Marigold Way, Pflugerville, TX 78660, USA
Spellman, John D *Governor, WA*
7048 51st Ave NE, Seattle, WA 98115, USA
Spence, A Michael *Nobel Economics Laureate*
768 Mayfield Ave, Stanford, CA 94305, USA
Spence, Dave *Labor Leader*
%Horseshoers Union, RR 2 Box 71C, Englishtown, NJ 07726, USA
Spence, Gerry *Attorney*
%Spence Moriarity Schuster, 15 S Jackson St, Jackson, WY 83001, USA
Spence, Roger F *Religious Leader*
%Reformed Episcopal Church, 2001 Frederick Road, Baltimore, MD 21228, USA
Spence, Sebastian *Actor*
1005 Cambie St, Vancouver BC V6B 5L7, Canada

Spencer, Bud *Actor*
%Mistral Film Group, Via Archimede 24, 00187 Rome, Italy
Spencer, Danielle *Actress*
%Robert Barnham Mgmt, 432 Tygarah Road, Myocum NSW 2481, Australia
Spencer, Elizabeth *Writer*
402 Longleaf Dr, Chapel Hill, NC 27517, USA
Spencer, F Gilman *Editor*
%Denver Post, Editorial Dept, 1560 Broadway, Denver, CO 80202, USA
Spencer, Felton *Basketball Player*
%New York Knicks, Madison Square Garden, 2 Penn Plaza, New York, NY 10121, USA
Spencer, Jimmy *Auto Racing Driver*
18326 Mainsail Pointe Dr, Huntersville, NC 28078, USA
Spencer, John *Actor*
10316 Viretta Lane, Los Angeles, CA 90077, USA
Spencer, Tracie *Singer*
%Rogers & Cowan, 6340 Breckenridge Run, Rex, GA 30273, USA
Spencer-Devlin, Muffin *Golfer*
%Linda Stoick, 425 California St, #1900, San Francisco, CA 94104, USA
Sperber Carter, Paula *Bowler*
9895 SW 96th St, Miami, FL 33176, USA
Sperber, Wendie Jo *Actress*
%Bresler Kelly Assoc, 11500 W Olympic Blvd, #510, Los Angeles, CA 90064, USA
Spidla, Vladimir *Prime Minister, Czech Republic*
%Kancelar Presidenta Republiky, Hradecek, 119 08 Prague 1, Czech Republic
Spidlik, Tomas Cardinal *Religious Leader*
%Society of Jesus, Borgo S Spirito 4, CP 6139, 00195 Rome-Prati, Italy
Spiegelman, Art *Illustrator, Writer*
%Raw Books & Graphics, 27 Greene St, New York, NY 10013, USA
Spielberg, David *Actor*
10537 Cushdon Ave, Los Angeles, CA 90064, USA
Spielberg, Steven *Movie Director*
%DreamWorks SKG, 100 Universal City Plaza, Universal City, CA 91608, USA
Spielman, C Christopher (Chris) *Football Player, Sportscaster*
2094 Edgemont Road, Columbus, OH 43212, USA
Spikes, Jack E *Football Player*
9537 Highland View Dr, Dallas, TX 75238, USA
Spikes, Takeo *Football Player*
3475 Oak Valley Road NE, #130, Atlanta, GA 30326, USA
Spillane, Mickey *Writer, Actor*
PO Box 265, Murrells Inlet, SC 29576, USA
Spiller, Michael A *Cinematographer*
2418 Roscomare Road, Los Angeles, CA 90077, USA
Spindt, Capp *Inventor (Field Emission Display Screen)*
%SRI International, 333 Ravenswood Ave, Menlo Park, CA 94025, USA
Spinetta, Jean-Cyril *Businessman*
%Group Air France, 45 Rue de Paris, 95747 Roissy CDG Cedex, France
Spinetti, Victor *Actor*
15 Devonshire Place, Brighton, Sussex, England
Spinks, Leon *Boxer*
209 Jones St, Hollister, MO 65672, USA
Spinks, Michael *Boxer*
1240 Chateau Ave, Saint Louis, MO 63103, USA
Spinotti, Dante *Cinematographer*
%Smith/Gosnell/Nicholson, PO Box 1156, Studio City, CA 91614, USA
Spitz, Mark A *Swimmer*
383 Dalehurst Ave, Los Angeles, CA 90024, USA
Spitzer, Robert *Psychiatrist*
%Columbia University, Psychiatry School, New York, NY 10027, USA
Spizzirri, Angelo *Actor*
%Metropolitan Talent Agency, 4526 Wilshire Blvd, Los Angeles, CA 90010, USA
Splatt, Rachel *Auto Racing Driver*
12629 N Tatum Blvd, #184, Phoenix, AZ 85032, USA
Splittorff, Paul W, Jr *Baseball Player*
4204 Hickory Lane, Blue Springs, MO 64015, USA
Spohr, Arnold T *Ballet Director*
%Royal Winnipeg Ballet, 380 Graham Ave, Winnipeg MB R3C 4K2, Canada
Spong, John S *Religious Leader*
24 Puddingstone Road, Morris Plains, NJ 07950, USA
Spoonhour, Charles (Charlie) *Basketball Coach*
%University of Nevada, Athletic Dept, Las Vegas, NV 89154, USA
Sporkin, Stanley *Government Official, Judge*
%US District Court, Courthouse, 3rd & Constitution NW, Washington, DC 20001, USA
Spottiswoode, Roger *Movie Director*
132 Spaulding Dr, #217, Beverly Hills, CA 90212, USA
Spradlin, Danny *Football Player*
1011 Laurie St, Maryville, TN 37803, USA
Spradlin, G D *Actor*
%La Familia Ranch, PO Box 1294, San Luis Obispo, CA 93406, USA

Spratlan, Lewis *Composer*
%Amherst College, Music Dept, Amherst, MA 01002, USA
Sprayberry, James M *Vietnam War Army Hero*
426 Holiday Dr, Titus, AL 36080, USA
Sprewell, Latrell *Basketball Player*
4340 Purchase St, Purchase, NY 10577, USA
Spring, Sherwood C *Astronaut*
5427 Point Longstreet Way, Burke, VA 22015, USA
Springer, Jerry *Entertainer, Mayor*
454 N Columbus Dr, #200, Chicago, IL 60611, USA
Springer, Robert C *Astronaut*
202 Village Dr, Sheffield, AL 35660, USA
Springfield, Rick *Singer, Actor*
%Ron Weisner, 515 Ocean Ave, Santa Monica, CA 90402, USA
Springs, Alice *Photographer*
7 Ave Saint-Ramon, #T1008, Monte Carlo, Monaco
Springs, Shawn *Football Player*
%Seattle Seahawks, 11220 NE 53rd St, Kirkland, WA 98033, USA
Springsteen, Bruce *Singer, Songwriter*
1224 Benedict Canyon Dr, Beverly Hills, CA 90210, USA
Sprinkel, Beryl W *Government Official*
20140 Saint Andrews Dr, Olympia Fields, IL 60461, USA
Sprouse, James M *Judge*
%US Court of Appeals, PO Box 401, 122 N Court St, Lewisburg, WV 24901, USA
Spurrier, Stephen O (Steve) *Football Player, Coach*
17050 Silver Charm Place, Leesburg, VA 20176, USA
Spuzich, Sandra *Golfer*
%Ladies Pro Golf Assn, 100 International Golf Dr, Daytona Beach, FL 32124, USA
Squier, Billy *Singer, Songwriter*
PO Box 231251, New York, NY 10023, USA
Squirek, Jack *Football Player*
4051 Vezbar Dr, Seven Hills, OH 44131, USA
Sri Chinmoy *Religious Leader*
85-45 Sri Chinmoy St, Jamaica, NY 11432, USA
St Clair, Robert B (Bob) *Football Player*
%Clover Stornetta Farms, PO Box 750369, Petaluma, CA 94975, USA
St Florian, Friedrich G *Architect*
%Rhode Island School of Design, Architecture Dept, Providence, RI 02903, USA
St George, William R *Navy Admiral*
862 San Antonio Place, San Diego, CA 92106, USA
St James, Lyn *Auto Racing Driver*
%LSJ Racing, 57 Gasoline Alley, #D, Indianapolis, IN 46222, USA
St Jean, Garry *Basketball Coach, Executive*
%Golden State Warriors, 1001 Broadway, Oakland, CA 94607, USA
St John of Fawsley, Norman A F *Government Official, England*
Old Rectory, Preston Capes, Daventry, Northants NN11 6TE, England
St John, H Bernard *Prime Minister, Barbados*
3 Enterprise, Christchurch, Barbados
St John, Jill *Actress*
%Borinstein Oreck Bogart, 3172 Dona Susana Dr, Studio City, CA 91604, USA
St John, Kristoff *Actor*
3443 Violet Trail, Calabasas, CA 91302, USA
St John, Lara *Concert Violinist*
%Columbia Artists Mgmt Inc, 165 W 57th St, New York, NY 10019, USA
Stabler, Ken M (Kenny) *Football Player*
%Stabler Co, PO Box 460, Orange Beach, AL 36561, USA
Stacey Q *Singer, Actress*
641 S Palm St, #D, La Habra, CA 90631, USA
Stackhouse, Jerry *Basketball Player*
2124 Oakridge Dr, Kinston, NC 28504, USA
Stacy, Hollis *Golfer*
9400 W 10th Ave, Lakewood, CO 80215, USA
Stacy, James *Actor*
478 Severn Ave, Tampa, FL 33606, USA
Stadler, Craig R *Golfer*
1 Cantitoe Lane, Englewood, CO 80113, USA
Stadler, Sergei V *Concert Violinist, Conductor*
Kaiserstr 43, 80801 Munich, Germany
Stafford, Harrison *Football Player*
RR 1 Box 216, Edna, TX 77957, USA
Stafford, James Francis Cardinal *Religious Leader*
%Pontifical Council for the Laity, Piazza S Calisto 16, 00153 Rome, Italy
Stafford, Jim *Singer, Songwriter*
PO Box 6366, Branson, MO 65615, USA
Stafford, Jo *Singer*
2339 Century Hill, Los Angeles, CA 90067, USA
Stafford, John R *Businessman*
%American Home Products, 5 Giralda Farms, Madison, NJ 07940, USA

Stafford, Michelle *Actress*
606 N Larchmont Blvd, #210, Los Angeles, CA 90004, USA
Stafford, Nancy *Actress*
PO Box 11807, Marina del Rey, CA 90295, USA
Stafford, Robert T *Governor, Senator, VT*
1 Sugarwood Hill Road, RR 1 Box 3954, Rutland, VT 05701, USA
Stafford, Thomas P *Astronaut, Air Force General*
%AVD, PO Box 604, Glenn Dale, MD 20769, USA
Stager, Gus *Swimming Coach*
%University of Michigan, Athletic Dept, Ann Arbor, MI 48104, USA
Stahl, Lesley R *Commentator*
%CBS-TV, News Dept, 51 W 52nd St, New York, NY 10019, USA
Stahl, Lisa *Actress*
%Don Buchwald, 6500 Wilshire Blvd, #2200, Los Angeles, CA 90048, USA
Stahl, Nick *Actor*
1122 S Roxbury Dr, Los Angeles, CA 90035, USA
Stahl, Norman H *Judge*
%US Appeals Court, McCormack Federal Building, Boston, MA 02109, USA
Stahler, Jeff *Editorial Cartoonist*
%Cincinnati Post, Editorial Dept, 125 E Court St, Cincinnati, OH 45202, USA
Staley, Dawn M *Basketball Player, Coach*
1228 Callowhill St, #603, Philadelphia, PA 19123, USA
Staley, Gerald A (Gerry) *Baseball Player*
2517 NE 100th St, Vancouver, WA 98686, USA
Staley, Walter *Equestrian Rider*
214 Teal Lake Road, Mexico, MO 65265, USA
Stallings, George *Religious Leader*
%African American Catholic Congregation, 1015 I St NE, Washington, DC 20002, USA
Stallings, Larry *Football Player*
207 S Mason Road, Saint Louis, MO 63141, USA
Stallworth, Johnny L (John) *Football Player*
188 Boulton Court, Madison, AL 35756, USA
Stamm, Michael (Mike) *Swimmer*
23 Wildwood Road, Orinda, CA 94563, USA
Stamos, John *Actor*
%Shelter Entertainment, 9255 Sunset Blvd, #1010, Los Angeles, CA 90069, USA
Stamp, Terence *Actor*
%Markham & Froggatt, Julian House, 4 Windmill St, London W1P 1HF, England
Stanat, Dug *Artist*
46828 Bradley St, Fremont, CA 94539, USA
Standiford, Les *Writer*
%Harper/Collins, 10 E 53rd St, New York, NY 10022, USA
Standing, John *Actor*
%International Creative Mgmt, 76 Oxford St, London W1N 0AX, England
Stanfel, Richard (Dick) *Football Player, Coach*
1104 Juniper Parkway, Libertyville, IL 60048, USA
Stanfill, William T (Bill) *Football Player*
111 Amelia Lane, Leesburg, GA 31763, USA
Stang, Arnold *Actor*
PO Box 920386, Needham, MA 02492, USA
Stang, Peter J *Organic Chemist*
%University of Utah, Chemistry Dept, Salt Lake City, UT 84112, USA
Stankalla, Stefan *Alpine Skier*
Furstenstr 14, 82467 Garmisch-Partenkirchen, Germany
Stankovic, Borislav (Boris) *Basketball Executive*
PO Box 7005, 81479 Munich, Germany
Stankowski, Paul *Golfer*
%Cornerstone Sports, 14646 N Kierland Blvd, #230, Scottsdale, AZ 85254, USA
Stanley, Allan H *Hockey Player*
RR 3, Fennelon Falls ON K0M 1N0, Canada
Stanley, Marianne Crawford *Basketball Coach*
%Washington Mystics, MCI Center, 601 F St NW, Washington, DC 20004, USA
Stanley, Mitchell J (Mickey) *Baseball Player*
5319 Timberbend Dr, Brighton, MI 48116, USA
Stanley, Paul *Singer, Guitarist (Kiss)*
%McGhee Mgmt, 8730 Sunset Blvd, #195, Los Angeles, CA 90069, USA
Stanley, Ralph *Guitarist, Singer*
%Press Office, 2607 Westwood Dr, Nashville, TN 37204, USA
Stansfield Smith, Colin *Architect*
Three Ministers House, 76 High St, Winchester, Hants SO23 8UL, England
Stansfield, Lisa *Singer, Songwriter*
PO Box 59, Ashwell, Herts SG7 5NG, England
Stansky, Peter D L *Historian*
375 Pinehill Road, Hillsborough, CA 94010, USA
Stantis, Scott *Editorial Cartoonist (Buckets)*
%Birmingham News, Editorial Dept, 2200 4th Ave N, Birmingham, AL 35203, USA
Stanton, Andrew *Animator, Director, Writer*
%Pixar, 1200 Park Ave, Emeryville, CA 94608, USA

Stanton, Frank N *Broadcast Executive*
25 W 52nd St, New York, NY 10019, USA
Stanton, Harry Dean *Actor*
14527 Mulholland Dr, Los Angeles, CA 90077, USA
Stanton, Jeff *Motorcycle Racing Rider*
1137 Athens Road, Sherwood, MI 49089, USA
Stanton, Paul *Hockey Player*
39 Phillips St, Marblehood, MA 01945, USA
Stanton, Phil *Entertainer (Blue Man Group)*
%Blue Man Group, Luxor Hotel, 3900 Las Vegas Blvd S, Las Vegas, NV 89119, USA
Stapinski, Helene *Writer*
%Saint Martin's Press, 175 5th Ave, New York, NY 10010, USA
Staples, Mavis *Singer*
PO Box 498360, Chicago, IL 60649, USA
Stapleton, Jean *Actress*
%Bauman-Hiller, 5757 Wilshire Blvd, #512, Los Angeles, CA 90036, USA
Stapleton, Kevin *Actor*
%Gersh Agency, 232 N Canon Dr, Beverly Hills, CA 90210, USA
Stapleton, Maureen *Actress*
1 Morgan Manor, #14, Lenox, MA 01240, USA
Stapleton, Oliver *Cinematographer*
%MacCorkindale & Holton, 1640 5th St, #205, Santa Monica, CA 90401, USA
Stapleton, Walter K *Judge*
%US Court of Appeals, Federal Building, 844 N King St, Wilmington, DE 19801, USA
Stapp, Scott *Singer (Creed), Lyricist*
%Agency Group, 1776 Broadway, #430, New York, NY 10019, USA
Starbuck, Jo Jo *Figure Skater*
33 Pomeroy Road, Madison, NJ 07940, USA
Starck, Philippe *Architect, Industrial Designer*
3 Rue Faisans, 67300 Schiltigheim, France
Starfield, Barbara H *Physician*
%Johns Hopkins University, Hygiene School, 624 N Broadway, Baltimore, MD 21205, USA
Stark, Freya M *Writer, Explorer*
Via Canova, Asolo, Treviso, Italy
Stark, Graham *Actor*
%International Creative Mgmt, 76 Oxford St, London W1N 0AX, England
Stark, Koo *Actress*
%Rebecca Blond, 52 Shaftesbury Ave, London W1V 7DE, England
Stark, Melissa *Sportscaster, Commentator*
%NBC-TV, News Dept, 30 Rockefeller Plaza, New York, NY 10112, USA
Stark, Nathan J *Lawyer*
4000 Cathedral Ave NW, #132, Washington, DC 20016, USA
Stark, Ray *Movie Producer*
%MGM Studios, 10232 W Washington Blvd, Culver City, CA 90232, USA
Stark, Rohn T *Football Player*
PO Box 10067, Lahaina, HI 96761, USA
Starke, Anthony *Actor*
%Paradigm Agency, 10100 Santa Monica Blvd, #2500, Los Angeles, CA 90067, USA
Starker, Janos *Concert Cellist*
1241 Winfield Road, Bloomington, IN 47401, USA
Starkweather, Gary K *Optical Engineer*
10274 Parkwood Dr, #7, Cupertino, CA 95014, USA
Starling, James D *Army General*
5336 Dawn Oak Lane, Fair Oaks, CA 95628, USA
Starn, Douglas *Photographer*
%Stux Gallery, 163 Mercer St, #1, New York, NY 10012, USA
Starn, Mike *Photographer*
%Stux Gallery, 163 Mercer St, #1, New York, NY 10012, USA
Starner, Shelby *Singer*
%Morebarn Music, 30 Hillcrest Ave, Morristown, NJ 07960, USA
Starnes, Vaughn A *Surgeon*
%Stanford University, Med Center, Heart/Lung Transplant Dept, Stanford, CA 94305, USA
Starr, Albert *Cardiac Surgeon*
5050 SW Patton Road, Portland, OR 97221, USA
Starr, B Bartlett (Bart) *Football Player*
2065 Royal Fern Lane, Birmingham, AL 35244, USA
Starr, Brenda K *Singer*
%Brothers Mgmt, 141 Dunbar Ave, Fords, NJ 08863, USA
Starr, Chauncey *Electrical Engineer*
95 Stern Lane, Atherton, CA 94027, USA
Starr, Fredro *Rap Artist, Actor*
%Writers & Artists, 8383 Wilshire Blvd, #550, Beverly Hills, CA 90211, USA
Starr, Kay *Singer*
%Ira Okun Entertainment, 708 Palisades Dr, Pacific Palisades, CA 90272, USA
Starr, Kenneth W *Government Official, Judge*
%Pepperdine Law School, 24255 Pacific Coast Highway, Malibu, CA 90263, USA
Starr, Leonard *Cartoonist (Annie, Kelly Green)*
%Tribune Media Services, 435 N Michigan Ave, #1500, Chicago, IL 60611, USA

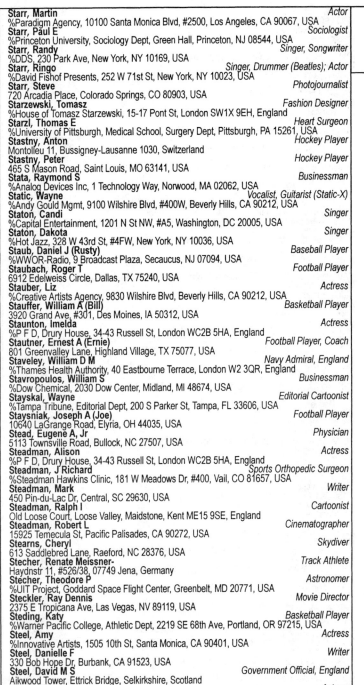

Starr, Martin *Actor*
%Paradigm Agency, 10100 Santa Monica Blvd, #2500, Los Angeles, CA 90067, USA
Starr, Paul E *Sociologist*
%Princeton University, Sociology Dept, Green Hall, Princeton, NJ 08544, USA
Starr, Randy *Singer, Songwriter*
%DDS, 230 Park Ave, New York, NY 10169, USA
Starr, Ringo *Singer, Drummer (Beatles); Actor*
%David Fishof Presents, 252 W 71st St, New York, NY 10023, USA
Starr, Steve *Photojournalist*
720 Arcadia Place, Colorado Springs, CO 80903, USA
Starzewski, Tomasz *Fashion Designer*
%House of Tomasz Starzewski, 15-17 Pont St, London SW1X 9EH, England
Starzl, Thomas E *Heart Surgeon*
%University of Pittsburgh, Medical School, Surgery Dept, Pittsburgh, PA 15261, USA
Stastny, Anton *Hockey Player*
Montolleu 11, Bussigney-Lausanne 1030, Switzerland
Stastny, Peter *Hockey Player*
465 S Mason Road, Saint Louis, MO 63141, USA
Stata, Raymond S *Businessman*
%Analog Devices Inc, 1 Technology Way, Norwood, MA 02062, USA
Static, Wayne *Vocalist, Guitarist (Static-X)*
%Andy Gould Mgmt, 9100 Wilshire Blvd, #400W, Beverly Hills, CA 90212, USA
Staton, Candi *Singer*
%Capital Entertainment, 1201 N St NW, #A5, Washington, DC 20005, USA
Staton, Dakota *Singer*
%Hot Jazz, 328 W 43rd St, #4FW, New York, NY 10036, USA
Staub, Daniel J (Rusty) *Baseball Player*
%WWOR-Radio, 9 Broadcast Plaza, Secaucus, NJ 07094, USA
Staubach, Roger T *Football Player*
6912 Edelweiss Circle, Dallas, TX 75240, USA
Stauber, Liz *Actress*
%Creative Artists Agency, 9830 Wilshire Blvd, Beverly Hills, CA 90212, USA
Stauffer, William A (Bill) *Basketball Player*
3920 Grand Ave, #301, Des Moines, IA 50312, USA
Staunton, Imelda *Actress*
%P F D, Drury House, 34-43 Russell St, London WC2B 5HA, England
Stautner, Ernest A (Ernie) *Football Player, Coach*
801 Greenvalley Lane, Highland Village, TX 75077, USA
Staveley, William D M *Navy Admiral, England*
%Thames Health Authority, 40 Eastbourne Terrace, London W2 3QR, England
Stavropoulos, William S *Businessman*
%Dow Chemical, 2030 Dow Center, Midland, MI 48674, USA
Stayskal, Wayne *Editorial Cartoonist*
%Tampa Tribune, Editorial Dept, 200 S Parker St, Tampa, FL 33606, USA
Staysniak, Joseph A (Joe) *Football Player*
10640 LaGrange Road, Elyria, OH 44035, USA
Stead, Eugene A, Jr *Physician*
5113 Townsville Road, Bullock, NC 27507, USA
Steadman, Alison *Actress*
%P F D, Drury House, 34-43 Russell St, London WC2B 5HA, England
Steadman, J Richard *Sports Orthopedic Surgeon*
%Steadman Hawkins Clinic, 181 W Meadows Dr, #400, Vail, CO 81657, USA
Steadman, Mark *Writer*
450 Pin-du-Lac Dr, Central, SC 29630, USA
Steadman, Ralph I *Cartoonist*
Old Loose Court, Loose Valley, Maidstone, Kent ME15 9SE, England
Steadman, Robert L *Cinematographer*
15925 Temecula St, Pacific Palisades, CA 90272, USA
Stearns, Cheryl *Skydiver*
613 Saddlebred Lane, Raeford, NC 28376, USA
Stecher, Renate Meissner- *Track Athlete*
Haydnstr 11, #526/38, 07749 Jena, Germany
Stecher, Theodore P *Astronomer*
%UIT Project, Goddard Space Flight Center, Greenbelt, MD 20771, USA
Steckler, Ray Dennis *Movie Director*
2375 E Tropicana Ave, Las Vegas, NV 89119, USA
Steding, Katy *Basketball Player*
%Warner Pacific College, Athletic Dept, 2219 SE 68th Ave, Portland, OR 97215, USA
Steel, Amy *Actress*
%Innovative Artists, 1505 10th St, Santa Monica, CA 90401, USA
Steel, Danielle F *Writer*
330 Bob Hope Dr, Burbank, CA 91523, USA
Steel, David M S *Government Official, England*
Aikwood Tower, Ettrick Bridge, Selkirkshire, Scotland
Steele, Barbara *Actress*
2460 Benedict Canyon Dr, Beverly Hills, CA 90210, USA
Steele, Larry *Basketball Player*
139 Del Prado St, Lake Oswego, OR 97035, USA

Steele, Richard *Boxing Referee*
2438 Antler Point Dr, Henderson, NV 89074, USA
Steele, Shelby *Writer*
%San Jose State University, English Dept, San Jose, CA 95192, USA
Steele, Tommy *Singer, Actor*
%IMG, Media House, 3 Burlington Lane, London W4 2TH, England
Steele, William M (Mike) *Army General*
Commanding General, Combined Arms Center, Fort Leavenworth, KS 66207, USA
Steele-Perkins, Christopher H *Photographer*
5 Saint John's Buildings, Canterbury St, London SW9 7QB, England
Steen, Jessica *Actress*
%Innovative Artists, 1505 10th St, Santa Monica, CA 90401, USA
Steenburgen, Mary *Actress*
165 Copper Cliff Lane, Sedona, AZ 86336, USA
Stefan, Greg *Hockey Player*
37648 Baywood Dr, #33, Farmington Hills, MI 48335, USA
Stefani, Gwen *Singer, Songwriter (No Doubt)*
PO Box 8899, Anaheim, CA 92812, USA
Stefanich, Jim *Bowler*
1025 N Prairie Ave, Joliet, IL 60435, USA
Stefanson, Leslie *Actress*
9271 1/2 W Norton Ave, West Hollywood, CA 90046, USA
Stefanyshyn-Piper, Heidemarie M *Astronaut*
3722 W Pine Brook Way, Houston, TX 77059, USA
Steffes, Kent *Volleyball Player*
11106 Ave de Cortez, Pacific Palisades, CA 90272, USA
Steffy, Joseph B (Joe), Jr *Football Player*
25 Water Way, Newburgh, NY 12550, USA
Steger, Joseph A *Educator*
%University of Cincinnati, President's Office, Cincinnati, OH 45221, USA
Steger, Will *Arctic Explorer*
%International Arctic Project, 990 3rd St E, Saint Paul, MN 55106, USA
Steiger, Ueli *Cinematographer*
2222 Kenilworth Ave, Los Angeles, CA 90039, USA
Stein, Ben *Actor, Comedian*
4549 Via Vienta, Malibu, CA 90265, USA
Stein, Bob *Basketball Executive*
%Minnesota Timberwolves, Target Center, 600 1st Ave N, Minneapolis, MN 55403, USA
Stein, Chris *Guitarist (Blondie)*
%Shore Fire Media, 32 Court St, #1600, Brooklyn, NY 11201, USA
Stein, Ed *Editorial Cartoonist*
%Rocky Mountain News, Editorial Dept, 400 W Colfax Ave, Denver, CO 80204, USA
Stein, Elias M *Mathematician*
132 Dodds Lane, Princeton, NJ 08540, USA
Stein, Gilbert (Gil) *Hockey Executive*
%National Hockey League, 650 5th Ave, #3300, New York, NY 10019, USA
Stein, Horst *Conductor*
%Mariedi Anders Artists, 535 El Camino del Mar, San Francisco, CA 94121, USA
Stein, Howard *Financier*
%Dreyfus Corp, 200 Park Ave, New York, NY 10166, USA
Stein, James *Businessman*
%Fluor Corp, 3353 Michelson Dr, Irvine, CA 92612, USA
Stein, Joseph *Writer*
1130 Park Ave, New York, NY 10128, USA
Stein, Mark *Singer, Keyboardist (Vanilla Fudge)*
%Future Vision, 280 Riverside Dr, #12L, New York, NY 10025, USA
Stein, Robert *Editor*
%McCall's Magazine, Editorial Dept, 375 Lexington Ave, New York, NY 10017, USA
Steinbach, Alice *Journalist*
%Baltimore Sun, Editorial Dept, 501 N Calvert St, Baltimore, MD 21202, USA
Steinbach, Terry L *Baseball Player*
750 Boone Ave N, #109, Golden Valley, MN 55427, USA
Steinberg, David *Actor, Comedian, Television Director*
15332 Longbow Dr, Sherman Oaks, CA 91403, USA
Steinberg, Leigh *Sports Attorney*
%Steinberg Moorad Dunn, 500 Newport Center Dr, #800, Newport Beach, CA 92660, USA
Steinberg, Leo *Historian*
165 W 66th St, New York, NY 10023, USA
Steinberg, Paul *Cartoonist*
%New Yorker Magazine, Editorial Dept, 4 Times Square, New York, NY 10036, USA
Steinberg, Saul P *Businessman*
%Reliance Group Holdings, 5 Hanover Square, #1700, New York, NY 10004, USA
Steinberger, Jack *Nobel Physics Laureate*
25 Chemin des Merles, 1213 Onex, Geneva, Switzerland
Steinbrenner, George M, III *Baseball Executive*
PO Box 25077, Tampa, FL 33622, USA
Steinem, Gloria *Social Activist, Editor*
118 E 73rd St, New York, NY 10021, USA

Steiner, George *Writer*
32 Barrow Road, Cambridge, England
Steiner, Paul *Cartoonist*
%Washington Times, 3600 New York Ave NE, Washington, DC 20002, USA
Steiner, Peter *Cartoonist*
%New Yorker Magazine, Editorial Dept, 4 Times Square, New York, NY 10036, USA
Steiner, Tommy Shane *Singer*
%Collinsworth, 50 Music Square W, #702, Nashville, TN 37203, USA
Steinfeld, Jake *Actor, Body Builder*
622 Toyopa Dr, Pacific Palisades, CA 90272, USA
Steinhardt, Arnold *Violinist (Guarneri String Quartet)*
%Herbert Barrett, 266 W 37th St, #2000, New York, NY 10018, USA
Steinhardt, Paul J *Physicist*
1000 Cedargrove Road, Wynnewood, PA 19096, USA
Steinhardt, Richard *Biologist*
%University of California, Biology Dept, Berkeley, CA 94720, USA
Steinhauer, Sherri *Golfer*
%Rick Lepley, 4675 SW 74th St, Coral Gables, FL 33143, USA
Steinkraus, William (Bill) *Equestrian Rider*
PO Box 3038, Darien, CT 06820, USA
Steinkuhler, Dean E *Football Player*
1135 Oak St, Syracuse, NE 68446, USA
Steinman, Jim *Songwriter*
%DAS Communications, 83 Riverside Dr, New York, NY 10024, USA
Steinsaltz, Adin *Religious Leader*
%Israel Talmudic Publications Institute, PO Box 1458, Jerusalem, Israel
Steinseifer Bates, Carrie *Swimmer*
9309 Benzon Dr, Pleasanton, CA 94588, USA
Steitz, Joan A *Biochemist*
45 Prospect Hill Road, Branford, CT 06405, USA
Stella, Frank P *Artist, Sculptor*
17 Jones St, New York, NY 10014, USA
Stelle, Kellogg S *Physicist*
%Imperial College, Prince Consort Road, London SW7 2BZ, England
Stempel, Robert C *Businessman*
%Energy Conversion Devices, 1647 W Maple Road, Troy, MI 48084, USA
Stenerud, Jan *Football Player*
3180 Shieks Place, Colorado Springs, CO 80904, USA
Stenmark, Ingemar *Alpine Skier*
Residence l'Annonciade, 17 Av de l'Anncenciade, 98000 Monte Carlo, Monaco
Stent, Gunther S *Molecular Biologist*
145 Purdue Ave, Kensington, CA 94708, USA
Stepanova, Maria *Basketball Player*
%Phoenix Mercury, American West Arena, 201 E Jefferson St, Phoenix, AZ 85004, USA
Stepashin, Sergei V *Prime Minister, Russia; Army General*
Government of Russia, Kasnopresneskaya Embankment 2, 103274 Moscow, Russia
Stephanie *Princess, Monaco*
Maison Clos Saint Martin, Saint Remy de Provence, France
Stephanopolous, Constantine (Costis) *President, Greece*
%Presidential Palace, 7 Vas Georgiou B, Odos Zalokosta 10, Athens, Greece
Stephanopoulos, George R *Journalist, Government Official*
151 E 83rd St, #6E, New York, NY 10028, USA
Stephens, Olin James, II *Naval Architect, Yacht Designer*
80 Lyme Road, #160, Hanover, NH 03755, USA
Stephens, Robert *Businessman*
%Adaptec Inc, 691 S Milpitas Blvd, Milpitas, CA 95035, USA
Stephens, Stanley G (Stan) *Governor, MT*
4 Capitol Court, Helena, MT 59601, USA
Stephens, Toby *Actor*
%International Creative Mgmt, 76 Oxford St, London W1N 0AX, England
Stephenson, Dwight E *Football Player*
1180 S Powerline Road, #208, Pompano Beach, FL 33069, USA
Stephenson, Garrett *Baseball Player*
503 Gem Dr, Kimberly, ID 83341, USA
Stephenson, Gordon *Architect*
55/14 Albert St, Claremont WA 6010, Australia
Stephenson, Jan L *Golfer*
PO Box 705, Windermere, FL 34786, USA
Stephenson, Neal T *Writer*
%Avon Books, 1350 Ave of Americas, New York, NY 10019, USA
Stephenson, Van *Singer, Songwriter (BlackHawk)*
%Vector Mgmt, 1607 17th Ave S, Nashville, TN 37212, USA
Stepnoski, Mark M *Football Player*
3001 Shelton Way, Plano, TX 75093, USA
Steppling, John *Writer*
%William Morris Agency, 151 El Camino Dr, Beverly Hills, CA 90212, USA
Steranko, Jim *Cartoonist (Captain America)*
PO Box 974, Reading, PA 19603, USA

S

Sterban - Stevens

Sterban, Richard A *Singer (Oak Ridge Boys)*
329 Rockland Road, Hendersonville, TN 37075, USA
Sterkel, Jill *Swimmer*
3025 Snoddy Road, Bloomington, IN 47401, USA
Sterling, Annette *Singer (Martha & Vandellas)*
%Soundedge Personal Mgmt, 332 Southdown Road, Lloyd Harbor, NY 11743, USA
Sterling, Jan *Actress*
3959 Hamilton St, #11, San Diego, CA 92104, USA
Sterling, Mindy *Actress*
7307 Melrose Ave, Los Angeles, CA 90046, USA
Sterling, Robert *Actor*
121 S Bentley Ave, Los Angeles, CA 90049, USA
Sterling, Tisha *Actress*
PO Box 788, Ketchum, ID 83340, USA
Stern, Andrew L *Labor Leader*
%Service Employees International Union, 1313 L St NW, Washington, DC 20005, USA
Stern, Bert *Photographer*
330 E 39th St, New York, NY 10016, USA
Stern, Daniel *Actor*
PO Box 6788, Malibu, CA 90264, USA
Stern, David J *Basketball Executive*
%National Basketball Assn, Olympic Tower, 122 E 55th St, New York, NY 10022, USA
Stern, Fritz R *Historian*
15 Claremont Ave, New York, NY 10027, USA
Stern, Gary H *Financier, Government Official*
%Federal Reserve Bank, PO Box 291, Minneapolis, MN 55480, USA
Stern, Gerald *Writer*
%W W Norton, 500 5th Ave, New York, NY 10110, USA
Stern, Howard A *Entertainer*
%Don Buchwald, 10 E 44th St, New York, NY 10017, USA
Stern, Leonard B *Television, Movie Producer*
1709 Angelo Dr, Beverly Hills, CA 90210, USA
Stern, Michael (Mike) *Jazz Guitarist*
%Tropix International, 163 3rd Ave, #206, New York, NY 10003, USA
Stern, Richard G *Writer*
%University of Chicago, English Dept, Chicago, IL 60637, USA
Stern, Robert A M *Architect*
%Robert A M Stern Architects, 460 W 34th St, New York, NY 10001, USA
Sternbach, Leo H *Chemist*
10 Woodmont Road, Montclair, NJ 07043, USA
Sternberg, Thomas *Businessman*
%Staples Inc, PO Box 9265, Framingham, MA 01701, USA
Sternecky, Neal *Cartoonist (Pogo)*
52 Bluebird Lane, Naperville, IL 60565, USA
Sternfeld, Reuben *Financier*
%Inter-American Development Bank, 1300 New York Ave NW, Washington, DC 20577, USA
Sternhagen, Frances *Actress*
152 Sutton Manor Road, New Rochelle, NY 10801, USA
Sterrett, Samuel B *Judge*
%US Tax Court, 400 2nd St NW, Washington, DC 20217, USA
Sterzinsky, Georg Maximilian Cardinal *Religious Leader*
%Archdiocese of Berlin, Wundstr 48/50, 14057 Berlin, Germany
Stetter, Karl *Microbiologist*
%Universtat Regensburg, Universitatsstr 31, 93053 Regensburg, Germany
Steussie, Todd E *Football Player*
34793 Emigrant Trail, Shingletown, CA 96088, USA
Stevens, Andrew *Actor*
%Irv Schechter, 9300 Wilshire Blvd, #410, Beverly Hills, CA 90212, USA
Stevens, April *Singer*
19530 Superior St, Northridge, CA 91324, USA
Stevens, Brinke *Actress*
PO Box 8900, Universal City, CA 91618, USA
Stevens, Cat (Yusef Islam) *Singer, Songwriter*
Ariola Steinhauser Str 3, 81667 Munich, Germany
Stevens, Chuck *Photographer*
PO Box 422782, San Francisco, CA 94142, USA
Stevens, Connie *Singer, Actress*
%Forever Spring, 426 S Robertson Blvd, Los Angeles, CA 90048, USA
Stevens, Dorit *Actress, Model*
206 S Brand Blvd, Glendale, CA 91204, USA
Stevens, Eileen *Social Activist*
126 Marion St, Sayville, NY 11782, USA
Stevens, Fisher *Actor*
329 N Orange Grove, Los Angeles, CA 90036, USA
Stevens, Gary *Thoroughbred Racing Jockey*
%Thoroughbred Racing Assn, 3000 Marcus Ave, New Hyde Park, NY 11042, USA
Stevens, George, Jr *Movie Producer*
%New Liberty Productions, John F Kennedy Center, Washington, DC 20566, USA

Stevens, John Paul *Supreme Court Justice*
%US Supreme Court, 1 1st St NE, Washington, DC 20543, USA

Stevens, Kaye *Singer, Actress*
%Ruth Webb, 10580 Des Moines Ave, Northridge, CA 91326, USA

Stevens, Kenneth N *Electrical Engineer*
7 Larchwood Lane, Natick, MA 01760, USA

Stevens, Kevin M *Hockey Player*
38 Bay Pond Road, Duxbury, MA 02332, USA

Stevens, Ray *Singer, Songwriter*
%William Morris Agency, 2100 W End Ave, #1000, Nashville, TN 37203, USA

Stevens, Rise *Opera Singer*
930 5th Ave, New York, NY 10021, USA

Stevens, Robert B *Educator*
%Covington/Burling, Leconfield House, Curzon St, London W1Y 8AS, England

Stevens, Robert M *Cinematographer*
1920 S Beverly Glen Blvd, #106, Los Angeles, CA 90025, USA

Stevens, Rogers *Guitarist (Blind Melon)*
%Shapiro Co, 9229 Sunset Blvd, #607, Los Angeles, CA 90069, USA

Stevens, Ronnie *Actor*
%Caroline Dawson, 19 Sydney Mews, London SW3 6HL, England

Stevens, Scott *Hockey Player*
102 Oval Road, Essex Falls, NJ 07021, USA

Stevens, Shadoe *Actor, Radio Personality*
2934 N Beverly Glen Circle, #399, Los Angeles, CA 90077, USA

Stevens, Shakin' *Singer, Songwriter*
%Mgmt Gerd Kehren, Postfach 1455, 41804 Erkelenz, Germany

Stevens, Stella *Model, Actress*
%Stella Visions, 1608 N Cahuenga Blvd, #649, Los Angeles, CA 90028, USA

Stevens, Steven *Actor*
%Stevens Group, 3518 Cahuenga Blvd W, Los Angeles, CA 90068, USA

Stevens, Tony *Bassist (Foghat)*
%Lustig Talent, PO Box 770850, Orlando, FL 32877, USA

Stevens, Warren *Actor*
14155 Magnolia Blvd, #27, Sherman Oaks, CA 91423, USA

Stevenson Lorenzo, Teofilo *Boxer*
%Comite Olimppicu, Hotel Havana, Libre, Havana, Cuba

Stevenson, Adlai E, III *Senator, IL*
20 N Clark St, #750, Chicago, IL 60602, USA

Stevenson, DeShawn *Basketball Player*
%Utah Jazz, Delta Center, 301 W South Temple, Salt Lake City, UT 84101, USA

Stevenson, Juliet *Actress*
68 Pall Mall, London SW1Y 5ES, England

Stevenson, Parker *Actor*
10100 Santa Monica Blvd, #400, Los Angeles, CA 90067, USA

Stever, H Guyford *Aeronautical Engineer, Educator*
59 Randolph Hill Road, Randolph, NH 03593, USA

Steward, Emanuel *Boxing Trainer, Manager*
19244 Bretton Dr, Detroit, MI 48223, USA

Stewart, Al *Singer, Songwriter*
%Chapman & Co, 14011 Ventura Blvd, #405, Sherman Oaks, CA 91423, USA

Stewart, Alana *Actress*
13480 Firth Dr, Beverly Hills, CA 90210, USA

Stewart, Alec *Cricketer*
%Surrey County Cricket Club, Kennington Oval, London SE11 5SS, England

Stewart, Bill *Jazz Drummer*
%Blue Note Records, 6920 Sunset Blvd, Los Angeles, CA 90028, USA

Stewart, Catherine Mary *Actress*
350 DuPont St, Toronto ON M5R 1Z9, Canada

Stewart, David A (Dave) *Keyboardist, Guitarist (Eurythmics)*
%Arista Records, 8750 Wilshire Blvd, #300, Beverly Hills, CA 90211, USA

Stewart, David K (Dave) *Baseball Player*
17762 Vineyeard Lane, Poway, CA 92064, USA

Stewart, French *Actor*
%United Talent Agency, 9560 Wilshire Blvd, #500, Beverly Hills, CA 90212, USA

Stewart, Gary *Singer*
%Entertainment Artists, 2409 21st Ave S, #100, Nashville, TN 37212, USA

Stewart, Ian *Government Official, England*
%House of Commons, Westminster, London SW1A 0AA, England

Stewart, James *Football Player*
%Detroit Lions, 222 Republic Dr, Allen Park, MI 48101, USA

Stewart, James B *Journalist*
%Wall Street Journal, Editorial Dept, 200 Liberty St, New York, NY 10281, USA

Stewart, James C *WW II Army Air Corps Hero*
8793 Grape Wagon Circle, San Jose, CA 95135, USA

Stewart, Jermaine *Singer*
%Richard Walters, 1800 Argyle Ave, #408, Los Angeles, CA 90028, USA

Stewart, John *Singer (Kingston Trio)*
%Fuji Productions, 2480 Williston Dr, Charlottesville, VA 22901, USA

Stewart, John Y (Jackie) *Auto Racing Driver*
%Stewart GP, 16 Tanners Dr, Blakelands, Milton Keynes MK14 5BW, England
Stewart, Jon *Actor, Comedian*
%Gold-Miller Mgmt, 9220 Sunset Blvd, #320, Los Angeles, CA 90069, USA
Stewart, Kordell *Football Player*
%Chicago Bears, 1000 Football Dr, Lake Forest, IL 60045, USA
Stewart, Lisa *Singer*
%Friedman & LaRosa, 1344 Lexington Ave, New York, NY 10128, USA
Stewart, Martha K *Entertainer, Publisher*
19 Newtown Turnpike, #6, Westport, CT 06880, USA
Stewart, Mary *Writer*
House of Letterawe, Lock Awe, Argyll PA33 1AH, Scotland
Stewart, Melvin, Jr *Swimmer*
1311 Lake Lauden Blvd, Knoxville, TN 37916, USA
Stewart, Natalie *Singer (Floetry), Songwriter*
%DreamWorks Records, 9268 W 3rd St, Beverly Hills, CA 90210, USA
Stewart, Patrick *Actor*
%William Morris Agency, 151 El Camino Dr, Beverly Hills, CA 90212, USA
Stewart, Peggy *Actress*
11139 Hortense St, Toluca Lake, CA 91602, USA
Stewart, Potter *Judge*
%US Court of Appeals, US Courthouse, 100 E 5th St, Cincinnati, OH 45202, USA
Stewart, Robert L *Astronaut, Army General*
815 Sun Valley Dr, Woodland Park, CO 80863, USA
Stewart, Roderick D (Rod) *Singer, Songwriter*
23 Beverly Park Terrace, Beverly Hills, CA 90210, USA
Stewart, Shannon H *Baseball Player*
18460 SW 78th Place, Miami, FL 33157, USA
Stewart, Thomas J, Jr *Opera Singer*
%Columbia Artists Mgmt Inc, 165 W 57th St, New York, NY 10019, USA
Stewart, Tonea *Actress*
%Alabama State University, Theater Arts Dept, Montgomery, AL 36101, USA
Stewart, Tony *Auto Racing Driver*
13415 Reese Blvd W, Huntersville, NC 28078, USA
Stewart, Tyler *Drummer (Barenaked Ladies)*
%Nettwerk Mgmt, 8730 Wilshire Blvd, #304, Beverly Hills, CA 90211, USA
Stewart, Will Foster *Actor*
8730 Santa Monica Blvd, #1, Los Angeles, CA 90069, USA
Stewart-Hardway, Donna *Actress*
PO Box 777, Pinch, WV 25156, USA
Stezer, Philip *Violinist (Emerson String Quartet)*
%I M G Artists, 3 Burlington Lane, Chiswick, London W4 2TH, England
Stich, Michael *Tennis Player*
Ernst-Barlach-Str 44, 25336 Elmshorn, Germany
Sticht, J Paul *Businessman*
11732 Lake House Court, North Palm Beach, FL 33408, USA
Stickel, Fred A *Publisher*
%Portland Oregonian, 1320 SW Broadway, Portland, OR 97201, USA
Stickler, Alfons M Cardinal *Religious Leader*
Piazza del S Uffizio 11, 00193 Rome, Italy
Stickles, Montford (Monty) *Football Player*
1363 3rd Ave, San Francisco, CA 94122, USA
Stickles, Ted *Swimmer*
1142 Sharynwood Dr, Baton Rouge, LA 70808, USA
Sticky Fingaz *Rap Artist (Onyx)*
%International Creative Mgmt, 8942 Wilshire Blvd, #219, Beverly Hills, CA 90211, USA
Stieb, David A (Dave) *Baseball Player*
10860 Shay Lane, Reno, NV 89511, USA
Stieber, Tamar *Journalist*
%Albuquerque Journal, Editorial Dept, 7777 Jefferson NE, Albuquerque, NM 87109, USA
Stiefel, Ethan *Ballet Dancer*
%American Ballet Theatre, 890 Broadway, New York, NY 10003, USA
Stiegler, Josef (Pepi) *Alpine Skier*
PO Box 290, Teton Village, WY 83025, USA
Stiers, David Ogden *Actor*
%Stubbs, 8675 W Washington Blvd, #203, Culver City, CA 90232, USA
Stigers, Curtis *Singer, Saxophonist*
%C Winston Simone Mgmt, 1790 Broadway, #1000, New York, NY 10019, USA
Stiglitz, Joseph E *Nobel Economics Laureate*
%Columbia University, International Affairs Building, New York, NY 10027, USA
Stigwood, Robert C *Movie, Theater, Music Producer*
%Barton Manor, Whippingham, East Cowes, PO32 6LB, Isle of Wight, England
Stiles, Jackie *Basketball Player*
%Patrick J Stiles, 115 E Hamilton, Claflin, KS 67525, USA
Stiles, Julia *Actress*
%Bryan Zuriss, 409 N Camden Dr, #202, Beverly Hills, CA 90210, USA
Stilgoe, Richard *Lyricist*
%Noel Gray Artists, 24 Denmark St, London WC2H 8NJ, England

Still, Arthur B (Art) *Football Player*
20002 Missouri City Road, Liberty, MO 64068, USA
Still, Ken *Golfer*
1210 Princeton St, Fircrest, WA 98466, USA
Still, Ray *Concert Oboist, Conductor*
858 Scenic Hills Way, Annapolis, MD 21401, USA
Still, Susan L *Astronaut*
%NASA, Johnson Space Center, 2101 NASA Road, Houston, TX 77058, USA
Still, William C, Jr *Chemist*
%Columbia University, Chemistry Dept, New York, NY 10027, USA
Stiller, Ben *Actor, Comedian, Director*
%United Talent Agency, 9560 Wilshire Blvd, #500, Beverly Hills, CA 90212, USA
Stiller, Jerry *Actor, Comedian*
118 Riverside Dr, #5A, New York, NY 10024, USA
Stills, Stephen *Singer, Guitarist (Crosby Stills Nash)*
17525 Ventura Blvd, #210, Encino, CA 91316, USA
Stillwagon, Jim R *Football Player*
3999 Parkway Lane, Hilliard, OH 43026, USA
Stillwell, Roger *Football Player*
25 Woodland Court, Novato, CA 94947, USA
Stilwell, Richard D *Opera Singer*
1969 Rockingham St, McLean, VA 22101, USA
Stine, Richard *Editorial Cartoonist*
PO Box 4699, Rollingbay, WA 98061, USA
Stine, Robert L (R L) *Writer*
%Scholastic Book Services, 555 Broadway, New York, NY 10012, USA
Sting *Singer, Actor, Bassist, Songwriter*
%Outlandos, 2 Grove, Highgate Village, London N16, England
Stingley, Darryl *Football Player, Executive*
400 E Randolph St, #K125, Chicago, IL 60601, USA
Stipe, Michael *Singer (REM), Songwriter*
%REM/Athens Ltd, 170 College Ave, Athens, GA 30601, USA
Stiritz, William P *Businessman*
%Ralston Purina Co, Checkerboard Square, Saint Louis, MO 63164, USA
Stirling, Steve *Hockey Coach*
%New York Islanders, Nassau Coliseum, Hempstead Turnpike, Uniondale, NY 11553, USA
Stitch, Stephen P *Philosopher*
%Rutgers University, Philosophy Dept, New Brunswick, NJ 08901, USA
Stith, Bryant *Basketball Player*
20697 Governor Harrison Parkway, Freeman, VA 23856, USA
Stobbs, Charles K (Chuck) *Baseball Player*
1731 Rivera Circle, Sarasota, FL 34232, USA
Stock, Barbara *Actress*
19045 Sprague St, Tarzana, CA 91356, USA
Stockdale, James B *Vietnam War Navy Hero (CMH), Admiral*
547 A Ave, Coronado, CA 92118, USA
Stockhausen, Karlheinz *Composer*
Stockhausen-Verlag, 51515 Kurten, Germany
Stockman, David A *Government Official, Financier*
%Blackstone Group, 345 Park Ave, New York, NY 10154, USA
Stockman, Shawn *Singer (Boyz II Men)*
%Southpaw Entertainment, 10675 Santa Monica Blvd, Los Angeles, CA 90025, USA
Stockmayer, Walter H *Physical Chemist*
Willey Hill, Norwich, VT 05055, USA
Stockton, Dave K *Golfer*
222 Escondido Dr, Redlands, CA 92373, USA
Stockton, Dick *Sportscaster*
2519 NW 59th St, Boca Raton, FL 33496, USA
Stockton, Richard L (Dick) *Tennis Player*
715 Stadium Dr, San Antonio, TX 78212, USA
Stockwell, Dean *Actor*
95723 Highway 99 W, Junction City, OR 97448, USA
Stockwell, John *Actor*
%United Talent Agency, 9560 Wilshire Blvd, #500, Beverly Hills, CA 90212, USA
Stoicheff, Boris P *Physicist*
66 Collier St, #6B, Toronto ON M4W 1L9, Canada
Stoitchkov, Hristo *Soccer Player*
%DC United, 14120 Newbrook Dr, Chantilly, VA 20151, USA
Stojko, Elvis *Figure Skater*
%Mentor Marketing, 2 Saint Clair Ave E, Toronto ON M4T 2T, Canada
Stoklos, Randy *Volleyball Player*
%Assn of Volleyball Pros, 330 Washington Blvd, #400, Marina del Rey, CA 90292, USA
Stole, Mink *Actress*
3155 Ettrick St, Los Angeles, CA 90027, USA
Stolle, Frederick S *Tennis Player*
%Turnberry Isle Yacht & Racquet Club, 19735 Turnberry Way, Miami, FL 33180, USA
Stoller, Mike *Composer*
%Leiber/Stoller Entertainment, 9000 W Sunset Blvd, West Hollywood, CA 90069, USA

Stolley, Paul D *Physician*
6424 Brass Knob, Columbia, MD 21044, USA
Stolley, Richard B *Editor*
%Time Inc, Time-Life Building, Rockefeller Center, New York, NY 10020, USA
Stolojan, Theodor *Prime Minister, Romania*
%World Bank, 1818 H St NW, Washington, DC 20433, USA
Stolper, Pinchas *Religious Leader*
%Orthodox Jewish Congregations Union, 11 Broadway, New York, NY 10004, USA
Stoltz, Eric *Actor*
7575 Mulholland Dr, Los Angeles, CA 90046, USA
Stoltzman, Richard L *Concert Clarinetist*
%Frank Salomon, 201 W 54th St, #1C, New York, NY 10019, USA
Stone, Andrew L *Movie Director*
2132 Century Park Lane, #212, Los Angeles, CA 90067, USA
Stone, Angie *Singer*
%Creative Artists Agency, 9830 Wilshire Blvd, Beverly Hills, CA 90212, USA
Stone, Dee Wallace *Actress*
23035 Cumorah Crest Dr, Woodland Hills, CA 91364, USA
Stone, Doug *Singer, Songwriter*
PO Box 943, Springfield, TN 37172, USA
Stone, Edward C, Jr *Space Physicist*
%Jet Propulsion Laboratory, 4800 Oak Grove Dr, #180-904, Pasadena, CA 91109, USA
Stone, George H *Baseball Player*
1206 Eastland Ave, Ruston, LA 71270, USA
Stone, James L *Korean War Army Hero (CMH)*
1279 Cedarland Plaza Dr, Arlington, TX 76011, USA
Stone, Leonard *Actor*
%Capital Artists, 6404 Wilshire Blvd, #950, Los Angeles, CA 90048, USA
Stone, Matt *Animator, Writer*
%Barnes Morris Klein Young, 1424 2nd St, #3, Santa Monica, CA 90401, USA
Stone, Nikki *Freestyle Aerials Skier*
%Podium Enterprises, PO Box 680-332, Park City, UT 84068, USA
Stone, Oliver W *Movie Director, Writer*
%Steven Pines, 520 Broadway, #600, Santa Monica, CA 90401, USA
Stone, Robert A *Writer*
%Donadio & Ashworth, 121 W 27th St, #704, New York, NY 10001, USA
Stone, Roger D *Political Consultant*
34 W 88th St, New York, NY 10024, USA
Stone, Sharon *Actress*
%P M K Public Relations, 8500 Wilshire Blvd, #700, Beverly Hills, CA 90211, USA
Stone, Sly *Singer, Songwriter, Keyboardist*
%Richard Walters, 1800 Argyle Ave, #408, Los Angeles, CA 90028, USA
Stone, Steven M (Steve) *Baseball Player, Sportscaster*
8340 E Cheryl Dr, Scottsdale, AZ 85258, USA
Stonecipher, David A *Financier*
%Jefferson-Pilot Corp, 100 N Greene St, Greensboro, NC 27401, USA
Stones, Dwight E *Track Athlete*
4790 Irvine Blvd, #105, Irvine, CA 92620, USA
Stonesipher, Don *Football Player*
1502 Canberry Court, Wheeling, IL 60090, USA
Stookey, Paul *Singer (Peter Paul & Mary), Songwriter*
%Newworld, RR 175, South Blue Hill Falls, ME 04615, USA
Stoops, Bob *Football Coach*
%University of Oklahoma, Athletic Dept, 108 Brooks St, Norman, OK 73069, USA
Stoppard, Tom S *Writer*
%P F D, Drury House, 34-43 Russell St, London WC2B 5HA, England
Storaro, Vittorio *Cinematographer*
Via Divino Amore 2, 00040 Frattocchie Merino, Italy
Storch, Larry *Actor*
330 W End Ave, #17F, New York, NY 10023, USA
Storey, David M *Writer*
2 Lyndhurst Gardens, London NW3, England
Stork, Jeff *Volleyball Player*
%Pepperdine University, Athletic Dept, 24255 Pacific Coast Hwy, Malibu, CA 90263, USA
Storm, Gale *Actress, Singer*
23831 Bluehill Bay, Dana Point, CA 92629, USA
Storm, Hannah *Commentator, Sportscaster*
%CBS-TV, News Dept, 51 W 52nd St, New York, NY 10019, USA
Storm, Tempest *Exotic Dancer*
PO Box 2095, Helendale, CA 92342, USA
Stormare, Peter *Actor*
1129 Poinsettia Dr, West Hollywood, CA 90046, USA
Stormer, Horst L *Nobel Physics Laureate*
20 E 9th St, #14P, New York, NY 10003, USA
Story, Liz *Pianist, Songwriter*
%SRO Artists, PO Box 9532, Madison, WI 53715, USA
Stossel, John *Commentator*
%Beresford Apartments, 211 Central Park West, #15K, New York, NY 10024, USA

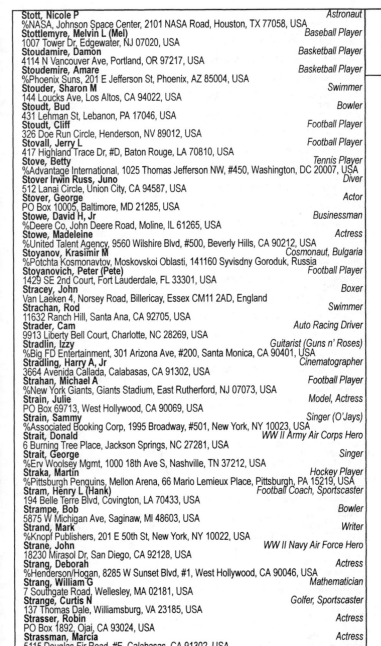

Stott, Nicole P *Astronaut*
%NASA, Johnson Space Center, 2101 NASA Road, Houston, TX 77058, USA
Stottlemyre, Melvin L (Mel) *Baseball Player*
1007 Tower Dr, Edgewater, NJ 07020, USA
Stoudamire, Damon *Basketball Player*
4114 N Vancouver Ave, Portland, OR 97217, USA
Stoudemire, Amare *Basketball Player*
%Phoenix Suns, 201 E Jefferson St, Phoenix, AZ 85004, USA
Stouder, Sharon M *Swimmer*
144 Loucks Ave, Los Altos, CA 94022, USA
Stoudt, Bud *Bowler*
431 Lehman St, Lebanon, PA 17046, USA
Stoudt, Cliff *Football Player*
326 Doe Run Circle, Henderson, NV 89012, USA
Stovall, Jerry L *Football Player*
417 Highland Trace Dr, #D, Baton Rouge, LA 70810, USA
Stove, Betty *Tennis Player*
%Advantage International, 1025 Thomas Jefferson NW, #450, Washington, DC 20007, USA
Stover Irwin Russ, Juno *Diver*
512 Lanai Circle, Union City, CA 94587, USA
Stover, George *Actor*
PO Box 10005, Baltimore, MD 21285, USA
Stowe, David H, Jr *Businessman*
%Deere Co, John Deere Road, Moline, IL 61265, USA
Stowe, Madeleine *Actress*
%United Talent Agency, 9560 Wilshire Blvd, #500, Beverly Hills, CA 90212, USA
Stoyanov, Krasimir M *Cosmonaut, Bulgaria*
%Potchta Kosmonavtov, Moskovskoi Oblasti, 141160 Syvisdny Goroduk, Russia
Stoyanovich, Peter (Pete) *Football Player*
1429 SE 2nd Court, Fort Lauderdale, FL 33301, USA
Stracey, John *Boxer*
Van Laeken 4, Norsey Road, Billericay, Essex CM11 2AD, England
Strachan, Rod *Swimmer*
11632 Ranch Hill, Santa Ana, CA 92705, USA
Strader, Cam *Auto Racing Driver*
9913 Liberty Bell Court, Charlotte, NC 28269, USA
Stradlin, Izzy *Guitarist (Guns n' Roses)*
%Big FD Entertainment, 301 Arizona Ave, #200, Santa Monica, CA 90401, USA
Stradling, Harry A, Jr *Cinematographer*
3664 Avenida Callada, Calabasas, CA 91302, USA
Strahan, Michael A *Football Player*
%New York Giants, Giants Stadium, East Rutherford, NJ 07073, USA
Strain, Julie *Model, Actress*
PO Box 69713, West Hollywood, CA 90069, USA
Strain, Sammy *Singer (O'Jays)*
%Associated Booking Corp, 1995 Broadway, #501, New York, NY 10023, USA
Strait, Donald *WW II Army Air Corps Hero*
6 Burning Tree Place, Jackson Springs, NC 27281, USA
Strait, George *Singer*
%Erv Woolsey Mgmt, 1000 18th Ave S, Nashville, TN 37212, USA
Straka, Martin *Hockey Player*
%Pittsburgh Penguins, Mellon Arena, 66 Mario Lemieux Place, Pittsburgh, PA 15219, USA
Stram, Henry L (Hank) *Football Coach, Sportscaster*
194 Belle Terre Blvd, Covington, LA 70433, USA
Strampe, Bob *Bowler*
5875 W Michigan Ave, Saginaw, MI 48603, USA
Strand, Mark *Writer*
%Knopf Publishers, 201 E 50th St, New York, NY 10022, USA
Strane, John *WW II Navy Air Force Hero*
18230 Mirasol Dr, San Diego, CA 92128, USA
Strang, Deborah *Actress*
%Henderson/Hogan, 8285 W Sunset Blvd, #1, West Hollywood, CA 90046, USA
Strang, William G *Mathematician*
7 Southgate Road, Wellesley, MA 02181, USA
Strange, Curtis N *Golfer, Sportscaster*
137 Thomas Dale, Williamsburg, VA 23185, USA
Strasser, Robin *Actress*
PO Box 1892, Ojai, CA 93024, USA
Strassman, Marcia *Actress*
5115 Douglas Fir Road, #E, Calabasas, CA 91302, USA
Stratas, Teresa *Opera Singer*
%Vincent Farrell Assoc, 481 8th Ave, #340, New York, NY 10001, USA
Strathairn, David *Actor*
%United Talent Agency, 9560 Wilshire Blvd, #500, Beverly Hills, CA 90212, USA
Stratham, Jason *Actor*
%International Creative Mgmt, 8942 Wilshire Blvd, #219, Beverly Hills, CA 90211, USA
Stratton, Frederick P, Jr *Businessman*
%Briggs & Stratton, PO Box 702, Milwaukee, WI 53201, USA

S

Straub - Struycken

Straub, Peter F *Writer*
53 W 85th St, New York, NY 10024, USA
Strauss, Robert S *Political Leader, Diplomat*
%Akin Gump Strauss Hauer Feld, 1700 Pacific Ave, #4100, Dallas, TX 75201, USA
Straw, John W (Jack) *Government Official, England*
%House of Commons, Westminster, London SW1A 0AA, England
Strawberry, Darryl E *Baseball Player*
5118 Rue Vendome, Lutz, FL 33558, USA
Strawser, Neil *Commentator*
130 E St SE, Washington, DC 20003, USA
Streep, Meryl *Actress*
%Creative Artists Agency, 9830 Wilshire Blvd, Beverly Hills, CA 90212, USA
Street, Picabo *Alpine Skier*
PO Box 321, Hailey, ID 83333, USA
Street, Rebecca *Actress*
225 S Gramercy Place, Los Angeles, CA 90004, USA
Streisand, Barbra *Singer, Actress, Director*
160 W 96th St, New York, NY 10025, USA
Strekalov, Gennadi M *Cosmonaut*
%Federation Peace Committee, 36 Mira Prospekt, 129090 Moscow, Russia
Stricker, Steve *Golfer*
1629 N Golf Glen, Madison, WI 53704, USA
Strickland de la Hunty, Shirley *Track Athlete*
22 Fraser Road, Applecross WA 6153, Australia
Strickland, Amzie *Actress*
1329 N Ogden Dr, West Hollywood, CA 90046, USA
Strickland, Gail *Actress*
14732 Oracle Place, Pacific Palisades, CA 90272, USA
Stringer, C Vivian *Basketball Coach*
%Rutgers University, Athletic Dept, New Brunswick, NJ 08903, USA
Stringfield, Sherry *Actress*
%Broder Kurland Webb Uffner, 9242 Beverly Blvd, #200, Beverly Hills, CA 90210, USA
Stritch, Elaine *Singer, Actress*
%Michael Whitehall, 125 Gloucester Road, London SW7 4TE, England
Strobel, Eric *Hockey Player*
6617 129th St W, Apple Valley, MN 55124, USA
Strock, Donald J (Don) *Football Player, Coach*
1512 Passion Vine Circle, Weston, FL 33326, USA
Strock, Herbert L *Movie Director*
1630 Hilts Ave, #205, Los Angeles, CA 90024, USA
Stroessner, Alfredo *President, Paraguay; Army General*
Lago Sul, Brasilia, Brazil
Strohmayer, Tod *Astronomer*
%Goddard Space Flight Center, NASA/GSFC, Greenbelt, MD 20771, USA
Strolz, Hubert *Alpine Skier*
6767 Warth 19, Austria
Strom, Brock T *Football Player*
4301 W 110th St, Leawood, KS 66211, USA
Strominger, Jack L *Biochemist*
%Dana Faber Cancer Institute, Biochemistry Dept, 44 Binney St, Boston, MA 02115, USA
Strong, Brenda *Actress*
%S D B Partners, 1801 Ave of Stars, #902, Los Angeles, CA 90067, USA
Strong, Maurice F *Government Official, Canada*
255 Consummers Road, #401, Toronto ON M2J 5B6, Canada
Strong, Rider *Actor*
%Yorke & Harper, 800 S Robertson Blvd, #2, Los Angeles, CA 90035, USA
Stroock, Daniel W *Mathematician*
55 Frost St, Cambridge, MA 02140, USA
Strossen, Nadine *Attorney, Association Executive*
57 Worth St, New York, NY 10013, USA
Stroud, Don *Actor*
1347 Gates Ave, Manhattan Beach, CA 90266, USA
Stroup, Theodore G (Ted), Jr *Army General*
2085 Hopewood Dr, Falls Church, VA 22043, USA
Strouse, Charles *Composer*
171 W 57th St, New York, NY 10019, USA
Strube, Juergen F *Businessman*
%BASF Corp, Carl-Bosch Str 38, 67063 Ludwigshafen, Germany
Struchkova, Raisa S *Ballerina*
%Sovetskiy Ballet, Tverskaya 22B, 103050 Moscow, Russia
Struever, Stuart M *Anthropologist*
2000 Sheridan Road, Evanston, IL 60208, USA
Strug, Kerri *Gymnast*
2801 N Camino Principal, Tucson, AZ 85715, USA
Struthers, Sally *Actress*
8721 W Sunset Blvd, #210, Los Angeles, CA 90069, USA
Struycken, Carel *Actor*
1665 E Mountain St, Pasadena, CA 91104, USA

Strykert, Ron *Guitarist (Men At Work)*
%TPA, PO Box 124, Round Corner NSW 2158, Australia
Stuart, Gloria *Actress*
884 S Bundy Dr, Los Angeles, CA 90049, USA
Stuart, Lyle *Publisher*
1530 Palisade Ave, #6L, Fort Lee, NJ 07024, USA
Stuart, Marty *Singer, Songwriter, Guitarist*
%Gurley Co, 1204B Cedar Lane, Nashville, TN 37212, USA
Stuart, Maxine *Actress*
%S D B Partners, 1801 Ave of Stars, #902, Los Angeles, CA 90067, USA
Stubblefield, Dana W *Football Player*
420 E State St, Columbus, OH 43215, USA
Stubbs, Imogen M *Actress*
%International Creative Mgmt, 76 Oxford St, London W1N 0AX, England
Stubbs, Levi *Singer (Four Tops)*
%William Morris Agency, 151 El Camino Dr, Beverly Hills, CA 90212, USA
Stuck, Hans-Joachim *Auto Racing Driver*
Harmstatt 3, 6352 Ellmau/Tirol, Austria
Studer, Cheryl *Opera Singer*
%Columbia Artists Mgmt Inc, 165 W 57th St, New York, NY 10019, USA
Studstill, Patrick L (Pat) *Football Player*
2235 Linda Flora Dr, Los Angeles, CA 90077, USA
Stuhr, Jerzy *Actor, Director*
%Graffutu Ltd, Ul SW Gertrudy 5, 31-107, Cracow, Poland
Stump, David *Cinematographer*
%HFWD Creative Representation, 394 E Glaucus St, Encinitas, CA 92024, USA
Stumpf, Kenneth E *Vietnam War Army Hero (CMH)*
16528 State Highway 131, Tomah, WI 54660, USA
Sturckow, Frederick W (Rick) *Astronaut*
RR 2 Box 14, Dickinson, TX 77539, USA
Sturdivant, John N *Labor Leader*
%American Government Employees Federation, 80 F St NW, Washington, DC 20001, USA
Sturdivant, Thomas V (Tom) *Baseball Player*
1324 SW 71st St, Oklahoma City, OK 73159, USA
Sturges, Shannon *Actress*
1223 Wilshire Blvd, #577, Santa Monica, CA 90403, USA
Sturm, Yfke *Model*
%Elite Model Mgmt, 111 E 22nd St, #200, New York, NY 10010, USA
Sturza, Ion *Prime Minister, Moldova*
%Premier's Office, Piaca Maril Atuner Nacional, 277033 Chishinev, Moldova
Styron, Alexandra *Writer*
%Little Brown, 3 Center Plaza, Boston, MA 02108, USA
Styron, William C, Jr *Writer*
12 Rucum Road, Roxbury, CT 06783, USA
Suarez Gonzalez, Adolfo *Prime Minister, Spain*
Sagasta, 33 Madrid 4, Spain
Suarez Rivera, Adolfo A Cardinal *Religious Leader*
Apartado Postal 7, Loma Larga 2429 Sierra Madre, Monterrey 64000, Mexico
Suau, Anthony *Photojournalist*
%Denver Post, PO Box 1709, Denver, CO 80201, USA
Subotnick, Morton L *Composer*
25 Minetta Lane, #4B, New York, NY 10012, USA
Such, Alec John *Drummer (Bon Jovi)*
%Bon Jovi Mgmt, 248 W 17th St, #501, New York, NY 10011, USA
Suchet, David *Actor*
%Ken McReddie, 91 Regent St, London W1R 7TB, England
Suchocka, Hanna *Prime Minister, Poland*
Urzad Rady Ministrow, Al Ujazdowskie 1/3, 00-567 Warsaw, Poland
Sudan, Madhu *Computer Scientist*
81 Benton Road, Somerville, MA 02143, USA
Sudduth, Jill *Synchronized Swimmer*
15910 Sunnyside Ave, Morgan Hill, CA 95037, USA
Sudharmono *Government Official, Indonesia; General*
Senopati St 44B, Jakarta Selatan, Indonesia
Sues, Alan *Actor*
9014 Dorrington Ave, West Hollywood, CA 90048, USA
Sugarman, Burt *Movie Producer*
%Giant Group, 9440 Santa Monica Blvd, #407, Beverly Hills, CA 90210, USA
Sugg, Diana K *Journalist*
%Baltimore Sun, Editorial Dept, 501 N Calvert St, Baltimore, MD 21202, USA
Suggs, M Louise *Golfer*
424 Royal Crescent Court, Saint Augustine, FL 32092, USA
Suggs, Terrell *Football Player*
%Baltimore Ravens, Ravens Stadium, 11001 Russell St, Baltimore, MD 21230, USA
Suharto, Mohamed *President, Indonesia; Army General*
8 Jalan Cendana, Jakarta, Indonesia
Suhey, Matthew J (Matt) *Football Player*
550 Carriage Way, Deerfield, IL 60015, USA

S

Suhl - Summers

Suhl, Harry *Physicist*
%University of California, Physics Dept, 9500 Gilman Dr, La Jolla, CA 92093, USA
Suhonen, Alpo *Hockey Coach*
%Chicago Blackhawks, United Center, 1901 W Madison St, Chicago, IL 60612, USA
Suhor, Yvonne *Actress*
%J Michael Bloom, 233 Park Ave S, #1000, New York, NY 10003, USA
Suhr, August R (Gus) *Baseball Player*
4516 E Marion Way, Phoenix, AZ 85018, USA
Suhrheinrich, Richard F *Judge*
%US Court of Appeals, 315 W Allegan, Lansing, MI 48933, USA
Sui, Anna *Fashion Designer*
%Anna Sui Corp, 275 W 39th St, New York, NY 10018, USA
Suits, Julia *Editorial Cartoonist*
%Creators Syndicate, 5777 W Century Blvd, #700, Los Angeles, CA 90045, USA
Sukarnoputri, Megawati *President, Indonesia*
%President's Office, Bharat Ka, Rashtrapti Bhavan, New Delhi 110004, India
Sukova, Helena *Tennis Player*
1 Ave Grande Bretagne, Monte Carlo, Monaco
Sukowa, Barbara *Actress*
%Artmedia, 20 Ave Rapp, 75007 Paris, France
Sukselainen, Vieno J *Prime Minister, Finland*
Paivattarenpolku 2, 02100 Tapiola, Finland
Sulaiman, Jose *Boxing Executive*
%World Boxing Council, Genova 33, Colonia Juarez, Cuahtetemoc 0660, Mexico
Suleymanoglu, Naim *Weightlifter*
%Olympic Committee, Sisli, Buyukdere Cad 18 Tankaya, Istanbul, Turkey
Suliotis, Elena *Opera Singer*
Villa il Poderino, Via Incontri 38, Florence, Italy
Sullivan, Danny *Auto Racing Driver*
434 E Cooper St, #201, Aspen, CO 81611, USA
Sullivan, Franklin L (Frank) *Baseball Player*
PO Box 1873, Lihue, HI 96766, USA
Sullivan, Kathleen *Commentator*
1025 N Kings Road, #202, West Hollywood, CA 90069, USA
Sullivan, Kathryn D *Astronaut*
795 Old Oak Trace, Columbus, OH 43235, USA
Sullivan, Kevin *Journalist*
%Washington Post, Editorial Dept, 1150 15th St NW, Washington, DC 20071, USA
Sullivan, Louis W *Secretary, Health & Human Services*
%Morehouse College, Medical School, 720 Westview Dr SW, Atlanta, GA 30310, USA
Sullivan, Michael J (Mike) *Governor, WY*
1140 S Center St, Casper, WY 82601, USA
Sullivan, Mike *Hockey Player, Coach*
9 Gardner Road, Duxbury, MA 02332, USA
Sullivan, Nicole *Actress*
%QDE, 5842 Sunset Blvd, Building 11, Beverly Hills, CA 90212, USA
Sullivan, Patrick J (Pat) *Football Player, Coach*
1717 Indian Creek Dr, Birmingham, AL 35243, USA
Sullivan, Susan *Actress*
8642 Allenwood Road, Los Angeles, CA 90046, USA
Sullivan, Timothy J *Educator*
%College of William & Mary, President's Office, Williamsburg, VA 23187, USA
Sulston, John E *Nobel Medicine Laureate*
39 Mingle Lane, Stapleford, Cambridge CB2 5BG, England
Sultan Salman Abdulaziz Al-Saud *Astronaut, Saudi Arabia*
PO Box 18368, Riyadh 11415, Saudi Arabia
Sultan, Donald K *Artist*
19 E 70th St, New York, NY 10021, USA
Sultonov, Outkir T *Prime Minister, Uzbekistan*
%Prime Minister's Office, Mustarilik 5, 70008 Tashkent, Uzbekistan
Sulzberger, Arthur O, Jr *Publisher, Businessman*
%New York Times Co, 229 W 43rd St, New York, NY 10036, USA
Sumaye, Frederick T *Prime Minister, Tanzania*
%Prime Minister's Office, PO Box 980, Dodoma, Tanzania
Sumino, Naoko *Astronaut*
%NASDA, Tsukuba Space Center, 2-1-1 Sengen, Tukubashi, Ibaraka 305, Japan
Summer, Donna *Singer*
18171 Eccles St, Northridge, CA 91325, USA
Summerall, George A (Pat) *Football Player, Sportscaster*
710 S White Chapel Blvd, Southlake, TX 76092, USA
Summers, Andy *Singer/Guitarist (Police)*
21A Noel St, London W1V 3PD, England
Summers, Carol *Artist*
2817 Smith Grade, Santa Cruz, CA 95060, USA
Summers, Dana *Cartoonist (Lug Nuts/Bound & Gagged)*
%Orlando Sentinel, Editorial Dept, 633 N Orange Ave, Orlando, FL 32801, USA
Summers, Jerry *Singer (Dovells)*
%American Promotions, 2011 Ferry Ave, #U19, Camden, NJ 08104, USA

Summers, Lawrence H (Larry) *Educator; Secretary, Treasury*
%Harvard University, President's Office, Cambridge, MA 02138, USA
Summers, Marc *Chef*
%Food Network, 1180 Ave of Americas, #1200, New York, NY 10036, USA
Summitt, Pat Head *Basketball Coach*
3720 River Trace Lane, Knoxville, TN 37920, USA
Sumners, Rosalynn *Figure Skater*
%International Management Group, 22 E 71st St, New York, NY 10021, USA
Sun Dao Lin *Actor, Director*
%Shanghai Film Studio, 595 Tsao Hsi North Road, Shanghai 200030, China
Sun Yun-Hsuan *Prime Minister, Taiwan*
10 Lane 6, Chung South Rd, Section 2, Taipei 100, Taiwan
Sundin, Mats *Hockey Player*
%Int'l Management Group, 801 6th St SW, #235, Calgary AB T2P 3V8, Canada
Sundlun, Bruce G *Governor, RI*
Seawood Cliff Ave, Newport, RI 02840, USA
Sundvold, Jon *Basketball Player*
2700 Westbrook Way, Columbia, MO 65203, USA
Sung, Elizabeth *Actress*
%GVA Talent, 9229 Sunset Blvd, #320, Los Angeles, CA 90069, USA
Sununu, John H *Governor, NH; Government Official*
24 Samoset Dr, Salem, NH 03079, USA
Supernaw, Doug *Singer, Songwriter*
%Red & Rio, PO Box 411, Bellville, TX 77418, USA
Suplee, Ethan *Actor*
%Don Buchwald, 6500 Wilshire Blvd, #2200, Los Angeles, CA 90048, USA
Suquia Goicoechea, Angel Cardinal *Religious Leader*
El Cardenal Arxobispo, San Justo 2, 28074 Madrid, Spain
Sura, Bob *Basketball Player*
%Detroit Pistons, Palace, 2 Championship Dr, Auburn Hills, MI 48326, USA
Surhoff, William J (B J) *Baseball Player*
221 Oakland Beach Ave, Rye, NY 10580, USA
Surin, Bruny *Track Athlete*
PO Box 2, Succ Saint Michel, Montreal QC H2A 3L8, Canada
Surovy, Nicolas *Actor*
%Susan Smith, 121A N San Vicente Blvd, Beverly Hills, CA 90211, USA
Surtain, Patrick *Football Player*
380 Sweet Bay Ave, Plantation, FL 33324, USA
Surtees, Bruce *Cinematographer*
36 Linda Vista Place, Monterey, CA 93940, USA
Surtees, John *Auto Racing Driver*
%Team Surtees, Fircroft Way, Edenbridge, Kent TN8 6EJ, England
Suschitzky, Wolfgang *Cinematographer*
Douglas House, 6 Maida Ave, #11, London W2 1TG, England
Suslick, Kenneth S *Chemist*
%University of Illinois, Chemistry Dept, Champaign, IL 61820, USA
Susman, Todd *Actor*
%Pakula/King, 9229 Sunset Blvd, #315, Los Angeles, CA 90069, USA
Sutcliffe, Richard L (Rick) *Baseball Player*
25911 99th St, Lees Summit, MO 64086, USA
Suter, Bob *Hockey Player*
4332 McConnell St, Fitchburg, WI 53711, USA
Suter, Gary *Hockey Player*
2128 County Road D, Lac du Flambu, WI 54538, USA
Sutherland, Donald *Actor*
%Creative Artists Agency, 9830 Wilshire Blvd, Beverly Hills, CA 90212, USA
Sutherland, Joan *Opera Singer*
Chalet Monet, Route de Son, ICH-18 Les Avants, Switzerland
Sutherland, Kiefer *Actor*
9056 Santa Monica Blvd, #100, Los Angeles, CA 90069, USA
Sutherland, Peter D *Government Official, Ireland*
68 Eglinton Road, Dublin 4, Ireland
Sutter, Brent *Hockey Player*
2551 Thaddeus Circle, #S, Glen Ellyn, IL 60137, USA
Sutter, Brian *Hockey Player, Coach*
%Chicago Blackhawks, United Center, 1901 W Madison St, Chicago, IL 60612, USA
Sutter, Darryl *Hockey Player, Coach*
%Calgary Flames, PO Box 1540, Station M, Calgary AB T2P 3B9, Canada
Sutter, Duane *Hockey Player, Coach*
3703 High Plne Dr, Coral Springs, FL 33065, USA
Sutter, H Bruce *Baseball Player*
1368 Hamilton Road, Kennesaw, GA 30152, USA
Sutton, Donald H (Don) *Baseball Player, Sportscaster*
14412 Club Circle, Alpharetta, GA 30004, USA
Sutton, Eddie *Basketball Coach*
%Oklahoma State University, Athletic Dept, Stillwater, OK 74078, USA
Sutton, Hal *Golfer*
212 Texas St, #117, Shreveport, LA 71101, USA

Sutton, Michael *Actor*
%Somers Teitelbaum David, 8840 Wilshire Blvd, #200, Beverly Hills, CA 90211, USA
Sutton, Percy E *Political Leader*
10 W 135th St, New York, NY 10037, USA
Suvari, Mena *Actress*
%United Talent Agency, 9560 Wilshire Blvd, #500, Beverly Hills, CA 90212, USA
Suwa, Gen *Anthropologist*
%University of California, Human Evolutionary Science Lab, Berkeley, CA 94720, USA
Suwyn, Mark A *Businessman*
%Louisiana-Pacific Corp, 111 SW 5th Ave, Portland, OR 97204, USA
Suzman, Janet *Actress*
Faircroft, 11 Keats Grove, Hampstead, London NW3, England
Suzuki, David T *Commentator, Geneticist, Writer*
211-3905 Springtree Dr, Vancouver BC V6L 2E2, Canada
Suzuki, Ichiro *Baseball Player*
%Seattle Mariners, Safeco Field, PO Box 4100, Seattle, WA 98194, USA
Suzuki, Robert *Educator*
%California State University, President's Office, Bakersfield, CA 93311, USA
Suzy *Columnist*
18 E 68th St, #1B, New York, NY 10021, USA
Svankmajer, Jan *Movie Director*
Cerninska 5, 118 00 Prague 1, Czech Republic
Svare, Harland *Football Player, Coach*
6127 Paseo Jaquita, Carlsbad, CA 92009, USA
Svenden, Birgitta *Concert Singer*
%Ulf Tornqvist, Sankt Eriksgatan 100, 113 31 Stockholm, Sweden
Svendsen, George *Football Player*
163 Wayzata Blvd W, #315, Wayzata, MN 55391, USA
Svendsen, Louise A *Museum Curator*
16 Park Ave, New York, NY 10016, USA
Sveningsson, Magnus *Bassist (Cardigans)*
%Motor SE, Gotabergs Gatan 2, 400 14 Gothenburg, Sweden
Svenson, Bo *Actor*
247 S Beverly Dr, #102, Beverly Hills, CA 90212, USA
Svensson, Peter *Guitarist (Cardigans), Songwriter*
%Motor SE, Gotabergs Gatan 2, 400 14 Gothenburg, Sweden
Sverak, Jan *Movie Director*
PO Box 33, 155 00 Prague 515, Czech Republic
Svoboda, Jiri *Movie Director*
Na Balkane 120, Prague 3, Czech Republic
Svoboda, Petr *Hockey Player*
1119 S Jefferson St, Allentown, PA 18103, USA
Swados, Elizabeth A *Writer, Composer*
360 Central Park West, #16G, New York, NY 10025, USA
Swagerty, Jane *Swimmer*
9128 N 70th St, Paradise Valley, AZ 85253, USA
Swaggart, Jimmy L *Evangelist*
8919 World Ministry Ave, Baton Rouge, LA 70810, USA
Swail, Julie *Water Polo Player, Coach*
%University of California, Athletic Dept, Irvine, CA 92697, USA
Swain, Dominique *Actress*
%International Creative Mgmt, 8942 Wilshire Blvd, #219, Beverly Hills, CA 90211, USA
Swaminathan, Monkombu S *Geneticist*
%MS Swaminathan Foundation, 3 Cross St, Taramani, Madras 600113, India
Swan, Billy *Singer, Songwriter*
%Muirhead Mgmt, 202 Fulham Road, Chelsea, London SW10 9PJ, England
Swan, John W D *Premier, Bermuda*
%Swan Building, 26 Victoria St, Hamilton HM12, Bermuda
Swan, Michael *Actor*
13576 Cheltenham Dr, Sherman Oaks, CA 91423, USA
Swan, Richard G *Mathematician*
700 Melrose Ave, #M3, Winter Park, FL 32789, USA
Swank, Hillary *Actress*
%Baker/Winokur/Ryder, 9100 Wilshire Blvd, #600, Beverly Hills, CA 90212, USA
Swann, Eric J *Football Player*
PO Box 790, Cornelius, NC 28031, USA
Swann, Lynn C *Football Player, Sportscaster*
%Swann Inc, 600 Grant St, #4870, Pittsburgh, PA 15219, USA
Swanson, August G *Physician*
3146 Portage Bay Place E, #H, Seattle, WA 98102, USA
Swanson, Jackie *Actress*
15155 Albright St, Pacific Palisades, CA 90272, USA
Swanson, Judith *Actress*
%Persona Mgmt, 40 E 9th St, New York, NY 10003, USA
Swanson, Kristy *Actress, Model*
2934 1/2 N Beverly Glen Circle, #416, Los Angeles, CA 90077, USA
Swanson, Steven R *Astronaut*
16403 Bougainville Lane, Friendswood, TX 77546, USA

Swartz, Jacob T *Scientist*
New York University, 251 Mercer St, New York, NY 10012, USA
Swayze, Patrick *Actor*
14960 Dickens St, #302, Sherman Oaks, CA 91403, USA
Swe, U Ba *Prime Minister, Myanmar*
84 Innes Road, Yangon, Myanmar
Swearingen, John E, Jr *Businessman*
1420 Lake Shore Dr, Chicago, IL 60610, USA
Sweat, Keith *Singer, Songwriter*
PO Box 1002, Bronx, NY 10466, USA
Swedberg, Heidi *Actress*
%Writers & Artists, 8383 Wilshire Blvd, #550, Beverly Hills, CA 90211, USA
Sweeney, D B *Actor*
%International Creative Mgmt, 8942 Wilshire Blvd, #219, Beverly Hills, CA 90211, USA
Sweeney, James (Jim) *Football Coach*
119 Justabout Road, Venetia, PA 15367, USA
Sweeney, John J *Labor Leader*
%AFL-CIO, 1750 New York Ave NW, Washington, DC 20006, USA
Sweeney, Julia *Actress, Comedienne*
137 N Larchmount Blvd, #214, Los Angeles, CA 90004, USA
Sweeney, Michael J (Mike) *Baseball Player*
2802 E Tam O'Shanter Court, Ontario, CA 91761, USA
Sweeney, Walter F (Walt) *Football Player*
1040 Martin Ave, #A, South Lake Tahoe, CA 96150, USA
Sweet, Matthew *Singer, Songwriter*
%Russell Carter Artists Mgmt, 315 W Ponce de Leon Ave, #755, Decatur, GA 30030, USA
Sweet, Sharon *Opera Singer*
%Columbia Artists Mgmt Inc, 165 W 57th St, New York, NY 10019, USA
Sweetney, Mike *Basketball Player*
%New York Knicks, Madison Square Garden, 2 Penn Plaza, New York, NY 10121, USA
Swensen, Joseph A *Conductor, Composer*
%Van Walsum Mgmt, 4 Addison Bridge Place, London W14 8XP, England
Swenson, Inga *Actress, Singer*
3351 Halderman St, Los Angeles, CA 90066, USA
Swenson, Rick *Dog Sled Racer*
PO Box 16205, Two Rivers, AK 99716, USA
Swenson, Robert C (Bob) *Football Player*
910 Cypress Lane, Louisville, CO 80027, USA
Swenson, Ruth Ann *Opera Singer*
%Columbia Artists Mgmt Inc, 165 W 57th St, New York, NY 10019, USA
Swensson, Earl S *Architect*
%Earl Swensson Assoc, 2100 W End Ave, #1200, Nashville, TN 37203, USA
Swett, James E *WW II Marine Corps Hero (CMH)*
PO Box 327, Trinity Center, CA 96091, USA
Swiatek, Kazimierz Cardinal *Religious Leader*
Pl Swobody 9, 220030 Minsk, Belarus
Swiczinsky, Helmut *Architect*
%Coop Himmelblau, Seilerstatte 16/11A, 81010 Vienna, Austria
Swienton, Gregory T *Businessman*
%Ryder System Inc, 3600 NW 82nd Ave, Miami, FL 33166, USA
Swift, Clive *Actor*
%Roxane Vacca Mgmt, 8 Silver Place, London W1R 3LJ, England
Swift, Graham C *Writer*
%AP Watt, 20 John St, London WC1N 2DR, England
Swift, Hewson H *Biologist*
%University of Chicago, Cell Biology Dept, Chicago, IL 60637, USA
Swift, Stephen J *Judge*
%US Tax Court, 400 2nd St NW, Washington, DC 20217, USA
Swift, Stromile *Basketball Player*
%Memphis Grizzlies, 175 Toyota Plaza, #150, Memphis, TN 38103, USA
Swift, William C (Bill) *Baseball Player*
5880 E Sapphire Lane, Paradise Valley, AZ 85253, USA
Swilling, Patrick T (Pat) *Football Player*
%Patrick's Place East, 6780 Bundy Road, New Orleans, LA 70127, USA
Swindell, F Gregory (Greg) *Baseball Player*
9625 N 55th St, Paradise Valley, AZ 85253, USA
Swindells, William, Jr *Businessman*
%Willamette Industries, 1300 SW 5th Ave, Portland, OR 97201, USA
Swindoll, Charles R *Evangelist, Writer*
%Insight for Living, 211 Imperial Highway, Fullerton, CA 92835, USA
Swingley, Doug *Dog Sled Racer*
General Delivery, Simms, MT 59477, USA
Swink, James E (Jim) *Football Player*
1201 8th Ave, Fort Worth, TX 76104, USA
Swinny, Wayne *Guitarist (Saliva)*
%Helter Skelter, Plaza, 535 Kings Road, London SW10 0S, England
Swinton, Tilda *Actress*
%Lorraine Hamilton, 76 Oxford St, London W1N 0AT, England

S

Swisher - Szymborska

Swisher, Carl C *Anthropologist*
%Institute of Human Origins, 1288 9th St, Berkeley, CA 94710, USA
Swit, Loretta *Actress*
23852 Pacific Coast Highway, Malibu, CA 90265, USA
Switzer, Barry *Football Player, Coach*
700 W Timberdell Road, Norman, OK 73072, USA
Swoopes, Sheryl *Basketball Player*
PO Box 43021, Lubbock, TX 79409, USA
Swygert, H Patrick *Educator*
%Howard University, President's Office, Washington, DC 20059, USA
Syberberg, Hans-Jurgen *Movie Director*
Genter Str 15A, 80805 Munich, Germany
Sybil *Singer*
%Mission Control, Business Center, Lower Road, London SE16 2XB, England
Sykes, Eric *Actor*
%Norma Farnes, 9 Orme Court, London W2 4RL, England
Sykes, Lynn R *Geologist*
RR 1 Box 248, 100 Washington Spring Road, Palisades, NY 10964, USA
Sykes, Peter *Movie Director*
%International Creative Mgmt, 76 Oxford St, London W1N 0AX, England
Sykes, Phil *Hockey Player*
2312 Hill Lane, Redondo Beach, CA 90278, USA
Sylbert, Anthea *Costume Designer*
13949 Ventura Blvd, #309, Sherman Oaks, CA 91423, USA
Sylvester, George H *Air Force General*
4571 Conicville Road, Mount Jackson, VA 22842, USA
Sylvester, Harold *Actor*
%International Creative Mgmt, 8942 Wilshire Blvd, #219, Beverly Hills, CA 90211, USA
Sylvester, Michael *Opera Singer*
%Columbia Artists Mgmt Inc, 165 W 57th St, New York, NY 10019, USA
Sylvia *Singer*
%So Much More Media, PO Box 120426, Nashville, TN 37212, USA
Symington, J Fife, III *Governor, AZ*
1700 W Washington St, Phoenix, AZ 85007, USA
Symms, Steven D *Senator, ID*
127 S Fairfax St, #137, Alexandria, VA 22314, USA
Syms, Sylvia *Actress*
%Barry Brown, 47 West Square, London SE11 4SP, England
Syron, Richard F *Financier, Government Official*
%American Stock Exchange, 86 Trinity Place, New York, NY 10006, USA
Sytsma, John F *Labor Leader*
%Locomotive Engineers Brotherhood, 1370 Ontario Ave, Cleveland, OH 44113, USA
Szabo, Istvan *Movie Director*
%Objektiv Fil Studio-MAFILM, Rona Utca 174, 1149 Budapest, Hungary
Szasz, Thomas S *Psychiatrist*
4739 Limberlost Lane, Manlius, NY 13104, USA
Szczerbiak, Wally *Basketball Player*
521 River St, Minneapolis, MN 55401, USA
Szekely, Eva *Swimmer*
Szepvolgyi Utca 4/B, 1025 Budapest, Hungary
Szekessy, Karen *Photographer*
Haynstr 2, 20249 Hamburg, Germany
Szep, Paul M *Editorial Cartoonist*
12760 Indian Rocks Road, #1071, Largo, FL 33774, USA
Szewczenko, Tanya *Figure Skater*
Niederbeerbacher Str 10, 64367 Muhltal, Germany
Szigmond, Vilmos *Cinematographer*
PO Box 2230, Los Angeles, CA 90078, USA
Szoka, Edmund C Cardinal *Religious Leader*
%Prefecture for Economic Affairs, 00120 Vatican City
Szymanski, Richard (Dick) *Football Player*
5270 Forest Edge Court, Lake Forest, FL 32771, USA
Szymborska, Wislawa *Nobel Literature Laureate*
Stowarzyszenie Pissarzy Polskich, Ul Kanonicza 7, 31-002 Cracow, Poland

T Hooft, Gerardus *Nobel Physics Laureate*
Leuvenlaan 4, Postbus 80.195, 3508 Utrecht, Netherlands
T, Mr *Actor*
15203 La Maida St, Sherman Oaks, CA 91403, USA
Tabachnik, Michel *Composer, Conductor*
%Garvey & Ivor, 59 Lansdowne Place, Hove BN3 1FL, England
Tabackin, Lewis B (Lew) *Jazz Flutist*
38 W 94th St, New York, NY 10025, USA
Tabai, Ieremia T *President, Kiribati*
%South Pacific Forum Secretariat, Ratu Su Kuna Rd, GPO Box 856, Suva, Fiji
Tabakov, Oleg P *Actor, Director*
Chernysherskogo 39, #3, 103062 Moscow, Russia
Tabaksblat, Morris *Businessman*
%Unilever NV, Weena 455, 3000 DK Rotterdam, Netherlands
Taber, Carol A *Publisher*
%Working Woman Magazine, 230 Park Ave, New York, NY 10169, USA
Tabitha 'Masentle *Princess, Lesotho*
%Royal Palace, PO Box 524, Maseru, Lesotho
Tabone, Anton *President, Malta*
33 Carmel St, Sliema, Malta
Tabor, David *Physicist*
8 Rutherford Road, Cambridge CB2 2HH, England
Tabor, Herbert *Biochemist*
%National Institutes of Health, 8 Center Dr, Bethesda, MD 20892, USA
Tabori, Kristoffer *Actor*
%International Artistes, 235 Regent St, London W1R 8AX, England
Tabori, Laszlo *Track Athlete*
2221 W Olive Ave, Burbank, CA 91506, USA
Tacha, Deanell R *Judge*
%US Court of Appeals, 4830 W 15th St, Lawrence, KS 66049, USA
Taco *Singer*
8124 W 3rd St, #204, Los Angeles, CA 90048, USA
Taddei, Giuseppe *Opera Singer*
%Metropolitan Opera Assn, Lincoln Center Plaza, New York, NY 10023, USA
Tademy, Lalita *Writer*
%Warner Books, 1271 Ave of Americas, New York, NY 10020, USA
Tafoya, Michele *Sportscaster*
%CBS-TV, Sports Dept, 51 W 52nd St, New York, NY 10019, USA
Taft, William H, IV *Government Official*
1001 Pennsylvania Ave NW, Washington, DC 20004, USA
Tagawa, Cary-Hiroyuki *Actor*
%Jerry Shandrew, 1050 S Stanley Ave, Los Angeles, CA 90019, USA
Tagliabue, Paul J *Football Executive*
%National Football League, 280 Park Ave, #12W, New York, NY 10017, USA
Taglianetti, Peter *Hockey Player*
67 Merion Court, Bridgeville, PA 15017, USA
Taillibert, Roger R *Architect*
163 Rue de la Pompe, 75116 Paris, France
Tait, John E *Businessman*
%Penn Mutual Life, Independence Square, Philadelphia, PA 19172, USA
Tait, Marissa *Actress*
3518 Cahuenga Blvd, #200, Los Angeles, CA 90068, USA
Tait, Tristan *Actor*
%Paradigm Agency, 10100 Santa Monica Blvd, #2500, Los Angeles, CA 90067, USA
Taittinger, Jean *Businessman*
58 Blvd Gouvion, Saint-Cyr, 75017 Paris, France
Takac, Robby *Bassist (Goo Goo Dolls)*
%Atlas/Third Rail Entertainment, 9200 W Sunset Blvd, West Hollywood, CA 90069, USA
Takacs, Tibor *Movie Director*
IP, 104 Richview Ave, Toronto ON M5P 3E9, Canada
Takacs-Nagy, Gabor *Concert Violinist*
Case Postale 196, 1245 Collonge-Bellerive, Switzerland
Takagi, Toranosuke *Auto Racing Driver*
%Nakajima Planing, 1-3-10 Higushi, Shivuyaku, Tokyo 150-0011, Japan
Takahashi, Joseph S *Neuroscientist*
%Northwestern University, Neurobiology Dept, 2153 N Campus Dr, Evanston, I 60208, USA
Takahashi, Michiaki *Immunologist*
%Osaka University, Microbe Diseases Research Institute, Osaka, Japan
Takamatsu, Shin *Architect*
%Shin Takamatsu Assoc, 195 Jobodaiincho Takeda, Fushimiku, Kyoto, Japan
Takei, George *Actor*
%Hosato Enterprises, 419 N Larchmont Blvd, #41, Los Angeles, CA 90004, USA
Takenouchi, Naoko *Artist*
%Kathleen Gaffney, Art Glass Int'l, PO Box 58922, Renton, WA 98058, USA
Takezawa, Kyoko *Concert Violinist*
%I C M Artists, 40 W 57th St, New York, NY 10019, USA
Tal, Josef *Composer, Concert Pianist*
3 Dvira Haneviyah St, Jerusalem, Israel

T

Talalay - Tani

Talalay, Paul *Pharmacologist*
5512 Boxhill Lane, Baltimore, MD 21210, USA
Talalay, Rachel *Movie Director*
1047 Grant St, Santa Monica, CA 90405, USA
Talavera, Tracee *Gymnast*
106 Mandala Court, Walnut Creek, CA 94598, USA
Talbot, Diron V *Football Player*
3803 B F Terry Blvd, Rosenberg, TX 77471, USA
Talbot, Don *Swimming Coach*
%Sports Federation, 333 River Road, Vanier, Ottawa ON K1L 8B9, Canada
Talbot, Nita *Actress*
3420 Merrimac Road, Los Angeles, CA 90049, USA
Talbot, Susan *Actress*
%Media Artists Group, 6300 Wilshire Blvd, #1470, Los Angeles, CA 90048, USA
Talbott, Gloria *Actress*
2066 Montecito Dr, Glendale, CA 91208, USA
Talbott, John H *Physician*
%Commodore Club, 177 Ocean Lane Dr, Key Biscayne, FL 33149, USA
Talbott, Michael *Actor*
10340 Santa Monica Blvd, Los Angeles, CA 90025, USA
Talbott, Strobe *Journalist*
%State Department, 2201 C St NW, Washington, DC 20520, USA
Talese, Gay *Writer*
154 E Atlantic Blvd, Ocean City, NJ 08226, USA
Taliaferro, George *Football Player*
%Innovative Health Systems, 3013 S Stratfield Dr, Bloomington, IN 47401, USA
Tallchief, Maria *Ballerina*
48 Prospect, Highland Park, IL 60035, USA
Talley, Darryl V *Football Player*
8713 Lake Tibet Court, Orlando, FL 32836, USA
Talley, Gary *Guitarist (Box Tops)*
%Horizon Mgmt, PO Box 8770, Endwell, NJ 13762, USA
Talley, Joel E *Vietnam War Air Force Hero*
20 Lakeshore Dr, Shalimar, FL 32579, USA
Tallman, Patricia *Actress*
%PMB 2161, 1801 E Tropicana, #9, Las Vegas, NV 89119, USA
Tallman, Richard C *Judge*
%US Court of Appeals, US Courthouse, 1010 5th Ave, Seattle, WA 98104, USA
Tam, Vivienne *Fashion Designer*
550 Fashion Ave, New York, NY 10018, USA
Tamahori, Lee *Movie Director*
%International Creative Mgmt, 8942 Wilshire Blvd, #219, Beverly Hills, CA 90211, USA
Tamayo Mendez, Arnaldo *Cosmonaut, Cuba*
Calle 16, #504, C/5A y 7MA, Miramar, Ciudad Havana 11300, Cuba
Tamberino, Paul *Soccer Referee*
349 Homeland Southway, Baltimore, MD 21212, USA
Tambiah, Stanley J *Anthropologist*
%Harvard University, Anthropology Dept, Cambirdge, MA 02138, USA
Tamblyn, Russ *Actor, Dancer*
1221 N King's Road, #PH 405, West Hollywood, CA 90069, USA
Tambor, Jeffrey *Actor*
%Brillstein/Grey, 9150 Wilshire Blvd, #350, Beverly Hills, CA 90212, USA
Tamia *Singer*
%International Creative Mgmt, 8942 Wilshire Blvd, #219, Beverly Hills, CA 90211, USA
Tamke, George W *Businessman*
%Emerson Electric Co, PO Box 4100, Saint Louis, MO 63136, USA
Tamm, Peter *Publisher*
Elbchaussee 277, 22605 Hamburg, Germany
Tan Dun *Composer*
%Columbia University, Arts School, Dodge Hall, New York, NY 10027, USA
Tan, Amy R *Writer*
215 S La Cienega Blvd, #PH, Beverly Hills, CA 90211, USA
Tan, Melvyn *Concert Pianist*
%Valerie Barber Mgmt, 4 Winsley St, #305, London W1N 7AR, England
Tanaev, Nikoly *Prime Minister, Kyrgyzstan*
%Prime Minister's Office, Ul Perromayskaya 57, Bishkek, Kyrgyzstan
Tanaka, Koichi *Nobel Chemistry Laureate*
%Shimadzu Corp, 1 Nishinokyo-Kuwabaracho, Nakagoku, Kyoto 604-8511, Japan
Tanaka, Shoji *Physicist*
%Superconductivity Laboratory, 1-10-13 Shinonome, Kotoku, Tokyo 135, Japan
Tanana, Frank D *Baseball Player*
28492 S Harwich Dr, Farmington Hills, MI 48334, USA
Tanford, Charles *Physiologist*
Tarlswood, Back Lane, Easingwold, York YO6 3BG, England
Tange, Kenzo *Architect, Pritzker Laureate*
%Kenzo Tange Assoc, 7-2-21 Akasaka, Minato-ku, Tokyo, Japan
Tani, Daniel M *Astronaut*
3703 Montvale Dr, Houston, TX 77059, USA

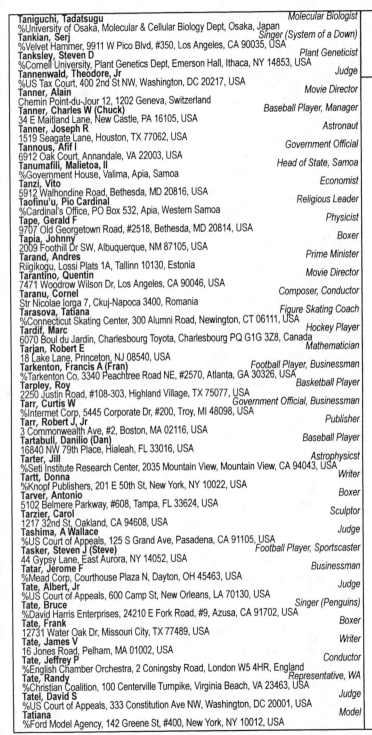

Taniguchi, Tadatsugu *Molecular Biologist*
%University of Osaka, Molecular & Cellular Biology Dept, Osaka, Japan
Tankian, Serj *Singer (System of a Down)*
%Velvet Hammer, 9911 W Pico Blvd, #350, Los Angeles, CA 90035, USA
Tanksley, Steven D *Plant Geneticist*
%Cornell University, Plant Genetics Dept, Emerson Hall, Ithaca, NY 14853, USA
Tannenwald, Theodore, Jr *Judge*
%US Tax Court, 400 2nd St NW, Washington, DC 20217, USA
Tanner, Alain *Movie Director*
Chemin Point-du-Jour 12, 1202 Geneva, Switzerland
Tanner, Charles W (Chuck) *Baseball Player, Manager*
34 E Maitland Lane, New Castle, PA 16105, USA
Tanner, Joseph R *Astronaut*
1519 Seagate Lane, Houston, TX 77062, USA
Tannous, Afif I *Government Official*
6912 Oak Court, Annandale, VA 22003, USA
Tanumafili, Malietoa, II *Head of State, Samoa*
%Government House, Valima, Apia, Samoa
Tanzi, Vito *Economist*
5912 Walhondine Road, Bethesda, MD 20816, USA
Taofinu'u, Pio Cardinal *Religious Leader*
%Cardinal's Office, PO Box 532, Apia, Western Samoa
Tape, Gerald F *Physicist*
9707 Old Georgetown Road, #2518, Bethesda, MD 20814, USA
Tapia, Johnny *Boxer*
2009 Foothill Dr SW, Albuquerque, NM 87105, USA
Tarand, Andres *Prime Minister*
Riigikogu, Lossi Plats 1A, Tallinn 10130, Estonia
Tarantino, Quentin *Movie Director*
7471 Woodrow Wilson Dr, Los Angeles, CA 90046, USA
Taranu, Cornel *Composer, Conductor*
Str Nicolae Iorga 7, Ckuj-Napoca 3400, Romania
Tarasova, Tatiana *Figure Skating Coach*
%Connecticut Skating Center, 300 Alumni Road, Newington, CT 06111, USA
Tardif, Marc *Hockey Player*
6070 Boul du Jardin, Charlesbourg Toyota, Charlesbourg PQ G1G 3Z8, Canada
Tarjan, Robert E *Mathematician*
18 Lake Lane, Princeton, NJ 08540, USA
Tarkenton, Francis A (Fran) *Football Player, Businessman*
%Tarkenton Co, 3340 Peachtree Road NE, #2570, Atlanta, GA 30326, USA
Tarpley, Roy *Basketball Player*
2250 Justin Road, #108-303, Highland Village, TX 75077, USA
Tarr, Curtis W *Government Official, Businessman*
%Intermet Corp, 5445 Corporate Dr, #200, Troy, MI 48098, USA
Tarr, Robert J, Jr *Publisher*
3 Commonwealth Ave, #2, Boston, MA 02116, USA
Tartabull, Danilio (Dan) *Baseball Player*
16840 NW 79th Place, Hialeah, FL 33016, USA
Tarter, Jill *Astrophysicst*
%Seti Institute Research Center, 2035 Mountain View, Mountain View, CA 94043, USA
Tartt, Donna *Writer*
%Knopf Publishers, 201 E 50th St, New York, NY 10022, USA
Tarver, Antonio *Boxer*
5102 Belmere Parkway, #608, Tampa, FL 33624, USA
Tarzier, Carol *Sculptor*
1217 32nd St, Oakland, CA 94608, USA
Tashima, A Wallace *Judge*
%US Court of Appeals, 125 S Grand Ave, Pasadena, CA 91105, USA
Tasker, Steven J (Steve) *Football Player, Sportscaster*
44 Gypsy Lane, East Aurora, NY 14052, USA
Tatar, Jerome F *Businessman*
%Mead Corp, Courthouse Plaza N, Dayton, OH 45463, USA
Tate, Albert, Jr *Judge*
%US Court of Appeals, 600 Camp St, New Orleans, LA 70130, USA
Tate, Bruce *Singer (Penguins)*
%David Harris Enterprises, 24210 E Fork Road, #9, Azusa, CA 91702, USA
Tate, Frank *Boxer*
12731 Water Oak Dr, Missouri City, TX 77489, USA
Tate, James V *Writer*
16 Jones Road, Pelham, MA 01002, USA
Tate, Jeffrey P *Conductor*
%English Chamber Orchestra, 2 Coningsby Road, London W5 4HR, England
Tate, Randy *Representative, WA*
%Christian Coalition, 100 Centerville Turnpike, Virginia Beach, VA 23463, USA
Tatel, David S *Judge*
%US Court of Appeals, 333 Constitution Ave NW, Washington, DC 20001, USA
Tatiana *Model*
%Ford Model Agency, 142 Greene St, #400, New York, NY 10012, USA

Tatrai, Vilmos *Concert Violinist*
R Wallenberg Utca 4, 1136 Budapest XIII, Hungary

Tattersall, David *Cinematographer*
%Lucasfilm, PO Box 2459, San Rafael, CA 94912, USA

Tatum, John D (Jack) *Football Player*
10620 Mark St, Oakland, CA 94605, USA

Tatupu, Mosi *Football Player*
71 Walnut St, Plainville, MA 02762, USA

Taube, Henry *Nobel Chemistry Laureate*
441 Gerona Road, Stanford, CA 94305, USA

Taubman, A Alfred *Businessman*
%Taubman Co, 200 E Long Lake Road, Bloomfield Hills, MI 48304, USA

Taufa'ahau Tupou IV *King, Tonga*
%Royal Palace, PO Box 6, Nuku'alofa, Tonga

Taupin, Bernie *Singer, Songwriter*
2905 Roundup Road, Santa Ynez, CA 93460, USA

Tauran, Jean-Louis Cardinal *Religious Leader*
Palazzo Apostolico, Vatican City 00120

Taurel, Sidney *Businessman*
%Eli Lilly Co, Lilly Corporate Center, Indianapolis, IN 46285, USA

Tauscher, Hansjorg *Alpine Skier*
Schwand 7, 87561 Oberstdorf, Germany

Tauziat, Nathalie *Tennis Player*
%Federation de Tennis, 1 Ave Gordon Bennett, 75016 Paris, France

Tavard, Georges H *Theologian*
330 Market St, Brighton, MA 02135, USA

Tavener, John H *Football Player*
241 N Oregon St, Johnstown, OH 43031, USA

Tavener, John K *Composer*
%Chester Music, 8-9 Firth St, London W1V 5TZ, England

Taverner, Sonia *Ballerina*
PO Box 129, Stony Plain AB, Canada

Tavernier, Bertrand R M *Movie Director*
%Little Bear Productions, 7-9 Rue Arthur Groussier, 75010 Paris, France

Taviani, Paolo *Movie Director*
%Instituto Luce SPA, Via Tuscolana 1055, 00173 Rome, Italy

Taviani, Vittorio *Movie Director*
%Instituto Luce SPA, Via Tuscolana 1055, 00173 Rome, Italy

Taxier, Arthur *Actor*
%Pakula/King, 9229 Sunset Blvd, #315, Los Angeles, CA 90069, USA

Taya, Maawiya Ould Sid'Ahmed *President, Mauritania; Army Officer*
%President's Office, Boite Postale 184, Nouakchott, Mauritania

Taylor, Andy *Guitarist (Duran Duran)*
%DD Productions, 93A Westbourne Park Villas, London W2 5ED, England

Taylor, Arthur R *Educator, Businessman*
%Muhlenburg College, President's Office, Allentown, PA 18104, USA

Taylor, Brian *Basketball Player*
3622 Green Vista Dr, Encino, CA 91436, USA

Taylor, Bruce L *Football Player*
6 Cascade Court W, Burr Ridge, IL 60527, USA

Taylor, Buck *Actor*
1305 Clyde Dr, Marrero, LA 70072, USA

Taylor, Carl E *Physician*
Bittersweet Acres, 1201 Hollins Lane, Baltimore, MD 21209, USA

Taylor, Cecil P *Jazz Pianist, Composer*
%Joel Chriss, 300 Mercer St, #3J, New York, NY 10003, USA

Taylor, Chad *Musician (Live)*
%Freedman & Smith, 1790 Broadway, #131, New York, NY 10019, USA

Taylor, Charles R (Charley) *Football Player, Executive*
12032 Canter Lane, Reston, VA 20191, USA

Taylor, Christine *Actress*
%United Talent Agency, 9560 Wilshire Blvd, #500, Beverly Hills, CA 90212, USA

Taylor, Christy *Actress*
10990 Massachusetts Ave, #3, Los Angeles, CA 90024, USA

Taylor, Clarice *Actress*
380 Elkwood Terrace, Englewood, NJ 07631, USA

Taylor, Dana *Actress*
100 S Sunrise Way, #468, Palm Springs, CA 92262, USA

Taylor, Dave *Hockey Player, Executive*
18920 Pasadero Dr, Tarzana, CA 91356, USA

Taylor, Delores *Actress*
PO Box 840, Moorpark, CA 93020, USA

Taylor, Elizabeth *Actress*
PO Box 55995, Sherman Oaks, CA 91413, USA

Taylor, Eric *Artist*
13 Tredgold Ave, Branhope near Leeds, West Yorkshire LS16 9BS, England

Taylor, Femi *Actress*
%Paul Telford Mgmt, 23 Noel St, London W1V 3RD, England

Taylor, Fred *Football Player*
13750 Bromley Point Dr, Jacksonville, FL 32225, USA
Taylor, Gilbert *Cinematographer*
%Cinematography Society, 11 Croft, Gerrards Cross, Bucks SL9 9E, England
Taylor, Glen *Basketball Executive*
%Minnesota Timberwolves, Target Center, 600 1st Ave N, Minneapolis, MN 55403, USA
Taylor, Henry S *Writer*
6930 Selkirk Dr, Bethesda, MD 20817, USA
Taylor, Holland *Actress*
2676 Hollyridge Dr, Los Angeles, CA 90068, USA
Taylor, J Herbert *Botanist*
110 Wood Road, #H210, Los Gatos, CA 95030, USA
Taylor, J T *Singer (Kool & the Gang)*
%Famous Artists Agency, 250 W 57th St, New York, NY 10107, USA
Taylor, Jackie Lynn *Actress*
PO Box 3182, Citrus Heights, CA 95611, USA
Taylor, James *Singer, Songwriter*
%Borman Entertainment, 1250 6th St, #401, Santa Monica, CA 90401, USA
Taylor, James A *Vietnam War Army Hero (CMH)*
PO Box 284, Trinity Center, CA 96091, USA
Taylor, James C (Jim) *Football Player*
7840 Walden Road, Baton Rouge, LA 70808, USA
Taylor, Jason *Football Player*
2342 SW 132nd St, Davie, FL 33325, USA
Taylor, Jay *Businesman*
%Placer Dome Inc, 1600-1055 Dunsmuir St, Vancouver BC V7X 1P1, Canada
Taylor, John *Bassist (Duran Duran)*
%Left Bank Mgmt, 9255 Sunset Blvd, #200, West Hollywood, CA 90069, USA
Taylor, Joseph H, Jr *Nobel Physics Laureate*
272 Hartley St, Princeton, NJ 08540, USA
Taylor, Josh *Actor*
422 S California Ave, Burbank, CA 91505, USA
Taylor, Judson H *Educator*
%State University of New York College, President's Office, Cortland, NY 13045, USA
Taylor, Kenneth N *Publisher*
1515 E Forest Ave, Wheaton, IL 60187, USA
Taylor, Kitrick L *Football Player*
18215 Foothill Blvd, #94, Fontana, CA 92335, USA
Taylor, Koko *Singer*
PO Box 60234, Chicago, IL 60660, USA
Taylor, Lance J *Economist*
PO Box 378, Old County Road, Washington, ME 04574, USA
Taylor, Lauriston S *Physicist*
10450 Lottsford Road, #1-5, Bowie, MD 20721, USA
Taylor, Lawrence *Football Player*
122 Canterburg Place, Williamsburg, VA 23188, USA
Taylor, Lili *Actress*
%William Morris Agency, 1325 Ave of Americas, New York, NY 10019, USA
Taylor, Lionel *Football Player, Coach*
6593 Sahchu Lane, Cochiti Lake, NM 87083, USA
Taylor, Livingston *Singer*
%Fat City Artists, 1906 Chet Atkins Place, #502, Nashville, TN 37212, USA
Taylor, Marianne *Actress*
%Jack Scagnatti, 5118 Vineland Ave, #102, North Hollywood, CA 91601, USA
Taylor, Mark L *Actor*
7919 Norton Ave, West Hollywood, CA 90046, USA
Taylor, Maurice *Basketball Player*
%Houston Rockets, Toyota Center, 2 E Greenway Plaza, Houston, TX 77046, USA
Taylor, Meldrick *Boxer*
1158 N York Road, Warminster, PA 18974, USA
Taylor, Meshach *Actor*
6300 Wilshire Blvd, #900, Los Angeles, CA 90048, USA
Taylor, Mick *Guitarist (Rolling Stones)*
%Jacobson & Colin, 19 W 21st St, #603A, New York, NY 10010, USA
Taylor, Nicole R (Niki) *Model*
8362 Pines Blvd, #334, Pembroke Pines, FL 33024, USA
Taylor, Noah *Actor*
%June Cann Mgmt, 110 Queen St, Woollahra NSW 2025, Australia
Taylor, Paul B *Dancer, Choreographer*
%Paul Taylor Dance Co, 552 Broadway, New York, NY 10012, USA
Taylor, Penny *Basketball Player*
%Cleveland Rockers, Gund Arena, 1 Center Court, Cleveland, OH 44115, USA
Taylor, Regina *Actress*
PO Box 2015, North Highlands, CA 95660, USA
Taylor, Renee *Actress*
%Judy Schoen, 606 N Larchmont Blvd, #309, Los Angeles, CA 90004, USA
Taylor, Richard E *Nobel Physics Laureate*
757 Mayfield Ave, Stanford, CA 94305, USA

T

Taylor - Tekulve

Taylor, Rip — *Actor, Comedian*
1133 N Clark Dr, Los Angeles, CA 90035, USA
Taylor, Robert — *Track Athlete*
1010 S Glenwood Blvd, Tyler, TX 75701, USA
Taylor, Rod — *Actor*
2375 Bowmont Dr, Beverly Hills, CA 90210, USA
Taylor, Roger — *Tennis Player*
39 Newstead Way, Wimbledon SW19, England
Taylor, Roger — *Drummer (Duran Duran)*
%DD Productions, 93A Westbourne Park Villas, London W2 5ED, England
Taylor, Roger M — *Drummer (Queen)*
%Neal Levin, 15260 Ventura Blvd, #1700, Sherman Oaks, CA 91403, USA
Taylor, Roosevelt — *Football Player*
1821 Arts St, New Orleans, LA 70117, USA
Taylor, Sandra — *Actress, Model*
%IPA Network, 231 E Alessandro Blvd, #A355, Riverside, CA 92508, USA
Taylor, Vince — *Body Builder*
20160 NW 9th Dr, Pembroke Pines, FL 33029, USA
Taylor, William (Billy), Jr — *Jazz Pianist, Composer*
555 Kappock St, Bronx, NY 10463, USA
Taylor, William O — *Publisher*
%Affiliated Publications, 135 William Morrissey Blvd, Dorchester, MA 02125, USA
Taylor, Wilson H — *Businessman*
%CIGNA Corp, 1 Liberty Place, 1650 Market St, Philadelphia, PA 19192, USA
Taylor-Taylor, Courtney — *Singer, Guitarist (Dandy Warhols)*
%Monqui Records, PO Box 5908, Portland, OR 97228, USA
Taylor-Young, Leigh — *Actress*
11300 W Olympic Blvd, #610, Los Angeles, CA 90064, USA
Taymor, Julie — *Theater, Movie Director, Lyricist*
%International Creative Mgmt, 40 W 57th St, #1800, New York, NY 10019, USA
Tchaikovsky, Aleksandr V — *Composer, Concert Pianist*
Leningradsky Prosp 14, #4, 125040 Moscow, Russia
Tcherina, Ludmila — *Ballerina*
42 Cours Albert 1er, 75008 Paris, France
Tcherkassky, Marianna — *Ballerina*
%American Ballet Theatre, 890 Broadway, New York, NY 10003, USA
Te Kanawa, Kiri — *Opera Singer*
%Jules Haefliger Impressario, Postfach 4113, 6002 Lucerne, Switzerland
Teaff, Grant — *Football Coach, Executive*
8265 Forest Ridge Dr, Waco, TX 76712, USA
Teagle, Terry — *Basketball Player*
2111 Heatherwood Dr, Missouri City, TX 77489, USA
Teannaki, Teatao — *President, Kiribati*
%President's Office, PO Box 68, Bairiki, Tarawa Atoll, Kiribati
Tear, Robert — *Opera Singer, Conductor*
11 Ravenscourt Court, London W6, England
Teasdale, Joseph P — *Governor, MO*
Commerce Tower, 911 Main St, #1210, Kansas City, MO 64105, USA
Teasley, Nikki — *Basketball Player*
%Los Angeles Sparks, Staples Center, 1111 S Figueroa St, Los Angeles, CA 90015, USA
Tebaldi, Renata — *Opera Singer*
Piazzetta della Guastella 1, 20122 Milan, Italy
Tebbit of Chingford, Norman B — *Government Official, England*
%House of Lords, Westminster, London SW1A 0PW, England
Tebbutt, Arthur R — *Statistician*
1511 Pelican Point Dr, Sarasota, FL 34231, USA
Techine, Andre J F — *Movie Director*
%Artmedia, 20 Ave Rapp, 75007 Paris, France
Tedeschi, Susan — *Singer*
%Blue Sky Artists, 761 Washington Ave N, Minneapolis, MN 55401, USA
Teevens, Buddy — *Football Coach*
%Stanford University, Athletic Dept, Stanford, CA 94395, USA
Tegart Dalton, Judy — *Tennis Player*
72 Grange Road, Toorak VIC 3142, Australia
Teich, Malvin C — *Electrical Engineer*
%Boston University, Electrical/Computer Engineering Dept, Boston, MA 02215, USA
Teicher, Louis (Lou) — *Pianist (Ferrante & Teicher)*
%Avant-Garde Records, 12224 Avila Dr, Kansas City, MO 64145, USA
Teichner, Helmut — *Skier*
4250 Marine Dr, #2101, Chicago, IL 60613, USA
Teitelbaum, Philip — *Psychologist*
%University of Florida, Psychology Dept, Gainesville, FL 32611, USA
Teitell, Conrad L — *Attorney*
16 Marlow Court, Riverside, CT 06878, USA
Tejada, Miguel O M — *Baseball Player*
%Oakland Athletics, NA Coliseum, 7000 Coliseum Way, Oakland, CA 94621, USA
Tekulve, Kenton C (Kent) — *Baseball Player*
1531 Sequoia Dr, Pittsburgh, PA 15241, USA

Telegdi, Valentine L *Physicist*
Eidgenossische Technische Hochschule, Houggerberg, Zurich, Switzerland
Tellep, Daniel M *Businessman*
%Lockheed Corp, PO Box 5118, Thousand Oaks, CA 91359, USA
Teller *Comedian, Illusionist (Penn & Teller)*
%William Morris Agency, 151 El Camino Dr, Beverly Hills, CA 90212, USA
Telnaes, Ann *Editorial Cartoonist*
%Tribune Media Services, 435 N Michigan Ave, #1500, Chicago, IL 60611, USA
Teltscher, Eliot *Tennis Player, Coach*
%Pepperdine University, Athletic Dept, Malibu, CA 90265, USA
Temesvari, Andrea *Tennis Player*
%ProServe, 1101 Woodrow Wilson Blvd, #1800, Arlington, VA 22209, USA
Temirkanov, Yuri K *Conductor*
%State Philharmonia, Mikhailovskaya 2, Saint Petersburg, Russia
Temko, Allan B *Journalist*
%San Francisco Chronicle, Editorial Dept, 901 Mission, San Francisco, CA 94103, USA
Templeman of White Lackington, Sydney W *Judge*
Manor Heath, Knowl Hill, Woking, Surrey GU22 7HL, England
Templeton, Ben *Cartoonist (Motley's Crew)*
%Tribune Media Services, 435 N Michigan Ave, #1500, Chicago, IL 60611, USA
Templeton, Garry L *Baseball Player*
13552 Del Poniente Road, Poway, CA 92064, USA
Templeton, John M *Financier*
%Lyford Cay Club, Box N7776, Nassau, Bahamas
Tenace, F Gene *Baseball Player*
2650 Cliff Hawk Court, Redmond, OR 97756, USA
Tenet, George J *Government Official*
%Central Intelligence Agency, Director's Office, Washington, DC 20505, USA
Tengbom, Anders *Architect*
Kornhamnstorg 6, 111 27 Stockholm, Sweden
Tenison, Renee *Model, Actress*
%Tenison Group, 171 Pier Ave, #403, Santa Monica, CA 90405, USA
Tennant, Stella *Model*
%Select Model Mgmt, Archer House, 43 King St, London WC2E 8RJ, England
Tennant, Veronica *Ballerina*
%National Ballet of Canada, 157 King St E, Toronto ON M5C 1G9, Canada
Tennant, Victoria *Actress*
PO Box 929, Beverly Hills, CA 90213, USA
Tenney, Jon *Actor*
%United Talent Agency, 9560 Wilshire Blvd, #500, Beverly Hills, CA 90212, USA
Tennille, Toni *Singer (Captain & Tennille)*
7123 Franktown Road, Carson City, NV 89704, USA
Tennison, Chalee *Singer*
%Tanasi Entertainment, 1204 17th Ave S, Nashville, TN 37212, USA
Tenorio, Pedro P *Governor, Northern Mariana Islands*
%Governor's Office, Capitol Hill, Chalan Kanoa, Saipan, CM 96950, USA
Tenuta, Judy *Actress, Comedienne*
%Super Artists, 12021 Wilshire Blvd, #612, Los Angeles, CA 90025, USA
Tepper, Lou *Football Coach*
%University of Illinois, Assembly Hall, Champaign, IL 61820, USA
Ter Horst, Jerald F *Government Official, Journalist*
7815 Evening Lane, Alexandria, VA 22306, USA
Ter-Petrosyan, Levon A *President, Armenia*
Marshal Baghramian Prospect 19, 375016 Yerevan, Armenia
Teraoka, Masami *Artist*
41-048 Kaulu St, Waimanalo, HI 96795, USA
Terekhova, Margarita B *Actress*
Bolshaya Gruzinskaya Str 57, #92, 123056 Moscow, Russia
Terentyeva, Nina N *Opera Singer*
%Bolshoi Theater, Teatralnaya Pl 1, 103009 Moscow, Russia
Tereschenko, Sergei A *Prime Minister, Kazakhstan*
%Prime Minister's Office, Dom Pravieelstra, 148008 Alma-Ata, Kazakhstan
Tereshkova, Valentina V *Cosmonaut*
%Int'l Co-operation Assn, Vozdvizhenka Str 14-18, 103885 Moscow, Russia
Tergesen, Lee *Actor*
%Gersh Agency, 232 N Canon Dr, Beverly Hills, CA 90210, USA
Terkel, Studs L *Writer*
850 W Castlewood Terrace, Chicago, IL 60640, USA
Terlesky, John *Actor*
14229 Dickens, #5, Sherman Oaks, CA 91423, USA
Termeer, Henricus A *Businessman*
%Genzyme Corp, 1 Kendall Square, Cambridge, MA 02139, USA
Terminator X *Rap Artist (Public Enemy)*
%William Morris Agency, 151 El Camino Dr, Beverly Hills, CA 90212, USA
Termo, Leonard *Actor*
%Baumgarten/Prophet, 1041 N Formosa Ave, #200, West Hollywood, CA 90046, USA
Terrace, Herbert S *Anthropologist*
17 Campfire Road, Chappaqua, NY 10514, USA

T

Terranova - Thaddeus

Terranova, Joe *Singer (Danny and the Juniors)*
%Joe Taylor Mgmt, PO Box 1017, Turnersville, NJ 08012, USA
Terranova, Phil *Boxer*
30 Bogardus Place, New York, NY 10040, USA
Terrasson, Jacky *Jazz Pianist*
%Joel Chriss, 300 Mercer St, #3J, New York, NY 10003, USA
Terrazas Sandoval, Julio Cardinal *Religious Leader*
Arzobispado, Casilla 25, Calle Ingavi 49, Santa Cruz, Bolivia
Terrell, David *Football Player*
196 N Main St, Roanoke, IN 46783, USA
Terreri, Chris *Hockey Player*
170 Dezenso Lane, West Orange, NJ 07052, USA
Terrile, Richard *Astronomer*
2121 E Woodlyn Road, Pasadena, CA 91104, USA
Terrio, Deney *Dancer, Entertainer*
%Paramount Entertainment, PO Box 12, Far Hills, NJ 07931, USA
Terry, Clark *Jazz Trumpeter, Singer*
420 Ivy Ave, Haworth, NJ 07641, USA
Terry, Hilda *Cartoonist (Teena)*
8 Henderson Place, New York, NY 10028, USA
Terry, Jason *Basketball Player*
%Atlanta Hawks, 190 Marietta St SW, Atlanta, GA 30303, USA
Terry, John *Actor*
25 W 5200 N, Park City, UT 84098, USA
Terry, John Q *Architect*
Old Exchange, Dedham, Colchester, Essex CO7 6HA, England
Terry, Megan D *Writer*
2309 Hanscom Blvd, Omaha, NE 68105, USA
Terry, Ralph W *Baseball Player*
801 Park St, Larned, KS 67550, USA
Terry, Randall A *Social Activist*
%Operation Rescue National, PO Box 360221, Melbourne, FL 32936, USA
Terry, Richard E *Businessman*
%Peoples Energy Corp, 130 E Randolph Dr, Chicago, IL 60601, USA
Terry, Ruth *Singer, Actress*
622 Hospitality Dr, Rancho Mirage, CA 92270, USA
Terry, Tony *Singer*
%Richard Walters, 1800 Argyle Ave, #408, Los Angeles, CA 90028, USA
Terzian, Jacques *Sculptor*
PO Box 883753, San Francisco, CA 94188, USA
Terzieff, Laurent D A *Actor, Theater Director*
8 Rue du Dragon, 75006 Paris, France
Tesh, John *Composer, Pianist, Entertainer*
PO Box 6010, Sherman Oaks, CA 91413, USA
Teske, Rachel *Golfer*
%Gaylord Sports Mgmt, 14646 N Kierland Blvd, #230, Scottsdale, AZ 85254, USA
Tessier-Lavigne, Marc *Neurobiologist*
361 Ridgeway Road, Woodside, CA 94062, USA
Testa, M David *Financier*
%T Rowe Price Assoc, 100 E Pratt St, Baltimore, MD 21202, USA
Testaverde, Vincent F (Vinny) *Football Player*
15 Tall Oak Court, Syosset, NY 11791, USA
Testi, Fabio *Actor*
Via Siacci 38, 00197 Rome, Italy
Tetley, Glen *Ballet Director, Choreographer*
15 W 9th St, New York, NY 10011, USA
Tetrault, Roger E *Businessman*
%McDermott International, 1450 Polydras St, New Orleans, LA 70112, USA
Tettamanzi, Dionigi Cardinal *Religious Leader*
%Arcivescovado, Piazza Matteotti 4, 16123 Genoa, Italy
Tettleton, Mickey L *Baseball Player*
52 W Royal Oak Road, Pauls Valley, OK 73075, USA
Tetzlaff, Christian *Concert Violinist*
%Shuman Assoc, 120 W 58th St, #8D, New York, NY 10019, USA
Tewell, Doug *Golfer*
6301 Oak Tree Dr, Edmond, OK 73003, USA
Tewes, Lauren *Actress*
157 W 57th St, #604, New York, NY 10019, USA
Tewkesbury, Joan F *Movie Director, Writer*
201 Ocean Ave, #B1702, Santa Monica, CA 90402, USA
Tews, Andreas *Boxer*
Hamburger Allee 1, 19063 Schwerin, Germany
Thacker, Brian M *Vietnam War Army Hero (CMH)*
11413 Monterey Dr, Wheaton, MD 20902, USA
Thackery, Jimmy *Singer, Guitarist*
%Mongrel Music, 743 Center Blvd, Fairfax, CA 94930, USA
Thaddeus, Patrick *Physicist*
58 Garfield St, Cambridge, MA 02138, USA

Thagard, Norman E *Astronaut, Physician*
502 N Ride, Tallahassee, FL 32303, USA
Thaksin Shinawatra *Prime Minister, Thailand*
%Premier's Office, Gov't House, Luke Land Road, Bangkok 10300/2, Thailand
Thalia *Singer, Actress*
%William Morris Agency, 151 El Camino Dr, Beverly Hills, CA 90212, USA
Than Shwe *Prime Minister, Myanmar; Army General*
%Prime Minister's Office, Theinbyu Road, Botahtaung, Yangon, Myanmar
Thani, Sheikh Abdul Aziz ibn Khalifa al- *Prime Minister, Qatar*
%Prime Minister's Office, Dohar, Qatar
Thani, Sheikh Hamad bin Khalifa al- *Emir, Qatar*
%Royal Palace, PO Box 923, Dohar, Qatar
Thapa, Surya Bahadur *Prime Minister, Nepal*
Tangal, Kathmandu, Nepal
Tharp, Twyla *Dancer, Choreographer*
%Twyla Tharp Productions, 336 Central Park West, #17B, New York, NY 10025, USA
Thatcher of Lincolnshire, Margaret H *Prime Minister, England*
11 Dulwich Gate, Dulwich, London SE12, England
Thaves, Bob *Cartoonist (Frank & Ernest)*
PO Box 67, Manhattan Beach, CA 90267, USA
Thaxter, Phyllis *Actress*
716 Riomar Dr, Vero Beach, FL 32963, USA
Thayer, Bill *Explorer*
PO Box 233, Snohomish, WA 98291, USA
Thayer, Brynn *Actress*
%House of Representatives, 400 S Beverly Dr, #101, Beverly Hills, CA 90212, USA
Thayer, Helen *Explorer, Skier*
PO Box 233, Snohomish, WA 98291, USA
Thayer, W Paul *Government Official, Businessman*
10200 Hollow Way, Dallas, TX 75229, USA
Theberge, James D *Diplomat*
4462 Cathedral Ave NW, Washington, DC 20016, USA
Theile, David *Swimmer*
84 Woodville St, Hendea, Brisbane QLD 4011, Australia
Theismann, Joseph R (Joe) *Football Player, Sportscaster*
5661 Columbia Pike, #200, Falls Church, VA 22041, USA
Theodorakis, Mikis *Composer*
Epifanous 1, Akropolis, Athens, Greece
Theodore, Jose *Hockey Player*
%Montreal Canadiens, 1260 de la Gauchetiere W, Montreal QC H3B 5E8, Canada
Theodorescu, Monica *Equestrian Athlete*
Gestit Lindenhof, 48336 Sassenberg, Germany
Theodosakis, Jason *Physician, Writer*
%Saint Martin's Press, 175 5th Ave, New York, NY 10010, USA
Theodosius, Primate Metropolitan *Religious Leader*
%Orthodox Church in America, PO Box 675 RR 25A, Syosset, NY 11791, USA
Theron, Charlize *Actress, Model*
%United Talent Agency, 9560 Wilshire Blvd, #500, Beverly Hills, CA 90212, USA
Theroux, Paul E *Writer*
35 Elsynge Road, London SW18 2NR, England
Theus, Reggie *Basketball Player*
%Sanders Agency, 241 Ave of Americas, #11H, New York, NY 10014, USA
Thewlis, David *Actor*
%International Creative Mgmt, 76 Oxford St, London W1N 0AX, England
Thiandoum, Hyacinthe Cardinal *Religious Leader*
Archeveche, Ave Jean XXIII, BP 1908, Dakar, Senegal
Thibaudet, Jean-Yves *Concert Pianist*
3601 Griffith Park Blvd, Los Angeles, CA 90027, USA
Thibault, Charles *Physiologist*
4 Place Jussieu, 75005 Paris, France
Thibiant, Aida *Fashion Expert*
%Institut de Beaute, 449 N Canon Dr, Beverly Hills, CA 90210, USA
Thicke, Alan *Actor*
10505 Sarah St, Toluca Lake, CA 91602, USA
Thiedemann, Fritz *Equestrian Rider*
Ostreherweg 28, 25746 Heide, Germany
Thiele, Gerhard P J *Astronaut, Germany*
%ESA/EAC, Linder Hohe, 51147 Cologne, Germany
Thielemann, Ray C (R C) *Football Player*
210 Rose Meadow Lane, Alpharetta, GA 30005, USA
Thielemans, Jean B (Toots) *Jazz Harmonica Player, Guitarist*
%Peter Levinson Communications, 2575 Palisade Ave, #11H, Bronx, NY 10463, USA
Thielen, Gunter *Businessman*
%Bertelsmann AG, Carl-Bertelsmann-Str 270, 33311 Guetersloh, Germany
Thiemann, Charles Lee *Financier*
%Federal Home Loan Bank, PO Box 598, Cincinnati, OH 45201, USA
Thieme, Paul *Indologist*
%Tubingen University, Wilhelmstr 7, 72074 Tubingen, Germany

T

Thier, Samuel O *Educator, Physician*
99-20 Florence St, #4B, Chestnut Hill, MA 02467, USA
Thierry, John F *Football Player*
1431 Federal Road, Opelousas, LA 70570, USA
Thiess, Ursula *Actress*
1940 Bel Air Road, Los Angeles, CA 90077, USA
Thiessen, Tiffani *Actress*
3523 Wrightwood Court, Studio City, CA 91604, USA
Thigpen, Yancey D *Football Player*
3305 Greystone Dr, Rocky Mountain, NC 27804, USA
Thimmesch, Nicholas *Journalist*
6301 Broad Branch Road, Chevy Chase, MD 20815, USA
Thinnes, Roy *Actor*
%Mail Center, 1910 Madison Ave, Memphis, TN 38104, USA
Thirsk, Robert B *Astronaut, Canada*
%Space Agency, 6767 Route de Aeroport, Saint-Hubert QC J3Y 8Y9, Canada
Thode, Henry G *Chemist*
%McMaster University, Nuclear Research Dept, Hamilton ON L8S 4M1, Canada
Thoma, Georg *Nordic Combined Skier*
Bisten 6, 79856 Hinterzarten, Germany
Thomalla, Georg *Actor*
Hans Nefer, 5640 Bad Gastein, Austria
Thomas of Swynnerton, Hugh S *Historian*
Well House, Sudbourne, Suffolk, England
Thomas, Andrew S W (Andy) *Astronaut*
%NASA, Johnson Space Center, 2101 NASA Road, Houston, TX 77058, USA
Thomas, Aurelius *Football Player*
PO Box 91157, Columbus, OH 43209, USA
Thomas, B Clendon *Football Player*
7508 Runsey Road, Oklahoma City, OK 73132, USA
Thomas, B J *Singer, Songwriter*
%Gloria Thomas, 1324 Crownhill Dr, Arlington, TX 76012, USA
Thomas, Barbara S *Government Official*
%News International, 1 Virginia St, London E1 9XY, England
Thomas, Betty *Actress, Director*
%Creative Artists Agency, 9830 Wilshire Blvd, Beverly Hills, CA 90212, USA
Thomas, Billy M *Army General*
2387 Spanish Oak Terrace, Colorado Springs, CO 80920, USA
Thomas, Blair *Football Player*
723 Belvoir Road, Plymouth Meeting, PA 19462, USA
Thomas, Broderick *Football Player*
16123 Padons Trace Court, Missouri City, TX 77489, USA
Thomas, Carla *Singer*
%Talent Consultants International, 1560 Broadway, #1308, New York, NY 10036, USA
Thomas, Caroline Bedell *Physician*
2401 Calvert St NW, #503, Washington, DC 20008, USA
Thomas, Chris *Jazz Bassist*
%Associated Booking Corp, 1995 Broadway, #501, New York, NY 10023, USA
Thomas, Clarence *Supreme Court Justice*
%US Supreme Court, 1 1st St NE, Washington, DC 20543, USA
Thomas, David *Concert Singer*
74 Hyde Vale, Greenwich, London SE10 8HP, England
Thomas, David Clayton *Singer (Blood Sweat & Tears)*
%Music Avenue Inc, 43 Washington St, Groveland, MA 01834, USA
Thomas, Debra J (Debi) *Figure Skater*
%Mentor Mgmt, 202 S Michigan St, #810, South Bend, IN 46601, USA
Thomas, Dennis (D T) *Singer (Kool & the Gang)*
%Pyramid Entertainment, 89 5th Ave, #700, New York, NY 10003, USA
Thomas, Dominic R *Religious Leader*
%Church of Jesus Christ, 6th & Lincoln Sts, Monongahela, PA 15063, USA
Thomas, Donald A *Astronaut*
311 Shadow Creek Dr, Seabrook, TX 77586, USA
Thomas, Donald Michael (D M) *Writer*
Coach House, Rashleigh Vale, Tregolls Rd, Truro, Cornwall TR1 1TJ, England
Thomas, E Donnall *Nobel Medicine Laureate*
%Hutchinson Cancer Research Center, PO Box 19024, Seattle, WA 98109, USA
Thomas, Elizabeth Marshall *Writer*
80 E Mountain Road, Peterborough, NH 03458, USA
Thomas, Ernest *Actor*
%Coast to Coast Talent, 3350 Barham Blvd, Los Angeles, CA 90068, USA
Thomas, Etan *Basketball Player*
%Washington Wizards, MCI Centre, 601 F St NW, Washington, DC 20004, USA
Thomas, Frank E *Baseball Player*
2521 N Bosworth Ave, Chicago, IL 60614, USA
Thomas, Frank J *Baseball Player*
118 Doray Dr, Pittsburgh, PA 15237, USA
Thomas, Franklin R (Frank) *Animator*
%Animation Celection, 1002 Prospect St, La Jolla, CA 92037, USA

Thomas, Fred *Law Enforcement Official*
%Metropolitan Police Dept, 300 Indiana Ave NW, Washington, DC 20001, USA
Thomas, Gareth *Engineer*
%University of California, Materials Science Dept, Berkeley, CA 94720, USA
Thomas, Heather *Actress*
%Lymberopoulos, 13601 Ventura Blvd, #354, Sherman Oaks, CA 91423, USA
Thomas, Heidi *Actress*
%Lichtman/Salners, 12216 Moorpark St, Studio City, CA 91604, USA
Thomas, Helen A *Journalist*
2501 Calvert St NW, Washington, DC 20008, USA
Thomas, Henry *Actor*
%International Creative Mgmt, 8942 Wilshire Blvd, #219, Beverly Hills, CA 90211, USA
Thomas, Henry L, Jr *Football Player*
16811 Southern Oaks Dr, Houston, TX 77068, USA
Thomas, Henry W *Writer*
3214 Warder St NW, Washington, DC 20010, USA
Thomas, Irma *Singer*
%Emile Jackson, PO Box 26126, New Orleans, LA 70186, USA
Thomas, Isiah L, III *Basketball Player, Executive, Coach*
PO Box 43136, Detroit, MI 48243, USA
Thomas, J Gorman *Baseball Player*
759 Tallwood Road, Charleston, SC 29412, USA
Thomas, Jack Ward *Government Official, Biologist*
%University of Montana, Biology Dept, Missoula, MT 59812, USA
Thomas, Jake *Actor*
%Stan Rogow Productions, 846 N Cahuenga Blvd, Bldg D, Los Angeles, CA 90038, USA
Thomas, Jay *Actor*
%Gersh Agency, 232 N Canon Dr, Beverly Hills, CA 90210, USA
Thomas, Jean *Ceramist*
1427 Summit Road, Berkeley, CA 94708, USA
Thomas, Jeremy *Movie Producer*
%Recorded Picture Co, 8-12 Broadwick St, London W1V 1FH, England
Thomas, John *Basketball Player*
%Toronto Raptors, Air Canada Center, 40 Bay St, Toronto ON M5J 2N8, Canada
Thomas, John C *Track Athlete*
51 Mulberry St, Brockton, MA 02302, USA
Thomas, John M *Chemist*
%Royal Institution, 21 Albemarle St, London W1X 4BS, England
Thomas, Jonathan Taylor *Actor*
%Industry Entertainment, 955 Carillo Dr, #300, Los Angeles, CA 90048, USA
Thomas, Kurt *Gymnast*
1184 N Hillcrest Road, Beverly Hills, CA 90210, USA
Thomas, Kurt *Basketball Player*
1826 Brook Terrace Trail, Dallas, TX 75232, USA
Thomas, LaToya *Basketball Player*
%Cleveland Rockers, Gund Arena, 1 Center Court, Cleveland, OH 44115, USA
Thomas, Mark A *Football Player*
556 Hillsboro St, Monticello, GA 31064, USA
Thomas, Marlo *Actress*
420 E 54th St, #28G, New York, NY 10022, USA
Thomas, Mary *Singer (Crystals)*
%Superstars Unlimited, PO Box 371371, Las Vegas, NV 89137, USA
Thomas, Michael Tilson *Conductor, Concert Pianist*
%San Francisco Symphony, Davies Symphony Hall, San Francisco, CA 94102, USA
Thomas, Pat *Football Player*
612 Middle Cove Dr, Plano, TX 75023, USA
Thomas, Philip Michael *Actor*
PO Box 3714, Brooklyn, NY 11202, USA
Thomas, Ray *Flutist, Singer (Moody Blues)*
%Insight Mgmt, 1222 16th Ave S, #300, Nashville, TN 37212, USA
Thomas, Richard *Actor*
3219 Fairpoint St, Pasadena, CA 91107, USA
Thomas, Rob *Singer (Matchbox 20), Songwriter*
%Creative Artists Agency, 9830 Wilshire Blvd, Beverly Hills, CA 90212, USA
Thomas, Robert D *Publisher*
223 Mariomi Road, New Canaan, CT 06840
Thomas, Rozonda (Chili) *Rap Artist (TLC)*
%Creative Artists Agency, 9830 Wilshire Blvd, Beverly Hills, CA 90212, USA
Thomas, Sean Patrick *Actor*
%Paradigm Agency, 200 W 57th St, #900, New York, NY 10019, USA
Thomas, Serena Scott *Actress*
%S M S Talent, 8730 Sunset Blvd, #440, Los Angeles, CA 90069, USA
Thomas, Steve *Entertainer*
%This Old House Show, PO Box 2284, South Burlington, VT 05407, USA
Thomas, Thurman L *Football Player*
7018 Robertson Road, Missouri City, TX 77489, USA
Thomas, Tra *Football Player*
%Philadelphia Eagles, 1 Novacare Way, Philadelphia, PA 19145, USA

T

Thomas - Thompson

Thomas, Wayne *Hockey Player*
%Cleveland Barons, 200 Hudson Road E, Cleveland, OH 44115, USA
Thomas, William H, Jr *Football Player*
2401 Echo Dr, Amarillo, TX 79107, USA
Thomas, Zach *Football Player*
1051 NW 122nd Ave, Plantation, FL 33323, USA
Thomason, Harry Z *Television Producer*
10732 Riverside Dr, North Hollywood, CA 91602, USA
Thomassin, Florence *Actress*
%Artmedia, 20 Ave Rapp, 75007 Paris, France
Thome, James H (Jim) *Baseball Player*
6137 Greenhill Road, New Hope, PA 18938, USA
Thomerson, Tim *Actor*
2635 28th St, #14, Santa Monica, CA 90405, USA
Thomopoulos, Anthony *Businessman*
10727 Wilshire Blvd, #1602, Los Angeles, CA 90024, USA
Thompson, Anthony *Football Player, Coach*
%Indiana University, Athletic Dept, Bloomington, IN 47405, USA
Thompson, Bennie *Football Player*
%Baltimore Ravens, Ravens Stadium, 11001 Russell St, Baltimore, MD 21230, USA
Thompson, Brooks *Basketball Player*
%Orlando Magic, Waterhouse Center, 8701 Maitland Summit Blvd, Orlando, FL 32810, USA
Thompson, Caroline W *Writer, Movie Director*
%William Morris Agency, 151 El Camino Dr, Beverly Hills, CA 90212, USA
Thompson, Christopher *Astrophysicist*
%University of North Carolina, Astrophysics Dept, Chapel Hill, NC 27599, USA
Thompson, Clifford *Hockey Player, Coach*
3 Summit Dr, #16, Reading, MA 01867, USA
Thompson, David O *Basketball Player, Executive*
5045 Strawberry Hill Dr, #C, Charlotte, NC 28211, USA
Thompson, David R *Judge*
%US Court of Appeals, 940 Front St, San Diego, CA 92101, USA
Thompson, David W *Space Scientist*
%Orbital Science Corp, 21839 Atlantic Blvd, Sterling, VA 20166, USA
Thompson, Edward K *Editor*
Rock Ledge Farm, RR 8 Box 350, Union Valley Road, Mahopac, NY 10541, USA
Thompson, Edward T *Editor*
11 Cotswold Dr, North Salem, NY 10560, USA
Thompson, Emma *Actress*
%Hamilton Asper Mgmt, 24 Hanway St, London W1P 9DD, England
Thompson, F M (Daley) *Track Athlete*
%Olympic Assn, 1 Wadsworth Plain, London SW18 1EH, England
Thompson, G Kennedy *Financier*
%First Union Corp, 1 First Union Center, Charlotte, NC 28288, USA
Thompson, G Ralph *Religious Leader*
%Seventh-Day Adventists, 12501 Old Columbia Pike, Silver Spring, MD 20904, USA
Thompson, Gary *Basketball Player*
2531 Park Vista Circle, Ames, IA 50014, USA
Thompson, Gina *Singer*
%Richard Walters, 1800 Argyle Ave, #408, Los Angeles, CA 90028, USA
Thompson, Hank *Singer, Songwriter*
2000 Vista Road, Roanoke, TX 76262, USA
Thompson, Hugh L *Educator*
%Washburn University, President's Office, Topeka, KS 66621, USA
Thompson, Hunter S *Journalist, Writer*
PO Box 220, Woody Creek, CO 81656, USA
Thompson, Jack *Football Player*
2507 29th Ave W, Seattle, WA 98199, USA
Thompson, Jack *Actor*
%June Cann Mgmt, 110 Queen St, Woollahra NSW 2025, Australia
Thompson, Jack E *Businessman*
%Homestake Mining Co, 650 California St, San Francisco, CA 94108, USA
Thompson, James B, Jr *Geologist*
1010 Waltham St, #F1, Lexington, MA 02421, USA
Thompson, James R (Jim), Jr *Governor, IL*
%Winston & Strawn, 35 W Wacker Dr, Chicago, IL 60601, USA
Thompson, James R, Jr *Space Administrator*
416 Randolph Ave SE, Huntsville, AL 35801, USA
Thompson, Jason D *Baseball Player*
1358 Forest Bay Dr, Waterford, MI 48328, USA
Thompson, Jennifer (Jenny) *Swimmer*
%USA Swimming, 1 Olympia Plaza, Colorado Springs, CO 80909, USA
Thompson, Jill *Cartoonist*
%DC Comics, 1700 Broadway, New York, NY 10019, USA
Thompson, John B *Basketball Player, Coach, Sportscaster*
3636 16th St NW, #B1161, Washington, DC 20010, USA
Thompson, John G *Mathematician*
%University of Florida, Mathematics Dept, Gainesville, FL 32611, USA

Thompson, John M *Businessman*
%IBM Corp, 1 N Castle Dr, Armonk, NY 10504, USA
Thompson, Kenneth L *Computer Scientist*
%AT&T Bell Lucent Laboratory, 600 Mountain Ave, New Providence, NJ 07974, USA
Thompson, Lea *Actress*
6061 Longridge Ave, Van Nuys, CA 91401, USA
Thompson, Leonard *Golfer*
9010 Marsh View Court, Ponte Vedra, FL 32082, USA
Thompson, Linda *Actress*
25254 Eldorado Meadows Road, Hidden Hills, CA 91302, USA
Thompson, Linda *Singer*
%High Road, 751 Bridgeway, #300, Sausalito, CA 94965, USA
Thompson, Lonnie *Glaciologist*
%Ohio State University, Geology Dept, Columbus, OH 43210, USA
Thompson, Mike *Editorial Cartoonist*
%Detroit Free Press, Editorial Dept, 600 W Fort St, Detroit, MI 48226, USA
Thompson, Obadele *Track Athlete*
%Amateur Athletics Assn, PO Box 46, Bridgetown, Barbados
Thompson, Paul H *Educator*
%Weber State University, President's Office, Ogden, UT 84408, USA
Thompson, Richard *Singer, Songwriter, Guitarist*
%Elizabeth Rush Agency, 100 Park St, #4, Montclair, NJ 07042, USA
Thompson, Richard K *Religious Leader*
%African Methodist Episcopal Zion Church, PO Box 32843, Charlotte, NC 28232, USA
Thompson, Robert G K *Army General, England*
Pitcott House, Winsford Minehead, Somerset, England
Thompson, Robert R (Robby) *Baseball Player*
4438 Gun Club Road, West Palm Beach, FL 33406, USA
Thompson, Sada *Actress*
PO Box 490, Southbury, CT 06488, USA
Thompson, Sophie *Actress*
%Jonathan Altaras, 13 Shorts Gardens, London WC2H 9AT, England
Thompson, Starley L *Climatologist*
%National Atmospheric Research Center, PO Box 3000, Boulder, CO 80307, USA
Thompson, Sue *Singer*
%Curb Entertainment, 3907 W Alameda Ave, #200, Burbank, CA 91505, USA
Thompson, Tina *Basketball Player*
%Houston Comets, 2 Greenway Plaza, #400, Houston, TX 77046, USA
Thompson, Tommy *Football Player*
PO Box 687, Calico Rock, AR 72519, USA
Thompson, Tommy G *Secretary, Health & Human Services*
%Health/Human Service Department, 200 Independence SW, Washington, DC 20201, USA
Thompson, Wilbur (Moose) *Track Athlete*
11372 Martha Ann, Los Alamitos, CA 90720, USA
Thompson, William P *Religious Leader*
%World Council of Churches, 475 Riverside Dr, New York, NY 10115, USA
Thomsen, Ulrich *Actor*
%Paradigm Agency, 10100 Santa Monica Blvd, #2500, Los Angeles, CA 90067, USA
Thomson of Fleet, Kenneth R *Publisher*
%Thomson Newspapers, 65 Queen St W, Toronto ON M5H 2M8, Canada
Thomson, Anna *Actress*
%Innovative Artists, 1505 10th St, Santa Monica, CA 90401, USA
Thomson, Brian E *Movie, Theater, Opera Designer*
5 Little Dowling St, Paddington NSW 2021, Australia
Thomson, Cyndi *Singer*
%The Firm, 9100 Wilshire Blvd, #100W, Beverly Hills, CA 90210, USA
Thomson, Gordon *Actor*
3914 Fredonia Dr, Los Angeles, CA 90068, USA
Thomson, H C (Hank) *Harness Racing Official*
PO Box 38, Mullett Lake, MI 49761, USA
Thomson, James A *Biologist, Anatomist*
%University of Wisconsin, Medical School, Biology Dept, Madison, WI 53706, USA
Thomson, June *Commentator*
%KNBC-TV, News Dept, 3000 W Alameda Ave, Burbank, CA 91523, USA
Thomson, Peter W *Golfer*
Carmel House, 44 Mathoura Road, Toorak VIC 3142, Australia
Thomson, Robert B (Bobby) *Baseball Player*
122 Sunlit Dr, Watchung, NJ 07069, USA
Thon, Olaf *Soccer Player*
%FC Schalke 04, Postfach 200861, 45843 Gelsenkirchen, Germany
Thone, Charles *Governor, NE*
%Erickson & Sederstrom, 301 S 13th St, #400, Lincoln, NE 68508, USA
Thoni, Gustav *Alpine Skier, Coach*
39026 Prato Allo Stelvio-Prao BZ, Italy
Thora *Actress*
%CunninghamEscottDipene, 10635 Santa Monica Blvd, #130, Los Angeles, CA 90025, USA
Thorburn, Clifford C D (Cliff) *Snooker Player*
31 West Side Dr, Markham ON L3P 7J5, Canada

Thorin, Donald E, Sr *Cinematographer*
15260 Ventura Blvd, #1040, Sherman Oaks, CA 91403, USA
Thorn, Christopher *Guitarist (Blind Melon)*
%Shapiro Co, 9229 Sunset Blvd, #607, Los Angeles, CA 90069, USA
Thorn, Gaston *Prime Minister, Luxembourg*
1 Rue de la Forge, Luxembourg
Thorn, George W *Physician*
89 Herrick St, #327, Beverly, MA 01915, USA
Thorn, Rod *Basketball Player, Executive*
20 Loewen Court, Rye, NY 10580, USA
Thorn, Tracey *Singer (Everything But the Girl)*
%JFD Mgmt, Acklam Workshops, 10 Aklam Road, London W10 5QZ, England
Thornburgh, Richard L (Dick) *Attorney General; Governor, PA*
%Kirkpatrick & Lockhart, 1800 Massachusetts Ave NW, #900, Washington, DC 20036, USA
Thorne, Dyanne *Actress*
8721 Sunset Blvd, #101, Los Angeles, CA 90069, USA
Thorne, Frank *Cartoonist (Moonshine McJuggs)*
1967 Grenville Road, Scotch Plains, NJ 07076, USA
Thorne, Gary *Commentator*
%ABC-TV, Sports Dept, 77 W 66th St, New York, NY 10023, USA
Thorne, Kip S *Physicist*
%California Institute of Technology, Physics Dept, Pasadena, CA 91125, USA
Thorne-Smith, Courtney *Actress, Model*
%Paradigm Agency, 10100 Santa Monica Blvd, #2500, Los Angeles, CA 90067, USA
Thornell, Jack R *Photojournalist*
6815 Madewood Dr, Metairie, LA 70003, USA
Thornhill, Arthur H, Jr *Publisher*
50 S School St, Portsmouth, NH 03801, USA
Thornhill, Leeroy *Dancer (Prodigy)*
%Midi Mgmt, Jenkins Lane, Great Hallinsbury, Essex CM22 9QL, England
Thornhill, Lisa *Actress*
208-11 Anin St, Bedford Nova Scotia B4A 4E3, Canada
Thornton, Billy Bob *Actor, Director*
%Industry Entertainment, 955 Carillo Dr, #300, Los Angeles, CA 90048, USA
Thornton, Frank *Actor*
%David Daly, 586A King Road, London SW6 2DX, England
Thornton, Kathryn C *Astronaut*
100 Bedford Place, Charlottesville, VA 22903, USA
Thornton, Sigrid *Actress*
%International Casting Services, 147 King St, Sydney NSW 2000, Australia
Thornton, William E *Astronaut*
7640 Pimilco Lane, Boerne, TX 78015, USA
Thornton, Zach *Soccer Player*
%Chicago Fire, 980 N Michigan Ave, #1998, Chicago, IL 60611, USA
Thorogood, George *Singer, Guitarist*
%Michael Donahue Mgmt, PO Box 807, Lewisburg, VA 24901, USA
Thorpe, Ian *Swimmer*
PO Box 427, Milsons Point NSW 2061, Australia
Thorpe, J Jeremy *Government Official, England*
2 Orme Square, Bayswater, London W2, England
Thorpe, James *Library, Art Gallery Director*
20 Loeffler Road, #T320, Bloomfield, CT 06002, USA
Thorpe, Jim *Golfer*
1612 Kersley Circle, Heathrow, FL 32746, USA
Thorpe, Otis H *Basketball Player*
PO Box 400, Canfield, OH 44406, USA
Thorsell, William *Editor*
%Toronto Globe & Mail, 444 Front St W, Toronto ON M5V 2S9, Canada
Thorsness, Leo K *Vietnam Air Force Hero (CMH)*
64915 E Brassie Dr, Tucson, AZ 85739, USA
Thorson, Linda *Actress*
%S M S Talent, 8730 Sunset Blvd, #440, Los Angeles, CA 90069, USA
Threadgill, Henry L *Jazz Saxophonist, Composer*
%Joel Chriss, 300 Mercer St, #3J, New York, NY 10003, USA
Threatt, Sedale *Basketball Player*
5359 Newcastle Lane, Calabasas, CA 91302, USA
Threlkeld, Richard D *Commentator*
%CBS-TV, News Dept, 51 W 52nd St, New York, NY 10019, USA
Threshie, R David, Jr *Publisher*
%Orange County Register, 625 N Grand Ave, Santa Ana, CA 92701, USA
Throne, Malachi *Actor*
11805 Mayfield Ave, #306, Los Angeles, CA 90049, USA
Thulin, Ingrid *Actress*
Kevingestrand 7B, 182 31 Danderyd, Sweden
Thunman, Nils R *Navy Admiral*
1516 S Willemore Ave, Springfield, IL 62704, USA
Thuot, Pierre J *Astronaut*
6606 Patrick Court, Centreville, VA 20120, USA

Thurm, Maren *Actress*
%ZBF Agentur, Ordensmeisterstr 15-16, 12099 Berlin, Germany
Thurman, Dennis L *Football Player*
3447 W 59th Place, Los Angeles, CA 90043, USA
Thurman, William E *Air Force General*
10 Firestone Dr, Pinehurst, NC 28374, USA
Thurmond, Nate *Basketball Player, Executive*
5094 Diamond Heights Blvd, #B, San Francisco, CA 94131, USA
Thurow, Lester C *Economist*
%Massachusetts Institute of Technology, Economics Dept, Cambridge, MA 02139, USA
Thurston, Frederick C (Fuzzy) *Football Player*
2 Watercolor Way, Naples, FL 34113, USA
Thyssen, Greta *Actress*
444 E 82nd St, New York, NY 10028, USA
Tian Jiyun *Government Official, China*
%Vice Premier's Office, State Council, Beijing, China
Tiant, Luis C *Baseball Player*
67 Pine Hill Road, Southborough, MA 01772, USA
Tibbets, Paul W, Jr *WW II Army Air Corps Hero*
5574 Knollwood Dr, Columbus, OH 43232, USA
Tice, George A *Photographer*
581 Kings Highway E, Atlantic Hills, NJ 07716, USA
Tice, Michael P (Mike) *Football Player*
6708 Galway Dr, Minneapolis, MN 55439, USA
Tichnor, Alan *Religious Leader*
%United Synagogues of Conservative Judaism, 155 5th Ave, New York, NY 10010, USA
Tickner, Charles (Charlie) *Figure Skater*
5410 Sunset Dr, Littleton, CO 80123, USA
Tidwell, Moody R, III *Judge*
%US Claims Court, 717 Madison Place NW, Washington, DC 20439, USA
Tiegs, Cheryl *Model*
457 Cuesta Way, Los Angeles, CA 90077, USA
Tiemann, Norbert T *Governor, NE*
7511 Pebblestone Dr, Dallas, TX 75230, USA
Tierney, Maura *Actress*
%Creative Artists Agency, 9830 Wilshire Blvd, Beverly Hills, CA 90212, USA
Tiffany *Singer, Model*
%Universal Attractions, 225 W 57th St, #500, New York, NY 10019, USA
Tiffin, Pamela *Actress*
15 W 67th St, New York, NY 10023, USA
Tigar, Kenneth *Actor*
642 Etta St, Los Angeles, CA 90065, USA
Tiger, Lionel *Social Scientist, Anthropologist*
248 W 23rd St, #400, New York, NY 10011, USA
Tigerman, Stanley *Architect*
%Tigerman McCurry Architects, 444 N Wells St, Chicago, IL 60610, USA
Tighe, Kevin *Actor*
PO Box 453, Sedro Woolley, WA 98284, USA
Tikkanen, Esa *Hockey Player*
%New York Rangers, Madison Square Garden, 2 Penn Plaza, New York, NY 10121, USA
Tilghman, Shirley M C *Educator, Molecular Biologist*
%Princeton University, President's Office, Princeton, NJ 08544, USA
Tilker, Ewald *Rowing Athlete*
2767 40th Ave, San Francisco, CA 94116, USA
Tiller, Joe *Football Coach*
%Purdue University, Athletic Dept, West Layafette, IN 47907, USA
Tiller, Nadja *Actress*
Via Tamporiva 26, 6976 Castagnola, Switzerland
Tilley, Patrick L (Pat) *Football Player, Coach*
3 Lake Point Place, Shreveport, LA 71119, USA
Tillis, Mel *Singer, Songwriter*
%Mel Tillis Enterprises, 2527 State Highway 248, Branson, MO 65616, USA
Tillis, Pam *Singer, Songwriter*
%Fitzgerald Hartley Co, 1908 Wedgewood Ave, Nashville, TN 37212, USA
Tillman, George, Jr *Movie Director*
%Creative Artists Agency, 9830 Wilshire Blvd, Beverly Hills, CA 90212, USA
Tillman, Robert L *Businessman*
%Lowe's Companies, 1605 Curtis Bridge Road, Wilkesboro, NC 28697, USA
Tillotson, Johnny *Singer*
%American Mgmt, 19948 Mayall St, Chatsworth, CA 91311, USA
Tilly, Jennifer *Actress*
1050 Stone Canyon Road, Los Angeles, CA 90077, USA
Tilly, Meg *Actress*
321 S Beverly Dr, #M, Beverly Hills, CA 90212, USA
Tilson, Joseph (Joe) *Artist*
2 Brook Street Mansions, 41 Davies St, London W1Y 1FJ, England
Tilton, Charlene *Actress*
%Wilkinson/Lipsman, 8075 W 3rd St, #500, Los Angeles, CA 90048, USA

T

Tilton - Tisch

Tilton, Glenn F *Businessman*
%UAL Corp, 1200 E Algonquin Road, Arlington Heights, IL 60005, USA
Tilton, Martha *Singer, Actress*
2257 Mandeville Canyon Road, Los Angeles, CA 90049, USA
Tilton, Robert *Evangelist*
%Robert Tilton Ministries, PO Box 819000, Dallas, TX 75381, USA
Timberlake, Justin *Singer ('N Sync)*
%Sunshine Consultants, 75 9th Ave, New York, NY 10011, USA
Timberlake, Robert W (Bob) *Football Player*
2219 E Jarvis St, Milwaukee, WI 53211, USA
Timchal, Cindy *Lacrosse Coach*
%University of Maryland, Athletic Dept, College Park, MD 20742, USA
Timken, William R, Jr *Businessman*
%Timken Co, 1835 Dueber Ave SW, Canton, OH 44706, USA
Timme, Robert *Architect*
%Taft Architects, 2370 Rice Blvd, #112, Houston, TX 77005, USA
Timmermann, Ulf *Track Athlete*
Conrad Blenkle Str 34, 1055 Berlin, Germany
Timmins, Cali *Actress*
%The Agency, 1800 Ave of Stars, #400, Los Angeles, CA 90067, USA
Timmons, Jeff *Singer (98 Degrees)*
%DAS Communications, 83 Riverside Dr, New York, NY 10024, USA
Timmons, Margo *Singer (Cowboy Junkies)*
%Macklam Feldman Mgmt, 1505 W 2nd Ave, #200, Vancouver BC V6H 3Y4, Canada
Timmons, Michael *Guitarist (Cowboy Junkies), Songwriter*
%Macklam Feldman Mgmt, 1505 W 2nd Ave, #200, Vancouver BC V6H 3Y4, Canada
Timmons, Peter *Musician (Cowboy Junkies)*
%Macklam Feldman Mgmt, 1505 W 2nd Ave, #200, Vancouver BC V6H 3Y4, Canada
Timms, Michele *Basketball Player*
%Phoenix Mercury, American West Arena, 201 E Jefferson St, Phoenix, AZ 85004, USA
Timofeev, Valeri *Artist*
464 Blue Mountain Lake, East Stroudsburg, PA 18301, USA
Timofeyeva, Nina V *Ballerina*
%Bolshoi Theater, Teatralnaya Pl 1, 103009 Moscow, Russia
Timonen, Kimmo *Hockey Player*
920 Cherry Plum Court, Nashville, TN 37215, USA
Timpson, Michael D *Football Player*
4722 Saint Simon Dr, Coconut Creek, FL 33073, USA
Tindemans, Leo *Prime Minister, Belgium*
Jan Verbertlei 24, 2520 Edegem, Belgium
Tindle, David *Artist*
%Redfern Gallery, 20 Cork St, London W1, England
Ting, Samuel C C *Nobel Physics Laureate*
2 Eliot Place, Jamaica Plain, MA 02130, USA
Ting, Walasse *Artist*
100 W 25th St, New York, NY 10001, USA
Tinglehoff, H Michael (Mick) *Football Player*
19288 Judicial Road, Prior Lake, MN 55372, USA
Tinker, Grant A *Businessman*
10727 Wilshire Blvd, #1604, Los Angeles, CA 90024, USA
Tinkham, Michael *Physicist*
98 Rutledge Road, Belmont, MA 02478, USA
Tinsley, Bruce *Editorial Cartoonist*
%King Features Syndicate, 888 7th Ave, New York, NY 10106, USA
Tinsley, Jackson B (Jack) *Editor*
%Fort Worth Star-Telegram, Editorial Dept, 400 W 7th St, Fort Worth, TX 76102, USA
Tinsley, Jamaal *Basketball Player*
%Indiana Pacers, Conseco Fieldhouse, 125 S Pennsylvania, Indianapolis, IN 46204, USA
Tippett, Andre B *Football Player*
17 Knob Hill St, Sharon, MA 02067, USA
Tippett, Dave *Hockey Player, Coach*
260 Breakers Lane, Stratford, CT 06615, USA
Tippin, Aaron *Singer, Songwriter*
%LGB Media, 1228 Pineview Lane, Nashville, TN 37211, USA
Tipton, Daniel *Religious Leader*
%Churches of Christ in Christian Union, PO Box 30, Circleville, OH 43113, USA
Tiriac, Ion *Tennis Player, Coach*
Blvd d'Italie 44, Monte Carlo, Monaco
Tirico, Mike *Sportscaster*
%ABC-TV, Sports Dept, 77 W 66th St, New York, NY 10023, USA
Tirimo, Martino *Concert Pianist, Conductor*
1 Romeyn Road, London SW16 2NU, England
Tirole, Jean M *Economist*
%Institut D'Economie Industrielle, Toulouse, France
Tisby, Dexter *Singer (Penguins)*
%David Harris Enterprises, 24210 E Fork Road, #9, Azusa, CA 91702, USA
Tisch, James S *Businessman*
%Loews Corp, 667 Madison Ave, New York, NY 10021, USA

Tisch, Laurence A	*Businessman*
%Loews Corp, 667 Madison Ave, New York, NY 10021, USA	
Tisch, Preston R	*Businessman, Government Official*
%Loews Corp, 667 Madison Ave, New York, NY 10021, USA	
Tisch, Steve	*Writer*
1162 Tower Road, Beverly Hills, CA 90210, USA	
Tisdale, Wayman	*Basketball Player*
4710 S Wheeling Ave, Tulsa, OK 74105, USA	
Tishchenko, Boris I	*Composer*
79 Rimsky-Korsakoff Ave, #10, 190121 Saint Petersburg, Russia	
Tito, Dennis	*Astronaut*
1800 Alta Mura Road, Pacific Palisades, CA 90272, USA	
Tito, Teburoro	*President, Kiribati*
%President's Office, Tarawa, Kiribati	
Titov, German	*Hockey Player*
%Anaheim Mighty Ducks, 2000 E Gene Autry Way, Anaheim, CA 92806, USA	
Titov, Vladimir G	*Cosmonaut*
%Potchta Kosmonavtov, Moskovskoi Oblasti, 141160 Syvisdny Goroduk, Russia	
Titov, Yuri E	*Gymnast*
Kolokolnikov Per 6, #19, 103045 Moscow, Russia	
Tits, Jacques L	*Mathematician*
12 Rue du Moulin des Pres, 75013 Paris, France	
Tittle, Yelberton A (Y A)	*Football Player*
2500 E Camino Real, Palo Alto, CA 94306, USA	
Titus-Carmel, Gerard	*Artist*
La Grand Maison, 02210 Oulchy Le Chateau, France	
Tizard, Catherine A	*Governor General, New Zealand*
12A Wallace St, Herne Bay, Auckland 1, New Zealand	
Tizon, Albert	*Journalist*
%Seattle Times, Editorial Dept, 1120 John St, Seattle, WA 98109, USA	
Tizzio, Thomas R, Sr	*Businessman*
%American Int'l Group, 70 Pine St, New York, NY 10270, USA	
Tjeknavorian, Loris-Zare	*Composer, Conductor*
%State Philharmonia, Mashtotsi Prospekt 46, Yerevan, Armenia	
Tjoflat, Gerald B	*Judge*
%US Court of Appeals, 311 W Monroe St, Jacksonville, FL 32202, USA	
Tkachuk, Keith	*Hockey Player*
11243 Hunters Pond Road, Creve Coeur, MO 63141, USA	
Tkaczuk, Ivan	*Religious Leader*
%Ukrainian Orthodox Church, 3 Davenport Ave, #2A, New Rochelle, NY 10805, USA	
Tkaczuk, Walter R (Walt)	*Hockey Player*
%River Valley Golf & Country Club, RR 3, Saint Mary's ON N0M 2G0, Canada	
Toback, James	*Movie Director*
%International Creative Mgmt, 8942 Wilshire Blvd, #219, Beverly Hills, CA 90211, USA	
Tober, Barbara D	*Editor*
%Bride Magazine, Editorial Dept, 4 W 42nd St, New York, NY 10036, USA	
Tobey, David (Dave)	*Basketball Referee, Player, Coach*
%Naismith Basketball Hall of Fame, 1150 W Columbus Ave, Springfield, MA 01105, USA	
Tobey, James	*Actor*
%Paradigm Agency, 10100 Santa Monica Blvd, #2500, Los Angeles, CA 90067, USA	
Tobian, Gary M	*Diver*
9171 Belted Kingfisher Road, Blaine, WA 98230, USA	
Tobias, Andrew	*Writer*
%Micro Education Corp of America, 285 Riverside Ave, Westport, CT 06880, USA	
Tobias, Oliver	*Actor*
%Gavin Barker Assoc, 2D Wimpole St, London W1G 0EB, England	
Tobias, Phillip V	*Anatomist*
%Witwatersrand University, 7 York Road, Johannesburg 2193 South Africa	
Tobias, Randall L	*Businessman*
%Eli Lilly Co, Lilly Corporate Center, Indianapolis, IN 46285, USA	
Tobias, Robert M	*Labor Leader*
%National Treasury Employees Union, 901 E St NW, Washington, DC 20004, USA	
Tobias, Stephen C	*Businessman*
%Norfolk Southern Corp, 3 Commercial Place, Norfolk, VA 23510, USA	
Tobin, Don	*Cartoonist (Little Woman)*
12312 Ranchwood Road, Santa Ana, CA 92705, USA	
Tobin, Vince	*Football Coach*
16359 N 109th Way, Scottsdale, AZ 85255, USA	
Tobolowsky, Stephen	*Actor*
%William Morris Agency, 151 El Camino Dr, Beverly Hills, CA 90212, USA	
Tocchet, Rick	*Hockey Player*
692 Highpointe Dr, Pittsburgh, PA 15220, USA	
Tochi, Brian	*Actor*
247 S Beverly Dr, #102, Beverly Hills, CA 90212, USA	
Toczyska, Stefania	*Opera Singer*
%Columbia Artists Mgmt Inc, 165 W 57th St, New York, NY 10019, USA	
Todd, Hallie	*Actress*
%Ann Morgan Guilbert, 550 Erskine Dr, Pacific Palisades, CA 90272, USA	

T

Todd, James R (Jim) *Baseball Player*
21639 Hill Gail Way, Parker, CO 80138, USA
Todd, Josh *Singer (Buckcherry)*
%The Firm, 9100 Wilshire Blvd, #100W, Beverly Hills, CA 90210, USA
Todd, Mark *Equestrian Rider*
PO Box 507, Cambridge, New Zealand
Todd, Rachel *Actress*
6310 San Vicente Blvd, #520, Los Angeles, CA 90048, USA
Todd, Richard *Actor*
Chinham Farm, Faringdon, Oxon SN7 8EZ, England
Todd, Richard *Football Player*
PO Box 471, Sheffield, AL 35660, USA
Todd, Tony *Actor*
%Innovative Artists, 1505 10th St, Santa Monica, CA 90401, USA
Todd, Virgil H *Religious Leader*
%Memphis Theological Seminary, 168 E Parkway S, Memphis, TN 38104, USA
Todorov, Stanko *Prime Minister, Bulgaria*
Narodno Sobranie, Sofia, Bulgaria
Todorovsky, Piotr Y *Movie Director*
Vernadskogo Prospect 70A, #23, 117454 Moscow, Russia
Toennies, Jan Peter *Physicist*
Ewaldstr 7, 37075 Gottingen, Germany
Toews, Jeffrey M (Jeff) *Football Player*
11924 SW 44th St, Davie, FL 33330, USA
Tofani, Loretta A *Journalist*
%Philadelphia Inquirer, Editorial Dept, 400 N Broad St, Philadelphia, PA 19130, USA
Toffler, Alvin *Writer*
%Random House, 1745 Broadway, #B1, New York, NY 10019, USA
Toft, Rod *Bowler*
11350 12th St N, Lake Elmo, MN 55042, USA
Tognini, Michel *Cosmonaut, France*
5413 Newcastle St, Bellaire, TX 77401, USA
Togunde, Victor *Actor*
%Christopher Nassif Agency, 1925 Century Park West, #750, Los Angeles, CA 90067, USA
Tokarev, Valeri I *Cosmonaut*
%Potchta Kosmonavtov, Moskovskoi Oblasti, 141160 Syvisdny Goroduk, Russia
Tokes, Laszlo *Religious Leader, Political Activist*
Calvin Str 1, 3700 Oradea, Romania
Tokody, Ilona *Opera Singer*
%Hungarian State Opera, Andrassy Utca 22, 1062 Budapest, Hungary
Tolan, Robert (Bobby) *Baseball Player*
804 Woodstock St, Bellaire, TX 77401, USA
Toland, John W *Writer*
1 Long Ridge Road, Danbury, CT 06810, USA
Tolbert, Tony L *Football Player*
475 S White Chapel Blvd, Southlake, TX 76092, USA
Toledo, Alejandro *President, Peru*
%Palacio de Gobierno S/N, Plaza de Armas S/N, Lima 1, Peru
Toles, Thomas G (Tom) *Editorial Cartoonist*
4625 46th St NW, Washington, DC 20016, USA
Tolkan, James *Actor*
%Paradigm Agency, 10100 Santa Monica Blvd, #2500, Los Angeles, CA 90067, USA
Tolsky, Susan *Actress*
10815 Acama St, North Hollywood, CA 91602, USA
Tom, Heather *Actress*
740 N Evergreen, Burbank, CA 91505, USA
Tom, Kiana *Physical Fitness Trainer, Model*
PO Box 1111, Sunset Beach, CA 90742, USA
Tom, Lauren *Actress*
%Gersh Agency, 232 N Canon Dr, Beverly Hills, CA 90210, USA
Tom, Nicholle *Actress*
3033 Vista Crest Drive, Los Angeles, CA 90068, USA
Tomasic, Andrew J (Andy) *Football, Baseball Player*
677 Maryland Ave, Whitehall, PA 18052, USA
Tomasson, Helgi *Ballet Dancer, Director*
%San Francisco Ballet, 455 Franklin St, San Francisco, CA 94102, USA
Tomba, Alberto *Alpine Skier*
Castel dei Britti, 40100 Bologna, Italy
Tomczak, Michael J (Mike) *Football Player*
108 Bell Acres Estate, Sewickley, PA 15143, USA
Tomei, Concetta *Actress*
765 Linda Flora Dr, Los Angeles, CA 90049, USA
Tomei, Marisa *Actress*
%Three Arts Entertainment, 9460 Wilshire Blvd, #700, Beverly Hills, CA 90212, USA
Tomey, Dick *Football Coach*
%San Francisco 49ers, 4949 Centennial Blvd, Santa Clara, CA 95054, USA
Tomfohrde, Heinn F *Businessman*
%GAF Corp, 1361 Alps Road, Wayne, NJ 07470, USA

Tomita, Stan *Photographer*
2439 Saint Louis Dr, Honolulu, HI 96816, USA
Tomjanovich, Rudolph (Rudy) *Basketball Player, Coach*
3142 Canterbury Lane, Montgomery, TX 77356, USA
Tomko, Jozef Cardinal *Religious Leader*
Villa Betania, Via Urbano VIII-16, 00165 Rome, Italy
Tomlin, Lily *Actress, Comedienne*
1800 Argyle Ave, #300, Los Angeles, CA 90028, USA
Tomlinson, Charles *Writer*
%Bristol University, English Dept, Bristol BS8 1TH, England
Tomlinson, John *Opera Singer*
%Music International, 13 Ardilaun Road, Highbury, London N5 2QR, England
Tomlinson, LaDainian *Football Player*
%San Diego Chargers, 4020 Murphy Canyon Road, San Diego, CA 92123, USA
Tomlinson, Mel A *Ballet Dancer*
790 Riverside Dr, #6B, New York, NY 10032, USA
Tomowa-Sintow, Anna *Opera Singer*
%Columbia Artists Mgmt Inc, 165 W 57th St, New York, NY 10019, USA
Tompkins, Angel *Actress*
%Hurkos, 11935 Kling St, #10, Valley Village, CA 91607, USA
Tompkins, Darlene *Actress*
15413 Hall Road, #230, Macomb, MI 48044, USA
Tompkins, Susie *Fashion Designer*
2500 Steiner St, #PH, San Francisco, CA 94115, USA
Toms, David *Golfer*
820 S MacArthur Blvd, #105-383, Coppell, TX 75019, USA
Tomsco, George *Musician (Fireballs)*
%Fireballs Entertainment, 1224 Cottonwood, Raton, NM 87740, USA
Tomsic, Dubravka *Concert Pianist*
%Trawick Artists, 1926 Broadway, New York, NY 10023, USA
Tomsic, Ronald (Ron) *Basketball Player*
448 Isabella Terrace, Corona del Mar, CA 92625, USA
Toneff, Robert (Bob) *Football Player*
18 Dutch Valley Lane, San Anselmo, CA 94960, USA
Tonegawa, Susumu *Nobel Medicine Laureate*
%Massachusetts Institute of Technology, Biology Dept, Cambridge, MA 02139, USA
Toner, Mike *Journalist*
%Atlanta Journal-Constitution, Editorial Dept, 72 Marietta, Atlanta, GA 30303, USA
Toney, Andrew *Basketball Player*
%Philadelphia 76ers, 1st Union Center, 3601 S Broad St, Philadelphia, PA 19148, USA
Toney, Sedric *Basketball Player*
3831 Sweetwater Dr, Cleveland, OH 44141, USA
Tonini, Ersilio Cardinal *Religious Leader*
Via Santa Teresa 8, 48100 Ravenna, Italy
Too $hort *Rap Artist*
%Pyramid Entertainment, 89 5th Ave, #700, New York, NY 10003, USA
Too Slim *Bassist (Riders in the Sky)*
%New Frontier Mgmt, 1921 Broadway, Nashville, TN 37203, USA
Tooker, George *Artist*
PO Box 385, Hartland, VT 05048, USA
Toomey, William A (Bill) *Track Athlete*
1755 Hi Mountain Road, Arroyo Grande, CA 93420, USA
Toon, Al *Football Player*
4827 Enchanted Valley Road, Middleton, WI 53562, USA
Toon, Malcolm *Diplomat*
375 PeeDee Road, Southern Pines, NC 28387, USA
Topfer, Morton L *Businessman*
%Dell Computer Corp, 1 Dell Way, Round Rock, TX 78682, USA
Topol, Chaim *Actor*
22 Vale Court, Maidville, London W9 1RT, England
Topper, John *Singer (Blues Traveler)*
%Monterey Peninsula Artists, 509 Hartnell St, Monterey, CA 93940, USA
Topping, Seymour *Editor*
5 Heathcote Road, Scarsdale, NY 10583, USA
Toppo, Telesphore P Cardinal *Religious Leader*
%Archdiocese, PO Box 5, Purulia Road, Ranchi 834001, Jharkland, India
Toradze, Alexander *Concert Pianist*
%Columbia Artists Mgmt Inc, 165 W 57th St, New York, NY 10019, USA
Torborg, Jeffrey A (Jeff) *Baseball Player, Manager*
5208 Siesta Cove Dr, Sarasota, FL 34242, USA
Torgensen, Paul E *Educator*
%Virginia Polytechnic Institute, President's Office, Blacksburg, VA 24061, USA
Torgeson, LaVern *Football Player*
17672 Gainsford Lane, Huntington Beach, CA 92649, USA
Tork, Peter *Singer, Bassist (Monkees)*
524 Anselmo Ave, #102, San Anselmo, CA 94960, USA
Torn, Rip *Actor*
118 S Beverly Blvd, #504, Beverly Hills, CA 90212, USA

T

Torp - Toussaint

Torp, Niels A *Architect*
Industrigaten 59, PO Box 5387, 0304 Oslo, Norway
Torrance, Sam *Golfer*
%Carnegie Sports, Glassmill, Battersea Bridge Rd, London SW11 3BZ, England
Torrance, Thomas F *Religious Leader, Educator*
37 Braid Farm Road, Edinburgh EH10 6LE, Scotland
Torre, Joseph P (Joe) *Baseball Player, Manager*
20 Lawrence Lane, Harrison, NY 10528, USA
Torrence, Dean *Singer (Jan & Dean), Songwriter*
221 Main St, #P, Huntington Beach, CA 92648, USA
Torrence, Gwendolyn (Gwen) *Track Athlete*
%Gold Medal Mgmt, 1750 14th St, Boulder, CO 80302, USA
Torres, Dara *Swimmer, Model*
%Wilhelmina Models, 300 Park Ave S, #200, New York, NY 10010, USA
Torres, Diego *Singer*
%Fenix Prod, Av Figueroa Alcorta 3221, Buenos Aires 1215, Argentina
Torres, Gina *Actress*
%Badgley Connor Talent, 9229 Sunset Blvd, #311, Los Angeles, CA 90069, USA
Torres, Harold *Singer (Crests)*
%Brothers Mgmt, 141 Dunbar Ave, Fords, NJ 08863, USA
Torres, Jose *Boxer*
364 Greenwich St, #B, New York, NY 10013, USA
Torres, Liz *Singer, Actress*
%Siegel, 1680 N Vine St, #617, Hollywood, CA 90028, USA
Torres, Raffi *Hockey Player*
%Edmonton Oilers, 11230 110th St, Edmonton AB T5G 3H7, Canada
Torres, Tico *Drummer (Bon Jovi)*
%Bon Jovi Mgmt, 248 W 17th St, #501, New York, NY 10011, USA
Torretta, Gino L *Football Player*
%All American Speakers, 365 W King Road, #200, Ithaca, NY 14850, USA
Torrey, Bill *Hockey Executive*
2740 Clubhouse Pointe, West Palm Beach, FL 33409, USA
Torrey, Rich *Cartoonist (Hartland)*
%King Features Syndicate, 888 7th Ave, New York, NY 10106, USA
Torrissen, Birger *Nordic Skier*
PO Box 216, Lakeville, CT 06039, USA
Torruella, Juan R *Judge*
%US Court of Appeals, 150 Ave Carlos Chardon, #119, San Juan, PR 00918, USA
Torry, Guy *Actor*
%William Morris Agency, 151 El Camino Dr, Beverly Hills, CA 90212, USA
Tortelier, Yan Pascal *Conductor, Concert Violinist*
%MA de Valmalete, Building Gaceau, 11 Ave Delcasse, 75635 Paris, France
Torti, Robert *Actor*
5722 Ranchito Ave, Van Nuys, CA 91401, USA
Tortorella, John *Hockey Coach*
2801 Northwood Hills Dr, Valrico, FL 33594, USA
Torvalds, Linus *Computer Software Designer*
%Transmeta Corp, 3990 Freedom Circle, Santa Clara, CA 95054, USA
Torvill, Jayne *Ice Dancer*
%Sue Young, PO Box 32, Heathfield, East Sussex TN21 0BW, England
Tosca, Carlos *Baseball Manager*
2831 Timber Knoll Dr, Valrico, FL 33594, USA
Toski, Bob *Golfer*
160 Essex St, Newark, OH 43055, USA
Totenberg, Nina *Commentator*
%National Public Radio, News Dept, 615 Main Ave NW, Washington, DC 20024, USA
Totten, Robert *Movie Director*
PO Box 7180, Big Bear Lake, CA 92315, USA
Totter, Audrey *Actress*
%Motion Picture Country Home, 23388 Mulholland Dr, Woodland Hills, CA 91364, USA
Totushek, John B *Navy Admiral*
Commander, Naval Reserve Force, HqUSN, Pentagon, Washington, DC 20350, USA
Toulouse, Gerard *Physicist*
%Laboratoire de Physique de l'ENS, 24 Rue Lhomond, 75231, Paris, France
Tountas, Pete *Bowler*
10100 N Calle del Carnero, Tucson, AZ 85737, USA
Touraine, Jean-Louis *Immunologist*
%Edouard-Herriot Hopital, Place d'Arsonval, 69437 Lyons Cedex 03, France
Toure, Younoussi *Prime Minister, Mali*
%Union Economique/Monetaire, 01 BP 543, Ouagadougou 01, Burkina Faso
Tournier, Michel *Writer*
Le Presbytere, Choisel, 78460 Chevreuse, France
Toussaint Coleman, Beth *Actress*
%Don Buchwald, 6500 Wilshire Blvd, #2200, Los Angeles, CA 90048, USA
Toussaint, Allen *Jazz Pianist, Composer*
3264 Frey Place, New Orleans, LA 70119, USA
Toussaint, Lorraine *Actress*
%William Morris Agency, 151 El Camino Dr, Beverly Hills, CA 90212, USA

Tovar, Steven E (Steve) *Football Player*
17203 Sandalwood Dr, Wildwood, FL 34785, USA
Tovoli, Luciano *Cinematographer*
%United Talent Agency, 9560 Wilshire Blvd, #500, Beverly Hills, CA 90212, USA
Towe, Monte *Basketball Player, Coach*
7434 Canal Blvd, New Orleans, LA 70124, USA
Tower, Joan P *Composer*
%Bard College, Music Dept, Annandale-on-Hudson, NY 12504, USA
Towers, Constance *Actress*
2100 Century Park W, #10263, Los Angeles, CA 90067, USA
Towers, Kenneth *Editor*
%Chicago Sun-Times, Editorial Dept, 401 N Wabash, Chicago, IL 60611, USA
Towle, Stephen R (Steve) *Football Player*
609 NE Lake Pointe Dr, Lees Summit, MO 64064, USA
Towne, Katharine *Actress*
%United Talent Agency, 9560 Wilshire Blvd, #500, Beverly Hills, CA 90212, USA
Towne, Robert *Movie Director, Writer*
1417 San Remo Dr, Pacific Palisades, CA 90272, USA
Towner, Ralph N *Jazz Guitarist, Pianist*
%Ted Kurland, 173 Brighton Ave, Boston, MA 02134, USA
Townes, Charles H *Nobel Physics Laureate*
1988 San Antonio Ave, Berkeley, CA 94707, USA
Townsend, Colleen *Actress*
%National Presbyterian Church, 4101 Nebraska Ave NW, Washington, DC 20016, USA
Townsend, John W, Jr *Space Scientist*
6532 79th St, Cabin John, MD 20818, USA
Townsend, Robert *Actor*
2934 1/2 N Beverly Glen Circle, #407, Los Angeles, CA 90077, USA
Townsend, Roscoe *Religious Leader*
%Evangelical Friends, 2018 Maple St, Wichita, KS 67213, USA
Townsend, Stuart *Actor*
%International Creative Mgmt, 76 Oxford St, London W1N 0AX, England
Townshend, Peter D B *Singer, Guitarist (Who), Songwriter*
Boathouse, Ranelagh Dr, Twickenham, Middx TW1 1QZ, England
Toye, Wendy *Choreographer, Ballerina*
%London Mgmt, 2-4 Noel St, London W1V 3RB, England
Toyoda, Shoichiro *Businessman*
%Keidanren, 1-9-4 Ohtemachi, Chuyodaku, Tokyo 100, Japan
Tozzi, Giorgio *Opera Singer*
%BMG Ricordi SpA, Via Berchet 2, 20100 Milan, Italy
Traa *Bassist (POD)*
%East West America Records, 75 Rockefeller Plaza, New York, NY 10019, USA
Trabert, M Anthony (Tony) *Tennis Player*
115 Knotty Pine Trail, Ponte Vedra Beach, FL 32082, USA
Tracey, Margaret *Ballerina*
%New York City Ballet, Lincoln Center Plaza, New York, NY 10023, USA
Trachsel, Stephen P (Steve) *Baseball Player*
4141 Ricardo Dr, Yorba Linda, CA 92886, USA
Trachta, Jeff *Actor*
1327 Cordova Ave, Glendale, CA 91207, USA
Trachte, Don *Cartoonist (Henry)*
%King Features Syndicate, 888 7th Ave, New York, NY 10106, USA
Trachtenberg, Michelle *Actress*
%United Talent Agency, 9560 Wilshire Blvd, #500, Beverly Hills, CA 90212, USA
Trachtenberg, Stephen J *Educator*
%George Washington University, President's Office, Washington, DC 20052, USA
Tracy, James E (Jim) *Baseball Player, Manager*
3535 Arlington Ave, Hamilton, OH 45015, USA
Tracy, Michael C *Artistic Director, Dancer*
%Pilobolus Dance Theater, PO Box 388, Washington Depot, CT 06794, USA
Tracy, Paul *Auto Racing Driver*
9700 Highridge Dr, Las Vegas, NV 89134, USA
Trager, Milton *Physical Therapist*
%Trager Institute, 3800 Park East Dr, #100, Beachwood, OH 44122, USA
Trager, William *Parasitologist*
%Rockefeller University, Parasitology Lab, 1230 York Ave, New York, NY 10021, USA
Train, Harry D, II *Navy Admiral*
401 College Place, #10, Norfolk, VA 23510, USA
Train, Russell E *Government Official, Environmentalist*
%World Wildlife Fund, 1250 24th St NW, Washington, DC 20037, USA
Trainor, Bernard E *Marine Corps General*
80 Potter Pond, Lexington, MA 02421, USA
Trajkovski, Boris *President, Macedonia*
%President's Office, Skopje, Macedonia
Trammell, Alan S *Baseball Player, Manager*
191 22nd St, Del Mar, CA 92014, USA
Trammell, Terry *Sports Orthopedic Surgeon*
%Orthopedics-Indianapolis, 1801 N Senate Blvd, #200, Indianapolis, IN 46202, USA

T

Tran Duc Luong *President, Vietnam*
%President's Office, Hoang Hoa Tham St, Hanoi, Vietnam
Trani, Eugene P *Educator*
%Virginia Commonwealth University, President's Office, Richmond, VA 23284, USA
Trask, Thomas E *Religious Leader*
%Assemblies of God, 1445 Boonville Ave, Springfield, MO 65802, USA
Traub, Charles *Photographer*
39 E 10th St, New York, NY 10003, USA
Trautmann, Richard *Judo Athlete*
Horemansstr 29, 80636 Munich, Germany
Trautwig, Al *Sportscaster*
%ABC-TV, Sports Dept, 77 W 66th St, New York, NY 10023, USA
Travalena, Fred *Actor, Comedian*
4515 White Oak Place, Encino, CA 91316, USA
Travanti, Daniel J *Actor*
1077 Melody Road, Lake Forest, IL 60045, USA
Travers, Mary *Singer (Peter Paul & Mary)*
%Fritz/Byers Mgmt, 1455 N Doheny Dr, Los Angeles, CA 90069, USA
Travers, Pat *Singer, Guitarist*
%ARM, 1257 Arcade St, Saint Paul, MN 55106, USA
Travis, Cecil H *Baseball Player*
2260 Highway 138, Riverdale, GA 30296, USA
Travis, Kylie *Model, Actress*
1196 Summit Dr, Beverly Hills, CA 90210, USA
Travis, Nancy *Actress*
231 S Cliffwood Ave, Los Angeles, CA 90049, USA
Travis, Randy *Singer, Songwriter, Guitarist*
%Elizabeth Travis Mgmt, 1610 16th Ave S, Nashville, TN 37212, USA
Travis, Stacey *Actress*
6100 Wilshire Blvd, #1170, Los Angeles, CA 90048, USA
Travolta, Ellen *Actress*
5923 Wilbur Ave, Tarzana, CA 91356, USA
Travolta, John *Actor*
1504 Live Oak Lane, Santa Barbara, CA 93105, USA
Traylor, B Keith *Football Player*
%Chicago Bears, 1000 Football Dr, Lake Forest, IL 60045, USA
Traylor, Robert *Basketball Player*
%New Orleans Hornets, New Orleans Arena, 1501 Girod St, New Orleans, LA 70113, USA
Traylor, Susan *Actress*
%Propaganda Films Mgmt, 1741 Ivar Ave, Los Angeles, CA 90028, USA
Traynor, Jay *Singer (Jay & the Americans)*
%Jet Music, 17 Pauline Court, Rensselaer, NY 12144, USA
Treach *Rap Artist (Naughty By Nature)*
%International Creative Mgmt, 8942 Wilshire Blvd, #219, Beverly Hills, CA 90211, USA
Treacy, Philip *Fashion Designer*
%Philip Treacy Ltd, 69 Elizabeth St, London SW1W 9PJ, England
Treadway, Edward A *Labor Leader*
%Elevator Constructors Union, 5565 Sterret Place, Columbia, MD 21044, USA
Treadway, James C, Jr *Government Official*
Laurel Ledge Farm, Croton Lake Road, RR 4, Mount Kisco, NY 10549, USA
Treadway, Kenneth *Swimming Executive*
%Phillips Petroleum Co, Adams Building, Bartlesville, OK 74003, USA
Trebek, Alex *Entertainer*
3405 Fryman Road, Studio City, CA 91604, USA
Trebelhorn, Thomas L (Tom) *Baseball Player, Manager*
4344 SE 26th Ave, Portland, OR 97202, USA
Tree, Michael *Violist (Guarneri String Quartet)*
45 E 89th St, New York, NY 10128, USA
Treen, David C *Governor, LA*
%Deutsch Kerrigan Stile, 755 Magazine St, New Orleans, LA 70130, USA
Trefilov, Andrei *Hockey Player*
%Calgary Flames, PO Box 1540, Station M, Calgary AB T2P 3B9, Canada
Trejo, Danny *Actor*
%Amsel Eisenstadt Frazier, 5757 Wilshire Blvd, #510, Los Angeles, CA 90036, USA
Trejos Fernandez, Jose J *President, Costa Rica*
Apartado 10 096, 1000 San Jose, Costa Rica
Trelford, Donald G *Editor*
15 Fowler Road, London N1 2EA, England
Tremayne, Les *Actor*
901 S Barrington Ave, Los Angeles, CA 90049, USA
Tremblay, Mario *Hockey Player, Coach*
714 Mistassini, Lachenaie QC J6W 5H2, Canada
Tremblay, Michel *Writer*
294 Carre Saint Louis, #5E, Montreal QC H2X 1A4, Canada
Tremlett, David R *Artist*
Broadlawns, Chipperfield Road, Bovingdon, Herts, England
Tremont, Ray C *Religious Leader*
%Volunteers of America, 3939 N Causeway Blvd, #400, Metairie, LA 70002, USA

Tremonti, Mark *Guitarist (Creed), Songwriter*
%Agency Group, 1776 Broadway, #430, New York, NY 10019, USA
Trent, Gary *Basketball Player*
2905 Bookout St, Dallas, TX 75201, USA
Treschev, Sergei Y *Cosmonaut*
%Potchta Kosmonavtov, Moskovskoi Oblasti, 141160 Syvisdny Goroduk, Russia
Tressel, Jim *Football Coach*
%Ohio State University, Athletic Dept, Columbus, OH 43210, USA
Tretiak, Vladislav *Hockey Player, Coach*
%Transglobal Sports, 94 Festival Dr, Toronto ON M2R 3V1, Canada
Tretyak, Ivan *Army General, Russia*
%Ministry of Defense, 34 Nanerezhnaya M Thoreza, Moscow, Russia
Trevanian *Writer*
%Jove Books, Berkley Publishing Group, 375 Hudson St, New York, NY 10014, USA
Trever, John *Editorial Cartoonist*
%Albuquerque Journal, Editorial Dept, 717 Silver Ave SW, Albuquerque, NM 87102, USA
Trevi, Gloria *Singer*
%Leisil Ent, Ave Parque 67 Napoles, Mexico City DF 03810, Mexico
Trevino, Lee B *Golfer*
1901 W 47th Place, #200, Westwood, KS 66205, USA
Trevino, Rick *Singer*
%William Morris Agency, 2100 W End Ave, #1000, Nashville, TN 37203, USA
Trevor, William *Writer*
%P F D, Drury House, 34-43 Russell St, London WC2B 5HA, England
Triandos, C Gus *Baseball Player*
165 Blossom Hill Road, #488, San Jose, CA 95123, USA
Tribbitt, Sherman W *Governor, DE*
39 Hazel Road, Dover, DE 19901, USA
Tribe, Laurence H *Attorney, Educator*
%Harvard University, Law School, Griswold Hall, Cambridge, MA 02138, USA
Trible, Paul S, Jr *Senator, VA; Educator*
%Christopher Newport University, 50 University Place, Newport News, VA 23606, USA
Trickle, Dick *Auto Racing Driver*
PO Box 645, Skyland, NC 28776, USA
Tricky *Rap Artist, Songwriter*
%Little Big Man, 155 Ave of Americas, #700, New York, NY 10013, USA
Triffle, Carol *Theater Director*
%Imago Theater, 17 SE 8th Ave, Portland, OR 97214, USA
Trigger, Sarah *Actress*
%Paradigm Agency, 10100 Santa Monica Blvd, #2500, Los Angeles, CA 90067, USA
Trillin, Calvin M *Writer*
%New Yorker Magazine, Editorial Dept, 4 Times Square, New York, NY 10036, USA
Trimble, David *Nobel Peace Laureate*
2 Queen St, Lurgen, County Armagh BT66 8BQ, Northern Ireland
Trimble, Vance H *Editor*
25 Oakhurst St, Wewoka, OK 74884, USA
Trimble, Vivian *Keyboardist (Luscious Jackson)*
%Metropolitan Entertainment, 2 Penn Plaza, #2600, New York, NY 10121, USA
Trinh, Eugene *Astronaut*
%NASA Headquarters, 300 E St SW, Washington, DC 20546, USA
Trinidad, Felix (Tito) *Boxer*
RR 6 Box 11479, Rio Piedras, PR 00926, USA
Trinkaus, Erik *Paleontologist*
%Washington University, Paleontolgy Dept, Saint Louis, MO 63130, USA
Trintignant, Jean-Louis *Actor*
%Artmedia, 20 Ave Rapp, 75007 Paris, France
Triplet, Kirk *Golfer*
8141 E Overlook Dr, Scottsdale, AZ 85255, USA
Trippi, Charles L (Charlie) *Football Player*
125 Riverhill Court, Athens, GA 30606, USA
Tripplehorn, Jean *Actress*
%Kelly Bush, 3859 Cardiff Ave, #200, Culver City, CA 90232, USA
Tripucka, Frank *Football Player*
23 Avon Dr, Essex Fells, NJ 07021, USA
Tripucka, Kelly *Basketball Player*
14 Devon Road, Boonton, NJ 07005, USA
Tritt, Travis *Singer, Songwriter*
PO Box 2044, Hiram, GA 30141, USA
Troccoli, Kathy *Singer, Songwriter*
%William Morris Agency, 2100 W End Ave, #1000, Nashville, TN 37203, USA
Troger, Christian-Alexander *Swimmer*
%I Muncher SC, Josefstr 26, 82941 Deisenhofen, Germany
Troisgros, Pierre E R *Restauranteur*
%Place Jean Troisgros, 42300 Roanne, France
Troitskaya, Natalia L *Opera Singer*
Klostergasse 37, 1170 Vienna, Austria
Trollope, Joanna *Writer*
%P F D, Drury House, 34-43 Russell St, London WC2B 5HA, England

T

Trone - Tsantiris

Trone, Roland (Don) *Singer (Don & Juan)*
%Mars Talent, 27 L'Ambiance Court, Bardonia, NY 10954, USA
Trost, Barry M *Chemist*
24510 Amigos Court, Los Altos Hills, CA 94024, USA
Trost, Carlisle A H *Navy Admiral*
11 Compromise St, Annapolis, MD 21401, USA
Trott, Stephen S *Judge*
%US Court of Appeals, US Courthouse, 550 W Fort St, Boise, ID 83724, USA
Trottier, Bryan J *Hockey Player, Executive, Coach*
356 Birdsong Way, Doylestown, PA 18901, USA
Trouble Valli *Guitarist (Crazy Town)*
%Q Prime, 729 7th Ave, #1600, New York, NY 10019, USA
Troupe, Tom *Actor*
8829 Ashcroft Ave, West Hollywood, CA 90048, USA
Troutt, William E *Educator*
%Belmont University, President's Office, Nashville, TN 37212, USA
Trova, Ernest T *Sculptor*
6 Layton Terrace, Saint Louis, MO 63124, USA
Trowbridge, Alexander B, Jr *Secretary, Commerce*
1823 23rd St NW, Washington, DC 20008, USA
Trower, Robin *Singer, Guitarist*
%Stardust Enterprises, 4600 Franklin Ave, Los Angeles, CA 90027, USA
Troxel, Gary *Singer (Fleetwoods)*
11471 Earle Dr, Mount Vernon, WA 98273, USA
Troyat, Henri *Writer*
%Academie Francaise, 23 Quai de Conti, 75006 Paris, France
Troyer, Verne *Actor*
%Simanton/Fondacaro Mgmt, 18032 Lenon Dr, #C, Yorba Linda, CA 92886, USA
Truax, Billy *Football Player*
PO Box 96, Gulfport, MS 39502, USA
Trucco, Michael *Actor*
%Rising Stars, PO Box 99, China Springs, TX 76633, USA
Trucks, Virgil O (Fire) *Baseball Player*
1016 Waterford Trail, Calera, AL 35040, USA
Trudeau, Garry B *Cartoonist (Doonesbury)*
459 Columbus Ave, #200, New York, NY 10024, USA
Trudeau, Jack F *Football Player*
9150 Timberwolf Lane, Zionsville, IN 46077, USA
Trufant, Marcus *Football Player*
%Seattle Seahawks, 11220 NE 53rd St, Kirkland, WA 98033, USA
Truitt, Anne D *Sculptor*
3506 35th St NW, Washington, DC 20016, USA
Trujillo, Chadwick *Astronomer*
%California Institute of Technology, Astronomy Dept, Pasadena, CA 91125, USA
Trujillo, Solomon D *Businessman*
%US West Inc, 1801 California St, Denver, CO 80202, USA
Truly, Richard H *Astronaut, Space Administrator, Admiral*
25078 Foothills Dr N, Lakewood, CO 80401, USA
Truman, Dan *Pianist, Keyboardist (Diamond Rio)*
%Dreamcatcher Artists Mgmt, 2908 Poston Ave, Nashville, TN 37203, USA
Truman, James *Editor*
%Conde Nast Publications, Editorial Office, 4 Times Square, New York, NY 10036, USA
Trumka, Richard L *Labor Leader*
%AFL-CIO, 1750 New York Ave NW, Washington, DC 20006, USA
Trump, Donald J *Businessman*
%Trump Organization, 725 5th Ave, New York, NY 10022, USA
Trump, Ivana *Businesswoman, Model*
PO Box 8104, West Palm Beach, FL 33407, USA
Trump, Ivanka *Model*
PO Box 8095, West Palm Beach, FL 33407, USA
Trumpy, Robert T (Bob), Jr *Football Player, Sportscaster*
75 Oak St, Cincinnati, OH 45246, USA
Trundy, Natalie *Actress*
2109 S Wilbur Ave, Walla Walla, WA 99362, USA
Truran, James W, Jr *Astrophysicist*
210 Wysteria Dr, Olympia Fields, IL 60461, USA
Truscott, Lucian K, IV *Writer*
%Avon/William Morrow, 1350 Ave of Americas, New York, NY 10019, USA
Tryggvason, Bjarni V *Astronaut, Canada*
%Space Agency, 6767 Route de Aeroport, Saint Hubert QC J3Y 8Y9, Canada
Trynin, Jennifer *Singer, Songwriter, Guitarist*
%Vector Mgmt, 1607 17th Ave S, Nashville, TN 37212, USA
Tsakalidis, Iakovos (Jake) *Basketball Player*
%Memphis Grizzlies, 175 Toyota Plaza, #150, Memphis, TN 38103, USA
Tsang, Bion *Concert Cellist*
%Columbia Artists Mgmt Inc, 165 W 57th St, New York, NY 10019, USA
Tsantiris, Len *Soccer Coach*
%University of Connecticut, Athletic Dept, Storrs Mansfield, CT

Tsao, I Fu *Chemical Engineer*
%University of Michigan, Chemical Engineering Dept, Ann Arbor, MI 48109, USA
Tschetter, Kris *Golfer*
%Legends Inc, 7458 Sommerset Shores Court, Orlando, FL 32819, USA
Tschumi, Bernard *Architect*
7 Rue Pecquay, 75004 Paris, France
Tsibliyev, Vasili V *Cosmonaut*
%Potchta Kosmonavtov, Moskovskoi Oblasti, 141160 Syvisdny Goroduk, Russia
Tskitishvili, Nikoloz *Basketball Player*
%Denver Nuggets, Pepsi Center, 1000 Chopper Circle, Denver, CO 80204, USA
Tsoucalas, Nicholas *Judge*
%US Court of International Trade, 1 Federal Plaza, New York, NY 10278, USA
Tsui, Daniel C *Nobel Physics Laureate*
2 Newlin Road, Princeton, NJ 08540, USA
Tsui, Lap-Chee *Molecular Geneticist*
%Sick Children Hospital, 555 University Ave, Toronto ON M5G 1X8, Canada
Tuanka Salehuddin Abdul Aziz Shah *Ruler, Malaysia*
%Sultan's Palace, Istana Bukit Serene, 50502 Kuala Lumpur, Malaysia
Tubbs, Billy *Basketball Coach*
%Lamar University, Athletic Dept, Beaumont, TX 77710, USA
Tubbs, Gerald J (Jerry) *Football Player*
3813 Centenary Ave, Dallas, TX 75225, USA
Tuberville, Tommy *Football Coach*
%Auburn University, Athletic Dept, Auburn University, AL 36849, USA
Tucci, Michael *Actor*
1435 Irving Ave, Glendale, CA 91201, USA
Tucci, Roberto Cardinal *Religious Leader*
Palazzo Pio, Piazza Pia 3, 00193 Rome, Italy
Tucci, Stanley *Actor, Director*
%Creative Artists Agency, 9830 Wilshire Blvd, Beverly Hills, CA 90212, USA
Tuchman, Maurice *Museum Curator*
150 E 57th St, #PH 1A, New York, NY 10022, USA
Tuck, Jessica *Actress*
%Brett Adams, 448 W 44th St, New York, NY 10036, USA
Tucker, Bill *Bowler*
26126 Meadowcrest Blvd, Huntington Woods, MI 48070, USA
Tucker, Chris *Actor, Comedian*
19133 Briarfield Way, Tarzana, CA 91356, USA
Tucker, Corin *Singer, Guitarist (Sleater-Kinney)*
%Legends of 21st Century, 7 Trinity Row, Florence, MA 01062, USA
Tucker, Marcia *Museum Official*
%New Museum of Contemporary Art, 583 Broadway, New York, NY 10012, USA
Tucker, Michael *Actor*
197 Oakdale Ave, Mill Valley, CA 94941, USA
Tucker, Michael *Fertility Biologist*
%Reproductive Biology Assoc, 5505 Peachtree Dunwoody, Atlanta, GA 30342, USA
Tucker, Robert L (Bob), Jr *Football Player*
8 Hunter Road, Hazleton, PA 18201, USA
Tucker, Tanya *Singer*
%Curtis Co, 109 Westpark Dr, #400, Brentwood, TN 37027, USA
Tucker, Tony *Boxer*
%Club Prana, 1619 7th Ave, Ybor City, Tampa, FL 33605, USA
Tucker, William E *Educator*
%Texas Christian University, Chancellor's Office, Fort Worth, TX 76129, USA
Tucker, Y Arnold *Football Player*
10835 SW 86th Ave, Ocala, FL 34481, USA
Tuckwell, Barry E *Concert French Hornist, Conductor*
13140 Fountain Head Road, Hagerstown, MD 21742, USA
Tudor, John T *Baseball Player*
31 Upton Hills Lane, Middleton, MA 01949, USA
Tueting, Sarah *Hockey Player*
488 Ash St, Winnetka, IL 60093, USA
Tuilaepa Sailele Maljelegaio *Prime Minister, Samoa*
%Prime Minister's Office, PO Box 193, Apia, Samoa
Tulbahadur Pun *WW II Nepal Army Hero (VC)*
%Victoria Cross Assn, Old Admiralty Building, London SW1A 2BL, England
Tully, Darrow *Publisher*
9862 Bridgeton Dr, Tampa, FL 33626, USA
Tulving, Endel *Psychologist*
45 Baby Point Crescent, York ON M6S 2B7, Canada
Tumi, Christian W Cardinal *Religious Leader*
Archveche, BP 179, Douala, Cameroon
Tune, Thomas J (Tommy) *Dancer, Actor*
1501 Broadway, #1508, New York, NY 10036, USA
Tung Chee-Hwa *Chief Executive, Hong Kong*
%Asia Pacific Finance Tower, 3 Garden Road, Hong Kong, China
Tunney, John V *Senator, CA*
304 Chautauqua Blvd, Pacific Palisades, CA 90272, USA

T

Tunney, Robin *Actress*
%Borinstein Oreck Bogart, 3172 Dona Susana Dr, Studio City, CA 91604, USA
Tunnick, George *Association Executive*
%National Assn of Female Executives, 127 W 24th St, New York, NY 10011, USA
Tupa, Thomas J (Tom) *Football Player*
6542 Lloyd Dr, Brecksville, OH 44141, USA
Tupouto'a *Crown Prince, Tonga*
%Royal Palace, PO Box 6, Nuku'alofa, Tonga
Turco, Marty *Hockey Player*
841 Shorewood Dr, Coppell, TX 75019, USA
Turco, Paige *Actress*
%Gersh Agency, 232 N Canon Dr, Beverly Hills, CA 90210, USA
Turco, Richard P *Atmospheric Scientist*
%R&D Assoc, 4640 Admiralty Way, Marina del Rey, CA 90292, USA
Turcotte, Donald L (Don) *Geophysicist*
27104 Middle Golf Dr, El Macero, CA 95618, USA
Turcotte, Jean-Claude Cardinal *Religious Leader*
1071 Rue de la Cathedrale, Montreal QC H2B 2V4, Canada
Turcotte, Ron *Thoroughbred Racing Jockey*
82 Seattle Slew Dr, Howell, NJ 07731, USA
Turgeon, Pierre *Hockey Player*
4073 Bryn Mawr Dr, Dallas, TX 75225, USA
Turk, Stephen *Cartoonist*
927 Westbourne Dr, Los Angeles, CA 90069, USA
Turkel, Ann *Actress*
9877 Beverly Grove Dr, Beverly Hills, CA 90210, USA
Turkoglu, Hidayet *Basketball Player*
%San Antonio Spurs, Alamodome, 1 SBC Center, San Antonio, TX 78219, USA
Turkson, Peter K A Cardinal *Religious Leader*
%Archdiocese, PO Box 112, Cape Coast, Ghana
Turley, Robert L (Bob) *Baseball Player*
11053 Big Canoe, Big Canoe, GA 30143, USA
Turlington, Christy *Model*
%United Talent Agency, 9560 Wilshire Blvd, #500, Beverly Hills, CA 90212, USA
Turnage, Mark-Anthony *Composer*
%Schott Co, 48 Great Marlborough St, London W1V 2BN, England
Turnbull, David *Physicist*
29 Concord Ave, #715, Cambridge, MA 02138, USA
Turnbull, Renaldo A *Football Player*
88 Oriole St, New Orleans, LA 70124, USA
Turnbull, Wendy *Tennis Player*
822 Boylston Dt, #203, Chestnut Hill, MA 02467, USA
Turnbull, William *Artist*
%Waddington Galleries, 11 Cork St, London W1, England
Turner, Bree *Actress*
%Osbrink, 4343 Lankershim, #100, North Hollywood, CA 91602, USA
Turner, Cathy *Speedskater*
251 East Ave, Hilton, NY 14468, USA
Turner, Cecil *Football Player*
4820 Scott St, Houston, TX 77004, USA
Turner, Edwin L *Astrophysicist*
%Princeton University, Astrophysical Sciences Dept, Princeton, NJ 08544, USA
Turner, Fred L *Businessman*
%McDonald's Corp, McDonald's Plaza, 1 Kroc Dr, Oak Brook, IL 60523, USA
Turner, Guinevere *Actress*
%Gersh Agency, 41 Madison Ave, #3300, New York, NY 10010, USA
Turner, Hamp *Football Player*
430172 Milledge Terrace, Athens, GA 30605, USA
Turner, Ike *Singer, Songwriter*
905 Viewpoint Dr, San Marcos, CA 92069, USA
Turner, James A (Jim) *Football Player*
14155 W 59th Place, Arvada, CO 80004, USA
Turner, James T *Judge*
%US Claims Court, 717 Madison Place NW, Washington, DC 20439, USA
Turner, James, Jr *Businessman*
%General Dynamics, 3190 Fairview Park Dr, Falls Church, VA 22042, USA
Turner, Janine *Actress, Model*
%Patricola Lust, 8271 Melrose Ave, #110, Los Angeles, CA 90046, USA
Turner, John N *Prime Minister, Canada*
27 Dunloe Road, Toronto ON M4V 2W4, Canada
Turner, Karri *Actress*
%Premiere Artists Agency, 1875 Century Park E, #2250, Los Angeles, CA 90067, USA
Turner, Kathleen *Actress*
163 Amsterdam Ave, #210, New York, NY 10023, USA
Turner, Keena *Football Player, Coach*
8200 W Erb Way, Tracy, CA 95304, USA
Turner, Morrie *Cartoonist (Wee Pals)*
PO Box 3004, Berkeley, CA 94703, USA

Turner, R E (Ted), III *Sports Executive, Businessman*
%Turner Foundation, 133 Luckie St NW, # 200, Atlanta, GA 30303, USA
Turner, R Gerald *Educator*
%University of Mississippi, Chancellor's Office, University, MS 38677, USA
Turner, Ron *Football Coach*
%San Jose State University, Athletic Dept, San Jose, CA 95192, USA
Turner, Ronald L *Businessman*
%Ceridian Corp, 3311 E Old Shakopee Road, Minneapolis, MN 55425, USA
Turner, Sherri *Golfer*
5729 19th Ave S, Minneapolis, MN 55417, USA
Turner, Stansfield *Navy Admiral, Government Official*
600 New Hampshire Ave NW, #800, Washington, DC 20037, USA
Turner, Steve *Guitarist (Mudhoney)*
%Legends of 21st Century, 7 Trinity Row, Florence, MA 01062, USA
Turner, Tina *Singer, Actress*
Villa Anna Fleur, 06230 Villefr sur Mer, France
Turnley, David C *Photojournalist*
34 Rue des Frances Bourgeois, 75003 Paris, France
Turnovsky, Martin *Conductor*
%Gerhild Baron, Dornbacher Str 41/III/2, 1170 Vienna, Austria
Turnquest, Orville A *Governor General, Bahamas*
%Government House, Government Hill, PO Box N8301, Nassau NP, Bahamas
Turow, Scott F *Writer*
%Sonnenschein Carlin Nath Rosenthal, 8000 Sears Tower, Chicago, IL 60606, USA
Turpin, Melvin *Basketball Player*
1524 Bal Harbor Court, Lexington, KY 40517, USA
Turre, Steve *Jazz Trombonist*
%Columbia Artists Mgmt Inc, 165 W 57th St, New York, NY 10019, USA
Turrell, James *Artist*
%Skystone Foundation, 114 N San Francisco St, #206, Flagstaff, AZ 86001, USA
Turro, Nicholas J *Chemist*
125 Downey Dr, Tenafly, NJ 07670, USA
Turteltaub, Jon *Movie Director*
%Endeavor Talent Agency, 9701 Wilshire Blvd, #1000, Beverly Hills, CA 90212, USA
Turturro, Aida *Actress*
%Mindel/Donigan, 9057 Nemo St, #C, West Hollywood, CA 90069, USA
Turturro, John *Actor, Director*
987 Terracina St, Santa Paula, CA 93060, USA
Turturro, Nicholas *Actor*
PO Box 570824, Tarzana, CA 91357, USA
Tushingham, Rita *Actress*
%Lip Service, 4 Kingly St, London W1R 5LF, England
Tusquets Blanca, Oscar *Architect*
%Tusquets Diaz Assoc, Cavallers 50, 08034 Barcelona, Spain
Tuten, Richard L (Rick) *Football Player*
1315 SE 22nd Ave, Ocala, FL 34471, USA
Tutone, Tommy *Singer, Dancer*
%Lustig Talent, PO Box 770850, Orlando, FL 32877, USA
Tuttle, O Frank *Geochemist*
PO Box 16, Greer, AZ 85927, USA
Tuttle, Perry *Football Player*
14224 King Elder Drive, Charlotte, NC 28273, USA
Tuttle, William G T, Jr *Army General*
9707 Ceralene Dr, Fairfax, VA 22032, USA
Tutu, Desmond M *Nobel Peace Laureate, Religious Leader*
PO Box 1092, Milnerton 744, Cape Town, South Africa
Tverdovsky, Oleg *Hockey Player*
63 Briarwood Terrace, Cedar Grove, NJ 07009, USA
Twain, Shania *Singer, Songwriter, Model*
%Q Prime, 729 7th Ave, #1600, New York, NY 10019, USA
Twardzik, Dave *Basketball Player, Executive*
%Orlando Magic, Waterhouse Center, 8701 Maitland Summit Blvd, Orlando, FL 32810, USA
Tway, Bob *Golfer*
6300 Oak Heritage Trail, Edmond, OK 73003, USA
Tweed, John N *Religious Leader*
%Reformed Presbyterian Church, 1117 E Devonshire Ave, Phoenix, AZ 85014, USA
Tweed, Shannon *Model, Actress*
11300 W Olympic Blvd, #619, Los Angeles, CA 90064, USA
Tweedy, Jeff *Singer (Wilco)*
%Monterey Peninsula Artists, 509 Hartnell St, Monterey, CA 93940, USA
Tweet *Singer, Songwriter*
%Violator Mgmt, 36 W 25th St, New York, NY 10010, USA
Twibell, Roger *Sportscaster*
%ABC-TV, Sports Dept, 77 W 66th St, New York, NY 10023, USA
Twiggy *Model, Actress*
4 Saint Georges House, Hanover Square, London W1R 9AJ, England
Twilley, Dwight *Singer, Songwriter*
%Paradise Artists, 108 E Matilija St, Ojai, CA 93023, USA

T

Twilley - Tzekova

Twilley, Howard J, Jr *Football Player*
3109 S Columbia Circle, Tulsa, OK 74105, USA
Twohy, Mike *Cartoonist*
605 Beloit Ave, Kensington, CA 94708, USA
Twohy, Robert *Cartoonist*
%New Yorker Magazine, Editorial Dept, 4 Times Square, New York, NY 10036, USA
Twombly, Cy *Artist*
%Gagosian Gallery, 980 Madison Ave, New York, NY 10021, USA
Twyman, John K (Jack) *Businessman, Basketball Player*
8955 Indian Ridge Lane, Cincinnati, OH 45243, USA
Tydings, Alexandra *Actress*
%Writers & Artists, 8383 Wilshire Blvd, #550, Beverly Hills, CA 90211, USA
Tydings, Joseph D *Senator, MD*
2705 Pocock Road, Monkton, MD 21111, USA
Tyers, Kathy *Writer*
%Martha Millard Agency, 204 Park Ave, Madison, NJ 07940, USA
Tykwer, Tom *Movie Director, Writer, Actor*
%Creative Artists Agency, 9830 Wilshire Blvd, Beverly Hills, CA 90212, USA
Tyler, Aisha *Actress, Comedian*
%Endeavor Talent Agency, 9701 Wilshire Blvd, #1000, Beverly Hills, CA 90212, USA
Tyler, Anne *Writer*
222 Tunbridge Road, Baltimore, MD 21212, USA
Tyler, Bonnie *Singer, Songwriter*
%David Aspden Mgmt, Coach House, S Holmwood, Dorking RH5 4LJ, England
Tyler, Harold R, Jr *Attorney*
%Patterson Belknap Webb Tyler, 30 Rockefeller Plaza, New York, NY 10112, USA
Tyler, Liv *Actress, Model*
%William Morris Agency, 151 El Camino Dr, Beverly Hills, CA 90212, USA
Tyler, Richard *Fashion Designer*
%Richard Tyler Couture, 727 Washington St, New York, NY 10014, USA
Tyler, Robert *Actor*
%Innovative Artists, 1505 10th St, Santa Monica, CA 90401, USA
Tyler, Steven *Singer (Aerosmith), Songwriter*
%Monterey Peninsula Artists, 509 Hartnell St, Monterey, CA 93940, USA
Tyler, Wendell A *Football Player*
2541 Still Meadow Lane, Lancaster, CA 93536, USA
Tylo, Hunter *Actress, Model*
11684 Ventura Blvd, #910, Studio City, CA 91604, USA
Tylo, Michael *Actor*
11684 Ventura Blvd, #910, Studio City, CA 91604, USA
Tyner, Charles *Actor*
%Dade/Schultz, 6442 Coldwater Canyon Ave, #206, Valley Green, CA 91606, USA
Tyner, McCoy *Jazz Pianist, Composer*
%Abby Hoffer, 223 1/2 E 48th St, New York, NY 10017, USA
Tyra, Charles (Charlie) *Basketball Player*
901 Stoneykirk Dr, Louisville, KY 40223, USA
Tyrese *Singer, Songwriter, Actor*
%William Morris Agency, 151 El Camino Dr, Beverly Hills, CA 90212, USA
Tyrrell, Susan *Actress*
%Abrams Artists, 9200 Sunset Blvd, #1125, Los Angeles, CA 90069, USA
Tysoe, Ronald W *Businessman*
%Federated Department Stores, 151 W 34th Ave, New York, NY 10001, USA
Tyson, Cathy *Actress*
%P F D, Drury House, 34-43 Russell St, London WC2B 5HA, England
Tyson, Cicely *Actress*
315 W 70th St, New York, NY 10023, USA
Tyson, Michael G (Mike) *Boxer*
%Jeff Wald, 3000 W Olympic Blvd, #1400-2, Santa Monica, CA 90404, USA
Tyson, Neil de Grasse *Astrophysicist*
%Hayden Planetarium, W 81st St & Central Park W, New York, NY 10024, USA
Tyson, Richard *Actor*
%Kritzer, 12200 W Olympic Blvd, #400, Los Angeles, CA 90064, USA
Tyurin, Mikhail *Cosmonaut*
%Potchta Kosmonavtov, Moskovskoi Oblasti, 141160 Syvisdny Goroduk, Russia
Tyus, Wyomia *Track Athlete*
1102 Keniston Ave, Los Angeles, CA 90019, USA
Tyzack, Margaret *Actress*
%Joyce Edwards, 275 Kennington Road, London SE1 6BY, England
Tzadua, Paulos Cardinal *Religious Leader*
PO Box 2141, Addis Abeba, Ethiopia
Tzekova, Polina *Basketball Player*
%Houston Comets, 2 Greenway Plaza, #400, Houston, TX 77046, USA

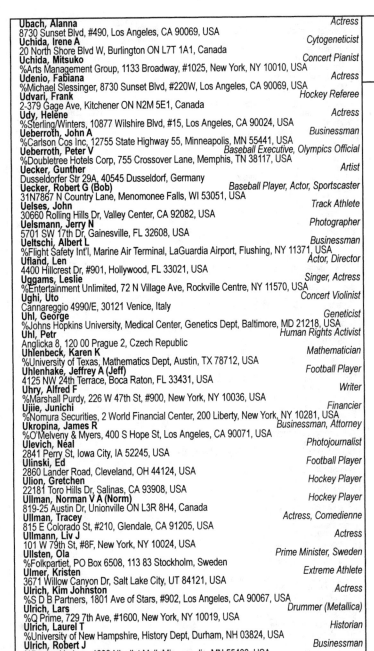

Ubach, Alanna *Actress*
8730 Sunset Blvd, #490, Los Angeles, CA 90069, USA

Uchida, Irene A *Cytogeneticist*
20 North Shore Blvd W, Burlington ON L7T 1A1, Canada

Uchida, Mitsuko *Concert Pianist*
%Arts Management Group, 1133 Broadway, #1025, New York, NY 10010, USA

Udenio, Fabiana *Actress*
%Michael Slessinger, 8730 Sunset Blvd, #220W, Los Angeles, CA 90069, USA

Udvari, Frank *Hockey Referee*
2-379 Gage Ave, Kitchener ON N2M 5E1, Canada

Udy, Helene *Actress*
%Sterling/Winters, 10877 Wilshire Blvd, #15, Los Angeles, CA 90024, USA

Ueberroth, John A *Businessman*
%Carlson Cos Inc, 12755 State Highway 55, Minneapolis, MN 55441, USA

Ueberroth, Peter V *Baseball Executive, Olympics Official*
%Doubletree Hotels Corp, 755 Crossover Lane, Memphis, TN 38117, USA

Uecker, Gunther *Artist*
Dusseldorfer Str 29A, 40545 Dusseldorf, Germany

Uecker, Robert G (Bob) *Baseball Player, Actor, Sportscaster*
31N7867 N Country Lane, Menomonee Falls, WI 53051, USA

Uelses, John *Track Athlete*
30660 Rolling Hills Dr, Valley Center, CA 92082, USA

Uelsmann, Jerry N *Photographer*
5701 SW 17th Dr, Gainesville, FL 32608, USA

Ueltschi, Albert L *Businessman*
%Flight Safety Int'l, Marine Air Terminal, LaGuardia Airport, Flushing, NY 11371, USA

Ufland, Len *Actor, Director*
4400 Hillcrest Dr, #901, Hollywood, FL 33021, USA

Uggams, Leslie *Singer, Actress*
%Entertainment Unlimited, 72 N Village Ave, Rockville Centre, NY 11570, USA

Ughi, Uto *Concert Violinist*
Cannareggio 4990/E, 30121 Venice, Italy

Uhl, George *Geneticist*
%Johns Hopkins University, Medical Center, Genetics Dept, Baltimore, MD 21218, USA

Uhl, Petr *Human Rights Activist*
Anglicka 8, 120 00 Prague 2, Czech Republic

Uhlenbeck, Karen K *Mathematician*
%University of Texas, Mathematics Dept, Austin, TX 78712, USA

Uhlenhake, Jeffrey A (Jeff) *Football Player*
4125 NW 24th Terrace, Boca Raton, FL 33431, USA

Uhry, Alfred F *Writer*
%Marshall Purdy, 226 W 47th St, #900, New York, NY 10036, USA

Ujiie, Junichi *Financier*
%Nomura Securities, 2 World Financial Center, 200 Liberty, New York, NY 10281, USA

Ukropina, James R *Businessman, Attorney*
%O'Melveny & Myers, 400 S Hope St, Los Angeles, CA 90071, USA

Ulevich, Neal *Photojournalist*
2841 Perry St, Iowa City, IA 52245, USA

Ulinski, Ed *Football Player*
2860 Lander Road, Cleveland, OH 44124, USA

Ulion, Gretchen *Hockey Player*
22181 Toro Hills Dr, Salinas, CA 93908, USA

Ullman, Norman V A (Norm) *Hockey Player*
819-25 Austin Dr, Unionville ON L3R 8H4, Canada

Ullman, Tracey *Actress, Comedienne*
815 E Colorado St, #210, Glendale, CA 91205, USA

Ullmann, Liv J *Actress*
101 W 79th St, #8F, New York, NY 10024, USA

Ullsten, Ola *Prime Minister, Sweden*
%Folkpartiet, PO Box 6508, 113 83 Stockholm, Sweden

Ulmer, Kristen *Extreme Athlete*
3671 Willow Canyon Dr, Salt Lake City, UT 84121, USA

Ulrich, Kim Johnston *Actress*
%S D B Partners, 1801 Ave of Stars, #902, Los Angeles, CA 90067, USA

Ulrich, Lars *Drummer (Metallica)*
%Q Prime, 729 7th Ave, #1600, New York, NY 10019, USA

Ulrich, Laurel T *Historian*
%University of New Hampshire, History Dept, Durham, NH 03824, USA

Ulrich, Robert J *Businessman*
%Dayton Hudson, 1000 Nicollet Mall, Minneapolis, MN 55403, USA

Ulrich, Skeet *Actor*
%International Creative Mgmt, 8942 Wilshire Blvd, #219, Beverly Hills, CA 90211, USA

Ulrich, Thomas *Boxer*
Brunsbutteler Damm 29, 13581 Berlin, Germany

Ultang, Don *Photojournalist*
3500 Lower West Branch Road, #121, Iowa City, IA 52245, USA

Ultra Nate *Singer*
%Peach Bisquit, 451 Washington Ave, #5A, Brooklyn, NY 11238, USA

U

Ulufa'alu - Urban

Ulufa'alu, Bartholomew *Prime Minister, Solomon Islands*
%Premier's Office, Legakiki Ridge, Honiara, Guadacanal, Solomon Islands
Ulusu, Bulent *Prime Minister, Turkey; Navy Admiral*
Ciftehavuzlar Yesilbahar 50K 8/27, Kadikoy/Istanbul, Turkey
Ulvaeus, Bjorn *Singer (ABBA), Composer*
%Gorel Hanser, Sodra Brobanken 41A, Skeppsholmen, 111 49 Stockholm, Sweden
Ulvang, Vegard *Cross Country Skier*
Fjellveien 53, 9900 Kirkenes, Norway
Ulyanov, Mikhail A *Actor, Director*
%Theater Vakhtangov, 26 Arbat, 121002 Moscow, Russia
Umar Bin Hassan *Rap Artist (Last Poets)*
%Agency Group, 1775 Broadway, #433, New York, NY 10019, USA
Umemoto, Nanako *Architect*
118 E 59th St, New York, NY 10022, USA
Umrao Singh *WW II India Army Hero (VC)*
%Victoria Cross Assn, Old Admiralty Building, London SW1A 2BL, England
Unanue, Emil R *Immunopathologist*
%Washington University, Medical School, Pathology Dept, Saint Louis, MO 63110, USA
Underwood, Blair *Actor*
PO Box 55665, Sherman Oaks, CA 91413, USA
Underwood, Jacob *Singer (O-Town)*
%Trans Continental Records, 7380 Sand Lake Road, #350, Orlando, FL 32819, USA
Underwood, Jay *Actor*
6100 Wilshire Blvd, #1170, Los Angeles, CA 90048, USA
Underwood, Ron *Movie Director*
%United Talent Agency, 9560 Wilshire Blvd, #500, Beverly Hills, CA 90212, USA
Underwood, Scott *Drummer (Train)*
%Jon Landau, 80 Mason St, Greenwich, CT 06830, USA
Ungaro, Emanuel M *Fashion Designer*
2 Ave du Montaigne, 75008 Paris, France
Ungaro, Susan Kelliher *Editor*
%Family Circle Magazine, Editorial Dept, 375 Lexington Ave, New York, NY 10017, USA
Unger, Deborah Kara *Actress*
%International Creative Mgmt, 8942 Wilshire Blvd, #219, Beverly Hills, CA 90211, USA
Unger, Garry D *Hockey Player*
5315 E 93rd St, Tulsa, OK 74137, USA
Unger, Jim *Cartoonist (Herman)*
%Universal Press Syndicate, 4520 Main St, Kansas City, MO 64111, USA
Unger, Kay *Fashion Designer*
%Saint Gillian Sportswear, 498 Fashion Ave, New York, NY 10018, USA
Unger, Leonard *Diplomat*
31 Amherst Road, Belmont, MA 02478, USA
Ungers, Oswald M *Architect*
Belvederestr 60, 50933 Cologne, Germany
Union, Gabrielle *Actress*
%International Creative Mgmt, 8942 Wilshire Blvd, #219, Beverly Hills, CA 90211, USA
Unkefer, Ronald A *Businessman*
%Good Guys Inc, 1600 Harbor Bay Parkway, Alameda, CA 94502, USA
Uno, Osamu *Businessman*
1-46 Showacho, Hamadera Sakai, Osaka 592, Japan
Unruh, James A *Businessman*
5426 E Morrison Lane, Paradise Valley, AZ 85253, USA
Unseld, Westley S (Wes) *Basketball Player, Coach, Executive*
2210 Cedar Circle Dr, Baltimore, MD 21228, USA
Unser, Alfred (Al) *Auto Racing Driver*
7625 Central Ave NW, Albuquerque, NM 87121, USA
Unser, Alfred (Al), Jr *Auto Racing Driver*
PO Box 56696, Albuquerque, NM 87187, USA
Unser, Robert W (Bobby) *Auto Racing Driver*
7700 Central Ave SW, Albuquerque, NM 87121, USA
Upatnieks, Juris *Optical Engineer*
%Applied Optics, 2662 Valley Dr, Ann Arbor, MI 48103, USA
Upchurch, Rickie (Rick) *Football Player*
988 S Avenida del Oro W, Pueblo, CO 81007, USA
Updike, John H *Writer*
675 Hale St, Beverly Farms, MA 01915, USA
Uphoff-Becker, Nicole *Equestrian Rider*
Freiherr-von-Lanen-Str 15, 48231 Warendorf, Germany
Upshaw, Dawn *Opera Singer*
%Columbia Artists Mgmt Inc, 165 W 57th St, New York, NY 10019, USA
Upshaw, Eugene (Gene) *Football Player, Labor Leader*
1102 Pepper Tree Dr, Great Falls, VA 22066, USA
Upshaw, Regan *Football Player*
%Washington Redskins, 21300 Redskin Park Dr, Ashburn, VA 20147, USA
Upton, Arthur C *Physician*
7743 S Galileo Lane, Tucson, AZ 85747, USA
Urban, Karl *Actor*
%Auckland Actors, PO Box 56460, Dominion Road, Auckland 1030, New Zealand

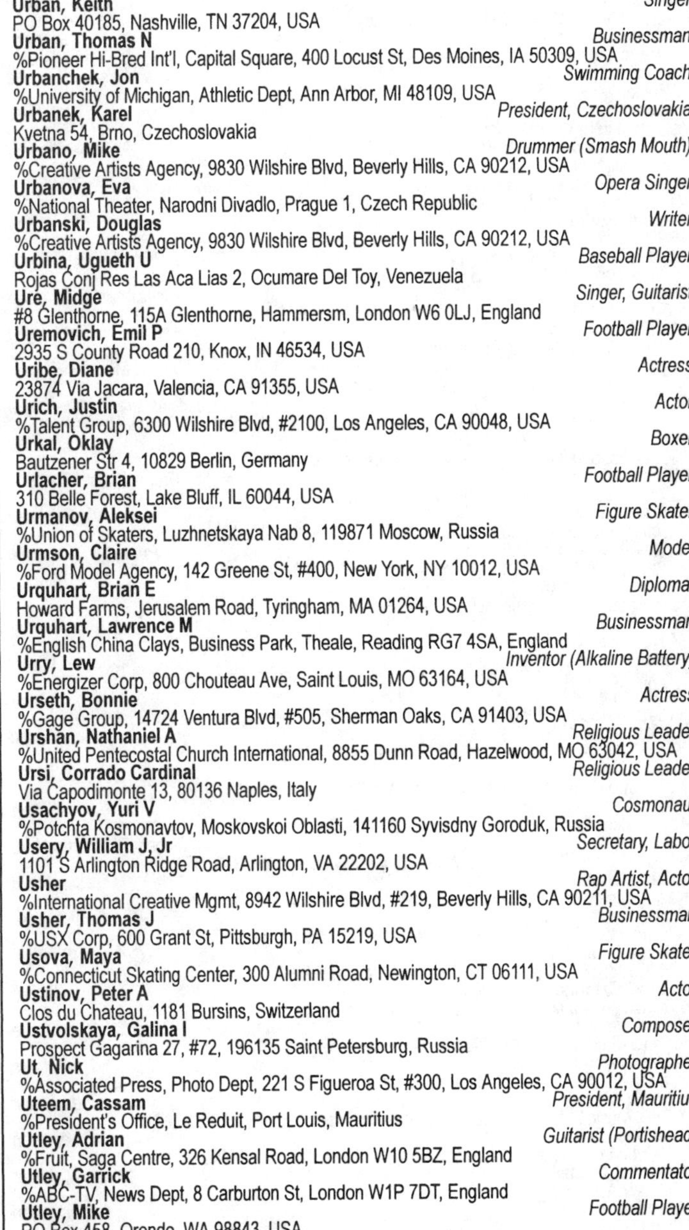

Urban, Keith — *Singer*
PO Box 40185, Nashville, TN 37204, USA

Urban, Thomas N — *Businessman*
%Pioneer Hi-Bred Int'l, Capital Square, 400 Locust St, Des Moines, IA 50309, USA

Urbanchek, Jon — *Swimming Coach*
%University of Michigan, Athletic Dept, Ann Arbor, MI 48109, USA

Urbanek, Karel — *President, Czechoslovakia*
Kvetna 54, Brno, Czechoslovakia

Urbano, Mike — *Drummer (Smash Mouth)*
%Creative Artists Agency, 9830 Wilshire Blvd, Beverly Hills, CA 90212, USA

Urbanova, Eva — *Opera Singer*
%National Theater, Narodni Divadlo, Prague 1, Czech Republic

Urbanski, Douglas — *Writer*
%Creative Artists Agency, 9830 Wilshire Blvd, Beverly Hills, CA 90212, USA

Urbina, Ugueth U — *Baseball Player*
Rojas Conj Res Las Aca Lias 2, Ocumare Del Toy, Venezuela

Ure, Midge — *Singer, Guitarist*
#8 Glenthorne, 115A Glenthorne, Hammersm, London W6 0LJ, England

Uremovich, Emil P — *Football Player*
2935 S County Road 210, Knox, IN 46534, USA

Uribe, Diane — *Actress*
23874 Via Jacara, Valencia, CA 91355, USA

Urich, Justin — *Actor*
%Talent Group, 6300 Wilshire Blvd, #2100, Los Angeles, CA 90048, USA

Urkal, Oklay — *Boxer*
Bautzener Str 4, 10829 Berlin, Germany

Urlacher, Brian — *Football Player*
310 Belle Forest, Lake Bluff, IL 60044, USA

Urmanov, Aleksei — *Figure Skater*
%Union of Skaters, Luzhnetskaya Nab 8, 119871 Moscow, Russia

Urmson, Claire — *Model*
%Ford Model Agency, 142 Greene St, #400, New York, NY 10012, USA

Urquhart, Brian E — *Diplomat*
Howard Farms, Jerusalem Road, Tyringham, MA 01264, USA

Urquhart, Lawrence M — *Businessman*
%English China Clays, Business Park, Theale, Reading RG7 4SA, England

Urry, Lew — *Inventor (Alkaline Battery)*
%Energizer Corp, 800 Chouteau Ave, Saint Louis, MO 63164, USA

Urseth, Bonnie — *Actress*
%Gage Group, 14724 Ventura Blvd, #505, Sherman Oaks, CA 91403, USA

Urshan, Nathaniel A — *Religious Leader*
%United Pentecostal Church International, 8855 Dunn Road, Hazelwood, MO 63042, USA

Ursi, Corrado Cardinal — *Religious Leader*
Via Capodimonte 13, 80136 Naples, Italy

Usachyov, Yuri V — *Cosmonaut*
%Potchta Kosmonavtov, Moskovskoi Oblasti, 141160 Syvisdny Goroduk, Russia

Usery, William J, Jr — *Secretary, Labor*
1101 S Arlington Ridge Road, Arlington, VA 22202, USA

Usher — *Rap Artist, Actor*
%International Creative Mgmt, 8942 Wilshire Blvd, #219, Beverly Hills, CA 90211, USA

Usher, Thomas J — *Businessman*
%USX Corp, 600 Grant St, Pittsburgh, PA 15219, USA

Usova, Maya — *Figure Skater*
%Connecticut Skating Center, 300 Alumni Road, Newington, CT 06111, USA

Ustinov, Peter A — *Actor*
Clos du Chateau, 1181 Bursins, Switzerland

Ustvolskaya, Galina I — *Composer*
Prospect Gagarina 27, #72, 196135 Saint Petersburg, Russia

Ut, Nick — *Photographer*
%Associated Press, Photo Dept, 221 S Figueroa St, #300, Los Angeles, CA 90012, USA

Uteem, Cassam — *President, Mauritius*
%President's Office, Le Reduit, Port Louis, Mauritius

Utley, Adrian — *Guitarist (Portishead)*
%Fruit, Saga Centre, 326 Kensal Road, London W10 5BZ, England

Utley, Garrick — *Commentator*
%ABC-TV, News Dept, 8 Carburton St, London W1P 7DT, England

Utley, Mike — *Football Player*
PO Box 458, Orondo, WA 98843, USA

Utley, Stan — *Golfer*
PO Box 6024, Columbia, MO 65205, USA

Utzon, Jorn — *Architect*
%General Delivery, 3150 Hellebaek, Denmark

Uyeda, Seiya — *Geophysicist*
2-39-6 Daizawa, Setagayaku, Tokyo 113, Japan

Uzawa, Hirofumi — *Economist*
Higashi 1-3-6, Hoya, Tokyo, Japan

V

Vacano, Jost *Cinematographer*
Leoprechtingstr 18, 81739 Munich, Germany
Vacanti, Charles A *Surgeon*
%Massachusetts University Med Center, Anesthesiology Dept, Worcester, MA 02139, USA
Vacariou, Nicolae *Prime Minister, Romania*
%Romanian Senate, Piata Revolutiei, 71243 Bucharest, Romania
Vaccaro, Brenda *Actress*
%Gold Marshak Liedtke, 3500 W Olive Ave, #1400, Burbank, CA 91505, USA
Vachon, Louis-Albert Cardinal *Religious Leader*
%Seminaire de Quebec, 1 Rue des Remparts, Quebec QC G1R 5LY, Canada
Vachon, Rogatien R (Rogie) *Hockey Player, Coach, Executive*
47385 Via Florence, La Quinta, CA 92253, USA
Vachss, Andrew H *Writer*
299 Broadway, #1800, New York, NY 10007, USA
Vaea of Houma, Baron *Prime Minister, Tonga*
%Prime Minister's Office, Nuku'alofa, Tonga
Vagelos, P Roy *Businessman, Biochemist*
1 Crossroads Dr, 500 Building A, Bedminster, NJ 07921, USA
Vago, Constantin *Pathologist*
%University of Sciences, Place Eugene Bataillon, 34095 Montpellier, France
Vahi, Tiit *Prime Minister, Estonia*
%Coalition Party Eesti Koonderakond, Kuhlbarsi 1, Tallinn 0104, Estonia
Vai, Steve *Guitarist (Alcatraz, Whitesnake)*
%Septys Entertainment, 1223 Wilshire Blvd, #804, Santa Monica, CA 90403, USA
Vail, Justina *Actress*
%UPN, 5555 Melrose Ave, Los Angeles, CA 90038, USA
Vajiralongkorn *Crown Prince, Thailand*
%Royal Residence, Chirtalad a Villa, Bangkok, Thailand
Vajna, Andrew *Movie Producer*
%Cinergi Productions, 2308 Broadway, Santa Monica, CA 90404, USA
Vajpayee, Atal Bihari *Prime Minister, India*
6 Raisina Road, New Delhi 110011, India
Valandrey, Charlotte *Actress*
%Artmedia, 20 Ave Rapp, 75007 Paris, France
Valar, Paul *Skier*
34 Hubertus Ring, Franconia, NH 03580, USA
Valderrama, Carlos *Soccer Player*
%Colorado Rapids, 555 17th St, #3350, Denver, CO 80202, USA
Valderrama, Wilmer *Actor*
%Rigberg Roberts Rugolo, 1180 S Beverly Dr, #601, Los Angeles, CA 90035, USA
Valdes, Jesus (Chucho) *Jazz Pianist*
%DL Media, 51 Oakland Terrace, Bala Cynwyd, PA 19004, USA
Valdez, Luis *Writer*
%El Teatro Capesino, 705 4th St, San Juan Bautista, CA 95045, USA
Vale, Jerry *Singer*
40960 Glenmore Dr, Palm Desert, CA 92260, USA
Vale, Tina *Singer (Redmon & Vale)*
%DreamWorks Records, 9268 W 3rd St, Beverly Hills, CA 90210, USA
Valek, Vladimir *Conductor*
Na Vapennem 6, 140 00 Prague 4, Czech Republic
Valen, Nancy *Actress*
%Metropolitan Talent Agency, 4526 Wilshire Blvd, Los Angeles, CA 90010, USA
Valensi, Nick *Guitarist (Strokes)*
%MVO Ltd, 370 7th Ave, #807, New York, NY 10001, USA
Valente, Catarina *Singer*
Villa Corallo, Via ai Ronci 12, 6816 Bissone, Switzerland
Valenti, Jack J *Association Executive*
%Motion Picture Assn, 4635 Ashby St NW, Washington, DC 20007, USA
Valentin, Barbara *Actress*
Hans-Sachs-Str 22, 80469 Munich, Germany
Valentin, Dave *Jazz Flutist*
%Turi's Music Enterprises, 103 Westwood Dr, Miami Springs, FL 33166, USA
Valentine, Dan *Businessman*
%C-Cube Microsystems, 1551 McCarthy Blvd, Milpitas, CA 95035, USA
Valentine, Darnell *Basketball Player*
7546 SW Ashford St, Tigard, OR 97224, USA
Valentine, Donald T *Businessman*
%Network Appliance Inc, 495 E Java Dr, Sunnyvale, CA 94089, USA
Valentine, Gary *Bassist (Blondie)*
%Shore Fire Media, 32 Court St, #1600, Brooklyn, NY 11201, USA
Valentine, James W *Paleobiologist*
1351 Glendale Ave, Berkeley, CA 94708, USA
Valentine, Karen *Actress*
PO Box 1410, Washington Depot, CT 06793, USA
Valentine, Robert J (Bobby) *Baseball Player, Manager*
71 Wynnewood Lane, Stamford, CT 06903, USA
Valentine, Scott *Actor*
17465 Flanders St, Granada Hills, CA 91344, USA

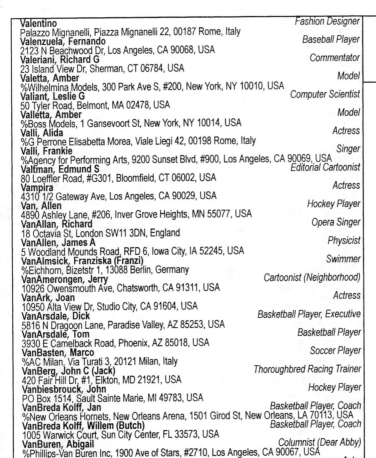

Valentino — *Fashion Designer*
Palazzo Mignanelli, Piazza Mignanelli 22, 00187 Rome, Italy

Valenzuela, Fernando — *Baseball Player*
2123 N Beachwood Dr, Los Angeles, CA 90068, USA

Valeriani, Richard G — *Commentator*
23 Island View Dr, Sherman, CT 06784, USA

Valetta, Amber — *Model*
%Wilhelmina Models, 300 Park Ave S, #200, New York, NY 10010, USA

Valiant, Leslie G — *Computer Scientist*
50 Tyler Road, Belmont, MA 02478, USA

Valletta, Amber — *Model*
%Boss Models, 1 Gansevoort St, New York, NY 10014, USA

Valli, Alida — *Actress*
%G Perrone Elisabetta Morea, Viale Liegi 42, 00198 Rome, Italy

Valli, Frankie — *Singer*
%Agency for Performing Arts, 9200 Sunset Blvd, #900, Los Angeles, CA 90069, USA

Valtman, Edmund S — *Editorial Cartoonist*
80 Loeffler Road, #G301, Bloomfield, CT 06002, USA

Vampira — *Actress*
4310 1/2 Gateway Ave, Los Angeles, CA 90029, USA

Van, Allen — *Hockey Player*
4890 Ashley Lane, #206, Inver Grove Heights, MN 55077, USA

VanAllan, Richard — *Opera Singer*
18 Octavia St, London SW11 3DN, England

VanAllen, James A — *Physicist*
5 Woodland Mounds Road, RFD 6, Iowa City, IA 52245, USA

VanAlmsick, Franziska (Franzi) — *Swimmer*
%Eichhorn, Bizetstr 1, 13088 Berlin, Germany

VanAmerongen, Jerry — *Cartoonist (Neighborhood)*
10926 Owensmouth Ave, Chatsworth, CA 91311, USA

VanArk, Joan — *Actress*
10950 Alta View Dr, Studio City, CA 91604, USA

VanArsdale, Dick — *Basketball Player, Executive*
5816 N Dragoon Lane, Paradise Valley, AZ 85253, USA

VanArsdale, Tom — *Basketball Player*
3930 E Camelback Road, Phoenix, AZ 85018, USA

VanBasten, Marco — *Soccer Player*
%AC Milan, Via Turati 3, 20121 Milan, Italy

VanBerg, John C (Jack) — *Thoroughbred Racing Trainer*
420 Fair Hill Dr, #1, Elkton, MD 21921, USA

Vanbiesbrouck, John — *Hockey Player*
PO Box 1514, Sault Sainte Marie, MI 49783, USA

VanBreda Kolff, Jan — *Basketball Player, Coach*
%New Orleans Hornets, New Orleans Arena, 1501 Girod St, New Orleans, LA 70113, USA

VanBreda Kolff, Willem (Butch) — *Basketball Player, Coach*
1005 Warwick Court, Sun City Center, FL 33573, USA

VanBuren, Abigail — *Columnist (Dear Abby)*
%Phillips-Van Buren Inc, 1900 Ave of Stars, #2710, Los Angeles, CA 90067, USA

Vance, Courtney B — *Actor*
%Creative Artists Agency, 9830 Wilshire Blvd, Beverly Hills, CA 90212, USA

Vance, Robert S — *Judge*
%US Court of Appeals, 1800 5th Ave N, Birmingham, AL 35203, USA

VanCulin, Samuel — *Religious Leader*
%All Hallows Church, 43 Trinity Square, London EC3N 4DJ, England

VanDam, Jose — *Opera Singer*
%Zurich Artists, Rutistr 52, 8044 Zurich-Gockhausen, Switzerland

VanDamme, Jean-Claude — *Actor*
%International Creative Mgmt, 8942 Wilshire Blvd, #219, Beverly Hills, CA 90211, USA

VanDantzig, Rudi — *Choreographer*
Emma-Straat 27, Amsterdam, Netherlands

VandenBerg, Lodewijk — *Astronaut*
%Constellation Technology Corp, 7887 Bryan Dairy Road, #100, Largo, FL 33777, USA

Vander Jagt, Guy — *Representative, MI*
%Baker & Hostetler, 1050 Connecticut Ave NW, Washington, DC 20036, USA

Vander, Musetta — *Actress*
%Agency for Performing Arts, 9200 Sunset Blvd, #900, Los Angeles, CA 90069, USA

VanDerBeek, James — *Actor*
2945 S Barrington Ave, Los Angeles, CA 90025, USA

Vanderberg Shaw, Helen — *Synchronized Swimming Coach*
%Heaven's Fitness, 301 14th St NW, Calgary AB T2N 2A1, Canada

Vanderhoef, Larry N — *Educator*
%University of California, President's Office, Davis, CA 95616, USA

Vanderloo, Mark — *Model*
%Wilhelmina Models, 300 Park Ave S, #200, New York, NY 10010, USA

VanDerMeer, Simon — *Nobel Physics Laureate*
4 Chemin des Corbillettes, 1218 GD-Saconnex, Switzerland

Vandermeersch, Bernard — *Anthropologist*
%University of Bordeaux, Anthropology Dept, Bordeaux, France

V

Vanderveen, Loet *Sculptor*
Lime Creek 5, Big Sur, CA 93920, USA
VanDerveer, Tara *Basketball Coach*
1036 Cascade Dr, Menlo Park, CA 94025, USA
VandeSande, Theo A *Cinematographer*
2337 High Oak Dr, Los Angeles, CA 90068, USA
VandeVen, Monique *Actress, Director*
%Features Creative Mgmt, Entrepotdok 76A, 101 AD Amsterdam, Netherlands
VanDevere, Trish *Actress*
3211 Retreat Court, Malibu, CA 90265, USA
VandeWeghe, Albert *Swimmer*
7712 W Skyline Dr, Tulsa, OK 74107, USA
Vandeweghe, Ernie *Basketball Player, Physician*
PO Box 1216, Rancho Santa Fe, CA 92067, USA
Vandeweghe, Kiki *Basketball Player*
2109 E 9th Ave, Denver, CO 80206, USA
VanDien, Casper *Actor*
3601 W Verdugo Ave, #121, Burbank, CA 91505, USA
Vandiver, S Ernest *Governor, GA*
109 Hartwell Dr, Lavonia, GA 30553, USA
VanDoren, Mamie *Actress*
3414 Via Lido, #184, Newport Beach, CA 92663, USA
Vandross, Luther *Singer, Songwriter*
%Artist Group International, 9560 Wilshire Blvd, #400, Beverly Hills, CA 90212, USA
VanDusen, Granville *Actor*
2161 Ridgemont Dr, Los Angeles, CA 90046, USA
VanDuyn, Mona J *Writer*
7505 Teasdale Ave, Saint Louis, MO 63130, USA
VanDyke, Barry *Actor*
27800 Blythdale Road, Agoura, CA 91301, USA
VanDyke, Dick *Actor*
21315 Mariposa de Oro, Malibu, CA 90265, USA
VanDyke, Jerry *Actor, Comedian*
%American Mgmt, 19948 Mayall St, Chatsworth, CA 91311, USA
VanDyke, Jerry *Actor*
PO Box 2130, Benton, AR 72018, USA
VanDyke, Leroy *Singer*
%Leroy Van Dyke Enterprises, 29000 Highway V, Smithton, MO 65350, USA
VanDyken, Amy *Swimmer*
19947 N 84th Way, Scottsdale, AZ 85255, USA
Vane, John R *Nobel Medicine Laureate*
%Harvey Research Institute, Charterhouse Square, London EC1M 6BQ, England
VanEeghen, Mark *Football Player*
90 Woodstock Lane, Cranston, RI 02920, USA
Vanek, John *Basketball Referee*
9th St, RD 1, Nesquehoning, PA 18240, USA
Vaness, Carol *Opera Singer*
%I C M Artists, 40 W 57th St, New York, NY 10019, USA
Vanessa-Mae *Concert, Rock Violinist*
%Mel Bush, Stratford Saye, 20 Wellington Rd, Bournemouth BH8 8JN, England
VanExcel, Nick *Basketball Player*
4209 50th St, #2, Kenosha, WI 53144, USA
Vangelis *Composer*
%Gorfaine/Schwartz, 13245 Riverside Dr, #450, Sherman Oaks, CA 91423, USA
Vangen, Scott D *Astronaut*
%NASA, Johnson Space Center, 2101 NASA Road, Houston, TX 77058, USA
VanGorkum, Harry *Actor*
%Don Buchwald, 6500 Wilshire Blvd, #2200, Los Angeles, CA 90048, USA
VanGorp, Michele *Basketball Player*
%Minnesota Lynx, Target Center, 600 1st Ave N, Minneapolis, MN 55403, USA
VanGraafeiland, Ellsworth A *Judge*
%US Court of Appeals, Federal Building, 100 State St, Rochester, NY 14614, USA
VanGrunsven, Anky *Equestrian Rider*
Bonengang 1, 5421 BZ Gemert, Netherlands
VanGundy, Jeff *Basketball Coach, Sportscaster*
%Houston Rockets, Toyota Center, 2 E Greenway Plaza, Houston, TX 77046, USA
VanHalen, Alex *Drummer (Van Halen)*
12024 Summit Circle, Beverly Hills, CA 90210, USA
VanHalen, Eddie *Singer, Guitarist (Van Halen)*
12024 Summit Circle, Beverly Hills, CA 90210, USA
VanHamel, Martine *Ballerina*
%American Ballet Theatre, 890 Broadway, New York, NY 10003, USA
VanHellmond, Andy *Hockey Referee*
71 Hyde Road, Stratford ON N5A 7Z3, Canada
VanHoften, James C D A *Astronaut*
%Bechtel National Inc, 50 Beale St, San Francisco, CA 94105, USA
VanHolt, Brian *Actor*
%William Morris Agency, 151 El Camino Dr, Beverly Hills, CA 90212, USA

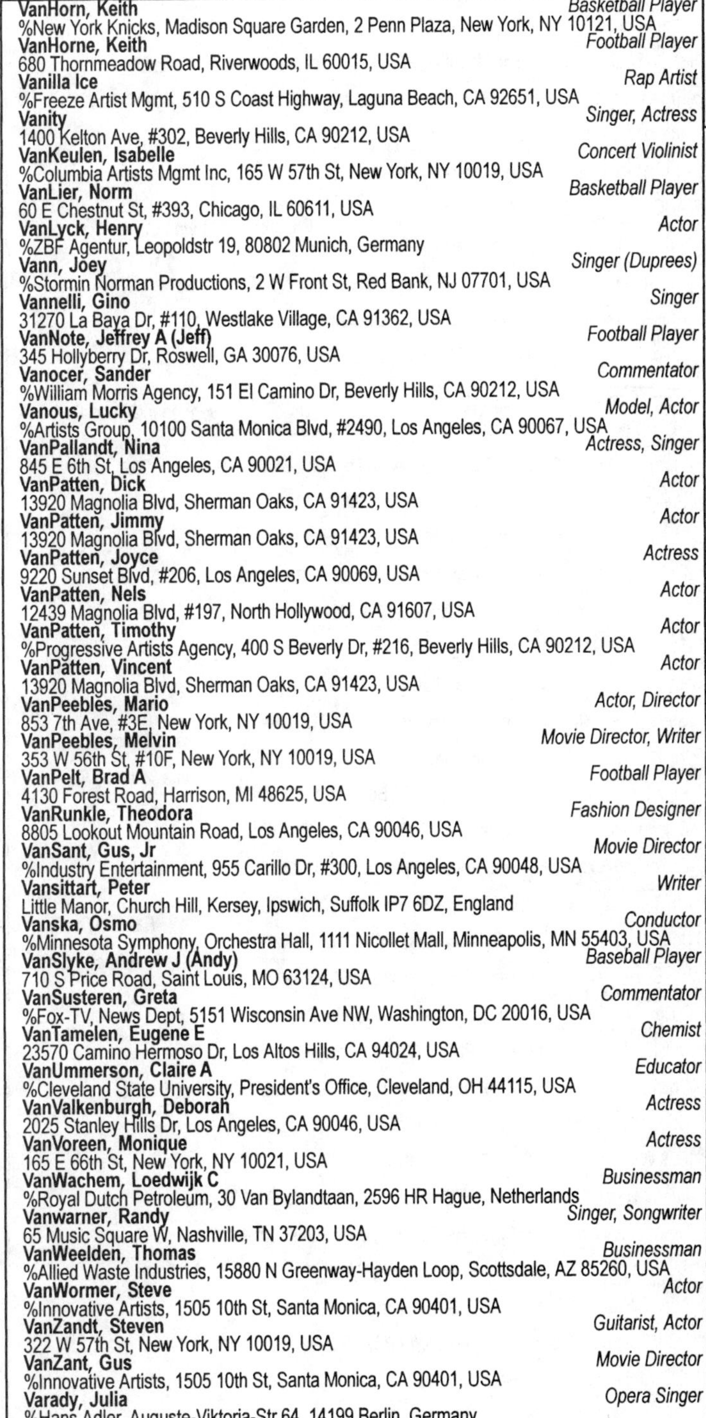

VanHorn, Keith *Basketball Player*
%New York Knicks, Madison Square Garden, 2 Penn Plaza, New York, NY 10121, USA
VanHorne, Keith *Football Player*
680 Thornmeadow Road, Riverwoods, IL 60015, USA
Vanilla Ice *Rap Artist*
%Freeze Artist Mgmt, 510 S Coast Highway, Laguna Beach, CA 92651, USA
Vanity *Singer, Actress*
1400 Kelton Ave, #302, Beverly Hills, CA 90212, USA
VanKeulen, Isabelle *Concert Violinist*
%Columbia Artists Mgmt Inc, 165 W 57th St, New York, NY 10019, USA
VanLier, Norm *Basketball Player*
60 E Chestnut St, #393, Chicago, IL 60611, USA
VanLyck, Henry *Actor*
%ZBF Agentur, Leopoldstr 19, 80802 Munich, Germany
Vann, Joey *Singer (Duprees)*
%Stormin Norman Productions, 2 W Front St, Red Bank, NJ 07701, USA
Vannelli, Gino *Singer*
31270 La Baya Dr, #110, Westlake Village, CA 91362, USA
VanNote, Jeffrey A (Jeff) *Football Player*
345 Hollyberry Dr, Roswell, GA 30076, USA
Vanocer, Sander *Commentator*
%William Morris Agency, 151 El Camino Dr, Beverly Hills, CA 90212, USA
Vanous, Lucky *Model, Actor*
%Artists Group, 10100 Santa Monica Blvd, #2490, Los Angeles, CA 90067, USA
VanPallandt, Nina *Actress, Singer*
845 E 6th St, Los Angeles, CA 90021, USA
VanPatten, Dick *Actor*
13920 Magnolia Blvd, Sherman Oaks, CA 91423, USA
VanPatten, Jimmy *Actor*
13920 Magnolia Blvd, Sherman Oaks, CA 91423, USA
VanPatten, Joyce *Actress*
9220 Sunset Blvd, #206, Los Angeles, CA 90069, USA
VanPatten, Nels *Actor*
12439 Magnolia Blvd, #197, North Hollywood, CA 91607, USA
VanPatten, Timothy *Actor*
%Progressive Artists Agency, 400 S Beverly Dr, #216, Beverly Hills, CA 90212, USA
VanPatten, Vincent *Actor*
13920 Magnolia Blvd, Sherman Oaks, CA 91423, USA
VanPeebles, Mario *Actor, Director*
853 7th Ave, #3E, New York, NY 10019, USA
VanPeebles, Melvin *Movie Director, Writer*
353 W 56th St, #10F, New York, NY 10019, USA
VanPelt, Brad A *Football Player*
4130 Forest Road, Harrison, MI 48625, USA
VanRunkle, Theodora *Fashion Designer*
8805 Lookout Mountain Road, Los Angeles, CA 90046, USA
VanSant, Gus, Jr *Movie Director*
%Industry Entertainment, 955 Carillo Dr, #300, Los Angeles, CA 90048, USA
Vansittart, Peter *Writer*
Little Manor, Church Hill, Kersey, Ipswich, Suffolk IP7 6DZ, England
Vanska, Osmo *Conductor*
%Minnesota Symphony, Orchestra Hall, 1111 Nicollet Mall, Minneapolis, MN 55403, USA
VanSlyke, Andrew J (Andy) *Baseball Player*
710 S Price Road, Saint Louis, MO 63124, USA
VanSusteren, Greta *Commentator*
%Fox-TV, News Dept, 5151 Wisconsin Ave NW, Washington, DC 20016, USA
VanTamelen, Eugene E *Chemist*
23570 Camino Hermoso Dr, Los Altos Hills, CA 94024, USA
VanUmmerson, Claire A *Educator*
%Cleveland State University, President's Office, Cleveland, OH 44115, USA
VanValkenburgh, Deborah *Actress*
2025 Stanley Hills Dr, Los Angeles, CA 90046, USA
VanVoreen, Monique *Actress*
165 E 66th St, New York, NY 10021, USA
VanWachem, Loedwijk C *Businessman*
%Royal Dutch Petroleum, 30 Van Bylandtaan, 2596 HR Hague, Netherlands
Vanwarner, Randy *Singer, Songwriter*
65 Music Square W, Nashville, TN 37203, USA
VanWeelden, Thomas *Businessman*
%Allied Waste Industries, 15880 N Greenway-Hayden Loop, Scottsdale, AZ 85260, USA
VanWormer, Steve *Actor*
%Innovative Artists, 1505 10th St, Santa Monica, CA 90401, USA
VanZandt, Steven *Guitarist, Actor*
322 W 57th St, New York, NY 10019, USA
VanZant, Gus *Movie Director*
%Innovative Artists, 1505 10th St, Santa Monica, CA 90401, USA
Varady, Julia *Opera Singer*
%Hans Adler, Auguste-Viktoria-Str 64, 14199 Berlin, Germany

V

Varda - Vaughn

Varda, Agnes *Movie Director*
%Cine-Tamaris, 86 Rue Daguerre, 75014 Paris, France
Vardalos, Nia *Actress*
%United Talent Agency, 9560 Wilshire Blvd, #500, Beverly Hills, CA 90212, USA
Varella, Leonor *Actress*
%Endeavor Talent Agency, 9701 Wilshire Blvd, #1000, Beverly Hills, CA 90212, USA
Varga, Imre *Sculptor*
Bartha Utca 1, Budapest XII, Hungary
Vargas Llosa, Mario *Writer*
Las Magnolias 295, 6 Piso, Barranco, Lima 4, Peru
Vargas, Elizabeth *Commentator*
%ABC-TV, News Dept, 77 W 66th St, New York, NY 10023, USA
Vargas, Jay R *Vietnam War Marine Corps Hero (CMH)*
12466 Thornbrush Court, San Diego, CA 92131, USA
Vargas, Ramon *Opera Singer*
%Columbia Artists Mgmt Inc, 165 W 57th St, New York, NY 10019, USA
Vargas, Valentina *Actress*
%Artists Agency, 1180 S Beverly Dr, #301, Los Angeles, CA 90035, USA
Vargo, Tim *Businessman*
%AutoZone Inc, 123 S Front St, Memphis, TN 38103, USA
Varian, Hal R *Economist*
1198 Estates Dr, Lafayette, CA 94549, USA
Varley of Chesterfield, Eric G *Government Official, England*
%Coalite Group, Buttermilk Lane, Bolsover, Derbyshire S44 6AB, England
Varmus, Harold E *Nobel Medicine Laureate*
%Memorial Sloan-Kettering Cancer Center, 1275 York Ave, New York, NY 10021, USA
Varo, Marton *Sculptor*
%Phillips Gallery, PO Box 5807, Carmel, CA 93921, USA
Varrichone, Frank *Football Player*
55 Dinsmore Ave, #103, Framingham, MA 01702, USA
Varshavsky, Alexander *Cell Biologist*
%California Institute of Technology, Cell Biology Dept, Pasadena, CA 91125, USA
Vartan, Michael *Actor*
252 N Larchmont Blvd, #201, Los Angeles, CA 90004, USA
Varton, Sylvie *Singer*
%Scotti, 706 N Beverly Dr, Beverly Hills, CA 90210, USA
Varty, Keith *Fashion Designer (Byblos)*
Bosco di San Francesco #6, Sirolo, Italy
Varvatos, John *Fashion Designer*
%Soho New York, 149 Mercer St, New York, NY 10012, USA
Vasary, Tamas *Concert Pianist, Conductor*
9 Village Road, London N3, England
Vasile, Radu *Prime Minister, Romania*
%Premier's Office, Piata Vicotriei 1, 71201 Bucharest, Romania
Vasilyev, Vladimir V *Ballet Dancer, Executive*
%Bolshoi Theater, Teatralnaya Pl 1, 103009 Moscow, Russia
Vasquez Rana, Mario *Publisher*
%El Sol de Mexico, Guillermo Prieto 7, Mexico City DF, Mexico
Vasquez, Juan F *Judge*
%US Tax Court, 400 2nd St NW, Washington, DC 20217, USA
Vass, Joan *Fashion Designer*
%Joan Vass Inc, 36 E 31st St, New York, NY 10016, USA
Vasser, Jimmy *Auto Racing Driver*
2398 Broadway St, San Francisco, CA 94115, USA
Vassiliou, George V *President, Cyprus*
PO Box 874, 21 Academiou Ave, Aglandjia, Nicosia, Cyprus
Vasyuchenko, Yuri *Ballet Dancer*
%Bolshoi Theater, Teatralnaya Pl 1, 103009 Moscow, Russia
Vasyutin, Vladimir V *Cosmonaut*
%Potchta Kosmonavtov, Moskovskoi Oblasti, 141160 Syvisdny Goroduk, Russia
Vaughan, Denis E *Conductor, Concert Organist*
%Schofer/Gold, 50 Riverside Dr, New York, NY 10024, USA
Vaughan, Martha *Biochemist*
11608 W Hill Dr, Rockville, MD 20852, USA
Vaughan, Peter *Actor*
%International Creative Mgmt, 76 Oxford St, London W1N 0AX, England
Vaughn, David *Basketball Player*
%New Jersey Nets, 390 Murray Hill Parkway, East Rutherford, NJ 07073, USA
Vaughn, Gregory L (Greg) *Baseball Player*
6309 Thresher Court, Elk Grove, CA 95758, USA
Vaughn, Jacque *Basketball Player*
%Atlanta Hawks, 190 Marietta St SW, Atlanta, GA 30303, USA
Vaughn, Jimmie *Guitarist*
%Mark I Mgmt, PO Box 29480, Austin, TX 78755, USA
Vaughn, Jonathan S (Jon) *Football Player*
2263 Franham Lane, Florissant, MO 63033, USA
Vaughn, Linda *Auto Racing*
2865 S Eagle Road, Newtown, PA 18940, USA

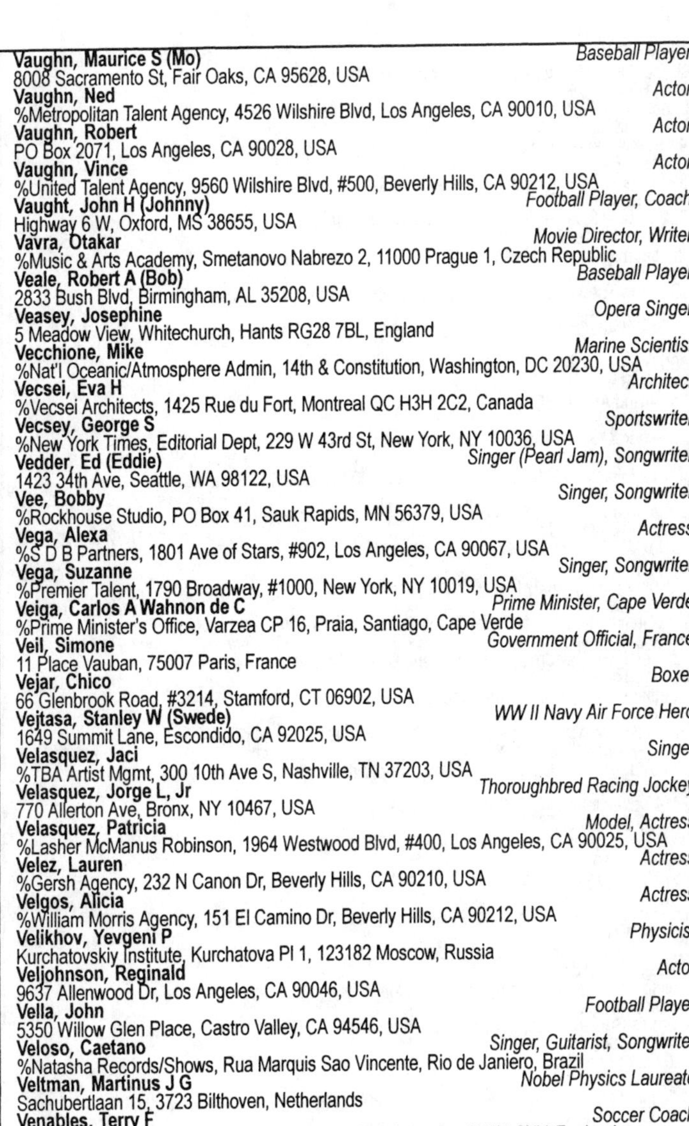

Vaughn, Maurice S (Mo) *Baseball Player*
8008 Sacramento St, Fair Oaks, CA 95628, USA
Vaughn, Ned *Actor*
%Metropolitan Talent Agency, 4526 Wilshire Blvd, Los Angeles, CA 90010, USA
Vaughn, Robert *Actor*
PO Box 2071, Los Angeles, CA 90028, USA
Vaughn, Vince *Actor*
%United Talent Agency, 9560 Wilshire Blvd, #500, Beverly Hills, CA 90212, USA
Vaught, John H (Johnny) *Football Player, Coach*
Highway 6 W, Oxford, MS 38655, USA
Vavra, Otakar *Movie Director, Writer*
%Music & Arts Academy, Smetanovo Nabrezo 2, 11000 Prague 1, Czech Republic
Veale, Robert A (Bob) *Baseball Player*
2833 Bush Blvd, Birmingham, AL 35208, USA
Veasey, Josephine *Opera Singer*
5 Meadow View, Whitechurch, Hants RG28 7BL, England
Vecchione, Mike *Marine Scientist*
%Nat'l Oceanic/Atmosphere Admin, 14th & Constitution, Washington, DC 20230, USA
Vecsei, Eva H *Architect*
%Vecsei Architects, 1425 Rue du Fort, Montreal QC H3H 2C2, Canada
Vecsey, George S *Sportswriter*
%New York Times, Editorial Dept, 229 W 43rd St, New York, NY 10036, USA
Vedder, Ed (Eddie) *Singer (Pearl Jam), Songwriter*
1423 34th Ave, Seattle, WA 98122, USA
Vee, Bobby *Singer, Songwriter*
%Rockhouse Studio, PO Box 41, Sauk Rapids, MN 56379, USA
Vega, Alexa *Actress*
%S D B Partners, 1801 Ave of Stars, #902, Los Angeles, CA 90067, USA
Vega, Suzanne *Singer, Songwriter*
%Premier Talent, 1790 Broadway, #1000, New York, NY 10019, USA
Veiga, Carlos A Wahnon de C *Prime Minister, Cape Verde*
%Prime Minister's Office, Varzea CP 16, Praia, Santiago, Cape Verde
Veil, Simone *Government Official, France*
11 Place Vauban, 75007 Paris, France
Vejar, Chico *Boxer*
66 Glenbrook Road, #3214, Stamford, CT 06902, USA
Vejtasa, Stanley W (Swede) *WW II Navy Air Force Hero*
1649 Summit Lane, Escondido, CA 92025, USA
Velasquez, Jaci *Singer*
%TBA Artist Mgmt, 300 10th Ave S, Nashville, TN 37203, USA
Velasquez, Jorge L, Jr *Thoroughbred Racing Jockey*
770 Allerton Ave, Bronx, NY 10467, USA
Velasquez, Patricia *Model, Actress*
%Lasher McManus Robinson, 1964 Westwood Blvd, #400, Los Angeles, CA 90025, USA
Velez, Lauren *Actress*
%Gersh Agency, 232 N Canon Dr, Beverly Hills, CA 90210, USA
Velgos, Alicia *Actress*
%William Morris Agency, 151 El Camino Dr, Beverly Hills, CA 90212, USA
Velikhov, Yevgeni P *Physicist*
Kurchatovskiy Institute, Kurchatova Pl 1, 123182 Moscow, Russia
Veljohnson, Reginald *Actor*
9637 Allenwood Dr, Los Angeles, CA 90046, USA
Vella, John *Football Player*
5350 Willow Glen Place, Castro Valley, CA 94546, USA
Veloso, Caetano *Singer, Guitarist, Songwriter*
%Natasha Records/Shows, Rua Marquis Sao Vincente, Rio de Janiero, Brazil
Veltman, Martinus J G *Nobel Physics Laureate*
Sachubertlaan 15, 3723 Bilthoven, Netherlands
Venables, Terry F *Soccer Coach*
%Terry Venables Holdings, 213 Putney Bridge Road, London SW15 2NY, England
Vendela *Model*
%I M G Models, 304 Park Ave S, #1200, New York, NY 10010, USA
Veneman, Ann *Secretary, Agriculture*
%Agriculture Department, 14th St & Independence Ave SW, Washington, DC 20250, USA
Venet, Bernar *Sculptor*
533 Canal St, New York, NY 10013, USA
Vengerov, Maxim *Concert Violinist*
%Lies Askonas, 6 Henrietta St, London WC2E 8LA, England
Venitucci, Michele *Actor*
%Carol Levi Co, Via Giuseppe Pisanelli, 00196 Rome, Italy
Venkataraman, Ramaswamy *President, India*
Pothigai, Greenways Road, Madras 600 028, India
Venora, Diane *Actress*
%Innovative Artists, 1505 10th St, Santa Monica, CA 90401, USA
Ventura, Robin M *Baseball Player*
106 Dingletown Road, Greenwich, CT 06830, USA
Venturi, Ken *Golfer*
161 Waterford Circle, Rancho Mirage, CA 92270, USA

V

Venturi - Vest

Venturi, Robert *Architect, Pritzker Laureate*
%Venturi Scott Brown Assoc, 4236 Main St, Philadelphia, PA 19127, USA
Vera, Billy *Singer, Songwriter, Actor*
%Agency for Performing Arts, 9200 Sunset Blvd, #900, Los Angeles, CA 90069, USA
Verba, Sidney *Political Scientist*
142 Summit Ave, Brookline, MA 02446, USA
Verbeek, Pat *Hockey Player*
789 Wallace St, Birmingham, MI 48009, USA
Verchota, Philip (Phil) *Hockey Player*
5852 County Road 9 NE, Willmar, MN 56201, USA
Verdan, Claude E *Surgeon*
%Museum of Human Hand, 21 Rue du Bugnon, 1005 Lausanne, Switzerland
Verdi, Bob *Sportswriter*
%Chicago Tribune, Editorial Dept, 435 N Michigan Ave, Chicago, IL 60611, USA
Verdugo, Elena *Actress*
PO Box 2048, Chula Vista, CA 91912, USA
Verdy, Violette *Ballerina*
2000 Broadway, #2B, New York, NY 10023, USA
Vereen, Ben *Actor, Dancer, Singer*
424 W End Ave, #18C, New York, NY 10024, USA
Verhoeven, Paul *Movie Director*
%Brenner & Glassberg, 2049 Century Park East, #950, Los Angeles, CA 90067, USA
Verhofstadt, Guy *Prime Minister, Belgium*
%Prime Minister's Office, 16 Rue de la Loi, 1000 Brussels, Belgium
Verica, Tom *Actor*
%I F A Talent Agency, 8730 Sunset Blvd, #490, Los Angeles, CA 90069, USA
Verity, C William, Jr *Secretary, Commerce*
PO Box 42220, Middletown, OH 45042, USA
Verkaik, Petra *Model, Actress*
PO Box 10134, Beverly Hills, CA 90213, USA
Verma, Inder M *Molecular Biologist*
%Salk Institute, 10100 N Torrey Pines Road, La Jolla, CA 92037, USA
Vermeij, Geerat J *Evolutionary Biologist, Paleontologist*
%University of California, Geology Dept, Davis, CA 95616, USA
Vermeil, Richard A (Dick) *Football Coach*
%Kansas City Chiefs, 1 Arrowhead Dr, Kansas City, KS 64129, USA
Vermes, Peter *Soccer Player*
%Kansas City Wizards, 2 Arrowhead Dr, Kansas City, MO 64129, USA
Vernier-Palliez, Bernard M A *Diplomat, France*
25 Grande Rue, 78170 La Celle Saint Cloud, France
Vernon, Glen *Actor*
12914 Valleyheart Dr, #2, Studio City, CA 91604, USA
Vernon, James B (Mickey) *Baseball Player*
100 E Rose Valley Road, Wallingford, PA 19086, USA
Vernon, John *Actor*
5751 Stansbury Ave, Van Nuys, CA 91401, USA
Vernon, Kate *Actress*
%Innovative Artists, 1505 10th St, Santa Monica, CA 90401, USA
Vernon, Mike *Hockey Player*
6781 NW 81st Court, Parkland, FL 33067, USA
Vernon, Richard *Actor*
%Julian Belfarge, 46 Albermarle St, London W1X 4PP, England
Veronis, John J *Publisher*
%Veronis Suhler Assoc, 350 Park Ave, New York, NY 10022, USA
Verplank, Scott *Golfer*
1800 Oak Forest Dr, Edmond, OK 73003, USA
Verrell, Cec *Actress*
%Michael Slessinger, 8730 Sunset Blvd, #220W, Los Angeles, CA 90069, USA
Verrett, Shirley *Opera Singer*
%International Management Group, 22 E 71st St, New York, NY 10021, USA
Versace, Dick *Basketball Coach*
%Memphis Grizzlies, 175 Toyota Plaza, #150, Memphis, TN 38103, USA
Versace, Donatella *Fashion Designer*
%Gianni Versace Spa, Via Della Spige 25, 20221 Milan, Italy
Verser, David *Football Player*
688 Riddle Road, #200, Cincinnati, OH 45220, USA
Vesser, Dale A *Army General*
1313 Merchant Lane, McLean, VA 22101, USA
Vessey, John W, Jr *Army General*
27650 Little Whitefish Road, Garrison, MN 56450, USA
Vessey, Tricia *Actress*
%United Talent Agency, 9560 Wilshire Blvd, #500, Beverly Hills, CA 90212, USA
Vest, Charles M *Educator*
%Massachusetts Institute of Technology, President's Office, Cambridge, MA 02138, USA
Vest, George S *Diplomat*
5307 Iroquois Road, Bethesda, MD 20816, USA
Vest, Jake *Cartoonist (That's Jake)*
PO Box 350757, Grand Island, FL 32735, USA

Vest, R Lamar *Religious Leader*
%Church of God, PO Box 2430, Cleveland, TN 37320, USA

Vetri, Victoria *Actress*
7045 Hawthorn Ave, #206, Los Angeles, CA 90028, USA

Vetrov, Aleksandr *Ballet Dancer*
%Bolshoi Theater, Teatralnaya Pl 1, 103009 Moscow, Russia

Vettori, Ernst *Ski Jumper*
Fohrenweg 1, 6060 Absam-Eichat, Austria

Vettrus, Richard J *Religious Leader*
%Church of Lutheran Brethren, 707 Crestview Dr, West Union, IA 52175, USA

Viardo, Vladimir V *Concert Pianist*
457 Piedmont Road, Cresskill, NJ 07626, USA

Vick, Michael *Football Player*
%Atlanta Falcons, 4400 Falcon Parkway, Flowery Branch, GA 30542, USA

Vickers, Brian *Auto Racing Driver*
27 High Tech Blvd, Thomasville, NC 27360, USA

Vickers, Jonathan S (Jon) *Opera Singer*
Collingtree, 18 Riddells Bay Road, Warwick WK 04, Bermuda

Vickers, Steve *Hockey Player*
209 Washington Ave, Batavia, NY 14020, USA

Victoria *Crown Princess, Sweden*
%Royal Palace, Kung Slottet, Stottsbacken, 111 30 Stockholm, Sweden

Victorin (Ursache), Archbishop *Religious Leader*
%Romanian Orthodox Church, 19959 Riopelle St, Detroit, MI 48203, USA

Vidal, Deborah *Golfer*
%Tony Criscuolo, 8425 NW 222nd Ave, Alachua, FL 32615, USA

Vidal, Gore *Writer*
Via Fusco 20, 84010 Ravello/SA, Italy

Vidal, Jean-Pierre *Alpine Skier*
%Ski Federation, 50 Rue de Marquisats, BP 51, 74011 Annecy Cedex, France

Vidal, Ricardo J Cardinal *Religious Leader*
Chancery, PO Box 52, Cebu City 6401, Philippines

Vidali, Lynn *Swimmer*
14750 Mosegard, Morgan Hill, CA 95037, USA

Vidmar, Peter *Gymnast*
23832 Via Roble, Coto De Caza, CA 92679, USA

Vidro, Jose A C *Baseball Player*
%Montreal Expos, Olympic Stadium, Montreal QC H1V 3N7, Canada

Vie, Richard C *Businessman*
PO Box 191, Lake Forest, IL 60045, USA

Viehboeck, Franz *Cosmonaut, Austria*
Brunnerbergstr 3021, 2380 Perchtoldsdorf, Austria

Vieillard, Roger *Artist*
7 Rue de l'Estrapade, 75005 Paris, France

Vieira, Meredith *Commentator*
%ABC-TV, News Dept, 77 W 66th St, New York, NY 10023, USA

Viereck, Peter *Writer*
12 Silver St, South Hadley, MA 01075, USA

Vig, Butch *Drummer (Garbage)*
%Borman Entertainment, 1250 6th St, #401, Santa Monica, CA 90401, USA

Vigil, Selene *Singer (Seven Year Bitch)*
%Rave Booking, PO Box 310780, Jamaica, NY 11431, USA

Vigneault, Alain *Hockey Player, Coach*
%Saint Louis Blues, Sawis Center, 1401 Clark Ave, Saint Louis, MO 63103, USA

Vigneron, Thierry *Track Athlete*
%Adidas USA, 5675 N Blackstock Road, Spartanburg, SC 29303, USA

Vigoda, Abe *Actor*
%Craig Mgmt, 125 S Sycamore Ave, Los Angeles, CA 90036, USA

Viguerie, Richard A *Publisher*
%Viguerie Co, 7777 Leesburg Pike, Falls Church, VA 22043, USA

Vike-Freibrga, Vaira *President, Latvia*
%President's Office, Supreme Council, 11 Jeraba St, Riga 22681 DDP, Latvia

Viktorenko, Aleksandr S *Cosmonaut*
%Potchta Kosmonavtov, Moskovskoi Oblasti, 141160 Syvisdny Goroduk, Russia

Vila, Bob *Entertainer, Writer*
115 Kingston St, #300, Boston, MA 02111, USA

Vilanch, Bruce *Actor, Comedian, Writer*
%William Morris Agency, 151 El Camino Dr, Beverly Hills, CA 90212, USA

Vilar, Tracy *Actress*
%Abrams Artists, 9200 Sunset Blvd, #1125, Los Angeles, CA 90069, USA

Vilas, Guillermo *Tennis Player*
%Guy Cromwell Betz, Pembroke One Building, #525, Virginia Beach, VA 23462, USA

Vilenkin, Alex *Physicist, Astronomer*
%Tufts University, Physics & Astronomy Dept, Medford, MA 02155, USA

Viljoen, Marais *President, South Africa*
PO Box 5555, Pretoria 0001, South Africa

Villapiano, Phillip J (Phil) *Football Player*
21 Riverside Dr, Rumson, NJ 07760, USA

Villarroel, Vernoica *Opera Singer*
%Columbia Artists Mgmt Inc, 165 W 57th St, New York, NY 10019, USA
Villella, Edward J *Ballet Dancer, Choreographer*
%Miami City Ballet, 2200 Liberty Ave, Miami Beach, FL 33139, USA
Villeneuve, Jacques *Auto Racing Driver*
%BAR Team, PO Box 5014, Brackley, Northants NN13 7YY, England
Villiers, Christopher *Actor*
%Michael Whitehall, 125 Gloucester Road, London SW7 4TE, England
Villiers, James *Actor*
%International Creative Mgmt, 76 Oxford St, London W1N 0AX, England
Vimond, Paul M *Architect*
91 Ave Niel, 75017 Paris, France
Vinatieri, Adam *Football Player*
PO Box 2779, Attleboro Falls, MA 02763, USA
Vince, Pruitt Taylor *Actor*
520 Salerno Dr, Pacific Palisades, CA 90272, USA
Vincent, Amy *Cinematographer*
5932 Graciosa Dr, Los Angeles, CA 90068, USA
Vincent, Jan-Michael *Actor*
%Artists Group, 10100 Santa Monica Blvd, #2490, Los Angeles, CA 90067, USA
Vincent, Jay *Basketball Player*
PO Box 27459, Lansing, MI 48909, USA
Vincent, Rhonda *Singer*
%Keith Case Assoc, 1025 17th Ave S, #200, Nashville, TN 37212, USA
Vincent, Richard F *Army Field Marshal, England*
%House of Lords, Westminster, London SW1A 0PW, England
Vincent, Sam *Basketball Player*
PO Box 27459, Lansing, MI 48909, USA
Vincent, Troy *Football Player*
460 Roeloffs Road, Yardley, PA 19067, USA
Vincent, Virginia *Actress*
1001 Hammond St, Los Angeles, CA 90069, USA
Vincz, Melanie *Actress*
2212 Earle Court, Redondo Beach, CA 90278, USA
Vines, C Jerry *Religious Leader*
%First Baptist Church, 124 W Ashley St, Jacksonville, FL 32202, USA
Vining, David *Gastroenterologist*
1725 Briar Lake Road, Winston Salem, NC 27103, USA
Vinnie *Rap Artist (Naughty By Nature)*
%International Creative Mgmt, 8942 Wilshire Blvd, #219, Beverly Hills, CA 90211, USA
Vinogradov, Oleg M *Ballet Director*
%Mariinsky Theater, Teatralnaya Square 1, 190000 Saint Petersburg, Russia
Vinogradov, Pavel V *Cosmonaut*
%Potchta Kosmonavtov, Moskovskoi Oblasti, 141160 Syvisdny Goroduk, Russia
Vinoly, Rafael *Architect*
1016 5th Ave, New York, NY 10028, USA
Vinson, James S *Educator*
%University of Evansville, President's Office, Evansville, IN 47722, USA
Vint, Jesse Lee, III *Actor*
%Film Artists, 13563 1/2 Ventura Blvd, #200, Sherman Oaks, CA 91423, USA
Vinton, Bobby *Singer*
%MPI Talent Agency, 9255 Sunset Blvd, #804, Los Angeles, CA 90069, USA
Vinton, Will *Animator*
%William Morris Agency, 151 El Camino Dr, Beverly Hills, CA 90212, USA
Viola, Bill *Sculptor, Video Artist*
282 Granada Ave, Long Beach, CA 90803, USA
Viola, Frank J, Jr *Baseball Player*
9868 Kilgore Road, Orlando, FL 32836, USA
Viola, Lisa *Dancer*
%Paul Taylor Dance Co, 552 Broadway, New York, NY 10012, USA
Virata, Cesar E *Prime Minister, Philippines*
63 E Maya Dr, Quezon City, Philippines
Virdon, William C (Bill) *Baseball Player, Manager*
1311 E River Road, Springfield, MO 65804, USA
Viren, Lasse *Track Athlete*
Suomen Urheilulitto Ry, Box 25202, 00250 Helsinki 25, Finland
Virts, Terry W, Jr *Astronaut*
1904 Edgewater Court, Friendswood, TX 77546, USA
Virtue, Frank *Guitarist*
8309 Rising Sun Ave, Philadelphia, PA 19111, USA
Virzaladze, Elizo K *Concert Pianist*
%Moscow Conservatory, Bolshaya Nikitskaya Str 13, Moscow, Russia
Vis, Anthony *Religious Leader*
%Reformed Church in America, 475 Riverside Dr, New York, NY 10115, USA
Viscardi Johnston, Catherine *Publisher*
%Mirabella Magazine, 200 Madison Ave, New York, NY 10016, USA
Viscuso, Sal *Actor*
6491 Ivarene Ave, Los Angeles, CA 90068, USA

V

Vise - Voight

Vise, David A *Journalist*
%Washington Post, Editorial Dept, 1150 15th St NW, Washington, DC 20071, USA
Vishnevskaya, Galina P *Opera Singer*
Gazetny Per 13, #79, 103009 Moscow, Russia
Vishnyova, Diana V *Ballerina*
%Mariinsky Theater, Teatralnaya Square 1, 190000 Saint Petersburg, Russia
Visitor, Nana *Actress*
%Gersh Agency, 232 N Canon Dr, Beverly Hills, CA 90210, USA
Visnjic, Goran *Actor*
%United Talent Agency, 9560 Wilshire Blvd, #500, Beverly Hills, CA 90212, USA
Viso, Michel *Spatinaut, France*
7 Domaine Chateau-Gaillard, 94700 Maisons-d'Alfort, France
Visscher, Maurice B *Physiologist*
120 Melbourne Ave SE, Minneapolis, MN 55414, USA
Visser, Lesley *Sportscaster*
%CBS-TV, Sports Dept, 51 W 52nd St, New York, NY 10019, USA
Vitale, Carol *Actress, Model*
1516 S Bundy Dr, #309, Los Angeles, CA 90025, USA
Vitale, Dick *Sportscaster, Basketball Coach*
%ESPN-TV, Sports Dept, ESPN Plaza, 935 Middle St, Bristol, CT 06010, USA
Vitamin C *Singer, Actress*
%International Creative Mgmt, 8942 Wilshire Blvd, #219, Beverly Hills, CA 90211, USA
Viterbi, Andrew J *Electrical Engineer, Computer Scientist*
%QUALCOMM Inc, 5775 Morehouse Dr, San Diego, CA 92121, USA
Vitez, Michael *Journalist*
%Philadelphia Inquirer, Editorial Dept, 400 N Broad St, Philadelphia, PA 19130, USA
Vithayathil, Varkey Cardinal *Religious Leader*
Syro-Malabar Archiepiscopal Curia, Bharath Matha College, Kerala, India
Vitolo, Dennis *Auto Racing Driver*
2130 Intracoastal Dr, Fort Lauderdale, FL 33305, USA
Vitousek, Peter M *Botanist, Ecologist*
%Stanford University, Biological Science Dept, Stanford, CT 94305, USA
Vittadini, Adrienne *Fashion Designer*
%Adrienne Vittadini Inc, 575 Fashion Ave, New York, NY 10018, USA
Vitti, Monica *Actress*
%IPC, Via F Siacci 38, 00197 Rome, Italy
Vittori, Roberto *Astronaut*
%Europe Astronaut Center, Linder Hole, Box 906096, 51127 Cologne, Germany
Vitukhnovskaya, Alina A *Writer*
Leningradskoye Shosse 80, #89, 125565 Moscow, Russia
Viviano, Joseph P *Businessman*
%Hershey Foods Corp, 100 Crystal A Dr, Hershey, PA 17033, USA
Vizquel, Omar E *Baseball Player*
Blvd Del Cafetel, Res Adroana 6 Pisa, Caracas, Venezuela
Vlacil, Frantisek *Movie Director*
Cinska 5, 160 00 Prague 6, Czech Republic
Vladeck, Judith P *Attorney*
%Vladeck Waldman Elias Engelhard, 1501 Broadway, New York, NY 10036, USA
Vlady, Marina *Actress*
10 Ave de Marivaux, 78800 Mission Lafitte, France
Vlk, Miloslav Cardinal *Religious Leader*
Arcibiskupstvi, Hradcanske Nam 16/56, 119 02 Prague 1, Czech Republic
Vo Nguyen Giap *Army General, Vietnam*
Dang Cong San Vietnam, 1C Blvd Hoang Van Thu, Hanoi, Vietnam
Vo Van Kiet *Prime Minister, Vietnam*
%Prime Minister's Office, Hoang Hoa Thum, Hanoi, Vietnam
Voevodsky, Vladimir *Mathematician*
22 Earle Lane, Princeton, NJ 08540, USA
Vogel, Darlene *Actress*
%Michael Slessinger, 8730 Sunset Blvd, #220W, Los Angeles, CA 90069, USA
Vogel, Hans-Jochen *Government Official, West Germany*
Stresemanstr 6, 53123 Bonn-Bad Godesberg, Germany
Vogel, Mark *Composer*
%Gorfaine/Schwartz, 13245 Riverside Dr, #450, Sherman Oaks, CA 91423, USA
Vogel, Mitch *Actor*
3335 Honeysuckle Ave, Palmdale, CA 93550, USA
Vogelstein, Bert *Geneticist, Oncologist*
%Johns Hopkins University, Medical School, Oncology Center, Baltimore, MD 21218, USA
Vogt, Lars *Concert Pianist*
%I C M Artists, 40 W 57th St, New York, NY 10019, USA
Vogt, Peter K *Virologist*
%LA County/USC Medical School, 2011 Zonal Ave, Los Angeles, CA 90089, USA
Vogt, Rochus E *Physicist, Astronomer*
%California Institute of Technology, Bridge Laboratory, Pasadena, CA 91125, USA
Vogts, Hans-Hubert (Berti) *Soccer Player*
Mozartweg 2, 41352 Korschenbroich, Germany
Voight, Jon *Actor*
9660 Oak Pass Road, Beverly Hills, CA 90210, USA

Voigt, Cynthia *Writer*
%Atheneum Publishers, 866 3rd Ave, New York, NY 10022, USA

Voigt, Deborah *Opera Singer*
%Columbia Artists Mgmt Inc, 165 W 57th St, New York, NY 10019, USA

Voinovich, George V *Governor, Senator, OH*
601 Lakeside Ave E, Cleveland, OH 44114, USA

Voiselle, William S (Bill) *Baseball Player*
105 Lowell St, Ninety Six, SC 29666, USA

Volberding, Paul *Cancer Researcher*
%General Hospital AIDS Activities Dept, 995 Potrero Ave, San Francisco, CA 94110, USA

Volcker, Paul A *Government Official*
151 E 79th St, New York, NY 10021, USA

Voldstad, John *Actor*
24812 Van Owen St, West Hills, CA 91300, USA

Volk, Igor P *Cosmonaut*
%Potchta Kosmonavtov, Moskovskoi Oblasti, 141160 Syvisdny Goroduk, Russia

Volk, Patricia *Writer*
%Gloria Loomis, 133 E 35th St, New York, NY 10016, USA

Volk, Phil *Guitarist (Paul Revere & the Raiders)*
%Paradise Artists, 108 E Matilija St, Ojai, CA 93023, USA

Volk, Richard R (Rick) *Football Player*
13605 Bardon Road, Phoenix, MD 21131, USA

Volker, Sandra *Swimmer*
%DESG, Mensingen Str 68, 80992 Munich, Germany

Volkert, Stephan *Rowing Athlete*
Semmelweisstr 42, 51061 Cologne, Germany

Volkmann, Elisabeth *Opera Singer*
Sonnenstr 20, 80331 Munich, Germany

Volkov, Aleksandr A *Cosmonaut*
%Potchta Kosmonavtov, Moskovskoi Oblasti, 141160 Syvisdny Goroduk, Russia

Vollbracht, Michaele *Fashion Designer, Artist*
%General Delivery, Safety Harbor, FL 34695, USA

Vollebak, Knut *Government Official, Norway*
%Royal Norwegian Embassy, 2720 34th St NW, Washington, DC 20008, USA

Vollenweider, Andreas *Concert Harpist*
Sempacher Str 16, 8032 Zurich, Switzerland

Volodos, Arcadi *Concert Pianist*
%Columbia Artists Mgmt Inc, 165 W 57th St, New York, NY 10019, USA

Volpe, Joseph (Joe) *Opera Executive*
%Metropolitan Opera Assn, Lincoln Center Plaza, New York, NY 10023, USA

Volynov, Boris V *Cosmonaut*
%Potchta Kosmonavtov, Moskovskoi Oblasti, 141160 Syvisdny Goroduk, Russia

VonAroldingen, Karin *Ballerina*
%New York City Ballet, Lincoln Center Plaza, New York, NY 10023, USA

VonBulow, Vicco (Loriot) *Actor*
Hohenweg 19, 82451 Munsing-Ammerland, Germany

VonDerHeyden, Karl I M *Businessman*
%PepsiCo Inc, 700 Anderson Hill Road, Purchase, NY 10577, USA

VonDetten, Erik *Actor*
%William Morris Agency, 151 El Camino Dr, Beverly Hills, CA 90212, USA

VonDohnanyi, Christoph *Conductor*
%Cleveland Orchestra, Severance Hall, Cleveland, OH 44106, USA

VonErich, Waldo *Wrestler*
%Columbia Sports Med Center, 9-145 Columbia W, Waterloo ON N2L 3L2, Canada

VonEschenbach, Andrew *Surgeon, Medical Administrator*
%National Cancer Institute, 9000 Rockville Pike, Bethesda, MD 20892, USA

VonFurstenberg, Betsy *Actress*
230 Central Park West, New York, NY 10024, USA

VonFurstenberg, Diane *Fashion Designer*
389 W 12th St, New York, NY 10014, USA

VonFurstenberg, Egon *Fashion Designer*
50 E 72nd St, New York, NY 10021, USA

VonGarnier, Katja *Movie Director*
%Creative Artists Agency, 9830 Wilshire Blvd, Beverly Hills, CA 90212, USA

VonGerkan, Manon *Model*
%Shamballa Jewels, 92 Thompson St, New York, NY 10012, USA

VonGerkan, Meinhard *Architect*
Elbchaussee 139, 22763 Hamburg, Germany

VonGrunigen, Michael *Alpine Skier*
Chalet Sunneblick, 3778 Schonried, Switzerland

VonHabsburg-Lothringem, Otto *Government Official, Germany*
Hindenburgstr 14, 82343 Pocking, Germany

VonHippel, Peter H *Chemist*
1900 Crest Dr, Eugene, OR 97405, USA

Vonk, Hans *Conductor*
%Intermusic Artists, 16 Duncan Terrace, London N1 8BZ, England

VonKlitzing, Klaus *Nobel Physics Laureate*
%Max Planck Institute, Heisenbergstr 1, 70569 Stuttgart, Germany

VonMehren, Arthur T *Attorney, Educator*
68 Sparks St, Cambridge, MA 02138, USA
VonMehren, Arthur T *Attorney*
925 Park Ave, New York, NY 10028, USA
Vonnegut, Kurt, Jr *Writer*
%Washington Square/Simon & Schuster, 1230 Ave of Americas, New York, NY 10020, USA
VonOtter, Anne Sofie *Opera Singer*
%I C M Artists, 40 W 57th St, New York, NY 10019, USA
VonOy, Jenna *Actress*
19 Saddle Ridge Road, Newtown, CT 06470, USA
VonPierer, Heinrich *Businessman*
%Siemens AG, Wittelsbacherplatz 2, 80333 Munich, Germany
VonQuast, Veronika *Actress*
%ZBF Agentur, Leopoldstr 19, 80802 Munich, Germany
VonRunkle, Theodora *Costume Designer*
8805 Lookout Mountain Road, Los Angeles, CA 90046, USA
VonSaltza Olmstead, S Christine (Chris) *Swimmer*
7060 Fairway Place, Carmel, CA 93923, USA
VonStade, Frederica *Opera Singer*
1200 San Antonio Ave, Alameda, CA 94501, USA
VonStraaten, Frans *Sculptor*
Samuel Muller Plein 17C, 3023 Rotterdam, Denmark
VonSydow, Max *Actor*
%Risberg, PO Box 5209, 102 45 Stockholm, Sweden
VonTrotta, Margarethe *Movie Director*
%Bioskop-Film, Turkenstr 91, 80799 Munich, Germany
VonWeizsacker, Carl Friedrich *Philosopher*
Aplenstr 15, 82319 Socking, Germany
VonWeizsacker, Richard *President, Germany*
Meisenstr 6, 14195 Berlin, Germany
Voog, Ana *Singer/Songwriter*
%MCA Records, 1755 Broadway, New York, NY 10019, USA
Voorhees, John J *Dermatologist*
3965 Waldenwood Dr, Ann Arbor, MI 48105, USA
Voorhies, Lark *Actress*
10635 Santa Monica Blvd, #130, Los Angeles, CA 90025, USA
Vorgan, Gigi *Actress*
3637 Stone Canyon, Sherman Oaks, CA 91403, USA
Voris, Roy M (Butch) *Navy Aviator (Blue Angels), Hero*
14 Greenwood Way, Monterey, CA 93940, USA
Voronin, Vladimir *President, Moldova*
%President's Office, 23 Nicolae lorge Str, 277033 Chishinev, Moldova
Vosloo, Arnold *Actor*
804 E 16th St, Los Angeles, CA 90021, USA
Voss, Brian *Bowler*
340 Banyon Brook Point, Roswell, GA 30076, USA
Voss, James S *Astronaut*
4207 Indian Sunrise Court, Houston, TX 77059, USA
Voss, Janice E *Astronaut*
14803 Flowerwood Dr, Houston, TX 77062, USA
VosSavant, Marilyn *Writer*
%Parade Publications, 711 3rd Ave, New York, NY 10017, USA
Votaw, Ty *Golf Executive*
%Ladies Pro Golf Assn, 100 International Golf Dr, Daytona Beach, FL 32124, USA
Voznesensky, Andrei A *Writer*
Kotelnicheskaya Nab 1/15, Bl W, #62, 109240 Moscow, Russia
Vraa, Sanna *Model, Actress*
%Irv Schechter, 9300 Wilshire Blvd, #410, Beverly Hills, CA 90212, USA
Vraciu, Alexander (Alex) *WW II Navy Air Force Hero*
309 Merrille Place, Danville, CA 94526, USA
Vranes, Danny *Basketball Player*
7105 Highland Dr, Salt Lake City, UT 84121, USA
Vuarnet, Jean *Alpine Skier*
Chalet Squaw Peak, 74110 Auoriaz, France
Vuckovich, Peter D (Pete) *Baseball Player*
309 Keiper Lane, Johnstown, PA 15909, USA
Vuitton, Henri-Louis *Fashion Designer*
78 Bis Ave Marceau, 75000 Paris, France
Vujtek, Vladimir *Hockey Player*
%Pittsburgh Penguins, Mellon Arena, 66 Mario Lemieux Place, Pittsburgh, PA 15219, USA
Vuono, Carl E *Army General*
5796 Westchester St, Alexandria, VA 22310, USA
Vyent, Louise *Model*
%Pauline's Talent Corp, 379 W Broadway, #502, New York, NY 10012, USA

W

Waakataar, Paar *Singer, Guitarist (A-Ha)*
%Banada Mgmt, 11 Elvaston Place, #300, London SW7 5QC, England
Wachtel, Christine *Track Athlete*
Helmut-Just-Str 5, 17036 Neubrandenburg, Germany
Wachter, Anita *Alpine Skier*
Gantschierstr 579, 6780 Schruns, Austria
Waddell, John Henry *Artist*
Star Route 2273, Oak Creek Village Road, Cornville, AZ 86325, USA
Waddell, Justine *Actress*
%International Creative Mgmt, 8942 Wilshire Blvd, #219, Beverly Hills, CA 90211, USA
Waddington of Read, David *Governor General, Bermuda*
Stable House, Sabden, Clitheroe, Lanc BB7 9HP, England
Waddington, Steven *Actor*
%Kerry Gardner, 15 Kensington High St, London W8 5NP, England
Wade, Abdoulaye *President, Senegal*
%President's Office, Ave Roume, BPI 168, Dakar, Senegal
Wade, Adam *Singer*
118 E 25th St, #600, New York, NY 10010, USA
Wade, Dwyane *Basketball Player*
%Miami Heat, American Airlines Arena, 601 Biscayne Blvd, Miami, FL 33132, USA
Wade, Jason *Singer, Guitarist (Lifehouse)*
%DreamWorks Records, 9268 W 3rd St, Beverly Hills, CA 90210, USA
Wade, S Virginia *Tennis Player*
Sharstead Court, Sittingbourne, Kent, England
Wade, William J (Bill), Jr *Football Player*
PO Box 210124, Nashville, TN 37221, USA
Wadhams, Wayne *Singer, Keyboardist (Fifth Estate)*
73 Hemenway, Boston, MA 02115, USA
Wadkins, Bobby *Golfer*
5815 Harbour Hill Place, Midlothian, VA 23112, USA
Wadkins, Lanny *Golfer*
6002 Kettering Court, Dallas, TX 75248, USA
Wadsworth, Charles W *Concert Pianist*
PO Box 157, Charleston, SC 29402, USA
Waelsch, Salome G *Geneticist*
90 Morningside Dr, New York, NY 10027, USA
Wages, Robert E *Labor Leader*
%Oil Chemical Atomic Workers International Union, PO Box 2812, Denver, CO 80201, USA
Wages, William *Cinematographer*
%Innovative Artists, 1505 10th St, Santa Monica, CA 90401, USA
Waggoner, Lyle *Actor*
1124 Oak Mirage Place, Westlake Village, CA 91362, USA
Waggoner, Paul E *Agronomist*
314 Vineyard Point Road, Guilford, CT 06437, USA
Wagner, Bruce *Writer*
%United Talent Agency, 9560 Wilshire Blvd, #500, Beverly Hills, CA 90212, USA
Wagner, Chuck *Actor, Singer*
1200 Maldonado Dr, Pensacola Beach, FL 32561, USA
Wagner, Dajuan *Basketball Player*
%Cleveland Cavaliers, Gund Arena, 1 Center Court, Cleveland, OH 44115, USA
Wagner, Fred *Cartoonist (Grin & Bear It)*
%North American Syndicate, 235 E 45th St, New York, NY 10017, USA
Wagner, Jack *Actor, Singer*
314 Waverly Place Court, Chesterfield, MO 63017, USA
Wagner, John *Cartoonist (Maxine)*
%Hallmark Cards, Shoebox Division, 101 McDonald Dr, Lawrence, KS 66044, USA
Wagner, Lindsay *Actress*
%Bartels Co, PO Box 57593, Sherman Oaks, CA 91413, USA
Wagner, Lou *Actor*
21224 Celtic St, Chatsworth, CA 91311, USA
Wagner, Louis C, Jr *Army General*
6309 Chaucer Lane, Alexandria, VA 22304, USA
Wagner, Matt *Cartoonist*
%DC Comics, 1700 Broadway, New York, NY 10019, USA
Wagner, Melinda *Composer*
%Theodore Presser, 588 N Gulph Road, King of Prussia, PA 19406, USA
Wagner, Michael R (Mike) *Football Player*
%McCandless, 800 Wyngold Dr, Pittsburgh, PA 15237, USA
Wagner, Philip M *Columnist*
32 Montgomery St, Boston, MA 02116, USA
Wagner, Robert *Actor*
1485 Lindacrest Dr, Beverly Hills, CA 90210, USA
Wagner, Robert T *Educator*
24497 N Playhouse Road, Keystone, SD 57751, USA
Wagner, Robin S A *Stage, Set Designer*
%Robin Wagner Studio, 890 Broadway, New York, NY 10003, USA
Wagner, William E (Billy) *Baseball Player*
2607 Iris Court, Pearland, TX 77584, USA

W

Wagner, Wolfgang M M *Opera Director*
%Bayreuth Festival, Postfach 100262, 95402 Bayreuth, Germany
Wagoner, Dan *Dancer, Choreographer*
%Contemporary Dance Theater, 17 Duke's Road, London WC1H 9AB, England
Wagoner, David R *Writer*
5416 154th Place SW, Edmonds, WA 98026, USA
Wagoner, G Richard *Businessman*
%General Motors Corp, 100 Renaissance Center, Detroit, MI 48243, USA
Wagoner, Harold E *Architect*
331 Lindsey Dr, Berwyn, PA 19312, USA
Wagoner, Porter *Singer, Songwriter*
%Porter Wagoner Enterprises, PO Box 290785, Nashville, TN 37229, USA
Wahl, Ken *Actor*
%William Morris Agency, 151 El Camino Dr, Beverly Hills, CA 90212, USA
Wahlberg, Donnie *Singer, Actor*
6441 Langdon Ave, Van Nuys, CA 91406, USA
Wahlberg, Mark *Singer, Actor, Model*
%Leverage Mgmt, 3030 Pennsylvania Ave, Santa Monica, CA 90404, USA
Wahlen, George E *WW II Navy Hero (CMH)*
3437 W 5700 South, Roy, UT 84067, USA
Wahlgren, Olof G C *Editor*
Nicoloviusgatan 5B, 217 57 Malmo, Sweden
Wahlstrom, Jarl H *Religious Leader*
Borgstrominkuja 1A10, 00840 Helsinki 84, Finland
Waigel, Theodor *Government Official, Germany*
Oberrohr, 86513 Ursberg, Germany
Waihee, John D, III *Governor, HI*
745 Fort Street Mall, #600, Honolulu, HI 96813, USA
Wain, Bea *Singer*
9955 Durant Dr, #305, Beverly Hills, CA 90212, USA
Wainwright, James *Actor*
7060 Hollywood Blvd, #610, Los Angeles, CA 90028, USA
Wainwright, Loudon, III *Singer, Songwriter*
%Teddy Wainwright, 521 SW Halpatiokee St, Stuart, FL 34994, USA
Wainwright, Rufus *Singer, Songwriter*
%Primary Talent, 2-12 Petonville Road, London N1 9PL, England
Waite, John *Singer, Songwriter*
%Rascoff/Zysblat, 110 W 57th St, #300, New York, NY 10019, USA
Waite, Ralph *Actor*
73317 Ironwood St, Palm Desert, CA 92260, USA
Waite, Terence H (Terry) *Religious Leader*
Wheelrights, Green Harvest, Bury Saint Edmunds, Suffolk IP29 4DH, England
Waits, Tom *Singer, Songwriter, Pianist*
%Mitch Schneider Organization, 14724 Ventura Blvd, #410, Sherman Oaks, CA 91403, USA
Waitt, Theodore W (Ted) *Businessman*
%Gateway Inc, 4545 Towne Centre Court, PO Box 2000, San Diego, CA 92121, USA
Waitz, Grete *Track Athlete*
Birgitte Hammers Vei 15G, 1169 Oslo, Norway
Waitz, Richard H *Cinematographer*
405 Zenith Ave, Lafayette, CO 80026, USA
Wajda, Andrzej *Movie Director*
Ul Konopnickiej 26, 30-302 Cracow, Poland
Wakasugi, Hiroshi *Conductor*
%Astrid Schoerke, Monckebergallee 41, 30453 Hanover, Germany
Wakata, Koichi *Astronaut, Japan*
%NASA, Johnson Space Center, 2101 NASA Road, Houston, TX 77058, USA
Wakeham of Maldon, John *Government Official, England*
%House of Lords, Westminster, London SW1A 0PW, England
Wakeley, Amanda *Fashion Designer*
79-91 New Kings Road, London SW6 4SQ, England
Wakeman, Frederic E, Jr *Historian*
702 Gonzalez Dr, San Francisco, CA 94132, USA
Wakeman, Rick *Keyboardist, Songwriter*
Bajonor House, 2 Bridge St, Peel, Isle of Man, United Kingdom
Wako, Gabriel Zubeir Cardinal *Religious Leader*
%Archdiocese, PO Box 49, Khartoum, Sudan
Wakoski, Diane *Writer*
607 Division St, East Lansing, MI 48823, USA
Waks, Aisha *Actress*
%Writers & Artists, 8383 Wilshire Blvd, #550, Beverly Hills, CA 90211, USA
Walcott, Derek A *Nobel Literature Laureate*
71 Saint Mary's Court, Brookline, MA 02446, USA
Walcott, Gregory *Actor*
22246 Saticoy St, Canoga Park, CA 91303, USA
Wald, Charles F *Air Force General*
Deputy CofS for Air/Space Operations, HqUSAF, Pentagon, Washington, DC 20330, USA
Wald, Patricia M *Judge*
%US Court of Appeals, 3rd & Constitution NW, Washington, DC 20001, USA

W

Waldegrave, William *Government Official, England*
66 Palace Gardens Terrace, London W8 4RR, England
Walden, Lynette *Actress*
%Metropolitan Talent Agency, 4526 Wilshire Blvd, Los Angeles, CA 90010, USA
Walden, Robert *Actor*
1450 Arroyo View Dr, Pasadena, CA 91103, USA
Walden, Robert E (Bobby) *Football Player*
1403 E Douglas Dr, Bainbridge, GA 39819, USA
Waldheim, Kurt *President, Austria; Sec-Gen, UN*
1 Lobkowitz Platz, 1010 Vienna, Austria
Waldhorn, Gary *Actor*
%London Mgmt, 2-4 Noel St, London W1V 3RB, England
Waldie, Marc *Volleyball Player*
13290 Ocean Vista Road, San Diego, CA 92130, USA
Waldman, Myron *Cartoonist (Casper the Friendly Ghost)*
3660 Lufberry Ave, Wantagh, NY 11793, USA
Waldner, Jan-Ove *Table Tennis Athlete*
%Banda, Skjulstagatan 1O, 632 29 Eskilstuna, Sweden
Waldorf, Duffy *Golfer*
%International Golf Partners, 3300 PGA Blvd, #820, West Palm Beach, FL 33410, USA
Waldron, Jeremy J *Educator*
1061 Keith Ave, Berkeley, CA 94708, USA
Wales, Ross *Swimmer*
2730 Walsh Road, Cincinnati, OH 45208, USA
Walesa, Lech *Nobel Peace Laureate; President, Poland*
Ul Polanki 54, 80-308 Gdansk-Oliwa, Poland
Walheim, Rex J *Astronaut*
142 Hidden Lake Dr, League City, TX 77573, USA
Walken, Christopher *Actor*
%International Creative Mgmt, 40 W 57th St, #1800, New York, NY 10019, USA
Walker of Worchester, Peter E *Government Official, England*
Abbots Morton Manor, Grooms Hill, Abbots Morton, Worc WR7 4LT, England
Walker, Alan *Anthropologist*
%Johns Hopkins, Medical School, Cell Biology/Anatomy Dept, Baltimore, MD 21205, USA
Walker, Alice M *Social Activist, Writer*
670 San Luis Road, Berkeley, CA 94707, USA
Walker, Ally *Actress*
%More/Medavoy, 7920 W Sunset Blvd, #400, Los Angeles, CA 90046, USA
Walker, Antoine *Basketball Player*
%Dallas Mavericks, 2909 Taylor St, Dallas, TX 75226, USA
Walker, Arnetia *Actress*
19551 Turtle Ridge Lane, Northridge, CA 91326, USA
Walker, B J *Financier*
%First Union Corp, 1 First Union Center, Charlotte, NC 28288, USA
Walker, Billy *Singer*
PO Box 618, Hendersonville, TN 37077, USA
Walker, Brian *Cartoonist (Hi & Lois)*
%King Features Syndicate, 888 7th Ave, New York, NY 10106, USA
Walker, Butch *Singer, Guitarist (Marvelous 3)*
%Progressive Global Agency, 103 W Tyne Dr, Nashville, TN 37205, USA
Walker, Catherine *Fashion Designer*
65 Sydney St, Chelsea, London SW3 6PX, England
Walker, Charles D *Astronaut*
%Boeing Co, 1200 Wilson Blvd, MC RS00, Arlington, VA 22209, USA
Walker, Charlie *Singer*
%Tessier-Marsh Talent, 2825 Blue Book Dr, Nashville, TN 37214, USA
Walker, Charls E *Economist*
10120 Chapel Road, Potomac, MD 20854, USA
Walker, Chet *Basketball Player*
124 Fleet St, Marina del Rey, CA 90292, USA
Walker, Chris *Actor*
%Rolf Kruger, 121 Gloucester Place, London W1H 3PJ, England
Walker, Clay *Singer*
%TBA Ent, 300 10th Ave S, Nashville, TN 37203, USA
Walker, Clint *Actor*
10175 Joerschke Dr, #1, Grass Valley, CA 95945, USA
Walker, Colleen *Golfer*
%Players Group, 5 Cathy Place, Menlo Park, CA 94025, USA
Walker, Darrell *Basketball Player, Coach*
16122 Patriot Dr, Little Rock, AR 72212, USA
Walker, David *Government Official*
%General Accounting Office, 441 G St NW, Washington, DC 20548, USA
Walker, Derek *Architect*
2 General Sage Dr, Santa Fe, NM 87505, USA
Walker, Derrick *Auto Racing Executive*
%Walker Racing, 147 Midland Rd, Royston, Barnsley, S York S71 4B1, England
Walker, Eamonn *Actor*
%William Morris Agency, 151 El Camino Dr, Beverly Hills, CA 90212, USA

Walker, George T, Jr *Composer*
323 Grove St, Montclair, NJ 07042, USA
Walker, Greg *Cartoonist (Hi & Lois)*
%King Features Syndicate, 888 7th Ave, New York, NY 10106, USA
Walker, Herschel J *Football Player*
1360 E 9th St, Cleveland, OH 44114, USA
Walker, Hezekiah *Singer*
%Covenant Agency, 1011 4th St, #315, Santa Monica, CA 90403, USA
Walker, James E *Educator*
%Middle Tennessee State University, President's Office, Murfreesboro, TN 37132, USA
Walker, James L (Jimmy) *Labor Leader*
%Fireman & Oilers Brotherhood, 1100 Circle 75 Parkway, Atlanta, GA 30339, USA
Walker, Jerry Jeff *Singer, Songwriter, Guitarist*
%Tried & True Music, PO Box 39, Austin, TX 78767, USA
Walker, Jimmie (J J) *Actor, Comedian*
%Nationwide Entertainment, 2756 N Green Valley Parkway, Henderson, NV 89014, USA
Walker, Joe Louis *Singer, Guitarist*
%Rick Bates Mgmt, 714 Brookside Lane, Sierra Madre, CA 91024, USA
Walker, John *Track Athlete*
Jeffs Road, RD Papatoetoe, New Zealand
Walker, John E *Nobel Chemistry Laureate*
%MRC Molecular Biology Laboratory, Hills Road, Cambridge CB2 2QH, England
Walker, Kenny *Basketball Player*
2252 Terrace Woods Park, Lexington, KY 40513, USA
Walker, Kenyatta *Football Player*
%Tampa Bay Buccaneers, 1 W Buccaneer Place, Tampa, FL 33607, USA
Walker, Larry K R *Baseball Player*
21642 River Road, Maple Ridge BC V2X 2B7, Canada
Walker, LeRoy T *Track Coach, Executive, Educator*
1208 Red Oak Ave, Durham, NC 27707, USA
Walker, Marcy *Actress*
%Leslie Bader, 19162 Index St, #4, Northridge, CA 91326, USA
Walker, Mort *Cartoonist (Beetle Bailey, Sarge)*
61 Studio Court, Stamford, CT 06903, USA
Walker, Paul *Actor*
%International Creative Mgmt, 8942 Wilshire Blvd, #219, Beverly Hills, CA 90211, USA
Walker, Paul L *Religious Leader*
%Church of God, PO Box 2430, Cleveland, TN 37320, USA
Walker, Peter *Movie Director*
23 Bentick St, London W1, England
Walker, Polly *Actress*
%Markham & Froggatt, Julian House, 4 Windmill St, London W1P 1HF, England
Walker, Robert M *Physicist*
1 Brookings Dr, #CB1105, Saint Louis, MO 63130, USA
Walker, Robert, Jr *Actor*
%TOPS, 23410 Civic Center Way, #C1, Malibu, CA 90265, USA
Walker, Roger N *Architect*
8 Brougham St, Mount Victoria, Wellington, New Zealand
Walker, Ronald C *Publisher*
%Smithsonian Magazine, 900 Jefferson Dr SW, Washington, DC 20560, USA
Walker, Sandra *Opera Singer*
%Columbia Artists Mgmt Inc, 165 W 57th St, New York, NY 10019, USA
Walker, Sarah E B *Opera Singer*
152 Inchmery Road, London SE6 1DF, England
Walker, Wally *Basketball Player*
154 Lombard St, #58, San Francisco, CA 94111, USA
Walker, Wesley D *Football Player*
PO Box 20438, Huntington Station, NY 11746, USA
Walker, William D *Businessman*
%Tektronix Inc, 26600 Southwest Parkway, Wilsonville, OR 97070, USA
Wall, Brian A *Sculptor*
306 Lombard St, San Francisco, CA 94133, USA
Wall, Carolyn *Publisher*
%Newsweek Magazine, 251 W 57th St, New York, NY 10019, USA
Wall, David *Ballet Dancer*
%Royal Ballet, Covent Garden, Bow St, London WC2E 9DD, England
Wall, Frederick T *Physical Chemist*
8515 Costa Verde Blvd, #606, San Diego, CA 92122, USA
Wall, John F *Army General*
507 Hanover St, Fredericksburg, VA 22401, USA
Wallace, Anthony F C *Anthropologist*
%University of Pennsylvania, Anthropology Dept, Philadelphia, PA 19014, USA
Wallace, B Steven (Steve) *Football Player*
4455 Harris Trail NW, Atlanta, GA 30327, USA
Wallace, Ben *Basketball Player*
%Detroit Pistons, Palace, 2 Championship Dr, Auburn Hills, MI 48326, USA
Wallace, Bruce *Geneticist*
940 McBryde Dr, Blacksburg, VA 24060, USA

W

Wallace, Carol *Editor*
%People Magazine, Editorial Dept, Time-Life Building, New York, NY 10020, USA
Wallace, Christopher (Chris) *Commentator*
%Fox-TV, News Dept, 205 E 67th St, New York, NY 10021, USA
Wallace, Craig K *Physician*
%National Institutes of Health, 9000 Rockville Pike, Bethesda, MD 20892, USA
Wallace, David Foster *Writer*
%Illinois State University, English Dept, Normal, IL 61761, USA
Wallace, Gerald *Basketball Player*
%Sacramento Kings, Arco Arena, 1 Sports Parkway, Sacramento, CA 95834, USA
Wallace, Ian *Opera Singer, Actor*
%P F D, Drury House, 34-43 Russell St, London WC2B 5HA, England
Wallace, Jane *Entertainer*
%Cosgrove-Meurer Productions, 4303 W Verdugo Ave, Burbank, CA 91505, USA
Wallace, Julie T *Actress*
%Annette Stone, 9 Newburgh St, London W1V 1LH, England
Wallace, Kenny *Auto Racing Driver*
8929 Harris Road, Concord, NC 28027, USA
Wallace, Marcia *Actress*
%Artists Group, 10100 Santa Monica Blvd, #2490, Los Angeles, CA 90067, USA
Wallace, Mike *Commentator*
%CBS-TV, News Dept, 51 W 52nd St, New York, NY 10019, USA
Wallace, Rasheed *Basketball Player*
01905 SW Greenwood Road, Portland, OR 97219, USA
Wallace, Rusty *Auto Racing Driver*
%Penske Racing, 136 Knob Hill Road, Mooresville, NC 28117, USA
Wallace, Tommy Lee *Movie Director*
%Innovative Artists, 1505 10th St, Santa Monica, CA 90401, USA
Wallace, William *Army General*
Commanding General, V Corps, APO, AE 09079, USA
Wallach, Eli *Actor*
%Paradigm Agency, 200 W 57th St, #900, New York, NY 10019, USA
Wallach, Evan J *Judge*
%US International Trade Court, 1 Federal Plaza, New York, NY 10278, USA
Wallach, Timothy C (Tim) *Baseball Player*
10762 Holly Dr, Garden Grove, CA 92840, USA
Wallechinsky, David *Writer*
%Avon/William Morrow, 1350 Ave of Americas, New York, NY 10019, USA
Waller, Charlie *Guitarist (Classic Country Gentlemen)*
%Lendel Agency, 9188 James Madison Highway, Warrenton, VA 20186, USA
Waller, Gordon *Singer (Peter & Gordon)*
7 Passage St, Powey, Cornwell PL23 1DE, England
Waller, Michael *Editor*
%Hartford Courant Co, 285 Broad St, Hartford, CT 06115, USA
Waller, Robert James *Writer*
%Aaron Priest Literary Agency, 708 3rd Ave, #2300, New York, NY 10017, USA
Waller, Ron *Football Player*
900 Concord Road, Seaford, DE 19973, USA
Waller, William L *Governor, MS*
220 S President St, Jackson, MS 39201, USA
Wallerstein, Ralph G *Hematologist*
3447 Clay St, San Francisco, CA 94118, USA
Walling, Cheves T *Chemist*
PO Box 537, Jaffrey, NH 03452, USA
Wallis, Shani *Actress*
15460 Vista Haven, Sherman Oaks, CA 91403, USA
Walliser, Maria *Alpine Skier*
Selfwingert, 7208 Malans, Switzerland
Wallop, Malcolm *Senator, WY*
58 Canyon Ranch Road, Big Horn, WY 82833, USA
Walls, Denise (Nee-C) *Singer (Annointed), Songwriter*
2113 South Ave, Youngstown, OH 44502, USA
Walls, Everson C *Football Player*
5927 Tree Shadow Court, Dallas, TX 75252, USA
Walmsley, Jon *Actor*
13810 Magnolia Blvd, Sherman Oaks, CA 91423, USA
Walpot, Heike *Astronaut, Germany*
%DLR, Abt Raumflugbetrieb, 51170 Cologne, Germany
Walser, Don *Singer, Songwriter, Yodeler*
%Nancy Fly Agency, 6618 Wolfcreek Pass, Austin, TX 78749, USA
Walsh, David M *Cinematographer*
15436 Valley Vista Blvd, Sherman Oaks, CA 91403, USA
Walsh, Diana Chapman *Educator*
%Wellesley College, President's Office, Wellesley, MA 02181, USA
Walsh, Don *Underwater Explorer*
%International Maritime Inc, 14758 Sitkum Lane, Myrtle Point, OR 97458, USA
Walsh, Donnie *Basketball Coach, Executive*
%Indiana Pacers, Conseco Fieldhouse, 125 S Pennsylvania, Indianapolis, IN 46204, USA

Walsh, Dylan *Actor*
%McGowan Agency, 370 Lexington Ave, #802, New York, NY 10017, USA
Walsh, Gwynyth *Actress*
12304 Santa Monica Blvd, #104, Los Angeles, CA 90025, USA
Walsh, Joe *Singer, Songwriter, Guitarist (Eagles)*
%ARM, 1257 Arcade St, Saint Paul, MN 55106, USA
Walsh, John *Television Host*
3111 S Dixie Highway, #244, West Palm Beach, FL 33405, USA
Walsh, John, Jr *Museum Curator*
%J Paul Getty Museum, Getty Center, 1200 Getty Center Dr, Los Angeles, CA 90049, USA
Walsh, Kate *Actress*
PO Box 261067, Encino, CA 91426, USA
Walsh, Lawrence E *Government Official, Attorney*
1902 Bedford St, Nichols Hills, OK 73116, USA
Walsh, M Emmet *Actor*
4173 Motor Ave, Culver City, CA 90232, USA
Walsh, Martin *Association Executive*
%National Organization on Disability, 910 16th St NW, Washington, DC 20006, USA
Walsh, Patrick C *Urologist*
%Johns Hopkins University, Brady Urological Institute, Baltimore, MD 21205, USA
Walsh, Stephen J (Steve) *Football Player*
1921 Flagler Estates Dr, West Palm Beach, FL 33411, USA
Walsh, Sydney *Actress*
%Innovative Artists, 1505 10th St, Santa Monica, CA 90401, USA
Walsh, Tom *Sculptor*
PO Box 133, Philomath, OR 97370, USA
Walsh, William E (Bill) *Football Coach*
12 Vineyard Hill Road, Woodside, CA 94062, USA
Walske, Steven *Businessman*
%Parametric Technology, 140 Kendrick St, Needham Heights, MA 02494, USA
Walter, Jessica *Actress*
27 W 87th St, #2, New York, NY 10024, USA
Walter, Lisa Ann *Actress, Comedian*
%United Talent Agency, 9560 Wilshire Blvd, #500, Beverly Hills, CA 90212, USA
Walter, Paul H L *Labor Leader*
3 Benedictine Retreat, Savannah, GA 31411, USA
Walter, Robert D *Businessman*
%Cardinal Health, 7000 Cardinal Place, Dublin, OH 43017, USA
Walter, Tracey *Actress*
257 N Rexford Dr, Beverly Hills, CA 90210, USA
Walter, Ulrich *Astronaut, Germany*
%IBM Germany, Schonaicherstr 220, 71032 Boblingen, Germany
Walters, Barbara *Commentator*
33 W 60th St, New York, NY 10023, USA
Walters, Charles *Movie Director*
23922 De Ville Way, #A, Malibu, CA 90265, USA
Walters, David L *Governor, OK*
RR 2, Watts, OK 74964, USA
Walters, Harry N *Government Official*
%DHC Holdings Corp, 125 Thomas Dale, Williamsburg, VA 23185, USA
Walters, Jamie *Actor, Singer*
4702 Ethel Ave, Sherman Oaks, CA 91423, USA
Walters, Julie *Actress*
%International Creative Mgmt, 76 Oxford St, London W1N 0AX, England
Walters, Melora *Actress*
%United Talent Agency, 9560 Wilshire Blvd, #500, Beverly Hills, CA 90212, USA
Walters, Minette *Writer*
%G P Putnam's Sons, 375 Hudson St, New York, NY 10014, USA
Walters, Peter I *Businessman*
22 Hill St, London W1X 7FU, England
Walters, Roger T *Architect*
46 Princess Road, London NW1 8JL, England
Walters, Susan *Actress*
%Innovative Artists, 1505 10th St, Santa Monica, CA 90401, USA
Walters, Tome H, Jr *Air Force General*
Defense Security Cooperation Agency, 1111 Davis Highway, Arlington, VA 22202, USA
Walther, Herbert *Physicist*
Egenhoferstr 7A, 81243 Munich, Germany
Walton, Anthony J (Tony) *Scenic Designer, Illustrator*
%International Creative Mgmt, 40 W 57th St, #1800, New York, NY 10019, USA
Walton, Cedar A, Jr *Jazz Pianist*
%Bridge Agency, 35 Clark St, #A5, Brooklyn Heights, NY 11201, USA
Walton, Helen R *Businesswoman*
%Wal-Mart Stores, 702 SW 8th St, Bentonville, AR 72716, USA
Walton, Jess *Actress*
4702 Ethel Ave, Sherman Oaks, CA 91423, USA
Walton, Joseph (Joe) *Football Player, Coach*
8 Windy Crest Dr, Beaver Falls, PA 15010, USA

W

Walton, S Robson (Rob) *Businessman*
%Wal-Mart Stores, 702 SW 8th St, Bentonville, AR 72716, USA
Walton, William T (Bill), III *Basketball Player, Sportscaster*
1010 Myrtle Way, San Diego, CA 92103, USA
Waltrip, Darrell L *Auto, Truck Racing Driver*
PO Box 381, Harrisburg, NC 28075, USA
Waltrip, Michael (Mike) *Auto Racing Driver*
PO Box 5065, Concord, NH 28027, USA
Waltrip, Robert L *Businessman*
%Service Corp International, 1929 Allen Parkway, Houston, TX 77019, USA
Waltz, Lisa *Actress*
%Writers & Artists, 8383 Wilshire Blvd, #550, Beverly Hills, CA 90211, USA
Walworth, Arthur *Writer*
North Hill, 865 Central Ave E, #206, Needham, MA 02492, USA
Walz, Carl E *Astronaut*
129 Lake Point Dr, League City, TX 77573, USA
Wamala, Emmanuel Cardinal *Religious Leader*
PO Box 14125, Mengo, Kampala, Uganda
Wambaugh, Joseph *Writer*
3520 Kellogg Way, San Diego, CA 92106, USA
Wambold, Richard L *Businessman*
%Pactiv Corp, 1900 W Field Court, Lake Forest, IL 60045, USA
Wan Li *Government Official, China*
%State Council, People's Congress, Tian An Men Square, Beijing, China
Wanamaker, Zoe *Actress*
%Conway Van Gelder Robinson, 18-21 Jermyn St, London SW1Y 6NB, England
Wang Jida *Sculptor*
7612 35th Ave, #3E, Jackson Heights, NY 11372, USA
Wang Junxia *Track Athlete*
%Athletic Assn, 9 Tiyuguan Road, Chongwen District, 10061 Beijing, China
Wang Tian-Ren *Sculptor*
%Shaanxi Sculpture Institute, Longshoucun, Xi'am, Shaanxi 710016, China
Wang Zhi Zhi *Basketball Player*
%Dallas Mavericks, 2909 Taylor St, Dallas, TX 75226, USA
Wang, Garrett *Actor*
7049 Macapa Dr, Los Angeles, CA 90068, USA
Wang, Henry Y *Chemical Engineer*
%University of Michigan, Chemical Engineering Dept, Ann Arbor, MI 48109, USA
Wang, Taylor G *Astronaut, Physicist*
1224 Arno Dr, Sierra Madre, CA 91024, USA
Wang, Vera *Fashion Designer*
%Vera Wang Bridal House, 225 W 39th St, #1000, New York, NY 10018, USA
Wang, Wayne *Movie Director*
%International Creative Mgmt, 8942 Wilshire Blvd, #219, Beverly Hills, CA 90211, USA
Wang, Zhen-Yi *Hematologist*
%Hopital de Shanghai, Rui Jin Road 11, Shanghai 200025, China
Wangchuck, Dasho Jigme Khesar Namgyal *Crown Prince, Bhutan*
%Royal Palace, Tashichhodzong, Thimphu, Bhutan
Wangchuk, Jigme Singye *King, Bhutan*
%Royal Palace, Tashichhodzong, Thimphu, Bhutan
Wannamaker, Zoe *Actress*
%Conway Van Gelder Robinson, 18-21 Jermyn St, London SW1Y 6NB, England
Wanner, H Eric *Foundation Executive*
%Russell Sage Foundation, 112 E 64th St, New York, NY 10021, USA
Wannstedt, David R (Dave) *Football Coach*
12600 N Stonebrook Circle, Davie, FL 33330, USA
Wansel, Dexter *Keyboardist, Pianist*
%Walt Reeder Productions, PO Box 27641, Philadelphia, PA 19118, USA
Wanzer, Robert F (Bobby) *Basketball Player*
28 Greenwood Park, Pittsford, NY 14534, USA
Waples, Keith *Harness Racing Driver*
PO Box 632, Durham ON N0G 1R0, Canada
Waples, Ron *Harness Racing Driver, Trainer*
7 Mill Run W, Hightstown, NJ 08520, USA
Wapner, Joseph A *Judge, Actor*
2388 Century Hill, Los Angeles, CA 90067, USA
Warburton, Patrick *Actor*
%Innovative Artists, 1505 10th St, Santa Monica, CA 90401, USA
Ward, Bill *Drummer (Black Sabbath)*
%Creative Artists Agency, 9830 Wilshire Blvd, Beverly Hills, CA 90212, USA
Ward, Burt *Actor*
%Flick East-West, 9057 Nemo St, #A, West Hollywood, CA 90069, USA
Ward, Burton *Auto Racing Driver*
%Bill Davis Racing, 301 Old Thomasville Road, Winston Salem, NC 27107, USA
Ward, Charlie *Basketball, Football Player*
109 Heisman Way, Thomasville, GA 31792, USA
Ward, Christopher L (Chris) *Football Player*
PO Box 1365, Inglewood, CA 90308, USA

Ward, Dale *Singer*
%A Crosse the World, PO Box 23066, London W11 3FR, England
Ward, David *Opera Singer*
1 Kennedy Crescent, Lake Wanaka, New Zealand
Ward, Fred *Actor*
1215 Cabrillo Ave, Venice, CA 90291, USA
Ward, Hines *Football Player*
150 Acadian Dr, Stockbridge, GA 30281, USA
Ward, John F *Businessman*
%Russell Corp, 755 Lee St, Alexander City, AL 35010, USA
Ward, John Milton *Educator*
20 Follen St, Cambridge, MA 02138, USA
Ward, Jon P *Businessman*
%RR Donnelley & Sons, 77 W Wacker Dr, Chicago, IL 60601, USA
Ward, Mary *Actress*
%Melbourne Artists, 643 Saint Kilda Road, Melbourne VIC 3004, Australia
Ward, Mary B *Actress*
%Innovative Artists, 1505 10th St, Santa Monica, CA 90401, USA
Ward, Megan *Actress*
PO Box 481219, Los Angeles, CA 90036, USA
Ward, Michael P *Mountaineer, Surgeon*
%Saint Andrews's Hospital, Bow St, London E3 3NT, England
Ward, R Duane *Baseball Player*
4505 Pacific St, Farmington, NM 87402, USA
Ward, Rachel *Actress*
%Himber Entertainment, 211 S Beverly Dr, #208, Beverly Hills, CA 90212, USA
Ward, Robert *Composer*
2701 Pickett Road, #4022, Durham, NC 27705, USA
Ward, Robert R (Bob) *Football Player*
PO Box 535, Riva, MD 21140, USA
Ward, Rodger *Auto Racing Driver*
24701 Raymond Way, #29, Lake Forest, CA 92630, USA
Ward, Ronald L (Ron) *Hockey Player*
3178 W 140th St, Cleveland, OH 44111, USA
Ward, Sela *Actress*
289 S Robertson Blvd, #469, Beverly Hills, CA 90211, USA
Ward, Simon *Actor*
%Shepherd & Ford, 13 Radner Walk, London SW3 4BP, England
Ward, Sterling *Religious Leader*
%Brethren Church, 524 College Ave, Ashland, OH 44805, USA
Ward, Susan *Actress*
%Howie Simon, 8219 Norton Ave, #6, West Hollywood, CA 90046, USA
Ward, Turner M *Baseball Player*
232 Autumn Dr, Saraland, AL 36571, USA
Ward, Vincent *Movie Director*
PO Box 423, Kings Cross, Sydney NSW 2011, Australia
Ward, Wendy *Golfer*
12845 Sassin Station Road N, Edwall, WA 99008, USA
Warden, Jack *Actor*
23604 Malibu Colony Road, Malibu, CA 90265, USA
Warden, John *Attorney*
%Sullivan & Cromwell 125 Broad St, New York NY 10004, USA
Wardlaw, Kim McLane *Judge*
%US Court of Appeals, 125 S Grand Ave, Pasadena, CA 91105, USA
Ware, Andre *Football Player*
3910 Wood Park, Sugar Land, TX 77479, USA
Ware, Herta *Actress*
PO Box 151, Topanga Canyon, CA 90290, USA
Warfield, Paul D *Football Player*
%Jamesco Inc, 15476 NW 77th Court, #347, Hialeah, FL 33016, USA
Wargo, Tom *Golfer*
2801 Putter Lane, Centralia, IL 62801, USA
Warhols, James *Writer, Illustrator*
PO Box 748, Rhinebeck, NY 12572, USA
Wariner, Steve *Singer, Songwriter*
%Steve Wariner Productions, PO Box 1647, Franklin, TN 37065, USA
Waring, Todd *Actor*
%Artists Agency, 1180 S Beverly Dr, #301, Los Angeles, CA 90035, USA
Wark, Robert R *Museum Curator*
%Huntington Library & Art Gallery, 1151 Oxford Road, San Marino, CA 91108, USA
Warlock, Billy *Actor*
%Pakula/King, 9229 Sunset Blvd, #315, Los Angeles, CA 90069, USA
Warmenhoven, Daniel *Businessman*
%Network Appliance Inc, 495 E Java Dr, Sunnyvale, CA 94089, USA
Warnecke, John Carl *Architect*
300 Broadway St, San Francisco, CA 94133, USA
Warnecke, Mark *Swimmer*
Am Schichtmeister 100, 58453 Witten, Germany

Warner, Chris *Cartoonist (Black Cross)*
%Dark Horse Publishing, 10956 SE Main St, Portland, OR 97216, USA
Warner, Curt *Football Player*
%Curt Warner Chevrolet, 10811 SE Mill Plain Blvd, Vancouver, WA 98664, USA
Warner, David *Actor*
%Julian Belfarge, 46 Albermarle St, London W1X 4PP, England
Warner, Douglas A, III *Financier*
%JP Morgan Chase, 270 Park Ave, New York, NY 10017, USA
Warner, Julie *Actress*
5850 W 3rd St, #128, Los Angeles, CA 90036, USA
Warner, Kurt *Football Player*
PO Box 249, Chesterfield, MO 63006, USA
Warner, Malcolm-Jamal *Actor*
PO Box 69646, Los Angeles, CA 90069, USA
Warner, Margaret *Commentator*
%News Hour Show, 2700 S Quincy St, Arlington, VA 22206, USA
Warner, T C *Actress*
%S D B Partners, 1801 Ave of Stars, #902, Los Angeles, CA 90067, USA
Warner, Todd *Sculptor*
8799 Boyne City Road, Charlevoix, MI 49720, USA
Warner, Tom *Television Producer*
%Carsey-Warner Productions, 4024 Radford Ave, Building 3, Studio City, CA 91604, USA
Warner, Ty *Toy Designer*
%Ty Inc, PO Box 5377, Oak Brook, IL 60522, USA
Warner, William W *Writer*
2243 47th St NW, Washington, DC 20007, USA
Warnes, Jennifer *Singer, Songwriter*
%Donald Miller, 12746 Kling St, Studio City, CA 91604, USA
Warnock, John *Businessman*
%Adobe Systems, 345 Park Ave, San Jose, CA 95110, USA
Warren G *Rap Artist*
%Richard Walters, 1800 Argyle Ave, #408, Los Angeles, CA 90028, USA
Warren, Christopher C (Chris), Jr *Football Player*
1020 W Casino Road, Everett, WA 98204, USA
Warren, Diane *Songwriter*
1896 Rising Glen Road, Los Angeles, CA 90069, USA
Warren, Estella *Model, Actress*
%AGS, 200 Park Ave, #800, New York, NY 10036, USA
Warren, Fran *Singer*
%Richard Barz, 21 Cobble Creek Dr, Tannersville, PA 18372, USA
Warren, Frederick M *Architect*
65 Cambridge Terrace, Christchurch 1, New Zealand
Warren, Gerard *Football Player*
%Cleveland Browns, 76 Lou Groza Blvd, Berea, OH 44017, USA
Warren, Gloria *Singer, Actress*
16872 Bosque Dr, Encino, CA 91436, USA
Warren, Jennifer *Actress*
1675 Old Oak Road, Los Angeles, CA 90049, USA
Warren, Kenneth S *Immunologist*
%Picower Medical Research Institute, 350 Community Dr, Manhasset, NY 11030, USA
Warren, Kiersten *Actress*
%Stubbs, 8675 W Washington Blvd, #203, Culver City, CA 90232, USA
Warren, L D *Editorial Cartoonist*
1815 William Howard Taft Road, #203, Cincinnati, OH 45206, USA
Warren, Lesley Ann *Actress*
%Mindel/Donegan Mgmt, 9057 Nemo St, #C, West Hollywood, CA 90069, USA
Warren, Michael (Mike) *Actor, Basketball Player*
21216 Escondido St, Woodland Hills, CA 91364, USA
Warren, Rosanna *Writer*
11 Robinwood Ave, Needham, MA 02492, USA
Warren, Thomas L *Association Executive*
%National Wildlife Federation, 11100 Wildlife Center Dr, Reston, VA 20190, USA
Warren, Tom *Triathlete*
2393 La Marque St, San Diego, CA 92109, USA
Warren, Ty *Football Player*
%New England Patriots, Gillette Stadium, RR 1, 60 Washington, Foxboro, MA 02035, USA
Warren-Green, Christopher *Conductor, Violinist*
%Columbia Artists Mgmt Inc, 165 W 57th St, New York, NY 10019, USA
Warrick, Peter *Football Player*
2166 Wastern Ave, Cincinnati, OH 45214, USA
Warrick, Ruth *Actress*
903 Park Ave, New York, NY 10021, USA
Warwick, Dionne *Singer*
%World Entertainment Assoc, 297101 Kinderkamack Road, #128, Oradell, NJ 07649, USA
Was, Don *Composer, Bassist (Was Not Was)*
10984 Bellagio Road, Los Angeles, CA 90077, USA
Washburn, Barbara *Cartographer*
1010 Waltham St, #F22, Lexington, MA 02421, USA

Washburn, Beverly — *Actress*
215 Chiquis Court, Henderson, NV 89074, USA

Washburn, H Bradford, Jr — *Museum Official, Explorer*
1010 Waltham St, #F22, Lexington, MA 02421, USA

Washburn, Jarrod M — *Baseball Player*
4334 E Deerpath Road, Danbury, WI 54830, USA

Washburn, Ray C — *Baseball Player*
19001 131st Dr SE, Snohomish, WA 98296, USA

Washington, Alonzo — *Cartoonist (Omega Man)*
%Omega 7, PO Box 171046, Kansas City, KS 66117, USA

Washington, Baby — *Singer, Pianist*
%Headline Talent, 1650 Broadway, #508, New York, NY 10019, USA

Washington, Claudell — *Baseball Player*
4067 Hardwick St, Lakewood, CA 90712, USA

Washington, Denzel — *Actor*
10153 1/2 Riverside Dr, PO Box 130, Toluca Lake, CA 91602, USA

Washington, Dwayne (Pearl) — *Basketball Player*
206 Grenadier Dr, #206C, Liverpool, NY 13090, USA

Washington, Eugene (Gene) — *Football Player*
2625 N Jewell Lane, Plymouth, MN 55447, USA

Washington, Gene A — *Football Player*
4087 Scripps Ave, Palo Alto, CA 94306, USA

Washington, Isaiah — *Actor*
%International Creative Mgmt, 8942 Wilshire Blvd, #219, Beverly Hills, CA 90211, USA

Washington, Joe D — *Football Player*
1204 Devonshire Dr, Desoto, TX 75115, USA

Washington, Kermit — *Basketball Player*
2242 NW 45th Ave, Camas, WA 98607, USA

Washington, Lionel — *Football Player*
%Green Bay Packers, PO Box 10628, Green Bay, WI 54307, USA

Washington, MaliVai — *Tennis Player*
5 S Roscoe Blvd, Ponte Vedra Beach, FL 32082, USA

Washington, Mike L — *Football Player*
3235 Hemon Road, Montgomery, AL 36106, USA

Washington, Theodore (Ted) — *Football Player*
3522 E 26th Ave, Tampa, FL 33605, USA

Wasim Akram — *Cricketer*
%Lancashire Cricket Club, Old Trafford, Manchester M16 0PX, England

Waskow, Thomas C — *Air Force General*
Commander, US Forces Japan & 5th Air Force, Unit 5068, APO, AP 96328, USA

Wasmeier, Markus — *Alpine Skier*
Breitensteinstr 14B, 83727 Schliersee-Neuhaus, Germany

Wass, Ted — *Actor*
3354 Longridge Terrace, Sherman Oaks, CA 91423, USA

Wasserburg, Gerald J — *Geophysicist*
1207 Arden Road, Pasadena, CA 91106, USA

Wasserman, Dale — *Writer*
Casa Blanca Estates, #37, Paradise Valley, AZ 95253, USA

Wasserman, Dan — *Editorial Cartoonist*
%Boston Globe, Editorial Dept, 135 William Morrissey Blvd, Dorchester, MA 02125, USA

Wasserman, Rob — *Jazz Bassist*
%Leslie Wiener Financial Services, PO Box 245, Sausalito, CA 94966, USA

Wasserman, Robert H — *Physiologist, Veterinarian*
%Cornell University, Veterinary Medicine College, Ithaca, NY 14853, USA

Wasserstein, Wendy — *Writer*
%Royce Carlton Inc, 866 United Nations Plaza, #4030, New York, NY 10017, USA

Wasson, Craig — *Actor*
9355 Sunset Blvd, #710, Los Angeles, CA 90069, USA

Wasson, Erin — *Model*
%I M G Models, 304 Park Ave S, #1200, New York, NY 10010, USA

Watanabe, Milio — *Computer Scientist*
%Nippon Electric Co, Computer Labs, 5-33-1 Shiba, Tokyo, Japan

Watanabe, Sadao — *Jazz Saxophonist*
%International Music Network, 278 S Main St, #400, Gloucester, MA 01930, USA

Watanabe, Youji — *Architect*
1-6-13 Hirakawacho, Chiyodaku, Tokyo, Japan

Waterman, Denis — *Actor*
%D&J Arlon, Pinewood Studios, Iverheath, Iver SL0 0NH, England

Waterman, Felicity — *Actress*
280 Mott St, #4R, New York, NY 10012, USA

Waters, Alice — *Chef*
%Chez Panisse, 1517 Shattuck Ave, Berkeley, CA 94709, USA

Waters, Charles T (Charlie) — *Football Player, Coach*
2838 Woodside St, Dallas, TX 75204, USA

Waters, Crystal — *Singer*
270 Lafayette St, #602, New York, NY 10012, USA

Waters, Frank (Muddy) — *Football Coach*
5337 E Hidden Lake Dr, East Lansing, MI 48823, USA

W

Waters - Watson

Waters, John *Movie Director*
10 W Highfield Road, Baltimore, MD 21218, USA
Waters, John B *Government Official*
405 Burridge Waters Edge, Sevierville, TN 37862, USA
Waters, Lou *Commentator*
%Cable News Network, News Dept, 1050 Techwood Dr NW, Atlanta, GA 30318, USA
Waters, Mark *Movie Director*
%Miramax Films, 11 Beach St, New York, NY 10013, USA
Waters, Richard *Publisher*
20 Somerset Downs, Saint Louis, MO 63124, USA
Waters, Roger *Singer, Bassist (Pink Floyd)*
%Agency Group, 370 City Road, London EC1V 2QA, England
Waterston, Robert *Biologist*
%Washington University Medical School, Biology Dept, Saint Louis, MO 63130, USA
Waterston, Sam *Actor*
RR Box 197, Easton St, West Cornwall, CT 06796, USA
Wathan, John D *Baseball Player, Manager*
1401 Deer Run Trail, Blue Springs, MO 64015, USA
Watkin, David *Cinematographer*
6 Sussex Mews, Brighton BN2 1GZ, England
Watkins, Carlene *Actress*
104 Fremont Place W, Los Angeles, CA 90005, USA
Watkins, Dean A *Inventor (Electron Tubes), Businessman*
%Watkins-Johnson Co, 401 River Oaks Parkway, San Jose, CA 95134, USA
Watkins, James D *Secretary, Energy; Navy Admiral*
2021 Indian Circle, Saint Leonard, MD 20685, USA
Watkins, Lloyd I *Economist*
PO Box 111, Bloomington, IL 61702, USA
Watkins, Michelle *Actress*
%Capital Artists, 6404 Wilshire Blvd, #950, Los Angeles, CA 90048, USA
Watkins, Tasker *WW II British Army Hero (VC), Judge*
5 Pump Court, Middle Temple, London EC4, England
Watkins, Tionne (T-Boz) *Rap Artist (TLC)*
%Creative Artists Agency, 9830 Wilshire Blvd, Beverly Hills, CA 90212, USA
Watkins, William D *Businessman*
%Seagate Technology, 920 Disc Dr, Scotts Valley, CA 95066, USA
Watkinson of Woking, Harold A *Government Official, England*
Tyma House, Bosham near Chichester, Sussex, England
Watley, Jody *Singer*
%Baker Winokur Rider, 9100 Wilshire Blvd, #600, Beverly Hills, CA 90212, USA
Watrous, William R (Bill), Jr *Jazz Trombonist*
%GNP/Crescendo Records, 8480 Sunset Blvd, #A, Los Angeles, CA 90069, USA
Watson Richardson, Lillian (Pokey) *Swimmer*
4960 Maunalani Circle, Honolulu, HI 96816, USA
Watson, A J *Auto Racing Engineer*
5420 Crawfordsville Road, Indianapolis, IN 46224, USA
Watson, Albert M *Photographer*
777 Washington St, New York, NY 10014, USA
Watson, Alexander F *Diplomat*
%Nature Conservancy International, 4245 Fairfax Dr, #100, Arlington, VA 22203, USA
Watson, Cecil J *Physician*
%Abbott Northwestern Hospital, 2727 Chicago Ave, Minneapolis, MN 55407, USA
Watson, Dale *Singer*
%Crowley Artist Mgmt, 602 Wayside Dr, Wimberley, TX 78676, USA
Watson, Doc *Singer, Guitarist, Banjoist*
%CM Mgmt, 5479 Larryon Dr, Woodland Hills, CA 91367, USA
Watson, Elizabeth M *Law Enforcement Official*
%Houston Police Department, Chief's Office, 1200 Travis St, Houston, TX 77002, USA
Watson, Emily *Actress*
%William Morris Agency, 151 El Camino Dr, Beverly Hills, CA 90212, USA
Watson, Emma *Actress*
PO Box 3000, Laevesden, Herts, London WD25 ZLF, England
Watson, Gene *Singer*
%Joe Taylor Agency, 2802 Columbine Place, Nashville, TN 37204, USA
Watson, Jack H, Jr *Government Official*
%Long Aldridge Norman, 1900 K St NW, Washington, DC 20006, USA
Watson, James D *Nobel Medicine Laureate*
Bungtown Road, Cold Spring Harbor, NY 11724, USA
Watson, Kenneth M *Physicist, Oceanographer*
8515 Costa Verde Blvd, #2008, San Diego, CA 92122, USA
Watson, Martha *Track Athlete*
5509 Royal Vista Lane, Las Vegas, NV 89149, USA
Watson, Max P, Jr *Businessman*
%BMC Software, 2101 CityWest Blvd, Houston, TX 77042, USA
Watson, Mills *Actor*
2824 Dell Ave, Venice, CA 90291, USA
Watson, Paul *Environmental Activist*
%Sea Shepherd Conservation Society, 1314 2nd St, Santa Monica, CA 90401, USA

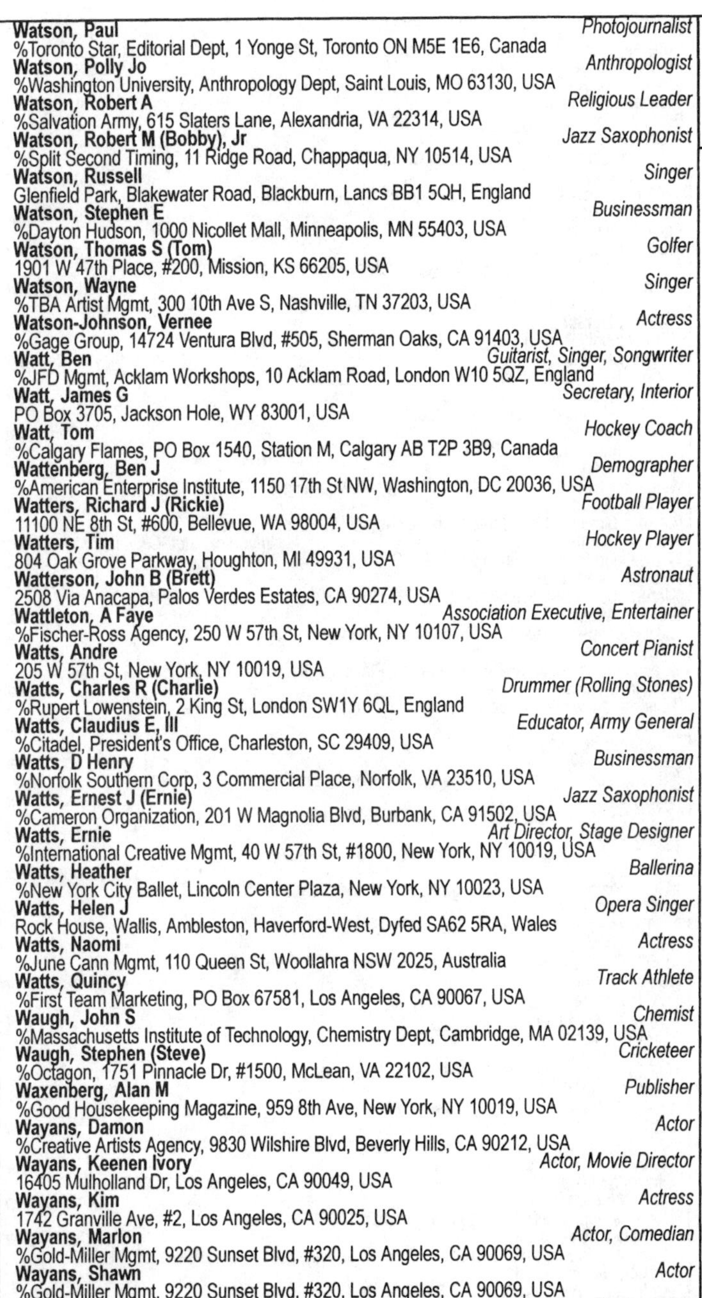

Watson, Paul — *Photojournalist*
%Toronto Star, Editorial Dept, 1 Yonge St, Toronto ON M5E 1E6, Canada

Watson, Polly Jo — *Anthropologist*
%Washington University, Anthropology Dept, Saint Louis, MO 63130, USA

Watson, Robert A — *Religious Leader*
%Salvation Army, 615 Slaters Lane, Alexandria, VA 22314, USA

Watson, Robert M (Bobby), Jr — *Jazz Saxophonist*
%Split Second Timing, 11 Ridge Road, Chappaqua, NY 10514, USA

Watson, Russell — *Singer*
Glenfield Park, Blakewater Road, Blackburn, Lancs BB1 5QH, England

Watson, Stephen E — *Businessman*
%Dayton Hudson, 1000 Nicollet Mall, Minneapolis, MN 55403, USA

Watson, Thomas S (Tom) — *Golfer*
1901 W 47th Place, #200, Mission, KS 66205, USA

Watson, Wayne — *Singer*
%TBA Artist Mgmt, 300 10th Ave S, Nashville, TN 37203, USA

Watson-Johnson, Vernee — *Actress*
%Gage Group, 14724 Ventura Blvd, #505, Sherman Oaks, CA 91403, USA

Watt, Ben — *Guitarist, Singer, Songwriter*
%JFD Mgmt, Acklam Workshops, 10 Acklam Road, London W10 5QZ, England

Watt, James G — *Secretary, Interior*
PO Box 3705, Jackson Hole, WY 83001, USA

Watt, Tom — *Hockey Coach*
%Calgary Flames, PO Box 1540, Station M, Calgary AB T2P 3B9, Canada

Wattenberg, Ben J — *Demographer*
%American Enterprise Institute, 1150 17th St NW, Washington, DC 20036, USA

Watters, Richard J (Rickie) — *Football Player*
11100 NE 8th St, #600, Bellevue, WA 98004, USA

Watters, Tim — *Hockey Player*
804 Oak Grove Parkway, Houghton, MI 49931, USA

Watterson, John B (Brett) — *Astronaut*
2508 Via Anacapa, Palos Verdes Estates, CA 90274, USA

Wattleton, A Faye — *Association Executive, Entertainer*
%Fischer-Ross Agency, 250 W 57th St, New York, NY 10107, USA

Watts, Andre — *Concert Pianist*
205 W 57th St, New York, NY 10019, USA

Watts, Charles R (Charlie) — *Drummer (Rolling Stones)*
%Rupert Lowenstein, 2 King St, London SW1Y 6QL, England

Watts, Claudius E, III — *Educator, Army General*
%Citadel, President's Office, Charleston, SC 29409, USA

Watts, D Henry — *Businessman*
%Norfolk Southern Corp, 3 Commercial Place, Norfolk, VA 23510, USA

Watts, Ernest J (Ernie) — *Jazz Saxophonist*
%Cameron Organization, 201 W Magnolia Blvd, Burbank, CA 91502, USA

Watts, Ernie — *Art Director, Stage Designer*
%International Creative Mgmt, 40 W 57th St, #1800, New York, NY 10019, USA

Watts, Heather — *Ballerina*
%New York City Ballet, Lincoln Center Plaza, New York, NY 10023, USA

Watts, Helen J — *Opera Singer*
Rock House, Wallis, Ambleston, Haverford-West, Dyfed SA62 5RA, Wales

Watts, Naomi — *Actress*
%June Cann Mgmt, 110 Queen St, Woollahra NSW 2025, Australia

Watts, Quincy — *Track Athlete*
%First Team Marketing, PO Box 67581, Los Angeles, CA 90067, USA

Waugh, John S — *Chemist*
%Massachusetts Institute of Technology, Chemistry Dept, Cambridge, MA 02139, USA

Waugh, Stephen (Steve) — *Cricketeer*
%Octagon, 1751 Pinnacle Dr, #1500, McLean, VA 22102, USA

Waxenberg, Alan M — *Publisher*
%Good Housekeeping Magazine, 959 8th Ave, New York, NY 10019, USA

Wayans, Damon — *Actor*
%Creative Artists Agency, 9830 Wilshire Blvd, Beverly Hills, CA 90212, USA

Wayans, Keenen Ivory — *Actor, Movie Director*
16405 Mulholland Dr, Los Angeles, CA 90049, USA

Wayans, Kim — *Actress*
1742 Granville Ave, #2, Los Angeles, CA 90025, USA

Wayans, Marlon — *Actor, Comedian*
%Gold-Miller Mgmt, 9220 Sunset Blvd, #320, Los Angeles, CA 90069, USA

Wayans, Shawn — *Actor*
%Gold-Miller Mgmt, 9220 Sunset Blvd, #320, Los Angeles, CA 90069, USA

Wayda, Stephen — *Photographer*
%Playboy Magazine, Reader Service, 680 N Lake Shore Dr, Chicago, IL 60611, USA

Wayne, June — *Artist*
1108 N Tamarind Ave, Los Angeles, CA 90038, USA

Wayne, Patrick — *Actor*
10502 Whipple St, Toluca Lake, CA 91602, USA

Wayne, Reggie — *Football Player*
%Indianapolis Colts, 7001 W 56th St, Indianapolis, IN 46254, USA

W

Wazed, Sheik Hasina *Prime Minister, Bangladesh*
%Sere-e Bangla Nagar, Gono, Bhaban, Sher-e-Banglanagar, Dakar, Bangladesh

Weah, George *Soccer Player*
%AC Milan, Via Turati 3, 20221 Milan, Italy

Weatherill, B Bruce *Government Official, England*
Emmets House, Ide Hill, Kent TN14 6BA, England

Weatherly, Shawn *Actress, Beauty Queen*
135 N Westgate Ave, Los Angeles, CA 90049, USA

Weathers, Carl *Actor, Football Player*
4241 Redwood Ave, #2205, Los Angeles, CA 90066, USA

Weatherspoon, Clarence *Basketball Player*
PO Box 117, Crawford, MS 39743, USA

Weatherspoon, Teresa G *Basketball Player*
%New York Liberty, Madison Square Garden, 2 Penn Plaza, New York, NY 10121, USA

Weatherwax, Jim *Football Player*
636 Cucharas Mountain Dr, Livermore, CO 80536, USA

Weaver, Dennis *Actor*
13869 County Road 1, Ridgway, CO 81432, USA

Weaver, Earl S *Baseball Player, Manager*
501 Cypress Pointe Dr W, Pembroke Pines, FL 33027, USA

Weaver, Fritz *Actor*
161 W 75th St, New York, NY 10023, USA

Weaver, James *Cartoonist*
3438 Admiralty Lane, Indianapolis, IN 46240, USA

Weaver, Reg *Labor Leader*
%National Education Assn, 1201 16th St NW, Washington, DC 20036, USA

Weaver, Robby *Actor*
%Artists Group, 10100 Santa Monica Blvd, #2490, Los Angeles, CA 90067, USA

Weaver, Rufus *Inventor (Stair Climbing Wheelchair)*
77 Adelaide St, New London, CT 06320, USA

Weaver, Sigourney *Actress*
%International Creative Mgmt, 40 W 57th St, #1800, New York, NY 10019, USA

Weaver, Warren E *Chemist*
7607 Horsepen Road, Richmond, VA 23229, USA

Weaver, Wayne *Football Executive*
%Jacksonville Jaguars, 1 AllTel Stadium Place, Jacksonville, FL 32202, USA

Weaving, Hugo *Actor*
%Shanahan Mgmt, PO Box 1509, Darlinghurst NSW 1300, Australia

Webb, Chloe *Actress*
1015 Main St, Venice, CA 90291, USA

Webb, Christiaan *Singer, Musician, Songwriter*
%SuperVision Mgmt, 109B Regents Park Road, London NW1 8UR, England

Webb, James R (Jimmy) *Football Player*
1319 S Prairie Flower Road, Turlock, CA 95380, USA

Webb, Jimmy *Songwriter, Singer*
1560 N Laurel Ave, #109, Los Angeles, CA 90046, USA

Webb, Justin *Singer, Musician, Songwriter*
%SuperVision Mgmt, 109B Regents Park Road, London NW1 8UR, England

Webb, Karrie *Golfer*
725 Presidential Dr, Boynton Beach, FL 33435, USA

Webb, Lucy *Actress, Comedienne*
1360 N Crescent Heights, #38, West Hollywood, CA 90046, USA

Webb, Richmond J *Football Player*
4120 Humphrey Dr, Dallas, TX 75216, USA

Webb, Russell (Russ) *Water Polo Player*
2362 Walnut Ave, Upland, CA 91784, USA

Webb, Tamilee *Physical Fitness Instructor*
PO Box 676107, Rancho Santa Fe, CA 92067, USA

Webb, Veronica *Model, Actress*
%Ford Model Agency, 142 Greene St, #400, New York, NY 10012, USA

Webb, Wayne *Bowler*
4413 McGuire St, North Las Vegas, NV 89031, USA

Webb, Wellington E *Mayor*
%Mayor's Office, City-County Building, 1437 Bannock St, Denver, CO 80202, USA

Webb, William H *Businessman*
%Altria Group, 120 Park Ave, New York, NY 10017, USA

Webber, Chris *Basketball Player*
%Sacramento Kings, Arco Arena, 1 Sports Parkway, Sacramento, CA 95834, USA

Webber, Julian Lloyd *Concert Cellist*
%Columbia Artists Mgmt Inc, 165 W 57th St, New York, NY 10019, USA

Webber, Mark *Actor*
%Handprint Entertainment, 1100 Glendon Ave, #1000, Los Angeles, CA 90024, USA

Webber, Tristan *Fashion Designer*
%Brower Lewis, 74 Gloucester Place, London W1H 3HN, England

Weber, Arnold R *Educator*
%Northwestern University, Chancellor's Office, Evanston, IL 60208, USA

Weber, Bob, Jr *Cartoonist (Slylock Fox)*
%King Features Syndicate, 888 7th Ave, New York, NY 10106, USA

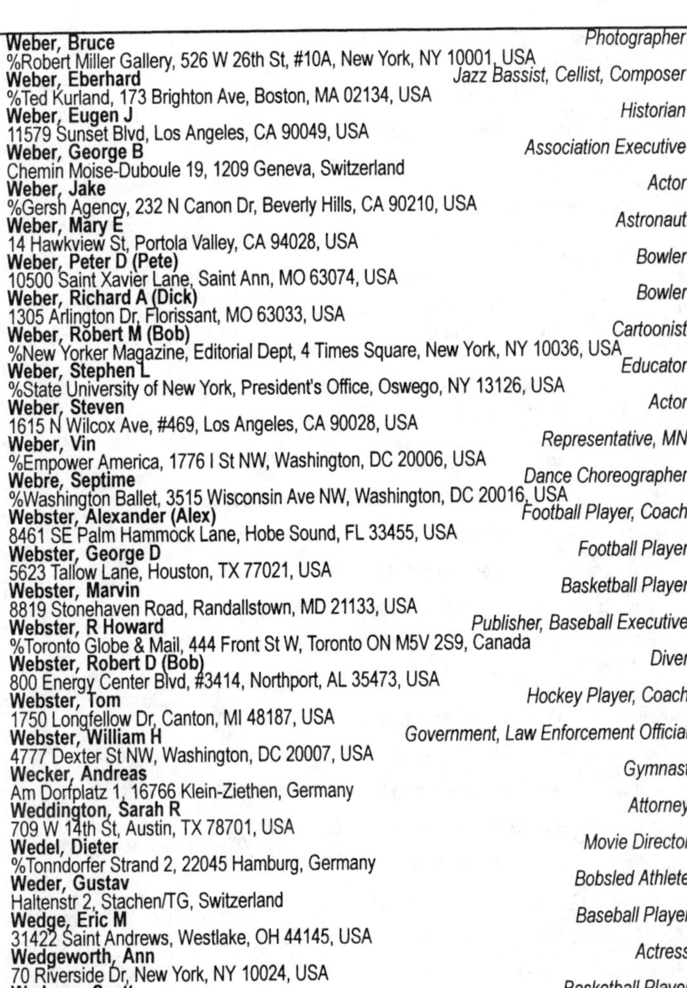

Weber, Bruce *Photographer*
%Robert Miller Gallery, 526 W 26th St, #10A, New York, NY 10001, USA

Weber, Eberhard *Jazz Bassist, Cellist, Composer*
%Ted Kurland, 173 Brighton Ave, Boston, MA 02134, USA

Weber, Eugen J *Historian*
11579 Sunset Blvd, Los Angeles, CA 90049, USA

Weber, George B *Association Executive*
Chemin Moise-Duboule 19, 1209 Geneva, Switzerland

Weber, Jake *Actor*
%Gersh Agency, 232 N Canon Dr, Beverly Hills, CA 90210, USA

Weber, Mary E *Astronaut*
14 Hawkview St, Portola Valley, CA 94028, USA

Weber, Peter D (Pete) *Bowler*
10500 Saint Xavier Lane, Saint Ann, MO 63074, USA

Weber, Richard A (Dick) *Bowler*
1305 Arlington Dr, Florissant, MO 63033, USA

Weber, Robert M (Bob) *Cartoonist*
%New Yorker Magazine, Editorial Dept, 4 Times Square, New York, NY 10036, USA

Weber, Stephen L *Educator*
%State University of New York, President's Office, Oswego, NY 13126, USA

Weber, Steven *Actor*
1615 N Wilcox Ave, #469, Los Angeles, CA 90028, USA

Weber, Vin *Representative, MN*
%Empower America, 1776 I St NW, Washington, DC 20006, USA

Webre, Septime *Dance Choreographer*
%Washington Ballet, 3515 Wisconsin Ave NW, Washington, DC 20016, USA

Webster, Alexander (Alex) *Football Player, Coach*
8461 SE Palm Hammock Lane, Hobe Sound, FL 33455, USA

Webster, George D *Football Player*
5623 Tallow Lane, Houston, TX 77021, USA

Webster, Marvin *Basketball Player*
8819 Stonehaven Road, Randallstown, MD 21133, USA

Webster, R Howard *Publisher, Baseball Executive*
%Toronto Globe & Mail, 444 Front St W, Toronto ON M5V 2S9, Canada

Webster, Robert D (Bob) *Diver*
800 Energy Center Blvd, #3414, Northport, AL 35473, USA

Webster, Tom *Hockey Player, Coach*
1750 Longfellow Dr, Canton, MI 48187, USA

Webster, William H *Government, Law Enforcement Official*
4777 Dexter St NW, Washington, DC 20007, USA

Wecker, Andreas *Gymnast*
Am Dorfplatz 1, 16766 Klein-Ziethen, Germany

Weddington, Sarah R *Attorney*
709 W 14th St, Austin, TX 78701, USA

Wedel, Dieter *Movie Director*
%Tonndorfer Strand 2, 22045 Hamburg, Germany

Weder, Gustav *Bobsled Athlete*
Haltenstr 2, Stachen/TG, Switzerland

Wedge, Eric M *Baseball Player*
31422 Saint Andrews, Westlake, OH 44145, USA

Wedgeworth, Ann *Actress*
70 Riverside Dr, New York, NY 10024, USA

Wedman, Scott *Basketball Player*
7912 NW Scenic Dr, Kansas City, MO 64152, USA

Wee Kim Wee *President, Singapore*
25 Siglap Plain, Singapore 456014, Singapore

Weed, Maurice James *Composer*
308 Overlook Road, #55, Asheville, NC 28803, USA

Weege, Reinhold *Television Producer*
2035 Via Don Benito, La Jolla, CA 92037, USA

Weeks, John D *Chemist*
15301 Watergate Road, Silver Spring, MD 20905, USA

Weeks, John R *Architect*
39 Jackson's Lane, Highgate, London N6 5SR, England

Weese, Miranda *Ballerina*
%New York City Ballet, Lincoln Center Plaza, New York, NY 10023, USA

Wefald, Jon *Educator*
%Kansas State University, President's Office, Manhattan, KS 66506, USA

Wegman, William G *Artist, Photographer*
239 W 18th St, New York, NY 10011, USA

Wegner, Hans J *Furniture Designer*
Tinglevej 17, 2820 Gentof'tte, Denmark

Wehling, Ulrich *Nordic Combined Athlete*
%Skiverband, Hubertusstr 1, 81477 Munich, Germany

Wehrli, Roger R *Football Player*
46 Fox Meadows Court, Saint Charles, MO 63303, USA

Wei Hui *Writer*
%Pocket Books, 1230 Ave of Americas, New York, NY 10020, USA

W

Wei, Dan-Wen *Concert Pianist*
%Columbia Artists Mgmt Inc, 165 W 57th St, New York, NY 10019, USA
Wei, James *Chemical Engineer*
571 Lake St, Princeton, NJ 08540, USA
Weibel, Robert *Pediatrician*
%University of Pennsylvania, Med School, Pediatrics Dept, Philadelphia, PA 19104, USA
Weibring, D A *Golfer*
1315 Garden Grove Court, Plano, TX 75075, USA
Weicker, Lowell P, Jr *Governor, Senator, CT*
200 Duke St, Alexandria, VA 22314, USA
Weida, Johnny *Air Force General, Educator*
Superintendent, US Air Force Academy, Colorado Springs, CO 80840, USA
Weidemann, Jakob *Artist*
Ringsveen, 2600 Lillehammer, Norway
Weidenbaum, Murray L *Government Official, Economist*
6231 Rosebury Ave, Saint Louis, MO 63105, USA
Weidenfeld of Chelsea, Arthur G *Publisher*
9 Chelsea Embankment, London SW3 4LE, England
Weider, Joe *Publisher*
%Weider Health & Fitness, 21100 Erwin St, Woodland Hills, CA 91367, USA
Weidinger, Christine *Opera Singer*
%John J Miller, 801 W 181st St, #20, New York, NY 10033, USA
Weidlinger, Paul *Civil Engineer*
%Weidlinger Assoc, 375 Hudson Ave, New York, NY 10014, USA
Weigel, Teri *Model, Actress*
6433 Topanga Canyon Blvd, #103, Woodland Hills, CA 91303, USA
Weight, Doug *Hockey Player*
%Saint Louis Blues, Sawis Center, 1401 Clark Ave, Saint Louis, MO 63103, USA
Weihenmayer, Erik *Mountaineer*
682 Partridge Circle, Golden, CO 80403, USA
Weikel, M Keith *Businessman*
%Manor Care Inc, 333 N Summit St, Toledo, OH 43604, USA
Weikl, Bernd *Opera Singer*
%Ulf Tornqvist, Sankt Eriksgatan 100, 113 31 Stockholm, Sweden
Weil, Andrew *Physician*
%University of Arizona, Medical Center, 1501 N Campbell Ave, Tucson, AZ 85724, USA
Weil, Bruno *Conductor, Composer*
%Kaylor Mgmt, 130 W 57th St, #8G, New York, NY 10019, USA
Weil, Cynthia *Songwriter*
%Gorfaine/Schwartz, 13245 Riverside Dr, #450, Sherman Oaks, CA 91423, USA
Weil, Frank A *Association Executive*
%Smithsonian Institution, 900 Jefferson Dr SW, Washington, DC 20560, USA
Weil, Liza *Actress*
%Creative Artists Agency, 9830 Wilshire Blvd, Beverly Hills, CA 90212, USA
Weiland, Scott *Singer (Stone Temple Pilots), Songwriter*
%Q Prime, 729 7th Ave, #1600, New York, NY 10019, USA
Weill, Claudia B *Movie Director*
2800 Seattle Dr, Los Angeles, CA 90046, USA
Weill, David (Dave) *Track Athlete*
120 Mountain Spring Ave, San Francisco, CA 94114, USA
Weill, Sanford I (Sandy) *Businessman*
%Citigroup Inc, 399 Park Ave, New York, NY 10022, USA
Wein, George *Musical Producer*
%Festival Productions, 311 W 74th St, New York, NY 10023, USA
Weinbach, Arthur F *Businessman*
%Automatic Data Processing, 1 ADP Blvd, Roseland, NJ 07068, USA
Weinbach, Lawrence A *Businessman*
%Unisys Corp, Unisys Way, Blue Bell, PA 19424, USA
Weinberg, Alvin M *Physicist*
111 Moylan Lane, Oak Ridge, TN 37830, USA
Weinberg, John L *Financier*
%Goldman Sachs Co, 85 Broad St, New York, NY 10004, USA
Weinberg, Max *Drummer (E-Street Band)*
%Panacea Entertainment, 12020 Chandler Blvd, #300, North Hollywood, CA 91607, USA
Weinberg, Robert A *Cancer Researcher, Biochemist*
%Whitehead Institute, 9 Cambridge Center, Cambridge, MA 02142, USA
Weinberg, Steven *Nobel Physics Laureate*
%University of Texas, Physics Dept, 2613 Wichita St, Austin, TX 78712, USA
Weinberger, Caspar W *Secretary, Defense & HEW; Publisher*
%Rogers & Wells, 2001 K St NW, Washington, DC 20006, USA
Weinbrecht, Donna *Freestyle Moguls Skier*
%General Delivery, West Milford, NJ 07480, USA
Weiner, Art E *Football Player*
404 Kimberly Dr, Greensboro, NC 27408, USA
Weiner, Gerry *Government Official, Canada*
40 Fredmir St, Dollard-des-Ormeaux PQ H9A 2R3, Canada
Weiner, Timothy E (Tim) *Journalist*
%New York Times, Editorial Dept, 1627 I St NW, Washington, DC 20006, USA

Weingarten, David M *Architect*
%Ace Architects, 330 2nd St, Oakland, CA 94607, USA
Weingarten, Reid *Attorney*
%Steptoe & Johnson, 4603 Harrison St, Chevy Chase, MD 20815, USA
Weinger, Scott *Actor*
9255 Sunset Blvd, #1010, West Hollywood, CA 90069, USA
Weinke, Chris *Football Player*
%Carolina Panthers, Ericsson Stadium, 800 S Mint St, Charlotte, NC 28202, USA
Weinstein, Arnold A *Writer, Lyricist*
%Columbia University, English Dept, New York, NY 10027, USA
Weinstein, Diane Gilbert *Judge*
%US Court of Claims, 717 Madison Place NW, Washington, DC 20439, USA
Weinstein, Harvey *Movie Producer*
%Miramax Films, 1995 Broadway, New York, NY 10023, USA
Weinstein, Robert (Bob) *Movie Producer*
%Miramax Films, 7920 Sunset Blvd, Los Angeles, CA 90046, USA
Weinstein, Sidney T *Army General*
11936 Holly Branch Court, Great Falls, VA 22066, USA
Weintraub, Jerry *Movie Producer*
27740 Pacific Coast Highway, Malibu, CA 90265, USA
Weir, Bob *Guitarist (Grateful Dead)*
%Grateful Dead, PO Box 1073, San Rafael, CA 94915, USA
Weir, Gillian C *Concert Organist, Harpsichordist*
78 Robin Way, Tilehurst, Berks RG3 5SW, England
Weir, Judith *Composer*
%Chester Music, 8/9 Frith St, London W1V 5TZ, England
Weir, Mike *Golfer*
%Taboo Muskoka Sands, Muskoka Beach Road, Gravenhurst ON P1P 1R1, Canada
Weir, Peter L *Movie Director*
%Salt Pan Films, PO Box 29, Palm Beach NSW 2108, Australia
Weis, Joseph F, Jr *Judge*
%US Court of Appeals, US Courthouse, 700 Grant St, Pittsburgh, PA 15219, USA
Weisberg, Ruth *Artist*
11452 W Washington Blvd, Los Angeles, CA 90066, USA
Weisberg, Tim *Jazz Flutist*
%Pyramid Entertainment, 89 5th Ave, #700, New York, NY 10003, USA
Weisel, Heidi *Fashion Designer*
%Heidi Weisel Inc, 260 W 35th St, New York, NY 10001, USA
Weiser-Most, Franz *Conductor*
%Van Walsum Mgmt, 4 Addison Bridge Place, London W14 8XP, England
Weishoff, Paula *Volleyball Player*
20021 Colgate Circle, Huntington Beach, CA 92646, USA
Weiskopf, Tom *Golfer*
7580 E Gray Road, Scottsdale, AZ 85260, USA
Weiskrantz, Lawrence *Psychologist*
%Oxford University, Experimental Psychology Dept, Oxford OX1 3UD, England
Weisman, Ben *Composer*
4527 Alla Road, #3, Marina del Rey, CA 90292, USA
Weisman, Sam *Actor, Director*
4448 Tujunga Ave, North Hollywood, CA 91602, USA
Weisner, Maurice F *Navy Admiral*
351 Woodbine Dr, Pensacola, FL 32503, USA
Weiss, Janet *Singer, Drummer (Sleater-Kinney)*
%Legends of 21st Century, 7 Trinity Row, Florence, MA 01062, USA
Weiss, Melvyn I *Attorney*
%Milberg Weiss Bershad, 1 Pennsylvania Plaza, New York, NY 10119, USA
Weiss, Michael T *Actor*
%Endeavor Talent Agency, 9701 Wilshire Blvd, #1000, Beverly Hills, CA 90212, USA
Weiss, Morry *Businessman*
%American Greetings Corp, 1 American Road, Cleveland, OH 44144, USA
Weiss, Robert W (Bob) *Basketball Player, Coach*
1600 Windermere Dr E, Seattle, WA 98112, USA
Weiss, Roberta *Actress*
%Sarnoff Co, 3500 W Olive Ave, #300, Burbank, CA 91505, USA
Weiss, Walter W *Baseball Player*
1275 Castlepoint Circle, Castle Rock, CO 80108, USA
Weissenberg, Alexis *Concert Pianist*
%Michael Schmidt, 59 E 54th St, #83, New York, NY 10022, USA
Weissflog, Jens *Ski Jumper*
Markt 2, 09484 Kurort Oberwiesenthal, Germany
Weissman, Irving L *Cancer Biologist, Pathologist*
%Stanford University, Pathology Dept, Beckman Center, Stanford, CA 94305, USA
Weissman, Robert *Businessman*
%IMS Health Inc, 1499 Post Road, Fairfield, CT 06824, USA
Weisz, Paul B *Chemical Engineer, Physicist*
%University of Pennsylvania, Bio-Engineering Dept, Philadelphia, PA 19104, USA
Weisz, Rachel *Actress*
%Creative Artists Agency, 9830 Wilshire Blvd, Beverly Hills, CA 90212, USA

W

Weithaas, Antje *Concert Violinist*
%Harrison/Parrott, 12 Penzance Place, London W11 4PA England
Weitz, Bruce *Actor*
18826 Erwin St, Tarzana, CA 91335, USA
Weitz, Paul J *Astronaut*
3086 N Tam Oshanter Dr, Flagstaff, AZ 86004, USA
Weitzman, Howard L *Attorney*
%Katten Muchin Zavis Weitzman, 1999 Ave of Stars, #1400, Los Angeles, CA 90067, USA
Weizman, Ezer *President, Israel; Air Force General*
Beit Amot Mishpat, 8 Shaul Hamelech Blvd, Tel-Aviv 64733, Israel
Welch, Gillian *Singer*
%Keith Case Assoc, 1025 17th Ave S, #200, Nashville, TN 37212, USA
Welch, Jack *Astronomer*
%University of California, Electrical Engineering Dept, Berkeley, CA 94720, USA
Welch, John F, Jr *Businessman*
%General Electric Co, 3135 Easton Turnpike, Fairfield, CT 06828, USA
Welch, Justin *Drummer (Elastica)*
%CMO Mgmt, Ransomes Dock, 35037 Parkgate Road, London SW11 4NP, England
Welch, Kevin *Singer, Songwriter*
%Press Network, 1035 16th Ave S, #200, Nashville, TN 37212, USA
Welch, Lenny *Singer*
%Brothers Mgmt, 141 Dunbar Ave, Fords, NJ 08863, USA
Welch, Raquel *Actress*
9903 Santa Monica Blvd, #514, Beverly Hills, CA 90212, USA
Welch, Robert L (Bob) *Baseball Player*
11055 E Gold Dust Ave, Scottsdale, AZ 85259, USA
Welch, Tahnee *Actress, Model*
PO Box 823, Beverly Hills, CA 90213, USA
Weld, William F *Governor, MA*
%Hale & Dorr, 60 State St, Boston, MA 02109, USA
Weldon, Fay *Writer*
24 Ryland Road, London NW5 3EA, England
Weldon, Joan *Actress*
67 E 78th St, New York, NY 10021, USA
Weldon, W Casey *Football Player*
%Washington Redskins, 21300 Redskin Park Dr, Ashburn, VA 20147, USA
Welland, Colin *Actor, Writer*
%Peter Charlesworth, 68 Old Brompton Road, London SW7 3LQ, England
Weller, Freddie *Singer, Songwriter*
%Ace Productions, PO Box 428, Portland, TN 37148, USA
Weller, Mary Louise *Actress*
1416 N Hayvenhurst Dr, #11, West Hollywood, CA 90046, USA
Weller, Michael *Writer*
%Rosenstone/Wender, 38 E 29th St, New York, NY 10016, USA
Weller, Peter *Actor*
8401 Cresthill Road, Los Angeles, CA 90069, USA
Weller, Thomas H *Nobel Medicine Laureate*
56 Winding River Road, Needham, MA 02492, USA
Weller, Walter *Conductor, Concert Violinist*
Doblinger Hauptstr 40, 1190 Vienna, Austria
Wellford, Harry W *Judge*
%US Court of Appeals, Federal Building, 167 N Main St, Memphis, TN 38103, USA
Welling, Tom *Actor*
%Lori Marshall, 6228 Beresford St, Burnaby BC V5J 1K2, Canada
Wellington, Harry H *Educator*
%New York Law School, 57 Worth St, New York, NY 10013, USA
Welliver, Titus *Actor*
%Innovative Artists, 1505 10th St, Santa Monica, CA 90401, USA
Wellman, William, Jr *Actor*
410 N Barrington Ave, Los Angeles, CA 90049, USA
Wells, Annie *Photojournalist*
%Press Democrat, Editorial Dept, 427 Mendocino Ave, Santa Rosa, CA 95401, USA
Wells, Audrey *Writer, Movie Director*
%Endeavor Talent Agency, 9701 Wilshire Blvd, #1000, Beverly Hills, CA 90212, USA
Wells, Carole *Actress*
%Burton Moss, 8827 Beverly Blvd, #L, Los Angeles, CA 90048, USA
Wells, Cory *Singer (Three Dog Night)*
3853 Carbon Canyon Road, Malibu, CA 90265, USA
Wells, David L (Dave) *Baseball Player*
2519 N McMullen Booth Road, #510-198, Clearwater, FL 33761, USA
Wells, Dawn *Actress*
4616 Ledge Ave, Toluca Lake, CA 91602, USA
Wells, Kitty *Singer*
%Midnight Special Productions, PO Box 916, Hendersonville, TN 37077, USA
Wells, Mark *Hockey Player*
27619 Harrison Woods Lane, Harrison Township, MI 48045, USA
Wells, Patricia *Journalist*
%Harper Collins Publishers, 10 E 53rd St, New York, NY 10022, USA

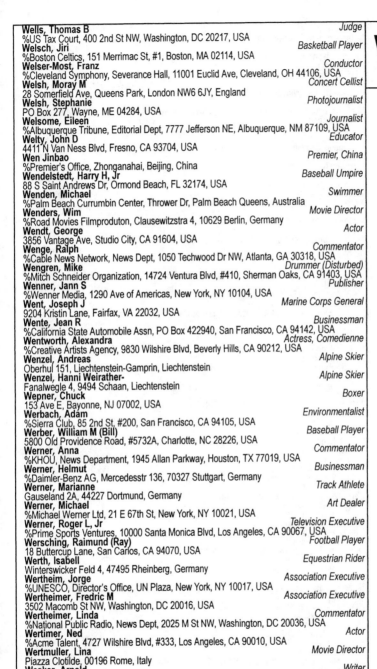

Wells, Thomas B *Judge*
%US Tax Court, 400 2nd St NW, Washington, DC 20217, USA
Welsch, Jiri *Basketball Player*
%Boston Celtics, 151 Merrimac St, #1, Boston, MA 02114, USA
Welser-Most, Franz *Conductor*
%Cleveland Symphony, Severance Hall, 11001 Euclid Ave, Cleveland, OH 44106, USA
Welsh, Moray M *Concert Cellist*
28 Somerfield Ave, Queens Park, London NW6 6JY, England
Welsh, Stephanie *Photojournalist*
PO Box 277, Wayne, ME 04284, USA
Welsome, Eileen *Journalist*
%Albuquerque Tribune, Editorial Dept, 7777 Jefferson NE, Albuquerque, NM 87109, USA
Welty, John D *Educator*
4411 N Van Ness Blvd, Fresno, CA 93704, USA
Wen Jinbao *Premier, China*
%Premier's Office, Zhonganahai, Beijing, China
Wendelstedt, Harry H, Jr *Baseball Umpire*
88 S Saint Andrews Dr, Ormond Beach, FL 32174, USA
Wenden, Michael *Swimmer*
%Palm Beach Currumbin Center, Thrower Dr, Palm Beach Queens, Australia
Wenders, Wim *Movie Director*
%Road Movies Filmproduton, Clausewitzstra 4, 10629 Berlin, Germany
Wendt, George *Actor*
3856 Vantage Ave, Studio City, CA 91604, USA
Wenge, Ralph *Commentator*
%Cable News Network, News Dept, 1050 Techwood Dr NW, Atlanta, GA 30318, USA
Wengren, Mike *Drummer (Disturbed)*
%Mitch Schneider Organization, 14724 Ventura Blvd, #410, Sherman Oaks, CA 91403, USA
Wenner, Jann S *Publisher*
%Wenner Media, 1290 Ave of Americas, New York, NY 10104, USA
Went, Joseph J *Marine Corps General*
9204 Kristin Lane, Fairfax, VA 22032, USA
Wente, Jean R *Businessman*
%California State Automobile Assn, PO Box 422940, San Francisco, CA 94142, USA
Wentworth, Alexandra *Actress, Comedienne*
%Creative Artists Agency, 9830 Wilshire Blvd, Beverly Hills, CA 90212, USA
Wenzel, Andreas *Alpine Skier*
Oberhul 151, Liechtenstein-Gamprin, Liechtenstein
Wenzel, Hanni Weirather- *Alpine Skier*
Fanalwegle 4, 9494 Schaan, Liechtenstein
Wepner, Chuck *Boxer*
153 Ave E, Bayonne, NJ 07002, USA
Werbach, Adam *Environmentalist*
%Sierra Club, 85 2nd St, #200, San Francisco, CA 94105, USA
Werber, William M (Bill) *Baseball Player*
5800 Old Providence Road, #5732A, Charlotte, NC 28226, USA
Werner, Anna *Commentator*
%KHOU, News Department, 1945 Allan Parkway, Houston, TX 77019, USA
Werner, Helmut *Businessman*
%Daimler-Benz AG, Mercedesstr 136, 70327 Stuttgart, Germany
Werner, Marianne *Track Athlete*
Gauseland 2A, 44227 Dortmund, Germany
Werner, Michael *Art Dealer*
%Michael Werner Ltd, 21 E 67th St, New York, NY 10021, USA
Werner, Roger L, Jr *Television Executive*
%Prime Sports Ventures, 10000 Santa Monica Blvd, Los Angeles, CA 90067, USA
Wersching, Raimund (Ray) *Football Player*
18 Buttercup Lane, San Carlos, CA 94070, USA
Werth, Isabell *Equestrian Rider*
Winterswicker Feld 4, 47495 Rheinberg, Germany
Wertheim, Jorge *Association Executive*
%UNESCO, Director's Office, UN Plaza, New York, NY 10017, USA
Wertheimer, Fredric M *Association Executive*
3502 Macomb St NW, Washington, DC 20016, USA
Wertheimer, Linda *Commentator*
%National Public Radio, News Dept, 2025 M St NW, Washington, DC 20036, USA
Wertimer, Ned *Actor*
%Acme Talent, 4727 Wilshire Blvd, #333, Los Angeles, CA 90010, USA
Wertmuller, Lina *Movie Director*
Piazza Clotilde, 00196 Rome, Italy
Wesker, Arnold *Writer*
37 Ashley Road, London N19 3AG, England
Wesley, Norman *Businessman*
%Fortune Brands Inc, 300 Tower Parkway, Lincolnshire, IL 60069, USA
Wesselmann, Tom *Artist*
RR 1 Box 36, Long Eddy, NY 12760, USA
West, Adam *Actor*
PO Box 1668, Ketchum, ID 83340, USA

W

West, Cornel *Theologian, Sociologist*
%Harvard University, Afro American Studies Dept, Cambridge, MA 02138, USA
West, David *Basketball Player*
%New Orleans Hornets, New Orleans Arena, 1501 Girod St, New Orleans, LA 70113, USA
West, Doug *Basketball Player*
15 Holly Road, Wheeling, WV 26003, USA
West, Ernest E *Korean War Army Hero (CMH)*
912 Adams Ave, Wurtland, KY 41144, USA
West, Jake *Labor Leader*
%International Assn of Iron Workers, 1750 New York Ave NW, Washington, DC 20006, USA
West, James E *Inventor (Telephone Microphone)*
724 Berkeley Ave, Plainfield, NJ 07062, USA
West, Jerome A (Jerry) *Basketball Player, Executive*
%Memphis Grizzlies, 175 Toyota Plaza, #150, Memphis, TN 38103, USA
West, Joel *Model*
%William Morris Agency, 1325 Ave of Americas, New York, NY 10019, USA
West, John C *Governor, SC; Diplomat*
PO Box 13, Hilton Head Island, SC 29938, USA
West, Jon Fredric *Opera Singer*
%Opera et Concert, Maximilianstr 22, 80539 Munich, Germany
West, Leslie *Singer, Guitarist*
%James Faith Entertainment, 318 Wynne Lane, Port Jefferson, NY 11777, USA
West, Lizzie *Singer*
%Warner Bros Records, 3300 Warner Blvd, Burbank, CA 91505, USA
West, Mark *Basketball Player*
715 E Forest Hills Dr, Phoenix, AZ 85022, USA
West, Paul *Writer*
%Elaine Markson, 44 Greenwich Ave, New York, NY 10011, USA
West, Richard L *WW II Army Air Corps Hero*
1603 Morningside Dr, Chillicothe, MO 64601, USA
West, Samuel *Actor*
%P F D, Drury House, 34-43 Russell St, London WC2B 5HA, England
West, Shane *Actor*
%Strong/Morrone, 9100 Wilshire Blvd, #503E, Beverly Hills, CA 90212, USA
West, Shelly *Singer*
%West Hood Entertainment, PO Box 158718, Nashville, TN 37215, USA
West, Timothy L *Actor*
%Gavin Barker Assoc, 2D Wimpole St, London W1G 0EB, England
West, Togo D, Jr *Secretary, Veterans Affairs*
922 N Cameron Ave, Winston Salem, NC 27101, USA
Westbrook, Bryant *Football Player*
7710 Hunters Point Dr, Sugar Land, TX 77479, USA
Westbrook, Michael *Football Player*
%Cincinnati Bengals, 1 Paul Brown Stadium, Cincinnati, OH 45202, USA
Westerberg, Paul *Singer, Songwriter*
%Mitch Schneider Organization, 14724 Ventura Blvd, #410, Sherman Oaks, CA 91403, USA
Westerfield, Putney *Publisher*
10 Green View Lane, Hillsborough, CA 94010, USA
Westfall, V Edward (Ed) *Hockey Player*
699 Hillside Ave, New Hyde Park, NY 11040, USA
Westhead, Paul *Basketball Coach*
2217 Via Alamitos, Palos Verdes Estates, CA 90274, USA
Westheimer, David K *Writer*
11722 Darlington Ave, #2, Los Angeles, CA 90049, USA
Westheimer, Frank H *Organic Chemist*
3 Berkeley St, Cambridge, MA 02138, USA
Westheimer, Gerald *Optometrist*
582 Santa Barbara Road, Berkeley, CA 94707, USA
Westheimer, Ruth S *Sex Therapist, Psychologist*
900 W 190th St, New York, NY 10040, USA
Westlake, Donald E *Writer*
%Knox Burger Assoc, 425 Madison Ave, New York, NY 10017, USA
Westling, Jon *Educator*
285 Goddard Ave, Brookline, MA 02445, USA
Westmoreland, James *Actor*
8019 1/2 W Norton Ave, West Hollywood, CA 90046, USA
Westmoreland, William C *Army General*
1 Gadsden Way, #CTG, Charleston, SC 29412, USA
Weston, Celia *Actress*
%Innovative Artists, 1505 10th St, Santa Monica, CA 90401, USA
Weston, J Fred *Educator*
258 Tavistock Ave, Los Angeles, CA 90049, USA
Weston, P John *Government Official, England*
13 Denbigh Gardens, Richmond, Surrey TW10 6EN, England
Weston, Randolph (Randy) *Jazz Pianist*
PO Box 749, Maplewood, NJ 07040, USA
Westphal, James A *Space Scientist*
%California Institute of Technology, Planetary Sciences Dept, Pasadena, CA 91125, USA

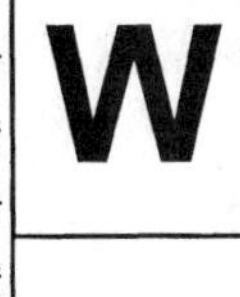

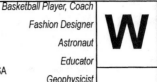

Westphal, Paul D *Basketball Player, Coach*
16640 Cumbre Verde Court, Pacific Palisades, CA 90272, USA
Westwood, Vivienne *Fashion Designer*
%Westwood Studios, 9-15 Elcho St, London SW11 4AU, England
Wetherbee, James D *Astronaut*
710 Huntercrest St, Seabrook, TX 77586, USA
Wetherell, T R *Educator*
%Florida State University, Athletic Dept, Tallahassee, FL 32306, USA
Wetherill, George W *Geophysicist*
%Carnegie Institution, Terrestrial Magnetism Dept, Washington, DC 20015, USA
Wethington, Charles T, Jr *Educator*
2926 Four Pines Dr, Lexington, KY 40502, USA
Wetnight, Ryan S *Football Player*
2752 E Fremont Ave, Fresno, CA 93710, USA
Wetter, Friedrich Cardinal *Religious Leader*
Kardinal-Faulhaber-Str 7, 80333 Munich, Germany
Wettig, Patricia *Actress*
522 Arbamar Place, Pacific Palisades, CA 90272, USA
Wetton, John *Singer, Bassist*
%Entourage Talent, 133 W 25th St, #500, New York, NY 10001, USA
Wetzel, Gary G *Vietnam War Army Hero (CMH)*
PO Box 84, Oak Creek, WI 53154, USA
Wetzel, John *Basketball, Player Coach*
13011 N Sunrise Canyon Lane, Marana, AZ 85653, USA
Wetzel, Robert L *Army General*
1425 Dartmouth Road, Columbus, GA 31904, USA
Wexler, Anne *Government Official*
1317 F St NW, #600, Washington, DC 20004, USA
Wexler, Haskell *Cinematographer*
1247 Lincoln Blvd, #585, Santa Monica, CA 90401, USA
Wexler, Jacqueline G *Educator*
222 Park Ave S, New York, NY 10003, USA
Wexner, Leslie H *Businessman*
%Limited Inc, 3 Limited Parkway, PO Box 16000, Columbus, OH 43216, USA
Weyand, Frederick C *Army General*
5002 Maunalani Circle, Honolulu, HI 96816, USA
Weyerhaeuser, George *Businessman*
%Weyerhaeuser Co, 33663 32nd Ave S, Federal Way, WA 98023, USA
Weymouth, Tina *Bassist (Talking Heads, Tom Tom Club)*
%Premier Talent, 3 E 54th St, #1100, New York, NY 10022, USA
Whalen, Laurence J *Judge*
%US Tax Court, 400 2nd St NW, Washington, DC 20217, USA
Whaley, Suzi *Golfer*
1 Essex Court, Farmington, CT 06032, USA
Whalley, Joanne *Actress*
1435 Lindacrest Dr, Beverly Hills, CA 90210, USA
Whalum, Kirk *Jazz Saxophonist*
%Cole Classic Mgmt, PO Box 231, Canoga Park, CA 91305, USA
Wharton, Bernard *Architect*
%Shope Reno Wharton, 18 W Putnam Ave, Greenwich, CT 06830, USA
Wheatley, E H *Publisher*
%Vancouver Sun, 2250 Granville St, Vancouver BC V6H 3G2, Canada
Wheatley, Tyrone *Football Player*
4794 Woodrose Circle, Dublin, CA 94568, USA
Wheaton, David *Tennis Player*
20045 Cottagewood Ave, Excelsior, MN 55331, USA
Wheaton, Wil *Actor*
2603 Seapine Lane, La Crescenta, CA 91214, USA
Wheeler, Charles F *Cinematographer*
79125 Jack Rabbit Trail, La Quinta, CA 92253, USA
Wheeler, Cheryl *Singer, Songwriter*
%Morningstar Mgmt, PO Box 1770, Hendersonville, TN 37077, USA
Wheeler, Daniel S *Editor*
%American Legion Magazine, 700 N Pennsylvania St, Indianapolis, IN 46204, USA
Wheeler, H Anthony *Architect*
Hawthornbank House, Dean Village, Edinburgh EH4 3BH, Scotland
Wheeler, John *Actor*
%Levin Agency, 8484 Wilshire Blvd, #745, Beverly Hills, CA 90211, USA
Wheeler, John A *Physicist*
1904 Meadow Lane, Hightstown, NJ 08520, USA
Whelan, Bill *Composer*
%Sony Records, 2100 Colorado Ave, Santa Monica, CA 90404, USA
Whelan, Wendy *Ballerina*
%New York City Ballet, Lincoln Center Plaza, New York, NY 10023, USA
Whelchel, Lisa *Actress*
8221 Navisota Dr, Lantana, TX 76226, USA
Wheless, Jamy *Animator*
405 Fair St, Petaluma, CA 94952, USA

W

Whicker, Alan D *Commentator*
Le Gallais Chambers, Saint Helier, Jersey, United Kingdom
Whinnery, Barbara *Actress*
%Baier/Kleinman, 3575 Cahuenga Blvd, #500, Los Angeles, CA 90068, USA
Whinnery, John R *Electrical Engineer*
1804 Wales Dr, Walnut Creek, CA 94595, USA
Whipple, Fred L *Astronomer*
35 Elizabeth Road, Belmont, MA 02478, USA
Whishaw, Anthony *Artist*
7A Albert Place, Victoria Road, London W8 5PD, England
Whisler, J Steven *Businessman*
%Phelps Dodge Corp, 1 N Central Ave, Phoenix, AZ 85004, USA
Whiston, Don *Hockey Player*
2 Jeffreys Neck, Ipswich, MA 01938, USA
Whitacre, Edward E, Jr *Businessman*
%SBC Communications, 175 E Houston, San Antonio, TX 78205, USA
Whitaker, Forest *Actor, Director*
%Three Arts Entertainment, 9460 Wilshire Blvd, #700, Beverly Hills, CA 90212, USA
Whitaker, Jack *Sportscaster*
500 Berwyn Baptist Road, #L-Fleur, Devon, PA 19333, USA
Whitaker, Jack *Golfer*
%Int'l Golf Partners, 3300 PGA Blvd, #820, West Palm Beach, FL 33410, USA
Whitaker, Louis R (Lou), Jr *Baseball Player*
803 Pipe St, Martinsville, VA 24112, USA
Whitaker, Mark *Editor*
%Newsweek Magazine, Editorial Dept, 251 W 57th St, New York, NY 10019, USA
Whitaker, Meade *Judge*
%US Tax Court, 400 2nd St NW, Washington, DC 20217, USA
Whitaker, Pernell *Boxer*
3808 Cranberry Court, Virginia Beach, VA 23456, USA
Whitbread, Fatima *Track Athlete*
%Chafford Information Ctr, Elizabeth Road, Grays, Essex RM16 6QZ, England
Whitcomb, Bob *Auto Racing Executive*
%Whitcomb Racing, 9201 Garrison Road, Charlotte, NC 28278, USA
Whitcomb, Edgar D *Governor, IN*
15415 Rome Road, Rome, IN 47574, USA
Whitcomb, Richard T *Inventor (Supercritical Wing)*
119 Tide Mill Lane, Hampton, VA 23666, USA
White of Rhymney, Eirene L *Government Official, England*
64 Vandon Court, Petty France, London SW1H 9HF, England
White, Alan *Drummer (Oasis)*
%Ignition Mgmt, 54 Linhope St, London NW1 6HL, England
White, Alvin S (Al) *Test Pilot*
14254 N Fawnbrooke Dr, Tucson, AZ 85737, USA
White, Betty *Actress, Comedienne*
PO Box 491965, Los Angeles, CA 90049, USA
White, Bryan *Singer, Songwriter*
%Holly Co, 3415 W End Ave, #101G, Nashville, TN 37203, USA
White, Charles R *Football Player, Administrator*
51 Foxtail Lane, Dove Canyon, CA 92679, USA
White, Chris *Bassist (Zombies)*
%Lustig Talent, PO Box 770850, Orlando, FL 32877, USA
White, Devon M *Baseball Player*
6440 E Sierra Vista Dr, Paradise Valley, AZ 85253, USA
White, Dwight *Football Player, Financier*
406 Landon Gate, Pittsburgh, PA 15238, USA
White, Edmund V *Writer*
%Maxine Groffsky, 2 5th Ave, New York, NY 10011, USA
White, Edward A (Ed) *Football Player*
PO Box 1437, Julian, CA 92036, USA
White, Frank *Baseball Player*
5335 W 96th St, Shawnee Mission, KS 66207, USA
White, Gilbert F *Geographer*
624 Pearl St, #302, Boulder, CO 80302, USA
White, Jaleel *Actor*
8916 Ashcroft Ave, West Hollywood, CA 90048, USA
White, James B *Attorney, Educator*
1606 Morton Ave, Ann Arbor, MI 48104, USA
White, John H *Photojournalist*
%Chicago Sun-Times, Editorial Dept, 401 N Wabash Ave, Chicago, IL 60611, USA
White, John Patrick *Actor*
%Metropolitan Talent Agency, 4526 Wilshire Blvd, Los Angeles, CA 90010, USA
White, Josh, Jr *Singer*
23625 Ripple Creek, Novi, MI 48375, USA
White, Joy Lynn *Singer*
%Buddy Lee, 38 Music Square E, #300, Nashville, TN 37203, USA
White, Judith M *Biologist*
%University of San Francisco, Biology Dept, San Francisco, CA 94117, USA

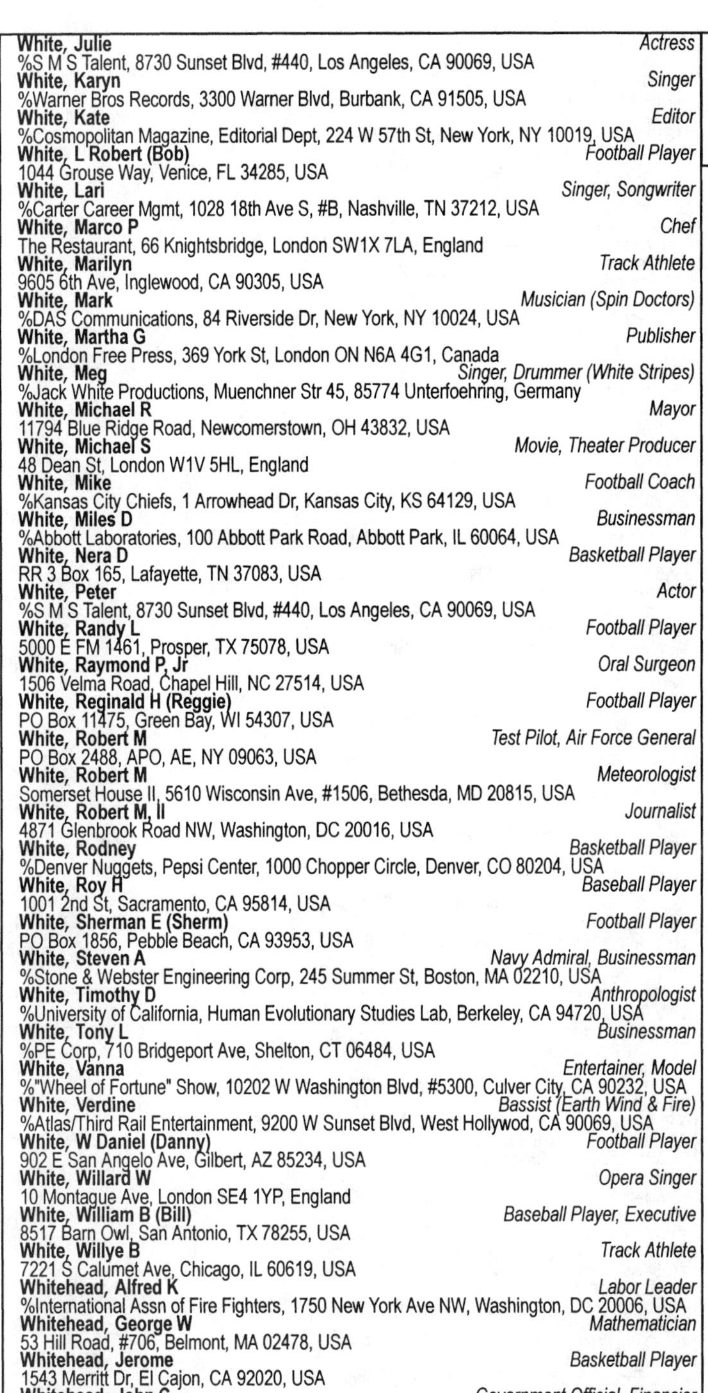

White, Julie *Actress*
%S M S Talent, 8730 Sunset Blvd, #440, Los Angeles, CA 90069, USA
White, Karyn *Singer*
%Warner Bros Records, 3300 Warner Blvd, Burbank, CA 91505, USA
White, Kate *Editor*
%Cosmopolitan Magazine, Editorial Dept, 224 W 57th St, New York, NY 10019, USA
White, L Robert (Bob) *Football Player*
1044 Grouse Way, Venice, FL 34285, USA
White, Lari *Singer, Songwriter*
%Carter Career Mgmt, 1028 18th Ave S, #B, Nashville, TN 37212, USA
White, Marco P *Chef*
The Restaurant, 66 Knightsbridge, London SW1X 7LA, England
White, Marilyn *Track Athlete*
9605 6th Ave, Inglewood, CA 90305, USA
White, Mark *Musician (Spin Doctors)*
%DAS Communications, 84 Riverside Dr, New York, NY 10024, USA
White, Martha G *Publisher*
%London Free Press, 369 York St, London ON N6A 4G1, Canada
White, Meg *Singer, Drummer (White Stripes)*
%Jack White Productions, Muenchner Str 45, 85774 Unterfoehring, Germany
White, Michael R *Mayor*
11794 Blue Ridge Road, Newcomerstown, OH 43832, USA
White, Michael S *Movie, Theater Producer*
48 Dean St, London W1V 5HL, England
White, Mike *Football Coach*
%Kansas City Chiefs, 1 Arrowhead Dr, Kansas City, KS 64129, USA
White, Miles D *Businessman*
%Abbott Laboratories, 100 Abbott Park Road, Abbott Park, IL 60064, USA
White, Nera D *Basketball Player*
RR 3 Box 165, Lafayette, TN 37083, USA
White, Peter *Actor*
%S M S Talent, 8730 Sunset Blvd, #440, Los Angeles, CA 90069, USA
White, Randy L *Football Player*
5000 E FM 1461, Prosper, TX 75078, USA
White, Raymond P, Jr *Oral Surgeon*
1506 Velma Road, Chapel Hill, NC 27514, USA
White, Reginald H (Reggie) *Football Player*
PO Box 11475, Green Bay, WI 54307, USA
White, Robert M *Test Pilot, Air Force General*
PO Box 2488, APO, AE, NY 09063, USA
White, Robert M *Meteorologist*
Somerset House II, 5610 Wisconsin Ave, #1506, Bethesda, MD 20815, USA
White, Robert M, II *Journalist*
4871 Glenbrook Road NW, Washington, DC 20016, USA
White, Rodney *Basketball Player*
%Denver Nuggets, Pepsi Center, 1000 Chopper Circle, Denver, CO 80204, USA
White, Roy H *Baseball Player*
1001 2nd St, Sacramento, CA 95814, USA
White, Sherman E (Sherm) *Football Player*
PO Box 1856, Pebble Beach, CA 93953, USA
White, Steven A *Navy Admiral, Businessman*
%Stone & Webster Engineering Corp, 245 Summer St, Boston, MA 02210, USA
White, Timothy D *Anthropologist*
%University of California, Human Evolutionary Studies Lab, Berkeley, CA 94720, USA
White, Tony L *Businessman*
%PE Corp, 710 Bridgeport Ave, Shelton, CT 06484, USA
White, Vanna *Entertainer, Model*
%"Wheel of Fortune" Show, 10202 W Washington Blvd, #5300, Culver City, CA 90232, USA
White, Verdine *Bassist (Earth Wind & Fire)*
%Atlas/Third Rail Entertainment, 9200 W Sunset Blvd, West Hollywod, CA 90069, USA
White, W Daniel (Danny) *Football Player*
902 E San Angelo Ave, Gilbert, AZ 85234, USA
White, Willard W *Opera Singer*
10 Montague Ave, London SE4 1YP, England
White, William B (Bill) *Baseball Player, Executive*
8517 Barn Owl, San Antonio, TX 78255, USA
White, Willye B *Track Athlete*
7221 S Calumet Ave, Chicago, IL 60619, USA
Whitehead, Alfred K *Labor Leader*
%International Assn of Fire Fighters, 1750 New York Ave NW, Washington, DC 20006, USA
Whitehead, George W *Mathematician*
53 Hill Road, #706, Belmont, MA 02478, USA
Whitehead, Jerome *Basketball Player*
1543 Merritt Dr, El Cajon, CA 92020, USA
Whitehead, John C *Government Official, Financier*
131 Old Chester Road, Essex Fells, NJ 07021, USA
Whitehead, John C *Research Executive*
%Brookings Institute, 1775 Massachusetts Ave NW, Washington, DC 20036, USA

W

Whitehead, Paxton *Actor*
%Abrams Artists, 9200 Sunset Blvd, #1125, Los Angeles, CA 90069, USA
Whitehead, Richard F *Navy Admiral*
%American Cage & Machine Co, 135 S LaSalle St, Chicago, IL 60674, USA
Whitehurst, C David *Football Player*
11010 Linbrook Lane, Duluth, GA 30097, USA
Whitelaw, Billie *Actress*
Rose Cottage, Plum St, Glensford, Suffolk C010 7PX, England
Whitemore, Willet F, Jr *Cancer Researcher*
2 Hawthorne Lane, Plandome, NY 11030, USA
Whiteread, Rachel *Sculptor*
%Anthony d'Offay, 22 Dering St, London W1R 9AA, England
Whitesides, George M *Chemist*
124 Grasmere St, Newton, MA 02458, USA
Whitfield, Dondre T *Actor*
%Writers & Artists, 8383 Wilshire Blvd, #550, Beverly Hills, CA 90211, USA
Whitfield, Lynn *Actress*
%William Morris Agency, 151 El Camino Dr, Beverly Hills, CA 90212, USA
Whitfield, Malvin G (Mal) *Track Athlete*
1225 Harvard St NW, Washington, DC 20009, USA
Whitford, Brad *Guitarist (Aerosmith)*
PO Box 869, Norwell, MA 02061, USA
Whiting, Margaret *Singer*
41 W 58th St, #5A, New York, NY 10019, USA
Whitlam, E Gough *Prime Minister, Australia*
Westfield Towers, 100 William St, Sydney NSW 2011, Australia
Whitley, Chris *Singer, Songwriter*
%Feinstein Mgmt, 420 Lexington Ave, #2150, New York, NY 10170, USA
Whitman, Kari *Actress, Model*
1155 N La Cienega Blvd, #104, West Hollywood, CA 90069, USA
Whitman, Mae *Actress*
%CunninghamEscottDipene, 10635 Santa Monica Blvd, #130, Los Angeles, CA 90025, USA
Whitman, Marina Von Neumann *Economist*
%University of Michigan, Public Policy School, Ann Arbor, MI 48109, USA
Whitman, Meg *Businesswoman*
%eBay, 2145 Hamilton Ave, San Jose, CA 95125, USA
Whitman, Slim *Singer*
3830 Old Jennings Road, Middleburg, FL 32068, USA
Whitman, Stuart *Actor*
749 San Ysidro Road, Santa Barbara, CA 93108, USA
Whitmore, James *Actor*
4990 Puesta del Sol, Malibu, CA 90265, USA
Whitmore, James, Jr *Actor*
1284 La Brea St, Thousand Oaks, CA 91362, USA
Whitmore, Kay *Hockey Player*
16 Springwood Road, Farmington, CT 06032, USA
Whitney, Ashley *Swimmer*
125 Villa View Court, Brentwood, TN 37027, USA
Whitney, CeCe *Actress*
1145 Barham Dr, #217, San Marcos, CA 92078, USA
Whitney, Grace Lee *Actress*
PO Box 79, Coarsegold, CA 93614, USA
Whitney, Jane *Entertainer*
5 TV Place, Needham, MA 02494, USA
Whitson, Peggy A *Astronaut*
306 Lakeview Circle, Seabrook, TX 77586, USA
Whittaker, James (Jim) *Mountaineer*
2023 E Sims Way, #277, Port Townsend, WA 98368, USA
Whittaker, Roger *Singer, Songwriter*
%BML Mgmt, 426 Marsh Point Circle, Saint Augustine, FL 32080, USA
Whittingham, Charles A *Publisher*
11 Woodmill Road, Chappaqua, NY 10514, USA
Whitton, Margaret *Actress*
%William Morris Agency, 151 El Camino Dr, Beverly Hills, CA 90212, USA
Whitwam, David R *Businessman*
%Whirlpool Corp, 2000 N State St, RR 63, Benton Harbor, MI 49022, USA
Whitworth, Kathrynne A (Kathy) *Golfer*
1735 Misletoe Dr, Flower Mound, TX 75022, USA
Whyte, Sandra *Hockey Player*
81 Golden Hills Road, Saugus, MA 01906, USA
Wiberg, Kenneth B *Chemist*
160 Carmalt Road, Hamden, CT 06517, USA
Wiberg, Pernilla *Alpine Skier*
Katterunsvagen 32, 60 210 Norrkopping, Sweden
Wick, Charles Z *Government Official*
%US Information Agency, 400 C St SW, Washington, DC 20024, USA
Wicker, Thomas G (Tom) *Writer, Journalist*
PO Box 361, Rochester, VT 05767, USA

Wickham, John A, Jr — *Army General*
13590 N Fawnbrooke Dr, Tucson, AZ 85737, USA

Wicki-Fink, Agnes — *Actress*
Weisgerberstr 2, 80805 Munich, Germany

Wickman, Robert J (Bob) — *Baseball Player*
PO Box 105, Abrams, MI 54101, USA

Wicks, Ben — *Editorial Cartoonist*
38 Yorkville Ave, Toronto ON M4W 1L5, Canada

Wicks, Sidney — *Basketball Player*
1030 S La Jolla Ave, Los Angeles, CA 90035, USA

Wicks, Sue — *Basketball Player*
%New York Liberty, Madison Square Garden, 2 Penn Plaza, New York, NY 10121, USA

Widby, G Ronald (Ron) — *Football, Basketball Player*
542 Mahler Road, Wichita Falls, TX 76310, USA

Widdoes, Kathleen — *Actress*
%"As the World Turns" Show, CBS-TV, 524 W 57th St, #5330, New York, NY 10019, USA

Widdrington, Peter N T — *Businessman*
%Laidlaw Inc, 3221 N Service Road, Burlington ON L7R 3Y8, Canada

Wideman, John Edgar — *Writer*
%University of Massachusetts, English Dept, Amherst, MA 01003, USA

Widener, H Emory, Jr — *Judge*
%US Court of Appeals, PO Box 868, Abingdon, VA 24212, USA

Widman, Herbert (Herb) — *Water Polo Player*
844 Monarch Circle, San Jose, CA 95138, USA

Widmark, Richard — *Actor*
PO Box 232, Woodland Hills, CA 91365, USA

Widom, Benjamin — *Chemist*
204 The Parkway, Ithaca, NY 14850, USA

Wiebe, Susanne — *Fashion Designer*
Amalienstr 39, 80799 Munich, Germany

Wiedemann, Josef — *Architect*
Im Eichgeholz 11, 80997 Munich, Germany

Wiedlin, Jane — *Musician (Go-Go's)*
%Nick Ben-Meir, 652 N Doheny Dr, Los Angeles, CA 90069, USA

Wiedorfer, Paul J — *WW II Army Hero (CMH)*
2506 Moore Ave, Baltimore, MD 21234, USA

Wiegert, Zach — *Football Player*
3747 Saltmeadow Court S, Jacksonville, FL 32224, USA

Wielicki, Krzysztof — *Mountaineer*
Ul A Frycza Modrzewskiego 21, 43-100 Tychy, Poland

Wieman, Carl E — *Nobel Physics Laureate*
%University of Colorado, 440 Physics Campus Box, Boulder, CO 80309, USA

Wiener, Jacques L, Jr — *Judge*
%US Court of Appeals, Federal Building, 500 Fannin St, Shreveport, LA 71101, USA

Wier, Murray — *Basketball Player, Coach*
118 Goodwater St, Georgetown, TX 78628, USA

Wieschaus, Eric F — *Nobel Medicine Laureate*
11 Pelham St, Boston, MA 02118, USA

Wiese, John P — *Judge*
%US Claims Court, 717 Madison Place NW, Washington, DC 20439, USA

Wiesel, Elie — *Writer, Nobel Peace Laureate*
200 E 64th St, New York, NY 10021, USA

Wiesen, Bernard — *Movie Director*
Weisgerberstr 2, 80805 Munich, Germany

Wiesenthal, Simon — *War Crimes Activist*
%Jewish Documentation Center, Salztorgasse 6, 1010 Vienna, Austria

Wiesner, Kenneth (Ken) — *Track Athlete*
3601 Meta Lake Road, Eagle River, WI 54521, USA

Wiest, Dianne — *Actress*
59 E 54th St, #22, New York, NY 10022, USA

Wiggin, Paul — *Football Player, Coach*
5013 Ridge Road, Edina, MN 55436, USA

Wiggins, Audrey — *Singer*
%William Morris Agency, 2100 W End Ave, #1000, Nashville, TN 37203, USA

Wiggins, John — *Singer*
%William Morris Agency, 2100 W End Ave, #1000, Nashville, TN 37203, USA

Wigglesworth, Marian McKean — *Skier*
%General Delivery, Wilson, WY 83014, USA

Wightman, Arthur S — *Mathematician, Physicist*
16 Balsam Lane, Princeton, NJ 08540, USA

Wightman, Donald E — *Labor Leader*
%Utility Workers Union, 815 16th Ave NW, Washington, DC 20006, USA

Wigle, Ernest D — *Cardiologist*
101 College St, Toronto ON M56 1L7, Canada

Wiik, Sven — *Skier*
PO Box 774484, Steamboat Springs, CO 80477, USA

Wijdenbosch, Jules A — *President, Suriname*
%Presidential Palace, Onafhankelikheidsplein 1, Paramaribo, Suriname

W

Wilander - Wilhelm

Wilander, Mats *Tennis Player*
%Einar Wilander, Vickersvagen 2, 352 53 Vaxjo, Sweden
Wilber, Doreen V H *Archery Athlete*
1401 W Lincoln Way, Jefferson, IA 50129, USA
Wilbraham, John H G *Concert Cornetist, Trumpeter*
9 D Cuthbert St, Wells, Somerset BA5 2AW, England
Wilbur, Richard C *Judge*
%US Tax Court, 400 2nd St NW, Washington, DC 20217, USA
Wilbur, Richard P *Writer*
88 Dodswell Road, Cummington, MA 01026, USA
Wilbur, Richard S *Physician, Association Executive*
985 Hawthorne Place, Lake Forest, IL 60045, USA
Wilby, James *Actor*
%International Creative Mgmt, 76 Oxford St, London W1N 0AX, England
Wilcox, Chris *Basketball Player*
%Los Angeles Clippers, Staples Center, 1111 S Figueroa St, Los Angeles, CA 90015, USA
Wilcox, Christopher *Editor*
%Reader's Digest Magazine, Reader's Digest Road, Pleasantville, NY 10570, USA
Wilcox, David *Singer, Songwriter*
%Elizabeth Rush Agency, 100 Park St, #4, Montclair, NJ 07042, USA
Wilcox, Davie (Dave) *Football Player*
94471 Willamette Dr, Junction City, OR 97448, USA
Wilcox, Larry *Actor*
10 Appaloosa Lane, Bell Canyon, CA 91307, USA
Wilcox, Lisa *Actress*
%Stone Manners, 6500 Wilshire Blvd, #550, Los Angeles, CA 90048, USA
Wilcox, Shannon *Actress*
1753 Centinela Ave, #A, Santa Monica, CA 90404, USA
Wilcutt, Terence W (Terry) *Astronaut*
1216 Red Wing Dr, Friendswood, TX 77546, USA
Wild, Earl *Concert Pianist, Composer*
2233 Fernleaf Lane, Columbus, OH 43235, USA
Wild, Jack *Actor*
%A Jay, Hawthorns, L Littleworth, Amberley, Stroud Glouc GL5 5AW, England
Wilde, Kim *Singer, Songwriter*
%Dance Crazy Mgmt, 294-296 Nether St, Finchley, London N31 RJ, England
Wilde, Patricia *Ballerina, Artistic Director*
%Pittsburgh Ballet Theater, 2900 Liberty Ave, Pittsburgh, PA 15201, USA
Wilder, Alan *Synthesizer Musician (Depeche Mode)*
%Reach Media, 295 Greenwich St, #109, New York, NY 10007, USA
Wilder, Don *Cartoonist (Crock)*
%North American Syndicate, 235 E 45th St, New York, NY 10017, USA
Wilder, Gene *Actor, Movie Director*
10930 Chalon Road, Los Angeles, CA 90077, USA
Wilder, James *Football Player*
14406 Burgundy Square, Tampa, FL 33613, USA
Wilder, James *Actor*
%Metropolitan Talent Agency, 4526 Wilshire Blvd, Los Angeles, CA 90010, USA
Wilder, L Douglas *Governor, VA; Educator*
3650 Monon St, #313, Los Angeles, CA 90027, USA
Wildman, George *Cartoonist (Popeye)*
1640 Shepard Ave, Hamden, CT 06518, USA
Wildman, Valerie *Actress*
110 Hurricane St, #305, Marina del Rey, CA 90292, USA
Wildmon, Donald *Social Activist*
%National Federation of Decency, PO Box 1398, Tupelo, MS 38802, USA
Wildung, Richard K (Dick) *Football Player*
10368 Rich Road, Bloomington, MN 55437, USA
Wiles, Andrew J *Mathematician*
%Princeton University, Mathematics Dept, Princeton, NJ 08544, USA
Wiles, Jason *Actor*
2381 Kimridge Road, Beverly Hills, CA 90210, USA
Wiley, Lee *Singer*
%Country Crossroads, 7787 Monterey St, Gilroy, CA 95020, USA
Wiley, Marcellus *Football Player*
%San Diego Chargers, 4020 Murphy Canyon Road, San Diego, CA 92123, USA
Wiley, Michael E *Businessman*
%Atlantic Richfield Co, 333 S Hope St, Los Angeles, CA 90071, USA
Wiley, Richard E *Government Official*
3818 Woodrow St, Arlington, VA 22207, USA
Wiley, William T *Artist*
PO Box 661, Forest Knolls, CA 94933, USA
Wilford, John Noble, Jr *Journalist*
232 W 10th St, New York, NY 10014, USA
Wilhelm, John W *Labor Leader*
%Hotel & Restaurant Employees Union, 1219 28th St NW, Washington, DC 20007, USA
Wilhelm, Kati *Biathlete*
%SC Motor Zella-Mehlis, Bierbachstr 68, 98544 Zella-Mehlis, Germany

Wilk, Brad *Drummer (Rage Against the Machine)*
%GAS Entertainment, 8935 Lindblade St, Culver City, CA 90232, USA

Wilkening, Laurel L *Educator*
%University of California, Chancellor's Office, Irvine, CA 92717, USA

Wilkens, Leonard R (Lenny), Jr *Basketball Player, Coach*
3429 Evergreen Point Road, Medina, WA 98039, USA

Wilkerson, Bobby *Basketball Player*
814 Rustic Road, Anderson, IN 46013, USA

Wilkerson, Brad *Baseball Player*
%Montreal Expos, Olympic Stadium, Montreal QC H1V 3N7, Canada

Wilkerson, Isabel *Journalist*
%New York Times, Editorial Dept, 229 W 43rd St, New York, NY 10036, USA

Wilkes, Glenn *Basketball Coach*
%Stetson University, Athletic Dept, Campus Box 8359, DeLand, FL 32720, USA

Wilkes, Jamaal *Basketball Player*
7846 W 81st St, Playa del Rey, CA 90293, USA

Wilkes, Maurice V *Computer Engineer*
%Olivetti Research Ltd, 24A Trumpington St, Cambridge CB2 1QA, England

Wilkie, Chris *Guitarist (Dubstar)*
%Primary Talent Int'l, 2-12 Petonville Road, London N1 9PL, England

Wilkie, David *Swimmer*
Oaklands, Queens Hill, Ascot, Berkshire, England

Wilkin, Richard E *Religious Leader*
%Winebrenner Theological Seminary, 950 N Main St, Findlay, OH 45840, USA

Wilkins, J Dominique *Basketball Player*
%Atlanta Hawks, 190 Marietta St SW, Atlanta, GA 30303, USA

Wilkins, Maurice (Mac) *Track Athlete*
PO Box 1058, 328 Coldbrook Lane, Soquel, CA 95073, USA

Wilkins, Maurice H F *Nobel Medicine Laureate*
30 Saint John's Park, London SE3, England

Wilkins, Roger *Journalist*
%George Mason University, 207 East Building, Fairfax, VA 22030, USA

Wilkins, William W, Jr *Judge*
%US Court of Appeals, PO Box 10857, Greenville, SC 29603, USA

Wilkinson, Amanda *Singer (Wilkinsons)*
%Fitzgerald-Hartley, 1908 Wedgewood Ave, Nashville, TN 37212, USA

Wilkinson, Dan *Football Player*
%Detroit Lions, 222 Republic Dr, Allen Park, MI 48101, USA

Wilkinson, Geoffrey *Nobel Chemistry Laureate*
%Imperial College, Chemistry Dept, London SW7 2AY, England

Wilkinson, J Harvie, III *Judge*
%US Court of Appeals, 255 W Main St, Charlottesville, VA 22902, USA

Wilkinson, Joseph B, Jr *Navy Admiral*
340 Chesapeake Dr, Great Falls, VA 22066, USA

Wilkinson, June *Model, Actress*
1025 N Howard St, Glendale, CA 91207, USA

Wilkinson, Laura *Diver*
14606 Falling Creek Dr, Houston, TX 77068, USA

Wilkinson, Leon *Bassist (Lynyrd Skynyrd)*
%Alliance Artists, 6025 Comers Parkway, #202, Norcross, GA 30092, USA

Wilkinson, Signe *Editorial Cartoonist*
%Philadelphia Daily News, Editorial Dept, 400 N Broad, Philadelphia, PA 19130, USA

Wilkinson, Steve *Singer (Wilkinsons)*
%Fitzgerald Hartley, 1908 Wedgewood Ave, Nashville, TN 37212, USA

Wilkinson, Tom *Actor*
6220 Del Valle Dr, Los Angeles, CA 90048, USA

Wilkinson, Tyler *Singer (Wilkinsons)*
%Fitzgerald Hartley, 1908 Wedgewood Ave, Nashville, TN 37212, USA

Will, George F *Columnist*
9 Grafton St, Chevy Chase, MD 20815, USA

Will-Halpin, Maggie *Golfer*
178 Tall Trees Court, Sarasota, FL 34232, USA

Willard, Fred C *Actor, Comedian*
%William Morris Agency, 151 El Camino Dr, Beverly Hills, CA 90212, USA

Willard, Kenneth H (Ken) *Football Player*
%Ken Willard Assoc, 3071 Viewpoint Road, Midlothian, VA 23113, USA

Willcocks, David V *Concert Organist, Conductor*
13 Grange Road, Cambridge CB3 9AS, England

Willebrands, Johannes Cardinal *Religious Leader*
%Council for Promoting Christian Unity, Via dell'Erba I, 00120 Rome, Italy

Willem-Alexander *Crown Prince, Netherlands*
%Huis ten Bosch, Hague, Netherlands

Willet, E Crosby *Stained Glass Artist*
%Willet Stained Glass Studios, 10 E Moreland Ave, Philadelphia, PA 19118, USA

Willett, Malcolm *Cartoonist (Tight Corner)*
%Universal Press Syndicate, 4520 Main St, Kansas City, MO 64111, USA

Willett, Walter *Epidemiologist*
%Harvard Medical School, 25 Shattuck St, Boston, MA 02115, USA

W

Willhite, Gerald — *Football Player*
10464 Iliff Court, Rancho Cordova, CA 95670, USA
William — *Prince, England*
%Clarence House, Stable Yard Gate, London SW1, England
William, David — *Actor, Theater Director*
194 Langarth St E, London ON N6C 1Z5, Canada
William, Edward — *Religious Leader*
%Bible Way Church, 5118 Clarendon Road, Brooklyn, NY 11203, USA
Williams of Crosby, Shirley V T B — *Government Official, England*
%House of Lords, Westminster, London SW1A 0PW, England
Williams of Elvel, Charles C P — *Government Official, England*
48 Thurloe Square, London SW7 2SX, England
Williams, Adrian — *Basketball Player*
%Phoenix Mercury, American West Arena, 201 E Jefferson St, Phoenix, AZ 85004, USA
Williams, Aeneas D — *Football Player*
11978 Charter House Lane, Saint Louis, MO 63146, USA
Williams, Alfred H — *Football Player*
7602 Las Flores Dr, Houston, TX 77083, USA
Williams, Alvin — *Basketball Player*
%Toronto Raptors, Air Canada Center, 40 Bay St, Toronto ON M5J 2N8, Canada
Williams, Andy — *Singer*
161 Berms Circle, #3, Branson, MO 65616, USA
Williams, Anson — *Actor*
24615 Skyline View Dr, Malibu, CA 90265, USA
Williams, Anthony A — *Mayor*
%Mayor's Office, District Building, 14th & E Sts NW, Washington, DC 20004, USA
Williams, B John, Jr — *Attorney, Judge*
%Morgan Lewis Bockius, 1800 M St NW, Washington, DC 20036, USA
Williams, Barbara — *Actress*
%Innovative Artists, 1505 10th St, Santa Monica, CA 90401, USA
Williams, Barry — *Actor, Singer*
2337 Roscomare Road, #2-242, Los Angeles, CA 90077, USA
Williams, Bernabe (Bernie) — *Baseball Player*
5 Hallock Place, Armonk, NY 10504, USA
Williams, Bert — *Actor*
%Susan Nathe, 8281 Melrose Ave, #200, Los Angeles, CA 90046, USA
Williams, Betty — *Nobel Peace Laureate*
Orchardville Gardens, Finaghy, Belfast 10, Northern Ireland
Williams, Billy — *Cinematographer*
%Coach House, Hawkshill Place, Esher, Surrey KT10 9HY, England
Williams, Billy Dee — *Actor*
18411 Hatteras St, #204, Tarzana, CA 91356, USA
Williams, Billy L — *Baseball Player*
586 Prince Edward Road, Glen Ellyn, IL 60137, USA
Williams, Bob A — *Football Player*
602 Stone Barn Road, Towson, MD 21286, USA
Williams, Brian — *Commentator*
%NBC-TV, News Dept, 30 Rockefeller Plaza, New York, NY 10112, USA
Williams, Bruce — *Entertainer*
PO Box 547, Elfers, FL 34680, USA
Williams, C K — *Writer*
%Princeton University, English Dept, Princeton, NJ 08544, USA
Williams, Cara — *Actress*
%Dann, 9903 Santa Monica Blvd, #606, Beverly Hills, CA 90212, USA
Williams, Christy — *Artist*
PO Box 849, Lopez Island, WA 98261, USA
Williams, Cindy — *Actress*
6149 Tapia Dr, Malibu, CA 90265, USA
Williams, Clarence — *Photojournalist*
%Los Angeles Times, Editorial Dept, 202 W 1st St, Los Angeles, CA 90012, USA
Williams, Clarence, III — *Actor*
%Flick East-West, 9057 Nemo St, #A, West Hollywood, CA 90069, USA
Williams, Cliff — *Bassist (AC/DC)*
11 Leominster Road, Morden, Surrey SA4 6HN, England
Williams, Clyde — *Religious Leader*
%Christian Methodist Episcopal Church, 4466 E Presley Blvd, Memphis, TN 38116, USA
Williams, Colleen — *Commentator*
%KNBC-TV, News Dept, 3000 W Alameda Ave, Burbank, CA 91523, USA
Williams, Curtis — *Singer (Penguins)*
%Neal Hollander Agency, 9966 Majorca Place, Boca Raton, FL 33434, USA
Williams, Dafydd R (David) — *Astronaut*
%NASA, Johnson Space Center, 2101 NASA Road, Houston, TX 77058, USA
Williams, Dana — *Bassist, Drummer (Diamond Rio)*
%Dreamcatcher Artists Mgmt, 2908 Poston Ave, Nashville, TN 37203, USA
Williams, Daniel — *Governor General, Grenada*
%Governor General's Office, Botanical Gardens, Saint George's, Grenada
Williams, Darnell — *Actor*
%Stone Manners, 6500 Wilshire Blvd, #550, Los Angeles, CA 90048, USA

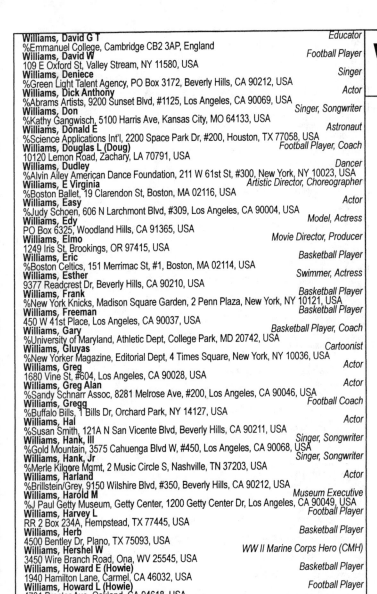

Williams, David G T *Educator*
%Emmanuel College, Cambridge CB2 3AP, England
Williams, David W *Football Player*
109 E Oxford St, Valley Stream, NY 11580, USA
Williams, Deniece *Singer*
%Green Light Talent Agency, PO Box 3172, Beverly Hills, CA 90212, USA
Williams, Dick Anthony *Actor*
%Abrams Artists, 9200 Sunset Blvd, #1125, Los Angeles, CA 90069, USA
Williams, Don *Singer, Songwriter*
%Kathy Gangwisch, 5100 Harris Ave, Kansas City, MO 64133, USA
Williams, Donald E *Astronaut*
%Science Applications Int'l, 2200 Space Park Dr, #200, Houston, TX 77058, USA
Williams, Douglas L (Doug) *Football Player, Coach*
10120 Lemon Road, Zachary, LA 70791, USA
Williams, Dudley *Dancer*
%Alvin Ailey American Dance Foundation, 211 W 61st St, #300, New York, NY 10023, USA
Williams, E Virginia *Artistic Director, Choreographer*
%Boston Ballet, 19 Clarendon St, Boston, MA 02116, USA
Williams, Easy *Actor*
%Judy Schoen, 606 N Larchmont Blvd, #309, Los Angeles, CA 90004, USA
Williams, Edy *Model, Actress*
PO Box 6325, Woodland Hills, CA 91365, USA
Williams, Elmo *Movie Director, Producer*
1249 Iris St, Brookings, OR 97415, USA
Williams, Eric *Basketball Player*
%Boston Celtics, 151 Merrimac St, #1, Boston, MA 02114, USA
Williams, Esther *Swimmer, Actress*
9377 Readcrest Dr, Beverly Hills, CA 90210, USA
Williams, Frank *Basketball Player*
%New York Knicks, Madison Square Garden, 2 Penn Plaza, New York, NY 10121, USA
Williams, Freeman *Basketball Player*
450 W 41st Place, Los Angeles, CA 90037, USA
Williams, Gary *Basketball Player, Coach*
%University of Maryland, Athletic Dept, College Park, MD 20742, USA
Williams, Gluyas *Cartoonist*
%New Yorker Magazine, Editorial Dept, 4 Times Square, New York, NY 10036, USA
Williams, Greg *Actor*
1680 Vine St, #604, Los Angeles, CA 90028, USA
Williams, Greg Alan *Actor*
%Sandy Schnarr Assoc, 8281 Melrose Ave, #200, Los Angeles, CA 90046, USA
Williams, Gregg *Football Coach*
%Buffalo Bills, 1 Bills Dr, Orchard Park, NY 14127, USA
Williams, Hal *Actor*
%Susan Smith, 121A N San Vicente Blvd, Beverly Hills, CA 90211, USA
Williams, Hank, III *Singer, Songwriter*
%Gold Mountain, 3575 Cahuenga Blvd W, #450, Los Angeles, CA 90068, USA
Williams, Hank, Jr *Singer, Songwriter*
%Merle Kilgore Mgmt, 2 Music Circle S, Nashville, TN 37203, USA
Williams, Harland *Actor*
%Brillstein/Grey, 9150 Wilshire Blvd, #350, Beverly Hills, CA 90212, USA
Williams, Harold M *Museum Executive*
%J Paul Getty Museum, Getty Center, 1200 Getty Center Dr, Los Angeles, CA 90049, USA
Williams, Harvey L *Football Player*
RR 2 Box 234A, Hempstead, TX 77445, USA
Williams, Herb *Basketball Player*
4500 Bentley Dr, Plano, TX 75093, USA
Williams, Hershel W *WW II Marine Corps Hero (CMH)*
3450 Wire Branch Road, Ona, WV 25545, USA
Williams, Howard E (Howie) *Basketball Player*
1940 Hamilton Lane, Carmel, CA 46032, USA
Williams, Howard L (Howie) *Football Player*
4731 Proctor Ave, Oakland, CA 94618, USA
Williams, Hype *Movie Director*
%Creative Artists Agency, 9830 Wilshire Blvd, Beverly Hills, CA 90212, USA
Williams, Ivy *Writer*
%Mediachase, 834 N Harper Ave, Los Angeles, CA 90046, USA
Williams, Jack K *Medical Administrator*
%Texas Medical Center, 1133 M D Anderson Blvd, Houston, TX 77030, USA
Williams, Jamal *Football Player*
%San Diego Chargers, 4020 Murphy Canyon Road, San Diego, CA 92123, USA
Williams, James *Jazz Pianist*
%Joanne Klein Entertainment, 130 W 28th St, New York, NY 10001, USA
Williams, James A *Army General*
8928 Maurice Lane, Annandale, VA 22003, USA
Williams, James A (Froggy) *Football Player*
296 Sugarberry Circle, Houston, TX 77024, USA
Williams, James D *Navy Admiral*
1111A N Stuart St, Arlington, VA 22201, USA

Williams, James F (Jimy) *Baseball Player, Manager*
1401 Olde Post Road, Palm Harbor, FL 34683, USA
Williams, James O *Football Player*
330 S Western Ave, Lake Forest, IL 60045, USA
Williams, Jay *Basketball Player*
%Chicago Bulls, United Center, 1901 W Madison St, Chicago, IL 60612, USA
Williams, Jayson *Basketball Player, Sportscaster*
%NBC-TV, Sports Dept, 30 Rockefeller Plaza, New York, NY 10112, USA
Williams, Jeffrey N *Astronaut*
2721 Moss Court, Seabrook, TX 77586, USA
Williams, Jerome *Basketball Player*
%Toronto Raptors, Air Canada Center, 40 Bay St, Toronto ON M5J 2N8, Canada
Williams, Jerry *Football Player*
1501 E Riviera Dr, Chandler, AZ 85249, USA
Williams, Jessica *Jazz Pianist*
%T-Best Talent Agency, 508 Honey Lake Court, Danville, CA 94506, USA
Williams, JoBeth *Actress*
%Innovative Artists, 1505 10th St, Santa Monica, CA 90401, USA
Williams, Jody *Nobel Peace Laureate*
115 Earls Way, Putney, VT 05346, USA
Williams, John *Concert Guitarist*
%Askonas Holt Ltd, 27 Chancery Lane, London WC2A 1PF, England
Williams, John A *Writer*
693 Forest Ave, Teaneck, NJ 07666, USA
Williams, John C *Archery Athlete*
718 David Road, Santa Maria, CA 93455, USA
Williams, John L *Football Player*
1709 Husson Ave, Palatka, FL 32177, USA
Williams, John M *Football Player*
2222 Victory Memorial Dr, Minneapolis, MN 55412, USA
Williams, John T *Conductor, Composer*
333 Loring Ave, Los Angeles, CA 90024, USA
Williams, Joseph R *Publisher*
%Memphis Commerical Appeal, 495 Union Ave, Memphis, TN 38103, USA
Williams, Kameelah *Singer (702)*
%Creative Artists Agency, 9830 Wilshire Blvd, Beverly Hills, CA 90212, USA
Williams, Kelli *Actress, Singer*
%Innovative Artists, 1505 10th St, Santa Monica, CA 90401, USA
Williams, Kevin *Football Player*
%Minnesota Vikings, 9520 Viking Dr, Eden Prairie, MN 55344, USA
Williams, Kiely *Singer (3LW)*
%Pyramid Entertainment, 89 5th Ave, #700, New York, NY 10003, USA
Williams, Kimberly *Actress*
%Beyond Talent Agency, 330 Bob Hope Dr, #C109, Burbank, CA 91523, USA
Williams, Lee E *Football Player*
11651 NW 4th St, Plantation, FL 33325, USA
Williams, Lewis T *Medical Researcher*
%Howard Hughes Medical Institute, 5323 Harry Hines Blvd, Dallas, TX 75390, USA
Williams, Lorenzo *Basketball Player*
2731 Via Capri, #924, Clearwater, FL 33764, USA
Williams, Lucinda *Singer, Songwriter*
%High Road, 751 Bridgeway, #300, Sausalito, CA 94965, USA
Williams, Lynn R *Labor Leader*
%Harvard University, Politics Institute, 79 Kennedy St, Cambridge, MA 02138, USA
Williams, Mark *Bowler*
%Professional Bowlers Assn, 719 2nd Ave, #701, Seattle, WA 98104, USA
Williams, Mary Alice *Commentator*
%NYNEX Corp, Public Relations Dept, 1113 Westchester Ave, White Plains, NY 10604, USA
Williams, Mason *Singer, Guitarist, Composer*
PO Box 25, Oakridge, OR 97463, USA
Williams, Matt *Writer*
%Zeiderman, 211 E 48th St, New York, NY 10017, USA
Williams, Maurice J *Association Executive*
%Overseas Development Council, 1875 Connecticut Ave NW, Washington, DC 20009, USA
Williams, Michael *Actor*
%Michael Whitehall, 125 Gloucester Road, London SW7 4TE, England
Williams, Michael D (Mike) *Baseball Player*
240 Horseshoe Farm Road, Pembroke, VA 24136, USA
Williams, Michael J *Marine Corps General*
Assistant Commander in Chief, HqUSMC, 2 Navy St, Washington, DC 20380, USA
Williams, Michael L *Actor*
%Julian Belfarge, 46 Albermarle St, London W1X 4PP, England
Williams, Micheal *Basketball Player*
1415 Reynoldston Lane, Dallas, TX 75232, USA
Williams, Michelle *Actress*
%Untitled Entertainment, 8436 W 3rd St, #650, Los Angeles, CA 90048, USA
Williams, Michelle *Singer (Destiny's Child)*
%Creative Artists Agency, 9830 Wilshire Blvd, Beverly Hills, CA 90212, USA

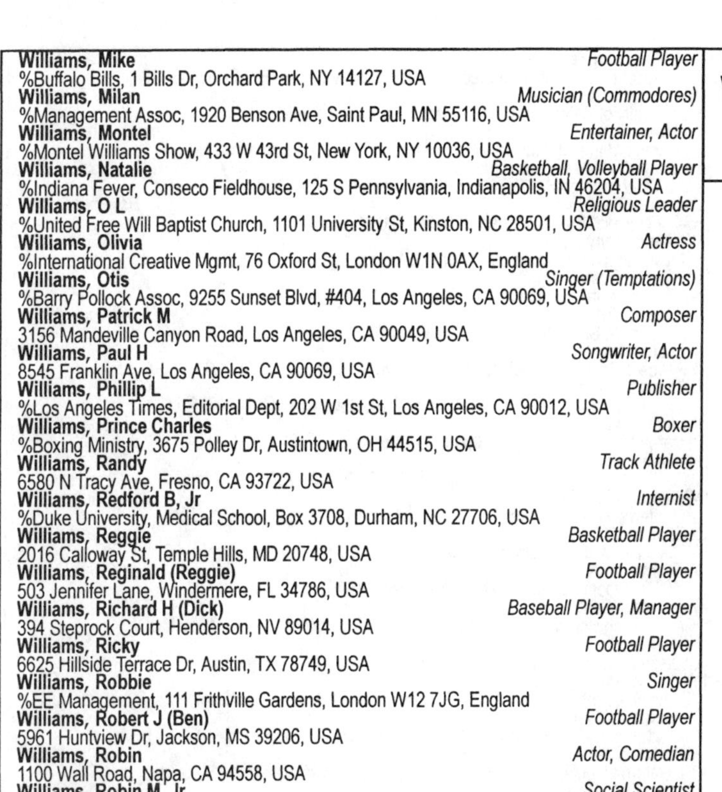

Williams, Mike *Football Player*
%Buffalo Bills, 1 Bills Dr, Orchard Park, NY 14127, USA
Williams, Milan *Musician (Commodores)*
%Management Assoc, 1920 Benson Ave, Saint Paul, MN 55116, USA
Williams, Montel *Entertainer, Actor*
%Montel Williams Show, 433 W 43rd St, New York, NY 10036, USA
Williams, Natalie *Basketball, Volleyball Player*
%Indiana Fever, Conseco Fieldhouse, 125 S Pennsylvania, Indianapolis, IN 46204, USA
Williams, O L *Religious Leader*
%United Free Will Baptist Church, 1101 University St, Kinston, NC 28501, USA
Williams, Olivia *Actress*
%International Creative Mgmt, 76 Oxford St, London W1N 0AX, England
Williams, Otis *Singer (Temptations)*
%Barry Pollock Assoc, 9255 Sunset Blvd, #404, Los Angeles, CA 90069, USA
Williams, Patrick M *Composer*
3156 Mandeville Canyon Road, Los Angeles, CA 90049, USA
Williams, Paul H *Songwriter, Actor*
8545 Franklin Ave, Los Angeles, CA 90069, USA
Williams, Phillip L *Publisher*
%Los Angeles Times, Editorial Dept, 202 W 1st St, Los Angeles, CA 90012, USA
Williams, Prince Charles *Boxer*
%Boxing Ministry, 3675 Polley Dr, Austintown, OH 44515, USA
Williams, Randy *Track Athlete*
6580 N Tracy Ave, Fresno, CA 93722, USA
Williams, Redford B, Jr *Internist*
%Duke University, Medical School, Box 3708, Durham, NC 27706, USA
Williams, Reggie *Basketball Player*
2016 Calloway St, Temple Hills, MD 20748, USA
Williams, Reginald (Reggie) *Football Player*
503 Jennifer Lane, Windermere, FL 34786, USA
Williams, Richard H (Dick) *Baseball Player, Manager*
394 Steprock Court, Henderson, NV 89014, USA
Williams, Ricky *Football Player*
6625 Hillside Terrace Dr, Austin, TX 78749, USA
Williams, Robbie *Singer*
%EE Management, 111 Frithville Gardens, London W12 7JG, England
Williams, Robert J (Ben) *Football Player*
5961 Huntview Dr, Jackson, MS 39206, USA
Williams, Robin *Actor, Comedian*
1100 Wall Road, Napa, CA 94558, USA
Williams, Robin M, Jr *Social Scientist*
414 Oak Ave, Ithaca, NY 14850, USA
Williams, Roderick *Opera Singer*
%Van Walsum Mgmt, 4 Addison Bridge Place, London W14 8XP, England
Williams, Roger *Pianist*
16150 Clear Valley Place, Encino, CA 91436, USA
Williams, Ron *Bowler*
5700 Westchase Dr, North Richland Hills, TX 76180, USA
Williams, Ron *Basketball Player*
610 Arcadia Terrace, #302, Sunnyvale, CA 94085, USA
Williams, Rowan *Religious Leader*
%Lambert Palace, London SE1 9JU, England
Williams, Roy *Basketball Coach*
%University of North Carolina, PO Box 2126, Chapel Hill, NC 27515, USA
Williams, Roy *Football Player*
%Dallas Cowboys, 1 Cowboys Parkway, Irving, TX 75063, USA
Williams, Sam B *Inventor (Fanjet Engine)*
%Williams International, 2280 W Maple Road, Walled Lake, MI 48390, USA
Williams, Scott *Basketball Player*
%Phoenix Suns, 201 E Jefferson St, Phoenix, AZ 85004, USA
Williams, Serena *Tennis Player*
313 Grand Key Terrace, West Palm Beach, FL 33418, USA
Williams, Simon *Actor*
%Jonathan Altaras, 13 Shorts Gardens, London WC2H 9AT, England
Williams, Stanley W (Stan) *Baseball Player*
4702 Hayter Ave, Lakewood, CA 90712, USA
Williams, Stephanie E *Actress*
%S M S Talent, 8730 Sunset Blvd, #440, Los Angeles, CA 90069, USA
Williams, Stephen *Anthropologist*
1017 Foothills Trail, Santa Fe, NM 87505, USA
Williams, Stephen F *Judge*
%US Court of Appeals, 333 Constitution NW, Washington, DC 20001, USA
Williams, Steven *Actor*
%Geddes Agency, 8430 Santa Monica Blvd, #200, West Hollywood, CA 90069, USA
Williams, Sunita L *Astronaut*
16810 Clear Oak Way, Houston, TX 77058, USA
Williams, T Franklin *Physician*
%Monroe Community Hospital, Director's Office, Rochester, NY 14620, USA

W

Williams - Willis

Williams, Tamika *Basketball Player*
%Minnesota Lynx, Target Center, 600 1st Ave N, Minneapolis, MN 55403, USA
Williams, Terrie *Biologist*
%University of California, Biology Dept, Santa Cruz, CA 95064, USA
Williams, Terry *Drummer (Dire Straits)*
%Damage Mgmt, 16 Lambton Place, London W11 2SH, England
Williams, Thomas S Cardinal *Religious Leader*
Viard, 21 Eccleston Hill, PO Box 198, Wellington 1, New Zealand
Williams, Todd *Baseball Player*
6244 Fly Road, East Syracuse, NY 13057, USA
Williams, Tonya Lee *Actress*
%Artists Agency, 1180 S Beverly Dr, #301, Los Angeles, CA 90035, USA
Williams, Treat *Actor*
1244 11th St, #A, Santa Monica, CA 90401, USA
Williams, Ulis *Track Athlete*
2511 29th St, Santa Monica, CA 90405, USA
Williams, Van *Actor*
%Pierce & Shelly, 612 Lighthouse Ave, #220, Pacific Grove, CA 93950, USA
Williams, Vanessa *Actress*
%Creative Artists Agency, 9830 Wilshire Blvd, Beverly Hills, CA 90212, USA
Williams, Vanessa L *Actress, Singer, Beauty Queen*
%Morey Mgmt, 9255 Sunset Blvd, #600, Los Angeles, CA 90069, USA
Williams, Venus *Tennis Player*
313 Grand Key Terrace, West Palm Beach, FL 33418, USA
Williams, Victoria *Singer, Songwriter*
%Monterey Peninsula Artists, 509 Hartnell St, Monterey, CA 93940, USA
Williams, W Clyde *Religious Leader*
%Christian Methodist Episcopal Church, 4466 E Presley Blvd, Memphis, TN 38116, USA
Williams, Walt *Basketball Player*
3240 Beaumont St, Temple Hills, MD 20748, USA
Williams, Walter *Singer (O'Jays)*
%Associated Booking Corp, 1995 Broadway, #501, New York, NY 10023, USA
Williams, Walter Ray, Jr *Bowler*
6503 NW 223rd St, Micanopy, FL 32667, USA
Williams, Wendy Lian *Diver*
%Advantage International, 1025 Thomas Jefferson NW, #450, Washington, DC 20007, USA
Williams, William A *Astronaut*
%Environmental Protection Agency, 200 SW 35th St, Corvallis, OR 97333, USA
Williams-Dourdan, Roshumba *Model*
%Bethann Model Mgmt, 36 N Moore St, #36N, New York, NY 10013, USA
Williamson, Corliss *Basketball Player*
%Detroit Pistons, Palace, 2 Championship Dr, Auburn Hills, MI 48326, USA
Williamson, Fred R *Actor, Football Player*
%H David Moss, 733 Seward St, #PH, Los Angeles, CA 90038, USA
Williamson, Keith A *Air Force Marshal, England*
%National Westminster Bank, Fakenham, Norfolk, England
Williamson, Marianne *Psychotherapist, Writer*
%Los Angeles Center for Living, 8265 W Sunset Blvd, West Hollywood, CA 90046, USA
Williamson, Matthew *Fashion Designer*
%Beverly Cable, 11 Saint Christopher's Place, London W1M 5HB, England
Williamson, Michael *Writer*
10400 Hutting Place, Silver Spring, MD 20902, USA
Williamson, Michael *Photojournalist*
%Washington Post, Editorial Dept, 1150 15th St NW, Washington, DC 20071, USA
Williamson, Mykelti T *Actor*
%William Morris Agency, 151 El Camino Dr, Beverly Hills, CA 90212, USA
Williamson, Nicol *Actor*
%Jonathan Altaras, 13 Shorts Gardens, London WC2H 9AT, England
Williamson, Oliver E *Economist*
%University of California, Economics Dept, Berkeley, CA 94720, USA
Williamson, Samuel R, Jr *Educator*
%University of the South, President's Office, Sewanee, TN 37375, USA
Willingham, Tyrone *Football Coach*
%Notre Dame University, Athletic Dept, PO Box 518, Notre Dame, IN 46556, USA
Willis, Bruce W *Actor*
%Rogers & Cowan, 6340 Breckenridge Run, Rex, GA 30273, USA
Willis, Gordon *Cinematographer*
11849 W Olympic Blvd, #100, Los Angeles, CA 90064, USA
Willis, Jim *Artist*
5323 SW 53rd Court, Portland, OR 97221, USA
Willis, Kelly *Singer, Songwriter*
4007 Lullwood Road, Austin, TX 78722, USA
Willis, Kevin A *Basketball Player*
4970 Carriage Lake Dr, Roswell, GA 30075, USA
Willis, Pete *Guitarist (Def Leppard)*
%Q Prime Mgmt, 729 7th Ave, #1400, New York, NY 10019, USA
Willis, William K (Bill) *Football Player*
1158 S Waverly St, Columbus, OH 43227, USA

Willison, Mike *Bassist (Fig Dish)*
%Metropolitan Entertainment Group, 2 Penn Plaza, #2600, New York, NY 10121, USA
Willman, David *Journalist*
%Los Angeles Times, Editorial Dept, 202 W 1st St, Los Angeles, CA 90012, USA
Willms, Andre *Rowing Athlete*
Rennebogen 94, 39130 Magdeburg, Germany
Willoch, Kare I *Prime Minister, Norway*
Fr Nansens V 17, 1324 Lysaker, Norway
Willoughby, Bill *Basketball Player*
350 W Englewood Ave, Englewood, NJ 07631, USA
Wills, Garry *Writer, Historian*
%Northwestern University, History Dept, Evanston, IL 60201, USA
Wills, Mark *Singer*
%Rasky-Baerlein Group, 1808 W End Ave, #516, Nashville, TN 37203, USA
Wills, Maurice M (Maury) *Baseball Player*
3200 La Rotonda Dr, #303, Rancho Palos Verdes, CA 90275, USA
Wills, Rick *Bassist (Foreigner)*
%Hard to Handle Mgmt, 16501 Ventura Blvd, #602, Encino, CA 91436, USA
Willson, John *Businessman*
%Placer Dome Inc, 1600-1055 Dunsmuir St, Vancouver BC V7X 1P1, Canada
Willson-Piper, Marty *Guitarist (Church)*
%Globeshine, 101 Chamberlayne Road, London NW10 3ND, England
Willumstad, Robert *Financier*
%Citigroup Inc, 399 Park Ave, New York, NY 10022, USA
Wilmarth, Dick *Dog Sled Racer*
1111 F St, Anchorage, AK 99501, USA
Wilmer, Douglas *Actor*
%Julian Belfarge, 46 Albermarle St, London W1X 4PP, England
Wilmer, Harry A *Psychiatrist*
%Texas Health Science Center, Psychiatric Dept, San Antonio, TX 78284, USA
Wilmore, Barry E *Astronaut*
1502 Regency Court, Friendswood, TX 77546, USA
Wilmut, Ian *Geneticist, Embryologist*
%Roslin Institute, Roslin Bio Centre, Midlothian EH25 9PS, Scotland
Wilson of Tillyorn, David C *Government Official, England; Diplomat*
%House of Lords, Westminster, London SW1A 0PW, England
Wilson, A N *Writer*
21 Arlington Road, London NW1 7ER, England
Wilson, Al *Singer*
%Talent Consultants International, 1560 Broadway, #1308, New York, NY 10036, USA
Wilson, Alexander G (Sandy) *Composer, Writer*
2 Southwell Gardens, #4, London SW7 4SB, England
Wilson, Allan B *Molecular Biologist*
%University of California, Molecular Biology Dept, Berkeley, CA 94724, USA
Wilson, Ann *Singer (Heart)*
%H K Mgmt, 9200 W Sunset Blvd, #530, Los Angeles, CA 90069, USA
Wilson, August *Writer*
600 1st Ave, #301, Seattle, WA 98104, USA
Wilson, Billy *Football Player*
%Whitehawk Ranch, PO Box 84, Clio, CA 96106, USA
Wilson, Blenda J *Educator*
%California State University, President's Office, Northridge, CA 91330, USA
Wilson, Brian D *Singer (Beach Boys), Songwriter*
14042 Aubrey Road, Beverly Hills, CA 90210, USA
Wilson, C A S John *Architect*
%John Wilson Assoc, 27 Horsell Road, London N5 1XL, England
Wilson, Carnie *Singer (Wilson Phillips/Wilsons)*
13601 Ventura Blvd, #286, Sherman Oaks, CA 91423, USA
Wilson, Cassandra *Jazz Singer*
%Dream Street Mgmt, 4346 Redwood Ave, #307, Marina del Rey, CA 90292, USA
Wilson, Cindy *Singer (B-52's)*
%Direct Management Group, 947 N La Cienega Blvd, #2, Los Angeles, CA 90069, USA
Wilson, Colin H *Writer*
Tetherdown, Trewallock Lane, Gorran Haven, Cornwall, England
Wilson, Craig *Water Polo Player*
1423 Lake Blvd, Davis, CA 95616, USA
Wilson, Dan *Singer, Guitarist, Songwriter*
%Monterey Peninsula Artists, 509 Hartnell St, Monterey, CA 93940, USA
Wilson, Daniel A (Dan) *Baseball Player*
1933 E Blaine St, Seattle, WA 98112, USA
Wilson, David *Actor*
%Susan Smith, 121A N San Vicente Blvd, Beverly Hills, CA 90211, USA
Wilson, David Mackenzie *Museum Director*
%Lifeboat House, Castletown IM9 1LD, Isle of Man, England
Wilson, Doug *Hockey Player*
18580 Petunia Court, Saratoga, CA 95070, USA
Wilson, Earle L *Religious Leader*
%Wesleyan Church, PO Box 50434, Indianapolis, IN 46250, USA

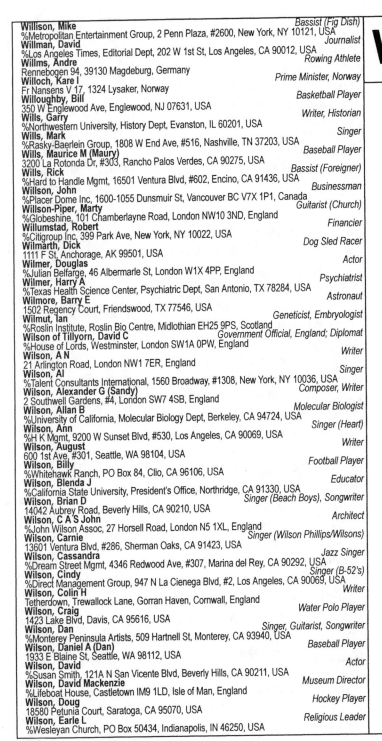

W

Wilson, Edward O *Zoologist, Writer*
1010 Waltham St, #A208, Lexington, MA 02421, USA
Wilson, Eric C T *WW II British Army Hero (VC)*
Woodside Cottage, Stowell, Sherborne, Dorset, England
Wilson, Eugene *Skier*
2775 Ranchview Lane N, #1, Plymouth, MN 55447, USA
Wilson, F Paul *Writer*
PO Box 33, Allenwood, NJ 08720, USA
Wilson, F Perry *Chemical Engineer*
225 N 56th St, #217, Lincoln, NE 68504, USA
Wilson, Frank *Auto Racing Executive*
%North Carolina Motor Speedway, PO Box 500, Rockingham, NC 28380, USA
Wilson, Gahan *Cartoonist, Writer*
%New Yorker Magazine, Editorial Dept, 4 Times Square, New York, NY 10036, USA
Wilson, George *Basketball Player*
3900 Rose Hill Ave, Cincinnati, OH 45229, USA
Wilson, George B (Mike), Jr *Football Player, Army General*
1062 E Lancaster Ave, Bryn Mawr, PA 19010, USA
Wilson, Georges *Movie, Theater Director*
Moulin de Vilgris, 78120 Rambouillet, France
Wilson, Gerald S *Jazz Trumpeter, Composer*
4625 Brynhurst Ave, Los Angeles, CA 90043, USA
Wilson, Harry C *Religious Leader*
%Wesleyan Church Int'l Center, 6060 Castleway West Dr, Indianapolis, IN 46250, USA
Wilson, Hugh *Movie Director*
%William Morris Agency, 151 El Camino Dr, Beverly Hills, CA 90212, USA
Wilson, J Tylee *Businessman*
PO Box 2057, Ponte Vedra Beach, FL 32004, USA
Wilson, James B *Navy Admiral*
40 Windermere Way, Kennett Square, PA 19348, USA
Wilson, James M *Geneticist*
%University of Pennsylvania, Med Center, Genetics Dept, Philadelphia, PA 19104, USA
Wilson, James Q *Government, Management Educator*
%University of California, Graduate Management School, Los Angeles, CA 90024, USA
Wilson, Jean D *Endocrinologist*
%Texas Southwestern Medical Center, 5323 Harry Hines Blvd, Dallas, TX 75390, USA
Wilson, Jeannie *Actress*
General Delivery, Ketchum, ID 83340, USA
Wilson, Julie *Singer, Actress*
%Stan Scotland Entertainment, 157 E 57th St, #18B, New York, NY 10022, USA
Wilson, Justin *Drummer (Reveille)*
%David Levin Mgmt, 200 W 57th St, #308, New York, NY 10019, USA
Wilson, Kenneth G *Nobel Physics Laureate*
%Ohio State University, Physics Dept, 174 W 18th Ave, Columbus, OH 43210, USA
Wilson, Kim *Singer (Fabulous Thunderbird)*
%Ricci Assoc, 28205 Agoura Road, Agoura Hills, CA 91301, USA
Wilson, Lanford *Writer*
PO Box 891, Sag Harbor, NY 11963, USA
Wilson, Lawrence F (Larry) *Football Player, Executive*
11834 N Blackheath Road, Scottsdale, AZ 85254, USA
Wilson, Louis H, Jr *WW II Marine Corps Hero (CMH); General*
100 University Park Dr, Birmingham, AL 35209, USA
Wilson, Luke *Actor*
%Creative Artists Agency, 9830 Wilshire Blvd, Beverly Hills, CA 90212, USA
Wilson, Marc D *Football Player*
113113 Mount Wallace Court, Alta Loma, CA 91737, USA
Wilson, Mary *Singer (Supremes)*
163 Amsterdam Ave, #125, New York, NY 10023, USA
Wilson, Mary *Singer (Heart)*
%Borman Entertainment, 1250 6th St, #401, Santa Monica, CA 90401, USA
Wilson, Melanie *Actress*
%Irv Schechter, 9300 Wilshire Blvd, #410, Beverly Hills, CA 90212, USA
Wilson, Michael H *Government Official, Canada*
%Industry & Science Dept, 235 Queen's St, Ottawa ON K1A OH5, Canada
Wilson, Nancy *Singer*
2819 W Charleston Blvd, #G72, Las Vegas, NV 89102, USA
Wilson, Nancy *Singer, Guitarist (Heart, Lovemongers)*
%H K Mgmt, 9200 W Sunset Blvd, #530, Los Angeles, CA 90069, USA
Wilson, Neal C *Religious Leader*
%Seventh-Day Adventists, 12501 Old Columbus Pike, Silver Spring, MD 20904, USA
Wilson, Olin C *Astronomer*
1508 Circa del Lago, B110, San Marcos, CA 92069, USA
Wilson, Peta *Actress*
%June Cann Mgmt, 73 Jersey Road, Woollahra NSW 2025, Australia
Wilson, Preston J R *Baseball Player*
%Colorado Rockies, Coors Field, 2001 Blake St, Denver, CO 80205, USA
Wilson, Ralph C, Jr *Football Executive*
%Buffalo Bills, 1 Bills Dr, Orchard Park, NY 14127, USA

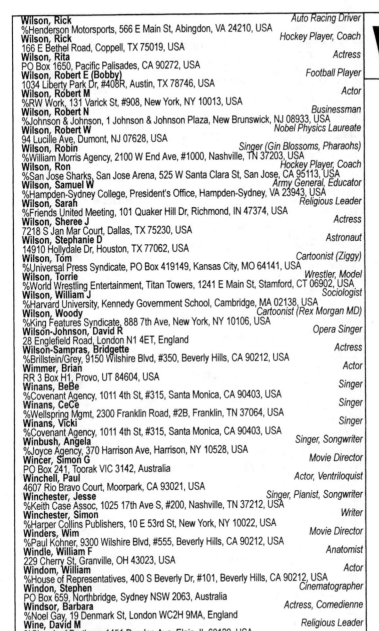

Wilson, Rick *Auto Racing Driver*
%Henderson Motorsports, 566 E Main St, Abingdon, VA 24210, USA
Wilson, Rick *Hockey Player, Coach*
166 E Bethel Road, Coppell, TX 75019, USA
Wilson, Rita *Actress*
PO Box 1650, Pacific Palisades, CA 90272, USA
Wilson, Robert E (Bobby) *Football Player*
1034 Liberty Park Dr, #408R, Austin, TX 78746, USA
Wilson, Robert M *Actor*
%RW Work, 131 Varick St, #908, New York, NY 10013, USA
Wilson, Robert N *Businessman*
%Johnson & Johnson, 1 Johnson & Johnson Plaza, New Brunswick, NJ 08933, USA
Wilson, Robert W *Nobel Physics Laureate*
94 Lucille Ave, Dumont, NJ 07628, USA
Wilson, Robin *Singer (Gin Blossoms, Pharaohs)*
%William Morris Agency, 2100 W End Ave, #1000, Nashville, TN 37203, USA
Wilson, Ron *Hockey Player, Coach*
%San Jose Sharks, San Jose Arena, 525 W Santa Clara St, San Jose, CA 95113, USA
Wilson, Samuel W *Army General, Educator*
%Hampden-Sydney College, President's Office, Hampden-Sydney, VA 23943, USA
Wilson, Sarah *Religious Leader*
%Friends United Meeting, 101 Quaker Hill Dr, Richmond, IN 47374, USA
Wilson, Sheree J *Actress*
7218 S Jan Mar Court, Dallas, TX 75230, USA
Wilson, Stephanie D *Astronaut*
14910 Hollydale Dr, Houston, TX 77062, USA
Wilson, Tom *Cartoonist (Ziggy)*
%Universal Press Syndicate, PO Box 419149, Kansas City, MO 64141, USA
Wilson, Torrie *Wrestler, Model*
%World Wrestling Entertainment, Titan Towers, 1241 E Main St, Stamford, CT 06902, USA
Wilson, William J *Sociologist*
%Harvard University, Kennedy Government School, Cambridge, MA 02138, USA
Wilson, Woody *Cartoonist (Rex Morgan MD)*
%King Features Syndicate, 888 7th Ave, New York, NY 10106, USA
Wilson-Johnson, David R *Opera Singer*
28 Englefield Road, London N1 4ET, England
Wilson-Sampras, Bridgette *Actress*
%Brillstein/Grey, 9150 Wilshire Blvd, #350, Beverly Hills, CA 90212, USA
Wimmer, Brian *Actor*
RR 3 Box H1, Provo, UT 84604, USA
Winans, BeBe *Singer*
%Covenant Agency, 1011 4th St, #315, Santa Monica, CA 90403, USA
Winans, CeCe *Singer*
%Wellspring Mgmt, 2300 Franklin Road, #2B, Franklin, TN 37064, USA
Winans, Vicki *Singer*
%Covenant Agency, 1011 4th St, #315, Santa Monica, CA 90403, USA
Winbush, Angela *Singer, Songwriter*
%Joyce Agency, 370 Harrison Ave, Harrison, NY 10528, USA
Wincer, Simon G *Movie Director*
PO Box 241, Toorak VIC 3142, Australia
Winchell, Paul *Actor, Ventriloquist*
4607 Rio Bravo Court, Moorpark, CA 93021, USA
Winchester, Jesse *Singer, Pianist, Songwriter*
%Keith Case Assoc, 1025 17th Ave S, #200, Nashville, TN 37212, USA
Winchester, Simon *Writer*
%Harper Collins Publishers, 10 E 53rd St, New York, NY 10022, USA
Winders, Wim *Movie Director*
%Paul Kohner, 9300 Wilshire Blvd, #555, Beverly Hills, CA 90212, USA
Windle, William F *Anatomist*
229 Cherry St, Granville, OH 43023, USA
Windom, William *Actor*
%House of Representatives, 400 S Beverly Dr, #101, Beverly Hills, CA 90212, USA
Windon, Stephen *Cinematographer*
PO Box 659, Northbridge, Sydney NSW 2063, Australia
Windsor, Barbara *Actress, Comedienne*
%Noel Gay, 19 Denmark St, London WC2H 9MA, England
Wine, David M *Religious Leader*
%Church of Brethren, 1451 Dundee Ave, Elgin, IL 60120, USA
Winfield, David M (Dave) *Baseball Player*
2235 Stratford Circle, Los Angeles, CA 90077, USA
Winfield, Paul *Actor*
5693 Holly Oak Dr, Los Angeles, CA 90068, USA
Winfrey, Oprah *Entertainer, Actress*
%Harpo Productions, 110 N Carpenter St, Chicago, IL 60607, USA
Winger, Debra *Actress*
20220 Inland Ave, Malibu, CA 90265, USA
Winger, Kip *Singer*
%Joseph Minkes Assoc, 2740 W Magnolia Blvd, #204, Burbank, CA 91505, USA

W

Wink - Wirth

Wink, Chris *Entertainer (Blue Man Group)*
%Blue Man Group, Luxor Hotel, 3900 Las Vegas Blvd S, Las Vegas, NV 89119, USA
Winkler, David *Movie Director*
%Rigberg Roberts Rugolo, 1180 S Beverly Dr, #601, Los Angeles, CA 90035, USA
Winkler, Gerard *Actor*
Alsertra 26-3A, 1090 Vienna, Austria
Winkler, Hans-Gunter *Equestrian Rider*
Dr Rau Allee 48, 48231 Warendorf, Germany
Winkler, Henry *Actor, Television Producer*
PO Box 49914, Los Angeles, CA 90049, USA
Winkler, Irwin *Movie Director, Producer*
%Irwin Winkler Productions, 211 S Beverly Dr, #220, Beverly Hills, CA 90212, USA
Winkles, Bobby B *Baseball Manager*
78452 Calle Huerta, La Quinta, CA 92253, USA
Winn, D Randolph (Randy) *Baseball Player*
59 Leeds Court E, Danville, CA 94526, USA
Winner, Michael R *Movie Director, Producer*
31 Melbury Road, London W14 8AB, England
Winningham, Mare *Actress*
%William Morris Agency, 151 El Camino Dr, Beverly Hills, CA 90212, USA
Winograd, Shmuel *Mathematician, Computer Scientist*
235 Glendale Road, Scarsdale, NY 10583, USA
Winslet, Kate *Actress*
%P F D, Drury House, 34-43 Russell St, London WC2B 5HA, England
Winslow, Kellen B *Football Player*
5173 Waring Road, #312, San Diego, CA 92120, USA
Winslow, Michael *Actor, Comedian*
1327 Ocean Ave, #J, Santa Monica, CA 90401, USA
Winsor, Jackie *Artist*
%Paula Cooper Gallery, 534 W 21st St, New York, NY 10011, USA
Winston, George *Pianist, Composer*
%Dancing Cat Productions, PO Box 639, Santa Cruz, CA 95061, USA
Winston, Hattie *Actress*
13025 Jarvis Ave, Los Angeles, CA 90061, USA
Winston, Patrick H *Computer Scientist*
%Massachusetts Institute of Technology, Technology Square, Cambridge, MA 02139, USA
Winston, Roland *Physicist (Nonimaging Optics)*
3384 Locksley Court, Merced, CA 95340, USA
Winston, Roy C *Football Player*
1541 S Elaine Dr, Baton Rouge, LA 70815, USA
Winston, Stan *Movie Director, Make-Up Artist*
7032 Valjean Ave, Van Nuys, CA 91406, USA
Winter, Edgar *Singer, Keyboardist*
%Hooker Enterprises, 26033 Mulholland Highway, Calabasas, CA 91302, USA
Winter, Edward D *Actor*
4230 Whitsett Ave, #1, Studio City, CA 91604, USA
Winter, Fred (Tex) *Basketball Coach*
%Los Angeles Lakers, Staples Center, 1111 S Figueroa St, Los Angeles, CA 90015, USA
Winter, Frederick T *Thorougbred Racing Jockey, Trainer*
Montague House, Eastbury, Newbury, Berks RG16 7JL, England
Winter, Harrison L *Judge*
%US Court of Appeals, 101 W Lombard St, Baltimore, MD 21201, USA
Winter, Johnny *Singer, Guitarist*
%Slatus Mgmt, 35 Hayward Ave, Colchester, CT 06415, USA
Winter, Olaf *Canoeing Athlete*
An der Pirschheide 28, 14471 Potsdam, Germany
Winter, Paul T *Jazz/New Age Musician*
%Living Music Records, PO Box 72, Litchfield, CT 06759, USA
Winter, Ralph K, Jr *Judge*
%US Court of Appeals, 55 Whitney Ave, New Haven, CT 06510, USA
Winter, William F *Governor, MS*
633 N State St, Jackson, MS 39202, USA
Winters, Brian *Basketball Player, Coach*
%Golden State Warriors, 1001 Broadway, Oakland, CA 94607, USA
Winters, Jonathan *Actor, Comedian*
945 Lilac Dr, Santa Barbara, CA 93108, USA
Winters, Shelley *Actress*
%Gladys Hart Assoc, 1244 11th St, #A, Santa Monica, CA 90401, USA
Wintour, Anna *Editor*
%Vogue Magazine, Editorial Dept, 350 Madison Ave, New York, NY 10017, USA
Winwood, Steve *Singer, Songwriter, Keyboardist*
%Trinley Cottage, Tirley, Gloucs GL19 4EU, England
Winzenried, Jesse D *Financier*
%Securities Investor Protection, 805 15th St NW, Washington, DC 20005, USA
Wire, William S, II *Businessman*
6119 Stonehaven Dr, Nashville, TN 37215, USA
Wirth, Billy *Actor, Director*
%Michael Slessinger, 8730 Sunset Blvd, #220W, Los Angeles, CA 90069, USA

Wirth, Timothy E *Senator, CO*
%United Nations Foundation, 1301 Connecticut Ave NW, Washington, DC 20036, USA

Wirtz, W Willard *Secretary, Labor*
1211 Connecticut Ave NW, Washington, DC 20036, USA

Wirtz, William W (Bill) *Hockey Executive*
181 De Windt Road, Winnetka, IL 60093, USA

Wisdom, Norman *Actor, Comedian*
%Eric Glass Ltd, 28 Berkeley Square, London W1X 6HD, England

Wise, Ray *Actor*
%Gold Marshak Liedtke, 3500 W Olive Ave, #1400, Burbank, CA 91505, USA

Wise, Richard C (Rick) *Baseball Player*
662 SW 201st Ave, #66, Beaverton, OR 97006, USA

Wise, Robert E *Movie Director, Producer*
%Robert Wise Productions, 2222 Ave of Stars, #2303, Los Angeles, CA 90067, USA

Wise, William A *Businessman*
%El Paso Energy Corp, 1001 Louisiana St, Houston, TX 77002, USA

Wise, Willie *Basketball Player*
5232 215th St SE, Woodinville, WA 98072, USA

Wiseman, Frederick *Movie Producer*
%Zipporah Films, 1 Richdale Ave, #4, Cambridge, MA 02140, USA

Wiseman, Joseph *Actor*
382 Central Park West, New York, NY 10025, USA

Wish Bone *Rap Artist (Bone Thugs-N-Harmony)*
%Creative Artists Agency, 9830 Wilshire Blvd, Beverly Hills, CA 90212, USA

Wishart, Leonard P, III *Army General*
19360 Magnolia Grove Square, #315, Leesburg, VA 20176, USA

Wisner, Frank G *Diplomat*
%American International Group, 70 Pine St, #1800, New York, NY 10270, USA

Wisniewski, Andreas *Actor*
%Gage Group, 14724 Ventura Blvd, #505, Sherman Oaks, CA 91403, USA

Wisniewski, Stephen A (Steve) *Football Player*
36 El Alamo Court, Danville, CA 94526, USA

Wisoff, Peter J K (Jeff) *Astronaut*
4268 Brindisi Place, Pleasanton, CA 94566, USA

Wistert, Albert A (Ox) *Football Player*
256 Gunnell Road, Grants Pass, OR 97526, USA

Wistert, Alvin L (Moose) *Football Player*
10250 W Seven Mile Road, Northville, MI 48167, USA

Wistrom, Grant *Football Player*
683 Spyglass Summit Dr, Chesterfield, MO 63017, USA

Withers, Bill *Singer, Songwriter*
PO Box 16698, Beverly Hills, CA 90209, USA

Withers, Googie *Actress*
%Larry Dalzall, 17 Broad Court, London WC2B 5QN, England

Withers, Jane *Actress*
1830 Valpreda St, Burbank, CA 91504, USA

Withers, Pick *Drummer (Dire Straits)*
%Damage Mgmt, 16 Lambton Place, London W11 2SH, England

Witherspoon, John *Actor*
%T-Boyds Boy Inc, 12400 Ventura Blvd, Box 354, Studio City, CA 91604, USA

Witherspoon, Reese *Actress*
%Nancy Ryder, 9111 Wilshire Blvd, #600W, Beverly Hills, CA 90210, USA

Witkin, Isaac *Sculptor*
%Bennington College, Art Dept, Bennington, VT 05201, USA

Witkin, Joel-Peter *Photographer*
1707 Five Points Road SW, Albuquerque, NM 87105, USA

Witkop, Bernhard *Chemist*
3807 Montrose Driveway, Chevy Chase, MD 20815, USA

Witt, Alicia *Actress*
%Booh Schut, 11350 Ventura Blvd, #206, Studio City, CA 91604, USA

Witt, Katarina *Figure Skater*
Reichenheimer Str, 09023 Chemnitz, Germany

Witt, Michael A (Mike) *Baseball Player*
37 Poppy Hills Road, Laguna Nigel, CA 92677, USA

Witt, Paul J *Writer*
16032 Valley Vista Blvd, Encino, CA 91436, USA

Witt, Robert E *Educator*
%University of Texas, President's Office, Arlington, TX 76019, USA

Witten, Edward *Theoretical Physicist*
%Institute for Advanced Study, Einstein Lane, Princeton, NJ 08540, USA

Wittman, Randy *Basketball Player, Coach*
8646 French Curve, Eden Prairie, MN 55347, USA

Wobst, Frank *Financier*
%Huntington Bancshares, Huntington Center, 41 S High St, Columbus, OH 43287, USA

Wockel-Eckert, Barbel *Track Athlete*
Im Bangert 61, 64750 Lutzelbach, Germany

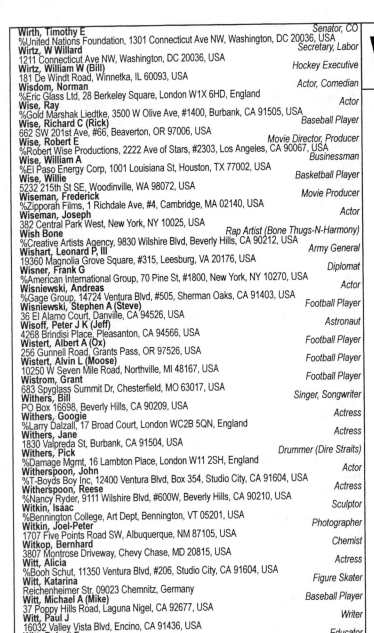

Woese, Carl R *Microbiologist*
806 W Delaware Ave, Urbana, IL 61801, USA

W

Woessner - Wolfowitz

Woessner, Mark M — *Businessman, Publisher*
Erich-Kastner-Str 25, 33332 Gutersloh, Germany
Woetzel, Damian — *Ballet Dancer, Choreographer*
%New York City Ballet, Lincoln Center Plaza, New York, NY 10023, USA
Wofford, Harris L — *Senator, PA*
260 Burch Dr, Coraopolis, PA 15108, USA
Wogan, Gerald N — *Toxicologist*
%Massachusetts Institute of Technology, Toxicology Div, Cambridge, MA 02139, USA
Woggon, Bill — *Cartoonist (Katy Keene)*
2724 Cabot Court, Thousand Oaks, CA 91360, USA
Wohl, Dave — *Basketball Player, Coach, Executive*
23 Tompkins Road, East Brunswick, NJ 08816, USA
Wohlers, Mark E — *Baseball Player*
135 Old Cedar Lane, Alpharetta, GA 30004, USA
Wohlhuter, Richard C (Rick) — *Track Athlete*
175 Dickinson Dr, Wheaton, IL 60187, USA
Woit, Dick — *Physical Fitness Expert*
%Lehmann Sports Center, 2700 N Lehmann Court, Chicago, IL 60614, USA
Woiwode, Larry — *Writer*
%State University of New York, English Dept, Binghamton, NY 13901, USA
Wojtowicz, R P — *Labor Leader*
%Railway Carmen Union, 3 Research Place, Rockville, MD 20850, USA
Wolaner, Robin P — *Publisher*
%Sunset Publishing Corp, 80 Willow Road, Menlo Park, CA 94025, USA
Wolf, David A — *Astronaut*
1714 Neptune Lane, Houston, TX 77062, USA
Wolf, Dick — *Television Producer*
%United Talent Agency, 9560 Wilshire Blvd, #500, Beverly Hills, CA 90212, USA
Wolf, Frank — *Publisher*
%Seventeen Magazine, 850 3rd Ave, New York, NY 10022, USA
Wolf, Naomi — *Writer*
%Random House, 1745 Broadway, #B1, New York, NY 10019, USA
Wolf, Peter — *Singer (J Geils Band)*
%Nick Ben-Meir, 652 N Doheny Dr, Los Angeles, CA 90069, USA
Wolf, Randall C (Randy) — *Baseball Player*
7266 Angela Ave, West Hills, CA 91307, USA
Wolf, Scott — *Actor*
6930 Calhoun Ave, Van Nuys, CA 91405, USA
Wolf, Sigrid — *Alpine Skier*
6652 Elbigenalp 45A, Austria
Wolf, Stephen M — *Businessman*
%US Airways Group, 2345 Crystal Dr, Arlington, VA 22202, USA
Wolfe, George C — *Theater Director*
%Shakespeare Festival, 425 Lafayette St, New York, NY 10003, USA
Wolfe, Kenneth L — *Businessman*
%Hershey Foods Corp, 100 Crystal A Dr, Hershey, PA 17033, USA
Wolfe, Naomi — *Writer*
%Royce Carlton Inc, 866 United Nations Plaza, New York, NY 10017, USA
Wolfe, Ralph S — *Microbiologist*
%University of Illinois, Microbiology Dept, Burrill Hall, Urbana, IL 61801, USA
Wolfe, Sterling — *Actor*
2609 Wyoming Ave, #A, Burbank, CA 91505, USA
Wolfe, Thad A — *Air Force General*
5207 Dunleigh Dr, Burke, VA 22015, USA
Wolfe, Thomas K (Tom), Jr — *Writer*
21 E 79th St, New York, NY 10021, USA
Wolfenden of Westcott, John F — *Educator*
White House, Guildford Road, Westcott near Dorking, Surrey, England
Wolfensohn, James D — *Financier*
%World Bank Group, 1818 H St NW, Washington, DC 20433, USA
Wolfenstein, Lincoln — *Physicist*
%Carnegie-Mellon University, Physics Dept, Pittsburgh, PA 15213, USA
Wolfermann, Klaus — *Track Athlete*
Fasanenweg 13A, 91074 Herzogenaurach, Germany
Wolff, Christoph J — *Educator*
182 Washington St, Belmont, MA 02478, USA
Wolff, Hugh — *Conductor*
%Van Walsum Mgmt, 4 Addison Bridge Place, London W14 8XP, England
Wolff, Jon A — *Geneticist*
1122 University Bay Dr, Madison, WI 53705, USA
Wolff, Sanford I — *Labor Leader*
8141 Broadway, New York, NY 10023, USA
Wolff, Tobias J A — *Writer*
%Stanford University, English Dept, Stanford, CA 94305, USA
Wolff, Torben — *Biologist, Zoologist*
Hesseltoften, 2900 Hellerup, Denmark
Wolfowitz, Paul D — *Government Official*
%Defense Department, Pentagon, Washington, DC 20301, USA

Wolfson, Louis E — *Businessman, Thoroughbred Racing Owner*
10205 Collins Ave, Bal Harbour, FL 33154, USA

Wolken, Jonathan — *Dance Artistic Director*
%Pilobolus Dance Theater, PO Box 388, Washington Depot, CT 06794, USA

Wollman, Harvey L — *Governor, SD*
RR 1 Box 43, Hitchcock, SD 57348, USA

Wollman, Roger L — *Judge*
%US Court of Appeals, Federal Building, 400 S Phillips, Sioux Falls, SD 57104, USA

Wolman, M Gordon — *Geographer*
2104 W Rogers Ave, Baltimore, MD 21209, USA

Wolper, David L — *Movie Producer*
617 N Rodeo Dr, Beverly Hills, CA 90210, USA

Wolpert, Julian — *Geographer*
188 E 64th St, #2304, New York, NY 10021, USA

Wolszczan, Aleksander — *Astronomer*
%Pennsylvania State University, Astronomy Dept, University Park, PA 16802, USA

Wolters, Kara — *Basketball Player*
137 Westfield Dr, Holliston, MA 01746, USA

Womack, Bobby — *Singer, Songwriter*
%GHR Entertainment, 6014 N Pointe Place, Woodland Hills, CA 91367, USA

Womack, James E — *Agricultural Researcher*
2105 Farley, College Station, TX 77845, USA

Womack, Lee Ann — *Singer*
%Erv Woolsey, 1000 18th Ave S, Nashville, TN 37212, USA

Wonder, Stevie — *Singer, Songwriter*
%Steveland Morris Music, 4616 W Magnolia Blvd, Burbank, CA 91505, USA

Wonders, Rich — *Bowler*
720 Augusta St, Racine, WI 53402, USA

Wong, Albert — *Computer Engineer*
26796 Vista Terrace, Lake Forest, CA 92630, USA

Wong-Staal, Flossie — *Molecular Biologist*
%University of California, Molecular Biology Dept, La Jolla, CA 92093, USA

Woo, John — *Movie Director*
%Endeavor Talent Agency, 9701 Wilshire Blvd, #1000, Beverly Hills, CA 90212, USA

Wood, Brenton — *Singer*
PO Box 4127, Inglewood, CA 90309, USA

Wood, C Norman — *Air Force General*
5440 Mount Corcoran Place, Burke, VA 22015, USA

Wood, Carolyn — *Swimmer*
4380 SW 86th Ave, Portland, OR 97225, USA

Wood, Charles G — *Writer*
%London Mgmt, 2-4 Noel St, London W1V 3RB, England

Wood, Elijah — *Actor*
PO Box 10459, Burbank, CA 91510, USA

Wood, Evan Rachel — *Actress*
%International Creative Mgmt, 8942 Wilshire Blvd, #219, Beverly Hills, CA 90211, USA

Wood, Glen — *Auto Racing Executive*
57 Rhody Creek Loop, Stuart, VA 24171, USA

Wood, Gordon S — *Historian*
77 Keense St, Providence, RI 02906, USA

Wood, Harlington, Jr — *Judge*
%US Court of Appeals, 600 E Monroe St, Springfield, IL 62701, USA

Wood, James — *Businessman*
%Great A&P Tea Co, 2 Paragon Dr, Montvale, NJ 07645, USA

Wood, James N — *Museum Director*
%Art Institute of Chicago, 111 S Michigan Ave, Chicago, IL 60603, USA

Wood, Janet — *Actress*
%Acme Talent, 4727 Wilshire Blvd, #333, Los Angeles, CA 90010, USA

Wood, John — *Actor*
%Royal Shakespeare Co, Barbican Center, Silk St, London EC2Y 8DS, England

Wood, John A — *Astrophysicist, Geologist*
1716 Cambridge St, #16, Cambridge, MA 02138, USA

Wood, Jon — *Auto, Truck Racing Driver*
%Hendrick Motorsports, 4400 Papa Joe Hendrick Blvd, Charlotte, NC 28262, USA

Wood, Kerry L — *Baseball Player*
15832 E Richwood Ave, Fountain Hills, AZ 85268, USA

Wood, Kimba M — *Judge*
%US District Court House, 40 Foley Square, New York, NY 10007, USA

Wood, Lana — *Actress*
868 Masterson Dr, Thousand Oaks, CA 91360, USA

Wood, Leon — *Basketball Player*
4217 Faculty Ave, Long Beach, CA 90808, USA

Wood, Maurice — *Physician*
RR 2 Box 543B, Hot Springs, VA 24445, USA

Wood, Nigel — *Astronaut, England*
Church Crookham, Aldershot, England

Wood, Oliver — *Cinematographer*
2018 N Vine St, Los Angeles, CA 90068, USA

W

Wood, Robert C *Secretary, Housing & Urban Development*
66 Pinewood Ave, Sudbury, MA 01776, USA
Wood, Robert E *Publisher*
%Peninsula Times Tribune, 435 N Michigan Ave, #1609, Chicago, IL 60611, USA
Wood, Robert J *Astronaut*
%McDonnell Douglas Corp, PO Box 516, Saint Louis, MO 63166, USA
Wood, Ronald (Ron) *Guitarist (Rolling Stones)*
%Monroe Sounds, 5 Church Row, Wandsworth Plain, London SW18 1ES, England
Wood, Sharon *Mountaineer*
PO Box 1482, Canmore AB T0L 0M0, Canada
Wood, Sidney B B *Tennis Player*
300 Murray Place, Southampton, NY 11968, USA
Wood, Stuart (Woody) *Guitarist (Bay City Rollers)*
27 Preston Grange Road, Preston Pans E, Lothian, Scotland
Wood, Thomas H *Publisher*
%Atlanta Constitution, 72 Marietta St NW, Atlanta, GA 30303, USA
Wood, Wilbur F *Baseball Player*
3 Elmsbrook Road, Bedford, MA 01730, USA
Wood, William B, III *Biologist*
%University of Colorado, Molecular Biology Dept, Boulder, CO 80309, USA
Wood, William V (Willie) *Football Player*
%Willie Wood Mechanical Systems, 7941 16th St NW, Washington, DC 20012, USA
Woodall, Jerry M *Electrical Engineer, Inventor*
%Yale University, Microelectronic Materials Ctr, 105 Wall, New Haven, CT 06511, USA
Woodard, Alfre *Actress*
602 Bay St, Santa Monica, CA 90405, USA
Woodard, Charlayne *Actress, Writer*
%Agency for Performing Arts, 9200 Sunset Blvd, #900, Los Angeles, CA 90069, USA
Woodard, Lynette *Basketball Player*
%University of Kansas, Allen Fieldhouse, Lawrence, KS 66045, USA
Woodard, Rickey *Jazz Saxophonist*
%JVC Music, 3800 Barham Blvd, #409, Los Angeles, CA 90068, USA
Woodard, Steven L (Steve) *Baseball Player*
800 Frost Court SW, Hartselle, AL 35640, USA
Woodbine, Bokeem *Actor*
19351 Ventura Blvd, Tarzana, CA 91356, USA
Woodbridge, Todd *Tennis Player*
%Advantage International, PO Box 3297, North Burnley, VIC 3121, Australia
Wooden, John R *Basketball Player, Coach*
17711 Margate St, #102, Encino, CA 91316, USA
Woodforde, Mark *Tennis Player*
%Octagon, 1751 Pinnacle Dr, #1500, McLean, VA 22102, USA
Woodhead, Cynthia *Swimmer*
PO Box 1193, Riverside, CA 92502, USA
Woodiwiss, Kathleen E *Writer*
%Avon Books, 959 8th Ave, New York, NY 10019, USA
Woodmansee, John W, Jr *Army General*
6609 Shady Creek Circle, Plano, TX 75024, USA
Woodring, Wendell P *Geologist, Paleontologist*
6647 El Colegio Road, Goleta, CA 93117, USA
Woodruff, Bob *Singer, Songwriter*
%Jim Della Croce Mgmt, 1229 17th Ave S, Nashville, TN 37212, USA
Woodruff, John Y *Track Athlete*
9 Dennison Dr, #J, East Windsor, NJ 08520, USA
Woodruff, Judy C *Commentator*
%Cable News Network, News Dept, 820 1st St NE, Washington, DC 20002, USA
Woods, Aubrey *Actress*
%James Sharkey, 21 Golden Square, London W1R 3PA, England
Woods, Barbara Alyn *Actress*
%David Shapira, 15821 Ventura Blvd, #235, Encino, CA 91436, USA
Woods, Elbert (Ickey) *Football Player*
7031 Fairpark Ave, Cincinnati, OH 45216, USA
Woods, Eldrick T (Tiger) *Golfer*
%Tiger Woods Foundation, 4281 Katella Ave, #111, Los Alamitos, CA 90720, USA
Woods, George *Track Athlete*
7631 Green Hedge Road, Edwardsville, IL 62025, USA
Woods, James *Actor*
%Guttman Assoc, 118 S Beverly Dr, #201, Beverly Hills, CA 90212, USA
Woods, Jerome *Football Player*
%Kansas City Chiefs, 1 Arrowhead Dr, Kansas City, KS 64129, USA
Woods, Michael *Actor*
%David Shapira, 15821 Ventura Blvd, #235, Encino, CA 91436, USA
Woods, Philip (Phil) *Jazz Clarinetist, Saxophonist, Composer*
PO Box 278, Delaware Water Gap, PA 18327, USA
Woods, Qyntel *Basketball Player*
%Portland Trail Blazers, Rose Garden, 1 Center Court St, Portland, OR 97227, USA
Woods, Robert S *Actor*
%ITA, 227 Central Park West, #5A, New York, NY 10024, USA

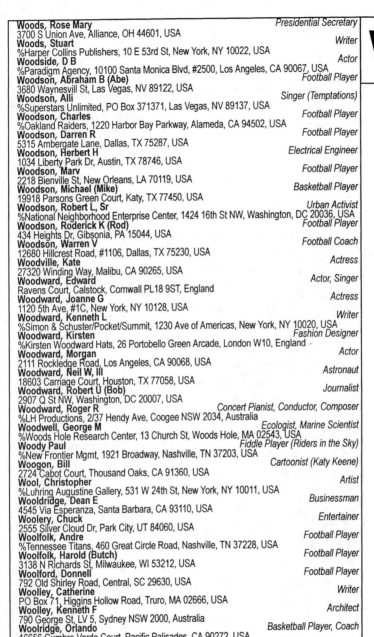

Woods, Rose Mary *Presidential Secretary*
3700 S Union Ave, Alliance, OH 44601, USA
Woods, Stuart *Writer*
%Harper Collins Publishers, 10 E 53rd St, New York, NY 10022, USA
Woodside, D B *Actor*
%Paradigm Agency, 10100 Santa Monica Blvd, #2500, Los Angeles, CA 90067, USA
Woodson, Abraham B (Abe) *Football Player*
3680 Waynesvill St, Las Vegas, NV 89122, USA
Woodson, Alli *Singer (Temptations)*
%Superstars Unlimited, PO Box 371371, Las Vegas, NV 89137, USA
Woodson, Charles *Football Player*
%Oakland Raiders, 1220 Harbor Bay Parkway, Alameda, CA 94502, USA
Woodson, Darren R *Football Player*
5315 Ambergate Lane, Dallas, TX 75287, USA
Woodson, Herbert H *Electrical Engineer*
1034 Liberty Park Dr, Austin, TX 78746, USA
Woodson, Marv *Football Player*
2218 Bienville St, New Orleans, LA 70119, USA
Woodson, Michael (Mike) *Basketball Player*
19918 Parsons Green Court, Katy, TX 77450, USA
Woodson, Robert L, Sr *Urban Activist*
%National Neighborhood Enterprise Center, 1424 16th St NW, Washington, DC 20036, USA
Woodson, Roderick K (Rod) *Football Player*
434 Heights Dr, Gibsonia, PA 15044, USA
Woodson, Warren V *Football Coach*
12680 Hillcrest Road, #1106, Dallas, TX 75230, USA
Woodville, Kate *Actress*
27320 Winding Way, Malibu, CA 90265, USA
Woodward, Edward *Actor, Singer*
Ravens Court, Calstock, Cornwall PL18 9ST, England
Woodward, Joanne G *Actress*
1120 5th Ave, #1C, New York, NY 10128, USA
Woodward, Kenneth L *Writer*
%Simon & Schuster/Pocket/Summit, 1230 Ave of Americas, New York, NY 10020, USA
Woodward, Kirsten *Fashion Designer*
%Kirsten Woodward Hats, 26 Portobello Green Arcade, London W10, England
Woodward, Morgan *Actor*
2111 Rockledge Road, Los Angeles, CA 90068, USA
Woodward, Neil W, III *Astronaut*
18603 Carriage Court, Houston, TX 77058, USA
Woodward, Robert U (Bob) *Journalist*
2907 Q St NW, Washington, DC 20007, USA
Woodward, Roger R *Concert Pianist, Conductor, Composer*
%LH Productions, 2/37 Hendy Ave, Coogee NSW 2034, Australia
Woodwell, George M *Ecologist, Marine Scientist*
%Woods Hole Research Center, 13 Church St, Woods Hole, MA 02543, USA
Woody Paul *Fiddle Player (Riders in the Sky)*
%New Frontier Mgmt, 1921 Broadway, Nashville, TN 37203, USA
Woogon, Bill *Cartoonist (Katy Keene)*
2724 Cabot Court, Thousand Oaks, CA 91360, USA
Wool, Christopher *Artist*
%Luhring Augustine Gallery, 531 W 24th St, New York, NY 10011, USA
Wooldridge, Dean E *Businessman*
4545 Via Esperanza, Santa Barbara, CA 93110, USA
Woolery, Chuck *Entertainer*
2555 Silver Cloud Dr, Park City, UT 84060, USA
Woolfolk, Andre *Football Player*
%Tennessee Titans, 460 Great Circle Road, Nashville, TN 37228, USA
Woolfolk, Harold (Butch) *Football Player*
3138 N Richards St, Milwaukee, WI 53212, USA
Woolford, Donnell *Football Player*
792 Old Shirley Road, Central, SC 29630, USA
Woolley, Catherine *Writer*
PO Box 71, Higgins Hollow Road, Truro, MA 02666, USA
Woolley, Kenneth F *Architect*
790 George St, LV 5, Sydney NSW 2000, Australia
Woolridge, Orlando *Basketball Player, Coach*
16656 Cumbre Verde Court, Pacific Palisades, CA 90272, USA
Woolsey, Elizabeth D *Skier*
Trail Creek Ranch, Wilson, WY 83014, USA
Woolsey, R James *Law Enforcement Official*
%Shea & Gardner, 1800 Massachusetts Ave NW, Washington, DC 20036, USA
Woolsey, Ralph A *Cinematographer*
23388 Mulholland Dr, #109, Woodland Hills, CA 91364, USA
Woomble, Roddy *Singer (Idlewild)*
%Agency Group Ltd, 370 City Road, London EC1V 2QA, England
Woosnam, Ian H *Golfer*
Dyffryn, Morda Road, Oswestry, Shropshire SY11 2AY, Wales

W

Woosnam, Phil *Soccer Executive*
1255 Fairfield E, Atlanta, GA 30338, USA
Wooten, Jim *Commentator*
%ABC-TV, News Dept, 5010 Creston St, Hyattsville, MD 20781, USA
Wootten, Morgan *Basketball Coach*
%De Matha High School, Athletic Dept, Hyattsville, MD 20781, USA
Wootton, Charles G *Diplomat*
%Chevron Corp, 555 Market St, San Francisco, CA 94105, USA
Wopat, Tom *Actor, Singer*
2614 Woodlawn Dr, Nashville, TN 37212, USA
Word, Weldon R *Engineer (Paveway Smart Bomb)*
633 Private Road 7908, Hawkins, TX 75765, USA
Worden, Alfred M *Astronaut*
PO Box 8065, Vero Beach, FL 32963, USA
Worgull, David *Religious Leader*
%Wisconsin Evangelical Lutheran Synod, 1270 N Dobson Road, Chandler, AZ 85224, USA
Worley, Darryl *Singer*
%William Morris Agency, 2100 W End Ave, #1000, Nashville, TN 37203, USA
Worley, Jo Anne *Actress*
PO Box 2054, Toluca Lake, CA 91610, USA
Worndl, Frank *Alpine Skier*
Burgsiedlung 19C, 87527 Sonthofen, Germany
Woronov, Mary *Actress*
4350 1/4 Beverly Blvd, Los Angeles, CA 90004, USA
Worsley, Lorne J (Gump) *Hockey Player*
421 Bonaire Ave, Beloeil QC H3G L1L, Canada
Worth, Maurice *Businessman*
%Delta Air Lines, Hartsfield International Airport, Atlanta, GA 30320, USA
Worthen, John E *Educator*
%Ball State University, President's Office, Muncie, IN 47306, USA
Worthington, Melvin L *Religious Leader*
%Free Will Baptists, PO Box 5002, Antioch, TN 37011, USA
Worthy, James A *Basketball Player, Sportscaster*
11821 Henley Lane, Los Angeles, CA 90077, USA
Wottle, David J (Dave) *Track Athlete*
9245 Forest Hill Lane, Germantown, TN 38139, USA
Wouk, Herman *Writer*
303 W Crestview Dr, Palm Springs, CA 92264, USA
Woytowicz-Rudnicka, Stefania *Concert Singer*
Al Przyjaciol 3 m 13, 00-565 Warsaw, Poland
Wozniak, Steve *Computer Designer, Inventor*
300 Santa Rosa Dr, Los Gatos, CA 95032, USA
Wragg, John *Sculptor*
6 Castle Lane, Devizes, Wilts SN10 1HJ, England
Wray, Fay *Actress*
2160 Century Park East, #1901, Los Angeles, CA 90067, USA
Wray, Gordon R *Engineering Designer*
Stonestack, Rempstone, Loughborough, Leics LE12 6RH, England
Wray, Link *Guitarist*
%Absolute Artists, 8490 W Sunset Blvd, #403, West Hollywood, CA 90069, USA
Wregget, Ken *Hockey Player*
176 Fieldgate Dr, Pittsburgh, PA 15241, USA
Wright Penn, Robin *Actress, Model*
%Creative Artists Agency, 9830 Wilshire Blvd, Beverly Hills, CA 90212, USA
Wright, Ben *Sportscaster*
%CBS-TV, Sports Dept, 51 W 52nd St, New York, NY 10019, USA
Wright, Betty *Singer*
%Rodgers Redding, 1048 Tatnall St, Macon, GA 31201, USA
Wright, Bonnie *Actress*
%P F D, Drury House, 34-43 Russell St, London WC2B 5HA, England
Wright, Bruce A *Air Force General*
Vice Commander, Air Combat Command, Langley Air Force Base, VA 23665, USA
Wright, Charles P, Jr *Writer*
940 Locust Ave, Charlottesville, VA 22901, USA
Wright, Chely *Singer*
%TBA Artist Mgmt, 300 10th Ave S, Nashville, TN 37203, USA
Wright, Clyde *Baseball Player*
528 S Jeanine St, Anaheim, CA 92806, USA
Wright, Cobina, Jr *Actress*
1326 Dove Meadow Road, Solvange, CA 93463, USA
Wright, Craig M *Architect*
%C M Wright Inc, 700 N La Cienega Blvd, Los Angeles, CA 90069, USA
Wright, Dick *Editorial Cartoonist*
%Columbus Dispatch, Editorial Dept, 34 S 3rd St, Columbus, OH 43215, USA
Wright, Donald C (Don) *Editorial Cartoonist*
PO Box 1176, Palm Beach, FL 33480, USA
Wright, Ernie H *Football Player*
1414 Lauren Court, Encinitas, CA 92024, USA

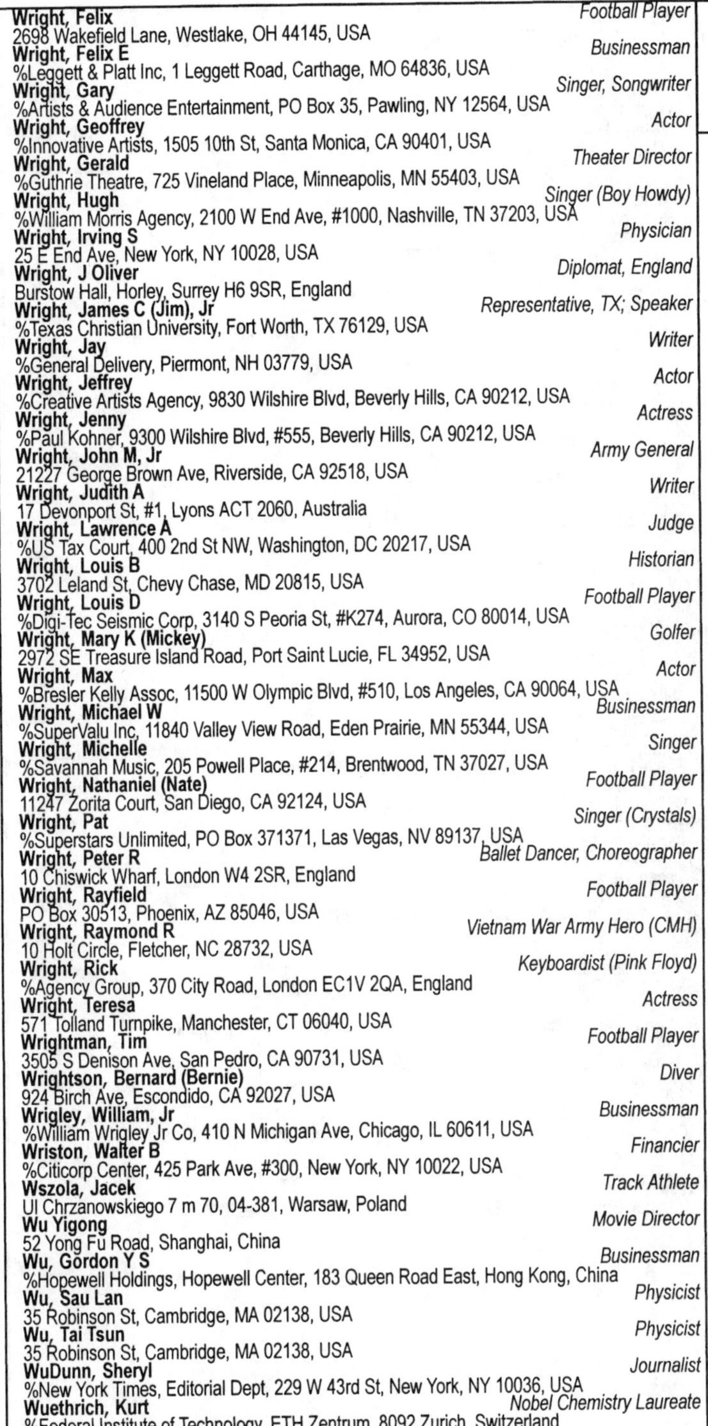

Wright, Felix *Football Player*
2698 Wakefield Lane, Westlake, OH 44145, USA

Wright, Felix E *Businessman*
%Leggett & Platt Inc, 1 Leggett Road, Carthage, MO 64836, USA

Wright, Gary *Singer, Songwriter*
%Artists & Audience Entertainment, PO Box 35, Pawling, NY 12564, USA

Wright, Geoffrey *Actor*
%Innovative Artists, 1505 10th St, Santa Monica, CA 90401, USA

Wright, Gerald *Theater Director*
%Guthrie Theatre, 725 Vineland Place, Minneapolis, MN 55403, USA

Wright, Hugh *Singer (Boy Howdy)*
%William Morris Agency, 2100 W End Ave, #1000, Nashville, TN 37203, USA

Wright, Irving S *Physician*
25 E End Ave, New York, NY 10028, USA

Wright, J Oliver *Diplomat, England*
Burstow Hall, Horley, Surrey H6 9SR, England

Wright, James C (Jim), Jr *Representative, TX; Speaker*
%Texas Christian University, Fort Worth, TX 76129, USA

Wright, Jay *Writer*
%General Delivery, Piermont, NH 03779, USA

Wright, Jeffrey *Actor*
%Creative Artists Agency, 9830 Wilshire Blvd, Beverly Hills, CA 90212, USA

Wright, Jenny *Actress*
%Paul Kohner, 9300 Wilshire Blvd, #555, Beverly Hills, CA 90212, USA

Wright, John M, Jr *Army General*
21227 George Brown Ave, Riverside, CA 92518, USA

Wright, Judith A *Writer*
17 Devonport St, #1, Lyons ACT 2060, Australia

Wright, Lawrence A *Judge*
%US Tax Court, 400 2nd St NW, Washington, DC 20217, USA

Wright, Louis B *Historian*
3702 Leland St, Chevy Chase, MD 20815, USA

Wright, Louis D *Football Player*
%Digi-Tec Seismic Corp, 3140 S Peoria St, #K274, Aurora, CO 80014, USA

Wright, Mary K (Mickey) *Golfer*
2972 SE Treasure Island Road, Port Saint Lucie, FL 34952, USA

Wright, Max *Actor*
%Bresler Kelly Assoc, 11500 W Olympic Blvd, #510, Los Angeles, CA 90064, USA

Wright, Michael W *Businessman*
%SuperValu Inc, 11840 Valley View Road, Eden Prairie, MN 55344, USA

Wright, Michelle *Singer*
%Savannah Music, 205 Powell Place, #214, Brentwood, TN 37027, USA

Wright, Nathaniel (Nate) *Football Player*
11247 Zorita Court, San Diego, CA 92124, USA

Wright, Pat *Singer (Crystals)*
%Superstars Unlimited, PO Box 371371, Las Vegas, NV 89137, USA

Wright, Peter R *Ballet Dancer, Choreographer*
10 Chiswick Wharf, London W4 2SR, England

Wright, Rayfield *Football Player*
PO Box 30513, Phoenix, AZ 85046, USA

Wright, Raymond R *Vietnam War Army Hero (CMH)*
10 Holt Circle, Fletcher, NC 28732, USA

Wright, Rick *Keyboardist (Pink Floyd)*
%Agency Group, 370 City Road, London EC1V 2QA, England

Wright, Teresa *Actress*
571 Tolland Turnpike, Manchester, CT 06040, USA

Wrightman, Tim *Football Player*
3505 S Denison Ave, San Pedro, CA 90731, USA

Wrightson, Bernard (Bernie) *Diver*
924 Birch Ave, Escondido, CA 92027, USA

Wrigley, William, Jr *Businessman*
%William Wrigley Jr Co, 410 N Michigan Ave, Chicago, IL 60611, USA

Wriston, Walter B *Financier*
%Citicorp Center, 425 Park Ave, #300, New York, NY 10022, USA

Wszola, Jacek *Track Athlete*
Ul Chrzanowskiego 7 m 70, 04-381, Warsaw, Poland

Wu Yigong *Movie Director*
52 Yong Fu Road, Shanghai, China

Wu, Gordon Y S *Businessman*
%Hopewell Holdings, Hopewell Center, 183 Queen Road East, Hong Kong, China

Wu, Sau Lan *Physicist*
35 Robinson St, Cambridge, MA 02138, USA

Wu, Tai Tsun *Physicist*
35 Robinson St, Cambridge, MA 02138, USA

WuDunn, Sheryl *Journalist*
%New York Times, Editorial Dept, 229 W 43rd St, New York, NY 10036, USA

Wuethrich, Kurt *Nobel Chemistry Laureate*
%Federal Institute of Technology, ETH Zentrum, 8092 Zurich, Switzerland

Wuhl, Robert *Actor*
%Paradigm Agency, 10100 Santa Monica Blvd, #2500, Los Angeles, CA 90067, USA
Wunderlich, Paul *Artist*
Haynstr 2, 20949 Hamburg, Germany
Wunsch, Carl I *Oceanographer*
78 Washington Ave, Cambridge, MA 02140, USA
Wuorinen, Charles P *Composer*
%Howard Stokar Mgmt, 870 W End Ave, New York, NY 10025, USA
Wurz, Alexander *Auto Racing Driver*
%McLaren Int'l, Working Park, Albert Dr, Woking, Surrey GU21 5JY, England
Wuycik, Dennis *Basketball Player*
31 Rogerson Dr, Chapel Hill, NC 27517, USA
Wyatt, Jane *Actress*
651 Siena Way, Los Angeles, CA 90077, USA
Wyatt, Jennifer *Golfer*
%Carolina Group, 2321 Devine St, #A, Columbia, SC 29205, USA
Wyatt, Leslie *Educator*
%Arkansas State University, President's Office, State University, AR 72467, USA
Wyatt, Oscar S, Jr *Businessman*
%Coastal Corp, 6955 Union Park Ave, #540, Midvale, UT 84047, USA
Wyatt, Shannon *Actress*
8949 Falling Creek Court, Annandale, VA 22003, USA
Wyatt, Sharon *Actress*
16830 Ventura Blvd, #300, Encino, CA 91436, USA
Wyche, Samuel D (Sam) *Football Coach, Sportscaster*
PO Box 1570, Pickens, SC 29671, USA
Wycheck, Frank *Football Player*
4674 Sunrise Ave, Bensalem, PA 19020, USA
Wyeth, Andrew N *Artist*
10000 Brintons Bridge Road, Chadds Ford, PA 19317, USA
Wyeth, James Browning *Artist*
Lookout Farm, 701 Smiths Bridge Road, Wilmington, DE 19807, USA
Wyle, Noah *Actor*
PO Box 27380, Los Angeles, CA 90027, USA
Wyler, Gretchen *Actress*
11754 Barranca Road, Camarillo, CA 93012, USA
Wylie, Paul *Figure Skater*
170 Estey Ave, Hyannis, MA 02601, USA
Wyludda, Ilke *Track Athlete*
%LAC Chemnitz, Reichenhainer Str 154, 09125 Chemnitz, Germany
Wyman, Bill *Bassist (Rolling Stones)*
%Ripple Productions, 344 Kings Road, London SW3 5UR, England
Wyman, Jane *Actress*
14 Kavenish Dr, Rancho Mirage, CA 92270, USA
Wymore, Patrice *Actress*
Port Antonio, Jamaica, British West Indies
Wyn-Davies, Geraint *Actor*
%Oscars Abrams Zimel, 438 Queen St E, Toronto ON M5A 1T4, Canada
Wynalda, Eric *Soccer Player*
2313 Stormcroft Court, Westlake Village, CA 91361, USA
Wyner, George *Actor*
3450 Laurie Place, Studio City, CA 91604, USA
Wyngaarden, James B *Physician*
%NAS, 2101 Columbus Ave NW, Washington, DC 20418, USA
Wyngarde, Peter *Actor*
%International Creative Mgmt, 76 Oxford St, London W1N 0AX, England
Wynn, Bob *Golfer*
78455 Calle Orense, La Quinta, CA 92253, USA
Wynn, Renaldo *Football Player*
19805 Rothschild Court, Ashburn, VA 20147, USA
Wynn, Stephen A *Businessman*
%Desert Inn Hotel, 3245 Las Vegas Blvd S, Las Vegas, NV 89109, USA
Wynter, Dana *Actress*
%Contemporary Artists, 610 Santa Monica Blvd, #202, Santa Monica, CA 90401, USA
Wyss, Amanda *Actress*
%Badgley Connor Talent, 9229 Sunset Blvd, #311, Los Angeles, CA 90069, USA

Xie Bingxin *Writer*
%Central Nationalities Institute, Residential Qtrs, Beijing 100081, China
Xie Jin *Movie Director*
%Shanghai Film Studio, 595 Caoxi Beilu, Shanghai, China
Xu Shuyang *Sculptor*
%Zhejiang Academy of Fine Arts, PO Box 169, Hangzhou, China
Xue Wei *Concert Violinist*
134 Sheaveshill Ave, London NW9, England
Xuereb, Salvator *Actor*
%Metropolitan Talent Agency, 4526 Wilshire Blvd, Los Angeles, CA 90010, USA
Yablans, Frank *Movie Producer*
88 Bull Path, East Hampton, NY 11937, USA
Yablokov, Alexey V *Biololgist*
%Koltsove Biology Institute, Vaviloca Str 26, 117808, Moscow, Russia
Yaeger, Andrea *Tennis Player*
1490 S Ute Ave, Aspen, CO 81611, USA
Yager, Faye *Social Activist*
%Children of the Underground, 902 Curlew Court NW, Atlanta, GA 30327, USA
Yager, Rick *Cartoonist (Buck Rogers)*
%North American Syndicate, 235 E 45th St, New York, NY 10017, USA
Yaguda, Stan *Singer (Jay & the Americans)*
%Joyce Agency, 370 Harrison Ave, Harrison, NY 10528, USA
Yagudin, Alexei *Figure Skater*
%Connecticut Skating Center, 300 Alumni Road, Newington, CT 06111, USA
Yake, Terry *Hockey Player*
3 Stratford Park, Bloomfield, CT 06002, USA
Yakovlev, Aleksandr N *Government Official, Russia*
%Prisoner Rehabilitation Commission, Ul Iljinka 8/4, 103132 Moscow, Russia
Yallop, Frank *Soccer Coach*
%San Jose Earthquakes, 3550 Stevens Creek Blvd, #200, San Jose, CA 95117, USA
Yalow, Rosalyn S *Nobel Medicine Laureate*
3242 Tibbett Ave, Bronx, NY 10463, USA
Yamagata, Hiro *Artist*
1050 Ave D, Redondo Beach, CA 90277, USA
Yamaguchi, Kristi T *Figure Skater*
2500 E Las Olas Blvd, #502, Fort Lauderdale, FL 33301, USA
Yamaguchi, Roy *Restauranteur*
%Roy's Restaurant, Kai Corporate Plaza, 6600 Kalaniaole Hwy, Honolulu, HI 96825, USA
Yamame, Marlene Mitsuko *Actress*
%Herb Tannen, 10801 National Blvd, #101, Los Angeles, CA 90064, USA
Yamamoto, Keith R *Molecular Biologist*
332 Douglass St, San Francisco, CA 94114, USA
Yamamoto, Kenichi *Businessman*
%Mazda Motor Corp, 4-6-19 Funairi-Minami, Minamiku, Hiroshima, Japan
Yamamoto, Takuma *Businessman*
%Fujitsu Ltd, 1-6-1 Marunouchi, Chiyodaku, Tokyo 100, Japan
Yamamoto, Yohji *Fashion Designer*
14-15 Conduit St, London W1R 9TG, England
Yamanaka, Tsuyoshi *Swimmer*
6-10-33-212 Akasaka, Minatoku, Tokyo, Japan
Yamani, Sheikh Ahmed Zaki *Government Official, Saudi Arabia*
Chermignon near Crans-Montana, Valais, Switzerland
Yamasaki, Taro M *Photojournalist*
%People Magazine, Editorial Dept, Time-Life Building, New York, NY 10020, USA
Yamashita, Yasuhiro *Judo Athlete, Coach*
1117 Kitakaname, Hitatsuka Kanagawa 259-1207, Japan
Yancy, Emily *Actress*
%Henderson/Hogan, 8285 W Sunset Blvd, #1, West Hollywood, CA 90046, USA
Yang Liwei *Taikonaut, China*
%Satellite Launch Center, Jiuquan, Gansu Province, China
Yang, Chen Ning *Nobel Physics Laureate*
3 Victoria Court, Saint James, NY 11780, USA
Yang, Chuan-Kwang (C K) *Track Athlete*
PO Box 7855-39, Tsoying, Kaohsking, Taiwan
Yang, Jerry *Businessman, Computer Programmer*
%Yahoo!, 701 First Ave, Sunnyvale, CA 94089, USA
Yang, Shang-Fa *Biochemist*
118 Villanova Dr, Davis, CA 95616, USA
Yankelovich, Daniel *Social Scientist*
%Public Agenda Foundation, 6 E 39th St, #900, New York, NY 10016, USA
Yankovic, Al (Weird Al) *Actor, Comedian, Singer, Songwriter*
1631 Magnetic Terrace, Los Angeles, CA 90069, USA
Yankovsky, Oleg I *Actor*
Komsomolsky Prospekt 41, #10, 119270 Moscow, Russia
Yannas, I V *Mechanical Engineer, Medical Researcher*
%Massachusetts Institute of Technology, Engineering School, Cambridge, MA 02139, USA
Yanni *Keyboardist, Songwriter*
PO Box 46996, Eden Prairie, MN 55344, USA

Yanofsky, Charles *Biologist*
725 Mayfield Ave, Stanford, CA 94305, USA
Yanukovich, Victor *Prime Minister, Ukraine*
%Prime Minister's Office, Hrushevskoga 12/2, 252008 Kiev, Ukraine
Yao Ming *Basketball Player*
%Houston Rockets, Toyota Center, 2 E Greenway Plaza, Houston, TX 77046, USA
Yarborough, W Caleb (Cale) *Auto Racing Driver*
%Yarborough Racing, 2723 W Palmetto St, Florence, SC 29501, USA
Yarborough, William P *Army General*
160 Hillside Road, Southern Pines, NC 28387, USA
Yarbrough, Curtis *Religious Leader*
%General Baptists Assn, 100 Stinson Dr, Poplar Bluff, MO 63901, USA
Yarbrough, Glenn *Singer, Songwriter (Limelighters)*
150 Avenida Presidio, San Clemente, CA 92672, USA
Yardley, George *Basketball Player*
%George Yardley Co, 17260 Newhope St, Fountain Valley, CA 92708, USA
Yared, Gabriel *Composer*
%Gorfaine/Schwartz, 13245 Riverside Dr, #450, Sherman Oaks, CA 91423, USA
Yarlett, Claire *Actress*
1540 Skylark Lane, Los Angeles, CA 90069, USA
Yarnall, Celeste *Actress*
2899 Agoura Road, #315, Westlake, CA 91361, USA
Yarnell, Lorene *Mime (Shields & Yarnell)*
%Arthur Shafman International, PO Box 352, Pawling, NY 12564, USA
Yarrow, Peter *Singer (Peter Paul & Mary), Songwriter*
27 W 67th St, #5E, New York, NY 10023, USA
Yary, A Ronald (Ron) *Football Player*
15650 El Prado Road, Chino, CA 91710, USA
Yasbeck, Amy *Actress*
11601 Wilshire Blvd, #2200, Los Angeles, CA 90025, USA
Yashin, Alexei *Hockey Player*
%New York Islanders, Nassau Coliseum, Hempstead Turnpike, Uniondale, NY 11553, USA
Yastrzemski, Carl M *Baseball Player*
8 Whittier Place, #7C, Boston, MA 02114, USA
Yates, Albert C *Educator*
%Colorado State University System, President's Office, Denver, CO 80202, USA
Yates, Bill *Cartoonist (Redeye)*
%King Features Syndicate, 888 7th Ave, New York, NY 10106, USA
Yates, Cassie *Actress*
260 S Beverly Dr, #210, Beverly Hills, CA 90212, USA
Yates, Jim *Auto Racing Driver*
%Commonwealth Service & Supply, 4740 Eisenhower Ave, Alexandria, VA 22304, USA
Yates, Peter J *Movie Director*
334 Caroline Ave, Culver City, CA 90232, USA
Yates, Ronald W (Ron) *Air Force General*
525 Silhouette Way, Monument, CO 80132, USA
Yau, Shing-Tung *Mathematician*
%Harvard University, Mathematics Dept, 1 Oxford St, Cambridge, MA 02138, USA
Yauch, Adam (MCA) *Rap Artist (Beastie Boys)*
%GAS Entertainment, 8935 Lindblade St, Culver City, CA 90232, USA
Ybarra y Churruca, Emilio de *Financier*
%Banco Bilbao-Vizcaya, Plaza de San Nicolas 4, 48005 Bilboa, Spain
Yeager, Bunny *Photographer, Model*
9301 NE 6th Ave, #B201, Miami Shores, FL 33138, USA
Yeager, Charles E (Chuck) *Test Pilot, Air Force General*
PO Box 579, Penn Valley, CA 95946, USA
Yeager, Cheryl L *Ballerina*
%American Ballet Theatre, 890 Broadway, New York, NY 10003, USA
Yeager, Jeana *Experimental Airplane Pilot*
3695 Highway 50, Campbell, TX 75422, USA
Yeager, Stephen W (Steve) *Baseball Player*
PO Box 34184, Granada Hills, CA 91394, USA
Yeagley, Jerry *Soccer Coach*
1418 S Sare Road, Bloomington, IN 47401, USA
Yeakel, G Scott *Astronaut*
12184 E Poinsettia Dr, Scottsdale, AZ 85259, USA
Yearley, Douglas C *Businessman*
%Phelps Dodge Corp, 1 N Central Ave, Phoenix, AZ 85004, USA
Yearwood, Trisha *Singer*
4636 Lebanon Pike, #316, Hermitage, TN 37076, USA
Yeliseyev, Aleksei S *Cosmonaut*
%Bauman Higher Technical School, Baumanskaya Ul 5, 107005 Moscow, Russia
Yellen, Janet L *Financier, Government Official*
683 San Luis Road, Berkeley, CA 94707, USA
Yellen, Linda B *Television Producer, Director*
3 Sheridan Square, New York, NY 10014, USA
Yeltsin, Boris N *President, Russian Federation*
Belji Don, Krascnopresneskaj Nab 2, 103274 Moscow, Russia

Yeoh, Michelle *Actress*
%William Morris Agency, 151 El Camino Dr, Beverly Hills, CA 90212, USA
Yeohlee *Fashion Designer*
%Yeohlee Designs, 530 Fashion Ave, New York, NY 10018, USA
Yeoman, William F (Bill) *Football Player, Coach*
3030 Country Club Blvd, Sugar Land, TX 77478, USA
Yeosock, John J *Army General*
223 Newport Dr, Peachtree City, GA 30269, USA
Yepremian, Garabed S (Garo) *Football Player*
1 E Mount Vernon St, Oxford, PA 19363, USA
Yerman, Jack *Track Athlete*
753 Camellia, Paradise, CA 95969, USA
Yeston, Maury *Composer*
%Yale University, Music Dept, New Haven, CT 06520, USA
Yeutter, Clayton K *Secretary, Agriculture*
10955 Martingale Court, Potomac, MD 20854, USA
Yevtushenko, Yevgeny A *Writer*
Kutuzovski Prospekt 2/1, #101, 121248 Moscow, Russia
Yewcic, Thomas (Tom) *Baseball, Football Player*
31 Cherokee Road, Arlington, MA 02474, USA
Yilmaz, A Mesut *Prime Minister, Turkey*
Basbakanlik, Bakanliklar, Ankara, Turkey
Ylonen, Juha *Hockey Player*
%Ottawa Senators, 1000 Palladium Dr, Kanata ON K2V 1A4, Canada
Yma Sumac *Singer*
%Absolute Artists, 8490 W Sunset Blvd, #403, West Hollywood, CA 90069, USA
Yo-Yo *Rap Artist*
%William Morris Agency, 1325 Ave of Americas, New York, NY 10019, USA
Yoakam, Dwight *Singer, Songwriter*
%Fitzgerald Hartley, 1908 Wedgewood Ave, Nashville, TN 37212, USA
Yoccoz, Jean-Christophe *Mathematician*
%University of Paris-Sud (Orsey), 91405 Orsay-Cedex-Bait 425, France
Yock, Robert J *Judge*
%US Claims Court, 717 Madison Place NW, Washington, DC 20439, USA
Yodoyman, Joseph *Prime Minister, Chad*
%Prime Minister's Office, N'Djamena, Chad
Yoken, Mel B *Writer*
261 Carroll St, New Bedford, MA 02740, USA
Yonaker, John *Football Player*
20450 Lake Shore Blvd, Cleveland, OH 44123, USA
York, Francine *Actress*
6430 Sunset Blvd, #1205, Los Angeles, CA 90028, USA
York, Glen P *Vietnam War Air Force Hero*
1620 E Driftwood Dr, Tempe, AZ 85283, USA
York, Herbert F *Physicist*
6110 Camino de la Costa, La Jolla, CA 92037, USA
York, John J *Actor*
4804 Laurel Canyon Blvd, #212, Valley Village, CA 91607, USA
York, Kathleen *Actress*
%Bresler Kelly Assoc, 11500 W Olympic Blvd, #510, Los Angeles, CA 90064, USA
York, Michael *Actor*
9100 Cordell Dr, Los Angeles, CA 90069, USA
York, Michael (Mike) *Hockey Player*
%Edmonton Oilers, 11230 110th St, Edmonton AB T5G 3H7, Canada
York, Michael M *Journalist*
%Lexington Herald-Leader, Editorial Dept, Main & Midland, Lexington, KY 40507, USA
York, Ray *Thoroughbred Racing Jockey*
27918 Taft Highway, Taft, CA 93268, USA
York, Susannah *Actress*
%P F D, Drury House, 34-43 Russell St, London WC2B 5HA, England
Yorke, Thom *Singer (Radiohead)*
%Nasty Little Man, 72 Spring St, #1100, New York, NY 10012, USA
Yorkin, Alan (Bud) *Movie Producer, Director*
%Bud Yorkin Productions, 250 Delfern Dr, Los Angeles, CA 90077, USA
Yorkin, Peg *Political Activist*
%Fund for Feminist Majority, 1600 Wilson Blvd, #704, Arlington, VA 22209, USA
Yorn, Peter *Singer, Songwriter*
%The Firm, 9100 Wilshire Blvd, #100W, Beverly Hills, CA 90210, USA
Yorzyk, William A (Bill) *Swimmer*
162 W Sturbridge Road, #7, East Brookfield, MA 01515, USA
Yoseliani, Otar D *Movie Director*
Mitskewitch 1 Korp, 1 #38, 380060 Tbilisi, Georgia
Yost, E Frederick (Ned) *Baseball Player, Manager*
N46W28654 Willow Brook Court, Hartland, WI 53029, USA
Yost, Edward F J (Eddie) *Baseball Player*
48 Oakridge Road, Wellesley, MA 02481, USA
Yost, Paul A, Jr *Coast Guard Admiral*
%James Madison Memorial Foundation, 200 K St NW, Washington, DC 20001, USA

Y

Yothers, Tina *Actress, Singer*
12368 Apple Dr, Chino, CA 91710, USA
Young MC *Rap Artist*
%Evolution Talent, 1776 Broadway, #1500, New York, NY 10019, USA
Young Ochowicz, Sheila G *Speed Skater, Cyclist*
2805 N University Dr, Waukesha, WI 53188, USA
Young, Aden *Actor*
%June Cann Mgmt, 110 Queen St, Woollahra NSW 2025, Australia
Young, Adrian *Drummer (No Doubt)*
%Rebel Waltz Inc, 31652 2nd Ave, Laguna Beach, CA 92651, USA
Young, Alan *Actor*
24072 La Hermosa, Laguna Niguel, CA 92677, USA
Young, Andrew *Diplomat, Mayor, Religious Leader*
%National Council of Churches, 924 N Magnolia Ave, #304, Orlando, FL 32803, USA
Young, Angus *Guitarist (AC/DC), Songwriter*
%East-West Records, 46 Kensington Court St, London W8 5DP, England
Young, Bob *Cartoonist (Tim Tyler's Luck)*
%King Features Syndicate, 888 7th Ave, New York, NY 10106, USA
Young, Boyd *Labor Leader*
%United Paperworkers Union, 3340 Perimeter Hill Dr, Nashville, TN 37211, USA
Young, Brian *Singer, Guitarist (Fountains of Wayne)*
%MOB Agency, 6404 Wilshire Blvd, #505, Los Angeles, CA 90048, USA
Young, Bryant C *Football Player*
601 Primrose Lane, Matteson, IL 60443, USA
Young, Burt *Actor*
%Agency for Performing Arts, 9200 Sunset Blvd, #900, Los Angeles, CA 90069, USA
Young, Charle E *Football Player*
16035 Mink Road NE, Woodinville, WA 98077, USA
Young, Christopher *Composer*
%Kraft-Benjamin-Engel, 15233 Ventura Blvd, #200, Sherman Oaks, CA 91403, USA
Young, Colville N *Governor General, Belize*
%Governor General's Office, Belize House, Belnopan, Belize
Young, Dean *Cartoonist (Blondie)*
%King Features Syndicate, 888 7th Ave, New York, NY 10106, USA
Young, Earl *Track Athlete*
4344 Livingston Ave, Dallas, TX 75205, USA
Young, Eric O *Baseball Player*
28 Regina Dr, Hattiesburg, MS 39402, USA
Young, Frank E *Research Scientist, Government Official*
%Food & Drug Administration, 5600 Fishers Lane, Rockville, MD 20852, USA
Young, Fred *Singer, Musician (Kentucky Headhunters)*
%Mitchell Fox Mgmt, 212 3rd Ave N, #301, Nashville, TN 37201, USA
Young, Fredd *Football Player*
4200 Real del Sur, Las Cruces, NM 88011, USA
Young, George L *Track Athlete*
8926 N Cox Road, Casa Grande, AZ 85222, USA
Young, H Edwin *Religious Leader*
%Southern Baptist Convention, 901 Commerce St, Nashville, TN 37203, USA
Young, Howard (Howie) *Hockey Player*
5527 N 22nd Dr, Phoenix, AZ 85015, USA
Young, J Steven (Steve) *Football Player*
261 E Broadway, Salt Lake City, UT 84111, USA
Young, J Warren *Publisher*
%Boys Life Magazine, 1325 Walnut Hill Road, Irving, TX 75038, USA
Young, James *Guitarist (Styx)*
%Alliance Artists, 1225 Northmeadow Parkway, #100, Roswell, GA 30076, USA
Young, Jerry *Religious Leader*
%Grace Brethren Church Fellowship, 855 Turnbull St, Deltona, FL 32725, USA
Young, Jesse Colin *Singer, Songwriter*
%Skyline Music, PO Box 31, Lancaster, NH 03584, USA
Young, Jewell L *Basketball Player*
4480 Fairways Blvd, Building 8, #203, Bradenton, FL 34209, USA
Young, Jim *Football Coach*
%US Military Academy, Athletic Dept, West Point, NY 10966, USA
Young, John A *Businessman*
%Norvell Inc, 122 E 1700 S, Provo, UT 84606, USA
Young, John W *Astronaut*
%NASA, Johnson Space Center, 2101 NASA Road, Houston, TX 77058, USA
Young, John Zachary *Zoologist*
1 Crossroads, Brill, Bucks HP18 9TL, England
Young, Kathy *Singer*
%Cape Entertainment, 1161 NW 76th Ave, Plantation, FL 33322, USA
Young, Keone *Actor*
%Gage Group, 14724 Ventura Blvd, #505, Sherman Oaks, CA 91403, USA
Young, Kevin *Track Athlete*
8860 Corban Ave, Northridge, CA 91324, USA
Young, Laurence Retman *Astronaut*
217 Thorndike St, #108, Cambridge, MA 02141, USA

Young, M Adrian 10300 4th St, #100, Rancho Cucamonga, CA 91730, USA	*Football Player*
Young, Malcolm 11 Leominster Road, Morden, Surrey SA4 6HN, England	*Guitarist (AC/DC), Songwriter*
Young, Martin D 1110 Marshall Road, #2007, Greenwood, SC 29646, USA	*Parasitologist*
Young, Melissa %Badgley Connor Talent, 9229 Sunset Blvd, #311, Los Angeles, CA 90069, USA	*Actress*
Young, Mighty Joe %Jay Reil, 3430 Bayberry Dr, Northbrook, IL 60062, USA	*Singer, Guitarist*
Young, Neil PO Box 410, Holualoa, HI 96725, USA	*Singer, Songwriter*
Young, Paul %What Mgmt, PO Box 1463, Culver City, CA 90232, USA	*Singer*
Young, Ray 3360 Barham Blvd, Los Angeles, CA 90068, USA	*Test Pilot*
Young, Richard E %Jet Propulsion Laboratory, 4800 Oak Grove Dr, Pasadena, CA 91109, USA	*Space Scientist*
Young, Richard S 137 Saint Croix Ave, Cocoa Beach, FL 32931, USA	*Space Administrator, Educator*
Young, Richard S 110 Highlever Road, London W10 6PL, England	*Photographer*
Young, Robert (Bob) 8705 Fairfield Dr, Bakersfield, CA 93311, USA	*Track Athlete*
Young, Scott 17 Sandy Ridge Road, Sterling, MA 01564, USA	*Hockey Player*
Young, Steve %American Federation of Musicians, 1501 Broadway, #800, New York, NY 10036, USA	*Labor Leader*
Young, Tom %Washington Wizards, MCI Centre, 601 F St NW, Washington, DC 20004, USA	*Basketball Coach*
Young, Vincent %Don Buchwald, 6500 Wilshire Blvd, #2200, Los Angeles, CA 90048, USA	*Actor*
Young, Walter R, Jr %Champion Enterprises, 2710 University Dr, Auburn Hills, MI 48326, USA	*Businessman*
Young, William Allen 5519 S Holt Ave, Los Angeles, CA 90056, USA	*Actor*
Young, Wise %Rutgers University, Collaborative Neuroscience Center, New Brunswick, NJ 08901, USA	*Neuroscientist*
Youngblood, H Jackson (Jack) 4377 Steed Terrace, Winter Park, FL 32792, USA	*Football Player, Sportscaster*
Youngblood, Jimmy L (Jim) 534 N Manhattan Place, Los Angeles, CA 90004, USA	*Football Player*
Youngerman, Jack PO Box 508, Bridgehampton, NY 11932, USA	*Artist*
Younis, Waqar %Surrey County Cricket Club, Kennington Oval, London SE11 5SS, England	*Cricketer*
Yount, Robin R 5001 E Arabian Way, Paradise Valley, AZ 85253, USA	*Baseball Player*
Youssoufi, Abderrahmane El %Prime Minister's Office, Rabat, Morocco	*Prime Minister, Morocco*
Yu Chuan Yong %Urban/Rural Construction Committee, 149 Guangming Road, Weihai PR, China	*Architect*
Yuan Enfeng %Provincial Broadcasting/TV Station, Xian, Shaanxi, China	*Singer*
Yuan Zhongyi %Qin Shi Huang's Terracotta Army Museum, Lintong, Xi'an, China	*Archaeologist, Museum Official*
Yuasa, Joji 1517 Shields Ave, Encinitas, CA 92024, USA	*Composer*
Yudof, Mark G %University of Minnesota, President's Office, Minneapolis, MN 55455, USA	*Educator*
Yue Jingyu %Physical Culture/Sports Bureau, 9 Tiyuguan Road, Beijing, China	*Swimmer*
Yulin, Harris 40 W 86th St, #5C, New York, NY 10024, USA	*Actor*
Yune, Rick %Innovative Artists, 1505 10th St, Santa Monica, CA 90401, USA	*Actor*
Yunis, Jorge J %Thomas Jefferson University, Jefferson Medical College, Philadelphia, PA 19107, USA	*Geneticist, Pathologist*
Yurchikhin, Fyodor N %NASA, Johnson Space Center, 2101 NASA Road, Houston, TX 77058, USA	*Cosmonaut*
Yushkevich, Dmitri %International Sports Advisors, 878 Ridge View Way, Franklin Lakes, NJ 07417, USA	*Hockey Player*
Yzaguirre, Raul %National Council of La Raza, 1111 19th St NW, #1000, Washington, DC 20036, USA	*Social Activist*
Yzerman, Steve PO Box 488, Bloomfield Hills, MI 48303, USA	*Hockey Player*

Z

Zabaleta - Zanuck

Zabaleta, Nicanor *Concert Harpist*
Villa Izar, Aldapeta, 20009 San Sebasatian, Spain
Zabel, Mark *Canoeing Athlete*
Grosse Fischerei 18A, 39240 Calbe/Saale, Germany
Zabel, Steven G (Steve) *Football Player*
6000 Oak Tree Road, Edmond, OK 73003, USA
Zaborowski, Robert R J M *Religious Leader*
%Mariavite Old Catholic Church, 2803 10th St, Wyandotte, MI 48192, USA
Zabriskie, Grace *Actress*
1800 S Robertson Blvd, #426, Los Angeles, CA 90035, USA
Zachara, Jan *Boxer*
Sladkovicova 13, 018 51 Nova Dubnica, Czech Republic
Zacharius, Walter *Publisher*
475 Park Ave S, New York, NY 10016, USA
Zacherle, John *Actor*
125 W 96th St, #4B, New York, NY 10025, USA
Zadeh, Lofti A *Computer Scientist (Fuzzy Logic)*
904 Mendocino Ave, Berkeley, CA 94707, USA
Zadel, C William *Businessman*
%Millipore Corp, 80 Ashby Road, Bedford, MA 01730, USA
Zadora, Pia *Actress, Singer, Model*
1143 Summit Dr, Beverly Hills, CA 90210, USA
Zaentz, Saul *Movie Producer*
%Saul Zaentz Co, 2600 10th St, Berkeley, CA 94710, USA
Zaffaroni, Alejandro C *Biochemist*
%Alza Corp, 1950 Charleston Road, Mountain View, CA 94043, USA
Zafferani, Rosa *Co-Regent, San Marino*
%Co-Regent's Office, Government Palace, 47031 San Marino
Zagaria, Anita *Actress*
%Carol Levi Co, Via Giuseppe Pisanelli, 00196 Rome, Italy
Zaglmann-Willinger, Cornelia *Movie Director*
Siegfriedstr 9, 80802 Munich, Germany
Zagorin, Perez *Historian*
2990 Beaumont Farm Road, Charlottesville, VA 22901, USA
Zahn, Geoffrey C (Geof) *Baseball Player*
6536 Walsh Road, Dexter, MI 48130, USA
Zahn, Paula A *Commentator*
%Cable News Network, News Dept, 1050 Techwood Dr NW, Atlanta, GA 30318, USA
Zahn, Steve *Actor*
%Lasher McManus Robinson, 1964 Westwood Blvd, #400, Los Angeles, CA 90025, USA
Zahn, Wayne *Bowler*
2143 E Center Lane, Tempe, AZ 85281, USA
Zaklinsky, Konstantin *Ballet Dancer*
%Mariinsky Theater, Teatralnaya Square 1, 190000 Saint Petersburg, Russia
Zaks, Jerry *Theater Director*
%Helen Merrill, 337 W 22nd St, New York, NY 10011, USA
Zal, Roxana *Actress*
%P M K Public Relations, 8500 Wilshire Blvd, #700, Beverly Hills, CA 90211, USA
Zalapski, Zarley *Hockey Player*
308 Kingsberry Circle, Pittsburgh, PA 15234, USA
Zale, Richard N *Chemist*
724 Santa Ynez St, Stanford, CA 94305, USA
Zalyotin, Sergei V *Cosmonaut*
%Potchta Kosmonavtov, Moskovskoi Oblasti, 141160 Syvisdny Goroduk, Russia
Zamba, Frieda *Surfer*
2706 S Central Ave, Flagler Beach, FL 32136, USA
Zamecnik, Paul *Onocologist*
101 Chestnut St, Boston, MA 02108, USA
Zamecnik, Paul C *Physician*
%Worcester Experimental Biology Foundation, 222 Maple St, Shrewsbury, MA 01545, USA
Zamka, George D *Astronaut*
144 Lake Point Dr, League City, TX 77573, USA
Zanardi, Alex *Auto Racing Driver*
%Target Canassi Racing, 7777 Woodland Dr, Indianapolis, IN 46278, USA
Zander, Robin *Singer, Guitarist (Cheap Trick)*
%Monterey Peninsula Artists, 509 Hartnell St, Monterey, CA 93940, USA
Zander, Thomas *Greco-Roman Wrestler*
Grundfeldstr 23, 73432 Aalen, Germany
Zane, Billy *Actor*
450 N Rossmore Ave, #1001, Los Angeles, CA 90004, USA
Zane, Lisa *Actress*
209 S Orange Dr, Los Angeles, CA 90036, USA
Zanes, Dan *Singer, Songwriter*
%Harriet Sternberg Mgmt, 4530 Gloria Ave, Encino, CA 91436, USA
Zanuck, Lili Fini *Movie Producer, Director*
%Zanuck Co, 9465 Wilshire Blvd, #308, Beverly Hills, CA 90212, USA
Zanuck, Richard D *Movie Producer*
%Zanuck Co, 9465 Wilshire Blvd, #308, Beverly Hills, CA 90212, USA

Zanussi, Krzysztof Ul Kaniowska 114, 01-529, Warsaw, Poland	*Movie Director*
Zapata, Carmen 6107 Ethel Ave, Van Nuys, CA 91401, USA	*Actress*
Zappa, Dweezil 7885 Woodrow Wilson Dr, Los Angeles, CA 90046, USA	*Singer, Guitarist, Actor*
Zappa, Moon Unit 10377 Oletha Lane, Los Angeles, CA 90077, USA	*Singer, Actress*
Zarate, Carlos %Gene Aguilera, PO Box 113, Montebello, CA 90640, USA	*Boxer*
Zarnas, August C (Gust) 850 Jennings St, Bethlehem, PA 18017, USA	*Football Player*
Zaslow, Jeffrey L (Jeff) %Chicago Sun-Times, Editorial Dept, 401 N Wabash, Chicago, IL 60611, USA	*Columnist*
Zatopkova, Dana Nad Kazankov 3, 171 00 Prague 7, Czech Republic	*Track Athlete*
Zawinul, Josef (Joe) %International Music Network, 278 S Main St, #400, Gloucester, MA 01930, USA	*Jazz Synthesizer, Composer*
Zawoluk, Robert (Zeke) 325 W 17th St, New York, NY 10011, USA	*Basketball Player*
Zayak, Elaine 298 McHenry Dr, Paramus, NJ 07652, USA	*Figure Skater*
Zeamer, Jay, Jr PO Box 602, Boothbay Harbor, ME 04538, USA	*WW II Army Air Corps Hero (CMH)*
Zeckendorf, William, Jr 502 Park Ave, New York, NY 10022, USA	*Businessman*
Zeckhauser, Richard J 138 Irving St, Cambridge, MA 02138, USA	*Economist*
Zedillo Ponce de Leon, Ernesto %Institutional Revolutionary, Insurges N 61, 06350 Mexico City DF, Mexico	*President, Mexico*
Zeffirelli, G Franco Via Appia Pignatelli 448, 00178 Rome, Italy	*Theater, Movie, Opera Director*
Zegers, Kevin %Agency for Performing Arts, 9200 Sunset Blvd, #900, Los Angeles, CA 90069, USA	*Actor*
Zeglis, John D %AT&T Corp, 32 Ave of Americas, New York, NY 10013, USA	*Businessman*
Zeh, Geoffrey N %Maintenance of Way Employees Brotherhood, 12050 Woodward, Detroit, MI 48203, USA	*Labor Leader*
Zeidler, Eberard H %Zeidler Roberts Architects, 315 Queen St W, Toronto ON M5V 2X2, Canada	*Architect*
Zeigler, Heidi %Mary Grady Agency, 221 E Walnut St, #130, Pasadena, CA 91101, USA	*Actress*
Zeile, Todd E %New York Yankees, Yankee Stadium, 161st St & River Ave, Bronx, NY 10451, USA	*Baseball Player*
Zeitlin, Zvi 204 Warren Ave, Rochester, NY 14618, USA	*Concert Pianist*
Zelensky, Igor %New York City Ballet, Lincoln Center Plaza, New York, NY 10023, USA	*Ballet Dancer*
Zelepukin, Valeri %Chicago Blackhawks, United Center, 1901 W Madison St, Chicago, IL 60612, USA	*Hockey Player*
Zelezny, Jan Rue Armady 683, Boleslav, Czech Republic	*Track Athlete*
Zell, Samuel %Itel Corp, 2 N Riverside Plaza, Chicago, IL 60606, USA	*Businessman*
Zellweger, Renee %Creative Artists Agency, 9830 Wilshire Blvd, Beverly Hills, CA 90212, USA	*Actress*
Zelmani, Sophie %United Stage Artists, PO Box 11029, 100 61 Stockholm, Sweden	*Singer*
Zeman, Jacklyn %Stone Manners, 6500 Wilshire Blvd, #550, Los Angeles, CA 90048, USA	*Actress*
Zeman, Milos %Premier's Office, Nabrezi E Benese 4, 118 01 Prague 1, Czech Republic	*Prime Minister, Czech Republic*
Zembriski, Walter 7231 Moss Leaf Lane, Orlando, FL 32819, USA	*Golfer*
Zemeckis, Robert L 100 Universal City Plaza, #Building 484, Universal City, CA 91608, USA	*Movie Director*
Zenawi, Hailu %Prime Minister's Office, PO Box 1013, Addis Ababa, Ethiopia	*Prime Minister, Ethiopia*
Zenawi, Meles %President's Office, PO Box 5707, Addis Ababa, Ethiopia	*President, Ethiopia*
Zender, Hans Am Rosenheck, 65812 Bad Soden, Germany	*Conductor, Composer*
Zender, Stuart %Searles, Chapel, 26A Munster St, London SW6 4EN, England	*Bassist (Jamiroquai)*
Zentmyer, George A, Jr 955 S El Camino Real, #216, San Mateo, CA 94402, USA	*Plant Pathologist*
Zerbe, Anthony 411 W 115th St, #51, New York, NY 10025, USA	*Actor*

Z

Zerhouni - Zikarsky

Zerhouni, Elias A *Government Official, Physician*
%National Institutes of Health, 9000 Rockville Pike, Bethesda, MD 20892, USA

Zernial, Gus E *Baseball Player*
687 Coventry Ave, Clovis, CA 93611, USA

Zero, Mark *Singer (Randy & the Rainbows)*
PO Box 656507, Fresh Meadows, NY 11365, USA

Zervas, Nicholas T *Neurosurgeon*
100 Canton Ave, Milton, MA 02186, USA

Zeta-Jones, Catherine *Actress, Model*
%William Morris Agency, 151 El Camino Dr, Beverly Hills, CA 90212, USA

Zettler, Michael E *Air Force General*
Deputy Chief of Staff for Logistics, HqUSA, Pentagon, Washington, DC 20310, USA

Zettler, Rob *Hockey Player*
31 Tadcaster Place, Saulte Sainte Marie ON P6B 5E3, Canada

Zewail, Ahmed H *Nobel Chemist Laureate*
871 Winston Ave, San Marino, CA 91108, USA

Zhamnov, Alexei *Hockey Player*
1950 N Orchard St, Chicago, IL 60614, USA

Zhang Aiping *Government Official, China; Army General*
%Ministry of Defense, State Council, Beijing, China

Zhang Xianliang *Writer*
%Ningxia Writers' Assn, Yinchuan City, China

Zhang Yimou *Movie Director*
%Xi'an Film Studio, Xi'an City, Shanxi Province, China

Zhang Ziyi *Actress*
%William Morris Agency, 151 El Camino Dr, Beverly Hills, CA 90212, USA

Zhe-Xi Lo *Antropologist*
%Carnegie Natural History Museum, 4400 Forbes Ave, Pittsburgh, PA 15213, USA

Zhenan Bao *Chemist, Inventor (Molecule Transistor)*
%AT&T Bell Lucent Laboratory, 600 Mountain Ave, New Providence, NJ 07974, USA

Zheng, Wei *Astronomer*
%Johns Hopkins Universities, Astronomy Dept, Baltimore, MD 21218, USA

Zhirinovsky, Vladimir V *Government Leader, Russia*
%Liberal Democratic Party, 1st Basmanny Per 3, 103045 Moscow, Russia

Zhislin, Grigory Y *Concert Violinist*
25 Whitehall Gardens, London W3 9RD, England

Zhitnik, Alexei *Hockey Player*
%Buffalo Sabres, HSBC Arena, 1 Seymour St, Buffalo, NY 14210, USA

Zholobov, Vitali M *Cosmonaut*
Ul Yanvarskovo Vostaniya D 12, 252010 Kiev, Ukraine

Zhou Long *Composer*
%University of Missouri, Music Dept, Kansas City, MO 64110, USA

Zhudov, Vyacheslav D *Cosmonaut*
%Potchta Kosmonavtov, Moskovskoi Oblasti, 141160 Syvisdny Goroduk, Russia

Zhumaliyev, Kubanychbek M *Prime Minister, Kyrgyzstan*
%Parliament Buildings, 720003 Bishkek, Kyrgyzstan

Zhvanetsky, Mikhail M *Writer, Actor*
Lesnaya Str 4, #63, 125047 Moscow, Russia

Zia, B Khaleda *Prime Minister, Bangladesh*
%Sere-e Bangla Nagar, Gono, Bhaban, Sher-e-Banglanagar, Dakar, Bangladesh

Ziblijew, Wassili *Cosmonaut*
%Potchta Kosmonavtov, Moskovskoi Oblasti, 141160 Syvisdny Goroduk, Russia

Zidane, Zinedine *Soccer Player*
%Real Madrid FC, Avda Concha Espina 1, 28036 Madrid, Spain

Ziegler, Dolores *Opera Singer*
%Lynda Kay, 2702 Crestworth Lane, Buford, GA 30519, USA

Ziegler, Jack *Cartoonist*
%New Yorker Magazine, Editorial Dept, 4 Times Square, New York, NY 10036, USA

Ziegler, John A, Jr *Hockey Executive*
%Dickinson Wright, 38525 Woodward Ave, Bloomfield, MI 48304, USA

Ziegler, Larry *Golfer*
10315 Luton Court, Orlando, FL 32836, USA

Ziemann, Sonja *Actress*
Via del Alp Dorf, 7500 Saint Moritz, Switzerland

Ziering, Ian *Actor*
2700 Jalmia Dr, West Hollywood, CA 90046, USA

Ziff, William B, Jr *Publisher*
%Ziff-Davis Publishing Co, 1 Park Ave, New York, NY 10016, USA

Ziffren, Kenneth *Attorney*
%Ziffren Brittenham Branca, 1801 Century Park West, Los Angeles, CA 90067, USA

Ziglar, Zig *Businessman*
%Success '94 Seminars, General Delivery, Hawkins, TX 75765, USA

Zigler, Edward F *Educator*
%Yale University, Bush Child Development Center, New Haven, CT 06520, USA

Zikarsky, Bengt *Swimmer*
%SV Wurzburg 05, Oberer Bogenweg 1, 97074 Wurzburg, Germany

Zikarsky, Bjorn *Swimmer*
555 California St, #2600, San Francisco, CA 94104, USA

Zikes, Les *Bowler*
424 S Stuart Lane, Palatine, IL 60067, USA
Zilinskas, Annette *Bassist (Bangles, Ringling Sisters)*
%Creative Artists Agency, 9830 Wilshire Blvd, Beverly Hills, CA 90212, USA
Zils, John *Structural Engineer*
N1513 Shore Haven Dr, Fontana, WI 53125, USA
Zim Zum *Guitarist (Marilyn Manson)*
%Mitch Schneider Organization, 14724 Ventura Blvd, #410, Sherman Oaks, CA 91403, USA
Zimbalist, Efrem, III *Businessman*
%Times Mirror Co, Times Mirror Square, Los Angeles, CA 90053, USA
Zimbalist, Efrem, Jr *Actor*
1448 Holsted Dr, Solvang, CA 93463, USA
Zimbalist, Stephanie *Actress*
%Blake Agency, 1333 Ocean Ave, Santa Monica, CA 90401, USA
Zimerman, Krystian *Concert Pianist*
%Columbia Artists Mgmt Inc, 165 W 57th St, New York, NY 10019, USA
Zimm, Bruno H *Chemist*
2522 Horizon Way, La Jolla, CA 92037, USA
Zimmer, Donald W (Don) *Baseball Player, Manager*
10124 Yacht Club Dr, Treasure Island, FL 33706, USA
Zimmer, Hans *Composer*
1547 14th St, Santa Monica, CA 90404, USA
Zimmer, Kim *Actress*
15561 Almendra Dr, Santa Clarita, CA 91355, USA
Zimmerer, Wolfgang *Bobsled Athlete*
Schwaigangerstr 22, 82418 Murnau, Germany
Zimmerman, Gary W *Football Player*
17450 Skyliners Road, Bend, OR 97701, USA
Zimmerman, H Leroy *Football Player*
808 Willis Ace, Madera, CA 93637, USA
Zimmerman, Howard E *Chemist*
7813 Westchester Dr, Middleton, WI 53562, USA
Zimmerman, James M *Businessman*
%Federated Department Stores, 151 W 34th St, New York, NY 10001, USA
Zimmerman, John T *Neuroscientist*
%University of Colorado, Medical School, Neurology Dept, Denver, CO 80202, USA
Zimmerman, Kent *Publisher*
%Friendly Exchange Magazine, 1999 Shepard Road, Saint Paul, MN 55116, USA
Zimmerman, Mary Beth *Golfer*
%Ladies Pro Golf Assn, 100 International Golf Dr, Daytona Beach, FL 32124, USA
Zimmerman, Philip (Phil) *Computer Software Designer*
%Network Assoc, 4677 Old Ironside Dr, Santa Clara, CA 95054, USA
Zimmermann, Egon *Alpine Skier*
%Hotel Kristberg, 67644 Am Arlberg, Austria
Zimmermann, Frank P *Concert Violinist*
%Riaskoff Mgmt, Concertgebouwplein 15, 1071 LL Amsterdam, Netherlands
Zimmermann, Markus *Bobsled Athlete*
Waldhauserstr 51-53, 83471 Schonau am Konigsee, Germany
Zimmermann, Udo *Composer*
%Operhaus Leipzig, Augustusplatz, 04109 Leipzig, Germany
Zinder, Norton D *Geneticist*
450 E 63rd St, New York, NY 10021, USA
Zindler, Marvin *Commentator*
%KTRK-TV, News Dept, 3310 Bissonnet, Houston, TX 77005, USA
Zinke, Olaf *Speedskater*
Johannes Bobrowski Str 22, 12627 Berlin, Germany
Zinkernagel, Rolf M *Nobel Medicine Laureate*
Rebhusstr 47, 8126 Zumikon, Switzerland
Zinman, David J *Conductor*
%Baltimore Symphony, 1212 Cathedral St, Baltimore, MD 21201, USA
Zippel, David *Lyricist*
%Kraft-Benjamin-Engel, 15233 Ventura Blvd, #200, Sherman Oaks, CA 91403, USA
Zisk, Richard W (Richie) *Baseball Player*
4231 NE 26th Terrace, Lighthouse Point, FL 33064, USA
Zito, Barry *Baseball Player*
10175 Spring Mountain Road, Las Vegas, NV 89117, USA
Zivkovic, Zoran *Prime Minister, Serbia*
%Prime Minister's Office, Nemanjina 11, 11000 Belgrade, Serbia
Zlatoper, Ronald J (Zap) *Navy Admiral*
1001 Kamokila Blvd, Kapolei, HI 96707, USA
Zmed, Adrian *Actor*
12186 Laurel Terrace, Studio City, CA 91604, USA
Zmeskal, Kim *Gymnast*
%Cincinnati Gymnastics Academy, 3635 Woodridge, Fairfield, OH 45014, USA
Zmievskaya Petrenko, Galina (Nina) *Figure Skating Coach*
%International Skating Center, PO Box 577, Simsbury, CT 06070, USA
Zoeller, Frank (Fuzzy) *Golfer*
4146 Lakeside Dr, Sellersburg, IN 47172, USA

Zoellick, Robert *Government Official*
%US Trade Representative Office, 600 17th St NW, Washington, DC 20506, USA
Zoffinger, George R *Financier*
%CoreStates (NJ) Bank, 370 Scotch Road, Pennington, NJ 08534, USA
Zook, John E *Football Player*
9425 Riviera Road, Roswell, GA 30075, USA
Zook, Ron *Football Coach*
9425 Rivera Road, Roswell, GA 30075, USA
Zoran *Fashion Designer*
157 Chambers St, #1200 , New York, NY 10007, USA
Zorich, Christopher R (Chris) *Football Player*
1429 S Clark St, Chicago, IL 60605, USA
Zorich, Louis *Actor*
%Susan Smith, 121A N San Vicente Blvd, Beverly Hills, CA 90211, USA
Zorn, James A (Jim) *Football Player, Coach*
2006 W Mercer Way, Mercer Island, WA 98040, USA
Zorrilla, Alberto *Swimmer*
580 Park Ave, New York, NY 10021, USA
Zou Jiahua *Government Official, China*
%Communist Party Central Committee, Jhong Nan Hai, Beijing, China
Zsigmond, Vilmos *Cinematographer*
%Spyros Skouras, 631 Wilshire Blvd, #2C, Santa Monica, CA 90401, USA
Zubak, Kresimir *Co-President, Bosnia-Herzegovina*
%Presidency, Marsala Titz 7A, 71000 Sarajevo, Bosnia-Herzegovina
Zuber, Maria *Geophysicist*
%Massachusetts Institute of Technology, Geophysics Dept, Cambridge, MA 02139, USA
Zucker, David *Movie Director, Producer*
%Creative Artists Agency, 9830 Wilshire Blvd, Beverly Hills, CA 90212, USA
Zucker, Jerry *Movie Director, Producer*
481 Denslow Ave, Los Angeles, CA 90049, USA
Zuckerman, Mortimer B *Publisher*
%Boston Properties, 599 Lexington Ave, New York, NY 10022, USA
Zugsmith, Albert *Movie Director*
23388 Mulholland Dr, Woodland Hills, CA 91364, USA
Zukav, Gary *Writer*
%Fireside/Simon & Schuster, 1230 Ave of Americas, New York, NY 10020, USA
Zukerman, Eugenia *Concert Flutist*
%Brooklyn College of Music, Bedford & H Aves, Brooklyn, NY 11210, USA
Zukerman, Pinchas *Concert Violinist, Conductor*
%Shirley Kirshbaum Assoc, 711 W End Ave, #5KN, New York, NY 10025, USA
Zullo, Alan *Cartoonist (Hall of Shame)*
%Tribune Media Services, 435 N Michigan Ave, #1500, Chicago, IL 60611, USA
Zuniga, Daphne *Actress*
%Murphy, 2401 Main St, Santa Monica, CA 90405, USA
Zuniga, Jose *Actor*
%Paradigm Agency, 10100 Santa Monica Blvd, #2500, Los Angeles, CA 90067, USA
Zuniga, Miles *Singer, Guitarist (Fastball)*
%Russell Carter Artists, 315 Ponce de Leon Ave, #755, Decatur, GA 30030, USA
Zurbriggen, Pirmin *Alpine Skier*
%Hotel Larchenhof, 3905 Saas-Almagell, Switzerland
Zvereva, Natalya *Tennis Player*
%Women's Tennis Assn, 1 Progress Plaza, #1500, Saint Petersburg, FL 33701, USA
Zwanzig, Robert W *Chemical Physicist*
5314 Sangamore Road, Bethesda, MD 20816, USA
Zweig, George *Theoretical Physicist*
%Los Alamos National Laboratory, MS B276, PO Box 1663, Los Alamos, NM 87544, USA
Zwerling, Darrell *Actor*
%CLInc Talent, 843 N Sycamore Ave, Los Angeles, CA 90038, USA
Zwick, Charles J *Financier*
4210 Santa Maria St, Coral Gables, FL 33146, USA
Zwick, Edward M *Movie Director, Producer*
1 Latimer Road, Santa Monica, CA 90402, USA
Zwilich, Ellen Taaffe *Composer*
%Music Assoc of America, 224 King St, Englewood, NJ 07631, USA
Zycinski, Jozef *Religious Leader*
Ul Prumasa St Wyszynskiego 2, Skr Poczt 198, 20-950 Lublin, Poland
Zydeco, Buckwheat *Singer, Accordionist*
%Concerted Efforts, 59 Parsons St, West Newton, MA 02465, USA
Zykina, Lyudmila G *Singer, Theater Director*
Kotelnicheskaya Nab Y15 Korp B, #64, Moscow, Russia
Zylberstein, Elsa *Actress*
%Agence Intertalent, 5 Rue Clement Marot, 75008 Paris, France
Zylis-Gara, Teresa *Opera Singer*
16A Blvd de Belgique, Monaco-Ville, Monaco

NECROLOGY

Listees of previous editions of the **V.I.P. Address Book** and the **V.I.P. Address Book Update** whose deaths have been reported prior to close of the compilation are listed below.

Adams, Lucian *Army Hero (CMH)*
Adams, W E (Smiley) *Horse Racing Trainer*
Aga Khan, Sadruddin *Prince, Iran*
Agnelli, Giovanni A *Businessman*
Ali Haider, Jemadar *Pakistan Army Hero (VC)*
Allen, Ivan, Jr *Mayor*
Aller, Lawrence H *Astronomer*
Almond, Gabriel A *Political Scientist*
Alves de Santa Rosa, Edvalodo *Soccer Player*
Amateau, Rodney *Movie, TV Director*
Amies, E Hardy *Fashion Designer*
Amin Dada, Idi *President, Uganda*
Amir, Israel *Air Force General, Israel*
Anderson, Michael P *Astronaut*
Anderson, Roy A *Businessman*
Anderson, William C *Writer, Hero*
Andros, Dee *Football Coach*
Applegate, Royce *Actor*
Aptheker, Herbert *Historian*
Arledge, Roone P, Jr *TV Executive*
Armstrong, Garner Ted *Evangelist*
Atherton, Alfred L, Jr *Diplomat*
Atkins, Robert C *Nutritionist*
Auchincloss, Kenneth *Editor*
Augstein, Rudolf *Publisher*
Babcock, Horace W *Astronomer*
Baer, Parley *Actor*
Ballard, Hank *Singer, Songwriter*
Bar-Illan, David *Concert Pianist*
Barbieri, Fedora *Opera Singer*
Bayer, George *Golfer*
Beach, Edward L *Navy Hero, Writer*
Bean, William D (Billy) *Baseball Player*
Beedle, Lynn S *Civil Engineer*
BenKhedda, Benyoussef *Premier, Algeria*
Bennett, Charles E *Representative, FL*
Bennett, Ward *Interior Designer*
Bennett, William G *Businessman*
Berg, Robert (Bob) *Jazz Saxophonist*
Berger, Arthur V *Composer*
Bergson, Abram *Economist*
Berio, Luciano *Composer, Conductor*
Berjer, Barbara *Actress*
Berlinger, Bernard E (Barney) *Track Athlete*
Berrigan, Philip F *Social Activist*
Berry, Fred *Actor*
Bettger, Lyle *Actor*
Biesheuvel, Barend *Premier, Netherlands*
Bille, Louis-Marie Cardinal *Religious Leader*
Biller, Morris (Moe) *Labor Leader*
Bird, Billie *Actress*
Bittle, Jerry *Cartoonist (Geech)*
Black, Stanley *Conductor, Composer*
Blackwell, Lucien E *Representative, PA*
Blassie, Freddie *Wrestler*
Blix, Herman *Gov't Official, Sweden*
Bloodworth, James H (Jim) *Baseball Player*
Boeker, Paul H *Diplomat*
Boggs, J Caleb *Governor, Senator, DE*
Bonds, Bobby L *Baseball Player*
Borel, Armand *Mathematician*
Bottari, Vic *Football Player*
Bower, Marvin *Businessman*
Bracken, Eddie *Actor*
Braidwood, Robert J *Archaeologist*
Brand, Paul W *Surgeon*
Brasher, Christopher (Chris) *Track Athlete*
Braunn, Erik *Singer, Guitarist (Iron Butterfly)*
Brawne, Michael *Architect*
Breathitt, Edward T (Ned), Jr *Governor, KY*
Brian, Mary *Actress*
Bright, Clarita Heath *Skier*
Bright, William R (Bill) *Religious Leader*
Brinkley, David *Commentator*
Brockhouse, Bertram N *Nobel Physics Laureate*
Bronson, Charles *Actor*
Brooks, Hadda *Singer, Pianist, Actress*
Brooks, Herbert P (Herb) *Hockey Coach*
Brooks, Rand *Actor*
Brown, David M *Astronaut*
Brown, Dorris A (Dee) *Writer*
Browne, Kathie *Actress*
Browning, John *Concert Pianist*
Brumel, Valery *Track Athlete*
Bruscantini, Sesto *Opera Singer*
Brymer, Jack *Concert Clarinetist*
Buchholz, Horst *Actor*
Budge, Hamer H *Representative, ID*
Burk, Adrian *Football Player*
Burton, Ron E *Football Player*
Caglayangil, Ihsan S *President, Turkey*
Cahill, Joseph T *Educator*
Calverly, Ernie *Basketball Player, Coach*
Campbell, Jeannette *Swimmer*
Cantlay, George G *Army General*
Carney, Art *Actor*
Carroll, Vinnette *Actress, Writer*
Carter, Gerald E Cardinal *Religious Leader*
Carter, Nell *Actress, Singer*
Caruso, Anthony *Actor*
Cash, Johnny *Singer, Songwriter*
Cash, June Carter *Singer, Guitarist*
Causley, Charles S *Writer*
Cayton, Bill *Boxing Manager*
Chadwick, Lynn R *Sculptor*
Chailly, Luciano *Composer*
Chamberlain, Charles E *Representative, MI*
Charles, Clive *Soccer Player, Coach*
Chawla, Kalpana *Astronaut*
Cheung, Leslie *Singer, Actor*
Chiang-Kai Shek, Madame *Gov't Official, China*
Christian, George E *Gov't Official*
Clark, Laurel B S *Astronaut*
Clarkson, Lana *Actress*
Coburn, James *Actor*
Codd, Edgar F *Computer Scientist*
Coit, M Louise *Writer*
Colasuonno, Francesco Cardinal *Religious Leader*
Colville, Mathew (Mac) *Hockey Player*
Conner, Nadine *Opera Singer*
Conniff, Ray *Conductor, Composer*
Connor, George L *Football Player*
Cook, Fielder *TV Producer, Director*
Cooper, Arthur M *Editor*
Coors, Joseph, Sr *Businessman*
Corelli, Franco *Opera Singer*
Craft, Clarence B *Army Hero (CMH)*
Cramer, William C *Representative, FL*
Crane, L Stanley *Businessman*
Crenna, Richard *Actor*
Cronyn, Hume *Actor*
Crosby, John O *Conductor*
Cruz, Celia *Singer, Actress*
Cuff, Ward *Football Player*
Cunningham, Briggs S *Yachtsman*
Daddah, Moktar Ould *President, Mauritania*
Dangel, Richard (Rich) *Guitarist, Composer*
Dargie, William A *Artist*
Dascalescu, Constantin *Premier, Romania*
Davey, Charles P (Chuck) *Boxer*
Davidson, Donald H *Philosopher*
Davis, Jacob E *Representative, OH*
Davis, Kenneth C *Attorney, Educator*
Davis, Raymond G *Marine Corps General (CMH)*
Dean, Clyde D *Marine Corps General*
DeBusschere, David A (Dave) *Basketball Player*

Dellenback, John R	*Representative, OR*
Densen-Gerber, Judianne	*Psychiatrist*
Deray, Jacques	*Movie Director*
DeTomaso, Alejandro	*Businessman*
DeToth, Andre	*Movie Director, Writer*
DeWeldon, Felix	*Sculptor*
Dexter, Brad	*Actor*
Dillon, C Douglas	*Secretary, Treasury*
Dinitz, Simcha	*Gov't Official, Israel*
Djindjic, Zoran	*Premier, Serbia*
Dobbs, Glenn	*Football Player*
Dobkin, Lawrence (Larry)	*TV Director, Actor*
Doby, Lawrence E (Larry)	*Baseball Player*
Doerr, Harriet	*Writer*
Donnegan, Lonnie	*Guitarist*
Dow, John G	*Representative, NY*
Dowiyogo, Bernard	*President, Nauru*
Downey, Edward	*Theologist*
Draper, Rusty	*Singer, Actor*
Dudinskyaya, Natalia	*Ballerina*
Dugan, Alan	*Writer*
Dunlop, John T	*Secretary, Labor*
Dunn, Carroll H	*Army General*
Dutt, James L	*Businessman*
Duvall, George	*Physicist*
Eban, Abba	*Gov't Official, Israel*
Ebsen, Buddy	*Actor, Dancer*
Edelmann, Otto K	*Opera Singer*
Edley, Christopher F	*Association Director*
Edwards, George	*Aeronautical Engineer*
Edwards, Teddy	*Jazz Saxphonist*
Elam, Jack	*Actor*
Ellis, Mary	*Actress, Singer*
Elworthy, Charles	*Air Force Marshal, England*
Ely, John H	*Attorney, Educator*
Engelmore, Robert	*Computer Scientist*
Enright, Dennis J	*Writer, Educator*
Erwin, Henry	*Army Air Corps Hero (CMH)*
Eyt, Pierre Cardinal	*Religious Leader*
Fafara, Stanley	*Actor*
Faith, Adam	*Singer, Actor*
Falkenburg McCrary, Jinx	*Model, Actress*
Fast, Howard M	*Writer*
Feifel, Herman	*Psychologist*
Ferre, Luis A	*Governor, PR*
Fiedler, Leslie A	*Writer, Critic*
Fiers, A Dale	*Religious Leader*
Finley, James D	*Businessman*
Fithian, Floyd	*Representative, IN*
Fitzpatrick, Thomas B	*Dermatologist*
Flexner, James T	*Writer*
Fong Chun, Kam	*Actor*
Formby, Margaret	*Rodeo Executive*
Foss, Joseph F	*Marine Air Hero (CMH)*
Fox, Noel	*Singer (Oak Ridge Boys)*
Freda, Vincent J	*Obstetrician*
Freeman, Marshall	*Singer (Oak Ridge Quartet)*
Freeman, Orville L	*Secretary, Agriculture*
Fresson, Bernard	*Actor*
Fukasaku, Kinji	*Movie Director*
Gabriel, Charles A	*Air Force General*
Gallagher, Kimberly A	*Track Athlete*
Galtieri, Leopold F	*President, Argentina*
Gardner, Herb	*Writer*
Gardner, Philip	*British Army Hero (VC)*
Gavilan, Kid	*Boxer*
Gayle, Jackie	*Actor, Comedian*
Gaylord, Edward L	*Publisher*
Gelber, Jack	*Writer*
Gelin, Daniel Y	*Actor*
Gentry, Jerald R (Jerry)	*Test Pilot*
Geraldine	*Queen, Albania*
Getty, John Paul, Jr	*Philanthropist*
Gibb, Maurice	*Singer (Bee Gees), Songwriter*
Gibson, Althea	*Tennis Player*
Gibson, Eleanor J	*Psychologist*
Gilbert, Herschel	*Composer*
Gillman, Sidney (Sid)	*Football Coach*
Ginsberg, Harold S	*Microbiologist, Virologist*
Ginzberg, Eli	*Economist*
Gionfriddo, Albert F (Al)	*Baseball Player*
Giroud, Francoise	*Writer, Journalist*
Glenn, William	*Heart Surgeon*
Goddard, Trevor	*Actor*
Goldhirsh, Bernard A	*Publisher*
Goldman-Rakic, Patricia	*Neuroscientist*
Gomes, Francisco da Costa	*President, Portugal*
Good, Robert A	*Immunologist*
Goode, William J	*Sociologist*
Goodwin, Ron	*Composer, Conductor*
Grace, Roy	*Businessman*
Granlund, Paul T	*Sculptor*
Graves, Howard D	*Army General, Educator*
Greene, David	*TV Director*
Greene, Wallace M, Jr	*Marine Corps General*
Greenstein, Jesse L	*Astronomer*
Gregg, Hugh	*Governor, NH*
Griffith, Harry A	*Army General*
Griffiths, Martha	*Representative, MI*
Grimsley, Will	*Sportswriter*
Groer, Hans Hermann Cardinal	*Religious Leader*
Guest, George H	*Concert Organist*
Gumede, Josiah Z	*President, Zimbabwe*
Guy, Billy	*Singer (Coasters)*
Guyton, Arthur C	*Physiologist*
Gwynne, Anne	*Actress*
Haavelmo, Trygve	*Nobel Economics Laureate*
Hackett, Buddy	*Actor, Comedian*
Haensel, Vladimir	*Chemical Engineer*
Hair, Jay D	*Foundation Executive*
Hakulinen, Veikko	*Nordic Skier*
Halaby, Najeeb	*Gov't Official, Businessman*
Hale, Sue Sally	*Polo Rider, Coach*
Hall, Conrad L	*Cinematographer*
Hanley, James M	*Representative, NY*
Hanna, Roland P	*Jazz Pianist, Composer*
Hansen, Mary	*Singer, Guitarist (Stereolab)*
Hardin, Garrett J	*Ecologist*
Hardy, James D	*Surgeon*
Harris, Billy	*Hockey Player*
Harris, Jonathan	*Actor*
Harrison, Lou	*Composer*
Hartke, Vance	*Senator, IN*
Hartley, Al	*Cartoonist (Archie)*
Haslam of Bolton, Robert	*Businessman*
Hasler, Arthur D	*Zoologist*
Hatfield, Bobby	*Singer (Righteous Brothers)*
Hauspurg, Arthur	*Businessman*
Haya	*Princess, Saudi Arabia*
Heilbrun, Carolyn G (Amanda Cross)	*Writer*
Heineken, Alfred H	*Businessman*
Heiskell, Andrew	*Publisher*
Heldman, Gladys	*Tennis Executive, Editor*
Helmick, Robert H	*Sports Official*
Hendrix, James R	*Army Hero (CMH)*
Henschel, Milton	*Religious Leader*
Hepburn, Katharine	*Actress*
Herskowitz, Ira	*Geneticist*
Hertz, Roy	*Obstetrician, Pharmacologist*
Hester, Jim	*Football Player*
Hicks, Louise Day	*Representative, MA; Activist*
Higginson, Frederick W	*British Air Force Ace*
Higham, John	*Historian*
Hill, Bobby Joe	*Basketball Player*
Hill, George Roy	*Movie Director*
Hiller, Wendy	*Actress*
Hines, Gregory O	*Dancer, Actor*
Hines, Jerome	*Opera Singer*
Hird, Thora	*Actress*
Hirschfeld, Albert (Al)	*Artist, Illustrator*

Hnatyshyn, Ramon — *Governor General, Canada*
Hod, Modechai — *Air Force General, Israel*
Hodges, Joy — *Singer, Actress, Dancer*
Hoffman, Norman — *Parachutist*
Hope, Bob — *Actor, Comedian*
Hopp, John L (Johnny) — *Baseball Player*
Houtte, Jean Van — *Premier, Belgium*
Houtteman, Arthur J (Art) — *Baseball Player*
Hovis, Larry — *Actor*
Howe, Harold, II — *Educator*
Hoyte, Hugh Desmond — *President, Guyana*
Hudec, Robert E — *Attorney*
Hughes, Vernon W — *Physicist*
Hulten, Vivi-Anne — *Figure Skater*
Hupp, Robert P — *Religious Leader, Social Worker*
Husband, Rick D — *Astronaut*
Hyder, John C (Whack) — *Basketball Coach*
Ienaga, Saburo — *Historian, Social Activist*
Illich, Ivan — *Educator, Writer, Theologian*
Ishii, Maki — *Composer, Conductor*
Istomin, Eugene G — *Concert Pianist*
Ivy, Frank (Pop) — *Football Player, Coach*
Izetbegovic, Alija — *President, Bosnia-Herzegovina*
Jackson, Maynard — *Mayor*
Jackson, Tony — *Singer, Bassist (Searchers)*
Jacques, Elliott — *Psychoanalyst*
Jacunski, Harry — *Football Player*
James, Harold L — *Geologist*
Janeway, Charles, Jr — *Immunobiolgist*
Jarvis, Graham P — *Actor*
Jenkins, Howard, Jr — *Gov't Official*
Jenkins, Roy H — *Gov't Official, England*
Jergens, Adele — *Actress, Model*
Jeter, Michael — *Actor*
Johnson, Donald J (Don) — *Bowler*
Johnston, Chester (Swede) — *Football Player*
Jump, Gordon — *Actor*
Juran, Nathan H — *Movie Director*
Justice, Charlie (Choo Choo) — *Football Player*
Katz, Bernard — *Nobel Medicine Laureate*
Katzin, Lee H — *Movie Director*
Kaye, Buddy — *Lyricist*
Kazan, Elia — *Movie Director*
Keach, Stacy, Sr — *Movie Producer, Actor*
Kelk, Jack — *Actor*
Kelley, Thomas W (Tom) — *Photographer*
Kelly, Michael — *Editor*
Kerr, Jean — *Writer*
Kindleberger, Charles P, II — *Economist*
King, Andrea — *Actress*
King, Earl — *Singer, Songwriter*
Kitur, Samson — *Track Athlete*
Klimov, Elem G — *Movie Director*
Kling, Karl — *Auto Racing Driver*
Kobart, Ruth — *Actress*
Kolobov, Yevgeny V — *Conductor*
Konvitz, Milton R — *Attorney, Educator*
Koppett, Leonard — *Sportswriter*
Korry, Edward M — *Diplomat*
Kroc, Joan B — *Philanthropist, Businesswoman*
Kuharic, Franjo Cardinal — *Religious Leader*
Kullberg, John F — *Association Executive*
Kupferman, Theodore — *Representative, NY*
Kyl, John — *Representative, IA*
Lacy, Sam — *Sportswriter*
Ladynina, Marina — *Actress, Comedienne*
Lagardere, Jean-Luc — *Publisher*
Lahar, Harold — *Football Player, Coach*
Lanchbery, John A — *Conductor*
Langton, Basil — *Actor, Theater Director*
Lankford, Richard E — *Representative, MD*
Larrabee, Michael (Mike) — *Track Athlete*
Larsen, Niels — *Ballet Director*
Leburton, Edmond — *Premier, Belgium*
Lee, John Marhsall — *Navy Admiral, Hero*
LeFrak, Samuel J — *Businessman*
Lemos, Carlos — *President, Colombia*
Lerner, Alfred — *Businessman*
LeSueur, Larry — *Commentator*
Levy, Bernard-Henri — *Philosopher*
Levy, Leon — *Financier*
Lewis, Allen — *Sportswriter*
Lewis, David H — *Yachtsman*
Lewis, Thomas F (Tom), Jr — *Representative, FL*
Liedtke, J Hugh — *Businessman*
Lindh, Anna — *Gov't Official, Sweden*
Little Eva — *Singer*
Little, Bernie — *Boat Racing Executive*
Loeb, David S — *Financier*
Loiseau, Bernard — *Chef*
Long, Olivier — *Gov't Official, Switzerland*
Long, Russell B — *Senator, LA*
Longden, Johnny — *Horse Racing Jockey*
Longmire, William P, Jr — *Physician*
Losee, Thomas P, Jr — *Publisher*
Luisetti, Angelo (Hank) — *Basketball Player*
Lyng, Richard E — *Secretary, Agriculture*
Mack, William P — *Navy Admiral, Writer*
MacKenzie, Gisele — *Singer, Violinist*
MacLeod, Robert F — *Football Player*
MacNaughton, Donald S — *Businessman*
MacNaughton, Ian — *TV, Movie Director*
Maddox, Lester G — *Governor, GA*
Magliochetti, Joseph — *Businessman*
Makarov, Oleg G — *Cosmonaut*
Malmin, John — *Photojournalist*
Maloney, George P — *Baseball Umpire*
Mann, Herbie — *Jazz Flutist*
Manning, Max — *Baseball Player*
Mantley, John — *Writer*
Marden, Luis — *Photographer, Writer*
Marhefka, Joseph C (Duke) — *Football Player*
Marion, Beth — *Actress*
Marshall, Burke — *Attorney*
Marshall, John — *Premier, New Zealand*
Marshall, William — *Actor*
Martin, James R — *Football Player*
Matta Echaurren, Roberto S (Matta) — *Artist*
Matthews, Harry (Kid) — *Boxer*
Mauldin, William H (Bill) — *Editorial Cartoonist*
McCarthy, Lin — *Actor*
McCloskey, Frank — *Representative, IN*
McCloskey, Robert — *Writer*
McCool, William C — *Astronaut*
McCormack, Mark H — *Sports Attorney*
McDermott, Maurice J (Mickey) — *Baseball*
McDonald, Wesley — *Navy Admiral*
McDonough, Will — *Sportswriter*
McLucas, John L — *Gov't Official, Businessman*
McMath, Sidney S — *Governor, AR*
McNally, David A — *Baseball Player*
McReynolds, Jim — *Guitarist (Jim & Jessie)*
Mechem, Edwin L — *Governor, Senator, NM*
Meehl, Paul — *Psychologist*
Merrill, E Durwood — *Baseball Umpire*
Merryman, James H — *Army General*
Merton, Robert K — *Sociologist*
Metcalfe, E Bennett — *Environmental Activist*
Meyer, Jean — *Actor, Director*
Michaels, Leonard — *Writer*
Miller, James G — *Psychiatrist*
Millichip, Bert — *Soccer Executive*
Miroshnichenko, Aleksandr — *Boxer*
Mitchell, Donald J — *Representative, NY*
Mitchell, Gordon — *Actor*
Mitchell, William J (Billy) — *Singer (Clovers)*
Mizell, Jason — *Rap Artist (Run-DMC)*
Modigliani, Franco — *Nobel Economics Laureate*
Mollemann, Jurgen — *Gov't Official, Germany*
Momoh, Joseph — *President, Ivory Coast*

Monash, Paul	Writer
Moore, Paul, Jr	Religious Leader
Moran, Peggy	Actress
Morinigo, Higinio	President, Paraguay
Morley, Karen	Actress
Moss, Frank E	Senator, UT
Mota Pinto, Carlos	Premier, Portugal
Mountfort, Guy	Enviromentalist
Moynihan, Daniel Patrick	Senator, NY
Mullaney, Robert	Aeronautical Engineer
Murie, Margaret	Conservationist
Murphy, Brianne	Cinematographer
Muzenda, Simon V	Prime Minister, Zimbabwe
Ne Win, U	President, Burma
Nelson, Richard	Army Air Corps Hero
Neustadt, Richard E	Political Scientist, Educator
Newman, David	Writer
Nixon, Joan Lowery	Writer
Norton, Cliff	Actor, Comedian
Noyelle, Andre	Cyclist
O'Bannon, Frank L	Governor, IN
O'Connor, Donald	Actor, Dancer
Oddi, Silvio Cardinal	Religious Leader
Okutsu, Yukio	WW II Army Hero (CMH)
Olatunji, Babtunde	Drummer, Band Leader
Oldham, Arthur W	Composer
Omarr, Sydney	Astrologer, Columnist
Ong, Walter J	Religious Leader, Educator
Orrick, William H, Jr	Judge
Osborne, Adam	Computer Scientist
Otunga, Maurice M Cardinal	Religious Leader
Owens, Wayne	Representative, UT
Palmer, Robert	Singer, Songwriter
Papp, Lazlo	Boxer
Parker, Fred I	Judge
Parker, Suzy	Model, Actress
Pascal, William (Bill)	Football Player
Passeau, Claude W	Baseball Player
Pavlov, Valentin S	Premier, USSR
Paycheck, Johnny	Singer, Songwriter
Peake, Felicity	British Air Force Commodore
Peck, Gregory	Actor
Pender, Paul	Boxer
Perez Godoy, Ricardo P	President, Peru
Petrassi, Goffredo	Composer
Petroff, Peter D	Inventor (Digital Wristwatch)
Peugeot, Pierre	Businessman
Phillips, Peg	Actress
Phillips, Sam	Record Company Executive
Plimpton, George A	Writer
Pogue, L Welch	Attorney
Pountain, Eric J	Businessman
Prigogine, V Ilya	Nobel Chemistry Laureate
Quillen, James H (Jimmy)	Representative, TN
Quilley, Denis	Actor
Quinn, Glenn	Actor
Quo, Beulah	Actress
Racamier, Henry	Businessman
Raffensberger, Kenneth D	Baseball Player
Rahn, Helmut	Soccer Player
Raine, Kathleen J	Writer
Ralston, Vera Hruba	Actress
Ramon, Ilan	Astronaut
Ramos de Oliveira, Mauro	Soccer Player
Rasmussen, Norman C	Nuclear Engineer
Rawls, John B	Philosopher
Reber, Grote	Radio Astronomer
Reeves, Connie D	Rodeo Riding Instructor
Regan, Donald T	Secretary, Treasury
Regan, Richie	Basketball Player, Coach
Reid, Ptolemy	Prime Minister, Guyana
Reina Idiaquez, Carlos R	President, Honduras
Reinhardt, Max	Publisher
Reisz, Karel	Movie Director
Reynolds, William D (Bill)	Football Player
Rhodes, John J	Representative, AZ
Riefenstahl, Leni	Movie Director, Photographer
Ritter, John	Actor
Ritts, Herb	Photographer
Roach, John R	Religious Leader
Robbins, Frederick C	Nobel Medicine Laureate
Robertshaw, Louis B	Marine Corps General
Rocco, Louis R	Army Hero (CMH)
Rockwell, Robert	Actor
Roddy, Rod	Actor
Rogell, William G (Bill)	Baseball Player
Rogers, Fred M	TV Producer, Host
Roncalio, Teno	Representative, WY
Rosenbluth, Marshall N	Fusion Theorist, Physicist
Rosenthal, Franz	Educator
Rosenthal, Manuel	Composer, Conductor
Rostow, Eugene V	Economist
Rostow, Walt W	Economist, Gov't Official
Rousselot, John H	Representative, CA
Rowberry, Dave	Keyboardist (Animals)
Rowling, Wallace E	Premier, New Zealand
Rule, Janice	Actress
Russell, Fred M	Sportswriter
Russell, William L	Geneticist
Russo, William	Composer
Sabattani, Aurelio Cardinal	Religious Leader
Sadler, Laura	Actress
Safar, Peter	Surgeon
Said, Edward W	Educator
Samwell, Ian	Guitarist
Sanchez, Ivan A	Businessman, Physicist
Sanford, John	Psychoanalyst, Writer
Sankoh, Foday	Gov't Official, Sierra Leone
Santamaria, Mongo	Jazz Congo Drummer
Sawyer, Harold	Representative, MI
Scharf, Walter	Composer
Schell, Jeff	Microbiologist
Scherle, William J	Representative, IA
Schiaffino, Juan A	Soccer Player
Schlesinger, John R	Movie Director
Schonberg, Harold C	Music Critic
Schramm, Texas E (Tex)	Football Executive
Scolari, Fred	Basketball Player
Scott, Martha	Actress
Scribner, Belding H	Medical Researcher
Self, Kenneth W	Businessman
Selover, John L	Publisher
Semm, Kurt K S	Gynecologist, Engineer
Sensi, Giuseppe Cardinal	Religious Leader
Shanklin, Ron	Football Player
Shawcross, H William	Gov't Official, England
Shearman, John K G	Art Historian
Sheene, Barry	Motorcycle Racing Rider
Shettles, Landrum B	Obstetrician
Shields, Carol A	Writer
Shinto, Hisashi	Businessman
Shipley, George E	Representative, IL
Shoemaker, William L	Racing Jockey/Trainer
Simmons, Richard W	Actor
Simone, Nina	Singer, Songwriter
Sisson, Charles Hubert (C H)	Writer
Sisulu, Walter	Gov't Official, South Africa
Slater, Joseph E	Educator
Smight, Jack	Movie Director
Smith, Delbert (Del)	Sculptor
Smith, Elliott	Singer, Songwriter
Smith, Preston E	Governor, TX
Smith, Ray F	Entomologist
Smithson, Peter D	Architect
Smythe, Quenton	South Africa Hero (VC)
Solomon, Ezra	Economist
Sonobe, Takashi	Businessman
Stack, Robert	Actor, Marksman
Stambolic, Ivan	President, Serbia
Stanley, Florence	Actress

NECROLOGY

Starr, Edwin	*Singer*
Stasinopoulos, Michalis	*President, Greece*
Steers, Lester (Les)	*Track Athlete*
Steig, William	*Writer, Artist*
Steiner, John E	*Aeronautical Engineer*
Stephens, Robert G	*Representative, GA*
Stewart, Redd	*Singer, Songwriter*
Stone, Peter H	*Writer*
Straub, Robert W	*Governor, OR*
Streshinsky, Ted	*Photographer*
Strummer, Joe	*Singer (Clash), Songwriter*
Stuart, Richard L (Dick)	*Baseball Player*
Stump, Bob	*Representative, AZ*
Sullivan, Haywood C	*Baseball Player*
Sunderman, F William	*Physician*
Swendry, Albert	*Composer*
Talic, Momir	*Army General, Bosnia*
Tannenbaum, Robert	*Educator*
Tarbell, Dean S	*Chemist*
Teller, Edward	*Physicist*
Temu, Naftali	*Track Athlete*
Thesiger, Wilfred P	*Explorer*
Thigpen, Lynne	*Actress*
Thompson, John P	*Businessman*
Thurmond, J Strom	*Governor, Senator, SC*
Tidbury, Charles H	*Businessman*
Tien, Chang-Lin	*Educator*
Tighe, John T (Jack)	*Baseball Player*
Tillman, Floyd	*Singer, Guitarist*
Tinsley, Gaynell C (Gus)	*Football Player*
To Huu	*Gov't Official, Vietnam*
Tobey, Kenneth	*Actor*
Tolar, Charles G (Charlie)	*Football Player*
Tonelli, Annalena	*Social Activist*
Tonelli, Mario (Motts)	*Football Player*
Tose, Leonard H	*Football Executive*
Townsend, Ed	*Songwriter*
Trang, Thuy	*Actress*
Trevor-Roper, Hugh R	*Historian*
Trintignant, Marie	*Actress*
Truman, David B	*Political Scientist*
Tureck, Rosalyn	*Concert Pianist*
Ulland, Olav H	*Ski Jumper, Coach*
Upham, Charles	*New Zealand Hero (VC)*
Uris, Leon M	*Writer*
Vago, Pierre	*Architect, Town Planner*
Vallone, Raf	*Actor*
Varnedoe, J Kirk T	*Museum Director*
Vathis, Paul	*Photojournalist*
Velasco Garcia, Ignacio Cardinal	*Religious Leader*
Vesco, Don	*Auto, Motorcycle Racer*
Vieira deMello, Sergio	*Diplomat, Brazil*
Vigorito, Joseph P	*Representative, PA*
Villas Boas, Orlando	*Anthropologist, Explorer*
Volz, Nedra	*Actress*
VonBrauchitsch, Manfred	*Auto Racing Driver*
Wacker, Jim	*Football Coach*
Wade, Benjamin S	*Baseball Player*
Walker, Zena	*Actress*
Warren, Frank W, III	*Football Player*
Warwick, Earl L	*Inventor (Silly Putty)*
Washington, Walter E	*Mayor*
Watson, Harry P	*Hockey Player*
Wayne, Michael	*Movie Producer*
Weiss, Theodore R	*Writer*
Welch, Elisabeth	*Actress, Singer*
Weller, George	*Journalist*
Wells, Billy	*Football Player*
Weston, Cole	*Photographer, Artist*
Whitacre, John J	*Businessman*
White, Frank D	*Governor, AR*
Whiting, Beatrice B	*Antropologist*
Wietecha, Ray	*Football Player*
Wilberforce, Richard O	*Judge*
Wilkins, Graham J	*Businessman*
Wilkins, Robert W	*Medical Researcher*
Williams, George H	*Educator*
Williamson, Malcolm B G C	*Composer*
Wilson, C Kemmons	*Businessman*
Wilson, Ross	*Hockey Player*
Wilson, Sloan	*Writer*
Wilzig, Siggi B	*Financier*
Winsor, Kathleen	*Writer*
Woodley, David (Dave) E	*Football Player*
Wooley, Sheb	*Singer, Songwriter, Actor*
Wright, Peter H	*British Army Hero (VC)*
Wyland VanDerWoude, Wendy	*Diver*
Wyle, George	*Songwriter*
Wyman, Thomas H	*Financier*
Wysocki, Pete	*Football Player*
Yanne, Jean	*Actor*
Yanovsky, Zal	*Guitarist (Lovin' Spoonful)*
Yatron, Gus	*Representative, PA*
Yoder, Hatten S, Jr	*Petrologist*
Yordan, Philip	*Writer*
Zapp, Walter	*Inventor (Minicamera)*
Zevon, Warren	*Singer, Songwriter*
Ziegler, Ronald L	*Gov't Official, Journalist*
Zindel, Paul	*Writer*
Zorina, Vera	*Actress, Ballet Dancer*

US SENATE

The men and women below are current members of the US Senate. They can all be reached by writing them in care of **US Senate, Washington, DC 20510.**

Letters should be addressed **The Honorable Jane/John Doe**
US Senator from - - -

Salutations in letters should be **Dear Mr/Ms Senator - - -**

Alabama	Sessions, Jeff
Alabama	Shelby, Richard C
Alaska	Murkowski, Lisa
Alaska	Stevens, Theodore F
Arizona	Kyl, Jon L
Arizona	McCain, John S, III
Arkansas	Lincoln, Blanche Lambert
Arkansas	Pryor, Mark
California	Boxer, Barbara
California	Feinstein, Dianne
Colorado	Allard, Wayne
Colorado	Campbell, Ben Nighthorse
Connecticut	Dodd, Christopher J
Connecticut	Lieberman, Joseph I
Delaware	Biden, Joseph R, Jr
Delaware	Carper, Thomas R.
Florida	Graham, D Robert (Bob)
Florida	Nelson, William (Bill)
Georgia	Chambliss, Saxby
Georgia	Miller, Zell
Hawaii	Akaka, Daniel K
Hawaii	Inouye, Daniel K
Idaho	Craig, Larry E
Idaho	Crapo, Michael
Illinois	Durbin, Richard J
Illinois	Fitzgerald, Peter G

US SENATE

Indiana	Bayh, Evan
Indiana	Lugar, Richard G
Iowa	Grassley, Charles E
Iowa	Harkin, Thomas R
Kansas	Brownback, Sam
Kansas	Roberts, Pat
Kentucky	Bunning, James
Kentucky	McConnell, Mitch
Louisiana	Breaux, John B
Louisiana	Landrieu, Mary L
Maine	Collins, Susan M
Maine	Snowe, Olympia J
Maryland	Mikulski, Barbara A
Maryland	Sarbanes, Paul S
Massachusetts	Kennedy, Edward M (Ted)
Massachusetts	Kerry, John F
Michigan	Levin, Carl
Michigan	Stabenow, Debbie
Minnesota	Coleman, Norm
Minnesota	Dayton, Mark
Mississippi	Cochran, Thad
Mississippi	Lott, Trent
Missouri	Bond, Christopher (Kit)
Missouri	Talent, Jim
Montana	Baucus, Max S
Montana	Burns, Conrad
Nebraska	Hagel, Chuck
Nebraska	Nelson, Benjamin E (Ben)
Nevada	Ensign, John
Nevada	Reid, Harry M
New Hampshire	Gregg, Judd A
New Hampshire	Sununu, John
New Jersey	Corzine, Jon S
New Jersey	Lautenberg, Frank
New Mexico	Bingaman, Jeff
New Mexico	Domenici, Pete V
New York	Clinton, Hillary Rodham
New York	Schumer, Charles E
North Carolina	Dole, Elizabeth
North Carolina	Edwards, John
North Dakota	Conrad, Kent
North Dakora	Dorgan, Byron L
Ohio	DeWine, Michael
Ohio	Voinovich, George V
Oklahoma	Inhofe, James M
Oklahoma	Nickles, Donald L
Oregon	Smith, Gordon
Oregon	Wyden, Ron
Pennsylvania	Santorum, Richard J (Rick)
Pennsylvania	Specter, Arlen
Rhode Island	Chafee, Lincoln D
Rhode Island	Reed, John F
South Carolina	Graham, Lindsey
South Carolina	Hollings, Ernest F (Fritz)
South Dakota	Daschle, Thomas A
South Dakota	Johnson, Tim
Tennessee	Alexander, Lamar
Tennessee	Frist, Bill
Texas	Cornyn, John
Texas	Hutchison, Kay Bailey
Utah	Bennett, Robert F (Rob)
Utah	Hatch, Orrin G
Vermont	Jeffords, James M (Jim)
Vermont	Leahy, Patrick J
Virginia	Allen, George
Virginia	Warner, John W
Washington	Cantwell, Maria
Washington	Murray, Patty
West Virginia	Byrd, Robert C.
West Virginia	Rockefeller, John D, IV
Wisconsin	Feingold, Russell D
Wisconsin	Kohl, Herbert H
Wyoming	Enzi, Michael B
Wyoming	Thomas, Craig

US HOUSE OF REPRESENTATIVES

The men and women below are current members of the US House of Representatives. They can all be reached by writing them in care of **US House of Representatives, Washington, DC 20515**.

Letters should be addressed to **The Honorable Jane/John Doe**
US Representative from - - -

Salutations in letters should be **Dear Mr/Ms Representative - - -**

Alabama	Aderholt, Robert B
Alabama	Bachus, Spencer T, III
Alabama	Bonner, Jo
Alabama	Cramer, Robert E (Bud), Jr
Alabama	Davis, Artur
Alabama	Everett, Terry
Alabama	Rogers, Mike
Alaska	Young, Donald E
American Samoa	Faleomavaega, Eni F H
Arizona	Flake, Jeff
Arizona	Franks, Trent
Arizona	Grijalva, Raul
Arizona	Hayworth, J D
Arizona	Kolbe, James T (Jim)
Arizona	Pastor, Ed
Arizona	Renzi, Rick
Arizona	Shadegg, John B
Arkansas	Berry, Marion
Arkansas	Boozman, John
Arkansas	Ross, Michael A
Arkansas	Snyder, Vic
California	Baca, Joe
California	Becerra, Xavier
California	Berman, Howard L
California	Bono, Mary
California	Calvert, Ken
California	Capps, Lois
California	Cardoza, Dennis
California	Cox, C Christopher
California	Cunningham, Randall (Duke)
California	Davis, Susan A
California	Dooley, Calvin M, Jr
California	Doolittle, John T
California	Dreier, David T
California	Eshoo, Anna G
California	Farr, Sam
California	Filner, Robert (Bob)
California	Gallegly, Elton W
California	Harmon, Jane
California	Herger, Wally W, Jr
California	Honda, Michael M
California	Hunter, Duncan L

US HOUSE OF REPRESENTATIVES

California	Issa, Darrell E
California	Lewis, Jerry
California	Lantos, Thomas P
California	Lee, Barbara
California	Lofgren, Zoe
California	Matsui, Robert T
California	McKeon, Howard P (Buck)
California	Millender-McDonald, Juanita M
California	Miller, Gary G
California	Miller, George
California	Napolitano, Grace F
California	Nunes, Devin
California	Ose, Douglas
California	Pelosi, Nancy
California	Pombo, Richard W
California	Radanovich, George P
California	Rohrabacher, Dana
California	Roybal-Allard, Lucille
California	Royce, Edward R (Ed)
California	Sanchez, Linda
California	Sanchez, Loretta
California	Schiff, Adam B
California	Sherman, Brad
California	Solis, Hilda L
California	Stark, Fortney N (Pete)
California	Tauscher, Ellen O
California	Thomas, William M
California	Thompson, Mike
California	Waters, Maxine
California	Watson, Diane E
California	Waxman, Henry A
California	Woolsey, Lynn C
Colorado	Beauprez, Bob
Colorado	DeGette, Diana
Colorado	Hefley, Joel M
Colorado	McInnis, Scott S
Colorado	Musgrave, Marilyn
Colorado	Tancredo, Thomas G (Tom)
Colorado	Udall, Mark
Connecticut	DeLauro, Rosa L
Connecticut	Johnson, Nancy L
Connecticut	Larson, John B
Connecticut	Shays, Christopher
Connecticut	Simmons, Robert
Delaware	Castle, Michael N
District of Columbia	Norton, Eleanor H
Florida	Bilirakis, Michael
Florida	Boyd, Allen
Florida	Brown, Corrine
Florida	Brown-Waite, Virginia
Florida	Crenshaw, Ander
Florida	Davis, Jim
Florida	Deutsch, Peter
Florida	Diaz-Balart, Mario
Florida	Diaz-Balart, Lincoln
Florida	Feeney, Tom
Florida	Foley, Mark
Florida	Goss, Porter J
Florida	Harris, Katherine
Florida	Hastings, Alcee L
Florida	Keller, Ric
Florida	Meek, Kendrick
Florida	Mica, John L
Florida	Miller, Jeff
Florida	Putnam, Adam H
Florida	Ros-Lehtinen, Ileana
Florida	Shaw, E Clay, Jr
Florida	Stearns, Clifford B (Cliff)
Florida	Weldon, Dave
Florida	Wexler, Robert
Florida	Young, C W (Bill)
Georgia	Bishop, Sanford
Georgia	Burns, Max
Georgia	Collins, Michael A (Mac)
Georgia	Deal, John Nathan
Georgia	Gingrey, Phil
Georgia	Isakson, Johnny
Georgia	Kingston, Jack
Georgia	Lewis, John R
Georgia	Linder, John E
Georgia	Majette, Denise
Georgia	Marshall, Jim
Georgia	Norwood, Charles, Jr
Georgia	Scott, David
Guam	Bordallo, Madeleine
Hawaii	Abercrombie, Neil
Hawaii	Case, Ed
Idaho	Otter, C L (Butch)
Idaho	Simpson, Michael K (Mike)
Illinois	Biggert, Judy
Illinois	Costello, Jerry F
Illinois	Crane, Philip M
Illinois	Davis, Danny K
Illinois	Emanuel, Rahm
Illinois	Evans, Lane A
Illinois	Gutierrez, Luis V
Illinois	Hastert, J Dennis
Illinois	Hyde, Henry J
Illinois	Johnson, Timothy V
Illinois	Kirk, Mark S
Illinois	LaHood, Ray
Illinois	Lipinski, William O
Illinois	Manzullo, Donald A
Illinois	Rush, Bobby L
Illinois	Schakowsky, Janice
Illinois	Shimkus, John M
Illinois	Weller, Gerald C (Jerry)
Indiana	Burton, Dan L
Indiana	Buyer, Stephen E
Indiana	Carson, Julia M
Indiana	Chocola, Chris
Indiana	Hill, Baron P
Indiana	Hostettler, John N
Indiana	Pence, Mike
Indiana	Souder, Mark Edward
Indiana	Visclosky, Peter J
Iowa	Boswell, Leonard L
Iowa	King, Steve
Iowa	Latham, Thomas
Iowa	Leach, James A S (Jim)
Iowa	Nussle, James A (Jim)
Kansas	Moore, Dennis
Kansas	Moran, Jerry
Kansas	Ryun, Jim
Kansas	Tiahrt, Todd
Kentucky	Fletcher, Ernie
Kentucky	Lewis, Ron
Kentucky	Lucas, Kenneth
Kentucky	Northup, Anne M
Kentucky	Rogers, Harold (Hal)

Kentucky	Whitfield, Edward
Louisiana	Alexander, Rodney
Louisiana	Baker, Richard H
Louisiana	Jefferson, William J (Jeff)
Louisiana	John, Christopher (Chris)
Louisiana	McCrery, Jim
Louisiana	Tauzin, Wilbert J (Billy)
Louisiana	Vitter, David
Maine	Allen, Thomas H
Maine	Michaud, Michael
Maryland	Bartlett, Roscoe G
Maryland	Cardin, Benjamin L
Maryland	Cummings, Elijah E
Maryland	Gilchrest, Wayne T
Maryland	Hoyer, Steny H
Maryland	Ruppersberger, C A (Dutch)
Maryland	Van Hollen, Chris
Maryland	Wynn Albert R
Massachusetts	Capuano, Michael E
Massachusetts	Delahunt, William D
Massachusetts	Frank, Barney
Massachusetts	Lynch, Stephen F
Massachusetts	Markey, Edward J
Massachusetts	McGovern, James P
Massachusetts	Meehan, Martin T
Massachusetts	Neal, Richard E
Massachusetts	Olver, John W
Massachusetts	Tierney, John F
Michigan	Camp, Dave
Michigan	Conyers, John, Jr
Michigan	Dingell, John D, Jr
Michigan	Ehlers, Vernon J
Michigan	Hoekstra, Peter
Michigan	Kildee, Dale E
Michigan	Kilpatrick, Carolyn Cheeks
Michigan	Knollenberg, Joseph (Joe)
Michigan	Levin, Sander M
Michigan	McCotter, Thaddeus
Michigan	Miller, Candice
Michigan	Rogers, Michael J
Michigan	Smith, Nick
Michigan	Stupak, Bart T
Michigan	Upton, Frederick S
Minnesota	Gutknecht, Gil
Minnesota	Kennedy, Mark R
Minnesota	Kline, John
Minnesota	McCollum, Betty
Minnesota	Oberstar, James L
Minnesota	Peterson, Collin C
Minnesota	Ramstad, Jim
Minnesota	Sabo, Martin O
Mississippi	Pickering, Charles W (Chip), Jr
Mississippi	Taylor, Gene
Mississippi	Thompson, Bennie G
Mississippi	Wicker, Roger F
Missouri	Akin, W Todd
Missouri	Blunt, Roy
Missouri	Clay, William L (Bill), Jr
Missouri	Emerson, Jo Ann
Missouri	Gephardt, Richard A
Missouri	Graves, Samuel B
Missouri	Hulshof, Kenny C
Missouri	McCarthy, Karen
Missouri	Skelton, Ike
Montana	Rehberg, Dennis R
Nebraska	Bereuter, Douglas K
Nebraska	Osborne, Thomas W
Nebraska	Terry, Lee
Nevada	Berkley, Shelley
Nevada	Gibbons, Jim
Nevada	Porter, Joe
New Hampshire	Bass, Charles F
New Hampshire	Bradley, Jeb
New Jersey	Andrews, Robert E
New Jersey	Ferguson, Michael A
New Jersey	Frelinghuysen, Rodney P
New Jersey	Garrett, Scott
New Jersey	Holt, Rush D
New Jersey	LoBiondo, Frank A
New Jersey	Menendez, Robert
New Jersey	Pallone, Frank, Jr
New Jersey	Pascrell, William J, Jr
New Jersey	Payne, Donald M
New Jersey	Rothman, Steven R
New Jersey	Saxton, H James
New Jersey	Smith, Christopher H
New Mexico	Pearce, Steve
New Mexico	Udall, Thomas
New Mexico	Wilson, Heather
New York	Ackerman, Gary L
New York	Bishop, Timothy
New York	Boehlert, Sherwood L
New York	Crowley, Joseph
New York	Engel, Eliot L
New York	Fossella, Vito
New York	Hinchey, Maurice D, Jr
New York	Houghton, Amory, Jr
New York	Israel, Steve
New York	Kelly, Sue W
New York	King, Peter T
New York	Lowey, Nita M
New York	Maloney, Carolyn B
New York	McCarthy, Carolyn
New York	McHugh, John M
New York	McNulty, Michael R
New York	Meeks, Gregory W
New York	Nadler, Jerrold L (Jerry)
New York	Owens, Major R
New York	Quinn, Jack
New York	Rangel, Charles B
New York	Reynolds, Thomas M
New York	Serrano, José E
New York	Slaughter, Louise M
New York	Sweeney, John E
New York	Towns, Edolphus
New York	Velazquez, Nydia M
New York	Walsh, James T
New York	Weiner, Anthony D
North Carolina	Balance, Frank Jr
North Carolina	Ballenger, T Cass
North Carolina	Burr, Richard M
North Carolina	Coble, Howard
North Carolina	Etheridge, Bob
North Carolina	Hayes, Robert (Robin)
North Carolina	Jones, Walter B, Jr
North Carolina	McIntyre, Mike
North Carolina	Miller, Brad
North Carolina	Myrick, Sue W
North Carolina	Price, David E
North Carolina	Taylor, Charles H

U.S. HOUSE OF REPRESENTATIVES

North Carolina	Watt, Melvin L	Tennessee	Tanner, John S
North Dakota	Pomeroy, Earl R	Tennessee	Wamp, Zach
Ohio	Boehner, John	Texas	Barton, Joe L
Ohio	Brown, Sherrod	Texas	Bell, Chris
Ohio	Chabot, Steve	Texas	Bonilla, Henry
Ohio	Gillmor, Paul E	Texas	Brady, Kevin
Ohio	Hobson, David L	Texas	Burgess, Michael
Ohio	Jones, Stephanie T	Texas	Carter, John
Ohio	Kaptur, Marcy	Texas	Culberson, John A
Ohio	Kucinich, Dennis J	Texas	DeLay, Thomas D (Tom)
Ohio	LaTourette, Steven C	Texas	Doggett, Lloyd
Ohio	Ney, Robert W (Bob)	Texas	Edwards, Chet
Ohio	Oxley, Michael G	Texas	Frost, J Martin
Ohio	Portman, Rob	Texas	Gonzalez, Charlie A
Ohio	Pryce, Deborah	Texas	Granger, Kay
Ohio	Regula, Ralph	Texas	Green, Gene
Ohio	Ryan, Timothy	Texas	Hall, Ralph M
Ohio	Strickland, Ted	Texas	Hensarling, Jeb
Ohio	Tiberi, Patrick J	Texas	Hinojosa, Ruben
Ohio	Turner, Michael	Texas	Johnson, Eddie Bernice
Oklahoma	Carson, Brad	Texas	Johnson, Samuel (Sam)
Oklahoma	Cole, Tom	Texas	Lampson, Nick
Oklahoma	Istook, Ernest J (Jim), Jr	Texas	Lee, Sheila Jackson
Oklahoma	Lucas, Frank D	Texas	Neugebauer, Randy
Oklahoma	Sullivan, John	Texas	Ortiz, Solomon P
Oregon	Blumenauer, Earl	Texas	Paul, Ron
Oregon	DeFazio, Peter A	Texas	Reyes, Silvestre
Oregon	Hooley, Darlene	Texas	Rodriguez, Ciro D
Oregon	Walden, Greg	Texas	Sandlin, Max
Oregon	Wu, David	Texas	Sessions, Pete
Pennsylvania	Brady, Robert A	Texas	Smith, Lamar S
Pennsylvania	Doyle, Michael F (Mike)	Texas	Stenholm, Charles W
Pennsylvania	English, Phillip	Texas	Thornberry, William M (Mac)
Pennsylvania	Fattah, Chaka	Texas	Turner, Jim
Pennsylvania	Gerlach, Jim	Utah	Bishop, Rob
Pennsylvania	Greenwood, James C	Utah	Cannon, Christopher B
Pennsylvania	Hart, Melissa A	Utah	Matheson, James D
Pennsylvania	Hoeffel, Joseph M	Vermont	Sanders, Bernard (Bernie)
Pennsylvania	Holden, Tim	Virgin Islands	Christensen, Donna M
Pennsylvania	Kanjorski, Paul E	Virginia	Boucher, Frederick C (Rick)
Pennsylvania	Murphy, Tim	Virginia	Cantor, Eric I
Pennsylvania	Murtha, John P	Virginia	Davis, Jo Ann S
Pennsylvania	Peterson, John E	Viriginia	Davis, Thomas M
Pennsylvania	Pitts, Joseph R	Virginia	Forbes, J Randy
Pennsylvania	Platts, Todd R	Virginia	Goode, Virgil H, Jr
Pennsylvania	Sherwood, Donald	Virginia	Goodlatte, Robert W (Bob)
Pennsylvania	Shuster, Bill	Virginia	Moran, James P, Jr
Pennsylvania	Toomey, Patrick J	Virginia	Schrock, Edward L
Pennsylvania	Weldon, W Curtis	Virginia	Scott, Robert C (Bobby)
Puerto Rico	Acevedo-Vila, Anibal	Virginia	Wolf, Frank R
Rhode Island	Kennedy, Patrick J	Washington	Baird, Brian
Rhode Island	Langevin, James R	Washington	Dicks, Norman D
South Carolina	Barrett, J Gresham	Washington	Dunn, Jennifer B
South Carolina	Brown, Henry E, Jr	Washington	Hastings, Doc
South Carolina	Clyburn, James E	Washington	Inslee, Jay
South Carolina	DeMint, James	Washington	Larson, Richard R
South Carolina	Spratt, John M, Jr	Washington	McDermott, James A (Jim)
South Carolina	Wilson, Joe	Washington	Nethercutt, George R, Jr
South Dakota	Janklow, William	Washington	Smith, Adam
Tennessee	Blackburn, Marsha	West Virginia	Capito, Shelly Moore
Tennessee	Cooper, Jim	West Virginia	Mollohan, Alan B
Tennessee	Davis, Lincoln	West Virginia	Rahall, Nick Joe, II
Tennessee	Duncan, John J, Jr	Wisconsin	Baldwin, Tammy
Tennessee	Ford, Harold E, Jr	Wisconsin	Green, Mark
Tennessee	Gordon, Bart	Wisconsin	Kind, Ron
Tennessee	Jenkins, William L (Bill)	Wisconsin	Kleczka, Gerald D

U.S. HOUSE OF REPRESENTATIVES

Wisconsin	Obey, David R
Wisconsin	Petri, Thomas E
Wisconsin	Ryan, Paul
Wisconsin	Sensenbrenner, F James, Jr
Wyoming	Cubin, Barbara

US GOVERNORS

The men and women below are current Governors of their respective states. They can all be reached by writing them in care of the **Governors Office** at the addresses below.

Letters should be addressed — **The Honorable Jane/John Doe**
Governor of - - -

Salutations in letters should be — **Dear Governor - - -**

Alabama	Riley, Bob	State Capitol, 600 Dexter Ave, Montgomery, AL 36130, USA
Alaska	Murkowski, Frank	State Capitol Building, PO Box 110001, Juneau, AK 99811, USA
American Samoa	Tulafono, Togiola	Executive Office Bldg, #300, Pago Pago, AS 96799, USA
Arizona	Napolitano, Janet	State Capitol, 1700 W Washington St, Phoenix, AZ 85007, USA
Arkansas	Huckabee, Michael	State Capitol, #250, Little Rock, AR 72201, USA
California	Schwartzenegger, Arnold	State Capitol, #100, Sacramento, CA 95814, USA
Colorado	Owens, Bill	State Capitol, #136, Denver, CO 80203, USA
Connecticut	Rowland, John G	State Capitol, 210 Capitol Ave, Hartford, CT 06106, USA
Delaware	Minner Ruth Ann	Tatnall Bldg, William Penn St, Dover, DE 19901, USA
Florida	Bush, J E	State Capitol, Tallahassee, FL 32399, USA
Georgia	Perdue, Sonny	State Capitol, #203, Atlanta, GA 30334, USA
Guam	Camacho, Felix	Executive Chamber, PO Box 2950, Agana, GU 96932, USA
Hawaii	Lingle, Linda	State Capitol, #500, Honolulu, HI 96813, USA
Idaho	Kempthorne, Dirk A	State Capitol, 700 W Jefferson, #200, Boise, ID 83720, USA
Illinois	Blagojevich, Rod	State House, 207 E Capitol Ave, #206, Springfield, IL 62706, USA
Indiana	Kernan, Joseph	State House, 200 Wwashington St, Indianapolis, IN 46204, USA
Iowa	Vilsack, Tom	State Capitol, Des Moines, IA 50319, USA
Kansas	Sebelius, Kathleen	State Capitol, #200, Topeka, KS 66612, USA
Kentucky	Fletcher, Ernie	State Capitol, 700 Capitol Ave, Frankfort, KY 40601, USA
Louisiana	Blanco, Kathleen	State Capitol, PO Box 94004, Baton Rouge, LA 70804, USA
Maine	Baldacci, John	Blaine House, 1 State House Station, Augusta, ME 04333, USA
Maryland	Ehrlich, Robert Jr	State House, 100 State Circle, Annapolis, MD 21401, USA
Massachusetts	Romney, Mitt	State House, #360, Boston, MA 02133, USA
Michigan	Granholm, Jennifer	State Capitol, PO Box 30013, Lansing, MI 48909, USA
Minnesota	Pawlenty, Tim	130 State Capitol, 75 Constitution Ave, St Paul, MN 55155, USA
Mississippi	Barbour, Haley	State Capitol, PO Box 139, Jackson, MS 39205, USA
Missouri	Holden, Bob	State Capitol, 201 W Capitol Ave,#216, Jefferson City, MO 65101, U
Montana	Martz, Judy	State Capitol, PO Box 0801, Helena, MT 59624, USA
Nebraska	Johanns, Mike	State Capitol, PO Box 94848, Lincoln, NE 68509, USA
Nevada	Guinn, Kenny	State Capitol, 101 N Carson St, Carson City, NV 89701, USA
New Hampshire	Benson, Craig	State House, #208, Concord, NH 03301, USA
New Jersey	McGreevey, Jim	State House, 125 W State St, PO Box 001, Trenton, NJ 08625, USA
New Mexico	Richardson, Bill	State Capitol, #400, Santa Fe, NM 87503, USA
New York	Pataki, George E	State Capitol, Albany, NY 12224, USA
North Carolina	Easley, Mike	State Capitol, 20301 Mail Service Center, Raleigh, NC 27699, USA
North Dakota	Hoeven, John	State Capitol, 600 East Blvd Ave, #101, Bismarck, ND 58505, USA
Ohio	Taft, Robert (Bob)	State House, 77 S High St, #3000, Columbus, OH 43266, USA
Oklahoma	Henry, Brad	State Capitol, #212, Oklahoma City, OK 73105, USA
Oregon	Kulongoski, Ted	State Capitol, 900 Court St, #254, Salem, OR 97301, USA
Pennsylvania	Rendell, Ed	Main Capitol, #225, Harrisburg, PA 17120, USA
Puerto Rico	Calderon, Sila	La Fortaleza, PO Box 9020082, San Juan, PR 00902, USA
Rhode Island	Carcieri, Donald	State House, Providence, RI 02903, USA
South Carolina	Sanford, Mark	State Capitol, PO Box 11829, Columbia, SC 29211, USA
South Dakota	Rounds, Mike	State Capitol, 500 E Capitol Ave, Pierre, SD 57501, USA
Tennessee	Bredesen, Phil	State Capitol, Nashville, TN 37243, USA
Texas	Perry, Rick	State Capitol, PO Box 12428, Austin, TX 78711, USA
Utah	Walker, Olene	State Capitol, #210, Salt Lake City, UT 81114, USA
Vermont	Douglas, Jim	Pavilion Building, 109 State St, Montpelier, VT 05609, USA
Virgin Islands	Turnbull, Charles	21-22 Kongens Gade, Charlotte Amalie, St. Thomas, VI 23219, USA
Virginia	Warner, Mark	State Capitol, Richmond, VA 23219, USA
Washington	Locke, Gary	State Capitol, PO Box 40002, Olympia, WA 98504, USA
West Virginia	Wise, Bob	State Capitol Complex, Charleston, WV 25305, USA
Wisconsin	Doyle, Jim	State Capitol, PO Box 7863, Madison, WI 53707, USA
Wyoming	Freudenthal, Dave	State Capitol, #124, Cheyenne, WY 82002, USA

Abrams Artists & Associates	9200 Sunset Blvd, #1125	Los Angeles, CA 90069, USA
Abrams-Rubaloff & Lawrence	8075 W 3rd St, #303	Los Angeles, CA 90048, USA
Agency For Performing Arts	9200 Sunset Blvd, #900	Los Angeles, CA 90069, USA
Agency, The	1800 Ave of Stars, #400	Los Angeles, CA 90067, USA
Agents Associes Beaume	201 Faubourg Saint Honore	75008 Paris, France
Agentur Killer	54 Harthauser Str	81545 Munich, Germany
Agentur Mattes	14 Merzstr	81679 Munich, Germany
Altaras, Jonathan	13 Shorts Gardens	London WC2H 9AT, England
Ambrosio/Mortimer & Associates	PO Box 16758	Beverly Hills, CA 90209, USA
Amsel Eisenstadt & Frazier	5757 Wilshire Blvd, #510	Los Angeles, CA 90036, USA
Artists Agency	10000 Santa Monica Blvd, #305	Los Angeles, CA 90067, USA
Artists Group	1180 S. Beverly Drive	Los Angeles, CA 90035, USA
Artists Management Group	9465 Wilshire Blvd, #419	Beverly Hills, CA 90212, USA
Artmedia	20 av Rapp	F-75007 Paris, France
Associated Booking Agency	1995 Broadway, #501	New York, NY 10023, USA
Associated Talent International	1320 Armacost Ave, #2	Los Angeles, CA 90025, USA
Badgley Connor King	9229 Sunset Blvd, #311	Los Angeles, CA 90069, USA
Baier/Kleinman Int'l	3575 Cahuenga Blvd, #500	Los Angeles, CA 90068, USA
Bauman Associates	5750 Wilshire Blvd, #473	Los Angeles, CA 90036, USA
Belfrage, Julian	46 Albermarle St	London W1X 4PP, England
Bethann Model Management	36 N Moore St, #36N	New York, NY 10013, USA
Bikoff Agency, Yvette	1040 1st Ave, #1126	New York, NY 10022, USA
Blake Agency	1333 Ocean Ave	Santa Monica, CA 90401, USA
Blanchard, Enterprises Nina	8826 Burton Way	Beverly Hills, CA 90211, USA
Bloom Ltd, J Michael	9255 Sunset Blvd, #710	Los Angeles, CA 90069, USA
Bloom Ltd, J Michael	233 Park Ave S, #1000	New York, NY 10003, USA
Borinstein Oreck Bogart Agency	3172 Dona Susana Dr	Studio City, CA 91604, USA
Boss Models	1 Gansevoort St	New York, NY 10014, USA
Bresler Kelly & Associates	11500 W Olympic Blvd, #510	Los Angeles, CA 90064, USA
Breslin, Herbert	119 W 57th St, #1505	New York, NY 10019, USA
Brillstein/Grey Entertainment	9150 Wilshire Blvd, #350	Beverly Hills, CA 90212, USA
Broder Kurland Webb Uffner	9242 Beverly Blvd, #200	Beverly Hills, CA 90210, USA
Buchwald & Associates, Don	6500 Wilshire Blvd, #2200	Los Angeles, CA 90048, USA
Burton Agency, Iris	1450 Belfast Dr	Los Angeles, CA 90069, USA
Camden ITG Talent Agency	1501 Main St, #204	Venice, CA 90291, USA
Carroll Agency, William	11360 Brill Dr	Studio City, CA 91604, USA
Cassidy Inc, Thomas	11761 E Speedway Blvd	Tucson, AZ 85748, USA
Cavaleri & Associates	178 S Victory Blvd, #205	Burbank, CA 91502, USA
Century Artists	PO Box 59747	Santa Barbara, CA 93150, USA
Chasin Agency	8899 Beverly Blvd, #716	Los Angeles, CA 90048, USA
Chatto & Linnit	Prince of Wales, Coventry St	London W1V 7FE, England
Circle Talent Associates	433 N Camden Dr, #400	Beverly Hills, CA 90210, USA
Click Model Management	881 7th Ave	New York, NY 10019, USA
CLInc Talent Agency	843 N Sycamore Ave	Los Angeles, CA 90038, USA
CNA & Associates	1925 Century Park E, #750	Los Angeles, CA 90067, USA
Coast To Coast Talent Group	3350 Barham Blvd	Los Angeles, CA 90068, USA
Commercials Unlimited	8383 Wilshire Blvd, #850	Beverly Hills, CA 90211, USA
Conner Agency, Hall	9169 Sunset Blvd	Los Angeles, CA 90069, USA
Contemporary Artists	610 Santa Monica Blvd, #202	Santa Monica, CA 90401, USA
Cosden Agency, Robert	3518 Cahuenga Blvd W, #200	Los Angeles, CA 90068, USA
Creative Artists Agency	9830 Wilshire Blvd	Beverly Hills, CA 90212, USA
Creative Entertainment Associates	2201 S 21st St	Philadelphia, PA 19145, USA
Cunningham-Escott-Dipene	10635 Santa Monica Blvd, #130	Los Angeles, CA 90025, USA
Dade/Schultz Agency	6442 Coldwater Canyon Ave, #206	North Hollywood, CA91606, USA
Daish Associates, Judy	2 St Charles Place	London M10 6EG, England
DH Talent Agency	1800 N Highland Ave, #300	Los Angeles, CA 90028, USA
Elite Model Management	111 E 22nd St, #200	New York, NY 10010, USA
Endeavor Talent Agency	9701 Wilshire Blvd, #1000	Beverly Hills, CA 90212, USA
Entertainment Talent Agency	PO Box 1821	Ojai, CA 93024, USA
Epstein-Wyckoff & Associates	280 S Beverly Dr, #400	Beverly Hills, CA 90212, USA
Evolution Entertainment	7722 Sunset Blvd	Los Angeles, CA 90046, USA
Famous Artists Agency	250 W 57th St	New York, NY 10107, USA
Film Artists Associates	13563 1/2 Ventura Blvd, #200	Sherman Oaks, CA 91423, USA
Firm, The	9100 Wilshire Blvd, #100W	Beverly Hills, CA 90212, USA
First Artists Agency	1631 N Bristol St, #B20	Santa Ana, CA 92706, USA
Flick East-West Talents	9057 Nemo St, #A	West Hollywood, CA 90069, USA

Ford Model Agency	142 Green St	New York, NY 10012, USA
Front Line Management	8900 Wilshire Blvd, #300	Beverly Hills, CA 90211, USA
Gage Group	14724 Ventura Blvd, #505	Sherman Oaks, CA 91403, USA
Geddes Agency	8430 Sunset Blvd, #200	West Hollywood, CA 90069, USA
Gersh Agency	232 N Canon Dr	Beverly Hills, CA 90210, USA
Gold/Marshak/Liedtke	3500 W Olive Ave, #1400	Burbank, CA 91505, USA
Gordon & Associates, Michelle	260 S Beverly Dr, #308	Beverly Hills, CA 90212, USA
Gorfaine/Schwarz/Roberts	13245 Riverside Dr, #450	Sherman Oaks, CA 91423, USA
Grady Agency, Mary	221 E Walnut St, #130	Pasadena, CA 91101, USA
Greene & Associates	7080 Hollywood Blvd, #1017	Los Angeles, CA 90028, USA
Halliday & Associates, Buzz	8899 Beverly Blvd, #620	Los Angeles, CA 90048, USA
Hallmark Entertainment	8033 Sunset Blvd, #1000	Los Angeles, CA 90046, USA
Halpern & Associates	P.O. Box 5597	Santa Monica, CA 90409, USA
Handprint Entertainment	1100 Glendon Ave, #1000	Los Angeles, CA 90024, USA
Henderson/Hogan Agency	8285 W Sunset Blvd, #1	West Hollywood, CA 90046, USA
Hervey/Grimes Talent Agency	PO Box 64249	Los Angeles, CA 90064, USA
House of Representatives	400 S Beverly Dr, #101	Beverly Hills, CA 90212, USA
HTM/Headliner Talent Mgmt	7200 France Ave S, #330	Edina, MN 55435, USA
IFA Talent Agency	8730 Sunset Blvd, #490	Los Angeles, CA 90069, USA
Imagine Entertainment	9465 Wilshire Blvd, #700	Beverly Hills, CA 90212, USA
Innovative Artists	1505 10th Street	Santa Monica, CA 91401, USA
International Creative Management	8942 Wilshire Blvd, #219	Beverly Hills, CA 90211, USA
International Talent Group	729 7th Ave, #1600	New York, NY 10019, USA
Joyce Agency	370 Harrison Ave	Harrison, NY 10528, USA
Karg/Weissenbach Associates	329 N Wetherly Dr, #101	Beverly Hills, CA 90211, USA
Katz Enterprises, Raymond	345 N Maple Dr, #205	Beverly Hills, CA 90210, USA
Kazarian/Spencer Associates	11365 Ventura Blvd, #100	Studio City, CA 91604, USA
Kohner Inc, Paul	9300 Wilshire Blvd, #555	Beverly Hills, CA 90212, USA
Kosden Agency, Robert	7135 Hollywood Blvd, #PH2	Los Angeles, CA 90046, USA
Kraft-Benjamin-Engel	15233 Ventura Blvd, #200	Sherman Oaks, CA 91403, USA
Kurland Associates, Ted	173 Brighton Ave	Boston, MA 02134, USA
LA Talent	8335 Sunset Blvd, #200	Los Angeles, CA 90069, USA
Lee Attractions, Buddy	38 Music Square E, #300	Nashville, TN 37203, USA
Light, Robert	6404 Wilshire Blvd	Los Angeles, CA 90048, USA
London Management	2-4 Noel St	London W1V 3RB, England
Lovell Associates	7095 Hollywood Blvd, #1006	Los Angeles, CA 90028, USA
Majestic Tours	29701 Kinderkarmack Road	Oradell, NJ 07649, USA
Management Javonovic	24 Kathi-Kobus-Str	80797 Munich, Germany
Markham & Froggatt	Julian House, 4 Windmill St	London W1P 1HF, England
Marshak Wycoff Associates	280 S Beverly Dr, #400	Beverly Hills, CA 90212, USA
MAX Agency	166 N Canon Dr	Beverly Hills, CA 90210, USA
MCA Concerts	100 Universal City Plaza	Universal City, CA 91608, USA
Media Artists Group, Inc	6300 Wilshire Blvd, #1470	Los Angeles, CA 90048, USA
Metropolitan Talent Agency	4526 Wilshire Blvd	Los Angeles, CA 90010, USA
MEW Inc	8489 W 3rd St, #1100	Los Angeles, CA 90048, USA
Miskin Agency	2355 Benedict Canyon	Beverly Hills, CA 90210, USA
Monterey Peninsula Artists	509 Hartnell St	Monterey, CA 93940, USA
More/Medovoy	7920 W Sunset Blvd, #400	Los Angeles, CA 90046, USA
Morris Agency, William	151 S El Camino Dr	Beverly Hills, CA 90212, USA
Moss Agency, Burton	8827 Beverly Blvd, #L	Los Angeles, CA 90048, USA
Nathe & Associates, Susan	8281 Melrose Ave, #200	Los Angeles, CA 90046, USA
Nationwide Entertainment	2756 N Green Valley Parkway, #449	Henderson, NV 89014, USA
Next Model Management	23 Watts St	New York, NY 10013, USA
Pakula/King & Associates	9229 Sunset Blvd, #315	Los Angeles, CA 90069, USA
Paradigm Agency	10100 Santa Monica Blvd, #2500	Los Angeles, CA 90067, USA
Pauline's Talent Corp	379 W Broadway, #502	New York, NY 10012, USA
Peters Fraser Dunlop	Drury House, 34-43 Russell St	London WC2B 5HA, England
PMK Public Relations	8500 Wilshire Blvd, #700	Beverly Hills, CA 90211, USA
Premier Artists Agency	1875 Century Park E, #2250	Los Angeles, CA 90067, USA
Premier Talent Agency	3 E 54th St, #1100	New York, NY 10022, USA
Progressive Artists Agency	400 S Beverly Dr, #216	Beverly Hills, CA 90212, USA
ProServe	1100 Woodrow Wilson Blvd, #1800	Arlington, VA 22209, USA
Ramsay, M	14A Goodwins Court, St Martin's Lane	London WC2N 4LL, England
Rascoff/Zysblat Organization	110 W 57th St, #300	New York, NY 10019, USA
Redway Associates, John	5 Denmark St	London WC2H 8LP, England
Reid Entertainment, John	Singes House, 32 Galena Road	London W6 0LT, England

AGENCY ADDRESSES

Rich Management, Elaine	2400 Whitman Place	Los Angeles, CA 90068, USA
Robinson Management, Dolores	9250 Wilshire Blvd, #220	Beverly Hills, CA 90212, USA
Rogers & Cowan Agency	6340 Breckenridge Run	Rex, GA 30273, USA
Rollins Joffe Morra Brezner	10201 Pico Blvd, #58	Los Angeles, CA 90064, USA
Rosenberg Office, Marion	8428 Melrose Place, #B	Los Angeles, CA 90069, USA
Rothberg, Arlyne	349 S Linden Dr, #C	Beverly Hills, CA 90212, USA
Ruffalo Management, Joseph	9655 Wilshire Blvd, #850	Beverly Hills, CA 90212, USA
Rush Artists Management	1600 Varick St	New York, NY 10013, USA
Russo, Lynne	3624 Mound View Ave	Studio City, CA 91604, USA
Sanders Agency	2120 Colorado Ave, #120	Santa Monica, CA 90404, USA
Sanders Agency	1204 Broadway, #304	New York, NY 10001, USA
Sanford-Beckett-Skouras	1015 Gayley Ave, #300	Los Angeles, CA 90024, USA
Savage Agency	6212 Banner Ave	Los Angeles, CA 90038, USA
Schechter Co, Irv	9300 Wilshire Blvd, #410	Beverly Hills, CA 90212, USA
Schiowitz/Clay/Rose	1680 Vine St, #1016	Los Angeles, CA 90028, USA
Schoen & Associates, Judy	606 N Larchmont Blvd, #309	Los Angeles, CA 90004, USA
Schwartz Associates, Don	1604 N Cahuenga Blvd, #101	Los Angeles, CA 90028, USA
SDB Partners, Inc	1801 Ave of Stars, #902	Los Angeles, CA 90067, USA
Sekura/A Talent Agency	PO Box 931779	Los Angeles, CA 90093, USA
Selected Artists Agency	3900 W Alameda Ave, #345	Burbank, CA 91505, USA
Shapira & Associates, David	15821 Ventura Blvd, #235	Encino, CA 91436, USA
Shapiro-Lichtman Agency	8827 Beverly Blvd	Los Angeles, CA 90048, USA
Sharkey Associates, James	21 Golden Square	London W1R 3PA, England
Shaw Concerts	Lincoln Center, 1900 Broadway, #200	New York, NY 10023, USA
Sherrell Agency, Lew	937 N Sinova	Mesa, AZ 85205, USA
Shriver PR, Evelyn	830 E Hillview Dr	Brentwood, TN 37027, USA
Silver Massetti & Szatmary	8730 Sunset Blvd, #440	Los Angeles, CA 90069, USA
Sindell & Associates, Richard	1910 Holmby Ave, #1	Los Angeles, CA 90025, USA
Slessinger & Associates, Michael	8730 Sunset Blvd, #220W	Los Angeles, CA 90069, USA
Smith & Associates, Susan	121A N San Vicente Blvd	Beverly Hills, CA 90211, USA
Smith/Gosnell/Nicholson	PO Box 1156	Studio City, CA 91614, USA
Somers Teitelbaum David	8840 Wilshire Blvd, #200	Beverly Hills, CA 90211, USA
Special Artists Agency	345 N Maple Dr, #302	Beverly Hills, CA 90210, USA
Starwil Talent	433 N Camden Dr, #400	Beverly Hills, CA 90210, USA
Sterling/Winters	10877 Wilshire Blvd, #15	Los Angeles, CA 90024, USA
Stone Manners Agency	6500 Wilshire Blvd, #550	Los Angeles, CA 90048, USA
Strain & Associates, Peter	5724 W 3rd St, #302	Los Angeles, CA 90036, USA
Subrena Artists	330 W 56th St, #18M	New York, NY 10019, USA
Talent Entertainment Group	9111 Wilshire Blvd	Beverly Hills, CA 90210, USA
Talent Group Inc	6300 Wilshire Blvd, #2110	Los Angeles, CA 90048, USA
Tannen & Associates, Herb	10801 National Blvd, #101	Los Angeles, CA 90064, USA
Thomas Agency, Robert	28051 Dequindre Road	Madison Heights, MI 48071, USA
Tisherman Agency	6767 Forest Lawn Dr, #101	Los Angeles, CA 90068, USA
Twentieth Century Artists	4605 Lankershim Blvd, #305	North Hollywood, CA 91602, USA
United Talent Agency	9560 Wilshire Blvd, #500	Beverly Hills, CA 90212, USA
Variety Artists International	1942 Spring St	Paso Robles, CA 93446, USA
Webb Enterprises, Ruth	10580 Des Moines Ave	Northridge, CA 91326, USA
Wilder Agency	3151 Cahuenga Blvd W, #310	Los Angeles, CA 90068, USA
Wilhelmina Artists	8383 Wilshire Blvd, #650	Beverly Hills, CA 90211, USA
Wolf/Kasteller	132 S Rodeo Dr, #300	Beverly Hills, CA 90212, USA
Wolfman Jack Entertainment	RR 1, PO Box 56	Belvidere, NC 27919, USA
Writers & Artists Agency	8383 Wilshire Blvd, #550	Beverly Hills, CA 90211, USA
ZBF Agentur	Ordensmeisterstr 15-16	12099 Berlin, Germany
Zealous Artists	139 S Beverly Dr, #225	Beverly Hills, CA 90212, USA

SYNDICATE ADDRESSES

Associated Press	50 Rockefeller Plaza	New York, NY 10020, USA
Creators Syndicate	5777 W Century Blvd, #700	Los Angeles, CA 90045, USA
King Features Syndicate	235 E 45th St	New York, NY 10106, USA
North American Syndicate	235 E 45th St	New York, NY 10017, USA
Times-Mirror Syndicate	Times-Mirror Square	Los Angeles, CA 90053, USA
Tribune Media Services	435 N Michigan Ave, #1500	Chicago, IL 60611, USA
United Feature Syndicate	200 Madison Ave	New York, NY 10016, USA
United Media Syndicate	200 Park Ave	New York, NY 10016, USA
United Press International	2 Pennsylvania Plaza, #1800	New York, NY 10121, USA
Universal Press Syndicate	4400 Fairway Dr	Fairway, KS 66205, USA

MAJOR TELEVISION STATION ADDRESSES

American Broadcasting Company

ABC-LA	500 S Buena Vista St	Burbank, CA 91521, USA
ABC-NY	77 W 66th St	New York, NY 10023, USA
KABC-TV	4151 Prospect Ave	Los Angeles, CA 90027, USA
KGO-TV	900 Front St	San Francisco, CA 94111, USA
KTRK-TV	3310 Bissonnet Dr	Houston, TX 77005, USA
WABC-TV	7 Lincoln Square	New York, NY 10023, USA
WCVB-TV (Boston)	5 TV Place	Needham, MA 02194, USA
WFAA-TV	606 Young St	Dallas, TX 75202, USA
WJLA-TV	3007 Tilden St NW	Washington, DC 20008, USA
WLS-TV	190 N State St	Chicago, IL 60601, USA
WPIV-TV	4100 City Line Ave	Philadelphia, PA 19131, USA
WPLG-TV	3900 Biscayne Blvd	Miami, FL 33137, USA
WSB-TV	1801 W Peachtree St NE	Atlanta, GA 30309, USA
WVUE-TV	1025 S Jefferson Davis Parkway	New Orleans, LA 70125, USA
WXYZ-TV (Detroit)	20777 W Ten-Mile Road	Southfield, MI 48037, USA

Columbia Broadcasting System

CBS-LA	7800 Beverly Blvd	Los Angeles, CA 90036, USA
CBS-NY	51 W 52nd St	New York, NY 10019, USA
KCBS-TV	6121 Sunset Blvd	Los Angeles, CA 90028, USA
KHOU-TV	1945 Allen Parkway	Houston, TX 77019, USA
KPIX-TV	855 Battery St	San Francisco, CA 94111, USA
KYW-TV	101 S Independence Mall E	Philadelphia, PA 19106, USA
WBBM-TV	630 N McClurg Court	Chicago, IL 60611, USA
WBZ-TV	1170 Soldiers Field Road	Boston, MA 02134, USA
WCBS-TV	524 W 57th St	New York, NY 10019, USA
WCIX-TV	8900 NW 18th Terrace	Miami, FL 33172, USA
WUSA-TV	4100 Wisconsin Ave NW	Washington, DC 20016, USA
WWL-TV	1024 N Rampart St	New Orleans, LA 70116, USA

Fox Television

Fox	10201 W Pico Blvd	Los Angeles, CA 90035, USA
KDFW-TV	400 N Griffin St	Dallas, TX 75202, USA
KRIV-TV	3935 Westheimer Road	Houston, TX 77027, USA
KTTV-TV	5746 W Sunset Blvd	Los Angeles, CA 90028, USA
KTVU-TV (San Francisco)	PO Box 22222	Oakland, CA 94623, USA
WAGA-TV	1551 Briarcliff Road NE	Atlanta, GA 30306, USA
WFLD-TV	205 N Michigan Ave	Chicago, IL 60601, USA
WFXT-TV (Boston)	1000 Providence Highway	Dedham, MA 02026, USA
WJBK-TV (Detroit)	16550 W Nine-Mile Road	Southfield, MI 48075, USA
WNOL-TV	1661 Canal St	New Orleans, LA 70112, USA
WNYW-TV	205 E 67th St	New York, NY 10021, USA
WSVN-TV	1401 79th St Causeway	Miami, FL 33141, USA
WTTG-TV	5151 Wisconsin Ave NW	Washington, DC 20016, USA
WTXF-TV	330 Market St	Philadelphia, PA 19106, USA

National Broadcasting Company

KNBC-TV (Los Angeles)	3000 W Alameda Ave	Burbank, CA 91523, USA
KPRC-TV	8181 Southwest Freeway	Houston, TX 77074, USA
KRON-TV	1001 Van Ness Ave	San Francisco, CA 94109, USA
KXAS-TV	3900 Barnett St	Fort Worth, TX 76103, USA
WDIV-TV	550 W Lafayette Blvd	Detroit, MI 48231, USA
WDSU-TV	520 Royal St	New Orleans, LA 70130, USA
WMAG-TV	454 N Columbus Dr	Chicago, IL 60611, USA
WMGM-TV (Philadelphia)	1601 New Road	Linwood, NJ 08221, USA
WNBC-TV	30 Rockefeller Plaza	New York, NY 10112, USA
WRC-TV	4001 Nebraska Ave NW	Washington, DC 20016, USA
WTVJ-TV	316 N Miami Ave	Miami, FL 33128, USA
WXIA-TV	1611 W Peachtree St NE	Atlanta, GA 30309, USA

CABLE TELEVISION CHANNEL ADDRESSES

American Christian Television	6350 West Freeway	Fort Worth, TX 76150, USA
American Movie Classics	150 Crossways Park W	Woodbury, NY 11797, USA
Arts & Entertainment	235 E 45th St	New York, NY 10017, USA
Black Entertainment Network	One BET Plaza, 1900 W Place NE	Washington, DC 20018, USA
British Broadcasting Company	Wood Lane	London W12 8Q, England
Cable News Network (CNN)	100 International Blvd NW	Atlanta, GA 30303, USA

CABLE TELEVISION STATION ADDRESSES

Canadian Broadcasting Company	1500 Bronson Ave	Ottawa ON K1G 3J5, Canada
Canadian Television Network	42 Charles St E	Toronto ON M4Y 1T5, Canada
Capital Cities/ABC	77 W 66th St	New York, NY 10023, USA
Cartoon Network	1050 Techwood Dr NW	Atlanta, GA 30318, USA
Christian Broadcasting Network	1000 Centerville Turnpike	Virginia Beach, VA 23463, USA
Cinemax	1100 6th Ave	New York, NY 10036, USA
Columbia Broadcasting System	51 W 52nd St	New York, NY 10019, USA
Comedy Central	1775 Broadway	New York, NY 10019, USA
Consumer News & Business	2200 Fletcher Ave	Fort Lee, NJ 07024, USA
Country Music Television	2806 Opryland Dr	Nashville, TN 37214, USA
Court TV	600 Third Ave	New York, NY 10016, USA
C-SPAN	400 N Capitol St NW, #650	Washington, DC 20001, USA
Discovery Channel	7700 Wisconsin Ave	Bethesda, MD 20814, USA
Disney Channel	3800 W Alameda Ave	Burbank, CA 91505, USA
E! (Entertainment Television)	5750 Wilshire Blvd	Los Angeles, CA 90036, USA
ESPN (Entertainment & Sports)	ESPN Plaza, 935 Middle St	Bristol, CT 06010, USA
Family Channel	PO Box 64549	Virginia Beach, VA 23467, USA
Food Network	1180 Ave of Americas, #1200	New York, NY 10036, USA
Fox Broadcasting Co	10201 W Pico Blvd	Los Angeles, CA 90035, USA
FX (Fox Net)	PO Box 900	Beverly Hills, CA 90213, USA
Game Show Network	10202 W Washington Blvd	Culver City, CA 90232, USA
Granada Television	36 Golden Square	London W1R 2AX, England
HGTV (Home & Garden TV)	PO Box 50970	Knoxville, TN 37950, USA
Home Box Office (HBO)	1100 Ave of Americas	New York, NY 10036, USA
Home Shopping Network	PO Box 9090	Clearwater, FL 34618, USA
Independent Film Channel	150 Crossways Park W	Woodbury, NY 11797, USA
Learning Channel	7700 Wisconsin Ave	Bethesda, MD 20814, USA
Lifetime	390 W 49th St	New York, NY 10019, USA
Madison Square Garden Network	2 Pennsylvania Plaza	New York, NY 10001, USA
Movie Channel (TMC)	1633 Broadway	New York, NY 10019, USA
MTV (Music Television)	1515 Broadway	New York, NY 10036, USA
National Broadcasting Company	30 Rockefeller Plaza	New York, NY 10112, USA
Nickelodeon	1515 Broadway	New York, NY 10036, USA
PBS (Public Broadcasting System)	1320 Braddock Place	Alexandria, VA 22314, USA
Playboy Channel	9242 Beverly Blvd	Beverly Hills, CA 90210, USA
Prime Ticket Network	10000 Santa Monica Blvd	Los Angeles, CA 90067, USA
QVC Inc	1365 Enterprise Dr	West Chester, PA 19380, USA
Sci-Fi Channel	1230 Ave of Americas	New York, NY 10020, USA
Showtime Network	1633 Broadway	New York, NY 10019, USA
TBN (Trinity Broadcast Network)	PO Box A	Tustin, CA 92711, USA
TBS (Turner Broadcasting System)	1 CNN Center, PO Box 105366	Atlanta, GA 30348, USA
Telemundo Group	1740 Broadway	New York, NY 10019, USA
TNN (The Nashville Network)	2806 Opryland Dr	Nashville, TN 37214, USA
TNT (Turner Network Television)	1050 Techwood Dr NW	Atlanta, GA 30318, USA
TVA	1600 de Maisonneuve Blvd E	Montreal QC H2L 4P2, Canada
Univision Network	605 3rd Ave	New York, NY 10158, USA
UPN	11800 Wilshire Blvd	Los Angeles, CA 90025
USA Cable Network	1230 Ave of Americas	New York, NY 10020, USA
VH-1 (Video Hits One)	1515 Broadway	New York, NY 10036, USA
Viewer's Choice	909 3rd Ave	New York, NY 10022, USA
WB	4000 Warner Blvd, Building 34R	Burbank, CA 91522, USA
Weather Channel	2600 Cumberland Parkway NW	Atlanta, GA 30339, USA

RECORD COMPANY ADDRESSES

A&M Records	70 University City Plaza	Universal City, CA 91608, USA
Angel Records	1750 N Vine St	Los Angeles, CA 90028, USA
Angel Records	150 5th Ave	New York, NY 10011, USA
Arista Records	8750 Wilshire Blvd, #300	Beverly Hills, CA 90211, USA
Arista Records	6 W 57th St	New York, NY 10019, USA
Asylum Records	9229 Sunset Blvd, #718	Los Angeles, CA 90069, USA
Asylum Records	75 Rockefeller Plaza	New York, NY 10019, USA
Atlantic Records	9229 Sunset Blvd, #900	Los Angeles, CA 90069, USA
Atlantic Records	1290 Ave of Americas	New York, NY 10104, USA
Blue Note Records	6920 Sunset Blvd	Los Angeles, CA 90028, USA
Capitol Records	1750 N Vine St	Los Angeles, CA 90028, USA

RECORD COMPANY ADDRESSES

Capitol Records	810 7th Ave	New York, NY 10019, USA
Chrysalis Records	8730 Sunset Blvd	Los Angeles, CA 90069, USA
Chrysalis Records	810 7th Ave, #4	New York, NY 10019, USA
Deutsche Grammaphon Records	810 7th Ave	New York, NY 10019, USA
Elektra Records	75 Rockefeller Plaza	New York, NY 10019, USA
EMI America Records	6920 Sunset Blvd	Los Angeles, CA 90028, USA
EMI America Records	810 7th Ave	New York, NY 10019, USA
Epic Records	1211 S Highland Ave	Los Angeles, CA 90019, USA
Epic Records	550 Madison Ave	New York, NY 10022, USA
Geffen Records	10900 Wilshire Blvd, #1000	Los Angeles, CA 90024, USA
Geffen Records	1755 Broadway	New York, NY 10019, USA
Island Records	8920 Sunset Blvd, #200	Los Angeles, CA 90069, USA
Island Records	925 8th St	New York, NY 10019, USA
LaFace Records	3350 Peach Tree Road	Atlanta, GA 30326, USA
London Records	810 7th Ave	New York, NY 10019, USA
MCA Records	70 Universal City Plaza	Universal City, CA 91608, USA
MCA Records	1755 Broadway	New York, NY 10019, USA
Mercury Records	54 Music Square E, #300	Nashville, TN 37203, USA
Motown Records	6255 Sunset Blvd	Los Angeles, CA 90028, USA
Nonesuch Records	75 Rockefeller Plaza	New York, NY 10019, USA
Phillips Records	810 7th Ave	New York, NY 10019, USA
Polydor Records	70 Universal City Plaza	Universal City, CA 91608, USA
Polydor Records	810 7th Ave	New York, NY 10019, USA
Polygram Records	3800 W Alameda Ave, #1500	Burbank, CA 91505, USA
Polygram Records	Worldwide Plaza, 825 8th Ave	New York, NY 10019, USA
RCA Records	6363 Sunset Blvd, #429	Los Angeles, CA 90028, USA
RCA Records	1540 Broadway, #3500	New York, NY 10036, USA
Reprise Records	3300 Warner Blvd	Burbank, CA 91505, USA
Reprise Records	75 Rockefeller Plaza	New York, NY 10019, USA
Rhino Records	10635 Santa Monica Blvd	Los Angeles, CA 90025, USA
Sire Records	3300 Warner Blvd	Burbank, CA 91505, USA
Sire Records	75 Rockefeller Plaza	New York, NY 10019, USA
Sony/Columbia/CBS Records	2100 Colorado Ave	Santa Monica, CA 90404, USA
Sony/Columbia/CBS Records	550 Madison Ave	New York, NY 10022, USA
Verve Records	Worldwide Plaza, 825 8th Ave	New York, NY 10019, USA
Virgin Records	338 N Foothill Road	Beverly Hills, CA 90210, USA
Virgin Records	150 5th Ave	New York, NY 10011, USA
Warner Bros Records	3300 Warner Blvd	Burbank, CA 91505, USA
Warner Bros Records	75 Rockefeller Plaza	New York, NY 10019, USA
Windham Hill Records	PO Box 5501	Beverly Hills, CA 90209, USA

PUBLISHER ADDRESSES

Atheneum Publishers	866 3rd Ave	New York, NY 10022
Avon Books	1350 Ave of Americas	New York, NY 10019, USA
Berkley Publishing	375 Hudson St	New York, NY 10014, USA
Crown Publishers	225 Park Ave S	New York, NY 10003, USA
Delacorte/Bantam/Dell/Doubleday	1540 Broadway	New York, NY 10036, USA
Dodd Mead	6 Ram Ridge Road	Spring Valley, NY 10977, USA
Dutton, EP/Penguin	375 Hudson St	New York, NY 10014, USA
Farrar Straus Giroux	19 Union Square W	New York, NY 10003, USA
Grove Press	841 Broadway	New York, NY 10003, USA
Harcourt Brace	525 B St	San Diego, CA 92101, USA
Harper Collins	10 E 53rd St	New York, NY 10022, USA
Henry Holt	115 W 18th St	New York, NY 10011, USA
Houghton Mifflin	215 Park Ave S	New York, NY 10003, USA
Hyperion Books	114 5th Ave	New York, NY 10011, USA
Knopf/Ballatine/Fawcett	201 E 50th St	New York, NY 10022, USA
Little Brown	1271 Ave of Americas	New York, NY 10020, USA
Little Brown	3 Center Plaza	Boston, MA 02108, USA
McGraw Hill	1221 Ave of Americas	New York, NY 10011, USA
MacMillan	1177 Ave of Americas, #1965	New York, NY 10036, USA
Morrow, William	1350 Ave of Americas	New York, NY 10019, USA
Mysterious Press/Warner Books	1271 6th Ave	New York, NY 10020, USA
New American Library	1633 Broadway	New York, NY 10019, USA
Norton, WW	500 5th Ave	New York, NY 10110, USA

PUBLISHER ADDRESSES

Oxford University Press	198 Madison Ave	New York, NY 10016, USA
Pocket Books	1230 Ave of Americas	New York, NY 10020, USA
Prentice-Hall	RR 9W	Englewood Cliffs, NJ 07632, USA
Putnam's Sons, GP	375 Hudson St, Basement	New York, NY 10014, USA
Random House	1745 Broadway, # B1	New York, NY 10019, USA
Scholastic Press	555 Broadway	New York, NY 10012, USA
Scribner's Sons, Charles	866 3rd Ave	New York, NY 10022, USA
Simon & Schuster	1230 Ave of Americas	New York, NY 10020, USA
Saint Martin's Press	175 5th Ave	New York, NY 10010, USA
Viking Press	375 Hudson St	New York, NY 10014, USA

PROFESSIONAL SPORTS TEAM ADDRESSES

BASEBALL

Anaheim Angels	Edison Field, 2000 Gene Autry Way	Anaheim, CA 92806, USA
Arizona Diamondbacks	Bank One Ballpark, 401 E Jefferson St	Phoenix, AZ 85004, USA
Atlanta Braves	Turner Field, 755 Hank Aaron Drive	Atlanta, GA 30315, USA
Baltimore Orioles	Oriole Park, 333 W Camden St	Baltimore, MD 21201, USA
Boston Red Sox	Fenway Park, 4 Yawkey Way	Boston, MA 02215, USA
Chicago Cubs	Wrigley Field, 1060 W Addison St	Chicago, IL 60613, USA
Chicago White Sox	Comiskey Park, 333 W 35th St	Chicago, IL 60616, USA
Cincinnati Reds	Cinergy Field, 100 Cinergy Field	Cincinnati, OH 45202, USA
Cleveland Indians	Jacobs Field, 2401 Ontario St	Cleveland, OH 44115, USA
Colorado Rockies	Coors Field, 2001 Blake St	Denver, CO 80205, USA
Detroit Tigers	Comerica Park, 2100 Woodward Ave	Detroit, MI 48201, USA
Florida Marlins	2269 Dan Marino Blvd	Miami, FL 33056, USA
Houston Astros	Astros Field, 501 Crawford St	Houston, TX 77002, USA
Kansas City Royals	Kauffman Stadium, 1 Royal Way	Kansas City, MO 64129, USA
Los Angeles Dodgers	Stadium, 1000 Elysian Park Ave	Los Angeles, CA 90012, USA
Milwaukee Brewers	Miller Park, 1 Brewers Way	Milwaukee, WI 5321, USA
Minnesota Twins	Metrodome, 34 Kirby Punkett Place	Minneapolis, MN 55415, USA
Montreal Expos	PO Box 500, Station M	Montreal QC H1V 3P2, Canada
New York Mets	Shea Stadium, 123-01 Roosevelt Ave	Flushing, NY 11368, USA
New York Yankees	Yankee Stadium, 161st & River	Bronx, NY 10451, USA
Oakland Athletic	7000Coliseum Way	Oakland, CA 94621, USA
Philadelphia Phillies	Veterans Stadium, 3501 S Broad St	Philadelphia, PA 19148, USA
Pittsburgh Pirates	PNC Park, 115 Federal St	Pittsburgh, PA 15212, USA
San Diego Padres	8880 Rio San Diego Drive, #400	San Diego, CA 92108, USA
San Francisco Giants	Pacific Bell Park, 24 Willie Mays Plaza	San Francisco, CA 94103, USA
Seattle Mariners	Safeco Field, PO Box 4100	Seattle, WA 98194, USA
Saint Louis Cardinals	Busch Stadium, 250 Stadium Plaza	Saint Louis, MO 63102, USA
Tampa Bay Devil Rays	Tropicana Field, 1 Tropicana Dr	Saint Petersburg, FL 33705, USA
Texas Rangers	The Ballpark, 1000Ballpark Way	Arlington, TX 76011, USA
Toronto Blue Jays	Skydome, 1 Blue Jay Way, #3200	Toronto ON M5V 1J1, Canada

MEN'S BASKETBALL

Atlanta Hawks	1 CNN Center, #405	Atlanta, GA 30303, USA
Boston Celtics	151 Merrimac St, #1	Boston, MA 02114, USA
Charlotte Bobcats	129 W Trade St, #700	Charlotte, NC 28202, USA
Chicago Bulls	United Center, 1901 W Madison St	Chicago, IL 60612, USA
Cleveland Cavaliers	Gund Arena, 1 Center Court	Cleveland, OH 44115, USA
Dallas Mavericks	2909 Taylor St	Dallas, TX 75226, USA
Denver Nuggets	Pepsi Center, 1000 Chopper Circle	Denver, CO 80204, USA
Detroit Pistons	Palace, 2 Championship Dr	Auburn Hills, MI 48326, USA
Golden State Warriors	1011 Broadway	Oakland, CA 94607, USA
Houston Rockets	2 E Greenway Plaza, #400	Houston, TX 77046, USA
Indiana Pacers	125 S Pennsylvania St	Indianapolis, IN 46204, USA
Los Angeles Clippers	Staples Center, 1111 S Figueroa St	Los Angeles, CA 90015, USA
Los Angeles Lakers	Staples Center, 1111 S Figueroa St	Los Angeles, CA 90015, USA
Memphis Grizzlies	175 Toyota Plaza, #150	Memphis, TN 38103, USA
Miami Heat	AA Arena, 601 Biscayne Blvd	Miami, FL 33132, USA
Milwaukee Bucks	Bradley Center, 1001 N 4th St	Milwaukee, WI 53203, USA
Minnesota Timberwolves	Target Center, 600 1st Ave N	Minneapolis, MN 55403, USA
New Jersey Nets	390 Murray Hill Parkway	East Rutherford, NJ 07073, USA
New Orleans Hornets	New Orleans Arena, 1501 Girod St	New Orleans, LA 70113, USA
New York Knicks	Madison Square Garden, 4 Penn Plaza	New York, NY 10121, USA
Orlando Magic	8701 Maitland Summit Blvd	Orlando, FL 32810, USA

Philadelphia 76ers	1st Union Center, 3601 S Broad St	Philadelphia, PA 19148, USA
Phoenix Suns	201 E Jefferson St	Phoenix, AZ 85004, USA
Portland Trail Blazers	Rose Garden, 1 Center Court, #200	Portland, OR 97227, USA
Sacramento Kings	Arco, Arena, 1 Sports Parkway	Sacramento, CA 95834, USA
San Antonio Spurs	1 SBC Center	San Antonio, TX 78219, USA
Seattle Supersonics	351 Elliott Ave W, #500	Seattle, WA 98119, USA
Toronto Raptors	20 Bay St, #1702	Toronto ON M5J 2N8, Canada
Utah Jazz	Delta Center, 301 W South Temple	Salt Lake City, UT 84101, USA
Washington Wizards	MCI Center, 601 F St, NW	Washington, DC 20004, USA

WOMEN'S BASKETBALL (WNBA)

Charlotte Sting	100 Hive Drive	Charlotte, NC 28217, USA
Cleveland Rockers	Gund Arena, 1 Center Court	Cleveland, OH 48326, USA
Connecticut Sun	Mohegan Sun Arena	Uncasville, CT 06382, USA
Detroit Shock	Palace, 2 Championship Dr	Auburn Hills, MI 48326, USA
Houston Comets	2 Greenway Plaza, #400	Houston, TX 77046, USA
Indiana Fever	125 S Pennsylvania St	Indianapolis, IN 46204, USA
Los Angeles Sparks	Staples Center, 1111 S Figueroa St	Los Angeles, CA 90015, USA
Minnesota Lynx	Target Center, 600 1st Ave N	Minneapolis, MN 55403, USA
New York Liberty	Madison Square Garden, 2 Penn Plaza	New York, NY 10121, USA
Phoenix Mercury	America West Arena, 201 E Jefferson St	Phoenix, AZ 85004, USA
Sacramento Monarchs	Arco Arena, 1 Sports Parkway	Sacramento, CA 95834, USA
San Antonio Silver Stars	1 SBC Center	San Antonio, TX 78219
Seattle Storm	351 Elliott Ave W, #500	Seattle, WA 98119, USA
Washington Mystics	MCI Center, 601 F St, NW	Washington, DC 20004, USA

FOOTBALL

Arizona Cardinals	PO Box 888	Phoenix, AZ 85001, USA
Atlanta Falcons	4400 Falcon Pkwy	Flowery Branch, GA 30542, USA
Baltimore Ravens	11001 Owings Mills Blvd	Owings Mills, MD 21117, USA
Buffalo Bills	1 Bills Dr	Orchard Park, NY 14127, USA
Carolina Panthers	Ericsson Stadium, 800 S Mint St	Charlotte, NC 28202, USA
Chicago Bears	1000 Football Dr	Lake Forest, IL 60045, USA
Cincinnati Bengals	1 Paul Brown Stadium	Cincinnati, OH 45202, USA
Cleveland Browns	76 Lou Groza Blvd	Berea, OH 44017, USA
Dallas Cowboys	1 Cowboys Parkway	Irving, TX 75063, USA
Denver Broncos	13655 Broncos Parkway	Englewood, CO 80112, USA
Detroit Lions	222 Republic Drive	Allen Park, MI 48101, USA
Green Bay Packers	PO Box 10628	Green Bay, WI 54307, USA
Houston Texans	4400 Post Oak Pkwy, #1400	Houston, TX 77027, USA
Indianapolis Colts	7001 W 56th St	Indianapolis, IN 46254, USA
Jacksonville Jaguars	1 AllTel Stadium Place	Jacksonville, FL 32202, USA
Kansas City Chiefs	1 Arrowhead Dr	Kansas City, KS 64129, USA
Miami Dolphins	7500 SW 30th St	Davie, FL 33314, USA
Minnesota Vikings	9520 Viking Dr	Eden Prairie, MN 55344, USA
New England Patriots	Gillette Stadium, 60 Washington St	Foxboro, MA 02035, USA
New Orleans Saints	5800 Airline Highway	Metairie, LA 70003, USA
New York Giants	Giants Stadium	East Rutherford, NJ 07073, USA
New York Jets	1000 Fulton Ave	Hempstead, NY 11550, USA
Oakland Raiders	1220 Harbor Bay Parkway	Alameda, CA 94502, USA
Philadelphia Eagles	1 NovaCare Way	Philadelphia, PA 19145, USA
Pittsburgh Steelers	3400 S Water St	Pittsburgh, PA 15203, USA
Saint Louis Rams	901 N Broadway	Saint Louis, MO 63101, USA
San Diego Chargers	4020 Murphy Canyon Rd	San Diego, CA 92123, USA
San Francisco 49ers	4949 Centennial Blvd	Santa Clara, CA 95054, USA
Seattle Seahawks	11220 NE 53rd St	Kirkland, WA 98033, USA
Tampa Bay Buccaneers	1 Buccaneer Place	Tampa, FL 33607, USA
Tennessee Oilers	460 Great Circle Road	Nashville, TN 37228, USA
Washington Redskins	21300 Redskin Park Dr	Ashburn, VA 20147, USA

ICE HOCKEY

Anaheim Mighty Ducks	2000 E Gene Autry Way	Anaheim, CA 92803, USA
Atlanta Thrashers	Philips Arena, 1 CNN Center	Atlanta, GA 30315, USA
Boston Bruins	1 Fleet Center	Boston, MA 02114, USA
Buffalo Sabres	HSBC Arena, 1 Seymour Knox Plaza	Buffalo, NY 14210, USA
Calgary Flames	PO Box 1540, Station M	Calgary AB T2P 3B9, Canada
Carolina Hurricanes	E&S Arena, 1400 Edwards Mill Road	Raleigh, NC 27607, USA

PROFESSIONAL SPORTS TEAM ADDRESSES

Chicago Blackhawks	United Center, 1901 W Madison St	Chicago, IL 60612, USA
Colorado Avalanche	Pepsi Center, 1000 Chopper Circle	Denver, CO 80204, USA
Columbus Blue Jackets	200 W Nationwide Blvd	Columbus, OH 43215, USA
Dallas Stars	211 Cowboys Parkway	Irving, TX 75063, USA
Detroit Red Wings	Joe Louis Arena, 600 Civic Center Dr	Detroit, MI 48226, USA
Edmonton Oilers	Edmonton Coliseum, 11230-110 St	Edmonton AB T5G 3G8, Canada
Florida Panthers	1 Panthers Parkway	Sunrise, FL 33323, USA
Hartford Whalers	Coliseum, 242 Trumbull St, #800	Hartford, CT 06103, USA
Los Angeles Kings	Staples Center, 1111 S Figueroa St	Los Angeles, CA 90015, USA
Minnesota Wild	Xcel Energy Center, 175 W Kellogg Blvd	Saint Paul, MN 55102, USA
Montreal Canadiens	1260 de la Gauchetiere St W	Montreal QC H3B 5E8, Canada
Nashville Predators	501 Broadway	Nashville, TN 37203, USA
New Jersey Devils	Continental Arena, 50 Route 120 N	East Rutherford, NJ 07073, USA
New York Islanders	1255 Hempstead Turnpike	Uniondale, NY 11553, USA
New York Rangers	Madison Square Garden, 2 Penn Plaza	New York, NY 10121, USA
Ottawa Senators	Corel Center, 1000 Palladium Dr	Kanata ON K2V 1A4, Canada
Philadelphia Flyers	1st Union Center, 3601 S Broad St	Philadelphia, PA 19148, USA
Phoenix Coyotes	Alltel Ice Den, 9375 E Bell Road	Phoenix, AZ 85260, USA
Pittsburgh Penguins	Mellon Arena, 66 Mario Lemieux Place	Pittsburgh, PA 15219, USA
Saint Louis Blues	Kiel Center, 1401 Clark Ave	Saint Louis, MO 63103, USA
San Jose Sharks	525 W Santa Clara St	San Jose, CA 95113, USA
Tampa Bay Lightning	Ice Palace, 401 Channelside Dr	Tampa, FL 33602, USA
Toronto Maple Leafs	AirCanada Center, 40 Bay St, #400	Toronto ON M5J 2X2, Canada
Vancouver Canucks	800 Griffiths Way	Vancouver BC V6B 6G1, Canada
Washington Capitals	MCI Center, 601 F St, NW	Washington, DC 20004, USA

SOCCER

Chicago Fire	980 N Michigan Ave, #1998	Chicago, IL 60611, USA
Colorado Rapids	555 17th St, #3350	Denver, CO 80202, USA
Columbus Crew	2121 Velman Ave	Columbus, OH 43211, USA
Dallas Burn	14800 Quorum Dr, #300	Dallas, TX 75254, USA
DC United	14120 Newbrook Dr	Chantilly, VA 20151, USA
Kansas City Wizards	2 Arrowhead Dr	Kansas City, MO 64129, USA
Los Angeles Galaxy	1010 Rose Bowl Dr	Los Angeles, CA 91103, USA
Miami Fusion FC	1350 NW 55th St	Fort Lauderdale, FL 33309, USA
New England Revolution	CMGI Field, 1 Patriot Place	Foxboro, MA 02035, USA
New York/New Jersey MetroStars	1 Harmon Plaza, #300	Secaucus, NJ 07094, USA
San Jose Earthquakes	3550 Stevens Creek Blvd, #200	San Jose, CA 95117, USA

OTHER SPORTS ORGANIZATION ADDRESSES

Amateur Athletic Union	PO Box 10000	Lake Buena Vista, FL 32830, USA
Amateur Softball Assn	2801 NE 50th St	Oklahoma City, OK 73111, USA
American Bicycle Assn	1645 W Sunrise Blvd	Gilbert, AZ 85233, USA
American Bowling Congress	5301 S 76th St	Greendale, WI 53129, USA
American Horse Show Assn	220 E 42nd St	New York, NY 10017, USA
American Hot Rod Assn	111 N Hayford Road	Spokane, WA 99224, USA
American Kennel Club	260 Madison Ave	New York, NY 10016, USA
American League Baseball	350 Park Ave, #1800	New York, NY 10022, USA
American Motorcycle Assn	13515 Yarmouth Dr	Pickerington, OH 43147, USA
American Power Boat Assn	17640 E Nine Mile Road	East Detroit, MI 48021, USA
American Prof Soccer League	122 C St, NW	Washington, DC 20001, USA
American Water Ski Assn	799 Overlook Dr	Winter Haven, FL 33884, USA
Assn of Int'l Amateur Boxing	Postamt Volkrdstr, Postlagernd	10319 Berlin, Germany
Assn of Int'l Marathon/Road Races	20 Trongate	Glasgow G1 5ES, England
Assn of Ski Racing Professionals	148 Porters Point Road	Colchester, VT 05446, USA
Assn of Surfing Professionals	16691 Gothard St	Huntington Beach, CA 92648, USA
Assn of Tennis Professionals	200 Tournament Road	Ponte Vedra Beach, FL 32082, USA
Assn of Volleyball Professionals	330 Washington Blvd, #400	Marina del Rey, CA 90292, USA
Canadian Football League	110 Eglinton Ave	Toronto, ON M4R 1A3, Canada
Canadian Nat'l Sports/Rec Center	1600 James Naismith Dr	Gloucestor ON KJB 5N4, Canada
Fedn de Int'l Hockey	Avenue des Arts 1 (bte 5)	1040 Brussels, Belgium
Fedn de Int'l Ski	Worbstr 210, 3073 Gumligen B	Berne, Switzerland
Fedn Int'l de Canoe	G Massaia 59	50134 Florence, Italy
Fedn Int'l de Football Assn	PO Box 85, Hitzigweg 11	8030 Zurich, Switzerland
Fedn Int'l de Gymnastics	Juraweg 12	3250 Lyss, Switzerland
Fedn Int'l de Tir a l'Arc (Archery)	Via Cerva 30	20122 Milan, Italy

OTHER SPORTS ORGANIZATION ADDRESSES

Fedn of Int'l Volleyball	Ave de la Gare 12	1001 Lausanne, Switzerland
Fedn of Int'l Amateur Cycling	Via Cassia N 490	00198 Rome, Italy
Fedn of Int'l Basketball	PO Box 700607, Kistlerhofstr 168	81379 Munich, Germany
Fedn of Int'l Bobsleigh/Toboggan	Via Piranesi 44/b	20137 Milan, Italy
Fedn of Int'l du Sport Automobiles	8 Place de la Concorde	75008 Paris, France
Fedn of Int'l Equestrian	PO Box 3000, Bolligenstr 54	32 Berne, Switzerland
FIFA Women's Football Assn	37 Sussex Road, Ickenham	Middx UB10 8PN, England
Formula One Driver's Assn	2 Rue Jean Jaures	1836 Luxembourg
Indy Racing League	4565 W 16th St	Indianapolis, IN 46222, USA
Int'l Badminton Federation	24 Winchcombe House	Cheltenham, Glos GL52 2NA, England
Int'l Baseball Assn	201 S Capitol Ave, #490	Indianapolis, IN 46225, USA
Int'l Boxing Federation	134 Evergreen Place	East Orange, NJ 07018, USA
Int'l Cricket Council	Lord's Cricket Ground	London NW8 8QN, England
Int'l Curling Federation	2 Coates Crescent	Edinburgh EH3 7AN, England
Int'l Game Fish Assn	1301 E Atlantic Blvd	Pompano Beach, FL 33060, USA
Int'l Hot Rod Assn	Highway 11E	Bristol, TN 37620, USA
Int'l Ice Hockey Federation	Bellevuestr 8	1190 Vienna, Austria
Int'l Jai Alai Assn	5 Calle Aldamar	San Sebastian 3, Spain
Int'l Judo Federation	Avenida del Trabajo 2666,	CP 1406, Buenos Aires, Argentina
Int'l Luge Federation	Olympiadestr 168	8786 Rottenmann, Austria
Int'l Motor Sports Assoc	1394 Broadway Ave	Braselton, GA 30517, USA
Int'l Olympic Committee	Chateau de Vidy	1007 Lausanne, Switzerland
Int'l Roller Skating Federation	1500 S 70th St	Lincoln, NE 68506, USA
Int'l Rugby Football Board	PO Box 902	Auckland, New Zealand
Int'l Skating Union	Promenade 73	7270 Davos-Platz, Switzerland
Int'l Sled Dog Racing Assn	PO Box 446	Nordman, ID 83848, USA
Int'l Softball Federation	2801 NE 59th St	Oklahoma City, OK 73111, USA
Int'l Sport Automobile Fed	8 Rue de la Concorde	70008-E Paris, France
Int'l Surfing Assn	Winston Ave, Branksome People	Dorset, England
Int'l Table Tennis Federation	53 London Road, St Leonards-on-Sea	East Sussex TN37 6AY, England
Int'l Tennis Federation	Palliser Road, Barons Court	London W14 9EN, England
Int'l Volleyball Federation	Ave de la Gare 12	1003 Lausanne, Switzerland
Int'l Weightlifting Federation	Rosemberg Hp U1	1374 Budapest PF 614, Hungary
Int'l Yacht Racing Union	60 Knightsbridge, Westminster	London SWEX 7JX, England
Ladies Professional Bowlers Tour	7171 Cherryvales Blvd	Rockford, IL 61112, USA
Ladies Professional Golf Assn	100 International Golf Dr	Daytona Beach, FL 32124, USA
Little League Baseball	PO Box 3485	Williamsport, PA 17701, USA
Major Indoor Lacrosse League	2310 W 75th St	Shawnee Mission, KS 66208, USA
Major League Baseball	350 Park Ave	New York, NY 10022, USA
National Archery Assn	1 Olympic Plaza	Colorado Springs, CO 80909, USA
National Assn of Stock Car Racing	1801 Speedway Blvd	Daytona Beach, FL 32015, USA
National Assn/Intercoll Athletics	1221 Baltimore Ave	Kansas City, MO 64105, USA
National Basketball Assn	645 5th Ave, #1000	New York, NY 10022, USA
National Collegiate Athletic Assn	70 W Washington St	Indianapolis, IN 46204, USA
National Football League	280 Park Ave	New York, NY 10017, USA
National Hockey League	1251 Ave of Americas	New York, NY 10020, USA
National Hot Rod Assn	2023 Financial Way	Glendora, CA 91741, USA
National League Baseball	350 Park Ave, #1800	New York, NY 10022, USA
National Pro Soccer League	229 3rd St NW	Canton, OH 44702, USA
National Rifle Assn	11250 Waples Mill Road	Fairfax, VA 22030, USA
National Tractor Pullers Assn	6155 Huntley Road, #B	Columbus, OH 43229, USA
PGA Seniors Tour	112 PGA Tour Blvd	Ponte Vedra Beach, FL 32082, USA
Professional Bowlers Assn	1720 Merriman Road	Akron, OH 44313, USA
Professional Golfers Assn	100 Ave of Champions	Palm Beach Gardens, FL 33410, USA
Professional Rodeo Cowboys	101 Pro Rodeo Dr	Colorado Springs, CA 80919, USA
Professional Sports Car Racing	1394 Broadway Ave	Braselton, GA 30517, USA
Special Olympics	1325 G St NW, #500	Washington, DC 20005, USA
Thoroughbred Racing Assn	420 Fair Hill Dr, #1	Elkton, MD 21921, USA
Union Int'l de Tir (Rifle)	Bavariaring 21	80336 Munich, Germany
United Syst of Indp Soccer	14497 N Dale Mabry Highway, #2011	Tampa, FL 33618, USA
US Auto Club	1720 Ruskin St	South Bend, IN 46604, USA
US Bobsled Federation	421 Old Military Road	Lake Placid, NY 12946, USA
US Cycling Federation	1 Olympic Plaza, Bldg 4	Colorado Springs, CO 80909, USA
US Figure Skating Assn	20 1st St	Colorado Springs, CO 80906, USA
US Luge Assn	35 Church St	Lake Placid, NY 12946, USA

OTHER SPORTS ORGANIZATIONS ADDRESSES

US Olympic Committee	1 Olympic Plaza	Colorado Springs, CO 80909, USA
US Polo Assn	4059 Iron Works Pike	Lexington, KY 40511, USA
US Skiing Assn	PO Box 100	Park City, UT 84060, USA
US Soccer Federation	1801 S Prarie Ave, #11	Chicago, IL 60616, USA
US Tennis Assn	Flushing Meadow	Flushing, NY 11368, USA
US Trotting Assn	750 Michigan Ave	Columbus, OH 43215, USA
US Youth Soccer Assn	PO Box 18404	Memphis, TN 38181, USA
USA Rugby	3595 E Fountain Blvd, #M2	Colorado Springs, CO 80910, USA
USA Track & Field	4341 Starlight Dr	Indianapolis, IN 46239, USA
Virginia Slims Women's Tennis	3135 Texas Commerce Tower	Houston, TX 77002, USA
Women's Basketball Assn	4011 N Bennington	Kansas City, MO 64117, USA
Women's Int'l Bowling Congress	5301 S 76th St	Greendale, WI 53129, USA
Women's Int'l Surfing Assn	PO Box 512	San Juan Capistrano, CA 92675, USA
Women's Pro Volleyball Assn	840 Apollo St, #204	El Segundo, CA 90245, USA
Women's Tennis Assn	1 Progress Plaza, #1500	Saint Petersburg, FL 33701, USA
World Boardsailing Assn	Feldafinger Platz 2	81477 Munich, Germany
World Boxing Assn	Rodrigo Sazagy, Apartado	4070 Panama City, Panama
World Boxing Council	Genova 33, Colonia Juarez	Cuahtemoc 0660, Mexico
World Taekwondo Federation	San 76 Yuksam-Dong	Kangnam-Ku, Seoul, Korea
World Team Tennis	445 N Wells St	Chicago, IL 60610, USA
World Union of Karate Orgs	1-15-16 Toranomon, Minato-ku	Tokyo 105, Japan
World Wrestling Federation	1055 Summer St	Stamford, CT 06902, USA

HALLS OF FAME ADDRESSES

Academy of Sports	4 Rue de Teheran	75008 Paris, France
Amateur Athletic Foundation of LA	2141 W Adams Blvd	Los Angeles, CA 90018, USA
American Water Ski	799 Overlook Dr SE	Winter Park, FL 33884, USA
Auto Racing	4790 W 16th St	Speedway, IN 46224, USA
Classical Music	4 E 4th St	Cincinnati, OH 45202, USA
College Football	1111 S Saint Joseph	South Bend, IN 46601, USA
Hockey	Exhibition Place	Toronto ON M6K 3C3, Canada
Int'l Boxing	PO Box 425	Canastota, NY 13032, USA
Int'l Gymnastics	227 Brooks St	Oceanside, CA 92054, USA
Int'l Motor Sports	PO Box 1018	Talladega, AL 35160, USA
Int'l Surfing	5580 La Jolla Blvd, #373	La Jolla, CA 92037, USA
Int'l Swimming	1 Hall of Fame Dr	Fort Lauderdale, FL 33316, USA
Int'l Tennis	194 Bellevue Ave	Newport, RI 02840, USA
Int'l Volleyball	PO Box 1895, 444 Dwight St	Holyoke, MA 01040, USA
Int'l Women's Sports	342 Madison Ave, #728	New York, NY 10173, USA
Lacrosse Foundation	White Athletic Center, Homewood	Baltimore, MD 21218, USA
Lawn Tennis Museum	All England Lawn Tennis Club	Wimbledon, England
LPGA	2570 Volusia Ave	Daytona Beach, FL 32114, USA
Naismith Basketball	1150 W Columbus Ave	Springfield, MA 01105, USA
Nat'l Baseball	PO Box 590	Cooperstown, NY 13326, USA
Nat'l Bowling Museum	111 Stadium Plaza	Saint Louis, MO 63102, USA
Nat'l Cowboy	Heritage Center, 1700 NE 63rd St	Oklahoma City, OK 73111, USA
Nat'l Cowgirl	111 W 4th St, #300	Fort Worth, TX 76102, USA
Nat'l Football Found	1865 Palmer Ave	Larchmont, NY 10538, USA
Nat'l Museum of Racing	Union Ave	Saratoga Springs, NY 12866, USA
Nat'l Ski	PO Box 191, Poplar & Mather	Ishpeming, MI 49849, USA
Nat'l Soccer	18 Stadium Circle	Oneonta, NY 13870, USA
Nat'l Softball	2801 NE 50th St	Oklahoma City, OK 73111, USA
Nat'l Sportcaster/Sportswriter	322 E Innes St	Salisbury, NC 28144, USA
Nat'l Sprint Car	1402 N Lincoln Ave	Knoxville, IA 50138, USA
Nat'l Track & Field	200 S Capital Ave	Indianapolis, IN 46225, USA
Nat'l Wrestling	405 W Hall of Fame Ave	Stillwater, OK 74074, USA
PGA Tour	112 Tournament Players Club Blvd	Ponte Vedra, FL 32082, USA
PGA World Golf	PGA Blvd, PO Box 1908	Pinehurst, NC 28374, USA
Pro Football	2121 George Halas Dr, NW	Canton, OH 44708, USA
Pro Rodeo Hall of Champions	101 Pro Rodeo Dr	Colorado Springs, CO 80919, USA
Professional Bowlers Assn	719 2nd Ave, #701	Seattle, WA 98104, USA
Professional Golfers Assn	PO Box 109601	Palm Beach Gardens, FL 33410, USA
Trapshooting	601 W Vandalia Road	Vandalia, OH 45377, USA
Trotter Horse Museum &	PO Box 590	Goshen, NY 10924, USA
US Bicycling	145 W Main Street	Somerville, NJ 08876, USA
US Figure Skating Assn	20 1st St	Colorado Springs, CO 80906, USA

OTHER SPORTS ORGANIZATION ADDRESSES

US Golf Assn Museum	Golf House	Far Hills, NJ 07931, USA
US Hockey	PO Box 657, Hat Trick Ave	Eveleth, MN 55734, USA
US Olympic Committee	1750 E Boulder St	Colorado Springs, CO 80909, USA
Women's Bowling	5301 S 76th St	Greendale, WI 53129, USA
Yachting	PO Box 129	Newport, RI 02840, USA

BIBLIOGRAPHY

Academy Players Directory, Academy of Motion Picture Arts/Sciences, 8949 Wilshire Blvd, Beverly Hills, CA 90211, USA
African Who's Who, African Journal Ltd, 54A Tottenham Court Road, London W1P 08T, England
Biographical Dictionary of Governors of the US, Meckler Publishing, Ferry Lane W, Westport, CT 06880, USA
Biographical Dictionary of US Executive Branch, Greenwood Press, 51 Riverside Ave, Westport, CT 06880, USA
Congressional Directory, Superintendent of Documents, US Government Printing Office, Washington, DC 20402, USA
Contemporary Architects, Saint Martin's Press, 175 5th Ave, New York, NY 10010, USA
Contemporary Designers, Gale Research Co, Book Tower, Detroit, MI 48226, USA
Contemporary Theatre, Film & Television, Gale Research Co, Book Tower, Detroit, MI 48226, USA
Corporate 1000, Washington Monitor, 1301 Pennsylvania Ave NW, Washington, DC 20004, USA
Editor & Publisher International Yearbook, 575 Lexington Ave, New York, NY 10022, USA
International Directory of Films & Filmmakers, Saint James Press, 175 5th Ave, New York, NY 10010, USA
International Who's Who, Europa Publications Ltd, 18 Bedford Square, London WC1B 3JN, England
International Who's Who in Music, Biddles Ltd, Walnut Tree House, Guildford, Surrey GU1 1DA, England
Kraks BlaBog, Nytorv 17, 1450 Copenhagen K, Denmark
Major Companies of Europe, Graham & Trotman Ltd, 66 Wilton Road, London SW1V 1DE, England
Major Companies of the Far East, Graham & Trotman Ltd, 66 Wilton Road, London SW1V 1DE, England
Martindale-Hubbell Law Directory, Reed Publishing, Summit, NJ 07902, USA
Moody's International Manual, Moody's Investors Service, 99 Church St, New York, NY 10007, USA
Notable Australians, Paul Hamlyn Pty Ltd, 31 176 S Creek Road, Dee Why, WA 2099, Australia
Notable New Zealanders, Paul Hamlyn Pty Ltd, 31 Airedale St, Auckland, New Zealand
Prominent Personalities in USSR, Scarecrow Press, Metuchen, NJ 08840, USA
US Court Directory, Government Printing Office, Washington, DC 20401, USA
US Gov't Manual, National Archives & Records Service, General Services Administration, Washington, DC 20408, USA
VIP Autogramm-Magazin, Postfach 11 05, 35112 Fronhausen, Germany
Who's Who, A & C Black Ltd, Saint Martin's Press, 175 5th Ave, New York, NY 10010, USA
Who's Who in America, Marquis Who's Who, 200 E Ohio St, Chicago, IL 60611, USA
Who's Who in American Art, R R Bowker Co, 1180 Ave of Americas, New York, NY 10003, USA
Who's Who in American Politics, R R Bowker Co, 1180 Ave of Americas, New York, NY 10036, USA
Who's Who in Canada, Global Press, 164 Commanden Blvd, Agincourt ON M1S 3C7, Canada
Who's Who in France, Editions Jacques Lafitte SA, 75008 Paris, France
Who's Who in Germany, Verlag AG Zurich, Germany
Who's Who in Israel, Bronfman Publishers Ltd, 82 Levinsky St, Tel Aviv 61010, Israel
Who's Who in Poland, Graphica Comense Srl, 22038 Taverreiro, Italy
Who's Who in Scandinavia, A Sutter Druckerei GmbH, 4300 Essen, Germany
Who's Who in Switzerland, Nagel Publishers, 5-5 bis de l'Orangeris, Geneva, Switzerland
Who's Who in the Theatre, Pitman Press, 39 Parker St, London WC2B 5PB, England
Who's Who in Washington, Tiber Reference Press, 4340 East-West Highway, Bethesda, MD 20814, USA

Book design by Lee Ann Nelson.
Cover logo is Corvinus Skyline, Body type is Swiss Narrow.
Production by Nelson Design, 9 Ridgeview Court, San Ramon, California 94583

FREE Autographs & Much More!

For ten years, ***Autograph Collector*** magazine has been the leading publication in its field. And it's no wonder when you consider what each monthly issue features.

Every month we give you over 100 addresses of celebrities who are known to send **FREE** autographs through the mail to those who ask! Our readers have written for and received thousands of dollars worth of autographs using our addresses!

Plus, the autograph industry's top experts write articles on how to spot fakes, where to find the bargains and much, much more! Learn what your autographs are worth ... read what today's hottest celebrities have to say about autographs. Each issue also features thousands of autographs for sale.

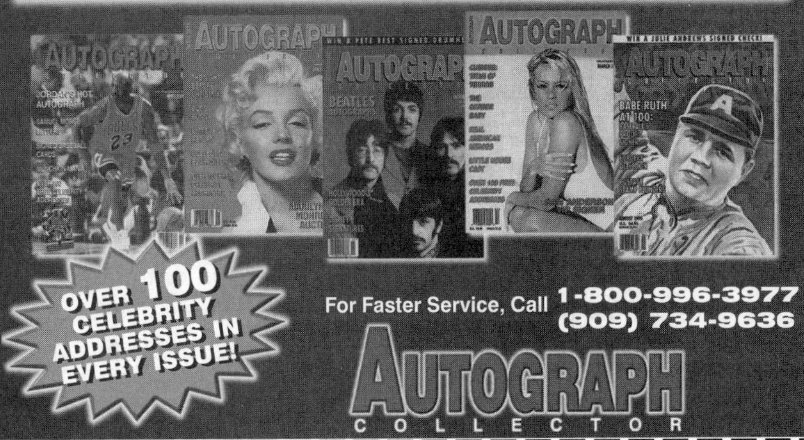

OVER 100 CELEBRITY ADDRESSES IN EVERY ISSUE!

For Faster Service, Call 1-800-996-3977 (909) 734-9636

AUTOGRAPH COLLECTOR

YES! Send me **12** issues of **Autograph Collector** so I can keep up on the current prices and trends of autographs and much more!

Name ______________________________ AM

Address ______________________________

City ______________________ State ______ Zip______

SUBSCRIPTIONS (Check appropriate boxes)

❍ U.S. $38.00 ❍ Canada/Mexico $72.00 ❍ All other Countries $94.00

❍ Cash, Check or Money Order enclosed ❍ Bill me

❍ Bill my Credit Card: ❍ VISA ❍ MC ❍ American Express

Card # ______________________________ Exp.______

Signature ______________________________

Make checks payable and mail to:

Autograph Collector, 510-A South Corona Mall, Corona, CA 92879-1420

An Invitation to Join the

The Universal Autograph Collectors Club, Inc. is a federally approved non-profit organization dedicated to the **education** of the autograph collector. For over thirty years the **UACC** has been serving the autograph collecting community by its publications, programs and passion. The organization sponsors autograph shows worldwide as well as publishing the award-winning ***Pen and Quill*** journal for its members.
The **UACC** is an organization for collectors run by collectors.
For more information and a **FREE** brochure, write:

UACC
Dept. AT
P.O. Box 6181
Washington, DC 20044-6181
or visit our website at ***www.uacc.org***

Dues are $26 in the U.S., $29 in Canada and Mexico and $37 everywhere else.

The UACC now accepts Visa and Mastercard

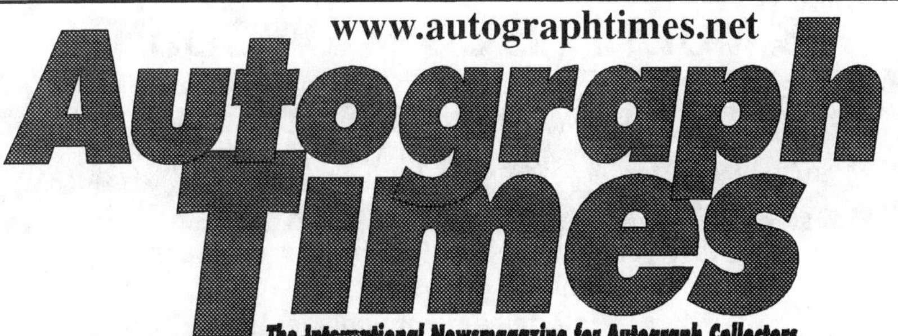

If you enjoy collecting autographs, then *Autograph Times* can help you enhance your collection. Each month brings you articles and features covering a variety of collecting categories and enough addresses to help you grow your collection quickly. Whether you are a novice or a seasoned collector, there's something for everyone in *Autograph Times*. You'll find more useful information in these pages than anywhere else and you can subscribe *risk free*. Your satisfaction is 100% guaranteed with full money back if you are ever dissatisfied in any way.

FREE
Inside Secrets of Collecting Autographs with paid subscription

Try Autograph Times for FREE!

Get the next available issue of Autograph Times for free.

Send your request to:

Autograph Times Trial
Dept. AM
P.O. Box 5790
Peoria, AZ 85385

For fastest service:

Call Toll Free
1-877-860-0349
or call 623-544-4037
or fax to: 623-214-5419
or e-mail request to:
info@autographtimes.net

Now available on the world wide web!

Autograph Times is now available — fully downloadable — on the world wide web. Take advantage of special online pricing and start enjoying Autograph Times *immediately!* Log on to:

www.autographtimes.net

V.I.P. ADDRESS BOOK UPDATE & MULTIPLE COPY DISCOUNTS

Keep Up To Date With the V.I.P. Address Book Update Only $24.95!

Every year 20% of people change residences

- **Athletes get traded**
- **Entertainers change agents**
- **Business people change jobs**
- **Politicians leave or change office**

Changed Addresses	The mid-year V.I.P. ADDRESS BOOK UPDATE lists changes since publication of the basic volume.
Bad Addresses	The UPDATE identifies addresses which are no longer accurate and for which corrections are not available.
New Addresses	The UPDATE even has addresses for new entrants!
Deaths	And a list of people who have died since the V.I.P. ADDRESS BOOK was published is included.

Foreign orders add $4.00 for overseas shipping

Multiple Copy Discounts

The V.I.P. ADDRESS BOOK offers the following multiple copy discounts:

1 - 2 Copies	**$94.95 each**
3 - 5 Copies	**$85.45 each**
6 - 12 Copies	**$80.71 each**
13 - 49 Copies	**$75.96 each**
50 - 99 Copies	**$71.21 each**
100 - 199 Copies	**$66.47 each**
200 Copies or More	**$56.97 each**

Order Information

Use your MasterCard, Visa, Discover or American Express or a company purchase order and call toll-free 1-800-258-0615

Or send your check or money order to:

Associated Media Companies
P.O. Box 489
Gleneden Beach, OR 97388-0489
Phone/Fax Number - (541) 764-4233
Internet Users - VIPADDRESS@HARBORSIDE.COM

ORDER A COPY FOR YOURSELF OR A FRIEND

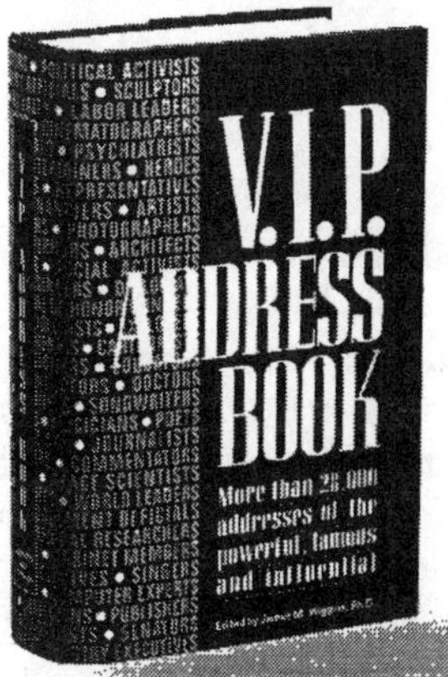

Put 28,000 essential V.I.P. addresses at your fingertips —for less than a penny each!

No matter what your need, you'll find virtually any address you may be looking for. Many of the names and addresses are not available in any other publication. That's why the Publisher's Marketing Association voted the V.I.P. Address Book the Benjamin Franklin Award for Directory of the Year and the American Reference Books Annual says "The format is excellent for easy consultation. Libraries will find it a useful addition to their collections."

What the experts say about the
V.I.P. ADDRESS BOOK:

"A **valuable resource** for many types of business. Researchers, publicists, fund raisers and marketing specialists are just a few of the professions that would benefit from owning this book." —Rainbo Electronic Reviews

"**Fantastic!** Every company's marketing, personnel, advertising and research departments should have copies." —Gail Watson, Watson Products

"The Benjamin Franklin Award winner as **Directory of the Year!**" —Publishers Marketing Association

SAVE $10.00! Order the mid-August Update at the same time you order the V.I.P. ADDRESS BOOK and take $10 off your order!

V.I.P. ADDRESS BOOK

Addresses of musicians, entertainers, government leaders, athletes, scientists, business leaders, artists, military leaders, publishers, activists and more...

$94.95 5½"x8½" LCCN 89-656029
(Foreign orders add $12.50 postage)

V.I.P. ADDRESS UPDATE

The perfect complement to the V.I.P. ADDRESS BOOK. The Bureau of Statistics says 20% of people move each year. The mid-August UPDATE keeps you abreast of address changes and also adds new addresses to the basic volume.

$24.95 ISBN 0-939731-10-6 5½"x8½" LCCN 89-30776
(Foreign orders add $4.00 postage)

Order toll-free 800-258-0615 or for more information 541-764-4233

To order by mail, complete this coupon and return with check, money order or credit card information (no C.O.D. orders) to:

V.I.P. Address Book
c/o Associated Media Companies
P.O. Box 489
Gleneden Beach, OR 97388 USA
Web site: www.vipaddress.com
Email: vipaddress@harborside.com

Save $10.00! Order book AND update for ONLY $109.90
(Foreign orders add postage: $16.50 for Book/Update)

☐ Yes, please send ________ copies of the V.I.P. ADDRESS BOOK at $94.95 each.
• *Foreign orders add $12.50 per copy for postage.*

☐ Yes, please send ________ copies of the V.I.P. ADDRESS BOOK UPDATE at $24.95 each.
• *Foreign orders add $4.00 for postage.*

Charge: ☐ VISA ☐ MasterCard ☐ Discover ☐ American Express

Account Number: ☐☐☐☐-☐☐☐☐-☐☐☐☐-☐☐☐☐

Expiration date: ☐☐-☐☐

Cardholder phone number (________) ____________

Cardholder signature ____________

Name ____________

Address ____________

City ____________ State _____ Zip ________

Country ____________

Library P.O. # ____________

Multiple copy discounts available! Call or write for details.

Here's What People Are Saying . . .

"Ideal for creative fund raisers! Whether it is for schools, hospitals or political candidates —this book is a must. If you need endorsements, referrals or donors, the book will be a boon to your efforts."

THOMAS L. HALL, TOM HALL & ASSOCIATES PUBLIC RELATIONS

"The book is the writer-researcher's best friend. This is a resource tool I can't afford to be without"

HANK NUWER, AUTHOR, REPORTER, EDUCATOR

"I'm an autograph collector and love the book. I've had great results."

MARK J. QUILLING, COLLECTOR

"Celebrity hounds may find much to peruse in this directory."

CHRONICLE OF PHILANTHROPY

"A public relations expert's dream . . . No office of a public relations professional should be without this vast resource."

PHILIP O. SPELMAN, PH.D., SPELMAN PUBLIC RELATIONS

"The book ranks high for accuracy —especially compared to other reference works. Ideally suited for organizations and media."

PAM KEYES, MIAMI NEWS-RECORD

"This publication is the most thorough, accurate and meticulously edited book of its kind. It is a must for any individual who wants to contact anyone of celebrity status."

JACK MASSEE MCKINLEY, COLLECTOR

"Absolutely indispensable for enterprising professional journalists"

LARRY MEYER, AUTHOR, EDITOR, EDUCATOR

"A valuable reference for anyone desirous of reaching people who daily appear on the national or international scene from every walk of life. An excellent addition to any library."

ANNE THOMPSON, ROCKY FORD DAILY GAZETTE